APR 4 2012

WITHDRAWN

CHILTON®

FORD
SERVICE MANUAL
2012 EDITION
VOLUME I

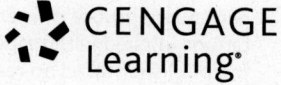
CENGAGE
Learning®

Australia • Brazil • Japan • Korea • Mexico • Singapore • Spain • United Kingdom • United States

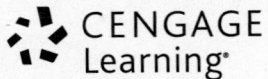

CHILTON®
Ford Service Manual
2010 Edition
Volume I

**Vice President,
Technology Professional
Business Unit:**
Gregory L. Clayton

**Publisher,
Technology Professional
Business Unit:**
David Koontz

Director of Marketing:
Beth A. Lutz

Senior Production Director:
Wendy Troeger

Production Manager:
Sherondra Thedford

Marketing Manager:
Jennifer Barbic

Marketing Coordinator:
Rachael Torres

Editorial Assistant:
Lisa Staib

Chilton Content Specialist:
Paula Baillie

Graphical Designer:
Melinda Possinger

Art Director:
Benj Gleeksman

Sr. Content Project Manager:
Mike Tubbert

Senior Editors:
Eugene F. Hannon, Jr., A.S.E.

Ryan Lee Price

Richard J. Rivele

Christine L. Sheeky

Editors:
Jim Bailey

Dennis Bailey

Maureen Lazarz

Kyla Nyjordet

Lance Williams

For product information and technology assistance, contact us at
Professional & Career Group customer Support, 1-800-648-7450.
For permission to use material from this text or product,
submit all requests online at
www.cengage.com/permissions.
Further permissions questions can be e-mailed to
permissionrequest@cengage.com.

ISBN-13: 978-1-4354-6166-6
ISBN-10: 1-4354-6166-5
ISSN: 1548-0887

Chilton
5 Maxwell Drive
Clifton Park, NY 12065-2919
USA

Cengage Learning is a leading provider of customized learning solutions with office locations around the globe, including Singapore, the United Kingdom, Australia, Mexico, Brazil, and Japan. Locate your local office at: **international.cengage.com/region**

Cengage Learning products are represented in Canada by Nelson Education, Ltd.

NOTICE TO THE READER

Printed in the United States of America
1 2 3 4 5 6 7 17 16 15 14 13 12

Table of Contents

Sections

1   Crown Victoria, Grand Marquis, Town Car

2   Edge, MKX

3   E-Series

4   Escape, Escape Hybrid, Mariner, Mariner Hybrid

5   Expedition, Navigator

6   Explorer, Mountaineer, Sport Trac

7   F-150, SVT Raptor

8   F-250, F-350

9   Fiesta

DTC   Diagnostic Trouble Codes

Model Index

Model	Section No.
C	
Crown Victoria	1-1
E	
E-Series	3-1
Edge	2-1
Escape	4-1
Escape Hybrid	4-1
Expedition	5-1
Explorer	6-1

Model	Section No.
F	
F-150	7-1
F-250	8-1
F-350	8-1
Fiesta	9-1
G	
Grand Marquis	1-1
M	
Mariner	4-1
Mariner Hybrid	4-1
MKX	2-1
Mountaineer	6-1

Model	Section No.
N	
Navigator	5-1
S	
Sport Trac	6-1
SVT Raptor	7-1
T	
Town Car	1-1

USING THIS INFORMATION

Organization

To find where a particular model section or procedure is located, look in the Table of Contents. Main topics are listed with the page number on which they may be found. Following the main topics is an alphabetical listing of all of the procedures within the section and their page numbers.

Manufacturer and Model Coverage

This product covers 2010-11 Ford Motor Company models that are produced in sufficient quantities to warrant coverage, and which have technical content available from the vehicle manufacturers before our publication date. Although this information is as complete as possible at the time of publication, some manufacturers may make changes which cannot be included here. While striving for total accuracy, the publisher cannot assume responsibility for any errors, changes, or omissions that may occur in the compilation of this data.

Part Numbers and Special Tools

Part numbers and special tools are recommended by the publisher and vehicle manufacturer to perform specific jobs. Before substituting any part or tool for the one recommended, you must be completely satisfied that neither your personal safety, nor the performance of the vehicle will be endangered.

ACKNOWLEDGEMENT

This product contains material that is reproduced and distributed under license from Ford Motor Company. No further reproduction or distribution of the Ford Motor Company material is allowed without express written permission from Ford Motor Company.

PRECAUTIONS

Before servicing any vehicle, please be sure to read all of the following precautions, which deal with personal safety, prevention of component damage, and important points to take into consideration when servicing a motor vehicle:

- Always wear safety glasses or goggles when drilling, cutting, grinding or prying.
- Steel-toed work shoes should be worn when working with heavy parts. Pockets should not be used for carrying tools. A slip or fall can drive a screwdriver into your body.
- Work surfaces, including tools and the floor should be kept clean of grease, oil or other slippery material.
- When working around moving parts, don't wear loose clothing. Long hair should be tied back under a hat or cap, or in a hair net.
- Always use tools only for the purpose for which they were designed. Never pry with a screwdriver.
- Keep a fire extinguisher and first aid kit handy.
- Always properly support the vehicle with approved stands or lift.
- Always have adequate ventilation when working with chemicals or hazardous material.
- Carbon monoxide is colorless, odorless and dangerous. If it is necessary to operate the engine with vehicle in a closed area such as a garage, always use an exhaust collector to vent the exhaust gases outside the closed area.

- When draining coolant, keep in mind that small children and some pets are attracted by ethylene glycol antifreeze, and are quite likely to drink any left in an open container, or in puddles on the ground. This will prove fatal in sufficient quantity. Always drain the coolant into a sealable container.
- To avoid personal injury, do not remove the coolant pressure relief cap while the engine is operating or hot. The cooling system is under pressure; steam and hot liquid can come out forcefully when the cap is loosened slightly. Failure to follow these instructions may result in personal injury. The coolant must be recovered in a suitable, clean container for reuse. If the coolant is contaminated it must be recycled or disposed of correctly.
- When carrying out maintenance on the starting system be aware that heavy gauge leads are connected directly to the battery. Make sure the protective caps are in place when maintenance is completed. Failure to follow these instructions may result in personal injury.
- Do not remove any part of the engine emission control system. Operating the engine without the engine emission control system will reduce fuel economy and engine ventilation. This will weaken engine performance and shorten engine life. It is also a violation of Federal law.
- Due to environmental concerns, when the air conditioning system is drained, the

refrigerant must be collected using refrigerant recovery/recycling equipment. Federal law requires that refrigerant be recovered into appropriate recovery equipment and the process be conducted by qualified technicians who have been certified by an approved organization, such as MACS, ASI, etc. Use of a recovery machine dedicated to the appropriate refrigerant is necessary to reduce the possibility of oil and refrigerant incompatibility concerns. Refer to the instructions provided by the equipment manufacturer when removing refrigerant from or charging the air conditioning system.

- Always disconnect the battery ground when working on or around the electrical system.
- Batteries contain sulfuric acid. Avoid contact with skin, eyes, or clothing. Also, shield your eyes when working near batteries to protect against possible splashing of the acid solution. In case of acid contact with skin or eyes, flush immediately with water for a minimum of 15 minutes and get prompt medical attention. If acid is swallowed, call a physician immediately. Failure to follow these instructions may result in personal injury.
- Batteries normally produce explosive gases. Therefore, do not allow flames, sparks or lighted substances to come near the battery. When charging or working near a battery, always shield your face and protect your eyes. Always provide ventilation. Failure to follow these instructions may result in personal injury.

• When lifting a battery, excessive pressure on the end walls could cause acid to spew through the vent caps, resulting in personal injury, damage to the vehicle or battery. Lift with a battery carrier or with your hands on opposite corners. Failure to follow these instructions may result in personal injury.

• Observe all applicable safety precautions when working around fuel. Whenever servicing the fuel system, always work in a well-ventilated area. Do not allow fuel spray or vapors to come in contact with a spark, open flame, or excessive heat (a hot drop light, for example). Keep a dry chemical fire extinguisher near the work area. Always keep fuel in a container specifically designed for fuel storage; also, always properly seal fuel containers to avoid the possibility of fire or explosion. Do not smoke or carry lighted tobacco or open flame of any type when working on or near any fuel-related components.

• Fuel injection systems often remain pressurized, even after the engine has been turned OFF. The fuel system pressure must be relieved before disconnecting any fuel lines. Failure to do so may result in fire and/or personal injury.

• The evaporative emissions system contains fuel vapor and condensed fuel vapor. Although not present in large quantities, it still presents the danger of explosion or fire. Disconnect the battery ground cable from the battery to minimize the possibility of an electrical spark occurring, possibly causing a fire or explosion if fuel vapor or liquid fuel is present in the area. Failure to follow these instructions can result in personal injury.

• The EPA warns that prolonged contact with used engine oil may cause a number of skin disorders, including cancer! You should make every effort to minimize your exposure to used engine oil. Protective gloves should be worn when changing oil. Wash your hands and any other exposed skin areas as soon as possible after exposure to used engine oil. Soap and water, or waterless hand cleaner should be used.

• Some vehicles are equipped with an air bag system, often referred to as a Supplemental Restraint System (SRS) or Supplemental Inflatable Restraint (SIR) system. The system must be disabled before performing service on or around system components, steering column, instrument panel components, wiring and sensors. Failure to follow safety and disabling procedures could result in accidental air bag deployment, possible personal injury and unnecessary system repairs.

• Always wear safety goggles when working with, or around, the air bag system. When carrying a non-deployed air bag, be sure the bag and trim cover are pointed away from your body. When placing a non-deployed air bag on a work surface, always face the bag and trim cover upward, away from the surface. This will reduce the motion of the module if it is accidentally deployed.

• Electronic modules are sensitive to electrical charges. The ABS module can be damaged if exposed to these charges.

• Brake pads and shoes may contain asbestos, which has been determined to be a cancer-causing agent. Never clean brake surfaces with compressed air. Avoid inhaling brake dust. Clean all brake surfaces with a commercially available brake cleaning fluid.

• When replacing brake pads, shoes, discs or drums, replace them as complete axle sets.

• When servicing drum brakes, disassemble and assemble one side at a time, leaving the remaining side intact for reference.

• Brake fluid often contains polyglycol ethers and polyglycols. Avoid contact with the eyes and wash your hands thoroughly after handling brake fluid. If you do get brake fluid in your eyes, flush your eyes with clean, running water for 15 minutes. If eye irritation persists, or if you have taken brake fluid internally, immediately seek medical assistance.

• Clean, high quality brake fluid from a sealed container is essential to the safe and proper operation of the brake system. You should always buy the correct type of brake fluid for your vehicle. If the brake fluid becomes contaminated, completely flush the system with new fluid. Never reuse any brake fluid. Any brake fluid that is removed from the system should be discarded. Also, do not allow any brake fluid to come in contact with a painted or plastic surface; it will damage the paint.

• Never operate the engine without the proper amount and type of engine oil; doing so will result in severe engine damage.

• Timing belt maintenance is extremely important! Many models utilize an interference-type, non-freewheeling engine. If the timing belt breaks, the valves in the cylinder head may strike the pistons, causing potentially serious (also time-consuming and expensive) engine damage.

• Disconnecting the negative battery cable on some vehicles may interfere with the functions of the on-board computer system (s) and may require the computer to undergo a relearning process once the negative battery cable is reconnected.

• Steering and suspension fasteners are critical parts because they affect performance of vital components and systems and their failure can result in major service expense. They must be replaced with the same grade or part number or an equivalent part if replacement is necessary. Do not use a replacement part of lesser quality or substitute design. Torque values must be used as specified during reassembly.

FORD, LINCOLN AND MERCURY

Crown Victoria • Grand Marquis • Town Car

BRAKES 1-10

ANTI-LOCK BRAKE SYSTEM (ABS) 1-10
General Information 1-10
  Precautions 1-10
Speed Sensors 1-10
  Removal & Installation 1-10

BLEEDING THE BRAKE SYSTEM 1-11
Bleeding Procedure 1-11
  Bleeding Procedure 1-11
  Bleeding the ABS System 1-12
  Fluid Fill Procedure 1-12

FRONT DISC BRAKES 1-13
Brake Caliper 1-13
  Removal & Installation 1-13
Disc Brake Pads 1-13
  Removal & Installation 1-13

PARKING BRAKE 1-15
Parking Brake Cables 1-15
  Adjustment 1-15
Parking Brake Shoes 1-16
  Adjustment 1-16
  Removal & Installation 1-16

REAR DISC BRAKES 1-14
Brake Caliper 1-14
  Removal & Installation 1-14
Disc Brake Pads 1-15
  Removal & Installation 1-15

CHASSIS ELECTRICAL 1-17

AIR BAG (SUPPLEMENTAL RESTRAINT SYSTEM) 1-17
General Information 1-17
  Arming the System 1-18
  Clockspring Centering 1-18
  Disarming the System 1-18
  Service Precautions 1-17

DRIVE TRAIN 1-18

Automatic Transaxle Fluid 1-18
  Drain and Refill 1-18
  Filter Replacement 1-18
Driveshaft 1-19
  Removal & Installation 1-19

Rear Axle Fluid 1-20
  Drain & Refill 1-20
Rear Axle Housing Cover 1-20
  Removal & Installation 1-20
Rear Axle Shaft 1-21
  Removal & Installation 1-21
Rear Axle Shaft Bearing & Seal 1-22
  Removal & Installation 1-22
Rear Pinion Seal 1-23
  Removal & Installation 1-23

ENGINE COOLING 1-24

Engine Coolant 1-24
  Bleeding 1-24
  Drain & Refill Procedure 1-24
Engine Fan 1-25
  Removal & Installation 1-25
Radiator 1-25
  Removal & Installation 1-25
Thermostat 1-26
  Removal & Installation 1-26
Water Pump 1-27
  Removal & Installation 1-27

ENGINE ELECTRICAL 1-28

BATTERY SYSTEM 1-28
Battery 1-28
  Battery Reconnect/Relearn Procedure 1-28
  Removal & Installation 1-28
CHARGING SYSTEM 1-29
Alternator 1-29
  Removal & Installation 1-29
IGNITION SYSTEM 1-30
Firing Order 1-30
Ignition Coil 1-30
  Removal & Installation 1-30
Ignition Timing 1-30
  Adjustment 1-30
Spark Plugs 1-30
  Inspection 1-30
  Removal & Installation 1-30
STARTING SYSTEM 1-32
Starter 1-32
  Removal & Installation 1-32

ENGINE MECHANICAL 1-33

Accessory Drive Belts 1-33
  Accessory Belt Routing 1-33
  Adjustment 1-33
  Inspection 1-33
  Removal & Installation 1-33
Air Cleaner 1-33
  Filter/Element Replacement .. 1-33
  Removal & Installation 1-33
Camshaft and Valve Lifters 1-33
  Inspection 1-33
  Removal & Installation 1-34
Catalytic Converter 1-35
  Removal & Installation 1-35
Crankshaft Front Seal 1-38
  Removal & Installation 1-38
Cylinder Head 1-38
  Removal & Installation 1-38
Engine Oil & Filter 1-40
  Replacement 1-40
Exhaust Manifold 1-41
  Removal & Installation 1-41
Intake Manifold 1-43
  Removal & Installation 1-43
Oil Pan 1-44
  Removal & Installation 1-44
Oil Pump 1-44
  Removal & Installation 1-44
Piston and Ring 1-45
  Positioning 1-45
Rear Main Seal 1-46
  Removal & Installation 1-46
Timing Chain & Sprockets 1-47
  Removal & Installation 1-47
Timing Chain Front Cover 1-46
  Removal & Installation 1-46
Valve Covers 1-49
  Removal & Installation 1-49

ENGINE PERFORMANCE & EMISSION CONTROLS 1-51

Camshaft Position (CMP) Sensor 1-51
  Location 1-51
  Removal & Installation 1-51

Crankshaft Position (CKP)
Sensor 1-51
  Location 1-51
  Removal & Installation.....1-51
Electronic Control Module
(ECM) 1-51
  Removal & Installation.........1-51
Heated Oxygen (HO2S)
Sensor 1-52
  Location 1-52
  Removal & Installation.........1-52
Knock Sensor (KS)..............1-52
  Location 1-52
  Removal & Installation.........1-52
Mass Air Flow (MAF)
Sensor 1-52
  Removal & Installation.........1-52
Throttle Position Sensor
(TPS) 1-52
  Location 1-52
  Removal & Installation.........1-52

FUEL............................1-53

**GASOLINE FUEL INJECTION
SYSTEM........................1-53**
Fuel Filter.........................1-54
  Removal & Installation.........1-54
Fuel Injectors 1-54
  Removal & Installation.........1-54
Fuel Pump.........................1-55
  Removal & Installation.........1-55
Fuel System Service
Precautions 1-53
Fuel Tank..........................1-56
  Draining.........................1-56
  Removal & Installation.........1-56
Idle Speed 1-57
  Adjustment 1-57
Relieving Fuel System
Pressure...........................1-54

Throttle Body....................1-57
  Removal & Installation.........1-57

**HEATING & AIR CONDITIONING
SYSTEM........................1-57**

Blower Motor 1-57
  Removal & Installation.........1-57
Heater Core 1-58
  Removal & Installation.........1-58

PRECAUTIONS 1-10

**SPECIFICATIONS AND
MAINTENANCE CHARTS 1-3**

Brake Specifications 1-7
Camshaft Specifications 1-5
Capacities 1-4
Crankshaft and Connecting
Rod Specifications 1-5
Engine and Vehicle
Identification 1-3
Engine Tune-Up Specifications ...1-3
Fluid Specifications....................1-4
General Engine Specifications.....1-3
Piston and Ring Specifications ...1-6
Scheduled Maintenance
Intervals 1-8,9
Tire, Wheel and Ball Joint
Specifications 1-7
Torque Specifications.................1-6
Valve Specifications 1-5
Wheel Alignment......................1-6

STEERING 1-60

Power Steering Gear................1-60
  Removal & Installation..........1-60
Power Steering Pump...............1-61
  Bleeding & Flushing............1-61

Fluid Fill Procedure 1-62
Purging...........................1-62
  Removal & Installation.........1-61

SUSPENSION.................1-63

FRONT SUSPENSION.........1-63
Coil Spring............................1-63
  Removal & Installation.........1-63
Control Links 1-64
  Removal & Installation.........1-64
Lower Ball Joint 1-64
  Removal & Installation.........1-64
Lower Control Arm..................1-64
  Removal & Installation.........1-64
Stabilizer Bar 1-65
  Removal & Installation.........1-65
Steering Knuckle 1-66
  Removal & Installation.........1-66
Strut & Spring Assembly 1-66
  Removal & Installation.........1-66
Upper Control Arm..................1-68
  Removal & Installation.........1-68
Wheel Bearings 1-68
  Removal & Installation.........1-68
REAR SUSPENSION 1-69
Coil Spring............................1-69
  Removal & Installation.........1-69
Lower Control Arm..................1-70
  Removal & Installation.........1-70
Stabilizer Bar 1-71
  Removal & Installation.........1-71
Strut Assembly 1-71
  Removal & Installation.........1-71
Upper Control Arm..................1-72
  Removal & Installation.........1-72

SPECIFICATIONS AND MAINTENANCE CHARTS

ENGINE AND VEHICLE IDENTIFICATION

Code ①	Engine						Model Year	
	Liters (cc)	Cu. In.	Cyl.	Fuel Sys.	Engine Type	Eng. Mfg.	Code ②	Year
W	4.6	4600	8	MFI	SOHC	Ford	A	2010
V	4.6	4600	8	MFI	SOHC	Ford	B	2011

① 8th position of VIN

② 10th position of VIN

25759_CVIC_C0001

GENERAL ENGINE SPECIFICATIONS

All measurements are given in inches.

Year	Model	Engine Displacement Liters	Engine ID/VIN	Fuel System Type	Net Horsepower @ rpm	Net Torque @ rpm (ft. lbs.)	Bore x Stroke (in.)	Com-pression Ratio	Oil Pressure @ rpm
2010	Crown Victoria	4.6	W	MFI	239@4800	286@3500	3.55x3.54	9.4:1	40-75@2000
		4.6	V	MFI	297@4500	350@2500	3.55x3.54	9.4:1	40-75@2000
	Grand Marquis	4.6	W	MFI	239@4800	286@3500	3.55x3.54	9.4:1	40-75@2000
		4.6	V	MFI	297@4500	350@2500	3.55x3.54	9.4:1	40-75@2000
	Town Car	4.6	W	MFI	239@4800	286@3500	3.55x3.54	9.4:1	40-75@2000
		4.6	V	MFI	297@4500	350@2500	3.55x3.54	9.4:1	40-75@2000
2011	Crown Victoria	4.6	W	MFI	239@4800	286@3500	3.55x3.54	9.4:1	40-75@2000
		4.6	V	MFI	297@4500	350@2500	3.55x3.54	9.4:1	40-75@2000
	Grand Marquis	4.6	W	MFI	239@4800	286@3500	3.55x3.54	9.4:1	40-75@2000
		4.6	V	MFI	297@4500	350@2500	3.55x3.54	9.4:1	40-75@2000
	Town Car	4.6	W	MFI	239@4800	286@3500	3.55x3.54	9.4:1	40-75@2000
		4.6	V	MFI	297@4500	350@2500	3.55x3.54	9.4:1	40-75@2000

25759_CVIC_C0002

ENGINE TUNE-UP SPECIFICATIONS

Year	Engine Displacement Liters	Engine ID/VIN	Spark Plug Gap (in.)	Ignition Timing (deg.)	Fuel Pump (psi)	Idle Speed (rpm)	Valve Clearance	
							Intake	Exhaust
2010	4.6	W	0.043-0.047	①	②	2,000	0.0008-0.0027	0.0018-0.0037
	4.6	V	0.043-0.047	①	②	2,000	0.0008-0.0027	0.0018-0.0037
2011	4.6	W	0.043-0.047	①	②	2,000	0.0008-0.0027	0.0018-0.0037
	4.6	V	0.043-0.047	①	②	2,000	0.0008-0.0027	0.0018-0.0037

NE: Not Equipped

① 10 degrees Before Top Dead Center (BTDC) and is not adjustable

② Key ON Engine Running (KOER): 28-45 psi

Key On Engine OFF (KOEO): 35-45 psi

25759_CVIC_C0003

CAPACITIES

Year	Model	Engine Displacement Liters	Engine ID/VIN	Engine Oil with Filter	Transmission/axle (pts.) Auto.	Manual	Drive Axle (pts.) Front	Rear	Transfer Case (pts.)	Fuel Tank (gal.)	Cooling System (qts.)
2010	Crown Victoria	4.6	W	6	26	NE	NA	5	NA	19	19
		4.6	V	6	26	NE	NA	5	NA	19	19
	Grand Marquis	4.6	W	6	26	NE	NA	5	NA	19	19
		4.6	V	6	26	NE	NA	5	NA	19	19
	Town Car	4.6	W	6	26	NE	NA	5	NA	19	19
		4.6	V	6	26	NE	NA	5	NA	19	19
2011	Crown Victoria	4.6	W	6	26	NE	NA	5	NA	19	19
		4.6	V	6	26	NE	NA	5	NA	19	19
	Grand Marquis	4.6	W	6	26	NE	NA	5	NA	19	19
		4.6	V	6	26	NE	NA	5	NA	19	19
	Town Car	4.6	W	6	26	NE	NA	5	NA	19	19
		4.6	V	6	26	NE	NA	5	NA	19	19

NA: Not Available

NE: Not Equipped

NOTE: All capacities are approximate. Add fluid gradually and ensure a proper fluid level is obtained.

25759_CVIC_C0004

FLUID SPECIFICATIONS

Year	Model	Engine Disp. Liters	Engine ID/VIN	Engine Oil	Auto. Trans.	Rear Drive Axle	Power Steering Fluid	Brake Master Cylinder	Cooling System
2010	Crown Victoria	4.6	W	5W-20	XT-10-QLV	①	ATF XT-5-QM	DOT 3	②
		4.6	V	5W-20	XT-10-QLV	①	ATF XT-5-QM	DOT 3	②
	Grand Marquis	4.6	W	5W-20	XT-10-QLV	①	ATF XT-5-QM	DOT 3	②
		4.6	V	5W-20	XT-10-QLV	①	ATF XT-5-QM	DOT 3	②
	Town Car	4.6	W	5W-20	XT-10-QLV	①	ATF XT-5-QM	DOT 3	②
		4.6	V	5W-20	XT-10-QLV	①	ATF XT-5-QM	DOT 3	②
2011	Crown Victoria	4.6	W	5W-20	XT-10-QLV	①	ATF XT-5-QM	DOT 3	②
		4.6	V	5W-20	XT-10-QLV	①	ATF XT-5-QM	DOT 3	②
	Grand Marquis	4.6	W	5W-20	XT-10-QLV	①	ATF XT-5-QM	DOT 3	②
		4.6	V	5W-20	XT-10-QLV	①	ATF XT-5-QM	DOT 3	②
	Town Car	4.6	W	5W-20	XT-10-QLV	①	ATF XT-5-QM	DOT 3	②
		4.6	V	5W-20	XT-10-QLV	①	ATF XT-5-QM	DOT 3	②

NE: Not Equipped

① Synthetic: 75W-140

   Normal: 80W-90

② Motorcraft® Premium Gold Engine Coolant with Bittering Agent

25759_CVIC_C0005

VALVE SPECIFICATIONS

Year	Engine Displacement Liters	VIN	Seat Angle (deg.)	Face Angle (deg.)	Spring Test Pressure (lbs. @ in.)	Spring Free-Length (in.)	Spring Installed Height (in.)	Stem-to-Guide Clearance (in.)		Stem Diameter (in.)	
								Intake	Exhaust	Intake	Exhaust
2010	4.6	W	45.5	45.25-45.75	131.994 lb@1.1032	1.951	1.5630-1.5866	0.0008-0.0027	0.0018-0.0037	0.2746-0.2754	0.2736-0.2744
	4.6	V	45.5	45.25-45.75	131.994 lb@1.1032	1.951	1.5630-1.5866	0.0008-0.0027	0.0018-0.0037	0.2746-0.2754	0.2736-0.2744
2011	4.6	W	45.5	45.25-45.75	131.994 lb@1.1032	1.951	1.5630-1.5866	0.0008-0.0027	0.0018-0.0037	0.2746-0.2754	0.2736-0.2744
	4.6	V	45.5	45.25-45.75	131.994 lb@1.1032	1.951	1.5630-1.5866	0.0008-0.0027	0.0018-0.0037	0.2746-0.2754	0.2736-0.2744

25759_CVIC_C0006

CAMSHAFT SPECIFICATIONS

All measurements in inches unless noted

Year	Engine Displacement Liters	Engine Code/VIN	Journal Diameter	Brg. Oil Clearance	Shaft End-play	Runout	Journal Bore	Lobe Height	
								Intake	Exhaust
2010	4.6	W	1.0605-1.0615	0.0010-0.0030	0.001-0.007	0.003	1.0625-1.0635	0.2799	0.2951
	4.6	V	1.0605-1.0615	0.0010-0.0030	0.001-0.007	0.003	1.0625-1.0635	0.2799	0.2951
2011	4.6	W	1.0605-1.0615	0.0010-0.0030	0.001-0.007	0.003	1.0625-1.0635	0.2799	0.2951
	4.6	V	1.0605-1.0615	0.0010-0.0030	0.001-0.007	0.003	1.0625-1.0635	0.2799	0.2951

25759_CVIC_C0007

CRANKSHAFT AND CONNECTING ROD SPECIFICATIONS

All measurements are given in inches.

Year	Engine Displacement Liters	Engine ID/VIN	Crankshaft				Connecting Rod		
			Main Brg. Journal Dia.	Main Brg. Oil Clearance	Shaft End-play	Thrust on No.	Journal Diameter	Oil Clearance	Side Clearance
2010	4.6	W	2.65	0.0011-0.0026	0.0051-0.012	NA	NA	NA	0.002
	4.6	V	2.65	0.0011-0.0026	0.0051-0.012	NA	NA	NA	0.002
2011	4.6	W	2.65	0.0011-0.0026	0.0051-0.012	NA	NA	NA	0.002
	4.6	V	2.65	0.0011-0.0026	0.0051-0.012	NA	NA	NA	0.002

NA: Not Available

25759_CVIC_C0008

PISTON AND RING SPECIFICATIONS
All measurements are given in inches.

Year	Engine Displacement Liters	VIN	Piston Clearance	Ring Gap			Ring Side Clearance		
				Top Compression	Bottom Compression	Oil Control	Top Compression	Bottom Compression	Oil Control
2010	4.6	W	NA	0.010-0.020	0.010-0.020	0.006-0.026	0.002-0.610	0.060-0.0602	0.275-0.2844
	4.6	V	NA	0.010-0.020	0.010-0.020	0.006-0.026	0.002-0.610	0.060-0.0602	0.275-0.2844
2011	4.6	W	NA	0.010-0.020	0.010-0.020	0.006-0.026	0.002-0.610	0.060-0.0602	0.275-0.2844
	4.6	V	NA	0.010-0.020	0.010-0.020	0.006-0.026	0.002-0.610	0.060-0.0602	0.275-0.2844

NA: Not available

25759_CVIC_C0009

TORQUE SPECIFICATIONS
All readings in ft. lbs.

Year	Engine Disp. Liters	Engine ID/VIN	Cylinder Head Bolts	Main Bearing Bolts	Rod Bearing Bolts	Crankshaft Damper Bolts	Flywheel Bolts	Manifold		Spark Plugs	Oil Pan Drain Plug
								Intake	Exhaust		
2010	4.6	W	①	NA	NA	18	②	7	18	18	17
	4.6	V	①	NA	NA	18	②	7	18	18	17
2011	4.6	W	①	NA	NA	18	②	7	18	18	17
	4.6	V	①	NA	NA	18	②	7	18	18	17

① Stage 1: Tighten to 30 ft. lbs.

Stage 2: Tighten an additional 90 degrees (one-fourth turn)

Stage 3: Loosen a minimum of one full turn (360 degrees)

Stage 4: Tighten to 30 ft. lbs.

Stage 5: Tighten an additional 90 degrees (one-fourth turn)

Stage 6: Tighten an additional 90 degrees (one-fourth turn)

② First pass: 14 ft. lbs. (20 Nm)

Second pass: 59 ft. lbs. (80 Nm)

25759_CVIC_C0010

WHEEL ALIGNMENT

Year	Model		Caster		Camber		Toe-in (in.)
			Range (+/-Deg.)	Preferred Setting (Deg.)	Range (+/-Deg.)	Preferred Setting (Deg.)	
2010	Crown Victoria	LH	0.75	6.2	0.75	0.4	0.2
		RH	0.75	6.4	0.75	0.4	0.2
	Grand Marquis	LH	0.75	6.2	0.75	0.4	0.2
		RH	0.75	6.4	0.75	0.4	0.2
	Town Car	LH	0.75	6.2	0.75	0.6	0.2
		RH	0.75	6.4	0.75	0.6	0.2
2011	Crown Victoria	LH	0.75	6.2	0.75	0.4	0.2
		RH	0.75	6.4	0.75	0.4	0.2
	Grand Marquis	LH	0.75	6.2	0.75	0.4	0.2
		RH	0.75	6.4	0.75	0.4	0.2
	Town Car	LH	0.75	6.2	0.75	0.6	0.2
		RH	0.75	6.4	0.75	0.6	0.2

25759_CVIC_C0011

TIRE, WHEEL AND BALL JOINT SPECIFICATIONS

| Year | Model | OEM Tires | | Tire Pressures (psi) | | Wheel Size | Ball Joint Inspection | Lug Nut (ft. lbs.) |
		Standard	Optional	Front	Rear			
2010	Crown Victoria	NA	NA	NA	NA	NA	NA	100
	Grand Marquis	NA	NA	NA	NA	NA	NA	100
	Town Car	NA	NA	NA	NA	NA	NA	100
2011	Crown Victoria	NA	NA	NA	NA	NA	NA	100
	Grand Marquis	NA	NA	NA	NA	NA	NA	100
	Town Car	NA	NA	NA	NA	NA	NA	100

OEM: Original Equipment Manufacturer

PSI: Pounds Per Square Inch

NA: Information not available

25759_CVIC_C0012

BRAKE SPECIFICATIONS

All measurements in inches unless noted

| Year | Model | | Brake Disc | | | Minimum Pad/Lining Thickness | | Brake Caliper | |
			Original Thickness	Minimum Thickness	Max. Runout	Front	Rear	Bracket Bolts (ft. lbs.)	Mounting Bolts (ft. lbs.)
2010	Crown Victoria	F	NA	1.037	NA	0.118	0.118	27	NA
		R	NA	0.708	NA	0.118	0.118	27	NA
	Grand Marquis	F	NA	1.037	NA	0.118	0.118	27	NA
		R	NA	0.708	NA	0.118	0.118	27	NA
	Town Car	F	NA	1.037	NA	0.118	0.118	27	NA
		R	NA	0.708	NA	0.118	0.118	27	NA
2011	Crown Victoria	F	NA	1.037	NA	0.118	0.118	27	NA
		R	NA	0.708	NA	0.118	0.118	27	NA
	Grand Marquis	F	NA	1.037	NA	0.118	0.118	27	NA
		R	NA	0.708	NA	0.118	0.118	27	NA
	Town Car	F	NA	1.037	NA	0.118	0.118	27	NA
		R	NA	0.708	NA	0.118	0.118	27	NA

F: Front

R: Rear

NA: Information not available

25759_CVIC_C0013

SCHEDULED MAINTENANCE INTERVALS
2010-11 Ford Crown Victoria, Mercury Grand Marquis and Lincoln Town Car - Normal

Service Item	Service Action	7500	15000	22500	30000	37500	45000	52500	60000	67500	75000	82500	90000	97500	105000
Engine oil & filter	Service	✓	✓	✓	✓	✓	✓	✓	✓	✓	✓	✓	✓	✓	✓
Rotate tires, inspect tread wear, measure tread depth and check pressure	Rotate/ Inspect		✓		✓		✓		✓		✓		✓		✓
Inspect wheels and related components for abnomal noise, wear, looseness or drag	Inspect	✓	✓	✓	✓	✓	✓	✓	✓	✓	✓	✓	✓	✓	✓
Brake system (Inspect brake pads, shoes, rotors, drums, brake lines, hoses and parking brake system (adjust parking brake if required).	Inspect		✓		✓		✓		✓		✓		✓		✓
Engine coolant strength hoses & clamps	Inspect		✓		✓		✓		✓		✓		✓		✓
Steering linkage, suspension, driveshaft U-joints	Inspect/ Lubricate	✓	✓	✓	✓	✓	✓	✓	✓	✓	✓	✓	✓	✓	✓
Engine air filter	Replace				✓				✓				✓		✓
Fuel filter	Replace				✓				✓				✓		
Drive belt(s)	Inspect	✓	✓	✓	✓	✓	✓	✓	✓	✓	✓	✓	✓	✓	✓
Drive belt(s)	Replace														
Shocks struts and other suspension components for leaks and damage	Inspect	✓	✓	✓	✓	✓	✓	✓	✓	✓	✓	✓	✓	✓	✓
Engine air filter	Inspect	✓	✓	✓	✓	✓	✓	✓	✓	✓	✓	✓	✓	✓	✓
Oil and fluid leaks	Inspect	✓	✓	✓	✓	✓	✓	✓	✓	✓	✓	✓	✓	✓	✓
Windshield wiper spray and wiper operation	Inspect	✓	✓	✓	✓	✓	✓	✓	✓	✓	✓	✓	✓	✓	✓
Windshield for cracks, chips and pitting	Inspect	✓	✓	✓	✓	✓	✓	✓	✓	✓	✓	✓	✓	✓	✓
Radiator, coolers, heater and airconditioning hoses	Inspect	✓	✓	✓	✓	✓	✓	✓	✓	✓	✓	✓	✓	✓	✓
Horn, exterior lamps, turn signals and hazard warning light operation	Inspect	✓	✓	✓	✓	✓	✓	✓	✓	✓	✓	✓	✓	✓	✓
Battery	Inspect	✓	✓	✓	✓	✓	✓	✓	✓	✓	✓	✓	✓	✓	✓
Exhaust system (Leaks, damage, loose parts and foreign material)	Inspect	✓	✓	✓	✓	✓	✓	✓	✓	✓	✓	✓	✓	✓	✓
Fluid levels (all)	Top off	✓	✓	✓	✓	✓	✓	✓	✓	✓	✓	✓	✓	✓	✓
Engine coolant	Replace														✓
Spark plugs	Replace														✓

Use of E85 50% of the time or greater, change engine oil and filter every 5,000 miles or 6 months.

25759_CVIC_C0014

SCHEDULED MAINTENANCE INTERVALS
2010-11 Ford Crown Victoria, Mercury Grand Marquis and Lincoln Town Car - Severe

Service Item	Service Action	5000	10000	15000	20000	25000	30000	35000	40000	45000	50000	55000	60000	65000	70000
Rotate tires, inspect tread wear, measure tread depth and check pressure	Rotate/Inspect	✓	✓	✓	✓	✓	✓	✓	✓	✓	✓	✓	✓	✓	✓
Brake system (Inspect brake pads, shoes, rotors, drums, brake lines, hoses and parking brake system (adjust parking brake if required).	Inspect	✓	✓	✓	✓	✓	✓	✓	✓	✓	✓	✓	✓	✓	✓
Lubricate Drivetrain/Steering/Suspension grease fittings	Inspect/Lubricate	✓	✓	✓	✓	✓	✓	✓	✓	✓	✓	✓	✓	✓	✓
Fuel filter	Replace	✓	✓	✓	✓	✓	✓	✓	✓	✓	✓	✓	✓	✓	✓
Transmission fluid & filter	Replace	✓	✓	✓	✓	✓	✓	✓	✓	✓	✓	✓	✓	✓	✓
Spark plugs	Replace	✓	✓	✓	✓	✓	✓	✓	✓	✓	✓	✓	✓	✓	✓
Drive belt(s)	Inspect	✓	✓	✓	✓	✓	✓	✓	✓	✓	✓	✓	✓	✓	✓
Drive belt(s)	Replace														✓
Shocks struts and other suspension components for leaks and damage	Inspect	✓	✓	✓	✓	✓	✓	✓	✓	✓	✓	✓	✓	✓	✓
Air filter	Inspect	✓	✓	✓	✓	✓	✓	✓	✓	✓	✓	✓	✓	✓	✓
Oil and fluid leaks	Inspect	✓	✓	✓	✓	✓	✓	✓	✓	✓	✓	✓	✓	✓	✓
Windshield for cracks, chips and pitting	Inspect	✓	✓	✓	✓	✓	✓	✓	✓	✓	✓	✓	✓	✓	✓
Windshield wiper spray and wiper operation	Inspect	✓	✓	✓	✓	✓	✓	✓	✓	✓	✓	✓	✓	✓	✓
Radiator, coolers, heater and air conditioning hoses	Inspect	✓	✓	✓	✓	✓	✓	✓	✓	✓	✓	✓	✓	✓	✓
Horn, exterior lamps, turn signals and hazard warning light operation	Inspect	✓	✓	✓	✓	✓	✓	✓	✓	✓	✓	✓	✓	✓	✓
Battery performance	Inspect	✓	✓	✓	✓	✓	✓	✓	✓	✓	✓	✓	✓	✓	✓
Exhaust system (Leaks, damage, loose parts and foreign material)	Inspect	✓	✓	✓	✓	✓	✓	✓	✓	✓	✓	✓	✓	✓	✓
Fluid levels (all)	Top off	✓	✓	✓	✓	✓	✓	✓	✓	✓	✓	✓	✓	✓	✓
Air filter	Replace	✓	✓	✓	✓	✓	✓	✓	✓	✓	✓	✓	✓	✓	✓
Engine oil & filter	Inspect	✓	✓	✓	✓	✓	✓	✓	✓	✓	✓	✓	✓	✓	✓
Rear differential fluid	Replace	✓	✓	✓	✓	✓	✓	✓	✓	✓	✓	✓	✓	✓	✓
Engine coolant	Replace														✓

For extensive idling and or low speed driving, change engine oil and filter every 5,000 miles, 6 months or 200 hours of engine operation.

25759_CVIC_C0015

PRECAUTIONS

Before servicing any vehicle, please be sure to read all of the following precautions, which deal with personal safety, prevention of component damage, and important points to take into consideration when servicing a motor vehicle:

• Never open, service or drain the radiator or cooling system when the engine is hot; serious burns can occur from the steam and hot coolant.

• Observe all applicable safety precautions when working around fuel. Whenever servicing the fuel system, always work in a well-ventilated area. Do not allow fuel spray or vapors to come in contact with a spark, open flame, or excessive heat (a hot drop light, for example). Keep a dry chemical fire extinguisher near the work area. Always keep fuel in a container specifically designed for fuel storage; also, always properly seal fuel containers to avoid the possibility of fire or explosion. Refer to the additional fuel system precautions later in this section.

• Fuel injection systems often remain pressurized, even after the engine has been turned **OFF**. The fuel system pressure must be relieved before disconnecting any fuel lines. Failure to do so may result in fire and/or personal injury.

• Brake fluid often contains polyglycol ethers and polyglycols. Avoid contact with the eyes and wash your hands thoroughly after handling brake fluid. If you do get brake fluid in your eyes, flush your eyes with clean, running water for 15 minutes. If eye irritation persists, or if you have taken brake fluid internally, IMMEDIATELY seek medical assistance.

• The EPA warns that prolonged contact with used engine oil may cause a number of skin disorders, including cancer. You should make every effort to minimize your exposure to used engine oil. Protective gloves should be worn when changing oil. Wash your hands and any other exposed skin areas as soon as possible after exposure to used engine oil. Soap and water, or waterless hand cleaner should be used.

• All new vehicles are now equipped with an air bag system, often referred to as a Supplemental Restraint System (SRS) or Supplemental Inflatable Restraint (SIR) system. The system must be disabled before performing service on or around system components, steering column, instrument panel components, wiring and sensors. Failure to follow safety and disabling procedures could result in accidental air bag deployment, possible personal injury and unnecessary system repairs.

• Always wear safety goggles when working with, or around, the air bag system. When carrying a non-deployed air bag, be sure the bag and trim cover are pointed away from your body. When placing a non-deployed air bag on a work surface, always face the bag and trim cover upward, away from the surface. This will reduce the motion of the module if it is accidentally deployed. Refer to the additional air bag system precautions later in this section.

• Clean, high quality brake fluid from a sealed container is essential to the safe and proper operation of the brake system. You should always buy the correct type of brake fluid for your vehicle. If the brake fluid becomes contaminated, completely flush the system with new fluid. Never reuse any brake fluid. Any brake fluid that is removed from the system should be discarded. Also, do not allow any brake fluid to come in contact with a painted surface; it will damage the paint.

• Never operate the engine without the proper amount and type of engine oil; doing so WILL result in severe engine damage.

• Timing belt maintenance is extremely important. Many models utilize an interference-type, non-freewheeling engine. If the timing belt breaks, the valves in the cylinder head may strike the pistons, causing potentially serious (also time-consuming and expensive) engine damage. Refer to the maintenance interval charts for the recommended replacement interval for the timing belt, and to the timing belt section for belt replacement and inspection.

• Disconnecting the negative battery cable on some vehicles may interfere with the functions of the on-board computer system(s) and may require the computer to undergo a relearning process once the negative battery cable is reconnected.

• When servicing drum brakes, only disassemble and assemble one side at a time, leaving the remaining side intact for reference.

• Only an MVAC-trained, EPA-certified automotive technician should service the air conditioning system or its components.

BRAKES

GENERAL INFORMATION

PRECAUTIONS

• Certain components within the ABS system are not intended to be serviced or repaired individually.

• Do not use rubber hoses or other parts not specifically specified for and ABS system. When using repair kits, replace all parts included in the kit. Partial or incorrect repair may lead to functional problems and require the replacement of components.

• Lubricate rubber parts with clean, fresh brake fluid to ease assembly. Do not use shop air to clean parts; damage to rubber components may result.

• Use only DOT 3 brake fluid from an unopened container.

• If any hydraulic component or line is removed or replaced, it may be necessary to bleed the entire system.

• A clean repair area is essential. Always clean the reservoir and cap thoroughly before removing the cap. The slightest amount of dirt in the fluid may plug an orifice and impair the system function. Perform repairs after components have been thoroughly cleaned; use only denatured alcohol to clean components. Do not allow ABS components to come into contact with any substance containing mineral oil; this includes used shop rags.

• The Anti-Lock control unit is a microprocessor similar to other computer units in the vehicle. Ensure that the ignition switch is **OFF** before removing or installing controller harnesses. Avoid static electricity discharge at or near the controller.

• If any arc welding is to be done on the vehicle, the control unit should be unplugged before welding operations begin.

ANTI-LOCK BRAKE SYSTEM (ABS)

SPEED SENSORS

REMOVAL & INSTALLATION

Front

The front wheel speed sensor is integrated with the wheel hub & bearing assembly. Refer to the Wheel Hub & Bearing Assembly in the Front Suspension section.

Rear

See Figure 1.

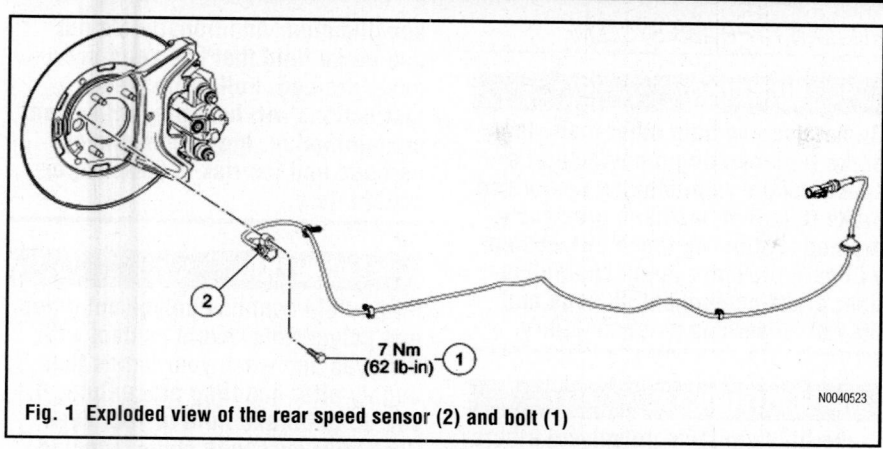

Fig. 1 Exploded view of the rear speed sensor (2) and bolt (1)

7 Nm
(62 lb-in)

N0040523

1. Disconnect the negative battery cable and wait one minute.
2. Remove the rear seat cushion.
3. Disconnect the rear wheel speed sensor electrical connector.
4. Push the wheel speed sensor harness grommet through the passenger compartment floor.
5. Disconnect the wheel speed sensor harness clips.
6. Remove the rear wheel speed sensor bolt and the sensor.
7. To install, reverse the removal procedure.

BRAKES   BLEEDING THE BRAKE SYSTEM

BLEEDING PROCEDURE

BLEEDING PROCEDURE

Pressure Bleeding

> ❊❊ **WARNING**
>
> **Do not use any fluid other than clean brake fluid meeting manufacturer's specification. Additionally, do not use brake fluid that has been previously drained. Following these instructions will help prevent system contamination, brake component damage and the risk of serious personal injury.**

> ❊❊ **CAUTION**
>
> **Brake fluid contains polyglycol ethers and polyglycols. Avoid contact with the eyes and wash your hands thoroughly after handling brake fluid. If you do get brake fluid in your eyes, flush your eyes with clean, running water for 15 minutes. If eye irritation persists, or if you have taken brake fluid internally, IMMEDIATELY seek medical assistance.**

➡ **When any part of the hydraulic system has been disconnected for repair or installation of new components, air can get into the system and cause spongy brake pedal action. This requires bleeding of the hydraulic system after it has been correctly connected.**

➡ **The Hydraulic Control Unit (HCU) bleeding procedure must be carried out if the HCU or any components upstream of the HCU are installed new.**

➡ **Pressure bleed the brake system at 30-50 psi.**

1. If equipped with a fire suppression system, depower the system, disconnect the negative battery cable and wait one minute.
2. Clean all dirt from and remove the brake master cylinder filler cap. Fill the brake master cylinder reservoir with clean, specified brake fluid.

➡ **Master cylinder pressure bleeder adapter tools are available from various manufacturers of pressure bleeding equipment. Follow the instructions of the manufacturer when installing the adapter.**

3. Install the bleeder adapter to the brake master cylinder reservoir and attach the bleeder tank hose to the fitting on the adapter.
4. Place a box-end wrench on the master cylinder bleeder screw. Attach a rubber drain hose to the bleeder screw and submerge the free end of the hose in a container partially filled with clean, specified brake fluid.

➡ **Make sure the bleeder tank contains enough clean, specified brake fluid to complete the bleeding operation.**

5. Open the valve on the bleeder tank.
6. Apply 30-50 psi to the brake system.
7. Loosen the bleeder screw and leave open until clear, bubble-free brake fluid flows into the container.
8. Remove the brake caliper bleeder screw cap and place a box-end wrench on the bleeder screw. Attach a rubber drain hose to the RH rear brake caliper bleeder screw, and submerge the free end of the hose in a container partially filled with clean, specified brake fluid.
9. Loosen the bleeder screw and leave open until clear, bubble-free brake fluid flows into the container.
10. Remove the rubber hose and install the bleeder screw cap. Tighten the brake caliper bleeder screw to specification.

11. Repeat Steps 5 through 7 for the LH rear, RH front and LH front bleeder screws in this order.
12. Release the bleeder tank pressure and close the bleeder tank valve. Remove the tank hose from the adapter and remove the adapter.
13. Install the reservoir cap.

➡ **If the brake pedal remains spongy, air may be trapped in the HCU .**

14. If the brake pedal remains spongy after pressure bleeding, carry out the ABS HCU bleeding procedure in this section with the scan tool.
15. If equipped with a fire suppression system, repower the system by connecting the negative battery calbe.

Manual Bleeding

> ❊❊ **WARNING**
>
> **Do not use any fluid other than clean brake fluid meeting manufacturer's specification. Additionally, do not use brake fluid that has been previously drained. Following these instructions will help prevent system contamination, brake component damage and the risk of serious personal injury.**

> ❊❊ **CAUTION**
>
> **Brake fluid contains polyglycol ethers and polyglycols. Avoid contact with the eyes and wash your hands thoroughly after handling brake fluid. If you do get brake fluid in your eyes, flush your eyes with clean, running water for 15 minutes. If eye irritation persists, or if you have taken brake fluid internally, IMMEDIATELY seek medical assistance.**

1. If equipped with a fire suppression system, depower the system, disconnect the negative battery cable and wait one minute.

2. Clean all dirt from the brake master cylinder filler cap and remove the filler cap.

3. Fill the brake master cylinder reservoir with clean, specified brake fluid.

4. Place a box-end wrench on the master cylinder bleeder screw. Attach a rubber drain hose to the bleeder screw and submerge the free end of the hose in a container partially filled with clean, specified brake fluid.

5. Loosen the bleeder screw and leave open until clear, bubble-free brake fluid flows into the container.

6. Remove the rubber hose.

7. Remove the brake caliper bleeder screw cap and place a box end wrench on the RH rear bleeder screw. Attach a rubber drain hose to the bleeder screw and submerge the free end of the hose in a container partially filled with clean, specified brake fluid.

8. Have an assistant pump the brake pedal and then hold firm pressure on the brake pedal.

9. Loosen the bleeder screw until a stream of brake fluid comes out. While the assistant maintains pressure on the brake pedal, tighten the bleeder screw.

10. Repeat until clear, bubble-free fluid comes out.

11. Refill the brake master cylinder reservoir as necessary.

12. Tighten the brake caliper bleeder screw to specification.

13. Remove the rubber hose and install the bleeder screw cap.

14. Repeat Steps 7 through 13 for the LH rear, RH front and LH front bleeder screws in this order.

15. If equipped with a fire suppression system, repower the system. Connect the negative battery cable.

BLEEDING THE ABS SYSTEM

※ WARNING

Do not use any fluid other than clean brake fluid meeting manufacturer's specification. Additionally, do not use brake fluid that has been previously drained. Following these instructions will help prevent system contamination, brake component damage and the risk of serious personal injury.

※ CAUTION

Brake fluid contains polyglycol ethers and polyglycols. Avoid contact with the eyes and wash your hands thoroughly after handling brake fluid. If you do get brake fluid in your eyes, flush your eyes with clean, running water for 15 minutes. If eye irritation persists, or if you have taken brake fluid internally, IMMEDIATELY seek medical assistance.

➡ Follow the Pressure Bleeding or Manual Bleeding procedure steps to bleed the system.

1. If equipped with a fire suppression system, depower the system, disconnect the negative battery cable and wait one minute.

2. Connect the scan tool and follow the ABS Service Bleed instructions.

3. Repeat the Pressure Bleeding or Manual Bleeding procedure steps to bleed the system.

4. If equipped with a fire suppression system, repower the system. Connect the negative battery cable.

FLUID FILL PROCEDURE

See Figure 2.

※ WARNING

Do not use any fluid other than clean brake fluid meeting manufacturer's specification. Additionally, do not use brake fluid that has been previously drained. Following these instructions will help prevent system contamination, brake component damage and the risk of serious personal injury.

※ CAUTION

Brake fluid contains polyglycol ethers and polyglycols. Avoid contact with the eyes and wash your hands thoroughly after handling brake fluid. If you do get brake fluid in your eyes, flush your eyes with clean, running water for 15 minutes. If eye irritation persists, or if you have taken brake fluid internally, IMMEDIATELY seek medical assistance.

1. Clean all dirt from the brake master cylinder filler cap and remove the filler cap.

2. Fill the brake master cylinder reservoir with clean, specified brake fluid.

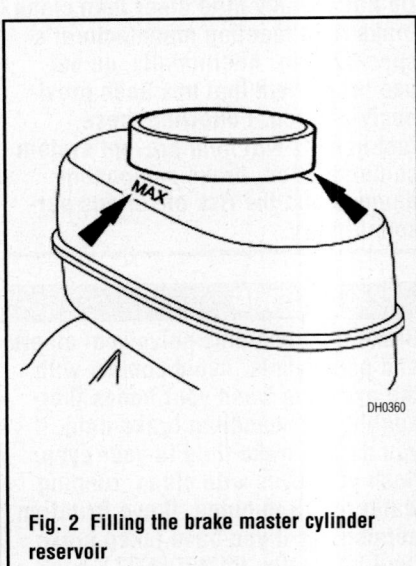

Fig. 2 Filling the brake master cylinder reservoir

BRAKES | **FRONT DISC BRAKES**

BRAKE CALIPER

REMOVAL & INSTALLATION
See Figure 3.

✳ WARNING

Do not use any fluid other than clean brake fluid meeting manufacturer's specification. Additionally, do not use brake fluid that has been previously drained. Following these instructions will help prevent system contamination, brake component damage and the risk of serious personal injury.

✳ CAUTION

Brake fluid contains polyglycol ethers and polyglycols. Avoid contact with the eyes and wash your hands thoroughly after handling brake fluid. If you do get brake fluid in your eyes, flush your eyes with clean, running water for 15 minutes. If eye irritation persists, or if you have taken brake fluid internally, IMMEDIATELY seek medical assistance.

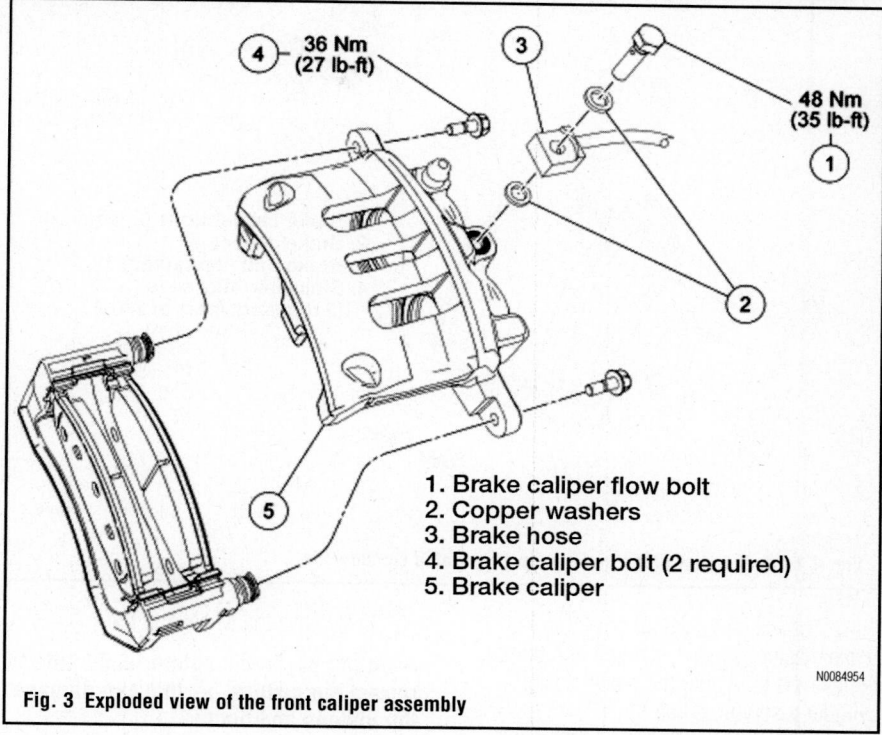

1. Brake caliper flow bolt
2. Copper washers
3. Brake hose
4. Brake caliper bolt (2 required)
5. Brake caliper

Fig. 3 Exploded view of the front caliper assembly

N0084954

1. If equipped with a fire suppression system, depower the system, disconnect the negative battery cable and wait one minute.
2. Remove the wheel and tire.
3. Remove the brake caliper flow bolt.
4. Discard the 2 copper washers.
5. Remove the 2 brake guide pin caliper bolts and the brake caliper.
6. Disconnect the brake pads from the caliper and remove the caliper.
7. Inspect the brake caliper for wear or damage. Inspect the guide pins and locating pins for wear or damage.
8. If leaks or damage are found, install a new brake caliper.

To install:

➡ Make sure guide pin boots are correctly seated or damage to guide pins may occur.

➡ Tighten the lower brake caliper bolt first.

9. Install the brake caliper to the anchor plate and install the 2 brake caliper guide pin bolts. Tighten to 27 ft. lbs. (36 Nm).
10. Using 2 new copper washers, position the brake hose and install the brake caliper flow bolt. Tighten to 35 ft. lbs. (48 Nm).
11. Bleed the brake caliper.
12. Install the wheel and tire.
13. If equipped with a fire suppression system, repower the system. Connect the negative battery cable.

DISC BRAKE PADS

REMOVAL & INSTALLATION
See Figure 4.

✳ WARNING

Do not use any fluid other than clean brake fluid meeting manufacturer's specification. Additionally, do not use brake fluid that has been previously drained. Following these instructions will help prevent system contamination, brake component damage and the risk of serious personal injury.

✳ CAUTION

Brake fluid contains polyglycol ethers and polyglycols. Avoid contact with the eyes and wash your hands thoroughly after handling brake fluid. If you do get brake fluid in your eyes, flush your eyes with clean, running water for 15 minutes. If eye irritation persists, or if you have taken brake fluid internally, IMMEDIATELY seek medical assistance.

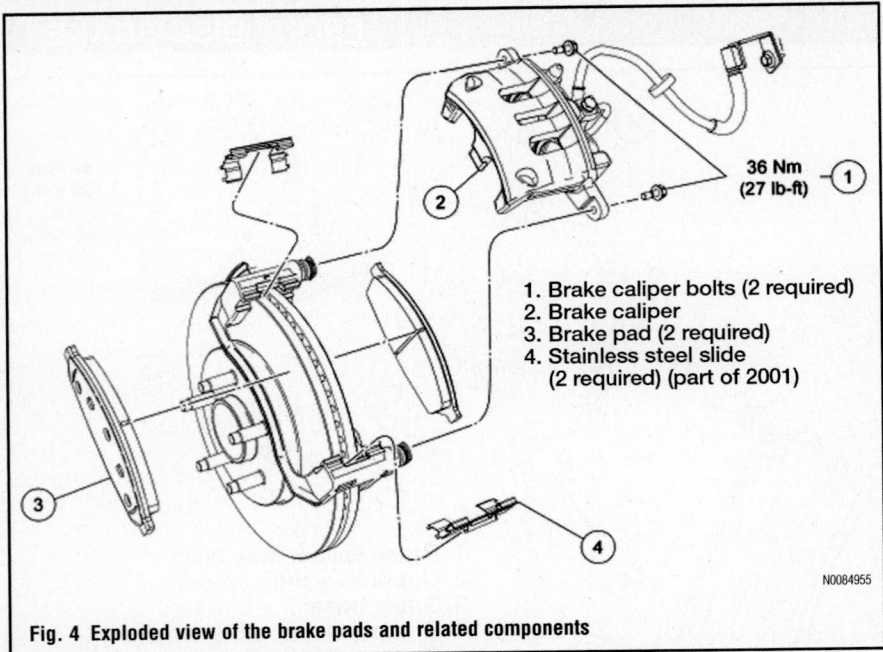

1. Brake caliper bolts (2 required)
2. Brake caliper
3. Brake pad (2 required)
4. Stainless steel slide
   (2 required) (part of 2001)

36 Nm
(27 lb-ft) — 1

N0084955

Fig. 4 Exploded view of the brake pads and related components

1. Check the brake fluid level in the brake master cylinder reservoir. If required, remove the fluid until the brake master cylinder reservoir is half full.

2. If equipped with a fire suppression system, depower the system, disconnect the negative battery cable and wait one minute.

3. Remove the wheel and tire.

➡ Do not pry in the caliper sight hole to retract the pistons, as this can damage the pistons and boots.

➡ Do not allow the brake caliper to hang from the brake hose or damage to the hose may occur.

4. Remove the 2 brake caliper guide pin bolts and position the caliper aside.

5. Support the caliper using mechanic's wire.

6. Remove the pads and stainless steel slides from the anchor plate.

7. Discard the slides.

➡ Protect the piston and boots when pushing the caliper piston into the caliper piston bores or damage to components may occur.

8. If installing new brake pads, using a suitable tool and a worn brake pad, compress the disc brake caliper pistons into the caliper.

9. To install, reverse the removal procedure. Tighten the caliper guide pin bolts to 27 ft. lbs. (36 Nm).

10. Install new slides.

11. Fill the brake master cylinder reservoir with clean specified brake fluid. Install the brake master cylinder filler cap.

If equipped with a fire suppression system, repower the system.

12. Apply brakes several times to verify correct brake operation.

13. If equipped with a fire suppression system, repower the system. Connect the negative battery cable.

BRAKES

❋❋ CAUTION

Dust and dirt accumulating on brake parts during normal use may contain asbestos fibers from production or aftermarket brake linings. Breathing excessive concentrations of asbestos fibers can cause serious bodily harm. Exercise care when servicing brake parts. Do not sand or grind brake lining unless equipment used is designed to contain the dust residue. Do not clean brake parts with compressed air or by dry brushing. Cleaning should be done by dampening the brake components with a fine mist of water, then wiping the brake components clean with a dampened cloth. Dispose of cloth and all residue containing asbestos fibers in an impermeable container with the appropriate label. Follow practices prescribed by the Occupational Safety and Health Administration (OSHA) and the Environmental Protection Agency (EPA) for the handling, processing, and disposing of

dust or debris that may contain asbestos fibers.

BRAKE CALIPER

REMOVAL & INSTALLATION

❋❋ WARNING

Do not use any fluid other than clean brake fluid meeting manufacturer's specification. Additionally, do not use brake fluid that has been previously drained. Following these instructions will help prevent system contamination, brake component damage and the risk of serious personal injury.

❋❋ CAUTION

Brake fluid contains polyglycol ethers and polyglycols. Avoid contact with the eyes and wash your hands thoroughly after handling brake fluid. If you do get brake fluid in your eyes, flush your eyes with clean, running

REAR DISC BRAKES

water for 15 minutes. If eye irritation persists, or if you have taken brake fluid internally, IMMEDIATELY seek medical assistance.

1. If equipped with a fire suppression system, depower the system, disconnect the negative battery cable and wait one minute.

2. Remove the wheel and tire.

3. Remove the brake caliper flow bolt.

4. Discard the 2 copper washers.

5. Remove the 2 brake guide pin caliper bolts and the brake caliper.

6. Disconnect the brake pads from the caliper and remove the caliper.

7. Inspect the brake caliper for wear or damage. Inspect the guide pins and locating pins for wear or damage.

8. If leaks or damage are found, install a new brake caliper.

To install:

➡ Make sure guide pin boots are correctly seated or damage to guide pins may occur.

➡**Tighten the lower brake caliper bolt first.**

9. Install the brake caliper to the anchor plate and install the 2 brake caliper guide pin bolts. Tighten to 27 ft. lbs. (36 Nm).

10. Using 2 new copper washers, position the brake hose and install the brake caliper flow bolt. Tighten to 35 ft. lbs. (48 Nm).

11. Bleed the brake caliper.

12. Install the wheel and tire.

13. If equipped with a fire suppression system, repower the system. Connect the negative battery cable.

DISC BRAKE PADS

REMOVAL & INSTALLATION

✳✳ WARNING

Do not use any fluid other than clean brake fluid meeting manufacturer's specification. Additionally, do not use brake fluid that has been previously drained. Following these instructions will help prevent system contamination, brake component damage and the risk of serious personal injury.

✳✳ CAUTION

Brake fluid contains polyglycol ethers and polyglycols. Avoid contact with the eyes and wash your hands thoroughly after handling brake fluid. If you do get brake fluid in your eyes, flush your eyes with clean, running water for 15 minutes. If eye irritation persists, or if you have taken brake fluid internally, IMMEDIATELY seek medical assistance.

1. Check the brake fluid level in the brake master cylinder reservoir. If required, remove the fluid until the brake master cylinder reservoir is half full.

2. If equipped with a fire suppression system, depower the system, disconnect the negative battery cable and wait one minute.

3. Remove the wheel and tire.

➡**Do not pry in the caliper sight hole to retract the pistons, as this can damage the pistons and boots.**

➡**Do not allow the brake caliper to hang from the brake hose or damage to the hose may occur.**

4. Remove the 2 brake caliper guide pin

bolts and position the caliper aside. To install, tighten to 27 ft. lbs. (36 Nm).

5. Support the caliper using mechanic's wire.

6. Remove the pads and stainless steel slides from the anchor plate.

7. Discard the slides.

➡**Protect the piston and boots when pushing the caliper piston into the caliper piston bores or damage to components may occur.**

8. If installing new brake pads, using a suitable tool and a worn brake pad, compress the disc brake caliper pistons into the caliper.

9. To install, reverse the removal procedure.

10. Install new slides.

11. Fill the brake master cylinder reservoir with clean specified brake fluid. Install the brake master cylinder filler cap.

If equipped with a fire suppression system, repower the system.

12. Apply brakes several times to verify correct brake operation.

13. If equipped with a fire suppression system, repower the system. Connect the negative battery cable.

BRAKES

PARKING BRAKE

PARKING BRAKE CABLES

ADJUSTMENT

See Figures 5 and 6.

1. If equipped with a fire suppression system, depower the system, disconnect the negative battery cable and wait one minute.

➡**Make sure the parking brake is fully released.**

2. Using the parking brake release handle, release the parking brake control.

3. With the vehicle in NEUTRAL, position it on a hoist.

4. Pull the parking brake cable adjuster clip downward. The tensioner spring will take up the cable slack and preload the cables.

5. Push upward on the bottom of the clip to lock the adjustment. If the clip does not slide upward, move the assembly slightly to align the closest groove on the parking brake cable adjuster rod with the clip.

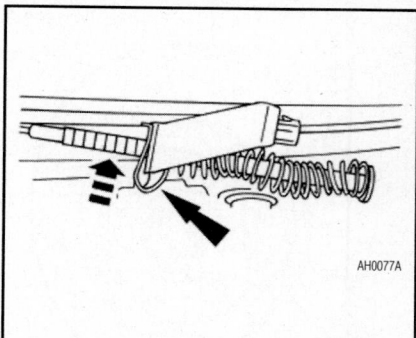

Fig. 6 Push upward on the bottom of the clip to lock the adjustment

➡**If new cables are installed, allow 20 minutes prior to releasing the parking brake control.**

6. Apply the parking brake control fully and release using the parking brake release handle.

7. Repeat Steps 5 and 6 to complete the adjustment procedure.

8. If equipped with a fire suppression system, repower the system. Connect the negative battery cable.

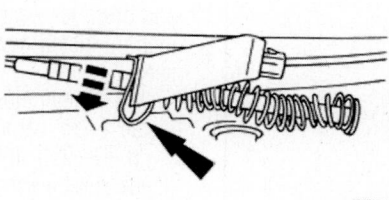

Fig. 5 Pull the parking brake cable adjuster clip downward

PARKING BRAKE SHOES

REMOVAL & INSTALLATION

See Figure 7.

❊❊ CAUTION

Brake fluid contains polyglycol ethers and polyglycols. Avoid contact with the eyes and wash your hands thoroughly after handling brake fluid. If you do get brake fluid in your eyes, flush your eyes with clean, running water for 15 minutes. If eye irritation persists, or if you have taken brake fluid internally, IMMEDIATELY seek medical assistance.

➡ **When servicing drum brakes, only dissemble and assemble one side at a time, leaving the remaining side intact for reference.**

❊❊ WARNING

Clean, high quality brake fluid is essential to the safe and proper operation of the brake system. You should always buy the highest quality brake fluid that is available. If the brake fluid becomes contaminated, drain and flush the system, then refill the master cylinder with new fluid. Never reuse any brake fluid. Any brake fluid that is removed from the system should be discarded. Also, do not allow any brake fluid to come in contact with a painted surface; it will damage the paint.

1. If equipped with a fire suppression system, depower the system, disconnect the negative battery cable and wait one minute.

2. Remove the brake disc.
Remove the adjuster by removing the brake shoe return spring and the adjusting spring.
A sharp-pointed tool such as a scratch awl is useful in removing and installing the springs.

3. Remove the parking brake actuator.

4. Push the parking brake shoes toward each other then pull the parking brake actuator out. Unhook the parking brake cable end.

5. Remove the brake shoe hold-down springs.

6. Remove the parking brake shoes.

7. Inspect the components for excessive wear or damage and install new components as necessary.

8. To install, reverse the removal procedure.

9. Using the specified anti-seize lubricant, lubricate the brake shoe contact point before installation of the rear brake shoes.

10. Lubricate the adjusting screw threads with the specified anti-seize lubricant.

11. Adjust the parking brake shoes.

12. Adjust the parking brake cable tension.

13. If equipped with a fire suppression system, repower the system. Connect the negative battery cable.

ADJUSTMENT

See Figure 8.

➡ **Make sure the parking brake is fully released.**

1. Using the release handle, release the parking brake control.

2. Remove the wheel and tire.

➡ **Do not allow the brake caliper and brake pads to hang from the brake hose or damage to the hose may occur.**

3. Remove the 2 brake caliper guide pin bolts and position the caliper and brake pads aside.

4. Support the caliper using mechanic's wire.

➡ **If the brake disc binds on the rear parking brake shoes, remove the adjustment hole access plug and retract the parking brake shoes using an adjusting tool.**

5. Insert the tool at the end of the access plug slot farthest from the brake caliper. Engage the adjuster and rotate by raising the end of the tool toward the backing plate. Remove the brake disc.

6. Inspect the parking brake shoes and drum for wear, damage or oil contamination. Install new components as necessary.

7. If the linings are oil contaminated, install a new rear axle oil seal.

8. Using a suitable brake adjusting gauge, measure the inside diameter of the drum portion of the rear brake disc. Record the measurement.

9. Using a suitable brake adjusting gauge, set the rear brake shoe and lining

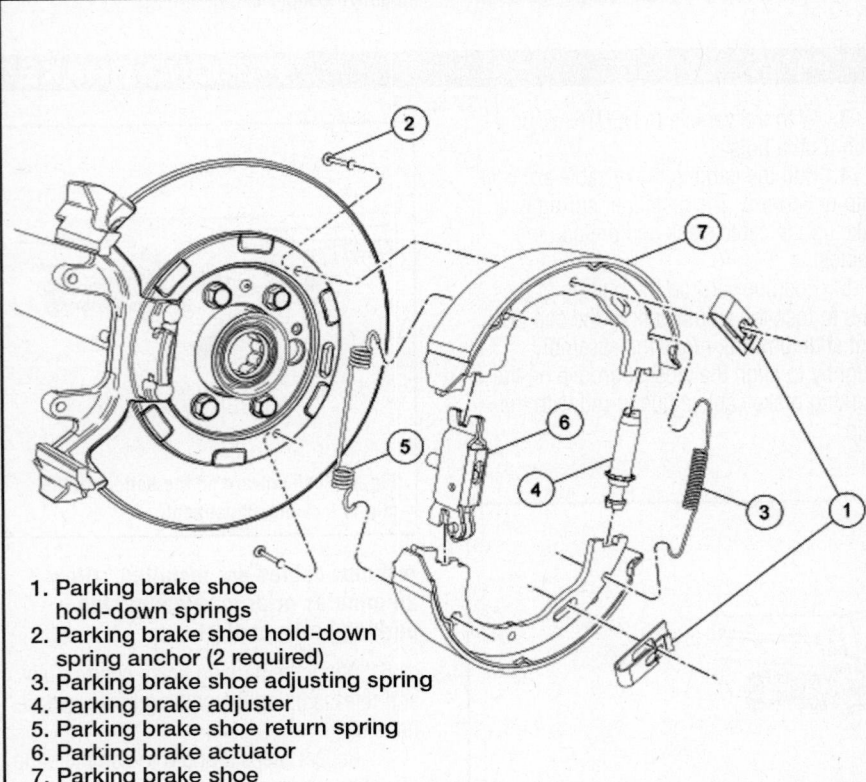

1. Parking brake shoe hold-down springs
2. Parking brake shoe hold-down spring anchor (2 required)
3. Parking brake shoe adjusting spring
4. Parking brake adjuster
5. Parking brake shoe return spring
6. Parking brake actuator
7. Parking brake shoe

N0085416

Fig. 7 Exploded view of the parking brake shoe assembly—With hub assembly removed

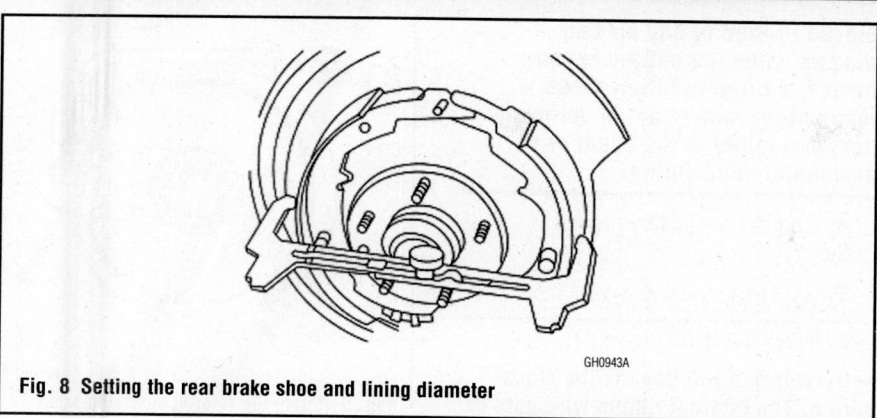

Fig. 8 Setting the rear brake shoe and lining diameter

GH0943A

diameter to 0.020 inches less than the inside diameter of the drum portion of the rear brake disc.

10. Position the brake disc onto the hub.

11. Position the brake caliper and brake pads onto the anchor plate and install the 2 brake caliper guide pin bolts. Tighten to 18 ft. lbs. (25 Nm).

12. Test the parking brake for normal operation.

13. If equipped with a fire suppression system, repower the system. Connect the negative battery cable.

CHASSIS ELECTRICAL — AIR BAG (SUPPLEMENTAL RESTRAINT SYSTEM)

GENERAL INFORMATION

✳✳ CAUTION

These vehicles are equipped with an air bag system. The system must be disarmed before performing service on, or around, system components, the steering column, instrument panel components, wiring and sensors. Failure to follow the safety precautions and the disarming procedure could result in accidental air bag deployment, possible injury and unnecessary system repairs.

SERVICE PRECAUTIONS

Disconnect and isolate the battery negative cable before beginning any airbag system component diagnosis, testing, removal, or installation procedures. Allow system capacitor to discharge for two minutes before beginning any component service. This will disable the airbag system. Failure to disable the airbag system may result in accidental airbag deployment, personal injury, or death.

Do not place an intact undeployed airbag face down on a solid surface. The airbag will propel into the air if accidentally deployed and may result in personal injury or death.

When carrying or handling an undeployed airbag, the trim side (face) of the airbag should be pointing away from the body to minimize possibility of injury if accidental deployment occurs. Failure to do this may result in personal injury or death.

Replace airbag system components with OEM replacement parts. Substitute parts may appear interchangeable, but internal differences may result in inferior occupant protection. Failure to do so may result in occupant personal injury or death.

Wear safety glasses, rubber gloves, and long sleeved clothing when cleaning powder residue from vehicle after an airbag deployment. Powder residue emitted from a deployed airbag can cause skin irritation. Flush affected area with cool water if irritation is experienced. If nasal or throat irritation is experienced, exit the vehicle for fresh air until the irritation ceases. If irritation continues, see a physician.

Do not use a replacement airbag that is not in the original packaging. This may result in improper deployment, personal injury, or death.

The factory installed fasteners, screws and bolts used to fasten airbag components have a special coating and are specifically designed for the airbag system. Do not use substitute fasteners. Use only original equipment fasteners listed in the parts catalog when fastener replacement is required.

During, and following, any child restraint anchor service, due to impact event or vehicle repair, carefully inspect all mounting hardware, tether straps, and anchors for proper installation, operation, or damage. If a child restraint anchor is found damaged in any way, the anchor must be replaced. Failure to do this may result in personal injury or death.

Deployed and non-deployed airbags may or may not have live pyrotechnic material within the airbag inflator.

Do not dispose of driver/passenger/curtain airbags or seat belt tensioners unless you are sure of complete deployment. Refer to the Hazardous Substance Control System for proper disposal.

Dispose of deployed airbags and tensioners consistent with state, provincial, local, and federal regulations.

After any airbag component testing or service, do not connect the battery negative cable. Personal injury or death may result if the system test is not performed first.

If the vehicle is equipped with the Occupant Classification System (OCS), do not connect the battery negative cable before performing the OCS Verification Test using the scan tool and the appropriate diagnostic information. Personal injury or death may result if the system test is not performed properly.

Never replace both the Occupant Restraint Controller (ORC) and the Occupant Classification Module (OCM) at the same time. If both require replacement, replace one, then perform the Airbag System test before replacing the other.

Both the ORC and the OCM store Occupant Classification System (OCS) calibration data, which they transfer to one another when one of them is replaced. If both are replaced at the same time, an irreversible fault will be set in both modules and the OCS may malfunction and cause personal injury or death.

If equipped with OCS, the Seat Weight Sensor is a sensitive, calibrated unit and must be handled carefully. Do not drop or handle roughly. If dropped or damaged, replace with another sensor. Failure to do so may result in occupant injury or death.

If equipped with OCS, the front passenger seat must be handled carefully as well. When removing the seat, be careful when setting on floor not to drop. If dropped, the sensor may be inoperative, could result in occupant injury, or possibly death.

If equipped with OCS, when the passenger front seat is on the floor, no one should sit in the front passenger seat. This uneven force may damage the sensing ability of the seat weight sensors. If sat on and damaged, the sensor may be inoperative, could result in occupant injury, or possibly death.

DISARMING THE SYSTEM

1. Turn all vehicle accessories OFF.
2. Turn the ignition to OFF.
3. At the Central Junction Box (CJB), located below the LH side of the instrument panel, remove the cover and the RCM fuse 22 (10A) from the CJB.
4. Turn the ignition ON and monitor the air bag warning indicator for at least 30 seconds. The air bag warning indicator will remain lit continuously (no flashing) if the correct RCM fuse has been removed. If the air bag warning indicator does not remain lit continuously, remove the correct RCM fuse before proceeding.
5. Turn the ignition OFF.
6. Disconnect the negative battery cable.

ARMING THE SYSTEM

1. Make sure all Restraint System Diagnostic Tool(s) that may have been installed during the repair have been removed from the vehicle and all SRS components are connected.
2. Turn the ignition from OFF to ON.
3. Install the RCM fuse 22 (10A) to the CJB and install the cover.

✳✳ WARNING

Make sure no one is in the vehicle and there is nothing blocking or placed in front of any air bag module when the battery is connected. Failure to follow these instructions may result in serious personal injury in the event of an accidental deployment.

4. Connect the battery ground cable.

CLOCKSPRING CENTERING

See Figures 9 and 10.

➡**Overturning will destroy the clockspring. The internal ribbon wire acts as the stop and may be broken from its internal connection.**

1. Rotate the rotor counterclockwise until it stops.
2. While rotating the rotor counterclockwise, carefully feel for the ribbon wire to run out of length. Stop when a slight resistance is felt.
3. Rotate the rotor clockwise and stop when the arrows line up.
4. Rotate the rotor clockwise 2 complete turns and line up the arrows. Stop rotating at this point. This is the center point of the clockspring.
5. Do not allow the rotor to move from this position.

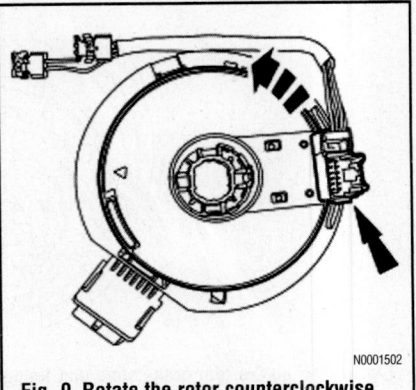

Fig. 9 Rotate the rotor counterclockwise

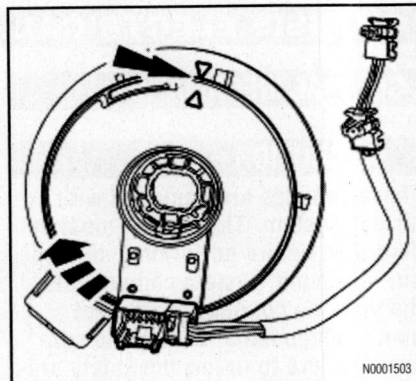

Fig. 10 Rotate the rotor clockwise and stop when the arrows line up

DRIVE TRAIN

AUTOMATIC TRANSAXLE FLUID

DRAIN AND REFILL

Drain

1. With the vehicle in NEUTRAL, position it on a hoist.
2. Loosen the transmission fluid pan bolts and allow the fluid to drain. After the fluid has drained, remove the transmission fluid pan.

➡**Do not remove the transmission fluid filter. It is not necessary to change the transmission fluid filter during a normal maintenance fluid change.**

3. Clean and inspect the transmission fluid pan, transmission fluid pan gasket and magnet.
4. Thoroughly flush the transmission fluid cooler tubes.

Refill

See Figure 11.

1. Position the magnet into the transmission fluid pan.

➡**The transmission fluid pan gasket is reusable. Clean and inspect for damage. If not damaged, the gasket should be reused.**

2. Install the transmission fluid pan and gasket.
3. Position the transmission fluid pan with the gasket in place.
4. Install the bolts. Tighten to 14 ft. lbs. (20 Nm).

➡**The use of any other transmission fluid may result in the transmission failing to operate in a normal manner or transmission failure.**

5. Fill the transmission. Add 5 quarts of automatic transmission fluid to the transmission through the fluid filler tube.
6. Start the engine. Move the transmission selector lever through all the gear ranges, checking for engagements.
7. Fill the transmission to the correct level.
8. Using the scan tool, start and run the engine until the transmission is at normal operating temperature 150-170°F, check and adjust the transmission fluid

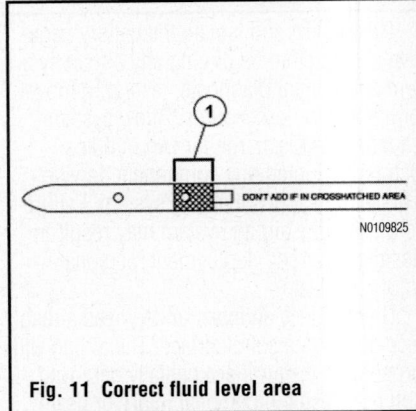

Fig. 11 Correct fluid level area

level, and check for any leaks. If transmission fluid is needed, add fluid in increments of 0.5 pints until the correct level is achieved (fluid should be in the crosshatched area of the fluid level indicator).

FILTER REPLACEMENT

See Figure 12.

➡**Do not use any supplemental transmission fluid additives or cleaning agents. The use of these products**

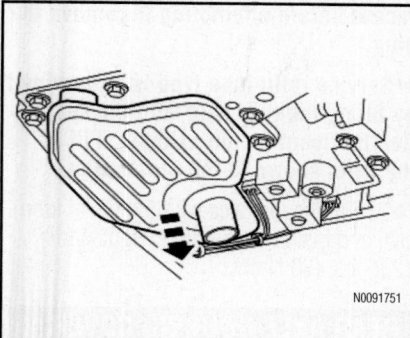

Fig. 12 Remove the transmission fluid filter and seal

could cause internal transmission components to fail; this will affect the operation of the transmission. Using fluid other than specified may result in transmission failure.

➡Normal maintenance requires periodic transmission fluid changes. If a major repair, such as a clutch, band or bearing is required, the automatic transmission must be removed for repair.

1. With the vehicle in NEUTRAL, position it on a hoist.
2. Loosen the transmission fluid pan bolts and allow the fluid to drain. After the fluid has drained, remove the bolts. Remove the transmission fluid pan and transmission fluid pan gasket.
3. Pull down evenly and remove the transmission fluid filter and seal.
4. Clean and inspect the transmission fluid pan, transmission fluid pan gasket and the magnet.

To install:

➡If installing a new transmission fluid filter, and the seal remains in the main control bore, carefully use a small screwdriver to remove the seal. Use care not to damage the main control bore.

➡If transmission is being serviced for a contamination-related failure, use a new transmission fluid filter and seal. The filter may be reused if no excessive contamination is present.

Install a new transmission fluid filter and seal as required.

5. Position the pan magnet into the transmission fluid pan.

➡The transmission fluid pan gasket is reusable, clean and inspect for damage, if not damaged, the gasket should be reused.

6. Install the transmission fluid pan and gasket.
7. Position the transmission fluid pan and gasket in place.
8. Install the transmission fluid pan bolts. Tighten to 14 ft. lbs. (20 Nm).

➡Start by filling the transmission with 5 quarts of transmission fluid.

9. Fill the transmission to the correct fluid level, using transmission fluid.

DRIVESHAFT

REMOVAL & INSTALLATION

See Figures 13 through 15.

➡Use caution when handling the driveshaft. Any slight dent in the driveshaft could result in a vibration.

➡The driveshaft has the following features:

- A fully retained U-joint pinion flange for a positive engagement with the rear axle.
- A splined slip-yoke permits the driveshaft to move forward and rearward on the transmission output shaft during drivetrain movement to maintain the required varying driveshaft length during normal vehicle operation.
- Conventional U-joints that allow a smooth rotation of the driveshaft through the constantly varying angles the driveshaft encounters during jounce and rebound.

➡The driveshaft is a tubular shaft that transfers the rotational torque from the transmission to the rear drive axle. The tube can be aluminium or steel and the diameter of the tubes can vary, depending on the application. All driveshafts are balanced as assemblies. If the vehicle is to be undercoated, cover the driveshaft assembly to prevent overspray of any undercoating material.

1. With the vehicle in NEUTRAL, position it on a hoist.
2. Index-mark the rear axle pinion flange and the driveshaft centering socket yoke.
3. Index-mark the transmission extension housing and driveshaft tube.

➡If new driveshaft flange bolts are not available, coat the threads of the origi-

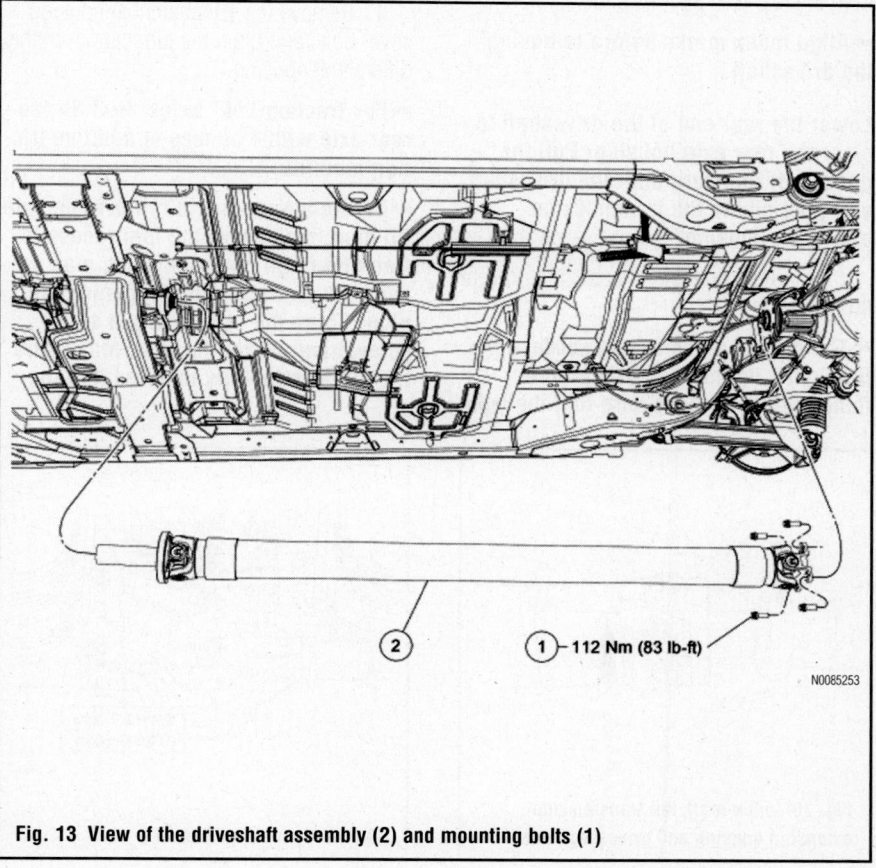

Fig. 13 View of the driveshaft assembly (2) and mounting bolts (1)

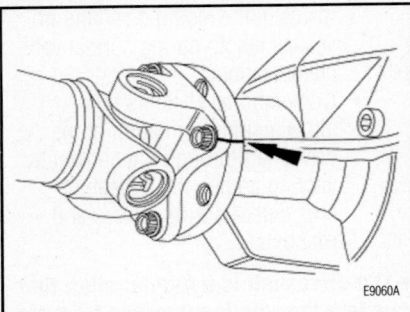

Fig. 14 Index-mark the rear axle pinion flange and the driveshaft centering socket yoke

nal bolts with the threadlock and sealer.

4. Remove and discard the 4 bolts. To install, tighten to 83 ft. lbs. (112 Nm).

➤The driveshaft centering socket yoke fits tightly on the rear axle pinion flange pilot. Never hammer on the driveshaft or any of its components to disconnect the yoke from the flange. Pry only in the area shown, with a suitable tool, to disconnect the yoke from the flange.

5. Using a suitable tool as shown, disconnect the driveshaft centering socket yoke from the rear axle pinion flange.

➤Align index marks before removing the driveshaft.

Lower the rear end of the driveshaft to clear the rear axle housing. Pull the driveshaft rearward until the driveshaft slip yoke clears the transmission extension housing.

6. Plug the extension housing to prevent fluid loss.

➤The driveshaft centering socket yoke fits tightly on the rear axle pinion flange pilot. To make sure that the yoke

seats squarely on the flange, tighten the bolts evenly in a cross pattern as shown or damage to the component may occur.

➤Lubricate the slip-yoke spline with long-life grease.

➤If, after installing a new driveshaft, a vibration is encountered, align the factory-made yellow paint mark at the rear of the driveshaft tube with the factory-made yellow paint mark on the rear axle pinion flange as closely as possible.

➤Inspect the mating surfaces on the rear axle pinion flange and the driveshaft centering socket yoke for foreign material and for damage from nicks or burrs that could prevent the flanges from fitting tightly together.

7. Repair damaged areas or install new components as necessary to make sure a tight fit is obtained.

8. To install, reverse the removal procedure.

REAR AXLE FLUID

DRAIN & REFILL

See Figure 16.

1. Remove the 10 differential housing cover bolts and drain the lubricant from the differential housing.

➤For Traction-Lok® axles, first fill the rear axle with 4 ounces of additive friction modifier.

➤Before attempting to remove the axle fill plug, make sure the tool recess is free of foreign material which may keep the tool from fully engaging the plug. Clean the recess with a small screwdriver or similar tool. Make sure the tool can be fully inserted into the

recess before attempting to remove the plug.

➤Service refill lube type is determined by filling the rear axle with the specified lubricant on the axle tag. Fill to the level shown in the illustration.

2. Fill the rear axle with 5 pints of lubricant and install the fill plug. Tighten to 22 ft. lbs. (30 Nm).

REAR AXLE HOUSING COVER

REMOVAL & INSTALLATION

See Figures 17 and 18.

1. With the vehicle in NEUTRAL, position it on a hoist.
2. Remove the differential housing cover.
3. Remove the 10 differential housing cover bolts and drain the lubricant from the differential housing.
4. Remove the differential housing cover.

To install:

➤The machined surfaces on the differential housing and the differential housing cover must be clean and free of oil before applying the silicone sealant. Cover the inside of the rear axle prior to cleaning the machined surface to prevent contamination.

5. Clean the gasket mating surfaces.

➤Install the differential housing cover within 15 minutes of applying the silicone or it will be necessary to apply new sealant.

6. Apply a continuous bead of silicone gasket and sealant to the differential housing cover.

➤If possible, allow at least one hour before filling the axle with lubricant to allow the silicone sealant to cure.

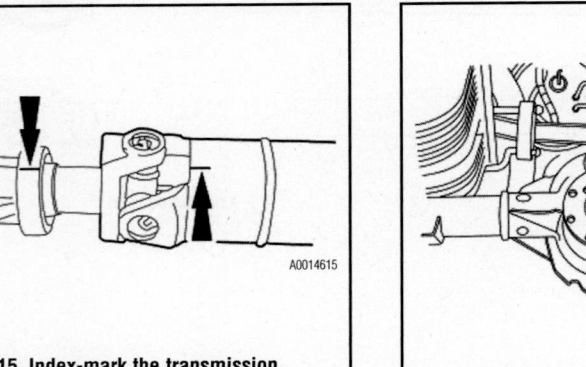

Fig. 15 Index-mark the transmission extension housing and driveshaft tube

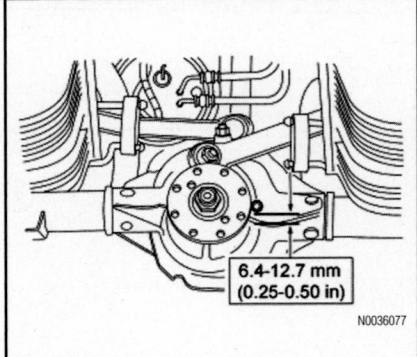

6.4-12.7 mm
(0.25-0.50 in)

Fig. 16 Rear axle fill level

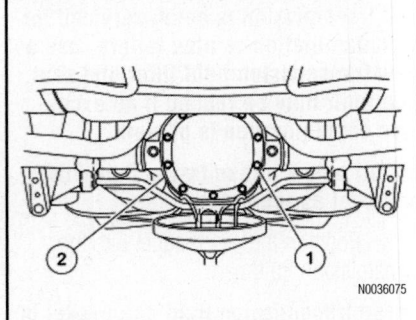

Fig. 17 Differential housing cover bolts (1) and differential housing cover (2)

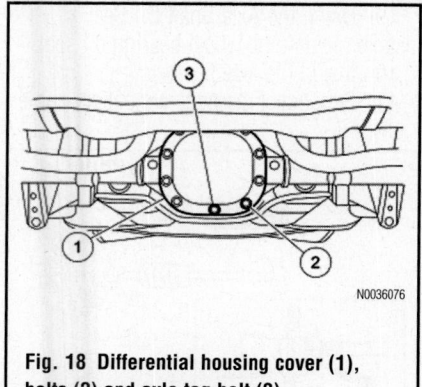

Fig. 18 Differential housing cover (1), bolts (2) and axle tag bolt (3)

7. Install the differential housing cover.

8. Position the differential housing cover. Install the 9 bolts. Tighten to 33 ft. lbs. (46 Nm).

9. Install the axle tag bolt. Tighten to 22 ft. lbs. (30 Nm).

➡ **For Traction-Lok® axles, first fill the rear axle with 118 ml (4 oz) of additive friction modifier.**

➡ **Before attempting to remove the axle fill plug, make sure the tool recess is free of foreign material which may keep the tool from fully engaging the plug. Clean the recess with a small screwdriver or similar tool. Make sure the tool can be fully inserted into the recess before attempting to remove the plug.**

➡ **Service refill lube type is determined by filling the rear axle with the specified lubricant on the axle tag.**

10. Fill the rear axle with 5 pints of lubricant and install the fill plug. Tighten to 22 ft. lbs. (30 Nm).

REAR AXLE SHAFT

REMOVAL & INSTALLATION

See Figures 19 through 23.

1. Disconnect the negative battery cable.

➡ **When removing the rear brake caliper in this procedure, it is not necessary to disconnect the hydraulic lines.**

2. Remove the brake disc.

3. Remove the the rear brake anti-lock sensor and bolt and position it aside.

4. Remove the differential housing cover.

➡ **Once the differential pinion shaft has been removed, turning the differential**

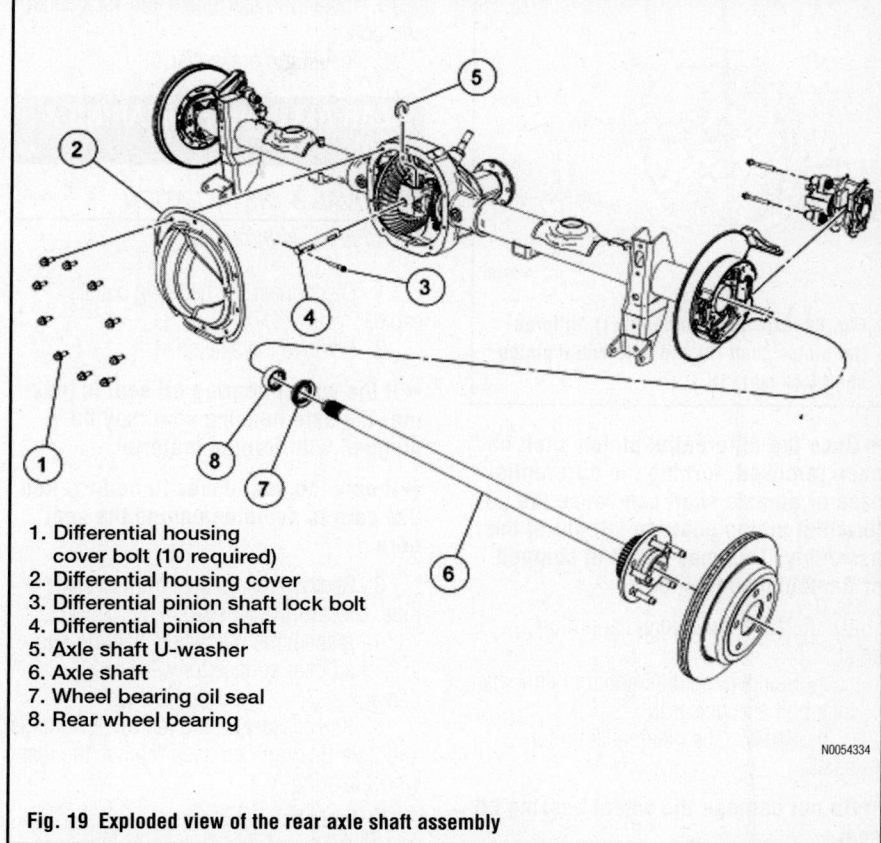

1. Differential housing cover bolt (10 required)
2. Differential housing cover
3. Differential pinion shaft lock bolt
4. Differential pinion shaft
5. Axle shaft U-washer
6. Axle shaft
7. Wheel bearing oil seal
8. Rear wheel bearing

Fig. 19 Exploded view of the rear axle shaft assembly

case or an axle shaft can cause the differential pinion gears to fall out of the assembly. This may result in damage to the component.

5. Remove the differential pinion shaft.
   a. Remove the differential pinion shaft lock bolt.
   b. Remove the differential pinion shaft.

➡ **Do not damage the rubber O-ring in the axle shaft U-washer groove.**

6. Remove the axle shaft U-washer.
   a. Push the axle shaft inboard.

b. Remove the U-washer.

7. Reinstall the differential pinion shaft.
   a. Push the axle shaft outboard.
   b. Install the differential pinion shaft.
   c. Install the differential pinion shaft lock bolt finger-tight.

➡ **Do not damage the wheel bearing oil seal.**

8. Remove the axle shaft.

To install:

9. Lubricate the lip of the wheel bearing oil seal with grease.

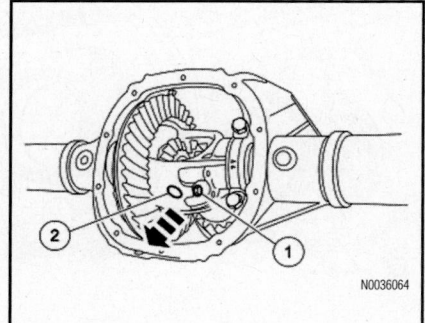

Fig. 20 Remove the differential pinion shaft lock bolt (1) and O-ring

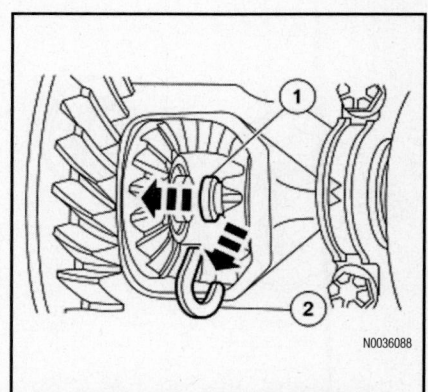

Fig. 21 Axle shaft (1) and U-washer (2)

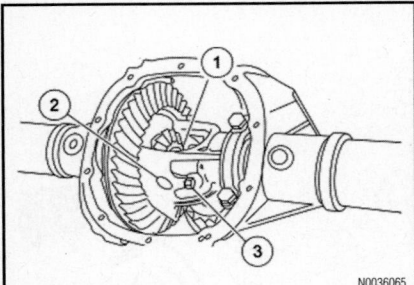

Fig. 22 Axle shaft outboard (1), differential pinion shaft (2) and differential pinion shaft lock bolt (3)

➡**Once the differential pinion shaft has been removed, turning the differential case or an axle shaft can cause the differential pinion gears to fall out of the assembly. This may result in chipped or damaged components.**

10. Remove the differential pinion shaft.

   a. Remove the differential pinion shaft lock bolt and discard.

   b. Remove the differential pinion shaft.

➡**Do not damage the wheel bearing oil seal.**

11. Install the axle shaft.

➡**Do not damage the rubber O-ring in the axle shaft U-washer groove.**

12. Install the axle shaft U-washer.

   a. Position the U-washer on the button end of the axle shaft.

   b. Pull the axle shaft outward to seat the U-washer in the side gear.

13. Install the differential pinion shaft.

   a. Align the hole in the differential pinion shaft with the lock bolt hole.

   b. Install a new differential pinion shaft lock bolt. Tighten to 22 ft. lbs. (30 Nm).

14. Install the differential housing cover.

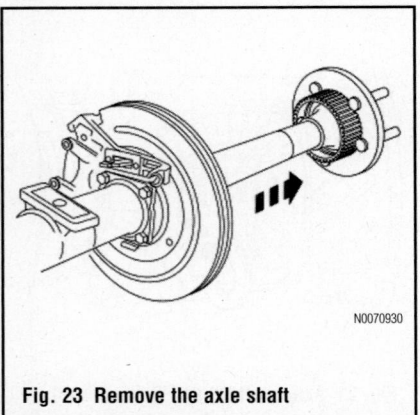

Fig. 23 Remove the axle shaft

15. Install the rear brake anti-lock sensor and bolt.

16. Install the brake disc.

REAR AXLE SHAFT BEARING & SEAL

REMOVAL & INSTALLATION

See Figures 24 through 27.

1. Disconnect the negative battery cable.

2. Remove the axle shaft.

➡**If the wheel bearing oil seal is leaking, the axle housing vent may be plugged with foreign material.**

➡**If only the seal needs to be installed, use care to avoid damaging the seal bore.**

3. Remove the oil seal from the axle tube. Discard the oil seal.

4. Inspect the rear wheel bearing and axle shaft bear surface for wear or damage.

5. If necessary, using the Slide Hammer and Axle Bearing Remover, remove the rear wheel bearing.

To install:

6. Using rear axle lubricant, lubricate the new rear wheel bearing.

7. Using the Axle Shaft Bearing Installer, install the rear wheel bearing.

8. Using long-life grease, lubricate the lip of the new wheel bearing oil seal.

9. Using the Axle Shaft Oil Seal Installer, install the wheel bearing oil seal.

10. Install the axle shaft.

11. Reconnect the negative battery cable.

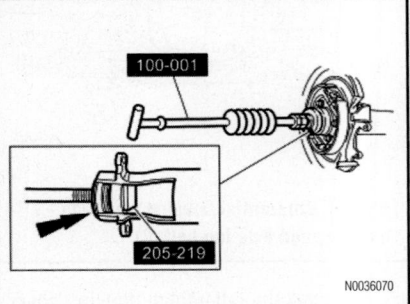

Fig. 25 Uusing the Slide Hammer and Axle Bearing Remover, remove the rear wheel bearing

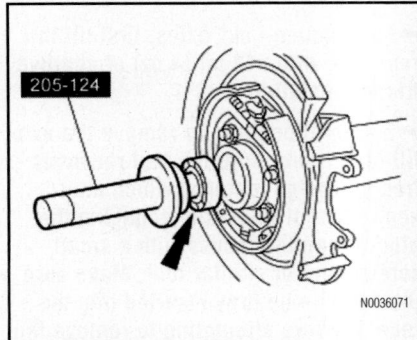

Fig. 26 Using the Axle Shaft Bearing Installer, install the rear wheel bearing

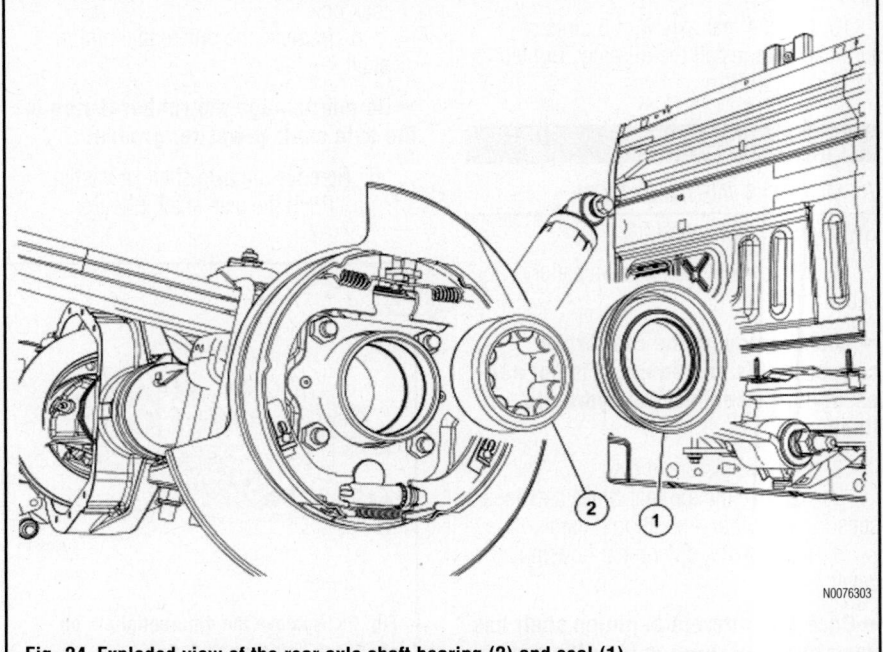

Fig. 24 Exploded view of the rear axle shaft bearing (2) and seal (1)

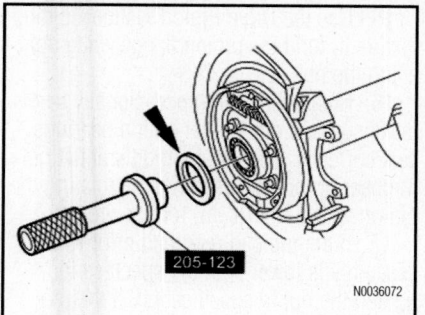

Fig. 27 Using the Axle Shaft Oil Seal Installer, install the wheel bearing oil seal

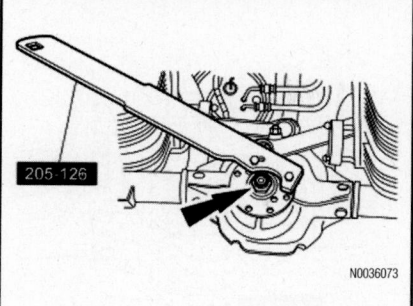

Fig. 29 Use the Drive Pinion Flange Holding Fixture

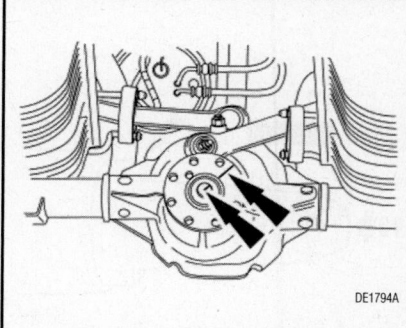

Fig. 30 Index-mark the pinion flange and the drive pinion stem

REAR PINION SEAL

REMOVAL & INSTALLATION

See Figures 28 through 33.

➡**Remove the rear brake discs to prevent brake drag during drive pinion bearing preload adjustment.**

➡**When removing the rear brake caliper in this procedure, it is not necessary to disconnect the hydraulic lines.**

1. Remove the brake discs.
2. Remove the driveshaft and position the driveshaft aside.

3. Install a torque wrench on the nut and record the torque necessary to maintain rotation of the pinion through several revolutions.
4. Use the Drive Pinion Flange Holding Fixture to hold the pinion flange while removing the nut.
   Discard the nut.
5. Index-mark the pinion flange and the drive pinion stem for correct alignment during installation.
6. Using the 2 Jaw Puller, remove the pinion flange.
7. Force up on the metal flange of the drive pinion seal. Install gripping pliers and

strike with a hammer until the drive pinion seal is removed.
8. Discard the seal.

To install:

9. Coat the new rear axle drive pinion seal lips with grease.

➡**If the rear axle drive pinion seal becomes misaligned during installation, remove the seal and install a new seal.**

10. Using the Drive Pinion Oil Seal Installer, install the rear axle drive pinion seal.
11. Lubricate the pinion flange splines with rear axle lubricant.

➡**Disregard the index marks if installing a new pinion flange.**

12. Position the pinion flange.
13. Using the Drive Pinion Flange Installer, install the pinion flange.
14. Position the new drive pinion nut.

➡**Do not, under any circumstance, loosen the nut to reduce preload or component damage may occur. If it is necessary to reduce preload, install a new collapsible spacer and nut.**

➡**Remove the Drive Pinion Flange Holding Fixture while taking preload readings with the torque wrench.**

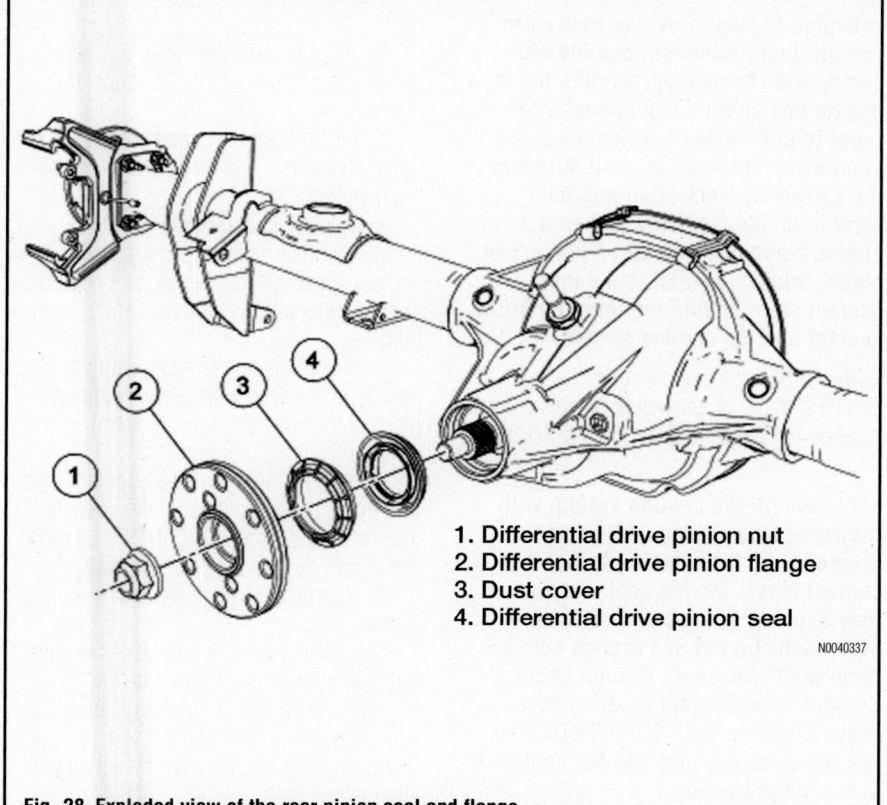

1. Differential drive pinion nut
2. Differential drive pinion flange
3. Dust cover
4. Differential drive pinion seal

Fig. 28 Exploded view of the rear pinion seal and flange

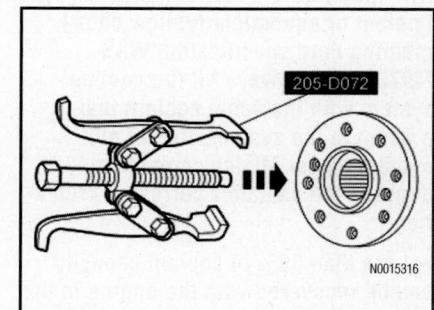

Fig. 31 Using the 2 Jaw Puller, remove the pinion flange

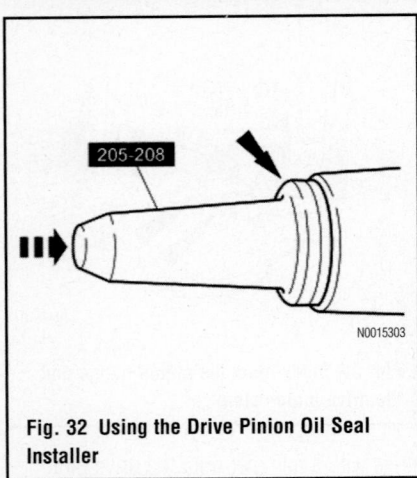

**Fig. 32 Using the Drive Pinion Oil Seal
Installer**

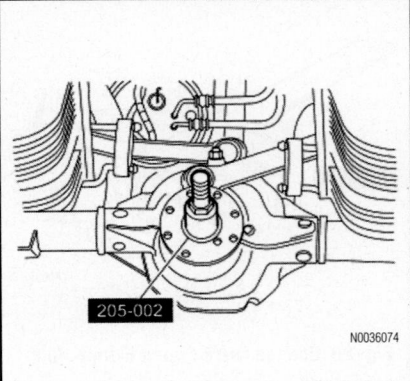

**Fig. 33 Using the Drive Pinion Flange
Installer**

15. Use the Drive Pinion Flange Holding Fixture to hold the pinion flange while tightening the nut.

16. Rotate the pinion occasionally to make sure the differential pinion bearings seat correctly. Take frequent differential pinion bearing preload readings by rotating the pinion with a Nm (lb-in) torque wrench.

17. If the preload recorded prior to disassembly is lower than the specification, tighten the nut to specification. If the preload recorded prior to disassembly is higher than the specification, tighten the nut to the original reading as recorded.

18. Install the drive shaft.

19. Install the brake discs.

20. Connect the negative battery cable.

ENGINE COOLING

ENGINE COOLANT

DRAIN & REFILL PROCEDURE

✳✳ WARNING

Always allow the engine to cool before opening the cooling system. Do not unscrew the coolant pressure relief cap when the engine is operating or the cooling system is hot. The cooling system is under pressure; steam and hot liquid can come out forcefully when the cap is loosened slightly. Failure to follow these instructions may result in serious personal injury.

➡**The coolant must be recovered in a suitable, clean container for reuse. If the coolant is contaminated it must be recycled or disposed of correctly and replaced. Using contaminated coolant may damage cooling system components or the engine.**

➡**Vehicle cooling systems are filled with Motorcraft® Premium Gold Engine Coolant or equivalent (yellow color) meeting Ford specification WSS-M97B51-A1. Always fill the cooling system with the same coolant that is present in the system. Do not mix coolant types. Mixing coolants may degrade the coolant's corrosion protection.**

➡**Less than 80% of coolant capacity can be recovered with the engine in the vehicle. Dirty, rusty or contaminated coolant requires the system flush and replacement.**

Release the pressure in the cooling system by slowly turning the pressure relief cap 1/2 turn counterclockwise. When the pressure is released, remove the pressure relief cap.

1. Connect the negative battery cable.

2. Place a suitable container below the radiator draincock and drain the radiator.

3. Close the radiator draincock.

➡**Engine coolant provides freeze protection, boil protection, cooling efficiency and corrosion protection to the engine and cooling components. In order to obtain these protections, the engine coolant must be maintained at the correct concentration and fluid level in the degas bottle. When adding engine coolant, use a 50/50 mixture of clean, drinkable water and engine coolant. To maintain the integrity of the coolant and the cooling system:**

4. Add Motorcraft® Premium Gold Engine Coolant or equivalent (yellow color) meeting Ford specification WSS-M97B51-A1.

➡**Always fill the cooling system with the same type of coolant that was drained from the system. Do not mix coolant types. Mixing coolant types may degrade the coolant's corrosion protection. Do not add orange-colored Motorcraft® Specialty Orange Engine Coolant or equivalent meeting Ford** ➡**specification WSS-M97B44-D. Mixing coolants may degrade the coolant's corrosion protection.**

➡**Do not add alcohol, methanol, brine or any engine coolants mixed with alcohol or methanol antifreeze. These can cause engine damage from overheating or freezing.**

Ford Motor Company does NOT recommend the use of recycled engine coolant in vehicles.

BLEEDING

1. Disconnect the negative battery cable.

2. Remove the thermostat. For additional information, refer to Thermostat in this section.

3. Disconnect the heater core coolant supply hose from the fitting at the rear of the manifold.

4. Add the coolant/water mixture through the thermostat opening until coolant appears at the heater core coolant supply outlet fitting at the rear of the manifold.

5. Install the heater hose, using an appropriately sized worm style clamp in place of the constant tension clamp.

6. Install the thermostat.

7. Add the correct engine coolant mixture to the degas bottle until the coolant level is between the COOLANT FILL LEVEL marks and replace the pressure cap.

8. Connect the negative battery cable.

9. Select the maximum heater temperature and blower motor speed settings. Position the control to discharge air at the A/C vents in the instrument panel.

10. Run the engine until it reaches operating temperature.

➡ **If air discharge remains cool and the engine coolant temperature gauge does not move, the engine coolant level is low in the engine and must be filled. Stop the engine, allow it to cool and fill the cooling system. Failure to follow these instructions may result in damage to the engine.**

Add the correct engine coolant mixture to the degas bottle until the coolant level is between the COOLANT FILL LEVEL marks.

11. Repeat the 2 previous steps until the engine coolant mixture is between the COOLANT FILL LEVEL marks on the degas bottle. Turn off the engine and allow it to cool.

12. Check the freeze protection of the engine coolant mixture with the Battery/Antifreeze Tester or equivalent. Adjust freezing point range if necessary.

ENGINE FAN

REMOVAL & INSTALLATION

See Figure 34.

1. Drain the cooling system. For additional information, refer to Cooling System Draining, Filling and Bleeding in this section.

2. Remove the bolt and position aside the power steering reservoir.

3. Disconnect the degas bottle overflow hose and the supply hose and position aside.

4. Remove the bolt and the degas bottle.

5. Disconnect the upper radiator hose and position aside.

6. Detach the transmission cooler tubes from the cooling fan motor and shroud.

7. Disconnect the cooling fan motor and shroud electrical connector.

➡ **Position the lower radiator hose away from the cooling fan motor and shroud.**

8. Remove the 2 bolts and the cooling fan motor and shroud assembly.

9. To install, reverse the removal procedure.

10. Connect the negative battery cable.

11. Fill and bleed the cooling system.

RADIATOR

REMOVAL & INSTALLATION

See Figures 35 through 37.

1. Disconnect the negative battery cable.

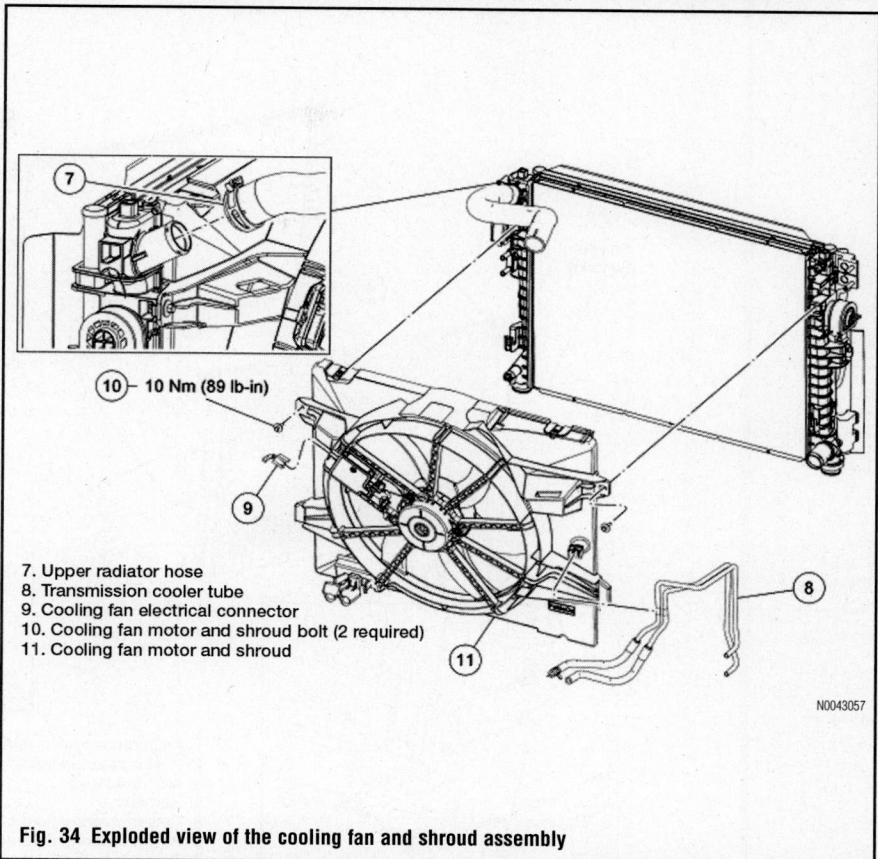

7. Upper radiator hose
8. Transmission cooler tube
9. Cooling fan electrical connector
10. Cooling fan motor and shroud bolt (2 required)
11. Cooling fan motor and shroud

10 Nm (89 lb-in)

N0043057

Fig. 34 Exploded view of the cooling fan and shroud assembly

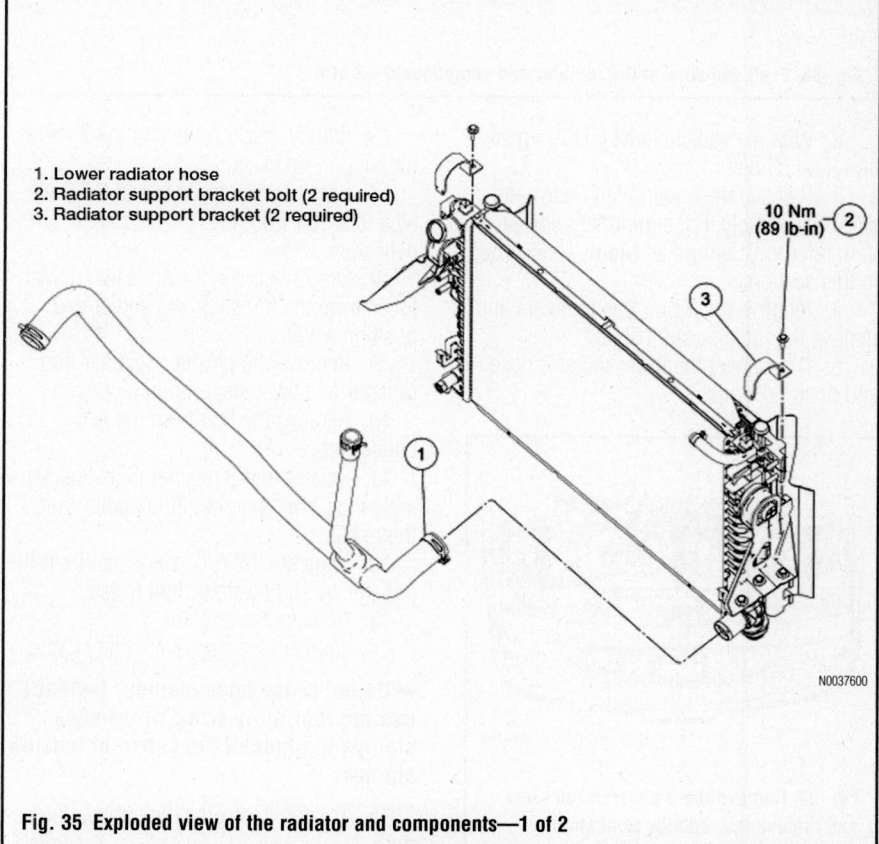

1. Lower radiator hose
2. Radiator support bracket bolt (2 required)
3. Radiator support bracket (2 required)

10 Nm (89 lb-in)

N0037600

Fig. 35 Exploded view of the radiator and components—1 of 2

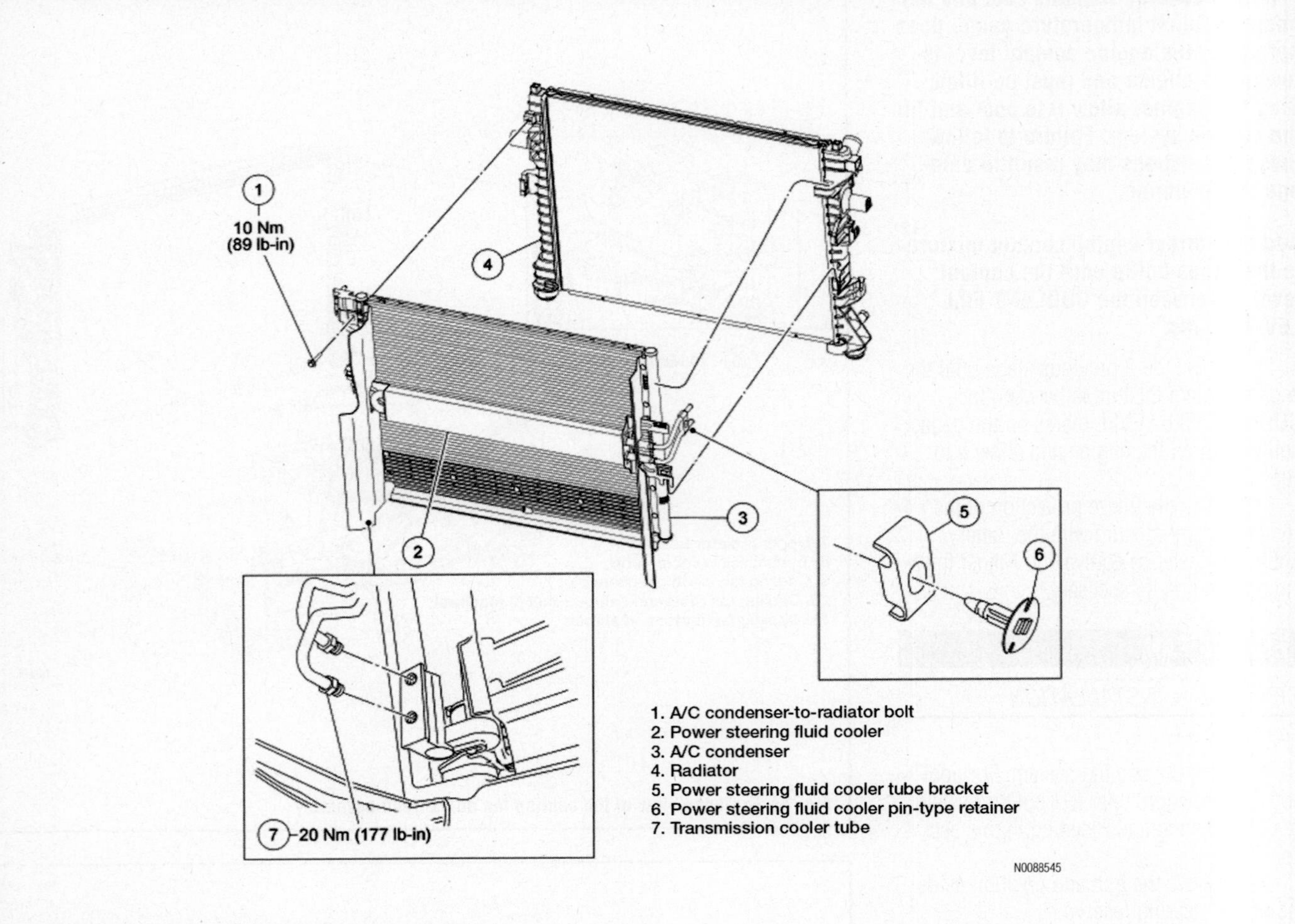

1. A/C condenser-to-radiator bolt
2. Power steering fluid cooler
3. A/C condenser
4. Radiator
5. Power steering fluid cooler tube bracket
6. Power steering fluid cooler pin-type retainer
7. Transmission cooler tube

N0088545

Fig. 36 Exploded view of the radiator and components—2 of 2

2. With the vehicle in NEUTRAL, position it on a hoist.

3. Remove the cooling fan motor and shroud assembly. For additional information, refer to Cooling Fan Motor and Shroud in this section.

4. Remove the 3 pin-type retainers and remove the radiator sight shield.

5. Disconnect the lower radiator hose and position aside.

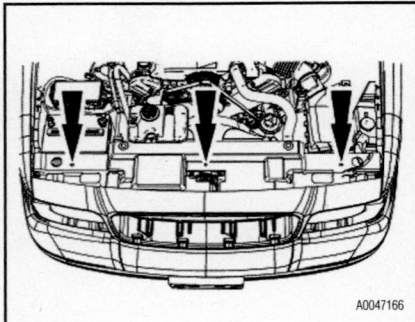

Fig. 37 Remove the 3 pin-type retainers and remove the radiator sight shield

A0047166

6. Remove the 2 bolts and the 2 radiator support brackets.

7. Remove the top 2 LH and 2 RH pin-type retainers from the A/C condenser air deflectors.

8. Disconnect the transmission cooler tubes from the transmission cooler and position aside.

9. Remove the pin-type retainer from radiator-to-power steering fluid cooler.

10. Remove the bolt from the A/C condenser.

11. Release the 2 retainer clips and separate the power steering fluid cooler from the radiator.

12. Separate the A/C condenser from the radiator by sliding from right to left.

13. Remove the radiator.

14. Connect the negative battery cable.

➡**Do not reuse hose clamps. Instead, use appropriately sized worm-style clamps in place of the constant tension clamps.**

15. To install, reverse the removal procedure.

16. Fill and bleed the cooling system. For additional information, refer to Cooling System Draining, Filling and Bleeding in this section.

17. Fill the transmission to the correct fluid level. For additional information, refer to Automatic Transaxle/Transmission.

THERMOSTAT

REMOVAL & INSTALLATION

See Figure 38.

1. Disconnect the negative battery cable.

2. Drain the cooling system. For additional information, refer to Cooling System Draining, Filling and Bleeding in this section.

3. Remove the 2 bolts and position aside the coolant outlet adapter and hose.

4. Remove the O-ring seal and the coolant thermostat from the intake manifold.

5. Discard the O-ring seal.

6. Clean all sealing surfaces with metal surface prep.

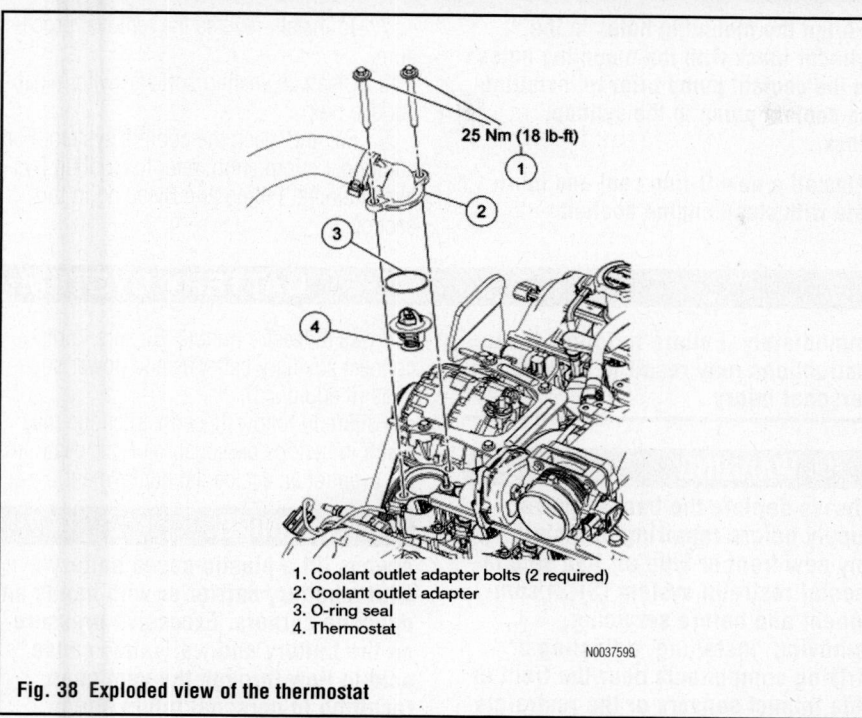

25 Nm (18 lb-ft)

1. Coolant outlet adapter bolts (2 required)
2. Coolant outlet adapter
3. O-ring seal
4. Thermostat

N0037599

Fig. 38 Exploded view of the thermostat

7. To install, reverse the removal procedure. If equipped with a fire suppression system, repower the system.

Fill and bleed the cooling system.

8. Connect the negative battery cable.

WATER PUMP

REMOVAL & INSTALLATION

See Figure 39.

1. Drain the cooling system. For additional information, refer to Cooling System Draining, Filling and Bleeding in this section.

2. Loosen the 4 coolant pump pulley bolts.

3. Remove the accessory drive belt. For additional information, refer to Accessory Drive.

4. Remove the 4 bolts and the coolant pump pulley. To install, tighten to 18 ft. lbs. (25 Nm).

5. Remove the 4 bolts and the coolant pump.

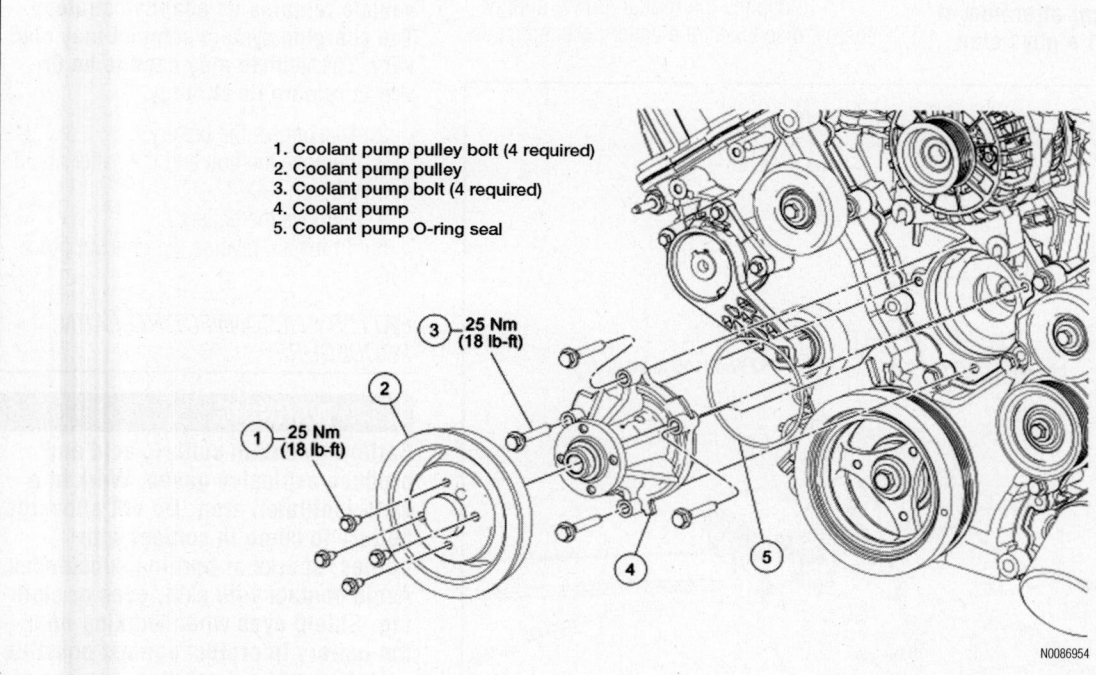

1. Coolant pump pulley bolt (4 required)
2. Coolant pump pulley
3. Coolant pump bolt (4 required)
4. Coolant pump
5. Coolant pump O-ring seal

3 — 25 Nm (18 lb-ft)

1 — 25 Nm (18 lb-ft)

N0086954

Fig. 39 Exploded view of the water pump

6. Discard the O-ring seal. To install, tighten to 18 ft. lbs. (25 Nm).

➡ Do not rotate the coolant pump housing once installed in the engine. Damage to the O-ring seal can occur, causing the coolant pump to leak.

➡ Align the mounting holes in the cylinder block with the mounting holes on the coolant pump prior to installing the coolant pump in the cylinder block.

➡ Install a new O-ring seal and lubricate with clean engine coolant.

7. To install, reverse the removal procedure.

8. Clean all sealing surfaces with metal surface prep.

9. Fill and bleed the cooling system. For additional information, refer to Cooling System Draining, Filling and Bleeding in this section.

ENGINE ELECTRICAL

BATTERY

REMOVAL & INSTALLATION
See Figure 40.

✳✳ WARNING

Batteries contain sulfuric acid and produce explosive gases. Work in a well-ventilated area. Do not allow the battery to come in contact with flames, sparks or burning substances. Avoid contact with skin, eyes or clothing. Shield eyes when working near the battery to protect against possible splashing of acid solution. In case of acid contact with skin or eyes, flush immediately with water for a minimum of 15 minutes, then get prompt medical attention. If acid is swallowed, call a physician immediately. Failure to follow these instructions may result in serious personal injury.

✳✳ WARNING

Always deplete the backup power supply before repairing or installing any new front or side air bag supplemental restraint system (SRS) component and before servicing, removing, installing, adjusting or striking components near the front or side impact sensors or the restraints control module (RCM). Nearby components include doors, instrument panel, console, door latches, strikers, seats and hood latches.

1. To deplete the backup power supply energy, disconnect the battery ground cable

BATTERY SYSTEM

and wait at least 1 minute. Be sure to disconnect auxiliary batteries and power supplies (if equipped).

Failure to follow these instructions may result in serious personal injury or death in the event of an accidental deployment.

✳✳ WARNING

Always lift a plastic-cased battery with a battery carrier or with hands on opposite corners. Excessive pressure on the battery end walls may cause acid to flow through the vent caps, resulting in personal injury and/or damage to the vehicle or battery.

➡ When the battery (or PCM) is disconnected and connected, some abnormal drive symptoms may occur while the vehicle relearns its adaptive strategy. The charging system setpoint may also vary. The vehicle may need to be driven to relearn its strategy.

2. Disconnect the battery.
3. Remove the bolt and the battery hold-down clamp.
4. Remove the battery.
5. To install, reverse the removal procedure.

BATTERY RECONNECT/RELEARN PROCEDURE

✳✳ WARNING

Batteries contain sulfuric acid and produce explosive gases. Work in a well-ventilated area. Do not allow the battery to come in contact with flames, sparks or burning substances. Avoid contact with skin, eyes or clothing. Shield eyes when working near the battery to protect against possible splashing of acid solution. In case of acid contact with skin or eyes, flush immediately with water for a minimum of 15 minutes, then get prompt medical attention. If acid is swallowed, call a physician immediately. Failure to follow these instructions may result in serious personal injury.

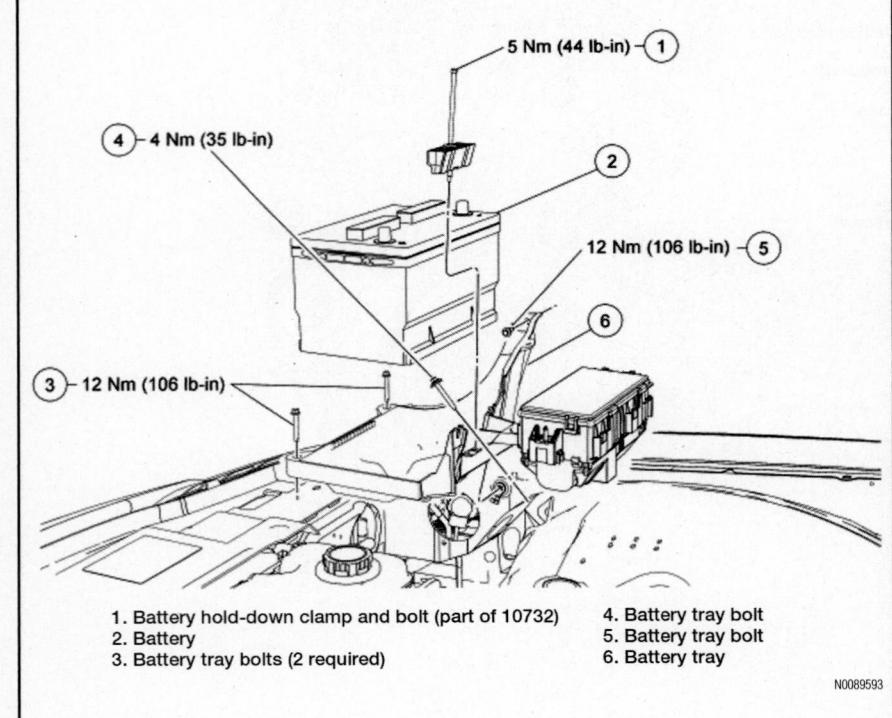

1. Battery hold-down clamp and bolt (part of 10732)
2. Battery
3. Battery tray bolts (2 required)
4. Battery tray bolt
5. Battery tray bolt
6. Battery tray

N0089593

Fig. 40 Exploded view of the battery and tray

❋❋ WARNING

Always deplete the backup power supply before repairing or installing any new front or side air bag supplemental restraint system (SRS) component and before servicing, removing, installing, adjusting or striking components near the front or side impact sensors or the restraints control module (RCM). Nearby components include doors, instrument panel, console, door latches, strikers, seats and hood latches.

To deplete the backup power supply energy, disconnect the battery ground cable and wait at least 1 minute. Be sure to disconnect auxiliary batteries and power supplies (if equipped). Failure to follow these instructions may result in serious personal injury or death in the event of an accidental deployment.

❋❋ WARNING

Always lift a plastic-cased battery with a battery carrier or with hands on opposite corners. Excessive pressure on the battery end walls may cause acid to flow through the vent caps, resulting in personal injury and/or damage to the vehicle or battery.

➡When the battery (or PCM) is disconnected and connected, some abnormal drive symptoms may occur while the vehicle relearns its adaptive strategy. The charging system setpoint may also vary. The vehicle may need to be driven to relearn its strategy.

ENGINE ELECTRICAL

ALTERNATOR

REMOVAL & INSTALLATION

See Figure 41.

1. Disconnect the battery.
2. Remove the nut and the engine cover.
3. Rotate the accessory drive belt ten-

CHARGING SYSTEM

sioner clockwise and position the accessory drive belt aside.

4. Disconnect the generator electrical connector.

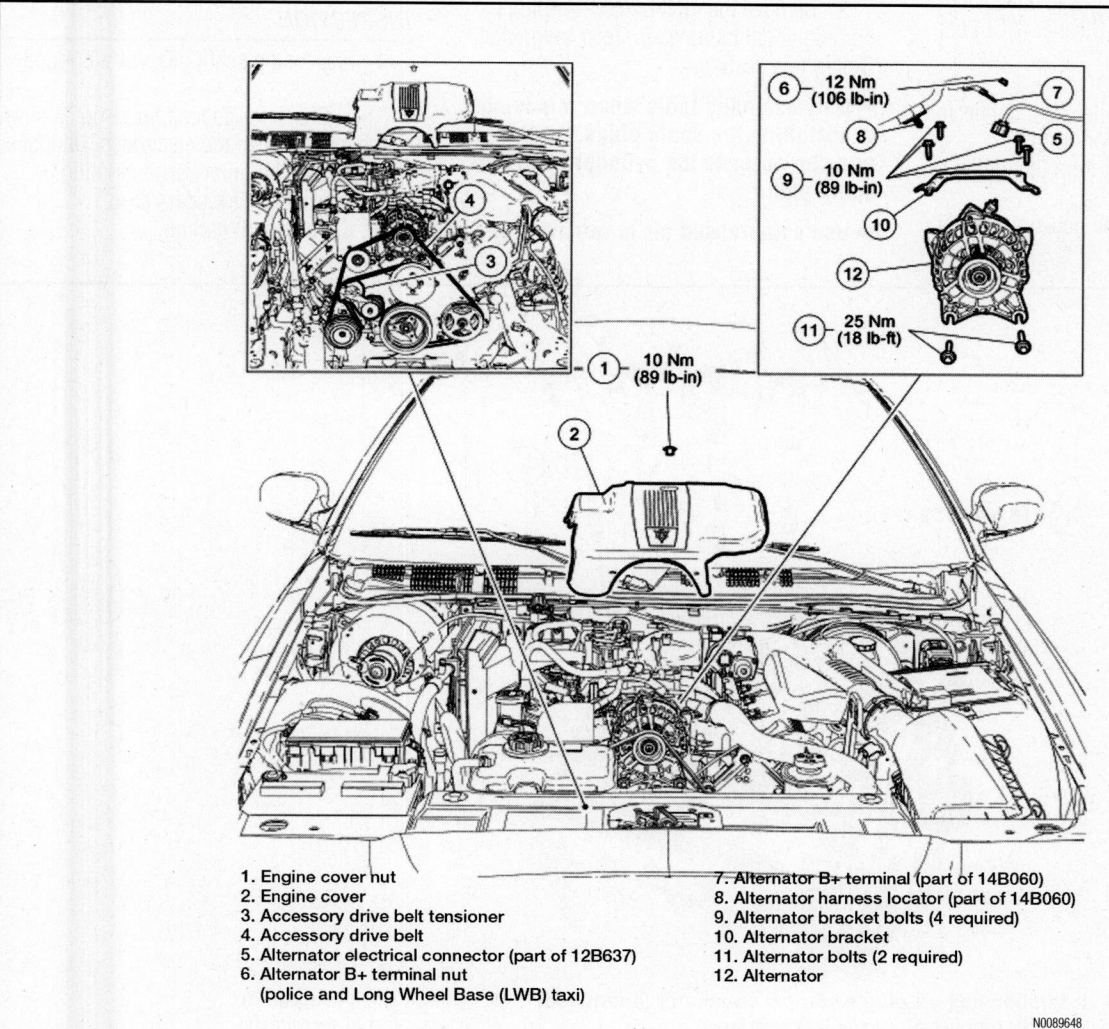

1. Engine cover nut
2. Engine cover
3. Accessory drive belt tensioner
4. Accessory drive belt
5. Alternator electrical connector (part of 12B637)
6. Alternator B+ terminal nut
   (police and Long Wheel Base (LWB) taxi)
7. Alternator B+ terminal (part of 14B060)
8. Alternator harness locator (part of 14B060)
9. Alternator bracket bolts (4 required)
10. Alternator bracket
11. Alternator bolts (2 required)
12. Alternator

N0089648

Fig. 41 Exploded view of the alternator and related components

5. Position the protective boot aside, remove the nut and position the generator B+ terminal aside.

6. Remove the battery cable harness pushpin from the generator bracket.

7. Remove the 4 bolts and the generator bracket.

8. Remove the 2 bolts and the generator.

9. If necessary, remove the cap, nut and the radial adapter.

10. To install, reverse the removal procedure.

11. Refer to illustration for torque values.

ENGINE ELECTRICAL

See Figures 42 and 43.

FIRING ORDER

See Figure 44.

Firing order: 1-3-7-2-6-5-4-8.

IGNITION COIL

REMOVAL & INSTALLATION

See Figures 42 and 43.

1. Disconnect the negative battery cable.
2. LH side
   a. Remove the Air Cleaner (ACL) outlet pipe.
3. Both sides
   a. Disconnect the electrical connector from the ignition coil-on-plug.
   b. Remove the bolt from the ignition coil-on-plug.
4. Remove the ignition coil-on-plug.

5. To install, reverse the removal procedure.

IGNITION TIMING

ADJUSTMENT

10 degrees Before Top Dead Center (BTDC) (not adjustable).

SPARK PLUGS

REMOVAL & INSTALLATION

1. Disconnect the negative battery cable.
2. Remove the ignition coil-on-plugs. For additional information, refer to Ignition Coil in this section.

➡ **Only use hand tools when removing or installing the spark plugs, or damage can occur to the cylinder head or spark plug.**

➡ **Use compressed air to remove any**

IGNITION SYSTEM

foreign material from the spark plug well before removing the spark plugs.

3. Remove the spark plugs. For installation, tighten to 13 ft. lbs. (18 Nm).
4. Inspect the spark plugs.
5. To install, reverse the removal procedure.
6. Adjust the spark plug gap on gasoline engines to 0.052-0.056 inches (1.32-1.42 mm).
7. Adjust the spark plug gap on flexible fuel engines to 0.041-0.047 inches (1.04-1.19 mm).

INSPECTION

1. Inspect the spark plug for a bridged gap.
   a. Check for deposit build-up closing the gap between the electrodes. Deposits are caused by oil or carbon fouling.
   b. Install a new spark plug.
2. Check for oil fouling.

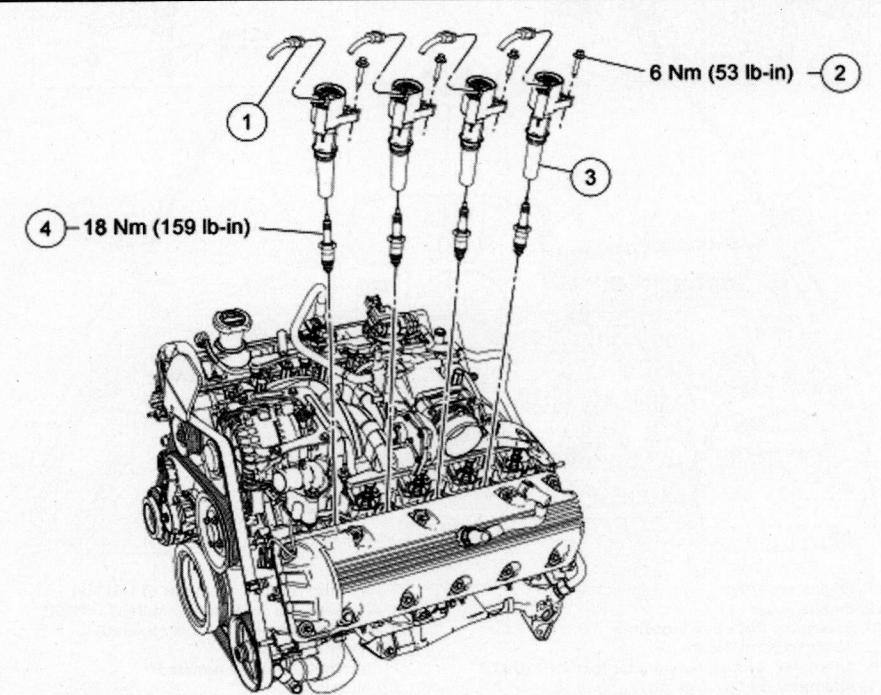

1. Ignition coil-on-plug electrical connector (4 required)
2. Ignition coil-on-plug bolt (4 required)
3. Ignition coil (4 required)
4. Spark plug (4 required)

N0087594

Fig. 42 Exploded view of the engine ignition system components—1 of 2

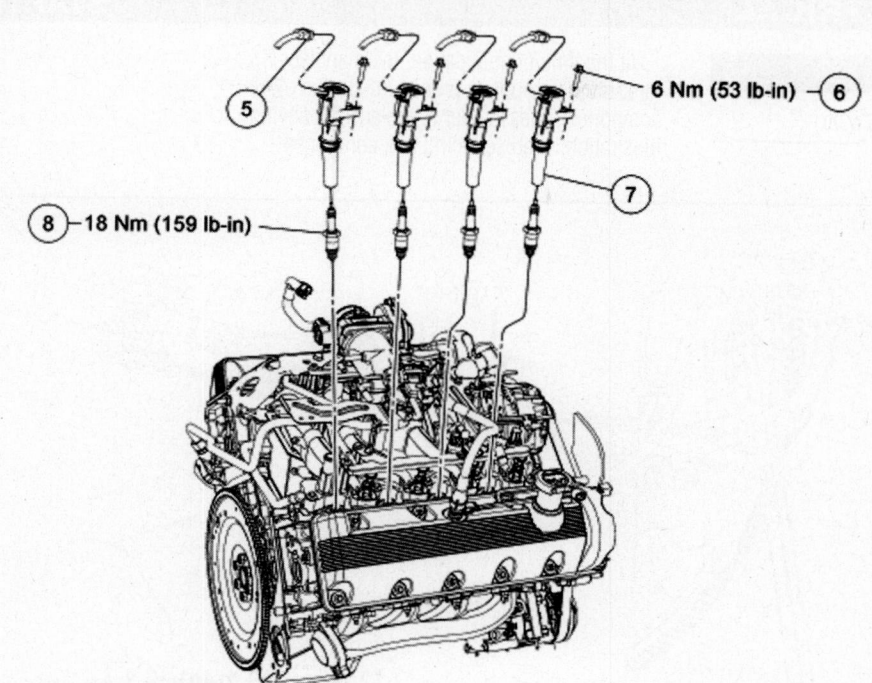

5. Ignition coil-on-plug electrical connector (4 required)
6. Ignition coil-on-plug bolt (4 required)
7. Ignition coil (4 required)
8. Spark plug (4 required)

N0087595

Fig. 43 Exploded view of the engine ignition system components—2 of 2

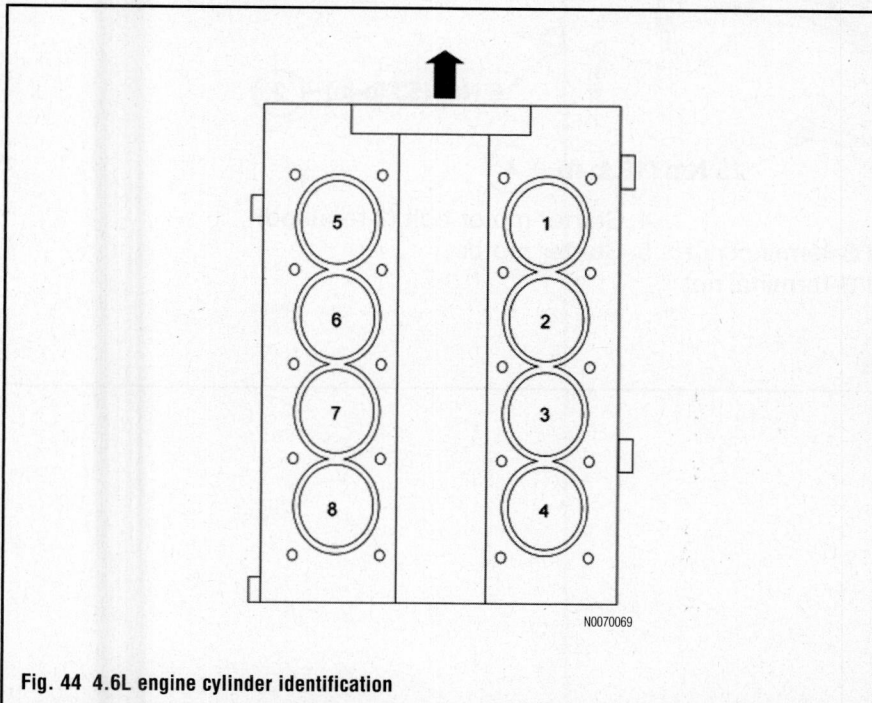

N0070069

Fig. 44 4.6L engine cylinder identification

a. Check for wet, black deposits on the insulator shell bore electrodes, caused by excessive oil entering the combustion chamber through worn rings and pistons, excessive valve-to-guide clearance or worn or loose bearings.

b. Correct the oil leak concern.

c. Install a new spark plug.

3. Inspect for carbon fouling. Look for black, dry, fluffy carbon deposits on the insulator tips, exposed shell surfaces and electrodes, caused by a spark plug with an incorrect heat range, dirty air cleaner, too rich a fuel mixture or excessive idling.

a. Install new spark plugs.

4. Inspect for normal burning.

a. Check for light tan or gray deposits on the firing tip.

5. Inspect for pre-ignition, identified by melted electrodes and a possibly damaged insulator. Metallic deposits on the insulator indicate engine damage. This may be caused by incorrect ignition timing, wrong type of fuel or the unauthorized installation of a heli-coil insert in place of the spark plug threads.

a. Install a new spark plug.

6. Inspect for overheating, identified by white or light gray spots and a bluish-burnt appearance of electrodes. This is caused by engine overheating, wrong type of fuel, loose spark plugs, spark plugs with an incorrect heat range, low fuel pump pressure or incorrect ignition timing.

a. Install a new spark plug.

7. Inspect for fused deposits, identified by melted or spotty deposits resembling bubbles or blisters. These are caused by sudden acceleration.

a. Install new spark plugs.

ENGINE ELECTRICAL   **STARTING SYSTEM**

STARTER

REMOVAL & INSTALLATION

See Figure 45.

At the time of publication, the manufacturer did not supply a procedure for this component. Please refer to the accompanying illustration when servicing this component

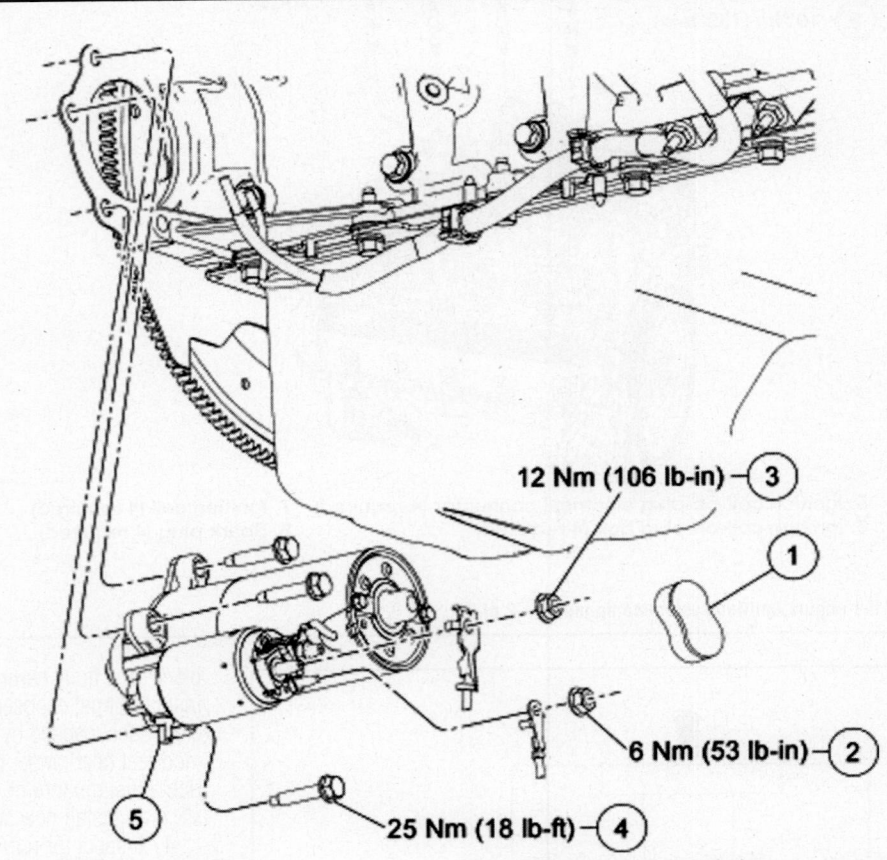

12 Nm (106 lb-in) — 3

1

6 Nm (53 lb-in) — 2

25 Nm (18 lb-ft) — 4

5

1. Terminal cover
2. Starter solenoid S-terminal nut
3. Starter solenoid B-terminal nut
4. Starter motor bolt (3 required)
5. Starter motor

N0087572

Fig. 45 Exploded view of the starter and components

ENGINE MECHANICAL

➠Disconnecting the negative battery cable may interfere with the functions of the on board computer systems and may require the computer to undergo a relearning process, once the negative battery cable is reconnected.

ACCESSORY DRIVE BELTS

ACCESSORY BELT ROUTING

See Figure 46.

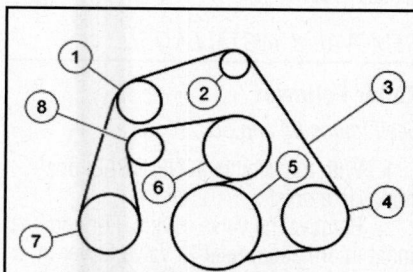

1. Accessory drive belt idler pulley
2. Generator pulley
3. Accessory drive belt
4. Power steering pump pulley
5. Crankshaft pulley
6. Coolant pump pulley
7. A/C clutch pulley
8. Accessory drive belt tensioner pulley

N0037351

Fig. 46 Accessory belt routing

INSPECTION

Inspect for glazing, cracking, splitting, delaminating and shredding. Replace as necessary.

ADJUSTMENT

Adjustment is not possible or necessary.

REMOVAL & INSTALLATION

See Figure 47.

1. Rotate the tensioner clockwise and remove the accessory drive belt.

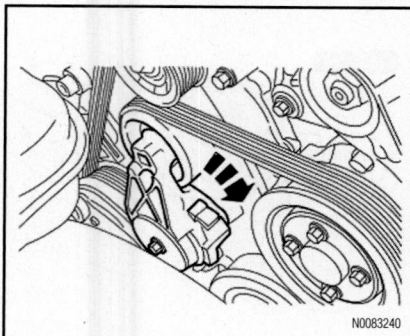

N0083240

Fig. 47 Rotate the tensioner clockwise

2. To install, reverse the removal procedure.

AIR CLEANER

REMOVAL & INSTALLATION

See Figure 48.

1. Disconnect the negative battery cable.
2. Disconnect the Mass Air Flow (MAF) sensor electrical connector.
3. Loosen the clamp and disconnect the Air Cleaner (ACL) outlet pipe from the ACL cover.
4. Remove the 3 nuts and the engine ACL assembly.
5. To install, reverse the removal procedure.

FILTER/ELEMENT REPLACEMENT

1. Release the 2 Air Cleaner (ACL) cover retaining clips from the ACL cover.
2. Lift the ACL cover and remove the ACL element.
3. Installation:
   a. Lift the ACL cover and install the ACL element.

➠It is important that all hinge features are fully engaged from the cover to the

tray after servicing the air filter element.

   b. Install the 2 ACL cover retaining clips to the ACL cover.

CAMSHAFT AND VALVE LIFTERS

INSPECTION

Camshaft Bearing Journal Diameter

See Figure 49.

➠Refer to the spec charts for specifications.

Camshaft End Play

See Figure 50.

➠Refer to the spec charts for specifications.

1. Using the Dial Indicator Gauge with Holding Fixture, measure the camshaft end play.
2. Position the camshaft to the rear of the cylinder head.
3. Zero the Dial Indicator Gauge.
4. Move the camshaft to the front of the

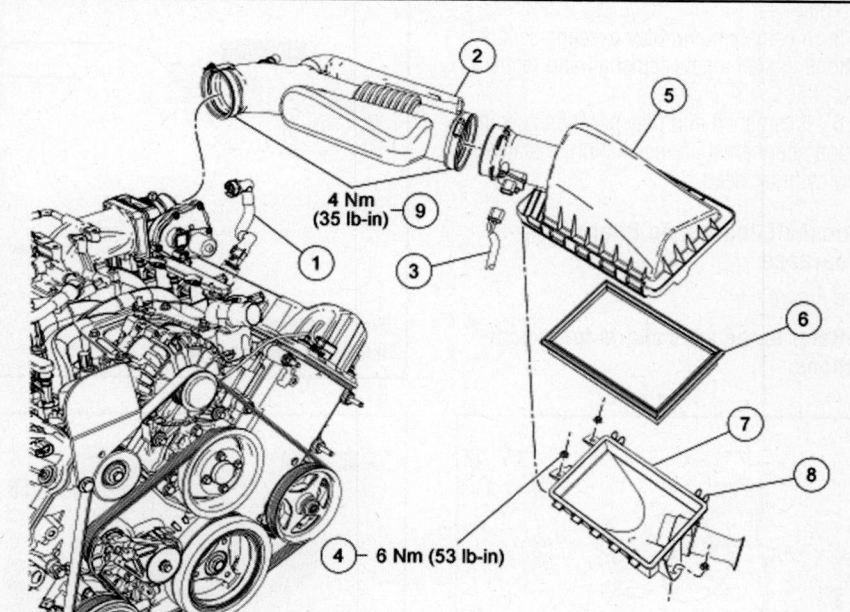

4 Nm (35 lb-in)

6 Nm (53 lb-in)

1. Crankcase ventilation hose
2. Air Cleaner (ACL) outlet pipe
3. Mass Air Flow (MAF) sensor electrical connector
4. ACL retainer nut (3 required)
5. ACL cover
6. ACL element
7. ACL tray (part of 9600)
8. ACL cover retaining clip (2 required)
9. ACL outlet pipe clamps

N0076674

Fig. 48 Exploded view of the air cleaner assembly

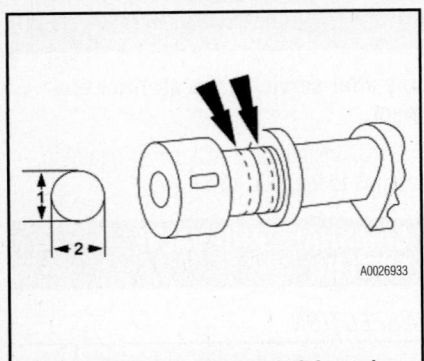

Fig. 49 Measure each camshaft journal diameter in 2 directions.

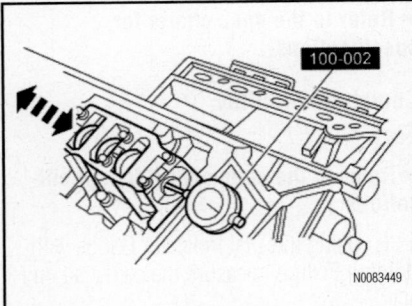

Fig. 50 Using the Dial Indicator Gauge with Holding Fixture, measure the camshaft end play

cylinder head. Note and record the camshaft end play.

5. If camshaft end play exceeds specifications, install a new camshaft and recheck end play.

6. If camshaft end play exceeds specification after camshaft installation, install a new cylinder head.

Camshaft Journal To Bearing Clearance

See Figure 51.

➡**Refer to the spec charts for specifications.**

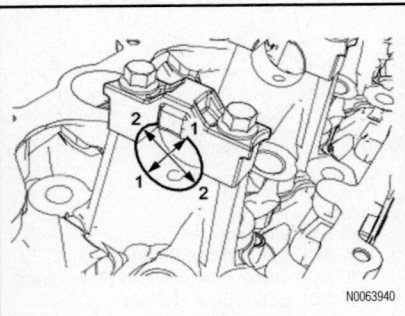

Fig. 51 Subtract the camshaft journal diameter from the camshaft bearing diameter.

➡**The camshaft journals must meet specifications before checking camshaft journal clearance.**

1. Measure each camshaft bearing in 2 directions.

2. Subtract the camshaft journal diameter from the camshaft bearing diameter.

Camshaft Lobe Lift

See Figure 52.

➡**Refer to the spec charts for specifications.**

1. Use the Dial Indicator Gauge with Holding Fixture to measure camshaft intake/exhaust lobe lift.

2. Rotate the camshaft and subtract the lowest Dial Indicator Gauge reading from the highest Dial Indicator Gauge reading to figure the camshaft lobe lift.

Camshaft Runout

See Figure 53.

➡**Refer to the spec charts for specifications.**

➡**Camshaft journals must be within specifications before checking runout.**

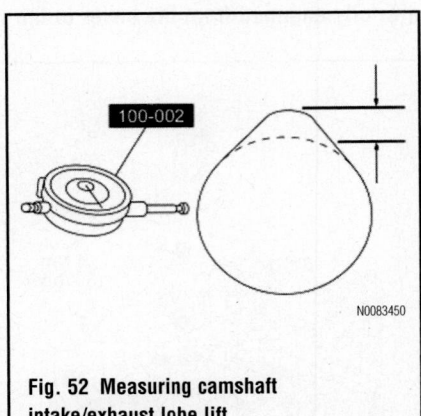

Fig. 52 Measuring camshaft intake/exhaust lobe lift

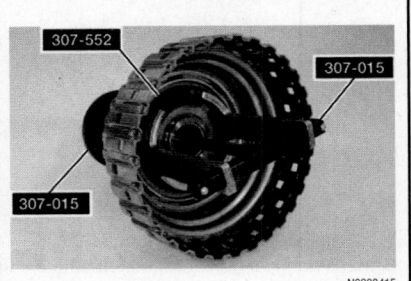

Fig. 53 Using the Dial Indicator Gauge with Holding Fixture, measure the camshaft runout

1. Using the Dial Indicator Gauge with Holding Fixture, measure the camshaft runout.

2. Rotate the camshaft and subtract the lowest Dial Indicator Gauge reading from the highest Dial Indicator Gauge reading.

Camshaft Surface Inspection

See Figure 54.

Inspect the camshaft lobes for pitting or damage in the contact area. Minor pitting is acceptable outside the contact area.

REMOVAL & INSTALLATION

Roller Follower

See Figures 55 and 56.

1. With the vehicle in NEUTRAL, position it on a hoist.

2. Remove the valve covers. For additional information, refer to Valve Cover in this section.

3. Position the piston of the cylinder being repaired at the bottom of the stroke.

4. Install the Valve Spring Compressor Spacer between the valve spring

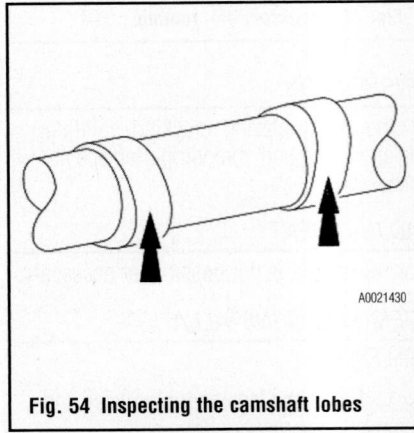

Fig. 54 Inspecting the camshaft lobes

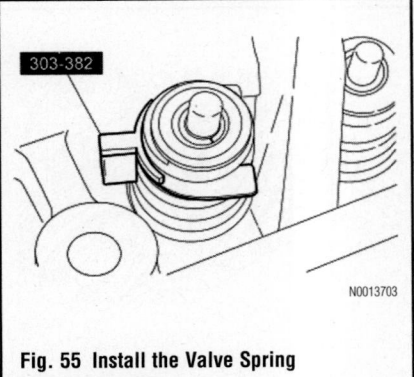

Fig. 55 Install the Valve Spring Compressor Spacer

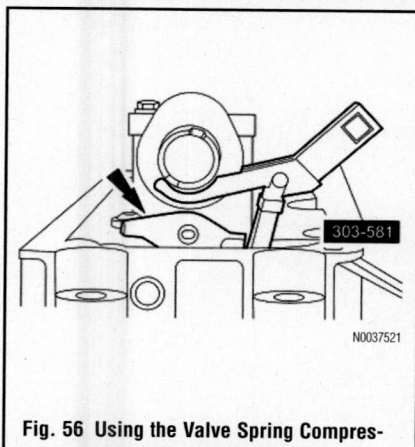

Fig. 56 Using the Valve Spring Compressor, compress the valve springs

coils to prevent valve stem seal damage.

5. Using the Valve Spring Compressor, compress the valve springs and remove the camshaft roller followers.

To install:

6. Using the Valve Spring Compressor, compress the valve spring and install the camshaft roller followers.

7. Remove the Valve Spring Compressor from between the valve spring.

8. Install the valve covers.

Camshaft

See Figure 57.

1. Disconnect the negative battery cable.

2. With the vehicle in NEUTRAL, position it on a hoist.

➡**At no time, when the timing chains are removed and the cylinder heads are installed, may the crankshaft or camshaft be rotated. Severe piston and valve damage will occur.**

3. Remove the camshaft roller followers.

4. Remove the timing chain. For additional information, refer to Timing Chain in this section.

5. Remove the bolt and the camshaft sprocket and spacer.

6. Remove the 13 camshaft bearing cap bolts.

7. Remove the camshaft bearing cap.

8. Remove the camshaft from the cylinder head.

To install:

9. Lubricate the camshaft journals with clean engine oil.

10. Install the camshaft onto the cylinder head.

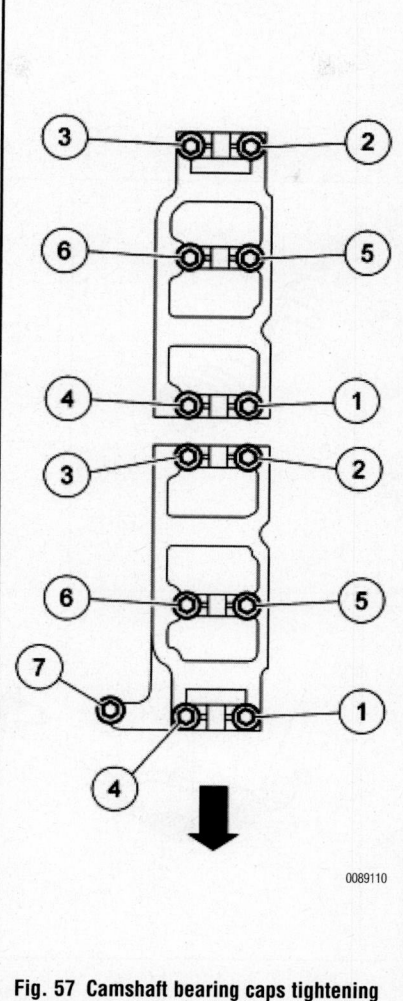

Fig. 57 Camshaft bearing caps tightening sequence

11. Lubricate the camshaft bearing cap with clean engine oil.

12. Install the camshaft bearing caps and loosely install the bolts. Tighten the bolts in the sequence shown. Tighten to 7 ft. lbs. (10 Nm).

13. Install the camshaft sprocket and bolt. Tighten the bolt in 2 stages.

   a. Stage 1: Tighten to 40 Nm (30 lb-ft).

   b. Stage 2: Tighten an additional 90 degrees (one-fourth turn).

14. Install the timing chains.

15. Install the roller followers.

16. If equipped with a fire suppression system, repower the system. Connect the negative battery cable.

CATALYTIC CONVERTER

REMOVAL & INSTALLATION

See Figures 58 and 59.

1. Disconnect the negative battery cable.

2. With the vehicle in NEUTRAL, position it on a hoist.

✳✳ WARNING

WARNING: Shut off the electrical power to the air suspension system prior to hoisting or jacking an air suspension equipped vehicle. Failure to do so may result in unexpected inflation or deflation of the air springs, which may result in shifting of the vehicle during these operations. Failure to follow this instruction may result in serious personal injury.

3. If equipped, turn the air suspension switch OFF.

4. For RH catalytic converter removal, disconnect the Heated Oxygen Sensor (HO2S) electrical connector.

5. Disconnect the Catalyst Monitor Sensor (CMS) electrical connector.

➡**To correctly seat the converter, alternately tighten the catalytic converter-to-exhaust manifold nuts to specification.**

6. Remove and discard the 2 catalytic converter-to-exhaust manifold nuts. To install, alternately tighten the new nuts to 40 Nm (30 lb-ft).

➡**Alternate tightening the catalytic converter-to-exhaust inlet pipe bolts to specifications to draw the flanges together evenly.**

7. Remove the 2 catalytic converter-to-inlet pipe bolts, the 2 flagnuts, the damper (if equipped) and the catalytic converter.

8. Discard the bolts, the flagnuts and the gaskets. To install, alternately tighten the new bolts to 40 Nm (30 lb-ft).

➡**Prior to Installation, Inspect the HO2S and the CMS wiring harness for damage.**

➡**Clean the mating surfaces of the exhaust manifold, the outlet pipe and the catalytic converter.**

➡**Always install new exhaust system fasteners and gaskets. Do not tighten the fasteners until all components are assembled. Make sure to tighten all fasteners beginning at the front of the vehicle.**

9. To install, reverse the removal procedure.

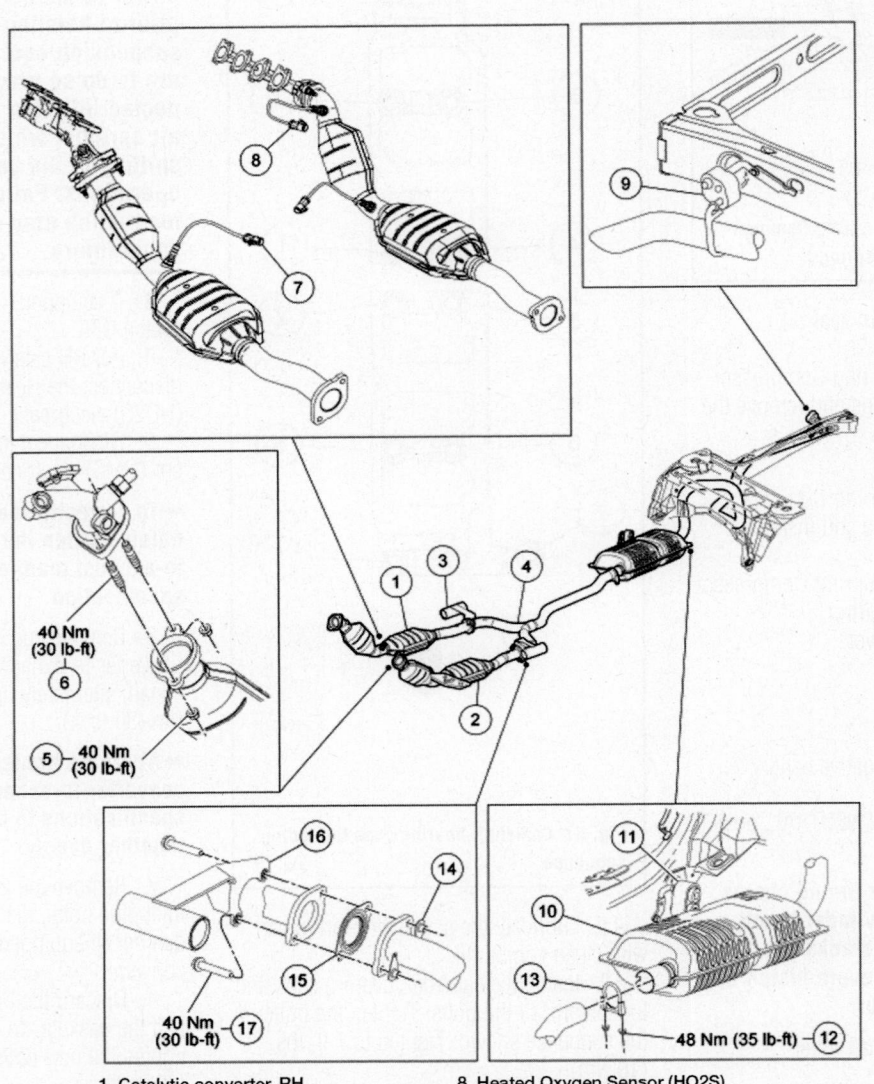

1. Catalytic converter, RH
2. Catalytic converter, LH
3. Damper — RH (except police vehicles)
4. Exhaust inlet pipe
5. Catalytic converter-to-exhaust
   manifold nut (4 required)
6. Catalytic converter-to-exhaust
   manifold stud (4 required)
7. Catalyst Monitor Sensor (CMS)
   electrical connector (2 required)
8. Heated Oxygen Sensor (HO2S)
   electrical connector
9. Tailpipe isolator and bracket
10. Muffler
11. Muffler isolator and bracket
12. Clamp nut (2 required)
13. Clamp
14. Flagnut (4 required)
15. Gasket
16. Damper — LH (except police vehicles)
17. Catalytic converter-to-exhaust
    inlet pipe bolt (4 required)

N0089710

Fig. 58 Exploded view of the exhaust system—Single exhaust

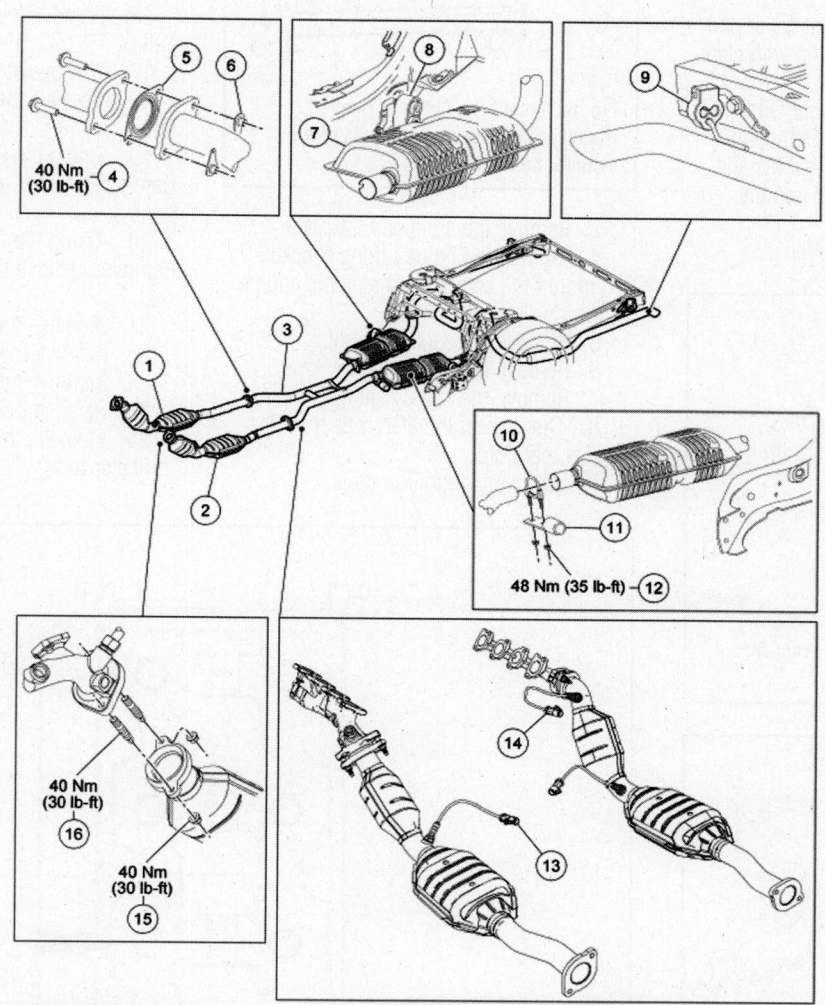

1. Catalytic converter, RH
2. Catalytic converter, LH
3. Exhaust inlet pipe
4. Converter-to-exhaust manifold nut (4 required)
5. Gasket
6. Flagnut (4 required)
7. Muffler (2 required)
8. Muffler isolator and bracket (2 required)
9. Tailpipe isolator and bracket (2 required)
10. Clamp (2 required)
11. Damper — RH/LH
12. Clamp nut (4 required)
13. Catalyst Monitor Sensor (CMS) electrical
    connector (2 required)
14. Heated Oxygen Sensor (HO2S) electrical connector
15. Catalytic converter-to-exhaust manifold nut (4 required)
14. Catalytic converter-to-exhaust manifold stud (4 required)

N0089711

Fig. 59 Exploded view of the exhaust system—Dual exhaust

CRANKSHAFT FRONT SEAL

REMOVAL & INSTALLATION

See Figures 60 and 61.

1. Remove the crankshaft pulley.
2. Using the Crankshaft Front Oil Seal Remover, remove the crankshaft front seal.

To install:

3. Lubricate the engine front cover and the crankshaft front seal inner lip with clean engine oil.
4. Using the Crankshaft Front Oil Seal Installer, Crankshaft Vibration Damper Installer and Front Cover Oil Seal Installer, install the crankshaft front seal into the engine front cover.
5. Install the crankshaft pulley.

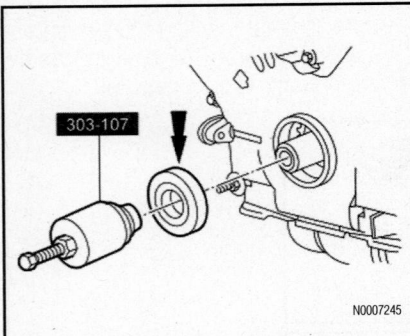

Fig. 60 Using the Crankshaft Front Oil Seal Remover

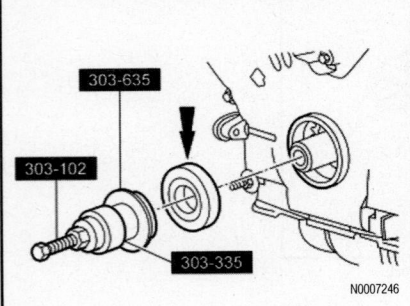

Fig. 61 Using the Crankshaft Front Oil Seal Installer, Crankshaft Vibration Damper Installer and Front Cover Oil Seal Installer

CYLINDER HEAD

REMOVAL & INSTALLATION

See Figures 62 through 65.

1. Disconnect the negative battery cable.
2. Remove the engine from the vehicle. Refer to Engine Assembly in this section.

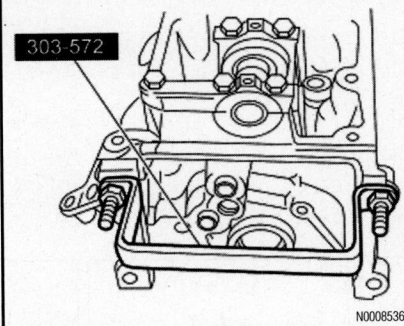

Fig. 62 Install the Cylinder Head Remover/Installer on both ends of the cylinder heads

3. Remove the bolts and flexplate.
4. Using the Engine Lifting Bracket Set, mount the engine on a suitable engine stand.
5. Remove the engine mounts.
6. Remove the drain plugs.
7. Remove the battery cables.
8. Disconnect the EGR tube from the exhaust manifold.
9. Remove the ignition coils.

10. Remove the alternator.
11. Remove the 8 bolts and the intake manifold.
12. Remove the coolant bypass tube.
13. Remove the valve covers.
14. Remove the camshaft roller followers.
15. Remove the 16 hydraulic lash adjusters.
16. Remove the bolt and the belt idler pulley.
17. Remove the coolant pump pulley.
18. Remove the crankshaft pulley bolt.
19. Using the Crankshaft Vibration Damper Remover, remove the crankshaft pulley.
20. Using the Crankshaft Front Oil Seal Remover, remove the crankshaft front oil seal.
21. Remove the front 4 oil pan bolts.
22. Remove the timing chain cover.
23. Remove the timing chains.
24. Remove the exhaust manifolds.
25. Remove the bolt and the oil level indicator tube.

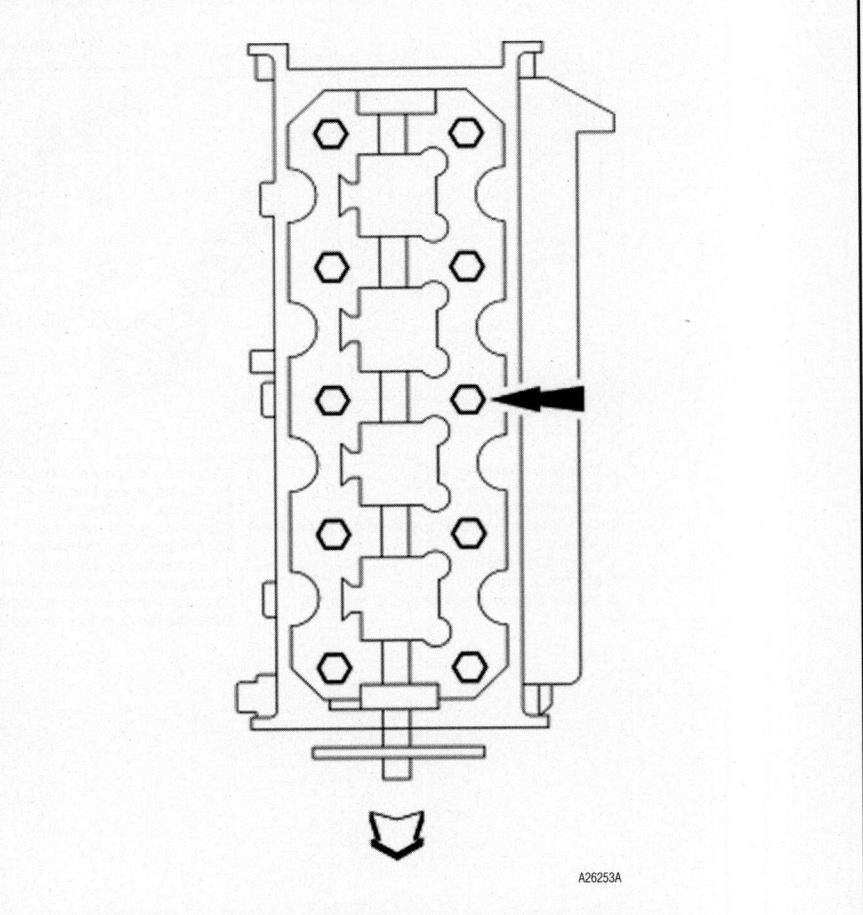

Fig. 63 Remove the bolts and the—RH cylinder head shown, LH similar

26. Remove the cylinder head insert from the LH cylinder head.

27. Clean and inspect the exhaust manifolds.

28. Install the Cylinder Head Remover/Installer on both ends of the cylinder head.

29. RH cylinder head:

➡The cylinder head must be cool before removing it from the engine. Cylinder head warpage may result if a warm or hot cylinder head is removed.

➡Aluminum surfaces are soft and can be scratched easily. Never place the cylinder head gasket surface, unprotected, on a bench surface. The scratches may cause leak paths.

➡Do not use metal scrapers, wire brushes, power abrasive discs or other abrasive means to clean the sealing surfaces. These tools cause scratches and gouges that make leak paths. Use a plastic scraping tool to remove all traces of the head gasket.

➡Place clean shop towels over exposed engine cavities. Carefully remove the towels so foreign material is not dropped into the engine.

➡The cylinder head bolts must be discarded and new bolts installed. They are a tighten-to-yield design and cannot be reused.

    a. Remove the bolts and the RH cylinder head.

    b. Discard the cylinder head gasket.

    c. Discard the cylinder head bolts.

30. LH cylinder head

➡The cylinder head must be cool before removing it from the engine. Cylinder head warpage may result if a warm or hot cylinder head is removed.

➡Aluminum surfaces are soft and can be scratched easily. Never place the cylinder head gasket surface, unprotected, on a bench surface. The scratches may cause leak paths.

➡Do not use metal scrapers, wire brushes, power abrasive discs or other abrasive means to clean the sealing surfaces. These tools cause scratches and gouges that make leak paths. Use a plastic scraping tool to remove all traces of the head gasket.

➡Place clean shop towels over exposed engine cavities. Carefully remove the towels so foreign material is not dropped into the engine.

➡The cylinder head bolts must be discarded and new bolts installed. They are a tighten-to-yield design and cannot be reused.

    a. Remove the bolts and the LH cylinder head.

    b. Discard the cylinder head gasket.

    c. Discard the cylinder head bolts.

31. Both cylinder heads

➡Do not use metal scrapers, wire brushes, power abrasive discs or other abrasive means to clean the sealing surfaces. These tools cause scratches and gouges that make leak paths. Use a plastic scraping tool to remove all traces of the head gasket.

➡Observe all warnings or cautions and follow all application directions contained on the packaging of the silicone gasket remover and the metal surface prep.

➡If there is no residual gasket material present, metal surface prep can be used to clean and prepare the surfaces.

    a. Clean the cylinder head-to-cylinder block mating surfaces of both the cylinder head and the cylinder block in the following sequence.

    b. Remove any large deposits of silicone or gasket material with a plastic scraper.

    c. Apply silicone gasket remover, following package directions, and allow to set for several minutes.

    d. Remove the silicone gasket remover with a plastic scraper. A second application of silicone gasket remover may be required if residual traces of silicone or gasket material remain.

    e. Apply metal surface prep, following package directions, to remove any remaining traces of oil or coolant, and to prepare the surfaces to bond with the new gasket. Do not attempt to make the metal shiny. Some staining of the metal surfaces is normal.

➡LH shown, RH similar.

32. Support the cylinder heads on a bench with the head gasket side up. Check the cylinder head distortion and the cylinder block distortion, paying particular attention to the oil pressure feed area.

To install:

➡The gasket sealing surfaces on the cylinder head and cylinder block must be clean.

➡The use of sealing aids (aviation cement, copper spray and glue) is not permitted. The gasket must be installed dry.

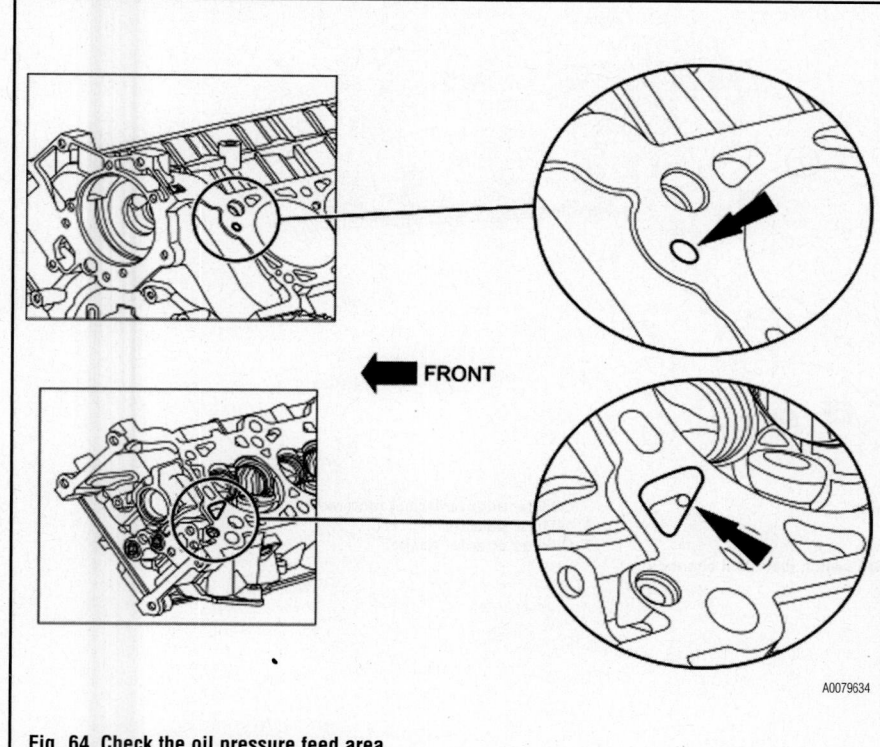

← FRONT

A0079634

Fig. 64 Check the oil pressure feed area

➡The new gasket has a film coating which is crucial to the gasket's ability to seal correctly. Do not scratch the gasket.

➡RH head gasket shown, LH head gasket similar.

33. Install the new head gasket over the dowel pins.

➡Cylinder head machining or milling is not authorized by the Ford Motor Company. Cylinder head flatness must be within 0.0254 mm (0.001 in) across a 38.1 mm (1.5 in) square area.

➡The gasket sealing surfaces on the cylinder head and cylinder block must be clean.

➡The use of sealing aids (aviation cement, copper spray and glue) is not permitted. The gasket must be installed dry.

➡Do not allow the dowels to scratch the sealing surface of the cylinder head during cylinder head installation.

➡RH cylinder head shown, LH cylinder head similar.

34. Install the cylinder head on the

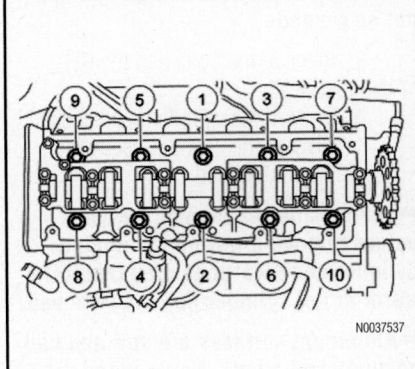

Fig. 65 Cylinder head tightening sequence

dowels and the head gasket. Loosely install new bolts.

35. Tighten the cylinder head bolts in 6 stages, in sequence:
   a. Stage 1: Tighten to 40 Nm (30 lb-ft).
   b. Stage 2: Tighten an additional 90 degrees (one-fourth turn).
   c. Stage 3: Loosen a minimum of one full turn (360 degrees).
   d. Stage 4: Tighten to 40 Nm (30 lb-ft).
   e. Stage 5: Tighten an additional 90 degrees (one-fourth turn).
   f. Stage 6: Tighten an additional 90 degrees (one-fourth turn).

36. Remove the Cylinder Head Remover/Installer from both ends of the cylinder head.

37. Complete the installation, reverse the remaining removal procedure.

ENGINE OIL & FILTER

REPLACEMENT

See Figures 66 and 67.

1. Remove the oil cap on top of the engine.
2. With the vehicle in NEUTRAL, position it on a hoist.
3. Position a oil receptacle under the vehicle.
4. Remove the oil pan drain plug until all the oil has fully drained. Install the oil pan plug.
5. Remove the oil filter.
6. Lubricate the new oil filter seal with clean engine oil.
7. Install the oil filter.
8. Fill the engine with the recommended oil.
9. Check the dipstick for accurate fill levels.

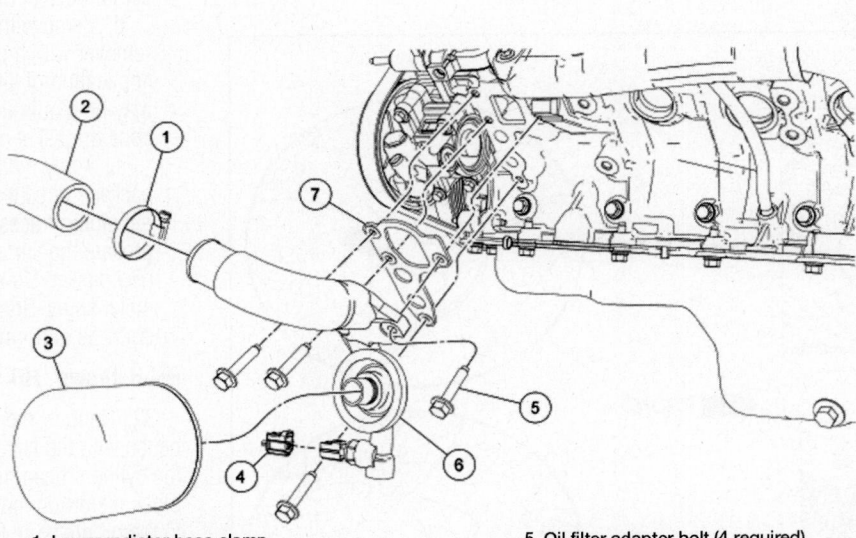

1. Lower radiator hose clamp
2. Lower radiator hose
3. Oil filter
4. Engine Oil Pressure (EOP) switch electrical connector
5. Oil filter adapter bolt (4 required)
6. Oil filter adapter
7. Oil filter adapter gasket

Fig. 66 Oil filter location—Without oil cooler

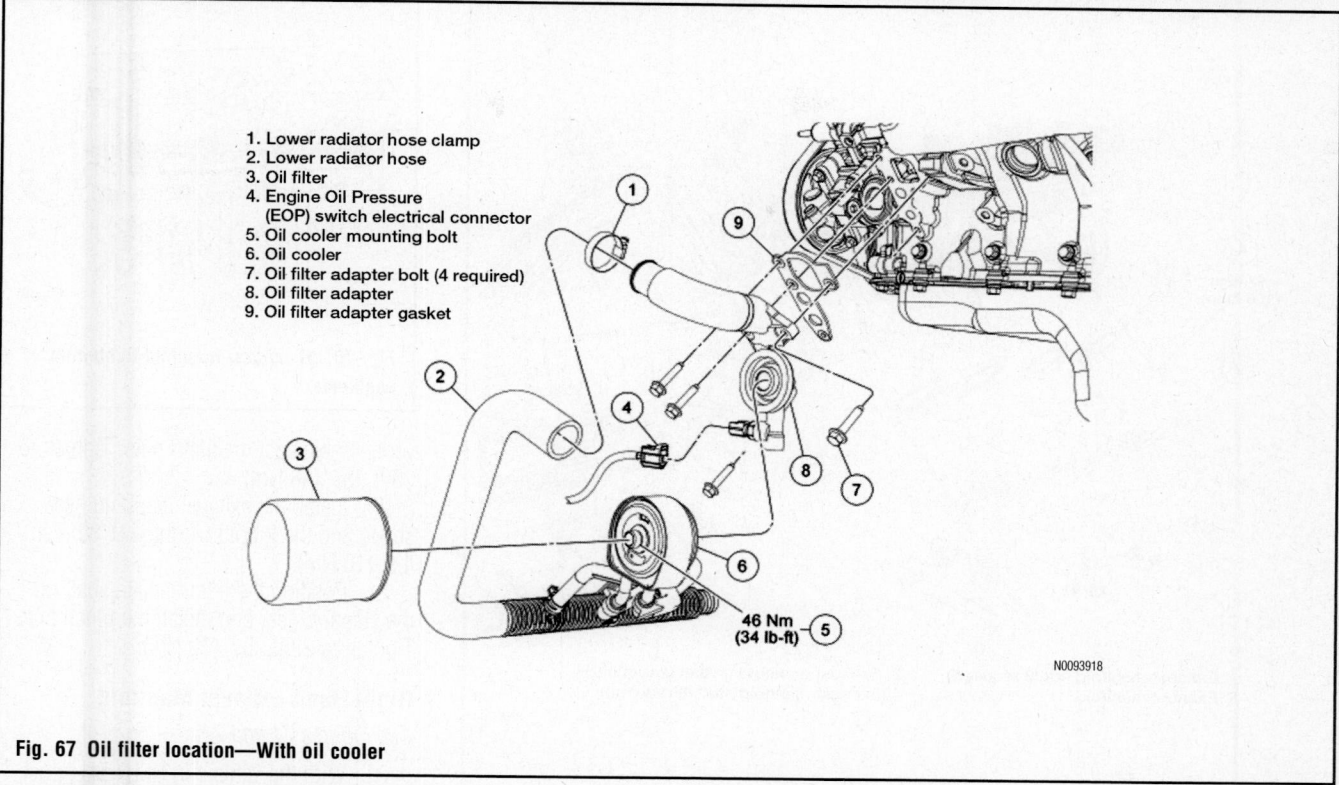

1. Lower radiator hose clamp
2. Lower radiator hose
3. Oil filter
4. Engine Oil Pressure
   (EOP) switch electrical connector
5. Oil cooler mounting bolt
6. Oil cooler
7. Oil filter adapter bolt (4 required)
8. Oil filter adapter
9. Oil filter adapter gasket

46 Nm
(34 lb-ft)

N0093918

Fig. 67 Oil filter location—With oil cooler

EXHAUST MANIFOLD

REMOVAL & INSTALLATION

Left Hand Exhaust Manifold

See Figures 68 through 70.

1. Disconnect the negative battery cable.

2. With the vehicle in NEUTRAL, position it on a hoist..

➡**Use a steering wheel holding device (such as Hunter® 28-75-1 or equivalent).**

3. Using a suitable holding device, hold the steering wheel in the straight-ahead position.

➡**Do not allow the intermediate shaft to rotate while it is disconnected from the steering gear or damage to the clockspring may result. If there is evidence that the intermediate shaft has rotated, the clockspring must be removed and recentered. For additional information, refer to Supplemental Restraint System.**

4. Remove the intermediated shaft pinch bolt and detach the intermediate shaft from the steering gear and position aside.

5. Remove the 2 exhaust manifold heat shield bolts and the shield.

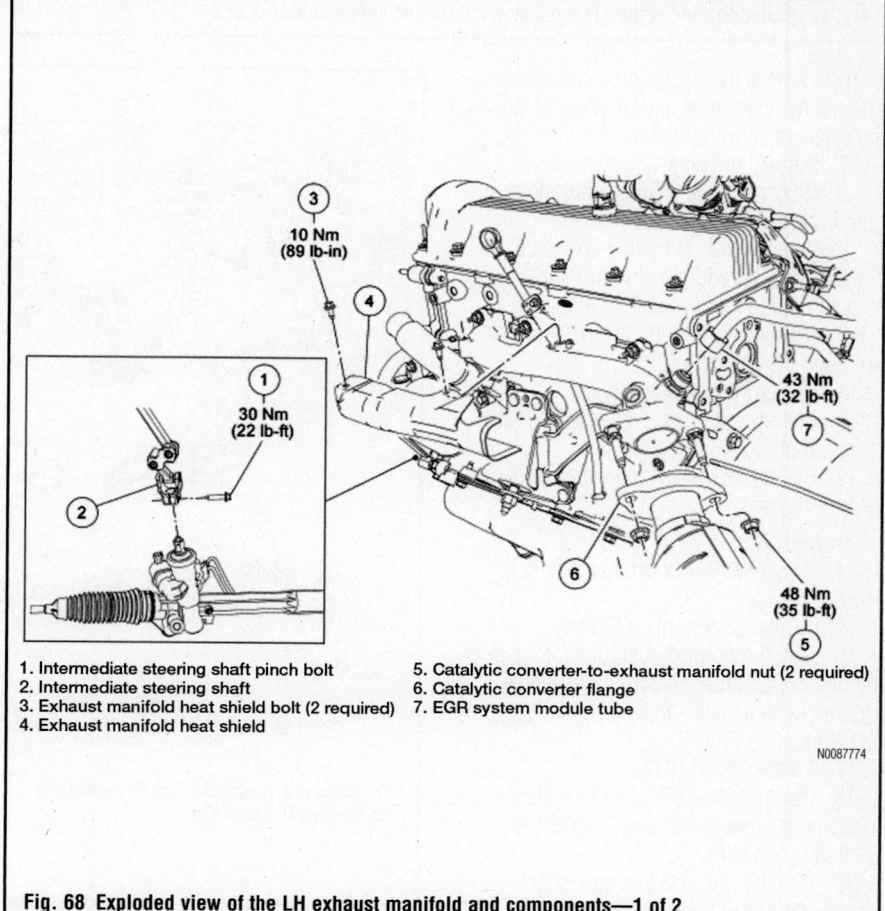

3
10 Nm
(89 lb-in)

4

1
30 Nm
(22 lb-ft)

2

43 Nm
(32 lb-ft)
7

6

48 Nm
(35 lb-ft)
5

1. Intermediate steering shaft pinch bolt
2. Intermediate steering shaft
3. Exhaust manifold heat shield bolt (2 required)
4. Exhaust manifold heat shield
5. Catalytic converter-to-exhaust manifold nut (2 required)
6. Catalytic converter flange
7. EGR system module tube

N0087774

Fig. 68 Exploded view of the LH exhaust manifold and components—1 of 2

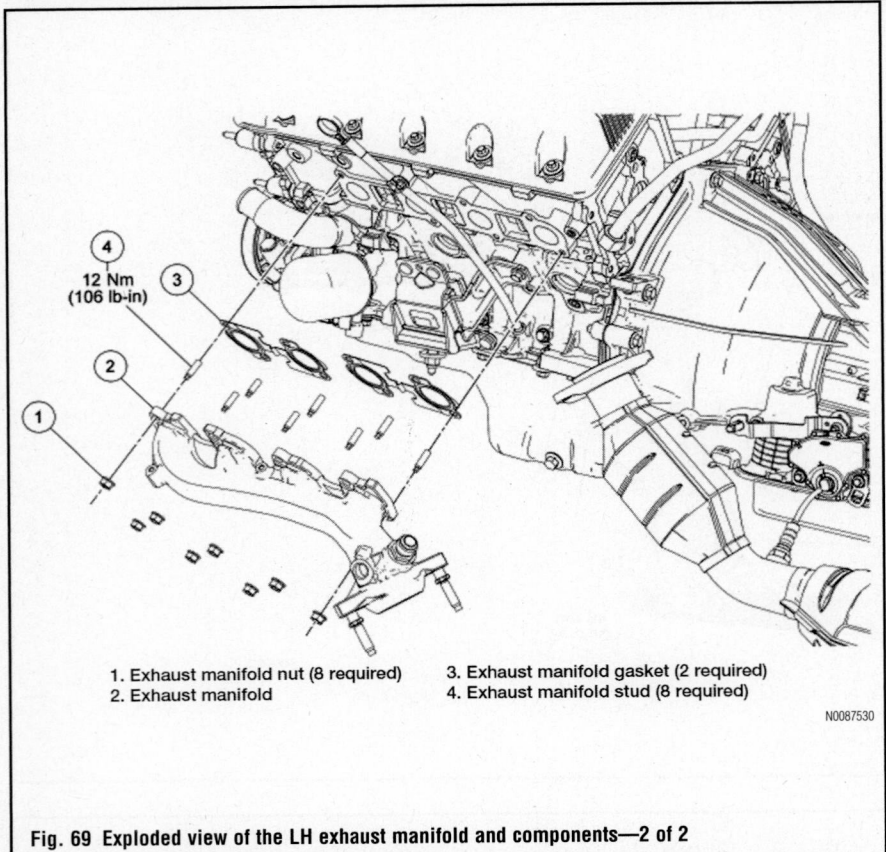

1. Exhaust manifold nut (8 required)
2. Exhaust manifold
3. Exhaust manifold gasket (2 required)
4. Exhaust manifold stud (8 required)

N0087530

Fig. 69 Exploded view of the LH exhaust manifold and components—2 of 2

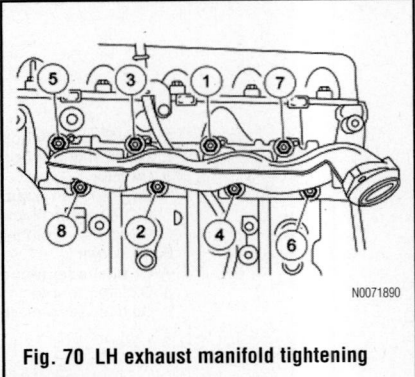

N0071890

Fig. 70 LH exhaust manifold tightening sequence

verter-to-exhaust manifold nuts. Tighten to 35 ft. lbs. (48 Nm).

20. Install the exhaust manifold heat shield and the 2 bolts. Tighten to 89 inch lbs. (10 Nm).

21. Position the intermediate shaft on the steering gear and install the pinch bolt. Tighten to 22 ft. lbs. (30 Nm).

Right Hand Exhaust Manifold

See Figures 71 and 72.

1. With the vehicle in NEUTRAL, position it on a hoist.

2. Disconnect the battery ground cable..

6. Remove the 2 catalytic converter-to-exhaust manifold nuts and position aside the catalytic converter flange.

7. Discard the nuts.

8. Disconnect the EGR system module tube from the exhaust manifold.

9. Remove the LH Heated Oxygen Sensor (HO2S). For additional information, refer to Engine Performance.

10. Remove the 8 nuts, the exhaust manifold and the gasket.

11. Discard the nuts and gasket.

12. Remove and discard the 8 exhaust manifold studs.

13. Clean and inspect the exhaust manifold for flatness.

To install:

14. Install the 8 new exhaust manifold studs.

15. Tighten to 9 ft. lbs. (12 Nm).

16. Install a new exhaust manifold gasket, the exhaust manifold and 8 new nuts. Tighten in sequence shown to 15 ft. lbs. (20 Nm).

17. Install the LH HO2S.

18. Connect the EGR system module tube to the exhaust manifold. Tighten to 32 ft. lbs. (43 Nm).

19. Position the catalytic converter flange and install the new catalytic con-

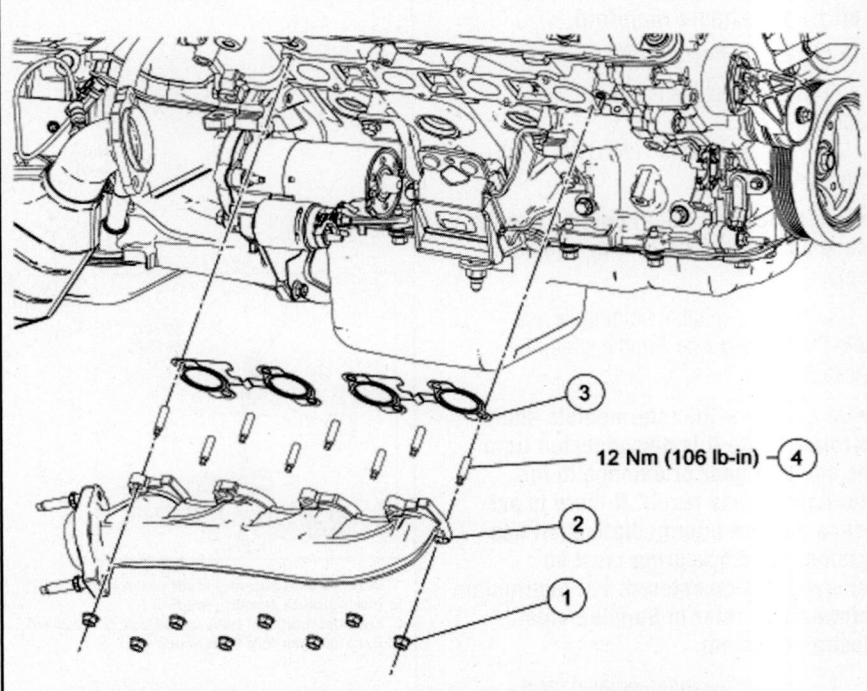

1. Exhaust manifold nut (8 required)
2. Exhaust manifold
3. Exhaust manifold gasket (2 required)
4. Exhaust manifold stud (8 required)

N0087529

Fig. 71 Exploded view of the RH exhaust manifold and components

3. Rotate the drive belt tensioner clockwise and remove the drive belt.

4. Disconnect the Crankshaft Position (CKP) sensor electrical connector.

5. Disconnect the A/C compressor electrical connector.

6. Remove the bolt from the transmission cooler tube bracket.

7. Remove the nut and position aside the transmission cooler tube assembly.

8. Remove the 3 bolts and position aside the A/C compressor.

9. Remove the catalytic converter-to-exhaust manifold nuts and position aside the catalytic converter flange.

10. Discard the nuts.

11. Remove the 8 nuts, the exhaust manifold and the gasket.

12. Discard the nuts and gasket.

13. Remove and discard the 8 exhaust manifold studs.

14. Clean and inspect the exhaust manifold for flatness.

To install:

15. Install the 8 new exhaust manifold studs. Tighten to 9 ft. lbs. (12 Nm).

16. Install a new exhaust manifold gasket, the exhaust manifold and 8 new nuts. Tighten in sequence shown to 15 ft. lbs. (20 Nm).

17. Position the catalytic converter flange and install the new catalytic converter-to-exhaust manifold nuts. Tighten to 35 ft. lbs. (48 Nm).

18. Position the A/C compressor and install the 3 bolts. Tighten to 18 ft. lbs. (25 Nm).

19. Position the transmission cooler tube assembly and install the nut. To install, tighten to 80 inch lbs. (9 Nm).

20. Install the transmission cooler tube bracket bolt. To install, tighten to 11 ft. lbs. (15 Nm).

21. Connect the A/C compressor electrical connector.

22. Connect the CKP sensor electrical connector.

23. Rotate the drive belt tensioner clockwise and install the drive belt.

24. Connect the battery ground cable.

INTAKE MANIFOLD

REMOVAL & INSTALLATION

See Figures 73 and 74.

1. Disconnect the negative battery cable.

2. With the vehicle in NEUTRAL, position it on a hoist.

3. Disconnect the fuel tube spring lock coupling. For additional information, refer to Fuel System.

4. Disconnect the battery ground cable.

5. Drain the engine cooling system. For additional information, refer to Engine Cooling.

6. Remove the Air Cleaner (ACL) and outlet pipe.

7. Remove the wiper mounting arm and pivot shaft.

8. Disconnect the 8 fuel injector electrical connectors.

9. Remove the 8 ignition coil-on-plugs. For additional information, refer to Engine Ignition.

10. Remove the 2 bolts and the intake manifold shield.

11. Disconnect the brake booster vacuum hose from the intake manifold.

12. Disconnect the quick connect coupling Evaporative Emission (EVAP) canister purge valve hoses from the Throttle Body (TB) spacer and from the EVAP canister purge valve. For additional information, refer to Fuel System.

13. Disconnect the quick connect coupling PCV tube from the TB spacer. For additional information, refer to Fuel System.

14. Disconnect the EGR system module vacuum and electrical connectors.

15. Disconnect the intake manifold-to-TB spacer vacuum hose.

16. Disconnect the generator electrical connector.

17. Detach the 2 generator wiring harness retainers from the generator bracket.

18. Remove the 4 generator bracket bolts and the bracket.

19. Remove the coolant thermostat. For additional information, refer to Engine Cooling.

20. Disconnect the throttle control and the Throttle Position (TP) sensor electrical connectors.

21. Release the heater hose spring clamp and disconnect the heater hose.

22. Remove the EGR system module tube.

23. If equipped, detach the wire harness retainer from the intake manifold crash bracket.

24. Remove the intake manifold crash bracket bolt and prevent the bolt from contacting the cylinder head with a rubber band or tie strap.

25. Remove the intake manifold crash bracket bolt.

26. Disconnect the fuel rail pressure and temperature sensor vacuum and electrical connectors.

27. Remove the wire harness retainer from the rear of the intake manifold.

28. Remove the 8 bolts and the intake manifold.

29. Remove and discard the intake manifold gaskets.

30. Clean the sealing surfaces.

To install:

➡ **Align the gasket locator tabs with the slots in the cylinder head.**

31. Install new intake manifold gaskets.

32. Install the intake manifold and hand-tighten the 8 bolts.

33. Install the 8 ignition coil-on-plugs.

34. Position the intake manifold crash bracket and loosely install the bolt and stud bolt.

35. Tighten the bolts in the sequence shown. Tighten to 18 ft. lbs. (25 Nm).

36. Tighten the intake manifold crash bracket bolt. Tighten to 18 ft. lbs. (25 Nm).

37. Install the EGR system module tube.

38. Install the intake manifold shield and the 2 bolts. Tighten to 89 inch lbs. (10 Nm).

39. To complete the installation, reverse remaining removal procedure.

40. Connect the battery ground cable.

41. Fill and bleed the engine cooling

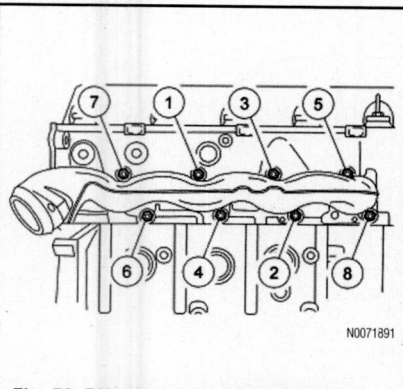

Fig. 72 RH exhaust manifold tightening sequence

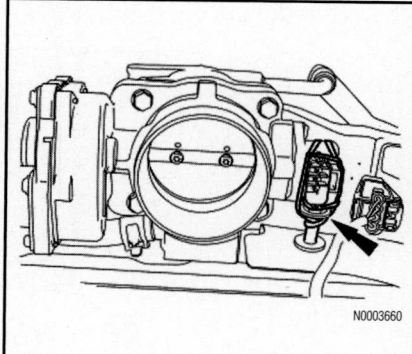

Fig. 73 Remove the intake manifold crash bracket bolt

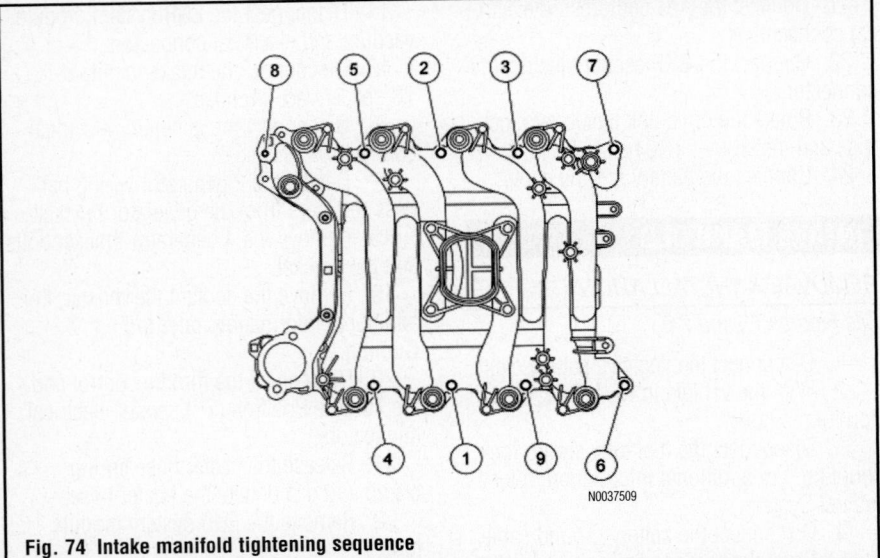

Fig. 74 Intake manifold tightening sequence

system. For additional information, refer to Engine Cooling.

OIL PAN

REMOVAL & INSTALLATION

See Figure 75.

1. Disconnect the negative battery cable.
2. With the vehicle in NEUTRAL, position it on a hoist.
3. Remove the front crossmember. Refer to Front Suspension.
4. Remove the bolt and the nut. Position the transmission cooler tubes aside.
5. Drain the engine oil.
6. Install the drain plug when finished.
7. Detach the 2 pin-type wire harness retainers.
8. Remove the oil pan bolts in the sequence shown.
9. Remove the oil pan and the gasket.

To install:

➡**Do not use metal scrapers, wire brushes, power abrasive discs or other abrasive means to clean the gasket mating surfaces. These tools cause scratches and gouges, which make leak paths. Use a plastic scraping tool to remove all traces of old sealant.**

Clean and inspect the mating surfaces.

➡**If not secured within 4 minutes, the sealant must be removed and the sealing area cleaned. To clean the sealing area, use silicone gasket remover and metal surface prep. Follow the directions on the packaging. Failure to fol-**

low this procedure can cause future oil leakage.

10. Apply silicone gasket and sealant at the rear seal retainer-to-cylinder block sealing surface.

➡**If not secured within 4 minutes, the sealant must be removed and the sealing area cleaned. To clean the sealing area, use silicone gasket remover and metal surface prep. Follow the directions on the packaging. Failure to follow this procedure can cause future oil leakage.**

11. Apply silicone gasket and sealant at the engine front cover-to-cylinder block mating surface.

12. Position the oil pan gasket and the oil pan.
13. Tighten the bolts in 2 stages, in the sequence shown in the removal procedure.
    Stage 1: Tighten to 15 ft. lbs. (20 Nm).
    Stage 2: Rotate an additional 60 degrees.
14. Attach the 2 pin-type wire harness retainers.
15. Position the transmission cooler tubes and install the bolt and the nut.
16. Install the front crossmember.
17. Fill the engine with clean engine oil.
18. Connect the negative battery cable.
19. Start the engine and check for leaks.

OIL PUMP

REMOVAL & INSTALLATION

1. Disconnect the negative battery cable.
2. With the vehicle in NEUTRAL, position it on a hoist.
3. Remove the oil pan.
4. Remove the timing chain and components. For additional information, refer to Timing Chain Components in this section.
5. Remove the 3 bolts, the oil pump screen and pickup tube.
6. Discard the O-ring seal.
7. Remove the 3 bolts and the oil pump.

To install:

➡**Do not use metal scrapers, wire brushes, power abrasive discs or other abrasive means to clean the sealing surfaces. These tools cause scratches**

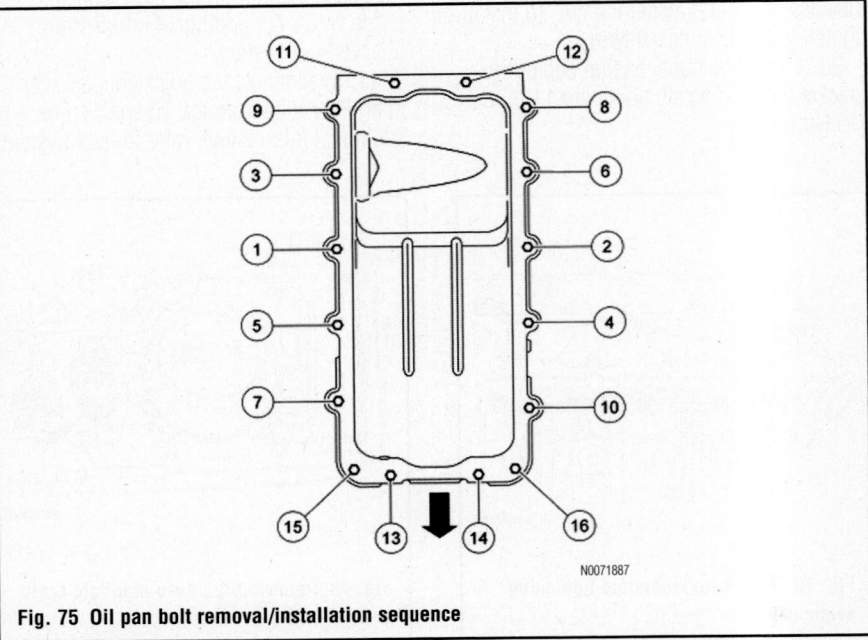

Fig. 75 Oil pan bolt removal/installation sequence

and gouges which make leak paths. Use a plastic scraping tool to remove all traces of old sealant.

8. Clean the sealing surfaces with metal surface prep. Follow the directions on the packaging. Inspect the mating surfaces.

9. Position the oil pump and install the 3 bolts. Tighten to 89 inch lbs. (10 Nm).

➡**Make sure the O-ring seal is in place and not damaged. A missing or damaged O-ring seal can cause foam in the** lubrication system, low oil pressure and severe engine damage.

➡**Clean and inspect the mating surfaces and install a new O-ring seal. Lubricate the O-ring seal with clean engine oil prior to installation.**

10. Position the oil pump screen and pickup tube and install the bolts.

11. Tighten the oil pump screen and pickup tube-to-oil pump bolts to 89 inch (10 Nm).

12. Tighten the oil pump screen and pickup tube-to-spacer bolt to 18 ft. lbs. (25 Nm).

13. Install the timing chain components.

14. Install the oil pan.

PISTON AND RING

POSITIONING

See Figure 76.

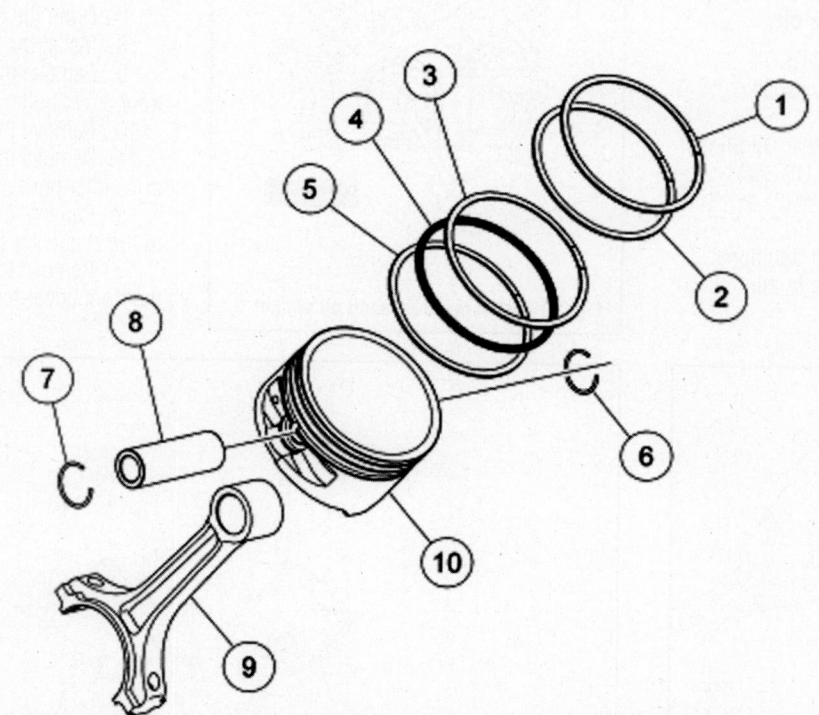

1. Piston compression upper ring
2. Piston compression lower ring
3. Piston oil control upper segment ring
4. Piston oil control spacer
5. Piston oil control lower segment ring
6. Piston pin retainer
7. Piston pin retainer
8. Piston pin
9. Connecting rod
10. Piston

N0004114

Fig. 76 Exploded view of the piston and ring

REAR MAIN SEAL

REMOVAL & INSTALLATION

See Figures 77 through 80.

1. With the vehicle in NEUTRAL, position it on a hoist.

2. Remove the flexplate. For additional information, refer to Flexplate in this section.

3. Using the Crankshaft Rear Oil Slinger Remover and Slide Hammer, remove the crankshaft oil slinger.

4. Using the Crankshaft Rear Oil Seal Remover and Slide Hammer, remove the crankshaft rear seal.

To install:

➡ **Lubricate the inner lip of the crankshaft rear seal with engine oil.**

5. Using the Crankshaft Rear Oil Seal Installers, install the crankshaft rear seal.

6. Using the Crankshaft Rear Oil Slinger Installer and Crankshaft Rear Oil Seal Installers, install the crankshaft oil slinger.

7. Install the flexplate. For additional information, refer to Flexplate in this section.

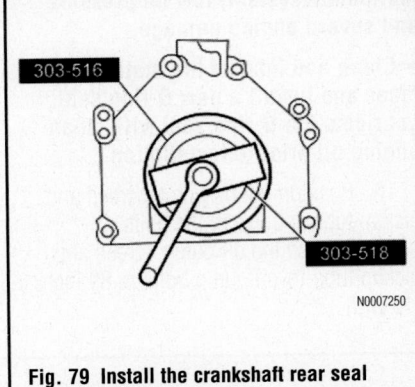

Fig. 79 Install the crankshaft rear seal

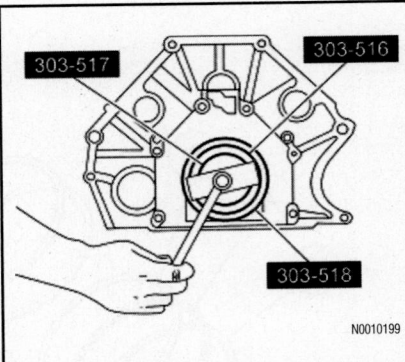

Fig. 80 Install the crankshaft oil slinger

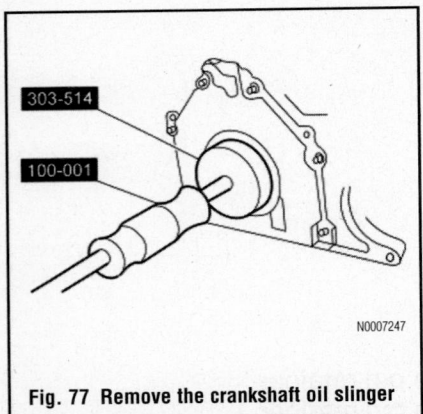

Fig. 77 Remove the crankshaft oil slinger

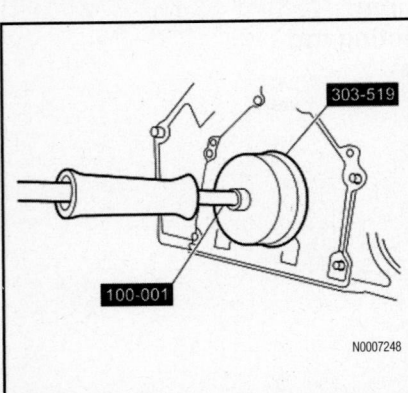

Fig. 78 Remove the crankshaft rear seal

TIMING CHAIN FRONT COVER

REMOVAL & INSTALLATION

See Figures 81 and 82.

1. Disconnect the negative battery cable.

2. With the vehicle in NEUTRAL, position it on a hoist.

3. Remove both valve covers. For additional information, refer to Valve Cover in this section.

4. Remove the water pump. For additional information, refer to Engine Cooling.

5. Remove the crankshaft front seal. For additional information, refer to Front Seal in this section.

6. Remove the 3 bolts and position the power steering pump aside.

7. Drain the engine oil.

8. Install the drain plug when finished.

9. Remove the 4 front oil pan-to-engine front cover bolts.

10. Remove the bolt and the shield.

11. Remove the bolt and the accessory drive idler pulley.

12. Remove the bolts and the stud bolts in the sequence shown.

13. Remove the engine front cover from the front cover-to-cylinder block dowel.

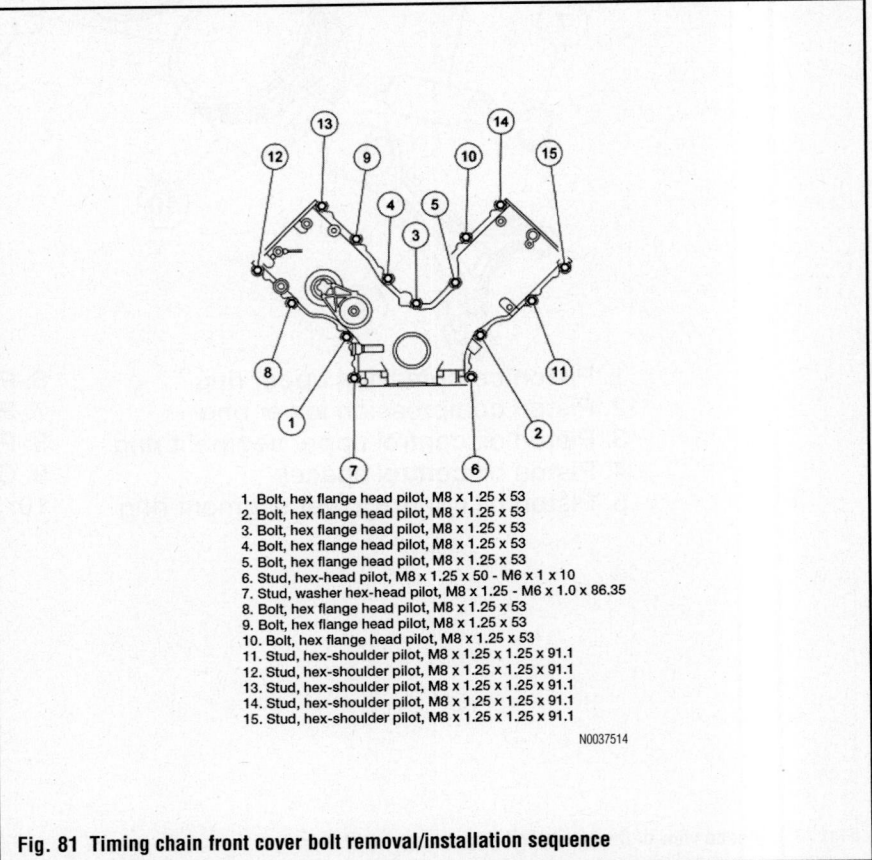

1. Bolt, hex flange head pilot, M8 x 1.25 x 53
2. Bolt, hex flange head pilot, M8 x 1.25 x 53
3. Bolt, hex flange head pilot, M8 x 1.25 x 53
4. Bolt, hex flange head pilot, M8 x 1.25 x 53
5. Bolt, hex flange head pilot, M8 x 1.25 x 53
6. Stud, hex-head pilot, M8 x 1.25 x 50 - M6 x 1 x 10
7. Stud, washer hex-head pilot, M8 x 1.25 - M6 x 1.0 x 86.35
8. Bolt, hex flange head pilot, M8 x 1.25 x 53
9. Bolt, hex flange head pilot, M8 x 1.25 x 53
10. Bolt, hex flange head pilot, M8 x 1.25 x 53
11. Stud, hex-shoulder pilot, M8 x 1.25 x 1.25 x 91.1
12. Stud, hex-shoulder pilot, M8 x 1.25 x 1.25 x 91.1
13. Stud, hex-shoulder pilot, M8 x 1.25 x 1.25 x 91.1
14. Stud, hex-shoulder pilot, M8 x 1.25 x 1.25 x 91.1
15. Stud, hex-shoulder pilot, M8 x 1.25 x 1.25 x 91.1

Fig. 81 Timing chain front cover bolt removal/installation sequence

➥Do not use metal scrapers, wire brushes, power abrasive discs or other abrasive means to clean the sealing surface. These tools cause scratches and gouges that make leak paths. Use a plastic scraping tool to remove all traces of the gasket material.

14. Clean the gasket surfaces with a plastic scraping tool and metal surface prep.

To install:

➥If not secured within 4 minutes, the sealant must be removed and the sealing area cleaned. To clean the sealing area, use silicone gasket remover and metal surface prep. Follow the directions on the packaging. Failure to follow this procedure can cause future oil leakage.

15. Apply silicone gasket and sealant along the cylinder head-to-block surface and the oil pan-to-cylinder block surface.

16. Position the new engine front cover gaskets.

17. Install the engine front cover on the front cover-to-cylinder block dowel and loosely install the bolts.

18. Tighten the front cover fasteners in the sequence shown to 25 Nm (18 lb-ft).

19. Install the accessory drive idler pulley and the bolt.

20. Install the shield and the bolts.

21. Install the oil pan.

➥The front lower hole in the power steering pump is not used.

22. Position the power steering pump and install the 3 bolts.

23. Install a new crankshaft front seal.

24. Install the water pump. For additional information, refer to Engine Cooling.

25. Install the valve covers.

26. Fill the engine with clean engine oil.

27. Disconnect the negative battery cable.

TIMING CHAIN & SPROCKETS

REMOVAL & INSTALLATION

See Figures 83 through 87.

1. With the vehicle in NEUTRAL, position it on a hoist.

2. Remove the Timing Chain Front Cover. For additional information, refer to Timing Chain Front Cover in this section.

3. Remove the crankshaft sensor ring from the crankshaft.

4. Disconnect the 8 ignition coil electrical connectors and ignition coils.

➥Only use hand tools when removing or installing the spark plugs, damage may occur to the cylinder head or spark plug.

➥Use compressed air to remove any foreign material from the spark plug wells before removing the spark plugs.

5. Remove the 8 spark plugs.

6. Position the lobe of the camshaft up.

7. Install the Valve Spring Compressor Spacer between the valve spring coils to prevent valve stem seal damage.

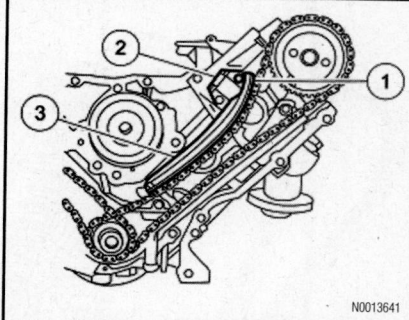

Fig. 83 Remove the bolts (1), tensioners (2) and tensioner arms (3)— LH shown, RH similar

➥If the components are to be reinstalled, they must be installed in the same positions. Mark the components for installation into their original locations. Failure to follow these instructions may result in engine damage.

8. Using the Valve Spring Compressor, compress the valve spring and remove the camshaft roller followers.

9. Position the crankshaft with the keyway at the 12 o'clock position.

➥LH shown, RH similar.

10. Remove the timing chain tensioning system from both timing chains.
   a. Remove the bolts.
   b. Remove the timing chain tensioners.
   c. Remove the timing chain tensioner arms.

11. Remove the LH and RH timing chains and the crankshaft sprocket.
   a. Remove the RH timing chain from the camshaft sprocket.
   b. Remove the RH timing chain from the crankshaft sprocket.
   c. Repeat for the LH timing chain and crankshaft sprocket.

12. Remove the timing chain guides.
   a. Remove the bolts.
   b. Remove the LH timing chain guide.
   c. Remove the bolts.
   d. Remove the RH timing chain guide.

13. Install the Camshaft Position Aligner.

14. Remove the bolt and the camshaft gear.

To install:

15. For engines with ratcheting timing chain tensioners:

➥Timing chain procedure must be followed exactly or damage to valves and pistons will result.

➥Do not compress the ratchet assembly. This will damage the ratchet assembly.

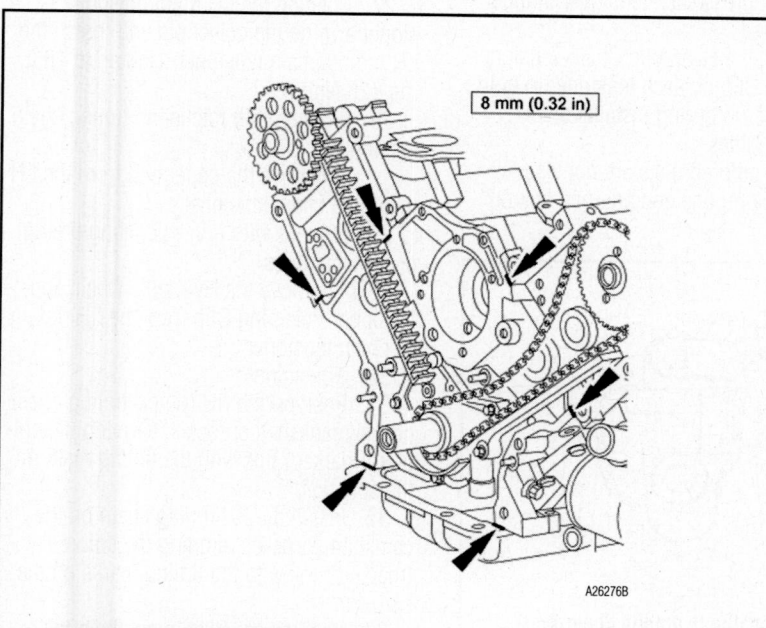

8 mm (0.32 in)

Fig. 82 Silicone gasket application areas

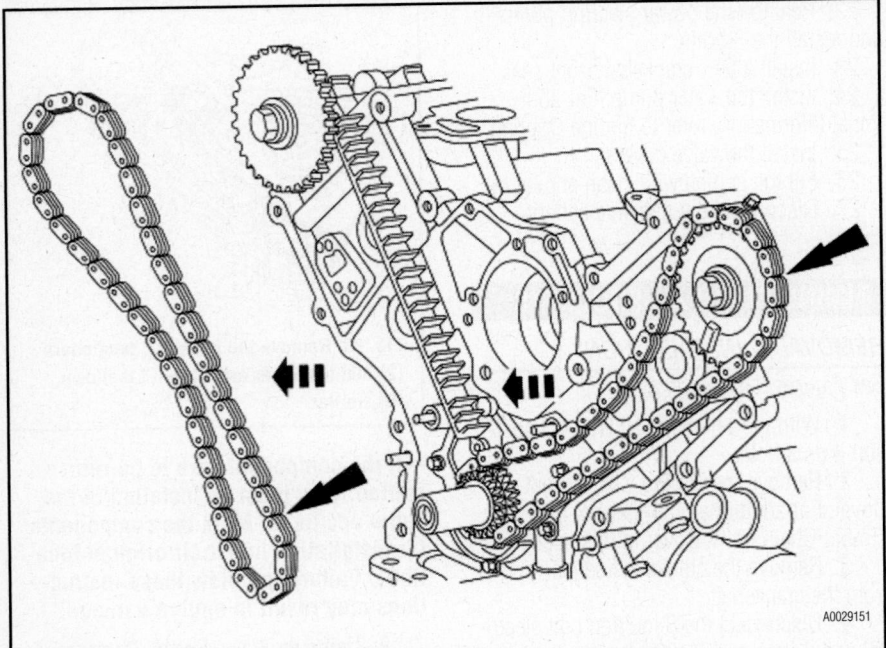

Fig. 84 Remove the LH and RH timing chains and the crankshaft sprocket

a. Compress each tensioner plunger, using an edge of a vise.

b. Using a small screwdriver or pick, push back and hold the ratchet mechanism.

c. While holding the ratchet mechanism, push the ratchet arm back into the tensioner housing.

d. Install a paper clip into the hole of each tensioner housing to hold the ratchet assembly and plunger in during installation.

e. Remove the tensioner from the vise.

16. Engines with non-ratcheting timing chain tensioners:

➡**If one or both tensioner mounting bolts are loosened or removed, the tensioner-sealing bead must be inspected for seal integrity. If cracks, tears, sepa-**ration from the tensioner body or permanent compression of the seal bead is observed, install a new tensioner or engine damage may occur.**

a. Inspect the RH and LH timing chain tensioners.

b. Install new tensioners as necessary.

➡**The timing chain procedure must be followed exactly or damage to valves and pistons will result.**

c. Compress each tensioner plunger, using a vise.

d. Install a Hydraulic Chain Tensioner Retaining Clip on each tensioner to hold the plunger in during installation.

17. All engines:

18. If the colored links are not visible, mark one link on one end and one link on the other end, and use as timing marks.

19. Install the camshaft sprockets and new bolts. Tighten the bolts in 2 stages.

a. Tighten to 30 ft. lbs. (40 Nm).

b. Tighten an additional 90 degrees (one-fourth turn).

20. Using the Crankshaft Holding Tool, position the crankshaft so the No. 1 cylinder is at Top Dead Center (TDC).

21. Install the crankshaft sprocket, making sure the flange faces forward.

22. Install the timing chain guide.

a. Position the LH timing chain guide.

b. Install and tighten the LH bolts to 89 inch lbs. (10 Nm).

c. Position the RH timing chain guide.

d. Install and tighten the RH bolts to 89 inch lbs. (10 Nm).

23. Rotate the RH camshaft sprocket until the timing mark is approximately at the 11 o'clock position.

24. Rotate the LH camshaft sprocket until the timing mark is approximately at the 1 o'clock position.

25. Position the LH (inner) timing chain on the crankshaft sprocket, aligning the colored (marked) link with the timing mark on the sprocket.

26. Install the LH timing chain on the sprocket, aligning the colored (marked) link with the timing marks on the sprocket.

➡**The LH timing chain tensioner arm has a bump near the dowel hole for identification.**

27. Position the LH timing chain tensioner arm on the dowel pin and install the LH timing chain tensioner. Tighten to 18 ft. lbs. (25 Nm).

28. Engines with ratcheting timing chain tensioners

a. Remove the paper clip from the LH timing chain tensioner.

29. Engines with non-ratcheting timing chain tensioners

a. Remove the Hydraulic Chain Tensioner Retaining Clip from the LH timing chain tensioner.

30. All engines:

31. Position the RH (outer) timing chain on the crankshaft sprocket, aligning the colored (marked) link with the timing mark on the sprocket.

32. Install the RH timing chain on the camshaft sprocket, aligning the colored (marked) link with the timing marks on the sprocket.

33. Position the RH timing chain tensioner arm on the dowel pin and install the

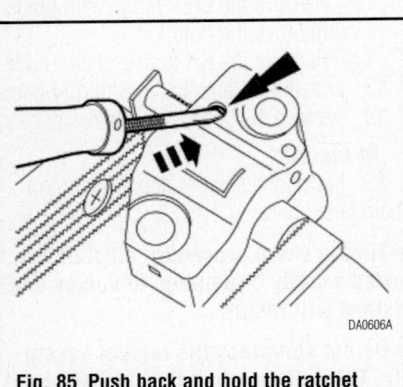

Fig. 85 Push back and hold the ratchet mechanism

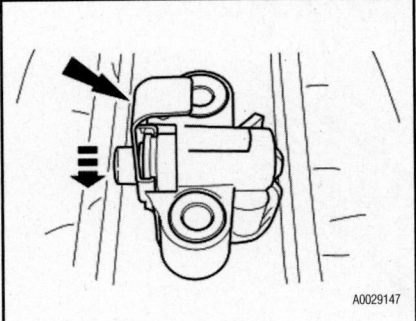

Fig. 86 Install a Hydraulic Chain Tensioner Retaining Clip on each tensioner

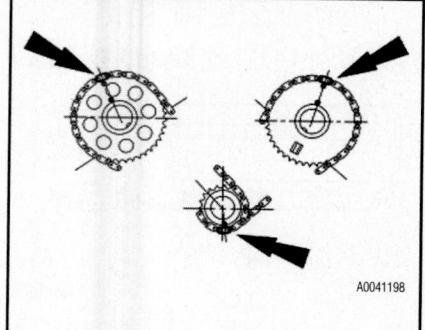

Fig. 87 Timing chain and sprocket orientation

RH timing chain tensioner. Tighten to 18 ft. lbs. (25 Nm).

34. Engines with ratcheting timing chain tensioners:

    a. Remove the paper clip from the RH timing chain tensioner.

35. Engines with non-ratcheting timing chain tensioners:

    a. Remove the Hydraulic Chain Tensioner Retaining Clip from the RH timing chain tensioner.

36. All engines:

37. Make sure that the colored (marked) chain links are lined up with the dots on the crankshaft sprocket and the camshaft sprockets.

38. Rotate the camshaft until the lobe is in the up position.

39. Install the Valve Spring Compressor Spacer between the valve spring coils to prevent valve stem seal damage.

➡**Lubricate the camshaft roller followers using clean engine oil.**

40. Install the camshaft roller followers.

41. Install the Valve Spring Compressor.

42. Compress the valve spring.

43. Install the camshaft roller followers in their original locations.

44. To complete the installation, reverse the remaining removal procedure.

VALVE COVERS

REMOVAL & INSTALLATION

LH Valve Cover

See Figures 88 and 89.

1. Disconnect the negative battery cable.

2. Remove the Air Cleaner.

3. Disconnect the 4 wiring harness retainers from the valve cover and position the wire harness aside.

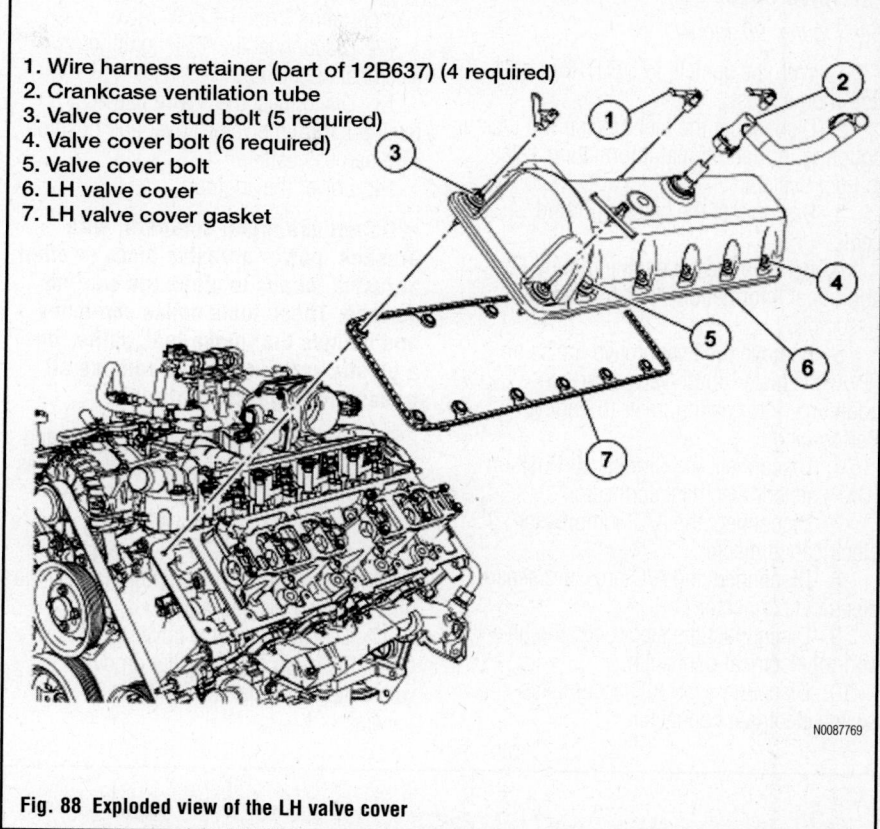

1. Wire harness retainer (part of 12B637) (4 required)
2. Crankcase ventilation tube
3. Valve cover stud bolt (5 required)
4. Valve cover bolt (6 required)
5. Valve cover bolt
6. LH valve cover
7. LH valve cover gasket

Fig. 88 Exploded view of the LH valve cover

4. Disconnect the crankcase ventilation tube quick connect coupling from the valve cover.

➡**Do not use metal scrapers, wire brushes, power abrasive discs or other abrasive means to clean the sealing surface. These tools cause scratches and gouges that make leak paths. Use a plastic scraping tool to remove all traces of the gasket material.**

5. Loosen the 11 fasteners and remove the LH valve cover and gasket.

6. Clean the valve cover mating surface of the cylinder head with silicone gasket remover and metal surface prep. Follow the directions on the packaging.

7. Discard the valve cover gasket. Clean the valve cover gasket groove with soap and water or a suitable solvent.

To install:

➡**If the valve cover is not installed and the fasteners tightened within 4 minutes, the sealant must be removed and the sealing area cleaned. To clean the sealing area, use silicone gasket remover and metal surface prep. Failure to follow this procedure can cause future oil leakage.**

8. Apply a bead of silicone gasket and sealant in 2 locations shown where the engine front cover meets the cylinder head.

9. Position the LH valve cover and new gasket on the cylinder head.

10. Tighten the fasteners in the sequence shown to 10 Nm (89 lb-in).

11. Connect the crankcase ventilation tube quick connect coupling to the valve cover.

12. Position the wire harness and connect the 4 wiring harness retainers to the valve cover.

13. Install the ACL and outlet pipe.

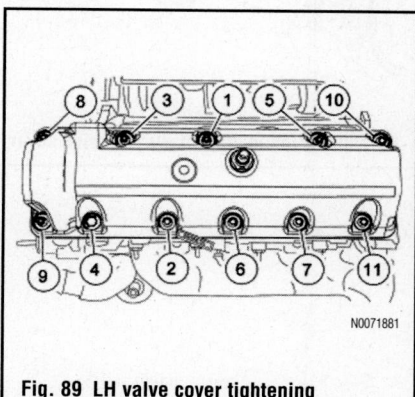

Fig. 89 LH valve cover tightening sequence

RH Valve Cover

See Figures 90 and 91.

1. With the vehicle in NEUTRAL, position it on a hoist.

2. Disconnect the fuel tube spring lock coupling. For additional information, refer to Fuel System.

3. Disconnect the battery ground cable.

4. Remove the LH engine mount. For additional information, refer to Engine Assembly.

5. Remove the Evaporative Emission (EVAP) canister purge valve. For additional information, refer to Engine Performance.

6. Disconnect the Crankshaft Position (CKP) sensor electrical connector.

7. Disconnect the A/C compressor electrical connector.

8. Disconnect the A/C pressure sensor electrical connector.

9. Disconnect the electronic engine control electrical connector.

10. Disconnect the A/C accumulator switch electrical connector.

11. Disconnect the PCV tube quick connect coupling from the PCV valve.

12. Disconnect the 4 RH ignition coil electrical connectors.

13. Disconnect the 3 wire harness retainers from the valve cover and position wire harness aside.

14. Lower the engine.

➡**Do not use metal scrapers, wire brushes, power abrasive discs or other abrasive means to clean the sealing surface. These tools cause scratches and gouges that make leak paths. Use a plastic scraping tool to remove all traces of the gasket material.**

15. Loosen the 8 studs, the 3 bolts and remove the valve cover and discard the gasket.

16. Clean the valve cover mating surface of the cylinder head with silicone gasket remover and metal surface prep. Follow the directions on the packaging.

17. Discard the valve cover gasket. Clean the valve cover gasket groove with soap and water or a suitable solvent.

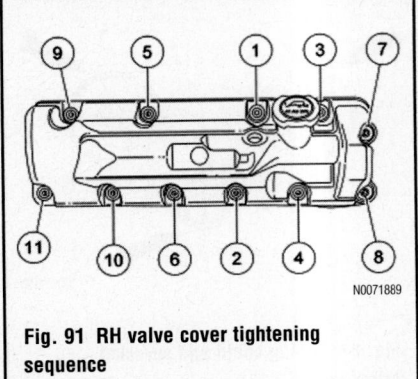

Fig. 91 RH valve cover tightening sequence

To install:

➡**If the valve cover is not installed and the fasteners tightened within 4 minutes, the sealant must be removed and the sealing area cleaned. To clean the sealing area, use silicone gasket remover and metal surface prep. Failure to follow this procedure can cause future oil leakage.**

18. Apply a bead of silicone gasket and sealant in 2 locations shown where the engine front cover meets the cylinder head.

19. Install a new valve cover gasket and the valve cover.

20. Tighten the fasteners in the sequence shown to 10 Nm (89 lb-in).

21. Raise the engine.

22. Position wire harness and connect the 3 wire harness retainers to the valve cover.

23. Connect the 4 RH ignition coil electrical connectors.

24. Connect the PCV tube quick connect coupling to the PCV valve.

25. Connect the A/C accumulator switch electrical connector.

26. Connect the 3 electronic engine control electrical connectors.

27. Connect the A/C pressure sensor electrical connector.

28. Connect the A/C compressor electrical connector.

29. Connect the CKP sensor electrical connector.

30. To complete installation, reverse the remaining removal procedure.

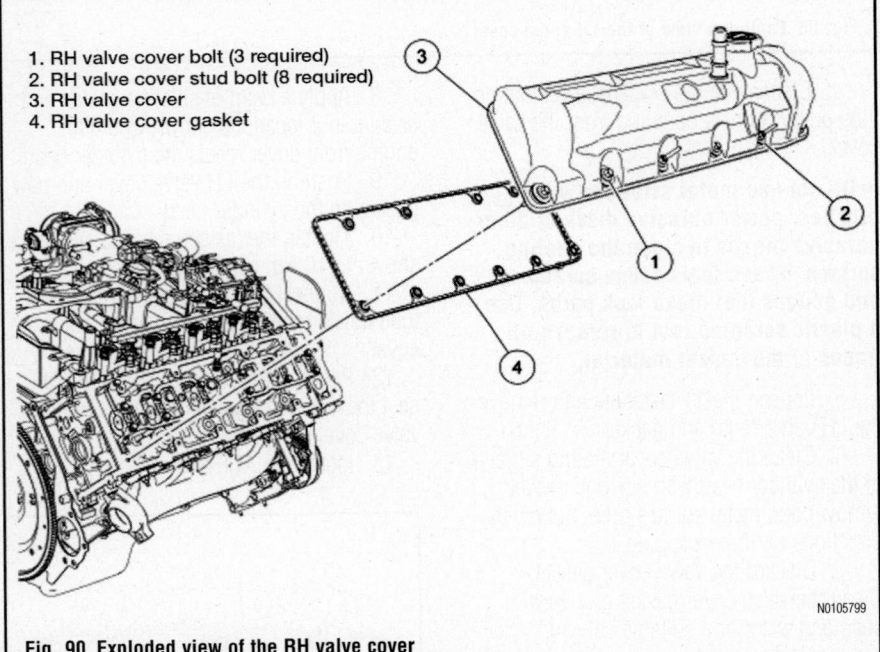

1. RH valve cover bolt (3 required)
2. RH valve cover stud bolt (8 required)
3. RH valve cover
4. RH valve cover gasket

Fig. 90 Exploded view of the RH valve cover

ENGINE PERFORMANCE & EMISSION CONTROLS

CAMSHAFT POSITION (CMP) SENSOR

LOCATION

See Figure 92.

REMOVAL & INSTALLATION

1. Disconnect the negative battery cable.
2. Disconnect the Camshaft Position (CMP) sensor electrical connector.
3. Remove the bolt and the CMP sensor.
4. To install, reverse the removal procedure.

CRANKSHAFT POSITION (CKP) SENSOR

LOCATION

See Figure 93.

REMOVAL & INSTALLATION

1. Disconnect the negative battery cable.
2. With the vehicle in NEUTRAL, position it on a hoist.
3. Rotate the tensioner and remove the drive belt from the A/C compressor pulley.
4. Disconnect the A/C compressor field coil electrical connector.
5. Disconnect the Crankshaft Position (CKP) sensor electrical connector.
6. Remove the nut and detach the 2 wiring harness clips.

➡**NOTE: It is not necessary to remove the A/C compressor stud bolts.**

7. Loosen the 3 A/C compressor stud bolts enough to slide the compressor down one inch, allowing access for CKP sensor removal.
8. Remove the bolt and the CKP sensor.
9. To install, reverse the removal procedure.

POWERTRAIN CONTROL MODULE (PCM)

REMOVAL & INSTALLATION

See Figure 94.

➡**Any PCM replacement will require that ALL customer keys are available to be programmed at the time of installation. PCM replacement DOES NOT require new keys. Retrieve the module configuration. Carry out the module configuration retrieval steps of the Programmable Module Installation (PMI) procedure.**

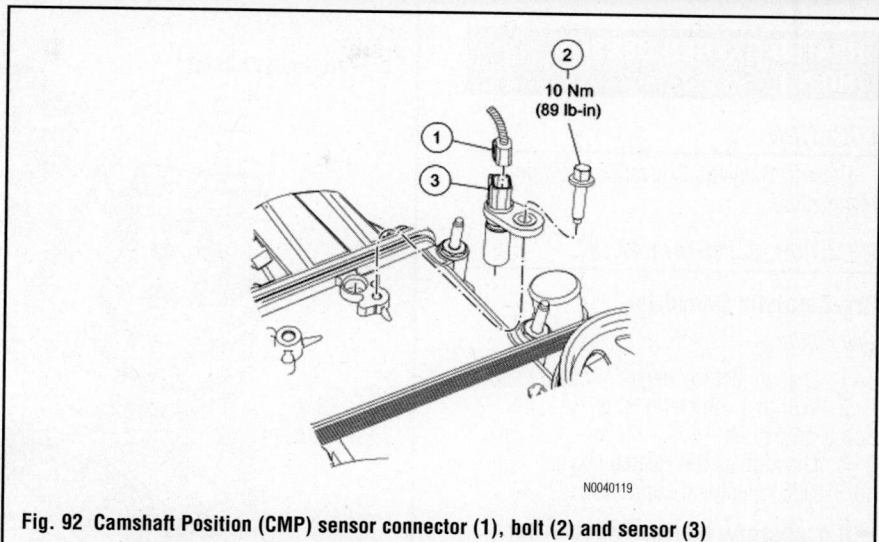

Fig. 92 Camshaft Position (CMP) sensor connector (1), bolt (2) and sensor (3)

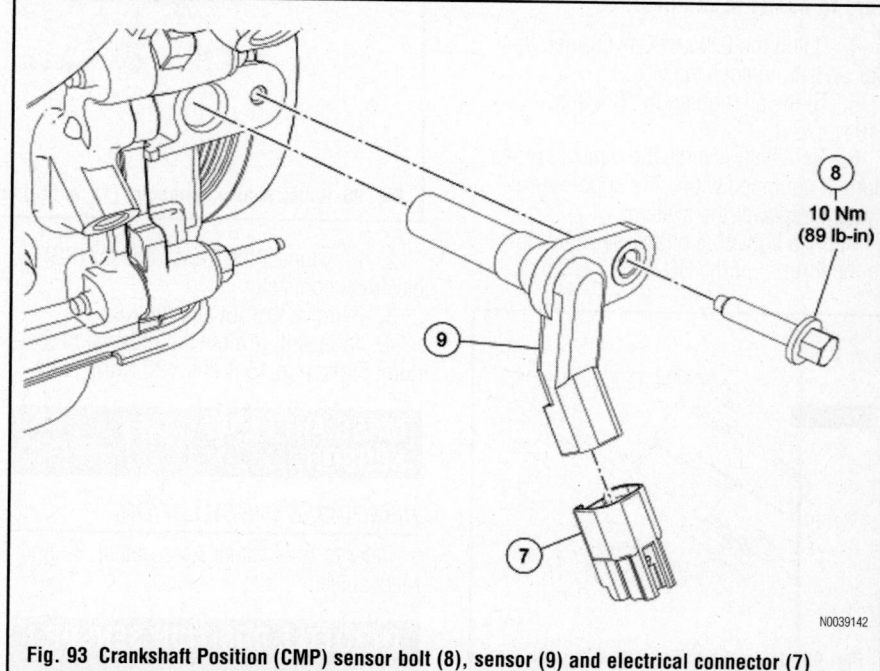

Fig. 93 Crankshaft Position (CMP) sensor bolt (8), sensor (9) and electrical connector (7)

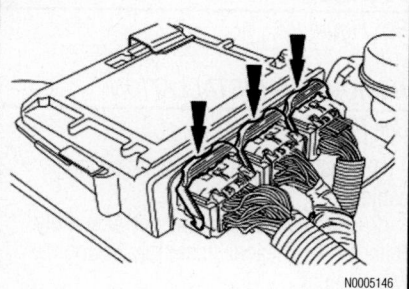

Fig. 94 Release the clips and disconnect the 3 PCM electrical connectors

1. Disconnect the negative battery cable.
2. Release the clips and disconnect the 3 PCM electrical connectors.
3. Remove the bolt and the PCM.

To install:
4. Install the PCM and the bolt.
5. Connect the 3 PCM electrical connectors and install the clips.
6. Restore the module configuration. Carry out the module configuration restore steps of the Programmable Module Installation (PMI) procedure.
7. Reprogram the Passive Anti-Theft System (PATS). Carry out the Key

Programming Using Two Programmed Keys procedure.

HEATED OXYGEN SENSOR (HO2S)

LOCATION

Refer to Catalytic Converter in Engine Mechanical.

REMOVAL & INSTALLATION

Pre-Catalytic Converter

See Figure 95.

1. Disconnect the negative battery cable.
2. With the vehicle in NEUTRAL, position it on a hoist.
3. Disconnect the Heated Oxygen Sensor (HO2S) electrical connector.

➡**If necessary, lubricate the sensor threads with penetrating and lock lubricant to assist in removal.**

4. Using the Exhaust Gas Oxygen Sensor Socket, remove the HO2S.
5. To install, tighten to 30 ft. lbs. (40 Nm).
6. To install, reverse the removal procedure. If equipped with a fire suppression system, repower the system.

Apply a light coat of anti-seize lubricant to the threads of the HO2S.

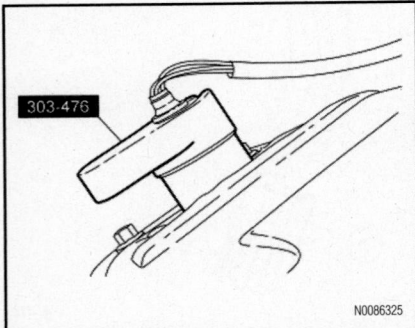

Fig. 95 Using the Exhaust Gas Oxygen Sensor Socket

Post Catalytic Converter

Refer to Catalytic Converter in Engine Mechanical.

KNOCK SENSOR (KS)

LOCATION

See Figure 96.

REMOVAL & INSTALLATION

1. Remove the intake manifold.

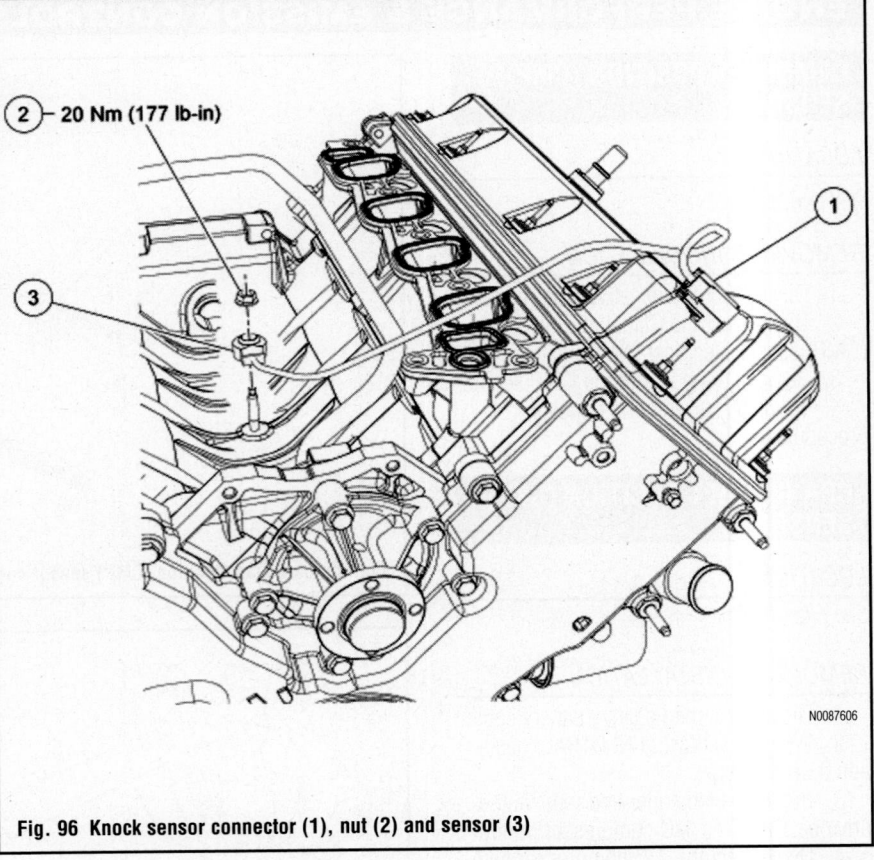

Fig. 96 Knock sensor connector (1), nut (2) and sensor (3)

2. Disconnect the Knock Sensor (KS) electrical connector.
3. Remove the nut and the KS.
4. To install, reverse the removal procedure. Tighten to 15 ft. lbs. (20 Nm).

MASS AIR FLOW (MAF) SENSOR

REMOVAL & INSTALLATION

Refer to Air Cleaner Assembly in Engine Mechanical.

THROTTLE POSITION SENSOR (TPS)

LOCATION

See Figure 97.

REMOVAL & INSTALLATION

See Figure 98.

1. Disconnect the negative battery cable.
2. Remove the Air Cleaner Assembly. Refer to Air Cleaner Assembly in Engine Mechanical.
3. Disconnect the Throttle Position (TP) sensor electrical connector.

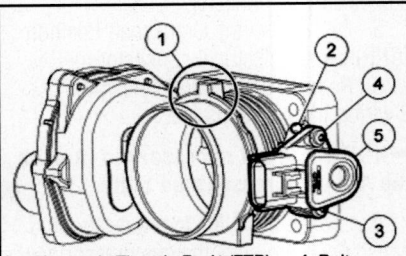

1. Electronic Throttle Body (ETB)
2. TP sensor bolt ear
3. Bolt
4. Bolt
5. TP sensor

Fig. 97 Locating the TPS sensor and components

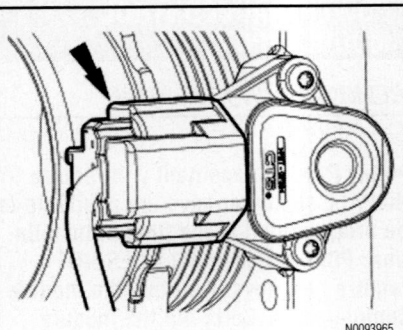

Fig. 98 Disconnect the Throttle Position (TP) sensor electrical connector

➡Do not put direct heat on the Throttle Position (TP) sensor or any other plastic parts because heat damage may occur. Damage may also occur if Electronic Throttle Body (ETB) temperature exceeds 120°C (248°F).

➡Do not use power tools.

4. Remove the TP sensor.

a. Using a suitable heat gun, apply heat to the top of the Electronic Throttle Body (ETB) until the top TP sensor bolt ear reaches approximately 55°C (130°F), this should take no more than 3 minutes using an 1,100-watt heat gun. The heat gun should be about 25.4 mm (1 in) away from the ETB .

b. Monitor the temperature of the top TP sensor bolt ear on the ETB with a suitable temperature measuring device, such as a digital temperature laser or infrared thermometer, while heating the ETB .

c. Using hand tools, quickly remove the bolt farthest from the heat source first and discard.

d. Using hand tools, remove the remaining bolt and discard.

e. Remove and discard the TP sensor.

To install:

➡When installing the new TP sensor, make sure that the radial locator tab on the TP sensor is aligned with the radial locator hole on the ETB .

➡Do not use power tools.

5. Install the new TP sensor.
6. Using hand tools, install the 2 new bolts.
7. Connect the TP sensor electrical connector.
8. Install the Air Cleaner Assembly. Refer to Air Cleaner Assembly in Engine Mechanical.
9. Connect the negative battery cable.

FUEL   GASOLINE FUEL INJECTION SYSTEM

FUEL SYSTEM SERVICE PRECAUTIONS

✳✳ WARNING

Observe all applicable safety precautions when working around fuel. Whenever servicing the fuel system, always work in a well ventilated area. Do not allow fuel spray or vapors to come in contact with a spark or open flame. Keep a dry chemical fire extinguisher near the work area. Always keep fuel in a container specifically designed for fuel storage; also, always properly seal fuel containers to avoid the possibility of fire or explosion.

Safety is the most important factor when performing not only fuel system maintenance but any type of maintenance. Failure to conduct maintenance and repairs in a safe manner may result in serious personal injury or death. Maintenance and testing of the vehicle's fuel system components can be accomplished safely and effectively by adhering to the following rules and guidelines.

• To avoid the possibility of fire and personal injury, always disconnect the negative battery cable unless the repair or test procedure requires that battery voltage be applied.

• Always relieve the fuel system pressure prior to disconnecting any fuel system component (injector, fuel rail, pressure regulator, etc.), fitting or fuel line connection. Exercise extreme caution whenever relieving fuel system pressure to avoid exposing skin, face and eyes to fuel spray. Please be advised that fuel under pressure may penetrate the skin or any part of the body that it contacts.

• Always place a shop towel or cloth around the fitting or connection prior to loosening to absorb any excess fuel due to spillage. Ensure that all fuel spillage (should it occur) is quickly removed from engine surfaces. Ensure that all fuel soaked cloths or towels are deposited into a suitable waste container.

• Always keep a dry chemical (Class B) fire extinguisher near the work area.

• Do not allow fuel spray or fuel vapors to come into contact with a spark or open flame.

• Always use a back-up wrench when loosening and tightening fuel line connection fittings. This will prevent unnecessary stress and torsion to fuel line piping.

• Always replace worn fuel fitting O-rings with new Do not substitute fuel hose or equivalent where fuel pipe is installed.

Before servicing the vehicle, make sure to also refer to the precautions in the beginning of this section as well.

✳✳ WARNING

Do not smoke, carry lighted tobacco or have an open flame of any type when working on or near any fuel-related component. Highly flammable mixtures are always present and may be ignited. Failure to follow these instructions may result in serious personal injury.

✳✳ WARNING

Do not carry personal electronic devices such as cell phones, pagers or audio equipment of any type when working on or near any fuel-related component. Highly flammable mixtures are always present and may be ignited. Failure to follow these instructions may result in serious personal injury.

✳✳ WARNING

Before working on or disconnecting any of the fuel tubes or fuel system components, relieve the fuel system pressure to prevent accidental spraying of fuel. Fuel in the fuel system remains under high pressure, even when the engine is not running. Failure to follow this instruction may result in serious personal injury.

✳✳ WARNING

When handling fuel, always observe fuel handling precautions and be prepared in the event of fuel spillage. Spilled fuel may be ignited by hot vehicle components or other ignition sources. Failure to follow these instructions may result in serious personal injury.

✳✳ WARNING

Always disconnect the battery ground cable at the battery when working on an evaporative emission (EVAP) system or fuel-related component. Highly flammable mixtures are always present and may be ignited. Failure to follow these instructions may result in serious personal injury.

⁜ WARNING

Shut off the electrical power to the air suspension system prior to hoisting or jacking an air suspension equipped vehicle. Failure to do so may result in unexpected inflation or deflation of the air springs, which may result in shifting of the vehicle during these operations. Failure to follow this instruction may result in serious personal injury.

⁜ WARNING

Do not carry personal electronic devices such as cell phones, pagers or audio equipment of any type when working on or near any fuel-related component. Highly flammable mixtures are always present and may be ignited. Failure to follow these instructions may result in serious personal injury.

⁜ WARNING

Before working on or disconnecting any of the fuel tubes or fuel system components, relieve the fuel system pressure to prevent accidental spraying of fuel. Fuel in the fuel system remains under high pressure, even when the engine is not running. Failure to follow this instruction may result in serious personal injury.

RELIEVING FUEL SYSTEM PRESSURE

See Figure 99.

➡The Fuel Pump (FP) module fuse is located in the Battery Junction Box (BJB), location F4.

1. Remove the FP module fuse.
2. Start the engine and allow it to idle until it stalls.
3. After the engine stalls, crank the engine for approximately 5 seconds to make sure the fuel system pressure has been released.
4. Turn the ignition switch to the OFF position.
5. When fuel system service is complete, install the FP module fuse.

➡It may take more than one key cycle to pressurize the fuel system.

6. Cycle the ignition key and wait 3 seconds to pressurize the fuel system.

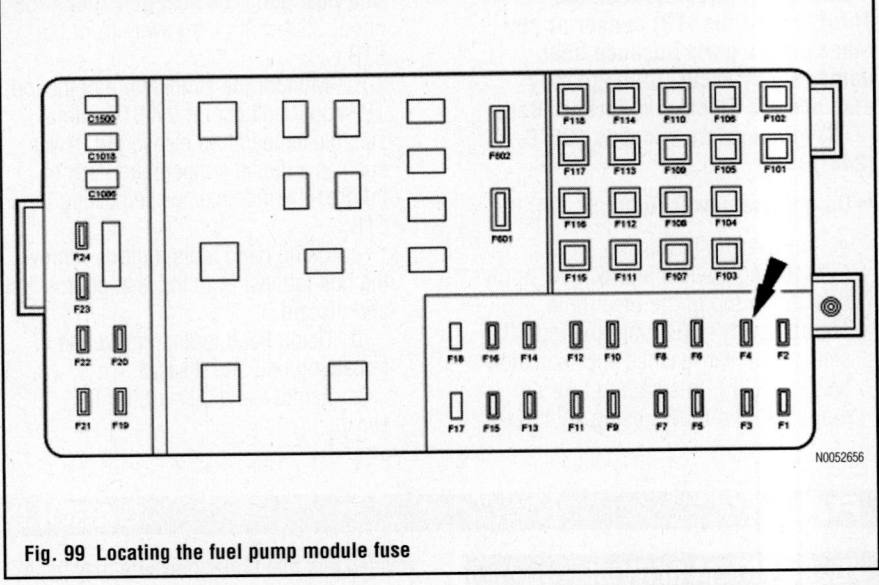

Fig. 99 Locating the fuel pump module fuse

➡Carry out a Key ON Engine OFF (KOEO) visual inspection for fuel leaks prior to starting the engine.

7. Start the vehicle and check the fuel system for leaks.

FUEL FILTER

REMOVAL & INSTALLATION

1. With the vehicle in NEUTRAL, position it on a hoist.
2. Release the fuel system pressure.
3. Disconnect the battery ground cable.

➡Some residual fuel may remain in the fuel tubes and fuel filter after releasing the fuel system pressure. Upon disconnecting or removing any fuel-related component, carefully drain residual fuel into a suitable container.

4. Disconnect the fuel tube-to-fuel filter inlet and outlet spring lock couplings.
5. Remove the fuel filter.
6. Release the fuel filter bracket clamp and remove the fuel filter.
7. To install, reverse the removal procedure.

FUEL INJECTORS

REMOVAL & INSTALLATION

See Figure 100.

1. With vehicle in NEUTRAL, position it on a hoist.
2. Release the fuel system pressure.
3. Disconnect the battery ground cable.
4. Disconnect the fuel supply tube-to-fuel rail spring lock coupling.
5. Remove the Throttle Body (TB).

6. Remove the EGR system module tube.
7. Release the clamp and disconnect the brake booster vacuum hose from the TB spacer.
8. Disconnect the Evaporative Emission (EVAP) vapor tube-to- TB spacer quick connect coupling.
9. Disconnect the crankcase ventilation tube-to- TB spacer quick connect coupling.
10. Disconnect the intake manifold vacuum hose from the TB spacer.
11. If equipped, release the wire harness retainer from the crash bracket.
12. Remove the 2 bolts and the crash bracket.
13. Disconnect the 8 fuel injector electrical connectors.
14. Disconnect the fuel rail pressure and temperature sensor vacuum hose and electrical connector.
15. Disconnect the EGR module vacuum and electrical connectors.
16. Remove the 2 bolts and the intake manifold shield.
17. Remove the 4 fuel rail bolts.
18. Remove the fuel rail and fuel injectors as an assembly.

➡O-ring seals are made of special fuel-resistant material. Fuel will damage ordinary O-ring seals, and may cause the fuel system to leak.

➡Do not reuse O-ring seals. The removal and installation process may damage the used O-ring seals, and may cause the fuel system to leak.

19. Remove the fuel injectors and O-ring seals.

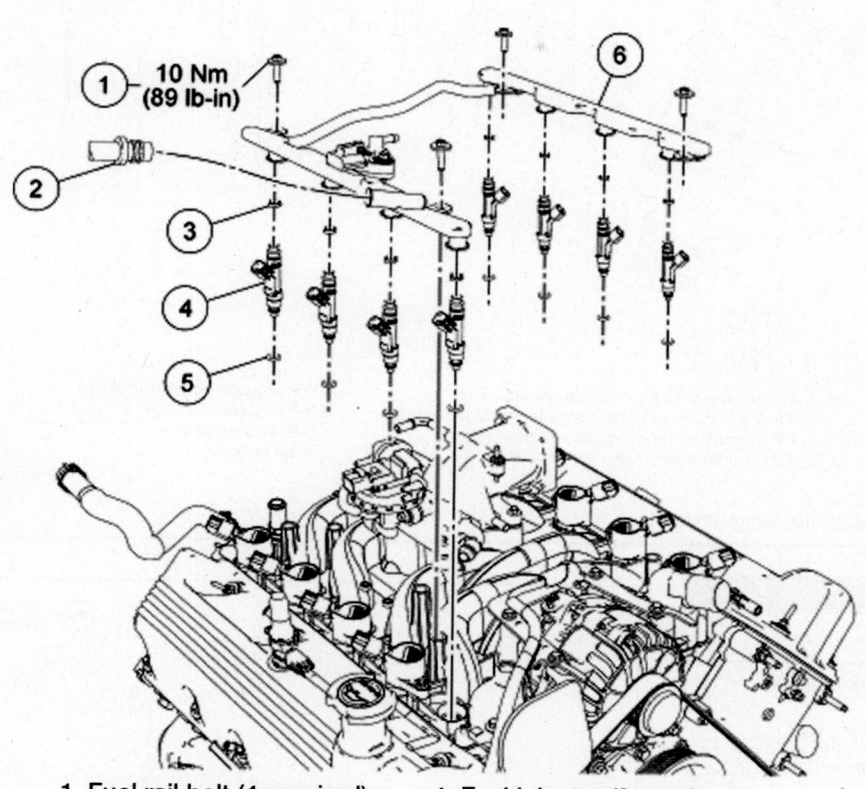

1. Fuel rail bolt (4 required)
2. Fuel tube-to-fuel rail spring lock coupling
3. Fuel injector upper O-ring seal (8 required)
4. Fuel injector (8 required)
5. Fuel injector lower O-ring seal (8 required)
6. Fuel rail

N0092687

Fig. 100 Exploded view of the fuel rail and fuel injectors

20. Discard the O-ring seals.
21. To install, reverse the removal procedure.
22. Install new upper and lower fuel injector O-ring seals and lubricate with clean engine oil prior to installation.

FUEL PUMP

REMOVAL & INSTALLATION

See Figure 101.

1. Remove the fuel tank. Refer to Fuel Tank in this section.

2. Disconnect the Fuel Pump (FP) module harness-to-Fuel Tank Pressure (FTP) sensor electrical connector.

3. Release the 2 FP module wiring harness retainers.

4. Clean the FP module mounting flange and immediate surrounding area of any dirt or foreign material.

➡The Fuel Pump (FP) module must be handled carefully to avoid damage to the float arm and the filter.

5. Remove the 6 bolts and the FP module.

6. Remove and discard the FP module seal.

➡Inspect the surfaces of the FP module flange and fuel tank seal contact surfaces. Do not polish or adjust the seal contact area of the FP module flange or fuel tank. Install a new FP module or fuel tank if the seal contact area is bent, scratched or corroded.

➡Install a new FP module seal.

7. To install, reverse the removal procedure.

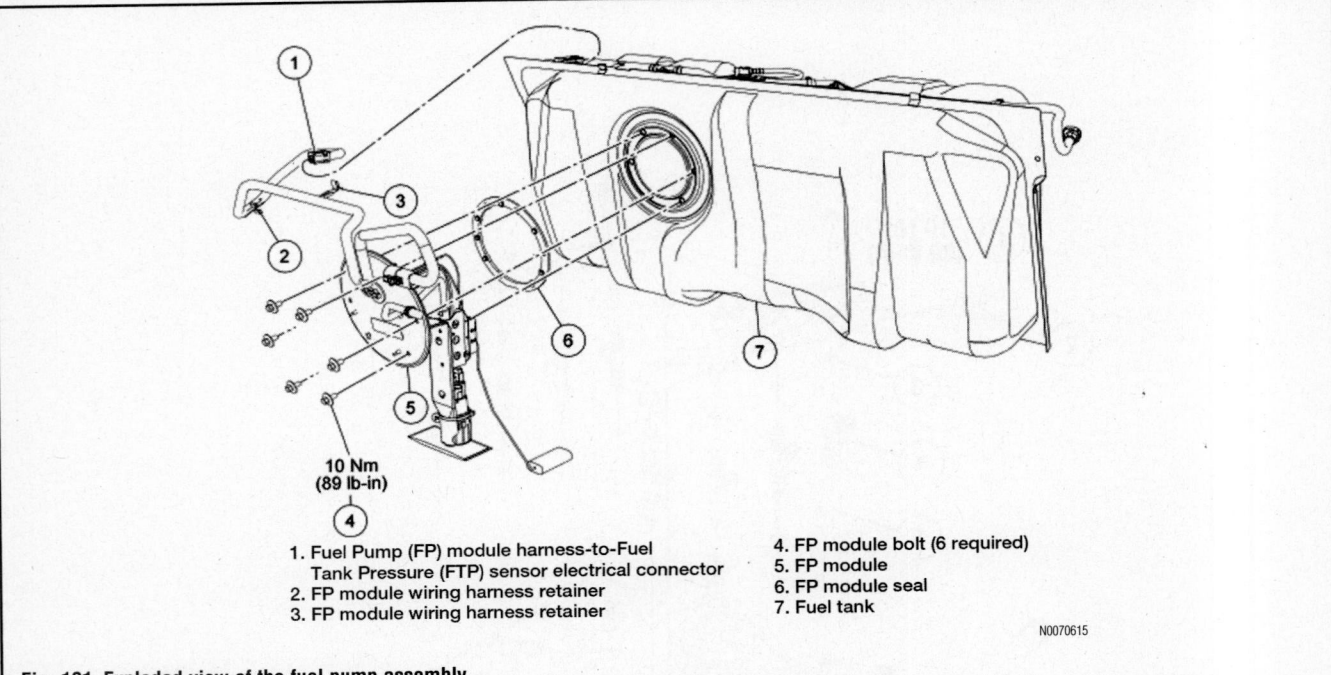

1. Fuel Pump (FP) module harness-to-Fuel Tank Pressure (FTP) sensor electrical connector
2. FP module wiring harness retainer
3. FP module wiring harness retainer
4. FP module bolt (6 required)
5. FP module
6. FP module seal
7. Fuel tank

N0070615

Fig. 101 Exploded view of the fuel pump assembly

FUEL TANK

DRAINING

1. Remove the fuel tank from the vehicle.
2. Remove the fuel tank filler pipe.
3. Using the Fuel Storage Tanker and a suitable fuel drain tube, extract the remaining fuel from the fuel tank.

REMOVAL & INSTALLATION

See Figure 102.

1. Release the fuel system pressure.
2. Disconnect the battery ground cable.
3. Drain the fuel tank.
4. Disconnect the Fuel Pump (FP) module electrical connector and release the retainer clip.
5. Disconnect the fuel tube-to- FP module spring lock coupling.
6. Disconnect the fuel vapor tube assembly-to-fuel vapor tube quick connect coupling.
7. Disconnect the fuel vapor tube-to-fuel vapor tube assembly quick connect coupling.
8. Completely lower and remove the fuel tank.

➡The fuel tank strap studs are manufactured as a break-off style. After installing the new fuel tank strap studs and fuel tank installation is completed, break-off the excess length at the recess in the studs.

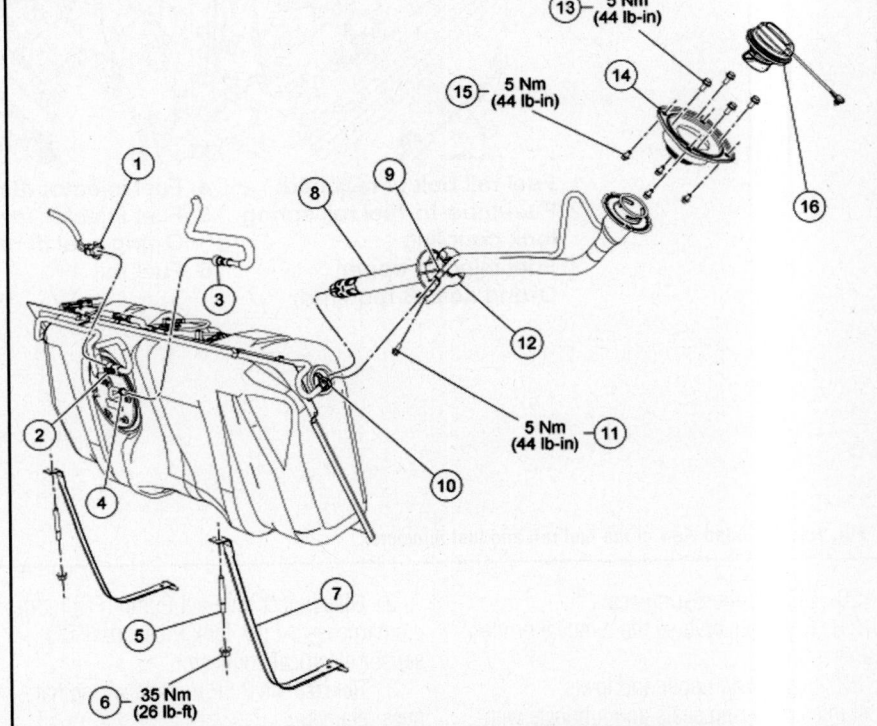

1. Fuel Pump (FP) module electrical connector
2. FP module electrical connector retainer clip
3. Fuel tube-to- FP module spring lock coupling
4. FP module
5. Fuel tank strap stud (2 required)
6. Fuel tank strap nut (2 required)
7. Fuel tank strap (2 required)
8. Fuel tank filler pipe
9. Fuel tank filler pipe recirculation tube
10. Fuel vapor tube assembly-to-fuel tank filler pipe recirculation tube quick connect coupling
11. Fuel tank filler pipe bracket bolt
12. Fuel tank filler pipe bracket
13. Fuel tank filler pipe flange bolt (4 required)
14. Fuel tank filler pipe seal
15. Fuel tank filler pipe seal bolt (4 required)
16. Fuel tank filler cap

N0087576

Fig. 102 Exploded view of the fuel tank and fuel filler pipe

9. Remove and discard the fuel tank strap studs.

10. To install, reverse the removal procedure.

IDLE SPEED

ADJUSTMENT

Idle speed adjustment is not necessary or possible.

THROTTLE BODY

REMOVAL & INSTALLATION

See Figure 103.

1. Remove the Air Cleaner (ACL) outlet pipe.

2. Disconnect the electronic throttle control and the Throttle Position (TP) sensor electrical connectors.

3. Remove the 4 bolts and the Throttle Body (TB).

4. Discard the TB gasket.

To install:

5. Install a new gasket, the TB and the 4 bolts.

6. Tighten the bolts in 2 stages.

   a. Stage 1: Tighten to 80 inch lbs. (9 Nm).

   b. Stage 2: Rotate an additional 90 degrees.

7. Connect the electronic throttle control and the TP sensor electrical connectors. Install the ACL outlet pipe.

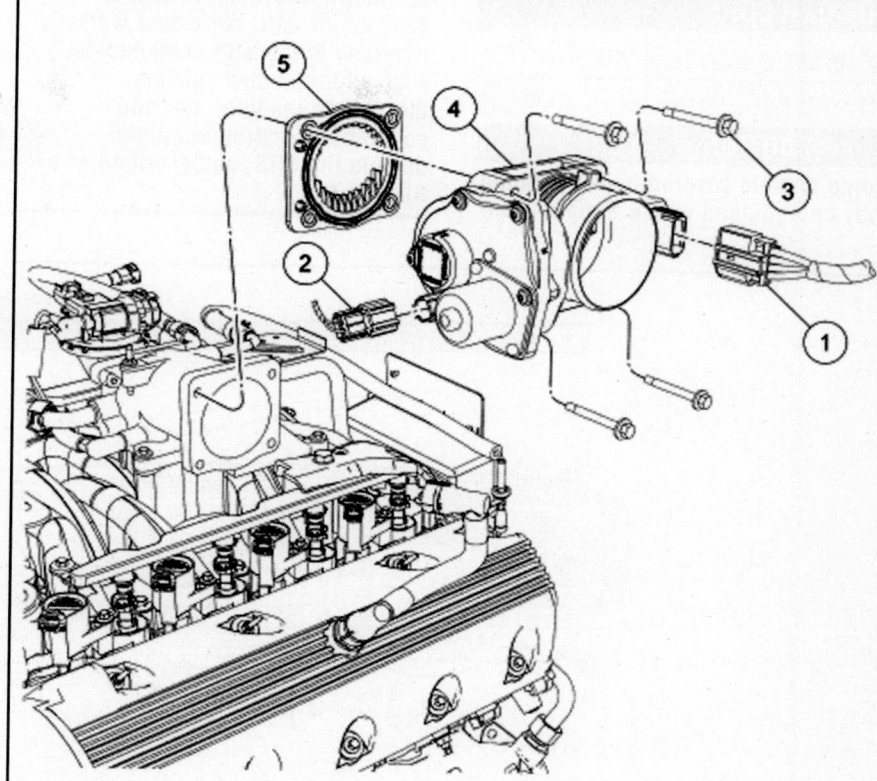

1. Throttle Position (TP) sensor electrical connector
2. Electronic throttle control electrical connector
3. Throttle Body (TB) bolt (4 required)
4. TB
5. TB gasket

N0092644

Fig. 103 Exploded view of the throttle body

HEATING & AIR CONDITIONING SYSTEM

BLOWER MOTOR

REMOVAL & INSTALLATION

See Figure 104.

1. Disconnect the negative battery cable.

2. Disconnect the blower motor electrical connector.

3. Detach the wire harness pin-type retainer above the blower motor.

4. Remove the blower motor vent tube.

5. Remove 4 blower motor screws.

6. Remove the blower motor.

➡**Prior to removing a wheel that is to be reused, clean any corrosion from the blower motor shaft to prevent damage to the wheel mounting shaft.**

7. Remove the blower motor wheel clip.

8. Remove the blower motor wheel.

9. To install, reverse the removal procedure.

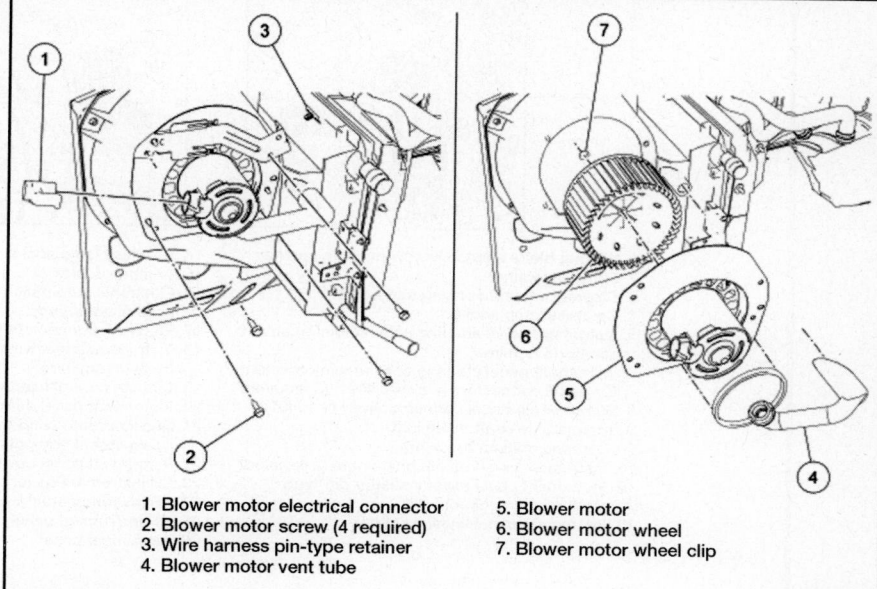

1. Blower motor electrical connector
2. Blower motor screw (4 required)
3. Wire harness pin-type retainer
4. Blower motor vent tube
5. Blower motor
6. Blower motor wheel
7. Blower motor wheel clip

N0039147

Fig. 104 Exploded view of the blower motor

HEATER CORE

REMOVAL & INSTALLATION

See Figures 105 through 107.

※※ CAUTION

Some models covered by this manual may be equipped with a Supplemental Restraint System (SRS), which uses an air bag. Whenever working near any of the SRS components, such as the impact sensors, the air bag module, steering column and instrument panel, disable the SRS, as described in Section 6.

1. **Remove the Instrument Panel:**
2. Place the selector lever in the No. 1 position.
3. Disconnect the negative battery cable.
4. Remove the steering wheel.
5. From under the hood, loosen the bolt and disconnect the LH bulkhead electrical connector.

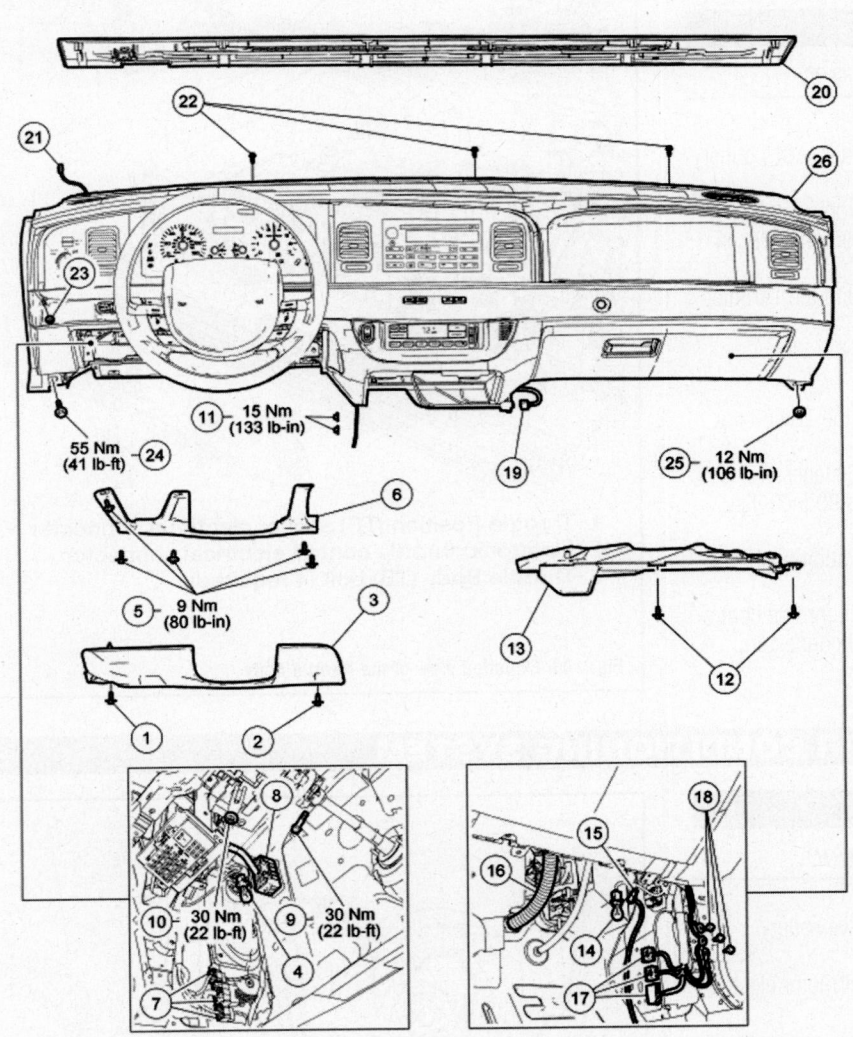

1. Parking brake release handle pushpin retainer
2. Pin-type retainer
3. Steering column opening trim panel
4. Courtesy lamp socket
5. Instrument panel steering column reinforcement screws (5 required)
6. Instrument panel steering column reinforcement
7. Electrical connectors (part of 14401) (3 required)
8. Bulkhead electrical connector (part of 14401)
9. Intermediate shaft pinch bolt
10. Steering column brace nut
11. Instrument panel tunnel brace nuts (2 required)
12. Instrument panel lower insulator pin-type retainers (2 required)
13. Instrument panel lower insulator
14. Courtesy lamp socket (part of 14401)
15. Antenna cable
16. Electronic automatic temperature control hose (if equipped)
17. Electrical connectors (3 required)
18. Instrument panel wiring harness ground bolts (3 required)
19. Climate control head vacuum harness connector
20. Instrument panel defroster opening grille
21. Sun load/auto lamp sensor electrical connector (if equipped)
22. Instrument panel cowl top screws (3 required)
23. LH instrument panel cowl side nut
24. LH instrument panel cowl side lower bolt
25. RH instrument panel cowl side lower nut
26. Instrument panel

N0090928

Fig. 105 Exploded view of the instrument panel

6. Release the retainers and position the bulkhead electrical connector through the dash panel.

7. Vehicles with Police option:

a. Remove the Battery Junction Box (BJB) wiring harness ties, disconnect the electrical connector and position the harness aside.

8. All vehicles:

9. Remove the 2 pin-type retainers, disconnect the power point electrical connector and remove the RH instrument panel lower insulator.

10. Disconnect the RH lower instrument panel courtesy lamp.

11. Position the LH and RH front door weatherstrip seals aside.

12. Remove the LH and RH scuff plates.

13. Remove the LH and RH A-pillar lower trim panels.

14. Disconnect the antenna cable in-line connector.

15. Remove the 3 RH instrument panel wiring harness ground bolts.

16. Disconnect the 3 RH instrument panel wiring harness electrical connectors.

17. If equipped, disconnect the Electronic Automatic Temperature Control (EATC) hose from the evaporator housing.

18. Disconnect the climate control head vacuum harness connector.

19. Remove the pin-type retainer and the steering column opening trim panel.

20. Remove the 5 screws and the instrument panel steering column reinforcement.

21. Remove the nut and position the steering column brace aside.

22. Remove and discard the intermediate shaft pinch bolt.

23. Separate the intermediate shaft from the steering column shaft. Install a new intermediate shaft pinch bolt and tighten to 30 Nm (22 lb-ft).

24. Disconnect the selector lever cable from the steering column.

25. Disconnect the cable from the steering column shift tube lever.

26. Disconnect the cable from the steering column bracket.

27. Disconnect the 3 LH instrument panel wiring harness electrical connectors.

28. Remove the pin-type retainer and the instrument panel tunnel brace cover.

29. Remove the 2 nuts and the instrument panel tunnel brace.

30. Remove the defroster opening grille.

31. If equipped, disconnect the electrical connectors.

32. Remove the 3 instrument panel cowl top screws.

33. Remove the RH instrument panel cowl side lower nut.

34. To install, tighten to 12 Nm (106 lb-in).

35. Remove the LH instrument panel cowl side upper nut.

36. Remove the LH instrument panel cowl side lower bolt.

➡**An assistant is needed to carry out this step.**

37. Remove the instrument panel from the vehicle.

38. **Remove the Plenum chamber:**

39. Drain and recycle the engine coolant.

40. Release the 2 heater hose clamps and disconnect the heater hoses at the heater core.

41. Detach the plenum chamber vacuum harness from the plenum chamber.

42. Disconnect the temperature blend door actuator electrical connector.

43. Disconnect the 2 air suspension control module electrical connectors.

44. Remove the 3 plenum chamber nuts.

➡**Do not excessively cut the rear footwell duct. Make sure to only cut the rear footwell duct to the point that allows the heater floor duct to be removed with the plenum chamber as an assembly.**

45. Position back the carpet from the plenum chamber. Cut each side of the rear footwell duct and bend back the duct.

46. Remove the in-vehicle temperature sensor aspirator hose (if equipped).

47. Remove the plenum chamber.

48. **Remove the heater core:**

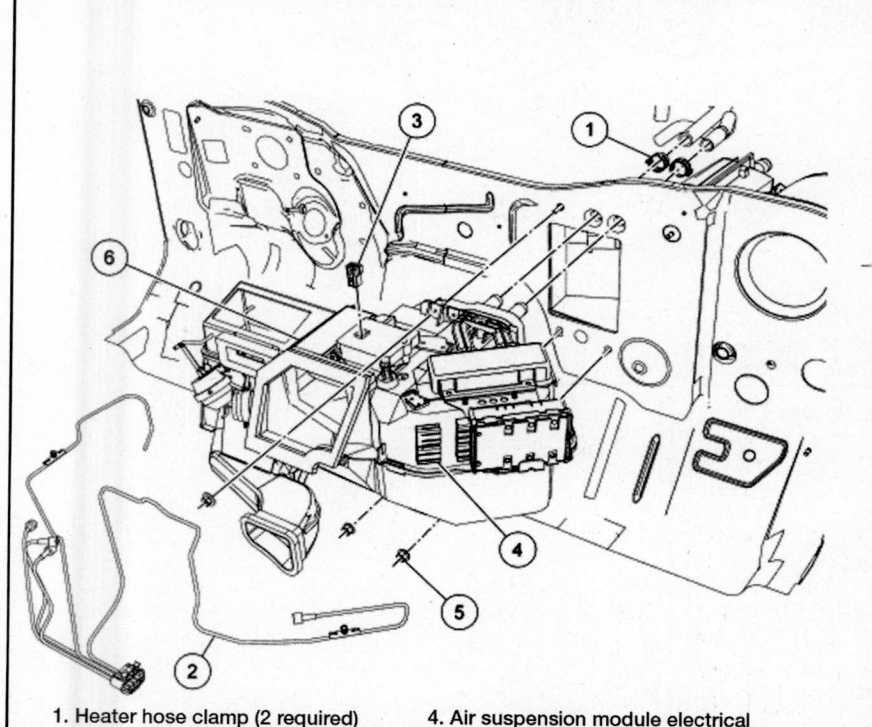

1. Heater hose clamp (2 required)
2. Plenum chamber vacuum harness
3. Temperature blend door actuator electrical connector
4. Air suspension module electrical connector (2 required)
5. Plenum chamber nut (3 required)
6. Plenum chamber

N0039154

Fig. 106 Exploded view of the plenum chamber

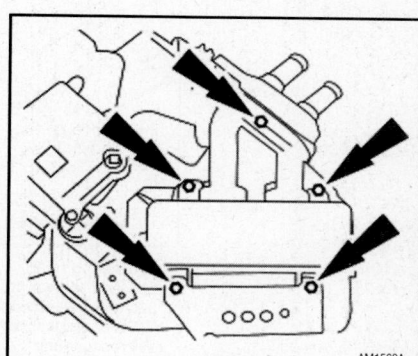

AM1560A

Fig. 107 Locating the heater core cover screws

➥If a heater core leak is suspected, the heater core must be leak tested before it is removed from the vehicle.

49. Remove the screws and the heater core cover.

50. Carefully cut the seal above the heater core inlet and outlet tubes and remove the heater core.

51. To install, reverse the removal procedure.

➥Make sure to sufficiently seal the rear footwell duct to the heater outlet floor duct.

52. Clean and lubricate the coolant hose with plain water only if needed.

53. Close the rear footwell duct around the heater outlet floor duct, install a tie strap and position back the carpet.

54. Fill the engine cooling system.

STEERING

POWER STEERING GEAR

REMOVAL & INSTALLATION

See Figure 108.

1. With the vehicle in NEUTRAL, position it on a hoist.

2. Using a suitable holding device, hold the steering wheel in the straight-ahead position.

➥Do not allow the steering column shaft to rotate while the steering column is disconnected from the steering gear or damage to the clockspring may result. If there is evidence that the intermediate shaft has rotated, the clockspring must be removed and recentered.

3. From the engine compartment,

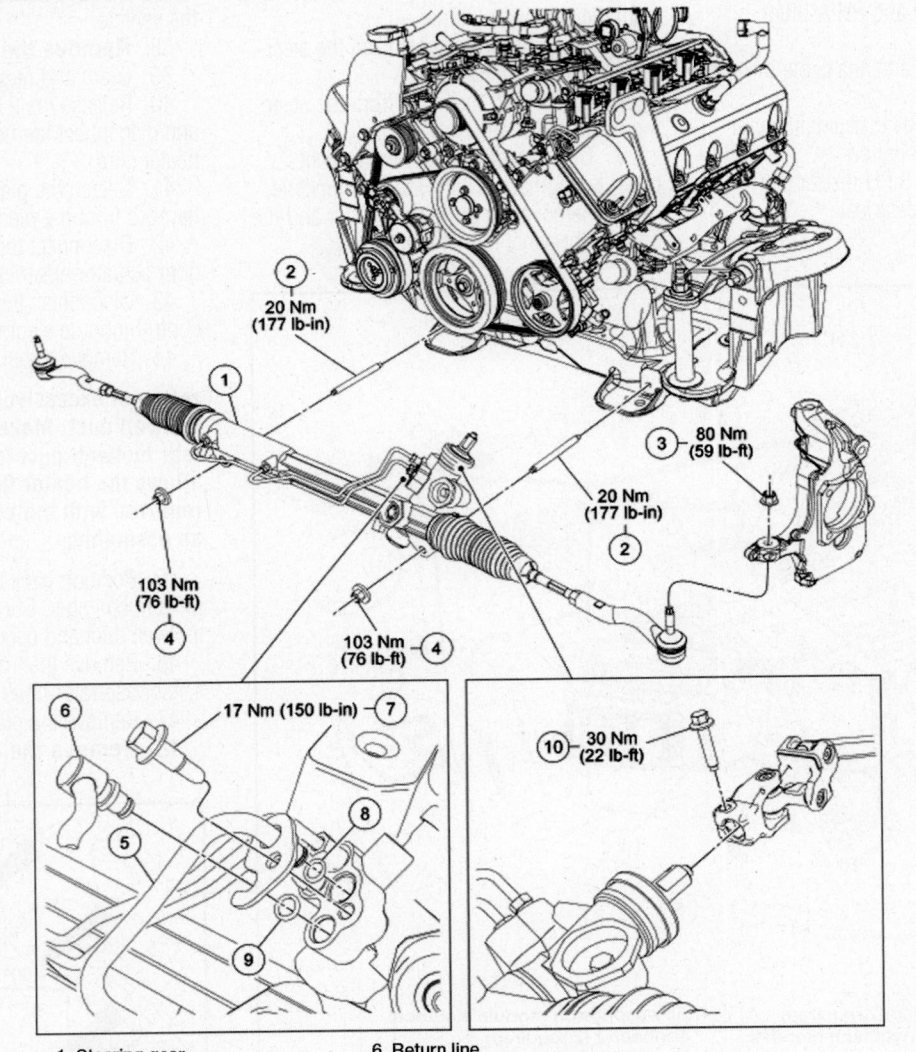

1. Steering gear
2. Steering gear studs (2 required)
3. Outer tie-rod end nut
4. Steering gear nuts (2 required)
5. Pressure line
6. Return line
7. Steering line clamp plate bolt
8. High-pressure O-ring seal
9. Low-pressure O-ring seal
10. Steering column shaft-to-steering gear coupling bolt

N0089257

Fig. 108 Exploded view of the power steering gear

remove the steering column shaft-to-steering gear coupling bolt and detach the shaft from the steering gear.

➡ **The hex-holding feature can be used to prevent turning of the stud while removing the nut.**

4. Remove the nuts and detach the outer tie-rod ends from the wheel knuckles.

➡ **New O-ring seals must be installed any time the lines are disconnected from the steering gear or a leak may occur.**

5. Remove the steering line clamp plate bolt and disconnect the pressure and return lines.

6. Discard the O-ring seals.

7. Remove the steering gear nuts.

8. Remove the steering gear studs and the steering gear.

➡ **When connecting a fitting with an O-ring seal, a new seal must be installed.**

9. To install, reverse the removal procedure. Refer to illustration for torque values.

10. Fill the power steering system. For additional information, refer to Power Steering Pump.

POWER STEERING PUMP

REMOVAL & INSTALLATION

See Figure 109.

➡ **While repairing the power steering system, care should be taken to prevent the entry of foreign material or failure of the power steering components may result.**

1. Disconnect the negative battery cable.

2. Using a suitable suction device, remove the power steering fluid from the reservoir.

3. Remove the power steering pump pulley.

4. Release the clamp and disconnect the power steering pump supply hose.

5. Remove the pressure line bracket-to-engine nut.

6. Disconnect the pressure line-to-pump fitting.

7. Discard the Teflon® seal.

8. Remove the 3 bolts and the power steering pump.

➡ **When connecting a fitting with a Teflon® seal, a new Teflon® seal must be installed.**

9. To install, reverse the removal proce-

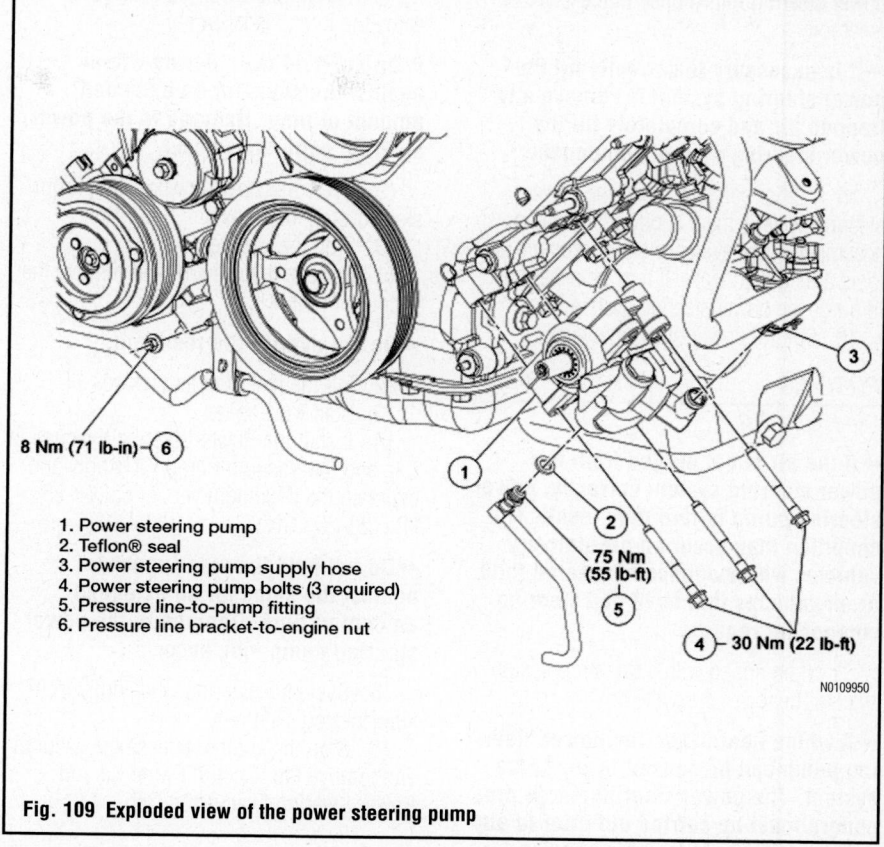

8 Nm (71 lb-in)–6

1. Power steering pump
2. Teflon® seal
3. Power steering pump supply hose
4. Power steering pump bolts (3 required)
5. Pressure line-to-pump fitting
6. Pressure line bracket-to-engine nut

75 Nm (55 lb-ft)

4 — 30 Nm (22 lb-ft)

N0109950

Fig. 109 Exploded view of the power steering pump

dure. Refer to the illustration for torque values.

10. Using the Teflon® Seal Installer Set, install a new Teflon® seal on the pressure line-to-pump fitting.

11. Fill the power steering system.

BLEEDING & FLUSHING

1. Remove the power steering fluid reservoir cap.

2. Using a suitable suction device, remove the power steering fluid from the reservoir.

3. Release the clamp and disconnect the return hose from the reservoir.

a. Remove the clamp from the hose and allow the remaining fluid to drain out of the reservoir.

4. Plug the power steering fluid reservoir inlet port.

5. Attach an extension hose to the return hose.

➡ **Do not reuse the power steering fluid that has been flushed from the power steering system.**

6. Place the open end of the extension hose into a suitable container.

7. If equipped with Hydro-Boost®, apply the brake pedal 4 times.

➡ **Do not overfill the reservoir.**

8. Fill the reservoir as needed with the specified fluid.

➡ **Do not allow the power steering pump to run completely dry of power steering fluid. Damage to the power steering pump may occur.**

9. Start the engine while simultaneously turning the steering wheel to lock and then immediately turn the ignition switch to the OFF position.

➡ **Avoid turning the steering wheel without the engine running as this may cause air to be pulled into the steering gear.**

➡ **Do not overfill the reservoir.**

10. Fill the reservoir as needed with the specified fluid.

11. Repeat Steps 8 and 9, turning the steering wheel in the opposite direction each time, until the fluid exiting the power steering fluid return hose is clean and clear of foreign material.

12. Remove the extension hose from the return hose.

13. Remove the plug from the fluid reservoir inlet port.

14. Install the clamp and connect the

power steering return hose to the reservoir.

➡**It is necessary to correctly fill the power steering system to remove any trapped air and completely fill the power steering system components.**

15. If, after correctly filling the power steering system, there is power steering noise accompanied by evidence of aerated fluid and there are no fluid leaks, it may be necessary to purge the power steering system.

16. Fill the power steering system.

PURGING

See Figure 110.

➡**If the air is not purged from the power steering system correctly, power steering pump failure may result. The condition may occur on pre-delivery vehicles with evidence of aerated fluid or on vehicles that have had steering component repairs.**

1. If equipped with a fire suppression system, depower the system.

➡**A whine heard from the power steering pump can be caused by air in the system. The power steering purge procedure must be carried out prior to any component repair for which power steering noise complaints are accompanied by evidence of aerated fluid.**

2. Remove the power steering fluid reservoir cap.

3. Fill the reservoir as needed with the specified fluid.

4. Raise the front wheels off the floor.

5. Tightly insert the Power Steering Evacuation Cap into the reservoir and connect the Vacuum Pump Kit.

6. Start the engine.

7. Using the Vacuum Pump Kit, apply vacuum and maintain the maximum vacuum of 68-85 kPa (20-25 in-Hg).

8. If equipped with Hydro-Boost®, apply the brake pedal twice.

➡**Do not hold the steering wheel against the stops for an extended amount of time. Damage to the power steering pump may occur.**

9. Cycle the steering wheel fully from stop-to-stop 10 times.

10. Stop the engine.

11. Release the vacuum and remove the Vacuum Pump Kit.

➡**Do not overfill the reservoir.**

12. Fill the reservoir as needed.

13. Start the engine.

14. Install the Power Steering Evacuation Cap and the Vacuum Pump Kit. Apply and maintain the maximum vacuum of 68-85 kPa (20-25 in-Hg).

➡**Do not hold the steering wheel against the stops for an extended amount of time. Damage to the power steering pump may occur.**

15. Cycle the steering wheel fully from stop-to-stop 10 times.

16. Stop the engine, release the vacuum and remove the Vacuum Pump Kit and Power Steering Evacuation Cap.

➡**Do not overfill the reservoir.**

17. Fill the reservoir as needed and install the reservoir cap.

18. Visually inspect the power steering system for leaks.

FLUID FILL PROCEDURE

See Figure 111.

➡**If the air is not purged from the power steering system correctly, premature power steering pump failure may result. The condition can occur on pre-delivery vehicles with evidence of aerated fluid or on vehicles that have had steering component repairs.**

1. Remove the power steering fluid reservoir cap.

2. Install the Power Steering Evacuation Cap, Power Steering Fill Adapter Manifold and Vacuum Pump Kit as shown in the illustration.

➡**The Power Steering Fill Adapter Manifold control valves are in the OPEN position when the points of the handles face the center of the Power Steering Fill Adapter Manifold.**

3. Close the Power Steering Fill Adapter Manifold control valve (fluid side).

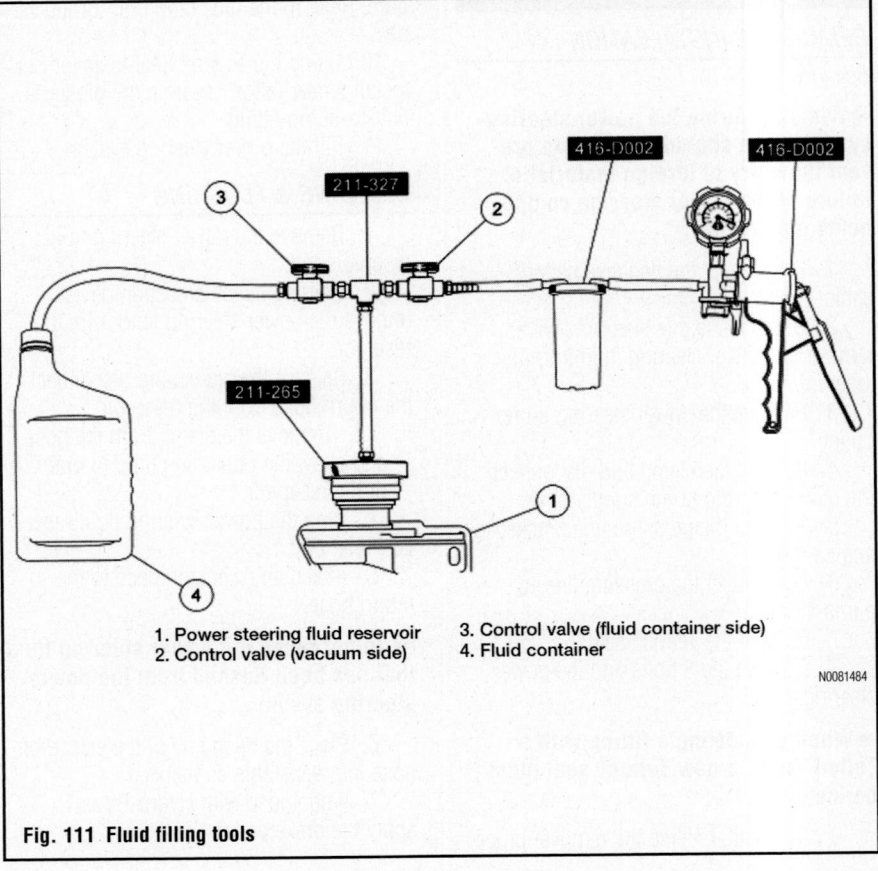

1. Power steering fluid reservoir
2. Control valve (vacuum side)
3. Control valve (fluid container side)
4. Fluid container

N0081484

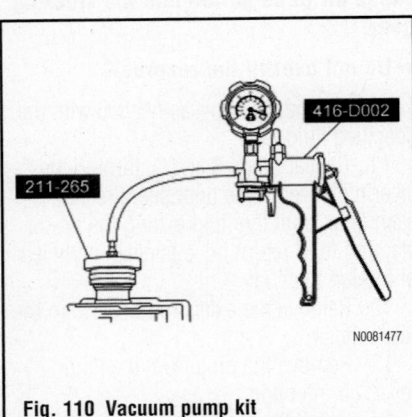

Fig. 110 Vacuum pump kit

Fig. 111 Fluid filling tools

4. Open the Power Steering Fill Adapter Manifold control valve (vacuum side).

5. Using the Vacuum Pump Kit, apply 68-85 kPa (20-25 in-Hg) of vacuum to the power steering system.

6. Observe the Vacuum Pump Kit gauge for 30 seconds.

7. If the Vacuum Pump Kit gauge reading drops more than 3 kPa (0.88 in-Hg), correct any leaks in the power steering system or the Power Steering Evacuation Cap, Power Steering Fill Adapter Manifold and Vacuum Pump Kit before proceeding.

➡**The Vacuum Pump Kit gauge reading will drop slightly during this step.**

8. Slowly open the Power Steering Fill Adapter Manifold control valve (fluid side) until power steering fluid completely fills the hose and then close the control valve.

9. Using the Vacuum Pump Kit, apply 68-85 kPa (20-25 in-Hg) of vacuum to the power steering system.

10. Close the Power Steering Fill Adapter Manifold control valve (vacuum side).

11. Slowly open the Power Steering Fill Adapter Manifold control valve (fluid side).

12. Once power steering fluid enters the fluid reservoir and reaches the minimum fluid level indicator line on the reservoir, close the Power Steering Fill Adapter Manifold control valve (fluid side).

13. Remove the Power Steering Evacuation Cap, Power Steering Fill Adapter Manifold and Vacuum Pump Kit.

14. Install the reservoir cap.

➡**Do not hold the steering wheel against the stops for an extended amount of time. Damage to the power steering pump may occur.**

➡**There will be a slight drop in the power steering fluid level in the reservoir when the engine is started.**

Start the engine and turn the steering wheel from stop-to-stop.

Turn the ignition switch to the OFF position.

➡**Do not overfill the reservoir.**

15. Remove the reservoir cap and fill the reservoir with the specified fluid.

16. Install the reservoir cap.

SUSPENSION   FRONT SUSPENSION

COIL SPRING

REMOVAL & INSTALLATION

See Figure 112.

> ❊❊ **WARNING**
>
> **Do not apply heat or flame to the shock absorber or strut tube. The shock absorber and strut tube are gas pressurized and could explode if heated. Failure to follow this instruction may result in serious personal injury.**

> ❊❊ **WARNING**
>
> **Keep all body parts clear of shock absorbers or strut rods. Shock absorbers or struts can extend unassisted. Failure to follow this instruction may result in serious personal injury.**

> ❊❊ **WARNING**
>
> **Do not remove the shock absorber center nut. Removal of this nut releases the spring tension and may result in serious personal injury.**

➡**Suspension fasteners are critical parts because they affect performance of vital components and systems and their failure may result in major service expense. New parts must be installed with the same part numbers or equivalent part, if replacement is necessary. Do not use a replacement part of lesser quality or substitute design. Torque values must be used as specified during reassembly to make sure correct retention of these parts.**

1. Remove the shock absorber and spring assembly. For additional information, refer to Strut and Spring Assembly in this section.

➡**Overtightening the vise may damage the shock absorber tube.**

2. Mount and mark the shock absorber and spring assembly.

3. Position the shock absorber and spring assembly in a suitable holding device.

4. Mark the upper mounting bracket, spring and shock absorber for assembly reference.

➡**If installing a new spring, make sure the part number is correct.**

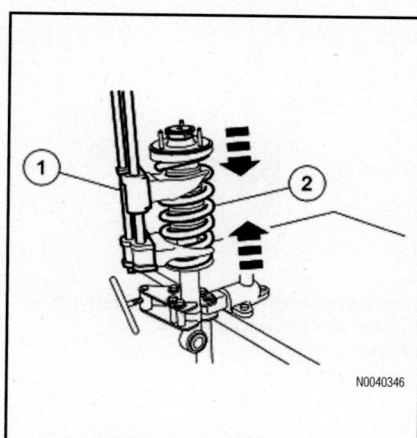

Fig. 112 Removing the spring

5. Compress the spring.

a. Install an appropriate spring compressor.

b. Compress the spring.

6. While holding the shock absorber rod, remove and discard the nut.

7. Remove the mounting bracket and dust boot as an assembly.

8. Carefully remove the spring and spring compressor.

To install:

➡**If a new shock absorber, spring or upper mount is installed, the new part should be marked in the same place as the old part to make sure the assembly is correctly aligned.**

9. Inspect the lower and upper spring seats for damage.

10. Inspect the spring insulator for wear or damage. Install a new mounting bracket if necessary.

➡**If installing a new spring, make sure the part number is correct.**

11. Inspect the spring for nicked or scratched paint. If the paint is nicked or scratched, install a new spring.

12. If removed, place the shock absorber into the vise.

13. Position the shock and spring compressor onto the strut.

14. Position the mounting bracket and dust boot onto the spring. Make sure the marks made during Disassembly,

15. Install a new shock rod nut. To install, tighten to 37 ft. lbs. (50 Nm).

16. Remove the spring compressor.

CONTROL LINKS

REMOVAL & INSTALLATION

See Figure 113.

➡Suspension fasteners are critical parts because they affect performance of vital components and systems and their failure may result in major service expense. New parts must be installed with the same part numbers or equivalent part, if replacement is necessary. Do not use a replacement part of lesser quality or substitute design. Torque values must be used as specified during reassembly to make sure correct retention of these parts.

1. Disconnect the negative battery cable.
2. Remove the wheel and tire.

➡Do not allow the caliper and anchor plate assembly to hang from the brake hose or damage to the hose may occur.

3. Remove the bolts and position the caliper, pads and anchor plate assembly aside.
4. Support the caliper and anchor plate assembly using mechanic's wire.
5. Remove the brake disc.

➡Use the hex-holding feature to prevent the stud from turning while removing the nut.

6. Remove the stabilizer link upper nut.
7. Discard the nut.

➡Use the hex-holding feature to prevent the stud from turning while removing the nut.

8. Remove the stabilizer link lower nut and the stabilizer bar link.
9. Discard the nut.
10. To install, reverse the removal procedure. Refer to the illustration for torque values.

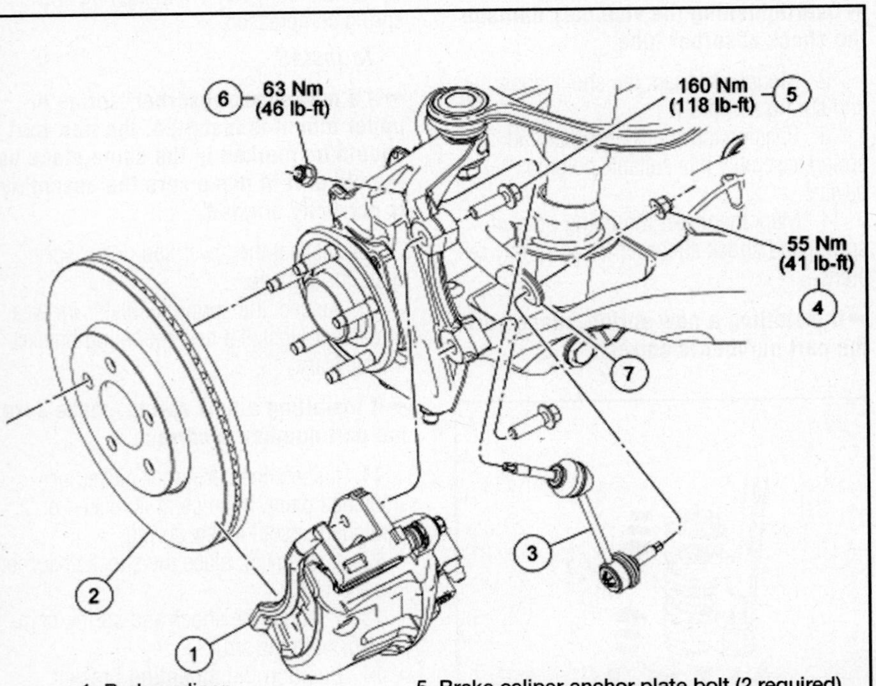

LOWER BALL JOINT

REMOVAL & INSTALLATION

See Figures 114 and 115.

1. Disconnect the negative battery cable.
2. Remove the Steering Knuckle. Refer to Steering Knuckle in this section.
3. Remove and discard the lower ball joint snap ring.
4. Using the C-Frame and Screw Installer/Remover and Ball Joint Installer/Remover, remove the lower ball joint.

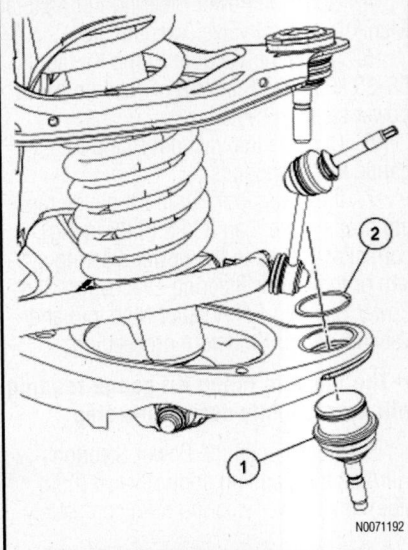

Fig. 114 View of the lower ball joint (1) and lower ball joint snap ring (2)

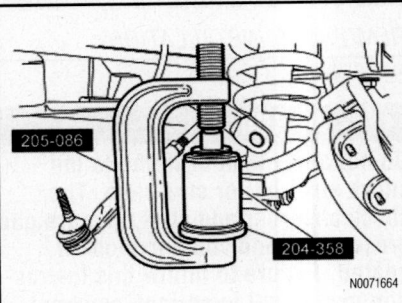

Fig. 115 Using the C-Frame and Screw Installer/Remover and Ball Joint Installer/Remover

To install:

➡Do not damage the lower ball joint boot when installing the ball joint or premature failure of the ball joint may occur.

➡Make sure the ball joint snap ring is fully seated.

5. Using the C-Frame and Screw Installer/Remover and Ball Joint Installer/Remover, install the lower ball joint.
6. Install the ball joint snap ring.
7. Install the wheel knuckle.

LOWER CONTROL ARM

REMOVAL & INSTALLATION

See Figure 116.

➡Suspension fasteners are critical parts because they affect performance

Fig. 113 Exploded view of the control links

1. Brake caliper
2. Brake disc
3. Stabilizer bar link
4. Stabilizer bar link lower nut
5. Brake caliper anchor plate bolt (2 required)
6. Stabilizer bar link upper nut
7. Stabilizer bar

6. 63 Nm (46 lb-ft)
5. 160 Nm (118 lb-ft)
4. 55 Nm (41 lb-ft)

N0081144

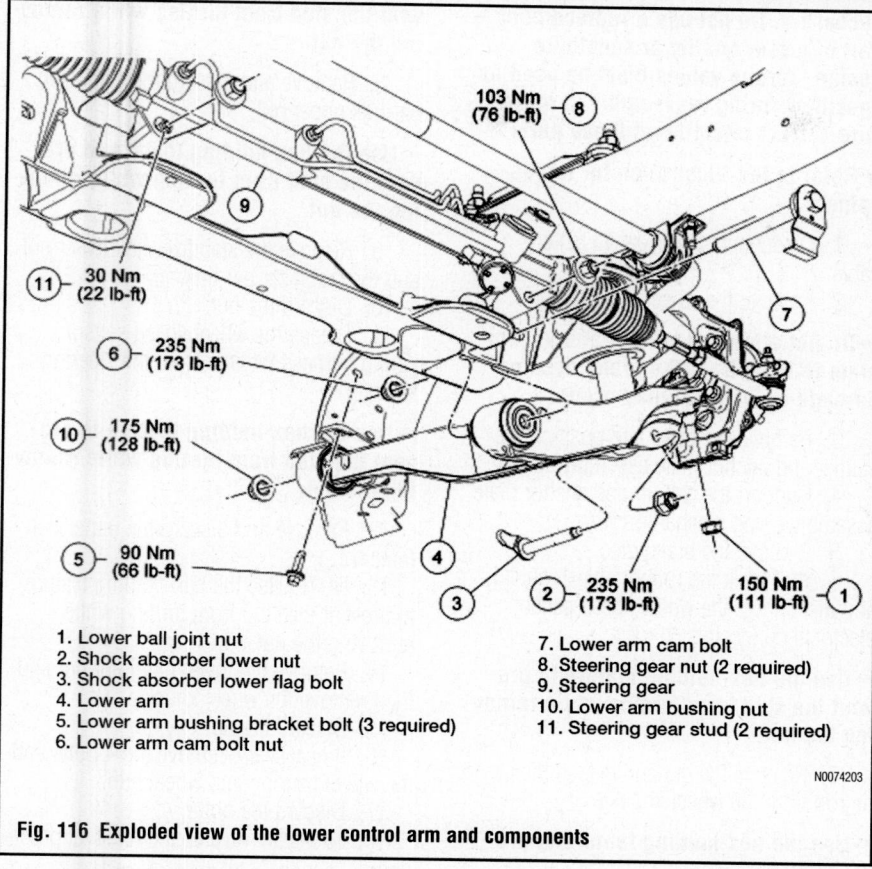

30 Nm
(22 lb-ft)

103 Nm
(76 lb-ft)

235 Nm
(173 lb-ft)

175 Nm
(128 lb-ft)

90 Nm
(66 lb-ft)

235 Nm
(173 lb-ft)

150 Nm
(111 lb-ft)

1. Lower ball joint nut
2. Shock absorber lower nut
3. Shock absorber lower flag bolt
4. Lower arm
5. Lower arm bushing bracket bolt (3 required)
6. Lower arm cam bolt nut
7. Lower arm cam bolt
8. Steering gear nut (2 required)
9. Steering gear
10. Lower arm bushing nut
11. Steering gear stud (2 required)

Fig. 116 Exploded view of the lower control arm and components

of vital components and systems and their failure may result in major service expense. New parts must be installed with the same part numbers or equivalent part, if replacement is necessary. Do not use a replacement part of lesser quality or substitute design. Torque values must be used as specified during reassembly to make sure correct retention of these parts.

1. Disconnect the negative battery cable.
2. Remove the wheel and tire.

➡ Use the hex-holding feature to prevent the stud from turning while removing the nut.

3. Remove and discard the lower ball joint nut.
4. Remove and discard the shock absorber lower nut and the flag bolt.

➡ Do not remove the cam bolt at this time or damage to the steering bellows boot will result.

5. Remove and discard the lower arm cam bolt nut.
6. Remove and discard the 3 lower arm bushing bracket bolts.
7. Remove and discard the 2 steering gear-to-crossmember stud nuts.

8. Remove the steering gear crossmember studs and move the steering gear upward to access the cam bolt.
9. Remove the cam bolt and the lower arm.
10. Discard the cam bolt.

To install:

➡ Refer to the illustration for torque values.

11. Position the lower arm and loosely install the new cam bolt and nut.
12. Position the steering gear and install the gear crossmember studs.
13. Install the 2 new steering gear-to-crossmember nuts.
14. Install the 3 new lower arm bushing bracket bolts.
15. Loosely install the new lower arm cam nut.
16. Loosely install the new shock absorber lower nut and flag bolt.
17. Install the new lower ball joint nut.
18. Install the wheel and tire.
19. With the weight of the vehicle on the wheel and tire assemblies, tighten the lower arm cam bolt and nut to 173 ft. lbs. (235 Nm).
20. With the weight of the vehicle on the wheel and tire assemblies, tighten the shock absorber lower nut to 173 ft. lbs. (235 Nm).
21. If a new lower control arm is being installed, tighten the new bushing nut to 128 ft. lbs. (175 Nm).
22. Check and if necessary, align the front end.

STABILIZER BAR

REMOVAL & INSTALLATION

See Figure 117.

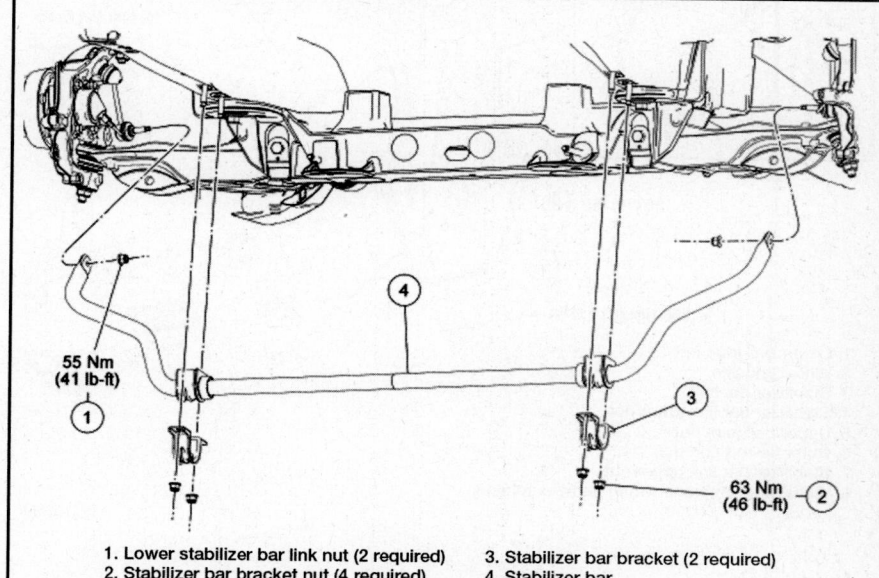

55 Nm
(41 lb-ft)

63 Nm
(46 lb-ft)

1. Lower stabilizer bar link nut (2 required)
2. Stabilizer bar bracket nut (4 required)
3. Stabilizer bar bracket (2 required)
4. Stabilizer bar

Fig. 117 View of the stabilizer bar assembly

→Refer to the illustration for torque values.

1. With the vehicle in NEUTRAL, position it on a hoist.

→Use the hex-holding feature to prevent the stud from turning while removing the nut.

2. Remove the 2 lower nuts and disconnect the stabilizer bar links from the stabilizer bar.
3. Discard the nuts.
4. Remove the 4 nuts, the 2 brackets and the stabilizer bar.
5. Discard the nuts.
6. To install, reverse the removal procedure.

STEERING KNUCKLE

REMOVAL & INSTALLATION
See Figure 118.

→Suspension fasteners are critical parts because they affect performance of vital components and systems and their failure may result in major service expense. New parts must be installed with the same part numbers or equivalent part, if replacement is necessary. Do not use a replacement part of lesser quality or substitute design. Torque values must be used as specified during reassembly to make sure correct retention of these parts.

→Refer to the illustration for torque values.

1. Disconnect the negative battery cable.
2. Remove the wheel and tire.

→Do not allow the caliper and anchor plate to hang from the brake hose or damage to the hose may occur.

3. Remove the bolts and position the caliper and anchor plate assembly aside.
4. Support the caliper and anchor plate assembly using mechanic's wire.
5. Remove the brake disc.
6. Pull back the rubber splash shield and disconnect the wheel speed sensor electrical connector.

→Use the hex-holding feature to prevent the stud from turning while removing the nut.

7. Remove the nut and detach the outer tie rod from the wheel knuckle.

→Use the hex-holding feature to pre-

vent the stud from turning while removing the nut.

8. Remove and discard the stabilizer bar link upper nut.

→Use the hex-holding feature to prevent the stud from turning while removing the nut.

9. Remove the stabilizer link lower nut and the stabilizer bar link.
10. Discard the nut.
11. Detach the wheel speed sensor wiring harness retainer from the steering knuckle.

→Use the hex-holding feature to prevent the stud from turning while removing the nut.

12. Remove and discard the upper ball joint nut.
13. NOTE: Use the hex-holding feature to prevent the stud from turning while removing the nut.
14. Remove the lower ball joint nut and then remove the wheel knuckle.
15. Discard the nut.
16. If necessary, remove the 4 bolts and the wheel bearing and wheel hub.
17. Discard the bolts.
18. To install, reverse the removal procedure.
19. Check and, if necessary, align the front end.

STRUT & SPRING ASSEMBLY

REMOVAL & INSTALLATION
See Figure 119.

→Suspension fasteners are critical parts because they affect performance of vital components and systems and their failure may result in major service expense. New parts must be installed with the same part numbers or equivalent part, if replacement is necessary. Do not use a replacement part of lesser quality or substitute design. Torque values must be used as specified during reassembly to make sure correct retention of these parts.

1. Disconnect the negative battery cable.
2. Remove the wheel and tire.

✳ WARNING
Do not remove the shock absorber center nut. Removal of this nut releases the spring tension and may result in serious personal injury.

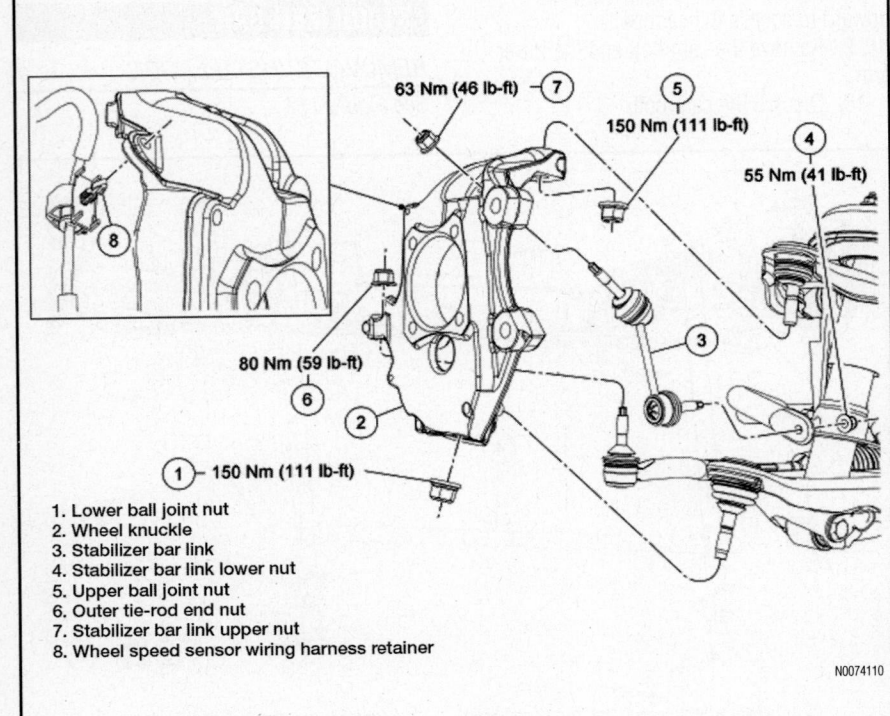

63 Nm (46 lb-ft) — ⑦
⑤
150 Nm (111 lb-ft)
④
55 Nm (41 lb-ft)
⑧
③
80 Nm (59 lb-ft)
⑥
②
① — 150 Nm (111 lb-ft)

1. Lower ball joint nut
2. Wheel knuckle
3. Stabilizer bar link
4. Stabilizer bar link lower nut
5. Upper ball joint nut
6. Outer tie-rod end nut
7. Stabilizer bar link upper nut
8. Wheel speed sensor wiring harness retainer

N0074110

Fig. 118 Exploded view of the steering knuckle and components

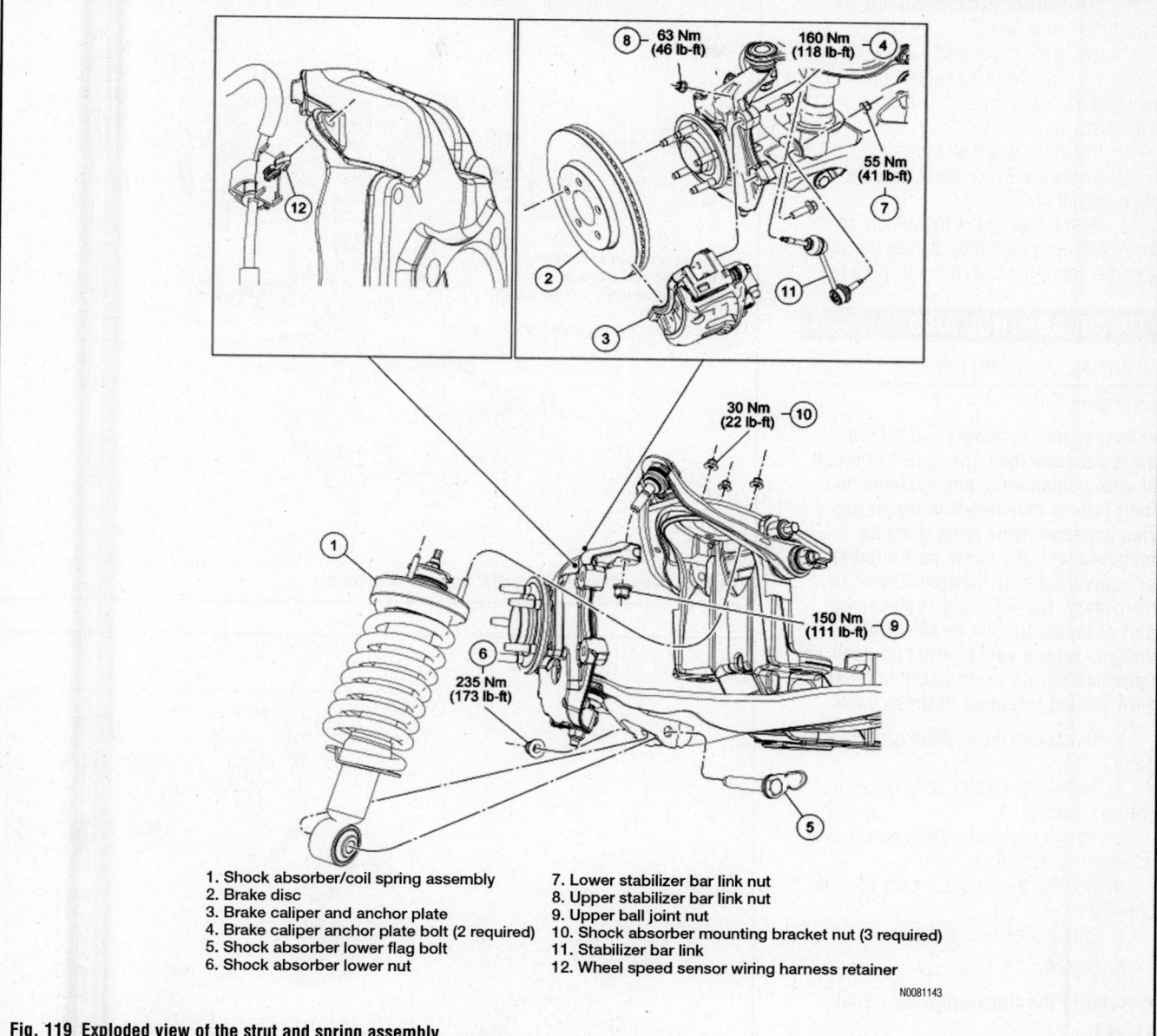

1. Shock absorber/coil spring assembly
2. Brake disc
3. Brake caliper and anchor plate
4. Brake caliper anchor plate bolt (2 required)
5. Shock absorber lower flag bolt
6. Shock absorber lower nut
7. Lower stabilizer bar link nut
8. Upper stabilizer bar link nut
9. Upper ball joint nut
10. Shock absorber mounting bracket nut (3 required)
11. Stabilizer bar link
12. Wheel speed sensor wiring harness retainer

N0081143

Fig. 119 Exploded view of the strut and spring assembly

3. Remove and discard the 3 shock absorber upper mount nuts.

➡**Do not allow the caliper and anchor plate assembly to hang from the brake hose or damage to the hose may occur.**

4. Remove the 2 bolts and position the caliper, pads and anchor plate assembly aside.

5. Support the caliper and anchor plate assembly using mechanic's wire.

6. Remove the brake disc.

➡**Use the hex-holding feature to prevent the stud from turning while removing the nut.**

7. Remove and discard the stabilizer bar upper link nut.

➡**Use the hex-holding feature to prevent the stud from turning while removing the nut.**

8. Remove and discard the stabilizer bar link lower nut and the stabilizer bar link.

9. Detach the wheel speed sensor wiring harness retainer from the wheel knuckle.

➡**Use the hex-holding feature to prevent the stud from turning while removing the nut.**

10. Remove and discard the upper ball joint nut.

11. Remove and discard the shock absorber lower nut and flag bolt.

12. Remove the shock absorber and spring assembly.

To install:

➡**Refer to the illustration for torque values.**

➡**Do not tighten the nut at this time.**

13. Install the shock absorber and spring assembly and loosely install the new lower nut and flag bolt.

14. Install the new upper ball joint nut and tighten.

15. Attach the wheel speed sensor wiring harness to the wheel knuckle.

16. Position the stabilizer bar link and install the 2 new nuts.

17. Install the brake disc.

18. Position the brake caliper and anchor plate assembly and install the 2 anchor plate bolts.

19. Install the wheel and tire.

20. Install the 3 new shock absorber upper mount nuts.

21. With the weight of the vehicle on the wheel and tire assemblies, tighten the shock absorber lower nut to 173 ft. lbs. (235 Nm).

UPPER CONTROL ARM

REMOVAL & INSTALLATION

See Figure 120.

➡**Suspension fasteners are critical parts because they affect performance of vital components and systems and their failure may result in major service expense. New parts must be installed with the same part numbers or equivalent part, if replacement is necessary. Do not use a replacement part of lesser quality or substitute design. Torque values must be used as specified during reassembly to make sure correct retention of these parts.**

1. Disconnect the negative battery cable.

2. Remove the shock absorber and spring assembly.

3. Detach the wheel speed sensor retainers from the upper arm.

4. Remove the 2 nuts, 2 bolts and the upper arm.

5. Discard the nuts and bolts.

To install:

➡**Refer to the illustration for torque values.**

6. Position the upper arm and loosely install the 2 new bolts and nuts.

7. Attach the wheel speed sensor retainers to the upper arm.

8. Install the shock absorber and spring assembly.

9. Install the wheel and tire.

10. With the weight of the vehicle on the wheel and tire assemblies, tighten the 2 new upper arm nuts to 111 ft. lbs. (150 Nm).

11. Check and if necessary, align the front end.

12. Connect the negative battery cable.

WHEEL BEARINGS

REMOVAL & INSTALLATION

See Figure 121.

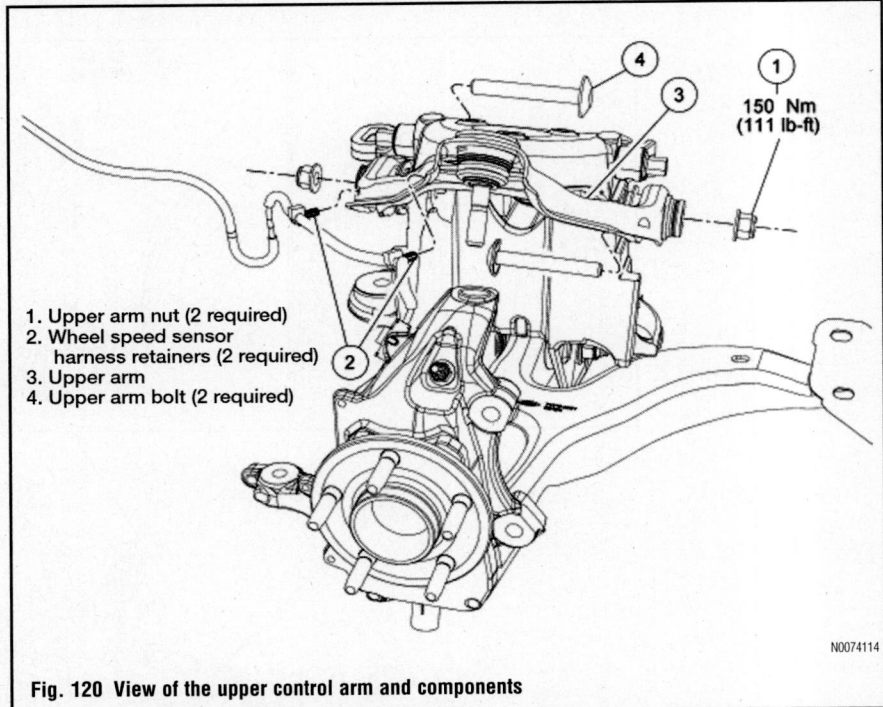

1. Upper arm nut (2 required)
2. Wheel speed sensor harness retainers (2 required)
3. Upper arm
4. Upper arm bolt (2 required)

Fig. 120 View of the upper control arm and components

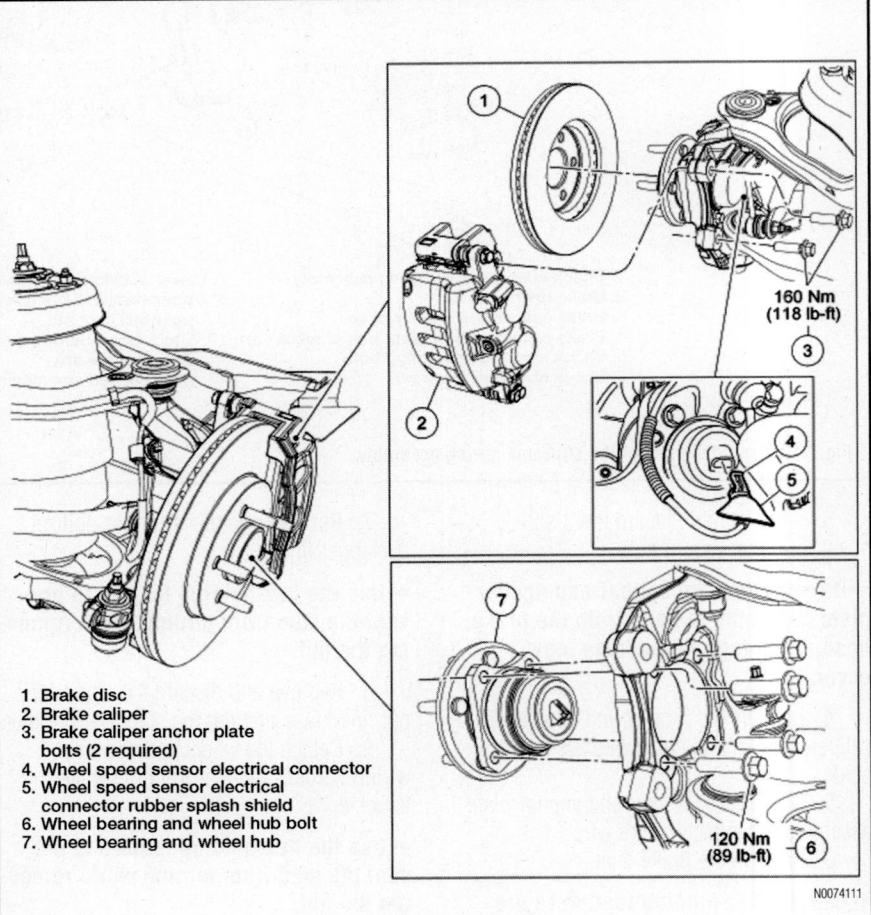

1. Brake disc
2. Brake caliper
3. Brake caliper anchor plate bolts (2 required)
4. Wheel speed sensor electrical connector
5. Wheel speed sensor electrical connector rubber splash shield
6. Wheel bearing and wheel hub bolt
7. Wheel bearing and wheel hub

Fig. 121 Exploded view of the wheel bearing and hub assembly

➡Suspension fasteners are critical parts because they affect performance of vital components and systems and their failure may result in major service expense. New parts must be installed with the same part numbers or equivalent part, if replacement is necessary. Do not use a replacement part of lesser quality or substitute design. Torque values must be used as specified during reassembly to make sure correct retention of these parts.

➡Refer to the illustration for torque values.

1. Disconnect the negative battery cable.
2. Remove the wheel and tire.

➡Do not allow the caliper and anchor plate to hang from the brake hose or damage to the hose may occur.

3. Remove the bolts and position the caliper and anchor plate assembly aside.
4. Support the caliper and anchor plate assembly using mechanic's wire.
5. Remove the brake disc.
6. Peel back the rubber splash shield and disconnect the wheel speed sensor electrical connector.

7. Remove and discard the bolts and the wheel bearing and wheel hub.

➡To avoid sensor or wiring damage, be sure to correctly route the wheel speed sensor wiring in front of the stabilizer bar link.

➡During reassembly, verify that the wheel speed sensor electrical connector is fully seated with an audible click, and that the rubber splash shield is positioned back into place.

8. To install, reverse the removal procedure.

SUSPENSION

COIL SPRING

REMOVAL & INSTALLATION

See Figure 122.

➡Suspension fasteners are critical parts because they affect the performance of vital components and their failure may result in major service expense. Install new fasteners with the same part number or an equivalent part if installation is necessary. Do not

install a part of lesser quality or substitute design. Torque values must be used as specified during reassembly to ensure correct retention of these parts.

1. For reference during the installation procedure, measure the distance from the lip of the fender to the center of the wheel hub with the vehicle in a static level ground position.
2. Disconnect the negative battery cable.

REAR SUSPENSION

3. With the vehicle in NEUTRAL, position it on a hoist.
4. Disconnect the stabilizer bar from the stabilizer bar links in the following sequence.
   a. Remove the nuts and the bushings.
   b. Rotate the stabilizer bar off the links.
   c. Discard the nuts.
5. Use a suitable jack or jackstands to support the rear axle.
6. Remove the nuts and bolts and disconnect the lateral arms from the frame.
7. Discard the nuts and bolts.

✳✳ WARNING

Keep all body parts clear of shock absorbers or strut rods. Shock absorbers or struts can extend unassisted. Failure to follow this instruction may result in serious personal injury.

8. Remove the nuts and bolts, and disconnect the shock absorbers from the axle.
9. Discard the nuts and bolts.
10. Carefully lower the jack or jackstands.
11. Remove the springs and spring insulators.

To install:

➡Refer to the illustration for torque values.

12. Inspect the spring insulators for wear or damage.
13. Install new insulators, if necessary.
14. Install the spring insulators on the springs.

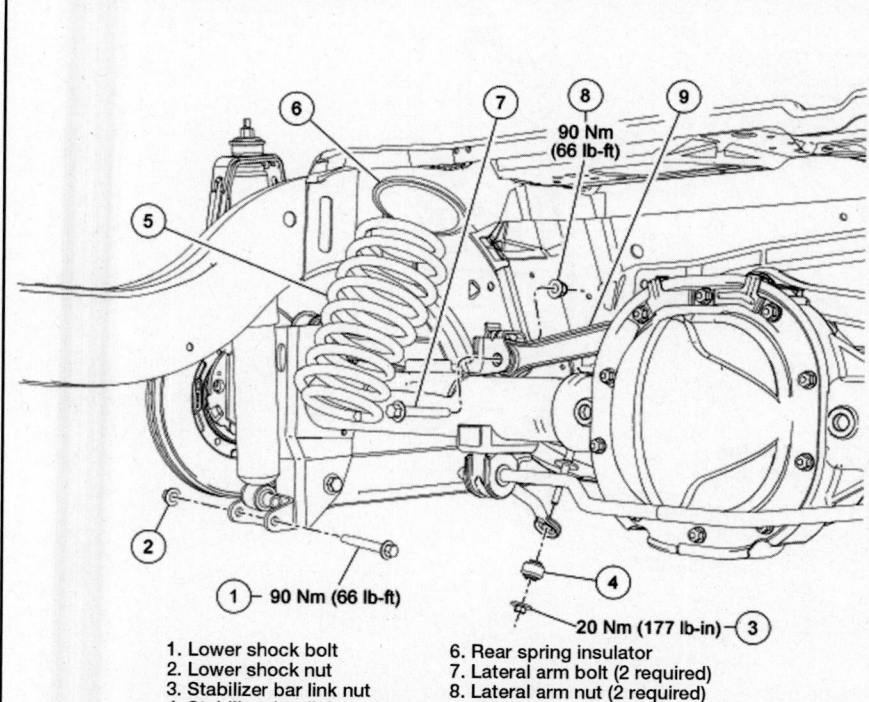

1. Lower shock bolt
2. Lower shock nut
3. Stabilizer bar link nut
4. Stabilizer bar link bushing
5. Rear spring
6. Rear spring insulator
7. Lateral arm bolt (2 required)
8. Lateral arm nut (2 required)
9. Lateral arm (2 required)

90 Nm (66 lb-ft)
90 Nm (66 lb-ft)
20 Nm (177 lb-in)

N0084897

Fig. 122 Exploded view of the coil spring assembly

15. Install the springs and the spring insulators in the vehicle.

16. Make sure that the springs are correctly seated.

17. Raise the axle using the jack or jackstands.

18. Connect the shock absorbers to the axle and install new bolts and nuts.

19. Make sure that the bolts are installed from the inboard side.

20. Connect the lateral arms to the frame and loosely install new bolts and nuts.

21. Do not tighten at this time.

22. Using the jack, raise the suspension until the distance between the lip of the fender and the center of the wheel hub is equal to the measurement taken in the removal procedure.

23. Tighten the lateral arm-to-frame bolts to 66 ft. lbs. (90 Nm).

24. Lower the axle and remove the suitable jack or jackstands.

25. Connect the stabilizer bar to the stabilizer bar links in the following sequence.

26. Rotate the stabilizer bar onto the links and install the bushings.

27. Install the new nuts.

LOWER CONTROL ARM

REMOVAL & INSTALLATION

See Figure 123.

➡**Suspension fasteners are critical parts because they affect performance of vital components and systems and their failure may result in major service expense. New fasteners must be installed with the same part number or an equivalent part if installation is necessary. Do not use a replacement part of lesser quality or substitute design. Torque values must be used as specified during reassembly to make sure of correct retention of these parts. Orientation of the fasteners is also important on all rear suspension arms.**

1. Make sure the fasteners are installed in the same direction as they were in when removed.

2. For reference during the installation procedure, measure the distance from the lip of the fender to the center of the wheel hub with the vehicle in a static level ground position.

3. Disconnect the negative battery cable.

4. Remove the wheel and tire.

5. Remove and discard the lower arm-to-axle nut and bolt.

6. Remove the lower arm-to-frame bolt, flagnut and the lower arm.

7. Discard the flagnut and bolt.

To install:

➡Refer to the illustration for torque values.

➡The rear suspension lower arms are interchangeable from side-to-side, with OUTBOARD stamped on one side of the arms for positioning during installation.

8. Position the lower arm and loosely install the new lower arm-to-frame bolt and flagnut.

9. Loosely install the new lower arm-to-axle nut and bolt.

10. Before tightening the fasteners, use a suitable jack to raise the suspension until the distance between the lip of the fender and the center of the wheel hub is equal to the measurement taken in the removal procedure.

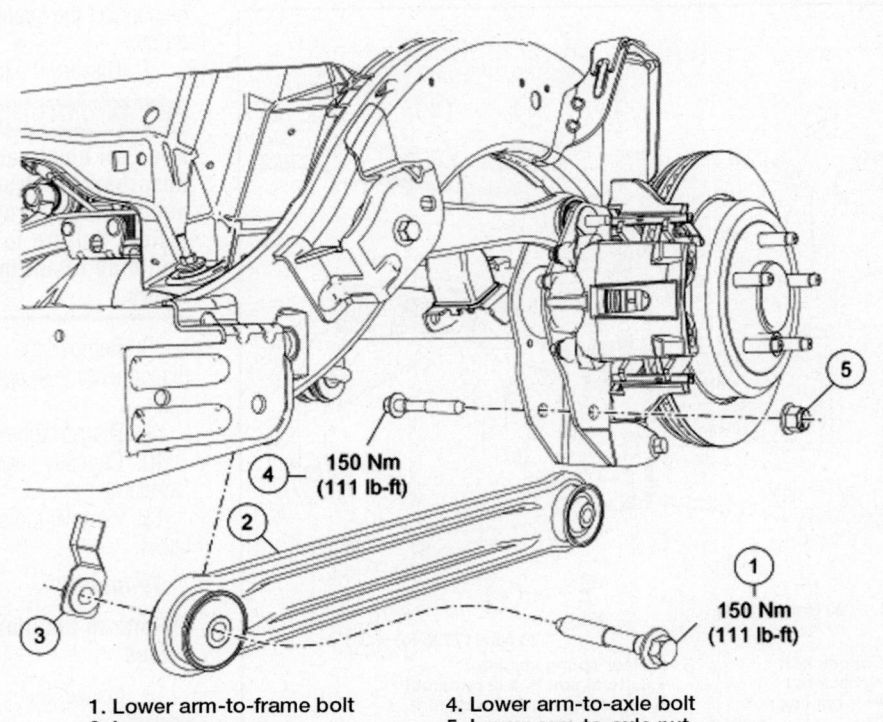

150 Nm
(111 lb-ft)

150 Nm
(111 lb-ft)

1. Lower arm-to-frame bolt
2. Lower arm
3. Lower arm-to-frame flagnut
4. Lower arm-to-axle bolt
5. Lower arm-to-axle nut

N0044378

Fig. 123 Exploded view of the lower control arm

11. Tighten the lower arm-to-frame nut.

12. Tighten the lower arm-to-axle nut.

13. Install the wheel and tire.

STABILIZER BAR

REMOVAL & INSTALLATION

See Figure 124.

➡Suspension fasteners are critical parts because they affect performance of vital components and systems and their failure may result in major service expense. New fasteners with the same part number or an equivalent part must be installed if installation is necessary. Do not use a replacement part of lesser quality or substitute design. Torque values must be used as specified during reassembly to make sure of correct retention of these parts. Orientation of the fasteners is also important on all rear suspension arms. Make sure the fasteners are installed in the same direction as they were in when removed.

➡Refer to the illustration for torque values.

1. Disconnect the negative battery cable.

2. With the vehicle in NEUTRAL, position it on a hoist.

3. Remove the 2 lower stabilizer bar link nuts, washers and bushings.

4. Discard the nuts.

5. Remove the 2 upper stabilizer bar link nuts, the washers and bushings, and the stabilizer bar links.

6. Discard the nuts.

7. Remove the 2 stabilizer bar bracket bolts, 2 brackets and the stabilizer bar.

8. Discard the 2 bracket bolts.

9. To install, reverse the removal procedure.

STRUT ASSEMBLY

REMOVAL & INSTALLATION

See Figure 125.

✳✳ WARNING

Keep all body parts clear of shock absorbers or strut rods. Shock absorbers or struts can extend unassisted. Failure to follow this instruction may result in serious personal injury.

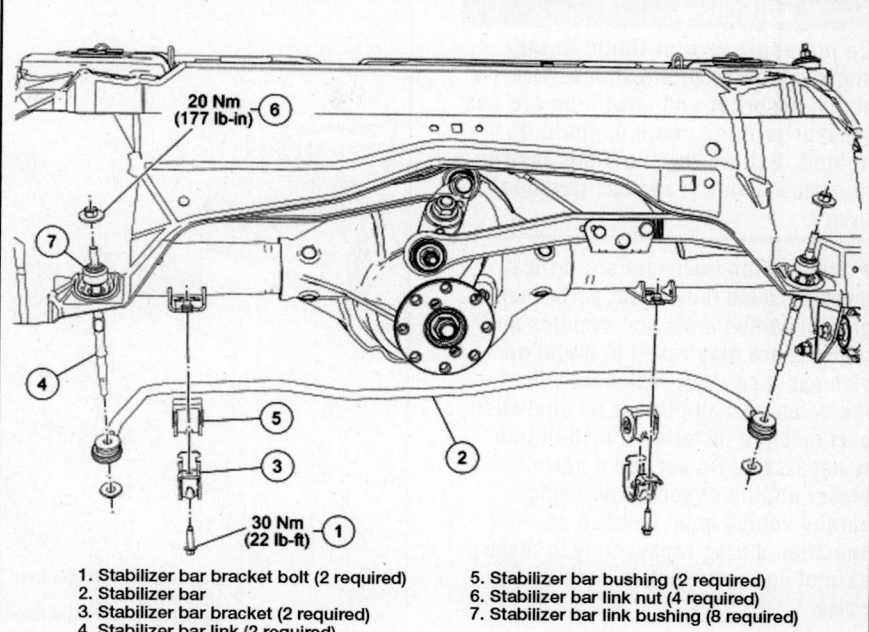

1. Stabilizer bar bracket bolt (2 required)
2. Stabilizer bar
3. Stabilizer bar bracket (2 required)
4. Stabilizer bar link (2 required)
5. Stabilizer bar bushing (2 required)
6. Stabilizer bar link nut (4 required)
7. Stabilizer bar link bushing (8 required)

20 Nm (177 lb-in)
30 Nm (22 lb-ft)

N0084896

Fig. 124 Exploded view of the stabilizer bar assembly

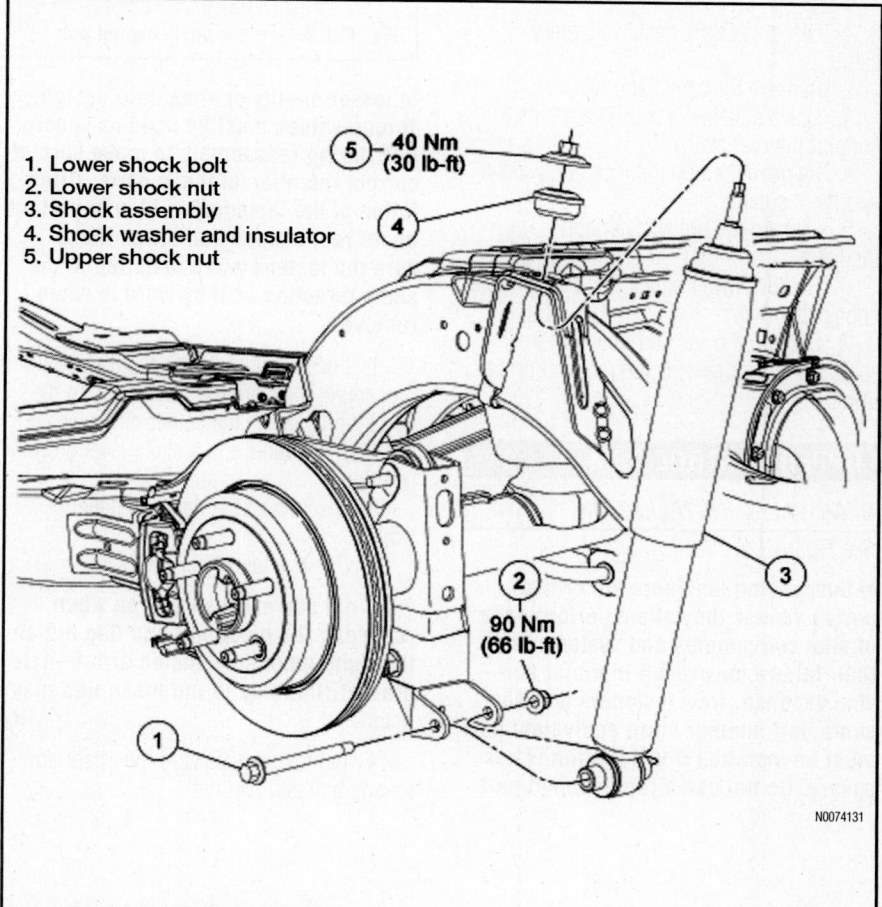

1. Lower shock bolt
2. Lower shock nut
3. Shock assembly
4. Shock washer and insulator
5. Upper shock nut

40 Nm (30 lb-ft)
90 Nm (66 lb-ft)

N0074131

Fig. 125 View of the strut assembly

❋❋ WARNING

Do not apply heat or flame to the shock absorber or strut tube. The shock absorber and strut tube are gas pressurized and could explode if heated. Failure to follow this instruction may result in serious personal injury.

➡Suspension fasteners are critical parts because they affect performance of vital components and systems and their failure may result in major service expense. New fasteners with the same part number or an equivalent part must be installed if installation is necessary. Do not use a part of lesser quality or substitute design. Torque values must be used as specified during reassembly to make sure of correct retention of these parts.

➡Install shock absorbers individually as required. It is not necessary to install in pairs.

➡Refer to the illustration for torque values.

1. Disconnect the negative battery cable.
2. Remove the wheel and tire.
3. Use a suitable jack or jackstands to support the rear axle.
4. Remove the upper shock nut, washer and the insulator.
5. Discard the nut, washer and insulator.
6. Remove lower shock nut, bolt and the shock absorber.
7. Discard the nut and bolt.
8. To install, reverse the removal procedure.

UPPER CONTROL ARM

REMOVAL & INSTALLATION

See Figure 126.

➡Suspension fasteners are critical parts because they affect performance of vital components and systems and their failure may result in major service expense. New fasteners with the same part number or an equivalent part must be installed if installation is necessary. Do not use a replacement part

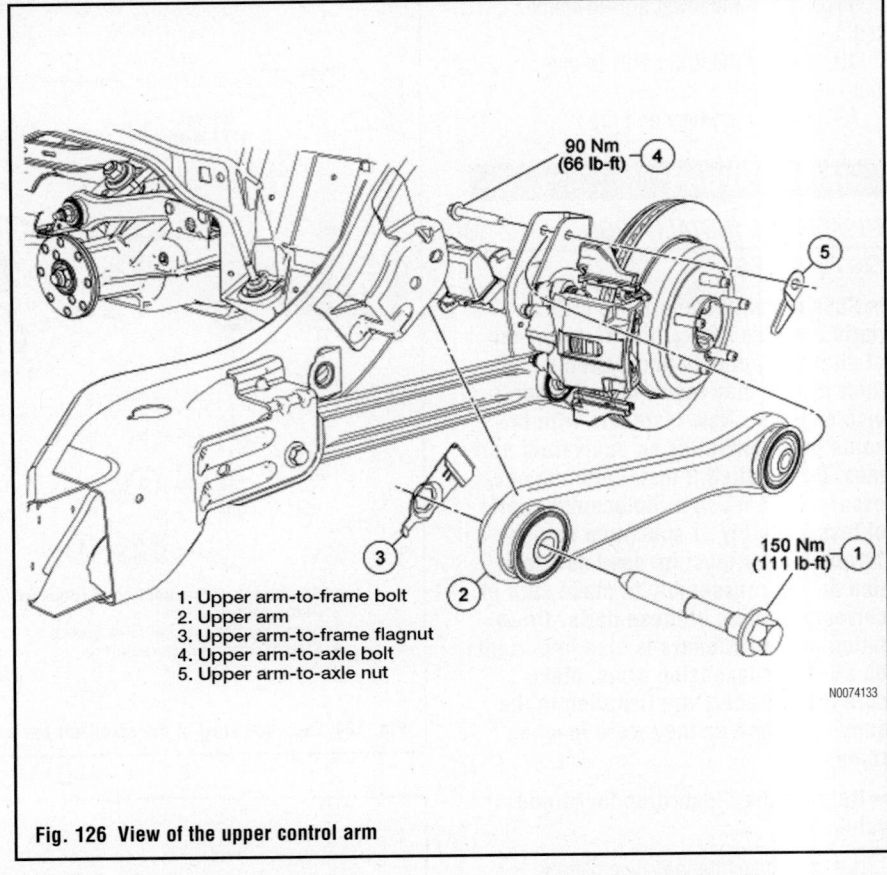

1. Upper arm-to-frame bolt
2. Upper arm
3. Upper arm-to-frame flagnut
4. Upper arm-to-axle bolt
5. Upper arm-to-axle nut

N0074133

Fig. 126 View of the upper control arm

of lesser quality or substitute design. Torque values must be used as specified during reassembly to make sure of correct retention of these parts. Orientation of the fasteners is also important on all rear suspension arms. Make sure the fasteners are installed in the same direction as they were in when removed.

1. For reference during the installation procedure, measure the distance from the lip of the fender to the center of the wheel hub with the vehicle in a static level ground position.
2. Disconnect the negative battery cable.
3. Remove the wheel and tire.

➡Do not use excessive force when removing the pivot bolt and flag nut on the right upper suspension arm-to-axle bracket. Damage to the brake line may occur.

4. Remove and discard the upper arm-to-axle bolt and flag nut.

5. Remove the upper arm-to-frame bolt and the upper arm.
6. Discard the nut and bolt.

To install:

➡The rear suspension upper arms are interchangeable from side-to-side, with FRONT and OUTBOARD stamped on the side of the arms for positioning during installation.

7. Position the upper arm and loosely install the new upper arm-to-frame bolt.
8. Loosely install the new upper arm-to-axle bolt and flag nut.
9. Before tightening the fasteners, use a suitable jack to raise the suspension until the distance between the lip of the fender and the center of the wheel hub is equal to the measurement taken in the removal procedure.
10. Tighten the upper arm-to-frame bolt.
11. Tighten the upper arm-to-axle bolt.
12. Install the wheel and tire.

FORD AND LINCOLN

Edge • MKX

2

BRAKES 2-12

**ANTI-LOCK BRAKE
SYSTEM (ABS)** 2-12
General Information..................2-12
  Precautions............................2-12
Speed Sensors 2-12
  Removal & Installation..........2-12
**BLEEDING THE BRAKE
SYSTEM**.......................2-15
Bleeding Procedure 2-15
  Bleeding Procedure 2-15
  Bleeding the ABS System 2-16
  Master Cylinder Bleeding 2-16
FRONT DISK BRAKES 2-16
Brake Caliper...........................2-17
  Removal & Installation..........2-17
Disc Brake Pads 2-17
  Removal & Installation..........2-17
PARKING BRAKE 2-20
Parking Brake Cables 2-20
  Adjustment 2-20
Parking Brake Shoes 2-20
  Removal & Installation..........2-20
REAR DISC BRAKES 2-18
Brake Caliper...........................2-18
  Removal & Installation..........2-18
Disc Brake Pads 2-19
  Removal & Installation..........2-19

CHASSIS ELECTRICAL 2-20

**AIR BAG (SUPPLEMENTAL
RESTRAINT SYSTEM)** 2-20
General Information..................2-20
  Arming the System 2-24
  Disarming the System...........2-21
  Service Precautions 2-20

DRIVE TRAIN 2-27

Automatic Transaxle Fluid 2-27
  Drain and Refill.....................2-27
Front Halfshaft.........................2-31
  Removal & Installation..........2-31
Rear Axle Stub Shaft Bearing
  and Seal 2-34
  Removal & Installation..........2-34

Rear Driveshaft........................2-34
  Removal & Installation..........2-34
Rear Halfshaft..........................2-34
  Removal & Installation..........2-34
Transfer Case Assembly
  (Power Transfer Unit) 2-27
  Removal & Installation..........2-27

ENGINE COOLING 2-37

Engine Coolant........................2-37
  Bleeding 2-37
  Drain & Refill Procedure.......2-37
  Flushing................................2-37
Engine Fan 2-38
  Removal & Installation..........2-38
Radiator 2-38
  Removal & Installation..........2-38
Thermostat 2-39
  Removal & Installation..........2-39

ENGINE ELECTRICAL.........2-41

BATTERY SYSTEM 2-41
Battery.....................................2-41
  Removal & Installation..........2-41
CHARGING SYSTEM 2-42
Alternator 2-42
  Removal & Installation..........2-42
IGNITION SYSTEM 2-44
Firing Order.............................2-44
Ignition Coil 2-44
  Removal & Installation..........2-44
Spark Plugs.............................2-45
  Removal & Installation..........2-45
STARTING SYSTEM 2-46
Starter 2-46
  Removal & Installation..........2-46

ENGINE MECHANICAL 2-47

Accessory Drive Belts 2-47
  Accessory Belt Routing..........2-47
  Removal & Installation..........2-47
Air Cleaner 2-48
  Removal & Installation..........2-48
Camshaft and Valve Lifters.......2-48
  Removal & Installation..........2-48

Catalytic Converter...................2-59
  Removal & Installation..........2-59
Crankshaft Front Seal...............2-60
  Removal & Installation..........2-60
Cylinder Head 2-60
  Removal & Installation..........2-60
Exhaust Manifold 2-66
  Removal & Installation..........2-66
Intake Manifold 2-67
  Removal & Installation..........2-67
Oil Pan 2-71
  Removal & Installation..........2-71
Oil Pump 2-77
  Removal & Installation..........2-77
Piston and Ring........................2-79
  Positioning 2-79
Rear Main Seal 2-79
  Removal & Installation..........2-79
Timing Chain & Sprockets 2-79
  Removal & Installation..........2-79
Valve Covers 2-82
  Removal & Installation..........2-82

**ENGINE PERFORMANCE &
EMISSION CONTROLS** 2-84

Camshaft Position (CMP)
  Sensor 2-84
  Removal & Installation..........2-84
Crankshaft Position (CKP)
  Sensor 2-84
  Removal & Installation..........2-84
Heated Oxygen Sensor
  (HO2S)..................................2-85
  Removal & Installation..........2-85
Knock Sensor (KS)...................2-85
  Removal & Installation..........2-85

FUEL............................2-86

**GASOLINE FUEL INJECTION
SYSTEM**.......................2-86
Fuel Injectors 2-86
  Removal & Installation..........2-86
Fuel Pump...............................2-87
  Removal & Installation..........2-87
Fuel System Service
  Precautions 2-86

Fuel Tank.....................................2-88
   Draining.................................2-88
   Removal & Installation..........2-89
Relieving Fuel System
  Pressure................................2-86
Throttle Body..........................2-89
   Removal & Installation..........2-89

HEATING & AIR CONDITIONING SYSTEM.....................2-90

Blower Motor 2-90
   Removal & Installation..........2-90
Heater Core 2-90
   Removal & Installation...........2-90

PRECAUTIONS 2-12

SPECIFICATIONS AND MAINTENANCE CHARTS 2-3

Brake Specifications...................2-7
Camshaft Specifications.............2-5
Capacities 2-4
Crankshaft and Connecting
  Rod Specifications 2-5
Engine and Vehicle
  Identification 2-3

Engine Tune-Up
  Specifications 2-3
Fluid Specifications...................2-4
General Engine
  Specifications 2-3
Piston and Ring
  Specifications 2-5
Scheduled Maintenance
  Intervals 2-8–2-11
Tire, Wheel and Ball Joint
  Specifications 2-7
Torque Specifications.................2-6
Valve Specifications 2-4
Wheel Alignment.......................2-6

STEERING 2-91

Power Steering Gear.................2-91
   Removal & Installation..........2-91
Power Steering Pump................2-92
   Bleeding 2-94
   Fluid Fill Procedure..............2-94
   Removal & Installation..........2-92

SUSPENSION..................2-95

FRONT SUSPENSION..........2-95
Lower Control Arm....................2-95
   Removal & Installation..........2-95

Shock Absorber & Spring
  Assembly 2-99
   Removal & Installation..........2-99
Stabilizer Bar & Link 2-96
   Removal & Installation..........2-96
Steering Knuckle 2-98
   Removal & Installation..........2-98
Wheel Bearings 2-100
   Removal & Installation........2-100

REAR SUSPENSION 2-100
Coil Spring............................2-100
   Removal & Installation........2-100
Lower Control Arm..................2-103
   Removal & Installation........2-103
Shock Absorber......................2-104
   Removal & Installation........2-104
Stabilizer Bar & Link 2-103
   Removal & Installation........2-103
Toe Link 2-105
   Removal & Installation........2-105
Trailing Arm 2-105
   Removal & Installation........2-105
Upper Control Arm..................2-105
   Removal & Installation........2-105
Wheel Bearings & Wheel
  Hub.......................................2-107
   Removal & Installation........2-107

SPECIFICATIONS AND MAINTENANCE CHARTS

ENGINE AND VEHICLE IDENTIFICATION

	Engine						Model Year	
Code ①	Liters (cc)	Cu. In.	Cyl.	Fuel Sys.	Engine Type	Eng. Mfg.	Code ②	Year
C	3.5 (3500)	214	6	SFI	Gas	Ford	A	2010
K	3.7 (3700)	226	6	SFI	Gas	Ford	B	2011

① 8th position of VIN

② 10th position of VIN

25759_EDGE_C0001

GENERAL ENGINE SPECIFICATIONS

All measurements are given in inches.

Year	Model	Engine Displacement Liters (cc)	Engine ID/VIN	Fuel System Type	Net Horsepower @ rpm	Net Torque @ rpm (ft. lbs.)	Bore x Stroke (in.)	Com- pression Ratio	Oil Pressure @ rpm
2010	Edge	3.5 (3500)	C	SFI	NA	NA	3.64x3.41	10.3:1	30 psi@1,500
	MKX	3.5 (3500)	C	SFI	NA	NA	3.64x3.41	10.3:1	30 psi@1,500
2011	Edge	3.5 (3500)	C	SFI	NA	NA	3.64x3.41	10.8:1	30 psi@1,500
	MKX	3.5 (3500)	C	SFI	NA	NA	3.64x3.41	10.8:1	30 psi@1,500
	Edge	3.7 (3700)	K	SFI	NA	NA	3.76x3.41	10.5:1	30 psi@1,500
	MKX	3.7 (3700)	K	SFI	NA	NA	3.76x3.41	10.5:1	30 psi@1,500

NA: Not Available

25759_EDGE_C0002

ENGINE TUNE-UP SPECIFICATIONS

Year	Engine Displacement Liters	Engine ID/VIN	Spark Plug Gap (in.)	Ignition Timing (deg.) MT	AT	Fuel Pump (psi)	Idle Speed (rpm) MT	AT	Valve Clearance Intake	Exhaust
2010	3.5	C	0.051-0.057	①	①	65	②	②	0.006-0.010	0.0142-0.0181
2011	3.5	C	0.049-0.053	①	①	58	②	②	0.006-0.010	0.0142-0.0181
	3.7	K	0.049-0.053	①	①	58	②	②	0.006-0.010	0.0142-0.0181

① Engines equipped with Distributorless Ignition System (DIS). Ignition timing is not adjustable

② Refer to the Vehicle Emission Control Information label

25759_EDGE_C0003

CAPACITIES

Year	Model	Engine Displacement Liters	Engine ID/VIN	Engine Oil with Filter	Transmission/axle (pts.) Auto.	Transmission/axle (pts.) Manual	Drive Axle (pts.) Front	Drive Axle (pts.) Rear	Transfer Case (pts.)	Fuel Tank (gal.)	Cooling System (qts.)
2010	Edge	3.5	C	5.5	18.8	NA	NA	2.43	0.93675	①	②
	MKX	3.5	C	5.5	18.8	NA	NA	2.43	0.93675	①	②
2011	Edge	3.5	C	NA	NA	NA	NA	2.43	0.93675	③	②
	MKX	3.5	C	NA	NA	NA	NA	2.43	0.93675	③	②
	Edge	3.7	K	NA	NA	NA	NA	2.43	0.93675	③	②
	MKX	3.7	K	NA	NA	NA	NA	2.43	0.93675	③	②

NOTE: All capacities are approximate. Add fluid gradually and ensure a proper fluid level is obtained.

① AWD: 20 gal
   FWD: 19 gal

② Without trailer tow option 11.7
   With trailer tow option 12.7

③ AWD: 19.2
   FWD: 18.3

25759_EDGE_C0004

FLUID SPECIFICATIONS

Year	Model	Engine Disp. Liters	Engine Oil	Manual Trans.	Auto. Trans.	Drive Axle Rear	Transfer Case	Power Steering Fluid	Brake Master Cylinder	Cooling System
2010	Edge	3.5	①	MERCON® LV	MERCON® LV	②	MERCON® V	MERCON® V	DOT 3	③
	MKX	3.5	①	MERCON® LV	MERCON® LV	②	MERCON® V	MERCON® V	DOT 3	③
2011	Edge	3.5	①	MERCON® LV	MERCON® LV	②	MERCON® V	MERCON® V	DOT 3	③
	MKX	3.5	①	MERCON® LV	MERCON® LV	②	MERCON® V	MERCON® V	DOT 3	③
	Edge	3.7	①	MERCON® LV	MERCON® LV	②	MERCON® V	MERCON® V	DOT 3	③
	MKX	3.7	①	MERCON® LV	MERCON® LV	②	MERCON® V	MERCON® V	DOT 3	③

DOT: Department Of Transpotation

① Motorcraft SAE 5W-20 Premium Synthetic Blend Motor Oil

② Motorcraft SAE 80W-90 Premium Rear Axle Lubricant

③ Motorcraft Specialty Green Engine Coolant

25759_EDGE_C0005

VALVE SPECIFICATIONS

Year	Engine Displacement Liters	Engine ID/VIN	Seat Angle (deg.)	Face Angle (deg.)	Spring Test Pressure (lbs. @ in.)	Spring Free-Length (in.)	Spring Installed Height (in.)	Stem-to-Guide Clearance (in.) Intake	Stem-to-Guide Clearance (in.) Exhaust	Stem Diameter (in.) Intake	Stem Diameter (in.) Exhaust
2010	3.5	C	44.5-45.5	44.5-45.5	53 @ 1.45	1.889	1.45	0.0008-0.0027	0.0013-0.0320	0.2157-0.2164	0.2151-0.2159
2011	3.5	C	44.5-45.5	44.5-45.5	114.7 @1.06	1.889	1.450	0.0008-0.0027	0.0013-0.0320	0.2157-0.2166	0.2151-0.2159
	3.7	K	44.5-45.5	44.5-45.5	114.7 @ 1.06	1.889	1.450	0.0008-0.0027	0.0013-0.0320	0.2157-0.2164	0.2151-0.2159

25759_EDGE_C0006

CAMSHAFT SPECIFICATIONS

All measurements in inches unless noted

Year	Engine Displacement Liters	Engine Code/VIN	Journal Diameter	Brg. Oil Clearance	Shaft End-play	Runout	Journal Bore	Lobe Height Intake	Lobe Height Exhaust
2010	3.5	C	①	②	0.0012-0.0066	0.0015	NA	0.380	0.380
2011	3.5	C	③	②	0.0012-0.0066	0.0015	④	0.394	0.380
	3.7	K	③	②	0.0012-0.0066	0.0015	④	0.380	0.0380

① 1st Journal: 1.221-1.222
   Intermediate: 1.023-1.024
② 1st Journal: 0.0027 MAX
   Intermediate: 0.0029 MAX
④ 1st journal: 1.537-1.537
   Intermediate journals: 1.023-1.024
③ 1st Journal: 1.537-1.538
   Intermediate: 1.023-1.024

25759_EDGE_C0007

CRANKSHAFT AND CONNECTING ROD SPECIFICATIONS

All measurements are given in inches.

Year	Engine Displacement Liters	Engine ID/VIN	Crankshaft Main Brg. Journal Dia.	Crankshaft Main Brg. Oil Clearance	Crankshaft Shaft End-play	Crankshaft Thrust on No.	Connecting Rod Journal Diameter	Connecting Rod Oil Clearance	Connecting Rod Side Clearance
2010	3.5	C	2.657	0.0010-0.0016	0.0039-0.0114	NA	2.204-2.2050	NA	NA
2011	3.5	C	2.6570	0.0010-0.0016	0.0039-0.0114	NA	2.204-2.2050	NA	0.0002
	3.7	K	2.6570	0.0010-0.0016	0.0020-0.0114	NA	2.204-2.2050	NA	0.0002

25759_EDGE_C0008

PISTON AND RING SPECIFICATIONS

All measurements are given in inches.

Year	Engine Displacement Liters	Engine ID/VIN	Piston Clearance	Ring Gap Top Compression	Ring Gap Bottom Compression	Ring Gap Oil Control	Ring Side Clearance Top Compression	Ring Side Clearance Bottom Compression	Ring Side Clearance Oil Control
2010	3.5	C	0.0003-0.0017	0.0059-0.0098	0.0118-0.0216	0.0059-0.0177	0.0484-0.0492	0.0602-0.0610	0.0996-0.1003
2011	3.5	C	0.003-0.0017	0.0066-0.0106	0.0118-0.0216	0.0059-0.0177	0.0484-0.0492	0.0602-0.0610	0.0996-0.1003
	3.7	K	0.0003-0.0017	0.0066-0.0106	0.0118-0.0216	0.0059-0.0177	0.0460-0.0468	0.0578-0.0586	0.0996-0.1004

25759_EDGE_C0009

TORQUE SPECIFICATIONS
All readings in ft. lbs.

Year	Engine Disp. Liters	Engine ID/VIN	Cylinder Head Bolts	Main Bearing Bolts	Rod Bearing Bolts	Crankshaft Damper Bolts	Flywheel Bolts	Manifold Intake	Manifold Exhaust	Spark Plugs	Oil Pan Drain Plug
2010	3.5	C	NA	NA	NA	NA	59	7	9	11	20
2011	3.5	C	①	NA	NA	NA	59	7	9	11	20
	3.7	K	①	6	NA	②	59	7	9	11	20

NA: Not Available

① Stage 1: 20 ft. lbs. (27 Nm)

Stage 2: 26 ft. lbs. (35 Nm)

Stage 3: Tighten 90 degrees

Stage 4: Tighten 90 degrees

Stage 5: Tighten 45 degrees

② Stage 1: Tighten to 89 ft. lbs. (120 Nm)

Stage 2: Loosen one full turn

Stage 3: Tighten to 37 ft. lbs. (50 Nm)

Stage 4: Tighten an additional 90 degrees

25759_EDGE_C0010

WHEEL ALIGNMENT

Year	Model		Caster Range (+/-Deg.)	Caster Preferred Setting (Deg.)	Camber Range (+/-Deg.)	Camber Preferred Setting (Deg.)	Toe-in (in.)
2010	Edge/	F	.75	①	.75	②	NA
	MKX	R	.75	NA	.75	-0.45	NA
2011	Edge/	F	.75	①	.75	③	NA
	MKX	R	.75	NA	.75	-0.45	NA

① Left Front: 4.3

Right Front: 4.5

② Left Front: -0.1

Right Front: -0.6

③ Left Front: -0.04

Right Front: -0.54

25759_EDGE_C0011

TIRE, WHEEL AND BALL JOINT SPECIFICATIONS

| Year | Model | OEM Tires | | Tire Pressures (psi) | | Wheel Size | Ball Joint Inspection | Lug Nut (ft. lbs.) |
		Standard	Optional	Front	Rear			
2010	Edge/ MKX	①	①	①	①	NA	NA	NA
2011	Edge/ MKX	①	①	①	①	NA	0-0.08 inch	NA

OEM: Original Equipment Manufacturer

PSI: Pounds Per Square Inch

NA: Information not available

① See safety certification sticker located on driver door jamb.

25759_EDGE_C0012

BRAKE SPECIFICATIONS

All measurements in inches unless noted

| Year | Model | | Brake Disc | | | Brake Drum Diameter | | | Minimum Pad/Lining Thickness | | Brake Caliper | |
			Original Thickness	Minimum Thickness	Max. Runout	Original Inside Diameter	Max. Wear Limit	Maximum Machine Diamter	Front	Rear	Bracket Bolts (ft. lbs.)	Mounting Bolts (ft. lbs.)
2010	Edge/	F	NA	1.023	0.1180	NA	NA	NA	0.118		NA	NA
	MKX	R	NA	0.629	0.1180	NA	NA	NA		0.118	NA	NA
2011	Edge/	F	NA	1.023	0.1180	NA	NA	NA	0.118		15	98
	MKX	R	NA	0.039	NA	NA	NA	NA		0.118	NA	76

NA: Information not available

F: Front

R: Rear

25759_EDGE_C0013

SCHEDULED MAINTENANCE INTERVALS
2010 Ford Edge/Lincoln MKX - Normal

TO BE SERVICED	TYPE OF SERVICE	VEHICLE MILEAGE INTERVAL (x1000)												
		7.5	15	22.5	30	37.5	45	52.5	60	67.5	75	82.5	90	97.5
Engine oil & filter	Replace	✓	✓	✓	✓	✓	✓	✓	✓	✓	✓	✓	✓	✓
Rotate and inspect tires	Service	✓	✓	✓	✓	✓	✓	✓	✓	✓	✓	✓	✓	✓
Inspect wheels and related components for abnomal noise, wear, looseness or drag	Inspect	✓	✓	✓	✓	✓	✓	✓	✓	✓	✓	✓	✓	✓
Fluid levels (all)	Top off	✓	✓	✓	✓	✓	✓	✓	✓	✓	✓	✓	✓	✓
Exhaust system (Leaks, damage, loose parts and foreign material)	Inspect		✓		✓		✓		✓		✓		✓	
Cabin air filter	Replace		✓		✓		✓		✓		✓		✓	
Cooling system and hoses	Inspect		✓		✓		✓		✓		✓		✓	
Brake system (Pads/shoes/rotors/drums, brake lines and hoses, and parking brake system)	Inspect		✓		✓		✓		✓		✓		✓	
Halfshaft & U-joints	Inspect		✓		✓		✓		✓		✓		✓	
Climate-controlled seat filter (if equipped)	Replace				✓				✓				✓	
Engine air filter	Replace				✓				✓				✓	
Spark plugs	Replace												✓	
Drive belt(s)	Inspect	✓	✓	✓	✓	✓	✓	✓	✓	✓	✓	✓	✓	✓
Shocks struts and other suspension components for leaks and damage	Inspect	✓	✓	✓	✓	✓	✓	✓	✓	✓	✓	✓	✓	✓
Oil and fluid leaks	Inspect	✓	✓	✓	✓	✓	✓	✓	✓	✓	✓	✓	✓	✓
Windshield for cracks, chips and pitting	Inspect	✓	✓	✓	✓	✓	✓	✓	✓	✓	✓	✓	✓	✓
Windshield wiper spray and wiper operation	Inspect	✓	✓	✓	✓	✓	✓	✓	✓	✓	✓	✓	✓	✓
Radiator, coolers, heater and airconditioning hoses	Inspect	✓	✓	✓	✓	✓	✓	✓	✓	✓	✓	✓	✓	✓
Horn, exterior lamps, turn signals and hazard warning light operation	Inspect	✓	✓	✓	✓	✓	✓	✓	✓	✓	✓	✓	✓	✓
Battery performance	Inspect	✓	✓	✓	✓	✓	✓	✓	✓	✓	✓	✓	✓	✓
Engine air filter	Inspect	✓	✓	✓	✓	✓	✓	✓	✓	✓	✓	✓	✓	✓
Drive belt(s)	Replace	Every 150,000 miles												
Engine coolant	Replace	At 6 years or 105,000 miles; then every 3 years or 45,000 miles												
Automatic transmision fluid	Replace	Every 150,000 miles												
Rear differential fluid	Replace	Every 150,000 miles												
Steering linkage, ball joints, suspension and tie-rod ends, lubricate if equipped with greases fittings	Inspect/ Lubricate	✓	✓	✓	✓	✓	✓	✓	✓	✓	✓	✓	✓	✓

25759_EDGE_C0014

SCHEDULED MAINTENANCE INTERVALS
2010 Ford Edge/Lincoln MKX - Severe

TO BE SERVICED	TYPE OF SERVICE	VEHICLE MILEAGE INTERVAL (x1000)											
		5	10	15	20	25	30	35	40	45	50	55	60
Battery performance	Inspect	✓	✓	✓	✓	✓	✓	✓	✓	✓	✓	✓	✓
Halfshaft boots	Inspect	✓	✓	✓	✓	✓	✓	✓	✓	✓	✓	✓	✓
Horn, exterior lamps, turn signals and hazard warning light operation	Inspect	✓	✓	✓	✓	✓	✓	✓	✓	✓	✓	✓	✓
Inspect wheels and related components for abnomal noise, wear, looseness or drag	Inspect	✓	✓	✓	✓	✓	✓	✓	✓	✓	✓	✓	✓
Shocks struts and other suspension components for leaks and damage	Inspect	✓	✓	✓	✓	✓	✓	✓	✓	✓	✓	✓	✓
Oil and fluid leaks	Inspect	✓	✓	✓	✓	✓	✓	✓	✓	✓	✓	✓	✓
Radiator, coolers, heater and airconditioning hoses	Inspect	✓	✓	✓	✓	✓	✓	✓	✓	✓	✓	✓	✓
Rotate and inspect tires	Service	✓	✓	✓	✓	✓	✓	✓	✓	✓	✓	✓	✓
Spark plugs	Replace												✓
Auto transaxle fluid & filter	Replace						✓						✓
Rear axle (If non-synthetic)	Replace												✓
Windshield wiper spray and wiper operation	Inspect	✓	✓	✓	✓	✓	✓	✓	✓	✓	✓	✓	✓
Windshield for cracks, chips and pitting	Inspect	✓	✓	✓	✓	✓	✓	✓	✓	✓	✓	✓	✓
Exhaust system (Leaks, damage, loose parts and foreign material)	Inspect	✓	✓	✓	✓	✓	✓	✓	✓	✓	✓	✓	✓
Engine oil and filter	Replace	✓	✓	✓	✓	✓	✓	✓	✓	✓	✓	✓	✓
Fluid levels (all)	Top off	✓	✓	✓	✓	✓	✓	✓	✓	✓	✓	✓	✓
Air filter	Inspect	✓	✓	✓	✓	✓	✓	✓	✓	✓	✓	✓	✓
Air filter	Replace						✓						✓
Drive belt(s)	Inspect	✓	✓	✓	✓	✓	✓	✓	✓	✓	✓	✓	✓
Cooling system & hoses	Inspect	✓	✓	✓	✓	✓	✓	✓	✓	✓	✓	✓	✓
Climate-controlled seat filter (if equipped)	Replace						✓						✓
Brake system (Inspect brake pads/shoes/rotors/drums, brake lines and hoses, and parking brake system)	Inspect	✓	✓	✓	✓	✓	✓	✓	✓	✓	✓	✓	✓
Cabin air filter (If equipped)	Inspect/ Service	✓	✓	✓	✓	✓	✓	✓	✓	✓	✓	✓	✓
Engine coolant	Replace	At 6 years or 105,000 miles; then every 3 years or 45,000 miles											
Drive belt(s)	Replace	Every 150,000 miles											
Steering linkage, ball joints, suspension and tie-rod ends, lubricate if equipped with greases fittings	Inspect/ Lubricate	✓	✓	✓	✓	✓	✓	✓	✓	✓	✓	✓	✓

For extensive idling and or low speed driving, change engine oil and filter every 5,000 miles, 6 months or 200 hours of engine operation.

SCHEDULED MAINTENANCE INTERVALS
2011 Ford Edge/Lincoln MKX - Normal

Service Item	Service Action	1	2	3	4	5	6	7	8	9	10	11	12	13	14	15
Drive belt(s)	Inspect	✓	✓	✓	✓	✓	✓	✓	✓	✓	✓	✓	✓	✓	✓	✓
Cabin air filter	Inspect	✓	✓	✓	✓	✓	✓	✓	✓	✓	✓	✓	✓	✓	✓	✓
Engine oil & filter	Replace	✓	✓	✓	✓	✓	✓	✓	✓	✓	✓	✓	✓	✓	✓	✓
Rotate tires, inspect tread wear, measure tread depth and check pressure	Inspect/ Rotate	✓	✓	✓	✓	✓	✓	✓	✓	✓	✓	✓	✓	✓	✓	✓
Inspect wheels and related components for abnomal noise, wear, looseness or drag	Inspect	✓	✓	✓	✓	✓	✓	✓	✓	✓	✓	✓	✓	✓	✓	✓
Fluid levels (all)	Top off	✓	✓	✓	✓	✓	✓	✓	✓	✓	✓	✓	✓	✓	✓	✓
Brake system (Pads/shoes/rotors/drums, brake lines and hoses, and parking brake system)	Inspect	✓	✓	✓	✓	✓	✓	✓	✓	✓	✓	✓	✓	✓	✓	✓
Cooling system, hoses, clamps & coolant strength	Inspect	✓	✓	✓	✓	✓	✓	✓	✓	✓	✓	✓	✓	✓	✓	✓
Exhaust system (Leaks, damage, loose parts and foreign material)	Inspect	✓	✓	✓	✓	✓	✓	✓	✓	✓	✓	✓	✓	✓	✓	✓
Halfshaft boots	Inspect	✓	✓	✓	✓	✓	✓	✓	✓	✓	✓	✓	✓	✓	✓	✓
Steering linkage, ball joints, suspension, tie-rod ends, driveshaft and u-joints: lubricate if equipped with grease fittings	Inspect/ Lubricate	✓	✓	✓	✓	✓	✓	✓	✓	✓	✓	✓	✓	✓	✓	✓
Battery performance	Inspect	✓	✓	✓	✓	✓	✓	✓	✓	✓	✓	✓	✓	✓	✓	✓
Horn, exterior lamps, turn signals and hazard warning light operation	Inspect	✓	✓	✓	✓	✓	✓	✓	✓	✓	✓	✓	✓	✓	✓	✓
Radiator, coolers, heater and air conditioning hoses	Inspect	✓	✓	✓	✓	✓	✓	✓	✓	✓	✓	✓	✓	✓	✓	✓
Windshield wiper spray and wiper operation	Inspect	✓	✓	✓	✓	✓	✓	✓	✓	✓	✓	✓	✓	✓	✓	✓
Windshield for cracks, chips and pitting	Inspect	✓	✓	✓	✓	✓	✓	✓	✓	✓	✓	✓	✓	✓	✓	✓
Suspension components for leaks and damage	Inspect	✓	✓	✓	✓	✓	✓	✓	✓	✓	✓	✓	✓	✓	✓	✓
Cabin air filter (If equipped)	Replace		√		√		√		√		√		√		√	
Rear differential fluid	Replace															✓
Spark plugs	Replace										✓					
Drive belt(s)	Replace															✓
Engine coolant	Replace										✓					✓
Engine air filter	Replace			✓			✓			✓			✓			✓
Engine air filter	Inspect	✓	✓	✓	✓	✓	✓	✓	✓	✓	✓	✓	✓	✓	✓	✓
Climate-controlled seat filter (if equipped)	Replace			✓			✓			✓			✓			✓
Auto transmisison fluid	Replace															✓

Oil change service intervals should be completed as indicated by the message center (Can be up to 1 year or 10,000 miles) If the message center is prematurely reset or is inoperative, perform the oil change interval at 6 months or 5,000 miles from your last oil change

25759_EDGE_C0016

SCHEDULED MAINTENANCE INTERVALS
2011 Ford Edge/Lincoln MKX - Severe

Service Item	Service Action	1	2	3	4	5	6	7	8	9	10	11	12	13	14	15
Engine oil & filter	Replace	✓	✓	✓	✓	✓	✓	✓	✓	✓	✓	✓	✓	✓	✓	✓
Auto transmission fluid	Replace			✓			✓			✓			✓			✓
Battery performance	Inspect	✓	✓	✓	✓	✓	✓	✓	✓	✓	✓	✓	✓	✓	✓	✓
Brake system (Pads/shoes/rotors/drums, brake lines and hoses, and parking brake system)	Inspect	✓	✓	✓	✓	✓	✓	✓	✓	✓	✓	✓	✓	✓	✓	✓
Cabin air filter (If equipped)	Inspect/Service	✓	✓	✓	✓	✓	✓	✓	✓	✓	✓	✓	✓	✓	✓	✓
Climate-controlled seat filter (if equipped)	Replace			✓			✓			✓			✓			✓
Cooling system, hoses, clamps & coolant strength	Inspect	✓	✓	✓	✓	✓	✓	✓	✓	✓	✓	✓	✓	✓	✓	✓
Drive belt(s)	Inspect	✓	✓	✓	✓	✓	✓	✓	✓	✓	✓	✓	✓	✓	✓	✓
Drive belt(s)	Replace															✓
Engine air filter	Inspect/Service	✓	✓	✓	✓	✓	✓	✓	✓	✓	✓	✓	✓	✓	✓	✓
Engine coolant	Replace										✓					✓
Exhaust system	Inspect	✓	✓	✓	✓	✓	✓	✓	✓	✓	✓	✓	✓	✓	✓	✓
Fluid levels (all)	Top off	✓	✓	✓	✓	✓	✓	✓	✓	✓	✓	✓	✓	✓	✓	✓
Halfshaft & U-joints	Inspect	✓	✓	✓	✓	✓	✓	✓	✓	✓	✓	✓	✓	✓	✓	✓
Horn, exterior lamps, turn signals and hazard warning light operation	Inspect	✓	✓	✓	✓	✓	✓	✓	✓	✓	✓	✓	✓	✓	✓	✓
Inspect wheels and related components for abnomal noise, wear, looseness or drag	Inspect	✓	✓	✓	✓	✓	✓	✓	✓	✓	✓	✓	✓	✓	✓	✓
Oil and fluid leaks	Inspect	✓	✓	✓	✓	✓	✓	✓	✓	✓	✓	✓	✓	✓	✓	✓
Radiator, coolers, heater and air conditioning hoses	Inspect	✓	✓	✓	✓	✓	✓	✓	✓	✓	✓	✓	✓	✓	✓	✓
Rear axle fluid (Non-synthetic)	Replace										✓					
Rotate tires, inspect tread wear, measure tread depth and check pressure	Inspect/Rotate	✓	✓	✓	✓	✓	✓	✓	✓	✓	✓	✓	✓	✓	✓	✓
Shocks struts and other suspension components for leaks and damage	Inspect	✓	✓	✓	✓	✓	✓	✓	✓	✓	✓	✓	✓	✓	✓	✓
Spark plugs	Replace										✓					
Steering linkage, ball joints, suspension and tie-rod ends, lubricate if equipped with greases fittings	Inspect/Lubricate	✓	✓	✓	✓	✓	✓	✓	✓	✓	✓	✓	✓	✓	✓	✓
Windshield for cracks, chips and pitting	Inspect	✓	✓	✓	✓	✓	✓	✓	✓	✓	✓	✓	✓	✓	✓	✓
Windshield wiper spray and wiper operation	Inspect	✓	✓	✓	✓	✓	✓	✓	✓	✓	✓	✓	✓	✓	✓	✓

For commercial use or extensive idling, change spark pluge at 60,000 miles.

For extensive idling and or low speed driving, change engine oil and filter every 5,000 miles, 6 months or 200 hours of engine operation.

PRECAUTIONS

Before servicing any vehicle, please be sure to read all of the following precautions, which deal with personal safety, prevention of component damage, and important points to take into consideration when servicing a motor vehicle:

• Never open, service or drain the radiator or cooling system when the engine is hot; serious burns can occur from the steam and hot coolant.

• Observe all applicable safety precautions when working around fuel. Whenever servicing the fuel system, always work in a well-ventilated area. Do not allow fuel spray or vapors to come in contact with a spark, open flame, or excessive heat (a hot drop light, for example). Keep a dry chemical fire extinguisher near the work area. Always keep fuel in a container specifically designed for fuel storage; also, always properly seal fuel containers to avoid the possibility of fire or explosion. Refer to the additional fuel system precautions later in this section.

• Fuel injection systems often remain pressurized, even after the engine has been turned **OFF**. The fuel system pressure must be relieved before disconnecting any fuel lines. Failure to do so may result in fire and/or personal injury.

• Brake fluid often contains polyglycol ethers and polyglycols. Avoid contact with the eyes and wash your hands thoroughly after handling brake fluid. If you do get brake fluid in your eyes, flush your eyes with clean, running water for 15 minutes. If eye irritation persists, or if you have taken brake fluid internally, IMMEDIATELY seek medical assistance.

• The EPA warns that prolonged contact with used engine oil may cause a number of skin disorders, including cancer. You should make every effort to minimize your exposure to used engine oil. Protective gloves should be worn when changing oil. Wash your hands and any other exposed skin areas as soon as possible after exposure to used engine oil. Soap and water, or waterless hand cleaner should be used.

• All new vehicles are now equipped with an air bag system, often referred to as a Supplemental Restraint System (SRS) or Supplemental Inflatable Restraint (SIR) system. The system must be disabled before performing service on or around system components, steering column, instrument panel components, wiring and sensors. Failure to follow safety and disabling procedures could result in accidental air bag deployment, possible personal injury and unnecessary system repairs.

• Always wear safety goggles when working with, or around, the air bag system. When carrying a non-deployed air bag, be sure the bag and trim cover are pointed away from your body. When placing a non-deployed air bag on a work surface, always face the bag and trim cover upward, away from the surface. This will reduce the motion of the module if it is accidentally deployed. Refer to the additional air bag system precautions later in this section.

• Clean, high quality brake fluid from a sealed container is essential to the safe and proper operation of the brake system. You should always buy the correct type of brake fluid for your vehicle. If the brake fluid becomes contaminated, completely flush the system with new fluid. Never reuse any brake fluid. Any brake fluid that is removed from the system should be discarded. Also, do not allow any brake fluid to come in contact with a painted surface; it will damage the paint.

• Never operate the engine without the proper amount and type of engine oil; doing so WILL result in severe engine damage.

• Timing belt maintenance is extremely important. Many models utilize an interference-type, non-freewheeling engine. If the timing belt breaks, the valves in the cylinder head may strike the pistons, causing potentially serious (also time-consuming and expensive) engine damage. Refer to the maintenance interval charts for the recommended replacement interval for the timing belt, and to the timing belt section for belt replacement and inspection.

• Disconnecting the negative battery cable on some vehicles may interfere with the functions of the on-board computer system(s) and may require the computer to undergo a relearning process once the negative battery cable is reconnected.

• When servicing drum brakes, only disassemble and assemble one side at a time, leaving the remaining side intact for reference.

• Only an MVAC-trained, EPA-certified automotive technician should service the air conditioning system or its components.

BRAKES

GENERAL INFORMATION

PRECAUTIONS

• Certain components within the ABS system are not intended to be serviced or repaired individually.

• Do not use rubber hoses or other parts not specifically specified for and ABS system. When using repair kits, replace all parts included in the kit. Partial or incorrect repair may lead to functional problems and require the replacement of components.

• Lubricate rubber parts with clean, fresh brake fluid to ease assembly. Do not use shop air to clean parts; damage to rubber components may result.

• Use only DOT 3 brake fluid from an unopened container.

• If any hydraulic component or line is removed or replaced, it may be necessary to bleed the entire system.

• A clean repair area is essential. Always clean the reservoir and cap thoroughly before removing the cap. The slightest amount of dirt in the fluid may plug an orifice and impair the system function. Perform repairs after components have been thoroughly cleaned; use only denatured alcohol to clean components. Do not allow ABS components to come into contact with any substance containing mineral oil; this includes used shop rags.

• The Anti-Lock control unit is a microprocessor similar to other computer units in

ANTI-LOCK BRAKE SYSTEM (ABS)

the vehicle. Ensure that the ignition switch is **OFF** before removing or installing controller harnesses. Avoid static electricity discharge at or near the controller.

• If any arc welding is to be done on the vehicle, the control unit should be unplugged before welding operations begin.

SPEED SENSORS

REMOVAL & INSTALLATION

Front

See Figure 1.

1. Remove the wheel and tire.
2. Remove the retainers and position the fender splash shield aside.

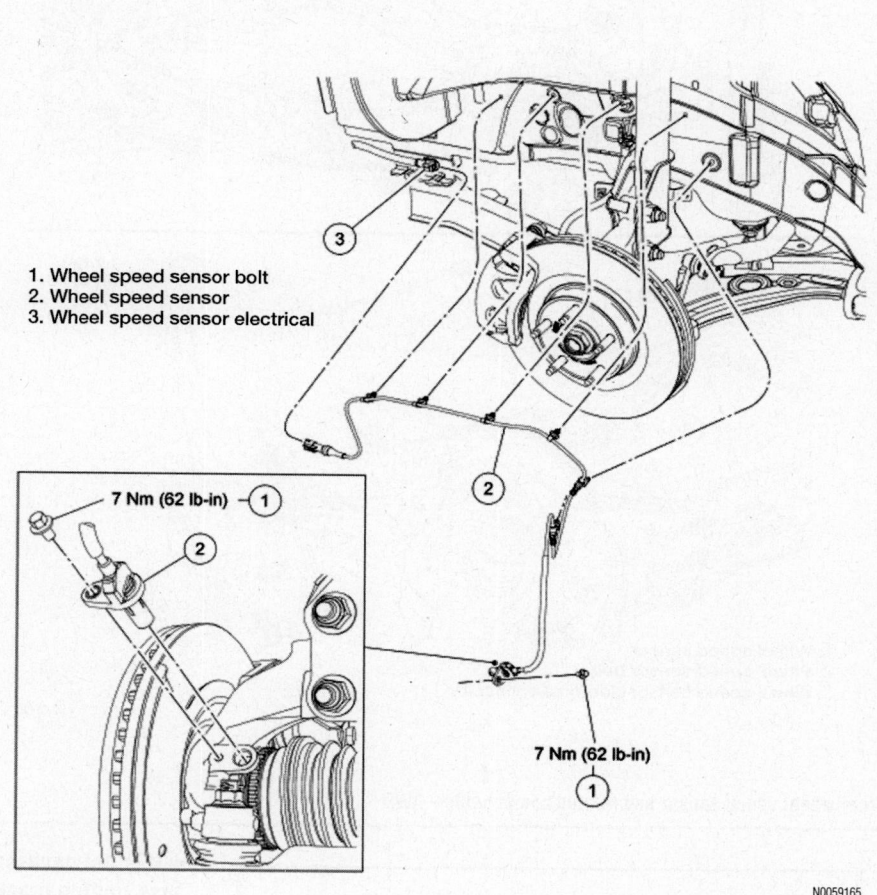

1. Wheel speed sensor bolt
2. Wheel speed sensor
3. Wheel speed sensor electrical

7 Nm (62 lb-in) ①
②

7 Nm (62 lb-in)
①

N0059165

Fig. 1 Exploded view of front speed sensor and related components

3. Disconnect the wheel speed sensor electrical connector.

4. Disconnect the 6 pushpin fasteners.

5. Remove the front wheel speed sensor bolt and the wheel speed sensor.

➡**The wheel speed sensor harness must be routed as shown or damage to**

the harness during vehicle jounce and rebound can occur.

To install:

6. To install, reverse the removal procedure. Tighten the wheel speed sensor to 62 inch lbs. (7 Nm).

Rear

See Figures 2 and 3.

1. Remove the wheel and tire.
2. Disconnect the wheel speed sensor electrical connector.

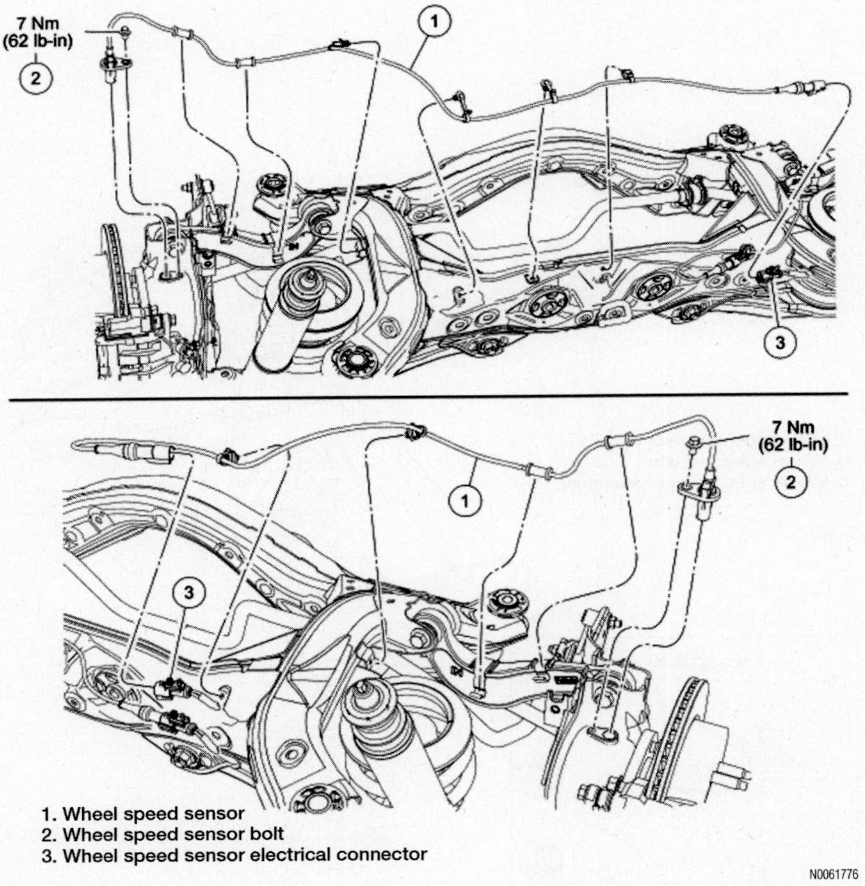

7 Nm
(62 lb-in)
②

①

③

7 Nm
(62 lb-in)
②

①

③

1. Wheel speed sensor
2. Wheel speed sensor bolt
3. Wheel speed sensor electrical connector

N0061776

Fig. 2 Exploded view of rear wheel speed sensor and related components—AWD

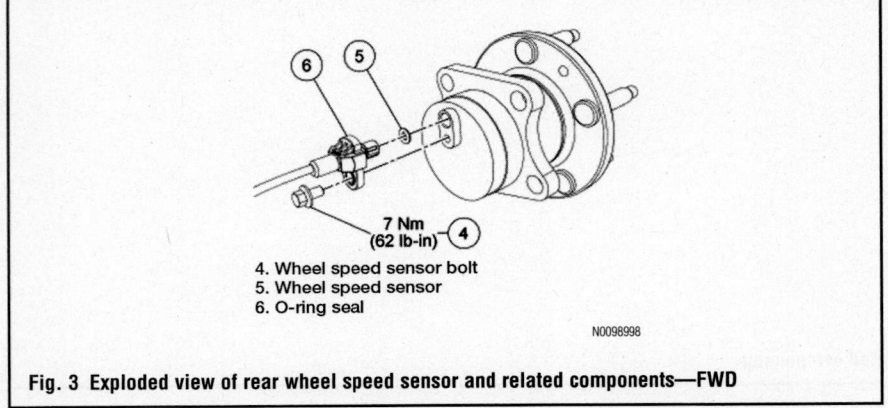

7 Nm
(62 lb-in) ④

4. Wheel speed sensor bolt
5. Wheel speed sensor
6. O-ring seal

N0098998

Fig. 3 Exploded view of rear wheel speed sensor and related components—FWD

➡It is not necessary to remove the harness routing brackets.

3. Disconnect the wheel speed sensor harness from the brackets.

4. Disconnect the pushpin fasteners.

5. Remove the wheel speed sensor bolt and the wheel speed sensor.

To install:

6. To install, reverse the removal procedure. Tighten the rear wheel speed sensor to 62 inch lbs. (7 Nm).

BRAKES

BLEEDING THE BRAKE SYSTEM

BLEEDING PROCEDURE

BLEEDING PROCEDURE

Pressure

See Figure 4.

✳✳ WARNING

Do not use any fluid other than clean brake fluid meeting manufacturer's specification. Additionally, do not use brake fluid that has been previously drained. Following these instructions will help prevent system contamination, brake component damage and the risk of serious personal injury.

✳✳ WARNING

Carefully read cautionary information on product label. For EMERGENCY MEDICAL INFORMATION seek medical advice. For additional information, consult the product Material Safety Data Sheet (MSDS) if available. Failure to follow these instructions may result in serious personal injury.

✳✳ WARNING

Do not allow the brake master cylinder to run dry during the bleeding operation. Master cylinder may be damaged if operated without fluid, resulting in degraded braking performance. Failure to follow this instruction may result in serious personal injury.

➡ Do not spill brake fluid on painted or plastic surfaces or damage to the surface may occur. If brake fluid is spilled onto a painted or plastic surface, immediately wash the surface with water.

➡ The Hydraulic Control Unit (HCU) bleeding procedure must be carried out if the HCU or any components upstream of the HCU are installed new.

➡ Pressure bleeding the brake system is preferred to manual bleeding.

1. Clean all dirt from the brake master cylinder filler cap and remove the filler cap.
   a. Fill the brake master cylinder with clean specified brake fluid.

➡ Master cylinder pressure bleeder adapter tools are available from various manufacturers of pressure bleeding equipment. Follow the instructions of

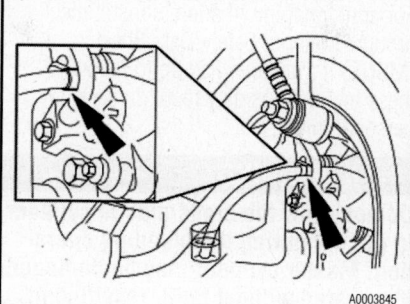

Fig. 4 Attaching the rubber drain tube to the RH rear bleeder screw

the equipment manufacturer when installing the adapter.

2. Install the bleeder adapter to the brake master cylinder reservoir and attach the bleeder tank hose to the fitting on the adapter.

➡ Make sure the bleeder tank contains enough clean, specified brake fluid to complete the bleeding operation.

3. Open the valve on the bleeder tank.
   a. Apply 30-50 psi (207-345 kPa) to the brake system.
4. Remove the RH rear bleeder cap and place a box-end wrench on the bleeder screw. Attach a rubber drain tube to the RH rear bleeder screw and submerge the free end of the tube in a container partially filled with clean, specified brake fluid.
5. Loosen the RH rear bleeder screw. Leave open until clear, bubble-free brake fluid flows, then tighten the RH rear bleeder screw and remove the rubber hose.
   a. Tighten to specifications. For additional information, refer to Brake Specifications.
   b. Install the bleeder screw cap.
6. Continue bleeding the system, going in order from the LH rear bleeder screw to the RH front bleeder screw ending with the LH front bleeder screw.
7. Release the bleeder tank pressure and close the bleeder tank valve. Remove the tank hose from the adapter and remove the adapter from the brake fluid reservoir.

Manual

See Figure 5.

✳✳ WARNING

Do not use any fluid other than clean brake fluid meeting manufacturer's specification. Additionally, do not use

brake fluid that has been previously drained. Following these instructions will help prevent system contamination, brake component damage and the risk of serious personal injury.

✳✳ WARNING

Carefully read cautionary information on product label. For EMERGENCY MEDICAL INFORMATION seek medical advice. For additional information, consult the product Material Safety Data Sheet (MSDS) if available. Failure to follow these instructions may result in serious personal injury.

✳✳ WARNING

Do not allow the brake master cylinder to run dry during the bleeding operation. Master cylinder may be damaged if operated without fluid, resulting in degraded braking performance. Failure to follow this instruction may result in serious personal injury.

➡ Do not spill brake fluid on painted or plastic surfaces or damage to the surface may occur. If brake fluid is spilled onto a painted or plastic surface, immediately wash the surface with water.

➡ The HCU bleeding procedure must be carried out if the HCU or any components upstream of the HCU are installed new.

➡ Pressure bleeding the brake system is preferred to manual bleeding.

1. Clean all dirt from the brake master cylinder filler cap and remove the filler cap.
   a. Fill the brake master cylinder with clean specified brake fluid.
2. Remove the bleeder screw cap and place a box-end wrench on the RH rear

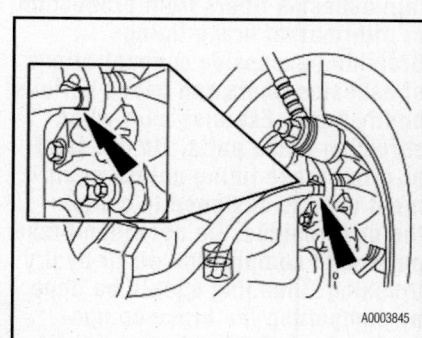

Fig. 5 Attaching the drain hose to the RH rear bleeder screw

bleeder screw. Attach a rubber drain hose to the RH rear bleeder screw and submerge the free end of the hose in a container partially filled with clean, specified brake fluid.

3. Have an assistant pump the brake pedal at least 3 times and then hold firm pressure on the brake pedal.

4. Loosen the RH rear bleeder screw until a stream of brake fluid comes out. While the assistant maintains pressure on the brake pedal, tighten the RH rear bleeder screw.

   a. Repeat until clear, bubble-free fluid comes out.

   b. Refill the brake master cylinder reservoir as necessary.

5. Remove the rubber hose and tighten the bleeder screw to specifications. For additional information, refer to Brake Specifications.

   a. Install the bleeder screw cap.

6. Repeat Steps 2 through 5 for the LH rear, RH front and LH front bleeder screws in this order.

MASTER CYLINDER BLEEDING

See Figure 6.

> ❊❊ **WARNING**
>
> **Do not use any fluid other than clean brake fluid meeting manufacturer's specification. Additionally, do not use brake fluid that has been previously drained. Following these instructions will help prevent system contamination, brake component damage and the risk of serious personal injury.**

1. Carefully read cautionary information on product label. For EMERGENCY MEDICAL INFORMATION seek medical advice. For additional information, consult the product Material Safety Data Sheet (MSDS) if available. Failure to follow these instructions may result in serious personal injury.

> ❊❊ **WARNING**
>
> **Do not allow the brake master cylinder to run dry during the bleeding operation. Master cylinder may be damaged if operated without fluid, resulting in degraded braking performance. Failure to follow this instruction may result in serious personal injury.**

➡ **Do not spill brake fluid on painted or plastic surfaces or damage to the surface may occur. If brake fluid is spilled onto a painted or plastic surface, immediately wash the surface with water.**

➡ **When a new brake master cylinder has been installed, or the system is emptied or partially emptied, it should be primed to prevent air from entering the system.**

2. Disconnect the brake tubes from the master cylinder.

3. Install short brake tubes with the ends submerged in the brake master cylinder reservoir.

4. Fill the brake master cylinder reservoir with clean, specified brake fluid.

5. Have an assistant pump the brake pedal until clear fluid flows from both brake tubes, without air bubbles.

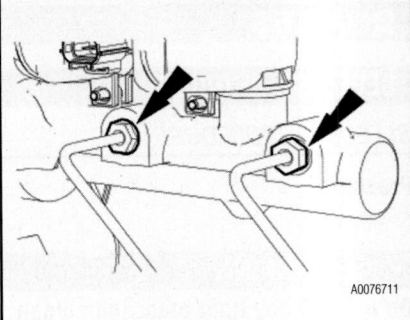

A0076711

Fig. 6 Disconnecting the brake tubes from the master cylinder

6. Remove the short brake tubes and install the brake outlet tubes.

7. Bleed the brake system. For additional information, refer to Brake System Bleeding.

BLEEDING THE ABS SYSTEM

➡ **The HCU bleeding procedure must be carried out if the HCU or any components upstream of the HCU are installed new.**

➡ **Pressure bleeding the brake system is preferred to manual bleeding.**

1. Follow the Pressure Bleeding or Manual Bleeding procedure steps to bleed the system.

2. Connect the scan tool and follow the ABS Service Bleed instructions.

3. Repeat the Pressure Bleeding or Manual Bleeding procedure steps to bleed the system.

BRAKES   FRONT DISC BRAKES

> ❊❊ **CAUTION**
>
> **Dust and dirt accumulating on brake parts during normal use may contain asbestos fibers from production or aftermarket brake linings. Breathing excessive concentrations of asbestos fibers can cause serious bodily harm. Exercise care when servicing brake parts. Do not sand or grind brake lining unless equipment used is designed to contain the dust residue. Do not clean brake parts with compressed air or by dry brushing. Cleaning should be done by dampening the brake components with a fine mist of water, then wiping the brake components clean with a dampened cloth. Dispose of**

cloth and all residue containing asbestos fibers in an impermeable container with the appropriate label. Follow practices prescribed by the Occupational Safety and Health Administration (OSHA) and the Environmental Protection Agency (EPA) for the handling, processing, and disposing of dust or debris that may contain asbestos fibers.

> ❊❊ **CAUTION**
>
> **Do not use any fluid other than clean brake fluid meeting manufacturer's specification. Additionally, do not use brake fluid that has been previ-**

ously drained. Following these instructions will help prevent system contamination, brake component damage and the risk of serious personal injury.

> ❊❊ **CAUTION**
>
> **Carefully read cautionary information on product label. For EMERGENCY MEDICAL INFORMATION seek medical advice. For additional information, consult the product Material Safety Data Sheet (MSDS) if available. Failure to follow these instructions may result in serious personal injury.**

BRAKE CALIPER

REMOVAL & INSTALLATION

See Figure 7.

❋❋ WARNING

Do not spill brake fluid on painted or plastic surfaces or damage to the surface may occur. If brake fluid is spilled onto a painted or plastic surface, immediately wash the surface with water.

1. Remove the wheel and tire assembly.
2. Remove the brake caliper flow bolt and position the hose aside.
   a. Discard the 2 copper washers.

➡**The guide pin bolts are different sizes. The longer/bigger bolt is the upper guide pin bolt.**

3. Remove the 2 brake caliper guide pin bolts.
4. Remove the brake caliper.

To install:

➡**During installation, make sure that the brake caliper hose is not twisted.**

5. To install, reverse the removal procedure. Tighten the brake caliper guide pin bolts to 65 ft. lbs. (88 Nm). Tighten the brake caliper flow bolt to 18 ft. lbs. (25 Nm). Bleed the brake caliper.

DISC BRAKE PADS

REMOVAL & INSTALLATION

See Figures 8 and 9.

❋❋ WARNING

Do not spill brake fluid on painted or plastic surfaces or damage to the surface may occur. If brake fluid is spilled onto a painted or plastic surface, immediately wash the surface with water.

1. Check the brake fluid level in the brake master cylinder reservoir.
   a. If required, remove the fluid until the brake master cylinder reservoir is one-half full.
2. Remove the wheel and tire.

➡**Do not pry in the caliper sight hole to retract the pistons as this can damage the pistons and boots.**

➡**Do not allow the brake caliper to hang from the brake hose or damage to the hose can occur.**

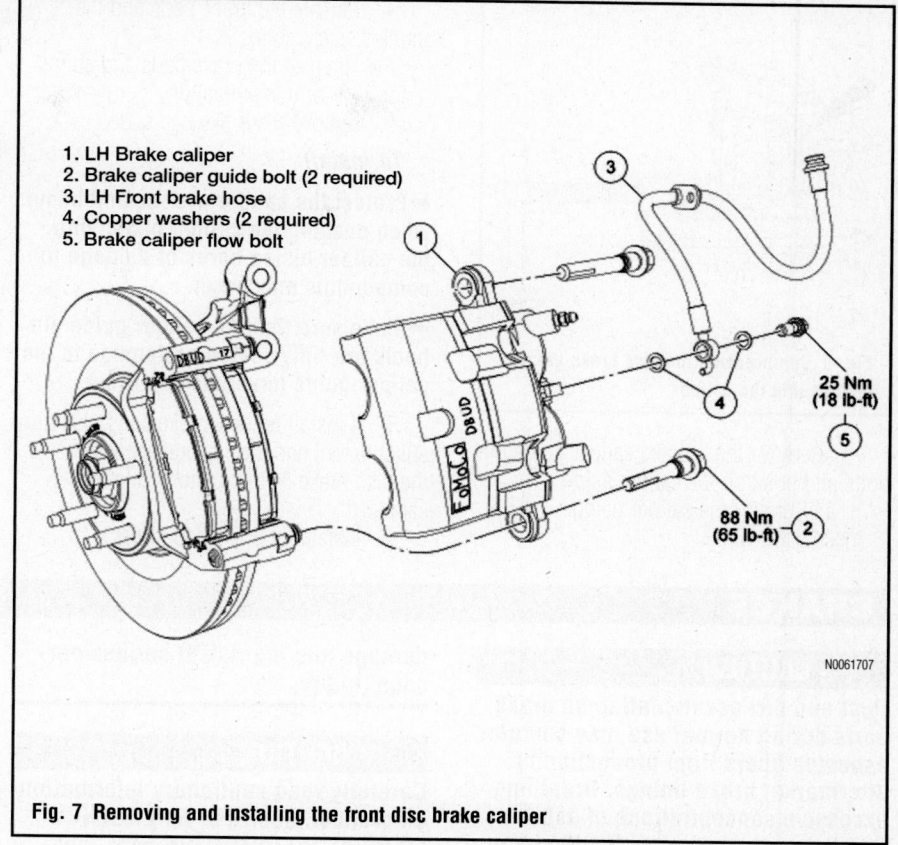

1. LH Brake caliper
2. Brake caliper guide bolt (2 required)
3. LH Front brake hose
4. Copper washers (2 required)
5. Brake caliper flow bolt

25 Nm (18 lb-ft)
88 Nm (65 lb-ft)

Fig. 7 Removing and installing the front disc brake caliper

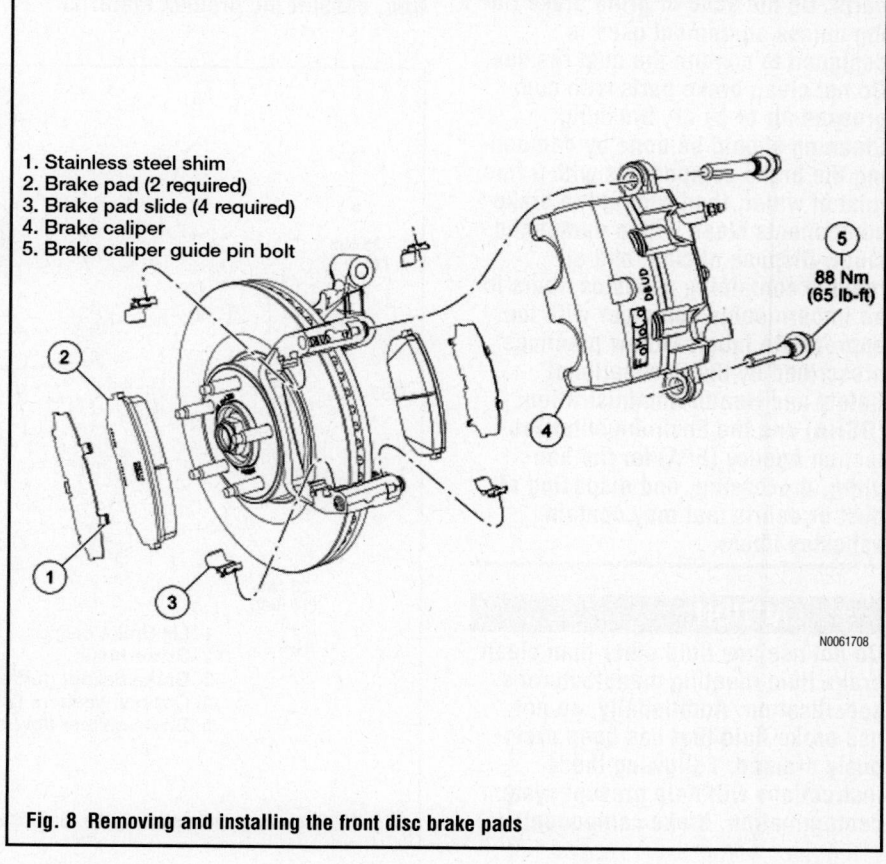

1. Stainless steel shim
2. Brake pad (2 required)
3. Brake pad slide (4 required)
4. Brake caliper
5. Brake caliper guide pin bolt

88 Nm (65 lb-ft)

Fig. 8 Removing and installing the front disc brake pads

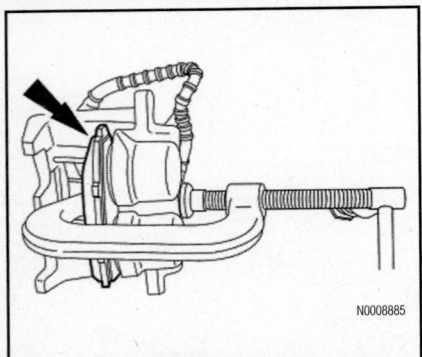

Fig. 9 Compressing the disc brake caliper pistons into the caliper

3. Remove the 2 brake caliper guide pin bolts and position the caliper aside.
   a. Support the caliper using mechanic's wire.

4. Remove the brake pads and the stainless steel shims.
   a. Inspect the brake pads and shims for wear or contamination.
5. Remove the brake pad slides.

To install:

➡️Protect the caliper pistons and boots when pushing the caliper piston into the caliper piston bores or damage to components may occur.

➡️Make sure that the caliper guide pin boots are fully seated or damage to the caliper guide pin boots can occur.

6. If installing new brake pads, using a suitable tool and a worn brake, compress the disc brake caliper pistons into the caliper.
7. Install the brake pad slides.

8. Apply a thin coating of the supplied grease to the shims and the shim contact area of the brake pads.
9. Install the stainless steel shims to the brake pads.

➡️The guide pin bolts are different sizes. The longer/bigger bolt is the upper guide pin bolt.

10. Position the brake caliper and install the 2 guide pin bolts.
    a. Tighten to 65 ft lbs. (88 Nm).
11. Install the wheel and tire.
12. Fill the brake master cylinder reservoir with clean, specified brake fluid.
    a. Apply brakes several times to verify correct brake operation.

BRAKES

⁜⁜ **CAUTION**

Dust and dirt accumulating on brake parts during normal use may contain asbestos fibers from production or aftermarket brake linings. Breathing excessive concentrations of asbestos fibers can cause serious bodily harm. Exercise care when servicing brake parts. Do not sand or grind brake lining unless equipment used is designed to contain the dust residue. Do not clean brake parts with compressed air or by dry brushing. Cleaning should be done by dampening the brake components with a fine mist of water, then wiping the brake components clean with a dampened cloth. Dispose of cloth and all residue containing asbestos fibers in an impermeable container with the appropriate label. Follow practices prescribed by the Occupational Safety and Health Administration (OSHA) and the Environmental Protection Agency (EPA) for the handling, processing, and disposing of dust or debris that may contain asbestos fibers.

⁜⁜ **CAUTION**

Do not use any fluid other than clean brake fluid meeting manufacturer's specification. Additionally, do not use brake fluid that has been previously drained. Following these instructions will help prevent system contamination, brake component

damage and the risk of serious personal injury.

⁜⁜ **CAUTION**

Carefully read cautionary information on product label. For EMERGENCY MEDICAL INFORMATION seek medical advice. For additional information, consult the product Material

REAR DISC BRAKES

Safety Data Sheet (MSDS) if available. Failure to follow these instructions may result in serious personal injury.

BRAKE CALIPER

REMOVAL & INSTALLATION
See Figure 10.

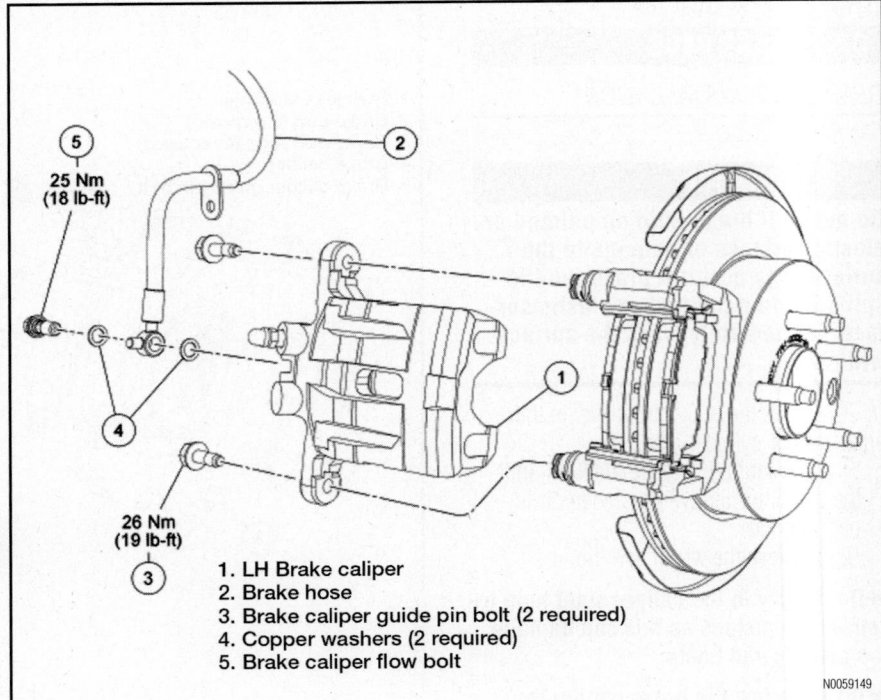

1. LH Brake caliper
2. Brake hose
3. Brake caliper guide pin bolt (2 required)
4. Copper washers (2 required)
5. Brake caliper flow bolt

25 Nm (18 lb-ft)

26 Nm (19 lb-ft)

Fig. 10 Removing and installing the rear disc brake caliper

✳✳ WARNING

Do not spill brake fluid on painted or plastic surfaces or damage to the surface may occur. If brake fluid is spilled onto a painted or plastic surface, immediately wash the surface with water.

1. Remove the wheel and tire.
2. Remove the brake caliper flow bolt and position the brake hose aside.
   a. Discard the 2 copper washers.
3. Remove the 2 brake caliper guide bolts and the brake caliper.
   a. If a leaking or damaged caliper piston boot is found, install a new disc brake caliper.

To install:

➡Make sure that the caliper guide pin boots are fully seated or damage to the caliper guide pin boots can occur.

➡Make sure that the brake caliper hose is not twisted during caliper installation.

4. Position the brake caliper onto the anchor plate and brake pads.
5. Install the 2 brake caliper guide pin bolts.
   a. To install, tighten to 19 ft. lbs. (26 Nm).
6. Using 2 new copper washers, position the brake hose and install the brake caliper flow bolt.
   a. Tighten to 18 ft. lbs. (25 Nm).
7. Install the wheel and tire.
8. Bleed the brake caliper.

DISC BRAKE PADS

REMOVAL & INSTALLATION
See Figures 9 and 11.

✳✳ WARNING

Do not spill brake fluid on painted or plastic surfaces or damage to the surface may occur. If brake fluid is spilled onto a painted or plastic surface, immediately wash the surface with water.

1. Check the brake fluid level in the brake master cylinder reservoir.

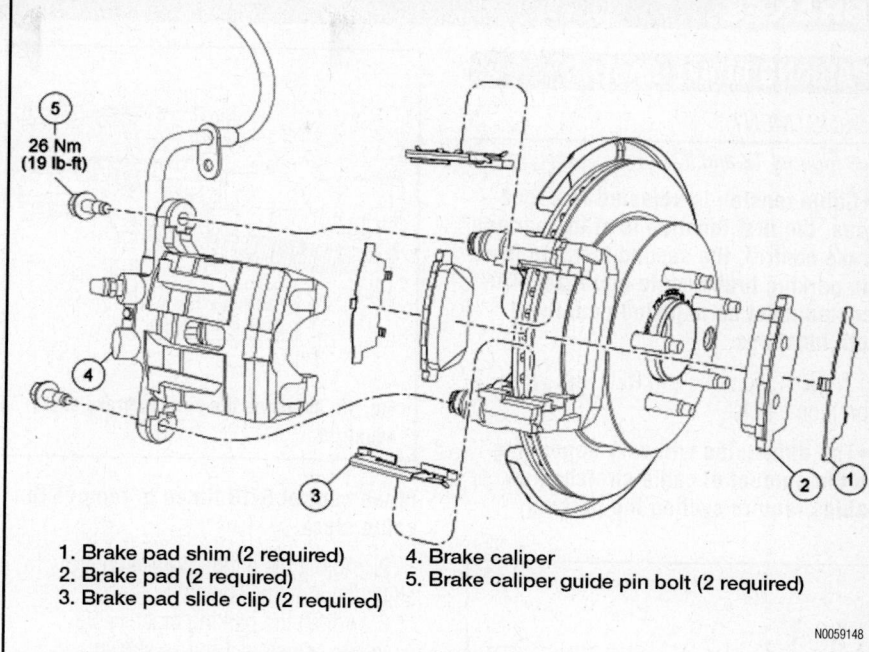

1. Brake pad shim (2 required)
2. Brake pad (2 required)
3. Brake pad slide clip (2 required)
4. Brake caliper
5. Brake caliper guide pin bolt (2 required)

N0059148

Fig. 11 Removing and installing the rear disc brake pads

a. If required, remove the fluid until the brake master cylinder reservoir is one-half full.
2. Remove the wheel and tire.

✳✳ WARNING

Do not pry in the caliper sight hole to retract the pistons, as this can damage the pistons and boots.

✳✳ WARNING

Do not allow the brake caliper to hang from the brake hose or damage to the hose can occur.

3. Remove the 2 brake caliper guide pin bolts and position the caliper aside.
   a. Support the caliper using mechanic's wire.
4. Remove the 2 brake pads, shims and slide clips.
   a. Discard the slide clips.

To install:

➡Protect the caliper pistons and boots when pushing the caliper piston into the caliper piston bores or damage to components may occur.

➡Make sure the caliper piston boot is clean and free of foreign material.

5. If installing new brake pads, using a suitable tool and a worn brake pad, compress the disc brake caliper pistons into the caliper.
6. Install the 2 brake pads, shims and new slide clips to the brake caliper anchor plate.

➡Make sure that the caliper guide pin boots are fully seated or damage to the caliper guide pin boots can occur.

➡Make sure that the brake caliper hose is not twisted during caliper installation.

7. Position the brake caliper on the anchor plate and install the 2 guide pin bolts.
   a. Tighten to 19 ft. lbs (26 Nm).
8. Install the wheel and tire.
9. Fill the brake master cylinder reservoir with clean, specified brake fluid.
   a. Apply brakes several times to verify correct brake operation.

BRAKES

PARKING BRAKE

PARKING BRAKE CABLES

ADJUSTMENT

See Figures 12 and 13.

➡Cable tension is adjusted in 2 locations, the first location is at the parking brake control, the second location is at the parking brake cable equalizer. The tension must be adjusted equally at both locations.

1. With the vehicle in NEUTRAL, position it on a hoist.

➡The dimension will vary depending on the amount of cable stretch. New cables require cycling the parking

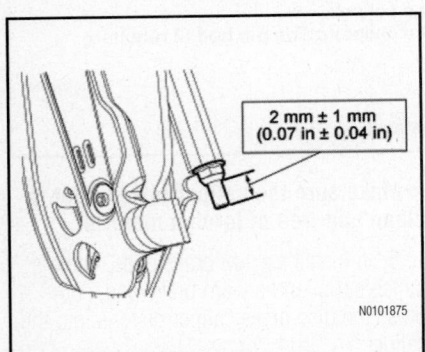

20 mm ± 1 mm
(0.78 in ± 0.04 in)

N0101874

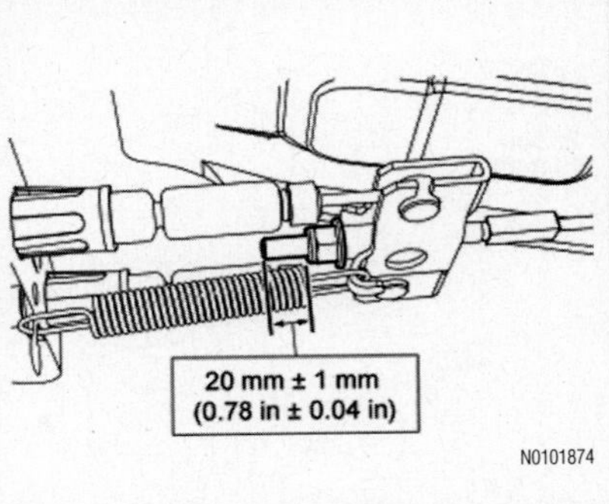

Fig. 13 Adjusting the parking brake cable equalizer

brake control 5-10 times to remove the cable slack.

2. Adjust the parking brake control adjustment nut as shown.
3. Adjust the parking brake cable equalizer adjustment nut as shown.
4. Fully apply the parking brake pedal 3 times to verify correct operation of the parking brake system.
   a. With the parking brake cable in the fully released position, brake drag should not be present.

PARKING BRAKE SHOES

REMOVAL & INSTALLATION

See Figure 14.

2 mm ± 1 mm
(0.07 in ± 0.04 in)

N0101875

Fig. 12 Adjusting the parking brake control nut

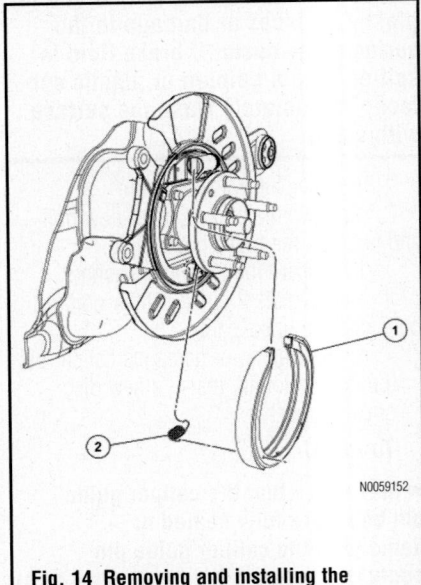

N0059152

Fig. 14 Removing and installing the parking brake shoe

1. Remove the rear brake disc.
2. Remove the parking brake shoe return spring.
3. Remove the parking brake shoe.

To install:

4. To install, reverse the removal procedure.
   a. Check the parking brake for normal operation.

CHASSIS ELECTRICAL

AIR BAG (SUPPLEMENTAL RESTRAINT SYSTEM)

GENERAL INFORMATION

✳✳ CAUTION

These vehicles are equipped with an air bag system. The system must be disarmed before performing service on, or around, system components, the steering column, instrument panel components, wiring and sensors. Failure to follow the safety precautions and the disarming procedure could result in accidental air bag deployment, possible injury and unnecessary system repairs.

SERVICE PRECAUTIONS

Disconnect and isolate the battery negative cable before beginning any airbag system component diagnosis, testing, removal, or installation procedures. Allow system

capacitor to discharge for two minutes before beginning any component service. This will disable the airbag system. Failure to disable the airbag system may result in accidental airbag deployment, personal injury, or death.

Do not place an intact undeployed airbag face down on a solid surface. The airbag will propel into the air if accidentally deployed and may result in personal injury or death.

When carrying or handling an undeployed airbag, the trim side (face) of the airbag should be pointing away from the body to minimize possibility of injury if accidental deployment occurs. Failure to do this may result in personal injury or death.

Replace airbag system components with OEM replacement parts. Substitute parts may appear interchangeable, but internal differences may result in inferior occupant

protection. Failure to do so may result in occupant personal injury or death.

Wear safety glasses, rubber gloves, and long sleeved clothing when cleaning powder residue from vehicle after an airbag deployment. Powder residue emitted from a deployed airbag can cause skin irritation. Flush affected area with cool water if irritation is experienced. If nasal or throat irritation is experienced, exit the vehicle for fresh air until the irritation ceases. If irritation continues, see a physician.

Do not use a replacement airbag that is not in the original packaging. This may result in improper deployment, personal injury, or death.

The factory installed fasteners, screws and bolts used to fasten airbag components have a special coating and are specifically designed for the airbag system. Do not use substitute fasteners. Use only original equipment fasteners listed in the parts catalog when fastener replacement is required.

During, and following, any child restraint anchor service, due to impact event or vehicle repair, carefully inspect all mounting hardware, tether straps, and anchors for proper installation, operation, or damage. If a child restraint anchor is found damaged in any way, the anchor must be replaced. Failure to do this may result in personal injury or death.

Deployed and non-deployed airbags may or may not have live pyrotechnic material within the airbag inflator.

Do not dispose of driver/passenger/curtain airbags or seat belt tensioners unless you are sure of complete deployment. Refer to the Hazardous Substance Control System for proper disposal.

Dispose of deployed airbags and tensioners consistent with state, provincial, local, and federal regulations.

After any airbag component testing or service, do not connect the battery negative cable. Personal injury or death may result if the system test is not performed first.

If the vehicle is equipped with the Occupant Classification System (OCS), do not connect the battery negative cable before performing the OCS Verification Test using the scan tool and the appropriate diagnostic information. Personal injury or death may result if the system test is not performed properly.

Never replace both the Occupant Restraint Controller (ORC) and the Occupant Classification Module (OCM) at the same time. If both require replacement, replace one, and then perform the Airbag System test before replacing the other.

Both the ORC and the OCM store Occupant Classification System (OCS) calibration data, which they transfer to one another when one of them is replaced. If both are replaced at the same time, an irreversible fault will be set in both modules and the OCS may malfunction and cause personal injury or death.

If equipped with OCS, the Seat Weight Sensor is a sensitive, calibrated unit and must be handled carefully. Do not drop or handle roughly. If dropped or damaged, replace with another sensor. Failure to do so may result in occupant injury or death.

If equipped with OCS, the front passenger seat must be handled carefully as well. When removing the seat, be careful when setting on floor not to drop. If dropped,

the sensor may be inoperative, could result in occupant injury, or possibly death.

If equipped with OCS, when the passenger front seat is on the floor, no one should sit in the front passenger seat. This uneven force may damage the sensing ability of the seat weight sensors. If sat on and damaged, the sensor may be inoperative, could result in occupant injury, or possibly death.

DISARMING THE SYSTEM

See Figures 15 through 31.

> ❋❋ **WARNING**
>
> **Always wear eye protection when servicing a vehicle. Failure to follow this instruction may result in serious personal injury.**

> ❋❋ **WARNING**
>
> **Always carry or place a live air bag module with the air bag and deployment door/trim cover/tear seam pointed away from the body. Do not set a live air bag module down with the deployment door/trim cover/tear seam face down. Failure to follow these instructions may result in serious personal injury in the event of an accidental deployment.**

> ❋❋ **WARNING**
>
> **Never probe the electrical connectors on air bag, Safety Canopy® or side air curtain modules. Failure to follow this instruction may result in the accidental deployment of these modules, which increases the risk of serious personal injury or death.**

> ❋❋ **WARNING**
>
> **Never disassemble or tamper with safety belt buckle/retractor pretensioners or adaptive load limiting retractors or probe the electrical connectors. Failure to follow this instruction may result in the accidental deployment of the safety belt pretensioners or adaptive load limiting retractors which increases the risk of serious personal injury or death.**

> ❋❋ **WARNING**
>
> **To reduce the risk of accidental deployment, do not use any memory**

saver devices. Failure to follow this instruction may result in serious personal injury or death.

➡The air bag warning indicator illuminates when the correct Restraints Control Module (RCM) fuse is removed and the ignition is ON.

➡The Supplemental Restraint System (SRS) must be fully operational and free of faults before releasing the vehicle to the customer.

All vehicles:
1. Turn all vehicle accessories OFF.
2. Turn the ignition OFF.
3. At the Smart Junction Box (SJB), located in the LH lower kick panel, remove the lower kick panel fuse cover and the RCM fuse 46 (7.5A) from the SJB . For additional information, refer to the Wiring Diagrams.
4. Turn the ignition ON and monitor the air bag warning indicator for at least 30 seconds. The air bag warning indicator will remain lit continuously (no flashing) if the correct RCM fuse has been removed. If the air bag warning indicator does not remain lit continuously, remove the correct RCM fuse before proceeding.
5. Turn the ignition OFF.

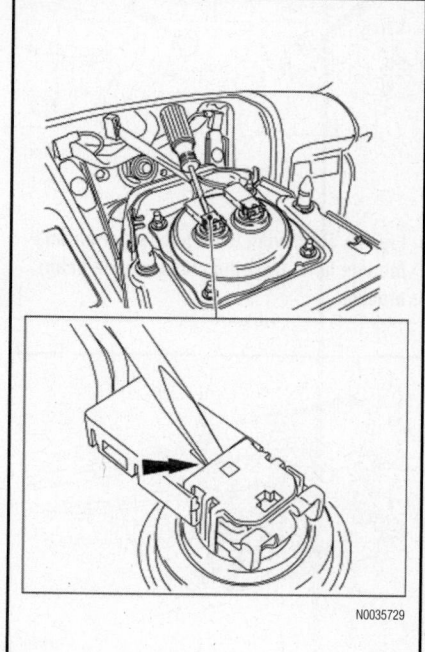

N0035729

Fig. 15 Removing the electrical connectors and driver air bag module

> ※※ **WARNING**
>
> Always deplete the backup power supply before repairing or installing any new front or side air bag supplemental restraint system (SRS) component and before servicing, removing, installing, adjusting or striking components near the front or side impact sensors or the restraints control module (RCM). Nearby components include doors, instrument panel, console, door latches, strikers, seats and hood latches.

> ※※ **WARNING**
>
> To deplete the backup power supply energy, disconnect the battery ground cable and wait at least 1 minute. Be sure to disconnect auxiliary batteries and power supplies (if equipped).

> ※※ **WARNING**
>
> Failure to follow these instructions may result in serious personal injury

or death in the event of an accidental deployment.

6. Disconnect the battery ground cable and wait at least one minute.

➡**Repeat this step for both locking pins.**

7. Using a 3-mm Allen wrench or a suitable tool through the access hole on the backside of the steering wheel, position the tool against the spring clip and push in, disengaging the clip from the locking pin. With the spring clip disengaged from the locking pin, gently pull back on that side of the driver air bag module to release it from the steering wheel.

➡**Do not pull the driver air bag module electrical connectors out by the locking buttons. Damage to the locking buttons may occur.**

8. Using a small screwdriver as shown, lift up and release the locking buttons on the driver air bag module electrical connectors. With the locking

buttons released, remove the electrical connectors and the driver air bag module.

9. Open and lower the glove compartment door. Then unhook the glove compartment door from the instrument panel.

   a. If equipped, detach the glove compartment door dampener.

Edge

10. Remove the 2 passenger air bag module bolts from the cross vehicle beam bracket.

➡**Do not handle the passenger air bag module by grabbing the edges of the air bag trim cover. Damage to the air bag module may occur.**

11. Through the glove compartment opening, release the 4 LH side air bag trim cover clips. Then, release the forward-most 5 air bag trim cover clips and separate the passenger air bag module from the instrument panel.

12. Using a small screwdriver as shown, lift up and release the locking button on the RH passenger air bag module electrical connector.

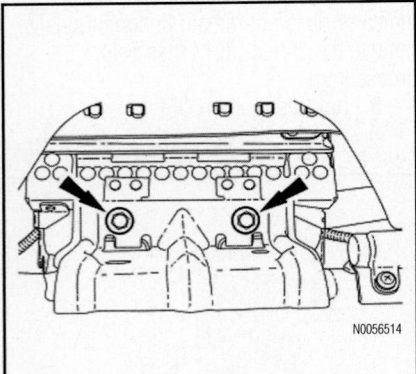

Fig. 16 Removing the 2 passenger air bag module bolts from the cross vehicle beam bracket

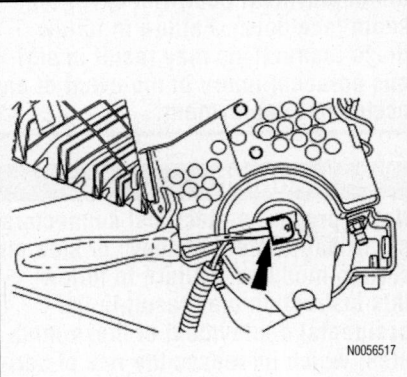

Fig. 18 Releasing the locking button on the LH passenger air bag module electrical connector

Fig. 20 Locating the screw for the LH duct assembly bracket

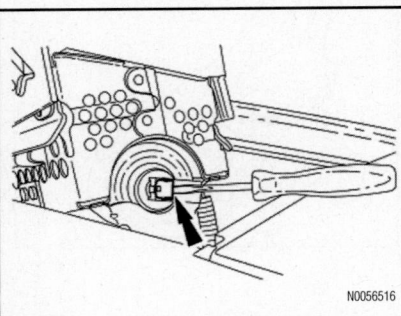

Fig. 17 Releasing the locking button on the RH passenger air bag module electrical connector

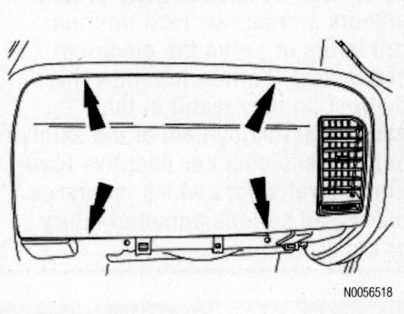

Fig. 19 Removing the RH instrument panel finish panel—MKX

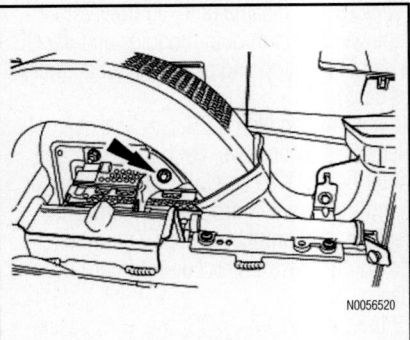

Fig. 21 Locating the LH duct assembly screw

➡**Do not pull the passenger air bag module electrical connector out by the locking button. Damage to the locking button may occur.**

13. With the RH locking button released, remove the RH electrical connector.

14. Using a small screwdriver as shown, lift up and release the locking button on the LH passenger air bag module electrical connector.

➡**Do not pull the passenger air bag module electrical connector out by the locking button. Damage to the locking button may occur.**

15. With the LH locking button released, remove the LH electrical connector and remove the passenger air bag module.

MKX

16. Pull straight out to release the 5 retaining clips and remove the RH instrument panel finish panel.

17. Remove the screw for the LH duct assembly bracket from the front of the instrument panel.

18. Through the glove compartment opening, remove the screw and the LH duct assembly.

19. Through the glove compartment opening, remove the screw and the RH duct assembly.

20. Remove the 4 bolts and the passenger air bag module support bracket.

21. Remove the 3 nuts from the passenger air bag module.

➡**Do not allow the passenger air bag module to hang from the wiring harness. Damage to the wiring harness and connectors may occur.**

22. Lower the rear of the passenger air bag module off the 3 mounting studs. Move the passenger air bag module rearward to release the 7 air bag trim cover hooks from the instrument panel and rest the module on the cross vehicle beam.

23. Using a small screwdriver as shown, lift up and release the locking button on the LH passenger air bag module electrical connector.

➡**Do not pull the passenger air bag module electrical connector out by the locking button. Damage to the locking button may occur.**

24. With the LH locking button released, remove the LH electrical connector from the passenger air bag module.

25. Using a small screwdriver as shown, lift up and release the locking button on the RH passenger air bag module electrical connector.

➡**Do not pull the passenger air bag module electrical connector out by the locking button. Damage to the locking button may occur.**

26. With the RH locking button released, remove the RH electrical connector. Remove the passenger air bag module from the glove compartment opening.

All vehicles

27. From under the rear of the front passenger seat, slide and disengage the passenger seat side air bag module electrical connector locking clip, and then release the tab and disconnect the passenger seat side air bag module electrical connector.

28. Remove the passenger side D-pillar trim panel.

➡**Do not pull the passenger Safety Canopy® module electrical connector out by the locking button. Damage to the locking button may occur.**

29. With the locking button released, remove the electrical connector from the passenger Safety Canopy® module.

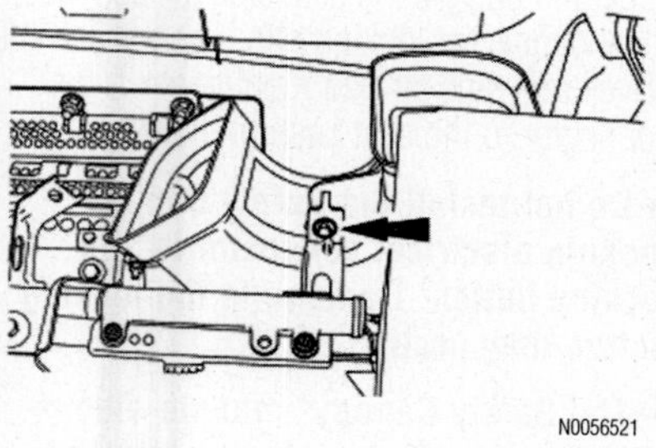

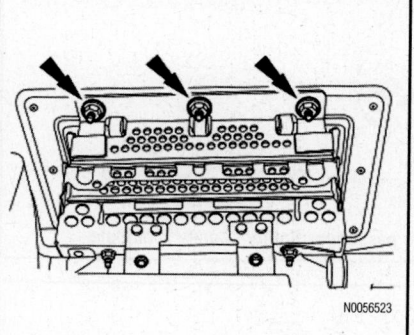

Fig. 22 Locating the RH duct assembly screw

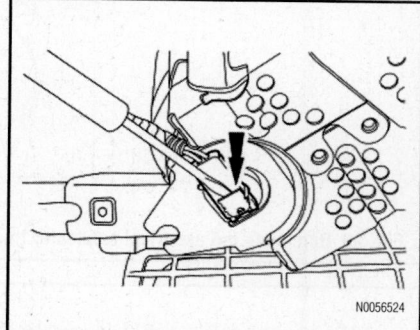

Fig. 24 Removing the 3 nuts from the passenger air bag module

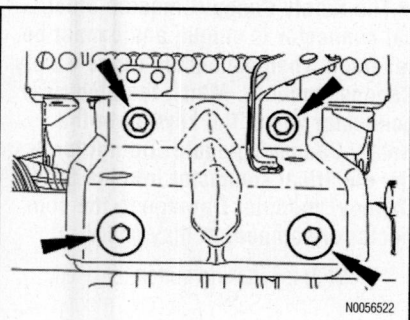

Fig. 26 Releasing the locking button on the LH passenger air bag module electrical connector

Fig. 23 Removing the passenger air bag module support bracket

Fig. 25 Releasing the air bag trim cover hooks

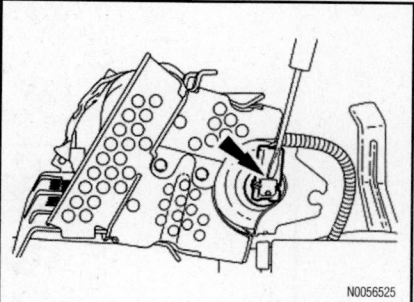

Fig. 27 Releasing the locking button on the RH passenger air bag module electrical connector

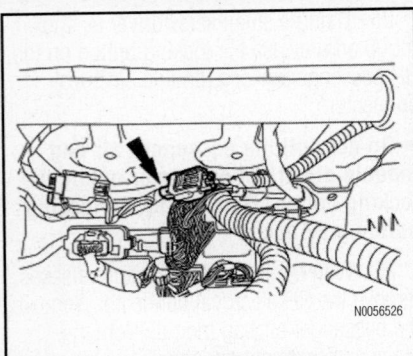

Fig. 28 Disengaging and disconnecting the passenger seat side air bag module electrical connector

30. Remove the driver side D-pillar trim panel.

➡**Do not pull the driver Safety Canopy® module electrical connector out by the locking button. Damage to the locking button may occur.**

31. With the locking button released, remove the electrical connector from the driver Safety Canopy® module.

32. From under the rear of the driver seat, detach the driver seat side air bag module electrical connector from the seat cushion frame. Then slide and disengage the driver seat side air bag electrical connector locking clip, and then

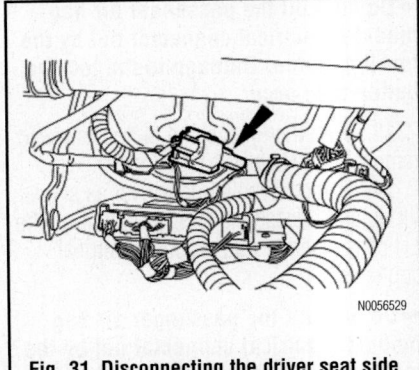

Fig. 31 Disconnecting the driver seat side air bag module electrical connector

release the tab and disconnect the driver seat side air bag module electrical connector.

33. Install RCM fuse 46 (7.5A) to the SJB.

34. Connect the battery ground cable.

ARMING THE SYSTEM

See Figures 32 through 39.

All vehicles

1. Remove RCM fuse 46 (7.5A) from the SJB.

2. Disconnect the battery ground cable and wait at least one minute.

3. Connect the driver seat side air bag module electrical connector and then slide and engage the seat side air bag electrical connector locking clip. Then attach the driver seat side air bag module electrical connector to the seat cushion frame.

➡**Do not install the Safety Canopy® module electrical connector by the locking button. Damage to the locking button may occur.**

➡**The Safety Canopy® module electrical connector locking button must be in the released position when the connector is being installed or connector damage may occur.**

➡**The Safety Canopy® module electrical connector is unique and cannot be reversed when connected to the Safety Canopy® module. Match the electrical connector key to the keyway in the Safety Canopy® module. Do not force the electrical connector into the Safety Canopy® module. Damage to the connector or component may occur.**

4. With the locking button released, install the driver Safety Canopy® module electrical connector fully into the driver Safety Canopy® module and seat the locking button.

5. Install the driver side D-pillar trim panel.

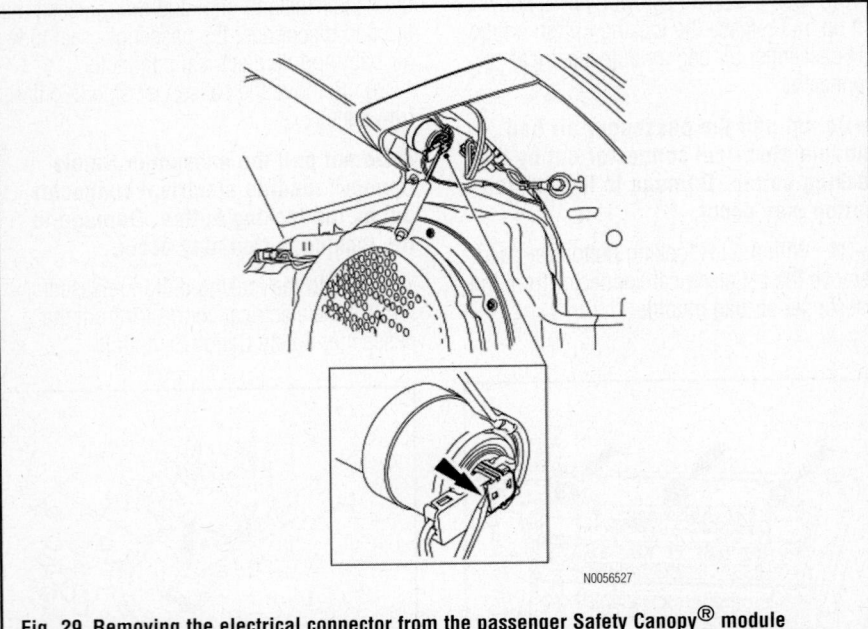

Fig. 29 Removing the electrical connector from the passenger Safety Canopy® module

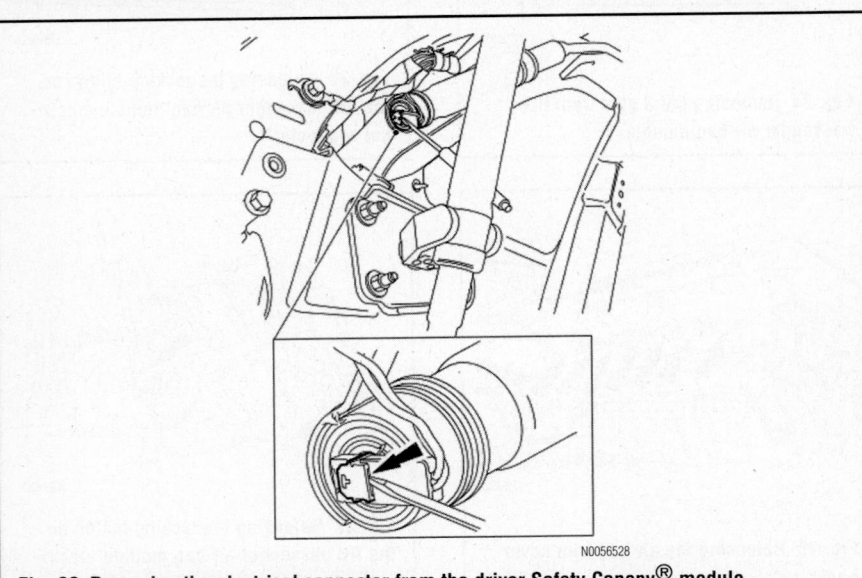

Fig. 30 Removing the electrical connector from the driver Safety Canopy® module

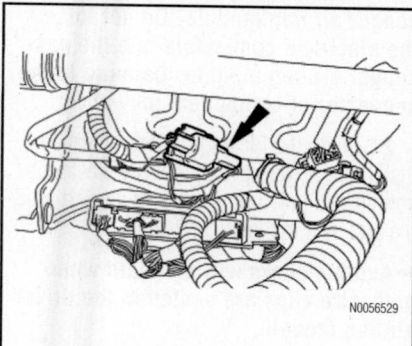

Fig. 32 Connecting the driver seat side air bag module electrical connector

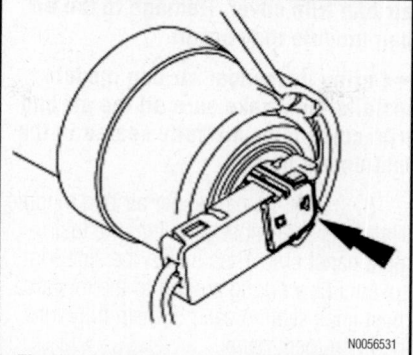

Fig. 34 Installing the passenger Safety Canopy® module electrical

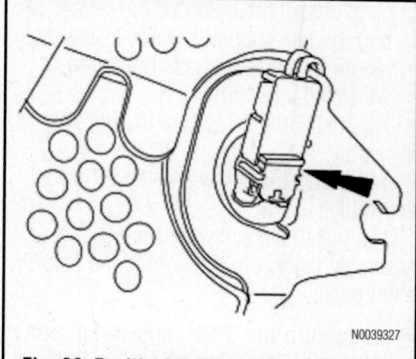

Fig. 36 Positioning the passenger air bag module on the cross vehicle beam

➡ Do not install the Safety Canopy® module electrical connector by the locking button. Damage to the locking button may occur.

➡ The Safety Canopy® module electrical connector locking button must be in the released position when the connector is being installed or connector damage may occur.

➡ The Safety Canopy® module electrical connector is unique and cannot be reversed when connected to the Safety Canopy® module. Match the electrical connector key to the keyway in the Safety Canopy® module. Do not force the electrical connector into the Safety Canopy® module. Damage to the connector or component may occur.

6. With the locking button released, install the passenger Safety Canopy® module electrical connector fully into the passenger Safety Canopy® module and seat the locking button.

7. Install the passenger side D-pillar trim panel.

8. Connect the passenger seat side air bag module electrical connector and then

slide and engage the seat side air bag electrical connector locking clip.

MKX

➡ Do not install the passenger air bag module electrical connectors by the locking buttons. Damage to the locking buttons may occur.

➡ The passenger air bag module electrical connector locking buttons must be in the released position when the connector is being installed or connector damage may occur.

➡ The passenger air bag module electrical connectors are unique and cannot be reversed when connected to the passenger air bag module. Match the electrical connector key to the keyway in the passenger air bag module. Do not force the electrical connectors into the passenger air bag module. Damage to the connector or component may occur.

➡ RH side shown, LH similar.

9. Position the passenger air bag module on the cross vehicle beam. With the locking buttons released, install the 2 passenger air bag module electrical connectors

fully into the passenger air bag module and seat the locking buttons.

➡ During the passenger air bag module installation, make sure all 7 of the air bag trim cover hooks are fully seated in the instrument panel.

10. Install the passenger 7 air bag trim cover hooks into the instrument panel. Raise the rear of the passenger air bag module onto the 3 mounting studs.

11. Install the 3 passenger air bag module nuts.

a. Tighten to 62 inch lbs. (7 Nm).

➡ To avoid a squeak or rattle condition, install the passenger air bag module bracket and passenger air bag module bolts in this order.

12. Install the passenger air bag module support bracket and the 4 bolts.

a. Install the passenger air bag module support bracket and 2 bolts to the cross vehicle beam. Tighten to 71 inch lbs. (8 Nm).

b. Install the inboard passenger air bag module support bracket-to-passenger air bag module bolt. Tighten to 71 inch lbs. (8 Nm).

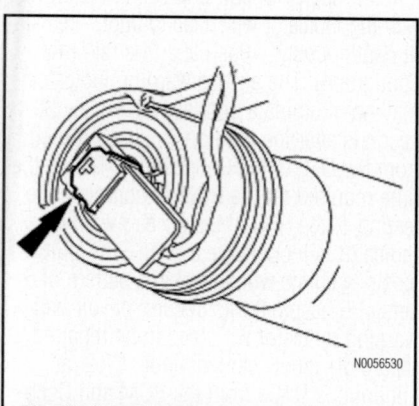

Fig. 33 Installing the driver Safety Canopy® module

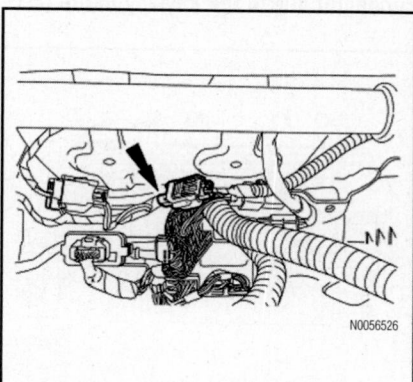

Fig. 35 Connecting the passenger seat side air bag module electrical connector

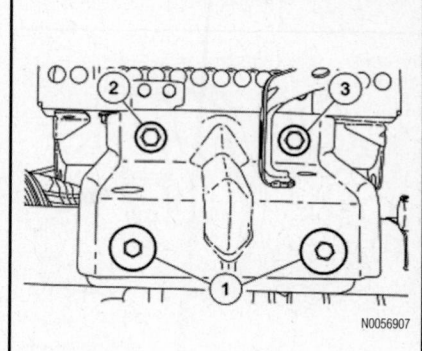

Fig. 37 Installing the passenger air bag module support bracket and the 4 bolts

c. Install the outboard passenger air bag module support bracket-to-passenger air bag module bolt. Tighten to 71 inch lbs (8 Nm).

13. Install the screw and the RH duct assembly.

14. Install the screw and the LH duct assembly.

15. Install the screw for the LH duct assembly bracket in the front of the instrument panel.

➡ **Make sure the 5 RH instrument panel finish panel retaining clips are fully seated in the instrument panel.**

16. Install the RH instrument panel finish panel.

Edge

➡ **Do not install the passenger air bag module electrical connectors by the locking buttons. Damage to the locking buttons may occur.**

➡ **The passenger air bag module electrical connector locking buttons must be in the released position when the connector is being installed or connector damage may occur.**

➡ **The passenger air bag module electrical connectors are unique and cannot be reversed when connected to the passenger air bag module. Match the electrical connector key to the keyway in the passenger air bag module. Do not force the electrical connectors into the passenger air bag module. Damage to the connector or component may occur.**

➡ **RH side shown, LH similar.**

17. With the locking buttons released, install the 2 passenger air bag module electrical connectors fully into the passenger air bag module and seat the locking buttons.

➡ **Do not handle the passenger air bag module by grabbing the edges of the air bag trim cover. Damage to the air bag module may occur.**

➡ **During passenger air bag module installation, make sure all the air bag trim cover clips are fully seated in the instrument panel.**

18. Install the passenger air bag module trim cover rear-most clips into the instrument panel first. Then install the side trim cover clips working around to the forward-most clips seating each of them fully into the instrument panel.

➡ **To avoid a squeak or rattle condition, install the 2 passenger air bag module bolts in this order.**

19. Install the 2 passenger air bag module bolts.

a. Install the inboard passenger air bag module bolt.
Tighten to 71 inch lbs. (8 Nm).
b. Install the outboard passenger air bag module bolt.
Tighten to 71 inch lbs (8 Nm).

All vehicles

20. Hook the glove compartment door to the instrument panel. Close the glove compartment door.

a. If equipped, attach the glove compartment door dampener.

➡ **Do not install the driver air bag module electrical connectors by the locking buttons. Damage to the locking buttons may occur.**

➡ **The driver air bag module electrical connector locking buttons must be in the released position when the connector is being installed or connector damage may occur.**

➡ **The driver air bag module electrical connectors are unique and cannot be reversed when connected to the driver air bag module. Match the electrical connector key to the keyway in the passenger air bag module. Do not force the electrical connectors into the passenger air bag module. Damage to the connector or component may occur.**

21. With the locking buttons released, install the driver air bag module electrical connectors fully into the driver air bag module and seat the locking buttons.

➡ **Audible clicks will be heard when both wire clips are seated in the driver air bag module.**

➡ **Align the driver air bag module locking pins to the steering wheel and, while pushing inward, seat the 2 driver air bag module locking pins to the steering wheel wire clips.**

a. When the 2 locking pins are seated in place, there should be an even gap between the driver air bag module trim cover and the steering wheel.

22. Turn the ignition from OFF to ON.

23. Install RCM fuse 46 (7.5A) to the SJB and install the lower kick panel fuse cover.

❊❊ WARNING

Make sure no one is in the vehicle and there is nothing blocking or placed in front of any air bag module when the battery is connected. Failure to follow these instructions may result in serious personal injury in the event of an accidental deployment.

24. Connect the battery ground cable.

25. Prove out the SRS as follows: Turn the ignition from ON to OFF. Wait 10 seconds, then turn the ignition back to ON and monitor the air bag warning indicator with the air bag modules installed. The air bag warning indicator will light continuously for approximately 6 seconds and then turn off. If an air bag SRS fault is present, the air bag warning indicator will: - fail to light. - remain lit continuously. - flash at a 5Hz rate (not configured). The air bag warning indicator may not illuminate until approximately 30 seconds after the ignition has been turned from the OFF to the ON position. This is the time required for the RCM to complete the testing of the SRS. If the air bag warning indicator is inoperative and an SRS fault exists, a chime will sound in a pattern of 5 sets of 5 beeps. If this occurs, the air bag warning indicator will need to be repaired before diagnosis can continue. Clear all continuous DTCs from the RCM and Occupant Classification System Module (OCSM) using a scan tool.

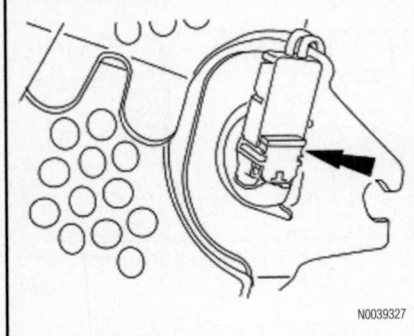

Fig. 38 Installing the passenger air bag module

N0039327

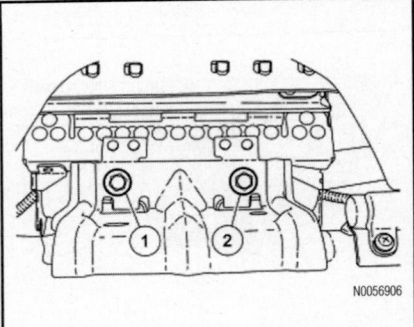

Fig. 39 Installing the passenger air bag module bolts

N0056906

DRIVE TRAIN

AUTOMATIC TRANSAXLE FLUID

DRAIN AND REFILL

See Figures 40 through 42.

1. With the vehicle in NEUTRAL, position it on a hoist. Jacking and Lifting.

➡ **If an internal problem is suspected, drain the transmission fluid through a paper filter. A small amount of metal or friction particles may be found from normal wear. If an excessive amount of metal or friction material is present, the transaxle will need to be overhauled.**

2. Remove the transmission fluid drain plug and allow the transmission fluid to drain.

3. Install the transmission fluid drain plug. Tighten to 80 inch lbs. (9 Nm).

4. Remove the transmission fluid level indicator.

5. If the transaxle was removed and disassembled, fill the transaxle with 6.5 qt (6.2L) of clean transmission fluid. If the main control cover was removed for in-vehicle repair, fill the transaxle with 4.5 qt (4.3L) of clean transmission fluid.

6. Start the engine and let it run for 3 minutes. Move the range selector lever into each gear position and allow engagement for a minimum of ten seconds. Check the transmission fluid level by installing and removing the transmission fluid level indicator. When installing the transmission fluid level indicator, be sure it is seated and rotate it clockwise to the locked position. Adjust the transmission fluid level.

 a. Correct transmission fluid level at normal operating temperature 180°F-200°F (82°C-93°C).

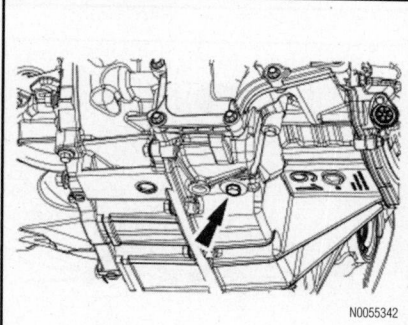

Fig. 40 Locating the transmission fluid drain plug

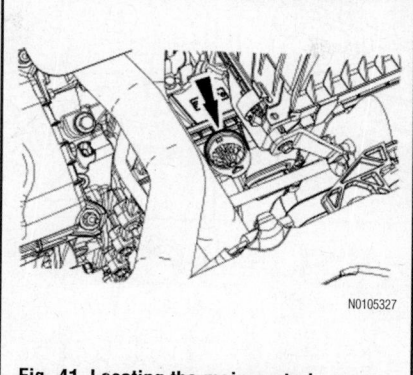

Fig. 41 Locating the main control cover

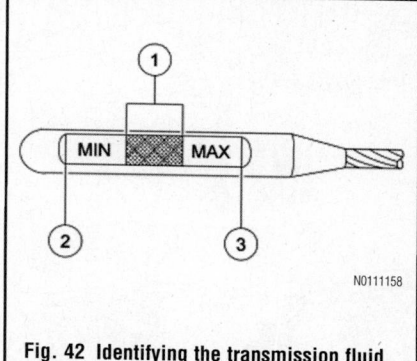

Fig. 42 Identifying the transmission fluid level

 b. Low transmission fluid level.
 c. High transmission fluid level.

TRANSFER CASE ASSEMBLY (POWER TRANSFER UNIT)

REMOVAL & INSTALLATION

2010 Models

See Figures 43 through 48.

➡ **A new intermediate shaft seal and deflector must be installed whenever the intermediate shaft or Power Transfer Unit (PTU) is removed from the vehicle.**

1. With the vehicle in NEUTRAL, position it on a hoist.

2. Remove the LH and RH wheel and tire.

3. Remove the intermediate shaft.

➡ **Index-mark the driveshaft for installation.**

4. Remove the 4 bolts and support the driveshaft with a length of mechanic's wire.

5. Remove the exhaust flexible pipe and the RH catalytic converter.

6. Remove the 2 roll restrictor nuts and the roll restrictor shield.

7. Remove the roll restrictor through bolt.

8. Remove the roll restrictor through bolt, 2 roll restrictor bracket bolts and the roll restrictor assembly.

9. Remove the 3 roll restrictor bracket-to-transaxle bolts and the roll restrictor-to-transaxle bracket.

10. Remove the 5 PTU support bracket bolts and the PTU support bracket.

11. Using a long extension, loosen but do not remove the 2 LH side PTU -to-transaxle bolts.

12. Remove the 3 RH side PTU -to-transaxle bolts and the 2 LH side PTU -to-transaxle bolts previously loosened.

13. Separate the PTU from the transaxle and remove it from the vehicle.

➡ **A new compression seal must be installed whenever the PTU is removed from the vehicle.**

14. Using a suitable tool, remove the compression seal and discard.

To install:

➡ **A new compression seal must be installed whenever the Power Transfer Unit (PTU) is removed from the vehicle.**

15. Using a suitable tool, install the new compression seal.

➡ **A new PTU intermediate shaft seal must be installed whenever the intermediate shaft or PTU is removed from the vehicle.**

16. Using a suitable pry bar, move the engine forward. Install a block of wood to hold the engine in the forward position. Install the PTU with the output flange facing the passenger side, filler plug facing upward. Rotate the PTU to the transaxle. Install the 5 PTU -to-transaxle bolts. Tighten to 66 ft. lbs (90 Nm).

17. Position the PTU support bracket into place and hand-tighten the 5 PTU support bracket bolts.

 a. Tighten the bolts to the transaxle to 52 ft. lbs (70 Nm).

 b. Tighten the bolts to the engine to 52 ft. lbs (70 Nm).

18. Install the roll restrictor-to-transmission bracket and the 3 roll restrictor bracket-to-transmission bolts. Tighten to 66 ft. lbs. (90 Nm).

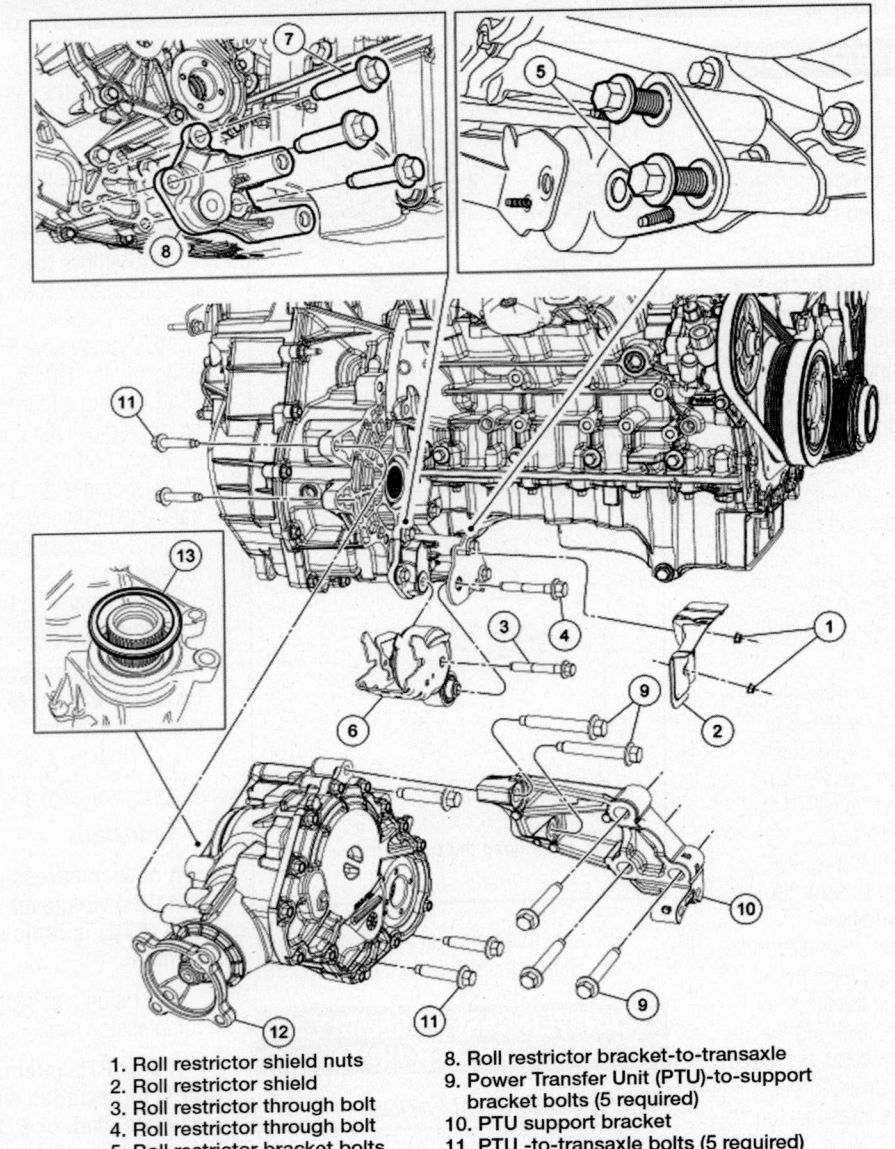

1. Roll restrictor shield nuts
2. Roll restrictor shield
3. Roll restrictor through bolt
4. Roll restrictor through bolt
5. Roll restrictor bracket bolts
6. Roll restrictor assembly
7. Roll restrictor bracket-to-transaxle bolt (3 required)
8. Roll restrictor bracket-to-transaxle
9. Power Transfer Unit (PTU)-to-support bracket bolts (5 required)
10. PTU support bracket
11. PTU-to-transaxle bolts (5 required)
12. PTU
13. Compression seal

N0077273

Fig. 43 Exploded view of the power transfer unit

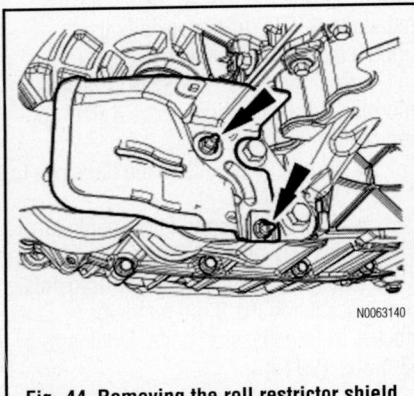

N0063140

Fig. 44 Removing the roll restrictor shield

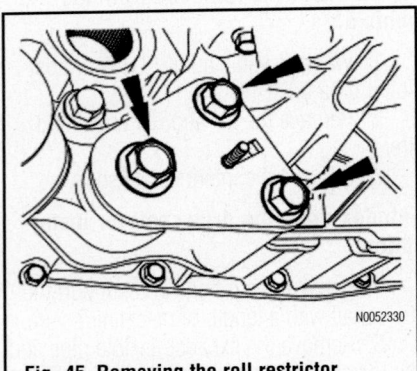

N0052330

Fig. 45 Removing the roll restrictor assembly

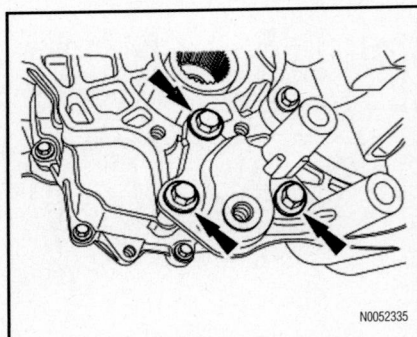

N0052335

Fig. 46 Removing the roll restrictor to transaxle bracket

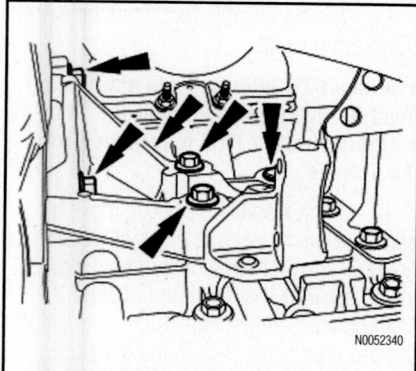

Fig. 47 Removing the PTU support bracket

19. Install the roll restrictor through bolt and the 2 roll restrictor bracket bolts. Tighten to 66 ft. lbs. (90 Nm).

20. Install the roll restrictor through bolt. Tighten to 76 ft. lbs. (103 Nm).

21. Install the roll restrictor shield and the 2 roll restrictor nuts. Tighten to 97 inch lbs. (11 Nm).

22. Install the exhaust flexible pipe and RH catalytic converter.

23. Install the intermediate shaft.

24. Line up the index marks on the driveshaft to the index marks on the PTU flange made during removal and install the 4 bolts. Tighten to 52 ft. lbs. (70 Nm).

25. Fill the PTU, if necessary.

26. Install the LH and RH wheel and tire.

2011 Models

See Figures 49 through 52.

1. With the vehicle in NEUTRAL, position it on a hoist.

2. Remove the intermediate shaft.

➡️ **Index-mark the driveshaft for installation.**

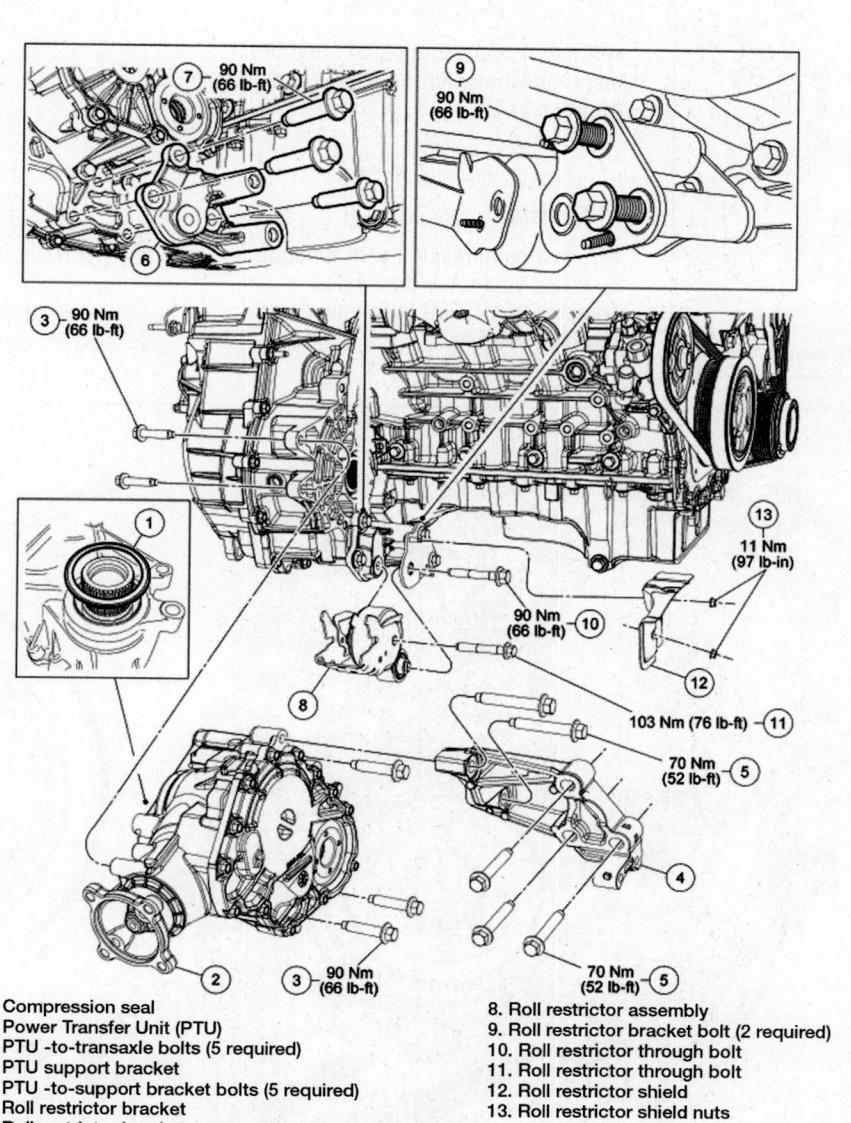

1. Compression seal
2. Power Transfer Unit (PTU)
3. PTU -to-transaxle bolts (5 required)
4. PTU support bracket
5. PTU -to-support bracket bolts (5 required)
6. Roll restrictor bracket
7. Roll restrictor bracket-to-transmission bolt (3 required)
8. Roll restrictor assembly
9. Roll restrictor bracket bolt (2 required)
10. Roll restrictor through bolt
11. Roll restrictor through bolt
12. Roll restrictor shield
13. Roll restrictor shield nuts

Fig. 48 Installing the PTU

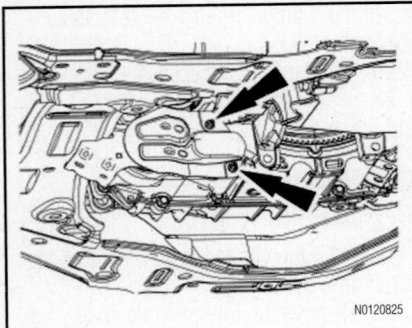

Fig. 49 Removing the 2 roll restrictor shield nuts and shield

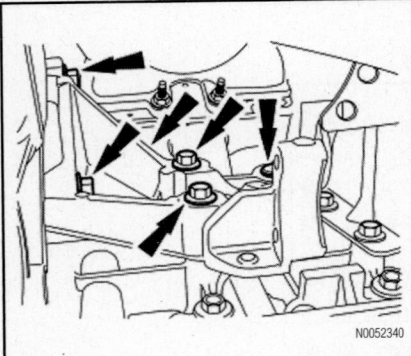

Fig. 50 Removing the PTU support bracket

3. Remove the 4 bolts and support the driveshaft with a length of mechanic's wire.

4. Remove the exhaust flexible pipe and the RH catalytic converter.

5. Remove the 2 roll restrictor shield nuts and the roll restrictor shield.

6. Remove the 2 roll restrictor through bolts and the roll restrictor.

7. Remove the 5 PTU support bracket bolts and the PTU support bracket.

8. Using a long extension, loosen but do not remove the 2 LH side PTU-to-transaxle bolts.

9. Remove the 3 RH side PTU-to-transaxle bolts and the 2 LH side PTU-to-transaxle bolts previously loosened.

10. Separate the PTU from the transaxle and remove it from the vehicle.

➡ **A new compression seal must be installed whenever the PTU is removed from the vehicle.**

11. Using a suitable tool, remove the compression seal and discard.

To install:

➡ **A new compression seal must be installed whenever the Power Transfer Unit (PTU) is removed from the vehicle.**

12. Using a suitable tool, install the new compression seal.

➡ **A new PTU intermediate shaft seal must be installed whenever the intermediate shaft or PTU is removed from the vehicle.**

13. Using a suitable pry bar, move the engine forward. Install a block of wood to hold the engine in the forward position. Install the PTU with the output flange facing the passenger side, filler plug facing upward. Rotate the PTU to the transaxle. Install the 5 PTU-to-transaxle bolts.
   a. Tighten to 66 ft. lbs. (90 Nm).

14. Position the PTU support bracket into place and hand-tighten the 5 PTU support bracket bolts.
   a. Tighten the bolts to the transaxle to 52 ft. lbs. (70 Nm).
   b. Tighten the bolts to the engine to 52 ft. lbs. (70 Nm).

15. Install the roll restrictor and the 2 roll restrictor through bolts.
   a. Tighten to 85 ft. lbs. (115 Nm).

16. Install the roll restrictor shield and the 2 roll restrictor shield nuts.
   a. Tighten to 80 inch lbs. (9 Nm).

17. Install the exhaust flexible pipe and RH catalytic converter.

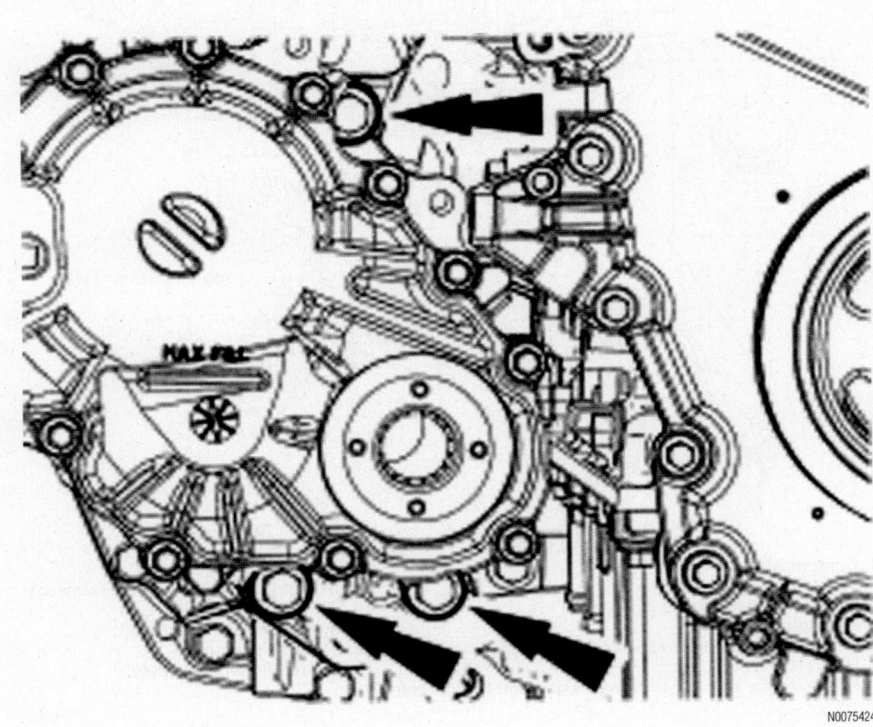

Fig. 51 Removing the PTU-to-transaxle bolts

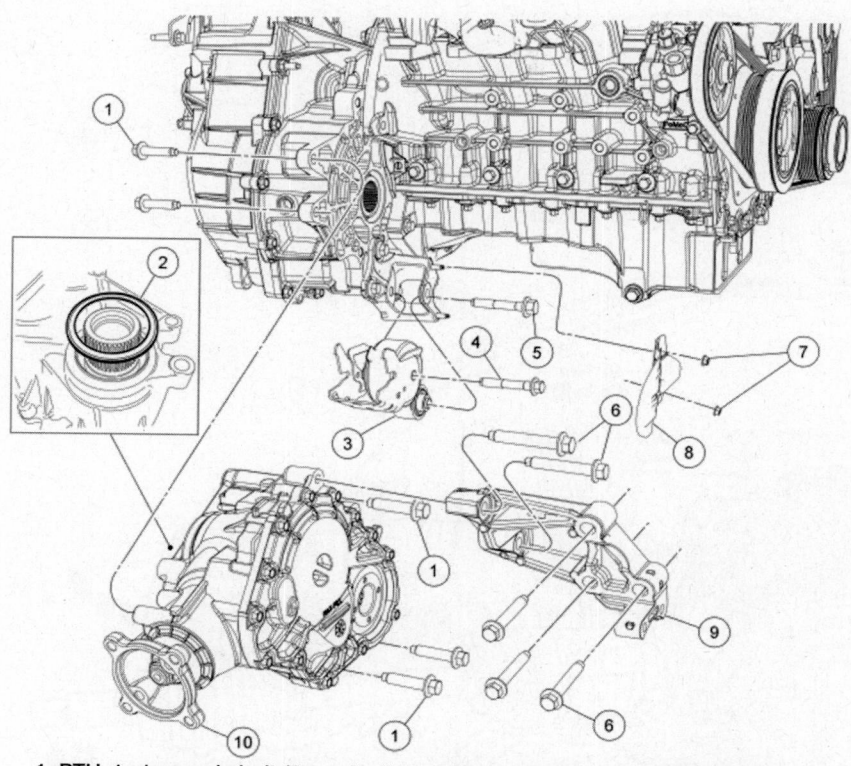

1. PTU -to-transaxle bolt (5 required)
2. Compression seal
3. Roll restrictor assembly
4. Roll restrictor through bolt
5. Roll restrictor through bolt
6. Power Transfer Unit (PTU)-to-support
   bracket bolt (5 required)
7. Roll restrictor shield nut (2 required)
8. Roll restrictor shield
9. PTU support bracket
10. PTU

N0120827

Fig. 52 Removing and installing the PTU

18. Install the intermediate shaft.
19. Line up the index marks on the driveshaft to the index marks on the PTU flange made during removal and install the 4 bolts.
   a. Tighten to 52 ft. lbs. (70 Nm).

➡**Clean the area around the filler plug before removing.**

20. Remove and discard the filler plug.
21. Fill the PTU, if necessary. The fluid must be even with the bottom of the fill opening.
22. Install a new filler plug and tighten to 15 ft. lbs. (20 Nm).

FRONT HALFSHAFT

REMOVAL & INSTALLATION

Left Side

See Figures 53 through 55.

➡**Suspension fasteners are critical parts because they affect performance of vital components and systems and their failure may result in major service expense. New parts must be installed with the same part numbers or equivalent part, if replacement is necessary. Do not use a replacement part of lesser quality or substitute design. Torque values must be used as** specified during reassembly to make sure of correct retention of these parts.

1. Remove the wheel and tire.

➡**Apply the brake to keep the halfshaft from rotating.**

2. Remove and discard the front wheel hub nut.
3. Remove and discard the ball joint bolt and nut.
   a. Separate the ball joint from the wheel knuckle.
4. Remove and discard the stabilizer bar link nut and position the link aside.
5. Using the Front Wheel Hub Remover, separate the halfshaft from the wheel hub.

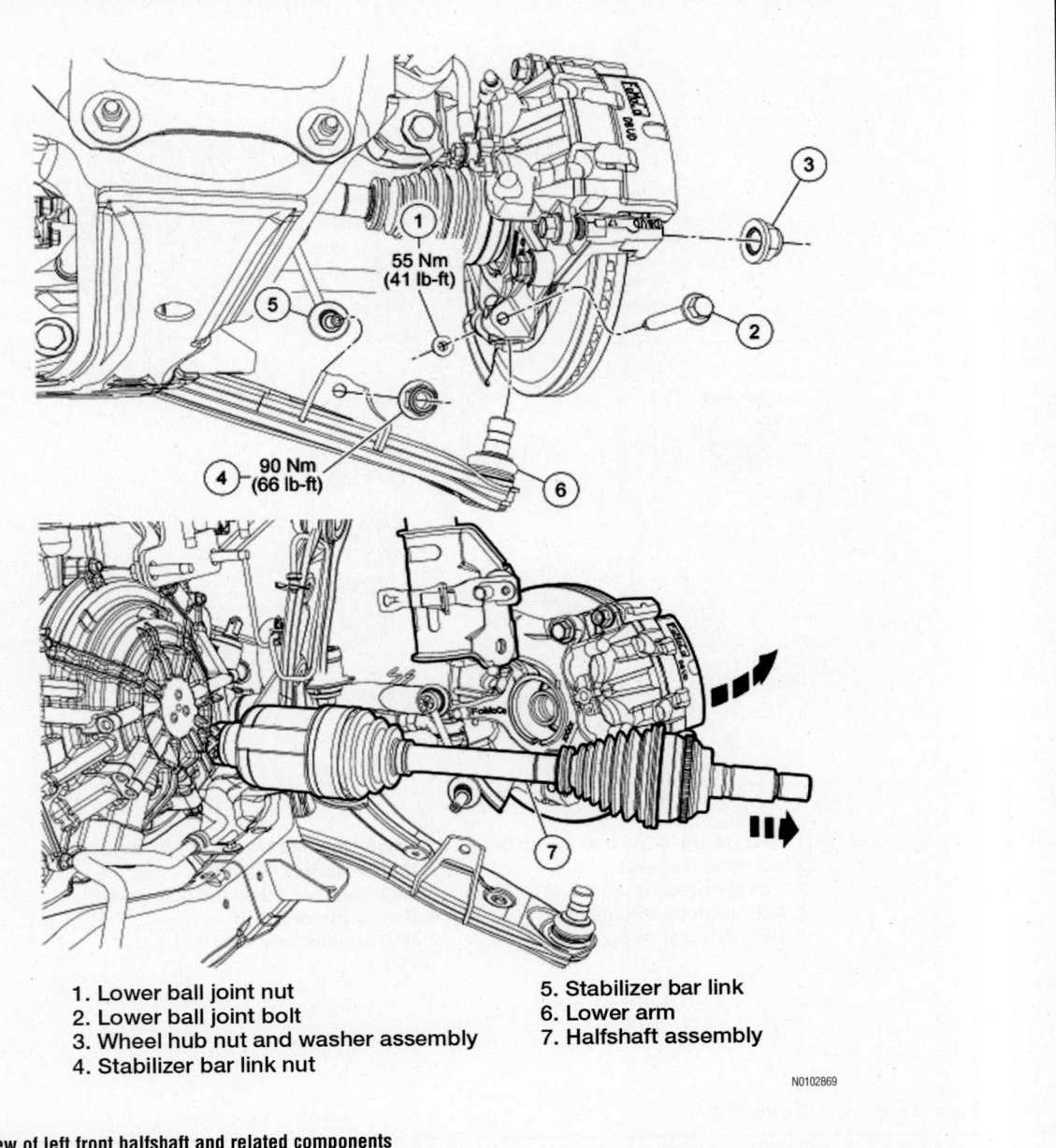

1. Lower ball joint nut
2. Lower ball joint bolt
3. Wheel hub nut and washer assembly
4. Stabilizer bar link nut
5. Stabilizer bar link
6. Lower arm
7. Halfshaft assembly

N0102869

Fig. 53 Exploded view of left front halfshaft and related components

6. Pull the knuckle outboard and rotate it toward the front of the vehicle.

  a. Secure the wheel knuckle.

7. Using the Halfshaft Remover, Halfshaft Remover (Plate) and Slide Hammer, remove the halfshaft from the transmission.

8. Remove and discard the circlip from the stub shaft.

To install:

9. Install a new stub shaft circlip.

10. Insert the halfshaft into the wheel hub.

➡**The sharp edges on the stub shaft splines can slice or puncture the oil seal. Use care when inserting the stub** shaft into the transmission to avoid oil seal damage.

➡**After insertion, pull the halfshaft inner end to make sure the circlip is locked.**

11. Push the stub shaft into the transmission so the circlip locks into the differential side gear.

12. Rotate the knuckle into position.

13. Position the halfshaft and ball joint in the wheel knuckle. Install the new ball joint bolt and nut. Tighten to 41 ft. lbs (55 Nm).

➡**Do not tighten the front wheel hub nut with the vehicle on the ground. The** nut must be tightened to specification before the vehicle is lowered onto the wheels. Wheel bearing damage will occur if the wheel bearing is loaded with the weight of the vehicle applied.

➡**Apply the brake to keep the halfshaft from rotating.**

14. Position the halfshaft in the hub and use the previously removed inner hub nut to seat the halfshaft. Tighten to 258 ft. lbs (350 Nm).

  a. Remove and discard the hub nut.

15. Position the stabilizer bar link and install the link nut.

Tighten to 66 ft. lbs. (90 Nm).

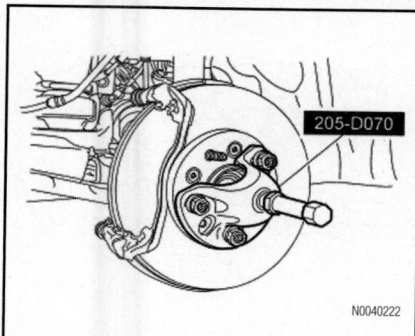

Fig. 54 Separating the halfshaft from the wheel hub

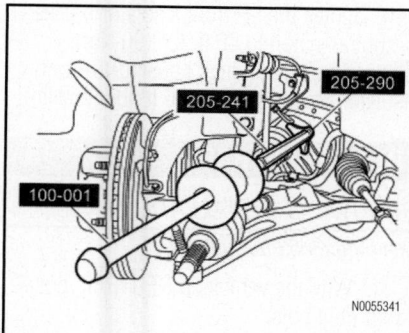

Fig. 55 Removing the halfshaft from the transmission

➡The wheel hub nut contains a one-time locking chemical that is activated by the heat created when it is tightened. Install and tighten the new wheel hub nut to specification within 5 minutes of starting it on the threads. Always install a new wheel hub nut after loosening or when not tightened within the specified time or damage to the components can occur.

➡Apply the brake to keep the halfshaft from rotating.

16. Install a new hub nut. Tighten to 258 ft. lbs. (350 Nm).
17. Install the front wheel and tire.

Right Side

See Figures 56 and 57.

➡Suspension fasteners are critical parts because they affect performance of vital components and systems and their failure may result in major service expense. New parts must be installed with the same part numbers or equivalent part, if replacement is necessary. Do not use a replacement part of lesser quality or substitute design. Torque values must be used as specified during reassembly to make

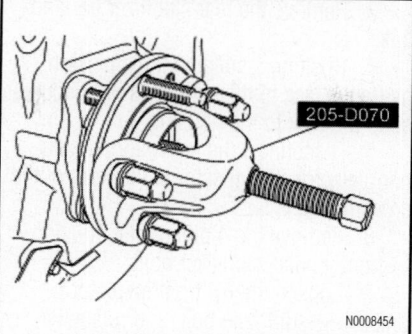

Fig. 56 Separating the halfshaft from the wheel hub

sure of correct retention of these parts.

1. Remove the wheel and tire.

➡Apply the brake to keep the halfshaft from rotating.

2. Remove the wheel hub nut.
   a. Do not discard at this time.
3. Remove the brake hose bracket bolt and disconnect the hose from the shock absorber.
4. Disconnect the wheel speed sensor harness from the shock absorber bracket.
5. Remove the brake disc.
6. Remove and discard the ball joint bolt and nut. Separate the ball joint from the wheel knuckle.
7. Remove and discard the stabilizer bar link nut and position the link aside.
8. Using the Front Wheel Hub Remover, separate the halfshaft from the wheel hub.
9. Pull the wheel knuckle outboard and rotate it toward the rear of the vehicle.
   a. Secure the wheel knuckle.
10. Use a brass drift to strike the right side halfshaft in the indicated area and separate the RH halfshaft from the intermediate shaft.
11. Remove and discard the circlip from the intermediate shaft.

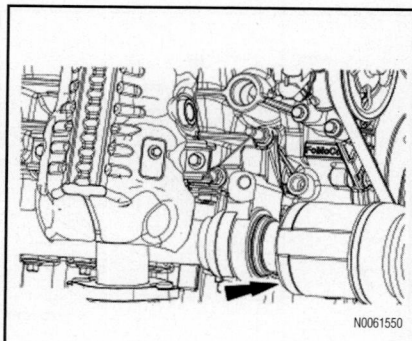

Fig. 57 Striking the right side halfshaft

To install:

12. Install a new 30 mm (1.181 in) intermediate shaft circlip.

➡Pull the right side inboard joint outward to make sure the circlip is locked.

13. Align the splines on the right side shaft with the intermediate shaft and push the stub shaft in until the circlip locks the shafts together.
14. Insert the halfshaft into the wheel hub.
15. Rotate the knuckle into position.
16. Position the halfshaft and ball joint in the wheel knuckle. Install the new ball joint bolt and nut. Tighten to 41 ft. lbs. (55 Nm).
17. Position the stabilizer bar link and install a new nut. Tighten to 66 ft. lbs. (90 Nm).
18. Install the brake disc.
19. Position the brake hose bracket and install the bolt. Tighten to 177 inch lbs. (20 Nm).
20. Connect the wheel speed sensor harness to the shock absorber bracket.

➡Do not tighten the front wheel hub nut with the vehicle on the ground. The nut must be tightened to specification before the vehicle is lowered onto the wheels. Wheel bearing damage will occur if the wheel bearing is loaded with the weight of the vehicle applied.

➡Apply the brake to keep the halfshaft from rotating.

21. Use the previously removed wheel hub nut to seat the halfshaft. Tighten to 258 ft. lbs. (350 Nm).
   a. Remove and discard the wheel hub nut.

➡The wheel hub nut contains a one-time locking chemical that is activated by the heat created when it is tightened. Install and tighten the new wheel hub nut to specification within 5 minutes of starting it on the threads. Always install a new wheel hub nut after loosening or when not tightened within the specified time or damage to the components can occur.

➡Apply the brake to keep the halfshaft from rotating.

22. Install a new wheel hub nut. Tighten to 258 ft. lbs. (350 Nm).
23. Install the front wheel and tire.

REAR AXLE STUB SHAFT BEARING AND SEAL

REMOVAL & INSTALLATION

See Figure 58.

→**The Rear Drive Unit (RDU) does not have stub shaft pilot bearings. It has stub shaft seals only.**

1. Remove the halfshaft.
2. Using the Torque Converter Fluid Seal Remover and Slide Hammer, remove the stub shaft seal.

To install:

→**Lubricate the new stub shaft seal with grease.**

3. Using the Front Axle Oil Seal Installer and Adapter Handle, install the stub shaft pilot bearing housing seal.
4. Install the halfshaft assembly.

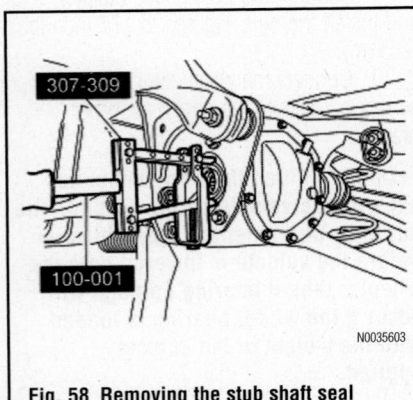

Fig. 58 Removing the stub shaft seal

REAR DRIVESHAFT

REMOVAL & INSTALLATION

See Figures 59 through 62.

1. Remove the driveshaft.
2. Remove the rear halfshafts.

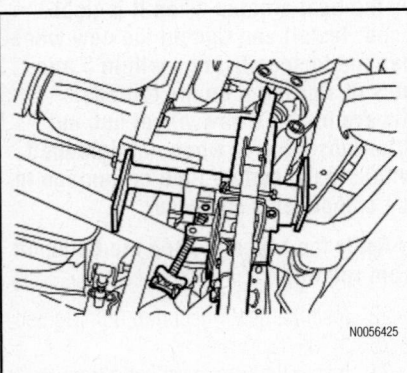

Fig. 59 Positioning the jack

3. Remove the rear stabilizer bar and link.
4. Position a suitable transmission hydraulic jack to the axle housing. Securely strap the jack to the housing.
5. Disconnect the active torque coupling electrical connector at the front of the crossmember.
6. Remove the 4 differential housing-to-front insulator bracket bolts.
7. Loosen the LH front insulator bracket-to-subframe bolt, and rotate the bracket aside.
8. Loosen the RH front insulator bracket-to-subframe bolt and the bracket, and rotate the bracket aside.
9. Remove the 2 RH side insulator bracket-to-rear axle differential bolts and the axle assembly.
10. Remove the 3 LH side insulator or bracket-to-rear axle differential bolts.
11. Lower the rear axle assembly.

To install:

12. To install, reverse the removal procedure. Tighten the 3 LH side insulator or bracket-to-rear axle differential bolts to 66 ft. lbs (90 Nm). Tighten the 2 RH side insulator bracket-to-rear axle differential bolts to 66 ft. lbs. (90 Nm). Tighten the RH front insulator bracket-to-subframe bolt to 66 ft. lbs. (90

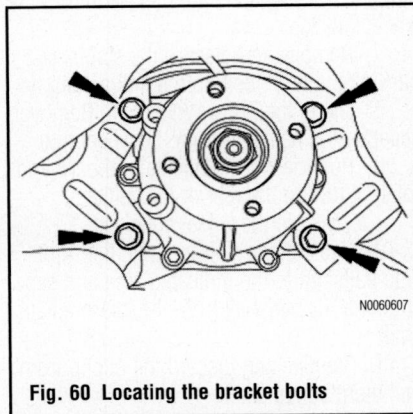

Fig. 60 Locating the bracket bolts

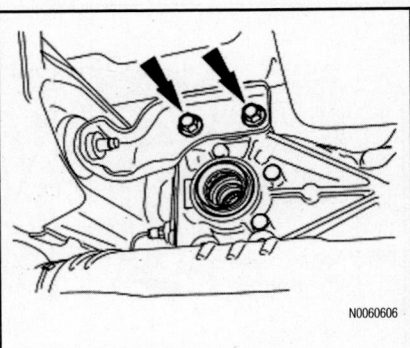

Fig. 61 Locating the RH side insulator bracket to rear axle differential bolts

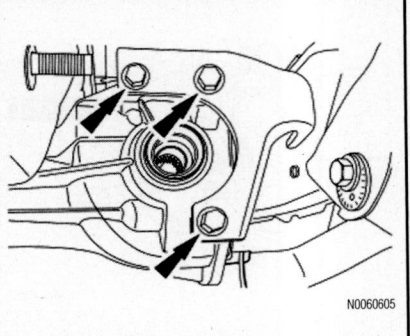

Fig. 62 Locating the LH side insulator bracket to rear axle differential bolts

Nm). Tighten the LH front insulator bracket-to-subframe bolt to 66 ft. lbs (90 Nm). Tighten the 4 differential housing-to-front insulator bracket bolts to 66 ft. lbs (90 Nm).

REAR HALFSHAFT

REMOVAL & INSTALLATION

See Figures 63 through 69.

1. With the vehicle in NEUTRAL, position it on a hoist.
2. Remove the rear wheel speed sensor.
3. Remove the inner and outer rear wheel hub nuts.
   a. Do not discard at this time.
4. Remove the brake caliper hose bracket bolt.
5. Remove the rear brake disc.

→**Suspension fasteners are critical parts because they affect performance of vital components and systems and their failure may result in major service expense. New parts must be installed with the same part numbers or equivalent part, if replacement is necessary. Do not use a replacement part of lesser quality or substitute design. Torque values must be used a specified during reassembly to make sure of correct retention of these parts.**

6. Remove and discard the upper arm outboard bolt.
7. Lift the upper arm from the knuckle.
8. Support the lower arm and remove the lower shock nut and bolt.
9. Remove and discard the stabilizer link upper nut.
10. Remove and discard the outer toe link nut and bolt.
11. Support the wheel knuckle and remove the lower arm nut and bolt and discard the nut and bolt.
12. Using the Front Hub Remover, separate the halfshaft from the rear axle hub assembly.

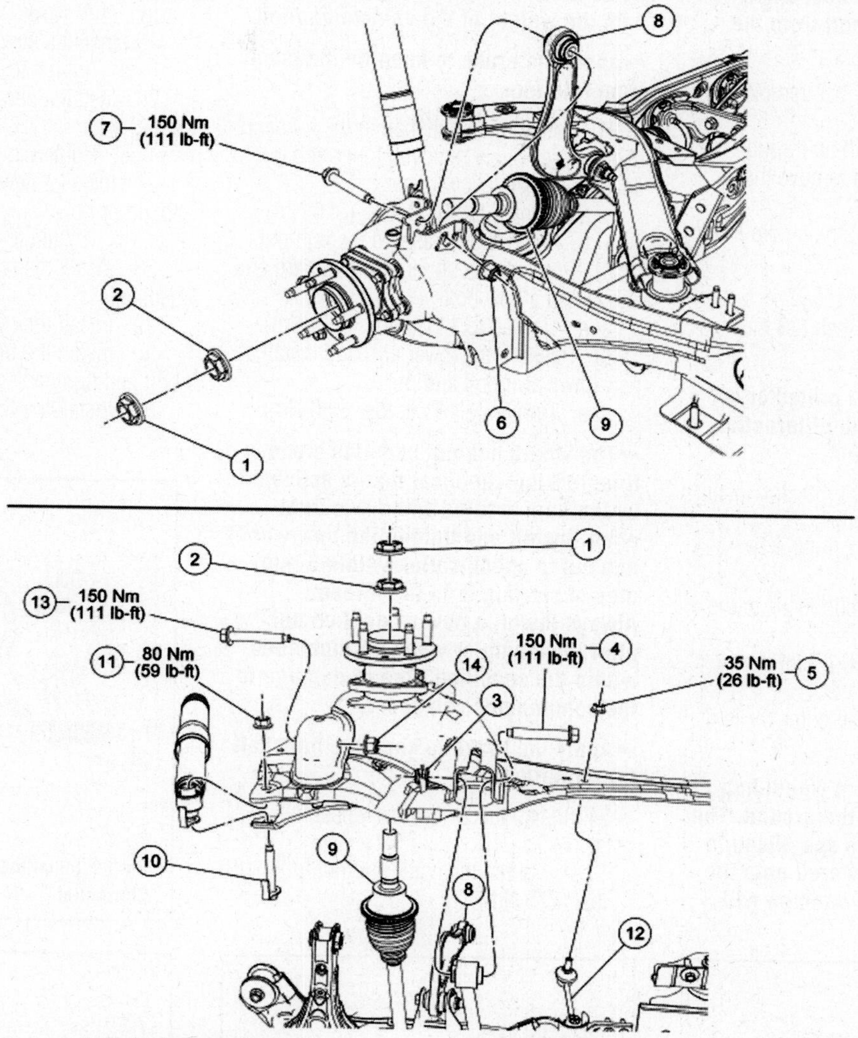

7 150 Nm
(111 lb-ft)

8

2

6   9

1

2   1

13 150 Nm
(111 lb-ft)

11 80 Nm
(59 lb-ft)

14   150 Nm
(111 lb-ft)   4

35 Nm
(26 lb-ft) 5

3

10

9   8

12

N0105311

1. Outer hub bearing nut
2. Inner hub bearing nut
3. Toe link outboard nut
4. Toe link outboard bolt
5. Stabilizer bar link nut
6. Upper arm outboard nut
7. Upper arm outboard bolt

8. Upper control arm
9. Halfshaft assembly
10. Lower shock absorber flag bolt
11. Lower shock absorber nut
12. Stabilizer bar link
13. Lower arm outboard bolt
14. Lower arm outboard nut

Fig. 63 Exploded view of the rear drive halfshafts and related components

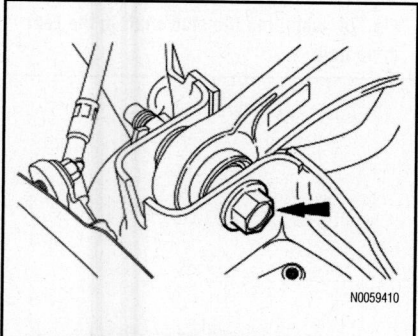

N0059410

Fig. 64 Removing the upper arm outboard bolt

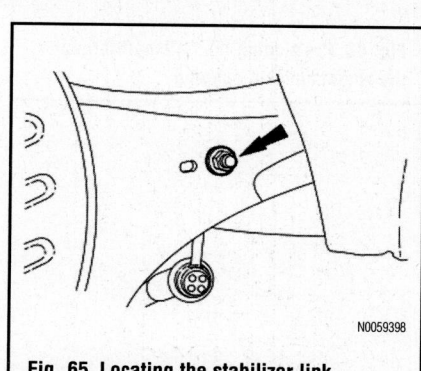

N0059398

Fig. 65 Locating the stabilizer link upper nut

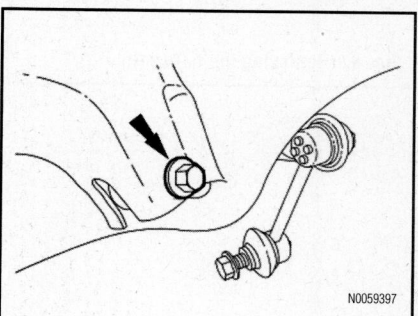

N0059397

Fig. 66 Identifying the outer toe link nut and bolt

➡️**Do not damage the oil seal when removing the axle halfshaft from the differential.**

13. Using a suitable pry bar, remove the halfshaft.

14. Position the halfshaft up through the wheel knuckle opening and remove the halfshaft.

15. Remove and discard the circlip from the stub shaft.

To install:

16. Install a new 1.102 inch (28 mm) circlip on the stub shaft.

➡️**Make sure the oil seal protector is correctly aligned with the differential oil seal during installation.**

17. Using the Axle Seal Protector, install the halfshaft in the differential.

18. Install the stub shaft in the rear drive unit.

   a. Make sure the circlip locks in the side gear.

19. Slide the outboard CV joint down through the knuckle.

20. Position the halfshaft outer CV joint through the hub bearing.

➡️**Do not tighten the front wheel hub nut with the vehicle on the ground. The nut must be tightened to specification before the vehicle is lowered onto the wheels. Wheel bearing damage will**

occur if the wheel bearing is loaded with the weight of the vehicle applied

➡️**Apply the brake to keep the halfshaft from rotating.**

21. Position the halfshaft in the hub and use the previously removed inner hub nut to seat the halfshaft.

   a. Tighten to 203 ft. lbs. (275 Nm).

   b. Remove and discard the hub nut.

22. Position the upper arm outboard end and install a new bolt.

   a. Tighten to 111 ft. lbs. (150 Nm).

23. Position the lower arm and install a new lower arm bolt and nut.

   a. Tighten to 111 ft. lbs. (150 Nm).

➡️**The wheel hub nut contains a one-time locking chemical that is activated by the heat created when it is tightened. Install and tighten the new wheel hub nut to specification within 5 minutes of starting it on the threads. Always install a new wheel hub nut after loosening or when not tightened within the specified time or damage to the components can occur.**

➡️**Apply the brake to keep the halfshaft from rotating.**

24. Install the 2 new rear wheel hub nuts.

   a. Tighten the inner hub nut to 203 ft. lbs. (275 Nm).

   b. Tighten the outer hub nut to 129 ft. lbs. (175 Nm).

25. Install a new rear toe link bolt.

   a. Tighten to 148 ft. lbs. (200 Nm).

26. Install a new stabilizer link upper nut.

   a. Tighten to 26 ft. lbs. (35 Nm).

27. Install a new lower shock absorber nut.

   a. Tighten to 59 ft. lbs. (80 Nm).

28. Install the rear wheel speed sensor.

29. Install the rear brake disc.

30. Install the brake caliper hose bracket bolt and tighten to 11 ft. lbs. (15 Nm).

31. Install the tire and wheel.

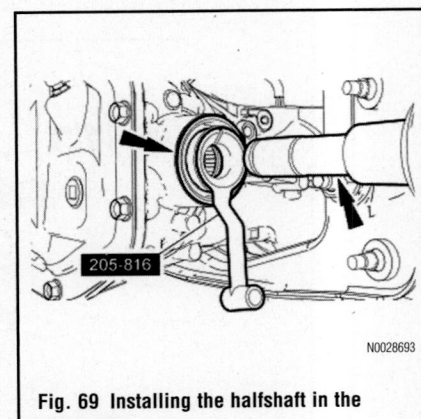

Fig. 69 Installing the halfshaft in the differential

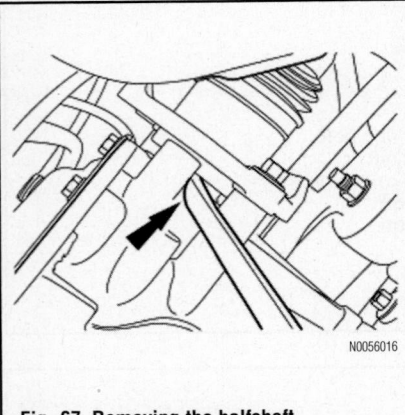

Fig. 67 Removing the halfshaft

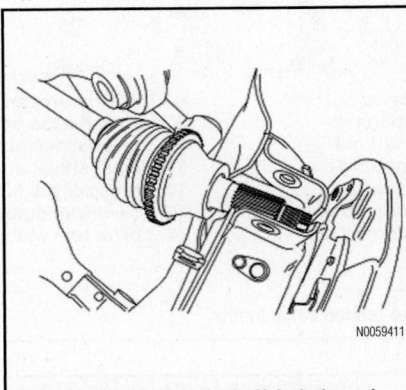

Fig. 68 Positioning the halfshaft through the wheel knuckle opening

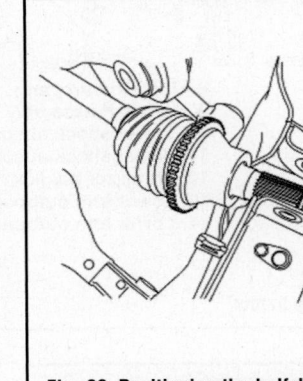

Fig. 70 Installing the stub shaft in the rear drive unit

ENGINE COOLING

ENGINE COOLANT

DRAIN & REFILL PROCEDURE

✳✳ WARNING

Always allow the engine to cool before opening the cooling system. Do not unscrew the coolant pressure relief cap when the engine is operating or the cooling system is hot. The cooling system is under pressure; steam and hot liquid can come out forcefully when the cap is loosened slightly. Failure to follow these instructions may result in serious personal injury.

➡The coolant must be recovered in a suitable, clean container for reuse. If the coolant is contaminated, it must be recycled or disposed of correctly. Using contaminated coolant may result in damage to the engine or cooling system components.

➡The engine cooling system is filled with Motorcraft® Specialty Green Engine Coolant. Mixing coolant types degrades the corrosion protection of the coolant. Do not mix coolant types. Failure to follow these instructions may result in engine or cooling system damage.

➡Genuine Mazda® Extended Life Coolant and Motorcraft® Specialty Green Engine Coolant are very sensitive to light. Do NOT allow these products to be exposed to ANY LIGHT for more than a day or two. Extended light exposure causes these products to degrade.

➡Stop-leak style pellets/products must not be used as an additive in this engine cooling system. The addition of stop-leak style pellets/products can clog or damage the cooling system resulting in degraded cooling system performance and/or failure.

➡Less than 80% of coolant capacity can be recovered with the engine in the vehicle. Dirty, rusty or contaminated coolant requires replacement.

1. With the vehicle in NEUTRAL, position it on a hoist.
2. Release the pressure in the cooling system by slowly turning the pressure relief cap one-half turn counterclockwise. When

the pressure is released, remove the pressure relief cap.
3. Place a suitable container below the radiator draincock.
   a. Open the draincock and allow to drain.
   b. Close the draincock after draining.
4. Open the degas bottle cap and fill the degas bottle to the MAX fill line.
   a. Recommended coolant concentration is 50/50 ethylene glycol to distilled water.
   b. Maximum coolant concentration is 60/40 for cold weather areas.
   c. Minimum coolant concentration is 40/60 for warm weather areas.
5. Idle the engine for 2 minutes with the degas bottle cap off, then turn the key to the OFF position.
6. If necessary, fill the degas bottle to the MAX fill line again.
7. Close the degas bottle cap.

BLEEDING

➡If the engine overheats or the fluid level drops below the minimum fill line, shut off the engine and add fluid to the degas bottle maximum fill line once the engine cools. Failure to follow these instructions may result in damage to the engine.

1. Start and run the engine at 2,500 rpm for 5 minutes.
2. Turn the key to the OFF position.

✳✳ WARNING

Always allow the engine to cool before opening the cooling system. Do not unscrew the coolant pressure relief cap when the engine is operating or the cooling system is hot. The cooling system is under pressure; steam and hot liquid can come out forcefully when the cap is loosened slightly. Failure to follow these instructions may result in serious personal injury.

3. Check the engine coolant level in degas bottle and fill as necessary.
   a. Recommended coolant concentration is 50/50 ethylene glycol to distilled water.
   b. Maximum coolant concentration is 60/40 for cold weather areas.
   c. Minimum coolant concentration is 40/60 for warm weather areas.

FLUSHING

✳✳ WARNING

Always allow the engine to cool before opening the cooling system. Do not unscrew the coolant pressure relief cap when the engine is operating or the cooling system is hot. The cooling system is under pressure; steam and hot liquid can come out forcefully when the cap is loosened slightly. Failure to follow these instructions may result in serious personal injury.

➡The engine cooling system is filled with Motorcraft® Specialty Green Engine Coolant. Mixing coolant types degrades the corrosion protection of the coolant. Do not mix coolant types. Failure to follow these instructions may result in engine or cooling system damage.

➡Genuine Mazda® Extended Life Coolant and Motorcraft® Specialty Green Engine Coolant are very sensitive to light. Do NOT allow these products to be exposed to ANY LIGHT for more than a day or two. Extended light exposure causes these products to degrade.

➡To remove rust, sludge and other foreign material from the cooling system, use cooling system flush that is safe for use with aluminum radiators. For additional information, refer to Specifications. This cleaning restores cooling system efficiency and helps prevent overheating. A pulsating or reversed direction of flushing water will loosen sediment more quickly than a steady flow in the normal coolant flow direction. In severe cases where cleaning solvents will not clean the cooling system efficiently, it will be necessary to use the pressure flushing method using cooling system flusher. Dispose of old coolant and flushing water contaminated with antifreeze and cleaning chemicals in accordance with local, state or federal laws.

1. Add premium cooling system flush to the cooling system and follow the directions on the package.
2. Drain the cooling system.
3. Remove the radiator.

➡️ **Radiator internal pressure must not exceed 20 psi (138 kPa). Damage to the radiator can result.**

4. Back flush the radiator with the radiator in an upside-down position with a high-pressure hose in the lower hose location and backflush.

5. Remove the thermostat.

6. Backflush the engine. Position the high-pressure water hose into the engine through the engine return and backflush the engine.

7. Install the thermostat.

8. Install the radiator.

9. Fill the cooling system.

ENGINE FAN

REMOVAL & INSTALLATION

See Figure 71.

1. Remove the Air Cleaner (ACL) assembly.

2. If equipped, detach the 2 block heater wiring clips from the radiator support.

3. Detach the wiring harness retainers and position the harness aside.

4. Position aside the upper radiator hose from the cooling fan motor and shroud.

5. Disconnect the cooling fan motor electrical connector.

6. Remove the 2 bolts and the cooling fan motor and shroud.

To install:

7. To install, reverse the removal procedure. Tighten the cooling fan motor and shroud bolts to 53 inch lbs. (6 Nm).

RADIATOR

REMOVAL & INSTALLATION

2010 Models

See Figures 72 and 73.

1. Drain the cooling system.

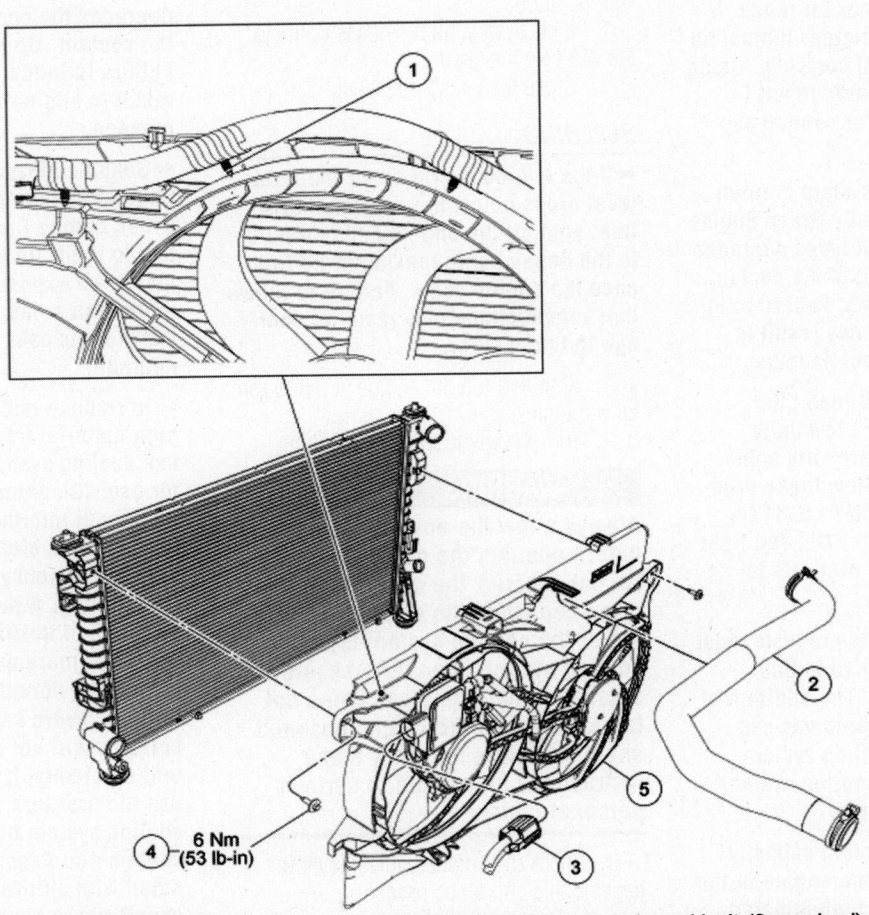

4. 6 Nm (53 lb-in)

1. Wiring harness retainer
2. Upper radiator hose
3. Cooling fan motor and shroud electrical connector
4. Cooling fan motor and shroud bolt (2 required)
5. Cooling fan motor and shroud

N0103216

Fig. 71 Removing and installing the engine fan and shroud

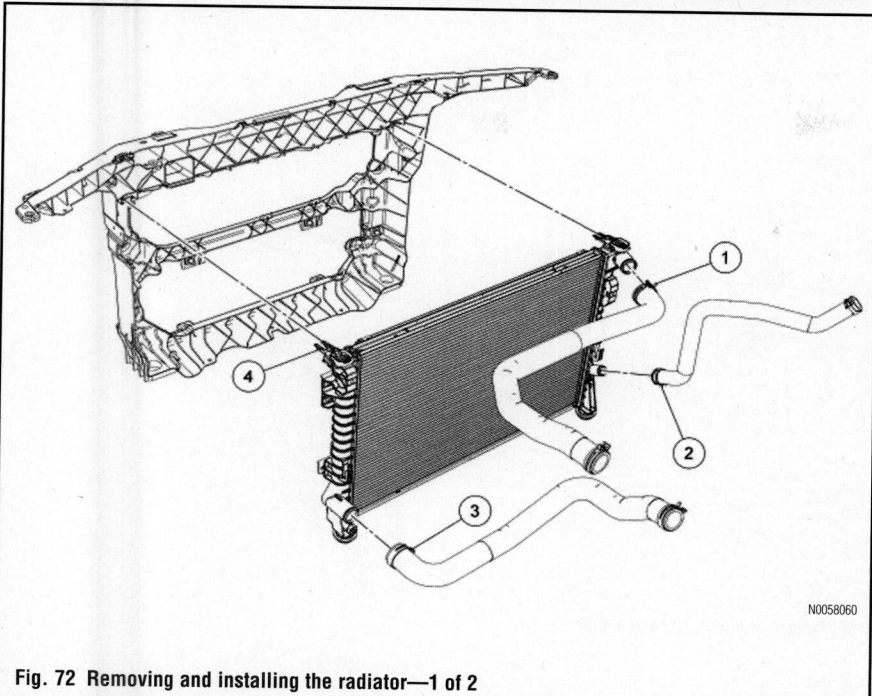

Fig. 72 Removing and installing the radiator—1 of 2

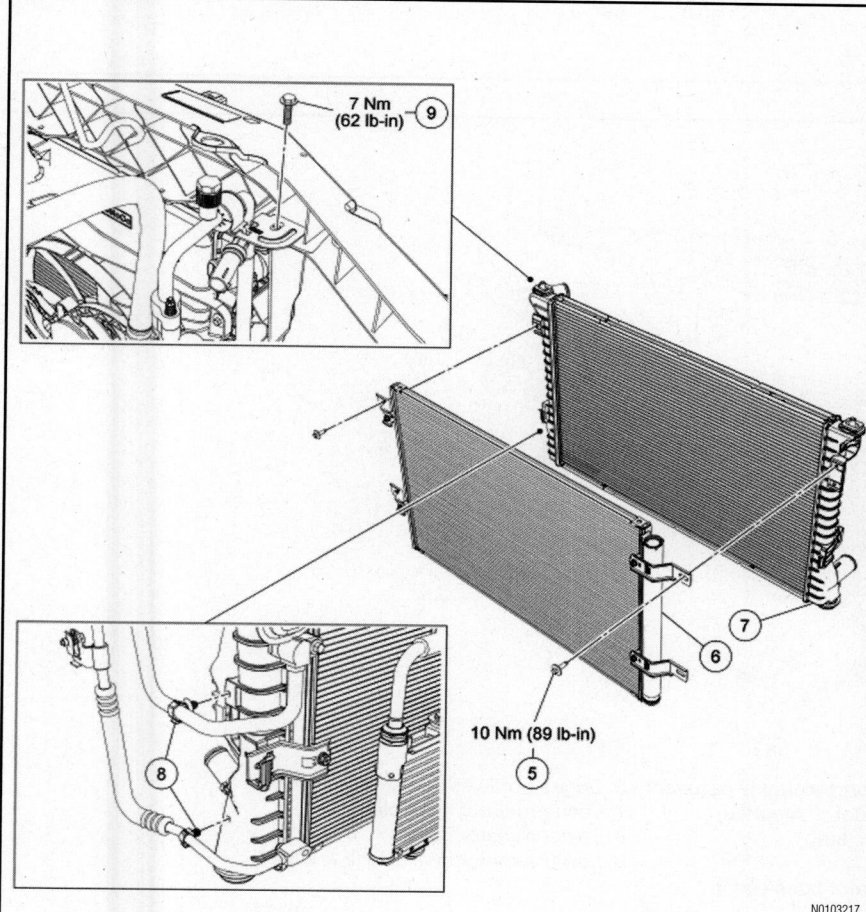

Fig. 73 Removing and installing the radiator—2 of 2

2. Remove the cooling fan motor and shroud.

3. Remove the front bumper cover.

4. Disconnect the upper radiator hose and lower degas bottle hose from the radiator.

5. Disconnect the lower radiator hose from the radiator.

6. Remove the compressor-to-condenser discharge line bracket bolt.

7. Lift and remove the tabs from the radiator support and position the radiator towards the engine.

8. Detach the 2 pin-type retainers from the radiator.

9. Remove the 2 A/C condenser bolts from the radiator and separate the condenser from the radiator.

10. Remove the radiator.

To install:

11. To install, reverse the removal procedure. Tighten the 2 A/C condenser bolts to 89 inch lbs. (10 Nm). Tighten the compressor-to-condenser discharge line bracket bolt to 62 inch lbs. (7 Nm).

12. Fill and bleed the cooling system.

2011 Models

See Figures 74 through 76.

➥ At the time of publication the manufacturer does not provide a specific Removal and Installation procedure for this component. Refer to the graphic(s) when servicing this component.

Items in the exploded views may not be listed in order of removal.

THERMOSTAT

REMOVAL & INSTALLATION

1. Drain the cooling system.

2. Remove the Air Cleaner (ACL) assembly and outlet pipe.

3. Remove the 2 bolts and position aside the thermostat housing cover.

4. Remove the O-ring seal and thermostat.

   a. Clean and inspect the O-ring seal. Install a new seal if necessary.

To install:

➥ The engine cooling system is filled with Motorcraft® Specialty Green Engine Coolant. Mixing coolant types degrades the corrosion protection of the coolant. Do not mix coolant types. Failure to follow these instructions may result in engine or cooling system damage.

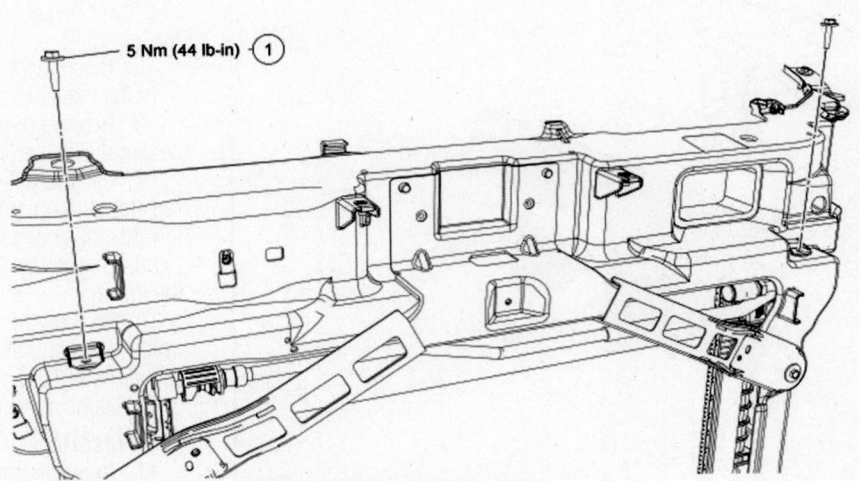

1. Upper radiator support bracket bolts (2 required)

N0119634

Fig. 74 Exploded view of radiator—1 of 3

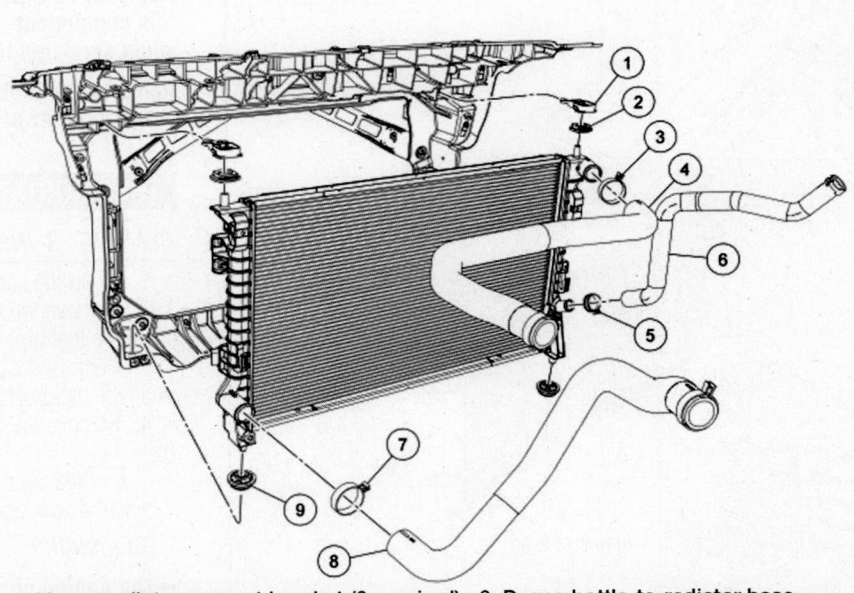

1. Upper radiator support bracket (2 required)
2. Upper radiator insulator (2 required)
3. Upper radiator hose clamp
4. Upper radiator hose
5. Degas bottle-to-radiator hose clamp
6. Degas bottle-to-radiator hose
7. Lower radiator hose clamp
8. Lower radiator hose
9. Lower radiator insulator (2 required)

N0119635

Fig. 75 Exploded view of radiator—2 of 3

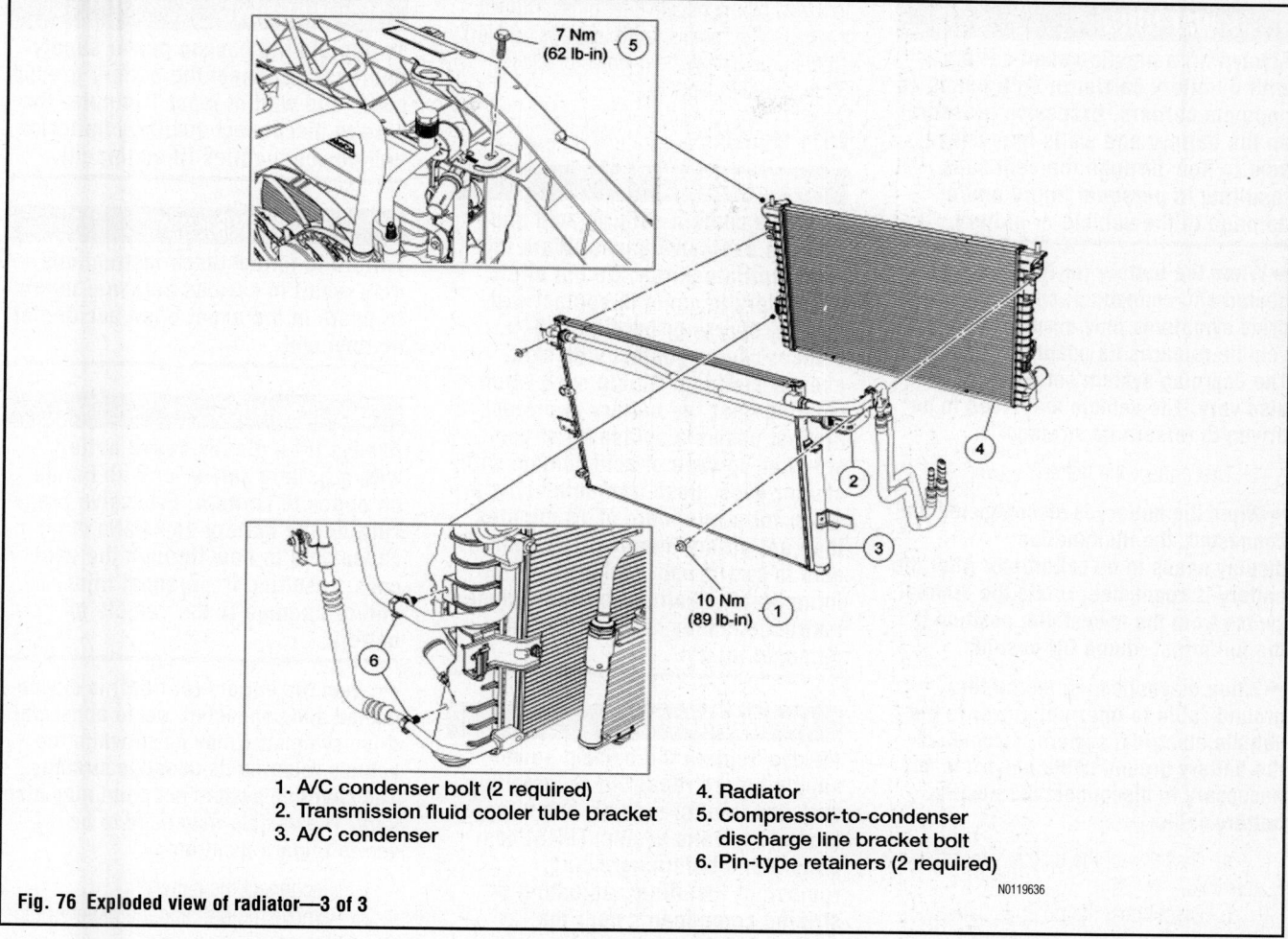

1. A/C condenser bolt (2 required)
2. Transmission fluid cooler tube bracket
3. A/C condenser
4. Radiator
5. Compressor-to-condenser discharge line bracket bolt
6. Pin-type retainers (2 required)

7 Nm (62 lb-in) ⑤
10 Nm (89 lb-in) ①

Fig. 76 Exploded view of radiator—3 of 3

N0119636

➡ Genuine Mazda® Extended Life Coolant and Motorcraft® Specialty Green Engine Coolant are very sensitive to light. Do NOT allow these products to be exposed to ANY LIGHT for more than a day or two. Extended light exposure causes these products to degrade.

➡ Lubricate the thermostat O-ring seal with clean engine coolant.

5. To install, reverse the removal procedure. Tighten the thermostat housing cover bolts to 89 inch lbs. (10 Nm).

6. Fill and bleed the cooling system.

ENGINE ELECTRICAL

BATTERY

REMOVAL & INSTALLATION

2010 Models

※ WARNING

Batteries contain sulfuric acid and produce explosive gases. Work in a well-ventilated area. Do not allow the battery to come in contact with flames, sparks or burning substances. Avoid contact with skin, eyes or clothing. Shield eyes when working near the battery to protect against possible splashing of acid solution. In case of acid contact with skin or eyes, flush immediately with water for a minimum of 15 minutes, then get prompt medical attention. If acid is swallowed, call a physician immediately. Failure to follow these instructions may result in serious personal injury.

※ WARNING

Always deplete the backup power supply before repairing or installing any new front or side air bag supplemental restraint system (SRS) component and before servicing, removing, installing, adjusting or striking components near the front or

BATTERY SYSTEM

side impact sensors or the restraints control module (RCM). Nearby components include doors, instrument panel, console, door latches, strikers, seats and hood latches.

※ WARNING

To deplete the backup power supply energy, disconnect the battery ground cable and wait at least 1 minute. Be sure to disconnect auxiliary batteries and power supplies (if equipped). Failure to follow these instructions may result in serious personal injury or death in the event of an accidental deployment.

✳✳ WARNING

Always lift a plastic-cased battery with a battery carrier or with hands on opposite corners. Excessive pressure on the battery end walls may cause acid to flow through the vent caps, resulting in personal injury and/or damage to the vehicle or battery.

➡When the battery (or PCM) is disconnected and connected, some abnormal drive symptoms may occur while the vehicle relearns its adaptive strategy. The charging system set point may also vary. The vehicle may need to be driven to relearn its strategy.

1. Disconnect the battery.

➡When the battery is disconnected and connected, the illumination display needs to be calibrated. After the battery is connected, rotate the dimmer switch from the lowest dim position to the full bright, dome ON position.

➡When disconnecting the battery ground cable to interrupt power to the vehicle electrical system, disconnect the battery ground cable only. It is not necessary to disconnect the positive battery cable.

    a. Disconnect the battery ground terminal.
    b. Disconnect the positive battery terminal.
2. Remove the bolt and the battery hold-down bracket.
3. Remove the battery.

To install:
4. To install, reverse the removal procedure. Connect the positive battery terminal

followed by the negative terminal. Tighten the battery terminals to 80 inch lbs. (9 Nm). Tighten the battery hold-down bracket to 62 inch lbs. (7 Nm).

2011 Models

✳✳ WARNING

Batteries contain sulfuric acid and produce explosive gases. Work in a well-ventilated area. Do not allow the battery to come in contact with flames, sparks or burning substances. Avoid contact with skin, eyes or clothing. Shield eyes when working near the battery to protect against possible splashing of acid solution. In case of acid contact with skin or eyes, flush immediately with water for a minimum of 15 minutes, then get prompt medical attention. If acid is swallowed, call a physician immediately. Failure to follow these instructions may result in serious personal injury.

✳✳ WARNING

Always deplete the backup power supply before repairing or installing any new front or side air bag supplemental restraint system (SRS) component and before servicing, removing, installing, adjusting or striking components near the front or side impact sensors or the restraints control module (RCM). Nearby components include doors, instrument panel, console, door latches, strikers, seats and hood latches.

✳✳ WARNING

To deplete the backup power supply energy, disconnect the battery ground cable and wait at least 1 minute. Be sure to disconnect auxiliary batteries and power supplies (if equipped).

✳✳ WARNING

Failure to follow these instructions may result in serious personal injury or death in the event of an accidental deployment.

✳✳ WARNING

Always lift a plastic-cased battery with a battery carrier or with hands on opposite corners. Excessive pressure on the battery end walls may cause acid to flow through the vent caps, resulting in personal injury and/or damage to the vehicle or battery.

➡When the battery (or PCM) is disconnected and connected, some abnormal drive symptoms may occur while the vehicle relearns its adaptive strategy. The charging system set point may also vary. The vehicle may need to be driven to relearn its strategy.

1. Disconnect the battery.
2. Remove the bolt and the battery hold-down bracket.
    a. To install, tighten to 62 inch lbs. (7 Nm).
3. Remove the battery.

To install:
4. To install, reverse the removal procedure.

ENGINE ELECTRICAL

ALTERNATOR

REMOVAL & INSTALLATION

See Figures 77 and 78.

➡The radial arm adapter is a serviceable item. Do not replace the generator if the radial arm adapter is the only concern.

1. Disconnect the battery.
2. Remove the cooling fan.

3. Rotate the accessory drive belt tensioner counterclockwise and position the accessory drive belt aside.
4. Position the generator B+ terminal protective cover aside, remove the nut and position the generator B+ terminal aside.
5. Disconnect the generator electrical connector.
    a. Detach the pin-type retainer and wiring harness.
6. Remove the generator stud nut.
7. Remove the generator stud.

CHARGING SYSTEM

8. Remove the RH fender splash shield.
9. Loosen the generator bolt and remove the generator.

To install:
10. To install, reverse the removal procedure. Tighten the generator stud to 71 inch lbs. (8 Nm).

Tighten the generator stud nut to 35 ft. lbs. (47 Nm). Tighten the generator B+ terminal to 150 inch lbs. (17 Nm). Tighten the generator to 35 ft. lbs. (47 Nm).

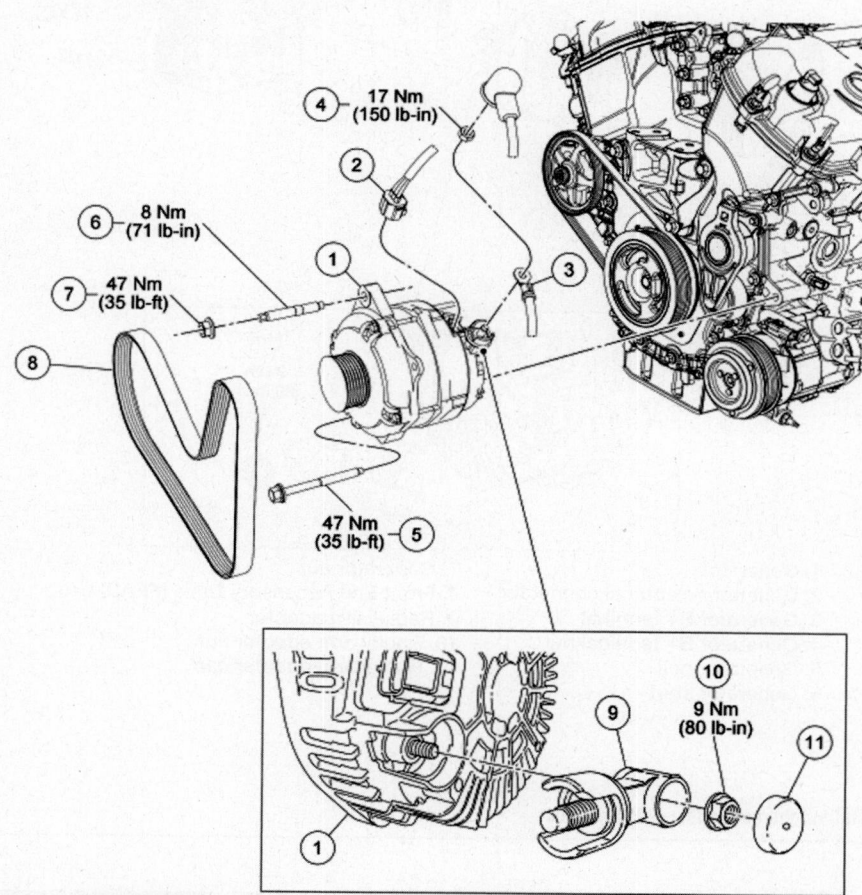

1. Generator
2. Generator electrical connector
3. Generator B+ terminal
4. Generator B+ terminal nut
5. Generator bolt
6. Generator stud
7. Generator nut
8. Front End Accessory Drive (FEAD) belt
9. Radial arm adapter
10. Radial arm adapter nut
11. Radial arm adapter cap

N0108671

Fig. 77 Removing and installing the generator—2010 models

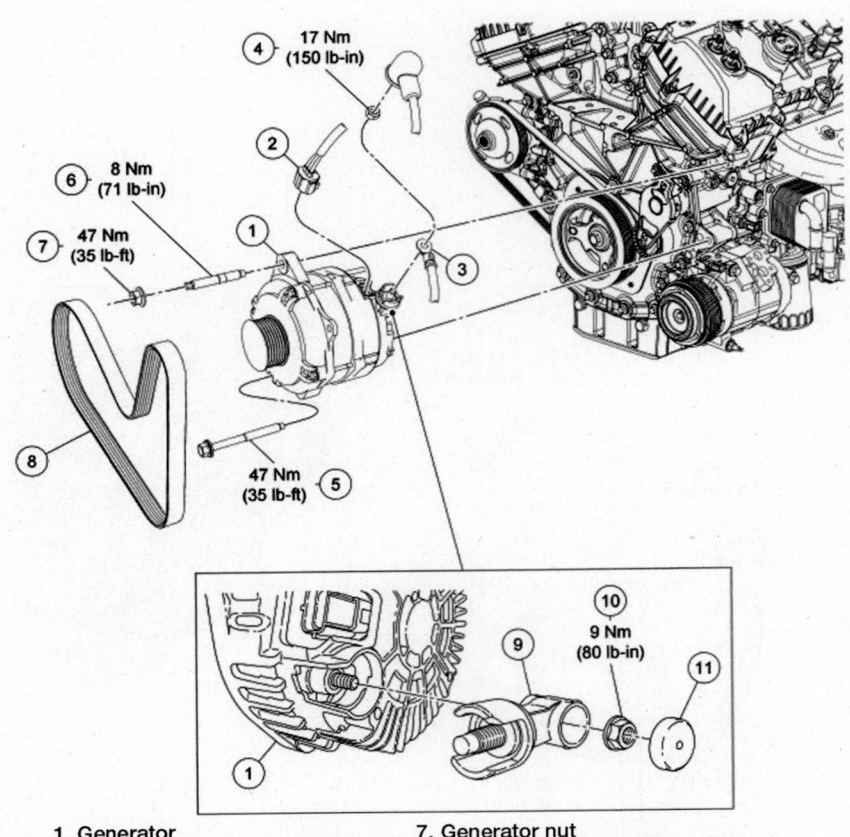

1. Generator
2. Generator electrical connector
3. Generator B+ terminal
4. Generator B+ terminal nut
5. Generator bolt
6. Generator stud
7. Generator nut
8. Front End Accessory Drive (FEAD) belt
9. Radial arm adapter
10. Radial arm adapter nut
11. Radial arm adapter cap

N0118621

Fig. 78 Removing and installing the generator—2011 models

ENGINE ELECTRICAL

FIRING ORDER

The 3.5L and the 3.7L engine firing order is 1-4-2-5-3-6.

IGNITION COIL

REMOVAL & INSTALLATION

2010 Models

LH side

1. Disconnect the crankcase vent tube quick connect coupling from the valve cover fitting and position aside.

RH side

➡ **The upper intake manifold must be removed to access the RH ignition coil-on-plugs.**

2. Remove the upper intake manifold.
Both sides
3. Disconnect the 6 ignition coil-on-plug electrical connectors.

➡ **When removing the ignition coil-on-plugs, a slight twisting motion will break the seal and ease removal.**

4. Remove the 6 bolts and the 6 ignition coil-on-plugs.

IGNITION SYSTEM

5. Inspect the coil seals for rips, nicks or tears. Remove and discard any damaged coil seals.

To install:

6. To install, reverse the removal procedure. Slide the new coil seal onto the coil until it is fully seated at the top of the coil. Apply a small amount of dielectric grease to the inside of the ignition coil-on-plug boots before attaching to the spark plugs. Tighten the 6 bolts and ignition coil on plugs to 62 inch lbs. (7 Nm).

2011 Models

RH side

➡ **The upper intake manifold must be removed to access the RH ignition coil-on-plugs.**

1. Remove the upper intake manifold.
Both sides
2. Disconnect the 6 ignition coil-on-plug electrical connectors.

➡ **When removing the ignition coil-on-plugs, a slight twisting motion will break the seal and ease removal.**

3. Remove the 6 bolts and the 6 ignition coil-on-plugs.
4. Inspect the coil seals for rips, nicks or tears. Remove and discard any damaged coil seals.

To install:

5. To install, reverse the removal procedure.
   a. To install, slide the new coil seal onto the coil until it is fully seated at the top of the coil.
   b. Apply a small amount of dielectric grease to the inside of the ignition coil-on-plug boots before attaching to the spark plugs.
   c. To install, tighten to 62 inch lbs. (7 Nm).

SPARK PLUGS

REMOVAL & INSTALLATION

See Figure 79.

RH side

➡ **The upper intake manifold must be removed to access the RH spark plugs only.**

1. Remove the upper intake manifold.
Both sides
2. Disconnect the 6 ignition coil-on-plug electrical connectors.

➡ **When removing the ignition coil-on-plugs, a slight twisting motion will break the seal and ease removal.**

3. Remove the 6 bolts and the 6 ignition coil-on-plugs.

➡ **Only use hand tools when removing or installing the spark plugs or damage can occur to the cylinder head or spark plug.**

➡ **Use compressed air to remove any foreign material in the spark plug well before removing the spark plugs.**

4. Remove the 6 spark plugs.

1. Deposits bridging spark plug gap
2. Wet black deposits (oil fouling)
3. Dry black deposits (carbon fouling)
4. Normal spark plug
5. Pre-ignition
6. Overheating
7. Fused spot deposits

DB0020A

Fig. 79 Inspecting the spark plugs

To install:
Both sides

5. Inspect the 6 spark plugs.
6. Adjust the spark plug gap as necessary.

➡Only use hand tools when removing or installing the spark plugs, or damage can occur to the cylinder head or spark plug.

7. Install the 6 spark plugs. Tighten to 133 inch lbs. (15 Nm).

➡**Apply a small amount of dielectric grease to the inside of the ignition coil-on-plug boots before attaching to the spark plugs.**

8. Install the 6 ignition coil-on-plugs and the 6 bolts. Tighten to 62 inch lbs. (7 Nm).

9. Connect the 6 ignition coil-on-plug electrical connectors.
   RH side
10. Install the upper intake manifold.
   LH side
11. Position and connect the crankcase vent tube quick connect coupling to the valve cover fitting.

ENGINE ELECTRICAL

STARTER

REMOVAL & INSTALLATION
See Figures 80 and 81.

❊❊ CAUTION

Always disconnect the battery ground cable at the battery before disconnecting the starter motor battery terminal lead. If a tool is shorted at the starter motor battery terminal, the tool can quickly heat enough to cause a skin burn. Failure to follow this instruction may result in serious personal injury.

1. Disconnect the battery ground cable.
2. Remove the Air Cleaner (ACL).
3. Disconnect the transmission shift cable and adjustment lock from the transmission manual control lever.
4. Disconnect the transmission shift cable rotating slide snap and position aside the transmission cable.
5. Remove the nut and the transmission manual control lever.
6. Remove the starter motor terminal cover.
7. Remove the starter motor solenoid battery cable nut.
8. Remove the starter motor solenoid wire nut.

STARTING SYSTEM

9. Detach the wiring harness retainer from the starter motor stud bolt and position the wiring harness aside.
10. Remove the starter motor bolt, stud bolt and the starter.

To install:
11. To install, reverse the removal procedure. Tighten the starter motor bolt and stud bolt to 20 ft. lbs. (27 Nm).
Tighten the starter motor solenoid wire nut to 44 inch lbs. (5 Nm). Tighten the starter motor solenoid battery cable nut to 106 inch lbs. (12 Nm). Tighten the transmission manual control lever nut to 159 inch lbs. (18 Nm).

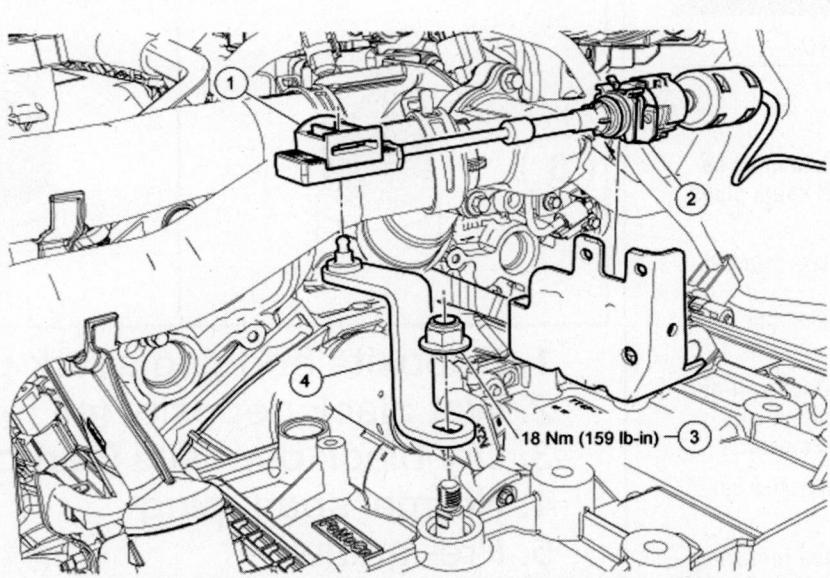

1. Transmission shift cable adjustment lock
2. Transmission shift cable rotating slide snap
3. Transmission manual control lever nut
4. Transmission manual control lever

N0089023

Fig. 80 Removing and installing the starter motor—1 of 2

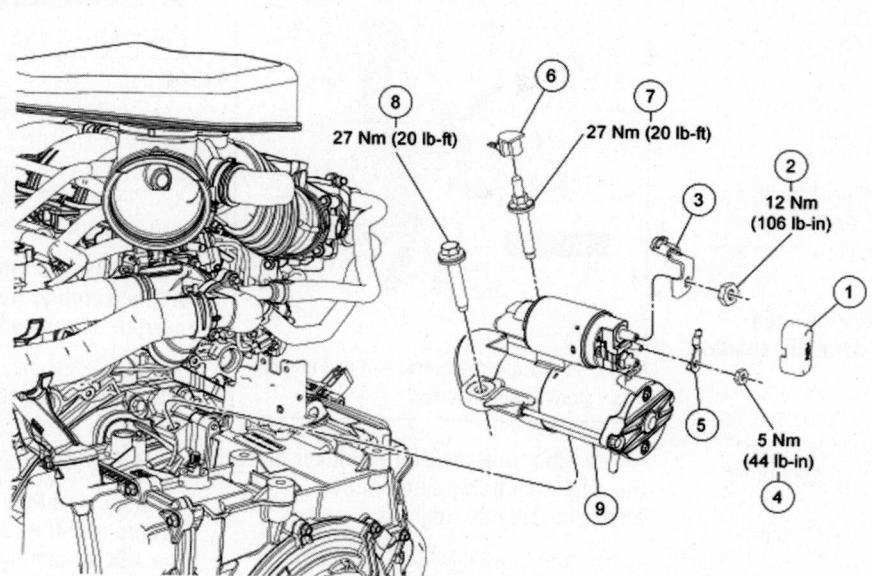

1. Starter motor solenoid battery cable terminal cover
2. Starter motor solenoid battery cable nut
3. Starter motor solenoid battery cable
4. Starter motor solenoid wire nut
5. Starter motor solenoid wire
6. Wire harness retainer
7. Starter motor stud bolt
8. Starter motor bolt
9. Starter motor

N0089024

Fig. 81 Removing and installing the starter motor—2 of 2

ENGINE MECHANICAL

→Disconnecting the negative battery cable may interfere with the functions of the on board computer systems and may require the computer to undergo a relearning process, once the negative battery cable is reconnected.

ACCESSORY DRIVE BELTS

ACCESSORY BELT ROUTING

See Figure 82.

Refer to the accompanying illustration

REMOVAL & INSTALLATION

Accessory Drive Belt

→Under no circumstances should the accessory drive belt, tensioner or pulleys be lubricated as potential damage to the belt material and tensioner damping mechanism will occur. Do not apply any fluids or belt dressing to the accessory drive belt or pulleys.

1. With the vehicle in NEUTRAL, position it on a hoist.
2. Working from the top of the vehicle, rotate the accessory drive belt tensioner

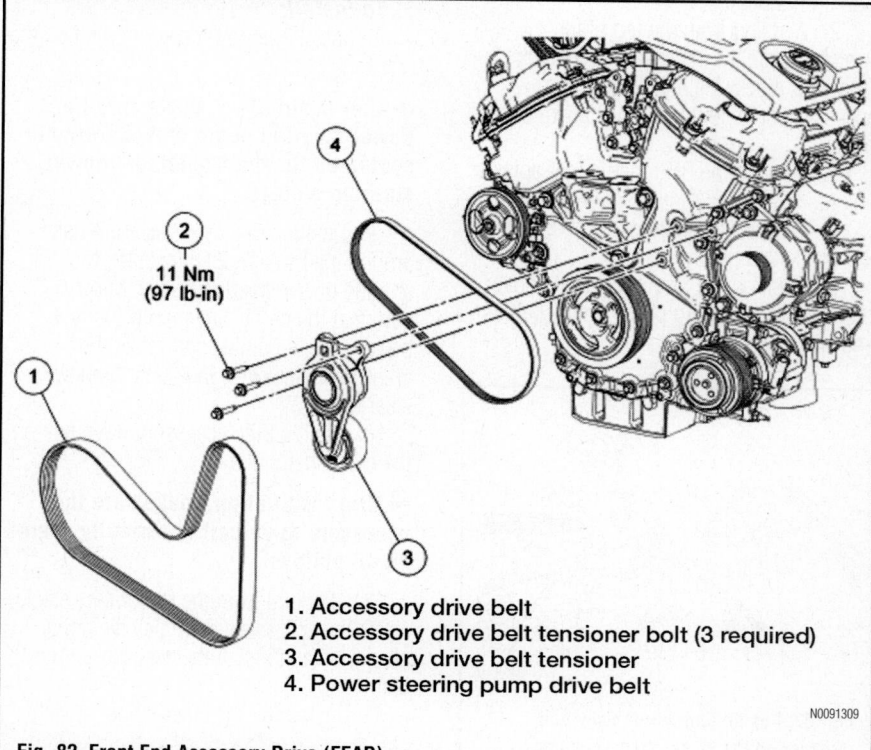

1. Accessory drive belt
2. Accessory drive belt tensioner bolt (3 required)
3. Accessory drive belt tensioner
4. Power steering pump drive belt

N0091309

Fig. 82 Front End Accessory Drive (FEAD)

clockwise and remove the accessory drive belt from the generator pulley.

3. Remove the RH inner fender splash shield.

4. Working from under the vehicle, remove the accessory drive belt.

To install:

5. Working from under the vehicle, position the accessory drive belt on all pulleys, with the exception of the generator pulley.

➡ **After installation, make sure the accessory drive belt is correctly seated on all pulleys.**

6. Working from the top of the vehicle, rotate the accessory drive belt tensioner clockwise and install the accessory drive belt.

7. Install the RH inner fender splash shield.

Power Steering Pump Belt

See Figures 83 and 84.

➡ **Under no circumstances should the accessory drive belt, tensioner or pulleys be lubricated as potential damage to the belt material and tensioner damping mechanism will occur. Do not apply any fluids or belt dressing to the accessory drive belt or pulleys.**

1. With the vehicle in NEUTRAL, position it on a hoist.

2. Working from the top of the vehicle, rotate the accessory drive belt tensioner clockwise and remove the accessory drive belt from the generator pulley.

3. Remove the RH inner fender splash shield.

4. Position the accessory drive belt off the crankshaft pulley.

5. Position the Stretchy Belt Remover on the power steering pump pulley belt as shown.

Fig. 83 Positioning the stretchy belt remover on the power steering pump pulley

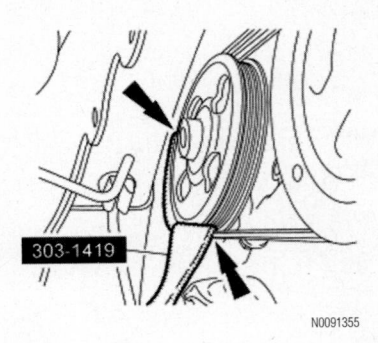

Fig. 84 Turning the crankshaft and feeding the stretchy belt remover

➡ **Feed the Stretchy Belt Remover on to the power steering pump pulley approximately 90 degrees.**

6. Turn the crankshaft clockwise and feed the Stretchy Belt Remover evenly on the power steering pump pulley as shown.

7. Remove the power steering pump belt.

   a. Fold the Stretchy Belt Remover under the inside of the power steering pump belt as shown.

   b. In one quick motion, firmly pull the Stretchy Belt Remover out the RH fender well removing the power steering pump belt.

To install:

8. Install the power steering belt on crankshaft pulley.

➡ **After installation, make sure the power steering pump belt is correctly seated on the crankshaft and power steering pulleys.**

9. Position the power steering belt around the Stretchy Belt Installer Tool and the power steering pulley. Make sure that the belt is engaged with the power steering pulley and rotate the crankshaft clockwise to install the power steering belt.

10. Position the accessory drive belt on the crankshaft pulley.

➡ **After installation, make sure the accessory drive belt is correctly seated on all pulleys.**

11. Working from the top of the vehicle, rotate the accessory drive belt tensioner clockwise and install the accessory drive belt.

12. Install the RH inner fender splash shield.

REMOVAL & INSTALLATION

See Figure 85.

1. Disconnect the Mass Air Flow (MAF) sensor electrical connector.

2. Loosen the clamp and disconnect the Air Cleaner (ACL) outlet pipe from the ACL.

3. Remove the ACL bolt.

➡ **No tools are needed to remove the ACL assembly. Removal should be carried out using hands only.**

4. Separate the 2 ACL feet from the rubber grommets and remove the ACL assembly.

To install:

➡ **Make sure that the 2 ACL feet are seated into the rubber grommets under the ACL assembly.**

➡ **The ACL outlet pipe should be securely sealed to prevent unmetered air from entering the engine.**

5. To install, reverse the removal procedure.

6. For 2010 models tighten the ACL bolt to 80 inch lbs. (9 Nm)

7. For 2011 models tighten the ACL bolts to 44 inch lbs. (5 Nm) (9 Nm).

8. Tighten the ACL outlet pipe to 44 inch lbs. (5 Nm).

REMOVAL & INSTALLATION

2010 Models

See Figures 86 through 112.

✳✳ WARNING

Do not smoke, carry lighted tobacco or have an open flame of any type when working on or near any fuel-related component. Highly flammable mixtures are always present and may be ignited. Failure to follow these instructions may result in serious personal injury.

➡ **During engine repair procedures, cleanliness is extremely important. Any foreign material, including any material created while cleaning gasket surfaces that enters the oil passages, coolant passages or the oil pan, can cause engine failure.**

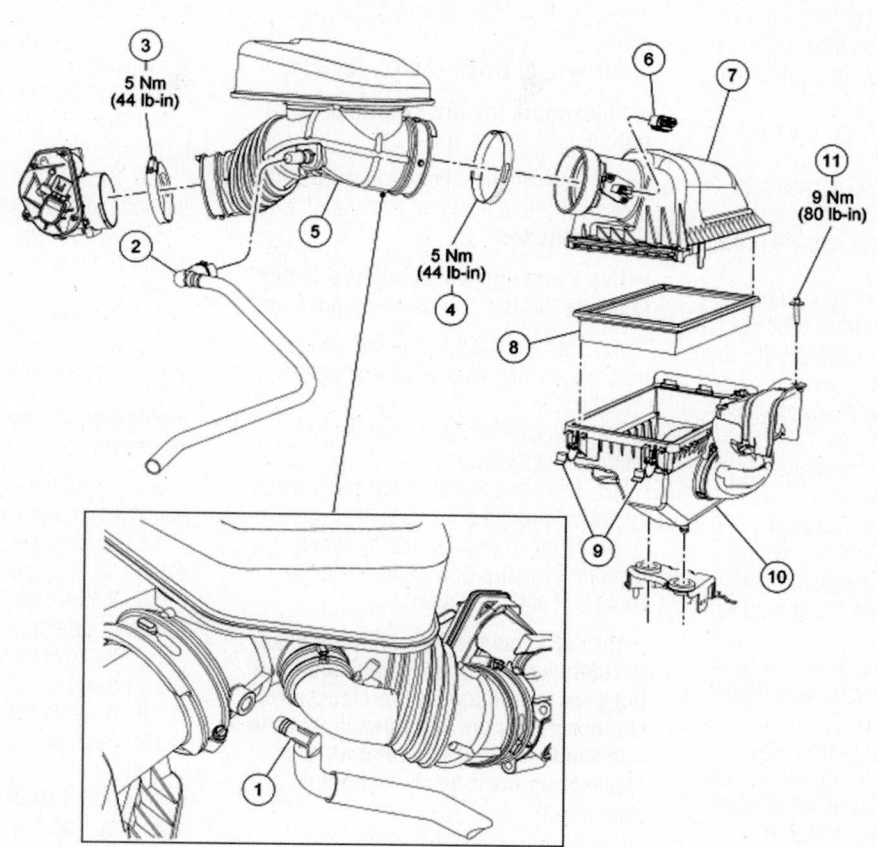

1. Vacuum tube
2. Crankcase vent tube
3. Air Cleaner (ACL) outlet pipe-to-Throttle Body (TB) clamp
4. ACL outlet pipe-to- ACL cover clamp
5. ACL outlet pipe
6. Mass Air Flow (MAF) sensor electrical connector
7. ACL cover
8. ACL element
9. ACL tray assembly-to- ACL cover clamps
10. ACL tray assembly
11. ACL bolt

N0060552

Fig. 85 Intake air system components

➡**Early build engines have 11 fastener valve covers; late build engines have 9 fastener valve covers. Do not attempt to install bolts in the 2 empty late build valve cover holes or damage to the valve cover will occur.**

➡**On early build engines, the timing chain rides on the inner side of the RH timing chain guide. Late build engines are equipped with a different design RH timing chain guide that requires the timing chain to ride on the outer side of the RH timing chain guide. For service, all replacement RH timing chain guides will be the late build design.**

All vehicles

1. With the vehicle in NEUTRAL, position it on a hoist.
2. Recover the A/C system.
3. Release the fuel system pressure.
4. Drain the engine cooling system.
5. Remove the accessory drive belt and the power steering belt.
6. Remove the LH halfshaft and intermediate shaft.
7. Disconnect the power steering cooler hose and drain the power steering fluid into a suitable drain pan.
8. Remove the degas bottle.
9. Remove the engine Air Cleaner (ACL) and ACL outlet pipe.
10. Remove the battery tray.
11. Disconnect the battery harness electrical connector.
12. Remove the nut and disconnect the power feed from the battery terminal.
13. Remove the bolt and the ground wire.

a. Detach the 2 wiring harness retainers from the cowl.
14. Disconnect the vacuum hose from the upper intake manifold.
15. Disconnect the Evaporative Emission (EVAP) tube quick connect coupling from the purge valve.
16. Disconnect the upper radiator hose, lower radiator hose and 2 heater hoses from the thermostat housing.
17. Detach the wiring harness retainer from the transaxle control cable bracket.
18. Disconnect the transaxle control cable from the control lever.

a. Detach the control cable from the bracket.
19. Disconnect the transaxle control electrical connector.

20. If equipped, detach the engine block heater harness retainers from the radiator support and the A/C suction tube.

21. Remove the nut and disconnect the A/C pressure tube fitting.

22. Remove the safety clip from the A/C fitting.

a. Disconnect the A/C suction tube fitting.

23. Disconnect the hose from the power steering reservoir.

24. Disconnect the fuel supply tube.

25. Disconnect the fuel hose routing clip from the transaxle stud and position the fuel hose aside.

26. Disconnect the 2 engine wiring harness electrical connectors.

a. Detach the electrical connector from the LH valve cover.

27. Remove the oil level indicator.

28. Detach the wiring harness retainer from the RH valve cover stud bolt.

29. Remove the bolt and the ground wire from the engine front cover.

30. Remove the nut, the ground wire and the radio interference capacitor wire from the engine front cover stud.

31. Loosen the exhaust flexible pipe clamp and disconnect the 2 exhaust hangers.

32. Remove the 4 nuts and the exhaust flexible pipe and Y-pipe as an assembly.

a. Discard the nuts and the gasket.

33. Remove the 3 pin-type retainers, the 7 screws and the radiator splash shield.

34. Remove the LH inner splash shield.

35. Remove the 2 secondary latches from the transmission fluid cooler tubes.

36. Using the Transmission Cooler Line Disconnect Tool, disconnect the transmission cooling tubes.

37. Remove the drain plug and drain the engine oil.

a. Install the drain plug and tighten to 20 ft. lbs. (27 Nm).

38. Remove and discard the engine oil filter.

39. Remove the power steering cooler bracket bolt from the RH side of the subframe.

All-Wheel Drive (AWD) vehicles

➡**Index-mark the driveshaft for installation.**

40. Remove the 4 bolts and support the driveshaft with a length of mechanic's wire.

All vehicles

➡**Use a steering wheel holding device (such as Hunter® 28-75-1 or equivalent).**

41. Using a suitable holding device, hold the steering wheel in the straight-ahead position.

42. Remove the 2 nuts and the roll restrictor heat shield.

43. Remove the engine roll restrictor-to-subframe through bolt.

44. Remove and discard the Power Steering Pressure (PSP) tube-to-pump banjo bolt and the 2 seals.

➡**Do not allow the intermediate shaft to rotate while it is disconnected from the gear or damage to the clockspring can occur. If there is evidence that the intermediate shaft has rotated, the clockspring must be removed and recentered.**

45. Remove and discard the steering intermediate shaft bolt.

a. Separate the steering intermediate shaft from the steering gear.

46. Remove and discard the cotter pins and tie-rod end nuts.

a. Using the Tie-Rod End Remover,

separate the tie-rod ends from the wheel knuckles.

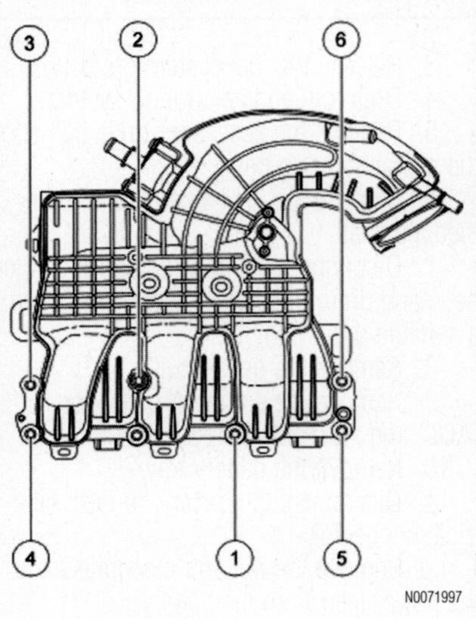

47. Remove the 3 RH subframe-to-lower bumper nuts.

48. Remove the 3 LH subframe-to-lower bumper nuts and separate the lower bumper from the subframe.

49. Position the Powertrain Lift under the subframe assembly.

50. Remove the 2 nuts, 4 bolts and the subframe support brackets.

51. Remove the 2 front subframe nuts.

52. Remove the 2 middle subframe nuts.

53. Using the Powertrain Lift, lower the subframe assembly from the vehicle.

➡**Position a block of wood under the transaxle.**

54. Install the Powertrain Lift and Universal Adapter Brackets.

55. Remove the transaxle support insulator through bolt and nut.

56. Remove the 3 nuts, the bolt and the transaxle support insulator bracket.

57. Remove the nut, bolt and engine mount brace.

58. Remove the 4 engine mount nuts.

59. Remove the 3 bolts and the engine mount.

60. Lower the engine and transaxle assembly from the vehicle.

61. If equipped, detach the engine block heater wiring harness retainers and position the harness aside.

62. Disconnect the PCV hose from the PCV valve.

63. Disconnect the Throttle Body (TB) electrical connector.

64. Detach the wiring harness retainers from the upper intake manifold.

65. Remove the upper intake manifold support bracket bolt.

➡**If the engine is repaired or replaced because of upper engine failure, typically including valve or piston damage, check the intake manifold for metal debris. If metal debris is found, install a new intake manifold. Failure to follow these instructions can result in engine damage.**

66. Remove the 6 bolts and the upper intake manifold in the following sequence.

a. Discard the gaskets.

67. Disconnect the RH Catalyst Monitor Sensor (CMS) electrical connector.

68. Disconnect the PSP switch electrical connector.

69. Disconnect the RH Variable Camshaft Timing (VCT) solenoid electrical connector.

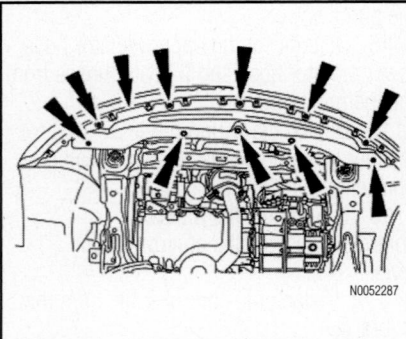

Fig. 86 Locating the pin type retainers and screws

N0052287

N0071997

Fig. 87 Identifying the upper intake manifold bolt removal sequence

70. Disconnect the 3 RH coil-on-plug electrical connectors.

71. Detach all of the wiring harness retainers from the RH valve cover and stud bolts.

72. Disconnect the LH VCT solenoid electrical connector.

73. Disconnect the 3 LH coil-on-plug electrical connectors.

74. Detach all of the wiring harness retainers from the LH valve cover and stud bolts.

75. Remove the 6 bolts and the 6 coil-on-plugs.

Early build vehicles

76. Loosen the 11 stud bolts and remove the LH valve cover.

   a. Discard the gasket.

77. Loosen the bolt, the 10 stud bolts and remove the RH valve cover.

   a. Discard the gasket.

Late build vehicles

78. Loosen the 9 stud bolts and remove the LH valve cover.

   a. Discard the gasket.

   b. Loosen the 9 stud bolts and remove the RH valve cover.

   c. Discard the gasket.

All vehicles

➡**VCT solenoid seal removal shown, spark plug tube seal removal similar.**

79. Inspect the VCT solenoid seals and the spark plug tube seals. Install new seals if damaged.

   a. Using the VCT Spark Plug Tube Seal Remover and Handle, remove the seal(s).

80. Remove the 3 bolts and the power steering pump.

81. Remove the 3 bolts and the accessory drive belt tensioner.

82. Using the Strap Wrench, remove the crankshaft pulley bolt and washer.

   a. Discard the bolt.

83. Using the 3 Jaw Puller, remove the crankshaft pulley.

84. Using the Oil Seal Remover, remove and discard the crankshaft front seal.

85. Remove the 2 bolts and the engine mount bracket.

➡**Only use hand tools to remove the studs.**

86. Remove the 2 engine mount studs.

87. Remove the 3 bolts and the engine mount bracket.

88. Remove the 22 engine front cover bolts.

89. Install 6 of the engine front cover bolts (finger-tight) into the 6 threaded holes in the engine front cover.

   a. Tighten the bolts one turn at a time in a crisscross pattern until the engine front cover-to-cylinder block seal is released.

   b. Remove the engine front cover.

➡**Only use a 3M(tm) Roloc® Bristle Disk (2-in white, part number 07528) to clean the engine front cover. Do not use metal scrapers, wire brushes or any other power abrasive disk to clean the engine front cover. These tools cause scratches and gouges that make leak paths.**

90. Clean the engine front cover using a 3M(tm) Roloc® Bristle Disk (2-in white) in a suitable tool turning at the recommended speed of 15,000 rpm.

   a. Thoroughly wash the engine front cover to remove any foreign material, including any abrasive particles created during the cleaning process.

➡**Place clean, lint-free shop towels over exposed engine cavities. Carefully remove the towels so foreign material is not dropped into the engine. Any foreign material (including any material created while cleaning gasket surfaces) that enters the oil passages or the oil pan, may cause engine failure.**

➡**Do not use wire brushes, power abrasive discs or 3M(tm) Roloc® Bristle Disk (2-in white) to clean the sealing surfaces. These tools cause scratches and gouges that make leak paths. They also cause contamination that will cause premature engine failure. Remove all traces of the gasket.**

91. Clean the sealing surfaces of the cylinder block in the following sequence.

   a. Remove any large deposits of silicone or gasket material.

   b. Apply silicone gasket remover and allow to set for several minutes.

   c. Remove the silicone gasket remover. A second application of silicone gasket remover may be required if residual traces of silicone or gasket material remain.

   d. Apply metal surface prep to remove any remaining traces of oil or coolant and to prepare the surfaces to bond. Do not attempt to make the metal shiny. Some staining of the metal surfaces is normal.

   e. Make sure the 2 locating dowel pins are seated correctly in the cylinder block.

Engines equipped with early build RH timing chain guides

92. Rotate the crankshaft clockwise and align the timing marks on the Variable Camshaft Timing (VCT) assemblies as shown.

Engines equipped with late build/replacement RH timing chain guides

93. Rotate the crankshaft clockwise and align the timing marks on the VCT assemblies as shown.

All vehicles

➡**The Camshaft Holding Tool will hold the camshafts in the Top Dead Center (TDC) position.**

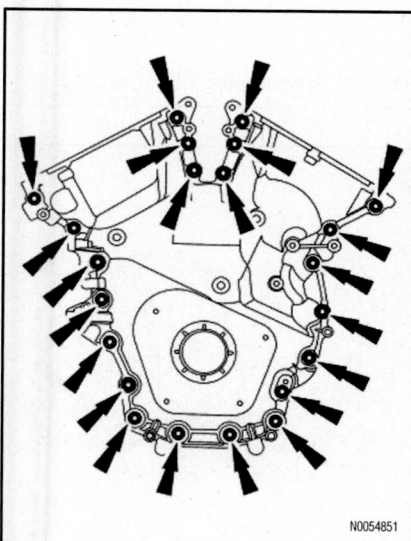

Fig. 88 Locating the 22 engine front cover bolts

N0054851

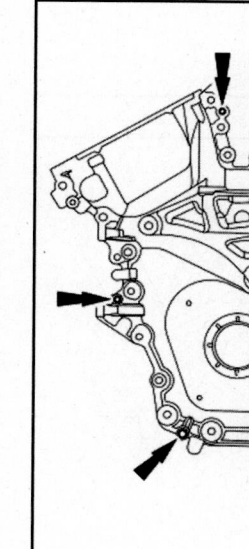

Fig. 89 Installing the 6 front cover bolts

N0082530

94. Install the Camshaft Holding Tool onto the flats of the LH camshafts.

➡**The Camshaft Holding Tool will hold the camshafts in the TDC position.**

95. Install the Camshaft Holding Tool onto the flats of the RH camshafts.

96. Remove the 3 bolts and the RH VCT housing.

97. Remove the 3 bolts and the LH VCT housing.

98. Remove the 2 bolts and the primary timing chain tensioner.

99. Remove the primary timing chain tensioner arm.

100. Remove the 2 bolts and the lower LH primary timing chain guide.

101. Remove the primary timing chain.

LH camshafts

102. Compress the LH secondary timing chain tensioner and install a suitable lock-pin to retain the tensioner in the collapsed position.

➡**The VCT bolt and the exhaust camshaft bolt must be discarded and new ones installed. However, the exhaust camshaft washer is reusable.**

103. Remove and discard the LH VCT assembly bolt and the LH exhaust camshaft sprocket bolt.

    a. Remove the LH VCT assembly, secondary timing chain and the LH exhaust camshaft sprocket as an assembly.

➡**When the Camshaft Holding Tool is removed, valve spring pressure will rotate the LH camshafts approximately 3 degrees to a neutral position.**

104. Remove the Camshaft Holding Tool from the LH camshafts.

➡**The camshafts must remain in the neutral position during removal or engine damage may occur.**

105. Verify the LH camshafts are in the neutral position.

➡**Cylinder head camshaft bearing caps are numbered to verify that they are assembled in their original positions.**

106. Remove the bolts and the LH camshaft bearing caps.

    a. Remove the LH camshafts.

RH camshafts

107. Compress the RH secondary timing chain tensioner and install a suitable lock-pin to retain the tensioner in the collapsed position.

➡**The VCT bolt and the exhaust camshaft bolt must be discarded and new ones installed. However, the exhaust camshaft washer is reusable.**

108. Remove and discard the RH VCT assembly bolt and the RH exhaust camshaft sprocket bolt.

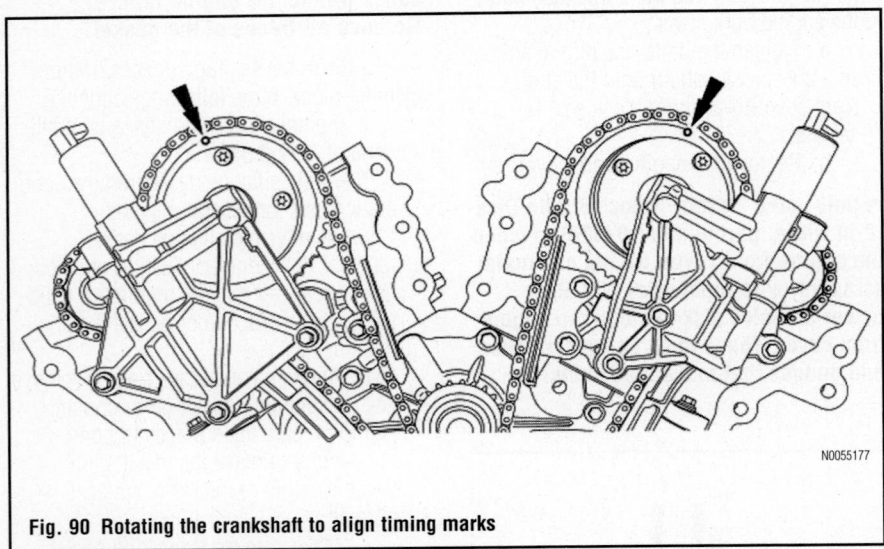

Fig. 90 Rotating the crankshaft to align timing marks

Fig. 92 Removing the RH VCT housing

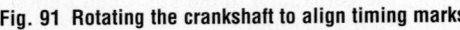

Fig. 91 Rotating the crankshaft to align timing marks

Fig. 93 Removing the LH VCT housing

a. Remove the RH VCT assembly, secondary timing chain and the RH exhaust camshaft sprocket as an assembly.

109. Remove the Camshaft Holding Tool from the RH camshafts.

➡The camshafts must remain in the neutral position during removal or engine damage may occur.

110. Rotate the RH camshafts counter-clockwise to the neutral position.

➡Cylinder head camshaft bearing caps are numbered to verify that they are assembled in their original positions.

111. Remove the bolts and the RH camshaft bearing caps.

a. Remove the RH camshafts.

To install:

❋❋ WARNING

Do not smoke, carry lighted tobacco or have an open flame of any type when working on or near any fuel-related component. Highly flammable mixtures are always present and

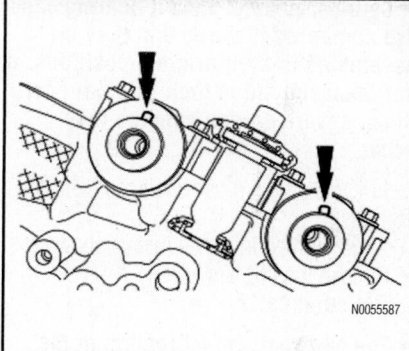

Fig. 96 Verifying the LH camshaft positioning

may be ignited. Failure to follow these instructions may result in serious personal injury.

➡During engine repair procedures, cleanliness is extremely important. Any foreign material, including any material created while cleaning gasket surfaces that enters the oil passages, coolant passages or the oil pan, can cause engine failure.

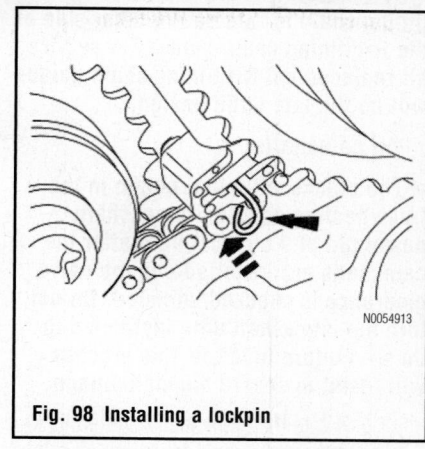

Fig. 98 Installing a lockpin

➡Early build engines have 11 fastener valve covers, late build engines have 9 fastener valve covers. Do not attempt to install bolts in the 2 empty late build valve cover holes or damage to the valve cover will occur.

➡On early build engines, the timing chain rides on the inner side of the RH timing chain guide. Late build engines are equipped with a different design RH timing chain guide that requires the

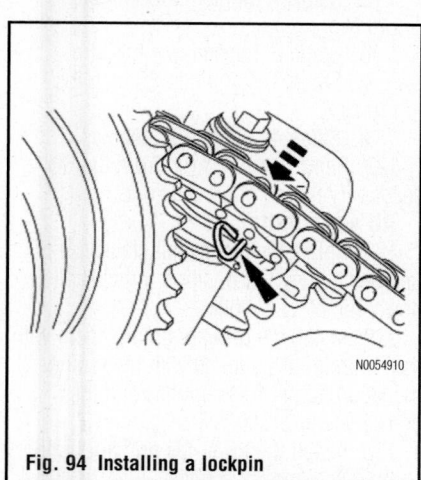

Fig. 94 Installing a lockpin

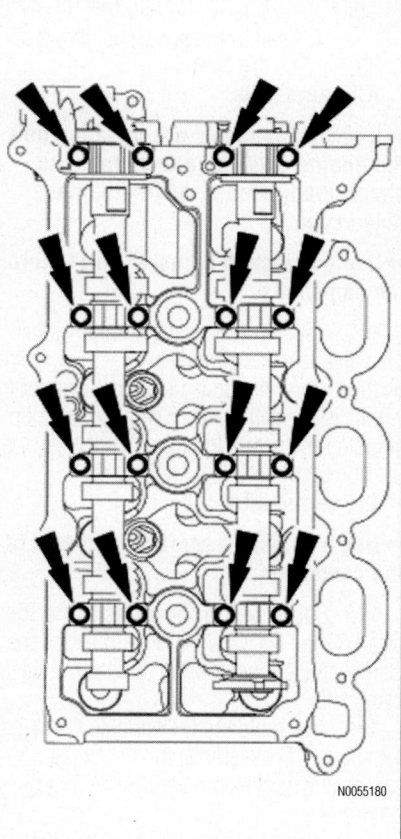

Fig. 97 Removing the LH camshafts

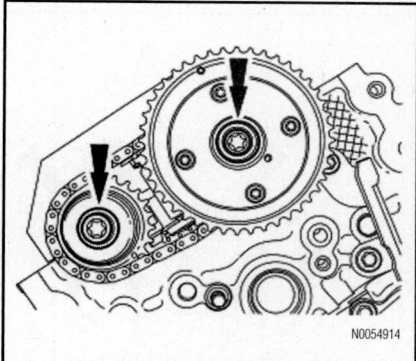

Fig. 99 Removing the RH VCT assembly, secondary timing chain and the RH exhaust camshaft sprocket as an assembly

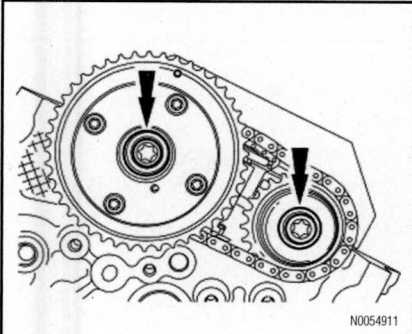

Fig. 95 Removing the LH VCT assembly, secondary timing chain and the LH exhaust camshaft sprocket as an assembly

Fig. 100 Rotating the RH camshafts

timing chain to ride on the outer side of the RH timing chain guide. For service, all replacement RH timing chain guides will be the late build design.

All camshafts

➡The crankshaft must remain in the freewheeling position (crankshaft dowel pin at 9 o'clock) until after the camshafts are installed and the valve clearance is checked/adjusted. Do not turn the crankshaft until instructed to do so. Failure to follow this process will result in severe engine damage.

112. Rotate the crankshaft counterclockwise until the crankshaft dowel pin is in the 9 o'clock position.

LH camshafts

➡The camshafts must remain in the neutral position during installation or engine damage may occur.

➡Coat the camshafts with clean engine oil prior to installation.

113. Position the camshafts onto the LH cylinder head in the neutral position as shown.

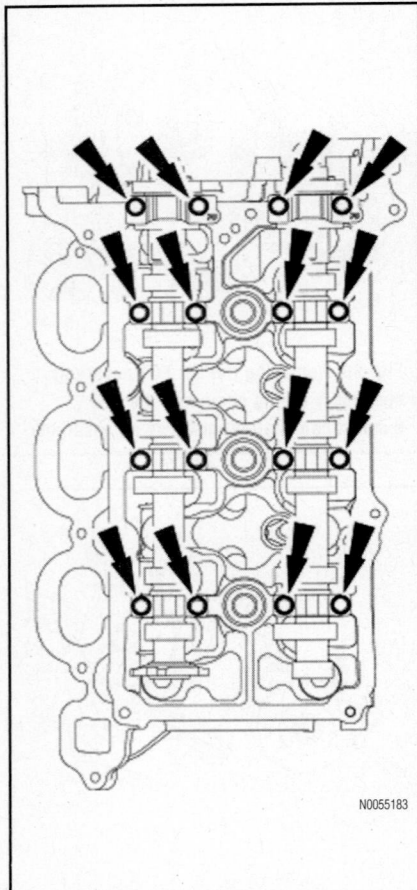

Fig. 101 Removing the RH camshafts

➡Cylinder head camshaft bearing caps are numbered to verify that they are assembled in their original positions. If not reassembled in their original positions, severe engine damage may occur.

114. Install the 8 camshaft caps and the 16 bolts.
   a. Tighten in the sequence shown to 89 inch lbs (10 Nm).

RH camshafts

➡The camshafts must remain in the neutral position during installation or engine damage may occur.

➡Coat the camshafts with clean engine oil prior to installation.

115. Position the camshafts onto the RH cylinder head in the neutral position as shown.

➡Cylinder head camshaft bearing caps are numbered to verify that they are assembled in their original positions. If not reassembled in their original positions, severe engine damage may occur.

116. Install the 8 camshaft caps and the 16 bolts.
   a. Tighten in the sequence shown to 89 inch lbs (10 Nm).

All camshafts

➡If any components are installed new, the engine valve clearance must be checked/adjusted or engine damage may occur.

➡Use a camshaft sprocket bolt to turn the camshafts.

117. Using a feeler gauge, confirm that the valve tappet clearances are within specification. If valve tappet clearances are not within specification, the clearance must be adjusted by installing new valve tappet(s) of the correct size.

LH camshafts

➡Use a camshaft sprocket bolt to turn the camshafts.

118. Rotate the LH camshafts to the Top Dead Center (TDC) position and install the Camshaft Holding Tool on the flats of the camshafts.

119. Assemble the LH Variable Camshaft Timing (VCT) assembly, the LH exhaust camshaft sprocket and the LH secondary timing chain.
   a. Align the colored links with the timing marks.

120. Position the LH secondary timing assembly onto the camshafts.

121. Install 2 new bolts and the original washer. Tighten in 4 stages.
   a. Stage 1: Tighten to 30 ft. lbs. (40 Nm).
   b. Stage 2: Loosen one full turn.
   c. Stage 3: Tighten to 89 inch lbs (10 Nm)
   d. Stage 4: Tighten 90 degrees.

122. Remove the lockpin from the LH secondary timing chain tensioner.

RH camshafts

➡Use a camshaft sprocket bolt to turn the camshafts.

123. Rotate the RH camshafts to the TDC position and install the Camshaft Holding Tool on the flats of the camshafts.

124. Assemble the RH VCT assembly, the RH exhaust camshaft sprocket and the RH secondary timing chain.
   a. Align the colored links with the timing marks.

125. Position the RH secondary timing assembly onto the camshafts.

126. Install 2 new bolts and the original washer. Tighten in 4 stages.
   a. Stage 1: Tighten to 30 ft. lbs. (40 Nm).
   b. Stage 2: Loosen one full turn.
   c. Stage 3: Tighten to 89 inch lbs (10 Nm).
   d. Stage 4: Tighten 90 degrees.

127. Remove the lockpin from the RH secondary timing chain tensioner.

All camshafts

128. Rotate the crankshaft clockwise 60 degrees to the TDC position (crankshaft dowel pin at 11 o'clock).

129. Install the primary timing chain with the colored links aligned with the timing marks on the VCT assemblies and the crankshaft sprocket.

130. Install the lower LH primary timing chain guide and the 2 bolts.
   a. Tighten to 89 inch lbs (10 Nm).

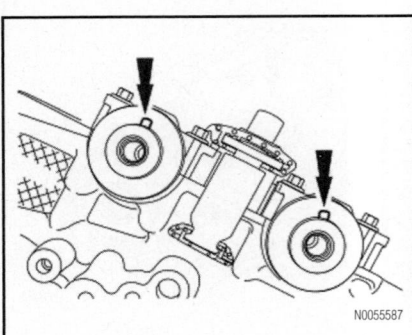

Fig. 102 Positioning the camshafts onto the LH cylinder head

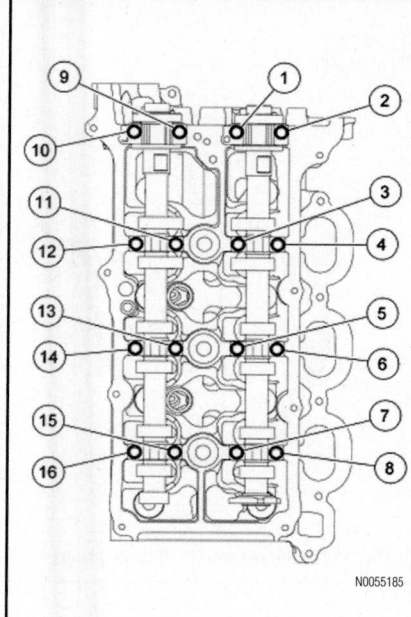

Fig. 103 Identifying the LH camshaft cap installation sequence

131. Install the primary timing chain tensioner arm.
132. Reset the primary timing chain tensioner.
   a. Rotate the lever counterclockwise.
   b. Using a soft-jawed vise, compress the plunger.
   c. Align the hole in the lever with the hole in the tensioner housing.
   d. Install a suitable lockpin.

➡It may be necessary to rotate the crankshaft slightly to remove slack from the timing chain and install the tensioner.

133. Install the primary tensioner and the 2 bolts.
   a. Tighten to 89 inch lbs. (10 Nm).
   b. Remove the lockpin.
134. As a post-check, verify correct alignment of all timing marks.
135. Inspect the VCT housing seals for damage and replace as necessary.

➡Make sure the dowels on the Variable Camshaft Timing (VCT) housing are fully engaged in the cylinder head prior to tightening the bolts. Failure to follow this process will result in severe engine damage.

136. Install the LH VCT housing and the 3 bolts.
   a. Tighten in the sequence shown to 89 inch lbs (10 Nm).

➡Make sure the dowels on the Variable Camshaft Timing (VCT) housing are fully engaged in the cylinder head prior to tightening the bolts. Failure to follow this process will result in severe engine damage.

137. Install the RH VCT housing and the 3 bolts.
   a. Tighten in the sequence shown to 89 inch lbs. (10 Nm).
138. Install the Alignment Pins.

➡Failure to use Motorcraft® High Performance Engine RTV Silicone may cause the engine oil to foam excessively and result in serious engine damage.

➡The engine front cover and bolts 17, 18, 19 and 20 must be installed within 4 minutes of the initial sealant application. The remainder of the engine front

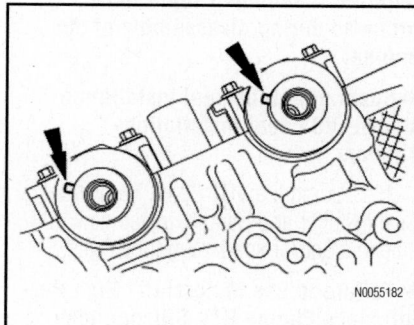

Fig. 104 Positioning the camshaft onto the RH cylinder head

cover bolts and the engine mount bracket bolts must be installed and tightened within 35 minutes of the initial sealant application. If the time limits are exceeded, the sealant must be removed, the sealing area cleaned and sealant reapplied. To clean the sealing area, use silicone gasket remover and metal surface prep. Follow the directions on the packaging. Failure to follow this procedure can cause future oil leakage.

139. Apply a 0.11 inch (3.0 mm) bead of Motorcraft® High Performance Engine RTV Silicone to the engine front cover sealing surfaces including the 3 engine mount bracket bosses.
   a. Apply a 0.21 inch (5.5 mm) bead of Motorcraft® High Performance Engine RTV Silicone to the oil pan-to-cylinder block joint and the cylinder head-to-cylinder block joint areas of the

engine front cover in 5 places as indicated.

➡Make sure the 2 locating dowel pins are seated correctly in the cylinder block.

140. Install the engine front cover and bolts 17, 18, 19 and 20.
   a. Tighten in sequence to 27 inch lbs. (3 Nm).
141. Remove the Alignment Pins.

➡Do not tighten the bolts at this time.

142. Install the engine mount bracket and the 3 bolts.

➡Do not expose the Motorcraft® High Performance Engine RTV Silicone to engine oil for at least 90 minutes after installing the engine front cover. Failure to follow this instruction may cause oil leakage.

143. Install the remaining engine front cover bolts. Tighten all of the engine front cover bolts and engine mount bracket bolts in the sequence shown in 2 stages:
   a. Stage 1: Tighten bolts 1 thru 22 to 89 inch lbs. (10 Nm) and bolts 23, 24 and 25 to 133 inch lbs. (15 Nm).
   b. Stage 2: Tighten bolts 1 thru 22 to 18 lb-ft (24 Nm) and bolts 23, 24 and 25 to 55 ft. lbs. (75 Nm).

➡The thread sealer on the engine mount studs (including new engine mount studs if applicable) must be

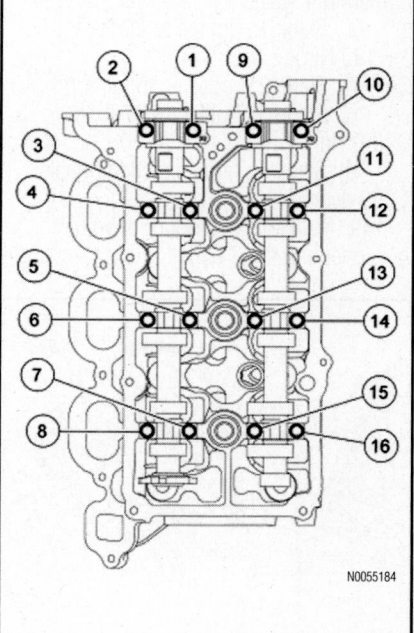

Fig. 105 Identifying the RH camshaft cap bolt tightening sequence

cleaned off with a wire brush and new Threadlock and Sealer applied prior to installing the engine mount studs. Failure to follow this procedure may result in damage to the engine mount studs or engine.

144. Install the engine mount studs in the following sequence.

a. Clean the front cover engine mount stud holes with pressurized air to remove any foreign material.

b. Clean all the thread sealer from the engine mount studs (old and new studs).

c. Apply new Threadlock and Sealer to the engine mount stud threads.

d. Install the 2 engine mount studs. Tighten to 177 inch lbs. (20 Nm).

145. Install the engine mount bracket and the 2 bolts.

a. Tighten to 22 ft. lbs. (30 Nm).

➡ Apply clean engine oil to the crankshaft front seal bore in the engine front cover.

146. Using the Crankshaft Vibration Damper Installer and Front Crankshaft Seal Installer, install a new crankshaft front seal.

➡ Lubricate the outside diameter sealing surfaces with clean engine oil.

147. Using the Crankshaft Vibration Damper Installer and Front Cover Oil Seal Installer, install the crankshaft pulley.

148. Using the Strap Wrench, install the crankshaft pulley washer and new bolt and tighten in 4 stages.

a. Stage 1: Tighten to 89 ft. lbs. (120 Nm).

b. Stage 2: Loosen one full turn.

c. Stage 3: Tighten to 37 ft. lbs. (50 Nm).

d. Stage 4: Tighten an additional 90 degrees.

149. Install the accessory drive belt tensioner and the 3 bolts.

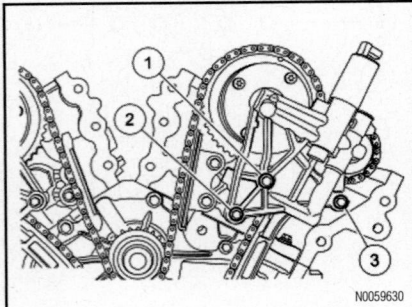

Fig. 106 Identifying the LH VCT bolt tightening sequence

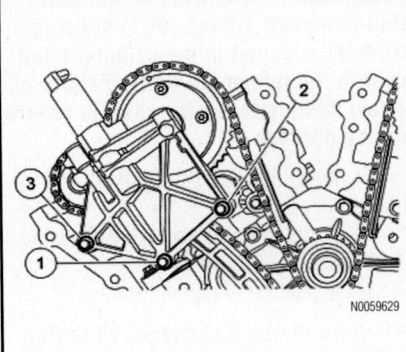

Fig. 107 Identifying the RH VCT bolt tightening sequence

a. Tighten to 97 inch lbs (11 Nm).

150. Install the power steering pump and the 3 bolts.

a. Tighten to 18 ft. lbs. (24 Nm).

➡ Installation of new seals is only required if damaged seals were removed during disassembly of the engine.

➡ Spark plug tube seal installation shown, VCT seal installation similar.

151. Using the VCT Spark Plug Tube Seal Installer and Handle, install new VCT solenoid and/or spark plug tube seals.

➡ Failure to use Motorcraft® High Performance Engine RTV Silicone may cause the engine oil to foam excessively and result in serious engine damage.

➡ If the valve cover is not installed and the fasteners tightened within 4 minutes, the sealant must be removed and the sealing area cleaned. To clean the sealing area, use silicone gasket remover and metal surface prep. Follow the directions on the packaging. Failure to follow this procedure can cause future oil leakage.

152. Apply a 0.31 inch (8 mm) bead of Motorcraft® High Performance Engine RTV Silicone to the engine front cover-to-RH cylinder head joints.

Early build vehicles

153. Using a new gasket, install the RH valve cover and tighten the bolt and 10 stud bolts.

a. Tighten in the sequence shown in the Valve Cover procedure to 89 inch lbs. (10 Nm).

Late build vehicles

154. Using a new gasket, install the RH valve cover and tighten the 9 stud bolts.

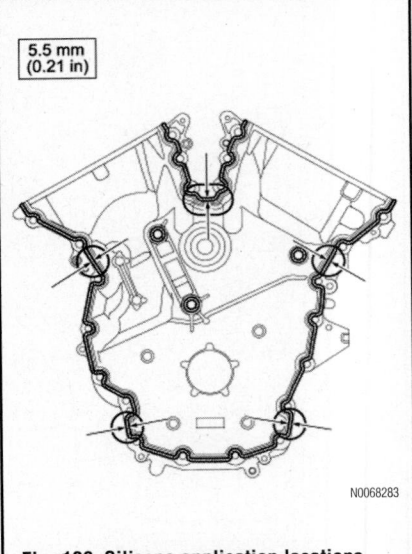

Fig. 108 Silicone application locations

a. Tighten in the sequence shown in the Valve Cover procedure to 89 inch lbs. (10 Nm).

All vehicles

➡ Failure to use Motorcraft® High Performance Engine RTV Silicone may cause the engine oil to foam excessively and result in serious engine damage.

➡ If the valve cover is not installed and the fasteners tightened within 4 minutes, the sealant must be removed and the sealing area cleaned. To clean the sealing area, use silicone gasket remover and metal surface prep. Follow the directions on the packaging.

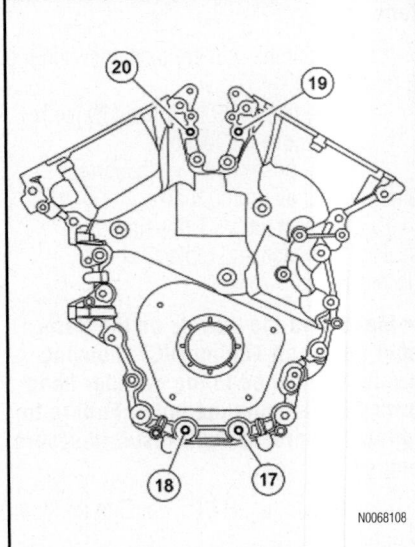

Fig. 109 Installing the engine front cover bolts 17, 18, 19 and 20

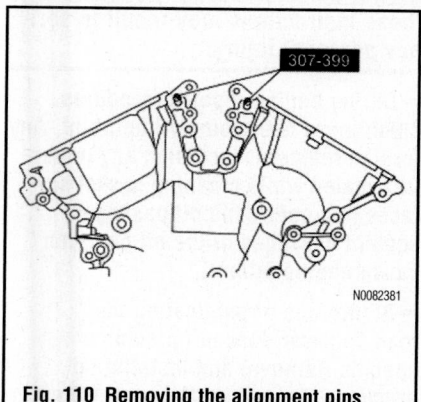

Fig. 110 Removing the alignment pins

Failure to follow this procedure can cause future oil leakage.

155. Apply a 0.31 inch (8 mm) bead of Motorcraft® High Performance Engine RTV Silicone to the engine front cover-to-LH cylinder head joints.

Early build vehicles
156. Using a new gasket, install the LH valve cover and tighten the 11 stud bolts.
    a. Tighten in the sequence shown in the Valve Cover procedure to 89 inch lbs. (10 Nm).
Late build vehicles
157. Using a new gasket, install the LH valve cover and tighten the 9 stud bolts.
    a. Tighten in the sequence shown in the Valve Cover procedure to 89 inch lbs. (10 Nm).

All vehicles
158. Install the 6 coil-on-plug assemblies and the 6 bolts.
    a. Tighten to 62 inch lbs. (7 Nm).
159. Attach all of the wiring harness retainers to the LH valve cover and stud bolts.
160. Connect the 3 LH coil-on-plug electrical connectors.
161. Connect the LH camshaft VCT solenoid electrical connector.
162. Attach all of the wiring harness retainers to the RH valve cover and stud bolts.
163. Connect the 3 RH coil-on-plug electrical connectors.
164. Connect the RH VCT solenoid electrical connector.
165. Connect the Power Steering Pressure (PSP) switch electrical connector.
166. Connect the RH Catalyst Monitor Sensor (CMS) sensor electrical connector.

➡ **If the engine is repaired or replaced because of upper engine failure, typically including valve or piston damage, check the intake manifold for metal**

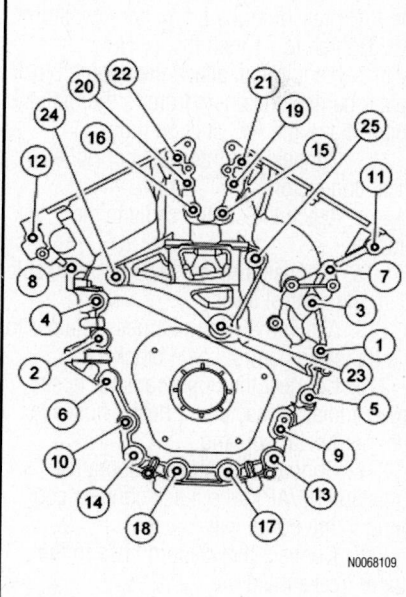

Fig. 111 Installing the remaining front cover bolts

debris. If metal debris is found, install a new intake manifold. Failure to follow these instructions can result in engine damage.

167. Using new gaskets, install the upper intake manifold and the 6 bolts.
    a. Tighten in the sequence shown to 89 inch lbs. (10 Nm).
168. Install the upper intake manifold support bracket bolt.
    a. Tighten to 89 inch lbs. (10 Nm).
169. Attach the wiring harness retainers to the upper intake manifold.
170. Connect the Throttle Body (TB) electrical connector.
171. Connect the PCV hose to the PCV valve.
172. If equipped, attach the engine block heater wiring harness retainers.
173. Raise the engine and transaxle assembly into the vehicle.
174. Install the engine mount and the 3 bolts. Tighten to 66 ft. lbs. (90 Nm).
175. Install the 4 engine mount nuts. Tighten to 46 ft. lbs. (63 Nm).
176. Install the engine mount brace, the nut and the bolt. Tighten to 177 inch lbs. (20 Nm).
177. Install the transaxle support insulator bracket, the 3 nuts and the bolt.
    a. Tighten the 3 nuts to 46 ft. lbs. (63 Nm).
    b. Tighten the bolt to 59 ft. lbs. (80 Nm).

178. Install the transaxle support insulator through bolt and nut. Tighten to 129 ft. lbs. (175 Nm).
179. Using the Powertrain Lift, raise the subframe into the installed position.
180. Install the 2 middle subframe nuts. Tighten to 98 ft. lbs. (133 Nm).
181. Install the 2 front subframe nuts. Tighten to 98 ft. lbs. (133 Nm).
182. Position the subframe support brackets in place and loosely install the 4 bolts.
183. Install the 2 rear subframe bracket nuts. Tighten to 98 ft. lbs. (133 Nm).
184. Tighten the 4 subframe support bracket bolts. Tighten to 66 ft. lbs. (90 Nm).
185. Position the lower bumper on the subframe and install the 3 LH nuts. Tighten to 80 inch lbs. (9 Nm).
186. Install the 3 RH lower bumper-to-subframe nuts. Tighten to 80 inch lbs. (9 Nm).
187. Install the tie-rod ends and nuts. Tighten to 35 ft. lbs. (48 Nm).
    a. Install new cotter pins.

➡ **Do not allow the intermediate shaft to rotate while it is disconnected from the gear or damage to the clockspring can occur. If there is evidence that the intermediate shaft has rotated, the clockspring must be removed and recentered.**

188. Install the intermediate shaft onto the steering gear and install a new bolt. Tighten to 17 ft. lbs. (23 Nm).
189. Using a new banjo bolt and 2 new seals, install the PSP tube. Tighten to 35 ft. lbs. (48 Nm).
190. Install the engine roll restrictor-to-subframe through bolt. Tighten to 76 ft. lbs. (103 Nm).
191. Install the roll restrictor heat shield and the 2 nuts. Tighten to 97 inch lbs. (11 Nm).

AWD vehicles
192. Line up the index marks on the rear driveshaft to the index marks on the PTU flange made during removal and install the 4 bolts. Tighten to 52 ft. lbs. (70 Nm).

All vehicles
193. Install the power steering cooler bracket bolt to the RH side of the subframe. Tighten to 80 inch lbs. (9 Nm).
194. Connect the power steering cooler hose.

➡ **Lubricate the engine oil filter gasket with clean engine oil prior to installing the oil filter.**

195. Install a new engine oil filter.

a. Tighten to 44 inch lbs. (5 Nm) and then rotate an additional 180 degrees.

196. Connect the 2 transmission fluid cooler tubes.

197. Install the 2 secondary latches onto the transmission fluid cooler tubes.

198. Install the LH inner splash shield.

199. Install the radiator splash shield, the 3 pin-type retainers and the 7 screws.

200. Using a new gasket, install the Y-pipe and exhaust flexible pipe assembly and 4 new nuts. Tighten to 30 ft. lbs. (40 Nm).

201. Install the 2 exhaust hangers and tighten the exhaust clamp. Tighten to 30 ft. lbs. (40 Nm).

202. Install the ground wire, the radio interference capacitor wire and the nut to the engine front cover stud. Tighten to 89 inch lbs. (10 Nm).

203. Install the ground wire and bolt to the engine front cover. Tighten to 89 inch lbs. (10 Nm).

204. Attach the wiring harness retainer to the RH valve cover stud bolt.

205. Install the oil level indicator.

206. Connect the 2 engine wiring harness electrical connectors.

a. Attach the electrical connector to the LH valve cover.

207. Connect the fuel hose routing clip to the transaxle stud.

208. Connect the fuel supply tube.

209. Connect the hose to the power steering reservoir.

210. Connect the A/C suction tube fitting.

a. Install the safety clip onto the A/C fitting.

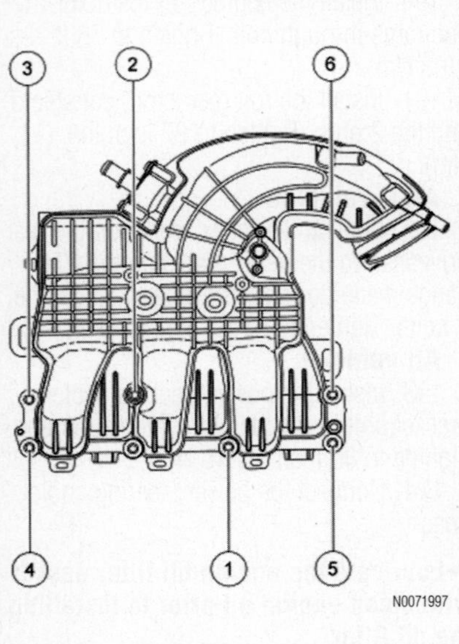

211. Using a new O-ring seal, connect the A/C pressure tube fitting and install the nut. Tighten to 71 inch lbs. (8 Nm).

212. If equipped, attach the engine block heater harness retainers from to the radiator support and the A/C suction tube.

213. Connect the transaxle control electrical connector.

214. Attach the control cable to the bracket.

a. Connect the transaxle control cable to the control lever.

215. Attach the wiring harness retainer to the transaxle control cable bracket.

216. Connect the upper radiator hose, lower radiator hose and 2 heater hoses to the thermostat housing.

217. Connect the upper Evaporative Emission (EVAP) tube quick connect coupling to the purge valve.

218. Connect the vacuum hose to the upper intake manifold.

219. Install the ground wire and the bolt. Tighten to 89 inch lbs. (10 Nm).

a. Attach the 2 wiring harness retainers to the cowl.

220. Connect the power feed to the battery terminal and install the nut. Tighten to 71 inch lbs. (8 Nm).

221. Connect the battery harness electrical connector.

222. Install the battery tray.

223. Install the engine Air Cleaner (ACL) and the ACL outlet pipe.

224. Install the degas bottle.

225. Install the LH halfshaft and intermediate shaft.

226. Install the accessory drive belt and the power steering belt.

➡Do not expose the Motorcraft® High Performance Engine RTV Silicone to engine oil for at least 90 minutes after installing the engine front cover. Failure to follow this instruction may cause oil leakage.

227. Fill the engine with clean engine oil.

228. Fill and bleed the cooling system.

229. Fill the power steering system.

230. Recharge the A/C system.

2011 Models

See Figures 113 through 118.

WARNING

Do not smoke, carry lighted tobacco or have an open flame of any type when working on or near any fuel-related component. Highly flammable mixtures are always present and may be ignited. Failure to follow

these instructions may result in serious personal injury.

➡During engine repair procedures, cleanliness is extremely important. Any foreign material, including any material created while cleaning gasket surfaces that enters the oil passages, coolant passages or the oil pan, can cause engine failure.

➡At the time of publication the manufacturer does not provide a specific Removal and Installation procedure for this component. Refer to the graphic(s) when servicing this component.

To install:

➡During installation, the camshaft seal gaps must be at the 12 o'clock position or damage to the engine may occur.

1. Install the camshafts and position the 4 camshaft seals gaps as shown.

RH camshafts

2. Install the 6 camshaft caps, mega cap, valve train oil tube and the 15 bolts in the sequence shown.

a. Tighten to 71 inch lbs. (8 Nm) then additional 45 degrees.

3. Loosen the 4 bolts.

4. Tighten the 4 bolts in the sequence shown.

a. Tighten bolts 8, 9, 10 and 11 to 71 inch lbs. (8 Nm) then additional 45 degrees.

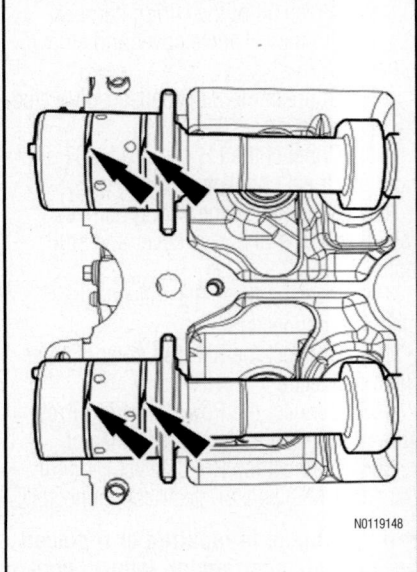

N0119148

Fig. 113 Installing the camshaft and positioning the camshaft seal gaps

N0071997

Fig. 112 Installing the upper intake manifold

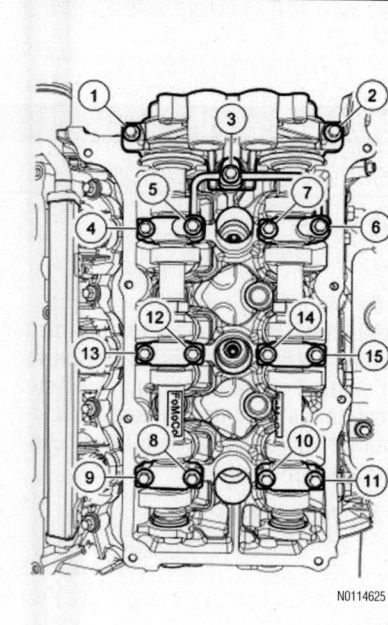

Fig. 114 Identifying the camshaft cap and bolt installation sequence

LH camshafts

5. Install the 6 camshaft caps, mega cap, valve train oil tube and the 15 bolts in the sequence shown.

　　a. Tighten to 71 inch lbs. (8 Nm) then additional 45 degrees.

6. Loosen the 4 bolts.

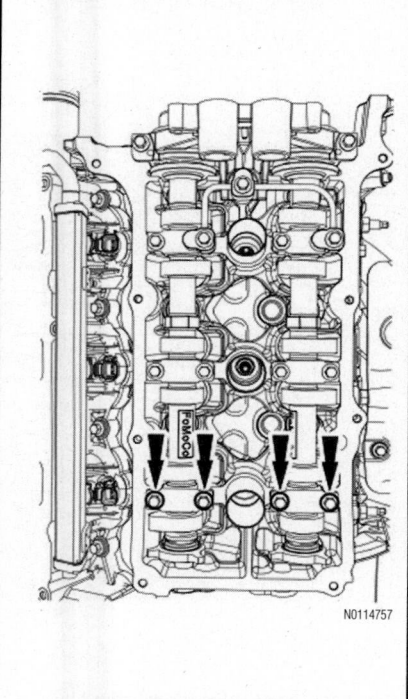

Fig. 115 Loosening the 4 bolts

7. Tighten the 4 bolts in the sequence shown.

　　a. Tighten bolts 8, 9, 10 and 11 to 71 inch lbs. (8 Nm) then additional 45 degrees.

CATALYTIC CONVERTER

REMOVAL & INSTALLATION

2010 Models

Left Side

➡**Always install new fasteners and gaskets. Clean flange faces prior to new gasket installation to make sure of correct sealing.**

1. With the vehicle in NEUTRAL, position it on a hoist.
2. Disconnect the Catalyst Monitor Sensor (CMS) electrical connector.
3. Remove the exhaust Y-pipe.
4. Remove the 2 catalytic converter support bracket-to-transmission bolts.
5. Remove the 4 nuts and the LH catalytic converter.

　　a. Discard the nuts and gasket.

6. Inspect the exhaust manifold studs for damage.

　　a. If damaged, replace stud(s), or if stud comes out when removing nut(s), replace the stud(s).

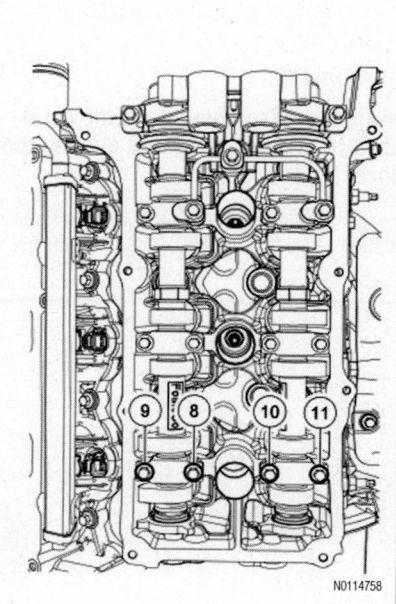

Fig. 116 Identifying the bolt tightening sequence

To install:

　To install, reverse the removal procedure. Tighten the exhaust manifold studs to 18 ft. lbs. (25 Nm). Tighten the 4 nuts to 30 ft. lbs. (40 Nm). Tighten the 2 catalytic converter support bracket-to-transmission bolts to 35 ft. lbs. (48 Nm). Install a new gasket and nuts.

Right Side

　All vehicles

➡**If necessary, the catalytic converter heat shield can be serviced separately.**

➡**Always install new fasteners and gaskets. Clean flange faces prior to new gasket installation to make sure of correct sealing.**

1. With the vehicle in NEUTRAL, position it on a hoist.
2. Remove the CMS.
3. Remove the exhaust Y-pipe.

　All-Wheel Drive (AWD) vehicles

➡**Index-mark the driveshaft for installation.**

4. Remove and discard the 4 U-joint flange bolts and separate the front driveshaft and secure it with a length of mechanic's wire.
5. Remove the intermediate shaft.
6. Remove the 2 catalytic converter support bracket-to-engine block bolts.

　All vehicles

7. Remove the 2 bolts and the power steering gear heat shield.

　Front Wheel Drive (FWD) vehicles

8. Remove the catalytic converter support bracket-to-engine block bolt and nut.

　All vehicles

9. Remove the 2 nuts and the roll restrictor shield.
10. Remove the roll restrictor bolt and rotate the engine forward.

　Tighten the roll restrictor bolt to 66 ft. lbs. (90 Nm).

11. Remove the 2 bracket-to-RH catalytic converter bolts.
12. Remove the 4 nuts and the RH catalytic converter.

　　a. Discard the 4 RH catalytic converter nuts and gasket.

To install:

➡**Prior to installation, inspect the CMS wiring harness for damage.**

13. To install, reverse the removal procedure.

a. Install a new gasket, nuts and studs.

b. Tighten the RH catalytic converter nuts to 30 ft. lbs. (40 Nm).

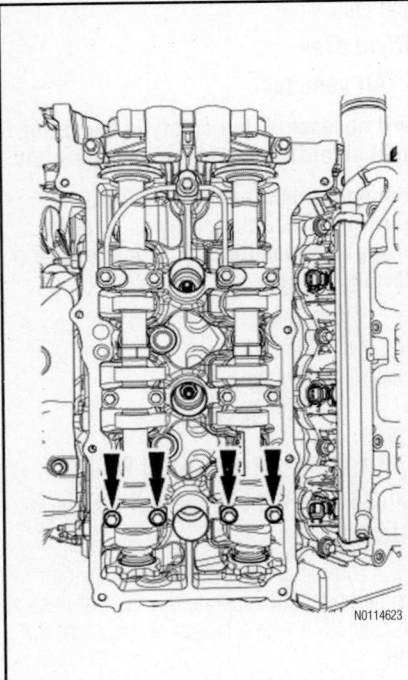

Fig. 117 Loosening the 4 bolts

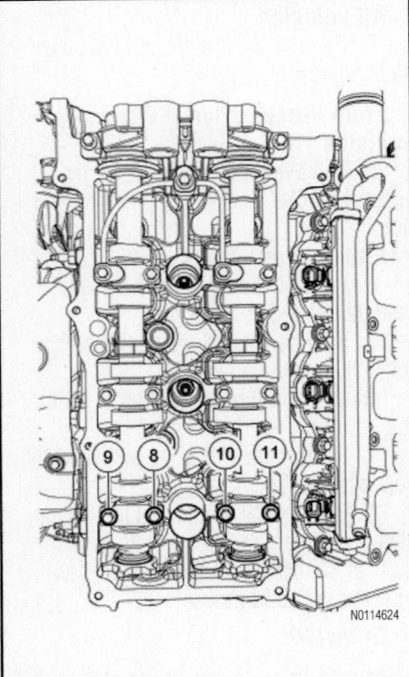

Fig. 118 Identifying the bolt tightening sequence

c. Tighten the bracket to RH catalytic converter bolts to 177 inch lbs. (20 Nm).

d. Tighten the roll restrictor bolt to 66 ft. lbs. (90 Nm).

e. Tighten the roll restrictor shield nuts to 97 inch lbs. (11 Nm).

f. Tighten the catalytic converter support bracket to engine block bolt and nut to 30 ft. lbs. (40 Nm).

g. Tighten the power steering gear heat shield bolts to 133 inch lbs. (15 Nm).

h. Tighten the 2 catalytic converter support bracket-to-engine block bolts to 30 ft. lbs. (40 Nm).

i. Tighten the 4 U-joint flange bolts to 52 ft. lbs. (70 Nm).

2011 Models

➡At the time of this publication, the manufacturer does not provide a procedure for this component.

➡Always install new fasteners and gaskets. Clean flange faces prior to new gasket installation to make sure of correct sealing.

CRANKSHAFT FRONT SEAL

REMOVAL & INSTALLATION

See Figure 119.

1. With the vehicle in NEUTRAL, position it on a hoist.

2. Remove the crankshaft pulley.

3. Using the Oil Seal Remover, remove and discard the crankshaft front seal.

a. Clean all sealing surfaces with metal surface prep.

To install:

➡Apply clean engine oil to the crankshaft front seal bore in the engine front cover.

4. Using the Front Crankshaft Seal Installer and Crankshaft Vibration Damper

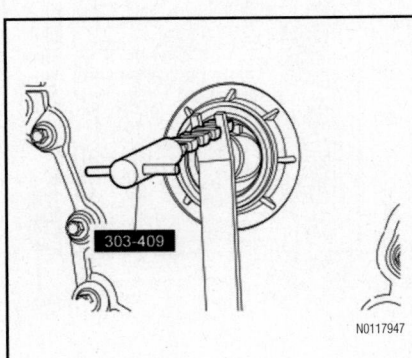

Fig. 119 Removing the crankshaft front seal

Installer, install a new crankshaft front seal.

5. Install the crankshaft pulley.

CYLINDER HEAD

REMOVAL & INSTALLATION

Left Side

See Figures 120 through 129.

➡During engine repair procedures, cleanliness is extremely important. Any foreign material, including any material created while cleaning gasket surfaces that enters the oil passages, coolant passages or the oil pan, can cause engine failure.

All vehicles

1. Remove the LH camshafts.

2. If equipped, remove the heat shield and disconnect the block heater electrical connector.

a. Remove the block heater wiring harness from the engine.

3. Disconnect the 6 fuel injector electrical connectors.

4. Disconnect the Cylinder Head Temperature (CHT) sensor electrical connector.

5. Disconnect the LH Camshaft Position (CMP) sensor electrical connector.

6. Disconnect the LH Heated Oxygen Sensor (HO2S) electrical connector.

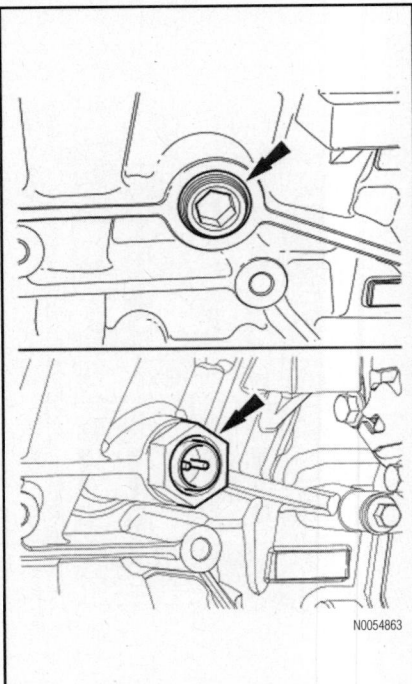

Fig. 120 Locating the RH cylinder block drain plug and/or block heater

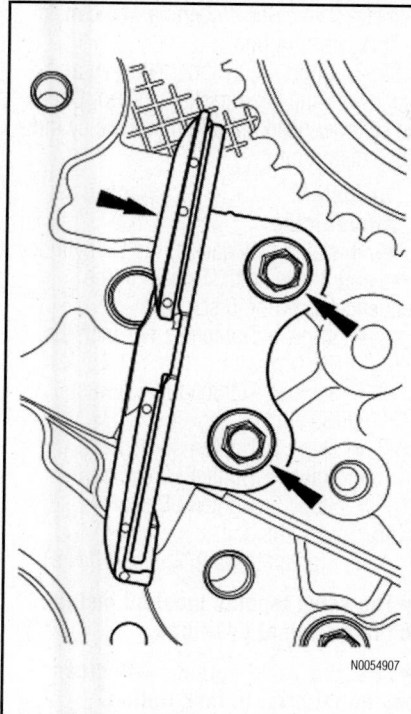

Fig. 121 Removing the upper LH primary timing chain guide

7. Disconnect the LH Catalyst Monitor Sensor (CMS) electrical connector.

8. Remove the wiring harness retainer bolt from the rear of the LH cylinder head.

9. Disconnect the A/C compressor electrical connector.

10. Remove the nut and disconnect the generator B+ cable.

11. Disconnect the generator electrical connector.

12. Detach the wiring harness retainer from the generator.

13. Disconnect the Engine Oil Pressure (EOP) switch electrical connector and the wiring harness pin-type retainer.

14. Remove the nut, 2 bolts and the A/C compressor.

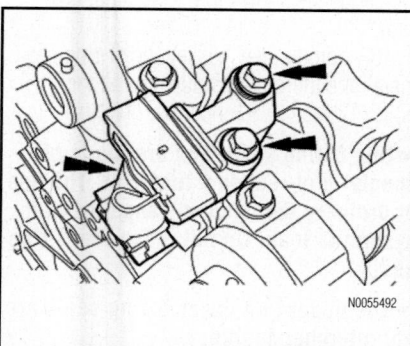

Fig. 122 Removing the LH secondary timing chain tensioner

15. Remove the nut, bolt and the generator.

16. Remove the 2 LH catalytic converter bracket bolts.

17. Remove the 4 nuts and the LH catalytic converter.

   a. Discard the nuts and the gasket.

18. Remove the 3 bolts and the LH exhaust manifold heat shield.

19. Remove the 6 nuts and the LH exhaust manifold.

   a. Discard the nuts and the exhaust manifold gasket.

20. Clean and inspect the LH exhaust manifold.

21. Remove and discard the 6 LH exhaust manifold studs.

22. Remove the LH cylinder block drain plug.

23. Allow coolant to drain from the cylinder block.

All-Wheel Drive (AWD) vehicles

24. Remove the 2 RH catalytic converter bracket bolts.

All vehicles

25. Remove the 4 nuts and the RH catalytic converter.

   a. Discard the nuts and the gasket.

26. Remove the RH cylinder block drain plug or, if equipped, the block heater.

27. Allow coolant to drain from the cylinder block.

28. Remove the 4 bolts and the fuel rail and injectors as an assembly.

29. Remove the 3 thermostat housing-to-lower intake manifold bolts.

   a. Remove the thermostat housing and discard the gasket and O-ring seal.

➡**If the engine is repaired or replaced because of upper engine failure, typically including valve or piston damage, check the intake manifold for metal debris. If metal debris if found, install a new intake manifold. Failure to follow these instructions can result in engine damage.**

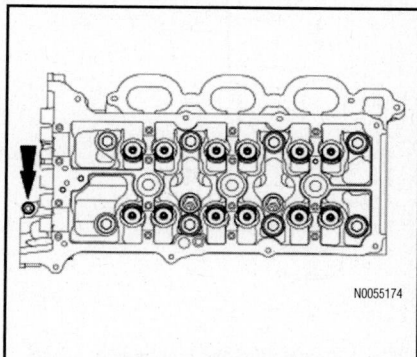

Fig. 123 Identifying the M6 bolt

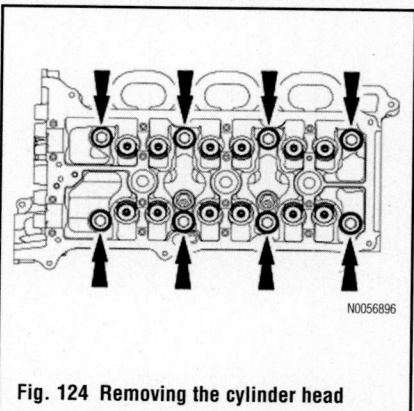

Fig. 124 Removing the cylinder head

30. Remove the 10 bolts and the lower intake manifold.

   a. Discard the gaskets.

31. Remove the bolt and the LH CMP sensor.

32. Remove the 2 bolts and the upper LH primary timing chain guide.

33. Remove the 2 bolts and the LH secondary timing chain tensioner.

➡**If the components are to be reinstalled, they must be installed in the same positions. Mark the components for installation into their original locations.**

34. Remove the valve tappets from the cylinder head.

35. Remove and discard the M6 bolt.

➡**Place clean shop towels over exposed engine cavities. Carefully remove the towels so foreign material is not dropped into the engine. Any foreign material (including any material created while cleaning gasket surfaces) that enters the oil passages or the oil pan, may cause engine failure.**

➡**Aluminum surfaces are soft and can be scratched easily. Never place the cylinder head gasket surface, unprotected, on a bench surface.**

➡**The cylinder head bolts must be discarded and new bolts must be installed. They are tighten-to-yield designed and cannot be reused.**

36. Remove and discard the 8 bolts from the cylinder head.

   a. Remove the cylinder head.

   b. Discard the cylinder head gasket.

➡**Do not use metal scrapers, wire brushes, power abrasive discs or other abrasive means to clean the sealing surfaces. These tools cause scratches and gouges that make leak paths. Use a plastic scraping tool to remove all traces of the head gasket.**

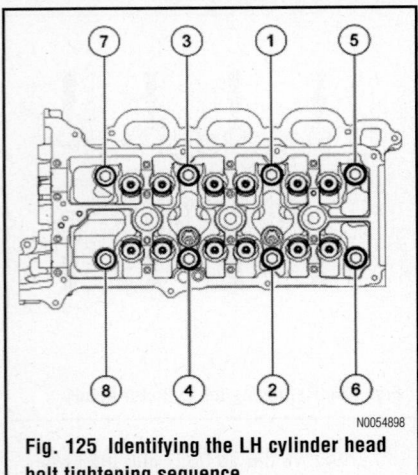

Fig. 125 Identifying the LH cylinder head bolt tightening sequence

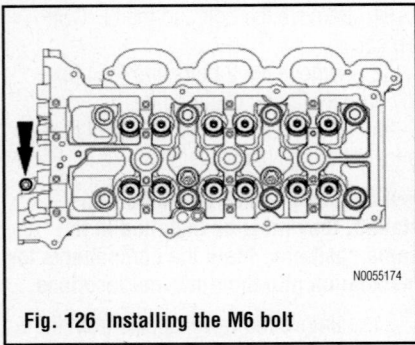

Fig. 126 Installing the M6 bolt

➡ Observe all warnings or cautions and follow all application directions contained on the packaging of the silicone gasket remover and the metal surface prep.

➡ If there is no residual gasket material present, metal surface prep can be used to clean and prepare the surfaces.

37. Clean the cylinder head-to-cylinder block mating surfaces of both the cylinder

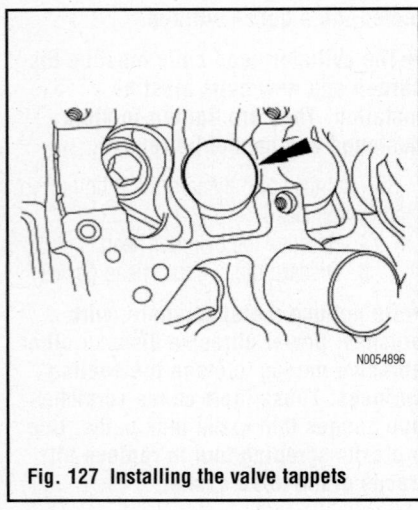

Fig. 127 Installing the valve tappets

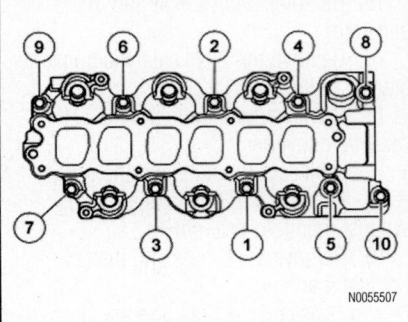

Fig. 128 Identifying the lower intake manifold bolt tightening sequence

heads and the cylinder block in the following sequence.

a. Remove any large deposits of silicone or gasket material with a plastic scraper.

b. Apply silicone gasket remover, following package directions, and allow to set for several minutes.

c. Remove the silicone gasket remover with a plastic scraper. A second application of silicone gasket remover may be required if residual traces of silicone or gasket material remain.

d. Apply metal surface prep, following package directions, to remove any remaining traces of oil or coolant and to prepare the surfaces to bond with the new gasket. Do not attempt to make the

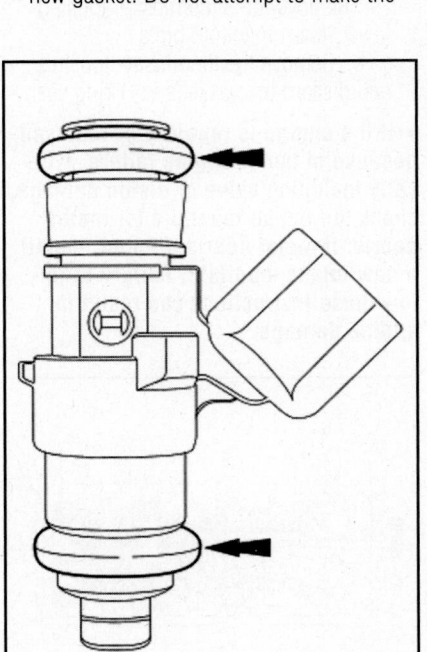

Fig. 129 Installing the fuel injector o-ring seals

metal shiny. Some staining of the metal surfaces is normal.

38. Support the cylinder head on a bench with the head gasket side up. Check the cylinder head distortion and the cylinder block distortion.

To install:
All vehicles

39. Install a new gasket, the LH cylinder head and 8 new bolts. Tighten in the sequence shown in 5 stages:

- Stage 1: Tighten to 177 inch lbs. (20 Nm).
- Stage 2: Tighten to 26 ft. lbs. (35 Nm).
- Stage 3: Tighten 90 degrees.
- Stage 4: Tighten 90 degrees.
- Stage 5: Tighten 90 degrees.

40. Install the bolt.

a. Tighten to 89 inch lbs. (10 Nm).

➡ The valve tappets must be installed in their original positions.

➡ Coat the valve tappets with clean engine oil prior to installation.

41. Install the valve tappets.

42. Install the LH secondary timing chain tensioner and the 2 bolts. Tighten to 89 inch lbs. (10 Nm).

43. Install the upper LH primary timing chain guide and the 2 bolts. Tighten to 89 inch lbs. (10 Nm).

44. Install LH Camshaft Position (CMP) sensor and the bolt. Tighten to 89 inch lbs. (10 Nm).

➡ If the engine is repaired or replaced because of upper engine failure, typically including valve or piston damage, check the intake manifold for metal debris. If metal debris is found, install a new intake manifold. Failure to follow these instructions can result in engine damage.

45. Using new gaskets, install the lower intake manifold and the 10 bolts. Tighten in the sequence shown to 89 inch lbs. (10 Nm).

46. Using a new gasket and O-ring seal, install the thermostat housing and the 3 bolts. Tighten to 89 inch lbs. (10 Nm).

➡ Use O-ring seals that are made of special fuel-resistant material. The use of ordinary O-rings can cause the fuel system to leak. Do not reuse the O-ring seals.

➡ The upper and lower O-ring seals are not interchangeable.

47. Install new fuel injector O-ring seals.

a. Remove the retaining clips and separate the fuel injectors from the fuel rail.

b. Remove and discard the O-ring seals.

c. Install new O-ring seals and lubricate with clean engine oil.

d. Install the fuel injectors and the retaining clips onto the fuel rail.

48. Install the fuel rail and injectors as an assembly and install the 4 bolts. Tighten to 89 inch lbs. (10 Nm).

49. Install the RH cylinder block drain plug or, if equipped, the block heater. Tighten to 30 ft. lbs. (40 Nm).

50. Using a new gasket, install the RH catalytic converter and 4 new nuts. Tighten to 30 ft. lbs. (40 Nm).

All-Wheel Drive (AWD) vehicles

51. Install the 2 RH catalytic converter bracket bolts.

a. Tighten the 4 catalytic converter nuts to 30 ft. lbs. (40 Nm).

b. Tighten the 2 catalytic converter brackets to 177 inch lbs. (20 Nm).

All vehicles

52. Install the LH cylinder block drain plug.

a. Tighten to 177 inch lbs. (20 Nm) plus an additional 180 degrees.

53. Install 6 new LH exhaust manifold studs.

a. Tighten to 106 inch lbs. (12 Nm).

➡**Failure to tighten the exhaust manifold nuts to specification a second time will cause the exhaust manifold to develop an exhaust leak.**

54. Using a new gasket, install the LH exhaust manifold and 6 new nuts. Tighten in 2 stages in the sequence shown:
- Stage 1: Tighten to 177 inch lbs. (20 Nm).
- Stage 2: Tighten to 18 ft. lbs. (25 Nm).

55. Install the LH exhaust manifold heat shield and the 3 bolts. Tighten to 89 inch lbs. (10 Nm).

56. Using a new gasket, install the LH catalytic converter and 4 new nuts.

a. Tighten to 30 ft. lbs. (40 Nm).

57. Install the 2 LH catalytic converter bracket bolts. Tighten to 177 inch lbs. (20 Nm).

58. Install the generator, the bolt and the nut. Tighten to 35 ft. lbs (47 Nm).

59. Install the A/C compressor, the nut and the 2 bolts. Tighten to 18 ft. lbs. (25 Nm).

60. Connect the Engine Oil Pressure (EOP) switch electrical connector and the wiring harness pin-type retainer.

61. Attach the wiring harness retainer to the generator.

62. Connect the generator electrical connector.

63. Connect the generator B+ cable and install the nut. Tighten to 150 inch lbs. (17 Nm).

64. Connect the A/C compressor electrical connector.

65. Install the wiring harness retainer bolt on the rear of the LH cylinder head. Tighten to 89 inch lbs. (10 Nm).

66. Connect the LH Catalyst Monitor Sensor (CMS) electrical connector.

67. Connect the LH Heated Oxygen Sensor (HO2S) electrical connector.

68. Connect the LH CMP sensor electrical connector.

69. Connect the Cylinder Head Temperature (CHT) sensor electrical connector.

70. Connect the 6 fuel injector electrical connectors.

71. If equipped, install the block heater wiring harness onto the engine.

a. Connect the block heater electrical connector and install the heat shield.

72. Install the LH camshafts.

Right Side

See Figures 130 through 139.

➡**During engine repair procedures, cleanliness is extremely important. Any foreign material, including any material created while cleaning gasket surfaces that enters the oil passages, coolant passages or the oil pan, can cause engine failure.**

All vehicles

1. Remove the RH camshafts.

2. If equipped, remove the heat shield and disconnect the block heater electrical connector.

a. Remove the block heater wiring harness from the engine.

3. Disconnect the RH Heated Oxygen Sensor (HO2S) electrical connector.

4. Disconnect the RH Camshaft Position (CMP) sensor electrical connector.

5. Remove the bolt and the ground cable from the RH cylinder.

6. Disconnect the 6 fuel injector electrical connectors.

7. Disconnect the Cylinder Head Temperature (CHT) sensor electrical connector.

8. Disconnect the LH Catalyst Monitor Sensor (CMS) electrical connector.

9. Remove the 2 LH catalytic converter bracket bolts.

10. Remove the 4 nuts and the LH catalytic converter.

a. Discard the nuts and the gasket.

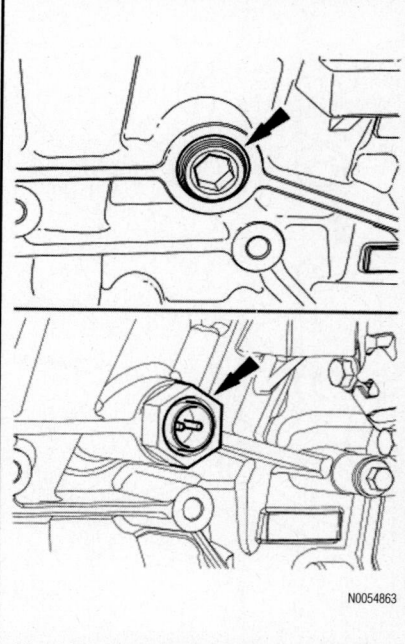

Fig. 130 Removing the RH cylinder block drain plug or block heater

11. Remove the LH cylinder block drain plug.

a. Allow coolant to drain from the cylinder block.

All-Wheel Drive (AWD) vehicles

12. Remove the 2 RH catalytic converter bracket bolts.

All vehicles

13. Remove the 4 nuts and the RH catalytic converter.

a. Discard the nuts and the gasket.

14. Remove the RH cylinder block drain plug or, if equipped, the block heater.

a. Allow coolant to drain from the cylinder block.

15. Remove the 3 bolts and the RH exhaust manifold heat shield.

16. Remove the 6 nuts and the RH exhaust manifold.

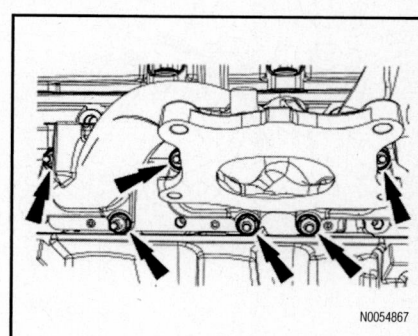

Fig. 131 Removing the RH exhaust manifold

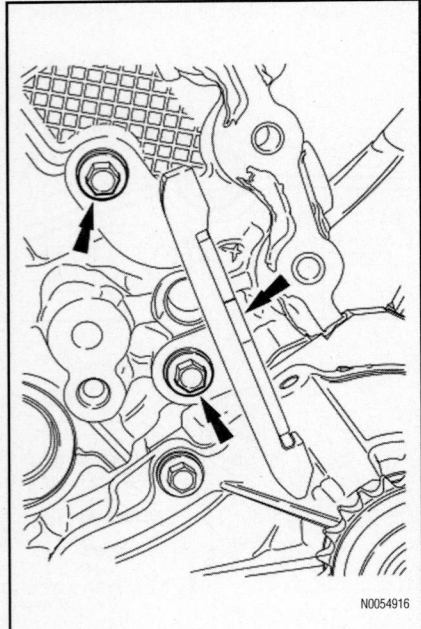

Fig. 132 Removing the RH primary timing chain guide

a. Discard the nuts and exhaust manifold gaskets.

17. Clean and inspect the RH exhaust manifold.

18. Remove and discard the 6 RH exhaust manifold studs.

Engines equipped with early build RH timing chain guides

19. Remove the 2 bolts and the RH primary timing chain guide.

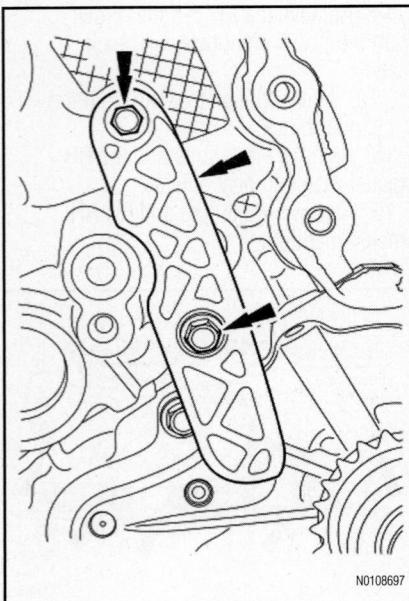

Fig. 133 Removing the RH primary timing chain guide

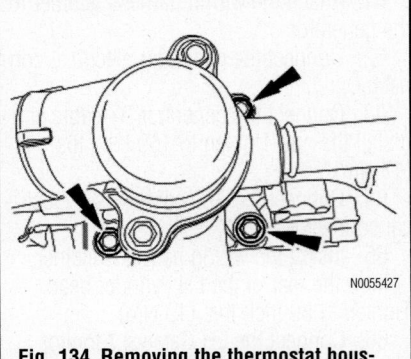

Fig. 134 Removing the thermostat housing to lower intake manifold bolts

Engines equipped with late build/replacement RH timing chain guides

20. Remove the 2 bolts and the RH primary timing chain guide.

All vehicles

21. Remove the 2 bolts and the RH secondary timing chain tensioner.

22. Remove the 2 bolts and the engine lifting eye.

➡️**Index-mark the location of the bracket on the cylinder head for installation.**

23. Remove the bolt and the upper intake manifold bracket.

24. Remove the bolt and the RH CMP sensor.

25. Remove the 4 bolts and the fuel rail and injectors as an assembly.

26. Remove the 3 thermostat housing-to-lower intake manifold bolts.

a. Remove the thermostat housing and discard the gasket and O-ring seal.

➡️**If the engine is repaired or replaced because of upper engine failure, typically including valve or piston damage, check the intake manifold for metal debris. If metal debris is found, install a new intake manifold. Failure to follow these instructions can result in engine damage.**

27. Remove the 10 bolts and the lower intake manifold.

a. Discard the gaskets.

28. Disconnect and remove the CHT sensor jumper harness.

➡️**If the components are to be reinstalled, they must be installed in the same positions. Mark the components for installation into their original locations.**

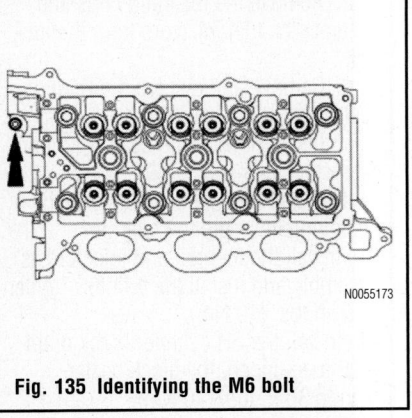

Fig. 135 Identifying the M6 bolt

29. Remove the valve tappets from the cylinder head.

30. Remove and discard the M6 bolt.

➡️**Place clean shop towels over exposed engine cavities. Carefully remove the towels so foreign material is not dropped into the engine. Any foreign material (including any material created while cleaning gasket surfaces) that enters the oil passages or the oil pan, may cause engine failure.**

➡️**Aluminum surfaces are soft and can be scratched easily. Never place the cylinder head gasket surface, unprotected, on a bench surface.**

➡️**The cylinder head bolts must be discarded and new bolts must be installed. They are tighten-to-yield designed and cannot be reused.**

31. Remove and discard the 8 bolts from the cylinder head.

a. Remove the cylinder head.

b. Discard the cylinder head gasket.

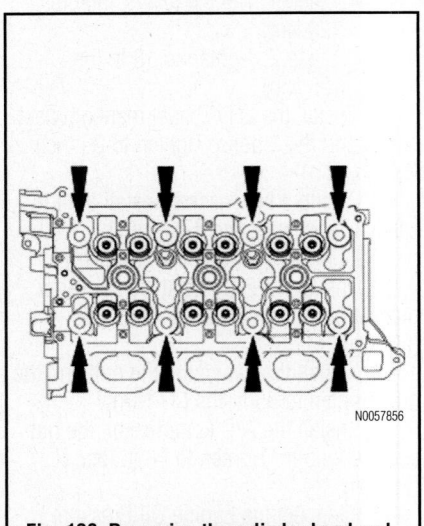

Fig. 136 Removing the cylinder head and gasket

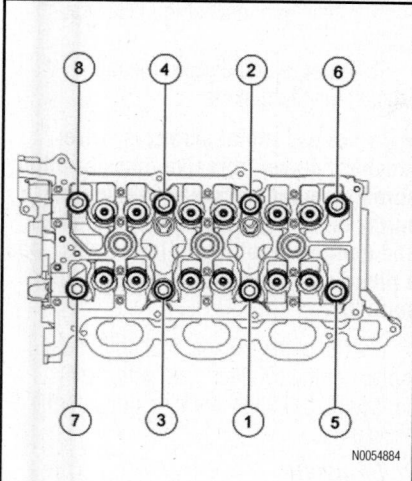

Fig. 137 Identifying the RH cylinder head bolt tightening sequence

➡ Do not use metal scrapers, wire brushes, power abrasive discs or other abrasive means to clean the sealing surfaces. These tools cause scratches and gouges that make leak paths. Use a plastic scraping tool to remove all traces of the head gasket.

➡ Observe all warnings or cautions and follow all application directions contained on the packaging of the silicone gasket remover and the metal surface prep.

➡ If there is no residual gasket material present, metal surface prep can be used to clean and prepare the surfaces.

32. Clean the cylinder head-to-cylinder block mating surfaces of both the cylinder heads and the cylinder block in the following sequence.

    a. Remove any large deposits of silicone or gasket material with a plastic scraper.

    b. Apply silicone gasket remover, following package directions, and allow to set for several minutes.

    c. Remove the silicone gasket remover with a plastic scraper. A second application of silicone gasket remover may be required if residual traces of silicone or gasket material remain.

    d. Apply metal surface prep, following package directions, to remove any remaining traces of oil or coolant and to prepare the surfaces to bond with the new gasket. Do not attempt to make the metal shiny. Some staining of the metal surfaces is normal.

33. Support the cylinder head on a bench with the head gasket side up. Check

the cylinder head distortion and the cylinder block distortion.

    To install:

➡ During engine repair procedures, cleanliness is extremely important. Any foreign material, including any material created while cleaning gasket surfaces that enters the oil passages, coolant passages or the oil pan, can cause engine failure.

➡ On early build engines, the timing chain rides on the inner side of the RH timing chain guide. Late build engines are equipped with a different design RH timing chain guide that requires the timing chain to ride on the outer side of the RH timing chain guide. For service, all replacement RH timing chain guides will be the late build design.

All vehicles

34. Install a new gasket, the RH cylinder head and 8 new bolts. Tighten in the sequence shown in 5 stages:

    a. Stage 1: Tighten to 177 inch lbs. (20 Nm).

    b. Stage 2: Tighten to 26 ft. lbs. (35 Nm).

    c. Stage 3: Tighten 90 degrees.

    d. Stage 4: Tighten 90 degrees.

    e. Stage 5: Tighten 90 degrees.

35. Install the bolt.

    a. Tighten to 89 inch lbs. (10 Nm).

➡ The valve tappets must be installed in their original positions.

➡ Coat the valve tappets with clean engine oil prior to installation.

36. Install the valve tappets.

37. Install and connect the Cylinder Head Temperature (CHT) sensor jumper harness.

➡ If the engine is repaired or replaced because of upper engine failure, typi-

cally including valve or piston damage, check the intake manifold for metal debris. If metal debris is found, install a new intake manifold. Failure to follow these instructions can result in engine damage.

38. Using new gaskets, install the lower intake manifold and the 10 bolts.

    a. Tighten in the sequence shown to 89 inch lbs. (10 Nm).

39. Using a new gasket and O-ring seal, install the thermostat housing and the 3 bolts. Tighten to 89 inch lbs. (10 Nm).

➡ Use O-ring seals that are made of special fuel-resistant material. The use of ordinary O-rings can cause the fuel system to leak. Do not reuse the O-ring seals.

➡ The upper and lower O-ring seals are not interchangeable.

40. Install new fuel injector O-ring seals.

    a. Remove the retaining clips and separate the fuel injectors from the fuel rail.

    b. Remove and discard the O-ring seals.

    c. Install new O-ring seals and lubricate with clean engine oil.

    d. Install the fuel injectors and the retaining clips onto the fuel rail.

41. Install the fuel rail and injectors as an assembly and install the 4 bolts. Tighten to 89 inch lbs. (10 Nm).

42. Install the RH Camshaft Position (CMP) sensor and the bolt. Tighten to 89 inch lbs. (10 Nm).

➡ Align the bracket with the index mark made during removal.

43. Install the upper intake manifold bracket and the bolt. Tighten to 89 inch lbs. (10 Nm).

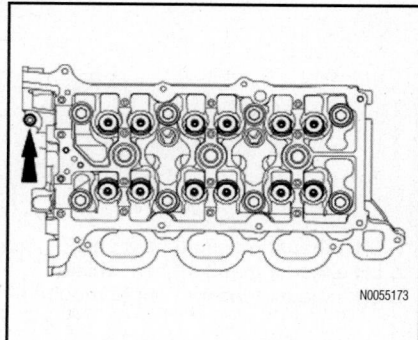

Fig. 138 Identifying the M6 bolt for installation

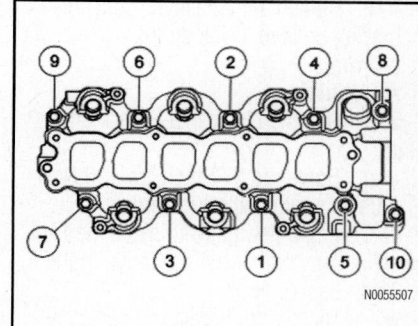

Fig. 139 Identifying the lower intake manifold bolt tightening sequence

44. Install the engine lifting eye and the 2 bolts. Tighten to 18 ft. lbs. (24 Nm).

45. Install the RH secondary timing chain tensioner and the 2 bolts. Tighten to 89 inch lbs. (10 Nm).

Engines equipped with late build/replacement RH timing chain guides

46. Install the RH primary timing chain guide and the 2 bolts. Tighten to 89 inch lbs. (10 Nm).

Engines equipped with early build RH timing chain guides

47. Install the RH primary timing chain guide and the 2 bolts. Tighten to 89 inch lbs. (10 Nm).

All vehicles

48. Install 6 new RH exhaust manifold studs. Tighten to 106 inch lbs. (12 Nm).

➡**Failure to tighten the exhaust manifold nuts to specification a second time will cause the exhaust manifold to develop an exhaust leak.**

49. Using a new gasket, install the RH exhaust manifold and 6 new nuts. Tighten in 2 stages in the sequence shown:

    a. Stage 1: Tighten to 177 inch lbs. (20 Nm).

    b. Stage 2: Tighten to 18 ft. lbs. (25 Nm).

50. Install the RH exhaust manifold heat shield and the 3 bolts. Tighten to 89 inch lbs. (10 Nm).

51. Install the RH cylinder block drain plug or, if equipped, the block heater. Tighten to 30 ft. lbs. (40 Nm).

➡**Do not tighten the 4 catalytic converter nuts at this time.**

52. Using a new gasket, install the RH catalytic converter and 4 new nuts.

All-Wheel Drive (AWD) vehicles

53. Install the 2 RH catalytic converter bracket bolts.

    a. Tighten the 4 catalytic converter nuts to 30 ft. lbs. (40 Nm).

    b. Tighten the 2 catalytic converter bracket bolts to 177 inch lbs. (20 Nm).

All vehicles

54. Install the LH cylinder block drain plug.

    a. Tighten to 177 inch lbs. (20 Nm) plus an additional 180 degrees.

55. Using a new gasket, install the LH catalytic converter and 4 new nuts. Tighten to 30 ft. lbs. (40 Nm).

56. Install the 2 LH catalytic converter bracket bolts. Tighten to 177 inch lbs. (20 Nm).

57. Connect the LH Catalyst Monitor Sensor (CMS) electrical connector.

58. Connect the CHT sensor electrical connector.

59. Connect the 6 fuel injector electrical connectors.

60. Install the ground cable and the bolt. Tighten to 89 inch lbs. (10 Nm).

61. Connect the RH CMP sensor electrical connector.

62. Connect the RH Heated Oxygen Sensor (HO2S) electrical connector.

63. If equipped, install the block heater wiring harness onto the engine.

    a. Connect the block heater electrical connector and install the heat shield.

64. Install the RH camshafts.

EXHAUST MANIFOLD

REMOVAL & INSTALLATION

Left Side

See Figures 140 and 141.

1. Remove the LH catalytic converter.
2. Remove the LH Heated Oxygen Sensor (HO2S).
3. Remove the 3 bolts and the LH exhaust manifold heat shield.
4. Remove the 6 nuts and the LH exhaust manifold.

    a. Discard the nuts and gasket.

5. Clean and inspect the LH exhaust manifold.

6. Remove and discard the 6 LH exhaust manifold studs.

➡**Do not use metal scrapers, wire brushes, power abrasive discs or other abrasive means to clean the sealing surfaces. These may cause scratches and gouges resulting in leak paths. Use a plastic scraper to clean the sealing surfaces.**

7. Clean the exhaust manifold mating surface of the cylinder head with metal surface prep. Follow the directions on the packaging.

To install:

8. Install 6 new LH exhaust manifold studs.

    a. Tighten to 106 inch lbs. (12 Nm).

➡**Failure to tighten the exhaust manifold nuts to specification a second time will cause the exhaust manifold to develop an exhaust leak.**

9. Using a new gasket, install the LH exhaust manifold and 6 new nuts. Tighten in 2 stages in the sequence shown:

- Stage 1: Tighten to 177 inch lbs. (20 Nm).
- Stage 2: Tighten to 18 ft. lbs. (25 Nm).

10. Install the LH exhaust manifold heat

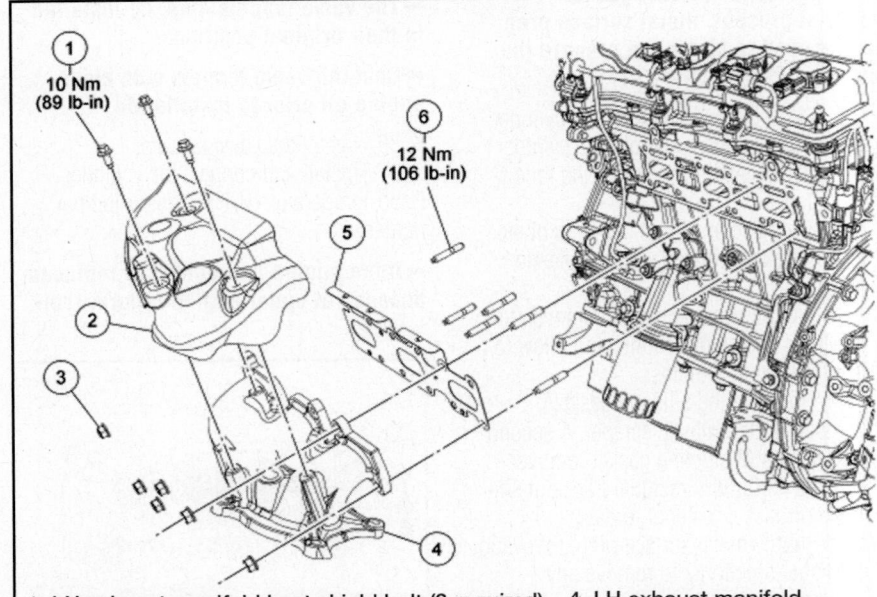

1. LH exhaust manifold heat shield bolt (3 required)
2. LH exhaust manifold heat shield
3. LH exhaust manifold nut (6 required)
4. LH exhaust manifold
5. LH exhaust manifold gasket
6. LH exhaust manifold stud (6 required)

N0103239

Fig. 140 Exploded view of LH side exhaust manifold and related components

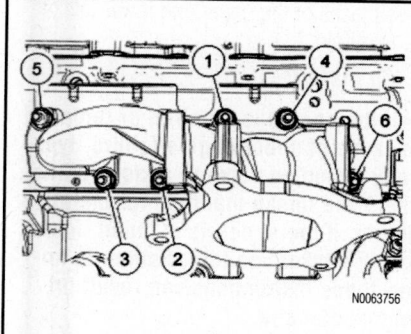

Fig. 141 Installing the new LH exhaust manifold studs

shield and the 3 bolts. Tighten to 89 inch lbs. (10 Nm).

11. Install the LH HO2S.
12. Install the LH catalytic converter.

Right Side

See Figure 142.

1. Remove the RH catalytic converter.
2. Disconnect the RH Heated Oxygen Sensor (HO2S) electrical connector.
3. Remove the 6 nuts and the RH exhaust manifold.
   a. Discard the nuts and gasket.
4. Clean and inspect the RH exhaust manifold.
5. Remove and discard the 6 RH exhaust manifold studs.

➡**Do not use metal scrapers, wire brushes, power abrasive discs or other abrasive means to clean the sealing surfaces. These may cause scratches and gouges resulting in leak paths. Use a plastic scraper to clean the sealing surfaces.**

6. Clean the exhaust manifold mating surface of the cylinder head with metal surface prep. Follow the directions on the packaging.

To install:

7. Install 6 new RH exhaust manifold studs. Tighten to 106 inch lbs. (12 Nm).

➡**Failure to tighten the exhaust manifold nuts to specification a second time will cause the exhaust manifold to develop an exhaust leak.**

8. Using a new gasket, install the RH exhaust manifold and 6 new nuts. Tighten in 2 stages in the sequence shown:
   • Stage 1: Tighten to 177 inch lbs. (20 Nm).
   • Stage 2: Tighten to 18 ft. lbs. (25 Nm).
9. Connect the RH HO2S electrical connector.

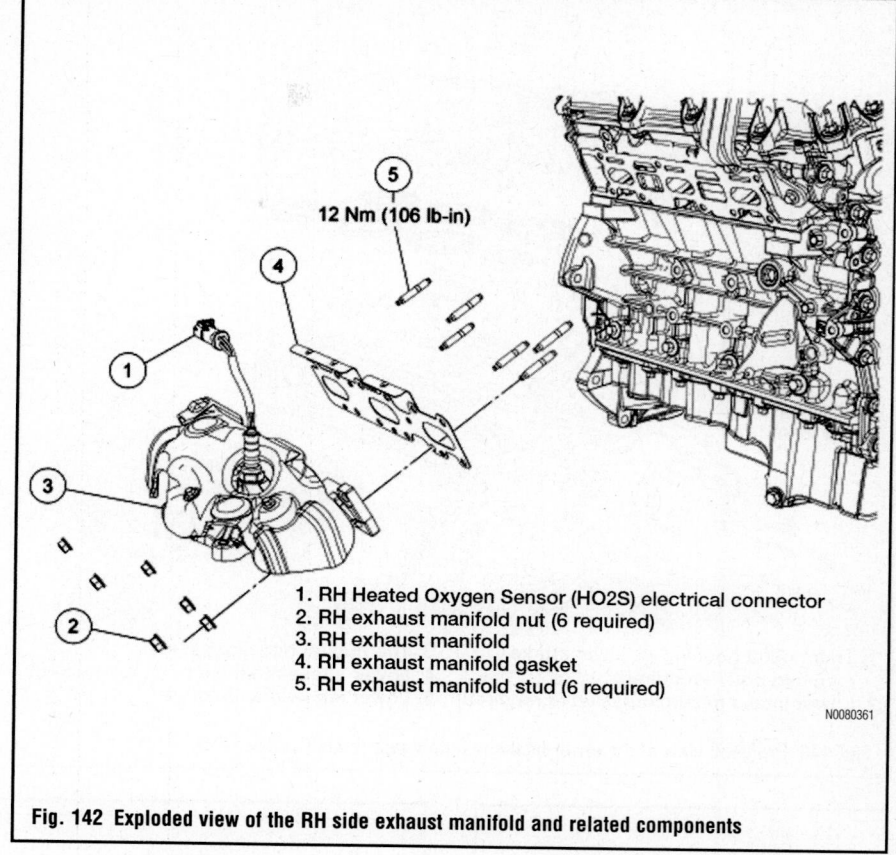

1. RH Heated Oxygen Sensor (HO2S) electrical connector
2. RH exhaust manifold nut (6 required)
3. RH exhaust manifold
4. RH exhaust manifold gasket
5. RH exhaust manifold stud (6 required)

12 Nm (106 lb-in)

Fig. 142 Exploded view of the RH side exhaust manifold and related components

10. Install the RH catalytic converter.

INTAKE MANIFOLD

REMOVAL & INSTALLATION

2010 Models

Lower

See Figures 143 and 144.

➡**During engine repair procedures, cleanliness is extremely important. Any foreign material, including any material created while cleaning gasket surfaces that enters the oil passages, coolant passages or the oil pan, can cause engine failure.**

1. With the vehicle in NEUTRAL, position it on a hoist.
2. Drain the cooling system.
3. Remove the fuel rail.
4. Remove the Air Cleaner (ACL) assembly.
5. Remove the 3 thermostat housing-to-lower intake manifold bolts.
6. Remove the 10 bolts and the lower intake manifold.
   a. Remove and discard the intake manifold and thermostat housing gaskets.

b. Clean and inspect all sealing surfaces.

To install:

➡**If the engine is repaired or replaced because of upper engine failure, typically including valve or piston damage, check the intake manifold for metal debris. If metal debris is found, install a new intake manifold. Failure to follow these instructions can result in engine damage.**

7. Using new intake manifold and thermostat housing gaskets, install the lower intake manifold and the 10 bolts.
   a. Tighten in the sequence shown to 89 inch lbs. (10 Nm).
8. Install the 3 thermostat housing-to-lower intake manifold bolts. Tighten to 89 inch lbs. (10 Nm).
9. Install the ACL assembly.
10. Install the fuel rail.
11. Fill and bleed the cooling system.

Upper

See Figures 145 through 147.

1. Remove the Air Cleaner (ACL) outlet pipe.
2. Disconnect the Throttle Body (TB) electrical connector.

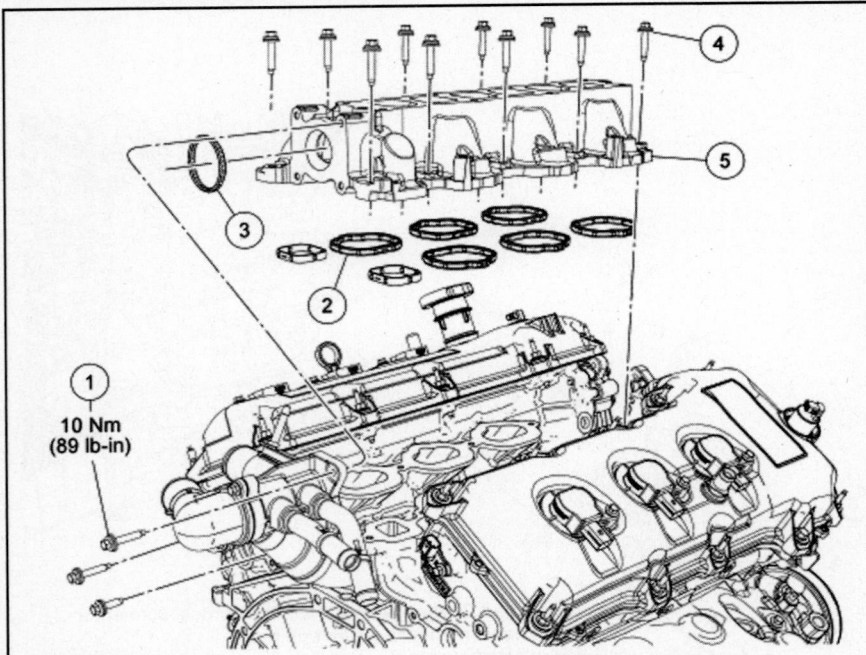

1. Thermostat housing-to-lower intake manifold bolt (3 required)
2. Lower intake manifold gasket (8 required)
3. Thermostat housing gasket
4. Lower intake manifold bolt (10 required)
5. Lower intake manifold

N0071967

Fig. 143 Exploded view of the lower intake manifold and related components

surfaces of the upper and lower intake manifold.

To install:

➡️**If the engine is repaired or replaced because of upper engine failure, typically including valve or piston damage, check the intake manifold for metal debris. If metal debris is found, install a new intake manifold. Failure to follow these instructions can result in engine damage.**

9. Using new gaskets, install the upper intake manifold and the 6 bolts. Tighten in the sequence shown to 89 inch lbs. (10 Nm).

10. Install the upper intake manifold support bracket bolt. Tighten to 89 inch lbs. (10 Nm).

11. Attach the wiring harness retainers to the upper intake manifold.

12. Connect the PCV tube to the PCV valve.

13. Connect the brake booster vacuum hose to the intake manifold.

14. Connect the EVAP tube to the intake manifold.

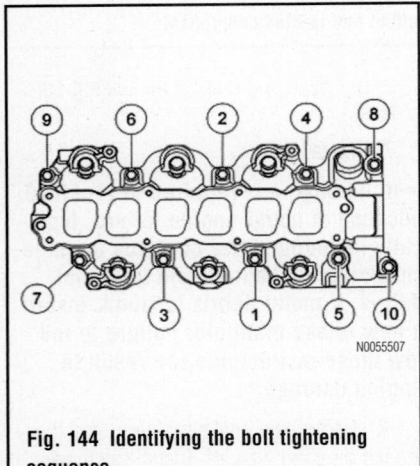

N0055507

Fig. 144 Identifying the bolt tightening sequence

3. Disconnect the Evaporative Emission (EVAP) tube from the intake manifold.

4. Disconnect the brake booster vacuum hose from the intake manifold.

5. Disconnect the PCV tube from the PCV valve.

6. Detach the wiring harness retainers from the upper intake manifold.

7. Remove the upper intake manifold support bracket bolt.

8. Remove the 6 bolts and remove the upper intake manifold.

   a. Remove and discard the gaskets.

   b. Clean and inspect all of the sealing

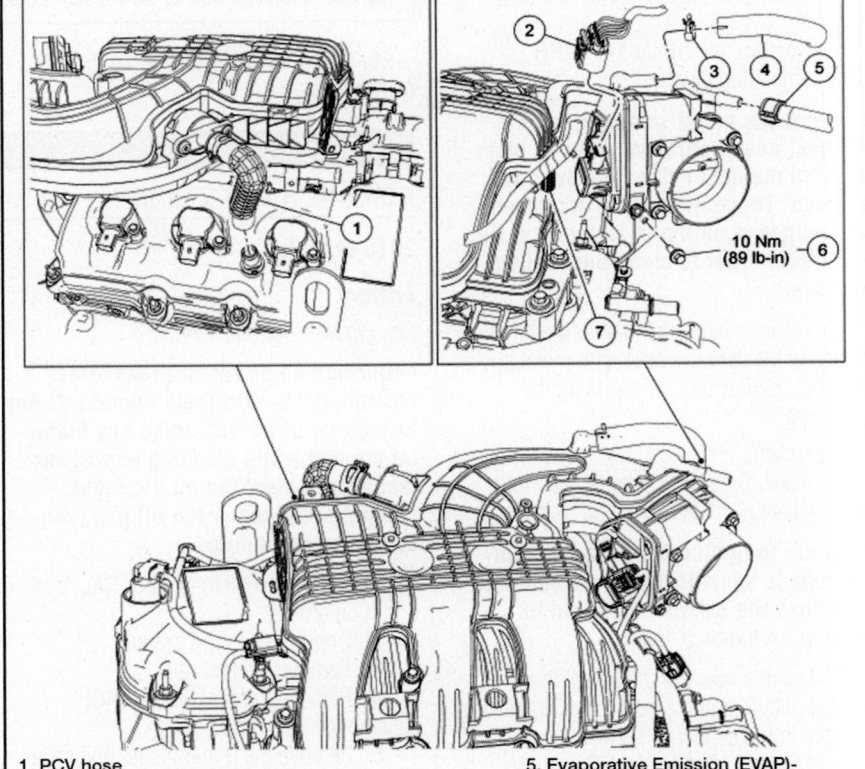

1. PCV hose
2. Throttle Body (TB) electrical connector
3. Brake booster-to-intake manifold vacuum hose clamp
4. Brake booster-to-intake manifold vacuum hose
5. Evaporative Emission (EVAP)-to-intake manifold tube
6. Upper intake manifold support bracket bolt
7. Engine control wiring harness retainer

N0071965

Fig. 145 Upper intake manifold and related components—1 of 2

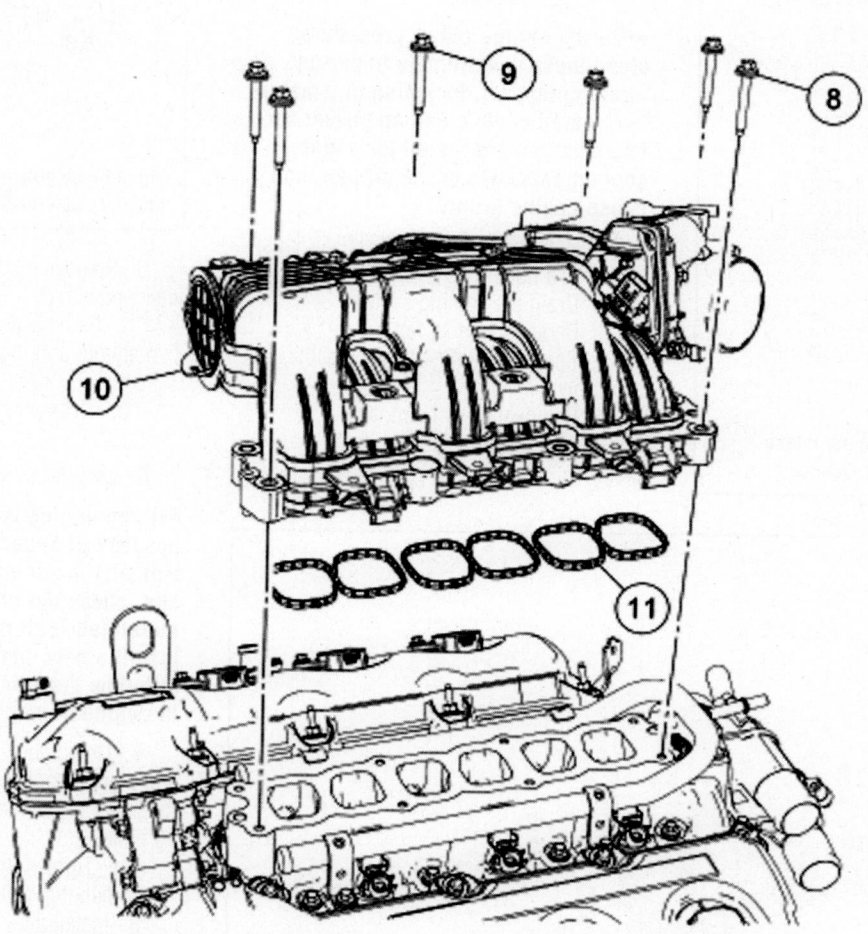

8. Upper intake manifold
    bolt (5 required)
9. Upper intake manifold bolt

10. Upper intake manifold
11. Upper intake manifold
    gasket (3 required)

N0076856

Fig. 146 Upper intake manifold and related components—2 of 2

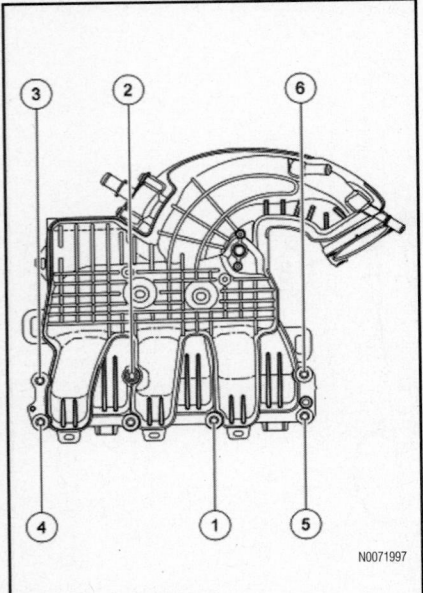

Fig. 147 Identifying the upper intake manifold bolt tightening sequence

15. Connect the TB electrical connector.
16. Install the ACL outlet pipe.

2011 Models

Lower

See Figures 148 and 149.

➡During engine repair procedures, cleanliness is extremely important. Any foreign material, including any material created while cleaning gasket surfaces that enters the oil passages, coolant passages or the oil pan, can cause engine failure.

1. With the vehicle in NEUTRAL, position it on a hoist.
2. Drain the cooling system.
3. Remove the fuel rail.
4. Remove the Air Cleaner (ACL) assembly.
5. Remove the 2 thermostat housing-to-lower intake manifold bolts.

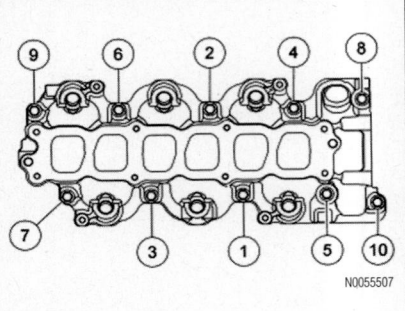

Fig. 149 Identifying the lower intake manifold bolt installation sequence

6. Remove the 10 bolts and the lower intake manifold.
   a. Remove and discard the intake manifold and thermostat housing gaskets.
   b. Clean and inspect all sealing surfaces.

To install:

➡If the engine is repaired or replaced because of upper engine failure, typically including valve or piston damage, check the intake manifold for metal debris. If metal debris is found, install a new intake manifold. Failure to follow these instructions can result in engine damage.

7. Using new intake manifold and thermostat housing gaskets, install the lower intake manifold and the 10 bolts.
   a. Tighten in the sequence shown to 89 inch lbs. (10 Nm).
8. Install the 2 thermostat housing-to-lower intake manifold bolts. Tighten to 71 inch lbs. (8 Nm) plus an additional 90 degrees.
9. Install the ACL assembly.
10. Install the fuel rail.
11. Fill and bleed the cooling system.

Upper

See Figures 150 and 151.

➡If the engine is repaired or replaced because of upper engine failure, typically including valve or piston damage, check the intake manifold for metal debris. If metal debris is found, install a new intake manifold. Failure to follow these instructions can result in engine damage.

1. At the time of publication, the manufacturer does not provide a procedure for this component. Refer

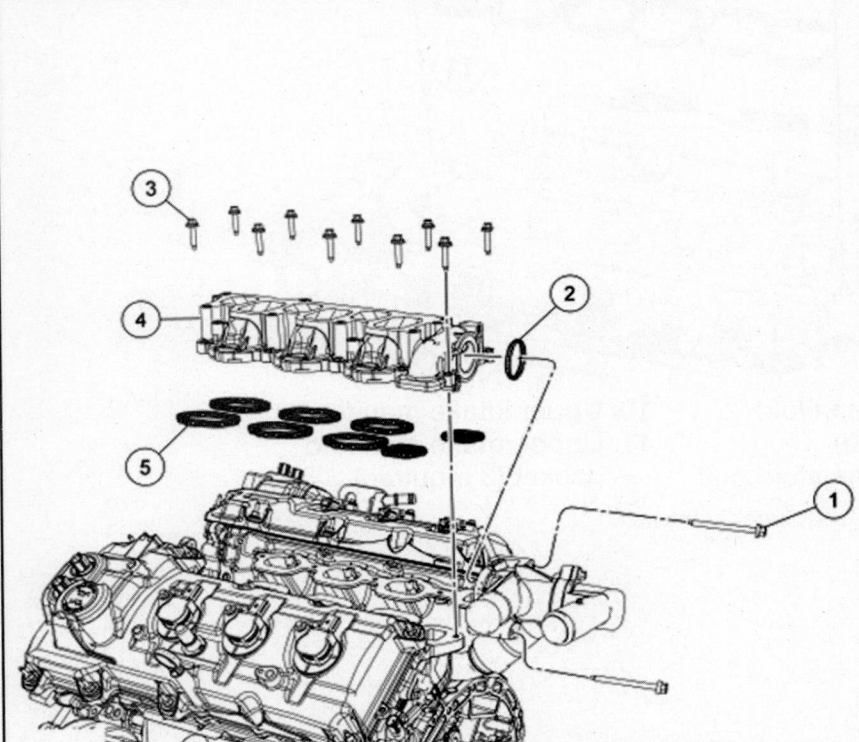

1. Thermostat housing-to-lower intake manifold bolt
2. Thermostat housing gasket
3. Lower intake manifold bolt (10 required)
4. Lower intake manifold
5. Lower intake manifold gasket (8 required)

Fig. 148 Exploded view of the lower intake manifold and related components

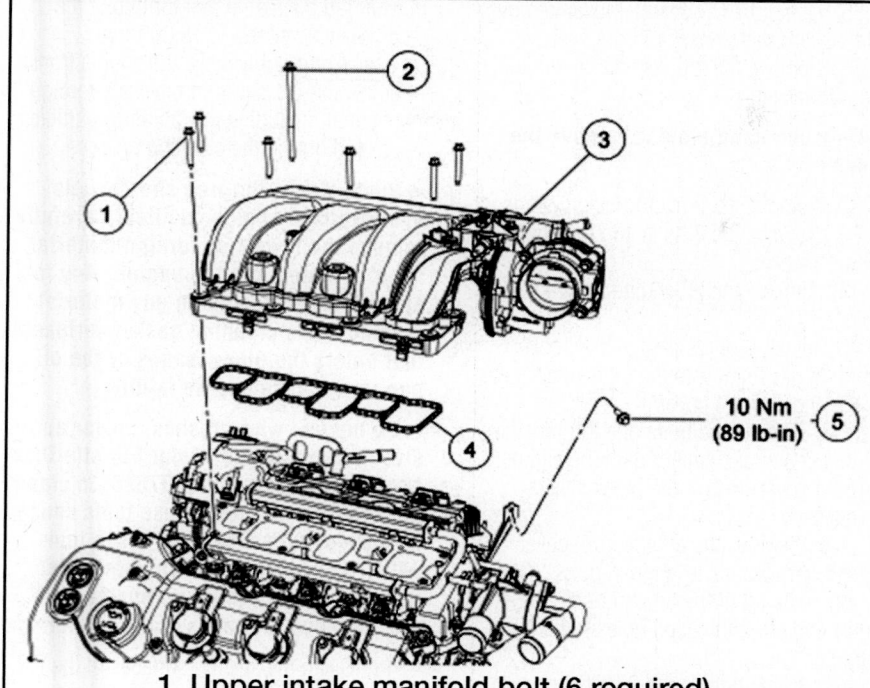

1. Upper intake manifold bolt (6 required)
2. Upper intake manifold bolt
3. Upper intake manifold
4. Upper intake manifold gasket
5. Upper intake manifold support bolt

N0117949

Fig. 150 Exploded view of the upper intake manifold

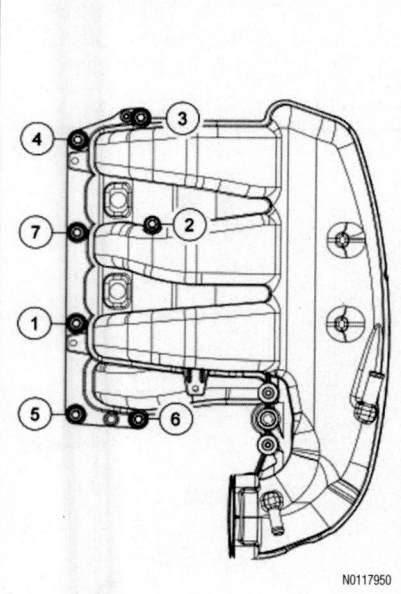

N0117950

Fig. 151 Identifying the upper intake manifold bolt tightening sequence

to the graphic(s) when servicing this component.

To install:

2. Tighten in the sequence shown in 2 stages.

a. Stage 1: Tighten to 89 inch lbs. (10 Nm).

b. Stage 2: Tighten an additional 45 degrees.

OIL PAN

REMOVAL & INSTALLATION

2010 Models

See Figures 152 through 164.

➥During engine repair procedures, cleanliness is extremely important. Any foreign material, including any material created while cleaning gasket surfaces that enters the oil passages, coolant passages or the oil pan, can cause engine failure.

➥Early build engines have 11 fastener valve covers, late build engines have 9 fastener valve covers. Do not attempt

to install bolts in the 2 empty late build valve cover holes or damage to the valve cover will occur.

All vehicles

1. Remove the engine from the vehicle.
2. Remove the 8 bolts and the flexplate.
3. Remove the crankshaft sensor ring.

➥Install the engine stand bolts into the cylinder block only. Do not install the bolts into the oil pan.

4. Mount the engine on a suitable engine stand.
5. If equipped, remove the heat shield and disconnect the block heater electrical connector.

a. Detach all of the engine block heater harness retainers and remove the harness.
6. Disconnect the PCV hose from the PCV valve.
7. Disconnect the Throttle Body (TB) electrical connector.
8. Detach the wiring harness retainers from the upper intake manifold.
9. Remove the upper intake manifold support bracket bolt.

➥If the engine is repaired or replaced because of upper engine failure, typically including valve or piston damage, check the intake manifold for metal debris. If metal debris if found, install a new intake manifold. Failure to follow these instructions can result in engine damage.

10. Remove the 6 bolts and the upper intake manifold in the sequence shown in the Intake Manifold procedure in this section.

a. Discard the gaskets.
11. Disconnect the Power Steering Pressure (PSP) switch electrical connector.

Front Wheel Drive (FWD) vehicles

12. Disconnect the RH Catalyst Monitor Sensor (CMS) electrical connector.

All vehicles

13. Disconnect the RH Variable Camshaft Timing (VCT) solenoid electrical connector.
14. Disconnect the 3 RH coil-on-plug electrical connectors.
15. Detach all of the wiring harness retainers from the RH valve cover and stud bolts.
16. Disconnect the LH CMS electrical connector.
17. Disconnect the LH VCT solenoid electrical connector.
18. Disconnect the 3 LH coil-on-plug electrical connectors.

19. Detach all of the wiring harness retainers from the LH valve cover and stud bolts.

➡**The A/C compressor must remain bolted to the engine block prior to installing the oil pan.**

20. Remove the A/C compressor nut and stud.

21. Remove the 3 bolts and the power steering pump.

22. Remove the 3 bolts and the accessory drive belt tensioner.

23. Remove the 4 nuts and the LH catalytic converter.
   a. Discard the nuts and the gasket.
   FWD vehicles

24. Remove the 4 nuts and the RH catalytic converter.
   a. Discard the nuts and the gasket.
   All vehicles

25. Remove the RH cylinder block drain plug or, if equipped, the block heater.
   a. Allow coolant to drain from the cylinder block.

26. Remove the LH cylinder block drain plug.
   a. Allow coolant to drain from the cylinder block.

27. Remove the 6 bolts and the 6 coil-on-plugs.
   Early build vehicles

28. Loosen the 11 stud bolts and remove the LH valve cover.
   a. Discard the gasket.

29. Loosen the bolt, the 10 stud bolts and remove the RH valve cover.
   a. Discard the gasket.
   Late build vehicles

30. Loosen the 9 stud bolts and remove the LH valve cover.
   a. Discard the gasket.

31. Loosen the 9 stud bolts and remove the RH valve cover.
   a. Discard the gasket.
   All vehicles

➡**VCT solenoid seal removal shown, spark plug tube seal removal similar.**

32. Inspect the VCT solenoid seals and the spark plug tube seals. Remove any damaged seals.
   a. Using the VCT Spark Plug Tube Seal Remover and Handle, remove the seal(s).

33. Using the Strap Wrench, remove the crankshaft pulley bolt and washer.
   a. Discard the bolt.

34. Using the 3 Jaw Puller, remove the crankshaft pulley.

35. Using the Oil Seal Remover, remove and discard the crankshaft front seal.

36. Remove the 2 bolts and the engine mount bracket.

➡**Only use hand tools to remove the studs.**

37. Remove the 2 engine mount studs.

38. Remove the 3 bolts and the engine mount bracket.

39. Remove the 22 engine front cover bolts.

40. Install 6 of the engine front cover bolts (finger-tight) into the 6 threaded holes in the engine front cover.
   a. Tighten the bolts one turn at a time in a crisscross pattern until the engine front cover-to-cylinder block seal is released.
   b. Remove the engine front cover.

41. Remove the 16 oil pan bolts.

42. Install 2 of the oil pan bolts (finger-tight) into the 2 threaded holes in the oil pan.
°Alternately tighten the 2 bolts one turn at a time until the oil pan-to-cylinder block seal is released.
   a. Remove the oil pan.

➡**Only use a 3M(tm) Roloc® Bristle Disk (2-in white) to clean the engine front cover and oil pan. Do not use metal scrapers, wire brushes or any other power abrasive disk to clean the engine front cover. These tools cause scratches and gouges that make leak paths.**

43. Clean the engine front cover and oil pan using a 3M(tm) Roloc® Bristle Disk (2-

in white) in a suitable tool turning at the recommended speed of 15,000 rpm.
   a. Thoroughly wash the engine front cover and oil pan to remove any foreign material, including any abrasive particles created during the cleaning process.

➡**Place clean, lint-free shop towels over exposed engine cavities. Carefully remove the towels so foreign material is not dropped into the engine. Any foreign material (including any material created while cleaning gasket surfaces) that enters the oil passages or the oil pan, may cause engine failure.**

➡**Do not use wire brushes, power abrasive discs or 3M(tm) Roloc® Bristle Disk (2-in white part number 07528) to clean the sealing surfaces. These tools cause scratches and gouges that make leak paths. They also cause contamination that will cause premature engine failure. Remove all traces of the gasket.**

44. Clean the sealing surfaces of the cylinder block in the following sequence.
   a. Remove any large deposits of silicone or gasket material.
   b. Apply silicone gasket remover and allow to set for several minutes.
   c. Remove the silicone gasket remover. A second application of silicone gasket remover may be required if residual traces of silicone or gasket material remain.
   d. Apply metal surface prep to remove any remaining traces of oil or coolant and to prepare the surfaces to bond. Do not attempt to make the metal shiny.

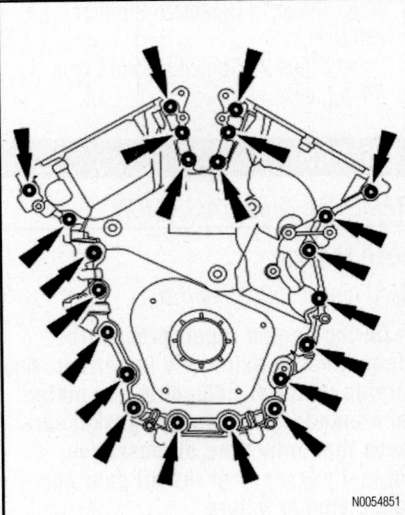

Fig. 152 Locating the 22 engine front cover bolts

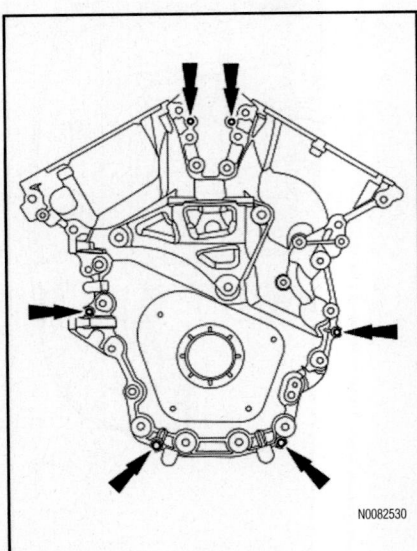

Fig. 153 Installing 6 of the engine front cover bolts finger tight

Some staining of the metal surfaces is normal.

e. Make sure the 2 locating dowel pins are seated correctly in the cylinder block.

To install:

➤During engine repair procedures, cleanliness is extremely important. Any foreign material, including any material created while cleaning gasket surfaces that enters the oil passages, coolant passages or the oil pan, can cause engine failure.

➤Early build engines have 11 fastener valve covers, late build engines have 9 fastener valve covers. Do not attempt to install bolts in the 2 empty late build valve cover holes or damage to the valve cover will occur.

All vehicles

➤Failure to use Motorcraft® High Performance Engine RTV Silicone may cause the engine oil to foam excessively and result in serious engine damage.

➤The oil pan and the 4 specified bolts must be installed and the oil pan aligned to the cylinder block and A/C compressor within 4 minutes of sealant application. Final tightening of the oil pan bolts must be carried out within 60 minutes of sealant application.

45. Apply a 0.11 inch (3 mm) bead of Motorcraft® High Performance Engine RTV

Silicone to the sealing surface of the oil pan.

a. Apply a 0.21 inch (5.5 mm) bead of Motorcraft® High Performance Engine RTV Silicone to the 2 crankshaft seal retainer plate-to-cylinder block joint areas on the sealing surface of the oil pan.

➤The oil pan and the 4 specified bolts must be installed within 4 minutes of the start of sealant application.

46. Install the oil pan and bolts 10, 11, 13 and 14.

a. Tighten the bolts in the sequence shown to 27 inch lbs. (3 Nm).

b. Loosen the bolts 180 degrees.

47. Align the oil pan to the cylinder block and the A/C compressor.

a. Position the oil pan so the mounting boss is against the A/C compressor and using a straightedge, align the oil pan flush with the rear of the cylinder block at the 2 areas shown.

48. Tighten bolts 10, 11, 13 and 14 in the sequence shown to 27 inch lbs. (3 Nm).

49. Install the remaining oil pan bolts. Tighten all the oil pan bolts in the sequence shown.

a. Tighten the large bolts (1-14) to 18 ft. lbs. (24 Nm).

b. Tighten the small bolts (15 and 16) to 89 inch lbs. (10 Nm).

50. Install the A/C compressor mounting stud and nut.

a. Tighten the stud to 80 inch lbs. (9 Nm) and the nut to 18 ft. lbs. (25 Nm).

51. Install the Alignment Pins.

➤Failure to use Motorcraft® High Performance Engine RTV Silicone may cause the engine oil to foam excessively and result in serious engine damage.

➤The engine front cover and bolts 17, 18, 19 and 20 must be installed within 4 minutes of the initial sealant application. The remainder of the engine front cover bolts and the engine mount bracket bolts must be installed and tightened within 35 minutes of the initial sealant application. If the time limits are exceeded, the sealant must be removed, the sealing area cleaned and sealant reapplied. To clean the sealing area, use silicone gasket remover and metal surface prep. Failure to follow this procedure can cause future oil leakage.

52. Apply a 0.11 inch (3.0 mm) bead of Motorcraft® High Performance Engine RTV Silicone to the engine front cover sealing surfaces including the 3 engine mount bracket bosses.

a. Apply a 0.21 inch (5.5 mm) bead of Motorcraft® High Performance Engine RTV Silicone to the oil pan-to-cylinder block joint and the cylinder head-to-cylinder block joint areas of the engine front cover in 5 places as indicated.

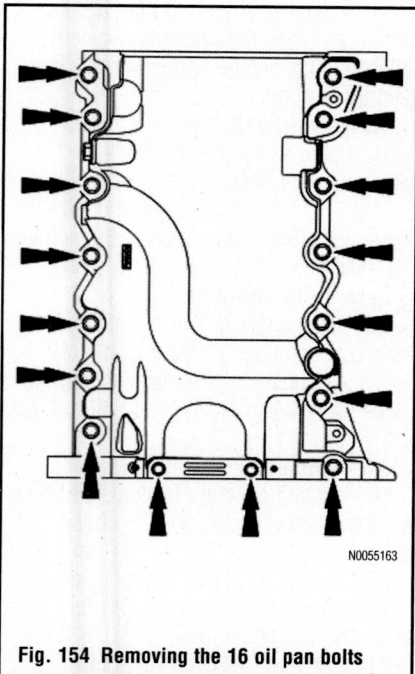

Fig. 154 Removing the 16 oil pan bolts

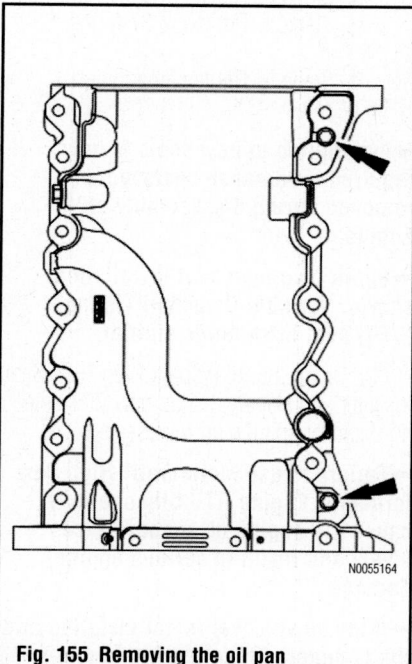

Fig. 155 Removing the oil pan

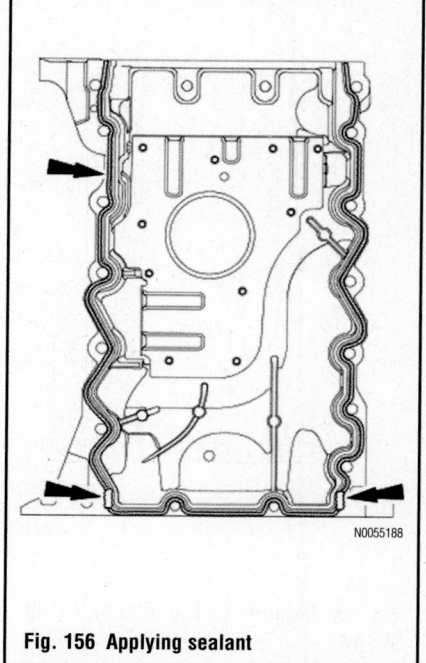

Fig. 156 Applying sealant

➡ **Make sure the 2 locating dowel pins are seated correctly in the cylinder block.**

53. Install the engine front cover and bolts 17, 18, 19 and 20.
    a. Tighten in sequence to 27 inch lbs. (3 Nm).
54. Remove the Alignment Pins.

➡ **Do not tighten the bolt at this time.**

55. Install the engine mount bracket and the 3 bolts.

➡ **Do not expose the Motorcraft® High Performance Engine RTV Silicone to engine oil for at least 90 minutes after installing the engine front cover. Failure to follow this instruction may cause oil leakage.**

56. Install the remaining engine front cover bolts. Tighten all of the engine front cover bolts and engine mount bracket bolts in the sequence shown in 2 stages:
    a. Stage 1: Tighten bolts 1 thru 22 to 89 inch lbs. (10 Nm) and bolts 23, 24 and 25 to 133 inch lbs. (15 Nm).
    b. Stage 2: Tighten bolts 1 thru 22 to 18 ft. lbs. (24 Nm) and bolts 23, 24 and 25 to 55 ft. lbs. (75 Nm).

➡ **The thread sealer on the engine mount studs (including new engine mount studs if applicable) must be cleaned off with a wire brush and new Threadlock and Sealer applied prior to**

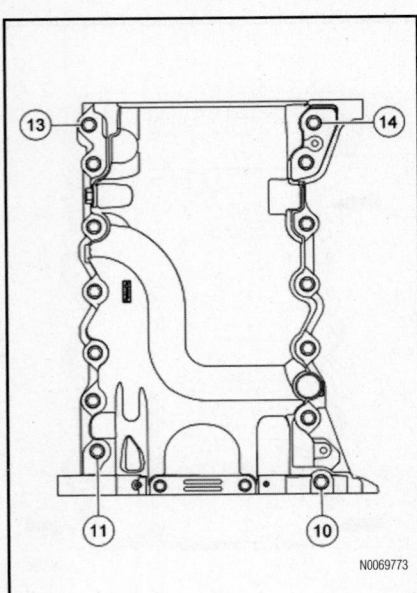

Fig. 157 Installing oil pan bolts 10, 11, 13 and 14

installing the engine mount studs. Failure to follow this procedure may result in damage to the engine mount studs or engine.

57. Install the engine mount studs in the following sequence.
    a. Clean the front cover engine mount stud holes with pressurized air to remove any foreign material.
    b. Clean all the thread sealer from the engine mount studs (old and new studs).
    c. Apply new Threadlock and Sealer to the engine mount stud threads.
    d. Install the 2 engine mount studs. Tighten to 177 inch lbs. (20 Nm).
58. Install the engine mount bracket and the 2 bolts. Tighten to 22 ft. lbs. (30 Nm).

➡ **Apply clean engine oil to the crankshaft front seal bore in the engine front cover.**

59. Using the Crankshaft Vibration Damper Installer and Front Crankshaft Seal Installer, install a new crankshaft front seal.

➡ **Lubricate the outside diameter sealing surfaces with clean engine oil.**

60. Using the Crankshaft Vibration Damper Installer and Front Cover Oil Seal Installer, install the crankshaft pulley.
61. Using the Strap Wrench, install the crankshaft pulley washer and new bolt and tighten in 4 stages.
    a. Stage 1: Tighten to 89 ft. lbs. (120 Nm).
    b. Stage 2: Loosen one full turn.
    c. Stage 3: Tighten to 37 ft. lbs. (50 Nm).
    d. Stage 4: Tighten an additional 90 degrees.

➡ **Installation of new seals is only required if damaged seals were removed during disassembly of the engine.**

➡ **Spark plug tube seal installation shown, Variable Camshaft Timing (VCT) seal installation similar.**

62. Using the VCT Spark Plug Tube Seal Installer and Handle, install new VCT solenoid and/or spark plug tube seals.

➡ **Failure to use Motorcraft® High Performance Engine RTV Silicone may cause the engine oil to foam excessively and result in serious engine damage.**

➡ **If the valve cover is not installed and the fasteners tightened within 4 min-**

utes, the sealant must be removed and the sealing area cleaned. To clean the sealing area, use silicone gasket remover and metal surface prep. Failure to follow this procedure can cause future oil leakage.

63. Apply a 0.31 inch (8 mm) bead of Motorcraft® High Performance Engine RTV Silicone to the engine front cover-to-RH cylinder head joints.

Early build vehicles
64. Using a new gasket, install the RH valve cover and tighten the bolt and 10 stud bolts.
    a. Tighten in the sequence shown in the Valve Cover procedure to 89 inch lbs. (10 Nm).

Late build vehicles
65. Using a new gasket, install the RH valve cover and tighten the 9 stud bolts.
    a. Tighten in the sequence shown in the Valve Cover procedure to 89 inch lbs. (10 Nm).

➡ **Failure to use Motorcraft® High Performance Engine RTV Silicone may cause the engine oil to foam excessively and result in serious engine damage.**

➡ **If the valve cover is not installed and the fasteners tightened within 4 minutes, the sealant must be removed and the sealing area cleaned. To clean the sealing area, use silicone gasket remover and metal surface prep. Failure to follow this procedure can cause future oil leakage.**

66. Apply a 0.31 inch (8 mm) bead of Motorcraft® High Performance Engine RTV Silicone to the engine front cover-to-LH cylinder head joints.

Early build vehicles
67. Using a new gasket, install the LH valve cover and tighten the 11 stud bolts.
    a. Tighten in the sequence shown in the Valve Cover procedure to 89 inch lbs. (10 Nm).

Late build vehicles
68. Using a new gasket, install the LH valve cover and tighten the 9 stud bolts.
    a. Tighten in the sequence shown in the Valve Cover procedure to 89 inch lbs. (10 Nm).

All vehicles
69. Install the 6 coil-on-plug assemblies and the 6 bolts. Tighten to 62 inch lbs. (7 Nm).
70. Install the LH cylinder block drain plug. Tighten to 177 inch lbs. (20 Nm) plus an additional 180 degrees.
71. Install the RH cylinder block drain

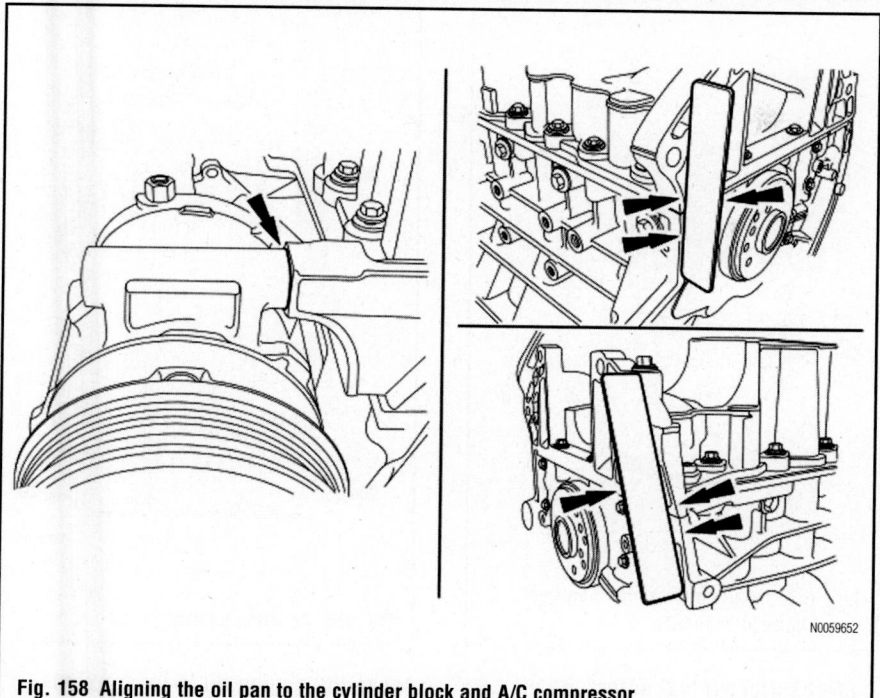

Fig. 158 Aligning the oil pan to the cylinder block and A/C compressor

plug or, if equipped, the block heater. Tighten to 30 ft. lbs. (40 Nm).

Front Wheel Drive (FWD) vehicles

72. Using a new gasket, install the RH catalytic converter and 4 new nuts. Tighten to 30 ft. lbs. (40 Nm).

All vehicles

73. Using a new gasket, install the LH catalytic converter and 4 new nuts. Tighten to 30 ft. lbs. (40 Nm).

74. Install the accessory drive belt ten-sioner and the 3 bolts. Tighten to 97 inch lbs. (11 Nm).

75. Install the power steering pump and the 3 bolts. Tighten to 18 ft. lbs. (24 Nm).

76. Attach all of the wiring harness retainers to the LH valve cover and stud bolts.

77. Connect the 3 LH coil-on-plug electrical connectors.

78. Connect the LH camshaft VCT solenoid electrical connector.

79. Connect the LH Catalyst Monitor Sensor (CMS) electrical connector.

80. Attach all of the wiring harness retainers to the RH valve cover and stud bolts.

81. Connect the 3 RH coil-on-plug electrical connectors.

82. Connect the RH VCT solenoid electrical connector.

FWD vehicles

83. Connect the RH CMS electrical connector.

All vehicles

84. Connect the Power Steering Pressure (PSP) switch electrical connector.

➡️**If the engine is repaired or replaced because of upper engine failure, typically including valve or piston damage, check the intake manifold for metal debris. If metal debris is found, install a new intake manifold. Failure to follow these instructions can result in engine damage.**

85. Using new gaskets, install the upper intake manifold and the 6 bolts.
    a. Tighten in the sequence shown to 89 inch lbs. (10 Nm).

86. Install the upper intake manifold support bracket bolt.
    a. Tighten to 89 inch lbs. (10 Nm).

87. Attach the wiring harness retainers to the upper intake manifold.

88. Connect the Throttle Body (TB) electrical connector.

89. Connect the PCV hose to the PCV valve.

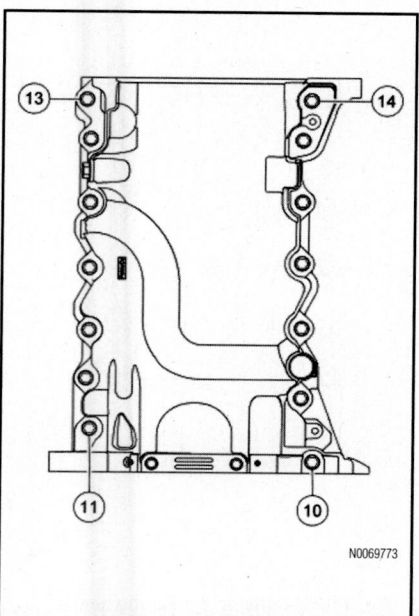

Fig. 159 Tightening the bolts in sequence

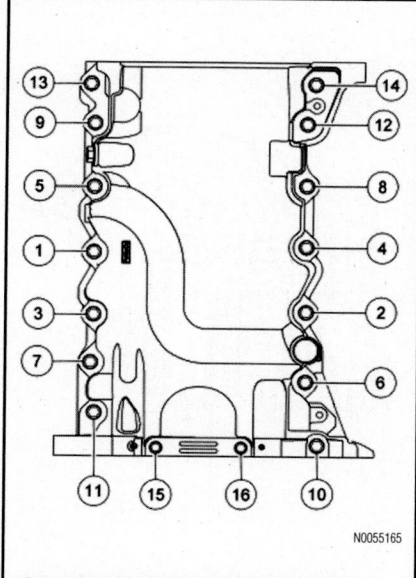

Fig. 160 Identifying the oil pan bolt tightening sequence

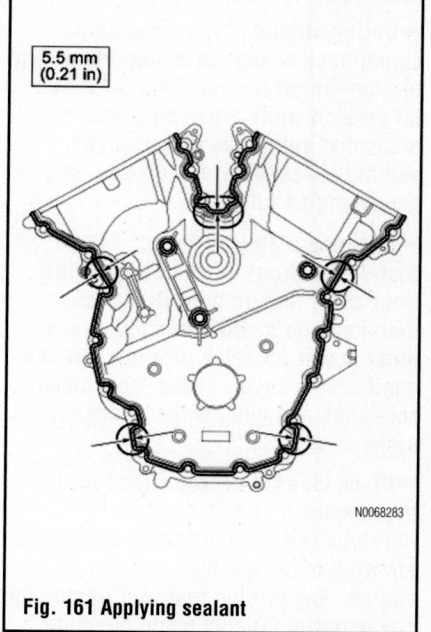

Fig. 161 Applying sealant

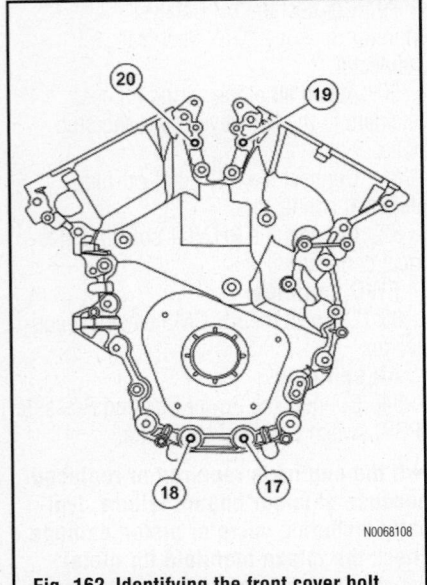

Fig. 162 Identifying the front cover bolt installation sequence

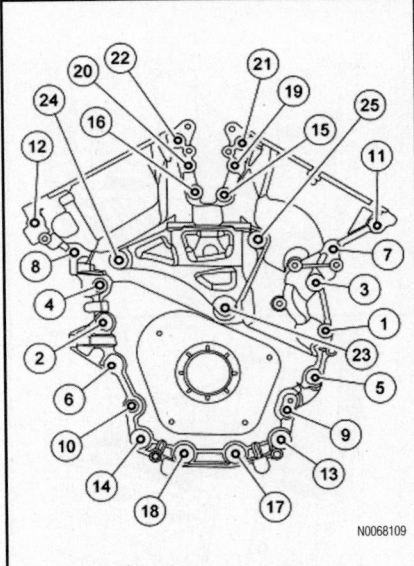

Fig. 163 Installing the remaining front cover bolts in sequence

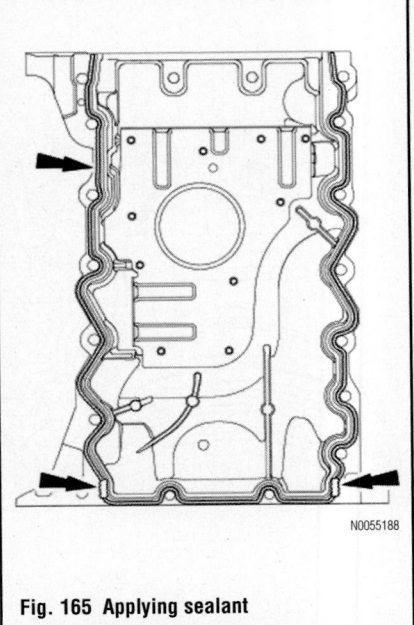

Fig. 165 Applying sealant

90. If equipped, position the engine block heater harness on the engine and attach all of the harness retainers.

   a. Connect the engine block heater electrical connector and install the heat shield.

91. Using the Heavy Duty Floor Crane and Spreader Bar, remove the engine from the stand.

92. Install the crankshaft sensor ring.

93. Install the flexplate and the 8 bolts.

   a. Tighten to 59 ft. lbs. (80 Nm).

94. Install the engine in the vehicle.

2011 Models

See Figures 165 through 168.

➡During engine repair procedures, cleanliness is extremely important. Any foreign material, including any material created while cleaning gasket surfaces that enters the oil passages, coolant passages or the oil pan, can cause engine failure.

➡Only use a 3M(tm) Roloc® Bristle Disk (2-in white) to clean the engine front cover and oil pan. Do not use metal scrapers, wire brushes or any other power abrasive disk to clean the engine front cover. These tools cause scratches and gouges that make leak paths.

➡Place clean, lint-free shop towels over exposed engine cavities. Carefully remove the towels so foreign material is not dropped into the engine. Any foreign material (including any material created while cleaning

gasket surfaces) that enters the oil passages or the oil pan, may cause engine failure.

➡At the time of publication the manufacturer does not provide a specific Removal and Installation procedure for this component. Refer to the graphic(s) when servicing this component. Items in the exploded views may not be listed in order of removal.

To install:

➡Failure to use Motorcraft® High Performance Engine RTV Silicone may

cause the engine oil to foam excessively and result in serious engine damage.

➡The oil pan and the 4 specified bolts must be installed and the oil pan aligned to the cylinder block and A/C compressor within 4 minutes of sealant application. Final tightening of the oil pan bolts must be carried out within 60 minutes of sealant application.

1. Apply a 0.11 inch (3 mm) bead of Motorcraft® High Performance Engine RTV

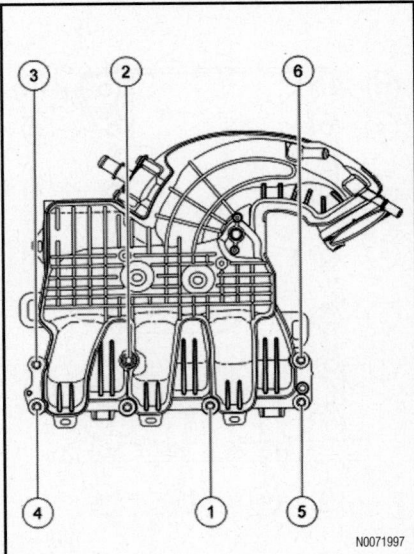

Fig. 164 Installing the upper intake manifold

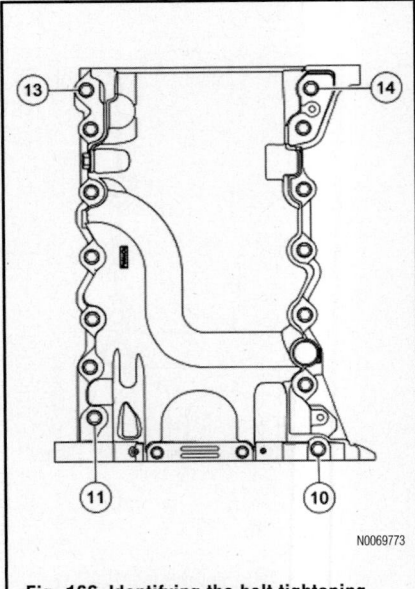

Fig. 166 Identifying the bolt tightening sequence

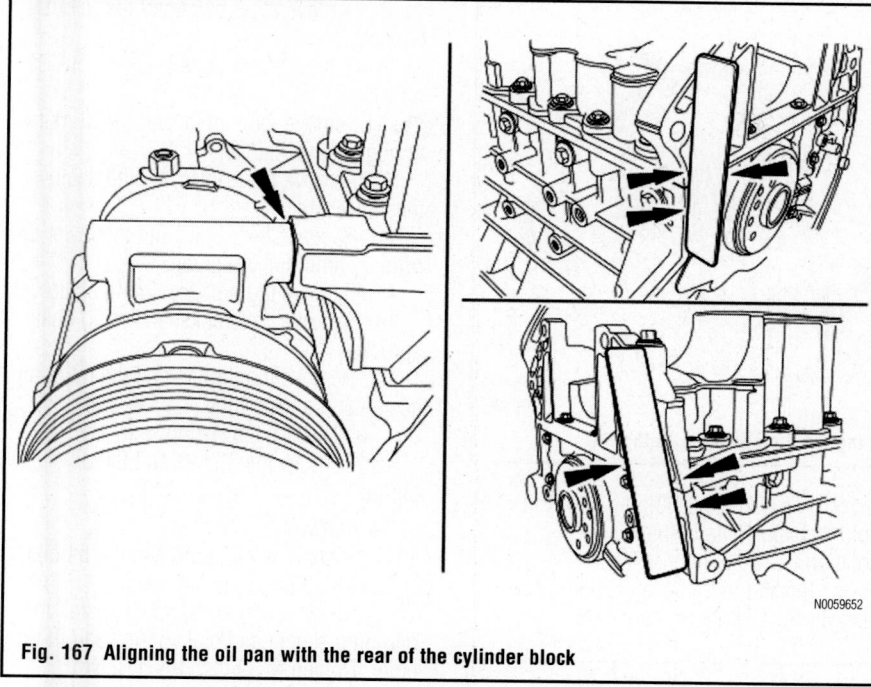

Fig. 167 Aligning the oil pan with the rear of the cylinder block

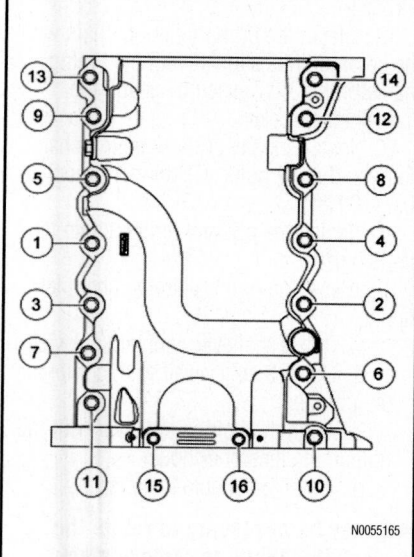

Fig. 168 Installing the remaining oil pan bolts

Silicone to the sealing surface of the oil pan.

    a. Apply a 0.21 inch (5.5 mm) bead of Motorcraft® High Performance Engine RTV Silicone to the 2 crankshaft seal retainer plate-to-cylinder block joint areas on the sealing surface of the oil pan.

➡**The oil pan and the 4 specified bolts must be installed within 4 minutes of the start of sealant application.**

2. Install the oil pan and bolts 10, 11, 13 and 14.

    a. Tighten the bolts in the sequence shown to 27 inch lbs. (3 Nm).

    b. Loosen the bolts 180 degrees.

3. Align the oil pan to the cylinder block and the A/C compressor.

    a. Position the oil pan so the mounting boss is against the A/C compressor and using a straightedge; align the oil pan flush with the rear of the cylinder block at the 2 areas shown.

4. Tighten bolts 10, 11, 13 and 14 in the sequence shown, to 27 inch lbs.

(3 Nm).

5. Install the remaining oil pan bolts. Tighten all the oil pan bolts in the sequence shown.

    a. Tighten the large bolts (1-14) to 18 ft. lbs. (24 Nm).

    b. Tighten the small bolts (15 and 16) to 89 inch lbs. (10 Nm).

OIL PUMP

REMOVAL & INSTALLATION

2010 Models

See Figures 169 through 175.

➡**During engine repair procedures, cleanliness is extremely important. Any foreign material, including any material created while cleaning gasket surfaces that enters the oil passages, coolant passages or the oil pan may cause engine failure.**

➡**On early build engines, the timing chain rides on the inner side of the RH timing chain guide. Late build engines are equipped with a different design RH timing chain guide that requires the timing chain to ride on the outer side of the RH timing chain guide. For service, all replacement RH timing chain guides will be the late build design.**

    All vehicles
1. Remove the engine front cover.
    Engines equipped with early build RH timing chain guides
2. Rotate the crankshaft clockwise and align the timing marks on the Variable Camshaft Timing (VCT) assemblies as shown.
    Engines equipped with late

Fig. 169 Rotating the crankshaft clockwise and aligning the timing marks on the VCT

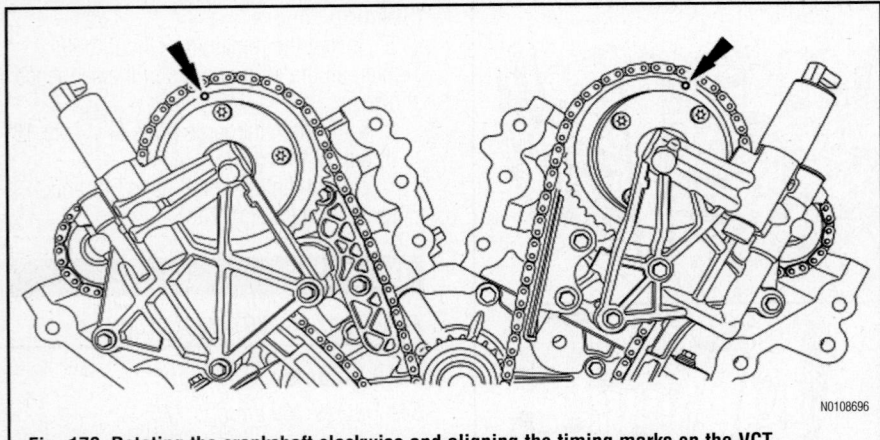

Fig. 170 Rotating the crankshaft clockwise and aligning the timing marks on the VCT

N0108696

build/replacement RH timing chain guides

3. Rotate the crankshaft clockwise and align the timing marks on the VCT assemblies as shown.

All vehicles

→ **The Camshaft Holding Tool will hold the camshafts in the Top Dead Center (TDC) position.**

4. Install the Camshaft Holding Tool onto the flats of the LH camshafts.

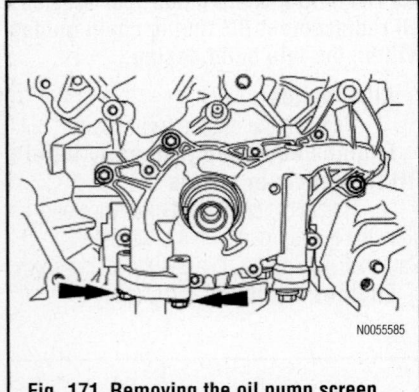

Fig. 171 Removing the oil pump screen and pickup tube

N0055585

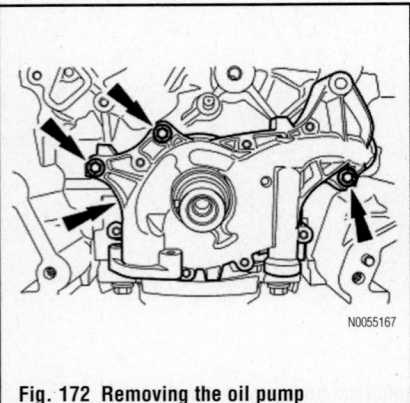

Fig. 172 Removing the oil pump

N0055167

5. The Camshaft Holding Tool will hold the camshafts in the TDC position.

6. Install the Camshaft Holding Tool onto the flats of the RH camshafts.

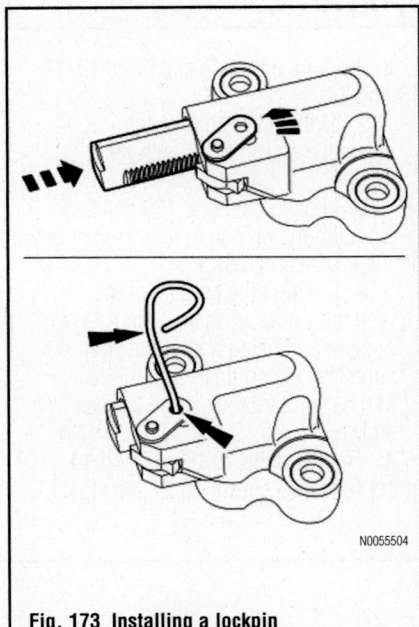

Fig. 173 Installing a lockpin

N0055504

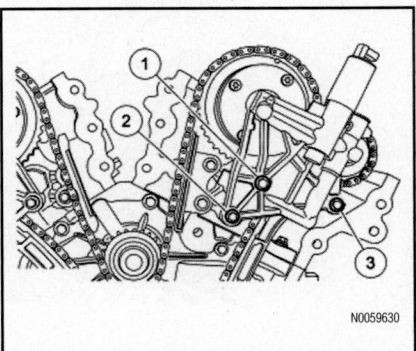

Fig. 174 Identifying the LH VCT housing bolt tightening sequence

N0059630

7. Remove the 3 bolts and the RH VCT housing.

8. Remove the 3 bolts and the LH VCT housing.

9. Remove the 2 bolts and the primary timing chain tensioner.

10. Remove the primary timing chain tensioner arm.

11. Remove the 2 bolts and the lower LH primary timing chain guide.

12. Remove the primary timing chain.

13. Remove the crankshaft timing chain sprocket.

14. Remove the 2 bolts and the oil pump screen and pickup tube.

   a. Discard the O-ring seal.

15. Remove the 3 bolts and the oil pump.

To install:

16. Install the oil pump and the 3 bolts. Tighten to 89 inch lbs. (10 Nm).

17. Using a new O-ring seal, install the oil pump screen and pickup tube and the 2 bolts. Tighten to 89 inch lbs. (10 Nm).

18. Install the crankshaft timing chain sprocket.

19. Install the primary timing chain with the colored links aligned with the timing marks on the VCT assemblies and the crankshaft sprocket.

20. Install the LH primary timing chain guide and the 2 bolts. Tighten to 89 inch lbs. (10 Nm).

21. Install the primary timing chain tensioner arm.

22. Reset the primary timing chain tensioner.

   a. Rotate the lever counterclockwise.

   b. Using a soft-jawed vise, compress the plunger.

   c. Align the hole in the lever with the hole in the tensioner housing.

   d. Install a suitable lockpin.

→ **It may be necessary to rotate the crankshaft slightly to remove slack from the timing chain and install the tensioner.**

23. Install the primary tensioner and the 2 bolts. Tighten to 89 inch lbs. (10 Nm).

   a. Remove the lockpin.

24. As a post-check, verify correct alignment of all timing marks.

25. Inspect the VCT housing seals for damage and replace as necessary.

→ **Make sure the dowels on the Variable Camshaft Timing (VCT) housing are fully engaged in the cylinder head prior to tightening the bolts. Failure to follow this process will result in severe engine damage.**

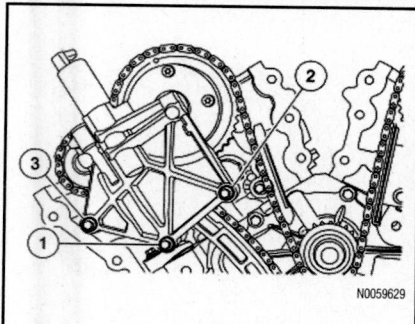

Fig. 175 Identifying the RH VCT housing bolt tightening sequence

26. Install the LH VCT housing and the 3 bolts. Tighten in the sequence shown to 89 inch lbs. (10 Nm).

➡**Make sure the dowels on the Variable Camshaft Timing (VCT) housing are fully engaged in the cylinder head prior to tightening the bolts. Failure to follow this process will result in severe engine damage.**

27. Install the RH VCT housing and the 3 bolts. Tighten in the sequence shown to 89 inch lbs. (10 Nm).
28. Install the engine front cover.

2011 Models

See Figure 176.

➡**During engine repair procedures, cleanliness is extremely important. Any foreign material, including any material created while cleaning gasket surfaces, that enters the oil passages, coolant passages or the oil pan may cause engine failure.**

At the time of publication the manufacturer does not provide a specific Removal and Installation procedure for this component. Refer to the graphic(s) when servicing this component. Items in the exploded views may not be listed in order of removal.

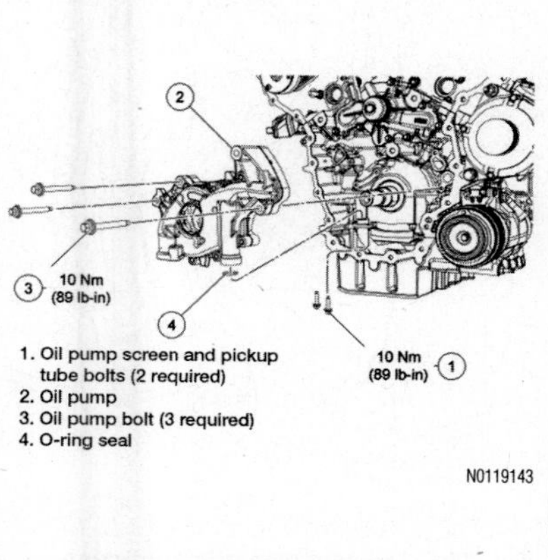

PISTON AND RING

POSITIONING
See Figure 177.

➡**The piston compression upper and lower ring should be installed with the "O" mark on the ring face pointing up toward the top of the piston.**

1. Install the piston rings onto the piston as shown.
2. Center line of the piston parallel to the wrist pin bore
3. Upper compression ring gap location
4. Upper oil control segment ring gap location
5. Lower oil control segment ring gap location
6. Expander ring and lower compression ring gap location

REAR MAIN SEAL

REMOVAL & INSTALLATION
See Figure 178.

1. With the vehicle in NEUTRAL, position it on a hoist.
2. Remove the flexplate.
3. Remove the crankshaft sensor ring.
4. Using the Crankshaft Rear Oil Seal Remover and Slide Hammer, remove and discard the crankshaft rear seal.
   a. Clean all sealing surfaces with metal surface prep.

To install:

➡**Lubricate the seal lips and bore with clean engine oil prior to installation.**

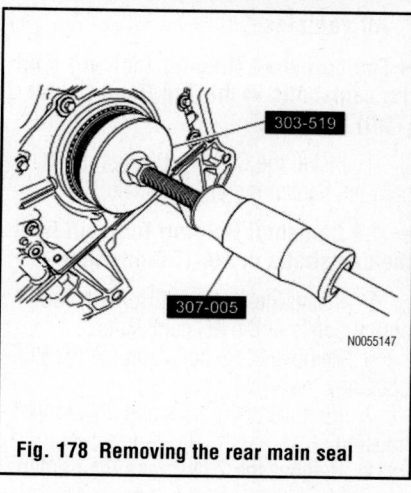

Fig. 178 Removing the rear main seal

5. Position the Rear Main Seal Installer onto the end of the crankshaft and slide a new crankshaft rear seal onto the tool.
6. Using the Rear Main Seal Installer and Handle, install the new crankshaft rear seal.
7. Install the crankshaft sensor ring.
8. Install the flexplate.

TIMING CHAIN & SPROCKETS

REMOVAL & INSTALLATION
See Figures 179 through 193.

➡**During engine repair procedures, cleanliness is extremely important. Any foreign material, including any material created while cleaning gasket surfaces that enters the oil passages, coolant passages or the oil pan may cause engine failure.**

➡**On early build engines, the timing chain rides on the inner side of the RH timing chain guide. Late build engines are equipped with a different design RH timing chain guide that requires the timing chain to ride on the outer side of the RH timing chain guide. For service, all replacement RH timing chain guides will be the late build design.**

All vehicles
1. Remove the engine front cover.
Engines equipped with early build RH timing chain guides
2. Rotate the crankshaft clockwise and align the timing marks on the Variable Camshaft Timing (VCT) assemblies as shown.
Engines equipped with late build/replacement RH timing chain guides
3. Rotate the crankshaft clockwise and align the timing marks on the VCT assemblies as shown.

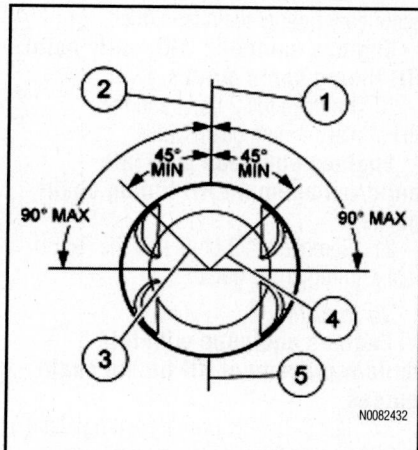

1. Oil pump screen and pickup tube bolts (2 required)
2. Oil pump
3. Oil pump bolt (3 required)
4. O-ring seal

Fig. 176 Exploded view of the oil pump

Fig. 177 Positioning the piston and ring

All vehicles

➡**The Camshaft Holding Tool will hold the camshafts in the Top Dead Center (TDC) position.**

4. Install the Camshaft Holding Tool onto the flats of the LH camshafts.

➡**The Camshaft Holding Tool will hold the camshafts in the TDC position.**

5. Install the Camshaft Holding Tool onto the flats of the RH camshafts.

6. Remove the 3 bolts and the RH VCT housing.

7. Remove the 3 bolts and the LH VCT housing.

8. Remove the 2 bolts and the primary timing chain tensioner.

9. Remove the primary timing chain tensioner arm.

10. Remove the 2 bolts and the lower LH primary timing chain guide.

11. Remove the primary timing chain.

12. Remove the crankshaft timing chain sprocket.

13. Remove the 2 bolts and the upper LH primary timing chain guide.

14. Compress the LH secondary timing chain tensioner and install a suitable lock-pin to retain the tensioner in the collapsed position.

➡**The VCT bolt and the exhaust camshaft bolt must be discarded and new ones installed. However, the exhaust camshaft washer is reusable.**

15. Remove and discard the LH VCT assembly bolt and the LH exhaust camshaft sprocket bolt.

a. Remove the LH VCT assembly, secondary timing chain and the LH exhaust camshaft sprocket as an assembly.

➡**It is necessary to tilt the Camshaft Holding Tool toward the rear of the engine to access the rearmost secondary timing chain tensioner bolt.**

16. Remove the 2 bolts and the LH secondary timing chain tensioner.

17. Compress the RH secondary timing chain tensioner and install a suitable lock-pin to retain the tensioner in the collapsed position.

➡**The VCT bolt and the exhaust camshaft bolt must be discarded and new ones installed. However, the exhaust camshaft washer is reusable.**

18. Remove and discard the RH VCT assembly bolt and the RH exhaust camshaft sprocket bolt.

a. Remove the RH VCT assembly,

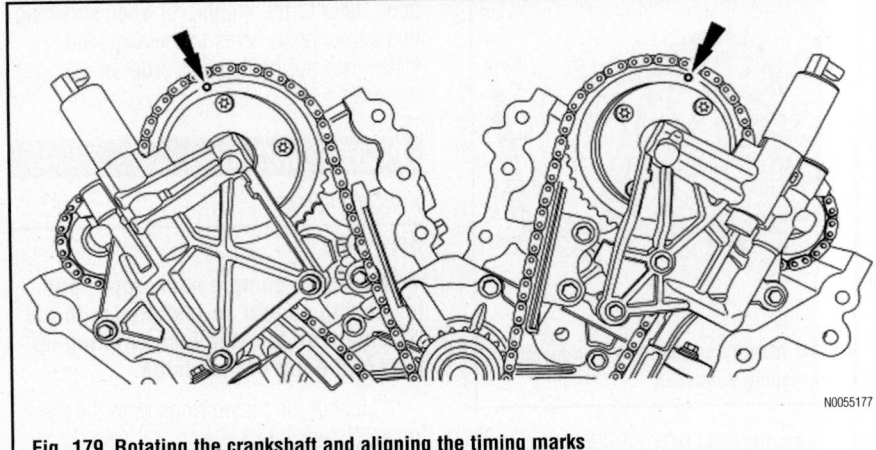

Fig. 179 Rotating the crankshaft and aligning the timing marks

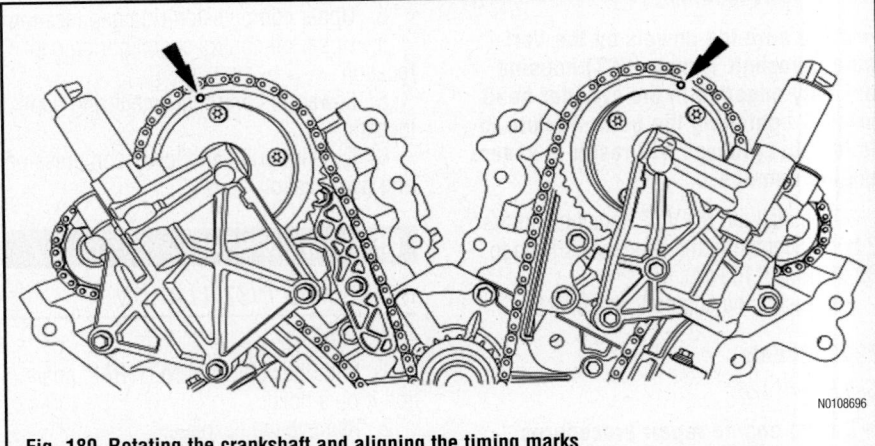

Fig. 180 Rotating the crankshaft and aligning the timing marks

secondary timing chain and the RH exhaust camshaft sprocket as an assembly.

➡**It is necessary to tilt the Camshaft Holding Tool toward the rear of the engine to access the rearmost secondary timing chain tensioner bolt.**

19. Remove the 2 bolts and the RH secondary timing chain tensioner.

Engines equipped with early build RH timing chain guides

20. Remove the 2 bolts and the RH primary timing chain guide.

Engines equipped with late build/replacement RH timing chain guides

21. Remove the 2 bolts and the RH primary timing chain guide.

To install:

Engines equipped with late build/replacement RH timing chain guides

22. Install the RH primary timing chain guide and the 2 bolts.

a. Tighten to 89 inch lbs. (10 Nm).

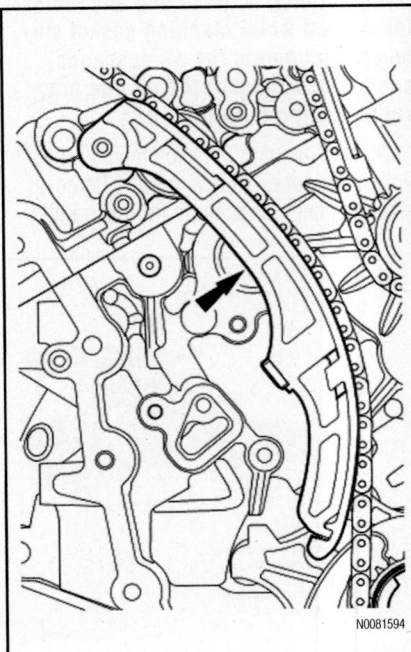

Fig. 181 Removing the primary timing chain tensioner arm

Engines equipped with early build RH timing chain guides

23. Install the RH primary timing chain guide and the 2 bolts.

    a. Tighten to 89 inch lbs. (10 Nm).

All vehicles

➡ **It is necessary to tilt the Camshaft Holding Tool toward the rear of the engine to access the rearmost secondary timing chain tensioner bolt.**

24. Install the RH secondary timing chain tensioner and the 2 bolts.

    a. Tighten to 89 inch lbs. (10 Nm).

25. Assemble the RH VCT assembly, the RH exhaust camshaft sprocket and the RH secondary timing chain.

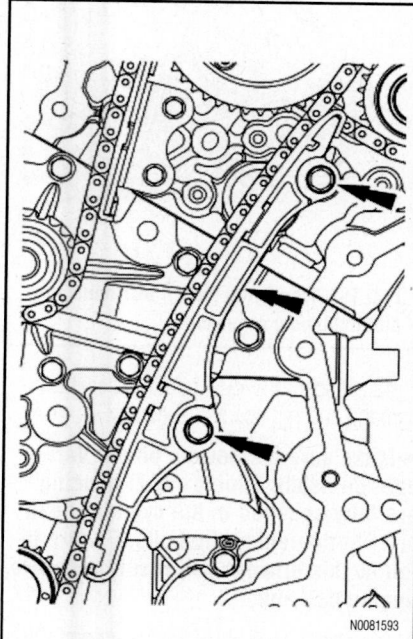

Fig. 182 Removing the LH primary timing chain guide

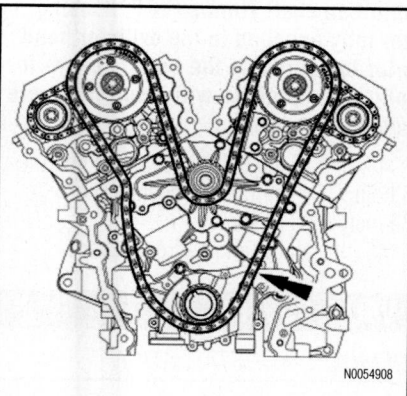

Fig. 183 Removing the primary timing chain

    a. Align the colored links with the timing marks.

26. Position the RH secondary timing assembly onto the camshafts.

27. Install the new VCT bolt and new exhaust camshaft bolt and the original washer. Tighten in 4 stages.

    a. Stage 1: Tighten to 30 ft. lbs. (40 Nm).

    b. Stage 2: Loosen one full turn.

    c. Stage 3: Tighten to 89 inch lbs. (10 Nm).

    d. Stage 4: Tighten 90 degrees.

28. Remove the lockpin from the RH secondary timing chain tensioner.

➡ **It is necessary to tilt the Camshaft Holding Tool toward the rear of the engine to access the rearmost secondary timing chain tensioner bolt.**

29. Install the LH secondary timing chain tensioner and the 2 bolts.

    a. Tighten to 89 inch lbs. (10 Nm).

30. Assemble the LH VCT assembly, the LH exhaust camshaft sprocket and the LH secondary timing chain.

    a. Align the colored links with the timing marks.

31. Position the LH secondary timing assembly onto the camshafts.

32. Install the new VCT bolt and new exhaust camshaft bolt and the original washer. Tighten in 4 stages.

    a. Stage 1: Tighten to 30 ft0 lbs. (40 Nm).

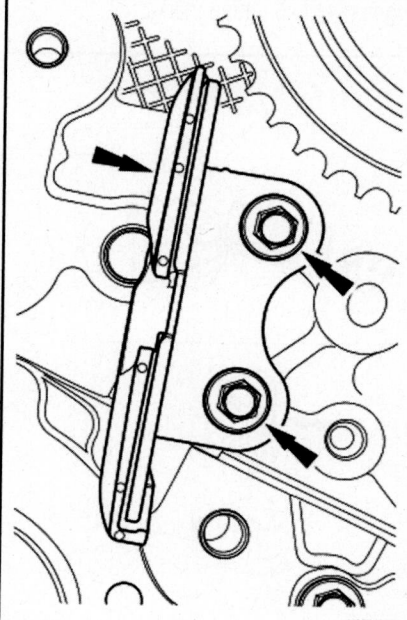

Fig. 184 Removing the LH primary timing chain guide

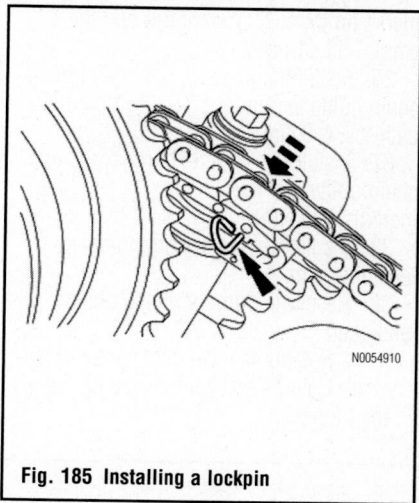

Fig. 185 Installing a lockpin

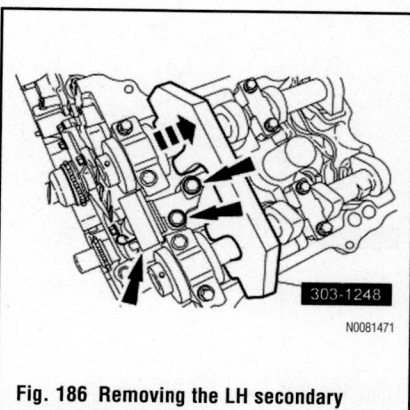

Fig. 186 Removing the LH secondary timing chain tensioner

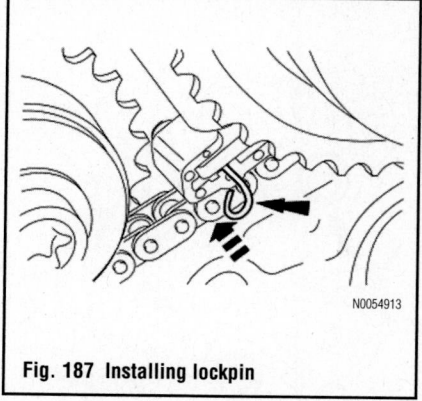

Fig. 187 Installing lockpin

    b. Stage 2: Loosen one full turn.

    c. Stage 3: Tighten to 89 inch lbs. (10 Nm).

    d. Stage 4: Tighten 90 degrees.

33. Remove the lockpin from the LH secondary timing chain tensioner.

34. Install the crankshaft timing chain sprocket.

35. Install the primary timing chain with the colored links aligned with the timing

marks on the VCT assemblies and the crankshaft sprocket.

36. Install the upper LH primary timing chain guide and the 2 bolts. Tighten to 89 inch lbs. (10 Nm).

37. Install the lower LH primary timing chain guide and the 2 bolts. Tighten to 89 inch lbs. (10 Nm).

38. Install the primary timing chain tensioner arm.

39. Reset the primary timing chain tensioner.

    a. Rotate the lever counterclockwise.

    b. Using a soft-jawed vise, compress the plunger.

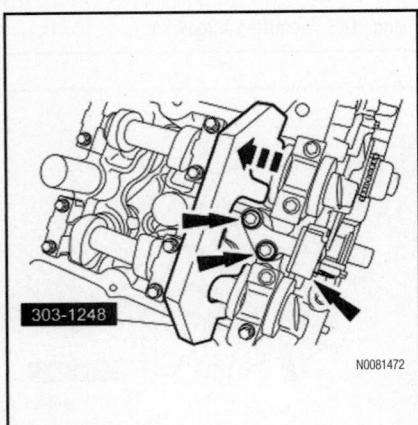

Fig. 188 Removing the RH secondary timing chain tensioner

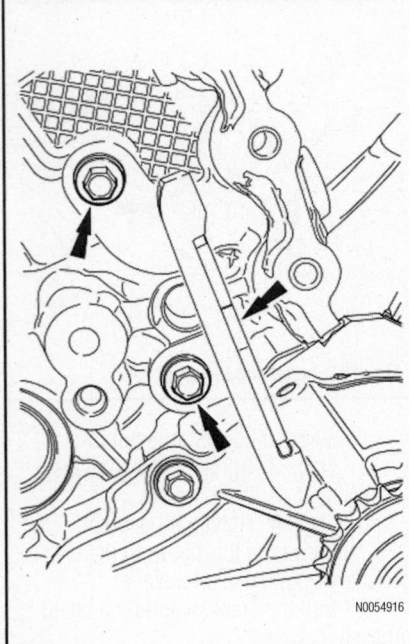

Fig. 189 Removing the primary timing chain guide

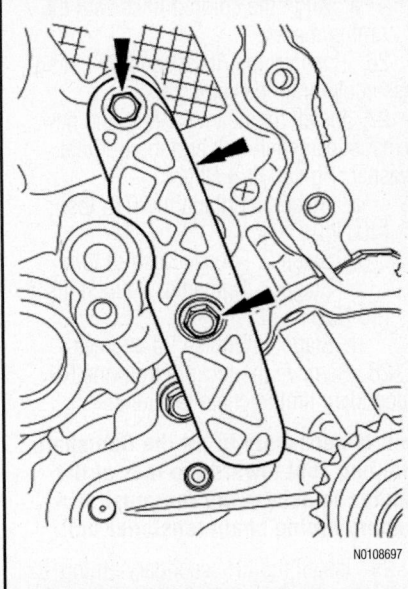

Fig. 190 Removing the RH primary timing chain guide

    c. Align the hole in the lever with the hole in the tensioner housing.

    d. Install a suitable lockpin.

➡**It may be necessary to rotate the crankshaft slightly to remove slack from the timing chain and install the tensioner.**

40. Install the primary tensioner and the 2 bolts. Tighten to 89 inch lbs. (10 Nm).

    a. Remove the lockpin.

41. As a post-check, verify correct alignment of all timing marks.

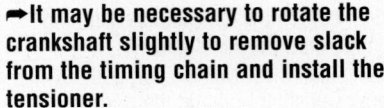

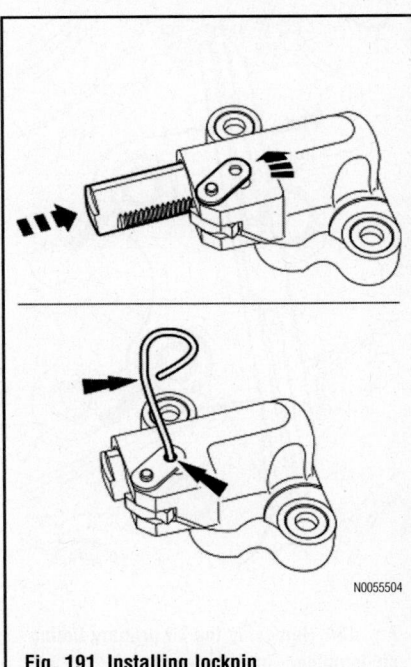

Fig. 191 Installing lockpin

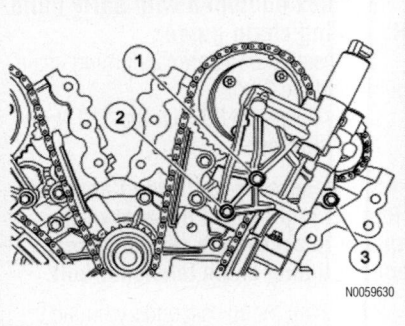

Fig. 192 Identifying the LH VCT housing bolt tightening sequence

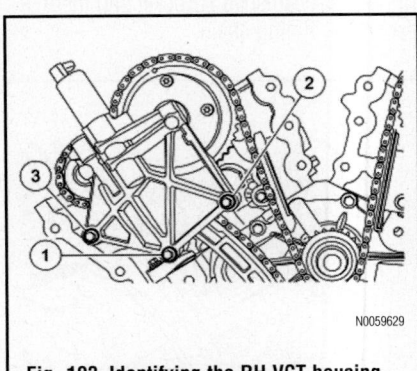

Fig. 193 Identifying the RH VCT housing bolt tightening sequence

42. Inspect the VCT housing seals for damage and replace as necessary.

➡**Make sure the dowels on the Variable Camshaft Timing (VCT) housing are fully engaged in the cylinder head prior to tightening the bolts. Failure to follow this process will result in severe engine damage.**

43. Install the LH VCT housing and the 3 bolts. Tighten in the sequence shown to 89 inch lbs. (10 Nm).

➡**Make sure the dowels on the Variable Camshaft Timing (VCT) housing are fully engaged in the cylinder head prior to tightening the bolts. Failure to follow this process will result in severe engine damage.**

44. Install the RH VCT housing and the 3 bolts. Tighten in the sequence shown to 89 inch lbs. (10 Nm).

45. Install the engine front cover.

VALVE COVERS

REMOVAL & INSTALLATION

Left Side

See Figures 194 through 197.

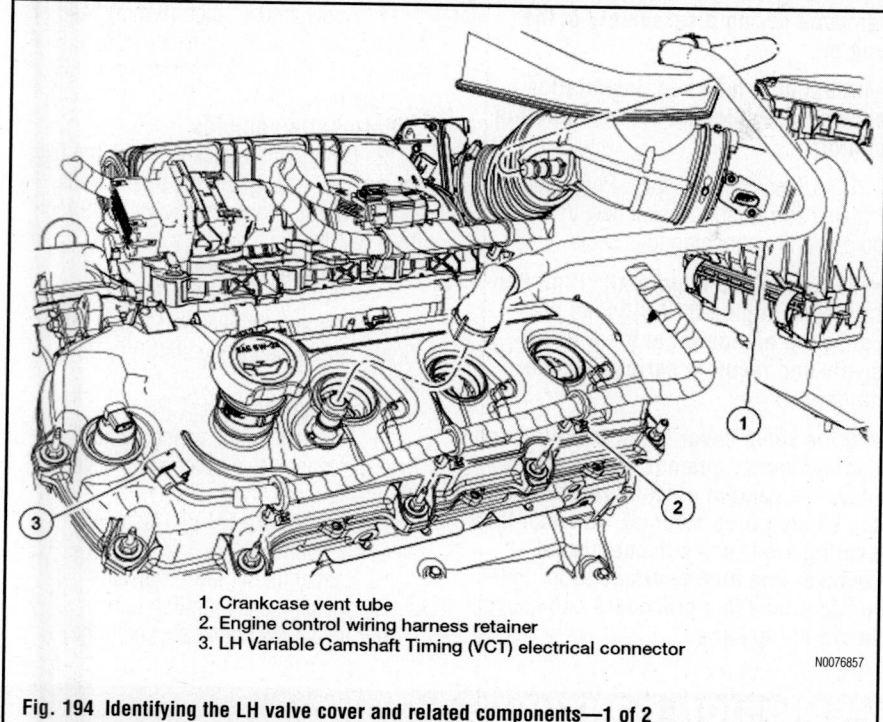

1. Crankcase vent tube
2. Engine control wiring harness retainer
3. LH Variable Camshaft Timing (VCT) electrical connector

N0076857

Fig. 194 Identifying the LH valve cover and related components—1 of 2

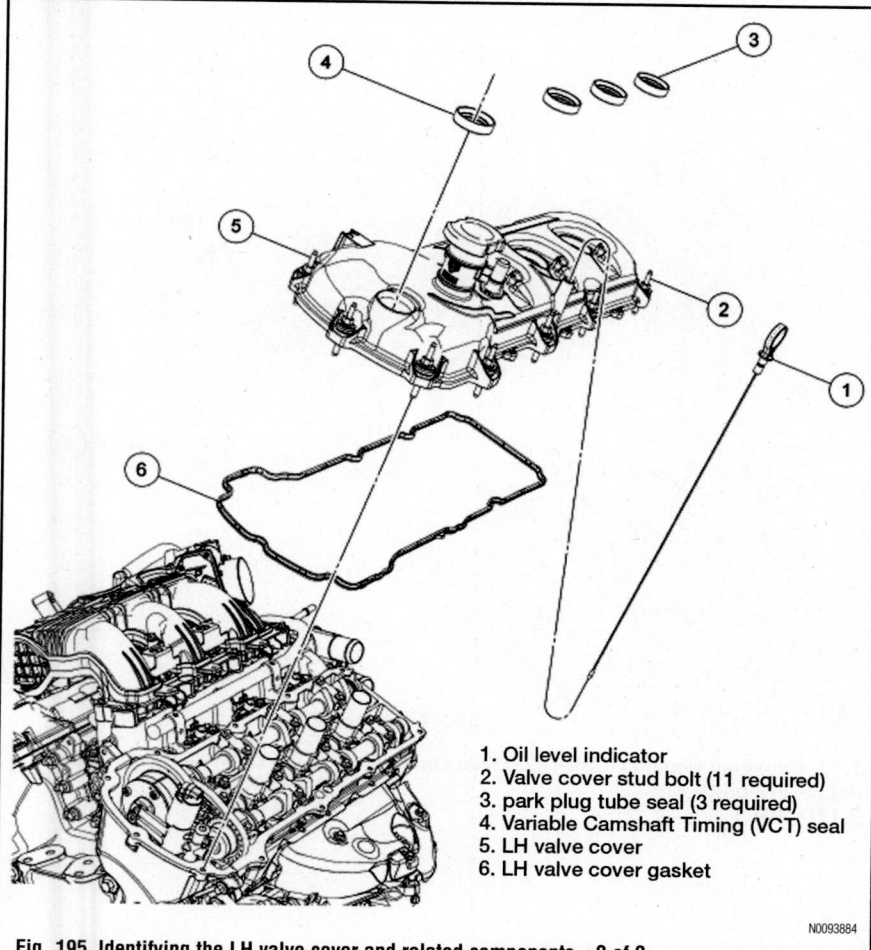

1. Oil level indicator
2. Valve cover stud bolt (11 required)
3. park plug tube seal (3 required)
4. Variable Camshaft Timing (VCT) seal
5. LH valve cover
6. LH valve cover gasket

N0093884

Fig. 195 Identifying the LH valve cover and related components—2 of 2

➡During engine repair procedures, cleanliness is extremely important. Any foreign material, including any material created while cleaning gasket surfaces that enters the oil passages, coolant passages or the oil pan, can cause engine failure.

➡Early build engines have 11 fastener valve covers, late build engines have 9 fastener valve covers. Do not attempt to install bolts in the 2 empty late build valve cover holes or damage to the valve cover will occur.

All vehicles

1. Remove the crankcase vent tube.
2. Remove the LH ignition coils.
3. Remove the oil level indicator.
4. Disconnect the LH Variable Camshaft Timing (VCT) solenoid electrical connector.
5. Detach all of the wiring harness retainers from the valve cover and the stud bolts.

Early build vehicles

6. Loosen the 11 stud bolts and remove the LH valve cover.
   a. Discard the gasket.

➡Early build shown, late build similar.

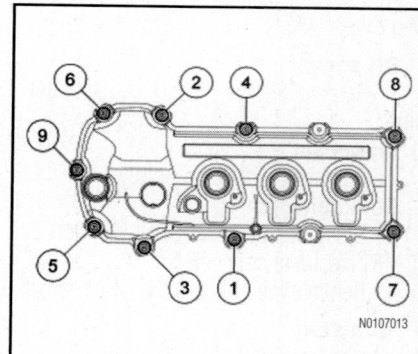

N0107013

Fig. 196 Identifying LH valve cover bolt installation sequence

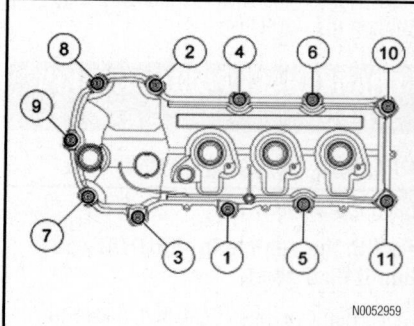

N0052959

Fig. 197 Identifying LH valve cover bolt installation sequence

Late build vehicles

7. Loosen the 9 stud bolts and remove the LH valve cover.

   a. Discard the gasket.

All vehicles

➡**VCT solenoid seal removal shown, spark plug tube seal removal similar.**

8. Inspect the VCT solenoid seals and the spark plug tube seals. Remove any damaged seals.

   a. Using the VCT Spark Plug Tube Seal Remover and Handle, remove the seal(s).

9. Clean the valve cover, cylinder head and engine front cover sealing surfaces with metal surface prep.

To install:
All vehicles

➡**Installation of new seals is only required if damaged seals were** removed during disassembly of the engine.

➡**Spark plug tube seal installation shown, VCT solenoid seal installation similar.**

10. Using the VCT Spark Plug Tube Seal Installer and Handle, install new VCT solenoid and/or spark plug tube seals.

➡**Failure to use Motorcraft® High Performance Engine RTV Silicone may cause the engine oil to foam excessively and result in serious engine damage.**

➡**If the valve cover is not installed and the fasteners tightened within 4 minutes, the sealant must be removed and the sealing area cleaned. To clean the sealing area, use silicone gasket remover and metal surface prep. Failure to follow this procedure can cause future oil leakage.**

11. Apply an 0.31 inch (8 mm) bead of Motorcraft® High Performance Engine RTV Silicone to the engine front cover-to-LH cylinder head joints.

Late build vehicles

12. Using a new gasket, install the LH valve cover and tighten the 9 stud bolts. Tighten in the sequence shown to 89 inch lbs. (10 Nm).

Early build vehicles

13. Using a new gasket, install the LH valve cover and tighten the 11 stud bolts. Tighten in the sequence shown to 89 inch lbs. (10 Nm).

All vehicles

14. Attach all of the wiring harness retainers to the valve cover and the stud bolts.

15. Connect the LH VCT solenoid electrical connector.

16. Install the oil level indicator.

17. Install the LH ignition coils.

18. Install the crankcase vent tube.

ENGINE PERFORMANCE & EMISSION CONTROLS

CAMSHAFT POSITION (CMP) SENSOR

REMOVAL & INSTALLATION

See Figure 198.

RH sensor

1. Remove the Air Cleaner (ACL) outlet pipe.

LH sensor

2. Remove the ACL assembly.

Both sensors

3. Disconnect the Camshaft Position (CMP) electrical connector.

4. Remove the bolt and the CMP sensor.

To install:

➡**Lubricate the CMP O-ring seal with clean engine oil.**

5. To install, reverse the removal procedure. Tighten the CMP sensor bolt to 89 inch lbs. (10 Nm).

CRANKSHAFT POSITION (CKP) SENSOR

REMOVAL & INSTALLATION

See Figure 199.

➡**With the vehicle in NEUTRAL, position it on a hoist.**

1. Remove the LH catalytic converter.

2. Remove the bolt, nut and the heat shield.

3. Remove the rubber grommet cover.

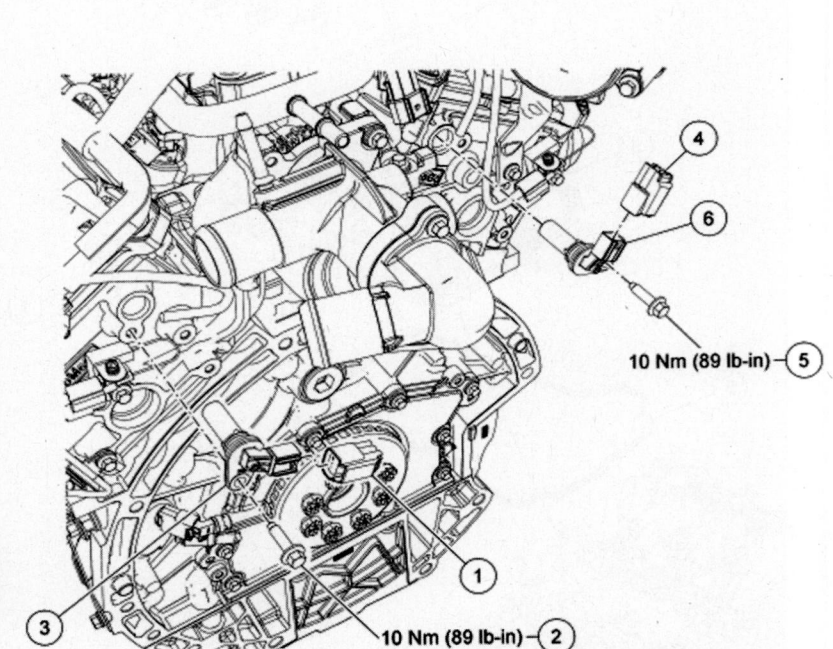

1. LH Camshaft Position (CMP) electrical connector
2. LH CMP bolt
3. LH CMP
4. RH CMP electrical connector
5. RH CMP bolt
6. RH CMP

N0056892

Fig. 198 Removing and installing the CMP sensor

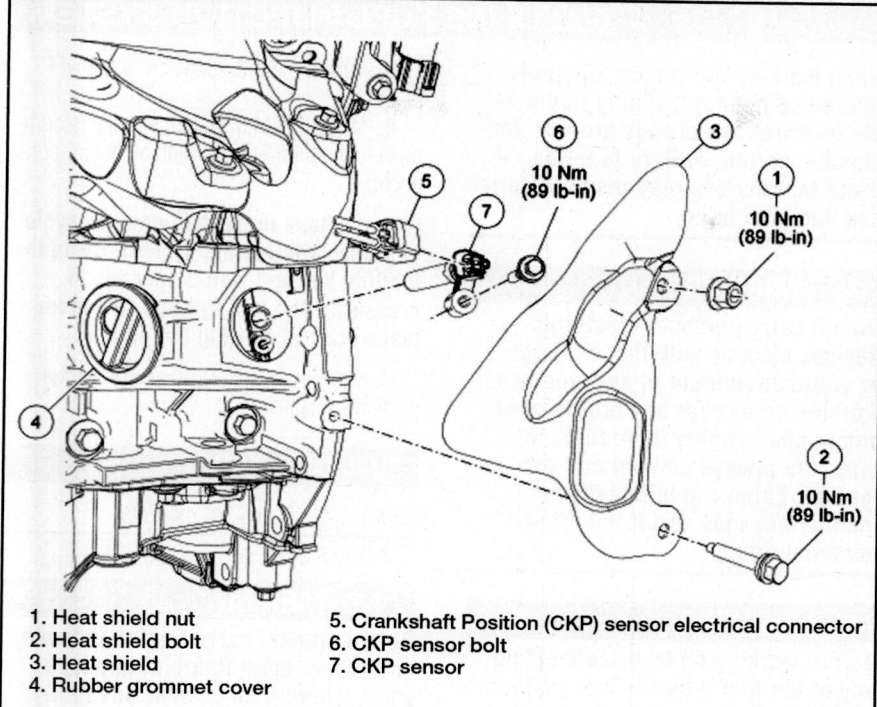

1. Heat shield nut
2. Heat shield bolt
3. Heat shield
4. Rubber grommet cover
5. Crankshaft Position (CKP) sensor electrical connector
6. CKP sensor bolt
7. CKP sensor

N0055318

Fig. 199 Removing and installing the CKP sensor

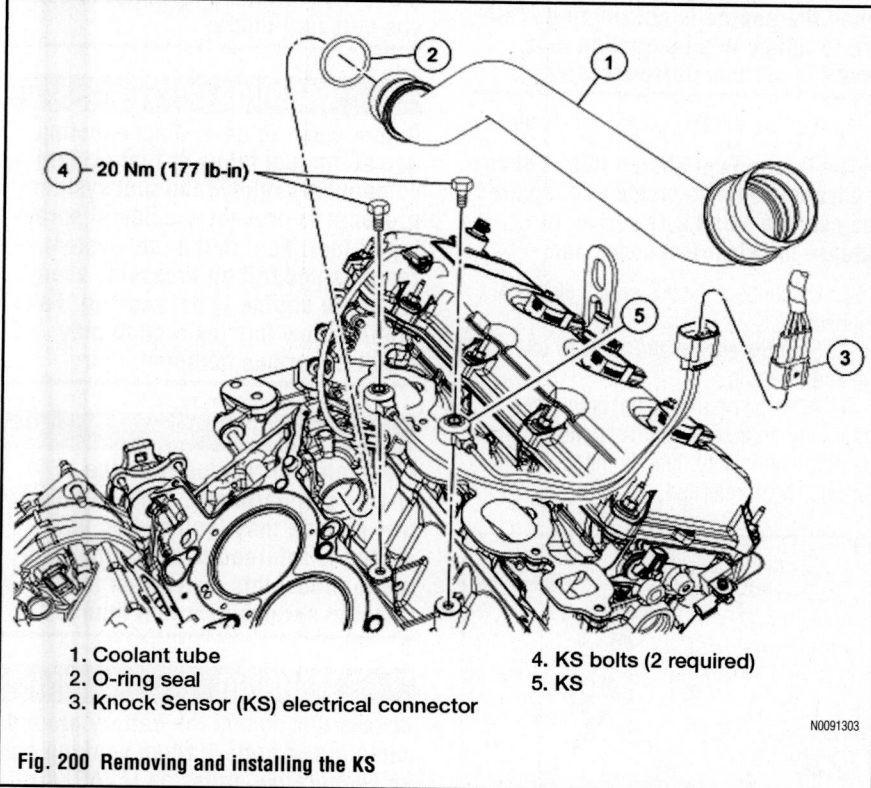

1. Coolant tube
2. O-ring seal
3. Knock Sensor (KS) electrical connector
4. KS bolts (2 required)
5. KS

N0091303

Fig. 200 Removing and installing the KS

4. Disconnect the Crankshaft Position (CKP) sensor electrical connector.

5. Remove the bolt and the CKP sensor.

To install:

6. To install, reverse the removal procedure.

    a. Tighten the CKP sensor bolt to 89 inch lbs. (10 Nm).

    b. Tighten the heat shield bolt and nut to 89 inch lbs. (10 Nm).

HEATED OXYGEN SENSOR (HO2S)

REMOVAL & INSTALLATION

1. With the vehicle in NEUTRAL, position it on a hoist.

2. Disconnect the Heated Oxygen Sensor (HO2S) electrical connector.

➡**If necessary, lubricate the sensor threads with penetrating and lock lubricant to assist in removal.**

3. Using the Exhaust Gas Oxygen Sensor Socket, remove the HO2S.

    a. Calculate the correct torque wrench setting for the following torque.

To install:

➡**Apply a light coat of anti-seize lubricant to the threads of the HO2S.**

4. To install, reverse the removal procedure. Tighten the HO2S to 35 ft. lbs. (48 Nm).

KNOCK SENSOR (KS)

REMOVAL & INSTALLATION

See Figure 200.

1. Remove the thermostat housing.

2. Remove the lower intake manifold.

3. Remove the coolant tube.

    a. Discard the O-ring seal.

4. Disconnect the Knock Sensor (KS) electrical connector.

5. Remove the 2 bolts and the KS.

To install:

6. To install, reverse the removal procedure.

    a. Lubricate the new O-ring seal with clean engine coolant.

    b. Tighten the KS bolts to 177 inch lbs. (20 Nm).

FUEL   **GASOLINE FUEL INJECTION SYSTEM**

FUEL SYSTEM SERVICE PRECAUTIONS

Safety is the most important factor when performing not only fuel system maintenance but any type of maintenance. Failure to conduct maintenance and repairs in a safe manner may result in serious personal injury or death. Maintenance and testing of the vehicle's fuel system components can be accomplished safely and effectively by adhering to the following rules and guidelines.

• To avoid the possibility of fire and personal injury, always disconnect the negative battery cable unless the repair or test procedure requires that battery voltage be applied.

• Always relieve the fuel system pressure prior to disconnecting any fuel system component (injector, fuel rail, pressure regulator, etc.), fitting or fuel line connection. Exercise extreme caution whenever relieving fuel system pressure to avoid exposing skin, face and eyes to fuel spray. Please be advised that fuel under pressure may penetrate the skin or any part of the body that it contacts.

• Always place a shop towel or cloth around the fitting or connection prior to loosening to absorb any excess fuel due to spillage. Ensure that all fuel spillage (should it occur) is quickly removed from engine surfaces. Ensure that all fuel soaked cloths or towels are deposited into a suitable waste container.

• Always keep a dry chemical (Class B) fire extinguisher near the work area.

• Do not allow fuel spray or fuel vapors to come into contact with a spark or open flame.

• Always use a back-up wrench when loosening and tightening fuel line connection fittings. This will prevent unnecessary stress and torsion to fuel line piping.

• Always replace worn fuel fitting O-rings with new Do not substitute fuel hose or equivalent where fuel pipe is installed.

Before servicing the vehicle, make sure to also refer to the precautions in the beginning of this section as well.

RELIEVING FUEL SYSTEM PRESSURE

See Figure 201.

❄❄ WARNING

Do not smoke, carry lighted tobacco or have an open flame of any type when working on or near any fuel-related component. Highly flammable mixtures are always present and may be ignited. Failure to follow these instructions may result in serious personal injury.

❄❄ WARNING

Do not carry personal electronic devices such as cell phones, pagers or audio equipment of any type when working on or near any fuel-related component. Highly flammable mixtures are always present and may be ignited. Failure to follow these instructions may result in serious personal injury.

❄❄ WARNING

Before working on or disconnecting any of the fuel tubes or fuel system components, relieve the fuel system pressure to prevent accidental spraying of fuel. Fuel in the fuel system remains under high pressure, even when the engine is not running. Failure to follow this instruction may result in serious personal injury.

1. Remove the LR quarter trim panel.

➡ **The Inertia Fuel Shutoff (IFS) switch is located behind a shield and requires the use of a small screwdriver to release the electrical connector.**

2. Disconnect the IFS switch electrical connector.
3. Start the engine and allow to idle until the engine stalls.
4. After the engine stalls, crank the engine for approximately 5 seconds to make sure the fuel injector supply manifold pressure has been released.

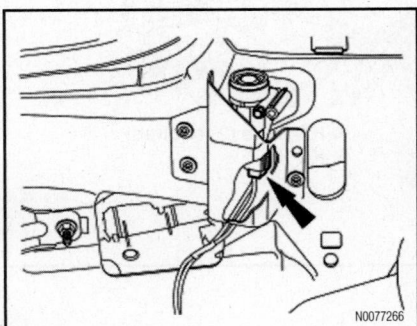

Fig. 201 Disconnecting the IFS switch electrical connector

5. Turn the ignition switch to the OFF position.
6. When the fuel system service is complete, connect the IFS switch electrical connector.

➡ **It may take more than one key cycle to pressurize the fuel system. Cycle the ignition key and wait 3 seconds to pressurize the fuel system. Check for leaks prior to starting the engine.**

7. Start the vehicle and check the fuel system for leaks.

FUEL INJECTORS

REMOVAL & INSTALLATION
See Figure 202.

❄❄ WARNING

Do not smoke, carry lighted tobacco or have an open flame of any type when working on or near any fuel-related component. Highly flammable mixtures are always present and may be ignited. Failure to follow these instructions may result in serious personal injury.

❄❄ WARNING

Before working on or disconnecting any of the fuel tubes or fuel system components relieve the fuel system pressure to prevent accidental spraying of fuel. Fuel in the fuel system remains under high pressure, even when the engine is not running. Failure to follow this instruction may result in serious personal injury.

❄❄ WARNING

Clean all fuel residue from the engine compartment. If not removed, fuel residue may ignite when the engine is returned to operation. Failure to follow this instruction may result in serious personal injury.

❄❄ WARNING

Always disconnect the battery ground cable at the battery when working on an evaporative emission (EVAP) system or fuel-related component. Highly flammable mixtures are always present and may be ignited. Failure to follow these instructions may result in serious personal injury.

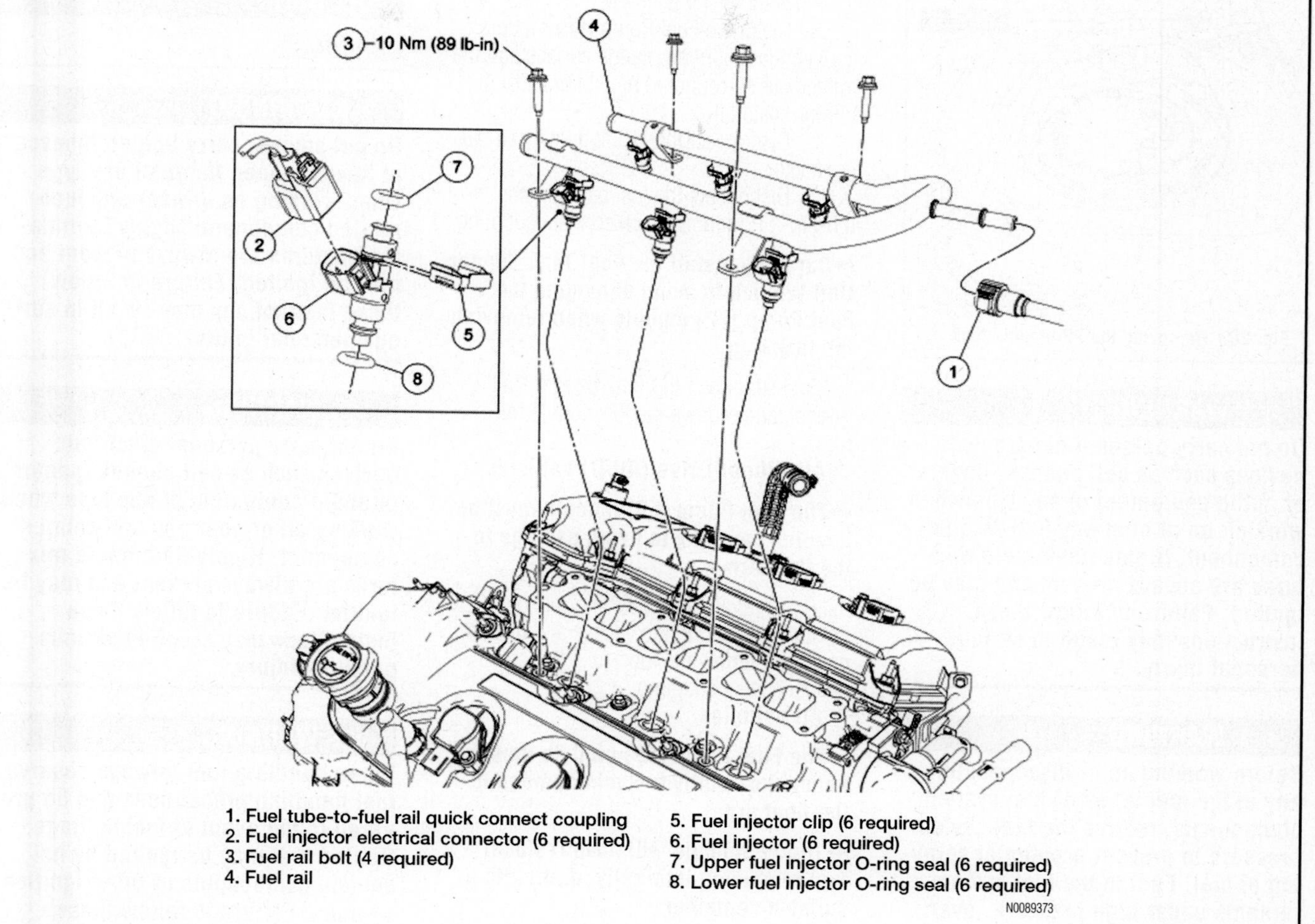
3
10 Nm (89 lb-in)
4
7
2
6
5
8
1
1. Fuel tube-to-fuel rail quick connect coupling
2. Fuel injector electrical connector (6 required)
3. Fuel rail bolt (4 required)
4. Fuel rail
5. Fuel injector clip (6 required)
6. Fuel injector (6 required)
7. Upper fuel injector O-ring seal (6 required)
8. Lower fuel injector O-ring seal (6 required)
N0089373

Fig. 202 Exploded view of the fuel rail and fuel injector

1. Release the fuel system pressure.
2. Disconnect the battery ground cable.
3. Remove the upper intake manifold.
4. Disconnect the fuel tube-to-fuel rail quick connect coupling.
5. Disconnect the 6 fuel injector electrical connectors.
6. Remove the 4 fuel rail bolts.
7. Remove the fuel rail and injectors as an assembly.
8. Remove the 6 fuel injector clips and the 6 fuel injectors.
    a. Remove and discard the 12 fuel injector O-ring seals.

To install:

➡Use O-ring seals that are made of special fuel-resistant material. The use of ordinary O-rings seals can cause the fuel system to leak. Do not reuse the O-ring seals.

➡The upper and lower fuel injector O-ring seals are similar in appearance but are not interchangeable.

➡Install new fuel injector O-ring seals and lubricate them with clean engine oil.

9. Install the 6 fuel injectors and the 6 fuel injector clips into the fuel rail.
10. Install the fuel rail and fuel injectors as an assembly.
11. Install the 4 fuel rail bolts.
    a. Tighten to 89 inch lbs. (10 Nm).
12. Connect the 6 fuel injector electrical connectors.
13. Connect the fuel tube-to-fuel rail quick connect coupling.
14. Install the upper intake manifold.
15. Connect the battery ground cable.

FUEL PUMP

REMOVAL & INSTALLATION

See Figure 203.

⁂ WARNING

Do not smoke, carry lighted tobacco or have an open flame of any type when working on or near any fuel-related component. Highly flammable mixtures are always present and may be ignited. Failure to follow these instructions may result in serious personal injury.

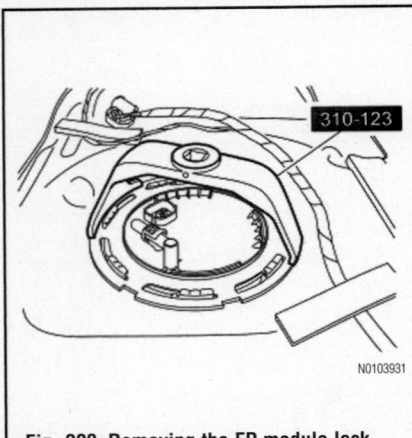

Fig. 203 Removing the FP module lock

❋❋ WARNING

Do not carry personal electronic devices such as cell phones, pagers or audio equipment of any type when working on or near any fuel-related component. Highly flammable mixtures are always present and may be ignited. Failure to follow these instructions may result in serious personal injury.

❋❋ WARNING

Before working on or disconnecting any of the fuel tubes or fuel system components, relieve the fuel system pressure to prevent accidental spraying of fuel. Fuel in the fuel system remains under high pressure, even when the engine is not running. Failure to follow this instruction may result in serious personal injury.

❋❋ WARNING

When handling fuel, always observe fuel handling precautions and be prepared in the event of fuel spillage. Spilled fuel may be ignited by hot vehicle components or other ignition sources. Failure to follow these instructions may result in serious personal injury.

❋❋ WARNING

1. Always disconnect the battery ground cable at the battery when working on an evaporative emission (EVAP) system or fuel-related component. Highly flammable mixtures are always present and may be ignited. Failure to follow these instructions may result in serious personal injury.

➡The Fuel Pump (FP) module has a serviceable fuel level sender.

All vehicles

2. Release the fuel system pressure.
3. Disconnect the battery ground cable.
4. Remove the fuel tank.
5. Clean the Fuel Pump (FP) module connection, coupling, flange surface and the immediate surrounding area of any dirt or foreign material.
6. Disconnect the FP module electrical connector.
7. Disconnect the fuel tank jumper tube-to- FP module quick connect coupling.

➡Carefully install the Fuel Tank Sender Unit Wrench to avoid damaging the Fuel Pump (FP) module when removing the lock ring.

8. Install the Fuel Tank Sender Unit Wrench and remove the FP module lock ring.

All-Wheel Drive (AWD) vehicles

➡The Fuel Pump (FP) module must be handled carefully to avoid damage to the float arm.

9. Carefully lift the FP module out of the fuel tank enough to access and disconnect the internal fuel tube-to- FP module quick connect coupling.

All vehicles

➡The Fuel Pump (FP) module must be handled carefully to avoid damage to the float arm.

➡The FP module will have residual fuel remaining internally, drain into a suitable container.

10. Completely remove the FP module from the fuel tank.

➡Inspect the mating surfaces of the FP module flange and the fuel tank O-ring seal contact surfaces. Do not polish or adjust the O-ring seal contact area of the fuel tank flange or the fuel tank. Install a new FP module or fuel tank if the O-ring seal contact area is bent, scratched or corroded.

11. Remove the FP module O-ring seal.

To install:

➡To install, apply clean engine oil to the O-ring seal.

➡Install a new lock ring if it is bent, damaged or corroded.

➡Make sure the alignment tab on the FP module and the fuel tank meet before tightening the FP module lock ring.

12. To install, reverse the removal procedure.

a. Install a FP module O-ring seal.

FUEL TANK

DRAINING

❋❋ WARNING

Do not smoke, carry lighted tobacco or have an open flame of any type when working on or near any fuel-related component. Highly flammable mixtures are always present and may be ignited. Failure to follow these instructions may result in serious personal injury.

❋❋ WARNING

Do not carry personal electronic devices such as cell phones, pagers or audio equipment of any type when working on or near any fuel-related component. Highly flammable mixtures are always present and may be ignited. Failure to follow these instructions may result in serious personal injury.

❋❋ WARNING

When handling fuel, always observe fuel handling precautions and be prepared in the event of fuel spillage. Spilled fuel may be ignited by hot vehicle components or other ignition sources. Failure to follow these instructions may result in serious personal injury.

❋❋ WARNING

Remove the fuel filler cap slowly. The fuel system may be under pressure. If the fuel filler cap is venting vapor or if you hear a hissing sound, wait until it stops before completely removing the fuel filler cap. Otherwise, fuel may spray out. Failure to follow these instructions may result in serious personal injury.

❋❋ WARNING

Always disconnect the battery ground cable at the battery when working on an evaporative emission (EVAP) system or fuel-related component. Highly flammable mixtures are always present and may be ignited. Failure to follow these instructions may result in serious personal injury.

1. Disconnect the battery ground cable.

2. Carefully turn the fuel tank filler cap counterclockwise approximately one-fourth turn until the thread disengages and position aside.

3. Insert a semi-rigid fuel drain tube (approximately 120-in long) into the fuel tank filler pipe.

4. Attach the Fuel Storage Tanker to the fuel drain tube and drain as much fuel as possible from the fuel tank filler pipe, lowering the fuel level below the fuel tank inlet spout.

➡**Some residual fuel may remain in the fuel tank filler pipe. Carefully drain into a suitable container.**

5. Release the clamp and remove the fuel tank filler pipe hose from the fuel tank.

   a. To install, tighten to 35 inch lbs. (4 Nm).

6. Insert the fuel drain tube into the fuel tank inlet spout, attach the Fuel Storage Tanker and drain as much fuel as possible from the fuel tank.

REMOVAL & INSTALLATION

All vehicles

1. Disconnect the battery ground cable.

2. Drain the fuel tank.

All-Wheel Drive (AWD) vehicles

3. Remove the muffler and tailpipe.

4. Remove the driveshaft.

All vehicles

5. Disconnect the fuel tank wiring harness electrical connector.

6. Disconnect the Fuel Tank Pressure (FTP) electrical connector and release the pin-type wire harness retainer from the fuel tank.

7. Disconnect the fuel vapor tube assembly-to-fuel tank quick connect coupling.

➡**Some residual fuel may remain in the fuel tubes. Carefully drain into a suitable container.**

8. Disconnect the fuel tank jumper tube-to-fuel tube quick connect coupling.

9. Remove the 2 bracket bolts and position parking brake cables aside.

10. Install the Powertrain Lift under the fuel tank.

➡**Remove all bolts prior to lowering the fuel tank. Fuel tank damage can occur if all the bolts are not removed prior to lowering.**

11. Remove the 2 fuel tank bracket bolts and the 4 fuel tank bolts.

12. Completely lower and remove the fuel tank from the vehicle.

  To install:

13. To install, reverse the removal procedure.

   a. Tighten the fuel tank bracket bolts to 18 ft. lbs. (25 Nm).

   b. Tighten the parking brake cable bracket bolts to 17 ft. lbs. (23 Nm).

THROTTLE BODY

REMOVAL & INSTALLATION

See Figure 204.

1. Remove the Air Cleaner (ACL) outlet pipe.

2. Disconnect the electronic throttle control electrical connector.

3. Remove the 4 bolts and the Throttle Body (TB).

   a. Discard the TB gasket.

  To install:

➡**Install a new TB gasket.**

4. To install, reverse the removal procedure.

   a. Tighten the TB bolts to 89 inch lbs. (10 Nm).

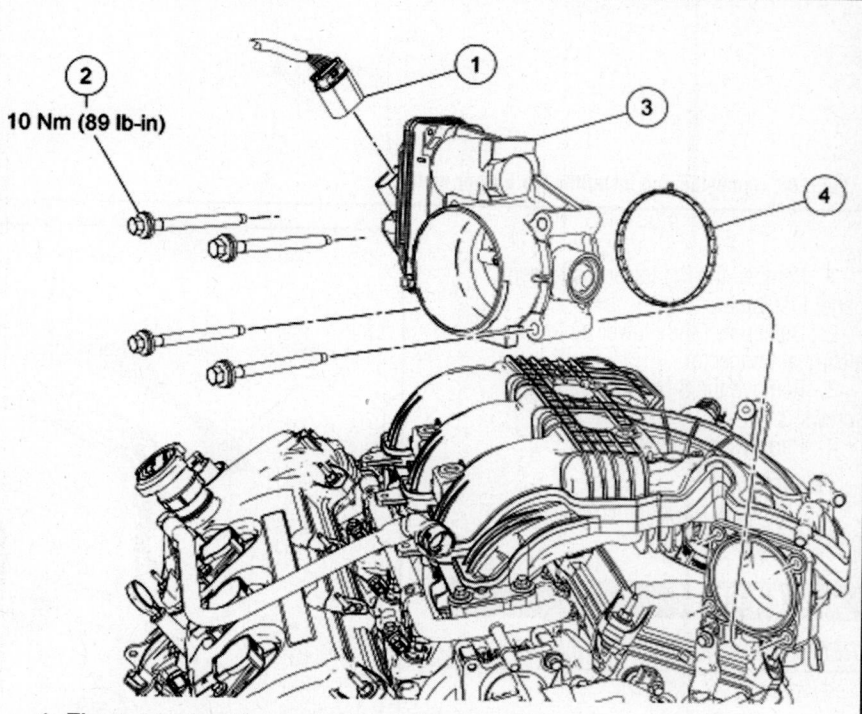

1. Electronic throttle control electrical connector
2. Throttle Body (TB) bolt (4 required)
3. TB
4. TB gasket

N0081636

Fig. 204 Removing and installing the TB

HEATING & AIR CONDITIONING SYSTEM

BLOWER MOTOR

REMOVAL & INSTALLATION

See Figure 205.

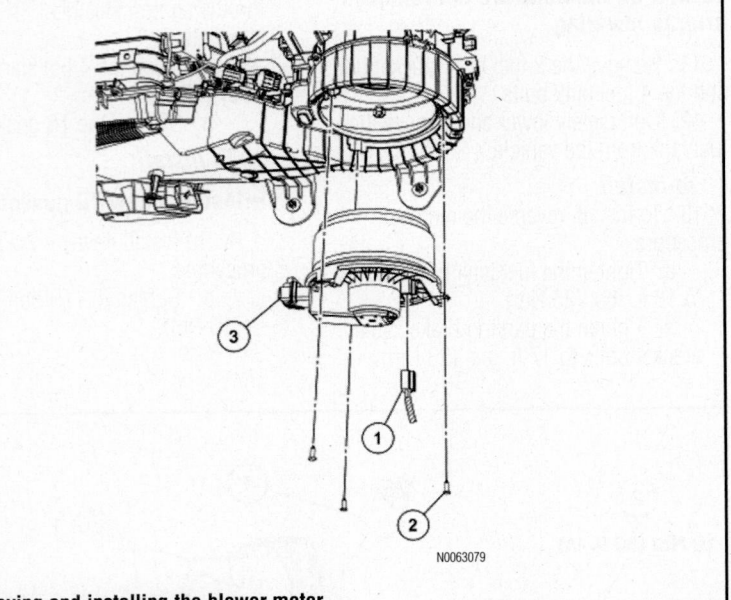

Fig. 205 Removing and installing the blower motor

1. Remove the RH lower instrument panel insulator.
2. Disconnect the blower motor electrical connector.
3. Remove the 3 blower motor screws.
4. Remove the blower motor.

To install:

5. To install, reverse the removal procedure.

HEATER CORE

REMOVAL & INSTALLATION

See Figures 206 and 207.

➡**If a heater core leak is suspected, the heater core must be pressure leak tested before it is removed from the vehicle.**

1. Remove the heater core and evaporator core housing.
2. Remove the 6 floor duct screws and the floor duct.
3. Remove the heater core tube dash panel seal.
4. Remove the heater tube bracket screw and the heater tube bracket.

5. Remove the 5 fresh air inlet duct screws and the fresh air inlet duct.
6. Disconnect the wire harness from the plenum chamber.

7. Remove the 7 lower facing plenum chamber screws.
8. Orient the heater core and evaporator core housing with the plenum chamber upright.
9. Remove the upper facing plenum chamber screw.
10. Remove the 2 plenum chamber clips and remove the plenum chamber being careful not to allow the evaporator core to become dislodged from the installed position.

➡**Do not handle the heater core by the inlet and/or outlet tube to remove. Handling the heater core by the tubes may damage the joints and lead to failure of the heater core.**

11. Remove the heater core in the following sequence.
    a. Grasp the heater core by the core-side of the heater tube connections and partially remove it from the plenum chamber.
    b. Grasp the heater core by the top of the core and remove it from the plenum chamber.

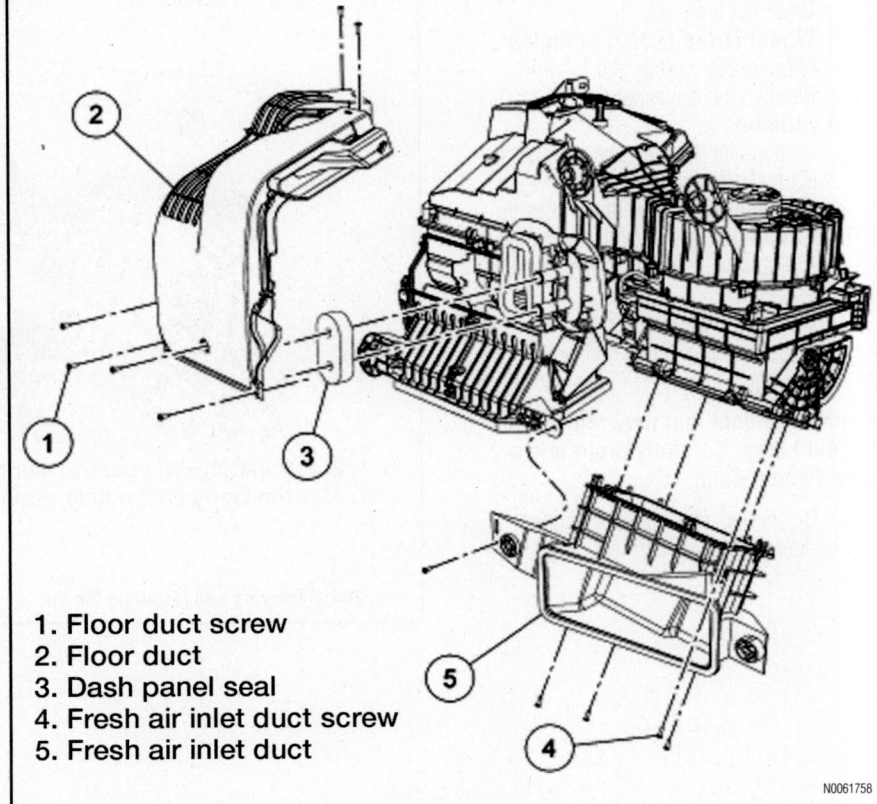

1. Floor duct screw
2. Floor duct
3. Dash panel seal
4. Fresh air inlet duct screw
5. Fresh air inlet duct

Fig. 206 Removing and installing the heater core—1 of 2

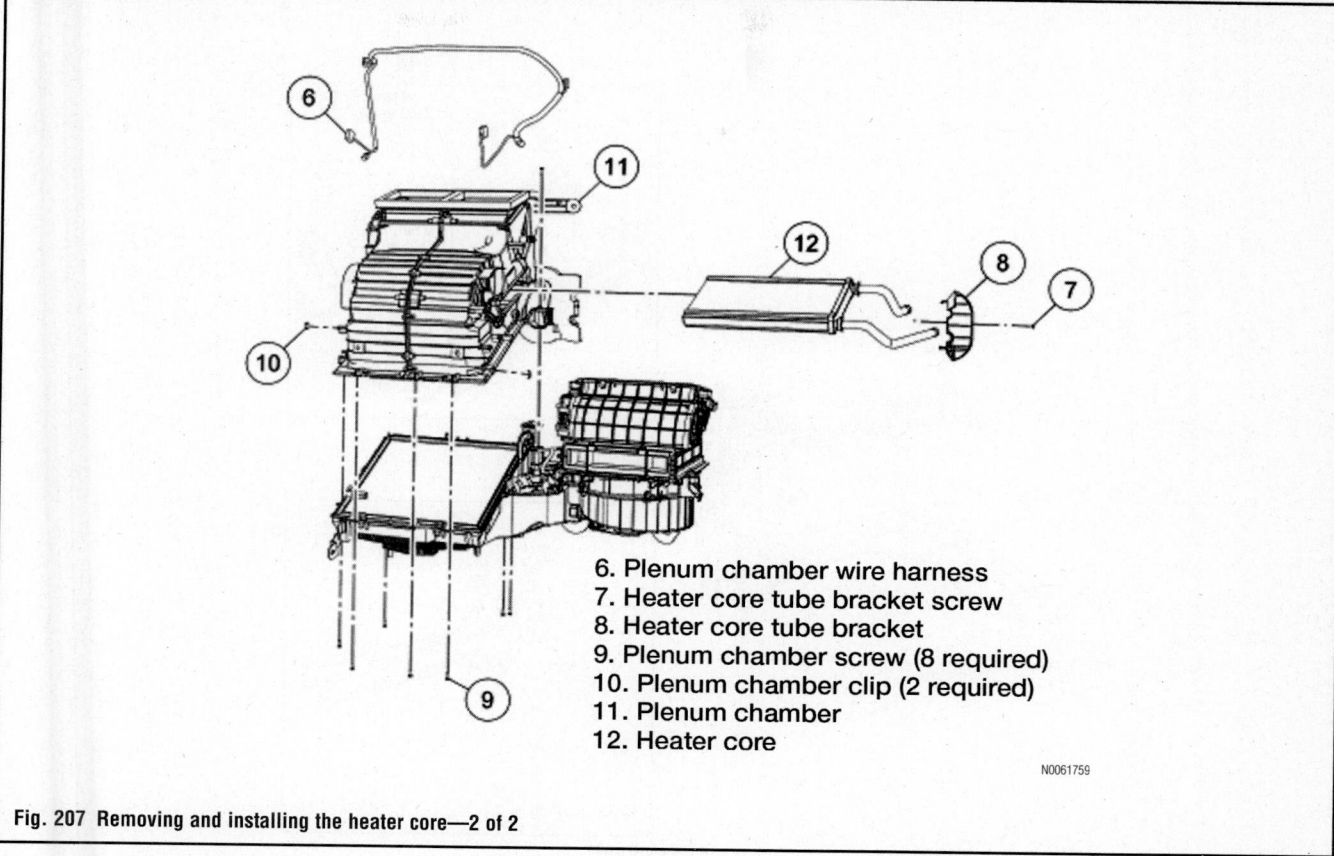

6. Plenum chamber wire harness
7. Heater core tube bracket screw
8. Heater core tube bracket
9. Plenum chamber screw (8 required)
10. Plenum chamber clip (2 required)
11. Plenum chamber
12. Heater core

N0061759

Fig. 207 Removing and installing the heater core—2 of 2

➡It is not necessary to carry out this step if the evaporator core has not become dislodged from the installed position during this procedure.

12. If the evaporator core has been moved at any point during heater core removal, remove the evaporator core, verify that the drain seal is installed in the correct position and

install the evaporator core in the correct position.

To install:

13. To install, reverse the removal procedure.

STEERING

POWER STEERING GEAR

REMOVAL & INSTALLATION

See Figures 208 and 209.

➡When repairing the power steering system, care should be taken to prevent the entry of foreign material or failure of the power steering components may result.

➡Use a steering wheel holding device (such as Hunter® 28-75-1 or equivalent).

1. Using a suitable holding device, hold the steering wheel in the straight-ahead position.
2. Remove the stabilizer bar.
3. Remove the pressure line-to-steering gear banjo bolt.
   a. Discard the 2 seals.

4. Release the clamp and disconnect the return hose from the steering gear.
5. Remove the 2 bolts and the steering gear heat shield.
6. Remove the 3 pressure line bracket-to-steering gear bolts.
7. Remove and discard the 4 steering gear bolts.
   a. Remove the steering gear.

To install:

➡When installing a new steering gear, install a new steering gear turn tube heat wrap.

8. Position the steering gear and tighten the 4 steering gear bolts to 76 ft. lbs. (103 Nm) in the sequence shown.

➡New seals must be installed any time the pressure line is disconnected from the power steering pump and/or the steering gear or a fluid leak may occur.

9. Install the pressure line-to-steering gear banjo bolt. Tighten to 35 ft. lbs. (48 Nm).
10. Install the 3 pressure line bracket-to-steering gear bolts. Tighten to 80 inch lbs. (9 Nm).
11. Release the clamp and connect the return hose to the steering gear.
12. Install the steering gear heat shield and the 2 bolts. Tighten to 53 inch lbs. (6 Nm).
13. Install the stabilizer bar.
14. Fill the power steering system.

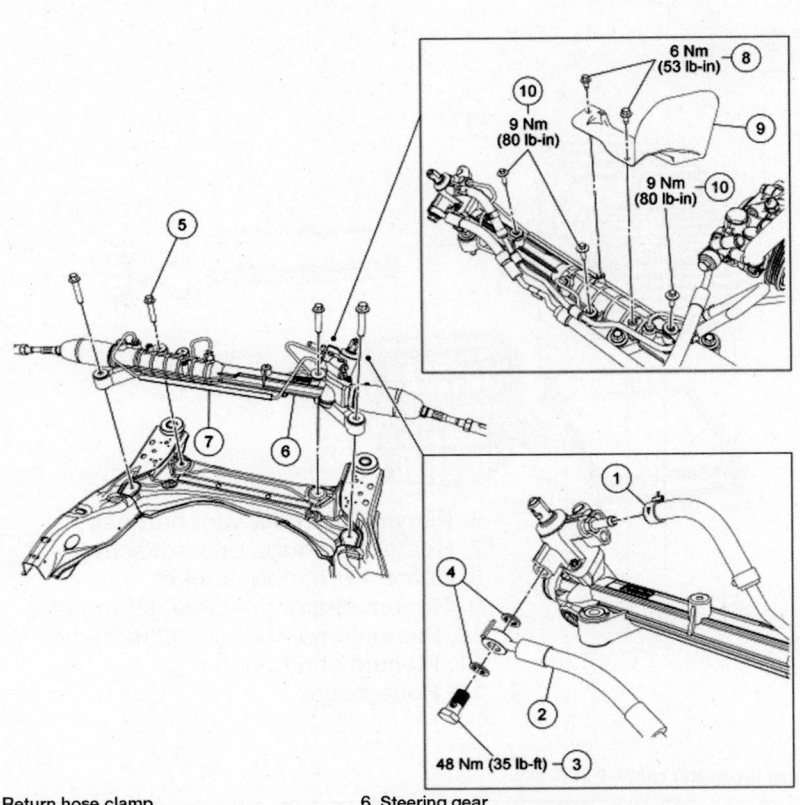

1. Return hose clamp
2. Pressure line kit
3. Pressure line-to-steering gear banjo bolt
4. Pressure line seals (2 required)
5. Steering gear bolt (4 required)
6. Steering gear
7. Steering gear turn tube heat wrap
8. Steering gear heat shield bolts (2 required)
9. Steering gear heat shield
10. Pressure line bracket-to-steering gear bolts (3 required)

N0105310

Fig. 208 Removing and installing the power steering gear

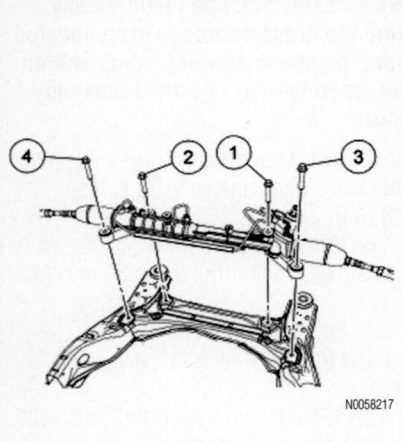

N0058217

Fig. 209 Identifying the steering gear bolt tightening sequence

POWER STEERING PUMP

REMOVAL & INSTALLATION

See Figures 210 through 212.

➡While repairing the power steering system, care should be taken to prevent the entry of foreign material or failure of the power steering components may result.

All vehicles
1. With the vehicle in NEUTRAL, position it on a hoist.
2. Using a suitable suction device, remove the power steering fluid from the fluid reservoir.
3. Remove the RH inner fender splash shield.
4. Position the Stretchy Belt Remover on the power steering pump pulley belt as shown.

➡Feed the Stretchy Belt Remover on to the power steering pump pulley approximately 5.984 inch (152 mm).

5. Turn the crankshaft clockwise and feed the Stretchy Belt Remover evenly on the power steering pump pulley.

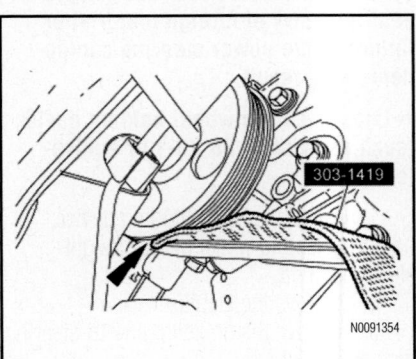

N0091354

Fig. 210 Positioning the stretchy belt remover

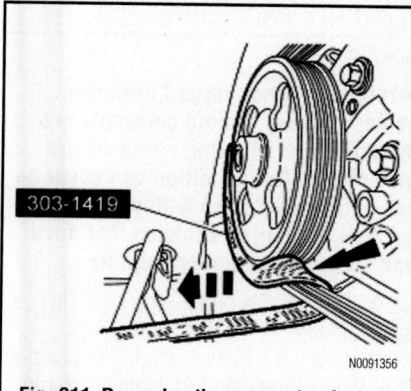

Fig. 211 Removing the power steering pump belt

6. Remove the power steering pump belt.

a. Fold the Stretchy Belt Remover under the inside of the power steering pump belt as shown.

b. In one quick motion, firmly pull the Stretchy Belt Remover out of the RH fender well, removing the power steering pump belt.

All-Wheel Drive (AWD) vehicles

7. Remove the 4 bolts and position the driveshaft aside.

All vehicles

8. Using a suitable jack, support the rear of the subframe.

9. Remove the 2 nuts, 4 bolts and the subframe support brackets.

10. Remove the 2 middle subframe nuts.

11. Lower the rear of the subframe.

12. Release the clamp and disconnect the power steering pump supply hose from the power steering pump.

13. Disconnect the Power Steering Pressure (PSP) switch electrical connector.

14. Remove the pressure line-to-power steering pump banjo bolt and disconnect the pressure line from the pump.

a. Discard the 2 seals.

b. Remove the 3 power steering pump bolts and the pump.

To install:
All vehicles

15. Position the power steering pump and install the 3 bolts. Tighten to 18 ft. lbs. (24 Nm).

➡**New seals must be installed any time the power steering pressure line is disconnected from the power steering pump, or a fluid leak may occur.**

16. Position the pressure line and install the pressure line-to-power steering pump banjo bolt and seals. Tighten to 35 ft. lbs. (48 Nm).

17. Connect the Power Steering Pressure (PSP) switch electrical connector.

18. Connect the power steering pump supply hose and secure the clamp.

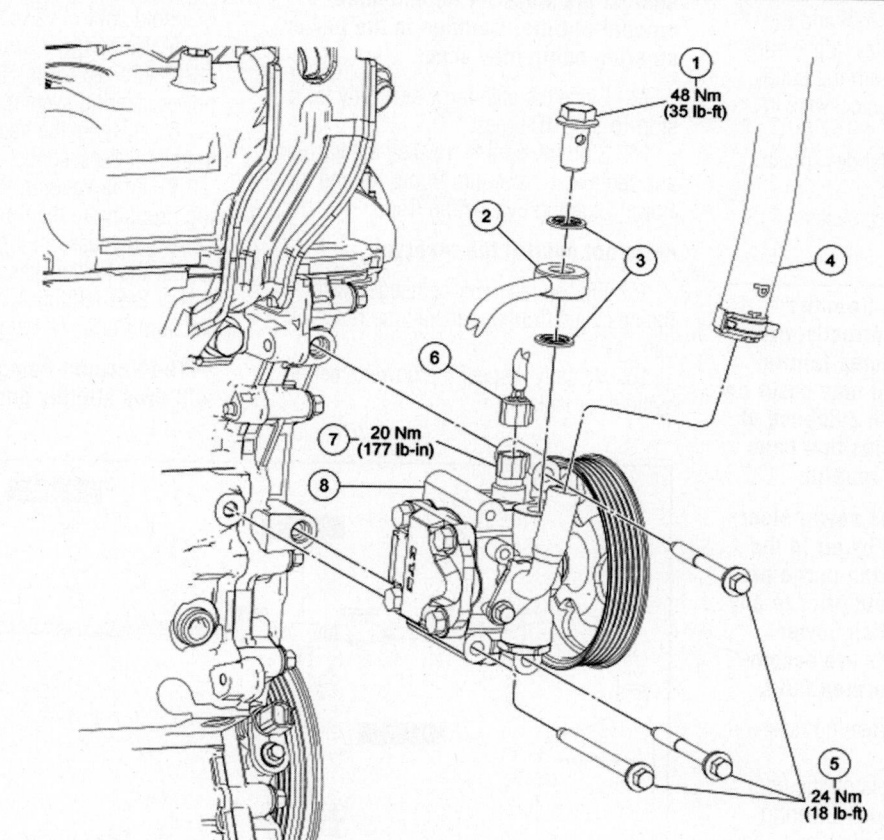

1. Pressure line-to-power steering pump banjo bolt
2. Pressure line kit
3. Pressure line seals (2 required)
4. Power steering pump supply hose
5. Power steering pump bolts (3 required)
6. Power Steering Pressure (PSP) switch electrical connector
7. PSP switch
8. Power steering pump

Fig. 212 Removing and installing the power steering pump

19. Using the jack, raise the rear of the subframe.

20. Install the 2 middle subframe nuts. Tighten to 111 ft. lbs. (150 Nm).

21. Install the 2 nuts, 4 bolts and the subframe support brackets.

   a. Tighten the nuts to 111 ft. lbs. (150 Nm).

   b. Tighten the bolts to 76 ft. lbs. (103 Nm).

AWD vehicles

22. Position the driveshaft and install the 4 bolts. Tighten to 52 ft. lbs. (70 Nm).

All vehicles

➡**After installation, make sure the belt is correctly seated on the crankshaft and power steering pulley or damage to the belt may occur.**

23. Using the Power Steering Belt Installation Tool, install the power steering belt onto the power steering pump pulley.

   a. Position the belt around the Power Steering Belt Installation Tool and the power steering pump pulley. Make sure that the belt is engaged with the pulley and rotate the crankshaft clockwise to install the belt.

24. Install the RH inner fender splash shield.

25. Fill the power steering system.

BLEEDING

➡**If the air is not purged from the power steering system correctly, premature power steering pump failure may result. The condition may occur on pre-delivery vehicles with evidence of aerated fluid or on vehicles that have had steering component repairs.**

➡**A whine heard from the power steering pump can be caused by air in the system. The power steering purge procedure must be carried out prior to any component repair for which power steering noise complaints are accompanied by evidence of aerated fluid.**

1. Remove the power steering reservoir cap. Check the fluid.

2. Raise the front wheels off the floor.

3. Tightly insert the Power Steering Evacuation Cap into the reservoir and connect the Vacuum Pump Kit.

4. Start the engine.

5. Using the Vacuum Pump Kit, apply vacuum and maintain the maximum vacuum of 68–85 kPa (20–25 in-Hg).

   a. If the Vacuum Pump Kit does not maintain vacuum, check the power steering system for leaks before proceeding.

6. If equipped with Hydro-Boost®, apply the brake pedal 4 times.

➡**Do not hold the steering wheel against the stops for an extended amount of time. Damage to the power steering pump may occur.**

7. Cycle the steering wheel fully from stop-to-stop 10 times.

8. Stop the engine.

9. Release the vacuum and remove the Vacuum Pump Kit and the Power Steering Evacuation Cap.

➡**Do not overfill the reservoir.**

10. Fill the reservoir as needed with the specified fluid.

11. Start the engine.

12. Install the Power Steering Evacuation Cap and the Vacuum Pump Kit. Apply and maintain the maximum vacuum of 68-85 kPa (20-25 in-Hg).

➡**Do not hold the steering wheel against the stops for an extended amount of time. Damage to the power steering pump may occur.**

13. Cycle the steering wheel fully from stop-to-stop 10 times.

14. Stop the engine, release the vacuum and remove the Vacuum Pump Kit and the Power Steering Evacuation Cap.

➡**Do not overfill the reservoir.**

15. Fill the reservoir as needed with the specified fluid and install the reservoir cap.

16. Visually inspect the power steering system for leaks.

FLUID FILL PROCEDURE

See Figure 213.

➡**If the air is not purged from the power steering system correctly, premature power steering pump failure may result. The condition can occur on pre-delivery vehicles with evidence of aerated fluid or on vehicles that have had steering component repairs.**

1. Remove the power steering fluid reservoir cap.

2. Install the Power Steering Evacuation Cap, Power Steering Fill Adapter Manifold and Vacuum Pump Kit.

➡**The Power Steering Fill Adapter Manifold control valves are in the OPEN position when the points of the handles face the center of the Power Steering Fill Adapter Manifold.**

3. Close the Power Steering Fill Adapter Manifold control valve (fluid side).

4. Open the Power Steering Fill Adapter Manifold control valve (vacuum side).

5. Using the Vacuum Pump Kit, apply 68-85 kPa (20-25 in-Hg) of vacuum to the power steering system.

6. Observe the Vacuum Pump Kit gauge for 30 seconds.

7. If the Vacuum Pump Kit gauge reading drops more than 3 kPa (0.88 in-Hg), correct any leaks in the power steering system or the Power Steering Evacuation Cap, Power Steering Fill Adapter Manifold and Vacuum Pump Kit before proceeding.

➡**The Vacuum Pump Kit gauge reading will drop slightly during this step.**

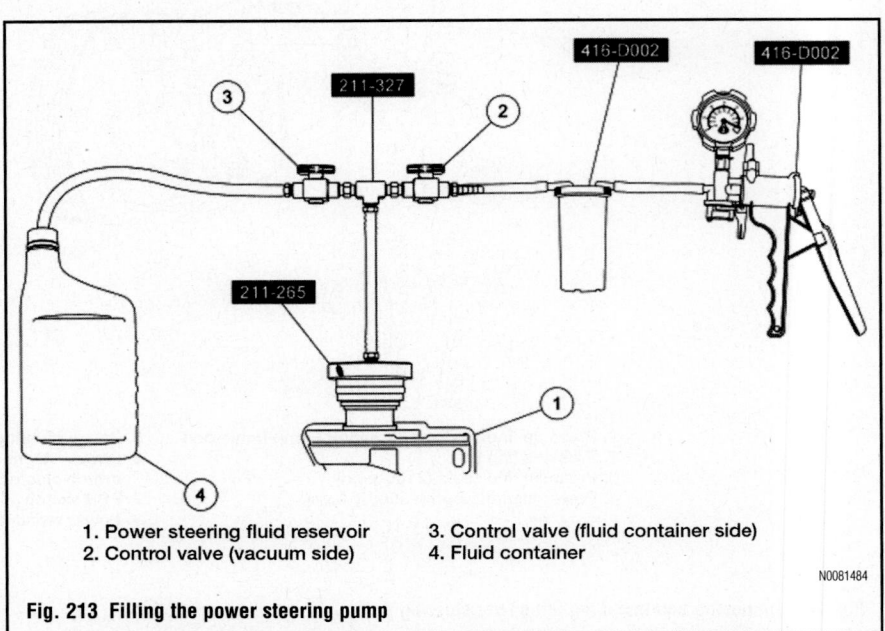

1. Power steering fluid reservoir
2. Control valve (vacuum side)
3. Control valve (fluid container side)
4. Fluid container

Fig. 213 Filling the power steering pump

N0081484

8. Slowly open the Power Steering Fill Adapter Manifold control valve (fluid side) until power steering fluid completely fills the hose and then close the control valve.

9. Using the Vacuum Pump Kit, apply 68-85 kPa (20-25 in-Hg) of vacuum to the power steering system.

10. Close the Power Steering Fill Adapter Manifold control valve (vacuum side).

11. Slowly open the Power Steering Fill Adapter Manifold control valve (fluid side).

12. Once power steering fluid enters the fluid reservoir and reaches the minimum fluid level indicator line on the reservoir, close the Power Steering Fill Adapter Manifold control valve (fluid side).

13. Remove the Power Steering Evacuation Cap, Power Steering Fill Adapter Manifold and Vacuum Pump Kit.

14. Install the reservoir cap.

➡ **Do not hold the steering wheel against the stops for an extended amount of time. Damage to the power steering pump may occur.**

➡ **There will be a slight drop in the power steering fluid level in the reservoir when the engine is started.**

15. Start the engine and turn the steering wheel from stop-to-stop.

16. Turn the ignition switch to the OFF position.

➡ **Do not overfill the reservoir.**

17. Remove the reservoir cap and fill the reservoir with the specified fluid.

18. Install the reservoir cap.

SUSPENSION

FRONT SUSPENSION

LOWER CONTROL ARM

REMOVAL & INSTALLATION

See Figure 214.

➡ Suspension fasteners are critical parts because they affect performance of vital components and systems and their failure may result in major service expense. New parts must be installed with the same part numbers or equivalent part, if replacement is necessary. Do not use a replacement part of lesser quality or substitute design. Torque values must be used as specified during reassembly to make sure of correct retention of these parts.

1. Remove the wheel and tire.

2. Remove and discard the stabilizer bar link lower nut.

3. Remove and discard the lower ball joint nut and bolt.

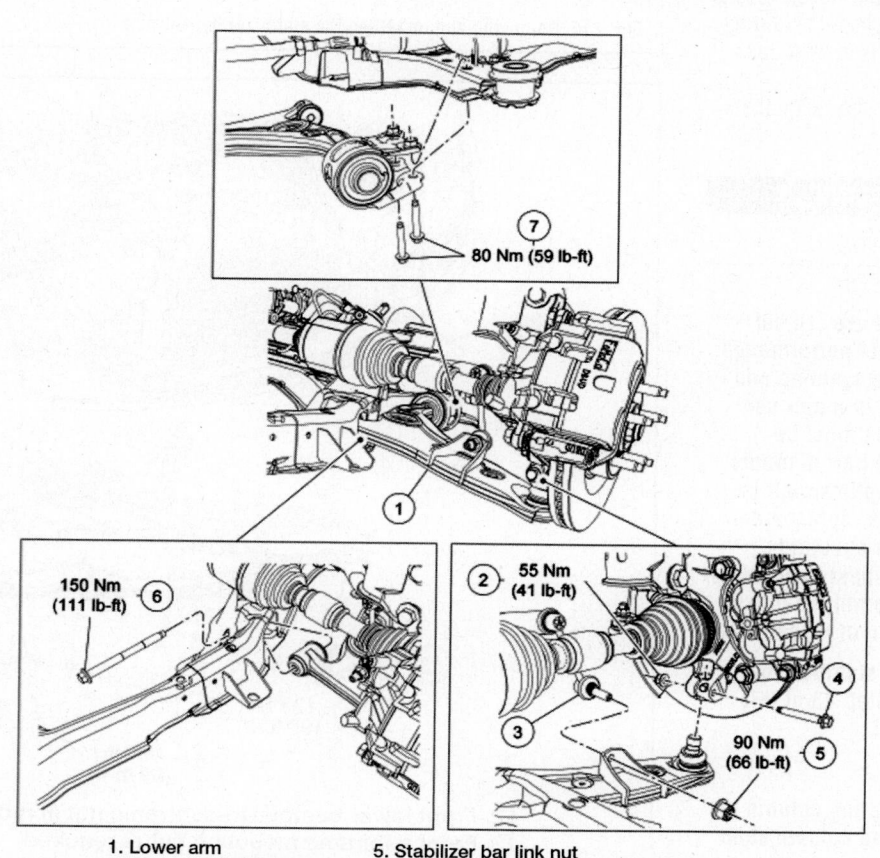

1. Lower arm
2. Lower ball joint nut
3. Stabilizer bar link
4. Lower ball joint bolt
5. Stabilizer bar link nut
6. Lower arm-to-frame forward bolt
7. Lower arm-to-frame rearward bolts (2 required)

150 Nm (111 lb-ft)
55 Nm (41 lb-ft)
80 Nm (59 lb-ft)
90 Nm (66 lb-ft)

N0108523

Fig. 214 Removing and installing the lower control arm

4. Remove the lower arm-to-frame forward bolt and spacer.

    a. Discard the bolt.

5. Remove the 2 lower arm-to-frame rearward bolts and the lower arm.

    a. Discard the 2 bolts.

To install:

➡ **Do not tighten the bolt at this time.**

6. Position the lower arm and loosely install the 2 new lower arm-to-frame rearward bolts.

➡ **Do not tighten the bolts at this time.**

7. Loosely install the new lower arm-to-frame forward bolt and install the spacer.

8. Install the new lower arm ball joint bolt and nut. Tighten to 41 ft. lbs. (55 Nm).

9. Install the new stabilizer bar link lower nut. Tighten to 66 ft. lbs. (90 Nm).

10. Install the wheel and tire.

11. With the weight of the vehicle resting on the wheels and tires, tighten the lower arm-to-frame forward bolts to 111 ft. lbs. (150 Nm).

12. With the weight of the vehicle resting on the wheels and tires, tighten the 2 lower arm-to-frame rearward bolts to 59 ft. lbs. (80 Nm).

13. Check and, if necessary, align the front end.

STABILIZER BAR & LINK

REMOVAL & INSTALLATION

See Figures 215 through 218.

➡ **Suspension fasteners are critical parts because they affect performance of vital components and systems and their failure may result in major service expense. New parts must be installed with the same part numbers or equivalent part, if replacement is necessary. Do not use a replacement part of lesser quality or substitute design. Torque values must be used as specified during reassembly to make sure of correct retention of these parts.**

➡ **If replacing only the stabilizer bar bushings, proceed to Step 23 of this procedure.**

All vehicles

➡ **Do not allow the steering column to rotate while the steering column shaft is disconnected, or damage to the clockspring may occur. If there is evidence that the steering column has rotated, the clockspring must be removed and recentered.**

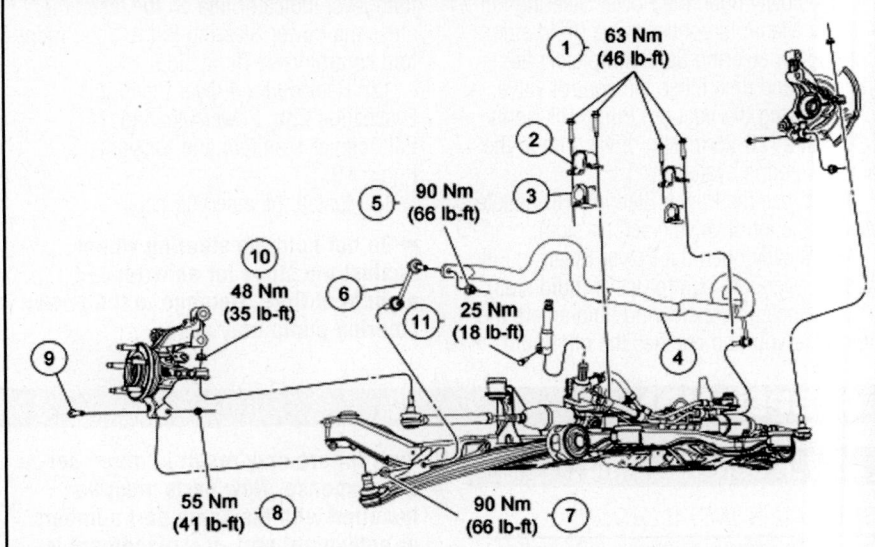

1. Stabilizer bar bracket bolts (4 required)
2. Stabilizer bar bracket (2 required)
3. Stabilizer bar bushing (2 required)
4. Stabilizer bar
5. Stabilizer bar link upper nut (2 required)
6. Stabilizer bar link (2 required)
7. Stabilizer bar link lower nut (2 required)
8. Lower ball joint nut (2 required)
9. Lower ball joint bolt
10. Outer tie-rod end nut (2 required)
11. Steering column shaft bolt

Fig. 215 Removing and installing the stabilizer bar—1 of 4

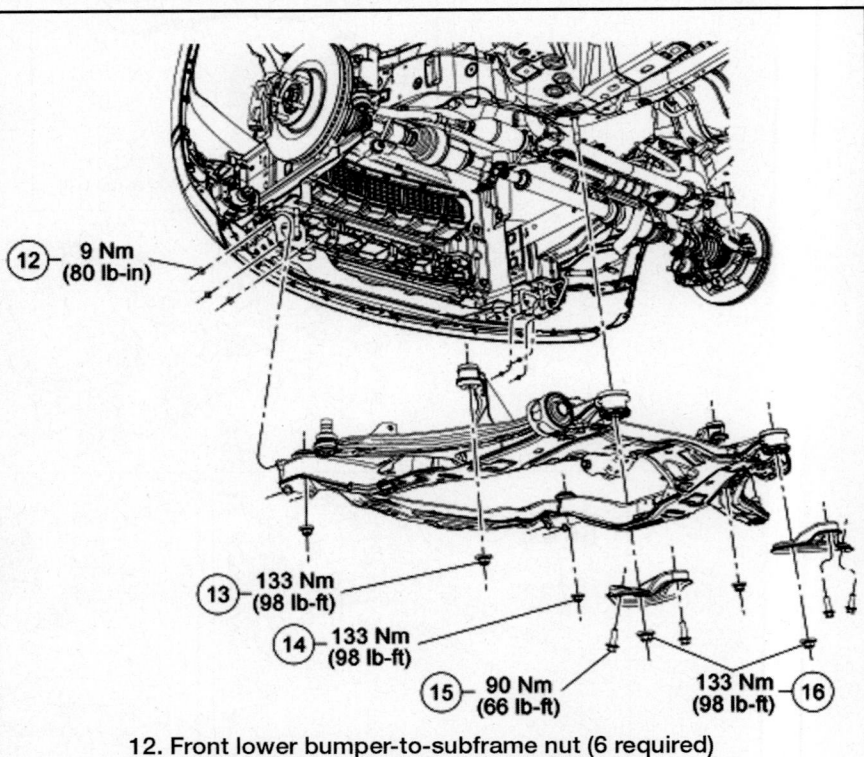

12. Front lower bumper-to-subframe nut (6 required)
13. Front subframe mounting nut (2 required)
14. Front subframe mounting nut (2 required)
15. Subframe support bracket bolt (4 required)
16. Subframe support bracket nuts (2 required)

Fig. 216 Removing and installing the stabilizer bar—2 of 4

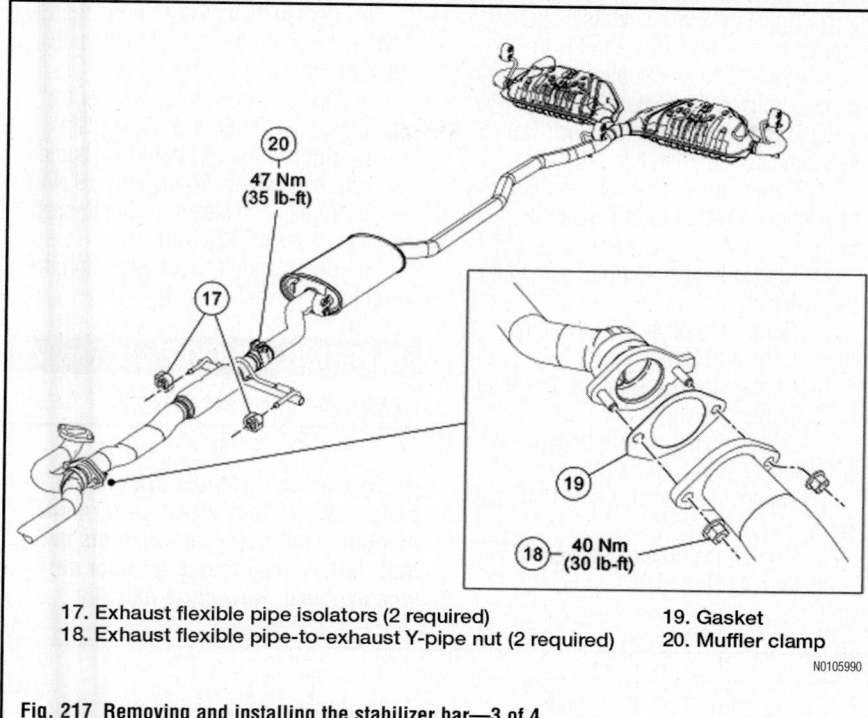

17. Exhaust flexible pipe isolators (2 required)
18. Exhaust flexible pipe-to-exhaust Y-pipe nut (2 required)
19. Gasket
20. Muffler clamp

N0105990

Fig. 217 Removing and installing the stabilizer bar—3 of 4

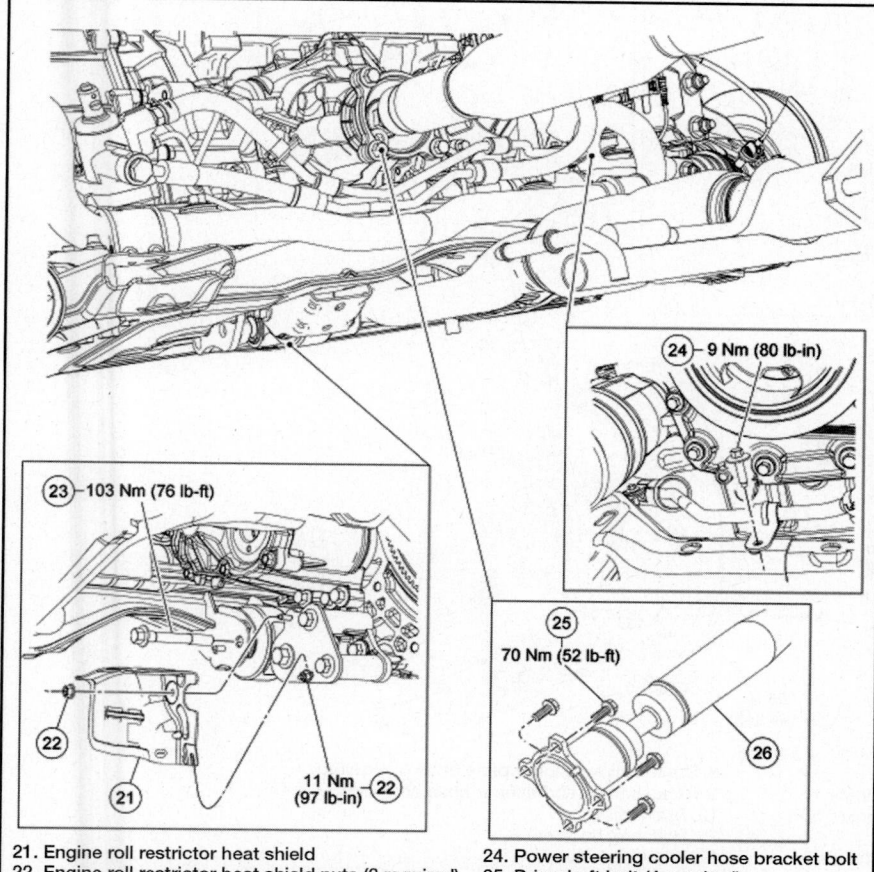

21. Engine roll restrictor heat shield
22. Engine roll restrictor heat shield nuts (2 required)
23. Engine roll restrictor-to-subframe bolt
24. Power steering cooler hose bracket bolt
25. Driveshaft bolt (4 required)
26. Driveshaft assembly

N0105989

Fig. 218 Removing and installing the stabilizer bar—4 of 4

➡Use a steering wheel holding device (such as Hunter® 28-75-1 or equivalent).

1. Using a suitable holding device, hold the steering wheel in the straight-ahead position.
2. Remove the wheel and tire.
3. Remove the steering column shaft bolt and disconnect the shaft from the steering gear.
4. Index-mark the relationship of the front subframe to the underbody at the mounting locations.
5. Remove the 4 pin-type retainers and the RH fender splash shield.
6. Remove the 3 pushpin fasteners, the 7 screws and the front splash shield.
7. Remove the 3 RH front lower bumper-to-subframe nuts.
8. Remove the 3 LH front lower bumper-to-subframe nuts and separate the lower bumper from the subframe.
9. Remove the power steering fluid cooler hose bracket bolt.
10. Loosen the muffler clamp and disconnect the 2 exhaust hangers.
11. Remove the 2 nuts and separate the flex pipe from the Y-pipe assembly.

All-Wheel Drive (AWD) vehicles
12. Index-mark the driveshaft, remove the 4 bolts and position the driveshaft aside.

All vehicles

➡Use the holding feature to prevent the ball stud from turning while removing or installing the stabilizer bar link nuts.

13. Remove the stabilizer link upper and lower nuts and the stabilizer links.
   a. Discard the nuts.
14. Remove the 2 outer tie-rod end nuts.
15. Using the Tie-Rod End Remover, separate the outer tie-rod ends from the wheel knuckles.
16. Remove the 2 lower ball joint bolts and nuts and separate the lower ball joints from the wheel knuckles.
   a. Discard the bolts and nuts.
17. Remove the upper nut, loosen the lower nut and remove the engine roll restrictor heat shield.
18. Remove the engine roll restrictor-to-subframe bolt.
19. Using a suitable jack, support the subframe.
   a. Support the subframe in the center rear area of the subframe.

➡During installation, the subframe brackets are loosely installed with the support bracket bolts. Align the index marks made in Step 2, then tighten the

rear subframe nuts prior to tightening the support bracket bolts.

20. Remove the 2 nuts, 4 bolts and the subframe support brackets.

    a. Discard the nuts and bolts.

21. Remove and discard the 4 subframe nuts.

22. Using the jack, lower the subframe approximately 3 inches (76.2 mm).

23. Remove the 4 bolts, 2 stabilizer bar brackets and bushings.

    a. Discard the bolts.

    b. Tighten the new stabilizer bar bracket bolts to 46 ft. lbs. (63 Nm).

24. Remove the stabilizer bar.

To install:

25. To install, reverse the removal procedure and note the following torque specifications:

    a. Tighten the new subframe nuts to 98 ft. lbs. (133 Nm).

    b. Tighten the new subframe support bracket nuts to 98 ft. lbs. (133 Nm).

    c. Tighten the new subframe support bracket bolts to 66 ft. lbs. (90 Nm).

    d. Tighten the engine roll restrictor to subframe bolt to 76 ft. lbs. (103 Nm).

    e. Tighten the engine roll restrictor heat shield upper nut to 97 inch lbs. (11 Nm).

    f. Tighten the ball joint nuts to 41 ft. lbs. (55 Nm).

    g. Tighten the outer tie rod end nuts to 35 ft. lbs. (48 Nm).

    h. Tighten the new stabilizer link nuts to 66 ft. lbs. (90 Nm).

    i. Tighten the driveshaft bolts to 52 ft. lbs. (70 Nm).

    j. Tighten the flex pipe nuts to 35 ft. lbs. (47 Nm).

    k. Tighten the exhaust hangers to 35 ft. lbs. (47 Nm).

    l. Tighten the power steering fluid cooler hose to bracket bolt to 80 inch lbs. (9 Nm).

    m. Tighten the LH front bumper to subframe nuts to 80 inch lbs. (9 Nm).

    n. Tighten the RH front lower bumper to subframe nuts to 80 inch lbs. (9 Nm).

    o. Tighten the steering column shaft bolt to 18 ft. lbs. (25 Nm).

    p. Check and, if necessary, align the front end.

STEERING KNUCKLE

REMOVAL & INSTALLATION

See Figure 219.

➡**Suspension fasteners are critical parts because they affect performance of vital components and systems and their failure may result in major service expense. New parts must be**

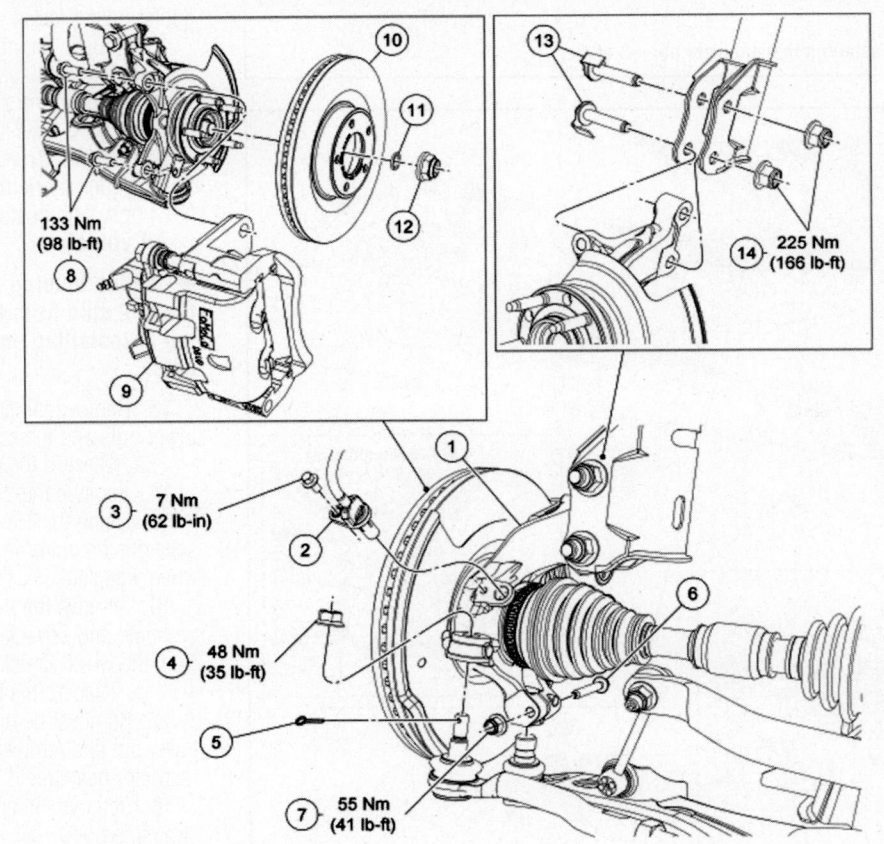

1. Wheel knuckle
2. Wheel speed sensor
3. Wheel speed sensor bolt
4. Tie-rod end nut
5. Tie-rod end cotter pin
6. Lower ball joint bolt
7. Lower ball joint nut
8. Brake caliper anchor plate bolts (2 required)
9. Brake caliper and anchor plate assembly
10. Brake disc
11. Halfshaft hub seal
12. Wheel hub nut
13. Lower shock absorber flag bolts (2 required)
14. Lower shock absorber nuts (2 required)

N0108521

Fig. 219 Removing and installing the steering knuckle

installed with the same part numbers or equivalent part, if replacement is necessary. Do not use a replacement part of lesser quality or substitute design. Torque values must be used as specified during reassembly to make sure of correct retention of these parts.

1. Remove the wheel and tire.

➡ **Apply the brake to keep the halfshaft from rotating.**

➡ **Do not discard the wheel hub nut and washer at this time.**

2. Remove the wheel hub nut and washer and the halfshaft hub seal.
   a. Discard the seal.
3. Remove the wheel speed sensor bolt and position the wheel speed sensor aside.

➡ **Do not allow the caliper and anchor plate assembly to hang from the brake hose or damage to the hose can occur.**

4. Remove the 2 bolts and position the caliper and anchor plate assembly aside.
   a. Support the caliper and anchor plate assembly using mechanic's wire.
5. Remove the brake disc.
6. Using the Front Hub Remover, separate the halfshaft from the wheel hub.
7. Remove and discard the tie-rod end cotter pin and nut.

➡ **Do not use a hammer to separate the tie-rod end from the wheel knuckle or damage to the wheel knuckle can result.**

8. Using the Tie-Rod End Remover, separate the tie-rod end from the wheel knuckle.
9. Remove the shock absorber lower nuts and flag bolts.
   a. Discard the nuts and flag bolts.
10. Remove the lower ball joint bolt, nut and the wheel knuckle.
   a. Discard the bolt and nut.

To install:
11. Position the wheel knuckle and install the new lower ball joint bolt and nut. Tighten the nut to 41 ft. lbs. (55 Nm).
12. Install the new shock absorber lower nuts and flag bolts. Tighten to 166 ft. lbs. (225 Nm).
13. Position the tie-rod end and install the new nut and cotter pin. Tighten to 35 ft. lbs. (48 Nm).
14. Position the wheel speed sensor and install the bolt. Tighten to 62 inch lbs. (7 Nm).
15. Install the brake disc.
16. Position the brake caliper and anchor plate assembly and install the

2 bolts. Tighten to 98 ft. lbs. (133 Nm).

➡ **Do not tighten the front wheel hub nut with the vehicle on the ground. The nut must be tightened to specification before the vehicle is lowered onto the wheels. Wheel bearing damage will occur if the bearing is loaded with the weight of the vehicle applied.**

➡ **Apply the brake to keep the halfshaft from rotating.**

17. Position the halfshaft in the hub and use the previously removed wheel hub nut and washer to seat the halfshaft.
   a. Tighten to 258 ft. lbs. (350 Nm).
   b. Remove and discard the wheel hub nut and washer.

➡ **The wheel hub nut contains a one-time locking chemical that is activated by the heat created when it is tightened. Install and tighten the new wheel hub nut to specification within**

5 minutes of starting it on the threads. Always install a new wheel hub nut after loosening or when not tightening within the specified time or damage to the components may occur.

➡ **Apply the brake to keep the halfshaft from rotating.**

18. Install a new wheel hub nut and washer. Tighten to 258 ft. lbs. (350 Nm).
19. Install the wheel and tire.
20. Check and, if necessary, align the front end.

SHOCK ABSORBER & SPRING ASSEMBLY

REMOVAL & INSTALLATION

See Figure 220.

➡ **Suspension fasteners are critical parts because they affect performance of vital components and systems and their failure may result in major**

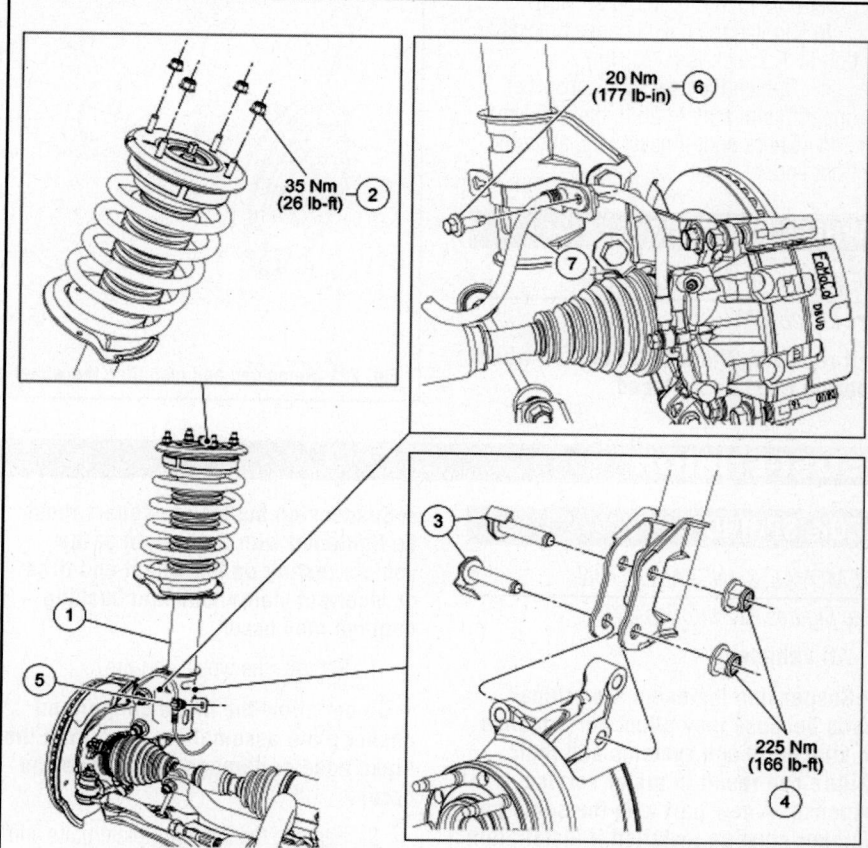

1. Shock absorber and spring assembly
2. Shock absorber upper mount nut (4 required)
3. Shock absorber lower flag bolts (2 required)
4. Shock absorber lower nuts (2 required)
5. Wheel speed sensor harness clip
6. Brake flexible hose bracket bolt
7. Brake flexible hose

N0091983

Fig. 220 Removing and installing the shock absorber and spring assembly

service expense. New parts must be installed with the same part numbers or equivalent part, if replacement is necessary. Do not use a replacement part of lesser quality or substitute design. Torque values must be used as specified during reassembly to make sure of correct retention of these parts.

1. Remove and discard the 4 shock absorber upper mount nuts.
2. Remove the wheel and tire.
3. Remove the brake flexible hose bracket bolt and disconnect the hose from the shock absorber.
4. Disconnect the wheel speed sensor harness from the shock absorber bracket.
5. Remove the shock absorber lower nuts, flag bolts and the shock absorber and spring assembly.
  a. Discard the nuts and flag bolts.

To install:

6. To install, reverse the removal procedure and note the following:
  a. Tighten the new shock absorber lower nuts to 166 ft. lbs. (225 Nm).
  b. Tighten the flexible hose bracket bolt to 177 inch lbs. (20 Nm).
  c. Tighten the new shock absorber upper mount nuts to 26 ft. lbs. (35 Nm).
  d. Check and, if necessary, align the front end.

WHEEL BEARINGS

REMOVAL & INSTALLATION
See Figure 221.

➡If removing the wheel hub, the wheel bearing must be replaced.

1. Remove the wheel knuckle.
2. Using the Step Plate and a suitable press, remove the wheel hub from the wheel bearing.

➡This step may not be necessary if the inner wheel bearing race remains in the wheel knuckle after removing the wheel hub.

3. Using the Pinion Bearing Cone Remover and a suitable press, remove the inner wheel bearing race from the wheel hub.
4. Remove the snap ring.
5. Using the Wheel Hub Cup

Remover/Installer and a suitable press, remove the outer wheel bearing race from the wheel knuckle.

To install:

6. Using the Wheel Hub Bearing Cup Installer and a suitable press, install the wheel bearing into the wheel knuckle.
7. Install the snap ring.
8. Using the Wheel Hub Bearing Cup Installer, Step Plate and a suitable press, install the wheel hub into the wheel bearing.
9. Install the wheel knuckle.

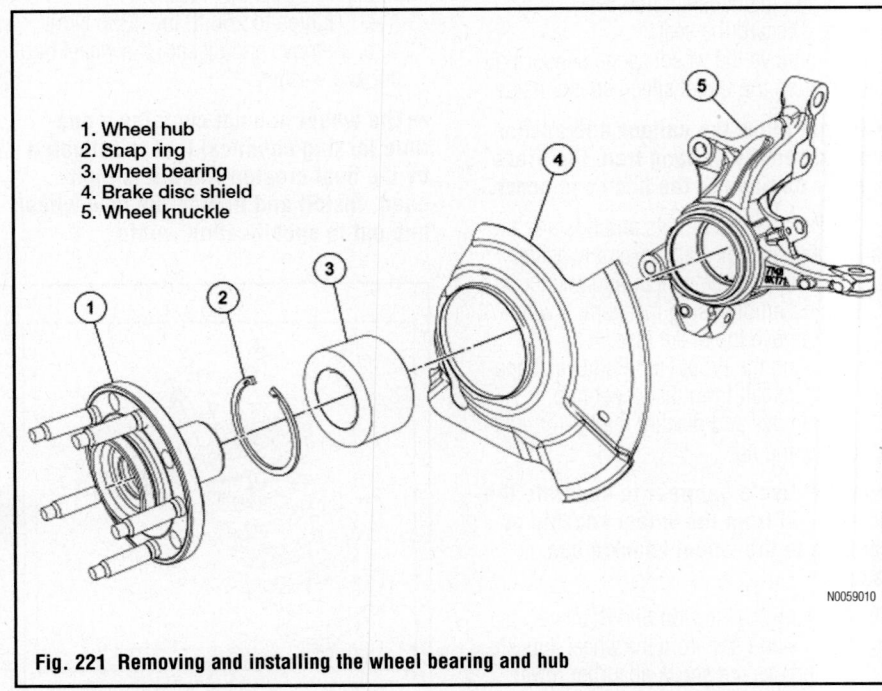

1. Wheel hub
2. Snap ring
3. Wheel bearing
4. Brake disc shield
5. Wheel knuckle

N0059010

Fig. 221 Removing and installing the wheel bearing and hub

SUSPENSION

COIL SPRING

REMOVAL & INSTALLATION
See Figures 222 through 224.

All vehicles

➡Suspension fasteners are critical parts because they affect performance of vital parts and systems and their failure can result in major service expense. A new part with the same part number must be installed if installation becomes necessary. Do not use a replacement part of lesser quality or substitute design. Torque values must be used as specified during reassembly to make sure of correct retention of these parts.

➡Suspension bushing fasteners must be tightened with the weight of the vehicle resting on the wheel and tires or incorrect clamp load and bushing damage may occur.

1. Remove the wheel and tire.

➡Do not allow the brake caliper and anchor plate assembly to hang from the brake hose or damage to the hose can occur.

2. Remove the 2 anchor plate bolts and position the brake caliper and anchor plate assembly aside.
  a. Support the brake caliper and anchor plate assembly using mechanic's wire.
3. Remove the brake disc.

REAR SUSPENSION

4. Remove the nut and disconnect the stabilizer bar link and parking brake cable bracket from the wheel knuckle.
  a. Discard the nut.
5. Remove the bolt and position the wheel speed sensor aside.
  a. If equipped, unclip the 2 retainers from the upper arm.
6. Remove the brake hose bracket bolt and position the hose aside.

All-Wheel Drive (AWD) vehicles

➡Do not discard the wheel hub nuts at this time.

7. Remove the outer and inner wheel hub nuts.
8. Using the Front Hub Remover, separate the halfshaft from the hub and bearing.

All vehicles

9. Position a suitable jackstand under the lower arm.

10. Remove and discard the shock absorber lower nut and flag bolt.

11. Remove and discard the upper arm outboard bolt and nut.

12. Remove and discard the toe link outboard bolt and nut.

13. Remove and discard the lower arm outboard bolt and nut.

AWD vehicles

14. Position the halfshaft through the wheel knuckle opening and secure the halfshaft aside.

All vehicles

15. The coil spring is under extreme load. Care must be taken at all times when removing or installing a loaded spring. Failure to follow this instruction may result in serious personal injury.

16. Pull outward on the wheel knuckle while lowering the jackstand and remove the spring.

    a. Inspect the spring upper and lower seats, remove and discard seats as necessary.

To install:
All vehicles

17. If removed, position a new lower seat into the lower arm with the recess in the seat aligned with the projection on the lower arm.

18. Position the spring onto the lower arm with the end of the spring 0-10 mm (0-0.39 in) from the step on the spring seat.

>✳✳ **WARNING**

The coil spring is under extreme load. Care must be taken at all times when removing or installing a loaded spring. Failure to follow this instruction may result in serious personal injury.

19. Pull outward on the wheel knuckle and install the spring.

AWD vehicles

20. Position the halfshaft into the wheel bearing and wheel hub.

All vehicles

21. Raise the jackstand and loosely install the new lower arm outboard bolt and nut.

22. Position the toe link and loosely install the new toe link outboard bolt and nut.

23. Position the upper arm and loosely install the new upper arm outboard bolt and nut.

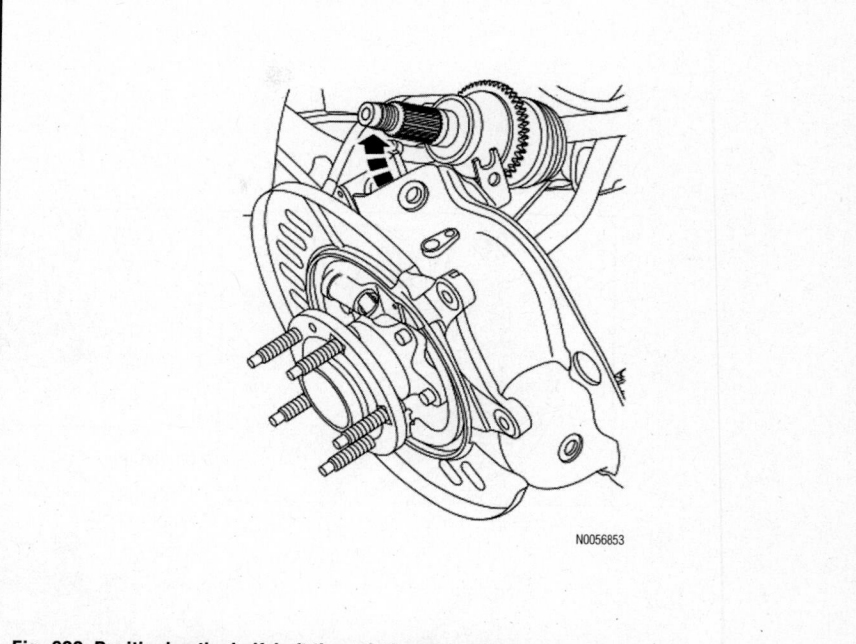

Fig. 222 Positioning the halfshaft through the wheel knuckle opening

24. Loosely install the new lower shock nut and flag bolt.

25. Lower and remove the jackstand.

AWD vehicles

➥**Do not tighten the rear wheel hub nut with the vehicle on the ground. The nut must be tightened to specification before the vehicle is lowered onto the wheels. Wheel bearing damage will occur if the bearing is loaded with the weight of the vehicle applied.**

➥**Apply the brake to keep the halfshaft from rotating.**

26. Position the halfshaft in the hub and use the previously removed wheel hub nut to seat the halfshaft.

    a. Tighten to 203 ft. lbs. (275 Nm).

    b. Remove and discard the wheel hub nut.

➥**The wheel hub nut contains a one-time locking chemical that is activated by the heat created when it is tightened. Install and tighten the new wheel hub nut to specification within 5 minutes of starting it on the threads. Always install a new wheel hub nut after loosening or when not tightening within the specified time or damage to the components may occur.**

➥**Apply the brake to keep the halfshaft from rotating.**

27. Install a new inner wheel hub nut. Tighten to 203 ft. lbs. (275 Nm).

28. Install a new outer wheel hub nut. Tighten to 129 ft. lbs. (175 Nm).

All vehicles

29. Install the brake hose bracket bolt. Tighten to 62 inch lbs. (7 Nm).

30. Position the wheel speed sensor and install the bolt. Tighten to 62 inch lbs. (7 Nm).

    a. If equipped, clip the 2 retainers to the upper arm.

31. Connect the parking brake cable bracket and stabilizer bar link to the wheel knuckle and install the nut. Tighten the nut to 30 ft. lbs. (40 Nm).

32. Install the brake disc.

33. Position the brake caliper and anchor plate assembly and install the 2 anchor plate bolts. Tighten to 41 ft. lbs. (55 Nm).

34. Install the wheel and tire.

35. With the weight of the vehicle on the wheel and tire, tighten the lower shock nut to 59 ft. lbs. (80 Nm).

36. With the weight of the vehicle on the wheel and tire, tighten the upper arm outboard bolt to 129 ft. lbs. (175 Nm).

37. With the weight of the vehicle on the wheel and tire, tighten the toe link outboard bolt to 129 ft. lbs. (175 Nm).

38. With the weight of the vehicle on the wheel and tire, tighten the lower arm outboard bolt in the following stages.

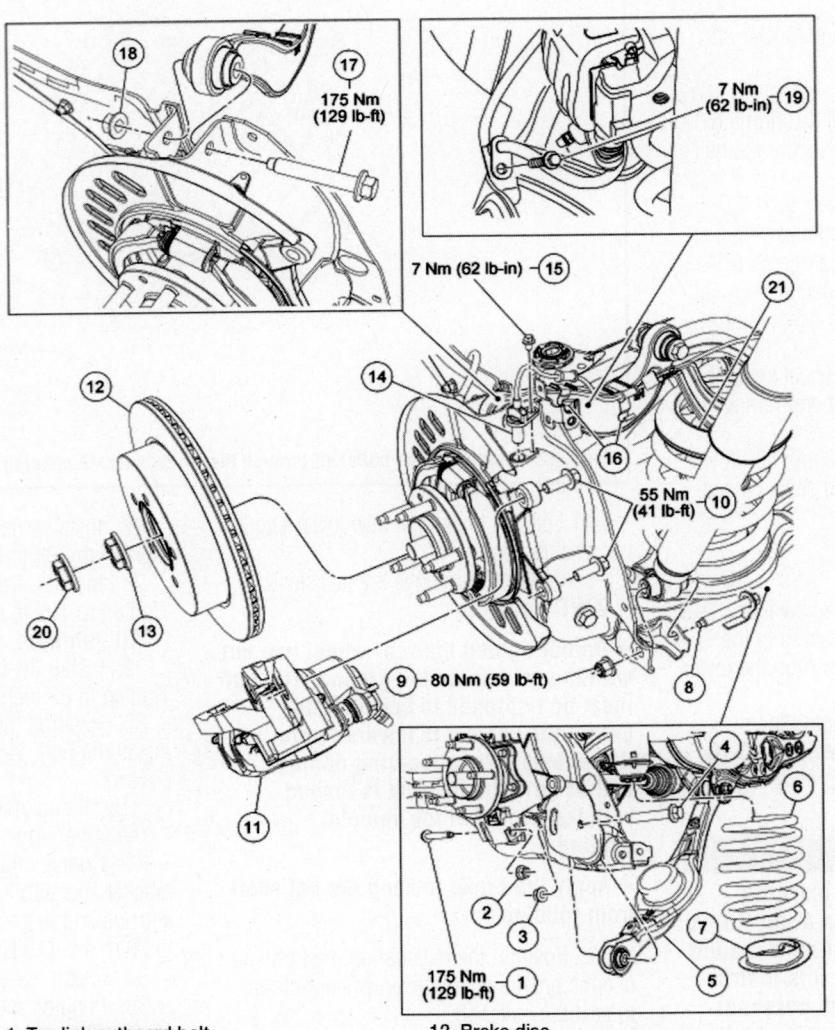

1. Toe link outboard bolt
2. Toe link outboard nut
3. Lower arm outboard nut
4. Lower arm outboard bolt
5. Lower arm
6. Spring
7. Spring lower seat
8. Shock absorber lower flag bolt
9. Shock absorber lower nut
10. Brake caliper anchor plate bolts (2 required)
11. Brake caliper and anchor plate assembly

12. Brake disc
13. Wheel hub nut (inner) (All-Wheel Drive (AWD))
14. Wheel speed sensor (AWD)
15. Wheel speed sensor bolt (AWD)
16. Wheel speed sensor harness
    clips (2 required) (AWD)
17. Upper arm outboard bolt
18. Upper arm outboard nut
19. Wheel speed sensor bolt (part of 2C190) (AWD)

N0098825

Fig. 223 Removing the coil spring—AWD

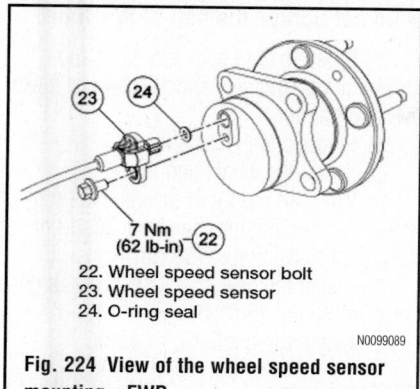

7 Nm
(62 lb-in)
22. Wheel speed sensor bolt
23. Wheel speed sensor
24. O-ring seal

N0099089

Fig. 224 View of the wheel speed sensor mounting—FWD

   a. Stage 1: Tighten to 59 ft. lbs. 80 Nm).
   b. Stage 2: Tighten an additional 90 degrees.
  39. Check and if necessary, align the vehicle.

LOWER CONTROL ARM

REMOVAL & INSTALLATION

See Figure 225.

  1. Remove the spring.
  2. Remove the cam adjuster nut, cam adjuster and cam bolt.
   a. Discard the cam bolt and nut.

To install:

  3. To install, reverse the removal procedure and tighten the new nut to 111 ft. lbs. (150 Nm).

STABILIZER BAR & LINK

REMOVAL & INSTALLATION

See Figure 226.

➡**Suspension fasteners are critical parts because they affect performance of vital components and systems and their failure may result in major service expense. New parts must be installed with the same part numbers or equivalent part, if replacement is necessary. Do not use a replacement part of lesser quality or substitute design. Torque values must be used as specified during reassembly to make sure of correct retention of these parts.**

  1. With the vehicle in NEUTRAL, position it on a hoist.
  2. Remove and discard the stabilizer bar link upper nuts.
  3. Remove and discard the stabilizer bar link lower nuts and remove the stabilizer bar links.

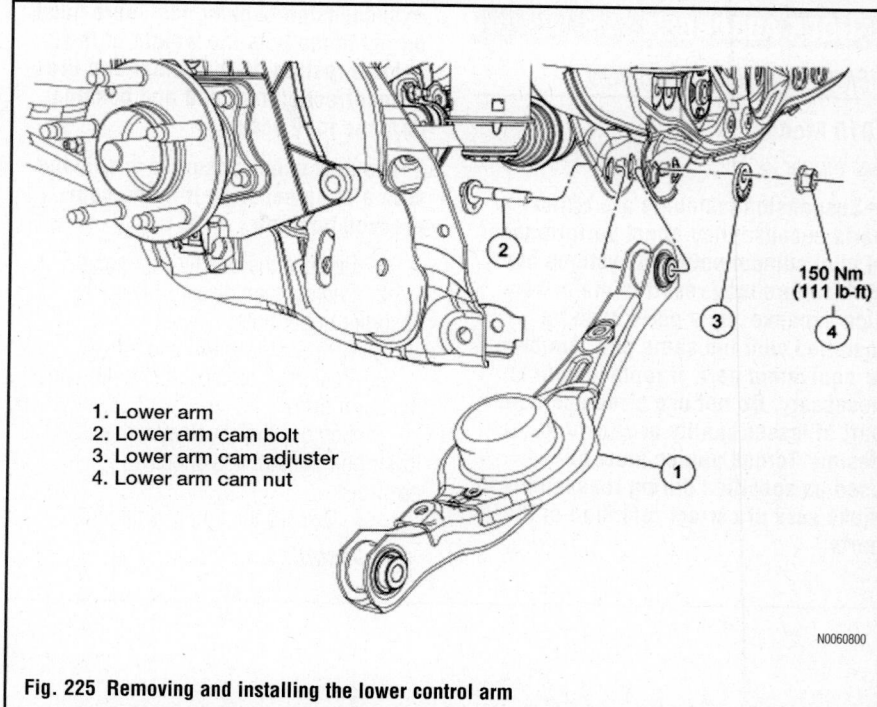

1. Lower arm
2. Lower arm cam bolt
3. Lower arm cam adjuster
4. Lower arm cam nut

150 Nm
(111 lb-ft)

N0060800

Fig. 225 Removing and installing the lower control arm

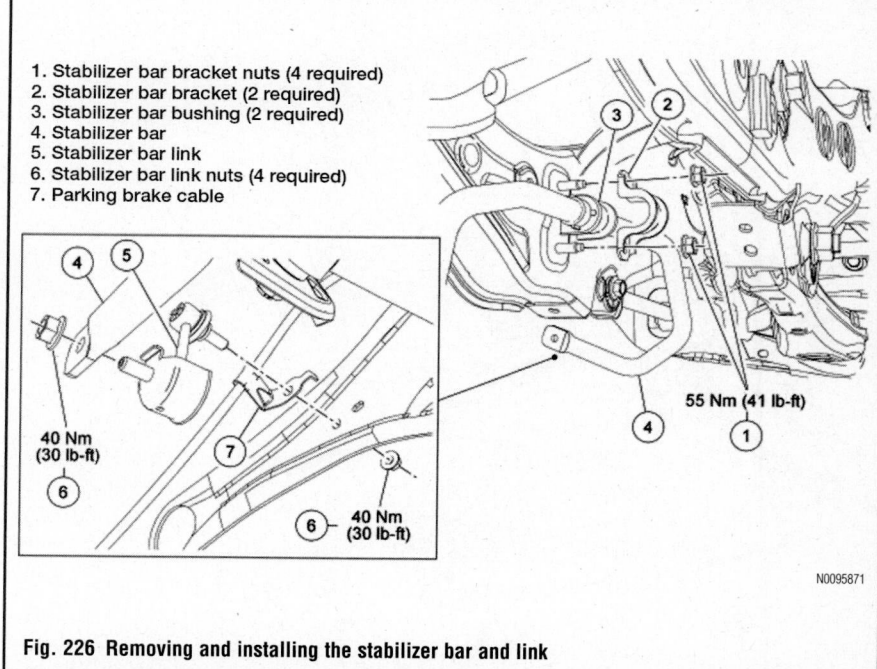

1. Stabilizer bar bracket nuts (4 required)
2. Stabilizer bar bracket (2 required)
3. Stabilizer bar bushing (2 required)
4. Stabilizer bar
5. Stabilizer bar link
6. Stabilizer bar link nuts (4 required)
7. Parking brake cable

40 Nm
(30 lb-ft)

40 Nm
(30 lb-ft)

55 Nm (41 lb-ft)

N0095871

Fig. 226 Removing and installing the stabilizer bar and link

  4. Remove and discard the stabilizer bar bracket nuts and remove the stabilizer bar brackets and the stabilizer bar.
   a. Tighten the new stabilizer bar bracket nuts to 41 ft. lbs. (55 Nm).
  5. Inspect the stabilizer bar bushings and install a new bushing(s), if necessary.

To install:

  6. To install, reverse the removal procedure and note the following:
   a. Tighten the stabilizer bar link new nuts to 30 ft. lbs. (40 Nm).
   b. Tighten the stabilizer bar link new upper nuts to 30 ft. lbs. (40 Nm).

SHOCK ABSORBER

REMOVAL & INSTALLATION

2010 Models

See Figure 227.

→Suspension fasteners are critical parts because they affect performance of vital components and systems and their failure may result in major service expense. New parts must be installed with the same part numbers or equivalent part, if replacement is necessary. Do not use a replacement part of lesser quality or substitute design. Torque values must be used as specified during reassembly to make sure of correct retention of these parts.

→Suspension bushing fasteners must be tightened with the weight of the vehicle resting on the wheel and tires or incorrect clamp load and bushing damage may occur.

→The new shock absorber is shipped with a strap securing it in the compressed position.

1. Remove the quarter trim panel.
2. Remove and discard the shock absorber upper nuts.
3. Remove the wheel and tire.
4. Position a suitable jackstand under the lower arm.
5. Remove the shock absorber lower bolt, flagnut and shock absorber.
   a. Discard the bolt and flagnut.

To install:

→Do not tighten the bolt at this time.

6. Position the shock absorber and loosely install the new shock absorber lower bolt and flagnut.
7. Remove the jackstand.
8. Install the wheel and tire.
9. With the weight of the vehicle on the wheel and tire, tighten the shock absorber lower bolt to 59 ft. lbs. (80 Nm).
10. Install the new shock absorber upper nuts. Tighten to 18 ft. lbs. (25 Nm).
11. Install the quarter trim panel.

2011 Models

See Figure 228.

→Suspension fasteners are critical parts because they affect performance of vital components and systems and their failure may result in major service expense. New parts must be installed with the same part numbers or equivalent part, if replacement is necessary. Do not use a replacement part of lesser quality or substitute design. Torque values must be used as specified during reassembly to make sure of correct retention of these parts.

→Suspension bushing fasteners must be tightened with the weight of the vehicle resting on the wheel and tires or incorrect clamp load and bushing damage may occur.

→The new shock absorber is shipped with a strap securing it in the compressed position.

1. Remove the quarter trim panel.
2. Remove and discard the shock absorber upper nuts.
3. Remove the wheel and tire.
4. Position a suitable jackstand under the lower arm.
5. Remove the shock absorber lower bolt, nut and shock absorber.
   a. Discard the bolt and nut.

To install:

→Do not tighten the bolt at this time.

6. Position the shock absorber and loosely install the new shock absorber lower bolt and nut.
7. Remove the jackstand.
8. Install the wheel and tire.
9. With the weight of the vehicle on the wheel and tire, tighten the shock absorber lower nut to 166 ft. lbs. (225 Nm).
10. Install the new shock absorber upper nuts. Tighten to 18 ft. lbs. (25 Nm).
11. Install the quarter trim panel.

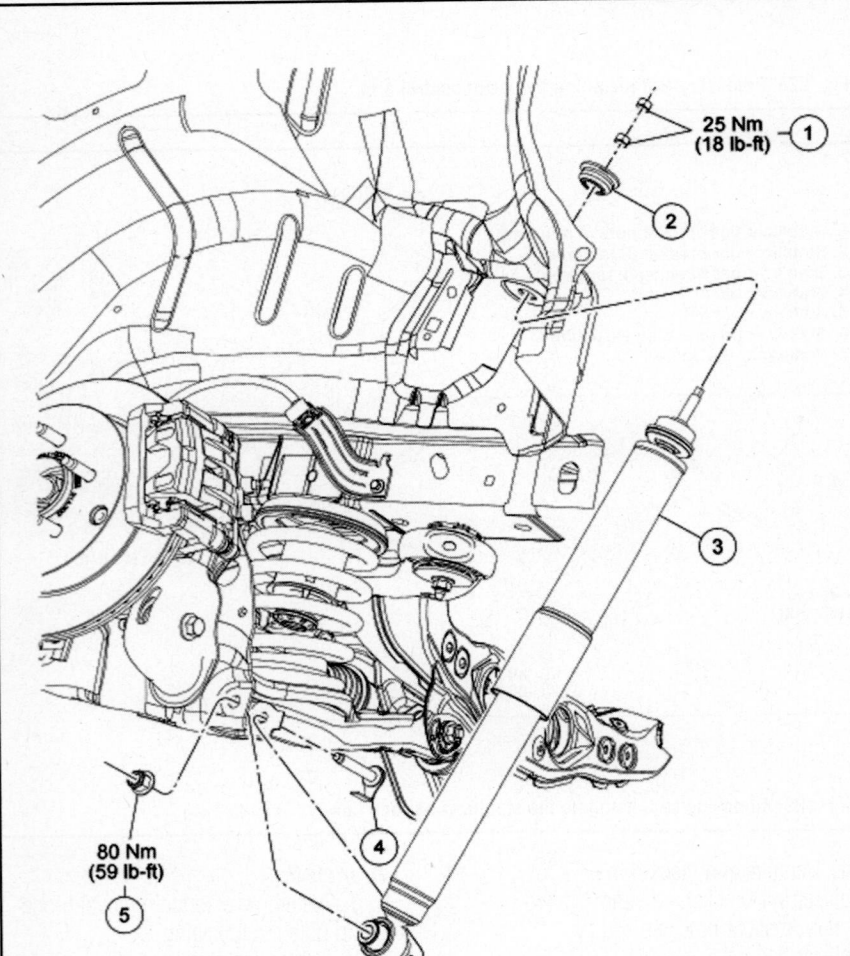

25 Nm (18 lb-ft) — 1

80 Nm (59 lb-ft) — 5

1. Shock absorber upper nuts (2 required)
2. Shock absorber
3. Shock absorber upper bushing
4. Shock absorber lower flag bolt
5. Shock absorber lower nut

N0060566

Fig. 227 Removing and installing the shock absorber

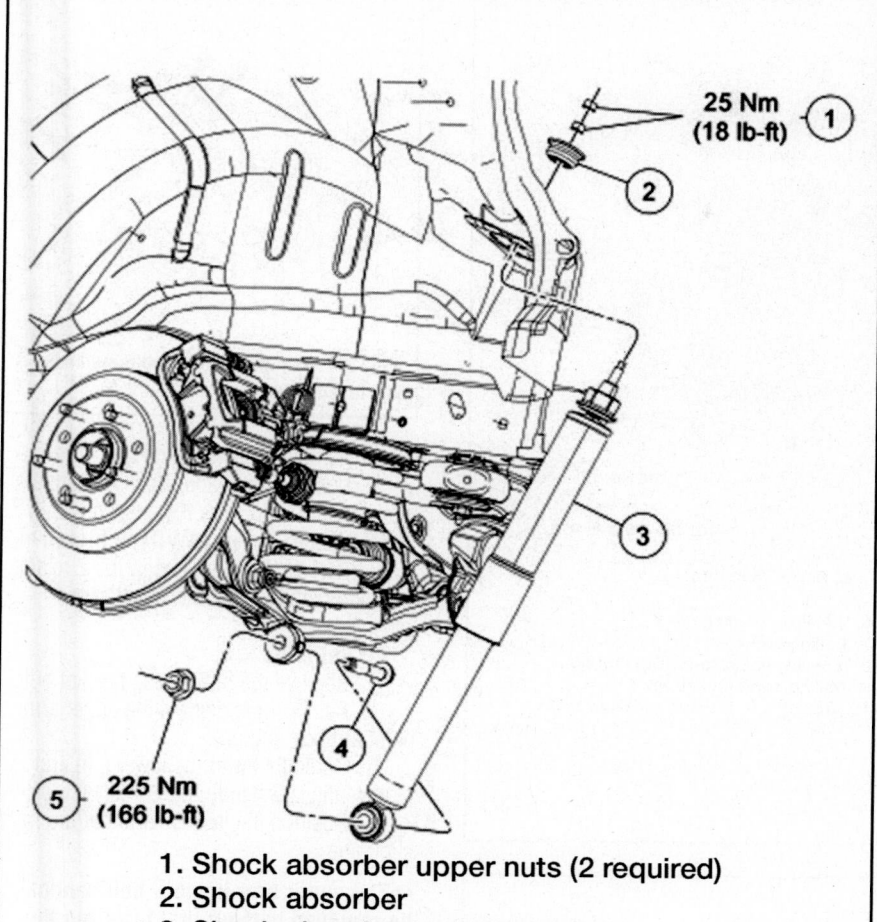

1. Shock absorber upper nuts (2 required)
2. Shock absorber
3. Shock absorber upper bushing
4. Shock absorber lower bolt
5. Shock absorber lower nut

N0111708

Fig. 228 Removing and installing the shock absorber

TRAILING ARM

REMOVAL & INSTALLATION

See Figure 229.

➡Suspension fasteners affect performance of vital components and systems and their failure may result in major service expense. If replacement is necessary install new parts with the same part numbers or equivalent part. Do not use a replacement part of lesser quality or substitute design. Tighten the fasteners to specification during reassembly.

➡Tighten the suspension bushing fasteners with the weight of the vehicle resting on the wheels and tires or incorrect clamp load and bushing damage may occur.

1. Remove the wheel and tire.
At the time of publication the manufacturer does not provide a specific Removal and Installation procedure for this component. Refer to the graphic(s) when servicing this component.

Items in the exploded views may not be listed in order of removal.

TOE LINK

REMOVAL & INSTALLATION

See Figure 230.

➡Suspension fasteners are critical parts because they affect performance of vital components and systems and their failure may result in major service expense. New parts must be

installed with the same part numbers or equivalent part, if replacement is necessary. Do not use a replacement part of lesser quality or substitute design. Torque values must be used as specified during reassembly to make sure of correct retention of these parts.

➡Suspension bushing fasteners must be tightened with the weight of the vehicle resting on the wheel and tires or incorrect clamp load and bushing damage may occur.

1. Remove the wheel and tire.
2. Remove and discard the toe link inboard nut, cam adjuster and cam bolt.
3. Remove and discard the toe link outboard bolt and nut then remove the toe link.

To install:

➡**Do not tighten the bolt at this time.**

4. Position the toe link and loosely install the new toe link outboard bolt and nut.

➡**Do not tighten the bolt at this time.**

5. Loosely install the new toe link inboard bolt and nut.
6. Install the wheel and tire.
7. With the weight of the vehicle on the wheel and tire, tighten the toe link outboard bolt to 129 ft. lbs. (175 Nm).
8. With the weight of the vehicle on the wheel and tire, tighten the toe link inboard nut to 148 ft. lbs. (200 Nm).

UPPER CONTROL ARM

REMOVAL & INSTALLATION

See Figures 231 and 232.

All vehicles

➡Suspension fasteners are critical parts because they affect performance of vital components and systems and their failure may result in major service expense. New parts must be installed with the same part numbers or equivalent part, if replacement is necessary. Do not use a replacement part of lesser quality or substitute design. Torque values must be used as specified during reassembly to make sure of correct retention of these parts.

➡Suspension bushing fasteners must be tightened with the weight of the vehicle resting on the wheel and tires or incorrect clamp load and bushing damage may occur.

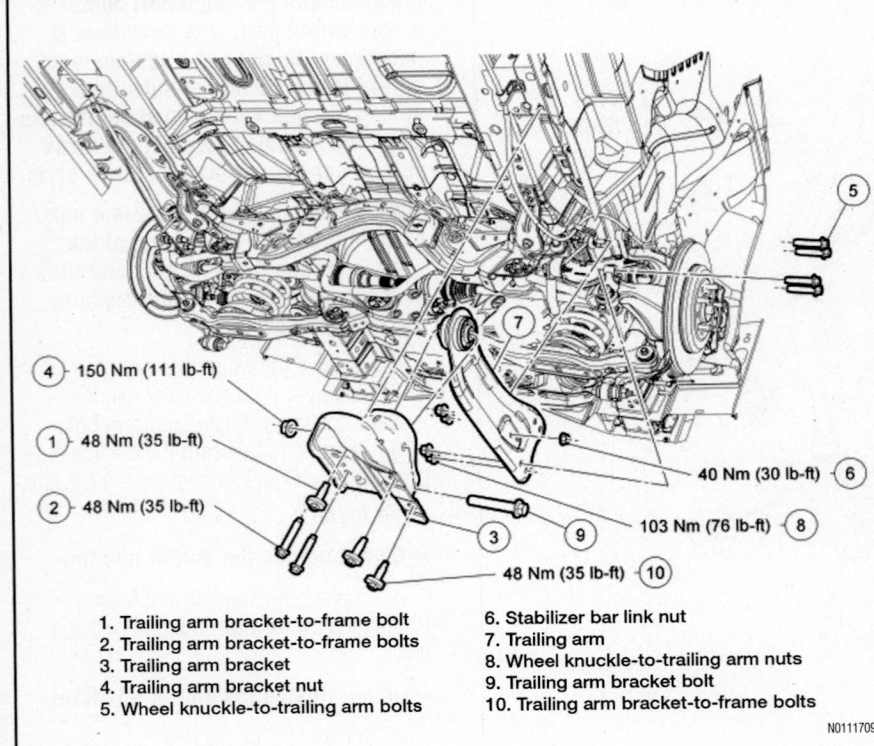

4 — 150 Nm (111 lb-ft)

1 — 48 Nm (35 lb-ft)

2 — 48 Nm (35 lb-ft)

40 Nm (30 lb-ft) — 6

3   9   103 Nm (76 lb-ft) — 8

48 Nm (35 lb-ft) — 10

1. Trailing arm bracket-to-frame bolt
2. Trailing arm bracket-to-frame bolts
3. Trailing arm bracket
4. Trailing arm bracket nut
5. Wheel knuckle-to-trailing arm bolts
6. Stabilizer bar link nut
7. Trailing arm
8. Wheel knuckle-to-trailing arm nuts
9. Trailing arm bracket bolt
10. Trailing arm bracket-to-frame bolts

N0111709

Fig. 229 Removing and installing the trailing arm

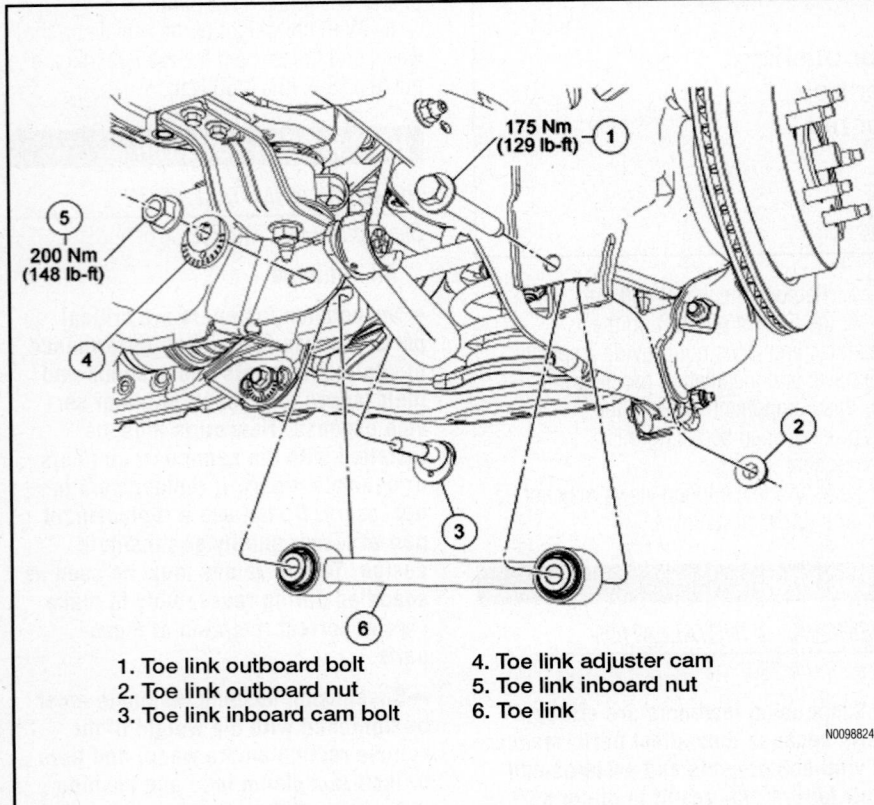

175 Nm (129 lb-ft) — 1

5 — 200 Nm (148 lb-ft)

4

3

2

6

1. Toe link outboard bolt
2. Toe link outboard nut
3. Toe link inboard cam bolt
4. Toe link adjuster cam
5. Toe link inboard nut
6. Toe link

N0098824

Fig. 230 Removing and installing the toe link

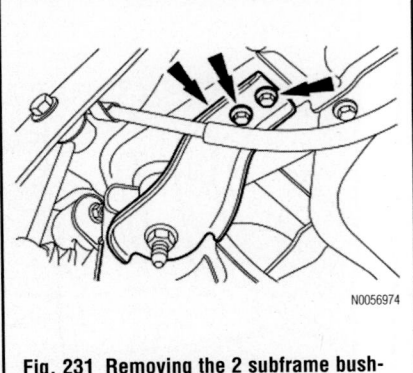

N0056974

Fig. 231 Removing the 2 subframe bushing brace bolts

1. Remove the wheel and tire.
2. Position a suitable jackstand under the lower arm and raise the suspension.

All-Wheel Drive (AWD) vehicles

3. Remove the bolt, unclip the 2 retainers and position aside the wheel speed sensor.

All vehicles

4. Remove the brake hose bracket bolt.
5. Remove and discard the upper arm outboard bolt and nut.
6. Carefully lower the lower arm and remove the jackstand.
7. Position the jackstand under the subframe.

➡ The upper arm inboard bolt cannot be removed without first lowering the subframe.

8. Remove and discard the 2 subframe bushing brace bolts.
9. Remove the subframe forward nut.

➡ The rear springs are under pressure. The jack must be lowered slowly while relieving the spring pressure or component damage may occur.

➡ The upper arm inboard bolt cannot be removed without first lowering the subframe.

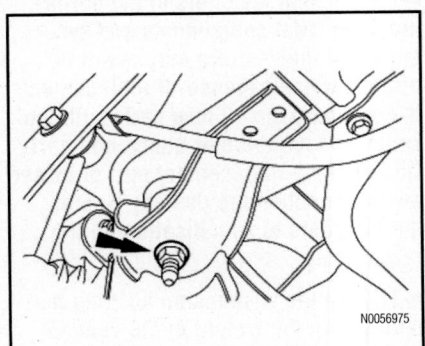

N0056975

Fig. 232 Removing the subframe forward nut

10. Remove the subframe rearward nut and lower the jackstand.

11. Remove and discard the upper arm inboard bolt and nut and remove the upper arm.

To install:
All vehicles

➡ **Do not tighten the bolt at this time.**

12. Position the upper arm and loosely install the new upper arm inboard bolt and nut.

13. Raise the jackstand and install the subframe rearward nut. Tighten to 66 ft. lbs. (90 Nm).

14. Install the subframe forward nut. Tighten to 66 ft. lbs. (90 Nm).

15. Install the 2 subframe bushing brace bolts. Tighten to 18 ft. lbs. (25 Nm).

16. Reposition the jack under the lower arm and raise the jack.

17. Loosely install the new upper arm outboard bolt and nut.

18. Remove the jackstand.

19. Install the wheel and tire.

All-Wheel Drive (AWD) vehicles

20. Position the wheel speed sensor, clip the 2 retainers to the upper arm and install the bolt. Tighten to 62 inch lbs. (7 Nm).

All vehicles

21. Install the brake hose bracket bolt.

22. With the weight of the vehicle on the wheel and tire, tighten the upper arm outboard bolt to 129 ft. lbs. (175 Nm).

23. With the weight of the vehicle on the wheel and tire, tighten the upper arm inboard bolt to 129 ft. lbs. (175 Nm).

WHEEL BEARINGS & WHEEL HUB

REMOVAL & INSTALLATION

2010 Models
See Figures 233 and 234.

All vehicles

➡ **Suspension fasteners are critical parts because they affect performance of vital components and systems and their failure may result in major service expense. New parts must be installed with the same part numbers or equivalent part, if replacement is necessary. Do not use a replacement part of lesser quality or substitute design. Torque values must be used as specified during reassembly to make sure of correct retention of these parts.**

1. Remove the wheel and tire.

➡ **Do not allow the brake caliper and anchor plate assembly to hang from the brake hose or damage to the hose can occur.**

2. Remove the 2 anchor plate bolts and position the brake caliper and anchor plate assembly aside.

a. Support the brake caliper and anchor plate assembly using mechanic's wire.

3. Remove the brake disc.

All-Wheel Drive (AWD) vehicles

➡ **Do not discard the inner nut at this time.**

4. Remove the outer and inner halfshaft nuts.

a. Discard the outer nut.

5. Using the Front Hub Remover, separate the halfshaft from the hub and bearing assembly.

6. Remove the brake hose bracket bolt.

7. Remove the wheel speed sensor bolt and detach the sensor from the wheel knuckle.

8. Unclip the wheel speed sensor harness from the upper arm and position the wheel speed sensor assembly aside.

9. Remove and discard the upper arm outboard bolt and nut.

a. Separate the upper arm from the wheel knuckle.

10. Position a suitable screw-type jackstand under the lower arm.

11. Remove and discard the shock absorber lower bolt and nut.

12. Remove and discard the stabilizer bar link upper nut.

13. Remove and discard the toe link outboard bolt and nut.

14. With the wheel knuckle supported by the screw-type jackstand, remove and discard the toe link outboard bolt and nut.

15. Position the halfshaft up through the wheel knuckle opening.

Front Wheel Drive (FWD) vehicles

16. Remove the wheel speed sensor bolt and detach the sensor from the wheel bearing and wheel hub.

All vehicles

17. Remove the 4 bolts and the wheel bearing and wheel hub.

a. Discard the bolts.

To install:
All vehicles

➡ **Before tightening the upper arm and lower arm bolts, use a jackstand to raise the rear suspension until the distance between the center of the hub and the lip of the fender is equal to the measurement taken in the removal procedure (curb height).**

18. Position the wheel bearing and wheel hub and install 4 new bolts. Tighten to 98 ft. lbs. (133 Nm).

AWD vehicles

19. Position the halfshaft through the wheel knuckle and into the wheel bearing and wheel hub.

20. Position the wheel knuckle onto the toe link and lower arm.

21. Loosely install the new toe link outboard bolt and nut.

22. Loosely install the new lower arm outboard bolt and nut.

23. Loosely install the new shock absorber lower bolt and nut.

24. Using the jack, raise the suspension and install the upper arm outboard bolt and nut. Tighten the bolt to 129 ft. lbs. (175 Nm).

25. Tighten the toe link outboard bolt to 129 ft. lbs. (175 Nm).

26. Tighten the lower arm outboard bolt in the following stages.

a. Stage 1: Tighten to 59 ft. lbs. (80 Nm).

b. Stage 2: Tighten an additional 90 degrees.

27. Tighten the shock absorber lower nut to 59 ft. lbs. (80 Nm).

28. Position the stabilizer bar link and install the new upper link nut. Tighten the nut to 30 ft. lbs. (40 Nm).

29. Install the brake hose bracket bolt.

a. Tighten the bolt to 62 inch lbs. (7 Nm).

30. Position the wheel speed sensor and install the bolts.

a. Tighten the bolt to 62 inch lbs. (7 Nm).

b. Clip the 2 wheel speed sensor harness retainers to the upper arm.

FWD vehicles

31. Attach the wheel speed sensor to the wheel bearing and wheel hub and install the bolt.

a. Tighten to 62 inch lbs. (7 Nm).

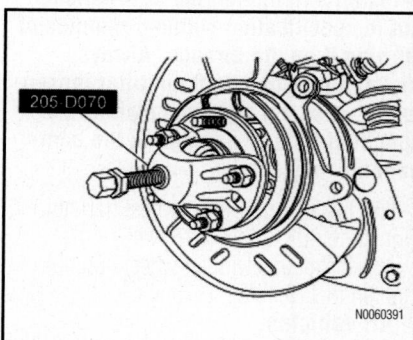

Fig. 233 Separating the halfshaft from the hub and bearing assembly

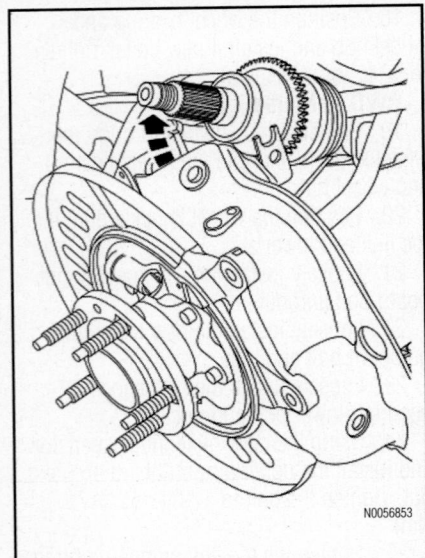

Fig. 234 Positioning the halfshaft through the wheel knuckle opening

All vehicles

32. Install the brake disc.

33. Position the brake caliper and anchor plate assembly and install the 2 bolts.

    a. Tighten to 41 ft. lbs. (55 Nm).

AWD vehicles

➡️**Do not tighten the rear halfshaft nut with the vehicle on the ground. The nut must be tightened to specification before the vehicle is lowered to the ground. Wheel bearing damage will occur if the wheel bearing is loaded with the weight of the vehicle applied.**

➡️**Apply the brake to keep the halfshaft from rotating.**

34. Position the halfshaft in the hub and use the previously removed wheel hub nut to seat the halfshaft.

    a. Tighten to 203 ft. lbs. (275 Nm).

    b. Remove and discard the nut.

➡️**Install and tighten the new halfshaft nut to specification within 5 minutes of starting it on the threads. Always install a new halfshaft nut after loosening or when not tightening within the specified time or damage to the components may occur.**

35. Install a new inner wheel hub nut. Tighten to 203 ft. lbs. (275 Nm).

36. Install a new outer wheel hub nut. Tighten to 129 ft. lbs. (175 Nm).

All vehicles

37. Install the wheel and tire.

2011 Models

See Figure 235.

➡️**Suspension fasteners affect performance of vital components and systems and their failure may result in major service expense. If replacement is necessary install new parts with the same part numbers or equivalent part. Do not use a replacement part of lesser quality or substitute design. Tighten the fasteners to specification during reassembly.**

At the time of publication the manufacturer does not provide a specific Removal and Installation procedure for this component. Refer to the graphic(s) when servicing this component.

➡️**Do not tighten the rear halfshaft with the vehicle on the ground. Tighten the nut to specification before the vehicle is lowered to the ground. Wheel bearing damage occurs if the wheel bearing is loaded with the weight of the vehicle applied.**

➡️**Install and tighten the new halfshaft nut to specification within 5 minutes of starting it on the threads. Always install a new halfshaft nut after loosening, or when not tightening within the specified time, or damage to the components may occur.**

➡️**Before tightening the upper and lower arm bolts, use a jackstand to raise the rear suspension until the distance between the center of the hub and the lip of the fender is equal to the measurement taken in the removal procedure (curb height).**

➡️**Apply the brake to keep the halfshaft from rotating.**

1. Remove the wheel and tire.
2. Remove the brake disc.

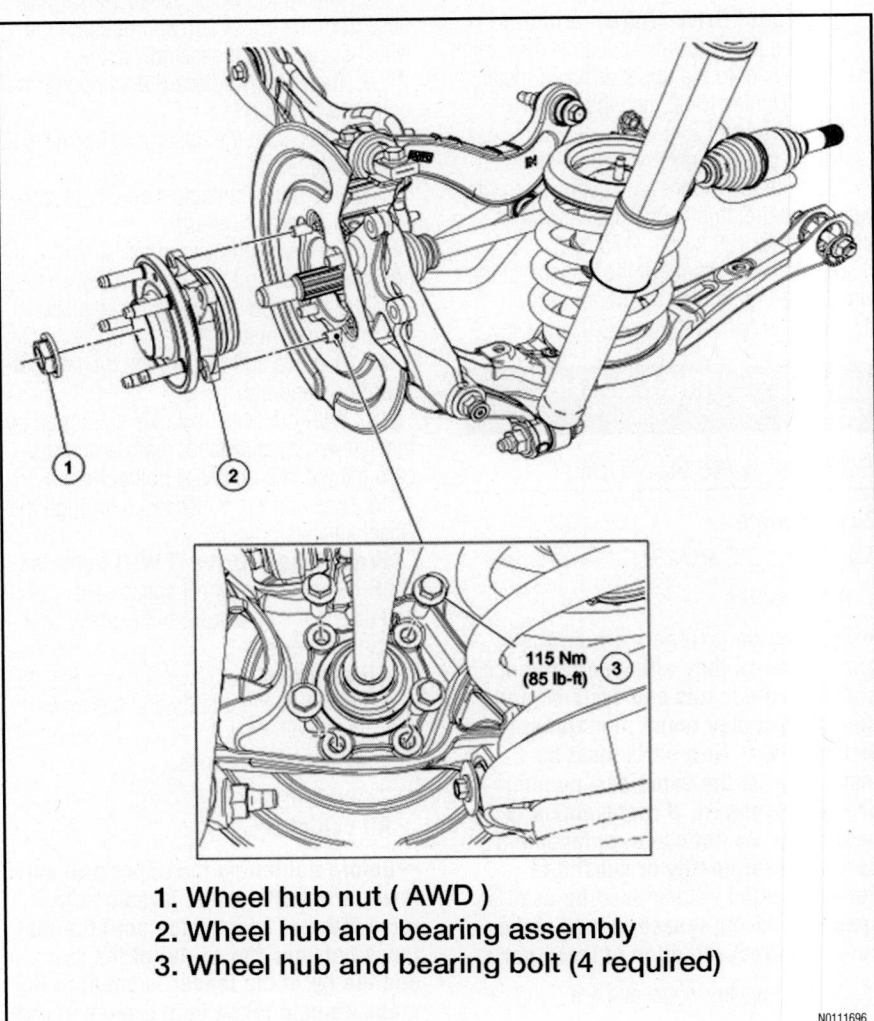

1. **Wheel hub nut (AWD)**
2. **Wheel hub and bearing assembly**
3. **Wheel hub and bearing bolt (4 required)**

Fig. 235 Exploded view of the wheel bearing and hub

FORD

E-Series

3

BRAKES 3-13

**ANTI-LOCK BRAKE SYSTEM
(ABS)** 3-13
General Information..................3-13
Precautions........................3-13
Speed Sensors 3-13
Removal & Installation..........3-13
**BLEEDING THE BRAKE
SYSTEM** 3-15
Bleeding Procedure..................3-15
Bleeding the ABS System 3-16
Fluid Fill Procedure 3-16
FRONT DISC BRAKES 3-17
Brake Caliper..........................3-17
Removal & Installation..........3-17
Disc Brake Pads 3-18
Removal & Installation..........3-18
PARKING BRAKE 3-20
Parking Brake Cables..............3-20
Cable Tension Release..........3-20
Parking Brake Shoes 3-20
Parking Brake Shoe
Adjustment 3-21
Removal & Installation..........3-20
REAR DISC BRAKES 3-18
Brake Caliper..........................3-18
Removal & Installation..........3-18
Disc Brake Pads 3-19
Removal & Installation..........3-19

CHASSIS ELECTRICAL 3-21

**AIR BAG (SUPPLEMENTAL
RESTRAINT SYSTEM)** 3-21
General Information..................3-21
Arming the System 3-22
Clockspring Centering 3-23
Disarming the System...........3-22
Service Precautions 3-21

DRIVE TRAIN 3-24

Automatic Transaxle Fluid 3-24
Drain and Refill 3-24
Filter Replacement 3-25
Rear Axle Housing...................3-26
Removal & Installation..........3-26

Rear Axle Shaft, Bearing & Seal ..3-27
Removal & Installation..........3-27
Rear Driveshaft.......................3-28
Removal & Installation..........3-28
Rear Pinion Seal.....................3-28
Removal & Installation..........3-28

ENGINE COOLING 3-29

Engine Coolant........................3-29
Drain, Bleeding & Refill
Procedure 3-29
Flushing............................3-30
Engine Fan 3-31
Removal & Installation..........3-31
Radiator..................................3-32
Removal & Installation..........3-32
Thermostat.............................3-33
Removal & Installation..........3-33
Water Pump 3-34
Removal & Installation..........3-34

ENGINE ELECTRICAL.........3-36

BATTERY SYSTEM 3-36
Battery...................................3-36
Battery Disconnect &
Reconnect........................3-36
Removal & Installation..........3-36
CHARGING SYSTEM 3-37
Alternator 3-37
Removal & Installation..........3-37
IGNITION SYSTEM 3-40
Firing Order............................3-40
Ignition Coil 3-40
Removal & Installation..........3-40
Ignition Timing........................3-40
Adjustment 3-40
Spark Plugs............................3-40
Removal & Installation..........3-40
STARTING SYSTEM 3-41
Starter 3-41
Removal & Installation..........3-41

ENGINE MECHANICAL 3-43

Accessory Drive Belts 3-43
Accessory Belt Routing........3-43

Adjustment 3-43
Inspection...........................3-43
Removal & Installation..........3-43
Air Cleaner.............................3-44
Filter/element Replacement...3-46
Removal & Installation..........3-44
Camshaft and Valve Lifters........3-46
Inspection...........................3-46
Removal & Installation..........3-48
Roller Followers...................3-47
Catalytic Converter 3-50
Removal & Installation..........3-50
Crankshaft Front Seal..............3-52
Removal & Installation..........3-52
Exhaust Manifold 3-52
Removal & Installation..........3-52
Intake Manifold 3-58
Removal & Installation..........3-58
Oil Pan 3-61
Removal & Installation..........3-61
Oil Pump................................3-63
Inspection...........................3-64
Removal & Installation..........3-63
Rear Main Seal.......................3-64
Removal & Installation..........3-64
Timing Chain & Sprockets........3-66
Removal & Installation..........3-66
Timing Chain Front Cover........3-64
Removal & Installation..........3-64
Valve Covers 3-68
Removal & Installation..........3-68

**ENGINE PERFORMANCE &
EMISSION CONTROLS** 3-74

Camshaft Position (CMP)
Sensor 3-74
Removal & Installation..........3-74
Component Locations 3-74
Crankshaft Position (CKP)
Sensor 3-76
Removal & Installation..........3-76
Electronic Control Module
(ECM) 3-81
Removal & Installation..........3-81
Engine Coolant Temperature
(ECT) Sensor 3-82
Removal & Installation..........3-82

Heated Oxygen (HO2S)
  Sensor 3-82
    Removal & Installation..........3-82
Intake Air Temperature (IAT)
  Sensor 3-82
    Removal & Installation..........3-82
Knock Sensor (KS)....................3-82
    Removal & Installation..........3-82
Manifold Absolute Pressure
  (MAP) Sensor 3-82
    Removal & Installation..........3-82
Mass Air Flow (MAF) Sensor....3-83
    Removal & Installation..........3-83
Throttle Position Sensor
  (TPS) 3-83
    Removal & Installation..........3-83

FUEL............................3-84

**DIESEL FUEL INJECTION
SYSTEM......................3-92**
Fuel Pressure Regulator 3-95
    Removal & Installation..........3-95
Fuel System Service
  Precautions 3-92
Glow Plugs..............................3-96
    Removal & Installation..........3-96
High Pressure Oil Pump
  Drive Gear 3-94
    Removal & Installation..........3-94
Injectors 3-93
    Removal & Installation..........3-93
Relieving Fuel System
  Pressure................................3-92
**GASOLINE FUEL INJECTION
SYSTEM......................3-84**
Fuel Injectors 3-84
    Removal & Installation..........3-84
Fuel Pump...............................3-88
    Removal & Installation..........3-88

Fuel System Service
  Precautions 3-84
Fuel Tank................................3-88
    Draining..............................3-88
    Removal & Installation..........3-89
Relieving Fuel System
  Pressure................................3-84
Throttle Body..........................3-90
    Removal & Installation..........3-90

**HEATING & AIR CONDITIONING
SYSTEM......................3-97**

Blower Motor 3-97
    Removal & Installation..........3-97
Heater Core 3-97
    Removal & Installation..........3-97

PRECAUTIONS 3-13

**SPECIFICATIONS AND
MAINTENANCE CHARTS 3-3**

Brake Specifications....................3-8
Camshaft Specifications..............3-6
Capacities 3-4
Crankshaft and Connecting
  Rod Specifications 3-6
Engine and Vehicle
  Identification 3-3
Engine Tune-Up
  Specifications 3-4
Fluid Specifications....................3-5
General Engine Specifications.....3-3
Piston and Ring
  Specifications 3-6
Scheduled Maintenance
  Intervals 3-9–3-12
Tire, Wheel and Ball Joint
  Specifications 3-8

Torque Specifications..................3-7
Valve Specifications....................3-5
Wheel Alignment........................3-7

STEERING 3-98

Power Steering Gear..................3-98
    Removal & Installation..........3-98
Power Steering Pump................3-99
    Bleeding & Flushing...........3-100
    Fluid Fill Procedure 3-101
    Purging............................3-100
    Removal & Installation..........3-99

SUSPENSION 9-102
FRONT SUSPENSION 9-102
Coil Spring.............................3-102
    Removal & Installation........3-102
Control Links 3-102
    Removal & Installation........3-102
Lower & Upper Ball Joint........3-102
    Removal & Installation........3-102
Radius Arm 3-103
    Removal & Installation........3-103
Shock Absorber......................3-103
    Removal & Installation........3-103
Stabilizer Bar.........................3-104
    Removal & Installation........3-104
Steering Knuckle 3-105
    Removal & Installation........3-105
REAR SUSPENSION 3-106
Leaf Spring............................3-106
    Removal & Installation........3-106
Shock Absorber......................3-107
    Removal & Installation........3-107
Stabilizer Bar.........................3-107
    Removal & Installation........3-107
Wheel Bearings 3-108
    Removal & Installation........3-108

SPECIFICATIONS AND MAINTENANCE CHARTS

ENGINE AND VEHICLE IDENTIFICATION

			Engine					Model Year	
Code ①	Liters (cc)	Cu. In.	Cyl.	Fuel Sys.	Engine Type	Eng. Mfg.		Code ②	Year
W	4.6		8	MFI	SOHC	Ford		A	2010
L	5.4		8	MFI	SOHC	Ford		B	2011
P	6.0		8	DITD	OHC	Ford			
S	6.8		10	MFI	SOHC	Ford			

① 8th position of VIN

② 10th position of VIN

25759_ETRK_C0001

GENERAL ENGINE SPECIFICATIONS

All measurements are given in inches.

Year	Model	Engine Displacement Liters	Engine ID/VIN	Fuel System Type	Net Horsepower @ rpm	Net Torque @ rpm (ft. lbs.)	Bore x Stroke (in.)	Compression Ratio	Oil Pressure @ rpm
2010	E-150	4.6	W	MFI	225@4800	286@3500	3.55x3.54	9.4:1	40-75@2000
		5.4	L	MFI	255@4500	350@2500	3.55x4.17	9.0:1	40-75@2000
	E-250	4.6	W	MFI	225@4800	286@3500	3.55x3.54	9.4:1	40-75@2000
		5.4	L	MFI	255@4500	350@2500	3.55x4.17	9.0:1	40-75@2000
	E-350	5.4	L	MFI	255@4500	350@2500	3.55x4.17	9.0:1	40-75@2000
		6.0	P	DITD	NA	NA	3.74x4.13	18:01	①
		6.8	S	MFI	305@4250	420@3250	3.55x4.16	9.0:1	40-75@2000
	E-450	5.4	L	MFI	255@4500	350@2500	3.55x4.17	9.0:1	40-75@2000
		6.8	S	MFI	305@4250	420@3250	3.55x4.16	9.0:1	40-75@2000
2011	E-150	4.6	W	MFI	225@4800	286@3500	3.55x3.54	9.4:1	40-75@2000
		5.4	L	MFI	255@4500	350@2500	3.55x4.17	9.0:1	40-75@2000
	E-250	4.6	W	MFI	225@4800	286@3500	3.55x3.54	9.4:1	40-75@2000
		5.4	L	MFI	255@4500	350@2500	3.55x4.17	9.0:1	40-75@2000
	E-350	5.4	L	MFI	255@4500	350@2500	3.55x4.17	9.0:1	40-75@2000
		6.8	S	MFI	305@4250	420@3250	3.55x4.16	9.0:1	40-75@2000
	E-450	5.4	L	MFI	255@4500	350@2500	3.55x4.17	9.0:1	40-75@2000
		6.8	S	MFI	305@4250	420@3250	3.55x4.16	9.0:1	40-75@2000

NA: Not available

① 12 psi at 700 rpm, 24 psi at 1,200 rpm and 45 psi at 1,800 rpm

25759_ETRK_C0002

ENGINE TUNE-UP SPECIFICATIONS

Year	Engine Displacement Liters	Engine ID/VIN	Spark Plug Gap (in.)	Ignition Timing (deg.) AT	Fuel Pump (psi)	Idle Speed (rpm) AT	Valve Clearance Intake	Exhaust
2010	4.6	W	0.043-0.047	①	②	2,000	0.0008-0.0027	0.0018-0.0037
	5.4	L	0.050-0.057	①	②	2,000	0.0008-0.0027	0.0018-0.0037
	6.0	P	NA	NA	③	2,000	0.0055 ⑤	NA
	6.8	S	0.052-0.056	①	④	2,000	0.0007-0.0027	0.0017-0.0037
2011	4.6	W	0.043-0.047	①	②	2,000	0.0008-0.0027	0.0018-0.0037
	5.4	L	0.050-0.057	①	②	2,000	0.0008-0.0027	0.0018-0.0037
	6.8	S	0.052-0.056	①	④	2,000	0.0007-0.0027	0.0017-0.0037

NA: Not Available

NE: Not Equipped

① 10 degrees Before Top Dead Center (BTDC) and is not adjustable

② Key ON Engine Running (KOER): 28-45 psi

   Key On Engine OFF (KOEO): 35-45 psi

③ KOER: 38-51 psi

   KOEO: 0-51 psi

④ KOER: 55-65 psi

   KOEO: 40-50 psi

⑤ Diesel

25759_ETRK_C0003

CAPACITIES

Year	Model	Engine Displacement Liters	Engine ID/VIN	Engine Oil with Filter	Transmission (pts.) Auto.	Drive Axle (pts.) Front	Rear	Transfer Case (pts.)	Fuel Tank (gal.)	Cooling System (qts.)
2010	E-150	4.6	W	6.0	27.6	NA	0.375	NA	35	23.8 ①
		5.4	L	6.0	27.6	NA	0.375	NA	35	28.8 ②
	E-250	4.6	W	6.0	27.6	NA	0.375	NA	35	23.8 ①
		5.4	L	6.0	27.6	NA	0.375	NA	35	28.8 ②
	E-350	5.4	L	6.0	27.6	NA	0.375	NA	35	28.8 ②
		6.0	P	15.0	38.0	NA	0.375	NA	35	24.4 ③
		6.8	S	7.0	27.6	NA	0.375	NA	35	30.4 ④
	E-450	5.4	L	6.0	27.6	NA	0.375	NA	35	28.8 ②
		6.8	S	7.0	27.6	NA	0.375	NA	35	30.4 ④
2011	E-150	4.6	W	6.0	27.6	NA	0.375	NA	35	23.8 ①
		5.4	L	6.0	27.6	NA	0.375	NA	35	28.8 ②
	E-250	4.6	W	6.0	27.6	NA	0.375	NA	35	23.8 ①
		5.4	L	6.0	27.6	NA	0.375	NA	35	28.8 ②
	E-350	5.4	L	6.0	27.6	NA	0.375	NA	35	28.8 ②
		6.8	S	7.0	27.6	NA	0.375	NA	35	30.4 ④
	E-450	5.4	L	6.0	27.6	NA	0.375	NA	35	28.8 ②
		6.8	S	7.0	27.6	NA	0.375	NA	35	30.4 ④

NA: Not Available

NE: Not Equipped

NOTE: All capacities are approximate. Add fluid gradually and ensure a proper fluid level is obtained.

① With aux. rear heat: 26 qts

② With aux. rear heat: 30:8 qts

③ With aux. rear heat: 26 qts

④ With aux. rear heat: 32.6 qts

25759_ETRK_C0004

FLUID SPECIFICATIONS

Year	Model	Engine Disp. Liters	Engine Oil	Auto. Trans.	Drive Axle Front	Drive Axle Rear	Power Steering Fluid	Brake Master Cylinder	Cooling System
2010	E-150	4.6	5W-20	XT-10-QLV	NE	①	ATF XT-5-QM	DOT 3	②
		5.4	5W-20	XT-10-QLV	NE	①	ATF XT-5-QM	DOT 3	②
	E-250	4.6	5W-20	XT-10-QLV	NE	①	ATF XT-5-QM	DOT 3	②
		5.4	5W-20	XT-10-QLV	NE	①	ATF XT-5-QM	DOT 3	②
	E-350	5.4	5W-20	XT-10-QLV	NE	①	ATF XT-5-QM	DOT 3	②
		6.0	15W-40	XT-10-QLV	NE	①	ATF XT-5-QM	DOT 3	②
		6.8	5W-20	XT-10-QLV	NE	①	ATF XT-5-QM	DOT 3	②
	E-450	5.4	5W-20	XT-10-QLV	NE	①	ATF XT-5-QM	DOT 3	②
		6.8	5W-20	XT-10-QLV	NE	①	ATF XT-5-QM	DOT 3	②
2011	E-150	4.6	5W-20	XT-10-QLV	NE	①	ATF XT-5-QM	DOT 3	②
		5.4	5W-20	XT-10-QLV	NE	①	ATF XT-5-QM	DOT 3	②
	E-250	4.6	5W-20	XT-10-QLV	NE	①	ATF XT-5-QM	DOT 3	②
		5.4	5W-20	XT-10-QLV	NE	①	ATF XT-5-QM	DOT 3	②
	E-350	5.4	5W-20	XT-10-QLV	NE	①	ATF XT-5-QM	DOT 3	②
		6.8	5W-20	XT-10-QLV	NE	①	ATF XT-5-QM	DOT 3	②
	E-450	5.4	5W-20	XT-10-QLV	NE	①	ATF XT-5-QM	DOT 3	②
		6.8	5W-20	XT-10-QLV	NE	①	ATF XT-5-QM	DOT 3	②

NE: Not Equipped

① Synthetic: 75W-140

Normal: 80W-90

② Motorcraft® Premium Gold Engine Coolant with Bittering Agent

25759_ETRK_C0005

VALVE SPECIFICATIONS

Year	Engine Disp. Liters	Seat Angle (deg.)	Face Angle (deg.)	Spring Test Pressure (lbs. @ in.)	Spring Free-Length (in.)	Spring Installed Height (in.)	Stem-to-Guide Clearance (in.) Intake	Stem-to-Guide Clearance (in.) Exhaust	Stem Diameter (in.) Intake	Stem Diameter (in.) Exhaust
2010	4.6	45.5	45.25-45.75	131.994 lb@1.1032	1.9508	1.5630-1.5866	0.0008-0.0027	0.0018-0.0037	0.2746-0.2754	0.2736-0.2744
	5.4	45.5	45.25-45.75	161.862-179.847@1.1	2.1	1.6654-1.6890	0.0008-0.0028	0.0018-0.0038	0.2746-0.2755	0.2736-0.2745
	6.0	①	①	NA	2.045	NA	②	②	③	③
	6.8	44.50-45.00	45.25-45.75	171@1.13	2.1	NA	0.0007-0.0027	0.0017-0.0037	0.274-0.275	0.273-0.274
2011	4.6	45.5	45.25-45.75	131.994 lb@1.1032	1.9508	1.5630-1.5866	0.0008-0.0027	0.0018-0.0037	0.2746-0.2754	0.2736-0.2744
	5.4	45.5	45.25-45.75	161.862-179.847@1.1	2.1	1.6654-1.6890	0.0008-0.0028	0.0018-0.0038	0.2746-0.2755	0.2736-0.2745
	6.8	44.50-45.00	45.25-45.75	171@1.13	2.1	NA	0.0007-0.0027	0.0017-0.0037	0.274-0.275	0.273-0.274

NA: Not Available

① Intake: 30 degrees

Exhaust: 37.5 degrees

② 0.0055 inches

③ 0.2735-0.272

25759_ETRK_C0006

CAMSHAFT SPECIFICATIONS
All measurements in inches unless noted

Year	Engine Displacement Liters	Engine Code/VIN	Journal Diameter	Brg. Oil Clearance	Shaft End-play	Runout	Journal Bore	Lobe Height Intake	Lobe Height Exhaust
2010	4.6	W	1.0605-1.0615	0.0010-0.0030	0.001-0.007	0.002	1.0625-1.0635	①	①
	5.4	L	1.0605-1.0615	0.0010-0.0030	0.001-0.007	0.0012	1.0625-1.0635	①	①
	6.0	P	2.440-2.441	0.0015-0.0060	0.002-0.008	NA	2.443-2.446	0.2261	0.2296
	6.8	S	1.060-1.062	0.076-0.025	0.001-0.007	0.0035	1.062-1.063	0.279	0.295
2011	4.6	W	1.0605-1.0615	0.0010-0.0030	0.001-0.007	0.002	1.0625-1.0635	①	①
	5.4	L	1.0605-1.0615	0.0010-0.0030	0.001-0.007	0.0012	1.0625-1.0635	①	①
	6.8	S	1.060-1.062	0.076-0.025	0.001-0.007	0.0035	1.062-1.063	0.279	0.295

①: Lobe lift: 0.2560 inches

25759_ETRK_C0007

CRANKSHAFT AND CONNECTING ROD SPECIFICATIONS
All measurements are given in inches.

Year	Engine Displacement Liters	Engine ID/VIN	Crankshaft Main Brg. Journal Dia.	Crankshaft Main Brg. Oil Clearance	Crankshaft Shaft End-play	Crankshaft Thrust on No.	Connecting Rod Journal Diameter	Connecting Rod Oil Clearance	Connecting Rod Side Clearance
2010	4.6	W	2.65	0.0011-0.0026	0.0051-0.012	NA	NA	NA	0.002
	5.4	L	2.65	0.0009-0.0019	0.0030-0.0148	NA	NA	0.0010-0.0025	0.0049-0.0187
	6.0	P	3.188-3.150	0.008-0.0034	0.02	NA	NA	0.0008-0.0033	0.012-0.024
	6.8	S	2.6568-2.6576	0.0009-0.0019	0.0030-0.0148	NA	NA	NA	0.0049-0.0187
2011	4.6	W	2.65	0.0011-0.0026	0.0051-0.012	NA	NA	NA	0.002
	5.4	L	2.65	0.0009-0.0019	0.0030-0.0148	NA	NA	0.0010-0.0025	0.0049-0.0187
	6.8	S	2.6568-2.6576	0.0009-0.0019	0.0030-0.0148	NA	NA	NA	0.0049-0.0187

NA: Not Available

25759_ETRK_C0008

PISTON AND RING SPECIFICATIONS
All measurements are given in inches.

Year	Engine Displacement Liters	Engine ID/VIN	Piston Clearance	Ring Gap Top Compression	Ring Gap Bottom Compression	Ring Gap Oil Control	Ring Side Clearance Top Compression	Ring Side Clearance Bottom Compression	Ring Side Clearance Oil Control
2010	4.6	W	NA	0.010-0.020	0.010-0.020	0.006-0.026	0.002-0.610	0.060-0.0602	0.275-0.2844
	5.4	L	NA	0.0006-0.0012	0.0098-0.0197	0.0059-0.0256	0.0602-0.0610	0.0598-0.0606	0.1193-0.1201
	6.0	P	NA	0.011-0.021	0.055-0.065	0.009-0.019	NA	0.0598-0.0606	NA
	6.8	S	NA	0.0059-0.0118	0.0098-0.0196	0.0059-0.0256	0.0591-0.0592	0.0598-0.0606	0.1193-0.1201
2011	4.6	W	NA	0.010-0.020	0.010-0.020	0.006-0.026	0.002-0.610	0.060-0.0602	0.275-0.2844
	5.4	L	NA	0.0006-0.0012	0.0098-0.0197	0.0059-0.0256	0.0602-0.0610	0.0598-0.0606	0.1193-0.1201
	6.8	S	NA	0.0059-0.0118	0.0098-0.0196	0.0059-0.0256	0.0591-0.0592	0.0598-0.0606	0.1193-0.1201

NA: Not available

25759_ETRK_C0009

TORQUE SPECIFICATIONS
All readings in ft. lbs.

Year	Engine Disp. Liters	Engine ID/VIN	Cylinder Head Bolts	Main Bearing Bolts	Rod Bearing Bolts	Crankshaft Damper Bolts	Flywheel Bolts	Manifold Intake	Manifold Exhaust	Spark Plugs	Oil Pan Drain Plug
2010	4.6	W	30	NA	NA	18	①	7	18	18	17
	5.4	L	②	NA	NA	③	①	④	18	18	17
	6.0	P	⑤	NA	NA	50 ⑥	NA	⑦	28	NA	17
	6.8	S	⑧	⑨	NA	⑩	⑪	⑫	18	18	17
2011	4.6	W	30	NA	NA	18	①	7	18	18	17
	5.4	L	②	NA	NA	③	①	④	18	18	17
	6.0	P	⑤	NA	NA	50 ⑥	NA	⑦	28	NA	17
	6.8	S	⑧	⑨	NA	⑩	⑪	⑫	18	18	17

NA: Not Available

① First pass: 14 ft. lbs. (20 Nm)
Second pass: 59 ft. lbs. (80 Nm)

② First pass: 18 ft. lbs. (25 Nm)
Second pass: 35 ft. lbs. (48 Nm)

③ Stage 1: 66 ft. lbs.
Stage 2: Loosen one full turn
Stage 3: 37 ft. lbs. (50 Nm)
Stage 4: Tighten an additional 90 degrees

④ First pass: 18 inch lbs. (2 Nm)
Second pass: 18 ft. lbs. (25 Nm).

⑤ Stage 1: Tighten bolts 1 through 10 to 65 ft. lbs. (88 Nm)
Stage 2: Tighten bolts 1 through 10 to 85 ft. lbs. (115 Nm)
Stage 3: Tighten bolts 1 through 10 an additional 90 degrees
Stage 4: Tighten bolts 1 through 10, a second time, 90 degrees
Stage 5: Tighten bolts 1 through 10, a third time, 90 degrees
Stage 6: Tighten bolts 11 through 15 to 18 ft. lbs. (24 Nm)
Stage 7: Tighten bolts 11 through 15 to 23 ft. lbs. (31 Nm)
*Refer to appropriate illustration for bolt references

⑥ Tighten an additional 90 degrees

⑦ Stage 1: Loosely install bolts 1-8
Stage 2: Tighten bolts 9-16 to 8 ft. lbs. (11 Nm)
Stage 3: Tighten all bolts to 8 ft. lbs. (11 Nm)
*Refer to appropriate illustration for bolt references

⑧ Stage 1: Tighten to 30 ft. lbs. (40 Nm)
Stage 2: Tighten an additional 90 degrees
Stage 3: Tighten an additional 90 degrees

⑨ Stage 1: Tighten to 30 ft. lbs. (40 Nm)
Stage 2: Tighten an additional 90 degrees
Stage 3: Tighten to 22 ft. lbs. (30 Nm).
Stage 4: Tighten an additional 90 degrees

⑩ Stage 1: Tighten to 66 ft. lbs. (90 Nm)
Stage 2: Loosed nut one full turn
Stage 3: Tighten to 37 ft. lbs. (50 Nm)
Stage 4: Tighten an additional 90 degrees without exceeding 148 ft. lbs. (200 Nm)

⑪ Stage 1: Tighten to 15 ft. lbs. (20 Nm)
Stage 2: Tighten to 59 ft. lbs. (80 Nm)

⑫ Stage 1: Tighten to 18 inch lbs (2 Nm)
Stage 2: Tighten to 18 ft. lbs. (25 Nm)

25759_ETRK_C0010

WHEEL ALIGNMENT

Year	Model		Caster Range (+/-Deg.)	Caster Preferred Setting (Deg.)	Camber Range (+/-Deg.)	Camber Preferred Setting (Deg.)	Toe-in (Deg.)
2010	E-150/250/350 and E-150/350 Wagon	L	-0.4° ± 0.75°	3.5° ± 1.3°	0° ± 0.75°	0.50° ± 0.75°	0.06° ± 0.25°
		R	-0.4° ± 0.75°	3.9° ± 1.3°	0° ± 0.75°	0.50° ± 0.75°	0.06° ± 0.25°
	E-250 Cutaway	L	-0.4° ± 0.75°	4.5° ± 2.4°	0° ± 0.75°	0.50° ± 0.75°	0.06° ± 0.25°
		R	-0.4° ± 0.75°	4.9° ± 2.4°	0° ± 0.75°	0.50° ± 0.75°	0.06° ± 0.25°
	E-350/450 Cutaway and E-350/450 Stripped Chassis	L	-0.4° ± 0.75°	3.9° ± 2.9°	0° ± 0.75°	0.50° ± 0.75°	0.06° ± 0.25°
		R	-0.4° ± 0.75°	4.3° ± 2.9°	0° ± 0.75°	0.50° ± 0.75°	0.06° ± 0.25°
2011	E-150/250/350 and E-150/350 Wagon	L	-0.4° ± 0.75°	3.5° ± 1.3°	0° ± 0.75°	0.50° ± 0.75°	0.06° ± 0.25°
		R	-0.4° ± 0.75°	3.9° ± 1.3°	0° ± 0.75°	0.50° ± 0.75°	0.06° ± 0.25°
	E-250 Cutaway	L	-0.4° ± 0.75°	4.5° ± 2.4°	0° ± 0.75°	0.50° ± 0.75°	0.06° ± 0.25°
		R	-0.4° ± 0.75°	4.9° ± 2.4°	0° ± 0.75°	0.50° ± 0.75°	0.06° ± 0.25°
	E-350/450 Cutaway and E-350/450 Stripped Chassis	L	-0.4° ± 0.75°	3.9° ± 2.9°	0° ± 0.75°	0.50° ± 0.75°	0.06° ± 0.25°
		R	-0.4° ± 0.75°	4.3° ± 2.9°	0° ± 0.75°	0.50° ± 0.75°	0.06° ± 0.25°

25759_ETRK_C0011

TIRE, WHEEL AND BALL JOINT SPECIFICATIONS

Year	Model	OEM Tires		Tire Pressures (psi)		Wheel Size	Ball Joint Inspection	Lug Nut (ft. lbs.)
		Standard	Optional	Front	Rear			
2010	E-Series	①	①	35	35	①	NA	148
		①	①	35	35	①	NA	148
2011	E-Series	①	①	35	35	①	NA	148
		①	①	35	35	①	NA	148

OEM: Original Equipment Manufacturer

PSI: Pounds Per Square Inch

NA: Information not available

①: Refer to the Vehicle Certification (VC) label located on the driver door jamb.

25759_ETRK_C0012

BRAKE SPECIFICATIONS
All measurements in inches unless noted

Year	Model		Brake Disc			Brake Drum Diameter			Minimum Pad/Lining Thickness		Brake Caliper	
			Original Thickness	Minimum Thickness	Max. Runout	Original Inside Diameter	Max. Wear Limit	Maximum Machine Diamter	Front	Rear	Bracket Bolts (ft. lbs.)	Mounting Bolts (ft. lbs.)
2010	E-Series	F	NA	1.511	NA	NA	NA	NA	0.118	0.039	195	27
		R	NA	1.354 ①	NA	NA	NA	NA			129	166
2011	E-Series	F	NA	1.511	NA	NA	NA	NA	0.118	0.039	195	27
		R	NA	1.354 ①	NA	NA	NA	NA			129	166

F: Front

R: Rear

NA: Information not available

① E-450: 1.590 inches

25759_ETRK_C0013

SCHEDULED MAINTENANCE INTERVALS
2010 Ford E-Series, 6.0L Engines - Normal

SERVICE ITEM	TYPE OF SERVICE	VEHICLE MILEAGE INTERVAL (x1000)												
		7.5	15	22.5	30	37.5	45	52.5	60	67.5	75	82.5	90	97.5
Engine oil & filter	Replace	✓	✓	✓	✓	✓	✓	✓	✓	✓	✓	✓	✓	✓
Rotate tires, inspect tread wear, measure tread depth and check pressure	Rotate/ Inspect	✓	✓	✓	✓	✓	✓	✓	✓	✓	✓	✓	✓	✓
Inspect wheels and related components for abnomal noise, wear, looseness or drag	Inspect	✓	✓	✓	✓	✓	✓	✓	✓	✓	✓	✓	✓	✓
Fluid levels (all)	Top off	✓	✓	✓	✓	✓	✓	✓	✓	✓	✓	✓	✓	✓
Brake system	Inspect		✓		✓		✓		✓		✓		✓	
Cooling system, hoses, clamps & coolant strength	Inspect		✓		✓		✓		✓		✓		✓	
Exhaust system (Leaks, damage, loose parts and foreign material)	Inspect	✓	✓	✓	✓	✓	✓	✓	✓	✓	✓	✓	✓	✓
Steering linkage, ball joints, suspension, tie-rod ends, driveshaft and u-joints: lubricate if equipped with grease fittings	Inspect/ Lubricate	✓	✓	✓	✓	✓	✓	✓	✓	✓	✓	✓	✓	✓
Drive belt(s)	Inspect	✓	✓	✓	✓	✓	✓	✓	✓	✓	✓	✓	✓	✓
Battery performance	Inspect	✓	✓	✓	✓	✓	✓	✓	✓	✓	✓	✓	✓	✓
Horn, exterior lamps, turn signals and hazard warning light operation	Inspect	✓	✓	✓	✓	✓	✓	✓	✓	✓	✓	✓	✓	✓
Engine air filter	Inspect	✓	✓	✓	✓	✓	✓	✓	✓	✓	✓	✓	✓	✓
Windshield for cracks, chips and pitting	Inspect	✓	✓	✓	✓	✓	✓	✓	✓	✓	✓	✓	✓	✓
Engine air filter	Replace				✓				✓				✓	
Automatic transmission fluid, for vehicles equipped with TorqShift transmissions	Replace								✓					
Oil and fluid leaks	Inspect	✓	✓	✓	✓	✓	✓	✓	✓	✓	✓	✓	✓	✓
Rear differential fluid	Replace	Every 150,000 miles												
Transmission fluid and filter (All except 5-speed TorqShift)	Replace	Every 150,000 miles												
Drive belt(s)	Replace	Every 150,000 miles												
Engine coolant	Replace	At 6 years or 105,000 miles; then every 3 years or 45,000 miles												
Shocks struts and other suspension components for	Inspect	✓	✓	✓	✓	✓	✓	✓	✓	✓	✓	✓	✓	✓
Windshield wiper spray and wiper operation	Inspect	✓	✓	✓	✓	✓	✓	✓	✓	✓	✓	✓	✓	✓
Repack front wheel bearings and replace seals	Inspect/ Repack								✓					
Fuel filters (Frame and engine mounted)	Replace				✓				✓				✓	

Oil change service intervals should be completed as indicated by the message center (Can be up to 1 year or 10,000 miles) If the message center is prematurely reset or is inoperative, perform the oil change interval at 6 months or 5,000 miles from your last oil change.

25759_ETRK_C0014

SCHEDULED MAINTENANCE INTERVALS
2010 Ford E-Series, 6.0L Engines - Severe

SERVICE ITEM	TYPE OF SERVICE	VEHICLE MILEAGE INTERVAL (x1000)												
		5	10	15	20	25	30	35	40	45	50	55	60	65
Air filter restriction gauge, replace filter as required	Inspect/ Service	✓	✓	✓	✓	✓	✓	✓	✓	✓	✓	✓	✓	✓
Automatic transmission fluid, for vehicles equipped with TorqShift transmissions	Replace												✓	
Battery performance	Inspect	✓	✓	✓	✓	✓	✓	✓	✓	✓	✓	✓	✓	✓
Brake system	Inspect	✓	✓	✓	✓	✓	✓	✓	✓	✓	✓	✓	✓	
Drive belt	Inspect	✓	✓	✓	✓	✓	✓	✓	✓	✓	✓	✓	✓	✓
Drive belt	Replace	Every 150,000 miles												
Drive belt (if equipped with dual alternators)	Replace												✓	
Engine coolant and fuel coolant	Replace												✓	
Engine coolant nitrite level strength, install additive if	Inspect and				✓				✓				✓	
Engine oil & filter	Replace	✓	✓	✓	✓	✓	✓	✓	✓	✓	✓	✓	✓	✓
Exhaust system (Leaks, damage, loose parts and foreign material)	Inspect	✓	✓	✓	✓	✓	✓	✓	✓	✓	✓	✓	✓	✓
Fluid levels (all)	Inspect	✓	✓	✓	✓	✓	✓	✓	✓	✓	✓	✓	✓	
Fuel filter/water separator	Check and Drain	✓	✓	✓	✓	✓	✓	✓	✓	✓	✓	✓	✓	✓
Fuel filters (frame & engine mounted)	Replace		✓		✓		✓		✓		✓		✓	
Horn, exterior lamps, turn signals and hazard warning light operation	Inspect	✓	✓	✓	✓	✓	✓	✓	✓	✓	✓	✓	✓	✓
Inspect wheels and related components for abnomal noise, wear, looseness or drag	Inspect	✓	✓	✓	✓	✓	✓	✓	✓	✓	✓	✓	✓	✓
Oil and fluid leaks	Inspect	✓	✓	✓	✓	✓	✓	✓	✓	✓	✓	✓	✓	✓
Radiator, coolers, heater and air conditioning hoses	Inspect	✓	✓	✓	✓	✓	✓	✓	✓	✓	✓	✓	✓	✓
Rear differential fluid	Replace										✓			
Repack front wheel bearings, install new seals, 4x2 (if non-sealed bearings)	Service/ Inspect/ Lubricate						✓				✓		✓	
Rotate tires, inspect tread wear, measure tread depth and check pressure	Rotate/ Inspect	✓	✓	✓	✓	✓	✓	✓	✓	✓	✓	✓	✓	✓
Shocks struts and other suspension components for leaks and damage	Inspect	✓	✓	✓	✓	✓	✓	✓	✓	✓	✓	✓	✓	✓
Steering linkage, ball joints, suspension, tie-rod ends, driveshaft and u-joints: lubricate if equipped with grease fittings	Inspect/ Lubricate	✓	✓	✓	✓	✓	✓	✓	✓	✓	✓	✓	✓	✓
Windshield for cracks, chips and pitting	Inspect	✓	✓	✓	✓	✓	✓	✓	✓	✓	✓	✓	✓	✓
Windshield wiper spray and wiper operation	Inspect	✓	✓	✓	✓	✓	✓	✓	✓	✓	✓	✓	✓	✓

Oil change service intervals should be completed as indicated by the message center (Can be up to 1 year or 10,000 miles) If the message center is prematurely reset or is inoperative, perform the oil change interval at 6 months or 5,000 miles from your last oil change.

For extensive idling and or low speed driving, change engine oil and filter every 5,000 miles, 6 months or 200 hours of engine operation.

25759_ETRK_C0015

SCHEDULED MAINTENANCE INTERVALS
2010-2011 Ford E-Series, 4.6L, 5.4L, 6.8L Engiens - Normal

SERVICE ITEM	TYPE OF SERVICE	VEHICLE MILEAGE INTERVAL (x1000)												
		7.5	15	22.5	30	37.5	45	52.5	60	67.5	75	82.5	90	97.5
Engine oil & filter	Replace	✓	✓	✓	✓	✓	✓	✓	✓	✓	✓	✓	✓	✓
Rotate tires, inspect tread wear, measure tread depth and check pressure	Rotate/ Inspect	✓	✓	✓	✓	✓	✓	✓	✓	✓	✓	✓	✓	✓
Inspect wheels and related components for abnomal noise, wear, looseness or drag	Inspect	✓	✓	✓	✓	✓	✓	✓	✓	✓	✓	✓	✓	✓
Fluid levels (all)	Top off	✓	✓	✓	✓	✓	✓	✓	✓	✓	✓	✓	✓	✓
Brake system	Inspect	✓	✓	✓	✓	✓	✓	✓	✓	✓	✓	✓	✓	✓
Cooling system, hoses, clamps & coolant strength	Inspect		✓		✓		✓		✓		✓		✓	
Exhaust system (Leaks, damage, loose parts and foreign material)	Inspect	✓	✓	✓	✓	✓	✓	✓	✓	✓	✓	✓	✓	✓
Steering linkage, ball joints, suspension, tie-rod ends, driveshaft and u-joints: lubricate if equipped with grease fittings	Inspect/L ubricate	✓	✓	✓	✓	✓	✓	✓	✓	✓	✓	✓	✓	✓
Drive belt	Inspect	✓	✓	✓	✓	✓	✓	✓	✓	✓	✓	✓	✓	✓
Battery performance	Inspect	✓	✓	✓	✓	✓	✓	✓	✓	✓	✓	✓	✓	✓
Horn, exterior lamps, turn signals and hazard warning light operation	Inspect	✓	✓	✓	✓	✓	✓	✓	✓	✓	✓	✓	✓	✓
Engine air filter	Inspect	✓	✓	✓	✓	✓	✓	✓	✓	✓	✓	✓	✓	✓
Windshield for cracks, chips and pitting	Inspect	✓	✓	✓	✓	✓	✓	✓	✓	✓	✓	✓	✓	✓
Engine air filter	Replace					✓			✓				✓	
Automatic transmission fluid, for vehicles equipped with TorqShift transmissions	Replace								✓					
Repack front wheel bearings and replace seals	Inspect/ Repack								✓					
Oil and fluid leaks	Inspect	✓	✓	✓	✓	✓	✓	✓	✓	✓	✓	✓	✓	✓
Rear differential fluid	Replace													
Spark plugs	Replace												✓	
Drive belt	Replace	Every 150,000 miles												
Engine coolant	Replace	At 6 years or 105,000 miles; then every 3 years or 45,000 miles												
Shocks struts and other suspension components for leaks and damage	Inspect	✓	✓	✓	✓	✓	✓	✓	✓	✓	✓	✓	✓	✓
Windshield wiper spray and wiper operation	Inspect	✓	✓	✓	✓	✓	✓	✓	✓	✓	✓	✓	✓	✓

Oil change service intervals should be completed as indicated by the message center (Can be up to 1 year or 10,000 miles) If the message center is prematurely reset or is inoperative, perform the oil change interval at 6 months or 5,000 miles from your last oil change.

25759_ETRK_C0016

SCHEDULED MAINTENANCE INTERVALS
2010-2011 Ford E-Series, 4.6L, 5.4L, 6.8L Engines - Severe

SERVICE ITEM	TYPE OF SERVICE	VEHICLE MILEAGE INTERVAL (x1000)												
		5	10	15	20	25	30	35	40	45	50	55	60	65
Automatic transmission fluid, for vehicles equipped with TorqShift transmissions	Replace												✓	
Battery performance	Inspect	✓	✓	✓	✓	✓	✓	✓	✓	✓	✓	✓	✓	✓
Brake system	Inspect	✓	✓	✓	✓	✓	✓	✓	✓	✓	✓	✓	✓	✓
Cooling system, hoses, clamps & coolant strength	Inspect	✓	✓	✓	✓	✓	✓	✓	✓	✓	✓	✓	✓	✓
Drive belt	Inspect	✓	✓	✓	✓	✓	✓	✓	✓	✓	✓	✓	✓	✓
Drive belt	Replace	Every 150,000 miles												
Engine coolant	Replace	At 6 years or 105,000 miles; then every 3 years or 45,000 miles												
Engine oil & filter	Replace	✓	✓	✓	✓	✓	✓	✓	✓	✓				
Exhaust system (Leaks, damage, loose parts and foreign material)	Inspect	✓	✓	✓	✓	✓	✓	✓	✓	✓	✓	✓	✓	✓
Oil and fluid leaks	Inspect	✓	✓	✓	✓	✓	✓	✓	✓	✓	✓	✓	✓	✓
Fluid levels (all)	Top off	✓	✓	✓	✓	✓	✓	✓	✓	✓	✓	✓	✓	✓
Horn, exterior lamps, turn signals and hazard warning light operation	Inspect	✓	✓	✓	✓	✓	✓	✓	✓	✓	✓	✓	✓	✓
Inspect wheels and related components for abnomal noise, wear, looseness or drag	Inspect	✓	✓	✓	✓	✓	✓	✓	✓	✓	✓	✓	✓	✓
Rear differential fluid	Replace	Every 150,000 miles												
Repack front wheel bearings and replace seals	Inspect/ Repack						✓						✓	
Rotate tires, inspect tread wear, measure tread depth and check pressure	Rotate/ Inspect	✓	✓	✓		✓	✓	✓	✓	✓	✓	✓	✓	✓
Shocks struts and other suspension components for leaks and damage	Inspect	✓	✓	✓		✓	✓	✓	✓	✓	✓	✓	✓	✓
Spark plugs	Replace												✓	
Steering linkage, ball joints, suspension and tie-rod ends, lubricate if equipped with greases fittings	Inspect	✓	✓	✓	✓	✓	✓	✓	✓	✓	✓	✓	✓	✓
Transmission fluid and filter (All except 5-speed TorqShift)	Replace						✓						✓	
Windshield wiper spray and wiper operation	Inspect	✓	✓	✓	✓	✓	✓	✓	✓	✓	✓	✓	✓	✓
Windshield for cracks, chips and pitting	Inspect	✓	✓	✓	✓	✓	✓	✓	✓	✓	✓	✓	✓	✓

Oil change service intervals should be completed as indicated by the message center (Can be up to 1 year or 10,000 miles) If the message center is prematurely reset or is inoperative, perform the oil change interval at 6 months or 5,000 miles from your last oil change.

For extensive idling and or low speed driving, change engine oil and filter every 5,000 miles, 6 months or 200 hours of engine operation.

25759_ETRK_C0017

PRECAUTIONS

Before servicing any vehicle, please be sure to read all of the following precautions, which deal with personal safety, prevention of component damage, and important points to take into consideration when servicing a motor vehicle:

• Never open, service or drain the radiator or cooling system when the engine is hot; serious burns can occur from the steam and hot coolant.

• Observe all applicable safety precautions when working around fuel. Whenever servicing the fuel system, always work in a well-ventilated area. Do not allow fuel spray or vapors to come in contact with a spark, open flame, or excessive heat (a hot drop light, for example). Keep a dry chemical fire extinguisher near the work area. Always keep fuel in a container specifically designed for fuel storage; also, always properly seal fuel containers to avoid the possibility of fire or explosion. Refer to the additional fuel system precautions later in this section.

• Fuel injection systems often remain pressurized, even after the engine has been turned **OFF**. The fuel system pressure must be relieved before disconnecting any fuel lines. Failure to do so may result in fire and/or personal injury.

• Brake fluid often contains polyglycol ethers and polyglycols. Avoid contact with the eyes and wash your hands thoroughly after handling brake fluid. If you do get brake fluid in your eyes, flush your eyes with clean, running water for 15 minutes. If eye irritation persists, or if you have taken brake fluid internally, IMMEDIATELY seek medical assistance.

• The EPA warns that prolonged contact with used engine oil may cause a number of skin disorders, including cancer. You should make every effort to minimize your exposure to used engine oil. Protective gloves should be worn when changing oil. Wash your hands and any other exposed skin areas as soon as possible after exposure to used engine oil. Soap and water, or waterless hand cleaner should be used.

• All new vehicles are now equipped with an air bag system, often referred to as a Supplemental Restraint System (SRS) or Supplemental Inflatable Restraint (SIR) system. The system must be disabled before performing service on or around system components, steering column, instrument panel components, wiring and sensors. Failure to follow safety and disabling procedures could result in accidental air bag deployment, possible personal injury and unnecessary system repairs.

• Always wear safety goggles when working with, or around, the air bag system. When carrying a non-deployed air bag, be sure the bag and trim cover are pointed away from your body. When placing a non-deployed air bag on a work surface, always face the bag and trim cover upward, away from the surface. This will reduce the motion of the module if it is accidentally deployed. Refer to the additional air bag system precautions later in this section.

• Clean, high quality brake fluid from a sealed container is essential to the safe and proper operation of the brake system. You should always buy the correct type of brake fluid for your vehicle. If the brake fluid becomes contaminated, completely flush the system with new fluid. Never reuse any brake fluid. Any brake fluid that is removed from the system should be discarded. Also, do not allow any brake fluid to come in contact with a painted surface; it will damage the paint.

• Never operate the engine without the proper amount and type of engine oil; doing so WILL result in severe engine damage.

• Timing belt maintenance is extremely important. Many models utilize an interference-type, non-freewheeling engine. If the timing belt breaks, the valves in the cylinder head may strike the pistons, causing potentially serious (also time-consuming and expensive) engine damage. Refer to the maintenance interval charts for the recommended replacement interval for the timing belt, and to the timing belt section for belt replacement and inspection.

• Disconnecting the negative battery cable on some vehicles may interfere with the functions of the on-board computer system(s) and may require the computer to undergo a relearning process once the negative battery cable is reconnected.

• When servicing drum brakes, only disassemble and assemble one side at a time, leaving the remaining side intact for reference.

• Only an MVAC-trained, EPA-certified automotive technician should service the air conditioning system or its components.

BRAKES

GENERAL INFORMATION

PRECAUTIONS

• Certain components within the ABS system are not intended to be serviced or repaired individually.

• Do not use rubber hoses or other parts not specifically specified for and ABS system. When using repair kits, replace all parts included in the kit. Partial or incorrect repair may lead to functional problems and require the replacement of components.

• Lubricate rubber parts with clean, fresh brake fluid to ease assembly. Do not use shop air to clean parts; damage to rubber components may result.

• Use only DOT 3 brake fluid from an unopened container.

• If any hydraulic component or line is removed or replaced, it may be necessary to bleed the entire system.

• A clean repair area is essential. Always clean the reservoir and cap thoroughly before removing the cap. The slightest amount of dirt in the fluid may plug an orifice and impair the system function. Perform repairs after components have been thoroughly cleaned; use only denatured alcohol to clean components. Do not allow ABS components to come into contact with any substance containing mineral oil; this includes used shop rags.

ANTI-LOCK BRAKE SYSTEM (ABS)

• The Anti-Lock control unit is a microprocessor similar to other computer units in the vehicle. Ensure that the ignition switch is **OFF** before removing or installing controller harnesses. Avoid static electricity discharge at or near the controller.

• If any arc welding is to be done on the vehicle, the control unit should be unplugged before welding operations begin.

SPEED SENSORS

REMOVAL & INSTALLATION

Front

See Figure 1.

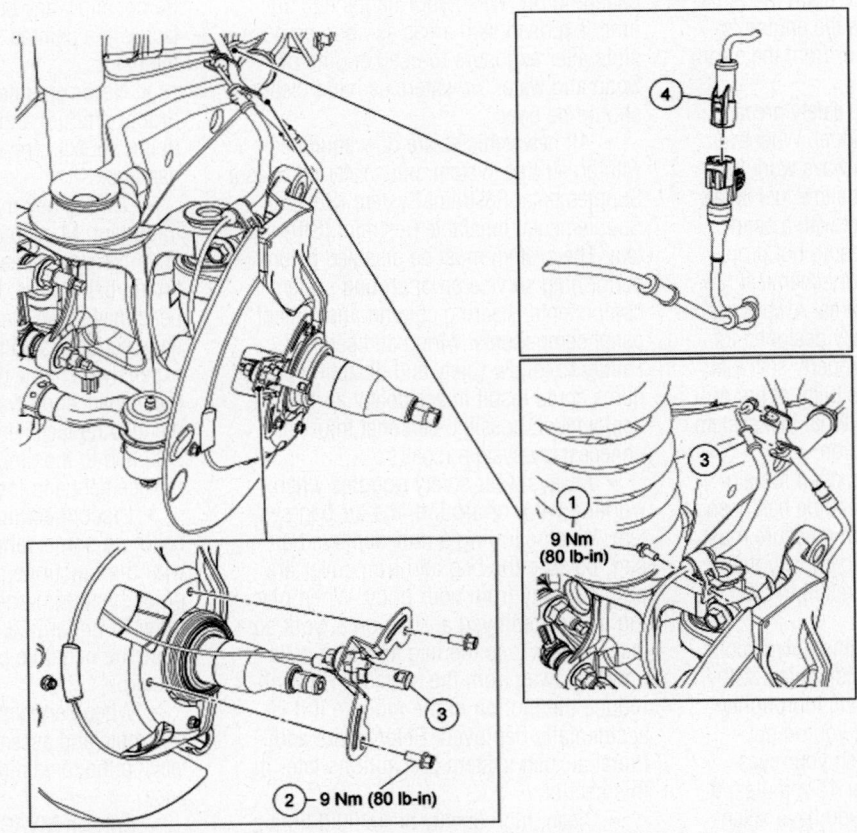

1. Front wheel speed sensor
   harness retainer bolt
2. Front wheel speed sensor bolt
3. Front wheel speed sensor
4. Front wheel speed sensor harness connector

N0076979

Fig. 1 Exploded view of the front speed sensor

1. Disconnect the negative battery cable.
2. Remove the brake disc.
3. Disconnect the front wheel speed sensor harness connector.
4. Disconnect the front wheel speed sensor wire from the front brake hose.
5. Remove the wheel speed sensor harness bolt.

6. Remove the 2 bolts and the front wheel speed sensor assembly.
7. To install, reverse the removal procedure.

Rear

See Figure 2.

1. With the vehicle in NEUTRAL, position it on a hoist.

2. Disconnect the negative battery cable.
3. Disconnect the wheel speed sensor electrical connector.
4. Disconnect the wheel speed sensor harness clips.
5. Remove the rear wheel speed sensor bolt, spacer and the sensor.
6. To install, reverse the removal procedure.

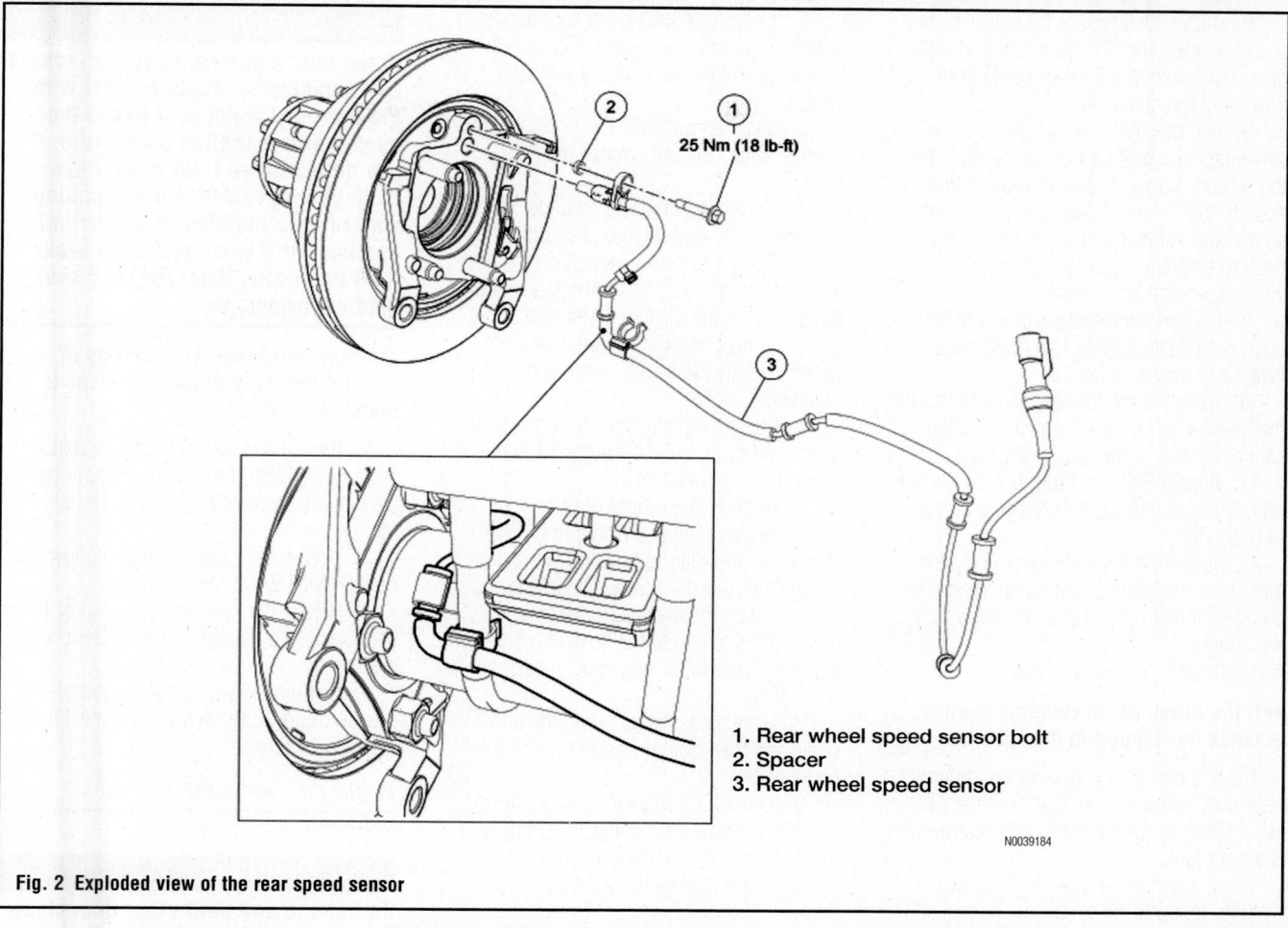

1. Rear wheel speed sensor bolt
2. Spacer
3. Rear wheel speed sensor

N0039184

Fig. 2 Exploded view of the rear speed sensor

BRAKES **BLEEDING THE BRAKE SYSTEM**

BLEEDING PROCEDURE

Pressure Bleeding

✻✻ WARNING

Do not use any fluid other than clean brake fluid meeting manufacturer's specification. Additionally, do not use brake fluid that has been previously drained. Following these instructions will help prevent system contamination, brake component damage and the risk of serious personal injury.

✻✻ CAUTION

Brake fluid contains polyglycol ethers and polyglycols. Avoid contact with the eyes and wash your hands thoroughly after handling brake fluid. If you do get brake fluid in your eyes, flush your eyes with clean, running water for 15 minutes. If eye irritation

persists, or if you have taken brake fluid internally, IMMEDIATELY seek medical assistance.

➡When any part of the hydraulic system has been disconnected for repair or installation of new components, air can get into the system and cause spongy brake pedal action. This requires bleeding of the hydraulic system after it has been correctly connected.

➡The Hydraulic Control Unit (HCU) bleeding procedure must be carried out if the HCU or any components upstream of the HCU are installed new.

➡Pressure bleed the brake system at 30-50 psi.

1. If equipped with a fire suppression system, depower the system, disconnect the negative battery cable and wait one minute.
2. Clean all dirt from and remove the brake master cylinder filler cap. Fill the

brake master cylinder reservoir with clean, specified brake fluid.

➡Master cylinder pressure bleeder adapter tools are available from various manufacturers of pressure bleeding equipment. Follow the instructions of the manufacturer when installing the adapter.

3. Install the bleeder adapter to the brake master cylinder reservoir and attach the bleeder tank hose to the fitting on the adapter.
4. Place a box-end wrench on the master cylinder bleeder screw. Attach a rubber drain hose to the bleeder screw and submerge the free end of the hose in a container partially filled with clean, specified brake fluid.

➡Make sure the bleeder tank contains enough clean, specified brake fluid to complete the bleeding operation.

5. Open the valve on the bleeder tank.

6. Apply 30-50 psi to the brake system.

7. Loosen the bleeder screw and leave open until clear, bubble-free brake fluid flows into the container.

8. Remove the brake caliper bleeder screw cap and place a box-end wrench on the bleeder screw. Attach a rubber drain hose to the RH rear brake caliper bleeder screw, and submerge the free end of the hose in a container partially filled with clean, specified brake fluid.

9. Loosen the bleeder screw and leave open until clear, bubble-free brake fluid flows into the container.

10. Remove the rubber hose and install the bleeder screw cap. Tighten the brake caliper bleeder screw to specification.

11. Repeat Steps 5 through 7 for the LH rear, RH front and LH front bleeder screws in this order.

12. Release the bleeder tank pressure and close the bleeder tank valve. Remove the tank hose from the adapter and remove the adapter.

13. Install the reservoir cap.

➡ **If the brake pedal remains spongy, air may be trapped in the HCU .**

14. If the brake pedal remains spongy after pressure bleeding, carry out the ABS HCU bleeding procedure in this section with the scan tool.

15. If equipped with a fire suppression system, repower the system by connecting the negative battery calbe.

Manual Bleeding

⁂ **WARNING**

Do not use any fluid other than clean brake fluid meeting manufacturer's specification. Additionally, do not use brake fluid that has been previously drained. Following these instructions will help prevent system contamination, brake component damage and the risk of serious personal injury.

⁂ **CAUTION**

Brake fluid contains polyglycol ethers and polyglycols. Avoid contact with the eyes and wash your hands thoroughly after handling brake fluid. If you do get brake fluid in your eyes, flush your eyes with clean, running water for 15 minutes. If eye irritation persists, or if you have taken brake fluid internally, IMMEDIATELY seek medical assistance.

1. If equipped with a fire suppression system, depower the system, disconnect the negative battery cable and wait one minute.

2. Clean all dirt from the brake master cylinder filler cap and remove the filler cap.

3. Fill the brake master cylinder reservoir with clean, specified brake fluid.

4. Place a box-end wrench on the master cylinder bleeder screw. Attach a rubber drain hose to the bleeder screw and submerge the free end of the hose in a container partially filled with clean, specified brake fluid.

5. Loosen the bleeder screw and leave open until clear, bubble-free brake fluid flows into the container.

6. Remove the rubber hose.

7. Remove the brake caliper bleeder screw cap and place a box end wrench on the RH rear bleeder screw. Attach a rubber drain hose to the bleeder screw and submerge the free end of the hose in a container partially filled with clean, specified brake fluid.

8. Have an assistant pump the brake pedal and then hold firm pressure on the brake pedal.

9. Loosen the bleeder screw until a stream of brake fluid comes out. While the assistant maintains pressure on the brake pedal, tighten the bleeder screw.

10. Repeat until clear, bubble-free fluid comes out.

11. Refill the brake master cylinder reservoir as necessary.

12. Tighten the brake caliper bleeder screw to specification.

13. Remove the rubber hose and install the bleeder screw cap.

14. Repeat Steps 7 through 13 for the LH rear, RH front and LH front bleeder screws in this order.

15. If equipped with a fire suppression system, repower the system. Connect the negative battery cable.

BLEEDING THE ABS SYSTEM

⁂ **WARNING**

Do not use any fluid other than clean brake fluid meeting manufacturer's specification. Additionally, do not use brake fluid that has been previously drained. Following these instructions will help prevent system contamination, brake component damage and the risk of serious personal injury.

⁂ **CAUTION**

Brake fluid contains polyglycol ethers and polyglycols. Avoid contact with the eyes and wash your hands thoroughly after handling brake fluid. If you do get brake fluid in your eyes, flush your eyes with clean, running water for 15 minutes. If eye irritation persists, or if you have taken brake fluid internally, IMMEDIATELY seek medical assistance.

➡**Follow the Pressure Bleeding or Manual Bleeding procedure steps to bleed the system.**

1. If equipped with a fire suppression system, depower the system, disconnect the negative battery cable and wait one minute.

2. Connect the scan tool and follow the ABS Service Bleed instructions.

3. Repeat the Pressure Bleeding or Manual Bleeding procedure steps to bleed the system.

4. If equipped with a fire suppression system, repower the system. Connect the negative battery cable.

FLUID FILL PROCEDURE

See Figure 3.

⁂ **WARNING**

Do not use any fluid other than clean brake fluid meeting manufacturer's specification. Additionally, do not use brake fluid that has been previously drained. Following these instructions will help prevent system contamination, brake component damage and the risk of serious personal injury.

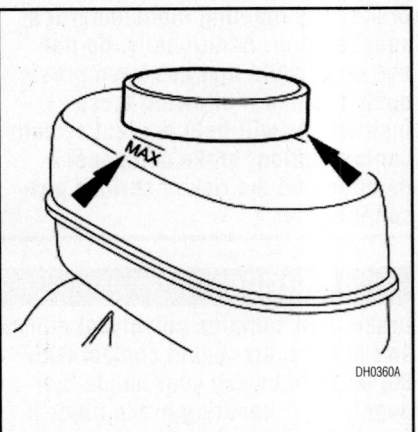

Fig. 3 Filling the brake master cylinder reservoir

❊❊ **CAUTION**

Brake fluid contains polyglycol ethers and polyglycols. Avoid contact with the eyes and wash your hands thoroughly after handling brake fluid. If you do get brake fluid in your eyes, flush your eyes with clean, running water for 15 minutes. If eye irritation persists, or if you have taken brake fluid internally, IMMEDIATELY seek medical assistance.

1. Clean all dirt from the brake master cylinder filler cap and remove the filler cap.
2. Fill the brake master cylinder reservoir with clean, specified brake fluid.

BRAKES

FRONT DISC BRAKES

❊❊ **CAUTION**

Dust and dirt accumulating on brake parts during normal use may contain asbestos fibers from production or aftermarket brake linings. Breathing excessive concentrations of asbestos fibers can cause serious bodily harm. Exercise care when servicing brake parts. Do not sand or grind brake lining unless equipment used is designed to contain the dust residue. Do not clean brake parts with compressed air or by dry brushing. Cleaning should be done by dampening the brake components with a fine mist of water, then wiping the brake components clean with a dampened cloth. Dispose of cloth and all residue containing asbestos fibers in an impermeable container with the appropriate label. Follow practices prescribed by the Occupational Safety and Health Administration (OSHA) and the Environmental Protection Agency (EPA) for the handling, processing, and disposing of dust or debris that may contain asbestos fibers.

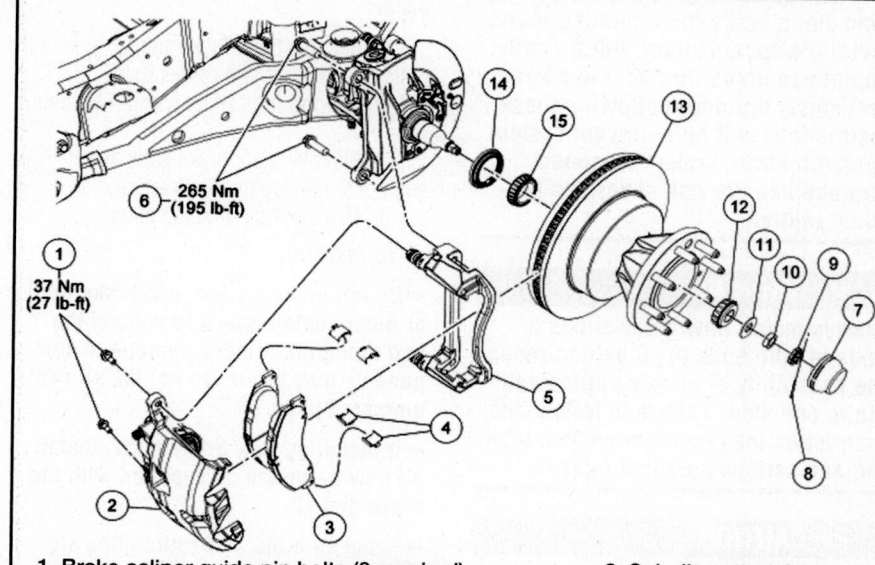

1. Brake caliper guide pin bolts (2 required)
2. Brake caliper
3. Brake pads
4. Brake pad anti-rattle clips (4 required)
5. Brake caliper anchor plate
6. Brake caliper anchor plate bolts (2 required)
7. Hub grease cap
8. Cotter pin
9. Spindle nut retainer
10. Spindle nut
11. Outer wheel bearing retainer washer
12. Outer wheel bearing
13. Brake disc and hub
14. Inner wheel bearing
15. Grease seal

N0074835

Fig. 4 Exploded view of the front brake assembly—dual rear wheel model, single rear wheel model similar

BRAKE CALIPER

REMOVAL & INSTALLATION
See Figure 4.

❊❊ **WARNING**

Do not use any fluid other than clean brake fluid meeting manufacturer's specification. Additionally, do not use brake fluid that has been previously drained. Following these instructions will help prevent system contamination, brake component damage and the risk of serious personal injury.

❊❊ **CAUTION**

Brake fluid contains polyglycol ethers and polyglycols. Avoid contact with the eyes and wash your hands thoroughly after handling brake fluid. If you do get brake fluid in your eyes, flush your eyes with clean, running water for 15 minutes. If eye irritation persists, or if you have taken brake fluid internally, IMMEDIATELY seek medical assistance.

1. Disconnect the negative battery cable.
2. Remove the wheel and tire.
3. Release the wheel speed sensor wiring harness from the brake flexible hose.
4. Remove the brake caliper flow bolt and position the brake flexible hose aside.
5. Discard the 2 copper washers.

➡Do not pry in the caliper sight hole to retract the pistons as this can damage the pistons and boots.

6. Remove the 2 brake caliper guide pin bolts and the brake caliper.

7. If leaks or damaged boots are found, install a new disc brake caliper.

To install:

➡Tighten the bottom caliper bolt before tightening the top caliper bolt or damage to guide pins may occur.

➡Make sure the caliper pin boots are correctly seated to prevent damage to the guide pins.

8. Position the brake caliper and install the 2 brake caliper guide pin bolts.
9. Using 2 new copper washers, position the brake flexible hose and install the brake caliper flow bolt.
10. Attach the wheel speed sensor wiring harness to the brake flexible hose.
11. Bleed the brake caliper.
12. Install the wheel and tire.

13. Apply brakes several times to verify correct brake operation.

DISC BRAKE PADS

REMOVAL & INSTALLATION

See Figure 5.

❊❊ WARNING

WARNING: Do not use any fluid other than clean brake fluid meeting manufacturer's specification. Additionally, do not use brake fluid that has been previously drained. Following these instructions will help prevent system contamination, brake component damage and the risk of serious personal injury.

❊❊ WARNING

Always install new brake shoes or pads at both ends of an axle to reduce the possibility of brakes pulling vehicle to one side. Failure to follow this instruction may result in uneven braking and serious personal injury.

❊❊ CAUTION

Do not spill brake fluid on painted or plastic surfaces or damage to the surface may occur. If brake fluid is spilled onto a painted or plastic surface, immediately wash the surface with water.

1. Check the brake fluid level in the brake master cylinder reservoir.
2. If required, remove the fluid until the brake master cylinder reservoir is half full.

3. Remove the wheel and tire.
4. Release the wheel speed sensor wiring harness from the brake flexible hose.

➡**Do not pry in the caliper sight hole to retract the pistons, as this can damage the pistons and boots.**

➡**Do not allow the brake caliper to hang from the brake caliper flexible hose or damage to the hose can occur.**

5. Remove the 2 brake caliper guide pin bolts and position the caliper aside.
6. Support the caliper using mechanic's wire.
7. Remove the 2 brake pads and if equipped, remove the 4 retraction clips.
8. Discard the retraction clips.

To install:

➡**Do not allow grease, oil, brake fluid or other contaminants to contact the pad lining material or damage to components may occur. Do not install contaminated pads.**

➡**If installing new brake pads, install all new hardware as supplied with the brake pad kit.**

➡**Make sure the anti-rattle clips are correctly seated (snapped) into the anchor plate.**

9. Install the 4 new anti-rattle clips and the 2 brake pads.

➡**Protect the caliper pistons and boots when pushing the caliper pistons into the caliper piston bores or damage to components may occur.**

10. If installing new brake pads, using a

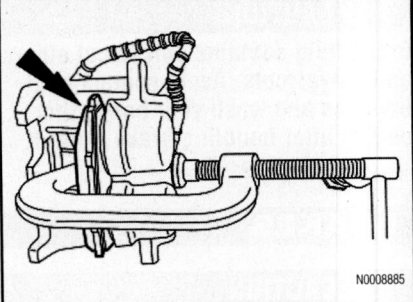

N0008885

Fig. 5 Using a C-clamp and a worn brake pad, compress the brake caliper pistons into the caliper

C-clamp and a worn brake pad, compress the brake caliper pistons into the caliper.

➡**To prevent deterioration of the caliper sleeve boots, do not use petroleum-based lubricant.**

11. Fill the rubber caliper sleeve boots with specified grease.
12. Install the brake pads.
13. Attach the wheel speed sensor wiring harness to the brake flexible hose.

➡**Tighten the bottom caliper bolt before tightening the top caliper bolt or damage to guide pins may occur.**

➡**Make sure the caliper pin boots are correctly seated to prevent damage to the guide pins.**

14. Position the brake caliper and install the 2 guide pin bolts.
15. Install the wheel and tire.
16. Fill the brake master cylinder reservoir with clean, specified brake fluid.
17. Apply brakes several times to verify correct brake operation.

BRAKES

❊❊ CAUTION

Dust and dirt accumulating on brake parts during normal use may contain asbestos fibers from production or aftermarket brake linings. Breathing excessive concentrations of asbestos fibers can cause serious bodily harm. Exercise care when servicing brake parts. Do not sand or grind brake lining unless equipment used is designed to contain the dust residue. Do not clean brake parts with compressed air or by dry brushing. Cleaning should be done by dampening the brake components with a fine mist of water, then wiping the brake components clean with a dampened cloth. Dispose of cloth and all residue containing asbestos fibers in an impermeable container with the appropriate label. Follow practices prescribed by the Occupational Safety and Health Administration (OSHA) and the Environmental Protection Agency (EPA) for the handling, processing, and disposing of dust or debris that may contain asbestos fibers.

BRAKE CALIPER

REMOVAL & INSTALLATION

See Figure 6.

REAR DISC BRAKES

❊❊ WARNING

Clean, high quality brake fluid is essential to the safe and proper operation of the brake system. You should always buy the highest quality brake fluid that is available. If the brake fluid becomes contaminated, drain and flush the system, then refill the master cylinder with new fluid. Never reuse any brake fluid. Any brake fluid that is removed from the system should be discarded. Also, do not allow any brake fluid to come in contact with a painted surface; it will damage the paint.

➡Do not spill brake fluid on painted or plastic surfaces or damage to the surface may occur. If brake fluid is spilled onto a painted or plastic surface, immediately wash the surface with water.

1. Remove the wheel and tire.

➡Use new copper washers on the brake caliper flow bolt.

2. Remove the brake caliper flow bolt and position the brake hose aside.
3. Discard the copper washers.
4. Remove the 2 brake caliper anchor plate bolts, the brake caliper and anchor plate as an assembly.
5. Remove the 2 brake caliper guide pin bolts and the brake caliper.
6. To install, reverse the removal procedure. Refer to the illustration for torque values.
7. Bleed the brake caliper. For additional information, refer to Brake System Bleeding for component bleeding.

DISC BRAKE PADS

REMOVAL & INSTALLATION

➡Do not spill brake fluid on painted or plastic surfaces or damage to the surface may occur. If brake fluid is spilled onto a painted or plastic surface, immediately wash the surface with water.

1. Remove the brake master cylinder filler cap. Check the brake fluid level in the brake master cylinder reservoir. Remove fluid until the brake master cylinder reservoir is half full.
2. Remove the wheel and tire.

➡Do not pry in the caliper sight hole to retract the pistons, as this can damage the pistons and boots.

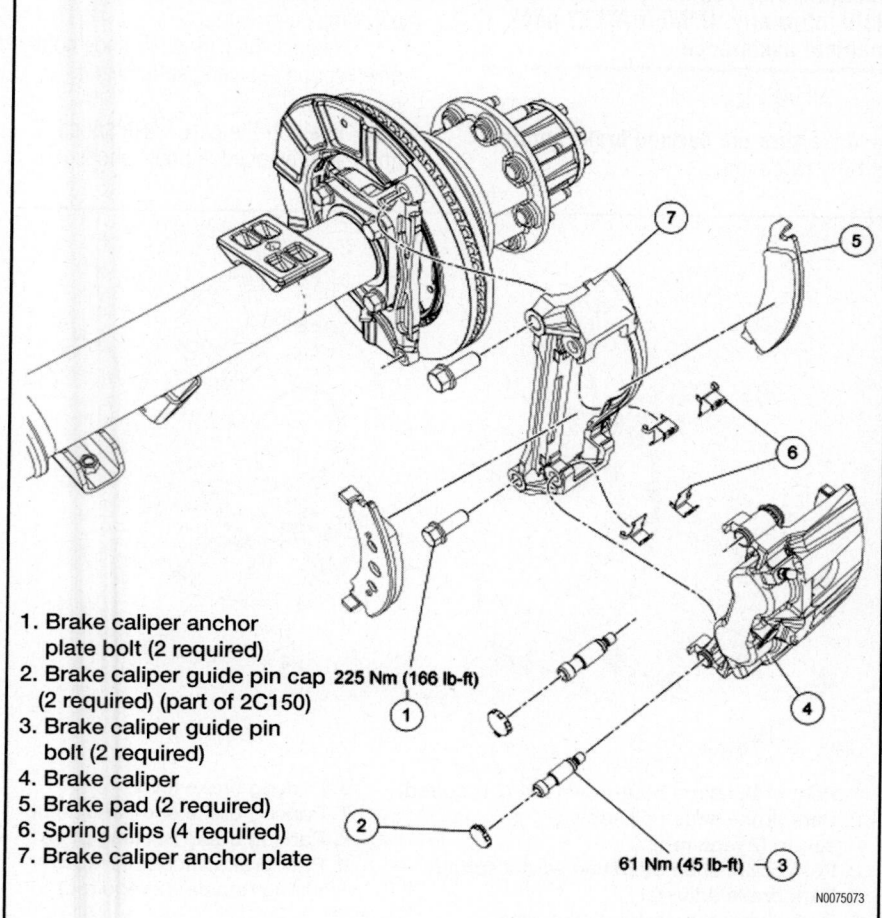

1. Brake caliper anchor plate bolt (2 required)
2. Brake caliper guide pin cap (2 required) (part of 2C150)
3. Brake caliper guide pin bolt (2 required)
4. Brake caliper
5. Brake pad (2 required)
6. Spring clips (4 required)
7. Brake caliper anchor plate

225 Nm (166 lb-ft)
61 Nm (45 lb-ft)
N0075073

Fig. 6 Exploded view of the rear brake system and components

3. Using a C-clamp, compress the caliper pistons into the caliper.

➡ **Do not allow the caliper to hang from the brake hose or damage to the hose can occur.**

4. Remove the 2 brake caliper anchor plate bolts and position the brake caliper and anchor plate assembly aside.

5. Support the caliper using mechanic's wire.

6. Remove the brake pads and 4 brake pad clips.

7. If new brake pads are being installed, discard brake pad clips.

8. To install, reverse the removal procedure. Refer to the Brake Caliper illustration for torque values.

9. If new brake pads are being installed, install new brake pad clips.

10. Check and fill the brake master cylinder reservoir as necessary with clean, specified brake fluid.

11. Apply the brake several times to verify correct brake operation.

BRAKES

PARKING BRAKE CABLES

CABLE TENSION RELEASE
See Figure 7.

1. Release the parking brake.

2. With the vehicle in NEUTRAL, position it on a hoist.

3. With an assistant, release the parking brake cable tension by pulling down on the intermediate cable at the cable-to-cable union until the parking brake control sector rotates to its stop and a 0.15 inches x 5.9 inches retainer pin can be inserted.

4. Disconnect the cable at the cable-to-cable union.

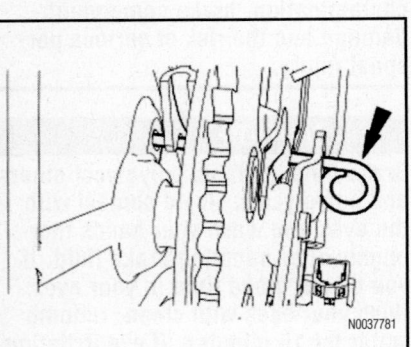

Fig. 7 Locating cable tension release pin

PARKING BRAKE SHOES

REMOVAL & INSTALLATION
See Figure 8.

✳✳ WARNING

Clean, high quality brake fluid is essential to the safe and proper operation of the brake system. You should always buy the highest quality brake fluid that is available. If the brake fluid becomes contaminated, drain and flush the system, then refill the master cylinder with new fluid. Never reuse any brake fluid. Any brake fluid that is removed from the system should be discarded. Also, do not allow any brake fluid to come in contact with a painted surface; it will damage the paint.

✳✳ CAUTION

Brake fluid contains polyglycol ethers and polyglycols. Avoid contact with the eyes and wash your hands thoroughly after handling brake fluid. If you do get brake fluid in your eyes, flush your eyes with clean, running water for 15 minutes. If eye irritation persists, or if you have taken brake fluid internally, IMMEDIATELY seek medical assistance.

1. All vehicles:

➡ **Make sure the parking brake control is fully released.**

PARKING BRAKE

a. Relieve the tension on the parking brake cable.

2. Vehicles with dual rear wheels (DRW):

   a. Remove the wheel hub. For additional information, refer to Wheel Hubs and Bearings.

3. Vehicles with Single Rear Wheel (SRW):

   a. Remove the brake disc.

4. All vehicles:

   a. Remove the park brake shoe adjusting screw.

   b. Remove the park brake shoe adjusting screw spring.

   c. Remove the park brake shoe hold-down spring retainers, springs and pins.

   d. Position the park brake shoes apart and remove the brake shoes

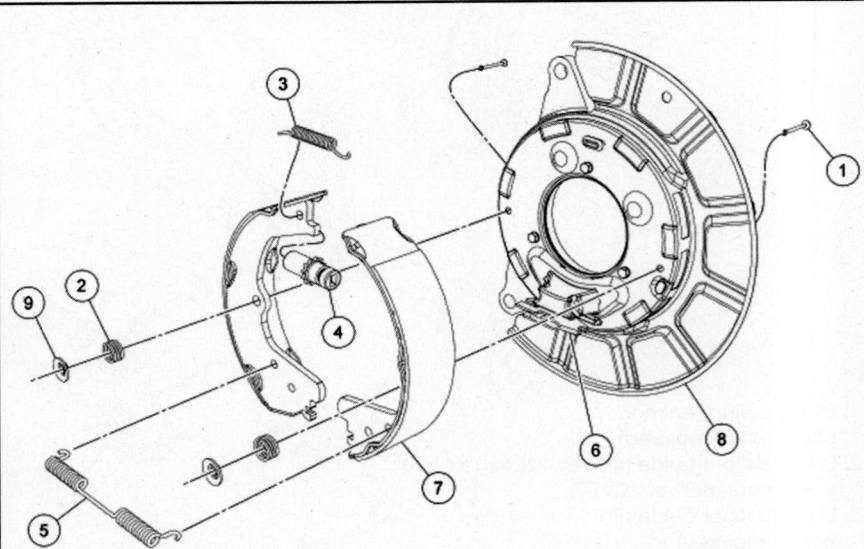

1. Park brake shoe hold-down pin (2 required)
2. Park brake shoe hold-down spring (2 required)
3. Park brake shoe adjusting screw spring
4. Park brake adjuster
5. Park brake shoe retracting spring
6. Parking brake lever
7. Parking brake shoe and lining
8. Parking brake backing plate
9. Park brake shoe hold-down spring retainer (2 required)

Fig. 8 Exploded view of the parking brake shoes

and the retracting spring from the axle.

To install:

➡**Lubricate the parking brake shoes where the shoe contacts the wear pad on the backing plate with the specified silicone grease.**

5. All vehicles:

  a. Install the retraction spring and position the parking brake shoe assembly on the axle.

  b. Position the 2 hold-down pins and install the 2 brake shoe hold-down springs and retainers.

  c. Install the brake shoe adjusting screw spring.

  d. Position the brake shoe adjusting screw.

  e. Adjust the parking brake shoes.

6. Vehicles with SRW:

  a. Install the rear brake disc.

  b. Install the wheel hub. For additional information, refer to Wheel Hubs and Bearings.

7. All vehicles:

  a. Reload the tension on the parking brake cable.

PARKING BRAKE SHOE ADJUSTMENT

See Figures 9 and 10.

➡**Make sure the parking brake is fully released.**

1. Release the parking brake control.

2. Remove the rear brake disc.

3. Using the Brake Adjusting Gauge, measure the inside diameter of the drum portion of the rear brake disc and set the locking screw.

4. Record the measurement.

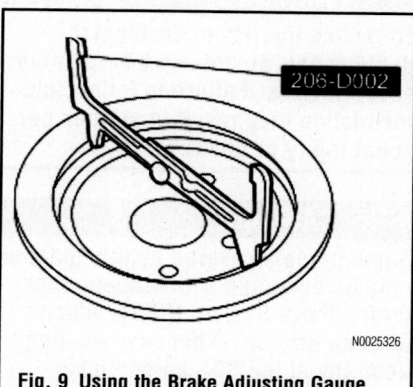

Fig. 9 Using the Brake Adjusting Gauge

5. Place the Brake Adjusting Gauge over the widest diameter of the parking brake shoes.

6. Adjust the parking brake shoe clearance to 0.6 mm (0.023 in) less than the inside diameter of the drum portion of the rear brake disc.

7. Rotate the parking brake shoe adjuster to achieve the correct parking brake shoe-to-brake disc clearance.

8. Install the rear brake disc.

9. Test the parking brake for normal operation.

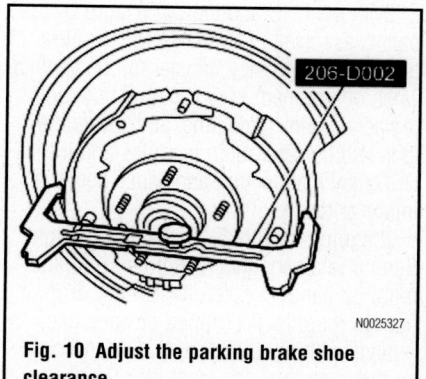

Fig. 10 Adjust the parking brake shoe clearance

CHASSIS ELECTRICAL

AIR BAG (SUPPLEMENTAL RESTRAINT SYSTEM)

GENERAL INFORMATION

✳✳ CAUTION

These vehicles are equipped with an air bag system. The system must be disarmed before performing service on, or around, system components, the steering column, instrument panel components, wiring and sensors. Failure to follow the safety precautions and the disarming procedure could result in accidental air bag deployment, possible injury and unnecessary system repairs.

SERVICE PRECAUTIONS

Disconnect and isolate the battery negative cable before beginning any airbag system component diagnosis, testing, removal, or installation procedures. Allow system capacitor to discharge for two minutes before beginning any component service. This will disable the airbag system. Failure to disable the airbag system may result in accidental airbag deployment, personal injury, or death.

Do not place an intact undeployed airbag face down on a solid surface. The airbag will propel into the air if accidentally deployed and may result in personal injury or death.

When carrying or handling an undeployed airbag, the trim side (face) of the airbag should be pointing away from the body to minimize possibility of injury if accidental deployment occurs. Failure to do this may result in personal injury or death.

Replace airbag system components with OEM replacement parts. Substitute parts may appear interchangeable, but internal differences may result in inferior occupant protection. Failure to do so may result in occupant personal injury or death.

Wear safety glasses, rubber gloves, and long sleeved clothing when cleaning powder residue from vehicle after an airbag deployment. Powder residue emitted from a deployed airbag can cause skin irritation. Flush affected area with cool water if irritation is experienced. If nasal or throat irritation is experienced, exit the vehicle for fresh air until the irritation ceases. If irritation continues, see a physician.

Do not use a replacement airbag that is not in the original packaging. This may result in improper deployment, personal injury, or death.

The factory installed fasteners, screws and bolts used to fasten airbag components have a special coating and are specifically designed for the airbag system. Do not use substitute fasteners. Use only original equipment fasteners listed in the parts catalog when fastener replacement is required.

During, and following, any child restraint anchor service, due to impact event or vehicle repair, carefully inspect all mounting hardware, tether straps, and anchors for proper installation, operation, or damage. If a child restraint anchor is found damaged in any way, the anchor must be replaced. Failure to do this may result in personal injury or death.

Deployed and non-deployed airbags may or may not have live pyrotechnic material within the airbag inflator.

Do not dispose of driver/passenger/curtain airbags or seat belt tensioners unless you are sure of complete deployment. Refer to the Hazardous Substance Control System for proper disposal.

Dispose of deployed airbags and tensioners consistent with state, provincial, local, and federal regulations.

After any airbag component testing or service, do not connect the battery negative cable. Personal injury or death may result if the system test is not performed first.

If the vehicle is equipped with the Occupant Classification System (OCS), do not connect the battery negative cable before performing the OCS Verification Test using the scan tool and the appropriate diagnostic information. Personal injury or death may result if the system test is not performed properly.

Never replace both the Occupant Restraint Controller (ORC) and the Occupant Classification Module (OCM) at the same time. If both require replacement, replace one, then perform the Airbag System test before replacing the other.

Both the ORC and the OCM store Occupant Classification System (OCS) calibration data, which they transfer to one another when one of them is replaced. If both are replaced at the same time, an irreversible fault will be set in both modules and the OCS may malfunction and cause personal injury or death.

If equipped with OCS, the Seat Weight Sensor is a sensitive, calibrated unit and must be handled carefully. Do not drop or handle roughly. If dropped or damaged, replace with another sensor. Failure to do so may result in occupant injury or death.

If equipped with OCS, the front passenger seat must be handled carefully as well. When removing the seat, be careful when setting on floor not to drop. If dropped, the sensor may be inoperative, could result in occupant injury, or possibly death.

If equipped with OCS, when the passenger front seat is on the floor, no one should sit in the front passenger seat. This uneven force may damage the sensing ability of the seat weight sensors. If sat on and damaged, the sensor may be inoperative, could result in occupant injury, or possibly death.

DISARMING THE SYSTEM

⁕⁕ WARNING

Always wear eye protection when servicing a vehicle. Failure to follow this instruction may result in serious personal injury.

⁕⁕ WARNING

Never disassemble or tamper with safety belt buckle/retractor pretensioners or adaptive load limiting retractors or probe the electrical connectors. Failure to follow this instruction may result in the accidental deployment of the safety belt pretensioners or adaptive load limiting

retractors which increases the risk of serious personal injury or death.

⁕⁕ WARNING

Never probe the electrical connectors on air bag, Safety Canopy® or side air curtain modules. Failure to follow this instruction may result in the accidental deployment of these modules, which increases the risk of serious personal injury or death.

⁕⁕ WARNING

To reduce the risk of accidental deployment, do not use any memory saver devices. Failure to follow this instruction may result in serious personal injury or death.

⁕⁕ CAUTION

Some models covered by this manual may be equipped with a Supplemental Restraint System (SRS), which uses an air bag. Whenever working near any of the SRS components, such as the impact sensors, the air bag module, steering column and instrument panel, disable the SRS, as described in Section 6.

➡ The air bag warning indicator illuminates when the correct Restraints Control Module (RCM) fuse is removed and the ignition is ON.

➡ The Supplemental Restraint System (SRS) must be fully operational and free of faults before releasing the vehicle to the customer.

1. Turn all vehicle accessories OFF.
2. Turn the ignition OFF.
3. At the Smart Junction Box (SJB), located below the LH side of the instrument panel, remove the cover and the RCM fuse 32 (10A) from the SJB . For additional information, refer to the Wiring Diagrams manual.
4. Turn the ignition ON and monitor the air bag warning indicator for at least 30 seconds. The air bag warning indicator will remain lit continuously (no flashing) if the correct RCM fuse has been removed. If the air bag warning indicator does not remain lit continuously, remove the correct RCM fuse before proceeding.
5. Turn the ignition OFF.

⁕⁕ WARNING

Always deplete the backup power supply before repairing or installing

any new front or side air bag supplemental restraint system (SRS) component and before servicing, removing, installing, adjusting or striking components near the front or side impact sensors or the restraints control module (RCM). Nearby components include doors, instrument panel, console, door latches, strikers, seats and hood latches.

To deplete the backup power supply energy, disconnect the battery ground cable and wait at least 1 minute. Be sure to disconnect auxiliary batteries and power supplies (if equipped).

Failure to follow these instructions may result in serious personal injury or death in the event of an accidental deployment.

6. Disconnect the battery ground cable and wait at least one minute.

ARMING THE SYSTEM

1. Turn the ignition from OFF to ON.
2. Install RCM fuse 32 (10A) to the SJB and install the cover.

⁕⁕ WARNING

Make sure no one is in the vehicle and there is nothing blocking or placed in front of any air bag module when the battery is connected. Failure to follow these instructions may result in serious personal injury in the event of an accidental deployment.

3. Connect the battery ground cable.
4. Prove out the SRS as follows:
   a. Turn the ignition from ON to OFF.
   b. Wait 10 seconds, then turn the ignition back ON and monitor the air bag warning indicator with all SRS components installed and connected.
   c. The air bag warning indicator will light continuously for approximately 6 seconds and then turn off.
   d. If an air bag SRS fault is present, the air bag warning indicator will: - fail to light. - remain lit continuously. - flash.
   e. The flashing might not occur until approximately 30 seconds after the ignition has been turned from the OFF to the ON position. This is the time required for the RCM to complete the testing of the SRS.
   f. If the air bag warning indicator is inoperative and a SRS fault exists, a chime will sound in a pattern of 5 sets of

5 beeps. If this occurs, the air bag warning indicator and any SRS fault discovered must be diagnosed and repaired. Clear all continuous DTCs from the RCM using a scan tool.

CLOCKSPRING CENTERING

See Figures 11 through 14.

→The air bag warning indicator illuminates when the correct Restraints Control Module (RCM) fuse is removed and the ignition is ON.

→The Supplemental Restraint System (SRS) must be fully operational and free of faults before releasing the vehicle to the customer.

1. Remove the driver air bag module.
2. Remove the steering column opening cover.
3. Pull outward on the steering column opening cover to release the retaining clips.
4. Detach the pin-type retainer and remove the electrical connector on the steering column opening lower finish panel reinforcement.
5. Remove the 2 Data Link Connector (DLC) screws and position aside.

6. Disconnect the clockspring electrical connectors and detach them from the bracket at the base of the steering column.
7. Place the road wheels in the straight-ahead position and remove the steering wheel.
8. If equipped, loosen the tilt lever/handle and remove.
9. Remove the ignition lock cylinder.
10. Turn the lock cylinder to the RUN position.
11. Using a suitable tool, push upward on the lock cylinder release tab through the hole in the lower shroud while pulling outward.
12. Remove the 3 screws and lower steering column shroud.
13. Remove the upper steering column shroud.

→Do not allow the clockspring to turn if it will be reused.

14. If reusing the clockspring, tape the rotor to the outer housing to prevent it from rotating.
15. If equipped, remove the key-in-ignition warning indicator switch.
16. Release the 3 clockspring retaining clips.

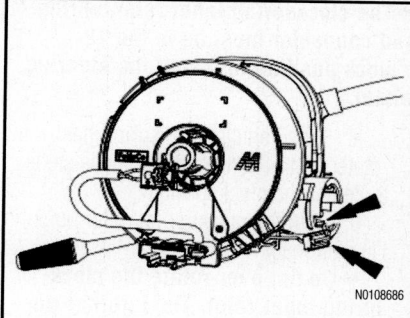

Fig. 12 If equipped, remove the key-in-ignition warning indicator switch

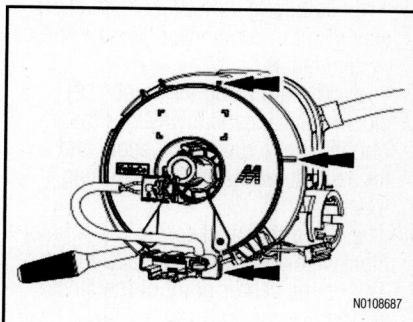

Fig. 13 Release the 3 clockspring retaining clips

17. Detach the 2 clockspring retaining clips holding the wire to the steering column.
18. Route the wiring through the instrument panel and remove the clockspring.

To install:

19. Installing a new clockspring:

→A new clockspring is supplied in a centralized position and held with a sealing key.

a. Remove the sealing key from the clockspring, holding the rotor in its centralized position.
b. Do not allow the clockspring rotor to turn.

20. Installing clockspring requiring recentering:

✳✳ WARNING

If the clockspring is not correctly centralized, it may fail prematurely. If in doubt, repeat the centralizing procedure. Failure to follow these instructions may increase the risk of serious personal injury or death in a crash.

→To prevent damage to the clockspring, make sure the road wheels are in the straight-ahead position.

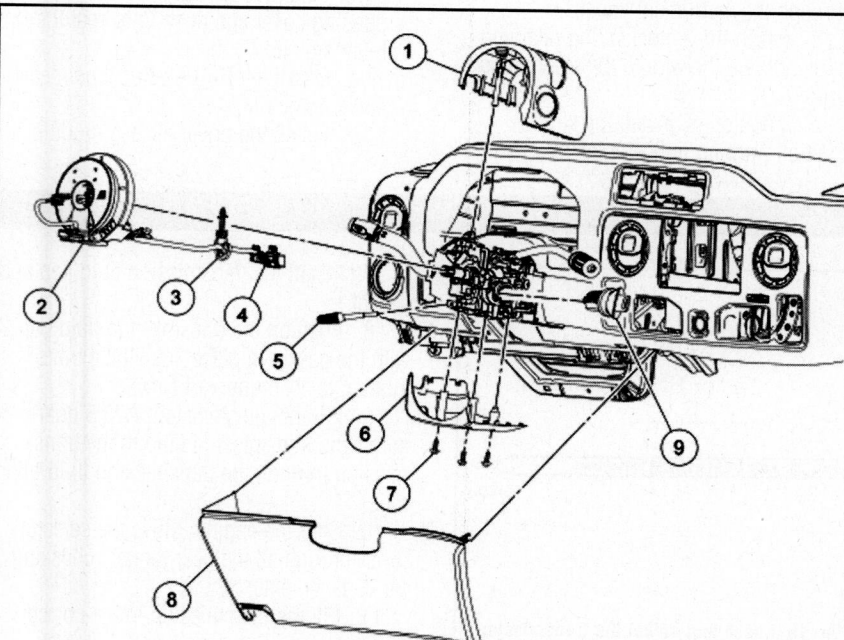

1. Upper steering column shroud
2. Clockspring
3. Clockspring wiring retaining clip (part of 14A664) (2 required)
4. Electrical connector (part of 14A664)
5. Tilt lever/handle
6. Lower steering column shroud
7. Lower steering column shroud screw (3 required)
8. Steering column opening cover
9. Ignition lock cylinder

Fig. 11 Exploded view of the clockspring assembly

➡The clockspring inner rotor, wiring and connector must be in the 12 o'clock position to install the steering wheel.

   a. If the vehicle clockspring has rotated out of center, follow these steps to center the clockspring.
   b. Hold the clockspring outer housing (1) stationary.

➡Do not over-rotate the clockspring inner rotor. The internal ribbon wire is connected to the clockspring rotor. The internal ribbon wire acts as a stop and can be broken from its internal connection.

   c. Failure to follow this instruction may result in component damage and/or system failure.
   d. While turning the rotor clockwise (2), carefully feel for the ribbon wire to run out of length and for a slight resistance. Stop turning at this point.
   e. Turn the clockspring (3) counterclockwise approximately 2.25 turns. This is the center point of the clockspring.
   f. Do not allow the rotor to turn from this position.
21. Installing original clockspring

➡When the tape is removed, do not allow the clockspring to turn.

   a. Remove the tape applied during clockspring removal.

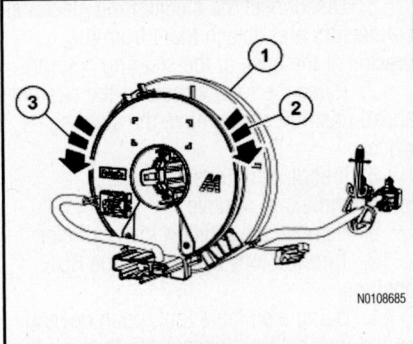

Fig. 14 Installing clockspring requiring re-centering

22. All clocksprings:

➡Slight turning of the clockspring rotor is allowable for alignment purposes to the steering column.

With the flats of the clockspring rotor aligned to the flats of the steering column shaft, slide the clockspring onto the steering column engaging the retaining tabs.

   a. Press at the 6, 12 and 3 o'clock positions to seat the clockspring.
   b. Route the clockspring wiring through the instrument panel.
   c. Attach the 2 clockspring retaining clips holding the wire to the steering column.
   d. If equipped, install the key-in-ignition warning indicator switch.

   e. Install the upper steering column shroud.
   f. Install the lower steering shroud and 3 screws.
   g. Install the ignition lock cylinder.
   • Put the ignition lock cylinder in the RUN position.
   • Insert the ignition lock cylinder into the steering column housing.
   • Make sure the ignition lock cylinder is fully seated and aligned in the interlocking washer before turning to the OFF position. This will allow the ignition lock cylinder retaining pin to extend into the steering column bore.
   h. Using the key, rotate the ignition lock cylinder through all of the switch positions.
   i. If equipped, install the tilt lever/handle.
   j. Install the steering wheel.
   k. Connect the clockspring electrical connectors. Install the pin-type retainers into the bracket.
   l. Install the steering column opening trim panel reinforcement and 6 bolts.
   m. Install the DLC and 2 screws.
   n. Install the steering column opening cover. Align the steering column opening cover and push in to seat the 6 retaining clips.
   o. Install the DLC electrical connector and 2 screws.
   p. Install the driver air bag module.

DRIVE TRAIN

AUTOMATIC TRANSAXLE FLUID

DRAIN AND REFILL
See Figure 15.

   1. With the vehicle in NEUTRAL, position it on a hoist.
   2. Loosen the transmission fluid pan bolts and allow the fluid to drain. After the fluid has drained, remove the transmission fluid pan.

➡Do not remove the transmission fluid filter. It is not necessary to change the transmission fluid filter during a normal maintenance fluid change.

   3. Clean and inspect the transmission fluid pan, transmission fluid pan gasket and magnet.
   4. Thoroughly flush the transmission fluid cooler tubes.
   5. Refill:

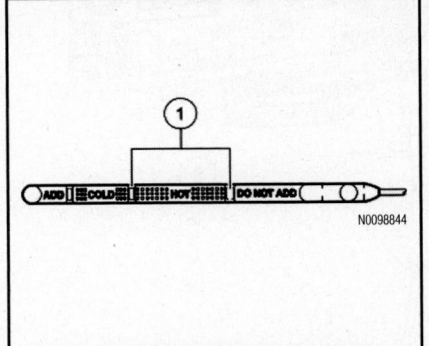

Fig. 15 Check and adjust the transmission fluid level

   6. Position the magnet into the transmission fluid pan.

➡The transmission fluid pan gasket is reusable. Clean and inspect for damage. If not damaged, the gasket should be reused.

   7. Install the transmission fluid pan and gasket.
   8. Position the transmission fluid pan with the gasket in place. Install the bolts. Tighten to 11 ft. lbs. (14 Nm).
   9. Fill the transmission. Add 5 quarts of automatic transmission fluid to the transmission through the transmission fluid filler tube.
   10. Start the engine. Move the selector lever through all the gear ranges, checking for engagements.
   11. Fill the transmission to the correct level.
   12. Using the scan tool, start and run the engine until the transmission is at normal operating temperature 150-170°F, check and adjust the transmission fluid level, and check for any leaks. If transmission fluid is needed, add fluid in increments of 0.5 pints until the correct level is achieved (fluid should be in the cross-hatched area of the fluid level indicator).

FILTER REPLACEMENT

4R70E/4R75E Transmission

See Figure 16.

➡ Do not use any supplemental transmission fluid additives or cleaning agents. The use of these products could cause internal transmission components to fail; this will effect the operation of the transmission. Use of a transmission fluid other than specified could result in transmission failure.

➡ Normal maintenance requires periodic transmission fluid changes. If a major repair, such as a clutch, band or bearing is required, the automatic transmission will need to be removed for repair. The transmission fluid needs to be changed if evidence of transmission fluid contamination is found.

1. With the vehicle in NEUTRAL, position it on a hoist.
2. Loosen the transmission fluid pan bolts and allow transmission fluid to drain. After the transmission fluid is drained, remove the bolts.
3. Remove the transmission fluid pan and transmission fluid pan gasket.
4. Pull down evenly and remove the transmission fluid filter and seal.
5. Clean and inspect the transmission fluid pan, gasket and magnet.

To install:

➡ If installing a new transmission fluid filter and the seal remains in the main control bore, carefully use a small screwdriver to remove the seal. Use care not to damage the main control bore.

➡ If transmission is being repaired for a contamination-related failure, use a new transmission fluid filter and seal.

The transmission fluid filter may be reused if no excessive contamination is present.

6. Install a new transmission fluid filter and seal as required.
7. Position the transmission fluid pan magnet into the transmission fluid pan.

➡ The transmission fluid pan gasket is reusable. Clean and inspect for damage; if not damaged, the transmission fluid pan gasket should be reused.

Install the transmission fluid pan and gasket.

8. Position the transmission fluid pan and gasket.
9. Install the transmission fluid pan bolts. Tighten to 9 ft. lbs. (14 Nm).

➡ When filling a dry transmission and torque converter, start with a minimum of 4.7L (5 qt).

10. Fill the transmission to the correct level with transmission fluid.

Torqshift Transmission

See Figures 17 and 18.

➡ This transmission utilizes an in-line filter.

➡ Use the following guidelines for installing the transmission fluid in-line filter:

- If the transmission was overhauled and the vehicle was equipped with a transmission fluid in-line filter, install a new transmission fluid in-line filter.
- If the transmission was overhauled and the vehicle was not equipped with a transmission fluid in-line filter, install a new transmission fluid in-line filter kit.

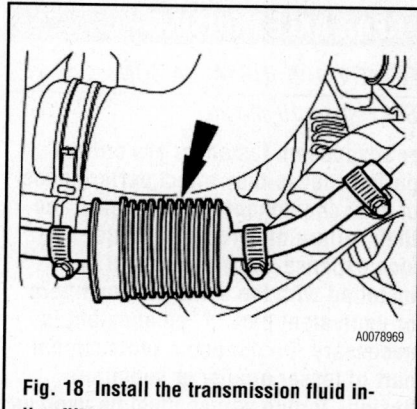

Fig. 18 Install the transmission fluid in-line filter

- If the transmission is being installed for a non-internal repair, do not install a transmission fluid in-line filter or filter kit.
- If installing a new or a Ford-authorized remanufactured transmission, install a transmission fluid in-line filter.

1. With the vehicle in NEUTRAL, position it on a hoist.
2. Remove the section of the rubber hose as illustrated.

➡ The transmission fluid in-line filter has a bypass valve in it. The arrow on the transmission fluid in-line filter indicates the direction of transmission fluid flow through the transmission fluid in-line filter. The transmission fluid in-line filter must be installed in the transmission fluid cooler return tube with the arrow on the transmission fluid in-line filter pointing away from the transmission fluid cooler and toward the transmission (the return tube has transmission fluid coming out of the cooler going to the transmission). If the transmission fluid in-line filter is not installed correctly, it will cause internal transmission damage.

➡ Do not install any rubber hoses or steel tubing with a bend entering the filter greater than 60 degrees. Doing so can block transmission fluid flow and cause internal transmission damage.

3. Install the transmission fluid in-line filter and tighten the clamps.
4. Clean a section of the transmission fluid pan and install the sticker.
5. Fill the transmission with transmission fluid.
6. Verify for correct operation.
7. Check the filter for leaks.

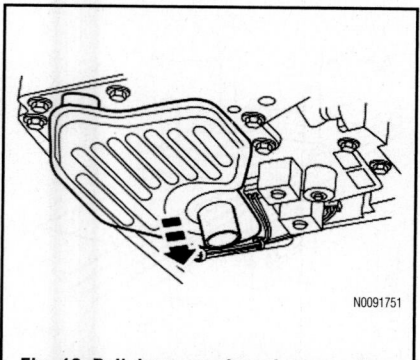

Fig. 16 Pull down evenly and remove the transmission fluid filter and seal

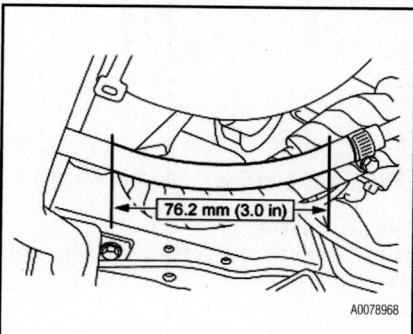

Fig. 17 Remove the section of the rubber hose

REAR AXLE HOUSING

REMOVAL & INSTALLATION

See Figures 19 and 20.

➡ Suspension fasteners are critical parts because they affect performance of vital components and systems and their failure may result in major service expense. New parts must be installed with the same part numbers or equivalent part, if replacement is necessary. Do not use a replacement part of lesser quality or substitute design. Torque values must be used as specified during reassembly to make sure of correct retention of these parts.

1. With the vehicle in NEUTRAL, position it on a hoist.

2. Remove the wheels and tires.

➡ Do not allow the caliper and anchor plate assembly to hang from the brake hose or damage to the hose can occur.

3. Remove the 2 brake caliper anchor plate bolts and position the brake caliper and anchor plate assembly aside.

4. Support the brake caliper and anchor plate assembly using mechanic's wire.

5. Disconnect the parking brake cable from the parking brake. Repeat for the opposite side. Position the cables aside.

6. Disconnect the axle vent tube.

7. Disconnect the axle vent.

8. Remove the brake tube bracket bolt.

9. Remove the park brake cable retainer bolt.

10. Disconnect the wheel speed sensor harness clips.

11. Remove the rear wheel speed sensor bolt, and position the sensor and spacer aside.

12. Position the brake tube, harness and cable aside.

13. Remove the driveshaft.

14. Use a suitable transmission jack to support the axle.

15. Remove and discard the shock absorber lower nuts and bolts.

➡ Watch for obstructions while lowering and raising the axle.

16. Lower the axle from the vehicle.

17. To install, reverse the removal procedure.

18. Install new fasteners where discarded.

➡ When installing new U-bolts, the measurement between A and B should be 107 mm (4.21 in) ± 3 mm (0.12 in) for E150/E250/E350 vehicles and 112 mm (4.41 in) ± 3 mm (0.12 in) for E450 vehicles. This is important for providing the correct U-bolt clamp load and retention of parts.

19. Remove and discard the 8 nuts and the 4 axle U-bolts.

20. To install, tighten until snug. Tighten the U-bolt nuts evenly in an X-type pattern in 5 stages.

    a. Stage 1: Tighten to 37 ft. lbs. (50 Nm).

    b. Stage 2: Tighten to 74 ft. lbs. (100 Nm).

    c. Stage 3: Tighten to 111 ft. lbs. (150 Nm).

    d. Stage 4: Tighten to148 ft. lbs. (200 Nm).

    e. Stage 5: Tighten to 166 ft. lbs. (225 Nm).

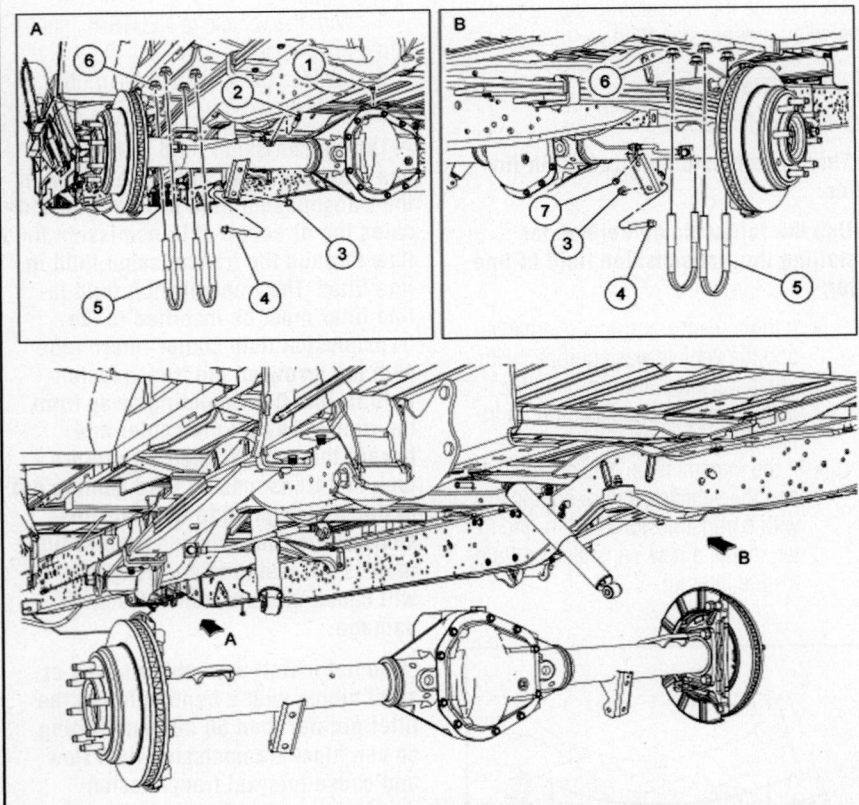

1. Brake tube bracket bolt
2. Axle housing vent
3. Lower shock absorber nuts
4. Lower shock absorber bolts
5. U-bolts (E-150, E-250 and E-350 Van and wagon) (2 required)
5. U-bolt (E-450) (2 required)
6. U-bolt (E-350 regular cab and cutaway) (2 required)
7. U-bolt nuts (4 required)

N0074317

Fig. 19 Rear axle assembly—Dana 60 and 70

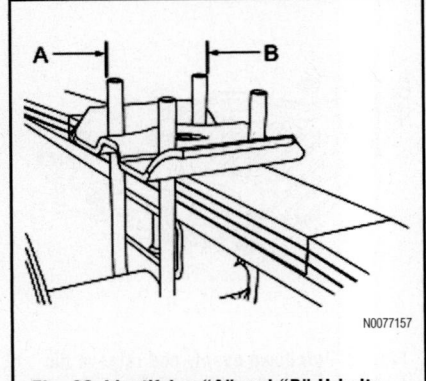

N0077157

Fig. 20 Identifying "A" and "B" U-bolts

REAR AXLE SHAFT, BEARING & SEAL

REMOVAL & INSTALLATION

Semi Floating Axle Shaft

See Figure 21.

1. Raise the vehicle on a hoist or raise the rear end of the vehicle with a jack. Install safety stands under the frame rails and lower the jack or hoist enough to allow the rear axle to drop into the rebound position for working clearance.

2. Remove the brake disc. For additional information, refer to Rear Disc Brake.

3. Remove the differential housing cover.

4. Vehicles equipped with RSC®; Remove the rear wheel speed sensor bolt and position the spacer and sensor aside.

➡**The differential assembly is equipped with a differential pinion shaft lock screw with torque prevailing threads and a 12-point drive head. This type of screw is reusable for no more than 4 installations.**

5. When in doubt about the number of installations of a torque prevailing differential pinion shaft lock screw, discard it and install a new screw.

6. Remove the lock screw.

➡**The pinion shaft is a slip-fit design and is removable by hand.**

7. Remove the differential pinion shaft.

8. Push the flanged end of the axle shaft toward the center of the axle and remove the U-washer.

➡**Do not damage the wheel bearing oil seal when removing the axle shaft.**

9. Remove the axle shaft.

10. Install the differential pinion shaft and the lock screw in the differential case.

To install:

11. Remove the lock screw and the differential pinion shaft.

➡**Do not damage the wheel bearing oil seal when installing the axle shaft.**

12. Push the axle shaft into the axle tube and engage the differential side gear with the shaft splines.

13. Push the axle shaft toward the center of the axle and install the U-washer. Pull the axle shaft outward until the U-washer locks into the differential side gear.

14. Align the differential pinion shaft lock screw hole with the hole in the differential case. Correctly position the differential pinion thrust washers. Install the differential pinion shaft.

➡**The threads in the differential case and on the lock screw must be free of dirt and oil.**

15. Install the new differential pinion shaft lock screw. Tighten to 20 ft. lbs. (27 Nm).

16. Install the differential housing cover.

17. Vehicles equipped with RSC®; Position the rear wheel speed sensor spacer, the sensor and install the bolt. Tighten to 18 ft. lbs. (25 Nm).

18. Install the brake disc.

Semi Floating Axle Bearing and Seal

See Figures 22 through 24.

1. Remove the axle shaft.

➡**If only a new axle shaft oil seal needs to be installed, use care to avoid damaging the axle shaft oil seal bore.**

2. Using a suitable seal remover, remove and discard the axle shaft oil seal.

3. Inspect the rear wheel bearing and axle shaft for wear or damage.

4. Using the Axle Bearing Remover and Slide Hammer, remove the rear wheel bearing.

To install:

5. Lubricate the new rear wheel bearing with axle lubricant. Refer to Specifications for the correct type.

6. Using the Rear Axle Bearing Installer and Handle, install the rear wheel bearing.

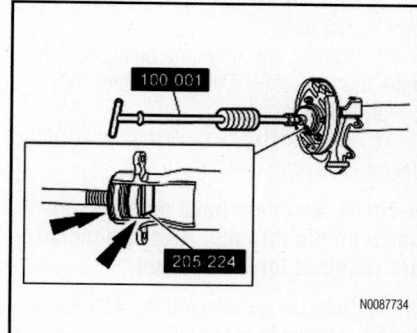

Fig. 22 Using the Axle Bearing Remover and Slide Hammer

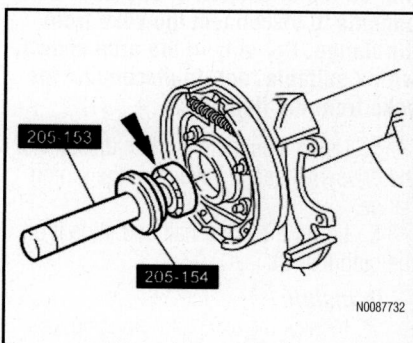

Fig. 23 Using the Rear Axle Bearing Installer and Handle

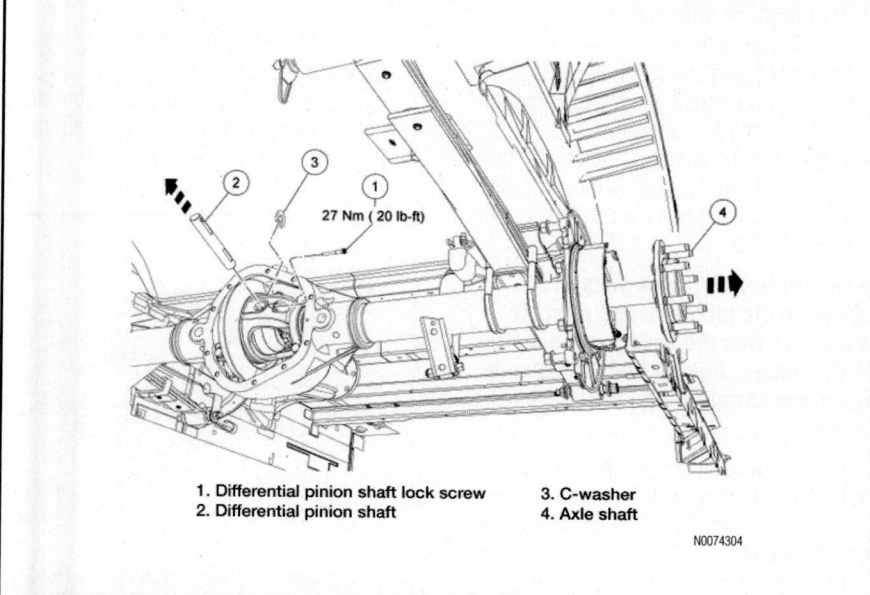

1. Differential pinion shaft lock screw
2. Differential pinion shaft
3. C-washer
4. Axle shaft

27 Nm (20 lb-ft)

N0074304

Fig. 21 Exploded view of the axle shaft assembly—Semi Floating

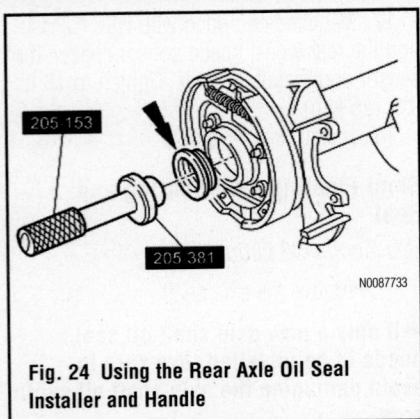

Fig. 24 Using the Rear Axle Oil Seal Installer and Handle

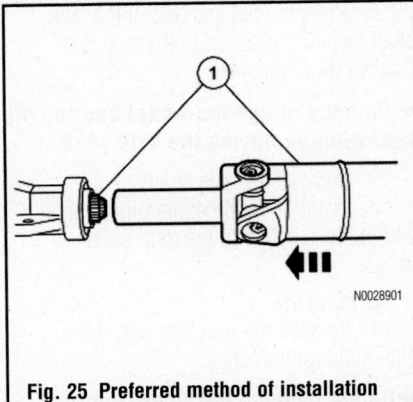

Fig. 25 Preferred method of installation

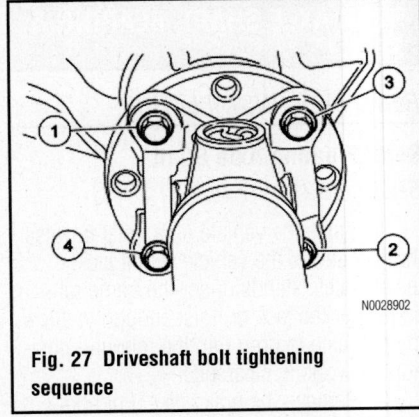

Fig. 27 Driveshaft bolt tightening sequence

7. Lubricate the lip of the new axle shaft oil seal with grease.

8. Using the Rear Axle Oil Seal Installer and Handle, install the new axle shaft oil seal.

9. Install the axle shaft.

REAR DRIVESHAFT

REMOVAL & INSTALLATION

See Figures 25 through 27.

➡**The following procedure is for the two piece drive shaft, one piece driveshaft procedure is similar.**

1. With the vehicle in NEUTRAL, position it on a hoist.

2. To maintain driveline balance, index-mark the driveshaft flange yoke and the pinion flange.

3. Index-mark the driveshaft yoke and the transmission tailshaft.

➡**These fasteners have an adhesive patch on the threads. New fasteners are required for installation.**

4. Remove and discard the 4 driveshaft-to-pinion flange bolts.

➡**The driveshaft flange yoke fits tightly on the pinion flange pilot. Never hammer on the driveshaft or any of its components to disconnect the yoke from the flange. Pry only in the area shown, with a suitable tool, to disconnect the yoke from the flange.**

5. Using a suitable pry bar, disconnect the driveshaft flange yoke from the pinion flange.

6. Lower the driveshaft and slide it off the output shaft.

To install:

7. Inspect the extension housing seal for damage. Install a new seal as necessary.

8. Lubricate the transmission output shaft spline with grease.

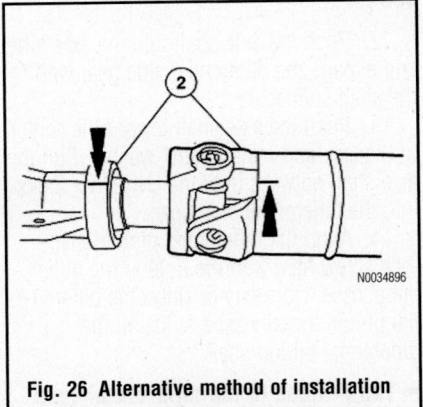

Fig. 26 Alternative method of installation

9. Check to see if a paint mark is present on the front of the driveshaft and on the end of the transmission output shaft.

➡**Depending on the paint markings, there are 2 methods of indexing the driveshaft and the output shaft.**

10. Install the driveshaft.

a. Preferred method: Align the factory-made paint marks on the output shaft and driveshaft and position the driveshaft in the transmission.

b. Alternate method: Align the index marks that were created in the removal process and position the driveshaft in the transmission.

➡**The driveshaft flange yoke fits tightly on the pinion flange pilot. To make sure that the yoke seats squarely on the flange, tighten the bolts evenly in a cross pattern in the sequence shown.**

11. Position the driveshaft flange yoke on the pinion flange with the index marks aligned and install 4 new driveshaft-to-pinion flange bolts.

12. Tighten the 4 new bolts in the sequence shown to 83 ft. lbs. (112 Nm).

REAR PINION SEAL

REMOVAL & INSTALLATION

See Figures 28 and 29.

1. Raise the vehicle on a hoist or raise the rear end of the vehicle with a jack. Install safety stands under the frame rails and lower the jack or hoist enough to allow the rear axle to drop into the rebound position for working clearance.

2. Remove the driveshaft. For additional information, refer to Rear Driveshaft.

➡**Index-mark the pinion flange to the pinion shaft prior to removal.**

3. Use the Drive Pinion Flange Holding Fixture to prevent the flange from turning while removing the locknut and washer.

4. Discard the locknut and washer.

5. Using the 2 Jaw Puller, remove the pinion flange.

6. Using the Bushing Remover and Slide Hammer; remove and discard the pinion seal.

7. Clean the pinion seal seat.

To install:

8. Lubricate the pinion seal rubber lips with axle lubricant. Refer to Specifications for the correct type.

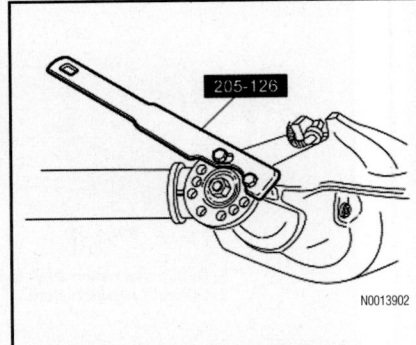

Fig. 28 Use the Drive Pinion Flange Holding Fixture

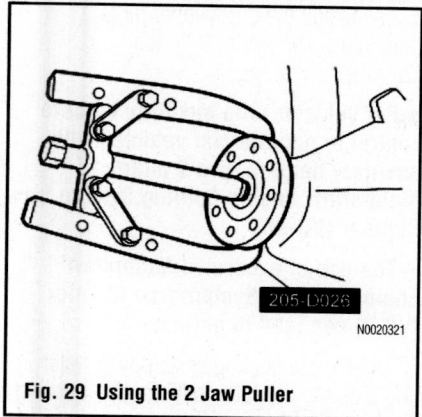

Fig. 29 Using the 2 Jaw Puller

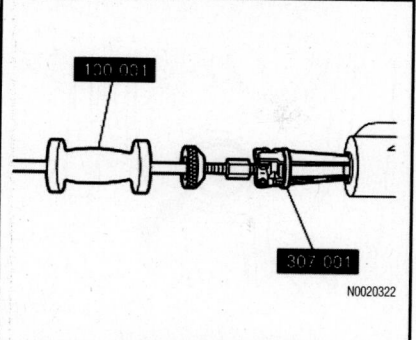

Fig. 30 Using the Bushing Remover and Slide Hammer

9. Using a suitable driver, install the pinion seal.

10. After installation, verify that the garter spring did not pop out of the seal. If the garter spring popped out, install a new pinion seal.

11. Coat the inside of the pinion flange with a small amount of axle lubricant. Refer to Specifications for the correct type.

12. Install the pinion flange.

➡**Always install a new washer and locknut or damage to the component may occur.**

13. Use the Drive Pinion Flange Holding Fixture to prevent the flange from turning while installing the new washer and locknut. Tighten to 250 ft. lbs. (339 Nm).

14. Install the driveshaft.

15. Check and as necessary, fill the axle with the specified type and amount of axle lubricant.

ENGINE COOLING

ENGINE COOLANT

DRAIN, BLEEDING & REFILL PROCEDURE

See Figure 31.

➡**Always fill the cooling system with the same coolant that is present in the system. Do not mix coolant types. Failure to follow these instructions may result in cooling system or engine damage.**

➡**The coolant must be recovered in a suitable, clean container for reuse. If the coolant is contaminated it must be disposed of correctly. Failure to follow these instructions may result in cooling system or engine damage.**

➡**Less than 80% of coolant capacity can be recovered with the engine in the vehicle. Dirty, rusty or contaminated coolant requires replacement.**

1. Release the pressure in the cooling system in the following sequence.

 a. Make sure the engine is cool.

 b. Wrap a thick cloth around the coolant pressure relief cap on the degas bottle. Slowly turn the cap counterclockwise (left) until the pressure begins to release.

 c. Step back while the pressure releases.

 d. When you are sure all the pressure has been released, use the cloth to turn and remove the cap.

2. Place a suitable container below the radiator draincock.

3. Open the radiator draincock and drain the coolant into a suitable container.

4. Close the radiator draincock when finished.

Filling and Bleeding with Radiator Refiller

➡**For diesel engine, do not add Motorcraft® Diesel Cooling System Additive when refilling the cooling system with new coolant. An excessive amount of additive may cause formation of gels that may cause coolant flow restriction, plugging of passages and overheating.**

➡**For diesel engine, when refilling the cooling system with new coolant, verify that the specified coolant is used. Not all coolants contain a nitrite additive package. Failure to have nitrite in the cooling system may result in major corrosive damage to the engine cooling system components.**

➡**For diesel engine, when reusing the coolant that was drained from the cooling system, check the antifreeze and anticorrosion level of the coolant.**

5. Install the RADIATOR REFILLER and follow the RADIATOR REFILLER manufacturer's instructions to fill and bleed the cooling system.

 a. Recommended coolant concentration is 50/50 ethylene glycol to distilled water.

 b. Maximum coolant concentration is 60/40 for cold weather areas.

 c. Minimum coolant concentration is 40/60 for warm weather areas.

Filling without RADIATOR REFILLER

➡**Always fill the cooling system with the same coolant that is present in the**

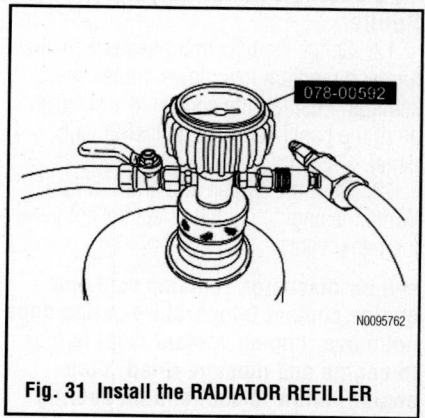

Fig. 31 Install the RADIATOR REFILLER

system. Do not mix coolant types. Failure to follow these instructions may result in cooling system or engine damage.

➡**For diesel engine, do not add Motorcraft® Diesel Cooling System Additive when refilling the cooling system with new coolant. An excessive amount of additive may cause formation of gels that may cause coolant flow restriction, plugging of passages and overheating.**

➡**For diesel engine, when refilling the cooling system with new coolant, verify that the specified coolant is used. Not all coolants contain a nitrite additive package. Failure to have nitrite in the cooling system may result in major corrosive damage to the engine cooling system components.**

➡**For diesel engine, when reusing the coolant that was drained from the cooling system, check the antifreeze and anticorrosion level of the coolant.**

6. Add the correct engine coolant mixture to the degas bottle.

   a. Recommended coolant concentration is 50/50 ethylene glycol to distilled water.

   b. Maximum coolant concentration is 60/40 for cold weather areas.

   c. Minimum coolant concentration is 40/60 for warm weather areas.

7. Move the temperature blend selector to the full warm position.

8. Run the engine until it reaches operating temperature.

9. Add the correct engine coolant mixture to the degas bottle until the coolant level is between the COOLANT FILL LEVEL marks.

10. Turn off the engine and allow the cooling system to cool.

11. Repeat Steps 1 through 5 until the degas bottle level is OK.

Bleeding without Radiator Refiller

12. Select the maximum heater temperature and medium low blower motor speed settings. Position the control to discharge air at the panel vents in the instrument panel.

13. Start the engine and allow to idle. While the engine is idling, feel for hot air at the panel vents.

➡️**If air discharge remains cool and engine coolant temperature gauge does not move, engine coolant level is low in engine and must be filled. Stop engine, allow to cool and fill cooling system. Failure to follow these instructions may result in cooling system or engine damage.**

14. Start engine and allow to idle until normal operating temperature is reached. Hot air should discharge from the panel vents. The engine coolant temperature gauge should maintain a stabilized reading in the middle of the NORMAL range and the upper radiator hose should feel hot to the touch.

15. Shut the engine off and allow to cool.

16. Check the engine for coolant leaks.

17. Check the engine coolant level in degas bottle and fill as necessary.

FLUSHING

Diesel Engines

See Figure 32.

➡️**This procedure should be used to clean and flush the diesel cooling system to make sure that all rust is removed from the system. Failure to**

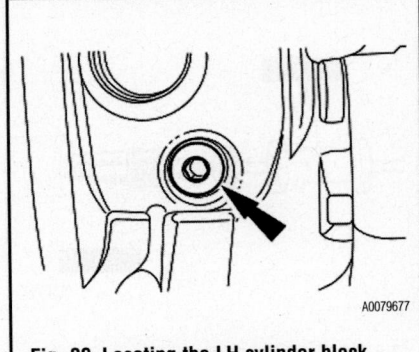

Fig. 32 Locating the LH cylinder block drain plug

follow these instructions may result in engine damage.

➡️**If oil or fuel is present in the cooling system, refer to the appropriate Technical Service Bulletins (TSBs) that pertain to 6.0L diesel engine cooling system concerns and follow the procedure outlined. Failure to remove all contaminants from the cooling system may result in engine damage.**

❈❈ WARNING
Always allow the engine to cool before opening the cooling system. Do not unscrew the coolant pressure relief cap when the engine is operating or the cooling system is hot. The cooling system is under pressure; steam and hot liquid can come out forcefully when the cap is loosened slightly. Failure to follow these instructions may result in serious personal injury.

1. Once pressure is released, remove the pressure relief cap.

2. Drain the cooling system.

3. Remove the thermostat housing assembly. For additional information, refer to Thermostat Diesel in this section.

4. Position the thermostat housing assembly in the vise. Press down on the thermostat crossbar and rotate the thermostat to remove it from the thermostat housing assembly.

5. Install the thermostat housing without the thermostat.

➡️**The RH cylinder block drain plug is not removed at this time.**

6. Remove the LH cylinder block drain plug and drain the cylinder block of coolant.

➡️**Lightly lubricate the O-ring seal on the cylinder block drain plug with clean engine oil before installing.**

7. Install the LH cylinder block drain plug. Tighten to 15 ft. lbs. (20 Nm).

➡️**For vehicles with auxiliary climate control or commercial vehicles with auxiliary heaters, use 3 quarts of Motorcraft® Engine Cooling System Iron Cleaner (VC-9).**

➡️**The use of excessive Motorcraft® Engine Cooling System Iron Cleaner (VC-9) can lead to gelling.**

8. Fill the cooling system with water and 2 quarts of Motorcraft® Engine Cooling System Iron Cleaner (VC-9).

➡️**Failure to allow the engine to run for one hour will result in insufficient cleaning of the cooling system.**

9. Using the scan tool, use the active command and set the engine rpm to 1,175. Run the engine for one hour.

❈❈ CAUTION
Always allow the engine to cool before opening the cooling system. Do not unscrew the coolant pressure relief cap when the engine is operating or the cooling system is hot. The cooling system is under pressure; steam and hot liquid can come out forcefully when the cap is loosened slightly. Failure to follow these instructions may result in serious personal injury.

10. Once pressure is released, remove the pressure relief cap.

11. Drain the cooling system.

12. Leave the radiator draincock open.

13. Remove the LH cylinder block drain plug.

14. Remove the starter. For additional information, refer to Starter in Engine Electrical.

15. Remove the RH cylinder block drain plug.

➡️**Failure to flush all the Motorcraft° Engine Cooling System Iron Cleaner (VC-9) from the cooling system will result in shortened coolant protection against corrosion.**

16. Flush the cooling system with clean water through the degas bottle to completely remove the Motorcraft® Engine Cooling System Iron Cleaner (VC-9) from the cooling system.

17. Flush the cooling system with clean water until no foam or discoloration is draining from the cooling system.

18. Backflush the heater core. For additional information, refer to Heater Core Back Flushing in this section.

➡**Failure to flush all the Motorcraft® Engine Cooling System Iron Cleaner (VC-9) from the cooling system will result in shortened coolant protection against corrosion.**

19. Flush the cooling system with clean water through the degas bottle to completely remove the Motorcraft® Engine Cooling System Iron Cleaner (VC-9) from the cooling system.

20. Flush the cooling system with clean water until no foam or discoloration is draining from the cooling system.

21. Close the radiator draincock.

➡**Do not fill the cooling system at this time.**

➡**Replace the thermostat housing assembly O-ring seal.**

22. Install the thermostat.

➡**Lightly lubricate the O-ring seal on the cylinder block drain plug with clean engine oil before installing.**

23. Install the RH cylinder block drain plug. Tighten to 15 ft. lbs. (20 Nm).

24. Install the starter.

➡**Lightly lubricate the O-ring seal on the cylinder block drain plug with clean engine oil before installing.**

25. Install the LH cylinder block drain plug. Tighten to 15 ft. lbs. (20 Nm).

26. Fill the cooling system.

Gasoline Engines

☀☀ WARNING

Always allow the engine to cool before opening the cooling system. Do not unscrew the coolant pressure relief cap when the engine is operating or the cooling system is hot. The cooling system is under pressure; steam and hot liquid can come out forcefully when the cap is loosened slightly. Failure to follow these instructions may result in serious personal injury.

1. Once pressure is released, remove the pressure relief cap. Drain the cooling system.

2. Remove the thermostat. For additional information, refer to Thermostat in this section.

3. Install the coolant hose connection without the thermostat.

➡**Refer to the cooling system Flush-All Operating Instructions for specific vehicle hook-up.**

4. Use cooling system Flush-All, Flush Kit Hardware Package and Drain Kit to flush the engine and radiator. Use Premium Cooling System Flush VC-1 or equivalent meeting Ford specification ESR-M14P7A.

5. Install the thermostat.

6. Fill the cooling system.

Heater Core Back Flushing

1. Once pressure is released, remove the pressure relief cap.

2. Partially drain the cooling system.

➡**Refer to the cooling system flusher operating instructions for particular vehicle hook-up.**

3. Use an appropriate cooling system flusher to backflush the heater core. Use Premium Cooling System

4. Flush VC-1 or equivalent meeting Ford specification ESR-M14P7-A.

5. Fill the cooling system.

ENGINE FAN

REMOVAL & INSTALLATION

4.6L, 5.4L and 6.8L Engines

See Figures 33 through 35.

➡**The fan, fan clutch and shroud must be removed and installed together due to insufficient clearance to remove them separately.**

1. With the vehicle in NEUTRAL, position it on a hoist.

2. Drain the engine cooling system.

3. Remove the Air Cleaner (ACL) assembly.

4. Disconnect and position the radiator

upper hose and the overflow hose from the radiator aside.

➡**The coolant hose must be mounted in the lower hole and power steering hose in the upper hole or damage to the hoses may occur.**

5. Disconnect the coolant degas bottle and power steering hose from the shroud.

6. Vehicles with 4.6L, 5.4L engine; Using the Fan Clutch Pulley Holding Wrench and Fan Clutch Hub Nut Wrench, loosen the fan clutch.

➡**The clutch assembly nut has a right-hand thread and must be rotated counterclockwise to remove it.**

7. Vehicles with 6.8L engine; Using the Fan Clutch Pulley Holding Wrench and Fan Clutch Hub Nut Wrench, loosen the fan clutch.

➡**The clutch assembly nut has a right-hand thread and must be rotated counterclockwise to remove it.**

8. Carefully rotate the fan and fan clutch assembly counterclockwise until the assembly is free from the coolant pump. Place the fan and fan clutch into the shroud opening.

9. Disconnect the lower radiator hose retaining clamp from the shroud.

10. If equipped, disconnect the underbody splash shield from the shroud.

➡**Use extreme care when removing or installing the fan, fan clutch and shroud. Failure to do so will cause damage to the radiator.**

11. Remove the mounting bolts and the fan, fan clutch and shroud.

12. If servicing the fan blade assembly or clutch, remove the 4 bolts and separate the cooling fan from the clutch.

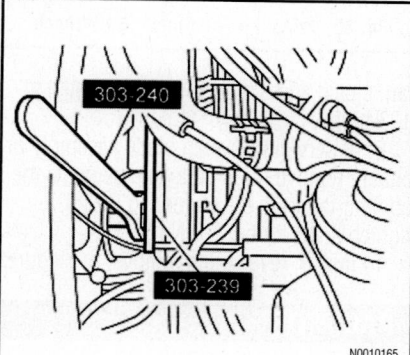

Fig. 33 Using the Fan Clutch Pulley Holding Wrench and Fan Clutch Hub Nut Wrench—4.6L, 5.4L engine

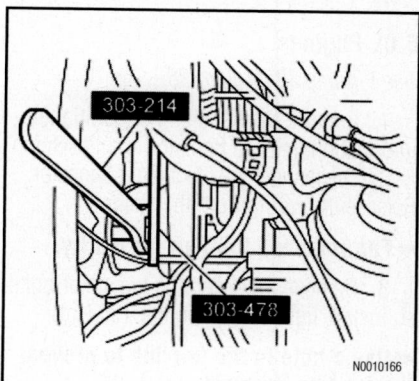

Fig. 34 Using the Fan Clutch Pulley Holding Wrench and Fan Clutch Hub Nut Wrench—6.8L Engine

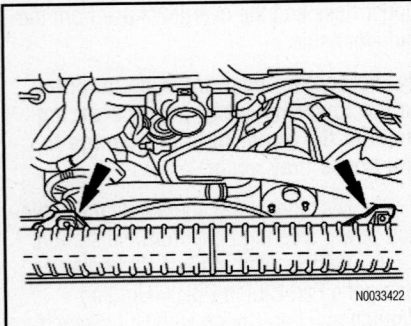

Fig. 35 Remove the mounting bolts and the fan, fan clutch and shroud

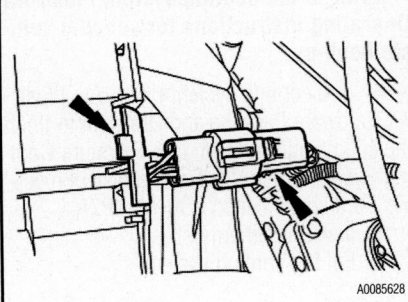

Fig. 36 Disconnect the electrical connector and release the wiring from the stator

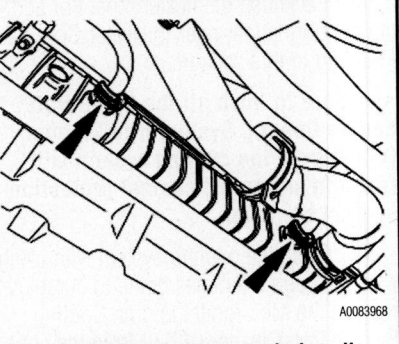

Fig. 39 Disconnect the transmission oil cooler hoses

To install:

13. If servicing the fan blade assembly or clutch, position the cooling fan onto the clutch and install the 4 bolts.

➡ **Use extreme care when installing the fan, fan clutch and shroud. Failure to do so will cause damage to the radiator.**

14. Carefully position the cooling fan, fan clutch and shroud into the vehicle as an assembly. Install the 2 fan shroud bolts.

15. Vehicles with 4.6L, 5.4L engine:
   a. Using the Fan Clutch Pulley Holding Wrench and the Fan Clutch Hub Nut Wrench, install the cooling fan.
   b. Calculate the correct torque wrench setting for the following torque. Tighten to 41 ft. lbs. (55 Nm).

16. Vehicles with 6.8L engine:
   a. Using the Fan Clutch Pulley Holding Wrench and the Fan Clutch Hub Nut Wrench, install the cooling fan.
   b. Calculate the correct torque wrench setting for the following torque. Tighten to 98 ft. lbs. (133).

17. To complete installation, reverse the remaining removal procedure.

18. Fill and bleed the engine cooling system.

6.0L Engines

See Figures 36 through 38.

1. Remove the radiator. For additional information, refer to Radiator in this section.

2. Disconnect the electrical connector. Release the wiring from the stator.

➡ **Fan removed from art for clarity.**

3. Remove the 4 cooling fan stator bolts. To install, tighten to 22 ft. lbs. (30 Nm).

➡ **Use a hole in the fan hub to prevent the fan from turning.**

4. Using the Fan Clutch Nut Wrench, loosen the fan clutch by turning the wrench counterclockwise. 5. Remove the cooling

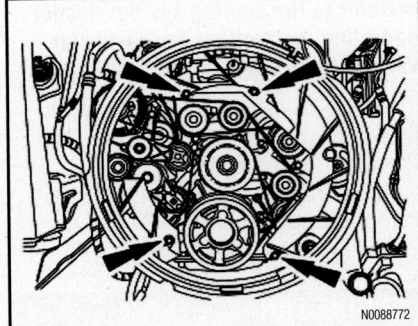

Fig. 37 Remove the 4 cooling fan stator bolts

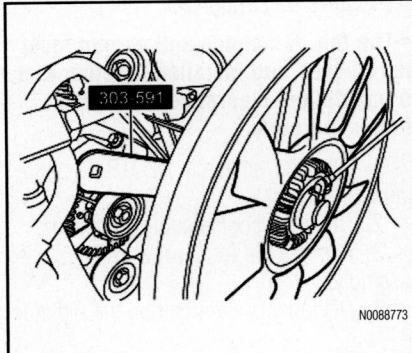

Fig. 38 Using the Fan Clutch Nut Wrench

fan, clutch and stator. To install, tighten to 133 ft. lbs. (180 Nm).

6. If servicing the fan blade assembly or clutch, remove the 6 bolts and separate the cooling fan from the clutch. To install, tighten to 15 ft. lbs. (20 Nm).

To install, reverse the removal procedure.

RADIATOR

REMOVAL & INSTALLATION

4.6L, 5.4L and 6.8L Engines

See Figure 39.

1. With the vehicle in NEUTRAL, position it on a hoist.

2. Remove the cooling fan.

3. If equipped, remove the underbody splash shield.

NOTE: Typical shown, others similar.

4. Disconnect the transmission oil cooler hoses.

5. Plug or cap the lines as needed.

6. Disconnect the lower radiator hose.

7. Remove the 4 bolts and the 2 radiator support brackets. To install, tighten to 15 ft. lbs. (20 Nm).

8. Remove the radiator from the vehicle.

9. To install, reverse the removal procedure.

10. If necessary, install new appropriately sized worm drive-type clamps.

6.0L Engines

See Figures 40 through 44.

1. With the vehicle in NEUTRAL, position it on a hoist.

2. Drain the cooling system.

3. Remove the 6 pushpin retainers and upper air deflector.

4. Remove the 4 bolts for the power steering reservoir bracket.

5. Remove the 3 bolts and power steering fluid indicator. Remove the power steering reservoir mounting bracket. Install the power steering fluid indicator and position aside.

6. Disconnect the coolant hoses from the Air Cleaner (ACL) outlet tube.

7. Loosen the 2 clamps and remove the ACL outlet pipe.

8. Disconnect the Mass Air Flow (MAF) sensor electrical connector. Disconnect the 3 clips and remove the ACL cover.

9. Loosen the clamps and remove the Charge Air Cooler (CAC) tube.

➡ **If there is any oil residue, clean both connecting ports and the inside surface**

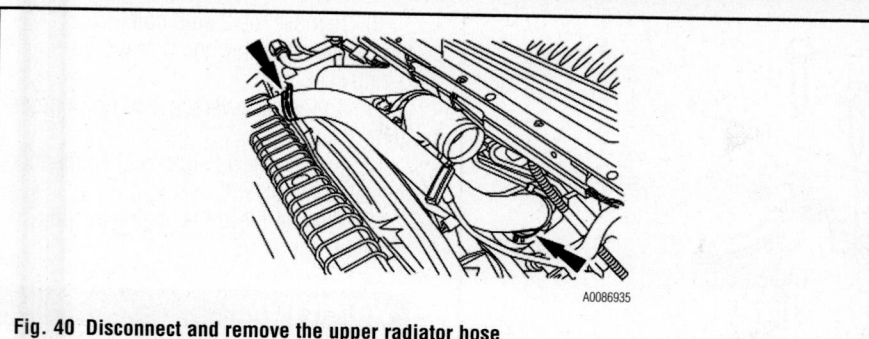
Fig. 40 Disconnect and remove the upper radiator hose

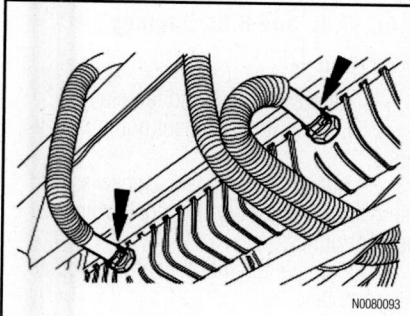
Fig. 41 Disconnect the transmission cooler hoses

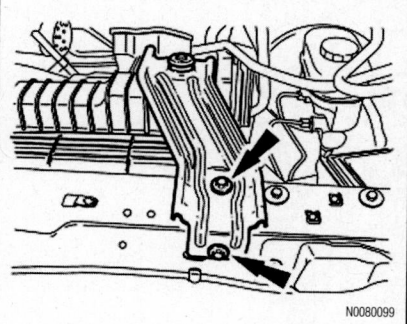
Fig. 43 Remove the 4 bolts and the radiator mounting brackets

of the CAC hose to prevent the hose from blowing off.

10. Loosen the clamps and remove the CAC hose.

11. Disconnect the radiator vent hose.

12. Disconnect and remove the upper radiator hose.

13. Remove the 4 bolts and lower air deflector.

14. Disconnect the transmission cooler hoses. Plug or cap the hoses as needed.

15. Disconnect the lower radiator hose.

16. Remove the 2 lower shroud bolts.

17. Disconnect the transmission cooler hoses from the lower shroud and remove the lower shroud.

18. Remove the 2 pushpin retainers and the closeout.

Fig. 44 Remove the 2 A/C condenser bolts

➡**LH side shown, RH side similar.**

19. Remove the 4 bolts and the radiator mounting brackets.

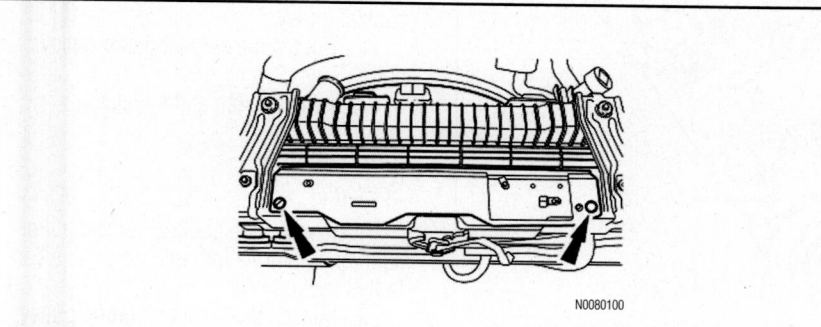
Fig. 42 Remove the 2 pushpin retainers and the closeout

20. Remove the 2 bolts and fan shroud.

➡**LH side shown, RH side similar.**

21. Remove the 2 A/C condenser bolts.

➡**Make sure the transmission cooler fittings on the radiator are not contacting the A/C condenser or damage to the A/C condenser may occur.**

22. With the help of an assistant, raise the radiator and CAC as an assembly enough to separate the A/C condenser from the CAC. Remove the radiator and CAC as an assembly from the vehicle.

To install:
23. With the help of an assistant, position the radiator and CAC into the vehicle.

24. From the bottom of the vehicle, connect the A/C condenser to the CAC and position the entire assembly into place.

25. Install the 2 A/C condenser bolts.

➡**Cooling module removed from vehicle for clarity.**

26. Install the fan shroud and 2 bolts.

27. Install the 4 bolts and the radiator mounting brackets. Tighten to 15 ft. lbs. (20 Nm).

28. To complete installation, reverse the remaining removal procedure.

29. Fill the cooling system.

THERMOSTAT

REMOVAL & INSTALLATION

4.6L, 5.4L and 6.8L Engines
See Figure 45.

1. Drain the engine cooling system.

2. Remove the Air Cleaner (ACL) outlet pipe.

3. If servicing the thermostat housing, disconnect the upper radiator hose.

4. Remove the 2 bolts and position the thermostat housing aside. Remove the thermostat and discard the O-ring seal.

5. Inspect and clean the sealing surfaces with metal surface prep. Follow the directions on the packaging.

6. Install a new O-ring seal.

7. To install, reverse the removal procedure.

8. Fill and bleed the engine cooling system.

6.0L Engines
See Figure 46.

1. Drain the cooling system.

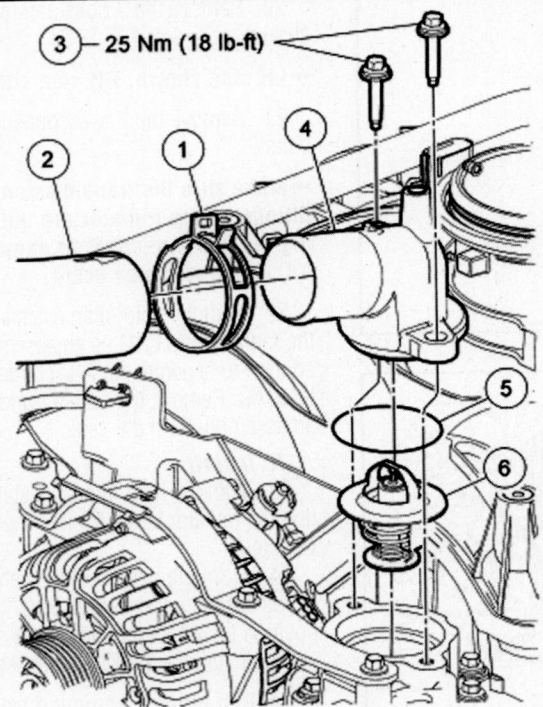

1. Upper radiator hose clamp
2. Upper radiator hose
3. Thermostat housing bolts
   (2 required) — 4.6L
3. Thermostat housing
   bolts (2 required) — 5.4L (2V), 6.8L
4. Thermostat housing
5. Thermostat O-ring
   seal
6. Thermostat

N0060250

Fig. 45 Exploded view of the thermostat assembly—4.6L, 5.4L and 6.8L Engines

2. Remove the 6 pushpin retainers and upper air deflector.

3. Remove the 4 bolts for the power steering reservoir bracket.

4. Remove the 3 bolts and power steering fluid indicator. Remove the power steering reservoir mounting bracket. Install the power steering fluid indicator and position aside. To install, tighten the 3 bolts to 8 ft. lbs. (11 Nm).

5. Disconnect the coolant hoses from the Air Cleaner (ACL) outlet pipe.

6. Loosen the 2 clamps and remove the ACL outlet pipe.

➡If there is any oil residue, clean both connecting ports and the inside surface of the Charge Air Cooler (CAC) tube to prevent the tube from blowing off.

7. Loosen the 2 clamps and remove the CAC tube.

8. Disconnect and position the upper radiator hose aside.

9. Remove the nut and position the fuel line retainer aside.

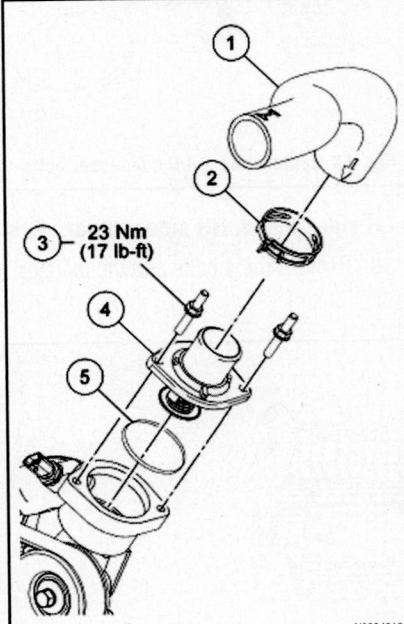

N0034816

Fig. 46 Exploded view of the thermostat assembly—6.0L Engines

10. Remove the 2 stud bolts, thermostat assembly and discard the O-ring seal.

11. To install, reverse the removal procedure.

12. Install a new O-ring seal on the thermostat assembly.

13. Fill and bleed the engine cooling system.

WATER PUMP

REMOVAL & INSTALLATION

4.6L, 5.4L and 6.8L Engines
See Figure 47.

1. Remove the fan and fan clutch.
2. Loosen the 4 coolant pump pulley bolts.
3. Rotate the tensioner clockwise and remove the accessory drive belt from the coolant pulley.
4. Remove the 4 bolts and the coolant pump pulley.
5. Remove the 4 coolant pump bolts and the coolant pump.
6. Discard the coolant pump O-ring seal.
7. Clean the sealing surfaces with metal surface prep. Follow the directions on the packaging.

To install:

➡Lubricate the new O-ring seal with clean engine coolant prior to installation into the cylinder block. Install a new O-ring on the coolant pump.

➡Do not rotate the coolant pump housing once the coolant pump has been positioned in the cylinder block. Damage to the O-ring seal will occur.

8. Position the coolant pump and install the 4 bolts.
9. Position the coolant pump pulley onto the coolant pump and install the bolts finger-tight.
10. Rotate the tensioner clockwise and install the accessory drive belt onto the coolant pulley.
11. Tighten the coolant pump pulley bolts.
12. Install the fan and fan clutch.

6.0L Engines
See Figure 48.

1. Remove the cooling fan stator. For additional information, refer to Engine Fan in this section.
2. Loosen the 4 coolant pump pulley bolts.
3. Rotate the drive belt tensioner clock-

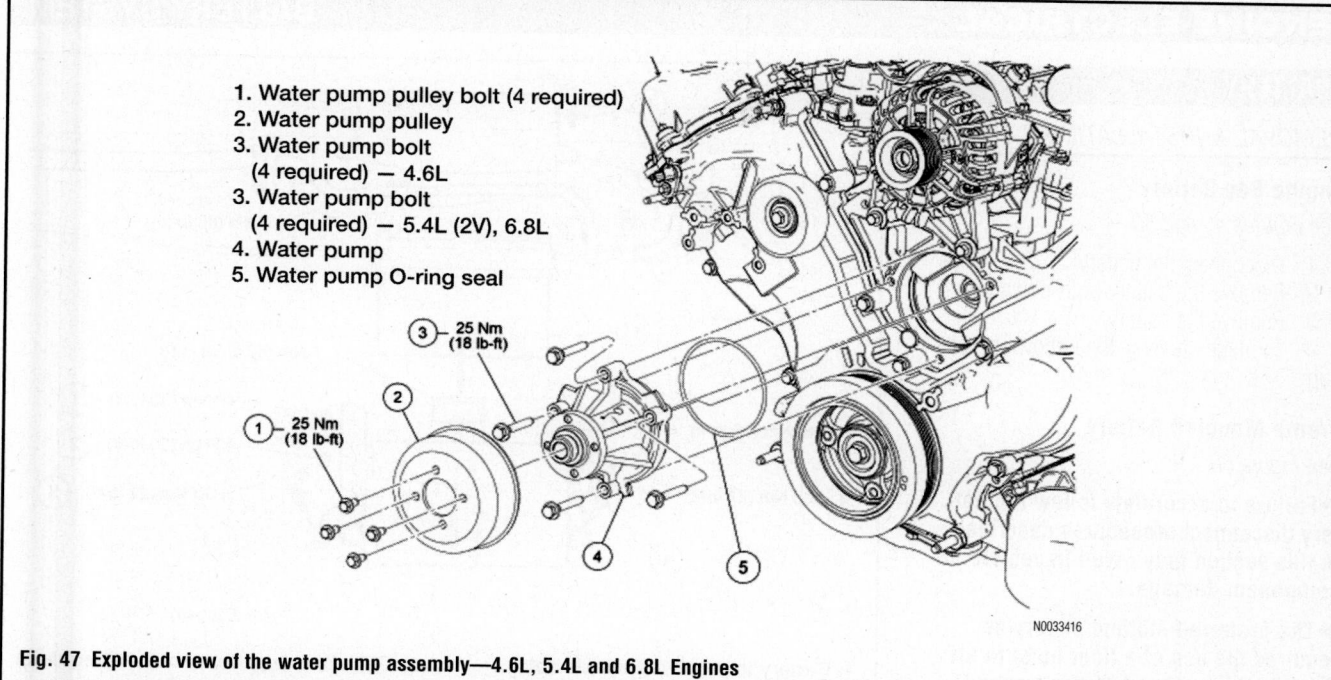

1. Water pump pulley bolt (4 required)
2. Water pump pulley
3. Water pump bolt
   (4 required) — 4.6L
3. Water pump bolt
   (4 required) — 5.4L (2V), 6.8L
4. Water pump
5. Water pump O-ring seal

3 — 25 Nm (18 lb-ft)
1 — 25 Nm (18 lb-ft)

Fig. 47 Exploded view of the water pump assembly—4.6L, 5.4L and 6.8L Engines

wise and remove the accessory drive belt from the coolant pump pulley.

4. Remove the 4 bolts and the coolant pump pulley.

5. Remove the 4 bolts and the coolant pump.

6. Discard the O-ring seal.

7. Clean and inspect the coolant pump sealing surfaces with metal surface prep.

To install:

→**Lubricate the new O-ring seal with clean engine coolant prior to installation.**

8. Install a new O-ring on the coolant pump.

→**Do not rotate the coolant pump housing once the coolant pump has been positioned in the cylinder block. Damage to the O-ring seal will occur.**

9. Position the coolant pump and install the 4 bolts.

10. Position the coolant pump pulley and install the 4 bolts finger-tight.

11. Rotate the drive belt tensioner clockwise and install the accessory drive belt onto the coolant pump pulley.

12. Tighten the 4 coolant pump pulley bolts.

13. Install the cooling fan stator.

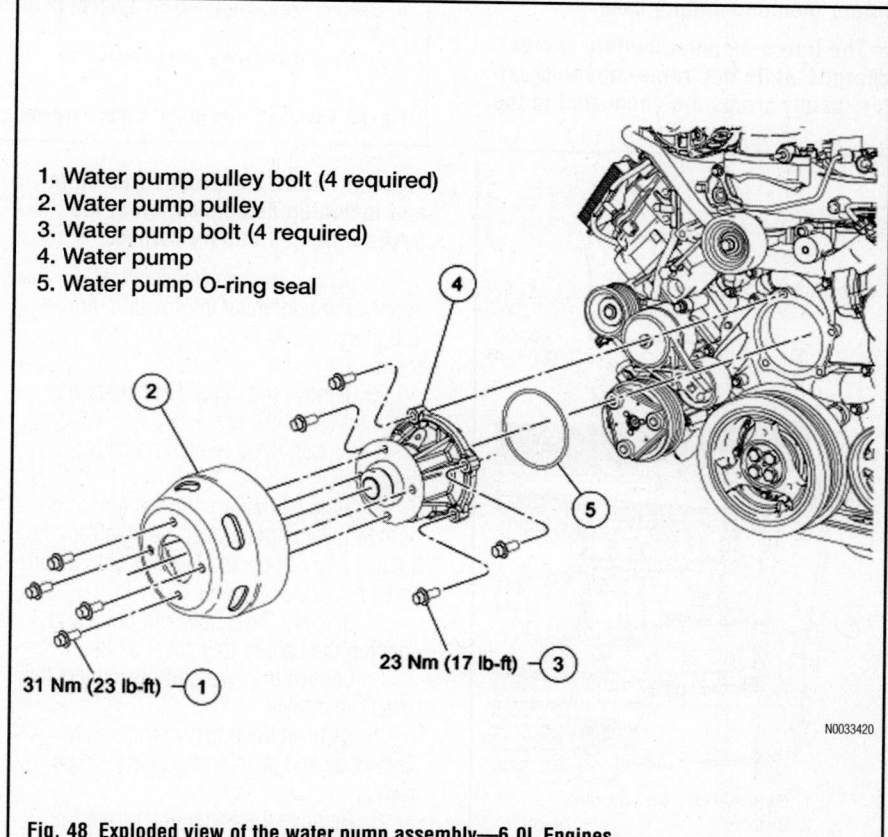

1. Water pump pulley bolt (4 required)
2. Water pump pulley
3. Water pump bolt (4 required)
4. Water pump
5. Water pump O-ring seal

31 Nm (23 lb-ft) — 1
23 Nm (17 lb-ft) — 3

Fig. 48 Exploded view of the water pump assembly—6.0L Engines

BATTERY

REMOVAL & INSTALLATION

Engine Bay Battery

See Figures 49 and 50.

1. Disconnect the battery.
2. Remove the battery hold-down bolt.
3. Remove the battery.
4. To install, reverse the removal procedure.

Frame Mounted Battery

See Figure 50.

➡Failure to accurately follow the battery disconnect procedures described in this section may result in vehicle or component damage.

➡The preferred method of service requires the use of a floor hoist to lift the vehicle overhead, and a transmission jack to support and lower the frame-mounted battery case.

➡The frame-mounted battery can be charged while the frame-mounted battery safety straps are connected to the

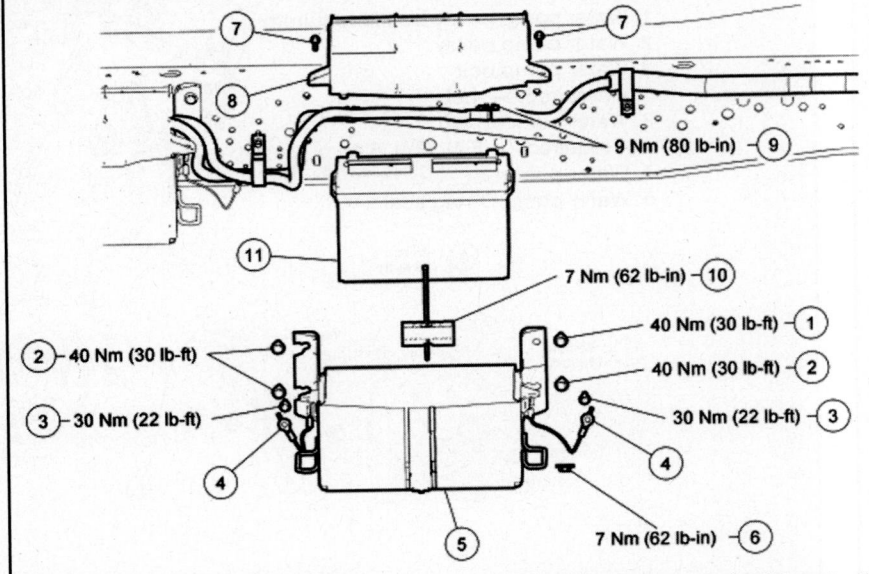

1. Battery tray bolt (upper RH bolt)
2. Battery tray bolts (3 required)
3. Battery tray safety strap bolts (2 required)
4. Battery tray safety strap eyelets (2 required)
5. Battery tray
6. Battery tray cover nut (2 required)
7. Battery tray cover bolts (2 required)
8. Battery tray cover
9. Battery terminal nuts (2 required)
10. Battery hold-down clamp and bolt
11. Battery

N0093929

Fig. 50 Exploded view of the battery assembly—Frame mounted

vehicle. Follow the procedures up to and including disconnection of the frame-mounted battery cables.

1. Disable the vehicle electrical supply. For additional information, refer to Battery Disconnect—Dual in this section.
2. Remove the upper RH battery tray bolt.
3. Loosen the 3 remaining battery tray bolts.
4. Slide the battery tray up and to the right to disengage the battery tray from the 3 battery tray bolts and lower it onto a suitable lifting device.
5. Remove the 2 nuts and bolts and position the battery tray cover aside.
6. Loosen the nuts and disconnect the battery terminals.
7. Remove the 2 battery tray safety strap bolts and position the safety straps aside.
8. Remove the battery tray from the vehicle and place on the work bench.
9. Remove the battery hold-down clamp and bolt.
10. Remove the battery.
11. To install, reverse the removal procedure.

BATTERY DISCONNECT & RECONNECT

Single

➡If equipped with the CD6 audio unit, precautions must be taken when the battery has been disconnected. When reconnecting the battery, make sure no interruption of power occurs for 30 seconds. If power is interrupted during the first 30 seconds, permanent damage to the CD6 audio unit will result.

➡When disconnecting the battery ground cable to interrupt power to the vehicle electrical system, disconnect the battery ground cable only. It is not necessary to disconnect the positive battery cable.

➡When the battery is disconnected and connected, some abnormal drive symptoms may occur while the vehicle relearns its adaptive strategy. The vehicle may need to be driven to relearn its strategy.

1. Disconnect the battery ground cable.
2. Disconnect the positive battery cable.
3. To connect, reverse the disconnect procedure.

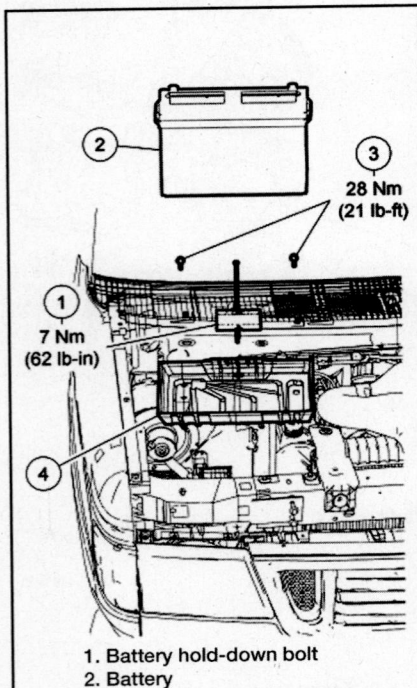

1. Battery hold-down bolt
2. Battery
3. Battery tray bolts (2 required)
4. Battery tray

N0026279

Fig. 49 Exploded view of the battery assembly—Engine bay mounted

中

Dual

➡️If equipped with the CD6 audio unit, precautions must be taken when the battery has been disconnected. When reconnecting the battery, make sure no interruption of power occurs for 30 seconds. If power is interrupted during the first 30 seconds, permanent damage to the CD6 audio unit will result.

➡️When the battery is disconnected and connected, some abnormal drive symptoms may occur while the vehicle relearns its adaptive strategy. The vehicle may need to be driven to relearn its strategy.

➡️When disconnecting the battery ground cable to interrupt power to the vehicle electrical system, disconnect the battery ground cable only. It is not necessary to disconnect the positive battery cable.

1. Loosen the nut and disconnect the battery ground cable.

➡️Make sure the frame-mounted battery negative cable does not contact the frame or damage to the cable may occur. If necessary, wrap the terminal with electrical tape.

2. Remove the bolt and disconnect the

auxiliary frame-mounted battery ground cable from the frame. To connect, tighten to 18 ft. lbs. (25 Nm).

➡️Make sure the frame-mounted battery negative cable does not contact the frame. If necessary, wrap the terminal with electrical tape.

3. Remove the bolt and disconnect the battery ground cable at the frame. To connect, tighten to 30 ft. lbs. (40 Nm).
4. Disconnect the positive battery cables.
5. To connect, reverse the disconnect procedure.

ENGINE ELECTRICAL

ALTERNATOR

REMOVAL & INSTALLATION

Diesel Engines

Dual

See Figure 51.

1. Disconnect the dual batteries.
2. Remove the bolt and position the

Manifold Absolute Pressure (MAP) sensor aside.
3. Remove the bolt and position the ground strap aside.
4. Remove the 2 bolts and position the power steering fluid reservoir bracket aside.
5. Remove the 3 bolts and position the cowl wiring harness aside.
6. Remove the 3 bracket screws from

CHARGING SYSTEM

the Charge Air Cooler (CAC) tube bracket.
7. Remove the 2 stud nuts and the CAC tube bracket. To install, tighten to 18 ft. lbs. (25 Nm).
8. Loosen the 2 clamps and remove the CAC tube.
9. Rotate the secondary accessory drive belt tensioner clockwise and position the accessory drive belt aside.
10. Disconnect the generator electrical connector.
11. Position the generator B+ protective cover aside, remove the B+ terminal nut and position the B+ terminal aside.
12. Remove the 3 bolts and the generator. To install, tighten to 35 ft. lbs. (47 Nm).
13. To install, reverse the removal procedure.

Single

See Figure 52.

1. Disconnect the dual batteries.
2. Remove the bolt and position the Manifold Absolute Pressure (MAP) sensor aside.
3. Remove the bolt and position the ground strap aside.
4. Remove the 2 bolts and position the power steering fluid reservoir bracket aside.
5. Remove the 3 bolts and position the cowl wiring harness aside.
6. Remove the 3 bracket screws from the Charge Air Cooler (CAC) tube bracket.
7. Remove the 2 stud nuts and the CAC tube bracket. To install, tighten to 18 ft. lbs. (25 Nm).

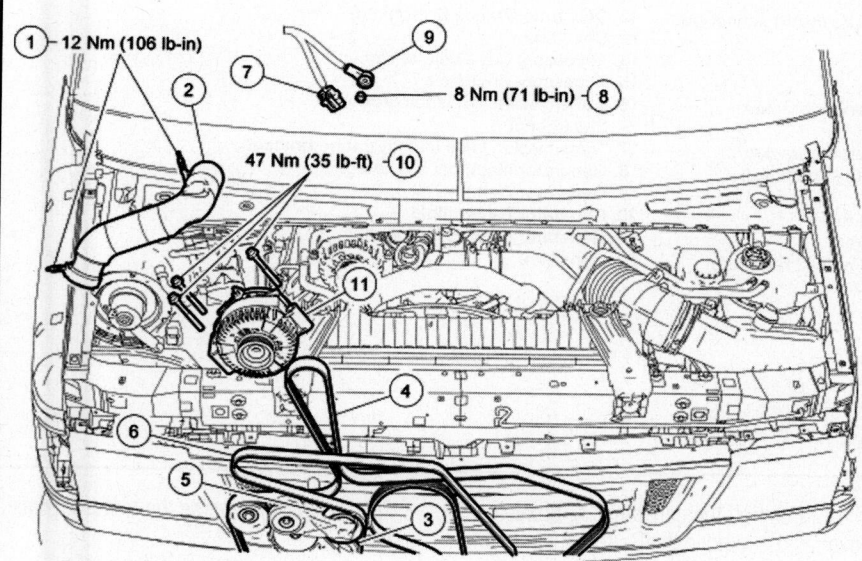

1. Charge Air Cooler (CAC) tube clamps (2 required)
2. CAC tube
3. Accessory drive belt tensioner (primary)
4. Accessory drive belt (primary)
5. Accessory drive belt tensioner (secondary)
6. Accessory drive belt (secondary)
7. Generator electrical connector
8. Generator B+ terminal nut
9. Generator B+ terminal
10. Generator bolts (3 required)
11. Generator

N0089861

Fig. 51 Exploded view of the dual alternator components

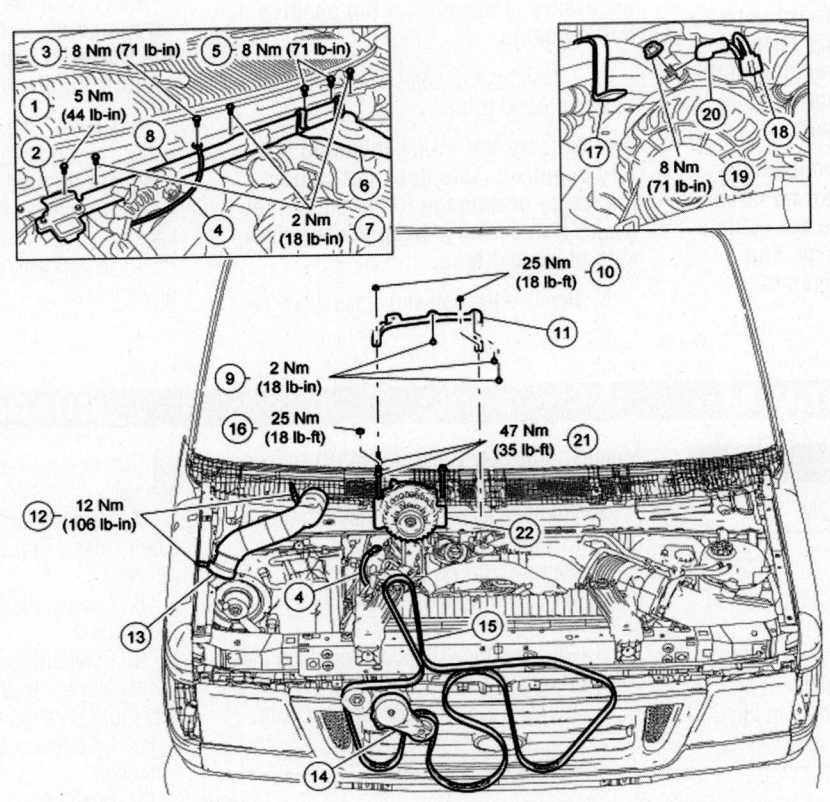

1. Manifold Absolute Pressure (MAP) sensor bolt
2. MAP sensor
3. Ground strap bolt
4. Ground strap
5. Power steering fluid reservoir bracket bolts (2 required)
6. Power steering fluid reservoir bracket
7. Cowl wiring harness bolts (3 required)
8. Cowl wiring harness
9. Charge Air Cooler (CAC) tube bracket screws (3 required)
10. CAC tube bracket stud nuts (2 required)
11. CAC tube bracket
12. CAC tube clamps (2 required)
13. CAC tube
14. Accessory drive belt tensioner
15. Accessory drive belt
16. Transmission level indicator tube bracket nut
17. Transmission level indicator tube bracket
18. Generator electrical connector
19. Generator B+ terminal nut
20. Generator B+ terminal
21. Generator bolts (3 required)
22. Generator

N0089862

Fig. 52 Exploded view of the single primary alternator

8. Loosen the 2 clamps and remove the CAC tube.

9. Rotate the accessory drive belt tensioner clockwise and position the accessory drive belt aside.

10. Remove the nut from the generator stud bolt and position the transmission level indicator tube bracket aside. To install, tighten to 18 ft. lbs. (25 Nm).

11. Disconnect the generator electrical connector.

12. Position the generator B+ protective cover aside, remove the B+ terminal nut and position the B+ terminal aside.

13. Remove the 3 bolts, the ground strap and the generator.

14. If necessary, remove the protective cap, the nut and the radial adapter.

➡**Make sure to install the engine-to-body ground strap under the front generator stud bolt.**

15. To install, reverse the removal procedure.

Gasoline Engines

See Figure 53.

1. Disconnect the battery.

2. 5.4L and 6.8L; Loosen the band clamp and remove the air filter element, tray and inlet snorkel.

3. 4.6L; Remove the air cleaner outlet pipe.

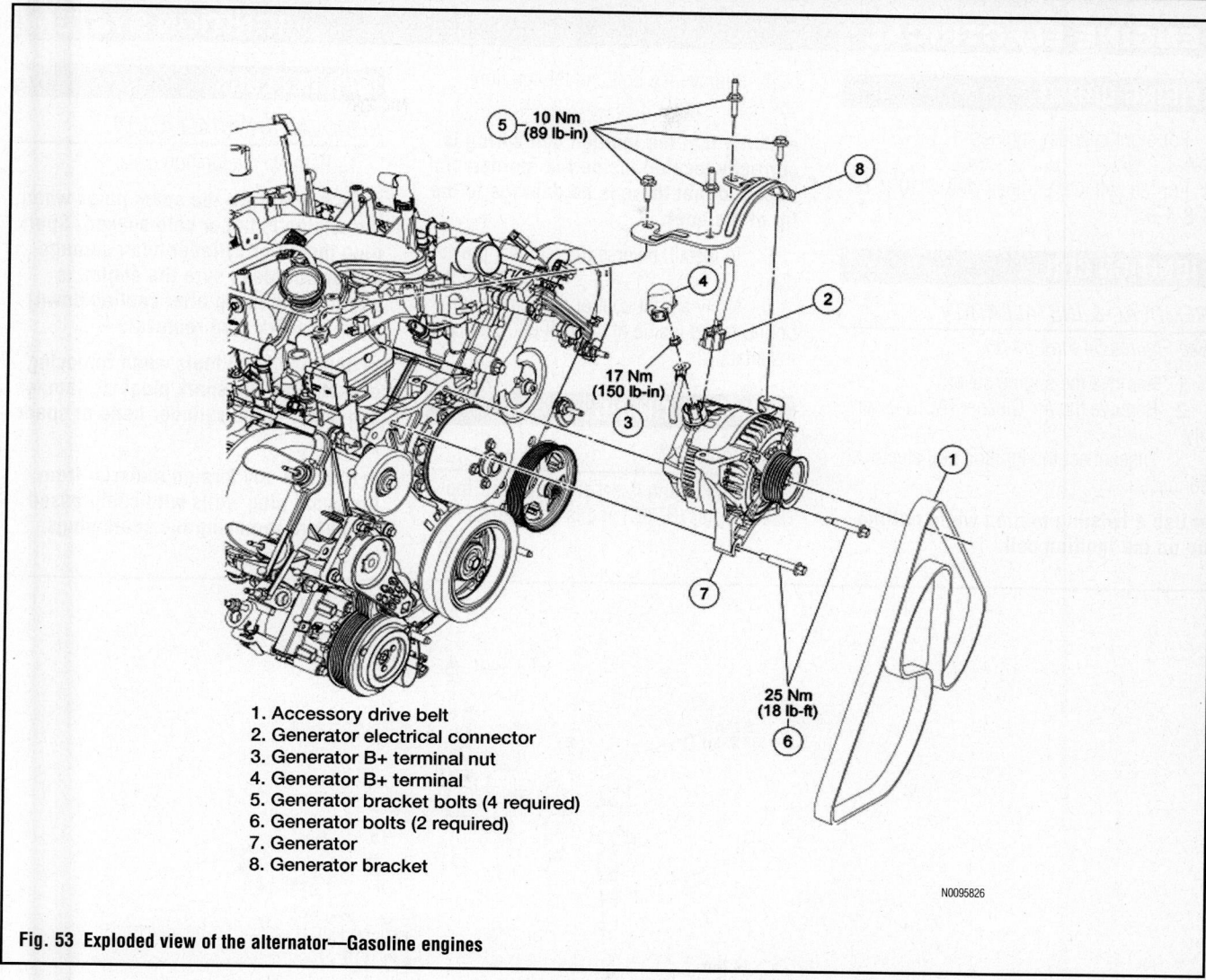

1. Accessory drive belt
2. Generator electrical connector
3. Generator B+ terminal nut
4. Generator B+ terminal
5. Generator bracket bolts (4 required)
6. Generator bolts (2 required)
7. Generator
8. Generator bracket

N0095826

Fig. 53 Exploded view of the alternator—Gasoline engines

4. Rotate the accessory drive belt tensioner clockwise (vehicles with A/C) or counterclockwise (vehicles without A/C) and position the accessory drive belt aside.

5. Disconnect the generator electrical connectors.

6. Position the generator B+ protective cover aside, remove the B+ terminal nut and position the B+ terminal aside.

7. Remove the 4 bolts and the generator bracket.

8. Remove the 2 bolts and the generator.

9. To install, reverse the removal procedure.

FIRING ORDER

For eight cylinder engines: 1-3-7-2-6-5-4-8.

For ten cylinder engines: 1-6-5-10-2-7-3-8-4-9.

IGNITION COIL

REMOVAL & INSTALLATION

See Figures 54 through 56.

1. Remove the engine cover.
2. Remove the Air Cleaner (ACL) assembly.
3. Disconnect the ignition coil electrical connector.

➡**Use a twisting motion while pulling up on the ignition coil.**

4. Remove the bolt and the ignition coil.

➡**Verify that the ignition coil spring is correctly located inside the ignition coil boot and that there is no damage to the tip of the boot.**

5. To install, reverse the removal procedure.
6. Apply a light coat of dielectric compound to the inside of the coil boots prior to installation.

IGNITION TIMING

ADJUSTMENT

Ignition timing is set at 10° Before Top Dead Center (BTDC) and is not adjustable.

SPARK PLUGS

REMOVAL & INSTALLATION

1. Remove the ignition coil.

➡**Do not remove the spark plugs when the engine is hot or cold soaked. Spark plug thread or cylinder head damage can occur. Make sure the engine is warm (hand touch after cooling down) prior to spark plug removal.**

➡**Only use hand tools when removing or installing the spark plugs or damage can occur to the cylinder head or spark plug.**

➡**Remove any foreign material from the spark plug wells with compressed air before removing the spark plugs.**

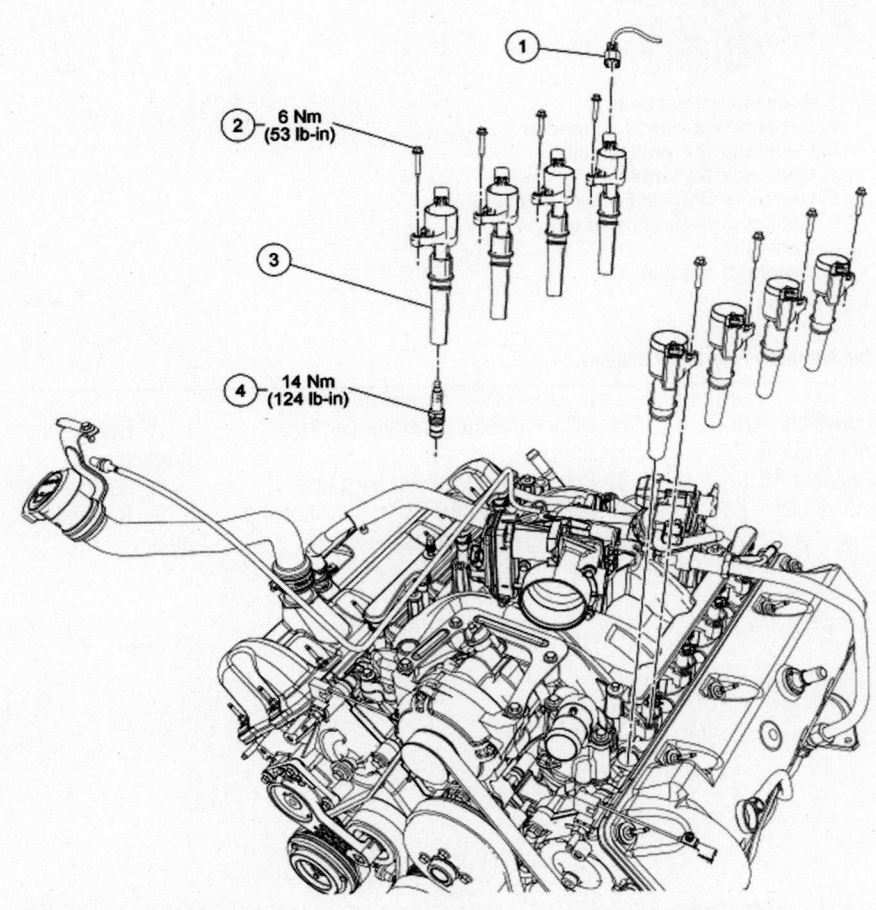

1. Ignition coil electrical connector (8 required)
2. Ignition coil retaining bolt (8 required)
3. Ignition coil (8 required)
4. Spark plug (8 required)

N0089253

Fig. 54 Exploded view of the engine ignition components—4.6L Engines

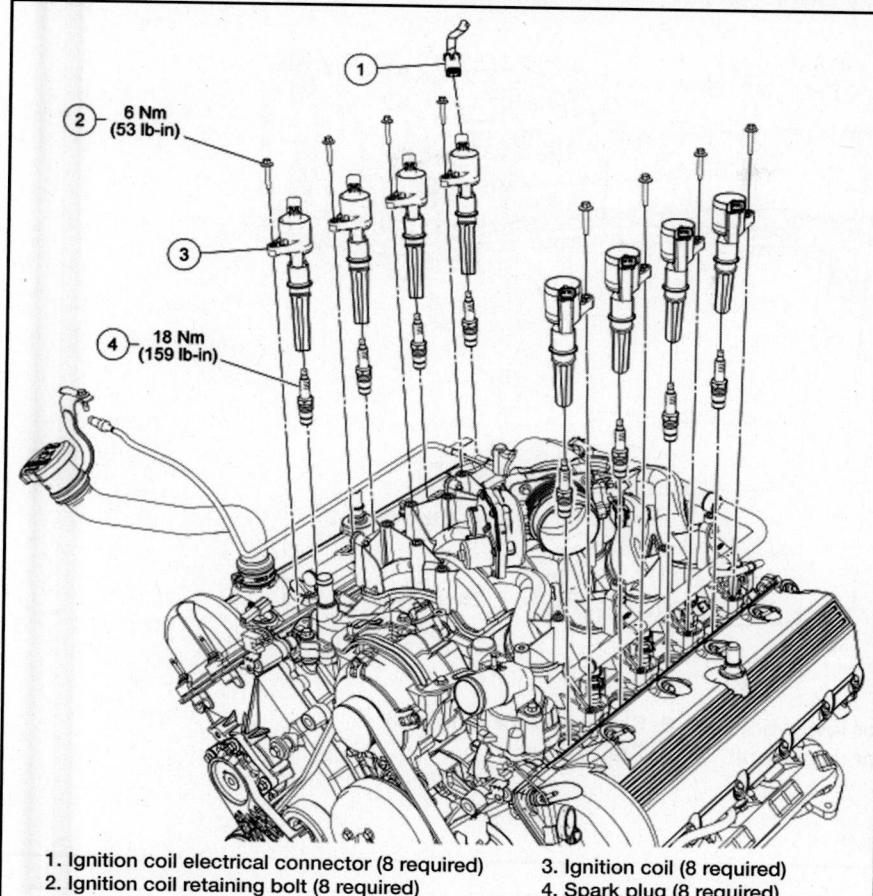

1. Ignition coil electrical connector (8 required)
2. Ignition coil retaining bolt (8 required)
3. Ignition coil (8 required)
4. Spark plug (8 required)

N0109748

Fig. 55 Exploded view of the engine ignition components—5.4L Engines

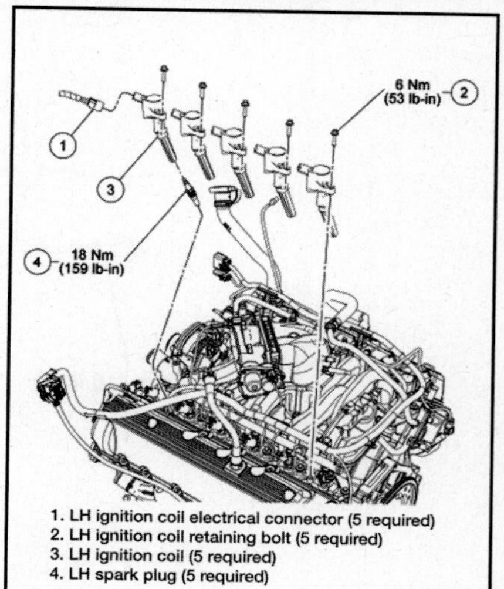

1. LH ignition coil electrical connector (5 required)
2. LH ignition coil retaining bolt (5 required)
3. LH ignition coil (5 required)
4. LH spark plug (5 required)

N0109084

Fig. 56 Exploded view of the engine ignition components—6.8L Engines

➡If an original spark plug is used, make sure it is installed in the same cylinder from which it was taken. New spark plugs can be used in any cylinder.

2. Remove the spark plugs. To install, tighten to 15 ft. lbs. (18 Nm).
3. Inspect the spark plugs.
4. To install, reverse the removal procedure.
5. Adjust the plug gap as necessary.

ENGINE ELECTRICAL

STARTER

REMOVAL & INSTALLATION

Diesel Engines

See Figure 57.

1. With the vehicle in NEUTRAL, position it on a hoist.

➡The 6.0L diesel uses 2 frame mount batteries. The ground path is through the frame.

2. Disconnect the battery ground cable from the frame.
3. Remove the nut and position the cable bracket aside.
4. Remove the starter solenoid protective cap.
5. Disconnect the starter motor electrical connections.
6. Remove the 2 bolts, the stud bolt and the starter.

To install:

7. Position the starter motor and install the 2 bolts and the stud bolt in 3 stages.
   a. Stage 1: Install the 2 bolts and the stud bolt finger tight.
   b. Stage 2: Tighten the upper bolt to 18 ft. lbs. (25 Nm).
   c. Stage 3: Tighten the lower bolt and stud bolt to 18 ft. lbs. (25 Nm).
8. Connect the starter motor electrical connection.
9. Connect the starter motor electrical connection.
   Tighten to 6 Nm (53 lb-in).
10. Install the starter solenoid protective cap.
11. Position the cable bracket and install the nut. Tighten to 18 ft. lbs. (25 Nm).

➡The 6.0L diesel uses 2 frame mount batteries. The ground path is through the frame.

12. Connect the battery ground cable.

STARTING SYSTEM

Gasoline Engines

See Figure 58.

1. With the vehicle in NEUTRAL, position it on a hoist.
2. Disconnect the battery ground cable.

➡The starter motor terminal cover is attached to the wiring harness.

3. Detach the starter motor solenoid terminal cover.
4. Remove the starter solenoid S-terminal nut and disconnect the S-terminal eyelet.
5. Remove the starter solenoid B-terminal nut and disconnect the B-terminal eyelet.
6. Remove the starter motor ground cable nut and disconnect the ground cable eyelet.
7. Remove the bolts, the stud bolt and the starter motor. To install, tighten the upper bolt before tightening the lower fasteners.
8. To install, reverse the removal procedure.

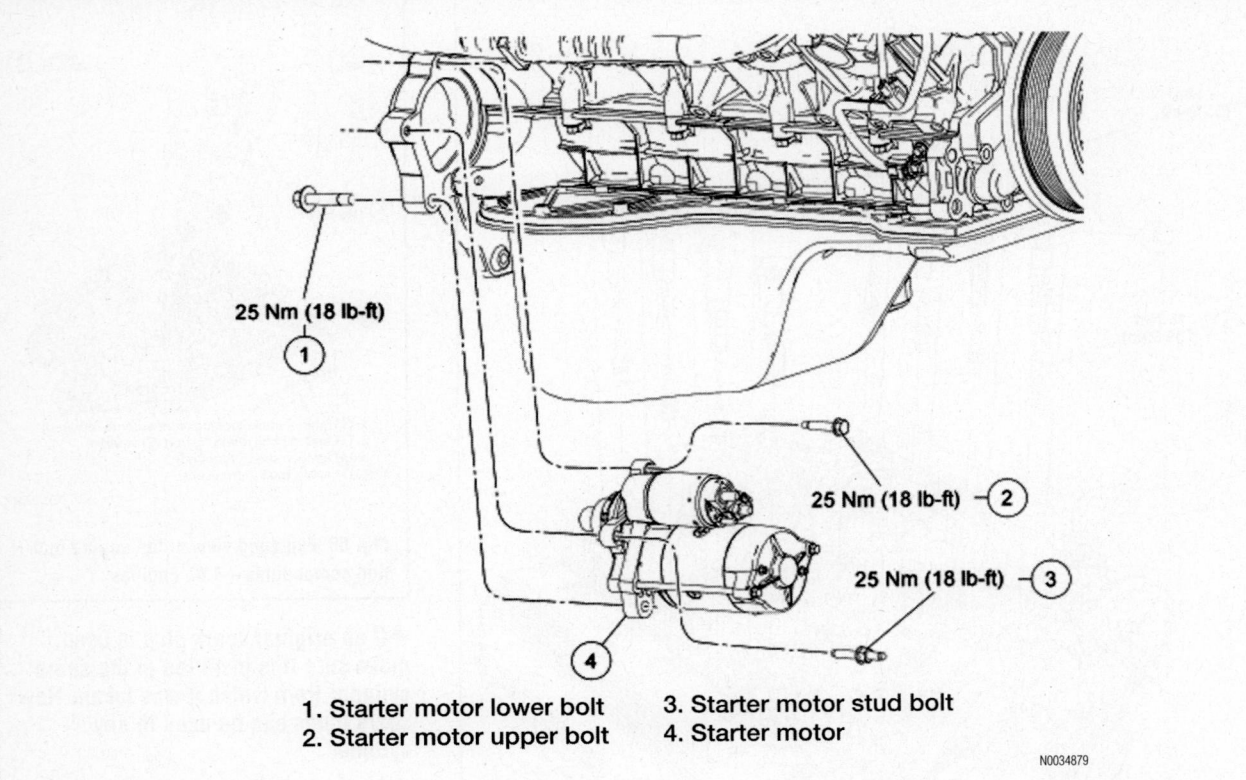

25 Nm (18 lb-ft)
1
25 Nm (18 lb-ft)
2
25 Nm (18 lb-ft)
3
4
1. Starter motor lower bolt
2. Starter motor upper bolt
3. Starter motor stud bolt
4. Starter motor
N0034879

Fig. 57 Exploded view of the starter assembly—Diesel

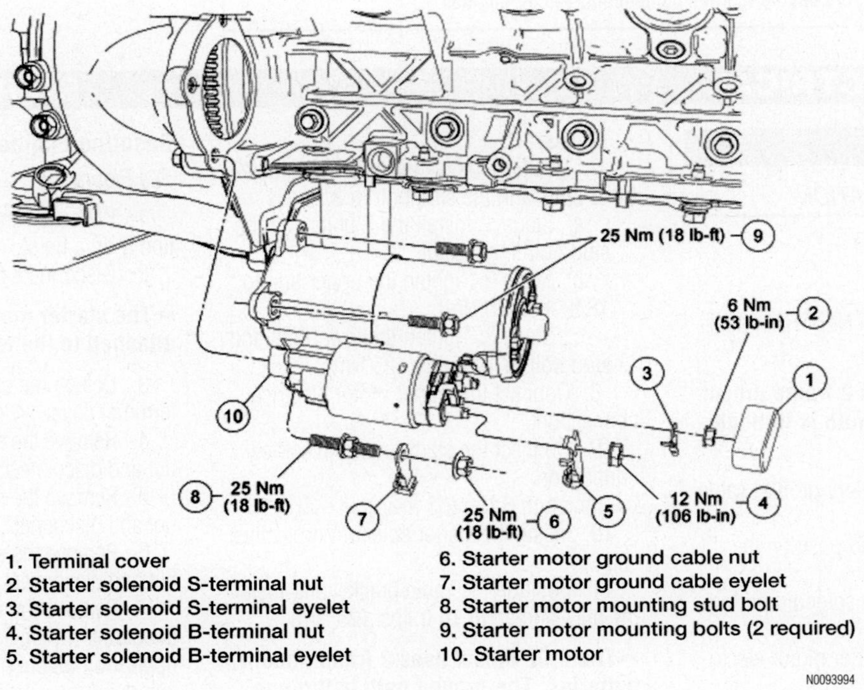

25 Nm (18 lb-ft)
9
6 Nm
(53 lb-in)
2
3
1
10
25 Nm
(18 lb-ft)
8
7
25 Nm
(18 lb-ft)
6
5
12 Nm
(106 lb-in)
4
1. Terminal cover
2. Starter solenoid S-terminal nut
3. Starter solenoid S-terminal eyelet
4. Starter solenoid B-terminal nut
5. Starter solenoid B-terminal eyelet
6. Starter motor ground cable nut
7. Starter motor ground cable eyelet
8. Starter motor mounting stud bolt
9. Starter motor mounting bolts (2 required)
10. Starter motor
N0093994

Fig. 58 Exploded view of the starter assembly—Gasoline engines

ENGINE MECHANICAL

→Disconnecting the negative battery cable may interfere with the functions of the on board computer systems and may require the computer to undergo a relearning process, once the negative battery cable is reconnected.

ACCESSORY DRIVE BELTS

ACCESSORY BELT ROUTING

See Figures 59 through 62.

INSPECTION

Inspect belts for glazing, cracking, tearing, splitting and shredding.

ADJUSTMENT

Tension is within specification if the tensioner is within the indicator markings

REMOVAL & INSTALLATION

See Figures 63 and 64.

1. Rotate the tensioner clockwise and remove the accessory drive belt.

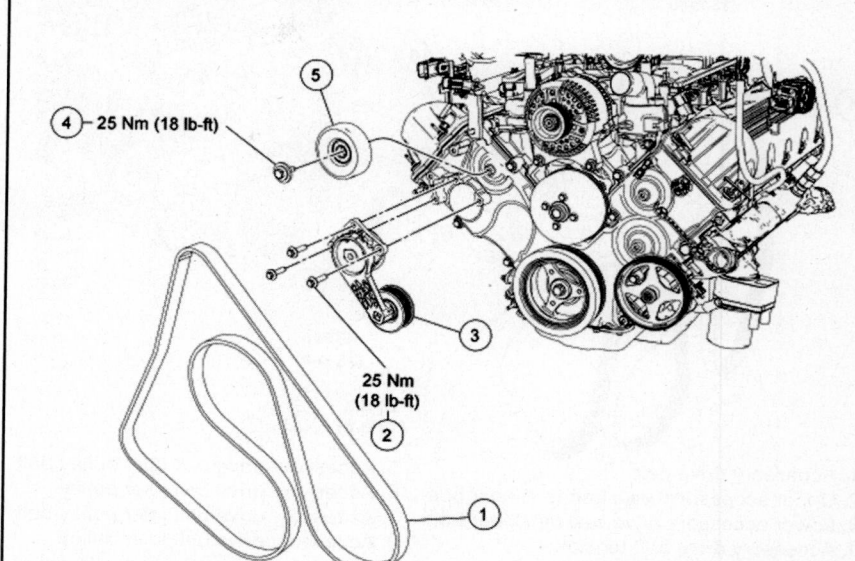

1. Accessory drive belt
2. Accessory drive belt tensioner bolt (3 required)
3. Accessory drive belt tensioner
4. Accessory drive belt idler pulley bolt
5. Accessory drive belt idler pulley

N0057662

Fig. 60 Accessory belt routing— 4.6L without A/C shown, 5.4L and 6.8L similar

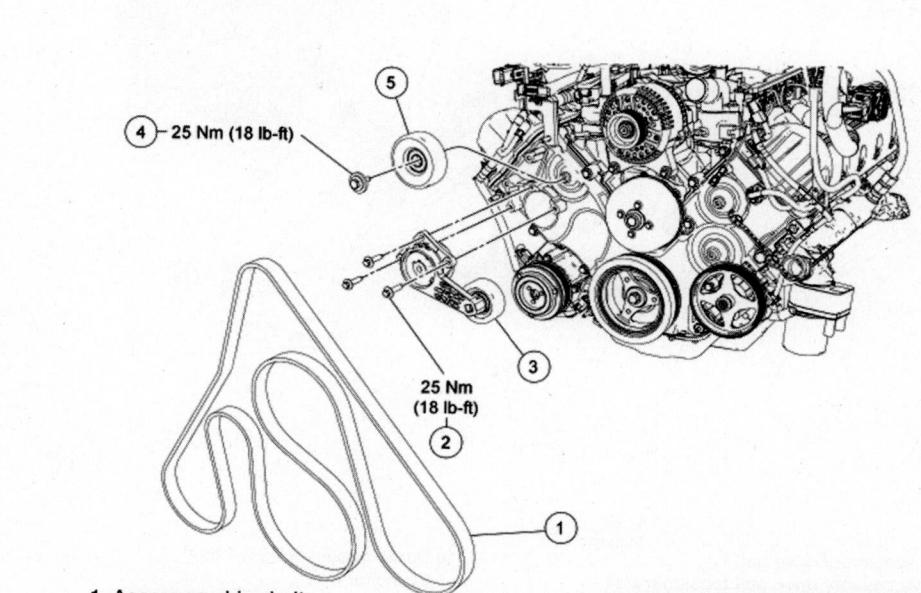

1. Accessory drive belt
2. Accessory drive belt tensioner bolt (3 required)
3. Accessory drive belt tensioner
4. Accessory drive belt idler pulley bolt
5. Accessory drive belt idler pulley

N0057661

Fig. 59 Accessory belt routing— 4.6L with A/C shown, 5.4L and 6.8L similar

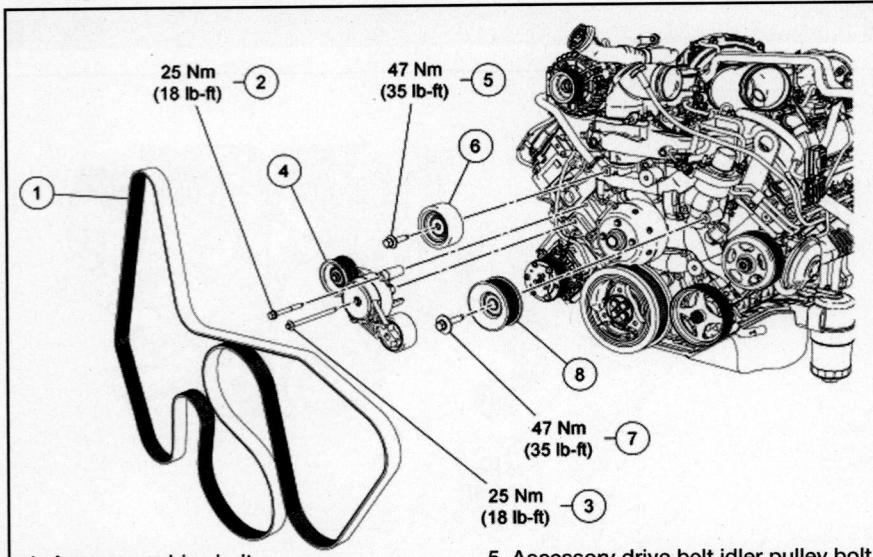

1. Accessory drive belt
2. Upper accessory drive belt tensioner bolt
3. Lower accessory drive belt tensioner bolt
4. Accessory drive belt tensioner
5. Accessory drive belt idler pulley bolt
6. Accessory drive belt idler pulley
7. Accessory drive belt idler pulley bolt
8. Accessory drive belt idler pulley

N0024897

Fig. 61 Accessory belt routing—6.0L single belt

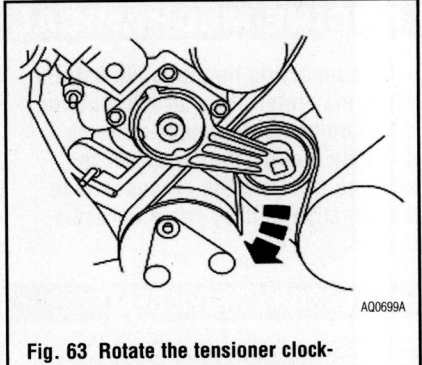

AQ0699A

Fig. 63 Rotate the tensioner clockwise—4.6L, 5.4L and 6.8L engines

AIR CLEANER

REMOVAL & INSTALLATION

4.6L, 5.4L and 6.8L Engines

See Figures 65 and 66.

1. Detach the Air Cleaner (ACL) inlet from the plastic seal on the radiator support.

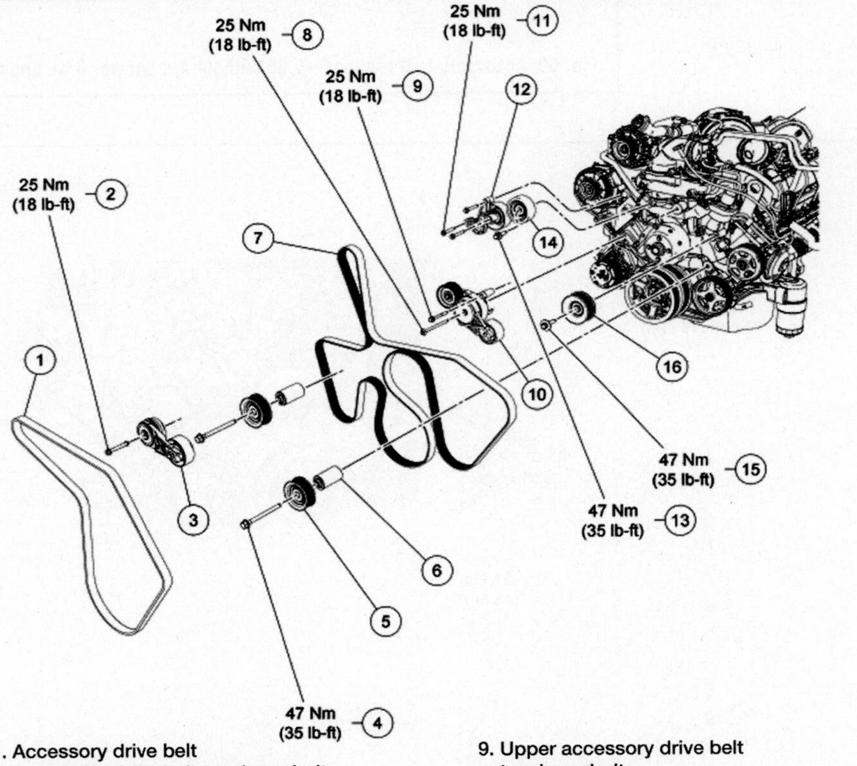

1. Accessory drive belt
2. Accessory drive belt tensioner bolt
3. Accessory drive belt tensioner
4. Accessory drive belt idler pulley bolt (2 required)
5. Accessory drive belt idler pulley (2 required)
6. Accessory drive belt idler pulley spacer (2 required)
7. Accessory drive belt
8. Lower accessory drive belt tensioner bolt
9. Upper accessory drive belt tensioner bolt
10. Accessory drive belt tensioner
11. Accessory drive belt idler pulley bracket bolt (3 required)
12. Accessory drive belt idler pulley
13. Accessory drive belt idler pulley bolt
14. Accessory drive belt idler pulley
15. Accessory drive belt idler pulley bolt
16. Accessory drive belt idler pulley

Fig. 62 Accessory belt routing—6.0L dual belt

N0024898

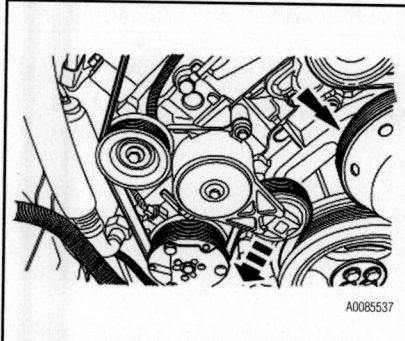

Fig. 64 Rotate the tensioner clockwise—
6.0L engines

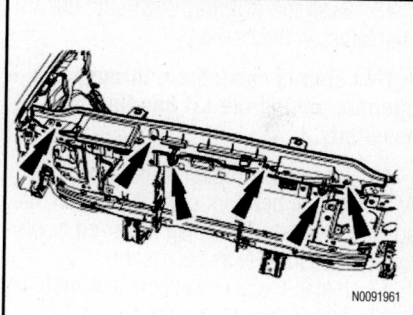

Fig. 66 Remove the 6 pushpins and the
upper air deflector

2. Loosen the ACL cover-to- ACL outlet pipe clamp. Remove the ACL outlet pipe from the ACL cover.

3. Remove the 6 pushpins and the upper air deflector.

4. Remove the 4 ACL cover bolts at the cowl and the radiator support.

5. Reposition the ACL and disconnect the Mass Air Flow (MAF) sensor electrical connector. Remove the ACL .

➡**Install the ACL bolts at the cowl first to aid in alignment of the ACL.**

6. To install, reverse the removal procedure.

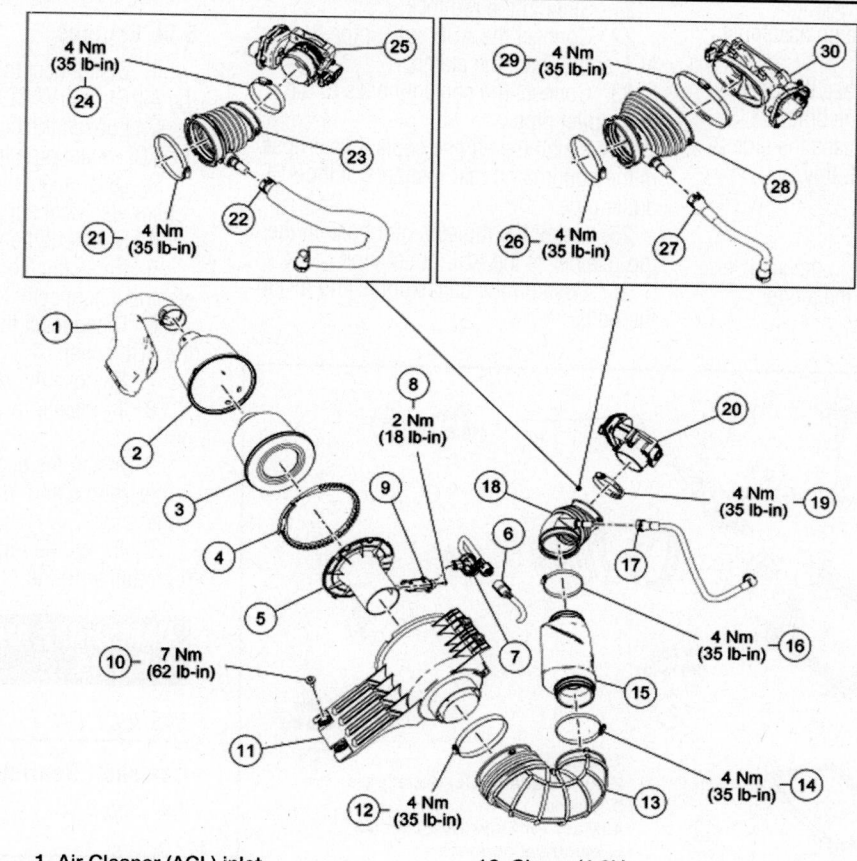

1. Air Cleaner (ACL) inlet
2. ACL tray
3. ACL element
4. ACL clamp
5. Mass Air Flow (MAF) sensor body
6. Engine harness-to- MAF sensor pigtail electrical connector
7. MAF sensor pigtail electrical connector
8. MAF sensor screw (2 required)
9. MAF sensor
10. ACL cover bolt (4 required)
11. ACL cover
12. Clamp
13. ACL outlet pipe
14. Clamp
15. Resonator
16. Clamp (4.6L)
17. Vapor tube quick connect fitting (4.6L)
18. Throttle Body (TB) inlet pipe (4.6L)
19. Clamp (4.6L)
20. TB (4.6L)
21. Clamp (5.4L)
22. Vapor tube quick connect fitting (5.4L)
23. TB inlet pipe (5.4L)
24. Clamp (5.4L)
25. TB (5.4L)
26. Clamp (6.8L)
27. Vapor tube quick connect fitting (6.8L)
28. TB inlet pipe (6.8L)
29. Clamp (6.8L)
30. TB (6.8L)

Fig. 65 Exploded view of the air cleaner assembly—4.6L, 5.4L and 6.8L Engines

6.0L Engines

See Figure 67.

1. Remove the bolts and position the degas bottle aside.

2. Disconnect the coolant hoses from the Air Cleaner (ACL) outlet pipe.

3. Loosen the clamp and disconnect the ACL outlet pipe from the ACL .

4. Disconnect the Mass Air Flow (MAF) sensor electrical connector.

5. Slide out the red lock.

6. Press the tab and disconnect the electrical connector.

7. Disconnect the 3 latches and remove the ACL cover.

8. Remove the ACL element.

9. Remove the LH headlamp assembly.

10. Remove the ACL tray.

11. Lift straight up to release the bottom legs from the 2 isolators in the bracket.

12. Move to the left to release the side 2 isolators and remove the ACL tray.

To install:

13. Install the ACL tray.

14. Position the ACL tray in the vehicle and move it to the right into the fender opening and 2 side isolators.

15. Push the ACL tray down into the 2 isolators in the bracket.

➡ **This step is carried out through the opening behind the LH headlamp assembly.**

16. Inspect the rubber seal flap on the ACL tray inlet bezel for correct position, flat against the body. If the flap is kinked or distorted, reposition it as necessary.

17. Install the LH headlamp assembly.

18. Install the ACL element.

19. Install the ACL cover and connect the 3 latches.

20. Connect the MAF sensor electrical connector.

21. Slide in the red lock.

22. Connect the ACL outlet pipe to the ACL and tighten the clamp.

23. Connect the coolant hoses to the ACL outlet pipe.

24. Install the engine coolant vent hose in the bottom and rear retainers of the ACL outlet pipe.

25. Install the radiator vent hose in the top retainer of the ACL outlet pipe.

26. Position the degas bottle and install the bolts.

FILTER/ELEMENT REPLACEMENT

4.6L, 5.4L and 6.8L Engines

1. Detach the Air Cleaner (ACL) inlet tube from the plastic seal on the radiator support, rotate the tube up and remove it.

2. Unlatch the clamp on the ACL assembly and remove the ACL tray.

3. Remove the ACL element.

4. To install, reverse the removal procedure.

5. Align the tab on the ACL cover with the slot in the tray assembly.

6. Make sure the band clamp is over both the tray and the cover and is latched closed.

6.0L Engines

1. Disconnect the coolant hoses from the Air Cleaner (ACL) outlet pipe.

2. Loosen the clamp and disconnect the ACL outlet pipe from the ACL .

3. Disconnect the Mass Air Flow (MAF) sensor electrical connector.

4. Slide out the red lock.

5. Press the tab and disconnect the electrical connector.

6. Disconnect the 3 latches and remove the ACL cover.

7. Remove the ACL element.

8. To install, reverse the removal procedure.

9. Install the engine coolant vent hose in the bottom and rear retainers of the ACL outlet pipe.

10. Install the radiator vent hose in the top retainer of the ACL outlet pipe.

CAMSHAFT AND VALVE LIFTERS

INSPECTION

Camshaft Bearing Journal Diameter

See Figure 68.

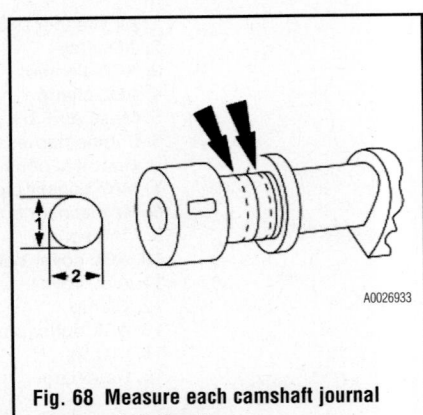

Fig. 68 Measure each camshaft journal diameter in 2 directions.

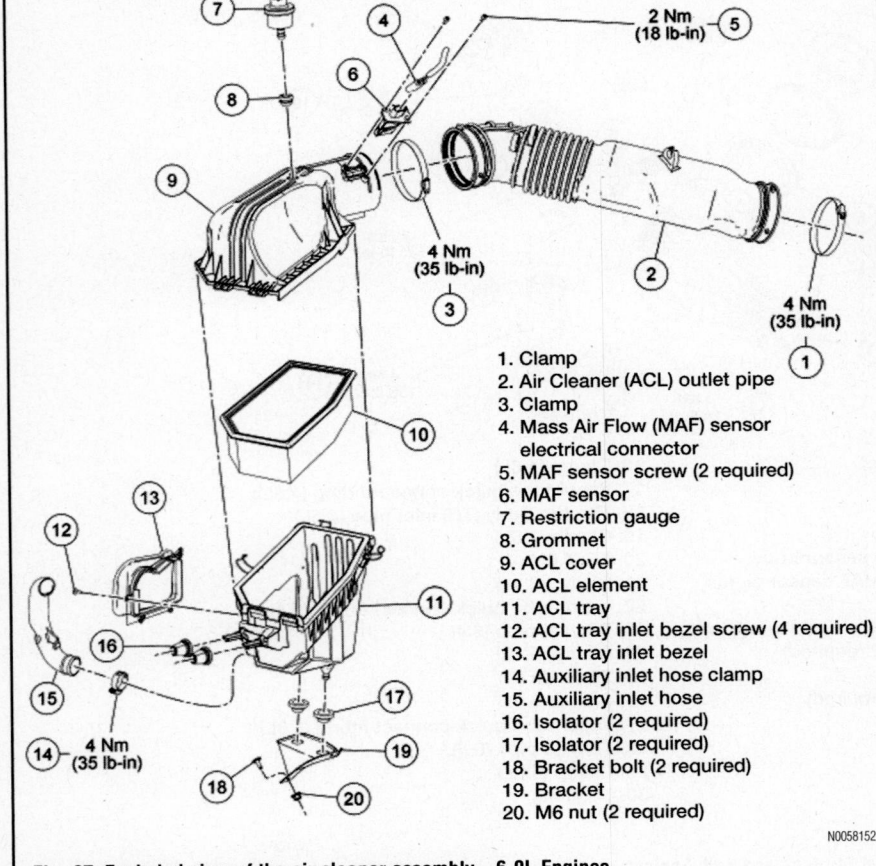

1. Clamp
2. Air Cleaner (ACL) outlet pipe
3. Clamp
4. Mass Air Flow (MAF) sensor electrical connector
5. MAF sensor screw (2 required)
6. MAF sensor
7. Restriction gauge
8. Grommet
9. ACL cover
10. ACL element
11. ACL tray
12. ACL tray inlet bezel screw (4 required)
13. ACL tray inlet bezel
14. Auxiliary inlet hose clamp
15. Auxiliary inlet hose
16. Isolator (2 required)
17. Isolator (2 required)
18. Bracket bolt (2 required)
19. Bracket
20. M6 nut (2 required)

Fig. 67 Exploded view of the air cleaner assembly—6.0L Engines

➡Refer to the spec charts for specifications.

Camshaft End Play

See Figure 69.

➡Refer to the spec charts for specifications.

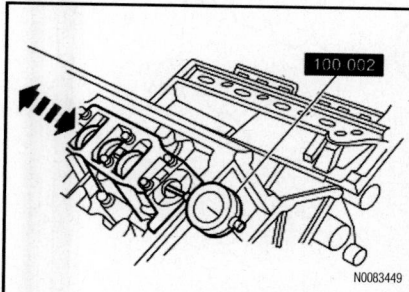

Fig. 69 Using the Dial Indicator Gauge with Holding Fixture, measure the camshaft end play

1. Using the Dial Indicator Gauge with Holding Fixture, measure the camshaft end play.
2. Position the camshaft to the rear of the cylinder head.
3. Zero the Dial Indicator Gauge.
4. Move the camshaft to the front of the cylinder head. Note and record the camshaft end play.
5. If camshaft end play exceeds specifications, install a new camshaft and recheck end play.
6. If camshaft end play exceeds specification after camshaft installation, install a new cylinder head.

Camshaft Journal To Bearing Clearance

See Figure 70.

➡Refer to the spec charts for specifications.

Fig. 70 Subtract the camshaft journal diameter from the camshaft bearing diameter.

➡The camshaft journals must meet specifications before checking camshaft journal clearance.

1. Measure each camshaft bearing in 2 directions.
2. Subtract the camshaft journal diameter from the camshaft bearing diameter.

Camshaft Lobe Lift

See Figure 71.

➡Refer to the spec charts for specifications.

1. Use the Dial Indicator Gauge with Holding Fixture to measure camshaft intake/exhaust lobe lift.
2. Rotate the camshaft and subtract the lowest Dial Indicator Gauge reading from the highest Dial Indicator Gauge reading to figure the camshaft lobe lift.

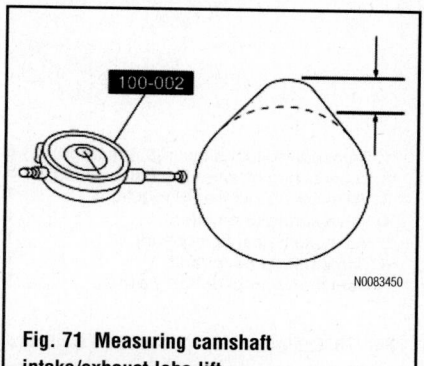

Fig. 71 Measuring camshaft intake/exhaust lobe lift

Camshaft Runout

See Figure 72.

➡Refer to the spec charts for specifications.

➡Camshaft journals must be within specifications before checking runout.

1. Using the Dial Indicator Gauge with Holding Fixture, measure the camshaft runout.

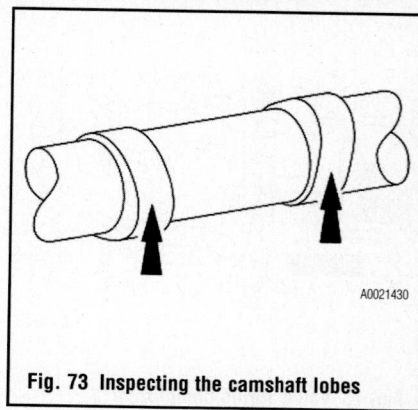

Fig. 73 Inspecting the camshaft lobes

2. Rotate the camshaft and subtract the lowest Dial Indicator Gauge reading from the highest Dial Indicator Gauge reading.

Camshaft Surface Inspection

See Figure 73.

Inspect the camshaft lobes for pitting or damage in the contact area. Minor pitting is acceptable outside the contact area.

ROLLER FOLLOWERS

See Figures 74 and 75.

1. If servicing the cylinder valvetrain components, remove the valve cover. For additional information, refer to Valve Cover in this section.
2. Position the piston of the cylinder being repaired at the bottom of the stroke.
3. Install the Valve Spring Compressor Spacer between the valve spring coils to protect the valve stem seal from damage.

➡The camshaft roller followers must be installed in their original locations. Record the camshaft roller follower locations. Failure to follow these instructions may result in engine damage.

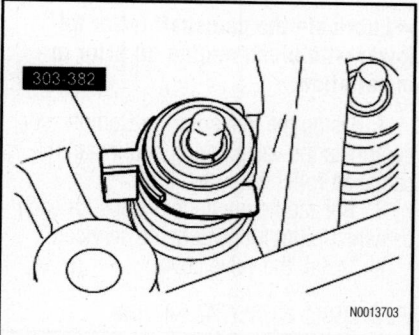

Fig. 74 Install the Valve Spring Compressor Spacer

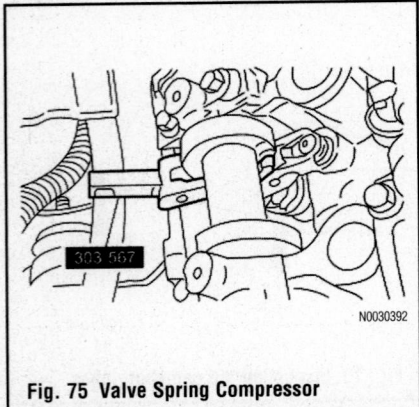

Fig. 75 Valve Spring Compressor

➡ Do not allow the valve keepers to fall off the valve or the valve may drop into the cylinder. If a valve drops into the cylinder, the cylinder head must be removed.

➡ It may be necessary to push the valve down while compressing the spring.

4. Using the Valve Spring Compressor, compress the valve spring and remove the camshaft roller follower.

5. Repeat the previous 3 steps for each of the roller followers being serviced.

To install:

6. Install the Valve Spring Compressor Spacer between the valve spring coils to protect the valve stem seal from damage.

➡ The camshaft roller followers must be installed in their original locations. Failure to follow these instructions may result in engine damage.

➡ Do not allow the valve keepers to fall off the valve or the valve may drop into the cylinder. If a valve drops into the cylinder, the cylinder head must be removed.

➡ It may be necessary to push the valve down while compressing the spring.

➡ Lubricate the camshaft roller follower with clean engine oil prior to installation.

7. Using the Valve Spring Compressor, compress the valve spring and install the camshaft roller follower.

8. Repeat the previous 3 steps for each camshaft roller follower being serviced.

9. Install the valve cover.

REMOVAL & INSTALLATION

4.6L Engines

See Figures 76 and 77.

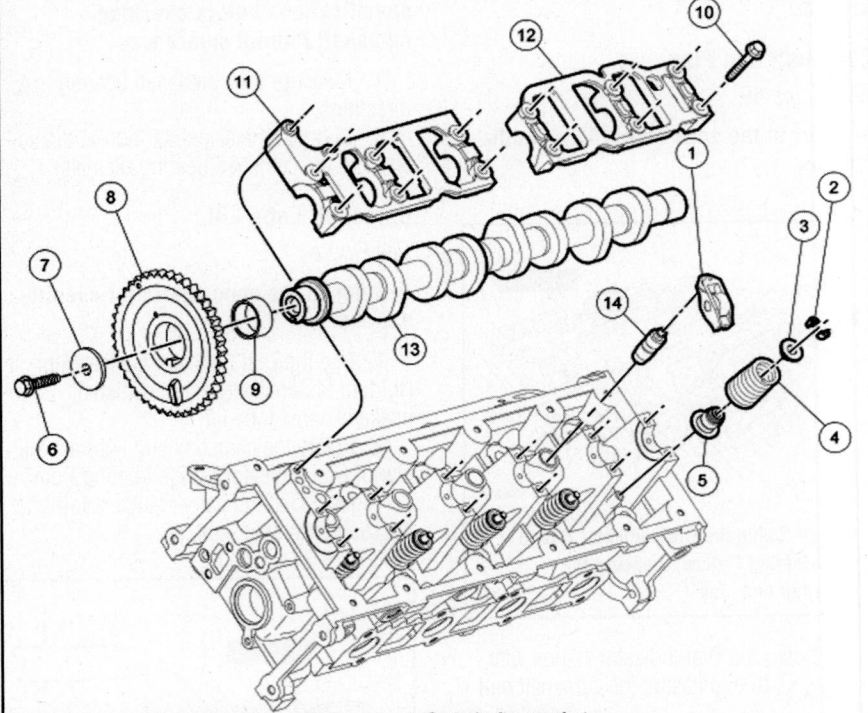

1. Camshaft roller follower (8 required)
2. Valve spring retainer key (16 required)
3. Valve spring retainer (8 required)
4. Valve spring (8 required)
5. Valve stem seal (8 required)
6. Camshaft sprocket bolt
7. Camshaft sprocket bolt washer
8. Camshaft sprocket
9. Camshaft gear spacer
10. Camshaft bearing cap assembly bolt (13 required)
11. Camshaft bearing cap
12. Camshaft bearing cap
13. Camshaft
14. Hydraulic lash adjuster (8 required)

Fig. 76 Exploded view of the valve train assembly—4.6L engines

➡ At no time, when the timing chains are removed and the cylinder heads are installed, may the crankshaft or camshaft be rotated. Severe piston and valve damage will occur.

1. Remove the camshaft roller followers.

2. Loosen the camshaft sprocket bolt.

3. Remove the timing chains. For additional information, refer to Timing Chain in this section.

4. Remove the bolt and the camshaft sprocket.

➡ The camshaft bearing caps must be installed in their original location. Record the camshaft bearing cap location.

5. Remove the 13 bolts, the 2 bearing caps and the camshaft.

6. Clean and inspect the camshaft bearing caps.

7. One of the bearing caps contains an oil flow restriction groove. Make sure the groove is free of foreign material.

To install:

8. Lubricate the camshaft journals with clean engine oil.

9. Install the camshaft and the 2 camshaft bearing caps in their original locations.

10. Lubricate the camshaft bearing caps with clean engine oil.

11. Position the 2 camshaft bearing caps.

12. Install the 13 bolts loosely.

➡ LH shown, RH similar.

13. Tighten the 13 bolts in the sequence shown. Tighten to 7 ft. lbs. (10 Nm).

14. Position the camshaft sprocket and install the bolt finger-tight.

15. Install the timing chains.

16. Tighten the camshaft sprocket bolt in 2 stages.

   a. Stage 1: Tighten to 30 ft. lbs. (40 Nm).

   b. Stage 2: Tighten an additional 90 degrees.

17. Install the camshaft roller followers.

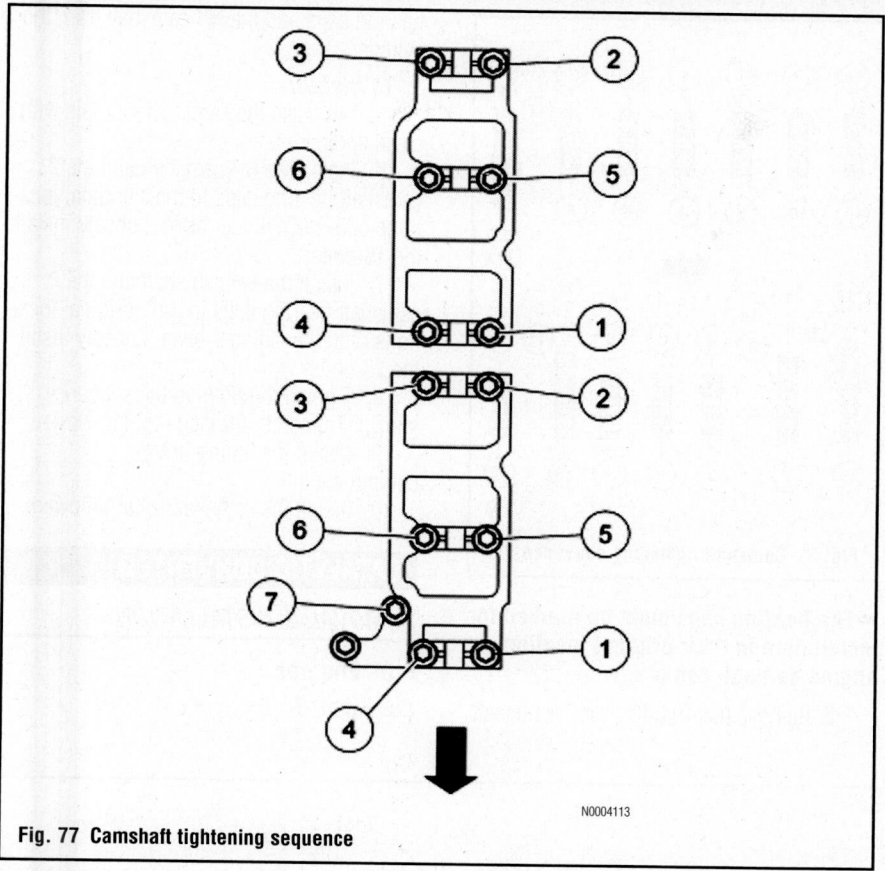

Fig. 77 Camshaft tightening sequence

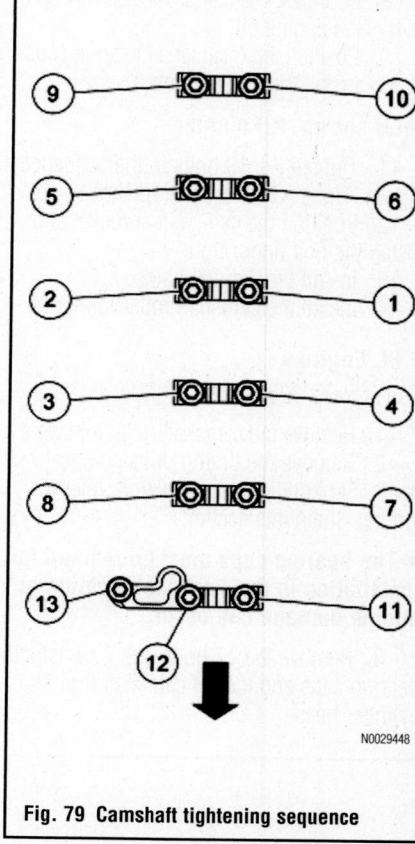

Fig. 79 Camshaft tightening sequence

5.4L Engines

See Figures 78 and 79.

➡ **At no time, when the timing chains are removed and the cylinder heads are installed, may the crankshaft or camshaft be rotated. Severe piston and valve damage will occur.**

1. Remove the camshaft roller followers.
2. Remove the timing chains. For additional information, refer to Timing Chain in this section.

➡ **The camshaft bearing caps must be installed in their original location. Record the camshaft bearing cap location.**

3. Remove the 13 bolts, the 6 bearing caps and the camshaft.
4. Clean and inspect the camshaft bearing caps.
5. One of the bearing caps contains an oil flow restriction groove. Make sure the groove is free of foreign material.

To install:

6. Lubricate the camshaft journals with clean engine oil.
7. Install the camshaft and the 6 camshaft bearing caps in their original locations.

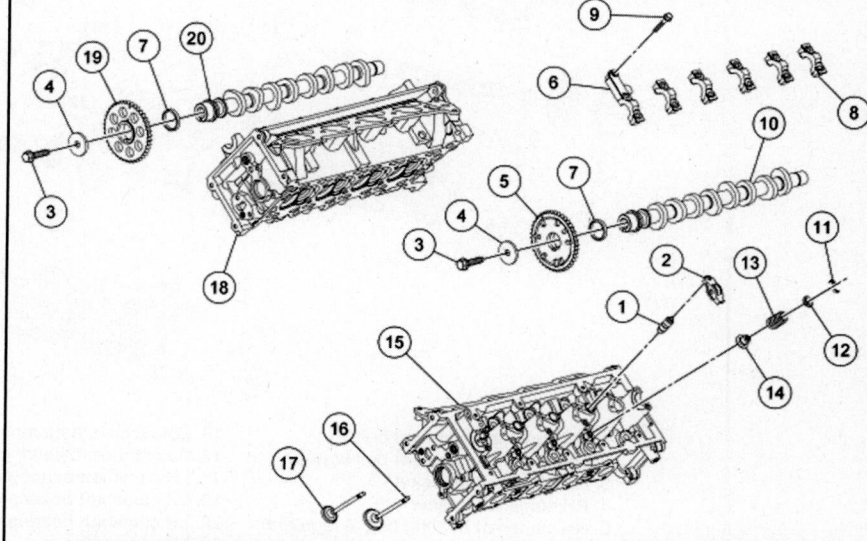

1. Hydraulic lash adjuster (16 required)
2. Roller follower (16 required)
3. Camshaft sprocket bolt (2 required)
4. Camshaft sprocket washer (2 required)
5. LH camshaft sprocket
6. Camshaft bearing cap (2 required)
7. Camshaft sprocket spacer (2 required)
8. Camshaft bearing cap (10 required)
9. Camshaft bearing cap bolt (26 required)
10. LH camshaft
11. Valve spring retainer key (32 required)
12. Valve spring retainer (16 required)
13. Valve spring (16 required)
14. Valve stem seal (16 required)
15. LH cylinder head
16. Intake valve (8 required)
17. Exhaust valve (8 required)
18. RH cylinder head
19. RH camshaft sprocket
20. RH camshaft

Fig. 78 Exploded view of the valve train components—5.4L Engines

8. Lubricate the camshaft bearing caps with clean engine oil.

9. Position the 6 camshaft bearing caps.

10. Install the 13 bolts loosely.

➡**LH shown, RH similar.**

11. Tighten the 13 bolts in the sequence shown. Tighten to 7 ft. lbs. (10 Nm).

12. Position the camshaft sprocket and install the bolt finger-tight.

13. Install the timing chains.

14. Install the camshaft roller followers.

6.8L Engines

See Figures 80 and 81.

1. Remove the camshaft roller followers.

2. Remove the timing drive components. For additional information, refer to Timing Chain this section.

➡**The bearing caps must be marked for installation in their original location or engine damage can occur.**

3. Remove the 17 bolts, the 7 camshaft bearing caps and the LH camshaft from the cylinder head.

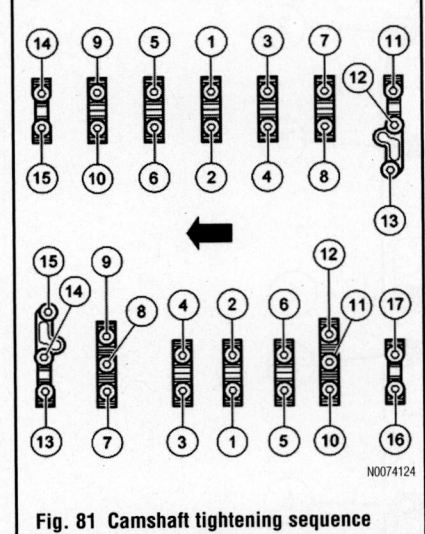

Fig. 81 Camshaft tightening sequence

➡**The bearing caps must be marked for installation in their original location or engine damage can occur.**

4. Remove the 15 bolts, the 7 camshaft

bearing caps and the RH camshaft from the cylinder head.

To install:

5. Lubricate the camshaft journals with clean engine oil.

6. Install the RH camshaft and the 7 camshaft bearing caps in their original locations onto the cylinder head. Loosely install the 15 bolts.

7. Install the LH camshaft and the 7 camshaft bearing caps in their original locations onto the cylinder head. Loosely install the 17 bolts.

8. Tighten the bolts in the sequence shown. Tighten to 89 inch lbs. (10 Nm).

9. Install the timing drive components.

10. Install the camshaft roller followers.

CATALYTIC CONVERTER

REMOVAL & INSTALLATION

6.0L Engines

See Figure 82.

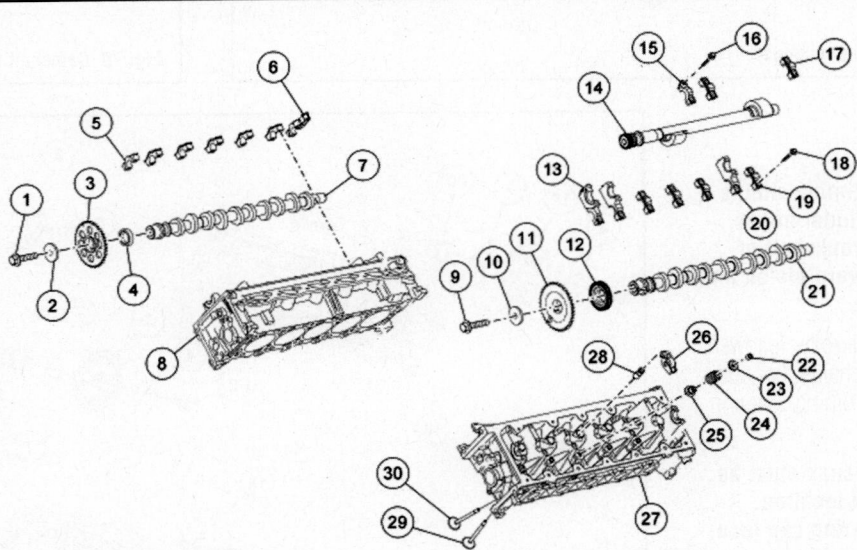

1. RH camshaft sprocket bolt
2. RH camshaft sprocket bolt washer
3. RH camshaft sprocket
4. RH camshaft spacer
5. RH camshaft bearing cap (6 required)
6. RH camshaft bearing cap
7. RH camshaft
8. RH cylinder head
9. LH camshaft sprocket bolt
10. LH camshaft sprocket bolt washer
11. LH camshaft sprocket
12. Balance shaft drive gear
13. LH camshaft bearing cap
14. Balance shaft
15. Balance shaft bearing cap
16. Balance shaft bearing cap bolt (6 required)
17. Balance shaft bearing cap (2 required)
18. LH camshaft bearing cap bolt (26 required)
19. LH camshaft bearing cap (4 required)
20. LH camshaft bearing cap (2 required)
21. LH camshaft
22. Valve key (40 required)
23. Valve spring retainer (20 required)
24. Valve spring (20 required)
25. Valve stem seal (20 required)
26. Camshaft roller follower (20 required)
27. LH cylinder head
28. Hydraulic lash adjuster (20 required)
29. Intake valve (10 required)
30. Exhaust valve (10 required)

Fig. 80 Exploded view of the valve train components—6.8L Engines

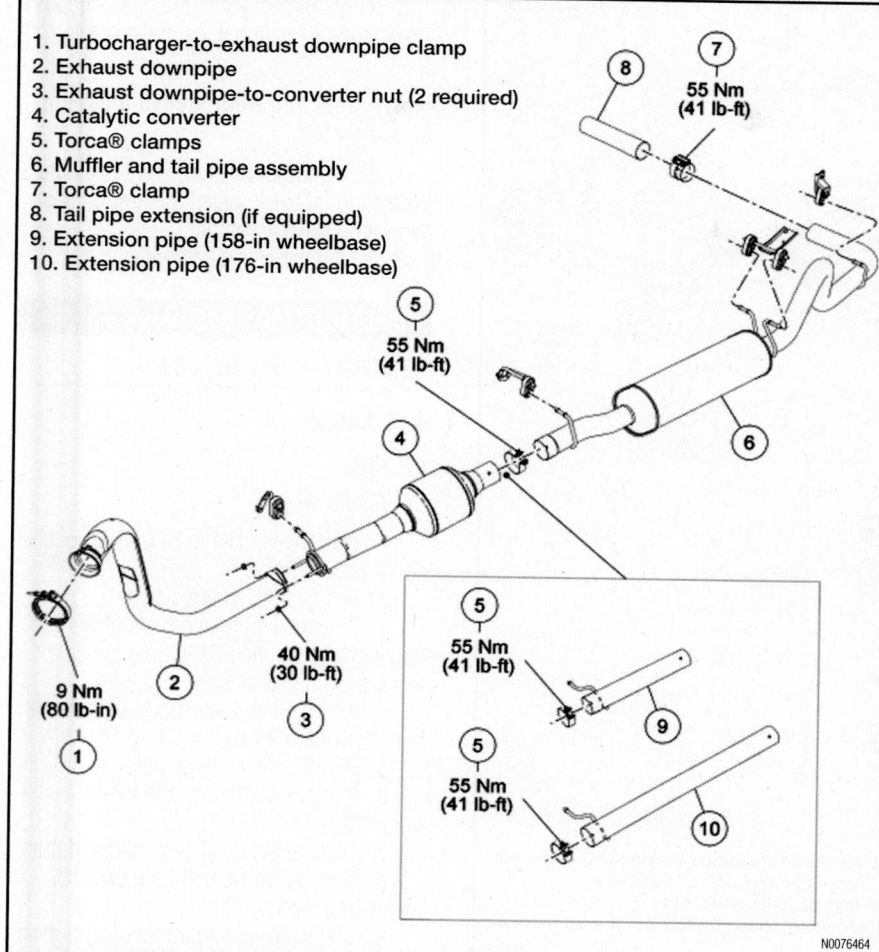

1. Turbocharger-to-exhaust downpipe clamp
2. Exhaust downpipe
3. Exhaust downpipe-to-converter nut (2 required)
4. Catalytic converter
5. Torca® clamps
6. Muffler and tail pipe assembly
7. Torca® clamp
8. Tail pipe extension (if equipped)
9. Extension pipe (158-in wheelbase)
10. Extension pipe (176-in wheelbase)

55 Nm
(41 lb-ft)

55 Nm
(41 lb-ft)

40 Nm
(30 lb-ft)

9 Nm
(80 lb-in)

55 Nm
(41 lb-ft)

55 Nm
(41 lb-ft)

55 Nm
(41 lb-ft)

N0076464

Fig. 82 Exploded view of the exhaust system—6.0L Engines

1. Exhaust fasteners are of a prevailing torque design. Use only new fasteners with the same part number as the original. Torque values must be used as specified during reassembly to make sure of correct retention of exhaust components.

2. With the vehicle in NEUTRAL, position it on a hoist.

3. Support the muffler and tail pipe assembly with a safety stand.

4. Release the front muffler and tail pipe assembly and, if equipped, the extension pipe hanger insulator(s).

5. Loosen the muffler and tail pipe assembly or, if equipped, the extension pipe-to-catalytic converter Torca® clamp. To install, tighten to 41 ft. lbs. (55 Nm).

6. Remove the muffler and tail pipe assembly and, if equipped, the extension pipe from the catalytic converter.

7. Release the catalytic converter hanger isolator.

8. Remove the 2 exhaust downpipe-to-catalytic converter nuts and discard. To

install, tighten the new nuts to 30 ft. lbs. (40 Nm).

9. Remove the catalytic converter from the exhaust downpipe.

10. To install, reverse the removal procedure.

4.6L, 5.4L and 6.8L Engines

See Figures 83 and 84.

1. Exhaust fasteners are of a prevailing torque design. Use only new fasteners with the same part number as the original. Torque values must be used as specified during reassembly to make sure of correct retention of exhaust components.

2. With the vehicle in NEUTRAL, position it on a hoist.

3. Support the muffler and tail pipe assembly with a safety stand.

4. Release the front muffler and tail pipe assembly and, if equipped, the extension pipe hanger insulator(s).

5. Loosen the muffler and tail pipe assembly or, if equipped, the extension

pipe-to-catalytic converter Torca® clamp. To install, tighten to 41 ft. lbs. (55 Nm).

6. Remove the muffler and tail pipe assembly and, if equipped, the extension pipe from the catalytic converter.

7. Disconnect the Catalyst Monitor Sensor (CMS) electrical connector.

8. Remove the 3 exhaust Y-pipe-to-catalytic converter nuts and discard. Remove the exhaust Y-pipe-to-catalytic converter support bracket.

9. Remove the catalytic converter from the exhaust Y-pipe and discard the gasket.

10. To install, reverse the removal procedure.

Y–Pipe

1. Exhaust fasteners are of a prevailing torque design. Use only new fasteners with the same part number as the original. Torque values must be used as specified during reassembly to make sure of correct retention of exhaust components.

2. With the vehicle in NEUTRAL, position it on a hoist.

3. Support the muffler and tail pipe assembly and catalytic converter with a safety stand.

4. Release the front muffler and tail pipe assembly and (if equipped, the extension pipe) isolators.

5. Remove the 3 exhaust Y-pipe-to-catalytic converter nuts and discard. Remove the exhaust Y-pipe-to-catalytic converter support bracket. To install, tighten the new nuts to 30 ft. lbs. (40 Nm).

6. Position the catalytic converter and muffler and tail pipe assembly rearward from the exhaust Y-pipe and discard the gasket.

7. Disconnect the Heated Oxygen Sensor (HO2S) and the Catalyst Monitor Sensor (CMS) electrical connectors.

8. Remove the 2 LH and 1 RH heat shield-to-crossmember bolts.

9. Remove the 2 crossmember-to-rear transmission mount nuts. To install, tighten to 70 ft. lbs. (95 Nm).

10. Support the rear of the transmission with a safety stand.

11. Remove the 2 RH and 2 LH transmission crossmember-to-frame nuts and 4 bolts and remove the transmission crossmember. To install, tighten to 60 ft. lbs. (81 Nm).

12. Remove the 4 exhaust Y-pipe-to-exhaust manifold nuts and discard. Remove the exhaust Y-pipe.

13. To install, tighten the new upper exhaust Y-pipe-to-exhaust manifold nuts to 30 ft. lbs. (40 Nm) then tighten the new lower exhaust Y-pipe-to-exhaust manifold nuts to 30 ft. lbs. (40 Nm).

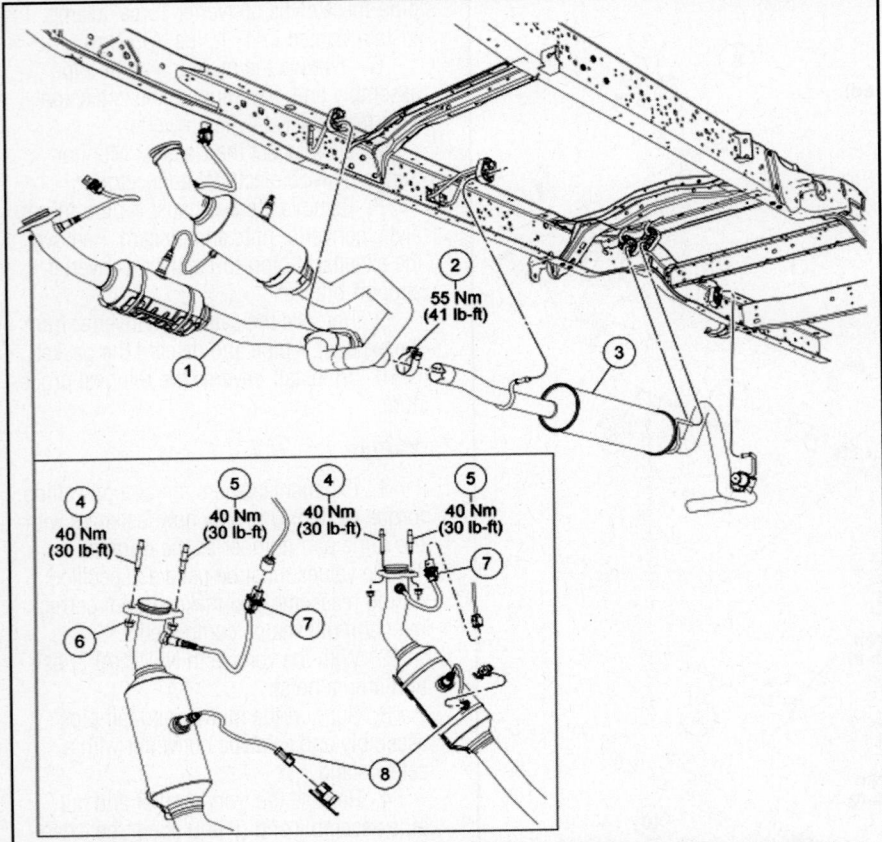

1. Exhaust Y-pipe
2. Torca® clamp
3. Muffler and tail pipe assembly
4. Exhaust manifold studs (2 required)
5. Exhaust manifold studs (2 required)
6. Exhaust manifold-to-exhaust Y-pipe nut (4 required)
7. Heated Oxygen Sensor (HO2S) electrical connectors (6.8L, 4.6L and 5.4L)
8. Catalyst Monitor Sensor (CMS) electrical connectors

N0108636

Fig. 83 Exploded view of the exhaust system—Van/Wagon models

14. To install, reverse the removal procedure.

CRANKSHAFT FRONT SEAL

REMOVAL & INSTALLATION

4.6L, 5.4L and 6.8L Engines
See Figures 85 and 86.

1. With the vehicle in NEUTRAL, position it on a hoist.
2. Remove the crankshaft pulley. For additional information, refer to Timing Chain in this section.
3. Using the Oil Seal Remover, remove and discard the crankshaft front seal.
4. Clean all sealing surfaces with metal surface prep.

To install:

➡ Apply clean engine oil to the crankshaft front seal bore in the engine front cover.

5. Using the Front Crankshaft Seal Installer and Crankshaft Vibration Damper Installer, install a new crankshaft front seal.
6. Install the crankshaft pulley.

6.0L Engines
See Figures 87 through 89.

1. Remove the crankshaft pulley. For additional information, refer to Timing Chain in this section.
2. Punch 2 holes in the seal.
3. Using the Oil Seal Remover, remove and discard the crankshaft seal.

➡ Production seals will not have a wear sleeve. If a service part has been installed, it will have a wear sleeve.

4. If equipped, using the Crankshaft Front Wear Ring Remover, remove and discard the crankshaft pulley wear sleeve.

To install:

5. Thoroughly clean the crankshaft front seal mounting surface.

6. Apply threadlock to the outer circumference of the leading edge of the crankshaft.

➡ New seal and wear sleeve must not be separated.

7. Using the Crankshaft Front Seal and Wear Ring Installer, install the new oil seal and wear sleeve assembly.
8. Install the crankshaft pulley.

EXHAUST MANIFOLD

REMOVAL & INSTALLATION

4.6L Engine

LH Side
See Figure 90.

1. With the vehicle in NEUTRAL, position it on a hoist.
2. Remove the engine cover.
3. Disconnect the upper and lower fitting and remove the EGR system module-to-exhaust manifold tube.
4. Remove the 4 exhaust Y-pipe flange nuts (2 RH and 2 LH).
5. Discard the 4 flange nuts.
6. Remove the 8 nuts and the exhaust manifold.
7. Discard the 8 exhaust manifold nuts.
8. Remove and discard the exhaust manifold gasket.
9. Clean the sealing surfaces with metal surface prep. Follow the directions on the packaging.
10. Remove and discard the 8 exhaust manifold-to-cylinder head studs.
11. Clean and inspect the exhaust manifold.

To install:

➡ Do not use metal scrapers, wire brushes, power abrasive discs, or other abrasive means to clean the sealing surfaces. These may cause scratches and gouges resulting in leak paths. Use a plastic scraper to clean the sealing surfaces.

12. Clean the sealing surfaces with metal surface prep.
13. Install 8 new exhaust manifold-to-cylinder head studs. Tighten to 9 ft. lbs. (12 Nm).
14. Using new exhaust manifold gaskets, position the LH exhaust manifold and install the 8 new nuts in the sequence shown. Tighten to 15 ft. lbs. (20 Nm).
15. Install the EGR system module-to-exhaust manifold tube and tighten the upper and lower fittings in 2 stages.

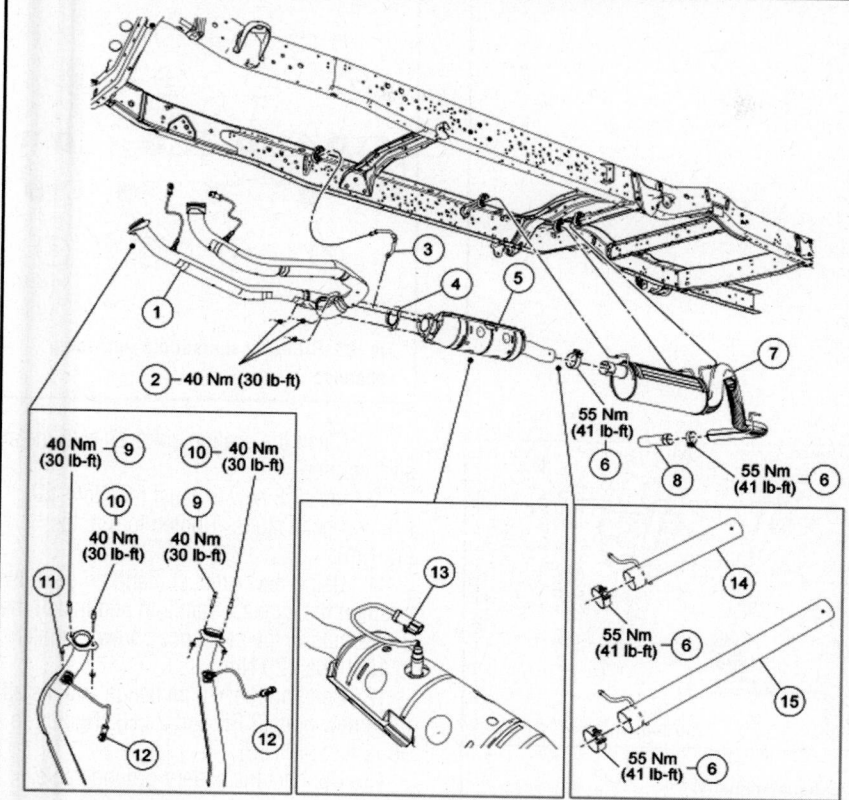

1. Exhaust Y-pipe
2. Exhaust Y-pipe-to-catalytic converter nuts (3 required)
3. Exhaust Y-pipe-to-catalytic converter support bracket
4. Exhaust Y-pipe-to-converter gasket
5. Catalytic converter
6. Torca® clamps
7. Muffler and tail pipe assembly
8. Tail pipe extension (if equipped)
9. Exhaust manifold-to-exhaust Y-pipe studs (2 required)
10. Exhaust manifold-to-exhaust Y-pipe studs (2 required)
11. Exhaust manifold-to-exhaust Y-pipe nut (4 required)
12. Heated Oxygen Sensor (HO2S) electrical connectors (6.8L and 5.4L)
13. Catalyst Monitor Sensor (CMS) electrical connector
14. Extension pipe (158-in wheelbase)
15. Extension pipe (176-in wheelbase)

Fig. 84 Exploded view of the exhaust system—Stripped Chassis (5-Speed Transmission)

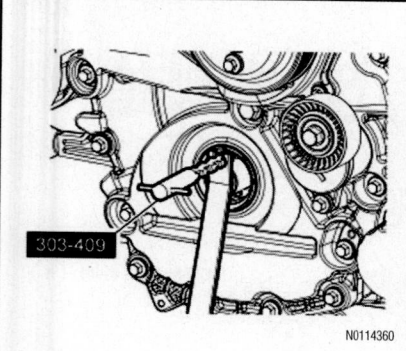

Fig. 85 Using the Oil Seal Remover

Fig. 86 Using the Front Crankshaft Seal Installer and Crankshaft Vibration Damper Installer

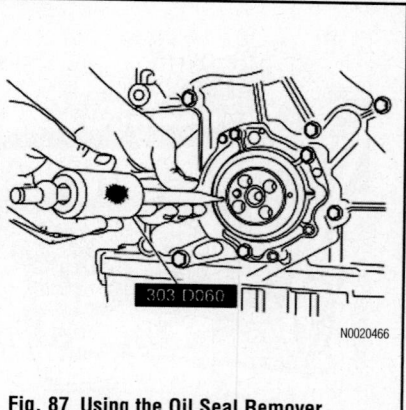

Fig. 87 Using the Oil Seal Remover

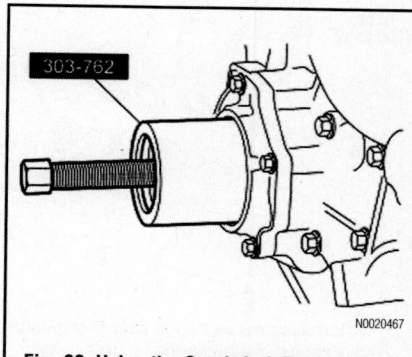

Fig. 88 Using the Crankshaft Front Wear Ring Remover

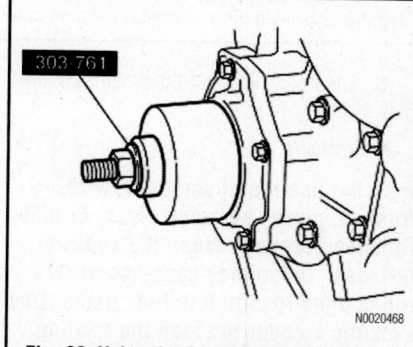

Fig. 89 Using the Crankshaft Front Seal and Wear Ring Installer

a. Stage 1: Connect the upper and lower fittings and hand-tighten.
b. Stage 2: Tighten to 31 ft. lbs. (42 Nm).
16. Install the engine cover.

RH Side

See Figure 92.

1. With the vehicle in NEUTRAL, position it on a hoist.
2. Disconnect the battery ground cable.

3. Remove the 4 exhaust Y-pipe flange nuts (2 RH and 2 LH).
4. Discard the 4 flange nuts.
5. Remove and discard the 8 exhaust manifold nuts.

➡️ **It may be necessary to raise the exhaust Y-pipe for additional clearance when removing the exhaust manifold from the vehicle.**

6. Remove the RH exhaust manifold and discard the gaskets.
7. Remove and discard the 8 exhaust manifold-to-cylinder head studs.

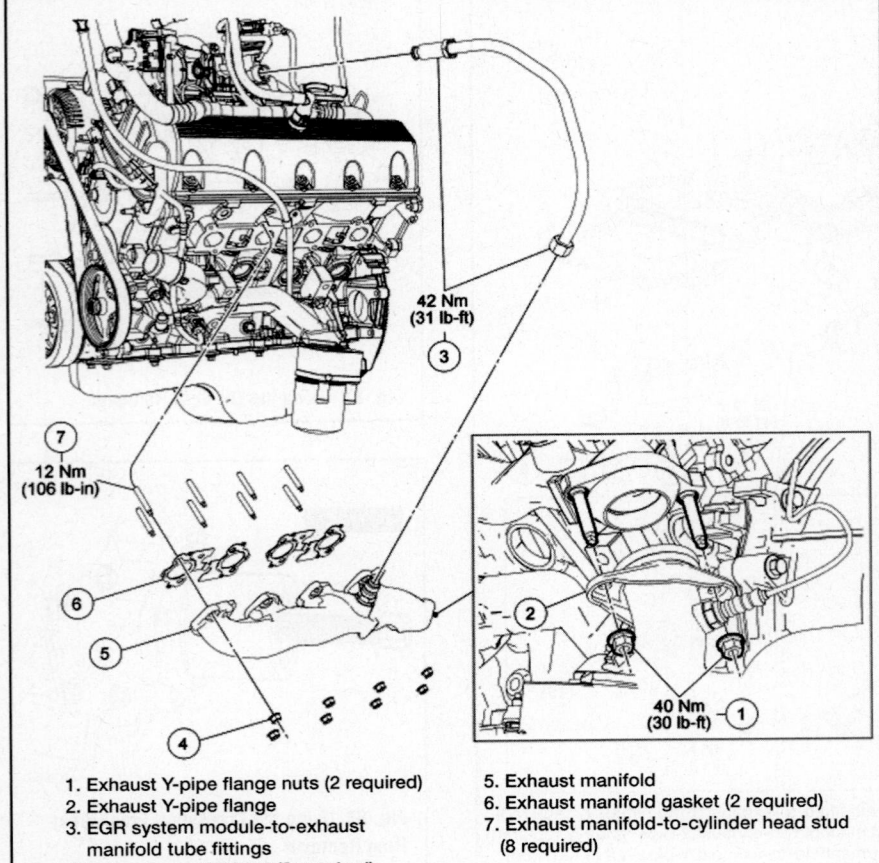

1. Exhaust Y-pipe flange nuts (2 required)
2. Exhaust Y-pipe flange
3. EGR system module-to-exhaust manifold tube fittings
4. Exhaust manifold nut (8 required)
5. Exhaust manifold
6. Exhaust manifold gasket (2 required)
7. Exhaust manifold-to-cylinder head stud (8 required)

Fig. 90 Exploded view of the LH exhaust manifold—4.6L Engine

8. Clean and inspect the exhaust manifold.

To install:

➥Do not use metal scrapers, wire brushes, power abrasive discs, or other abrasive means to clean the sealing surfaces. These may cause scratches and gouges resulting in leak paths. Use a plastic scraper to clean the sealing surfaces.

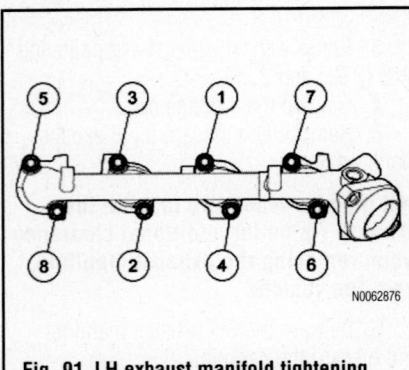

Fig. 91 LH exhaust manifold tightening sequence

Fig. 93 RH exhaust manifold tightening sequence

9. Clean the sealing surfaces with metal surface prep.
10. Install 8 new exhaust manifold-to-cylinder head studs. Tighten to 9 ft. lbs. (12 Nm).
11. Using new exhaust manifold gaskets, position the exhaust manifold and install the 8 new nuts in the sequence shown. Tighten to 15 ft. lbs. (20 Nm).
12. Position the Y-pipe flange and install the 4 new nuts (2 RH and 2 LH). Tighten to 30 ft. lbs. (40 Nm).
13. Connect the battery ground cable.

5.4L Engine

LH Side

See Figures 94 and 95.

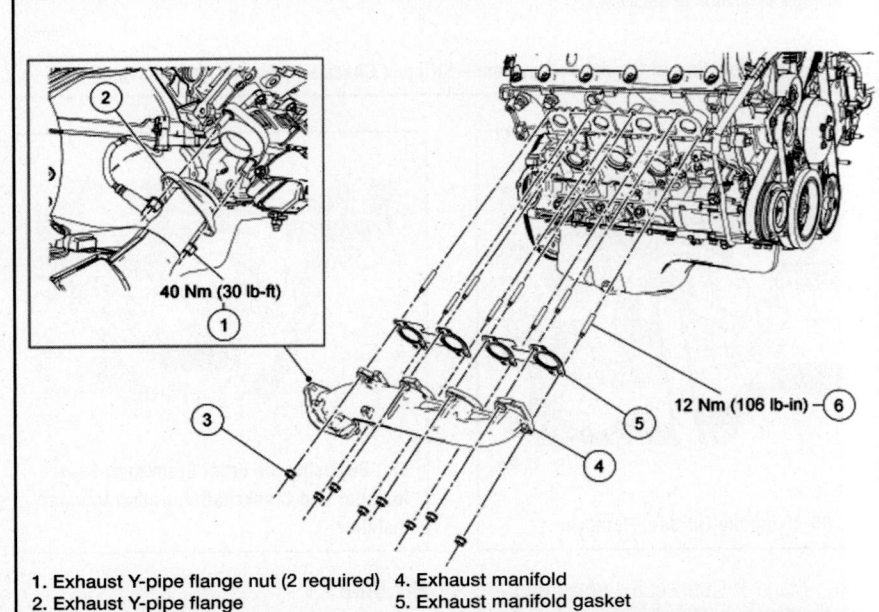

1. Exhaust Y-pipe flange nut (2 required)
2. Exhaust Y-pipe flange
3. Exhaust manifold nut (8 required)
4. Exhaust manifold
5. Exhaust manifold gasket
6. Exhaust manifold-to-cylinder head stud (8 required)

Fig. 92 Exploded view of the RH exhaust manifold

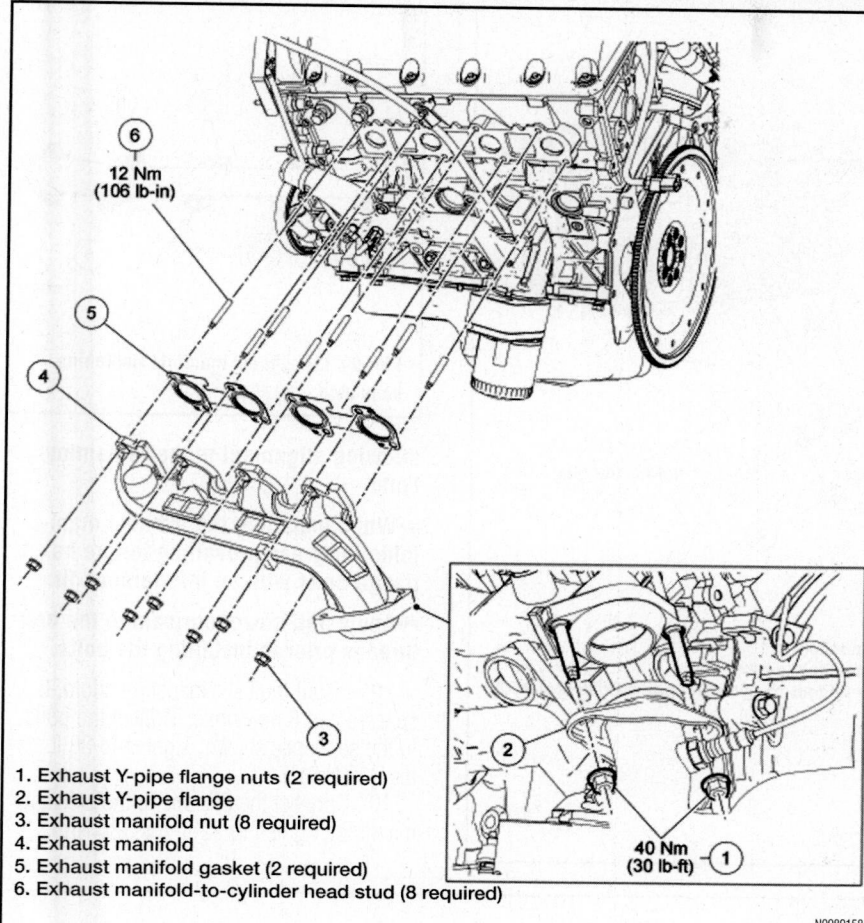

1. Exhaust Y-pipe flange nuts (2 required)
2. Exhaust Y-pipe flange
3. Exhaust manifold nut (8 required)
4. Exhaust manifold
5. Exhaust manifold gasket (2 required)
6. Exhaust manifold-to-cylinder head stud (8 required)

N0089158

Fig. 94 Exploded view of the LH exhaust manifold—5.4L Engines

1. With the vehicle in NEUTRAL, position it on a hoist.
2. Remove the engine cover.
3. Remove the 4 exhaust Y-pipe flange nuts (2 RH and 2 LH).
4. Discard the 4 flange nuts.
5. Remove the 8 nuts and the exhaust manifold.
6. Discard the 8 exhaust manifold nuts.
7. Remove and discard the exhaust manifold gasket.
8. Clean the sealing surfaces with metal surface prep. Follow the directions on the packaging.
9. Remove and discard the 8 exhaust manifold-to-cylinder head studs.
10. Clean and inspect the exhaust manifold.

To install:

➡**Do not use metal scrapers, wire brushes, power abrasive discs, or other abrasive means to clean the sealing surfaces. These may cause scratches**

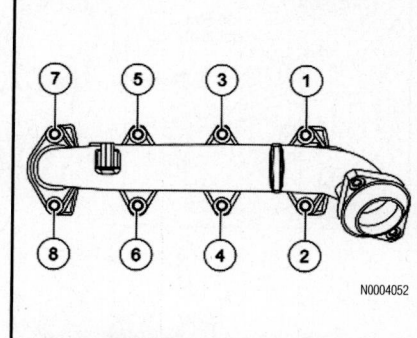

N0004052

Fig. 95 LH tightening exhaust manifold tightening sequence

and gouges resulting in leak paths. Use a plastic scraper to clean the sealing surfaces.

11. Clean the sealing surfaces with metal surface prep.
12. Install 8 new exhaust manifold-to-cylinder head studs. Tighten to 9 ft. lbs. (12 Nm).
13. Using new exhaust manifold gaskets, position the LH exhaust manifold and install

the 8 new nuts in the sequence shown. Tighten to 18 ft. lbs. (25 Nm).
14. Position the Y-pipe flange and install the 2 new RH and 2 new LH nuts. Tighten to 30 ft. lbs. (40 Nm).
15. Install the engine cover.

RH Side

See Figures 96 and 97.

1. With the vehicle in NEUTRAL, position it on a hoist.
2. Remove the engine cover.
3. Remove the 4 exhaust Y-pipe flange nuts (2 RH and 2 LH).
4. Discard the 4 flange nuts.
5. Remove the 8 nuts and the exhaust manifold.
6. Discard the 8 exhaust manifold nuts.
7. Remove and discard the exhaust manifold gasket.
8. Clean the sealing surfaces with metal surface prep. Follow the directions on the packaging.
9. Remove and discard the 8 exhaust manifold-to-cylinder head studs.
10. Clean and inspect the exhaust manifold.

To install:

➡**Do not use metal scrapers, wire brushes, power abrasive discs, or other abrasive means to clean the sealing surfaces. These may cause scratches and gouges resulting in leak paths. Use a plastic scraper to clean the sealing surfaces.**

11. Clean the sealing surfaces with metal surface prep.
12. Install 8 new exhaust manifold-to-cylinder head studs. Tighten to 9 ft. lbs. (12 Nm).
13. Using new exhaust manifold gaskets, position the LH exhaust manifold and install the 8 new nuts in the sequence shown. Tighten to 18 ft. lbs. (25 Nm).
14. Position the Y-pipe flange and install the 2 new RH and 2 new LH nuts. Tighten to 30 ft. lbs. (40 Nm).
15. Install the engine cover.

6.0L Engines

LH Side

See Figures 98 and 99.

1. With the vehicle in NEUTRAL, position it on a hoist.
2. Remove the engine cover.
3. Prior to removing the exhaust manifold, inspect the exhaust manifold for warpage with a feeler gauge between the manifold and the cylinder head. Record the

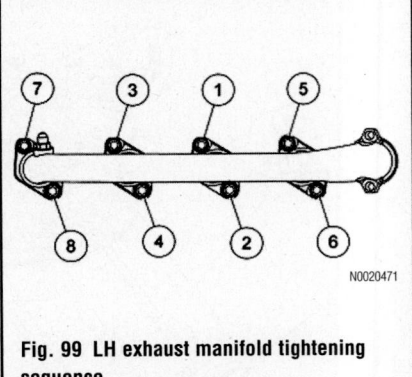

Fig. 99 LH exhaust manifold tightening sequence

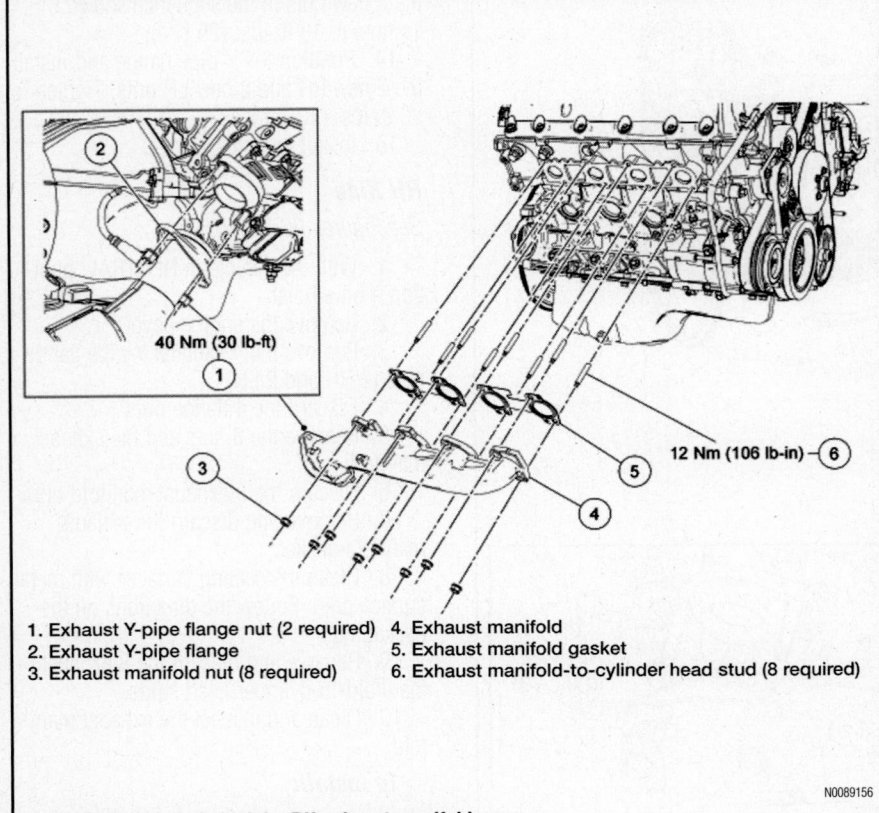

1. Exhaust Y-pipe flange nut (2 required)
2. Exhaust Y-pipe flange
3. Exhaust manifold nut (8 required)
4. Exhaust manifold
5. Exhaust manifold gasket
6. Exhaust manifold-to-cylinder head stud (8 required)

Fig. 96 Exploded view of the RH exhaust manifold

allowing alignment of the remaining bolts.

➡ **When installing the exhaust manifolds, only use prevailing torque hex flange bolts with an interference fit.**

➡ **Apply anti-seize lubricant to the bolt threads prior to installing the bolts.**

9. Install the LH exhaust manifold, 8 spacers and 8 new bolts. Tighten the bolts in the sequence shown. Tighten to 28 ft. lbs. (38 Nm).

10. Connect the EP tube to the exhaust manifold. Tighten to 22 ft. lbs. (30 Nm).

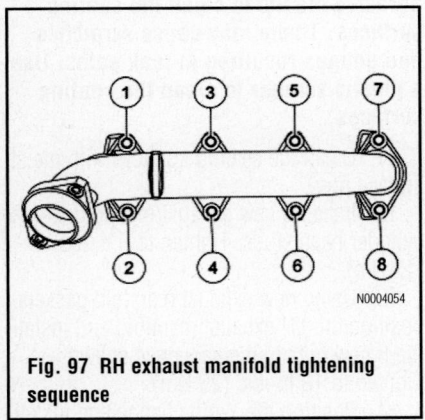

Fig. 97 RH exhaust manifold tightening sequence

measurement and compare with the specifications.

4. Remove the 2 LH exhaust manifold-to-turbocharger adapter pipe nuts.

5. Discard the nuts.

6. Disconnect the Exhaust Pressure (EP) tube from the LH exhaust manifold.

7. Remove the 8 bolts, 8 spacers and the LH exhaust manifold.

8. Discard the bolts.

To install:

➡ **Start installing the bolts with the second bolt from the rear on the top. The hole diameter is smaller, therefore**

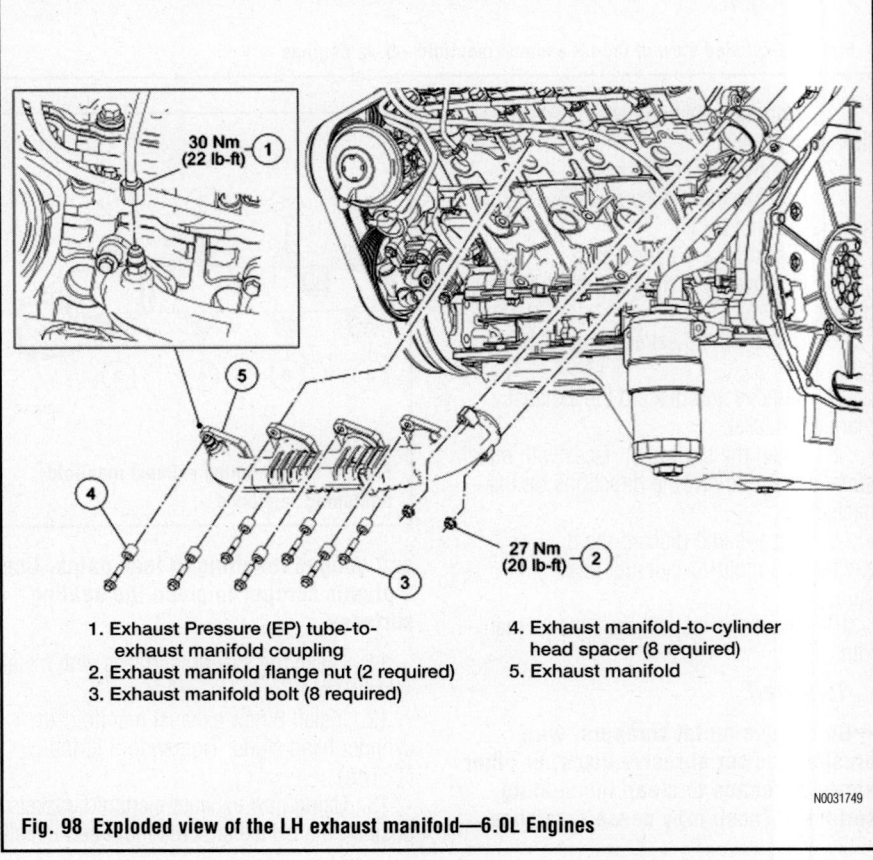

1. Exhaust Pressure (EP) tube-to-exhaust manifold coupling
2. Exhaust manifold flange nut (2 required)
3. Exhaust manifold bolt (8 required)
4. Exhaust manifold-to-cylinder head spacer (8 required)
5. Exhaust manifold

Fig. 98 Exploded view of the LH exhaust manifold—6.0L Engines

➡️**Apply anti-seize lubricant to the bolt threads prior to installing the bolts.**

11. Install the 2 new LH exhaust manifold-to-turbocharger adapter pipe nuts. Tighten to 20 ft. lbs. (27 Nm).

12. Install the engine cover.

RH Side

See Figures 100 and 101.

1. With the vehicle in NEUTRAL, position it on a hoist.

2. Disconnect the battery ground cable.

3. Remove the engine cover.

4. Prior to removing the exhaust manifold, inspect the exhaust manifold for warpage with a feeler gauge between the manifold and the cylinder head. Record the measurement and compare with the specifications.

5. Remove the 2 RH exhaust manifold-to-turbocharger adapter pipe nuts.

6. Discard the nuts.

7. Remove the 8 bolts, 8 spacers and the RH exhaust manifold.

8. Discard the bolts.

To install:

➡️**Start installing the bolts with the second bolt from the rear on the top.**

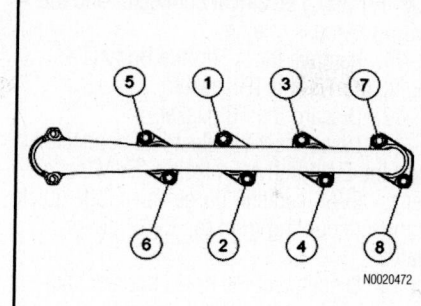

Fig. 101 RH exhaust manifold tightening sequence

The hole diameter is smaller, therefore allowing alignment of the remaining bolts.

➡️**When installing the exhaust manifolds, only use prevailing torque hex flange bolts with an interference fit.**

➡️**Apply anti-seize lubricant to the bolt threads prior to installing the bolts.**

9. Install the RH exhaust manifold, 8 spacers and 8 new bolts. Tighten the bolts in the sequence shown.

➡️**Apply anti-seize lubricant to the bolt threads prior to installing the bolts.**

10. Install the 2 new RH exhaust manifold-to-turbocharger adapter pipe nuts.

11. Install the engine cover.

12. Connect the battery ground cable.

6.8L Engines

See Figures 102 and 103.

➡️**Procedure below is for the LH exhaust manifold, RH is similar.**

1. With the vehicle in NEUTRAL, position it on a hoist.

2. Remove the engine cover.

3. Remove the 4 nuts.

4. Remove the 10 exhaust manifold nuts and the exhaust manifold.

5. Discard the exhaust manifold gaskets and the nuts.

6. Remove and discard the 10 exhaust manifold studs.

7. Clean and inspect the exhaust manifold.

To install:

➡️**Do not use metal scrapers, wire brushes, power abrasive discs or other abrasive means to clean the sealing surfaces. These may cause scratches and gouges resulting in leak paths. Use a plastic scraper to clean the sealing surfaces.**

8. Clean the sealing surfaces with metal surface prep. Follow the directions on the packaging.

9. Install 10 new exhaust manifold studs. Tighten to 9 ft. lbs. (12 Nm).

10. Position the new gaskets, the exhaust manifold and tighten the nuts in the sequence shown. Tighten to 18 ft. lbs. (25 Nm).

11. Position the exhaust Y-pipe flange and install the 4 nuts. Tighten to 30 ft. lbs. (40 Nm).

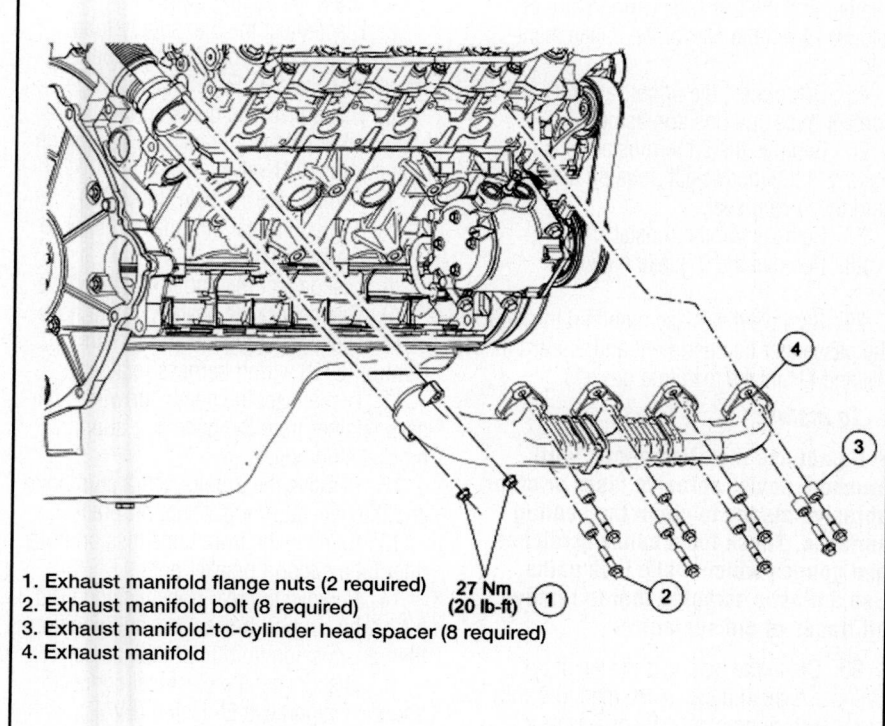

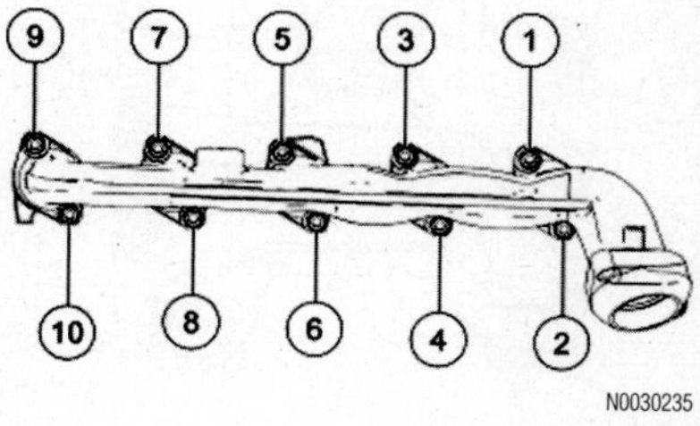

1. Exhaust manifold flange nuts (2 required)
2. Exhaust manifold bolt (8 required)
3. Exhaust manifold-to-cylinder head spacer (8 required)
4. Exhaust manifold

27 Nm (20 lb-ft)

Fig. 100 Exploded view of the RH exhaust manifold—6.0L Engines

Fig. 102 LH exhaust manifold tightening sequence

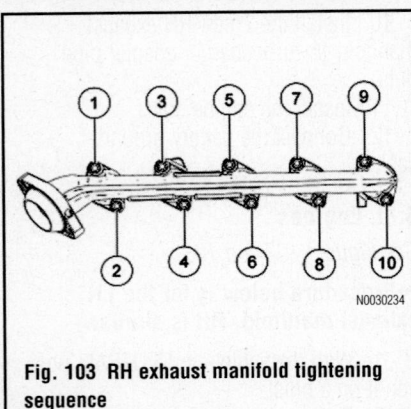

Fig. 103 RH exhaust manifold tightening sequence

INTAKE MANIFOLD

REMOVAL & INSTALLATION

4.6L Engine

See Figure 104.

1. Disconnect the battery ground cable.
2. Remove the engine cover.
3. Remove the Air Cleaner (ACL) assembly and the ACL outlet pipe.
4. Drain the cooling system.
5. Disconnect the fuel supply tube quick connect coupling. For additional information, refer to Fuel System.
6. Disconnect the quick connect couplings and remove the PCV tube.
7. Remove the front transmission fluid filler tube support bracket bolt.
8. Remove the rear transmission fluid filler tube bolt and position the transmission fluid filler tube aside.
9. If equipped, disconnect the auxiliary heater hoses and position them aside.
10. Disconnect the Electronic Throttle

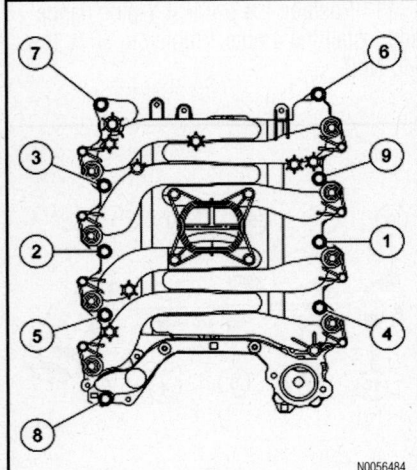

Fig. 104 Intake manifold tightening sequence—4.6L Engines

Control (ETC) electrical connector and the wiring harness retainer.

11. Remove the 4 Throttle Body (TB) bolts, the TB and TB gasket.
12. Discard the TB gasket.
13. Disconnect the electrical connector and the Evaporative Emission (EVAP) canister-to- EVAP canister purge valve tube quick connect coupling from the EVAP purge valve.
14. Disconnect the brake booster vacuum hose from the intake manifold.
15. Disconnect the EGR system module vacuum connector and position the vacuum tube assembly aside.
16. Disconnect the EGR system module electrical connector.
17. Disconnect the upper and lower fittings and remove the exhaust manifold-to-EGR system module tube.
18. Remove the 2 bolts and the EGR system module.
19. Discard the EGR system module gasket.
20. Remove the 8 ignition coils.
21. Remove the 4 bolts and the generator support bracket.
22. Disconnect the heater coolant hose and position aside.
23. Disconnect the 8 fuel injector electrical connectors.
24. Disconnect the Knock Sensor (KS) electrical connector, electrical connector retainer and the 2 engine wiring harness retainers from the rear of the intake manifold.
25. Disconnect the upper radiator coolant hose and position aside.
26. Remove the 2 thermostat housing bolts and the thermostat housing and discard the O-ring seal.
27. Remove the thermostat.
28. Remove the 9 intake manifold bolts.
29. Remove the intake manifold through the passenger compartment and discard the RH and LH intake manifold gaskets.

To install:

➡**Do not use metal scrapers, wire brushes, power abrasive discs or other abrasive means to clean the sealing surfaces. These tools cause scratches and gouges which make leak paths. Use a plastic scraping tool to remove all traces of old sealant.**

30. Clean the mating surfaces of the cylinder head and the intake manifold with metal surface prep and silicone gasket remover. Follow the directions on the packaging.

➡**If the engine is repaired or replaced because of upper engine failure, typically including valve or piston damage, check the intake manifold for metal debris. If metal debris is found, install a new intake manifold. Failure to follow these instructions can result in engine damage.**

31. Install the intake manifold in the following sequence.
32. Position the new intake manifold gaskets.
33. Position the intake manifold.
34. Loosely install the 9 intake manifold bolts.
35. Tighten the 9 intake manifold bolts in the sequence shown. Tighten to 89 inch lbs. (10 Nm).
36. To complete installation, reverse the remaining removal procedure. Refer to the appropriate sections for procedures and torque values.
37. Connect the battery ground cable.
38. Fill and bleed the engine cooling system.

5.4L Engine

See Figure 105.

1. Disconnect the battery ground cable.
2. Remove the engine cover.
3. Remove the Air Cleaner (ACL) assembly and the ACL outlet pipe.
4. Drain the cooling system.
5. Disconnect the fuel supply tube quick connect coupling. For additional information, refer to Fuel System.
6. Disconnect the quick connect coupling and remove the crankcase ventilation tube from the LH valve cover.
7. Remove the Throttle Body (TB) spacer. For additional information, refer to Engine Performance.
8. Disconnect the upper radiator hose.
9. Disconnect the heater coolant hose.
10. Disconnect the Electronic Throttle Control (ETC) wiring harness retainer.
11. Disconnect the generator wiring harness retainer from the generator support bracket stud bolt.
12. Remove the 2 bolts, the 2 stud bolts and the generator upper support bracket.
13. Remove the front transmission fluid filler tube support bracket bolt.
14. Remove the rear transmission fluid filler tube support bracket nut and position the transmission fluid filler tube aside.
15. Disconnect the electrical connector and the Evaporative Emission (EVAP) canister-to- EVAP canister purge valve tube quick connect coupling from the EVAP purge valve.

16. Remove the bolt and the EVAP canister purge valve.

17. If equipped, disconnect the auxiliary heater hoses and position aside.

18. Disconnect the quick connect coupling and remove the PCV tube from the RH valve cover.

19. Disconnect the 8 fuel injector electrical connectors.

20. Disconnect the 8 ignition coil electrical connectors.

➡️**Use a twisting motion while pulling up on the ignition coil.**

21. Remove the 8 bolts and the 8 ignition coils.

22. Remove the 2 bolts, the thermostat housing and the thermostat.

23. Discard the O-ring seal.

24. Remove the 9 bolts, the intake manifold assembly and discard the intake manifold gaskets.

To install:

➡️**Do not use metal scrapers, wire brushes, power abrasive discs or other abrasive means to clean the sealing surfaces. These tools cause scratches and gouges which make leak paths. Use a plastic scraping tool to remove all traces of old sealant.**

25. Clean the mating surfaces of the cylinder head and the intake manifold with metal surface prep and silicone gasket remover. Follow the directions on the packaging.

➡️**If the engine is repaired or replaced because of upper engine failure, typically including valve or piston damage, check the intake manifold for metal debris. If metal debris is found, install a new intake manifold. Failure to follow these instructions can result in engine damage.**

26. Install the intake manifold in the following sequence.

27. Position the new intake manifold gaskets.

28. Position the intake manifold.

29. Loosely install the 9 intake manifold bolts.

30. Using a new O-ring seal, install the thermostat.

➡️**The thermostat housing bolts are tightened in sequence with the intake manifold bolts.**

31. Loosely install the thermostat housing and the 2 bolts.

32. Tighten the 11 bolts in 2 stages in the sequence shown.

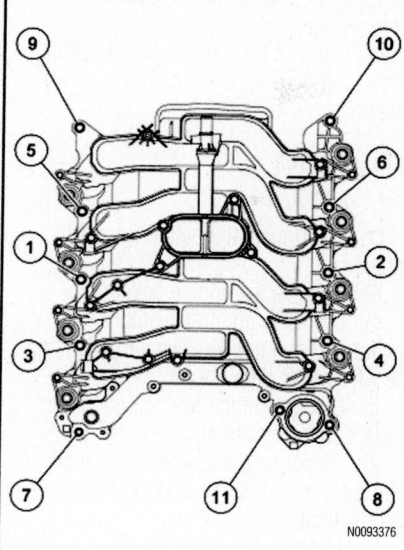

Fig. 105 Intake manifold tightening sequence

a. Stage 1: Tighten to 18 inch lbs (2 Nm).

b. Stage 2: Tighten to 18 ft. lbs. (25 Nm).

33. To complete installation, reverse the remaining removal procedure. Refer to the appropriate sections for procedures and torque values.

34. Connect the battery ground cable.

35. Fill and bleed the engine cooling system.

6.0L Engines

See Figure 106.

1. Disconnect the battery ground cable.

2. Remove the cooling fan stator.

3. Remove the turbocharger pedestal.

4. Vehicles with dual generator

a. Remove the accessory drive belt.

b. Remove the bolt and the accessory drive belt tensioner.

c. Remove the accessory drive belt.

d. Remove the 3 bolts, the bracket and the accessory drive belt idler pulley.

e. Remove the 2 bolts and the accessory drive belt tensioner.

f. Disconnect the generator electrical connector and the B+ wire.

g. Remove the 4 bolts and the generator and mounting bracket as an assembly.

5. Vehicles with single generator; Remove the accessory drive belt.

6. Disconnect the electrical connector pushpin and remove the bolt and position the ground wire aside.

7. Remove the bolt and position the

Manifold Absolute Pressure (MAP) assembly aside.

8. Remove the 3 bolts and position the wiring aside.

9. Remove the 3 bolts for the Charge Air Cooler (CAC) tube and oil fill tube.

10. Disconnect the oil fill tube at the valve cover.

11. Remove the 2 nuts, CAC tube, oil fill tube and bracket.

12. Disconnect the generator electrical connector, the B+ wire and the wiring pushpin.

13. Remove the transmission fluid indicator and tube nut.

14. Disconnect the pushpin retainer. Remove the retaining nut and position the transmission fluid indicator and tube aside.

15. Remove the 3 bolts, ground wire and the generator.

16. Remove the 2 bolts and position the heater hose tube aside.

17. Remove and discard the O-ring seal.

➡️**It will be necessary to position back or remove the heat insulating wrap.**

18. Disconnect the wiring retainer and the Fuel Injection Pressure Regulator (IPR) valve electrical connector.

19. Disconnect the EGR valve electrical connector.

20. Disconnect the Engine Oil Pressure (EOP) sensor electrical connector.

21. Disconnect the Engine Oil Temperature (EOT) sensor electrical connector.

22. Disconnect the pin-type retainer and Engine Coolant Temperature (ECT) sensor.

23. Remove the ECT sensor.

24. Plug or cap the opening as needed.

25. Disconnect the Intake Air Temperature 2 (IAT2) sensor electrical connector.

26. Remove the IAT2 sensor.

27. Plug or cap the opening as needed.

28. Disconnect the 8 fuel injector electrical connectors.

29. Disconnect the wiring harness retainers and position the engine wiring harness aside as needed for intake manifold removal.

30. Disconnect the MAP sensor hose.

31. Disconnect the engine coolant vent hose.

32. Remove the secondary fuel filter and remove all fuel from the filter housing.

33. Disconnect the fuel tubes and banjo bolt at the secondary fuel filter.

34. Remove and discard the sealing washers.

35. Disconnect the fuel tube at the fuel filter housing and remove the nut.

36. Remove the RH banjo bolt and fuel tube.

37. Discard the sealing washers.
38. Remove the 2 bolts and the secondary fuel filter assembly.

➡**Align the flat edge with the index feature located on the coolant supply port.**

39. Pull the EGR cooler clamp forward, twist and then slide the EGR cooler hose rearward to remove.
40. Remove the 11 bolts, the 5 stud bolts and the intake manifold.
41. Remove the intake manifold gaskets and the front module O-ring seal.
42. Discard the front module O-ring seal.
43. Clean and inspect the intake manifold gaskets. Install new gaskets if necessary.
44. Clean and inspect the sealing surfaces.

To install:

➡**The locating tabs on the gaskets must be positioned upward and toward the center of the engine, or a leak will occur.**

45. Install the intake manifold gaskets and the new front module O-ring seal.
46. Install the intake manifold, 5 stud bolts and 11 bolts. Tighten in 3 stages, in the sequence shown.
   a. Stage 1: Loosely install bolts 1-8.
   b. Stage 2: Tighten bolts 9-16 to 97 inch lbs. (11 Nm).
   c. Stage 3: Tighten all bolts to 97 inch lbs. (11 Nm).
47. To complete installation, reverse the remaining removal procedure. Refer to the

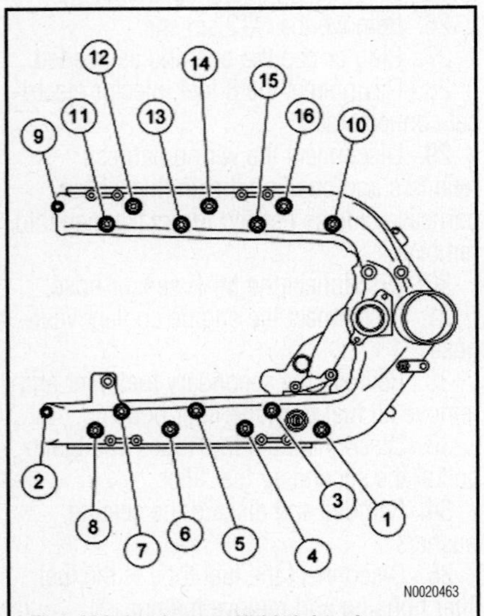

Fig. 106 Intake manifold tightening sequence—6.0L engine

N0020463

appropriate sections for procedures and torque values.

48. Connect the battery ground cable.
49. Fill and bleed the engine cooling system.

6.8L Engines

See Figure 107.

1. Disconnect the battery ground cable.
2. Remove the engine cover.
3. Drain the cooling system.
4. Remove the Air Cleaner (ACL) and the ACL outlet pipe.
5. Disconnect the fuel supply hose quick connect coupling.
6. Disconnect the generator electrical wiring harness retainer and the generator electrical connector.
7. Position the generator B+ protective boot aside and remove the generator B+ nut and terminal and position the generator harness aside.
8. Remove the 3 bolts, the stud bolt and the generator support bracket.
9. Compress and slide the hose clamp and disconnect the coolant hose.

➡**The red clip must be pulled out before disconnecting the electrical connector.**

10. Disconnect the electronic Electronic Throttle Control (ETC) electrical connector.

➡**The red clip must be pulled out before disconnecting the electrical connector.**

11. Disconnect the Throttle Position (TP) sensor electrical connector.
12. Disconnect the quick connect couplings and remove the PCV tube.
13. Disconnect the 2 coolant heated PCV fitting coolant hoses and the body vacuum tube connector.
14. Disconnect the brake booster vacuum hose and the Evaporative Emission (EVAP) hose quick connect coupling.
15. Disconnect the electrical connector, remove the bolt and position the EVAP canister purge valve aside.
16. Remove the 4 bolts and the Throttle Body (TB) and TB spacer as an assembly.
17. Discard the TB spacer gasket.
18. Disconnect the heater coolant hose.
19. Disconnect the 10 fuel injector electrical connectors.
20. Disconnect the 10 ignition coil electrical connectors.
21. Remove the transmission fluid indicator and tube support bracket nut.

22. Remove the transmission fluid level indicator tube support bracket nut and position the tube aside.
23. Disconnect the 2 RH engine wiring harness retainers and position the harness aside.
24. Disconnect the 3 LH engine wiring harness retainers and position the harness aside.
25. Remove the bolt and position the engine wiring harness support bracket aside.
26. Remove the 10 bolts and the 10 ignition coils.
27. Remove the 2 bolts, thermostat housing and thermostat.
28. Discard the O-ring seal.
29. Remove the 11 bolts, the intake manifold and the intake manifold gaskets.
30. Discard the intake manifold gaskets.

To install:

➡**Do not use metal scrapers, wire brushes, power abrasive discs or other abrasive means to clean the sealing surfaces. These tools cause scratches and gouges which make leak paths. Use a plastic scraping tool to remove all traces of old sealant.**

31. Clean the mating surfaces of the cylinder head and the intake manifold with silicone gasket remover and metal surface prep. Follow the directions on the packaging.

➡**If the engine is repaired or replaced because of upper engine failure, typically including valve or piston damage, check the intake manifold for metal debris. If metal debris is found, install a new intake manifold. Failure to follow these instructions can result in engine damage.**

32. Position new intake manifold gaskets and the intake manifold, and loosely install the 11 bolts.
33. Using a new O-ring seal, install the thermostat.

➡**The thermostat housing bolts are tightened in sequence with the intake manifold bolts.**

34. Position the thermostat housing and loosely install the 2 bolts.
35. Tighten the bolts in the sequence shown in 2 stages.
   a. Stage 1: Tighten to 18 inch lbs. (2 Nm).
   b. Stage 2: Tighten to 18 ft. lbs. (25 Nm).
36. To complete installation, reverse the remaining removal procedure. Refer to the appropriate sections for procedures and torque values.

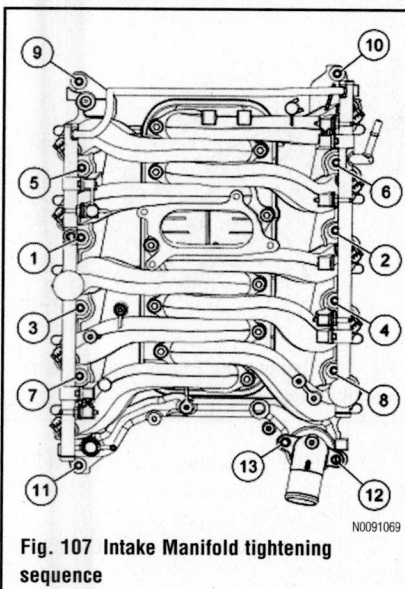

Fig. 107 Intake Manifold tightening sequence

37. Connect the battery ground cable.
38. Fill and bleed the engine cooling system.

OIL PAN

REMOVAL & INSTALLATION

4.6L, 5.4L & Engines

See Figures 108 through 113.

1. With the vehicle in NEUTRAL, position it on a hoist.
2. Remove the intake manifold. For additional information, refer to Intake Manifold in this section.
3. Remove the fan shroud and the engine cooling fan. For additional information, refer to Engine Cooling.
4. Remove the alternator.
5. Remove the retainers and the shield.
6. Disconnect the coolant hose from the heater outlet tube and remove the heater outlet tube stud.

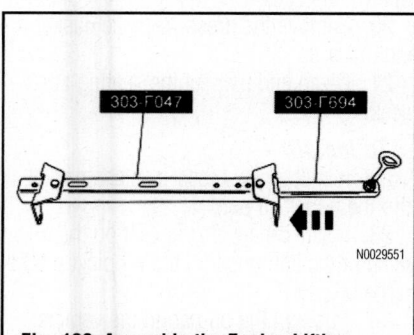

Fig. 108 Assemble the Engine Lifting Bracket and the Modular Engine Lift Bar Adapter

7. Remove the heater outlet tube.
8. For 5.4L Engines; Disconnect the Knock Sensor (KS) electrical connector and engine wiring harness retainers.
9. For 5.4L and 6.8L Engines; Remove the 2 heater outlet tube studs.
10. Discard the O-ring seals.
11. Remove the 2 upper transmission-to-engine bolts.
12. For 6.8L engines; Disconnect the oil fill tube from the RH valve cover. Remove the bolt and the oil fill tube.
13. Assemble the Engine Lifting Bracket and the Modular Engine Lift Bar Adapter.
14. Install the Engine Lifting Bracket and the Modular Engine Lift Bar Adapter.
15. Install the Engine Support Bar and support the engine.
16. Drain the engine oil, remove and discard the oil filter.
17. Remove the nut and position aside the transmission cooler tube support bracket and the starter wiring harness support bracket.
18. Remove the 4 engine support insulator-to-crossmember nuts.
19. Remove the 2 bolts and the flexplate inspection plate.

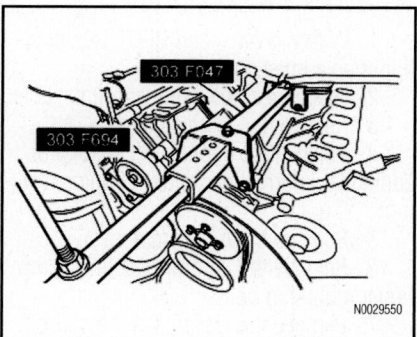

Fig. 109 Install the Engine Lifting Bracket and the Modular Engine Lift Bar Adapter

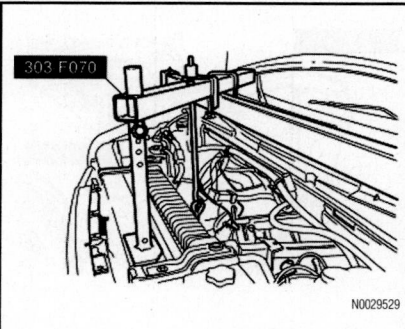

Fig. 110 Install the Engine Support Bar and support the engine

20. Using the Engine Support Bar, raise the engine 10.25 inches from the crankshaft pulley to the lower edge of the No. 1 cross-member.
21. Remove the 16 oil pan bolts and partially lower the oil pan.
22. Remove the 3 bolts retaining the oil pump screen and pickup tube. Position the bolts and the oil pump screen and pickup tube in the oil pan.
23. Remove the oil pan from the rear of the engine. Discard the oil pan gasket.

➡Do not use metal scrapers, wire brushes, power abrasive discs or other abrasive means to clean the sealing surfaces. These may cause scratches and gouges resulting in leak paths. Use a plastic scraper to clean the sealing surfaces.

24. Clean the sealing surfaces with silicone gasket remover and metal surface prep. Follow the directions on the packaging. Inspect the mating surfaces.

To install:

25. Position the oil pump screen and pickup tube and the 3 bolts into the oil pan and position the oil pan and new oil pan gasket onto the crossmember.
26. Position the oil pump screen and pickup tube and install the 3 bolts.
27. Tighten the 2 oil pump screen and pickup tube-to-oil pump bolts to 89 inch lbs. (10 Nm).
28. Tighten the oil pump screen and pickup tube-to-spacer bolt to 18 ft. lbs. (25 Nm).

➡If the oil pan is not secured within 4 minutes, the sealant must be removed and the sealing area cleaned with silicone gasket remover and metal surface prep. Follow the directions on the packaging.

29. Allow to dry until there is no sign of wetness, or 4 minutes, whichever is longer. Failure to follow this procedure can cause future oil leakage.
30. Apply the silicone gasket and sealant at the engine front cover-to-cylinder block mating surface.

➡If the oil pan is not secured within 4 minutes, the sealant must be removed and the sealing area cleaned with silicone gasket remover and metal surface prep. Follow the directions on the packaging.

31. Allow to dry until there is no sign of wetness, or 4 minutes, whichever is longer. Failure to follow this procedure can cause future oil leakage.

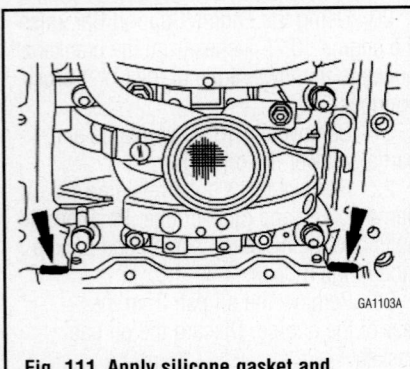

Fig. 111 Apply silicone gasket and sealant in the locations shown

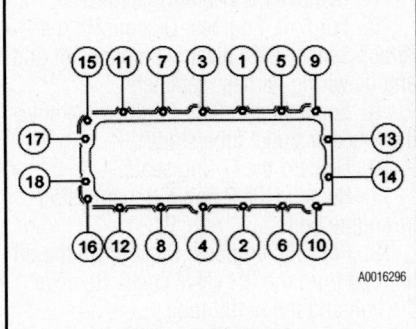

Fig. 113 Oil pan tightening sequence—6.8L engines

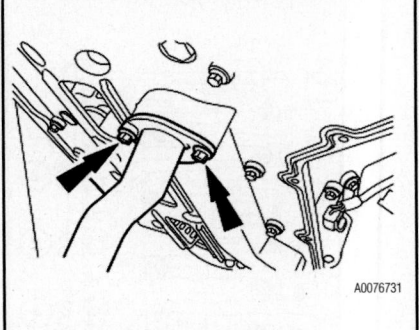

Fig. 115 Remove the 2 bolts and position the oil pickup tube

32. Apply the silicone gasket and sealant in the locations shown.

33. Position the new oil pan gasket and the oil pan and loosely install the 16 bolts.

34. Tighten the bolts in 3 stages in the sequence shown.

    a. Stage 1: Tighten to 18 inch lbs (2 Nm).

    b. Stage 2: Tighten to 15 ft. lbs. (20 Nm).

    c. Stage 3: Tighten an additional 60 degrees.

35. Install a new oil filter.

36. Lower the engine and remove the Engine Support Bar, Engine Lifting Bracket and the Modular Engine Lift Bar Adapter.

37. Install the 4 engine support insulator-to-crossmember nuts. Tighten to 66 ft. lbs. (90 Nm).

38. Position the flexplate inspection

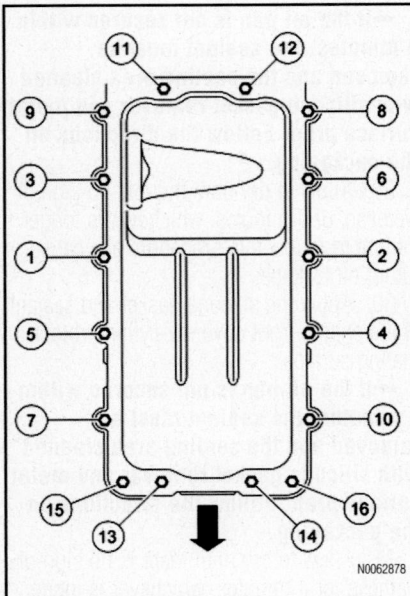

Fig. 112 Oil pan tightening sequence—4.6L and 5.4L engines

cover and install the 2 bolts. Tighten to 25 ft. lbs. (34 Nm).

39. Position the transmission cooler tube support bracket and the starter wiring harness support bracket and install the nut. Tighten to 7 ft. lbs. (10 Nm).

40. To complete installation, reverse the remaining removal procedure. Refer to the appropriate sections for procedures and torque values.

41. Fill the engine with clean engine oil.

42. Start the engine and check for leaks.

6.0L Engine

See Figures 114 through 116.

1. With the vehicle in NEUTRAL, position it on a hoist.

2. Disconnect the battery ground cable.

3. Remove the engine cover.

4. Remove the cooling fan stator. For additional information, refer to Engine Cooling.

5. Remove the A/C compressor.

6. Remove the 2 power steering pump upper mounting bolts.

7. Remove the LH fan stator stand-off.

➡**The front bolt will remain in the power steering pump.**

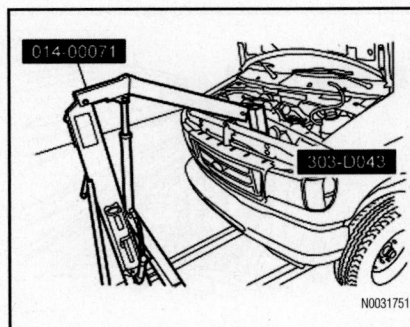

Fig. 114 Install the Engine Lifting Attachment and Heavy Duty Floor Crane

8. Remove the 2 bolts and position the power steering pump aside.

9. Remove the oil pan drain plug.

10. Remove and discard the 2 exhaust flange nuts.

11. Remove the 4 engine mount nuts.

12. Remove the bolt and position the cable aside and remove the RH fan stator stand-off.

13. Install the Adapter. Refer to Engine Assembly.

14. Install the Engine Lifting Attachment and Heavy Duty Floor Crane.

➡**Use care when raising the engine to avoid engine or body damage.**

15. Raise the engine.

16. Support the engine with jackstands or other suitable devices.

➡**The oil pan bolts must be reinstalled in their original positions. Mark the location of the longer bolts to aid in installation.**

17. Remove the 20 bolts and position back the oil pan until the oil pickup tube bolts are accessible.

18. Remove the 2 bolts and position the oil pickup tube into the oil pan. Remove the oil pan.

19. Remove and discard the oil pickup tube O-ring seal.

20. Remove the press-in-place gasket and discard.

21. Clean and inspect the sealing surfaces.

To install:

22. Install a new press-in-place gasket into the upper oil pan.

23. Install a new O-ring seal on the oil pickup tube and position the oil pickup tube in the oil pan.

24. Position the oil pan in the vehicle.

25. Install the oil pan pickup tube and the 2 bolts. Tighten to 10 ft. lbs. (13 Nm).

26. Install the oil pan and the 20 bolts.

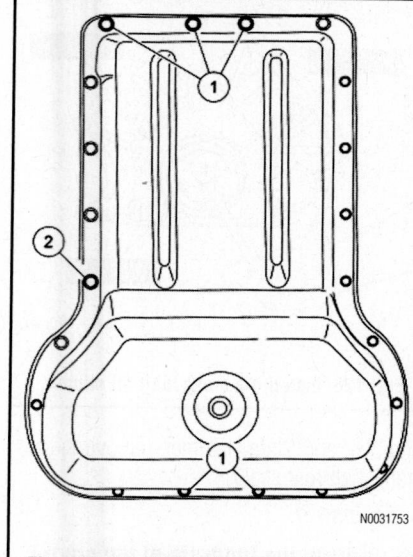

Fig. 116 Identifying the longer bolts (1) and remaining bolts (2)

27. Install the 5 longer oil pan bolts.
28. Install the remaining oil pan bolts. Tighten to 10 ft. lbs. (13 Nm).
29. Lower the engine.
30. Position back the cable and install the bolt. Install the RH fan stator stand-off. Tighten both to 35 ft. lbs. (47 Nm).

➡**Tighten the top retaining nut first.**

➡**Left side shown, right side similar.**

31. Install the 4 engine mount nuts. Tighten to 66 ft. lbs. (90 Nm).
32. Install the 2 new exhaust flange nuts. Tighten to 30 ft. lbs. (40 Nm).
33. Clean and inspect the oil pan drain plug and gasket. Install new, if necessary.
34. Install the oil drain plug. Tighten to 32 ft. lbs. (44 Nm).
35. Reposition the power steering pump and install the 2 bolts. Tighten to 25 Nm (18 lb-ft).
36. Install the LH fan stator stand-off. Tighten to 35 ft. lbs. (47 Nm).
37. Install the 2 upper power steering pump bolts. Tighten to 18 ft. lbs. (25 Nm).
38. Fill the engine with clean engine oil.
39. Install the engine cover.
40. Connect the battery ground cable.
41. Install the A/C compressor.
42. Install the cooling fan stator.
43. Run the engine and check for leaks.

OIL PUMP

REMOVAL & INSTALLATION

4.6L, 5.4L and 6.8L Engines

See Figures 117 and 118.

Fig. 117 Locating the 3 bolts

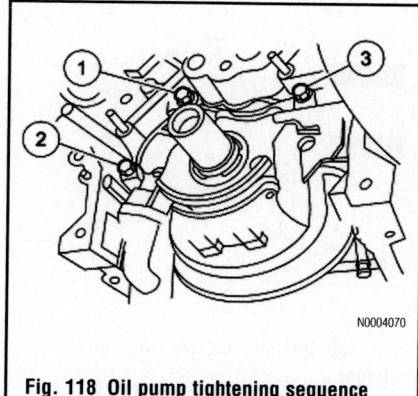

Fig. 118 Oil pump tightening sequence

1. Remove the oil pan. For additional information, refer to Oil Pan in this section.
2. Remove the crankshaft sprocket. For additional information, refer to Timing Chain in this section.
3. Remove the 3 bolts and the oil pump.

To install:

➡**Lubricate the new O-ring seal with clean engine oil.**

4. Clean and inspect the mating surfaces and install a new O-ring seal.
5. Install the oil pump and loosely install the 3 bolts.
6. Tighten the bolts in the sequence shown. Tighten to 89 inch lbs. (10 Nm).
7. Install the crankshaft sprocket. For additional information, refer to Timing Chain in this section.
8. Install the oil pan. For additional information, refer to Oil Pan in this section.

6.0L Engines

1. Remove the crankshaft front seal. For additional information, refer to Crankshaft Front Seal in this section.
2. Remove the 5 bolts and the oil pump cover.

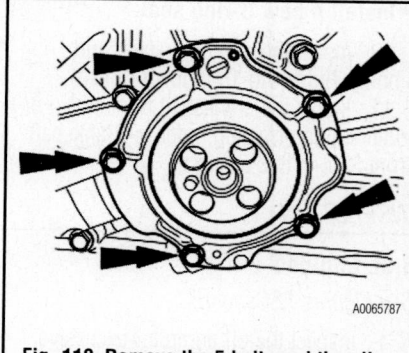

Fig. 119 Remove the 5 bolts and the oil pump cover

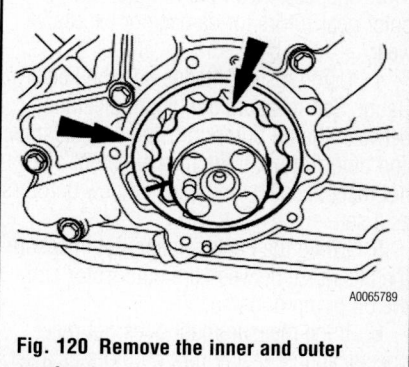

Fig. 120 Remove the inner and outer gerotors

3. Remove and discard the O-ring seal.

➡**Mark the front of the inner and outer gerotors for correct reassembly.**

4. Remove the inner and outer gerotors.
5. Inspect the oil pump components. Install new components, as necessary.
6. Inspect the oil pump for excessive metal particles.
7. Inspect the oil pump for gouges, cracks or deep scratches.
8. Inspect the oil pump inner and outer gear rotors for damage or excessive wear.

To install:

➡**If reusing the original oil pump drive rotors, install the oil pump drive rotors with the marking pointing outward. Replacement oil pump drive rotors will have no marks and orientation is not necessary.**

9. Lubricate the inner drive rotor with clean engine oil and install onto the crankshaft. Lubricate the outer drive rotor with clean engine oil and mesh with the inner drive rotor in the oil pump housing.

➡**Install a new O-ring seal.**

10. Install the oil pump cover and 5 bolts. Tighten to 10 ft. lbs. (13 Nm).

11. Install the crankshaft front seal. For additional information, refer to Crankshaft Front Seal in this section.

INSPECTION

6.0L Engines

See Figures 121 and 122.

1. Inspect the oil pump for excessive metal particles.

2. Inspect the oil pump for gouging, cracks or deep scratches.

3. Inspect the oil pump inner and outer gear rotors for damage or excessive wear.

4. Using a straightedge and the Feeler Gauge Set, measure the height clearance between the oil pump housing and the inner and outer rotors. If the measurement does not meet specifications, install new gerotors as a set.

5. Using the Feeler Gauge Set, measure the clearance between the outer rotor and the oil pump housing.

6. If the measurement does not meet specifications, install new gerotors as a set.

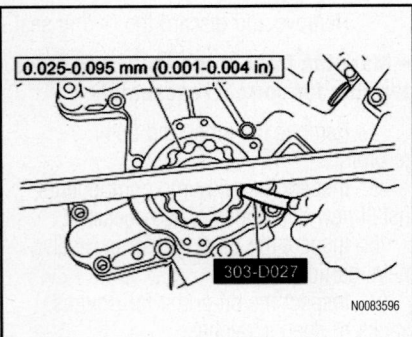

Fig. 121 Using a straightedge and the Feeler Gauge Set

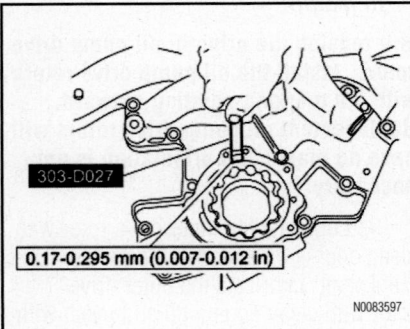

Fig. 122 Using the Feeler Gauge Set, measure the clearance

REAR MAIN SEAL

REMOVAL & INSTALLATION

4.6L, 5.4L and 6.8L Engines

See Figures 123 through 125.

1. With the vehicle in NEUTRAL, position it on a hoist.

2. Remove the flexplate.

3. Using the Crankshaft Rear Oil Slinger Remover and Slide Hammer, remove the crankshaft oil slinger.

4. Using the Crankshaft Rear Oil Seal

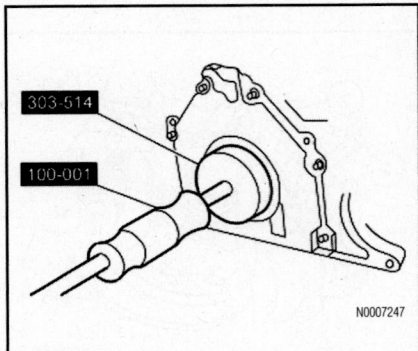

Fig. 123 Remove the crankshaft oil slinger

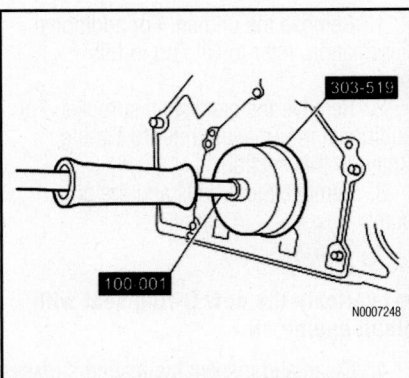

Fig. 124 Remove the crankshaft rear seal

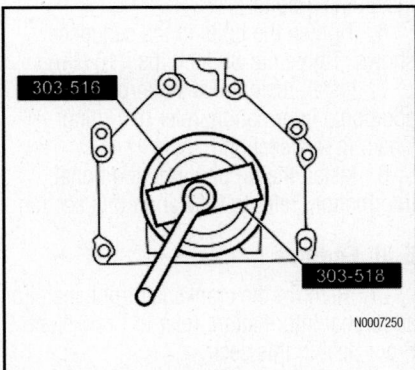

Fig. 125 Install the crankshaft rear seal

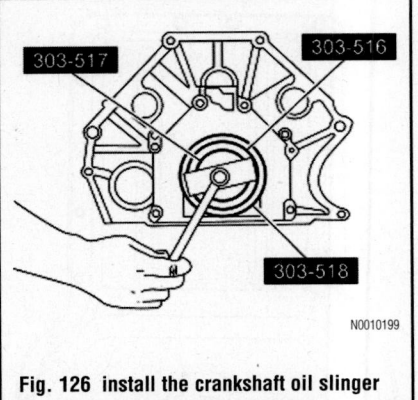

Fig. 126 install the crankshaft oil slinger

Remover and Slide Hammer, remove the crankshaft rear seal.

To install:

➡**Lubricate the inner lip of the crankshaft rear seal with engine oil.**

5. Using the Crankshaft Rear Oil Seal Installers, install the crankshaft rear seal.

6. Using the Crankshaft Rear Oil Slinger Installer and Crankshaft Rear Oil Seal Installers, install the crankshaft oil slinger.

7. Install the flexplate.

TIMING CHAIN FRONT COVER

REMOVAL & INSTALLATION

4.6L, 5.4L and 6.8L Engines

See Figures 127 through 129.

1. With the vehicle in NEUTRAL, position it on a hoist.

2. Remove the radiator.

3. Remove the LH and RH valve covers.

4. Remove the oil drain plug and drain the engine oil. Install the drain plug when finished.

5. Remove the nut and position the LH radio interference capacitor aside.

6. Remove the nut and position the RH radio interference capacitor aside.

7. Loosen the 4 coolant pump pulley bolts.

8. Rotate the tensioner clockwise and remove the accessory drive belt.

9. Remove the 4 coolant pump pulley bolts and the coolant pump pulley.

10. Remove the bolt and the accessory drive belt idler pulley.

11. Remove the 3 bolts and position the power steering pump aside.

12. Disconnect the A/C compressor electrical connector.

13. Disconnect the Crankshaft Position (CKP) sensor electrical connector.

14. Remove the nut and position aside

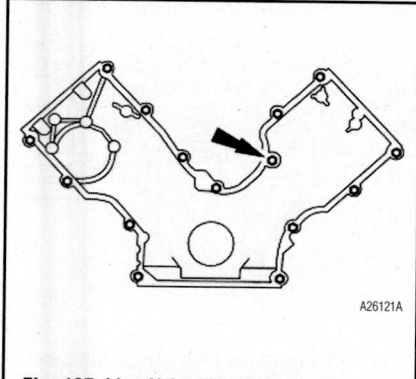

Fig. 127 Identifying the 15 fasteners

the transmission cooler tube support bracket and the starter wiring harness support bracket.

15. Disconnect the Camshaft Position (CMP) sensor electrical connector.

➡**This bolt is a torque-to-yield design and cannot be reused. Failure to follow these instructions may result in engine damage.**

16. Using the Strap Wrench, remove the bolt and washer and discard the bolt.

17. Remove the crankshaft pulley. Refer to Timing Chain in this Section.

18. Remove and discard the front crankshaft seal.

19. Remove the front 4 oil pan bolts.

20. Remove the 15 fasteners.

21. Remove the engine front cover from the front cover-to-cylinder block dowel.

22. Remove and discard the engine front cover gaskets.

➡**Do not use metal scrapers, wire brushes, power abrasive discs or other abrasive means to clean the sealing surfaces. These tools cause scratches and gouges which make leak paths. Use a plastic scraping tool to remove all traces of old sealant.**

23. Clean the mating surfaces with silicone gasket remover and metal surface prep. Follow the directions on the packaging.

24. Inspect the mating surfaces.

To install:

➡**Do not use metal scrapers, wire brushes, power abrasive discs or other abrasive means to clean the sealing surfaces. These tools cause scratches and gouges which make leak paths. Use a plastic scraping tool to remove all traces of old sealant.**

➡**If the engine front cover is not secured within 4 minutes, the sealant**

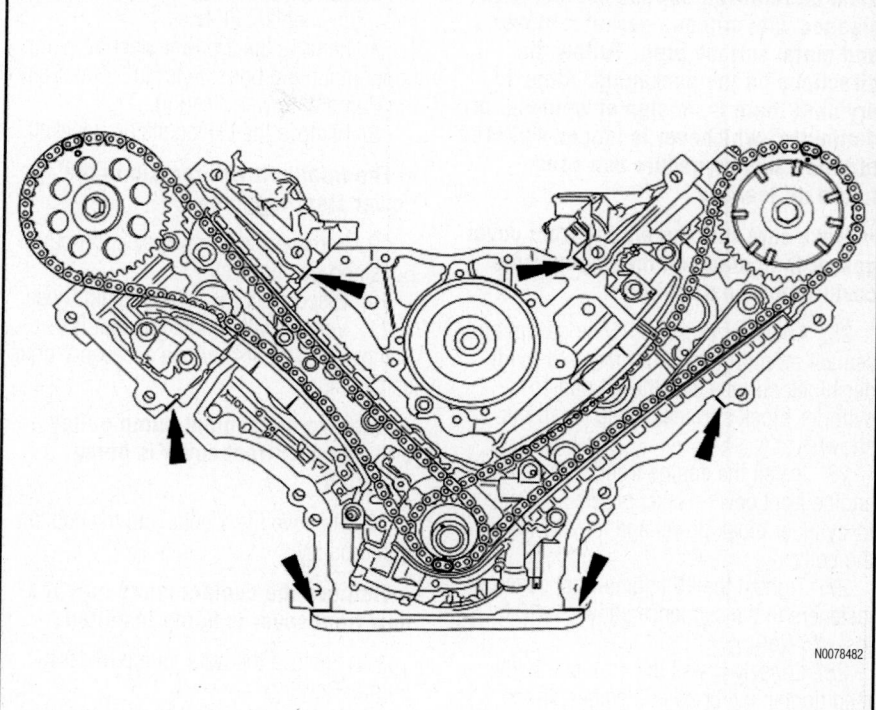

Fig. 128 Cylinder head-to-cylinder block surface and the oil pan-to-cylinder block surface locations

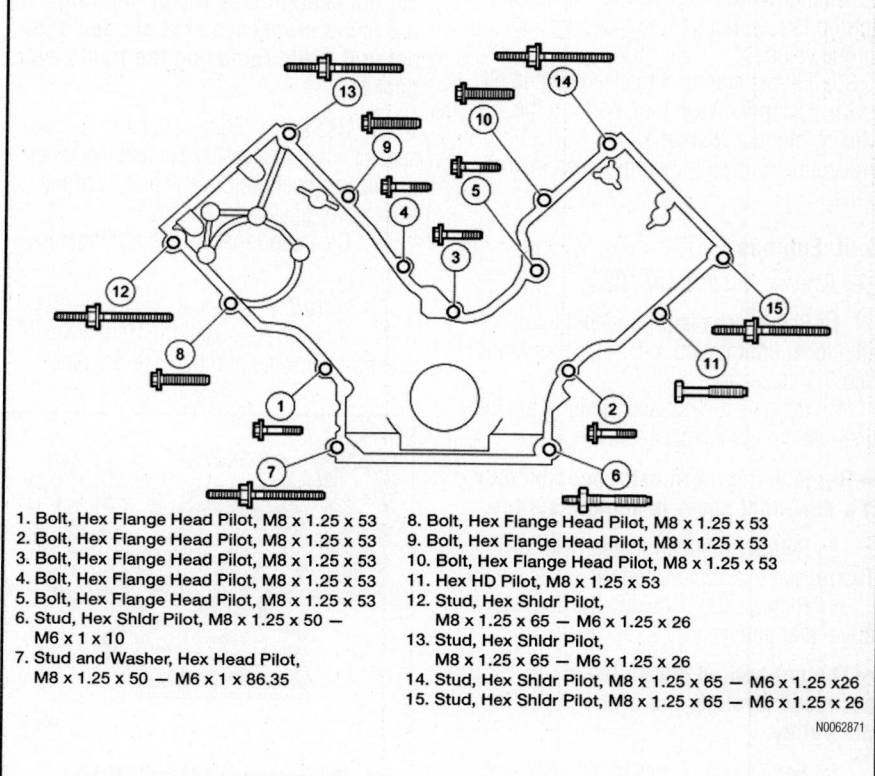

1. Bolt, Hex Flange Head Pilot, M8 x 1.25 x 53
2. Bolt, Hex Flange Head Pilot, M8 x 1.25 x 53
3. Bolt, Hex Flange Head Pilot, M8 x 1.25 x 53
4. Bolt, Hex Flange Head Pilot, M8 x 1.25 x 53
5. Bolt, Hex Flange Head Pilot, M8 x 1.25 x 53
6. Stud, Hex Shldr Pilot, M8 x 1.25 x 50 — M6 x 1 x 10
7. Stud and Washer, Hex Head Pilot, M8 x 1.25 x 50 — M6 x 1 x 86.35
8. Bolt, Hex Flange Head Pilot, M8 x 1.25 x 53
9. Bolt, Hex Flange Head Pilot, M8 x 1.25 x 53
10. Bolt, Hex Flange Head Pilot, M8 x 1.25 x 53
11. Hex HD Pilot, M8 x 1.25 x 53
12. Stud, Hex Shldr Pilot, M8 x 1.25 x 65 — M6 x 1.25 x 26
13. Stud, Hex Shldr Pilot, M8 x 1.25 x 65 — M6 x 1.25 x 26
14. Stud, Hex Shldr Pilot, M8 x 1.25 x 65 — M6 x 1.25 x26
15. Stud, Hex Shldr Pilot, M8 x 1.25 x 65 — M6 x 1.25 x 26

Fig. 129 Tighten the 15 engine front cover fasteners in the sequence shown

must be removed and the sealing area cleaned with silicone gasket remover and metal surface prep. Follow the directions on the packaging. Allow to dry until there is no sign of wetness, or 4 minutes, whichever is longer. Failure to follow this procedure can cause future oil leakage.

➡**Make sure that the engine front cover gasket is in place on the engine front cover before installation.**

25. Apply a bead of silicone gasket and sealant along the cylinder head-to-cylinder block surface and the oil pan-to-cylinder block surface, at the locations shown.
26. Install the engine front cover with the engine front cover gasket on the front cover-to-cylinder block dowel and loosely install the bolts.
27. Tighten the 15 engine front cover fasteners in the sequence shown to 18 ft. lbs. (25 Nm).
28. Loosely install the 4 oil pan bolts, then tighten the bolts in 2 stages, in the sequence shown.
    a. Stage 1: Tighten to 15 ft. lbs. (20 Nm).
    b. Stage 2: Tighten an additional 60 degrees.
29. To complete installation, reverse the remaining removal procedure. Refer to the appropriate sections for procedures and torque values.
30. Fill the engine with clean engine oil.
31. Using the scan tool, perform the Misfire Monitor Neutral Profile Correction procedure, following the on-screen instructions.

6.0L Engines

See Figures 130 through 132.

1. Remove the intake manifold. For additional information, refer to Intake Manifold in this section.
2. Remove the nut and position the fuel line retaining bracket aside.

➡**Remove the thermostat housing only if a new front cover is being installed.**

3. Remove the thermostat. Refer to Thermostat in Engine Cooling.
4. Remove the bolts and the accessory drive idler pulleys.

➡**The nut behind the pulley is accessed through one of the holes in the pulley.**

5. Remove the 2 nuts and the coolant hose shield.

6. Loosen the clamp and disconnect the engine coolant fill hose.
7. Remove the 2 power steering pump upper mounting bolts. Refer to Power Steering Pump in Power Steering.
8. Remove the LH fan stator stand-off.

➡**The front bolt will remain in the power steering pump.**

9. Remove the 2 power steering pump bolts and position aside.
10. Disconnect the lower radiator hose.
11. Vehicle with single generator; Remove the 2 bolts and the accessory drive belt tensioner.

➡**Remove the coolant pump pulley only if a new front cover is being installed.**

12. Remove the 4 bolts and the coolant pump pulley.

➡**Remove the coolant pump only if a new front cover is being installed.**

13. Remove the water pump. Refer to Engine Cooling.
14. Remove the oil pump. For additional information, refer to Oil Pump in this section.
15. Remove the 17 bolts and the front cover.

➡**Sealant is used where the crankcase and lower crankcase meet. Failure to cut the sealant may result in pulling the lower crankcase seal out and damaging it while removing the front cover gasket.**

16. Use a thin-blade scraper to cut the sealant where the crankcase and the lower crankcase meet. Remove and discard the front cover gasket.
17. Clean and inspect the sealing surfaces.

   To install:

18. If removed, install the front cover crankcase dowels into the cylinder block.

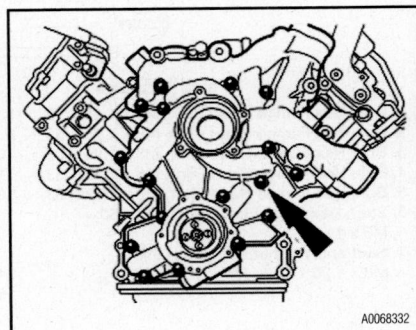

Fig. 130 Remove the 17 bolts and the front cover

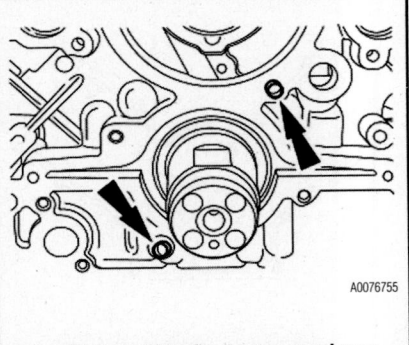

Fig. 131 Install the front cover crankcase dowels into the cylinder block

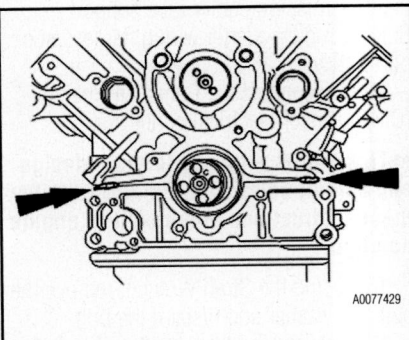

Fig. 132 Locating where the crankcase and the lower crankcase meet

➡**Use guide studs to aid in installation. Studs must be fabricated locally.**

19. Install the guide studs.
20. Apply a bead of sealant at the seam where the crankcase and the lower crankcase meet.
21. Install a new engine front cover gasket.
22. Install the 17 engine front cover and bolts. Tighten to 18 ft. lbs. (24 Nm).
23. To complete installation, reverse the remaining removal procedure. Refer to the appropriate sections for procedures and torque values.
24. Fill the engine with clean engine oil.
25. Using the scan tool, perform the Misfire Monitor Neutral Profile Correction procedure, following the on-screen instructions.

TIMING CHAIN & SPROCKETS

REMOVAL & INSTALLATION

4.6L, 5.4L and 6.8L Engines

See Figures 133 through 138.

➡**Since the engine is not free-wheeling, the timing procedures must be followed exactly or piston and valve damage can occur.**

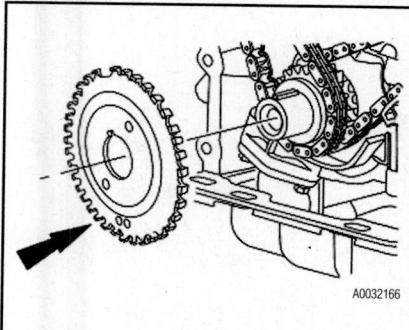

Fig. 133 Remove the crankshaft sensor ring from the crankshaft

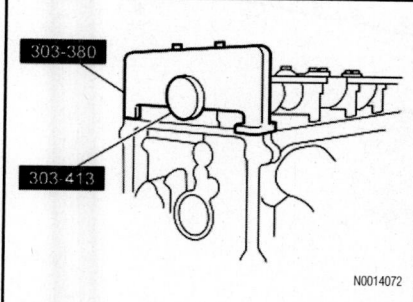

Fig. 134 Install the Camshaft Aligner and Camshaft Pulley Aligner

1. Remove the engine front cover. For additional information, refer to Timing Chain Front Cover in this section.

2. Remove the crankshaft sensor ring from the crankshaft.

3. Rotate the crankshaft until the timing mark on the RH camshaft sprocket is approximately at the 11 o'clock position and the timing mark on the LH camshaft sprocket is approximately at the 1 o'clock position.

4. Install the Camshaft Aligner and Camshaft Pulley Aligner on the camshaft.

➡️If one or both of the tensioner mounting bolts are loosened or removed, the tensioner-sealing bead must be inspected for seal integrity. If cracks, tears or separation from the tensioner body or permanent compression of the seal bead is observed, install a new tensioner or engine damage may occur.

5. Remove the timing chain tensioning system from both timing chains.
   a. Remove the 4 bolts.
   b. Remove the 2 timing chain tensioners.
   c. Remove the 2 timing chain tensioner arms.

6. Remove the 2 timing chains and crankshaft sprocket.

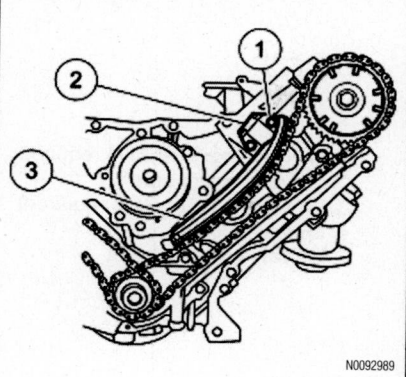

Fig. 135 Remove the 4 bolts (1), 2 timing chain tensioners (2) and 2 timing chain tensioner arms (3)

7. Remove the timing chain guides.
   a. Remove the 2 bolts.
   b. Remove the LH timing chain guide.
   c. Remove the 2 bolts.
   d. Remove the RH timing chain guide.

To install:

➡️Timing chain procedures must be followed exactly or damage to valves and pistons will result.

➡️Prior to installation, inspect the tensioner-sealing bead for seal integrity. If cracks, tears, separation from the tensioner body or permanent compression of the seal bead is observed, install a new tensioner or engine damage may occur.

8. Compress the tensioner plunger, using a vise.

9. Install a retaining clip on the tensioner to hold the plunger in during installation.

10. If the copper links are not visible, mark 1 link on one end and 1 link on the other end, and use as timing marks.

11. Install the crankshaft sprocket, making sure the flange faces forward.

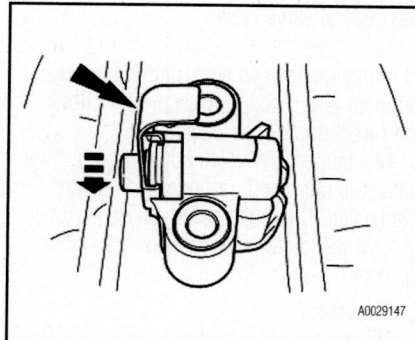

Fig. 136 Install a retaining clip on the tensioner

12. Install the timing chain guides.
13. Position the LH timing chain guide.
14. Install and tighten the 2 LH bolts.
15. Position the RH timing chain guide.
16. Install and tighten the 2 RH bolts. Tighten to 89 inch lbs. (10 Nm).

➡️Unless otherwise instructed, do not rotate either the crankshaft or the camshafts, when the timing chains are removed and the cylinder heads are installed. Severe piston and valve damage will occur.

➡️The No. 1 cylinder is at Top Dead Center (TDC) when the stud on the engine block fits into the slot in the handle of the special tool.

17. Using the Crankshaft Holding Tool, position the crankshaft so the No. 1 cylinder is at TDC.

18. Remove the Crankshaft Holding Tool.

19. Position the LH (inner) timing chain on the crankshaft sprocket, aligning the copper (marked) link with the timing mark on the sprocket.

20. Install the LH timing chain on the camshaft sprocket, aligning the copper (marked) link with the timing marks on the sprocket.

➡️The LH timing chain tensioner arm has a bump near the dowel hole for identification.

21. Position the LH timing chain tensioner arm on the dowel pin and install the LH timing chain tensioner and the 2 bolts. Tighten to 18 ft. lbs. (25 Nm).

22. Remove the retaining clip from the LH timing chain tensioner.

23. Position the RH (outer) timing chain on the crankshaft sprocket, aligning the copper (marked) link with the timing mark on the sprocket.

24. Install the RH timing chain on the camshaft sprocket, aligning the copper

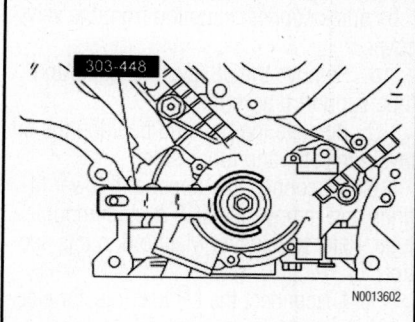

Fig. 137 Using the Crankshaft Holding Tool

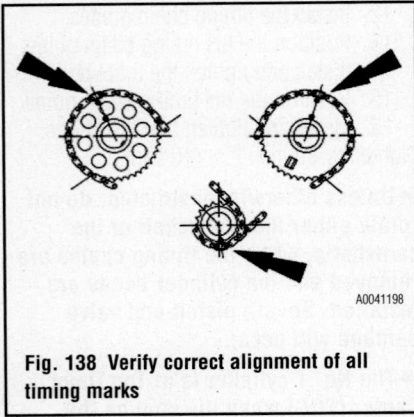

Fig. 138 Verify correct alignment of all timing marks

(marked) link with the timing marks on the sprocket.

25. Position the RH timing chain tensioner arm on the dowel pin and install the RH timing chain tensioner and the 2 bolts. Tighten to 18 ft. lbs. (25 Nm).

26. Remove the retaining clip from the RH timing chain tensioner.

27. Make sure that the copper (marked) chain links are lined up with the dots on the crankshaft sprockets and the camshaft sprocket.

28. Remove the Camshaft Aligner and Camshaft Pulley Aligner from the camshaft.

29. Install the crankshaft sensor ring on the crankshaft.

30. Install the engine front cover. For additional information, refer to Engine Front Cover in this section.

VALVE COVERS

REMOVAL & INSTALLATION

4.6L Engine

LH Valve Cover

See Figure 139.

1. Remove the Air Cleaner (ACL) assembly and the ACL outlet pipe.

2. Remove the engine cover.

3. Disconnect the crankcase ventilation tube quick connect coupling from the valve cover.

4. Remove the oil level indicator and tube support bracket net.

5. Remove the bolt and position the oil level indicator and tube aside.

6. Disconnect the upper and lower fittings and remove the EGR system module tube. Refer to Exhaust Manifold in this section.

7. Disconnect the LH fuel injector electrical connectors, ignition coil electrical connectors and the wire harness retainers.

8. Disconnect the wiring harness

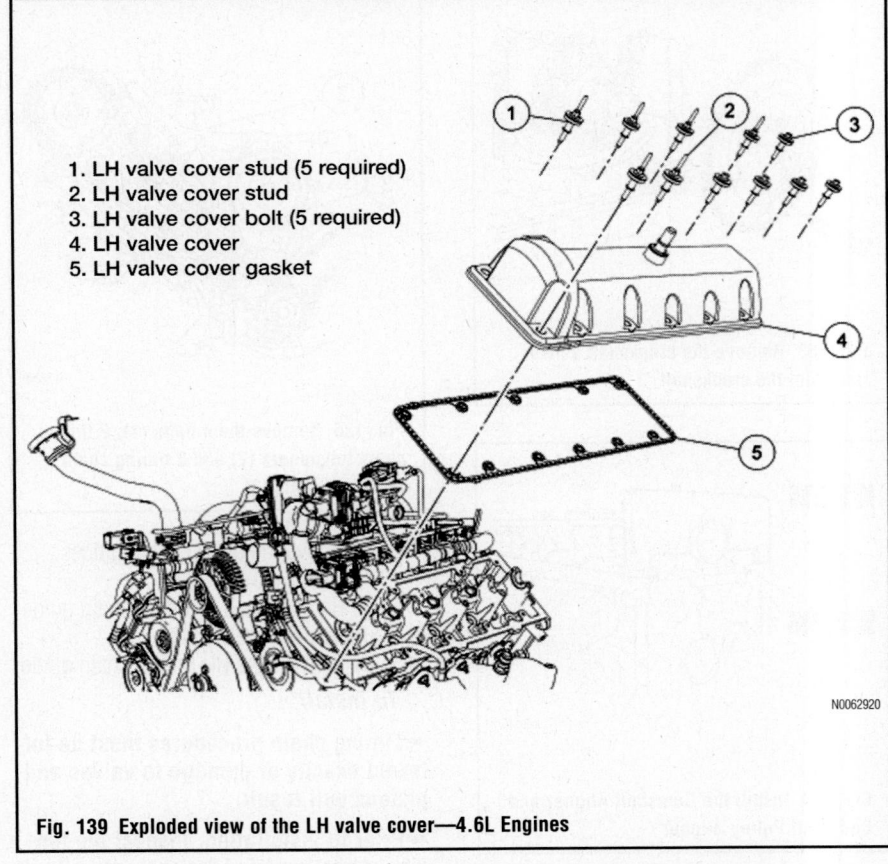

1. LH valve cover stud (5 required)
2. LH valve cover stud
3. LH valve cover bolt (5 required)
4. LH valve cover
5. LH valve cover gasket

Fig. 139 Exploded view of the LH valve cover—4.6L Engines

retainer and position the engine control wiring harness aside.

9. Disconnect the electrical connector.

10. Disconnect the engine wiring harness retainer and the 2 PCM electrical connectors.

➡**Do not use metal scrapers, wire brushes, power abrasive discs or other abrasive means to clean the sealing surfaces. These tools cause scratches and gouges which make leak paths. Use a plastic scraping tool to clean sealing surfaces.**

11. Remove the LH valve cover.

12. Fully loosen the fasteners and remove the valve cover.

13. Clean the valve cover mating surface of the cylinder head with silicone gasket remover and metal surface prep. Follow the directions on the packaging.

14. Inspect the valve cover gasket. If the gasket is damaged, remove and discard the gasket. Clean the valve cover gasket groove with soap and water or a suitable solvent.

To install:

15. Apply instant gel adhesive completely around the gasket groove in the valve cover. Install the new valve cover gasket.

➡**If not secured within 4 minutes, the sealant must be removed and the sealing area cleaned with silicone gasket remover and metal surface prep. Follow the directions on the packaging. Allow to dry until there is no sign of wetness, or 4 minutes, whichever is longer. Failure to follow this procedure can cause future oil leakage.**

16. Apply a bead of silicone gasket and sealant in 2 places where the engine front cover meets the cylinder head.

17. Position the valve cover and gasket on the cylinder head and loosely install all of the fasteners.

18. Position the valve cover and tighten the 11 fasteners in a criss-cross pattern to 89 inch lbs. (10 Nm).

19. To complete installation, reverse the remaining removal procedure. Refer to the appropriate sections for procedures and torque values.

RH Valve Cover

See Figure 140.

1. Remove the Air Cleaner (ACL) assembly and the ACL outlet pipe.

2. Remove the engine cover.

3. Remove the LH engine support insulator.

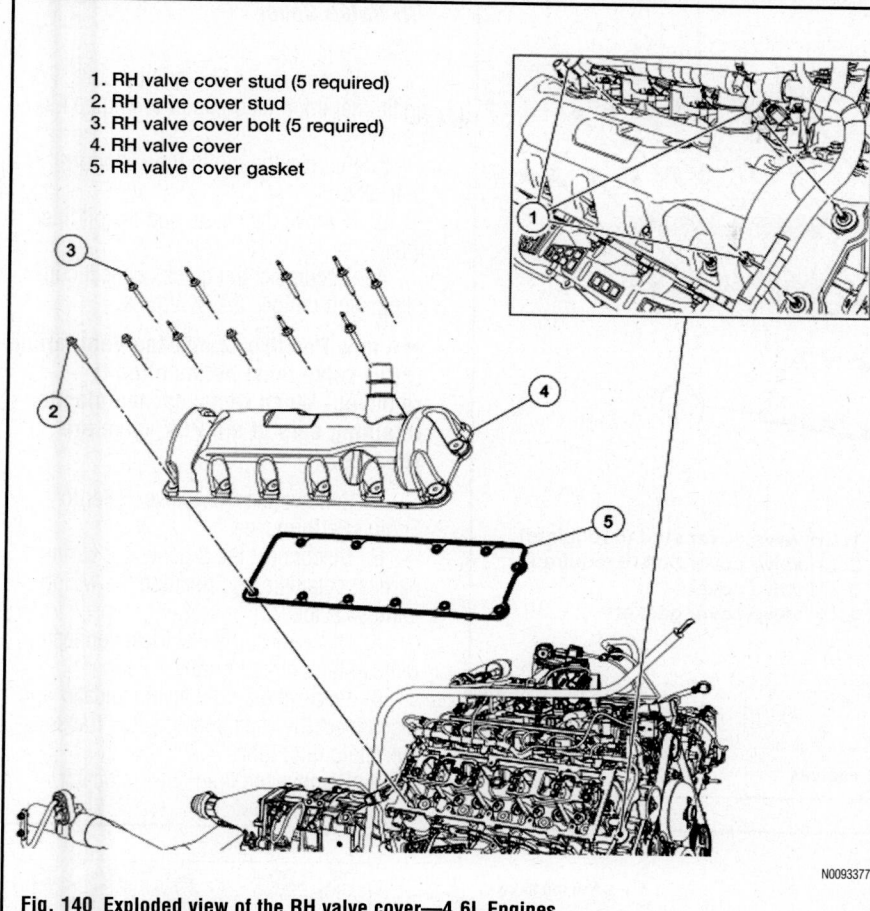

1. RH valve cover stud (5 required)
2. RH valve cover stud
3. RH valve cover bolt (5 required)
4. RH valve cover
5. RH valve cover gasket

Fig. 140 Exploded view of the RH valve cover—4.6L Engines

→**Do not use the oil pan to support the engine or damage to the oil pan may occur.**

4. Using a wood block to support the engine, slowly lower the engine and remove the jack.

5. Disconnect the quick connect couplings and remove the PCV tube.

→**A new Positive Crankcase Ventilation (PCV) valve must be installed if removed. When removed, the plastic retaining ears of the PCV valve are sheared.**

6. Remove the PCV valve. Refer to Engine Performance.

7. Remove the oil fill tube support bracket bolt.

8. Remove the clamp and the oil filler tube.

9. Disconnect the 2 generator wiring harness retainers and position the wiring harness aside.

10. Disconnect the electrical connector, remove the nut and ground strap.

11. Remove the fuel charging wiring harness from the valve cover studs and position the wiring harness and support bracket aside.

→**Do not use metal scrapers, wire brushes, power abrasive discs or other abrasive means to clean the sealing surfaces. These tools cause scratches and gouges which make leak paths. Use a plastic scraping tool to clean sealing surfaces.**

12. Remove the RH valve cover.

13. Fully loosen the fasteners and remove the valve cover.

14. Clean the valve cover mating surface of the cylinder head with silicone gasket remover and metal surface prep. Follow the directions on the packaging.

15. Inspect the valve cover gasket. If the gasket is damaged, remove and discard the gasket. Clean the valve cover gasket groove with soap and water or a suitable solvent.

To install:

16. Apply instant gel adhesive completely around the gasket groove in the valve cover. Install the new valve cover gasket.

→**If the valve cover is not secured within 4 minutes, the sealant must be removed and the sealing area cleaned with silicone gasket remover and metal surface prep. Follow the directions on the packaging.**

17. Allow to dry until there is no sign of wetness, or 4 minutes, whichever is longer. Failure to follow this procedure can cause future oil leakage.

18. Apply the silicone gasket and sealant in 2 places where the engine front cover meets the cylinder head.

19. Position the valve cover and tighten the 11 fasteners in the criss-cross to 89 inch lbs. (10 Nm).

20. To complete installation, reverse the remaining removal procedure. Refer to the appropriate sections for procedures and torque values.

5.4L Engine

LH Valve Cover

See Figure 141.

1. Remove the Air Cleaner (ACL) assembly and the ACL outlet pipe.

2. Remove the engine cover.

3. Disconnect the crankcase ventilation tube quick connect coupling from the valve cover.

4. Remove the oil level indicator and tube support bracket nut.

5. Remove the bolt and position the oil level indicator and tube aside.

6. Disconnect the 4 LH fuel injector electrical connectors, 4 LH ignition coil electrical connectors and the 4 LH wire harness retainers.

7. Disconnect the wiring harness retainer and position the engine control wiring harness aside.

8. Disconnect the electrical connector.

9. Disconnect the engine wiring harness retainer and the 2 PCM electrical connectors.

→**Do not use metal scrapers, wire brushes, power abrasive discs or other abrasive means to clean the sealing surfaces. These tools cause scratches and gouges which make leak paths. Use a plastic scraping tool to clean sealing surfaces.**

10. Remove the LH valve cover.

11. Fully loosen the fasteners and remove the valve cover.

12. Clean the valve cover mating surface of the cylinder head with silicone gasket remover and metal surface prep. Follow the directions on the packaging.

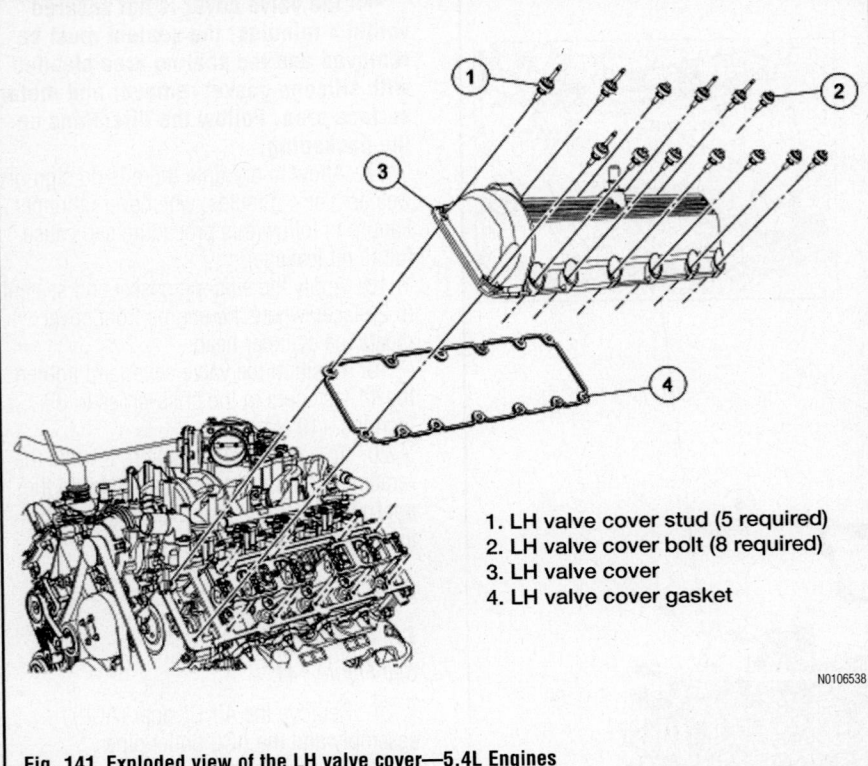

Fig. 141 Exploded view of the LH valve cover—5.4L Engines

1. LH valve cover stud (5 required)
2. LH valve cover bolt (8 required)
3. LH valve cover
4. LH valve cover gasket

N0106538

RH Valve Cover

See Figure 142.

1. Remove the 4 RH ignition coils. For additional information, refer to Engine Electrical.

2. Remove the oil fill tube support bracket bolt.

3. Remove the clamp and the oil filler tube.

4. Disconnect the quick connect couplings and remove the PCV tube.

➡**A new Positive Crankcase Ventilation (PCV) valve must be installed if removed. When removed, the plastic retaining ears of the PCV valve are sheared.**

5. Remove the PCV valve. Refer to Engine Performance

6. Disconnect the 2 generator wiring harness retainers and position the wiring harness aside.

7. Disconnect the electrical connector, remove the nut and ground strap.

8. Remove the fluid level indicator and disconnect the attachments at the transmission fluid filler tube.

9. Remove the fluid level indicator.

13. Inspect the valve cover gasket. If the gasket is damaged, remove and discard the gasket. Clean the valve cover gasket groove with soap and water or a suitable solvent.

To install:

14. Apply instant gel adhesive completely around the gasket groove in the valve cover. Install the new valve cover gasket.

➡**If not secured within 4 minutes, the sealant must be removed and the sealing area cleaned with silicone gasket remover and metal surface prep. Follow the directions on the packaging. Allow to dry until there is no sign of wetness, or 4 minutes, whichever is longer. Failure to follow this procedure can cause future oil leakage.**

15. Apply a bead of silicone gasket and sealant in 2 places where the engine front cover meets the cylinder head.

16. Position the valve cover and gasket on the cylinder head and loosely install all of the fasteners.

17. Tighten the 13 fasteners in a criss-cross pattern. Tighten to 89 inch lbs. (10 Nm).

18. To complete installation, reverse the remaining removal procedure. Refer to the appropriate sections for procedures and torque values.

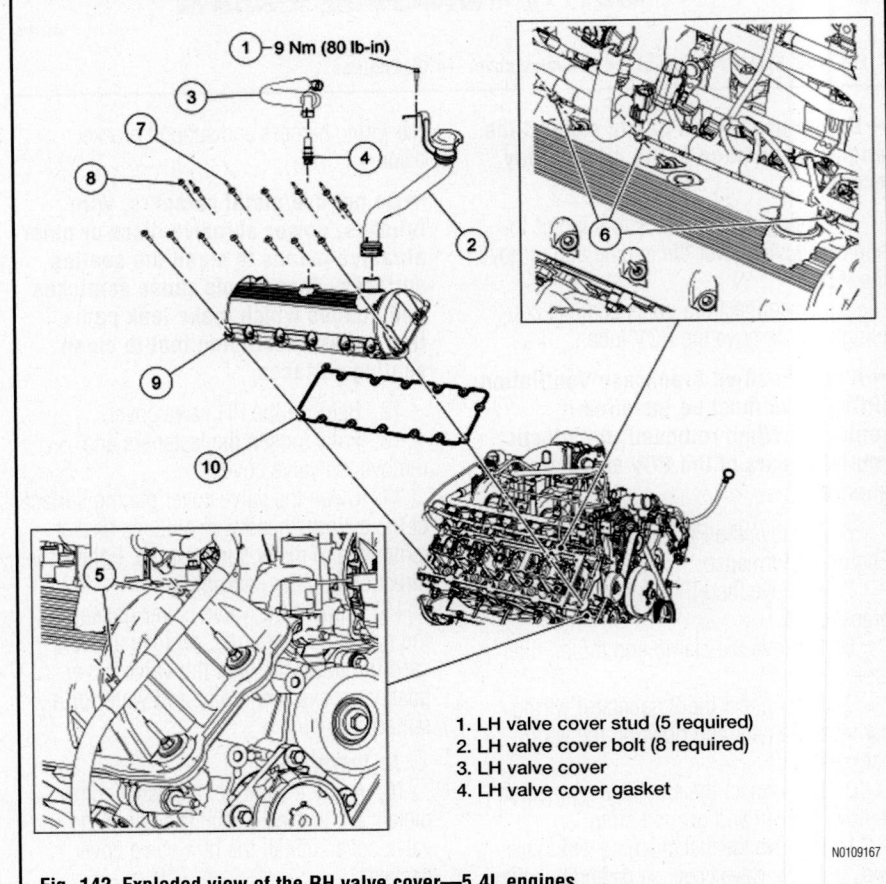

1. LH valve cover stud (5 required)
2. LH valve cover bolt (8 required)
3. LH valve cover
4. LH valve cover gasket

N0109167

Fig. 142 Exploded view of the RH valve cover—5.4L engines

10. Disconnect the rear heater hose hanger.

11. Remove the bolt, nut and position the transmission fluid filler tube aside.

12. Disconnect the 4 RH fuel injector electrical connectors.

13. Remove the fuel charging wiring harness from the valve cover studs and position the wiring harness and support bracket aside.

➡**Do not use metal scrapers, wire brushes, power abrasive discs or other abrasive means to clean the sealing surfaces. These tools cause scratches and gouges which make leak paths. Use a plastic scraping tool to clean sealing surfaces.**

14. Remove the RH valve cover.

15. Fully loosen the 14 fasteners and remove the valve cover.

16. Clean the valve cover mating surface of the cylinder head with silicone gasket remover and metal surface prep. Follow the directions on the packaging.

17. Inspect the valve cover gasket. If the gasket is damaged, remove and discard the gasket. Clean the valve cover gasket groove with soap and water or a suitable solvent.

To install:

18. Apply instant gel adhesive completely around the gasket groove in the valve cover. Install the new valve cover gasket.

➡**If not secured within 4 minutes, the sealant must be removed and the sealing area cleaned with silicone gasket remover and metal surface prep. Follow the directions on the packaging. Allow to dry until there is no sign of wetness, or 4 minutes, whichever is longer. Failure to follow this procedure can cause future oil leakage.**

19. Apply a bead of silicone gasket and sealant in 2 places where the engine front cover meets the cylinder head.

20. Position the valve cover on the cylinder head and loosely install the 14 fasteners.

21. Tighten the 14 fasteners in a criss-cross pattern. Tighten to 89 inch lbs. (10 Nm).

22. To complete installation, reverse the remaining removal procedure. Refer to the appropriate sections for procedures and torque values.

6.0L Engine

LH Valve Cover

See Figure 143.

1. Disconnect the battery ground cable.
2. Remove the engine cover.

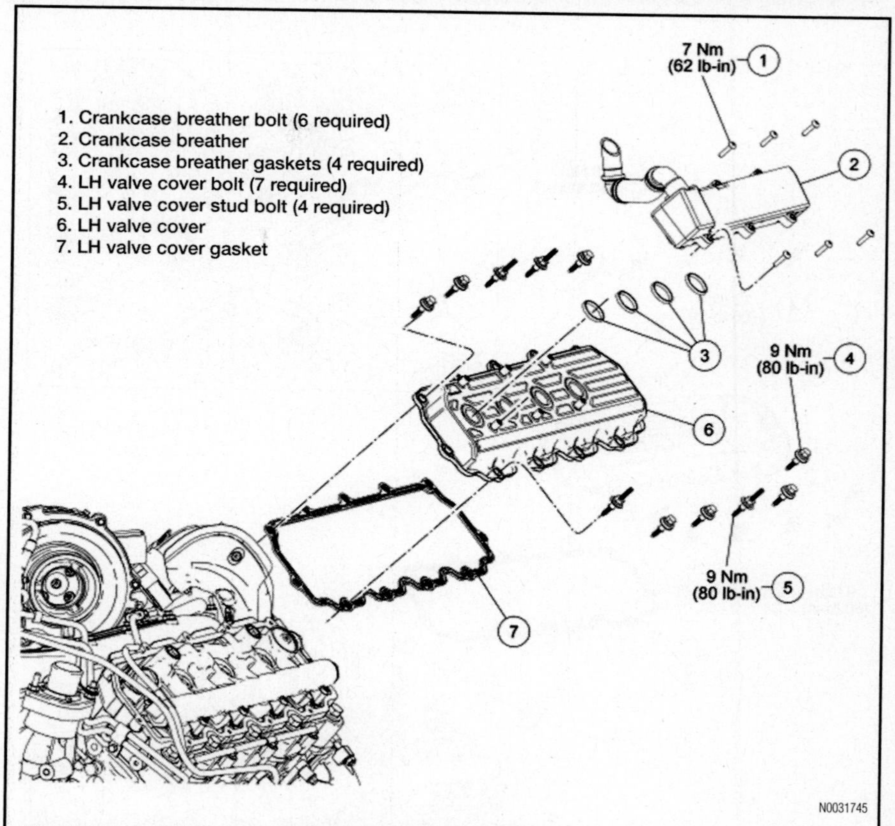

1. Crankcase breather bolt (6 required)
2. Crankcase breather
3. Crankcase breather gaskets (4 required)
4. LH valve cover bolt (7 required)
5. LH valve cover stud bolt (4 required)
6. LH valve cover
7. LH valve cover gasket

7 Nm (62 lb-in) — 1
9 Nm (80 lb-in) — 4
9 Nm (80 lb-in) — 5

N0031745

Fig. 143 Exploded view of the LH valve cover—6.0L engines

3. Remove the turbocharger inlet tube. Refer to Air Cleaner Assembly in this section.

➡**If there is any oil residue, clean both connecting ports and the inside surface of the Charge Air Cooler (CAC) pipe to prevent the pipe from blowing off.**

4. Loosen the clamps and remove the CAC pipe. Refer to Air Cleaner Assembly in this section.

5. Disconnect the oil level indicator and tube from the stator.

6. Disconnect the glow plug wire retainer, remove the nut and position the oil level indicator and tube aside.

7. Disconnect the glow plug module electrical connectors.

8. Disconnect the Exhaust Pressure (EP) sensor electrical connector and push-pin retainer.

9. Disconnect the EP tube at the exhaust manifold.

10. Remove the 2 nuts and the glow plug module. Refer to Engine Performance.

➡**To prevent engine damage, do not use air-powered tools when installing the crankcase breather.**

➡**Mark the position of the valve cover bolts for valve cover bolt installation.**

11. If servicing the crankcase breather, remove the 6 bolts and the crankcase breather.

12. Discard the 4 crankcase breather gaskets.

➡**To prevent engine damage, do not use air-powered tools when installing the valve cover.**

➡**Mark the position of the valve cover bolts for valve cover bolt installation.**

13. Remove the 11 retainers and the valve cover.

14. Clean and inspect the valve cover gasket. To install, tighten to 80 inch lbs. (9 Nm).

15. To install, reverse the removal procedure.

RH Valve Cover

See Figure 144.

1. Connect a Heavy Duty Floor Crane and lifting chain to the Adapter and raise the engine as needed to remove the motor mount. Refer to Engine Assembly.

2. Remove the 4 bolts and the LH motor mount. Carefully lower the engine. Refer to Engine Assembly.

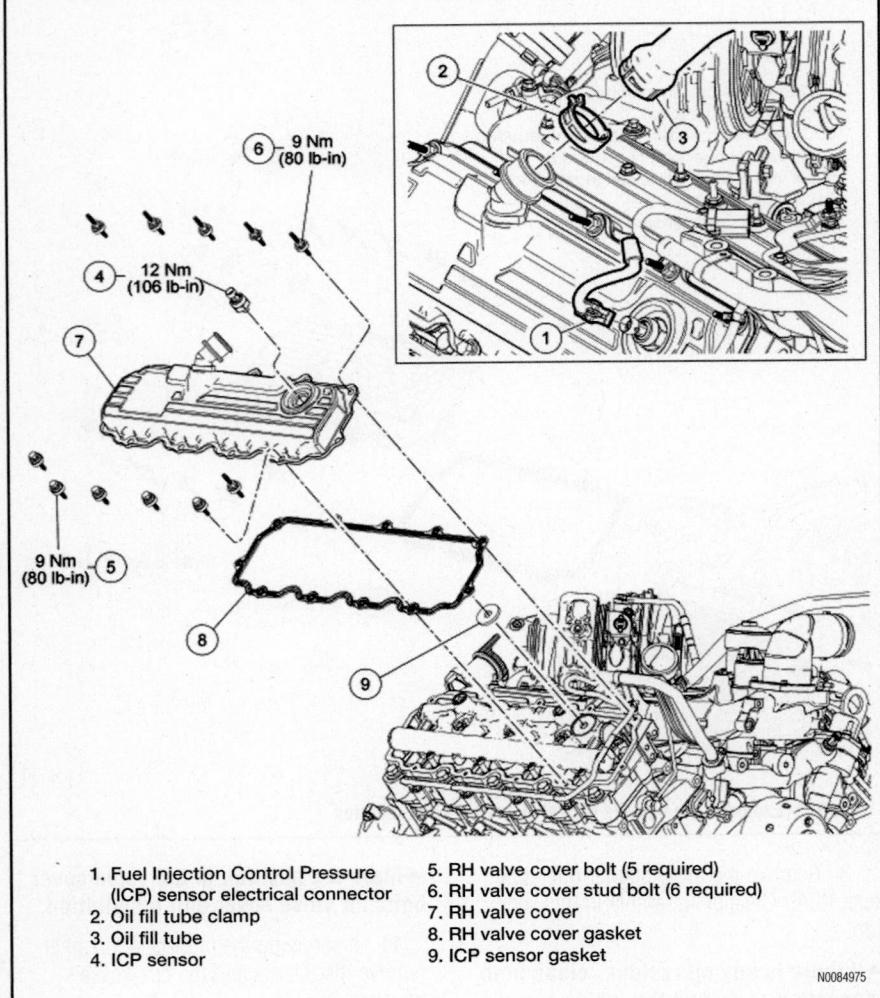

1. Fuel Injection Control Pressure (ICP) sensor electrical connector
2. Oil fill tube clamp
3. Oil fill tube
4. ICP sensor
5. RH valve cover bolt (5 required)
6. RH valve cover stud bolt (6 required)
7. RH valve cover
8. RH valve cover gasket
9. ICP sensor gasket

N0084975

Fig. 144 Exploded view of the RH valve cover—6.0L Engines

3. Remove the bolt and position the Manifold Absolute Pressure (MAP) sensor aside. Refer to Engine Performance.

4. Remove the 3 bolts for the Charge Air Cooler (CAC) pipe and oil fill tube.

5. Remove the nut and disconnect the pushpin retainer for the transmission fluid indicator and tube. To install, tighten to 10 ft. lbs. (13 Nm).

6. Remove the retaining nut for the transmission fluid level indicator and tube. Position the tube aside.

7. Loosen the clamp at the turbocharger outlet hose. Disconnect the CAC pipe from the turbocharger.

8. Refer to Air Cleaner assembly in this section.

9. Disconnect the oil fill tube at the valve cover.

10. Disconnect the Injection Control Pressure (ICP) sensor electrical connector and wire retainers.

11. Remove the ICP sensor. Refer to Engine Performance.

12. Position the wiring away from the valve cover as needed.

➡**To prevent engine damage, do not use air-powered tools when installing the valve cover.**

➡**Mark the position of the valve cover bolts for the valve cover bolt installation.**

13. Remove the 6 stud bolts, the 5 bolts and the valve cover.

14. Clean and inspect the valve cover gasket. To install, tighten to 80 inch lbs. (9 Nm).

15. Remove the high-pressure oil rail-to-valve cover gasket.

16. To install, reverse the removal procedure.

17. Tighten the top retaining nuts on the motor mount first.

6.8L Engines

LH Valve Cover

See Figure 145.

1. Remove the engine cover.

2. Remove the Air Cleaner (ACL) and the ACL outlet pipe.

3. Remove the engine fan. Refer to Engine Fan in Engine Cooling.

4. Disconnect the quick connect couplings and remove the PCV tube.

5. Remove the 4 exhaust Y-pipe flange nuts.

6. Loosen the 2 transmission insulator and retainer nuts. Refer to Drivetrain.

7. Loosen the 2 LH and RH engine support insulator nuts. Refer to Engine Assembly.

8. Using a utility stand positioned on the RH rear of the cylinder block, raise the engine 1 inch.

9. Remove the 2 RH engine support insulator-to-crossmember bracket nuts. Refer to Engine Assembly.

10. Remove the nut and the RH engine support insulator-to-crossmember bracket. Refer to Engine Assembly.

11. Using the utility stand positioned on the RH rear of the cylinder block, lower the engine 38 mm (1.5 in).

12. Disconnect the 2 PCM electrical connectors and the wiring harness retainer.

13. Disconnect the 3 LH engine wiring harness retainers.

14. Disconnect the engine wiring harness retainer from the LH valve cover stud bolt.

15. Disconnect the Camshaft Position (CMP) sensor electrical connector.

16. Disconnect the engine wiring harness retainer from the engine front cover stud bolt.

17. Disconnect the LH 5 fuel injector electrical connectors.

18. Disconnect the LH 5 ignition coil electrical connectors and position the engine wiring harness aside.

19. Remove the oil level indicator and tube support bracket nut.

20. Remove the bolt and position the oil level indicator and tube aside.

21. Disconnect the quick connect coupling and remove the crankcase vent tube.

➡**Do not use metal scrapers, wire brushes, power abrasive discs or other abrasive means to clean the sealing surfaces. These tools cause scratches and gouges which make leak paths. Use a plastic scraping tool to clean the sealing surfaces.**

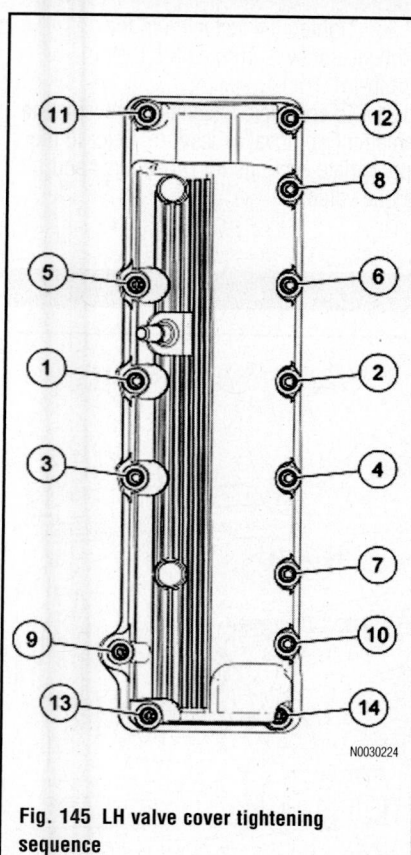

Fig. 145 LH valve cover tightening sequence

➡ **The fasteners are part of the valve cover and should not be removed.**

22. Remove the LH valve cover.

23. Fully loosen the fasteners and remove the valve cover.

24. Clean the valve cover mating surface of the cylinder head with silicone gasket remover and metal surface prep. Follow the directions on the packaging.

25. Discard the valve cover gasket. Clean the valve cover gasket groove with soap and water or a suitable solvent.

To install:

26. Apply instant gel adhesive completely around the gasket groove in the valve cover. Install the new valve cover gasket.

➡ **If not secured within 4 minutes, the sealant must be removed and the sealing area cleaned. To clean the sealing area, use silicone gasket remover and metal surface prep. Follow the directions on the packaging. Allow to dry until there is no sign of wetness, or 4 minutes, whichever is longer. Failure to follow this procedure can cause future oil leakage.**

27. Apply a bead of silicone gasket and sealant in 2 places where the engine front cover meets the cylinder head.

28. Position the valve cover and the valve cover gasket on the cylinder head and loosely install the 14 bolts.

29. Tighten the 14 bolts in the sequence shown. Tighten to 89 inch lbs. (10 Nm).

30. To complete installation, reverse the remaining removal procedure. Refer to the appropriate sections for procedures and torque values.

RH Valve Cover

See Figure 146.

1. Remove the engine cover.

2. Remove the Air Cleaner (ACL) and the ACL outlet pipe.

3. Remove the engine fan. Refer to Engine Fan in Engine Cooling.

4. Remove the 4 exhaust Y-pipe flange nuts. Refer to Catalytic Converter.

5. Loosen the 2 transmission insulator and retainer nuts. Refer to Drivetrain.

6. Remove the 2 LH engine support insulator nuts. Refer to Engine Assembly.

7. Loosen the 2 RH engine support insulator nuts. Refer to Engine Assembly.

8. Using a utility stand positioned on the LH rear of the cylinder block, raise the engine 25.4 mm (1 in).

9. Remove the 3 nuts and the LH

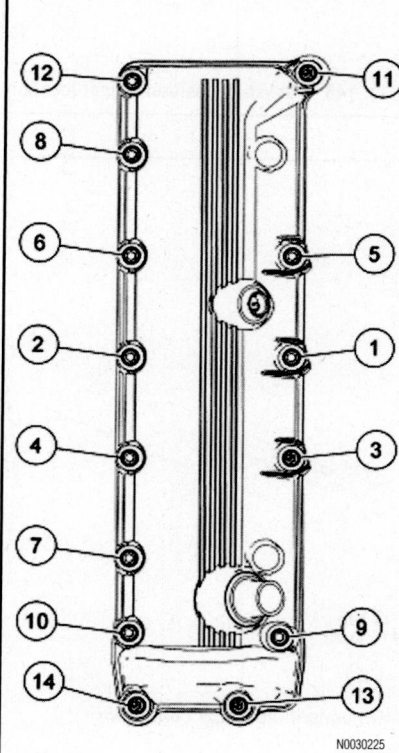

Fig. 146 RH valve cover tightening sequence—6.8L Engines

engine support insulator-to-crossmember bracket. Refer to Engine Assembly.

10. Using the utility stand positioned on the LH rear of the cylinder block, lower the engine 38 mm (1.5 in).

11. Disconnect the generator wiring harness retainer from the engine front cover stud bolt.

12. Disconnect the 2 electrical connectors.

13. Disconnect the electrical connector position retainers, remove the nut, ground strap and mounting bracket.

14. Disconnect the oil fill tube.

15. Remove the bolt and the oil fill tube.

16. Disconnect the quick connect couplings and remove the PCV tube.

17. Rotate the PCV valve counterclockwise and remove the PCV valve.

18. Disconnect the wiring harness retainer from the front RH valve cover stud bolt.

19. Remove the nut for the transmission fluid indicator and tube.

20. Remove the nut and position the transmission fluid indicator and tube aside.

21. Disconnect the RH 5 ignition coil electrical connectors.

22. Disconnect the RH 5 fuel injector electrical connectors.

23. Disconnect the 2 retainers and position the engine wiring harness aside.

24. Remove the 5 bolts and the 5 RH ignition coils.

➡ **Do not use metal scrapers, wire brushes, power abrasive discs or other abrasive means to clean the sealing surfaces. These tools cause scratches and gouges which make leak paths. Use a plastic scraping tool to remove all traces of old sealant.**

➡ **The fasteners are part of the valve cover and should not be removed.**

25. Remove the RH valve cover.

26. Fully loosen the fasteners and remove the valve cover.

27. Clean the valve cover mating surface of the cylinder head with silicone gasket remover and metal surface prep. Follow the directions on the packaging.

28. Discard the valve cover gasket. Clean the valve cover gasket groove with soap and water or a suitable solvent.

To install:

Apply instant gel adhesive completely around the gasket groove in the valve cover. Install the new valve cover gasket.

NOTE: If not secured within 4 minutes, the sealant must be removed and the sealing area cleaned. To clean the sealing area, use silicone gasket remover and metal surface prep. Follow the directions on the packaging. Allow to dry until there is no sign of wetness, or 4 minutes, whichever is longer. Failure to follow this procedure can cause future oil leakage.

Apply a bead of silicone gasket and sealant in 2 places where the engine front cover meets the cylinder head.

29. Position the valve cover and the valve cover gasket on the cylinder head and loosely install the 14 fasteners.

30. Tighten the fasteners in the sequence shown. Tighten to 10 Nm (89 lb-in).

31. To complete installation, reverse the remaining removal procedure. Refer to the appropriate sections for procedures and torque values.

ENGINE PERFORMANCE & EMISSION CONTROLS

COMPONENT LOCATIONS

Diesel System

See Figures 147 through 156.

Gasoline Systems

See Figures 157 through 168.

CAMSHAFT POSITION (CMP) SENSOR

REMOVAL & INSTALLATION

Diesel Systems

1. With the vehicle in NEUTRAL, position it on a hoist.
2. Turn the ignition switch to the OFF position.

➡**The Camshaft Position (CMP) sensor is located behind the power steering pump.**

3. Disconnect the CMP sensor electrical connector.

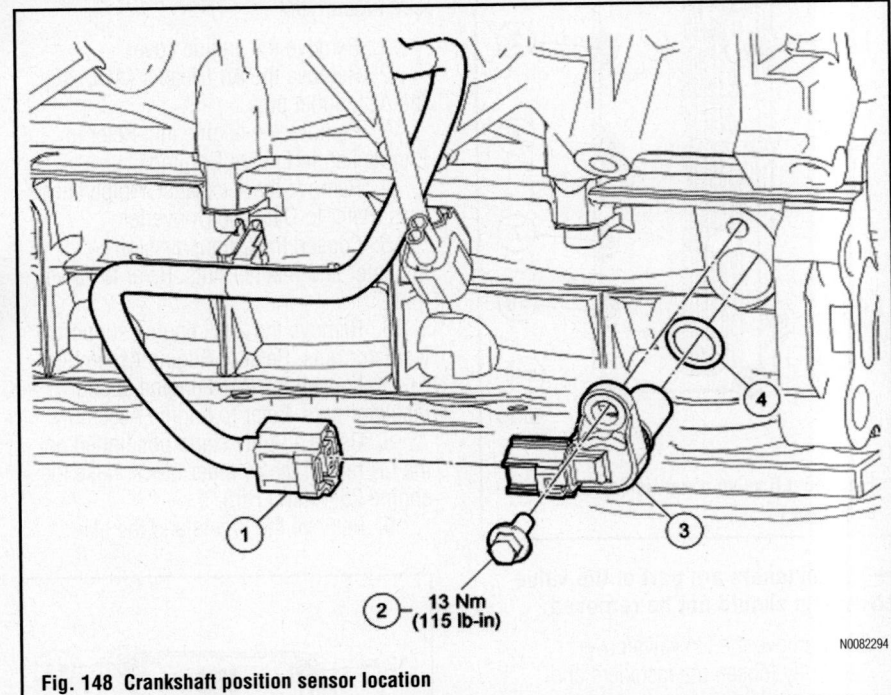

2 — 13 Nm (115 lb-in)

Fig. 148 Crankshaft position sensor location

N0082294

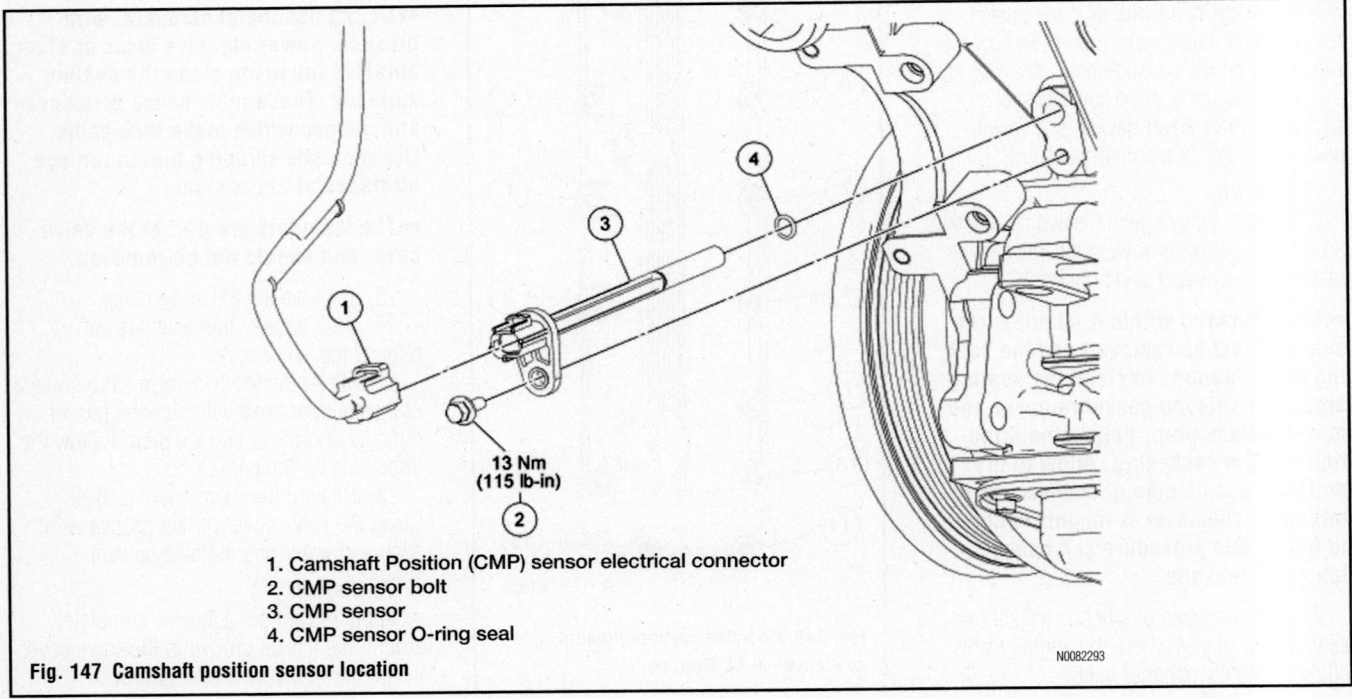

13 Nm (115 lb-in)

1. Camshaft Position (CMP) sensor electrical connector
2. CMP sensor bolt
3. CMP sensor
4. CMP sensor O-ring seal

Fig. 147 Camshaft position sensor location

N0082293

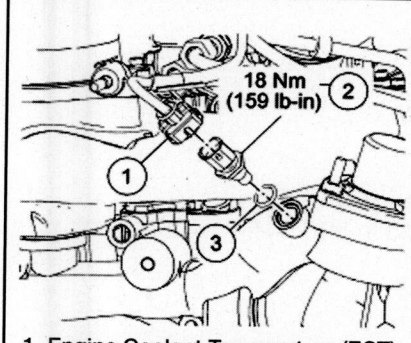

1. Engine Coolant Temperature (ECT) sensor electrical connector
2. ECT sensor
3. ECT sensor O-ring seal

N0082295

Fig. 149 Engine coolant temperature sensor location

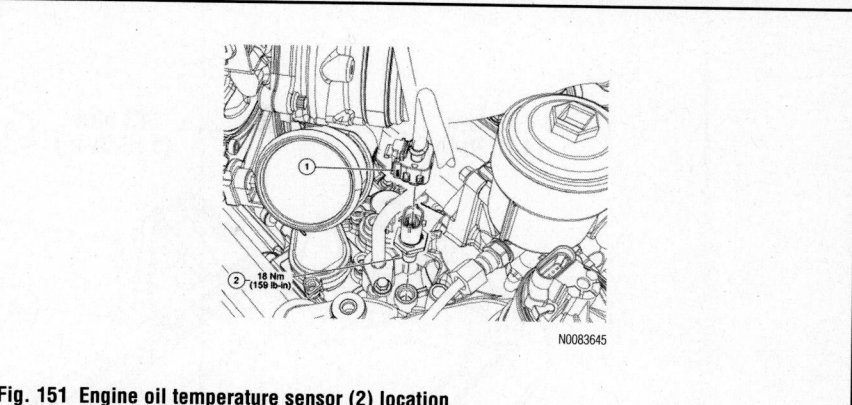

Fig. 151 Engine oil temperature sensor (2) location

4. Remove the bolt, the CMP sensor and discard the O-ring seal. To install, tighten to 10 ft. lbs. (13 Nm).

➡**Apply clean engine oil to the new O-ring seal prior to installation.**

5. To install, reverse the removal procedure.
6. Install a new O-ring seal.

Gasoline Systems

1. Remove the Air Cleaner (ACL) and ACL outlet pipe.
2. Disconnect the Camshaft Position (CMP) sensor electrical connector.
3. Remove the bolt and the CMP sensor. Inspect the O-ring seal for damage and install new if necessary.
4. Lubricate the O-ring seal and with clean engine oil prior to installation.

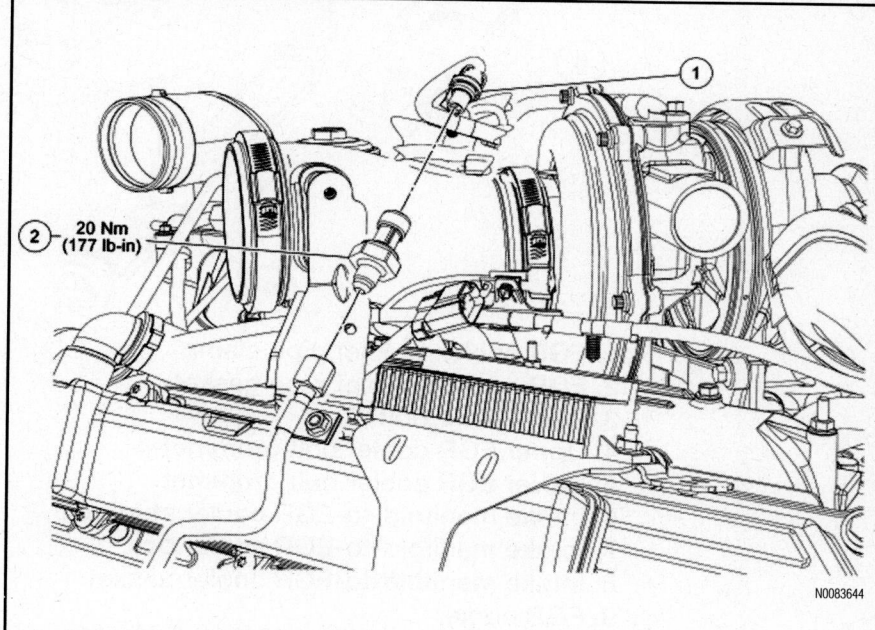

Fig. 152 Exhaust pressure sensor (2) location

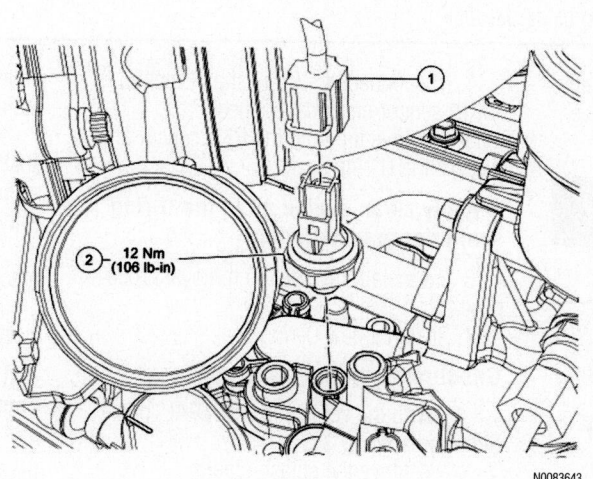

Fig. 150 Engine oil pressure switch (2) location

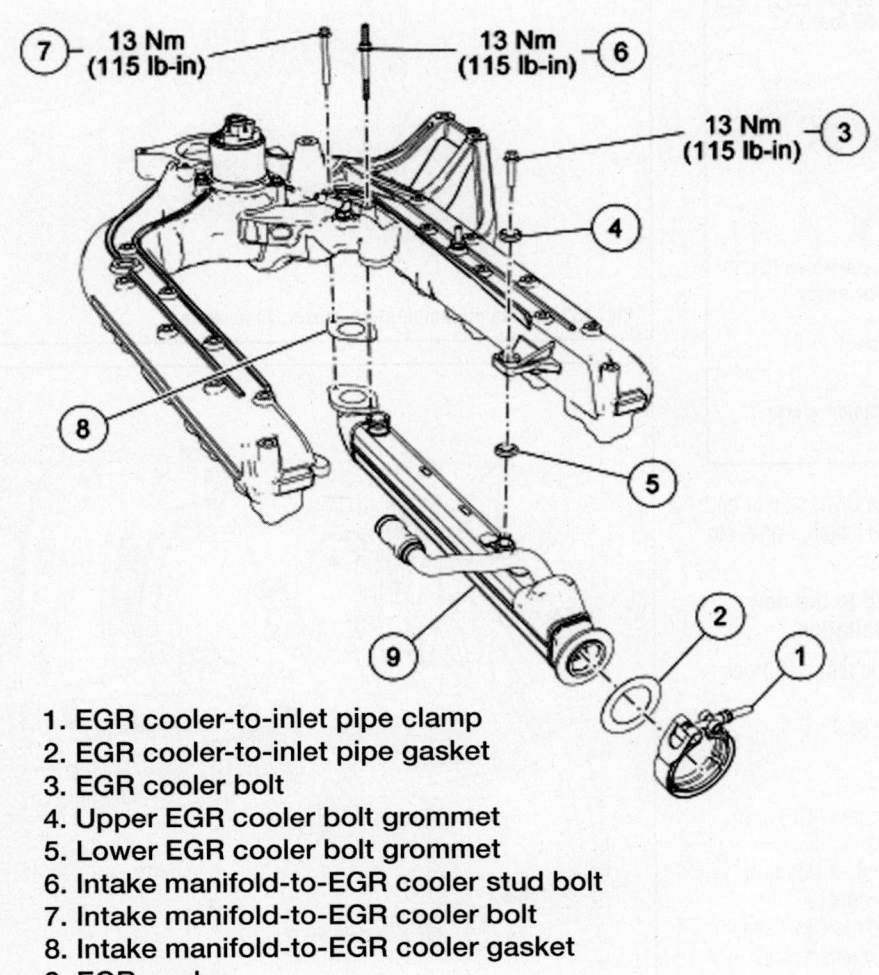

1. EGR cooler-to-inlet pipe clamp
2. EGR cooler-to-inlet pipe gasket
3. EGR cooler bolt
4. Upper EGR cooler bolt grommet
5. Lower EGR cooler bolt grommet
6. Intake manifold-to-EGR cooler stud bolt
7. Intake manifold-to-EGR cooler bolt
8. Intake manifold-to-EGR cooler gasket
9. EGR cooler

N0082298

Fig. 153 Exhaust Gas Recirculation (EGR) Cooler location

5. To install, tighten to 10 Nm (89 lb-in).
6. To install, reverse the removal procedure.

CRANKSHAFT POSITION (CKP) SENSOR

REMOVAL & INSTALLATION

Diesel Systems

1. With the vehicle in NEUTRAL, position it on a hoist.
2. Turn the ignition switch to the OFF position.
3. Remove the bolt and position the ground cable aside. To install, tighten to 35 ft. lbs. (47 Nm)

4. Disconnect the Crankshaft Position (CKP) sensor electrical connector.
5. Remove the bolt, the CKP sensor and discard the O-ring seal.

➡**Apply clean engine oil to the O-ring seal prior to installation.**

6. To install, reverse the removal procedure.
7. Install a new O-ring seal.

Gasoline Systems

1. With the vehicle in NEUTRAL, position it on a hoist.
2. Remove the splash shield.
3. Rotate the accessory drive belt tensioner clockwise and remove the accessory drive belt from the A/C compressor pulley.
4. Disconnect and detach the Crankshaft Position (CKP) sensor electrical connector and position the wiring harness aside.
5. Detach the wiring harness from the bracket.
6. Disconnect the A/C compressor electrical connector.

➡**It is not necessary to remove the A/C compressor bolts.**

7. Loosen the 3 bolts enough to slide the A/C compressor down 25.4 mm (1 in), allowing access for CKP sensor removal. To install, tighten to 18 ft. lbs. (25 Nm).

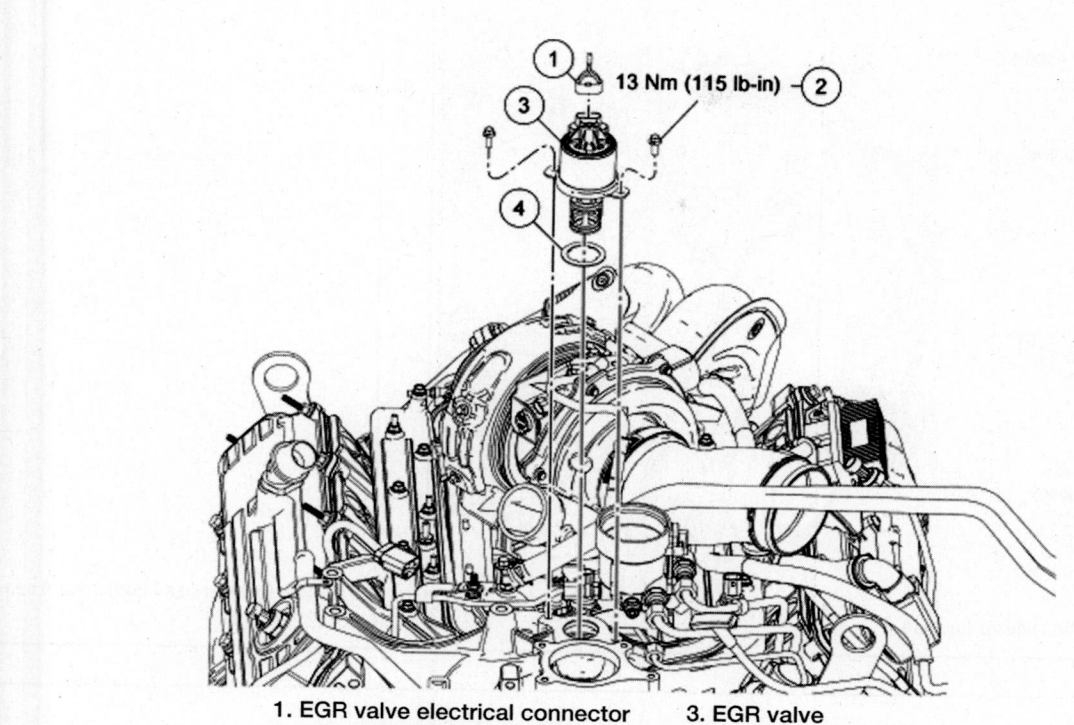

13 Nm (115 lb-in)

1. EGR valve electrical connector
2. EGR valve bolt (2 required)
3. EGR valve
4. EGR valve gasket

N0082297

Fig. 154 Exhaust Gas Recirculation (EGR) valve location

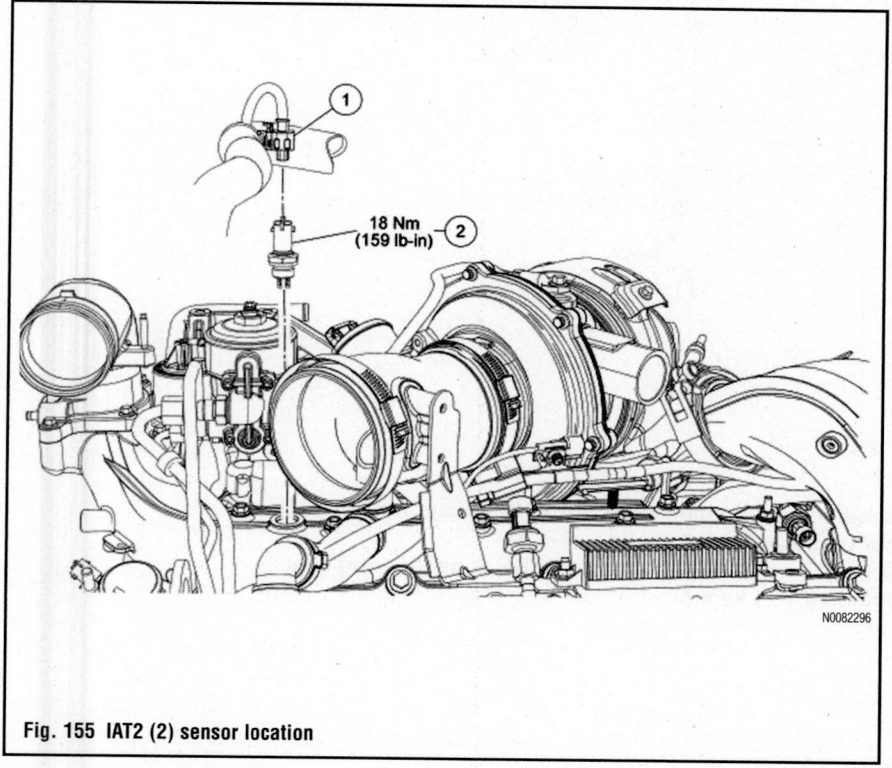

18 Nm (159 lb-in)

N0082296

Fig. 155 IAT2 (2) sensor location

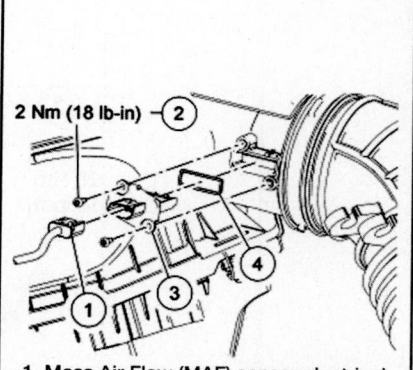

2 Nm (18 lb-in)

1. Mass Air Flow (MAF) sensor electrical
   connector
2. MAF sensor screw (2 required)
3. MAF sensor
4. MAF sensor gasket

N0033232

Fig. 156 MAF sensor location

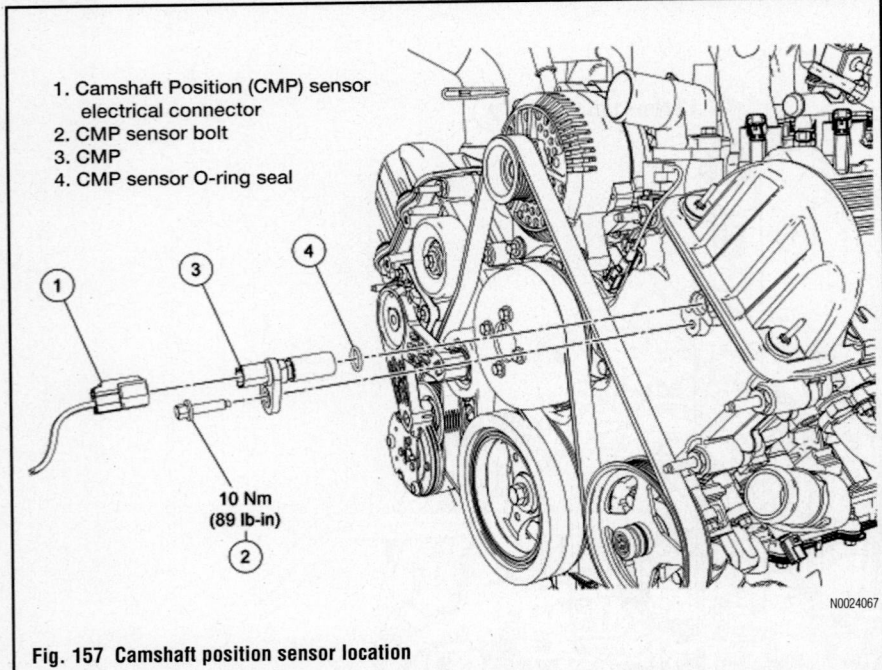

1. Camshaft Position (CMP) sensor electrical connector
2. CMP sensor bolt
3. CMP
4. CMP sensor O-ring seal

10 Nm (89 lb-in)

N0024067

Fig. 157 Camshaft position sensor location

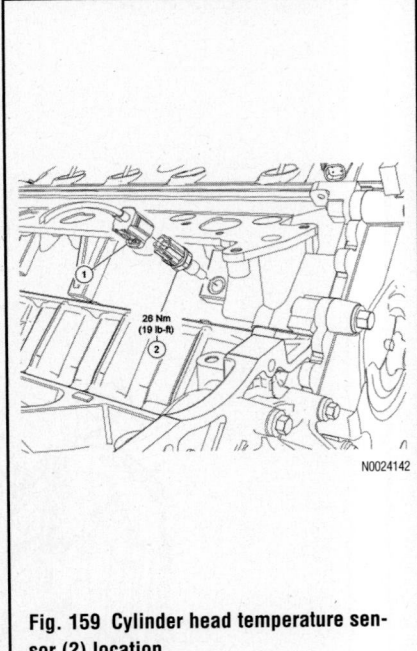

26 Nm (19 lb-ft)

N0024142

Fig. 159 Cylinder head temperature sensor (2) location

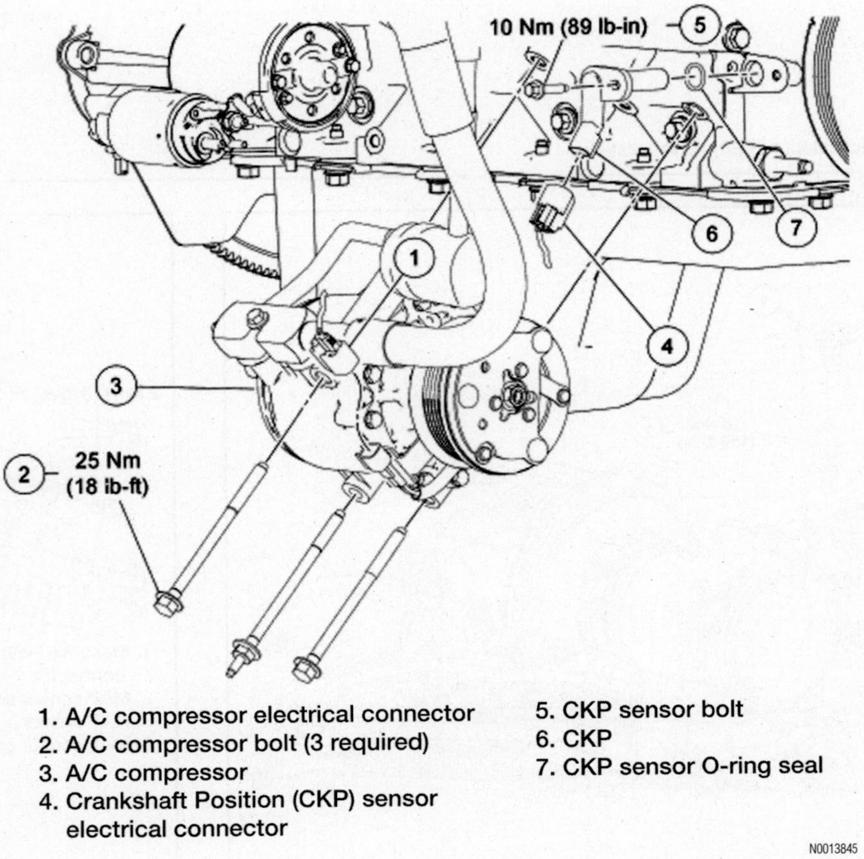

10 Nm (89 lb-in)

25 Nm (18 ib-ft)

1. A/C compressor electrical connector
2. A/C compressor bolt (3 required)
3. A/C compressor
4. Crankshaft Position (CKP) sensor electrical connector
5. CKP sensor bolt
6. CKP
7. CKP sensor O-ring seal

N0013845

Fig. 158 Crankshaft position sensor location

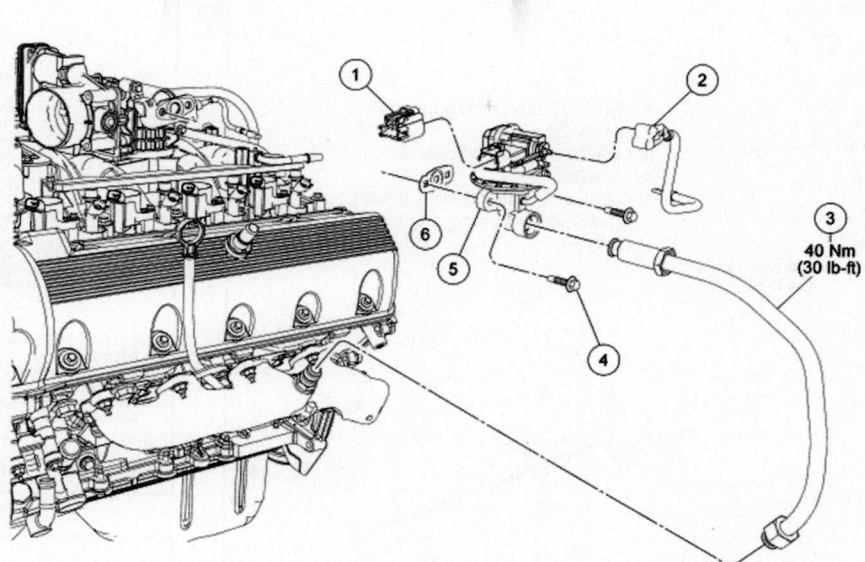

1. EGR system module electrical connector
2. EGR system module vacuum connector
3. Exhaust manifold-to-EGR system module tube
4. EGR system module bolt (2 required)
5. EGR system module
6. EGR system module gasket

N0105848

Fig. 160 EGR system components—4.6L Engines

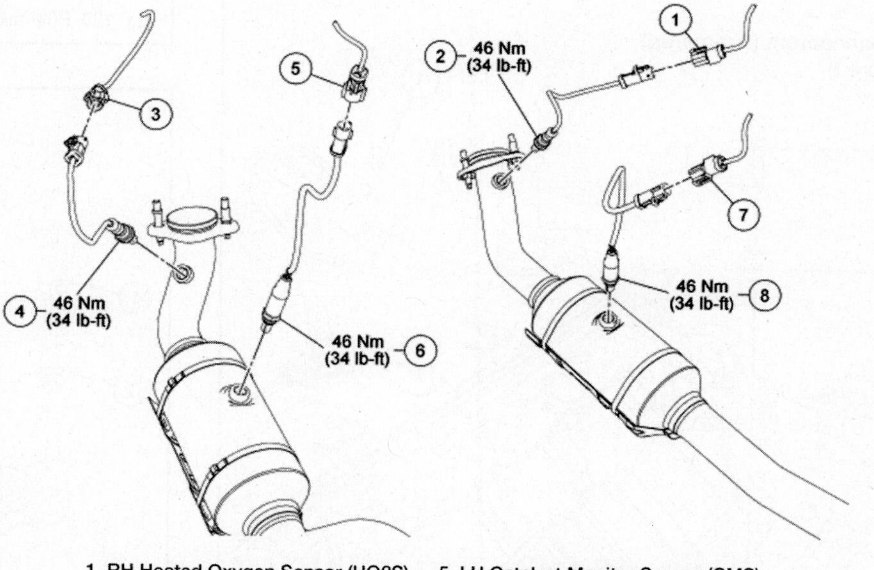

1. RH Heated Oxygen Sensor (HO2S) electrical connector
2. RH HO2S
3. LH HO2S electrical connector
4. LH HO2S
5. LH Catalyst Monitor Sensor (CMS) electrical connector
6. LH CMS
7. RH CMS electrical connector
8. RH CMS

N0089622

Fig. 161 HO2S and catalyst monitor sensor—E-150–E-350 vehicles

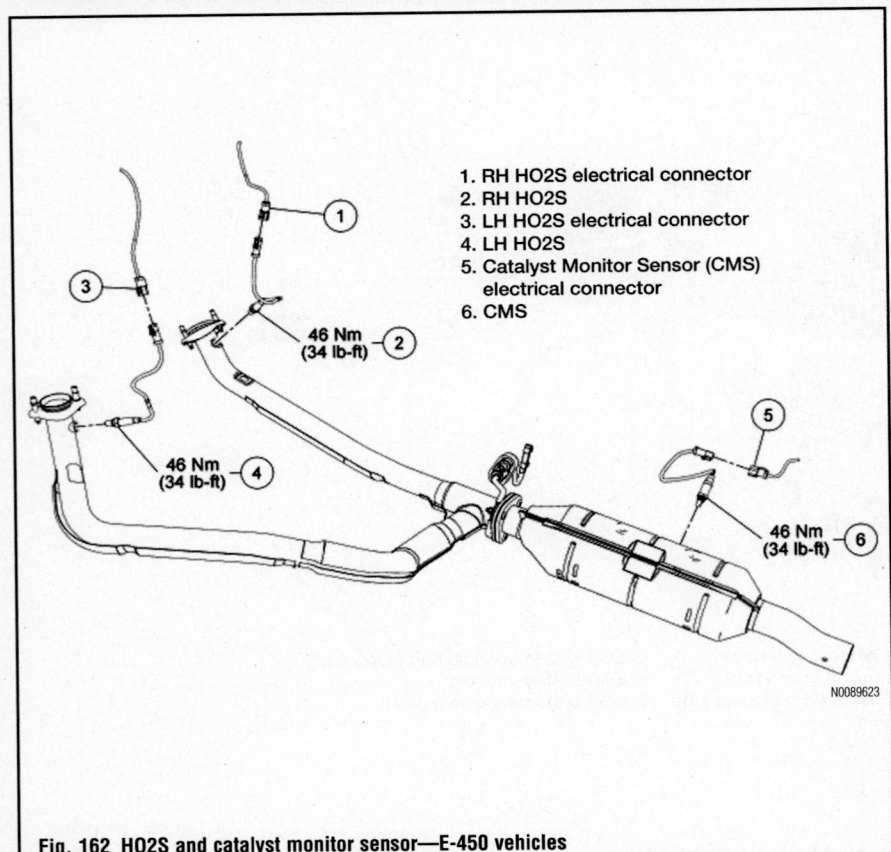

1. RH HO2S electrical connector
2. RH HO2S
3. LH HO2S electrical connector
4. LH HO2S
5. Catalyst Monitor Sensor (CMS) electrical connector
6. CMS

46 Nm (34 lb-ft)

Fig. 162 HO2S and catalyst monitor sensor—E-450 vehicles

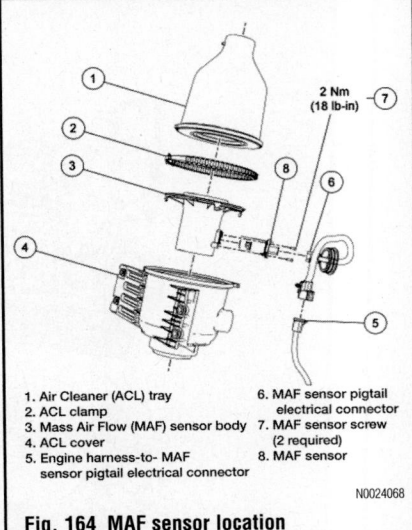

1. Air Cleaner (ACL) tray
2. ACL clamp
3. Mass Air Flow (MAF) sensor body
4. ACL cover
5. Engine harness-to- MAF sensor pigtail electrical connector
6. MAF sensor pigtail electrical connector
7. MAF sensor screw (2 required)
8. MAF sensor

2 Nm (18 lb-in)

Fig. 164 MAF sensor location

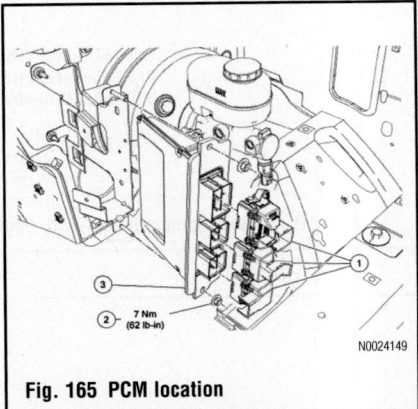

7 Nm (62 lb-in)

Fig. 165 PCM location

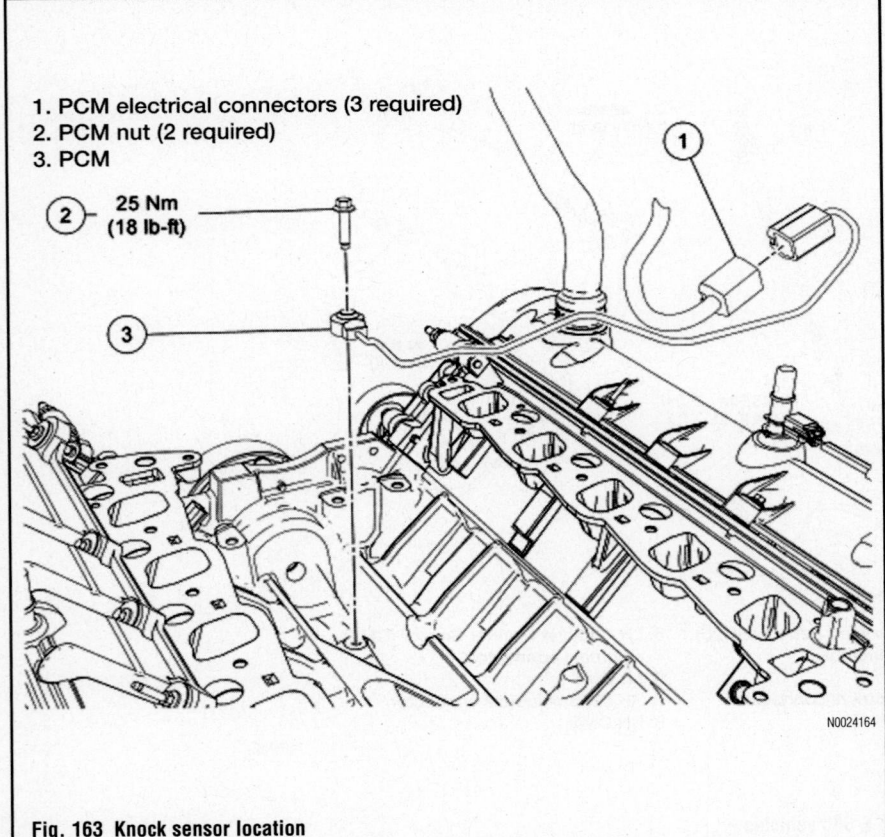

1. PCM electrical connectors (3 required)
2. PCM nut (2 required)
3. PCM

25 Nm (18 lb-ft)

Fig. 163 Knock sensor location

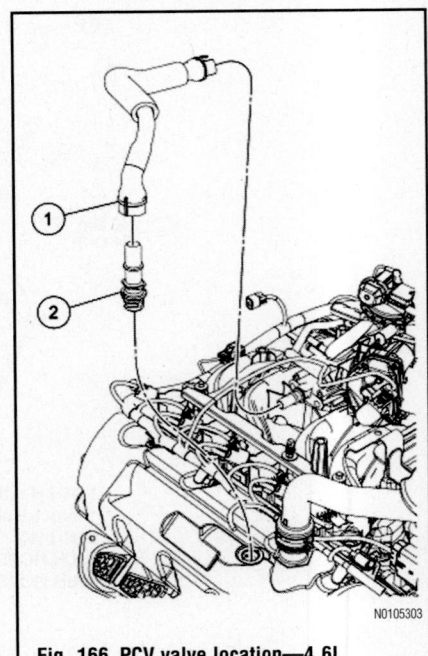

Fig. 166 PCV valve location—4.6L Engines

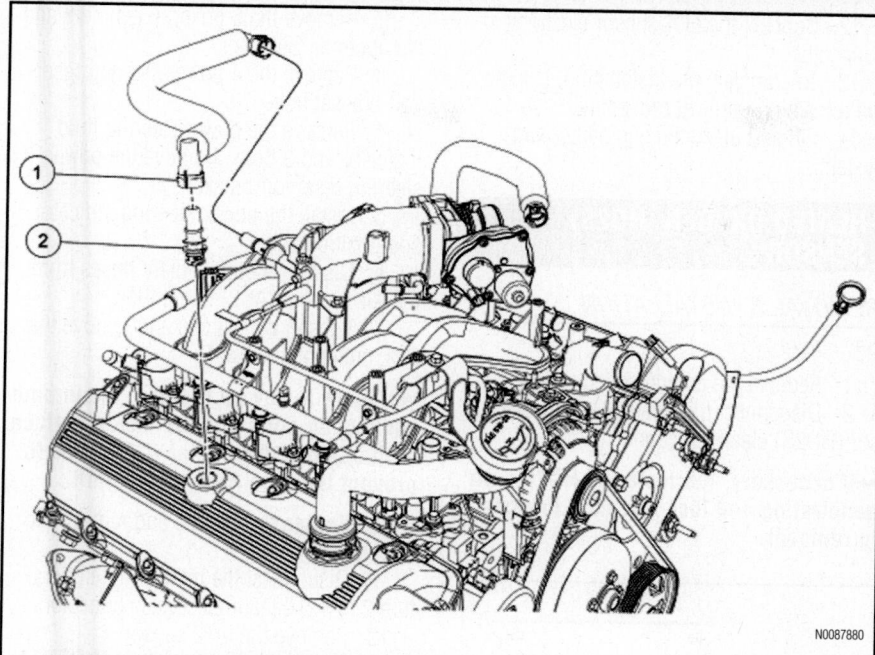

Fig. 167 PCV valve (2) location—5.4L Engines

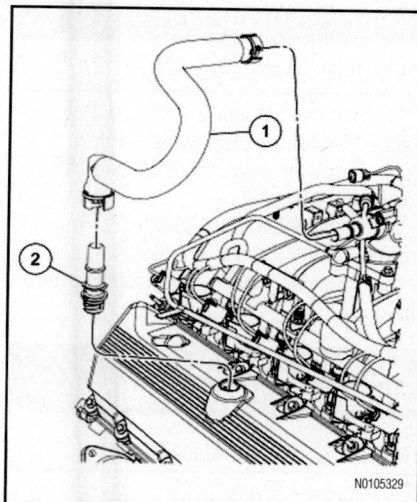

Fig. 168 PCV valve (2) location—6.8L Engines

8. Remove the CKP sensor bolt and the CKP sensor. Inspect the O-ring seal for damage and replace if necessary.

9. Lubricate the O-ring seal with clean engine oil prior to installation.

10. To install, reverse the removal procedure.

ELECTRONIC CONTROL MODULE (ECM)

REMOVAL & INSTALLATION

Diesel Systems

See Figures 169 and 170.

1. Turn the ignition switch to the OFF position.

2. Retrieve the module configuration. Carry out the module configuration retrieval steps of the Programmable Module Installation (PMI) procedure.

3. Remove the 6 pushpin retainers and the upper air deflector.

4. Remove the 4 power steering reservoir bracket bolts.

5. Remove the power steering fluid indicator and 3 bolts. Remove the power steering reservoir bracket.   6. Install the power steering indicator and position aside.

7. Disconnect the coolant hoses from the Air Cleaner (ACL) outlet pipe.

8. Loosen the clamps and remove the ACL outlet pipe.

9. Unlatch and disconnect the PCM electrical connectors.

10. Remove the bolt and PCM.

To install:

11. Install the PCM and the bolt.

➡**Fully seat the Powertrain Control Module (PCM) electrical connectors prior to latching them or damage to the connector pins may occur.**

12. Connect the PCM electrical connectors and latch.

13. To complete the installation, reverse the remaining removal procedure.

14. Restore the module configuration. Carry out the module configuration restore

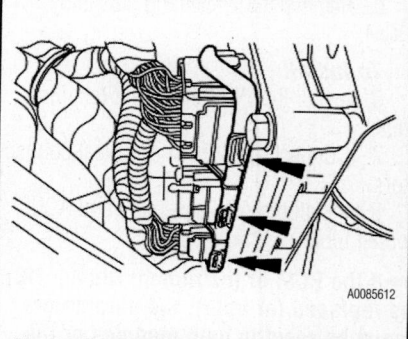

Fig. 169 Unlatch and disconnect the PCM electrical connectors

Fig. 170 Remove the bolt and PCM

steps of the Programmable Module Installation (PMI) procedure.

➡**If the Instrument Cluster (IC) or the PCM (or both) is being replaced, the parameters must be reset in both modules or the vehicle will experience a Passive Anti-Theft System (PATS) no start. This will occur even if the vehicle is not equipped with PATS .**

15. Carry out the Passive Anti-Theft System (PATS) Parameter Reset.

Gasoline Systems

➡**Refer to the Powertrain Control/Emissions Diagnosis (PC/ED) manual for correct Vehicle Communication Module (VCM) hook-up procedure.**

1. If servicing the PCM, connect the scan tool to the vehicle. Allow the scan tool to identify the vehicle and obtain configuration data.

2. All programmable module information will automatically be retrieved by the VCM .

3. Remove the Air Cleaner (ACL) assembly and ACL outlet tube.

4. Disconnect the 3 PCM electrical connectors.

5. Remove the 2 retaining nuts and PCM.

To install:

6. Install the PCM and the 2 retaining nuts.

7. Connect the 3 PCM electrical connectors.

8. Install the ACL assembly and ACL outlet tube.

➡ **If the PCM or Instrument Cluster (IC) is replaced (or both), the parameters must be reset in both modules or the vehicle will experience a Passive Anti-Theft System (PATS) no-start. This will occur even if the vehicle is not equipped with PATS .**

9. Restore the module configurations for the IC module and the PCM. Carry out the module configuration restore steps of the Programmable Module Installation (PMI) procedure.

ENGINE COOLANT TEMPERATURE (ECT) SENSOR

REMOVAL & INSTALLATION

Diesel Systems

1. Turn the ignition switch to the OFF position.

2. Drain the engine cooling system.

3. Remove the 6 pushpin retainers and the upper air deflector.

4. Remove the 4 power steering reservoir bracket bolts.

5. Remove the power steering fluid indicator and 3 bolts. Remove the power steering reservoir bracket. Install the power steering indicator and position aside.

6. Disconnect the coolant hoses from the Air Cleaner (ACL) outlet pipe.

7. Loosen the clamps and remove the ACL outlet pipe.

➡ **If there is any oil residue, clean both connecting ports and the inside surface of the Charge Air Cooler (CAC) tube to prevent the tube from blowing off.**

8. Loosen the clamps and remove the CAC tube.

9. Disconnect the Engine Coolant Temperature (ECT) electrical connector.

10. Remove the ECT sensor and discard the O-ring seal.

To install:

➡ **Apply clean engine oil to the new O-ring seal prior to installation.**

11. Using a new O-ring seal, install the ECT sensor.

12. Connect the ECT sensor electrical connector.

13. To complete the installation, reverse the remaining removal procedure.

14. Fill and bleed the engine cooling system.

HEATED OXYGEN (HO2S) SENSOR

REMOVAL & INSTALLATION

See Figure 171.

1. Remove the engine cover.

2. Disconnect the Heated Oxygen Sensor (HO2S) electrical connector.

➡ **If necessary, lubricate the HO2S with penetrating and lock lubricant to assist in removal.**

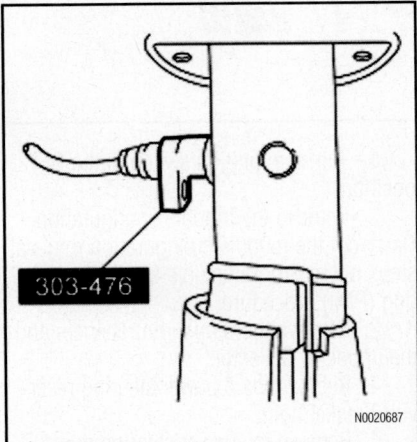

303-476

N0020687

Fig. 171 Using the Exhaust Gas Oxygen Sensor Socket

3. Using the Exhaust Gas Oxygen Sensor Socket, remove the HO2S.

To install:

4. Install the HO2S .

5. Apply a light coat of high temperature nickel anti-seize lubricant to the HO2S threads prior to installation.

6. Calculate the correct torque wrench setting for the following torque.

7. Using the Exhaust Gas Oxygen Sensor Socket, tighten to 34 ft. lbs. (46 Nm).

8. Connect the HO2S electrical connector.

9. Install the engine cover.

INTAKE AIR TEMPERATURE (IAT) SENSOR

REMOVAL & INSTALLATION

1. Turn the ignition switch to the OFF position.

2. Remove the 6 pushpin retainers and the upper air deflector.

3. Remove the 4 power steering reservoir bracket bolts.

4. Remove the power steering fluid indicator and 3 bolts. Remove the power steering reservoir bracket.

5. Install the power steering indicator and position aside.

6. Disconnect the coolant hoses from the Air Cleaner (ACL) outlet tube.

7. Loosen the clamps and remove the ACL outlet pipe.

➡ **If there is any oil residue, clean both connecting ports and the inside surface of the Charge Air Cooler (CAC) tube to prevent the tube from blowing off.**

8. Loosen the clamps and remove the CAC tube.

9. Disconnect the Intake Air Temperature 2 (IAT2) sensor electrical connector.

10. Remove the IAT2 sensor.

11. To install, reverse the removal procedure.

KNOCK SENSOR (KS)

REMOVAL & INSTALLATION

1. Remove the intake manifold. Refer to Intake Manifold in Engine Mechanical.

2. Disconnect the Knock Sensor (KS) electrical connector.

3. Remove the bolt and the KS. To install, tighten to 18 ft. lbs. (25 Nm).

4. To install, reverse the removal procedure.

MANIFOLD ABSOLUTE PRESSURE (MAP) SENSOR

REMOVAL & INSTALLATION

See Figures 172 and 173.

1. Turn the ignition switch to the OFF position.

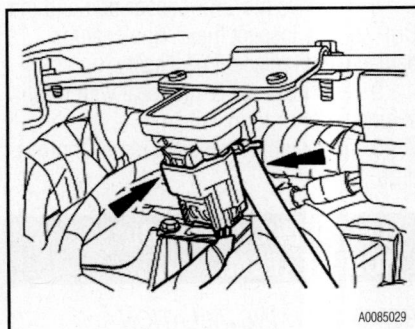

A0085029

Fig. 172 Disconnect the electrical connector

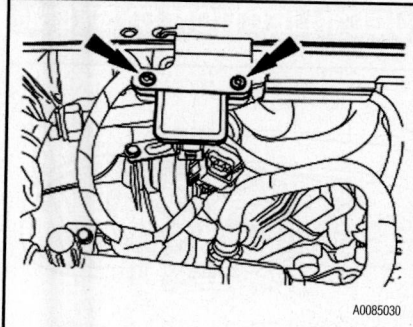

Fig. 173 Remove the 2 mounting screws and the MAP sensor

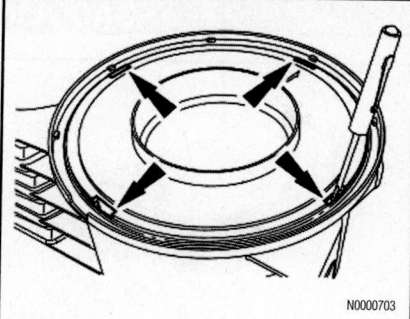

Fig. 174 Release the latches and remove the Mass Air Flow (MAF) assembly

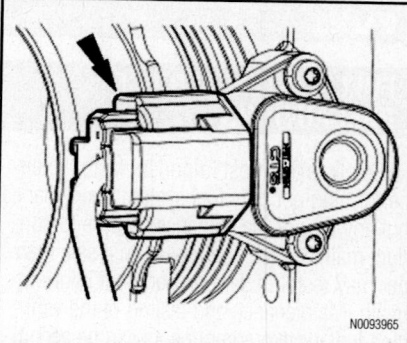

Fig. 175 Disconnect the TP sensor electrical connector

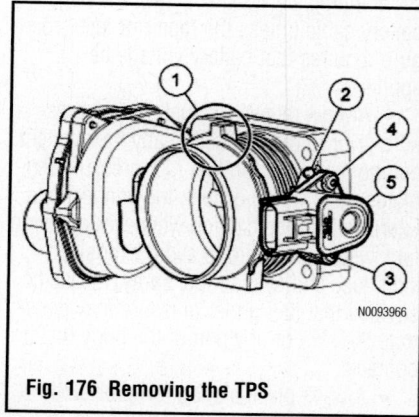

Fig. 176 Removing the TPS

2. Disconnect the Manifold Absolute Pressure (MAP) sensor.

3. Disconnect the pressure hose.

4. Disconnect the electrical connector.

5. Remove the 2 mounting screws and the MAP sensor.

6. To install, reverse the removal procedure.

MASS AIR FLOW (MAF) SENSOR

REMOVAL & INSTALLATION

Diesel Systems

1. Turn the ignition switch to the OFF position.

2. Disconnect the Mass Air Flow (MAF) sensor electrical connector.

3. Remove the 2 screws and the MAF sensor.

4. To install, reverse the removal procedure.

Gasoline Systems

1. Remove the Air Cleaner (ACL).

➡ **Do not tamper with the Mass Air Flow (MAF) sensing elements located in the airflow meter. Tampering can result in unit failure.**

2. Open the ACL.

3. Release the air box clamp.

4. Separate the inlet side from the outlet side of the ACL.

5. Release the latches and remove the Mass Air Flow (MAF) assembly.

➡ **The red clip must be pulled out before disconnecting the electrical connector.**

6. Disconnect the MAF sensor electrical connector.

7. Remove the 2 screws and MAF sensor.

➡ **The grommet used to seal the ACL housing at the extension harness must be fully seated. Failure to do so will result in unmetered air entering the engine.**

➡ **Use the alignment notch to correctly align the inlet side and the outlet side of the ACL .**

8. To install, reverse the removal procedure.

THROTTLE POSITION SENSOR (TPS)

REMOVAL & INSTALLATION

See Figures 175 and 176.

1. Remove the Air Cleaner (ACL) outlet pipe.

2. Disconnect the TP sensor electrical connector.

➡ **Do not put direct heat on the Throttle Position (TP) sensor or any other plastic parts because heat damage may occur. Damage may also occur if Electronic Throttle Body (ETB) temperature exceeds 248°F.**

➡ **Do not use power tools.**

3. Remove the TP sensor.

a. Using a suitable heat gun, apply heat to the top of the ETB until the top TP sensor bolt ear reaches approximately 130°F. This should take no more than 3 minutes using an 1,100-watt heat gun. The heat gun should be about 1 inch away from the ETB .

b. Monitor the temperature of the top TP sensor bolt ear on the ETB with a suitable temperature measuring device, such as a digital temperature laser or infrared thermometer, while heating the ETB .

c. Using hand tools, quickly remove the bolt farthest from the heat source first and discard.

d. Using hand tools, remove the remaining bolt and discard.

e. Remove and discard the TP sensor.

To install:

➡ **When installing the new TP sensor, make sure that the radial locator tab on the TP sensor is aligned with the radial locator hole on the ETB .**

➡ **Do not use power tools.**

4. Install the new TP sensor.

5. Using hand tools, install the 2 new bolts. Tighten to 27 inch lbs. (3 Nm).

6. Connect the TP sensor electrical connector.

7. Install the ACL outlet pipe.

FUEL SYSTEM SERVICE PRECAUTIONS

Safety is the most important factor when performing not only fuel system maintenance but any type of maintenance. Failure to conduct maintenance and repairs in a safe manner may result in serious personal injury or death. Maintenance and testing of the vehicle's fuel system components can be accomplished safely and effectively by adhering to the following rules and guidelines.

• To avoid the possibility of fire and personal injury, always disconnect the negative battery cable unless the repair or test procedure requires that battery voltage be applied.

• Always relieve the fuel system pressure prior to disconnecting any fuel system component (injector, fuel rail, pressure regulator, etc.), fitting or fuel line connection. Exercise extreme caution whenever relieving fuel system pressure to avoid exposing skin, face and eyes to fuel spray. Please be advised that fuel under pressure may penetrate the skin or any part of the body that it contacts.

• Always place a shop towel or cloth around the fitting or connection prior to loosening to absorb any excess fuel due to spillage. Ensure that all fuel spillage (should it occur) is quickly removed from engine surfaces. Ensure that all fuel soaked cloths or towels are deposited into a suitable waste container.

• Always keep a dry chemical (Class B) fire extinguisher near the work area.

• Do not allow fuel spray or fuel vapors to come into contact with a spark or open flame.

• Always use a back-up wrench when loosening and tightening fuel line connection fittings. This will prevent unnecessary stress and torsion to fuel line piping.

• Always replace worn fuel fitting O-rings with new Do not substitute fuel hose or equivalent where fuel pipe is installed.

Before servicing the vehicle, make sure to also refer to the precautions in the beginning of this section as well.

RELIEVING FUEL SYSTEM PRESSURE

See Figures 177 and 178.

✳✳ WARNING

Do not smoke, carry lighted tobacco or have an open flame of any type

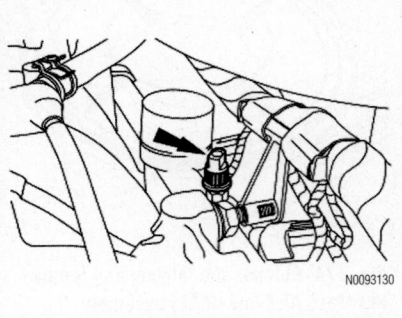

Fig. 177 Locating the fuel pressure relief valve

when working on or near any fuel-related component. Highly flammable mixtures are always present and may be ignited. Failure to follow these instructions may result in serious personal injury.

✳✳ WARNING

Before working on or disconnecting any of the fuel tubes or fuel system components, relieve the fuel system pressure to prevent accidental spraying of fuel. Fuel in the fuel system remains under high pressure, even when the engine is not running. Failure to follow this instruction may result in serious personal injury.

✳✳ WARNING

When handling fuel, always observe fuel handling precautions and be prepared in the event of fuel spillage. Spilled fuel may be ignited by hot vehicle components or other ignition sources. Failure to follow these instructions may result in serious personal injury.

✳✳ WARNING

Do not carry personal electronic devices such as cell phones, pagers or audio equipment of any type when working on or near any fuel-related component. Highly flammable mixtures are always present and may be ignited. Failure to follow these instructions may result in serious personal injury.

1. Disconnect the battery ground cable.
2. Remove the engine cover.

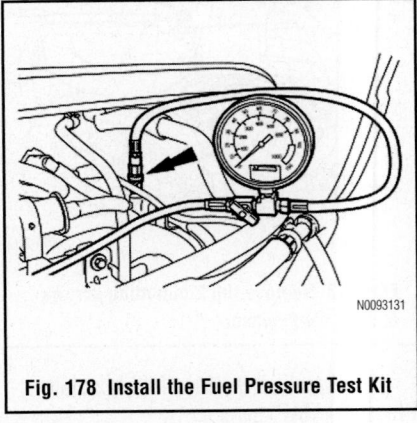

Fig. 178 Install the Fuel Pressure Test Kit

➡ **6.8L shown, 4.6L and 5.4L similar.**

3. Remove the cap from the fuel pressure relief valve located on the fuel rail.

➡ **6.8L shown, 4.6L and 5.4L similar.**

4. Install the Fuel Pressure Test Kit onto the fuel pressure relief valve.

➡ **Open the manual valve slowly to relieve the system pressure. This may drain fuel from the fuel system. Place fuel in a suitable container.**

5. Open the manual valve on the Fuel Pressure Test Kit and relive the fuel pressure.

6. Once fuel system service is complete, install the cap on the fuel pressure relief valve.

7. Connect the battery ground cable.

➡ **It may take more than one key cycle to pressurize the fuel system.**

8. Cycle the ignition key and wait 3 seconds to pressurize the fuel system. Check for leaks before starting the engine.

9. Start the vehicle and check the fuel system for leaks.

FUEL INJECTORS

REMOVAL & INSTALLATION

4.6L Engine

See Figure 179.

➡ **Do not smoke, carry lighted tobacco or have an open flame of any type when working on or near any fuel-related component. Highly flammable mixtures are always present and may be ignited. Failure to follow these instructions may result in serious personal injury.**

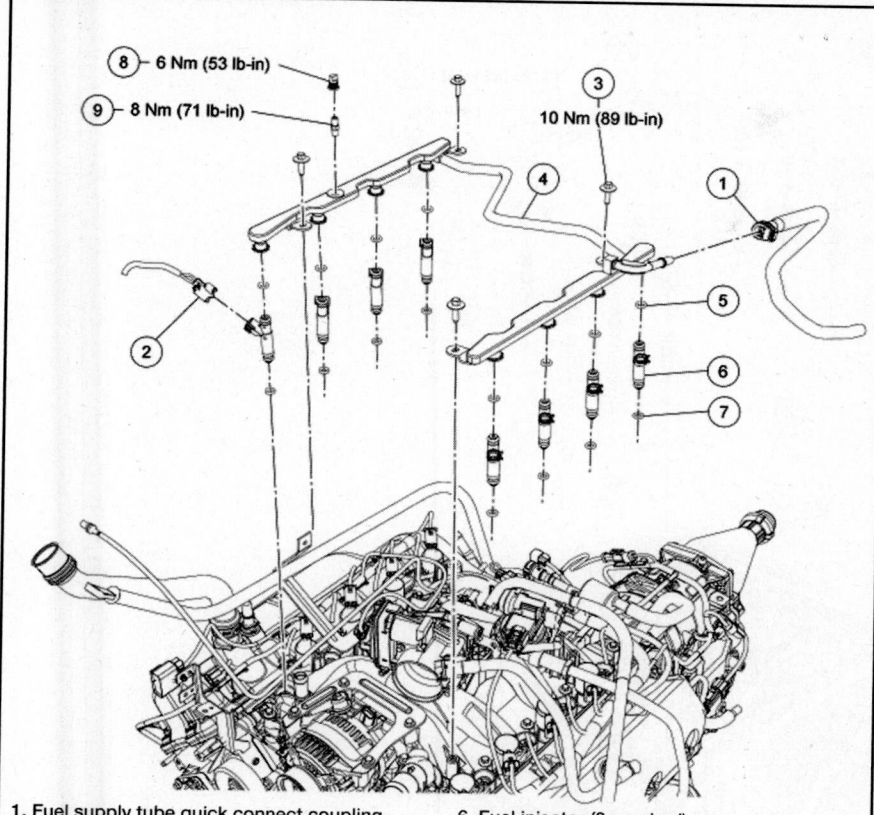

8 — 6 Nm (53 lb-in)

9 — 8 Nm (71 lb-in)

3

10 Nm (89 lb-in)

4

1

2

5

6

7

1. Fuel supply tube quick connect coupling
2. Fuel injector electrical connector (8 required)
3. Fuel rail bolt (4 required)
4. Fuel rail
5. Fuel injector-to-fuel rail O-ring seal (8 required)

6. Fuel injector (8 required)
7. Fuel injector-to-intake manifold O-ring seal (8 required)
8. Fuel pressure relief valve cap
9. Fuel pressure relief valve

N0106193

Fig. 179 Exploded view of the fuel rail assembly—4.6L Engines

11. Disconnect the 8 fuel injector electrical connectors.

12. Remove the 4 fuel rail bolts. To install, tighten to 89 inch lbs. (10 Nm).

➡ **When removing the fuel rail, leave the fuel injectors in the intake manifold. This will make removal of the fuel rail easier.**

13. Separate the fuel rail from the 8 fuel injectors and remove the fuel rail.

➡ **Install new fuel injector-to-fuel rail O-ring seals on the fuel injectors.**

➡ **Lubricate the new fuel injector-to-fuel rail O-ring seals with clean engine oil prior to installation.**

14. Remove the 8 fuel injectors from the intake manifold.

15. Remove and discard the fuel injector O-ring seals.

16. To install, reverse the removal procedure.

5.4L Engines

See Figure 180.

✳✳ WARNING

Do not smoke, carry lighted tobacco or have an open flame of any type when working on or near any fuel-related component. Highly flammable mixtures are always present and may be ignited. Failure to follow these instructions may result in serious personal injury.

✳✳ WARNING

Before working on or disconnecting any of the fuel tubes or fuel system components, relieve the fuel system pressure to prevent accidental spraying of fuel. Fuel in the fuel system remains under high pressure, even when the engine is not running. Failure to follow this instruction may result in serious personal injury.

➡ **Fuel injection equipment is manufactured to very precise tolerances and fine clearances. It is therefore essential that absolute cleanliness is observed when working with these components. Always install plugs to any open orifices or tubes. Failure to follow these instructions may result in fuel injection component damage.**

➡ **When reusing liquid or vapor tube connectors, make sure to use compressed air to remove any foreign**

✳✳ WARNING

Before working on or disconnecting any of the fuel tubes or fuel system components, relieve the fuel system pressure to prevent accidental spraying of fuel. Fuel in the fuel system remains under high pressure, even when the engine is not running. Failure to follow this instruction may result in serious personal injury.

➡ **Fuel injection equipment is manufactured to very precise tolerances and fine clearances. It is therefore essential that absolute cleanliness is observed when working with these components. Always install plugs to any open orifices or tubes. Failure to follow these instructions may result in fuel injection component damage.**

➡ **When reusing liquid or vapor tube connectors, make sure to use compressed air to remove any foreign**

clip area before separating from the tube. Failure to follow these instructions may result in fuel or vapor leaks and connector damage.

1. Disconnect the battery ground cable.

2. Remove the engine cover.

3. Relieve the fuel pressure.

4. Remove the Air Cleaner (ACL) and the ACL outlet tube.

5. Disconnect the fuel supply tube quick connect coupling.

6. Disconnect the Evaporative Emission (EVAP) purge valve tube quick connect coupling from the intake manifold.

7. Disconnect the EVAP canister purge valve electrical connector.

8. Disconnect the EVAP canister-to-EVAP canister purge valve tube quick connect coupling.

9. Remove the bolt and the EVAP canister purge valve.

10. Disconnect the quick connect couplings and remove the PCV tube.

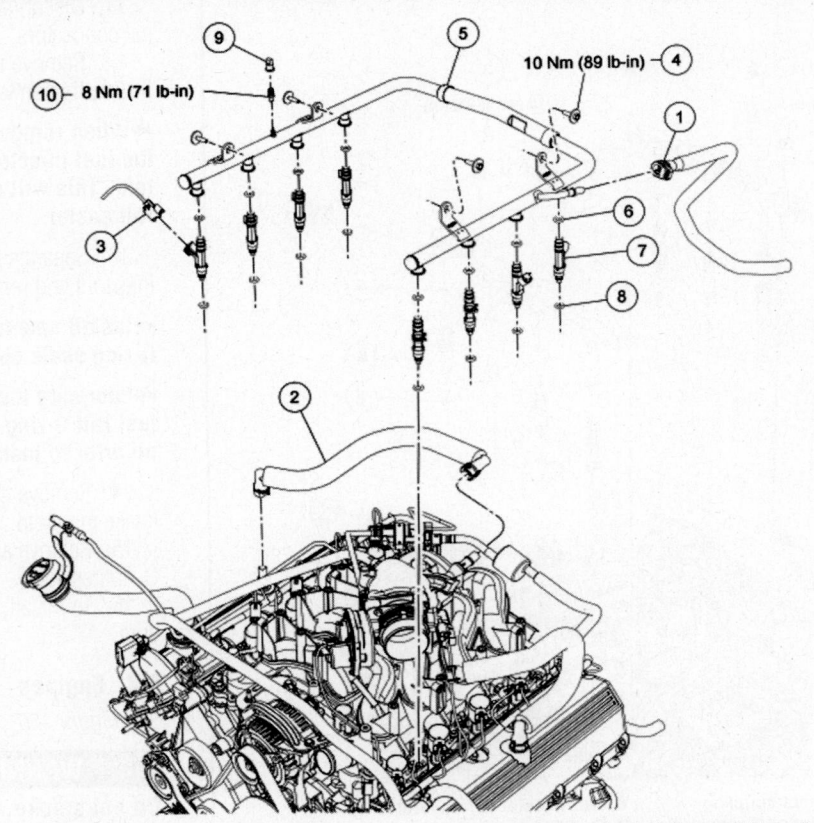

1. Fuel supply tube quick connect coupling
2. PCV tube
3. Fuel injector electrical connector (8 required)
4. Fuel rail bolt (4 required)
5. Fuel rail
6. Fuel injector-to-fuel rail O-ring seal (8 required)
7. Fuel injector (8 required)
8. Fuel injector-to-intake manifold O-ring seal (8 required)
9. Fuel pressure relief valve cap
10. Fuel pressure relief valve

N0109749

Fig. 180 Exploded view of the fuel rail assembly—5.4L Engines

material from the connector retaining clip area before separating from the tube. Failure to follow these instructions may result in fuel or vapor leaks and connector damage.

1. Disconnect the battery ground cable.
2. Remove the engine cover.
3. Relieve the fuel pressure.
4. Remove the Air Cleaner (ACL) and the ACL outlet tube.
5. Disconnect the fuel supply tube quick connect coupling.
6. Disconnect the quick connect couplings and remove the PCV tube.
7. Disconnect the 8 fuel injector electrical connectors.
8. Remove the 4 fuel rail bolts.

➡ When removing the fuel rail, leave the fuel injectors in the intake manifold. This will make removal of the fuel rail easier.

9. Separate the fuel rail from the 8 fuel injectors and remove the fuel rail.

➡ Install new fuel injector-to-fuel rail O-ring seals on the fuel injectors.

➡ Lubricate the new fuel injector-to-fuel rail O-ring seals with clean engine oil prior to installation.

10. Remove the 8 fuel injectors from the intake manifold.
11. Remove and discard the fuel injector O-ring seals.
12. To install, reverse the removal procedure.

6.8L Engines

See Figure 181.

⁂ WARNING

Do not smoke, carry lighted tobacco or have an open flame of any type when working on or near any fuel-related component. Highly flamma-

ble mixtures are always present and may be ignited. Failure to follow these instructions may result in serious personal injury.

⁂ WARNING

Before working on or disconnecting any of the fuel tubes or fuel system components, relieve the fuel system pressure to prevent accidental spraying of fuel. Fuel in the fuel system remains under high pressure, even when the engine is not running. Failure to follow this instruction may result in serious personal injury.

➡ Fuel injection equipment is manufactured to very precise tolerances and fine clearances. It is therefore essential that absolute cleanliness is observed when working with these components. Always install plugs to any open orifices or tubes. Failure to

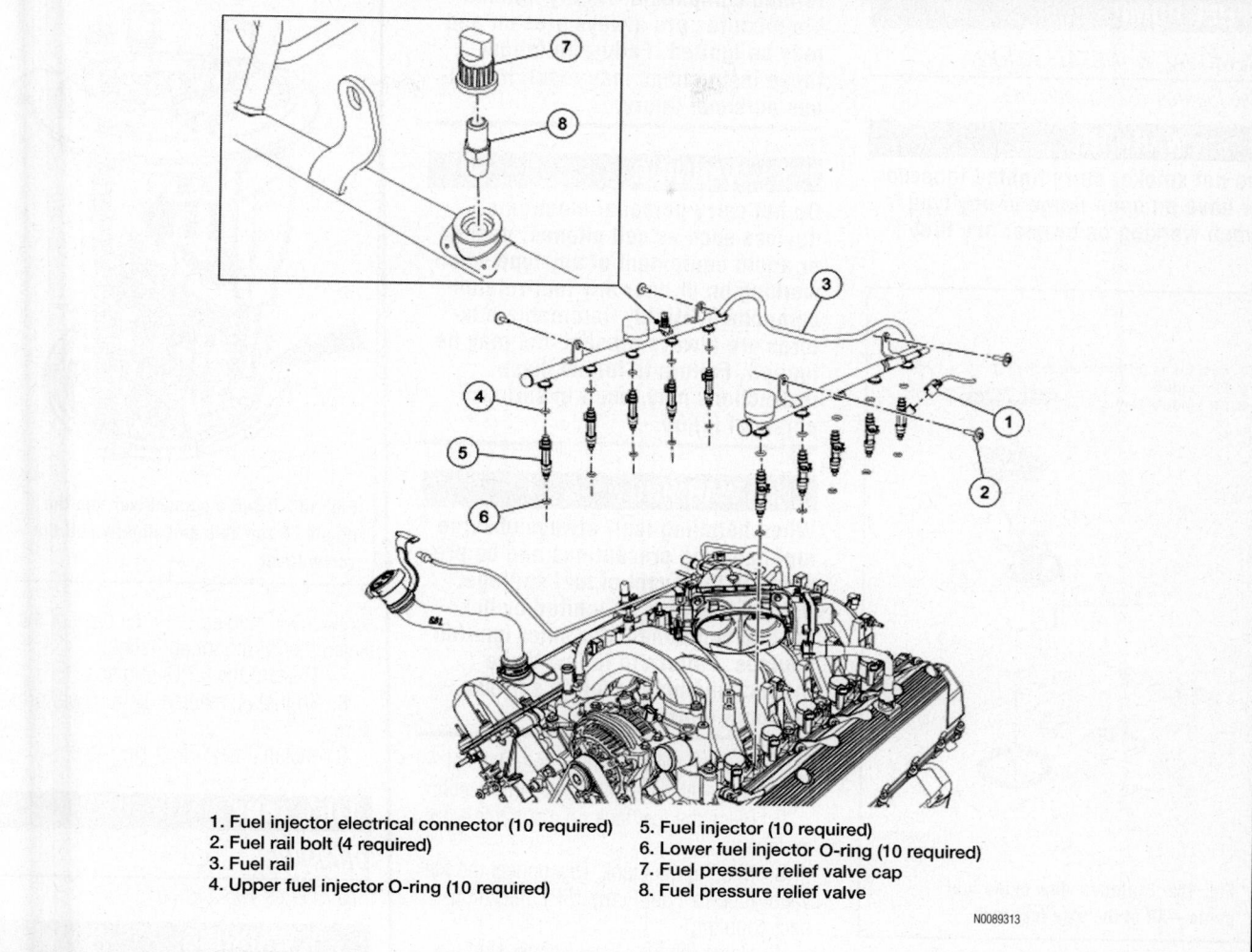

1. Fuel injector electrical connector (10 required)
2. Fuel rail bolt (4 required)
3. Fuel rail
4. Upper fuel injector O-ring (10 required)
5. Fuel injector (10 required)
6. Lower fuel injector O-ring (10 required)
7. Fuel pressure relief valve cap
8. Fuel pressure relief valve

N0089313

Fig. 181 Exploded view of the fuel rail assembly—6.8L Engines

follow these instructions may result in fuel injection component damage.

➡When reusing liquid or vapor tube connectors, make sure to use compressed air to remove any foreign material from the connector retaining clip area before separating from the tube. Failure to follow these instructions may result in fuel or vapor leaks and connector damage.

1. Disconnect the battery ground cable.
2. Remove the engine cover.
3. Remove the Air Cleaner (ACL) and the ACL outlet tube.
4. Release the fuel system pressure.
5. Disconnect the fuel tube quick connect coupling.
6. Disconnect the transmission wiring harness retainers from the engine wiring harness. Position the transmission wiring harness aside.

7. Disconnect the Throttle Position (TP) sensor electrical connector and the wiring harness retainer.
8. Disconnect the 10 fuel injector electrical connectors.
9. Disconnect the 10 ignition coil electrical connectors.
10. Disconnect the quick connect couplings and remove the PCV tube.
11. Disconnect the engine wiring harness retainer from the rear of the intake manifold.
12. Disconnect the 2 RH engine wiring harness retainers and position the wiring harness away from the fuel rail.
13. Disconnect the 3 LH engine wiring harness retainers and position the wiring harness away from the fuel rail.

➡When removing the fuel rail, leave the fuel injectors in the intake manifold. This will ease removal of the fuel rail.

14. Remove the 4 bolts, separate the fuel rail from the 10 fuel injectors and remove the fuel rail.
15. Remove the fuel injectors from the intake manifold and discard the upper and lower fuel injector O-ring seals.

To install:

➡Use O-ring seals that are made of special fuel-resistant material. Use of ordinary O-rings can cause the fuel system to leak.

➡Lubricate the new O-ring seals with clean engine oil prior to installation.

16. Install 20 new upper and lower O-ring seals onto the 10 fuel injectors.
17. Install the 10 fuel injectors into the intake manifold.
18. Position the fuel rail onto the fuel injectors and install the 4 bolts.
19. To install, reverse the removal procedure.

FUEL PUMP

REMOVAL & INSTALLATION

See Figures 182 through 185.

✳ WARNING

Do not smoke, carry lighted tobacco or have an open flame of any type when working on or near any fuel-

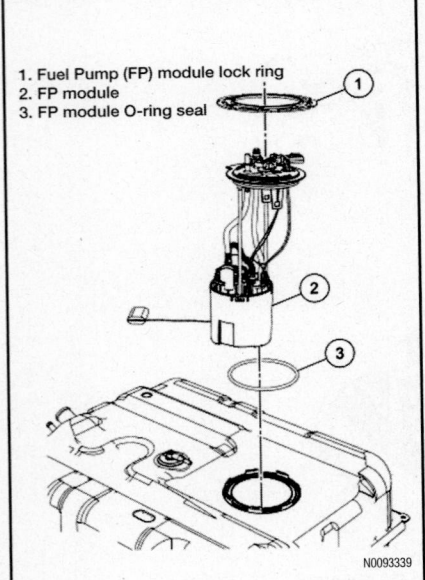

1. Fuel Pump (FP) module lock ring
2. FP module
3. FP module O-ring seal

N0093339

Fig. 182 Exploded view of the fuel pump—Aft of the axle fuel tank

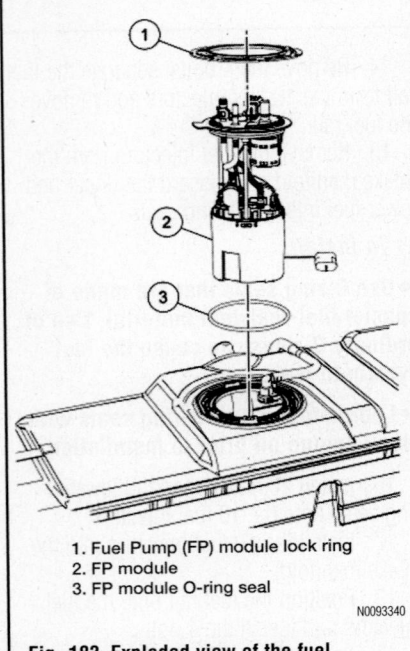

1. Fuel Pump (FP) module lock ring
2. FP module
3. FP module O-ring seal

N0093340

Fig. 183 Exploded view of the fuel pump—Midship fuel tank

related component. Highly flammable mixtures are always present and may be ignited. Failure to follow these instructions may result in serious personal injury.

✳ WARNING

Do not carry personal electronic devices such as cell phones, pagers or audio equipment of any type when working on or near any fuel-related component. Highly flammable mixtures are always present and may be ignited. Failure to follow these instructions may result in serious personal injury.

✳ WARNING

When handling fuel, always observe fuel handling precautions and be prepared in the event of fuel spillage. Spilled fuel may be ignited by hot vehicle components or other ignition sources. Failure to follow these instructions may result in serious personal injury.

1. Remove the fuel tank. For additional information, refer to Fuel Tank in this section.
2. Place the fuel tank on a suitable work surface.
3. Midship fuel tank; Disconnect the fuel vapor tube-to-Fuel Pump (FP) quick connect coupling.
4. Using the Fuel Tank Sender Unit Wrench, remove the FP module lock ring.

➡ If the FP does not clear the FP mounting flange on the fuel tank, the use of a screwdriver may be necessary.

5. Remove the FP and FP O-ring seal.
6. If necessary, insert a screwdriver into the empty FP rod hole and slightly pull the

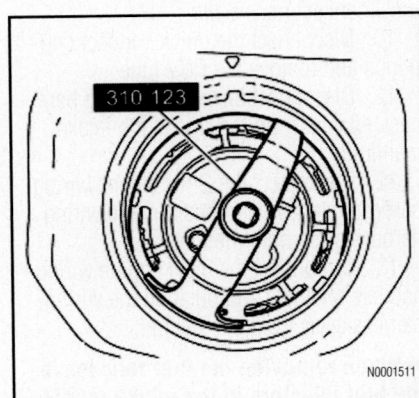

N0001511

Fig. 184 Using the Fuel Tank Sender Unit Wrench

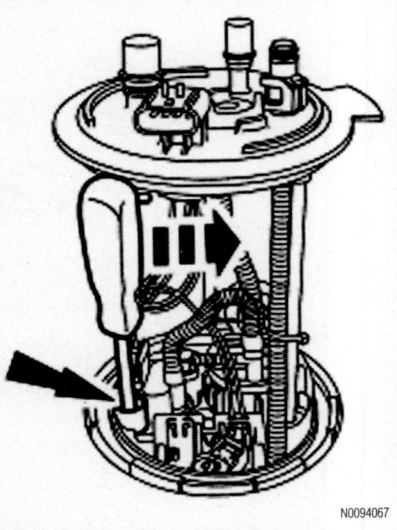

N0094067

Fig. 185 Insert a screwdriver into the empty FP rod hole and slightly pull the screwdriver

screwdriver inboard until the base of the FP clears the FP mounting flange.

7. Discard the FP O-ring seal.
8. To install, reverse the removal procedure.
9. Install a new FP O-ring seal.

FUEL TANK

DRAINING

See Figures 186 and 187.

✳ WARNING

Do not smoke, carry lighted tobacco or have an open flame of any type when working on or near any fuel-related component. Highly flammable mixtures are always present and may be ignited. Failure to follow these instructions may result in serious personal injury.

✳ WARNING

Do not carry personal electronic devices such as cell phones, pagers or audio equipment of any type when working on or near any fuel-related component. Highly flammable mixtures are always present and may be ignited. Failure to follow these instructions may result in serious personal injury.

✳ WARNING

When handling fuel, always observe fuel handling precautions and be pre-

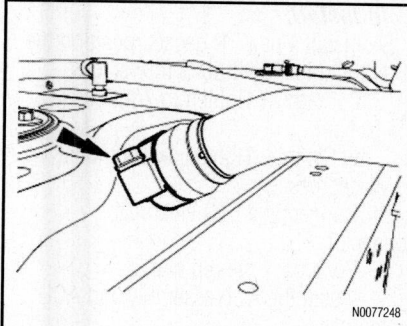

Fig. 186 Remove the fuel tank filler pipe hose

pared in the event of fuel spillage. Spilled fuel may be ignited by hot vehicle components or other ignition sources. Failure to follow these instructions may result in serious personal injury.

⁂ WARNING

Remove the fuel filler cap slowly. The fuel system may be under pressure. If the fuel filler cap is venting vapor or if you hear a hissing sound, wait until it stops before completely removing the fuel filler cap. Otherwise, fuel may spray out. Failure to follow these instructions may result in serious personal injury.

⁂ WARNING

Before working on or disconnecting any of the fuel tubes or fuel system components, relieve the fuel system pressure to prevent accidental spraying of fuel. Fuel in the fuel system remains under high pressure, even when the engine is not running. Failure to follow this instruction may result in serious personal injury.

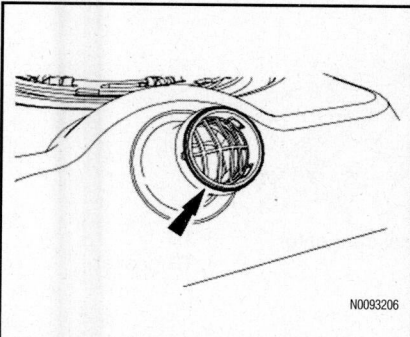

Fig. 187 Lubricate the O-ring seal on the new fuel tank inlet check valve

➡Midship fuel tank shown, aft-of-axle tank similar.

1. With the vehicle in NEUTRAL, position it on a hoist.
2. Release the fuel system pressure.
3. If connected, disconnect the battery ground cable.
4. Release the fuel tank filler cap and position aside.
5. Insert a suitable fuel drain tube into the fuel tank filler pipe until it stops.
6. Attach the 100 Gallon Manual Fuel Tanker to the fuel drain tube and remove as much fuel as possible from the fuel tank filler pipe.

➡Vehicle body removed from art for clarity.

7. Remove the fuel tank filler pipe hose at the fuel tank-to-fuel tank filler pipe hose connection. Loosen the clamp and disconnect the fuel tank filler pipe hose.

➡The fuel tank inlet check valve must be replaced after being removed.

8. Using an appropriate tool, remove the fuel tank inlet check valve.
9. Discard the fuel tank inlet check valve.
10. Lubricate the O-ring seal on the new fuel tank inlet check valve with clean engine oil.

➡Follow the operating instructions supplied by the equipment manufacturer.

11. Insert the hose from the 100 Gallon Manual Fuel Tanker and siphon the fuel through the fuel tank filler pipe opening in the fuel tank.

REMOVAL & INSTALLATION

⁂ WARNING

Do not smoke, carry lighted tobacco or have an open flame of any type when working on or near any fuel-related component. Highly flammable mixtures are always present and may be ignited. Failure to follow these instructions may result in serious personal injury.

⁂ WARNING

Do not carry personal electronic devices such as cell phones, pagers or audio equipment of any type when working on or near any fuel-related component. Highly flammable mixtures are always present and may be

ignited. Failure to follow these instructions may result in serious personal injury.

⁂ WARNING

When handling fuel, always observe fuel handling precautions and be prepared in the event of fuel spillage. Spilled fuel may be ignited by hot vehicle components or other ignition sources. Failure to follow these instructions may result in serious personal injury.

⁂ WARNING

Remove the fuel filler cap slowly. The fuel system may be under pressure. If the fuel filler cap is venting vapor or if you hear a hissing sound, wait until it stops before completely removing the fuel filler cap. Otherwise, fuel may spray out. Failure to follow these instructions may result in serious personal injury.

⁂ WARNING

Before working on or disconnecting any of the fuel tubes or fuel system components, relieve the fuel system pressure to prevent accidental spraying of fuel. Fuel in the fuel system remains under high pressure, even when the engine is not running. Failure to follow this instruction may result in serious personal injury.

Aft of Axle Tank

See Figure 188.

1. With the vehicle in NEUTRAL, position it on a hoist.
2. Release the fuel system pressure.
3. Disconnect the battery ground cable.
4. Drain the fuel tank.
5. Disconnect the fuel tank filler pipe and the filler vent tube from the fuel tank.
6. Position a suitable jack under the fuel tank.

➡The 40 gallon fuel tank has 2 cradle bracket bolts and the 55 gallon has 3 cradle bracket bolts.

7. Remove the 2 or 3 fuel tank cradle bracket bolts. To install, tighten to 76 ft. lbs. (103 Nm).

➡The 40 gallon fuel tank has 2 cradle bracket bolts and the 55 gallon has 3 cradle bracket nuts.

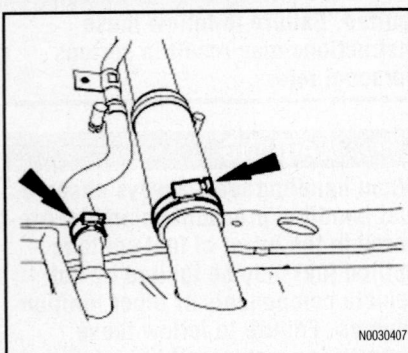

Fig. 188 Disconnect the fuel tank filler pipe and the filler vent tube

8. Remove the 2 or 3 fuel tank cradle bracket nuts. To install, tighten to 66 ft. lbs. (90 Nm).

➡The 40 gallon fuel tank has 2 fuel tank support strap nuts and the 55 gallon has 3 fuel tank support strap nuts.

9. Remove the 2 or 3 nuts and the fuel tank support straps.

10. Partially lower the fuel tank.

11. Disconnect the fuel vapor tube-to-fuel vapor vent valve(s) quick connect coupling(s).

12. Disconnect the fuel supply tube-to-Fuel Pump (FP) module quick connect coupling.

13. Disconnect the FP module and Fuel Tank Pressure (FTP) sensor electrical connectors.

14. Lower the fuel tank.

15. To install, reverse the removal procedure.

Midship Tank

1. With the vehicle in NEUTRAL, position it on a hoist.

2. Release the fuel system pressure.

3. Disconnect the battery ground cable.

4. Drain the fuel tank.

5. If connected, disconnect the fuel tank filler pipe hose.

6. Disconnect the fuel vapor tube quick connect coupling at the rear of the fuel tank.

7. Position a suitable jack under the fuel tank.

8. Remove the nut and the front fuel tank support strap. To install, tighten to 18 ft. lbs. (25 Nm).

9. Remove the nut and the rear fuel tank support strap. To install, tighten to 18 ft. lbs. (25 Nm).

10. Partially lower the fuel tank.

11. Disconnect the fuel tank filler pipe

vent hose-to-fuel vapor tube quick connect coupling.

12. Disconnect the Fuel Pump (FP) module/fuel level sensor electrical connector.

13. Disconnect the fuel supply tube-to-FP module quick connect coupling.

14. Lower the fuel tank.

15. To install, reverse the removal procedure.

THROTTLE BODY

REMOVAL & INSTALLATION

4.6L Engines

See Figure 189.

1. Remove the Air Cleaner (ACL) assembly and ACL outlet tube.

➡The red clip must be pulled out before disconnecting the electrical connector.

2. Disconnect the Electronic Throttle Control (ETC) electrical connector.

3. Remove the 4 bolts and the Throttle Body (TB).

4. Discard the TB gasket.

To install:

5. Install a new TB gasket, position the TB and tighten the 4 bolts in 2 stages.

a. Stage 1: Tighten to 7 ft. lbs. (10 Nm).

b. Stage 2: Tighten an additional 90 degrees.

6. Connect the ETC electrical connector.

7. Push back the red clip.

8. Install the ACL assembly and ACL outlet tube.

5.4L Engines

See Figure 190.

1. Remove the Air Cleaner (ACL) assembly and ACL outlet tube.

➡The red clip must be pulled out before disconnecting the electrical connector.

2. Disconnect the Electronic Throttle Control (ETC) electrical connector.

➡The red clip must be pulled out before disconnecting the electrical connector.

3. Disconnect the Throttle Position (TP) sensor electrical connector.

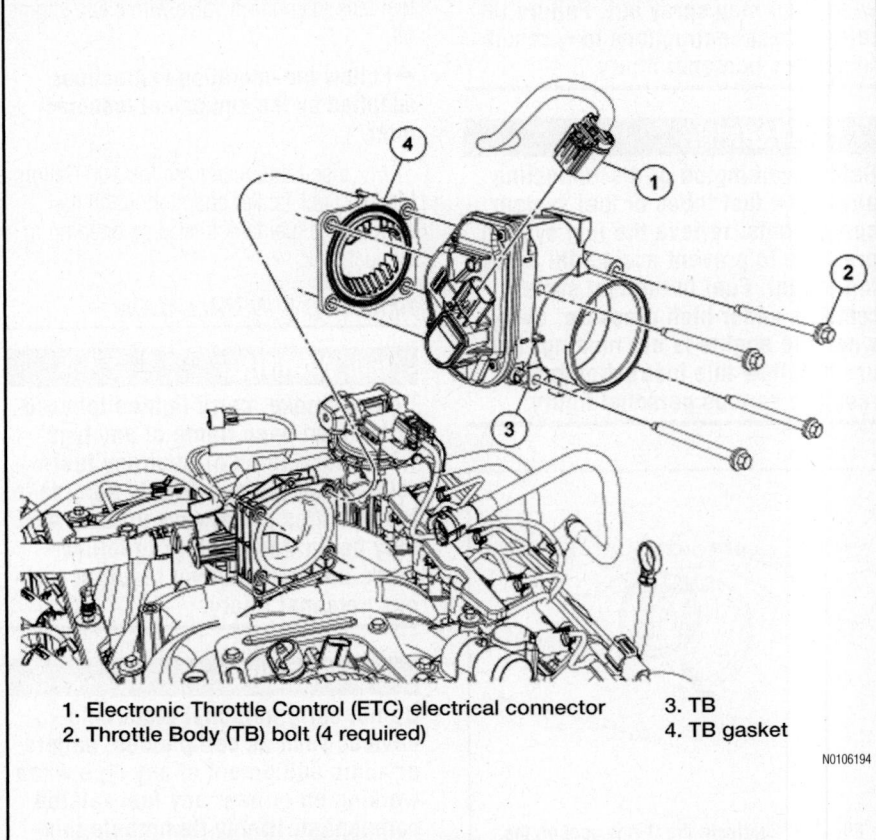

1. Electronic Throttle Control (ETC) electrical connector
2. Throttle Body (TB) bolt (4 required)
3. TB
4. TB gasket

Fig. 189 Exploded view of the throttle body—4.6L Engines

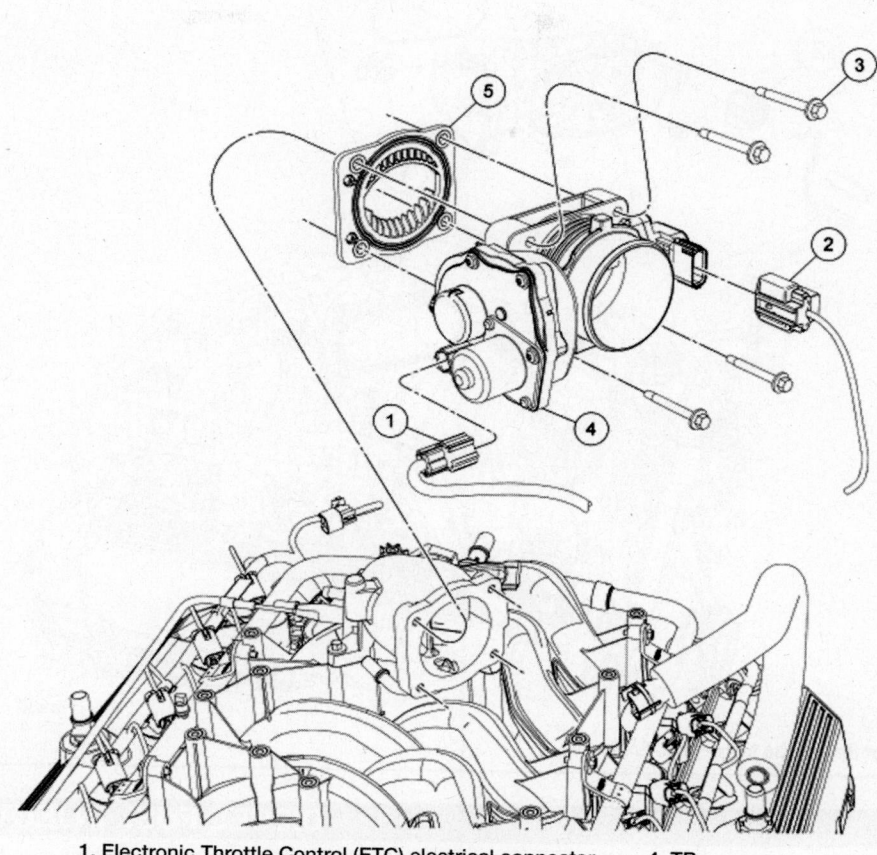

1. Electronic Throttle Control (ETC) electrical connector
2. Throttle Position (TP) sensor electrical connector
3. Throttle Body (TB) bolt (4 required)
4. TB
5. TB gasket

N0093151

Fig. 190 Exploded view of the throttle body—5.4L Engines

4. Remove the 4 bolts and the Throttle Body (TB).

5. Discard the TB gasket.

To install:

6. Install a new TB gasket, position the TB and tighten the 4 bolts in 2 stages.

   a. Stage 1: Tighten to 80 inch lbs. (9 Nm).

   b. Stage 2: Tighten an additional 90 degrees.

7. Connect the TP sensor electrical connector.

8. Push back the red clip.

9. Connect the ETC electrical connector.

10. Push back the red clip.

11. Install the ACL assembly and ACL outlet tube.

6.8L Engines

See Figure 191.

1. Remove the engine cover.

2. Remove the Air Cleaner (ACL) assembly and the ACL outlet tube.

➡**The red clip must be pulled out before disconnecting the electrical connector.**

3. Disconnect the Electronic Throttle Control (ETC) electrical connector.

➡**The red clip must be pulled out before disconnecting the electrical connector.**

4. Disconnect the Throttle Position (TP) sensor electrical connector.

5. Remove the 4 bolts and the TB assembly.

6. Discard the TB O-ring seal.

To install:

7. Using a new O-ring seal, install the TB and tighten the 4 bolts in 2 stages.

   a. Stage 1: Tighten to 80 inch lbs. (9 Nm).

   b. Stage 2: Tighten an additional 90 degrees (one-fourth turn).

8. Connect the TP sensor electrical connector.

9. Connect the ETC electrical connector.

10. Install the ACL assembly and the ACL outlet tube.

11. Install the engine cover.

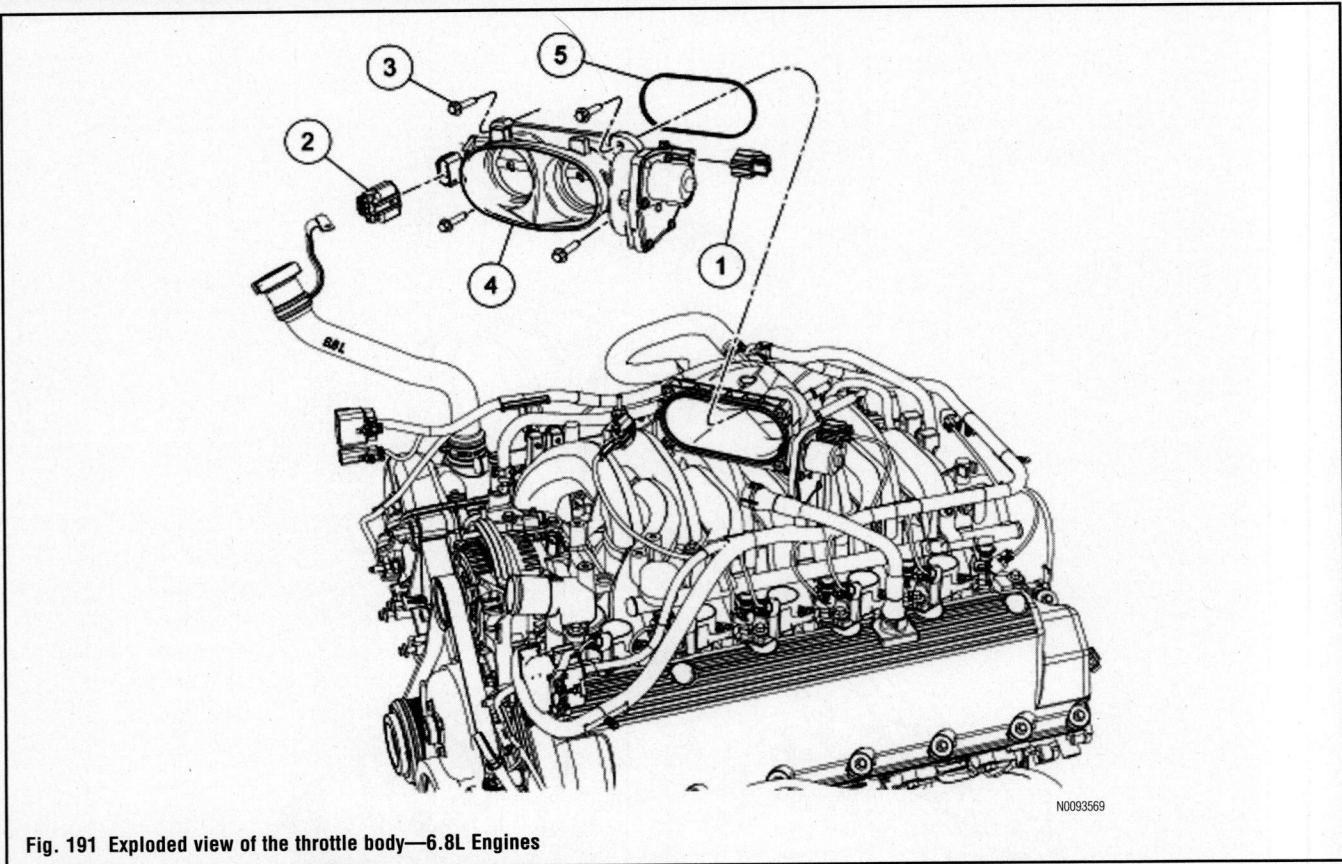

Fig. 191 Exploded view of the throttle body—6.8L Engines

N0093569

FUEL **DIESEL FUEL INJECTION SYSTEM**

FUEL SYSTEM SERVICE PRECAUTIONS

Safety is the most important factor when performing not only fuel system maintenance but any type of maintenance. Failure to conduct maintenance and repairs in a safe manner may result in serious personal injury or death. Maintenance and testing of the vehicle's fuel system components can be accomplished safely and effectively by adhering to the following rules and guidelines.

• To avoid the possibility of fire and personal injury, always disconnect the negative battery cable unless the repair or test procedure requires that battery voltage be applied.

• Always relieve the fuel system pressure prior to disconnecting any fuel system component (injector, fuel rail, pressure regulator, etc.), fitting or fuel line connection. Exercise extreme caution whenever relieving fuel system pressure to avoid exposing skin, face and eyes to fuel spray. Please be advised that fuel under pressure may penetrate the skin or any part of the body that it contacts.

• Always place a shop towel or cloth around the fitting or connection prior to loosening to absorb any excess fuel due to spillage. Ensure that all fuel spillage (should it occur) is quickly removed from engine surfaces. Ensure that all fuel soaked cloths or towels are deposited into a suitable waste container.

• Always keep a dry chemical (Class B) fire extinguisher near the work area.

• Do not allow fuel spray or fuel vapors to come into contact with a spark or open flame.

• Always use a back-up wrench when loosening and tightening fuel line connection fittings. This will prevent unnecessary stress and torsion to fuel line piping.

• Always replace worn fuel fitting O-rings with new. Do not substitute fuel hose or equivalent where fuel pipe is installed.

Before servicing the vehicle, make sure to also refer to the precautions in the beginning of this section as well.

RELIEVING FUEL SYSTEM PRESSURE

See Figure 192.

✳✳ WARNING

Do not smoke, carry lighted tobacco or have an open flame of any type when working on or near any fuel-related component. Highly flammable mixtures are always present and may be ignited. Failure to follow these instructions may result in serious personal injury.

✳✳ WARNING

When handling fuel, always observe fuel handling precautions and be prepared in the event of fuel spillage. Spilled fuel may be ignited by hot vehicle components or other ignition sources. Failure to follow these instructions may result in serious personal injury.

✳✳ WARNING

Before working on or disconnecting any of the fuel tubes or fuel system components, relieve the fuel system pressure to prevent accidental spray-

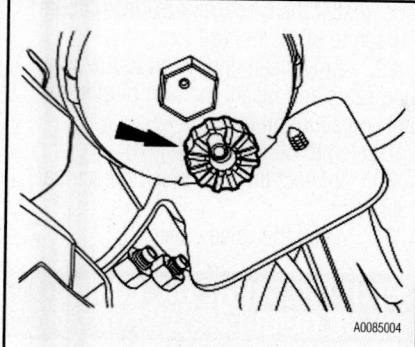

Fig. 192 Open the fuel/water separator
drain valve

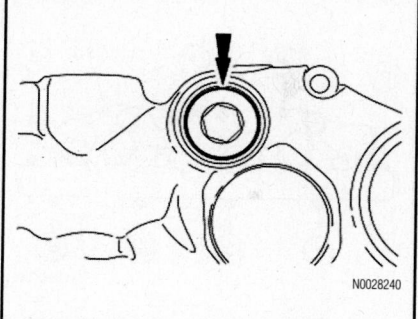

Fig. 194 Loosen the crankcase-to-head
tube

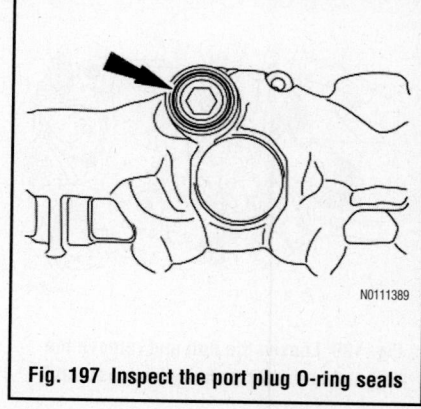

Fig. 197 Inspect the port plug O-ring seals

ing of fuel. Fuel in the fuel system
remains under high pressure, even
when the engine is not running. Failure to follow this instruction may
result in serious personal injury.

1. With the vehicle in NEUTRAL, position it on a hoist.
2. Disconnect the battery ground cable.
3. Open the fuel/water separator drain
valve to release the fuel pressure.

INJECTORS

REMOVAL & INSTALLATION

See Figures 193 through 201.

1. Remove the valve covers.
2. Disconnect the fuel injector electrical
connector.
3. Loosen the crankcase-to-head
tube(s).
4. Position the crankcase-to-head tube
and separate the tube.
5. Allow the lower section to go back
down.

➡**Do not remove the oil rail end plugs
or acoustic wave attenuator port fitting.
Service parts are not available to support these components.**

6. Remove the 9 bolts and the high-
pressure oil rail.

➡**Use a shop towel and metal brake
parts cleaner to remove the oil residue
prior to removing.**

7. If the crankcase-to-head tube separated, using the High Pressure Supply Tube
Remover, remove the lower crankcase-to-
head tube.
8. Inspect the D-ring seals for
damage (nicks, cuts and gouges). If damaged, replace the crankcase-to-head
tube.

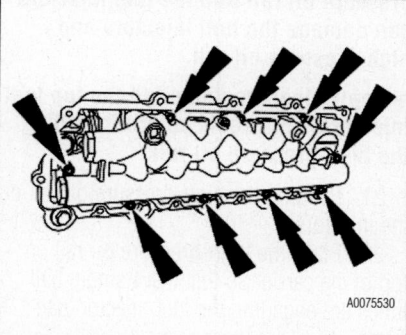

Fig. 195 Remove the 9 bolts and the high-
pressure oil rail

9. Remove the port plug from the high-
pressure oil rail.
10. Inspect the port plug O-ring seals for
damage (nicks, cuts and gouges). If damaged, replace the port plug.

➡**Do not attempt to apply battery voltage to the fuel injector or damage to
the fuel injector will occur.**

11. Using the Injector Connector Release
Tool, push the fuel injector electrical connector out of the rocker arm carrier.
12. Prior to removing the injector
assembly, insert clean shop towels in the oil
drain holes adjacent to each glow plug.

➡**To prevent engine damage, do not
use air tools to remove or install the
fuel injectors.**

➡**If engine coolant is found in the combustion chambers, it may be necessary
to install a new injector sleeve. For
additional information, refer to Fuel
Injector Sleeve in this section.**

➡**There is no need to drain the fuel rail.**

➡**The bolt is part of the fuel injector
hold-down assembly.**

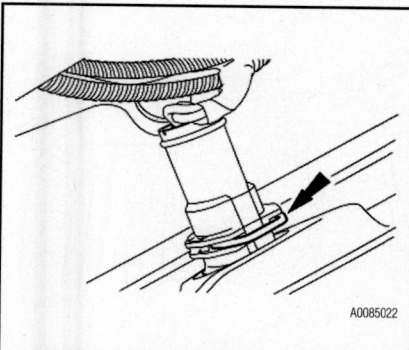

Fig. 193 Disconnect the fuel injector electrical connector

Fig. 196 Using the High Pressure Supply
Tube Remover

Fig. 198 Using the Injector Connector
Release Tool

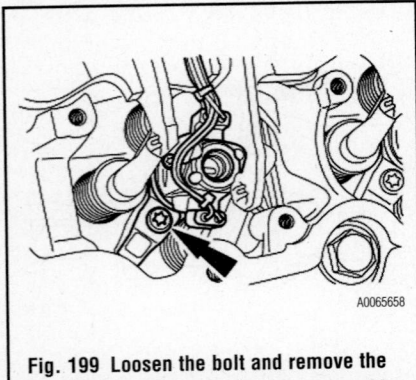

Fig. 199 Loosen the bolt and remove the bolt and fuel injector hold-down assembly

13. Loosen the bolt and remove the bolt and fuel injector hold-down assembly and the fuel injector.

14. Remove and discard the O-ring seals and copper washer.

To install:

➡**If the fuel injector oil inlet D-ring is damaged, a new fuel injector must be installed.**

➡**Lubricate the fuel injector and O-ring seals liberally with clean engine oil.**

15. Install new O-ring seals and a copper washer on the fuel injector.

➡**Failure to tighten the injector correctly can lead to engine failure.**

➡**To prevent engine damage, do not use air tools to remove or install the fuel injectors.**

16. Assemble the fuel injector hold down and bolt on the fuel injector and install the assembly. Tighten to 26 ft. lbs. (35 Nm).

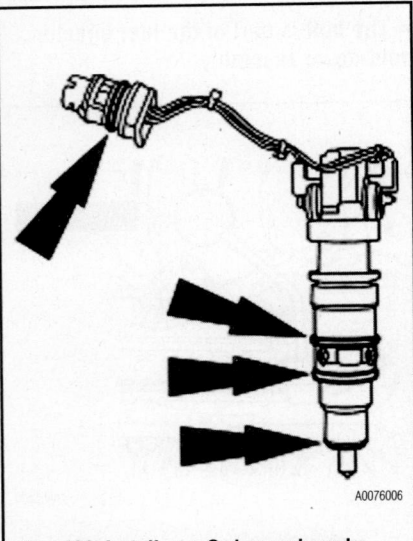

Fig. 200 Install new O-ring seals and a copper washer on the fuel injector

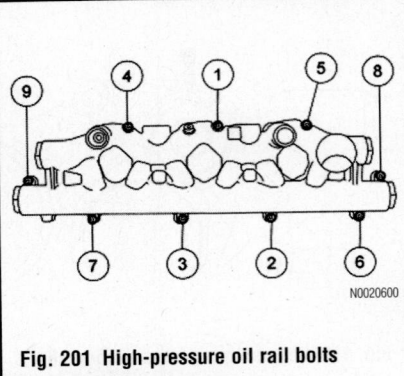

Fig. 201 High-pressure oil rail bolts tightening sequence

17. Remove the shop towels.

➡**Make sure the injector wiring is clear of all moving parts or engine damage can occur.**

18. Install the fuel injector electrical connector into the rocker carrier.

19. Apply clean engine oil to the top fuel injector O-ring seals.

➡**Apply clean engine oil to the D-ring seal, prior to installing.**

20. Position the lower section of the crankcase-to-head tube in the engine.

➡**Using the bolts to push the high-pressure oil rail into the fuel injectors can damage the fuel injectors and high-pressure oil rail.**

➡**Apply clean engine oil to the top fuel injector D-ring seals before installing the high-pressure oil rail.**

21. Position the high-pressure oil rail on the injectors.

22. Place the high-pressure oil rail on top of the carrier so that the 4 single ball tubes are engaging the fuel injector lead angle.

23. Insert 3 guide bolts, 2 on the ends of the straight side of the high-pressure oil rail and 1 in the middle of the wavy side of the high-pressure rail. Install the guide studs 6 to 7 turns.

24. Manually press the high-pressure oil rail into the fuel injectors.

25. Inspect that the high-pressure oil rail mounting feet are flat against the mounting surface.

26. Loosely install the 6 high-pressure oil rail bolts.

27. Remove the 3 guide bolts, install the remaining high-pressure oil rail bolts and tighten the 9 bolts in the sequence shown. Tighten to 13 Nm (115 lb-in).

28. Apply clean engine oil to the D-ring seals and reassemble the crankcase-to-head

tube. Install the crankcase-to-head tube(s). Tighten to 60 ft. lbs. (82 Nm).

29. Apply clean engine oil to the port plug seals and install the port plug in the high-pressure oil rail. Tighten to 60 ft. lbs. (82 Nm).

30. Connect the fuel injector electrical connector.

31. Install the valve covers.

HIGH PRESSURE OIL PUMP DRIVE GEAR

REMOVAL & INSTALLATION

See Figures 202 through 207.

1. Remove the turbocharger pedestal.

2. Position back the heat insulating wrap and disconnect the fuel Injection Pressure Regulator (IPR) valve electrical connector.

3. Using the Injector Pressure Regulator Socket, remove the IPR valve. Remove and discard the O-ring seals.

➡**Use care when removing the pump cover. The 3 bolts remaining in the pump cover under the EGR cooler can fall out of the pump cover and into the engine under the high-pressure pump.**

4. Remove or loosen the 8 bolts as needed.

➡**To prevent engine damage, do not pry off the high-pressure pump cover off the pump or damage to the cover can occur.**

5. Use a thin gasket scraper to separate the cover from the crankcase at the rear cover seam. Remove the high-pressure oil pump cover.

6. Remove and discard the press-in-place gasket.

7. Position the Dial Indicator Gauge

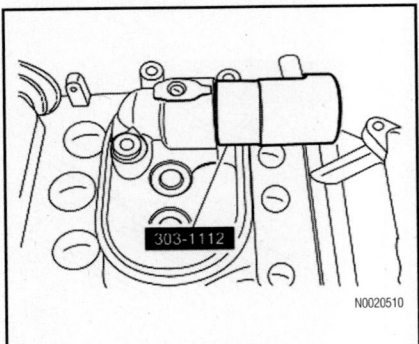

Fig. 202 Using the Injector Pressure Regulator Socket

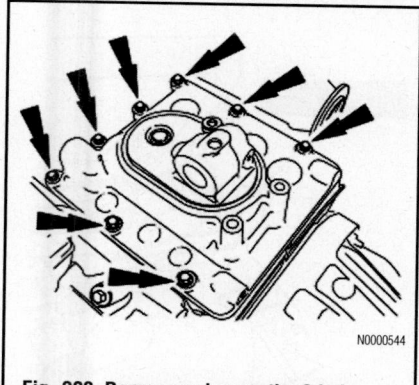

Fig. 203 Remove or loosen the 8 bolts

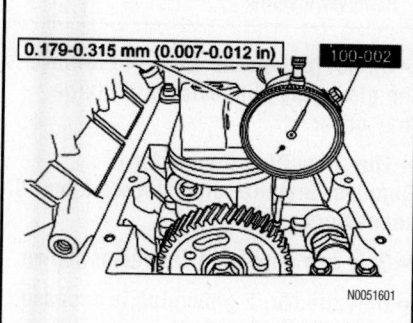

Fig. 204 Position the Dial Indicator Gauge with Holding Fixture

with Holding Fixture and check the oil pump drive gear backlash.

8. Loosen the 2 bolts on the high-pressure oil branch tube adapter.

9. Remove the 3 bolts and the high-pressure oil pump.

10. Remove and discard the lower O-ring seals.

11. Remove and discard the high-pressure oil pump O-ring seal.

To install:

➡**To prevent engine damage, use only an approved pump cover seal. Substi-**

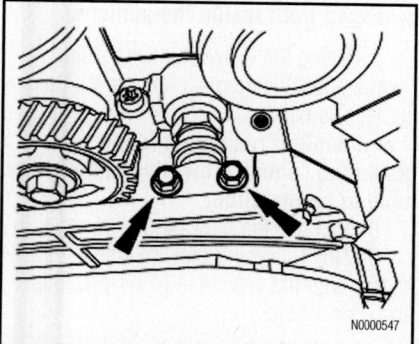

Fig. 205 Loosen the 2 bolts on the high-pressure oil branch tube adapter

Fig. 206 Remove the 3 bolts and the high-pressure oil pump

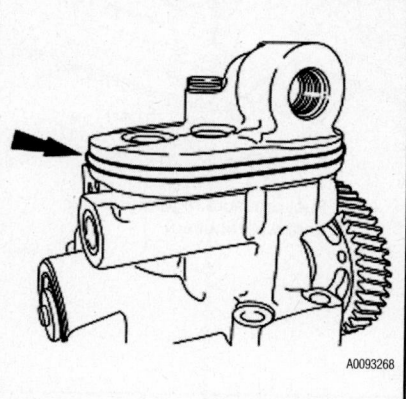

Fig. 207 Remove and discard the high-pressure oil pump O-ring seal

tution could cause damage to the pump cover.

12. Install a new O-ring seal on the high-pressure oil pump.

13. Install new lower O-ring seals.

14. Install the high-pressure pump and the 3 bolts. Tighten to 23 ft. lbs. (31 Nm).

15. Tighten the 2 high-pressure oil branch tube adapter bolts. Tighten to 10 ft. lbs. (14 Nm).

16. Position the Dial Indicator Gauge with Holding Fixture and check the oil pump drive gear backlash.

17. Install a new press-in-place gasket in the high-pressure pump cover.

18. Clean the cover mounting surface and apply sealer at the seams.

➡**To prevent engine damage, the high-pressure oil pump cover must be firmly seated on the O-ring seal to prevent cracking the cover plate.**

➡**Use care when installing the high-pressure pump cover with fasteners. The 3 bolts in the cover could fall out of the cover and fall down in the engine under the high-pressure pump.**

➡**Apply clean engine oil to the high-pressure oil pump O-ring seal prior to installing the high-pressure pump cover.**

19. Install the high-pressure oil pump cover and the 5 remaining bolts. Tighten to 8 ft. lbs. (11 Nm).

➡**Install new O-ring seals.**

20. Using the Injector Pressure Regulator Socket, install the IPR valve. Tighten to 37 ft. lbs. (50 Nm).

21. Connect the IPR valve electrical connector.

22. Position back the heat insulating wrap.

23. Install the turbocharger.

FUEL PRESSURE REGULATOR

REMOVAL & INSTALLATION

See Figures 208 through 211.

1. Remove the 6 pushpin retainers and the upper air deflector.

2. Remove the 4 power steering reservoir bracket bolts.

3. Remove the power steering fluid indicator and 3 bolts. Remove the power steering reservoir mounting bracket. Install the power steering fluid indicator and position the power steering reservoir aside.

4. Disconnect the coolant hoses from the Air Cleaner (ACL) outlet pipe.

5. Loosen the clamps and remove the ACL outlet pipe.

➡**If there is any oil residue, clean both connecting ports and the inside surface of the Charge Air Cooler (CAC) pipe to prevent the pipe from blowing off.**

6. Loosen the clamps and remove the CAC tube.

7. Remove the secondary fuel filter and remove all fuel from the filter housing. To install, tighten to 10 ft. lbs. (14 Nm).

8. Disconnect the fuel return tube from the regulator cover. To install, tighten to 32 ft. lbs. (43 Nm).

❖❖ WARNING

Clean all fuel residue from the engine compartment. If not removed, fuel residue may ignite when the engine is returned to operation. Failure to follow this instruction may result in serious personal injury.

9. Remove the 4 screws and the fuel pressure regulator cover.

10. Remove and discard the fuel pressure regulator cover O-ring seal.

11. Remove the spring and poppet valve.

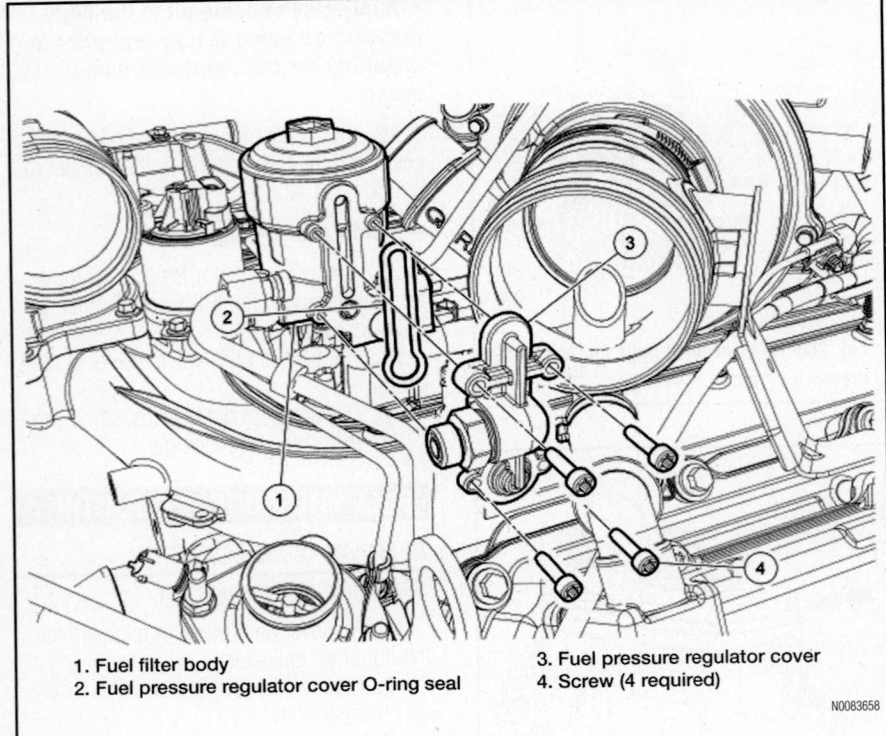

1. Fuel filter body
2. Fuel pressure regulator cover O-ring seal
3. Fuel pressure regulator cover
4. Screw (4 required)

N0083658

Fig. 208 Exploded view of the fuel pressure regulator

A0090509

Fig. 209 Remove the secondary fuel filter

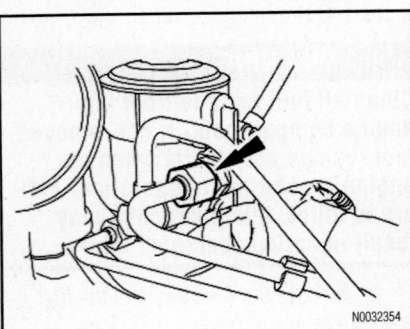

N0032354

Fig. 210 Disconnect the fuel return tube from the regulator cover

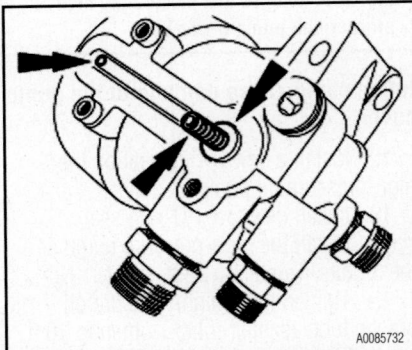

A0085732

Fig. 211 Inspect the fixed orifice for foreign material

12. Inspect the fixed orifice for foreign material.
13. Clean the fuel pressure regulator bore in the fuel filter housing.
14. To install, reverse the removal procedure.

GLOW PLUGS

REMOVAL & INSTALLATION
See Figures 212 and 213.

1. No. 2 glow plug:
2. Remove the ECU. Refer to Engine Performance.

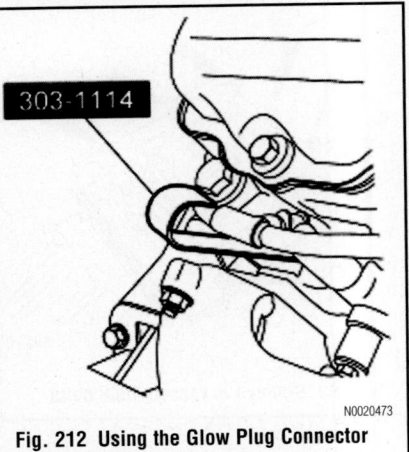

303-1114

N0020473

Fig. 212 Using the Glow Plug Connector Remover/Installer

→Do not pull on the wiring to remove the glow plug connector or damage may occur.

→The Glow Plug Connector Remover/Installer does not work on all connectors.

→Only one glow plug connector shown.

→Only the No. 2 glow plug is accessed from under the hood.

3. Using the Glow Plug Connector Remover/Installer, remove the glow plug harness as needed.

→If coolant residue is found on the glow plug, a new glow plug sleeve may have to be installed.

4. Remove the glow plug.
5. No. 7 and 8 glow plugs:
6. Remove the engine cover.

→Do not pull on the wiring to remove the glow plug connector or damage may occur.

→The Glow Plug Connector Remover/Installer does not work on all connectors.

→The No. 7 and 8 glow plugs are accessed from inside the vehicle.

7. Using the Glow Plug Connector Remover/Installer, remove the glow plug harness as needed.

→If coolant residue is found on the glow plug, a new glow plug sleeve may have to be installed.

8. Remove the glow plug.
9. No. 1, 3 and 5 glow plugs:
10. With the vehicle in NEUTRAL, position it on a hoist.

→Do not pull on the wiring to remove the glow plug connector or damage may occur.

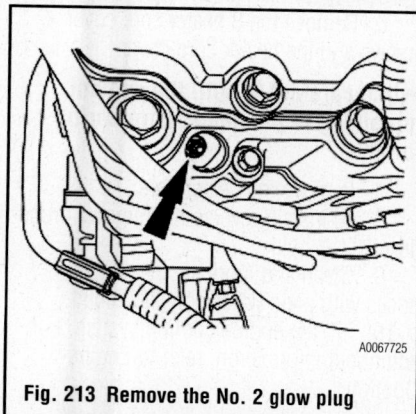

Fig. 213 Remove the No. 2 glow plug

➡ **The Glow Plug Connector Remover/Installer does not work on all connectors.**

➡ **The No. 1, 3 and 5 glow plugs are accessed through the wheel well.**

11. Using the Glow Plug Connector Remover/Installer, remove the glow plug harness as needed.

➡ **If coolant residue is found on the glow plug, a new glow plug sleeve may have to be installed.**

12. Remove the glow plug.

13. No. 4 and 6 glow plugs:
14. Remove the LH exhaust manifold. For additional information, refer to Engine Mechanical.

➡ **Do not pull on the wiring to remove the glow plug connector or damage may occur.**

➡ **The Glow Plug Connector Remover/Installer does not work on all connectors.**

➡ **The No. 4 and 6 glow plugs are accessed from under the vehicle.**

15. Using the Glow Plug Connector Remover/Installer, remove the glow plug harness as needed.

➡ **If coolant residue is found on the glow plug, a new glow plug sleeve may have to be installed.**

16. Remove the glow plug.
To install:
17. No. 4 and 6 glow plugs:
18. Install the glow plug. Tighten to 14 ft. lbs. (19 Nm).
19. Clean and apply clean engine oil to the O-ring seals prior to installation.
20. Using the Glow Plug Connector Remover/Installer, install the glow plug harness.

21. Install the LH exhaust manifold.
22. No. 1, 3 and 5 glow plugs:
23. Install the glow plug. Tighten to Tighten to 14 ft. lbs. (19 Nm).
24. Clean and apply clean engine oil to the O-ring seals prior to installation.
25. Using the Glow Plug Connector Remover/Installer, install the glow plug harness.
26. No. 7 and 8 glow plugs:
27. Install the glow plug. Tighten to 14 ft. lbs. (19 Nm).
28. Clean and apply clean engine oil to the O-ring seals prior to installation.
29. Using the Glow Plug Connector Remover/Installer, install the glow plug harness.
30. Install the engine cover.
31. No. 2 glow plug:
32. Install the glow plug. Tighten to 14 ft. lbs. (19 Nm).
33. Clean and apply clean engine oil to the O-ring seals prior to installation.
34. Using the Glow Plug Connector Remover/Installer, install the glow plug harness.
35. To complete the installation, reverse the remaining removal procedure.

HEATING & AIR CONDITIONING SYSTEM

BLOWER MOTOR

REMOVAL & INSTALLATION
See Figure 214.

1. Vehicles with 4.6L, 5.4L or 6.8L engine; remove the battery. Refer to Battery in Engine Electrical.
2. Vehicles equipped with 6.0L diesel: Remove the 3 bolts and position the junction box aside.
3. Vehicles equipped with A/C:
   a. Position the suction accumulator aside.

   b. Remove the 3 screws.
   c. Position the suction accumulator aside.

➡ **To ease removal, align the flat spot on the blower motor mounting plate with the accumulator.**

4. Remove the blower motor.
5. Disconnect the blower motor electrical connector.
6. Remove the vent tube.
7. Remove 4 screws.
8. Remove the retaining clip.
9. Remove the blower motor.
10. To install, reverse the removal procedure.

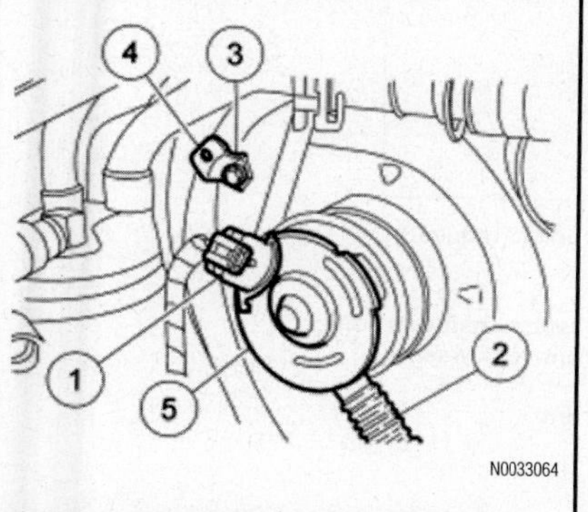

HEATER CORE

REMOVAL & INSTALLATION
See Figures 215 and 216.

1. Drain the engine coolant. For additional information, refer to Engine Cooling.
2. Disconnect the heater hoses at the heater core.
3. Remove the glove compartment.
4. Remove the 4 glove compartment screws.
5. Remove the glove compartment.

Fig. 214 Blower motor and components

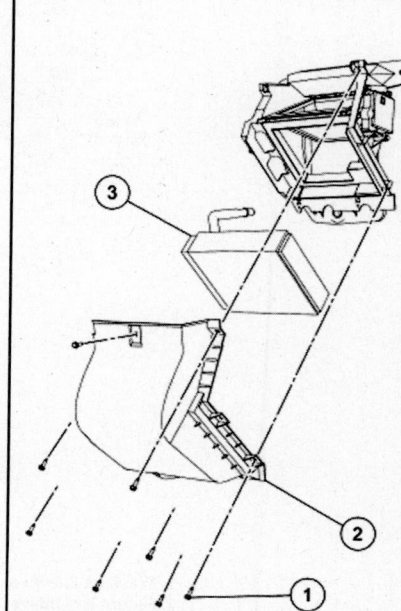

1. Heater core cover screw (8 required)
2. Heater core cover
3. Heater core

Fig. 215 Exploded view of the heater core and components

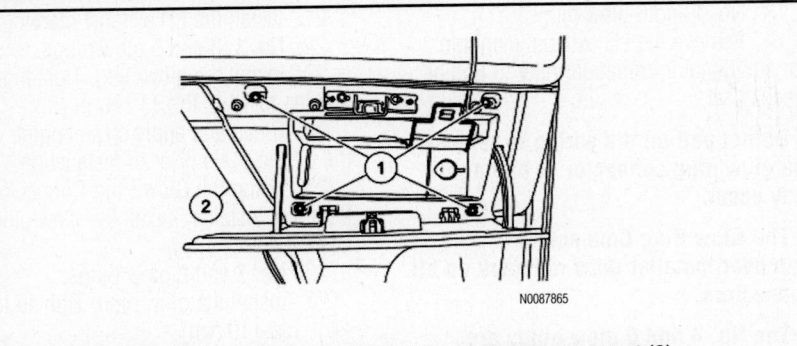

Fig. 216 Remove the 4 glove compartment screws (1) and glove compartment (2)

6. Remove the 8 heater core cover screws and the heater core cover.

➡**Use care not to spill the coolant remaining in the heater core during removal.**

7. Remove the heater core.
8. To install, reverse the removal procedure.
9. Clean and lubricate the coolant hoses with plain water only, if needed.
10. Fill the engine cooling system. For additional information, refer to Engine Cooling.

STEERING

POWER STEERING GEAR

REMOVAL & INSTALLATION
See Figures 217 through 219.

➡**New O-ring seals must be installed any time the pressure and return lines are disconnected from the steering gear.**

➡**Use a steering wheel holding device**

(such as Hunter® 28-75-1 or equivalent).

1. Using a suitable holding device, hold the steering wheel in the straight-ahead position.

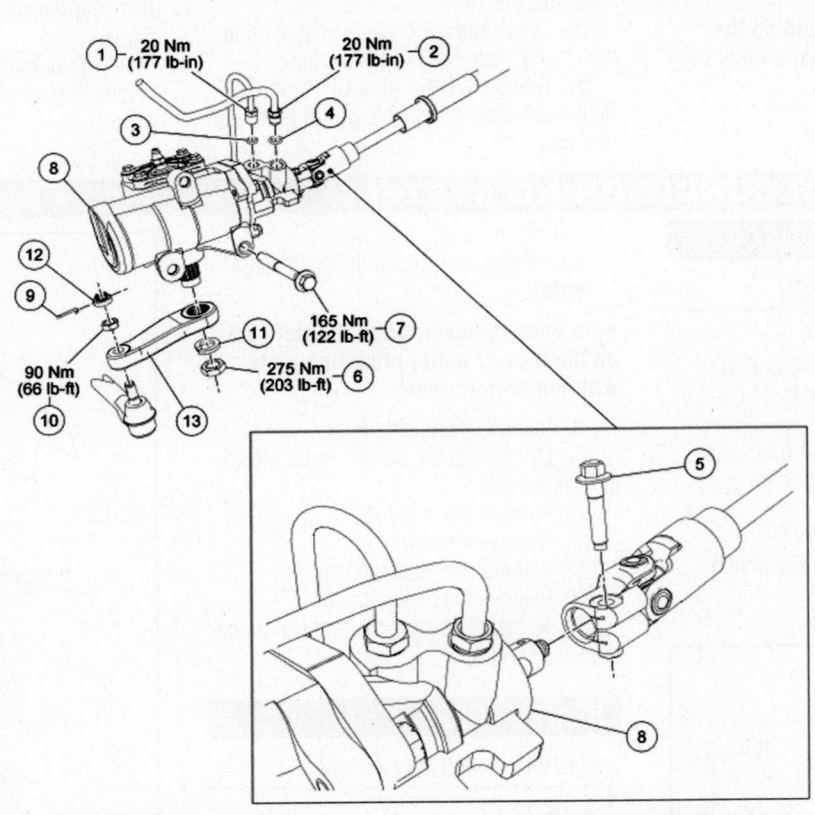

1. Pressure line-to-steering gear fitting
2. Return line fitting
3. O-ring seal
4. O-ring seal
5. Steering column shaft bolt (all except commercial chassis)
6. Steering column shaft bolt (commercial chassis)
7. Sector shaft arm nut
8. Steering gear bolt (3 required)
9. Steering gear
10. Cotter pin
11. Drag link-to-sector shaft arm nut
12. Sector shaft arm lock washer
13. Nut retainer
14. Sector shaft arm

Fig. 217 Exploded view of the power steering gear

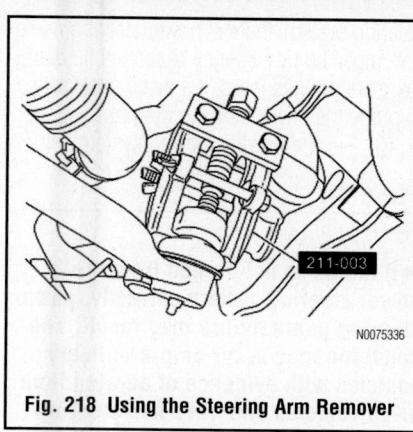

Fig. 218 Using the Steering Arm Remover

2. With the vehicle in NEUTRAL, position it on a hoist.

➡**Do not allow the steering column to rotate while the steering column shaft is disconnected or damage to the clockspring may result. If there is evidence that the steering column has rotated, the clockspring must be removed and recentered. For additional information, refer to Supplemental Restraint System.**

3. Remove the bolt and detach the steering column shaft from the gear. To install, tighten to 41 ft. lbs. (55 Nm) (commercial chassis). To install, tighten to 18 ft. lbs. (25 Nm) (non-commercial chassis).

4. Disconnect the pressure and return line fittings from the steering gear.

5. Remove and discard the O-ring seals. To install, tighten to 15 ft. lbs. (20 Nm).

6. Remove the drag link-to-sector shaft arm cotter pin, nut retainer and nut.

7. Discard the cotter pin. To install, tighten to 66 ft. lbs. (90 Nm).

8. Using the Steering Arm Remover, separate the sector shaft arm from the drag link.

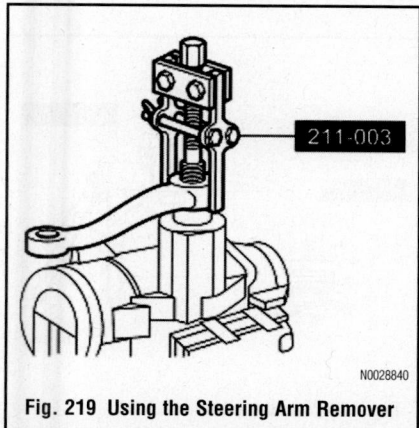

Fig. 219 Using the Steering Arm Remover

9. Remove the 3 steering gear bolts and the gear.

10. Secure the steering gear in a vise and remove the sector shaft arm nut and lock washer.

11. Using the Steering Arm Remover, remove the steering gear sector shaft arm.

➡**When connecting pressure and return line fittings with O-ring seals, new seals must be installed.**

12. To install, reverse the removal procedure.

13. Install new O-ring seals on the pressure and return line fittings.

14. Install a new cotter pin.

15. Fill the power steering system.

POWER STEERING PUMP

REMOVAL & INSTALLATION

See Figures 220 through 222.

1. Vehicles with 6.0L engine; Remove the engine cooling fan. For additional information, refer to Engine Cooling.

2. Rotate the tensioner clockwise and remove the accessory drive belt from the power steering pump pulley.

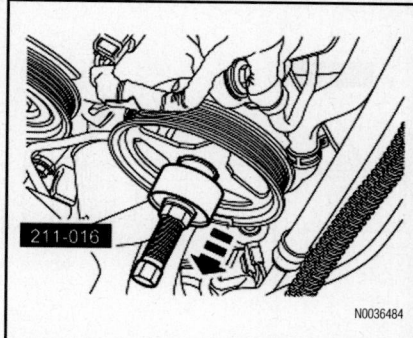

Fig. 221 Using the Power Steering Pump Pulley Remover

3. With the vehicle in NEUTRAL, position it on a hoist.

4. If equipped, remove the deflector shield.

5. Using the Power Steering Pump Pulley Remover, remove the pulley.

6. Using a suitable suction device, remove the power steering fluid from the fluid reservoir.

7. Disconnect the power steering pump supply hose.

8. Disconnect the pressure line-to-pump fitting.

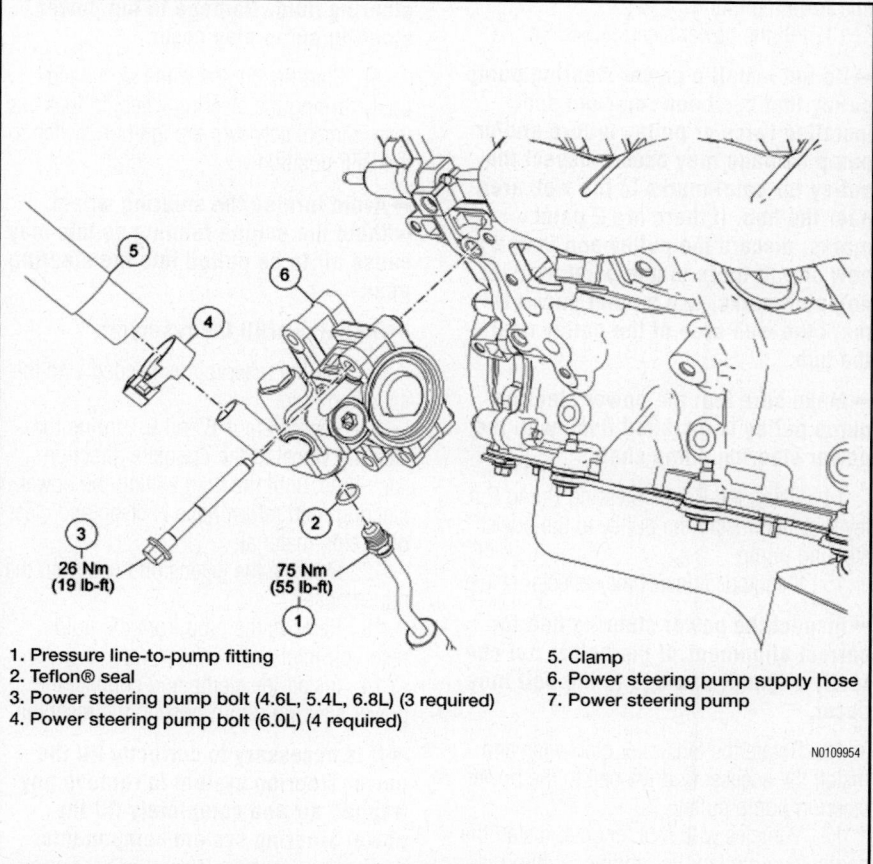

3. 26 Nm (19 lb-ft)
2. 75 Nm (55 lb-ft)

1. Pressure line-to-pump fitting
2. Teflon® seal
3. Power steering pump bolt (4.6L, 5.4L, 6.8L) (3 required)
4. Power steering pump bolt (6.0L) (4 required)
5. Clamp
6. Power steering pump supply hose
7. Power steering pump

Fig. 220 Exploded view of the power steering pump

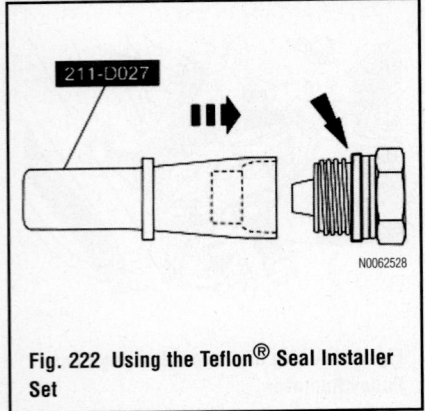

Fig. 222 Using the Teflon® Seal Installer Set

9. Remove and discard the Teflon® seal. To install, tighten to 55 ft. lbs. (75 Nm).

10. Remove the power steering pump bolts and the pump. To install, tighten to 19 ft. lbs. (26 Nm).

➡A new Teflon® seal must be installed on the pressure line-to-pump fitting anytime the line is disconnected from the pump.

11. To install, reverse the removal procedure.

12. Using the Teflon® Seal Installer Set, install a new Teflon® seal on the pressure line-to-pump fitting.

13. Fill the power steering system.

➡Do not install a power steering pump pulley that has been removed and installed twice or pulley failure and/or pump damage may occur. Inspect the pulley for paint marks in the web area near the hub. If there are 2 paint marks, discard the pulley and install a new one. If there is one paint mark or no paint marks, use a paint pencil to mark the web area of the pulley near the hub.

➡Make sure that the power steering pump pulley is installed flush with the power steering pump shaft.

14. Using the Power Steering Pump Pulley Installer, install the pulley to the power steering pump.

15. If equipped, install the deflector shield.

➡Inspect the power steering belt for correct alignment. If the belt is not correctly aligned, damage to the belt may occur.

16. Rotate the tensioner clockwise and install the accessory drive belt to the power steering pump pulley.

17. Vehicles with 6.0L engine; Install the engine cooling fan. For additional information, refer to Engine Cooling.

BLEEDING & FLUSHING

1. Remove the power steering fluid reservoir cap.

2. Using a suitable suction device, remove the power steering fluid from the reservoir.

3. Release the clamp and disconnect the return hose from the reservoir.

   a. Remove the clamp from the hose and allow the remaining fluid to drain out of the reservoir.

4. Plug the power steering fluid reservoir inlet port.

5. Attach an extension hose to the return hose.

➡Do not reuse the power steering fluid that has been flushed from the power steering system.

6. Place the open end of the extension hose into a suitable container.

7. If equipped with Hydro-Boost®, apply the brake pedal 4 times.

➡Do not overfill the reservoir.

8. Fill the reservoir as needed with the specified fluid.

➡Do not allow the power steering pump to run completely dry of power steering fluid. Damage to the power steering pump may occur.

9. Start the engine while simultaneously turning the steering wheel to lock and then immediately turn the ignition switch to the OFF position.

➡Avoid turning the steering wheel without the engine running as this may cause air to be pulled into the steering gear.

➡Do not overfill the reservoir.

10. Fill the reservoir as needed with the specified fluid.

11. Repeat Steps 8 and 9, turning the steering wheel in the opposite direction each time, until the fluid exiting the power steering fluid return hose is clean and clear of foreign material.

12. Remove the extension hose from the return hose.

13. Remove the plug from the fluid reservoir inlet port.

14. Install the clamp and connect the power steering return hose to the reservoir.

➡It is necessary to correctly fill the power steering system to remove any trapped air and completely fill the power steering system components.

15. If, after correctly filling the power

steering system, there is power steering noise accompanied by evidence of aerated fluid and there are no fluid leaks, it may be necessary to purge the power steering system.

16. Fill the power steering system.

PURGING

See Figure 223.

➡If the air is not purged from the power steering system correctly, power steering pump failure may result. The condition may occur on pre-delivery vehicles with evidence of aerated fluid or on vehicles that have had steering component repairs.

1. If equipped with a fire suppression system, depower the system.

➡A whine heard from the power steering pump can be caused by air in the system. The power steering purge procedure must be carried out prior to any component repair for which power steering noise complaints are accompanied by evidence of aerated fluid.

2. Remove the power steering fluid reservoir cap.

3. Fill the reservoir as needed with the specified fluid.

4. Raise the front wheels off the floor.

5. Tightly insert the Power Steering Evacuation Cap into the reservoir and connect the Vacuum Pump Kit.

6. Start the engine.

7. Using the Vacuum Pump Kit, apply vacuum and maintain the maximum vacuum of 68-85 kPa (20-25 in-Hg).

8. If equipped with Hydro-Boost®, apply the brake pedal twice.

➡Do not hold the steering wheel against the stops for an extended amount of time. Damage to the power steering pump may occur.

9. Cycle the steering wheel fully from stop-to-stop 10 times.

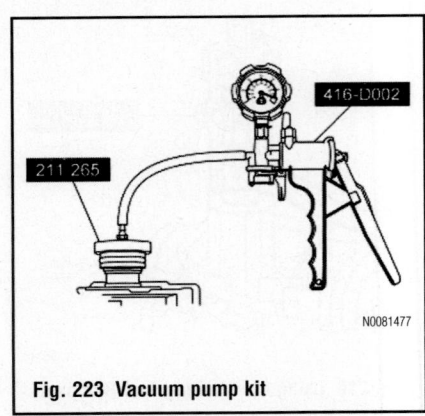

Fig. 223 Vacuum pump kit

10. Stop the engine.

11. Release the vacuum and remove the Vacuum Pump Kit.

➡**Do not overfill the reservoir.**

12. Fill the reservoir as needed.

13. Start the engine.

14. Install the Power Steering Evacuation Cap and the Vacuum Pump Kit. Apply and maintain the maximum vacuum of 68-85 kPa (20-25 in-Hg).

➡**Do not hold the steering wheel against the stops for an extended amount of time. Damage to the power steering pump may occur.**

15. Cycle the steering wheel fully from stop-to-stop 10 times.

16. Stop the engine, release the vacuum and remove the Vacuum Pump Kit and Power Steering Evacuation Cap.

➡**Do not overfill the reservoir.**

17. Fill the reservoir as needed and install the reservoir cap.

18. Visually inspect the power steering system for leaks.

FLUID FILL PROCEDURE

See Figure 224.

➡**If the air is not purged from the power steering system correctly, premature power steering pump failure may result. The condition can occur on pre-delivery vehicles with evidence of aerated fluid or on vehicles that have had steering component repairs.**

1. Remove the power steering fluid reservoir cap.

2. Install the Power Steering Evacuation Cap, Power Steering Fill Adapter Manifold and Vacuum Pump Kit as shown in the illustration.

➡**The Power Steering Fill Adapter Manifold control valves are in the OPEN position when the points of the handles face the center of the Power Steering Fill Adapter Manifold.**

3. Close the Power Steering Fill Adapter Manifold control valve (fluid side).

4. Open the Power Steering Fill Adapter Manifold control valve (vacuum side).

5. Using the Vacuum Pump Kit, apply 68-85 kPa (20-25 in-Hg) of vacuum to the power steering system.

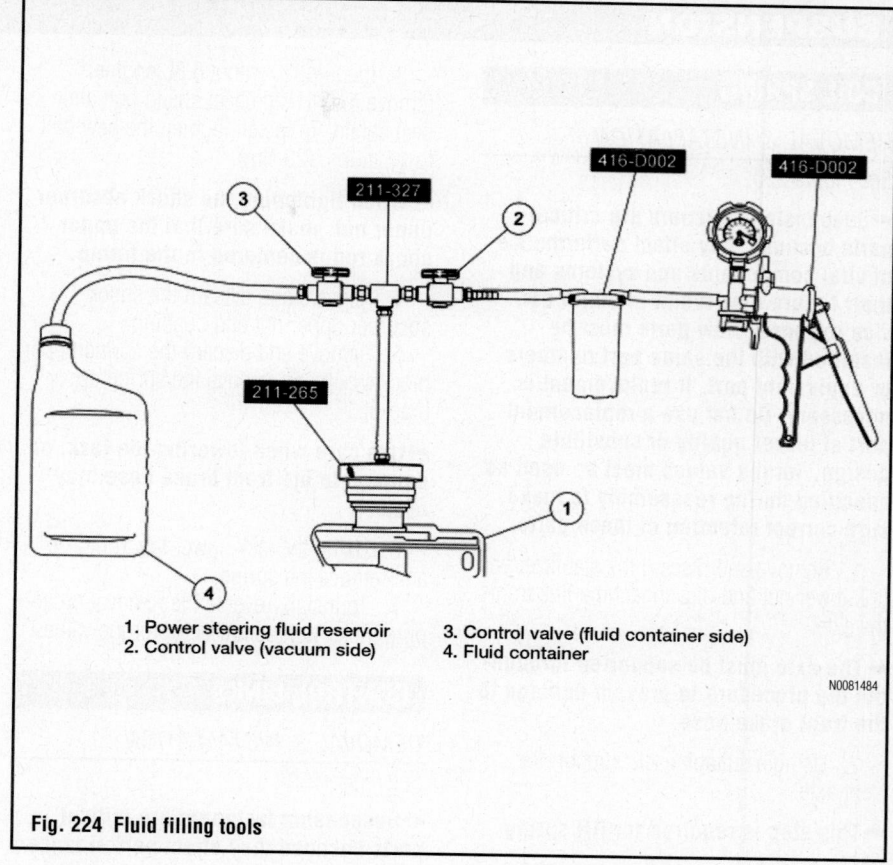

1. Power steering fluid reservoir
2. Control valve (vacuum side)
3. Control valve (fluid container side)
4. Fluid container

N0081484

Fig. 224 Fluid filling tools

6. Observe the Vacuum Pump Kit gauge for 30 seconds.

7. If the Vacuum Pump Kit gauge reading drops more than 3 kPa (0.88 in-Hg), correct any leaks in the power steering system or the Power Steering Evacuation Cap, Power Steering Fill Adapter Manifold and Vacuum Pump Kit before proceeding.

➡**The Vacuum Pump Kit gauge reading will drop slightly during this step.**

8. Slowly open the Power Steering Fill Adapter Manifold control valve (fluid side) until power steering fluid completely fills the hose and then close the control valve.

9. Using the Vacuum Pump Kit, apply 68-85 kPa (20-25 in-Hg) of vacuum to the power steering system.

10. Close the Power Steering Fill Adapter Manifold control valve (vacuum side).

11. Slowly open the Power Steering Fill Adapter Manifold control valve (fluid side).

12. Once power steering fluid enters the fluid reservoir and reaches the minimum fluid level indicator line on the reservoir,

close the Power Steering Fill Adapter Manifold control valve (fluid side).

13. Remove the Power Steering Evacuation Cap, Power Steering Fill Adapter Manifold and Vacuum Pump Kit.

14. Install the reservoir cap.

➡**Do not hold the steering wheel against the stops for an extended amount of time. Damage to the power steering pump may occur.**

➡**There will be a slight drop in the power steering fluid level in the reservoir when the engine is started.**

Start the engine and turn the steering wheel from stop-to-stop.

Turn the ignition switch to the OFF position.

➡**Do not overfill the reservoir.**

15. Remove the reservoir cap and fill the reservoir with the specified fluid.

16. Install the reservoir cap.

COIL SPRING

REMOVAL & INSTALLATION

See Figure 225.

➤Suspension fasteners are critical parts because they affect performance of vital components and systems and their failure may result in major service expense. New parts must be installed with the same part numbers or equivalent part, if replacement is necessary. Do not use a replacement part of lesser quality or substitute design. Torque values must be used as specified during reassembly to make sure correct retention of these parts.

1. Remove and discard the stabilizer bar link lower nut and disconnect the link from the axle.

➤The axle must be supported throughout the procedure to prevent damage to the front brake hose.

2. Using a suitable jack, support the front axle.

➤This step is required for RH spring only.

3. If equipped with a 6.8L engine, remove the RH side heat shield bolt and heat shield. To install, tighten the new bolt to 17 ft. lbs. (23 Nm).

➤When tightening the shock absorber upper nut, make sure that the upper shock rod is centered in the frame.

4. Remove and discard the shock absorber upper nut and bushing.
5. Remove and discard the spring upper bracket bolt and remove the spring upper bracket.

➤Use care when lowering the jack, or damage to the front brake hose may occur.

6. Using the jack, lower the front axle and remove the spring.
7. To install, reverse the removal procedure. Refer to illustration for torque values.

CONTROL LINKS

REMOVAL & INSTALLATION

See Figure 226.

➤Suspension fasteners are critical parts because they affect performance

of vital components and systems and their failure may result in major service expense. New parts must be installed with the same part numbers or equivalent part, if replacement is necessary. Do not use a replacement part of lesser quality or substitute design. Torque values must be used as specified during reassembly to make sure correct retention of these parts.

1. With the vehicle in NEUTRAL, position it on a hoist.

➤Use the hex-holding feature to prevent the stud from turning while removing the nut.

2. Remove and discard the stabilizer link upper nut.

➤Use the hex-holding feature to prevent the stud from turning while removing the nut.

3. Remove and discard the stabilizer link lower nut and remove the stabilizer bar link.
4. To install, reverse the removal procedure. Refer to illustration for torque values.

LOWER & UPPER BALL JOINT

REMOVAL & INSTALLATION

See Figures 227 and 228.

1. Remove the steering knuckle. For additional information, refer to Steering Knuckle in this section.
2. Remove the lower ball joint grease plug.
3. Position the wheel spindle in a vise and remove the snap ring from the lower ball joint.

➤To avoid damage to the components, do not use heat to aid ball joint removal.

4. Using the C-Frame and Screw Installer/Remover and Ball Joint Installer/Remover, remove the lower ball joint.
5. Using the C-Frame and Screw Installer/Remover and Ball Joint Installer/Remover, remove the upper ball joint.

To install:

➤To avoid damage to components, do not use heat to aid installation.

➤Clean the wheel knuckle ball joint bores.

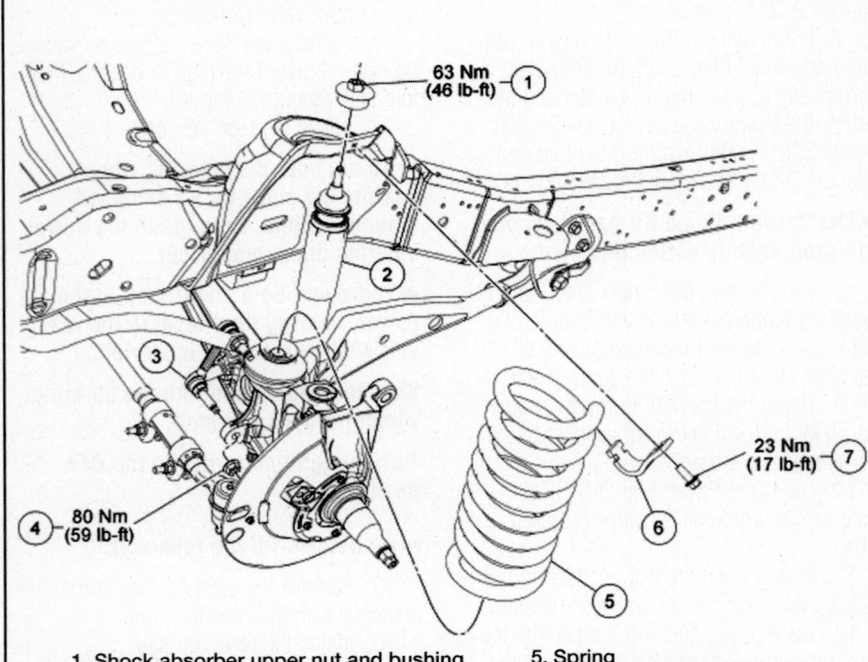

1. Shock absorber upper nut and bushing
2. Shock absorber
3. Stabilizer bar link
4. Stabilizer bar link nut
5. Spring
6. Spring upper bracket
7. Spring upper bracket bolt

N0077162

Fig. 225 Exploded view of the spring assembly

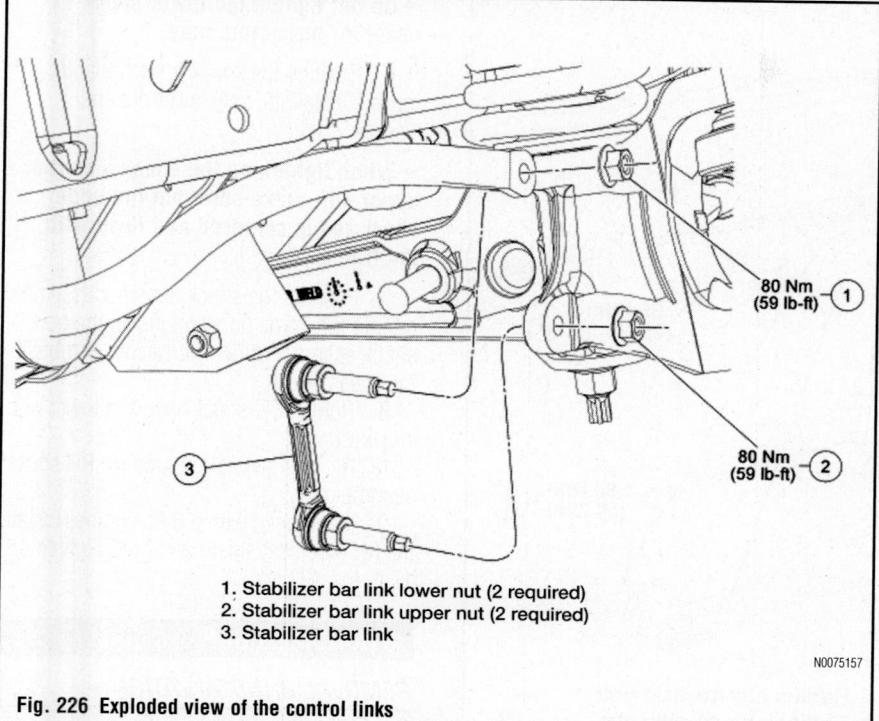

1. Stabilizer bar link lower nut (2 required)
2. Stabilizer bar link upper nut (2 required)
3. Stabilizer bar link

N0075157

Fig. 226 Exploded view of the control links

➡**The upper ball joint must be installed first.**

6. Using the C-Frame and Screw Installer/Remover and Ball Joint Installer/Remover, install the upper ball joint.

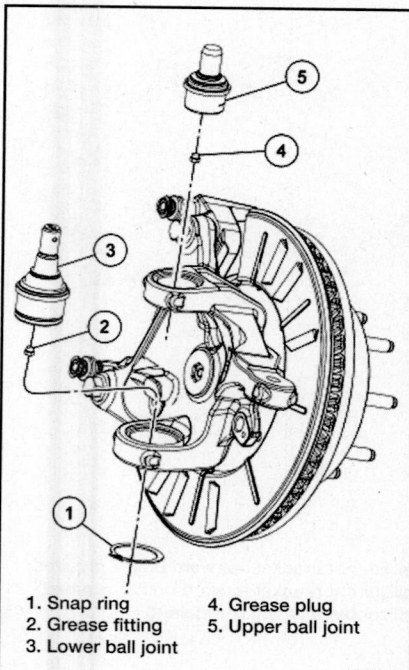

1. Snap ring
2. Grease fitting
3. Lower ball joint
4. Grease plug
5. Upper ball joint

N0105545

Fig. 227 Exploded view of the lower and upper ball joint

7. Using the C-Frame and Screw Installer/Remover and Ball Joint Installer/Remover, install the lower ball joint.
8. Install the snap ring in the groove at the bottom of the lower ball joint.
9. Install the lower ball joint grease plug.
10. Install the steering knuckle.

RADIUS ARM

REMOVAL & INSTALLATION
See Figure 229.

➡**Suspension fasteners are critical parts because they affect performance of vital components and systems and their failure may result in major service expense. New parts must be installed with the same part numbers or equivalent part, if replacement is necessary. Do not use a replacement part of lesser quality or substitute design. Torque values must be used as specified during reassembly to make sure correct retention of these parts.**

1. Remove the front spring. For additional information, refer to Coil Spring in this section.
2. Remove and discard the shock absorber lower nut and disconnect the shock absorber from the radius arm.
3. Remove and discard the radius arm rearward nut and flag bolt.

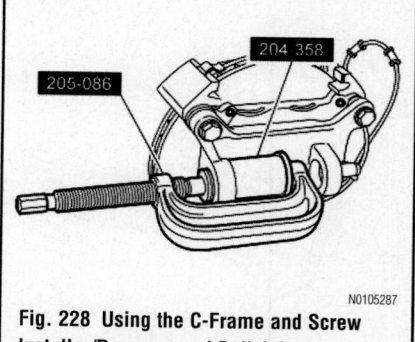

Fig. 228 Using the C-Frame and Screw Installer/Remover and Ball Joint Installer/Remover

4. Remove the radius arm-to-axle nut and bolt, the spring retainer and the insulator.
5. Discard the nut and bolt.

➡**Inspect the spring and radius arm insulators and install new as necessary.**

6. To install, reverse the removal procedure. Refer to illustration for torque values.

SHOCK ABSORBER

REMOVAL & INSTALLATION
See Figure 230.

➡**Suspension fasteners are critical parts because they affect performance of vital components and systems and their failure can result in major service expense. They must be replaced with the same part number or an equivalent part if replacement is necessary. Do not use a replacement part of lesser quality or substitute design. Torque values must be used as specified during reassembly to make sure of correct retention of these parts.**

➡**This step is required for RH shock absorber only.**

1. If equipped with a 6.8L engine, remove the RH side heat shield bolt and heat shield.
2. Remove and discard the shock absorber upper nut, washer and bushing assembly.
3. With the vehicle in NEUTRAL, position it on a hoist.
4. Remove and discard the shock absorber lower nut and washer.
5. Remove the shock absorber.

To install:

➡**Refer to illustration for torque values.**

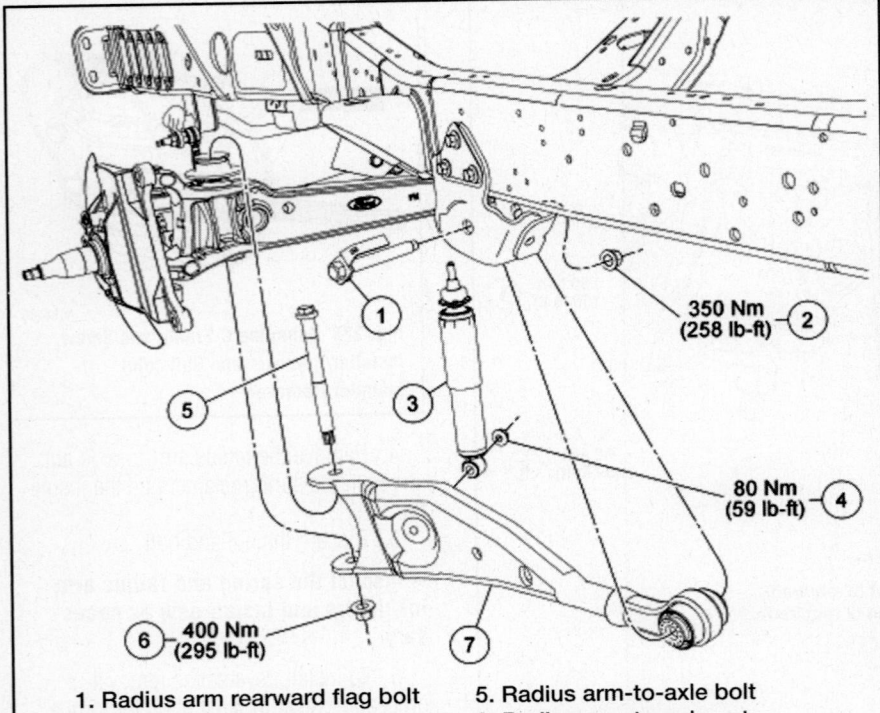

1. Radius arm rearward flag bolt
2. Radius arm rearward nut
3. Shock absorber
4. Shock absorber lower nut
5. Radius arm-to-axle bolt
6. Radius arm-to-axle nut
7. Radius arm

N0093012

Fig. 229 Exploded view of the radius arm

➡ Do not tighten the lower shock absorber nut at this time.

6. Position the shock absorber and loosely install the new lower nut and washer.

➡ When tightening the shock absorber upper nut, make sure that the upper shock rod is centered and flush with the frame.

7. Position the shock absorber assembly up into the frame hole and install the new shock absorber upper nut washer and bushing assembly.

8. Tighten the shock absorber lower nut and washer.

NOTE: This step is required for RH shock absorber only.

9. If equipped with a 6.8L engine, install the RH side heat shield and bolt. Tighten to 17 ft. lbs. (23 Nm).

STABILIZER BAR

REMOVAL & INSTALLATION

See Figure 231.

➡ Suspension fasteners are critical parts because they affect performance of vital components and systems and

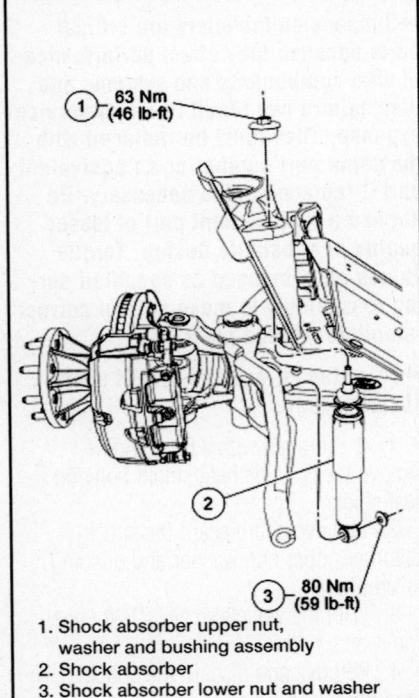

1. Shock absorber upper nut, washer and bushing assembly
2. Shock absorber
3. Shock absorber lower nut and washer

N0089223

Fig. 230 Exploded view of the shock absorber

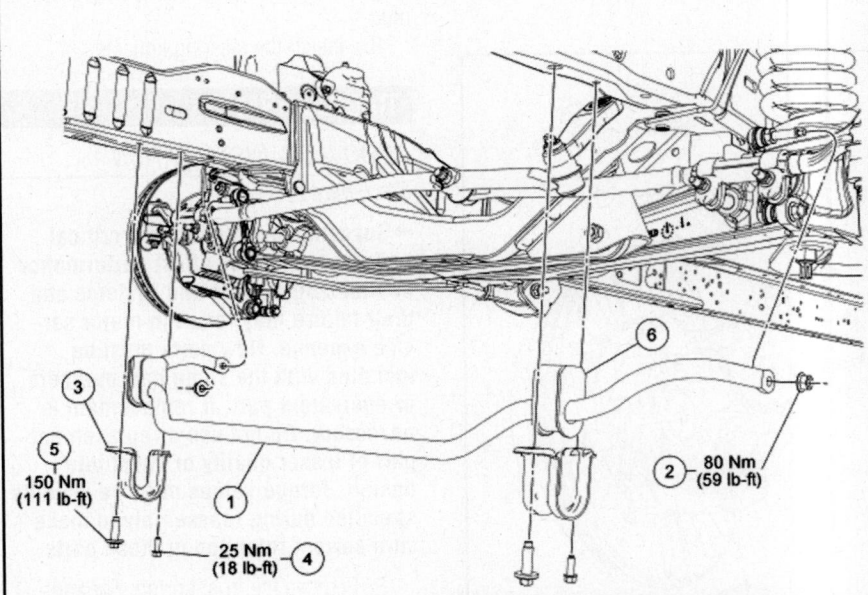

1. Stabilizer bar
2. Stabilizer bar link lower nut (2 required)
3. Stabilizer bar bracket (2 required)
4. Stabilizer bar bracket rearward bolt (2 required)
5. Stabilizer bar bracket forward bolt (2 required)
6. Stabilizer bar bushing (2 required)

N0089246

Fig. 231 Exploded view of the stabilizer bar

their failure may result in major service expense. New parts must be installed with the same part numbers or equivalent part, if replacement is necessary. Do not use a replacement part of lesser quality or substitute design. Torque values must be used as specified during reassembly to make sure correct retention of these parts.

1. With the vehicle in NEUTRAL, position it on a hoist.
2. Remove and discard the 2 stabilizer bar link lower nuts.
3. Remove the 2 stabilizer bar bracket rearward bolts.
4. Discard the 2 bolts.

5. Remove the 2 stabilizer bar bracket forward bolts and the 2 stabilizer bar brackets.
6. Discard the 2 bolts.
7. Remove the stabilizer bar.
8. To install, reverse the removal procedure. Refer to illustration for torque values.

STEERING KNUCKLE

REMOVAL & INSTALLATION
See Figure 232.

➡ **Suspension fasteners are critical parts because they affect performance of vital components and systems and their failure may result in major ser-**

vice expense. New parts must be installed with the same part numbers or equivalent part, if replacement is necessary. Do not use a replacement part of lesser quality or substitute design. Torque values must be used as specified during reassembly to make sure correct retention of these parts.

➡ **It is not necessary to remove the brake disc when removing the wheel spindle to service the ball joints.**

1. If installing a new wheel spindle, remove the brake disc. If the wheel spindle is being removed to service the ball joints, remove the brake pads. For additional information, refer to Front Disc Brake.

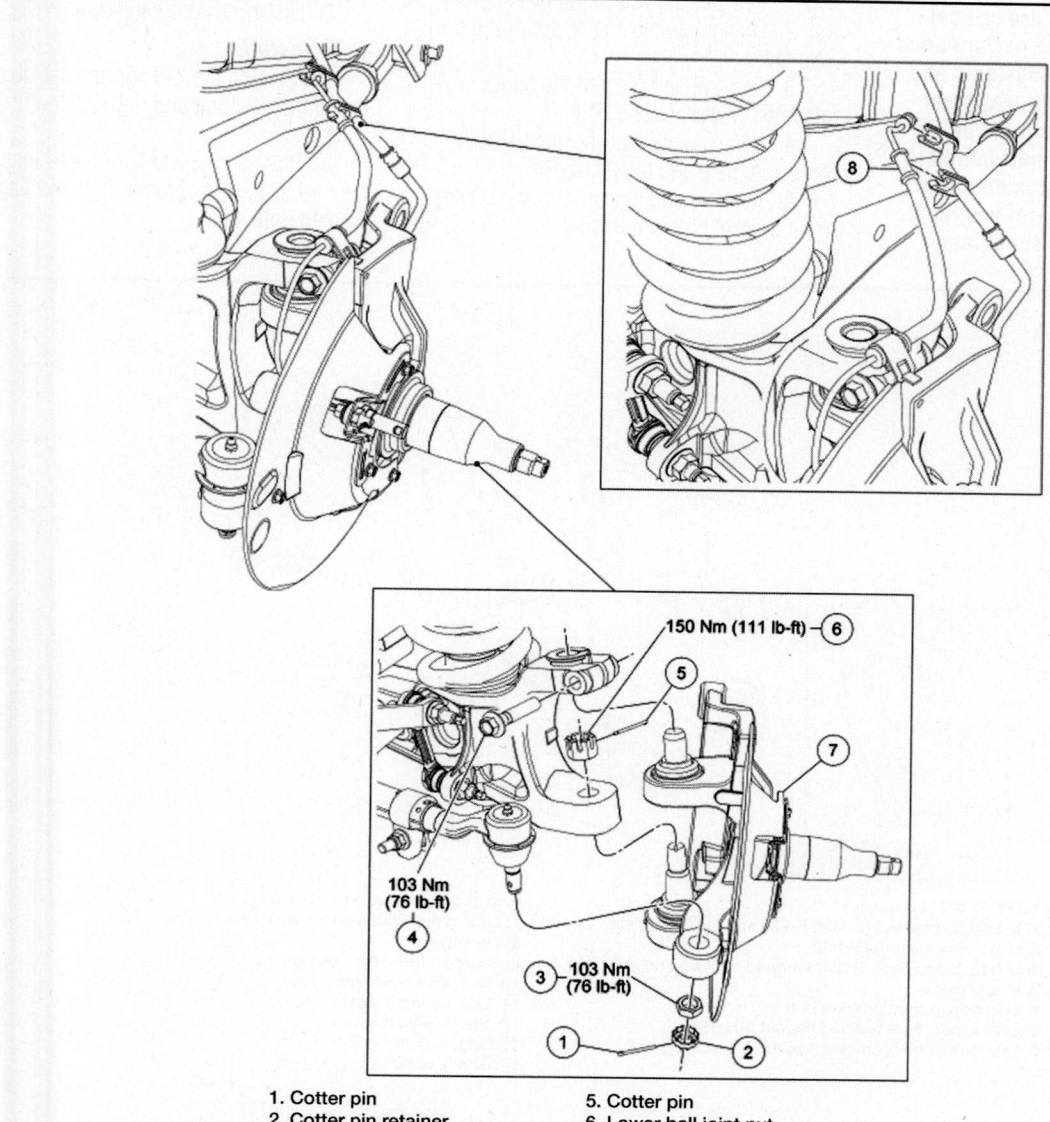

150 Nm (111 lb-ft) — 6

103 Nm (76 lb-ft) — 4

3 — 103 Nm (76 lb-ft)

1. Cotter pin
2. Cotter pin retainer
3. Outer tie-rod end nut
4. Upper ball joint bolt
5. Cotter pin
6. Lower ball joint nut
7. Wheel spindle
8. Wheel speed sensor harness

Fig. 232 Exploded view of the steering knuckle

N0105546

2. Disconnect the wheel speed sensor electrical connector and detach the sensor harness from the brake hose.

3. Remove the outer tie-rod end cotter pin, retainer and nut.

4. Discard the cotter pin.

5. Using the Ball Joint Separator, disconnect the outer tie-rod end.

6. Remove and discard the upper ball joint bolt.

7. Remove and discard the lower ball joint cotter pin and nut.

8. Install a new cotter pin.

➡**To prevent damage to the ball joint boot and socket, do not use a pickle fork-type remover to loosen the ball joints.**

9. Remove the wheel spindle in the following sequence.

10. Strike the lower end of the axle to loosen the ball joint.

11. Remove the wheel spindle.

12. To install, reverse the removal procedure. Refer to illustration for torque values.

13. Check and, if necessary, align the front end.

SUSPENSION

REAR SUSPENSION

LEAF SPRING

REMOVAL & INSTALLATION

See Figures 233 and 234.

➡**Suspension fasteners are critical parts because they affect performance of vital components and systems and their failure may result in major service expense. New parts must be installed with the same part numbers or equivalent part, if replacement is necessary. Do not use a replacement part of lesser quality or substitute** design. **Torque values must be used as specified during reassembly to make sure of correct retention of these parts.**

1. Remove the wheel and tire.
2. Using a suitable jack, support the rear axle.
3. Remove and discard the shock absorber lower nut and bolt.
4. Remove and discard the 4 U-bolt nuts, the plate and the 2 U-bolts.
5. Remove and discard the leaf spring front bracket bolt and flagnut.

6. Remove and discard the leaf spring shackle-to-bracket bolt and flagnut, then remove the leaf spring assembly.

7. Remove the shackle-to-leaf spring nut, bolt and shackle.

8. Discard the bolt and nut.

To install:

9. Position the leaf spring shackle and install the new bolt and nut. Tighten until snug.

10. Position the leaf spring and install the new shackle-to-bracket bolt and flagnut. Tighten until snug.

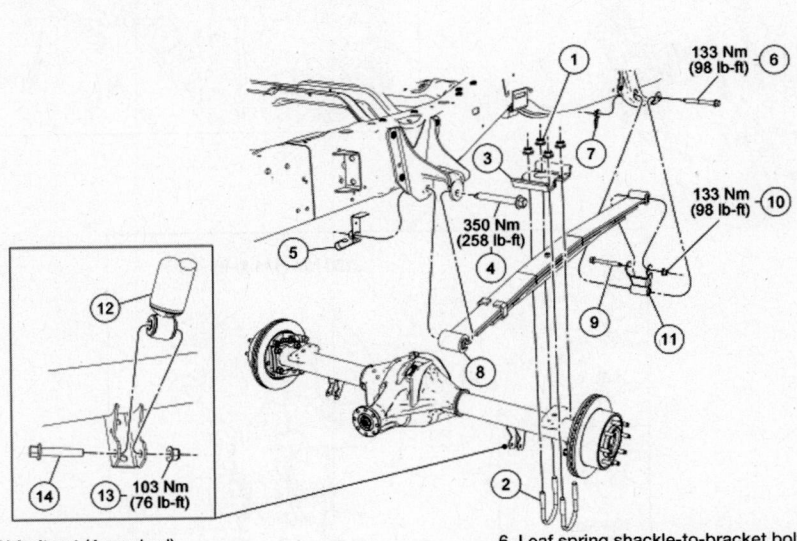

1. U-bolt nut (4 required)
2. U-bolt (2 required) (E-150, E-250 and E-350 van and wagon)
2. U-bolt (2 required) (E-450)
2. U-bolt (2 required) (E-350 stripped chassis and cutaway)
3. U-bolt plate
4. Leaf spring front bracket bolt
5. Leaf spring front bracket flagnut (RH side)
5. Leaf spring front bracket flagnut (LH side)

6. Leaf spring shackle-to-bracket bolt
7. Leaf spring shackle-to-bracket flagnut
8. Leaf spring
9. Leaf spring-to-shackle bolt
10. Shackle-to-leaf spring nut
11. Leaf spring shackle
12. Shock absorber
13. Shock absorber lower nut
14. Shock absorber lower bolt

N0105368

Fig. 233 Exploded view of the leaf spring assembly

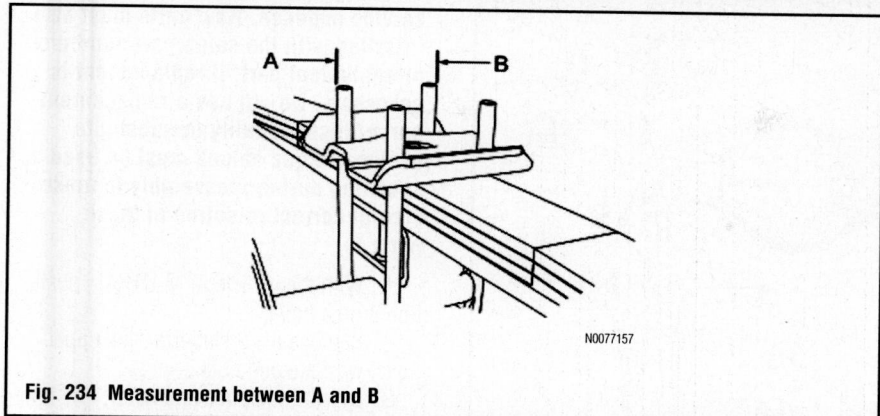

Fig. 234 Measurement between A and B

11. Install the new spring-to-front bracket bolt and flagnut. Tighten until snug.

➡️When installing new U-bolts, the measurement between A and B should be 4.21 inches ± 0.12 inches for E150/E250/E350 vehicles and 4.41 inches ± 0.12 inches for E450 vehicles. This is important for providing the correct U-bolt clamp load and retention of parts.

12. Position the spring upper plate and install the U-bolts and nuts. Tighten until snug.

13. Install the new shock absorber lower nut and bolt. Tighten until snug.

14. Install the wheel and tire.

15. Lower the vehicle until the weight of the vehicle is resting on the wheels and tires (curb height).

16. Tighten the new leaf spring shackle-to-bracket bolt to 98 ft. lbs. (133 Nm).

17. Tighten the shackle-to-leaf spring nut to 98 ft. lbs. (133 Nm).

18. Tighten the leaf spring front bracket bolt to 258 ft. lbs. (350 Nm).

19. Tighten the U-bolt nuts evenly in an X-type pattern in 5 stages.

　a. Stage 1: Tighten to 37 ft. lbs. (50 Nm).

　b. Stage 2: Tighten to 74 ft. lbs. (100 Nm).

　c. Stage 3: Tighten to 111 ft. lbs. (150 Nm).

　d. Stage 4: Tighten to 148 ft. lbs. (200 Nm).

　e. Stage 5: Tighten to 166 ft. lbs. (225 Nm).

20. Tighten the shock absorber lower nut to 76 ft. lbs. (103 Nm).

SHOCK ABSORBER

REMOVAL & INSTALLATION

See Figure 235.

⁕⁑ WARNING

Do not apply heat or flame to the shock absorber or strut tube. The shock absorber and strut tube are gas pressurized and could explode if heated. Failure to follow this instruction may result in serious personal injury.

➡️Suspension fasteners are critical components because they affect performance of vital components and systems and their failure can result in major service expense. Install new components with the same component number or an equivalent component if installation is necessary. Do not use an installation component of lesser quality or substitute design. Torque values must be used as specified during reassembly to make sure of correct retention of these components.

1. With the vehicle in NEUTRAL, position it on a hoist.

2. Using a suitable jack, support the rear axle.

3. Remove and discard the shock absorber lower nut and bolt.

4. Remove and discard the shock absorber upper nut and remove the shock absorber.

5. To install, reverse the removal procedure. . Refer to illustration for torque values.

STABILIZER BAR

REMOVAL & INSTALLATION

See Figure 236.

➡️Suspension fasteners are critical parts because they affect performance of vital components and systems and their failure may result in major

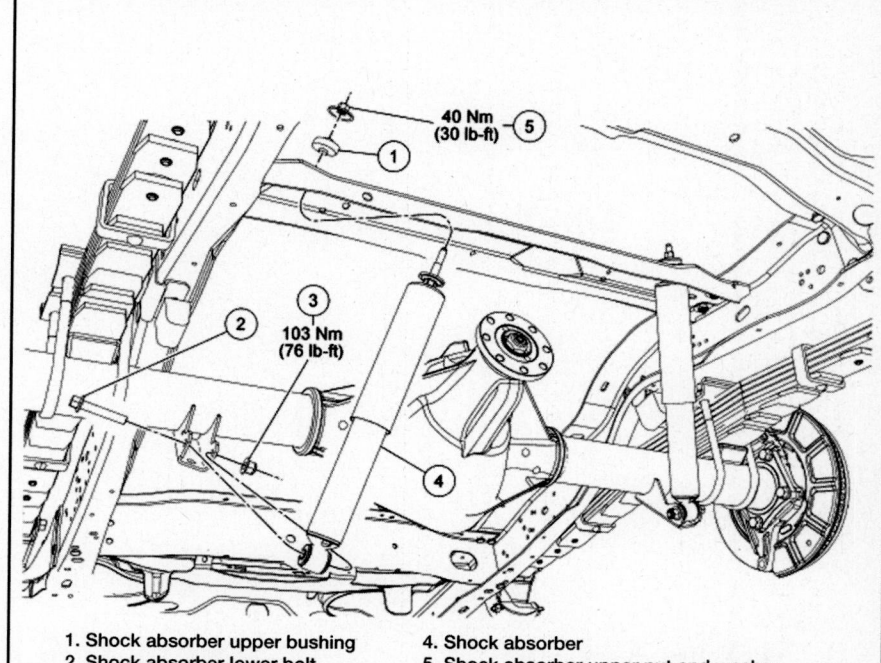

1. Shock absorber upper bushing
2. Shock absorber lower bolt
3. Shock absorber lower nut
4. Shock absorber
5. Shock absorber upper nut and washer

Fig. 235 Exploded view of the shock absorber

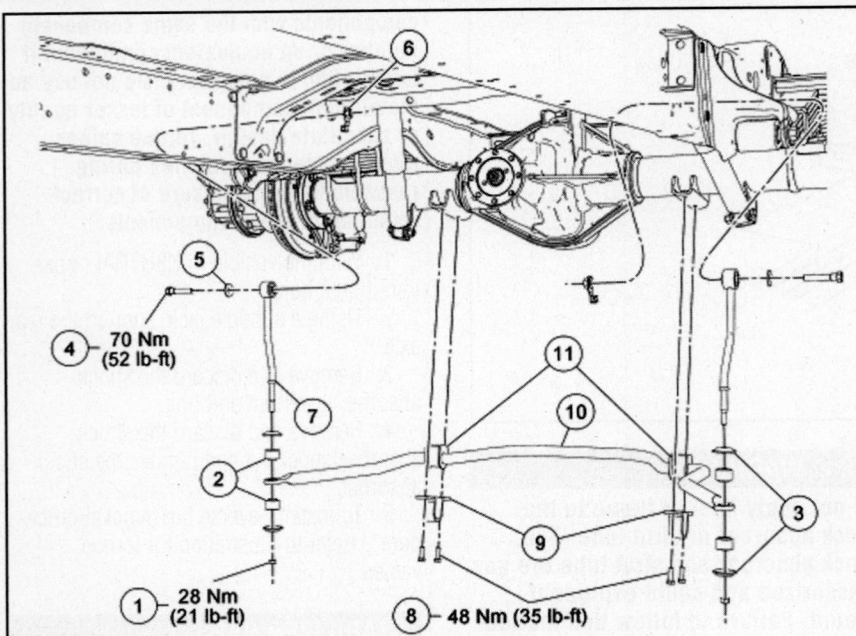

4 — 70 Nm
(52 lb-ft)

1 — 28 Nm
(21 lb-ft)

8 — 48 Nm (35 lb-ft)

1. Stabilizer link lower nut (2 required)
2. Link insulators (4 required)
3. Link washers (4 required)
4. Stabilizer link upper bolt (2 required)
5. Link upper washer (2 required)
6. Link upper nut (2 required)
7. Stabilizer bar link
8. Stabilizer bar bracket bolts (4 required)
9. Stabilizer bar brackets
10. Stabilizer bar
11. Stabilizer bar bushings (2 required)

N0106705

Fig. 236 Exploded view of the stabilizer bar

service expense. **New parts must be installed with the same part numbers or equivalent part, if replacement is necessary. Do not use a replacement part of lesser quality or substitute design. Torque values must be used as specified during reassembly to make sure of correct retention of these parts.**

1. With the vehicle in NEUTRAL, position it on a hoist.
2. Remove the 2 stabilizer link upper bolts, washers and nuts.
3. Discard the bolts and nuts.
4. Remove the 2 stabilizer link lower nuts, washers and insulators.
5. Discard the nuts.
6. Remove the 2 stabilizer bar links, washers and insulators.
7. Remove the 4 stabilizer bar bracket bolts, the 2 brackets and the stabilizer bar.
8. Discard the bolts.
9. To install, reverse the removal procedure. Refer to illustration for torque values.

WHEEL BEARINGS

REMOVAL & INSTALLATION

Refer to Rear Axle Housing in Drive Train.

FORD AND MERCURY

Escape • Escape Hybrid • Mariner • Mariner Hybrid

4

BRAKES 4-12

ANTI-LOCK BRAKE SYSTEM (ABS) **4-12**
ABS Module 4-14
 Removal & Installation 4-14
General Information 4-12
 Precautions 4-12
Hydraulic Control Unit (HCU) ...4-14
 Removal & Installation 4-14
Speed Sensors 4-13
 Removal & Installation 4-13
BLEEDING THE BRAKE SYSTEM **4-16**
Bleeding Procedure 4-16
 Brake System Bleeding
  Procedure 4-16
 Component Bleeding 4-17
 Fluid Fill Procedure 4-17
FRONT DISC BRAKES **4-18**
Brake Caliper 4-18
 Removal & Installation 4-18
Disc Brake Pads 4-18
 Removal & Installation 4-18
PARKING BRAKE **4-21**
Parking Brake Cables 4-21
 Relieving Cable Tension 4-22
 Removal & Installation 4-21
Parking Brake Control 4-22
 Removal & Installation 4-22
Parking Brake Shoes 4-22
 Removal & Installation 4-22
REAR DRUM BRAKES **4-19**
Brake Drum 4-19
 Removal & Installation 4-19
Brake Shoes 4-20
 Adjustment 4-20
 Removal & Installation 4-20

CHASSIS ELECTRICAL **4-24**

AIR BAG (SUPPLEMENTAL RESTRAINT SYSTEM) **4-24**
General Information 4-24
 Arming/Repowering the
  System 4-25
 Disarming/Depowering the
  System 4-24
Service Precautions 4-24

DRIVE TRAIN **4-20**

Automatic Transaxle Fluid 4-25
 Drain and Refill 4-25
 Filter Replacement 4-25
Clutch....................................4-27
 Bleeding 4-27
 Removal & Installation 4-26
Front Driveshaft 4-29
 Removal & Installation 4-29
Front Halfshaft 4-29
 Removal & Installation 4-29
Manual Transaxle Assembly 4-25
 Removal & Installation 4-25
Rear Axle Fluid 4-30
 Drain & Refill 4-30
Rear Axle Housing 4-30
 Removal & Installation 4-30
Rear Axle Stub Shaft Bearing
 and Seal 4-31
 Removal & Installation 4-31
Rear Halfshaft 4-31
 Removal & Installation 4-31
Rear Pinion Seal 4-32
 Removal & Installation 4-32
Transfer Case Assembly
 (Power Transfer Unit) 4-27
 Draining & Refilling 4-28
 Removal & Installation 4-27

ENGINE COOLING **4-33**

Engine Coolant 4-33
 Drain, Refill & Bleeding
  Procedure 4-33
 Flushing Procedure 4-34
Engine Fan 4-34
 Removal & Installation 4-34
Radiator 4-37
 Removal & Installation 4-37
Thermostat 4-37
 Removal & Installation 4-37
Water Pump 4-37
 Removal & Installation 4-37

ENGINE ELECTRICAL **4-38**

BATTERY SYSTEM **4-38**
12-Volt Battery 4-38

12-volt Battery Disconnect,
 Reconnect & Relearn
 Procedure 4-38
 Removal & Installation 4-29
High-Voltage Traction Battery....4-39
 High-voltage Traction
 Battery Depower/Repower
 Procedure 4-42
 Removal & Installation 4-39
CHARGING SYSTEM **4-43**
Alternating Current (AC)
 Powerpoint 4-45
 Removal & Installation 4-45
Direct Current/Alternating
 Current (DC/AC) Inverter 4-45
 Removal & Installation 4-45
Direct Current/Direct Current
 (DC/DC) Converter 4-46
 Removal & Installation 4-46
Generator 4-43
 Removal & Installation 4-43
IGNITION SYSTEM **4-47**
Firing Order.............................4-47
Ignition Coil 4-47
 Removal & Installation 4-47
Ignition Timing 4-47
 Adjustment 4-47
Spark Plugs.............................4-47
 Removal & Installation 4-47
STARTING SYSTEM **4-47**
Starter 4-47
 Removal & Installation 4-47

ENGINE MECHANICAL **4-49**

Accessory Drive Belts 4-49
 Accessory Belt Routing 4-49
 Adjustment 4-49
 Removal & Installation 4-49
Air Cleaner 4-50
 Filter/Element
  Replacement 4-51
 Removal & Installation 4-50
Camshaft & Valve Lifters...........4-51
 Removal & Installation 4-51
Catalytic Converter 4-60
 Removal & Installation 4-60
Crankshaft Front Seal 4-61
 Removal & Installation 4-61

Crankshaft Pulley 4-62
   Removal & Installation..........4-62
Cylinder Head 4-64
   Removal & Installation..........4-64
Exhaust Intermediate Pipe 4-68
   Removal & Installation..........4-68
Exhaust Manifold 4-68
   Removal & Installation..........4-68
Intake Manifold 4-70
   Removal & Installation..........4-70
Oil Pan...................................4-74
   Removal & Installation..........4-74
Oil Pump.................................4-76
   Removal & Installation..........4-76
Piston and Ring........................4-77
   Positioning 4-77
Rear Main Seal.........................4-78
   Removal & Installation..........4-78
Timing Chain & Sprockets 4-86
   Removal & Installation..........4-86
Timing Chain Front Cover.........4-80
   Removal & Installation..........4-80
Valve Covers 4-90
   Removal & Installation..........4-90
Valve Lash (Valve Clearance) 4-91
   Adjustment 4-91

ENGINE PERFORMANCE & EMISSION CONTROLS 4-92

Camshaft Position (CMP)
  Sensor 4-92
   Location..........................4-92
   Removal & Installation..........4-92
Catalyst Monitor Sensor (CMS) .4-93
   Location..........................4-93
   Removal & Installation..........4-93
Component Locations 4-92
Crankshaft Position (CKP)
  Sensor 4-93
   Location..........................4-93
   Removal & Installation..........4-94
Cylinder Head Temperature
  (CHT) Sensor..........................4-96
   Location..........................4-96
   Removal & Installation..........4-96
Heated Oxygen Sensor (HO2S) .4-96
   Location..........................4-96
   Removal & Installation..........4-97
Knock Sensor (KS)....................4-97
   Location..........................4-97
   Removal & Installation..........4-97
Manifold Absolute Pressure
  (MAP) Sensor 4-99
   Location..........................4-99
   Removal & Installation..........4-99

Mass Air Flow (MAF) Sensor ..4-100
   Location..........................4-100
   Removal & Installation........4-100
Powertrain Control Module
  (PCM) 4-100
   Location..........................4-100
   Removal & Installation........4-100
Variable Camshaft Timing
  (VCT) Oil Control Solenoid...4-101
   Location..........................4-101
   Removal & Installation........4-102

FUEL 4-102

GASOLINE FUEL INJECTION SYSTEM 4-102
Fuel Control Module 4-103
   Removal & Installation........4-103
Fuel Injectors & Fuel Rail........4-104
   Removal & Installation........4-104
Fuel Pump..............................4-106
   Removal & Installation........4-106
Fuel System Service
  Precautions 4-102
Fuel Tank................................4-107
   Draining..........................4-107
   Removal & Installation........4-107
Idle Speed 4-108
   Adjustment 4-108
Inertia Fuel Shutoff (IFS)
  Switch 4-108
   Removal & Installation........4-108
Relieving Fuel System
  Pressure................................4-102
   Relieving System
    Pressure 4-102
   Restoring System
    Pressure 4-103
Throttle Body..........................4-108
   Removal & Installation........4-108

HEATING & AIR CONDITIONING SYSTEM 4-109

Blower Motor 4-109
   Removal & Installation........4-109
Compressor 4-109
   Removal & Installation........4-109
Heater Core 4-113
   Removal & Installation........4-113
Heater Core & Evaporator
  Core Housing.........................4-114
   Removal & Installation........4-114

PRECAUTIONS 4-12

SPECIFICATIONS AND MAINTENANCE CHARTS 4-3

Brake Specifications 4-7
Camshaft Specifications 4-5
Capacities 4-4
Crankshaft and Connecting
  Rod Specifications 4-5
Engine and Vehicle Identification ...4-3
Engine Tune-Up Specifications ...4-3
Fluid Specifications....................4-4
General Engine Specifications.....4-3
Piston and Ring Specifications ...4-6
Scheduled Maintenance
  Intervals 4-8,9,10,11
Tire, Wheel and Ball Joint
  Specifications 4-00
Torque Specifications 4-6
Valve Specifications 4-11
Wheel Alignment 4-00

STEERING 4-115

Power Steering Gear................4-115
   Removal & Installation........4-115

SUSPENSION 4-116

FRONT SUSPENSION 4-116
Component Locations 4-116
Lower Control Arm..................4-116
   Removal & Installation........4-116
Stabilizer Bar..........................4-116
   Removal & Installation........4-116
Stabilizer Bar Bushing.............4-117
   Removal & Installation........4-117
Stabilizer Bar Link 4-117
   Removal & Installation........4-117
Steering Knuckle 4-117
   Removal & Installation........4-117
Strut & Spring Assembly 4-118
   Removal & Installation........4-118
Wheel Bearings & Hub............4-119
   Removal & Installation........4-119
REAR SUSPENSION 4-119
Coil Spring.............................4-119
   Removal & Installation........4-120
Stabilizer Bar..........................4-120
   Removal & Installation........4-120
Strut & Spring Assembly 4-121
   Removal & Installation........4-121
Upper Control Arm..................4-121
   Removal & Installation........4-121
Wheel Bearing 4-121
   Removal & Installation........4-121
Wheel Knuckle 4-123
   Removal & Installation........4-123

SPECIFICATIONS AND MAINTENANCE CHARTS

ENGINE AND VEHICLE IDENTIFICATION

Code ①	Liters (cc)	Cu. In.	Cyl.	Fuel Sys.	Engine Type	Eng. Mfg.
7	2.5	152	4	SFI	DOHC	Ford
3	2.5	152	4	PFI	DOHC	Ford
G	3.0	183	6	SFI	DOHC	Ford

Model Year	
Code ②	Year
A	2010
B	2011

25759_ESCA_C0001

GENERAL ENGINE SPECIFICATIONS

All measurements are given in inches.

Year	Model	Engine Displacement Liters	Engine ID/VIN	Fuel System Type	Net Horsepower @ rpm	Net Torque @ rpm (ft. lbs.)	Bore x Stroke (in.)	Com- pression Ratio	Oil Pressure @ rpm
2010	Escape/Mariner	2.5	7	SFI	171@6000	171@4500	3.5x3.9	9.7:1	NA
	Escape/Mariner	2.5	3	PFI	①	134@4500	3.5x3.9	12.3:1	NA
	Escape/Mariner	3.0	G	SFI	240@6550	233@4300	3.5x3.13	10.3:1	25@1500
2011	Escape/Mariner	2.5	7	SFI	171@6000	171@4500	3.5x3.9	9.7:1	NA
	Escape/Mariner	2.5	3	PFI	①	134@4500	3.5x3.9	12.3:1	NA
	Escape/Mariner	3.0	G	SFI	240@6550	233@4300	3.5x3.13	10.3:1	25@1500

NA: Not available

① Hybrid: 155@6000 (gas engine); 94@5000 (electric motor)

25759_ESCA_C0002

ENGINE TUNE-UP SPECIFICATIONS

Year	Engine Displacement Liters	Engine ID/VIN	Spark Plug Gap (in.)	Ignition Timing (deg.) MT	Ignition Timing (deg.) AT	Fuel Pump (psi)	Idle Speed (rpm) MT	Idle Speed (rpm) AT	Valve Clearance (in.) Intake	Valve Clearance (in.) Exhaust
2010	2.5	7	0.049-0.053	NA	NA	NA	NA	NA	0.00010	0.00011
	2.5	3	0.049-0.053	NA	NA	NA	NA	NA	0.00010	0.00011
	3.0	G	0.045-0.049	NA	NA	NA	NA	NA	0.0007-0.0027	0.0017-0.037
2011	2.5	7	0.049-0.053	NA	NA	NA	NA	NA	0.00010	0.00011
	2.5	3	0.049-0.053	NA	NA	NA	NA	NA	0.00010	0.00011
	3.0	G	0.045-0.049	NA	NA	NA	NA	NA	0.0007-0.0027	0.0017-0.037

NA: Not available

25759_EDGE_C0003

CAPACITIES

Year	Model	Engine Displacement Liters (VIN)	Engine Oil with Filter (qts.)	TransmissioNAxle (pts.) Auto.	Manual	Drive Axle (pts.) Front	Rear	Transfer Case (pts.)	Fuel Tank (gal.)	Cooling System (qts.)
2010	Escape/Mariner	2.5 (7)	4.5	①	5.0	NA	2.43	0.75	16.5	②
	Escape/Mariner	2.5 (3)	4.5	8.5 ③	5.0	NA	2.43	0.75	16.5	②
	Escape/Mariner	3.0 (G)	6.0	①	5.0	NA	2.43	0.75	16.5	10.5
2011	Escape/Mariner	2.5 (7)	4.5	①	5.0	NA	2.43	0.75	16.5	②
	Escape/Mariner	2.5 (3)	4.5	8.5 ③	5.0	NA	2.43	0.75	16.5	②
	Escape/Mariner	3.0 (G)	6.0	①	5.0	NA	2.43	0.75	16.5	10.5

① Fill and check multiple times on dipstick.

② To MAX fill line of reservoir

③ Transaxle cooling system fill: 3.7 qts.

25759_ESCA_C0004

FLUID SPECIFICATIONS

Year	Model	Engine Disp. Liters	Engine Oil	Manual Trans.	Auto. Trans.	Drive Axle Rear	Transfer Case ①	Power Steering Fluid	Brake Master Cylinder	Cooling System
2010	Escape/Mariner	2.5	5W-20	80W-90	Mercon®LV	80W-90	75W-140	NA	DOT 3	①
	Escape/Mariner	3.0	5W-20	80W-90	Mercon®LV	80W-90	75W-140	NA	DOT 3	①
2011	Escape/Mariner	2.5	5W-20	80W-90	Mercon®LV	80W-90	75W-140	NA	DOT 3	①
	Escape/Mariner	3.0	5W-20	80W-90	Mercon®LV	80W-90	75W-140	NA	DOT 3	①

NA: Not available

DOT: Department Of Transpotation

① Motorcraft® Premium Gold Engine Coolant with Bittering Agent (WSS-M97B51-A1)

25759_ESCA_C0005

VALVE SPECIFICATIONS

Year	Engine Displacement Liters	Engine ID/VIN	Seat Angle (deg.)	Face Angle (deg.)	Spring Compr. Pressure (lbs. @ in.)	Spring Free-Length (in.)	Spring Installed Height (in.)	Stem-to-Guide Clearance (in.) Intake	Exhaust	Stem Diameter (in.) Intake	Exhaust
2010	2.5	7	45	45	97@0.35	1.768	1.492	0.0010	0.0011	0.2153-0.2159	0.2151-0.2157
	2.5	3	45	45	97@0.35	1.768	1.492	0.0010	0.0011	0.2153-0.2159	0.2151-0.2157
	3.0	G	44.75	45.5	575@1.27	1.988	1.670	0.0007-0.0027	0.0017-0.0037	0.2353-0.2360	0.2343-0.2350
2011	2.5	7	45	45	97@0.35	1.768	1.492	0.0010	0.0011	0.2153-0.2159	0.2151-0.2157
	2.5	3	45	45	97@0.35	1.768	1.492	0.0010	0.0011	0.2153-0.2159	0.2151-0.2157
	3.0	G	44.75	45.5	575@1.27	1.988	1.670	0.0007-0.0027	0.0017-0.0037	0.2353-0.2360	0.2343-0.2350

25759_ESCA_C0006

CAMSHAFT SPECIFICATIONS

All measurements in inches unless noted

Year	Engine Displacement Liters	Engine Code/VIN	Journal Diameter	Brg. Oil Clearance	Shaft End-play	Runout	Journal Bore	Lobe Height	
								Intake	Exhaust
2010	2.5	7	0.982-0.983	0.001-0.003	0.003-0.009	0.001	0.984-0.985	0.324	0.307
	2.5	3	0.982-0.983	0.001-0.003	0.003-0.009	0.001	0.984-0.985	0.324	0.307
	3.0	G	1.060-1.061	0.0047	0.009	—	1.062-1.063	0.200	0.200
2011	2.5	7	0.982-0.983	0.001-0.003	0.003-0.009	0.001	0.984-0.985	0.324	0.307
	2.5	3	0.982-0.983	0.001-0.003	0.003-0.009	0.001	0.984-0.985	0.324	0.307
	3.0	G	1.060-1.061	0.0047	0.009	—	1.062-1.063	0.200	0.200

25759_ESCA_C0007

CRANKSHAFT AND CONNECTING ROD SPECIFICATIONS

All measurements are given in inches.

Year	Engine Displacement Liters	Engine ID/VIN	Crankshaft				Connecting Rod		
			Main Brg. Journal Dia.	Main Brg. Oil Clearance	Shaft End-play	Thrust on No.	Journal Diameter	Oil Clearance	Side Clearance
2010	2.5	7	2.0460-2.0470	0.0006-0.0015	0.0070-0.0180	NA	2.0460-2.0470	0.001-0.002	0.0760-0.1200
	2.5	3	2.0460-2.0470	0.0006-0.0015	0.0070-0.0180	NA	2.0460-2.0470	0.001-0.002	0.0760-0.1200
	3.0	G	2.4791-2.4800	0.0010-0.0018	0.0030-0.0010	3	2.0872-2.0879	0.0010-0.0025	0.0039-0.0118
2011	2.5	7	2.0460-2.0470	0.0006-0.0015	0.0070-0.0180	NA	2.0460-2.0470	0.001-0.002	0.0760-0.1200
	2.5	3	2.0460-2.0470	0.0006-0.0015	0.0070-0.0180	NA	2.0460-2.0470	0.001-0.002	0.0760-0.1200
	3.0	G	2.4791-2.4800	0.0010-0.0018	0.0030-0.0010	3	2.0872-2.0879	0.0010-0.0025	0.0039-0.0118

NA: Not available

25759_ESCA_C0008

PISTON AND RING SPECIFICATIONS

All measurements are given in inches.

Year	Engine Displacement Liters	Engine ID/VIN	Piston Clearance (in.)	Ring Gap			Ring Side Clearance		
				Top Compression	Bottom Compression	Oil Control	Top Compression	Bottom Compression	Oil Control
2010	2.5	7	0.0009-0.0017	0.0060-0.0120	0.0120-0.0180	0.0070-0.0270	NA	NA	NA
	2.5	3	0.0009-0.0017	0.0060-0.0120	0.0060-0.0120	0.0070-0.0270	NA	NA	NA
	3.0	G	0.0005-0.0009	0.0039-0.0098	0.0106-0.0165	0.0059-0.0256	0.0016-0.0030	0.0016-0.0033	NA
2011	2.5	7	0.0009-0.0017	0.0060-0.0120	0.0120-0.0180	0.0070-0.0270	NA	NA	NA
	2.5	3	0.0009-0.0017	0.0060-0.0120	0.0060-0.0120	0.0070-0.0270	NA	NA	NA
	3.0	G	0.0005-0.0009	0.0039-0.0098	0.0106-0.0165	0.0059-0.0256	0.0016-0.0030	0.0016-0.0033	NA

NA: Not available.

25759_ESCA_C0009

TORQUE SPECIFICATIONS

All readings in ft. lbs.

Year	Engine Disp. Liters	Engine ID/VIN	Cylinder Head Bolts	Main Bearing Bolts	Rod Bearing Bolts	Crankshaft Damper Bolts	Flywheel Bolts	Manifold		Spark Plugs	Oil Pan Drain Plug
								Intake	Exhaust		
2010	2.5	7	①	②	③	④	⑤ ⑥	13	35	11	21
	2.5	3	①	②	③	④	⑤ ⑥	13	35	11	21
	3.0	G	⑦	⑧	⑨	⑩	⑤ ⑥	⑪	15	11	19
2011	2.5	7	①	②	③	④	⑤ ⑥	13	35	11	21
	2.5	3	①	②	③	④	⑤ ⑥	13	35	11	21
	3.0	G	⑦	⑧	⑨	⑩	⑤ ⑥	⑪	15	11	19

NA: Information not available.

① Step 1: 44 inch lbs.
Step 2: 11 ft. lbs.
Step 3: 33 ft. lbs.
Step 4: Plus 90 degrees
Step 5: Plus 90 degrees
② Step 1: 44 inch lbs.
Step 2: 18 ft. lbs.
Step 3: Plus 90 degrees
③ Step 1: 21 ft. lbs.
Step 2: Plus 90 degrees
④ Step 1: 74 ft. lbs.
Step 2: Plus 90 degrees

⑤ For flexplate, refer to Flywheel Bolts.
⑥ Step 1: 37 ft. lbs.
Step 2: 59 ft. lbs.
Step 3: 83 ft. lbs.
⑦ Step 1: 30 ft. lbs.
Step 2: Tighten bolts 90 degrees
Step 3: Loosen bolts one full turn
Step 4: 30 ft. lbs.
Step 5: Tighten bolts 90 degrees
Step 6: Tighten bolts additional 90 degrees
⑧ Step 1: Fasteners 1-8: 18 ft. lbs.
Step 2: Fasteners 9-19: 30 ft. lbs.
Step 3: Fasteners 1-16: Plus 90 degrees
Step 4: Fasteners 17-22: 18 ft. lbs.

⑨ Step 1: 17 ft. lbs.
Step 2: 32 ft. lbs.
⑩ Step 1: 86 ft. lbs.
Step 2: Loosen one full turn
Step 3: 37 ft. lbs.
Step 4: Plus 90 degrees
⑪ Upper and Lower: 89 inch lbs.

25759_ESCA_C0010

WHEEL ALIGNMENT

Year	Model		Caster Range (+/-Deg.)	Caster Preferred Setting (Deg.)	Camber Range (+/-Deg.)	Camber Preferred Setting (Deg.)	Toe-in (in.)
2010	Escape/Mariner	F	0.5	1.6	0.5	-0.84	0.23+/-0.23
		R	NA	NA	0.70 ①	0	-0.18+/-0.20
2011	Escape/Mariner	F	0.5	1.6	0.5	-0.84	0.23+/-0.23
		R	NA	NA	0.70 ①	0	-0.18+/-0.20

NA: Not Available

① Left side: +/- 0.60

25759_ESCA_C0011

TIRE, WHEEL AND BALL JOINT SPECIFICATIONS

Year	Model	OEM Tires Standard	OEM Tires Optional	Tire Pressures (psi) Front	Tire Pressures (psi) Rear	Wheel Size	Ball Joint Inspection	Lug Nut (ft. lbs.)
2010	Escape	P235/70R16	none	①	①	NA	0.008 in.	100
	Mariner	P235/70R16	none	①	①	NA	0.008 in.	100
2010	Escape	P235/70R16	none	①	①	NA	0.008 in.	100
	Mariner	P235/70R16	none	①	①	NA	0.008 in.	100

OEM: Original Equipment Manufacturer

PSI: Pounds Per Square Inch

NA: Information not available

① See safety certification on driver's door jam

25759_ESCA_C0012

BRAKE SPECIFICATIONS

All measurements in inches unless noted

Year	Model		Brake Disc Original Thickness	Brake Disc Minimum Thickness	Brake Disc Max. Runout	Brake Drum Diameter Original Inside Diameter	Brake Drum Diameter Max. Wear Limit	Brake Drum Diameter Maximum Machine Diameter	Minimum Pad/Lining Thickness Front	Minimum Pad/Lining Thickness Rear	Brake Caliper Bracket Bolts (ft. lbs.)	Brake Caliper Mounting Bolts (ft. lbs.)
2010	Escape/	F	NA	0.944	0.0040	NA	NA	NA	0.118	—	129	37
	Mariner	R	NA	0.430	0.0040	NA	NA	10.090	—	0.039	NA	NA
2011	Escape/	F	NA	0.944	0.0040	NA	NA	NA	0.118	—	129	37
	Mariner	R	NA	0.430	0.0040	NA	NA	10.090	—	0.039	NA	NA

F: Front

R: Rear

NA: Information not available

25759_ESCA_C0013

SCHEDULED MAINTENANCE INTERVALS
2010 Ford Escape, Escape Hybrid/Mercury Mariner, Mariner Hybrid - Normal

TO BE SERVICED	TYPE OF SERVICE	VEHICLE MILEAGE INTERVAL (x1000)												
		7.5	15	22.5	30	37.5	45	52.5	60	67.5	75	82.5	90	97.5
Spark plugs	Replace												✓	
Accessory drive belt	Replace	Every 150,000 miles												
Rear differential fluid	Replace	Every 150,000 miles												
Cabin air filter	Replace		✓		✓		✓		✓		✓		✓	
Engine air filter	Replace				✓				✓					
Transmisison fluid	Replace	Every 150,000 miles												
Transfer case fluid	Replace	Every 150,000 miles												
Engine oil and filter	Replace	✓	✓	✓	✓	✓	✓	✓	✓	✓	✓	✓	✓	✓
Engine coolant	Replace	At 6 years or 105,000 miles; then every 3 years or 45,000 miles												
Inverter coolant (Hybrids only)	Replace	At 6 years or 105,000 miles; then every 3 years or 45,000 miles												
Brake system (Pads/shoes/rotors/drums, brake lines and hoses, and parking brake system)	Inspect		✓		✓		✓		✓		✓		✓	
Radiator, coolers, heater and air conditioning hoses	Inspect	✓	✓	✓	✓	✓	✓	✓	✓	✓	✓	✓	✓	✓
Inspect wheels and related components for abnomal noise, wear, looseness or drag	Inspect	✓	✓	✓	✓	✓	✓	✓	✓	✓	✓	✓	✓	✓
Exhaust system	Inspect	✓	✓	✓	✓	✓	✓	✓	✓	✓	✓	✓	✓	✓
Horn, exterior lamps, turn signals and hazard warning light operation	Inspect	✓	✓	✓	✓	✓	✓	✓	✓	✓	✓	✓	✓	✓
Oil and fluid leaks	Inspect	✓	✓	✓	✓	✓	✓	✓	✓	✓	✓	✓	✓	✓
Shocks struts and other suspension components for leaks and damage	Inspect	✓	✓	✓	✓	✓	✓	✓	✓	✓	✓	✓	✓	✓
Windshield & windshield wipers	Inspect	✓	✓	✓	✓	✓	✓	✓	✓	✓	✓	✓	✓	✓
Battery performance	Inspect	✓	✓	✓	✓	✓	✓	✓	✓	✓	✓	✓	✓	✓
Cooling system, hoses, clamps & coolant strength	Inspect	✓	✓	✓	✓	✓	✓	✓	✓	✓	✓	✓	✓	✓
Engine air filter	Inspect	✓	✓	✓	✓	✓	✓	✓	✓	✓	✓	✓	✓	✓
Halfshaft boots	Inspect	✓	✓	✓	✓	✓	✓	✓	✓	✓	✓	✓	✓	✓
Accessory drive belt	Inspect	✓	✓	✓	✓	✓	✓	✓	✓	✓	✓	✓	✓	✓
Steering linkage, ball joints, suspension, tie-rod ends, driveshaft and u-joints: lubricate if equipped with grease fittings	Inspect/ Lubricate	✓	✓	✓	✓	✓	✓	✓	✓	✓	✓	✓	✓	✓
Rotate tires, inspect tread wear, measure tread depth and check pressure	Rotate/ Inspect	✓	✓	✓	✓	✓	✓	✓	✓	✓	✓	✓	✓	✓
Fluid levels (all)	Top off	✓	✓	✓	✓	✓	✓	✓	✓	✓	✓	✓	✓	✓

Use of E85 50% of the time or greater, change engine oil and filter every 5,000 miles or 6 months.

For extensive idling and or low speed driving, change engine oil and filter every 5,000 miles, 6 months or 200 hours of engine operation.

WARNING: To prevent the risk of high-voltage shock, always follow precisely all warnings and service instructions, including instructions to depower the system. The high-voltage hybrid system utilizes approximately 300 volts DC, provided through high-voltage cables to its components and modules. The high-voltage cables and wiring are identified by orange harness tape or orange wire covering. All high-voltage components are marked with high-voltage warning labels with a high-voltage symbol. Failure to follow these instructions may result in serious personal injury or death.

SCHEDULED MAINTENANCE INTERVALS
2010 Ford Escape, Escape Hybrid/Mercury Mariner, Mariner Hybrid - Severe

TO BE SERVICED	TYPE OF SERVICE	VEHICLE MILEAGE INTERVAL (x1000)											
		5	10	15	20	25	30	35	40	45	50	55	60
Accessory drive belt	Inspect	✓	✓	✓	✓	✓	✓	✓	✓	✓	✓	✓	✓
Accessory drive belt	Replace					every 150,000 miles							
Transmision fluid	Replace						✓						✓
Battery performance	Inspect	✓	✓	✓	✓	✓	✓	✓	✓	✓	✓	✓	✓
Brake system (Pads/shoes/rotors/drums, brake lines and hoses, and parking brake system)	Inspect	✓	✓	✓	✓	✓	✓	✓	✓	✓	✓	✓	✓
Cabin air filter	Replace			✓			✓			✓			✓
Cooling system, hoses, clamps & coolant strength	Inspect	✓	✓	✓	✓	✓	✓	✓	✓	✓	✓	✓	✓
Engine air filter	Inspect	✓	✓	✓	✓	✓	✓	✓	✓	✓	✓	✓	✓
Engine air filter	Replace						✓						✓
Exhaust system	Inspect	✓	✓	✓	✓	✓	✓	✓	✓	✓	✓	✓	✓
Fluid levels (all)	Top off	✓	✓	✓	✓	✓	✓	✓	✓	✓	✓	✓	✓
Halfshaft boots	Inspect	✓	✓	✓	✓	✓	✓	✓	✓	✓	✓	✓	✓
Horn, exterior lamps, turn signals and hazard warning light operation	Inspect	✓	✓	✓	✓	✓	✓	✓	✓	✓	✓	✓	✓
Inspect wheels and related components for abnomal noise, wear, looseness or drag	Inspect	✓	✓	✓	✓	✓	✓	✓	✓	✓	✓	✓	✓
Oil and fluid leaks	Inspect	✓	✓	✓	✓	✓	✓	✓	✓	✓	✓	✓	✓
Radiator, coolers, heater and air conditioning hoses	Inspect	✓	✓	✓	✓	✓	✓	✓	✓	✓	✓	✓	✓
Rear differential fluid	Replace					every 150,000 miles							
Shocks struts and other suspension components for leaks and damage	Inspect	✓	✓	✓	✓	✓	✓	✓	✓	✓	✓	✓	✓
Spark plugs	Replace												✓
Steering linkage, ball joints, suspension, tie-rod ends, driveshaft and u-joints: lubricate if equipped with grease fittings	Inspect/ Lubricate	✓	✓	✓	✓	✓	✓	✓	✓	✓	✓	✓	✓
Transfer case fluid	Replace												✓
Windshield for cracks, chips and pitting	Inspect	✓	✓	✓	✓	✓	✓	✓	✓	✓	✓	✓	✓
Windshield wiper spray and wiper operation	Inspect	✓	✓	✓	✓	✓	✓	✓	✓	✓	✓	✓	✓
Engine coolant	Replace		At 6 years or 105,000 miles; then every 3 years or 45,000 miles										
Inverter coolant (Hybrid only)	Replace		At 6 years or 105,000 miles; then every 3 years or 45,000 miles										
Engine oil & filter	Replace	✓	✓	✓	✓	✓	✓	✓	✓	✓	✓	✓	✓
Rotate tires, inspect tread wear, measure tread depth and check pressure	Rotate/ Inspect	✓	✓	✓	✓	✓	✓	✓	✓	✓	✓	✓	✓

Use of E85 50% of the time or greater, change engine oil and filter every 5,000 miles or 6 months.

For extensive idling and or low speed driving, change engine oil and filter every 5,000 miles, 6 months or 200 hours of engine operation.

WARNING: To prevent the risk of high-voltage shock, always follow precisely all warnings and service instructions, including instructions to depower the system. The high-voltage hybrid system utilizes approximately 300 volts DC, provided through high-voltage cables to its components and modules. The high-voltage cables and wiring are identified by orange harness tape or orange wire covering. All high-voltage components are marked with high-voltage warning labels with a high-voltage symbol. Failure to follow these instructions may result in serious personal injury or death.

SCHEDULED MAINTENANCE INTERVALS
2011 Ford Escape, Escape Hybrid/Mercury Mariner, Mariner Hybrid - Normal

Service Item	Service Action	1	2	3	4	5	6	7	8	9	10	11	12	13	14	15
Drive belt	Inspect	✓	✓	✓	✓	✓	✓	✓	✓	✓	✓	✓	✓	✓	✓	✓
Cabin air filter	Inspect	✓	✓	✓	✓	✓	✓	✓	✓	✓	✓	✓	✓	✓	✓	✓
Engine oil & filter	Replace	✓	✓	✓	✓	✓	✓	✓	✓	✓	✓	✓	✓	✓	✓	✓
Rotate tires, inspect tread wear, measure tread depth and check pressure	Inspect/ Rotate	✓	✓	✓	✓	✓	✓	✓	✓	✓	✓	✓	✓	✓	✓	✓
Inspect wheels and related comp. for abnomal noise, wear, looseness or drag	Inspect	✓	✓	✓	✓	✓	✓	✓	✓	✓	✓	✓	✓	✓	✓	✓
Fluid levels (all)	Top off	✓	✓	✓	✓	✓	✓	✓	✓	✓	✓	✓	✓	✓	✓	✓
Brake system (Pads/shoes/rotors/drums, brake lines and hoses, and parking brake system)	Inspect	✓	✓	✓	✓	✓	✓	✓	✓	✓	✓	✓	✓	✓	✓	✓
Cooling system, hoses, clamps & coolant strength	Inspect	✓	✓	✓	✓	✓	✓	✓	✓	✓	✓	✓	✓	✓	✓	✓
Exhaust system	Inspect	✓	✓	✓	✓	✓	✓	✓	✓	✓	✓	✓	✓	✓	✓	✓
Halfshaft boots	Inspect	✓	✓	✓	✓	✓	✓	✓	✓	✓	✓	✓	✓	✓	✓	✓
Steering linkage, ball joints, suspension, tie-rod ends, driveshaft and u-joints: lubricate if equipped with grease fittings	Inspect / Lubricate	✓	✓	✓	✓	✓	✓	✓	✓	✓	✓	✓	✓	✓	✓	✓
Battery performance	Inspect	✓	✓	✓	✓	✓	✓	✓	✓	✓	✓	✓	✓	✓	✓	✓
Horn, exterior lamps, turn signals and hazard warning light operation	Inspect	✓	✓	✓	✓	✓	✓	✓	✓	✓	✓	✓	✓	✓	✓	✓
Radiator, coolers, heater and air conditioning hoses	Inspect	✓	✓	✓	✓	✓	✓	✓	✓	✓	✓	✓	✓	✓	✓	✓
Windshield, wipers and wiper spray	Inspect	✓	✓	✓	✓	✓	✓	✓	✓	✓	✓	✓	✓	✓	✓	✓
Suspension components for leaks and damage	Inspect	✓	✓	✓	✓	✓	✓	✓	✓	✓	✓	✓	✓	✓	✓	✓
Cabin air filter (If equipped)	Replace		✓		✓		✓		✓		✓		✓		✓	
Spark plugs	Replace										✓					
Drive belt	Replace															✓
Engine coolant	Replace										✓					✓
Inverter coolant (Hybrids)	Replace										✓					✓
Engine air filter	Replace			✓			✓			✓			✓			✓
Engine air filter	Inspect	✓	✓	✓	✓	✓	✓	✓	✓	✓	✓	✓	✓	✓	✓	✓
Climate-controlled seat filter (if equipped)	Replace			✓			✓			✓			✓			✓
Automatic transaxle fluid	Replace															✓
Transfer case fluid	Replace															✓
Rear differential fluid	Replace															✓

WARNING: To prevent the risk of high-voltage shock, always follow precisely all warnings and service instructions, including instructions to depower the system. The high-voltage hybrid system utilizes approximately 300 volts DC, provided through high-voltage cables to its components and modules. The high-voltage cables and wiring are identified by orange harness tape or orange wire covering. All high-voltage components are marked with high-voltage warning labels with a high-voltage symbol. Failure to follow these instructions may result in serious personal injury or death.

Oil change service intervals should be completed as indicated by the message center (Can be up to 1 year or 10,000 miles) If the message center is prematurely reset or is inoperative, perform the oil change interval at 6 months or 5,000 miles from your last oil change.

For extensive idling and or low speed driving, change engine oil and filter every 5,000 miles, 6 months or 200 hours of engine operation.

Use of E85 50% of the time or greater, change engine oil and filter every 5,000 miles or 6 months.

For commercial use or extensive idling, change spark plugs at 60,000 miles.

SCHEDULED MAINTENANCE INTERVALS
2011 Ford Escape, Escape Hybrid/Mercury Mariner, Mariner Hybrid - Normal

Service Item	Service Action	1	2	3	4	5	6	7	8	9	10	11	12	13	14	15
Engine oil & filter	Replace	✓	✓	✓	✓	✓	✓	✓	✓	✓	✓	✓	✓	✓	✓	✓
Automatic transaxle fluid	Replace			✓			✓			✓			✓			✓
Battery performance	Inspect	✓	✓	✓	✓	✓	✓	✓	✓	✓	✓	✓	✓	✓	✓	✓
Brake system (Pads/shoes/rotors/drums, brake lines and hoses, and parking brake system)	Inspect	✓	✓	✓	✓	✓	✓	✓	✓	✓	✓	✓	✓	✓	✓	✓
Cabin air filter (If equipped)	Inspect/Service	✓	✓	✓	✓	✓	✓	✓	✓	✓	✓	✓	✓	✓	✓	✓
Climate-controlled seat filter (if equipped)	Replace			✓			✓			✓			✓			✓
Cooling system, hoses, clamps & coolant strength	Inspect	✓	✓	✓	✓	✓	✓	✓	✓	✓	✓	✓	✓	✓	✓	✓
Drive belt	Inspect	✓	✓	✓	✓	✓	✓	✓	✓	✓	✓	✓	✓	✓	✓	✓
Drive belt	Replace															✓
Engine air filter	Inspect/Service	✓	✓	✓	✓	✓	✓	✓	✓	✓	✓	✓	✓	✓	✓	✓
Engine coolant	Replace										✓					✓
Inverter coolant (Hybrids)	Replace															
Exhaust system	Inspect	✓	✓	✓	✓	✓	✓	✓	✓	✓	✓	✓	✓	✓	✓	✓
Fluid levels (all)	Top off	✓	✓	✓	✓	✓	✓	✓	✓	✓	✓	✓	✓	✓	✓	✓
Halfshaft & U-joints	Inspect	✓	✓	✓	✓	✓	✓	✓	✓	✓	✓	✓	✓	✓	✓	✓
Horn, exterior lamps, turn signal and hazard operation	Inspect	✓	✓	✓	✓	✓	✓	✓	✓	✓	✓	✓	✓	✓	✓	✓
Inspect wheels and related comp. for abnomal noise, wear, looseness or drag	Inspect	✓	✓	✓	✓	✓	✓	✓	✓	✓	✓	✓	✓	✓	✓	✓
Oil and fluid leaks	Inspect	✓	✓	✓	✓	✓	✓	✓	✓	✓	✓	✓	✓	✓	✓	✓
Radiator, coolers, heater and air conditioning hoses	Inspect	✓	✓	✓	✓	✓	✓	✓	✓	✓	✓	✓	✓	✓	✓	✓
Rotate tires, inspect tread wear, measure tread depth and check pressure	Inspect/Rotate	✓	✓	✓	✓	✓	✓	✓	✓	✓	✓	✓	✓	✓	✓	✓
Shocks struts and other suspension components for leaks and damage	Inspect	✓	✓	✓	✓	✓	✓	✓	✓	✓	✓	✓	✓	✓	✓	✓
Spark plugs	Replace						✓						✓			
Steering linkage, ball joints, suspension and tie-rod ends, lubricate if equipped with grease fittings	Inspect/Lubricate	✓	✓	✓	✓	✓	✓	✓	✓	✓	✓	✓	✓	✓	✓	✓
Windshield, wipers and wiper spray	Inspect	✓	✓	✓	✓	✓	✓	✓	✓	✓	✓	✓	✓	✓	✓	✓
Rear differential fluid	Replace															✓
Transfer case fluid	Replace						✓						✓			

WARNING: To prevent the risk of high-voltage shock, always follow precisely all warnings and service instructions, including instructions to depower the system. The high-voltage hybrid system utilizes approximately 300 volts DC, provided through high-voltage cables to its components and modules. The high-voltage cables and wiring are identified by orange harness tape or orange wire covering. All high-voltage components are marked with high-voltage warning labels with a high-voltage symbol. Failure to follow these instructions may result in serious personal injury or death.

Oil change service intervals should be completed as indicated by the message center (Can be up to 1 year or 10,000 miles) If the message center is prematurely reset or is inoperative, perform the oil change interval at 6 months or 5,000 miles from your last oil change.

For extensive idling and or low speed driving, change engine oil and filter every 5,000 miles, 6 months or 200 hours of engine operation.

Use of E85 50% of the time or greater, change engine oil and filter every 5,000 miles or 6 months.

For commercial use or extensive idling, change spark plugs at 60,000 miles.

PRECAUTIONS

Before servicing any vehicle, please be sure to read all of the following precautions, which deal with personal safety, prevention of component damage, and important points to take into consideration when servicing a motor vehicle:

• Never open, service or drain the radiator or cooling system when the engine is hot; serious burns can occur from the steam and hot coolant.

• Observe all applicable safety precautions when working around fuel. Whenever servicing the fuel system, always work in a well-ventilated area. Do not allow fuel spray or vapors to come in contact with a spark, open flame, or excessive heat (a hot drop light, for example). Keep a dry chemical fire extinguisher near the work area. Always keep fuel in a container specifically designed for fuel storage; also, always properly seal fuel containers to avoid the possibility of fire or explosion. Refer to the additional fuel system precautions later in this section.

• Fuel injection systems often remain pressurized, even after the engine has been turned **OFF**. The fuel system pressure must be relieved before disconnecting any fuel lines. Failure to do so may result in fire and/or personal injury.

• Brake fluid often contains polyglycol ethers and polyglycols. Avoid contact with the eyes and wash your hands thoroughly after handling brake fluid. If you do get brake fluid in your eyes, flush your eyes with clean, running water for 15 minutes. If eye irritation persists, or if you have taken brake fluid internally, IMMEDIATELY seek medical assistance.

• The EPA warns that prolonged contact with used engine oil may cause a number of skin disorders, including cancer. You should make every effort to minimize your exposure to used engine oil. Protective gloves should be worn when changing oil. Wash your hands and any other exposed skin areas as soon as possible after exposure to used engine oil. Soap and water, or waterless hand cleaner should be used.

• All new vehicles are now equipped with an air bag system, often referred to as a Supplemental Restraint System (SRS) or Supplemental Inflatable Restraint (SIR) system. The system must be disabled before performing service on or around system components, steering column, instrument panel components, wiring and sensors. Failure to follow safety and disabling procedures could result in accidental air bag deployment, possible personal injury and unnecessary system repairs.

• Always wear safety goggles when working with, or around, the air bag system. When carrying a non-deployed air bag, be sure the bag and trim cover are pointed away from your body. When placing a non-deployed air bag on a work surface, always face the bag and trim cover upward, away from the surface. This will reduce the motion of the module if it is accidentally deployed. Refer to the additional air bag system precautions later in this section.

• Clean, high quality brake fluid from a sealed container is essential to the safe and proper operation of the brake system. You should always buy the correct type of brake fluid for your vehicle. If the brake fluid becomes contaminated, completely flush the system with new fluid. Never reuse any brake fluid. Any brake fluid that is removed from the system should be discarded. Also, do not allow any brake fluid to come in contact with a painted surface; it will damage the paint.

• Never operate the engine without the proper amount and type of engine oil; doing so WILL result in severe engine damage.

• Timing belt maintenance is extremely important. Many models utilize an interference-type, non-freewheeling engine. If the timing belt breaks, the valves in the cylinder head may strike the pistons, causing potentially serious (also time-consuming and expensive) engine damage. Refer to the maintenance interval charts for the recommended replacement interval for the timing belt, and to the timing belt section for belt replacement and inspection.

• Disconnecting the negative battery cable on some vehicles may interfere with the functions of the on-board computer system(s) and may require the computer to undergo a relearning process once the negative battery cable is reconnected.

• When servicing drum brakes, only disassemble and assemble one side at a time, leaving the remaining side intact for reference.

• Only an MVAC-trained, EPA-certified automotive technician should service the air conditioning system or its components.

BRAKES   ANTI-LOCK BRAKE SYSTEM (ABS)

GENERAL INFORMATION

PRECAUTIONS

• Certain components within the ABS system are not intended to be serviced or repaired individually.

• Do not use rubber hoses or other parts not specifically specified for and ABS system. When using repair kits, replace all parts included in the kit. Partial or incorrect repair may lead to functional problems and require the replacement of components.

• Lubricate rubber parts with clean, fresh brake fluid to ease assembly. Do not use shop air to clean parts; damage to rubber components may result.

• Use only DOT 3 brake fluid from an unopened container.

• If any hydraulic component or line is removed or replaced, it may be necessary to bleed the entire system.

• A clean repair area is essential. Always clean the reservoir and cap thoroughly before removing the cap. The slightest amount of dirt in the fluid may plug an orifice and impair the system function. Perform repairs after components have been thoroughly cleaned; use only denatured alcohol to clean components. Do not allow ABS components to come into contact with any substance containing mineral oil; this includes used shop rags.

• The Anti-Lock control unit is a microprocessor similar to other computer units in the vehicle. Ensure that the ignition switch is **OFF** before removing or installing controller harnesses. Avoid static electricity discharge at or near the controller.

• If any arc welding is to be done on the vehicle, the control unit should be unplugged before welding operations begin.

• Do not use any fluid other than clean brake fluid meeting manufacturer's specification. Additionally, do not use brake fluid that has been previously drained. Following these instructions will help prevent system contamination, brake component damage and the risk of serious personal injury.

• Do not spill brake fluid on painted or plastic surfaces or damage to the surface may occur. If brake fluid is spilled onto a painted or plastic surface, immediately wash the surface with water.

SPEED SENSORS

REMOVAL & INSTALLATION

Front

See Figure 1.

1. Before servicing the vehicle, refer to the Precautions Section.
2. Raise and safely support the vehicle.

➡**The harness connector is located in the engine compartment.**

3. Disconnect the electrical connector.

✷✷ CAUTION

Care must be taken during the removal of the plug to prevent damage. If the plug is damaged, a new sensor may need to be installed, even though the sensor is functional in all other aspects.

4. Remove the grommet from the body.
5. When removing the body plug, rotate the plug into a position which allows the use of a small screwdriver to release the tabs on the underside of the body plug. These 2 tabs are located at right angles to the sensor wire.
6. Remove the front wheel speed sensor wire from the retainer.
7. Remove the front wheel speed sensor wire-to-body bolt.
8. Remove the front wheel speed sensor wire bolt.
9. Remove the front wheel speed sensor bolt from the wheel knuckle.

➡**Clean off any foreign material that may have collected around the sensor before removal.**

10. Remove the front wheel speed sensor.

➡**Thoroughly clean the mounting surface.**

To install:

11. Installation is the reverse of the removal procedure, noting the following tightening specifications:

- Front wheel speed sensor-to-knuckle bolt: 80 inch lbs. (9 Nm)
- Front wheel speed sensor wire bolt: 11 ft. lbs. (15 Nm)
- Front wheel speed sensor wire-to-body bolt: 80 inch lbs. (9 Nm)

REMOVAL & INSTALLATION

See Figures 2 and 3.

1. Raise and safely support the vehicle.

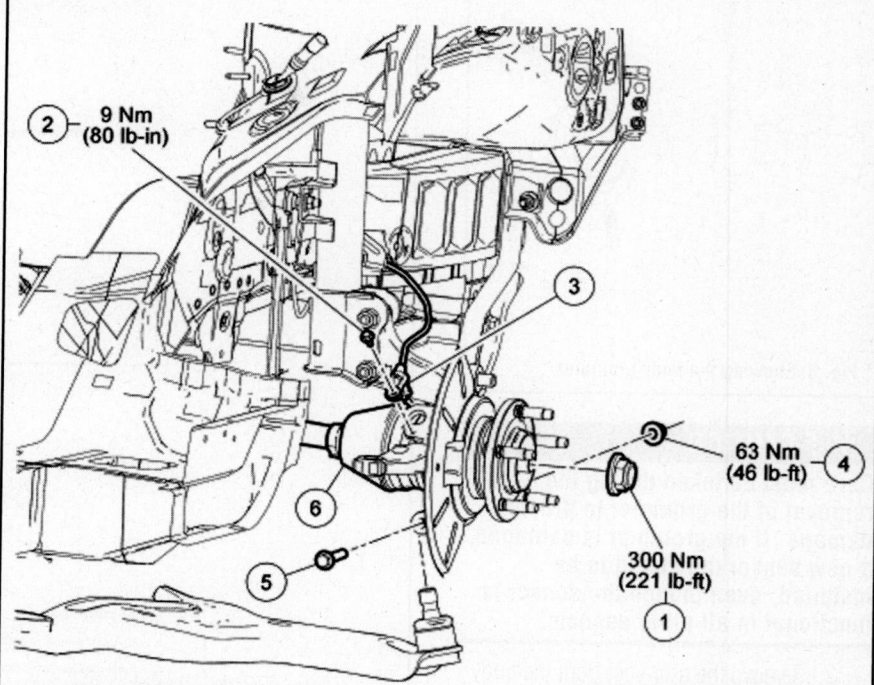

1. Wheel hub nut
2. Wheel speed sensor bolt
3. Wheel speed sensor
4. Lower ball joint nut
5. Lower arm bolt
6. Halfshaft assembly

N00096800

Fig. 1 Exploded view of the front ABS brake system components

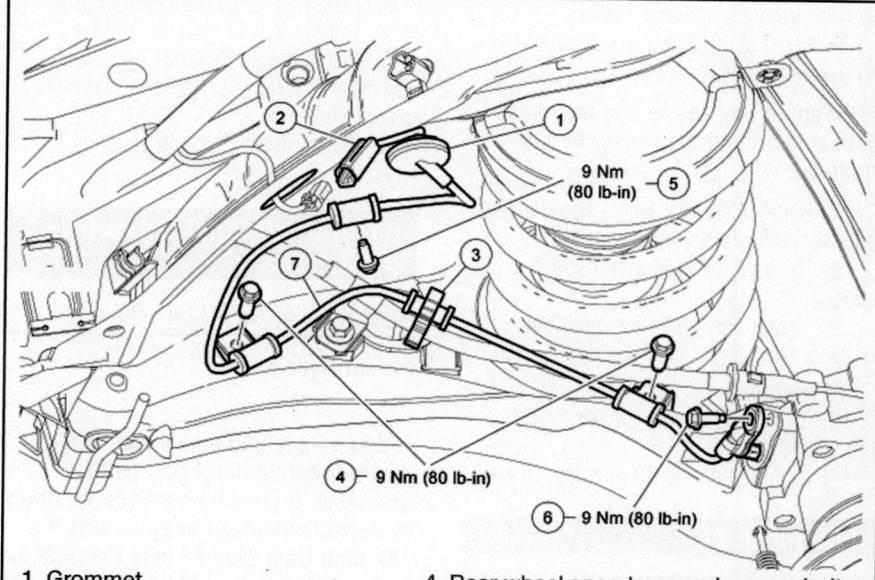

1. Grommet
2. Rear wheel speed sensor electrical connector
3. Rear wheel speed sensor harness retainer
4. Rear wheel speed sensor harness bolts (2 required)
5. Rear wheel speed sensor harness bolt
6. Rear wheel speed sensor bolt
7. Rear wheel speed sensor

N0029661

Fig. 2 Showing the rear wheel speed sensor layout

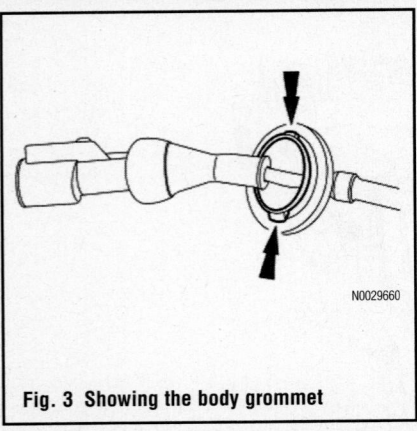

Fig. 3 Showing the body grommet

❊❊ CAUTION

Care must be taken during the removal of the grommet to prevent damage. If the grommet is damaged, a new sensor may need to be installed, even though the sensor is functional in all other aspects.

2. Remove the grommet from the body.

3. When removing the body grommet, rotate the grommet into a position which allows the use of a small screwdriver to release the tabs on the underside of the grommet. These 2 tabs are located at right angles to the sensor wire.

4. Disconnect the rear wheel speed sensor electrical connector.

5. Remove the rear wheel speed sensor harness from the harness retainer.

6. Remove the 3 rear wheel speed sensor harness bolts.

➡ **Clean off any debris that may have collected around the sensor before removal.**

7. Remove the rear wheel speed sensor bolt from the wheel knuckle.

8. Remove the rear wheel speed sensor.

9. Thoroughly clean the mounting surface.

To install:

10. To install, reverse the removal procedure.

11. Tighten bolts to 80 inch lbs. (9 Nm).

ABS MODULE

REMOVAL & INSTALLATION

See Figure 4.

The manufacturer does not provide a removal procedure. Please note the following when servicing this component.

1. Install the 4 ABS module and screws. Tighten to 18 inch lbs. (2 Nm).

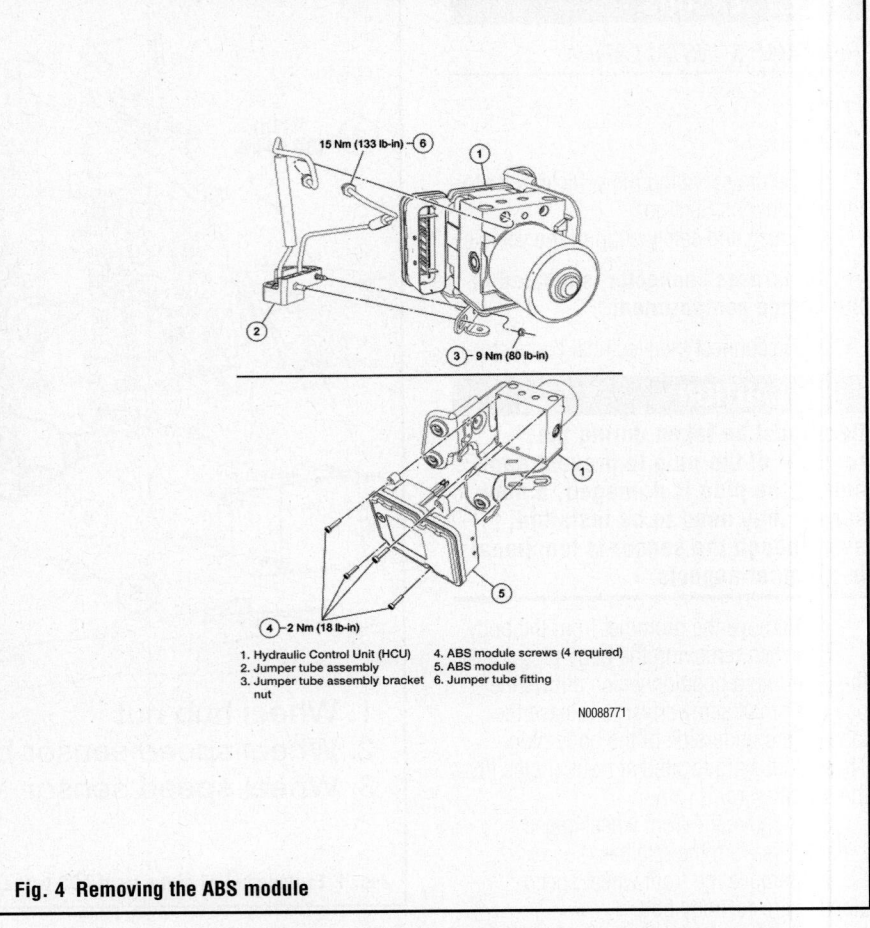

1. Hydraulic Control Unit (HCU)
2. Jumper tube assembly
3. Jumper tube assembly bracket nut
4. ABS module screws (4 required)
5. ABS module
6. Jumper tube fitting

Fig. 4 Removing the ABS module

2. Install the jumper tubes fittings to the HCU. Tighten to 133 inch lbs. (15 Nm).

3. Install the jumper tube assembly bracket nut. Tighten to 80 inch lbs. (9 Nm).

4. Test system, checking carefully for leaks.

HYDRAULIC CONTROL UNIT (HCU)

REMOVAL & INSTALLATION

Except Hybrid

See Figure 5.

➡ **When installing a new ABS module/Hydraulic Control Unit (HCU) assembly, it must be configured (either by download/upload or uploading the "As-Built Data Method" via the OEM or appropriate aftermarket equipment). This step is necessary only if a new ABS module is being installed.**

1. Connect the scan tool and upload the module configuration from the ABS module.

2. Remove the air cleaner and the outlet pipe.

3. Disconnect the master cylinder brake tube fittings from the HCU.

4. If equipped with 3.0L engine, disconnect the master cylinder brake tube fittings from the master cylinder and remove the brake tubes.

➡ **The brake tubes must be installed in the same location as removed.**

5. Disconnect the front brake tube fittings from the HCU.

6. Disconnect the rear brake tube fittings from the jumper tubes.

7. Disconnect the electrical connector by rotating the protective cover.

8. Remove the 3 HCU bracket-to-frame bolts and remove the HCU.

To install:

9. To install, reverse the removal procedure. Use the following tightening specifications:

- HCU bracket to frame bolts 15 ft. lbs. (20 Nm).
- Rear and front brake tube fittings, tighten to 133 inch lbs. (15 Nm).

10. If a new ABS module was installed, download the module configuration information from the scan tool. If a new ABS

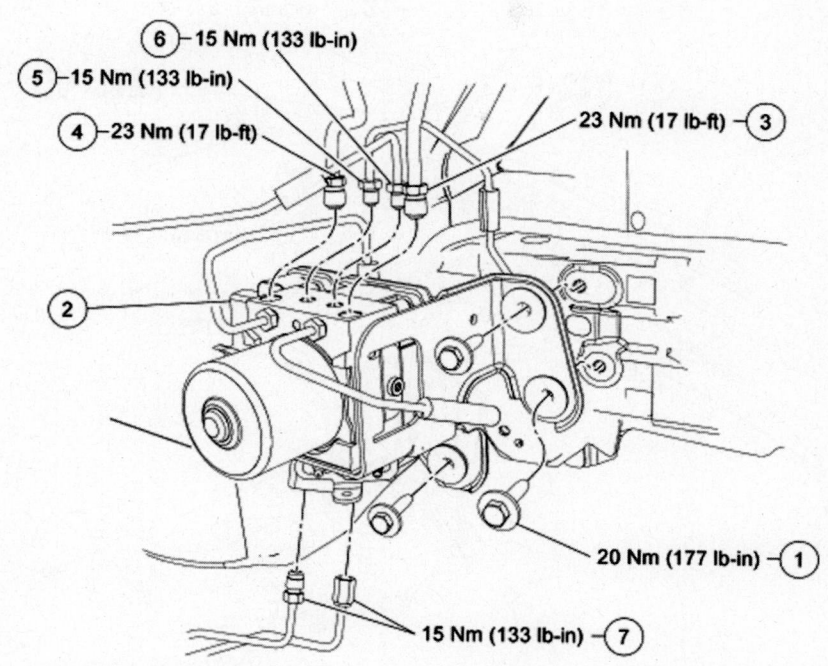

6 — 15 Nm (133 lb-in)
5 — 15 Nm (133 lb-in)
4 — 23 Nm (17 lb-ft)
23 Nm (17 lb-ft) — 3
2
20 Nm (177 lb-in) — 1
15 Nm (133 lb-in) — 7

1. Hydraulic Control Unit (HCU) bracket-to-frame bolt (3 required)
2. HCU
3. Master cylinder secondary brake tube fitting
4. Master cylinder primary brake tube fitting
5. LH front brake tube fitting
6. RH front brake tube fitting
7. Rear brake tube fittings

N0088774

Fig. 5 Removing/installing the hydraulic control unit (HCU)

module and/or a new HCU was installed, carry out the IVD Initialization sequence following the scan tool directions.

11. Bleed the brake system and check for leaks.

Hybrid

See Figure 6.

1. If a new ABS module is being installed, connect the scan tool and upload the module configuration information from the ABS module.

2. Remove the Hydraulic Control Unit (HCU) heat shield:

  a. Remove the 2 heat shield bolts.

  b. Release the 2 high-voltage cable retaining pins from the heat shield.

3. Disconnect the electrical connector by rotating the protective cover.

4. Disconnect the master cylinder brake tube fittings from the HCU:

5. Note the order of the brake tubes and then disconnect the brake tube-to- HCU fittings (12 mm).

6. Remove the 3 HCU bracket-to-frame bolts.

7. Disconnect the brake tube from the routing clip located at the bottom of the HCU bracket.

8. Remove the HCU assembly.

9. If a new HCU is being installed, remove the HCU bracket-to- HCU bolts.

❊❊ CAUTION

Use care not to cross the tubes during installation. If the brake tubes are crossed, the ABS module will set DTCs during an ABS event.

To install:

10. To install, reverse the removal procedure and note the following steps.

11. If a new HCU is being installed, install the HCU bracket-to- HCU bolts. Tighten to 80 inch lbs. (9 Nm).

12. Install the 3 HCU bracket-to-frame bolts. Tighten to 15 ft. lbs. (20 Nm).

13. Connect the brake tube-to- HCU fittings (12 mm), noting the proper locations as during removal. Tighten to 133 inch lbs. (15 Nm).

14. Connect the master cylinder brake tube fittings to the HCU. Tighten to 17 ft. lbs. (23 Nm).

15. If a new ABS module was installed, download the module configuration information from the scan tool.

16. If a new ABS module and/or a new HCU was installed, carry out the Multi-Calibration routine, following the scan tool directions.

17. Bleed the brake system.

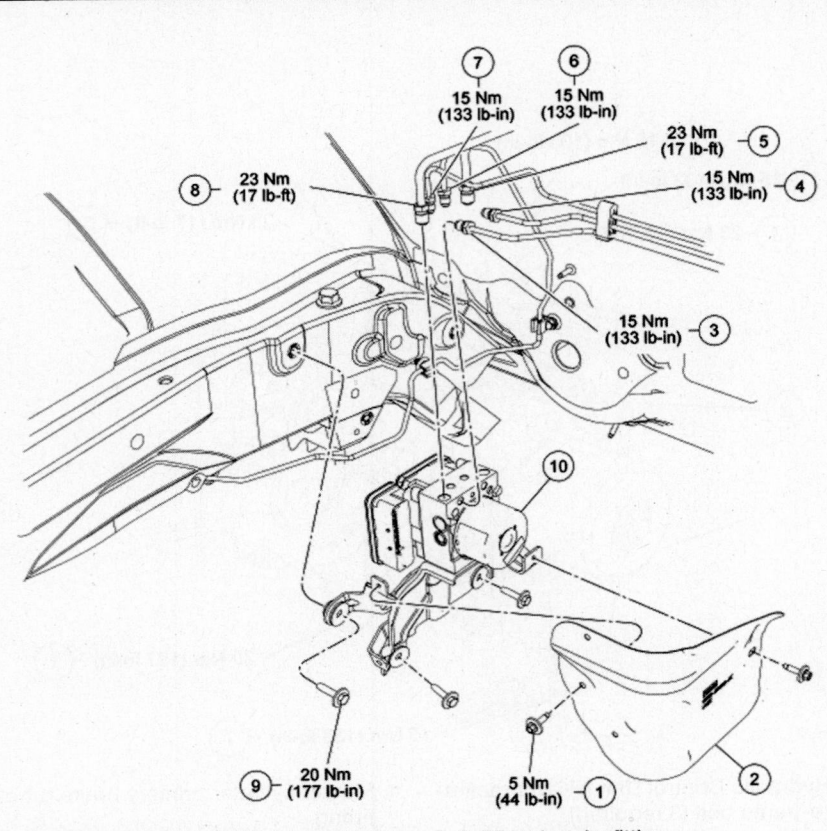

1. Hydraulic Control Unit (HCU) heat shield bolt
   (2 required)
2. HCU heat shield
3. LR brake tube fitting
4. RR brake tube fitting
5. Master cylinder secondary brake tube fitting
6. RF brake tube fitting
7. LF brake tube fitting
8. Master cylinder primary brake tube fitting
9. HCU bracket-to-frame bolt (3 required)
10. HCU

N0088726

Fig. 6 Removing the Hydraulic Control Unit—Hybrid

BRAKES

BLEEDING THE BRAKE SYSTEM

BLEEDING PROCEDURE

BRAKE SYSTEM BLEEDING PROCEDURE

Manual Bleeding

1. Clean all the dirt from the brake master cylinder filler cap and remove the filler cap.

2. Fill the brake master cylinder reservoir with clean, specified brake fluid.

3. Remove the RR bleeder screw cap and place a box-end wrench on the bleeder screw. Attach a rubber drain hose to the RR bleeder screw and submerge the free end of the hose in a container partially filled with clean, specified brake fluid.

4. Have an assistant pump and then hold firm pressure on the brake pedal.

5. Loosen the RR bleeder screw until a stream of brake fluid comes out. While an assistant maintains pressure on the brake pedal, tighten the RR bleeder screw.

6. Repeat until clear, bubble-free fluid comes out.

7. Refill the brake master cylinder reservoir as necessary.

8. Tighten the RR bleeder screw to 142 inch lbs. (16 Nm). Remove the rubber hose and install the bleeder screw cap.

9. Repeat above steps for the LR bleeder screw.

10. Remove the RF bleeder cap and place a box-end wrench on the bleeder screw. Attach a rubber drain hose to the RF bleeder screw and submerge the free end of the hose in a container partially filled with clean, specified brake fluid.

11. Have an assistant pump and then hold firm pressure on the brake pedal.

12. Loosen the RF bleeder screw until a stream of brake fluid comes out. While the assistant maintains pressure on the brake pedal, tighten the RF bleeder screw.

13. Repeat until clear, bubble-free fluid comes out.

14. Refill the brake master cylinder reservoir as necessary.

15. Tighten the RF bleeder screw to 142 inch lbs. (16 Nm). Remove the rubber hose and install the bleeder screw cap.

16. Repeat above steps for the LF bleeder screw.

Pressure Bleeding

1. Clean all dirt from the brake master cylinder filler cap and remove the filler cap.

2. Fill the brake master cylinder reservoir with clean, specified brake fluid.

➡**Master cylinder pressure bleeder adapter tools are available from various manufacturers of pressure bleeding equipment. Follow the instructions of the manufacturer when installing the adapter.**

3. Install the bleeder adapter to the brake master cylinder reservoir, and attach the bleeder tank hose to the fitting on the adapter.

➡**Make sure the bleeder tank contains enough clean, specified brake fluid to complete the bleeding operation.**

4. Open the valve on the bleeder tank.

5. Apply 30–50 psi (207–345 kPa) to the brake system.

6. Remove the RR bleeder screw cap and place a box-end wrench on the bleeder screw. Attach a rubber drain hose to the RR bleeder screw and submerge the free end of the hose in a container partially filled with clean, specified brake fluid.

7. Loosen the RR bleeder screw. Leave open until clear, bubble-free brake fluid flows, then tighten the RR bleeder screw to 142 inch lbs. (16 Nm). Remove the rubber hose. Install the cap.

8. Continue bleeding the rest of the system, going in order from the LR bleeder screw to the RF bleeder screw, ending with the LF bleeder screw. Tighten the bleeder screws to 142 inch lbs. (16 Nm).

9. Close the bleeder tank valve and release the pressure. Remove the tank hose from the adapter and remove the adapter. Fill the reservoir with clean, specified brake fluid and install the reservoir cap.

10. With the ignition off, press the brake pedal through the gap to seat the clevis pin against the brake booster push rod and then confirm the pedal is firm.

11. If the brake pedal feels spongy (soft), repeat the Pressure Bleeding procedure to remove any remaining air from the system.

COMPONENT BLEEDING

Hydraulic Control Unit (HCU) Bleeding

➡**The Hydraulic Control Unit (HCU) bleeding procedure must be carried out if the HCU or any components upstream of the HCU are installed new.**

➡**Due to the complexity of the fluid path within the hybrid brake system, it is necessary to pressure bleed this system.**

1. Follow the Pressure Bleeding or Manual Bleeding procedure to bleed the system, in this section.

2. Connect the scan tool and follow the ABS Hydraulic Control Unit (HCU) bleeding instructions.

3. Repeat the Pressure Bleeding or Manual Bleeding procedure to bleed the system.

Master Cylinder Bleeding

➡**The Hydraulic Control Unit (HCU) bleeding procedure must be carried out if the HCU or any components upstream of the HCU are installed new.**

➡**Due to the complexity of the fluid path within the hybrid brake system, it is necessary to pressure bleed this system.**

1. Place a box-end wrench on the master cylinder bleeder screw and attach a rubber drain hose to the bleeder screw. Submerge the free end of the rubber hose into the master cylinder reservoir.

2. Fill the master cylinder reservoir with clean, specified brake fluid.

3. Have an assistant pump the brake pedal until clear fluid flows from the rubber hose, without air bubbles.

4. Tighten the bleeder screw to 142 inch lbs. (16 Nm). Remove the rubber hose and install the bleeder screw cap.

5. Bleed the brake system.

Brake Caliper

➡**It is not necessary to do a complete brake system bleed if only the brake caliper was disconnected or installed new.**

1. Remove the bleeder screw cap and place a box-end wrench on the bleeder screw. Attach a rubber drain hose to the bleeder screw and submerge the free end of the hose in a container partially filled with clean, specified brake fluid.

2. Have an assistant pump the brake pedal at least 2 times and then hold firm pressure on the brake pedal.

3. Loosen the bleeder screw until a stream of brake fluid comes out. While the assistant maintains pressure on the brake pedal, tighten the bleeder screw.

4. Repeat until clear, bubble-free fluid comes out.

5. Refill the brake master cylinder reservoir as necessary.

6. Tighten the bleeder screw to 142 inch lbs. (16 Nm). Remove the rubber hose and install the bleeder screw cap.

7. Apply brakes several times to verify correct brake operation.

Wheel Cylinder

➡**It is not necessary to do a complete brake system bleed if only the wheel cylinder was disconnected or installed new.**

1. Remove the bleeder screw cap and place a box-end wrench on the bleeder screw. Attach a rubber drain hose to the bleeder screw and submerge the free end of the hose in a container partially filled with clean, specified brake fluid.

2. Have an assistant pump the brake pedal at least 2 times and then hold firm pressure on the brake pedal.

3. Loosen the bleeder screw until a stream of brake fluid comes out. While the assistant maintains pressure on the brake pedal, tighten the bleeder screw.

4. Repeat until clear, bubble-free fluid comes out.

5. Refill the brake master cylinder reservoir as necessary.

6. Tighten the bleeder screw to 142 inch lbs. (16 Nm). Remove the rubber hose and install the bleeder screw cap.

7. Apply brakes several times to verify correct brake operation.

FLUID FILL PROCEDURE

When master cylinder is refilled following any brake system component removal, fill to "MAX" line and then perform Brake System Bleeding and recheck fluid level.

BRAKES **FRONT DISC BRAKES**

❋❋ CAUTION

Dust and dirt accumulating on brake parts during normal use may contain asbestos fibers from production or aftermarket brake linings. Breathing excessive concentrations of asbestos fibers can cause serious bodily harm. Exercise care when servicing brake parts. Do not sand or grind brake lining unless equipment used is designed to contain the dust residue. Do not clean brake parts with compressed air or by dry brushing. Cleaning should be done by dampening the brake components with a fine mist of water, then wiping the brake components clean with a dampened cloth. Dispose of cloth and all residue containing asbestos fibers in an impermeable container with the appropriate label. Follow practices prescribed by the Occupational Safety and Health Administration (OSHA) and the Environmental Protection Agency (EPA) for the handling, processing, and disposing of dust or debris that may contain asbestos fibers.

BRAKE CALIPER

REMOVAL & INSTALLATION

See Figure 7.

➡The rear brake pads will wear at approximately twice the rate of the front brake pads.

1. Remove the wheel and tire.

❋❋ CAUTION

If the anchor housing spring is to be removed, do not force the spring off the brake caliper or damage to the spring can occur. Do not use any tools to remove the spring, use hand force only. Do not use excessive force or damage to the spring can occur.

➡The LH side brake pad anti-rattle spring must be installed with the 2-tabbed end in the upper brake caliper cavity.

2. For the LH brake caliper, release the lower portion of the brake pad anti-rattle spring.

3. Apply force to the center of the spring and pull outward at the bottom of the spring to remove it from the lower brake caliper cavity.

4. Rotate the spring upward and remove it from the brake caliper.

➡The RH side brake pad anti-rattle spring must be installed with the 2-tabbed end in the lower brake caliper cavity. For the RH brake caliper, release the upper portion of the brake pad anti-rattle spring.

5. Apply force to the center of the spring and pull outward at the top of the spring to remove it from the upper brake caliper cavity.

6. Rotate the spring downward and remove it from the brake caliper.

➡The brake caliper and brake flexible hose are removed as an assembly.

7. Disconnect the brake tube fitting from the brake flexible hose.

8. Remove and discard the retainer clip from the brake flexible hose.

9. Remove the 2 guide pin bushing caps and the 2 brake caliper guide pin bolts, position the caliper aside.

10. Support the caliper using mechanic's wire.

11. Remove the 2 brake pads from the caliper.

12. Remove the brake flexible hose from the brake caliper.

To install:

13. Install the brake pads onto the caliper and position the brake caliper onto the anchor plate.

14. Install the 2 brake caliper guide pin bolts and the 2 bushing caps. Tighten the bolts to 18 ft. lbs. (25 Nm).

➡If present, the 2-tabbed end of the brake pad anti-rattle spring must be installed first.

15. Install the brake pad anti-rattle spring using the following procedure:

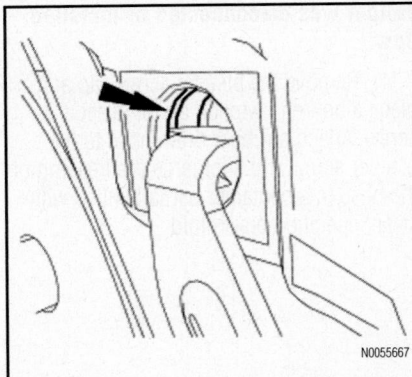

N0055667

Fig. 7 Showing installed position of the anti-rattle spring latch in the anchor plate

16. Insert the tab of the spring into the brake caliper cavity.

17. Twist the tab into the cavity (LH side in the upper brake caliper cavity, RH side in the lower brake caliper cavity).

18. Rotate the brake pad anti-rattle spring and position the upper portion onto the anchor plate.

19. Position the lower portion of the brake pad anti-rattle spring onto the anchor plate.

20. Push down and inward until the upper and lower ends of the brake pad anti-rattle spring are latched and seated in the brake caliper cavities.

❋❋ CAUTION

The latch MUST be positioned as shown, or damage to component may occur.

21. Verify that the brake pad anti-rattle spring is correctly latched by pulling on the spring.

➡Make sure that the brake flexible hose is not twisted.

22. Install the brake flexible hose to the brake caliper. Tighten to 15 ft. lbs. (20 Nm.

23. Position the brake flexible and install a new retainer clip.

24. Attach the brake tube fitting to the brake flexible hose. Tighten to 159 inch lbs. (18 Nm).

25. Bleed the brake caliper, as described in this section.

26. Install the wheel and tire.

DISC BRAKE PADS

REMOVAL & INSTALLATION

See Figure 8.

➡The rear brake pads will wear at approximately twice the rate of the front brake pads.

1. If necessary, using a suitable suction device, remove the brake fluid from the master cylinder reservoir until it is half filled.

2. Remove the wheel and tire.

❋❋ CAUTION

If the brake pad anti-rattle spring is to be removed, do not force the spring off the brake caliper or damage to the spring can occur. Do not use any tools to remove the spring, use hand force only. Do not use excessive force or damage to the spring can occur.

➡ **The LH side brake pad anti-rattle spring must be installed with the 2-tabbed end in the upper brake caliper cavity.**

3. For the LH brake caliper, release the lower portion of the brake pad anti-rattle spring.

4. Apply force to the center of the spring and pull outward at the bottom of the spring to remove it from the lower brake caliper cavity.

5. Rotate the spring upward and remove it from the brake caliper.

➡ **The RH side brake pad anti-rattle spring must be installed with the 2-tabbed end in the lower brake caliper cavity.**

6. For the RH brake caliper, release the upper portion of the brake pad anti-rattle spring.

7. Apply force to the center of the spring and pull outward at the top of the spring to remove it from the upper brake caliper cavity.

8. Rotate the spring downward and remove it from the brake caliper.

❋❋ **CAUTION**

Do not allow the caliper to hang from the brake hose or damage to the hose can occur.

9. Remove the 2 guide pin bushing caps and the 2 brake caliper guide pin bolts, position the caliper aside. Support the caliper using mechanic's wire.

10. Remove the 2 brake pads from the caliper.

To install:

11. Inspect the brake pads for wear and contamination, install new pads as necessary.

❋❋ **CAUTION**

Protect the piston and boots when pushing the caliper piston into the caliper piston bores or damage to the piston or boots may occur.

12. If installing new brake pads, using a C-clamp and worn brake pad, compress the brake caliper piston into the brake caliper.

13. Inspect the brake disc and resurface or install new as necessary.

14. Using specified brake parts cleaner, clean, dry and inspect the brake caliper anchor plate. Apply a light coat of specified lubricant to the 4 brake pad contact points on the anchor plate.

➡ **Make sure that the brake flexible hose is not twisted.**

15. Install the brake pads onto the caliper and position the brake caliper onto the anchor plate.

16. Install the 2 brake caliper guide pin bolts and the 2 bushing caps. Tighten the bolts to 18 ft. lbs. (25 Nm).

➡ **The 2-tabbed end of the brake pad anti-rattle spring must be installed first.**

17. Install the brake pad anti-rattle spring using the following procedure:

18. Insert the tab of the spring into the brake caliper cavity.

19. Twist the tab into the cavity (LH side in the upper brake caliper cavity, RH side in the lower brake caliper cavity).

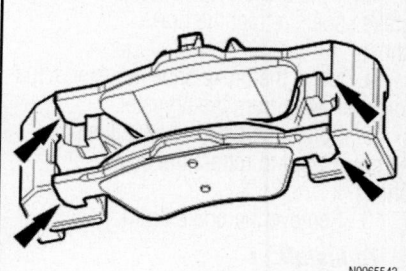

N0065543

Fig. 8 Using specified brake parts cleaner, clean, dry and inspect the brake caliper anchor plate. Apply a light coat of specified lubricant to the 4 brake pad contact points on the anchor plate.

20. Rotate the brake pad anti-rattle spring and position the upper portion onto the anchor plate.

21. Position the lower portion of the brake pad anti-rattle spring onto the anchor plate.

22. Push down and inward until the upper and lower ends of the brake pad anti-rattle spring are latched and seated in the brake caliper cavities.

➡ **The latch MUST be positioned as shown in the illustration in this section or damage to component may occur.**

23. Verify that the brake pad anti-rattle spring is correctly latched by pulling on the spring.

24. Install the wheel and tire.

25. Fill the brake master cylinder reservoir with clean, specified brake fluid.

26. Apply brakes several times to verify correct brake operation.

BRAKES

❋❋ **CAUTION**

Dust and dirt accumulating on brake parts during normal use may contain asbestos fibers from production or aftermarket brake linings. Breathing excessive concentrations of asbestos fibers can cause serious bodily harm. Exercise care when servicing brake parts. Do not sand or grind brake lining unless equipment used is designed to contain the dust residue. Do not clean brake parts with compressed air or by dry brushing. Cleaning should be done by

dampening the brake components with a fine mist of water, then wiping the brake components clean with a dampened cloth. Dispose of cloth and all residue containing asbestos fibers in an impermeable container with the appropriate label. Follow practices prescribed by the Occupational Safety and Health Administration (OSHA) and the Environmental Protection Agency (EPA) for the handling, processing, and disposing of dust or debris that may contain asbestos fibers.

REAR DRUM BRAKES

BRAKE DRUM

REMOVAL & INSTALLATION
See Figure 9.

1. Remove the wheel and tire.

❋❋ **CAUTION**

Use of a brake drum puller or a torch is not recommended. Brake drum distortion can result.

2. If the brake drum is seized to the wheel hub pilot diameter, tap the center of the brake drum between the wheel studs.

3. If the brake drum binds on the brake shoes, retract the brake shoes.

4. Move the brake shoe adjuster actuator lever away from the adjuster.

5. Rotate the brake shoe adjuster screw upward to retract the brake shoes.

6. Remove the brake drum.

To install:

7. Using the Brake Drum Gauge, measure the inside diameter of the brake drum.

8. Install a new brake drum if the inside diameter exceeds the specification stamped on the outside face of the brake drum.

9. Adjust the rear brakes.

10. Position the brake drum on the vehicle.

11. Install the wheel and tire.

BRAKE SHOES

REMOVAL & INSTALLATION

➡If new rear brake shoes and linings are being installed, resurface the brake drums to remove glazing and to provide an equal friction surface from side-to-side. Resurfacing also corrects out-of-round and bell conditions.

1. Remove the brake drum.

2. Remove the 2 brake shoe retaining springs and the 2 pins.

3. Remove the upper return spring.

4. Remove the self-adjuster and spring assembly.

5. Remove the lower return spring.

6. Remove the trailing brake shoe and parking brake actuator lever assembly.

7. Remove the leading brake shoe.

8. Using specified brake parts cleaner, clean and dry the brake shoe contact points on the backing plate.

9. Apply a thin coat of the specified silicone grease to the brake shoe contact points on the backing plate.

➡Adjust the self-adjuster to the full retracted position to ease the installation of the brake drum.

10. To install, reverse the removal procedure.

11. Adjust the rear brake shoes.

ADJUSTMENT

1. Remove the brake drum.

2. Using the Brake Adjustment Gauge, measure the inside diameter of the brake drum.

3. Position the Brake Adjustment Gauge on the brake shoes and linings and adjust accordingly.

4. Install the brake drum.

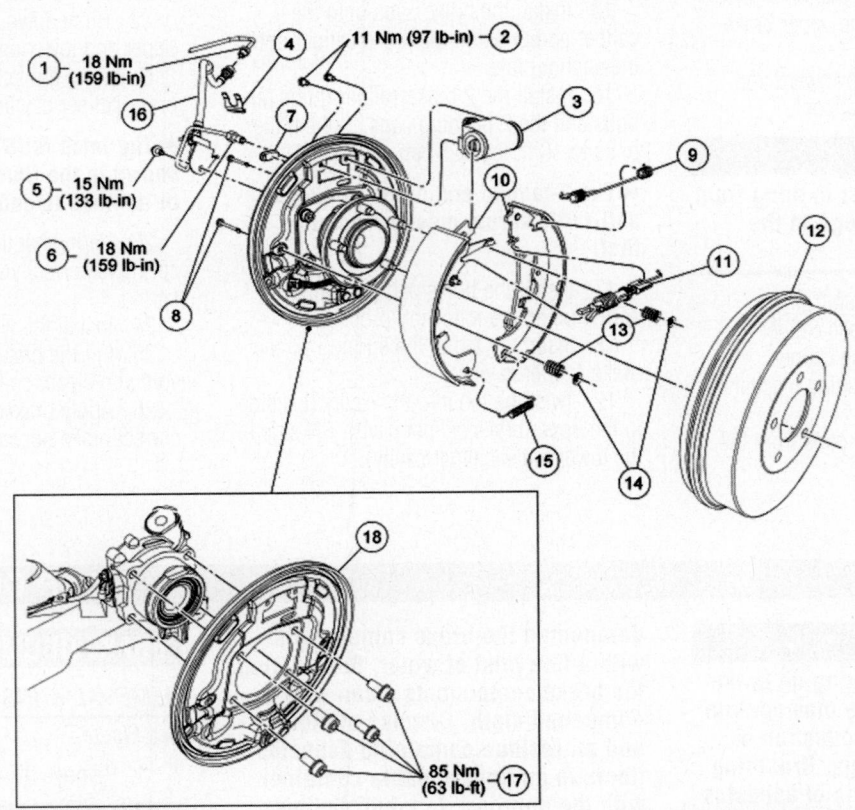

1. Brake tube fitting
2. Wheel cylinder bolts
3. Wheel cylinder
4. Brake flexible hose clip
5. Brake flexible hose bracket bolt
6. Brake flexible hose fitting
7. Plug
8. Brake shoe retaining pins
9. Upper return spring
10. Brake shoe (kit)
11. Self-adjuster assembly
12. Brake drum
13. Brake shoe retaining springs
14. Brake shoe retaining spring plates
15. Lower return spring
16. Brake flexible hose
17. Backing plate bolts
18. Backing plate

N0086552

Fig. 9 Exploded view of the rear drum brake assembly

BRAKES

PARKING BRAKE

PARKING BRAKE CABLES

REMOVAL & INSTALLATION

Front

See Figures 10 through 12.

1. Raise and safely support the vehicle.
2. Remove the parking brake control, as described in this section.
3. Remove the floor console.
4. Remove the driver side front seat.
5. Remove the 3 front parking brake cable bracket bolts.
6. Disconnect the front parking brake cable from the RR parking brake cable connector by releasing the locking tab.
7. Disconnect the front parking brake cable conduit from the LR parking brake cable.
8. Release the front parking brake cable pass-through grommet from the vehicle underbody.
9. To install, reverse the removal procedure.
10. Tighten the cable bolts to 17 ft. lbs. (23 Nm).

Right Rear Parking Brake Cable

See Figure 13.

1. Release the parking brake cable tension.

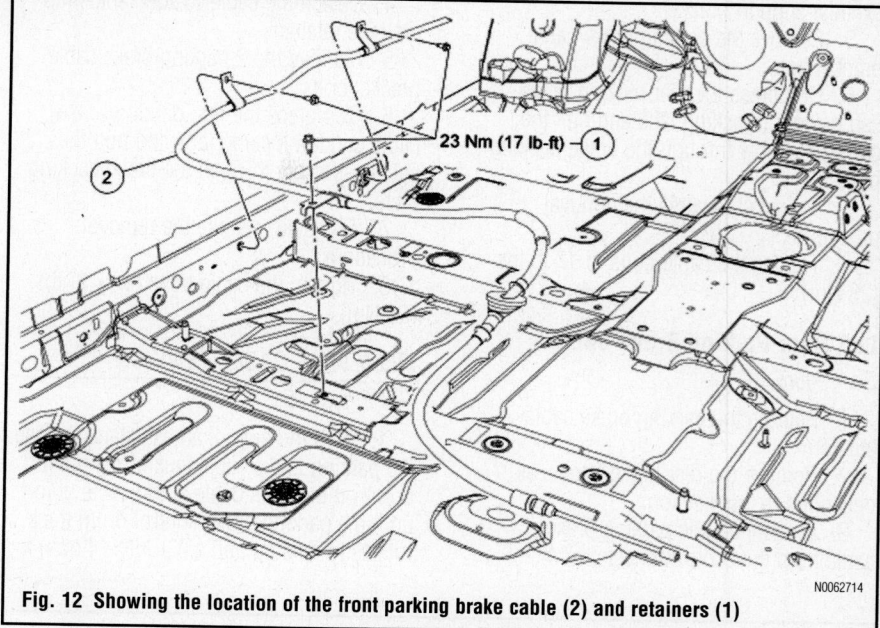

Fig. 12 Showing the location of the front parking brake cable (2) and retainers (1)

2. Remove the rear brake shoes, as described in this section.
3. Disconnect the parking brake cable from the cable connector and the equalizer bracket by compressing the cable conduit locking tabs.

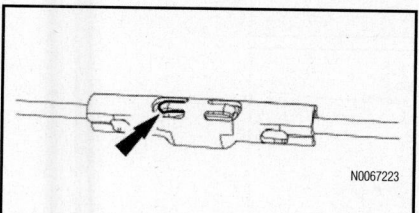

Fig. 10 Disconnect the front parking brake cable from the RR parking brake cable connector by releasing the locking tab.

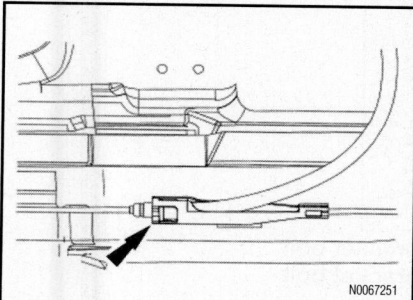

Fig. 11 Disconnect the front parking brake cable conduit from the LR parking brake cable.

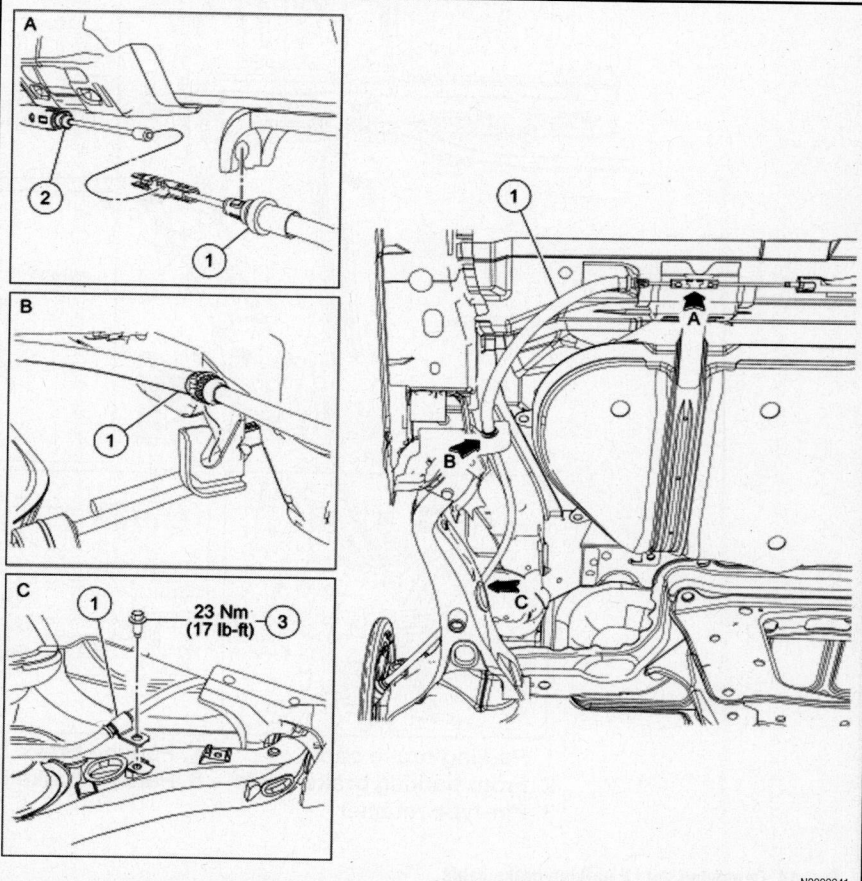

Fig. 13 Removing the RR parking brake cable (1), cable connector (2), and cable bolts (3)

4. Compress the retaining clip and detach the parking brake cable from the exhaust support bracket.

5. Remove the parking brake cable bracket bolt.

6. Compress the rear parking brake cable conduit locking tabs and pull the cable assembly through the brake backing plate.

7. To install, reverse the removal procedure.

8. Tighten the cable bolts to 17 ft. lbs. (23 Nm).

Left Rear Parking Brake Cable

See Figure 14.

1. Release the parking brake cable tension.

2. Remove the rear brake shoes, as described in this section.

3. Disconnect the parking brake cable from the cable connector and the

equalizer bracket by compressing the cable conduit locking tabs.

4. Detach the cable-to-fuel tank strap pin type retainer.

5. Remove the 2 parking brake cable bracket bolts.

6. Compress the rear parking brake cable conduit locking tabs and pull the cable assembly through the brake backing plate.

7. To install, reverse the removal procedure.

8. Tighten the cable bolts to 17 ft. lbs. (23 Nm).

RELIEVING CABLE TENSION

See Figure 15.

1. With the help of an assistant, release the parking brake cable tension by pulling down on the front cable at the cable union, until the parking brake control drum track rotates to its stop and a 0.15 IN. (4 mm) x

3.93 in. (100 mm) retainer pin can be inserted.

2. Before removing the brake control retaining pin, make sure all cable connections are secure and the cable tension is reloaded slowly.

3. To reload the tension on the parking brake cable, follow the release procedure in reverse.

PARKING BRAKE SHOES

REMOVAL & INSTALLATION

➡See "REAR DRUM BRAKES" in this section.

PARKING BRAKE CONTROL

REMOVAL & INSTALLATION

See Figure 16.

1. Remove the front driver side door scuff plate and kick panel.

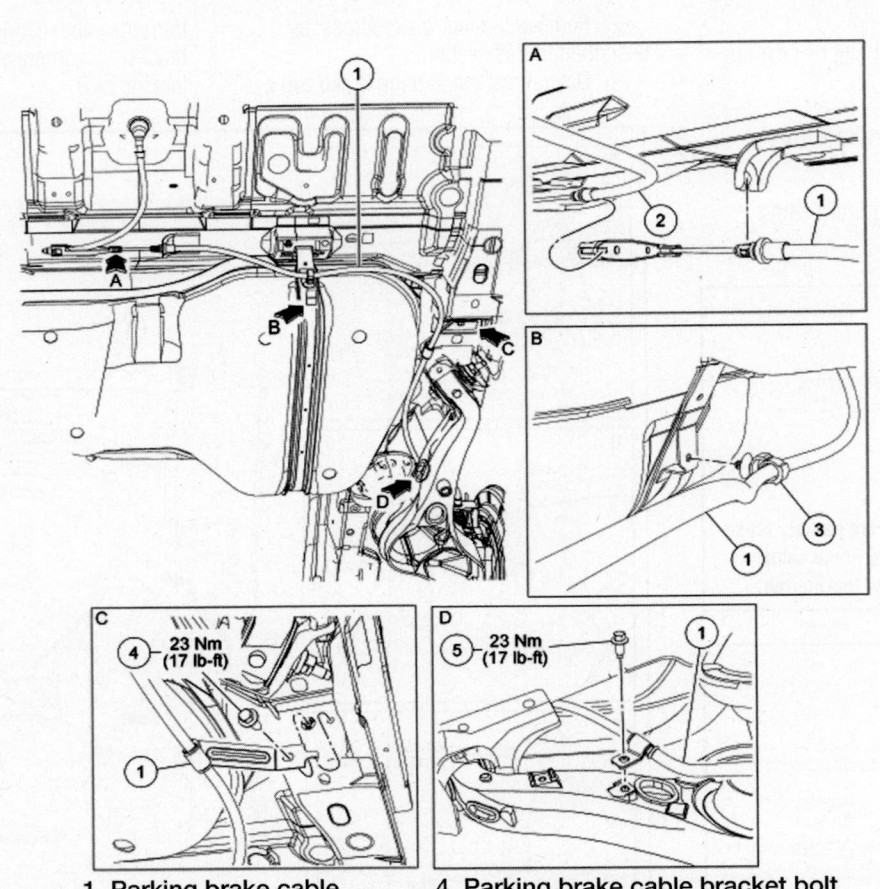

1. Parking brake cable
2. Front parking brake cable
3. Pin-type retainer
4. Parking brake cable bracket bolt
5. Parking brake cable bracket bolt

N0087799

Fig. 14 Removing the LF parking brake cable.

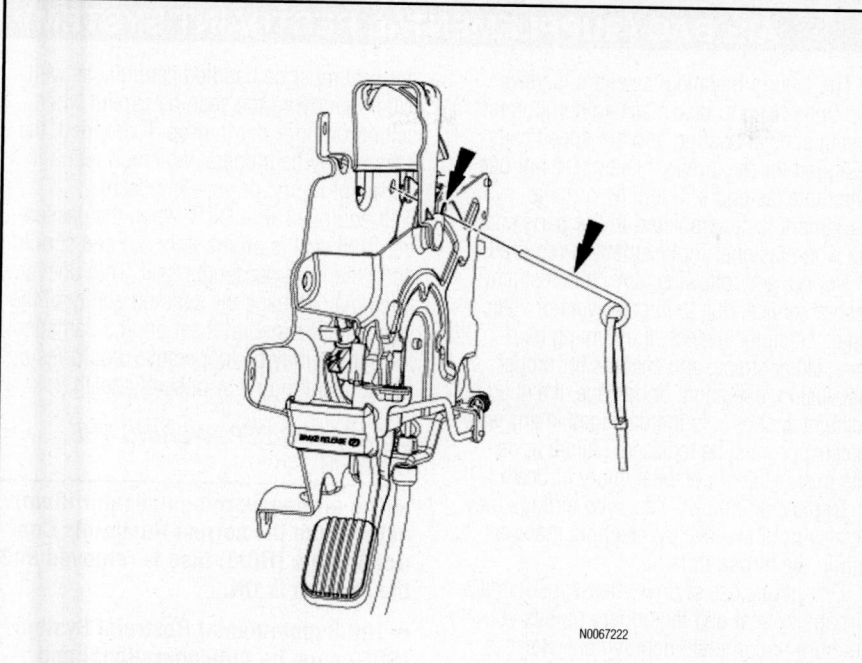

N0067222

Fig. 15 With the help of an assistant, release the parking brake cable tension by pulling down on the front cable at the cable union, until the parking brake control drum track rotates to its stop and a 0.15 IN. (4 mm) x 3.93 in. (100 mm) retainer pin can be inserted.

2. Release the parking brake cable tension as described in this section.

3. Remove the parking brake release handle bolt.

4. Disconnect the parking brake warning indicator switch electrical connector and detach the harness pin-type retainer from the parking brake control cover.

5. Remove the 2 parking brake control bolts.

6. Remove the 2 parking brake control nuts.

7. Remove the parking brake control.

8. Disconnect the front parking brake cable.

➡**Make sure that the cable is in the groove on the control wheel prior to final tightening of fasteners.**

To install:

9. To install, reverse the removal procedure.

10. Tighten parking brake control nuts and bolts to 20 ft. lbs. (27 Nm).

11. Tighten parking brake control nuts to 20 ft. lbs. (27 Nm).

12. Tighten the release handle bolt to 89 inch lbs. (10 Nm).

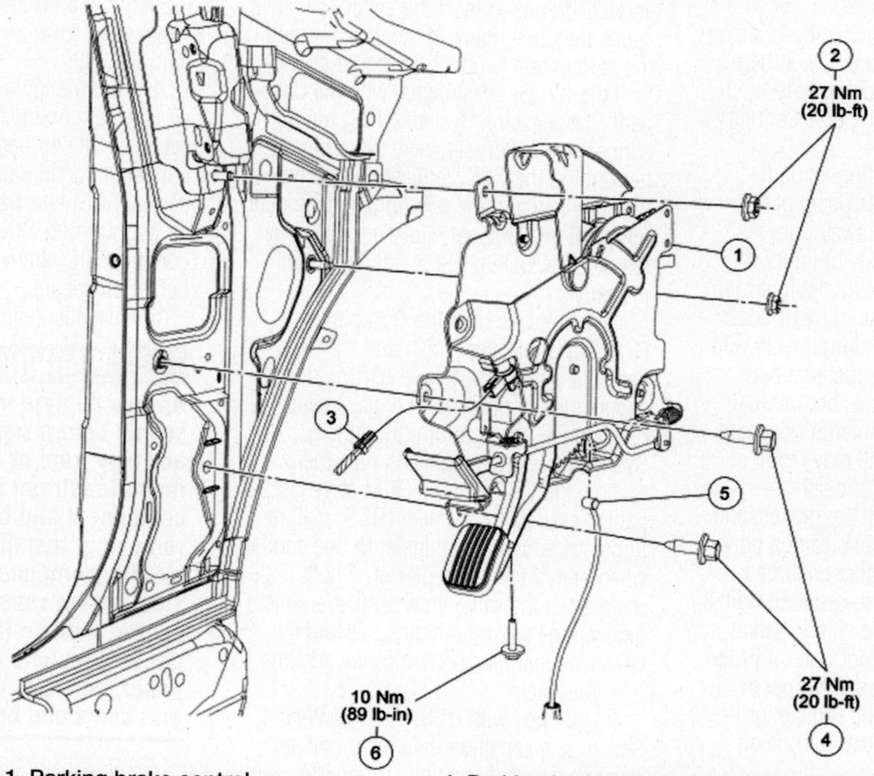

1. Parking brake control
2. Parking brake control nuts (2 required)
3. Parking brake warning indicator switch electrical connector
4. Parking brake control bolts (2 required)
5. Front parking brake cable
6. Parking brake release handle bolt

Fig. 16 Removing the parking brake control assembly

N0067231

CHASSIS ELECTRICAL | **AIR BAG (SUPPLEMENTAL RESTRAINT SYSTEM)**

GENERAL INFORMATION

✳✳ CAUTION

These vehicles are equipped with an air bag system. The system must be disarmed before performing service on, or around, system components, the steering column, instrument panel components, wiring and sensors. Failure to follow the safety precautions and the disarming procedure could result in accidental air bag deployment, possible injury and unnecessary system repairs.

SERVICE PRECAUTIONS

Disconnect and isolate the battery negative cable before beginning any airbag system component diagnosis, testing, removal, or installation procedures. Allow system capacitor to discharge for two minutes before beginning any component service. This will disable the airbag system. Failure to disable the airbag system may result in accidental airbag deployment, personal injury, or death.

Do not place an intact undeployed airbag face down on a solid surface. The airbag will propel into the air if accidentally deployed and may result in personal injury or death.

When carrying or handling an undeployed airbag, the trim side (face) of the airbag should be pointing away from the body to minimize possibility of injury if accidental deployment occurs. Failure to do this may result in personal injury or death.

Replace airbag system components with OEM replacement parts. Substitute parts may appear interchangeable, but internal differences may result in inferior occupant protection. Failure to do so may result in occupant personal injury or death.

Wear safety glasses, rubber gloves, and long sleeved clothing when cleaning powder residue from vehicle after an airbag deployment. Powder residue emitted from a deployed airbag can cause skin irritation. Flush affected area with cool water if irritation is experienced. If nasal or throat irritation is experienced, exit the vehicle for fresh air until the irritation ceases. If irritation continues, see a physician.

Do not use a replacement airbag that is not in the original packaging. This may result in improper deployment, personal injury, or death.

The factory installed fasteners, screws and bolts used to fasten airbag components have a special coating and are specifically designed for the airbag system. Do not use substitute fasteners. Use only original equipment fasteners listed in the parts catalog when fastener replacement is required.

During, and following, any child restraint anchor service, due to impact event or vehicle repair, carefully inspect all mounting hardware, tether straps, and anchors for proper installation, operation, or damage. If a child restraint anchor is found damaged in any way, the anchor must be replaced. Failure to do this may result in personal injury or death.

Deployed and non-deployed airbags may or may not have live pyrotechnic material within the airbag inflator.

Do not dispose of driver/passenger/curtain airbags or seat belt tensioners unless you are sure of complete deployment. Refer to the Hazardous Substance Control System for proper disposal.

Dispose of deployed airbags and tensioners consistent with state, provincial, local, and federal regulations.

After any airbag component testing or service, do not connect the battery negative cable. Personal injury or death may result if the system test is not performed first.

If the vehicle is equipped with the Occupant Classification System (OCS), do not connect the battery negative cable before performing the OCS Verification Test using the scan tool and the appropriate diagnostic information. Personal injury or death may result if the system test is not performed properly.

Never replace both the Occupant Restraint Controller (ORC) and the Occupant Classification Module (OCM) at the same time. If both require replacement, replace one, then perform the Airbag System test before replacing the other.

Both the ORC and the OCM store Occupant Classification System (OCS) calibration data, which they transfer to one another when one of them is replaced. If both are replaced at the same time, an irreversible fault will be set in both modules and the OCS may malfunction and cause personal injury or death.

If equipped with OCS, the Seat Weight Sensor is a sensitive, calibrated unit and must be handled carefully. Do not drop or handle roughly. If dropped or damaged, replace with another sensor. Failure to do so may result in occupant injury or death.

If equipped with OCS, the front passenger seat must be handled carefully as well. When removing the seat, be careful when setting on floor not to drop. If dropped, the sensor may be inoperative, could result in occupant injury, or possibly death.

If equipped with OCS, when the passenger front seat is on the floor, no one should sit in the front passenger seat. This uneven force may damage the sensing ability of the seat weight sensors. If sat on and damaged, the sensor may be inoperative, could result in occupant injury, or possibly death.

DISARMING/DEPOWERING THE SYSTEM

➡**The air bag warning indicator illuminates when the correct Restraints Control Module (RCM) fuse is removed and the ignition is ON.**

➡**The Supplemental Restraint System (SRS) must be fully operational and free of faults before releasing the vehicle to the customer.**

1. Turn all vehicle accessories OFF.
2. Turn the ignition OFF.
3. At the Smart Junction Box (SJB), located at the RH side of the center console, remove the cover and RCM fuse 31 (10A) from the SJB.
4. Turn the ignition ON and monitor the air bag warning indicator for at least 30 seconds. The air bag warning indicator will remain lit continuously (no flashing) if the correct RCM fuse has been removed. If the air bag warning indicator does not remain lit continuously, remove the correct RCM fuse before proceeding.
5. Turn the ignition OFF.

✳✳ WARNING

Always deplete the backup power supply before repairing or installing any new front or side air bag supplemental restraint system (SRS) component and before servicing, removing, installing, adjusting or striking components near the front or side impact sensors or the restraints control module (RCM). Nearby components include doors, instrument panel, console, door latches, strikers, seats and hood latches.

6. To deplete the backup power supply energy, disconnect the battery ground cable and wait at least 1 minute. Be sure to disconnect auxiliary batteries and power supplies (if equipped).

✳✳ WARNING

Failure to follow these instructions may result in serious personal injury or death in the event of an accidental deployment.

7. Disconnect the battery ground cable and wait at least one minute.

ARMING/REPOWERING THE SYSTEM

1. Turn the ignition from OFF to ON.
2. Install RCM fuse 31 (10A) to the SJB and install the cover.

✳✳ WARNING

Make sure no one is in the vehicle and there is nothing blocking or placed in front of any air bag module

when the battery is connected. Failure to follow these instructions may result in serious personal injury in the event of an accidental deployment.

3. Connect the battery ground cable.
4. Prove out the SRS as follows: Turn the ignition from ON to OFF. Wait 10 seconds, then turn the ignition back ON and monitor the air bag warning indicator with the air bag modules installed.

a. The air bag indicator will light continuously for approximately 6 seconds and then turn off.

b. If an air bag SRS fault is present, the air bag indicator will: - fail to light. - remain lit continuously. - flash.

c. The flashing might not occur until approximately 30 seconds after the ignition has been turned from the OFF to the ON position. This is the time required for the RCM to complete the testing of the SRS.

d. If the air bag indicator is inoperative and a SRS fault exists, a chime will sound in a pattern of 5 sets of 5 beeps.

e. If this occurs, the air bag warning indicator and any SRS fault discovered must be diagnosed and repaired.

f. Clear all continuous DTCs from the RCM and Occupant Classification System Module (OCSM) using a scan tool.

DRIVE TRAIN

AUTOMATIC TRANSAXLE FLUID

DRAIN AND REFILL

1. Raise and safely support the vehicle.

➡ **If an internal problem is suspected, drain the transaxle fluid through a paper filter. A small amount of metal or friction particles may be found from normal wear. If an excessive amount of metal or friction material is present, the transaxle will need to be overhauled.**

2. Remove the transaxle fluid drain plug and allow the transaxle fluid to drain.
3. Install the transaxle fluid drain plug. Tighten to 106 inch. lbs. (12 Nm).
4. Fill the transaxle with clean transaxle fluid.
5. Start the engine and let it run for 3 minutes. Move the range selector lever into each gear position.
6. Repeat Steps 2, 3, 4 and 5 two more times. After the transaxle fluid has been changed a total of 3 times, check the transaxle fluid level for a final time, making sure that the transaxle fluid is at the correct level.

FILTER REPLACEMENT

1. Note the orientation of the fluid filter to the fluid pump.
2. Remove the filter from the pump.
3. Rotate the filter 90 degrees clockwise.
4. Pull the filter out of the pump.
5. Remove the magnet from the filter.
6. Installation is the reverse of the removal procedure.

MANUAL TRANSAXLE ASSEMBLY

REMOVAL & INSTALLATION

See Figures 17 through 21.

1. Raise and safely support the vehicle.
2. Remove the air cleaner assembly.
3. Remove the battery tray.
4. Remove the wiring harness bracket nut.
5. Disconnect the reverse switch and Vehicle Speed Sensor (VSS) connectors. Detach the VSS pushpin retainers from the shift cable bracket.
6. Disconnect the shift cables at their connecting ends.
7. Remove the 3 shift cable bracket bolts. Position the bracket and shift cables aside.
8. Position the clutch hydraulic tube aside.

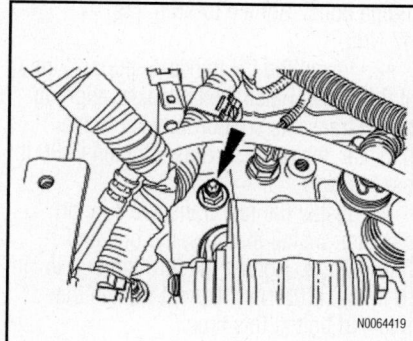

Fig. 17 Remove the wiring harness bracket nut.

9. Remove the clutch hydraulic tube bracket-to-transaxle bolt.
10. Disconnect the clutch hydraulic tube from the clutch slave cylinder.
11. Plug the hydraulic tube. Position the clutch hydraulic tube aside.
12. Using a proper set of engine support bar and adapters, support the engine.
13. Remove the 3 LH transaxle support insulator bracket nuts. Loosen, but do not remove the through bolt.
14. Remove the transaxle rear support insulator bolt and the 2 nuts.
15. Remove the RH engine mount bolt.
16. Remove the 3 upper transaxle-to-engine bolts.

✳✳ CAUTION

Do not use heat to loosen a seized wheel nut or damage to the wheel and wheel bearing can occur.

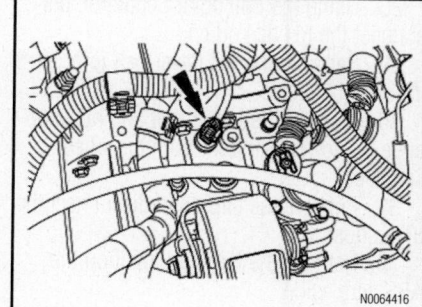

Fig. 18 Disconnect the reverse switch and Vehicle Speed Sensor (VSS) connectors. Detach the VSS pushpin retainers from the shift cable bracket.

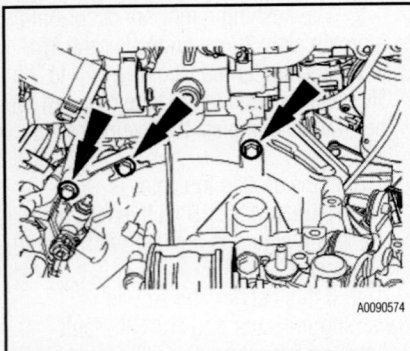

Fig. 19 Remove the 3 upper transaxle-to-engine bolts.

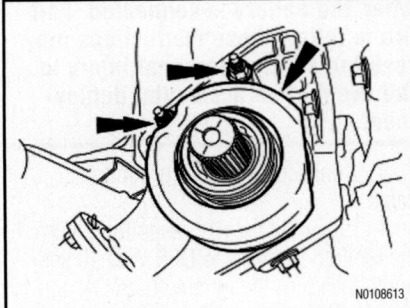

Fig. 20 Remove the 2 intermediate shaft retaining nuts. Remove the heat shield and intermediate shaft.

17. Remove the wheel and tire.

18. Remove the 6 LH splash shield screws. Remove the LH lower splash shield.

19. Remove the crossmember:

  a. Remove the 3 front-to-aft crossmember bolts and the transaxle front support insulator through bolt.

  b. Remove the front-to-aft crossmember and the transaxle front support insulator.

  c. Remove the transaxle right support insulator through bolt and the mount.

20. Remove the starter motor assembly.

21. Disconnect the LH stabilizer bar link.

22. Using the Ball Joint Separator, disconnect the LH tie-rod end. Separate the LH lower ball joint from the wheel knuckle.

23. Remove the lower pinch bolt and nut. Separate the lower ball joint from the wheel knuckle.

24. Remove the clip, then disconnect the brake hose.

25. Remove the bolt and position the ABS wire aside.

26. Using the Slide Hammer with the Halfshaft (Plate) Remover, remove the LH front drive halfshaft from the differential. Support the halfshaft with a length of mechanic's wire.

27. Disconnect the RH stabilizer bar link.

28. Using the Ball Joint Separator, disconnect the RH tie-rod end.

29. Separate the RH lower ball joint from the wheel knuckle.

30. Remove the pinch bolt and nut. Separate the lower ball joint from the wheel knuckle.

31. Remove the clip, then disconnect the brake hose.

32. Remove the bolt and position the ABS wire aside.

33. Using a brass drift to strike the RH halfshaft in the indicated area, separate and remove the halfshaft from the intermediate shaft. Support the halfshaft with a length of mechanic's wire.

34. Remove the 2 intermediate shaft retaining nuts. Remove the heat shield and intermediate shaft.

35. Working in the engine compartment, use the Engine Support Bar to raise the engine up 1.0 in. (25 mm), lowering the transaxle side downward.

36. Remove 2 lower transaxle-to-engine bolts.

✷✷ WARNING

Secure the assembly to the jack. Avoid any obstructions while lowering and raising the jack. Contact with obstructions may cause the assembly to fall off the jack, which may result in serious personal injury.

37. Position the transaxle jack under the transaxle.

38. Remove the remaining 4 transaxle-to-engine bolts.

39. Remove the transaxle.

To install:

➡**Do not lubricate the splines on the input shaft.**

40. Raise and position the transaxle to the engine.

41. Install the 2 short transaxle-to-engine bolts. Tighten to 35 ft. lbs. (47 Nm).

42. Install the LH transaxle support insulator bracket. Raise the transaxle, aligning the LH transaxle support bracket to the insulator. Install the 3 nuts. Tighten to 30 ft. lbs. (40 Nm).

43. Install the rear transaxle support insulator: install the nuts, the bolt and through bolt. Tighten the through bolt to 76 ft. lbs. (103 Nm). Do not tighten the nuts and bolt at this time.

44. After removing the transaxle jack, install 4 long transaxle-to-engine bolts. Tighten to 35 ft. lbs. (47 Nm).

45. Tighten the LH transaxle support insulator through bolt to specification. Tighten to 76 ft. lbs. (103 Nm).

46. Tighten the transaxle rear support insulator fasteners to 59 ft. lbs. (80 Nm).

47. Remove the Engine Support Bar.

48. Install the RH engine support bolt. Tighten to 66 ft. lbs. (90 Nm).

49. Install the 3 upper transaxle-to-engine bolts. Tighten to 35 ft. lbs. (47 Nm).

50. Install the intermediate shaft, heat shield and the 2 nuts. Tighten to 20 ft. lbs. (27 Nm).

51. Install the RH halfshaft onto the intermediate shaft.

52. Connect the RH ball joint. Tighten to 46 ft. lbs. (63 Nm).

53. Connect the RH stabilizer bar link. Tighten to 41 ft. lbs. (55 Nm).

54. Connect the RH tie-rod end. Tighten to 41 ft. lbs. (55 Nm).

55. Install the brake hose and the clip. Position the ABS wire then install the bolt.

56. Install the LH halfshaft.

57. Connect the LH ball joint. Tighten to 46 ft. lbs. (63 Nm).

58. Connect the stabilizer bar link. Tighten to 41 ft. lbs. (55 Nm).

59. Connect the RH tie-rod end. Tighten to 41 ft. lbs. (55 Nm).

60. Connect the brake hose and install the clip. Position the ABS wire then install the bolt.

61. Install the starter motor assembly.

62. Install the front-to-aft crossmember. Position the crossmember. Install the 2 bolts and a nut. Tighten the bolts to 66 ft. lbs. (90 Nm), and tighten the new nut to 129 ft. lbs. (175 Nm).

63. Install the transaxle front support insulator through bolt. Tighten to 85 ft. lbs. (115 Nm).

64. Install the crossmember.

65. Position the crossmember. Install the bolts. Tighten to 85 ft. lbs. (115 Nm).

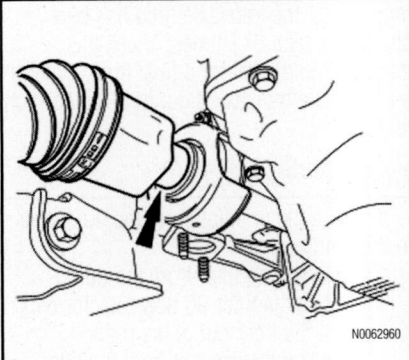

Fig. 21 Install the RH halfshaft onto the intermediate shaft.

66. Connect the clutch hydraulic tube. Connect the clutch hydraulic tube from the clutch slave cylinder.

67. Install the clutch hydraulic tube bracket-to-transaxle bolt. Tighten to 22 inch lbs. (2.5 Nm).

68. Install the shift cable bracket. Install the 3 bolts. Tighten to 16 ft. lbs. (22 Nm).

69. Connect the shift cables.

70. Connect the reverse switch and Vehicle Speed Sensor (VSS) connectors.

71. Install the wiring harness bracket nut. Tighten to 106 inch lbs. (12 Nm).

72. Install the battery tray.

73. Install the air cleaner assembly.

✳✳ CAUTION

Do not spill brake fluid on painted or plastic surfaces or damage to the surface may occur. If brake fluid is spilled onto a painted or plastic surface, immediately wash the surface with water.

74. Fill and bleed the clutch.

75. Install the LH side splash shield.

76. Install the wheel and tire.

CLUTCH

REMOVAL & INSTALLATION

See Figure 22.

1. Remove the transaxle. See "Manual Transaxle" section.

2. Using a flywheel holding tool (303-103, or equivalent), lock the flywheel to the engine.

3. Check the diaphragm spring fingers for discoloration, scoring, bent or broken segments and spring ends that are higher or lower than the rest.

✳✳ WARNING

The clutch disc and clutch pressure plate are heavy and may fall if not held when the bolts are removed. Failure to follow this instruction may result in serious personal injury.

➡**Loosen the bolts evenly to prevent pressure plate damage.**

4. Remove the 6 bolts, clutch pressure plate and clutch disc.

To install:

5. Use a suitable cleaning solution to remove any oil film from the clutch pressure plate friction surface.

Inspect the clutch pressure plate surface for burn marks, scores, flatness or ridges.

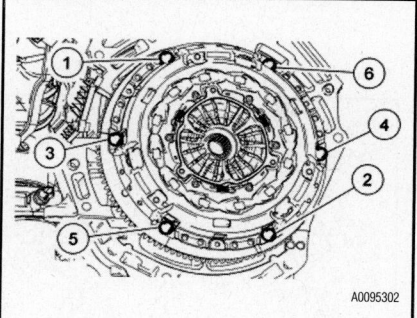

Fig. 22 Tighten to 21 ft. lbs. (29 Nm) in the sequence shown.

➡**If the clutch disc is saturated with oil, inspect the rear engine crankshaft seal for leakage. If leakage is found, install a new seal prior to clutch disc installation.**

6. Use an emery cloth to remove minor imperfections in the clutch disc lining surface.

7. Install a new clutch disc if any of the following conditions are present:
- Oil or grease saturation.
- Worn or loose facings.
- Warpage or loose rivets at the hub.
- Wear or rust on the splines.

8. Check the clutch disc runout and wear.

9. Using a clutch aligner tool (308-020, or equivalent), position the clutch disc on the flywheel.

10. Position the clutch pressure plate on the flywheel and install the 6 clutch pressure plate bolts. Tighten to 21 ft. lbs. (29 Nm) in the sequence shown.

11. Install the transaxle.

BLEEDING

✳✳ CAUTION

Do not spill brake fluid on painted or plastic surfaces or damage to the surface may occur. If brake fluid is spilled onto a painted or plastic surface, immediately wash the surface with water.

1. Raise and safely support the vehicle.

2. Check the fluid level of the brake/clutch reservoir. Fill the reservoir with the specified fluid to the MAX mark.

3. Remove the 7 splash shield bolts and the pushpin, then remove the splash shield.

4. Remove the bleeder screw cover and attach a rubber hose to the bleeder screw. Place the other end of the rubber hose into a clear container partially filled with the specified brake fluid.

5. Have an assistant depress and release the clutch pedal 5 to 7 times. Fully depress the clutch pedal to the floor and hold down.

6. With the clutch pedal depressed, loosen the bleeder screw until fluid and air escape the system. With the clutch being held to the floor, tighten the bleeder screw. Repeat Steps 5 and 6 until no air comes from the rubber hose.

7. Tighten the bleeder screw to 71 inch lbs. (8 Nm).

8. Install the bleeder screw cover.

9. Position the splash shield and install the 7 bolts and the pushpin.

10. Check the fluid level of the reservoir. Fill the reservoir with the specified fluid to the MAX mark. Install the reservoir cap.

11. Depress and release the clutch pedal several times.

12. Test the clutch system for normal operation.

TRANSFER CASE ASSEMBLY (POWER TRANSFER UNIT)

REMOVAL & INSTALLATION

See Figure 23.

1. Raise and safely support the vehicle.

2. Drain the Power Transfer Unit (PTU). See "Draining & Refilling" in this section.

3. Remove the front RH intermediate shaft.

4. Remove the driveshaft.

5. Remove the 4 bolts and the crossmember brace.

6. If equipped with 3.0L, remove the catalytic converter.

7. For all vehicles, remove the 3 PTU heat shield bolts and the PTU heat shield.

8. If equipped with 2.5L, remove the 2 exhaust bracket nuts. Remove the 2 bolts and the exhaust bracket.

9. For all vehicles, remove the 6 PTU-to-engine bracket bolts and the bracket. Disconnect the PTU vent tube and position it aside. Remove the 4 PTU-to-transaxle bolts.

10. Remove the PTU.

➡**If necessary, install a new RH differential fluid seal.**

11. Position the Power Transfer Unit (PTU) to the transaxle.

12. Install the 3 PTU-to-transaxle bolts. Tighten to 52 ft. lbs. (70 Nm).

13. Install the PTU-to-transaxle bolt (M10). Tighten to 35 ft. lbs. (48 Nm).

14. Connect the PTU vent tube.

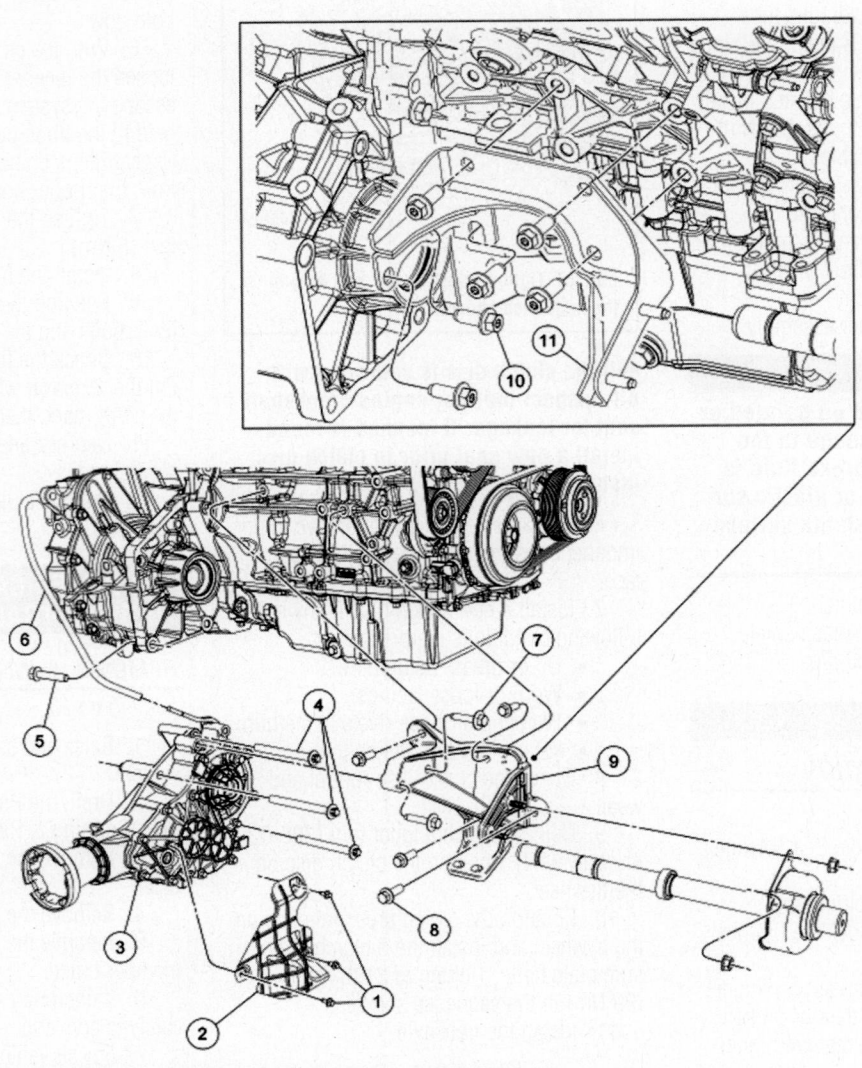

1. Power Transfer Unit (PTU) heat shield bolts (3 required)
2. PTU heat shield
3. PTU
4. PTU -to-transaxle bolts (3 required)
5. PTU -to-transaxle bolt (M10)
6. Vent tube
7. PTU bracket-to- PTU bolt (2.5L) (2 required)
8. PTU bracket-to-engine bolt (2.5L) (4 required)
9. PTU -to-engine bracket (2.5L)
10. PTU -to-engine bracket bolts (3.0L) (6 required)
11. PTU -to-engine bracket (3.0L)

N0092214

Fig. 23 Removing the Power Transfer Unit (PTU)/Transfer Case

15. Install the PTU -to-engine bracket and the 6 bracket bolts. Tighten to 35 ft. lbs. (48 Nm).

16. Install the catalytic converter.

17. Install the PTU heat shield and the 3 PTU heat shield bolts. Tighten to 97 inch lbs. (11 Nm).

18. Install the crossmember brace and the 4 bolts. Tighten to 30 ft. lbs. (40 Nm).

19. Install the driveshaft.

20. Install the front RH intermediate shaft.

21. Install the exhaust as required.

22. Fill the PTU.

23. Check the transaxle fluid level.

DRAINING & REFILLING

➡**The Power Transfer Unit (PTU) must be drained and refilled any time the PTU has been submerged in water.**

➡**This unit is lubricated for life and is not to be checked unless a leak is suspected or a repair is necessary.**

1. Raise and safely support the vehicle.

2. Remove the drain plug and drain the fluid.

3. Apply silicone sealant to the drain plug threads and install the drain plug. Tighten to 124 inch lbs. (14 Nm).

4. Check that the fluid level is even with

the bottom of the filler hole with the vehicle on flat, level ground.

5. Remove the fill plug and fill the PTU with specified lubricant.

6. Apply silicone sealant to the fill plug and install the plug. Tighten to 25 ft. lbs. (34 Nm).

FRONT DRIVESHAFT

REMOVAL & INSTALLATION

See Figure 24.

➡**The Escape Hybrid driveshaft is longer than the driveshaft in the Escape/Mariner and is not interchangeable.**

1. Raise and safely support the vehicle.
2. Remove the ground strap bolt.

➡**Do not reuse the Constant Velocity (CV) joint bolts and washers. Install new bolts and washers or damage to the vehicle may occur.**

3. Remove and discard the 6 CV joint-to-Power Transfer Unit (PTU) flange bolts and 3 washers.
4. Index-mark the front driveshaft to the center bearing.

➡**Do not reuse the bolts and cap straps for the center U-joint. Install new bolts and cap straps or damage to the vehicle may occur.**

➡**There is a difference in the length of the head of the replacement cap strap bolts from the production bolts. The longer head pinion bolts can be used in either location.**

5. Remove and discard the 4 U-joint cap strap bolts and 2 cap straps and remove the front driveshaft.
6. Index-mark the pinion and yoke to the driveshaft.

➡**Do not reuse the bolts for the rear U-joint flange. Install new bolts.**

7. Remove and discard the 4 rear driveshaft-to-pinion flange bolts.
8. With the help of an assistant, remove the center bearing support nuts and the driveshaft.

➡**If a driveshaft is installed and driveshaft vibration is encountered after installation, index the driveshaft.**

To install:

9. Installation is reverse of the removal procedure.
10. Tighten the new fasteners as follows:
    • Center bearing support nuts and the driveshaft: 41 ft. lbs. (55 Nm).

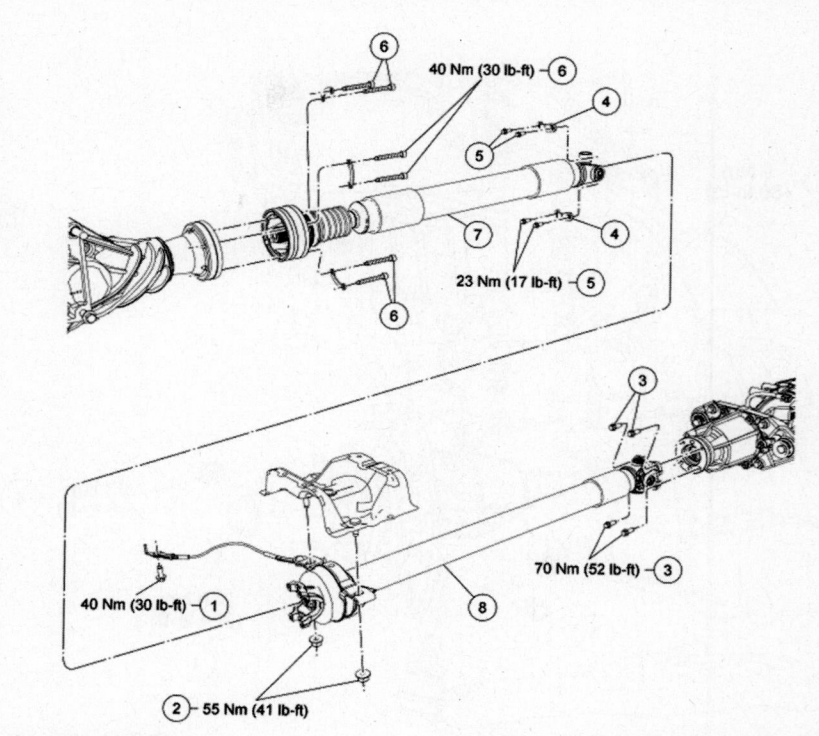

1. Ground strap bolt
2. Center bearing support nuts (2 required)
3. Rear driveshaft-to-pinion flange bolts (4 required)
4. U-joint cap straps (2 required)
5. U-joint cap strap bolts (4 required)
6. CV joint-to-Power Transfer Unit (PTU) flange bolt and washer assembly (3 required)
7. Front driveshaft
8. Rear driveshaft

N0067838

Fig. 24 Removing the driveshaft

• 4 rear driveshaft-to-pinion flange bolts: 52 ft. lbs. (70 Nm).
• 4 U-joint cap strap bolts and 2 cap straps: 17 ft. lbs. (23 Nm).
• CV joint-to-Power Transfer Unit (PTU) flange bolts and 3 washers: 30 ft. lbs. (40 Nm).
• Ground strap bolt: 30 ft. lbs. (40 Nm).

FRONT HALFSHAFT

REMOVAL & INSTALLATION

See Figures 25 through 27.

1. Raise and safely support the vehicle.
2. Remove the wheel and tire.
3. Remove and discard the wheel hub nut.
4. Remove the wheel speed sensor bolt and position the sensor aside.
5. Remove and discard the lower ball joint bolt and nut.

⁂⁂ **CAUTION**

Use care when releasing the lower arm and wheel knuckle into the resting position or damage to the ball joint seal and/or Constant Velocity (CV) joint boot may occur.

6. Separate the lower arm from the wheel knuckle.
7. Using a proper Front Hub Remover (205-D070 or equivalent), separate the halfshaft from the wheel hub.
8. For the left halfshaft, using a slide hammer, remove the LH halfshaft from the differential.
9. For the right halfshaft, using a brass drift to strike the RH halfshaft in the indicated area, separate and remove the halfshaft.

To install:

10. For the left halfshaft, position the LH halfshaft so the splines line up with the differential side gear splines. Push the halfshaft into the differential side gear.

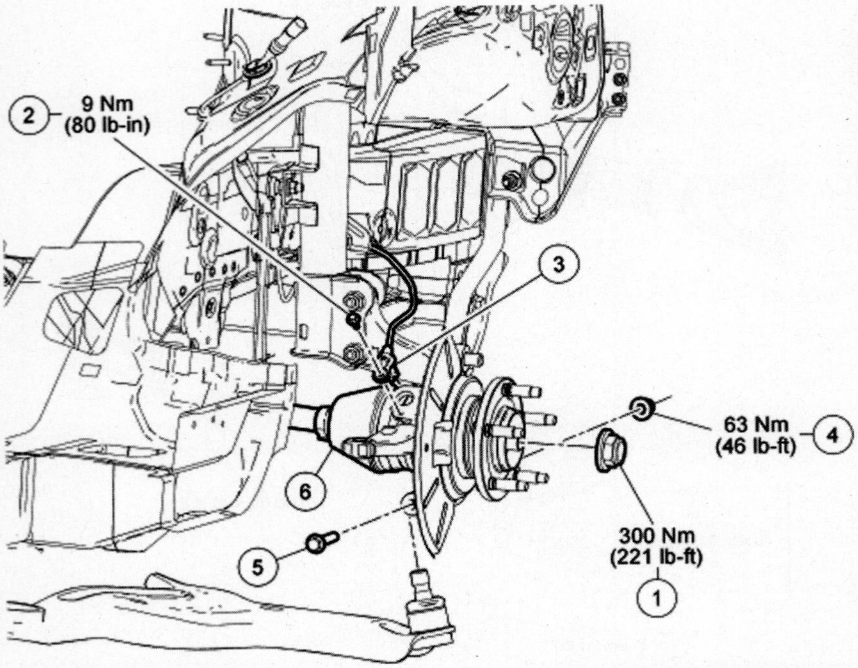

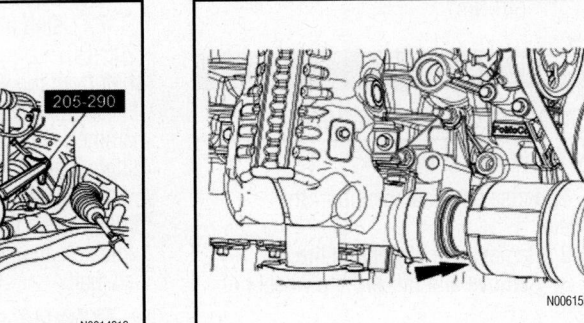

1. Wheel hub nut
2. Wheel speed sensor bolt
3. Wheel speed sensor
4. Lower ball joint nut
5. Lower arm bolt
6. Halfshaft assembly

N0096800

Fig. 25 Removing the front halfshaft (RH halfshaft shown; LH shaft similar)

➡**When seated correctly, the halfshaft bearing retainer circlip can be felt as it snaps into the differential side gear groove.**

11. For the right halfshaft, align the RH halfshaft with the splines of the intermediate shaft and push the halfshaft in until the cir-clip locks the shafts together. Apply a thin coat of the specified grease to the splines of the intermediate shaft.

12. For either halfshaft, using the half-shaft installer, install the halfshaft into the front wheel hub.

13. Position the lower arm into the front wheel knuckle.

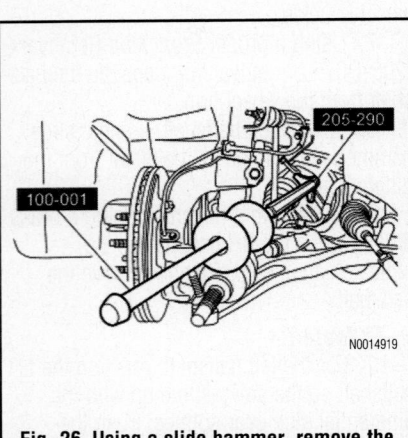

N0014919

Fig. 26 Using a slide hammer, remove the LH halfshaft from the differential.

Fig. 27 For the right halfshaft, using a brass drift to strike the RH halfshaft in the indicated area, separate and remove the halfshaft.

N0061550

14. Install the new lower ball joint bolt and nut. Tighten to 46 ft. lbs. (63 Nm).

15. Install the wheel speed sensor and bolt. Tighten to 80 inch lbs. (9 Nm).

✳✳ CAUTION

Do not tighten the front wheel hub nut with the vehicle on the ground. The nut must be tightened to specification before the vehicle is lowered onto the wheels. Wheel bearing damage will occur if the wheel bearing is loaded with the weight of the vehicle applied.

➡**Apply the brake to keep the halfshaft from rotating.**

16. Install the new wheel hub nut. Tighten to 222 ft. lbs. (300 Nm).

17. Install the front tires and wheels.

18. Check and fill the transaxle fluid as necessary.

REAR AXLE FLUID

DRAIN & REFILL

➡**These steps assume refilling the axle/differential housing following repair.**

1. Remove the filler plug and fill the rear axle with 2.43 pts. (1.15L) of rear axle lubricant.

2. Check that the fluid level is 0.118–0.196 in. (3–5 mm) below the bottom of the filler hole.

3. Install the filler plug and tighten to 20 ft. lbs. (27 Nm).

REAR AXLE HOUSING

REMOVAL & INSTALLATION

See Figures 28 and 29.

➡**The rear axle assembly is a balanced unit and is serviced only as an assembly. The only serviceable parts are the seals, cover and fasteners. If any other components are worn or damaged, the axle must be replaced.**

1. Raise and safely support the vehicle.

2. Index-mark the driveshaft flange and the pinion flange.

➡**Support the driveshaft.**

3. Remove and discard the 4 drive-shaft-to-drive pinion bolts and position aside the rear driveshaft.

4. Remove the rear halfshafts.

5. Position a suitable transaxle hydraulic jack to the axle housing. Securely strap the jack to the housing.

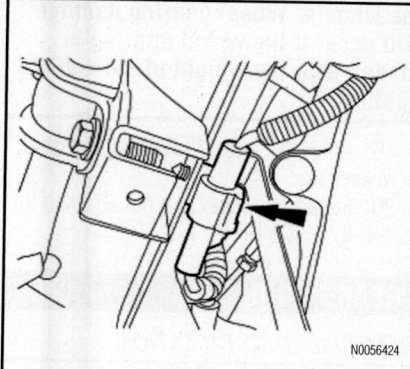

Fig. 28 Disconnect the active torque coupling electrical connector.

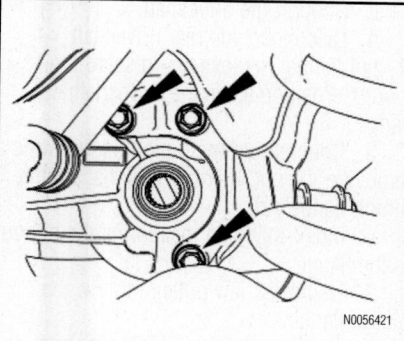

Fig. 29 Remove the 3 LH side insulator bracket-to-rear axle differential bolts.

6. Disconnect the active torque coupling electrical connector.

7. Remove the 4 differential housing-to-front insulator bracket bolts.

8. Remove and discard the LH front insulator bracket-to-subframe bolt and rotate the bracket aside.

9. Remove and discard the RH front insulator bracket-to-subframe bolt and the bracket.

10. Remove the 3 LH side insulator bracket-to-rear axle differential bolts.

11. Lower the rear axle assembly.

To install:

12. To install, reverse the removal procedure. Use only new bolts and tighten the fasteners as follows:
- 3 LH side insulator bracket-to-rear axle differential bolts: 66 ft. lbs. (90 Nm).
- RH and LH front insulator bracket-to-subframe bolt and the bracket: 66 ft. lbs. (90 Nm).
- 4 differential housing-to-front insulator bracket bolts: 66 ft. lbs. (90 Nm).
- 4 driveshaft-to-drive pinion bolts: 30 ft. lbs. (40 Nm).

REAR AXLE STUB SHAFT BEARING AND SEAL

REMOVAL & INSTALLATION
See Figure 30.

➡**There is no bearing for the stud shaft. There is a seal only.**

1. Remove the halfshaft assembly.

2. Use a Torque Converter Fluid Seal Remover and Slide Hammer to remove the stub shaft seal.

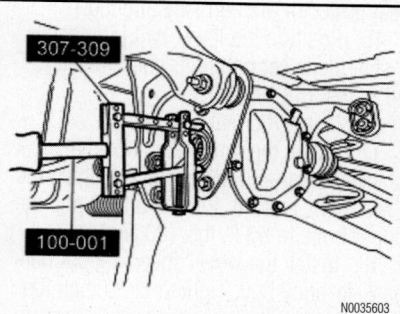

Fig. 30 Use a Torque Converter Fluid Seal Remover and Slide Hammer to remove the stub shaft seal.

To install:

3. Lubricate the new stub shaft seal with grease.

4. Using a suitable Front Axle Oil Seal Installer and Handle (205-350 and 205-153 or equivalent), install the stub shaft seal.

5. Inspect the inboard CV joint seal journal for rust or nicks/scratches prior to installing the halfshaft. If necessary, polish the seal journal with fine crocus cloth.

6. Install the halfshaft assembly.

REAR HALFSHAFT

REMOVAL & INSTALLATION
See Figures 31 through 33.

1. Note the following precautions before beginning work:
- Never pick up or hold the halfshaft by only the inner or outer Constant Velocity (CV) joint. Damage to the CV joint will occur.
- Never use a hammer to remove or install the halfshafts. Damage to the halfshaft may occur.
- Never use the halfshaft assembly as a lever to position other

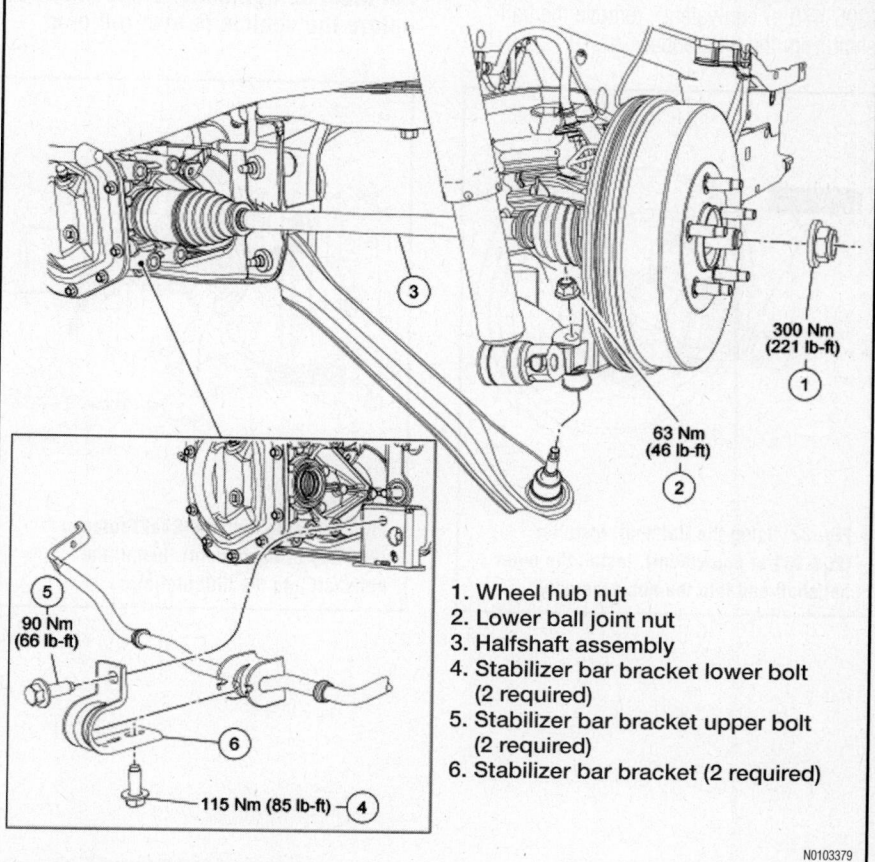

1. Wheel hub nut
2. Lower ball joint nut
3. Halfshaft assembly
4. Stabilizer bar bracket lower bolt (2 required)
5. Stabilizer bar bracket upper bolt (2 required)
6. Stabilizer bar bracket (2 required)

Fig. 31 Removing the rear halfshaft

components. Damage to the half-shaft or Constant Velocity (CV) joints may occur.

- Do not allow the boots to contact sharp edges or hot exhaust components. Damage to the halfshaft boots will occur.
- Do not drop assembled halfshafts. The impact may cut the boots from the inside without evidence of external damage.

2. Remove the coil spring. See "REAR SUSPENSION" section.

3. Remove and discard the wheel hub nut.

4. Remove the wheel speed sensor harness-to-body bolt.

5. Remove and discard the 4 stabilizer bar bracket upper and lower bolts.

6. Support the wheel knuckle.

7. Remove the nut and separate the lower ball joint.

❊❊ CAUTION

Use care and do not damage the oil seal when removing the axle half-shaft from the differential.

8. Support the halfshaft inner joint.

9. Using the Halfshaft Remover Tool (205-475 or equivalent), remove the half-shaft from the differential.

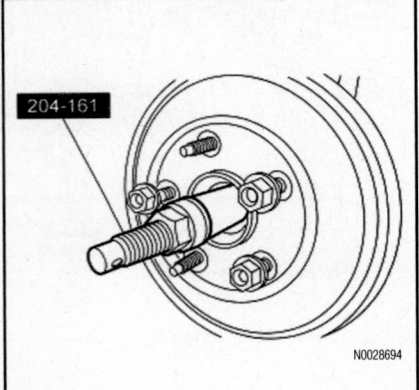

Fig. 32 Using the Halfshaft Installer (204-161 or equivalent), install the outer halfshaft end into the hub assembly.

10. Using the Front Hub Remover, separate the halfshaft from the rear wheel hub assembly.

11. Remove the halfshaft.

To install:

12. Using the Halfshaft Installer (204-161 or equivalent), install the outer halfshaft end into the hub assembly.

13. Using the Axle Seal Protector (205-816 or equivalent), install the halfshaft into the differential.

14. If the axle is equipped with the oil seal protector, make sure the oil seal lip and seal protector are correctly aligned.

15. Position the lower ball joint and install the lower ball joint nut. Tighten to 46 ft. lbs. (63 Nm).

16. Install the rear coil spring.

17. Install the 4 new stabilizer bar bracket upper and lower bolts. Tighten the lower bolts to 85 ft. lbs. (115 Nm) and the upper bolts to 66 ft. lbs. (90 Nm).

18. Install the wheel speed sensor harness-to-body bolt. Tighten to 80 inch lbs. (9 Nm).

❊❊ CAUTION

Do not tighten the rear wheel hub nut with the vehicle on the ground. The nut must be tightened to specification before the vehicle is lowered onto

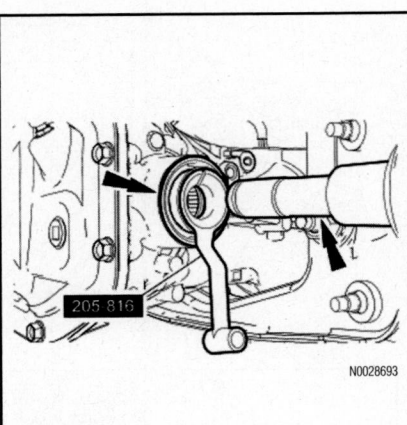

Fig. 33 Using the Axle Seal Protector (205-816 or equivalent), install the halfshaft into the differential.

the wheels. Wheel bearing damage will occur if the wheel bearing is loaded with the weight of the vehicle applied.

19. Apply the brake to keep the halfshaft from rotating.

20. Install the wheel hub nut. Tighten to 221 ft. lbs. (300 Nm).

REAR PINION SEAL

REMOVAL & INSTALLATION

1. Raise and safely support the vehicle.

2. Index-mark the driveshaft flange and the pinion flange.

3. Support the driveshaft.

4. Disconnect the rear driveshaft U-joint flange: Remove and discard the 4 bolts. Position aside the driveshaft and flange.

5. Counterhold the pinion flange while removing the nut. Remove and discard the pinion flange nut.

6. Index-mark the location of the pinion to the flange.

7. Using a 2-jaw puller, remove the pinion flange.

8. Using a proper seal remover and slide hammer, remove the pinion seal.

To install:

9. Make sure that the mating surface is clean before installing the new seal.

10. Using a proper pinion drive seal installer (205-133 or equivalent), install the pinion seal.

11. Lubricate the pinion flange with grease.

12. Line up the index marks and position the pinion flange.

13. While counterholding the drive pinion flange, install a new pinion nut. Tighten to 180 ft. lbs. (244 Nm).

14. Line up the index marks and position the rear driveshaft and U-joint flange.

15. Install the 4 new bolts. Tighten to 52 ft. lbs. (70 Nm).

ENGINE COOLING

ENGINE COOLANT

DRAIN, REFILL & BLEEDING PROCEDURE

Draining

> ❄ **CAUTION**
>
> Always allow the engine to cool before opening the cooling system. Do not unscrew the coolant pressure relief cap when the engine is operating or the cooling system is hot. The cooling system is under pressure; steam and hot liquid can come out forcefully when the cap is loosened slightly. Failure to follow these instructions may result in serious personal injury.

➡ The coolant must be recovered in a suitable, clean container for reuse. If the coolant is contaminated, it must be recycled or disposed of correctly. Using contaminated coolant may result in damage to the engine or cooling system components.

➡ Less than 80% of coolant capacity can be recovered with the engine in the vehicle. Dirty, rusty or contaminated coolant requires replacement.

1. Raise and safely support the vehicle.
2. Release the pressure in the cooling system by slowly turning the pressure relief cap one-half turn counterclockwise. When the pressure is released, remove the pressure relief cap.
3. Remove the retainers and the LH splash shield (2.5L and Hybrid engines).
4. Remove the retainers and the RH splash shield (3.0L engine).
5. Place a suitable container below the radiator draincock. Open the draincock and allow to drain. Close the draincock after draining.
6. Install the LH splash shield and the retainers (2.5L and Hybrid engines).
7. Install the RH splash shield and the retainers (3.0L engine).

Filling & Bleeding

See Figures 34 and 35.

➡ Engine coolant provides freeze protection, boil protection, cooling efficiency and corrosion protection to the engine and cooling components. In order to obtain these protections, the engine coolant must be maintained at the correct concentration and fluid level in the degas bottle. To maintain the integrity of the coolant and the cooling system:

> ❄ **WARNING**
>
> Do not add/mix orange-colored Motorcraft® Specialty Orange Engine Coolant or equivalent meeting Ford specification WSS-M97B44-D or green colored Motorcraft® Premium Engine Coolant. Mixing coolants may degrade the coolant's corrosion protection.

> ❄ **WARNING**
>
> Do not add alcohol, methanol, brine or any engine coolants mixed with alcohol or methanol antifreeze. These can cause engine damage from overheating or freezing.

1. On 2.5L engine, perform the following:
   a. Open the degas bottle cap and the bleed valve on the back of the engine water outlet (2.5L and Hybrid engines).

➡ Make sure the coolant flows from the radiator through the upper radiator hose and fills the engine.

   b. When full, coolant should flow from the bleed hole. Fill the degas bottle to the MAX fill line.

➡ Recommended coolant concentration is 50/50 ethylene glycol to distilled water. Maximum coolant concentration is 60/40 for cold weather areas. Minimum coolant concentration is 40/60 for warm weather areas.

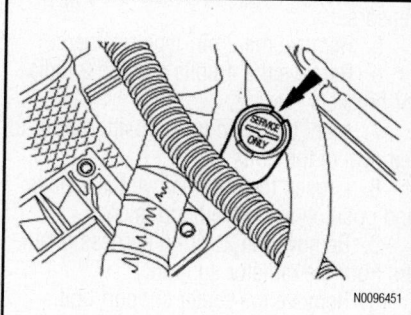

Fig. 34 Open the degas bottle cap and the bleed valve on the back of the engine water outlet—2.5L and Hybrid engines

   c. Close the degas bottle cap and the bleed valve.

> ❄ **WARNING**
>
> If the engine overheats or the fluid level drops below the minimum fill line, shut off the engine and add fluid to the degas bottle maximum fill line once the engine cools. Failure to follow these instructions may result in damage to the engine.

   d. Start the engine and let it idle for 30 minutes or until the engine reaches normal operating temperature.
   e. Allow the engine to cool and repeat the steps if necessary.
   f. Start the engine and turn the heater to the MAX position. Run the engine at 2,500 rpm for 10 minutes.
   g. Repeat steps as necessary.
   h. Check the engine coolant level in the degas bottle and fill as necessary.
2. For 3.0L engines, perform the following:
   a. Open the degas bottle cap and the bleed valve on the top of the coolant pump housing.
3. Make sure the coolant flows from the radiator through the upper radiator hose and fills the engine. When full, coolant should flow from the bleed hole.
4. Fill the degas bottle until the coolant level is between the COOLANT FILL LEVEL marks.

➡ Recommended coolant concentration is 50/50 ethylene glycol to distilled water. Maximum coolant concentration is 60/40 for cold weather areas. Minimum coolant concentration is 40/60 for warm weather areas.

   a. Close the degas bottle cap and the bleed valve.

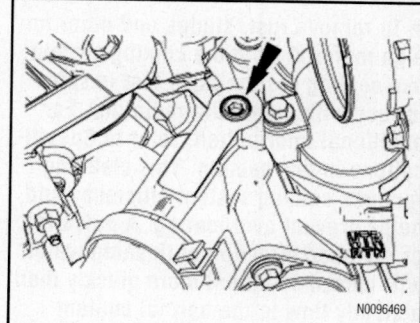

Fig. 35 Open the degas bottle cap and the bleed valve on the top of the coolant pump housing—3.0L engine

b. Select the maximum heater temperature and blower motor speed settings. Position the control to discharge air at vents in the instrument panel.

c. Start the engine and allow to idle. While engine is idling, feel for hot air at vents.

✳✳ CAUTION

If air discharge remains cool and engine coolant temperature gauge does not move, engine coolant level is low in engine and must be filled. Stop engine, allow to cool and fill cooling system. Failure to follow these instructions may result in damage to the engine.

d. Start the engine and allow to idle until normal operating temperature is reached. Hot air should discharge from vents. The engine coolant temperature gauge should maintain a stabilized reading in the middle of the NORMAL range and the upper radiator hose should feel hot to the touch.

e. Shut the engine OFF and allow to cool.

f. Check the engine for coolant leaks.

g. Check the engine coolant level in degas bottle and fill as necessary.

FLUSHING PROCEDURE

✳✳ WARNING

Always allow the engine to cool before opening the cooling system. Do not unscrew the coolant pressure relief cap when the engine is operating or the cooling system is hot. The cooling system is under pressure; steam and hot liquid can come out forcefully when the cap is loosened slightly. Failure to follow these instructions may result in serious personal injury.

➡ To remove rust, sludge and other foreign material from the cooling system, use cooling system flush that is safe for use with aluminum radiators. For additional information, refer to Specifications in this section. This cleaning restores cooling system efficiency and helps prevent overheating. A pulsating or reversed direction of flushing water will loosen sediment more quickly than a steady flow in the normal coolant flow direction. In severe cases where cleaning solvents will not clean the cooling system efficiently, it will be necessary to use the pressure flushing

method using cooling system flusher. Dispose of old coolant and flushing water contaminated with antifreeze and cleaning chemicals in accordance with local, state or federal laws.

1. Add appropriate cooling system flush to the cooling system and follow the directions on the package.

2. Drain the cooling system.

3. Remove the radiator. See "Radiator" in this section.

✳✳ CAUTION

Radiator internal pressure must not exceed 20 psi (138 kPa). Damage to the radiator can result.

4. Backflush the radiator with the radiator in an upside-down position with a high-pressure hose in the lower hose location.

➡ **On 2.5L and Hybrid engines, the thermostat and housing are serviced as an assembly.**

5. Remove the thermostat. See "Thermostat" in this section.

6. Backflush the engine. Position the high-pressure water hose into the engine through the engine return and backflush the engine.

7. Install the thermostat.

8. Install the radiator.

9. Fill and bleed the cooling system.

ENGINE FAN

REMOVAL & INSTALLATION

Except Hybrid

See Figure 36.

1. With vehicle in Neutral, position it on a hoist.

2. For the 2.5L engine, drain the cooling system.

3. Remove the front bumper cover.

4. Remove the 2 front impact severity sensors.

5. Remove the 2 pin-type retainers.

6. Remove the 4 bolts and the 2 radiator brackets.

7. Mark the hood latch position prior to removal of the bolts.

8. Loosen the nut, remove the 2 bolts and position aside the hood latch.

9. Remove the 2 wiring harness retainers from the radiator support.

10. Remove the center support bolt.

11. For the 2.5L engine, disconnect the cooling fan resistor electrical connector. Disconnect the coolant recovery hose from the radiator and position it aside.

12. Disconnect the 2 cooling fan electrical connectors and wire harness retainers.

13. Remove the 2 cooling fan bolts and the cooling fan motor and shroud.

To install:

14. To install, reverse the removal procedure.

15. Tighten the fasteners as follows:
- 2 cooling fan bolts and the cooling fan motor and shroud: 71 inch lbs. (8 Nm).
- Center support bolt: 89 inch lbs. (10 Nm).
- 2 bolts for hood latch: 80 inch lbs. (9 Nm).
- 4 bolts and the 2 radiator brackets: 89 inch lbs. (10 Nm).

16. For the 2.5L engine, fill and bleed the cooling system.

Hybrid Engines

See Figure 37.

1. With vehicle in NEUTRAL, position it on a hoist.

2. Remove the front bumper cover.

3. Remove the 2 front impact severity sensors.

4. Remove the 4 bolts and the 2 radiator brackets.

5. Mark the hood latch position prior to removal of the bolts.

6. Remove the 2 bolts, the nut and position aside the hood latch.

7. Remove the center support lower bolt.

8. Remove the bolt and the center support.

9. Remove the 2 bolts and position the auxiliary coolant pump aside.

10. Disconnect the cooling fan resistor electrical connector.

11. Disconnect the 2 cooling fan electrical connectors.

12. Remove the 6 cooling fan bolts.

➡ **Remove the LH cooling fan first and slide the RH cooling fan to the left side to remove.**

13. Remove the LH and the RH cooling fans.

To install:

14. To install, reverse the removal procedure.

15. Tighten the component fasteners as follows:
- Cooling fan bolts: 71 inch lbs. (8 Nm).
- Auxiliary coolant pump: 62 inch lbs. (7 Nm).
- Center support: 89 inch lbs. (10 Nm).

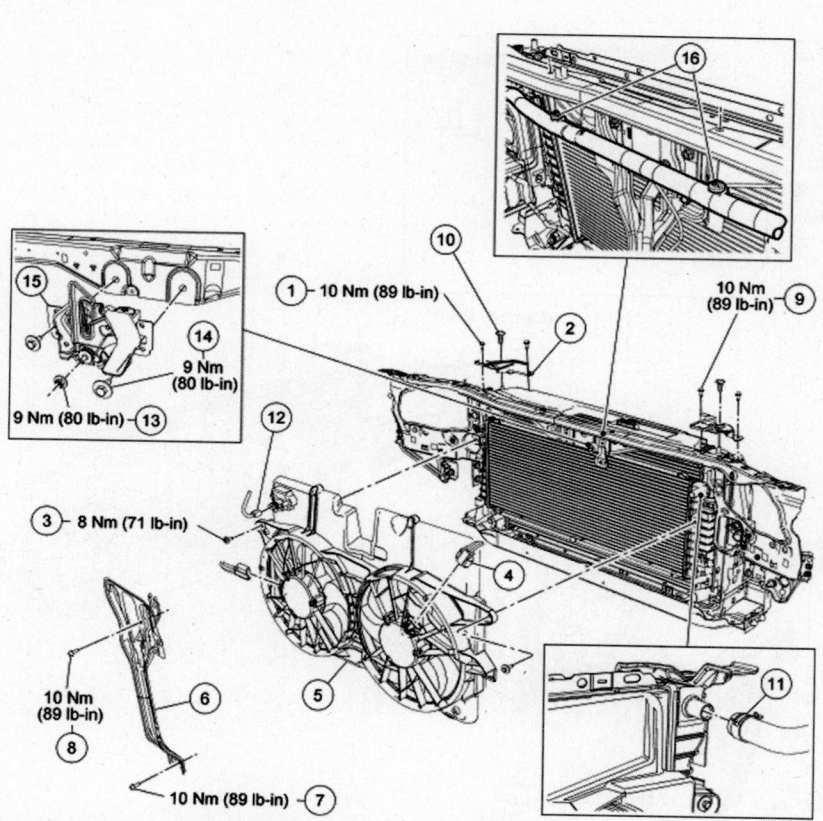

1. Radiator bracket bolt (4 required)
2. Radiator bracket (2 required)
3. Cooling fan bolt (2 required)
4. Cooling fan electrical connector (2 required)
5. Cooling fan motor and shroud
6. Center support
7. Center support lower bolt
8. Center support bolt
9. Front grille bolt (2 required)
10. Pin-type retainer (2 required)
11. Coolant recovery hose (2.5L only)
12. Cooling fan resistor electrical connector (2.5L only)
13. Hood latch nut
14. Hood latch bolt (2 required)
15. Hood latch
16. Wiring harness retainers (2 required)

N0085325

Fig. 36 Removing the engine cooling fan

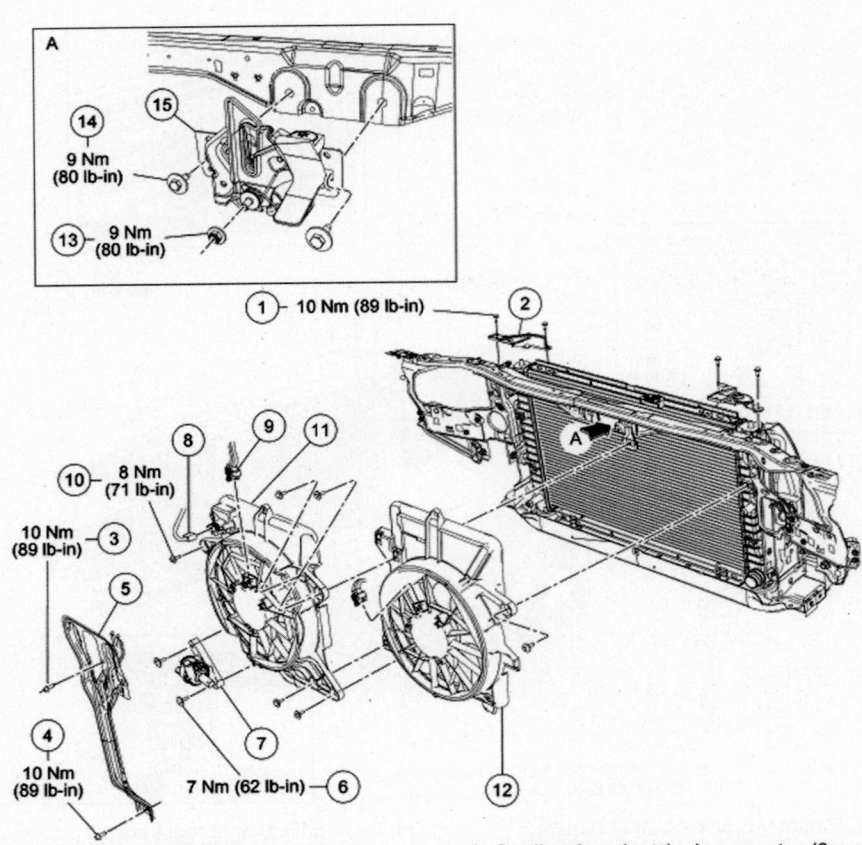

1. Radiator bracket bolt (4 required)
2. Radiator bracket (2 required)
3. Center support bolt
4. Center support lower bolt
5. Center support
6. Auxiliary coolant pump bolt (2 required)
7. Auxiliary coolant pump
8. Cooling fan resistor electrical connector
9. Cooling fan electrical connector (2 required)
10. Cooling fan bolt (6 required)
11. LH cooling fan
12. RH cooling fan
13. Hood latch nut
14. Hood latch bolt (2 required)
15. Hood latch

N0101345

Fig. 37 Exploded view of the cooling fan system—Hybrid engines

- Center support lower bolt: 89 inch lbs. (10 Nm).
- Hood latch: 80 inch lbs. (9 Nm).
- Radiator brackets: 89 inch lbs. (10 Nm).

RADIATOR

REMOVAL & INSTALLATION

2.5L Engine

1. With vehicle in Neutral, position it on a hoist.
2. Remove the cooling fan motor and shroud.
3. Disconnect the upper radiator hose from the radiator.
4. Disconnect the lower degas bottle-to-radiator hose from the radiator.
5. Disconnect the lower radiator hose from the radiator.
6. Remove the 2 A/C condenser-to-radiator bolts and position aside the A/C condenser.
7. Remove the radiator.
8. To install, reverse the removal procedure.
9. Tighten the 2 A/C condenser-to-radiator bolts to 71 inch lbs. (8 Nm).

3.0L Engine

1. Drain the cooling system.
2. Remove the cooling fan motor and shroud.
3. Disconnect the radiator-to-degas bottle hose and upper radiator hose from the radiator.
4. Disconnect the degas bottle-to-radiator hose from the radiator.
5. Disconnect the lower radiator hose from the radiator.
6. Remove the 2 A/C condenser-to-radiator bolts and position aside the A/C condenser from the radiator.
7. Remove the radiator.
8. To install, reverse the removal procedure.
9. Install 2 A/C condenser-to-radiator bolts and position aside the A/C condenser from the radiator. Tighten to 71 inch lbs. (8 Nm).
10. Fill and bleed the cooling system.

Hybrid Engines

1. Drain the cooling system.
2. Drain the Motor Electronics Cooling System (MECS).
3. Remove the cooling fan motor and shroud.
4. Disconnect the upper hose from the MECS radiator.

5. Remove the 2 MECS radiator-to-engine radiator bolts and position the MECS radiator aside.
6. Remove the 2 A/C condenser-to-radiator bolts and position the A/C condenser aside.
7. Disconnect the lower radiator hose from the radiator.
8. Disconnect the degas bottle return hose from the radiator.
9. Disconnect the engine coolant vent hose from the radiator.
10. Disconnect the upper radiator hose from the radiator.
11. Remove the radiator.

To install:

12. To install, reverse the removal procedure.
13. Tighten the component fasteners as follows:

- A/C condenser-to-radiator bolts: 89 inch lbs. (10 Nm).
- MECS radiator-to-engine radiator bolts: 53 inch lbs. (6 Nm).

14. Fill and bleed the cooling system.
15. Fill and bleed the MECS.

THERMOSTAT

REMOVAL & INSTALLATION

2.5L Engine

➡**The thermostat and thermostat housing are serviced as an assembly.**

1. Drain the cooling system.
2. Disconnect the heater hose from the thermostat housing.
3. Disconnect the lower radiator hose from the thermostat housing.

➡**The view of the thermostat housing bolts is obstructed by A/C and other engine components. However, the bolts can be removed by using 1/4-in drive hand tools.**

4. Remove the 3 bolts and thermostat housing.
5. Remove and discard the gasket.
6. To install, reverse the removal procedure.
7. Install a new gasket.
8. Tighten the 3 thermostat housing bolts to 89 inch lbs. (10 Nm).
9. Fill and bleed the cooling system.

3.0L Engine

1. Drain the cooling system.
2. Disconnect the lower radiator hose from the thermostat housing.
3. Remove the 2 bolts, thermostat housing cover, O-ring seal and thermostat.

4. To install, reverse the removal procedure.
5. Lubricate the thermostat housing O-ring seal with clean engine coolant.
6. Tighten the thermostat housing bolts to 89 inch lbs. (10 Nm).
7. Clean and inspect the O-ring seal. Install a new seal if necessary.
8. Fill and bleed the cooling system.

Hybrid Engines

➡**The thermostat and thermostat housing are serviced as an assembly.**

1. Drain the cooling system.
2. Remove the accessory drive belt tensioner.
3. Disconnect the Knock Sensor (KS) electrical connector. Detach the KS wiring harness pin-type retainer.
4. Disconnect the heater hose at the thermostat housing.
5. Disconnect the lower radiator hose at the thermostat housing.
6. Remove the 3 bolts and the thermostat housing. Remove and discard the gasket.

To install:

7. To install, reverse the removal procedure.
8. Tighten the thermostat housing bolts to 89 inch lbs. (10 Nm).
9. Install a new gasket.
10. Fill and bleed the cooling system.

WATER PUMP

REMOVAL & INSTALLATION

2.5L Engine

1. Drain the cooling system.
2. Loosen the 3 coolant pump bolts.
3. Remove the accessory drive belt.
4. Remove the 3 bolts and the coolant pump pulley.
5. Remove the 3 bolts and the coolant pump.
6. Remove and discard the O-ring seal.
7. To install, reverse the removal procedure.
8. Lubricate the new O-ring seal with clean engine coolant.

➡**Make sure the coolant pump is correctly seated to the engine block before installing and tightening the fasteners, or damage to the coolant pump may occur.**

9. Tighten the 3 coolant pump bolts to 15 ft. lbs. (20 Nm).
10. Tighten the 3 pulley bolts to 89 inch lbs. (10 Nm).

11. Fill and bleed the cooling system.

3.0L Engine

1. Drain the cooling system.
2. Remove the air cleaner outlet pipe.
3. Disconnect the lower radiator hose from the thermostat housing.
4. Remove the coolant pump belt.
5. Remove the 3 bolts and the coolant pump.
6. Remove and discard the gasket.

To install:

7. Using a new gasket, install the coolant pump and the 3 bolts. Tighten to 89 inch lbs. (10 Nm).
8. Install the coolant pump belt.
9. Connect the lower radiator hose to the thermostat housing.

10. Install the air cleaner outlet pipe.
11. Fill and bleed the cooling system.

Hybrid Engines

1. Drain the cooling system.
2. Remove the degas bottle.
3. Remove the accessory drive belt.
4. Remove the 3 bolts and the coolant pump pulley.

❋❋ CAUTION

Make sure the coolant pump is correctly seated to the engine block before installing and tightening the fasteners, or damage to the coolant pump may occur.

5. Remove the 3 bolts and the coolant pump. Remove and discard the O-ring seal.

To install:

6. To install, reverse the removal procedure.
7. Lubricate the O-ring seal with clean engine coolant.
8. Install the 3 bolts and the coolant pump, with a new O-ring seal. Tighten the bolts to 89 inch lbs. (10 Nm).
9. Install the 3 bolts and the coolant pump pulley. Tighten to 15 ft. lbs. (20 Nm).
10. Lubricate the O-ring seal with clean engine coolant.
11. Fill and bleed the cooling system.

ENGINE ELECTRICAL

12-VOLT BATTERY

REMOVAL & INSTALLATION

Except Hybrid

❋❋ WARNING

Batteries contain sulfuric acid and produce explosive gases. Work in a well-ventilated area. Do not allow the battery to come in contact with flames, sparks or burning substances. Avoid contact with skin, eyes or clothing. Shield eyes when working near the battery to protect against possible splashing of acid solution. In case of acid contact with skin or eyes, flush immediately with water for a minimum of 15 minutes, then get prompt medical attention. If acid is swallowed, call a physician immediately. Failure to follow these instructions may result in serious personal injury.

❋❋ WARNING

Always lift a plastic-cased battery with a battery carrier or with hands on opposite corners. Excessive pressure on the battery end walls may cause acid to flow through the vent caps, resulting in personal injury and/or damage to the vehicle or battery.

➡Because the engine is electronically controlled by the PCM, some control conditions are maintained by power from the battery. When the battery is disconnected or a new battery is

installed, the engine must relearn its idle and fuel trim strategy for optimum driveability and performance. Allow the engine to idle for one minute. The relearning process automatically completes as the vehicle is driven. The vehicle may need to be driven 10 mi. (16 km). If the engine is not allowed to relearn its idle trim, the idle quality may be adversely affected until the idle trim is eventually relearned. Additionally, to account for customer driving habits and conditions, the automatic transaxle must relearn its adaptive strategy. Optimal shifting resumes within a few hundred kilometers (miles) of operation. The clock and the preset radio stations must be reset once the battery is connected.

1. Disconnect the battery.
2. Remove the 2 battery hold-down nuts.
3. Remove the battery hold-down clamp.
4. Remove the battery cover (if equipped).
5. Remove the battery.
6. To install, reverse the removal procedure.
7. Tighten the hold-down nuts to 80 inch lbs. (9 Nm).

Hybrid

➡Because the engine is electronically controlled by the PCM, some control conditions are maintained by power from the battery. When the battery is disconnected or a new battery is installed, the engine must relearn its idle and fuel trim strategy for optimum

BATTERY SYSTEM

driveability and performance. Allow the engine to idle for one minute. The relearning process automatically completes as the vehicle is driven. The vehicle may need to be driven 16 km (10 mi). If the engine is not allowed to relearn its idle trim, the idle quality may be adversely affected until the idle trim is eventually relearned. Additionally, to account for customer driving habits and conditions, the automatic transmission must relearn its adaptive strategy. Optimal shifting resumes within a few hundred kilometers (miles) of operation. The clock and the preset radio stations must be reset once the battery is connected.

1. Disconnect the battery.
2. Remove the air cleaner assembly.
3. Remove the battery wedge clamp and bolt.
4. Remove the battery.
5. Remove the battery wedge clamp and bolt.
6. To install, reverse the removal procedure and tighten the battery bolt to 80 inch lbs. (9 Nm).

12-VOLT BATTERY DISCONNECT, RECONNECT & RELEARN PROCEDURE

❋❋ WARNING

Always deplete the backup power supply before repairing or installing any new front or side air bag supplemental restraint system (SRS) component and before servicing, removing, installing, adjusting or

striking components near the front or side impact sensors or the restraints control module (RCM). Nearby components include doors, instrument panel, console, door latches, strikers, seats and hood latches.

Refer to the "AIR BAG (SUPPLEMENTAL RESTRAINT SYSTEM" section for location of the RCM and impact sensor(s).

➡To deplete the backup power supply energy, disconnect the battery ground cable and wait at least 1 minute. Be sure to disconnect auxiliary batteries and power supplies (if equipped).

✲✲ WARNING

Failure to follow these instructions may result in serious personal injury or death in the event of an accidental deployment.

✲✲ WARNING

Always lift a plastic-cased battery with a battery carrier or with hands on opposite corners. Excessive pressure on the battery end walls may cause acid to flow through the vent caps, resulting in personal injury and/or damage to the vehicle or battery.

✲✲ WARNING

Batteries contain sulfuric acid and produce explosive gases. Work in a well-ventilated area. Do not allow the battery to come in contact with flames, sparks or burning substances. Avoid contact with skin, eyes or clothing. Shield eyes when working near the battery to protect against possible splashing of acid solution. In case of acid contact with skin or eyes, flush immediately with water for a minimum of 15 minutes, then get prompt medical attention. If acid is swallowed, call a physician immediately. Failure to follow these instructions may result in serious personal injury.

1. Battery posts, terminals and related accessories contain lead and lead components. Wash hands after handling. Failure to follow these instructions may result in serious personal injury.

✲✲ CAUTION

If equipped with the CD6 audio unit, precautions must be taken when the battery has been disconnected. When reconnecting the battery, make sure no interruption of power occurs for 30 seconds. If power is interrupted during the first 30 seconds, permanent damage to the CD6 audio unit will result.

➡When the battery is disconnected and connected, some abnormal drive symptoms may occur while the vehicle relearns its adaptive strategy. The vehicle may need to be driven to allow the PCM to relearn the adaptive strategy values. the hybrid vehicles, a 5-minute stable idle in PARK with the A/C turned off to allow the PCM to learn the adaptive airflow values is necessary.

➡When the battery is disconnected and connected, the illumination display needs to be calibrated. After the battery is connected, rotate the dimmer switch from the lowest dim position to the full bright, dome ON position.

2. When disconnecting the battery ground cable to interrupt power to the vehicle electrical system, disconnect the battery ground cable only. It is not necessary to disconnect the positive battery cable.
3. Disconnect the negative battery cable.
4. Disconnect the positive battery cable.
5. To connect, reverse the disconnect procedure.
6. Tighten both cable nuts to 44 inch lbs. (5 Nm).

HIGH-VOLTAGE TRACTION BATTERY

REMOVAL & INSTALLATION

Hybrid Engines
See Figures 38 through 41.

✲✲ CAUTION

To prevent the risk of high-voltage shock, always follow precisely all warnings and service instructions, including instructions to depower the system. The high-voltage hybrid system utilizes approximately 300 volts DC, provided through high-voltage cables to its components and modules. The high-voltage cables and wiring are identified by orange harness tape or orange wire covering. All high-voltage components are

marked with high-voltage warning labels with a high-voltage symbol. Failure to follow these instructions may result in serious personal injury or death.

✲✲ CAUTION

Before placing the vehicle in a paint booth, the High Voltage Traction Battery (HVTB) must be removed to avoid heat damage.

The vehicle is principally powered by an internal combustion engine, much like any ordinary vehicle. However, it also transforms the energy that is normally wasted during stop and go operations into electricity (regenerative braking), which is stored in the High Voltage Traction Battery (HVTB) until the moment it is needed by the Electronically Controlled Continuously Variable Transmission (eCVT) traction motor or the 12-volt system. The traction motor is used to support the engine during acceleration or uphill driving. In low-speed driving situations, the vehicle may move under only battery power, without the internal combustion engine running. The internal combustion engine may automatically shut off when the vehicle is stopped/idling or when coasting under 30 mph and will restart when the accelerator is depressed, when the traction motor needs assistance or if the HVTB state-of-charge is low. This avoids using excess fuel when the vehicle is not in motion. The vehicle does not need to be plugged into an external source of electricity to be recharged. The energy provided by the engine and the regenerative braking, via the eCVT traction motor and generator motor, charges the HVTB.

The HVTB , located in the floor of the rear cargo area, utilizes the following components:
- HVTB
- HVTB service disconnect plug

The high-voltage system also includes the following components:
- High-voltage cable assembly
- Electronically Controlled Continuously Variable Transaxle (eCVT), including motor generators and regenerative braking.

DC/DC converter, located on the RH side of the engine compartment, above the wheel housing.

Air Conditioning Compressor Module (ACCM) and A/C compressor assembly located on the lower LH side of the engine block.

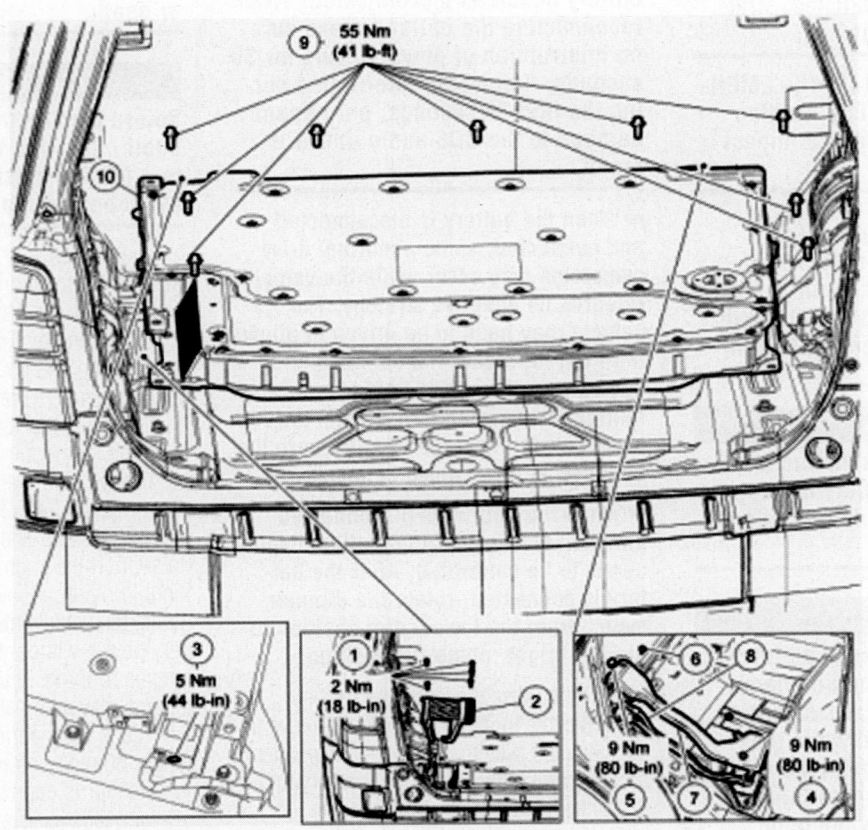

1. A/C return duct assembly screws
2. A/C return duct assembly
3. 40-pin low voltage connector bolt
4. High-voltage cables shield nuts
5. High-voltage cables shield bolt
6. High-voltage cables shield plastic rivet/screw
7. High-voltage cables shield
8. High-voltage cables electrical connector
9. High Voltage Traction Battery (HVTB) bolts
10. HVTB

N0091118

Fig. 38 Removing the High Voltage Traction Battery (HVTB)

➡**A replacement High Voltage Traction Battery (HVTB) may have a low state of charge that is insufficient to start the vehicle. If this occurs, follow the instructions for the jump start procedure in the Owner's Literature.**

1. Depower the HVTB. See "High Voltage Traction Battery Depower/Repower Procedure" in this section.

2. Remove the rear cargo area carpet insert.

3. Remove the 5 A/C return duct assembly screws. Remove the A/C return duct assembly.

➡**Due to clearance issues, the 40-pin connector must be disconnected last**

during the removal process and connected first during the installation process.

4. Loosen the bolt of the 40-pin low voltage connector.

➡**Access the shield nuts through the slotted opening in the carpet.**

5. From the right rear door opening, fold the right rear seat cushion forward and remove the 2 high-voltage cables shield nuts.

6. Fold the right rear seat backrest down and remove the high-voltage cables shield bolt, then remove the scrivet.

7. Remove the high-voltage cables shield.

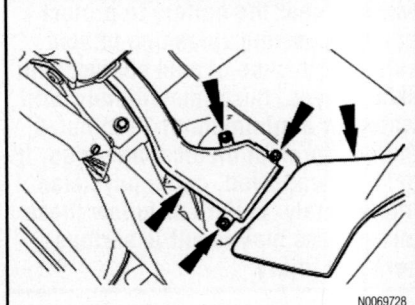

N0069728

Fig. 39 From the right rear door opening, fold the right rear seat cushion forward and remove the 2 high-voltage cables shield nuts.

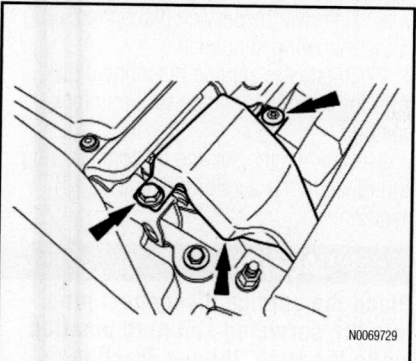

Fig. 40 Fold the right rear seat backrest down and remove the high-voltage cables shield bolt, then remove the scrivet.

8. Press the locking tab down and rotate the locking lever upward until the aligning dowels are disengaged from the locking lever to remove the high-voltage cables electrical connector.

The attaching bolts have a conductive coating on them and are serrated under the head flange. These features ground the HVTB to the vehicle, which is required for electro-magnetic compatibility. If a bolt(s) is lost or damaged, a new bolt(s) must be installed with the identical type of bolt.

9. Remove the 9 HVTB bolts.

➡**Make certain to reinstall this plug during the HVTB installation procedure to avoid NVH issues.**

10. Remove the cap plug to expose the center (rear) lifting attachment point.

11. Attach 3 M10 x 1.5 x 35 eyebolts to the 3 HVTB lift points. Install nuts onto the eye bolts to gain the proper eyebolt height. Obtain the eyebolts locally.

✷✷ CAUTION

Use chain lengths as specified. Changing the chain length may result in damage to the High Voltage Traction Battery (HVTB) or HVTB lifting points.

12. Attach the lengths of chain to the eyebolts and the lifting device.

59 cm (23 in)

34 cm (13 in)

59 cm (23 in)

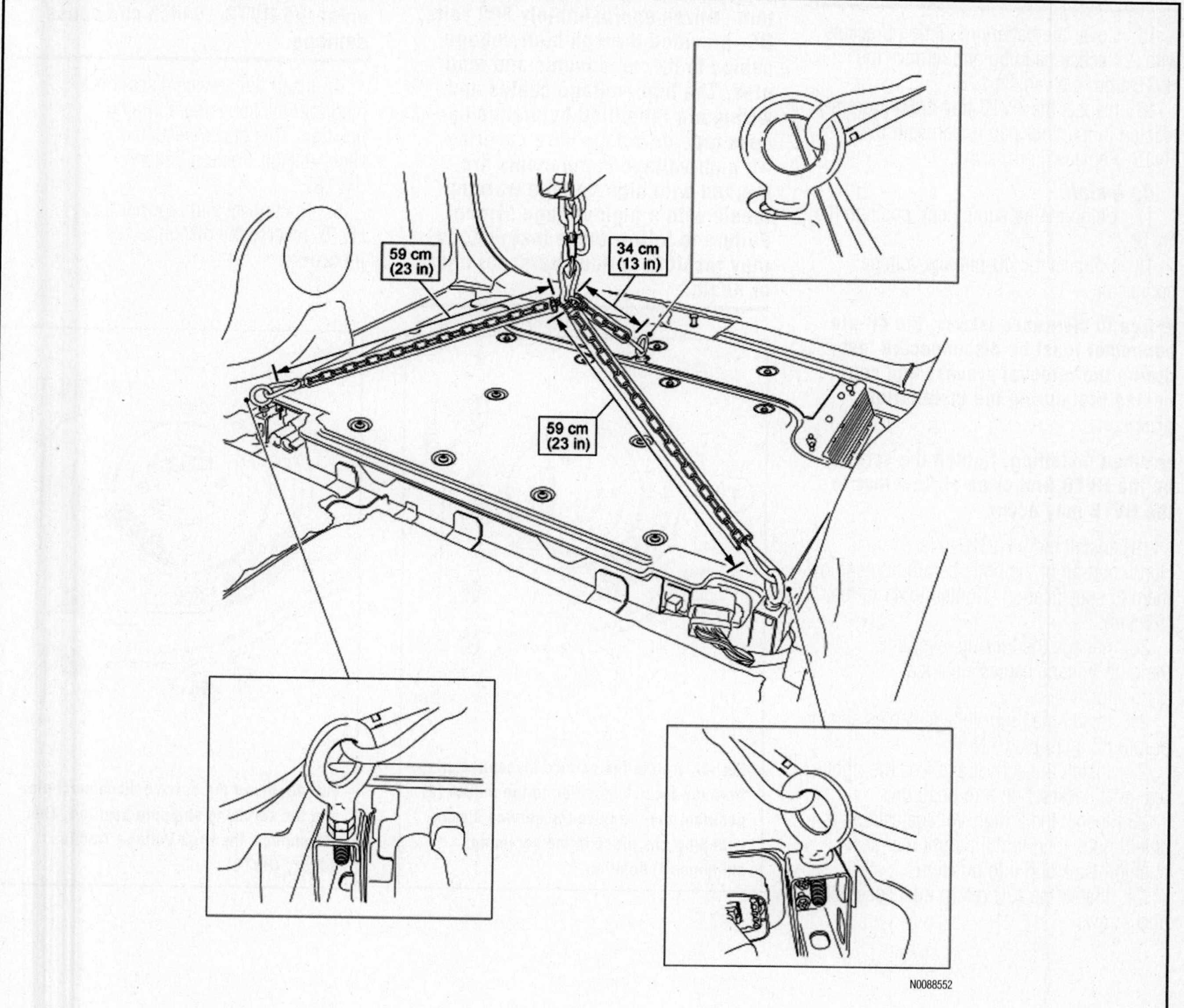

Fig. 41 Attach the lengths of chain to the eyebolts and the lifting device.

※※ CAUTION

Make certain the High Voltage Traction Battery (HVTB) does not mar or damage the interior panels during removal. There is only 6mm (0.23 in) clearance on each side.

13. With an assistant, lift the HVTB off the 2 alignment dowels using a floor crane.

14. Disconnect the 40-pin low voltage connector.

※※ CAUTION

Do not strike the headliner with the HVTB (or floor crane) during removal or damage to the headliner could occur.

15. Cover the battery mounting brackets with protective padding and remove the HVTB from the vehicle.

16. Inspect the HVTB tray drain grommet located in the floor pan underneath the HVTB. Replace if necessary.

To install:

17. Using the lift equipment, position the HVTB.

18. Connect the 40-pin low voltage connector.

➡Due to clearance issues, the 40-pin connector must be disconnected last during the removal process and connected first during the installation process.

➡When installing, tighten the screws on the HVTB first or an airflow loss to the HVTB may occur.

19. Install the 9 HVTB bolts. Hand-start all of the bolts before tightening them to specification. Tighten to 41 ft. lbs. (55 Nm).

20. Engage the locking lever and the high-voltage cables electrical connector.

21. Install the high-voltage cables shield bolt to 80 inch lbs. (9 Nm).

22. Install the scrivet and fold the right rear seat backrest up into position.

23. Install the 2 high-voltage cables shield nuts, then fold the right rear seat cushion back and into position.

24. Install the A/C return duct assembly and screws.

25. Install the rear cargo area carpet insert.

26. Repower the HVTB. See "High Voltage Traction Battery Depower/Repower Procedure" in this section.

HIGH-VOLTAGE TRACTION BATTERY DEPOWER/REPOWER PROCEDURE

Hybrid Engines

See Figures 42 and 43.

※※ CAUTION

To prevent the risk of high-voltage shock, always follow precisely all warnings and service instructions, including instructions to depower the system. The high-voltage hybrid system utilizes approximately 300 volts DC, provided through high-voltage cables to its components and modules. The high-voltage cables and wiring are identified by orange harness tape or orange wire covering. All high-voltage components are marked with high-voltage warning labels with a high-voltage symbol. Failure to follow these instructions may result in serious personal injury or death.

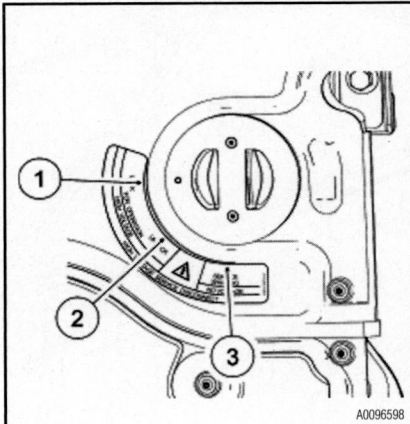

A0096598

Fig. 42 Rotate the service disconnect plug from the lock (1) position to the unlock (2) position, then remove the service disconnect plug and place in the servicing shipping (3) position.

1. Remove the service disconnect plug in the following sequence.

2. Rotate the service disconnect plug from the lock (1) position to the unlock (2) position.

3. Remove the service disconnect plug and place in the servicing shipping (3) position.

※※ CAUTION

Place the service disconnect plug into the servicing shipping position while the High Voltage Traction Battery (HVTB) is being removed and/or while the high-voltage system is having repairs carried out. If the service disconnect plug is left out and placed on the bench or toolbox, dirt or other contaminants may enter the HVTB , which can cause damage.

4. Insert the service disconnect plug into the servicing shipping position. This disconnects the High Voltage Traction Battery (HVTB).

5. To connect and repower the HVTB, reverse the disconnect procedure.

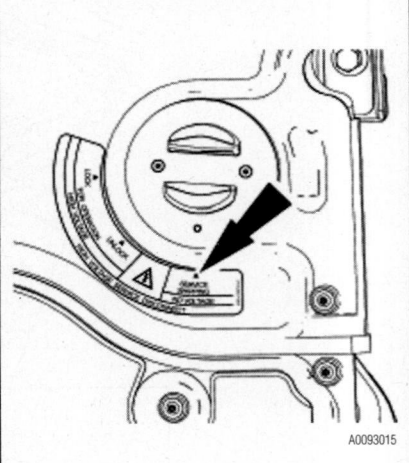

A0093015

Fig. 43 Insert the service disconnect plug into the servicing shipping position. This disconnects the High Voltage Traction Battery (HVTB).

ENGINE ELECTRICAL

CHARGING SYSTEM

GENERATOR

REMOVAL & INSTALLATION

2.5L & Hybrid Engines

See Figure 44.

❋❋ WARNING

Do not allow any metal object to come in contact with the generator housing and internal diode cooling fins. A short circuit may result and burn out the diodes. Failure to follow this instruction may result in component damage.

➡ **The radial arm adapter is a serviceable item. Do not replace the generator if the radial arm adapter is the only concern.**

1. Raise and safely support the vehicle.
2. Disconnect the battery.
3. Remove the 5 bolts, 1 pushpin and the RH lower splash shield.
4. Rotate the Front End Accessory Drive (FEAD) belt tensioner clockwise and position the accessory drive belt aside.
5. Remove the battery harness locator from the lower generator stud.
6. Remove the generator bolt.
7. Remove the 2 generator stud nuts.

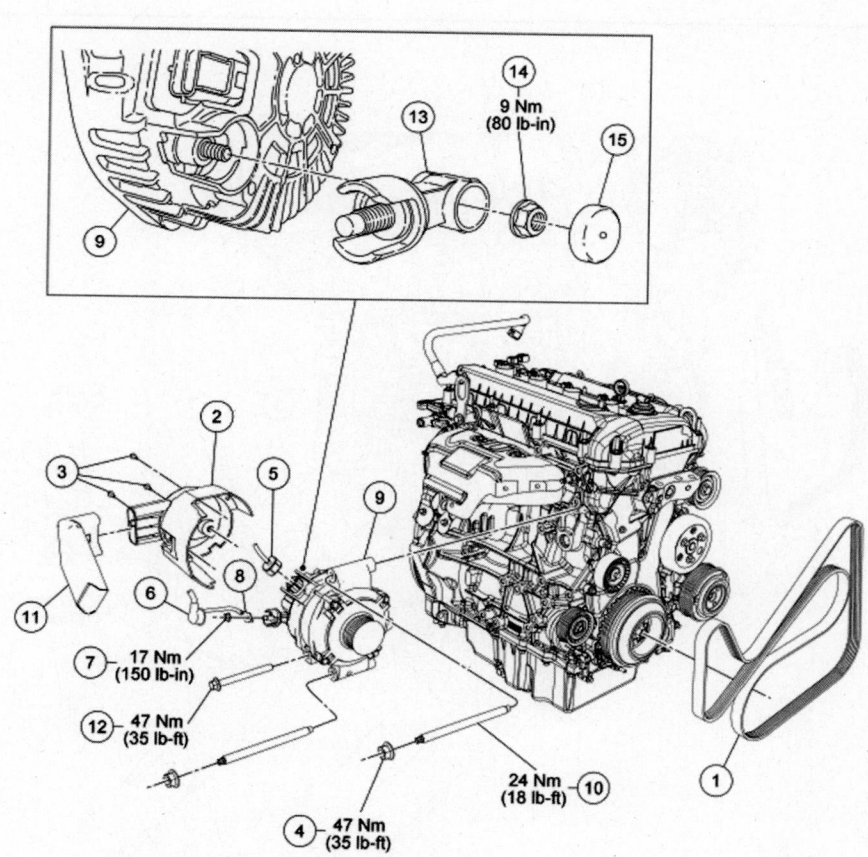

1. Front end accessory drive belt
2. Generator upper air duct
3. Generator upper air duct screws (3 required)
4. Generator stud nut (2 required)
5. Generator electrical connector
6. B+ protective cover
7. Generator B+ terminal nut
8. Generator B+ cable
9. Generator
10. Generator stud (2 required)
11. Generator lower air duct
12. Generator bolt
13. Radial arm adapter
14. Radial arm adapter nut
15. Radial arm adapter cap

N0109750

Fig. 44 Removing the generator—2.5L & Hybrid engine

8. Working from the top of the vehicle, press the locking tab to release the generator lower air duct from the generator and remove the lower air duct.

9. Position the generator B+ protective cover aside and remove the generator B+ terminal nut.

10. Position the generator B+ cable aside.

11. Disconnect the generator electrical connector.

12. Remove the generator.

13. Remove the 3 screws and the generator upper air duct.

To install:

14. Install the 3 screws and the generator upper air duct. Tighten to 35 inch lbs. (4 Nm).

15. Working from the top of the vehicle, install the generator and the generator stud.

16. Install the 2 generator stud nuts hand-tight.

17. Install the generator B+ cable and install the generator B+ terminal nut. Tighten to 150 inch lbs. (17 Nm).

18. Connect the generator electrical connector.

19. Position the generator B+ protective cover on the B+ terminal.

20. Working from under the vehicle, install the lower generator bolt hand-tight.

21. Tighten the 2 generator stud nuts. Tighten to 35 ft. lbs. (47 Nm).

22. Install the lower generator air duct.

23. Tighten the generator bolt. Tighten to 35 ft. lbs. (47 Nm).

24. Rotate the FEAD belt tensioner clockwise and position the accessory drive belt onto the pulleys.

25. Install the 5 bolts, 1 pushpin and the RH lower splash shield. Tighten to 71 inch lbs. (8 Nm).

26. Position the harness locator on the generator stud.

27. Connect the battery.

3.0L Engine

See Figure 45.

1. Raise and safely support the vehicle.

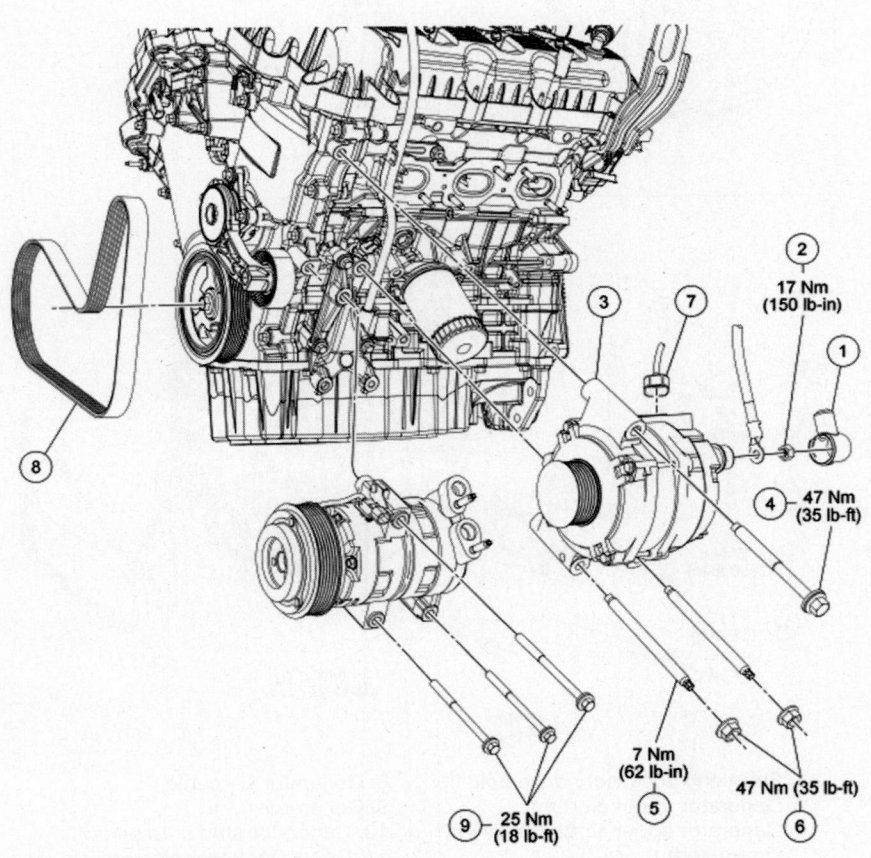

1. Generator B+ cable and B+ protective cover
2. Generator B+ terminal nut
3. Generator
4. Generator bolt
5. Generator stud (2 required)
6. Generator stud nuts (2 required)
7. Generator electrical connector
8. Front End Accessory Drive (FEAD) belt
9. A/C compressor bolts (3 required)

N0109022

Fig. 45 Removing the generator—3.0L engine

✳✳ CAUTION

Do not allow any metal object to come in contact with the generator housing and internal diode cooling fins. A short circuit may result and burn out the diodes. Failure to follow this instruction may result in component damage.

2. Disconnect the battery.

3. Remove the 5 RH lower splash shield bolts and the 1 pin-type retainer.

4. Remove the RH lower splash shield.

5. Rotate the Front End Accessory Drive (FEAD) tensioner counterclockwise and position the accessory drive belt aside.

6. Disconnect the generator electrical connector.

7. Position the generator B+ protective cover aside and remove the generator B+ terminal nut.

8. Remove the 3 A/C compressor bolts. Use a tie-strap and position the A/C compressor aside.

9. Loosen the 2 generator nuts.

10. Remove the 2 lower generator studs.

11. Remove the upper generator bolt and the generator.

To install:

12. To install, reverse the removal procedure.

13. Tighten the fasteners as follows:

- Upper generator bolt: 35 ft. lbs. (47 Nm)
- 2 lower generator studs: 62 inch lbs. (7 Nm)
- 2 generator nuts: 35 ft. lbs. (47 Nm)
- A/C compressor bolts: 18 ft. lbs. (25 Nm)
- Generator B+ terminal nut: 150 inch lbs. (17 Nm)

ALTERNATING CURRENT (AC) POWERPOINT

REMOVAL & INSTALLATION

Hybrid Engines

See Figure 46.

1. Disconnect the 12-volt battery.
2. Remove the console trim insert.
3. Disconnect the electrical connector and remove the AC power point.
4. To install, reverse the removal procedure.

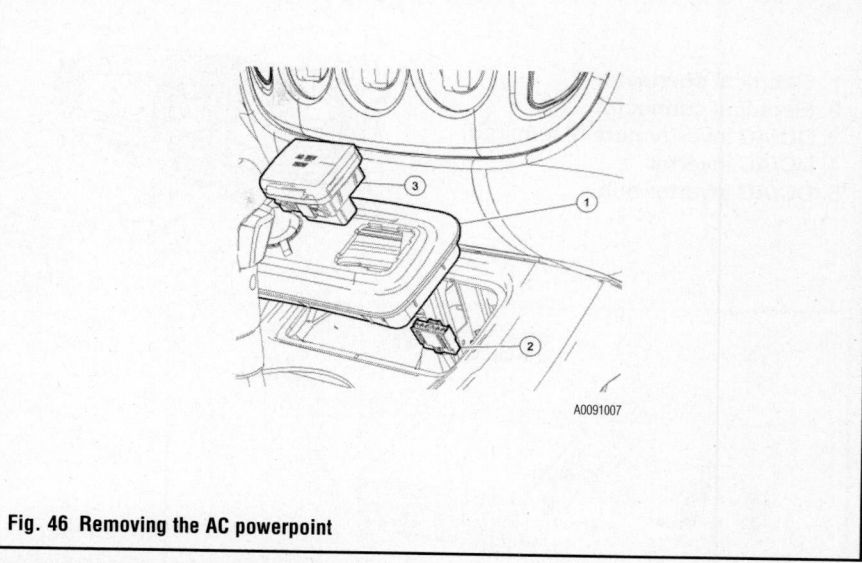

Fig. 46 Removing the AC powerpoint

DIRECT CURRENT/ ALTERNATING CURRENT (DC/AC) INVERTER

REMOVAL & INSTALLATION

Hybrid Engines

See Figures 47 and 48.

1. Disconnect the 12-volt battery.
2. Remove the lower LH center instrument panel finish panel.
3. Disconnect the electrical connectors from the DC/AC inverter.

4. Remove the 2 DC/AC inverter nuts.
5. Remove the DC/AC inverter bolt.
6. Remove the DC/AC inverter.

To install:

7. Install the DC/AC inverter.
8. Install the DC/AC inverter bolt. Tighten 97 inch lbs. (11 Nm).
9. Install the 2 DC/AC inverter nuts. Tighten to 80 inch lbs. (9 Nm).
10. Attach the connectors to the inverter.
11. Install the lower LH center instrument panel finish panel.
12. Connect the battery.

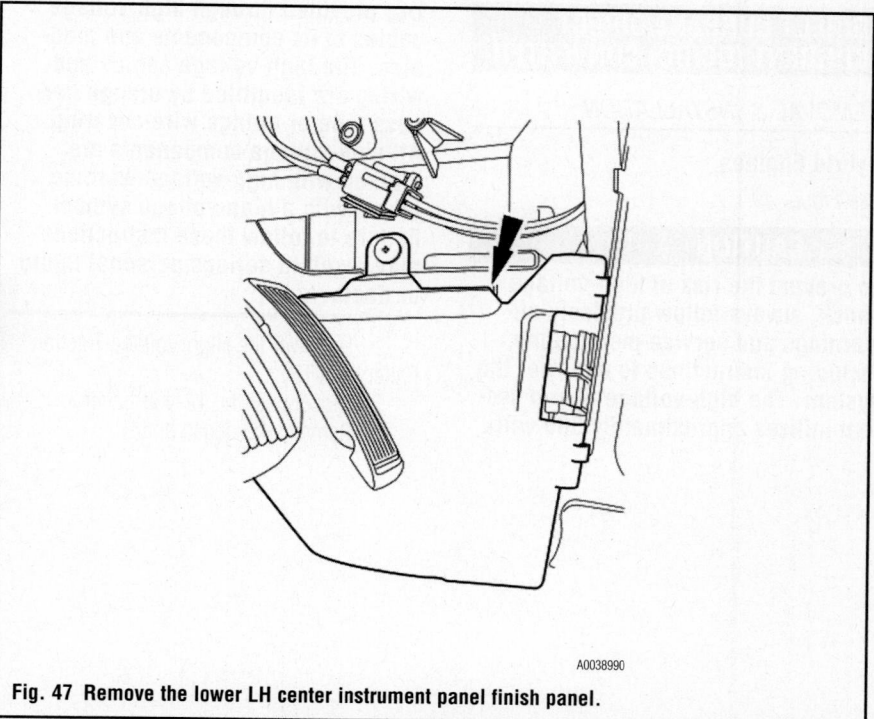

Fig. 47 Remove the lower LH center instrument panel finish panel.

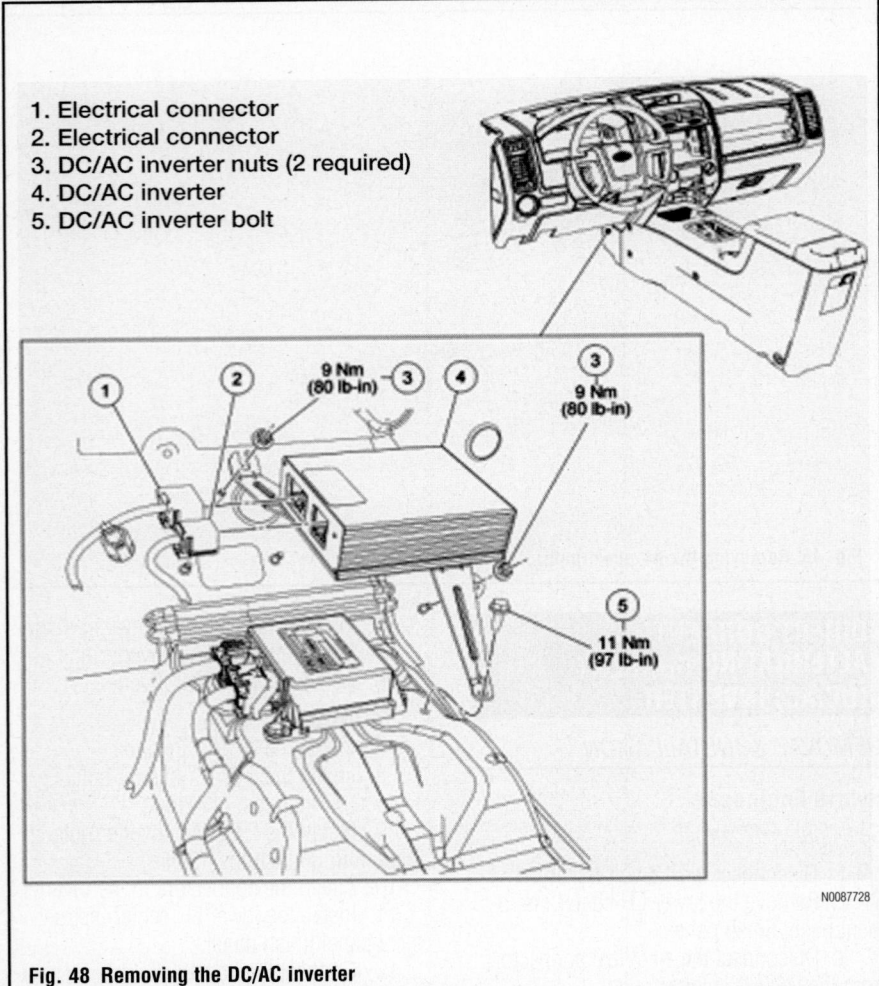

1. Electrical connector
2. Electrical connector
3. DC/AC inverter nuts (2 required)
4. DC/AC inverter
5. DC/AC inverter bolt

9 Nm (80 lb-in)
9 Nm (80 lb-in)
11 Nm (97 lb-in)

N0087728

Fig. 48 Removing the DC/AC inverter

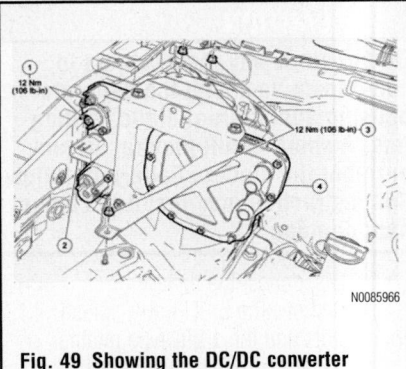

N0085966

Fig. 49 Showing the DC/DC converter location

DIRECT CURRENT/DIRECT CURRENT (DC/DC) CONVERTER

REMOVAL & INSTALLATION

Hybrid Engines
See Figure 49.

✳✳ CAUTION

To prevent the risk of high-voltage shock, always follow precisely all warnings and service instructions, including instructions to depower the system. The high-voltage hybrid system utilizes approximately 300 volts

DC, provided through high-voltage cables to its components and modules. The high-voltage cables and wiring are identified by orange harness tape or orange wire covering. All high-voltage components are marked with high-voltage warning labels with a high-voltage symbol. Failure to follow these instructions may result in serious personal injury or death.

1. Depower the High Voltage Traction Battery (HVTB).
2. Disconnect the 12-volt battery.
3. Remove the degas bottle.

4. Disconnect the 2 female pin-type retainers from the DC/DC converter bracket.
5. Press the locking clip to release the connector.
6. Clamp the Motor Electronics Cooling System (MECS) hoses to prevent coolant from leaking from the hoses during the repair.
7. Loosen the hose clamps and remove the MECS hoses from the DC/DC converter.

✳✳ WARNING

Always tighten the DC/DC converter low-voltage battery cable fasteners to specification. Loose connections may result in electrical arcing, which increases both the risk of fires and serious personal injury.

8. Remove the 2 DC/DC converter low voltage battery cable nuts and remove the low voltage battery cables.
9. Disconnect the DC/DC converter low voltage electrical connector.
10. Remove the 3 DC/DC converter nuts.
11. Remove the DC/DC converter assembly.

To install:
12. To install, reverse the removal procedure.
13. Install and tighten the 3 DC/DC converter nuts to 106 inch lbs. (12 Nm).
14. Install and tighten the 2 DC/DC converter low voltage battery cable nuts and low voltage battery cables to 106 inch lbs. (12 Nm).

ENGINE ELECTRICAL

IGNITION SYSTEM

FIRING ORDER

2.5L & Hybrid Engine

Firing order: 1–3–4–2

3.0L Engine

Firing order: 1–4–2–5–3–6

IGNITION COIL

REMOVAL & INSTALLATION

2.5L & Hybrid Engine

1. Disconnect the 4 ignition coil electrical connectors.

➡**When removing the ignition coil-on-plugs, a slight twisting motion will break the seal and ease removal.**

2. Remove the 4 bolts and the ignition coils.

3. Inspect the coil seals for rips, nicks or tears. Remove and discard any damaged coil seals.

4. To install, slide the new coil seal onto the coil until fully seated at the top of the coil.

5. Tighten the coil bolts to 71 inch lbs. (8 Nm).

6. Apply a small amount of dielectric grease to the inside of the ignition coil boots before attaching to the spark plugs.

3.0L Engine

1. On the left bank, remove the air cleaner

2. For the right bank, remove the upper intake manifold. See "Intake Manifold" in "ENGINE MECHANICAL" section.

3. Disconnect the ignition coil electrical connectors.

➡**When removing the ignition coils, a slight twisting motion will break the seal and ease removal.**

4. Remove the bolts and the ignition coils.

5. To install, reverse the removal procedure.

6. Tighten the coil bolts to 62 inch lbs. (7 Nm).

7. Apply a small amount of dielectric grease to the inside of the ignition coil boots before attaching to the spark plugs.

IGNITION TIMING

ADJUSTMENT

➡**The ignition timing is electronically controlled and no adjustment is required.**

SPARK PLUGS

REMOVAL & INSTALLATION

1. [Remove] the ignition coils. See "Ignition [Coil]" in this section.

[REMOVAL & INSTALLATION]

Only use hand tools when removing or installing the spark plugs, or damage can occur to the cylinder head or spark plug.

2. Use compressed air to remove any foreign material in the spark plug well prior to removing the spark plugs.

3. Remove the spark plugs.

4. Inspect the spark plugs for any signs of damage. Replace as needed.

5. To install, reverse the removal procedure.

6. Tighten the spark plug to:

- 2.5L & Hybrid: 106 inch lbs. (12 Nm).
- 3.0L: 133 inch lbs. (15 Nm).

7. Adjust the spark plug gap as necessary.

ENGINE ELECTRICAL

STARTING SYSTEM

STARTER

REMOVAL & INSTALLATION

2.5L & Hybrid Engine

See Figure 50.

1. Raise and safely support the vehicle.
2. Disconnect the battery ground cable.
3. Remove the 5 bolts, the pin-type retainer (not shown) and the RH splash shield.
4. Remove the starter solenoid wire nut.
5. Remove the starter solenoid battery cable nut and disconnect the starter motor solenoid terminal cover and cables.
6. Remove the ground wire nut and position aside the ground wire.
7. Remove the 2 stud bolts and the starter motor.

To install:

8. To install, reverse the removal procedure.

9. Tighten the fasteners as follows:
- Starter stud bolts: 26 ft. lbs. (35 Nm).
- Ground wire nut: 159 inch lbs. (18 Nm).
- Solenoid battery cable nut: 106 inch lbs. (12 Nm).
- Solenoid wire nut: 44 inch lbs. (5 Nm).
- Splash shield bolts: 80 inch lbs. (9 Nm).

3.0L Engine

See Figure 51.

1. Disconnect the battery ground cable.

2. Remove the starter motor solenoid wire nut.

3. Remove the starter motor solenoid battery cable nut and position aside the cables.

4. Remove the ground wire nut and position aside the ground wire.

5. Remove the 2 stud bolts and the starter motor.

To install:

6. To install, reverse the removal procedure.

7. Tighten the fasteners as follows:
- Starter bolts: 20 ft. lbs. (27 Nm).
- Ground wire nut: 159 inch lbs. (18 Nm).
- Solenoid battery cable nut: 106 inch lbs. (12 Nm).
- Solenoid wire nut: 44 inch lbs. (5 Nm).

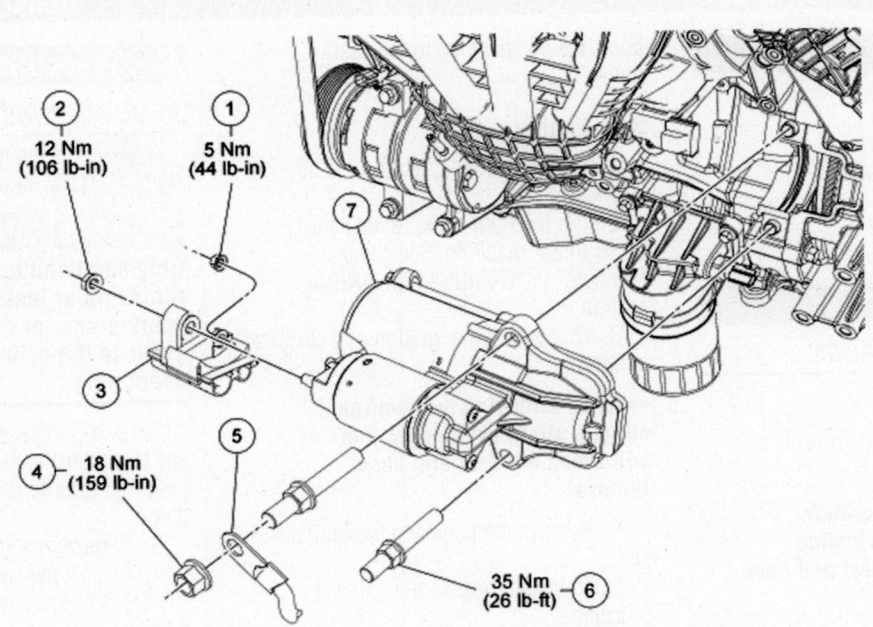

1. Starter motor solenoid wire nut
2. Starter motor solenoid battery cable nut
3. Starter motor solenoid terminal cover
4. Ground wire nut
5. Ground wire
6. Starter motor stud bolt (2 required)
7. Starter motor

N0101172

Fig. 50 Removing the starter—2.5L engine

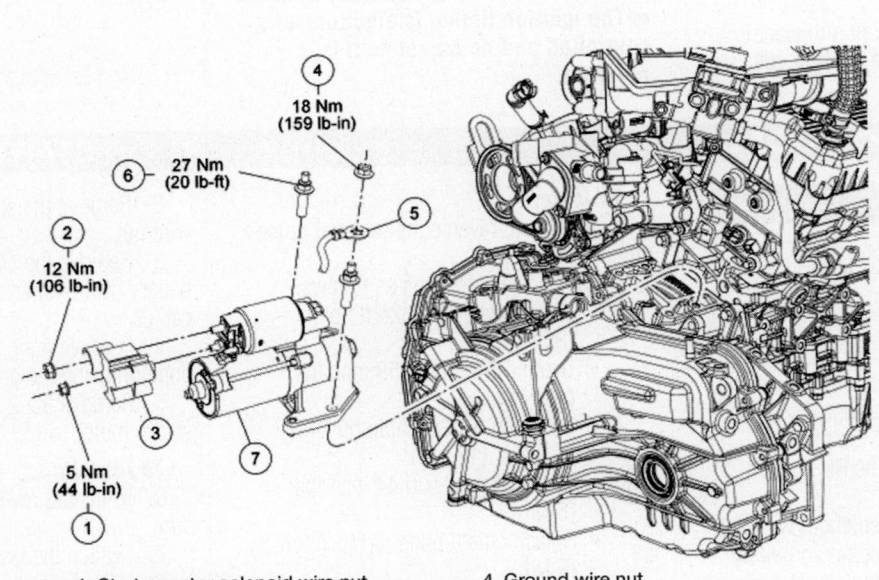

1. Starter motor solenoid wire nut
2. Starter motor solenoid battery cable nut
3. Starter motor solenoid wire terminal cover
4. Ground wire nut
5. Ground wire
6. Starter motor stud bolts (2 required)
7. Starter motor

N0086578

Fig. 51 Removing the starter—3.0L engine

ENGINE MECHANICAL

→Disconnecting the negative battery cable may interfere with the functions of the on board computer systems and may require the computer to undergo a relearning process, once the negative battery cable is reconnected.

ACCESSORY DRIVE BELTS

ACCESSORY BELT ROUTING

See Figures 52 through 54.

ADJUSTMENT

The serpentine belt utilizes a self-adjusting tensioner. No manual adjustment is required.

REMOVAL & INSTALLATION

2.5L & Hybrid Engine

See Figure 55.

1. Raise and safely support the vehicle.
2. Remove the pin-type retainer, 5 bolts and the RH splash shield.
3. Using the hex feature, rotate the accessory drive belt tensioner clockwise and remove the accessory drive belt from the coolant pump pulley.
4. Remove the accessory drive belt from the engine.
5. To install, reverse the removal procedure.

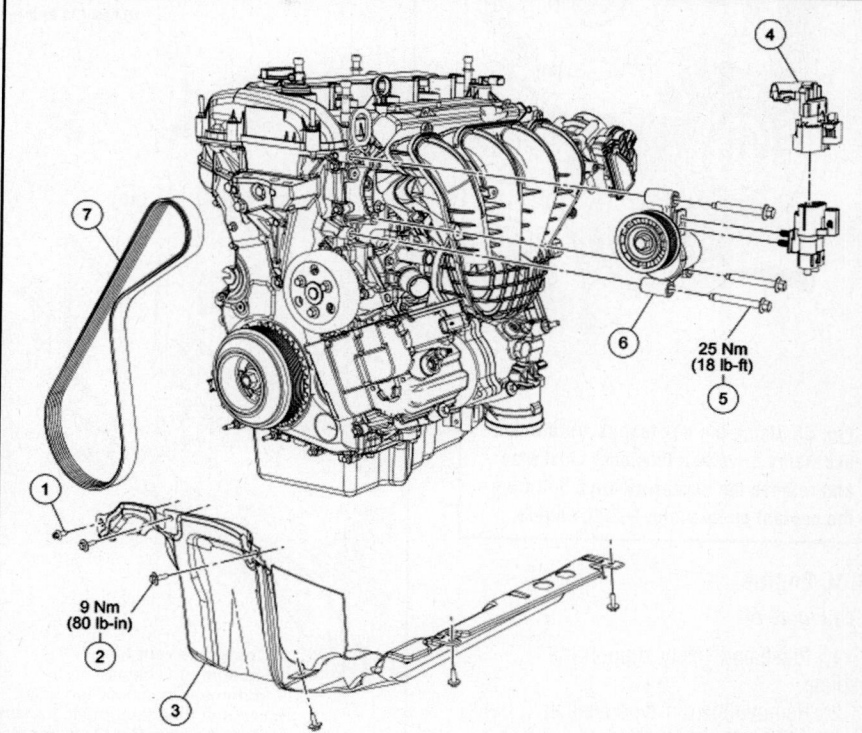

1. RH splash shield pin-type retainer
2. RH splash shield bolt (5 required)
3. RH splash shield
4. Vehicle high voltage electrical system electrical connector (2 required)
5. Accessory drive belt tensioner bolt (3 required)
6. Accessory drive belt tensioner
7. Accessory drive belt

Fig. 53 Accessory belt routing—Hybrid engine

N0101211

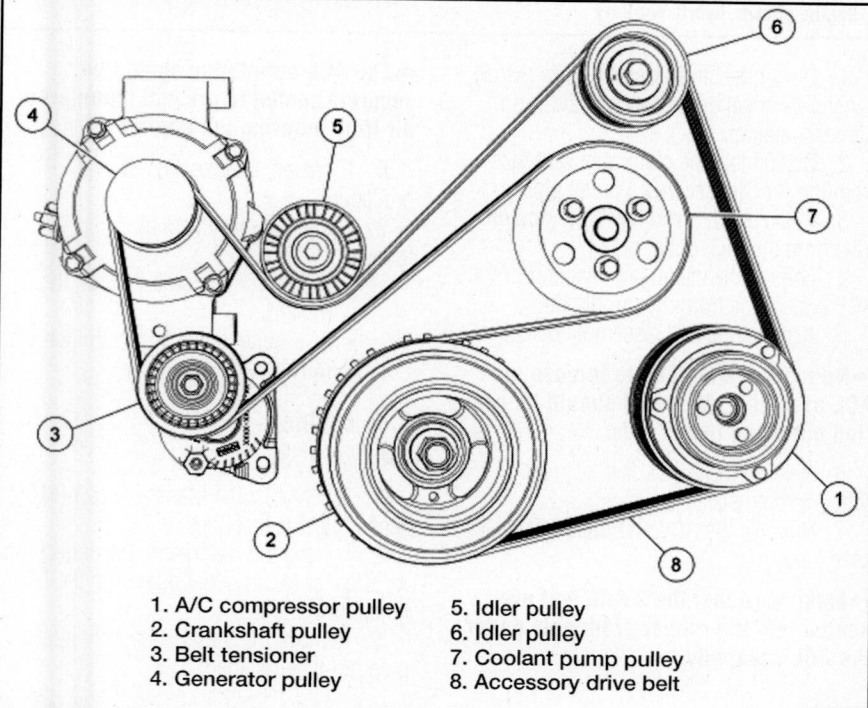

1. A/C compressor pulley
2. Crankshaft pulley
3. Belt tensioner
4. Generator pulley
5. Idler pulley
6. Idler pulley
7. Coolant pump pulley
8. Accessory drive belt

Fig. 52 Accessory belt routing—2.5L engine

N0087760

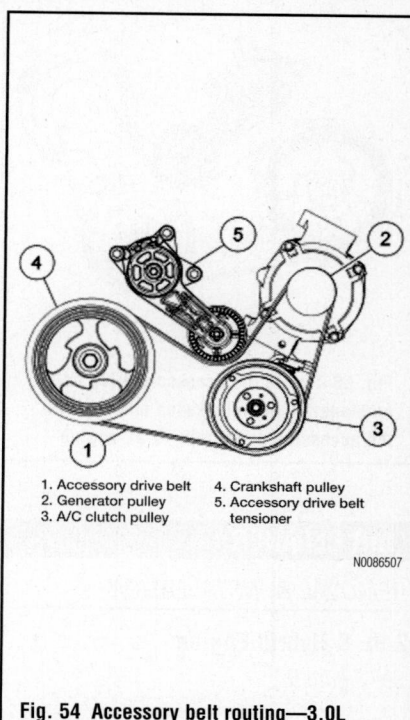

1. Accessory drive belt
2. Generator pulley
3. A/C clutch pulley
4. Crankshaft pulley
5. Accessory drive belt tensioner

Fig. 54 Accessory belt routing—3.0L engine

N0086507

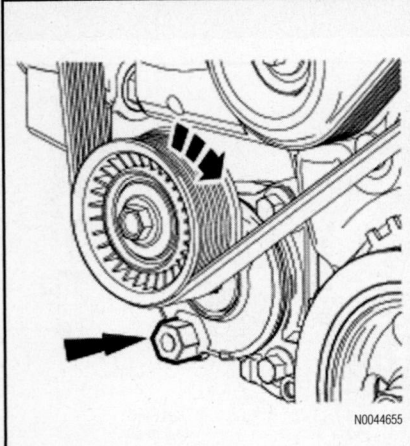

Fig. 55 Using the hex feature, rotate the accessory drive belt tensioner clockwise and remove the accessory drive belt from the coolant pump pulley—2.5L engine

3.0L Engine

See Figure 56.

1. Raise and safely support the vehicle.

2. Remove the pin-type retainer, 5 bolts and the RH lower splash shield.

3. Rotate the accessory drive belt tensioner counterclockwise and remove the accessory drive belt.

4. To install, reverse the removal procedure.

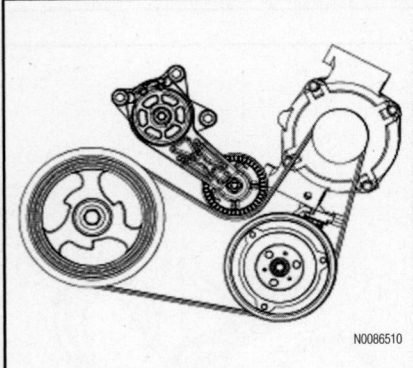

Fig. 56 Rotate the accessory drive belt tensioner counterclockwise and remove the accessory drive belt—3.0L engine

AIR CLEANER

REMOVAL & INSTALLATION

2.5L & Hybrid Engine

See Figure 57.

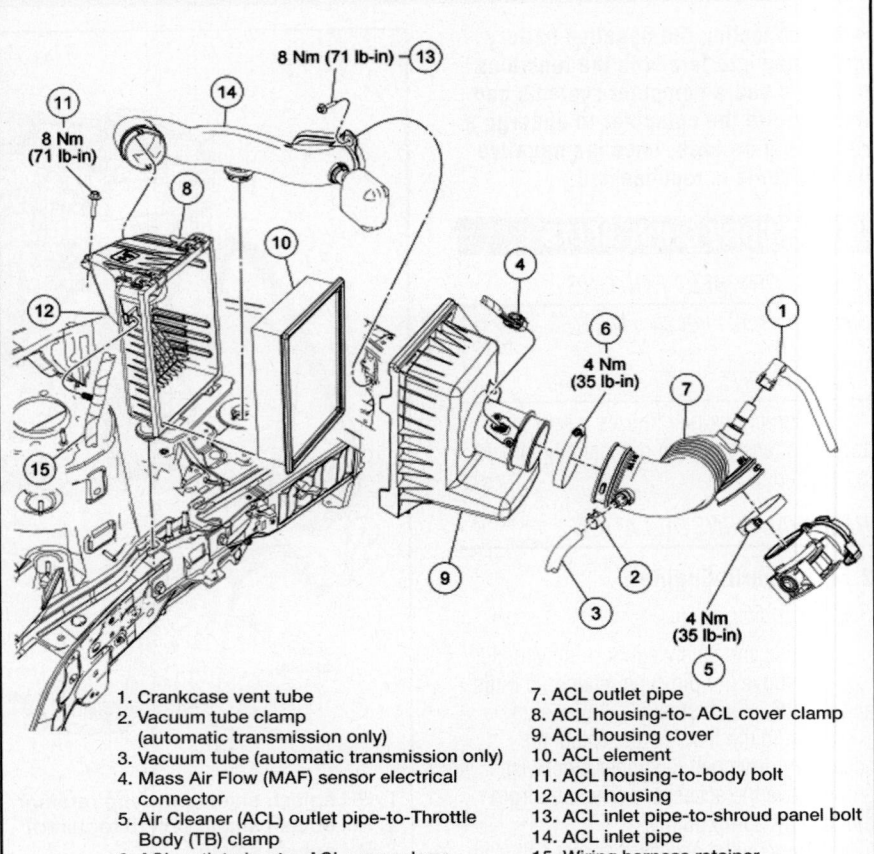

1. Crankcase vent tube
2. Vacuum tube clamp (automatic transmission only)
3. Vacuum tube (automatic transmission only)
4. Mass Air Flow (MAF) sensor electrical connector
5. Air Cleaner (ACL) outlet pipe-to-Throttle Body (TB) clamp
6. ACL outlet pipe-to- ACL cover clamp
7. ACL outlet pipe
8. ACL housing-to- ACL cover clamp
9. ACL housing cover
10. ACL element
11. ACL housing-to-body bolt
12. ACL housing
13. ACL inlet pipe-to-shroud panel bolt
14. ACL inlet pipe
15. Wiring harness retainer

Fig. 57 Exploded view of the air cleaner system components—2.5L & Hybrid engine (gasoline engine shown; hybrid similar)

1. Disconnect the Mass Air Flow (MAF) sensor electrical connector and the wiring harness retainer.

2. Disconnect the crankcase vent tube from the Air Cleaner (ACL) outlet pipe.

3. If equipped, disconnect the vacuum tube from the ACL outlet pipe.

4. Loosen the clamp and disconnect the ACL outlet pipe from the throttle body.

5. Remove the ACL assembly bolt.

➡**No tools are needed to remove the ACL assembly. Removal should be carried out using hands only.**

6. Release the 2 ACL feet from the rubber grommets.

7. Remove the ACL and outlet pipe assembly.

➡**Make sure that the 2 ACL feet are seated into the rubber grommets under the ACL assembly.**

➡**The ACL outlet pipe should be securely sealed to prevent unmetered air from entering the engine.**

8. To install, reverse the removal procedure.

9. Tighten the fasteners as follows:

- ACL assembly bolt: 71 inch lbs. (8 Nm).
- ACL outlet pipe clamp: 35 inch lbs. (4 Nm).

3.0L Engine

See Figure 58.

1. Disconnect the Mass Air Flow (MAF) sensor electrical connector.

2. Loosen the clamp and disconnect the Air Cleaner (ACL) outlet pipe from the ACL housing.

3. Remove the 3 ACL assembly intake pipe pin-type retainers.

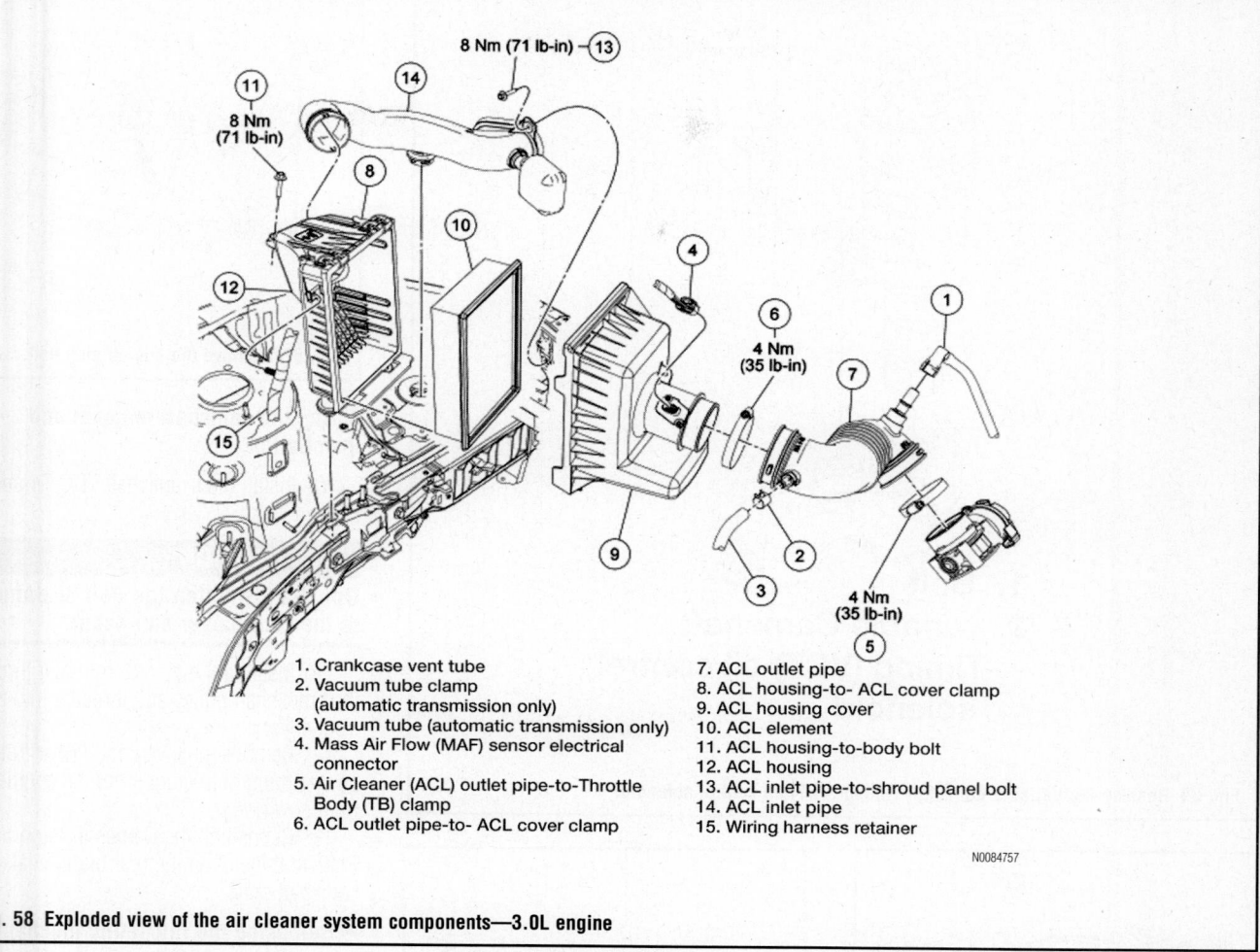

8 Nm (71 lb-in) —13

11
8 Nm
(71 lb-in)

14

8

13

12

10

4

6
4 Nm
(35 lb-in)

1

7

15

5

9

2

3

4 Nm
(35 lb-in)

5

1. Crankcase vent tube
2. Vacuum tube clamp
   (automatic transmission only)
3. Vacuum tube (automatic transmission only)
4. Mass Air Flow (MAF) sensor electrical
   connector
5. Air Cleaner (ACL) outlet pipe-to-Throttle
   Body (TB) clamp
6. ACL outlet pipe-to- ACL cover clamp

7. ACL outlet pipe
8. ACL housing-to- ACL cover clamp
9. ACL housing cover
10. ACL element
11. ACL housing-to-body bolt
12. ACL housing
13. ACL inlet pipe-to-shroud panel bolt
14. ACL inlet pipe
15. Wiring harness retainer

N0084757

Fig. 58 Exploded view of the air cleaner system components—3.0L engine

4. No tools are needed to remove the ACL assembly. Removal should be carried out using hands only.

5. By lifting upwards on the ACL assembly, release the 4 ACL rubber grommets from the LH valve cover and intake manifold.

6. Make sure that the 4 ACL rubber grommets are seated onto the LH valve cover and intake manifold.

➡ **The ACL outlet pipe should be securely sealed to prevent unmetered air from entering the engine.**

7. To install, reverse the removal procedure.

➡ **When installing the ACL assembly, install the ACL housing on the 2 intake manifold studs first, then install on the 2 LH valve cover studs.**

8. Tighten the ACL outlet pipe clamp to 35 inch lbs. (4 Nm).

FILTER/ELEMENT REPLACEMENT

➡ **Refer to appropriate illustration for filter replacement.**

CAMSHAFT & VALVE LIFTERS

REMOVAL & INSTALLATION

2.5L Engine
See Figures 59 through 70.

✳✳ WARNING

During engine repair procedures, cleanliness is extremely important. Any foreign material (including any material created while cleaning gasket surfaces) that enters the oil passages, coolant passages or the oil pan can cause engine failure.

✳✳ CAUTION

Do not rotate the camshafts unless instructed to in this procedure. Rotating the camshafts or crankshaft with

timing components loosened or removed can cause serious damage to the valves and pistons.

1. Raise and safely support the vehicle.
2. Remove the accessory drive belt.
3. Remove the valve cover and remove the Variable Camshaft Timing (VCT) oil control solenoid.
4. Remove the RF wheel and tire.
5. Check the valve clearance. See "Valve Lash (Valve Clearance)" in this section.

✳✳ CAUTION

Failure to position the No. 1 piston at Top Dead Center (TDC) can result in damage to the engine. Turn the engine in the normal direction of rotation only.

6. Using the crankshaft pulley bolt, turn the crankshaft clockwise to position the No. 1 piston at Top Dead Center (TDC).

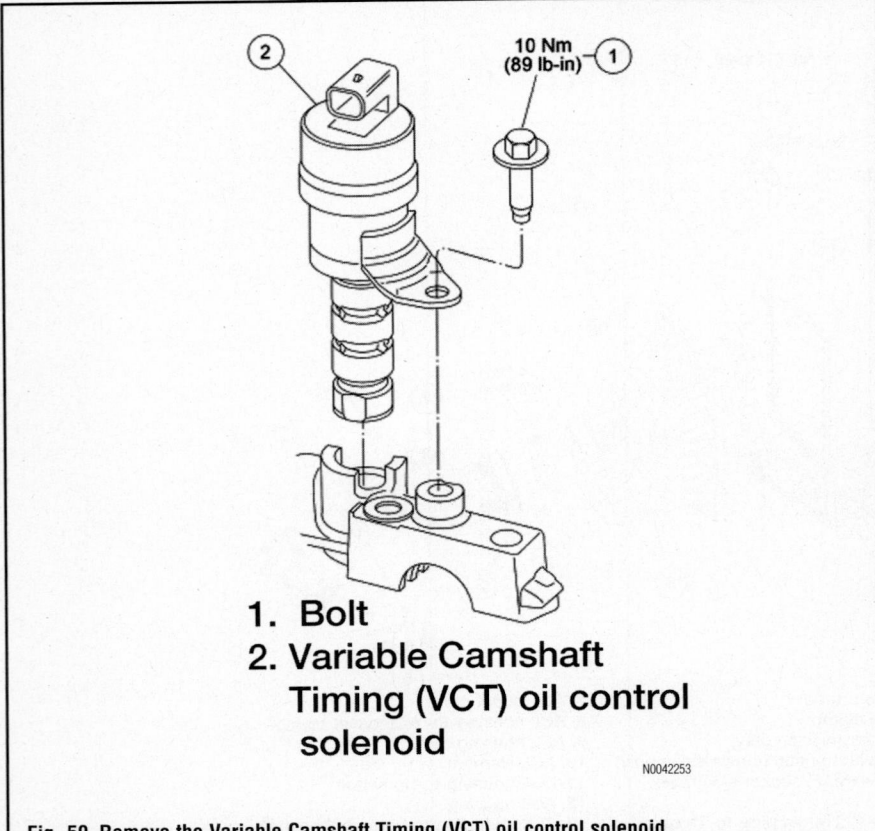

10 Nm
(89 lb-in) — 1

1. **Bolt**
2. **Variable Camshaft Timing (VCT) oil control solenoid**

N0042253

Fig. 59 Remove the Variable Camshaft Timing (VCT) oil control solenoid.

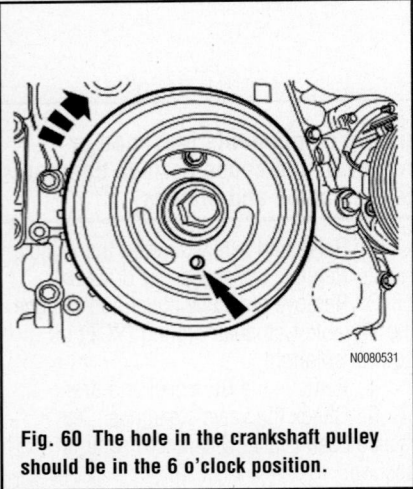

N0080531

Fig. 60 The hole in the crankshaft pulley should be in the 6 o'clock position.

7. The hole in the crankshaft pulley should be in the 6 o'clock position.

✳✳ CAUTION

The Camshaft Alignment Plate is for camshaft alignment only. Using this tool to prevent engine rotation can result in engine damage.

➡The camshaft timing slots are offset. If the Camshaft Alignment Plate cannot be installed, rotate the crankshaft one

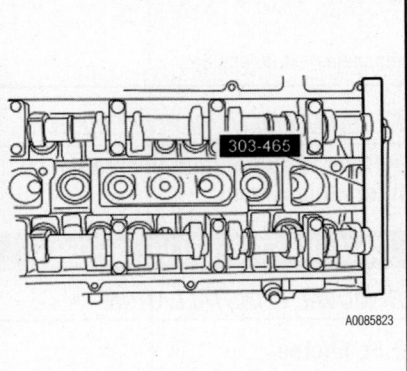

303-465

A0085823

Fig. 61 Install the Camshaft Alignment Plate in the slots on the rear of both camshafts.

complete revolution clockwise to correctly position the camshafts.

8. Install the Camshaft Alignment Plate in the slots on the rear of both camshafts.
9. Remove the engine plug bolt.

➡The Crankshaft TDC Timing Peg will contact the crankshaft and prevent it from turning past TDC. However, the crankshaft can still be rotated in the counterclockwise direction. The crankshaft must remain at the TDC position

A0032806

Fig. 62 Remove the engine plug bolt.

during the camshaft removal and installation.

10. Install the Crankshaft TDC Timing Peg.

✳✳ CAUTION

Only hand-tighten the bolt or damage to the front cover can occur.

11. Install a 6 mm x 18 mm bolt through the crankshaft pulley and thread it into the front cover.
12. Remove the lower and upper front cover timing hole plugs from the engine front cover.
13. Reposition the Camshaft Alignment Plate to the slot on the rear of the intake camshaft only.

➡Releasing the ratcheting mechanism in the timing chain tensioner allows the plunger to collapse and create slack in the timing chain. Installing an M6 x 30 mm bolt into the upper front cover timing hole will hold the tensioner arm in a retracted position and allow enough slack in the timing chain for removal of the exhaust camshaft gear.

14. Using a small pick tool, unlock the chain tensioner ratchet through the lower front cover timing hole.
15. Using the flats of the camshaft, have an assistant rotate the exhaust camshaft clockwise to collapse the timing chain tensioner plunger.
16. Insert an M6 x 30 mm bolt into the upper front cover timing hole to hold the tensioner arm in the retracted position.
17. Using the flats on the camshaft to prevent camshaft rotation, remove the bolt and the exhaust camshaft drive gear.
18. Remove the Camshaft Alignment Plate.
19. Remove the timing chain from the intake camshaft drive gear.

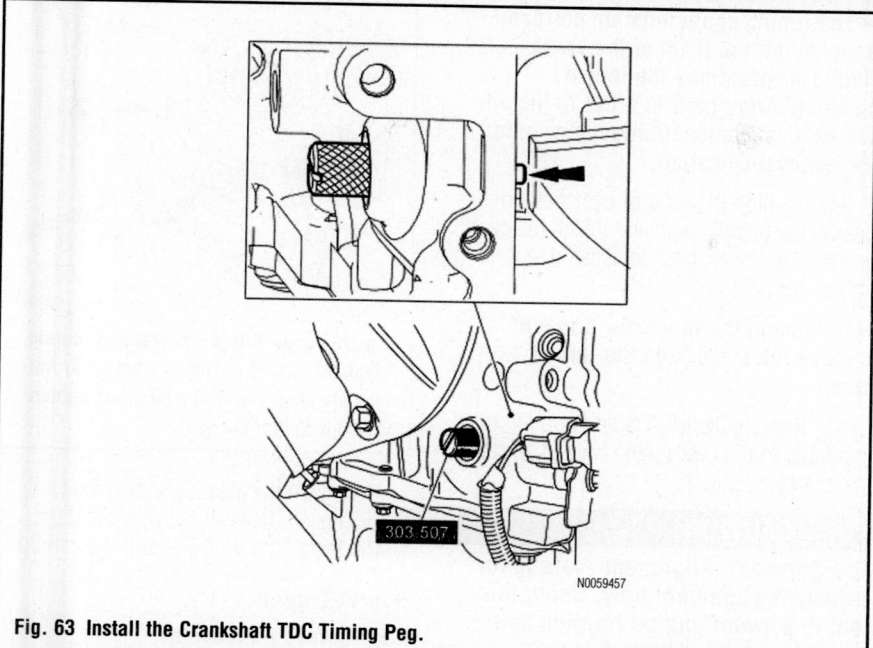

Fig. 63 Install the Crankshaft TDC Timing Peg.

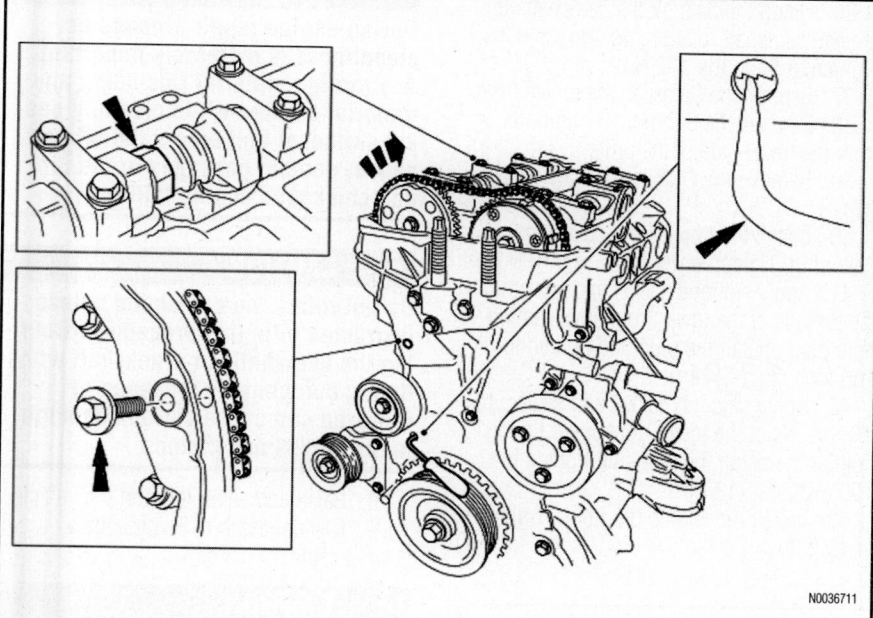

Fig. 64 Unlock the chain tensioner ratchet, with a small pick, through the lower front cover timing hole; rotate the exhaust camshaft clockwise to collapse the timing chain tensioner plunger; then, insert an M6 x 30 mm bolt into the upper front cover timing hole to hold the tensioner arm in the retracted position.

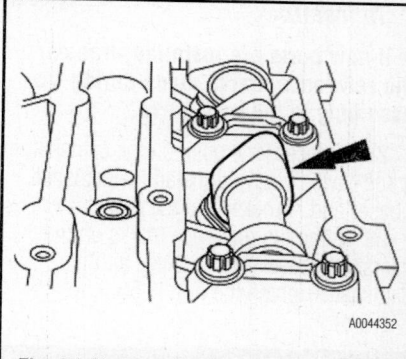

Fig. 65 Mark the position of the camshaft lobes on the No. 1 cylinder for installation reference.

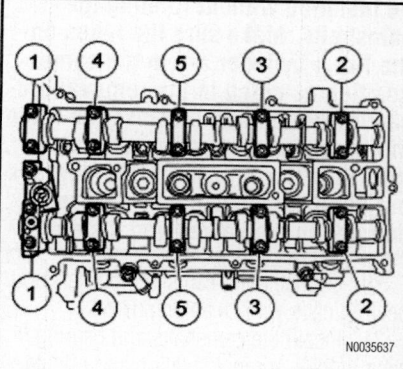

Fig. 66 Loosen the camshaft bearing cap bolts, in sequence, one turn at a time until all tension is released from the camshaft bearing caps.

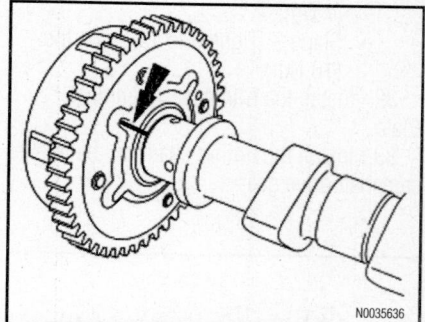

Fig. 67 If removal of the camshaft phaser and sprocket is necessary, mark the sprocket and camshaft for reference during installation.

20. Mark the position of the camshaft lobes on the No. 1 cylinder for installation reference.

⁂ CAUTION

Failure to follow the camshaft loosening procedure can result in damage to the camshafts.

21. Mark the location and orientation of each camshaft bearing cap.
22. Remove the camshafts from the engine.
23. Loosen the camshaft bearing cap bolts, in sequence, one turn at a time until all tension is released from the camshaft bearing caps.

24. Remove the bolts and the camshaft bearing caps.
25. Remove the camshafts.
26. If removal of the camshaft phaser and sprocket is necessary, mark the sprocket and camshaft for reference during installation.
27. If necessary, place the camshaft in a soft-jawed vise. Remove the bolt and the camshaft phaser and sprocket.

To install:

➡If new parts are installed, transfer the reference marks made during disassembly to the new parts.

28. If necessary, position the camshaft in a soft-jawed vise and install the camshaft phaser and sprocket and the bolt

29. Align the reference marks on the camshaft phaser and sprocket and the camshaft. Tighten the bolt to 53 ft. lbs. (72 Nm).

✳✳ CAUTION

Install the camshafts with the alignment slots in the camshafts lined up so the Camshaft Alignment Plate can be installed without rotating the camshafts. Make sure the lobes on the No. 1 cylinder are in the same position as noted in the removal procedure. Rotating the camshafts when the timing chain is removed, or installing the camshafts 180 degrees out of position can cause severe damage to the valves and pistons.

30. Lubricate the camshaft journals and bearing caps with clean engine oil.

31. Install the camshafts and bearing caps in their original location and orientation. Tighten the bearing caps in the sequence shown in 3 stages:
   • Stage 1: Tighten the camshaft bearing cap bolts one turn at a time, until finger-tight.
   • Stage 2: Tighten to 62 inch lbs. (7 Nm).
   • Stage 3: Tighten to 142 inch lbs. (16 Nm).

32. Install the Camshaft Alignment Plate.

33. Install the timing chain on the intake camshaft drive gear.

➡The timing chain must be correctly engaged on the teeth of the crankshaft timing sprocket and the intake camshaft drive gear in order to install the exhaust camshaft drive gear onto the exhaust camshaft.

34. Position the exhaust camshaft drive gear in the timing chain and install the gear and bolt on the exhaust camshaft. Hand-tighten the bolt.

➡Releasing the tensioner arm will remove the slack from the timing chain.

35. Remove the M6 x 30 mm bolt from the upper front cover timing hole to release the tensioner arm.

✳✳ CAUTION

The Camshaft Alignment Plate is for camshaft alignment only. Using this tool to prevent engine rotation can result in engine damage.

36. Using the flats on the camshafts to prevent camshaft rotation, tighten the bolts. Tighten to 53 ft. lbs. (72 Nm).

37. Remove the Camshaft Alignment Plate.

38. Remove the 6 mm x 18 mm bolt from the lower side of the pulley.

39. Remove the Crankshaft TDC Timing Peg.

40. Install the upper front cover timing hole plug. Tighten to 89 inch lbs. (10 Nm).

41. Apply silicone gasket and sealant to the threads of the lower front cover timing hole plug. Install the plug and tighten to 106 inch lbs. (12 Nm).

42. Apply silicone gasket and sealant to the threads of the lower front cover timing hole plug. Install the plug and tighten to 106 inch lbs. (12 Nm).

43. Install the engine plug bolt. Tighten to 15 ft. lbs. (20 Nm).

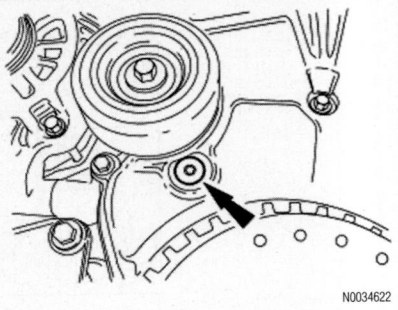

Fig. 70 Apply silicone gasket and sealant to the threads of the lower front cover timing hole plug. Install the plug and tighten to 106 inch lbs. (12 Nm).

44. Install the accessory drive belt.
45. Install the front RH wheel and tire.
46. Install the VCT oil control solenoid.

Hybrid Engine

See Figures 71 through 81.

✳✳ WARNING

During engine repair procedures, cleanliness is extremely important. Any foreign material (including any material created while cleaning gasket surfaces) that enters the oil passages, coolant passages or the oil pan can cause engine failure.

✳✳ CAUTION

Do not rotate the camshafts unless instructed to in this procedure. Rotating the camshafts or crankshaft with timing components loosened or removed can cause serious damage to the valves and pistons.

1. Raise and safely support the vehicle.
2. Disconnect the 12-volt battery ground cable.

✳✳ CAUTION

Before removing the high voltage cables, the vehicle electrical system must be completely shut down for at least 5 minutes to allow for the high voltage capacitors to discharge.

3. Depower the vehicle High Voltage Traction Battery (HVTB) electrical system. See "ENGINE ELECTRICAL" section.

4. Remove the degas bottle.

5. Remove the DC/DC converter. See "ENGINE ELECTRICAL" section.

6. Remove the Variable Camshaft Timing (VCT) oil control solenoid. See "ENGINE PERFORMANCE & EMISSION CONTROLS" section.

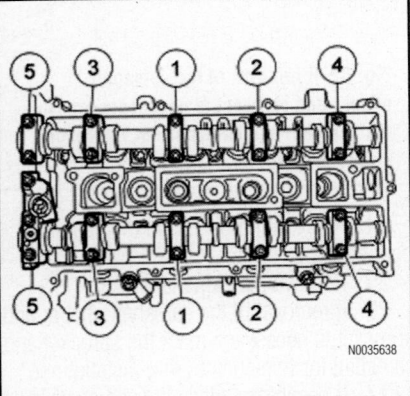

Fig. 68 Camshaft bolt tightening sequence

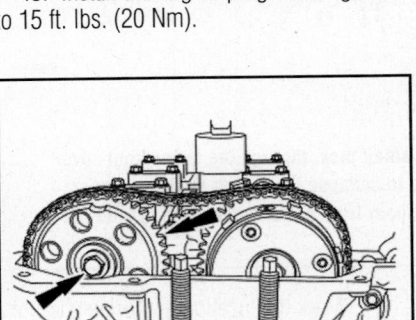

Fig. 69 Position the exhaust camshaft drive gear in the timing chain and install the gear and bolt on the exhaust camshaft. Hand-tighten the bolt.

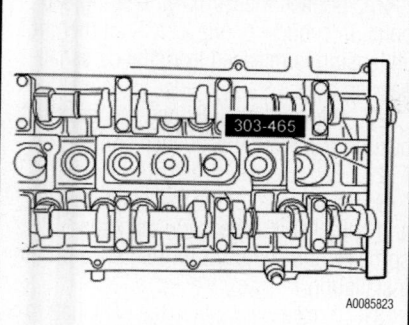

Fig. 71 Install the Camshaft Alignment Plate in the slots on the rear of both camshafts.

7. Check the valve clearance. See "Valve Clearance" in this section.
8. Remove the RF wheel and tire.
9. Remove the accessory drive belt.

✳✳ CAUTION

Failure to position the No. 1 piston at Top Dead Center (TDC) can result in damage to the engine. Turn the engine in the normal direction of rotation only.

10. Using the crankshaft pulley bolt, turn the crankshaft clockwise to position the No. 1 piston at Top Dead Center (TDC).

➡ **The hole in the crankshaft pulley should be in the 6 o'clock position.**

✳✳ CAUTION

The Camshaft Alignment Plate 303-465 is for camshaft alignment only. Using this tool to prevent engine rotation can result in engine damage.

➡ **The camshaft timing slots are offset. If the Camshaft Alignment Plate cannot be installed, rotate the crankshaft one**

complete revolution clockwise to correctly position the camshafts.

11. Install the Camshaft Alignment Plate in the slots on the rear of both camshafts.
12. Remove the engine plug bolt.

➡ **The Crankshaft TDC Timing Peg will contact the crankshaft and prevent it from turning past TDC. However, the crankshaft can still be rotated in the counterclockwise direction. The crankshaft must remain at the TDC position during the camshaft removal and installation.**

13. Install the Crankshaft TDC Timing Peg and turn the crankshaft clockwise until the crankshaft contacts the Crankshaft TDC Timing Peg.
14. Install, hand-tight only, a standard 6 mm x 18 mm bolt through the crankshaft pulley and thread it into the 6 o'clock hole in the front cover.

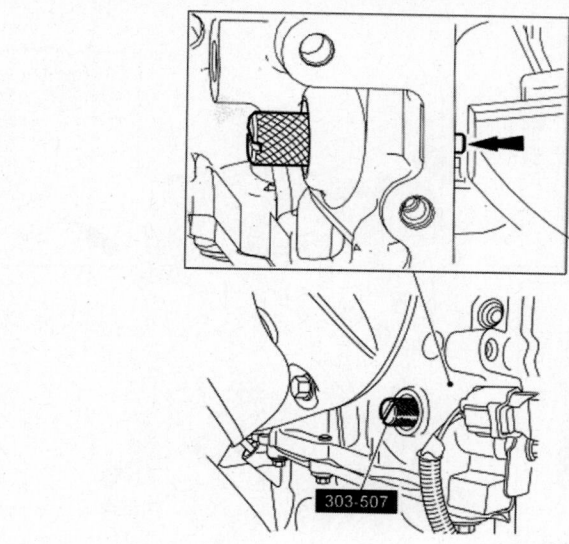

Fig. 73 Install the Crankshaft TDC Timing Peg and turn the crankshaft clockwise until the crankshaft contacts the Crankshaft TDC Timing Peg.

15. Remove the lower front cover timing hole plug from the engine front cover.
16. Remove the upper front cover timing hole plug from the engine front cover.
17. Reposition the Camshaft Alignment Plate to the slot on the rear of the intake camshaft only.

✳✳ CAUTION

Releasing the ratcheting mechanism in the timing chain tensioner allows the plunger to collapse and create slack in the timing chain. Installing an M6 x 30mm (1.18 in) bolt into the upper front cover timing hole will hold the tensioner arm in a retracted position and allow enough slack in the timing chain for removal of the exhaust camshaft gear.

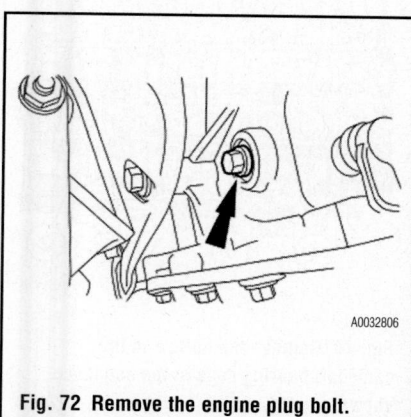

Fig. 72 Remove the engine plug bolt.

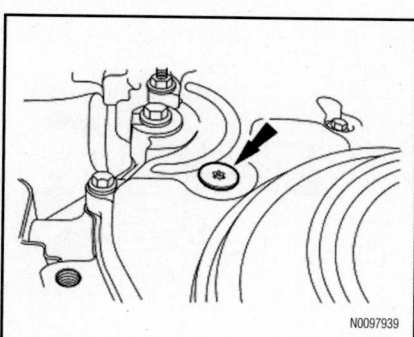

Fig. 74 Remove the lower front cover timing hole plug from the engine front cover.

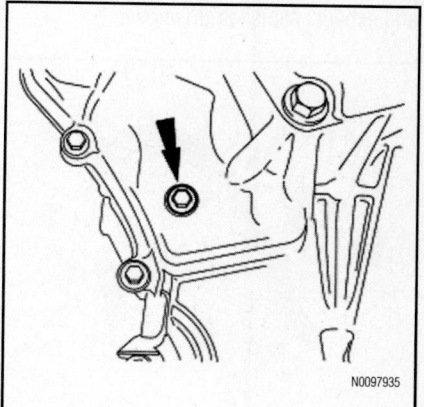

Fig. 75 Remove the upper front cover timing hole plug from the engine front cover.

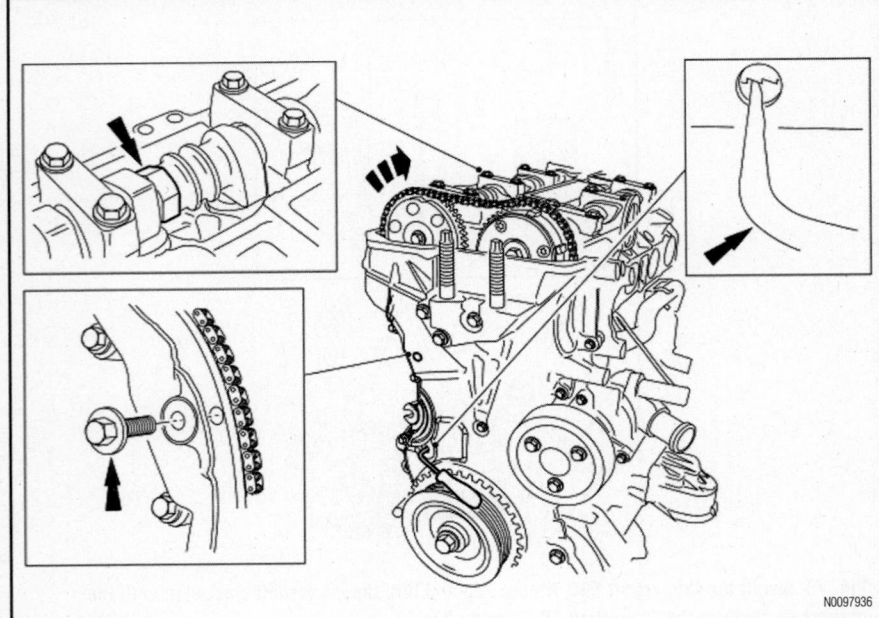

N0097936

Fig. 76 Using a small pick tool, unlock the chain tensioner ratchet through the lower front cover timing hole, have an assistant rotate the exhaust camshaft clockwise to collapse the timing chain tensioner plunger, then insert an M6 x 30mm (1.18 in) bolt into the upper front cover timing hole to hold the tensioner arm in the retracted position.

18. Using a small pick tool, unlock the chain tensioner ratchet through the lower front cover timing hole.

19. Using the flats of the camshaft, have an assistant rotate the exhaust camshaft clockwise to collapse the timing chain tensioner plunger.

20. Insert an M6 x 30mm (1.18 in) bolt into the upper front cover timing hole to hold the tensioner arm in the retracted position.

21. Remove the Camshaft Alignment Plate.

22. Using the flats on the camshaft to prevent camshaft rotation, remove the bolt and exhaust camshaft drive gear.

23. Remove the timing chain from the camshaft phaser and sprocket.

24. Mark the position of the camshaft lobes on the No. 1 cylinder for installation reference.

✳✳ CAUTION

Failure to follow the camshaft loosening procedure can result in damage to the camshafts.

25. Mark the location and orientation of each camshaft bearing cap for installation reference.

26. Remove the camshafts from the engine.

27. Loosen the camshaft bearing cap bolts, in sequence, one turn at a time until all tension is released from the camshaft bearing caps.

28. Remove the bolts and the camshaft bearing caps in the sequence shown.

29. Remove the camshafts.

30. If removal of the camshaft phaser and sprocket is necessary, mark the sprocket and camshaft for reference during installation.

31. If necessary, place the camshaft in a soft-jawed vise. Remove the bolt and the camshaft phaser and sprocket.

To install:

➡ **If new parts are installed, transfer the reference marks made during disassembly to the new parts.**

If necessary, position the camshaft in a soft-jawed vise and install the camshaft phaser and sprocket and the bolt.

32. Align the reference marks on the camshaft phaser and sprocket and the camshaft. Tighten the bolt to 53 ft. lbs. (72 Nm).

33. Install the camshafts with the alignment slots in the camshafts lined up so the Camshaft Alignment Plate can be installed without rotating the camshafts. Make sure the lobes on the No. 1 cylinder are in the same position as noted in the removal procedure. Rotating the camshafts when the timing chain is removed, or installing the camshafts 180 degrees out of position can cause severe damage to the valves and pistons.

34. Lubricate the camshaft journals and bearing caps with clean engine oil.

35. Install the camshafts and bearing caps in their original location and orienta-

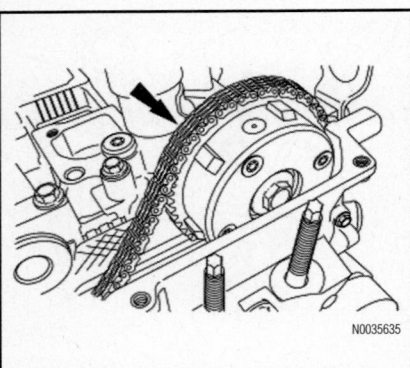

N0035635

Fig. 77 Remove the timing chain from the camshaft phaser and sprocket.

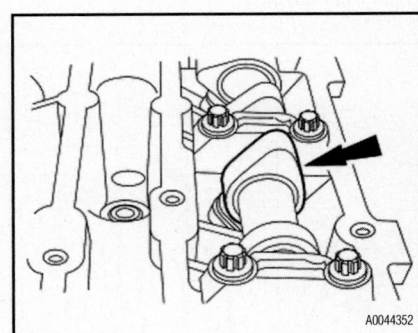

A0044352

Fig. 78 Mark the position of the camshaft lobes on the No. 1 cylinder for installation reference.

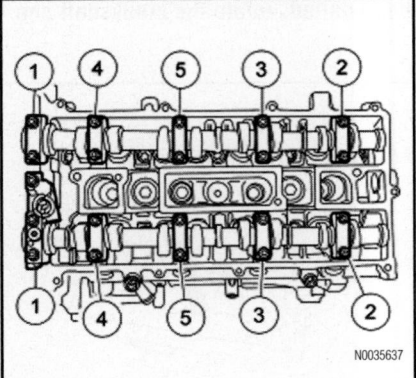

N0035637

Fig. 79 Remove the bolts and the camshaft bearing caps in the sequence shown.

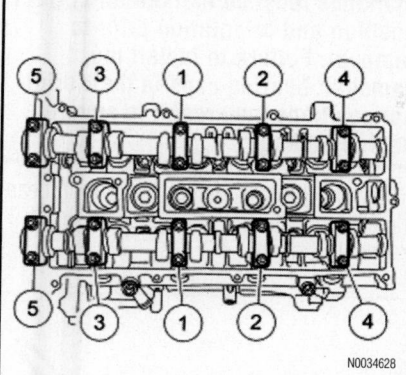

Fig. 80 Install the camshafts and bearing caps in their original location and orientation. Tighten the bearing caps in the sequence shown in 3 stages

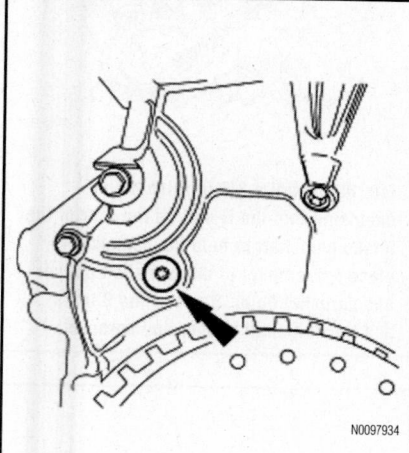

Fig. 81 Apply silicone gasket and sealant to the threads of the lower front cover timing hole plug. Install the plug and tighten to 106 inch lbs. (12 Nm).

tion. Tighten the bearing caps in the sequence shown in 3 stages:
- Stage 1: Tighten the camshaft bearing cap bolts one turn at a time, until finger-tight.
- Stage 2: Tighten to 62 inch lbs. (7 Nm).
- Stage 3: Tighten to 142 inch lbs. (16 Nm).

36. Install the Camshaft Alignment Plate onto both camshafts.
37. Install the timing chain on the camshaft phaser and sprocket.

➡ **The timing chain must be correctly engaged on the teeth of the crankshaft timing sprocket and the intake camshaft drive gear in order to install**

the exhaust camshaft drive gear onto the exhaust camshaft.

38. Position the exhaust camshaft drive gear in the timing chain and install the gear and bolt on the exhaust camshaft. Hand-tighten the bolt.

➡ **Releasing the tensioner arm will remove the slack from the timing chain release.**

39. Remove the M6 x 30 mm bolt from the upper front cover timing hole to release the tensioner arm.

✳✳ CAUTION

The Camshaft Alignment Plate 303-465 is for camshaft alignment only. Using this tool to prevent engine rotation can result in engine damage.

40. Using the flats on the camshaft to prevent camshaft rotation, tighten the bolt. Tighten to 53 ft. lbs. (72 Nm).
41. Remove the Camshaft Alignment Plate.
42. Remove the 6 mm x 18 mm bolt from the 6 o'clock hole in the crankshaft pulley.
43. Remove the Crankshaft TDC Timing Peg from the side of the engine block.
44. Install the upper front cover timing hole plug. Tighten to 89 inch lbs. (10 Nm).
45. Apply silicone gasket and sealant to the threads of the lower front cover timing

hole plug. Install the plug and tighten to 106 inch lbs. (12 Nm).
46. Install the engine plug bolt (from which timing peg was removed). Tighten to 15 ft. lbs. (20 Nm).
47. Install the accessory drive belt.
48. Install the RF wheel and tire.
49. Install the VCT oil control solenoid. See "ENGINE PERFORMANCE & EMISSION CONTROLS" section.
50. Install the valve cover.
51. Install the DC/DC converter. See "ENGINE ELECTRICAL" section.
52. Install the degas bottle.
53. Repower the vehicle HVTB electrical system. See "ENGINE ELECTRICAL" section.
54. Connect the battery ground cable.

3.0L Engine

See Figures 82 through 92.

➡ **This procedure applies to either cylinder bank.**

1. Remove the coolant pump belt.
2. Remove the timing drive components. See "Timing Chain Front Cover" in this section.

➡ **Failure to use the correct special tools, assembled as shown in the illustration, will result in damage to the coolant pump pulley and/or special tools.**

3. Using the Water Pump Pulley Plate,

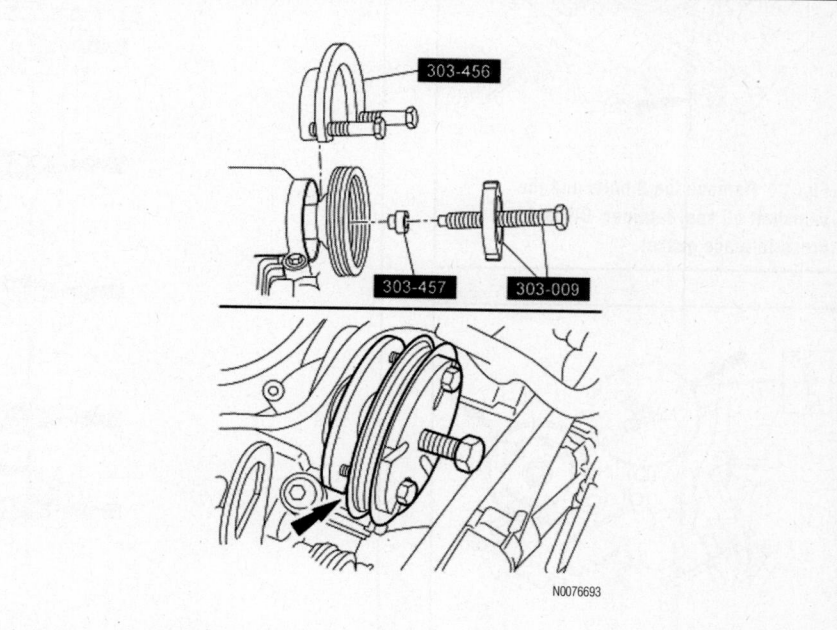

Fig. 82 Using the Water Pump Pulley Plate, Water Pump Shaft Protector and the Crankshaft Vibration Damper Remover, remove the coolant pump pulley.

Water Pump Shaft Protector and the Crankshaft Vibration Damper Remover, remove the coolant pump pulley.

> ❄❄ **CAUTION**
>
> **Do not scratch the camshaft sealing surface while removing the camshaft oil seal. If scratched, camshaft oil seal leakage may occur.**

4. Using the Oil Seal Remover, remove and discard the camshaft oil seal.

5. Remove the 2 bolts and the camshaft

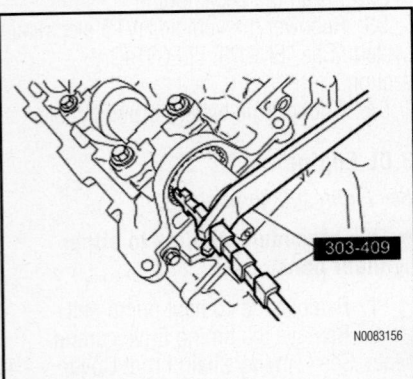

Fig. 83 Using the Oil Seal Remover, remove and discard the camshaft oil seal.

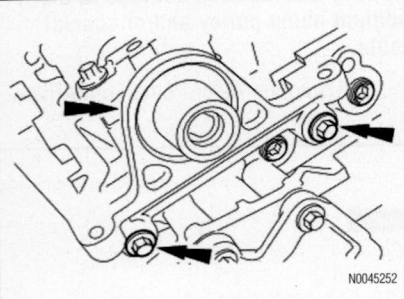

Fig. 84 Remove the 2 bolts and the camshaft oil seal retainer. Discard the press-in-place gasket.

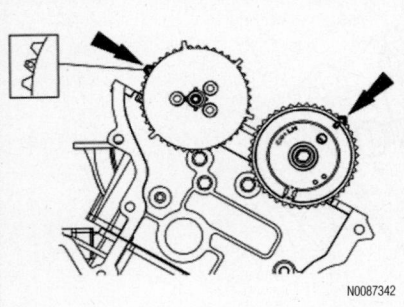

Fig. 85 Verify the camshafts are in the neutral position.

oil seal retainer. Discard the press-in-place gasket.

> ❄❄ **CAUTION**
>
> **The camshafts must be in the neutral position before removing the bearing caps or damage to the engine may occur.**

6. Verify the camshafts are in the neutral position.

> ❄❄ **CAUTION**
>
> **Do not allow the camshaft to rotate from the neutral position while removing the camshaft phaser and sprocket or damage to the engine may occur.**

7. Install a 3/8-in ratchet and extension into the D-slot on the rear of the intake camshaft to hold the camshaft in place for removal of the camshaft phaser and sprocket bolts. Remove the 3 bolts and the camshaft phaser and sprocket.

> ❄❄ **CAUTION**
>
> **Cylinder head camshaft bearing caps must be assembled in their original positions. Some engines have factory markings on the camshaft bearing caps (as shown in illustration). Engines that do not have the factory**

markings must be marked for correct position and orientation prior to removal. Failure to install the camshaft bearing caps in their original positions may result in severe engine damage.

8. If necessary, mark the camshaft bearing cap position and orientation as shown in the illustration.

Fig. 86 Install a 3/8-in ratchet and extension into the D-slot on the rear of the intake camshaft to hold the camshaft in place for removal of the camshaft phaser and sprocket bolts. Remove the 3 bolts and the camshaft phaser and sprocket.

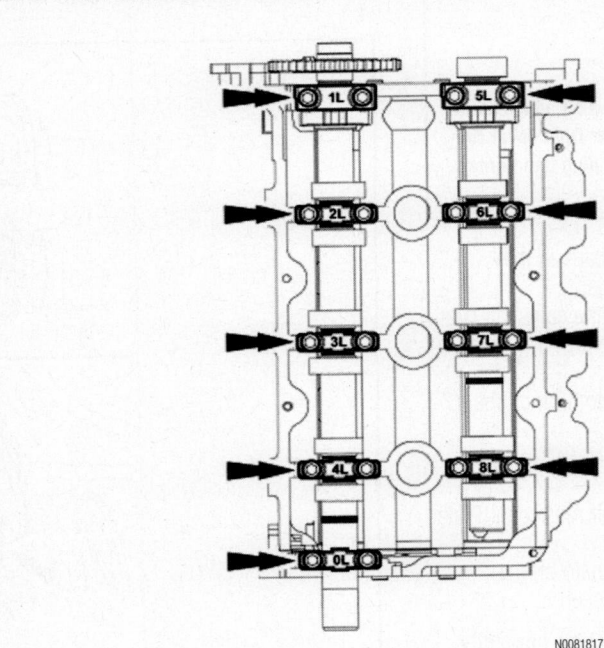

Fig. 87 If necessary, mark the camshaft bearing cap position and orientation as shown in the illustration.

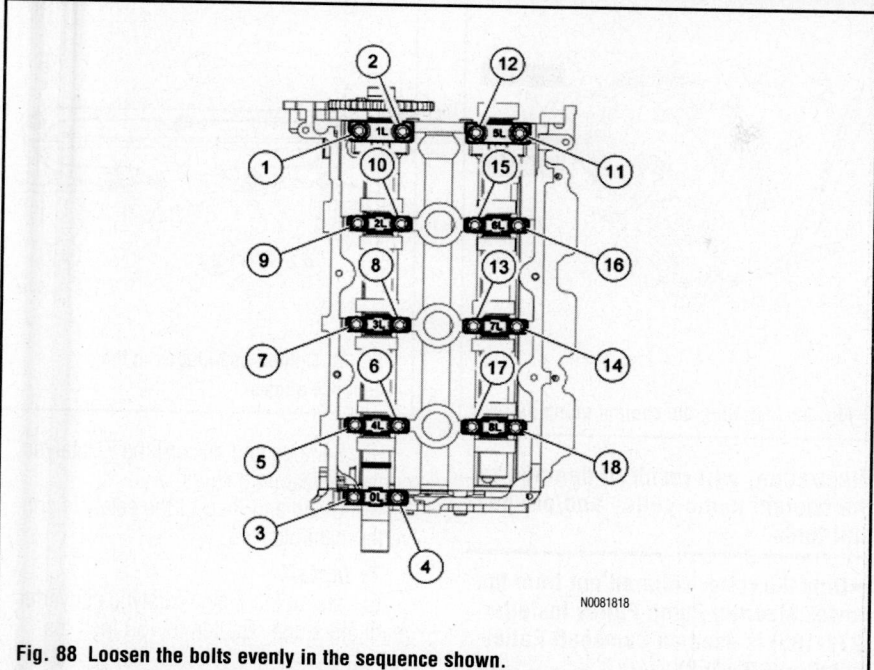

Fig. 88 Loosen the bolts evenly in the sequence shown.

✳✳ CAUTION

In the next steps, after loosening all of the camshaft bearing cap bolts, remove the camshaft bearing thrust caps (1L and 5L or 1R and 5R) first, or damage to the thrust caps may occur.

9. Loosen the bolts evenly in the sequence shown.

10. Remove the camshaft bearing thrust caps (1L and 5L or 1R and 5R). Remove the remaining camshaft bearing caps.

11. Remove the camshafts from the cylinder head.

To install:

12. Position the camshaft phaser and sprocket onto the intake camshaft.

13. Install the 3 bolts finger-tight.

14. Lubricate the camshafts with clean engine oil and carefully position the camshafts onto the cylinder head.

15. Align the camshafts in the neutral positions, as during removal.

✳✳ CAUTION

Cylinder head camshaft journal caps and cylinder heads are numbered to verify that they are assembled in their original positions. If not reassembled in their original positions, severe engine damage may occur.

✳✳ CAUTION

Do not install the camshaft journal thrust caps until all of the camshaft bearing caps have been installed or damage to the thrust caps can occur.

16. Lubricate the bearing surfaces of the camshaft bearing caps with clean engine oil and install the bearing caps. Loosely install the bolts.

17. Lubricate the bearing surfaces of the camshaft bearing thrust caps with clean engine oil and install the bearing thrust caps (1L and 5L or 1R and 5R). Loosely install the bolts.

18. Tighten the LH camshaft bearing cap bolts in the sequence shown in 2 stages:

- Stage 1: Tighten to 89 inch lbs. (10 Nm).
- Stage 2: Individually loosen and then tighten each camshaft bearing cap to 89 inch lbs. (10 Nm).

✳✳ CAUTION

Do not allow the camshaft to rotate from the neutral position while tightening the camshaft phaser and sprocket bolts or damage to the engine may occur.

19. Install a 3/8-in ratchet and extension into the D-slot on the rear of the intake camshaft to hold the camshaft in place for tightening of the camshaft phaser and sprocket bolts.

20. Tighten the 3 camshaft phaser and sprocket bolts to 159 inch lbs. (18 Nm).

21. Clean the sealing surfaces with metal surface prep before installing a new press-in-place gasket.

22. Install the camshaft oil seal retainer and the 2 bolts. Tighten to 89 inch lbs. (10 Nm).

23. Lubricate the camshaft oil seal with clean engine oil.

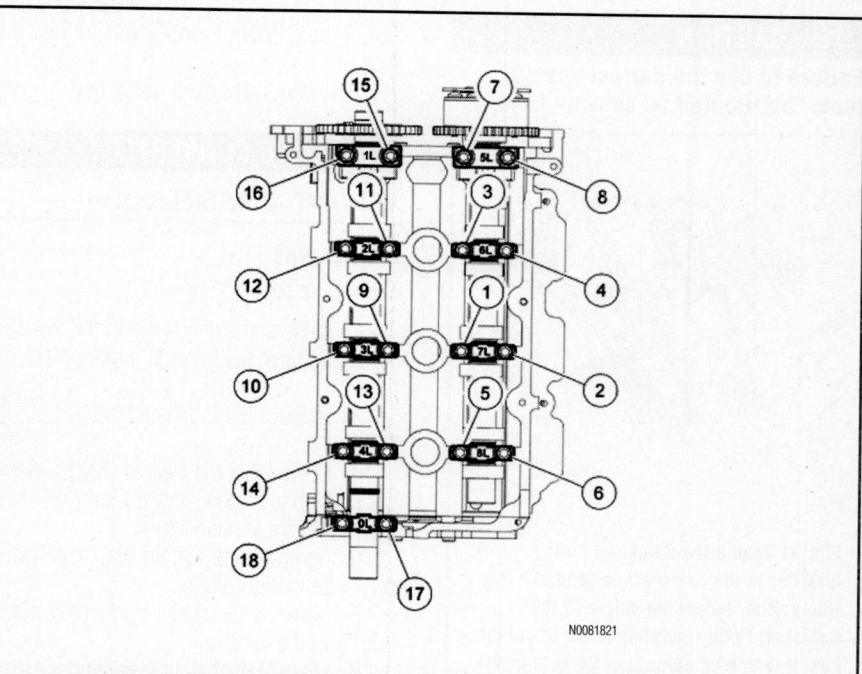

Fig. 89 Tighten the camshaft bearing cap bolts in the sequence shown in 2 stages

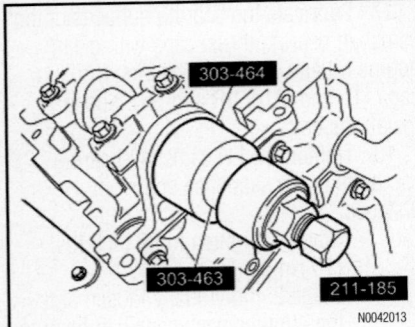

Fig. 90 Using the Camshaft Oil Seal Installer, Camshaft Oil Seal Protector and the Power Steering Pump Pulley Installer, install the camshaft oil seal.

24. Using the Camshaft Oil Seal Installer, Camshaft Oil Seal Protector and the Power Steering Pump Pulley Installer, install the camshaft oil seal.

> ✳✳ **CAUTION**
>
> **Failure to use the correct special tools, assembled as shown in the illustration, will result in damage to the coolant pump pulley and/or special tools.**

25. Install the Camshaft Pulley Installer in the camshaft as shown in the illustration. Adjust the collar on the Camshaft Pulley Installer screw to get the best thread engagement in the rear of the camshaft.

> ✳✳ **CAUTION**
>
> **Failure to use the correct special tools, assembled as shown in the**

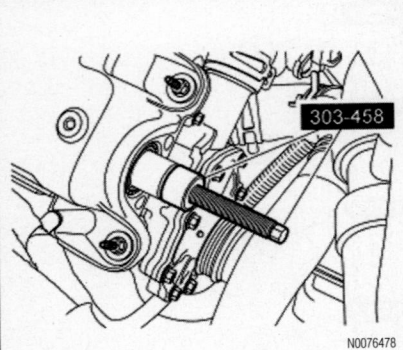

Fig. 91 Install the Camshaft Pulley Installer in the camshaft as shown in the illustration. Adjust the collar on the Camshaft Pulley Installer screw to get the best thread engagement in the rear of the camshaft.

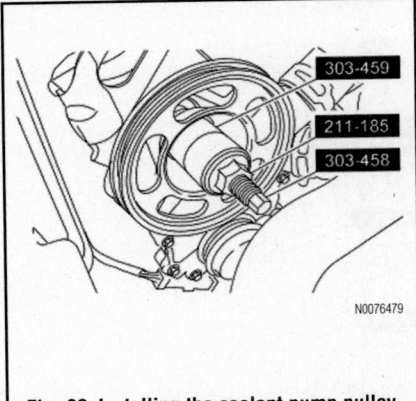

Fig. 92 Installing the coolant pump pulley

illustration, will result in damage to the coolant pump pulley and/or special tools.

➡ **Only the roller collared nut from the Power Steering Pump Pulley Installer (211-185) is used on Camshaft Pulley Installer (303-458).**

26. Position the coolant pump pulley over the previously installed Camshaft Pulley Installer and on the end of the camshaft. Install the Camshaft Pulley Installer, Power Steering Pump Pulley Installer and the Water Pump Pulley Spacer as shown in the illustration.

27. Using the Camshaft Pulley Installer, Power Steering Pump Pulley Installer and the Water Pump Pulley Spacer, install a new service coolant pump pulley flush with the end of the camshaft.

28. Install the timing drive components. See "Timing Chain Front Cover" in this section.

29. Install the coolant pump belt.

CATALYTIC CONVERTER

REMOVAL & INSTALLATION

2.5L Engine

See Figure 93.

1. Raise and safely support the vehicle.
2. Remove the exhaust intermediate pipe.
3. Remove the 2 exhaust bracket bolts.
4. Disconnect the Heated Oxygen Sensor (HO2S) and the Catalyst Monitor Sensor (CMS) electrical connectors.
5. Remove and discard the 7 catalytic converter manifold nuts.
6. Remove the catalytic converter manifold from the vehicle.
7. Discard the catalytic converter manifold gasket.

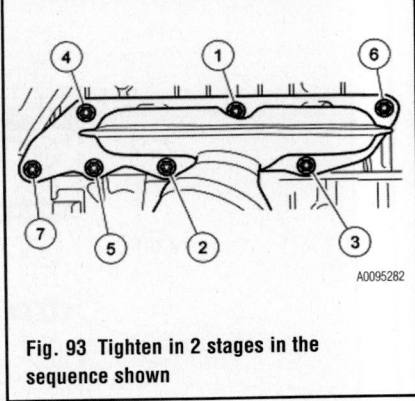

Fig. 93 Tighten in 2 stages in the sequence shown

8. Remove and discard the 7 catalytic converter manifold studs.
9. Clean and inspect the catalytic converter manifold.

To install:

10. Install the 7 new catalytic converter manifold studs. Tighten to 150 inch lbs. (17 Nm).
11. Failure to tighten the catalytic converter manifold nuts to specification before installing the converter bracket bolts will cause the converter to develop an exhaust leak.
12. Using a new gasket, install the catalytic converter and the 7 exhaust manifold nuts. Tighten in 2 stages in the sequence shown:
    - Stage 1: Tighten to 35 ft. lbs. (47 Nm).
    - Stage 2: Tighten to 35 ft. lbs. (47 Nm).
13. Connect the HO2S and the CMS electrical connectors.
14. Install the 2 exhaust bracket bolts. Tighten to 18 ft. lbs. (25 Nm).
15. Install the exhaust intermediate pipe.

Hybrid Engine

See Figure 94.

➡ **This procedure is for the exhaust manifold with the catalytic converter, as an assembly.**

1. Raise and safely support the vehicle.
2. Remove the exhaust intermediate pipe.
3. Remove the 2 exhaust bracket bolts.
4. Disconnect the Heated Oxygen Sensor (HO2S) and the Catalyst Monitor Sensor (CMS) electrical connectors.
5. Remove and discard the 7 catalytic converter manifold nuts.
6. Remove the catalytic converter manifold from the vehicle.
7. Discard the catalytic converter manifold gasket.
8. Remove and discard the 7 catalytic converter manifold studs.

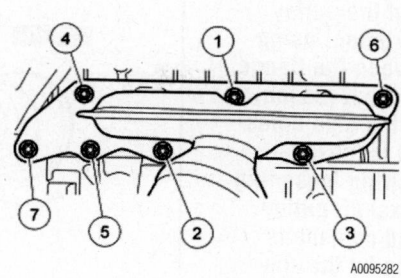

Fig. 94 Using a new gasket, install the catalytic converter and the 7 exhaust manifold nuts. Tighten in 2 stages in the sequence shown.

9. Clean and inspect the catalytic converter manifold.

To install:

10. Install the 7 new catalytic converter manifold studs. Tighten to 150 inch lbs. (17 Nm).

❊ CAUTION

Failure to tighten the catalytic converter manifold nuts to specification the first and second times before installing the converter bracket bolts will cause the converter to develop an exhaust leak.

11. Using a new gasket, install the catalytic converter and the 7 exhaust manifold nuts. Tighten in 2 stages in the sequence shown:
- Stage 1: Tighten to 35 ft. lbs. (47 Nm).
- Stage 2: Tighten to 35 ft. lbs. (47 Nm)

12. Connect the HO2S and the CMS electrical connectors.

13. Install the 2 exhaust bracket bolts. Tighten to 18 ft. lbs. (25 Nm).

14. Install the exhaust intermediate pipe.

3.0L Engine

Left Side

See Figure 95.

1. Raise and safely support the vehicle.

2. Remove the 6 retainers and the passenger side splash shield.

3. Remove the LH Heated Oxygen Sensor (HO2S).

4. Rotate the accessory drive belt tensioner counterclockwise and remove the accessory drive belt.

5. Disconnect the A/C compressor electrical connector.

6. Remove the 3 bolts and position the A/C compressor aside.

7. Remove the 3 bolts and the LH catalytic converter heat shield.

8. Remove exhaust Y-pipe.

9. Remove and discard the 6 LH catalytic converter manifold nuts.

10. Remove the LH catalytic converter manifold from the vehicle.

11. Discard the gasket.

12. Remove and discard the 6 LH catalytic converter manifold studs.

13. Clean and inspect the LH catalytic converter manifold.

To install:

14. Install the 6 new LH catalytic converter manifold studs. Tighten to 97 inch lbs. (11 Nm).

❊ CAUTION

Failure to tighten the catalytic converter nuts to specification before installing the exhaust Y-pipe will cause the converter to develop an exhaust leak.

15. Using a new gasket, install the LH catalytic converter and the 6 nuts.

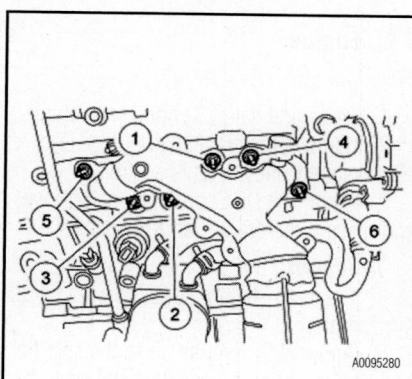

Fig. 95 Using a new gasket, install the LH catalytic converter and the 6 nuts. Tighten in 2 stages in the sequence shown

Tighten in 2 stages in the sequence shown:
- Stage 1: Tighten to 18 ft. lbs. (25 Nm).
- Stage 2: Tighten to 18 ft. lbs. (25 Nm).

16. Install the exhaust Y-pipe.

17. Install the LH catalytic converter heat shield and the 3 bolts. Tighten to 89 inch lbs. (10 Nm).

18. Position the A/C compressor and install the 3 bolts. Tighten to 18 ft. lbs. (25 Nm).

19. Connect the A/C compressor electrical connector.

20. Rotate the accessory drive belt tensioner counterclockwise and install the accessory drive belt.

21. Install the LH HO2S.

22. Install the passenger side splash shield and the 6 retainers.

Right Side

1. Remove the exhaust Y-pipe.

2. Disconnect the RH Catalyst Monitor Sensor (CMS) electrical connector.

3. Remove and discard the 3 RH catalytic converter nuts and remove the converter.

4. Discard the RH catalytic converter manifold gasket.

5. To install, reverse the removal procedure.

6. Tighten the new converter nuts to 30 ft. lbs. (40 Nm).

7. Install a new gasket and nuts.

CRANKSHAFT FRONT SEAL

REMOVAL & INSTALLATION

2.5L Engine

See Figure 96.

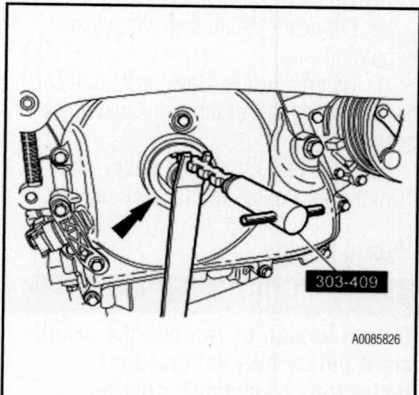

Fig. 96 Using the Oil Seal Remover, remove the crankshaft front oil seal.

✳✳ WARNING

Do not loosen or remove the crankshaft pulley bolt without first installing the special tools as instructed in this procedure. The crankshaft pulley and the crankshaft timing sprocket are not keyed to the crankshaft. The crankshaft, the crankshaft sprocket and the pulley are fitted together by friction, using diamond washers between the flange faces on each part. For that reason, the crankshaft sprocket is also unfastened if the pulley bolt is loosened. Before any repair requiring loosening or removal of the crankshaft pulley bolt, the crankshaft and camshafts must be locked in place by the special service tools, otherwise severe engine damage can occur.

✳✳ WARNING

During engine repair procedures, cleanliness is extremely important. Any foreign material (including any material created while cleaning gasket surfaces) that enters the oil passages, coolant passages or the oil pan can cause engine failure.

1. Remove the crankshaft pulley. See "Crankshaft Pulley" in this section.

✳✳ CAUTION

Use care not to damage the engine front cover or the crankshaft when removing the seal.

2. Using the Oil Seal Remover, remove the crankshaft front oil seal.

To install:

3. Remove the through-bolt from the Camshaft Front Oil Seal Installer.
4. Lubricate the oil seal with clean engine oil.
5. Using a proper Camshaft Front Oil Seal Installer, install the crankshaft front oil seal.
6. Install the crankshaft pulley. See "Crankshaft Pulley" in this section.

Hybrid Engine

✳✳ WARNING

Do not loosen or remove the crankshaft pulley bolt without first installing the special tools as instructed in this procedure. The crankshaft pulley and the crankshaft timing sprocket are not keyed to the

crankshaft. The crankshaft, the crankshaft sprocket and the pulley are fitted together by friction, using diamond washers between the flange faces on each part. For that reason, the crankshaft sprocket is also unfastened if the pulley bolt is loosened. Before any repair requiring loosening or removal of the crankshaft pulley bolt, the crankshaft and camshafts must be locked in place by the special service tools or severe engine damage can occur.

✳✳ WARNING

During engine repair procedures, cleanliness is extremely important. Any foreign material (including any material created while cleaning gasket surfaces) that enters the oil passages, coolant passages or the oil pan can cause engine failure.

1. Remove the crankshaft pulley. See "Crankshaft Pulley" in this section.

✳✳ CAUTION

Use care not to damage the engine front cover or the crankshaft when removing the seal.

2. Using a proper Oil Seal Remover, remove the crankshaft front seal.

To install:

3. Remove the through bolt from the Camshaft Front Oil Seal Installer, if equipped.
4. Lubricate the oil seal with clean engine oil.
5. Using a proper Camshaft Front Oil Seal Installer, install the crankshaft front oil seal.
6. Install the crankshaft pulley. See "Crankshaft Pulley" in this section.

3.0L Engine

See Figure 97.

1. Raise and safely support the vehicle.
2. Remove the crankshaft pulley. See "Crankshaft Pulley" in this section.
3. Using the Oil Seal Remover, remove and discard the crankshaft front seal.

To install:

4. Clean all sealing surfaces with metal surface prep.
5. Apply clean engine oil to the seal lip and seal bore before installing the seal.
6. Using the Front Cover Oil Seal Installer and the Crankshaft Vibration Damper Installer, install a new crankshaft front seal.

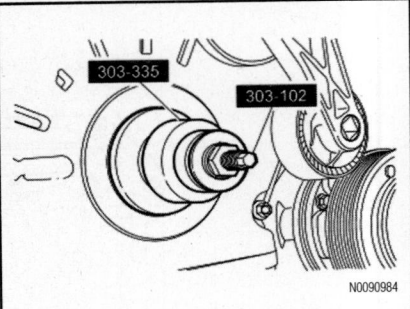

Fig. 97 Using the Front Cover Oil Seal Installer and the Crankshaft Vibration Damper Installer, install a new crankshaft front seal.

7. Install the crankshaft pulley.

CRANKSHAFT PULLEY

REMOVAL & INSTALLATION

2.5L & Hybrid Engines

See Figure 98.

✳✳ WARNING

Do not loosen or remove the crankshaft pulley bolt without first installing the special tools as instructed in this procedure. The crankshaft pulley and the crankshaft timing sprocket are not keyed to the crankshaft. The crankshaft, the crankshaft sprocket and the pulley are fitted together by friction, using diamond washers between the flange faces on each part. For that reason, the crankshaft sprocket is also unfastened if the pulley bolt is loosened. Before any repair requiring loosening or removal of the crankshaft pulley bolt, the crankshaft and camshafts must be locked in place by the special service tools, otherwise severe engine damage can occur.

✳✳ WARNING

During engine repair procedures, cleanliness is extremely important. Any foreign material (including any material created while cleaning gasket surfaces) that enters the oil passages, coolant passages or the oil pan can cause engine failure.

1. Raise and safely support the vehicle.
2. Remove the front RH wheel and tire.
3. Remove the accessory drive belt.
4. Remove the valve cover.

❋❋ CAUTION

Failure to position the No. 1 piston at Top Dead Center (TDC) can result in damage to the engine. Turn the engine in the normal direction of rotation only.

5. Using the crankshaft pulley bolt, turn the crankshaft clockwise to position the No. 1 piston at Top Dead Center (TDC). The hole in the crankshaft pulley should be in the 6 o'clock position.

❋❋ CAUTION

The Camshaft Alignment Plate is for camshaft alignment only. Using this tool to prevent engine rotation can result in engine damage.

➡The camshaft timing slots are offset. If the Camshaft Alignment Plate cannot be installed, rotate the crankshaft one complete revolution clockwise to correctly position the camshafts.

6. Install the Camshaft Alignment Plate in the slots on the rear of both camshafts.
7. Remove the engine plug bolt.

➡The Crankshaft TDC Timing Peg will contact the crankshaft and prevent it from turning past TDC. However, the crankshaft can still be rotated in the counterclockwise direction. The crankshaft must remain at the TDC position during the crankshaft pulley removal and installation.

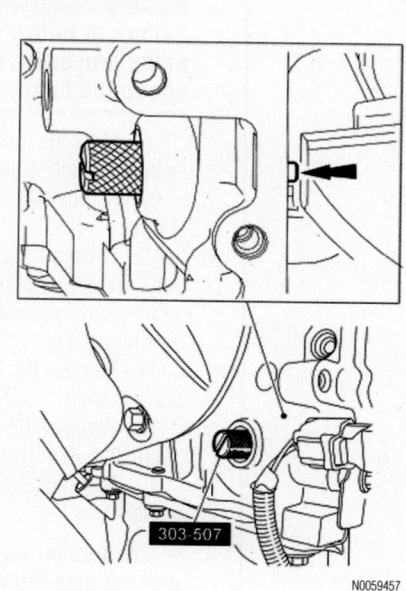

Fig. 98 Install the Crankshaft TDC Timing Peg.

8. Install the Crankshaft TDC Timing Peg.

❋❋ CAUTION

The crankshaft must remain in the Top Dead Center (TDC) position during removal of the pulley bolt or damage to the engine can occur. Therefore, the crankshaft pulley must be held in place with the Crankshaft Damper Holding Tool, and the bolt should be removed using an air impact wrench (1/2-in drive minimum).

❋❋ CAUTION

The crankshaft sprocket diamond washer may come off with the crankshaft pulley. The diamond washer must be replaced. Remove and discard the diamond washer. If the diamond washer is not installed, engine damage may occur.

9. Use the Crankshaft Damper Holding Tool and a suitable 1/2-in drive hand tool to hold the crankshaft pulley. Use an air impact wrench to remove the crankshaft pulley bolt.
10. Remove and discard the crankshaft pulley bolt and washer.
11. Remove the crankshaft pulley.
12. Remove the diamond washer and discard.

To install:
13. Install a new diamond washer.

➡Do not install the crankshaft pulley bolt at this time.

14. Apply clean engine oil on the seal area before installing.
15. Position the crankshaft pulley onto the crankshaft with the hole in the pulley at the 6 o'clock position.
16. Install, hand-tight only, a 6 mm x 18 mm bolt through the crankshaft pulley and thread it into the front cover.

❋❋ CAUTION

The crankshaft must remain in the Top Dead Center (TDC) position during installation of the pulley bolt or damage to the engine can occur. Therefore, the crankshaft pulley must be held in place with the Crankshaft Damper Holding Tool and the bolt should be installed using hand tools only.

➡Do not reuse the crankshaft pulley bolt.

17. Install a new crankshaft pulley bolt. Use the Crankshaft Damper Holding Tool and a suitable 1/2-in drive hand tool to hold the crankshaft pulley, tighten the crankshaft pulley bolt in 2 stages:
  • Stage 1: Tighten to 74 ft. lbs. (100 Nm).
  • Stage 2: Tighten an additional 90 degrees.
18. Remove the 6 mm x 18 mm bolt from hole in lower side of pulley.
19. Remove the Crankshaft TDC Timing Peg.
20. Remove the Camshaft Alignment Plate.

➡Only turn the engine in the normal direction of rotation.

21. Turn the crankshaft clockwise one and three-fourths turns.
22. Install the Crankshaft TDC Timing Peg.

➡Only turn the engine in the normal direction of rotation.

23. Turn the crankshaft clockwise until the crankshaft contacts the Crankshaft TDC Timing Peg.

❋❋ CAUTION

Only hand-tighten the bolt or damage to the front cover can occur.

24. Using the 6 mm x 18 mm bolt, check the position of the crankshaft pulley.
25. If it is not possible to install the bolt, the engine valve timing must be corrected by repeating this procedure.

26. Install the Camshaft Alignment Plate to check the position of the camshafts.

27. Remove the Camshaft Alignment Plate.

28. Remove the 6 mm x 18 mm bolt from lower hole in pulley.

29. Remove the Crankshaft TDC Timing Peg.

30. Install the engine plug bolt. Tighten to 15 ft. lbs. (20 Nm).

31. Install the accessory drive belt.

32. Install the front RH wheel and tire.

33. Install the valve cover.

34. Using the scan tool, perform the Misfire Monitor Neutral Profile Correction procedure, following the on-screen instructions.

3.0L Engine

See Figure 99.

1. Raise and safely support the vehicle.
2. Remove the accessory drive belt.
3. Remove the crankshaft pulley bolt and washer.
4. Discard the crankshaft pulley bolt.
5. Using a 3 Jaw Puller, remove the crankshaft pulley.

To install:

6. Lubricate the crankshaft front seal inner lip with clean engine oil.

7. Clean the keyway and slot using metal surface prep before applying silicone gasket and sealant.

➡The crankshaft pulley must be installed and the bolt tightened within

4 minutes of applying the silicone gasket and sealant.

8. Apply silicone gasket and sealant to the end of the keyway slot.

9. Lubricate the outside diameter sealing surface with clean engine oil.

10. Using a proper Crankshaft Vibration Damper Installer, install the crankshaft pulley.

11. Install the bolt and washer. Tighten the bolt in 4 stages:
- Stage 1: Tighten to 89 ft. lbs. (120 Nm).
- Stage 2: Loosen one full turn.
- Stage 3: Tighten to 37 ft. lbs. (50 Nm).
- Stage 4: Tighten an additional 90 degrees.

12. Install the accessory drive belt.

CYLINDER HEAD

REMOVAL & INSTALLATION

2.5L & Hybrid Engines

See Figures 100 through 103.

⁂ WARNING

Do not loosen or remove the crankshaft pulley bolt without first installing the special tools as instructed in this procedure. The crankshaft pulley and the crankshaft timing sprocket are not keyed to the crankshaft. The crankshaft, the

crankshaft sprocket and the pulley are fitted together by friction, using diamond washers between the flange faces on each part. For that reason, the crankshaft sprocket is also unfastened if the pulley bolt is loosened. Before any repair requiring loosening or removal of the crankshaft pulley bolt, the crankshaft and camshafts must be locked in place by the special service tools, otherwise severe engine damage can occur.

⁂ WARNING

During engine repair procedures, cleanliness is extremely important. Any foreign material (including any material created while cleaning gasket surfaces) that enters the oil passages, coolant passages or the oil pan may cause engine failure.

1. Raise and safely support the vehicle.
2. Release the fuel system pressure. See "GASOLINE FUEL INJECTION SYSTEMS" section.
3. Drain the engine cooling system.
4. Remove the Variable Camshaft Timing (VCT) oil control solenoid.
5. Remove the timing drive components.
6. Remove the Camshaft Alignment Plate.
7. Mark the position of the camshaft lobes on the No. 1 cylinder for installation reference.

⁂ CAUTION

Failure to follow the camshaft loosening procedure can result in damage to the camshafts.

8. Mark the location and orientation of each camshaft bearing cap.
9. Remove the camshafts from the engine.
10. Loosen the camshaft bearing cap bolts, in sequence, one turn at a time until all tension is released from the camshaft bearing caps.
11. Remove the bolts and the camshaft bearing caps.
12. Remove the camshafts. See "Camshaft & Valve Lifters" in this section.
13. Mark locations and remove the valve tappets.

➡The number on the valve tappets only reflects the digits that follow the decimal. For example, a tappet with the number 0.650 has the thickness of 3.650 mm.

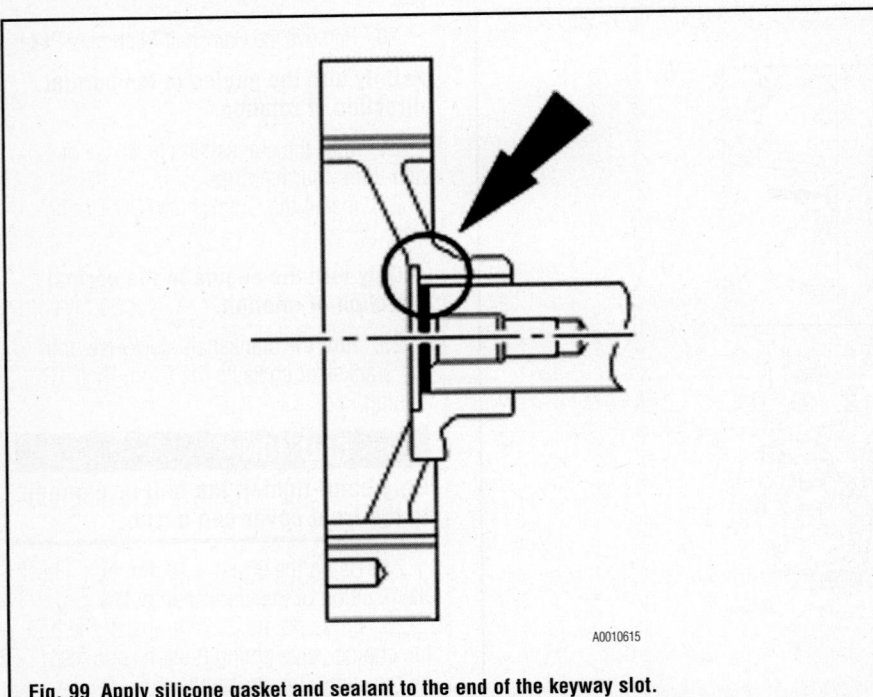

Fig. 99 Apply silicone gasket and sealant to the end of the keyway slot.

A0010615

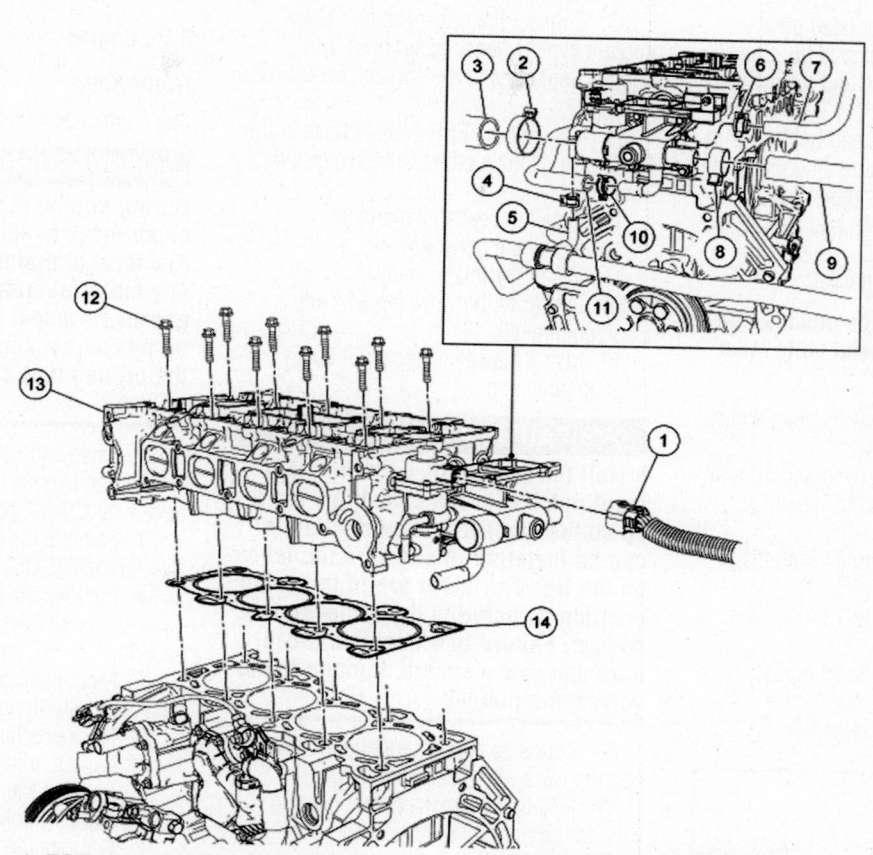

1. EGR valve electrical connector
   (part of 12B637)
2. Upper radiator hose clamp
3. Upper radiator hose
4. EGR coolant tube clamp
5. EGR coolant hose (part of heater hose)
6. Engine coolant vent hose clamp
   (part of 8W005)
7. Engine coolant vent hose
8. Heater hose clamp (part of 18K580)
9. Heater hose
10. Bypass hose clamp
11. Bypass hose
12. Cylinder head bolt (10 required)
13. Cylinder head
14. Cylinder head gasket

N0085930

Fig. 100 Exploded view of the cylinder head assembly—2.5L engine

14. Inspect the valve tappets for any signs of wear or damage.

15. Remove the intake manifold. See "Intake Manifold" in this section.

16. Remove the generator. See "ENGINE ELECTRICAL" section.

17. Remove the exhaust manifold. See "Exhaust Manifold" in this section.

18. Disconnect the EGR valve electrical connector. Disconnect the EGR coolant hose from the EGR valve.

19. Disconnect the upper radiator hose, coolant bypass hose, heater hose and coolant vent hose from the engine coolant outlet.

20. Remove the 10 bolts and the cylinder head.

21. Discard the bolts and the cylinder head gasket.

To install:

❊❊ CAUTION

Do not use metal scrapers, wire brushes, power abrasive discs or other abrasive means to clean the sealing surfaces. Use a plastic scraping tool to remove all traces of the head gasket.

➡**If there is no residual gasket material present, metal surface prep can be used to clean and prepare the surfaces.**

22. Clean the cylinder head-to-cylinder block mating surface of both the cylinder

head and the cylinder block in the following sequence.

23. Remove any large deposits of silicone or gasket material with a plastic scraper.

24. Apply silicone gasket remover, following package directions, and allow to set for several minutes.

25. Remove the silicone gasket remover with a plastic scraper. A second application of silicone gasket remover may be required if residual traces of silicone or gasket material remain.

26. Apply metal surface prep, following package directions, to remove any traces of oil or coolant, and to prepare the surfaces to bond with the new gasket. Do not attempt to

make the metal shiny. Some staining of the metal surfaces is normal.

27. Support the cylinder head on a bench with the head gasket side up. Check the cylinder head distortion and the cylinder block distortion.

28. Clean the cylinder head bolt holes in the cylinder block. Make sure all coolant, oil or other foreign material is removed.

29. Apply silicone gasket and sealant to the locations shown.

30. Install a new head gasket.

➡The cylinder head bolts must not be reused. New cylinder head bolts must be installed.

31. Lubricate the bolts with clean engine oil prior to installation.

32. Install the cylinder head and 10 new bolts. Tighten the bolts in the sequence shown in 5 stages:
- Stage 1: Tighten to 44 inch lbs. (5 Nm).
- Stage 2: Tighten to 133 inch lbs. (15 Nm).
- Stage 3: Tighten to 33 ft. lbs. (45 Nm).
- Stage 4: Turn 90 degrees.

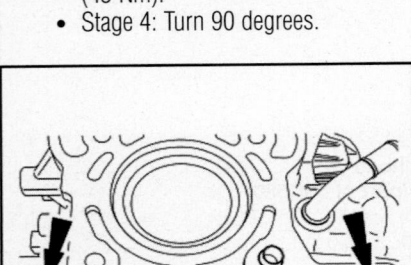

Fig. 101 Apply silicone gasket and sealant to the locations shown.

- Stage 5: Turn an additional 90 degrees.

33. Connect the upper radiator hose, coolant bypass hose, heater hose and coolant vent hose to the engine coolant outlet.

34. Connect the EGR coolant hose to the EGR valve. Connect the EGR valve electrical connector.

35. Install the exhaust manifold.

36. Install the generator.

37. Install the intake manifold.

38. Lubricate the valve tappets with clean engine oil.

39. Install the valve tappets in their original positions.

✳✳ **CAUTION**

Install the camshafts with the alignment notches in the camshafts lined up so the camshaft alignment plate can be installed. Make sure the lobes on the No. 1 cylinder are in the same position as noted in the removal procedure. Failure to follow this procedure can cause severe damage to the valves and pistons.

40. Lubricate the camshaft journals and bearing caps with clean engine oil.

41. Install the camshafts and bearing caps in their original location and orientation. Tighten the bearing caps in the sequence shown in 3 stages:
- Stage 1: Tighten the camshaft bearing cap bolts, one turn at a time, until finger-tight.
- Stage 2: Tighten to 7 Nm (62 lb-in).
- Stage 3: Tighten to 16 Nm (142 lb-in).

42. Install the Camshaft Alignment Plate.

43. Install the timing drive components.

44. Install the VCT oil control solenoid.

45. Fill and bleed the engine cooling system.

3.0L Engine

Right Bank

See Figures 104 and 105.

✳✳ **WARNING**

During engine repair procedures, cleanliness is extremely important. Any foreign material (including any material created while cleaning gasket surfaces) that enters the oil passages, coolant passages or the oil pan may cause engine failure.

1. Raise and safely support the vehicle.

2. Remove the lower intake manifold. See "Intake Manifold" in this section.

3. Remove the coolant pump housing. See "ENGINE COOLING" section.

4. Remove the RH camshafts. See "Camshafts & Valve Lifters" in this section.

5. Mark positions and remove the camshaft roller followers.

6. Mark positions and remove the hydraulic lash adjusters.

7. Remove the RH exhaust manifold. See "Exhaust Manifold" in this section.

8. Remove the bolts in the sequence shown.

9. Remove the cylinder head.

10. Discard the bolts and gasket.

11. Support the cylinder head on a bench with the head gasket side up. Check the cylinder head distortion and the cylinder block distortion.

To install:

➡New cylinder head bolts must be installed. They are a torque-to-yield design and cannot be reused.

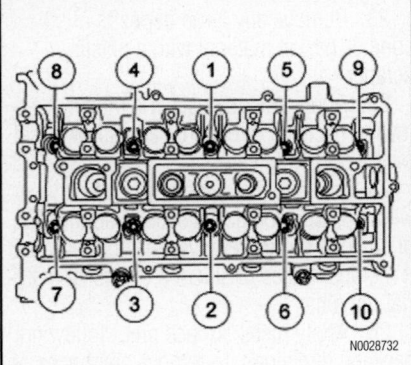

Fig. 102 Cylinder head bolt tightening sequence—2.5L engine

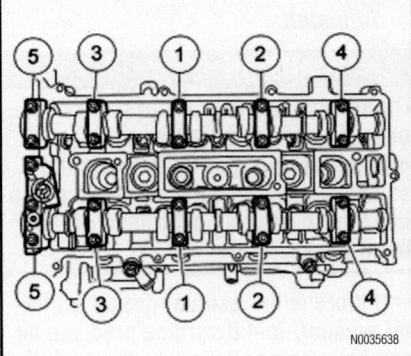

Fig. 103 Camshaft bearing cap bolt tightening sequence—2.5L engine

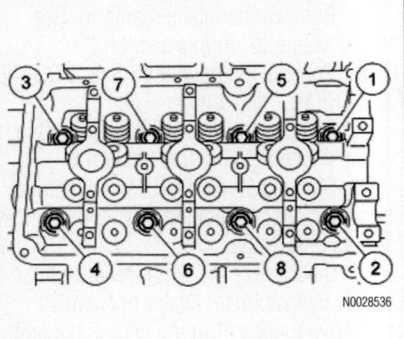

Fig. 104 Remove the bolts in the sequence shown.

⁂ CAUTION

Do not use metal scrapers, wire brushes, power abrasive discs or other abrasive means to clean the sealing surfaces. These tools cause scratches and gouges which make leak paths.

12. Use a plastic scraping tool to remove all traces of the head gasket. Clean all surfaces with metal surface prep.

13. Position a new gasket and the cylinder head.

14. Install the bolts and tighten in 6 stages in the sequence shown.
- Stage 1: Tighten to 30 ft. lbs. (40 Nm).
- Stage 2: Tighten 90 degrees.
- Stage 3: Loosen one full turn.
- Stage 4: Tighten to 30 ft. lbs. (40 Nm).
- Stage 5: Tighten 90 degrees.
- Stage 6: Tighten 90 degrees.

15. Install the RH exhaust manifold. See "Exhaust Manifold" in this section.

⁂ CAUTION

The hydraulic lash adjusters and camshaft roller followers must be installed in their original positions. If not reassembled in their original positions, severe engine damage may occur.

16. Install the hydraulic lash adjusters. Lubricate the hydraulic lash adjusters with clean engine oil.

17. Install the camshaft roller followers. Lubricate the camshaft roller followers with clean engine oil.

18. Install the RH camshafts. See "Camshafts & Valve Lifters" in this section.

19. Install the coolant pump housing. See "ENGINE COOLING" section.

20. Install the lower intake manifold. See "Intake Manifold" in this section.

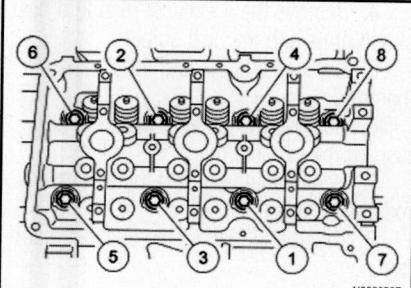

Fig. 105 Cylinder head bolt tightening sequence for right bank head—3.0L engine

Left Bank

See Figures 106 and 107.

⁂ WARNING

During engine repair procedures, cleanliness is extremely important. Any foreign material (including any material created while cleaning gasket surfaces) that enters the oil passages, coolant passages or the oil pan may cause engine failure.

1. Raise and safely support the vehicle.

2. Remove the lower intake manifold. See "Intake Manifold" in this section.

3. Remove the coolant pump housing. See "ENGINE COOLING" section.

4. Remove the LH camshafts. See "Camshafts & Valve Lifters" in this section.

5. Mark locations and remove the camshaft roller followers.

6. Mark locations and remove the hydraulic lash adjusters.

7. Remove the LH catalytic converter. See "Catalytic Converter" in this section.

8. Remove the 4 upper radiator support bracket bolts.

9. Remove the oil level indicator.

10. Remove the stud bolt and then remove the oil level indicator tube by guiding it between the radiator support and the cooling fan. Remove and discard the O-ring seal.

11. Remove the bolts in the sequence shown.

12. Clean the cylinder head gasket surfaces with a plastic scraping tool and metal surface prep.

13. Support the cylinder head on a bench with the head gasket side up. Check the cylinder head distortion and the cylinder block distortion.

To install:

14. Position a new gasket and the cylinder head.

➡**New cylinder head bolts must be installed. They are a torque-to-yield design and cannot be reused.**

15. Install the bolts and tighten in 6 stages in the sequence shown.
- Stage 1: Tighten to 30 ft. lbs. (40 Nm).
- Stage 2: Tighten 90 degrees.
- Stage 3: Loosen one full turn.
- Stage 4: Tighten to 30 ft. lbs. (40 Nm).
- Stage 5: Tighten 90 degrees.
- Stage 6: Tighten 90 degrees.

16. Install a new oil level indicator O-ring seal and lubricate with clean engine oil.

17. Guide the oil level indicator tube between the radiator support and the cooling fan and install it in the orifice, install the stud bolt. To install, tighten to 89 inch lbs. (10 Nm).

18. Install the oil level indicator.

19. Install the 4 upper radiator support bracket bolts. Tighten to 89 inch lbs. (10 Nm).

20. Install the LH catalytic converter.

⁂ CAUTION

The hydraulic lash adjusters and camshaft roller followers must be installed in their original positions. If not reassembled in their original positions, severe engine damage may occur.

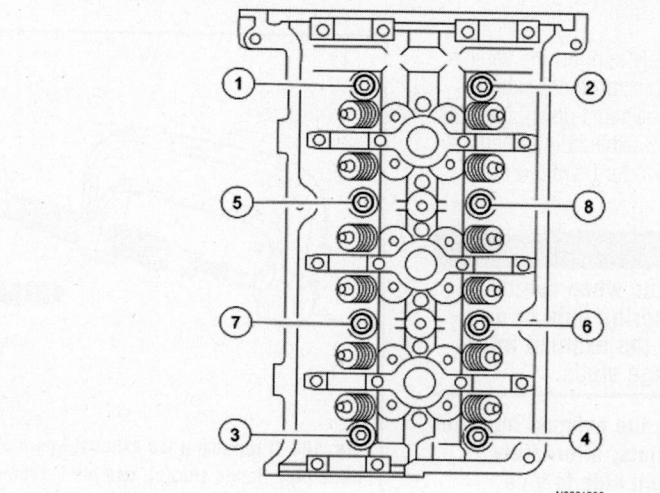

Fig. 106 LH cylinder head bolt loosening sequence—3.0L engine

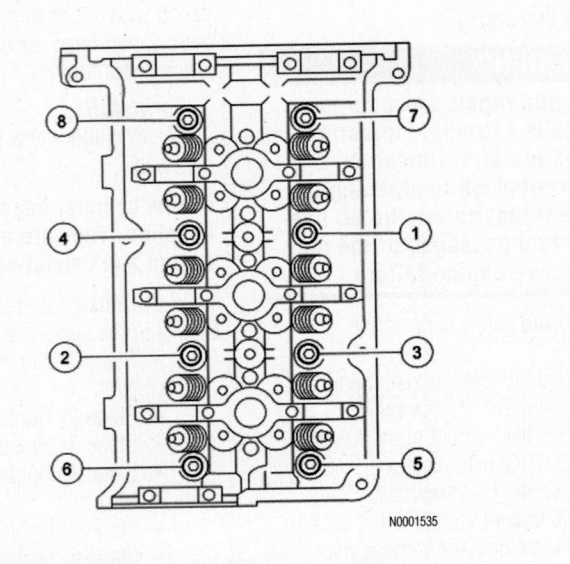

Fig. 107 LH cylinder head bolt tightening sequence—3.0L engine

21. Install the hydraulic lash adjusters. Lubricate the hydraulic lash adjusters with clean engine oil.

22. Install the camshaft roller followers. Lubricate the camshaft roller followers with clean engine oil.

23. Install the camshafts. See "Camshafts & Valve Lifters" in this section.

24. Install the coolant pump housing. See "ENGINE COOLING" section.

25. Install the lower intake manifold. See "Intake Manifold" in this section.

EXHAUST INTERMEDIATE PIPE

REMOVAL & INSTALLATION

2.5L & Hybrid Engines

See Figure 108.

1. Raise and safely support the vehicle.

2. Remove and discard the 3 exhaust intermediate pipe-to-exhaust downpipe nuts (2.5L engine) or the 3 exhaust intermediate pipe-to-catalytic converter manifold nuts (Hybrid engine).

※※ CAUTION

Only use hand tools when removing or installing the spring nuts or damage may occur to the exhaust intermediate pipe flange studs.

➡**When loosening the exhaust intermediate pipe spring nuts, alternately loosen the nuts from side to side.**

3. Remove and discard the two 10mm catalytic converter-to-exhaust intermediate

pipe spring nuts and remove the intermediate pipe.

To install:

4. Inspect the exhaust intermediate pipe flange studs for damage.

5. If damaged, replace stud(s), or if stud comes out when removing nut(s), replace the stud(s).

6. If replacing the exhaust intermediate pipe flange stud(s), use the C-Frame and Screw Installer/Remover to push the 10mm stud out of the flange.

➡**When positioning the new 10 mm stud in the exhaust intermediate flange, make sure to line up the new stud seat knurls with witness knurl grooves in the exhaust intermediate flange.**

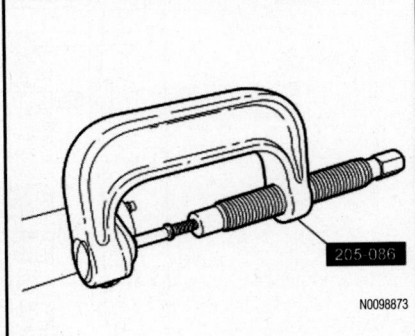

Fig. 108 If replacing the exhaust intermediate pipe flange stud(s), use the C-Frame and Screw Installer/Remover to push the 10mm stud out of the flange.

7. If replacing the exhaust intermediate pipe flange stud(s), use a C-clamp and a deep well socket to push the 10mm stud fully into the flange. Make sure the stud is fully and evenly seated into the flange.

➡**Replace the gasket by hand. Do not rotate the gasket back and forth during installation. Doing so may lessen the gaskets ability to seal and stay correctly positioned during assembly.**

8. Thoroughly clean the sealing surfaces of the flanges using a finishing pad. Inspect the cleaned sealing surface for nicks and scratches and replace as necessary.

9. Install a new converter-to-exhaust intermediate pipe gasket by hand.

10. Install the 2 new 10mm catalytic converter-to-exhaust intermediate pipe spring nuts and alternately tighten RH side to LH side in sequence in 3 stages:
- Stage 1: Tighten to 44 inch lbs. (5 Nm).
- Stage 2: Tighten to 133 inch lbs. (15 Nm).
- Stage 3: Tighten to 18 ft. lbs. (25 Nm).

11. For Hybrid engine, install 3 new exhaust intermediate pipe-to-catalytic converter manifold nuts. Tighten to 18 ft. lbs. (25 Nm).

12. For the 2.5L engine, install 3 new exhaust intermediate pipe-to-exhaust downpipe nuts. Tighten to 18 ft. lbs. (25 Nm).

EXHAUST MANIFOLD

REMOVAL & INSTALLATION

2.5L Engine (Exc. Hybrid)

See Figures 109 and 110

1. Raise and safely support the vehicle.

2. Remove the exhaust downpipe and exhaust intermediate pipe. See "Exhaust Intermediate Pipe" in this section.

3. Disconnect the Heated Oxygen Sensor (HO2S) electrical connector.

4. Remove the 4 exhaust manifold heat shield bolts and the heat shield.

5. Remove and discard the 7 exhaust manifold nuts.

6. Remove the exhaust manifold and discard the exhaust manifold gasket.

7. Remove and discard the 7 exhaust manifold studs.

8. Clean and inspect the exhaust manifold.

To install:

9. Install the 7 new exhaust manifold studs. Tighten to 150 inch lbs. (17 Nm).

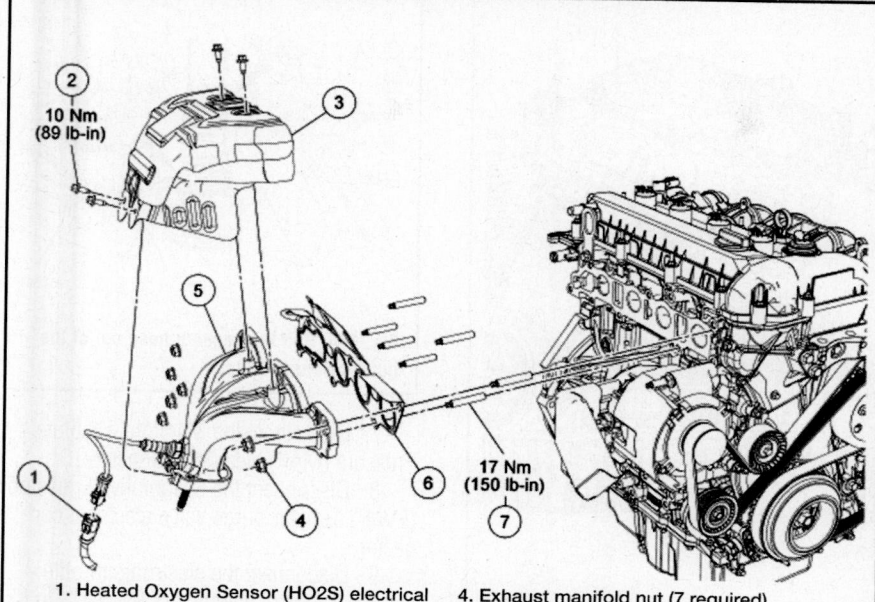

1. Heated Oxygen Sensor (HO2S) electrical connector
2. Exhaust manifold heat shield bolt (4 required)
3. Exhaust manifold heat shield
4. Exhaust manifold nut (7 required)
5. Exhaust manifold
6. Exhaust manifold gasket
7. Exhaust manifold stud (7 required)

N0086211

Fig. 109 Removing the exhaust manifold—2.5L engine

※ **CAUTION**

Failure to tighten the catalytic converter nuts to specification, including the second time, before installing the converter bracket bolts will cause the converter to develop an exhaust leak.

10. Install a new exhaust manifold gasket, the exhaust manifold and 7 new nuts in the sequence shown in 2 stages:
- Stage 1: Tighten to 35 ft. lbs. (48 Nm).
- Stage 2: Tighten to 35 ft. lbs. (48 Nm).

N0085944

Fig. 110 Exhaust manifold nut tightening sequence—2.5L engine

11. Install the exhaust manifold heat shield and the 4 bolts. Tighten to 89 inch lbs. (10 Nm).
12. Connect the HO2S electrical connector.
13. Install the exhaust downpipe and exhaust intermediate pipe. See "Exhaust Intermediate Pipe" in this section.

Hybrid Engine

See Figure 111.

1. Raise and safely support the vehicle.
2. Remove the exhaust intermediate pipe. See "Exhaust Intermediate Pipe" in this section.
3. Remove the 2 exhaust bracket bolts.
4. Disconnect the Heated Oxygen Sensor (HO2S) and the Catalyst Monitor Sensor (CMS) electrical connectors.
5. Remove and discard the 7 catalytic converter manifold nuts.
6. Remove the catalytic converter manifold from the vehicle.
7. Discard the catalytic converter manifold gasket.
8. Remove and discard the 7 catalytic converter manifold studs.
9. Clean and inspect the catalytic converter manifold.

To install:
10. Install the 7 new catalytic converter manifold studs. Tighten to 150 inch lbs. (17 Nm).

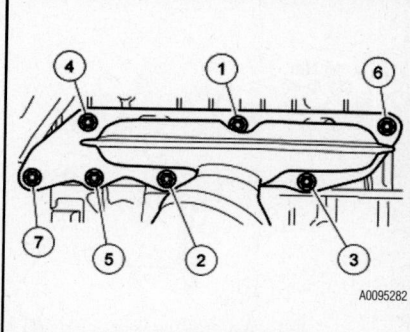

A0095282

Fig. 111 Manifold nut tightening sequence—Hybrid engine

※ **CAUTION**

Failure to tighten the catalytic converter manifold nuts to both the first step and second step specification before installing the converter bracket bolts will cause the converter to develop an exhaust leak.

11. Using a new gasket, install the catalytic converter and the 7 exhaust manifold nuts. Tighten in 2 stages in the sequence shown:
- Stage 1: Tighten to 35 ft. lbs. (47 Nm).
- Stage 2: Tighten to 35 ft. lbs. (47 Nm).
12. Connect the HO2S and the CMS electrical connectors.
13. Install the 2 exhaust bracket bolts. Tighten to 18 ft. lbs. (25 Nm).
14. Install the exhaust intermediate pipe. See "Exhaust Intermediate Pipe" in this section.

3.0L Engine

See Figures 112 and 113.

1. Raise and safely support the vehicle.
2. Remove the RH catalytic converter.
3. Disconnect the Heated Oxygen Sensor (HO2S) electrical connector.
4. Remove the 3 exhaust manifold heat shield bolts and the heat shield.
5. Remove the EGR tube fitting nut from the exhaust manifold.
6. Remove and discard the 6 exhaust manifold nuts.
7. Remove the exhaust manifold and discard the exhaust manifold gasket.
8. Remove and discard the 6 exhaust manifold studs.
9. Clean and inspect the exhaust manifold.

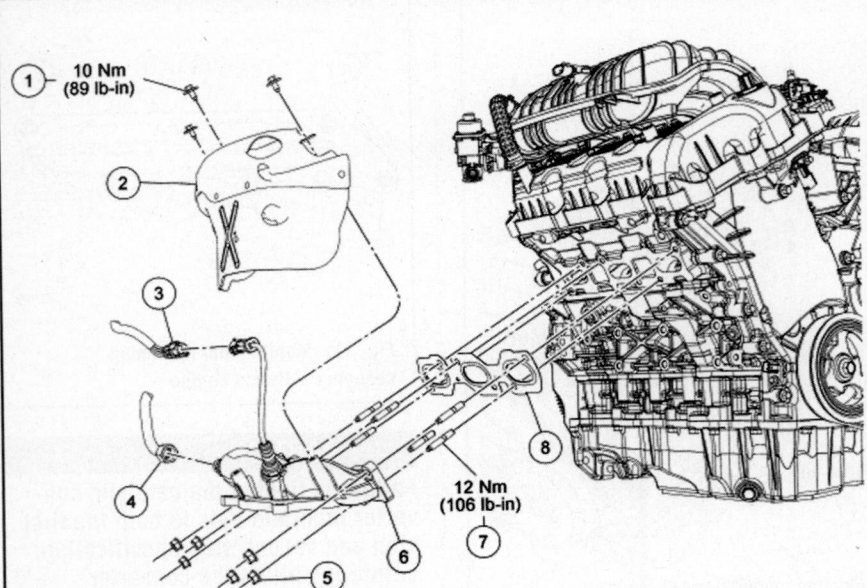

1. Exhaust manifold heat shield bolt (3 required)
2. Exhaust manifold heat shield
3. Heated Oxygen Sensor (HO2S) electrical connector
4. EGR tube nut
5. Exhaust manifold nut (6 required)
6. Exhaust manifold
7. Exhaust manifold stud (6 required)
8. Exhaust manifold gasket

N0087536

Fig. 112 Removing the exhaust manifold—3.0L engine

To install:

10. Install the 6 new exhaust manifold studs. Tighten to 106 inch lbs. (12 Nm).

❊❊ CAUTION

Failure to tighten the catalytic converter nuts to specifications, the first and second steps, before installing the converter bracket bolts will cause the converter to develop an exhaust leak.

11. Install a new exhaust manifold gasket, the exhaust manifold and 6 new nuts. Tighten the nuts in 2 stages in the sequence shown:

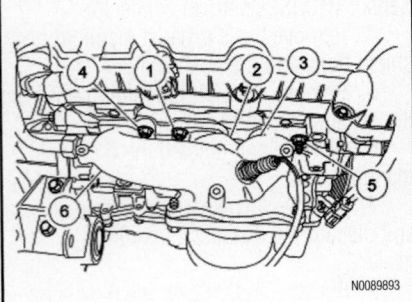

N0089893

Fig. 113 Exhaust manifold bolt tightening sequence—3.0L engine

- Stage 1: Tighten to 15 ft. lbs. (20 Nm).
- Stage 2: Tighten to 15 ft. lbs. (20 Nm).

12. Install the EGR tube fitting nut on the exhaust manifold. Tighten to 30 ft. lbs. (40 Nm).

13. Install the exhaust manifold heat shield and the 3 bolts. Tighten to 89 inch lbs. (10 Nm).

14. Connect the HO2S electrical connector.

15. Install the 3.0L RH catalytic converter.

INTAKE MANIFOLD

REMOVAL & INSTALLATION

2.5L Engine

See Figures 114 through 117.

1. With vehicle in Neutral, position it on a hoist.
2. Remove the fuel rail.
3. Disconnect the vacuum supply hose.
4. Depress the quick release locking ring.
5. Pull the vacuum hose out of the quick release fitting.
6. Disconnect the fuel vapor return hose from the intake manifold.

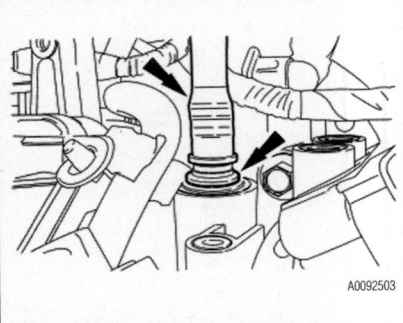

A0092503

Fig. 114 Pull the vacuum hose out of the quick release fitting.

7. Disconnect the Manifold Absolute Pressure (MAP) electrical connector.
8. Disconnect the Evaporative Emission (EVAP) canister purge valve electrical connector.
9. Disconnect the electronic throttle control electrical connector.
10. Disconnect the Knock Sensor (KS) electrical connector.
11. Detach the wire harness pin-type retainer.
12. Detach the heater hose pin-type retainer.
13. Detach all wiring harness pin-type retainers from the intake manifold and position the wiring harness aside.
14. Loosen the clamp and disconnect air cleaner outlet pipe from the throttle body.
15. Remove the intake manifold lower bolt.
16. Remove the intake manifold lower bolt.
17. Remove the 6 bolts and position the intake manifold aside to access the crankcase vent oil separator tube and the EGR tube.
18. Squeeze the 2 crankcase vent oil separator tube tabs and disconnect the tube from the intake manifold.
19. Remove the EGR tube.
20. Remove the intake manifold and gaskets.

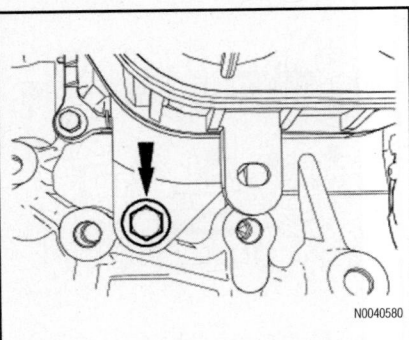

N0040580

Fig. 115 Remove the intake manifold lower bolt.

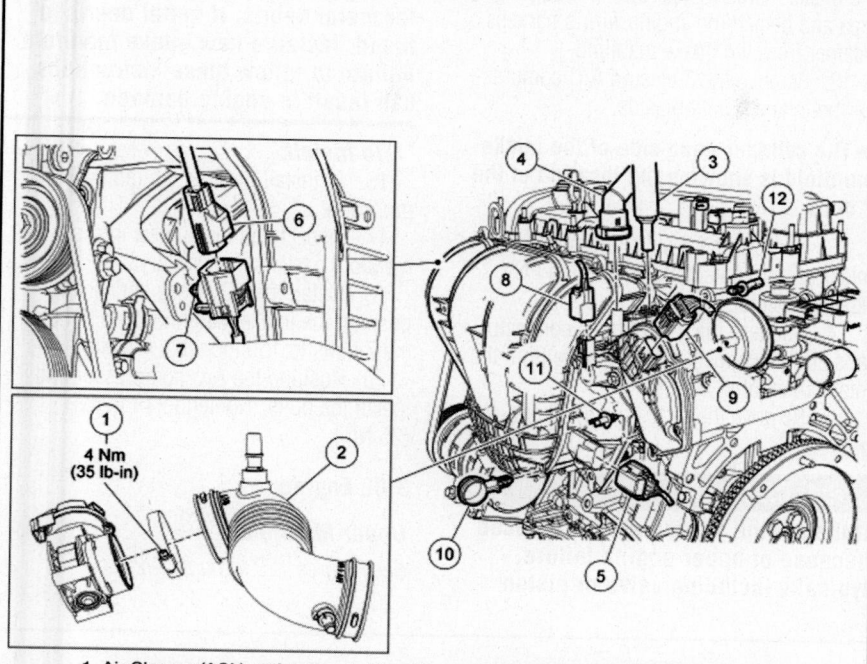

1. Air Cleaner (ACL) outlet pipe-to-Throttle Body (TB) clamp
2. ACL outlet pipe
3. Vacuum supply hose
4. Fuel vapor return hose
5. Manifold Absolute Pressure (MAP) sensor electrical connector
6. Knock Sensor (KS) electrical connector
7. Wire harness pin-type retainer
8. Evaporative Emission (EVAP) canister purge valve electrical connector
9. Electronic throttle control electrical connector
10. Heater hose retainer
11. Wire harness pin-type retainer
12. Wire harness pin-type retainer

N0097090

Fig. 116 Removing the intake manifold (1 of 2)—2.5L engine

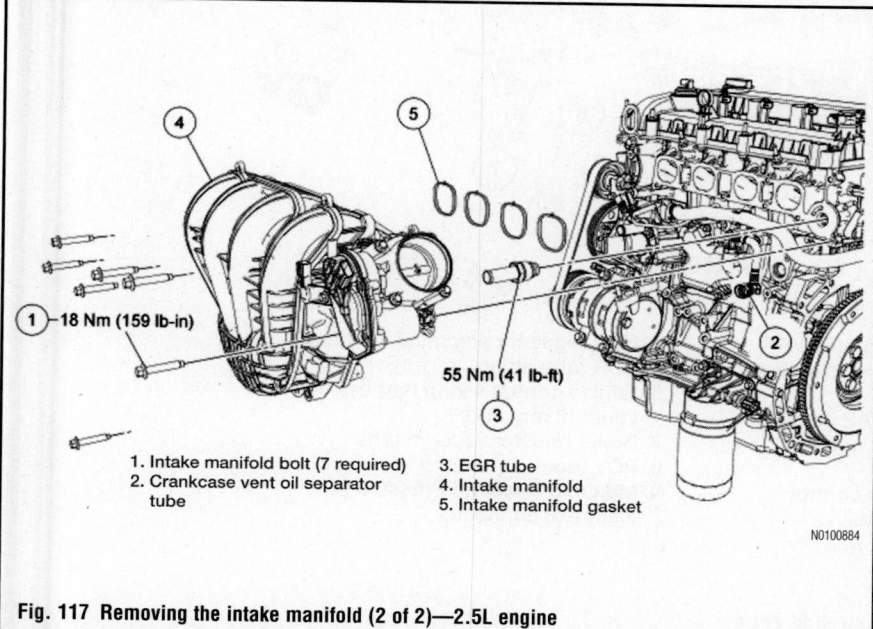

1. Intake manifold bolt (7 required)
2. Crankcase vent oil separator tube
3. EGR tube
4. Intake manifold
5. Intake manifold gasket

N0100884

Fig. 117 Removing the intake manifold (2 of 2)—2.5L engine

To install:

> **✱✱ CAUTION**
>
> If the engine is repaired or replaced because of upper engine failure, typically including valve or piston damage, check the intake manifold for metal debris. If metal debris is found, install a new intake manifold. Failure to follow these instructions can result in engine damage.

21. To install, reverse the removal procedure.

22. Inspect and install new intake manifold gaskets if necessary.

23. Tighten the fasteners as follows:
- EGR tube connection: 41 ft. lbs. (55 Nm)
- Intake manifold bolts: 159 inch lbs. (18 Nm).

Hybrid Engine

See Figures 118 and 119.

1. With vehicle in Neutral, position it on a hoist.

2. Remove the fuel rail. See "GASOLINE FUEL INJECTION SYSTEM" section.

3. Remove the cooling fan motor and shroud. See "ENGINE COOLING" section.

4. Remove the Throttle Body (TB). See "GASOLINE FUEL INJECTION SYSTEM" section.

5. Remove the accessory drive belt tensioner.

6. Disconnect the Engine Oil Pressure (EOP) switch electrical connector.

7. Disconnect the Manifold Absolute Pressure (MAP) sensor electrical connector.

8. Disconnect the Evaporative Emission (EVAP) canister purge valve electrical connector.

9. Disconnect the EVAP tube-to- EVAP canister purge valve quick connect coupling

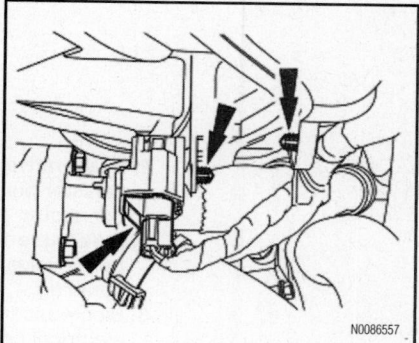

N0086557

Fig. 118 Disconnect the Knock Sensor (KS) electrical connector and detach the 2 pin-type retainers.

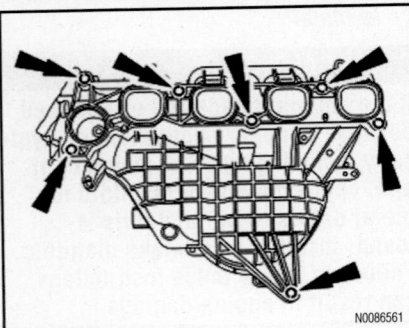

Fig. 119 Remove the 7 bolts and position the intake manifold aside to access the PCV hose connector.

and the brake booster vacuum tube from the intake manifold.

10. Disconnect the Knock Sensor (KS) electrical connector and detach the 2 pin-type retainers.

11. Detach the 2 wiring retainers from the intake manifold near the TB mounting area and detach the engine wiring harness retainer from the intake manifold.

12. Remove the 3 electric A/C compressor bolts and position aside.

➡**The cylinder head side of the intake manifold is showing the location of the 7 bolts.**

13. Remove the 7 bolts and position the intake manifold aside to access the PCV hose connector.

14. Squeeze the 2 PCV hose connector tabs and disconnect the PCV hose from the intake manifold.

15. Remove the intake manifold and gaskets.

✷✷ CAUTION

If the engine is repaired or replaced because of upper engine failure, typically including valve or piston damage, check the intake manifold for metal debris. If metal debris is found, install a new intake manifold. Failure to follow these instructions can result in engine damage.

To install:

16. To install, reverse the removal procedure.

17. Inspect and install new intake manifold gaskets if necessary.

18. Install the PCV hose connector, position the intake manifold, then tighten the 7 bolts to 159 inch lbs. (18 Nm).

19. Position the A/C compressor and install the bolts. Tighten to 18 ft. lbs. (25 Nm).

3.0L Engine

Upper Manifold

See Figures 120 through 122.

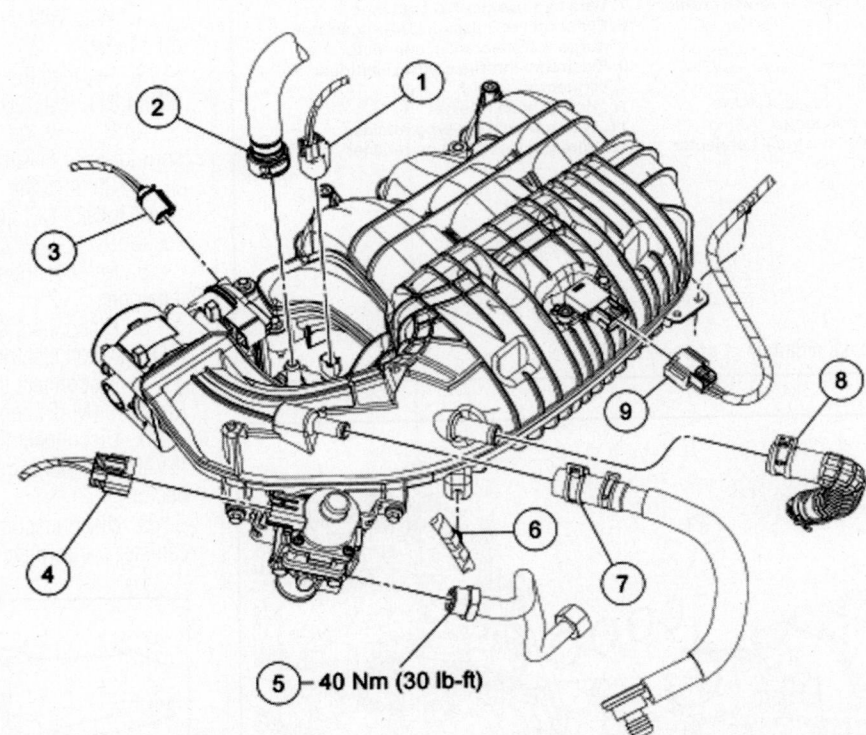

1. Evaporative Emission (EVAP) canister purge valve electrical connector
2. EVAP tube-to- EVAP canister purge valve quick connect coupling
3. Electronic throttle control electrical connector
4. EGR regulator electrical connector
5. EGR tube fitting
6. Engine control wiring harness retainer (2 required)
7. Brake booster vacuum tube
8. PCV tube
9. Manifold Absolute Pressure (MAP) electrical connector

5 – 40 Nm (30 lb-ft)

Fig. 120 Removing the upper intake manifold (1 of 2)—3.0L engine

Fig. 126 Working from under the vehicle, loosen the 2 RH engine bracket-to-Power Transfer Unit (PTU) 0.19 in. (5 mm).

pan-to-engine block and to the oil pan-to-engine front cover mating surface. Do not cover the bolt holes.

17. Position the oil pan onto the engine and install the oil pan bolts finger-tight.

➡**The engine front cover-to-oil pan bolts must be tightened first to align the front surface of the oil pan flush with the front surface of the engine block.**

18. Install the 4 engine front cover-to-oil pan bolts. Tighten to 89 inch lbs. (10 Nm).

19. Tighten the oil pan bolts in the sequence shown. Tighten to 18 ft. lbs. (25 Nm).

20. On FWD vehicles, perform the following:

a. Alternate tightening the 1 LH bellhousing-to-engine and 1 RH engine-to-bellhousing bolts to slide the transaxle and engine together. Tighten to 35 ft. lbs. (48 Nm).

b. Tighten the 1 remaining LH bellhousing-to-engine bolt. Tighten to 35 ft. lbs. (48 Nm).

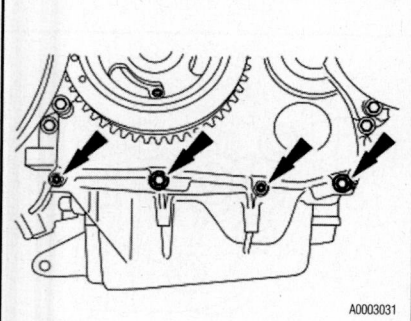

Fig. 127 Install the 4 engine front cover-to-oil pan bolts. Tighten to 89 inch lbs. (10 Nm).

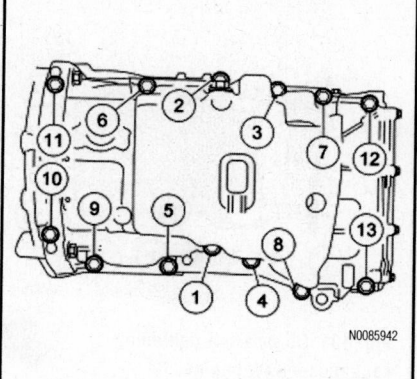

Fig. 128 Oil pan bolt tightening sequence

c. Tighten the 1 remaining RH engine-to-bellhousing bolt (automatic transaxle). Tighten to 35 ft. lbs. (48 Nm).

21. On AWD vehicles, perform the following:

a. Alternate tightening the 1 RH engine-to- PTU bracket bolt and 1 LH bellhousing-to-engine bolt to slide transaxle and engine together.

b. Tighten the PTU bracket bolt to 33 ft. lbs. (45 Nm).

c. Tighten the LH bellhousing bolt to 35 ft. lbs. (48 Nm).

d. Tighten the remaining RH engine-to- PTU bracket bolt. Tighten to 33 ft. lbs. (45 Nm).

e. Tighten the 1 remaining LH lower bolt. Tighten to 35 ft. lbs. (48 Nm).

22. Install the 2 bellhousing-to-oil pan bolts. Tighten to 35 ft. lbs. (48 Nm).

23. Install the 2 oil pan-to-bellhousing bolts. Tighten to 35 ft. lbs. (48 Nm).

24. Install the LH splash shield and the 7 retainers. Tighten to 80 inch lbs. (9 Nm).

25. On AWD vehicles, working from the top of vehicle, tighten the 2 RH engine-to-bellhousing bolts. Tighten to 35 ft. lbs. (48 Nm).

26. Tighten the 2 upper bellhousing-to-engine bolts. Tighten to 35 ft. lbs. (48 Nm).

27. Install the air cleaner outlet pipe.

28. Fill the engine with clean engine oil.

Hybrid Engine

See Figure 129.

1. Raise and safely support the vehicle.

2. Drain the engine oil, then install the drain plug. Tighten to 21 ft. lbs. (28 Nm).

3. Remove the engine front cover. See "Timing Chain Front Cover" in this section.

4. Remove the 4 oil pan-to-bellhousing bolts. Remove the 13 bolts and the oil pan.

To install:

> ❋❋❋ **CAUTION**

Do not use metal scrapers, wire brushes, power abrasive discs or other abrasive means to clean the sealing surfaces. These tools cause scratches and gouges, which make leak paths. Use a plastic scraping tool to remove traces of sealant.

5. Clean and inspect all mating surfaces.

➡**If the oil pan is not secured within 4 minutes of sealant application, the sealant must be removed and the sealing area cleaned with metal surface prep. Allow to dry until there is no sign of wetness, or 4 minutes, whichever is longer. Failure to follow this procedure can cause future oil leakage.**

6. Apply a 2.5mm (0.09 in) bead of silicone gasket and sealant to the oil pan mating edges (do not cover the bolt holes).

7. Position the oil pan and install the 2 rear oil pan bolts finger-tight.

8. Using a suitable straightedge, align the front surface of the oil pan flush with the front surface of the engine block.

9. Install the remaining oil pan bolts. Tighten in the sequence shown to 18 ft. lbs. (25 Nm).

10. Install the 4 oil pan-to-bellhousing bolts. Tighten to 35 ft. lbs. (48 Nm).

11. Install the engine front cover. See "Timing Chain Front Cover" in this section.

12. Fill the engine with clean engine oil.

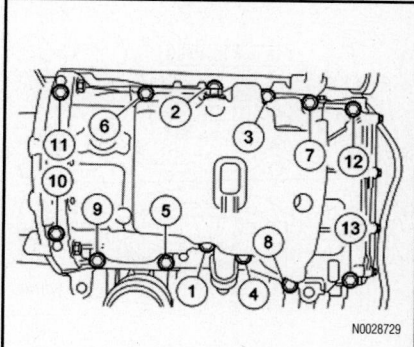

Fig. 129 Install the remaining oil pan bolts. Tighten in the sequence shown to 18 ft. lbs. (25 Nm).

3.0L Engine

See Figures 130 and 131.

> **✳✳ WARNING**
>
> **During engine repair procedures, cleanliness is extremely important. Any foreign material (including any material created while cleaning gasket surfaces) that enters the oil passages, coolant passages or the oil pan may cause engine failure.**

1. Raise and safely support the vehicle.
2. Remove the exhaust Y-pipe.
3. Drain the engine oil and install the drain plug. Tighten to 19 ft. lbs. (26 Nm).
4. Remove and discard the oil filter.
5. Remove the transaxle to torque converter access cover.
6. Remove the 2 oil pan-to-transaxle bolts.
7. Remove the 15 bolts and the oil pan.
8. Remove and discard the oil pan gasket.

To install:

> **✳✳ CAUTION**
>
> **Do not use metal scrapers, wire brushes, power abrasive discs or other abrasive means to clean the sealing surfaces. These tools cause scratches and gouges which make leak paths.**

9. Use a plastic scraping tool to remove all traces of the oil pan gasket.
10. Clean all sealing surfaces with metal surface prep and install a new oil pan gasket.

➡ **The oil pan must be installed and the bolts tightened within 4 minutes of sealant application.**

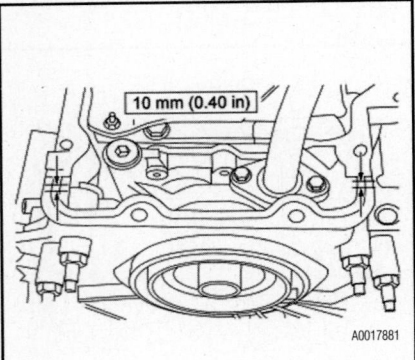

Fig. 130 Apply a 0.40 in. (10 mm) diameter dot of silicone sealant to the areas indicated.

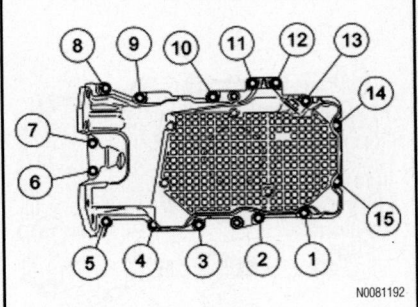

Fig. 131 Oil pan bolt tightening sequence—3.0L engine

11. Apply a 0.40 in. (10 mm) diameter dot of silicone sealant to the areas indicated.
12. Position the oil pan and loosely install the bolts.
13. Install the 2 oil pan-to-transaxle bolts. Tighten to 30 ft. lbs. (40 Nm).
14. Tighten the oil pan-to-engine bolts in the sequence shown to 18 ft. lbs. (25 Nm).
15. Install the transaxle access cover.
16. Lubricate the engine oil filter gasket with clean engine oil prior to installing.
17. Install a new oil filter. Tighten to 44 inch lbs. (5 Nm) and then rotate an additional 180 degrees.
18. Install the exhaust Y-pipe.
19. Fill the engine with clean engine oil.

OIL PUMP

REMOVAL & INSTALLATION

2.5L & Hybrid Engines

See Figures 132 through 136.

1. With the engine in Neutral, position it on a hoist.

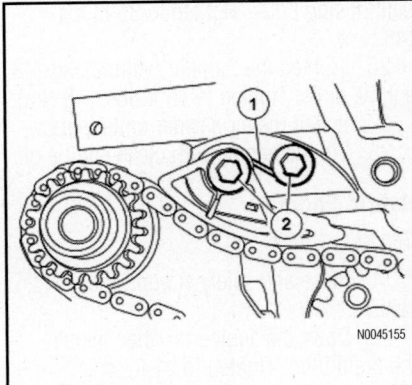

Fig. 132 Release the tension on the tensioner spring (1) and remove the 2 shoulder bolts (2) and the tensioner.

2. Remove the engine front cover. See "Timing Chain Front Cover" in this section.
3. Drain the engine oil, then install the drain plug. To install, tighten to 21 ft. lbs. (28 Nm).
4. Remove the 4 oil pan-to-bellhousing bolts.
5. Remove the 13 bolts and the oil pan.
6. Discard the gasket and clean and inspect the gasket mating surfaces.
7. Remove the 2 bolts and the oil pump screen and pickup tube.
8. Remove the oil pump drive chain tensioner.
9. Release the tension on the tensioner spring. Remove the 2 shoulder bolts and the tensioner.
10. Remove the chain from the oil pump sprocket.
11. Remove the bolt and oil pump sprocket.
12. Remove the 4 bolts and the oil pump.

To install:

13. Clean the oil pump and cylinder block mating surfaces with metal surface prep.
14. Install the oil pump assembly. Tighten the 4 bolts in the sequence shown in 2 stages:
    - Stage 1: Tighten to 89 inch lbs. (10 Nm).
    - Stage 2: Tighten to 15 ft. lbs. (20 Nm).
15. Install the oil pump sprocket and bolt. Tighten to 18 ft. lbs. (25 Nm).
16. Install the chain onto the oil pump sprocket.
17. Install the oil pump drive chain tensioner shoulder bolt. Tighten to 89 inch lbs. (10 Nm).
18. Install the oil pump drive chain tensioner and bolt. Hook the tensioner spring around the shoulder bolt. Tighten to 89 inch lbs. (10 Nm).
19. Install the oil pump drive chain tensioner and bolt. Hook the tensioner

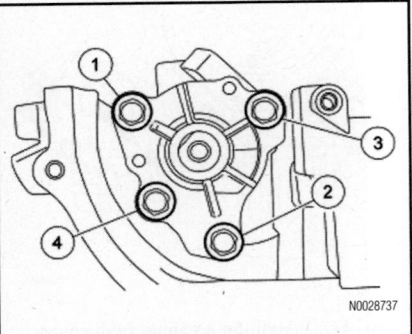

Fig. 133 Oil pump bolt tightening sequence—3.0L engine

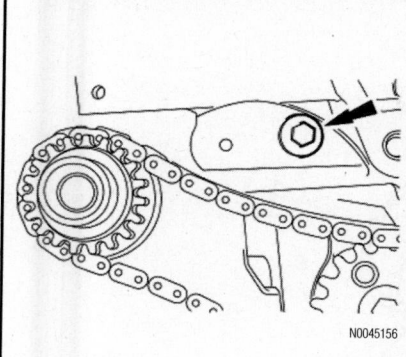

Fig. 134 Install the oil pump drive chain tensioner shoulder bolt. Tighten to 89 inch lbs. (10 Nm).

spring around the shoulder bolt. Tighten to 89 inch lbs. (10 Nm).

20. Install the oil pump screen and pickup tube and the 2 bolts. Tighten to 89 inch lbs. (10 Nm).

❋❋ CAUTION

Do not use metal scrapers, wire brushes, power abrasive discs or other abrasive means to clean the sealing surfaces. These tools cause scratches and gouges, which make leak paths. Use a plastic scraping tool to remove traces of sealant.

21. Clean all mating surfaces with metal surface prep.

➡ **If the oil pan is not secured within 10 minutes of sealant application, the sealant must be removed and the sealing area cleaned with metal surface prep. Allow to dry until there is no sign of wetness, or 10 minutes, whichever is longer. Failure to follow this procedure can cause future oil leakage.**

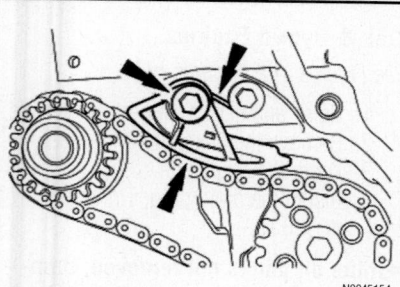

Fig. 135 Install the oil pump drive chain tensioner and bolt. Hook the tensioner spring around the shoulder bolt. Tighten to 89 inch lbs. (10 Nm).

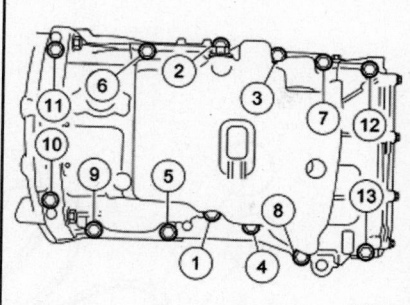

Fig. 136 Install the remaining oil pan bolts. Tighten in the sequence shown to 18 ft. lbs. (25 Nm).

22. Apply a 0.9 in. (2.5 mm) bead of sealant gasket and sealant to the oil pan.

23. Position the oil pan onto the engine and install the 2 rear oil pan bolts finger-tight.

24. Using a suitable straight edge, align the front surface of the oil pan flush with the front surface of the engine block.

25. Install the remaining oil pan bolts. Tighten in the sequence shown to 18 ft. lbs. (25 Nm).

26. Install the 4 oil pan-to-bellhousing bolts. Tighten to 35 ft. lbs. (48 Nm).

27. Install the engine front cover. See "Timing Chain Front Cover" in this section.

28. Fill the engine with clean engine oil.

3.0L Engine

See Figures 137 and 138.

❋❋ WARNING

During engine repair procedures, cleanliness is extremely important. Any foreign material (including any material created while cleaning gasket surfaces) that enters the oil passages, coolant passages or the oil pan may cause engine failure.

Fig. 138 Position the oil pump and install the bolts. Tighten in the sequence shown to 89 inch lbs. (10 Nm).

1. Raise and safely support the vehicle.

2. Remove the timing drive components. See "Timing Chain & Sprockets" in this section.

3. Remove the oil pump screen and pickup tube.

4. Remove the bolts in the sequence shown.

To install:

5. Position the oil pump and install the bolts. Tighten in the sequence shown to 89 inch lbs. (10 Nm).

6. Install the oil pump screen and pickup tube.

7. Install the timing drive components. See "Timing Chain & Sprockets" in this section.

PISTON AND RING

POSITIONING

See Figures 139 through 141.

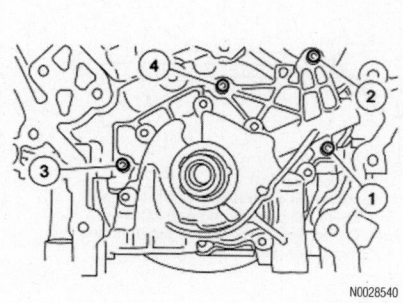

Fig. 137 Remove the bolts in the sequence shown.

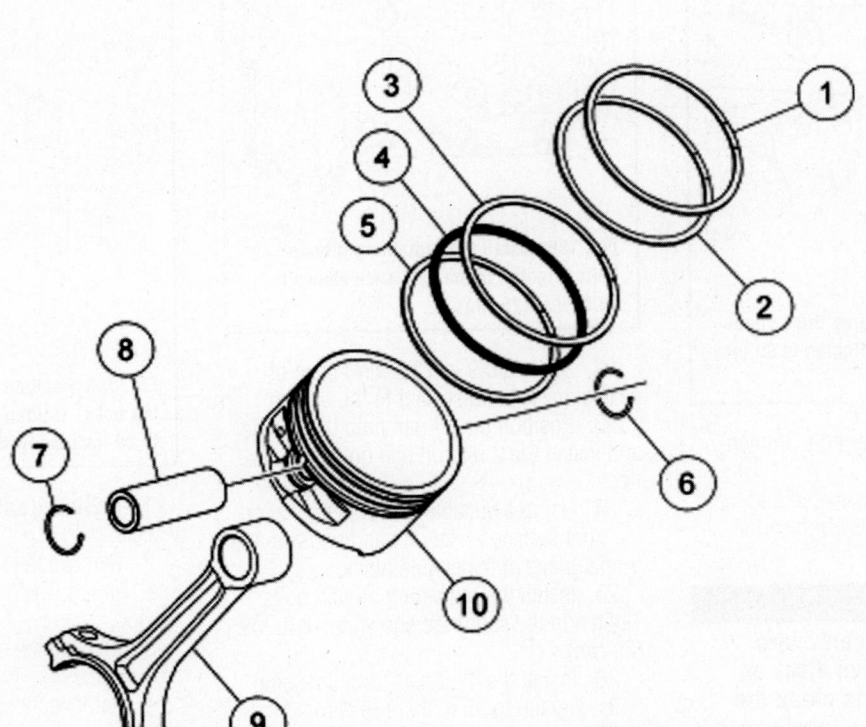

1. Piston compression upper ring
2. Piston compression lower ring
3. Piston oil control upper segment ring
4. Piston oil control spacer
5. Piston oil control lower segment ring
6. Piston pin retainer
7. Piston pin retainer
8. Piston pin
9. Connecting rod
10. Piston

N0010114

Fig. 139 Exploded view of the piston assembly—2.5L engine, Hybrid engine & 3.0L engine

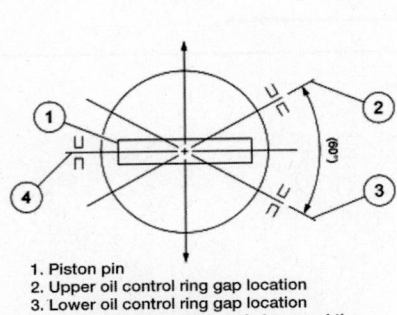

1. Piston pin
2. Upper oil control ring gap location
3. Lower oil control ring gap location
4. Center line of the piston pin bore and the expander gap

N0082528

Fig. 140 Showing the piston ring end gap positions—2.5L & Hybrid engines

REAR MAIN SEAL

REMOVAL & INSTALLATION

2.5L & Hybrid Engines

See Figures 142 through 144.

1. Raise and safely support the vehicle.
2. Remove the flexplate or flywheel.
3. Drain the engine oil.
4. Install the drain plug. Tighten to 21 ft. lbs. (28 Nm).

➡**If the oil pan is not removed, damage to the rear oil seal retainer joint can occur.**

5. Remove the 17 bolts and the oil pan.
6. Remove the 6 bolts and the crankshaft rear oil seal with retainer plate.

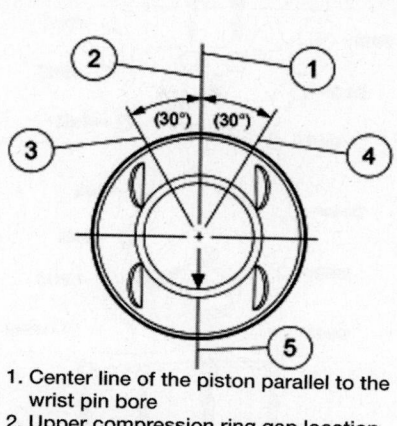

1. Center line of the piston parallel to the wrist pin bore
2. Upper compression ring gap location
3. Upper oil control segment ring gap location
4. Lower oil control segment ring gap location
5. Expander ring and lower compression ring gap location

N0082470

Fig. 141 Showing the piston ring end gap positions—3.0L engine

To install:

7. Using a proper oil seal installer, position the crankshaft rear oil seal with retainer plate onto the crankshaft.

8. Install the crankshaft rear oil seal with retainer plate and bolts. Tighten in the sequence shown to 89 inch lbs. (10 Nm).

✳✳ CAUTION

Do not use metal scrapers, wire brushes, power abrasive discs or other abrasive means to clean the sealing surfaces. These tools cause scratches and gouges, which make leak paths. Use a plastic scraping tool to remove traces of sealant.

9. Clean and inspect all the oil pan and cylinder block mating surfaces.

➡**If the oil pan is not secured within 4 minutes of sealant application, the sealant must be removed and the sealing area cleaned with metal surface prep. Allow to dry until there is no sign of wetness, or 4 minutes, whichever is longer. Failure to follow this procedure can cause future oil leakage.**

10. Apply a 0.09 in. (2.5 mm) bead of silicone gasket and sealant to the oil pan. Install the oil pan. Install the 2 oil pan bolts finger-tight.

11. Install the 4 bolts. Tighten to 89 inch lbs. (10 Nm).

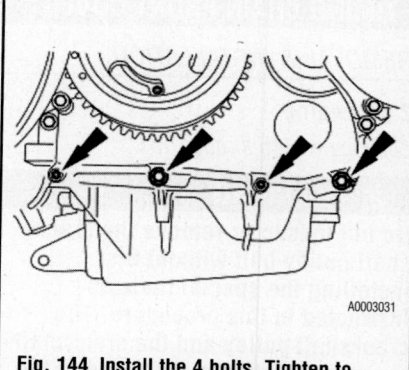

Fig. 144 Install the 4 bolts. Tighten to 89 inch lbs. (10 Nm).

12. Install the remaining oil pan bolts and tighten the oil pan bolts in the sequence shown to 18 ft. lbs. (25 Nm).

13. Install the flexplate or flywheel.

14. Fill the engine with clean engine oil.

3.0L Engine

See Figure 145.

1. Raise and safely support the vehicle.
2. Remove the flexplate.
3. Using a proper slide hammer and oil seal remover, remove and discard the crankshaft rear oil seal.

To install:

4. Clean all sealing surfaces with metal surface prep.

5. Apply clean engine oil to the seal lip and seal bore before installing the seal.

6. Using a proper seal installer with bolts, install the crankshaft rear oil seal.

7. Install the flexplate.

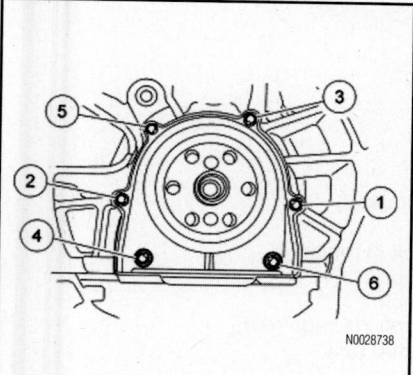

Fig. 142 Install the crankshaft rear oil seal with retainer plate and bolts. Tighten in the sequence shown to 89 inch lbs. (10 Nm).

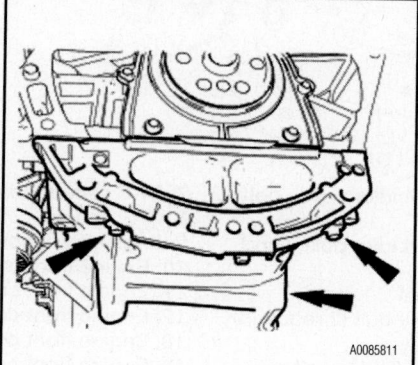

Fig. 143 Apply a 0.09 in. (2.5 mm) bead of silicone gasket and sealant to the oil pan. Install the oil pan. Install the 2 oil pan bolts finger-tight.

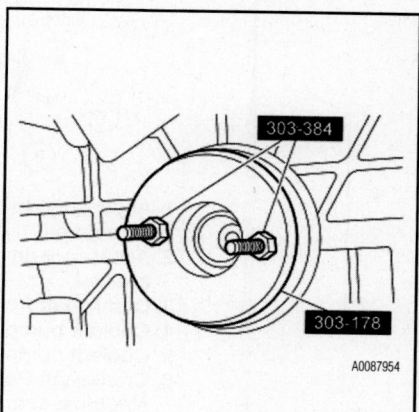

Fig. 145 Using a proper seal installer with bolts, install the crankshaft rear oil seal.

TIMING CHAIN FRONT COVER

REMOVAL & INSTALLATION

2.5L Engine

See Figures 146 through 151.

> **⁂ WARNING**
>
> Do not loosen or remove the crankshaft pulley bolt without first installing the special tools as instructed in this procedure. The crankshaft pulley and the crankshaft timing sprocket are not keyed to the crankshaft. The crankshaft, the crankshaft sprocket and the pulley are fitted together by friction, using diamond washers between the flange

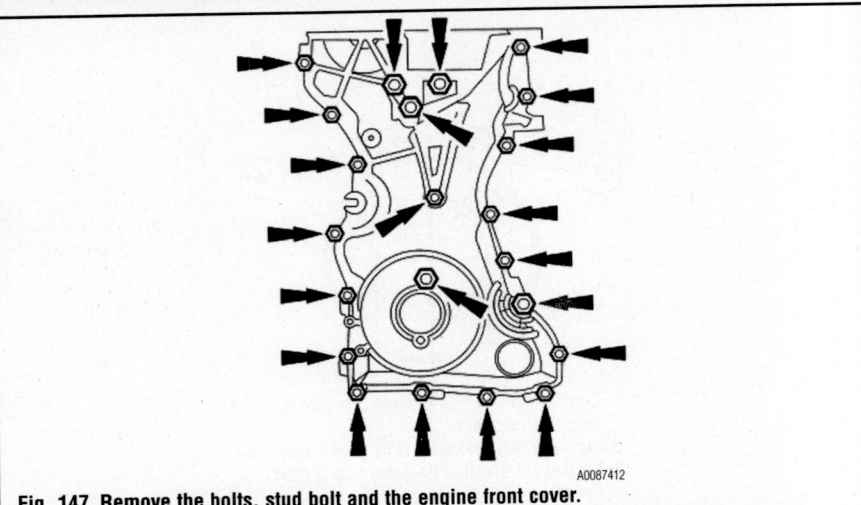

Fig. 147 Remove the bolts, stud bolt and the engine front cover.

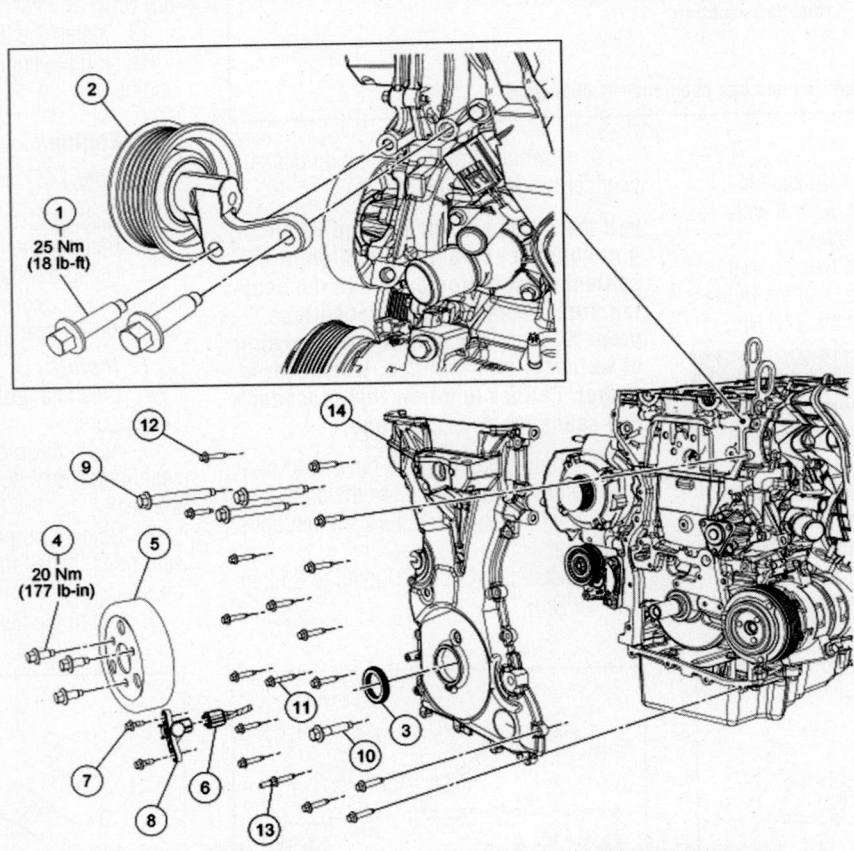

1. Accessory drive belt idler pulley bolt (2 required)
2. Accessory drive belt idler pulley and bracket
3. Crankshaft front seal
4. Coolant pump pulley bolt (3 required)
5. Coolant pump pulley
6. Crankshaft Position (CKP) sensor electrical connector
7. CKP sensor bolt (2 required)
8. CKP sensor
9. Engine front cover bolt (3 required)
10. Engine front cover bolt
11. Engine front cover bolt
12. Engine front cover bolt (16 required)
13. Engine front cover stud bolt
14. Engine front cover

Fig. 146 Exploded view of the timing chain cover (engine front cover)

faces on each part. For that reason, the crankshaft sprocket is also unfastened if the pulley bolt is loosened. Before any repair requiring loosening or removal of the crankshaft pulley bolt, the crankshaft and camshafts must be locked in place by the special service tools, otherwise severe engine damage can occur.

✳✳ WARNING

During engine repair procedures, cleanliness is extremely important. Any foreign material (including any material created while cleaning gasket surfaces) that enters the oil passages, coolant passages or the oil pan can cause engine failure.

1. Raise and safely support the vehicle.
2. Remove the accessory drive belt and the smooth idler pulley.
3. Remove the crankshaft pulley.
4. Remove the engine mount.

✳✳ CAUTION

Use care not to damage the engine front cover or the crankshaft when removing the seal.

5. Using a proper oil seal remover, remove the crankshaft front oil seal.
6. Remove the 3 bolts and the coolant pump pulley.
7. Remove the 2 bolts and the accessory drive belt idler pulley and bracket.
8. Disconnect the Crankshaft Position (CKP) sensor electrical connector. Remove and the 2 bolts and the CKP sensor.
9. Remove the bolts, stud bolt and the engine front cover.

To install:

✳✳ CAUTION

Do not use metal scrapers, wire brushes, power abrasive disks or other abrasive means to clean sealing surfaces. These tools cause scratches and gouges which make leak paths.

Clean and inspect the mounting surfaces of the engine and the front cover.

➡ The engine front cover must be installed and the bolts tightened within 4 minutes of applying the silicone gasket and sealant.

10. Apply a 2.5mm (0.09 in) bead of silicone gasket and sealant to the cylinder

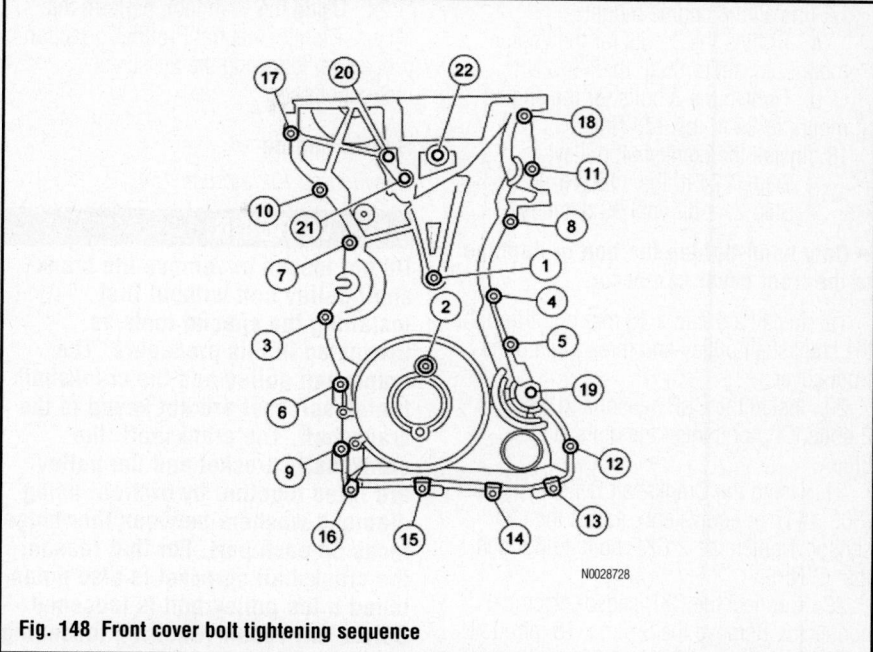

Fig. 148 Front cover bolt tightening sequence

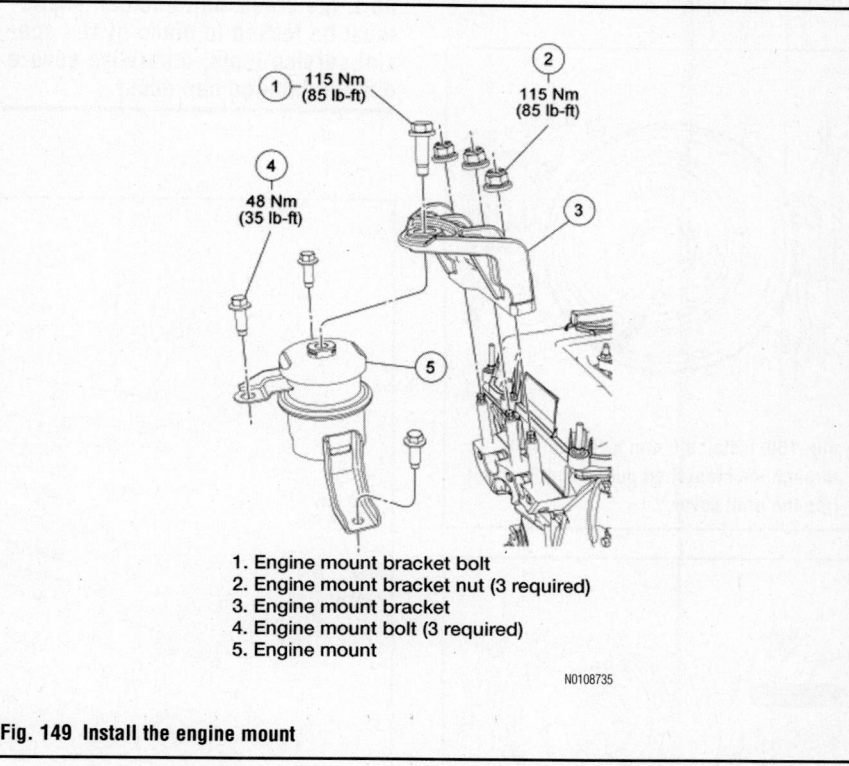

1. Engine mount bracket bolt
2. Engine mount bracket nut (3 required)
3. Engine mount bracket
4. Engine mount bolt (3 required)
5. Engine mount

Fig. 149 Install the engine mount

head and oil pan joint areas and to the front cover.

11. Install the engine front cover. Tighten the bolts in the sequence shown, to the following specifications:
- Tighten the 8mm bolts and stud bolt to 89 inch lbs. (10 Nm).
- Tighten the 13mm bolts to 35 ft. lbs. (48 Nm).

12. Install the accessory drive belt idler pulley and bracket and the 2 bolts. Tighten to 18 ft. lbs. (25 Nm).

13. Install the coolant pump pulley and bolts. Tighten to 15 ft. lbs. (20 Nm).

14. If installed, remove the through bolt from the Camshaft Front Oil Seal Installer.

15. Lubricate the oil seal with clean engine oil.

16. Using the Camshaft Front Oil Seal Installer, install the crankshaft front oil seal.

17. Install the engine mount:
  a. Tighten the 3 nuts for the engine mount bracket to 85 ft. lbs. (115 Nm).
  b. Tighten the 3 bolts for the engine mount to 35 ft. lbs. (48 Nm).
18. Install the crankshaft pulley:
  • Step 1: 74 ft. lbs. (100 Nm)
  • Step 2: additional 90 degrees

➡ Only hand-tighten the bolt or damage to the front cover can occur.

19. Install a 6 mm x 18 mm bolt through the crankshaft pulley and thread it into the front cover.
20. Install the CKP sensor and the 2 bolts. Do not tighten the bolts at this time.
21. Using the Crankshaft Sensor Aligner (303-1417 or equivalent), adjust the CKP sensor. Tighten the 2 CKP bolts to 62 inch lbs. (7 Nm).
22. Connect the CKP sensor electrical connector. Remove the 6 mm x 18 mm bolt.
23. Install the accessory drive belt and smooth idler pulley.

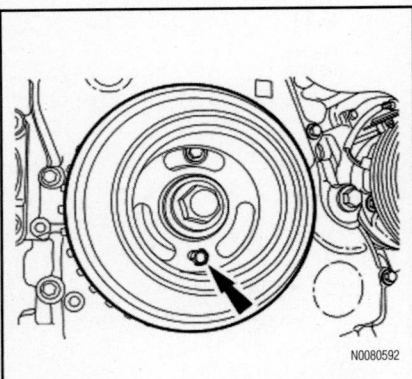

Fig. 150 Install a 6 mm x 18 mm bolt through the crankshaft pulley and thread it into the front cover.

Fig. 151 Using the Crankshaft Sensor Aligner (303-1417 or equivalent), adjust the CKP sensor. Tighten the 2 CKP bolts to 62 inch lbs. (7 Nm).

24. Using the scan tool, perform the Misfire Monitor Neutral Profile Correction procedure, following the on-screen instructions.

Hybrid Engine

See Figures 152 through 154.

✳✳ WARNING

Do not loosen or remove the crankshaft pulley bolt without first installing the special tools as instructed in this procedure. The crankshaft pulley and the crankshaft timing sprocket are not keyed to the crankshaft. The crankshaft, the crankshaft sprocket and the pulley are fitted together by friction, using diamond washers between the flange faces on each part. For that reason, the crankshaft sprocket is also unfastened if the pulley bolt is loosened. Before any repair requiring loosening or removal of the crankshaft pulley bolt, the crankshaft and camshafts must be locked in place by the special service tools, otherwise severe engine damage can occur.

✳✳ WARNING

During engine repair procedures, cleanliness is extremely important. Any foreign material (including any material created while cleaning gasket surfaces) that enters the oil passages, coolant passages or the oil pan can cause engine failure.

1. Raise and safely support the vehicle.
2. Remove the accessory drive belt and tensioner.
3. Remove the crankshaft pulley. See "Crankshaft Pulley" in this section.
4. Remove the engine mount.
5. Detach the transaxle selector lever cable fastener from the engine front cover stud bolt.

✳✳ CAUTION

Use care not to damage the engine front cover or the crankshaft when removing the seal.

6. Using a proper Oil Seal Remover, remove the crankshaft front seal.
7. Remove the 3 bolts and the coolant pump pulley.
8. Disconnect the Crankshaft Position (CKP) sensor electrical connector.

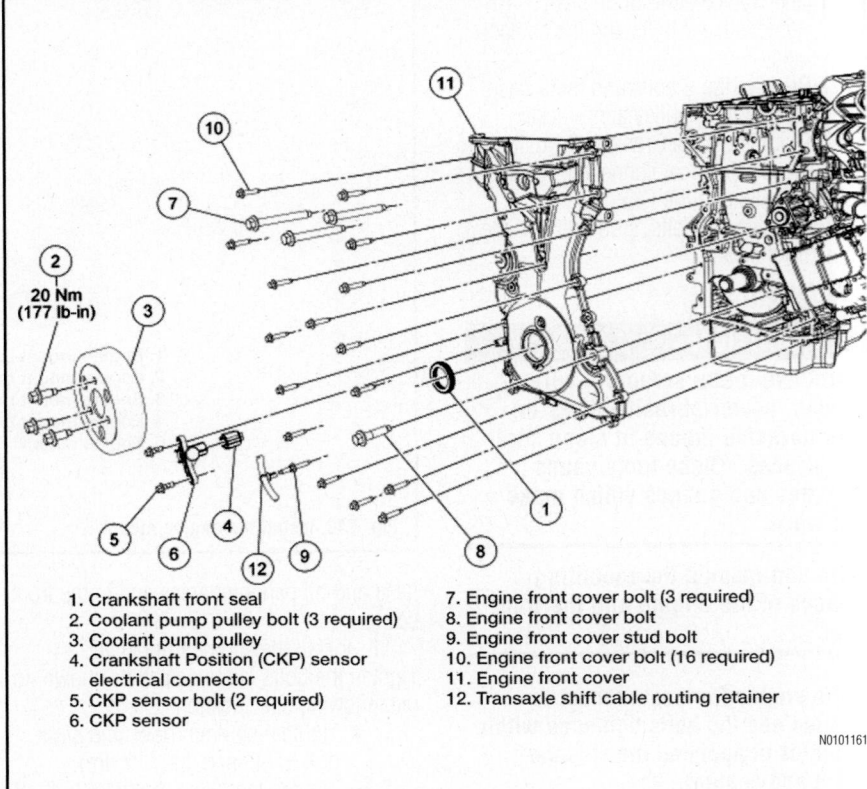

1. Crankshaft front seal
2. Coolant pump pulley bolt (3 required)
3. Coolant pump pulley
4. Crankshaft Position (CKP) sensor electrical connector
5. CKP sensor bolt (2 required)
6. CKP sensor
7. Engine front cover bolt (3 required)
8. Engine front cover bolt
9. Engine front cover stud bolt
10. Engine front cover bolt (16 required)
11. Engine front cover
12. Transaxle shift cable routing retainer

Fig. 152 Exploded view of the timing chain front cover—Hybrid engine

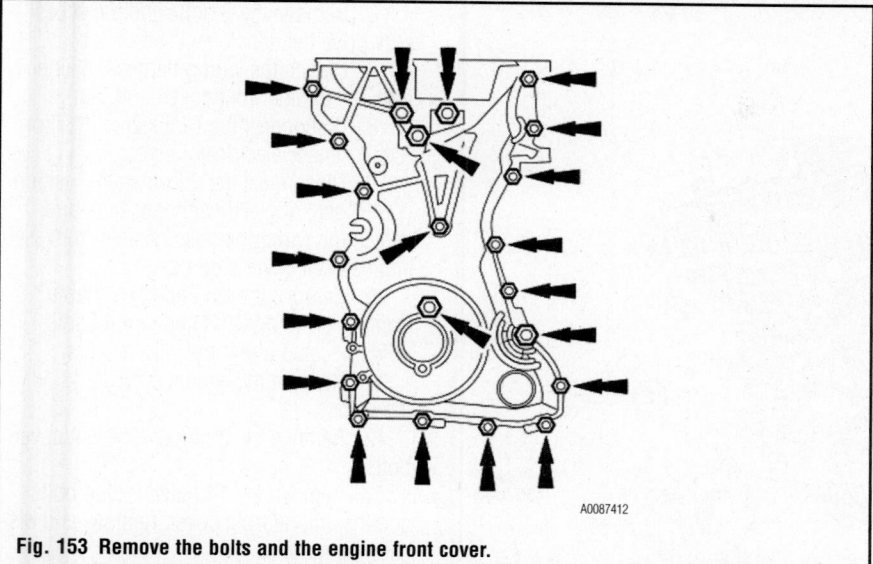

Fig. 153 Remove the bolts and the engine front cover.

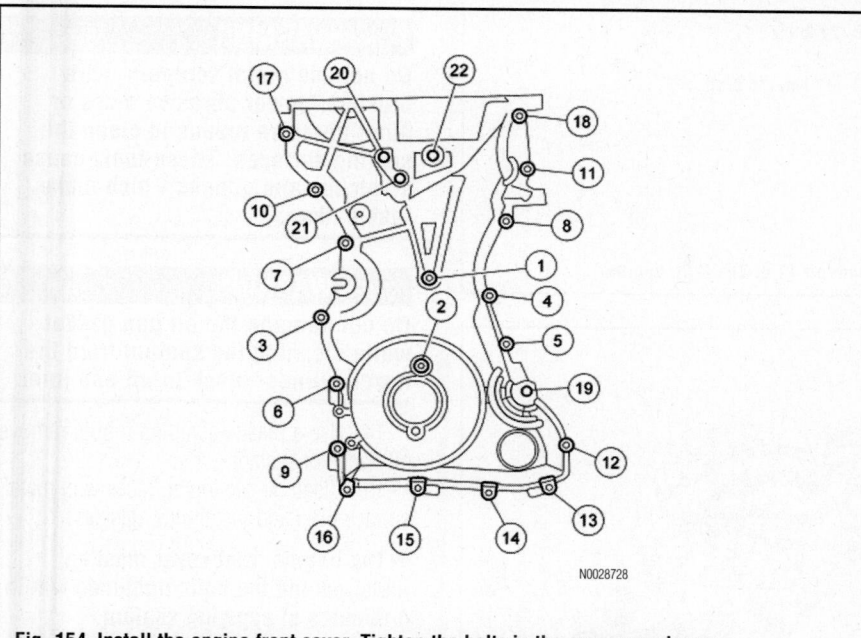

Fig. 154 Install the engine front cover. Tighten the bolts in the sequence shown.

Remove the 2 bolts and the CKP sensor.

9. Remove the bolts and the engine front cover.

To install:

✳✳ CAUTION

Do not use metal scrapers, wire brushes, power abrasive disks or other abrasive means to clean sealing surfaces. These tools cause scratches and gouges which make leak paths.

10. Clean and inspect the mounting surfaces of the engine and the front cover.

➡ **The engine front cover must be installed and the bolts tightened within 4 minutes of applying the silicone gasket and sealant.**

11. Apply a 2.5mm (0.09 in) bead of silicone gasket and sealant to the cylinder head and oil pan joint areas. Apply a 2.5mm (0.09 in) bead of silicone gasket and sealant to the front cover. Do not cover the bolt holes.

12. Install the engine front cover. Tighten the bolts in the sequence shown, to the following specifications:

- Tighten the 8mm bolts to 89 inch lbs. (10 Nm).
- Tighten the 13mm bolts to 35 ft. lbs. (48 Nm).

13. Install the engine front cover. Tighten the bolts in the sequence shown.

➡ **Remove the through bolt from the Camshaft Front Oil Seal Installer. Lubricate the oil seal with clean engine oil. Using a proper Camshaft Front Oil Seal Installer, install the crankshaft front seal.**

14. Install the coolant pump pulley and the 3 bolts. Tighten to 15 ft. lbs. (20 Nm).

15. Attach the transaxle selector lever cable fastener to the engine front cover stud bolt.

16. Install the engine mount. Tighten the bolt to 85 ft. lbs. (115 Nm).

17. Install the crankshaft pulley. See "Crankshaft Pulley" in this section.

✳✳ CAUTION

Only hand-tighten the bolt or damage to the front cover can occur.

18. Install a standard 6mm (0.23 in) x 18mm (0.7 in) bolt through the crankshaft pulley, with the small hole at the 6 o'clock position, and thread it into the front cover.

19. Install the CKP sensor and the 2 bolts. Do not tighten the bolts at this time.

20. Using the Crankshaft Sensor Aligner, adjust the CKP sensor. Tighten the 2 CKP bolts to 62 inch lbs. (7 Nm). Connect the CKP sensor electrical connector.

21. Remove the 6 mm x 18 mm bolt from the crankshaft pulley hole.

22. Install the accessory drive belt and tensioner.

3.0L Engine

See Figures 155 through 159.

✳✳ WARNING

During engine repair procedures, cleanliness is extremely important. Any foreign material (including any material created while cleaning gasket surfaces) that enters the oil passages, coolant passages or the oil pan can cause engine failure.

1. Raise and safely support the vehicle.
2. Release the fuel system pressure. See "GASOLINE FUEL INJECTION SYSTEMS" section.
3. Disconnect the battery ground cable.
4. Remove the crankshaft front seal. See "Crankshaft Front Seal" in this section.
5. Remove the generator bolt and the 2 nuts. Remove the stud and position the generator away from the engine.

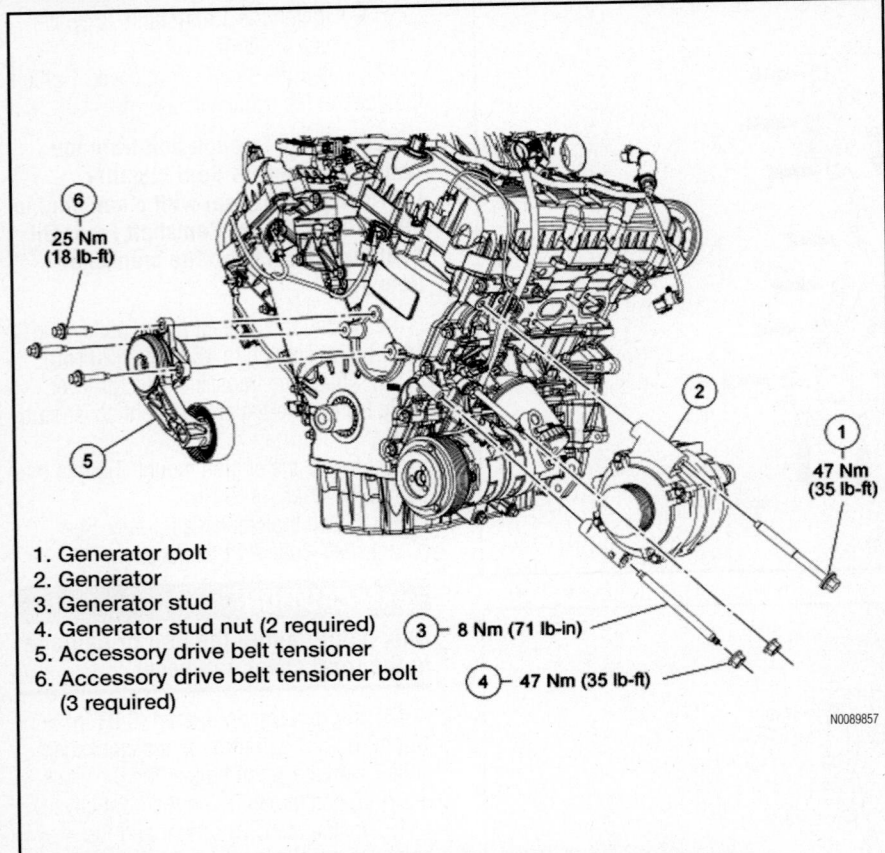

1. Generator bolt
2. Generator
3. Generator stud
4. Generator stud nut (2 required)
5. Accessory drive belt tensioner
6. Accessory drive belt tensioner bolt
   (3 required)

6. 25 Nm (18 lb-ft)
3. 8 Nm (71 lb-in)
4. 47 Nm (35 lb-ft)
1. 47 Nm (35 lb-ft)

N0089857

Fig. 155 Removing the engine front cover and components (1 of 3)—3.0L engine

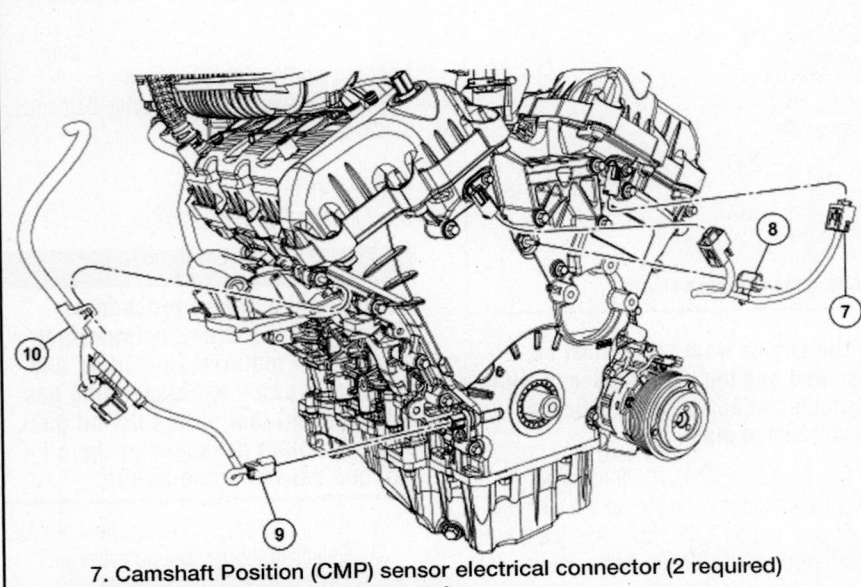

7. Camshaft Position (CMP) sensor electrical connector (2 required)
8. CMP sensor wiring harness retainer
9. Crankshaft Position (CKP) electrical connector
10. CKP wiring harness retainer

N0080728

Fig. 156 Removing the engine front cover and components (2 of 3)—3.0L engine

6. Remove the 3 bolts and the accessory drive belt tensioner.

7. Detach the wiring harness retainer from the engine front cover stud bolt.

8. Disconnect the Crankshaft Position (CKP) sensor electrical connector.

9. Disconnect the 2 Camshaft Position (CMP) sensor electrical connectors and detach the wiring harness retainer from the engine front cover stud bolt.

10. Remove the LH and RH Variable Camshaft Timing (VCT) oil control solenoids, located under the valve covers.

11. Remove the engine support insulator.

12. Remove the 2 oil pan-to-front cover bolts.

13. Remove the 14 bolts, 2 stud bolts and the engine front cover. Remove and discard the gaskets.

To install:

❋❋ WARNING

Do not use metal scrapers, wire brushes, power abrasive discs or other abrasive means to clean the sealing surfaces. These tools cause scratches and gouges which make leak paths.

❋❋ WARNING

Do not damage the oil pan gasket while cleaning the sealant from the lower cylinder block-to-oil pan joint.

14. Use a plastic scraping tool to remove all traces of sealant.

15. Clean all sealing surfaces with metal surface prep and install new gaskets.

➡**The engine front cover must be installed and the bolts tightened within 4 minutes of applying sealant.**

16. Apply a 0.23 in. (6 mm) diameter dot of silicone gasket and sealer to the cylinder block, lower cylinder block, cylinder head and oil pan mating surfaces.

17. Position the engine front cover and install the bolts. Tighten in the sequence shown to 18 ft. lbs. (25 Nm).

18. Install the 2 oil pan-to-front cover bolts. Tighten to 18 ft. lbs. (25 Nm).

19. Remove the oil pan drain plug and drain the engine oil. Install the plug and tighten to 19 ft. lbs. (26 Nm).

20. Install the engine support insulator:

a. Tighten the insulator nuts to 41 ft. lbs. (55 Nm).

b. Tighten the 3 bolts for the engine support insulator to 35 ft. lbs. (48 Nm).

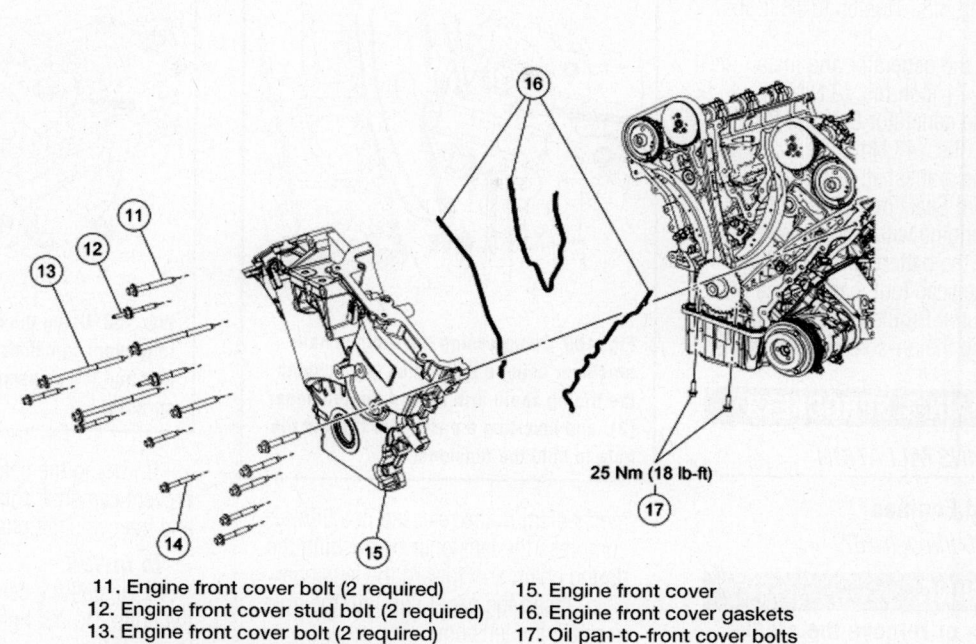

11. Engine front cover bolt (2 required)
12. Engine front cover stud bolt (2 required)
13. Engine front cover bolt (2 required)
14. Engine front cover bolt (10 required)

15. Engine front cover
16. Engine front cover gaskets
17. Oil pan-to-front cover bolts

N0089863

Fig. 157 Removing the engine front cover and components (3 of 3)—3.0L engine

21. Install the LH and RH VCT oil control solenoids. Tighten the bolts to 89 inch lbs. (10 Nm).

22. Connect the 2 CMP sensor electrical connectors and attach the wiring harness retainer to the engine front cover stud bolt.

23. Connect the CKP electrical connector.

24. Attach the wiring harness retainer to the engine front cover stud bolt.

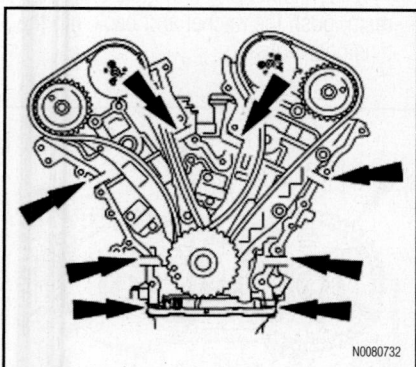

N0080732

Fig. 158 Apply a 0.23 in. (6 mm) diameter dot of silicone gasket and sealer to the cylinder block, lower cylinder block, cylinder head and oil pan mating surfaces.

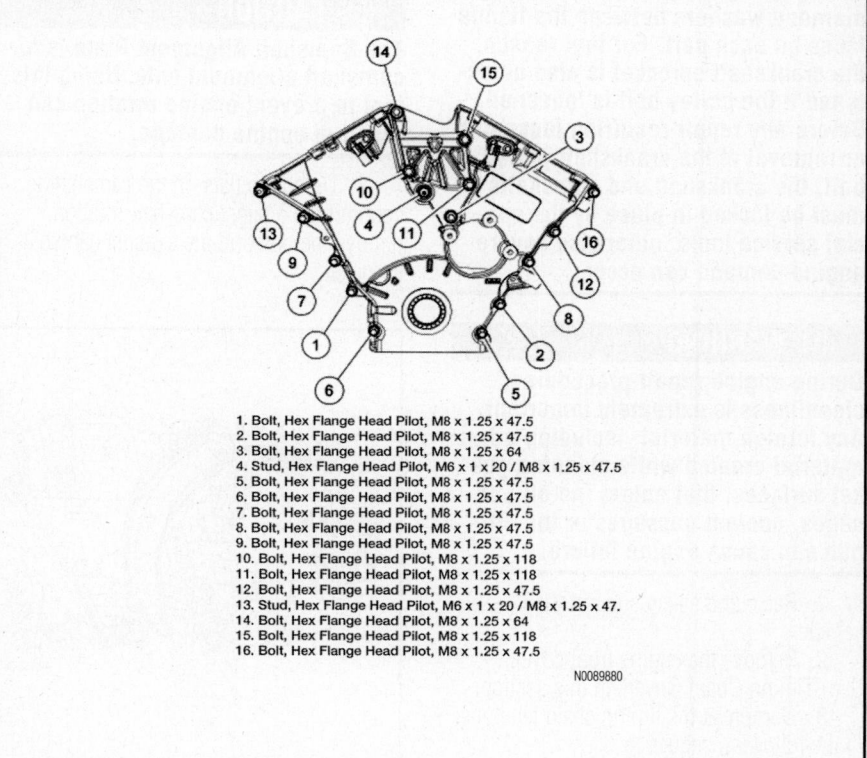

1. Bolt, Hex Flange Head Pilot, M8 x 1.25 x 47.5
2. Bolt, Hex Flange Head Pilot, M8 x 1.25 x 47.5
3. Bolt, Hex Flange Head Pilot, M8 x 1.25 x 64
4. Stud, Hex Flange Head Pilot, M6 x 1 x 20 / M8 x 1.25 x 47.5
5. Bolt, Hex Flange Head Pilot, M8 x 1.25 x 47.5
6. Bolt, Hex Flange Head Pilot, M8 x 1.25 x 47.5
7. Bolt, Hex Flange Head Pilot, M8 x 1.25 x 47.5
8. Bolt, Hex Flange Head Pilot, M8 x 1.25 x 47.5
9. Bolt, Hex Flange Head Pilot, M8 x 1.25 x 47.5
10. Bolt, Hex Flange Head Pilot, M8 x 1.25 x 118
11. Bolt, Hex Flange Head Pilot, M8 x 1.25 x 118
12. Bolt, Hex Flange Head Pilot, M8 x 1.25 x 47.5
13. Stud, Hex Flange Head Pilot, M6 x 1 x 20 / M8 x 1.25 x 47.
14. Bolt, Hex Flange Head Pilot, M8 x 1.25 x 64
15. Bolt, Hex Flange Head Pilot, M8 x 1.25 x 118
16. Bolt, Hex Flange Head Pilot, M8 x 1.25 x 47.5

N0089880

Fig. 159 Position the engine front cover and install the bolts. Tighten in the sequence shown to 18 ft. lbs. (25 Nm).

25. Install the accessory drive belt tensioner and the 3 bolts. Tighten to 18 ft. lbs. (25 Nm).

26. Position the generator and install the stud. Tighten to 71 inch lbs. (8 Nm).

27. Install the generator bolt and 2 nuts. Tighten to 35 ft. lbs. (47 Nm).

28. Install the crankshaft front seal. See "Crankshaft Front Seal" in this section.

29. Fill the engine with clean engine oil.

30. Connect the battery ground cable.

31. Using the scan tool, perform the Misfire Monitor Neutral Profile Correction procedure, following the on-screen instructions.

TIMING CHAIN & SPROCKETS

REMOVAL & INSTALLATION

2.5L & Hybrid Engines

See Figures 160 through 167.

✳✳ WARNING

Do not loosen or remove the crankshaft pulley bolt without first installing the special tools as instructed in this procedure. The crankshaft pulley and the crankshaft timing sprocket are not keyed to the crankshaft. The crankshaft, the crankshaft sprocket and the pulley are fitted together by friction, using diamond washers between the flange faces on each part. For that reason, the crankshaft sprocket is also unfastened if the pulley bolt is loosened. Before any repair requiring loosening or removal of the crankshaft pulley bolt, the crankshaft and camshafts must be locked in place by the special service tools, otherwise severe engine damage can occur.

✳✳ WARNING

During engine repair procedures, cleanliness is extremely important. Any foreign material, including any material created while cleaning gasket surfaces, that enters the oil passages, coolant passages or the oil pan can cause engine failure.

1. Raise and safely support the vehicle.

2. Remove the engine front cover. See "Timing Chain Cover" in this section.

3. Compress the timing chain tensioner in the following sequence:

   a. Using a small pick, release and hold the ratchet mechanism.

   b. While holding the ratchet

Fig. 160 Compressing the timing chain tensioner using a small pick (1), pushing the timing chain arm toward the tensioner (2), and inserting a paper clip (3) into the hole to hold the tensioner.

mechanism in the released position, compress the tensioner by pushing the timing chain arm toward the tensioner.

   c. Insert the paper clip into the hole to retain the tensioner.

4. Remove the 2 bolts and timing chain tensioner.

5. Remove the timing chain tensioner arm.

6. Remove the timing chain.

7. Remove the 2 bolts and the timing chain guide.

✳✳ CAUTION

The Camshaft Alignment Plate is for camshaft alignment only. Using this tool to prevent engine rotation can result in engine damage.

8. Using the flats on the camshaft to counterhold against camshaft rotation, remove the bolt and the exhaust camshaft sprocket.

Fig. 161 Remove the timing chain tensioner arm.

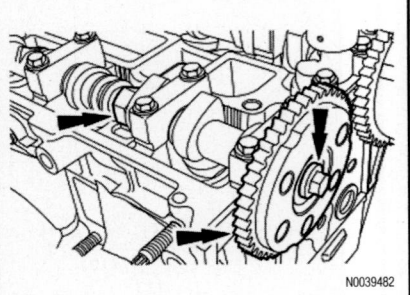

Fig. 162 Using the flats on the camshaft to prevent camshaft rotation, remove the bolt and the camshaft phaser and sprocket.

9. Using the flats on the camshaft to prevent camshaft rotation, remove the bolt and the camshaft phaser and sprocket.

To install:

10. Install the camshaft sprockets and the bolts. Do not tighten the bolts at this time.

11. Install the timing chain guide and the 2 bolts. Tighten to 89 inch lbs. (10 Nm).

12. Install the timing chain.

13. Install the timing chain tensioner arm.

14. If the timing chain plunger and ratchet assembly are not pinned in the compressed position, follow the next 4 steps:

✳✳ CAUTION

Do not compress the ratchet assembly. This will damage the ratchet assembly.

   a. Using the edge of a vise, compress the timing chain tensioner plunger.

   b. Using a small pick, push back and hold the ratchet mechanism.

   c. While holding the ratchet mechanism, push the ratchet arm back into the tensioner housing.

Fig. 163 Install the camshaft sprockets and the bolts. Do not tighten the bolts at this time.

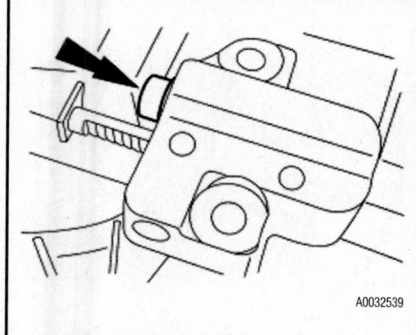

Fig. 164 Using the edge of a vise, compress the timing chain tensioner plunger.

d. Install a paper clip into the hole in the tensioner housing to hold the ratchet assembly and the plunger in during installation.

15. Install the timing chain tensioner and the 2 bolts. Remove the paper clip to release the piston. Tighten to 89 inch lbs. (10 Nm).

16. Using the flats on the camshafts to prevent camshaft rotation, tighten the camshaft sprocket bolts. Tighten to 53 ft. lbs. (72 Nm).

17. Install the engine front cover. See "Timing Chain Cover" in this section.

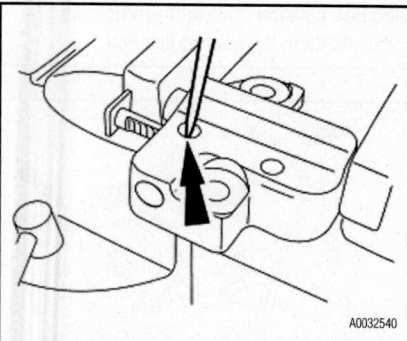

Fig. 165 Using a small pick, push back and hold the ratchet mechanism.

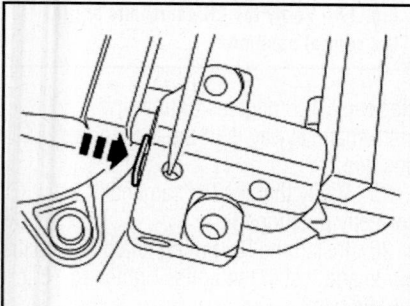

Fig. 166 While holding the ratchet mechanism, push the ratchet arm back into the tensioner housing.

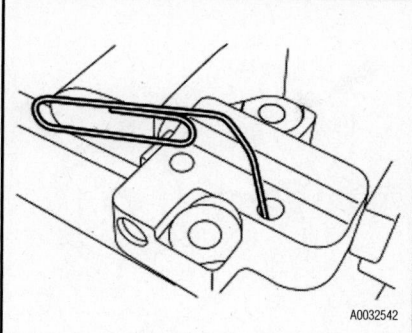

Fig. 167 Install a paper clip into the hole in the tensioner housing to hold the ratchet assembly and the plunger in during installation.

3.0L Engine

See Figures 168 through 180.

> ❋❋ **WARNING**
>
> **During engine repair procedures, cleanliness is extremely important. Any foreign material (including any material created while cleaning gasket surfaces) that enters the oil passages, coolant passages or the oil pan may cause engine failure.**

> ❋❋ **WARNING**
>
> **Failure to verify correct timing drive component alignment will result in severe engine damage.**

1. Remove the engine front cover. See "Timing Chain Cover" in this section.

2. Remove the LH and RH spark plugs.

3. Remove the ignition pulse wheel.

4. Install the crankshaft pulley bolt and washer.

5. Rotate the crankshaft clockwise to position the crankshaft keyway in the 11 o'clock position and position the camshafts in the correct position. This will position the

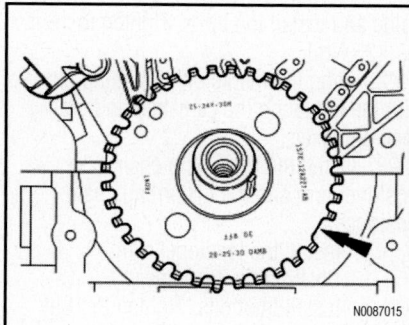

Fig. 168 Remove the ignition pulse wheel.

No. 1 cylinder at Top Dead Center (TDC).

6. Verify that the camshafts are correctly located. If not, rotate the crankshaft one additional turn and recheck.

7. Rotate the crankshaft clockwise 120 degrees to the 3 o'clock position to position the RH camshafts in the neutral position.

8. Verify that the RH camshafts are in the neutral position.

9. Remove the RH timing chain tensioner arm:

   a. Remove the 2 bolts.

   b. Remove the tensioner.

   c. Remove the tensioner arm.

10. Remove the 2 bolts and the RH timing chain guide. Remove the RH timing chain from the engine.

11. Rotate the crankcase clockwise 600 degrees (one and two-third turns) to position the crankcase keyway in the 11 o'clock position. This will position the LH camshafts in the neutral position.

12. Verify the LH camshafts are in the neutral position.

13. Remove the LH timing chain and tensioner arm:

   a. Remove the 2 bolts.

   b. Remove the tensioner.

   c. Remove the tensioner arm.

14. Remove the 2 bolts and the LH timing chain guide. Remove the LH timing chain from the engine.

15. Remove the crankshaft pulley bolt and the crankshaft sprocket.

To install:

> ❋❋ **WARNING**
>
> **Failure to verify correct timing drive component alignment will result in severe engine damage.**

16. Install the crankshaft sprocket with the timing mark facing out. The timing mark on the LH and RH timing chains will be aligned to this mark during assembly.

17. Position the chain tensioner in a soft-jawed vise (LH shown, RH similar).

18. Hold the chain tensioner ratchet lock mechanism away from the ratchet stem with a small pick.

> ❋❋ **CAUTION**
>
> **During tensioner compression, do not release the ratchet stem until the tensioner piston is fully bottomed in its bore or damage to the ratchet stem will result.**

19. Slowly compress the timing chain tensioner. Retain the tensioner piston with a

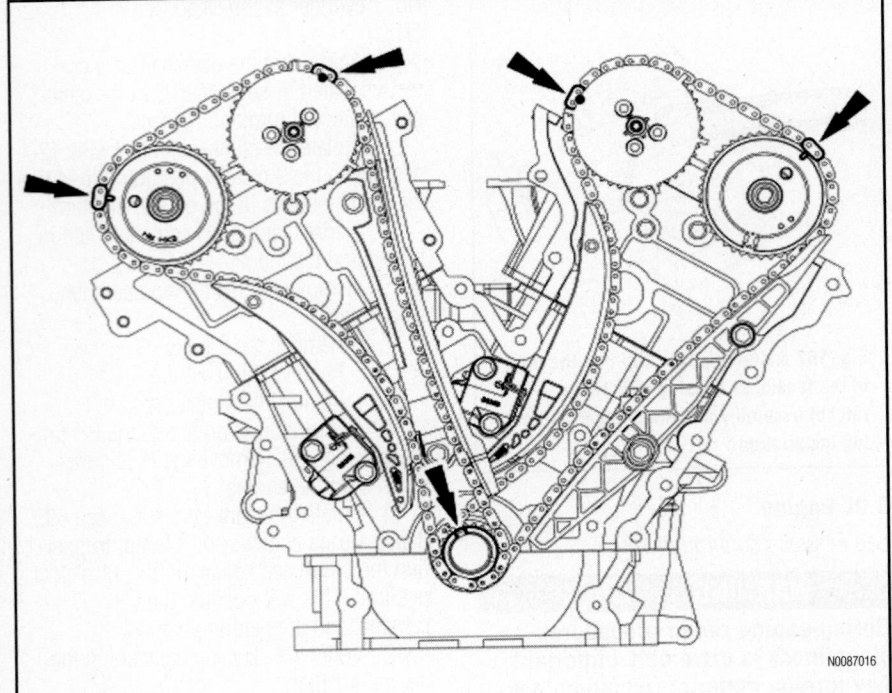

Fig. 169 Verify that the camshafts are correctly located. If not, rotate the crankshaft one additional turn and recheck.

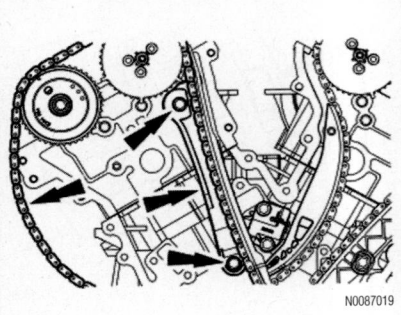

Fig. 172 Remove the 2 bolts and the RH timing chain guide. Remove the RH timing chain from the engine.

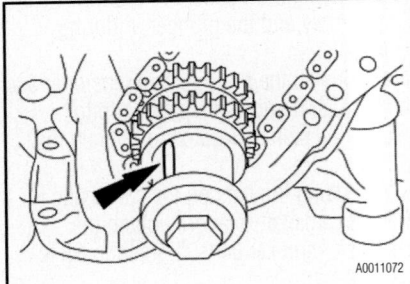

Fig. 173 Rotate the crankcase clockwise 600 degrees (one and two-third turns) to position the crankcase keyway in the 11 o'clock position. This will position the LH camshafts in the neutral position.

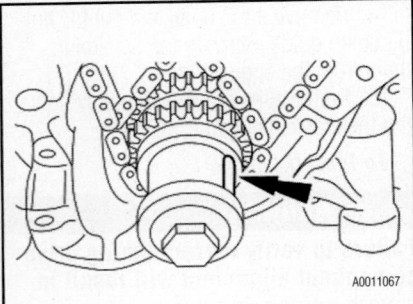

Fig. 170 Rotate the crankshaft clockwise 120 degrees to the 3 o'clock position to position the RH camshafts in the neutral position.

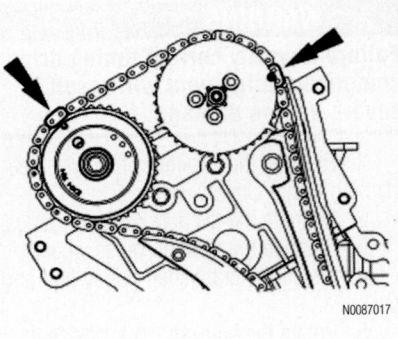

Fig. 171 Verify that the RH camshafts are in the neutral position.

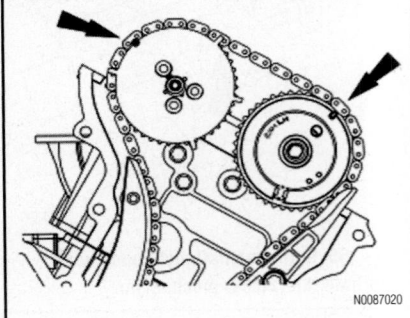

Fig. 174 Verify the LH camshafts are in the neutral position.

0.06 in. (1.5 mm) diameter wire or paper clip.

➡ If timing marks in the timing chains are not evident, use a permanent-type marker to mark the crankshaft and camshaft timing marks on the LH and RH timing chains. Mark any link to use as the crankshaft timing mark.

20. Starting with the crankshaft timing mark, count 29 links and mark the link. Continue counting to link 42 and mark the link.

21. Position the LH timing chain and

guide and install the bolts. Tighten to 18 ft. lbs. (25 Nm).

22. Align the marks on the timing chain with the marks on the camshaft and crankshaft sprockets.

23. Install the LH timing chain tensioner arm and the LH timing chain tensioner:

    a. Install the tensioner arm.
    b. Position the tensioner.
    c. Install the bolts. Tighten to 18 ft. lbs. (25 Nm).

24. Install the crankshaft pulley bolt and rotate the crankshaft

clockwise 120 degrees until the crankshaft keyway is in the 3 o'clock position.

25. Verify that the RH camshafts are correctly positioned.

26. Install the RH timing chain and chain guide and install the bolts. Tighten to 18 ft. lbs. (25 Nm).

27. Align the marks on the timing chain with the marks on the camshaft and crankshaft sprockets.

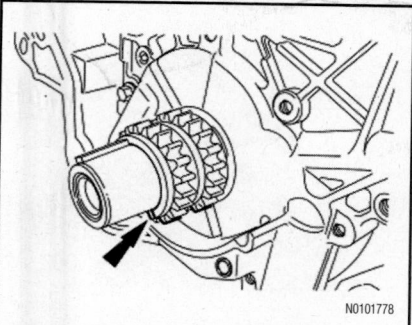

Fig. 175 Install the crankshaft sprocket with the timing mark facing out. The timing mark on the LH and RH timing chains will be aligned to this mark during assembly.

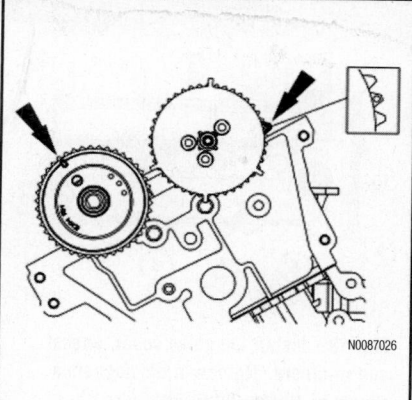

Fig. 178 Verify that the RH camshafts are correctly positioned.

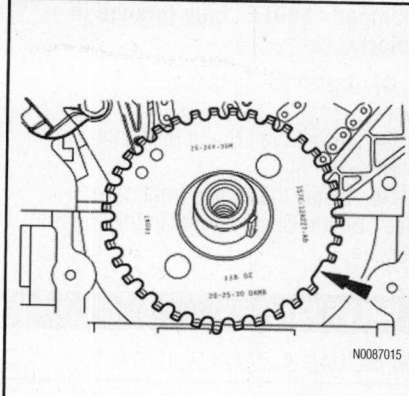

Fig. 180 Install the ignition pulse wheel, noting notch position.

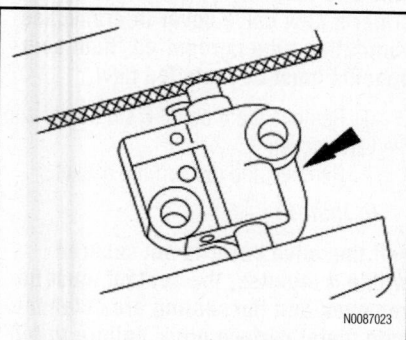

Fig. 176 Position the chain tensioner in a soft-jawed vise (LH shown, RH similar).

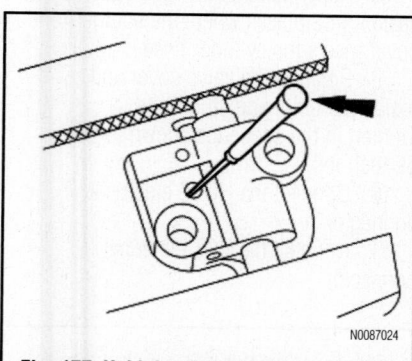

Fig. 177 Hold the chain tensioner ratchet lock mechanism away from the ratchet stem with a small pick.

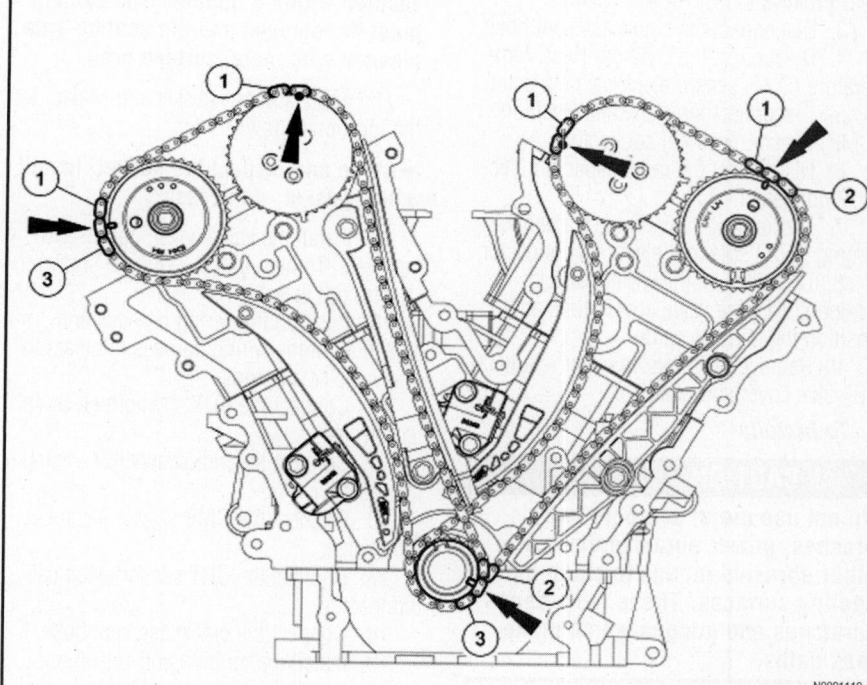

Fig. 179 Verifying timing chain position with 12 links (1) between timing marks, 27 links (2) between camshaft and crankshaft timing marks, and 30 links (3) between camshaft and crankshaft timing marks.

28. Install the RH timing chain tensioner and tensioner arm:
    a. Install the tensioner arm.
    b. Position the tensioner.
    c. Install the bolts. Tighten to 18 ft. lbs. (25 Nm).
29. Remove the LH and RH timing chain tensioner piston retaining wires.
30. Rotate the crankshaft counterclockwise 120 degrees to TDC.

✳✳ WARNING

Failure to verify correct timing drive component alignment will result in severe engine damage.

31. Verify the timing with the following steps:
    a. There should be 12 chain links between the camshaft timing marks.
    b. There should be 27 chain links between the camshaft and the crankshaft timing marks.
    c. There should be 30 chain links between the camshaft and the crankshaft timing marks.
32. Remove the crankshaft pulley bolt and washer.

➡ The pulse wheel is used in several different engines. Install the pulse wheel with the keyway in the slot stamped "30RFF" only (orange in color).

33. Install the ignition pulse wheel.

34. Install the LH and RH spark plugs.

35. Install the engine front cover. See "Timing Chain Cover" in this section.

VALVE COVERS

REMOVAL & INSTALLATION

2.5L & Hybrid Engines

See Figures 181 and 182.

1. Remove the oil level indicator.
2. Remove the ignition coil-on-plugs. See "ENGINE ELECTRICAL" section.
3. Disconnect the crankcase vent hose.
4. Disconnect the Cylinder Head Temperature (CHT) sensor electrical connector.
5. Disconnect the Camshaft Position (CMP) sensor electrical connector.
6. Disconnect the radio capacitor electrical connector.
7. Disconnect the Variable Camshaft Timing (VCT) solenoid electrical connector.
8. Detach all of the wiring harness retainers from the valve cover studs and position the harness aside.
9. Remove the 14 valve cover retainers, the valve cover and gasket.

To install:

✳✳ CAUTION

Do not use metal scrapers, wire brushes, power abrasive discs or other abrasive means to clean the sealing surfaces. These tools cause scratches and gouges which make leak paths.

10. Clean and inspect the sealing surfaces.

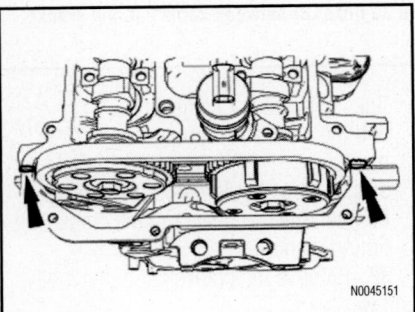

Fig. 181 Apply silicone gasket and sealant to the locations shown.

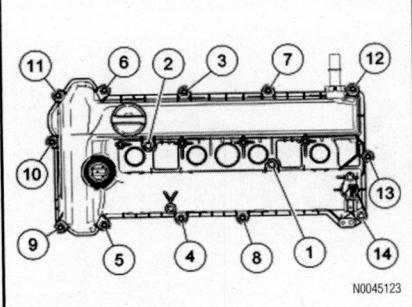

Fig. 182 Install the valve cover, gasket and retainers. Tighten in the sequence shown to 10 Nm (89 lb-in).

➡**The valve cover must be secured within 4 minutes of silicone gasket application. If the valve cover is not secured within 4 minutes, the sealant must be removed and the sealing area cleaned with metal surface prep.**

11. Apply silicone gasket and sealant to the locations shown.

➡**Clean and inspect the gasket. Install a new gasket, if necessary.**

12. Install the valve cover, gasket and retainers. Tighten in the sequence shown to 10 Nm (89 lb-in).
13. Position the wiring harness and attach all of the wiring harness retainers to the valve cover studs.
14. Connect the VCT solenoid electrical connector.
15. Connect the radio capacitor electrical connector.
16. Connect the CMP sensor electrical connector.
17. Connect the CHT sensor electrical connector.
18. Connect the crankcase vent hose.
19. Install the ignition coil-on-plugs.
20. Install the oil level indicator.

3.0L Engine

Left Bank

See Figures 183 and 184.

1. Remove the LH ignition coil-on-plugs. See "ENGINE ELECTRICAL" section.
2. Detach the upper radiator hose from the 2 retainers on the cooling fan shroud and position the hose aside.
3. Detach the 2 wiring retainers from the valve cover and the valve cover stud bolts.
4. Disconnect the Variable Camshaft Timing (VCT) electrical connector.
5. Disconnect the Heated Oxygen Sensor (HO2S) electrical connector.

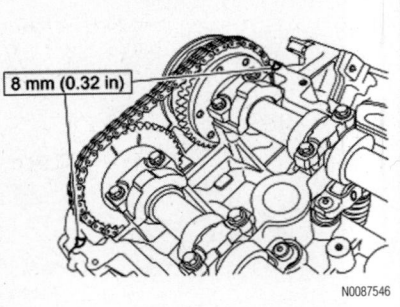

Fig. 183 Apply a bead of silicone gasket and sealant in 2 places where the engine front cover meets the cylinder head.

➡**Inspect the crankcase ventilation tube and valve cover sealing area. If either a new valve cover or crankcase ventilation tube is required, both components must be installed new.**

6. Remove the 8 bolts, 6 stud bolts and the valve cover.
7. Remove and discard the gasket.

To install:

➡**If the valve cover is not secured within 4 minutes, the sealant must be removed and the sealing area cleaned with metal surface prep. Failure to follow this procedure can cause future oil leakage.**

8. Apply a bead of silicone gasket and sealant in 2 places where the engine front cover meets the cylinder head.
9. Position the valve cover and install the bolts and stud bolts. Tighten in the sequence shown to 89 inch lbs. (10 Nm).
10. Connect the HO2S electrical connector.
11. Connect the VCT electrical connector.

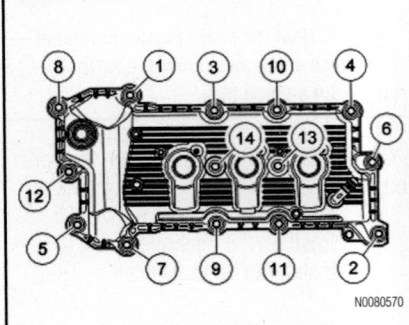

Fig. 184 Position the valve cover and install the bolts and stud bolts. Tighten in the sequence shown to 89 inch lbs. (10 Nm).

12. Attach the 2 wiring retainers to the valve cover stud bolts and valve cover.

13. Attach the upper radiator hose to the 2 retainers on the cooling fan shroud.

14. Install the LH ignition coil-on-plugs.

Right Bank

See Figure 185.

1. Remove the RH ignition coil-on-plugs. See "ENGINE ELECTRICAL" section.

2. Detach the 3 main engine control wiring harness retainers from the valve cover stud bolts and from the valve cover.

3. Disconnect the Variable Camshaft Timing (VCT) electrical connector.

4. Detach the Crankshaft Position (CKP) wiring harness retainer from the stud.

5. Remove the 11 bolts, 3 stud bolts and the valve cover.

6. Remove and discard the gasket.

To install:

➡ **If the valve cover is not secured within 4 minutes, the sealant must be removed and the sealing area cleaned with metal surface prep. Failure to follow this procedure can cause future oil leakage.**

7. Apply a bead of silicone gasket and sealant in 2 places where the engine front cover meets the cylinder head.

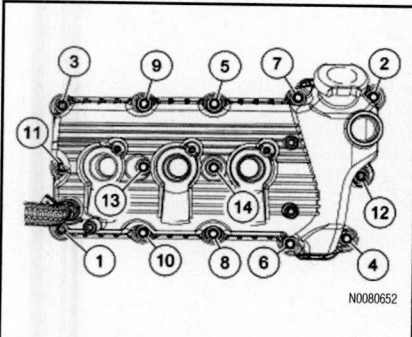

Fig. 185 Position the valve cover and install the 11 bolts and 3 stud bolts. Tighten in the sequence shown to 10 Nm (89 lb-in).

➡ **See illustration under "Right Bank" for same sealant location.**

8. Position the valve cover and install the 11 bolts and 3 stud bolts. Tighten in the sequence shown to 10 Nm (89 lb-in).

9. Attach the CKP wiring harness retainer on the stud.

10. Connect the VCT electrical connector. Attach the 3 main engine control wiring harness retainers to the valve cover and to the valve cover stud bolts.

11. Install the RH ignition coil-on-plugs.

VALVE LASH (VALVE CLEARANCE)

ADJUSTMENT

2.5L & Hybrid Engines

See Figure 186.

1. Remove the valve cover. See "Valve Cover" in this section.

2. Remove the 5 bolts, the pin-type retainer and the RH splash shield.

✳✳ CAUTION

Turn the engine clockwise only, and only use the crankshaft bolt.

3. Before removing the camshafts, measure the clearance of each valve at base

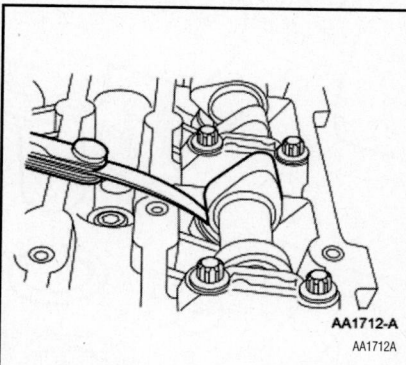

Fig. 186 Use a feeler gauge to measure the clearance of each valve and record its location.

circle, with the lobe pointed away from the tappet. Failure to measure all clearances prior to removing the camshafts will necessitate repeated removal and installation and wasted labor time.

4. Use a feeler gauge to measure the clearance of each valve and record its location.

➡ **The number on the valve tappet only reflects the digits that follow the decimal. For example, a tappet with the number 0.650 has the thickness of 3.650 mm.**

5. The nominal clearance is:
   - Intake: 0.0095 in. (0.25 mm)
   - Exhaust: 0.0115 in. (0.30 mm).

6. The acceptable clearances after being fully installed are:
   - Intake: 0.008–0.011 in. (0.22–0.28 mm)
   - Exhaust: 0.010–0.013 in.(0.27–0.33 mm)

7. Select tappets using this formula: tappet thickness = measured clearance + the existing tappet thickness - nominal clearance.

8. Select the closest tappet size to the ideal tappet thickness available and mark the installation location.

9. If any tappets do not measure within specifications, install new tappets in these locations.

3.0L Engine

➡ **This engine uses hydraulic lash adjusters and no clearance adjustment is needed.**

1. Hydraulic lash adjuster specifications should be:
   - Clearance to bore: 0.0007–0.0027 in. (0.018–0.069 mm)
   - Collapsed lash adjuster gap: (0.019–0.043 in. (0.50–1.11 mm)

ENGINE PERFORMANCE & EMISSION CONTROLS

COMPONENT LOCATIONS

➡️ Manufacturer does not provide a complete location view of all engine performance and emission control components. Refer to individual component sections.

CAMSHAFT POSITION (CMP) SENSOR

LOCATION

2.5L & Hybrid Engines

See Figure 187.

The CMP sensor is located on top of the valve cover.

3.0L Engine

See Figure 188.

This engine uses 2 CMP sensors (one for each bank). They are located on the front end of each camshaft, respectively.

REMOVAL & INSTALLATION

2.5L & Hybrid Engines

1. Disconnect the Camshaft Position (CMP) sensor electrical connector.
2. Remove the bolt and the CMP sensor.
3. Inspect the O-ring seal and install new as necessary.

➡️ Lubricate the CMP sensor O-ring seal with clean engine oil.

4. To install, reverse the removal procedure.
5. Tighten the CMP sensor bolt to 62 inch lbs. (7 Nm).

3.0L Engine

1. Disconnect the Camshaft Position (CMP) sensor electrical connector.
2. Remove the bolt and the CMP sensor.
3. Inspect the O-ring seal and install new as necessary.
4. Lubricate the CMP sensor O-ring seal with clean engine oil.
5. To install, reverse the removal procedure.
6. Tighten the sensor bolt to 89 inch lbs. (10 Nm).

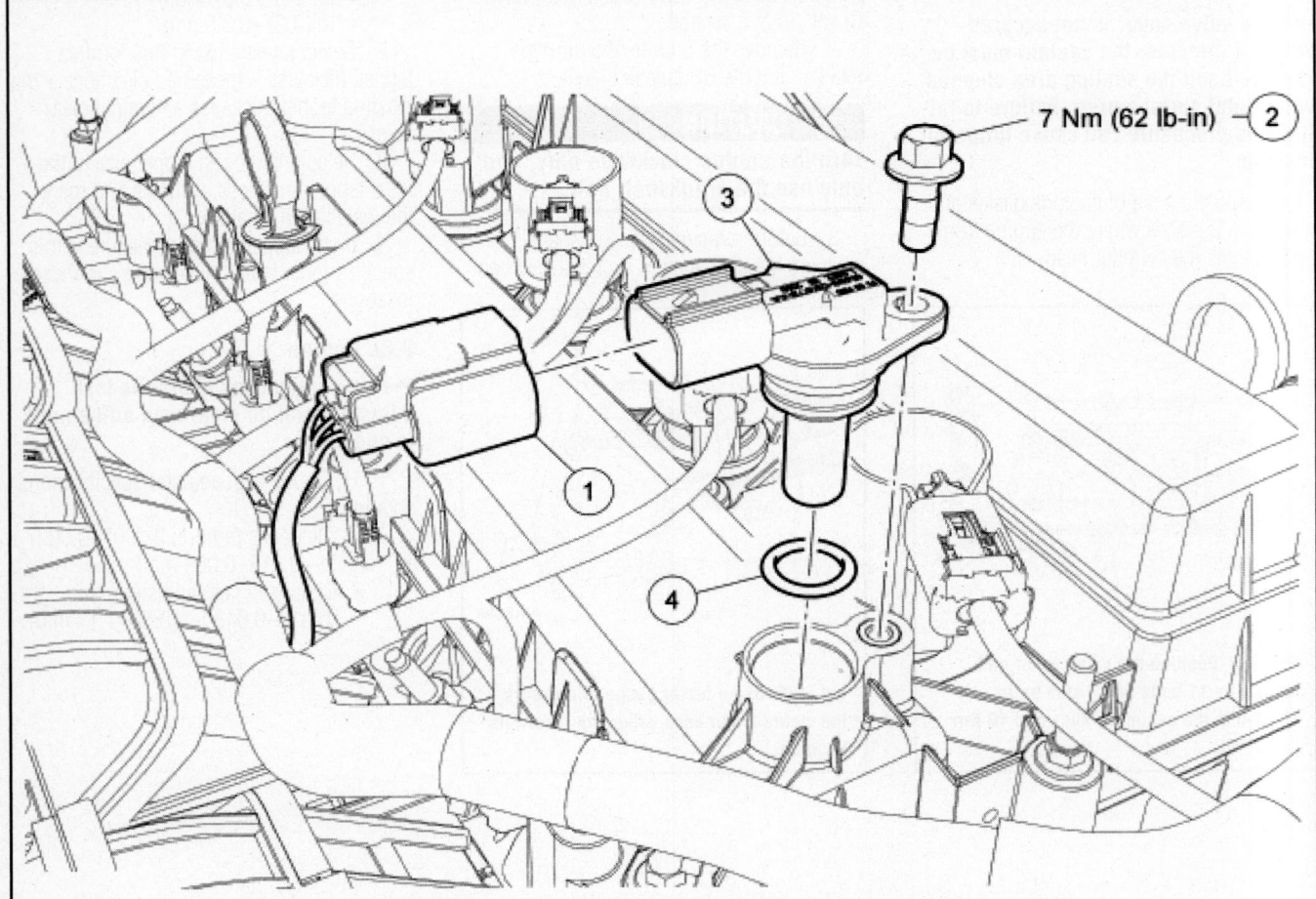

1. Camshaft Position (CMP) sensor electrical connector
2. CMP sensor bolt
3. CMP
4. CMP O-ring seal

N0086358

Fig. 187 Showing the location of the CMP sensor

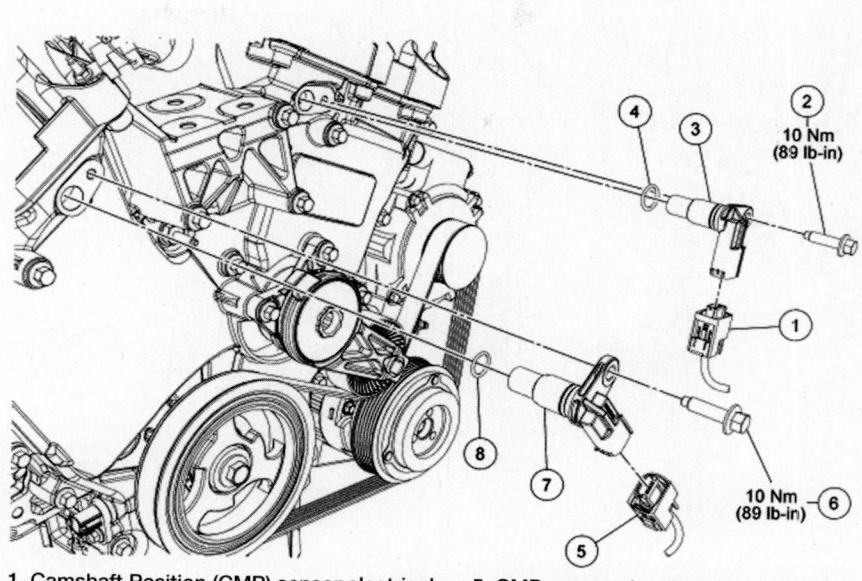

1. Camshaft Position (CMP) sensor electrical connector - LH
2. CMP sensor bolt - LH
3. CMP sensor - LH
4. CMP sensor O-ring seal - LH
5. CMP sensor electrical connector - RH
6. CMP sensor bolt - RH
7. CMP sensor - RH
8. CMP sensor O-ring seal – RH

Fig. 188 Showing the locations of the CMP sensors

CATALYST MONITOR SENSOR (CMS)

LOCATION

2.5L & Hybrid Engines

See Figure 189.

3.0L Engine

See Figure 190.

REMOVAL & INSTALLATION

2.5L & Hybrid Engines

1. Raise and safely support the vehicle.
2. Disconnect the Catalyst Monitor Sensor (CMS) electrical connector.

➡**If necessary, lubricate the sensor threads with penetrating and lock lubricant to assist in removal.**

3. Using the Exhaust Gas Oxygen Sensor Socket, remove the CMS.

To install:
4. Install the CMS to position.

➡**Apply a light coat of anti-seize lubricant to the threads of the CMS.**

5. Tighten the CMS to 35 ft. lbs. (48 Nm).

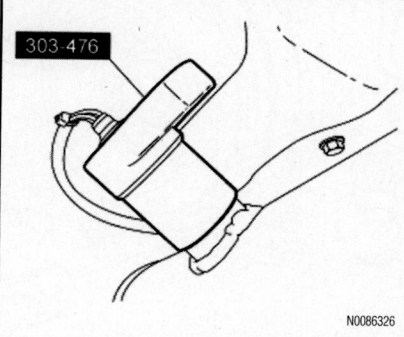

Fig. 189 Showing the CMS location—2.5L shown; Hybrid engine similar

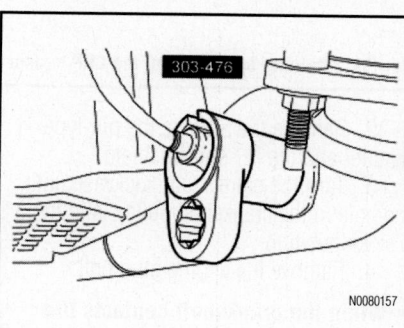

Fig. 190 Showing the CMS location (RH sensor shown; LH similar)—3.0L engine

6. Connect the electrical connector.

3.0L Engine

1. Raise and safely support the vehicle.
2. Disconnect the Catalyst Monitor Sensor (CMS) electrical connector.

➡**If necessary, lubricate the sensor threads with penetrating and lock lubricant to assist in removal.**

3. Using the Exhaust Gas Oxygen Sensor Socket, remove the CMS.

To install:
4. Position the CMS.
5. Apply a light coat of anti-seize lubricant to the threads of the CMS.
6. Tighten the CMS to 35 ft. lbs. (48 Nm).
7. Attach the electrical connector.

CRANKSHAFT POSITION (CKP) SENSOR

LOCATION

2.5L Engine

See Figure 191.

Hybrid Engine

See Figure 192.

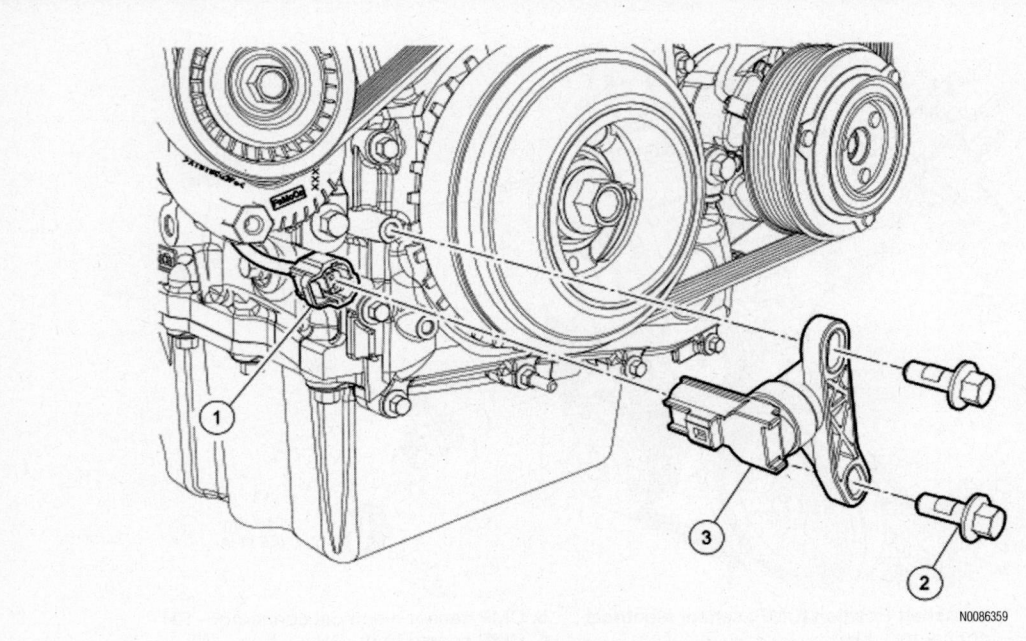

Fig. 191 Showing the CKP sensor electrical connector (1), retaining bolt (2) and the CKP sensor (3)—2.5L engine

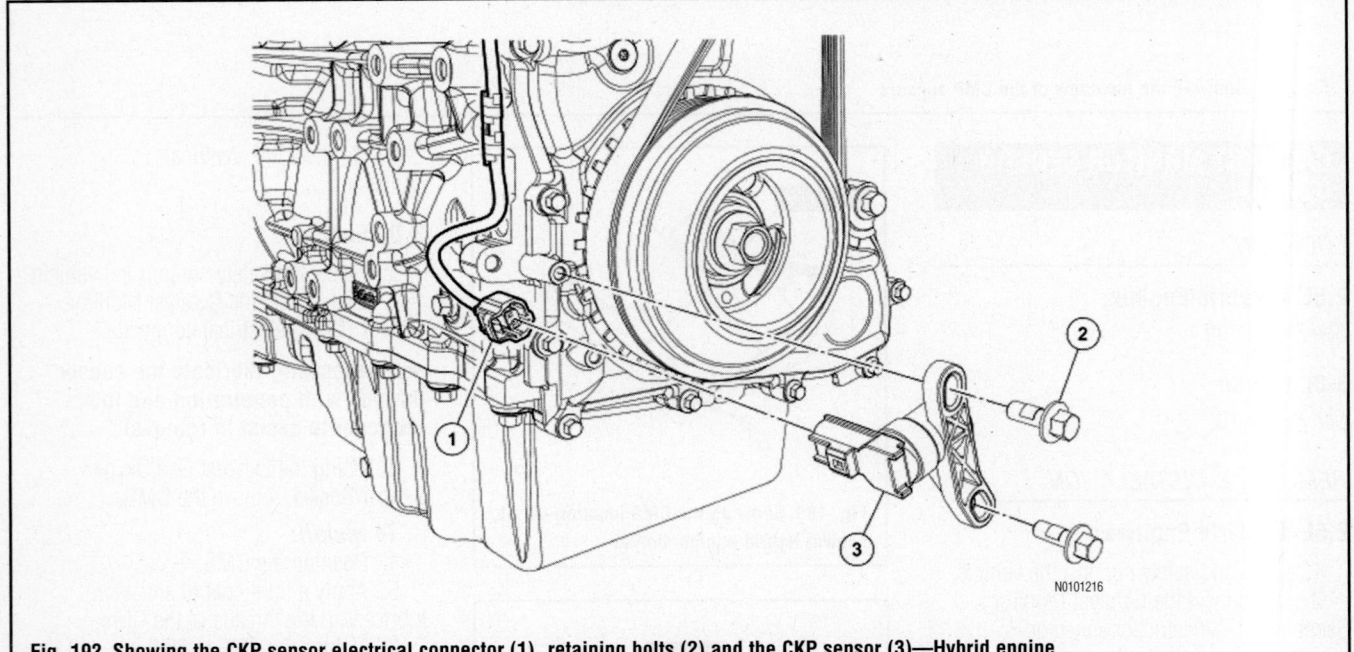

Fig. 192 Showing the CKP sensor electrical connector (1), retaining bolts (2) and the CKP sensor (3)—Hybrid engine

3.0L Engine

See Figure 193.

REMOVAL & INSTALLATION

2.5L & Hybrid Engines

See Figures 194 through 197.

1. Raise and safely support the vehicle.

2. Remove the 5 bolts, the pin-type retainer and the RH splash shield.

3. Turn the crankshaft clockwise until the hole in the crankshaft pulley is in the 3 o'clock position.

4. Remove the engine plug bolt.

➡**When the crankshaft contacts the Crankshaft TDC Timing Peg, the No. 1 cylinder will be at Top Dead Center (TDC).**

5. Install the Crankshaft TDC Timing Peg and turn the crankshaft clockwise until the crankshaft contacts the Crankshaft TDC Timing Peg.

6. Disconnect the Crankshaft Position (CKP) sensor electrical connector.

7. Remove the bolts and the CKP sensor.

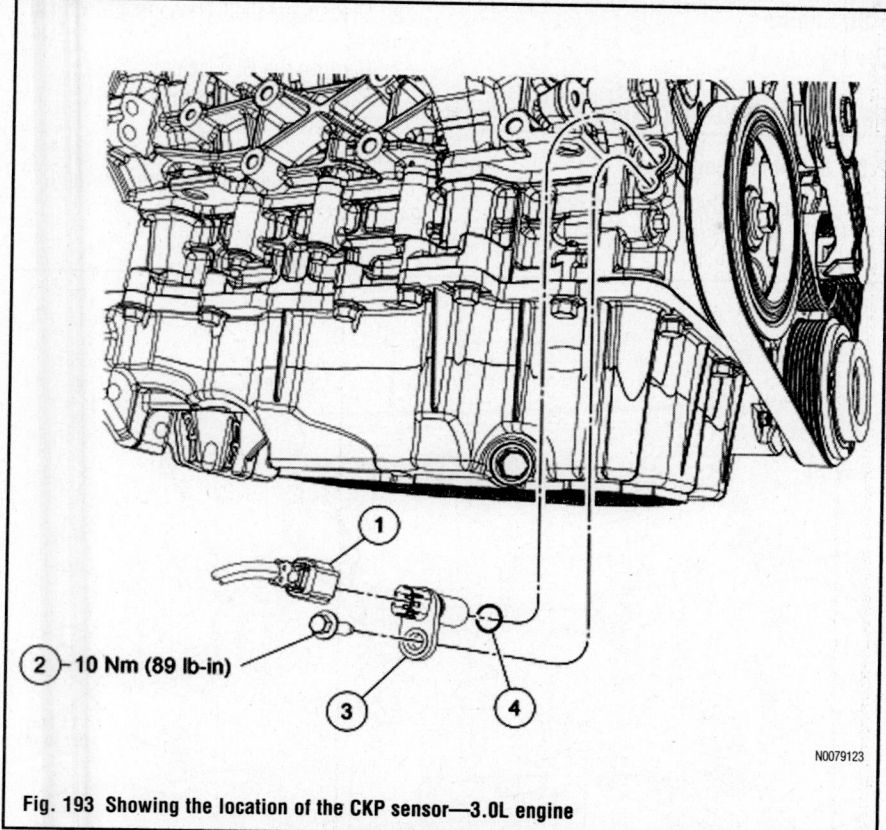

Fig. 193 Showing the location of the CKP sensor—3.0L engine

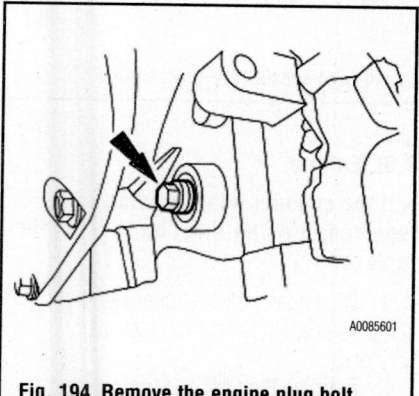

Fig. 194 Remove the engine plug bolt.

To install:

✳✳ CAUTION

Only hand-tighten the bolt or damage to the front cover can occur.

8. Install a 6 mm x 18 mm bolt into the crankshaft pulley hole and thread it into the front cover.

9. Install the CKP sensor and the 2 bolts, but do not tighten the bolts at this time.

10. Adjust the CKP sensor with the Crankshaft Sensor Aligner. Tighten the 2 bolts to 62 inch lbs. (7 Nm).

11. Connect the CKP sensor electrical connector.

12. Remove the 6 mm x 18 mm bolt from the crankshaft pulley.

13. Install the engine plug bolt. Tighten to 15 ft. lbs. (20 Nm).

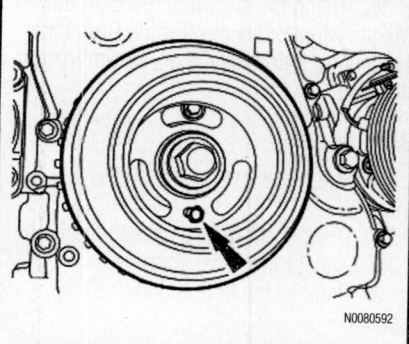

Fig. 196 Install a 6 mm x 18 mm bolt into the crankshaft pulley hole and thread it into the front cover.

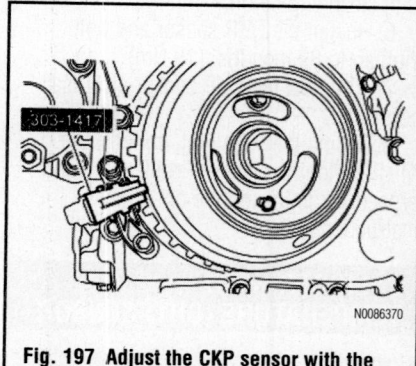

Fig. 197 Adjust the CKP sensor with the Crankshaft Sensor Aligner. Tighten the 2 bolts to 62 inch lbs. (7 Nm).

14. Install the RH splash shield with the 5 bolts and the pin-type retainer. Tighten the bolts to 80 inch lbs. (9 Nm).

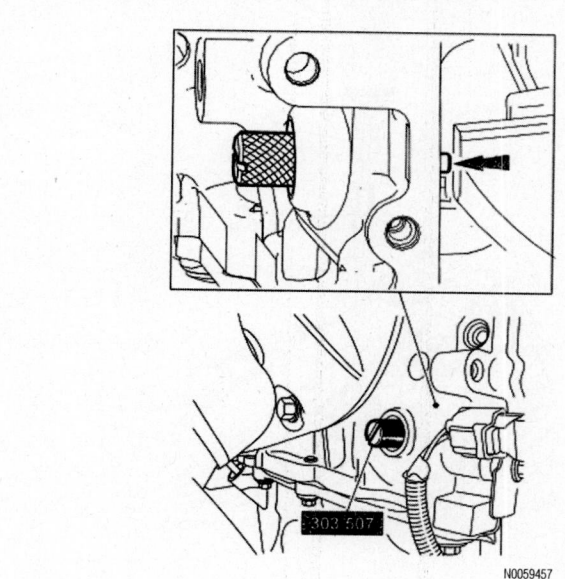

Fig. 195 Install the Crankshaft TDC Timing Peg and turn the crankshaft clockwise until the crankshaft contacts the Crankshaft TDC Timing Peg.

15. Using the scan tool, perform the Misfire Monitor Neutral Profile Correction procedure, following the on-screen instructions.

3.0L Engine

1. Raise and safely support the vehicle.
2. Disconnect the Crankshaft Position (CKP) sensor electrical connector.
3. Remove the bolt and the CKP sensor.

To install:

4. Inspect the O-ring seal and install new as necessary.
5. Lubricate the CKP sensor O-ring seal with clean engine oil.
6. Install the CKP sensor and bolt. Tighten to 89 inch lbs. (10 Nm).
7. Connect the CKP sensor electrical connector.
8. Using the scan tool, perform the Misfire Monitor Neutral Profile Correction procedure, following the on-screen instructions.

CYLINDER HEAD TEMPERATURE (CHT) SENSOR

LOCATION

2.5L & Hybrid Engines

See Figure 198.

3.0L Engine

See Figure 199.

REMOVAL & INSTALLATION

2.5L & Hybrid Engines

1. Detach the Cylinder Head Temperature (CHT) sensor cover and position aside.

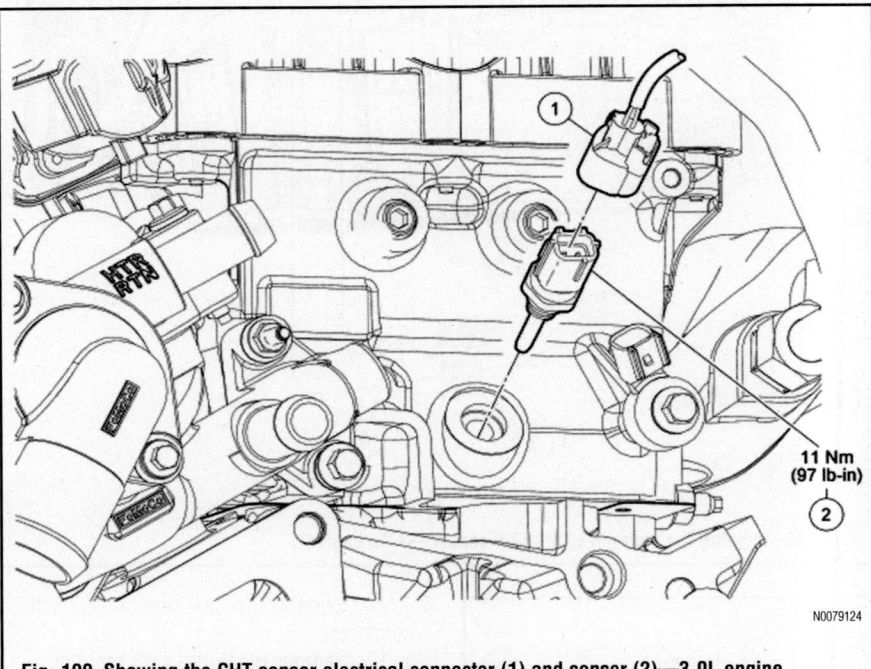

Fig. 199 Showing the CHT sensor electrical connector (1) and sensor (2)—3.0L engine

2. Disconnect the CHT sensor electrical connector.
3. Remove the CHT sensor.
4. Position the CHT sensor.
5. Tighten to 106 inch lbs. (12 Nm).
6. Attach the electrical connector and install the cover.

3.0L Engine

➡**If the cylinder head is being replaced, the CHT must be replaced.**

1. Disconnect the Cylinder Head Temperature (CHT) sensor electrical connector.
2. Remove the CHT sensor.
3. Install and tighten to 97 inch lbs. (11 Nm).
4. Attach the electrical connector.

HEATED OXYGEN SENSOR (HO2S)

LOCATION

2.5L & Hybrid Engines

See Figure 200.

3.0L Engine

See Figure 201.

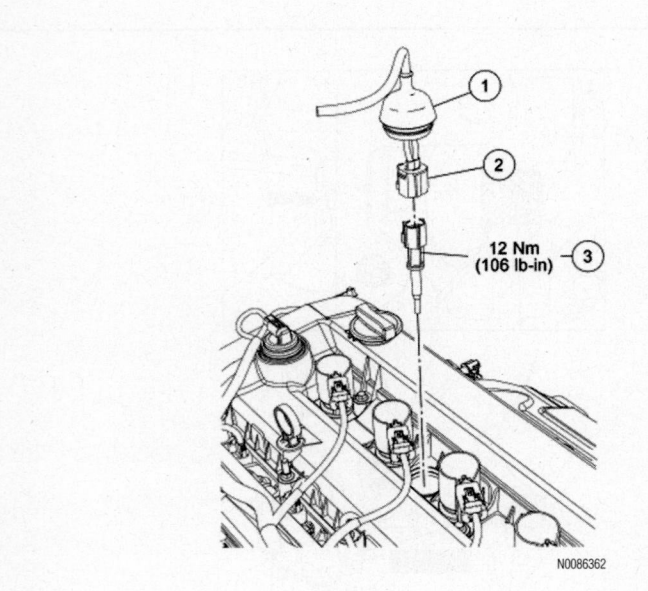

Fig. 198 Showing the CHT sensor cover (1), electrical connector (2) and sensor (3)—2.5L & Hybrid engines

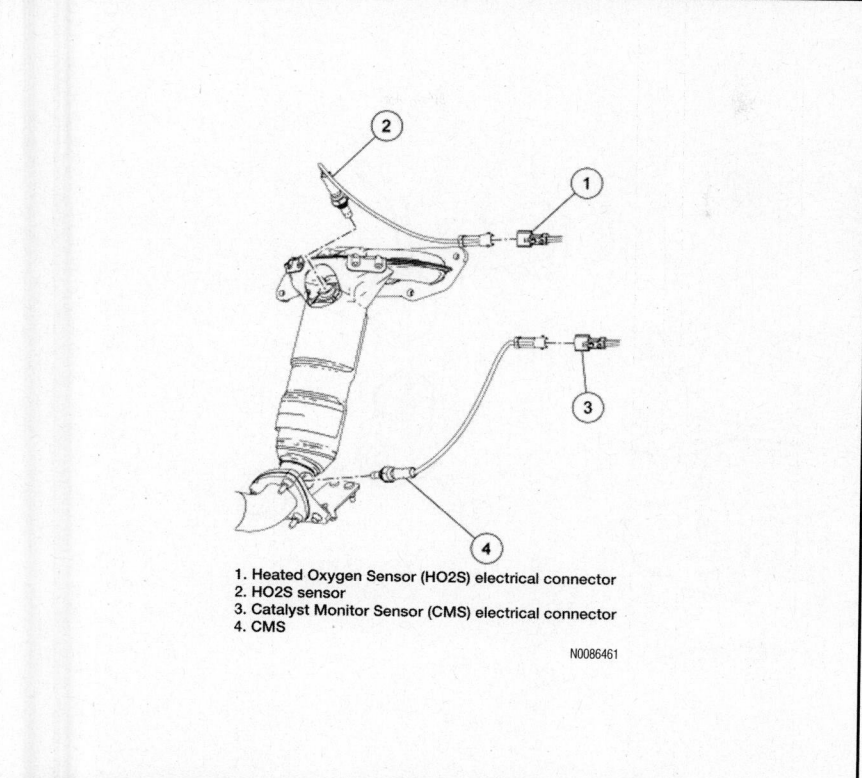

1. Heated Oxygen Sensor (HO2S) electrical connector
2. HO2S sensor
3. Catalyst Monitor Sensor (CMS) electrical connector
4. CMS

N0086461

Fig. 200 Showing the locations of the Heated Oxygen Sensor and the Catalyst Monitor Sensor—2.5L & Hybrid engines

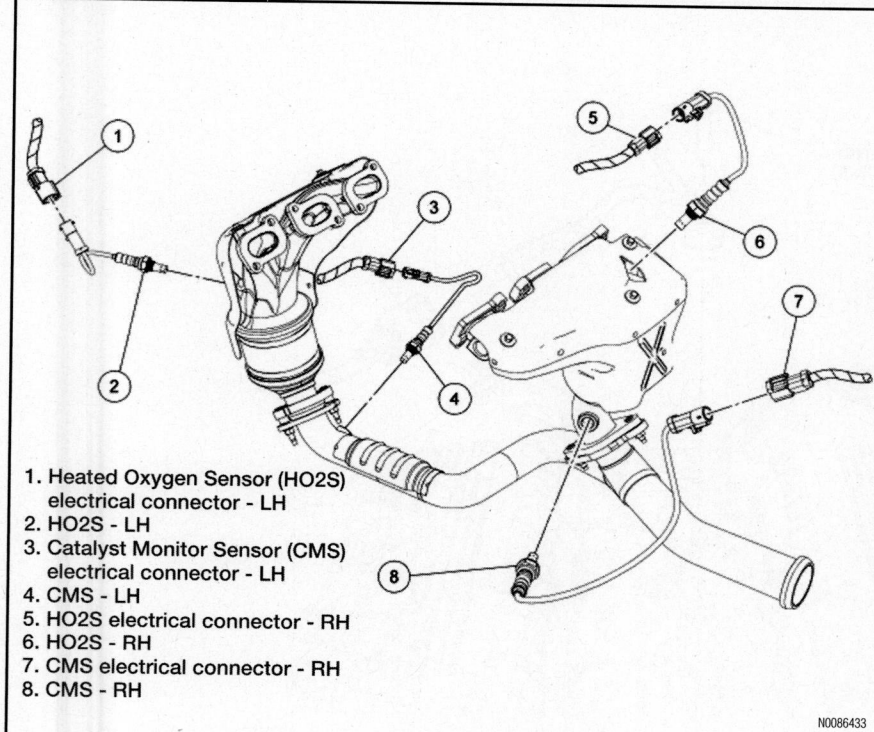

1. Heated Oxygen Sensor (HO2S) electrical connector - LH
2. HO2S - LH
3. Catalyst Monitor Sensor (CMS) electrical connector - LH
4. CMS - LH
5. HO2S electrical connector - RH
6. HO2S - RH
7. CMS electrical connector - RH
8. CMS - RH

N0086433

Fig. 201 Showing the locations of the Heated Oxygen Sensor and the Catalyst Monitor Sensor—3.0L engine

REMOVAL & INSTALLATION

2.5L & Hybrid Engines

1. Raise and safely support the vehicle.
2. Disconnect the Heated Oxygen Sensor (HO2S) electrical connector.

➡**If necessary, lubricate the sensor threads with penetrating and lock lubricant to assist in removal.**

3. Using the Exhaust Gas Oxygen Sensor Socket, remove the HO2S.

To install:

4. Apply a light coat of anti-seize lubricant to the threads of the HO2S.
5. Install the HO2S and tighten to 35 ft. lbs. (48 Nm).
6. Attach the electrical connector.

3.0L Engine

➡**This procedure is the same for both banks (except as indicated).**

1. Raise and safely support the vehicle.
2. Remove the 7 bolts and the LH splash shield.
3. Disconnect the LH Heated Oxygen Sensor (HO2S) electrical connector.

➡**If necessary, lubricate the sensor threads with penetrating and lock lubricant to assist in removal.**

4. Using the Exhaust Gas Oxygen Sensor Socket, remove the HO2S.

To install:

5. Apply a light coat of anti-seize lubricant to the threads of the HO2S.
6. Install the HO2S and tighten to 35 ft. lbs. (48 Nm).
7. Attach the electrical connector.

KNOCK SENSOR (KS)

LOCATION

See Figures 202 and 203.

➡**The locations shown are for 2.5L, Hybrid and 3.0L engines.**

REMOVAL & INSTALLATION

➡**This procedure applies to 2.5L, Hybrid and 3.0L engines.**

1. Remove the intake manifold.
2. Disconnect the KS electrical connector.
3. Remove the bolt and the KS.

To install:

4. Install the KS and the bolt. Tighten to 18 ft. lbs. (25 Nm).
5. Connect the KS electrical connector.

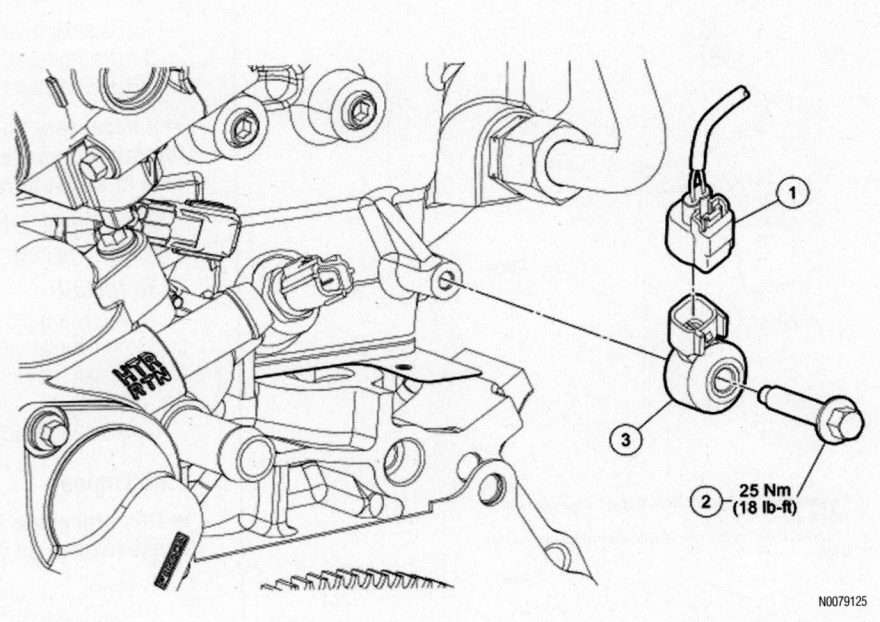

N0079125

Fig. 202 Showing the location of the Knock Sensor (3), retaining bolt (2) and electrical connector (1) for cylinder head mounted sensor

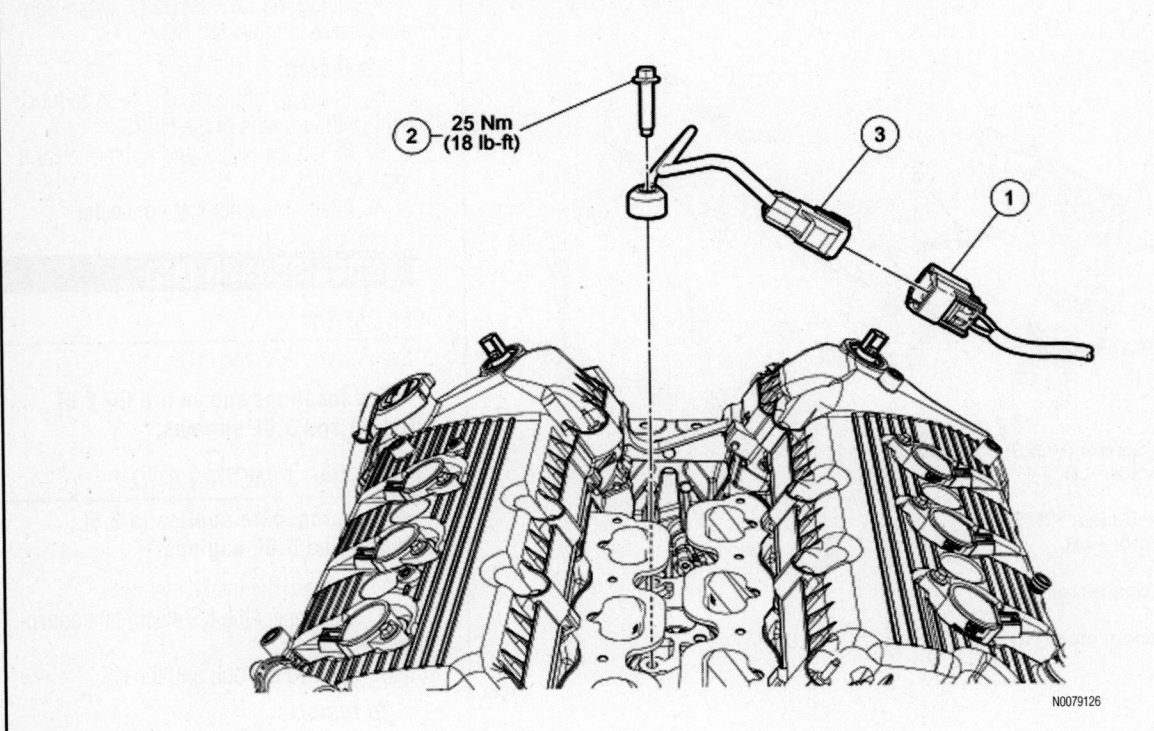

N0079126

Fig. 203 Showing the location of the Knock Sensor (3), retaining bolt (2) and electrical connector (1) for engine block mounted sensor

6. Install the lower intake manifold, if removed.

MANIFOLD ABSOLUTE PRESSURE (MAP) SENSOR

LOCATION

2.5L & Hybrid Engines

See Figure 204.

3.0L Engine

See Figure 205.

REMOVAL & INSTALLATION

2.5L & Hybrid Engines

1. Raise and safely support the vehicle.
2. Disconnect the Manifold Absolute Pressure (MAP) sensor electrical connector.

3. Using a tool like KD Tool #58181 or Lisle T25 Torx® Bit, remove the screw and the MAP sensor.
4. To install, tighten to 27 inch lbs. (3 Nm).
5. Lubricate the MAP sensor O-ring seal with clean engine oil.
6. To install, reverse the removal procedure.

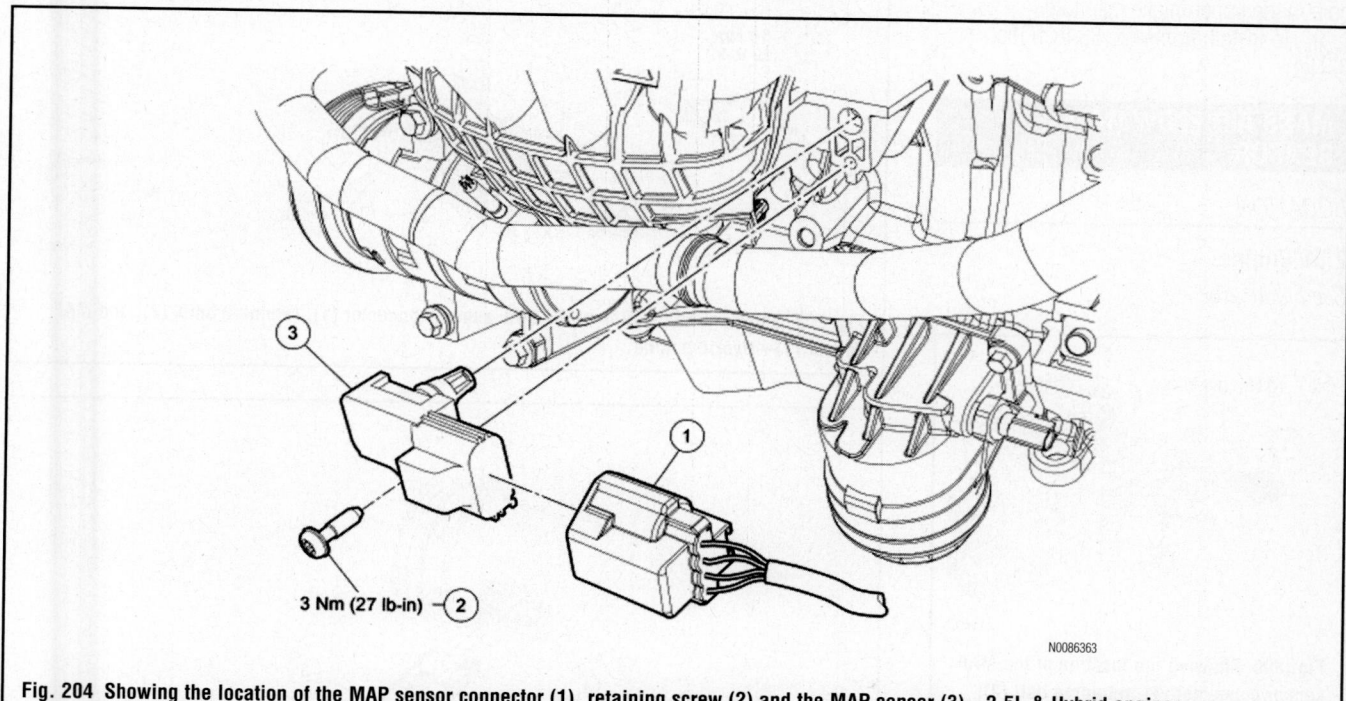

Fig. 204 Showing the location of the MAP sensor connector (1), retaining screw (2) and the MAP sensor (3)—2.5L & Hybrid engines

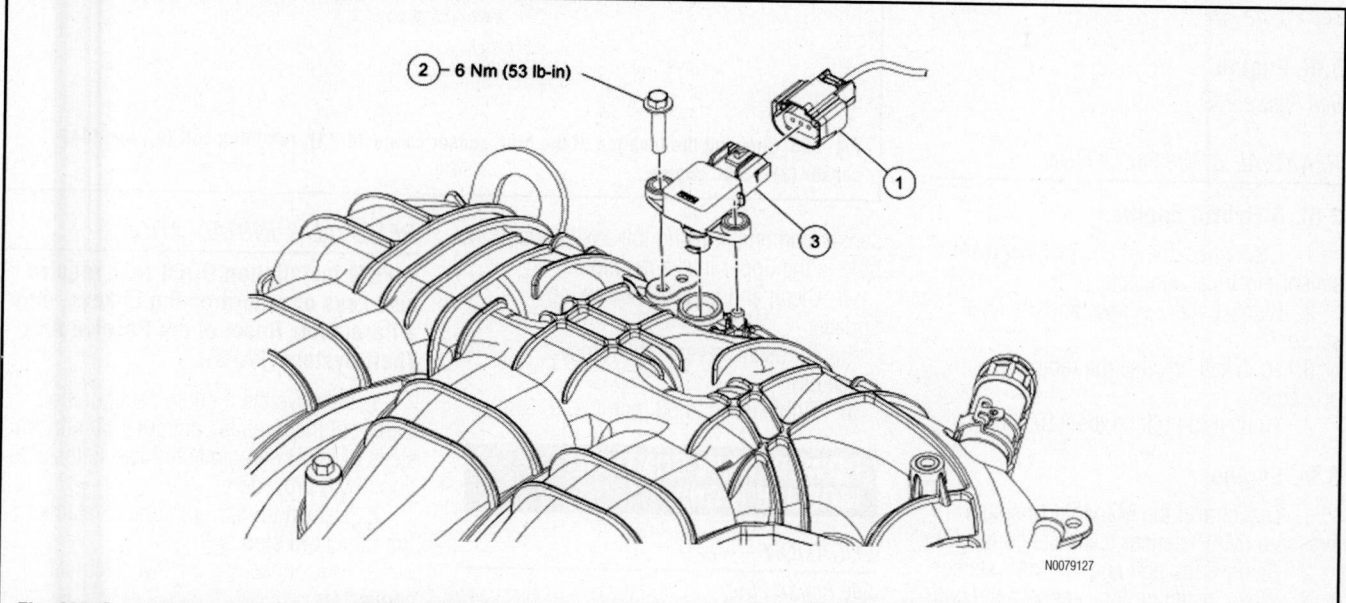

Fig. 205 Showing the location of the MAP sensor connector (1), retaining screw (2) and the MAP sensor (3)—3.0L engine

3.0L Engine

1. Disconnect the Manifold Absolute Pressure (MAP) sensor electrical connector.
2. Remove the bolt and the MAP sensor.
3. Clean and inspect the sealing surface.
4. To install, reverse the removal procedure.
5. When installing the sensor, if the bolt fails to hold specified torque, relocate the sensor and retain, using the auxiliary bolt hole in the upper intake manifold.
6. To install, tighten to 53 inch lbs. (6 Nm).

MASS AIR FLOW (MAF) SENSOR

LOCATION

2.5L Engine

See Figure 206.

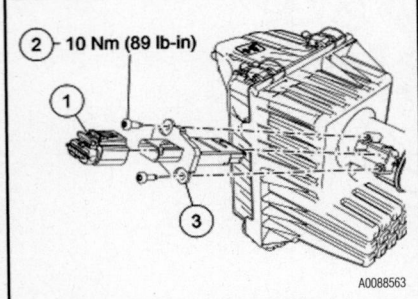

Fig. 206 Showing the location of the MAF sensor connector (1), retaining bolt (2), and MAF sensor (3)—2.5L engine

Hybrid Engine

See Figure 207.

3.0L Engine

See Figure 208.

REMOVAL & INSTALLATION

2.5L & Hybrid Engines

1. Disconnect the Mass Air Flow (MAF) sensor electrical connector.
2. Remove the 2 screws and the MAF sensor.
3. To install, reverse the removal procedure.
4. Tighten to 89 inch lbs. (10 Nm).

3.0L Engine

1. Disconnect the Manifold Absolute Pressure (MAP) sensor electrical connector.
2. Remove the bolt and the MAP sensor.
3. When installing the sensor, if the bolt fails to hold specified torque, relocate the

Fig. 207 Showing the location of the MAF sensor connector (1), retaining bolts (2), and MAF sensor (3)—Hybrid engine

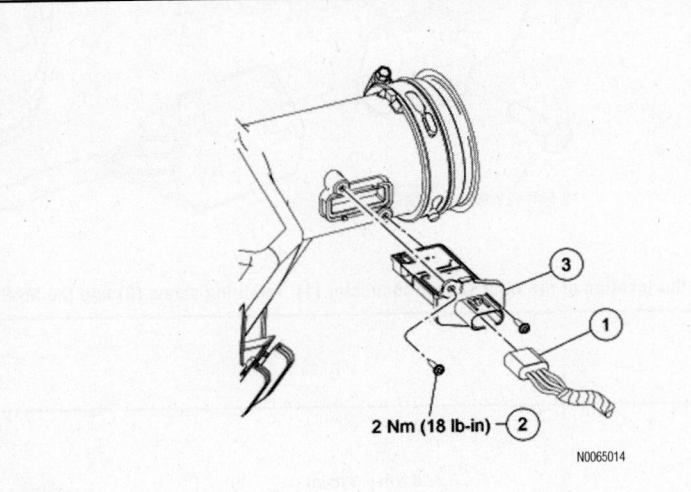

Fig. 208 Showing the location of the MAF sensor connector (1), retaining bolt (2), and MAF sensor (3)—3.0L engine

sensor and retain, using the auxiliary bolt hole in the upper intake manifold.
4. Clean and inspect the sealing surface.
5. To install, reverse the removal procedure.
6. Tighten bolt to 53 inch lbs. (6 Nm).

POWERTRAIN CONTROL MODULE (PCM)

LOCATION

See Figure 209.

REMOVAL & INSTALLATION

➡PCM installation DOES NOT require new keys or programming of keys, only a Parameter Reset of the Passive Anti-Theft System (PATS).

1. Retrieve the module configuration. Carry out the module configuration retrieval steps of the Programmable Module Installation (PMI) procedure.
2. Detach the wiring harness retainer from the cowl stud bolt.
3. Disconnect the 3 PCM electrical connectors.

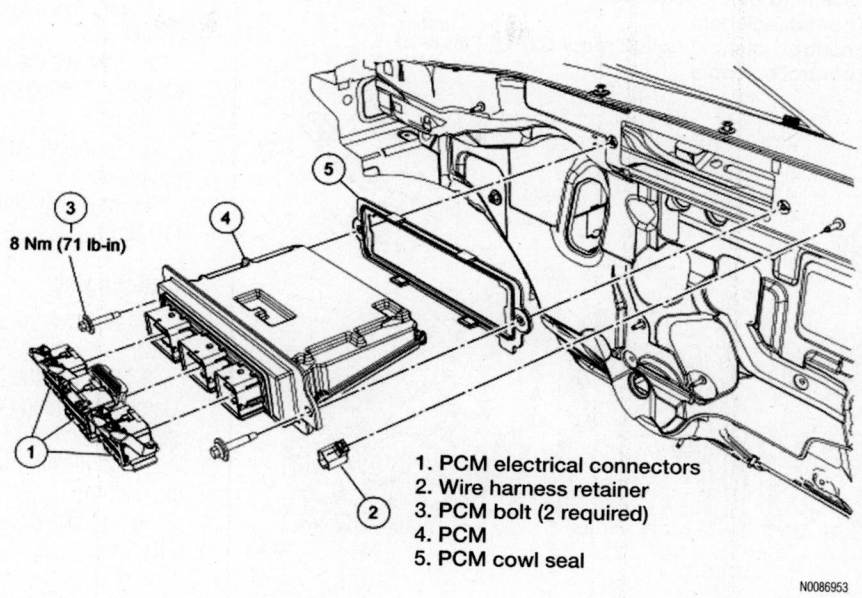

8 Nm (71 lb-in)

1. PCM electrical connectors
2. Wire harness retainer
3. PCM bolt (2 required)
4. PCM
5. PCM cowl seal

N0086953

Fig. 209 Showing the PCM location on the bulkhead—all engines

4. Remove the 2 bolts and the PCM.

5. Remove and inspect the PCM cowl seal; install new if damaged.

To install:

6. Install the PCM cowl seal.

7. Install the PCM and the 2 bolts. Tighten to 71 inch lbs. (8 Nm).

8. Connect the 3 PCM electrical connectors.

9. Attach the wiring harness retainer to the cowl stud bolt.

10. Restore the module configuration. Carry out the module configuration restore steps of the Programmable Module Installation (PMI) procedure.

11. Reprogram the PATS. Carry out the Parameter Reset procedure.

VARIABLE CAMSHAFT TIMING (VCT) OIL CONTROL SOLENOID

LOCATION

2.5L & Hybrid Engines

See Figure 210.

3.0L Engine

See Figure 211.

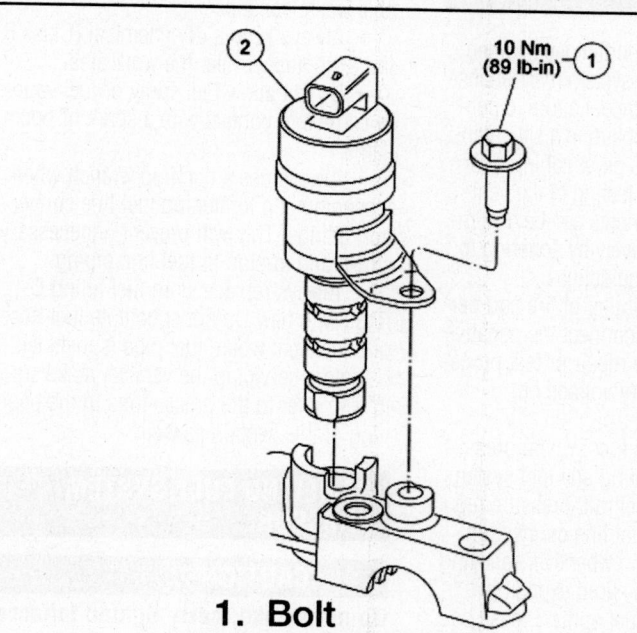

10 Nm (89 lb-in)

1. **Bolt**
2. **Variable Camshaft Timing (VCT) oil control solenoid**

N0042253

Fig. 210 Showing the location of the VCT solenoid (2) and retaining bolt (1)—2.5L & Hybrid engines

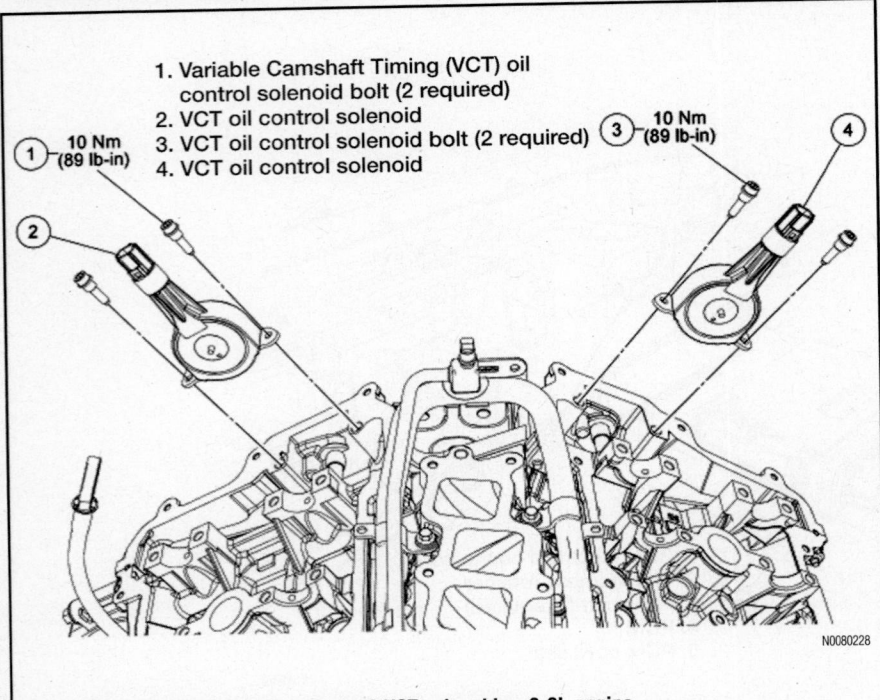

1. Variable Camshaft Timing (VCT) oil
   control solenoid bolt (2 required)
2. VCT oil control solenoid
3. VCT oil control solenoid bolt (2 required)
4. VCT oil control solenoid

10 Nm (89 lb-in)

Fig. 211 Showing the locations of the 2 VCT solenoids—3.0L engine

REMOVAL & INSTALLATION

2.5L & Hybrid Engines

1. Remove the valve cover.
2. Remove the bolt and the Variable Camshaft Timing (VCT) oil control solenoid.
3. To install, reverse the removal procedure.
4. To install, tighten to 89 inch lbs. (10 Nm).

3.0L Engine

1. Remove the LH or RH valve cover.
2. Remove the 2 bolts and the Variable Camshaft Timing (VCT) oil control solenoid.
3. To install, reverse the removal procedure.
4. Tighten retaining bolt to 89 inch lbs. (10 Nm).

FUEL

GASOLINE FUEL INJECTION SYSTEM

FUEL SYSTEM SERVICE PRECAUTIONS

Safety is the most important factor when performing not only fuel system maintenance but any type of maintenance. Failure to conduct maintenance and repairs in a safe manner may result in serious personal injury or death. Maintenance and testing of the vehicle's fuel system components can be accomplished safely and effectively by adhering to the following rules and guidelines.

• To avoid the possibility of fire and personal injury, always disconnect the negative battery cable unless the repair or test procedure requires that battery voltage be applied.

• Always relieve the fuel system pressure prior to disconnecting any fuel system component (injector, fuel rail, pressure regulator, etc.), fitting or fuel line connection. Exercise extreme caution whenever relieving fuel system pressure to avoid exposing skin, face and eyes to fuel spray. Please be advised that fuel under pressure may penetrate the skin or any part of the body that it contacts.

• Always place a shop towel or cloth around the fitting or connection prior to loosening to absorb any excess fuel due to spillage. Ensure that all fuel spillage (should it occur) is quickly removed from engine surfaces. Ensure that all fuel soaked cloths or towels are deposited into a suitable waste container.

• Always keep a dry chemical (Class B) fire extinguisher near the work area.

• Do not allow fuel spray or fuel vapors to come into contact with a spark or open flame.

• Always use a back-up wrench when loosening and tightening fuel line connection fittings. This will prevent unnecessary stress and torsion to fuel line piping.

• Always replace worn fuel fitting O-rings with new Do not substitute fuel hose or equivalent where fuel pipe is installed.

Before servicing the vehicle, make sure to also refer to the precautions in the beginning of this section as well.

RELIEVING FUEL SYSTEM PRESSURE

✳✳ CAUTION

Do not smoke, carry lighted tobacco or have an open flame of any type when working on or near any fuel-related component. Highly flammable mixtures are always present and may be ignited. Failure to follow these instructions may result in serious personal injury.

✳✳ CAUTION

Do not carry personal electronic devices such as cell phones, pagers or audio equipment of any type when working on or near any fuel-related component. Highly flammable mixtures are always present and may be ignited. Failure to follow these instructions may result in serious personal injury.

✳✳ CAUTION

Before working on or disconnecting any of the fuel tubes or fuel system components, relieve the fuel system pressure to prevent accidental spraying of fuel. Fuel in the fuel system remains under high pressure, even when the engine is not running. Failure to follow this instruction may result in serious personal injury.

✳✳ WARNING

The Fuel Pump (FP) module fuse is located in the Battery Junction Box (BJB), location 22.

RELIEVING SYSTEM PRESSURE

See Figure 212.

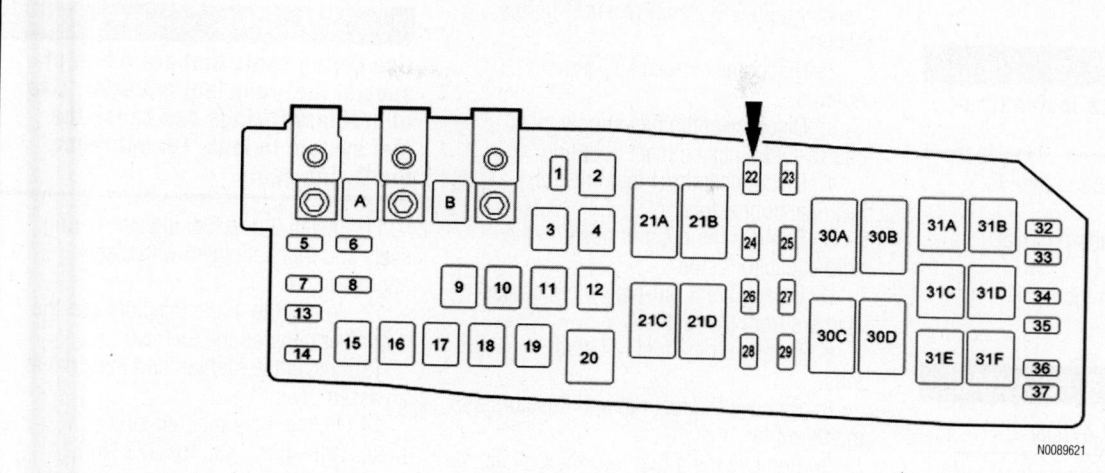

Fig. 212 Remove the FP fuse (No. 22)

1. Remove the FP fuse.
2. Start the engine and allow it to idle until it stalls.
3. After the engine stalls, crank the engine for approximately 5 seconds to make sure the fuel injection supply manifold pressure has been released.
4. Turn the ignition switch to the OFF position.

RESTORING SYSTEM PRESSURE

1. When the fuel system service is complete, install the FP module fuse.
2. Carry out a Key ON Engine OFF (KOEO) visual inspection for leaks prior to starting the engine.
3. Start the vehicle and check the fuel system for leaks.

FUEL CONTROL MODULE

REMOVAL & INSTALLATION

See Figure 213.

1. Raise and safely support the vehicle.

➡**The Fuel Pump (FP) control module is located near the left rear side of the fuel tank.**

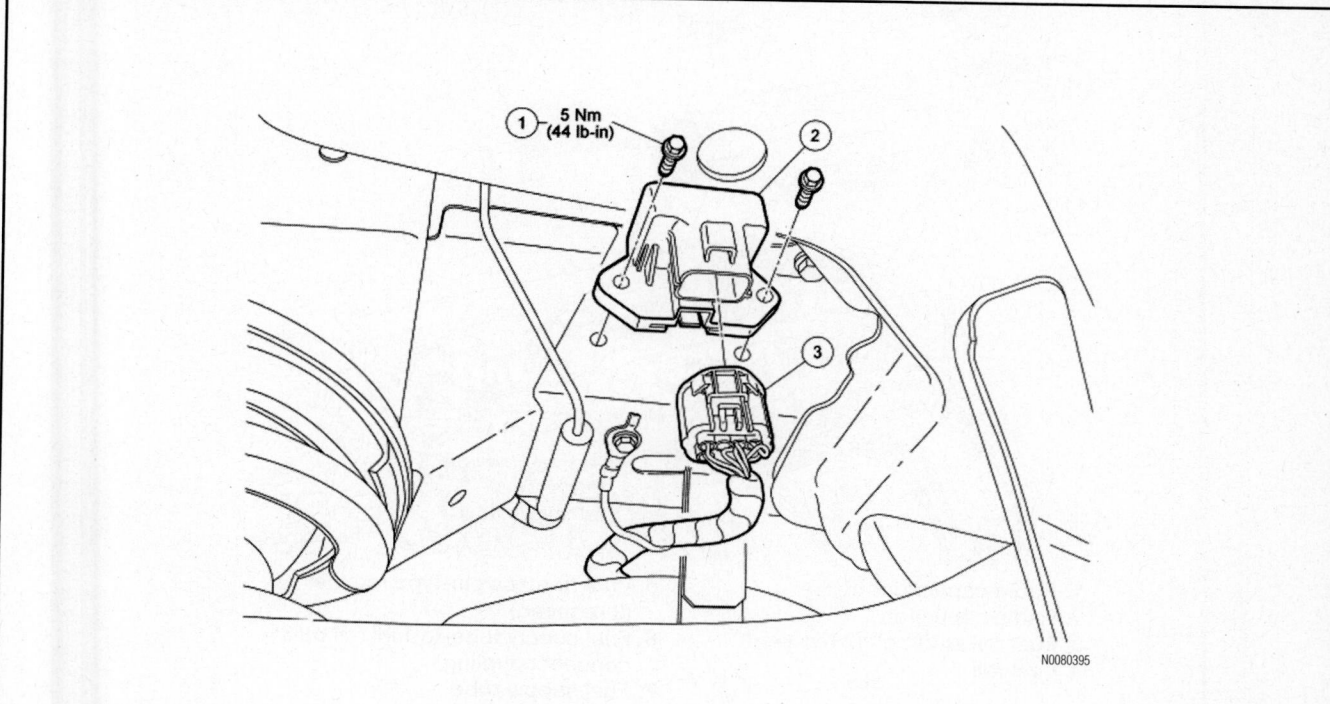

Fig. 213 Showing the fuel module control bolts (1), module (2), and electrical connector (3)—All engines

2. Disconnect the FP control module electrical connector.

Do not over-tighten the fasteners or damage will occur.

3. Remove the 2 bolts and the FP control module.

4. To install, reverse the removal procedure.

5. Tighten bolts to 44 inch lbs. (5 Nm).

FUEL INJECTORS & FUEL RAIL

REMOVAL & INSTALLATION

➡ **The fuel injectors are serviced with the fuel rail.**

2.5L & Hybrid Engines

See Figures 214 and 215.

1. Release the fuel pressure. See "Relieving Fuel System Pressure" in this section.

2. Disconnect the battery ground cable.

3. Disconnect the fuel supply tube-to-fuel quick connect coupling.

4. Disconnect the 4 fuel injector electrical connectors.

5. Remove the nut and position the radio capacitor aside.

6. Detach the 2 pin-type wire harness retainers from the fuel rail.

7. Remove the 2 fuel rail stud bolts.

8. Remove the fuel rail and injectors as an assembly.

9. Remove the 4 fuel injector retainer clips and the 4 fuel injectors.

10. Remove and discard the 8 fuel injector O-ring seals.

To install:

Use O-ring seals that are made of special fuel-resistant material. Use of ordinary O-rings can cause the fuel system to leak. Do not reuse the O-ring seals.

11. Install 8 new fuel injector O-ring seals and lubricate them with clean engine oil.

12. Install the 4 fuel injectors and the 4 retainer clips on the fuel rail.

13. Install the fuel rail and injectors as an assembly.

14. Install the 2 fuel rail stud bolts. Tighten to 17 ft. lbs. (23 Nm).

15. Attach the 2 pin-type wire harness retainers to the fuel rail.

16. Position the radio capacitor and install the nut. Tighten to 89 inch lbs. (10 Nm).

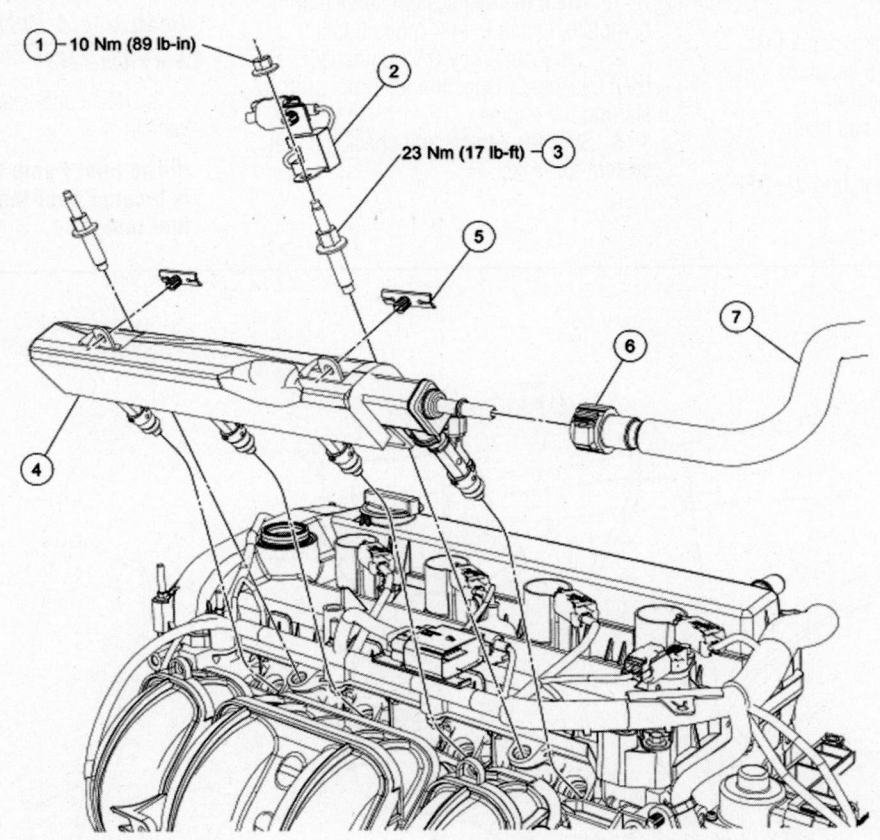

1. Radio capacitor nut
2. Radio capacitor
3. Fuel rail stud bolt (2 required)
4. Fuel rail
5. Wire harness pin-type retainer (2 required)
6. Fuel supply tube-to-fuel rail quick connect coupling
7. Fuel supply tube

N0080535

Fig. 214 Exploded view of the fuel rail assembly—2.5L & Hybrid engines

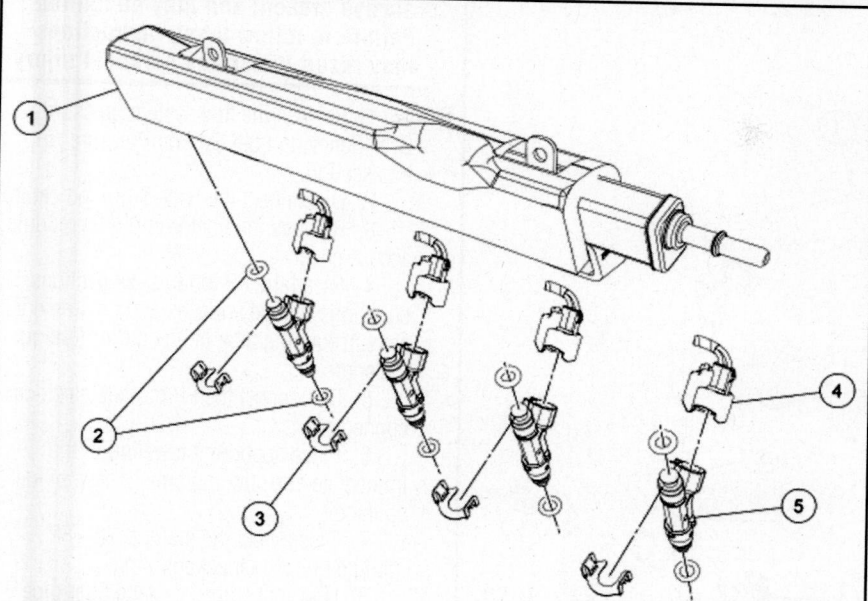

1. Fuel rail
2. Fuel injector O-ring seals (2 required per injector)
3. Fuel injector clip (4 required)
4. Fuel injector electrical connector (4 required)
5. Fuel injector (4 required)

N0086632

Fig. 215 Exploded view of the fuel injectors and rail—2.5L & Hybrid engines

11. Remove and discard the 12 fuel injector O-ring seals.

To install:

⁂ WARNING

Use O-ring seals that are made of special fuel-resistant material. Use of ordinary O-rings can cause the fuel system to leak. Do not reuse the O-ring seals.

➡ **The upper and lower fuel injector O-ring seals are similar in appearance, but are not interchangeable.**

12. Install new fuel injector O-ring seals and lubricate them with clean engine oil.
13. Install the 6 fuel injectors and clips on the fuel rail.
14. Position the fuel rail and install the bolts. Tighten to 89 inch lbs. (10 Nm).
15. Connect the engine wire harness and the fuel charging wire harness pin-type retainers to the fuel rail.
16. Connect the 4 wire harness pin-type retainers to the fuel rail.

17. Connect the 4 fuel injector electrical connectors.
18. Connect the fuel supply tube-to-fuel rail quick connect coupling.
19. Connect the battery ground cable.
20. Restore fuel system pressure. See "Relieving Fuel System Pressure" in this section.

3.0L Engine

See Figures 216 and 217.

1. Release the fuel system pressure. See "Relieving Fuel System Pressure" in this section.
2. Disconnect the battery ground cable.
3. Remove the upper intake manifold. See "Intake Manifold" in "ENGINE MECHANICAL" section.
4. Disconnect the fuel jumper tube-to-fuel rail quick connect coupling.
5. Release the 4 wire harness pin-type retainers from the fuel rail.
6. Release the engine wire harness and the fuel charging wire harness pin-type retainers from the fuel rail.
7. Disconnect the 6 fuel injector electrical connectors.
8. Remove the 4 fuel rail bolts.
9. Remove the fuel rail and injectors as an assembly.
10. Remove the 6 clips and the fuel injectors.

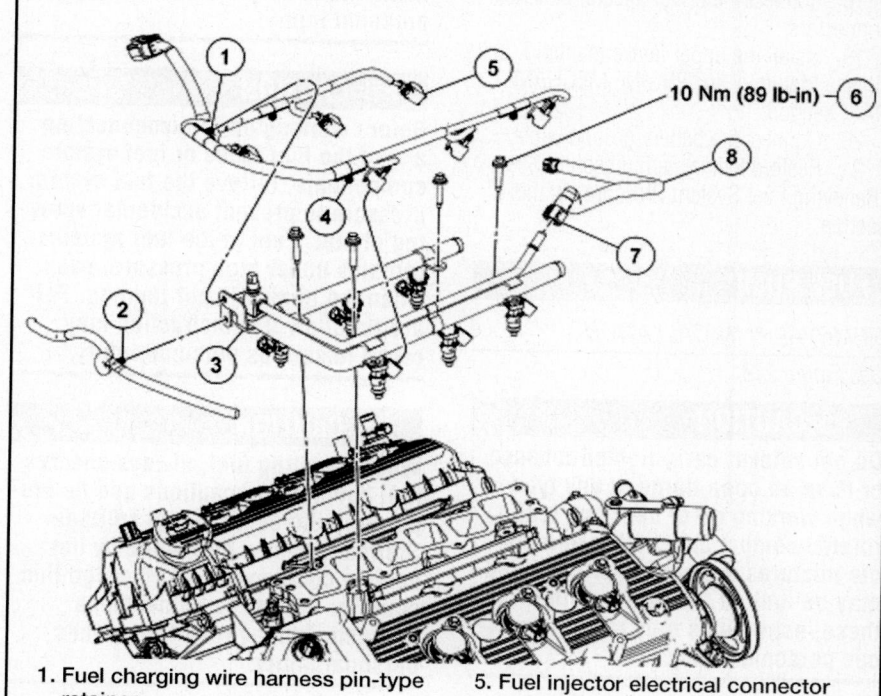

1. Fuel charging wire harness pin-type retainer
2. Engine wire harness pin-type retainer
3. Fuel rail
4. Wire harness pin-type retainer (4 required)
5. Fuel injector electrical connector (6 required)
6. Fuel rail bolt (4 required)
7. Fuel jumper tube-to-fuel rail quick connect coupling
8. Fuel jumper tube

10 Nm (89 lb-in)

N0101016

Fig. 216 Exploded view of the fuel rail assembly—3.0L engine

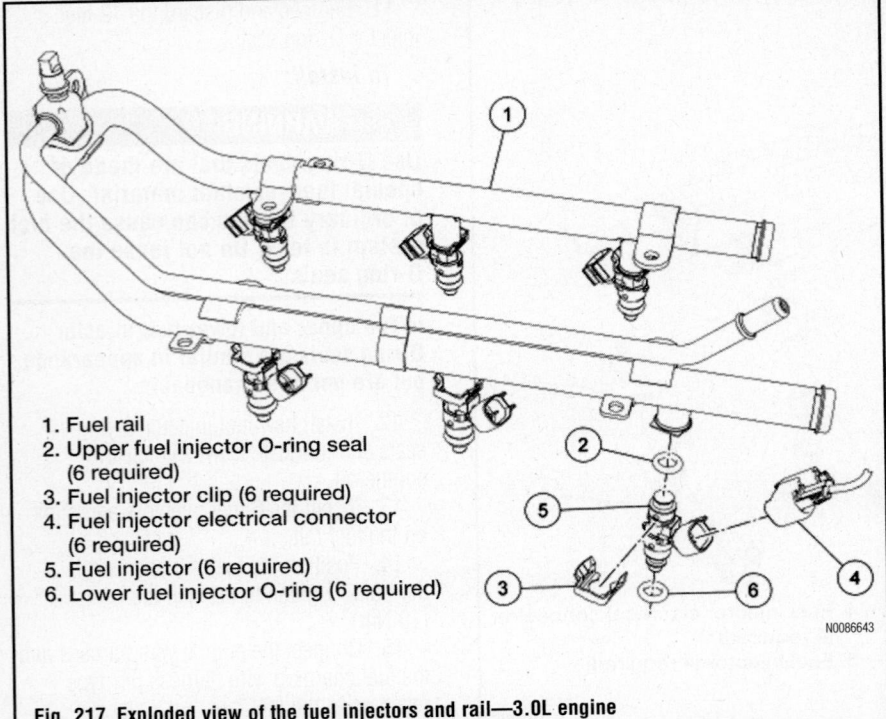

1. Fuel rail
2. Upper fuel injector O-ring seal
   (6 required)
3. Fuel injector clip (6 required)
4. Fuel injector electrical connector
   (6 required)
5. Fuel injector (6 required)
6. Lower fuel injector O-ring (6 required)

N0086643

Fig. 217 Exploded view of the fuel injectors and rail—3.0L engine

17. Connect the fuel jumper tube-to-fuel rail quick connect coupling.

18. Connect the 6 fuel injector electrical connectors.

19. Install the upper intake manifold. See "Intake Manifold" in "ENGINE MECHANICAL" section.

20. Connect the battery ground cable.

21. Restore fuel system pressure. See "Relieving Fuel System Pressure" in this section.

FUEL PUMP

REMOVAL & INSTALLATION

See Figure 218.

✳✳ CAUTION

Do not smoke, carry lighted tobacco or have an open flame of any type when working on or near any fuel-related component. Highly flammable mixtures are always present and may be ignited. Failure to follow these instructions may result in serious personal injury.

✳✳ CAUTION

Do not carry personal electronic devices such as cell phones, pagers or audio equipment of any type when working on or near any fuel-related component. Highly flammable mix-

tures are always present and may be ignited. Failure to follow these instructions may result in serious personal injury.

✳✳ CAUTION

Before working on or disconnecting any of the fuel tubes or fuel system components, relieve the fuel system pressure to prevent accidental spraying of fuel. Fuel in the fuel system remains under high pressure, even when the engine is not running. Failure to follow this instruction may result in serious personal injury.

✳✳ CAUTION

When handling fuel, always observe fuel handling precautions and be prepared in the event of fuel spillage. Spilled fuel may be ignited by hot vehicle components or other ignition sources. Failure to follow these instructions may result in serious personal injury.

✳✳ CAUTION

Always disconnect the battery ground cable at the battery when working on an evaporative emission (EVAP) system or fuel-related component. Highly flammable mixtures are

always present and may be ignited. Failure to follow these instructions may result in serious personal injury.

1. Release the fuel system pressure. See "Relieving Fuel System Pressure" in this section.

2. Disconnect the battery ground cable.

3. Remove the Fuel Pump (FP) module access cover.

4. Clean the FP module connections, couplings, flange surfaces and the immediate surrounding area of any dirt or foreign material.

5. Disconnect the FP module electrical connector.

6. Place absorbent toweling in the immediate surrounding area in case of fuel spillage.

7. Disconnect the fuel tube-to- FP module quick connect coupling.

8. Disconnect the fuel tank filler pipe recirculation tube-to- FP module quick connect coupling.

➡For initial draining on vehicles with a full tank of fuel, it is required to remove the fuel through the fuel tank filler pipe recirculation tube port on the FP module.

9. Connect a hose from an external storage tank to the fuel tank filler pipe recirculation tube port on the FP module and remove approximately one-fourth of the fuel from a completely full tank (approximately 4 gallons), lowering the fuel level below the FP module mounting flange.

10. Carefully install a proper fuel tank sender unit wrench to avoid damaging the

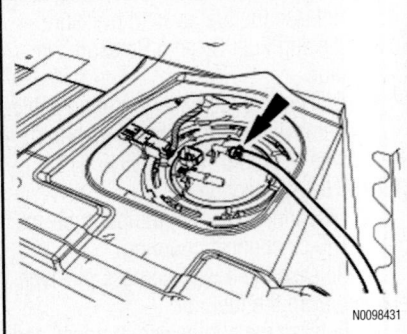

N0098431

Fig. 218 Connect a hose from an external storage tank to the fuel tank filler pipe recirculation tube port on the FP module and remove approximately one-fourth of the fuel from a completely full tank (approximately 4 gallons), lowering the fuel level below the FP module mounting flange.

fuel pump module when removing the lock ring.

11. Install the Fuel Tank Sender Unit Wrench (310-123 or equivalent) and remove the FP module lock ring.

✳✳ CAUTION

The Fuel Pump (FP) module must be handled carefully to avoid damage to the float arm.

➡ **Some residual fuel may remain in the FP module. Carefully drain into a suitable container.**

12. Completely remove the FP module from the fuel tank.

13. Inspect the surfaces of the FP module flange and fuel tank O-ring seal contact surfaces. Do not polish or adjust the O-ring seal contact area of the fuel tank flange or the fuel tank. Install a new FP module or fuel tank if the O-ring seal contact area is bent, scratched or corroded.

14. Remove and discard the FP module O-ring seal.

To install:

15. Install new FP module O-ring seal.

16. Completely install the FP module from the fuel tank.

➡ **Make sure the alignment tabs on the FP module and the fuel tank meet prior to tightening the FP module lock ring.**

17. Install the Fuel Tank Sender Unit Wrench (310-123 or equivalent) and tighten the FP module lock ring.

18. Install the fuel tank filler pipe recirculation tube-to- FP module quick connect coupling.

19. Connect the fuel tube-to-FP module using the quick connect coupling.

20. Connect the FP module electrical connector.

21. Install the Fuel Pump (FP) module access cover.

22. Install the battery ground cable.

23. Restore fuel system pressure. See "Relieving Fuel System Pressure" in this section.

FUEL TANK

DRAINING

See Figures 219 and 220.

1. Release the fuel system pressure. See "Relieving Fuel System Pressure" in this section.

2. Disconnect the battery ground cable.

3. Remove the Fuel Pump (FP) module access cover.

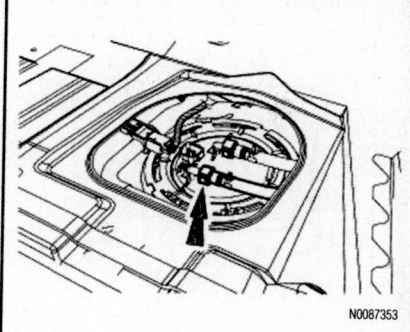

Fig. 219 Disconnect the fuel tube-to- FP module quick connect coupling.

4. Clean the FP module connections, couplings, flange surfaces and the immediate surrounding area of any dirt or foreign material.

5. Disconnect the FP module electrical connector.

6. Place absorbent toweling in the immediate surrounding area in case of fuel spillage.

7. Disconnect the fuel tube-to- FP module quick connect coupling.

8. Disconnect the fuel tank filler pipe recirculation tube-to- FP module quick connect coupling.

➡ **For initial fuel draining, it is required to remove the fuel through the fuel tank filler pipe recirculation tube port on the FP module.**

9. Connect an external fuel storage tank filler pipe on the FP module and remove approximately one-fourth of the fuel (from a completely full tank), lowering the fuel level below the FP module mounting flange.

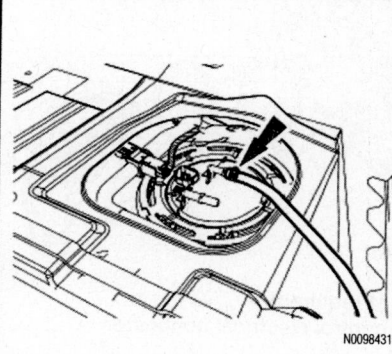

Fig. 220 Connect an external fuel storage tank filler pipe on the FP module and remove approximately one-fourth of the fuel (from a completely full tank), lowering the fuel level below the FP module mounting flange.

✳✳ CAUTION

Carefully install the Fuel Tank Sender Unit Wrench to avoid damaging the FP module when removing the lock ring.

10. Using a proper sending unit wrench (310-123 or equivalent), remove the FP module lock ring.

✳✳ CAUTION

The Fuel Pump (FP) module must be handled carefully to avoid damage to the float arm and filter.

11. Position the FP module aside, insert the tube from the external fuel storage tank into the FP module aperture and remove as much fuel as possible from the fuel tank.

REMOVAL & INSTALLATION

See Figure 221.

1. Raise and safely support the vehicle.

2. Drain the fuel tank.

3. Remove the exhaust muffler and resonator.

4. For AWD vehicles, remove the rear driveshaft. See "DRIVE TRAIN" section.

5. Release the clamp and remove the fuel tank filler pipe hose from the fuel tank.

6. Position a powertrain lift under the fuel tank.

7. Detach the parking brake cable pin-type retainer from the front of the LH fuel tank strap.

8. Detach the wire harness and fresh air tube pin-type retainers from the rear of LH fuel tank strap.

9. Remove the 2 bolts and position the 2 fuel tank straps aside.

10. Remove the 2 bolts and position the RR exhaust hanger aside.

11. Partially lower the fuel tank enough to disconnect the fuel vapor tube assembly-to-fuel tank quick connect coupling.

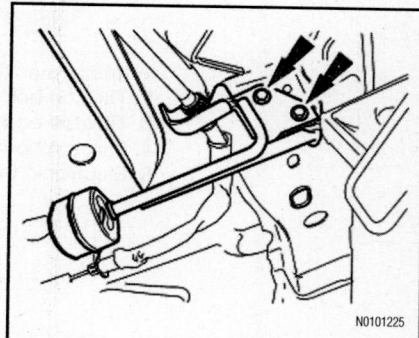

Fig. 221 Remove the 2 bolts and position the RR exhaust hanger aside.

12. Completely lower and remove the fuel tank from the vehicle.

To install:

13. To install, reverse the removal procedure.

14. Position the RR exhaust hanger and tighten to 17 ft. lbs. (23 Nm).

15. Position the 2 fuel tank straps and tighten to 41 ft. lbs. (55 Nm).

16. Install the fuel tank filler pipe hose to the fuel tank and tighten to 35 inch lbs. (4 Nm).

IDLE SPEED

ADJUSTMENT

➡ **Idle speed is electronically controlled and no adjustment is required.**

INERTIA FUEL SHUTOFF (IFS) SWITCH

REMOVAL & INSTALLATION

See Figure 222.

1. Remove the RH lower A-pillar trim panel.

2. Disconnect the Inertia Fuel Shutoff (IFS) switch electrical connector.

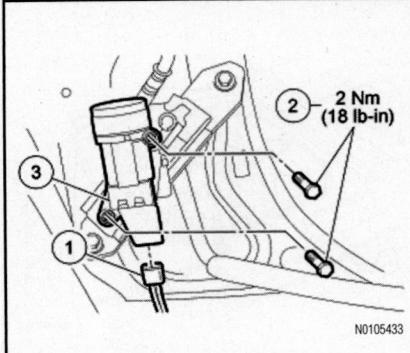

Fig. 222 Showing the IFS switch (3), mounting bolts (2) and electrical connector (1)

3. Remove the 2 bolts and the IFS switch.

4. To install, reverse the removal procedure.

5. Tighten the IFS switch bolts to 18 inch lbs. (2 Nm).

THROTTLE BODY

REMOVAL & INSTALLATION

2.5L & Hybrid Engines

See Figure 223.

1. Remove the air cleaner outlet pipe.

2. Disconnect the electrical throttle control electrical connector.

3. Remove the 4 bolts and the throttle body. Discard the gasket.

To install:

4. Install a new throttle body gasket.

5. Position the throttle body and install the bolts. Tighten to 89 inch lbs. (10 Nm).

6. Attach the electrical connector.

7. Install the air cleaner outlet pipe.

3.0L Engine

See Figure 224.

1. Remove the air cleaner outlet pipe.

2. Disconnect the electrical throttle control electrical connector.

3. Remove the 4 bolts and the throttle body. Discard the gasket.

To install:

4. Install a new throttle body gasket.

5. Position the throttle body and install the bolts. Tighten to 89 inch lbs. (10 Nm).

6. Attach the electrical connector.

7. Install the air cleaner outlet pipe.

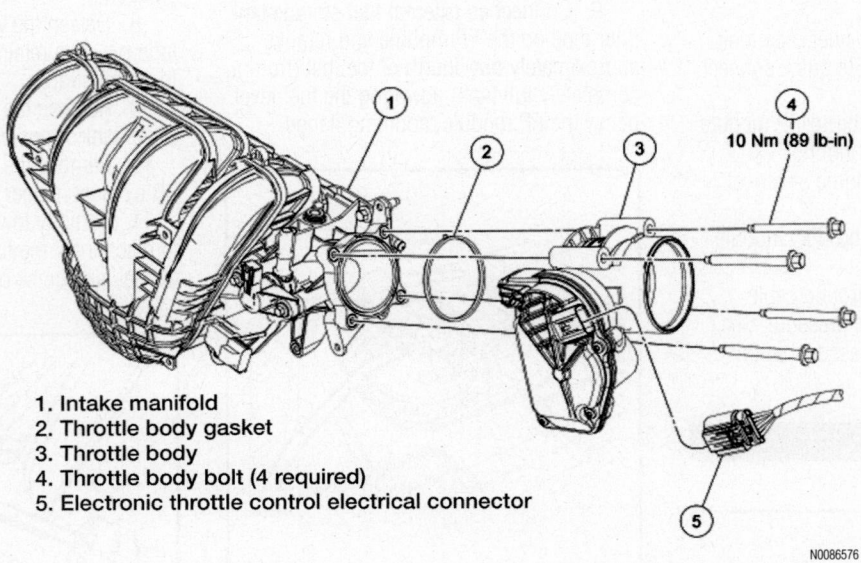

1. Intake manifold
2. Throttle body gasket
3. Throttle body
4. Throttle body bolt (4 required)
5. Electronic throttle control electrical connector

Fig. 223 Removing the throttle body—2.5L & Hybrid engines

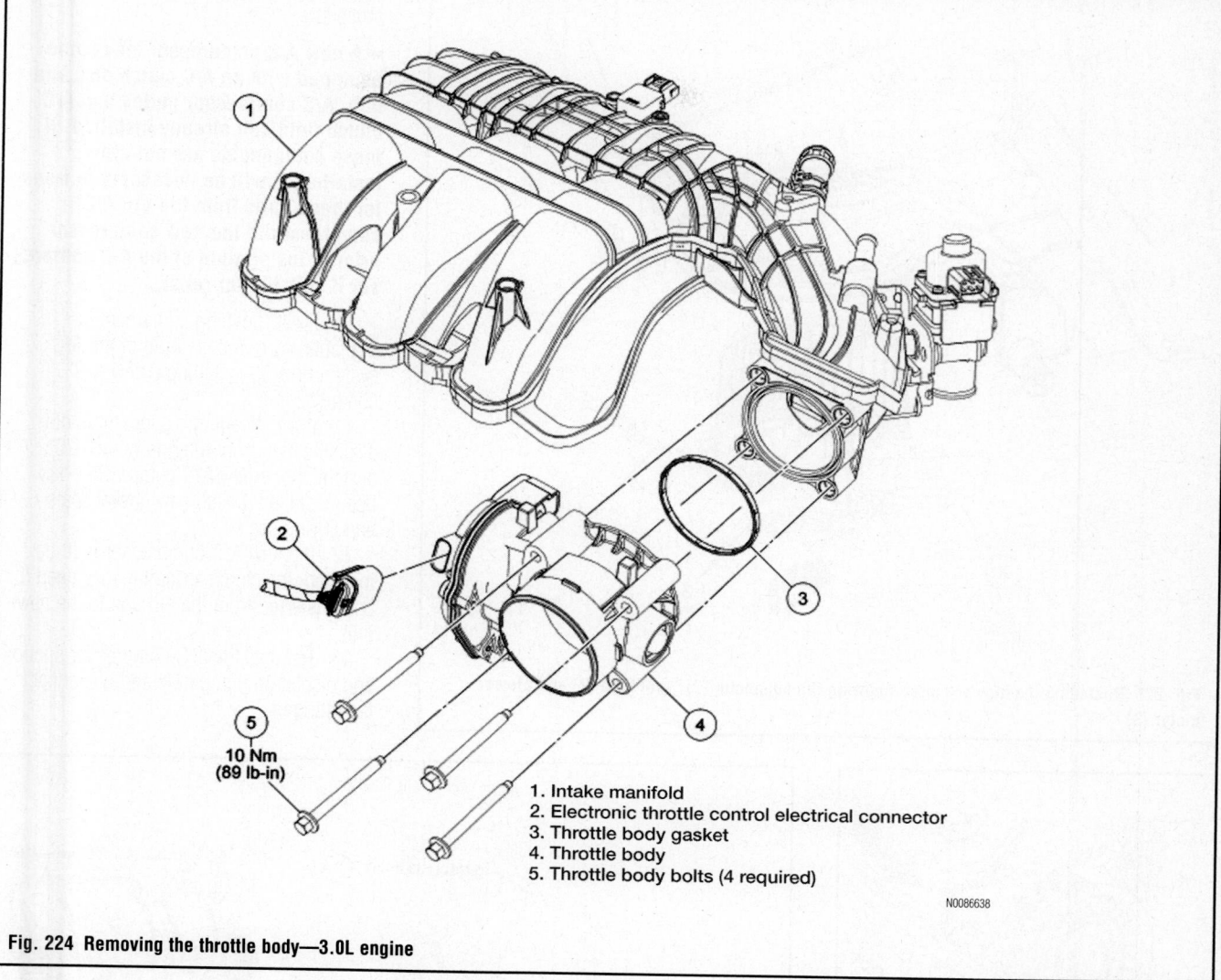

1. Intake manifold
2. Electronic throttle control electrical connector
3. Throttle body gasket
4. Throttle body
5. Throttle body bolts (4 required)

N0086638

Fig. 224 Removing the throttle body—3.0L engine

HEATING & AIR CONDITIONING SYSTEM

BLOWER MOTOR

REMOVAL & INSTALLATION
See Figure 225.

1. Disconnect the blower motor electrical connector.

2. Release the 2 blower motor vent tube clips and pull the vent tube down until it is disengaged from the heater core and evaporator core housing.

➡ **The carpet below the blower motor must be slightly repositioned to remove the blower motor.**

3. Rotate the blower motor counterclockwise to disengage it from the housing and remove the blower motor.

4. To install, reverse the removal procedure.

COMPRESSOR

REMOVAL & INSTALLATION

2.5L Engine
See Figures 226 and 227.

❊❊ WARNING

If installing a new Air Conditioning (A/C) compressor due to an internal failure of the old unit, carry out the following procedures to remove contamination from the A/C system. Failure to remove contamination from the A/C system, if present, will result in poor A/C performance and/or damage to the new A/C compressor and other components.

1. Raise and safely support the vehicle.

2. Recover the refrigerant, using a proper A/C service center.

3. Remove the RH lower engine splash shield.

4. Release the accessory drive belt tensioner and remove the drive belt from the A/C compressor pulley.

5. Disconnect the A/C clutch field coil electrical connector.

❊❊ CAUTION

Do not allow the Air Conditioning (A/C) compressor to hang from the A/C lines or damage to the A/C lines can occur.

6. Remove the 3 A/C compressor bolts and lower the A/C compressor to allow access to the suction and discharge fitting nuts.

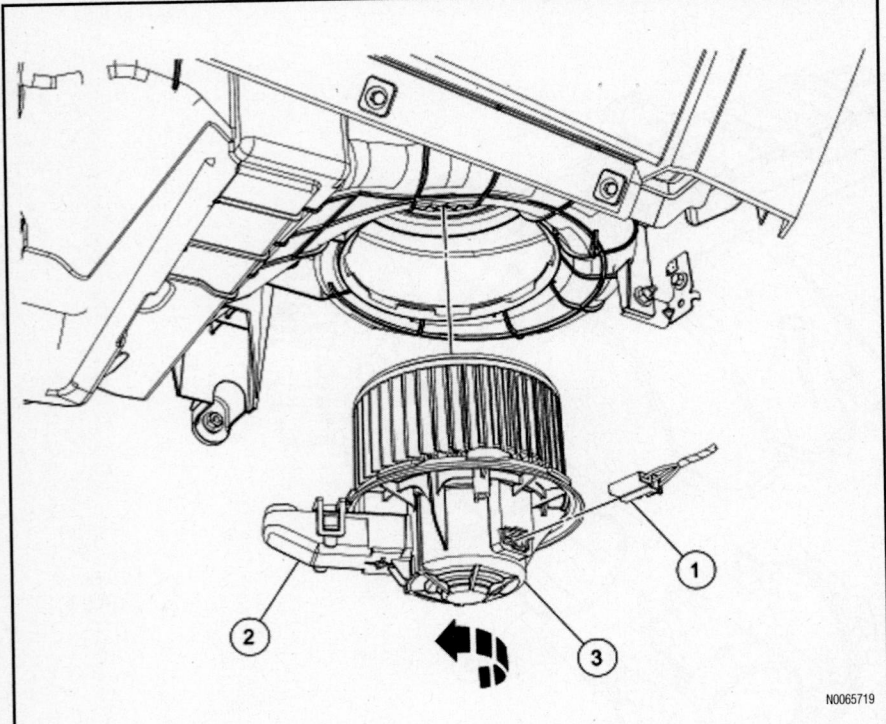

Fig. 225 Removing the blower motor; showing the connector (1), vent tube (2) and blower motor (3)

9. To install, reverse the removal procedure.

➡**A new A/C compressor may come equipped with an A/C clutch disc and hub, A/C compressor pulley and A/C clutch field coil already installed. If these components are not pre-installed, it will be necessary to transfer these parts from the old A/C compressor to the new compressor prior to installation of the A/C compressor if suitable for reuse.**

10. If A/C flushing equipment is available, carry out flushing of the A/C system prior to installing a new A/C compressor.

11. If A/C flushing equipment is not available, carry out filtering of the A/C system after a new A/C compressor has been installed. Install new gasket seals and O-ring seals.

12. If a new A/C compressor is to be installed, the clutch assembly may need to be transferred from the old unit to the new unit.

13. Remove the A/C compressor suction and discharge fitting nuts and disconnect the fittings.

Fig. 226 Release the accessory drive belt tensioner and remove the drive belt from the A/C compressor pulley.

7. Remove the A/C compressor suction and discharge fitting nuts and disconnect the fittings. Discard the O-ring seals and gasket seals.

8. Remove the A/C compressor.

To install:

➡**If installing a new A/C compressor, transfer the shipping caps from the new A/C compressor to the old A/C compressor after the refrigerant oil has been measured.**

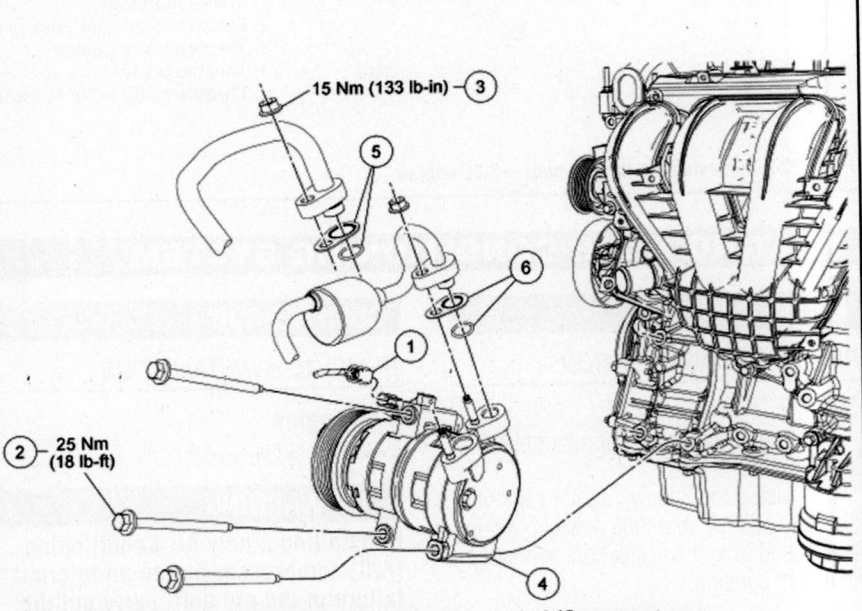

1. A/C clutch field coil electrical connector
2. A/C compressor bolt (3 required)
3. A/C compressor fitting nut (suction and discharge) (2 required)
4. A/C compressor
5. O-ring seal and gasket seal kit
6. O-ring seal and gasket seal kit

Fig. 227 Exploded view of the compressor mounting—2.5L engine

Discard the O-ring seals and gasket seals. Tighten to 133 inch lbs. (15 Nm).

14. Remove the 3 A/C compressor bolts and lower the A/C compressor to allow access to the suction and discharge fitting nuts. To install, tighten the A/C compressor bolts to 18 ft. lbs. (25 Nm).

15. Install a new Thermostatic Expansion Valve (TXV) as directed by the A/C flushing or filtering procedure.

16. If not filtering the A/C system, lubricate the refrigerant system with the correct amount of clean PAG oil.

17. Install a new receiver/drier as directed by the A/C flushing or filtering procedure.

➥Installation of a new receiver/drier is not required when repairing the A/C system except when there is physical evidence of system contamination from a failed A/C compressor or damage to the receiver/drier.

18. Evacuate, leak test and charge the refrigerant system.

Hybrid Engine

See Figures 228 through 230.

> ✳✳ **WARNING**
>
> **Service electric Air Conditioning (A/C) compressors are shipped with a small amount of electric compressor oil already installed which may not match the nominal amount required by the refrigerant system. Before installing a new service electric A/C compressor, the correct electric compressor oil level must be determined based on the amount of oil removed along with the oil electric A/C compressor. Failure to correctly match the electric compressor oil amount will result in damage to the electric A/C compressor and other refrigerant system components.**

1. Raise and safely support the vehicle.

2. Recover the refrigerant.

3. Depower the high-voltage traction battery system. See "ENGINE ELECTRICAL" section.

> ✳✳ **WARNING**
>
> **Failure to disconnect high-voltage cable connectors as instructed may result in damage to the connectors.**

4. Release the clips and locking tabs and disconnect the interlock connector and the high-voltage cable connector at the A/C Compressor Module (ACCM).

5. Press the locking clip in the white interlock connector and disengage the white connector before releasing the locking clip on the orange portion of the high-voltage connector. The white interlock connector will not come completely apart until the orange portion is released.

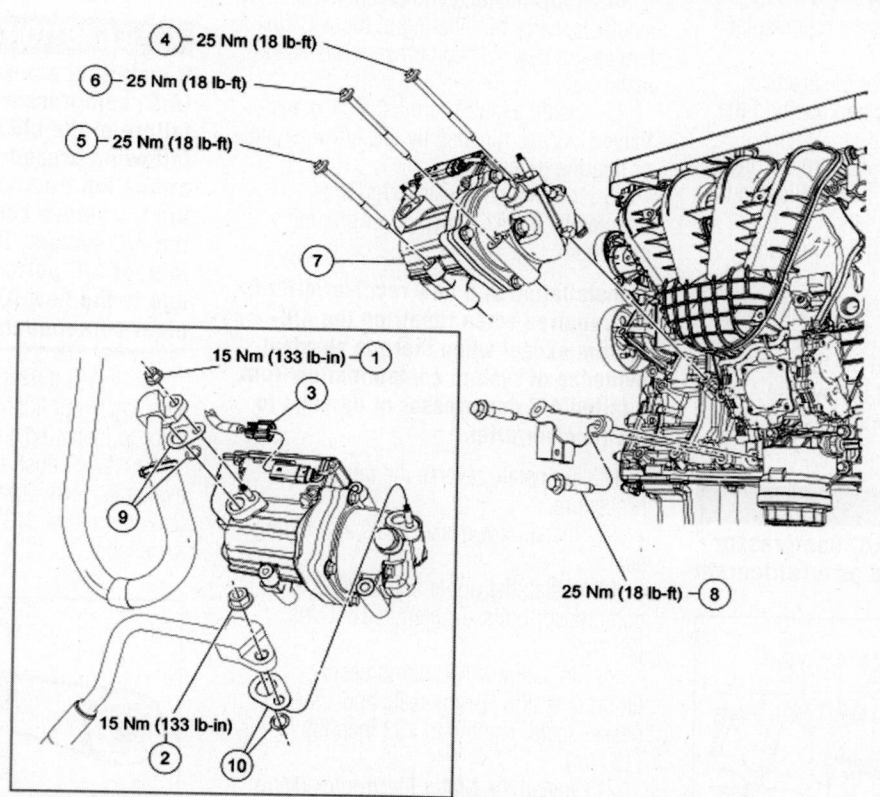

1. A/C compressor suction fitting nut
2. A/C compressor discharge fitting nut
3. A/C compressor electrical connector
4. Upper A/C compressor bolt
5. Lower front A/C compressor bolt
6. Lower rear A/C compressor bolt
7. A/C compressor
8. A/C compressor bracket bolt (2 required)
9. O-ring seal and gasket seal kit
10. O-ring seal and gasket seal kit

N0105986

Fig. 228 Exploded view of removing the A/C compressor—Hybrid engine

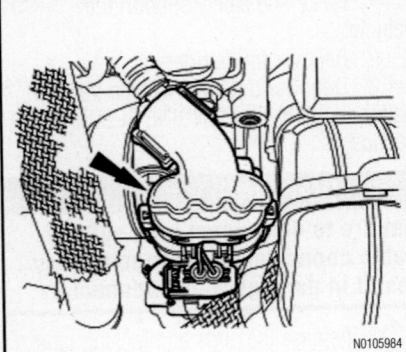

Fig. 229 Press the locking clip in the white interlock connector and disengage the white connector before releasing the locking clip on the orange portion of the high-voltage connector. The white interlock connector will not come completely apart until the orange portion is released.

6. Detach the ACCM high-voltage cable connector pin-type retainer.

7. Remove the RH lower engine splash shield.

8. Remove the 2 Motor Electronics (M/E) coolant pump bolts and position the pump aside.

9. Remove the 2 A/C compressor fitting nuts and disconnect the fittings. Discard the O-ring seals and gasket seals.

10. Disconnect the A/C compressor electrical connector.

11. Remove the upper and lower front A/C compressor bolts.

12. Completely loosen the lower rear A/C compressor bolt and remove the A/C compressor.

To install:

✳✳ CAUTION

Motorcraft® Electric A/C Compressor Oil only must be used as a refrigerant

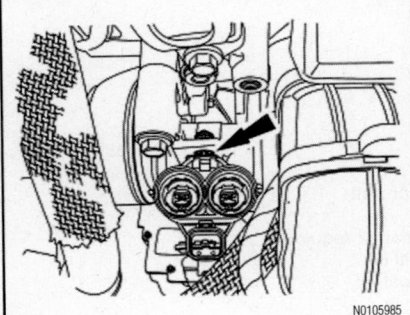

Fig. 230 Detach the ACCM high-voltage cable connector pin-type retainer.

system lubricant for hybrid vehicles. Addition of any oil other than Motorcraft® Electric A/C Compressor Oil to the hybrid vehicle refrigerant system will damage the electric Air Conditioning (A/C) compressor and contaminate the refrigerant system.

✳✳ CAUTION

If installing a new Air Conditioning (A/C) compressor due to an internal failure of the old unit, carry out the following procedures to remove contamination from the A/C system. Failure to remove contamination from the A/C system, if present, will result in poor A/C performance and/or damage to the new A/C compressor and other components.

13. If A/C flushing equipment is available, carry out flushing of the A/C system prior to installing a new A/C compressor.

14. If A/C flushing equipment is not available, carry out filtering of the A/C system after a new A/C compressor has been installed.

15. Install a new Thermostatic Expansion Valve (TXV) as directed by the A/C flushing or filtering procedure.

16. Install a new receiver/drier as directed by the A/C flushing or filtering procedure.

➡ Installation of a new receiver/drier is not required when repairing the A/C system except when there is physical evidence of system contamination from a failed A/C compressor or damage to the receiver/drier.

17. To install, reverse the removal procedure.

18. Install new gasket seals and O-ring seals.

19. Install the upper and lower A/C compressor bolts. Tighten to 18 ft. lbs. (25 Nm).

20. Install new A/C compressor fitting nuts and O-ring seals and gasket seals. Tighten to 133 inch lbs. (15 Nm).

21. Install the Motor Electronics (M/E) coolant pump and bolts. Tighten to 15 ft. lbs. (20 Nm).

22. Add the correct amount of clean electric A/C compressor oil to the refrigerant system.

23. Evacuate, leak test and charge the refrigerant system.

3.0L Engine

See Figures 231 and 232.

1. Raise and safely support the vehicle.

2. Recover the refrigerant using a proper A/C service center.

3. Remove the RH lower engine splash shield.

4. Release the tensioner and remove the drive belt from the A/C compressor pulley.

5. Remove the A/C compressor suction and discharge fitting nuts and disconnect the fittings. Discard the O-ring seals and gasket seals.

6. Disconnect the A/C clutch field coil electrical connector.

7. Remove the 3 A/C compressor bolts.

8. Remove the A/C compressor.

➡ If installing a new A/C compressor, transfer the shipping caps from the new A/C compressor to the old A/C compressor after the refrigerant oil has been measured.

To install:

✳✳ CAUTION

If installing a new Air Conditioning (A/C) compressor due to an internal failure of the old unit, carry out the following procedures to remove contamination from the A/C system. Failure to remove contamination from the A/C system, if present, will result in poor A/C performance and/or damage to the new A/C compressor and other components.

9. If A/C flushing equipment is available, carry out flushing of the A/C system prior to installing a new A/C compressor.

10. If A/C flushing equipment is not available, carry out filtering of the A/C system after a new A/C compressor has been installed.

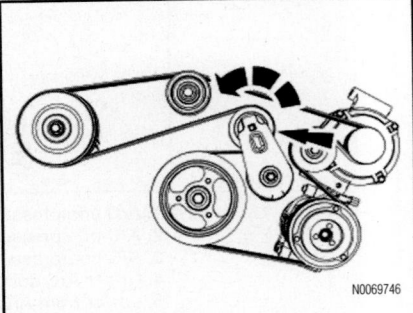

Fig. 231 Release the tensioner and remove the drive belt from the A/C compressor pulley.

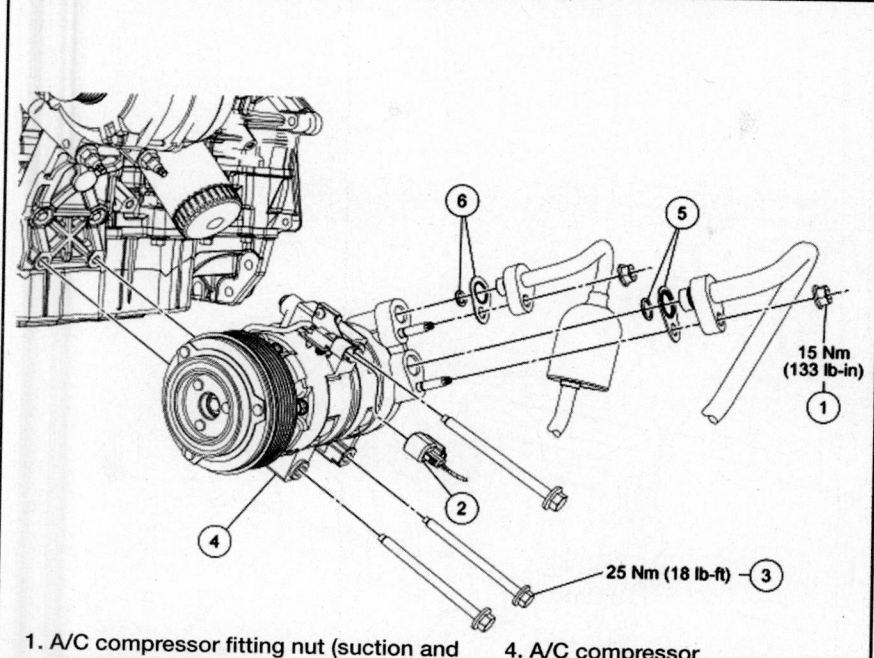

1. A/C compressor fitting nut (suction and discharge) (2 required)
2. A/C clutch field coil electrical connector
3. A/C compressor bolt (3 required)
4. A/C compressor
5. O-ring seal and gasket seal kit
6. O-ring seal and gasket seal kit

N0086250

Fig. 232 Removing the A/C compressor—3.0L engine

11. Install a new Thermostatic Expansion Valve (TXV) as directed by the A/C flushing or filtering procedure.

12. Install a new receiver/drier as directed by the A/C flushing or filtering procedure.

➡**Installation of a new receiver/drier is not required when repairing the A/C system except when there is physical evidence of system contamination from a failed A/C compressor or damage to the receiver/drier.**

➡**A new A/C compressor may come equipped with an A/C clutch disc and hub, A/C compressor pulley and A/C clutch field coil already installed. If these components are not pre-installed, it will be necessary to transfer these parts from the old A/C compressor to the new compressor prior to installation of the A/C compressor if suitable for reuse.**

13. Position the A/C compressor and install the bolts. Tighten to 18 ft. lbs. (25 Nm).

14. Attach the electrical connector.

15. Connect the A/C compressor suction and discharge fittings, using new O-ring seals and gasket seals. Tighten the nuts to 133 inch lbs. (15 Nm).

16. Install the drive belt to the A/C compressor pulley. Ensure the tensioner is set.

17. If not filtering the A/C system, lubricate the refrigerant system with the correct amount of clean PAG oil.

18. Evacuate, leak test and charge the refrigerant system.

19. Install the splash shield.

HEATER CORE

REMOVAL & INSTALLATION

See Figure 233.

➡**If a heater core leak is suspected, the heater core must be leak tested before the heater core is removed.**

➡**Use only the approved coolant for this vehicle.**

1. Remove the heater core and evaporator core housing.

2. Remove the dash panel seal.

3. Remove the heater core bracket screw and the heater core bracket.

4. Remove the heater core.

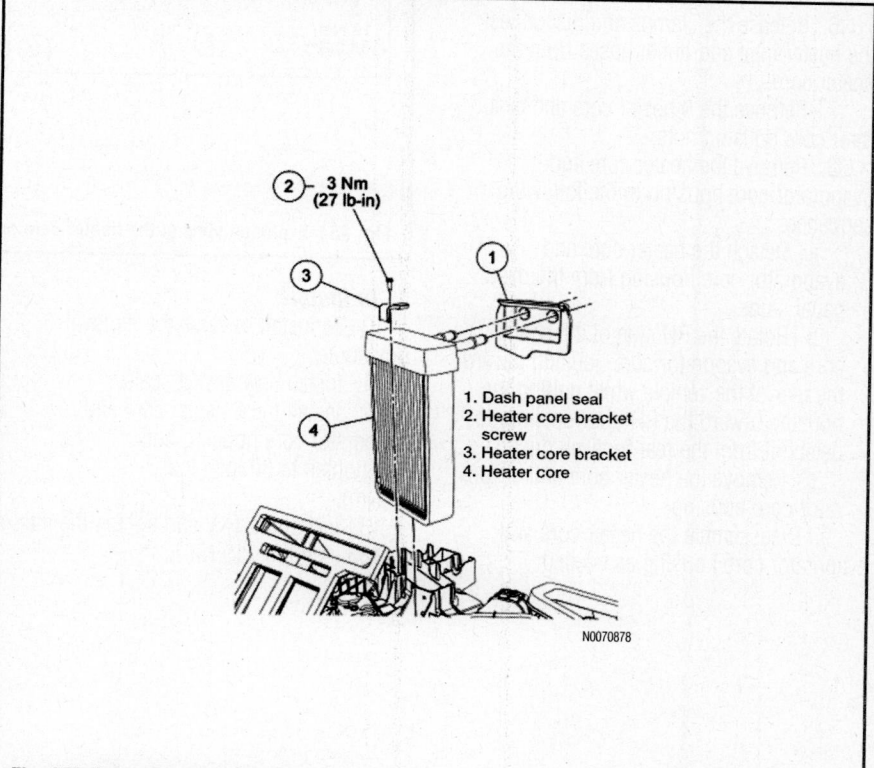

1. Dash panel seal
2. Heater core bracket screw
3. Heater core bracket
4. Heater core

N0070878

Fig. 233 Removing the heater core

5. To install, reverse the removal procedure.

6. Tighten the heater core bracket screw to 27 inch lbs.(3 Nm).

HEATER CORE & EVAPORATOR CORE HOUSING

REMOVAL & INSTALLATION

See Figure 234.

❄ WARNING

Motorcraft® Electric Compressor Oil only must be used as a refrigerant system lubricant for hybrid vehicles. Addition of any oil other than Motorcraft® Electric Compressor Oil to the hybrid vehicle refrigerant system will damage the electric Air Conditioning (A/C) compressor and contaminate the refrigerant system.

➡ **If a heater core leak is suspected, the heater core must be leak tested before the heater core is removed.**

1. Drain the engine coolant.
2. Recover the refrigerant, using a proper A/C service station.
3. Remove the instrument panel.
4. Remove the Thermostatic Expansion Valve (TXV) fitting nut and disconnect the fitting.
5. Discard the gasket seals.
6. Release the clamps and disconnect the heater inlet and outlet hoses from the heater core.
7. Remove the 6 heater core and evaporator core housing nuts.
8. Remove the heater core and evaporator core housing in the following sequence.

   a. Detach the heater core and evaporator core housing from the dash panel studs.

   b. Rotate the RH side of the heater core and evaporator core housing toward the rear of the vehicle while pulling the housing toward the RH door opening to detach it from the rear footwell duct.

   c. Remove the heater core and evaporator core housing.

9. Disassemble the heater core and evaporator core housing as needed.

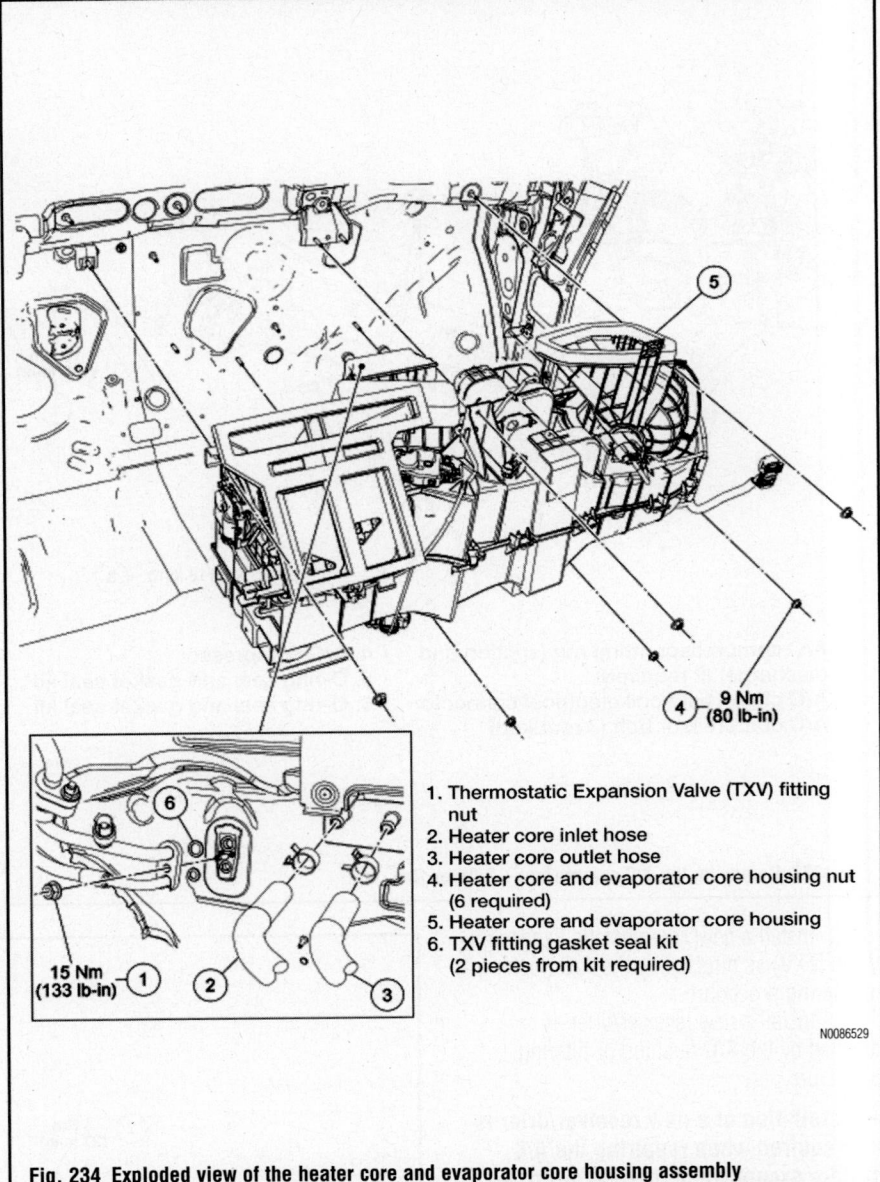

1. Thermostatic Expansion Valve (TXV) fitting nut
2. Heater core inlet hose
3. Heater core outlet hose
4. Heater core and evaporator core housing nut (6 required)
5. Heater core and evaporator core housing
6. TXV fitting gasket seal kit (2 pieces from kit required)

N0086529

Fig. 234 Exploded view of the heater core and evaporator core housing assembly

To install:

10. To install, reverse the removal procedure.
11. Install new gasket seals.
12. Install the 6 heater core and evaporator core housing nuts and tighten to 80 inch lbs. (9 Nm).
13. Install the TXV and tighten the fitting to 133 inch lbs. (15 Nm).

14. Add the correct amount of clean PAG oil (non-hybrid) or electric A/C compressor oil (hybrid) to the refrigerant system.
15. Fill and bleed the engine cooling system.
16. Evacuate, leak test and charge the refrigerant system.

STEERING

POWER STEERING GEAR

REMOVAL & INSTALLATION

See Figures 235 through 237.

1. Remove the front wheels and tires.
2. Turn the ignition key to the OFF position.
3. Remove the ignition key.

❊❊ CAUTION

Do not allow the steering wheel to rotate while the intermediate shaft is disconnected or damage to the clock spring can result. If there is evidence that the shaft has rotated, the clock-spring must be removed and recentered.

4. Remove and discard the steering column coupling-to-steering gear bolt and disconnect the coupling from the steering gear.
5. From the engine compartment, loosen the 2 steering gear bolts.
6. If equipped, remove the 3 pin-type retainers and the steering gear shield.
7. Remove and discard the 2 outer tie-rod end nuts.

❊❊ CAUTION

Do not use a hammer to separate the tie-rod end from the wheel knuckle or damage to the wheel knuckle can result.

8. Using the Ball Joint Separator, separate the tie-rod ends from the wheel knuckles.
9. For AWD vehicles, remove the rear transaxle insulator through bolt.
10. For FWD vehicles with A/T and 2.5L (including Hybrid), remove the 3 transaxle damper bolts and the transaxle damper.
11. It may be necessary to lower the rear of the front subframe slightly to provide clearance for removing the steering gear bolts.
12. Remove and discard the 2 steering gear bolts.

➡**For All-Wheel Drive (AWD) vehicles (except Hybrid), it is necessary to grasp the driveshaft by hand and apply slight downward pressure to obtain clearance for the removal of the steering gear.**

13. Rotate the steering gear 90 degrees clockwise and remove it from the LH side of the vehicle.

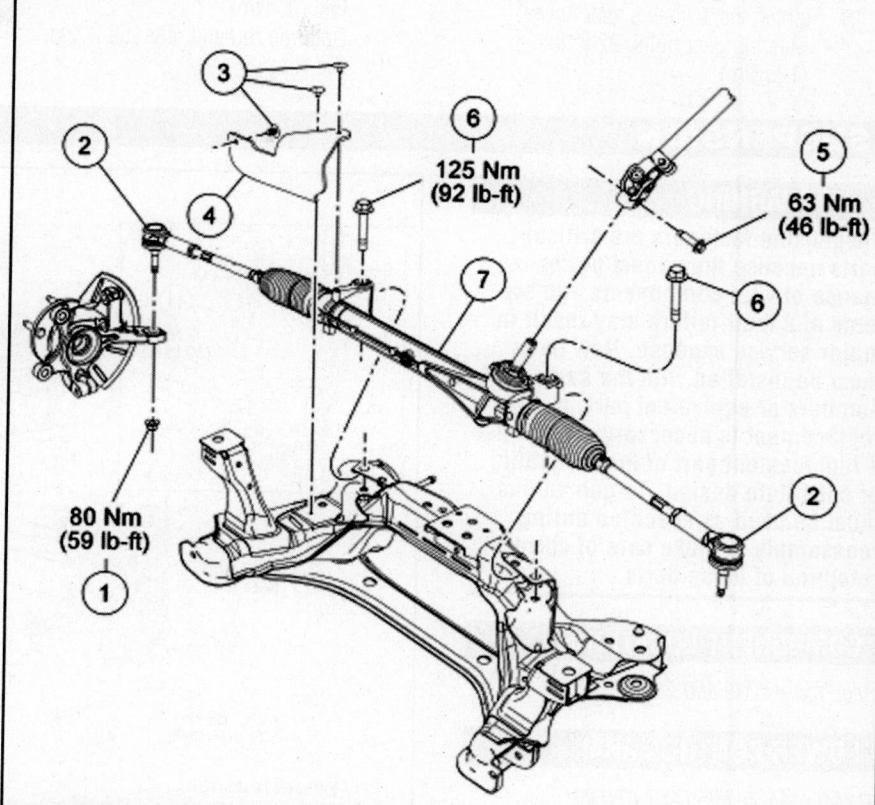

1. Outer tie-rod end nut (2 required)
2. Outer tie-rod ends
3. Pin-type retainers
4. Steering gear shield (3.0L engines and Hybrid vehicles only)
5. Steering column coupling-to-steering gear bolt
6. Steering gear bolts (2 required)
7. Steering gear

N0111176

Fig. 235 Exploded view of the power steering gear

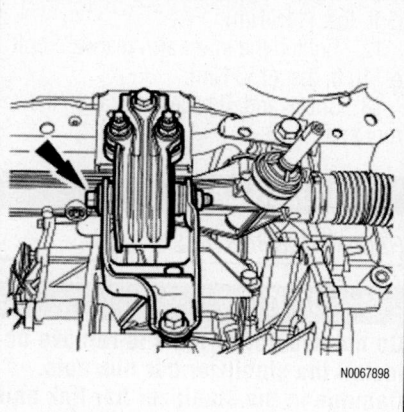

N0067898

Fig. 236 For AWD vehicles, remove the rear transaxle insulator through bolt.

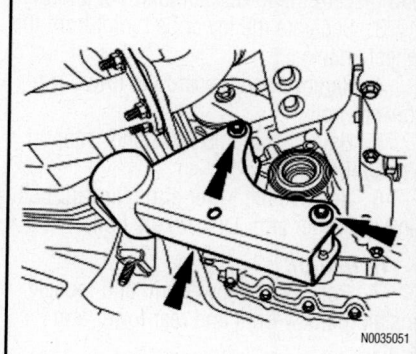

N0035051

Fig. 237 For FWD vehicles with A/T and 2.5L (including Hybrid), remove the 3 transaxle damper bolts and the transaxle damper.

To install:

14. To install, reverse the removal procedure.

15. Tighten the fasteners as follows:
- Steering gear bolts: 92 ft. lbs. (125 Nm)

- Transaxle damper bolts: 30 ft. lbs. (40 Nm)
- Rear transaxle insulator bolt: 66 ft. lbs. (90 Nm)
- Outer tie rod end nuts: 59 ft. lbs. (80 Nm)

- Steering gear coupling bolt: 46 ft. lbs. (63 Nm)

16. Check and, if necessary, align the front end.

SUSPENSION

FRONT SUSPENSION

✳✳ WARNING

Suspension fasteners are critical parts because they affect performance of vital components and systems and their failure may result in major service expense. New parts must be installed with the same part numbers or equivalent part, if replacement is necessary. Do not use a replacement part of lesser quality or substitute design. Torque values must be used as specified during reassembly to make sure of correct retention of these parts.

COMPONENT LOCATIONS

See Figures 238 and 239.

LOWER CONTROL ARM

REMOVAL & INSTALLATION

➡**The ride height is measured from the center of the halfshaft spindle to the edge of the fender.**

1. For reference during the installation of the lower arm, measure the distance between the center of the wheel hub and the lip of the fender with the weight of the vehicle resting on the wheel and tire assemblies.

2. Remove the wheel and tire. Remove and discard the lower ball joint nut and bolt.

3. Separate the lower ball joint from the wheel knuckle.

4. Remove and discard the lower arm forward bolt.

5. Using a suitable jackstand, support the subframe.

6. Remove the lower arm rearward bolt and the lower arm. Discard the bolt.

To install:

7. Position the lower arm and loosely install the new front and rear lower arm bolts.

8. Remove the jackstand.

9. Position the wheel knuckle on the lower ball joint and install the new lower ball joint bolt and nut. Tighten the bolt and nut to 46 ft. lbs. (63 Nm).

10. Position a floor jack under the lower

1. Wheel hub nut
2. Tie-rod end nut
3. Lower ball joint nut
4. Lower ball joint pinch bolt
5. Strut-to-knuckle nuts (2 required)
6. Strut-to-knuckle bolts (2 required)
7. Wheel knuckle
8. Lower arm forward bolt
9. Lower arm rearward bolt
10. Lower arm
11. Wheel speed sensor bolt

N0090751

Fig. 238 Exploded view of the front suspension assembly (1 of 2)

ball joint and raise it until the previously recorded ride height is achieved.

11. Tighten the lower arm forward bolt to 85 ft. lbs. (115 Nm).

12. Tighten the lower arm rearward bolt to 110 ft. lbs. (150 Nm).

13. Check and, if necessary, align the front end.

STABILIZER BAR

REMOVAL & INSTALLATION

✳✳ CAUTION

Do not use power tools to remove or install the stabilizer bar link nuts. Damage to the stabilizer bar link ball joints and boots may occur. Do not hold the stabilizer bar link boot with any tool or damage to the boot may occur.

➡**The stabilizer bar links are designed with low friction ball joints that have a low breakaway torque. When installing the stabilizer link to the stabilizer bar, make sure the stabilizer bar is perpendicular to the stabilizer link when tightening the link nut or the link nut may not seat properly.**

1. Remove the stabilizer bar bushings.
2. Remove the wheel and tire.

➡**Use the hex-holding feature to prevent the ball stud from turning while removing or installing the stabilizer link nut.**

3. Remove and discard the 2 lower stabilizer bar link nuts.

4. Remove the stabilizer bar through the LH wheel opening.

5. To install, reverse the removal procedure.

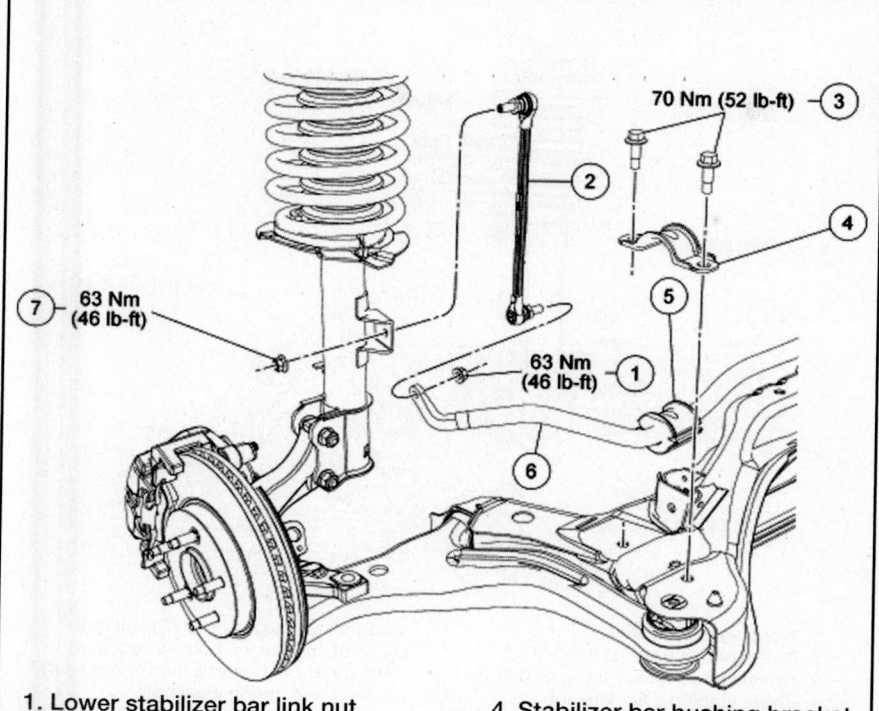

1. Lower stabilizer bar link nut
2. Stabilizer bar link
3. Stabilizer bar bushing bracket bolts (2 required)
4. Stabilizer bar bushing bracket
5. Stabilizer bar bushing
6. Stabilizer bar
7. Upper stabilizer bar link nut

N0098882

Fig. 239 Exploded view of the front suspension assembly (2 of 2)

6. Tighten the new stabilizer bar link nuts to 46 ft. lbs. (63 Nm).

STABILIZER BAR BUSHING

REMOVAL & INSTALLATION

✳✳ CAUTION

When installing the stabilizer bar bushings, make sure the bushings are correctly oriented with the bushing flanges in the up position and the bushing split pointing to the front of the vehicle.

1. Raise and safely support the vehicle.
2. Remove the 2 stabilizer bar bushing bracket bolts and the stabilizer bar bushing bracket.
3. Discard the bolts.
4. Remove the stabilizer bar bushing.
5. Inspect the stabilizer bar bushing for wear. If necessary, install a new part.
6. To install, reverse the removal procedure.

7. Tighten the new stabilizer bar bushing bracket bolts to 52 ft. lbs. (70 Nm).

STABILIZER BAR LINK

REMOVAL & INSTALLATION

✳✳ CAUTION

Do not use power tools to remove or install the stabilizer bar link nuts. Damage to the stabilizer bar link ball joints and boots may occur. Do not hold the stabilizer bar link boot with any tool or damage to the boot may occur.

➡**The stabilizer bar links are designed with low friction ball joints that have a low breakaway torque.**

➡**When installing the stabilizer link to the stabilizer bar, make sure the stabilizer bar is perpendicular to the stabilizer link when tightening the link nut or the link nut may not seat properly.**

1. Remove the wheel and tire.

➡**Use the hex-holding feature to prevent the ball stud from turning while removing or installing the stabilizer bar link nut.**

2. Remove and discard the upper stabilizer bar link nut.
3. Remove and discard the lower stabilizer bar link nut.
4. Remove the stabilizer bar link.
5. Inspect the stabilizer bar link ball joints and boots for wear. If necessary, install new parts.
6. To install, reverse the removal procedure.
7. Tighten the new lower stabilizer bar link nut and the new upper stabilizer bar link nut to 46 ft. lbs. (63 Nm).

STEERING KNUCKLE

REMOVAL & INSTALLATION
See Figure 240.

1. Remove the brake disc. See "BRAKES" section.
2. Remove and discard the wheel hub nut.
3. Using a proper puller, separate the halfshaft from the wheel hub.
4. Remove and discard the tie-rod end nut.

✳✳ CAUTION

Do not use a hammer to separate the tie-rod end from the wheel knuckle or damage to the wheel knuckle can result.

5. Separate the tie rod from the wheel knuckle.
6. Remove and discard the lower ball joint bolt and nut.
7. Remove the wheel speed sensor bolt and position the sensor aside.
8. Separate the lower ball joint from the wheel knuckle.
9. Remove the 2 strut-to-knuckle nuts, bolts and the wheel knuckle.
10. Discard the nuts and bolts.

To install:
11. Position the wheel knuckle and install the 2 new strut-to-knuckle bolts and nuts. Tighten to 85 ft. lbs. (115 Nm).
12. Position and align the ball joint stud into the wheel knuckle.
13. Install the new lower ball joint bolt and nut. Tighten to 46 ft. lbs. (63 Nm).
14. Install the wheel speed sensor and the bolt. Tighten to 80 inch lbs.(9 Nm).

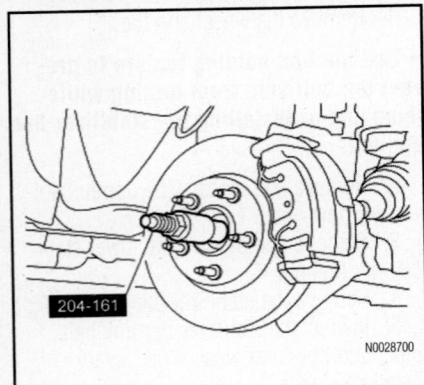

Fig. 240 Using a proper halfshaft installer tool (204-161 or equivalent), install the halfshaft into the wheel hub.

15. Position the tie-rod end into the wheel knuckle and install the new tie-rod end nut. Tighten to 59 ft. lbs. (80 Nm).

16. Using a proper halfshaft installer tool (204-161 or equivalent), install the halfshaft into the wheel hub.

17. Install the brake disc. See "BRAKES" section.

※※ CAUTION

Do not tighten the front wheel hub nut with the vehicle on the ground. The nut must be tightened to specification before the vehicle is lowered onto the wheels. Wheel bearing damage will occur if the wheel bearing is loaded with the weight of the vehicle applied.

18. Apply the brake to keep the halfshaft from rotating.

19. Install the new front wheel hub nut. Tighten to 221 ft. lbs. (300 Nm).

20. Check and, if necessary, align the front end.

STRUT & SPRING ASSEMBLY

REMOVAL & INSTALLATION

See Figures 241 and 242.

1. Verify the steering wheel is in the unlocked position before removal.

2. Remove the wheel and tire.

3. Remove the brake jounce hose clip.

4. Pull the brake jounce hose downward slightly to remove the hose from the bracket and position the brake jounce hose aside.

5. Remove the wheel speed sensor harness bolt.

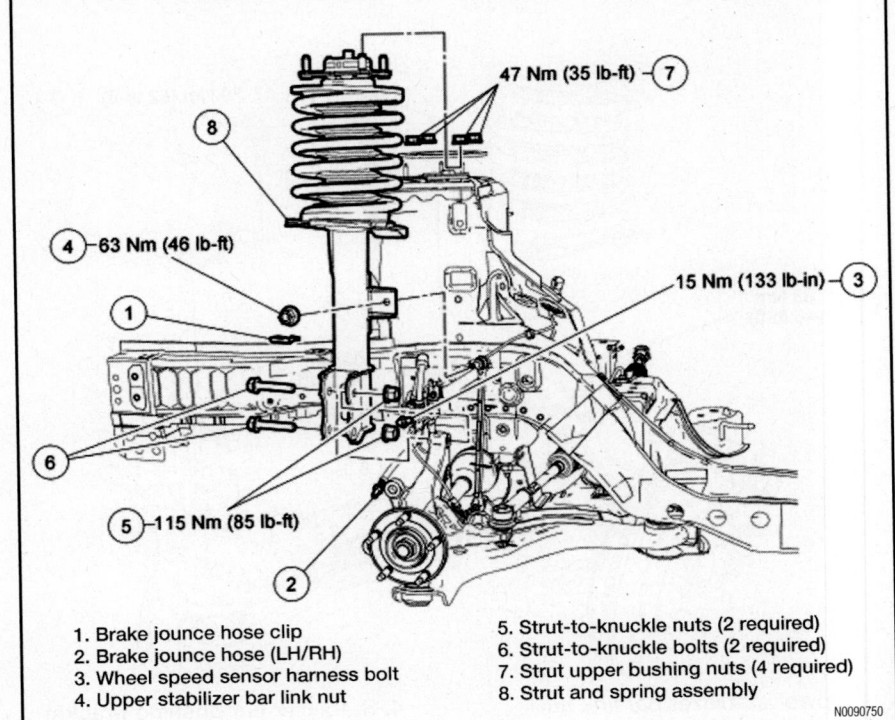

1. Brake jounce hose clip
2. Brake jounce hose (LH/RH)
3. Wheel speed sensor harness bolt
4. Upper stabilizer bar link nut
5. Strut-to-knuckle nuts (2 required)
6. Strut-to-knuckle bolts (2 required)
7. Strut upper bushing nuts (4 required)
8. Strut and spring assembly

Fig. 241 Showing the strut and spring assembly

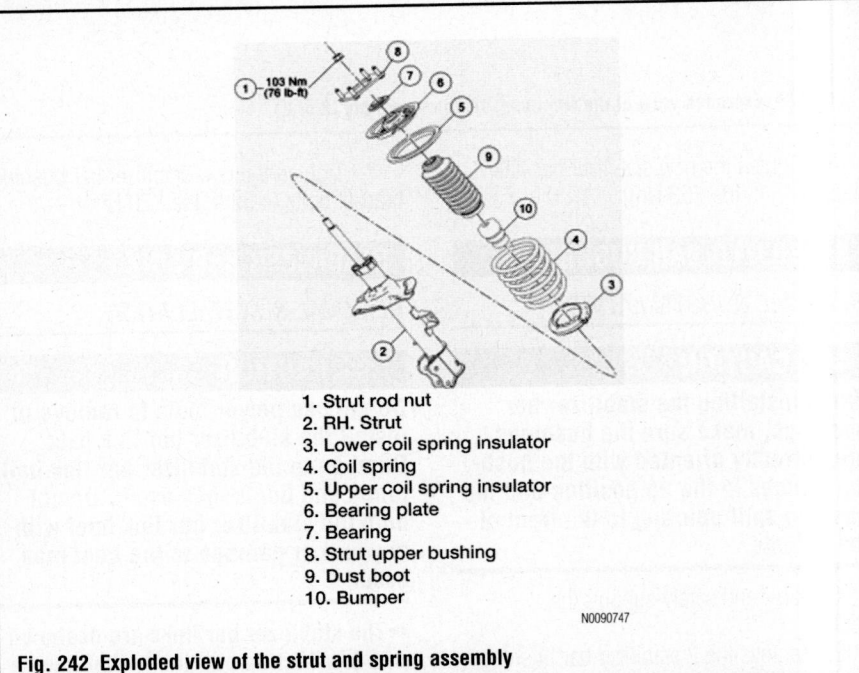

1. Strut rod nut
2. RH. Strut
3. Lower coil spring insulator
4. Coil spring
5. Upper coil spring insulator
6. Bearing plate
7. Bearing
8. Strut upper bushing
9. Dust boot
10. Bumper

Fig. 242 Exploded view of the strut and spring assembly

➡**Use the hex-holding feature to prevent the ball stud from turning while removing or installing the stabilizer bar link nut.**

6. Remove and discard the upper stabilizer bar link nut.

7. Remove and discard the 2 strut-to-knuckle nuts and bolts.

8. Reference mark the 4 strut upper bushing plate nuts.

9. Remove and discard the 4 strut upper bushing nuts.

❋❋ CAUTION

Do not allow the axle shaft to move outboard. Over-extension of the tripod Constant Velocity (CV) joint can result in the separation of internal parts, causing failure of the axle shaft.

10. Remove the strut and spring assembly.

To install:

11. Position the strut and spring assembly upper mounting plate into the inner fender.

12. Align the 4 new strut upper bushing nuts to the reference marks. Tighten to 35 ft. lbs. (47 Nm).

13. Install the 2 new strut-to-knuckle bolts and nuts. Tighten to 85 ft. lbs. (115 Nm).

14. Install the new upper stabilizer bar link nut. Tighten to 46 ft. lbs. (63 Nm).

15. Install the wheel speed sensor harness bolt. Tighten to 133 inch lbs. (15 Nm).

16. Position the brake jounce hose to the bracket and install the brake jounce hose clip.

17. Check the front end alignment and adjust as necessary.

WHEEL BEARINGS & HUB

REMOVAL & INSTALLATION

See Figures 243 through 246.

➡**This step may not be necessary if the inner wheel bearing race remains in the wheel knuckle after removing the wheel hub.**

1. Using the Pinion Bearing Cone Remover, press the inner wheel bearing race from the wheel hub.

2. Remove the snap ring.

3. Using the Pinion Bearing Cone Remover, Wheel Bearing Adapter and Han-

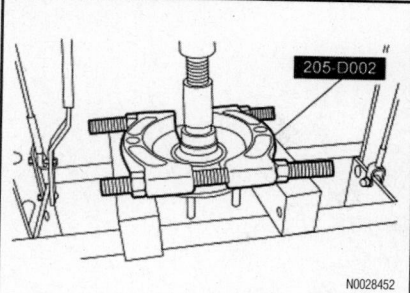

Fig. 243 Using the Pinion Bearing Cone Remover, press the inner wheel bearing race from the wheel hub.

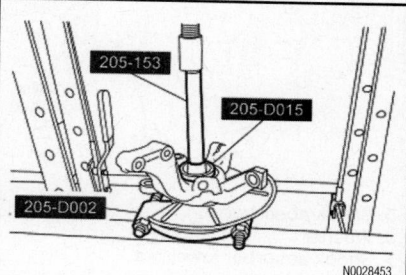

Fig. 244 Using the Pinion Bearing Cone Remover, Wheel Bearing Adapter and Handle, press the outer wheel bearing race from the wheel knuckle.

dle, press the outer wheel bearing race from the wheel knuckle.

To install:

4. Position the wheel knuckle in a vise.

➡**Step Plate 205-278 is not seen in place. It is located behind the wheel knuckle.**

5. Using the Pinion Bearing Cup Replacer and the 2 Step Plates, install the

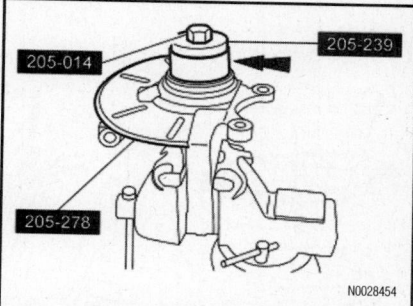

Fig. 245 Using the Pinion Bearing Cup Replacer and the 2 Step Plates, install the wheel bearing into the wheel knuckle.

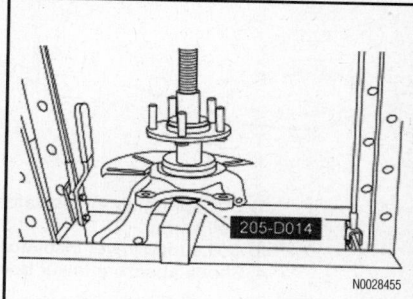

Fig. 246 Using the Pinion Bearing Cone Remover, Press the wheel hub into the wheel bearing

wheel bearing into the wheel knuckle.

6. Install the snap ring.

7. Using the Pinion Bearing Cone Remover, press the wheel hub into the wheel bearing.

8. Using the Pinion Bearing Cone Remover, press the wheel hub into the wheel bearing.

9. Install the wheel knuckle. See "Steering Knuckle" in this section.

SUSPENSION

❋❋ WARNING

Suspension fasteners are critical parts because they affect performance of vital components and systems and their failure may result in major service expense. New parts must be installed with the same part numbers or equivalent part, if replacement is necessary. Do not use a replacement part of lesser quality or substitute design. Torque values must be used as specified during reassembly to make sure of correct retention of these parts.

COIL SPRING

REMOVAL & INSTALLATION

See Figure 247.

➡**All-Wheel Drive (AWD) vehicle shown, Front Wheel Drive (FWD) vehicle similar.**

1. Remove the wheel and tire.

2. Remove the brake hose bracket-to-wheel knuckle bolt.

3. Disconnect the brake tube from the wheel cylinder and position the brake tube and bracket assembly aside.

REAR SUSPENSION

4. Using a suitable jackstand, support the wheel knuckle.

5. Remove and discard the shock absorber lower nut, washer and bolt.

6. Remove the upper arm. See "Upper Control Arm" in this section.

7. Loosen the lower arm inner bolt.

➡**Note the position of the coil spring insulators and coil spring for installation.**

8. Using the jackstand, carefully lower the wheel knuckle.

9. Remove the coil spring.

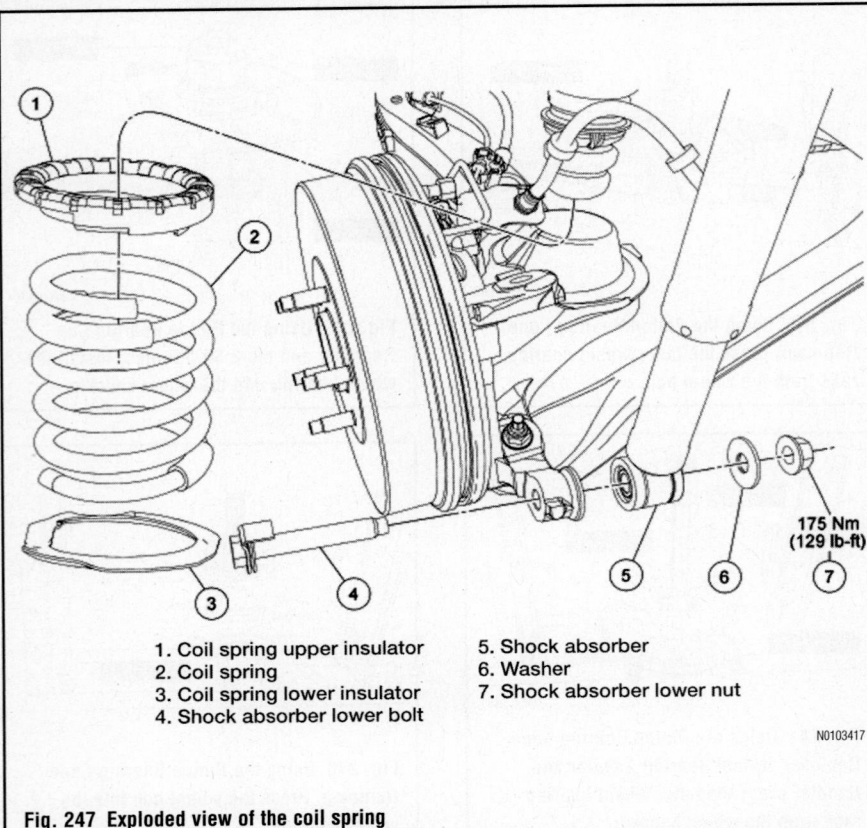

1. Coil spring upper insulator
2. Coil spring
3. Coil spring lower insulator
4. Shock absorber lower bolt
5. Shock absorber
6. Washer
7. Shock absorber lower nut

175 Nm (129 lb-ft)

N0103417

Fig. 247 Exploded view of the coil spring

To install:

10. Align the coil spring and coil spring insulators to the previously noted position.

11. Using a suitable jackstand, carefully raise the wheel knuckle.

12. Install the new shock absorber lower bolt, washer and nut. Tighten to 129 ft. lbs. (175 Nm).

13. Install the upper arm. See "Upper Control Arm" in this section.

14. Connect the brake tube fitting to the wheel cylinder. Tighten to 159 inch lbs. (18 Nm).

15. Install the brake hose bracket-to-wheel knuckle bolt. Tighten to 16 ft. lbs. (22 Nm).

16. Bleed the rear wheel cylinder.

STABILIZER BAR

REMOVAL & INSTALLATION

See Figure 248.

✳✳ CAUTION

Do not use power tools to remove or install the stabilizer bar link nuts. Damage to the stabilizer bar link ball joints and boots may occur.

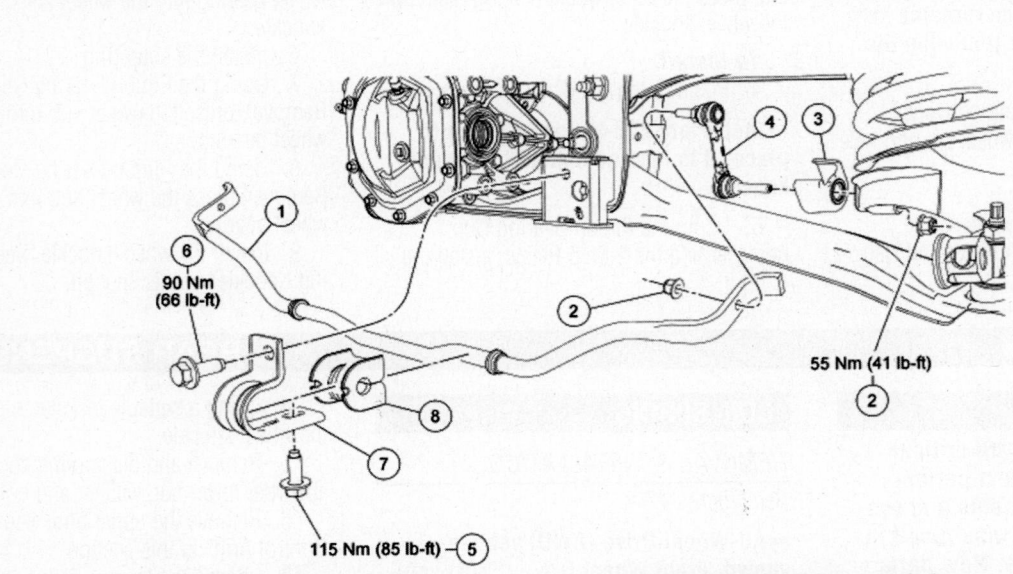

90 Nm (66 lb-ft)

55 Nm (41 lb-ft)

115 Nm (85 lb-ft)

1. Stabilizer bar
2. Stabilizer bar link nuts (2 required)
3. Stabilizer bar link shield (2 required)
4. Stabilizer bar link (2 required)
5. Stabilizer bar bracket lower bolt (4 required)
6. Stabilizer bar bracket upper bolt (4 required)
7. Stabilizer bar bracket (2 required)
8. Stabilizer bar bushing (2 required)

N0100886

Fig. 248 Removing the stabilizer bar

➡The stabilizer bar links are designed with low friction ball joints that have a low breakaway torque.

1. Raise and safely support the vehicle.

➡Do not hold the stabilizer bar link boot with any tool or damage to the boot may occur. Use the hex-holding feature to prevent the stud from turning while removing the nut.

2. Remove and discard the stabilizer bar link upper nut(s).
3. Remove the stabilizer bar link lower nut(s). Discard the nuts.
4. Remove the stabilizer bar links.
5. Remove and discard the stabilizer bar bracket upper and lower bolts.
6. Remove the stabilizer bar brackets and the stabilizer bar.

✳✳ CAUTION

When installing the stabilizer link to the stabilizer bar, make sure the stabilizer bar is perpendicular to the stabilizer link when tightening the link nut or the link nut may not seat properly.

7. Inspect and, if necessary, install new stabilizer bar bushings.

To install:
8. To install, reverse the removal procedure.
9. Install new stabilizer bar bracket upper and lower bolts:
- Tighten the new upper bolts to 66 ft. lbs. (90 Nm).
- Tighten the new lower bolts to 85 ft. lbs. (115 Nm).
10. Install the stabilizer bar links. Tighten the new nuts to 41 ft. lbs. (55 Nm).
11. Install stabilizer bar link upper nut(s). Tighten the new nuts to 41 ft. lbs. (55 Nm).

STRUT & SPRING ASSEMBLY

REMOVAL & INSTALLATION

➡See "Coil Spring" in this section.

UPPER CONTROL ARM

REMOVAL & INSTALLATION

See Figure 249.

1. Remove the wheel and tire.
2. Remove and discard the upper ball joint nut.
3. Remove the upper arm inner bolt and the upper arm. Discard the bolt.

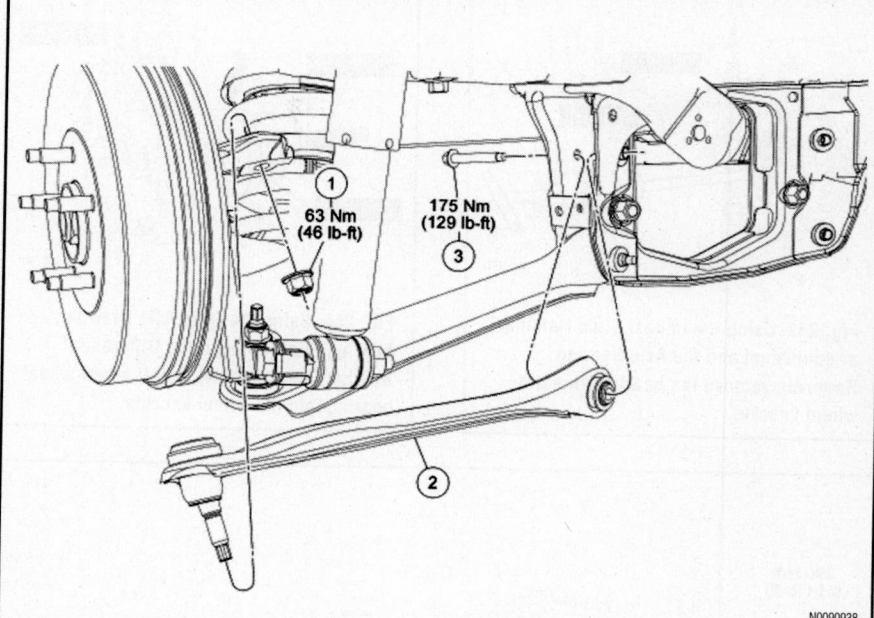

Fig. 249 Showing the upper ball joint nut (1), upper control arm (2) and the upper arm inner bolt (3)

To install:
4. To install, reverse the removal procedure.

➡Do not fully tighten the upper arm inner bolt until the weight of the vehicle is on the wheels and tires.

5. Install the upper arm and a new upper ball joint nut. Tighten the new nut to 46 ft. lbs. (63 Nm).
6. Install the new upper arm inner bolt. Tighten the new bolt to 129 ft. lbs. (175 Nm).

WHEEL BEARING

REMOVAL & INSTALLATION

Front Wheel Drive (FWD) Vehicles
See Figures 250 through 255.

1. Remove the wheel and tire.
2. Apply the brake to keep the halfshaft from rotating.
3. Remove and discard the wheel hub nut.
4. Remove the wheel speed sensor ring.
5. Remove the brake drum. See "BRAKES" section.
6. Using the Front Hub Remover and Impact Slide Hammer or equivalent tools, remove the wheel hub.

➡This step may not be necessary if the inner wheel bearing race remains in

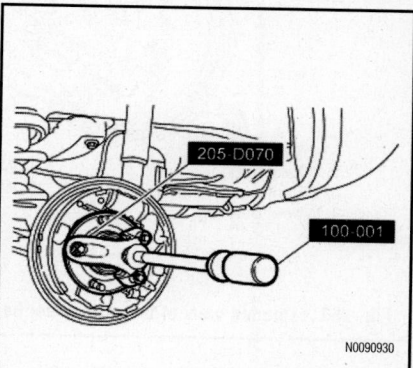

Fig. 250 Using the Front Hub Remover and Impact Slide Hammer or equivalent tools, remove the wheel hub.

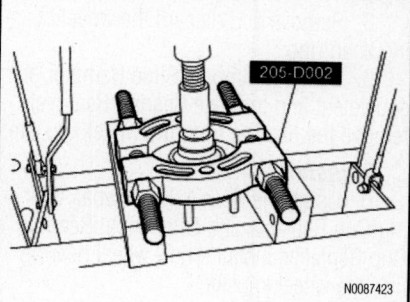

Fig. 251 Using a suitable press and the Pinion Bearing Cone Remover or equivalent, press the inner bearing race from the wheel knuckle.

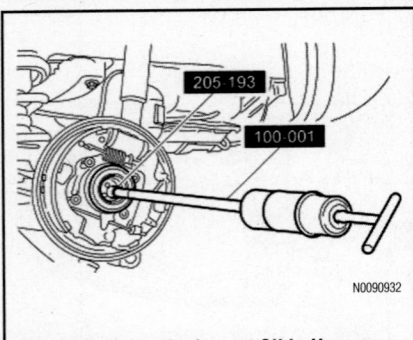

Fig. 252 Using the Impact Slide Hammer or equivalent and the Axle Bearing Remover, remove the bearing from the wheel knuckle.

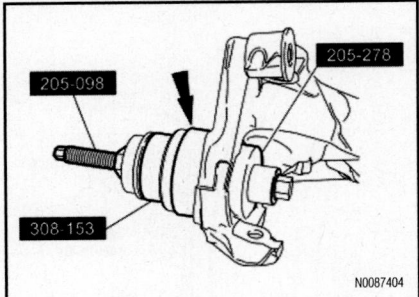

Fig. 254 Using the Rear Axle Drawbar, Bearing Cup Replacer and Differential Bearing Cup Replacer, install a new wheel bearing into the wheel knuckle.

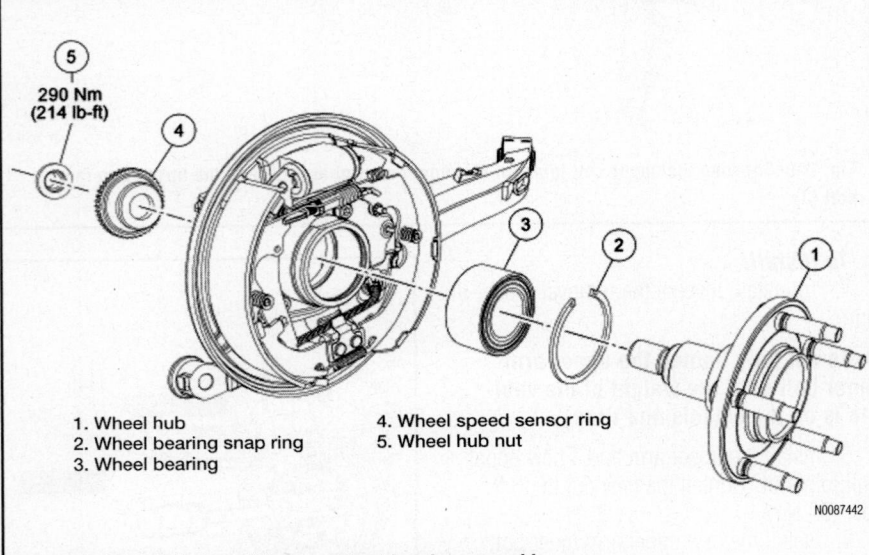

1. Wheel hub
2. Wheel bearing snap ring
3. Wheel bearing
4. Wheel speed sensor ring
5. Wheel hub nut

5. 290 Nm (214 lb-ft)

Fig. 253 Exploded view of the rear wheel bearing assembly

the wheel knuckle after removing the wheel hub.

7. Using a suitable press and the Pinion Bearing Cone Remover or equivalent, press the inner bearing race from the wheel knuckle.

8. Remove and discard the wheel bearing snap ring.

9. Using the Impact Slide Hammer or equivalent and the Axle Bearing Remover, remove the bearing from the wheel knuckle.

To install:

10. Using the Rear Axle Drawbar, Bearing Cup Replacer and Differential Bearing Cup Replacer, install a new wheel bearing into the wheel knuckle.

11. Install the new wheel bearing snap ring.

12. Using the Half Shaft Installer and Receiver Adapter, install the wheel hub into the wheel bearing.

13. Install the wheel speed sensor ring.

14. Install the brake drum.

➡ **Apply the brake to keep the halfshaft from rotating.**

15. Install the new wheel hub nut. Tighten to 214 ft. lbs. (290 Nm).

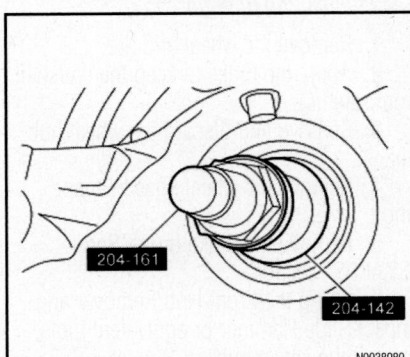

Fig. 255 Using the HalfShaft Installer and Receiver Adapter, install the wheel hub into the wheel bearing.

All Wheel Drive (AWD) Vehicles

See Figures 254 through 257.

1. Remove the wheel knuckle. See "Wheel Knuckle" in this section.

2. Remove the wheel bearing snap ring.

3. Remove the 4 bolts and the brake drum backing plate.

4. Position the wheel knuckle on a suitable press.

5. Using the PTO Driven Gear Oil Seal Installer, the Handle and the Pinion Bearing Cone Remover or equivalent, position the wheel knuckle on a suitable press and press the wheel bearing from the wheel knuckle.

To install:

6. Using the Rear Axle Drawbar, Bearing Cup Replacer and Differential Bearing Cup Replacer, install a new wheel bearing into the wheel knuckle.

7. Install the new wheel bearing snap ring.

8. Install the 4 bolts and the brake drum backing plate. Tighten to 63 ft. lbs. (85 Nm).

9. Using the Halfshaft Installer and Receiver Adapter, install the wheel hub into the wheel bearing.

10. Install the wheel knuckle.

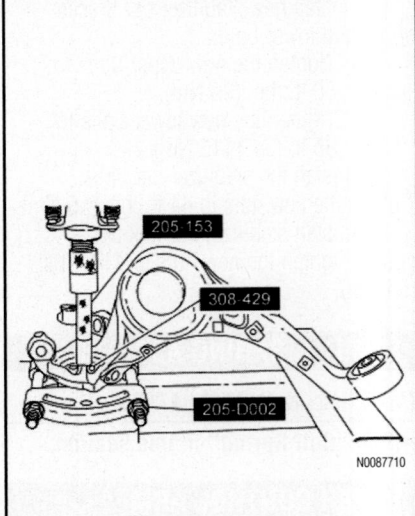

Fig. 256 Using the PTO Driven Gear Oil Seal Installer, the Handle and the Pinion Bearing Cone Remover or equivalent, position the wheel knuckle on a suitable press and press the wheel bearing from the wheel knuckle.

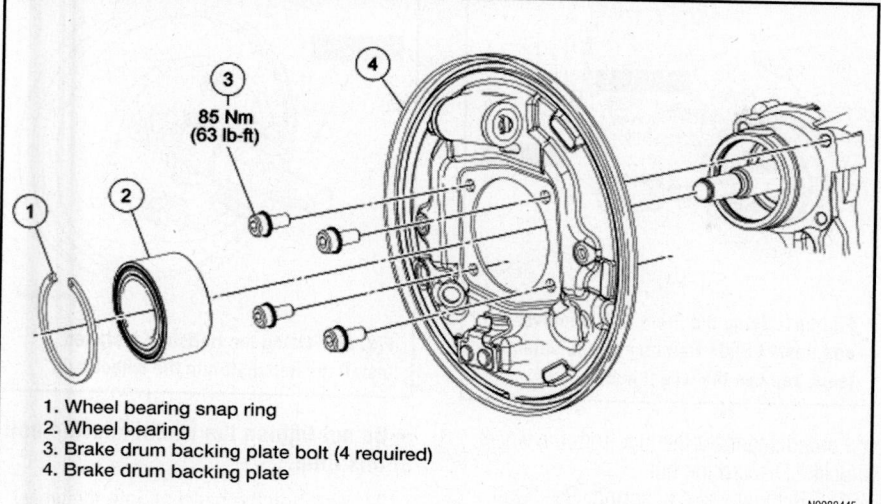

1. Wheel bearing snap ring
2. Wheel bearing
3. Brake drum backing plate bolt (4 required)
4. Brake drum backing plate

N0088445

Fig. 257 Exploded view of the rear wheel and bearing assembly

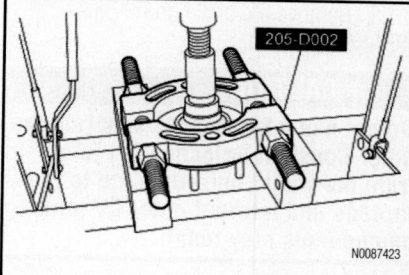

N0087423

Fig. 259 Using a suitable press and the Pinion Bearing Cone Remover or equivalent, press the inner bearing race from the wheel knuckle.

WHEEL KNUCKLE

REMOVAL & INSTALLATION

Front Wheel Drive (FWD) Vehicles

See Figures 258 and 259.

1. Remove the wheel and tire.

➡**Apply the brake to keep the wheel hub from rotating.**

2. Remove and discard the wheel hub nut.

3. Remove the wheel speed sensor ring.

4. Remove the brake drum. See "BRAKES" section.

5. Using the Front Hub Remover and Impact Slide Hammer or equivalent tools, remove the wheel hub.

➡**This step may not be necessary if the inner wheel bearing race remains in the wheel knuckle after removing the wheel hub.**

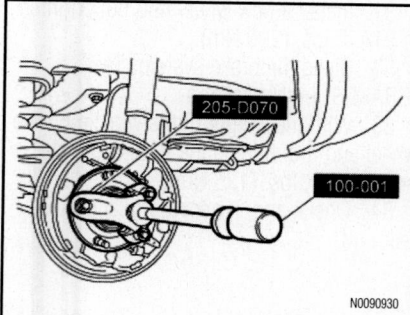

N0090930

Fig. 258 Using the Front Hub Remover and Impact Slide Hammer or equivalent tools, remove the wheel hub.

6. Using a suitable press and the Pinion Bearing Cone Remover or equivalent, press the inner bearing race from the wheel knuckle.

7. Remove the brake shoes. See "BRAKES" section.

8. Remove the parking brake cable bracket-to-control arm bolt.

9. Unclip the wheel speed harness retainer from the parking brake cable and disconnect the cable from the brake backing plate.

10. Remove the wheel speed sensor bolt and the 2 wheel speed sensor harness bolts.

11. Disconnect the wheel speed sensor from the wheel knuckle, and position the sensor and harness aside.

12. Remove the stabilizer bar link lower nut and disconnect the link from the wheel knuckle. Discard the nut.

13. Remove the coil spring. See "Coil Spring" in this section.

14. Remove and discard the lower ball joint nut.

15. Index-mark the notch on the cam nut adjustment cam.

16. Remove and discard the wheel knuckle bolt and cam nut.

17. Remove the wheel knuckle.

18. Remove the wheel bearing. See "Wheel Bearing" in this section.

To install:

19. Install the wheel bearing. See "Wheel Bearing" in this section.

➡**The joint area must be free of foreign material to make sure of correct clamping.**

20. Align the notch on the cam nut with the index marks.

21. Position the wheel knuckle and install a new wheel knuckle bolt and cam nut.

22. Using a suitable tool, hold the cam nut stationary while tightening the new wheel knuckle bolt. Tighten to 92 ft. lbs. (125 Nm).

23. Position the lower ball joint into the wheel knuckle and install the new lower ball joint nut. Tighten to 46 ft. lbs. (63 Nm).

24. Install the coil spring. See "Coil Spring" in this section.

25. Connect the stabilizer bar link and install the nut. Tighten to 41 ft. lbs. (55 Nm).

26. Position the wheel speed sensor harness and the sensor.

27. Install the wheel speed sensor bolt and the 2 wheel speed sensor harness bolts. Tighten the bolts to 80 inch lbs. (9 Nm).

28. Connect the brake tube to the wheel cylinder. Tighten to 150 inch lbs. (17 Nm).

29. Install the brake hose bracket bolt. Tighten to 16 ft. lbs. (22 Nm).

30. Connect the parking brake cable to the brake backing plate and install the parking brake cable bracket bolt. Tighten to 17 ft. lbs. (23 Nm).

31. Install the brake shoes and brake drum. See "BRAKES" section.

➡**Apply the brake to keep the wheel hub from rotating.**

32. Install a new wheel hub nut. Tighten the nut to 214 ft. lbs. (290 Nm).

33. Bleed the brake system. See "BRAKES" section.

34. Check and, if necessary, align the rear end.

All Wheel Drive (AWD) Vehicles

See Figures 260 through 263.

1. Remove the wheel and tire.

➡**Apply the brake to keep the halfshaft from rotating.**

2. Remove and discard the wheel hub nut.

3. Remove the brake drum. See "BRAKES" section.

✳✳ CAUTION

Do not use a hammer to separate the outer Constant Velocity (CV) joint from the wheel hub. Damage to the threads and internal outer CV joint components may result.

4. Using the Front Hub Remover or equivalent, separate the CV joint from the wheel hub.

5. Using the Front Hub Remover or equivalent and the Impact Slide Hammer or equivalent, separate the wheel hub from the wheel bearing.

➡ **This step may not be necessary if the inner wheel bearing race remains in the wheel bearing after removing the wheel hub.**

6. Using a suitable press and the Pinion Bearing Cone Remover or equivalent, press the inner bearing race from the wheel knuckle.

7. Remove the brake shoes. See "BRAKES" section.

8. Remove the parking brake cable bracket-to-control arm bolt.

9. Unclip the wheel speed harness retainer from the parking brake cable and disconnect the cable from the brake backing plate.

10. Remove the wheel speed sensor bolt and the 2 wheel speed sensor harness bolts.

11. Disconnect the wheel speed sensor from the wheel knuckle, and position the sensor and harness aside.

12. Remove the stabilizer bar link lower

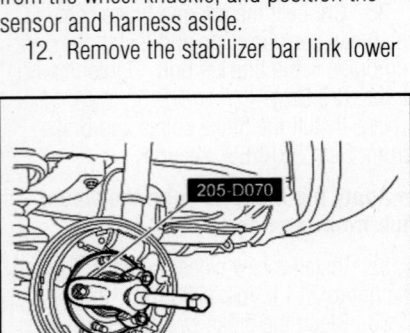

Fig. 260 Using the Front Hub Remover or equivalent, separate the CV joint from the wheel hub.

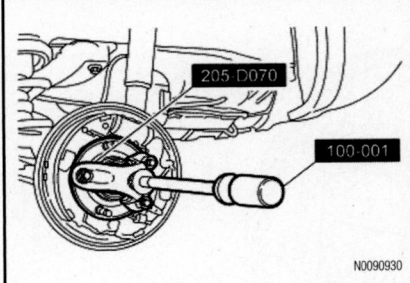

Fig. 261 Using the Front Hub Remover and Impact Slide Hammer or equivalent tools, remove the wheel hub.

nut and disconnect the link from the wheel knuckle. Discard the nut.

13. Remove the coil spring. See "Coil Spring" in this section.

14. Remove and discard the lower ball joint nut.

15. Index-mark the notch on the cam nut adjustment cam.

16. Remove and discard the wheel knuckle bolt and cam nut.

17. Remove the wheel knuckle.

18. Remove the wheel bearing. See "Wheel Bearing" in this section.

To install:

19. Install the wheel bearing. See "Wheel Bearing" in this section.

✳✳ CAUTION

The joint area must be free of foreign material to make sure of correct clamping.

20. Align the notch on the cam nut with the index marks.

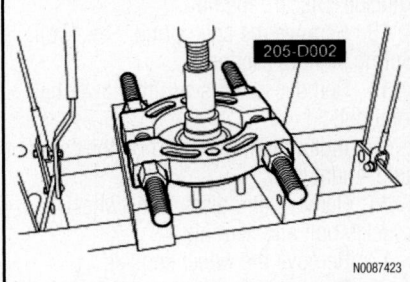

Fig. 262 Using a suitable press and the Pinion Bearing Cone Remover or equivalent, press the inner bearing race from the wheel knuckle.

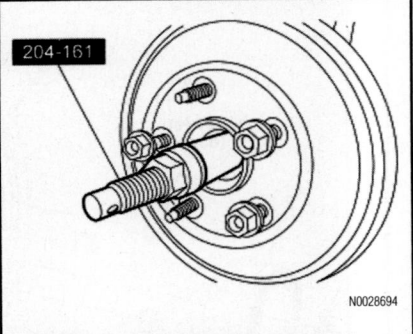

Fig. 263 Using the Halfshaft Installer, install the halfshaft into the wheel hub.

➡ **Do not tighten the wheel knuckle bolt at this time.**

21. Position the halfshaft into the wheel hub and install the wheel knuckle.

22. Hold the cam nut stationary and loosely install a new wheel knuckle bolt and cam nut.

23. Position the lower ball joint into the wheel knuckle and install the new lower ball joint nut. Tighten to 46 ft. lbs. (63 Nm).

24. Install the coil spring. See "Coil Spring" in this section.

25. Connect the stabilizer bar link and install the new nut. Tighten to 41 ft. lbs. (55 Nm).

26. Position the wheel speed sensor harness and the sensor.

27. Install the wheel speed sensor bolt and the 2 wheel speed sensor harness bolts. Tighten the bolts to 80 inch lbs. (9 Nm).

28. Connect the parking brake cable to the brake backing plate and install the parking brake cable bracket bolt. Tighten to 17 ft. lbs. (23 Nm).

29. Install the brake shoes and the brake drum. See "BRAKES" section.

30. Using the Halfshaft Installer, install the halfshaft into the wheel hub.

➡ **Apply the brake to keep the halfshaft from rotating.**

31. Install a new wheel hub nut. Tighten to 214 ft. lbs. (290 Nm).

32. Bleed the brake system. See "BRAKES" in this section.

33. With the weight of the vehicle on the wheel and tire, tighten the wheel knuckle bolt to 92 ft. lbs. (125 Nm).

34. Check and, if necessary, align the rear end.

FORD AND LINCOLN

Expedition • Navigator

5

AUXILIARY HEATING & AIR CONDITIONING SYSTEM 5-73

Blower Motor 5-73
   Removal & Installation..........5-73
Heater Core & Evaporator
Core 5-73
   Removal & Installation..........5-73

BRAKES 5-11

ANTI-LOCK BRAKE SYSTEM (ABS) 5-11
General Information...................5-11
   Precautions...........................5-11
Speed Sensors.........................5-11
   Removal & Installation..........5-11
BLEEDING THE BRAKE SYSTEM 5-13
Bleeding Procedure..................5-13
   Bleeding the Brake System ...5-13
   Brake Caliper 5-13
   Hydraulic Control Unit
   (HCU) 5-13
   Master Cylinder Bleeding 5-13
Precautions & Notes 5-13
FRONT DISC BRAKES 5-14
Brake Caliper..........................5-14
   Removal & Installation..........5-14
Brake Disc (Rotor)...................5-15
   Removal & Installation..........5-15
Disc Brake Pads 5-15
   Removal & Installation..........5-15
PARKING BRAKE 5-16
Parking Brake Cable Tension
Release 5-17
   Tension Release Procedure...5-17
Parking Brake Cables 5-16
   Removal & Installation.........5-16
Parking Brake Control 5-17
   Removal & Installation..........5-17
Parking Brake Shoes 5-18
   Removal & Installation..........5-18
REAR DISC BRAKES 5-15
Brake Caliper..........................5-15
   Removal & Installation..........5-15
Brake Disc (Rotor)...................5-15
   Removal & Installation..........5-15

Disc Brake Pads 5-16
   Removal & Installation..........5-16

CHASSIS ELECTRICAL 5-21

AIR BAG (SUPPLEMENTAL RESTRAINT SYSTEM)........5-21
General Information...................5-21
   Arming (Repowering) the
   System 5-22
   Disarming (Depowering)
   the System..........................5-21
   Service Precautions 5-21

DRIVE TRAIN 5-22

Automatic Transmission Fluid...5-22
   Drain & Refill 5-22
Front Driveshaft......................5-23
   Removal & Installation..........5-23
Front Halfshaft........................5-24
   Removal & Installation..........5-24
Front Pinion Seal 5-24
   Removal & Installation..........5-24
Rear Axle Housing....................5-26
   Removal & Installation..........5-26
Rear Axle Stub Shaft Bearing
and Seal 5-26
   Removal & Installation..........5-26
Rear Driveshaft 5-27
   Removal & Installation..........5-27
Rear Halfshaft.........................5-27
   Removal & Installation..........5-27
Rear Pinion Seal 5-28
   Removal & Installation..........5-28
Transfer Case Assembly 5-23
   Removal & Installation..........5-23

ENGINE COOLING 5-29

Cooling Fan Motor & Shroud ...5-29
   Removal & Installation.........5-29
Cooling Module 5-30
   Removal & Installation..........5-30
Engine Coolant........................5-33
   Drain, Refill & Bleeding
   Procedure...........................5-33
   Flushing..............................5-35

Radiator.................................5-35
   Removal & Installation..........5-35
Thermostat 5-35
   Removal & Installation..........5-35
Water Pump 5-35
   Removal & Installation..........5-35

ENGINE ELECTRICAL.........5-36

BATTERY SYSTEM 5-36
Battery...................................5-36
   Battery Reconnect/Relearn
   Procedure 5-35
   Removal & Installation..........5-35
CHARGING SYSTEM 5-36
Generator 5-36
   Removal & Installation..........5-36
IGNITION SYSTEM 5-36
Firing Order............................5-36
Ignition Coil-On Plug................5-36
   Removal & Installation..........5-36
Ignition Timing........................5-36
   Adjustment 5-36
Spark Plugs.............................5-36
   Removal & Installation..........5-36
STARTING SYSTEM 5-37
Starter 5-37
   Removal & Installation..........5-37

ENGINE MECHANICAL 5-38

Accessory Drive Belts 5-38
   Accessory Belt Routing.........5-38
   Adjustment 5-38
   Removal & Installation..........5-38
Air Cleaner Assembly...............5-38
   Filter/Element Replacement ..5-38
   Removal & Installation..........5-38
Camshaft & Valve Lifters..........5-38
   Removal & Installation..........5-39
Catalytic Converter 5-39
   Exhaust System Alignment
   Procedure 5-43
   Removal & Installation..........5-42
Crankshaft Front Seal...............5-44
   Removal & Installation..........5-44
Cylinder Head 5-44
   Removal & Installation..........5-44

Exhaust Manifold 5-47
   Removal & Installation..........5-47
Intake Manifold 5-47
   Removal & Installation..........5-47
Oil Pan...................................5-48
   Removal & Installation..........5-48
Oil Pump.................................5-50
   Removal & Installation..........5-50
Piston and Ring........................5-50
   Positioning 5-50
Rear Main Seal.........................5-50
   Removal & Installation..........5-50
Timing Chain & Sprockets 5-54
   Removal & Installation..........5-54
Timing Chain Front Cover
   (Engine Front Cover)..............5-51
   Removal & Installation..........5-51
Valve Covers 5-58
   Removal & Installation..........5-58
Variable Valve Timing
   Housing 5-60
   Removal & Installation..........5-60

**ENGINE PERFORMANCE &
EMISSION CONTROLS 5-60**

Camshaft Position (CMP)
   Sensor 5-60
   Location..............................5-60
   Removal & Installation..........5-60
Catalyst Monitor Sensor............5-60
   Location..............................5-60
   Removal & Installation..........5-60
Crankshaft Position (CKP)
   Sensor 5-61
   Location..............................5-61
   Removal & Installation..........5-61
Cylinder Head Temperature
   (CHT) Sensor 5-61
   Location..............................5-61
   Removal & Installation..........5-62
Evaporative Emission (EVAP)
   Canister Vent Solenoid 5-64
   Location..............................5-64
   Removal & Installation..........5-64
Evaporative Emissions (EVAP)
   Canister 5-62
   Location..............................5-62
   Removal & Installation..........5-62
Evaporative Emissions (EVAP)
   Canister Purge Valve...............5-63
   Location..............................5-63
   Removal & Installation..........5-63
Fuel Tank Pressure Sensor........5-64
   Location..............................5-64
   Removal & Installation..........5-65

Heated Oxygen (HO2S)
   Sensor 5-65
   Location..............................5-65
   Removal & Installation..........5-65
Knock Sensor (KS)....................5-65
   Location..............................5-65
   Removal & Installation..........5-65
Mass Air Flow (MAF) Sensor....5-66
   Location..............................5-66
   Removal & Installation..........5-66
Positive Crankcase
   Ventilation (PCV) 5-66
   Location..............................5-66
   Removal & Installation..........5-66
Powertrain Control Module
   (PCM) 5-67
   Location..............................5-67
   Removal & Installation..........5-67
Throttle Position Sensor
   (TPS) 5-67
   Location..............................5-67
   Removal & Installation..........5-67
Variable Camshaft Timing
   (VCT) Oil Control Solenoid.....5-68
   Location..............................5-68
   Removal & Installation..........5-68

FUEL............................5-69

**GASOLINE FUEL INJECTION
SYSTEM.......................5-69**
Fuel Injectors 5-69
   Removal & Installation..........5-69
Fuel Pump Module...................5-70
   Removal & Installation..........5-70
Fuel System Service
   Precautions 5-69
Fuel Tank...............................5-70
   Draining.............................5-70
   Removal & Installation..........5-70
Idle Speed 5-71
   Adjustment 5-71
Relieving Fuel System
   Pressure.............................5-69
Throttle Body.........................5-71
   Removal & Installation..........5-71

**HEATING & AIR
CONDITIONING SYSTEM 5-71**

Blower Motor 5-71
   Removal & Installation..........5-71
Condenser..............................5-71
   Removal & Installation..........5-71
Heater Core & Evaporator
   Core 5-71
   Removal & Installation..........5-71

PRECAUTIONS 5-11

**SPECIFICATIONS AND
MAINTENANCE CHARTS 5-4**

Brake Specifications...................5-8
Camshaft Specifications..............5-6
Capacities 5-5
Crankshaft and Connecting
   Rod Specifications 5-6
Engine and Vehicle
   Identification 5-4
Engine Tune-Up
   Specifications 5-4
Fluid Specifications....................5-5
General Engine Specifications.....5-4
Piston and Ring
   Specifications 5-6
Scheduled Maintenance
   Intervals 5-9
Tire Wheel and Ball Joint
   Specifications 5-7
Torque Specifications.................5-7
Valve Specifications...................5-5
Wheel Alignment.......................5-7

STEERING 5-74

Power Steering Gear.................5-74
   Removal & Installation..........5-74
Power Steering Pump................5-75
   Fluid Fill Procedure 5-76
   Removal & Installation..........5-75

SUSPENSION..................5-84

AIR SUSPENSION 5-89
Air Shock Absorber (Rear) 5-89
   Removal & Installation..........5-89
Air Spring Solenoid..................5-90
   Inflating/deflating AIR
   Spring 5-91
   Removal & Installation..........5-90
   Ride Height Adjustment 5-91
Air Suspension Compressor 5-91
   Removal & Installation..........5-91
Air Suspension Vehicle
   Dynamics Module 5-92
   Removal & Installation..........5-92
FRONT SUSPENSION 5-77
Lower Ball Joint 5-77
   Removal & Installation..........5-77
Lower Control Arm...................5-77
   Removal and & Installation...5-77
Stabilizer Bar..........................5-78
   Removal & Installation..........5-78

Steering Knuckle 5-79
   Removal & Installation..........5-79
Strut & Spring Assembly 5-80
   Removal & Installation..........5-80
Upper Control Arm....................5-82
   Removal & Installation..........5-82
Wheel Bearing & Hub 5-82
   Removal & Installation..........5-82

REAR SUSPENSION 5-84
  Lower Ball Joint 5-84
    Removal & Installation..........5-84
  Lower Control Arm....................5-84
    Removal & Installation..........5-84
  Stabilizer Bar 5-85
    Removal & Installation.........5-85
  Strut & Spring Assembly 5-85
    Removal & Installation..........5-85

Trailing Arm 5-85
   Removal & Installation..........5-85
Upper Control Arm....................5-86
   Removal & Installation..........5-86
Wheel Bearing & Hub 5-86
   Removal & Installation..........5-86
Wheel Knuckle 5-87
   Removal & Installation..........5-87

SPECIFICATIONS AND MAINTENANCE CHARTS

ENGINE AND VEHICLE IDENTIFICATION

		Engine						Model Year	
Code ①	Liters (cc)	Cu. In.	Cyl.	Fuel Sys.	Engine Type	Eng. Mfg.		Code ②	Year
5	5.4	330	6	EFI ③	SOHC	Ford		A	2010
								B	2011

① 8th position of VIN

② 10th position of VIN

③ Flex-Fuel system

25759_EXPD_C0001

GENERAL ENGINE SPECIFICATIONS

All measurements are given in inches.

Year	Model	Engine Displacement Liters (cc)	Engine ID/VIN	Fuel System Type	Net Horsepower @ rpm	Net Torque @ rpm (ft. lbs.)	Bore x Stroke (in.)	Compression Ratio	Oil Pressure @ rpm
2010	Expedition	5.4 (5400)	5	EFI	310@5100	365@3600	3.55x4.17	9.8:1	75@2000
	Navigator	5.4 (5400)	5	EFI	310@5100	365@3600	3,55x4,17	9.8:1	75@2000
2011	Expedition	5.4 (5400)	5	EFI	310@5100	365@3600	3.55x4.17	9.8:1	75@2000
	Navigator	5.4 (5400)	5	EFI	310@5100	365@3600	3,55x4,17	9.8:1	75@2000

25759_EXPD_C0002

ENGINE TUNE-UP SPECIFICATIONS

Year	Engine Displacement Liters	Engine ID/VIN	Spark Plug Gap (in.)	Ignition Timing (deg.) MT	AT ①	Fuel Pump (psi)	Idle Speed (rpm) MT	AT	Valve Clearance Intake	Exhaust
2010	5.4	5	0.0040-0.0050	N/A	10B	62-69	N/A	②	HYD	HYD
2011	5.4	5	0.0040-0.0050	N/A	10B	62-69	N/A	②	HYD	HYD

N/A: Not Available

HYD: Hydraulic

NOTE: The Vehicle Emission Control Information label often reflects specification changes made during production.

The label figures must be used if they differ from those in this chart.

① With engine running

② Idle speed is electronically controlled and cannot be adjusted

25759_EXPD_C0003

CAPACITIES

Year	Model	Engine Displacement Liters	Engine ID/VIN	Engine Oil with Filter	Transmission/axle (pts.)		Drive Axle (pts.)		Transfer Case (pts.)	Fuel Tank (gal.)	Cooling System (qts.)
					Auto.	Manual	Front	Rear			
2010	Expedition	5.4	5	7.0	7.0 ①	N/A	3.6	4.25	2.7-3.1	28.0	②
	Navigator	5.4	5	7.0	7.0 ①	N/A	3.6	4.25	2.7-3.1	28.0	②
2011	Expedition	5.4	5	7.0	7.0 ①	N/A	3.6	4.25	2.7-3.1	28.0	②
	Navigator	5.4	5	7.0	7.0 ①	N/A	3.6	4.35	2.7-3.1	28.0	②

NOTE: All capacities are approximate. Add fluid gradually and ensure a proper fluid level is obtained.

N/A: Not available

① After repair or replacement.

② Base radiator: 16.4 qts.

With auxiliary rear heater: 19.0 qts.

H.D. trailer tow w/o aux. heater: 16.9 qts.

H.D. trailer tow w/aux. rear heater: 19.5 qts.

25759_EXPD_C0004

FLUID SPECIFICATIONS

Year	Model	Engine Disp. Liters	Engine Oil	Auto. Trans.	Drive Axle		Transfer Case	Power Steering Fluid	Brake Master Cylinder	Cooling System
					Front	Rear				
2010	Expedition	5.4	5W-20	Mercon® LV	80W-90	75W-140	①	Mercon® V	DOT 3	②
	Navigator	5.4	5W-20	Mercon® LV	80W-90	75W-140	①	Mercon® V	DOT 3	②
2011	Expedition	5.4	5W-20	Mercon® LV	80W-90	75W-140	①	Mercon® V	DOT 3	②
	Navigator	5.4	5W-20	Mercon® LV	80W-90	75W-140	①	Mercon® V	DOT 3	②

DOT: Department Of Transpotation

① ESP-M2C166-H

② Motorcraft Premium Gold coolant with Bittering Agent (WSS-M97B51-A1)

25759_EXPD_C0005

VALVE SPECIFICATIONS

Year	Engine Displacement Liters	Engine ID/VIN	Seat Angle (deg.)	Face Angle (deg.)	Spring Test Pressure (lbs. @ in.)	Spring Free-Length (in.)	Spring Installed Height (in.)	Stem-to-Guide Clearance (in.)		Stem Diameter (in.)	
								Intake	Exhaust	Intake	Exhaust
2010	5.4	5	44.5-45.0	45.5	79@1.66	2.190	1.660	0.001-0.002	0.003-0.004	0.237-0.238	0.234-0.235
2011	5.4	5	44.5-45.0	45.5	79@1.66	2.190	1.660	0.001-0.002	0.003-0.004	0.237-0.238	0.234-0.235

25759_EXPD_C0006

CAMSHAFT SPECIFICATIONS

All measurements in inches unless noted

Year	Engine Displacement Liters	Engine Code/VIN	Journal Diameter	Brg. Oil Clearance	Shaft End-play	Runout	Journal Bore	Lobe Height Intake	Exhaust
2010	5.4	5	1.126-1.127	0.001-0.003	0.003-0.007	0.001	1.128-1.129	0.217	0.217
2011	5.4	5	1.126-1.127	0.001-0.003	0.003-0.007	0.001	1.128-1.129	0.217	0.217

25759_EXPD_C0007

CRANKSHAFT AND CONNECTING ROD SPECIFICATIONS

All measurements are given in inches.

Year	Engine Displacement Liters	Engine ID/VIN	Crankshaft Main Brg. Journal Dia.	Main Brg. Oil Clearance	Shaft End-play	Thrust on No.	Connecting Rod Journal Diameter	Oil Clearance	Side Clearance
2010	5.4	5	2.6567-2.6576	0.0009-0.0019	0.0030-0.0148	5	2.0885-2.0877	0.0010-0.0025	0.0187-0.0049
2011	5.4	5	2.6567-2.6576	0.0009-0.0019	0.0030-0.0148	5	2.0885-2.0877	0.0010-0.0025	0.0187-0.0049

25759_EXPD_C0008

PISTON AND RING SPECIFICATIONS

All measurements are given in inches.

Year	Engine Displacement Liters	Engine ID/VIN	Piston Clearance	Ring Gap Top Compression	Bottom Compression	Oil Control	Ring Side Clearance Top Compression	Bottom Compression	Oil Control
2010	5.4	5	0.0010-0.0018	0.006-0.0127	0.0098-0.0197	0.0059-0.0256	0.0008-0.0031	0.0012-0.0028	N/A
2011	5.4	5	0.0010-0.0018	0.006-0.0127	0.0098-0.0197	0.0059-0.0256	0.0008-0.0031	0.0012-0.0028	N/A

25759_EXPD_C0009

TORQUE SPECIFICATIONS
All readings in ft. lbs.

Year	Engine Disp. Liters	Engine ID/VIN	Cylinder Head Bolts	Main Bearing Bolts	Rod Bearing Bolts	Crankshaft Damper Bolts	Flywheel Bolts	Manifold Intake	Manifold Exhaust	Spark Plugs	Oil Pan Drain Plug
2010	5.4	5	①	②	③	④	59	⑤	18	25	10
2011	5.4	5	①	②	③	④	59	⑤	18	25	10

① Step 1: 30 ft. lbs.
   Step 2: Plus 90 degrees
   Step 3: Plus 90 degrees
② Vertical mounted bolts:
   Step 1: 30 ft. lbs.
   Step 2: Plus 90 degrees
   Side Bolts:
   Step 1: 22 ft. lbs.
   Step 2: Plus 90 degrees

③ Step 1: 32 ft. lbs.
   Step 2: Plus 105 degrees
④ Step 1: 66 ft. lbs.
   Step 2: Loosen bolts
   Step 3: 37 ft. lbs.
   Step 4: Plus 90 degrees
⑤ Step 1: 18 inch lbs.
   Step 2: 18 ft. lbs.

25759_EXPD_C0010

WHEEL ALIGNMENT

Year	Model	Suspension Type	Caster Range (+/-Deg.)	Caster Preferred Setting (Deg.)	Camber Range (+/-Deg.)	Camber Preferred Setting (Deg.)	Toe-in (in.)
2010	Expedition	Coil Spring	1.00	+4.3	0.75	-0.30	0.14 +/- 0.20
	Navigator	Air	1.00	+4.3	0.75	-0.30	0.14 +/- 0.20
2011	Expedition	Coil Spring	1.00	+4.3	0.75	-0.30	0.14 +/- 0.20
	Navigator	Air	1.00	+4.3	0.75	-0.30	0.14 +/- 0.20

25759_EXPD_C0011

TIRE, WHEEL AND BALL JOINT SPECIFICATIONS

Year	Model	OEM Tires Standard	OEM Tires Optional	Tire Pressures (psi) Front	Tire Pressures (psi) Rear	Wheel Size	Ball Joint Inspection	Lug Nut (ft. lbs.)
2010	Expedition	265/70-17	①	②	②	17 in. ③	0.030 in. ④	150
	Navigator	265/70-17	①	②	②	17 in. ③	0.030 in. ④	150
2011	Expedition	265/70-17	①	②	②	17 in. ③	0.030 in. ④	150
	Navigator	265/70-17	①	②	②	17 in. ③	0.030 in. ④	150

OEM: Original Equipment Manufacturer

PSI: Pounds Per Square Inch

N/A: Information not available or Not Applicable

① Multiple optional tire sizes are available; consult local dealer.
② See safety certification sticker located on driver door jamb.
③ 17 in. standard size; optional 18 in.
④ Both upper and lower arm ball joints

25759_EXPD_C0012

BRAKE SPECIFICATIONS

All measurements in inches unless noted

Year	Model		Brake Disc Original Thickness	Brake Disc Minimum Thickness	Brake Disc Max. Runout	Brake Drum Diameter Original Inside Diameter	Brake Drum Diameter Max. Wear Limit	Brake Drum Diameter Maximum Machine Diamter	Minimum Pad/Lining Thickness Front	Minimum Pad/Lining Thickness Rear	Brake Caliper Bracket Bolts (ft. lbs.)	Brake Caliper Mounting Bolts (ft. lbs.)
2010	Expedition	F	N/A	1.259	N/A	—	—	—	0.790	—	184	27
		R	N/A	0.787	N/A	—	—	—	—	0.790	184	27
	Navigator	F	N/A	1.259	N/A	—	—	—	0.790	—	184	27
		R	N/A	0.787	N/A	—	—	—	—	0.790	184	27
2011	Expedition	F	N/A	1.259	N/A	—	—	—	0.790	—	184	27
		R	N/A	0.787	N/A	—	—	—	—	0.790	184	27
	Navigator	F	N/A	1.259	N/A	—	—	—	0.790	—	184	27
		R	N/A	0.787	N/A	—	—	—	—	0.790	184	27

F: Front

R: Rear

N/A: Information not available

25759_EXPD_C0013

SCHEDULED MAINTENANCE INTERVALS

FORD EXPEDITION, LINCOLN NAVIGATOR - NORMAL SERVICE

TO BE SERVICED	TYPE OF SERVICE	VEHICLE MILEAGE INTERVAL (x1000)											
		75	15	22.5	30	37.5	45	52.5	60	67.5	75	82.5	90
Accessory drive belt	Inspect	✓	✓	✓	✓	✓	✓	✓	✓	✓	✓	✓	✓
Accessory drive belt	Replace												✓
Automatic transmission fluid & filter	Replace	every 150,000 miles											
Battery performance	Inspect	✓	✓	✓	✓	✓	✓	✓	✓	✓	✓	✓	✓
Brake system: Pads/shoes/rotors/drums, brake lines and hoses, and parking brake system)	Inspect		✓		✓		✓		✓		✓		✓
Cabin air filter (If equipped)	Replace		✓		✓		✓		✓		✓		
Cooling system, hoses, clamps & coolant strength	Inspect	✓	✓	✓	✓	✓	✓	✓	✓	✓	✓	✓	✓
Engine air filter	Inspect	✓	✓	✓	✓	✓	✓	✓	✓	✓	✓	✓	✓
Engine air filter	Replace				✓					✓			✓
Engine coolant	Replace	at 6 yrs or 105,000 miles; then every 3 years or 45,000 miles											
Engine oil and filter	Replace	✓	✓	✓	✓	✓	✓	✓	✓	✓	✓	✓	✓
Exhaust system (Leaks, damage, loose parts and foreign material)	Inspect	✓	✓	✓	✓	✓	✓	✓	✓	✓	✓	✓	✓
Fluid levels (all)	Top off	✓	✓	✓	✓	✓	✓	✓	✓	✓	✓	✓	✓
Front axle fluid (4x4)	Replace												
Halfshaft boots	Inspect	✓	✓	✓	✓	✓	✓	✓	✓	✓	✓	✓	✓
Horn, exterior lamps, turn signals and hazard warning light operation	Inspect	✓	✓	✓	✓	✓	✓	✓	✓	✓	✓	✓	✓
Inspect wheels and related components for abnomal noise, wear, looseness or drag	Inspect	✓	✓	✓	✓	✓	✓	✓	✓	✓	✓	✓	✓
Oil and fluid leaks	Inspect	✓	✓	✓	✓	✓	✓	✓	✓	✓	✓	✓	✓
Radiator, coolers, heater and air conditioning hoses	Inspect	✓	✓	✓	✓	✓	✓	✓	✓	✓	✓	✓	✓
Rear drive axle fluid	Replace	every 150,000 miles											
Rotate tires, inspect tread wear, measure tread depth and check pressure	Rotate/Inspect	✓	✓	✓	✓	✓	✓	✓	✓	✓	✓	✓	✓
Shocks struts and other suspension components for leaks and damage	Inspect	✓	✓	✓	✓	✓	✓	✓	✓	✓	✓	✓	✓
Spark plugs	Replace	every 105,000 miles											
Steering linkage, ball joints, suspension, tie-rod ends, driveshaft and u-joints: lubricate if equipped with grease fittings	Inspect/Lubricate	✓	✓	✓	✓	✓	✓	✓	✓	✓	✓	✓	✓
Transfer case oil (4x4)	Replace	every 150,000 miles											
Windshield for cracks, chips and pitting	Inspect	✓	✓	✓	✓	✓	✓	✓	✓	✓	✓	✓	✓
Windshield wiper spray and wiper operation	Inspect	✓	✓	✓	✓	✓	✓	✓	✓	✓	✓	✓	✓

Use of E85 50% of the time or greater, change engine oil and filter every 5,000 miles or 6 months.

SCHEDULED MAINTENANCE INTERVALS

FORD EXPEDITION, LINCOLN NAVIGATOR - SEVERE SERVICE

TO BE SERVICED	TYPE OF SERVICE	VEHICLE MILEAGE INTERVAL (x1000)											
		5	10	15	20	25	30	35	40	45	50	55	60
Accessory drive belt	Inspect	✓	✓	✓	✓	✓	✓	✓	✓	✓	✓	✓	✓
Accesory drive belts	Replace												
Automatic transmisison fluid & filter	Replace						✓						✓
Battery performance	Inspect	✓	✓	✓	✓	✓	✓	✓	✓	✓	✓	✓	✓
Brake system (Pads/shoes/rotors/drums, brake lines and hoses, and parking brake system)	Inspect			✓			✓			✓			✓
Cabin air filter (If equipped)	Replace			✓			✓			✓			✓
Cooling system, hoses, clamps & coolant strength	Inspect	✓	✓	✓	✓	✓	✓	✓	✓	✓	✓	✓	✓
Engine air filter	Inspect	✓	✓	✓	✓	✓	✓	✓	✓	✓	✓	✓	✓
Engine air filter	Replace						✓						✓
Engine coolant	Replace	at 6 years or 105,000 miles; then every 3 years or 45,000 miles											
Engine oil and filter	Replace	every 5,000 miles, 6 months or 200 hours of engine operation											
Exhaust system (Damage, leaks, loose parts & foreign material)	Inspect	✓	✓	✓	✓	✓	✓	✓	✓	✓	✓	✓	✓
Fluid levels (all)	Top off	✓	✓	✓	✓	✓	✓	✓	✓	✓	✓	✓	✓
Front axle fluid (4x4)	Replace												
Halfshaft boots	Inspect	✓	✓	✓	✓	✓	✓	✓	✓	✓	✓	✓	✓
Horn, exterior lamps, turn signals and hazard warning light operation	Replace	✓	✓	✓	✓	✓	✓	✓	✓	✓	✓	✓	✓
Inspect wheels and related components for abnomal noise, wear, looseness or drag	Inspect	✓	✓	✓	✓	✓	✓	✓	✓	✓	✓	✓	✓
Oil and fluid leaks	Inspect	✓	✓	✓	✓	✓	✓	✓	✓	✓	✓	✓	✓
Radiator, coolers, heater and air conditioning hoses	Inspect	✓	✓	✓	✓	✓	✓	✓	✓	✓	✓	✓	✓
Rear drive axle fluid	Replace												
Rotate tires, inspect tread wear, measure tread depth and check pressure	Rotate/ Inspect	every 7,500 miles											
Shocks struts and other suspension components for leaks and damage	Replace	✓	✓	✓	✓	✓	✓	✓	✓	✓	✓	✓	✓
Spark plugs	Replace												✓
Steering linkage, ball joints, suspension, tie-rod ends, driveshaft and u-joints: lubricate if equipped with grease fittings	Inspect	✓	✓	✓	✓	✓	✓	✓	✓	✓	✓	✓	✓
Transfer case lubricant (4x4)	Replace												✓
Windshield wiper spray and wiper operation	Inspect	✓	✓	✓	✓	✓	✓	✓	✓	✓	✓	✓	✓
Windshield for cracks, chips and pitting	Inspect	✓	✓	✓	✓	✓	✓	✓	✓	✓	✓	✓	✓

For extensive idling and or low speed driving, change engine oil and filter every 5,000 miles, 6 months or 200 hours of engine operation.

Use of E85 50% of the time or greater, change engine oil and filter every 5,000 miles or 6 months.

PRECAUTIONS

Before servicing any vehicle, please be sure to read all of the following precautions, which deal with personal safety, prevention of component damage, and important points to take into consideration when servicing a motor vehicle:

• Never open, service or drain the radiator or cooling system when the engine is hot; serious burns can occur from the steam and hot coolant.

• Observe all applicable safety precautions when working around fuel. Whenever servicing the fuel system, always work in a well-ventilated area. Do not allow fuel spray or vapors to come in contact with a spark, open flame, or excessive heat (a hot drop light, for example). Keep a dry chemical fire extinguisher near the work area. Always keep fuel in a container specifically designed for fuel storage; also, always properly seal fuel containers to avoid the possibility of fire or explosion. Refer to the additional fuel system precautions later in this section.

• Fuel injection systems often remain pressurized, even after the engine has been turned **OFF**. The fuel system pressure must be relieved before disconnecting any fuel lines. Failure to do so may result in fire and/or personal injury.

• Brake fluid often contains polyglycol ethers and polyglycols. Avoid contact with the eyes and wash your hands thoroughly after handling brake fluid. If you do get brake fluid in your eyes, flush your eyes with clean, running water for 15 minutes. If eye irritation persists, or if you have taken brake fluid internally, IMMEDIATELY seek medical assistance.

• The EPA warns that prolonged contact with used engine oil may cause a number of skin disorders, including cancer. You should make every effort to minimize your exposure to used engine oil. Protective gloves should be worn when changing oil. Wash your hands and any other exposed skin areas as soon as possible after exposure to used engine oil. Soap and water, or waterless hand cleaner should be used.

• All new vehicles are now equipped with an air bag system, often referred to as a Supplemental Restraint System (SRS) or Supplemental Inflatable Restraint (SIR) system. The system must be disabled before performing service on or around system components, steering column, instrument panel components, wiring and sensors. Failure to follow safety and disabling procedures could result in accidental air bag deployment, possible personal injury and unnecessary system repairs.

• Always wear safety goggles when working with, or around, the air bag system. When carrying a non-deployed air bag, be sure the bag and trim cover are pointed away from your body. When placing a non-deployed air bag on a work surface, always face the bag and trim cover upward, away from the surface. This will reduce the motion of the module if it is accidentally deployed. Refer to the additional air bag system precautions later in this section.

• Clean, high quality brake fluid from a sealed container is essential to the safe and proper operation of the brake system. You should always buy the correct type of brake fluid for your vehicle. If the brake fluid becomes contaminated, completely flush the system with new fluid. Never reuse any brake fluid. Any brake fluid that is removed from the system should be discarded. Also, do not allow any brake fluid to come in contact with a painted surface; it will damage the paint.

• Never operate the engine without the proper amount and type of engine oil; doing so WILL result in severe engine damage.

• Timing belt maintenance is extremely important. Many models utilize an interference-type, non-freewheeling engine. If the timing belt breaks, the valves in the cylinder head may strike the pistons, causing potentially serious (also time-consuming and expensive) engine damage. Refer to the maintenance interval charts for the recommended replacement interval for the timing belt, and to the timing belt section for belt replacement and inspection.

• Disconnecting the negative battery cable on some vehicles may interfere with the functions of the on-board computer system(s) and may require the computer to undergo a relearning process once the negative battery cable is reconnected.

• When servicing drum brakes, only disassemble and assemble one side at a time, leaving the remaining side intact for reference.

• Only an MVAC-trained, EPA-certified automotive technician should service the air conditioning system or its components.

BRAKES

GENERAL INFORMATION

PRECAUTIONS

• Certain components within the ABS system are not intended to be serviced or repaired individually.

• Do not use rubber hoses or other parts not specifically specified for and ABS system. When using repair kits, replace all parts included in the kit. Partial or incorrect repair may lead to functional problems and require the replacement of components.

• Lubricate rubber parts with clean, fresh brake fluid to ease assembly. Do not use shop air to clean parts; damage to rubber components may result.

• Use only DOT 3 brake fluid from an unopened container.

• If any hydraulic component or line is removed or replaced, it may be necessary to bleed the entire system.

• A clean repair area is essential. Always clean the reservoir and cap thoroughly before removing the cap. The slightest amount of dirt in the fluid may plug an orifice and impair the system function. Perform repairs after components have been thoroughly cleaned; use only denatured alcohol to clean components. Do not allow ABS components to come into contact with any substance containing mineral oil; this includes used shop rags.

• The Anti-Lock control unit is a microprocessor similar to other computer

ANTI-LOCK BRAKE SYSTEM (ABS)

units in the vehicle. Ensure that the ignition switch is **OFF** before removing or installing controller harnesses. Avoid static electricity discharge at or near the controller.

• If any arc welding is to be done on the vehicle, the control unit should be unplugged before welding operations begin.

SPEED SENSORS

REMOVAL & INSTALLATION

Front

See Figure 1.

1. Remove the wheel and tire.
2. Disconnect the wheel speed sensor electrical connector.

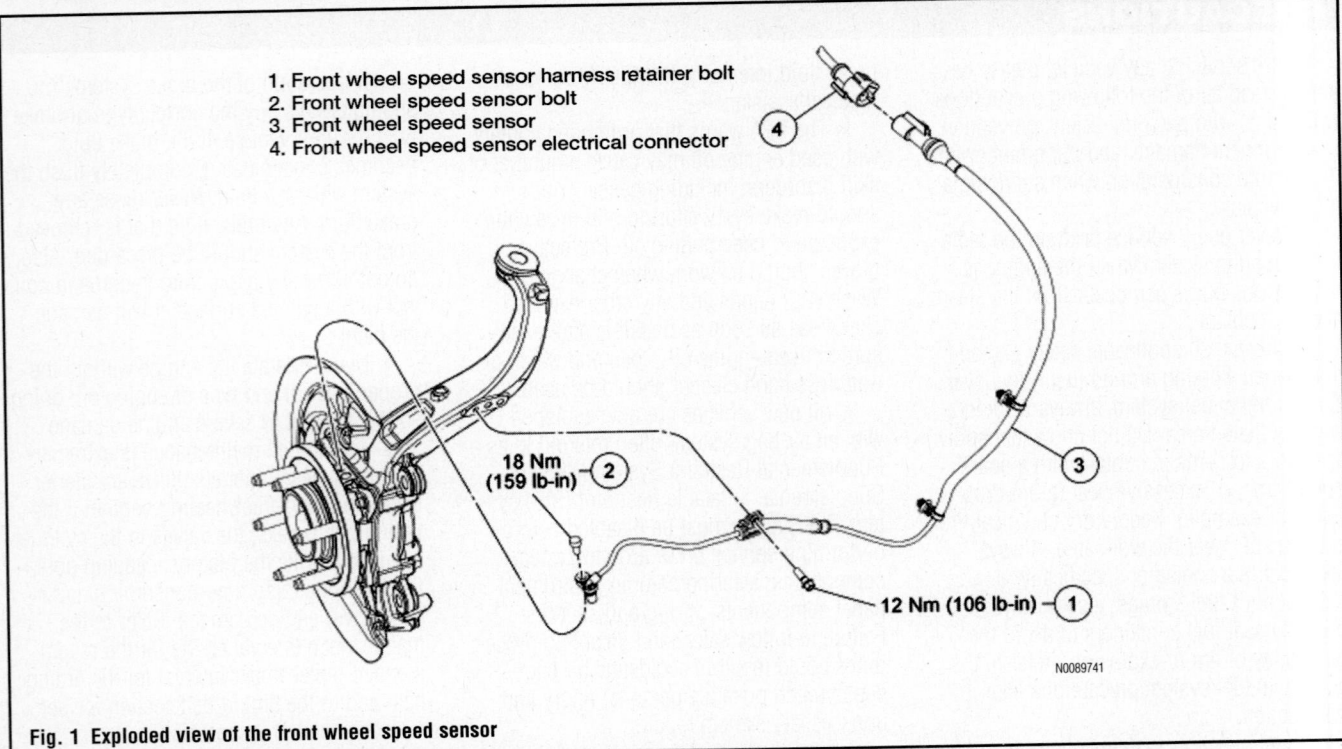

1. Front wheel speed sensor harness retainer bolt
2. Front wheel speed sensor bolt
3. Front wheel speed sensor
4. Front wheel speed sensor electrical connector

18 Nm (159 lb-in)

12 Nm (106 lb-in)

N0089741

Fig. 1 Exploded view of the front wheel speed sensor

3. Remove the wheel speed sensor harness bolt and detach the retainers.

✳✳ CAUTION

Do not allow the caliper to hang from the brake hose or damage to the hose can result.

4. Remove the 2 caliper anchor bolts and position the caliper, pads and anchor plate aside. Support the caliper with mechanic's wire.

5. Remove the brake disc.

6. Remove the front wheel speed sensor bolt and the sensor.

To install:

7. To install, reverse the removal procedure.

8. Install the front wheel speed sensor bolt and the sensor. Tighten to 13 ft. lbs. (18 Nm).

9. Position the caliper and install the 2 caliper anchor bolts Tighten to 148 ft. lbs. (200 Nm).

10. Install the wheel speed sensor harness bolt. Tighten to 106 inch lbs. (12 Nm).

Rear

See Figure 2.

1. Remove the parking brake shoes. See "PARKING BRAKE" section.

2. Disconnect the wheel speed sensor harness from the retaining clips.

3. Remove the rear wheel speed sensor bolt and the sensor.

4. To install, reverse the removal procedure.

5. Install and tighten the rear wheel speed sensor bolt to 13 ft. lbs. (18 Nm).

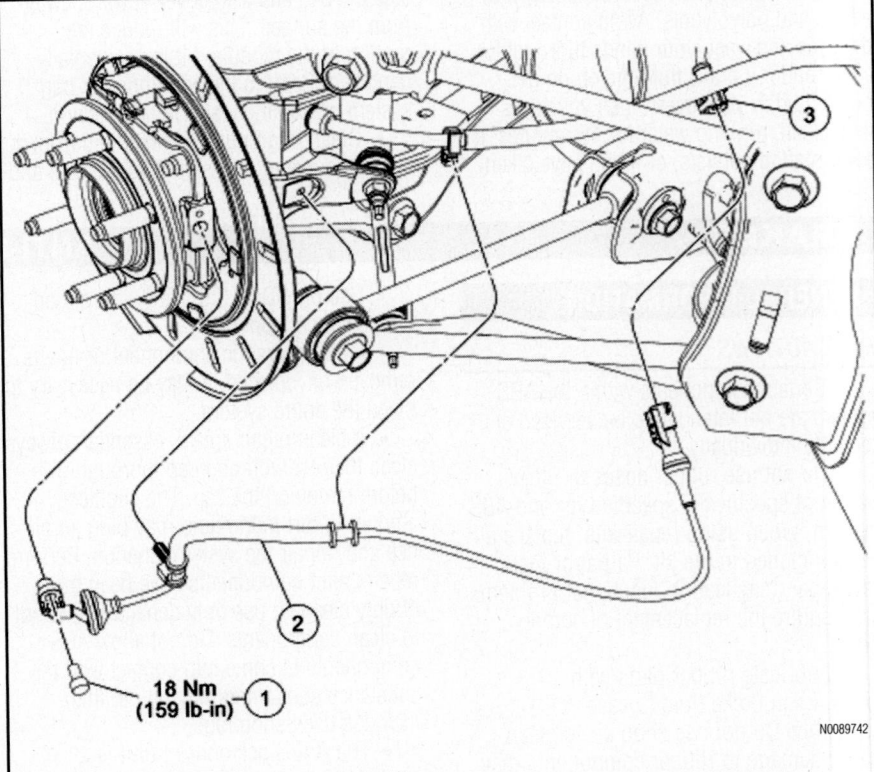

18 Nm (159 lb-in)

N0089742

Fig. 2 Removing the rear wheel speed sensor bolt (1), sensor (2) and electrical connector (3)

BRAKES

BLEEDING THE BRAKE SYSTEM

PRECAUTIONS & NOTES

❋❋ WARNING

Do not use any fluid other than clean brake fluid meeting manufacturer's specification. Additionally, do not use brake fluid that has been previously drained. Following these instructions will help prevent system contamination, brake component damage and the risk of serious personal injury.

1. Do not allow the brake master cylinder to run dry during the bleeding operation. Master cylinder may be damaged if operated without fluid, resulting in degraded braking performance. Failure to follow this instruction may result in serious personal injury.

❋❋ WARNING

Do not spill brake fluid on painted or plastic surfaces or damage to the surface may occur. If brake fluid is spilled onto a painted or plastic surface, immediately wash the surface with water.

➡The Hydraulic Control Unit (HCU) bleeding procedure must be carried out if the HCU or any components upstream of the HCU are installed new.

➡Pressure bleeding the brake system is preferred to manual bleeding.

BLEEDING PROCEDURE

BLEEDING THE BRAKE SYSTEM

1. Clean all dirt from the brake master cylinder filler cap and remove the filler cap.
2. Fill the brake master cylinder with clean specified brake fluid.

➡Master cylinder pressure bleeder adapter tools are available from various manufacturers of pressure bleeding

equipment. Follow the instructions of the equipment manufacturer when installing the adapter. Install the bleeder adapter to the brake master cylinder reservoir and attach the bleeder tank hose to the fitting on the adapter.

➡Make sure the bleeder tank contains enough clean, specified brake fluid to complete the bleeding operation.

3. Open the valve on the bleeder tank. Apply 30–50 psi to the brake system.
4. Remove the RH rear bleeder cap and place a box-end wrench on the bleeder screw. Attach a rubber drain tube to the RH rear bleeder screw and submerge the free end of the tube in a container partially filled with clean, specified brake fluid.
5. Loosen the RH rear bleeder screw. Leave open until clear, bubble-free brake fluid flows, then tighten the RH rear bleeder screw and remove the rubber hose.
6. Tighten the bleeder screw. Install the bleeder screw cap.
7. Continue bleeding the system, going in order from the LH rear bleeder screw to the RH front bleeder screw ending with the LH front bleeder screw.
8. Release the bleeder tank pressure and close the bleeder tank valve. Remove the tank hose from the adapter and remove the adapter from the brake fluid reservoir.

BRAKE CALIPER

➡It is not necessary to do a complete brake system bleed if only the brake caliper was disconnected or installed new.

1. Remove the bleeder screw cap and place a box-end wrench on the bleeder screw. Attach a rubber drain hose to the bleeder screw and submerge the free end of the hose in a container partially filled with clean, specified brake fluid.
2. Have an assistant pump the brake pedal at least 2 times and then hold firm pressure on the brake pedal.

3. Loosen the bleeder screw until a stream of brake fluid comes out. While the assistant maintains pressure on the brake pedal, tighten the bleeder screw.
4. Repeat until clear, bubble-free fluid comes out.
5. Refill the brake master cylinder reservoir as necessary.
6. Remove the rubber hose and tighten the bleeder screw.
7. Install the bleeder screw cap.

HYDRAULIC CONTROL UNIT (HCU)

➡The HCU bleeding procedure must be carried out if the HCU or any components upstream of the HCU are installed new.

➡Pressure bleeding the brake system is preferred to manual bleeding.

1. Follow the Pressure Bleeding procedure steps to bleed the brake system.
2. Connect the scan tool and follow the ABS Service Bleed instructions.
3. Repeat the Pressure Bleeding procedure steps to bleed the system.

MASTER CYLINDER BLEEDING

➡When a new brake master cylinder has been installed, or the system is emptied or partially emptied, it should be primed to prevent air from entering the system.

1. Disconnect the brake tubes from the master cylinder.
2. Install short brake tubes with the ends submerged in the brake master cylinder reservoir.
3. Fill the brake master cylinder reservoir with clean, specified brake fluid.
4. Have an assistant pump the brake pedal until clear fluid flows from both brake tubes, without air bubbles.
5. Remove the short brake tubes and install the brake outlet tubes.
6. Bleed the brake system. See ""Bleeding the Brake System" in this section.

BRAKES   **FRONT DISC BRAKES**

❋❋ CAUTION

Dust and dirt accumulating on brake parts during normal use may contain asbestos fibers from production or aftermarket brake linings. Breathing excessive concentrations of asbestos fibers can cause serious bodily harm. Exercise care when servicing brake parts. Do not sand or grind brake lining unless equipment used is designed to contain the dust residue. Do not clean brake parts with com-pressed air or by dry brushing. Cleaning should be done by dampening the brake components with a fine mist of water, then wiping the brake components clean with a dampened cloth. Dispose of cloth and all residue containing asbestos fibers in an impermeable container with the appropriate label. Follow practices prescribed by the Occupational Safety and Health Administration (OSHA) and the Environmental Protection Agency (EPA) for the handling, processing, and disposing of dust or debris that may contain asbestos fibers.

BRAKE CALIPER

REMOVAL & INSTALLATION

See Figure 3.

1. Remove the wheel and tire.
2. Remove the brake caliper flow bolt and discard the 2 copper washers.
3. Remove the 2 brake caliper guide pin bolts and the brake caliper.

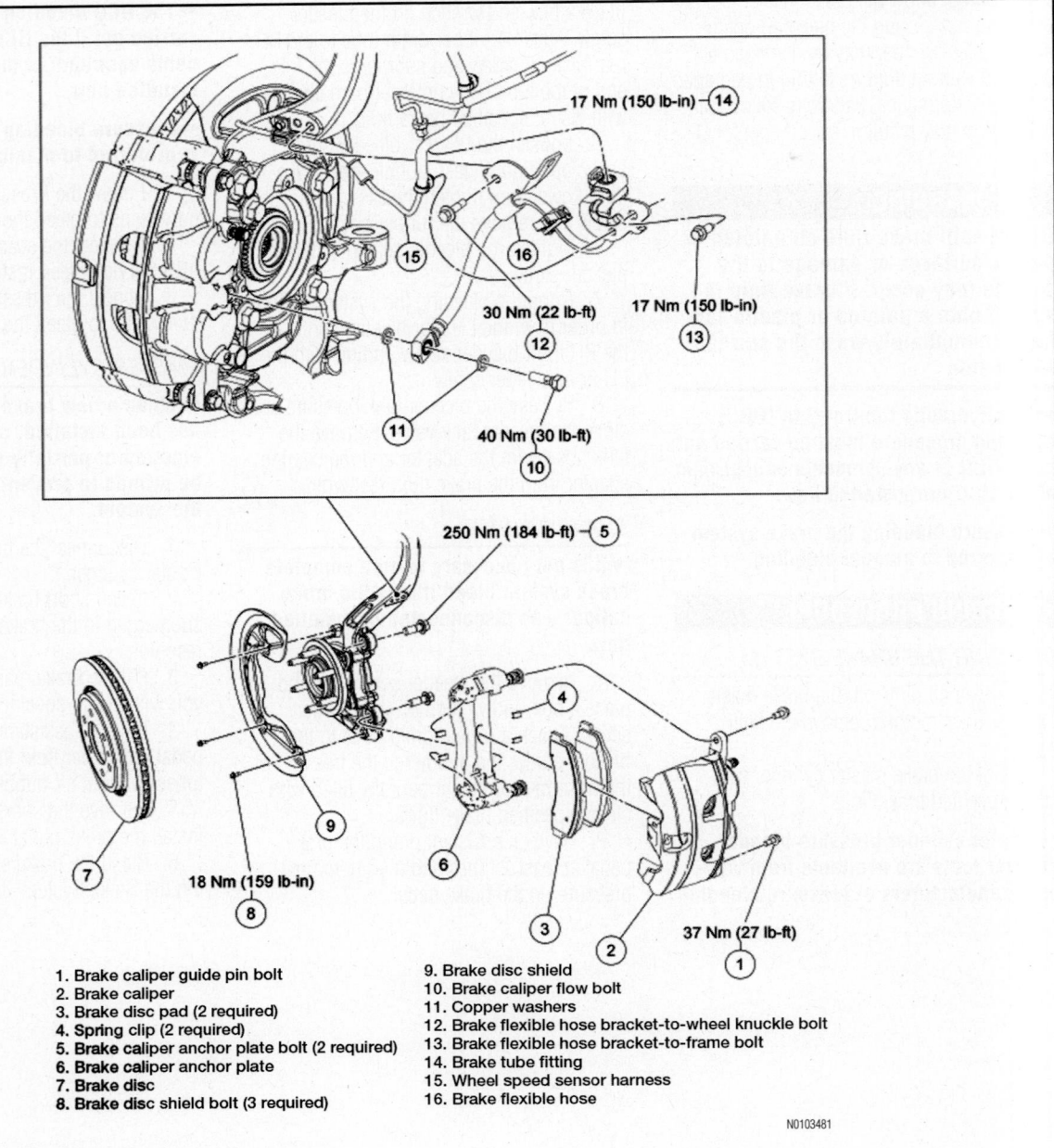

1. Brake caliper guide pin bolt
2. Brake caliper
3. Brake disc pad (2 required)
4. Spring clip (2 required)
5. Brake caliper anchor plate bolt (2 required)
6. Brake caliper anchor plate
7. Brake disc
8. Brake disc shield bolt (3 required)
9. Brake disc shield
10. Brake caliper flow bolt
11. Copper washers
12. Brake flexible hose bracket-to-wheel knuckle bolt
13. Brake flexible hose bracket-to-frame bolt
14. Brake tube fitting
15. Wheel speed sensor harness
16. Brake flexible hose

N0103481

Fig. 3 Exploded view of the front disc brake system

To install:

4. Using 2 new copper washers, position the brake flexible hose on the brake caliper and install the brake caliper flow bolt. Tighten to 30 ft. lbs. (40 Nm).

➡**Tighten the lower caliper guide pin bolt first.**

5. Position the brake caliper on the brake caliper anchor plate and install the 2 guide pin bolts. Tighten to 27 ft. lbs. (37 Nm).

6. Bleed the brake caliper. See "Bleeding Procedure" section.

7. Install the wheel and tire.

BRAKE DISC (ROTOR)

REMOVAL & INSTALLATION

1. Remove the wheel and tire.

✻✻ CAUTION

Do not allow the caliper and anchor plate assembly to hang from the brake hose or damage to the hose can occur.

2. Remove the 2 brake caliper anchor plate bolts and position the caliper and anchor plate assembly aside.

3. Support the caliper and anchor plate assembly using mechanic's wire.

4. Remove the front brake disc from the wheel hub.

To install:

5. Clean any rust or foreign material from the brake disc and wheel hub.

➡**Use specified parts cleaner to clean the front brake disc and hub surfaces.**

6. Install the brake disc on the wheel hub.

7. Position the brake caliper and anchor plate assembly on the wheel knuckle and install 2 new bolts. Tighten to 184 ft. lbs. (250 Nm).

8. Install the wheel and tire.

DISC BRAKE PADS

REMOVAL & INSTALLATION

✻✻ WARNING

Always install new brake shoes or pads at both ends of an axle to reduce the possibility of brakes pulling vehicle to one side. Failure to follow this instruction may result in uneven braking and serious personal injury.

1. Check the brake fluid level in the brake master cylinder reservoir. If necessary, remove fluid until the brake master cylinder reservoir is half full.

2. Remove the wheel and tire.

✻✻ CAUTION

Do not allow the caliper to hang from the brake hose or damage to the hose can occur.

3. Remove the 2 brake caliper guide pin bolts and position the caliper aside. Support the caliper using mechanic's wire.

4. Remove the brake pads and the 4 spring clips. Discard the spring clips.

To install:

➡**Protect the pistons and boots when compressing the piston into its bore.**

5. Using a C-clamp and a worn brake pad, compress the disc brake caliper pistons into the brake caliper bore.

6. Install the new spring clips and brake pads.

➡**Tighten the lower caliper guide pin bolt first.**

7. Position the brake caliper on the brake caliper anchor plate and install the 2 guide pin bolts. Tighten to 27 ft. lbs. (37 Nm).

8. Install the wheel and tire.

9. Apply brakes several times to verify correct brake operation.

10. Fill the master cylinder with clean, specified brake fluid.

BRAKES

✻✻ CAUTION

Dust and dirt accumulating on brake parts during normal use may contain asbestos fibers from production or aftermarket brake linings. Breathing excessive concentrations of asbestos fibers can cause serious bodily harm. Exercise care when servicing brake parts. Do not sand or grind brake lining unless equipment used is designed to contain the dust residue. Do not clean brake parts with compressed air or by dry brushing. Cleaning should be done by dampening the brake components with a fine mist of water, then wiping the brake components clean with a dampened cloth. Dispose of cloth and all residue containing asbestos fibers in an impermeable container with the appropriate label. Follow practices prescribed by the Occupational Safety and Health Administration (OSHA) and the Environmental Pro-tection Agency (EPA) for the handling, processing, and disposing of dust or debris that may contain asbestos fibers.

BRAKE CALIPER

REMOVAL & INSTALLATION

1. Remove the wheel and tire.

2. Remove the brake hose flow bolt and disconnect the hose.

3. Remove and discard the copper washers.

4. Remove the 2 brake caliper guide pin caps and bolts.

5. Inspect the guide pin threads for damage, install a new guide pin(s) as necessary.

6. Clean and dry guide pin threads as necessary.

7. Remove the brake caliper and remove the brake pads from the caliper.

8. Inspect the disc brake caliper dust boot for leaks and/or damage. If leaks or damage are found, install a new brake caliper.

REAR DISC BRAKES

➡**Do not apply lubricant to guide pin threads or incorrect tightening of the guide pins may result.**

To install:

9. To install, reverse the removal procedure.

10. Install new guide pin bushings. Apply supplied white lubricant to the inside of the guide pin bushings.

11. Install a new guide pin(s) as necessary. Tighten to 28 ft. lbs. (38 Nm).

12. Install caliper bolts. Tighten to 30 ft. lbs. (40 Nm).

13. Bleed the brake caliper. See "Bleeding Procedure" section.

BRAKE DISC (ROTOR)

REMOVAL & INSTALLATION

1. Remove the wheel and tire.

➡**Do not allow the brake caliper and anchor plate assembly to hang by the flexible brake hose or damage to the hose may occur.**

2. Remove the brake caliper anchor plate bolts and position the anchor plate and caliper assembly aside.

3. Support the caliper and anchor plate assembly with mechanic's wire.

4. Inspect the brake caliper anchor plate bolt threads for damage and foreign material.

➡ **If the brake disc binds on the parking brake shoe, remove the adjustment hole access plug and contract the parking brake shoe.**

5. Remove the brake disc.

6. Inspect the brake disc and resurface or install a new brake disc as necessary.

7. To install, reverse the removal procedure.

8. Install cleaned and dried anchor plate bolts or install new as necessary. Tighten to 140 ft. lbs. (190 Nm).

DISC BRAKE PADS

REMOVAL & INSTALLATION
See Figure 4.

✳✳ WARNING

Always install new brake shoes or pads at both ends of an axle to reduce the possibility of brakes pulling vehicle to one side. Failure to follow this instruction may result in uneven braking and serious personal injury.

1. Check the brake fluid level in the brake master cylinder reservoir. If required, remove the fluid until the brake master cylinder reservoir is half full.

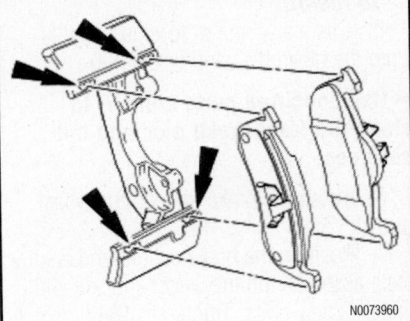

N0073960

Fig. 4 Using specified brake parts cleaner, dry and inspect the brake caliper anchor plate. Apply equal amounts of the supplied yellow lubricant to the 4 brake pad contact points on the anchor plate as shown.

2. Remove the wheel and tire.

✳✳ CAUTION

Do not allow the brake caliper to hang by the flexible brake hose or damage to the hose may occur.

3. Remove the 2 brake caliper guide pin caps and bolts and position the caliper and brake pad assembly aside. Support the caliper using mechanic's wire.

4. Remove and discard the guide pin bushings.

5. Inspect the guide pin threads for damage, install new guide pin(s) as necessary.

6. Remove the brake pads from the caliper.

7. Inspect the brake pads for wear or contamination.

8. Using a C-clamp and a worn brake pad, press the piston into the caliper.

9. Inspect the brake disc and resurface or install a new brake disc as necessary.

To install:

10. Using specified brake parts cleaner, dry and inspect the brake caliper anchor plate. Apply equal amounts of the supplied yellow lubricant to the 4 brake pad contact points on the anchor plate as shown.

✳✳ CAUTION

Do not apply lubricant to guide pin threads or incorrect tightening of the guide pins may result.

11. Install new brake hardware as follows:

   a. Apply equal amounts of the supplied white lubricant to the inside of the guide pin bushings.

   b. Install the guide pin bushings into the caliper bores.

   c. Install the guide pins into the bushings.

12. Install the brake pads to the caliper.

13. Position the caliper onto the anchor plate and install the 2 brake caliper guide pin bolts. Tighten to 28 ft. lbs. (38 Nm).

14. Clean and dry guide pin threads as necessary.

15. Fill the master cylinder with clean, specified brake fluid.

16. Install the wheel and tire.

17. Apply the brake several times to verify correct brake operation.

BRAKES

PARKING BRAKE

PARKING BRAKE CABLES

REMOVAL & INSTALLATION

Front Cable

See Figure 5.

1. Remove the parking brake control. See "Parking Brake Control" in this section.

2. With the vehicle in Neutral, position it on a hoist.

3. Remove the front park brake cable P-clip-to-frame bolt.

4. Remove the front parking brake cable and conduit.

5. Pry the rubber seal from the front floor pan.

6. Compress the retainer and release the conduit from the bracket.

7. Remove the front cable and conduit from the cable union.

8. To install, reverse the removal procedure.

9. Install the front park brake cable P-clip-to-frame bolt. Tighten to 13 ft. lbs. (18 Nm).

Left Rear Cable

See Figures 6 and 7.

1. Relieve the tension on the parking brake cable system.

2. With the vehicle in Neutral, position it on a hoist.

3. Separate the LH rear cable from the equalizer.

4. Compress the 2 tabs and remove the conduit from the bracket.

➡ **Be sure to correctly install the park brake cable retainer spring and route cables between suspension links.**

5. Disconnect the parking brake cable retainer spring from the cable.

6. Disconnect the LH rear cable from the retaining clip.

7. Disconnect the ABS wheel speed sensor wire from the retaining clip.

8. Release the parking brake cable from the LH bracket assembly.

9. Release the cable from the parking brake actuating lever and remove the cable.

10. To install, reverse the removal procedure.

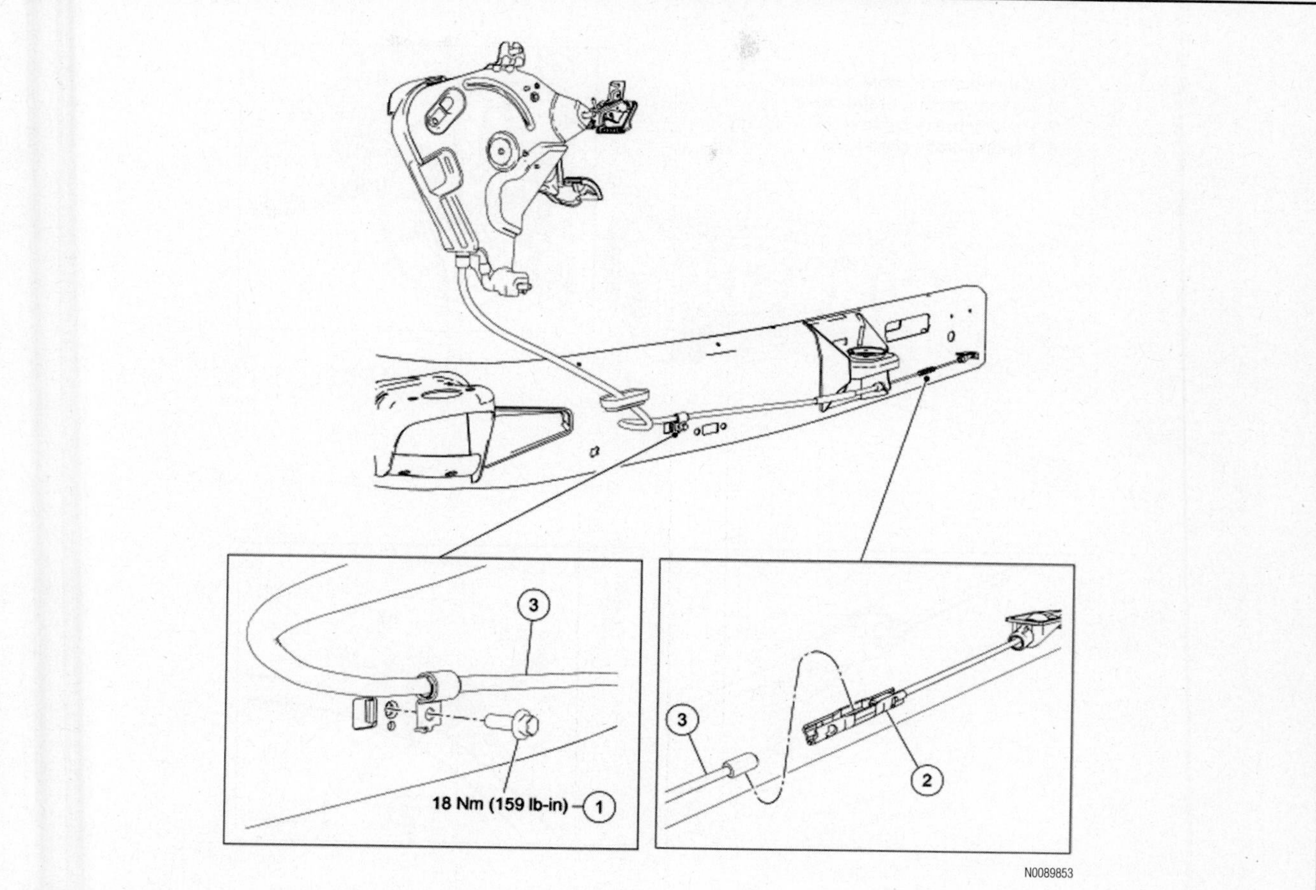

Fig. 5 Showing the front parking brake cable clip (1), cable union (2) and the cable (3)

18 Nm (159 lb-in)

N0089853

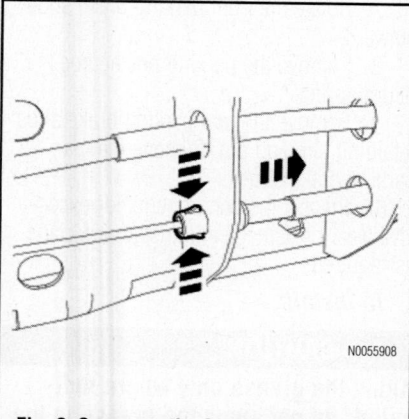

N0055908

Fig. 6 Compress the 2 tabs and remove the conduit from the bracket.

Right Rear Cable

See Figure 8.

1. Relieve the tension on the parking brake cable system.

2. With the vehicle in Neutral, position it on a hoist.

3. Disconnect the RH rear cable from the cable union.

4. Compress the 2 tabs and release the conduit from the equalizer.

5. Disconnect the RH rear cable from the retaining clip.

6. Remove the bolt and the wire form bracket from the LH side of the vehicle.

7. Remove the rear parking brake cable-to-crossmember bolt.

8. Remove the bolt and the wire form bracket from the RH side of the vehicle.

9. Release the parking brake cable from the RH bracket assembly.

10. Release the cable from the parking brake actuating lever and remove the cable.

To install:

11. To install, reverse the removal procedure. Tighten the fasteners as follows:

- RH wire form bracket bolt: 13 ft. lbs. (18 Nm).
- Rear parking brake cable-to-crossmember bolt: 13 ft. lbs. (18 Nm).
- LH wire form bracket bolt: 13 ft. lbs. (18 Nm).

PARKING BRAKE CABLE TENSION RELEASE

TENSION RELEASE PROCEDURE

1. Remove the LH cowl side trim panel.

2. With the help of an assistant, release the parking brake cable tension by pulling down on the intermediate cable at the cable-to-cable union until the parking brake control sector rotates to its stop and a 4 mm (0.15 in) x 150 mm (5.9 in) retainer pin can be inserted.

3. To reload the tension on the parking brake cable, follow the release procedure in reverse.

4. Make sure the cable tension is reloaded slowly.

PARKING BRAKE CONTROL

REMOVAL & INSTALLATION

See Figures 9 and 10.

1. Relieve tension on the parking brake cable system. See procedure in this section.

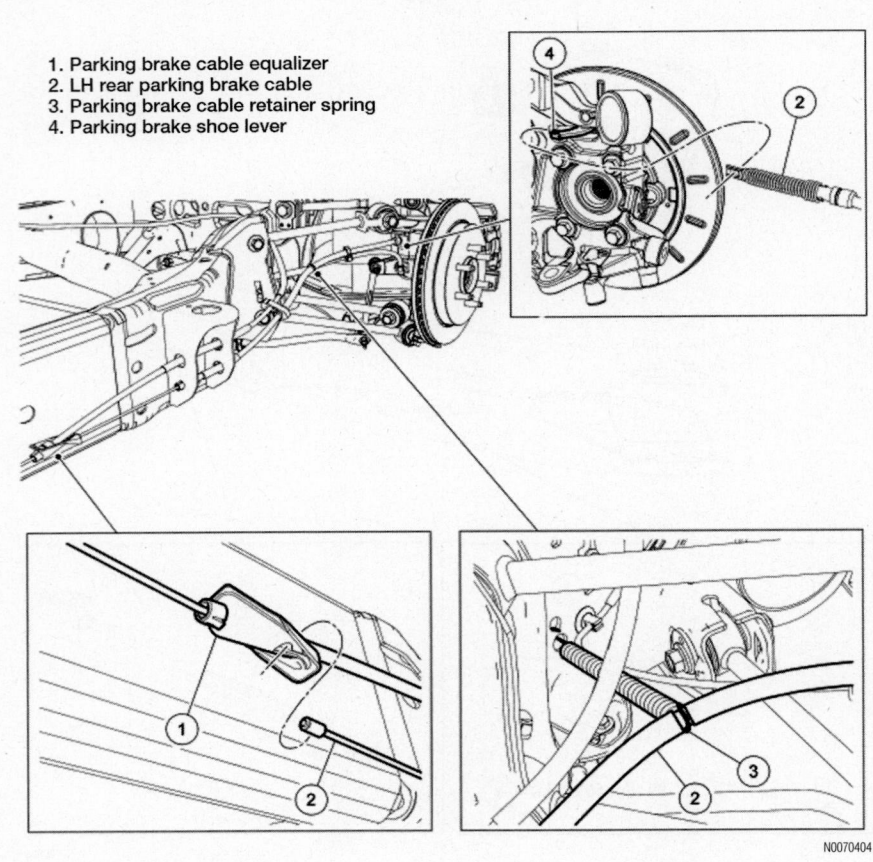

1. Parking brake cable equalizer
2. LH rear parking brake cable
3. Parking brake cable retainer spring
4. Parking brake shoe lever

Fig. 7 Showing the left rear parking brake cable and related components

2. Remove the front door scuff plate.

3. Remove the instrument panel steering column opening trim panel and if equipped, the instrument panel lower cover.

4. Remove the parking brake release handle bolt.

5. Remove the retainer and the cowl trim panel.

6. Compress the 2 tabs and disconnect the parking brake release cable from the parking brake control assembly.

7. Disconnect the parking brake release cable from the release lever and remove the parking brake release handle.

8. Disconnect the parking brake switch electrical connector.

9. Remove the 3 parking brake control assembly bolts.

10. Position the parking brake control assembly onto the floor.

11. Disconnect the parking brake cable from the take-up spool.

12. Compress the 2 tabs, disconnect the parking brake cable from the control assembly and remove the control assembly.

To install:

13. To install, reverse the removal procedure.

14. Install the 3 parking brake control assembly bolts. Tighten to 177 inch lbs. (20 Nm).

15. Install the parking brake release handle bolt. Tighten to 27 inch lbs. (3 Nm).

PARKING BRAKE SHOES

REMOVAL & INSTALLATION

See Figures 11 through 13.

1. Relieve the tension on the parking brake cable system. See procedure in this section.

2. Remove the brake disc. See "REAR DISC BRAKES" section.

3. Remove the front parking brake shoe retaining clip and pin.

4. Using a suitable tool, spread the bottom of the parking brake shoes apart.

5. Remove the parking brake shoe adjuster and spring.

6. Slide the front parking brake shoe up and out of the guide flange.

7. Rotate the front parking brake shoe outward.

8. Remove the parking brake shoe return spring.

9. Remove the rear parking brake shoe retaining clip and pin. Remove the rear parking brake shoe.

10. Inspect the components for excessive wear or damage and install new parts as required.

To install:

✳✳ CAUTION

Apply the grease only where indicated, do not apply the grease to the parking brake shoes. The grease will contaminate the brake shoe linings and damage to the linings will result.

11. Apply a light coat of the specified grease to the 6 parking brake shoe contact points on the disc brake shield.

12. Install the rear parking brake shoe:
   a. Hold the rear parking brake shoe in position.
   b. Install the retaining pin and clip.

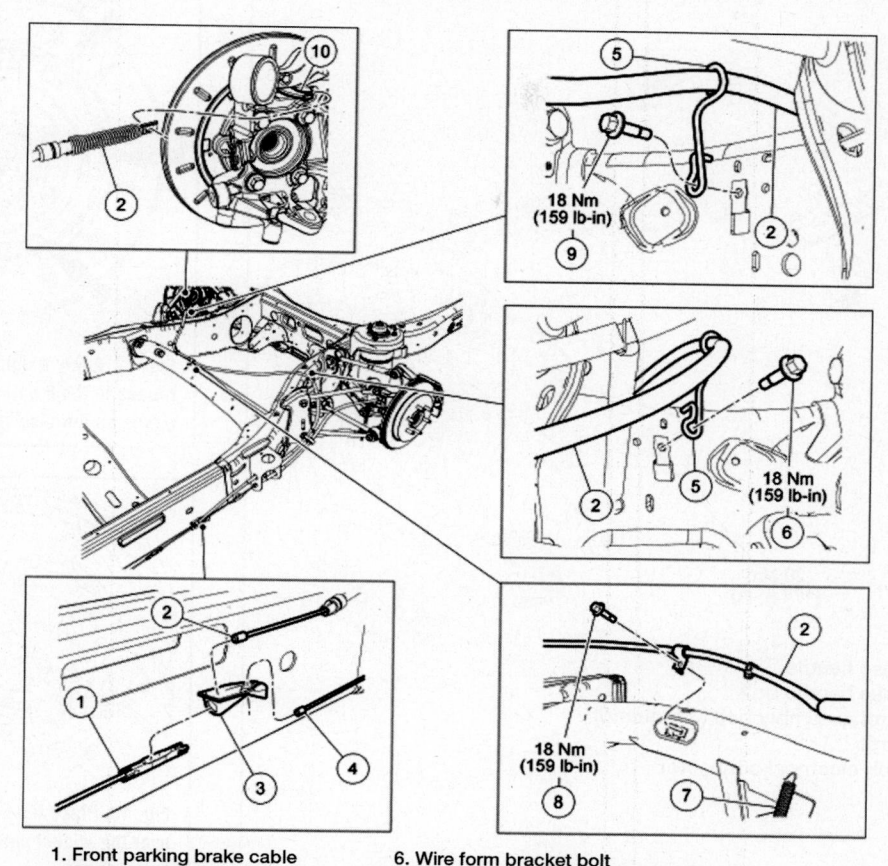

1. Front parking brake cable
2. RH parking brake cable
3. Parking brake cable equalizer
4. LH parking brake cable
5. Wire form bracket
6. Wire form bracket bolt
7. Parking brake cable retaining spring
8. Rear parking brake cable-to-crossmember bolt
9. Wire form bracket bolt
10. RH parking brake shoe lever

N0089852

Fig. 8 Showing the RR parking brake cable and related components

13. Install the front parking brake shoe:
   a. Install the parking brake shoe return spring to the rear parking brake shoe and to the front parking brake shoe.
   b. Rotate the front parking brake shoe into the guide flange.

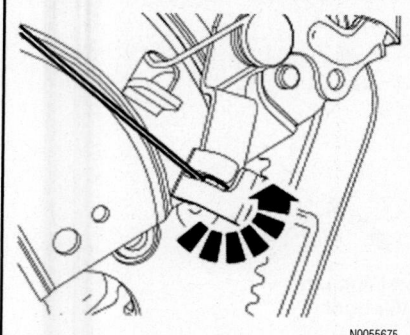

Fig. 9 Disconnect the parking brake release cable from the release lever and remove the parking brake release handle.

   c. Slide the front parking brake shoe down into position on the flange.
   d. Install the front parking brake shoe retaining pin and clip.
14. Install the parking brake shoe adjuster spring.
15. Install the parking brake shoe adjuster:
   a. Using a suitable tool, spread the bottom of the parking brake shoes apart.
   b. Install the parking brake shoe adjuster.
16. Adjust the parking brake shoes as follows:
   a. Make sure the parking brake is fully released.
   b. Using the release handle, release the parking brake control.
   c. Remove the rear brake disc.
   d. Using the Brake Adjusting Gauge, measure the inside diameter of the drum portion of the rear brake disc and set the locking screw.
   e. Record the measurement.

   f. Place the Brake Adjusting Gauge over the widest diameter of the parking brake shoes.
   g. Adjust the parking brake shoe clearance to 0.45 mm (0.02 in) less than the inside diameter of the drum portion of the rear brake disc.
   h. Rotate the parking brake shoe adjuster to achieve the correct parking brake shoe-to-brake disc clearance.
   i. Install the rear brake disc.
   j. Test the parking brake for normal operation.

➡**This step will require the aid of an assistant.**

17. Enable the parking brake cable system.
18. Pull down on the front parking brake cable at the coupler.
19. Remove the retaining pin from the parking brake lever.
20. Check the parking brake for correct operation.

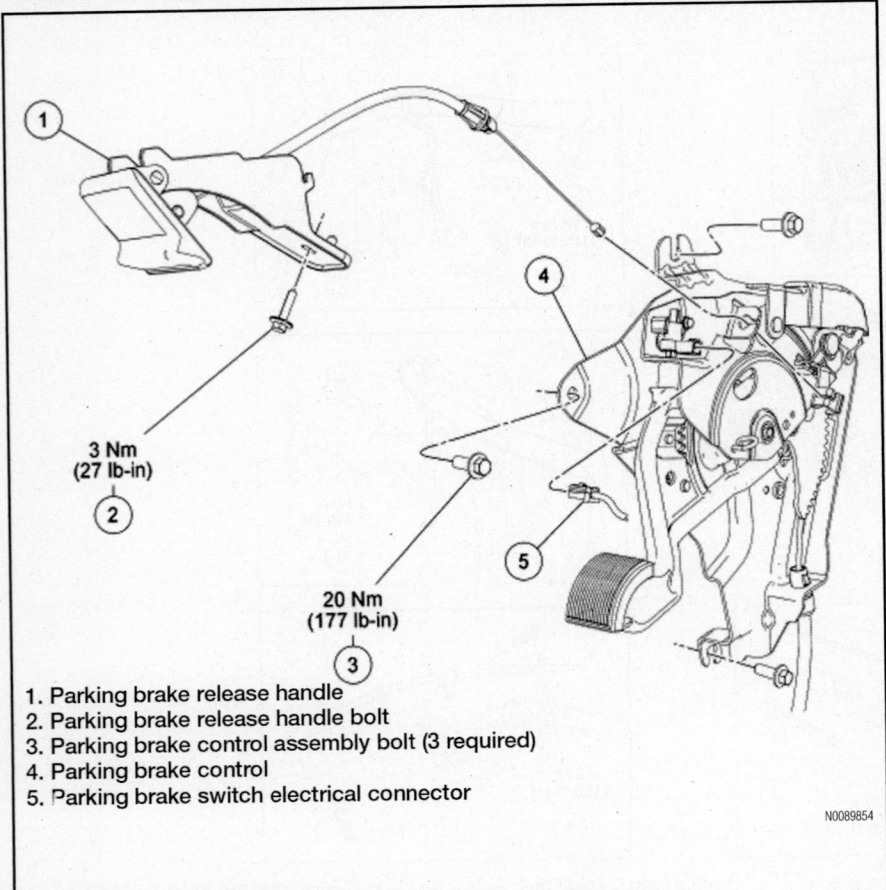

1. Parking brake release handle
2. Parking brake release handle bolt
3. Parking brake control assembly bolt (3 required)
4. Parking brake control
5. Parking brake switch electrical connector

N0089854

Fig. 10 Showing the parking brake control assembly

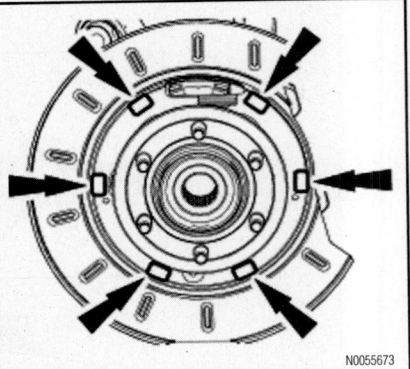

N0055673

Fig. 12 Apply a light coat of the specified grease to the 6 parking brake shoe contact points on the disc brake shield.

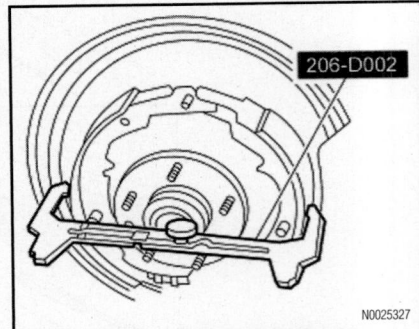

206-D002

N0025327

Fig. 13 Place the Brake Adjusting Gauge over the widest diameter of the parking brake shoes.

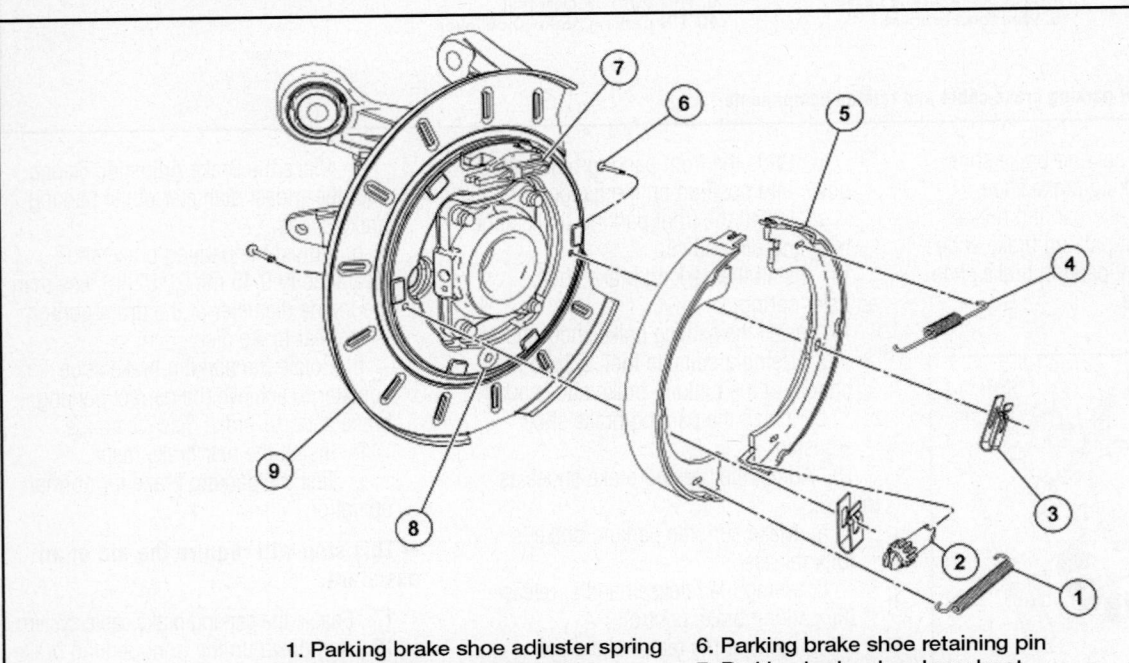

1. Parking brake shoe adjuster spring
2. Parking brake shoe adjuster
3. Parking brake shoe retaining clip
4. Parking brake shoe return spring
5. Parking brake shoe
6. Parking brake shoe retaining pin
7. Parking brake shoe lever boot
8. Adjuster hole plug
9. Brake disc shield

N0056021

Fig. 11 Showing the parking brake shoes and related components

CHASSIS ELECTRICAL

AIR BAG (SUPPLEMENTAL RESTRAINT SYSTEM)

GENERAL INFORMATION

❋❋ CAUTION

These vehicles are equipped with an air bag system. The system must be disarmed before performing service on, or around, system components, the steering column, instrument panel components, wiring and sensors. Failure to follow the safety precautions and the disarming procedure could result in accidental air bag deployment, possible injury and unnecessary system repairs.

SERVICE PRECAUTIONS

Disconnect and isolate the battery negative cable before beginning any airbag system component diagnosis, testing, removal, or installation procedures. Allow system capacitor to discharge for two minutes before beginning any component service. This will disable the airbag system. Failure to disable the airbag system may result in accidental airbag deployment, personal injury, or death.

Do not place an intact undeployed airbag face down on a solid surface. The airbag will propel into the air if accidentally deployed and may result in personal injury or death.

When carrying or handling an undeployed airbag, the trim side (face) of the airbag should be pointing away from the body to minimize possibility of injury if accidental deployment occurs. Failure to do this may result in personal injury or death.

Replace airbag system components with OEM replacement parts. Substitute parts may appear interchangeable, but internal differences may result in inferior occupant protection. Failure to do so may result in occupant personal injury or death.

Wear safety glasses, rubber gloves, and long sleeved clothing when cleaning powder residue from vehicle after an airbag deployment. Powder residue emitted from a deployed airbag can cause skin irritation. Flush affected area with cool water if irritation is experienced. If nasal or throat irritation is experienced, exit the vehicle for fresh air until the irritation ceases. If irritation continues, see a physician.

Do not use a replacement airbag that is not in the original packaging. This may result in improper deployment, personal injury, or death.

The factory installed fasteners, screws and bolts used to fasten airbag components have a special coating and are specifically designed for the airbag system. Do not use substitute fasteners. Use only original equipment fasteners listed in the parts catalog when fastener replacement is required.

During, and following, any child restraint anchor service, due to impact event or vehicle repair, carefully inspect all mounting hardware, tether straps, and anchors for proper installation, operation, or damage. If a child restraint anchor is found damaged in any way, the anchor must be replaced. Failure to do this may result in personal injury or death.

Deployed and non-deployed airbags may or may not have live pyrotechnic material within the airbag inflator.

Do not dispose of driver/passenger/curtain airbags or seat belt tensioners unless you are sure of complete deployment. Refer to the Hazardous Substance Control System for proper disposal.

Dispose of deployed airbags and tensioners consistent with state, provincial, local, and federal regulations.

After any airbag component testing or service, do not connect the battery negative cable. Personal injury or death may result if the system test is not performed first.

If the vehicle is equipped with the Occupant Classification System (OCS), do not connect the battery negative cable before performing the OCS Verification Test using the scan tool and the appropriate diagnostic information. Personal injury or death may result if the system test is not performed properly.

Never replace both the Occupant Restraint Controller (ORC) and the Occupant Classification Module (OCM) at the same time. If both require replacement, replace one, then perform the Airbag System test before replacing the other.

Both the ORC and the OCM store Occupant Classification System (OCS) calibration data, which they transfer to one another when one of them is replaced. If both are replaced at the same time, an irreversible fault will be set in both modules and the OCS may malfunction and cause personal injury or death.

If equipped with OCS, the Seat Weight Sensor is a sensitive, calibrated unit and must be handled carefully. Do not drop or handle roughly. If dropped or damaged, replace with another sensor. Failure to do so may result in occupant injury or death.

If equipped with OCS, the front passenger seat must be handled carefully as well. When removing the seat, be careful when setting on floor not to drop. If dropped, the sensor may be inoperative, could result in occupant injury, or possibly death.

If equipped with OCS, when the passenger front seat is on the floor, no one should sit in the front passenger seat. This uneven force may damage the sensing ability of the seat weight sensors. If sat on and damaged, the sensor may be inoperative, could result in occupant injury, or possibly death.

DISARMING (DEPOWERING) THE SYSTEM

➡ **The air bag warning indicator illuminates when the correct Restraints Control Module (RCM) fuse is removed and the ignition is ON.**

➡ **The Supplemental Restraint System (SRS) must be fully operational and free of faults before releasing the vehicle to the customer.**

1. Turn all vehicle accessories OFF.
2. Turn the ignition switch OFF.
3. At the Smart Junction Box (SJB), located in the RH lower kick panel, remove the cover and the RCM fuse 32 (10A) from the SJB.
4. Turn the ignition switch ON and visually monitor the air bag warning indicator for at least 30 seconds. The air bag warning indicator will remain lit continuously (no flashing) if the correct RCM fuse has been removed. If the air bag warning indicator does not remain lit continuously, remove the correct RCM fuse before proceeding.
5. Turn the ignition switch OFF.

❋❋ WARNING

Always deplete the backup power supply before repairing or installing any new front or side air bag supplemental restraint system (SRS) component and before servicing, removing, installing, adjusting or striking components near the front or side impact sensors or the restraints control module (RCM). Nearby components include doors, instrument panel, console, door latches, strikers, seats and hood latches.

6. To deplete the backup power supply energy, disconnect the battery ground cable and wait at least 1 minute. Be sure to disconnect auxiliary batteries and power supplies (if equipped).

❊❊ WARNING

Failure to follow these instructions may result in serious personal injury or death in the event of an accidental deployment.

7. Disconnect the battery ground cable and wait at least one minute.

ARMING (REPOWERING) THE SYSTEM

1. Make sure that all SRS components are connected.
2. Turn the ignition switch from OFF to ON.
3. Install RCM fuse 32 (10A) to the SJB and close the cover.

❊❊ WARNING

Make sure no one is in the vehicle and there is nothing blocking or placed in front of any air bag module when the battery is connected. Failure to follow these instructions may result in serious personal injury in the event of an accidental deployment.

4. Connect the battery ground cable.
5. Prove out the SRS as follows:
   a. Turn the ignition from ON to OFF. Wait 10 seconds, then turn the back to ON and visually monitor the air bag warning indicator with the air bag modules installed.
   b. The air bag warning indicator will illuminate continuously for approximately 6 seconds and then turn off.
   c. If an SRS fault is present, the air bag warning indicator will: - fail to light. - remain lit continuously. - flash.
   d. The flashing might not occur until approximately 30 seconds after the ignition has been turned from the OFF to the ON position.

➡ **This is the time required for the RCM to complete the testing of the SRS.**

   e. If the air bag warning indicator is inoperative and a SRS fault exists, a chime will sound in a pattern of 5 sets of 5 beeps. If this occurs, the air bag warning indicator and any SRS fault discovered must be diagnosed and repaired.
   f. Clear all continuous DTCs from the RCM using a scan tool.

DRIVE TRAIN

AUTOMATIC TRANSMISSION FLUID

DRAIN & REFILL

Drain

See Figure 14.

1. With the vehicle in NEUTRAL, position it on a hoist.

➡ **Some transmission fluid leakage may occur when removing the transmission fluid fill plug.**

2. Remove the transmission fluid fill plug fluid level indicator assembly located on the passenger side front portion of the transmission case.

➡ **Removal of the transmission fluid fill plug will relieve any vacuum that might** have built up in the transmission. This will aid in allowing the transmission fluid pan to be easily removed when the bolts are removed.

3. Remove the bolts and the transmission fluid pan and allow the transmission fluid to drain.

➡ **The transmission fluid pan gasket can be reused if not damaged.**

4. Install a new transmission fluid pan gasket, if required.
5. Install the transmission fluid pan and tighten the bolts in a crisscross pattern. Tighten to 106 inch lbs. (12 Nm).

Refill

See Figure 15.

➡ **This procedure contains the air purge steps required to purge air from the transmission fluid cooling system. This procedure is NOT intended for use with the Transmission Fluid Level Check.**

❊❊ CAUTION

The vehicle should not be driven if the transmission fluid level is low as internal failure could result.

❊❊ CAUTION

The use of any other transmission fluid than specified can result in the transmission failing to operate in a normal manner or transmission failure.

➡ **If the transmission starts to slip, shifts slowly or shows signs of trans-** mission fluid leaking, the transmission fluid level should be checked.

1. Using the Transmission Fluid Fill Tube, add 3.5 qts. (3.3L) of fluid through the transmission fluid fill hole.
2. Check the transmission fluid level cold.

➡ **The vehicle is safe to drive if the transmission fluid is in the cold level range: 90°F–110°F).**

3. Using the scan tool and with the engine running, place the selector lever in each gear position and hold approximately 5 seconds. Place the selector lever in PARK, with the engine at idle (600-750 rpm).
4. Separate the transmission fluid level indicator from the transmission fluid fill plug.

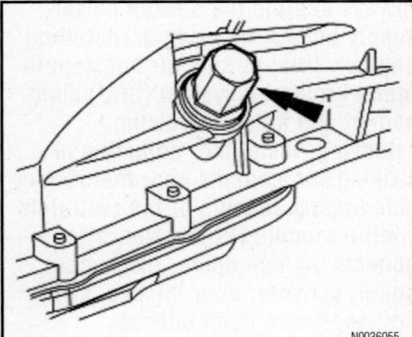

N0036055

Fig. 14 Remove the transmission fluid fill plug fluid level indicator assembly located on the passenger side front portion of the transmission case.

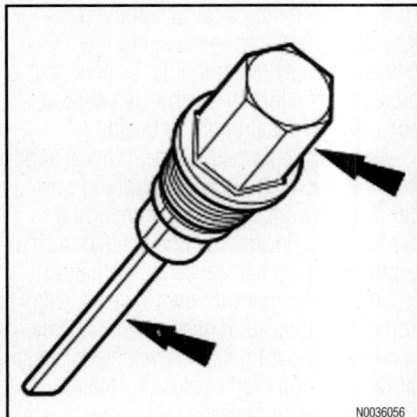

N0036056

Fig. 15 Separate the transmission fluid level indicator from the transmission fluid fill plug.

5. Wipe the fluid level indicator clean. Reinstall the level indicator back into the transmission fluid fill plug hole. Repeat this until a consistent reading is established.

6. Add transmission fluid to the cold level location as shown on the indicator stick.

7. Install the transmission fluid fill plug. Tighten to 26 ft. lbs. (35 Nm).

8. While driving the vehicle, use the scan tool to verify that the TFT has reached a temperature of 190°F. This will circulate the transmission fluid through the torque converter and the transmission fluid cooling system, eliminating any trapped air in the transmission fluid cooling system.

9. With the engine idling at 600–750 rpm in PARK, verify that the TFT is between 176°F–185°F.

10. Remove the transmission fluid fill plug transmission fluid level indicator assembly located on the passenger side front portion of the transmission case.

11. Separate the transmission fluid level indicator from the transmission fluid fill plug.

12. Wipe the transmission fluid level indicator clean. Reinstall the transmission fluid level indicator only back into the transmission fluid fill plug hole to check the transmission fluid level. Repeat this until a consistent reading is established.

13. With the TFT between 176°F–185°F, the transmission fluid level must be at the upper level of the crosshatch mark on the indicator stick.

➡ **If the transmission fluid is not at the correct level, follow the steps for "Adding Additional Transmission Fluid" in this procedure.**

14. Install the transmission fluid fill plug. Tighten to 26 ft. lbs. (35 Nm).

Adding Additional Transmission Fluid
See Figure 16.

➡ **To get an accurate transmission fluid level reading the engine should be idling at 600–750 rpm in PARK.**

1. Install the Transmission Fluid Fill Tube into the transmission fluid fill hole.

2. Fill a proper Transporter Fluid Evacuator/Injector (307-D465 or equivalent) with approximately 1 pt. of transmission fluid.

3. Connect the open end of the fluid hose from the Transporter Fluid Evacuator/Injector onto the Transmission Fluid Fill Tube from the transmission case.

4. Use a Rubber Tip Air Nozzle to apply a maximum of 30 psi to the open end of the vacuum/pressure hose from the Transporter

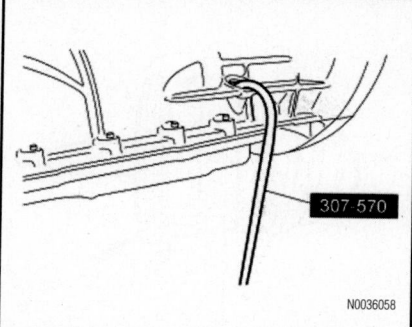

Fig. 16 Install the Transmission Fluid Fill Tube into the transmission fluid fill hole.

Fluid Evacuator/Injector. Transmission fluid will immediately start flowing out of the Transporter Fluid Evacuator/Injector into the transmission.

✳✳ CAUTION

Do not overfill the transmission. The transmission fluid level must be at the upper level of the crosshatch mark.

5. Reinstall the transmission fluid level indicator only back into the transmission fluid fill plug hole to check the transmission fluid level. Repeat this until a consistent reading is established.

6. Using the scan tool, verify that the TFT is between 176°F–185°F. The transmission fluid level must be at the upper level of the crosshatch mark.

➡ **If the transmission fluid is over full, use the same equipment, with a vacuum device attached, to draw excess fluid out of the transmission.**

7. Install the transmission fluid fill plug. Tighten to 26 ft. lbs. (35 Nm).

TRANSFER CASE ASSEMBLY

REMOVAL & INSTALLATION

➡ **Manufacturer does not provide a removal and installation procedure for this component.**

FRONT DRIVESHAFT

REMOVAL & INSTALLATION
See Figure 17.

1. With the vehicle in NEUTRAL, position the vehicle on a hoist.

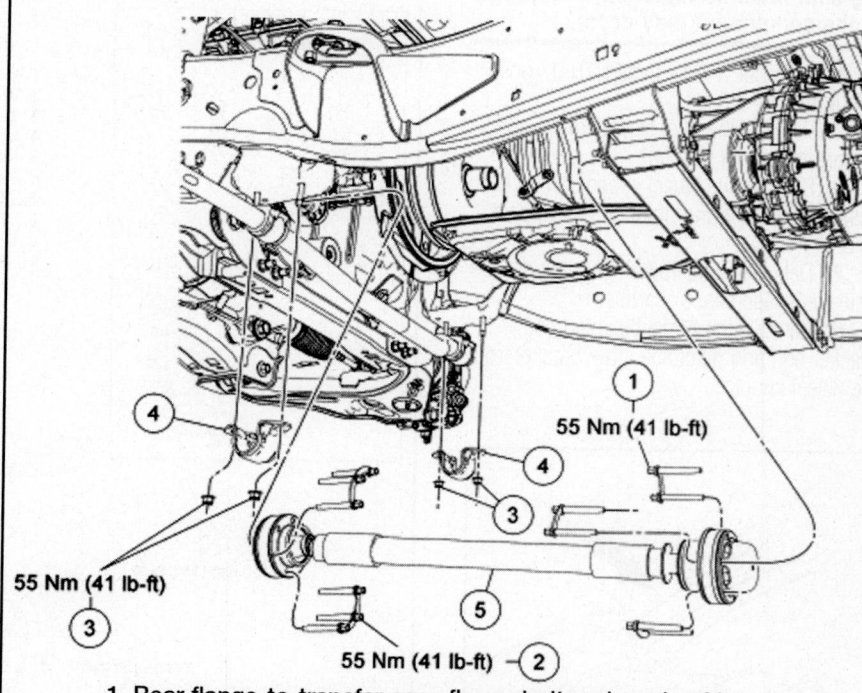

55 Nm (41 lb-ft)

55 Nm (41 lb-ft)

55 Nm (41 lb-ft)

1. Rear flange-to-transfer case flange bolt and washer kits
2. Front flange-to-pinion flange bolt and washer kits
3. Stabilizer bar bracket nuts (4 required)
4. Stabilizer bar brackets (2 required)
5. Driveshaft

Fig. 17 Removing the front driveshaft

2. Index-mark the front flange to the pinion flange.

3. Index-mark the rear flange to the transfer case flange.

4. Remove and discard the 6 rear flange-to-transfer case flange bolts and 3 washers.

5. Remove and discard the 6 front flange-to-pinion flange bolts and 2 washers.

6. Remove and discard the 4 stabilizer bar bracket nuts and allow the stabilizer bar to swing downward.

7. Remove the front driveshaft from the vehicle.

To install:

8. Install the stabilizer bar and install 4 new bracket nuts. Tighten to 41 ft. lbs. (55 Nm).

9. Install the driveshaft and install new front and rear flange bolts and washers. Tighten to 41 ft. lbs. (55 Nm).

FRONT HALFSHAFT

REMOVAL & INSTALLATION

See Figures 18 through 20.

✳✳ CAUTION

Whenever a halfshaft is removed, a new circlip and stub shaft pilot bearing seal must be installed or damage to the component may occur.

1. With the vehicle in NEUTRAL, position it on a hoist.

2. Remove the dust cap. Remove and discard the wheel hub nut.

3. Remove the wheel speed sensor harness bracket bolt and position the harness aside.

4. Detach the flexible hose retainer from the speed sensor harness.

5. Remove the brake flexible hose bracket bolt and disconnect the bracket from the wheel knuckle.

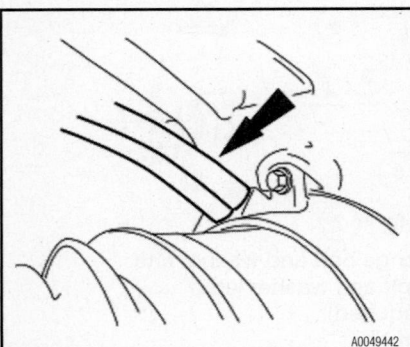

Fig. 18 Remove the vacuum/vent tube at the vacuum/vent port of the Integrated Wheel End (IWE) disconnect.

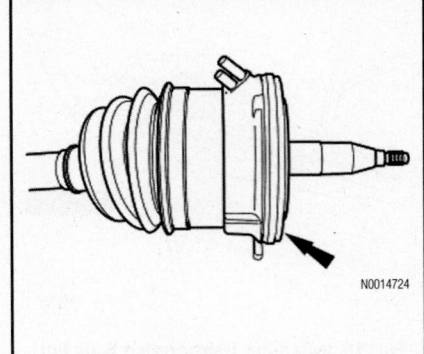

Fig. 19 Remove the IWE disconnect from the outboard CV joint housing.

6. Remove the vacuum/vent tube at the vacuum/vent port of the Integrated Wheel End (IWE) disconnect.

7. Remove the 3 IWE bolts.

8. Remove and discard the tie-rod end nut.

9. Disconnect the tie-rod end from the wheel knuckle.

10. Remove and discard the upper ball joint nut.

11. Disconnect the upper ball joint from the wheel knuckle.

12. Use care to not damage the hub seal.

➡**Allow the steering knuckle to swing outboard while keeping the CV shaft pushed inboard.**

13. Once clearance is available, remove the CV shaft joint outboard end and IWE disconnect from the steering knuckle hub bearing.

14. Remove the IWE disconnect from the outboard CV joint housing.

15. Using the Halfshaft Remover and Slide Hammer, remove the halfshaft from the differential and the intermediate shaft.

16. Remove and discard the circlip and the stub shaft seal.

To install:

✳✳ CAUTION

Verify the spline engagement by checking for spline lash before installing the halfshaft nut or component damage may occur.

17. Install a new stub shaft seal and circlip.

18. Ensure the IWE disconnect is properly attached to the outboard CV joint housing.

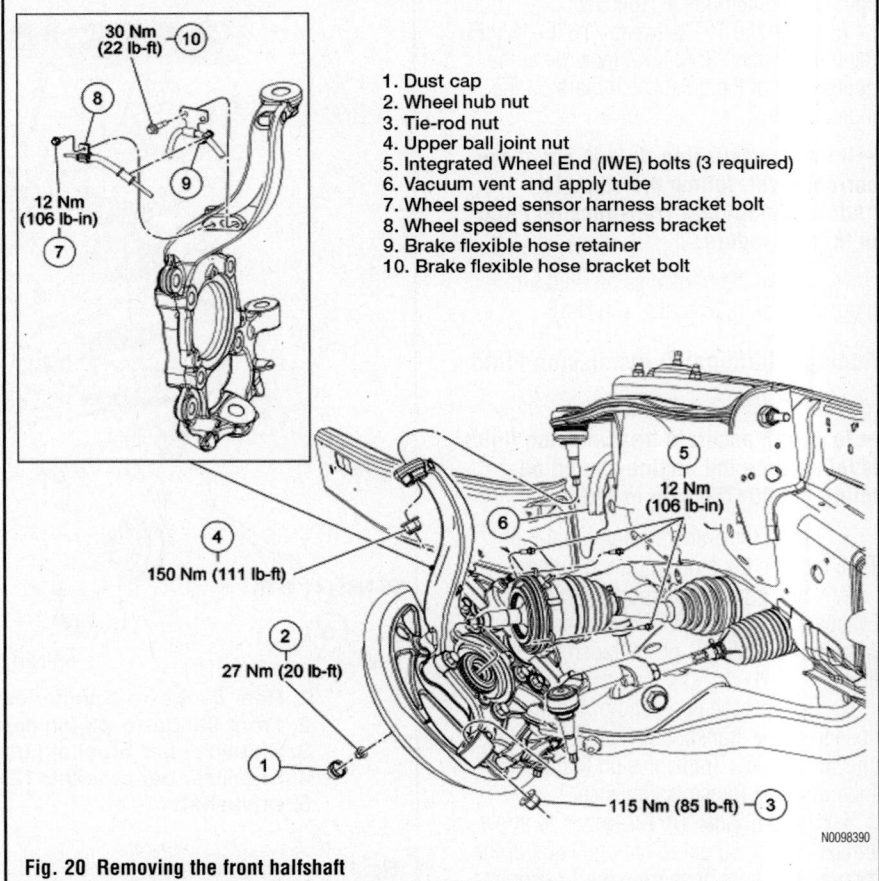

1. Dust cap
2. Wheel hub nut
3. Tie-rod nut
4. Upper ball joint nut
5. Integrated Wheel End (IWE) bolts (3 required)
6. Vacuum vent and apply tube
7. Wheel speed sensor harness bracket bolt
8. Wheel speed sensor harness bracket
9. Brake flexible hose retainer
10. Brake flexible hose bracket bolt

Fig. 20 Removing the front halfshaft

19. Position the halfshaft to the differential and intermediate shaft.

20. Install the upper ball joint to the wheel knuckle. Tighten the new nut to 111 ft. lbs. (150 Nm).

21. Connect the tie-rod end to the wheel knuckle. Tighten the new nut to 85 ft. lbs. (115 Nm).

22. Install the 3 IWE bolts. Tighten to 106 inch lbs. (12 Nm).

23. Connect the vacuum/vent tube at the vacuum/vent port of the Integrated Wheel End (IWE) disconnect.

24. Install the brake flexible hose bracket bolt and connect the bracket to the wheel knuckle. Tighten to 22 ft. lbs. (30 Nm).

25. Install the wheel speed sensor harness bracket bolt. Tighten to 106 inch lbs. (12 Nm).

26. Install a new wheel hub nut. Tighten the new nut to 20 ft. lbs. (27 Nm).

27. Install the wheel hub dust cap.

FRONT PINION SEAL

REMOVAL & INSTALLATION
See Figures 21 through 25.

❋❋ CAUTION

The color on the rear face of the drive pinion nut is critical to this repair. Use the same color new drive pinion nut for installation as the original. If a new collapsible spacer must be installed for pinion bearing preload reduction, install the nut supplied with the new spacer or damage to the component may occur.

➡ **This operation disturbs the pinion bearing preload. Carefully reset the pinion bearing preload during assembly.**

1. With the vehicle in NEUTRAL, position it on a hoist.

2. Remove the front brake pads. See "BRAKES" section.

3. Remove the front driveshaft. See "Front Driveshaft" in this section.

4. Measure and record the pinion bearing preload:

   a. Using an inch-lb. (Nm) torque wrench, rotate the pinion gear. Measure the torque required to maintain pinion gear rotation.

5. Index-mark the pinion flange and the drive pinion gear.

6. Install a new pinion nut with the same color as the original if not replacing the collapsible spacer. If a new collapsible spacer is installed, install the nut in the kit or damage to the component may occur.

7. Using the Drive Pinion Flange Holding Fixture to hold the pinion flange, remove and discard the pinion nut and washer.

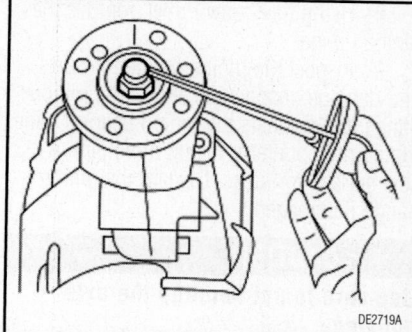

Fig. 22 Using an inch-lb. (Nm) torque wrench, rotate the pinion gear. Measure the torque required to maintain pinion gear rotation.

Fig. 23 Using the Drive Pinion Flange Holding Fixture to hold the pinion flange, remove and discard the pinion nut and washer.

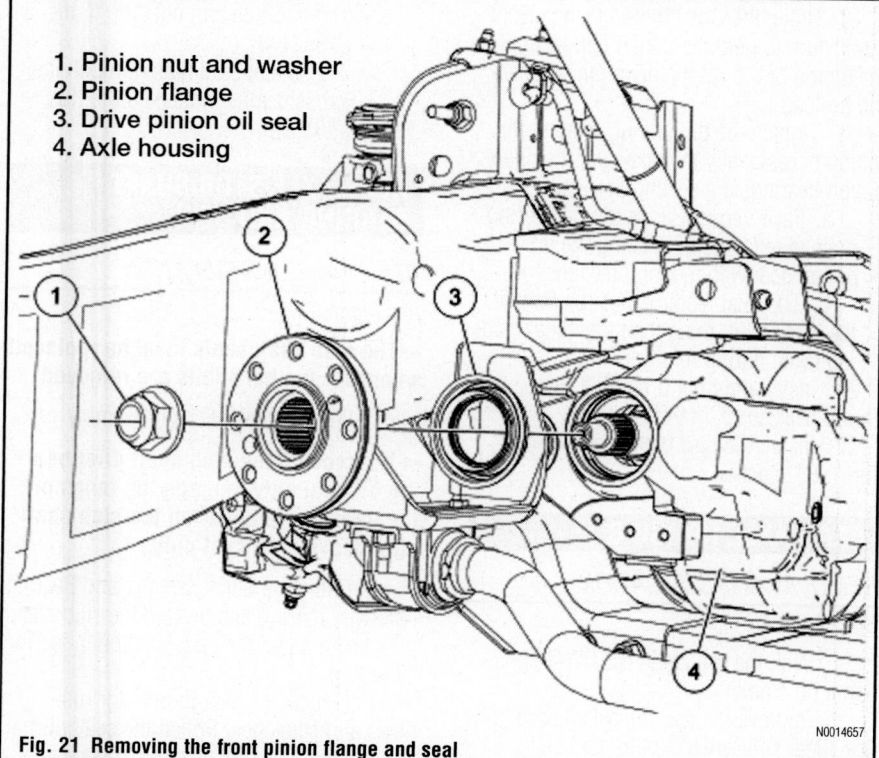

1. Pinion nut and washer
2. Pinion flange
3. Drive pinion oil seal
4. Axle housing

Fig. 21 Removing the front pinion flange and seal

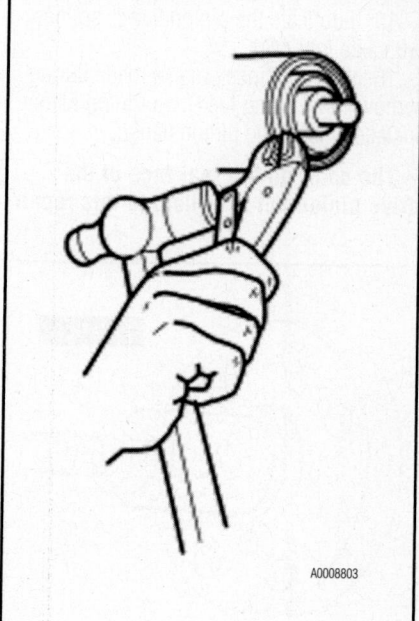

Fig. 24 Force up on the metal flange of the drive pinion seal. Install gripping pliers and strike with a hammer to remove the drive pinion seal.

8. Using the 2 Jaw Puller, remove the pinion flange.

9. Inspect the pinion flange for burrs and damage. Inspect the end of the pinion flange that contacts the pinion bearing cone, pinion nut counterbore and drive pinion seal surface for nicks. Discard the pinion flange if damaged.

✳✳ CAUTION

Use care to not damage the axle housing.

10. Force up on the metal flange of the drive pinion seal. Install gripping pliers and strike with a hammer to remove the drive pinion seal.

11. Verify the splines on the drive pinion gear are free of burrs. If burrs are evident, remove them with a fine crocus cloth.

12. Clean the drive pinion seal bore.

To install:

13. Lubricate the drive pinion seal lips with axle lubricant.

➡**Drive pinion seal must be fully seated all the way around or drive pinion seal damage will occur.**

14. Using a proper Drive Pinion Oil Seal Installer, install the drive pinion seal.

✳✳ CAUTION

Never use a hammer or install the pinion flange with power tools.

15. Lubricate the pinion flange splines with axle lubricant.

16. Align the index marks made during removal and, using the Drive Pinion Flange Installer, install the pinion flange.

➡**The color on the rear face of the drive pinion nut is critical to this repair.**

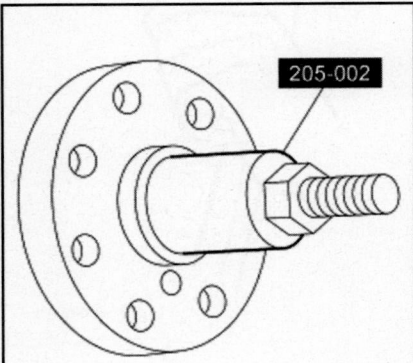

205-002

N0015176

Fig. 25 Align the index marks made during removal and, using the Drive Pinion Flange Installer, install the pinion flange.

Use the same color new drive pinion nut for installation as the original. If a new collapsible spacer must be installed for pinion bearing preload reduction, install the nut supplied with the new spacer or damage to the component may occur.

17. Select the correct 8.8 in. drive pinion nut for installation.

➡**A variety of nut applications is available. Consult your parts supplier for the proper nut.**

✳✳ CAUTION

Install a new pinion nut with the same color as the original if not replacing the collapsible spacer or damage to the component may occur.

18. Install the new washer and pinion nut. Only hand-tighten the pinion nut at this time.

✳✳ CAUTION

Do not loosen the pinion nut to reduce drive pinion bearing preload. Install a new drive pinion collapsible spacer and pinion nut if drive pinion bearing preload reduction is necessary. If a new collapsible spacer must be installed for pinion bearing preload reduction, install the nut supplied with the new spacer or damage to the component may occur.

19. Using the Drive Pinion Flange Holding Fixture to hold the pinion flange, tighten the pinion nut to set the drive pinion bearing preload.

20. Tighten the pinion nut, rotating the pinion occasionally to make sure the drive pinion bearings are seating correctly:

 a. Take frequent drive pinion bearing preload readings by rotating the drive pinion gear with the torque wrench.

 b. The final reading must be 5 inch lbs. (0.56 Nm) more than the initial reading taken during removal.

21. Install the front driveshaft. See "Front Driveshaft" in this section.

22. Install the disc brake pads. See "BRAKES" section.

REAR AXLE HOUSING

REMOVAL & INSTALLATION
See Figure 26.

1. With the vehicle in NEUTRAL, position it on a hoist.

2. Remove the rear driveshaft assembly. See "Rear Driveshaft" in this section.

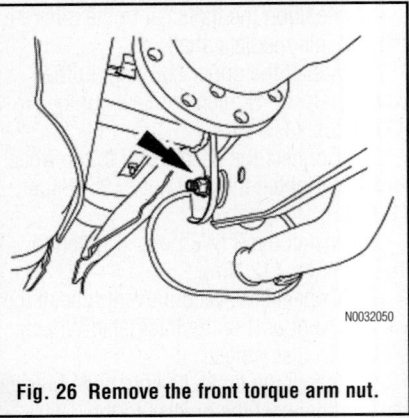

N0032050

Fig. 26 Remove the front torque arm nut.

3. Remove the halfshafts. See "Rear Halfshafts" in this section.

4. Remove the rear stabilizer bar. See "SUSPENSION" section.

5. Using a suitable jack, support the axle housing.

6. Remove the 2 insulator stud nuts, accessible through the crossmember holes.

7. Remove the front torque arm nut.

➡**Move the axle housing forward to clear the rear mounting studs from the bushings.**

8. Lower the axle housing from the vehicle.

To install:

9. To install, reverse the removal procedure.

10. Tighten the fasteners as follows:
 • Front torque arm nut: 100 ft. lbs. (135 Nm)
 • 2 insulator stud nuts (through the crossmember holes): 100 ft. lbs. (135 Nm)

REAR AXLE STUB SHAFT BEARING AND SEAL

REMOVAL & INSTALLATION
See Figure 27.

➡**The stub shaft seals must be replaced whenever the halfshafts are removed.**

1. Remove the halfshaft assembly.

➡**If removing the stub shaft pilot bearing oil seal only, engage the tangs of the Bearing Remover on the stub shaft pilot bearing oil seal only.**

2. Using the Slide Hammer and Bearing Remover, remove and discard the stub shaft pilot bearing and the stub shaft pilot bearing oil seal.

3. Inspect the seal journal for rust, nicks and scratches. Polish the seal journal surface with fine crocus cloth, if necessary.

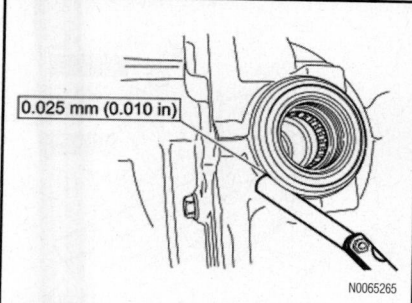

Fig. 27 Make sure the stub shaft oil seal is correctly seated in the differential housing.

To install:

4. Lubricate the new stub shaft pilot bearing with axle lubricant.

➡Installation of the stub shaft pilot bearing or stub shaft oil seal without the correct tools can result in early bearing or seal failure. If the stub shaft pilot bearing becomes cocked in the bore during installation, remove it and install a new one.

5. Place the stub shaft pilot bearing onto the Halfshaft Pilot Bearing Installer and Adapter.

6. Install the stub shaft pilot bearing into the rear axle housing bore.

➡Do not disassemble the new oil seal.

➡Use a tool like the Lisle LIS17850 to avoid interference with the suspension components.

7. Install the new seal onto a suitable installer.

✳✳ CAUTION

Strike only the handle. Directly striking the installer tool will damage the seal.

8. Carefully align the stub shaft pilot bearing seal with the housing bore and install the stub shaft pilot bearing seal flush in the differential housing.

➡If a feeler gauge of the specification shown in the illustration can be inserted between the stub shaft oil seal and the differential housing, the stub shaft seal is not seated correctly. Remove the stub shaft oil seal and install a new stub shaft oil seal.

9. Make sure the stub shaft oil seal is correctly seated in the differential housing.

➡Inspect the stub shaft seal journal for rust, nicks or scratches prior to installing the halfshaft. Polish the seal journal with fine crocus cloth, if required.

10. Install the halfshaft.

REAR DRIVESHAFT

REMOVAL & INSTALLATION
See Figure 28.

1. With the vehicle in NEUTRAL, position it on a hoist.
2. For 4-Wheel Drive (4WD) vehicles, perform the following:
    a. Index-mark the driveshaft flange to the pinion flange.
    b. Index-mark the driveshaft slip yoke to the transfer case housing.
    c. Remove and discard the 4 driveshaft flange bolts.

✳✳ CAUTION

The driveshaft flange fits tightly on the pinion flange pilot. Never hammer on the driveshaft or any of its components to disconnect the driveshaft from the pinion flange. Pry only in the area shown, with a suitable tool, to disconnect the driveshaft flange from the pinion flange or damage to the component may occur.

    d. Using a suitable prybar tool, disconnect the driveshaft flange from the pinion flange.
    NOTE: Align the original index-marks at the transfer case. Do not rotate the driveshaft when removing the slip yoke from the transfer case output shaft.
    e. Remove the driveshaft.
    f. Mark the transfer case output shaft to the transfer case housing after removing the driveshaft.
3. For Rear Wheel Drive (RWD) vehicles, perform the following:
    a. Index-mark the driveshaft flanges for correct alignment during installation.
    b. Remove and discard the 4 driveshaft front flange bolts.
    c. Remove and discard the 4 driveshaft rear flange bolts.

✳✳ CAUTION

The driveshaft flange fits tightly on the pinion flange pilot. Never hammer on the driveshaft or any of its components to disconnect the driveshaft from the pinion flange. Pry only in the area shown, with a suitable tool, to disconnect the driveshaft flange from the pinion flange or damage to the component may occur.

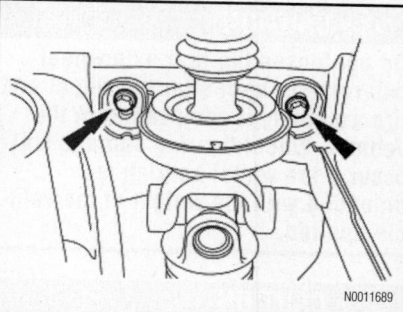

Fig. 28 Remove and discard the 2 driveshaft center bearing bolts, then remove the driveshaft.

    d. Using a suitable prybar tool, disconnect the driveshaft flange from the pinion flange.
    e. Remove and discard the 2 driveshaft center bearing bolts, then remove the driveshaft.

To install:

4. For 4WD vehicles, perform the following:
    a. Align all the index marks and install the driveshaft slip yoke into the transfer case housing.
    b. Align the index marks and install the driveshaft flange and the 4 driveshaft flange bolts. Tighten to 76 ft. lbs. (103 Nm).
5. For RWD vehicles, perform the following:

➡If new driveshaft center bearing bolts are not available, coat the threads of the original driveshaft center bearing bolts with threadlock sealer.

    a. Position the driveshaft center bearing and hand-tighten the 2 new center support bearing bracket bolts until the driveshaft is mounted to the flanges. Tighten to 35 ft. lbs. (48 Nm).
    b. Install the 4 new driveshaft front and then 4 rear flange bolts. Tighten the bolts to 76 ft. lbs. (103 Nm).

REAR HALFSHAFT

REMOVAL & INSTALLATION
See Figures 29 and 30.

➡This procedure applies to both rear halfshaft assemblies.

➡Always install a new differential stub shaft seal whenever a rear halfshaft is removed.

✷✷ CAUTION

Do not loosen the rear axle wheel hub retainer until after the wheel and tire assembly is removed from the vehicle. Wheel bearing damage will occur if the wheel bearing is unloaded with the weight of the vehicle applied.

✷✷ CAUTION

Suspension fasteners are critical parts because they affect performance of vital components and systems and their failure may result in major service expense. New parts must be installed with the same part numbers or equivalent part, if replacement is necessary. Do not use a replacement part of lesser quality or substitute design. Torque values must be used as specified during reassembly to make sure of correct retention of these parts.

1. With the vehicle in NEUTRAL, position it on a hoist.
2. Remove the wheel and tire.
3. Have an assistant press the brake pedal to keep the axle from rotating.

4. Remove and discard the wheel hub nut and the washer.
5. Separate the halfshaft from the knuckle.
6. Remove the brake disc. See "BRAKES" section.
7. Remove and discard the upper trailing arm-to-wheel knuckle bolt.
8. Remove and discard the upper arm-to-wheel knuckle nut.
9. Using the Ball Joint Separator, separate the upper arm from the wheel knuckle.
10. Remove and discard the stabilizer bar link nut.
11. Remove and discard the toe link-to-wheel knuckle bolt.
12. Disconnect the anti-lock brake sensor at the connector and open the wire retaining clips.
13. Compress the spring, depress the retaining tabs and detach the parking brake cable from the wheel knuckle.
14. Remove and discard the 2 lower trailing arm-to-wheel knuckle bolts.
15. Rotate the top of the knuckle assembly outboard and remove the halfshaft from the knuckle.
16. Using the Halfshaft Remover and Adapter (Handle), disengage the inboard CV joint housing from the differential side gear.

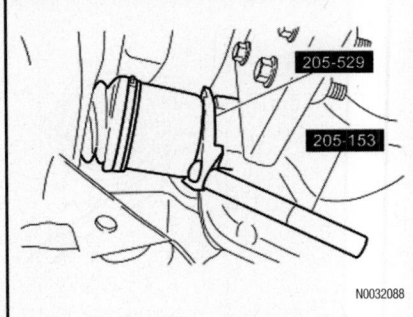

Fig. 30 Using the Halfshaft Remover and Adapter (Handle), disengage the inboard CV joint housing from the differential side gear.

17. Remove the halfshaft assembly from the vehicle.
18. Remove and discard the halfshaft retainer circlip.

To install:
19. To install, reverse the removal procedure.
20. Always install the halfshaft with a new retainer circlip and a new wheel hub nut.
21. Install a new differential stub shaft seal.
22. Tighten the fasteners as follows:
- 2 lower trailing arm-to-wheel knuckle bolts: 76 ft. lbs. (103 Nm)
- Toe link-to-wheel knuckle bolt: 166 ft. lbs. (225 Nm)
- Stabilizer bar link new nut: 46 ft. lbs. (63 Nm)
- Upper arm-to-wheel knuckle new nut: 76 ft. lbs. (103 Nm)
- upper trailing arm-to-wheel knuckle new bolt: 184 ft. lbs. (250 Nm)
- Wheel hub new nut and the washer: 184 ft. lbs. (250 Nm)

REAR PINION SEAL

REMOVAL & INSTALLATION

See Figure 31.

✷✷ CAUTION

This operation disturbs the pinion bearing preload. Carefully reset the pinion bearing preload during installation or damage to the component may occur.

➡Remove the rear wheel and tire assemblies, brake calipers and brake discs to prevent brake drag during the drive pinion bearing preload adjustment.

1. Remove the rear brake discs. See "BRAKES" section.
2. Remove the rear driveshaft assembly, as detailed in this section.

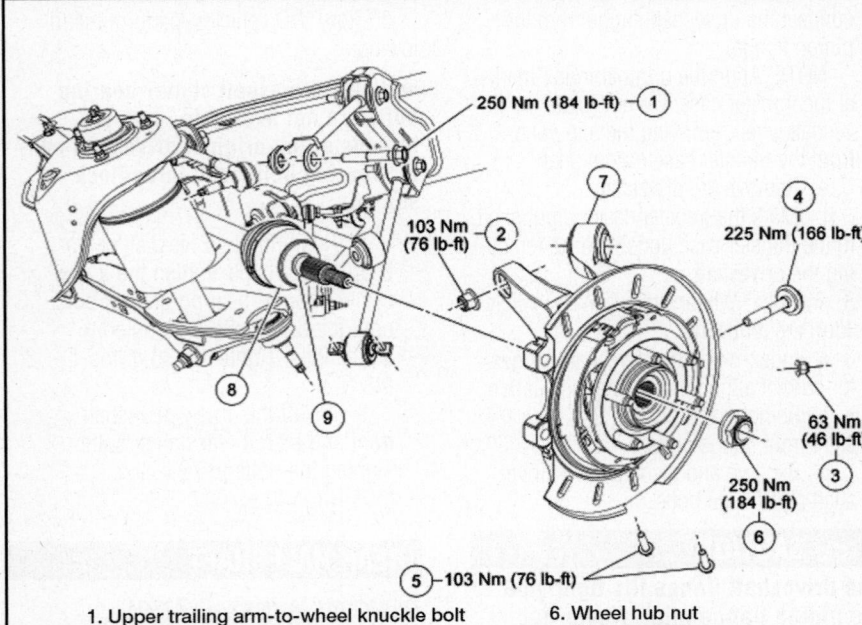

250 Nm (184 lb-ft) — ①
103 Nm (76 lb-ft) — ②
225 Nm (166 lb-ft) — ④
63 Nm (46 lb-ft) — ③
250 Nm (184 lb-ft) — ⑥
⑤—103 Nm (76 lb-ft)

1. Upper trailing arm-to-wheel knuckle bolt
2. Upper arm-to-wheel knuckle nut
3. Stabilizer bar link nut
4. Toe link-to-wheel knuckle bolt
5. Lower trailing arm-to-wheel knuckle bolts (2 required)
6. Wheel hub nut
7. Wheel knuckle
8. Rear halfshaft
9. Washer

Fig. 29 Exploded view of the rear halfshaft components

3. Install a proper torque wrench on the nut and record the torque necessary to maintain rotation of the drive pinion gear through several revolutions.

❄❄ CAUTION

Install a new pinion nut with the same color as the original if not replacing the collapsible spacer. If a new collapsible spacer is installed, install the nut in the kit or damage to the component may occur.

4. Using the Drive Pinion Flange Holding Fixture to hold the pinion flange, remove the pinion nut. Discard the nut.

5. Index-mark the drive pinion flange and the drive pinion gear stem to maintain initial balance during installation.

6. Using the 2 Jaw Puller, remove the drive pinion flange.

7. Force up on the metal flange of the drive pinion seal. Install gripping pliers and strike with a hammer until the pinion seal is removed.

To install:

8. Lubricate the lips of the new drive pinion seal with grease.

➡**If the drive pinion seal becomes misaligned during installation, remove it and install a new seal.**

9. Using a proper Drive Pinion Oil Seal Installer, install the drive pinion seal.

10. Lubricate the drive pinion flange splines, with rear axle lubricant.

➡**Disregard the index marks if installing a new drive pinion flange.**

11. Position the drive pinion flange.

12. Using a proper Drive Pinion Flange Installer, install the drive pinion flange.

➡**The color on the rear face of the drive pinion nut is critical to this repair. Use the same color new drive pinion nut for installation as the original. If a new collapsible spacer must be installed for pinion bearing preload reduction, install the nut supplied with the new spacer or damage to the component may occur.**

13. Select the correct drive pinion nut for installation.

14. Position the new drive pinion nut.

❄❄ CAUTION

Do not under any circumstance loosen the nut to reduce preload. If it is necessary to reduce preload, install a new drive pinion collapsible spacer. If a new collapsible spacer must be installed for pinion bearing preload reduction, install the nut supplied with the new spacer or damage to the component may occur.

➡**Remove the Drive Pinion Flange Holding Fixture while taking preload readings with the torque wrench.**

15. Using the Drive Pinion Flange Holding Fixture to hold the pinion flange, tighten the nut.

16. Rotate the pinion occasionally to make sure the pinion bearings seat correctly.

   a. Take frequent pinion bearing torque preload readings by rotating the drive pinion gear with a Nm (lb-in) torque wrench.

   b. If the preload recorded prior to disassembly is lower than the specification

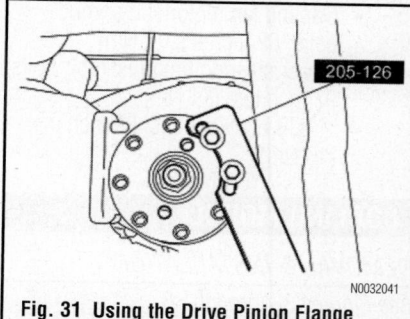

Fig. 31 Using the Drive Pinion Flange Holding Fixture to hold the pinion flange, remove the pinion nut.

for used bearings, tighten the nut to specification.

   c. If the preload recorded prior to disassembly is higher than the specification for used bearings, tighten the nut to the original reading as recorded.

   d. Refer to the torque specification for Rotational Torque Ranges:

- Minimum breakaway torque (Traction-Lok®): 20 ft. lbs. (27 Nm)
- Pinion bearing preload: 16–29 inch lbs. (1.8–3.3 Nm)

❄❄ CAUTION

The driveshaft flange yoke fits tightly on the pinion flange pilot. To make sure that the yoke seats squarely on the flange, tighten the bolts evenly in a cross pattern as shown or damage to the component may occur.

17. Align the index marks.

18. Install the rear driveshaft. See procedure in this section.

19. Install the rear brake discs. See "BRAKES" section.

20. Install the rear wheel and tire.

ENGINE COOLING

COOLING FAN MOTOR & SHROUD

REMOVAL & INSTALLATION

1. Disconnect the battery ground cable.

2. Remove the upper air deflector 12 upper air deflector pushpins and remove the deflector.

3. Release the 2 tabs and open the Battery Junction Box (BJB) cover. Remove the battery power cable nut and disconnect the battery power cable terminal.

4. Remove the air cleaner outlet tube.

5. Detach the power steering fluid cooler hose retainer from the cooling fan motor and shroud.

6. Detach the wiring harness retainer from the power steering fluid reservoir stud bolt.

7. Detach the wiring harness retainer from the LH side of the cooling fan motor and shroud.

8. Detach the wiring harness retainer from the top RH side of the radiator.

9. Detach the electrical connector retainer and the wiring harness retainer from the top RH side of the cooling fan motor and shroud.

10. Detach the 3 wiring harness retainers from the RH side of the cooling fan motor and shroud.

11. Detach the upper radiator hose retainer from the cooling fan motor and shroud.

12. Disconnect the 2 cooling fan electrical connectors.

13. Detach the 3 cooling fan wiring harness retainers.

14. Remove the 4 BJB bracket bolts.

15. Remove the power steering fluid reservoir stud bolt and position the power steering fluid reservoir and the wiring harness aside.

16. Remove the 2 bolts and the cooling fan motor and shroud.

To install:

17. To install, reverse the removal procedure.

18. Tighten the fasteners as follows:

- Cooling fan motor and shroud bolts: 62 inch lbs. (7 Nm)
- Power steering fluid reservoir bolts: 97 inch lbs. (11 Nm)
- 4 BJB bracket bolts: 89 inch lbs. (10 Nm)

COOLING MODULE

REMOVAL & INSTALLATION

See Figures 32 through 38.

1. With the vehicle in NEUTRAL, position it on a hoist.
2. Drain the engine cooling system.
3. Recover the A/C system refrigerant.
4. Disconnect the battery ground cable.

5. Remove the RH and LH headlamp assemblies.
6. Remove the front bumper cover as follows:

   a. Remove the 3 lower air deflector pin-type retainers. Position the air deflector aside.

   b. Remove the 2 front bumper cover lower pin-type retainers.

   c. Remove the 4 LH and RH front fender splash shield screws.

   d. Remove the 4 LH and RH front bumper cover-to-fender bolts.

   e. If equipped, disconnect the fog lamp electrical connector. If equipped, disconnect the park aid sensor electrical connector.

   f. Remove the upper air deflector.

   g. Remove the 10 pin-type retainers.

   h. Remove the 2 upper pin-type retainers for the lower air deflector.

   i. Remove the 4 grille-to-radiator support bolts. Remove the front bumper cover.

7. Release the 2 clamps and disconnect the 2 power steering fluid cooler hoses from the condenser core.

8. Release the 2 tabs and open the Battery Junction Box (BJB) cover. Remove the battery power cable nut and disconnect the battery power cable terminal.

9. Release the clamp and disconnect the upper radiator hose from the radiator. Detach the radiator hose retainer from the cooling fan motor and shroud.

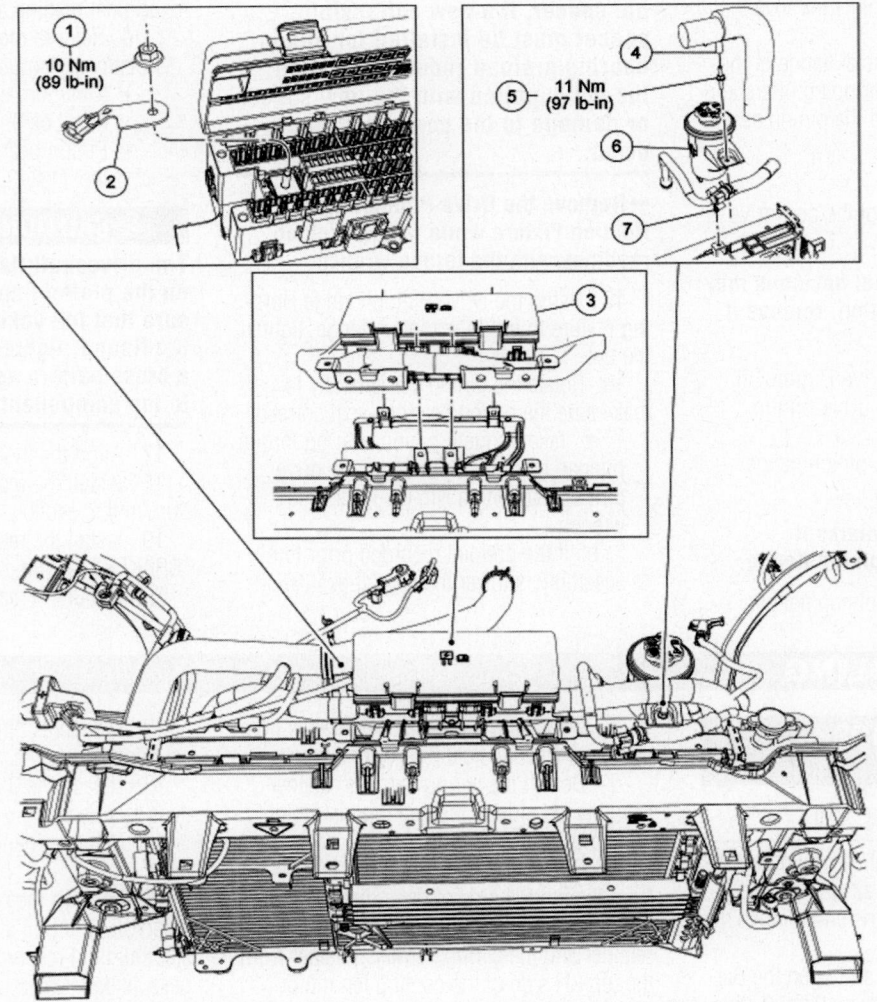

1. Battery power cable nut
2. Battery power cable terminal
3. Battery Junction Box (BJB)
4. Wiring harness retainer
5. Power steering fluid reservoir stud bolt
6. Power steering fluid reservoir
7. Power steering fluid cooler hose retainer

N0103491

Fig. 32 Component removal for cooling module (1 of 7)

10. Detach the wiring harness retainer from the top RH side of the radiator.

11. Detach the electrical connector retainer and the wiring harness retainer from the top RH side of the cooling fan motor and shroud.

12. Detach the 3 wiring harness retainers from the RH side of the cooling fan motor and shroud.

13. Detach the power steering fluid cooler hose from the LH side of the cooling fan motor and shroud.

14. Detach the wiring harness retainer from the power steering fluid reservoir stud bolt.

15. Detach the wiring harness retainer from the LH side of the cooling fan motor and shroud.

16. Remove the power steering fluid cooler stud bolt.

17. Disconnect the 2 cooling fan electrical connectors and detach the 3 cooling fan wiring retainers from the cooling fan motor and shroud.

18. Release the 4 BJB retaining tabs and detach the BJB from the bracket. Position the BJB , the wiring harness and the power steering fluid reservoir aside.

19. Remove the spring clip and disconnect the lower radiator hose from the radiator.

20. Remove the 2 hood latch assembly bolts.

21. Disconnect the 2 cable position retainers and position the hood latch assembly aside.

22. Remove the pushpin and move the air deflector aside.

23. Remove the 2 transmission cooler tube secondary latches.

24. Using the Transmission Cooler Line Disconnect Tool, disconnect the transmission fluid cooler tubes from the transmission fluid cooler hoses.

25. Remove the condenser inlet fitting bolt, the condenser outlet fitting nut and disconnect the 2 fittings. Discard the O-ring and gasket seals.

26. Disconnect the horn assembly electrical connector.

27. Disconnect the ambient temperature sensor electrical connector.

28. Remove the 6 cooling module bolts

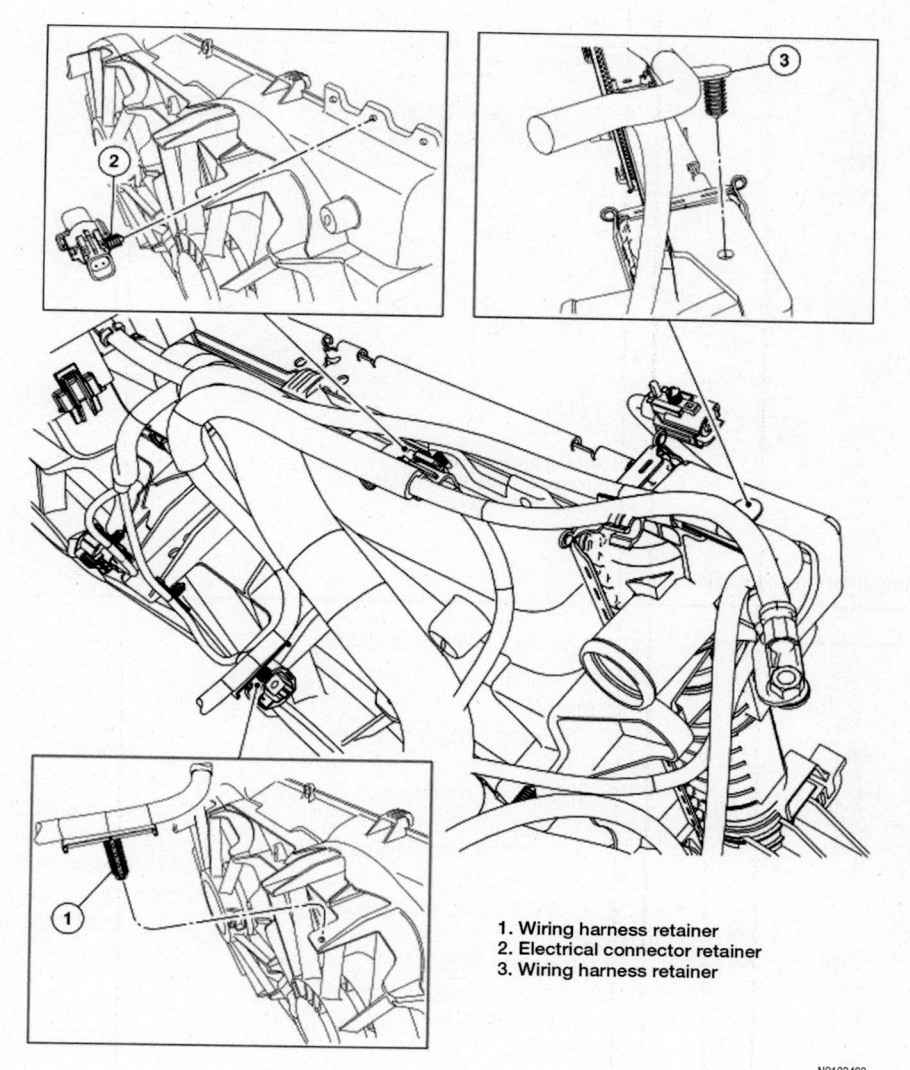

1. Wiring harness retainer
2. Electrical connector retainer
3. Wiring harness retainer

N0103493

Fig. 33 Component removal for cooling module (2 of 7)

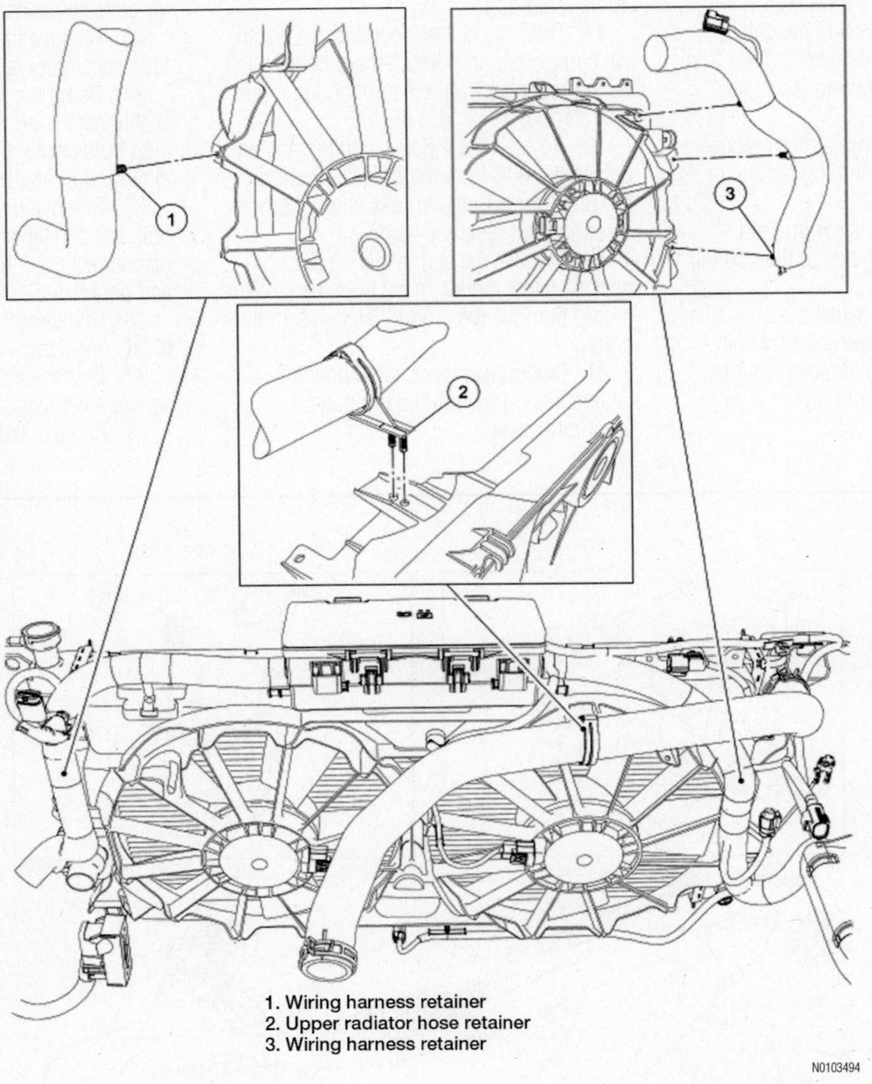

1. Wiring harness retainer
2. Upper radiator hose retainer
3. Wiring harness retainer

N0103494

Fig. 34 Component removal for cooling module (3 of 7)

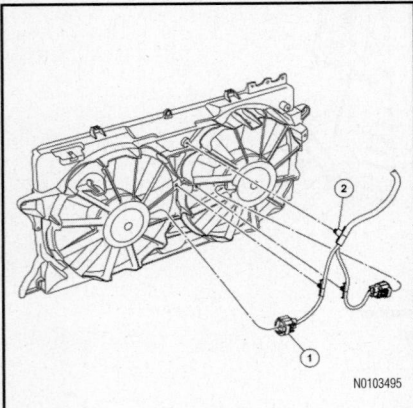

N0103495

Fig. 35 Component removal for cooling module (4 of 7)–showing cooling fan connector (1) and wiring retainer (2)

and remove the cooling module from the vehicle.

To install:

29. Position the cooling module in the vehicle.

30. Install the 6 cooling module bolts. Tighten to 18 ft. lbs. (25 Nm).

31. Connect the ambient temperature sensor electrical connector.

32. Connect the horn assembly electrical connector.

33. Using new O-ring seals and gaskets, connect the A/C condenser outlet and inlet fittings and install the nut and bolt. Tighten to 133 inch lbs. (15 Nm).

34. Connect the transmission fluid cooler tubes and install the 2 secondary latches.

35. Position the air deflector and install the pushpin.

36. Position the hood latch assembly and install the 2 hood latch assembly bolts. Tighten to 18 ft. lbs. (25 Nm).

37. Connect the 2 hood latch cable position retainers.

38. Connect the lower radiator hose to the radiator and install the spring clip.

39. Position the wiring harness, the BJB and the power steering fluid reservoir. Attach the BJB to the bracket.

40. Install the power steering fluid reservoir stud bolt. Tighten to 97 inch lbs. (11 Nm).

41. Attach the wiring harness retainer to the power steering fluid reservoir stud bolt.

42. Attach the power steering fluid cooler hose to the LH side of the cooling fan motor and shroud.

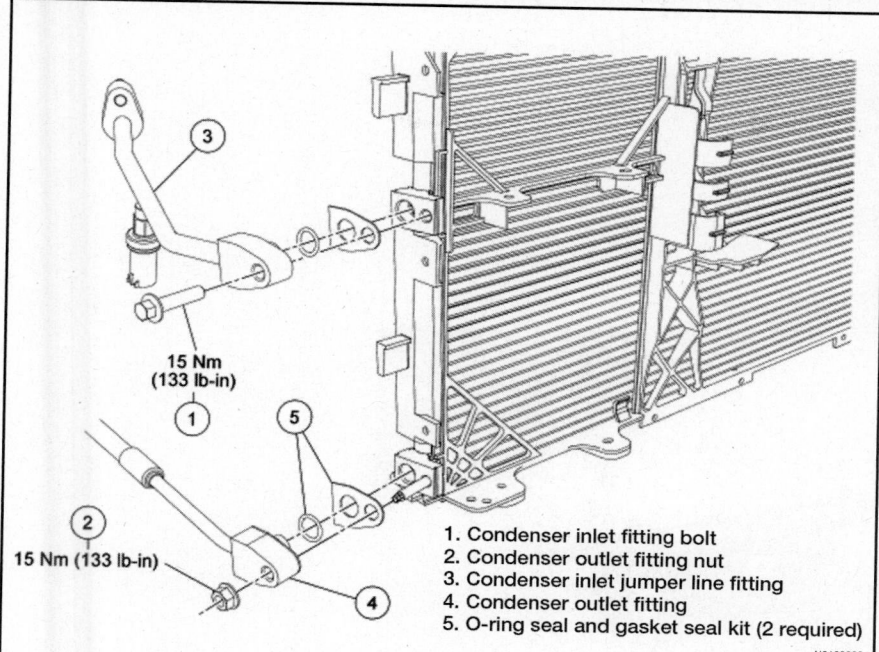

1. Condenser inlet fitting bolt
2. Condenser outlet fitting nut
3. Condenser inlet jumper line fitting
4. Condenser outlet fitting
5. O-ring seal and gasket seal kit (2 required)

15 Nm (133 lb-in)

15 Nm (133 lb-in)

N0103099

Fig. 36 Component removal for cooling module (5 of 7)

43. Attach the wiring harness retainer to the LH side of the cooling fan motor and shroud.

44. Attach the 3 cooling fan wiring harness retainers to the cooling fan and connect the 2 cooling fan electrical connectors.

45. Attach the 3 wiring harness retainers to the RH side of the cooling fan motor and shroud.

46. Attach the wiring harness retainer and the electrical connector retainer to the top RH side of the cooling fan motor and shroud.

47. Attach the wiring harness retainer to the top RH side of the radiator.

48. Connect the upper radiator hose to the radiator and position the clamp. Attach the upper radiator hose retainer to the cooling fan motor and shroud.

49. Connect the battery power cable terminal and install the nut. Close the BJB cover. Tighten to 89 inch lbs. (10 Nm).

50. Connect the 2 power steering fluid cooler hoses to the condenser core and position the clamps.

51. Install the front bumper cover and the RH and LH headlamp assemblies.

52. Connect the battery ground cable.

53. Fill and bleed the engine cooling system, as described in this section.

54. Fill and bleed the power steering system.

55. Fill the transmission with fluid and verify correct operation.

56. Evacuate, leak test and charge the refrigerant system.

ENGINE COOLANT

DRAIN, REFILL & BLEEDING PROCEDURE

✺✺ WARNING

Always allow the engine to cool before opening the cooling system. Do not unscrew the coolant pressure relief cap when the engine is operating or the cooling system is hot. The cooling system is under pressure; steam and hot liquid can come out forcefully when the cap is loosened slightly. Failure to follow these instructions may result in serious personal injury.

✺✺ CAUTION

The coolant must be recovered in a suitable, clean container for reuse. If the coolant is contaminated it must be recycled or disposed of correctly. Failure to follow these instructions may result in engine or cooling system damage.

✺✺ CAUTION

Vehicle cooling systems are filled with Motorcraft® Premium Gold Engine Coolant. Always fill the cooling system with the same type of coolant that is present in the system. Do not mix coolant types. Failure to follow these instructions may result in engine or cooling system damage.

➡Less than 80% of the coolant capacity can be recovered with the engine in the vehicle. Dirty, rusty or contaminated coolant requires replacement.

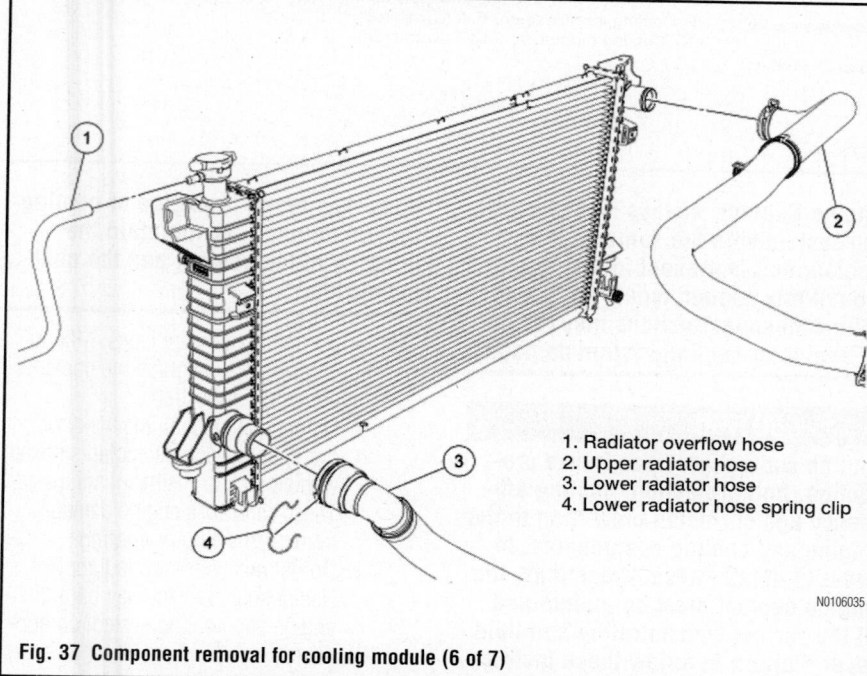

1. Radiator overflow hose
2. Upper radiator hose
3. Lower radiator hose
4. Lower radiator hose spring clip

N0106035

Fig. 37 Component removal for cooling module (6 of 7)

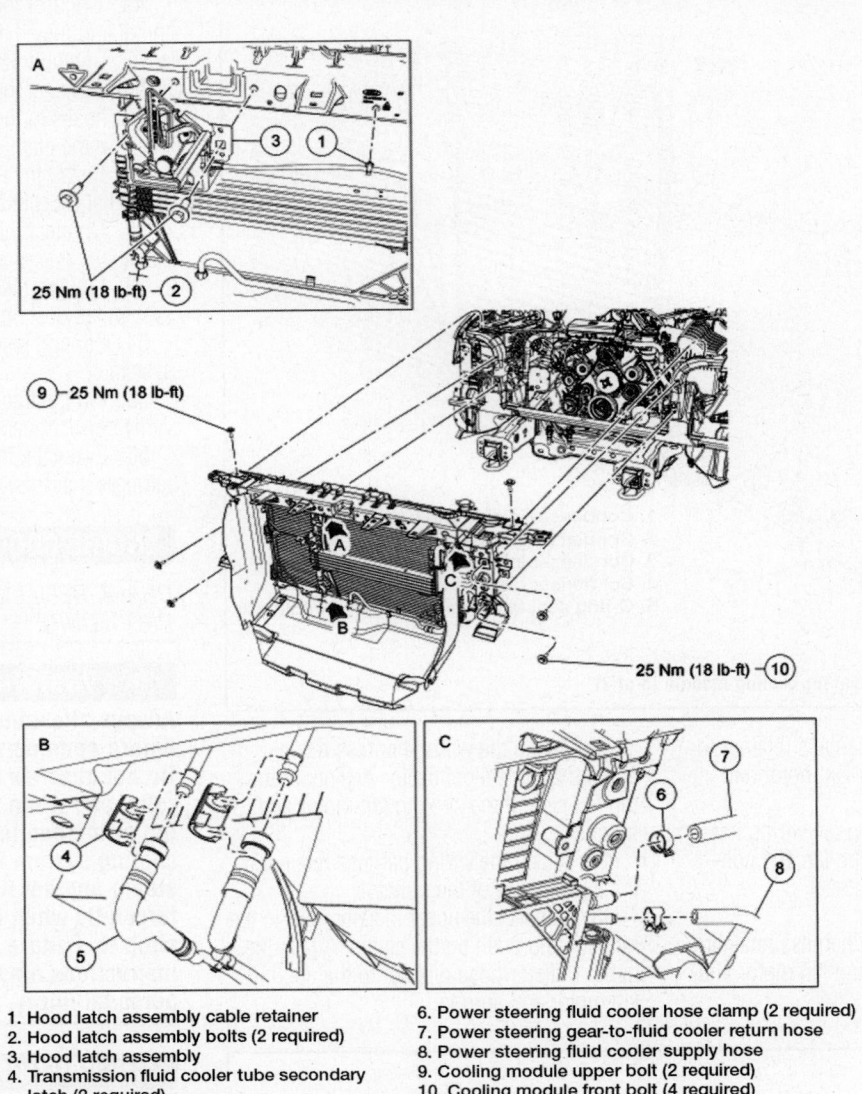

1. Hood latch assembly cable retainer
2. Hood latch assembly bolts (2 required)
3. Hood latch assembly
4. Transmission fluid cooler tube secondary latch (2 required)
5. Transmission fluid cooler tube (2 required)
6. Power steering fluid cooler hose clamp (2 required)
7. Power steering gear-to-fluid cooler return hose
8. Power steering fluid cooler supply hose
9. Cooling module upper bolt (2 required)
10. Cooling module front bolt (4 required)

N0092097

Fig. 38 Component removal for cooling module (7 of 7)

1. Make sure the engine is cool.

2. Wrap a thick cloth around the radiator cap. Slowly turn the cap counterclockwise until the pressure begins to release.

3. Step back while the pressure releases.

4. When sure all the pressure has been released, use the cloth to turn and remove the cap.

5. Place a suitable container below the radiator draincock. Drain the coolant.

6. Tighten the radiator draincock when finished.

❋❋ CAUTION

Vehicle cooling systems are filled with Motorcraft® Premium Gold

Engine Coolant. Always fill the cooling system with the same type of coolant that is present in the system. Do not mix coolant types. Failure to follow these instructions may result in engine or cooling system damage.

❋❋ CAUTION

Engine coolant provides freeze protection, boil protection, cooling efficiency and corrosion protection to the engine and cooling components. In order to obtain these protections, the engine coolant must be maintained at the correct concentration and fluid level. Failure to follow these instruc-

tions may result in engine or cooling system damage. To maintain the integrity of the coolant and the cooling system:

- Do not mix coolant types. Mixing coolants may degrade the coolant's corrosion protection.
- Do not add alcohol, methanol or brine, or any engine coolants mixed with alcohol or methanol antifreeze. These can cause engine damage from overheating or freezing.
- Do not mix with recycled coolant. Use of such coolant may harm the engine and cooling system components.

7. Fill the radiator through the radiator fill neck until the coolant level is at the bottom of the filler neck.

→**Recommended coolant concentration is 50/50 ethylene glycol to distilled water.**

8. Install the radiator cap.

9. Fill the coolant expansion tank until the coolant reaches the COLD FILL mark.

10. On the Electronic Manual Temperature Control (EMTC), move the temperature blend selector to the full WARM position. On the Electronic Automatic Temperature Control (EATC), set the temperature to 90°F (32°C).

❊❊ CAUTION

If the air discharge remains cool and the engine coolant temperature gauge does not move, the engine coolant level is low in the engine and must be filled. Stop the engine, allow it to cool and fill the cooling system. Failure to follow this instructions may result in damage to the engine.

11. Run the engine at idle until it reaches normal operating temperature.

12. Add more correct coolant mixture to the coolant expansion tank until the coolant level is at the COLD FILL mark.

13. Turn the engine off and allow it to cool.

14. Start the engine and allow it to idle until it reaches normal operating temperature. While the engine is idling, feel for hot air from the A/C vents.

15. Hot air should discharge from the A/C vents. The engine coolant temperature gauge should maintain a stabilized reading in the middle of the NORMAL range and the upper radiator hose should feel hot to the touch.

16. Check the engine coolant level in the coolant expansion tank and fill it as necessary.

17. Repeat the previous 5 steps as necessary.

FLUSHING

1. Drain the engine cooling system.

2. Remove the thermostat. See "Thermostat" in this section.

3. Install the thermostat housing without the thermostat.

→**Refer to the cooling system flusher manufacturer's operating instructions for specific vehicle hook-up.**

4. Use a cooling system flusher to flush the engine and radiator. Use Premium Cooling System Flush.

5. Install the thermostat.

6. Fill and bleed the cooling system.

RADIATOR

REMOVAL & INSTALLATION

1. With the vehicle in NEUTRAL, position it on a hoist.

2. Drain the cooling system.

3. Remove the RH and LH headlamp assemblies.

4. Remove the cooling fan motor and shroud.

5. Disconnect the radiator overflow hose from the radiator.

6. Release the clamp and disconnect the upper radiator hose from the radiator.

7. Remove the spring clip and disconnect the lower radiator hose from the radiator.

8. Remove the 2 radiator bolts.

9. Remove the 2 bolts and position the coolant expansion tank aside.

10. Disconnect the electrical connector and remove the bolt and the horn assembly.

11. Remove the 6 LH and RH air deflector-to-condenser core pin-type retainers.

12. Disconnect the 2 transmission fluid cooler-to-radiator hoses.

→**The cooling module must be positioned rearward to raise and detach the 4 condenser mounts from the radiator.**

13. Depress the retaining tabs on the 2 lower condenser mounting brackets and raise the condenser assembly until the 4 condenser mounting brackets detach from the radiator.

14. Remove the radiator.

To install:

15. To install, reverse the removal procedure.

16. Tighten the fasteners as follows:
- Horn retaining bolt: 89 inch lbs. (10 Nm)
- Coolant expansion tank bolts: 133 inch lbs. (15 Nm)

17. Radiator bolts: 133 inch lbs. (15 Nm)

18. Fill and bleed the cooling system.

19. Carry out the transmission fluid level check.

THERMOSTAT

REMOVAL & INSTALLATION

1. Drain the engine cooling system.

2. If servicing the thermostat housing, disconnect the upper radiator hose from the thermostat housing.

3. Remove the 2 bolts, the thermostat housing and the thermostat. Discard the O-ring seal.

4. Inspect the mating surfaces. Clean the sealing surfaces with metal surface prep and silicone gasket remover.

To install:

5. If necessary, install a new thermostat with the spring facing down.

6. Install a new O-ring seal.

7. Make sure the thermostat housing is seated evenly by hand tightening the 2 thermostat housing bolts prior to final tightening. Tighten to 89 inch lbs. (10 Nm).

8. Fill and bleed the cooling system.

WATER PUMP

REMOVAL & INSTALLATION

1. Drain the engine cooling system.

2. Loosen the 4 coolant pump pulley bolts.

3. Remove the accessory drive belt by rotating the belt tensioner.

4. Remove the 4 bolts and the coolant pump pulley.

5. Remove the 4 bolts and the coolant pump. Discard the O-ring seal.

6. Inspect the sealing surfaces and clean with metal surface prep. Follow the directions on the packaging.

To install:

❊❊ CAUTION

Align the bolt holes with the bosses prior to insertion of the coolant pump and insert the pump straight into the coolant pump cavity. Do not rotate the coolant pump once installed in the coolant pump cavity or damage to the O-ring seal can occur, causing the coolant pump to leak.

→**Install a new O-ring seal and lubricate with clean engine coolant.**

7. Install the coolant pump and 4 bolts. Tighten to 18 ft. lbs. (25 Nm).

8. Install the coolant pump pulley and 4 bolts.

9. Install the accessory drive belt.

10. Tighten the 4 bolts for the coolant pump pulley. Tighten to 18 ft. lbs. (25 Nm).

11. Fill the engine cooling system.

ENGINE ELECTRICAL

BATTERY

REMOVAL & INSTALLATION

➡When the battery (or PCM) is disconnected and connected, some abnormal drive symptoms may occur while the vehicle relearns its adaptive strategy. The charging system setpoint may also vary. The vehicle may need to be driven to relearn its strategy.

➡When the battery is disconnected and connected, the illumination display needs to be calibrated. After the battery is connected, rotate the dimmer switch from the lowest dim position to the full bright, dome ON position.

1. Disconnect the battery cables.
2. Loosen and remove the battery hold-down bolt and clamp.

❈❈ WARNING

Always lift a plastic-cased battery with a battery carrier or with hands on opposite corners. Excessive pressure on the battery end walls may cause acid to flow through the vent caps, resulting in personal injury and/or damage to the vehicle or battery.

3. Remove the battery and the heat shield.
4. To install, reverse the removal procedure.
5. Tighten the hold-down bolt to 62 inch lbs. (7 Nm).

BATTERY SYSTEM

6. Tighten the cable-to-battery bolts to 44 inch lbs. (5 Nm).

BATTERY RECONNECT/RELEARN PROCEDURE

➡When the battery (or PCM) is disconnected and connected, some abnormal drive symptoms may occur while the vehicle relearns its adaptive strategy. The charging system setpoint may also vary. The vehicle may need to be driven to relearn its strategy.

➡When the battery is disconnected and connected, the illumination display needs to be calibrated. After the battery is connected, rotate the dimmer switch from the lowest dim position to the full bright, dome ON position.

ENGINE ELECTRICAL

GENERATOR

REMOVAL & INSTALLATION

❈❈ CAUTION

Do not allow any metal object to come in contact with the generator housing and internal diode cooling fins. A short circuit may result and burn out the diodes.

1. Disconnect the battery.
2. For Navigator, release the 2 retainers and remove the engine cover.

3. Remove the air cleaner intake pipe.
4. Rotate the Front End Accessory Drive (FEAD) belt tensioner counterclockwise and position the accessory drive belt aside.
5. Remove the harness locator from the generator bracket.
6. Remove the 4 bolts and the generator bracket.
7. Remove the 2 bolts and position generator aside.
8. Disconnect the generator electrical connector.

CHARGING SYSTEM

9. Position the generator B+ protective cover aside, remove and discard the nut, then position the generator B+ terminal aside.
10. Remove the generator.

To install:

11. To install, reverse the removal procedure. Tighten the fasteners as follows:
- B+ terminal new nut: 150 inch lbs. (17 Nm)
- Generator bolts: 18 ft. lbs. (25 Nm)
- 4 generator bracket bolts: 89 inch lbs. (10 Nm)

ENGINE ELECTRICAL

FIRING ORDER

Firing order is: 1–3–7–2–6–5–4–8

IGNITION COIL-ON PLUG

REMOVAL & INSTALLATION

1. Disconnect the ignition coil-on-plug electrical connector.
2. Remove the bolt and the ignition coil-on-plug.
3. Remove the ignition coil-on-plug, using a twisting motion while pulling up on the ignition coil-on-plug.

➡Verify that the ignition coil-on-plug spring is correctly located inside the ignition coil-on-plug boot and that

there is no damage to the tip of the boot.

4. To install, reverse the removal procedure.
5. Apply a light coat of dielectric compound to the inside of the ignition coil boots.
6. Tighten the coil bolt to 53 inch lbs. (6 Nm).

IGNITION TIMING

ADJUSTMENT

➡Basic setting is 10° BTDC. The ignition timing is electronically controlled. No adjustment is required.

IGNITION SYSTEM

SPARK PLUGS

REMOVAL & INSTALLATION

❈❈ CAUTION

The spark plug procedure must be followed exactly or damage to the cylinder head and spark plug will result.

❈❈ CAUTION

Do not remove the spark plugs when the engine is hot or cold soaked. Spark plug thread or cylinder head damage can occur. Make sure the engine is warm (hand touch after

cooling down) prior to spark plug removal.

1. Remove the ignition coil-on-plug.

✳✳ CAUTION

Only use hand tools when removing or installing the spark plugs or dam-

age can occur to the cylinder head or spark plug.

➥Use compressed air to remove any foreign material from the spark plug well before removing the spark plugs.

2. Remove the spark plug.

3. Inspect the spark plug.

To install:
4. Adjust the spark plug gap as necessary: 0.039–0.043 in (1.00–1.10 mm).
5. Install the spark plug. Tighten to 106 inch lbs. (12 Nm).
6. Install the ignition coil-on-plug.

ENGINE ELECTRICAL   **STARTING SYSTEM**

STARTER

REMOVAL & INSTALLATION
See Figure 39.

✳✳ WARNING

Always disconnect the battery ground cable at the battery before disconnecting the starter motor battery ter-

minal lead. If a tool is shorted at the starter motor battery terminal, the tool can quickly heat enough to cause a skin burn. Failure to follow this instruction may result in serious personal injury.

1. With the vehicle in NEUTRAL, position it on a hoist.
2. Disconnect the battery ground cable.

3. Remove the starter terminal cover and remove the nut and the solenoid S-terminal electrical connection.
4. Remove the nut and the solenoid B-terminal electrical connection.
5. Remove the nut and the starter battery ground cable from the stud.
6. Remove the 2 bolts, the stud bolt and the starter motor.

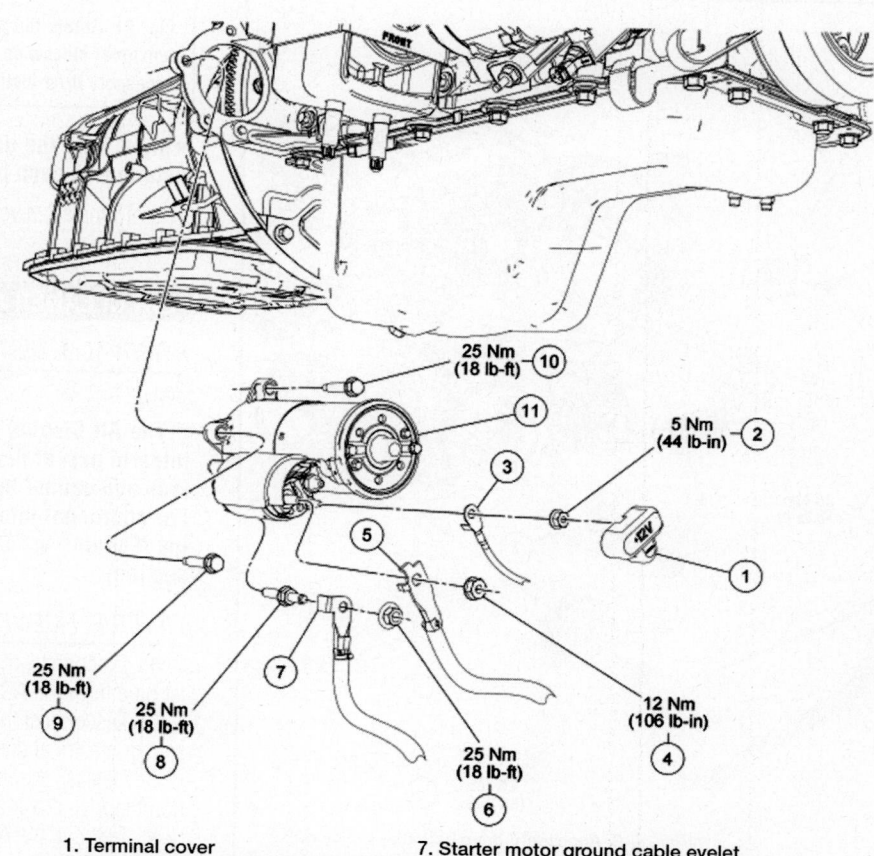

1. Terminal cover
2. Starter solenoid S-terminal nut
3. Starter solenoid S-terminal eyelet
4. Starter solenoid B-terminal nut
5. Starter solenoid B-terminal eyelet
6. Starter motor ground cable nut
7. Starter motor ground cable eyelet
8. Starter motor mounting stud bolt
9. Starter motor mounting bolt
10. Starter motor mounting bolt
11. Starter motor

N0105258

Fig. 39 Showing the starter mounting and related components

To install:

7. Position the starter and install the 2 bolts and the stud bolt in 3 stages:
- Stage 1: Install the 2 starter bolts and the stud bolt finger-tight.
- Stage 2: Tighten the upper bolt to 18 ft. lbs. (25 Nm).
- Stage 3: Tighten the lower bolt and stud bolt to 18 ft. lbs. (25 Nm).

8. Position the starter battery ground cable onto the stud and install the nut. Tighten to 18 ft. lbs. (25 Nm).

9. Connect the solenoid B-terminal electrical connection and install the nut. Tighten to 106 inch lbs. (12 Nm).

10. Connect the solenoid S-terminal electrical connection and install the nut and the starter terminal cover. Tighten to 44 inch lbs. (5 Nm).

11. Connect the battery ground cable.

ENGINE MECHANICAL

➡️Disconnecting the negative battery cable may interfere with the functions of the on board computer systems and may require the computer to undergo a relearning process, once the negative battery cable is reconnected.

ACCESSORY DRIVE BELTS

ACCESSORY BELT ROUTING

See Figure 40.

ADJUSTMENT

➡️The accessory drive belt is self-adjusted by the belt tensioner. No manual adjustment is required.

REMOVAL & INSTALLATION

See Figure 41.

1. Rotate the accessory drive belt tensioner clockwise and remove the accessory drive belt.

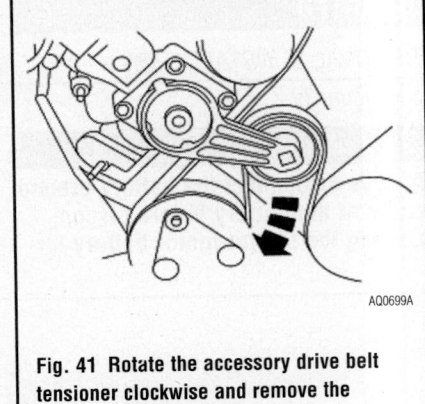

Fig. 41 Rotate the accessory drive belt tensioner clockwise and remove the accessory drive belt.

➡️Make sure the drive belt is correctly installed on each pulley.

2. To install, reverse the removal procedure.

AIR CLEANER ASSEMBLY

REMOVAL & INSTALLATION

See Figure 42.

➡️The Air Cleaner (ACL) housing is an integral part of the coolant expansion tank and cannot be serviced separately. For additional information, see "Cooling Module" in "ENGINE COOLING" section.

FILTER/ELEMENT REPLACEMENT

1. Disconnect the Air Cleaner (ACL) outlet pipe from the ACL cover.

2. Disconnect the Mass Air Flow (MAF) sensor electrical connector.

3. Release the retaining clips and position the ACL cover aside.

4. Remove the ACL element.

➡️The ACL element must be fully seated into the ACL housing. Failure to do so will result in unusual engine noise.

5. To install, reverse the removal procedure.

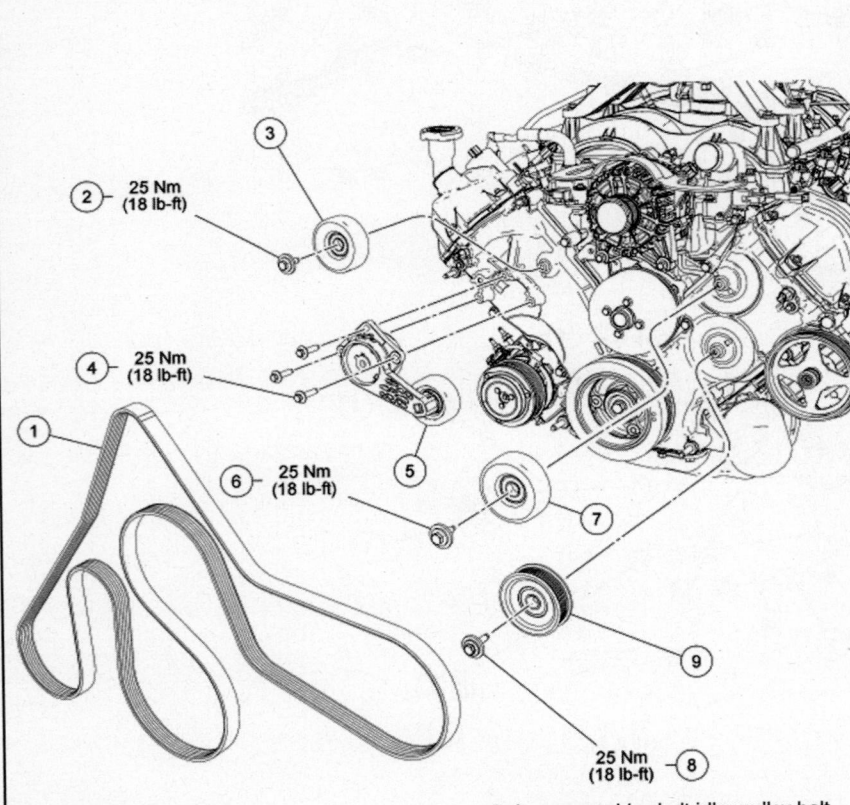

1. Accessory drive belt
2. Accessory drive belt idler pulley bolt
3. Accessory drive belt idler pulley
4. Accessory drive belt tensioner bolt (3 required)
5. Accessory drive belt tensioner
6. Accessory drive belt idler pulley bolt
7. Accessory drive belt idler pulley
8. Accessory drive belt idler pulley bolt
9. Accessory drive belt idler pulley

N0050286

Fig. 40 Showing the accessory drive belt routing and related components

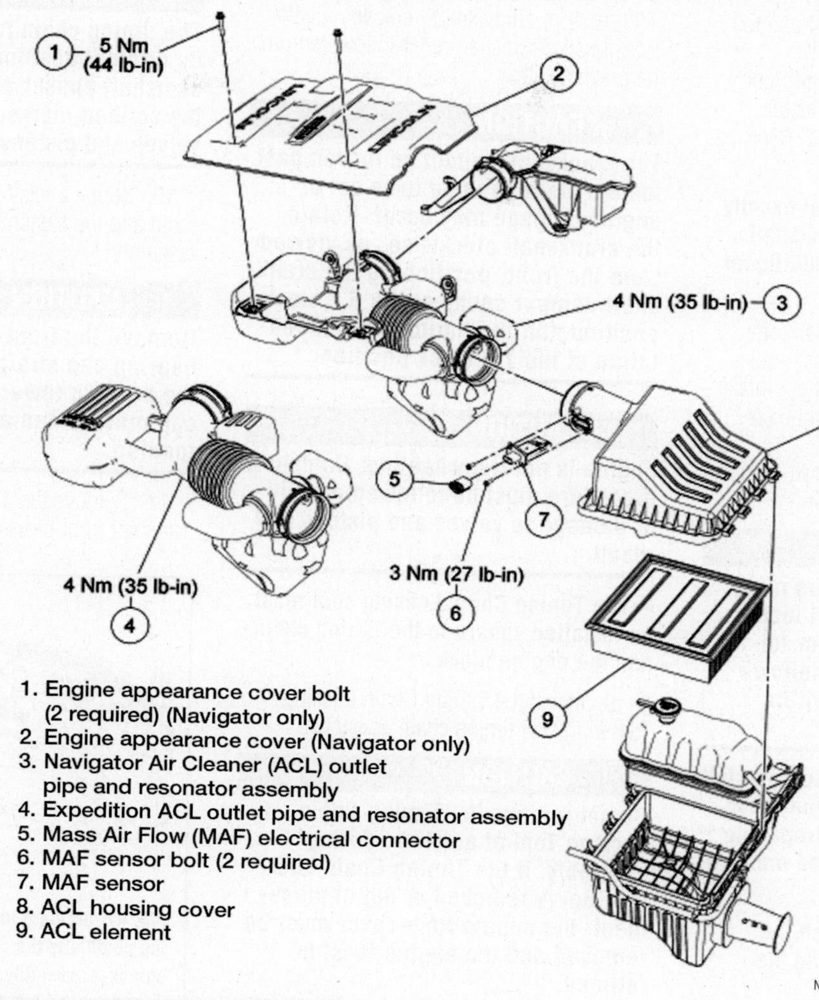

1. 5 Nm (44 lb-in)

4 Nm (35 lb-in) — 3

4 Nm (35 lb-in)
4

3 Nm (27 lb-in)
6

1. Engine appearance cover bolt
   (2 required) (Navigator only)
2. Engine appearance cover (Navigator only)
3. Navigator Air Cleaner (ACL) outlet
   pipe and resonator assembly
4. Expedition ACL outlet pipe and resonator assembly
5. Mass Air Flow (MAF) electrical connector
6. MAF sensor bolt (2 required)
7. MAF sensor
8. ACL housing cover
9. ACL element

N0092050

Fig. 42 Exploded view of the air intake system and components

CAMSHAFT & VALVE LIFTERS

REMOVAL & INSTALLATION

See Figures 43 through 52.

➥This procedure references components for the LH camshaft; however, RH camshaft procedure is similar.

✳ CAUTION

The camshaft procedure must be followed exactly or damage to the valves and pistons will result.

1. Position the crankshaft damper spoke at the 12 o'clock position and the timing mark indentation at the 1 o'clock position.
2. Remove the LH valve cover. See "Valve Covers" in this section.

✳ CAUTION

Damage to the camshaft phaser and sprocket assembly will occur if mis-

handled or used as a lifting or leveraging device.

✳ CAUTION

Only use hand tools to remove the camshaft phaser and sprocket

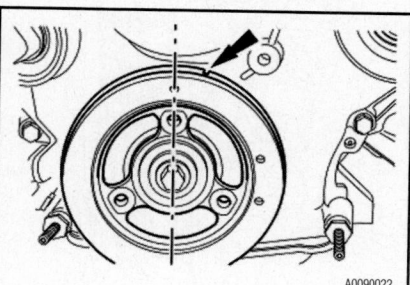

A0090022

Fig. 43 Position the crankshaft damper spoke at the 12 o'clock position and the timing mark indentation at the 1 o'clock position.

assembly or damage may occur to the camshaft or camshaft phaser and sprocket.

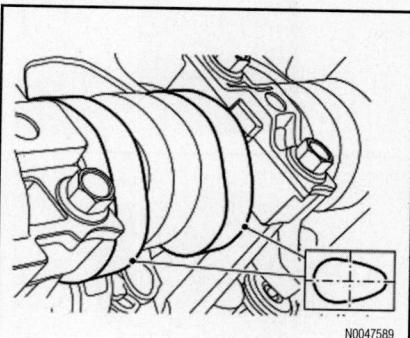

N0047589

Fig. 44 The No. 5 cylinder camshaft lobe must be coming up on the exhaust stroke. Verify by noting the position of the 2 intake camshaft lobes and the exhaust lobe on the No. 5 cylinder.

3. Loosen and back off the LH camshaft phaser and sprocket bolt one full turn.

4. Disconnect the LH Camshaft Position (CMP) sensor electrical connector.

5. Remove the bolt and the LH CMP sensor.

➡ If the camshaft lobes are not exactly positioned as shown, the crankshaft keyway will require one full additional rotation to 12 o'clock.

6. The No. 5 cylinder camshaft lobe must be coming up on the exhaust stroke. Verify by noting the position of the 2 intake camshaft lobes and the exhaust lobe on the No. 5 cylinder.

7. Remove only the 3 camshaft roller followers shown in the illustration.

❊❊ CAUTION

The camshaft roller followers must be installed in their original locations. Record camshaft roller follower locations. Failure to follow these instructions may result in engine damage.

➡ Do not allow the valve keepers to fall off of the valve or the valve may drop into the cylinder. If a valve drops into the cylinder, the cylinder head must be removed.

➡ It may be necessary to push the valve down while compressing the spring.

8. Using the Valve Spring Compressor (303-1039 or equivalent), remove only the 3 designated camshaft roller followers from the previous step.

❊❊ CAUTION

The crankshaft cannot be moved past the 6 o'clock position once set or engine damage may occur. Rotate the crankshaft clockwise, as viewed from the front, positioning the crankshaft damper spoke at the 6 o'clock position and the timing mark indentation at the 7 o'clock position.

❊❊ CAUTION

Engine is not freewheeling. Camshaft procedure must be followed exactly or damage to valves and pistons will result.

➡ The Timing Chain Locking Tool must be installed square to the timing chain and the engine block.

9. Install the Timing Chain Locking Tool in the LH timing chain as shown.

❊❊ CAUTION

Do not remove the Timing Chain Locking Tool at any time during assembly. If the Timing Chain Locking Tool is removed or out of placement, the engine front cover must be removed and the engine must be retimed.

❊❊ CAUTION

The timing chain must be installed in its original position onto the camshaft phaser and sprocket using the scribed marks, or damage to valves and pistons will result.

10. Scribe a location mark on the timing chain and the camshaft phaser and sprocket assembly.

❊❊ CAUTION

Remove the front thrust camshaft bearing cap straight upward from the bearing towers or the bearing cap may be damaged from side loading.

11. Remove the 2 bolts and the LH camshaft front bearing cap.

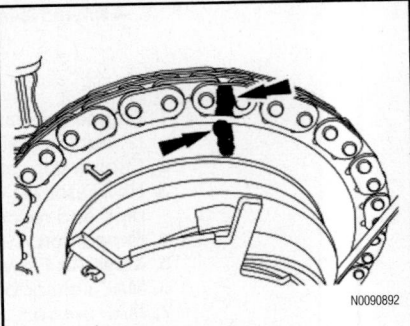

Fig. 47 Scribe a location mark on the timing chain and the camshaft phaser and sprocket assembly.

Fig. 45 Remove only the 3 camshaft roller followers shown in the illustration.

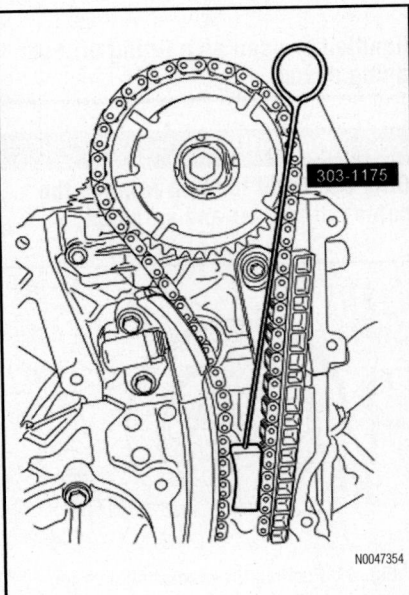

Fig. 46 Install the Timing Chain Locking Tool in the LH timing chain as shown.

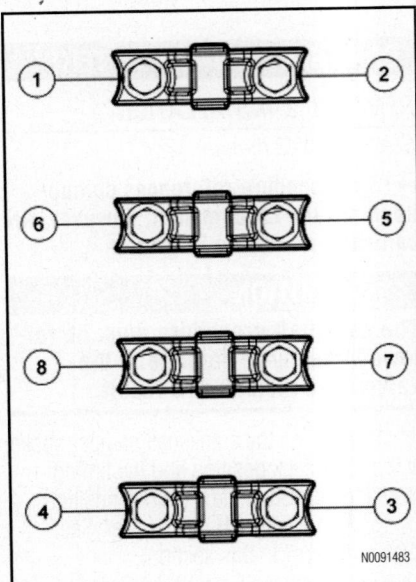

Fig. 48 Remove the remaining 8 bolts in the sequence shown and remove the 4 camshaft bearing caps.

✳ CAUTION

The camshaft bearing caps must be installed in their original locations. Record camshaft bearing cap locations. Failure to follow these instructions may result in engine damage.

12. Remove the remaining 8 bolts in the sequence shown and remove the 4 camshaft bearing caps.

13. Clean and inspect the LH camshaft bearing caps.

14. The camshaft front thrust bearing cap contains an oil metering groove. Make sure the groove is free of foreign material.

✳ CAUTION

Damage to the camshaft phaser and sprocket assembly will occur if mishandled or used as a lifting or leveraging device.

✳ CAUTION

Only use hand tools to remove the camshaft phaser and sprocket bolt or damage may occur to the camshaft or camshaft phaser and sprocket.

✳ CAUTION

Do not remove the Timing Chain Locking Tool at any time during assembly. If the Timing Chain Locking Tool is removed or out of placement, the engine front cover must be removed and the engine must be retimed.

15. Remove the bolt and the camshaft phaser and sprocket assembly from the camshaft. Discard the bolt and washer.

16. Remove the camshaft.

17. Remove and inspect the camshaft phaser and sprocket for damage.

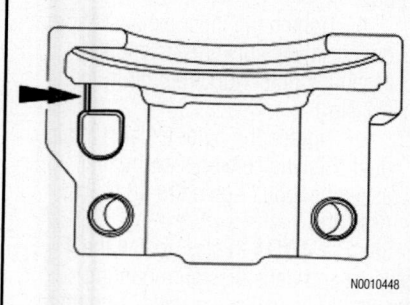

Fig. 49 The camshaft front thrust bearing cap contains an oil metering groove. Make sure the groove is free of foreign material.

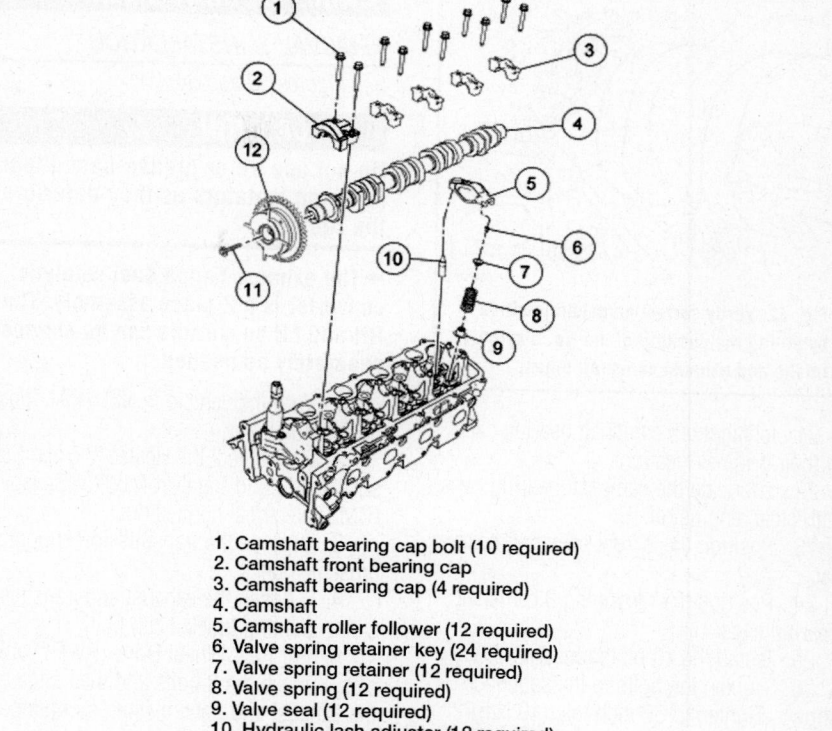

1. Camshaft bearing cap bolt (10 required)
2. Camshaft front bearing cap
3. Camshaft bearing cap (4 required)
4. Camshaft
5. Camshaft roller follower (12 required)
6. Valve spring retainer key (24 required)
7. Valve spring retainer (12 required)
8. Valve spring (12 required)
9. Valve seal (12 required)
10. Hydraulic lash adjuster (12 required)
11. Camshaft phaser and sprocket bolt
12. Camshaft phaser and sprocket

Fig. 50 Exploded view of the camshaft and valve assembly

To install:

➡ Do not allow the camshaft roller followers to move out of position when installing the camshaft.

18. Lubricate the camshaft and camshaft journals with clean engine oil and install the camshaft.

✳ CAUTION

The timing chain must be installed in its original position onto the camshaft phaser and sprocket using the scribed marks, or damage to valves and pistons will result.

➡ If replacement of the camshaft phaser and sprocket is necessary, transfer the scribe mark to the new camshaft phaser and sprocket.

19. Position the camshaft phaser and sprocket into the timing chain with the timing chain scribe marks in alignment.

✳ CAUTION

Damage to the camshaft phaser and sprocket assembly will occur if mishandled or used as a lifting or leveraging device.

20. Install the camshaft phaser and sprocket assembly onto the camshaft and install a new camshaft phaser and sprocket bolt finger-tight.

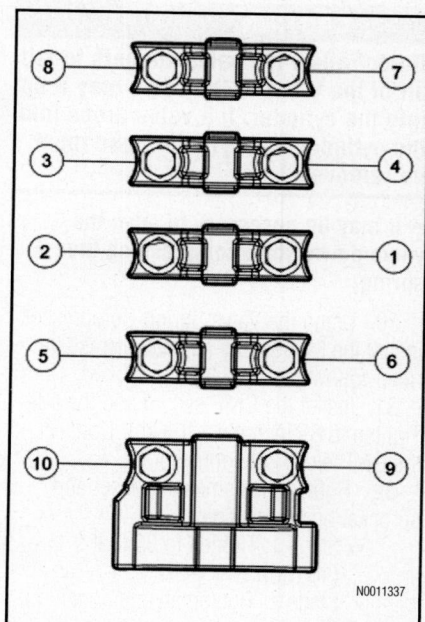

Fig. 51 Tighten the bolts in the sequence shown. Tighten to 89 inch lbs. (10 Nm).

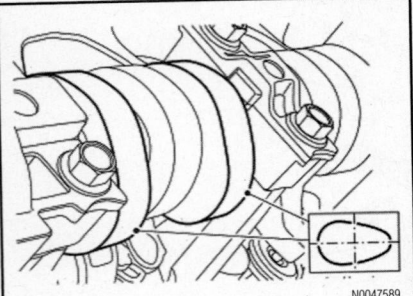

Fig. 52 Verify correct camshaft position by noting the position of the No. 5 cylinder intake and exhaust camshaft lobes.

21. Install the 5 camshaft bearing caps in their original locations.

22. Lubricate the camshaft bearing caps with clean engine oil.

23. Position the 2 front camshaft bearing cap.

24. Position the remaining 8 camshaft bearing caps.

25. Install the 10 bolts loosely.

26. Tighten the bolts in the sequence shown. Tighten to 89 inch lbs. (10 Nm).

27. Remove the Timing Chain Locking Tool.

28. Rotate the crankshaft a half turn counterclockwise and position the crankshaft damper spoke at the 12 o'clock position and the timing mark indentation at the 1 o'clock position.

29. Verify correct camshaft position by noting the position of the No. 5 cylinder intake and exhaust camshaft lobes.

✳✳ CAUTION

Do not allow the valve keepers to fall off of the valve or the valve may drop into the cylinder. If a valve drops into the cylinder, the cylinder head must be removed.

➡ **It may be necessary to push the valve down while compressing the spring.**

30. Using the Valve Spring Compressor, install the 3 originally removed camshaft roller followers.

31. Install the CMP sensor and the bolt. Tighten to 89 inch lbs. (10 Nm). Connect the CMP electrical connector.

32. Tighten the camshaft phaser and sprocket bolt in 2 stages:
- Stage 1: Tighten to 30 ft. lbs. (40 Nm).
- Stage 2: Tighten an additional 90 degrees.

33. Install the LH valve cover.

CATALYTIC CONVERTER

REMOVAL & INSTALLATION

See Figures 53 and 54.

✳✳ CAUTION

Do not use oil or grease-based lubricants on isolators as they deteriorate the rubber.

➡ **The exhaust Y-pipe dual catalytic converter is a 2-piece assembly. The RH and LH converters can be serviced separately as needed.**

1. With the vehicle in NEUTRAL, position it on a hoist.

2. Disconnect the Heated Oxygen Sensor (HO2S) and Catalyst Monitor Sensor (CMS) electrical connectors.

3. Remove the transmission support crossmember.

4. Loosen the exhaust and transmission mounting bracket cap bolt.

5. For Rear Wheel Drive (RWD) vehicles, remove the 3 bolts and then slide off the exhaust and transmission mounting bracket from the exhaust Y-pipe dual catalytic converter.

6. For 4-Wheel Drive (4WD) vehicles, remove the 4 bolts from the exhaust and transmission mounting bracket.

➡ **On 4WD vehicles, the exhaust and transmission mounting bracket will not slide off the exhaust Y-pipe dual catalytic converter until the exhaust Y-pipe dual catalytic converter is removed from the vehicle.**

7. For all vehicles, remove the 2 exhaust Y-pipe dual catalytic converter-to-muffler assembly bolts.

8. Remove the 4 exhaust Y-pipe dual catalytic converter-to-exhaust manifold nuts. Discard the nuts.

9. Remove the exhaust Y-pipe dual catalytic converter from the vehicle.

10. For 4WD vehicles, if necessary, remove the exhaust and transmission mounting bracket from the exhaust Y-pipe dual catalytic converter.

11. For all vehicles, if necessary, loosen the RH catalytic converter-to-LH catalytic converter Torca® clamp. If necessary, separate the RH catalytic converter from the LH catalytic converter.

To install:

✳✳ CAUTION

Do not tighten the fasteners until all components are assembled and aligned, making sure to tighten all fasteners beginning at the front of the vehicle.

12. Clean the mating surfaces of the exhaust manifold outlet flare and the exhaust Y-pipe dual catalytic converter inlet flares. Also clean the mating surfaces of the exhaust Y-pipe dual catalytic converter-to-muffler assembly.

13. If separated, install RH catalytic converter to the LH catalytic converter.

14. For 4WD vehicles, if removed, install the exhaust and transmission mounting bracket to the exhaust Y-pipe dual catalytic converter.

15. For all vehicles, position the exhaust Y-pipe dual catalytic converter into the vehicle.

16. Install the 2 new RH catalytic converter-to-exhaust manifold nuts and tighten in the following sequence:
- a. Tighten the RH lower catalytic converter-to-exhaust manifold nut. Tighten to 30 ft. lbs. (40 Nm).
- b. Tighten the RH upper catalytic converter-to-exhaust manifold nut. Tighten to 30 ft. lbs. (40 Nm).

17. Install the 2 new LH catalytic converter-to-exhaust manifold nuts and tighten in the following sequence:
- a. Snug the LH inner catalytic converter-to-exhaust manifold nut.
- b. Tighten the LH outer catalytic converter-to-exhaust manifold nut. Tighten to 30 ft. lbs. (40 Nm).
- c. Tighten the LH inner catalytic converter-to-exhaust manifold nut. Tighten to 30 ft. lbs. (40 Nm).

18. If loosened, tighten the RH catalytic converter-to-LH catalytic converter clamp. Tighten to 41 ft. lbs. (55 Nm).

19. Install the 2 exhaust Y-pipe dual catalytic converter-to-muffler assembly bolts and tighten in the following sequence:
- a. Snug the outer exhaust Y-pipe dual catalytic converter-to-muffler assembly bolt.
- b. Tighten the inner exhaust Y-pipe dual catalytic converter-to-muffler assembly bolt. Tighten to 46 ft. lbs. (63 Nm).
- c. Tighten the outer exhaust Y-pipe dual catalytic converter-to-muffler assembly bolt. Tighten to 46 ft. lbs. (63 Nm).

20. For 4WD vehicles, install the 4 exhaust and transmission mounting bracket-to-transmission bolts. Tighten to 66 ft. lbs. (90 Nm).

21. For RWD vehicles, slide on the exhaust and transmission mounting bracket to the exhaust Y-pipe dual catalytic

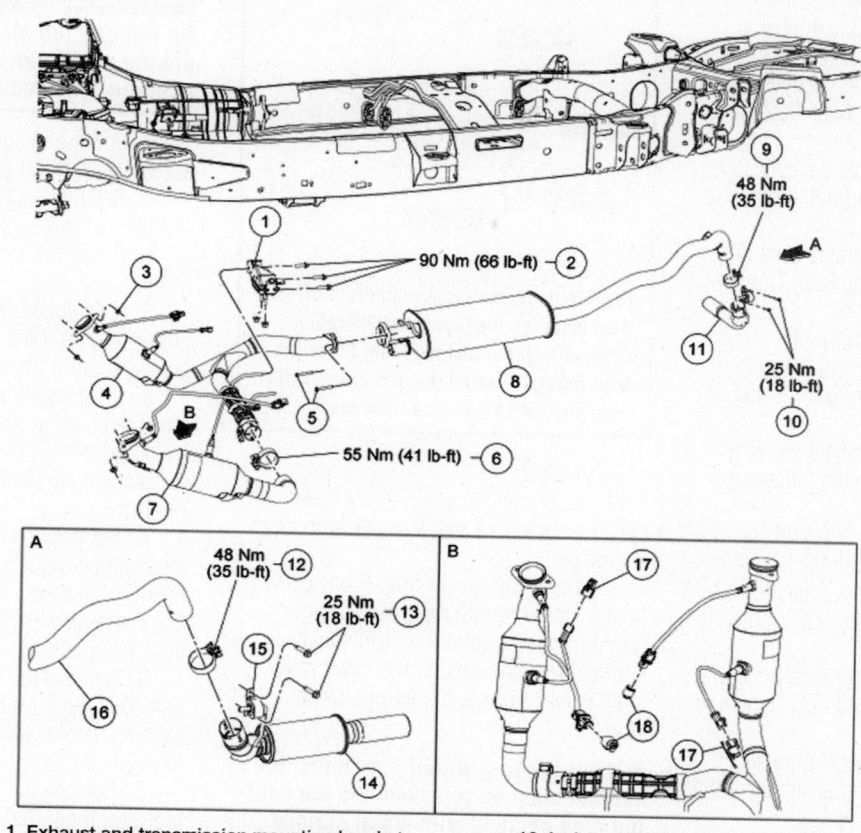

1. Exhaust and transmission mounting bracket
2. Exhaust and transmission mount bolts (3 required)
3. Exhaust Y-pipe dual catalytic converter-to-exhaust manifold nut (4 required)
4. RH catalytic converter
5. RH catalytic converter-to-muffler assembly bolts (2 required)
6. RH catalytic converter-to-LH catalytic converter clamp
7. LH catalytic converter
8. Muffler assembly
9. Muffler assembly-to-resonator clamp
10. Isolator and bracket assembly bolts
11. Tail pipe
12. Muffler assembly-to-tail pipe clamp
13. Isolator and bracket assembly bolts (2 required)
14. Resonator
15. Isolator and bracket assembly
16. Muffler assembly
17. Catalyst Monitor Sensor (CMS) electrical connectors (2 required)
18. Heated Oxygen Sensor (HO2S) electrical connectors (2 required)

N0101895

Fig. 53 Exploded view of the exhaust system components

converter and install the 3 exhaust and transmission mounting bracket-to-transmission bolts. Tighten to 66 ft. lbs. (90 Nm).

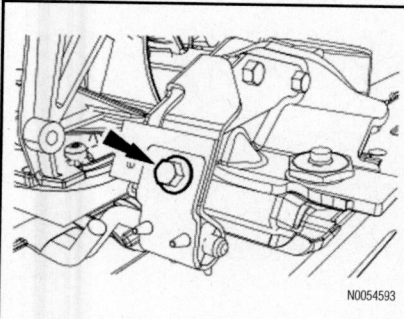

N0054593

Fig. 54 Loosen the exhaust and transmission mounting bracket cap bolt.

22. For all vehicles, Tighten the exhaust and transmission mounting bracket cap bolt. Tighten to 26 ft. lbs. (35 Nm).

23. Install the transmission support crossmember. Tighten bolts to 66 ft. lbs. (90 Nm).

24. Connect the HO2S and CMS electrical connectors.

25. Check to see if the exhaust system isolators are at zero load. If the exhaust system isolators are not at zero load, then carry out the exhaust system alignment procedure.

EXHAUST SYSTEM ALIGNMENT PROCEDURE

1. With the vehicle in NEUTRAL, position it on a hoist.

2. If equipped, remove the 6 bolts and transfer case skid plate.

3. Loosen all exhaust component fasteners from the exhaust manifolds to the muffler inlet pipe except the RH catalytic converter-to-LH catalytic converter clamp.

4. Verify that the RH catalytic converter-to-LH catalytic converter and tail pipe clamps are secure and pipes are fully inserted.

➡**Make sure the exhaust isolators are not torn, damaged or binding.**

5. Beginning at the front of the vehicle, align the exhaust system to establish the maximum clearance to surrounding components. Make sure that all slip fit pipes are pushed all the way into the preceding pipe and the notches are correctly lined up with the tabs.

6. Tighten the 2 RH catalytic converter-to-exhaust manifold nuts in the following sequence:

    a. Tighten the RH lower catalytic converter-to-exhaust manifold nut. Tighten to 30 ft. lbs. (40 Nm).

    b. Tighten the RH upper catalytic converter-to-exhaust manifold nut. Tighten to 30 ft. lbs. (40 Nm).

    c. Tighten the exhaust and transmission mounting bracket cap bolt. Tighten to 26 ft. lbs. (35 Nm).

    d. If loosened, tighten the RH catalytic converter-to-LH catalytic converter clamp. Tighten to 41 ft. lbs. (55 Nm).

7. Tighten the 2 LH catalytic converter-to-exhaust manifold nuts in the following sequence:

    a. Snug the LH inner catalytic converter-to-exhaust manifold nut.

    b. Tighten the LH outer catalytic converter-to-exhaust manifold nut. Tighten to 30 ft. lbs. (40 Nm).

    c. Tighten the LH inner catalytic converter-to-exhaust manifold nut. Tighten to 30 ft. lbs. (40 Nm).

8. Tighten the 2 exhaust Y-pipe dual catalytic converter-to-muffler assembly bolts in the following sequence:

    a. Snug the outer exhaust Y-pipe dual catalytic converter-to-muffler assembly bolt.

    b. Tighten the inner exhaust Y-pipe dual catalytic converter-to-muffler assembly bolt. Tighten to 46 ft. lbs. (63 Nm).

9. Start the engine and check the exhaust system for leaks.

10. If equipped, install the transfer case skid plate and 6 bolts. Tighten to 18 ft. lbs. (25 Nm).

CRANKSHAFT FRONT SEAL

REMOVAL & INSTALLATION

See Figure 55.

1. With the vehicle in NEUTRAL, position it on a hoist.

2. Rotate the tensioner clockwise and remove the accessory drive belt from the crankshaft pulley.

3. Remove the crankshaft pulley bolt and washer. Discard the crankshaft pulley bolt.

4. Using the 3 Jaw Puller, remove the crankshaft pulley.

5. Using the Crankshaft Front Oil Seal Remover (303-107 or equivalent), remove and discard the crankshaft seal.

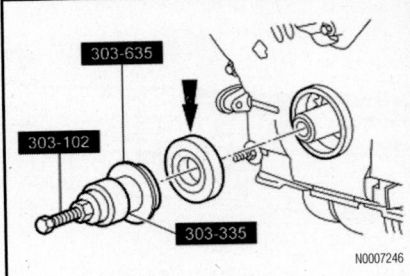

Fig. 55 Using the Crankshaft Front Oil Seal Installer, the Crankshaft Vibration Damper Installer and the Front Cover Oil Seal Installer, install the new crankshaft front seal into the engine front cover.

To install:

6. Lubricate the engine front cover and the new crankshaft seal inner lip with clean engine oil.

7. Using the Crankshaft Front Oil Seal Installer, the Crankshaft Vibration Damper Installer and the Front Cover Oil Seal Installer, install the new crankshaft front seal into the engine front cover.

➡️ **If not secured within 4 minutes, the sealant must be removed and the sealing area cleaned with metal surface prep and silicone gasket remover. Allow to dry until there is no sign of wetness, or 4 minutes, whichever is longer. Failure to follow this procedure can cause future oil leakage.**

8. Apply silicone gasket and sealant to the Woodruff key slot in the crankshaft pulley.

9. Using the Crankshaft Vibration Damper Installer (303-102 or equivalent), install the crankshaft pulley.

10. Using a new crankshaft pulley bolt, install the bolt and washer and tighten the bolt in 4 stages:

    a. Stage 1: Tighten to 66 ft. lbs. (90 Nm).

    b. Stage 2: Loosen 360 degrees

    c. Stage 3: Tighten to 37 ft. lbs. (50 Nm).

    d. Stage 4: Tighten an additional 90 degrees.

11. Rotate the tensioner clockwise and install the accessory drive belt onto the crankshaft pulley.

CYLINDER HEAD

REMOVAL & INSTALLATION

See Figures 56 through 64.

1. Remove the engine.

✳️✳️ CAUTION

Do not use the oil pan to support the engine or oil pan and oil pan gasket damage may occur.

2. Lower and support the engine assembly on wood blocks.

3. Remove the Engine Lifting Bracket installed during engine removal.

4. Install the engine onto an engine stand.

5. If equipped with cylinder block drain plugs, remove the 3 bolts and the RH engine support insulator.

6. If equipped, remove the cylinder block drain plugs and drain the coolant into a suitable container. Then, install the cylinder block drain plugs. Tighten to 18 ft. lbs. (24 Nm).

7. Remove the nut and the RH radio interference capacitor. Repeat for LH radio interference capacitor.

8. Remove the bolt and the intake manifold vacuum tube support bracket.

9. Remove the 8 bolts and the 8 ignition coils. Remove the ignition coil using a twisting motion while pulling up on the ignition coil.

10. Remove the bolt and the oil level indicator tube. Discard the O-ring seal.

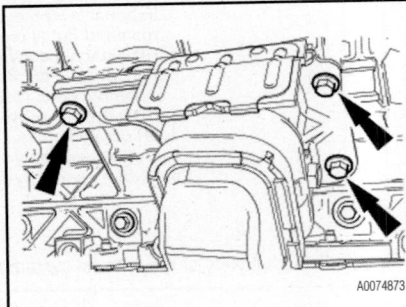

Fig. 56 If equipped with cylinder block drain plugs, remove the 3 bolts and the RH engine support insulator.

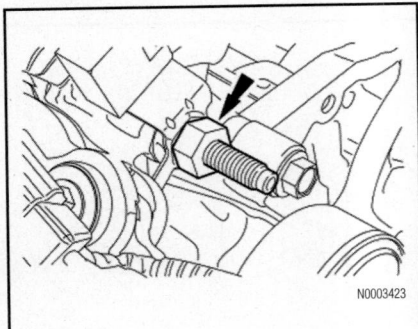

Fig. 57 Remove the nut and the radio interference capacitor.

Fig. 58 Remove the 7 bolts, the coolant pump pulley and the 3 accessory drive belt idler pulleys.

11. Loosen the bolts and remove the valve covers. See "Valve Covers" in this section.

12. Remove the 7 bolts, the coolant pump pulley and the 3 accessory drive belt idler pulleys.

13. Remove the 7 bolts, the coolant pump pulley and the 3 accessory drive belt idler pulleys.

14. Remove the 3 bolts and the accessory drive belt tensioner.

15. Remove the crankshaft front pulley and seal. See "Crankshaft Front Seal" in this section.

16. Remove the front 4 oil pan bolts.

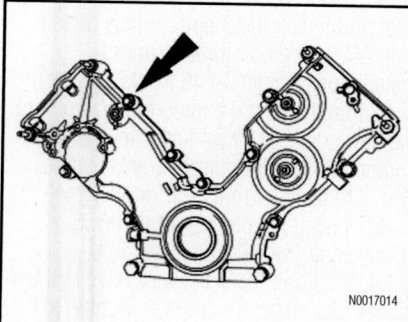

Fig. 59 Remove the 15 engine front cover fasteners.

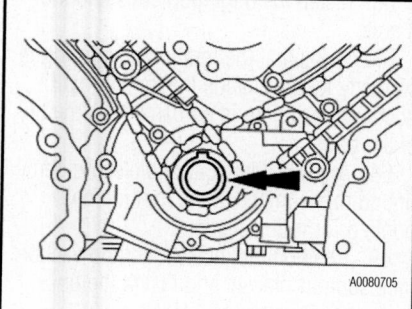

Fig. 60 Position the crankshaft keyway at the 12 o'clock position.

➡**Correct fastener location is essential for the assembly procedure. Record fastener location.**

17. Remove the 15 engine front cover fasteners.

18. Remove the engine front cover from the cylinder block.

19. Remove the crankshaft sensor ring from the crankshaft.

20. Position the crankshaft keyway at the 12 o'clock position.

➡**If the camshaft lobes are not exactly positioned as shown, the crankshaft will require one full additional rotation to 12 o'clock.**

21. Remove the camshafts. See "Camshafts & Valve Lifters" in this section.

22. Rotate the crankshaft clockwise and position the crankshaft keyway at the 6 o'clock position.

23. Remove the timing chains. See "Timing Chain & Sprocket" in this section.

✳✳ CAUTION

If the components are to be reused, they must be installed in the same positions. Mark the components for installation into their original locations. Failure to follow these instructions may result in engine damage.

24. Remove all of the remaining camshaft roller followers from the cylinder head.

25. Remove the hydraulic lash adjusters from the LH cylinder head.

26. Install the Cylinder Head Remover/Installer on the LH cylinder head.

27. Install the Cylinder Head Remover/Installer on the LH cylinder head.

28. Remove the LH exhaust manifold. See "Exhaust Manifold" in this section.

29. Remove and discard the 8 LH exhaust manifold-to-cylinder head studs.

30. Remove the RH camshaft. See "Camshaft & Valve Lifter" in this section.

31. Remove the hydraulic lash adjusters from the RH cylinder head.

32. Install the Cylinder Head Remover/Installer on the RH cylinder head.

33. Remove the RH exhaust manifold. See "Exhaust Manifold" in this section.

34. Remove and discard the 8 RH exhaust manifold-to-cylinder head studs.

35. Remove the nut and the ground strap from the cylinder head.

36. Remove the stud bolt and the coolant tube. Discard the O-ring seals.

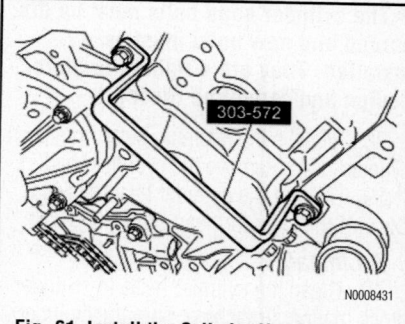

Fig. 61 Install the Cylinder Head Remover/Installer on the LH cylinder head.

37. Place clean shop towels over exposed engine cavities. Carefully remove the towels so foreign material is not dropped into the engine.

✳✳ CAUTION

Do not use metal scrapers, wire brushes, power abrasive discs or other abrasive means to clean the sealing surfaces. These tools cause scratches and gouges that make leak paths. Use a plastic scraping tool to remove all traces of the head gasket. Aluminum surfaces are soft and can be scratched easily. Never place the cylinder head gasket surface, unprotected, on a bench surface, or the cylinder head may be damaged.

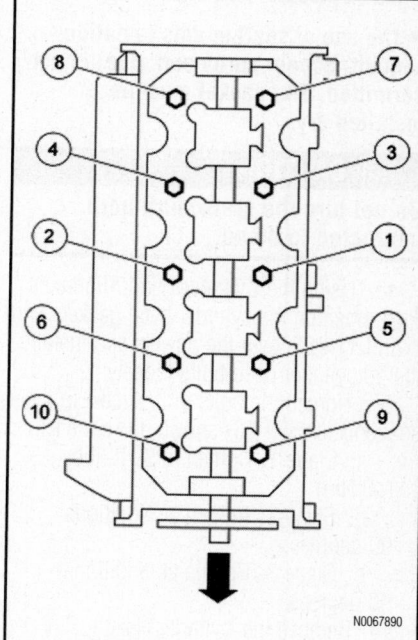

Fig. 62 Tighten the bolts in 3 stages, in the sequence shown (RH shown, LH similar)

➡The cylinder head bolts must be discarded and new bolts must be installed. They are a tighten-to-yield design and cannot be reused.

38. Remove the retaining bolts from each cylinder head. Remove the cylinder head(s).

39. Discard the cylinder head gaskets. Discard the cylinder head bolts.

To install:

40. Clean the cylinder head-to-cylinder block mating surfaces of both the cylinder head and the cylinder block in the following sequence.

41. Remove any large deposits of silicone or gasket material with a plastic scraper.

42. Apply silicone gasket remover, following package directions and allow to set for several minutes.

43. Remove the silicone gasket remover with a plastic scraper. A second application of silicone gasket remover may be required if residual traces of silicone or gasket material remain.

44. Apply metal surface prep, following package directions, to remove any remaining traces of oil or coolant and to prepare the surfaces to bond with the new gasket. Do not attempt to make the metal shiny. Some staining of the metal surfaces is normal.

45. Support the cylinder heads on a bench with the head gasket side up. Check the cylinder head distortion and the cylinder block distortion, paying particular attention to the oil pressure feed area.

➡The use of sealing aids (aviation cement, copper spray and glue) is not permitted. The gasket must be installed dry.

❄❄ CAUTION

Do not turn the crankshaft until instructed to do so.

46. Using the Cylinder Head Alignment Pins, position the cylinder head gaskets and cylinder heads over the dowels and install the 20 cylinder head bolts loosely.

47. Tighten the bolts in 3 stages, in the sequence shown (RH shown, LH similar):
   a. Stage 1: Tighten to 30 ft. lbs. (40 Nm).
   b. Stage 2: Tighten an additional 90 degrees.
   c. Stage 3: Tighten an additional 90 degrees.

48. Remove the Cylinder Head Remover/Installer from the cylinder head.

➡The hydraulic lash adjusters must be installed in their original locations.

Lubricate the hydraulic lash adjusters with clean engine oil prior to installation.

49. Install the hydraulic lash adjusters into the cylinder head.

50. Install 8 new exhaust manifold-to-cylinder head studs. Tighten to 106 inch lbs. (12 Nm).

51. Position new gaskets, the exhaust manifold and tighten 8 new nuts in the sequence shown. Tighten to 18 ft. lbs. (25 Nm).

52. Install 2 new O-ring seals and lubricate the O-ring seals with clean engine coolant. Install the coolant tube and the stud bolt. Tighten to 89 inch lbs. (10 Nm).

53. Position the ground strap and install the nut. Tighten to 89 inch lbs. (10 Nm).

54. Install the LH and RH camshafts. See "Camshaft & Valve Lifter" in this section.

➡Lubricate the camshaft and camshaft journals with clean engine oil prior to installation.

55. Install the timing chain. See "Timing Chain & Sprockets" in this section.

56. Loosely install the 4 oil pan front bolts, then tighten the bolts in 2 stages, in the sequence shown:

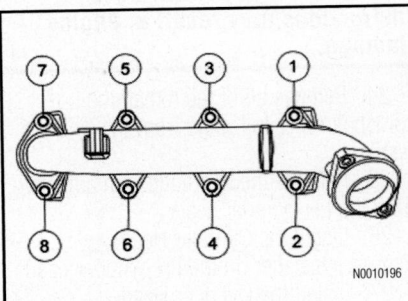

Fig. 63 Position new gaskets, the exhaust manifold and tighten 8 new nuts in the sequence shown. Tighten to 18 ft. lbs. (25 Nm)–LH shown; RH similar

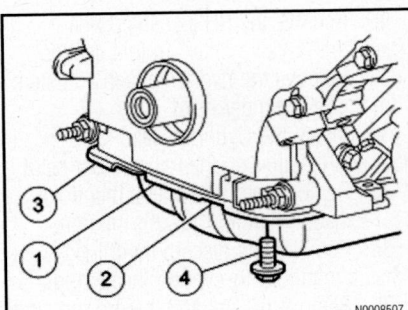

Fig. 64 Loosely install the 4 oil pan front bolts, then tighten the bolts in 2 stages, in the sequence shown

   a. Stage 1: Tighten to 177 inch lbs. (20 Nm).
   b. Stage 2: Tighten an additional 60 degrees.

57. Clean the valve cover mating surface with silicone gasket remover and metal surface prep. Follow the directions on the packaging.

➡If not secured within 4 minutes, the sealant must be removed and the sealing area cleaned. To clean the sealing area, use silicone gasket remover and metal surface prep. Failure to follow this procedure can cause future oil leakage.

58. Apply silicone gasket and sealant in 2 places where the engine front cover meets the cylinder head.

59. Install the valve covers. See "Valve Covers" in this section.

60. Position the oil level indicator tube and install the bolt. Install a new O-ring seal and lubricate the O-ring seal with clean engine oil prior to installation. Tighten to 89 inch lbs. (10 Nm).

➡Clean the engine support insulator-to-cylinder block mating surfaces of any dirt or foreign material prior to installation.

61. If equipped with cylinder block drain plugs, position the RH engine support insulator and install the 3 bolts. Apply threadlock 262 to the bolt threads prior to installation. Tighten to 46 ft. lbs. (63 Nm).

62. Lubricate the engine front cover and the new crankshaft seal inner lip with clean engine oil. Install the front crankshaft seal. See "Crankshaft Front Seal" in this section.

63. Install the crankshaft pulley. See "Crankshaft Pulley" in this section.

64. Position the accessory drive belt tensioner and install the 3 bolts. Tighten to 18 ft. lbs. (25 Nm).

65. Install the 3 accessory drive belt idler pulleys, the coolant pump pulley and the 7 bolts. Tighten to 18 ft. lbs. (25 Nm).

66. Install the 8 ignition coils and the 8 bolts.

67. Verify that the ignition coil spring is correctly located inside the ignition coil boot and that there is no damage to the tip of the boot.

68. Apply a light coat of dielectric compound to the inside of the ignition coil boots prior to installation.

69. Position the intake manifold vacuum tube support bracket and install the bolt. Tighten to 89 inch lbs. (10 Nm).

70. Install the LH and RH radio ignition interference capacitors and the nuts. Tighten to 18 ft. lbs. (25 Nm).

71. Using a floor crane, remove the engine from the engine stand.

> **⁑ CAUTION**
>
> **Do not use the oil pan to support the engine or oil pan and oil pan gasket damage may occur.**

72. Lower and support the engine assembly on wood blocks. Install the Engine Lifting Bracket.
73. Install the engine.

EXHAUST MANIFOLD

REMOVAL & INSTALLATION

Left Side

See Figure 65.

1. With the vehicle in NEUTRAL, position it on a hoist.
2. Remove the Air Cleaner (ACL) outlet pipe.
3. Remove the coolant expansion tank.

> **⁑ CAUTION**
>
> **Do not allow the steering column shaft to rotate while the intermediate shaft is disconnected or damage to the clockspring can result. If there is evidence that the shaft has rotated, the clockspring must be removed and recentered. See "AIR BAG (SUPPLEMENTAL RESTRAINT SYSTEM)" section.**

4. Remove the steering column pinch bolt and disconnect the steering shaft and position aside.
5. Remove the 4 (2 LH and 2 RH) exhaust manifold-to-catalytic converter nuts.
6. On 4WD vehicles, remove the front driveshaft. See "DRIVE TRAIN" section.
7. Remove the 8 exhaust manifold nuts, the 8 studs and the exhaust manifold. Discard the exhaust manifold nuts and studs.

> **⁑ CAUTION**
>
> **Do not use metal scrapers, wire brushes, power abrasive discs or other abrasive means to clean the sealing surfaces. These may cause scratches and gouges resulting in leak paths. Use a plastic scraper to clean the sealing surfaces.**

8. Remove and discard the 2 exhaust manifold gaskets. Clean the sealing surfaces with metal surface prep.
9. Inspect the exhaust manifold for any signs of cracks, distortion or damage.

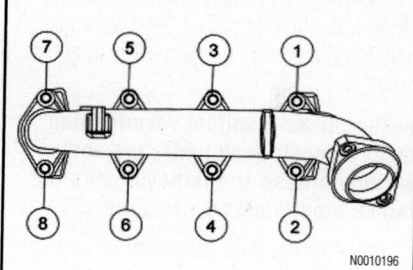

Fig. 65 Using new exhaust manifold nuts, install the 8 nuts. Tighten to 18 ft. lbs. (25 Nm) in the sequence shown.

To install:

10. Using 2 new exhaust manifold gaskets and 8 new studs, position the 2 gaskets and exhaust manifold and install the 8 studs. Tighten to 106 inch lbs. (12 Nm).
11. Using new exhaust manifold nuts, install the 8 nuts. Tighten to 18 ft. lbs. (25 Nm) in the sequence shown.
12. For 4WD vehicles, install the front driveshaft. See "DRIVE TRAIN" section.

> **⁑ CAUTION**
>
> **Do not allow the steering column shaft to rotate while the intermediate shaft is disconnected or damage to the clockspring can result. If there is evidence that the shaft has rotated, the clockspring must be removed and recentered. See "AIR BAG (SUPPLEMENTAL RESTRAINT SYSTEM)" section.**

13. Connect the steering shaft and install the bolt. Tighten to 22 ft. lbs. (30 Nm).
14. Install the 4 exhaust manifold-to-catalytic converter nuts.
15. Install the coolant expansion tank.
16. Install the ACL outlet tube.

Right Side

See Figure 66.

1. With the vehicle in NEUTRAL, position it on a hoist.
2. Remove the RH inner fenderwell.
3. Remove the RH engine support insulator.
4. Remove the 2 bolts and the exhaust manifold heat shield.
5. Remove the 8 exhaust manifold nuts, the 8 studs and the exhaust manifold. Discard the exhaust manifold nuts and studs.

> **⁑ CAUTION**
>
> **Do not use metal scrapers, wire brushes, power abrasive discs or other abrasive means to clean the**

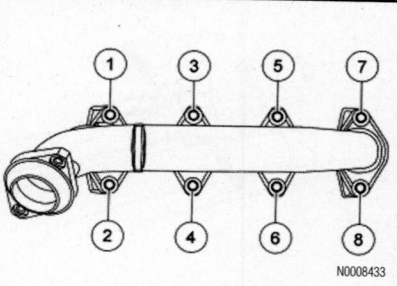

Fig. 66 Using 8 new exhaust manifold nuts, install the 8 nuts. Tighten to 18 ft. lbs. (25 Nm) in the sequence shown.

sealing surfaces. These may cause scratches and gouges resulting in leak paths. Use a plastic scraper to clean the sealing surfaces.

6. Remove and discard the 2 exhaust manifold gaskets. Clean the sealing surfaces with metal surface prep.
7. Inspect the exhaust manifold for cracks, distortion or signs of damage.

To install:

8. Using 2 new exhaust manifold gaskets and 8 new studs, position the 2 gaskets and exhaust manifold and install the 8 studs. Tighten to 106 inch lbs. (12 Nm (106 lb-in).
9. Using 8 new exhaust manifold nuts, install the 8 nuts. Tighten to 18 ft. lbs. (25 Nm) in the sequence shown.
10. Position the exhaust manifold heat shield and install the 2 bolts. Tighten to 89 inch lbs. (10 Nm).
11. Install the RH engine support insulator.
12. Install the RH inner fenderwell.

INTAKE MANIFOLD

REMOVAL & INSTALLATION

See Figures 67 and 68.

> **⁑ WARNING**
>
> **Before working on or disconnecting any of the fuel tubes or fuel system components, relieve the fuel system pressure to prevent accidental spraying of fuel. Fuel in the fuel system remains under high pressure, even when the engine is not running. Failure to follow this instruction may result in serious personal injury. See "FUEL" section.**

1. Drain the cooling system.
2. Remove the generator. See "ENGINE ELECTRICAL" section.

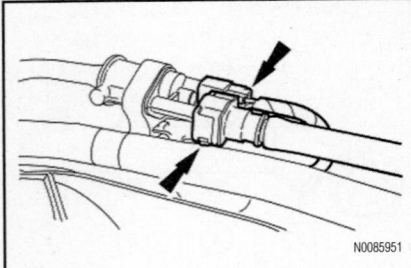

Fig. 67 Disconnect the electrical connector and the Evaporative Emission (EVAP) tube quick connect coupling from the EVAP canister purge valve.

3. Disconnect the quick connect couplings and remove the crankcase ventilation tube.

4. Remove the bolt, loosen the clamp and remove the air intake resonator assembly.

5. Remove the 3 bolts and the Throttle Body (TB)-to-Air Cleaner (ACL) outlet tube adapter.

6. Disconnect the quick connect couplings and remove the PCV tube.

7. Disconnect the fuel supply tube quick connect coupling.

8. Disconnect the electrical connector and the Evaporative Emission (EVAP) tube quick connect coupling from the EVAP canister purge valve.

9. Disconnect the upper radiator hose from the thermostat housing.

10. Disconnect the heater coolant hose from the coolant crossover manifold assembly.

11. Disconnect the 8 fuel injector electrical connectors.

12. Disconnect the Throttle Position (TP) sensor and Electronic Throttle Control (ETC) electrical connectors.

13. Disconnect the 4 LH ignition coil and the LH Variable Camshaft Timing (VCT) solenoid electrical connectors and detach the 2 engine wiring harness retainers from the LH valve cover studs.

14. Disconnect the intake manifold vacuum tube from the brake booster vacuum hose.

➡**The intake manifold vacuum tube must be removed with the intake manifold as an assembly.**

15. Disconnect the intake manifold vacuum tube from the LH valve cover stud bolt and the support bracket at the rear of the LH cylinder head.

16. Remove the 10 intake manifold bolts.

17. Remove the 3 bolts, the coolant crossover manifold assembly and discard the gaskets.

18. Clean and inspect the sealing surfaces with silicone gasket remover and metal surface prep, using plastic scrapers only.

➡**The intake manifold vacuum tube must be positioned under the engine wiring harness and removed with the intake manifold as an assembly.**

19. Position the intake forward to gain access to the wiring harness retainers.

20. Disconnect the 2 engine wiring harness retainers from the rear of the intake manifold.

21. Disconnect the Cylinder Head Temperature (CHT) sensor jumper harness electrical connector retainer.

22. Remove the intake manifold and discard the gaskets.

To install:

✴✴ WARNING

If the engine is repaired or replaced because of upper engine failure, typically including valve or piston damage, check the intake manifold for metal debris. If metal debris is found, install a new intake manifold. Failure to follow these instructions can result in engine damage.

➡**The intake manifold vacuum tube must be positioned under the engine wiring harness during installation of the intake manifold.**

23. Using new intake manifold gaskets, position the intake manifold. Position the intake manifold forward and connect the

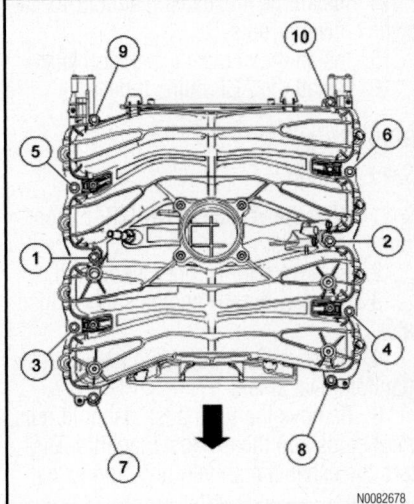

Fig. 68 Install the 10 intake manifold bolts and tighten in 2 stages in the sequence shown

CHT sensor jumper harness electrical connector retainer.

24. Connect the 2 engine wiring harness retainers to the rear of the intake manifold and position back the intake manifold assembly.

25. Using new gaskets, position the coolant crossover manifold assembly and install the 3 bolts. Tighten to 89 inch lbs. (10 Nm).

26. Install the 10 intake manifold bolts and tighten in 2 stages in the sequence shown:

   a. Stage 1: Tighten to 18 inch lbs. (2 Nm).

   b. Stage 2: Tighten to 89 inch lbs. (10 Nm).

27. Connect the intake manifold vacuum tube to the support bracket and the valve cover stud.

28. Connect the brake booster vacuum hose to the intake manifold vacuum tube and position the clamp.

29. Connect the 4 LH ignition coil and the LH VCT solenoid electrical connectors and attach the 2 engine wiring harness retainers to the LH valve cover studs.

30. Connect the TP sensor and electronic throttle control electrical connectors.

31. Connect the 8 fuel injector electrical connectors.

32. Connect the heater coolant hose to the coolant crossover manifold assembly.

33. Connect the upper radiator hose to the thermostat housing.

34. Connect the electrical connector and the EVAP tube quick connect coupling to the EVAP canister purge valve.

35. Connect the fuel supply tube quick connect coupling.

36. Position the PCV tube and connect the quick connect couplings.

37. Position the TB -to- ACL outlet tube adapter and install the 3 bolts. Tighten the bolt to 89 inch lbs. (10 Nm).

38. Position the air intake resonator assembly, install the bolt and the clamp. Tighten the bolt to 89 inch lbs. (10 Nm).

39. Position the crankcase ventilation tube and connect the quick connect couplings.

40. Install the generator. See "ENGINE ELECTRICAL" section.

41. Fill and bleed the engine cooling system.

OIL PAN

REMOVAL & INSTALLATION
See Figures 69 through 73.

1. With the vehicle in NEUTRAL, position it on a hoist.

2. For 4WD vehicles, if equipped, remove the 10 bolts and the 2 skid plates.

3. Remove the oil drain plug and drain the engine oil. Install the drain plug when finished. Tighten to 17 ft. lbs. (23 Nm).

4. Remove the 4 nuts, the 4 bolts and the crossmember under the oil pan.

5. On 4WD vehicles, perform the following:

  a. Position a suitable hydraulic jack under the front axle. Securely strap the jack to the axle.

  b. Rotate the steering column so the pinch bolt for the steering column coupling allows clearance for the axle carrier mounting bushing bolt and remove it.

  c. Remove the axle shaft housing carrier bushing bolt.

  d. Remove the lower front axle carrier mounting bushing bolt.

➡**Use care when lowering the front axle housing, or the vacuum lines to the axle solenoid may become disconnected or damaged.**

  e. Lower the axle to allow clearance for the oil pan to be removed.

6. Remove the starter wiring harness rear support bracket bolt.

7. Remove the nut and position the starter wiring harness and the transmission fluid cooler tubes aside.

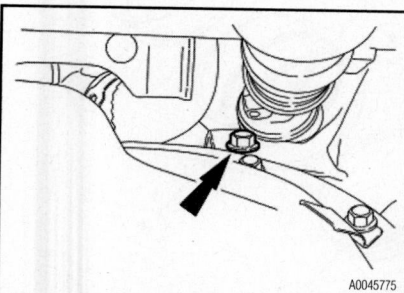

Fig. 69 Rotate the steering column so the pinch bolt for the steering column coupling allows clearance for the axle carrier mounting bushing bolt and remove it.

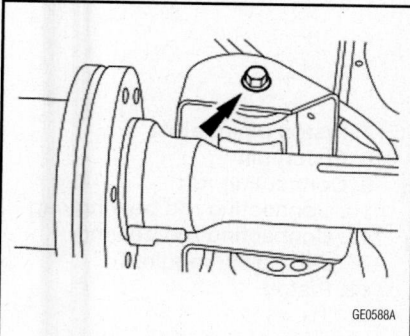

Fig. 70 Remove the axle shaft housing carrier bushing bolt.

8. Detach the oil pressure switch wiring harness from the oil pan bolt.

9. Remove the 16 bolts, the oil pan and the gasket. Discard the gasket.

✳✳ CAUTION

Do not use metal scrapers, wire brushes, power abrasive discs or other abrasive means to clean the sealing surfaces. These tools cause scratches and gouges, which make leak paths. Use a plastic scraping tool to remove all traces of old sealant.

10. Inspect the oil pan. Clean the gasket mating surfaces of the oil pan and engine block with silicone gasket remover and metal surface prep.

To install:

➡**If not secured within 4 minutes, the sealant must be removed and the sealing area cleaned with silicone gasket remover and metal surface**

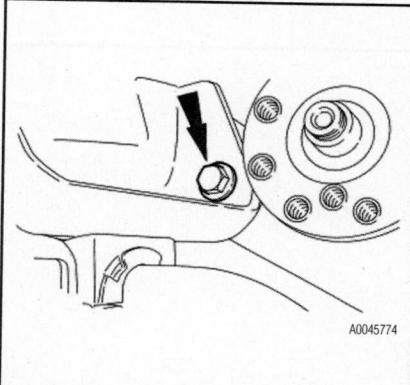

Fig. 71 Remove the lower front axle carrier mounting bushing bolt.

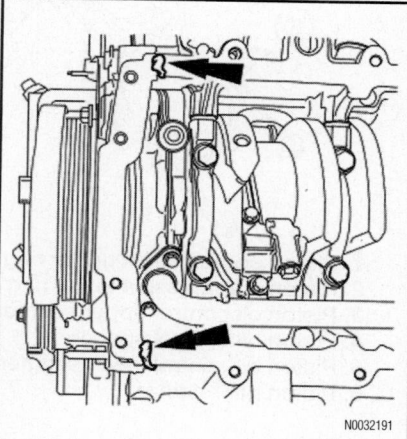

Fig. 72 Apply silicone gasket and sealant at the engine front cover-to-cylinder block sealing surface.

prep. Follow the directions on the packaging. Allow to dry until there is no sign of wetness, or 4 minutes, whichever is longer. Failure to follow this procedure can cause future oil leakage.

11. Apply silicone gasket and sealant at the outer edges of the crankshaft rear seal retainer plate-to-cylinder block sealing surface.

12. Apply silicone gasket and sealant at the engine front cover-to-cylinder block sealing surface.

13. Position a new gasket and the oil pan and install the 16 bolts. Tighten the bolts in the sequence shown in 3 stages.

  a. Stage 1: Tighten to 18 inch lbs. (2 Nm).

  b. Stage 2: Tighten to 177 inch lbs. (20 Nm).

  c. Stage 3: Tighten an additional 60 degrees.

14. Attach the oil pressure switch wiring harness to the oil pan bolt.

15. Position the transmission fluid cooler tube support bracket, the starter wiring harness support bracket and install the nut. Tighten to 89 inch lbs. (10 Nm).

16. Position the starter wiring harness and install the starter wiring harness rear support bracket bolt. Tighten to 89 inch lbs. (10 Nm).

17. Install the transmission fluid cooling tubes rear support bracket bolt. Tighten to 35 ft. lbs. (48 Nm).

18. On 4WD vehicles, perform the following:

✳✳ CAUTION

Use care when positioning the front axle housing, or the vacuum lines to the axle solenoid may become disconnected or damaged.

  a. Raise the front axle carrier into position.

  b. Install the lower front axle carrier mounting bushing bolt. Tighten to 85 ft. lbs. (115 Nm).

  c. Install the axle shaft housing carrier bushing bolt. Tighten to 85 ft. lbs. (115 Nm).

  d. Install the upper front axle carrier mounting bushing bolt. Tighten to 85 ft. lbs. (115 Nm).

19. Position the crossmember and install the 4 bolts and the 4 nuts. Tighten to 66 ft. lbs. (90 Nm).

20. On 4WD vehicles, if equipped, install the 2 skid plates and the 10 bolts. Tighten to 35 ft. lbs. (48 Nm).

21. Fill the engine with clean engine oil.

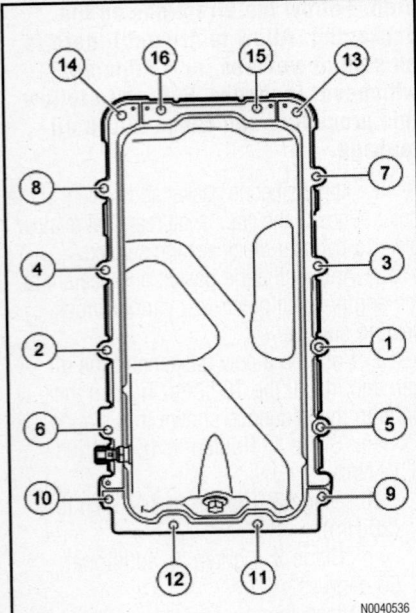

Fig. 73 Position a new gasket and the oil pan and install the 16 bolts. Tighten the bolts in the sequence shown in 3 stages.

OIL PUMP

REMOVAL & INSTALLATION

See Figure 74.

1. Remove the timing drive components. See "Timing Chain & Sprockets" in this section.
2. Remove the oil pan. See "Oil Pan" in this section.
3. Remove the 3 bolts and the oil pump screen and pickup tube.
4. Remove the 3 bolts and the oil pump.

To install:

✳✳ CAUTION

Do not use metal scrapers, wire brushes, power abrasive discs or

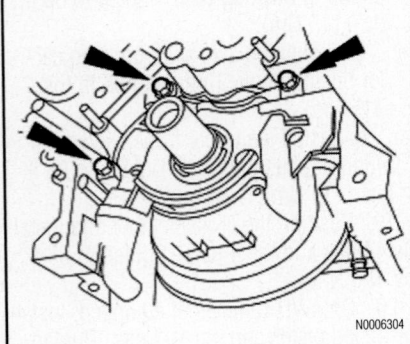

Fig. 74 Remove the 3 bolts and the oil pump.

other abrasive means to clean the sealing surfaces. These tools cause scratches and gouges which make leak paths. Use a plastic scraping tool to remove all traces of old sealant.

5. Clean the sealing surfaces with metal surface prep. Follow the directions on the packaging. Inspect the mating surfaces.
6. Position the oil pump and install the 3 bolts. Tighten to 89 inch lbs. (10 Nm).

➡**Make sure the O-ring is in place and not damaged. A missing or damaged O-ring can cause foam in the lubrication system, low oil pressure and severe engine damage.**

7. Position the oil pump screen and pickup tube and install the 3 bolts.
   a. Tighten the 2 oil pump screen and pickup tube-to-oil pump bolts to 89 inch lbs. (10 Nm).

   b. Tighten the oil pump screen and pickup tube-to-spacer bolt to 18 ft. lbs. (25 Nm).
8. Install the oil pan. See "Oil Pan" in this section.
9. Install the timing drive components. See "Timing Chain & Sprockets" in this section.

PISTON AND RING

POSITIONING

See Figure 75.

REAR MAIN SEAL

REMOVAL & INSTALLATION

See Figure 76.

1. Remove the transmission. See "DRIVE TRAIN" section.
2. Remove the 8 bolts and the flexplate.
3. Using the Slide Hammer and the Crankshaft Rear Oil Slinger Remover,

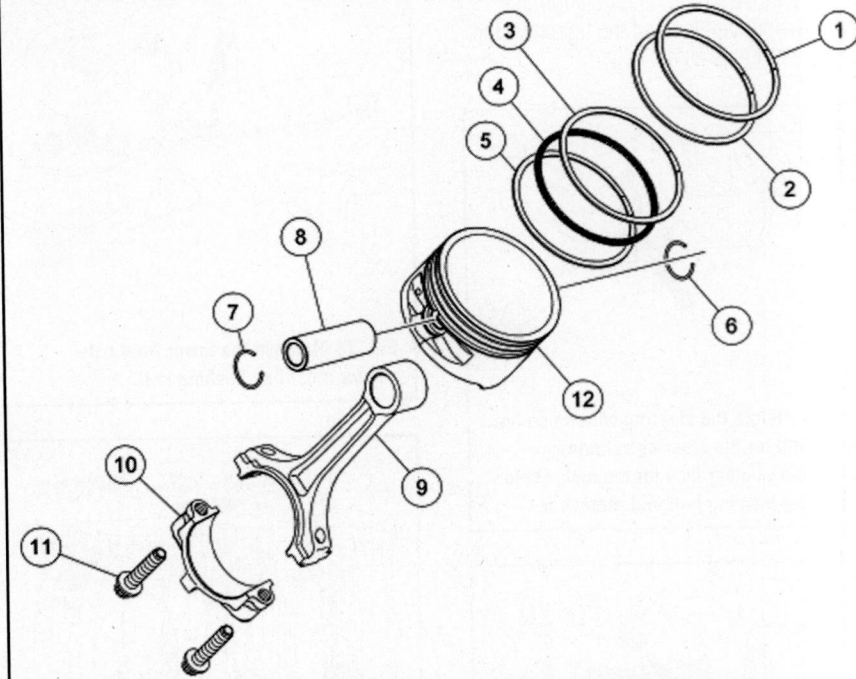

1. Piston compression upper ring
2. Piston compression lower ring
3. Piston oil control upper segment ring
4. Piston oil control spacer
5. Piston oil control lower segment ring
6. Piston pin retainer
7. Piston pin retainer
8. Piston pin
9. Connecting rod
10. Connecting rod bearing cap
11. Connecting rod bearing cap bolt (2 required)
12. Piston

Fig. 75 Exploded view of the piston assembly–ring end gaps should be equally offset from each other

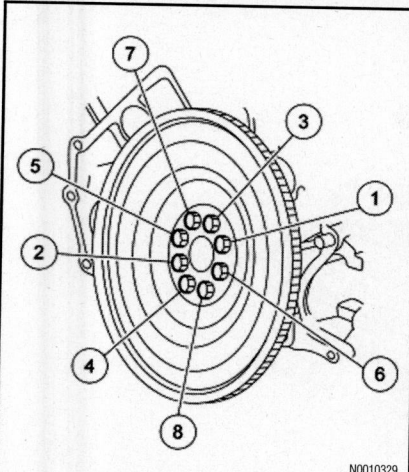

Fig. 76 Install the flexplate and tighten the 8 bolts in the sequence shown. Tighten to 59 ft. lbs. (80 Nm).

N0010329

remove and discard the crankshaft rear oil slinger.

4. Using the Slide Hammer and the Crankshaft Rear Oil Seal Remover, remove and discard the crankshaft rear seal.

To install:

➡ Lubricate the crankshaft rear seal with clean engine oil prior to installation.

5. Using the Crankshaft Rear Oil Seal Installers, install a new crankshaft rear seal.

6. Using the Crankshaft Rear Oil Seal Installers and the Crankshaft Rear Oil Slinger Installer, install a new crankshaft oil slinger, coated with clean engine oil.

7. Install the flexplate and tighten the 8 bolts in the sequence shown. Tighten to 59 ft. lbs. (80 Nm).

8. Install the transmission. See "DRIVE TRAIN" section.

TIMING CHAIN FRONT COVER (ENGINE FRONT COVER)

REMOVAL & INSTALLATION

See Figures 77 through 83.

1. With the vehicle in NEUTRAL, position it on a hoist.

2. Remove the RH and LH valve covers. See "Valve Covers" in this section.

3. Loosen the 4 coolant pump pulley bolts.

4. Rotate the tensioner clockwise and remove the accessory drive belt.

5. Remove the 4 bolts and the coolant pump pulley.

6. Drain the engine oil.

7. Remove the bolt and position the starter wiring harness and starter wiring harness rear support bracket aside.

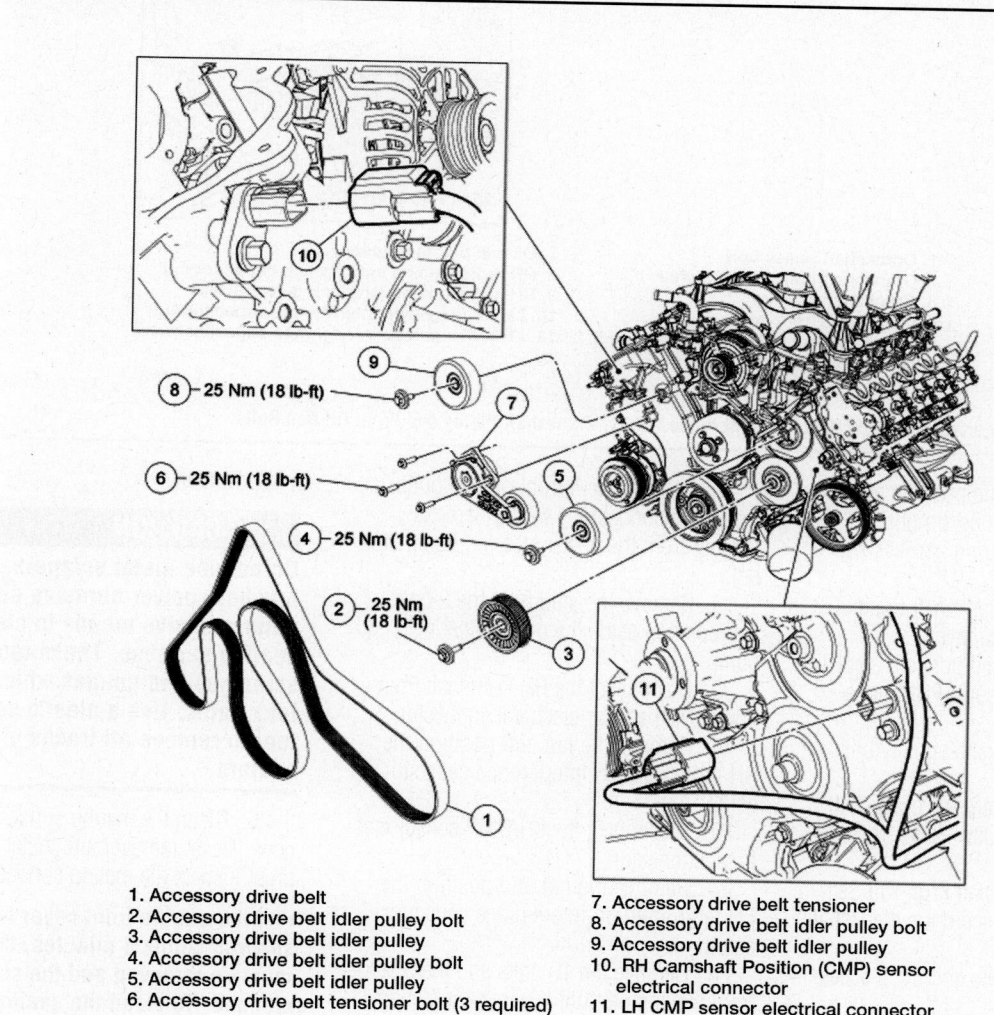

1. Accessory drive belt
2. Accessory drive belt idler pulley bolt
3. Accessory drive belt idler pulley
4. Accessory drive belt idler pulley bolt
5. Accessory drive belt idler pulley
6. Accessory drive belt tensioner bolt (3 required)
7. Accessory drive belt tensioner
8. Accessory drive belt idler pulley bolt
9. Accessory drive belt idler pulley
10. RH Camshaft Position (CMP) sensor electrical connector
11. LH CMP sensor electrical connector

N0102931

Fig. 77 Front End Accessory Drive (FEAD), LH and RH Camshaft Position (CMP) Sensors Electrical Connectors

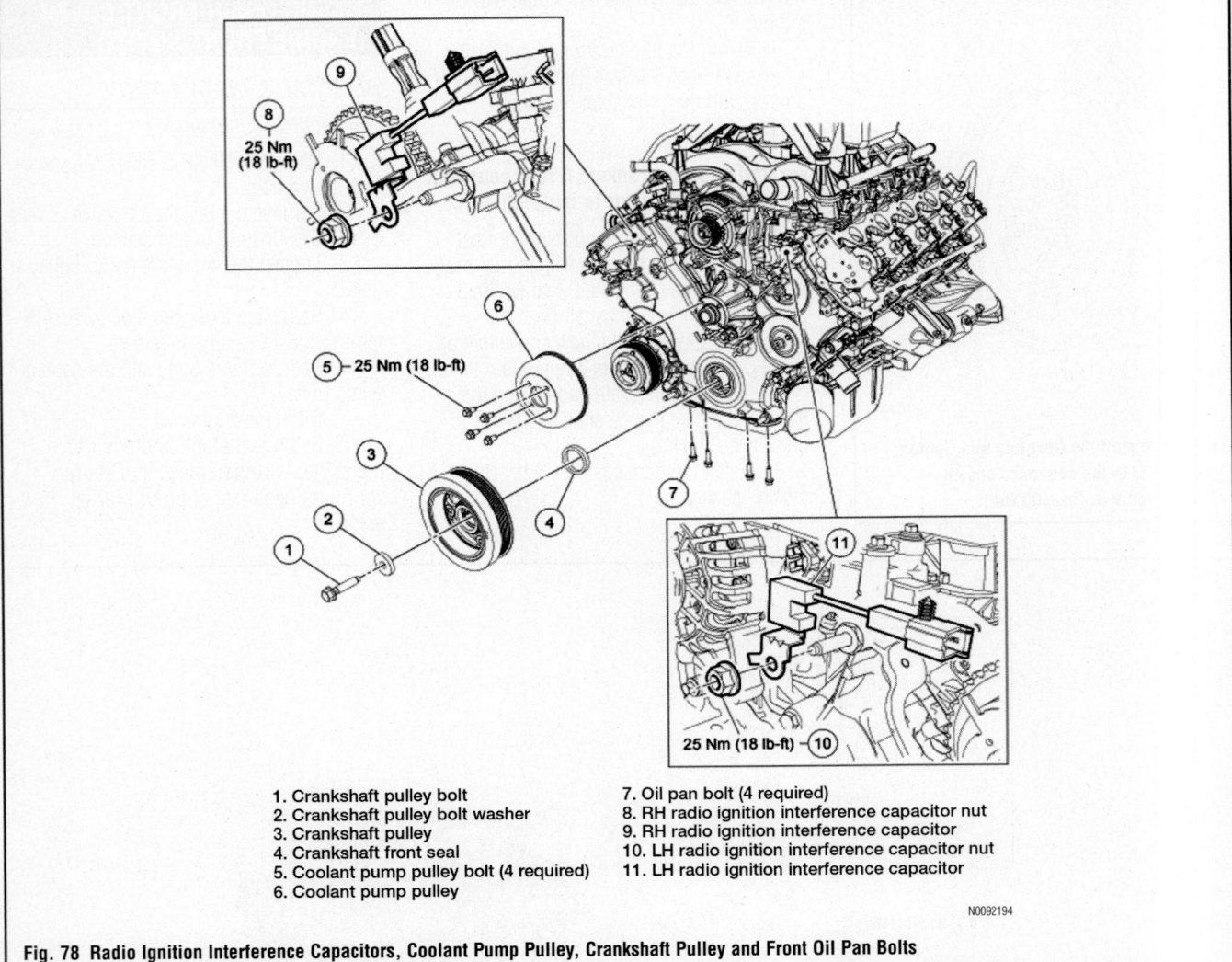

1. Crankshaft pulley bolt
2. Crankshaft pulley bolt washer
3. Crankshaft pulley
4. Crankshaft front seal
5. Coolant pump pulley bolt (4 required)
6. Coolant pump pulley
7. Oil pan bolt (4 required)
8. RH radio ignition interference capacitor nut
9. RH radio ignition interference capacitor
10. LH radio ignition interference capacitor nut
11. LH radio ignition interference capacitor

N0092194

Fig. 78 Radio Ignition Interference Capacitors, Coolant Pump Pulley, Crankshaft Pulley and Front Oil Pan Bolts

8. Remove the nut and position aside the transmission cooler tube support bracket and the starter wiring harness support bracket.

9. Disconnect the Crankshaft Position (CKP) sensor electrical connector.

10. Remove the nut and position aside the Power Steering Pressure (PSP) hose support bracket.

11. Remove the crankshaft pulley bolt and washer.

12. Remove and discard the crankshaft pulley bolt. Using the 3 Jaw Puller, remove the crankshaft pulley.

13. Using the Crankshaft Front Oil Seal Remover, remove and discard the crankshaft front seal.

14. Remove the 3 bolts and the 3 accessory drive idler pulleys.

15. Remove the 3 bolts and the accessory drive belt tensioner.

16. If equipped, remove the 4 bolts and the skid plate.

17. Remove the 4 front oil pan bolts.

18. Disconnect the wiring harness retainer from the power steering pump stud bolt.

19. Remove the stud bolt, the 2 bolts, and position aside the power steering pump.

20. Disconnect the RH Camshaft Position (CMP) sensor electrical connector.

21. Remove the nut and position the RH radio ignition interference capacitor aside.

22. Disconnect the LH CMP sensor electrical connector.

23. Remove the nut and position the LH radio ignition interference capacitor aside.

24. Remove the 10 bolts and the 5 studs from the engine front cover (timing chain cover).

25. Remove the engine front cover from the front cover-to-cylinder block dowel. Remove the engine front cover gaskets.

To install:

※※ **CAUTION**

Do not use metal scrapers, wire brushes, power abrasive discs or other abrasive means to clean the sealing surfaces. These tools cause scratches and gouges which make leak paths. Use a plastic scraping tool to remove all traces of old sealant.

26. Clean the mating surfaces with silicone gasket remover and metal surface prep. Inspect the mating surfaces.

➡**If the engine front cover is not secured within 4 minutes, the sealant must be removed and the sealing area cleaned. To clean the sealing area, use silicone gasket remover and metal surface prep. Allow to dry until there is no sign of wetness, or 4 minutes,**

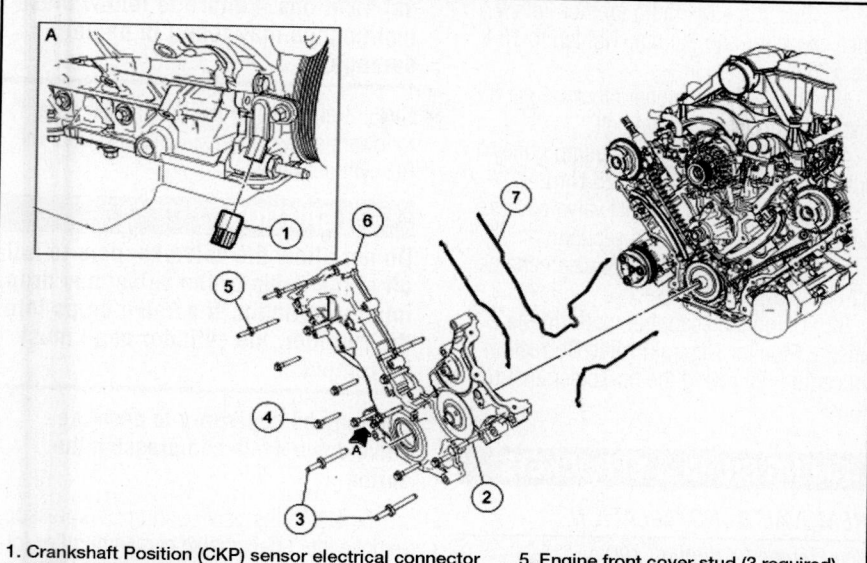

1. Crankshaft Position (CKP) sensor electrical connector
2. Engine front cover bolt
3. Engine front cover studs (2 required)
4. Engine front cover bolt (9 required)
5. Engine front cover stud (3 required)
6. Engine front cover
7. Engine front cover gasket (3 required)

N0102932

Fig. 79 Engine Front Cover, Gaskets and Crankshaft Position (CKP) Sensor Electrical Connector

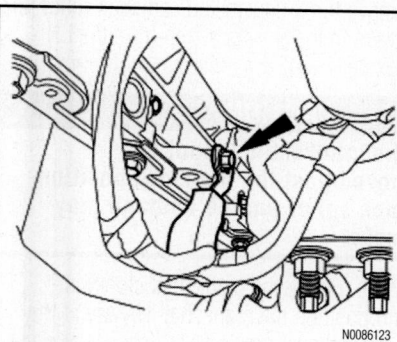

N0086123

Fig. 80 Remove the bolt and position the starter wiring harness and starter wiring harness rear support bracket aside.

whichever is longer. Failure to follow this procedure can cause future oil leakage.

➡ Make sure that the engine front cover gasket is in place on the engine front cover before installation.

27. Apply a bead of silicone gasket and sealant along the cylinder head-to-cylinder block surface and the oil pan-to-cylinder block surface, at the locations shown.

28. Install a new engine front cover gasket on the engine front cover. Position the engine front cover onto the dowels. Install the fasteners finger-tight.

29. Tighten the 15 engine front cover fasteners in the sequence shown in 2 stages:

    a. Stage 1: Tighten fasteners 1 through 15 to 18 ft. lbs. (25 Nm).

    b. Stage 2: Tighten fasteners 6 and 7 to 35 ft. lbs. (48 Nm).

30. Loosely install the 4 oil pan bolts, then tighten in 2 stages, in the sequence shown:

    a. Stage 1: Tighten to 177 inch lbs. (20 Nm).

    b. Stage 2: Tighten an additional 60 degrees.

31. Connect the CKP sensor electrical connector.

32. Position the starter wiring harness support bracket and the transmission cooler tube support bracket and tighten the nut. Tighten to 89 inch lbs. (10 Nm).

33. Position the starter wiring harness and starter wiring harness rear support bracket and install the bolt. Tighten to 89 inch lbs. (10 Nm).

34. Lubricate the engine front cover and the crankshaft seal inner lip with clean engine oil. Install the seal and oil slinger. See "Crankshaft Front Seal" in this section.

➡ If not secured within 4 minutes, the sealant must be removed and the sealing area cleaned with metal surface prep and silicone gasket remover. Allow to dry until there is no sign of wetness, or 4 minutes, whichever is longer. Failure to follow this procedure can cause future oil leakage.

35. Apply silicone gasket and sealant to the Woodruff key slot in the crankshaft pulley.

36. Use the Crankshaft Vibration Damper Installer to install the crankshaft pulley.

37. Tighten the new crankshaft pulley bolt in 4 stages:

    a. Stage 1: Tighten to 66 ft. lbs. (90 Nm).

    b. Stage 2: Loosen 360 degrees.

    c. Stage 3: Tighten to 37 ft. lbs. (50 Nm).

    d. Stage 4: Tighten an additional 90 degrees.

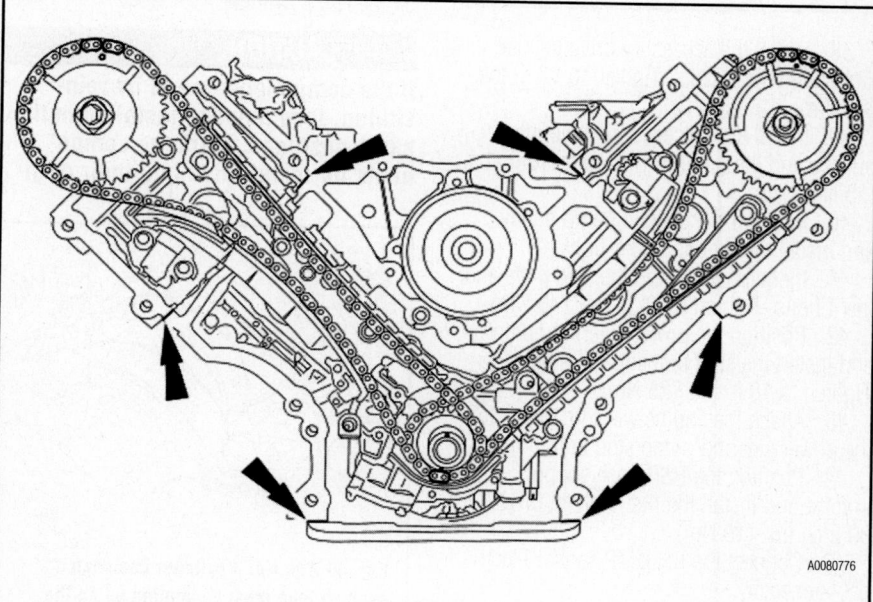

A0080776

Fig. 81 Apply a bead of silicone gasket and sealant along the cylinder head-to-cylinder block surface and the oil pan-to-cylinder block surface, at the locations shown.

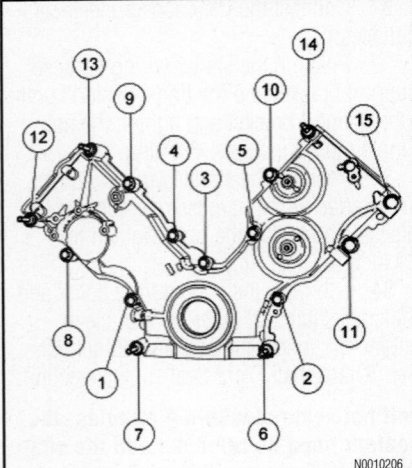

Fig. 82 Tighten the 15 engine front cover fasteners in the sequence shown in 2 stages

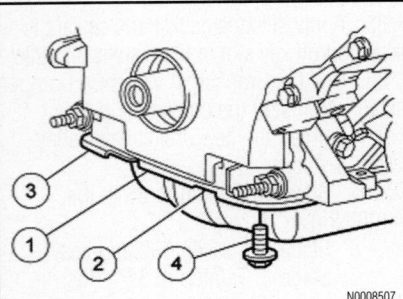

Fig. 83 Loosely install the 4 oil pan bolts, then tighten in 2 stages, in the sequence shown

38. Install the accessory drive belt tensioner and the 3 bolts. Tighten to 18 ft. lbs. (25 Nm).

39. Install the 3 accessory drive idler pulleys and the 3 bolts. Tighten to 18 ft. lbs. (25 Nm).

40. Position the coolant pump pulley and install the 4 bolts finger-tight.

41. If equipped, install the skid plate and the 4 bolts. Tighten to 35 ft. lbs. (48 Nm).

42. Position the power steering pump and install the stud bolt and the 2 bolts. Tighten to 18 ft. lbs. (25 Nm).

43. Attach the engine wiring harness to the power steering pump stud bolt.

44. Position the PSP hose support bracket and install the nut. Tighten to 89 inch lbs. (10 Nm).

45. Connect the RH CMP sensor electrical connector.

46. Install the LH radio ignition interference capacitor and the nut. Tighten to 18 ft. lbs. (25 Nm). Connect the LH CMP sensor electrical connector.

47. Install the RH radio ignition interference capacitor and the nut. Tighten to 18 ft. lbs. (25 Nm).

48. Rotate the tensioner clockwise and install the accessory drive belt.

49. Tighten the 4 coolant pump pulley bolts. Tighten to 18 ft. lbs. (25 Nm).

50. Install the LH and RH valve covers. See "Valve Covers" in this section.

51. Fill the crankcase with clean engine oil.

52. Using the scan tool, perform the Misfire Monitor Neutral Profile Correction procedure, following the on-screen instructions

TIMING CHAIN & SPROCKETS

REMOVAL & INSTALLATION
See Figures 84 through 100.

1. Remove the engine front cover. See "Timing Chain Cover (Engine Front Cover)" in this section.

2. Remove the crankshaft sensor ring from the crankshaft.

3. Position the crankshaft keyway at the 12 o'clock position.

➡**If the camshaft lobes are not exactly positioned as shown, the crankshaft will require one full additional rotation to 12 o'clock.**

4. The No. 1 cylinder camshaft exhaust lobe must be coming up on the exhaust stroke. Verify by noting the position of the 2 intake camshaft lobes and the exhaust lobe on the No. 1 cylinder.

❋❋ CAUTION
If the components are to be reinstalled, they must be installed in the same positions. Mark the components for installation into their origi-

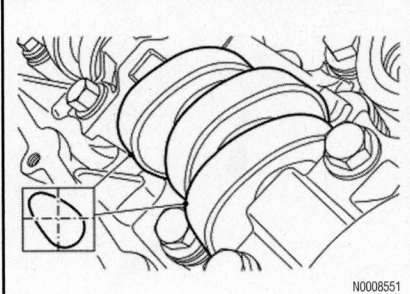

Fig. 84 The No. 1 cylinder camshaft exhaust lobe must be coming up on the exhaust stroke. Verify by noting the position of the 2 intake camshaft lobes and the exhaust lobe on the No. 1 cylinder.

nal locations. Failure to follow these instructions may result in engine damage.

5. Remove only the 3 camshaft roller followers shown in the illustration from the RH cylinder head.

❋❋ CAUTION
Do not allow the valve keepers to fall off of the valve or the valve may drop into the cylinder. If a valve drops into the cylinder, the cylinder head must be removed.

➡**It may be necessary to push the valve down while compressing the spring.**

6. Using the Valve Spring Compressor, remove the 3 designated camshaft roller followers in the previous step from the RH cylinder head.

7. Remove only the 3 camshaft roller followers shown in the illustration from the LH cylinder head.

8. Using the Valve Spring Compressor, remove the 3 designated camshaft roller followers in the previous step from the LH cylinder head.

❋❋ CAUTION
The crankshaft cannot be moved past the 6 o'clock position once set or engine damage may occur.

9. Rotate the crankshaft clockwise and position the crankshaft keyway at the 6 o'clock position.

❋❋ CAUTION
If one or both tensioner mounting bolts are loosened or removed, the tensioner-sealing bead must be inspected for seal integrity. If cracks, tears, separation from the tensioner body or permanent compression of the seal bead is observed, install a new tensioner or engine damage may occur.

10. Remove the 2 bolts, the LH timing chain tensioner and tensioner arm. Repeat for the RH side.

11. Remove the RH and LH timing chains and the crankshaft sprocket.

12. Remove the RH timing chain from the camshaft and crankshaft sprockets.

13. Repeat the above procedure for the LH timing chain.

14. Remove the 4 bolts and remove both timing chain guides.

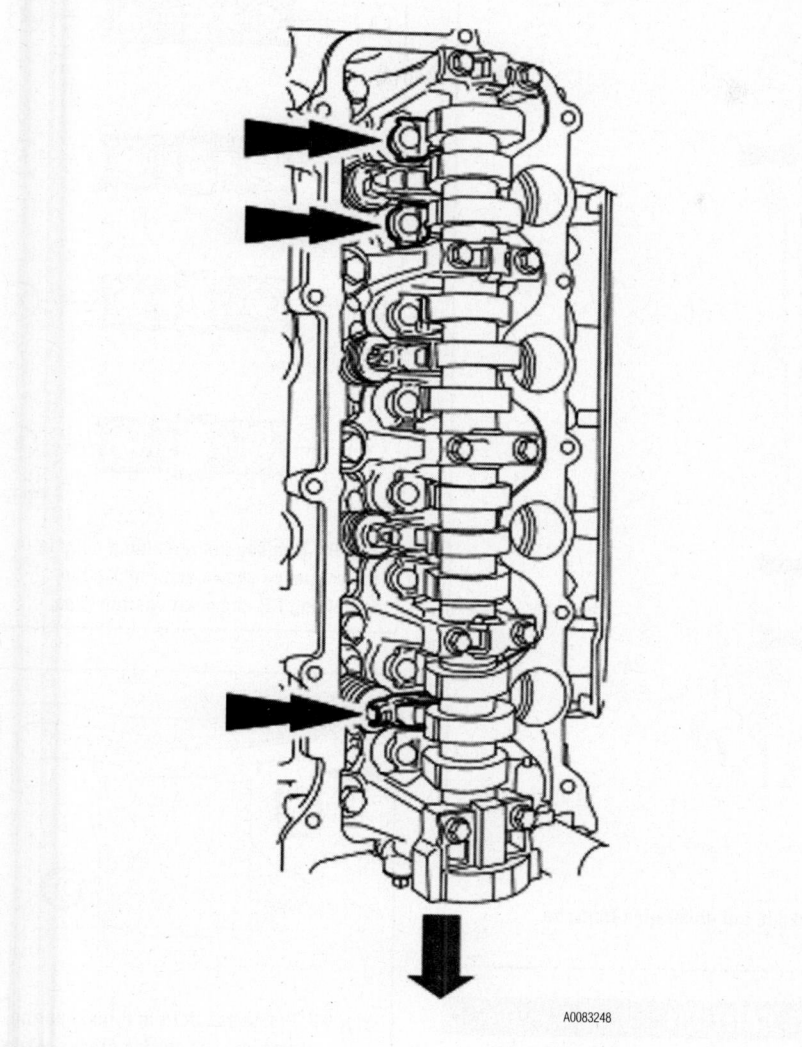

Fig. 85 Remove only the 3 camshaft roller followers shown in the illustration from the RH cylinder head.

Fig. 86 Using the Valve Spring Compressor, remove the 3 designated camshaft roller followers in the previous step from the RH cylinder head.

✳✳ CAUTION

Damage to the camshaft phaser and sprocket assembly will occur if mishandled or used as a lifting or leveraging device.

✳✳ CAUTION

Only use hand tools to remove the camshaft phaser and sprocket assembly or damage may occur to the camshaft or camshaft phaser and sprocket.

15. Using the Cam Phaser Locking Tool, remove the bolt and the RH camshaft phaser and sprocket assembly. Discard the camshaft phaser and sprocket bolt. Repeat for LH side.

✳✳ CAUTION

Remove the front thrust camshaft bearing cap straight upward from the bearing towers or the bearing cap may be damaged from side loading.

16. Remove the 2 bolts and the RH camshaft front bearing cap.

✳✳ CAUTION

The camshaft bearing caps must be installed in their original locations. Record camshaft bearing cap locations. Failure to follow these instructions may result in engine damage.

17. Remove the remaining bolts in the sequence shown and remove the remaining RH camshaft bearing caps.
18. Clean and inspect the RH camshaft bearing caps.

➡**The camshaft front thrust bearing cap contains an oil metering groove. Make sure the groove is free of foreign material.**

19. Remove the RH camshaft.
20. Repeat the above for the LH camshaft bearing caps and camshaft.
Remove all of the remaining camshaft roller followers from the cylinder heads.

To install:

✳✳ CAUTION

If the components are to be reinstalled, they must be installed in the same positions. Mark the components for installation into the original locations. Failure to follow these instructions may result in engine damage.

21. Lubricate the camshaft and camshaft journals with clean engine oil prior to installation.
22. Install the LH and RH camshaft bearing caps in their original locations.
23. Lubricate the camshaft bearing caps with clean engine oil.
24. Position the 2 front camshaft bearing caps.
25. Position the 8 remaining camshaft bearing caps. Install the 20 bolts loosely. Tighten to 89 inch lbs. (10 Nm) in the sequence shown.

✳✳ CAUTION

Damage to the camshaft phaser and sprocket assembly will occur if mishandled or used as a lifting or leveraging device.

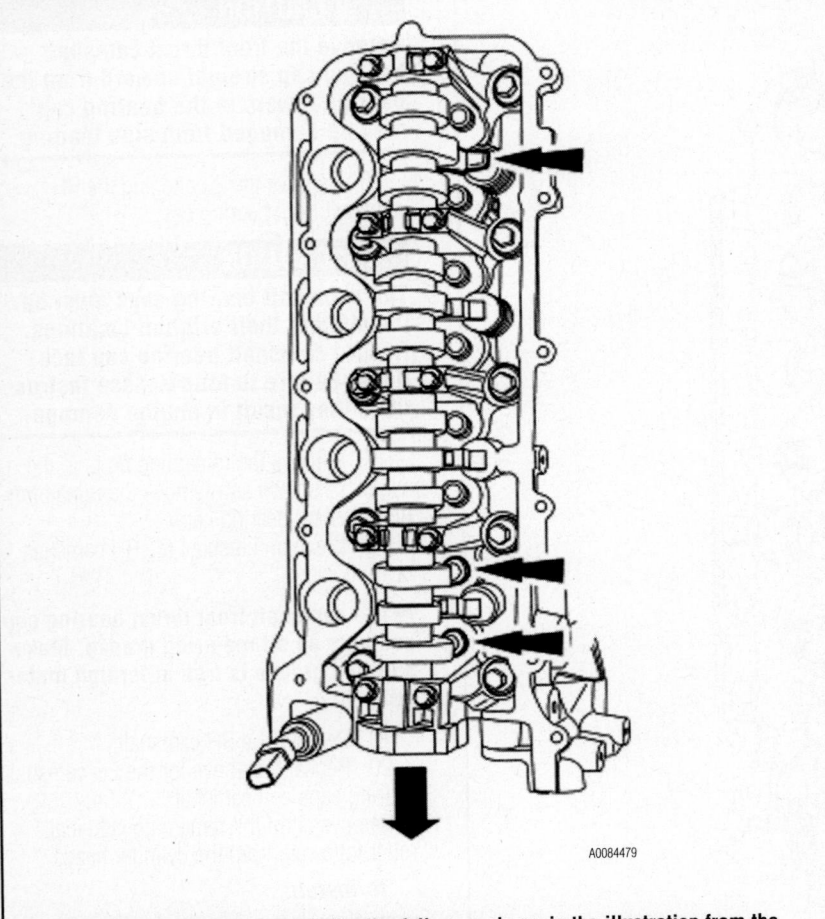

Fig. 87 Remove only the 3 camshaft roller followers shown in the illustration from the LH cylinder head.

26. Position the camshaft phaser and sprockets and install 2 new camshaft phaser and sprocket bolts finger-tight.

✳✳ CAUTION

Damage to the camshaft phaser and sprocket assembly will occur if mishandled or used as a lifting or leveraging device.

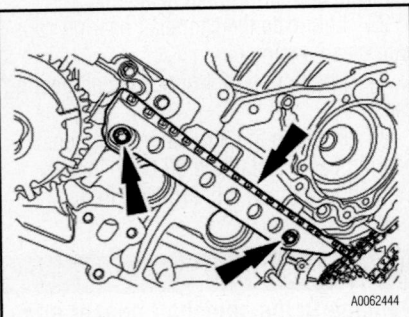

Fig. 88 Remove the 4 bolts and remove both timing chain guides.

✳✳ CAUTION

Only use hand tools to remove the camshaft phaser and sprocket assembly or damage may occur to the camshaft or camshaft phaser and sprocket.

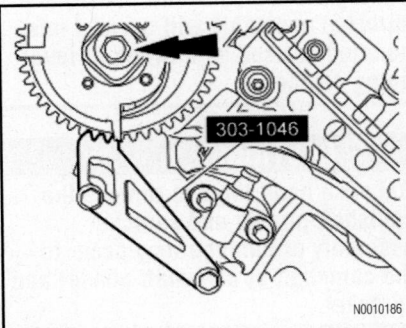

Fig. 89 Using the Cam Phaser Locking Tool, remove the bolt and the RH camshaft phaser and sprocket assembly. Discard the camshaft phaser and sprocket bolt. Repeat for LH side.

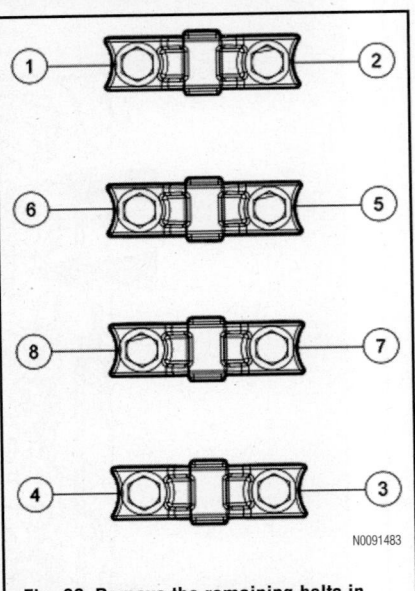

Fig. 90 Remove the remaining bolts in the sequence shown and remove the remaining RH camshaft bearing caps.

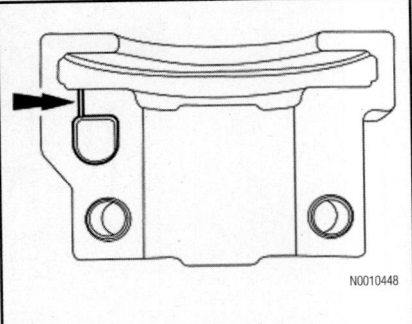

Fig. 91 The camshaft front thrust bearing cap contains an oil metering groove. Make sure the groove is free of foreign material.

27. Using the Cam Phaser Locking Tool, tighten the LH and RH camshaft phaser and sprocket bolts in 2 stages:
 a. Stage 1: Tighten to 30 ft. lbs. (40 Nm).
 b. Stage 2: Tighten an additional 90 degrees.
28. Position the crankshaft with the Crankshaft Holding Tool, then remove the tool.

✳✳ CAUTION

Timing chain procedures must be followed exactly or damage to valves and pistons will result.

✳✳ CAUTION

Prior to installation, inspect the tensioner-sealing bead for seal integrity. If cracks, tears, separation from the

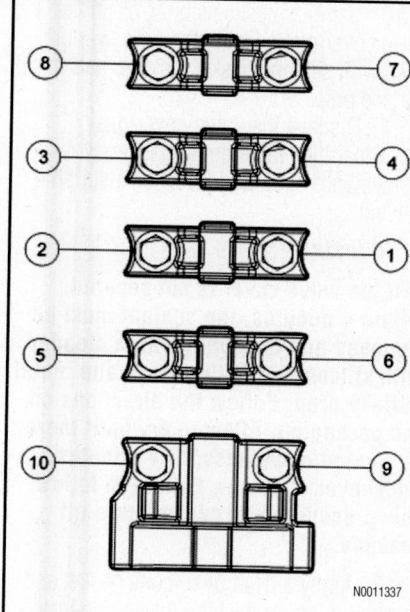

Fig. 92 Position the 8 remaining camshaft bearing caps. Install the 20 bolts loosely. Tighten to 89 inch lbs. (10 Nm) in the sequence shown.

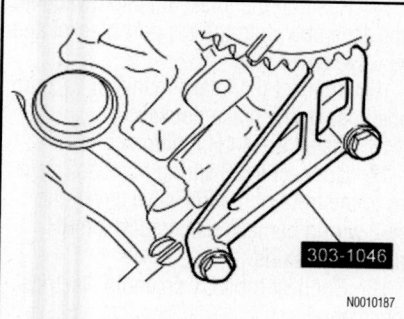

Fig. 93 Using the Cam Phaser Locking Tool, tighten the LH and RH camshaft phaser and sprocket bolts in 2 stages

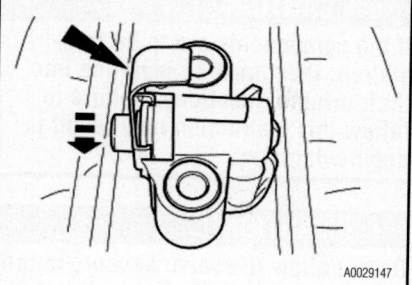

Fig. 94 Compress the tensioner plunger, using a vise. Install a retaining clip on the tensioner to hold the plunger in during installation.

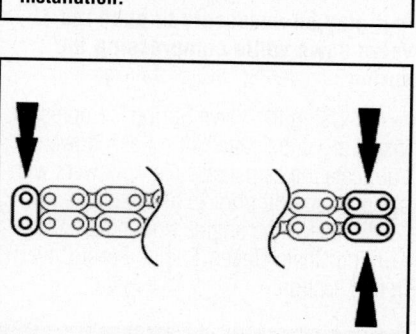

Fig. 95 If the copper links are not visible, mark 2 links on one end and 1 link on the other end, and use as timing marks.

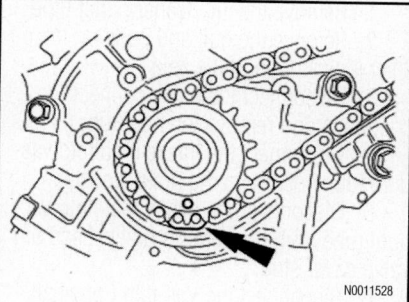

Fig. 96 Position the lower end of the LH (inner) timing chain on the crankshaft sprocket, aligning the timing mark on the outer flange of the crankshaft sprocket with the single copper (marked) link on the chain.

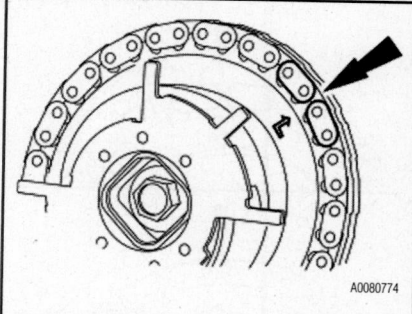

Fig. 97 Position the timing chain on the camshaft phaser and sprocket with the timing mark positioned between the 2 copper (marked) chain links.

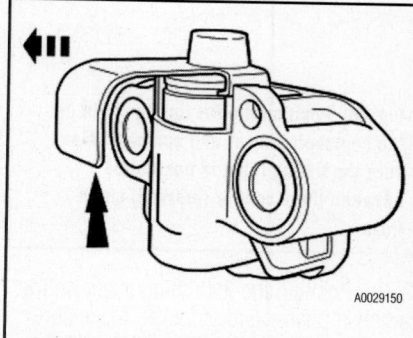

Fig. 98 Remove the retaining clip from the LH timing chain tensioner.

tensioner body or permanent compression of the seal bead is observed, install a new tensioner or engine damage may occur.

29. Compress the tensioner plunger, using a vise. Install a retaining clip on the tensioner to hold the plunger in during installation.
30. Remove the tensioner from the vise.
31. If the copper links are not visible, mark 2 links on one end and 1 link on the other end, and use as timing marks.
32. Install the crankshaft sprocket, making sure the flange faces forward.
33. Install the 4 bolts and the LH and RH timing chain guides. Tighten to 89 inch lbs. (10 Nm).

34. Position the lower end of the LH (inner) timing chain on the crankshaft sprocket, aligning the timing mark on the outer flange of the crankshaft sprocket with the single copper (marked) link on the chain.

➡️ **Make sure the upper half of the timing chain is below the tensioner arm dowel.**

35. Position the timing chain on the camshaft phaser and sprocket with the timing mark positioned between the 2 copper (marked) chain links.

➡️ **The LH timing chain tensioner arm has a bump near the dowel hole for identification.**

36. Position the LH timing chain tensioner arm on the dowel pin and install the LH timing chain tensioner and the 2 bolts. Tighten to 18 ft. lbs. (25 Nm).
37. Remove the retaining clip from the LH timing chain tensioner.
38. Position the lower end of the RH (outer) timing chain on the crankshaft sprocket, aligning the timing mark on the sprocket with the single copper (marked) chain link. (See LH timing chain illustration for reference.)

➡️ **The lower half of the timing chain must be positioned above the tensioner arm dowel.**

➡️ **The camshaft phaser and sprocket will be stamped with one of the illustrated timing marks for the RH camshaft.**

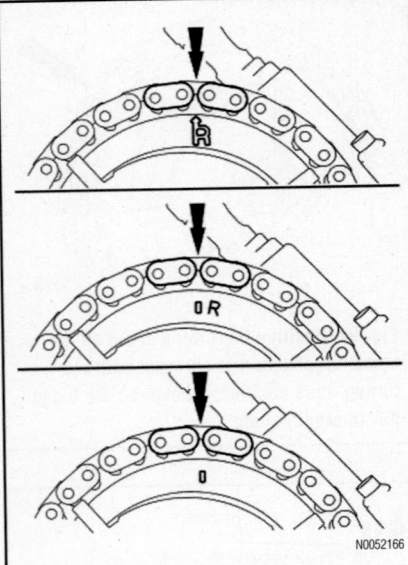

Fig. 99 Position the RH timing chain on the camshaft phaser and sprocket. Make sure the timing mark is positioned between the 2 copper (marked) chain links.

39. Position the RH timing chain on the camshaft phaser and sprocket. Make sure the timing mark is positioned between the 2 copper (marked) chain links.

40. Position the RH timing chain tensioner arm on the dowel pin and install the RH timing chain tensioner and the 2 bolts. Tighten to 18 ft. lbs. (25 Nm).

41. Remove the retaining clip from the RH timing chain tensioner.

42. As a post-check, verify correct alignment of all timing marks.

43. Install the crankshaft sensor ring on the crankshaft.

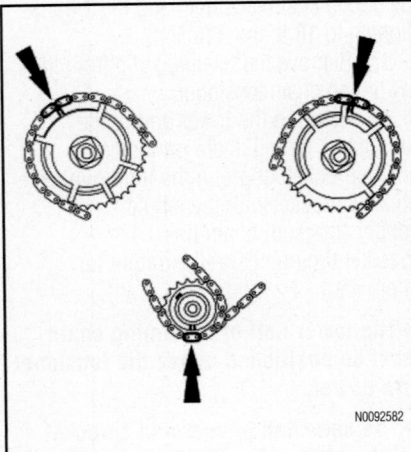

Fig. 100 As a post-check, verify correct alignment of all timing marks.

✳✳ CAUTION

If the components are to be reinstalled, they must be installed into their original locations. Failure to follow this instruction may result in engine damage.

✳✳ CAUTION

Do not allow the valve keepers to fall off of the valve or the valve may drop into the cylinder. If a valve drops into the cylinder, the cylinder head must be removed.

➡ It may be necessary to push the valve down while compressing the spring.

44. Using the Valve Spring Compressor, install all of the camshaft roller followers. Lubricate the camshaft roller followers with clean engine oil prior to installation.

45. Install the engine front cover. See "Timing Chain Cover (Engine Front Cover)" in this section.

VALVE COVERS

REMOVAL & INSTALLATION

Left Side

See Figures 101 and 102.

1. Remove the air cleaner outlet pipe.
2. Remove the bolt and position the oil level indicator and tube aside.
3. Disconnect the quick connect couplings and remove the PCV tube.
4. Disconnect the intake manifold vacuum tube hose from the brake booster.
5. Disconnect the intake manifold vacuum tube from the support bracket and the valve cover stud.
6. Disconnect the Variable Camshaft Timing (VCT) solenoid electrical connector.
7. Disconnect the 3 wiring harness retainers from the front of the LH valve cover and the 2 wiring harness retainers from the LH valve cover studs.
8. Remove the 4 LH ignition coils.

✳✳ CAUTION

When removing the valve cover, make sure to avoid damaging the Variable Camshaft Timing (VCT) solenoid.

➡ The fasteners are part of the valve cover and should not be removed.

9. Loosen the 10 fasteners and remove the LH valve cover and gasket.

10. Using a plastic scraper, clean the valve cover mating surface of the cylinder head with silicone gasket remover and metal surface prep.

11. Discard the valve cover gasket. Clean the valve cover gasket groove with soap and water or a suitable solvent.

To install:

➡ If the valve cover is not secured within 4 minutes, the sealant must be removed and the sealing area cleaned with silicone gasket remover and metal surface prep. Follow the directions on the packaging. Allow to dry until there is no sign of wetness, or 4 minutes, whichever is longer. Failure to follow this procedure can cause future oil leakage.

12. Apply a bead of silicone gasket and sealant in 2 places where the engine front cover meets the cylinder head.

13. Position the LH valve cover and new gasket on the cylinder head and tighten the 10 fasteners in the sequence shown. Tighten to 89 inch lbs. (10 Nm).

14. Position the intake manifold vacuum tube assembly onto the support bracket and the valve cover stud.

15. Connect the intake manifold vacuum tube hose to the brake booster.

16. Install the 4 LH ignition coils.

17. Connect the 3 wiring harness retainers to the front of the RH valve cover and the 2 wiring harness retainers to the RH valve cover studs.

18. Connect the VCT solenoid electrical connector.

19. Position the PCV tube and connect the quick connect couplings.

20. Position back the oil level indicator and tube and install the bolt. Tighten to 89 inch lbs. (10 Nm).

21. Install the ACL outlet pipe.

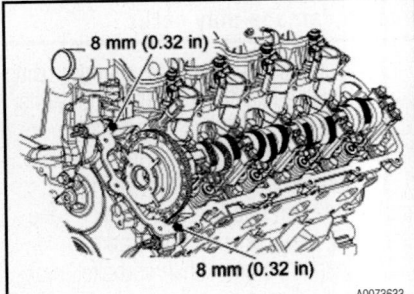

Fig. 101 Apply a bead of silicone gasket and sealant in 2 places where the engine front cover meets the cylinder head.

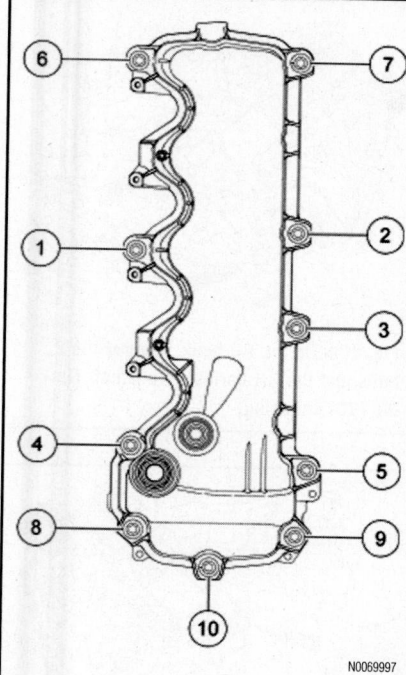

Fig. 102 Position the LH valve cover and new gasket on the cylinder head and tighten the 10 fasteners in the sequence shown. Tighten to 89 inch lbs. (10 Nm).

Right Side

See Figures 103 through 108.

1. For vehicles with auxiliary heat, drain the cooling system, then disconnect the 2 auxiliary heat coolant hoses and position the auxiliary heat coolant hoses aside.

2. Disconnect the quick connect couplings and remove the crankcase vent tube.

3. Disconnect the right PCM electrical connector and position aside.

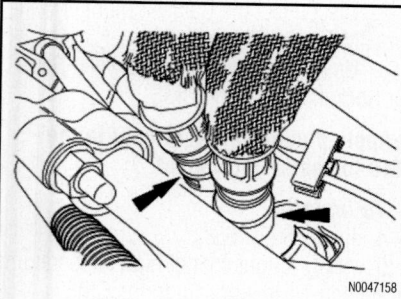

Fig. 103 For vehicles with auxiliary heat, drain the cooling system, then disconnect the 2 auxiliary heat coolant hoses and position the auxiliary heat coolant hoses aside.

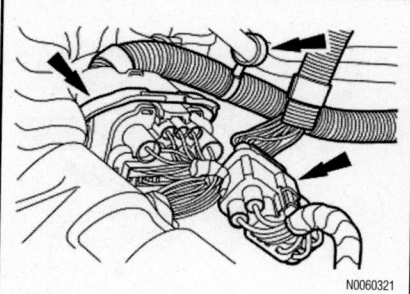

Fig. 104 Disconnect the 2 electrical connectors and the wiring harness retainer and position the wiring harness aside.

4. Remove the nut and the ground cable and disconnect the wiring harness retainer near the right PCM connector.

5. Disconnect the middle PCM electrical connector.

6. Disconnect the 2 electrical connectors and the wiring harness retainer and position the wiring harness aside.

7. Disconnect the RH radio ignition interference capacitor and engine cooling fan clutch electrical connectors.

8. Remove the 4 RH ignition coils.

9. Disconnect the RH Variable Camshaft Timing (VCT) solenoid electrical connector.

10. Disconnect the 2 engine wiring harness retainers from the RH valve cover studs and position the wiring harness aside.

✳✳ CAUTION

Do not use metal scrapers, wire brushes, power abrasive discs or other abrasive means to clean the sealing surfaces. These tools cause scratches and gouges which make leak paths. Use a plastic scraping tool to remove all traces of old sealant.

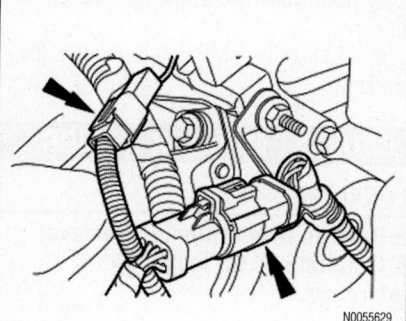

Fig. 105 Disconnect the RH radio ignition interference capacitor and engine cooling fan clutch electrical connectors.

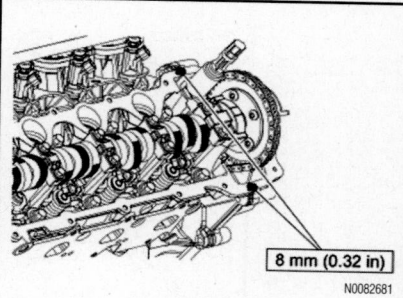

Fig. 106 Apply a bead of silicone gasket and sealant in 2 places where the engine front cover meets the cylinder head.

✳✳ CAUTION

When removing the valve cover, make sure to avoid damaging the Variable Camshaft Timing (VCT) solenoid.

➡The fasteners are part of the valve cover and should not be removed.

11. Loosen the 9 fasteners and remove the RH valve cover and gasket.

12. Clean the valve cover mating surface of the cylinder head with silicone gasket remover and metal surface prep.

13. Discard the valve cover gasket. Clean the valve cover gasket groove with soap and water or a suitable solvent.

To install:

➡If the valve cover is not secured within 4 minutes, the sealant must be removed and the sealing area cleaned with silicone gasket remover and metal surface prep. Follow the directions on the packaging. Allow to dry until there is no sign of wetness, or 4 minutes, whichever is longer. Failure to follow this procedure can cause future oil leakage.

14. Apply a bead of silicone gasket and sealant in 2 places where the engine front cover meets the cylinder head.

➡When installing the valve cover, make sure to avoid damaging the Variable Camshaft Timing (VCT) solenoid.

15. Position the RH valve cover and new gasket on the cylinder head and tighten the 9 fasteners in the sequence shown. Tighten to 89 inch lbs. (10 Nm).

16. Install the 4 RH ignition coils.

17. Position back the engine wiring harness and connect the 2 electrical connectors and the wiring harness retainer.

18. Connect the middle PCM electrical connector.

19. Connect the wiring harness retainer and ground cable and

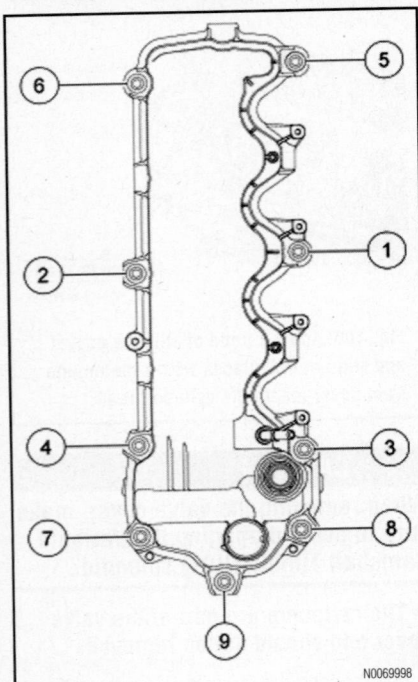

Fig. 107 Position the RH valve cover and new gasket on the cylinder head and tighten the 9 fasteners in the sequence shown. Tighten to 89 inch lbs. (10 Nm).

install the nut. Tighten to 89 inch lbs. (10 Nm).

20. Connect the right PCM electrical connector.

21. Connect the RH radio ignition interference capacitor and engine cooling fan clutch electrical connectors.

22. Connect the RH VCT solenoid electrical connector.

23. Connect the wiring harness retainers to the valve cover.

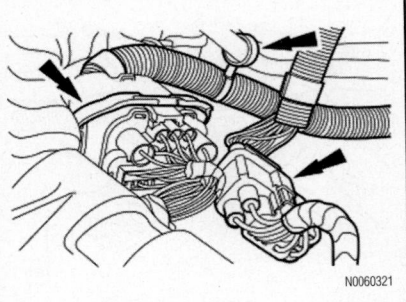

Fig. 108 Position back the engine wiring harness and connect the 2 electrical connectors and the wiring harness retainer.

24. Position the crankcase vent tube and connect the quick connect couplings.

25. Vehicles with auxiliary heat: connect the 2 auxiliary heat coolant hoses.

26. Fill and bleed the coolant system.

VARIABLE VALVE TIMING HOUSING

REMOVAL & INSTALLATION
See Figures 109 and 110.

1. Remove the timing drive components. See "Timing Chain & Sprockets" in this section.

2. On the RH bank, remove the 2 bolts and the RH Variable Camshaft Timing (VCT) housing.

3. On the LH bank, remove the 2 bolts and the LH VCT housing.

4. Remove and discard the VCT housing gasket.

5. Using a plastic scraper, clean and inspect the cylinder head sealing surfaces with metal surface prep.

6. Clean and inspect the VCT housing.

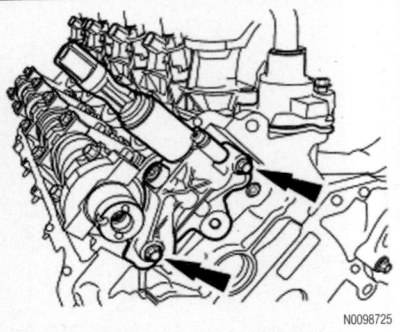

Fig. 109 On the RH bank, remove the 2 bolts and the RH Variable Camshaft Timing (VCT) housing.

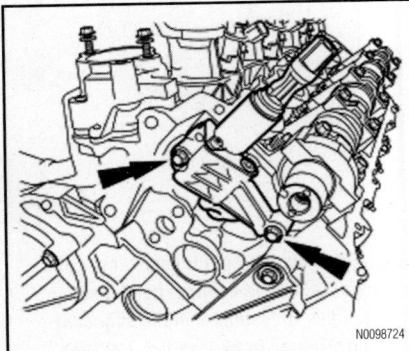

Fig. 110 On the LH bank, remove the 2 bolts and the LH VCT housing.

To install:

7. Install a new gasket onto the VCT housing.

8. Position the RH and LH VCT housings and install the bolts. Tighten to 89 inch lbs. (10 Nm).

9. Install the timing drive components. See "Timing Chain & Sprockets" in this section.

ENGINE PERFORMANCE & EMISSION CONTROLS

CAMSHAFT POSITION (CMP) SENSOR

LOCATION
See Figure 111.

Refer to the accompanying illustration.

REMOVAL & INSTALLATION

1. If removing the LH Camshaft Position (CMP) sensor, remove the air cleaner outlet pipe.

2. Disconnect the Camshaft Position (CMP) sensor electrical connector.

3. Remove the bolt and the CMP sensor.

4. Lubricate the O-ring seal with clean engine oil prior to installation.

5. To install, reverse the removal procedure.

6. Tighten the CMP bolt to 89 inch lbs. (10 Nm).

CATALYST MONITOR SENSOR

LOCATION
➡Refer to illustration in "Removal & Installation" for location reference.

REMOVAL & INSTALLATION
See Figure 112.

1. With the vehicle in NEUTRAL, position it on a hoist.

2. Disconnect the Catalyst Monitor Sensor (CMS) electrical connector.

3. Using the Exhaust Gas Oxygen Sensor Socket, remove the CMS.

➡Apply penetrating lubricant to the CMS to assist in removal.

To install:

4. Install the CMS.

5. Apply a light coat of high temperature nickel anti-seize lubricant to the CMS threads prior to installation.

6. Calculate the correct torque wrench setting for the following torque.

7. Using the Exhaust Gas Oxygen Sensor Socket, tighten to 34 ft. lbs. (46 Nm).

8. Connect the CMS electrical connector.

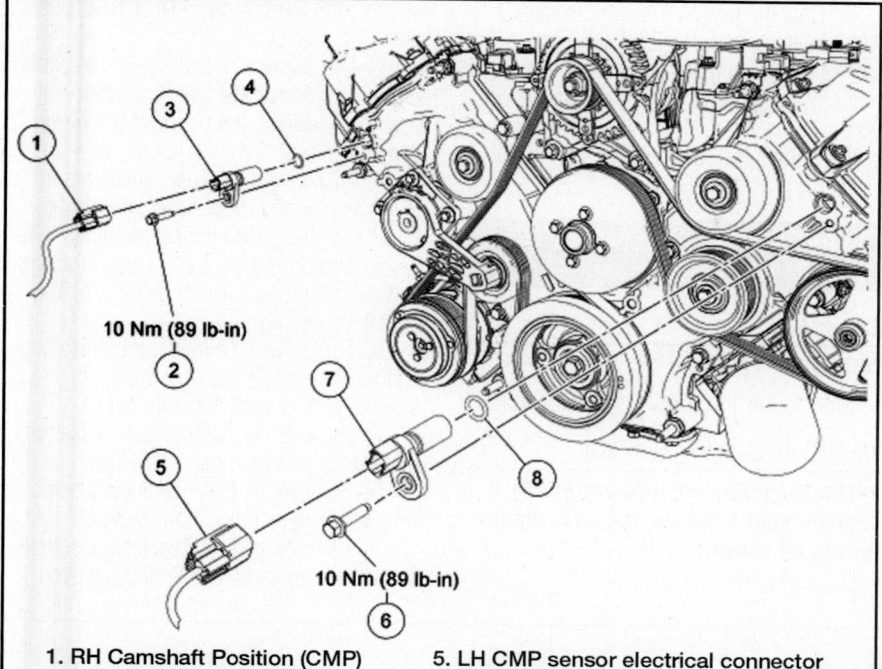

10 Nm (89 lb-in)

10 Nm (89 lb-in)

1. RH Camshaft Position (CMP) sensor electrical connector
2. RH CMP sensor bolt
3. RH CMP sensor
4. RH CMP sensor O-ring seal
5. LH CMP sensor electrical connector
6. LH CMP sensor bolt
7. LH CMP sensor
8. LH CMP sensor O-ring seal

N0050394

Fig. 111 Removing the CMP sensors and related components

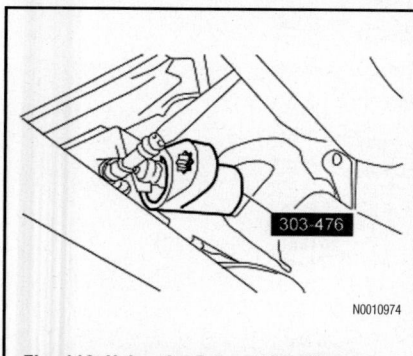

303-476

N0010974

Fig. 112 Using the Exhaust Gas Oxygen Sensor Socket, remove the CMS.

CRANKSHAFT POSITION (CKP) SENSOR

LOCATION

See Figure 113.

Refer to the accompanying illustration.

REMOVAL & INSTALLATION

1. With the vehicle in NEUTRAL, position it on a hoist.
2. Rotate the accessory drive belt tensioner clockwise and detach the accessory drive belt from the A/C compressor pulley.

3. Disconnect the A/C compressor electrical connector.

4. Disconnect the Crankshaft Position (CKP) sensor electrical connector.

5. Remove the 3 bolts and position the A/C compressor aside.

6. Remove the bolt and the CKP sensor.

7. Lubricate the O-ring seal with clean engine oil prior to installation.

To install:

8. To install, reverse the removal procedure.

9. Tighten the fasteners as follows:
   - Tighten the CKP sensor bolt to 89 inch lbs. (10 Nm).
   - Tighten the A/C compressor bolts to 18 ft. lbs. (25 Nm).

10. Using the scan tool, perform the Misfire Monitor Neutral Profile Correction procedure, following the on-screen instructions.

CYLINDER HEAD TEMPERATURE (CHT) SENSOR

LOCATION

See Figure 114.

Refer to the accompanying illustration.

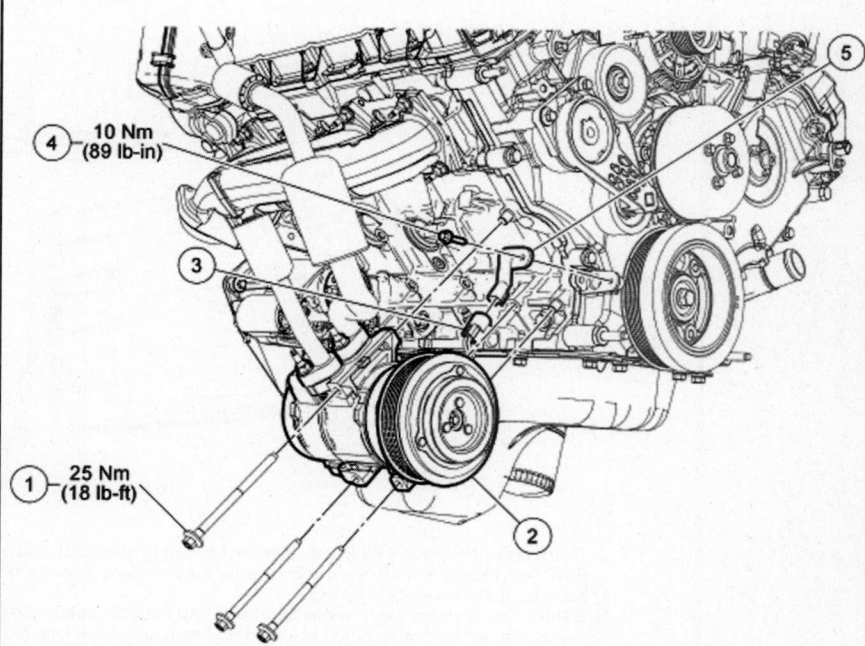

10 Nm (89 lb-in)

25 Nm (18 lb-ft)

1. A/C compressor bolt (3 required)
2. A/C compressor
3. Crankshaft Position (CKP) sensor electrical connector
4. CKP sensor bolt
5. CKP sensor

N0065047

Fig. 113 Showing removal of the CKP sensor

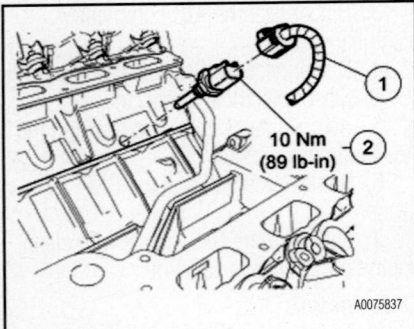

Fig. 114 Showing the CHT sensor connector (1) and sensor (2)

REMOVAL & INSTALLATION

1. Remove the intake manifold.
2. Disconnect the Cylinder Head Temperature (CHT) sensor electrical connector.
3. Remove the CHT sensor and discard.

4. Coat the new CHT sensor threads with high temperature nickel anti-seize lubricant prior to installation.
5. To install, reverse the removal procedure
6. Tighten the sensor to 89 inch lbs. (10 Nm).

EVAPORATIVE EMISSIONS (EVAP) CANISTER

LOCATION

See Figures 115 and 116.

Refer to the accompanying illustrations.

REMOVAL & INSTALLATION

➡**The Evaporative Emission (EVAP) canister vent solenoid and dust separator are an assembly.**

1. With the vehicle in NEUTRAL, position it on a hoist.
2. Disconnect the battery ground cable.
3. Disconnect the EVAP canister vent solenoid electrical jumper from the wiring harness.
4. Disconnect the Fuel Tank Pressure (FTP) sensor and vapor tube assembly-to-EVAP canister quick connect coupling.
5. Disconnect the EVAP canister purge valve vapor tube-to- EVAP canister quick connect coupling.
6. Disconnect the fresh air tube-to-canister vent solenoid and dust separator assembly quick connect coupling.
7. Remove the EVAP canister assembly bracket-to-frame rail bolt in the rear.
8. Remove the EVAP canister assembly bracket-to-frame rail bolt in the front.
9. Remove the EVAP canister assembly bracket and exhaust Y-pipe dual catalytic

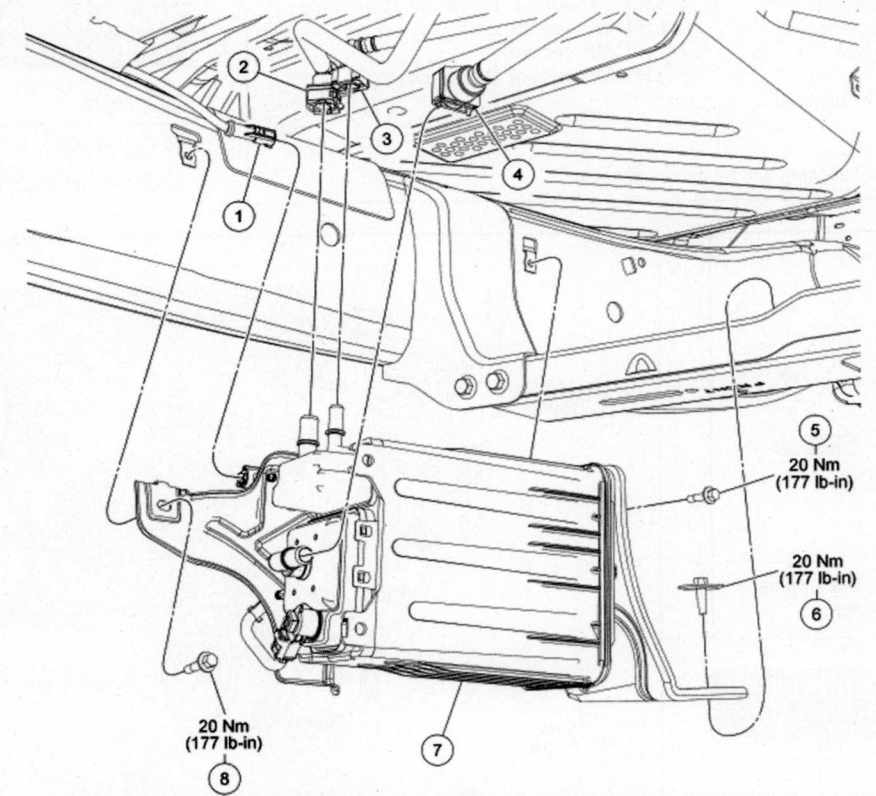

1. Evaporative Emission (EVAP) canister vent solenoid electrical connector
2. Fuel Tank Pressure (FTP) sensor and vapor tube assembly-to- EVAP canister quick connect coupling
3. EVAP canister purge valve vapor tube-to- EVAP canister quick connect coupling
4. Fresh air tube-to-canister vent solenoid and dust separator assembly quick connect coupling
5. EVAP canister assembly bracket-to-frame rail bolt
6. EVAP canister assembly bracket and exhaust Y-pipe dual catalytic converter heat shield-to-transmission crossmember bolt
7. EVAP canister assembly
8. EVAP canister assembly bracket-to-frame rail bolt

Fig. 115 Removing the EVAP canister—28 gal. fuel tank application shown; 33.5 gal. tank similar

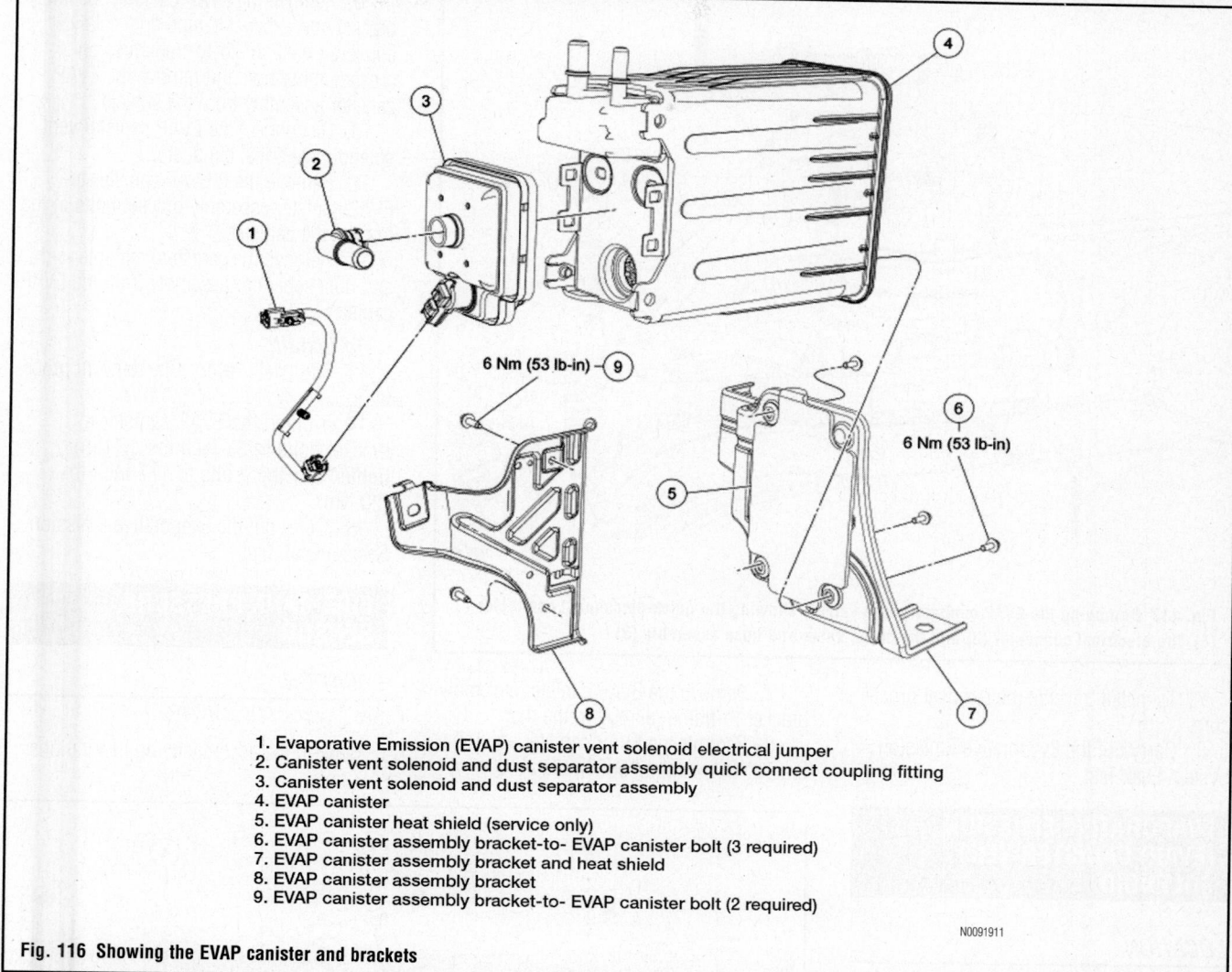

1. Evaporative Emission (EVAP) canister vent solenoid electrical jumper
2. Canister vent solenoid and dust separator assembly quick connect coupling fitting
3. Canister vent solenoid and dust separator assembly
4. EVAP canister
5. EVAP canister heat shield (service only)
6. EVAP canister assembly bracket-to- EVAP canister bolt (3 required)
7. EVAP canister assembly bracket and heat shield
8. EVAP canister assembly bracket
9. EVAP canister assembly bracket-to- EVAP canister bolt (2 required)

N0091911

Fig. 116 Showing the EVAP canister and brackets

converter heat shield-to-transmission crossmember bolt and remove the EVAP canister assembly from the vehicle.

10. Disconnect the EVAP canister vent solenoid electrical connector.

11. Remove the 5 EVAP canister-to-EVAP canister assembly bracket bolts.

12. Remove the EVAP canister assembly from the EVAP canister assembly brackets.

13. Remove the canister vent solenoid and dust separator assembly from the EVAP canister.

➡**Inspect the EVAP canister heat shield and if damaged, install a new EVAP canister heat shield.**

To install:

14. To install, reverse the removal procedure.

15. Tighten the EVAP canister to bracket bolts to 53 inch lbs. (6 Nm); tighten all other bolts to 177 inch lbs. (20 Nm).

16. Carry out the Evaporative Emission System Leak Test.

EVAPORATIVE EMISSIONS (EVAP) CANISTER PURGE VALVE

LOCATION

See Figure 117.

Refer to the accompanying illustration.

REMOVAL & INSTALLATION

❊❊ WARNING

Always disconnect the battery ground cable at the battery when working on an evaporative emission (EVAP) system or fuel-related component. Highly flammable mixtures are always present and may be ignited. Failure to follow these instructions may result in serious personal injury.

1. Do not smoke, carry lighted tobacco or have an open flame of any type when working on or near any fuel-related component. Highly flammable mixtures are always present and may be ignited. Failure to follow these instructions may result in serious personal injury.

2. Disconnect the battery ground cable.

3. Disconnect the Evaporative Emission (EVAP) canister purge valve and hose electrical connector.

4. Disconnect EVAP canister purge valve hose-to-intake manifold quick connect coupling.

5. Disconnect the EVAP canister-to-EVAP canister purge valve and hose assembly vapor tube quick connect coupling.

6. Slide the EVAP canister purge valve and hose assembly off the bracket.

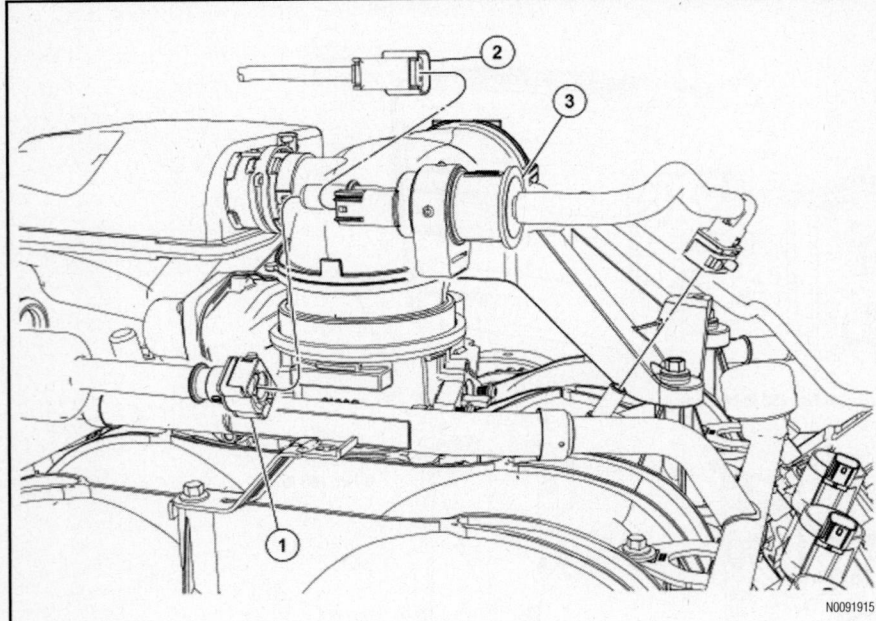

Fig. 117 Removing the EVAP canister purge valve—showing the quick-disconnect connector (1), the electrical connector (2) and the purge valve and hose assembly (3)

7. To install, reverse the removal procedure.

8. Carry out the Evaporative Emission System Leak Test.

EVAPORATIVE EMISSION (EVAP) CANISTER VENT SOLENOID

LOCATION

➡See illustration under "Evaporative Emissions (EVAP) Canister" in this section for location of this solenoid.

REMOVAL & INSTALLATION

➡The Evaporative Emission (EVAP) canister vent solenoid and dust separator are an assembly.

1. With the vehicle in NEUTRAL, position it on a hoist.

2. Disconnect the battery ground cable.

3. Disconnect the EVAP canister vent solenoid electrical jumper from the wiring harness.

4. Disconnect the Fuel Tank Pressure (FTP) sensor and vapor tube assembly-to- EVAP canister quick connect coupling.

5. Disconnect the EVAP canister purge valve vapor tube-to- EVAP canister quick connect coupling.

6. Disconnect the fresh air tube-to-canister vent solenoid and dust separator assembly quick connect coupling.

7. Remove the EVAP canister assembly bracket-to-frame rail bolt in the rear.

8. Remove the EVAP canister assembly bracket-to-frame rail bolt in the front.

9. Remove the EVAP canister assembly bracket and exhaust Y-pipe dual catalytic converter heat shield-to-transmission crossmember bolt and remove the EVAP canister assembly from the vehicle.

10. Disconnect the EVAP canister vent solenoid electrical connector.

11. Remove the 2 EVAP canister-to-EVAP canister assembly bracket bolts in the front of the canister.

12. Remove the canister vent solenoid and dust separator assembly from the EVAP canister.

To install:

13. To install, reverse the removal procedure.

14. Tighten the EVAP canister to bracket bolts to 53 inch lbs. (6 Nm); tighten all other bolts to 177 inch lbs. (20 Nm).

15. Carry out the Evaporative Emission System Leak Test.

FUEL TANK PRESSURE SENSOR

LOCATION

See Figures 118 and 119.

Refer to the accompanying illustrations.

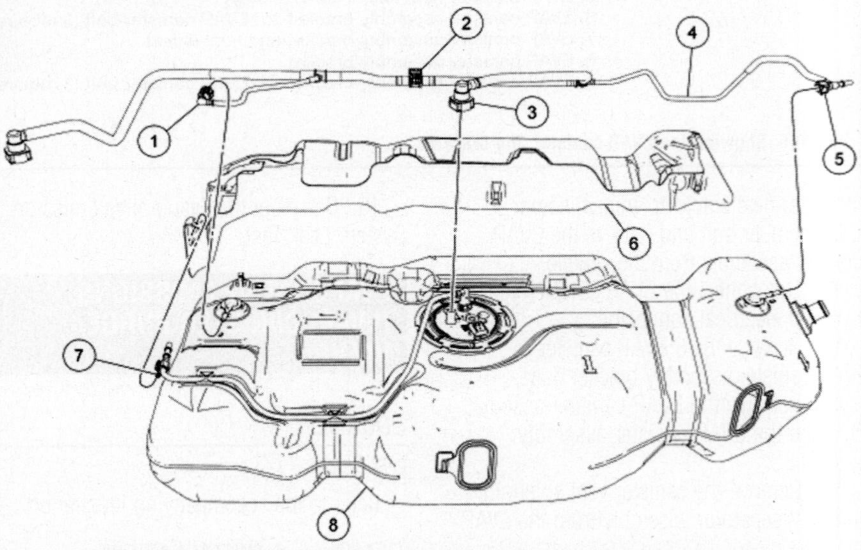

1. Fuel Tank Pressure (FTP) sensor and vapor tube assembly-to-fuel vapor/grade vent valve quick connect coupling
2. FTP sensor
3. FTP sensor and vapor tube assembly-to-fuel pump module quick connect coupling
4. FTP sensor and vapor tube assembly
5. FTP sensor and vapor tube assembly-to-fuel vapor/grade vent valve quick connect coupling
6. Heat shield
7. Fuel supply tube-to-heat shield pushpin retainer
8. Fuel tank

Fig. 118 Showing the location of the FTP sensor—with 28 gal. fuel tank

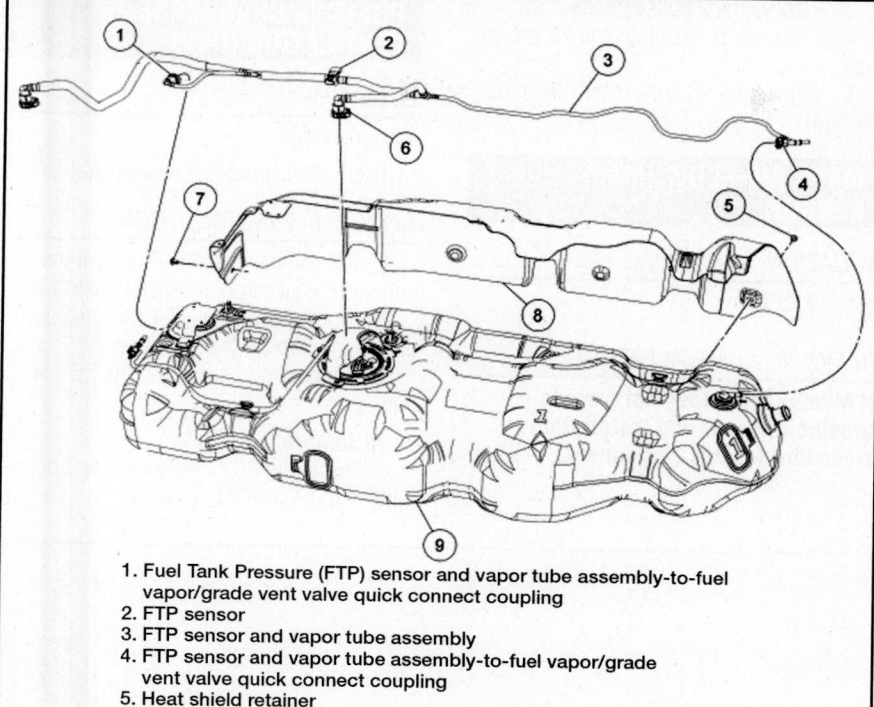

1. Fuel Tank Pressure (FTP) sensor and vapor tube assembly-to-fuel vapor/grade vent valve quick connect coupling
2. FTP sensor
3. FTP sensor and vapor tube assembly
4. FTP sensor and vapor tube assembly-to-fuel vapor/grade vent valve quick connect coupling
5. Heat shield retainer
6. FTP sensor and vapor tube assembly-to-fuel pump module quick connect coupling
7. Heat shield retainer
8. Heat shield
9. Fuel tank

N0102841

Fig. 119 Showing the location of the FTP sensor—with 33.5 gal. fuel tank

REMOVAL & INSTALLATION

1. Remove the fuel tank. See "Fuel Tank" in "GASOLINE FUEL INJECTION SYSTEM" section.
2. Disconnect the fuel supply tube-to-heat shield pushpin retainer.
3. For 33.5 gal. fuel tank, remove the fuel tank heat shield retainer(s).
4. Remove the fuel tank heat shield.
5. Disconnect the Fuel Tank Pressure (FTP) sensor and vapor tube assembly-to-fuel vapor/grade vent valves quick connect couplings.
6. Disconnect the FTP sensor and vapor tube assembly-to-fuel pump module quick connect coupling.
7. Remove the FTP sensor and vapor tube assembly from the fuel tank.
8. To install, reverse the removal procedure.
9. Carry out the Evaporative Emission System Leak Test.

HEATED OXYGEN (HO2S) SENSOR

LOCATION

See Figure 120.

REMOVAL & INSTALLATION

1. With the vehicle in NEUTRAL, position it on a hoist.
2. Disconnect the Heated Oxygen Sensor (HO2S) electrical connector.
3. Using the Exhaust Gas Oxygen Sensor Socket, remove the HO2S.
4. Apply penetrating lubricant to the HO2S to assist in removal.

To install:

5. Apply a light coat of high temperature nickel anti-seize lubricant to the HO2S threads prior to installation.
6. Install the HO2S.
7. Calculate the correct torque wrench setting and use the Exhaust Gas Oxygen Sensor Socket to tighten to 34 ft. lbs.(46 Nm).
8. Connect the HO2S electrical connector.

KNOCK SENSOR (KS)

LOCATION

See Figure 121.

Refer to the accompanying illustration.

REMOVAL & INSTALLATION

1. Remove the intake manifold. See "ENGINE MECHANICAL" section.
2. Disconnect the Knock Sensor (KS) electrical connectors.

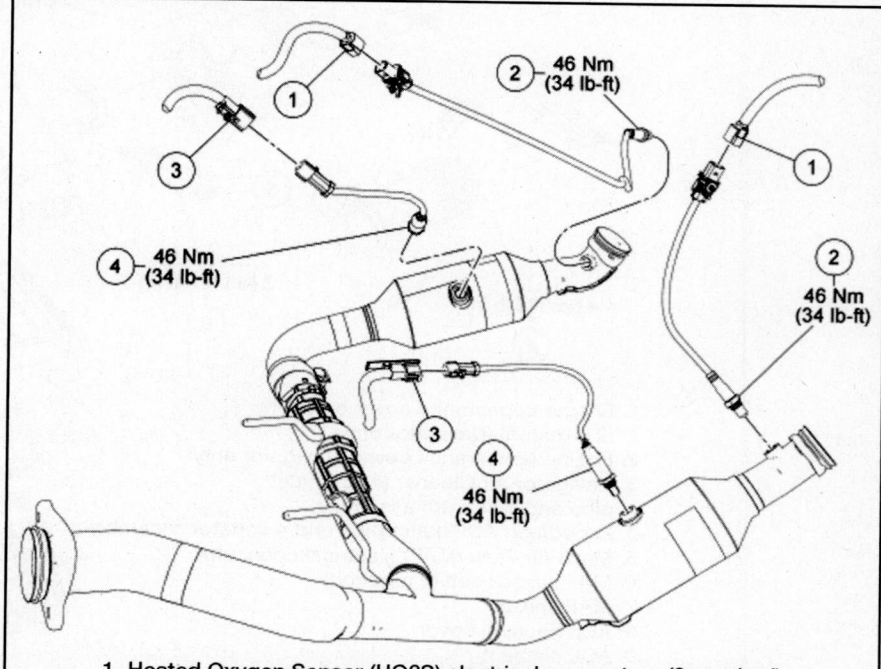

1. Heated Oxygen Sensor (HO2S) electrical connectors (2 required)
2. HO2S (2 required)
3. Catalyst Monitor Sensor (CMS) electrical connectors (2 required)
4. CMS (2 required)

N0091834

Fig. 120 Showing the location of the HO2S and catalyst monitor sensors

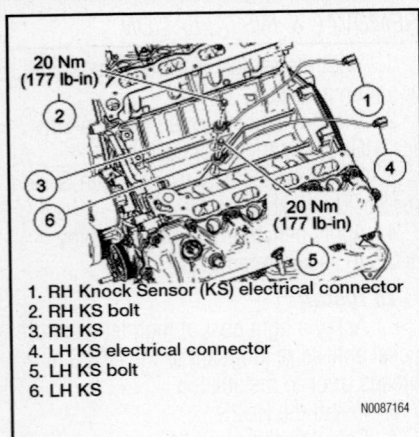

1. RH Knock Sensor (KS) electrical connector
2. RH KS bolt
3. RH KS
4. LH KS electrical connector
5. LH KS bolt
6. LH KS

N0087164

Fig. 121 Showing the locations of the knock sensors

3. Remove the 2 bolts and the 2 KS.
4. To install, reverse the removal procedure.
5. Tighten the KS bolts to 177 inch lbs. (20 Nm).

MASS AIR FLOW (MAF) SENSOR

LOCATION

See Figure 122.

REMOVAL & INSTALLATION

➡ **Manufacture does not provide a specific removal and installation procedure for this component.**

POSITIVE CRANKCASE VENTILATION (PCV)

LOCATION

See Figure 123.

Refer to the accompanying illustration.

REMOVAL & INSTALLATION

1. Release the clamp and remove the bolt and the air intake resonator assembly.
2. Disconnect the quick connect couplings and remove the PCV tube.
3. Remove the 2 bolts and the PCV fitting.

   To install:
4. Install the PCV fitting and the 2 bolts. Tighten to 54 inch lbs. (6 Nm).

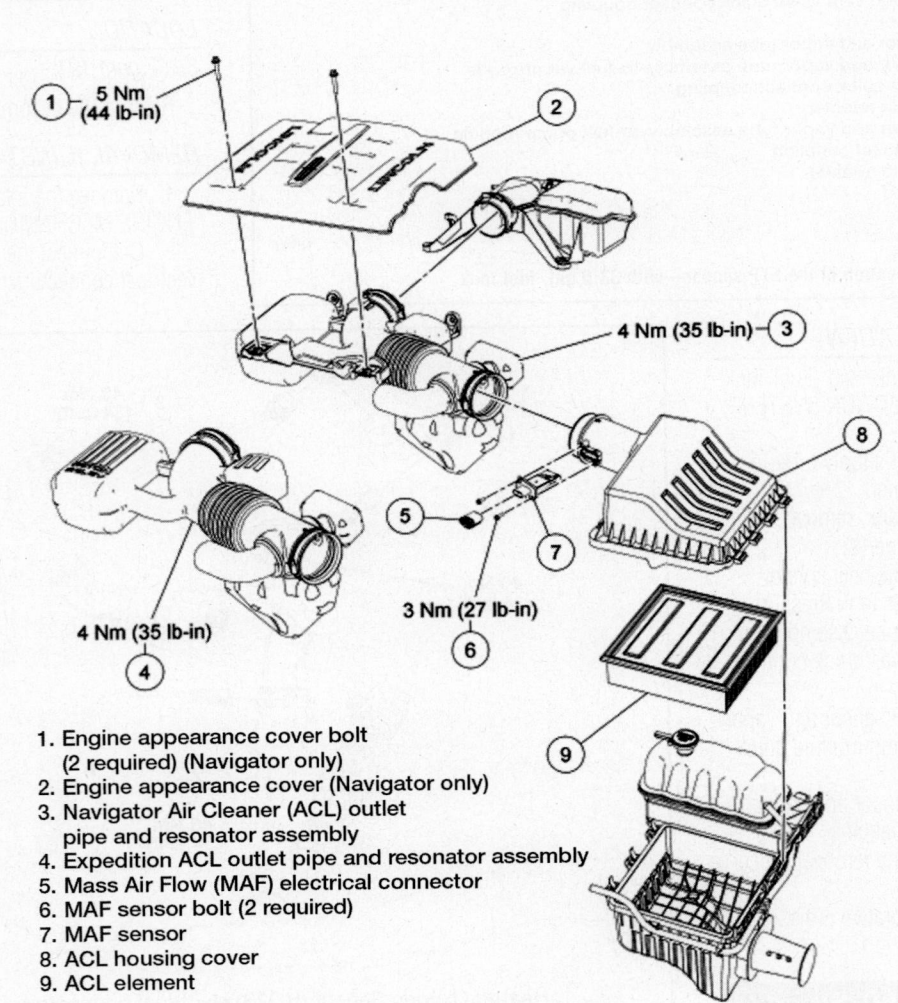

1. Engine appearance cover bolt (2 required) (Navigator only)
2. Engine appearance cover (Navigator only)
3. Navigator Air Cleaner (ACL) outlet pipe and resonator assembly
4. Expedition ACL outlet pipe and resonator assembly
5. Mass Air Flow (MAF) electrical connector
6. MAF sensor bolt (2 required)
7. MAF sensor
8. ACL housing cover
9. ACL element

N0092050

Fig. 122 Showing the air cleaner assembly and the location of the MAF sensor

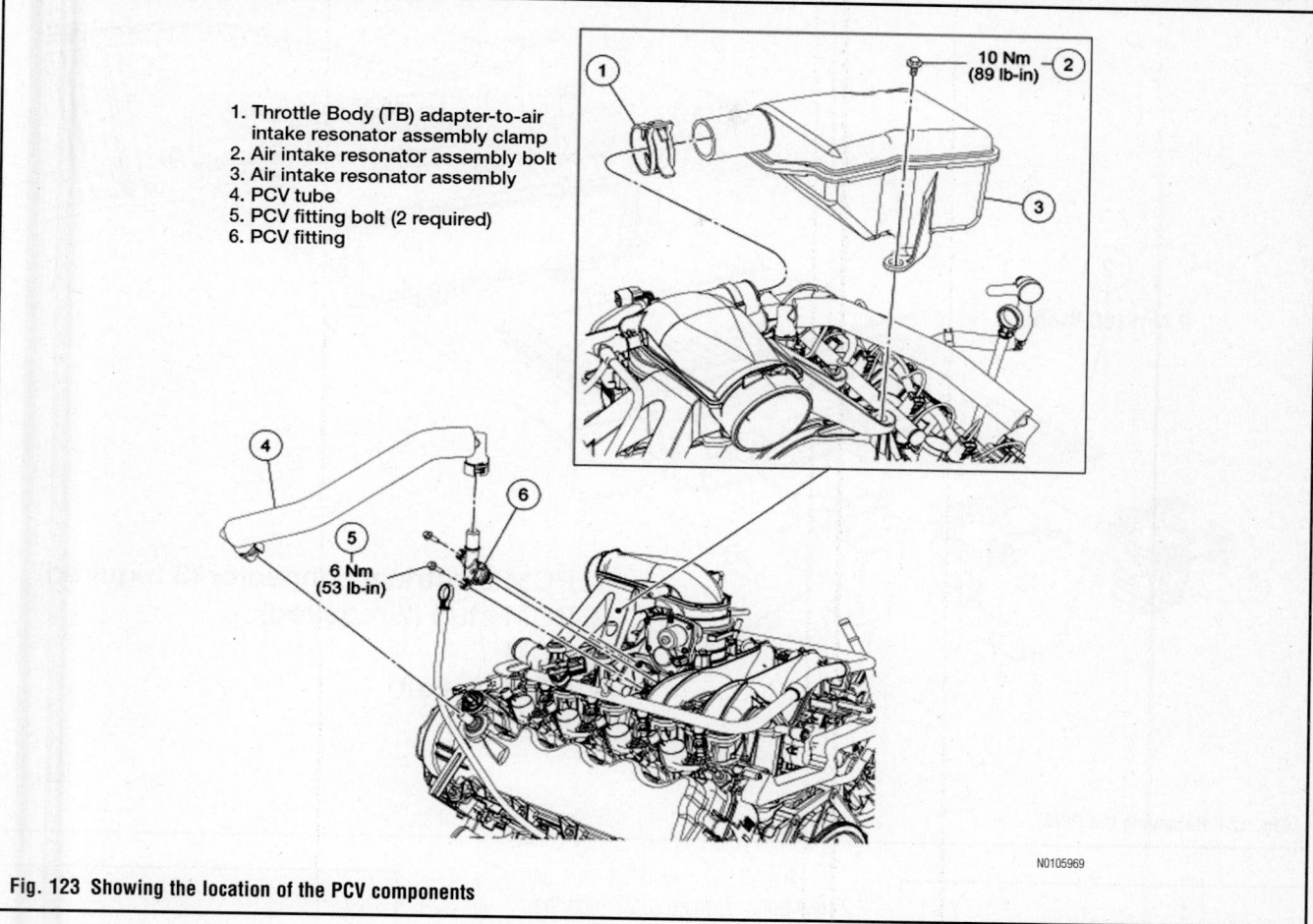

1. Throttle Body (TB) adapter-to-air
   intake resonator assembly clamp
2. Air intake resonator assembly bolt
3. Air intake resonator assembly
4. PCV tube
5. PCV fitting bolt (2 required)
6. PCV fitting

10 Nm
(89 lb-in)

6 Nm
(53 lb-in)

N0105969

Fig. 123 Showing the location of the PCV components

5. Position the PCV tube and connect the quick connect couplings.

6. Position the air intake resonator assembly, install the bolt and the clamp. Tighten to 89 inch lbs. (10 Nm).

POWERTRAIN CONTROL MODULE (PCM)

LOCATION

See Figure 124.

Refer to the accompanying illustration.

REMOVAL & INSTALLATION

1. If servicing the PCM, connect the scan tool to the vehicle. Allow the scan tool to identify the vehicle and obtain configuration data.

➡**All programmable module information will automatically be retrieved by the VCM.**

2. Disconnect the battery ground cable.
3. Disconnect the 3 PCM electrical connectors.
4. Remove the 2 stud bolts and the PCM.

➡**If the Instrument Cluster (IC) or the PCM is being replaced (or both), the parameters must be reset in both modules or the vehicle will experience a Passive Anti-Theft System (PATS) no-start. This will occur even if the vehicle is not equipped with PATS.**

5. To install, reverse the removal procedure.

6. Tighten the mounting bolts to 80 inch lbs. (9 Nm).

7. Using the scan tool, perform the Misfire Monitor Neutral Profile Correction procedure, following the on-screen instructions.

THROTTLE POSITION SENSOR (TPS)

LOCATION

See Figure 125.

Refer to the accompanying illustration.

REMOVAL & INSTALLATION

1. Remove the Throttle Body (TB). See "FUEL" section.

❊❊ **CAUTION**

Do not put direct heat on the Throttle Position (TP) sensor or any other plastic parts because heat damage may occur. Damage may also occur if Electronic Throttle Body (ETB) temperature exceeds 248°F (120°C).

➡**Do not use power tools.**

2. Remove the Throttle Position (TP) sensor.

3. Using a heat gun, apply heat to the top of the Electronic Throttle Body (ETB) until the top TP sensor bolt ear reaches approximately 130°F (55°C), this should take no more than 3 minutes using an 1,100-watt heat gun. The heat gun should be about 1 inch away from the ETB.

4. Monitor the temperature of the top TP sensor bolt ear on the ETB with a digital temperature laser or infrared thermometer, while heating the ETB.

5. Using hand tools, quickly remove the bolt farthest from the heat source first and discard, then, remove the remaining bolt and discard.

6. Remove and discard the TP sensor.

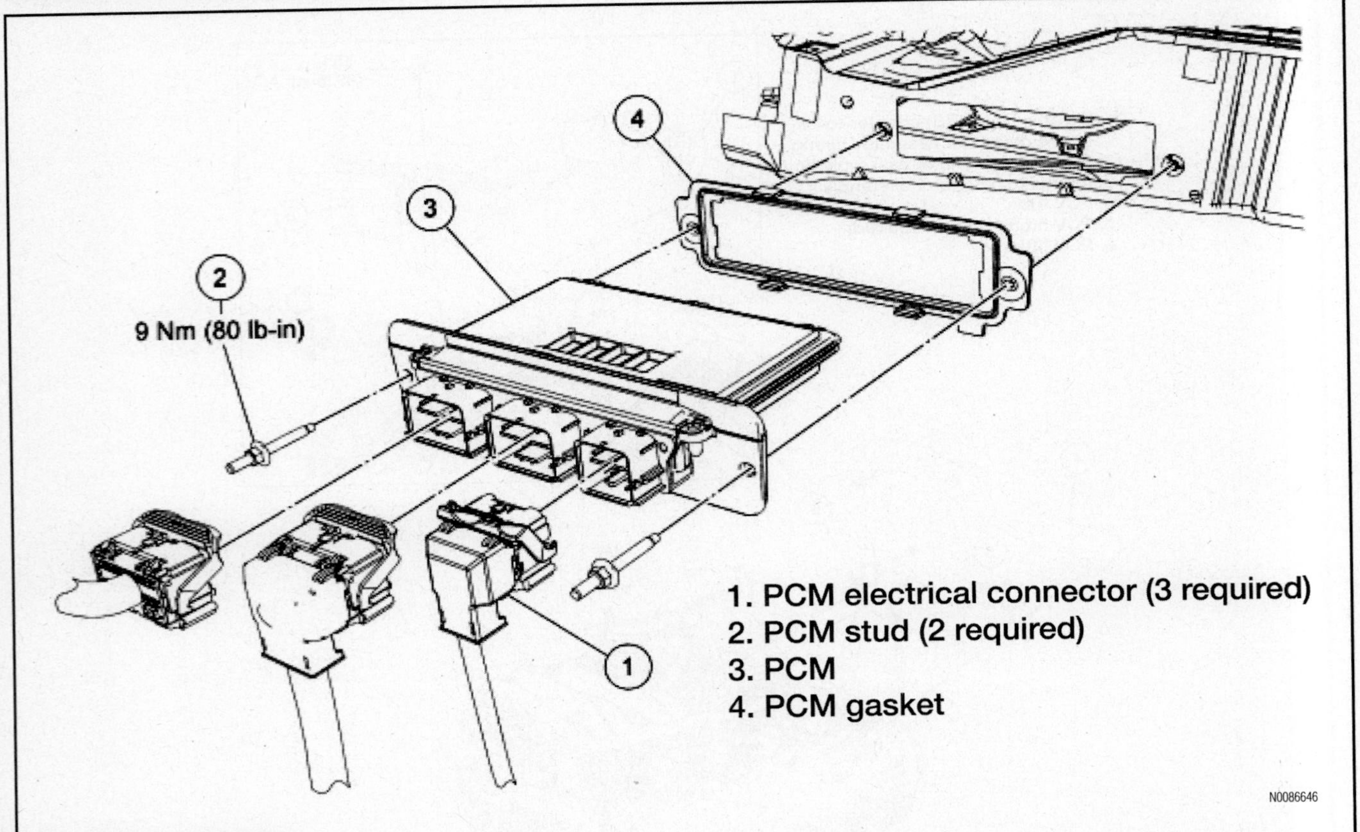

9 Nm (80 lb-in)

1. **PCM electrical connector (3 required)**
2. **PCM stud (2 required)**
3. **PCM**
4. **PCM gasket**

N0086646

Fig. 124 Removing the PCM

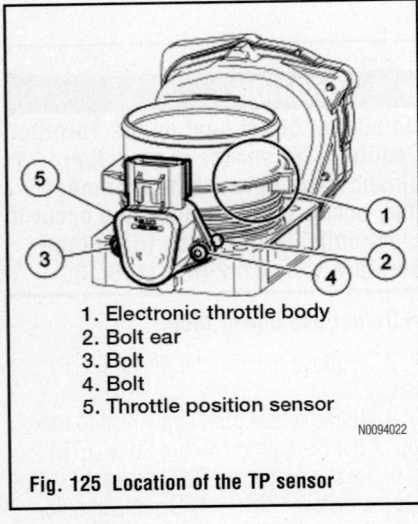

1. Electronic throttle body
2. Bolt ear
3. Bolt
4. Bolt
5. Throttle position sensor

N0094022

Fig. 125 Location of the TP sensor

To install:

➡**When installing the new TP sensor, make sure that the radial locator tab on the TP sensor is aligned with the radial locator hole on the ETB.**

7. Install the new TP sensor. using 2 new bolts. Tighten to 27 inch lbs. (3 Nm).

8. Install the throttle body. See "FUEL" section.

VARIABLE CAMSHAFT TIMING (VCT) OIL CONTROL SOLENOID

LOCATION

See Figure 126.

Refer to the accompanying illustration.

REMOVAL & INSTALLATION

1. Remove the valve cover. See "ENGINE MECHANICAL" section.

2. Remove the bolt and the Variable Camshaft Timing (VCT) oil control solenoid.

3. To install, reverse the removal procedure.

4. Tighten the bolt to 44 inch lbs. (5 Nm).

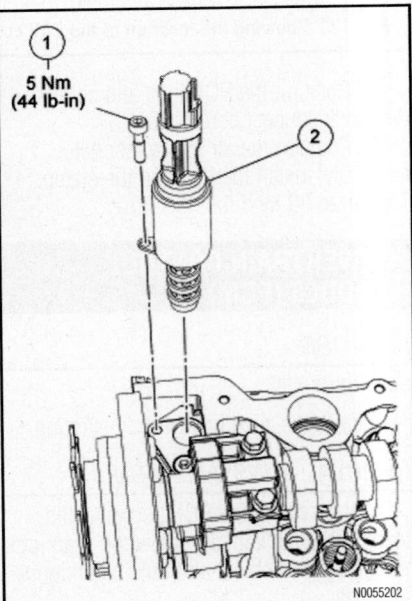

5 Nm (44 lb-in)

N0055202

Fig. 126 Removing the VCT oil control solenoid bolt (1) and solenoid (2)—left side solenoid shown; right side similar

FUEL   **GASOLINE FUEL INJECTION SYSTEM**

FUEL SYSTEM SERVICE PRECAUTIONS

Safety is the most important factor when performing not only fuel system maintenance but any type of maintenance. Failure to conduct maintenance and repairs in a safe manner may result in serious personal injury or death. Maintenance and testing of the vehicle's fuel system components can be accomplished safely and effectively by adhering to the following rules and guidelines.

• To avoid the possibility of fire and personal injury, always disconnect the negative battery cable unless the repair or test procedure requires that battery voltage be applied.

• Always relieve the fuel system pressure prior to disconnecting any fuel system component (injector, fuel rail, pressure regulator, etc.), fitting or fuel line connection. Exercise extreme caution whenever relieving fuel system pressure to avoid exposing skin, face and eyes to fuel spray. Please be advised that fuel under pressure may penetrate the skin or any part of the body that it contacts.

• Always place a shop towel or cloth around the fitting or connection prior to loosening to absorb any excess fuel due to spillage. Ensure that all fuel spillage (should it occur) is quickly removed from engine surfaces. Ensure that all fuel soaked cloths or towels are deposited into a suitable waste container.

• Always keep a dry chemical (Class B) fire extinguisher near the work area.

• Do not allow fuel spray or fuel vapors to come into contact with a spark or open flame.

• Always use a back-up wrench when loosening and tightening fuel line connection fittings. This will prevent unnecessary stress and torsion to fuel line piping.

• Always replace worn fuel fitting O-rings with new Do not substitute fuel hose or equivalent where fuel pipe is installed.

Before servicing the vehicle, make sure to also refer to the precautions in the beginning of this section as well.

RELIEVING FUEL SYSTEM PRESSURE

See Figure 127.

> **❊❊ CAUTION**
>
> **Do not smoke, carry lighted tobacco or have an open flame of any type when working on or near any**

fuel-related component. Highly flammable mixtures are always present and may be ignited. Failure to follow these instructions may result in serious personal injury.

> **❊❊ CAUTION**
>
> **Before working on or disconnecting any of the fuel tubes or fuel system components, relieve the fuel system pressure to prevent accidental spraying of fuel. Fuel in the fuel system remains under high pressure, even when the engine is not running. Failure to follow this instruction may result in serious personal injury.**

> **❊❊ CAUTION**
>
> **When handling fuel, always observe fuel handling precautions and be prepared in the event of fuel spillage. Spilled fuel may be ignited by hot vehicle components or other ignition sources. Failure to follow these instructions may result in serious personal injury.**

> **❊❊ CAUTION**
>
> **Do not carry personal electronic devices such as cell phones, pagers or audio equipment of any type when working on or near any fuel-related component. Highly flammable mixtures are always present and may be ignited. Failure to follow these instructions may result in serious personal injury.**

1. Disconnect the battery ground cable.
2. Remove the cap from the fuel pressure relief valve located on the fuel rail.

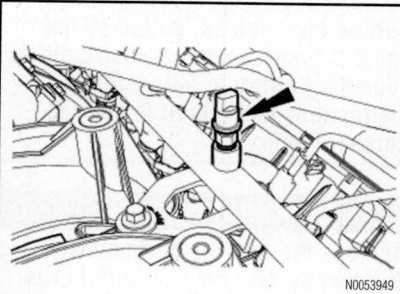

Fig. 127 Remove the cap from the fuel pressure relief valve located on the fuel rail.

3. Install the Fuel Pressure Test Kit onto the fuel pressure relief valve.

➡ **Open the manual valve slowly to relieve the system pressure. This may drain fuel from the fuel system. Place fuel in a suitable container.**

4. Open the manual valve on the Fuel Pressure Test Kit and relieve the fuel pressure.

➡ **It may take more than one key cycle to pressurize the fuel system.**

5. Cycle the ignition key and wait 3 seconds to pressurize the fuel system. Check for leaks before starting the engine.

FUEL INJECTORS

REMOVAL & INSTALLATION

See Figure 128.

> **❊❊ CAUTION**
>
> **Fuel injection equipment is manufactured to very precise tolerances and fine clearances. It is therefore essential that absolute cleanliness is observed when working with these components. Always install blanking plugs to any open orifices or tubes.**

➡ **When reusing liquid or vapor tube connectors, make sure to use compressed air to remove any foreign material from the connector retaining clip area before separating from the tube.**

1. Disconnect the battery ground cable.
2. Remove the air cleaner outlet pipe.
3. Disconnect the crankcase ventilation tube quick connect coupling from the ACL outlet pipe-to-throttle body (TB) adapter.
4. Release the clamp and remove the bolt and the air intake resonator assembly.

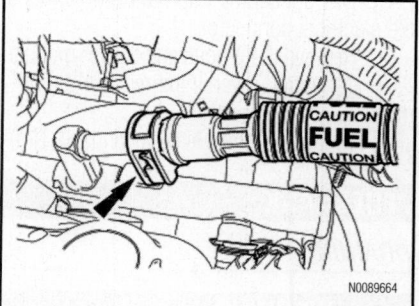

Fig. 128 Disconnect the fuel tube quick connect coupling.

5. Remove the 3 ACL outlet pipe-to-TB adapter bolts.

6. Remove the ACL outlet pipe-to-TB adapter.

7. Disconnect the Electronic Throttle Control (ETC) electrical connector.

8. Disconnect the Throttle Position (TP) sensor electrical connector.

9. Disconnect the Evaporative Emission (EVAP) tube quick connect coupling from the intake manifold.

10. Disconnect the fuel tube quick connect coupling.

11. Disconnect the 8 fuel injector electrical connectors.

12. Remove the 4 fuel rail bolts and the fuel rail and injectors as an assembly.

✳✳ CAUTION

Use O-ring seals that are made of special fuel-resistant material. Use of ordinary O-rings can cause the fuel system to leak.

13. Remove the fuel injector-to-fuel rail locks and separate the 8 fuel injectors from the fuel rail.

14. Discard the upper and lower fuel injector O-ring seals.

To install:

15. To install, reverse the removal procedure.

16. Lubricate the new O-ring seals with clean engine oil prior to installation.

17. Install the fuel rail and 4 new bolts. Tighten to 89 inch lbs. (10 Nm).

18. Install the 3 ACL outlet pipe-to-TB adapter bolts. Tighten to 89 inch lbs. (10 Nm).

19. Install the air intake resonator assembly. Tighten the clamp bolt to 89 inch lbs. (10 Nm).

FUEL PUMP MODULE

REMOVAL & INSTALLATION

See Figure 129.

1. Disconnect the Fuel Pump (FP) module electrical connector.

2. Remove the 2 bolts and the FP module.

3. To install, reverse the removal procedure.

4. To install, tighten to 80 inch lbs. (9 Nm).

FUEL TANK

DRAINING

✳✳ WARNING

Do not smoke, carry lighted tobacco or have an open flame of any type

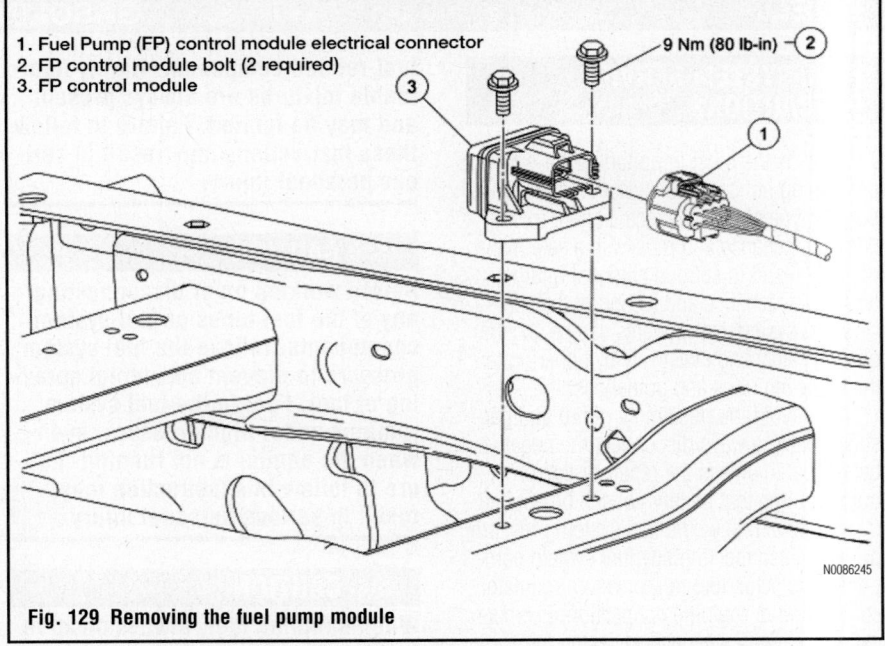

1. Fuel Pump (FP) control module electrical connector
2. FP control module bolt (2 required)
3. FP control module

9 Nm (80 lb-in) — 2

N0086245

Fig. 129 Removing the fuel pump module

when working on or near any fuel-related component. Highly flammable mixtures are always present and may be ignited. Failure to follow these instructions may result in serious personal injury.

✳✳ WARNING

Do not carry personal electronic devices such as cell phones, pagers or audio equipment of any type when working on or near any fuel-related component. Highly flammable mixtures are always present and may be ignited. Failure to follow these instructions may result in serious personal injury.

✳✳ WARNING

When handling fuel, always observe fuel handling precautions and be prepared in the event of fuel spillage. Spilled fuel may be ignited by hot vehicle components or other ignition sources. Failure to follow these instructions may result in serious personal injury.

✳✳ WARNING

Remove the fuel filler cap slowly. The fuel system may be under pressure. If the fuel filler cap is venting vapor or if you hear a hissing sound, wait until it stops before completely removing the fuel filler cap. Other-

wise, fuel may spray out. Failure to follow these instructions may result in serious personal injury.

1. If equipped, turn the air suspension switch OFF.

2. With the vehicle in NEUTRAL, position it on a hoist.

3. Release the fuel system pressure.

4. Disconnect the battery ground cable.

5. Disconnect the fuel tank filler pipe from the fuel tank.

➡**For draining, do not use a hose larger than 0.5 in. diameter.**

6. Using a proper gasoline hand pump and storage device, pump the fuel from the fuel tank.

REMOVAL & INSTALLATION

1. With the vehicle in NEUTRAL, position it on a hoist.

2. Drain the fuel tank.

3. Remove the 4 or 5 nuts (as equipped) and the fuel tank skid plate.

4. Disconnect the fuel tank filler pipe vent tube-to-Fuel Tank Pressure (FTP) sensor and vapor tube assembly quick connect coupling in the rear of the fuel tank.

5. Disconnect the FTP sensor and vapor tube assembly-to-Evaporative Emission (EVAP) canister quick connect coupling in the front of the fuel tank.

6. Disconnect the fuel tank fuel supply tube-to-front fuel supply tube quick connect coupling.

7. Remove the 4 sway bar bracket nuts and let the sway bar hang down.

※※ CAUTION

Do not support the fuel tank directly beneath the Fuel Pump (FP) mounting area. Damage to the FP assembly can occur.

8. Position a jack under the fuel tank.

9. If equipped, remove the center fuel tank support strap bolt.

10. Remove the 2 bolts from the front and rear fuel tank support straps. Remove the front fuel tank support strap.

➡ **To assist in removing the center fuel tank support strap, the front of the fuel tank may need to be pushed up slightly to get the center fuel tank support strap to clear the fuel tank.**

11. Lower the fuel tank slightly and rotate the center fuel tank support strap aside.

12. Rotate the rear fuel tank support strap aside.

13. Lower the fuel tank slightly. Disconnect the fuel pump module and fuel tank pressure sensor electrical connectors.

14. Remove the fuel tank from the vehicle.

15. If equipped, if installing a new center fuel tank support strap, remove the center fuel tank support strap from the vehicle.

16. If installing a new rear fuel tank support strap, remove the rear fuel tank support strap from the vehicle.

To install:

17. To install, reverse the removal procedure.

18. Install the front and rear fuel tank support straps. Tighten the bolts to 30 ft. lbs. (40 Nm).

19. Install the center fuel tank support strap and bolt (if equipped). Tighten to 30 ft. lbs. (40 Nm).

20. Install the sway bar and the 4 sway bar bracket nuts. Tighten to 35 ft. lbs. (48 Nm).

IDLE SPEED

ADJUSTMENT

➡ **Idle speed is electronically controlled and no adjustment is required.**

THROTTLE BODY

REMOVAL & INSTALLATION

1. Remove the bolt and disconnect the quick connect coupling and remove the Evaporative Emission (EVAP) purge valve assembly.

2. Remove the 4 bolts and the fuel rail.

3. Remove the 8 fuel injector-to-fuel rail locking clips and separate the 8 fuel injectors from the fuel rail.

4. Discard the 2 O-ring seals from each fuel injector.

5. Remove the vacuum tube assembly from the intake manifold.

6. Remove the 2 bolts and the PCV fitting.

7. Remove the 4 bolts, the vibration damper and the Throttle Body (TB).

To install:

※※ CAUTION

If the engine is repaired or replaced because of upper engine failure, typically including valve or piston damage, check the intake manifold for metal debris. If metal debris is found, install a new intake manifold.

8. Failure to follow these instructions can result in engine damage.

9. Lubricate the O-ring seal with clean engine oil prior to installation.

10. Install the PCV fitting and the 2 bolts. Tighten to 53 inch lbs. (6 Nm).

11. Install the vacuum tube assembly onto the intake manifold and position the clamp.

12. Install the throttle body, vibration damper and tighten the 4 bolts in 2 stages:
- Stage 1: Tighten to 80 inch lbs. (9 Nm).
- Stage 2: Tighten an additional 90 degrees.

➡ **Lubricate the new O-ring seals with clean engine oil prior to installation.**

13. Install 16 new O-ring seals on each of the fuel injectors.

14. Assemble the 8 fuel injectors onto the fuel rail and install the 8 locking clips.

15. Install the fuel rail and fuel injector as an assembly onto the intake manifold. Install the 4 fuel rail bolts. Tighten to 89 inch lbs. (10 Nm).

16. Position the Evaporative Emission (EVAP) purge valve assembly and connect the quick connect coupling and install the bolt. Tighten to 89 inch lbs. (10 Nm).

HEATING & AIR CONDITIONING SYSTEM

BLOWER MOTOR

REMOVAL & INSTALLATION
See Figure 130.

1. Remove the 2 RH lower instrument panel insulator pin-type retainers and remove the insulator (if equipped).

2. Remove the RH lower A-pillar junction box cover.

3. Disconnect the blower motor electrical connector.

4. Remove the 3 blower motor screws.

➡ **The carpet below the blower motor must be repositioned, the blower motor will have to be carefully manipulated along the dash panel insulator, and the dash panel insulator will have to be slightly deflected to allow the blower motor to clear the heater core and evaporator core housing.**

5. Remove the blower motor in the following sequence.

6. Rotate the blower motor housing until the vent tube opening is facing the rear of the vehicle.

7. Depress the ridges in the dash panel insulator to allow the blower motor to be removed.

8. Remove the blower motor.

9. To install, reverse the removal procedure.

CONDENSER

REMOVAL & INSTALLATION

1. With the vehicle in NEUTRAL, position it on a hoist.

2. Recover the refrigerant.

3. Disconnect the battery cables.

4. Remove the upper radiator sight shield.

5. Remove the RH and LH headlamp assemblies.

6. Remove the air cleaner outlet tube.

7. Remove the 4 junction box bolts and position the junction box aside.

8. Detach the power steering cooler line clip.

9. Remove the condenser inlet fitting bolt and disconnect the fitting. Discard the O-ring and gasket seals.

10. Remove the condenser outlet fitting nut and disconnect the fitting. Discard the O-ring and gasket seals.

11. Remove the 2 cooling module bolts.

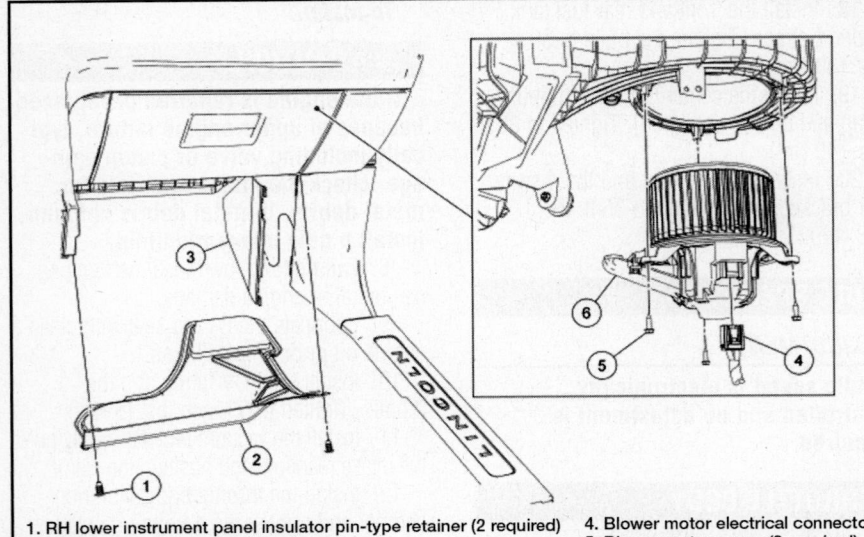

1. RH lower instrument panel insulator pin-type retainer (2 required)
2. RH lower instrument panel insulator
3. Junction box cover
4. Blower motor electrical connector
5. Blower motor screw (3 required)
6. Blower motor

N0087380

Fig. 130 Removing the main blower motor

12. Release the clamps and disconnect the 2 power steering cooler lines from the condenser core.

13. Remove the 3 pin-type retainers and detach the LH air deflector from the condenser bracket.

14. Remove the 2 RH outer air deflector pin-type retainers and position the air deflector aside.

15. Remove the 2 pin-type retainers and detach the RH air deflector from the condenser bracket.

16. Remove the 9 lower radiator splash shield pin-type retainers and position the shield aside.

17. Release the clamps and disconnect the 2 transmission cooler lines from the transmission cooler.

18. Detach the transmission cooler line pin-type retainer from the condenser core bracket.

➡**The cooling module must be positioned rearward to raise and detach the 4 condenser mounts from the cooling module.**

➡**The condenser must be removed from below the vehicle.**

19. Detach and remove the condenser core and transmission cooler as an assembly in the following sequence:

a. Position the cooling module rearward enough to allow the condenser to be lifted upward.

b. Depress the retaining tabs on the 2 lower condenser mounting brackets and detach the 4 condenser mounting brackets from the cooling module.

c. Position the top of the condenser forward to detach the top lip of the condenser bracket from the cooling module and remove the condenser core and bracket.

To install:

20. To install, reverse the removal procedure.

21. Install new gasket seals and O-ring seals.

22. Tighten all fasteners to 133 inch lbs. (15 Nm).

23. Lubricate the refrigerant system with the correct amount of clean PAG oil.

24. Fill the power steering fluid level.

25. Fill the transmission fluid level.

26. Evacuate, leak test and charge the refrigerant system.

HEATER CORE & EVAPORATOR CORE

REMOVAL & INSTALLATION

➡**If an evaporator core leak is suspected, the evaporator must be vacuum leak tested before it is removed from the vehicle.**

1. Recover the refrigerant.

2. Drain the engine coolant.

3. Remove the instrument panel.

4. Disconnect the 2 heater hose quick disconnect fittings at the heater core.

5. Remove the Thermostatic Expansion Valve (TXV) fitting nut and disconnect the fitting.

6. Discard the gasket seals.

7. Remove the 3 heater core and evaporator core housing nuts.

8. Detach the 4 satellite radio antenna cable pin-type retainers from the heater core and evaporator core housing (if equipped).

9. Detach the 3 body harness electrical connectors from the bracket below the air inlet duct.

10. Remove the air inlet duct bracket nut.

11. Remove the plenum chamber nut.

12. Remove the 4 tunnel instrument panel bracket bolts and the tunnel instrument panel bracket.

13. Detach the rear footwell duct from the heater core and evaporator core housing.

14. Remove the heater core and evaporator core housing.

To install:

15. To install, reverse the removal procedure.

16. Install new gasket seals.

17. Tighten the fasteners as follows:

- Plenum chamber nut: 62 inch lbs. (7 Nm).
- Air inlet duct bracket nut: 62 inch lbs. (7 Nm).
- 3 heater core and evaporator core housing nuts: 62 inch lbs. (7 Nm).
- TXV fitting nut: 133 inch lbs. (15 Nm).

18. Lubricate the refrigerant system with the correct amount of clean PAG oil.

19. Fill the engine coolant level.

20. Evacuate, leak test and charge the refrigerant system.

AUXILIARY HEATING & AIR CONDITIONING SYSTEM

BLOWER MOTOR

REMOVAL & INSTALLATION

1. Remove the RH quarter trim panel.
2. Remove the blower motor.
3. Disconnect the blower motor electrical connector.
4. Remove the blower motor screws. Remove the blower motor.
5. To install, reverse the removal procedure.

HEATER CORE & EVAPORATOR CORE

REMOVAL & INSTALLATION

See Figure 131.

1. With the vehicle in NEUTRAL, position it on a hoist.
2. Recover the refrigerant.
3. Drain the engine coolant.
4. Remove the RH quarter trim panel.

➡**Allow any residual coolant to drain from the auxiliary heater core after disconnecting the auxiliary heater hose fittings.**

5. Position a suitable drain pan and disconnect the 2 auxiliary heater hose fittings from the heater core at the floorpan connection.
6. Disconnect the 2 auxiliary evaporator line fittings at the floorpan connection.
7. Discard the O-ring seals.
8. Remove the 2 floorpan bracket bolts.
9. Remove the auxiliary headliner duct pin-type retainer and disconnect the duct.
10. Disconnect the auxiliary mode door actuator electrical connector.
11. Disconnect the auxiliary temperature blend door actuator electrical connector.

12. Disconnect the auxiliary blower motor resistor electrical connector.
13. Disconnect the auxiliary blower motor electrical connector and detach the wire harness from the housing.
14. Remove the 2 auxiliary heater core and evaporator core housing bolts.
15. Remove the auxiliary heater core and evaporator core housing.

To install:

16. To install, reverse the removal procedure.
17. Install new O-ring seals.
18. Tighten the 2 auxiliary heater core and evaporator core housing bolts 71 inch lbs. (8 Nm).
19. Lubricate the refrigerant system with the correct amount of clean PAG oil.
20. Fill the engine cooling system.
21. Evacuate, leak test and charge the refrigerant system.

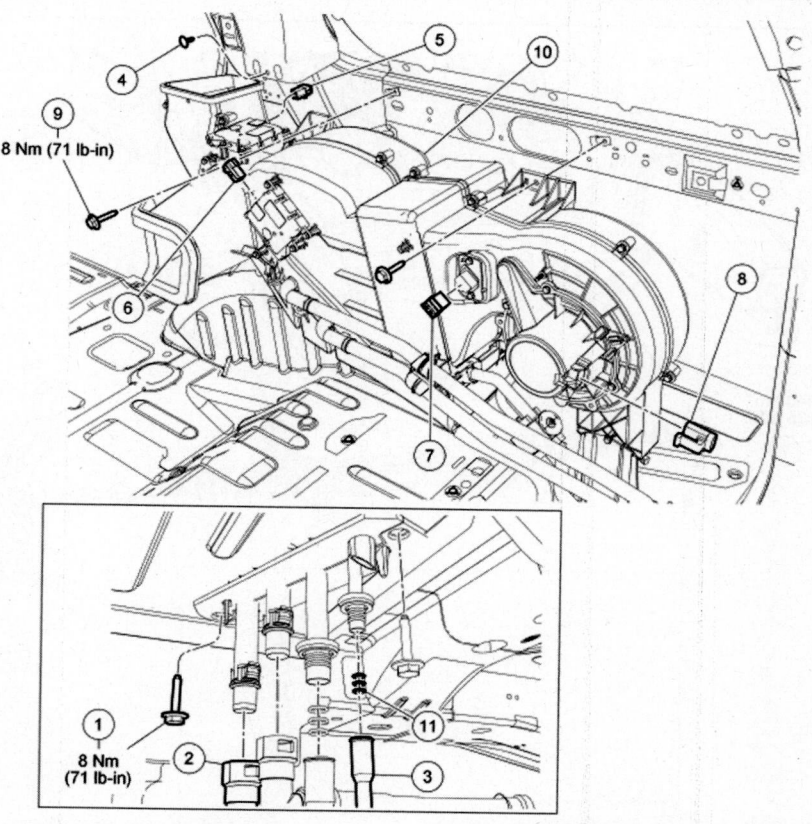

1. Floorpan bracket bolt (2 required)
2. Auxiliary heater hose fitting (2 required)
3. Auxiliary evaporator line fitting (2 required)
4. Auxiliary headliner duct pin-type retainer
5. Auxiliary mode door actuator electrical connector
6. Auxiliary temperature blend door actuator electrical connector
7. Blower motor resistor electrical connector
8. Blower motor electrical connector
9. Auxiliary heater core and evaporator core housing bolt (2 required)
10. Auxiliary heater core and evaporator core housing
11. O-ring seal (6 required)

N0077360

Fig. 131 Exploded view of the auxiliary heater core and evaporator core assembly

STEERING

POWER STEERING GEAR

REMOVAL & INSTALLATION

See Figures 132 and 133.

1. With the vehicle in NEUTRAL, position it on a hoist.

> ⁂ **CAUTION**
>
> **Do not allow the steering column shaft to rotate while disconnected from the gear or damage to the clockspring may occur. If there is evidence that the steering column shaft has rotated, the clockspring must be re-centered.**

2. Hold the steering wheel in the straight ahead position using a suitable holding device.

3. Remove the front wheels and tires.

4. If equipped, remove the 4 skid plate bolts and the skid plate.

5. Remove and discard the outer tie-rod end nuts.

> ⁂ **CAUTION**
>
> **Use care when installing the Ball Joint Tool Separator or damage to the tie-rod end boot may occur.**

6. Using the Ball Joint Tool Separator, disconnect the tie-rod ends from the wheel knuckles.

7. Release the lower cooling fan shroud tab and rotate the shroud upward.

8. Remove the 2 bolts and the oil drip shield.

> ⁂ **CAUTION**
>
> **Do not allow the steering column shaft to rotate while it is disconnected from the steering gear or damage to the clockspring may result. If there is evidence that the steering column shaft has rotated, the clockspring must be removed and re-centered.**

9. Remove the steering column shaft-to-steering gear bolt and disconnect the steering column shaft from the steering gear.

10. Discard the bolt.

11. Remove the power steering line clamp plate bolt, rotate the clamp plate and disconnect the power steering lines. Discard the O-ring seals.

12. Remove the 2 steering gear-to-crossmember bolts and remove the steering gear. Discard the bolts.

To install:

> ⁂ **CAUTION**
>
> **Make sure the LH steering gear bushing is seated correctly or failure of the steering gear may occur. The RH**

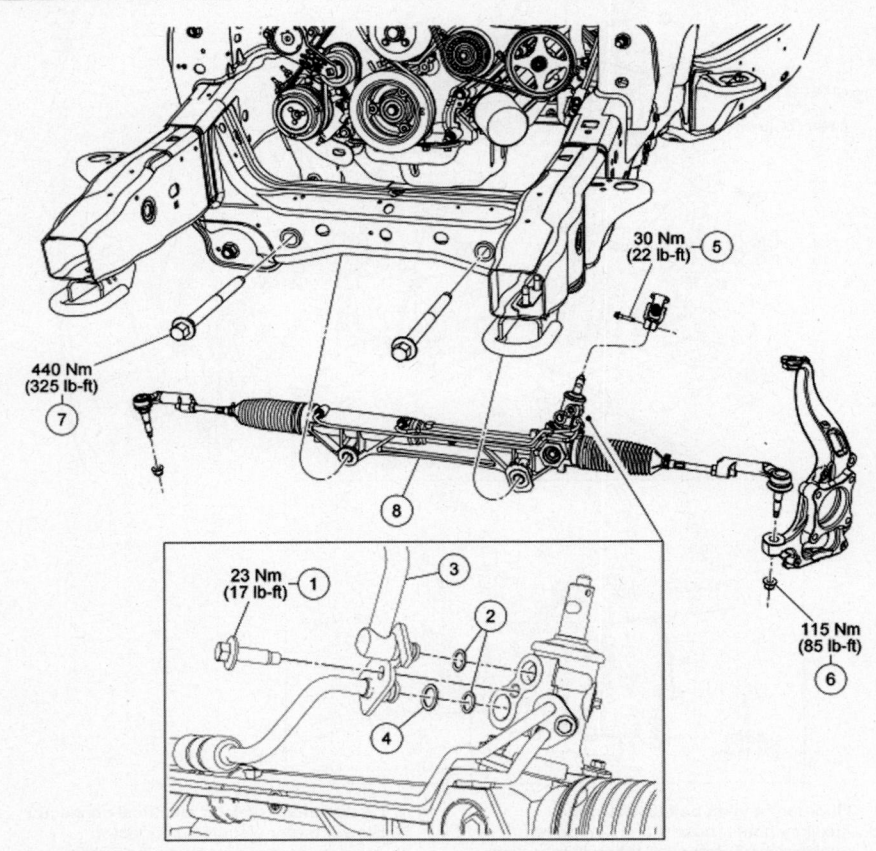

1. Power steering line clamp plate bolt
2. Power steering line O-ring seals (2 required)
3. Power steering return line
4. O-ring seal
5. Steering column shaft-to-steering gear bolt
6. Outer tie-rod end nut (2 required)
7. Steering gear-to-crossmember bolt (2 required)
8. Steering gear

N0072066

Fig. 132 Removing the power steering gear

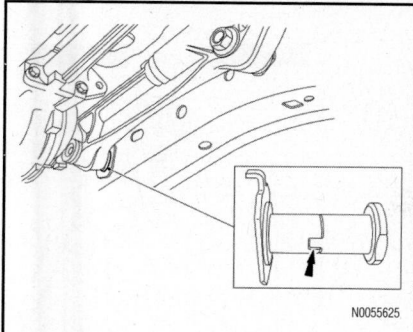

Fig. 133 Make sure the LH steering gear bushing is seated correctly or failure of the steering gear may occur. The RH side bushing does not have locking tabs.

side bushing does not have locking tabs.

13. Position the steering gear and install the 2 new steering gear-to-cross-member bolts. Tighten to 325 ft. lbs. (440 Nm).

14. Connect the steering column shaft and install a new bolt. Tighten to 22 ft. lbs. (30 Nm).

➡ **New O-ring seals must be installed any time the line is disconnected from the power steering gear.**

15. Connect the steering lines, rotate the clamp plate and install the clamp plate bolt. Tighten to 17 ft. lbs. (23 Nm).

16. Install the oil drip shield and the 2 bolts. Tighten to 62 inch lbs. (7 Nm).

17. Release the lower cooling fan shroud tab and rotate the shroud downward.

➡ **Make sure that the tie-rod end boots are seated correctly on the tie-rod ends or tie-rod end failure may occur.**

18. Connect the outer tie-rod ends to the wheel knuckles and install the new nuts. Tighten to 85 ft. lbs. (115 Nm).

19. If equipped, install the skid plate and the 4 bolts. Tighten to 18 ft. lbs. (25 Nm).

20. Install the front wheels and tires.

21. Fill the power steering system.

22. Check and, if necessary, adjust the front toe.

POWER STEERING PUMP

REMOVAL & INSTALLATION

See Figure 134.

✳✳ CAUTION

While repairing the power steering system, care should be taken to prevent the entry of foreign material or failure of the power steering components may result.

➡ **A new Teflon® seal must be installed any time the line is disconnected from the power steering pump.**

1. Remove the power steering pump pulley.

2. Using a suitable suction device, remove the power steering fluid from the fluid reservoir.

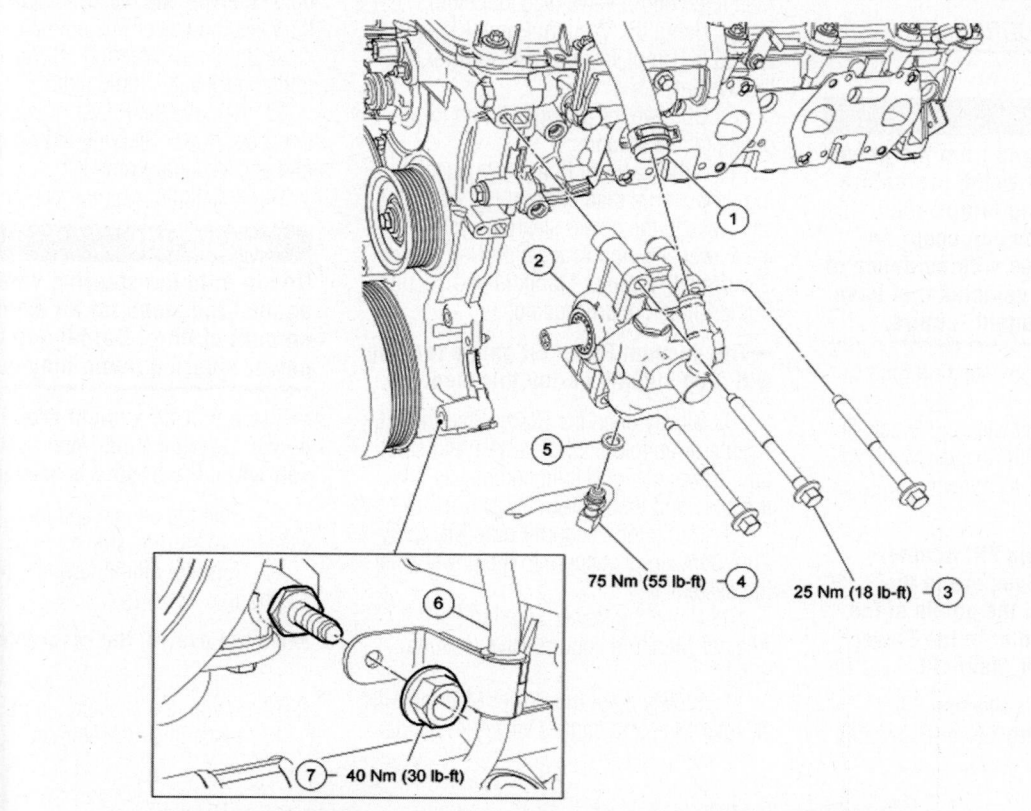

1. Power steering fluid reservoir-to-pump supply hose
2. Power steering pump
3. Power steering pump bolt (3 required)
4. Power steering pressure line-to-power steering pump fitting
5. Power steering pressure line Teflon® seal
6. Power steering pressure line
7. Power steering pressure line bracket-to-engine nut

Fig. 134 Exploded view of removing the power steering pump

3. Release the clamp and disconnect the power steering fluid reservoir-to-pump supply hose.

4. Remove the power steering pressure line bracket-to-engine nut.

5. Disconnect the power steering pressure line-to-power steering pump fitting. Discard the seal.

6. Remove the 3 bolts and the power steering pump.

To install:

7. To install, reverse the removal procedure.

8. Tighten the fasteners as follows:
- 3 power steering pump bolts: 18 ft. lbs. (25 Nm).
- Power steering pressure line-to-power steering pump fitting: 55 ft. lbs. (75 Nm).
- Power steering pressure line bracket-to-engine nut: 30 ft. lbs. (40 Nm).

9. Using the Teflon Seal Installer Set, install a new Teflon seal on the pressure line-to-pump fitting.

10. Fill the power steering system.

FLUID FILL PROCEDURE

See Figure 135.

✳✳ CAUTION

If the air is not purged from the power steering system correctly, premature power steering pump failure may result. The condition can occur on pre-delivery vehicles with evidence of aerated fluid or on vehicles that have had steering component repairs.

1. Remove the power steering fluid reservoir cap.

2. Install the Power Steering Evacuation Cap, Power Steering Fill Adapter Manifold and Vacuum Pump Kit as shown in the illustration.

➡**The Power Steering Fill Adapter Manifold control valves are in the OPEN position when the points of the handles face the center of the Power Steering Fill Adapter Manifold.**

3. Close the Power Steering Fill Adapter Manifold control valve (fluid side).

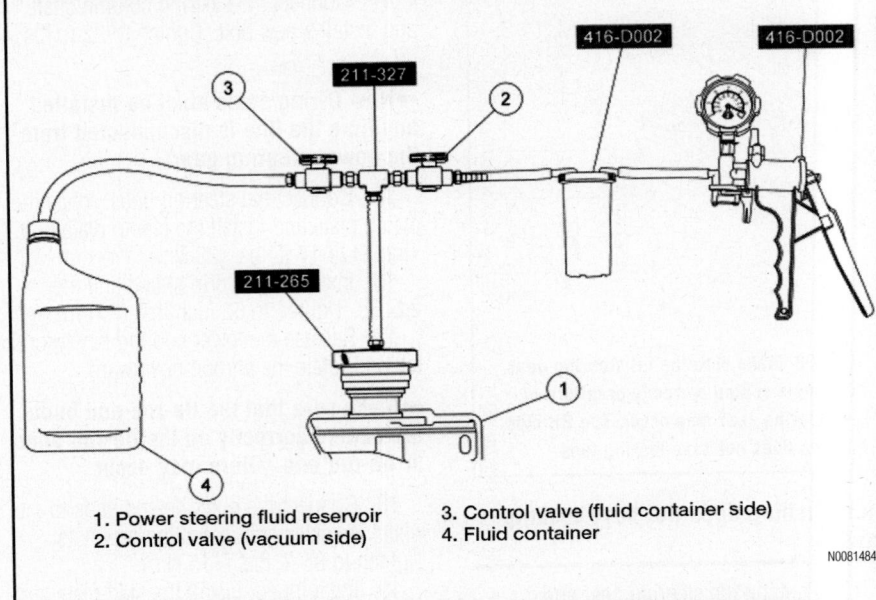

1. Power steering fluid reservoir
2. Control valve (vacuum side)
3. Control valve (fluid container side)
4. Fluid container

N0081484

Fig. 135 Install the Power Steering Evacuation Cap, Power Steering Fill Adapter Manifold and Vacuum Pump Kit as shown in the illustration.

4. Open the Power Steering Fill Adapter Manifold control valve (vacuum side).

5. Using the Vacuum Pump Kit, apply 20–25 in. Hg of vacuum to the power steering system.

6. Observe the Vacuum Pump Kit gauge for 30 seconds.

7. If the Vacuum Pump Kit gauge reading drops more than 0.88 in. Hg, correct any leaks in the power steering system or the Power Steering Evacuation Cap, Power Steering Fill Adapter Manifold and Vacuum Pump Kit before proceeding.

➡**The Vacuum Pump Kit gauge reading will drop slightly during this step.**

8. Slowly open the Power Steering Fill Adapter Manifold control valve (fluid side) until power steering fluid completely fills the hose and then close the control valve.

9. Using the Vacuum Pump Kit, apply 20–25 in. Hg of vacuum to the power steering system.

10. Close the Power Steering Fill Adapter Manifold control valve (vacuum side).

11. Slowly open the Power Steering Fill Adapter Manifold control valve (fluid side).

12. Once power steering fluid enters the fluid reservoir and reaches the minimum fluid level indicator line on the reservoir, close the Power Steering Fill Adapter Manifold control valve (fluid side).

13. Remove the Power Steering Evacuation Cap, Power Steering Fill Adapter Manifold and Vacuum Pump Kit.

14. Install the reservoir cap.

✳✳ CAUTION

Do not hold the steering wheel against the stops for an extended amount of time. Damage to the power steering pump may occur.

➡**There will be a slight drop in the power steering fluid level in the reservoir when the engine is started.**

15. Start the engine and turn the steering wheel from stop-to-stop.

16. Turn the ignition switch to the OFF position.

➡**Do not overfill the reservoir.**

17. Remove the reservoir cap and fill the reservoir with the specified fluid.

18. Install the reservoir cap.

SUSPENSION

LOWER BALL JOINT

REMOVAL & INSTALLATION

1. Remove the wheel knuckle. See "Steering Knuckle" in this section.
2. Remove and discard the lower ball joint snap ring.
3. On 4WD models, perform the following:

    a. Using the C-Frame and Screw Installer/Remover and Ball Joint Remover, remove the lower ball joint.

To install:

4. On 4WD models, perform the following:

✳✳ CAUTION

Do not damage the lower ball joint boot when installing the C-Frame and Screw Installer/Remover and Ball Joint Installer/Remover or pre-

mature failure of the ball joint may occur.

    a. Make sure the ball joint snap ring is fully seated.
    b. Using the C-Frame and Screw Installer/Remover and Ball Joint Installer/Remover, install the lower ball joint. Install the ball joint snap ring.
5. Install the wheel knuckle. See "Steering Knuckle" in this section.

LOWER CONTROL ARM

REMOVAL & INSTALLATION

See Figures 136 and 137.

✳✳ CAUTION

Suspension fasteners are critical parts because they affect performance of vital components and systems and

their failure may result in major service expense. New parts must be installed with the same part numbers or equivalent parts, if replacement is necessary. Do not use a replacement part of lesser quality or substitute design. Torque values must be used as specified during reassembly to make sure of correct retention of these parts.

1. Measure the distance from the center of the hub to the lip of the fender with the vehicle in a level, static ground position (curb height).
2. Remove the wheel and tire.
3. Use the hex-holding feature to prevent the stud from turning while removing the nut, then remove and discard the stabilizer bar link lower nut.
4. On RWD models, perform the following:
    a. Remove and discard the lower ball joint nut.

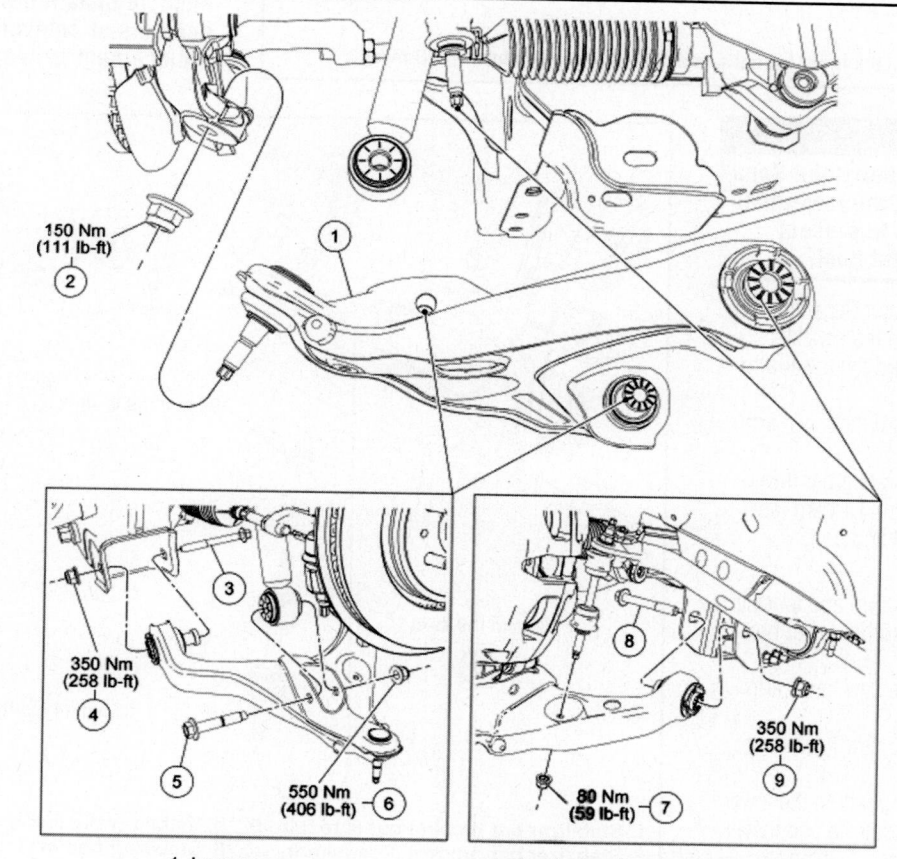

150 Nm (111 lb-ft) — 2

350 Nm (258 lb-ft) — 4

550 Nm (406 lb-ft) — 6

80 Nm (59 lb-ft) — 7

350 Nm (258 lb-ft) — 9

1. Lower arm
2. Lower ball joint nut
3. Lower arm forward bolt
4. Lower arm forward nut
5. Shock absorber lower bolt
6. Shock absorber lower nut
7. Stabilizer bar link lower nut
8. Lower arm rearward bolt
9. Lower arm rearward nut

N0091318

Fig. 136 Exploded view of the lower control arm and related components—RWD models

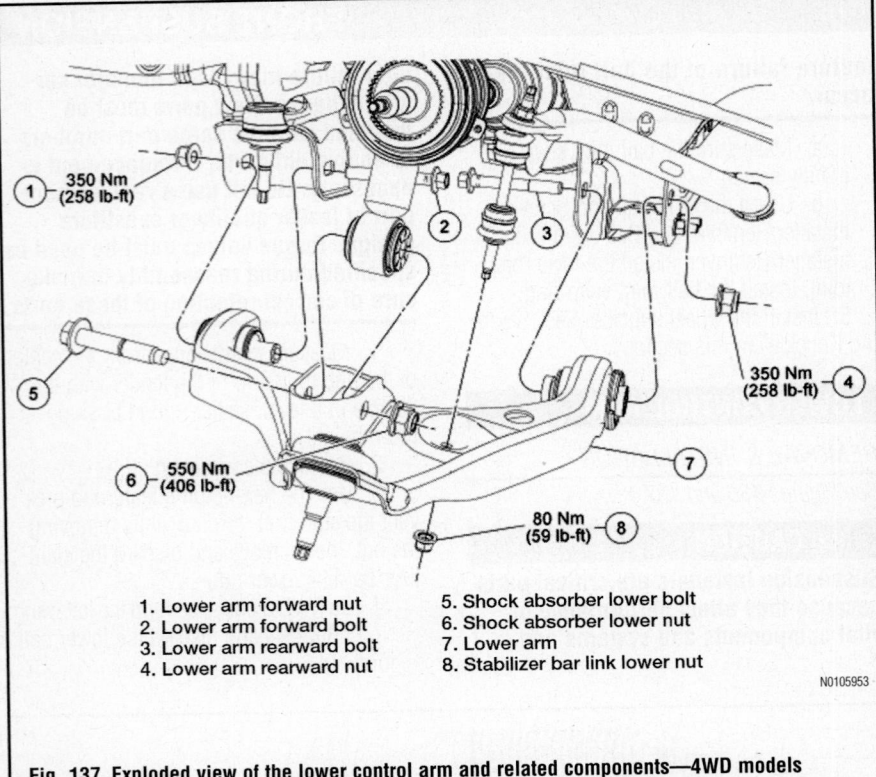

1. Lower arm forward nut
2. Lower arm forward bolt
3. Lower arm rearward bolt
4. Lower arm rearward nut
5. Shock absorber lower bolt
6. Shock absorber lower nut
7. Lower arm
8. Stabilizer bar link lower nut

N0105953

Fig. 137 Exploded view of the lower control arm and related components—4WD models

※ **CAUTION**

Make sure to use the Ball Joint Separator when separating the lower ball joint from the knuckle to prevent damage to the ball joint boot.

  b. Using the Ball Joint Separator, separate the ball joint from the knuckle.
  5. Remove and discard the lower arm rearward nut and bolt.
  6. Remove and discard the lower arm forward nut and bolt.
  7. Remove the shock absorber lower nut, bolt and the lower arm. Discard the shock absorber lower nut and bolt.

To install:

  8. Position the lower arm and loosely install the new shock absorber lower bolt and nut.
  9. Loosely install the new lower arm forward nut and bolt.
  10. Loosely install the new lower arm rearward nut and bolt.
  11. On RWD models, position the lower ball joint into the wheel knuckle and install the new lower ball joint nut. Tighten to 111 ft. lbs. (150 Nm).
  12. Install the new stabilizer bar link lower nut. Tighten to 59 ft. lbs. (80 Nm).
  13. Use a suitable jack to raise the suspension until the distance between the center of the hub and the lip of the fender is

equal to the measurement taken in Step 1 (curb height).

➡ **Use a crowfoot wrench to tighten the lower arm rearward nut.**

  14. Tighten the lower arm rearward nut, then the forward nut, each to 258 ft. lbs. (350 Nm).
  15. Install the wheel and tire.
  16. Tighten the shock absorber lower nut to 406 ft. lbs. (550 Nm).
  17. Check and, if necessary, align the front end.

STABILIZER BAR

REMOVAL & INSTALLATION

See Figure 138.

※ **CAUTION**

Suspension fasteners are critical parts because they affect performance of vital components and systems and their failure may result in major service expense. New parts must be installed with the same part numbers or equivalent parts, if replacement is necessary. Do not use

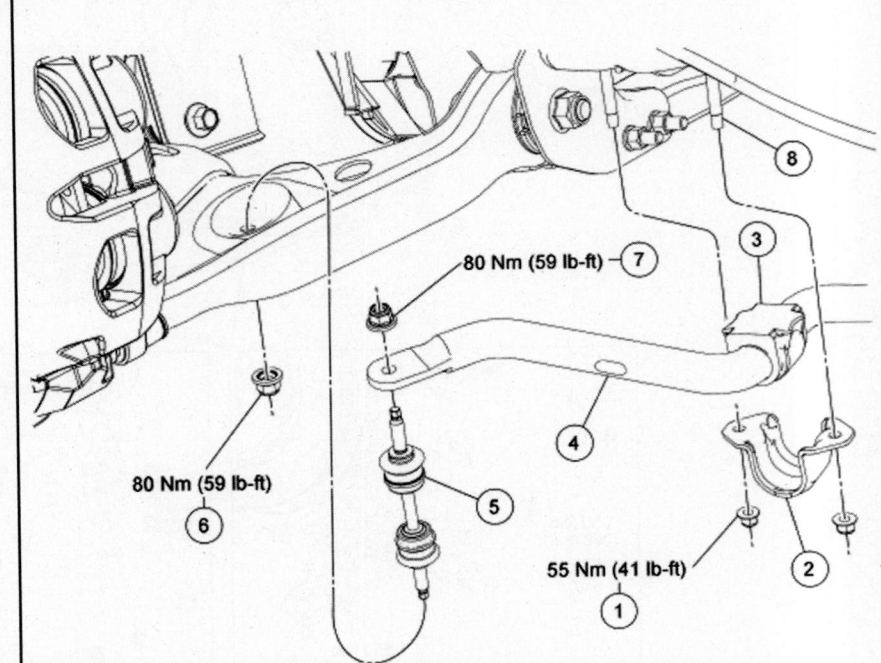

1. Stabilizer bar bracket nut (4 required)
2. Stabilizer bar bracket (2 required)
3. Stabilizer bar bushing (2 required)
4. Stabilizer bar
5. Stabilizer bar link (2 required)
6. Stabilizer bar link lower nut (2 required)
7. Stabilizer bar link upper nut (2 required)
8. Stabilizer bracket bolt plate

N0105926

Fig. 138 Exploded view of the stabilizer bar and link

a replacement part of lesser quality or substitute design. Torque values **must be used as specified during reassembly to make sure of correct retention of these parts.**

1. With the vehicle in NEUTRAL, position it on a hoist.

➡The hex-holding feature can be used to prevent turning of the stud while removing the nut.

2. Remove and discard the 2 stabilizer bar link upper nuts.

✳✳ CAUTION

Do not hold the stabilizer link boot with any tool as damage to the boot will occur.

3. Remove and discard the 2 stabilizer bar link lower nuts and remove the 2 stabilizer bar links.

4. Remove the 4 stabilizer bar bracket nuts, brackets and the stabilizer bar. Discard the nuts.

5. Remove and discard the stabilizer bracket bolt plates.

6. Inspect and, if necessary, install new stabilizer bar bushings.

To install:

7. To install, reverse the removal procedure.

➡**Make sure the stabilizer bar bushing upset is installed into the bracket groove.**

8. Tighten the fasteners as follows:
   - 4 new stabilizer bar bracket nuts: 41 ft. lbs. (55 Nm).
   - 2 new stabilizer bar link lower nuts: 59 ft. lbs. (80 Nm).
   - 2 new stabilizer bar link upper nuts: 59 ft. lbs. (80 Nm).

STEERING KNUCKLE

REMOVAL & INSTALLATION
See Figures 139 and 140.

✳✳ CAUTION

Suspension fasteners are critical parts because they affect performance of vital components and systems and their failure may result in major service expense. New parts must be installed with the same part numbers or equivalent part, if replacement is necessary. Do not use a replacement part of lesser quality or substitute design. Torque values must be used as specified during

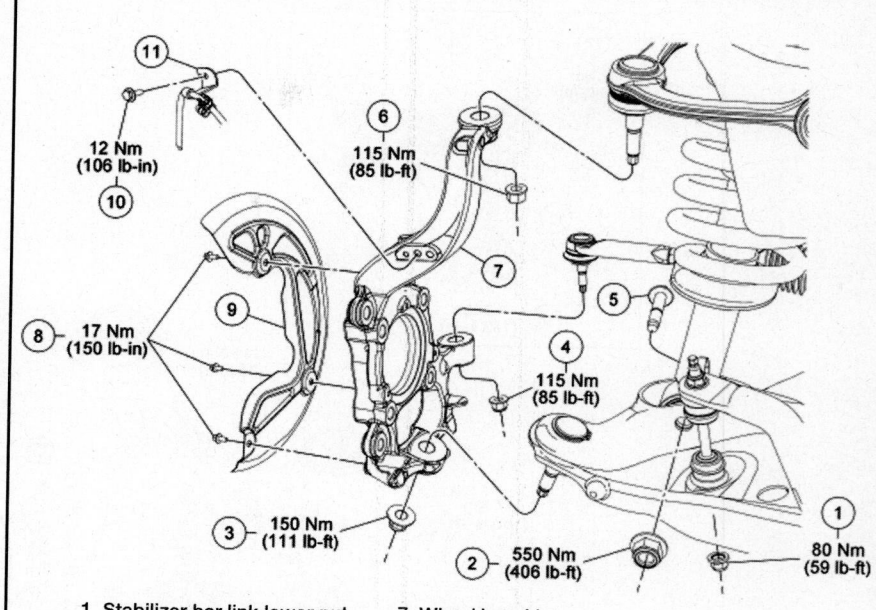

1. Stabilizer bar link lower nut
2. Shock absorber lower nut
3. Lower ball joint nut
4. Tie-rod end nut
5. Shock absorber lower bolt
6. Upper ball joint nut
7. Wheel knuckle
8. Brake disc shield bolts (3 required)
9. Brake disc shield
10. Wheel speed sensor harness bracket bolt
11. Wheel speed sensor harness bracket

N0091319

Fig. 139 Exploded view of the steering knuckle assembly—RWD models

reassembly to make sure of correct retention of these parts.

1. Remove the wheel bearing and wheel hub. See "Wheel Bearing & Hub" in this section.

2. Remove and discard the tie-rod end nut. Using the Ball Joint Separator, separate the tie-rod end from the wheel knuckle.

3. Remove the wheel speed sensor harness bracket bolt and position the harness aside.

➡**Use the hex-holding feature to prevent the stud from turning while removing the nut.**

4. Remove and discard the stabilizer bar link lower nut.

5. Remove and discard the shock absorber lower nut and bolt.

6. On 4WD models, remove the 3 Integrated Wheel End (IWE) bolts.

7. Remove and discard the upper ball joint nut.

✳✳ CAUTION

Be sure not to damage the ball joint boot when installing the Ball Joint Separator.

8. Using the Ball Joint Separator, separate the upper ball joint from the wheel knuckle.

9. Remove and discard the lower ball joint nut. Using the Ball Joint Separator, separate the lower ball joint from the wheel knuckle and remove the wheel knuckle.

10. If necessary, remove the 3 brake disc shield bolts and remove the brake disc shield.

To install:

✳✳ CAUTION

Do not tighten the lower shock nut until the installation procedure is complete and the weight of the vehicle is resting on the wheel and tire assemblies or incorrect clamp load and bushing damage may occur.

11. If necessary, install the brake disc shield and 3 brake disc shield bolts. Tighten to 150 inch lbs. (17 Nm).

12. Position the lower ball joint into the wheel knuckle and install the new nut. Tighten to 111 ft. lbs. (150 Nm).

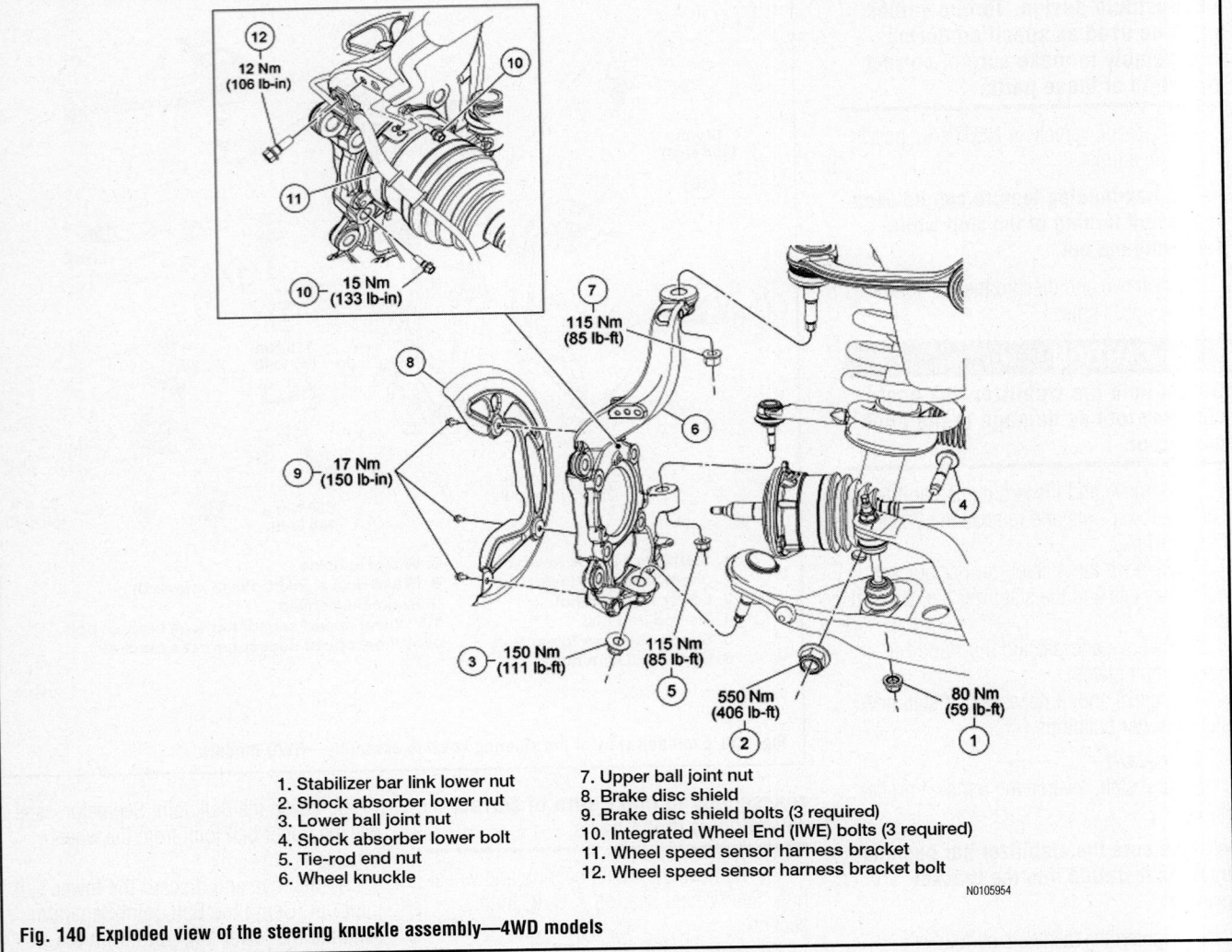

1. Stabilizer bar link lower nut
2. Shock absorber lower nut
3. Lower ball joint nut
4. Shock absorber lower bolt
5. Tie-rod end nut
6. Wheel knuckle
7. Upper ball joint nut
8. Brake disc shield
9. Brake disc shield bolts (3 required)
10. Integrated Wheel End (IWE) bolts (3 required)
11. Wheel speed sensor harness bracket
12. Wheel speed sensor harness bracket bolt

N0105954

Fig. 140 Exploded view of the steering knuckle assembly—4WD models

13. Position the upper ball joint and install the new nut. Tighten to 85 ft. lbs. (115 Nm).

14. For 4WD models, position the IWE and install the 3 IWE bolts. Tighten to 133 inch lbs. (15 Nm).

15. Loosely install the new shock absorber lower nut and bolt. Do not tighten the nut at this time.

16. Install the new stabilizer bar link lower nut. Tighten to 59 ft. lbs. (80 Nm).

17. Position the wheel speed sensor harness bracket and install the bolt. Tighten to 106 inch lbs. (12 Nm).

18. Install the new tie-rod end nut. Tighten to 85 ft. lbs. (115 Nm).

19. Install the wheel bearing and wheel hub. See "Wheel Bearing & Hub" in this section.

20. With the weight of the vehicle on the wheel and tire, tighten the shock absorber lower nut to 406 ft. lbs. (550 Nm).

21. Check and, if necessary, align the front end.

STRUT & SPRING ASSEMBLY

REMOVAL & INSTALLATION

See Figure 141.

✱✱ CAUTION

Suspension fasteners are critical parts because they affect performance of vital components and systems and their failure may result in major service expense. New parts must be installed with the same part numbers or equivalent parts, if replacement is necessary. Do not use a replacement part of lesser quality or substitute design. Torque values must be used as specified during reassembly to make sure of correct retention of these parts.

1. Remove and discard the shock absorber upper mount nuts.
2. Remove the wheel and tire.

3. Remove and discard the tie-rod end nut.

4. Using the Ball Joint Separator, separate the tie-rod end from the wheel knuckle.

5. Detach the flexible hose retainer from the speed sensor harness. Remove the brake flexible hose bracket bolt and disconnect the bracket from the wheel knuckle.

6. Remove and discard the upper ball joint nut.

7. Remove and discard the shock absorber lower nut and bolt. Using the Ball Joint Separator, disconnect the upper arm ball joint from the wheel knuckle and remove the shock absorber and spring assembly.

➡**If the individual spring and/or shock components are not being serviced, continue to the Installation procedure.**

➡**For reference during assembly, index-mark the upper mount, spring and shock absorber.**

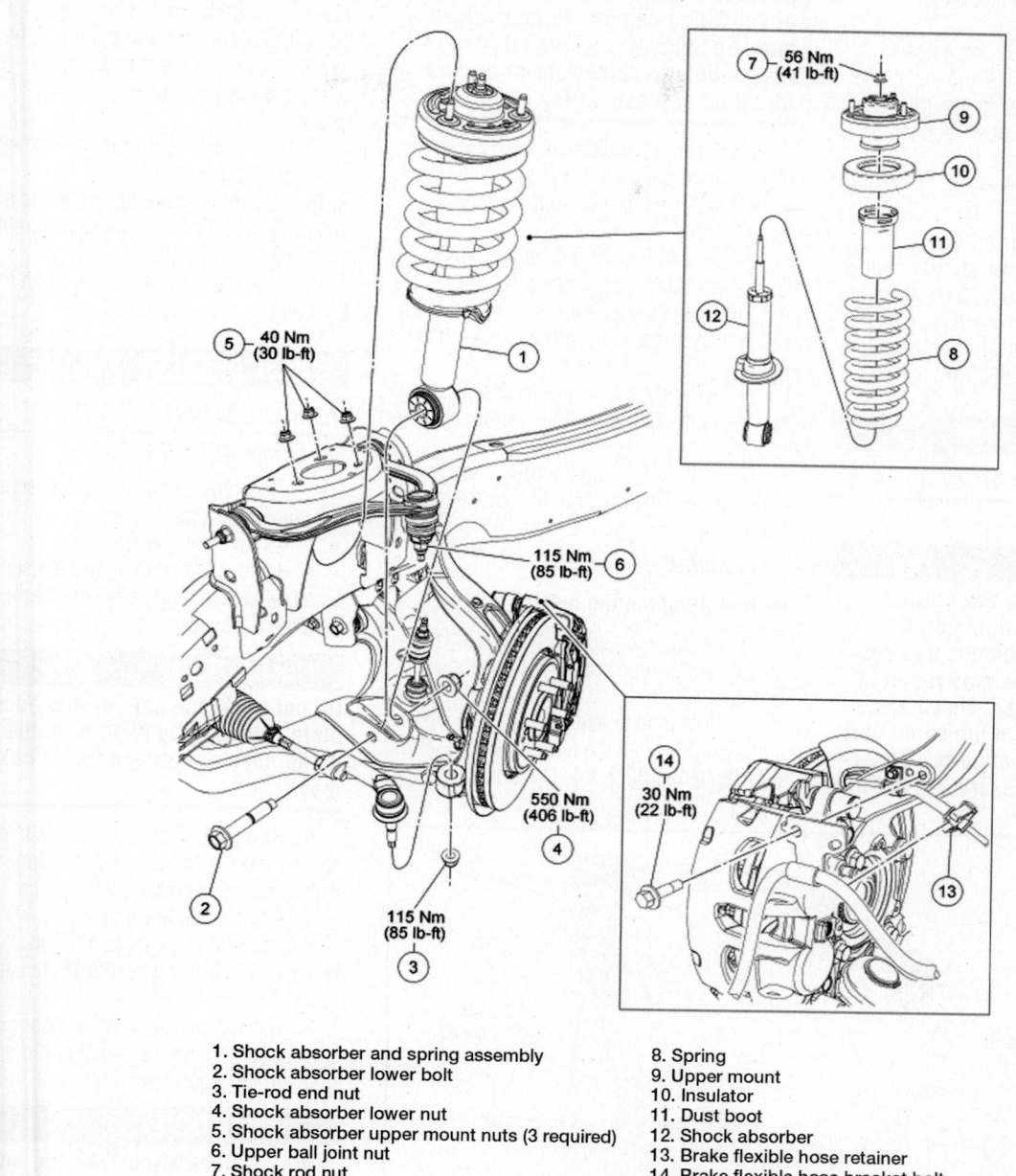

1. Shock absorber and spring assembly
2. Shock absorber lower bolt
3. Tie-rod end nut
4. Shock absorber lower nut
5. Shock absorber upper mount nuts (3 required)
6. Upper ball joint nut
7. Shock rod nut
8. Spring
9. Upper mount
10. Insulator
11. Dust boot
12. Shock absorber
13. Brake flexible hose retainer
14. Brake flexible hose bracket bolt

N0097808

Fig. 141 Exploded view of the strut and spring assembly

Using a suitable spring compressor, compress the spring until the tension is released from the shock absorber.

➡**Use the hex-holding feature to prevent the shock rod from turning while removing the nut.**

8. While holding the shock rod, remove the nut and the shock absorber. Discard the nut.

9. Remove the upper mount, dust boot and insulator.

To install:

✳✳ CAUTION

Do not tighten the lower shock nut until the installation procedure is complete and the weight of the vehicle is resting on the wheel and tire assemblies or incorrect clamp load and bushing damage may occur.

10. Position the shock absorber and spring and install the dust boot, insulator and the upper mount.

11. Align the index marks made during disassembly.

12. Using a suitable spring compressor, compress the spring until the tension is released from the shock absorber.

13. Using the hex-holding feature to hold the shock rod, install the shock absorber and the shock rod nut. Tighten the new nut to 41 ft. lbs. (56 Nm).

14. Install the shock absorber and spring assembly and connect the upper arm ball joint to the wheel knuckle. Tighten the new nut to 85 ft. lbs. (115 Nm).

15. Loosely install the new shock absorber lower nut and bolt.

16. Connect the brake flexible hose bracket to the wheel knuckle and install the bolt. Tighten the bolt to 22 ft. lbs. (30 Nm).

17. Attach the flexible hose retainer to the speed sensor harness.

18. Install the tie-rod end nut. Tighten to 111 ft. lbs. (150 Nm).

19. Install the wheel and tire.

20. Install the new shock absorber upper mount nuts. Tighten to 30 ft. lbs. (40 Nm).

21. With the weight of the vehicle on the wheel and tire, tighten the shock absorber lower nut to 406 ft. lbs. (550 Nm).

UPPER CONTROL ARM

REMOVAL & INSTALLATION

See Figure 142.

❊❊ CAUTION

Suspension fasteners are critical parts because they affect performance of vital components and systems and their failure may result in major service expense. New parts must be installed with the same part numbers or equivalent parts, if replacement is necessary. Do not use

a replacement part of lesser quality or substitute design. Torque values must be used as specified during reassembly to make sure of correct retention of these parts.

1. Measure the distance from the center of the hub to the lip of the fender with the vehicle in a level, static ground position (curb height).

2. Remove the shock absorber and spring assembly. See "Strut & Spring Assembly" in this section.

3. Remove and discard the upper ball joint nut.

4. Using the Ball Joint Separator, separate the upper ball joint from the wheel knuckle.

5. Remove the upper arm-to-frame nuts and bolts and the upper arm. Discard the bolts.

To install:

➡ **Do not tighten the nuts at this time.**

6. Position the upper arm and loosely install the new upper arm-to-frame bolts and nuts.

7. Position the ball joint into the wheel knuckle and install the new upper ball joint nut. Tighten to 85 ft. lbs. (115 Nm).

8. Use a suitable jack to raise the suspension until the distance between the center of the hub and the lip of the fender is equal to the measurement taken in during removal (curb height).

9. Tighten the upper arm-to-frame nuts to 111 ft. lbs. (150 Nm).

10. Install the shock absorber and spring assembly. See "Strut & Spring Assembly" in this section.

11. Check and, if necessary, align the front end.

WHEEL BEARING & HUB

REMOVAL & INSTALLATION

See Figures 143 and 144.

1. Disconnect the wheel speed sensor electrical connector.

2. Remove the wheel and tire.

3. Remove the wheel speed sensor harness bracket bolt and detach the harness from the retainers.

❊❊ CAUTION

Do not allow the caliper and anchor plate assembly to hang from the brake hose or damage to the hose may result.

4. Remove the 2 bolts and position the caliper and anchor plate aside. Support the caliper using mechanic's wire.

5. Remove the brake disc.

6. Remove the 4 bolts and the wheel bearing and wheel hub. Discard the bolts.

7. If installing a new wheel bearing and wheel hub, remove the wheel speed sensor bolt and the wheel speed sensor.

❊❊ CAUTION

If the original wheel bearing and wheel hub is being installed, a new O-ring seal must be installed or damage to the wheel bearing may occur.

To install:

8. To install, reverse the removal procedure.

9. Tighten the fasteners as follows:
- Wheel speed sensor bolt: 13 ft. lbs. (18 Nm).
- 4 wheel hub bolts: 129 ft. lbs. (175 Nm).
- 2 caliper and anchor plate bolts: 184 ft. lbs. (250 Nm).
- Wheel speed sensor harness bracket bolt: 106 inch lbs. (12 Nm).

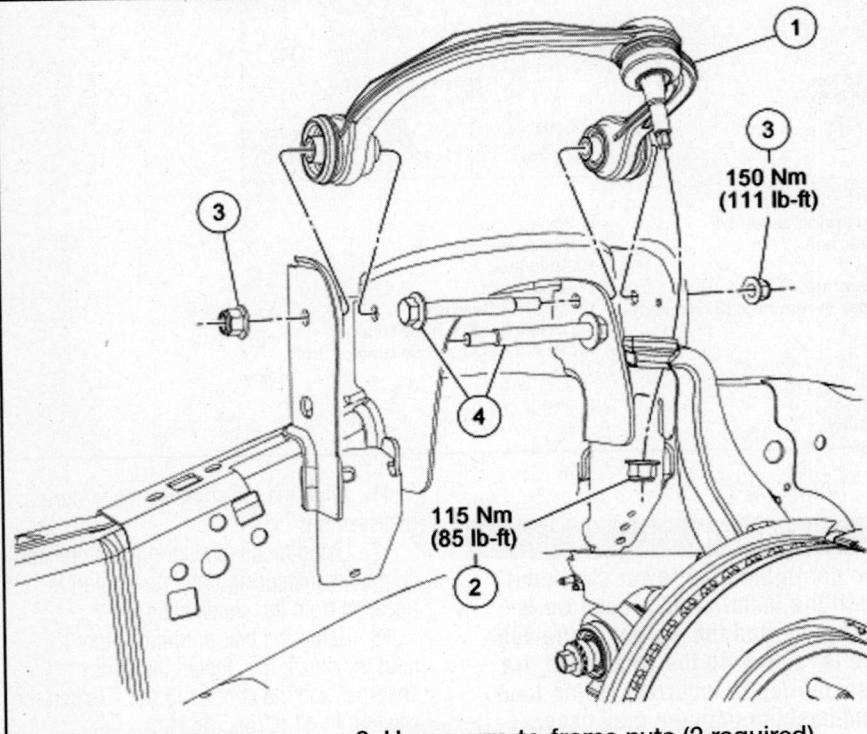

1. Upper arm
2. Upper ball joint nut
3. Upper arm-to-frame nuts (2 required)
4. Upper arm-to-frame bolts (2 required)

N0105923

Fig. 142 Removing the upper control arm

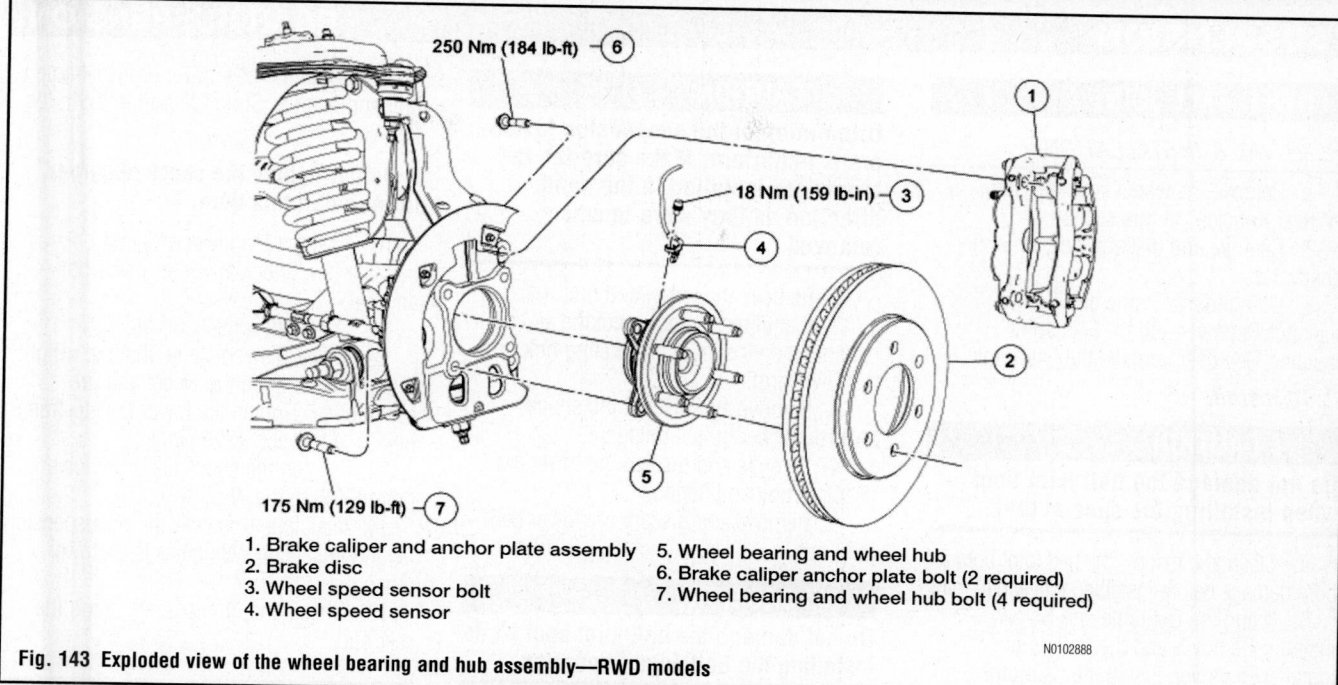

250 Nm (184 lb-ft) — 6

18 Nm (159 lb-in) — 3

175 Nm (129 lb-ft) — 7

1. Brake caliper and anchor plate assembly
2. Brake disc
3. Wheel speed sensor bolt
4. Wheel speed sensor
5. Wheel bearing and wheel hub
6. Brake caliper anchor plate bolt (2 required)
7. Wheel bearing and wheel hub bolt (4 required)

N0102888

Fig. 143 Exploded view of the wheel bearing and hub assembly—RWD models

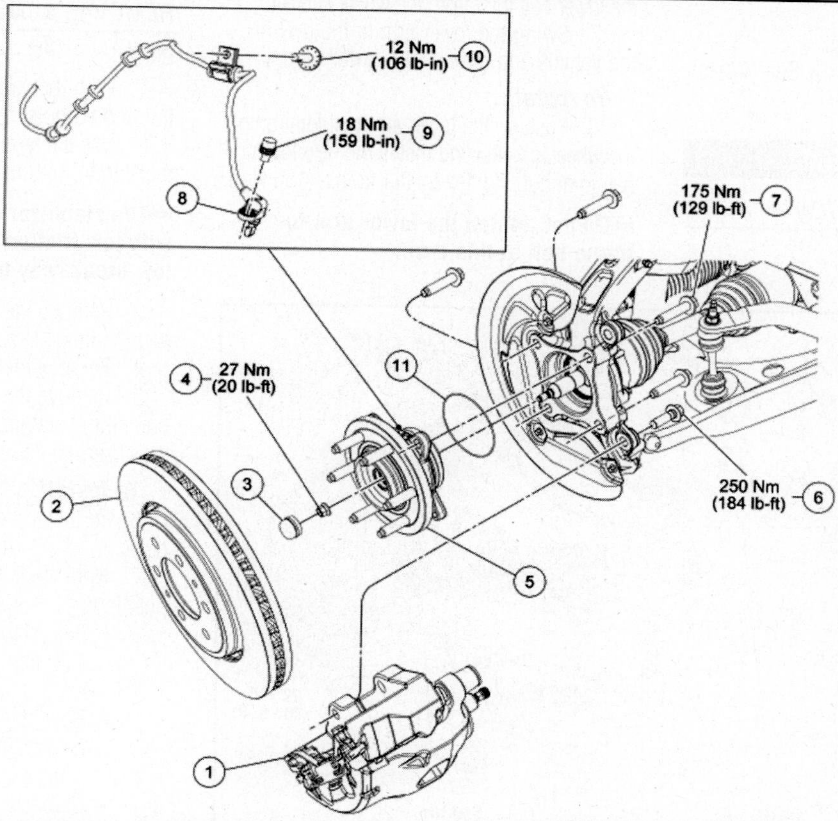

12 Nm (106 lb-in) — 10

18 Nm (159 lb-in) — 9

175 Nm (129 lb-ft) — 7

27 Nm (20 lb-ft) — 4

250 Nm (184 lb-ft) — 6

1. Brake caliper and anchor plate assembly
2. Brake disc
3. Dust cap
4. Halfshaft nut
5. Wheel bearing and wheel hub
6. Brake caliper anchor plate bolt (2 required)
7. Wheel bearing and wheel hub bolt (4 required)
8. Wheel speed sensor
9. Wheel speed sensor bolt
10. Wheel speed sensor harness bracket bolt
11. O-ring seal

N0102737

Fig. 144 Exploded view of the wheel bearing and hub assembly—4WD models

LOWER BALL JOINT

REMOVAL & INSTALLATION

1. Remove the wheel knuckle. See "Wheel Knuckle" in this section.
2. Remove and discard the ball joint snap ring.
3. Using the C-Frame and Screw Installer/Remover and the Ball Joint Installer/Remover, remove the ball joint.

To install:

❊❊ CAUTION

Do not damage the ball joint boot when installing the special tool.

4. Clean and inspect the ball joint bore for bore damage before installing a new ball joint.
5. Using the C-Frame and Screw Installer/Remover and the Ball Joint Installer/Remover, install the ball joint.

➡ **Always use a new ball joint snap ring.**

6. Install a new snap ring.
7. Install the wheel knuckle. See "Wheel Knuckle" in this section.

LOWER CONTROL ARM

REMOVAL & INSTALLATION

See Figure 145.

❊❊ CAUTION

Orientation of the suspension fasteners is important. Make sure the fasteners are installed in the same direction as they were in when removed.

1. Remove the wheel and tire.
2. If equipped, disconnect the air suspension height sensor connecting link from the lower arm.
3. Remove and discard the shock absorber lower bolt and flagnut.
4. Remove and discard the lower arm-to-frame bolt and flagnut.
5. Remove and discard the lower ball joint nut.

❊❊ CAUTION

Do not damage the ball joint boot while installing the Ball Joint Separator.

6. Using the Ball Joint Separator, separate the lower ball joint from the wheel knuckle.
7. Swing the lower arm to the rear of the vehicle and remove the lower arm.

To install:

8. Position the lower arm ball joint onto the wheel knuckle and install the new lower ball joint nut. Tighten to 111 ft. lbs. (150 Nm).

➡ **Do not tighten the lower arm-to-frame bolt at this time.**

9. Install the new lower arm-to-frame bolt and flagnut. Snug the bolt to 37 ft. lbs. (50 Nm).

➡ **Do not tighten the shock absorber lower nut at this time.**

10. Position the lower arm and install a new shock absorber lower bolt and nut.
11. Install the wheel and tire.
12. Lower the vehicle so that the weight of the vehicle is on the wheel and tire assemblies. Tighten the lower arm-to-frame bolt to 166 ft. lbs. (225 Nm).
13. Tighten the shock absorber lower bolt to 406 ft. lbs. (550 Nm).
14. If equipped, connect the air suspension height sensor connecting link to the lower arm.
15. Check and, if necessary, align the rear end.

STABILIZER BAR

REMOVAL & INSTALLATION

See Figure 146.

1. With the vehicle in NEUTRAL, position it on a hoist.
2. Use the hex-holding feature to prevent the stud from turning while removing the nut.

➡ **The stabilizer bar links are designed with low friction ball joints that have a low breakaway torque.**

3. Remove the 4 stabilizer bar link nuts and the links. Discard the nuts.
4. Remove the stone shields.
5. Remove the 4 stabilizer bar bracket nuts, the 2 stabilizer bar brackets and the stabilizer bar. Discard the nuts.

To install:

6. To install, reverse the removal procedure.
7. Note the following fasteners positions:
   - Rear stabilizer bar must be installed with the center hump facing downward.
   - Rear stabilizer bar bushings must be installed outboard of the upset rings on the stabilizer bar.
   - Stabilizer bar link stone shields must be installed on the stabilizer bar attachment point.
8. Tighten the fasteners as follows:
   - 4 stabilizer bar bracket nuts: 35 ft. lbs. (48 Nm).
   - Stone shields new nuts: 46 ft. lbs. (63 Nm).

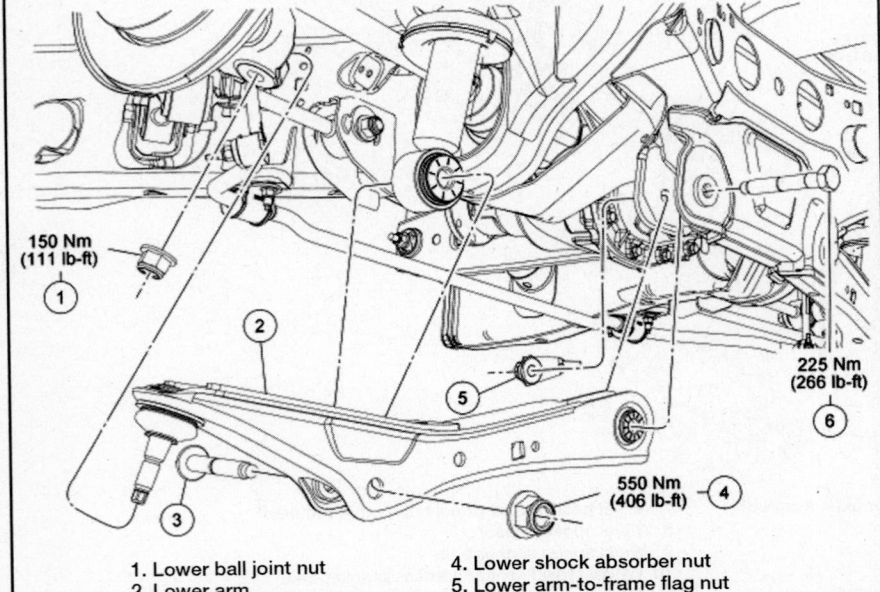

150 Nm (111 lb-ft) ①

②

③

⑤

225 Nm (266 lb-ft) ⑥

550 Nm (406 lb-ft) ④

1. Lower ball joint nut
2. Lower arm
3. Lower shock absorber bolt
4. Lower shock absorber nut
5. Lower arm-to-frame flag nut
6. Lower arm-to-frame bolt

N0097805

Fig. 145 Removing the lower control arm

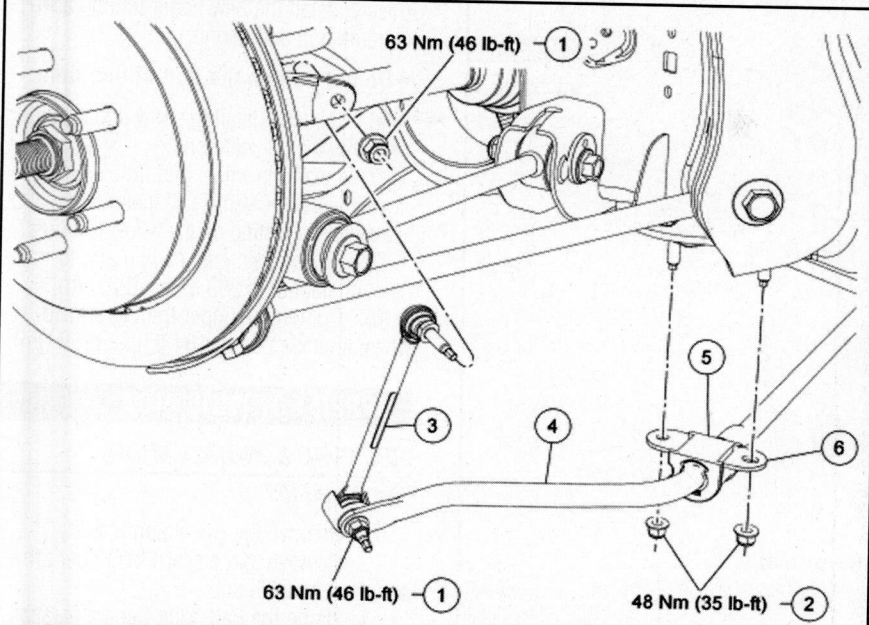

1. Stabilizer bar link nuts (4 required)
2. Stabilizer bar link lower nuts (4 required)
3. Stabilizer bar link (2 required)
4. Stabilizer bar
5. Stabilizer bar bushing (2 required)
6. Stabilizer bar bracket (2 required)

N0054437

Fig. 146 Removing the stabilizer bar

STRUT & SPRING ASSEMBLY

REMOVAL & INSTALLATION

See Figure 147.

✳✳ CAUTION

Suspension fasteners are critical parts because they affect performance of vital components and systems and their failure may result in major service expense. New parts must be installed with the same part numbers or equivalent part, if replacement is necessary. Do not use a replacement part of lesser quality or substitute design. Torque values must be used as specified during reassembly to make sure correct retention of these parts.

1. Remove the lower arm. See "Lower Control Arm" in this section.
2. Remove and discard the shock absorber upper mount nuts.
3. Remove the shock absorber and spring assembly.

➡️If the individual spring and/or shock components are not being serviced, continue with Step 5.

➡️For reference during assembly, index-mark the upper mount, spring and shock absorber.

4. Using a suitable spring compressor, compress the spring until the tension is released from the shock absorber.
5. While holding the shock rod, remove the nut and washer.
6. Remove the shock absorber. Discard the nut.

7. Remove the upper mount, dust boot and insulator.

To install:

8. To install, reverse the removal procedure.
9. Tighten the fasteners as follows:
   • Shock absorber new nut: 41 ft. lbs. (56 Nm).
   • Shock absorber upper mount new nuts: 30 ft. lbs. (40 Nm).

TRAILING ARM

REMOVAL & INSTALLATION

Lower

See Figure 148.

1. Remove the wheel and tire.
2. Remove and discard the 2 lower trailing arm-to-wheel knuckle bolts.
3. Remove and discard the lower trailing arm-to-frame bolt and flagnut.
4. Remove the lower trailing arm.

To install:

➡️**Do not tighten the bolt at this time.**

5. Install the lower trailing arm and loosely install the new lower trailing arm-to-frame bolt and flagnut.

➡️**Do not tighten the bolt at this time.**

6. Loosely install the 2 new lower trailing arm-to-wheel knuckle bolts.
7. Install the wheel and tire.

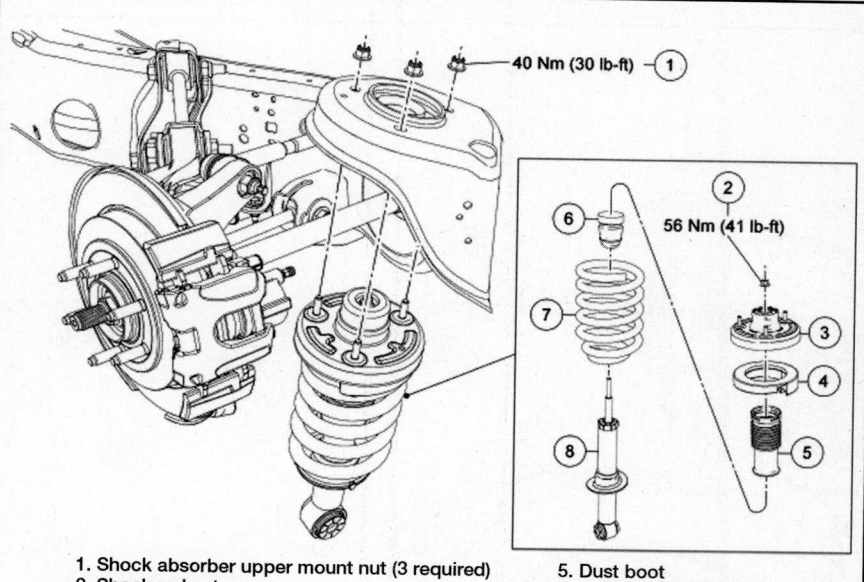

1. Shock absorber upper mount nut (3 required)
2. Shock rod nut
3. Upper mount
4. Insulator
5. Dust boot
6. Jounce bumper
7. Spring
8. Shock absorber

N0059390

Fig. 147 Exploded view of the shock absorber and spring assembly

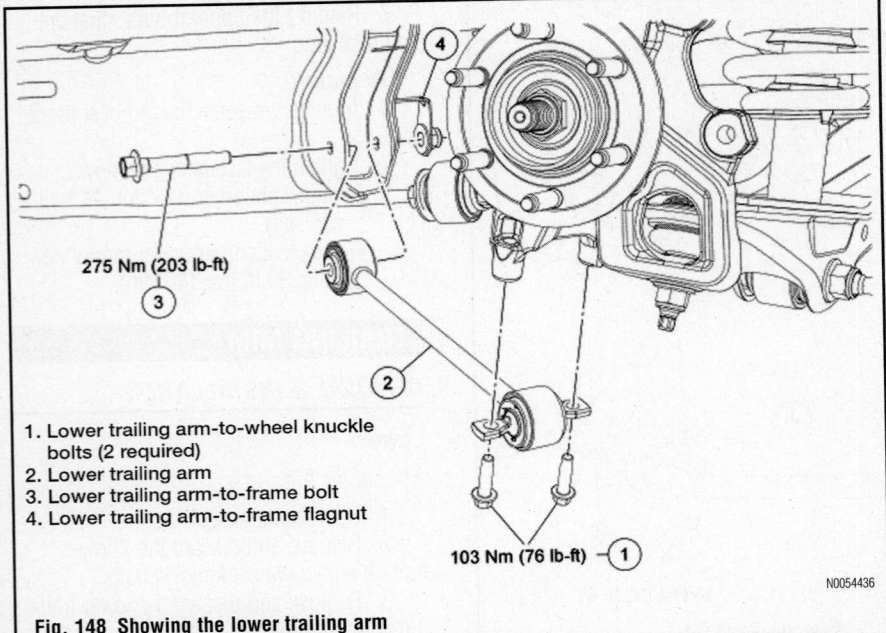

275 Nm (203 lb-ft)

1. Lower trailing arm-to-wheel knuckle bolts (2 required)
2. Lower trailing arm
3. Lower trailing arm-to-frame bolt
4. Lower trailing arm-to-frame flagnut

103 Nm (76 lb-ft)

N0054436

Fig. 148 Showing the lower trailing arm

8. Lower the vehicle so that the weight of the vehicle is resting on the wheel and tires.

9. Tighten the 2 lower trailing arm-to-wheel knuckle bolts to 76 ft. lbs. (103 Nm).

10. Tighten the lower trailing arm-to-frame bolt to 203 ft. lbs. (275 Nm).

Upper

See Figure 149.

1. Remove the wheel and tire.

2. Remove and discard the upper trailing arm-to-wheel knuckle bolt.

3. Remove and discard the upper trailing arm-to-frame bolt and flagnut.

➡**After removal of the upper trailing arm, inspect the knuckle bushing for excessive wear or damage and install new as necessary.**

4. Remove the upper trailing arm.

To install:

➡**Do not tighten the bolt at this time.**

5. Install the upper trailing arm and

1. Upper trailing arm
2. Upper trailing arm-to-wheel knuckle bolt
3. Upper trailing arm-to-frame flagnut
4. Upper trailing arm-to-frame bolt

250 Nm (184 lb-ft)

275 Nm (203 lb-ft)

N0054307

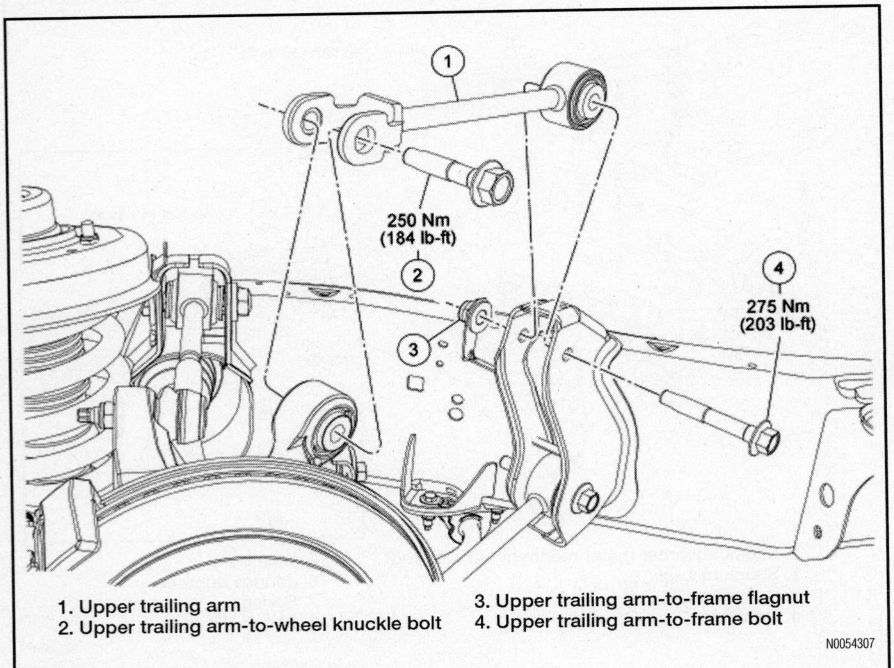

Fig. 149 Showing the upper trailing arm

loosely install the new upper trailing arm-to-frame bolt and flagnut.

➡**Do not tighten the bolt at this time.**

6. Loosely install the new upper trailing arm-to-wheel knuckle bolt.

7. Install the wheel and tire.

8. Lower the vehicle so that the weight of the vehicle is resting on the wheel and tires.

9. Tighten the upper trailing arm-to-frame bolt and flagnut to 203 ft. lbs. (275 Nm).

10. Tighten the upper trailing arm-to-wheel knuckle bolt to 184 ft. lbs. (250 Nm).

UPPER CONTROL ARM

REMOVAL & INSTALLATION

See Figure 150.

1. Remove the wheel and tire.

2. Remove and discard the upper arm-to-wheel knuckle nut.

3. Using the Ball Joint Separator, separate the upper arm from the wheel knuckle.

4. Remove and discard the upper arm-to-frame bolt, washer, camber set shim and flagnut.

5. Remove the upper arm.

To install:

➡**Do not tighten the nut at this time.**

6. Install the upper arm and loosely install the new upper arm-to-frame bolt, washer, camber set shim and flagnut.

➡**Do not tighten the nut at this time.**

7. Loosely install the new upper arm-to-wheel knuckle nut.

8. Install the wheel and tire.

9. With the weight of the vehicle on the wheel and tires, tighten the upper arm-to-frame bolt to 166 ft. lbs. (225 Nm).

10. With the weight of the vehicle on the wheel and tires, tighten the upper arm-to-wheel knuckle nut to 76 ft. lbs. (103 Nm).

11. Check and, if necessary, adjust the rear alignment.

WHEEL BEARING & HUB

REMOVAL & INSTALLATION

See Figure 151.

1. Remove the wheel and tire.

2. Have an assistant press the brake pedal to keep the axle from rotating.

3. Remove and discard the halfshaft nut.

4. Using a suitable hub puller, separate the outboard CV joint from the wheel hub.

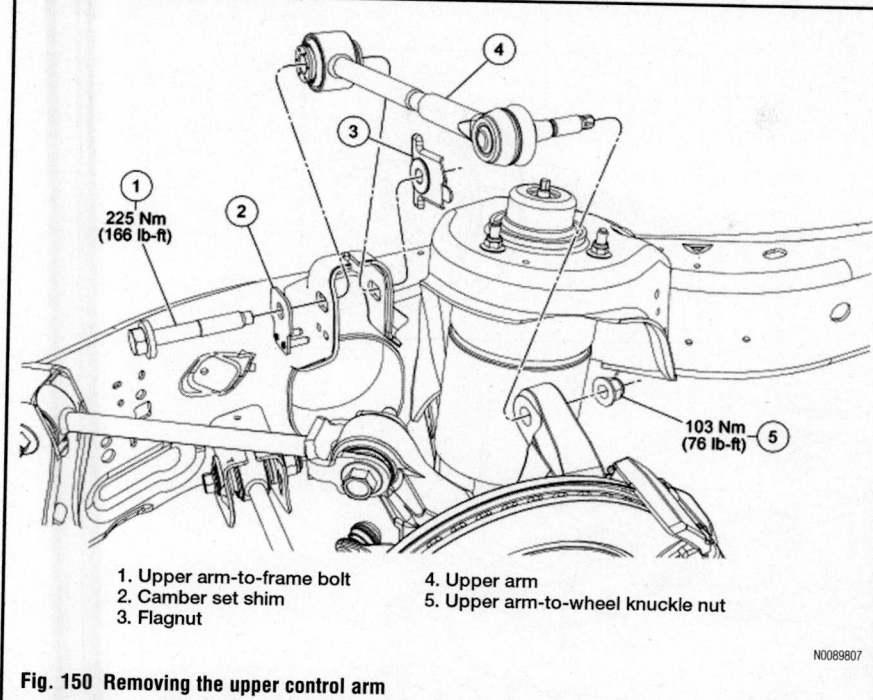

1. Upper arm-to-frame bolt
2. Camber set shim
3. Flagnut
4. Upper arm
5. Upper arm-to-wheel knuckle nut

225 Nm (166 lb-ft)

103 Nm (76 lb-ft)

N0089807

Fig. 150 Removing the upper control arm

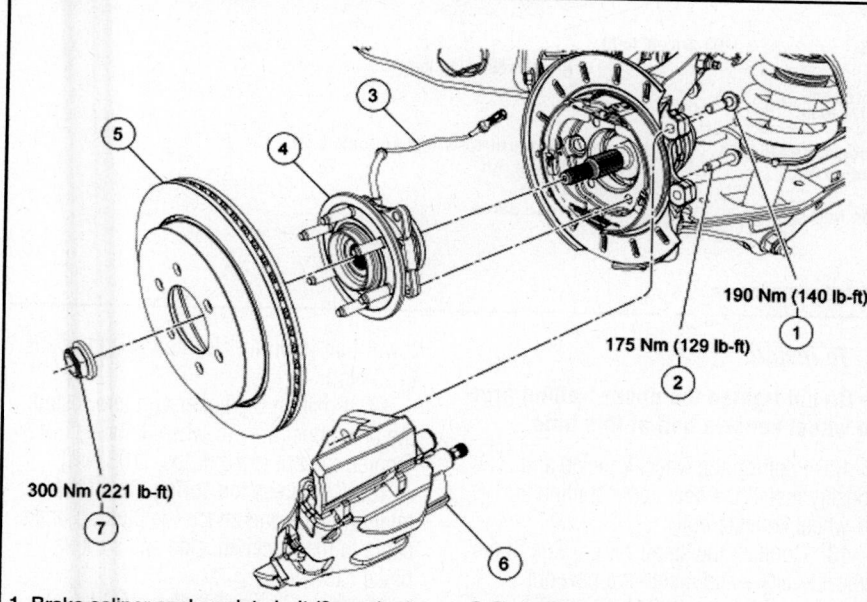

1. Brake caliper anchor plate bolt (2 required)
2. Wheel bearing and wheel hub bolt (4 required)
3. Rear wheel speed sensor bolt
4. Wheel bearing and wheel hub
5. Brake disc
6. Brake caliper and anchor plate assembly
7. Halfshaft nut

190 Nm (140 lb-ft)

175 Nm (129 lb-ft)

300 Nm (221 lb-ft)

N0089809

Fig. 151 Removing the wheel hub and bearing assembly

✳ CAUTION

Do not allow the caliper and anchor plate assembly to hang from the brake hose or damage to the hose may result.

5. Remove the bolts and position the caliper and anchor plate assembly aside.

6. Support the caliper and anchor plate assembly using mechanic's wire.

7. Remove the brake disc.

8. Detach the wheel speed sensor harness from the retainers and disconnect the wheel speed sensor electrical connector. Push the wheel speed sensor harness grommet through the brake disc shield.

9. Remove the 4 bolts, the wheel bearing and wheel hub, and the wheel speed sensor as an assembly.

10. Route the sensor wiring through the access hole in the brake disc shield. Discard the bolts.

11. If necessary, remove the wheel speed sensor bolt and the wheel speed sensor from the wheel bearing and wheel hub.

To install:

12. If necessary, install the wheel speed sensor and bolt. Tighten to 13 ft. lbs. (18 Nm).

13. Position the wheel bearing and wheel hub, and the wheel speed sensor. Install the 4 new wheel bearing and wheel hub bolts.

14. Route the sensor wiring through the access hole in the brake disc shield. Tighten to 129 ft. lbs. (175 Nm).

15. Attach the wheel speed sensor harness to the retainers and connect the wheel speed sensor electrical connector. Push the wheel speed sensor harness grommet through the brake disc shield.

16. Install the brake disc.

17. Position the caliper and anchor plate assembly and install the bolts. Tighten to 140 ft. lbs. (190 Nm).

18. Have an assistant press the brake pedal to keep the axle from rotating.

19. Install the new halfshaft nut. Tighten to 221 ft. lbs. (300 Nm).

20. Install the wheel and tire.

WHEEL KNUCKLE

REMOVAL & INSTALLATION

See Figure 152.

1. Remove the wheel bearing and wheel hub assembly.

2. Remove the parking brake shoes. See "BRAKES" section.

3. Compress the spring and depress the retaining tabs and detach the parking brake cable from the wheel knuckle and parking brake lever.

4. Remove and discard the upper arm-to-wheel knuckle nut.

5. Using the Ball Joint Separator, separate the upper arm from the wheel knuckle.

6. Remove and discard the lower ball joint nut.

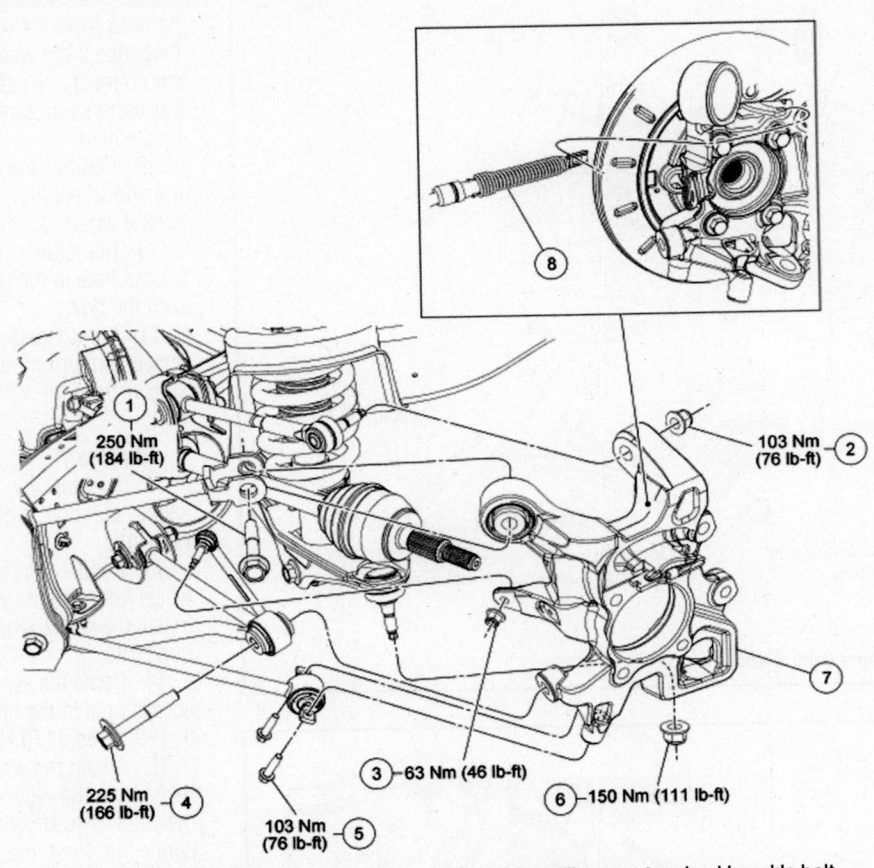

1. Upper trailing arm-to-wheel knuckle bolt
2. Upper arm-to-wheel knuckle nut
3. Stabilizer bar link nut
4. Toe link-to-wheel knuckle bolt
5. Lower trailing arm-to-wheel knuckle bolt
6. Lower ball joint nut
7. Wheel knuckle
8. Parking brake cable

N0074031

Fig. 152 Exploded view of the wheel knuckle and related components

7. Using the Ball Joint Separator, separate the lower ball joint from the wheel knuckle.

8. Remove and discard the 2 bolts and disconnect the lower trailing arm from the wheel knuckle.

9. Remove and discard the bolt and disconnect the toe link from the wheel knuckle.

➡Use the hex-holding feature to prevent the stud from turning while removing the nut.

10. Using the hex-holding feature, remove and discard the stabilizer bar link nut and disconnect the link from the wheel knuckle.

11. Remove the upper trailing arm-to-wheel knuckle bolt and the wheel knuckle. Discard the bolt.

To install:

➡Do not tighten the upper trailing arm-to wheel knuckle bolt at this time.

12. Position the wheel knuckle and loosely install the new upper trailing arm-to-wheel knuckle bolt.

13. Connect the stabilizer bar link to the wheel knuckle and install the new nut. Tighten to 46 ft. lbs. (63 Nm).

➡Do not tighten the toe link-to-wheel knuckle bolt at this time.

14. Connect the toe link-to-the wheel knuckle and loosely install the new bolt.

15. Connect the lower trailing arm to the wheel knuckle and install the 2 new bolts. Tighten to 76 ft. lbs. (103 Nm).

16. Position the lower ball joint onto the wheel knuckle and install the new

lower ball joint nut. Tighten to 111 ft. lbs. (150 Nm).

17. Position the upper arm and install the new upper arm-to-wheel knuckle nut. Tighten the nut to 76 ft. lbs. (103 Nm).

18. Compress the spring, insert the retaining tabs and attach the parking brake cable to the wheel knuckle and parking brake cable lever.

19. Install the brake disc shield.

20. Install the parking brake shoes. See "BRAKES" section.

21. Install the wheel bearing and wheel hub assembly. See "Wheel Bearing & Hub" in this section.

22. Lower the vehicle so that the weight of the vehicle is resting on the wheel and tires.

23. Tighten the toe link-to-the wheel knuckle bolt to 166 ft. lbs. (225 Nm).

24. Tighten the upper trailing arm-to-wheel knuckle bolt to 184 ft. lbs. (250 Nm).

SUSPENSION   **AIR SUSPENSION**

AIR SHOCK ABSORBER (REAR)

REMOVAL & INSTALLATION
See Figure 153.

※※ WARNING

Do not apply heat or flame to the shock absorber or strut tube. The shock absorber and strut tube are gas pressurized and could explode if heated. Failure to follow this instruction may result in serious personal injury.

※※ WARNING

Vent all air pressure from the air suspension system prior to disconnecting or removing any air suspension components. It is dangerous to remove air suspension components while under pressure. Failure to follow this instruction may result in serious personal injury.

➡Vehicles built prior to 12/03/2007 use a longer air spring and shock absorber than vehicles built after 12/03/2007. To prevent component damage, it is important to use the correct air spring and or shock absorber when replacing these parts.

※※ CAUTION

Suspension fasteners are critical parts because they affect performance of vital components and systems and their failure can result in major service expense. A new part with the same part number must be used if installation is necessary. Do not use a new part of lesser quality or substitute design. Torque values must be used as specified during reassembly to make sure of correct retention of these parts.

1. Using the scan tool, vent the appropriate air spring.
2. Remove the lower arm.
3. Disconnect the air spring solenoid valve electrical connector.
4. Disconnect the air line at the air valve.
5. Compress the orange quick connect lock ring, then pull downward on the air supply line.

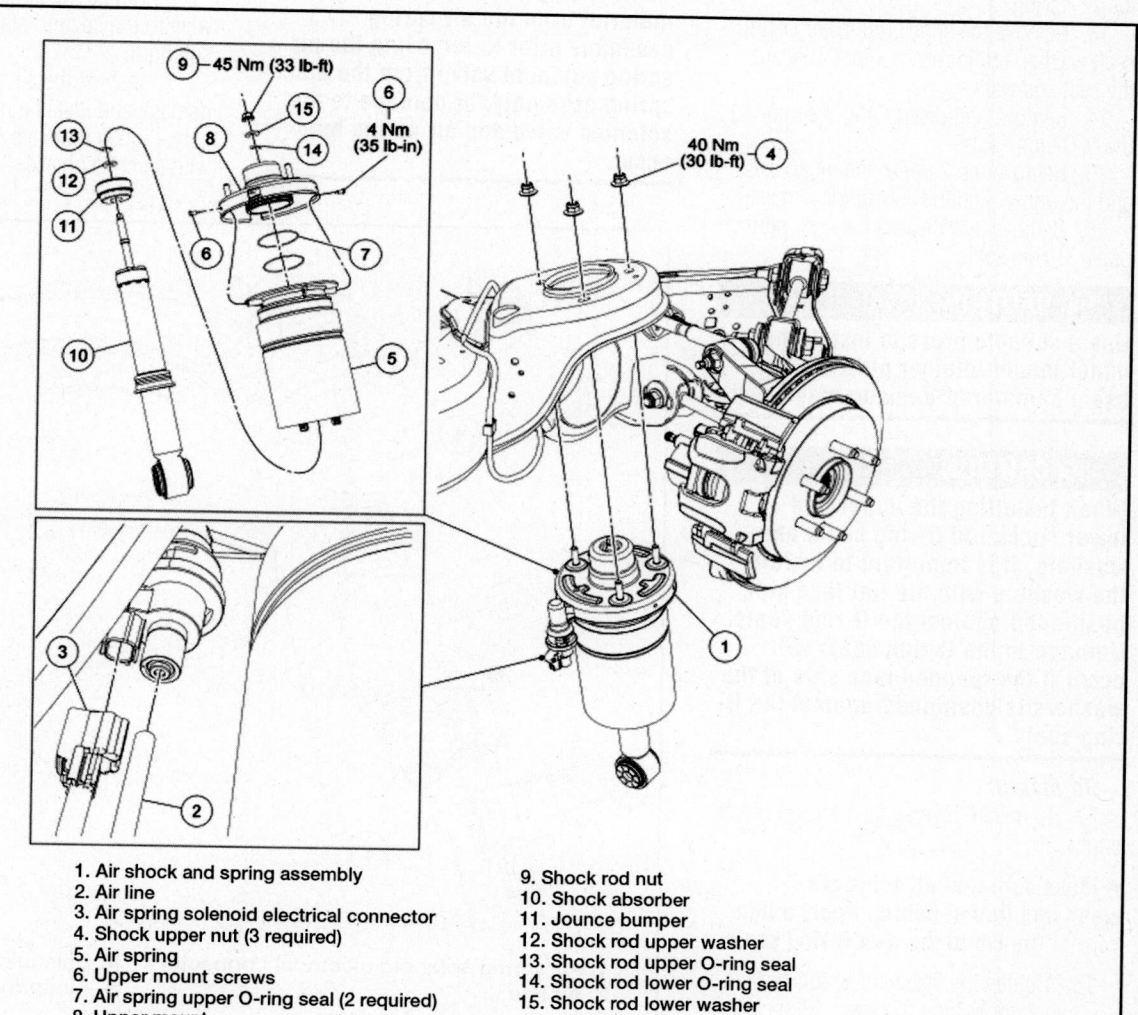

1. Air shock and spring assembly
2. Air line
3. Air spring solenoid electrical connector
4. Shock upper nut (3 required)
5. Air spring
6. Upper mount screws
7. Air spring upper O-ring seal (2 required)
8. Upper mount
9. Shock rod nut
10. Shock absorber
11. Jounce bumper
12. Shock rod upper washer
13. Shock rod upper O-ring seal
14. Shock rod lower O-ring seal
15. Shock rod lower washer

N0092579

Fig. 153 Removing the rear air shock absorber

6. Remove and discard the 3 shock absorber upper nuts.

7. Remove the air shock absorber.

8. Use the hex-holding feature to prevent the shock rod from turning while removing the nut.

9. Remove and discard the shock absorber rod nut.

10. Remove the shock rod upper washer and O-ring seal. Discard the O-ring seal washer.

❈❈ CAUTION

If the retainer tabs are broken, a new air spring must be installed, or failure of the air spring may occur.

11. Index-mark the air spring and shock absorber for reference during the installation procedure.

12. Depress the retainer tabs and remove the air spring.

13. Remove the shock rod lower O-ring seal, washer and jounce bumper. Discard the seal and washer.

14. Remove and discard the 2 air spring lower O-ring seals.

15. Remove the 2 upper mount screws and the upper mount. Discard the screws.

16. Remove and discard the 2 air spring upper O-ring seals.

❈❈ CAUTION

Use a suitable press to install the upper mount retainer pins. Do not use a hammer or damage may occur.

❈❈ CAUTION

When installing the upper and lower shock rod O-ring seals and washers, it is important to install the washers with the flat face side positioned against the O-ring seals. Damage to the O-ring seals will occur if the rounded face side of the washers is positioned against the O-ring seals.

To install:

17. To install, reverse the removal procedure.

➡**Make sure that all seals are clean and free of debris. Apply a thin coat of grease to the new O-ring seals.**

18. Tighten the fasteners as follows:
- 2 upper mount screws: 35 inch lbs. (4 Nm).
- Shock absorber rod nut: 33 ft. lbs. (45 Nm).

- 3 shock absorber upper nuts: 30 ft. lbs. (40 Nm).

AIR SPRING SOLENOID

REMOVAL & INSTALLATION

See Figure 154.

1. If the air spring solenoid valve is functional, use the scan tool to vent the appropriate air spring(s).

2. With the vehicle in NEUTRAL, position it on a hoist.

3. Disconnect the air spring solenoid valve electrical connector.

4. Disconnect the air line at the air valve.

5. Compress the orange quick connect lock ring, then pull downward on the air supply line.

❈❈ CAUTION

Remove any dirt or other foreign material from the air spring assembly prior to removing the air spring solenoid valve from the air spring assembly, or damage to the solenoid valve and air spring may occur.

Remove the air spring solenoid clip.

❈❈ WARNING

Vent all air pressure from the air suspension system prior to disconnecting or removing any air suspension components. It is dangerous to remove air suspension components while under pressure. Failure to follow this instruction may result in serious personal injury.

➡**The air spring solenoid valve has a 2-stage release. Vent the air spring using the following procedure: Carefully rotate the air spring solenoid counterclockwise until it reaches the first stage and allow the air in the spring to completely vent.**

6. Rotate the solenoid counterclockwise to the second stage and remove the solenoid.

7. Inspect the air spring O-ring for damage and install a new O-ring as necessary. Lightly lubricate the solenoid seal area with silicone grease.

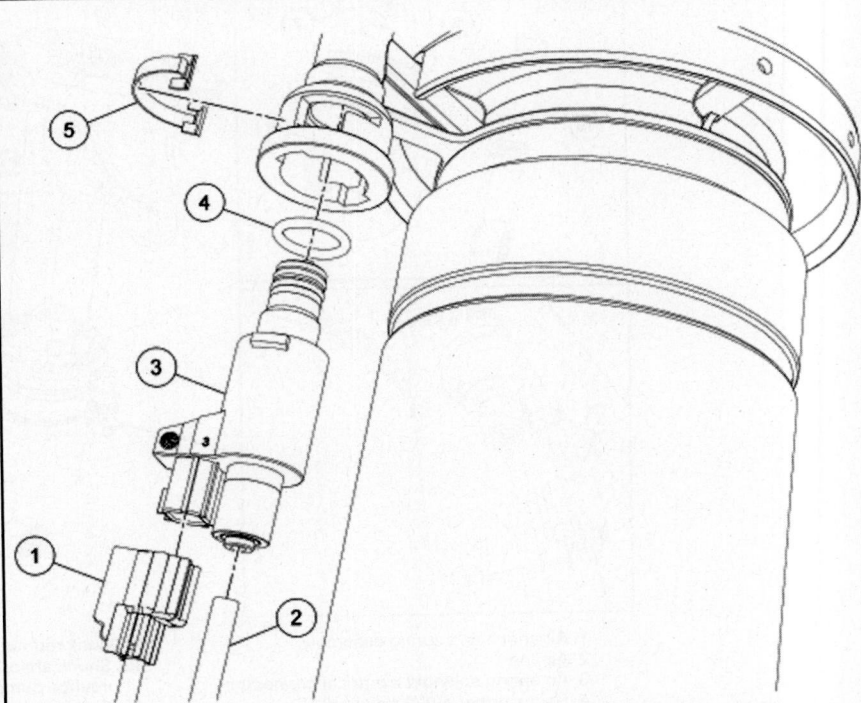

1. Air spring solenoid electrical connector
2. Air line
3. Air spring solenoid valve
4. Solenoid valve O-ring
5. Air spring solenoid clip

N0056483

Fig. 154 Showing the air spring solenoid

8. After installing the solenoid, it is necessary to inflate the air suspension system.

9. When installing the air spring solenoid, make sure that the electrical connector is positioned away from the air spring.

10. When installing the air lines, make sure the air line is fully inserted into the fitting for correct installation.

11. To install, reverse the removal procedure.

INFLATING/DEFLATING AIR SPRING

1. Turn the ignition switch to the RUN position.

2. Connect the scan tool to the Data Link Connector (DLC).

3. Select the air suspension control module active command LR_SOL (LR) or RR_SOL (RR) from OFF to ON.

➡When using the air suspension control module active command AS_COMP, do not run the air compressor for more than 3 minutes to prevent overheating and shutdown. If this occurs, wait for the system to cool down before resuming the inflation procedure.

4. Select the air suspension control module active command "AS VENT" to deflate the air springs or AS_COMP to inflate the air springs.

RIDE HEIGHT ADJUSTMENT

➡The Vehicle Dynamics Module (VDM) has a preprogrammed trim height. The vehicle must be on a level surface, such as a drive on alignment hoist.

❈❈ CAUTION

The vehicle ride height must be set to the correct dimensions to prevent vehicle damage.

➡Incorrect air suspension ride height can be caused by an air suspension system that is incorrectly set.

1. Position the vehicle on a level surface.

2. Using the vehicle message center, verify that the air suspension is in the ON mode.

3. Using the scan tool, run the accurate trim test.

4. Measure the ride height.

5. If the ride height is not within specification, use the scan tool to vent or fill the air suspension to the correct dimension.

6. Using the scan tool, save the vehicle trim height for both sensors.

AIR SUSPENSION COMPRESSOR

REMOVAL & INSTALLATION

See Figure 155.

❈❈ WARNING

Vent all air pressure from the air suspension system prior to disconnecting or removing any air suspension components. It is dangerous to remove air suspension components while under pressure. Failure to follow this instruction may result in serious personal injury.

1. Remove the inner fender splash shield.

2. Disconnect the air line from the compressor drier.

3. Compress the quick connect lock ring inward, then pull the line outward from the air drier.

4. Disconnect the air compressor air intake hose.

5. Disconnect the air compressor electrical connector.

6. Remove the 3 air compressor bracket bolts and remove the air compressor and bracket assembly.

➡When installing the air lines, make sure the white inner air line is fully inserted into the fitting for correct installation. Make sure that there are no objects trapped under or on the bracket. Make sure that the air compressor is not in contact with any surrounding components that could cause vibration noises. Make sure that the air compressor moves freely in the rubber isolators. Make sure that the bracket has no deformations that could cause the 3 rubber isolators to load against each other.

To install:

7. To install, reverse the removal procedure

8. Install the 3 air compressor bracket bolts and tighten to 133 inch lbs. (15 Nm).

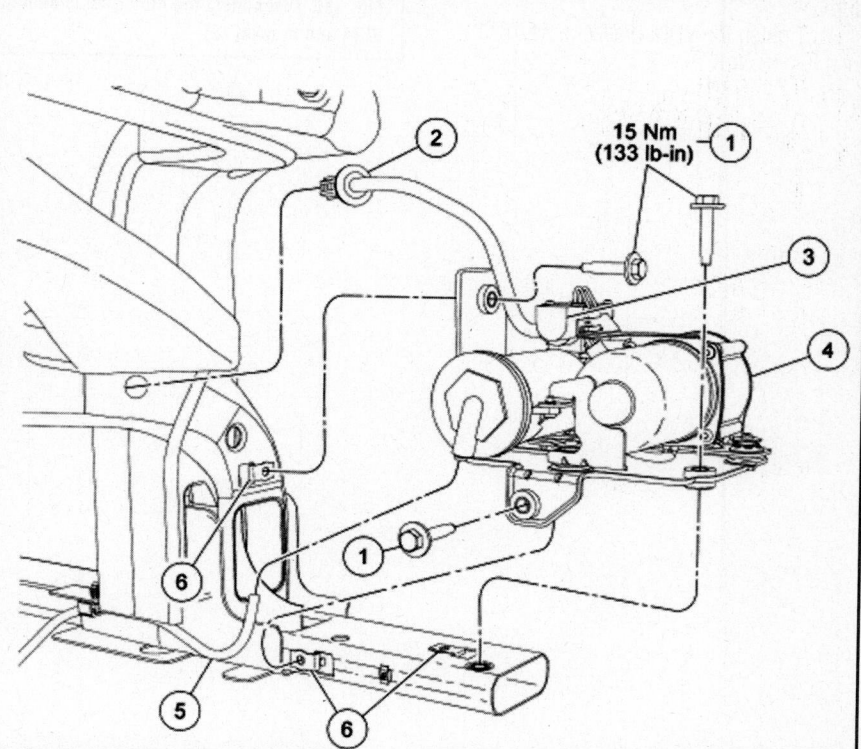

1. Compressor bolts (3 required)
2. Compressor air intake hose
3. Compressor electrical connector
4. Compressor and bracket assembly
5. Air line
6. Clip nuts (3 required)

N0086316

Fig. 155 Removing the air suspension compressor

AIR SUSPENSION VEHICLE DYNAMICS MODULE

REMOVAL & INSTALLATION

See Figure 156.

✳✳ CAUTION

Electronic modules are sensitive to static electrical charges. If exposed to these charges, damage may result.

➡**The Vehicle Dynamics Module (VDM) is mounted to the lower left side of the dash above the parking brake control.**

1. Disconnect the 2 VDM electrical connectors.
2. Remove the VDM bracket nuts and the module.

➡**The VDM is calibrated with information from the ride height sensors. A new or exchanged VDM requires that the LH and RH ride height sensors are calibrated and a Pneumatic Test is carried out.**

3. To install, reverse the removal procedure.
4. Tighten the VDM bracket nuts to 71 inch lbs. (8 Nm).

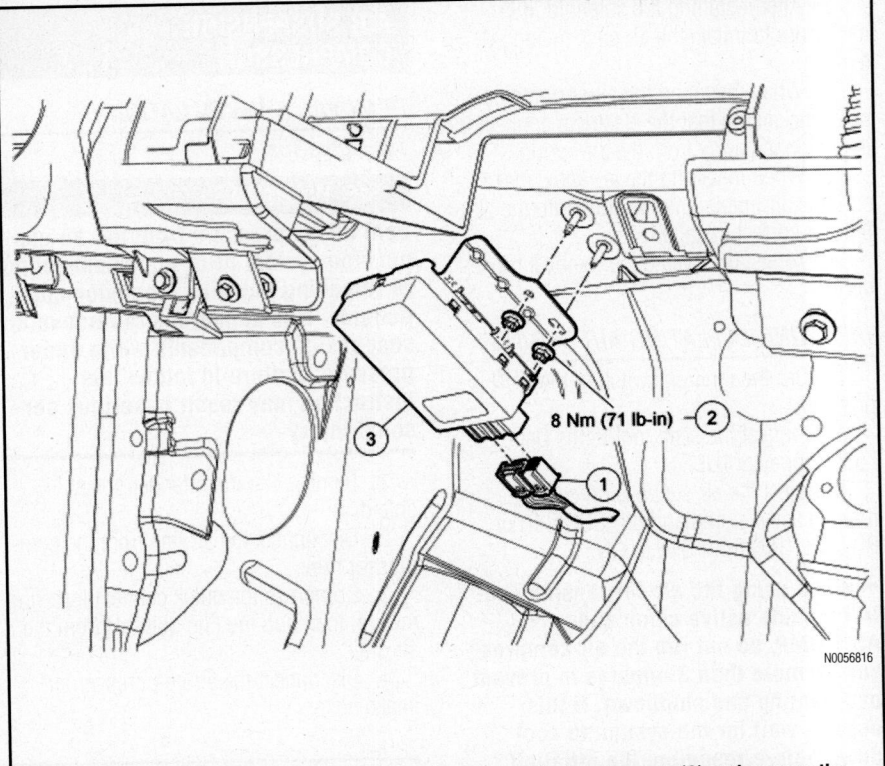

Fig. 156 Disconnect the electrical connector (1), remove the bracket nuts (2) and remove the VDM and bracket (3)

AUXILIARY HEATING & AIR CONDITIONING SYSTEM...6-132

Blower Motor 6-132
   Removal & Installation.......6-132
Heater Core 6-133
   Removal & Installation.......6-133

BRAKES 6-14

ANTI-LOCK BRAKE SYSTEM (ABS) 6-14
General Information...................6-14
   Precautions........................6-14
Wheel Speed Sensors 6-14
   Removal & Installation.........6-14
BLEEDING THE BRAKE SYSTEM.....................6-16
   Bleeding Procedure 6-16
   Bleeding the ABS System 6-17
FRONT DISC BRAKES 6-17
Brake Caliper.........................6-17
   Removal & Installation.........6-17
Disc Brake Pads 6-19
   Removal & Installation.........6-19
PARKING BRAKE 6-22
Parking Brake Cables 6-22
   Adjustment 6-22
Parking Brake Shoes 6-22
   Adjustment 6-23
   Removal & Installation.........6-22
REAR DISC BRAKES 6-20
Brake Caliper.........................6-20
   Removal & Installation.........6-20
Disc Brake Pads 6-21
   Removal & Installation.........6-21

CHASSIS ELECTRICAL 6-25

AIR BAG (SUPPLEMENTAL RESTRAINT SYSTEM).......6-25
General Information...................6-25
   Arming (Repowering) the System....................6-27
Clockspring Centering 6-29
Disarming (Depowering) the System....................6-26
Service Precautions 6-25

DRIVE TRAIN 6-32
Driveshaft.............................6-35
   Removal & Installation.........6-35
Front Driveshaft.....................6-36
   Removal & Installation.........6-36
Front Halfshafts 6-37
   Removal & Installation.........6-37
Front Pinion Seal 6-39
   Removal & Installation.........6-39
Rear Driveshaft......................6-40
   Removal & Installation.........6-40
Rear Halfshafts 6-42
   Removal & Installation.........6-42
Rear Pinion Seal 6-45
   Removal & Installation.........6-45
Transfer Case Assembly 6-32
   Removal & Installation.........6-32
Transfer Case Fluid 6-35
   Drain & Refill....................6-35

ENGINE COOLING 6-47

Engine Coolant......................6-47
   Draining, Filling and Bleeding..6-47
Engine Fan............................6-48
   Removal & Installation.........6-48
Radiator 6-48
   Removal & Installation.........6-48
Thermostat............................6-49
   Removal & Installation.........6-49
Water Pump...........................6-51
   Removal & Installation.........6-51

ENGINE ELECTRICAL.........6-53

CHARGING SYSTEM 6-53
Alternator 6-53
   Removal & Installation.........6-53
Voltage Regulator 6-57
   Adjustment 6-57
IGNITION SYSTEM 6-57
Firing Orders 6-57
Ignition Coil..........................6-57
   Removal & Installation.........6-57
Ignition Timing 6-58
   Inspection 6-58
Spark Plugs 6-58
   Removal & Installation.........6-58

STARTING SYSTEM 6-60
Starter..................................6-60
   Removal & Installation..........6-60
   Solenoid or Relay Replacement 6-60

ENGINE MECHANICAL 6-62

Accessory Drive Belts.............6-62
   Accessory Belt Routing.......6-62
   Adjustment........................6-62
   Inspection 6-62
   Removal & Installation..........6-62
Balance Shaft........................6-63
   Removal & Installation..........6-63
Camshaft and Valve Lifters 6-64
   Removal & Installation..........6-64
Catalytic Converter 6-73
   Removal & Installation..........6-73
Crankshaft Damper.................6-75
   Removal & Installation..........6-75
Crankshaft Front Seal 6-76
   Removal & Installation..........6-76
Cylinder Head 6-76
   Removal & Installation..........6-76
Exhaust Manifold....................6-85
   Removal & Installation..........6-85
Flexplate 6-87
   Removal & Installation..........6-87
Intake Manifold......................6-88
   Removal & Installation..........6-88
Oil Pan.................................6-92
   Removal & Installation..........6-92
Oil Pump 6-93
   Removal & Installation..........6-93
Piston and Ring......................6-97
   Positioning........................6-97
Rear Main Seal 6-97
   Removal & Installation..........6-97
Rocker Arms/Shafts 6-99
   Removal & Installation..........6-99
Timing Chain and Sprockets ...6-105
   Camshaft Timing Procedure...6-109
   Removal & Installation........6-105
Timing Chain Cover and Seal..6-101
   Removal & Installation........6-101
Valve Covers.........................6-112
   Removal & Installation........6-112

Valve Lash..................................6-114
  Adjustment.............................6-114

ENGINE PERFORMANCE & EMISSION CONTROLS 6-114

Accelerator Pedal Position
  (APP) Sensor.......................6-114
  Location...............................6-114
  Removal & Installation........6-114
Camshaft Position (CMP)
  Sensor.................................6-114
  Location...............................6-114
  Removal & Installation........6-114
Crankshaft Position (CKP)
  Sensor.................................6-114
  Location...............................6-114
  Removal & Installation........6-115
Engine Coolant Temperature
  (ECT) Sensor.....................6-116
  Location...............................6-116
  Removal & Installation........6-116
Evaporative Emissions
  (EVAP) Canister.................6-116
  Location...............................6-116
  Removal & Installation........6-116
Exhaust Gas Recirculation
  (EGR) Valve.......................6-117
  Location...............................6-117
  Removal & Installation........6-117
Heated Oxygen Sensor (HO2S)...6-117
  Location...............................6-117
  Removal & Installation........6-117
Intake Air Temperature
  (IAT) Sensor.......................6-118
  Location...............................6-118
  Removal & Installation........6-118
Knock Sensor (KS).................6-118
  Location...............................6-118
  Removal & Installation........6-118
Malfunction Indicator
  Light (MIL)...........................6-118
  Reset Procedure.................6-118
Mass Air Flow (MAF) Sensor...6-118
  Location...............................6-118
  Removal & Installation........6-118
Positive Crankcase
  Ventilation (PCV) Valve........6-119
  Location...............................6-119
  Removal & Installation........6-119
Powertrain Control
  Module (PCM).....................6-119
  Location...............................6-119
  Removal & Installation........6-119
Throttle Control Actuator (TAC)..6-120
  Location...............................6-120
  Removal & Installation........6-120

Throttle Position Sensor (TPS)...6-121
  Location...............................6-121
  Removal & Installation........6-121

FUEL 6-122

GASOLINE FUEL INJECTION SYSTEM 6-122
Fuel Filter................................6-122
  Removal & Installation........6-122
Fuel Pump/ Fuel Pump
  Module/Fuel Tank Module.....6-123
  Removal & Installation........6-123
Fuel Rail & Injectors.................6-124
  Removal & Installation........6-124
Fuel System Service
  Precautions.........................6-122
Fuel Tank................................6-126
  Removal & Installation........6-126
Idle Speed...............................6-127
  Adjustment..........................6-127
Relieving Fuel System Pressure..6-122
Throttle Body..........................6-127
  Removal & Installation........6-127

HEATING & AIR CONDITIONING SYSTEM...6-129

Blower Motor...........................6-129
  Removal & Installation........6-129
Heater Core.............................6-129
  Removal & Installation........6-129
Heater Core & Evaporator
  Core Housing......................6-131
  Removal & Installation........6-131
HVAC Unit...............................6-130
  Removal & Installation........6-130

PRECAUTIONS 6-14

SPECIFICATIONS AND MAINTENANCE CHARTS 6-3

Brake Specifications...............6-9
Camshaft and Bearing
  Specifications Chart.............6-5
Capacities..............................6-4
Crankshaft and Connecting
  Rod Specifications...............6-5
Engine and Vehicle Identification...6-3
Fluid Specifications................6-4
Gasoline Engine Tune-Up
  Specifications.....................6-3
General Engine Specifications.....6-3
Piston and Ring Specifications...6-5
Scheduled Maintenance
  Intervals.............................6-10–13

Tire, Wheel and Ball Joint
  Specifications.......................6-8
Torque Specifications...............6-6
Valve Specifications.................6-4
Wheel Alignment......................6-8

STEERING 6-135

Power Rack & Pinion
  Steering Gear.......................6-135
  Removal & Installation........6-135
Power Steering Pump..............6-138
  Bleeding..............................6-139
  Removal & Installation........6-138

SUSPENSION 6-140

FRONT SUSPENSION 6-140
Lower Control Arm...................6-140
  Lower Control Arm
  Bushing Replacement.......6-141
  Removal and & Installation...6-140
Stabilizer Bar..........................6-142
  Removal & Installation........6-142
Stabilizer Bar Link...................6-143
  Removal & Installation........6-143
Steering Knuckle.....................6-144
  Removal & Installation........6-144
Strut & Spring Assembly........6-145
  Removal & Installation........6-145
Upper Control Arm..................6-146
  Removal & Installation........6-146
Wheel Hub & Bearing.............6-147
  Adjustment..........................6-148
  Removal & Installation........6-147
REAR SUSPENSION 6-149
Knuckle..................................6-149
  Removal & Installation........6-149
Lower Control Arm...................6-152
  Removal & Installation........6-152
Shock Absorber.......................6-153
  Removal & Installation........6-153
Spring....................................6-153
  Removal & Installtion..........6-153
Stabilizer Bar..........................6-154
  Removal & Installation........6-154
Stabilizer Bar Link...................6-157
  Removal & Installation........6-157
Struts.....................................6-157
  Removal & Installation........6-157
Toe Link.................................6-157
  Removal & Installation........6-157
Trailing Arm............................6-159
  Removal & Installation........6-159
Upper Control Arm..................6-160
  Removal & Installation........6-160
Wheel Hub & Bearing.............6-162
  Removal & Installation........6-162

SPECIFICATIONS AND MAINTENANCE CHARTS

ENGINE AND VEHICLE IDENTIFICATION

		Engine						Model Year	
Code ①	Liters	Cu. In.	Cyl.	Fuel Sys.	Type	Eng. Mfg.		Code ②	Year
8	3.5	214	6	MFI	DOHC	Ford		A	2010
E	4.0	244	6	MFI	SOHC	Ford		B	2011
8	4.6	281	8	MFI	SOHC	Ford			

MFI: (Sequential) Multi-port Fuel Injection

DOHC: Dual Overhead Camshafts

SOHC: Single Overhead Camshaft

① 8th digit of the Vehicle Identification Number (VIN)

② 10th digit of the Vehicle Identification Number (VIN)

25759_EXPL_C0001

GENERAL ENGINE SPECIFICATIONS

Year	Model	Engine Displ. Liters	Engine VIN	Net Horsepower @ rpm	Net Torque @ rpm (ft. lbs.)	Bore x Stroke (in.)	Com- pression Ratio	Oil Pressure @ rpm
2010	Explorer/	4.0	E	210@5100	254@3700	3.95x3.32	9.7:1	15@2000
	Mountaineer	4.6	8	292@5700	315@4000	3.55x3.54	9.8:1	75@2000
2011	Explorer	3.5	8	290@6500	255@4100	3.64x3.41	10.8:1	30@1500

25759_EXPL_C0002

GASOLINE ENGINE TUNE-UP SPECIFICATIONS

Year	Engine Displacement Liters	Engine ID/VIN	Spark Plug Gap (in.)	Ignition Timing (deg.) ①		Fuel Pressure (psi) ②	Idle Speed (rpm)		Valve Clearance	
				MT	AT		MT	AT	In.	Ex.
2010	4.0	K	0.052-0.056	—	10B	30-40	—	①	HYD	HYD
	4.6	8	0.039-0.043	—	10B	30-40	—	①	HYD	HYD
2011	3.5	8	0.049-0.053	—	N/A	30-40	—	①	HYD	HYD

NOTE: The Vehicle Emission Control Information label often reflects specification changes changes made during production. The label figures must be used if they differ from those in this chart.

B: Before top dead center

HYD: Hydraulic

① Idle speed and ignition timing are electronically controlled and cannot be adjusted

② Key on; engine off

25759_EXPL_C0003

CAPACITIES

Year	Model	Engine Displ. Liters	Engine ID/VIN	Engine Oil with Filter (qts.)	Transmission (pts.) 5-Spd	Transmission (pts.) Auto.	Transfer Case (pts.)	Drive Axle Front (pts.)	Drive Axle Rear (pts.)	Fuel Tank (gal.)	Cooling System (qts.)
2010	Explorer/	4.0	K	5.0	—	①	3.0	2.70	3.50	22.5	②
	Mountaineer	4.6	8	6.5	—	①	3.0	2.70	3.50	22.5	③
2011	Explorer	3.5	8	6.0	—	④	1.02	2.70	3.50	18.6	12.2

NOTE: All capacities are approximate. Add fluid gradually and check to be sure a proper fluid level is obtained.

① 5R55S A/T: 25.4 pts. (dry fill spec)

  6R80 A/T: 23.9 pts. (dry fill spec)

② w/o auxiliary heater: 12.2 qts.

  w/auxiliary heater: 14.0 qts.

③ w/o auxiliary heater: 14.0 qts.

  w/auxiliary heater: 15.7 qts.

④ 25.4 pts. (dry fill spec)

25759_EXPL_C0004

FLUID SPECIFICATIONS

Year	Model	Engine Disp. Liters (VIN)	Engine Oil	Auto. Trans.	Drive Axle	Transfer Case	Power Steering Fluid	Brake Master Cylinder	Cooling System
2010	Explorer/	4.0 (K)	5W-30	① ②	③	75W-140	Mercon® V	DOT 3	④
	Mountaineer	4.6 (8)	5W-20	① ②	③	75W-140	Mercon® V	DOT 3	④
2011	Explorer	3.5 (8)	5W-20	⑤	⑥	75W-140	Mercon® V	DOT 3	④

DOT: Department Of Transpotation

① 5R55S: Mercon® V ATF

② 6R80: Mercon® LV ATF

③ Rear 75W-140 Synthetic Rear Axle Lubricant, Front 80W-90 Premium Lubricant

④ Motorcraft® Specialty Green Engine Coolant

⑤ 6R80: Mercon® LV ATF

⑥ Rear: 80W-90 Premium Rear Axle Lubricant

25759_EXPL_C0005

VALVE SPECIFICATIONS

Year	Engine Displ. Liters	Engine ID/VIN	Seat Angle (deg.)	Face Angle (deg.)	Spring Test Pressure (lbs. @ in.)	Spring Installed Height (in.)	Stem-to-Guide Clearance (in.) Intake	Stem-to-Guide Clearance (in.) Exhaust	Stem Diameter (in.) Intake	Stem Diameter (in.) Exhaust
2010	4.0	K	45	45	203-225@ 1.413-1.445	1.569- 1.609	0.0010- 0.0020	0.0010- 0.0030	0.2740- 0.2750	0.2730- 0.2740
	4.6	8	44.5- 45	45.5	163-179@ 1.22	1.660	0.0008- 0.0027	0.0018- 0.0037	0.2352- 0.2360	0.2343- 0.2351
2011	3.5	8	44.5- 45.5	44.5- 45.5	118@ 1.063	1.456	0.0009- 0.0028	0.2152 0.2159	0.2157- 0.2164	0.2152- 0.2159

25759_EXPL_C0006

CAMSHAFT AND BEARING SPECIFICATIONS CHART

All measurements are given in inches.

Year	Engine Displ. Liters	Engine VIN	Bearing Outside Dia.	Brg. Oil Clearance	Shaft End-play	Runout	Journal Bore	Lobe Height Intake	Lobe Height Exhaust
2010	4.0	K	1.099-1.101	0.002-0.004	0.003-0.007	0.002	1.102-1.104	0.259	0.259
	4.6	8	1.126-1.127	0.001-0.003	0.001-0.007 0.007	0.001	1.128-1.129	0.217	0.217
2011	3.5	8	①	0.002-0.004	0.0013-0.0067	0.0016	②	0.3937	0.3811

① First journal: 1.535-1.5358

Intermediate journals: 1.0222-1.0211

① First journal: 1.5369-1.5379 in.

Intermediate journals: 1.0222-1.0211 in.

25759_EXPL_C0007

CRANKSHAFT AND CONNECTING ROD SPECIFICATIONS

All measurements are given in inches.

Year	Engine Displ. Liters	Engine ID/VIN	Crankshaft Main Brg. Journal Dia.	Crankshaft Main Brg. Oil Clearance	Crankshaft Shaft End-play	Crankshaft Thrust on No.	Connecting Rod Journal Diameter	Connecting Rod Oil Clearance	Connecting Rod Side Clearance
2010	4.0	K	2.2430-2.2440	0.0003-0.0024	0.0020-0.0126	3	2.1250-2.1260	0.0008-0.0012	0.0036-0.0125
	4.6	8	2.6567-2.6576	0.0009-0.0019	0.0030-0.0148	3	2.0859-2.0867	0.0009-0.0026	0.0060-0.0200
2011	3.5	8	2.6575	0.0010-0.0016	0.0040-0.0115	N/A	2.2041-2.2048	0.0008-0.0021	0.0069-0.0167

NA: Not Available

25759_EXPL_C0009

PISTON AND RING SPECIFICATIONS

All measurements are given in inches.

Year	Engine Displ. Liters	Engine ID/VIN	Piston Clearance	Ring Gap Top Compression	Ring Gap Bottom Compression	Ring Gap Oil Control	Ring Side Clearance Top Compression	Ring Side Clearance Bottom Compression	Ring Side Clearance Oil Control
2010	4.0	K	0.0012-0.0020	0.009-0.015	0.016-0.028	—	0.0016-0.0030	0.0012-0.0026	SNUG
	4.6	8	0.0007-0.0019	0.006-0.012	0.0098-0.0197	0.006-0.0256	0.0008-0.0020	0.0008-0.0020	SNUG
2011	3.5	8	0.0004-0.0017	0.0067-0.0105	0.0118-0.022	0.0059-0.0177	N/A	N/A	N/A

NA: Not Available

25759_EXPL_C0008

TORQUE SPECIFICATIONS

All readings in ft. lbs.

Year	Engine Displ. Liters	Engine ID/VIN	Cylinder Head Bolts	Main Bearing Bolts	Rod Bearing Bolts	Crankshaft Damper Bolts	Flywheel/ Flexplate Bolts	Manifold Intake *	Manifold Exhaust	Spark Plugs	Oil Pan Drain Plug
2010	4.0	K	①	72	②	③	④	8	16	13	19
	4.6	8	⑤	⑥	⑦	⑧	59	⑨	18	9	17
2011	3.5	8	⑩	⑪	⑫	⑬	59	⑭	⑮	11	20

NA: Information not available

* NOTE: Applies to Lower Manifold only.

① Step 1: 12mm bolts: 9 ft. lbs.

Step 2: 12mm bolts: 18 ft. lbs.

Step 3: 8mm bolts: 24 ft. lbs.

Step 4: 12mm bolts: plus 90 degrees

Step 5: 12mm bolts: plus an additional 90 degrees

② Step 1: 15 ft. lbs.

Step 2: plus 90 degrees

③ Step 1: 41 ft. lbs.

Step 2: plus 85 degrees

④ Step 1: 37 ft. lbs.

Step 2: +90 degrees

⑤ Step 1: 30 ft. lbs.

Step 2: plus 90 degrees

Step 3: plus 90 additional degrees

⑥ Vertical Bolts:

Step 1: 30 ft. lbs.

Step 2: plus 90 degrees

Jack screws:

Step 1: 44 inch lbs.

Step 2: 89 inch lbs.

Cross bolts:

Step 1: 15 ft. lbs.

⑦ Step 1: 32 ft. lbs.

Step 2: plus 105 degrees

⑧ Step 1: 89 ft. lbs.

Step 2: back off 1 full turn

Step 3: 37 ft. lbs.

Step 4: plus 90 degrees

⑨ Step 1: 18 inch lbs.

Step 2: 89 inch lbs.

⑩ Step 1: 15 ft. lbs.

Step 2: 26 ft. lbs.

Step 3: plus 90 degrees

Step 4: plus an additional 90 degrees

Step 5: plus 45 degrees

⑪ Early built engines main bearing bolts:

Step 1: 44 ft. lbs.

Step 3: plus 90 degrees

Early built engines main bearing cap side bolts:

Step 1: 33 ft. lbs.

Step 2: plus 90 degrees

Late built engine main bearing bolts:

Step 1: 24 ft. lbs.

Step 3: plus 135 degrees

Late built engines main bearing cap side bolts:

Step 1: 18 ft. lbs.

Step 2: plus 180 degrees

⑫ Step 1: 17 ft. lbs.

Step 2: 32 ft. lbs.

Step 3: plus 90 degrees

⑬ Step 1: 89 ft. lbs.

Step 2: Loosen one full turn

Step 3: 37 ft. lbs.

Step 4: plus 90 degrees

⑭ 89 inch lbs.

⑮ Exhaust manifold studs: 106 inch lbs.

Exhaust manifold nuts:

Step 1: 15 ft. lbs.

Step 4: 18 ft. lbs.

25759_EXPL_C0010

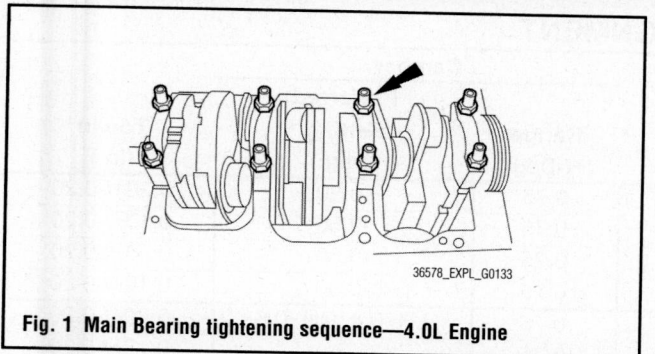

Fig. 1 Main Bearing tightening sequence—4.0L Engine

36578_EXPL_G0133

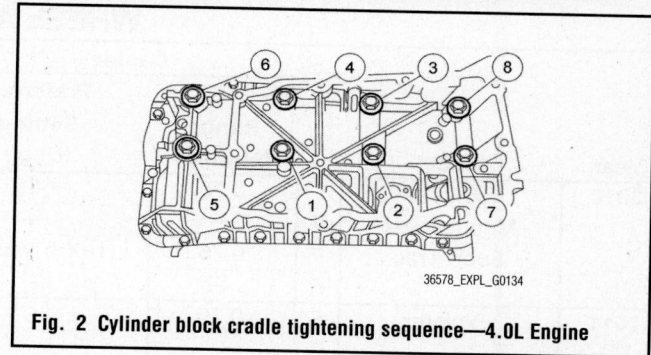

Fig. 2 Cylinder block cradle tightening sequence—4.0L Engine

36578_EXPL_G0134

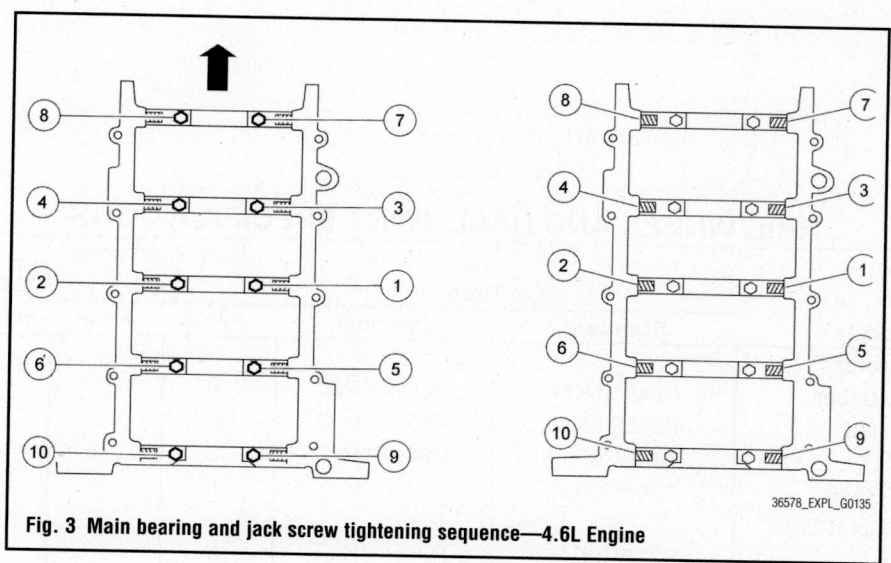

36578_EXPL_G0135

Fig. 3 Main bearing and jack screw tightening sequence—4.6L Engine

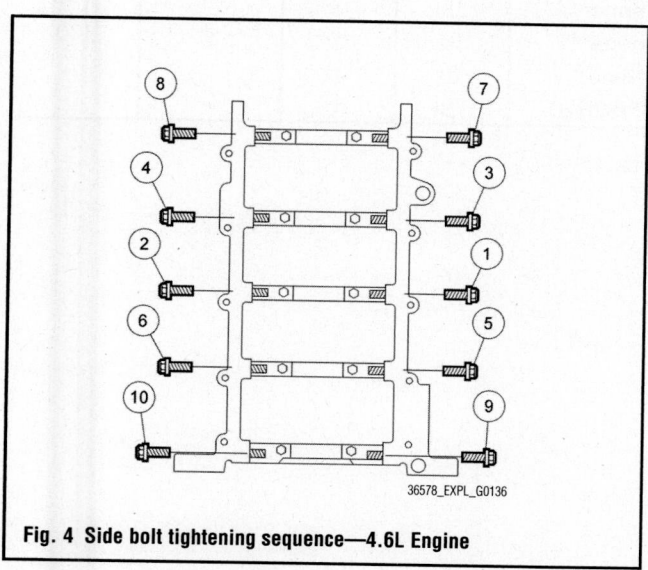

36578_EXPL_G0136

Fig. 4 Side bolt tightening sequence—4.6L Engine

WHEEL ALIGNMENT

Year	Model		Caster Range (+/-Deg.)	Caster Preferred Setting (Deg.)	Camber Range (+/-Deg.)	Camber Preferred Setting (Deg.)	Toe-in (in.)
2010	Explorer/	F	0.75	+4.6	0.75	-0.50	0.20+/-0.20
	Mountaineer	R	—	—	0.75	-0.50	0.10+/-0.20
	Sport Trac	F	0.75	LH +4.5, RH +4.7	0.75	-0.50	0.20+/-0.20
		R	—	—	0.75	-0.50	0.10+/-0.20
2011	Explorer	F	0.75	①	0.75	LH -0.4, RH -0.6	0.20+/-0.20
		R	—	—	0.75	②	0.12+/-0.20

① AWD vehicles: LH +3.3, RH +3.5
   FWD vehicles: LH +3.4, RH +3.6

② AWD vehicles: -0.70
   FWD vehicles: -0.85

25759_EXPL_C0012

TIRE, WHEEL AND BALL JOINT SPECIFICATIONS

Year	Model	OEM Tires Standard	OEM Tires Optional	Tire Pressures (psi) Front	Tire Pressures (psi) Rear	Ball Joint Inspection	Lug Nut Torque (ft. lbs.)
2010	Explorer					②	100
	Eddie Bauer	P245/65R17	P255/50R20	①	①		
	Limited	P235/65R18	P255/50R20	①	①		
	XLT	P235/70R16	P245/65R17	①	①		
	XLT Sport	P255/50R20	None	①	①		
	Explorer Sport-Trac					②	100
	XLT	P235/70R16	P245/65R17	①	①		
	Limited	P235/65R18	P235/65R18	①	①		
	Mountaineer					②	100
	V6	P245/65R17	none	①	①		
	Premier	P235/65R18	none	①	①		
2011	Explorer (base)	P245/65R17	none	①	①	②	100
	XLT	P245/60R18	None	①	①		
	Limited	P255/50R20	P245/50R20	①	①		

NS: Information not specified

OEM: Original Equipment Manufacturer

PSI: Pounds Per Square Inch

STD: Standard

OPT: Optional

① See placard on vehicle

② Upper: 0.008"; Lower: 0.32"

25759_EXPL_C0013

BRAKE SPECIFICATIONS

All measurements in inches unless noted

| Year | Model | | Brake Disc | | | Brake Drum Diameter | | | Minimum Lining Thickness | Brake Caliper | |
			Original Thickness	Min. Thickness	Max. Runout	Original Inside Dia.	Max. Wear Limit	Max. Machine Dia.		Bracket Bolts (ft. lbs.)	Mounting Bolts (ft. lbs.)
2010	Explorer/	F	NA	1.122	NS	—	—	—	0.118	122	53
	Mountaineer	R	NA	0.433	NS	—	—	—	0.118	—	24
2011	Explorer	F	NA	1.122	NS	—	—	—	0.118	111	53
		R	NA	0.394	NS	—	—	—	0.118	103	24

NS: Information not supplied

25759_EXPL_C0011

SCHEDULED MAINTENANCE INTERVALS
2010 Ford Explorer/Sport Trac and Mercury Mountaineer

TO BE SERVICED	TYPE OF SERVICE	VEHICLE MILEAGE INTERVAL (x1000)												
		7.5	15	22.5	30	37.5	45	52.5	60	67.5	75	82.5	90	97.5
Air cleaner filter	R				✓				✓				✓	
Auto. Trans. fluid level	I		✓		✓		✓		✓		✓		✓	
Auto. Trans. Fluid ①	R								✓					
Accessory drive belt ②	I	Every 150,000 miles												
Cabin air filter	R		✓		✓		✓		✓		✓		✓	
Cooling system hoses and clamps	S/I		✓		✓		✓		✓		✓		✓	
Driveshafts & halfshafts	S/I		✓		✓		✓		✓		✓		✓	
Engine coolant	R	At 6 years or 105,000 miles; then every 3 years or 45,000 miles												
Engine oil & filter	R	Every 7,500 miles												
Exhaust system & heat shields	I		✓		✓		✓		✓		✓		✓	
Fuel filter	R				✓				✓					
Tires	Rotate	Every 7,500 miles												
Steering linkage	S/I		✓		✓		✓		✓		✓		✓	
Spark plugs	R	Every 90,000 miles												
Suspension components and ball joints ③	S/I		✓		✓		✓		✓		✓		✓	
Multi-Point inspection	④	✓	✓	✓	✓	✓	✓	✓	✓	✓	✓	✓	✓	✓

R: Replace   S/I: Inspect and service, if necessary   L: Lubricate   A: Adjust   C: Clean

① TorqShift fluid and filter change at 60,000 miles, if not previously done

② Replace at 150,000 miles, if not previously done

③ Replace front bearing grease and seal on RWD vehicles at 60,000 miles.

④ Inspect the reservoir fluid level, rotor and or drum, brake lines, hoses, calipers and or wheel cylinders

Monthly Checks

Check each of the following items every month:

- All interior and exterior lights
- Tires for wear and correct air pressure, including spare tire
- Engine oil fluid level
- Windshield washer solvent fluid level

Six Month Checks

Check each of the following items at least every 6 months:

- Lap/shoulder belts and seat latches for wear and function
- External mounted spare is stowed correctly (tight to body)
- Parking brake for correct operation
- Safety warning lamps (brake, ABS, air bag, safety belt) for correct operation
- Engine coolant system fluid level and correct strength
- Power steering fluid
- Battery 12-volt connections. Clean if necessary
- Windshield washer spray, wiper operation, clean all wiper blades
- Lubricate all hinges, latches and outside locks. Inspect for correct operation
- Lubricate door rubber weatherstrips. Inspect for excessive wear
- Clean body and door drain holes. Inspect for clogs and obstructions

25759_EXPL_C0014

SCHEDULED MAINTENANCE INTERVALS
2010 Ford Explorer/Sport Trac and Mercury Mountaineer

④ **Multi-Point inspection**

The following inspections are recommended at every service interval:

Check and top off brake, coolant, manual and automatic transmission fluid power steering and washer fluid

Inspect tires for wear and correct air pressure, including spare tire

Check exhaust system for leaks, damage, loose parts and foreign material

Check battery performance

Check operation of horn, exterior lamps, turn signals and hazard warning lights

Check radiator, coolers, heater and air conditioning hoses

Inspect windshield wiper spray and wiper operation

Check windshield for cracks, chips and pitting

Inspect for oil and fluid leaks

Inspect air filter

Inspect halfshaft dust boots

Check shocks struts and other suspension components for leaks and damage

Inspect steering linkage

Inspect accessory drive belts

When operating in dusty conditions such as unpaved or dusty roads:

Change engine oil and install a new oil filter every 8,000 km (5,000 miles) or 6 months.

Install a new fuel filter every 24,000 km (15,000 miles).

Rotate tires every 8,000 km (5,000 miles) or 6 months.

Inspect and lubricate control arms, steering linkage, and drivetrain zerk fittings every 8,000 km (5,000 miles) or 6 months.

Change non-TorqShift automatic transmission fluid every 48,000 km (30,000 miles).

Change transfer case fluid every 96,000 km (60,000 miles).

Install a new engine air filter as required.

Replace wheel bearing grease and seals every 48,000 km (30,000 miles).

Install a new cabin air filter as required.

When operating in off-road conditions:

Change engine oil and install a new oil filter every 8,000 km (5,000 miles) or 6 months.

Rotate tires every 8,000 km (5,000 miles) or 6 months.

Inspect and lubricate control arms, steering linkage, and drivetrain zerk fittings every 8,000 km (5,000 miles) or 6 months.

Change non-TorqShift automatic transmission fluid every 48,000 km (30,000 miles). (not required on 6R60/6R75 transmissions).

Change transfer case fluid every 96,000 km (60,000 miles).

Replace wheel bearing grease and seals every 48,000 km (30,000 miles).

Install a new cabin air filter as required.

Inspect and lubricate steering linkage ball joints with zerk fittings.

Special Operating Condition Requirements

When towing a trailer or using a camper or car-top carrier:

Change engine oil and install a new oil filter every 8,000 km (5,000 miles) or 3 months.

Change non-TorqShift automatic transmission fluid every 48,000 km (30,000 miles). (not required on 6R60/6R75 transmissions).

Inspect and rotate tires 8,000 km (5,000 miles)

Change transfer case fluid every 96,000 km (60,000 miles).

Inspect and lubricate steering linkage ball joints with zerk fittings.

During extensive idling and/or low speed driving for long distances, as in heavy commercial use such as delivery, taxi, patrol car or livery:

Change engine oil and install a new oil filter every 8,000 km (5,000 miles) or 6 months.

Install a new fuel filter every 24,000 km (15,000 miles).

Rotate tires every 8,000 km (5,000 miles) or 6 months.

Inspect and lubricate control arms, steering linkage, and drivetrain zerk fittings every 8,000 km (5,000 miles) or 6 months.

Change non-TorqShift automatic transmission fluid every 48,000 km (30,000 miles).

Change transfer case fluid every 96,000 km (60,000 miles).

Replace wheel bearing grease and seals every 48,000 km (30,000 miles).

Install a new cabin air filter as required.

SCHEDULED MAINTENANCE INTERVALS
2011 Ford Explorer - Normal

Service Item	Service Action	1	2	3	4	5	6	7	8	9	10	11	12	13	14	15
Engine oil & filter	Replace	✓	✓	✓	✓	✓	✓	✓	✓	✓	✓	✓	✓	✓	✓	✓
Spark plugs	Replace										✓					
Engine coolant	Replace										✓					✓
Halfshaft boots	Inspect	✓	✓	✓	✓	✓	✓	✓	✓	✓	✓	✓	✓	✓	✓	✓
Drive belt(s)	Inspect	✓	✓	✓	✓	✓	✓	✓	✓	✓	✓	✓	✓	✓	✓	✓
Drive belt(s)	Replace															✓
Automatic transmission fluid	Replace															✓
Engine air filter	Replace			✓			✓			✓			✓			✓
Engine air filter	Inspect	✓	✓		✓	✓		✓	✓		✓	✓		✓	✓	
Cooling system, hoses, clamps & coolant strength	Inspect	✓	✓	✓	✓	✓	✓	✓	✓	✓	✓	✓	✓	✓	✓	✓
Battery performance	Inspect	✓	✓	✓	✓	✓	✓	✓	✓	✓	✓	✓	✓	✓	✓	✓
Climate-controlled seat filter (if equipped)	Replace			✓			✓			✓			✓			✓
Exhaust system (Leaks, damage, loose parts and foreign material)	Inspect	✓	✓	✓	✓	✓	✓	✓	✓	✓	✓	✓	✓	✓	✓	✓
Horn, exterior lamps, turn signals and hazard warning light operation	Inspect	✓	✓	✓	✓	✓	✓	✓	✓	✓	✓	✓	✓	✓	✓	✓
Windshield for cracks, chips and pitting	Inspect	✓	✓	✓	✓	✓	✓	✓	✓	✓	✓	✓	✓	✓	✓	✓
Windshield wiper spray and wiper operation	Inspect	✓	✓	✓	✓	✓	✓	✓	✓	✓	✓	✓	✓	✓	✓	✓
Fluid levels (all)	Top off	✓	✓	✓	✓	✓	✓	✓	✓	✓	✓	✓	✓	✓	✓	✓
Brake system (Pads/shoes/rotors/drums, brake lines and hoses, and parking brake system)	Inspect	✓	✓	✓	✓	✓	✓	✓	✓	✓	✓	✓	✓	✓	✓	✓
Inspect wheels and related components for abnormal noise, wear, looseness or drag	Inspect	✓	✓	✓	✓	✓	✓	✓	✓	✓	✓	✓	✓	✓	✓	✓
Steering linkage, ball joints, suspension, tie-rod ends, driveshaft and u-joints: lubricate if equipped with grease fittings	Inspect/ Lubricate	✓	✓	✓	✓	✓	✓	✓	✓	✓	✓	✓	✓	✓	✓	✓
Radiator, coolers, heater and air conditioning hoses	Inspect	✓	✓	✓	✓	✓	✓	✓	✓	✓	✓	✓	✓	✓	✓	✓
Rotate tires, inspect tread wear, measure tread depth and check pressure	Inspect/ Rotate	✓	✓	✓	✓	✓	✓	✓	✓	✓	✓	✓	✓	✓	✓	✓
Suspension components for leaks and damage	Inspect	✓	✓	✓	✓	✓	✓	✓	✓	✓	✓	✓	✓	✓	✓	✓
Transfer case fluid	Replace															✓

Oil change service intervals should be completed as indicated by the message center (Can be up to 1 year or 10,000 miles) If the message center is prematurely reset or is inoperative, perform the oil change interval at 6 months or 5,000 miles from your last oil change.

For extensive idling and or low speed driving, change engine oil and filter every 5,000 miles, 6 months or 200 hours of engine operation.

25759_EXPL_C0016

SCHEDULED MAINTENANCE INTERVALS
2011 Ford Explorer - Severe

Service Item	Service Action	1	2	3	4	5	6	7	8	9	10	11	12	13	14	15
Engine oil & filter	Replace	✓	✓	✓	✓	✓	✓	✓	✓	✓	✓	✓	✓	✓	✓	✓
Spark plugs	Replace						✓						✓			
Engine coolant	Replace										✓					✓
Rear differential fluid	Replace															✓
Drive belt(s)	Inspect	✓	✓	✓	✓	✓	✓	✓	✓	✓	✓	✓	✓	✓	✓	✓
Drive belt(s)	Replace															✓
Transfer case fluid	Replace															✓
Auto transmission fluid	Replace			✓			✓			✓			✓			✓
Engine air filter	Inspect/ Service	✓	✓	✓	✓	✓	✓	✓	✓	✓	✓	✓	✓	✓	✓	✓
Cooling system, hoses, clamps & coolant strength	Inspect	✓	✓	✓	✓	✓	✓	✓	✓	✓	✓	✓	✓	✓	✓	✓
Battery performance	Inspect	✓	✓	✓	✓	✓	✓	✓	✓	✓	✓	✓	✓	✓	✓	✓
Climate-controlled seat filter (if equipped)	Replace			✓			✓			✓			✓			✓
Exhaust system (Leaks, damage, loose parts and foreign material)	Inspect	✓	✓	✓	✓	✓	✓	✓	✓	✓	✓	✓	✓	✓	✓	✓
Horn, exterior lamps, turn signals and hazard warning light operation	Inspect	✓	✓	✓	✓	✓	✓	✓	✓	✓	✓	✓	✓	✓	✓	✓
Oil and fluid leaks	Inspect	✓	✓	✓	✓	✓	✓	✓	✓	✓	✓	✓	✓	✓	✓	✓
Shocks struts and other suspension components for leaks and damage	Inspect	✓	✓	✓	✓	✓	✓	✓	✓	✓	✓	✓	✓	✓	✓	✓
Windshield, wipers and washer	Inspect	✓	✓	✓	✓	✓	✓	✓	✓	✓	✓	✓	✓	✓	✓	✓
Halfshaft & U-joints	Inspect	✓	✓	✓	✓	✓	✓	✓	✓	✓	✓	✓	✓	✓	✓	✓
Fluid levels (all)	Top off	✓	✓	✓	✓	✓	✓	✓	✓	✓	✓	✓	✓	✓	✓	✓
Brake system (Pads/shoes/rotors/drums, brake lines and hoses, and parking brake system)	Inspect	✓	✓	✓	✓	✓	✓	✓	✓	✓	✓	✓	✓	✓	✓	✓
Inspect wheels and related components for abnormal noise, wear, looseness or drag	Inspect	✓	✓	✓	✓	✓	✓	✓	✓	✓	✓	✓	✓	✓	✓	✓
Cabin air filter (If equipped)	Inspect/ Service	✓	✓	✓	✓	✓	✓	✓	✓	✓	✓	✓	✓	✓	✓	✓
Radiator, coolers, heater and air conditioning hoses	Inspect	✓	✓	✓	✓	✓	✓	✓	✓	✓	✓	✓	✓	✓	✓	✓
Rotate tires, inspect tread wear, measure tread depth and check pressure	Inspect/ Rotate	✓	✓	✓	✓	✓	✓	✓	✓	✓	✓	✓	✓	✓	✓	✓
Steering linkage, ball joints, suspension and tie-rod ends, lubricate if equipped with greases fittings	Inspect/ Lubricate	✓	✓	✓	✓	✓	✓	✓	✓	✓	✓	✓	✓	✓	✓	✓
Front differential fluid	Replace															✓

Oil change service intervals should be completed as indicated by the message center (Can be up to 1 year or 10,000 miles) If the message center is prematurely reset or is inoperative, perform the oil change interval at 6 months or 5,000 miles from your last oil change.

For extensive idling and or low speed driving, change engine oil and filter every 5,000 miles, 6 months or 200 hours of engine operation.

PRECAUTIONS

Before servicing any vehicle, please be sure to read all of the following precautions, which deal with personal safety, prevention of component damage, and important points to take into consideration when servicing a motor vehicle:

• Never open, service or drain the radiator or cooling system when the engine is hot; serious burns can occur from the steam and hot coolant.

• Observe all applicable safety precautions when working around fuel. Whenever servicing the fuel system, always work in a well-ventilated area. Do not allow fuel spray or vapors to come in contact with a spark, open flame, or excessive heat (a hot drop light, for example). Keep a dry chemical fire extinguisher near the work area. Always keep fuel in a container specifically designed for fuel storage; also, always properly seal fuel containers to avoid the possibility of fire or explosion. Refer to the additional fuel system precautions later in this section.

• Fuel injection systems often remain pressurized, even after the engine has been turned **OFF**. The fuel system pressure must be relieved before disconnecting any fuel lines. Failure to do so may result in fire and/or personal injury.

• Brake fluid often contains polyglycol ethers and polyglycols. Avoid contact with the eyes and wash your hands thoroughly after handling brake fluid. If you do get brake fluid in your eyes, flush your eyes with clean, running water for 15 minutes. If eye irritation persists, or if you have taken brake fluid internally, IMMEDIATELY seek medical assistance.

• The EPA warns that prolonged contact with used engine oil may cause a number of skin disorders, including cancer. You should make every effort to minimize your exposure to used engine oil. Protective gloves should be worn when changing oil. Wash your hands and any other exposed skin areas as soon as possible after exposure to used engine oil. Soap and water, or waterless hand cleaner should be used.

• All new vehicles are now equipped with an air bag system, often referred to as a Supplemental Restraint System (SRS) or Supplemental Inflatable Restraint (SIR) system. The system must be disabled before performing service on or around system components, steering column, instrument panel components, wiring and sensors. Failure to follow safety and disabling procedures could result in accidental air bag deployment, possible personal injury and unnecessary system repairs.

• Always wear safety goggles when working with, or around, the air bag system. When carrying a non-deployed air bag, be sure the bag and trim cover are pointed away from your body. When placing a non-deployed air bag on a work surface, always face the bag and trim cover upward, away from the surface. This will reduce the motion of the module if it is accidentally deployed. Refer to the additional air bag system precautions later in this section.

• Clean, high quality brake fluid from a sealed container is essential to the safe and proper operation of the brake system. You should always buy the correct type of brake fluid for your vehicle. If the brake fluid becomes contaminated, completely flush the system with new fluid. Never reuse any brake fluid. Any brake fluid that is removed from the system should be discarded. Also, do not allow any brake fluid to come in contact with a painted surface; it will damage the paint.

• Never operate the engine without the proper amount and type of engine oil; doing so WILL result in severe engine damage.

• Timing belt maintenance is extremely important. Many models utilize an interference-type, non-freewheeling engine. If the timing belt breaks, the valves in the cylinder head may strike the pistons, causing potentially serious (also time-consuming and expensive) engine damage. Refer to the maintenance interval charts for the recommended replacement interval for the timing belt, and to the timing belt section for belt replacement and inspection.

• Disconnecting the negative battery cable on some vehicles may interfere with the functions of the on-board computer system(s) and may require the computer to undergo a relearning process once the negative battery cable is reconnected.

• When servicing drum brakes, only disassemble and assemble one side at a time, leaving the remaining side intact for reference.

• Only an MVAC-trained, EPA-certified automotive technician should service the air conditioning system or its components.

BRAKES

GENERAL INFORMATION

PRECAUTIONS

• Certain components within the ABS system are not intended to be serviced or repaired individually.

• Do not use rubber hoses or other parts not specifically specified for and ABS system. When using repair kits, replace all parts included in the kit. Partial or incorrect repair may lead to functional problems and require the replacement of components.

• Lubricate rubber parts with clean, fresh brake fluid to ease assembly. Do not use shop air to clean parts; damage to rubber components may result.

• Use only DOT 3 brake fluid from an unopened container.

• If any hydraulic component or line is removed or replaced, it may be necessary to bleed the entire system.

• A clean repair area is essential. Always clean the reservoir and cap thoroughly before removing the cap. The slightest amount of dirt in the fluid may plug an orifice and impair the system function. Perform repairs after components have been thoroughly cleaned; use only denatured alcohol to clean components. Do not allow ABS components to come into contact with any substance containing mineral oil; this includes used shop rags.

• The Anti-Lock control unit is a microprocessor similar to other computer units in the vehicle. Ensure that the ignition switch is **OFF** before removing or installing controller harnesses. Avoid static electricity discharge at or near the controller.

• If any arc welding is to be done on the vehicle, the control unit should be unplugged before welding operations begin.

ANTI-LOCK BRAKE SYSTEM (ABS)

WHEEL SPEED SENSORS

REMOVAL & INSTALLATION

Front

2010 Models

See Figure 5.

1. Remove the front brake disc. See Rotor in Front Disc Brakes.
2. Disconnect the wheel speed sensor electrical connector.
3. Remove the wheel speed sensor harness bolt.
4. Remove the wheel speed sensor harness pin-type retainers.
5. Remove the wheel speed sensor bolt.
6. Remove the wheel speed sensor and the harness.

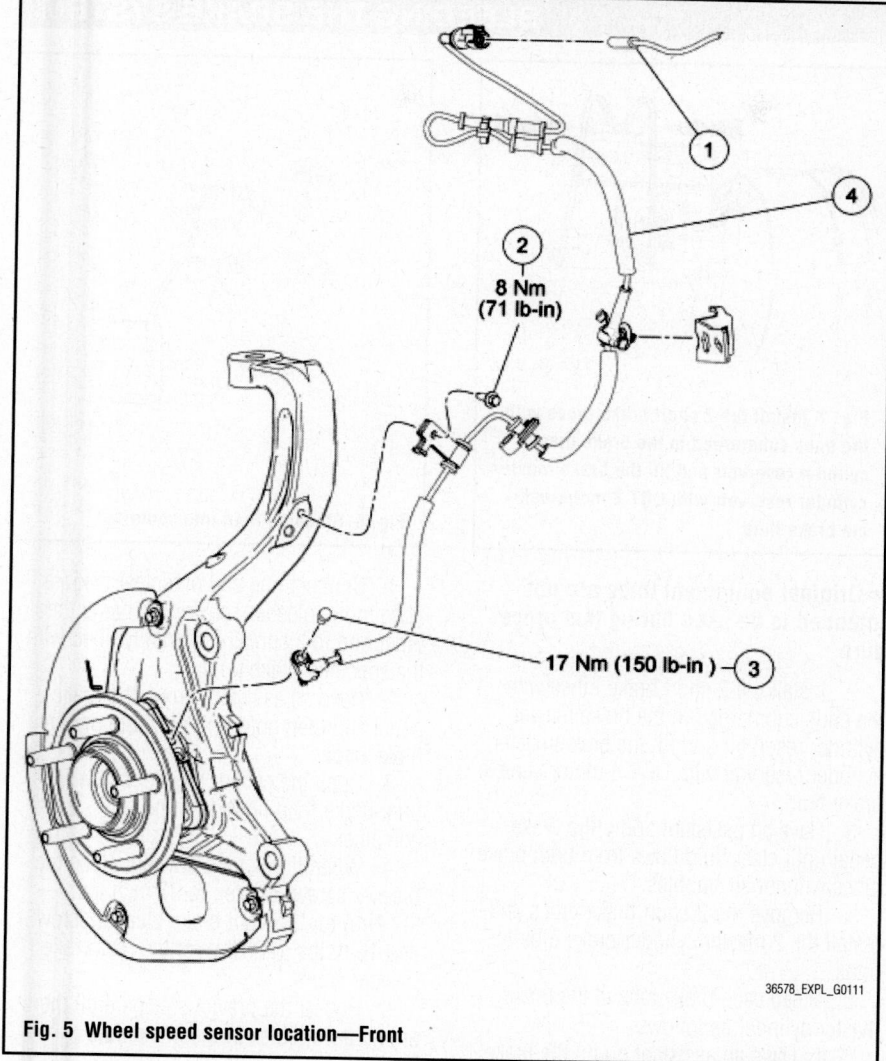

8 Nm
(71 lb-in)

17 Nm (150 lb-in)

36578_EXPL_G0111

Fig. 5 Wheel speed sensor location—Front

To install:

7. Installation is the reverse of the removal procedure, tighten the wheel speed sensor bolt to 13 ft. lbs. (17 Nm).

2011 Models

1. Raise and safely support the vehicle.
2. Remove the wheel and tire.
3. Remove the fender splash shield.
4. Disconnect the wheel speed sensor electrical connector.
5. Detach the 2 pin-type retainers.
6. Detach the 2 grommets from the routing brackets.
7. Remove the front wheel speed sensor bolt and the front wheel speed sensor.

To install:

8. Position the front wheel speed sensor and install the front wheel speed sensor bolt.
Tighten to 11 ft. lbs. (15 Nm).

9. Attach the 2 grommets to the routing brackets.
10. Attach the 2 pin-type retainers.

11. Connect the wheel speed sensor electrical connector.
12. Install the fender splash shield.
13. Install the wheel and tire, then lower the vehicle.

Rear

2010 Models

See Figure 6.

1. With the vehicle in NEUTRAL, position it on a hoist.
2. Disconnect the wheel speed sensor electrical connector.
3. Disconnect the wheel speed harness from the retainers.
4. Remove the wheel speed sensor bolt and the wheel speed sensor.

To install:

5. Installation is the reverse of the removal procedure.

2011 Models

1. Disconnect the wheel speed sensor electrical connector.
2. Detach the 2 pin-type retainers.
3. Detach the 2 grommets from the routing brackets.
4. Remove the rear wheel speed sensor bolt and the rear wheel speed sensor.

To install:

5. Position the rear wheel speed sensor and install the rear wheel speed sensor bolt.
Tighten to 11 ft. lbs. (15 Nm).
6. Attach the 2 grommets to the routing brackets.
7. Attach the 2 pin-type retainers.
8. Connect the wheel speed sensor electrical connector.

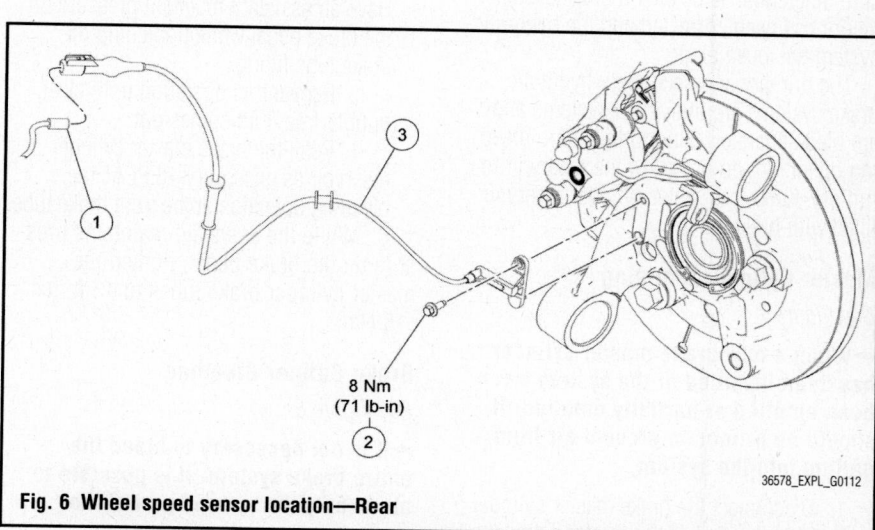

8 Nm
(71 lb-in)

36578_EXPL_G0112

Fig. 6 Wheel speed sensor location—Rear

BLEEDING PROCEDURE

1. Before servicing, refer to Precautions.

> ※ **WARNING**
>
> **Do not allow the brake master cylinder reservoir to run dry during the bleeding operation. Keep the brake master cylinder reservoir filled with the specified brake fluid. Never reuse brake fluid that has been drained from the hydraulic system.**

> ※ **WARNING**
>
> **Brake fluid is harmful to painted and plastic surfaces. If brake fluid is spilled onto a painted or plastic surface, immediately wash it with water.**

When any part of the hydraulic system has been disconnected for repair or replacement, air may get into the lines and cause spongy pedal action (because air can be compressed and brake fluid cannot). To correct this condition, it is necessary to bleed the hydraulic system after it has been properly connected to be sure all air is expelled from the brake cylinders and lines.

When bleeding the brake system, bleed one brake cylinder at a time, beginning at the cylinder with the longest hydraulic line (farthest from the master cylinder) first. ALWAYS Keep the master cylinder reservoir filled with brake fluid during the bleeding operation. Never use brake fluid that has been drained from the hydraulic system, no matter how clean it is.

It will be necessary to centralize the pressure differential value after a brake system failure has been corrected and the hydraulic system has been bled.

The primary and secondary hydraulic brake systems are individual systems and are bled separately. During the entire bleeding operation, do not allow the reservoir to run dry. Keep the master cylinder reservoir filled with brake fluid.

Master Cylinder Bleeding

See Figure 7.

➡ **When a new brake master cylinder has been installed or the system has been emptied or partially emptied, it should be primed to prevent air from getting into the system.**

1. Disconnect the brake master cylinder tubes from the side of the master cylinder.

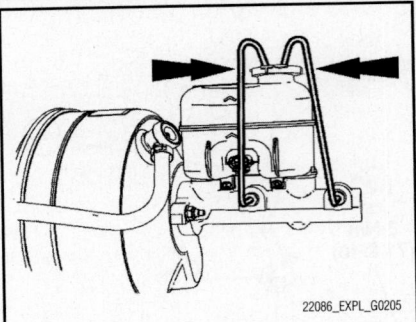

22086_EXPL_G0205

Fig. 7 Install the 2 short brake tubes with the ends submerged in the brake master cylinder reservoir and fill the brake master cylinder reservoir with DOT 3 motor vehicle brake fluid

➡ **Original equipment lines are not intended to be used during this procedure.**

2. Install the 2 short brake tubes with the ends submerged in the brake master cylinder reservoir and fill the brake master cylinder reservoir with DOT 3 motor vehicle brake fluid.

3. Have an assistant pump the brake pedal until clear fluid flows from both brake tubes without air bubbles.

4. Remove the 2 short brake tubes and install the 2 master cylinder brake tube fittings.

5. Bleed each brake tube at the brake master cylinder as follows:

   a. Have an assistant pump the brake pedal and then hold firm pressure on the brake pedal.

   b. Loosen the rear brake tube fittings until a stream of brake fluid comes out. Have an assistant maintain pressure on the brake pedal while tightening the brake tube fitting.

   c. Repeat this operation until clear, bubble-free fluid comes out.

   d. Refill the brake master cylinder reservoir as necessary. REPEAT the bleeding operation at the front brake tube.

6. While the assistant maintains pressure on the brake pedal, tighten the master cylinder brake tubes to 13 ft. lbs. (18 Nm).

Brake Caliper Bleeding

See Figure 8.

➡ **It is not necessary to bleed the entire brake system. It is possible to bleed only the opened part of the system.**

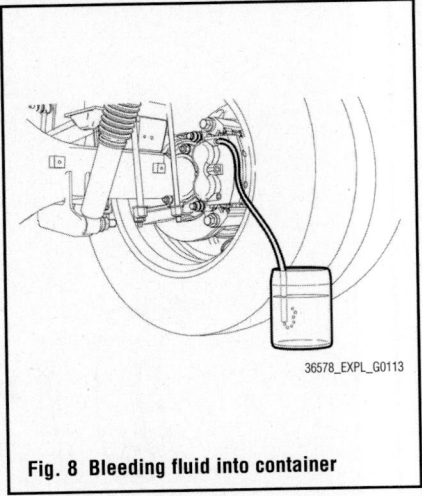

36578_EXPL_G0113

Fig. 8 Bleeding fluid into container

1. Connect one end of a clear flexible hose to the bleeder screw. Submerge the other end in a container partially filled with the specified brake fluid.

2. Have an assistant pump the brake pedal and then hold firm pressure on the brake pedal.

3. Open the caliper bleeder screw until brake fluid flows into the container.

4. When fluid stops flowing, close the bleeder screw. Tighten to 97 inch lbs. (11 Nm) for the front brake bleeder screw and 16 ft. lbs. (22 Nm) for the rear brake bleeder screw.

5. Repeat the previous steps until there are no air bubbles in the brake fluid.

Pressure Bleeding

➡ **Pressure bleeding the brake system is preferred to manual bleeding.**

1. Clean all dirt from and remove the brake master cylinder filler cap and fill the brake master cylinder reservoir with clean, specified brake fluid.

➡ **Master cylinder pressure bleeder adapter tools are available from various manufacturers of pressure bleeding equipment. Follow the instructions of the equipment manufacturer when installing the adapter.**

2. Install the bleeder adapter to the brake master cylinder reservoir and attach the bleeder tank hose to the fitting on the adapter.

➡ **Make sure the bleeder tank contains enough clean, specified brake fluid to complete the bleeding operation.**

3. Remove the RH rear bleeder cap and place a box-end wrench on the bleeder screw. Attach a rubber drain tube to the RH rear bleeder screw and submerge the free end of the tube in a container partially filled with clean, specified brake fluid.

4. Open the valve on the bleeder tank.

a. Set pressure to 30-50 psi (207-345 kPa).

5. Loosen the RH rear bleeder screw. Leave open until clear, bubble-free brake fluid flows, then tighten the RH rear bleeder screw and remove the rubber hose.

6. Tighten to specifications. Refer to Brake Caliper.

7. Continue bleeding the system, going in order from the LH rear bleeder screw to the RH front bleeder screw ending with the LH front bleeder screw.

8. Release the bleeder tank pressure and close the bleeder tank valve. Remove the tank hose from the adapter and remove the adapter from the brake fluid reservoir.

Manual Bleeding

> ✳✳ **CAUTION**
>
> **Do not allow the brake master cylinder to run dry during the bleeding**

operation. Master cylinder may be damaged if operated without fluid, resulting in degraded braking performance. Failure to follow this instruction may result in serious personal injury.

> ✳✳ **WARNING**
>
> **Do not spill brake fluid on painted or plastic surfaces or damage to the surface may occur. If brake fluid is spilled onto a painted or plastic surface, immediately wash the surface with water.**

➡ **The Hydraulic Control Unit (HCU) bleeding procedure must be carried out if the HCU or any components upstream of the HCU are installed new.**

➡ **Pressure bleeding the brake system is preferred to manual bleeding.**

1. Clean all dirt from and remove the brake master cylinder filler cap and fill the brake master cylinder reservoir with clean, specified brake fluid.

2. Remove the bleeder screw cap and place a box-end wrench on the RH rear

bleeder screw. Attach a rubber drain hose to the RH rear bleeder screw and submerge the free end of the hose in a container partially filled with clean, specified brake fluid.

3. Have an assistant pump the brake pedal at least 3 times and then hold firm pressure on the brake pedal.

4. Loosen the RH rear bleeder screw until a stream of brake fluid comes out. While the assistant maintains pressure on the brake pedal, tighten the RH rear bleeder screw.

5. Repeat until clear, bubble-free fluid comes out.

6. Refill the brake master cylinder reservoir as necessary.

7. Remove the rubber hose and tighten the bleeder screw to specifications. Refer to Brake Caliper.

8. Install the bleeder screw cap.

9. Repeat Steps 2 through 5 for the LH rear, RH front and LH front bleeder screws in this order.

BLEEDING THE ABS SYSTEM

Refer to Bleeding the Brake System.

BRAKES   **FRONT DISC BRAKES**

BRAKE CALIPER

REMOVAL & INSTALLATION

2010 Models

See Figure 9.

1. Before servicing the vehicle, refer to Precautions.

2. With the vehicle in NEUTRAL, position it on a hoist.

3. Remove the front wheels.

4. Remove the brake hose flow bolt and position the brake hose aside. Discard the 2 copper washers. Cap the fluid ports.

5. Remove the 2 brake caliper bolts and the brake caliper.

> ✳✳ **WARNING**
>
> **Do not pry in the brake caliper sight hole to retract the pistons as this can damage the pistons and boots.**

6. If leaks or damaged boots are found, install a new brake caliper.

To install:

7. Position the brake caliper and install the 2 bolts. Tighten the bottom locator pin brake caliper bolt before tightening the top

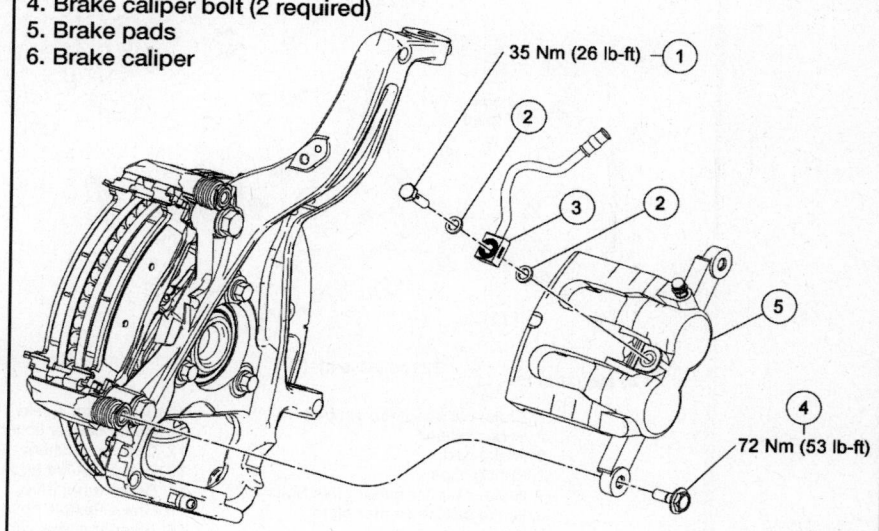

1. Brake hose flow bolt
2. Copper washers (2 required)
3. Brake hose
4. Brake caliper bolt (2 required)
5. Brake pads
6. Brake caliper

35 Nm (26 lb-ft)

72 Nm (53 lb-ft)

22086_EXPL_G0206

Fig. 9 Showing the brake caliper mounting, brake hose bolt (1), washer (2), hose connection (3), caliper bolts (4) and the brake caliper (5)—2010 model

guide pin brake caliper bolt. Torque the bolts to 53 ft. lbs. (72 Nm).

8. Using 2 new copper washers, position the brake hose and install the brake hose flow bolt. Tighten the bolt to 26 ft. lbs. (35 Nm).

9. Bleed the brake caliper. Refer to Bleeding the Brake System.

10. Install the wheels and lower the vehicle.

11. Test the brake system for normal operation.

2011 Models
See Figure 10.

> ❋❋ **WARNING**
>
> Do not use any fluid other than clean brake fluid meeting manufacturer's specification. Additionally, do not use brake fluid that has been previously drained. Following these instructions will help prevent system

contamination, brake component damage and the risk of serious personal injury.

> ❋❋ **CAUTION**
>
> Carefully read cautionary information on product label. For EMERGENCY MEDICAL INFORMATION seek medical advice. In the USA or Canada on Ford/Motorcraft products call: 1-800-959-3673. For additional information, consult the product Material Safety Data Sheet (MSDS), if available. Failure to follow these instructions may result in serious personal injury.

> ❋❋ **WARNING**
>
> Do not spill brake fluid on painted or plastic surfaces or damage to the

surface may occur. If brake fluid is spilled onto a painted or plastic surface, immediately wash the surface with water.

1. Remove the brake pads, as outlined in this section.

2. Remove the brake caliper flow bolt and position the brake hose aside. Discard the copper washers.

3. Remove the brake caliper.

To install:

4. Position the brake hose and install the brake caliper flow bolt. Install new copper washers. Tighten the brake caliper flow bolt to 35 ft. lbs. (47 Nm).

5. Install the brake pads, as outlined in this section.

6. Bleed the brake caliper.

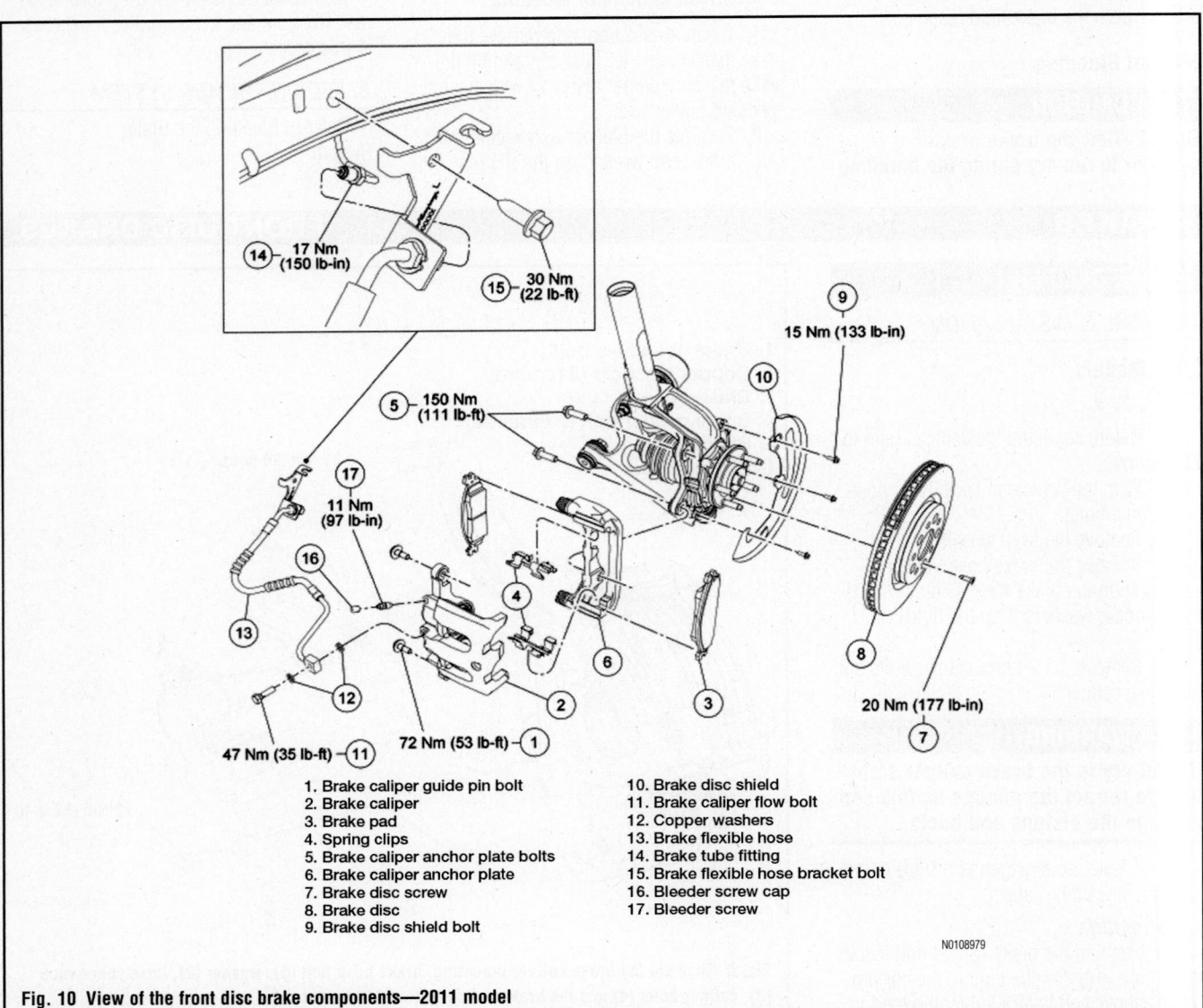

1. Brake caliper guide pin bolt
2. Brake caliper
3. Brake pad
4. Spring clips
5. Brake caliper anchor plate bolts
6. Brake caliper anchor plate
7. Brake disc screw
8. Brake disc
9. Brake disc shield bolt
10. Brake disc shield
11. Brake caliper flow bolt
12. Copper washers
13. Brake flexible hose
14. Brake tube fitting
15. Brake flexible hose bracket bolt
16. Bleeder screw cap
17. Bleeder screw

N0108979

Fig. 10 View of the front disc brake components—2011 model

DISC BRAKE PADS

REMOVAL & INSTALLATION

2010 Models

See Figure 11.

➡Install new brake pads if they are worn past the specified thickness above the metal backing plate or rivets. Install new brake pads in complete axle sets.

1. Before servicing the vehicle, refer to the Precautions.
2. Remove brake fluid in the master cylinder reservoir until the reservoir is half full.
3. Raise and support the vehicle.
4. Remove the wheel and tire assembly.
5. Remove the 2 brake caliper bolts and position the brake caliper aside. Support the caliper using mechanic's wire.
6. Inspect the brake pads for wear and contamination.
7. Inspect the brake disc, machine or install a new front brake disc as necessary.
8. Remove the brake pads and clips. Discard the clips.

To install:

9. Install the new brake pad clips and the brake pads.

❊❊ WARNING

Protect the piston and boots when pushing the caliper piston into the caliper piston bores.

10. Using a suitable tool (C-clamp) and a worn brake pad, compress the disc brake caliper pistons into the caliper.
11. Position the brake caliper and install the 2 bolts. Tighten the lower bolt and then the upper bolt to 53 ft. lbs. (72 Nm).
12. Install the wheel and tire assembly and lower the vehicle.
13. Fill the brake master cylinder reservoir with clean brake fluid.
14. Test the brakes for normal operation.

2011 Models

See Figure 10.

1. Check the brake fluid level in the brake master cylinder reservoir. If required, remove the fluid until the brake master cylinder reservoir is half full.
2. Raise and safely support the vehicle.
3. Remove the wheel and tire.
4. Using a C-clamp, compress the pistons into the caliper housing.

➡**Do not allow the brake caliper to hang from the brake hose or damage to the hose may occur.**

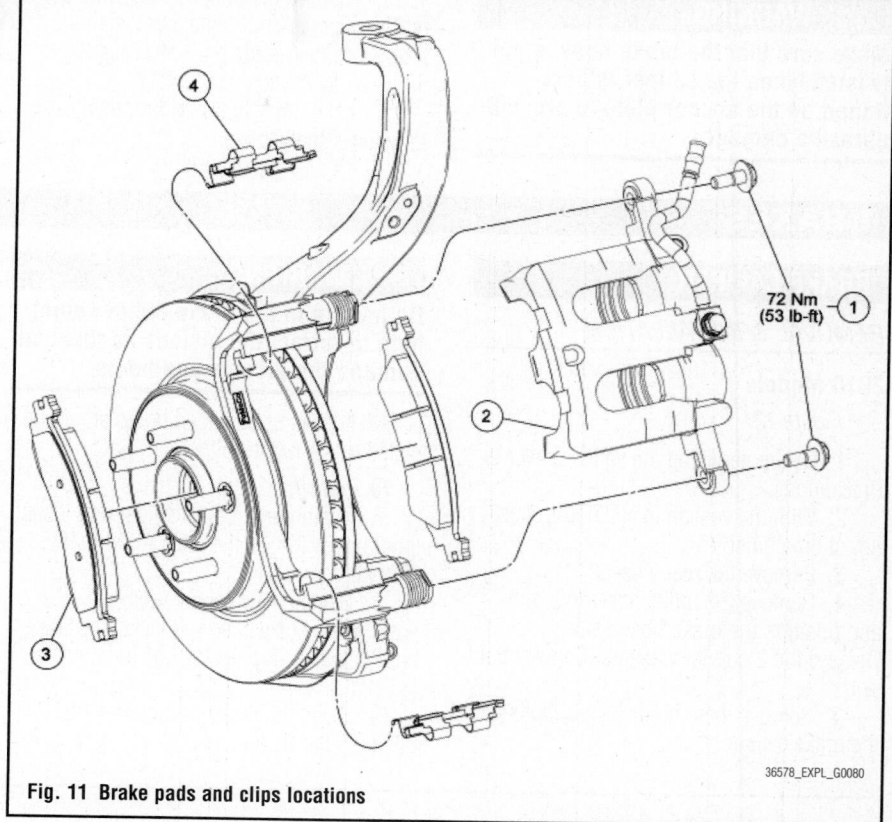

Fig. 11 Brake pads and clips locations

36578_EXPL_G0080

5. Remove the 2 brake caliper guide pin bolts and position the caliper aside. Support the caliper using mechanic's wire.
6. Remove the 2 brake pads, spring clips and wire spreader springs (if equipped) from the brake caliper anchor plate. Discard the spring clips and wire spreader springs (if equipped).
7. Inspect the brake caliper for leaks or damage. Install a new brake caliper if required.
8. Inspect the brake caliper anchor plate. Install a new brake caliper anchor plate if required. Inspect the guide pins and boots for binding or damage. Install new as necessary.

To install:

➡If installing new brake pads, make sure to install all new hardware and specified lubricant (8U7Z-19A506-A) supplied with the brake pad kit. Refer to the brake pad instruction sheet when applying lubricant.

9. Install the new spring clips and brake pads to the brake caliper anchor plate. Apply equal amounts of specified lubricant to the brake caliper-to-brake pad contact points as directed. Install the brake pads to the brake caliper anchor plate.

❊❊ WARNING

Do not allow grease, oil, brake fluid or other contaminants to contact the pad lining material, or damage to components may occur. Do not install contaminated pads.

➡If reusing the existing brake pads, be sure to apply equal amounts of the specified lubricant (8U7Z-19A506-A) to the caliper-to-brake pad contact points.

➡Do not grease or lubricate the brake pad spring clips.

10. Install the spring clips and brake pads to the brake caliper anchor plate.

➡The coil in the center of the wire spreader spring must lie against the anchor plate and must not be in the raised position. If the coil in the center of the wire spreader spring does not rest against the caliper anchor plate, the spring is installed incorrectly and must be repositioned.

11. Insert ends of wire spreader springs into holes in pad pressure plates.

➡Make sure the caliper pin boots are correctly seated to prevent corrosion to the guide pins.

BRAKES

BRAKE CALIPER

REMOVAL & INSTALLATION

2010 Models

See Figure 12.

1. Before servicing the vehicle, refer to Precautions.
2. With the vehicle in NEUTRAL, position it on a hoist.
3. Remove the rear wheels.
4. Remove the brake hose flow bolt and position the brake hose aside. Discard the 2 copper washers. Cap the fluid ports.
5. Remove the 2 brake caliper bolts and the brake caliper.

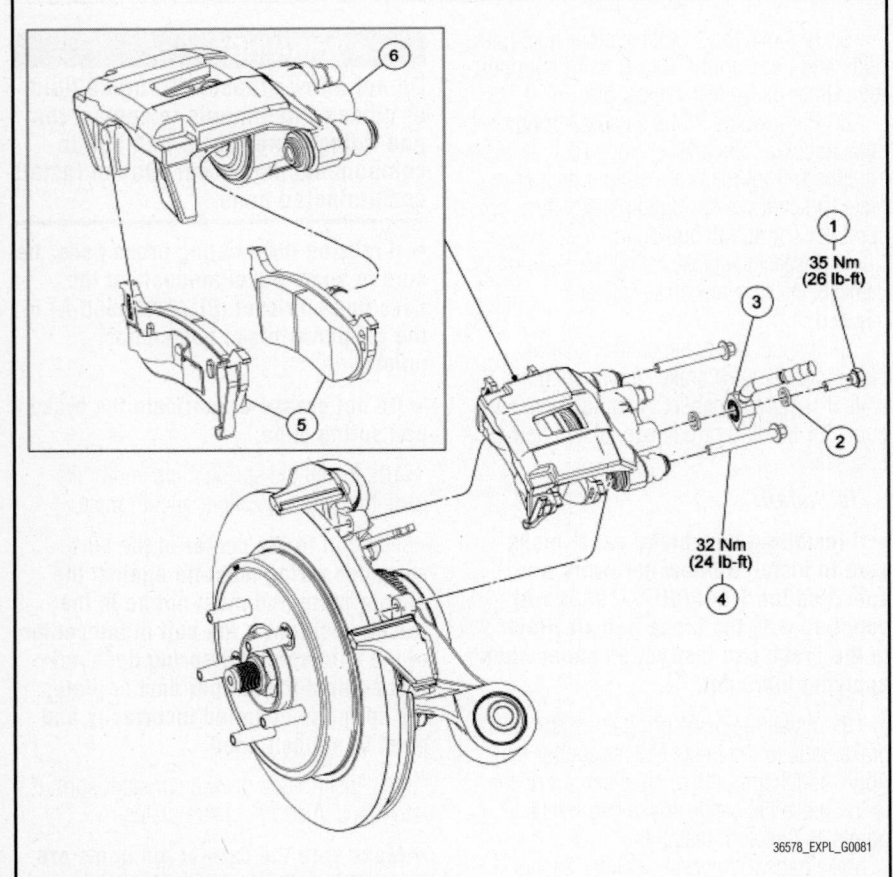

Fig. 12 Showing the rear brake caliper mounting

36578_EXPL_G0081

35 Nm (26 lb-ft)
32 Nm (24 lb-ft)

12. Position the brake caliper onto the brake caliper anchor plate and install the 2 brake caliper guide pin bolts. Tighten to 53 ft. lbs. (72 Nm).
13. Install the wheel and tire, then carefully lower the vehicle.

6. If leaks or damaged boots are found, install a new brake caliper.

To install:

7. Position the brake caliper and install the 2 bolts. Torque the bolts to 24 ft. lbs. (32 Nm).
8. Using 2 new copper washers, position the brake hose and install the brake hose flow bolt. Tighten the bolt to 26 ft. lbs. (35 Nm).
9. Bleed the brake caliper. Refer to Bleeding the Brake System.

14. If necessary, fill the brake master cylinder reservoir with clean, specified brake fluid. Apply brakes several times to verify correct brake operation.

REAR DISC BRAKES

10. Install the wheels and lower the vehicle.
11. Test the brake system for normal operation.

2011 Models

➡️Do not spill brake fluid on painted or plastic surfaces or damage to the surface may occur. If brake fluid is spilled onto a painted or plastic surface, immediately wash the surface with water.

1. Release the parking brake cable tension. REFER to Parking Brake Cable Tension Release.
2. Disconnect the parking brake cable from the subframe bracket and the caliper. Position the parking brake cable aside.
3. Remove and discard the brake pads, as outlined in this section.
4. Clean and inspect the disc brake caliper. If leaks or damaged boots are found, install a new disc brake caliper.
5. Disconnect the brake tube fitting from the brake flexible hose.

➡️The brake caliper and brake flexible hose are removed as an assembly.

6. Remove the retainer clip from the brake flexible hose.

To install:

✳✳ WARNING

During installation, make sure that the brake flexible hose does not become twisted or damage to hose may occur.

7. Install the brake pads, as outlined in this section.
8. Install the brake flexible hose retainer clip.
9. Connect the brake tube fitting to the brake flexible hose. Tighten to 13 ft. lbs. (17 Nm).
10. Connect the parking brake cable to the subframe and caliper.
11. Remove the retainer pin from the parking brake control.
12. Bleed the caliper.

DISC BRAKE PADS

REMOVAL & INSTALLATION

2010 Models
See Figure 13.

➤**Install new brake pads if they are worn past the specified thickness above the metal backing plate or rivets. Install new brake pads in complete axle sets.**

1. Before servicing the vehicle, refer to the Precautions.
2. Remove brake fluid in the master cylinder reservoir until the reservoir is half full.
3. Raise and support the vehicle.
4. Remove the wheel and tire assembly.
5. Remove the 2 brake caliper bolts and position the brake caliper aside. Support the caliper using mechanic's wire.
6. Inspect the brake pads for wear and contamination.
7. Inspect the brake disc, machine or install a new front brake disc as necessary.
8. Remove the brake pads and clips. Discard the clips.

To install:

9. Install the new brake pad clips and the brake pads.

✳✳ WARNING

Protect the piston and boots when pushing the caliper piston into the caliper piston bores.

10. Using a suitable tool (C-clamp) and a worn brake pad, compress the disc brake caliper pistons into the caliper.
11. Position the brake caliper and install the 2 bolts. Tighten the lower bolt and then the upper bolt to 24 ft. lbs. (32 Nm).
12. Install the wheel and tire assembly and lower the vehicle.
13. Fill the brake master cylinder reservoir with clean brake fluid.
14. Test the brakes for normal operation.

2011 Models
See Figures 14 and 15.

✳✳ CAUTION

Do not use any fluid other than clean brake fluid meeting manufacturer's specification. Additionally, do not use brake fluid that has been previously drained. Following these instructions will help prevent system contamination, brake component damage and the risk of serious personal injury.

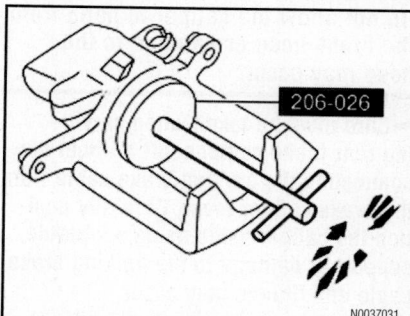

Fig. 14 Using the special tool to rotate the caliper piston clockwise to compress the piston into its cylinder

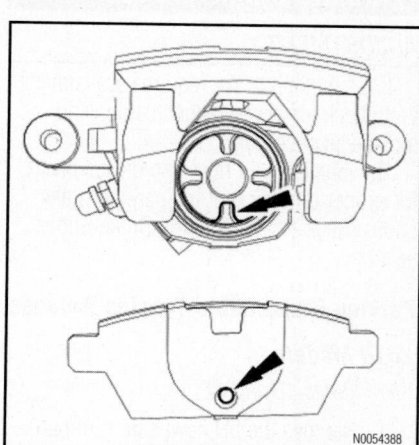

Fig. 15 Position the notch in the caliper piston so that it will correctly align with the pin on the backside of the inboard brake pad

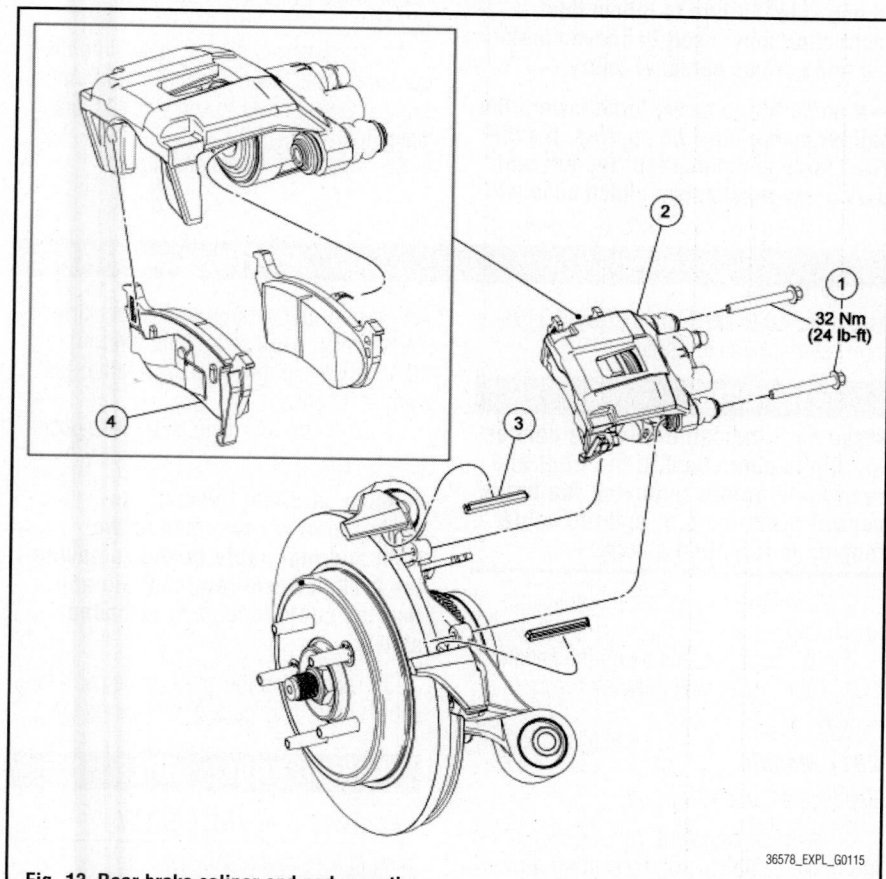

Fig. 13 Rear brake caliper and pad mounting

36578_EXPL_G0115

❋ CAUTION

Carefully read cautionary information on product label. For EMERGENCY MEDICAL INFORMATION seek medical advice. In the USA or Canada on Ford/Motorcraft products call: 1-800-959-3673. For additional information, consult the product Material Safety Data Sheet (MSDS), if available. Failure to follow these instructions may result in serious personal injury.

➡ **Do not spill brake fluid on painted or plastic surfaces or damage to the surface may occur. If brake fluid is spilled onto a painted or plastic surface, immediately wash the surface with water.**

1. Check the brake fluid level in the brake fluid reservoir. If required, remove fluid until the brake master cylinder reservoir is half full.
2. Remove the wheel and tire.
3. Remove the brake caliper bolts.

❋ WARNING

Do not allow the caliper to hang from the brake hose or damage to the hose may occur.

➡ **Care must be taken when servicing rear brake components without disconnecting the parking brake cable from the brake caliper lever. Carefully position the caliper aside using a suitable support or damage to the parking brake cable end fittings may occur.**

4. Using hand force and a rocking motion, separate the brake caliper from the anchor plate. Position the brake caliper aside, supported with mechanic's wire.

➡ **When the brake pads are separated from the brake caliper, new brake pads must be installed to prevent brake noise and shudder. The brake pads are one-time use only.**

5. Remove and discard the 2 brake pads and spring clips from the brake caliper anchor plate.

➡ **Do not remove the anchor plate guide pins. The guide pins are press fit to the brake caliper anchor plate. If the guide pins are damaged, a new anchor plate must be installed.**

6. Inspect the brake caliper anchor plate assembly:
   a. Check the guide pins and boots for binding or damage.
   b. Install a new brake caliper anchor plate if it is worn or damaged.

To install:

➡ **Always install new brake shoes or pads at both ends of an axle to reduce the possibility of brakes pulling vehicle to one side. Failure to follow this instruction may result in uneven braking and serious personal injury.**

➡ **A moderate to heavy force toward the caliper piston must be applied. If sufficient force is not applied, the internal park brake mechanism clutch cone will** not engage and the piston will not compress.

7. Using 206-026 (T87P-2588-A) (or equivalent such as OTC tool 7317A), rotate the caliper piston clockwise to compress the piston into its cylinder.
8. Clean the residual adhesive from the brake caliper fingers and piston using specified brake parts cleaner.
9. Position the notch in the caliper piston so that it will correctly align with the pin on the backside of the inboard brake pad.

➡ **Do not allow grease, oil, brake fluid or other contaminants to contact the pad lining material, or damage to components may occur. Do not install contaminated pads.**

10. Install the new spring clips and brake pads to the brake caliper anchor plate.

➡ **During installation, make sure brake flexible hose does not become twisted. A twisted brake hose may make contact with other components causing damage to the hose.**

11. Position the brake caliper and install the 2 bolts. Tighten to 24 ft. lbs. (33 Nm).
12. If necessary, fill the brake fluid reservoir with clean, specified brake fluid. Apply brakes several times to verify correct brake operation.
13. Install the wheel and tire.

BRAKES

PARKING BRAKE CABLES

ADJUSTMENT

If the parking brake requires adjustment first check for any damaged cables and replace as necessary.

On vehicles with rear disc brakes check for proper operation of the parking brake shoes. Refer to the "Parking Brake Shoes" section.

Parking Brake Cable Tension Release

2010 Models

See Figures 16 and 17.

1. Remove the LH cowl side trim panel.
2. With the help of an assistant, release the parking brake cable tension by pulling down on the intermediate cable at the cable-to-cable connector clip until the parking brake control sector rotates to its stop and a 0.15 inch (4 mm) x 5.9 inch (150 mm) retainer pin can be inserted.

❋ WARNING

Make sure the cable-to-cable connector clip is connected to the front and rear cable before removing the brake control retaining pin, and the cable tension is reloaded slowly.

3. Disconnect the cable-to-cable connector clip.
4. To reload the tension on the parking brake cable, follow the release procedure in reverse.

2011 Models

See Figures 18 and 19.

1. With an assistant, release the parking brake cable tension by pulling down on the front cable at the cable-to-cable

PARKING BRAKE

union until the parking brake control sector rotates to its stop and a 4 mm (0.15 in) x 150 mm (5.9 in) retainer pin can be inserted.

2. With the vehicle in NEUTRAL, position it on a hoist.

➡ **Make sure that the cable-to-cable union is connected to the front and rear cable before removing the brake control retaining pin and that the cable tension is reloaded slowly.**

3. Disconnect the cable at the cable-to-cable union by releasing the locking tab.

PARKING BRAKE SHOES

REMOVAL & INSTALLATION

See Figures 20 and 21.

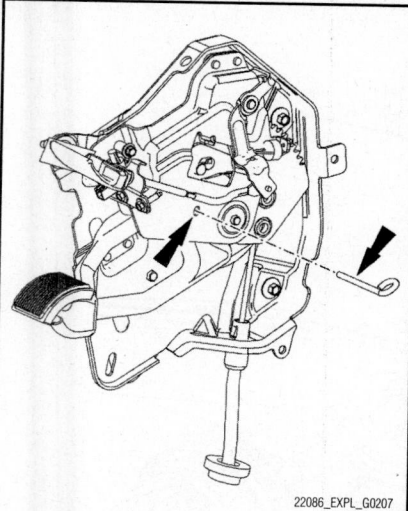

Fig. 16 With the help of an assistant, release the parking brake cable tension by pulling down on the intermediate cable at the cable-to-cable connector clip until the parking brake control sector rotates to its stop and a 0.15 inch (4 mm) x 5.9 inch (150 mm) retainer pin can be inserted—2010 Models

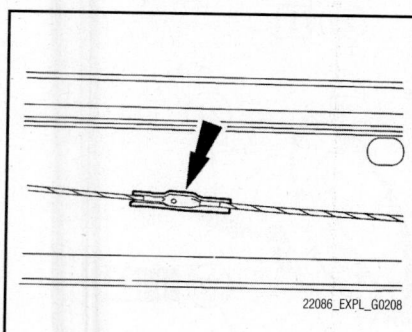

Fig. 17 Disconnect the cable-to-cable connector clip—2010 Models

1. Before servicing the vehicle, refer to the Precautions.
2. Remove the rear brake disc.
3. Remove the parking brake shoe adjusting screw.
4. Remove the parking brake shoe adjusting screw spring.
5. Remove the 2 parking brake shoe hold-down springs and pins.
6. Remove the parking brake shoe retracting spring and the parking brake shoes.

To install:
7. Position the parking brake shoes and attach the retracting spring.
8. Install the 2 parking brake shoe hold-down pins and springs.
9. Install the parking brake shoe adjusting screw spring.

➡ **Completely retract the parking brake adjusting screw before installation.**

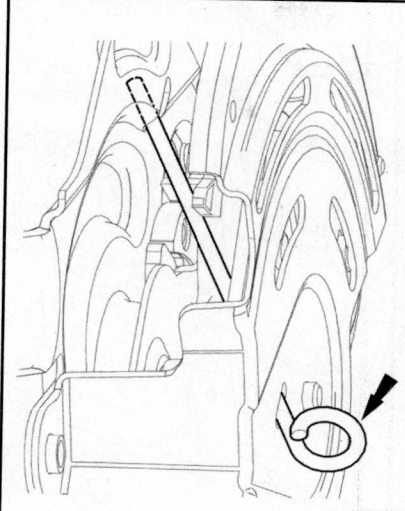

Fig. 18 With an assistant, release the parking brake cable tension by pulling down on the front cable at the cable-to-cable union until the parking brake control sector rotates to its stop and a 4 mm (0.15 in) x 150 mm (5.9 in) retainer pin can be inserted—2011 Models

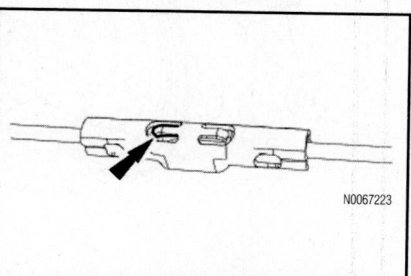

Fig. 19 Disconnect the cable at the cable-to-cable union by releasing the locking tab

10. Install the brake shoe adjusting screw.
11. Use a brake adjusting gauge to measure the inside diameter of the parking brake drum.
12. Adjust the parking brake shoe clearance of 0.04 inch (1.07 mm) less than the inside diameter of the parking brake drum. Make sure that the parking brake shoes are correctly centered and measure across the center point of the shoes. Rotate the parking brake shoe adjuster wheel to achieve the correct parking brake shoe-to-brake disc clearance.
13. Install the rear brake disc.
14. To reload the tension on the parking brake cable, follow the release procedure in reverse.

ADJUSTMENT

➡ **Make sure the parking brake is fully released.**

1. Using the release handle, release the parking brake control.
2. Remove the rear brake disc. Refer to Rotor in Rear Disc Brakes
3. Using the Brake Adjusting Gauge, measure the inside diameter of the drum portion of the rear brake disc and set the locking screw. Record the measurement.
4. Place the Brake Adjusting Gauge over the widest diameter of the parking brake shoes.
5. Adjust the parking brake shoe clearance to 0.021 inches (0.54 mm) less than the inside diameter of the drum portion of the rear brake disc.
6. Rotate the parking brake shoe adjuster to achieve the correct parking brake shoe-to-brake disc clearance.
7. Install the rear brake disc.
8. Test the parking brake for normal operation.

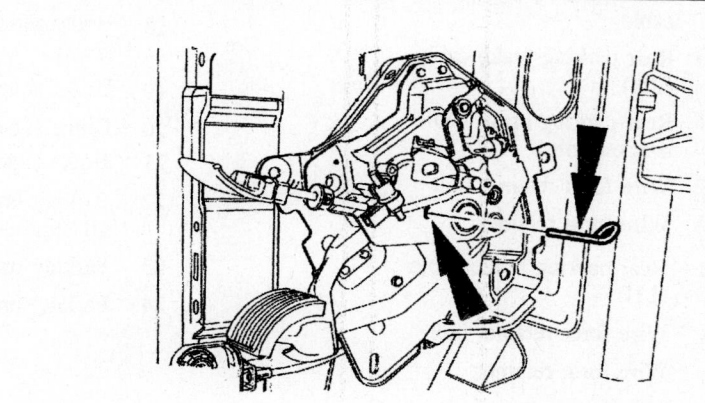

Fig. 20 Parking brake control

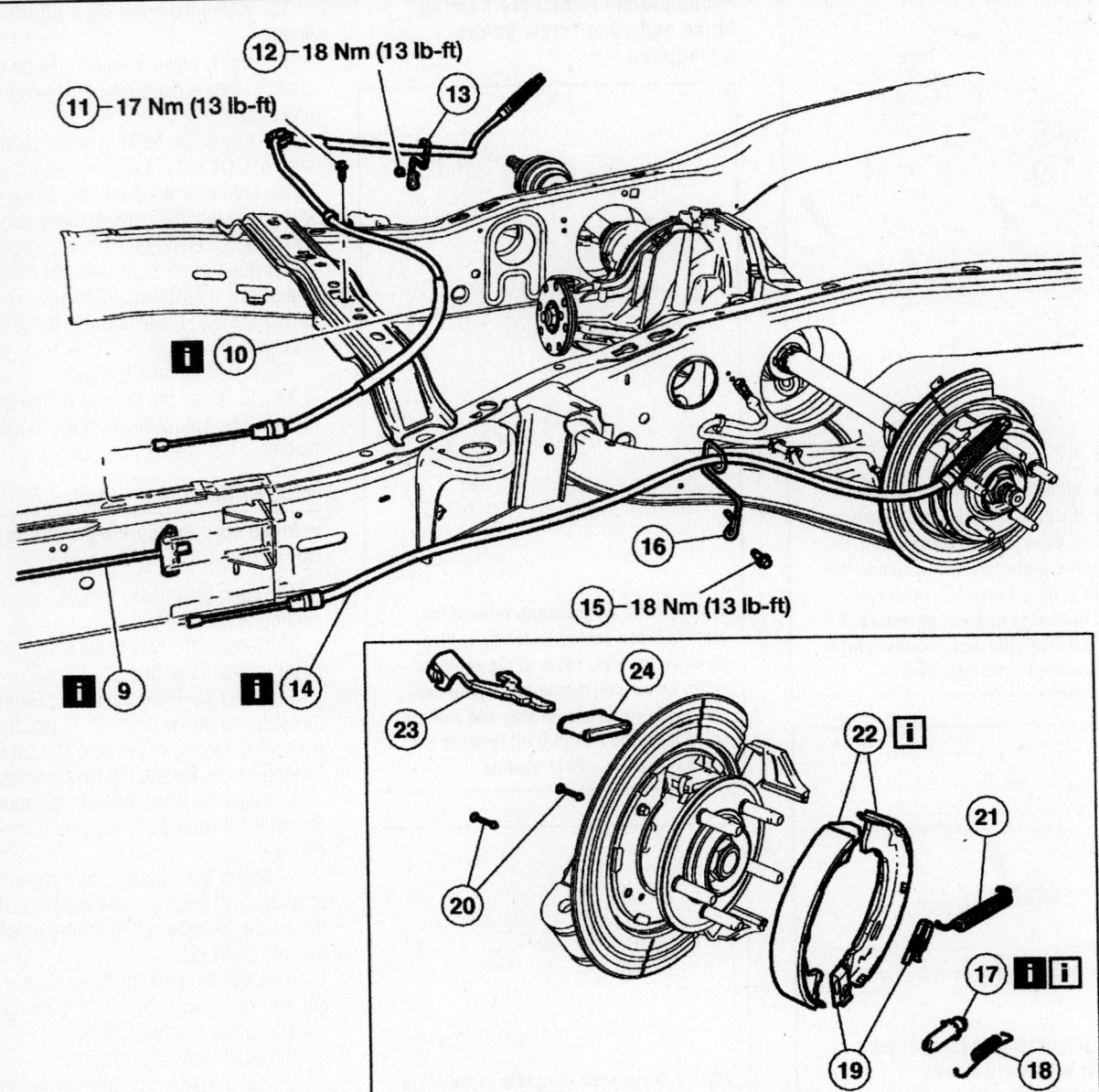

Fig. 21 Parking brake shoes and related parts

9 Intermediate parking brake cable
10 Rear parking brake cable (RH)
11 Rear parking brake cable bracket bolt
12 Wire form retainer bolt
13 Wire form retainer
14 Rear parking brake cable (LH)
15 Wire form retainer bolt
16 Wire form retainer

17 Brake shoe adjusting screw
18 Brake shoe adjusting screw spring
19 Brake shoe hold-down spring
20 Brake shoe hold-down pins
21 Brake shoe retracting spring
22 Parking brake shoe kit (one kit required)
23 Parking brake lever (RH/LH)
24 Parking brake lever boot

06017-EXPL-G164

CHASSIS ELECTRICAL
AIR BAG (SUPPLEMENTAL RESTRAINT SYSTEM)

GENERAL INFORMATION

SERVICE PRECAUTIONS

✳✳ CAUTION

Batteries contain sulfuric acid and produce explosive gases. Work in a well-ventilated area. Do not allow the battery to come in contact with flames, sparks or burning substances. Avoid contact with skin, eyes or clothing. Shield eyes when working near the battery to protect against possible splashing of acid solution. In case of acid contact with skin or eyes, flush immediately with water for a minimum of 15 minutes, then get prompt medical attention. If acid is swallowed, call a physician immediately. Failure to follow these instructions may result in serious personal injury.

✳✳ CAUTION

Always deplete the backup power supply before repairing or installing any new front or side air bag supplemental restraint system (SRS) component and before servicing, removing, installing, adjusting or striking components near the front or side impact sensors or the restraints control module (RCM). Nearby components include doors, instrument panel, console, door latches, strikers, seats and hood latches.

✳✳ CAUTION

To deplete the backup power supply energy, disconnect the battery ground cable and wait at least 1 minute. Be sure to disconnect auxiliary batteries and power supplies (if equipped). Failure to follow these instructions may result in serious personal injury or death in the event of an accidental deployment.

✳✳ CAUTION

Always lift a plastic-cased battery with a battery carrier or with hands on opposite corners. Excessive pressure on the battery end walls may cause acid to flow through the vent caps, resulting in personal injury and/or damage to the vehicle or battery.

✳✳ WARNING

If equipped with the CD6 audio unit, precautions must be taken when the battery has been disconnected. When reconnecting the battery, make sure no interruption of power occurs for 30 seconds. If power is interrupted during the first 30 seconds, permanent damage to the CD6 audio unit will result.

➡When the battery is disconnected and connected, some abnormal drive symptoms may occur while the vehicle relearns its adaptive strategy. The vehicle may need to be driven to relearn its strategy.

➡When disconnecting the battery ground cable to interrupt power to the vehicle electrical system, disconnect the battery ground cable only. It is not necessary to disconnect the positive battery cable.

✳✳ CAUTION

Disconnect and isolate the battery negative cable before beginning any airbag system component diagnosis, testing, removal, or installation procedures. Allow system capacitor to discharge for two minutes before beginning any component service. This will disable the airbag system. Failure to disable the airbag system may result in accidental airbag deployment, personal injury, or death.

✳✳ CAUTION

Do not place an intact undeployed airbag face down on a solid surface. The airbag will propel into the air if accidentally deployed and may result in personal injury or death.

✳✳ CAUTION

When carrying or handling an undeployed airbag, the trim side (face) of the airbag should be pointing away from the body to minimize possibility of injury if accidental deployment occurs. Failure to do this may result in personal injury or death.

✳✳ CAUTION

Replace airbag system components with original equipment replacement parts. Substitute parts may appear interchangeable, but internal differences may result in inferior occupant protection. Failure to do so may result in occupant personal injury or death.

✳✳ CAUTION

Wear safety glasses, rubber gloves, and long sleeved clothing when cleaning powder residue from vehicle after an airbag deployment. Powder residue emitted from a deployed airbag can cause skin irritation. Flush affected area with cool water if irritation is experienced. If nasal or throat irritation is experienced, exit the vehicle for fresh air until the irritation ceases. If irritation continues, see a physician.

✳✳ CAUTION

The safety belt pretensioner is a pyrotechnic device. Always wear safety glasses when repairing an air bag equipped vehicle and when handling a safety belt buckle pretensioner or safety belt retractor pretensioner. Never probe a pretensioner electrical connector. Doing so could result in pretensioner or air bag deployment and could result in personal injury.

✳✳ CAUTION

Do not use a replacement airbag that is not in the original packaging. This may result in improper deployment, personal injury, or death.

✳✳ CAUTION

To reduce the risk of personal injury, do not use any memory saver devices.

✳✳ CAUTION

The factory installed fasteners, screws and bolts used to fasten airbag components have a special coating and are specifically designed for the airbag system. Do not use substitute fasteners. Use only original equipment fasteners listed in the parts catalog when fastener replacement is required.

✳✳ CAUTION

During, and following, any child restraint anchor service, due to impact event or vehicle repair, carefully inspect all mounting hardware, tether straps, and anchors for proper installation, operation, or damage. If a child restraint anchor is found damaged in any way, the anchor must be replaced. Failure to do this may result in personal injury or death.

✳✳ CAUTION

Never probe the connectors on the air bag module or safety canopy module. Doing so can result in air bag deployment, which can result in personal injury.

Deployed and non–deployed airbags may or may not have live pyrotechnic material within the airbag inflator.

Do not dispose of driver/passenger/curtain airbags or seat belt tensioners unless you are sure of complete deployment.

Dispose of deployed airbags and tensioners consistent with state, provincial, local, and federal regulations.

✳✳ CAUTION

Anytime the Safety Canopy® or side air curtain module has deployed, a new headliner and new A-, B-, C- and D-pillar upper trim panels and attaching hardware must be installed. Remove any other damaged components and hardware and install new components and hardware as needed. Failure to follow these instructions may result in the Safety Canopy® or side air curtain module deploying incorrectly and increases the risk of serious personal injury or death in a crash.

✳✳ CAUTION

Always carry or place a live Safety Canopy®, or side air curtain module, with the module and tear seam pointed away from your body. Failure to follow this instruction may result in serious personal injury or death in the event of an accidental deployment.

✳✳ CAUTION

Do not obstruct or place objects in the deployment path of the Safety Canopy® or side air curtain module. Failure to follow this instruction may result in the Safety Canopy® or side air curtain module deploying incorrectly and increases the risk of serious personal injury or death in a crash.

✳✳ CAUTION

Never probe the electrical connectors on air bag, Safety Canopy® or side air curtain modules. Failure to follow this instruction may result in the accidental deployment of these modules, which increases the risk of serious personal injury or death.

DISARMING (DEPOWERING) THE SYSTEM

2010 Models

1. Before servicing the vehicle, refer to Precautions.

If a seat equipped with a seat mounted side air bag and/or a safety belt pretensioner (if equipped) system is being serviced, the supplemental restraint system (SRS) must be de-powered.

The air bag warning lamp illuminates when the RCM fuse is removed and the ignition switch is ON. This is normal operation and does not indicate a supplemental restraint system (SRS) fault.

2. Turn all vehicle accessories OFF.
3. Turn the ignition switch to OFF.
4. At the central junction box (CJB), located below the left side of the instrument panel, remove the restraints control module (RCM) fuse (10A) from the CJB.
5. Turn the ignition **ON** and visually monitor the air bag indicator for at least 30 seconds. The air bag indicator will remain lit continuously (no flashing) if the correct RCM fuse has been removed. If the air bag indicator does not remain lit continuously, remove the correct RCM fuse before proceeding.
6. Turn the ignition **OFF**.

✳✳ WARNING

To avoid accidental deployment and possible personal injury, the backup power supply must be depleted before repairing or replacing any front or side air bag supplemental restraint system (SRS) components and before servicing, replacing, adjusting or striking components

near the front or side air bag sensors or RCM, such as doors, instrument panel, console, door latches, strikers, seats and hood latches. The side impact sensors (if equipped) are located at or near the base of the B-pillars and C-pillars.

✳✳ CAUTION

To deplete the backup power supply energy, disconnect the battery ground cable and wait at least one minute. Be sure to disconnect auxiliary batteries and power supplies (if equipped). Disconnect the battery ground cable and wait at least one minute.

2011 Models

With Intelligent Access (IA)

✳✳ CAUTION

Always wear eye protection when servicing a vehicle. Failure to follow this instruction may result in serious personal injury.

✳✳ CAUTION

Never probe the electrical connectors on air bag, Safety Canopy® or side air curtain modules. Failure to follow this instruction may result in the accidental deployment of these modules, which increases the risk of serious personal injury or death.

✳✳ CAUTION

To reduce the risk of accidental deployment, do not use any memory saver devices. Failure to follow this instruction may result in serious personal injury or death.

➡The air bag warning indicator illuminates when the correct Restraints Control Module (RCM) fuse is removed and the ignition is ON.

1. Turn all vehicle accessories OFF.
2. Turn the ignition OFF.
3. At the Body Control Module (BCM), located in the Left Hand (LH) lower kick panel, remove the lower kick panel fuse cover and the Restraints Control Module (RCM) fuse 37 (10A) from the Body Control Module (BCM).
4. Turn the ignition ON and monitor the air bag warning indicator for at least 30 seconds. The air bag warning indicator remains lit continuously (no flashing) if the correct

Restraints Control Module (RCM) fuse is removed. If the air bag warning indicator is not lit continuously, remove the correct Restraints Control Module (RCM) fuse before proceeding.

5. Turn the ignition OFF.

✳✳ CAUTION

Always deplete the backup power supply before repairing or installing any new front or side air bag Supplemental Restraint System (SRS) component and before servicing, removing, installing, adjusting or striking components near the front or side impact sensors or the Restraints Control Module (RCM). Nearby components include doors, instrument panel, console, door latches, strikers, seats and hood latches. To deplete the backup power supply energy, disconnect the battery ground cable and wait at least 1 minute. Be sure to disconnect auxiliary batteries and power supplies (if equipped). Failure to follow these instructions may result in serious personal injury or death in the event of an accidental deployment.

6. Disconnect the battery ground cable and wait at least one minute.

Without Intelligent Access (IA)

✳✳ CAUTION

Always wear eye protection when servicing a vehicle. Failure to follow this instruction may result in serious personal injury.

✳✳ CAUTION

Never probe the electrical connectors on air bag, Safety Canopy® or side air curtain modules. Failure to follow this instruction may result in the accidental deployment of these modules, which increases the risk of serious personal injury or death.

✳✳ CAUTION

To reduce the risk of accidental deployment, do not use any memory saver devices. Failure to follow this instruction may result in serious personal injury or death.

➡ The air bag warning indicator illuminates when the correct Restraints Con-

trol Module (RCM) fuse is removed and the ignition is ON.

1. Turn all vehicle accessories OFF.
2. Turn the ignition OFF.
3. At the Body Control Module (BCM), located in the Left Hand (LH) lower kick panel, remove the lower kick panel fuse cover and the Restraints Control Module (RCM) fuse 37 (10A) from the Body Control Module (BCM).
4. Turn the ignition ON and monitor the air bag warning indicator for at least 30 seconds. The air bag warning indicator remains lit continuously (no flashing) if the correct Restraints Control Module (RCM) fuse is removed. If the air bag warning indicator is not lit continuously, remove the correct Restraints Control Module (RCM) fuse before proceeding.
5. Turn the ignition OFF.

✳✳ CAUTION

Always deplete the backup power supply before repairing or installing any new front or side air bag Supplemental Restraint System (SRS) component and before servicing, removing, installing, adjusting or striking components near the front or side impact sensors or the Restraints Control Module (RCM). Nearby components include doors, instrument panel, console, door latches, strikers, seats and hood latches. To deplete the backup power supply energy, disconnect the battery ground cable and wait at least 1 minute. Be sure to disconnect auxiliary batteries and power supplies (if equipped). Failure to follow these instructions may result in serious personal injury or death in the event of an accidental deployment.

6. Disconnect the battery ground cable and wait at least one minute.

ARMING (REPOWERING) THE SYSTEM

✳✳ CAUTION

The restraint system diagnostic tool is for restraint system service only. Remove from vehicle prior to road use. Failure to remove could result in injury and possible violation of vehicle safety standards.

Make sure all restraint system diagnostic tool(s) that may have been

installed during the repair have been removed from the vehicle and all SRS components are connected.

1. Before servicing the vehicle, refer to the Precautions.
2. Turn the ignition switch from **OFF** to **ON**.
3. Install the RCM fuse to the CJB.

✳✳ CAUTION

Be sure that nobody is in the vehicle and that there is nothing blocking or set in front of any air bag module when the battery ground cable is connected.

4. Connect the battery ground cable.
5. Prove out the supplemental restraint system (SRS) as follows:

   a. Turn the ignition key from **ON** to **OFF**. Wait 10 seconds, then turn the key back to ON and visually monitor the air bag indicator with the air bag modules installed. The air bag indicator will light continuously for approximately 6 seconds and then turn off. If an air bag supplemental restraint system (SRS) fault is present, the air bag indicator will:

   - Fail to light.
   - Remain lit continuously.
   - Flash.

   b. The flashing might not occur until approximately 30 seconds after the ignition switch has been turned from the **OFF** to the **ON** position. This is the time required for the restraints control module (RCM) to complete the testing of the SRS. If the air bag indicator is inoperative and a SRS fault exists, a chime will sound in a pattern of 5 sets of 5 beeps. If this occurs, the air bag indicator and any SRS fault discovered must be diagnosed and repaired.

6. Clear all continuous DTCs from the restraints control module using a scan tool.

2011 Models

With Intelligent Access (IA)

See Figures 22 and 23.

✳✳ CAUTION

Always wear eye protection when servicing a vehicle. Failure to follow this instruction may result in serious personal injury.

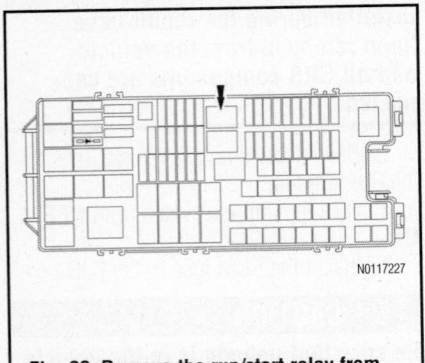

Fig. 22 Remove the run/start relay from the Battery Junction Box (BJB)

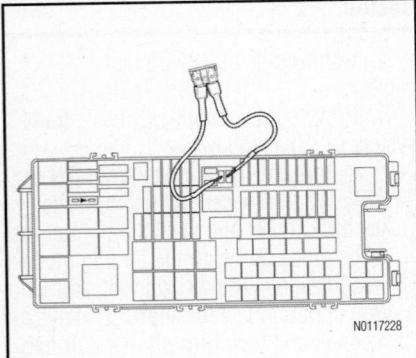

Fig. 23 Install a 30A fused jumper wire in Battery Junction Box (BJB) run/start relay cavities 3 and 5, as shown

✳✳ CAUTION

Never probe the electrical connectors on air bag, Safety Canopy® or side air curtain modules. Failure to follow this instruction may result in the accidental deployment of these modules, which increases the risk of serious personal injury or death.

✳✳ CAUTION

To reduce the risk of accidental deployment, do not use any memory saver devices. Failure to follow this instruction may result in serious personal injury or death.

→The air bag warning indicator illuminates when the correct Restraints Control Module (RCM) fuse is removed and the ignition is ON.

1. Install Restraints Control Module (RCM) fuse 37 (10A) to the Body Control Module (BCM) and close the cover.
2. Remove the run/start relay from the Battery Junction Box (BJB).

---

3. Install a 30A fused jumper wire in Battery Junction Box (BJB) run/start relay cavities 3 and 5, as shown.

✳✳ CAUTION

Make sure no one is in the vehicle and there is nothing blocking or placed in front of any air bag module when the battery is connected. Failure to follow these instructions may result in serious personal injury in the event of an accidental deployment.

4. Connect the battery ground cable.
5. Wait at least 30 seconds, then remove the fused jumper wire from the Battery Junction Box (BJB).
6. Install the run/start relay in the Battery Junction Box (BJB) and install the cover.
7. Prove out the Supplemental Restraint System (SRS): Wait 10 seconds, then turn the ignition ON and monitor the air bag warning indicator with the air bag modules installed. The air bag warning indicator illuminates continuously for approximately 6 seconds and then turns off. If a Supplemental Restraint System (SRS) fault is present, the air bag warning indicator:
   - fails to light.
   - remains lit continuously.
   - flashes.
8. The flashing may not occur until approximately 30 seconds after the ignition has been turned from OFF to ON. This is the time required for the Restraints Control Module (RCM) to complete the testing of the Supplemental Restraint System (SRS). If the air bag warning indicator is inoperative and a Supplemental Restraint System (SRS) fault exists, a chime sounds in a pattern of 5 sets of 5 beeps. If this occurs, diagnose and repair the air bag warning indicator and any Supplemental Restraint System (SRS) faults.
9. Clear all Continuous Memory Diagnostic Trouble Codes (CMDTCs) from the Restraints Control Module (RCM) and
10. Occupant Classification System Module (OCSM) using a scan tool.

Without Intelligent Access (IA)

✳✳ CAUTION

Always wear eye protection when servicing a vehicle. Failure to follow this instruction may result in serious personal injury.

✳✳ CAUTION

Never probe the electrical connectors on air bag, Safety Canopy® or side air curtain modules. Failure to follow this instruction may result in the accidental deployment of these modules, which increases the risk of serious personal injury or death.

✳✳ CAUTION

To reduce the risk of accidental deployment, do not use any memory saver devices. Failure to follow this instruction may result in serious personal injury or death.

→The air bag warning indicator illuminates when the correct Restraints Control Module (RCM) fuse is removed and the ignition is ON.

1. Turn the ignition from OFF to ON.
2. Install Restraints Control Module (RCM) fuse 37 (10A) to the Body Control Module (BCM) and close the cover.

✳✳ CAUTION

Make sure no one is in the vehicle and there is nothing blocking or placed in front of any air bag module when the battery is connected. Failure to follow these instructions may result in serious personal injury in the event of an accidental deployment.

3. Connect the battery ground cable.
4. Prove out the Supplemental Restraint System (SRS): Turn the ignition from ON to OFF. Wait 10 seconds, then turn the ignition back to ON and monitor the air bag warning indicator with the air bag modules installed. The air bag warning indicator illuminates continuously for approximately 6 seconds and then turns off. If a Supplemental Restraint System (SRS) fault is present, the air bag warning indicator:
   - fails to light.
   - remains lit continuously.
   - flashes.

→The flashing may not occur until approximately 30 seconds after the ignition has been turned from OFF to ON. This is the time required for the Restraints Control Module (RCM) to complete the testing of the Supplemental Restraint System (SRS). If the air bag warning indicator is inoperative and a Supplemental Restraint System (SRS) fault exists, a chime sounds in a pattern of 5 sets of 5 beeps. If this occurs, diagnose and repair the air bag warning indicator and any Supplemental Restraint System (SRS) faults.

5. Clear all continuous Diagnostic Trouble Codes (DTCs) from the Restraints Control Module (RCM) and Occupant Classification System Module (OCSM) using a scan tool.

CLOCKSPRING CENTERING

2010 Models

See Figures 24 through 28.

1. Before servicing the vehicle, refer to Precautions.

2. Disarm the system. Refer to Disarming the System.

3. Make sure the road wheels are in the straight-ahead position.

4. Remove the 2 steering wheel back cover plugs.

5. Remove the 2 driver air bag module bolts.

6. Partially remove the driver air bag module from the steering wheel.

7. Disconnect the driver air bag module electrical connectors and carefully remove the airbag to a proper location.

✳✳ WARNING

The clockspring electrical connectors are unique and cannot be reversed when connected to the driver air bag module. Match the electrical connector key to the keyway in the driver air bag module. Do not force the electrical connectors into the driver air bag module.

8. Disconnect the horn switch electrical connector and remove the driver air bag module.

9. Loosen the steering wheel bolt.

✳✳ WARNING

Removing the steering wheel without using a puller can damage the column bearings.

10. Using the special tool, separate the steering wheel from the steering column.

➡**A new bolt must be installed.**

11. Remove and discard the steering wheel bolt.

12. Remove the steering wheel.

13. Remove the 2 steering column opening cover screws.

14. Remove the steering column opening cover.

15. Remove the 3 lower steering column shroud screws.

16. Remove the lower steering column shroud.

17. Remove the upper steering column shroud. Lift where shown, releasing the retaining clips and rotate the upper steering column trim panel out of the instrument cluster finish panel. Remove the upper steering column shroud hard shell.

18. If installing the same clockspring, apply 2 strips of masking tape across the clockspring to prevent accidental rotation when the clockspring is removed.

19. Remove the multifunction switch screw.

20. While releasing the retaining tab at the top of the multifunction switch, slide the multifunction switch up and out of the way.

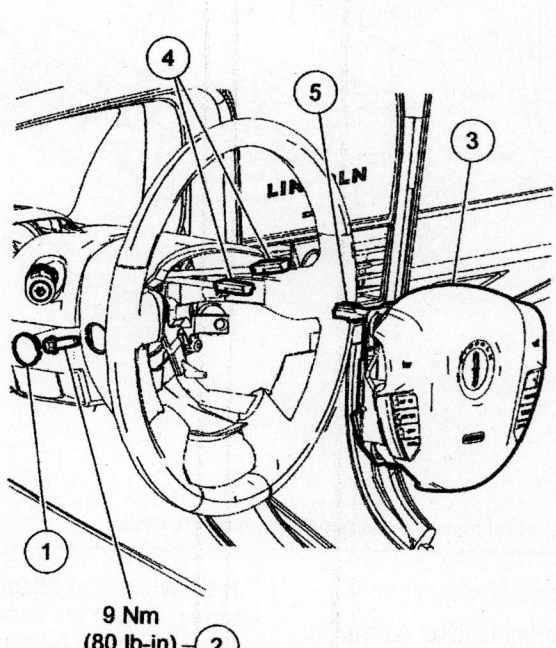

9 Nm
(80 lb-in) – 2

1 Steering wheel back cover plug (2 required)

2 Driver air bag module bolt (2 required)

3 Driver air bag module

4 Driver air bag module electrical connectors

5 Horn switch electrical connector

06017-EXPL-G125

Fig. 24 Air bag module—generic shown most are similar

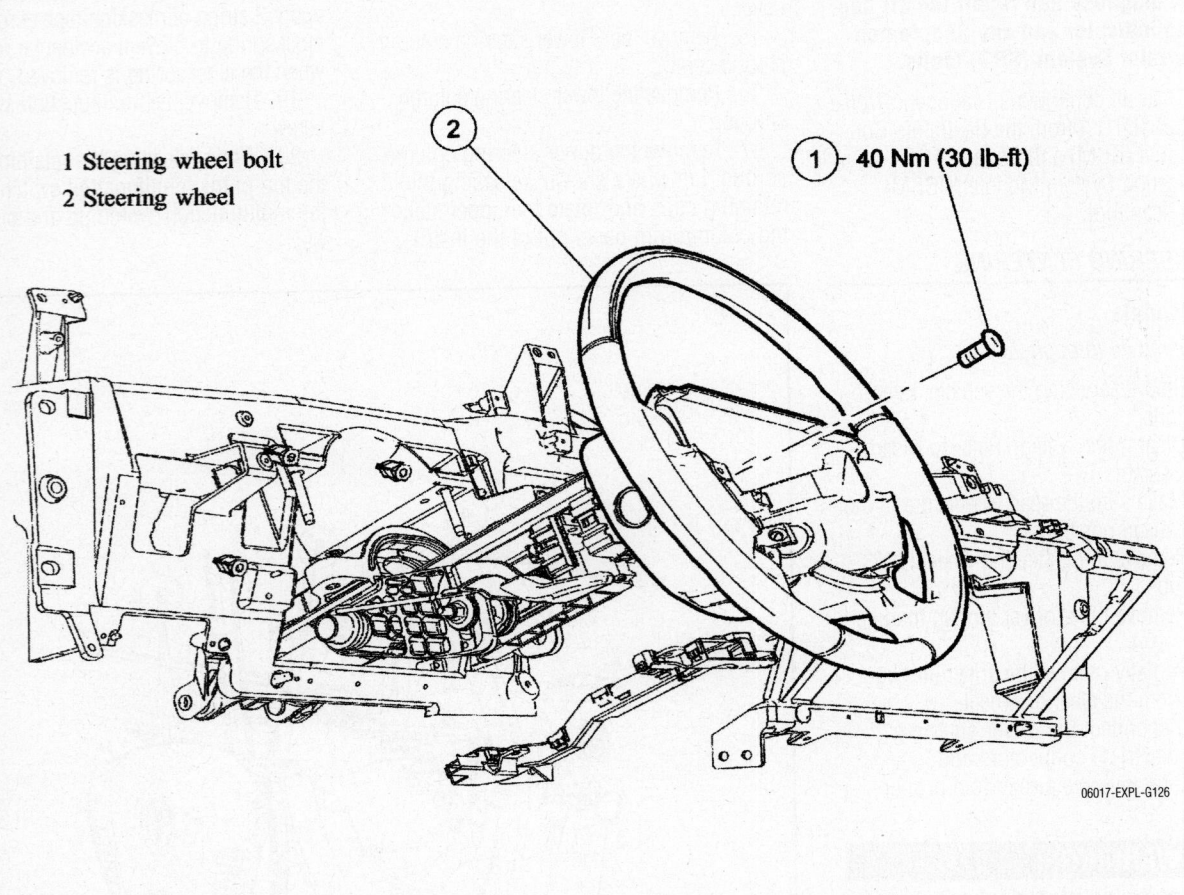

1 Steering wheel bolt
2 Steering wheel

1 — 40 Nm (30 lb-ft)

06017-EXPL-G126

Fig. 25 Steering wheel removal—generic shown, most are similar

21. Remove the 2 clockspring screws.

➡**If the clockspring is to be reinstalled, do not allow the clockspring to turn from its removal position.**

22. Disconnect the 3 clockspring electrical connectors and remove the clockspring.

23. Remove the 3 clockspring mounting bracket screws and discard the clockspring mounting bracket if damaged.

To install:

24. Position the clockspring mounting bracket, if removed.

25. Install the 3 clockspring mounting bracket screws.

26. Connect the 3 clockspring electrical connectors.

❋❋ CAUTION

Incorrect centralization may result in premature component failure. If in

doubt when centralizing the clock-spring, repeat the centralizing procedure. Failure to follow this instruction may result in personal injury.

❋❋ WARNING

Make sure the road wheels are in the straight-ahead position.

27. If the vehicle's clockspring has rotated out of the center position, follow these steps to center the clockspring.

a. Hold the clockspring outer housing stationary.

❋❋ WARNING

Overturning will destroy the clock-spring. The internal ribbon wire acts as the stop and can be broken from its internal connection.

b. While turning the clockspring rotor counterclockwise, carefully feel for the ribbon wire to run out of length and for a slight resistance. Stop turning at this point.

28. Starting with the clockspring inner rotor, wiring and connector in the 12 o'clock position, rotate the inner rotor clockwise through 2 revolutions to center the clock-spring.

29. The clockspring inner rotor, wiring and connector must be in the 12 o'clock position.

❋❋ WARNING

To prevent damage to the clock-spring, make sure the road wheels are in the straight-ahead position.

➡**The clockspring inner rotor, wiring and connector must be in the**

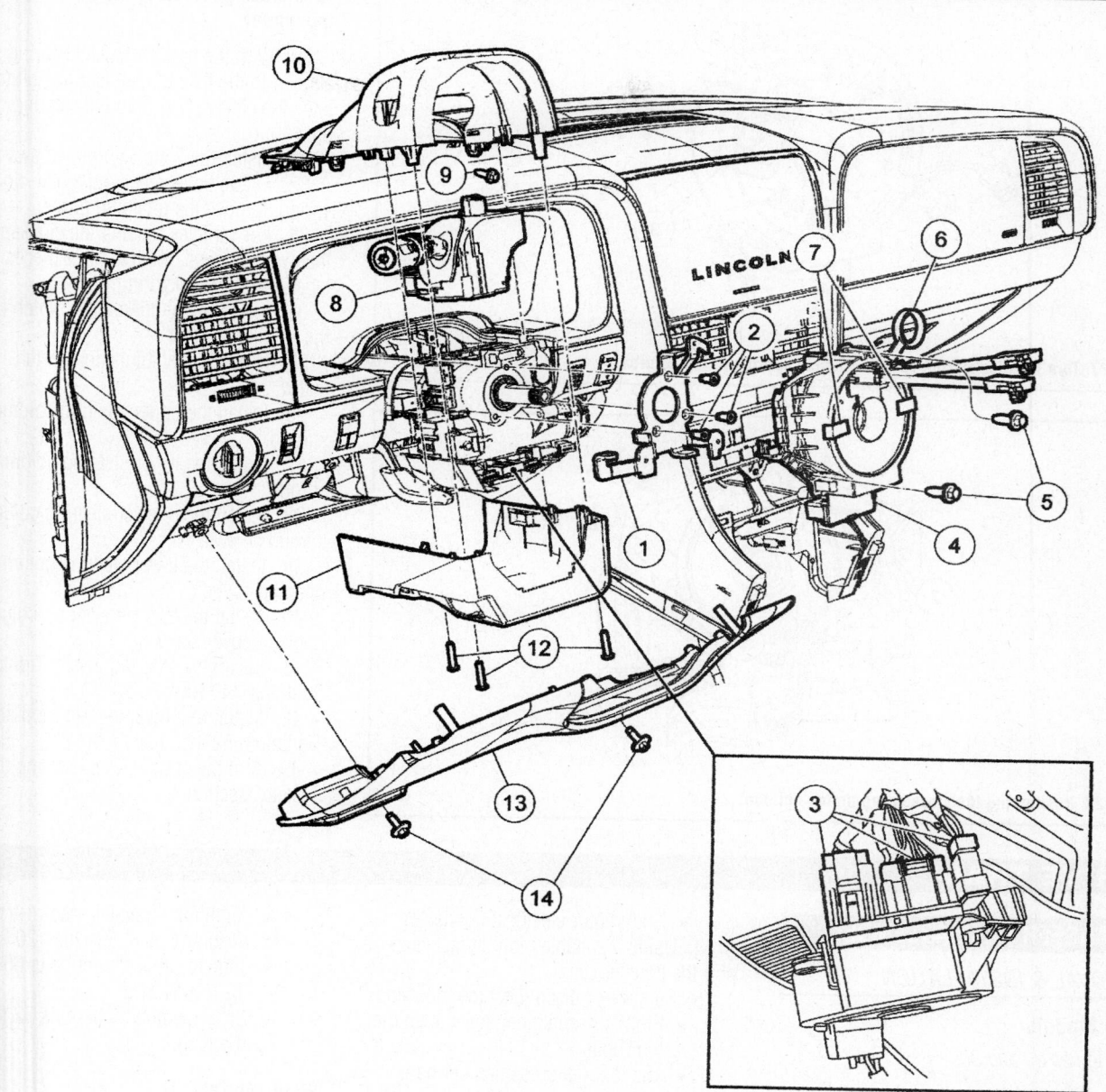

1 Clockspring mounting bracket

2 Clockspring mounting bracket screws (3 required)

3 Clockspring electrical connectors (3 required)

4 Clockspring

5 Clockspring screws (2 required)

6 Retaining pin

7 Tape

8 Multi-function switch

9 Multi-function switch screw

10 Upper steering column shroud

11 Lower steering column shroud

12 Lower steering column shroud screws (3 required)

13 Lower steering column opening cover

14 Lower steering column opening cover screws (2 required)

06017-EXPL-G127

Fig. 26 Clockspring removal—generic shown most are similar

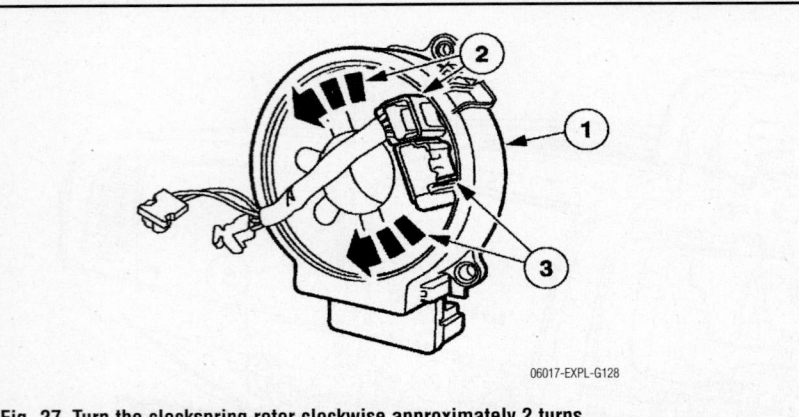

06017-EXPL-G128

Fig. 27 Turn the clockspring rotor clockwise approximately 2 turns

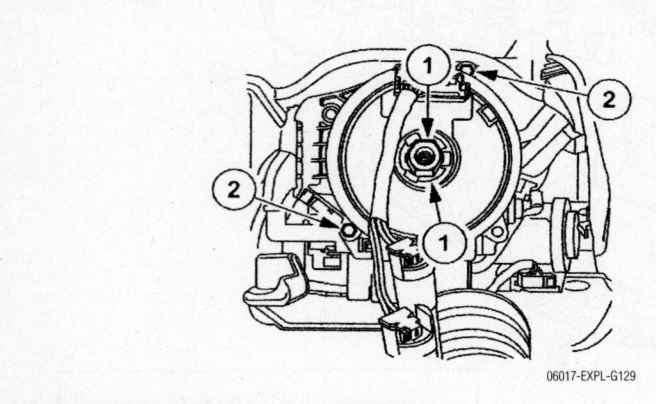

06017-EXPL-G129

Fig. 28 Positioning the clockspring on the column

12 o'clock position to install the steering wheel.

30. With the flats of the clockspring aligned to the flats of the steering column, slide the clockspring onto the steering column.

31. Install the 2 clockspring screws.

32. For vehicles receiving a new clockspring, remove the retaining pin.

33. For vehicles reusing the clockspring that was removed, remove the 2 pieces of tape from the clockspring.

34. Install the multifunction switch onto the steering column.

35. Install the multifunction switch screw.

36. Install the upper steering column shroud.

37. Install the lower steering column shroud.

38. Install the 3 lower steering column shroud screws.

39. Install the lower steering column opening cover.

40. Install the 2 lower steering column opening cover screws.

41. Install the steering wheel. Tighten to 30 ft. lbs. (40 Nm).

42. Install the driver air bag module. Tighten to 62 inch lbs. (7 Nm).

43. Arm the system. See "Arming the System" section.

DRIVE TRAIN

TRANSFER CASE ASSEMBLY

REMOVAL & INSTALLATION

2010 Models

See Figures 29 and 30.

1. Before servicing the vehicle, refer to Precautions.

2. Place the transmission in **Neutral**.

3. Remove or disconnect the following:
   - Negative battery cable
   - Skid plate, if equipped

➡️**Drain the transfer case if disassembly is necessary.**

➡️**Match-mark the front and rear driveshaft yokes and pinion flange and the rear driveshaft yoke and rear output flange.**

   - Rear driveshaft, refer to Driveshaft in Rear Drive Axle
   - Front driveshaft, refer to Driveshaft in Front Drive Axle
   - Vent tube

   - Shift motor electrical connector

4. Using a suitable high lift jack, support the transfer case.

5. Remove or disconnect the following:
   - Right crossmember cover, then the four bolts
   - The four left crossmember bolts
   - Heat shields from the crossmember
   - Transmission mount nuts
   - The seven bolts and separate the transfer case from the extension housing

6. Lower the transfer case from the vehicle.

7. Remove and discard the transfer case-to-extension housing gasket. Clean the gasket surfaces.

To install:

8. Installation is the reverse of the removal procedure.

9. Use a new transfer case gasket.

10. Replace aluminum transfer case-to-transmission bolts.

11. Observe the following tightening specifications:

   - Aluminum transfer case-to-transmission bolts 15 ft. lbs. (20 Nm).
   - Transmission mount bolts 66 ft. lbs. (90 Nm)
   - Crossmember bolts/nuts 72 ft. lbs. (98 Nm).

2011 Models

See Figures 31 through 33.

➡️**On 2011 Models, the transfer case is called the Power Transfer Unit (PTU).**

1. With the vehicle in NEUTRAL, position it on a hoist.

2. Remove the Right Hand (RH) halfshaft, as outlined in this section.

3. Remove the Right Hand (RH) catalytic converter, as outlined in the Engine Mechanical Section..

➡️**To maintain the initial driveshaft balance, index-mark the driveshaft flange and the output flange.**

4. Remove the 4 driveshaft-to-output flange bolts, then disconnect the driveshaft

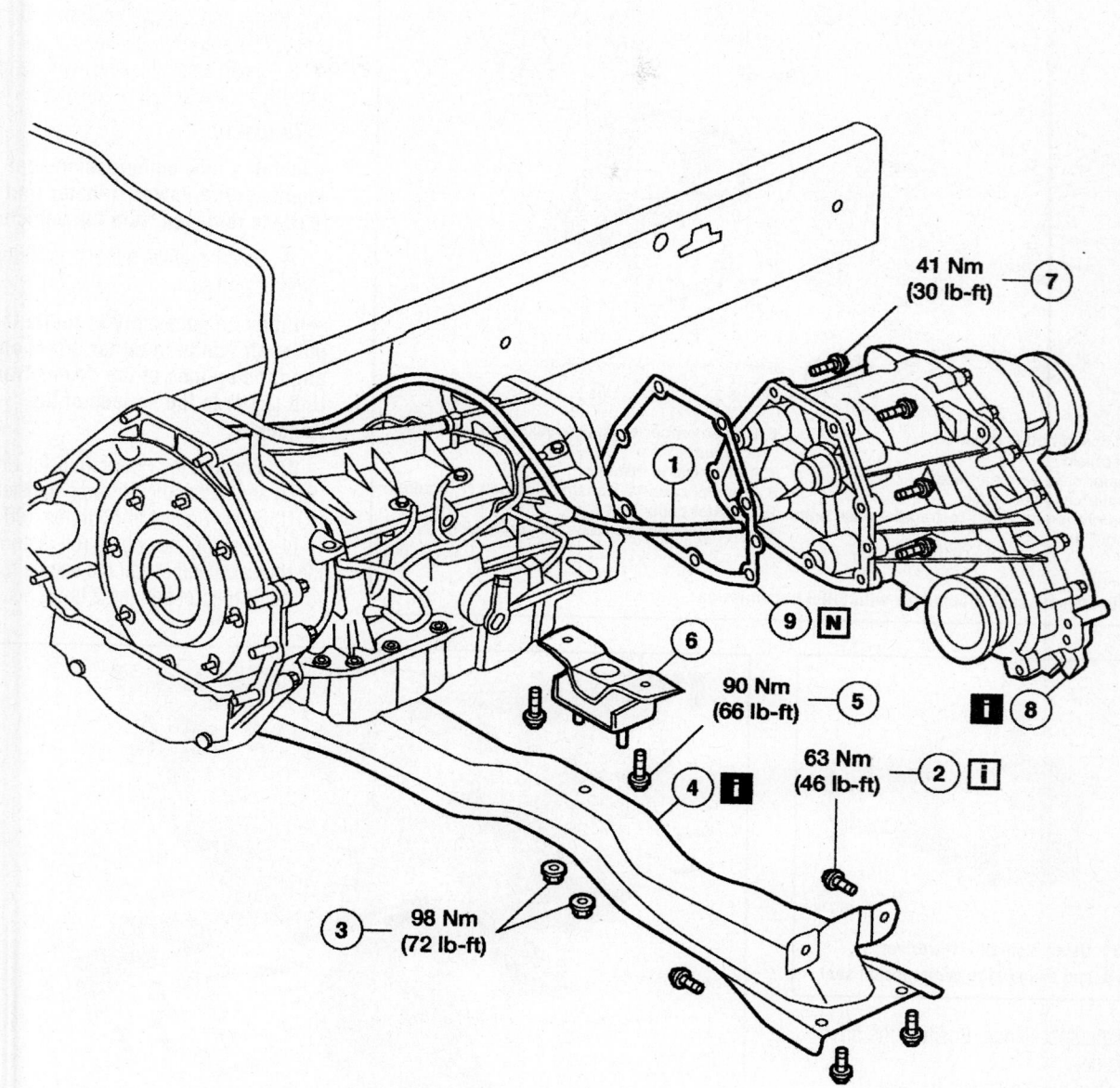

41 Nm
(30 lb-ft) — 7

1

9 N

90 Nm
(66 lb-ft) — 5

63 Nm
(46 lb-ft) — 2 i

i 8

4 i

3 — 98 Nm
(72 lb-ft)

1 Vent hose

2 Crossmember bolt (8
   required) Installation Note

3 Crossmember-to-transmission
   insulator nut (2 required)

4 Crossmember Removal Note

5 Transmission
   insulator-to-transfer case bolts
   (2 required)

6 Transmission insulator

7 Transfer case-to-transmission
   bolts (7 required)

8 Transfer case Removal Note

9 Transfer case-to-transmission
   gasket

06017-EXPL-G81

Fig. 29 Transfer case mounting—with 5R55 transmission

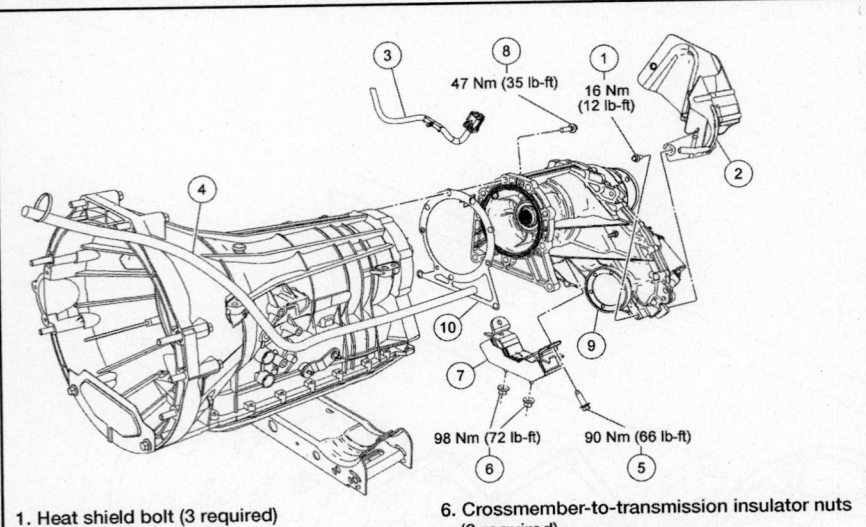

47 Nm (35 lb-ft)

16 Nm (12 lb-ft)

98 Nm (72 lb-ft)   90 Nm (66 lb-ft)

1. Heat shield bolt (3 required)
2. Heat shield
3. Transfer case wire harness
4. Transfer case vent tube
5. Transmission insulator-to-transfer case bolts (2 required)
6. Crossmember-to-transmission insulator nuts (2 required)
7. Transmission insulator
8. Transfer case-to-transmission bolt (7 required)
9. Transfer case
10. Transfer case-to-transmission gasket

22086_EXPL_G0169

Fig. 30 Transfer case mounting—with 6R80 transmission

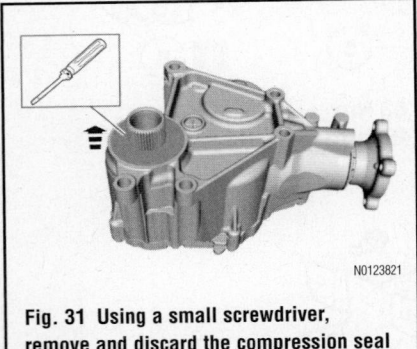

N0123821

Fig. 31 Using a small screwdriver, remove and discard the compression seal

from the output flange. Position the driveshaft aside.

5. Remove the Power Transfer Unit (PTU) support bracket:
- Remove the 2 Power Transfer Unit (PTU) support bracket-to-Power Transfer Unit (PTU) bolts.
- Remove the 3 Power Transfer Unit (PTU) support bracket-to-engine bolts.

6. Position the engine roll restrictor aside:
   a. Remove the 2 engine roll restrictor-to-transaxle bolts and the engine roll restrictor bracket.
   b. Loosen the rear engine roll restrictor bolt and pivot the engine roll restrictor downward.

➡**Position a drain pan under the vehicle.**

7. Remove the 5 Power Transfer Unit (PTU) bolts and pull the Power Transfer Unit

(PTU) outward and separate it from the transaxle. Rotate the output flange upward, then turn it and remove the Power Transfer Unit (PTU) from the vehicle.

8. Using a small screwdriver, remove and discard the compression seal.

   To install:

➡**Install a new compression seal whenever the Power Transfer Unit (PTU) is removed from the vehicle.**

9. Using a suitable tool, install the new compression seal.

➡**It may be necessary to rotate the output shaft flange in either direction to align the splines of the Power Transfer Unit (PTU) to the splines of the transaxle.**

10. Position the Power Transfer Unit (PTU) and install the 5 Power Transfer Unit (PTU) bolts. Tighten to 66 ft. lbs. (90 Nm).

11. Position the engine roll restrictor to the transaxle and install the engine roll restrictor bracket and the 2 bolts:

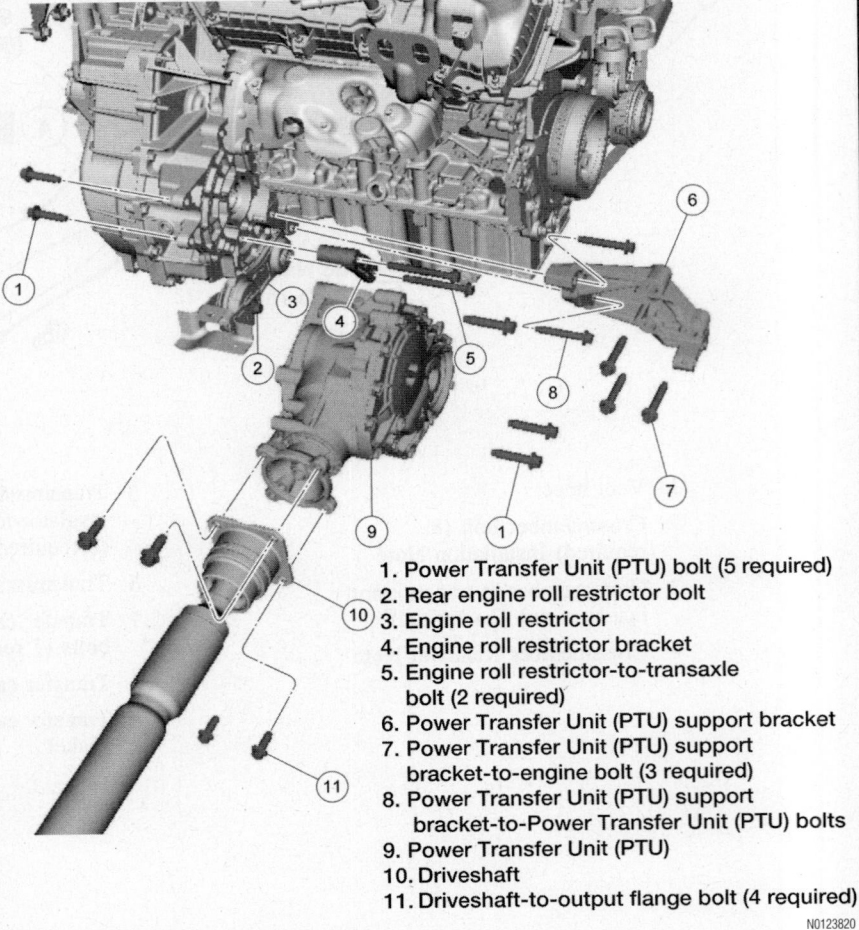

1. Power Transfer Unit (PTU) bolt (5 required)
2. Rear engine roll restrictor bolt
3. Engine roll restrictor
4. Engine roll restrictor bracket
5. Engine roll restrictor-to-transaxle bolt (2 required)
6. Power Transfer Unit (PTU) support bracket
7. Power Transfer Unit (PTU) support bracket-to-engine bolt (3 required)
8. Power Transfer Unit (PTU) support bracket-to-Power Transfer Unit (PTU) bolts
9. Power Transfer Unit (PTU)
10. Driveshaft
11. Driveshaft-to-output flange bolt (4 required)

N0123820

Fig. 32 Exploded view of the Power Transfer Unit (PTU)—2011 Models

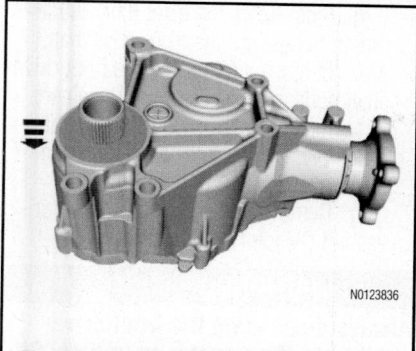

Fig. 33 Using a suitable tool, install the new compression seal

a. Tighten the engine roll restrictor-to-transaxle bolts to 76 ft. lbs. (103 Nm).

b. Tighten the rear engine roll restrictor bolt to 66 ft. lbs. (90 Nm).

12. Position the Power Transfer Unit (PTU) support bracket:

a. Install the 3 Power Transfer Unit (PTU) support bracket-to-engine bolts. Tighten to 35 ft. lbs. (48 Nm).

b. Install the 2 Power Transfer Unit (PTU) support bracket-to-Power Transfer Unit (PTU) bolts. Tighten to 35 ft. lbs. (48 Nm).

➡**Line up the index marks made during removal.**

13. Install the 4 driveshaft-to-output flange bolts. Tighten to 52 ft. lbs. (70 Nm).

14. Install the Right Hand (RH) catalytic converter.

15. Install the Right Hand (RH) halfshaft.

16. Inspect the transmission fluid level and add clean, specified fluid as necessary.

TRANSFER CASE FLUID

DRAIN & REFILL

2011 Models

See Figure 34.

➡**Install a new Power Transfer Unit (PTU) any time the Power Transfer Unit (PTU) has been submerged in water.**

➡**Do not drain the Power Transfer Unit (PTU) unless contamination is suspected. To drain the Power Transfer Unit (PTU) fluid, remove the Power Transfer Unit (PTU) from the vehicle. The fluid that is drained may appear black and have a pungent odor. Do not mistake this for contaminated fluid.**

➡**Fill level checks are done in-vehicle only. Let the vehicle sit 10 minutes**

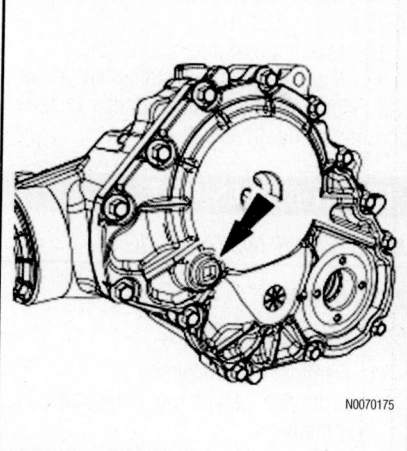

Fig. 34 Location of the PTU drain plug—2011 Models

after the road test before checking the fluid level.

1. With the vehicle in NEUTRAL, position it on a hoist. REFER to Lifting Points.

➡**NOTE: Clean the area around the fill plug before removing.**

2. Remove and discard the fill plug.

3. With the vehicle on a flat, level surface, fill the Power Transfer Unit (PTU). The fluid must be even with the bottom of the fill opening:

• Fluid capacity is 0.56 qt. (0.53 L).

4. Install a new fill plug and tighten to 15 ft. lbs. (20 Nm).

DRIVESHAFT

REMOVAL & INSTALLATION

2011 Models

See Figures 35 through 39.

➡**Index mark both driveshaft flanges.**

1. With the vehicle in NEUTRAL, position it on a hoist.

2. Remove the muffler and tailpipe.

3. Remove the 4 exhaust support brace bolts and the exhaust support brace.

➡**Do not reuse the bolt and washer assemblies for the rear Constant Velocity (CV) joint flange. Install new assemblies or damage to the vehicle may occur.**

4. Remove and discard the 3 Rear Drive Unit (RDU) pinion flange bolt and washer assemblies.

5. Using a flat blade screwdriver in the area shown, separate the driveshaft Con-

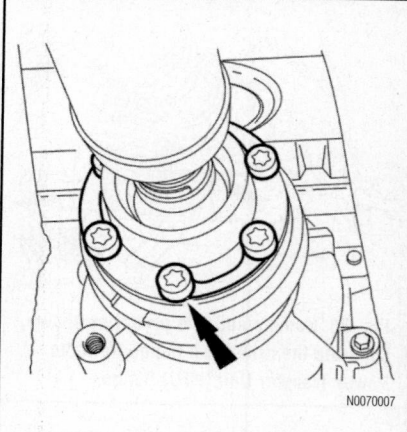

Fig. 35 Remove and discard the 3 Rear Drive Unit (RDU) pinion flange bolt and washer assemblies

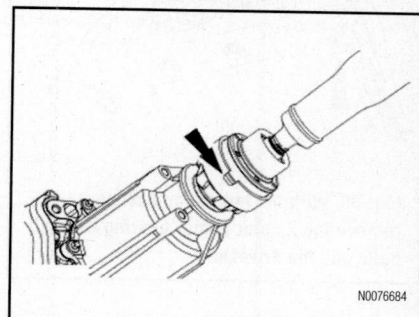

Fig. 36 Using a flat blade screwdriver in the area shown, separate the driveshaft Constant Velocity (CV) flange from the Rear Drive Unit (RDU) flange

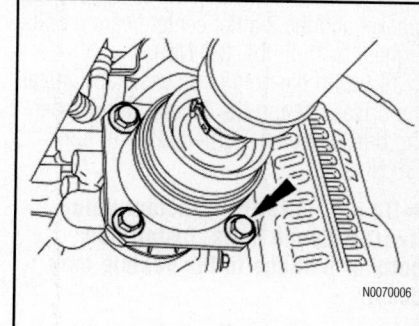

Fig. 37 Remove and discard the 4 Power Transfer Unit (PTU) flange bolts

stant Velocity (CV) flange from the Rear Drive Unit (RDU) flange.

6. Remove and discard the 4 Power Transfer Unit (PTU) flange bolts.

7. Using a suitable prybar as shown, separate the driveshaft flange from the Power Transfer Unit (PTU) flange.

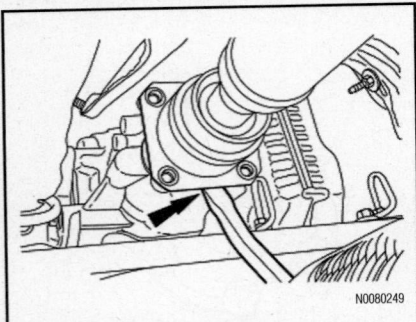

Fig. 38 Using a suitable prybar as shown, separate the driveshaft flange from the Power Transfer Unit (PTU) flange

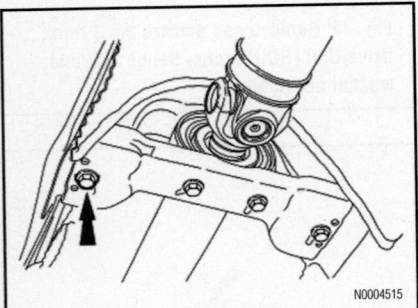

Fig. 39 With the help of an assistant, remove the 2 outer center bearing bracket bolts and the driveshaft

8. With the help of an assistant, remove the 2 outer center bearing bracket bolts and the driveshaft.

9. If necessary, remove the 2 inner center bearing bolts and remove the center bearing bracket.

To install:

10. If removed, install the center bearing bracket and the 2 inner center bearing bolts. Tighten to 15 ft. lbs. (20 Nm).

11. With the help of an assistant, install the driveshaft and the 2 outer center bearing bracket bolts. Tighten to 22 ft. lbs. (30 Nm).

➡ **Do not reuse the Constant Velocity (CV) flange bolts. Install new bolts or damage to the vehicle may occur.**

12. Install 4 new Power Transfer Unit (PTU) flange bolts.

➡ **Do not reuse the bolt and washer assemblies for the rear Constant Velocity (CV) joint flange.**

13. Install new assemblies or damage to the vehicle may occur.

14. Install 3 new Rear Drive Unit (RDU) pinion flange bolt and washer assemblies. Tighten to 18 ft. lbs. (25 Nm).

15. Install the exhaust support brace and the 4 exhaust support brace bolts. Tighten to 22 ft. lbs. (30 Nm).

16. Install the muffler and tailpipe.

17. If a driveshaft is installed and driveshaft vibration is encountered after installation, index the driveshaft.

FRONT DRIVESHAFT

REMOVAL & INSTALLATION

2010 Models

See Figures 40 through 42.

1. Remove the following:

   a. If necessary, remove the transmission insulator.

   b. Remove the cable shield by prying on the side of the shield closest to the boot, then sliding the shield away from the boot.

   c. Remove the shift cable and bracket.

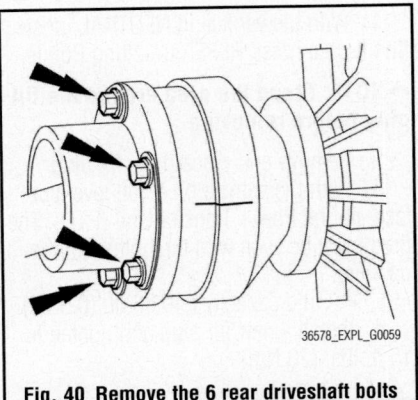

36578_EXPL_G0059

Fig. 40 Remove the 6 rear driveshaft bolts

d. Index-mark the front differential pinion flange and the front driveshaft.

e. Remove and discard the front driveshaft bolts and universal joint retainers.

f. Index-mark the front output shaft assembly and the front driveshaft constant velocity (CV) joint.

g. Remove and discard the front driveshaft CV joint bolts and washers.

❊❊ **WARNING**

Always disconnect the front driveshaft from the transfer case first. Otherwise, the weight of the driveshaft can pinch the boot between the shaft and the boot can and cause the boot to tear. Also, tape the bearing cups to the driveshaft to prevent them from falling off of the spider.

h. Remove the driveshaft.

i. Mark the rear driveshaft pinion

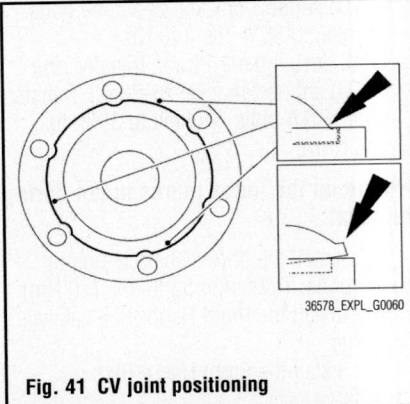

36578_EXPL_G0060

Fig. 41 CV joint positioning

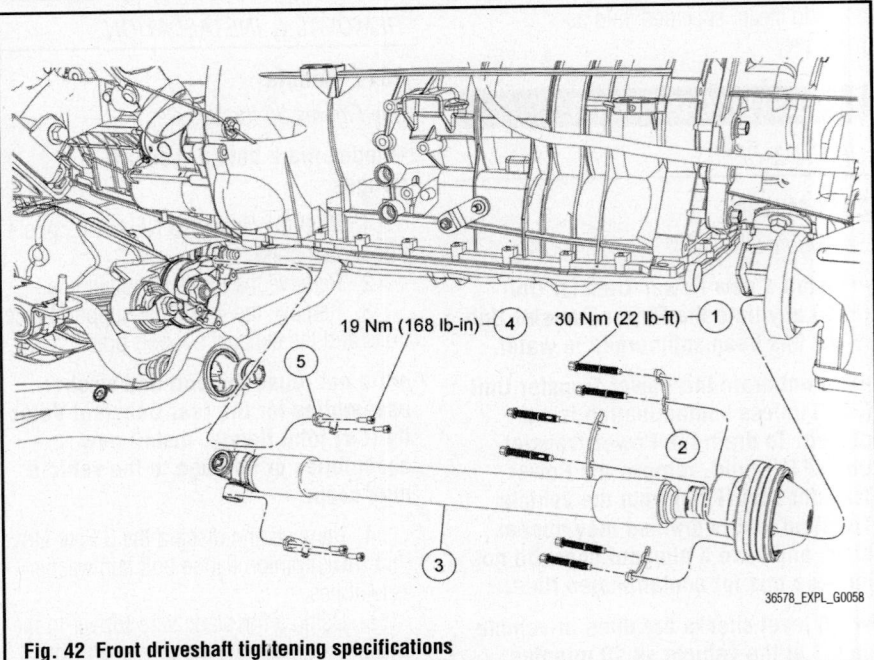

19 Nm (168 lb-in) — 4   30 Nm (22 lb-ft) — 1

36578_EXPL_G0058

Fig. 42 Front driveshaft tightening specifications

flange and the rear transfer case flange for correct alignment during assembly.

j. Remove the 6 rear driveshaft bolts.

k. Remove the rear driveshaft from the flange using a pry bar.

To install:

2. To install, reverse removal procedure.

➡**Tighten the Constant Velocity (CV) joint bolts evenly in a cross pattern or damage will occur to the CV joint. The can (domed CV joint housing cover) is pressed into the CV joint housing at the factory. When housed correctly, the can will appear as shown in the cut-away illustration (top box). Do not reseat the can in the CV joint housing if the can's flange is above the CV joint housing as shown in the cut-away illustration (bottom box), install a new driveshaft.**

FRONT HALFSHAFTS

REMOVAL & INSTALLATION

2010 Models

See Figure 43.

1. Before servicing the vehicle, refer to Precautions.

2. Remove or disconnect the following:

3. Loosen the front axle wheel hub retainer.

- Wheel and tire assembly

- Hub retainer and the washer. Discard the front axle wheel hub retainer.
- The two bolts and position the disc brake caliper aside. Refer to Caliper in Front Disc Brakes.
- Tie rod end from the knuckle. Discard the nut. Refer to Steering Knuckle in Suspension.
- Stabilizer bar link. Discard the nut. Refer to Stabilizer Bar in Suspension.

✳✳ WARNING

Do not allow the knuckle to hang freely. It is possible to overextend and internally separate each inner CV-joint from its housing.

- Upper ball joint from the knuckle

✳✳ WARNING

Do not use a hammer to separate the outboard CV-joint from the hub. Damage to the threads and internal CV-joint components may result.

4. Press the outboard CV-joint until it is loose in the hub.

5. Remove the outboard CV-joint from the hub.

✳✳ WARNING

Do not damage the axle shaft oil seal or the machined sealing surface on the inboard CV-joint housing.

➡**A circlip retains the inboard CV-joint housing to the differential side gear in the axle.**

6. On the left side, pry the left inboard CV-joint housing from the differential side gear.

7. On the right side, disengage the right inboard CV-joint housing from the axle tube.

8. Pull the halfshaft and the axle shaft away from the axle tube, and separate the inboard CV-joint housing from the axle shaft.

9. Remove the halfshaft assembly from the vehicle.

✳✳ WARNING

Do not damage the axle shaft oil seal, the machined sealing surface on the inboard CV-joint housing, or the axle shaft splines.

To install:

10. Installation is the reverse of the removal procedure.

11. Always install the halfshaft with a new retainer circlip and a new front axle wheel hub retainer.

12. On the right side, check the retainer circlip engagement after reseating the axle shaft and after installing the halfshaft in the axle. On the left side, check the retainer circlip engagement after installing the halfshaft in the axle. When seated, the retainer circlip will lock the axle shaft and the inboard CV-joint housing to the axle.

✳✳ WARNING

Never use power tools to tighten the front axle wheel hub retainer. Torque the retainer to 184 ft. lbs. (250 Nm).

➡**It may be necessary to support the front suspension lower arm to be able to connect the upper ball joint to the knuckle.**

2011 Models

Left Side

See Figures 44 and 45.

1. With the vehicle in NEUTRAL, position it on a hoist.

2. Remove the wheel and tire.

➡**Apply the brake to keep the halfshaft from rotating.**

3. Remove the wheel hub nut. Do not discard at this time.

➡**Use care when releasing the lower arm and knuckle into the resting position or damage to the ball joint seal or Constant Velocity (CV) boot may occur.**

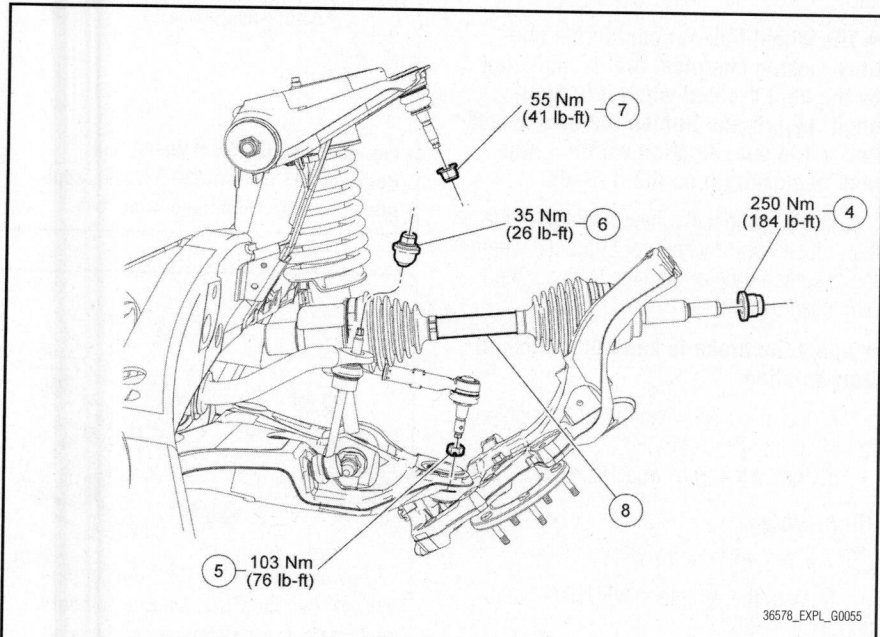

55 Nm (41 lb-ft) — 7
35 Nm (26 lb-ft) — 6
250 Nm (184 lb-ft) — 4
103 Nm (76 lb-ft) — 5
— 8

36578_EXPL_G0055

Fig. 43 Front axle halfshaft attachment locations and torques

➡Use the hex holding feature to prevent the stud from turning while removing the nut.

4. Remove and discard the lower ball joint nut. Separate the ball joint from the wheel knuckle.

5. Using the Front Wheel Hub Remover 205-D070 (D93P-1175-B), separate the halfshaft from the wheel hub.

6. Pull the wheel knuckle outboard and rotate it toward the rear of the vehicle.

➡The sharp edges on the stub shaft splines can slice or puncture the oil seal. Use care when inserting the stub shaft into the transmission or damage to the component may occur.

7. Using the Slide Hammer 100-001 (T50T-100-A) and Halfshaft Remover 205-832 , remove the halfshaft from the transmission.

8. Remove and discard the circlip from the stub shaft.

9. Inspect the halfshaft hub for wear or damage and install a new halfshaft, if necessary:

    a. Inspect the differential seal surface.

    b. Inspect the halfshaft bushing surface. If this surface is damaged, inspect the halfshaft bushing for damage.

    c. Inspect the differential side gear splines.

To install:

➡The circlips are unique in size and shape for each shaft. Make sure to use the specified circlip for the application or vehicle damage may occur.

10. Install the correct new circlip on the inboard stub shaft.

➡After insertion, pull the halfshaft inner end to make sure the circlip is locked.

11. Push the stub shaft into the transmission so the circlip locks into the differential side gear.

12. Rotate the wheel knuckle into position and insert the halfshaft into the wheel hub.

13. Position the lower ball joint into the wheel knuckle and install the new nut. Tighten to 148 ft. lbs. (200 Nm).

➡Do not tighten the wheel hub nut with the vehicle on the ground. The nut must be tightened to specification before the vehicle is lowered onto the wheels. Wheel bearing damage will occur if the wheel bearing is loaded with the weight of the vehicle applied.

➡Apply the brake to keep the halfshaft from rotating.

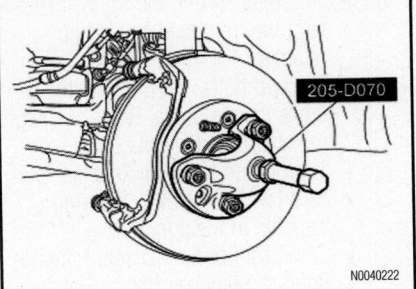

Fig. 44 Using the Front Wheel Hub Remover 205-D070 (D93P-1175-B), separate the halfshaft from the wheel hub

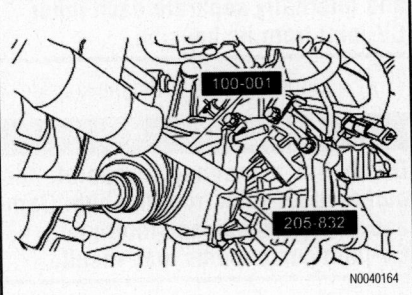

Fig. 45 Using the Slide Hammer 100-001 (T50T-100-A) and Halfshaft Remover 205-832 , remove the halfshaft from the transmission

14. Using the previously removed wheel hub nut, seat the halfshaft. Tighten to 258 ft. lbs. (350 Nm).

15. Remove and discard the wheel hub nut.

➡The wheel hub nut contains a one-time locking chemical that is activated by the heat created when it is tightened. Install and tighten the new wheel hub nut to specification within 5 minutes of starting it on the threads.

16. Always install a new wheel hub nut after loosening or when not tightened within the specified time or damage to the components can occur.

➡Apply the brake to keep the halfshaft from rotating.

17. Install a new wheel hub nut. Tighten to 258 ft. lbs. (350 Nm).

18. Install the front wheel and tire

Right Side

See Figures 46 through 48.

1. With the vehicle in NEUTRAL, position it on a hoist.

2. Remove the wheel and tire.

➡Apply the brake to keep the halfshaft from rotating.

3. Remove the wheel hub nut, but do discard at this time.

4. Remove the Right Hand (RH) brake disc.

5. Remove the bolt from the brake hose bracket.

➡Suspension fasteners are critical parts because they affect performance of vital components and systems and their failure may result in major service expense. New parts must be installed with the same part number or equivalent part, if replacement is necessary. Do not use a replacement part of lesser quality or substitute design. Torque values must be used as specified during reassembly to make sure of correct retention of these parts.

➡Use care when releasing the lower arm and knuckle into the resting position or damage to the ball joint seal or Constant Velocity (CV) boot may occur.

➡Use the hex holding feature to prevent the stud from turning while removing the nut.

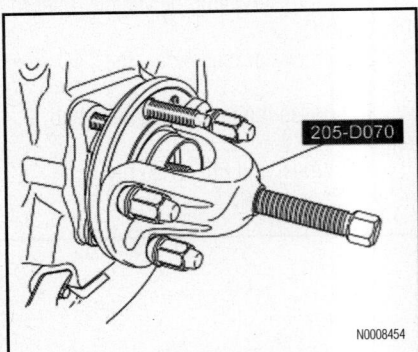

Fig. 46 Using the Front Wheel Hub Remover 205-D070 (D93P-1175-B), separate the halfshaft from the wheel hub

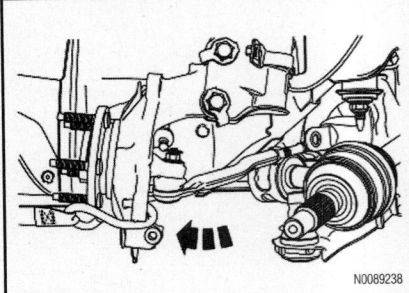

Fig. 47 Pull the wheel knuckle outboard and rotate it toward the rear of the vehicle. Secure the wheel knuckle assembly

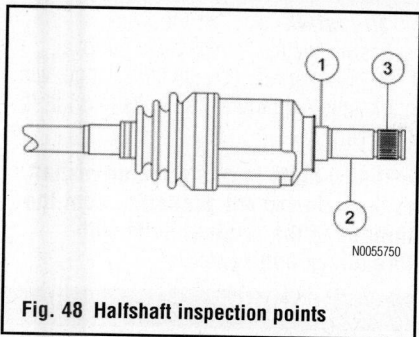

Fig. 48 Halfshaft inspection points

6. Remove and discard the lower ball joint nut. Separate the lower ball joint from the wheel knuckle.

7. Using the Front Wheel Hub Remover 205-D070 (D93P-1175-B), separate the halfshaft from the wheel hub.

8. Pull the wheel knuckle outboard and rotate it toward the rear of the vehicle. Secure the wheel knuckle assembly.

9. Remove the 2 lower scrivets from the rubber shield and position the shield aside.

10. Remove the 2 halfshaft bracket nuts.

11. Remove the halfshaft assembly, (if equipped with trailer tow) and the heat shield.

12. Inspect the halfshaft assembly for wear or damage and install a new halfshaft, if necessary:
- 1. Inspect the differential seal surface.
- 2. Inspect the halfshaft bearing.
- 3. Inspect the differential side gear splines.

To install:

➡For AWD models, a new Power Transfer Unit (PTU) shaft seal must be installed whenever the intermediate shaft is removed or damage to the components can occur.

13. For AWD models, install a new intermediate shaft seal and deflector.

14. Install the halfshaft assembly, (if equipped with trailer tow) the heat shield, and the 2 halfshaft bracket nuts. Tighten to 18 ft. lbs. (25 Nm).

15. Rotate the wheel knuckle into position and insert the halfshaft into the wheel hub.

16. Position the lower ball joint into the wheel knuckle and install the new nut. Tighten to 148 ft. lbs. (200 Nm).

17. Position the brake hose bracket and install the bolt. Tighten to 22 ft. lbs. (30 Nm).

18. Install the 2 scrivets in the rubber shield.

19. Install the Right Hand (RH) brake disc.

➡Do not tighten the front wheel hub nut with the vehicle on the ground. The nut must be tightened to specification

before the vehicle is lowered onto the wheels. Wheel bearing damage will occur if the wheel bearing is loaded with the weight of the vehicle applied.

➡Apply the brake to keep the halfshaft from rotating.

20. Using the previously removed wheel hub nut, seat the halfshaft. Tighten to 258 ft. lbs. (350 Nm). Remove and discard the wheel hub nut.

➡The wheel hub nut contains a one-time locking chemical that is activated by the heat created when it is tightened. Install and tighten the new wheel hub nut to specification within 5 minutes of starting it on the threads.

21. Always install a new wheel hub nut after loosening or when not tightened within the specified time or damage to the components can occur.

➡Apply the brake to keep the halfshaft from rotating.

22. Install a new wheel hub nut. Tighten to 258 ft. lbs. (350 Nm)

23. Install the wheel and tire.

FRONT PINION SEAL

REMOVAL & INSTALLATION

2010 Models

See Figures 49 through 51.

➡This operation disturbs the pinion bearing preload. Carefully reset the pinion bearing preload during assembly.

1. With the vehicle in NEUTRAL, position it on a hoist.

➡he front wheels and tires and brake calipers must be removed to prevent drag during the pinion bearing preload recording and adjustment.

2. Remove the front tires and wheels.

3. Remove the front driveshaft.

✴✴ WARNING

When removing the disc brake caliper, never allow it to hang from the brake hose or damage to the component may occur.

4. Remove the 4 disc brake caliper anchor bolts, then remove the disc brake calipers and disc brake caliper anchors as an assembly.

5. Using mechanic's wire, position and support the disc brake calipers and disc brake caliper anchors.

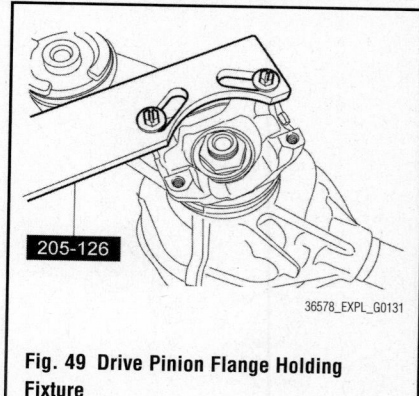

Fig. 49 Drive Pinion Flange Holding Fixture

6. Measure and record the pinion bearing preload.
- a. Using a Nm torque wrench, rotate the pinion gear. Measure the torque required to maintain pinion gear rotation.
- b. Index-mark the pinion flange and the pinion gear stem.

7. Using the Drive Pinion Flange Holding Fixture to hold the pinion flange, remove and discard the pinion nut.

8. Using the 2-Jaw Puller, remove the pinion flange.

9. Inspect the pinion flange for burrs and damage. Inspect the end of the pinion flange that contacts the pinion bearing cone, pinion nut counterbore and drive pinion oil seal surface for nicks. Discard the pinion flange if damaged.

10. Using gripping pliers and a hammer, remove the drive pinion oil seal.

11. Remove the drive pinion oil slinger and the outer pinion bearing.

12. Remove and discard the collapsible spacer.

13. Verify the splines on the pinion stem are free of burrs. If burrs are evident, remove them with a fine crocus cloth.

14. Clean the drive pinion oil seal bore.

To install:

15. Install a new collapsible spacer.

16. Install the outer pinion bearing and the drive pinion oil slinger.

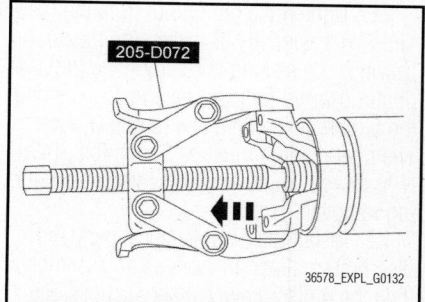

Fig. 50 Flange removal using 2-Jaw puller

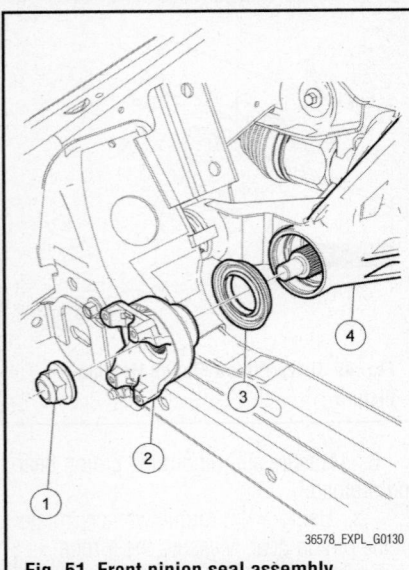

Fig. 51 Front pinion seal assembly

➡ **Lubricate the drive pinion oil seal lips with axle lubricant.**

17. Using the Drive Pinion Oil Seal Installer, install the drive pinion oil seal.

❊❊ WARNING

Never install the pinion flange with power tools or damage to the component may occur.

18. Align the index marks and using the special tool, install the pinion flange.

19. Install the new pinion nut. Only hand-tighten the pinion nut at this time.

❊❊ WARNING

Do not loosen the pinion nut to reduce pinion bearing preload. Install a new collapsible spacer and pinion nut if pinion bearing preload reduction is necessary or damage to the component may occur.

20. Using the Drive Pinion Flange Holding Fixture to hold the pinion flange, tighten the pinion nut to set the pinion bearing preload.

21. Tighten the pinion nut, rotating the pinion occasionally to make sure the pinion bearings are seating correctly. Take frequent pinion bearing preload readings by rotating the pinion gear with a Nm torque wrench. The final reading must be 5 inch lbs. (0.56 Nm) more than the initial reading taken during removal.

22. Install the disc brake calipers and disc brake caliper anchors as an assembly, then the 4 disc brake caliper anchor bolts and tighten to 80 ft. lbs. (108 Nm).

❊❊ WARNING

Always connect the front driveshaft to the axle first. Otherwise, the weight of the driveshaft may pinch the boot between the shaft and the flange and cause the boot to tear.

➡ **Install the driveshaft with new bolts and washers and new bolts and U-joint retainers. If new bolts are not available, coat the threads of the original bolts with threadlock and sealer.**

23. Install the front driveshaft.
24. Install the front tires and wheels.

REAR DRIVESHAFT

REMOVAL & INSTALLATION

2010 Models—One Piece

4.0L Engine

See Figure 52.

1. Perform the following:
    a. Index-mark the rear driveshaft flange and the rear pinion flange for proper realignment.
    b. Remove and discard the 4 rear driveshaft bolts.
    c. Remove and discard the bolts and universal joint retainers.
    d. Remove the rear driveshaft from the flange, using a pry bar; do not hammer on the flange or driveshaft.

To install:
2. Installation is reverse of removal.
3. Tighten rear driveshaft to flange, with marks aligned; tighten the bolts to 83 ft. lbs. (112 Nm).

➡ **If new bolts to retain the driveshaft to the axle are not available, coat the threads of the original bolts with threadlock and sealer.**

❊❊ WARNING

The driveshaft flange fits tightly on the rear axle pinion flange pilot. To make sure that the driveshaft flange seats squarely on the pinion flange, tighten the bolts evenly in a cross pattern.

4.6L Engine

See Figures 53 and 54.

1. With the vehicle in NEUTRAL, position it on a hoist.

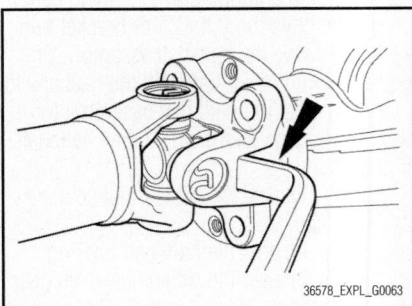

Fig. 53 Disconnecting the driveshaft flanges—4.6L Engine

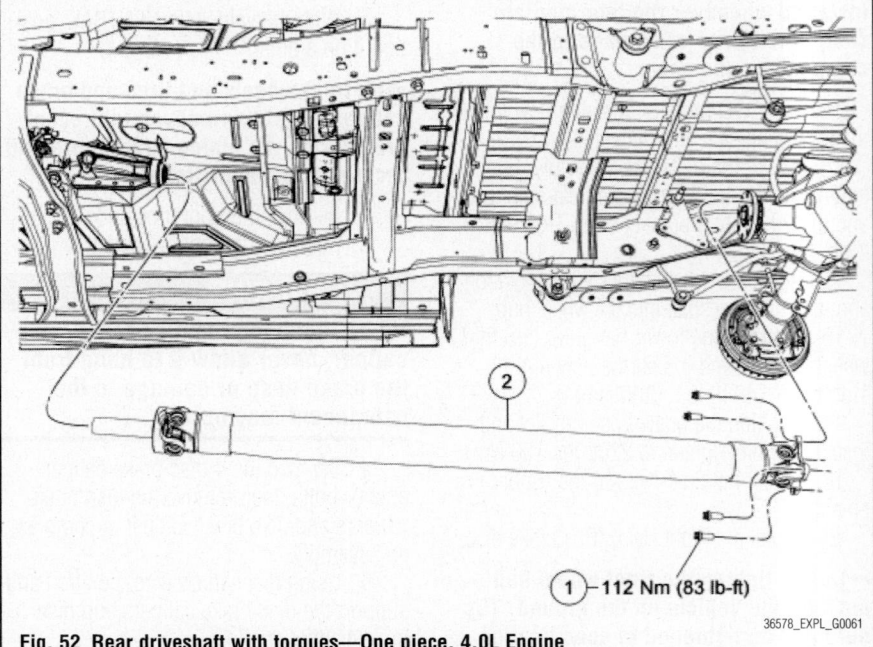

Fig. 52 Rear driveshaft with torques—One piece, 4.0L Engine

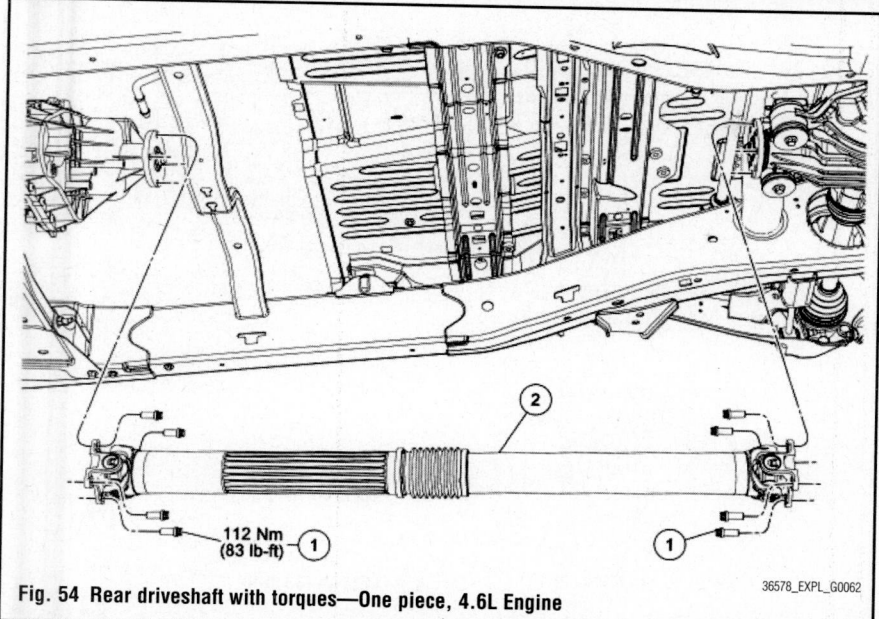

Fig. 54 Rear driveshaft with torques—One piece, 4.6L Engine

36578_EXPL_G0062

2. If equipped, remove the skid plate.

3. Index-mark the driveshaft flange to the transfer case rear output flange to maintain driveshaft balance.

4. Index-mark the driveshaft flange to the pinion flange to maintain driveshaft balance.

5. Remove and discard the 4 driveshaft flange bolts.

6. Remove and discard the 4 transfer case rear output flange bolts.

❋❋ WARNING

The driveshaft flange fits tightly on the axle pinion flange pilot and the transfer case output flange. Never hammer on the driveshaft, or any of its components, to disconnect the driveshaft flanges from the mating flanges. Pry only in the area shown with a suitable tool.

7. Using a suitable tool as shown, disconnect the driveshaft flanges and remove the driveshaft.

To install:

8. Installation is reverse of removal.

9. Tighten rear driveshaft to flange, with marks aligned; tighten the bolts to 83 ft. lbs. (112 Nm)

➡ **If new bolts to retain the driveshaft to the axle are not available, coat the threads of the original bolts with threadlock and sealer.**

❋❋ WARNING

The driveshaft flange fits tightly on the rear axle pinion flange pilot. To make sure that the driveshaft flange seats

squarely on the pinion flange, tighten the bolts evenly in a cross pattern.

2010 Models—Two Piece

2WD Models

See Figures 55 and 56.

1. With the vehicle in NEUTRAL, position it on a hoist.

2. Remove the 2 nuts from the driveshaft center bearing bracket.

3. Index-mark the rear U-joint flange to the differential pinion flange.

➡ **For 4.0L engine place an index mark on the transmission output shaft that**

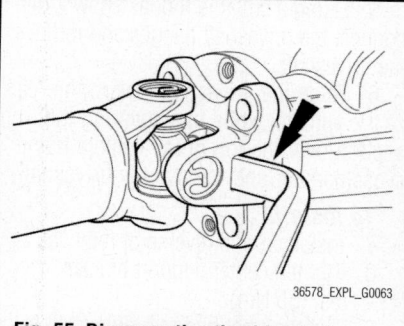

Fig. 55 Disconnecting the driveshaft flanges—Two Piece, 2WD

36578_EXPL_G0063

matches the transmission extension housing mark.

➡ **For 4.6L engine index-mark the front U-joint flange to the transmission output flange**

➡ **If new flange bolts are not available and the originals are not damaged, they can be reused if the threads are coated with threadlock and sealer.**

4. Remove and discard the 4 driveshaft flange bolts from the transmission output shaft flange.

❋❋ WARNING

The driveshaft flange fits tightly on the axle pinion flange pilot and the transfer case output flange. Never hammer on the driveshaft, or any of its components, to disconnect the driveshaft flanges from the mating flanges. Pry only in the area shown with a suitable tool.

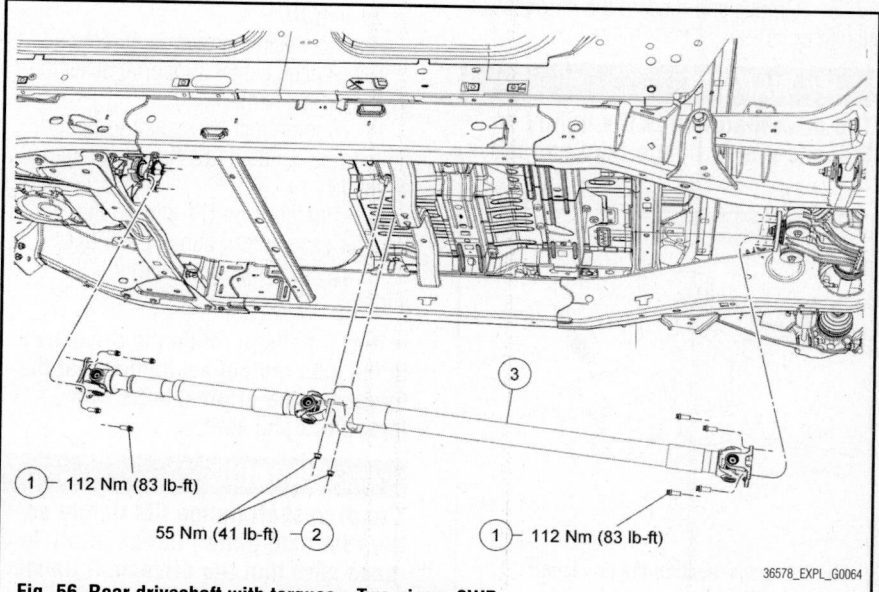

Fig. 56 Rear driveshaft with torques—Two piece, 2WD

36578_EXPL_G0064

5. Using a suitable tool as shown, disconnect the driveshaft flanges and remove the driveshaft.

6. Slide the driveshaft toward the rear of the vehicle, while maneuvering the front section over the top of the vehicle frame crossmember and remove the driveshaft.

To install:

7. Installation is reverse of removal.

8. Tighten center support bracket to 41 ft. lbs. (55 Nm).

9. Tighten front and rear driveshaft to flange, with marks aligned; tighten the bolts to 83 ft. lbs. (112 Nm).

➡If new bolts to retain the driveshaft to the axle are not available, coat the threads of the original bolts with threadlock and sealer.

✳✳ WARNING

The driveshaft flange fits tightly on the rear axle pinion flange pilot. To make sure that the driveshaft flange seats squarely on the pinion flange, tighten the bolts evenly in a cross pattern.

4WD Models

See Figures 57 and 58.

1. With the vehicle in NEUTRAL, position it on a hoist.

2. Remove the 2 nuts from the driveshaft center bearing bracket.

3. Index-mark the CV joint to the transfer case output flange.

4. Index-mark the rear U-joint flange to the differential pinion flange.

5. Remove and discard the 6 CV joint bolts and 3 CV joint washers.

6. Remove and discard the 4 driveshaft flange bolts.

✳✳ WARNING

The driveshaft flange fits tightly on the axle pinion flange pilot and the

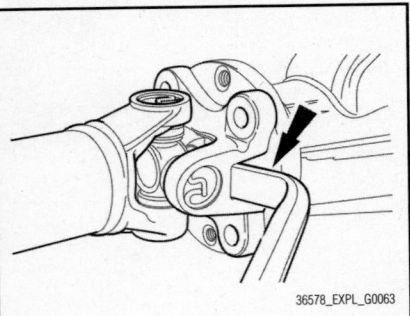

Fig. 57 Disconnecting the driveshaft flanges—Two piece, 4WD

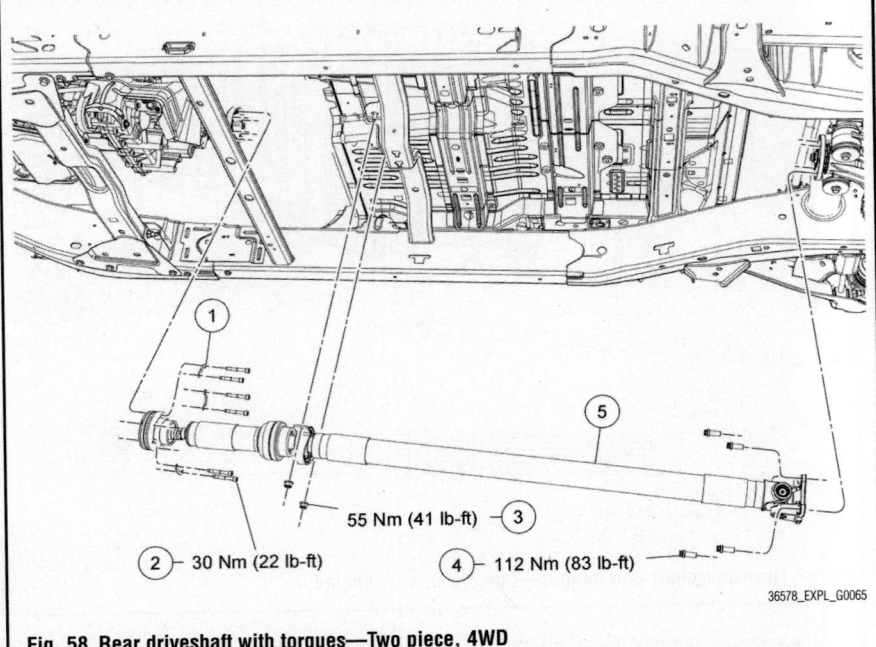

Fig. 58 Rear driveshaft with torques—Two piece, 4WD

55 Nm (41 lb-ft) — 3
2 — 30 Nm (22 lb-ft)
4 — 112 Nm (83 lb-ft)

36578_EXPL_G0065

transfer case output flange. Never hammer on the driveshaft, or any of its components, to disconnect the driveshaft flanges from the mating flanges. Pry only in the area shown with a suitable tool.

7. Using a suitable tool as shown, disconnect the driveshaft flanges and remove the driveshaft.

8. Slide the driveshaft toward the rear of the vehicle, while maneuvering the front section over the top of the vehicle frame crossmember and remove the driveshaft.

To install:

9. Installation is reverse of removal.

10. Tighten center support bracket to 41 ft. lbs. (55 Nm).

11. Tighten rear driveshaft to flange bolts to 83 ft. lbs. (112 Nm), with marks aligned.

12. Tighten front CV joint to the transfer case output flange bolts to 22 ft. lbs. (30 Nm), with marks aligned.

➡If new bolts to retain the driveshaft to the axle are not available, coat the threads of the original bolts with threadlock and sealer.

✳✳ WARNING

The driveshaft flange fits tightly on the rear axle pinion flange pilot. To make sure that the driveshaft flange seats squarely on the pinion flange,

tighten the bolts evenly in a cross pattern.

REAR HALFSHAFTS

REMOVAL & INSTALLATION

2010 Models

See Figures 59 through 64.

✳✳ WARNING

Do not loosen the rear axle wheel end nut until after the wheel and tire assembly are removed from the vehicle. Wheel bearing damage will occur if the wheel bearing is unloaded with the weight of the vehicle applied.

1. Before servicing the vehicle, refer to Precautions.

2. With the vehicle in NEUTRAL, position it on a hoist.

3. Remove the rear wheel and tire assembly.

4. Remove and discard the rear axle wheel end nut.

5. Using the special tool, press the outboard CV joint until it is loose in the hub.

6. Remove the brake cable retainer screw.

7. Remove and discard the outboard toe link nut and back out the bolt for clearance.

8. Remove and discard the lower arm outboard bolt.

9. Remove and discard the 3 wheel knuckle bolts.

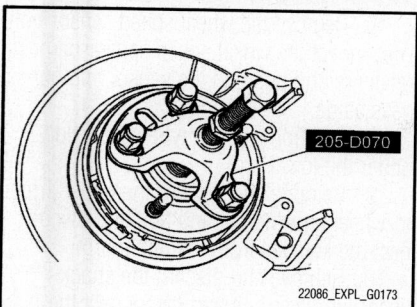

Fig. 59 Using the special tool, press the outboard CV joint until it is loose in the hub

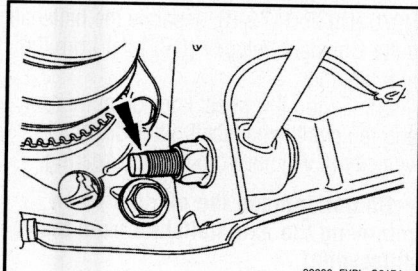

Fig. 60 Remove and discard the outboard toe link nut and back out the bolt for clearance

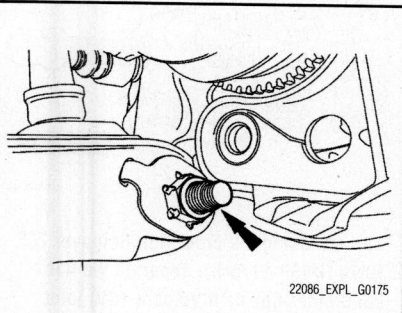

Fig. 61 Remove and discard the lower arm outboard bolt

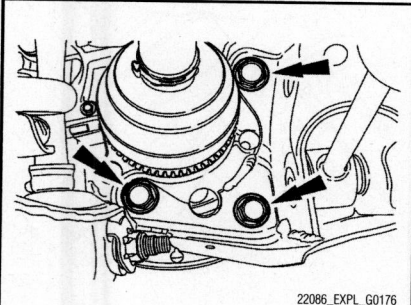

Fig. 62 Remove and discard the 3 wheel knuckle bolts

10. Pivot the wheel knuckle assembly upward on the upper arm outboard bolt. Loosen the upper arm bolt to prevent bushing damage.

> ❋❋ **WARNING**

Do not damage the stub shaft pilot bearing oil seal or the machined sealing surface on the inboard CV joint housing. Do not allow the splines on the inboard CV joint housing to touch the stub shaft pilot bearing oil seal.

➡A circlip retains the inboard CV joint housing to the differential side gear in the axle.

11. Using the special tool, disengage the

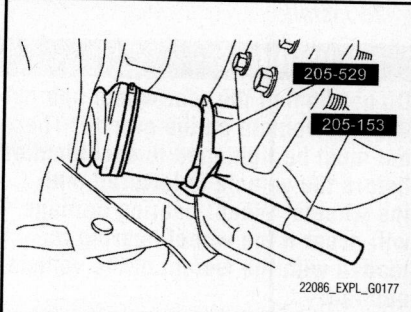

Fig. 63 Using the special tool, disengage the inboard CV joint housing from the differential side gear

inboard CV joint housing from the differential side gear.

12. Remove the halfshaft assembly.

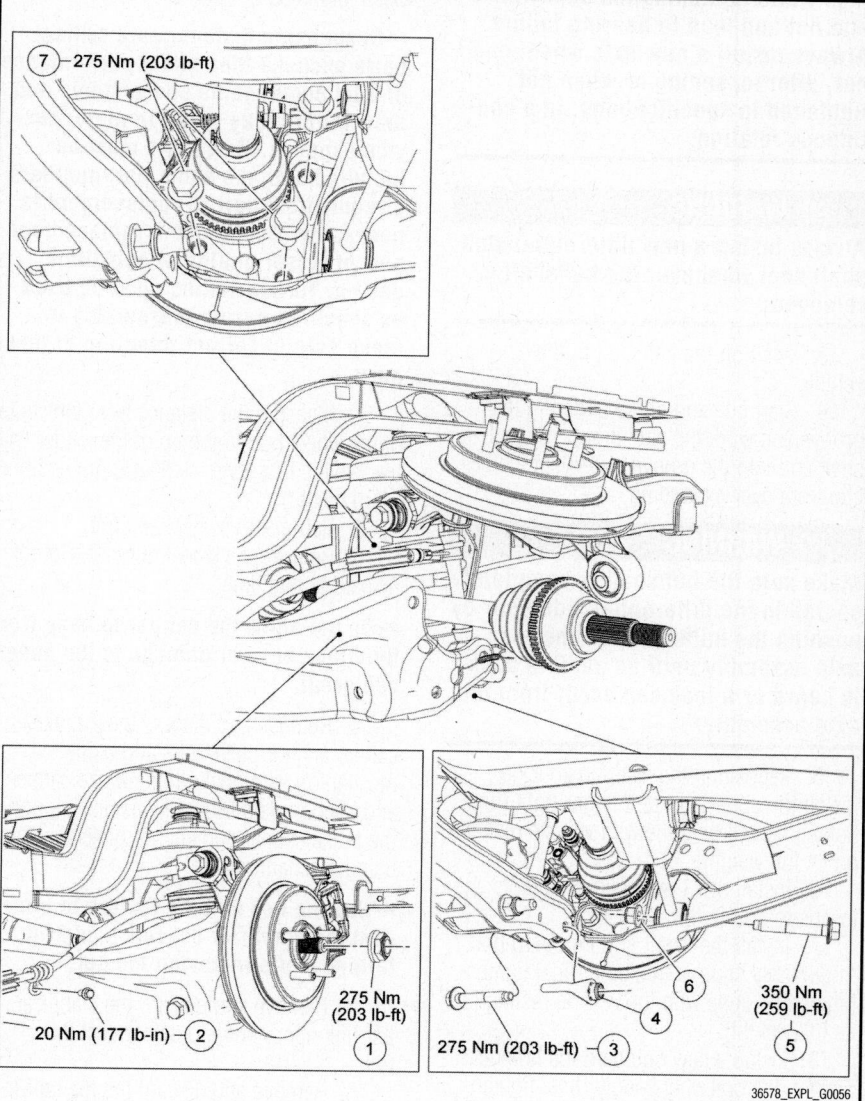

Fig. 64 Halfshaft complete view with torques

To install:

> ⁂ **WARNING**
>
> **Do not tighten the rear wheel hub nut with the vehicle on the ground. The nut must be tightened to specification before the vehicle is lowered onto the wheels. Wheel bearing damage will occur if the wheel bearing is loaded with the weight of the vehicle applied.**

> ⁂ **WARNING**
>
> **Install and tighten the new axle wheel end nut to specification in a continuous rotation. Stopping the rotation during installation will cause the nylon lock to seat incorrectly. This will cause incorrect torque readings while tightening the axle wheel end nut and lead to bearing failure. Always install a new axle wheel end nut, after loosening or when not tightened to specifications, in a continuous rotation.**

> ⁂ **WARNING**
>
> **Always install a new differential stub shaft seal whenever the halfshaft is removed.**

13. Position the halfshaft in the vehicle.

14. Start one end of the circlip in the groove and work the circlip over the half-shaft and into the groove to prevent the circlip from over-expanding.

> ⁂ **WARNING**
>
> **Make sure the halfshaft is completely seated in the differential side gear by pushing the halfshaft into the rear axle assembly until an audible click is heard or a leak can occur from the axle assembly.**

15. Reposition the steering knuckle. Install the upper arm bolt finger-tight (final tightening will be done with vehicle resting on its full weight).

16. Install the 3 wheel knuckle bolts and torque to 203 ft. lbs. (275 Nm).

17. Install the lower arm outboard bolt; torque only snug at this time (final tightening will be done with the vehicle resting on its full weight).

18. Install a new outboard toe link nut. Tighten the bolt only snugly (final tightening will be done with the vehicle resting on its full weight).

19. Install the brake cable retainer screw. Torque to 15 ft. lbs. (20 Nm).

20. Check that the outboard CV joint is properly fit into the hub.

21. Install a new rear axle wheel end nut. Tighten the nut to 258 ft. lbs. (350 Nm).

22. Install the wheel and tire assembly.

23. Lower the vehicle to its full resting weight.

24. Tighten the fasteners as follows:
   a. Wheel lug nuts: 100 ft. lbs. (135 Nm)
   b. Outboard toe link bolt: 259 ft. lbs. (350 Nm)
   c. Lower arm outboard bolt: 203 ft. lbs. (275 Nm)
   d. Upper arm bolt: 203 ft. lbs. (275 Nm)

2011 Models

See Figures 65 through 67.

➡ **Suspension fasteners are critical parts because they affect performance of vital components and systems and their failure may result in major service expense. New parts must be installed with the same part numbers or equivalent part, if replacement is necessary. Do not use a replacement part of lesser quality or substitute design. Torque values must be used as specified during reassembly to make sure of correct retention of these parts.**

1. Measure the distance from the center of the wheel hub to the lip of the fender with the vehicle in a level, static ground position (curb height).

2. Remove the wheel and tire.

3. Remove the wheel hub nut. Do not discard at this time.

➡ **Do not allow the caliper to hang from the brake hose or damage to the hose can occur.**

4. Remove and discard the 2 brake caliper anchor plate bolts and using mechanic's wire position the brake caliper and anchor plate assembly aside. Support the brake caliper and anchor plate assembly using mechanic's wire.

➡ **Use the hex holding feature to prevent the stabilizer bar link stud from turning while removing the nut.**

5. Remove and discard the stabilizer bar link upper nut and disconnect the link.

6. Remove and discard the toe link-to-wheel knuckle nut and bolt and disconnect the link.

7. Remove the wheel speed sensor bolt. Disconnect the wheel speed sensor harness retainers and position the sensor and harness aside.

8. Position a screw type jackstand under the lower arm.

9. Remove and discard the upper arm-to-wheel knuckle nut and bolt and disconnect the knuckle from the upper arm.

10. Remove and discard the shock absorber lower bolt and disconnect the shock absorber from the knuckle bracket.

11. Loosen, but do not remove the lower arm to wheel knuckle bolt.

12. Using the Front Hub Remover 205-D070 (D93P-1175-B), separate the halfshaft outer Constant Velocity (CV) joint from the hub bearing.

13. Swing the wheel knuckle outward and remove the halfshaft outer Constant Velocity (CV) joint from the hub bearing.

➡ **Do not damage the oil seal when removing the axle halfshaft from the differential.**

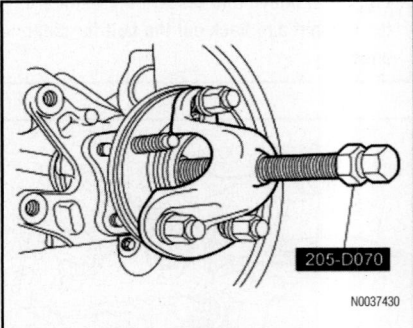

Fig. 65 Using the Front Hub Remover 205-D070 (D93P-1175-B), separate the half-shaft outer Constant Velocity (CV) joint from the hub bearing

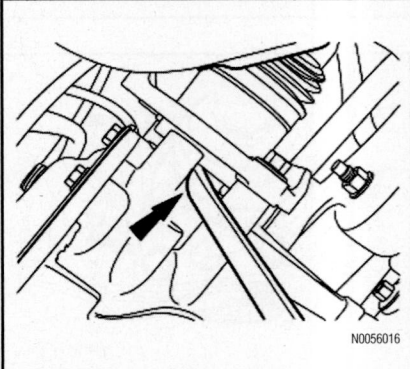

Fig. 66 Using a suitable pry bar, remove the halfshaft inner Constant Velocity (CV) joint from the differential

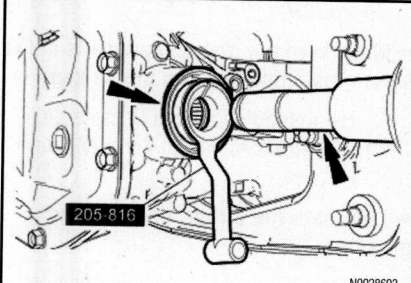

Fig. 67 Using the Axle Seal Protector 205-816 , install the halfshaft inner Constant Velocity (CV) joint into the differential. Make sure the circlip locks in the side gear

14. Using a suitable pry bar, remove the halfshaft inner Constant Velocity (CV) joint from the differential.

15. Remove the halfshaft from the vehicle.

16. Remove and discard the circlip from the halfshaft.

To install:

➡**Before tightening suspension bushing fasteners, use a jackstand to raise the rear suspension until the distance between the center of the hub and the lip of the fender is equal to the measurement taken in the removal procedure (curb height).**

➡**The circlips are unique in size and shape for each shaft. Make sure to use the specified circlip for the application or vehicle damage may occur.**

17. Install a new circlip on the halfshaft.

18. Using the Axle Seal Protector 205-816 , install the halfshaft inner Constant Velocity (CV) joint into the differential. Make sure the circlip locks in the side gear.

19. Swing the wheel knuckle inward and install the halfshaft outer Constant Velocity (CV) joint through the hub bearing.

20. Position the wheel knuckle to the upper arm and loosely install a new nut and bolt.

21. Position the shock absorber and loosely install a new bolt.

22. Position the wheel speed sensor harness in the retainers and install the sensor and bolt.
Tighten to 11 ft. lbs. (15 Nm).

23. Position the toe link and loosely install a new toe link-to-wheel knuckle bolt and nut.

24. Position a suitable jackstand under the lower control arm at the shock and

spring assembly attachment point and raise the rear suspension until the distance between the center of the hub and the lip of the fender is equal to the measurement taken in Step 1 of the Removal procedure (curb height) .

➡**A slotted upper arm allows for the rear suspension camber to be adjusted by pushing inward or pulling outward on the wheel knuckle while tightening the upper arm to wheel knuckle nut.**

25. With the wheel knuckle pushed inward for maximum negative camber, tighten the upper arm to wheel knuckle nut. Tighten to 148 ft. lbs. (200 Nm).

26. Tighten the lower arm-to-wheel knuckle bolt. Tighten to 195 ft. lbs. (265 Nm).

27. Tighten the shock absorber lower bolt. Tighten to 129 ft. lbs. (175 Nm).

28. Tighten the toe link-to-wheel knuckle nut. Tighten to 59 ft. lbs. (80 Nm).

➡**Use the hex holding feature to prevent the stabilizer bar link stud from turning while removing or installing the nut.**

29. Connect the stabilizer bar link and install a new stabilizer bar link upper nut. Tighten to 41 ft. lbs. (55 Nm).

30. Position the brake caliper and anchor plate assembly and install the 2 bolts. Tighten to 76 ft. lbs. (103 Nm).

➡**Do not tighten the wheel hub nut with the vehicle on the ground. The nut must be tightened to specification before the vehicle is lowered onto the wheels. Wheel bearing damage will occur if the wheel bearing is loaded with the weight of the vehicle applied.**

➡**Apply the brake to keep the halfshaft from rotating.**

31. Use the previously removed hub nut to seat the halfshaft. Tighten to 258 ft. lbs. (350 Nm). Remove and discard the hub nut.

➡**The wheel hub nut contains a one-time locking chemical that is activated by the heat created when it is tightened. Install and tighten the new wheel hub nut to specification within 5 minutes of starting it on the threads.**

32. Always install a new wheel hub nut after loosening or when not tightened within the specified time or damage to the components can occur.

➡**Apply the brake to keep the halfshaft from rotating.**

33. Install a new hub nut. Tighten to 258 ft. lbs. (350 Nm).

34. Install the wheel and tire.

35. Check and if necessary, adjust the rear toe.

REAR PINION SEAL

REMOVAL & INSTALLATION

2010 Models
See Figure 68.

1. Before servicing the vehicle, refer to Precautions.

2. Drain the axle housing fluid.

3. Remove or disconnect the following:
- Rear wheel and tire assemblies
- Brake caliper and support bracket from the knuckle as an assembly. Wire the caliper and support bracket assembly out of the way.

➡**Matchmark the driveshaft flange and rear axle pinion flange to maintain initial balance during installation.**

4. Disconnect and position the driveshaft out of the way.

5. Install an inch/pound torque wrench on the nut and record the torque necessary to maintain rotation of the drive pinion gear through several revolutions.

6. Remove and discard the pinion flange nut.

➡**Matchmark the rear axle pinion flange and drive pinion gear stem to maintain initial balance during installation.**

7. Remove the rear axle pinion flange.

8. Force up on the metal flange of the rear axle drive pinion seal. Install gripping pliers and strike with a hammer until the rear axle drive pinion seal is removed.

To install:

9. Lubricate the new rear drive pinion seal with grease.

➡**If the rear axle drive pinion seal becomes misaligned during installa-**

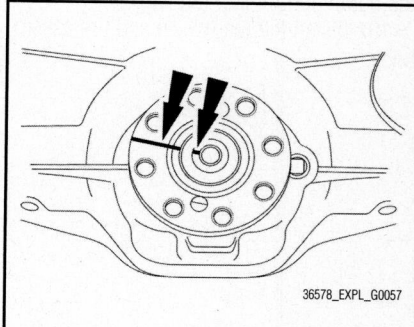

Fig. 68 Matchmark the rear axle pinion flange and drive pinion gear stem

tion, remove the rear axle drive pinion seal and install a new seal.

10. Drive in the rear axle drive pinion seal.

11. Inspect the rear axle pinion flange seal journal for rust, nicks and scratches prior to installing the flange. Polish the seal journal with fine crocus cloth, if necessary.

12. Lubricate the rear axle pinion flange splines.

13. Install the rear axle pinion flange, aligning the matchmarks made during disassembly.

➡**Disregard the index marks if installing a new pinion flange.**

✳✳ WARNING

Do not under any circumstance loosen the nut to reduce preload. If it is necessary to reduce preload, install a new differential drive pinion collapsible spacer and nut.

14. Rotate the pinion occasionally to make sure the pinion bearings seat correctly. Take frequent pinion bearing torque preload readings by rotating the drive pinion gear with an inch/pound torque wrench.

➡**Rotational torque must be at least the recorded original torque plus a maximum of 5 inch-pounds.**

15. If the preload recorded prior to disassembly is lower than the specification for used bearings, then tighten the nut to specification. If the preload recorded prior to disassembly is higher than the specification for used bearings, then tighten the nut to the original reading as recorded.
Pinion bearing preload: 16–29 inch lbs. (1.8–3.2 Nm).

16. Connect the driveshaft. Torque the bolts to 83 ft. lbs. (112 Nm).

17. Install the rear brake calipers. Torque the bolts to 24 ft. lbs. (32 Nm).

18. Install the rear wheel and tire assemblies.

2011 Models

See Figures 69 through 72.

1. Remove the driveshaft, as outlined in this section.

2. Using the Drive Pinion Flange Holding Fixture 205-126 (T78P-4851-A), hold the pinion flange and remove the nut. Discard the nut.

3. Index mark the location of the pinion to the pinion flange.

4. Using the 2 Jaw Puller 205-D072 (D97L-4221-A), remove the pinion flange.

5. Using the Torque Converter Fluid Seal Remover 307-309 (T94P-77001-BH) and Slide Hammer 100-001 (T50T-100-A), remove and discard the pinion seal.

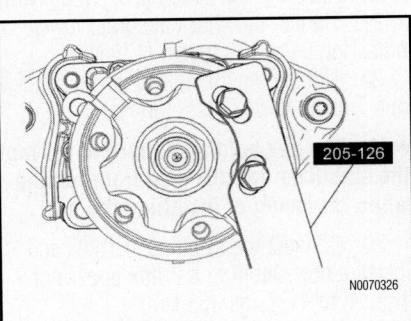

Fig. 69 Using the Drive Pinion Flange Holding Fixture 205-126 (T78P-4851-A), hold the pinion flange and remove the nut. Discard the nut.

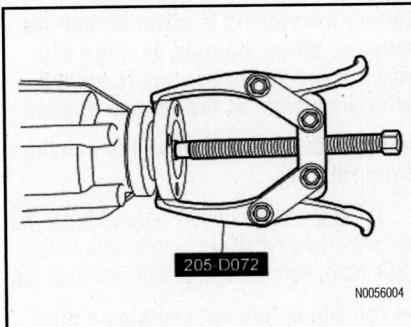

Fig. 70 Using the 2 Jaw Puller 205-D072 (D97L-4221-A), remove the pinion flange

To install:

➡**Make sure the mating surface is clean before installing the new pinion seal.**

6. Using the Pinion Seal Replacer 205-133 (T79P-4676-A), install the new pinion seal.

➡**Lubricate the pinion flange with grease.**

7. Align the index marks and position the pinion flange to the pinion.

8. Using the Drive Pinion Flange Holding Fixture 205-126 (T78P-4851-A), install the new pinion nut. Tighten to 180 ft. lbs. (244 Nm).

9. Install the driveshaft.

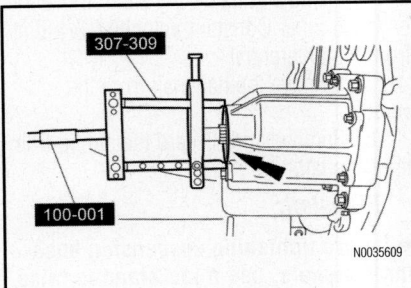

Fig. 71 Using the Torque Converter Fluid Seal Remover 307-309 (T94P-77001-BH) and Slide Hammer 100-001 (T50T-100-A), remove and discard the pinion seal

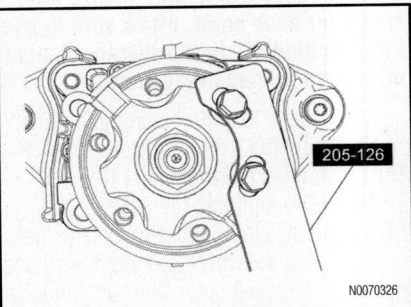

Fig. 72 Using the Drive Pinion Flange Holding Fixture 205-126 (T78P-4851-A), install the new pinion nut

ENGINE COOLING

ENGINE COOLANT

DRAINING, FILLING AND BLEEDING

2011 Models

➤The cooling system is filled with Motorcraft® Specialty Green Engine Coolant. Always fill the cooling system with the manufacturer's specified coolant. If a non-specified coolant has been used the cooling system must be chemically flushed. REFER to Cooling System Flushing. Failure to follow these instructions may damage the engine or cooling system.

➤Use Motorcraft® Specialty Green Engine Coolant. Use the same type of coolant that was originally used to fill the cooling system. Do not mix coolant types. Mixing coolant types degrades the coolant corrosion protection and may damage the engine or cooling system.

➤Motorcraft® Specialty Green Engine Coolant is very sensitive to light. Do NOT allow this product to be exposed to ANY LIGHT for more than a day or two. Extended light exposure causes this product to degrade.

To drain, perform the following steps:

1. With the vehicle in NEUTRAL, position it on a hoist. REFER to Lifting Points.

✳✳ CAUTION

Always allow the engine to cool before opening the cooling system. Do not unscrew the coolant pressure relief cap when the engine is operating or the cooling system is hot. The cooling system is under pressure; steam and hot liquid can come out forcefully when the cap is loosened slightly. Failure to follow these instructions may result in serious personal injury.

➤The coolant must be recovered in a suitable, clean container for reuse. If the coolant is contaminated it must be recycled or disposed of correctly. Using contaminated coolant may damage the engine or cooling system components.

➤Stop-leak style pellets/products must not be used as an additive in this engine cooling system. The addition of stop-leak style pellets/products may clog or damage the cooling system, resulting in degraded cooling system performance and/or failure.

➤Less than 80% of coolant capacity can be recovered with the engine in the vehicle. Dirty, rusty or contaminated coolant requires replacement.

2. Release the pressure in the cooling system by slowly turning the pressure relief cap 1/2 turn counterclockwise. When the pressure is released, remove the pressure relief cap.

3. Place a suitable container below the radiator draincock and drain the coolant.

4. Close the radiator draincock.

To fill and bleed, perform the following:

➤Use UVU550000 to fill the cooling system, then carry out the remaining steps to bleed all the air from the cooling system. Failure to follow these instructions can leave air in the cooling system which may damage the engine or cooling system.

➤The cooling system is filled with Motorcraft® Specialty Green Engine Coolant. Always fill the cooling system with the manufacturer's specified coolant. If a non-specified coolant has been used the cooling system must be chemically flushed.

➤Use Motorcraft® Specialty Green Engine Coolant. Use the same type of coolant that was originally used to fill the cooling system. Do not mix coolant types. Mixing coolant types degrades the coolant corrosion protection and may damage the engine or cooling system.

➤Motorcraft® Specialty Green Engine Coolant is very sensitive to light. Do NOT allow this product to be exposed to ANY LIGHT for more than a day or two. Extended light exposure causes this product to degrade.

➤Engine coolant provides boil protection, corrosion protection, freeze protection and cooling efficiency to the engine and cooling components. In order to obtain these protections, maintain the engine coolant at the correct concentration and fluid level in the degas bottle.

To maintain the integrity of the coolant and the cooling system:
• Add Motorcraft® Specialty Green Engine Coolant.
• Do not mix with any other type of engine coolant. Mixing coolant may degrade the coolant's corrosion protection.
• Do not add alcohol, methanol or brine, or any engine coolants mixed with alcohol or methanol antifreeze. These can cause engine damage from overheating or freezing.
• Ford Motor Company does NOT recommend the use of recycled engine coolant in vehicles originally equipped with Motorcraft® Specialty Green Engine Coolant since a Ford approved recycling process is not yet available.

➤Stop-leak pellets/products must not be used as an additive in this engine cooling system. The addition of stop-leak style pellets/products can clog or damage the cooling system resulting in degraded cooling system performance and/or failure.

Install UVU550000 and follow the manufacturer's instructions to fill the and bleed the cooling system. Recommended coolant concentration is 50/50 engine coolant to distilled water. For extremely cold climates less than -36.7 C (-34 F):
• It may be necessary to increase the coolant concentration above 50%
• NEVER increase the coolant concentration above 60%.
• Maximum coolant concentration is 60/40 for cold weather areas.
• A coolant concentration of 60% will provide freeze protection down to -50 C (-58 F).
• Engine coolant concentration above 60% will decrease the overheat protection characteristics of the engine coolant and may damage the engine.
For extremely hot climates:
• It is still necessary to maintain the coolant concentration above 40%.
• NEVER decrease the coolant concentration below 40%.
• Minimum coolant concentration is 40/60 for warm weather areas.
• A coolant concentration of 40% will provide freeze point protection down to -26.1 C (-15 F).
• Engine coolant concentration below 40% will decrease the corrosion and freeze protection characteristics of the

engine coolant and may damage the engine.

Vehicle driven year-round in non-extreme climates should use a 50/50 mixture of engine coolant and distilled water for optimum cooling system and engine protection.

Fill the degas bottle to 25 mm (1 in) above the COLD FILL line.

5. Install the degas bottle cap until at least 1 audible click is heard.

6. Turn the climate control system off.

7. Start the engine and increase the engine speed to 3,500 Revolutions Per Minute (RPM) and hold for 30 seconds.

8. Turn the engine off and wait for 1 minute to purge any large air pockets from the cooling system.

> ☀☀ **CAUTION**
>
> **Always allow the engine to cool before opening the cooling system. Do not unscrew the coolant pressure relief cap when the engine is operating or the cooling system is hot. The cooling system is under pressure; steam and hot liquid can come out forcefully when the cap is loosened slightly. Failure to follow these instructions may result in serious personal injury.**

9. Check the engine coolant level in the degas bottle and if necessary fill to 25 mm (1 in) above the top of the COLD FILL line on the degas bottle if the engine is warm or to the top of the COLD FILL line if the engine is cold.

10. Start the engine and let it idle until the engine reaches normal operating temperature and the thermostat is fully open. A fully open thermostat is verified by the cooling fan cycling on at least once.

11. Increase the engine speed to 3,500 Revolutions Per Minute (RPM) and hold for 30 seconds.

12. Allow the engine to idle for 30 seconds.

13. Turn the engine off for 1 minute.

14. Repeat the previous 3 steps, a total of 10 times to remove any remaining air trapped in the system.

> ☀☀ **CAUTION**
>
> **Always allow the engine to cool before opening the cooling system. Do not unscrew the coolant pressure relief cap when the engine is operating or the cooling system is hot. The cooling system is under pressure; steam and hot liquid can come out forcefully when the cap is loosened**

slightly. **Failure to follow these instructions may result in serious personal injury.**

15. Check the engine coolant level in the degas bottle and if necessary fill to 25 mm (1 in) above the top of the COLD

16. FILL line on the degas bottle if the engine is warm or to the top of the COLD FILL line if the engine is cold.

17. Install the degas bottle cap until at least 1 audible click is heard.

ENGINE FAN

REMOVAL & INSTALLATION

2010 Models
See Figure 73.

1. Remove the air cleaner outlet tube, on models with the 4.6L engine.

2. Remove the coolant expansion tank.

3. Remove the bolt and position the power steering fluid reservoir aside.

4. Remove the bolts, then unclip the upper fan shroud from the lower fan shroud and remove the upper fan shroud.

5. Disconnect the fan clutch electrical connector.

6. Remove the fan clutch wiring harness bracket bolt.

7. Remove the cooling fan.

To install:

8. Installation is the reverse of the removal procedure.

9. Torque the cooling fan bolts to 41 ft. lbs. (55 Nm).

10. Torque the power steering reservoir bolt to 89 inch lbs. (10 Nm).

2011 Models

1. With the vehicle in NEUTRAL, position it on a hoist.

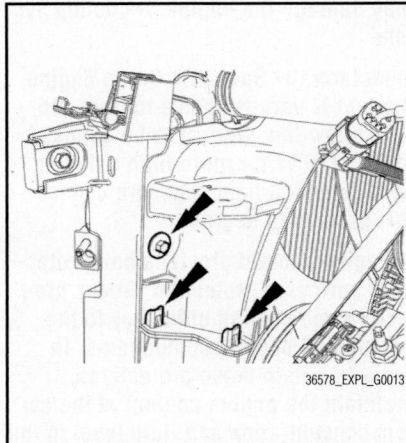

36578_EXPL_G0013

Fig. 73 Upper fan shroud bolt locations

2. Remove the Air Cleaner (ACL).

3. If equipped, detach the block heater wiring harness from the engine wiring harness.

4. Disconnect the cooling fan electrical connector.

5. Detach the 8 wiring harness retainers.

6. Detach the hood latch cable from the clip on the cooling fan motor and shroud.

7. Detach the upper radiator hose from the upper radiator hose support.

8. Release the tab through the access hole and remove the upper radiator hose support.

9. Remove the 2 bolts and the cooling fan motor and shroud.

To install:

10. Position the cooling fan motor and shroud and install the 2 bolts. Tighten to 53 inch lbs. (6 Nm).

11. Install the upper radiator hose support.

12. Attach the upper radiator hose to the support.

13. Attach the hood release cable to the clip on the cooling fan motor and shroud.

14. Attach the 8 wiring harness retainers.

15. Connect the cooling fan electrical connector.

16. If equipped, attach the block heater wiring harness to the engine wiring harness.

17. Install the Air Cleaner (ACL).

RADIATOR

REMOVAL & INSTALLATION

2010 Models
See Figures 73 and 74.

1. Drain the cooling system.

2. Remove or disconnect the following:

- Air cleaner outlet pipe (4.6L)
- Coolant expansion tank
- Power steering fluid reservoir; remove bolts and position aside
- Upper and lower radiator hoses
- Transmission cooling hose retainer from radiator support bracket
- 4 lower radiator air deflector push pins
- Latch assemblies from the transmission cooler tubes
- Transmission cooler tubes, using special tool 307-569
- Upper fan shroud
- Fan clutch electrical connector
- Fan clutch wiring harness bracket bolt

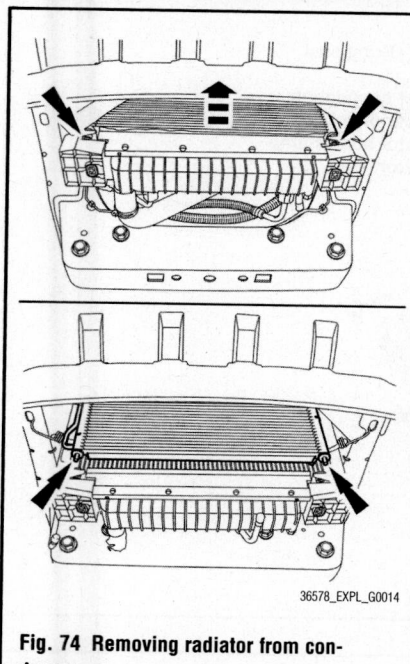

Fig. 74 Removing radiator from condenser

- Cooling fan
- Lower fan shroud
- A/C tube from the upper retainer
- Radiator support bracket-to-body bolts
- Radiator top seal

3. Deflect the A/C condenser seals and remove the A/C condenser-to-radiator support bracket bolts.

4. Remove the radiator and the radiator support brackets as an assembly.

5. Remove the bolts and separate the radiator support brackets and the radiator.

To install:

6. Install or connect the following:
- Support brackets to the radiator
- Radiator into position; tighten the bolts to 9 ft. lbs. (12 Nm)
- Reposition A/C condenser seals
- Radiator top seal
- Radiator support bracket-to-body bolts; tighten the bolts to 11 ft. lbs. (15 Nm)
- A/C tube from the upper retainer
- Lower fan shroud
- Cooling fan; tighten the bolts to 41 ft. lbs. (55 Nm)
- Fan clutch wiring harness bracket bolt
- Fan clutch electrical connector
- Upper fan shroud
- Transmission cooler tubes
- Upper and lower radiator hoses
- Power steering fluid reservoir; tighten bolts to 89 inch lbs. (10 Nm)

- Coolant expansion tank
- Air cleaner outlet pipe (4.6L)

2011 Models

See Figure 75.

1. Drain the cooling system.

2. Remove the cooling fan motor and shroud.

3. Remove the front bumper cover.

4. Release the clamp and disconnect the upper radiator hose from the radiator.

5. For early build vehicles, release the clamp and disconnect the degas bottle-to-radiator hose from the radiator.

6. Release the clamp and disconnect the lower radiator hose from the radiator.

7. Remove the 2 upper support bracket bolts and position the radiator toward the engine.

8. Remove the 2 upper radiator brackets.

9. Remove the Left Hand (LH) and Right Hand (RH) air deflectors from the Air Conditioning (A/C) condenser.

10. Remove the 2 Air Conditioning (A/C) condenser bolts and separate the condenser from the radiator.

11. Pry the clip up off the radiator and remove the upper radiator air deflector.

12. Remove the radiator.

13. Position the radiator in the vehicle, making sure the lower air deflector is under the Air Conditioning (A/C) condenser.

➡**The longer bolt goes on the Left Hand (LH) side.**

14. Attach the Air Conditioning (A/C) condenser to the radiator and install the 2 bolts. Tighten to 53 inch lbs. (6 Nm).

15. Install the upper radiator air

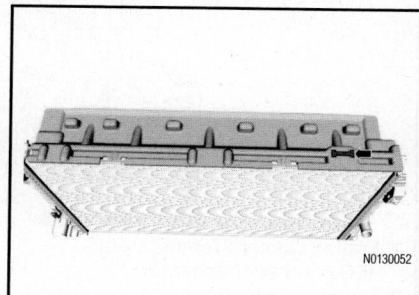

Fig. 75 Pry the clip up off the radiator and remove the upper radiator air deflector

deflector and attach the clip to the radiator.

16. Install the Left Hand (LH) and Right Hand (RH) air deflectors on the Air Conditioning (A/C) condenser.

17. Install the 2 upper radiator brackets.

18. Position the radiator and install the 2 upper radiator bracket bolts. Tighten to 44 inch lbs. (5 Nm).

19. Connect the lower radiator hose to the radiator and position the clamp.

20. For early build vehicles, connect the degas bottle-to-radiator hose to the radiator and position the clamp.

21. Connect the upper radiator hose to the radiator and position the clamp.

22. Install the front bumper cover.

23. Install the cooling fan motor and shroud.

24. Fill and bleed the cooling system.

THERMOSTAT

REMOVAL & INSTALLATION

3.5L Engine

See Figure 76.

1. Drain the cooling system, as outlined in this section.

2. Remove the Air Cleaner (ACL) outlet pipe.

3. Remove the 2 bolts and position the coolant inlet connection aside.

4. Remove the thermostat and the O-ring seal. Discard the O-ring seal.

To install:

➡**Use Motorcraft® Specialty Green Engine Coolant. Use the same type of coolant that was originally used to fill the cooling system. Do not mix coolant types. Mixing coolant types degrades the coolant corrosion protection and may damage the engine or cooling system.**

➡**Motorcraft® Specialty Green Engine Coolant is very sensitive to light. Do NOT allow this product to be exposed to ANY LIGHT for more than a day or two. Extended light exposure causes this product to degrade.**

5. Lubricate the O-ring seal with clean engine coolant, then install a new O-ring seal and the thermostat.

6. Position the coolant inlet connector and install the 2 bolts. Tighten to 89 inch lbs. (10 Nm).

7. Install the Air Cleaner (ACL) outlet pipe.

8. Fill and bleed the cooling system.

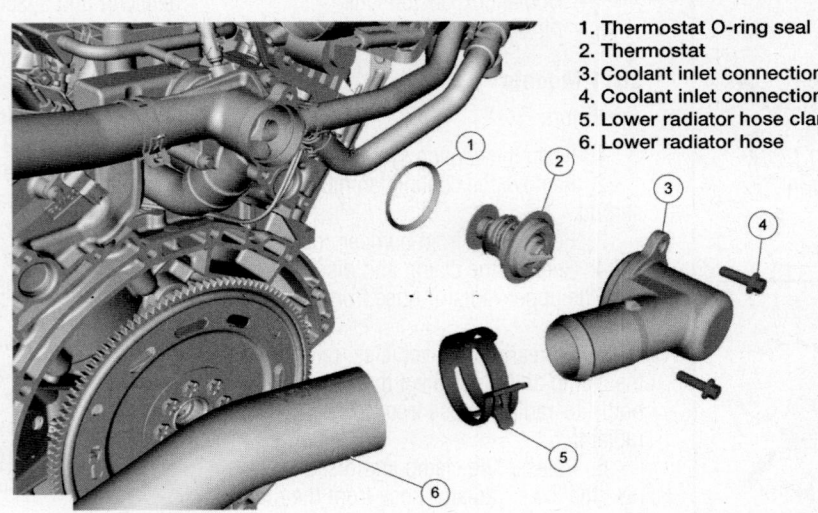

1. Thermostat O-ring seal
2. Thermostat
3. Coolant inlet connection
4. Coolant inlet connection bolt
5. Lower radiator hose clamp
6. Lower radiator hose

Fig. 76 Exploded view of the thermostat and related components—3.5L engine

4.0L Engine

See Figure 77.

1. Drain the cooling system.
2. Disconnect the upper radiator hose from the thermostat housing.
3. Remove the thermostat housing and the thermostat.

To install:

4. Installation is the reverse of the removal procedure.
5. Install a new O-ring seal in the thermostat housing.
6. Torque the thermostat housing bolts to 89 inch lbs. (10 Nm).
7. Fill and bleed the cooling system.

4.6L Engine

See Figure 78.

1. Drain the cooling system.
2. Remove the throttle body. See the "Fuel Systems" section.
3. Disconnect the fuel vapor tube near the thermostat housing.
4. Remove the bolts and position the thermostat housing cover aside.
5. Remove the O-ring seal and the thermostat.

To install:

6. Installation is the reverse of the removal procedure.
7. Install the thermostat with the spring facing downward.
8. Install a new O-ring seal and tighten the thermostat housing bolts to 89 inch lbs. (10 Nm).
9. Fill and bleed the cooling system.

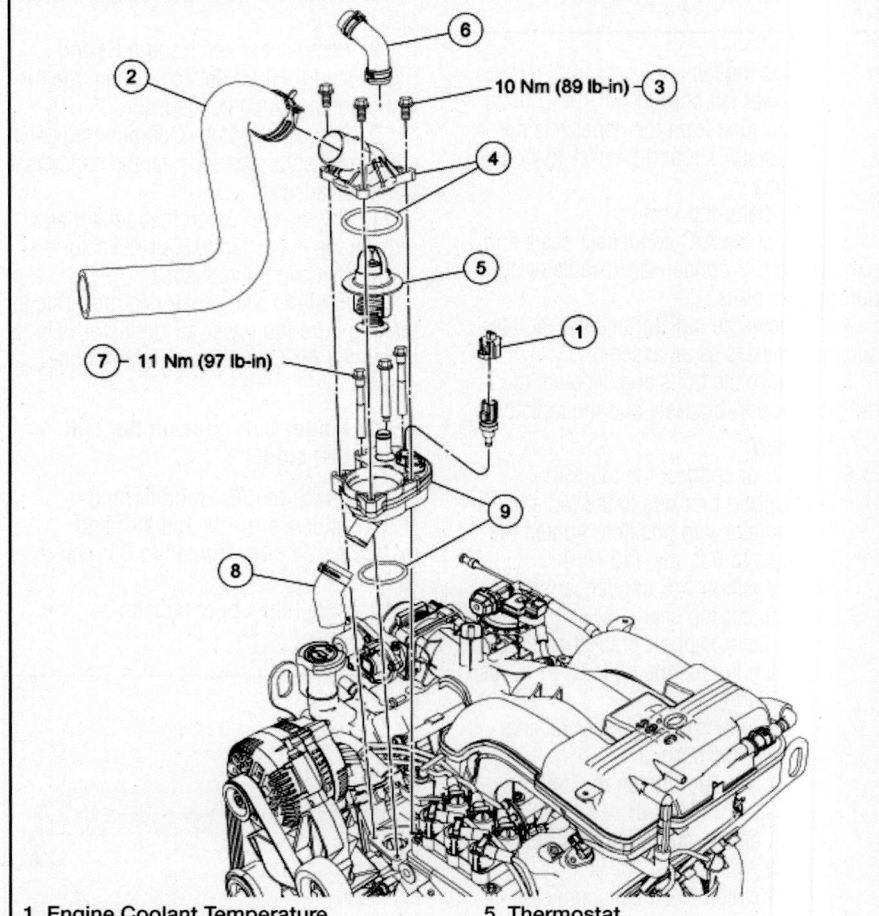

1. Engine Coolant Temperature (ECT) sensor connector
2. Upper radiator hose
3. Thermostat housing cover bolt (3 required)
4. Thermostat housing cover with)-ring seal
5. Thermostat
6. Heater hose
7. Thermostat housing bolt (3 required)
8. Bypass hose
9. Thermostat housing with)O-ring seal

Fig. 77 Thermostat housing assembly—4.0L Engine

36578_EXPL_G0206

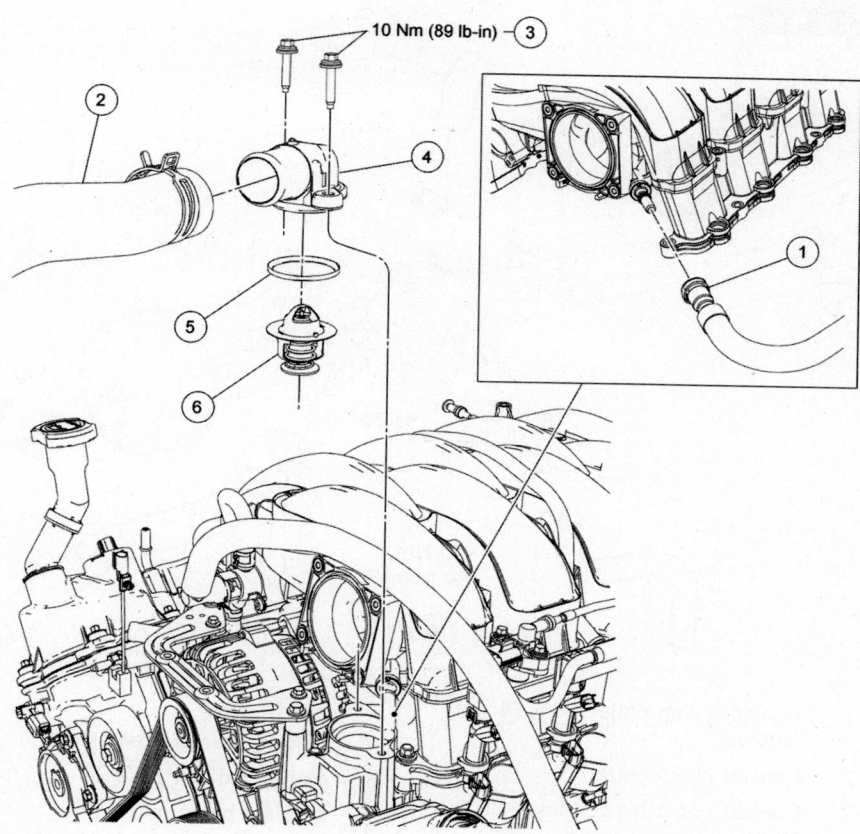

1. Fuel vapor tube
2. Upper radiator hose
3. Thermostat housing bolt
   (2 required)
4. Thermostat housing cover
5. Thermostat O-ring seal
6. Thermostat

36578_EXPL_G0015

Fig. 78 Thermostat bolt location—4.6L Engine

WATER PUMP

REMOVAL & INSTALLATION

4.0L Engine

See Figure 79.

1. Before servicing the vehicle, refer to Precautions.
2. Drain the cooling system.
3. Remove or disconnect the following:
   - Fan shroud and cooling fan
   - Accessory drive belt
   - Water pump pulley
   - Coolant by-pass hose
   - Lower radiator hose
   - Water pump

❊❊❊ WARNING

Use care when scraping the water pump-to-engine block mating surfaces. Gouges in the aluminum could form leak paths.

4. Clean all the sealing surfaces.

To install:

5. Installation is the reverse of the removal procedure.

6. Observe the following tightening specifications:
   - Water pump bolts: 89 inch lbs. (10 Nm)
   - Pulley bolts: 18 ft. lbs. (25 Nm)

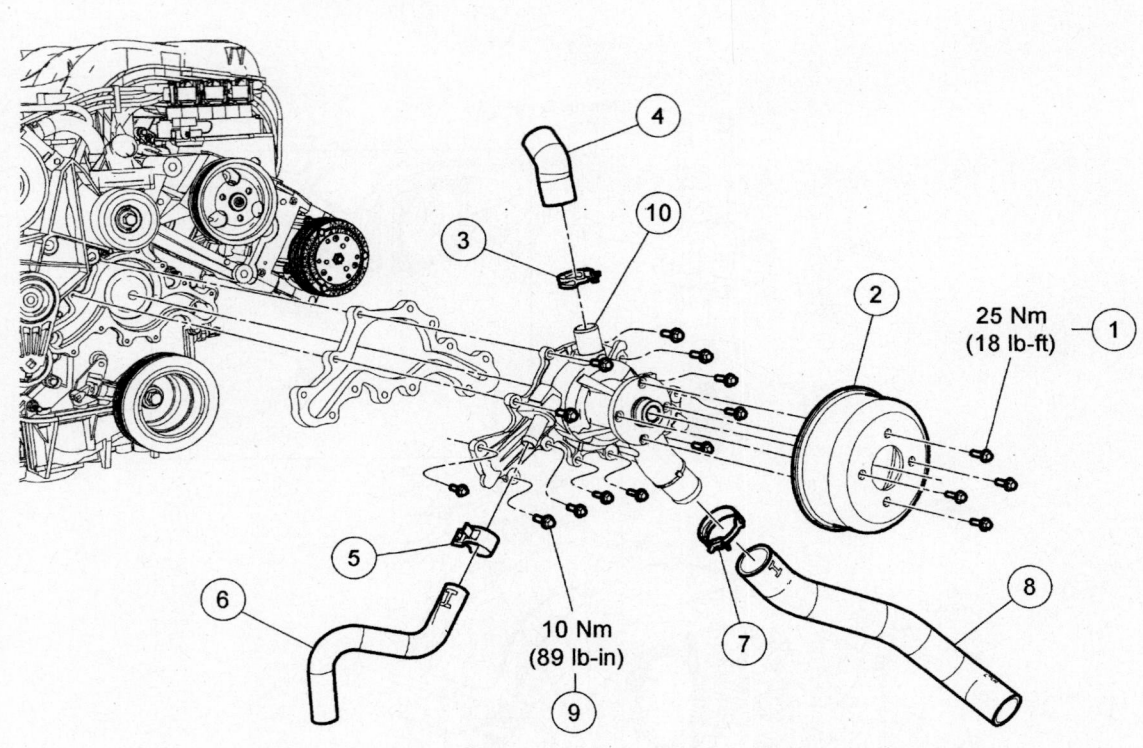

1	Coolant pump pulley bolts (4 required)		6	Heater hose
2	Coolant pump pulley		7	Lower radiator hose clamp
3	Coolant pump bypass hose clamp		8	Lower radiator hose
4	Coolant pump bypass hose		9	Coolant pump bolts (12 required)
5	Heater hose clamp		10	Coolant pump

06017-EXPL-G09

Fig. 79 Typical water pump installation—4.0L engine

4.6L Engine

See Figure 80.

1. Before servicing the vehicle, refer to Precautions.

2. Drain the cooling system.

3. Remove or disconnect the following:
   - Engine cooling fan
   - Upper fan shroud
   - Water pump pulley bolts (loosen only)
   - Accessory drive belt
   - Water pump pulley
   - Water pump

4. Discard the O-ring seal.

To install:

5. Installation is the reverse of the removal procedure.

6. Install a new O-ring seal and lubricate with engine coolant.

7. Observe the following tightening specifications:
   - Water pump mounting bolts: 18 ft. lbs. (25 Nm).
   - Water pump pulley bolts: 18 ft. lbs. (25 Nm).

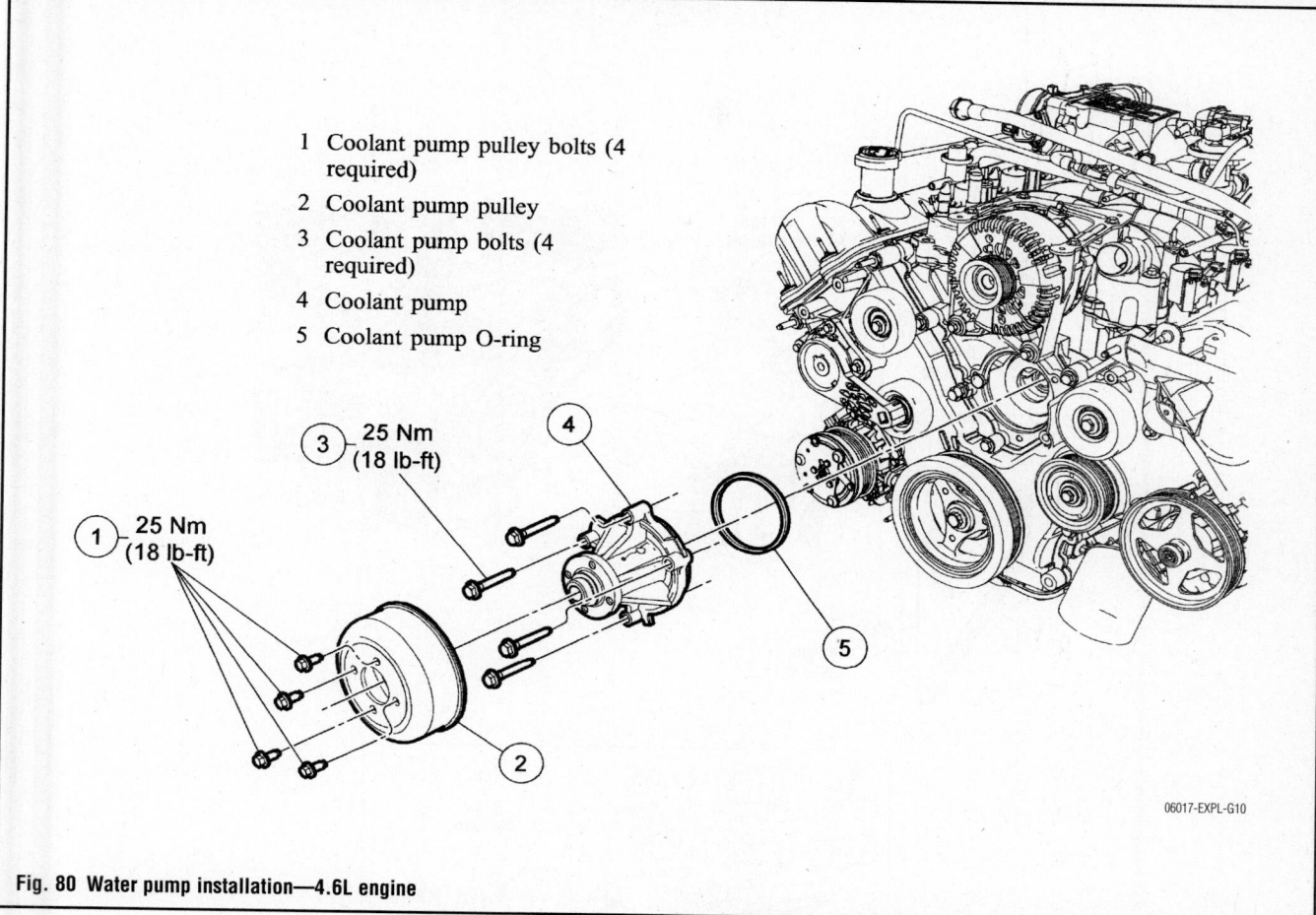

1 Coolant pump pulley bolts (4 required)
2 Coolant pump pulley
3 Coolant pump bolts (4 required)
4 Coolant pump
5 Coolant pump O-ring

3 25 Nm (18 lb-ft)

1 25 Nm (18 lb-ft)

06017-EXPL-G10

Fig. 80 Water pump installation—4.6L engine

ENGINE ELECTRICAL   **CHARGING SYSTEM**

ALTERNATOR

REMOVAL & INSTALLATION

3.5L Engine

See Figure 81.

➡The radial arm adapter is a serviceable item. Do not replace the generator if the radial arm adapter is the only concern.

1. Disconnect the battery.
2. Remove the cooling fan motor and shroud, as outlined in the Engine Cooling Section.
3. Rotate the accessory drive belt tensioner clockwise and position the accessory drive belt aside.
4. Position the generator B+ terminal protective cover aside, remove the nut and position the generator B+ terminal aside.
5. Disconnect the generator electrical connector.

6. Remove the Right Hand (RH) fender splash shield.
7. Fully loosen the generator bolt.
8. Remove the generator stud nut.
9. Remove the generator stud and the generator.

To install:
10. Installation is the reverse of the removal procedure, noting the following:
   a. Tighten the generator stud to 71 inch lbs. (8 Nm).
   b. Tighten the generator bolt to 35 ft. lbs. (47 Nm).
   c. Tighten the B+ terminal nut to 13 ft. lbs. (17 Nm).

4.0L Engine

See Figure 82.

1. Before servicing the vehicle, refer to the precautions in the beginning of this section.
2. Disconnect the battery.
3. Rotate the front end accessory drive

belt tensioner counterclockwise and position the front end accessory drive belt aside.
4. Position the protective cover aside and remove the alternator B+ terminal nut.
5. Disconnect the alternator B+ terminal and the 2 electrical connectors.
6. Remove the 3 bolts and the alternator.
7. If necessary, remove the nut and the alternator pulley.

To install:
8. If the alternator pulley was removed, install it and tighten the pulley bolt to 80 ft. lbs. (109 Nm).
9. Position the alternator and install the 3 mounting bolts. Tighten the mounting bolts to 35 ft. lbs. (47 Nm).
10. Connect the alternator B+ terminal and both electrical connectors.
11. Install the alternator B+ terminal nut. Tighten it to 80 inch lbs. (9 Nm).
12. Install the accessory drive belt and slowly release the tensioner.
13. Connect the battery cables.

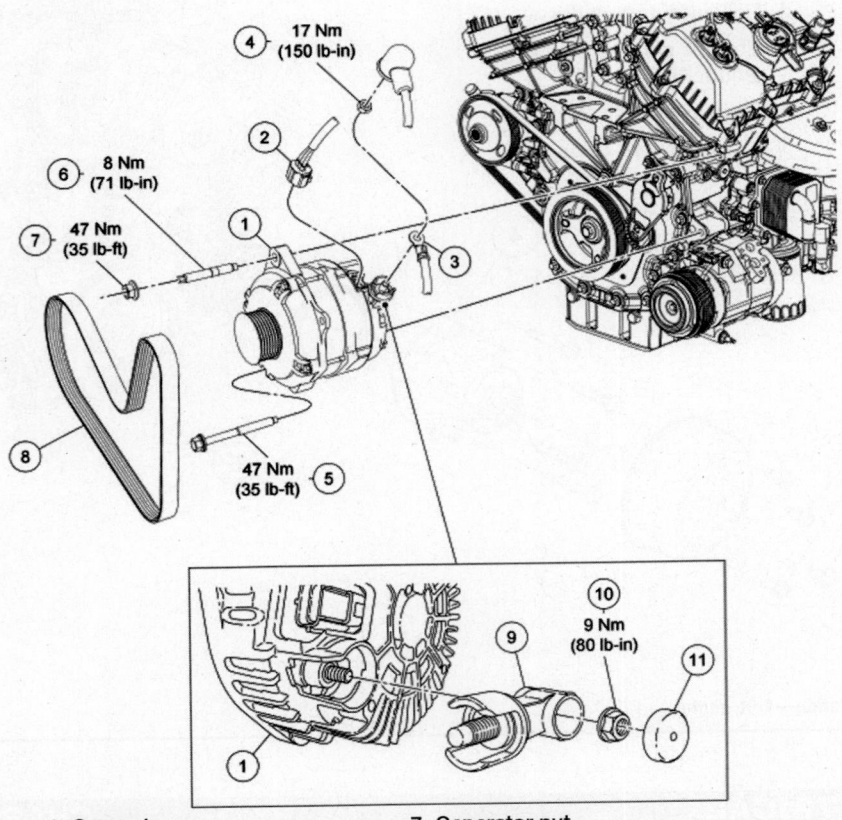

1. Generator
2. Generator electrical connector
3. Generator B+ terminal
4. Generator B+ terminal nut
5. Generator bolt
6. Generator stud
7. Generator nut
8. Front End Accessory Drive (FEAD) belt
9. Radial arm adapter
10. Radial arm adapter nut
11. Radial arm adapter cap

N0118621

Fig. 81 Exploded view of the alternator and related components—3.5L engine

4.6L Engine

See Figures 83 and 84.

1. Before servicing the vehicle, refer to the precautions in the beginning of this section.

2. Disconnect the battery.

3. Remove the throttle body as follows:

   a. Remove the air cleaner outlet pipe.

   b. Disconnect the electronic throttle control and throttle position (TP) sensor electrical connectors.

   c. Remove the bolts, the throttle body, and the gasket. Discard the gasket.

4. Rotate the front end accessory drive belt tensioner clockwise and position the front end accessory drive belt aside.

5. Remove or disconnect the following:

   • 4 bolts and the alternator bracket

   • 2 bolts and position the alternator aside

   • Protective cover and nut; position the alternator B+ terminal aside

   • Remove the alternator.

   • If necessary, remove the pulley from the alternator.

To install:

6. If removed, install the pulley onto the alternator. Tighten the pulley nut to 80 ft. lbs. (109 Nm).

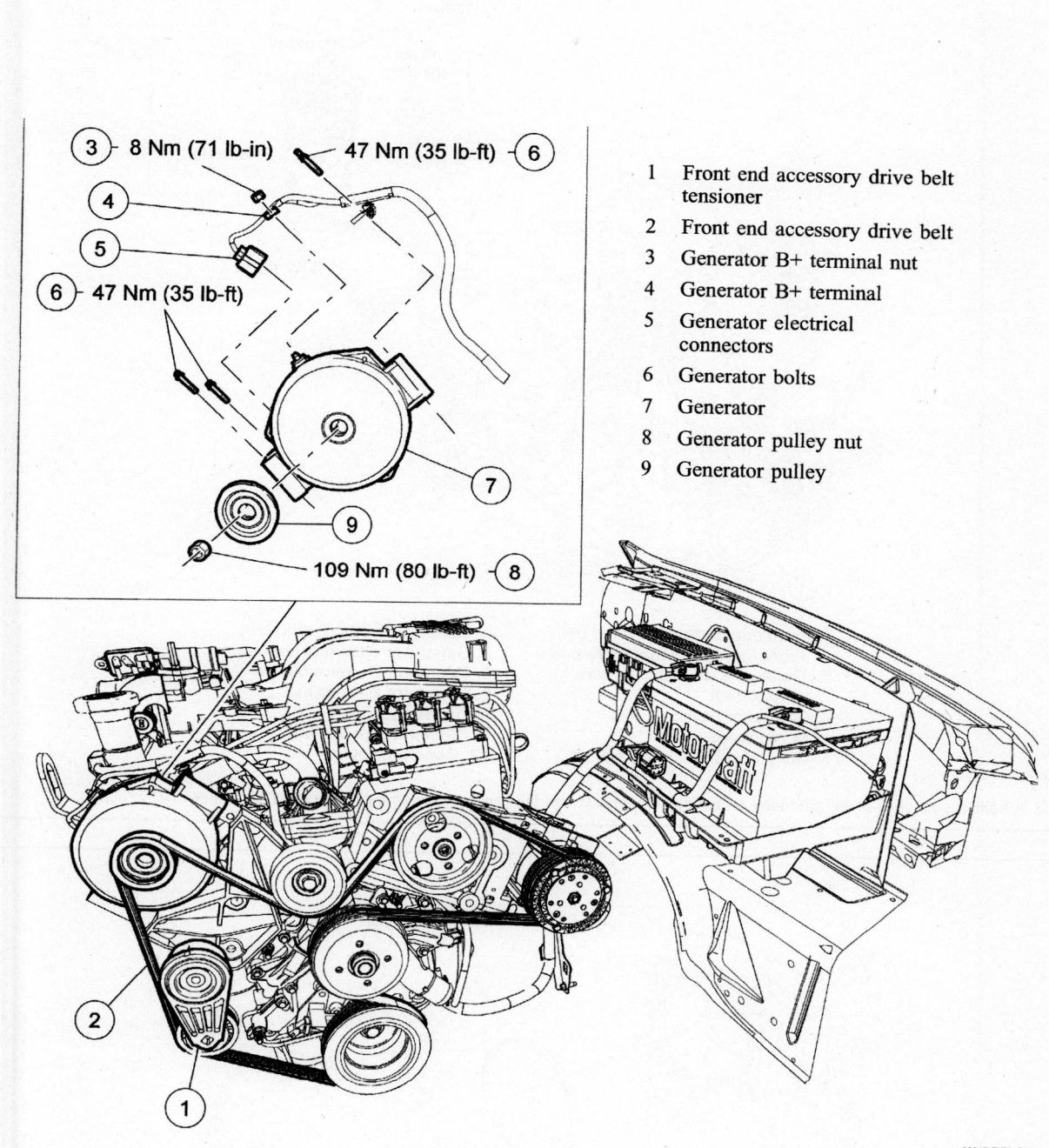

1   Front end accessory drive belt tensioner
2   Front end accessory drive belt
3   Generator B+ terminal nut
4   Generator B+ terminal
5   Generator electrical connectors
6   Generator bolts
7   Generator
8   Generator pulley nut
9   Generator pulley

06017-EXPL-G02

Fig. 82 Alternator mounting—4.0L engine

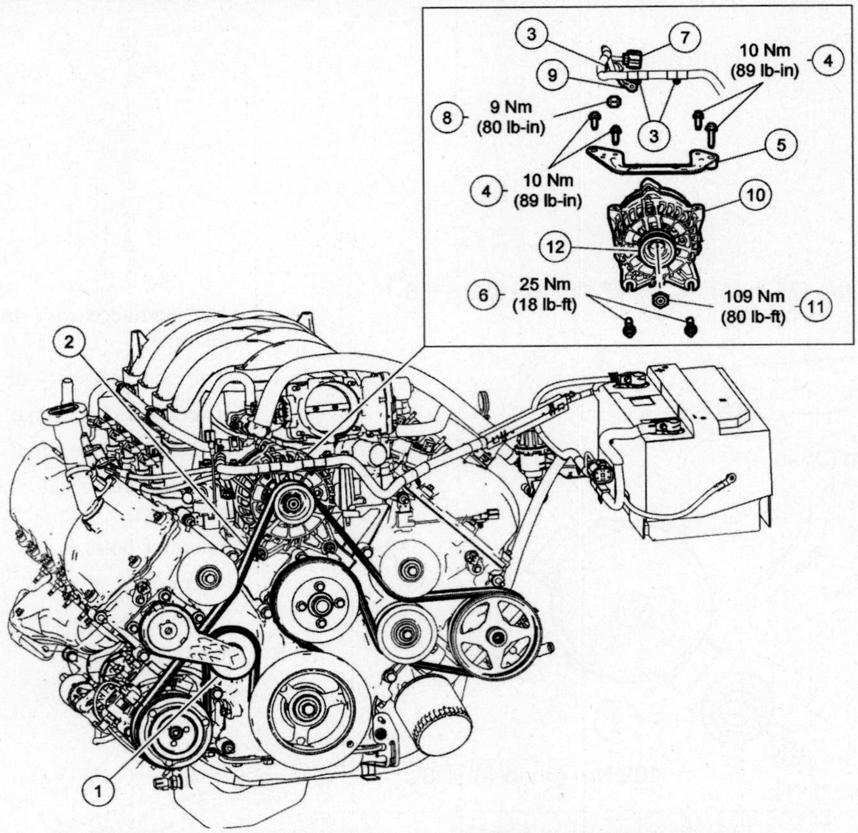

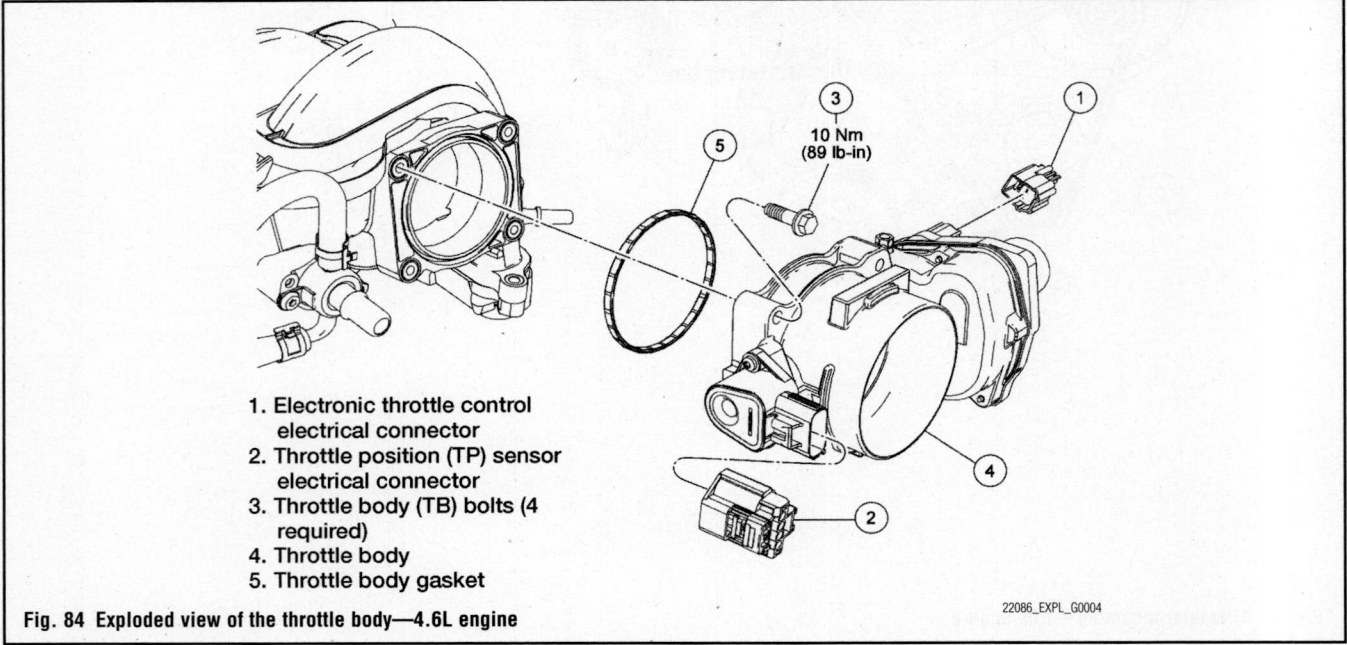

1. Front end accessory drive belt
2. Front end accessory drive belt
3. Generator harness locators (3 required)
4. Generator bracket bolts (4 required)
5. Generator bracket tensioner
6. Generator bolts (2 required)
7. Generator electrical connector
8. Generator B+ terminal nut
9. Generator B+ terminal
10. Generator
11. Generator pulley nut
12. Generator pulley

22086_EXPL_G0003

Fig. 83 A front engine view of the alternator mounting components and the accessory drive belt routing—4.6L engine

1. Electronic throttle control electrical connector
2. Throttle position (TP) sensor electrical connector
3. Throttle body (TB) bolts (4 required)
4. Throttle body
5. Throttle body gasket

22086_EXPL_G0004

Fig. 84 Exploded view of the throttle body—4.6L engine

7. Position the alternator. Install the mounting bolts and tighten to 18 lb. ft. (25 Nm).

8. Install the alternator B+ terminal and nut; reposition the protective cover.

9. Install the alternator bracket. Tighten the 4 bolts to 89 inch lbs. (10 Nm).

10. Install the accessory drive belt and release the tensioner.

11. Install the throttle body as follows:
a. Position the throttle body, with a new gasket. Install and tighten the mounting bolts to 89 inch lbs. (10 Nm).
b. Connect the TP sensor and electronic throttle control connectors.

c. Install the air cleaner outlet pipe.
12. Reconnect the battery.

VOLTAGE REGULATOR

ADJUSTMENT

The voltage regulator is an internal component of the alternator and cannot be serviced separately.

ENGINE ELECTRICAL

FIRING ORDERS

See Figures 85 and 86.

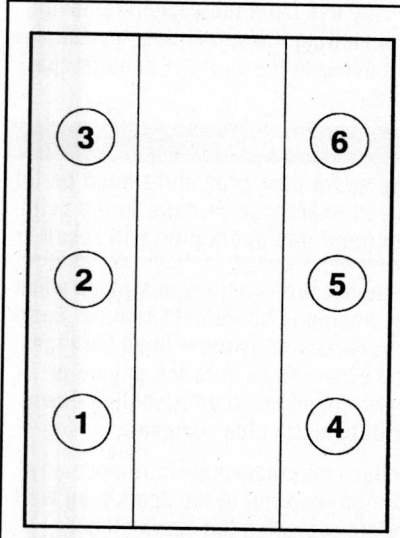

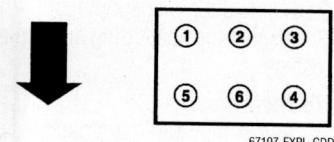

67197-EXPL-GDD

Fig. 85 4.0L Engine
Firing order: 1–4–2–5–3–6
Distributorless ignition system

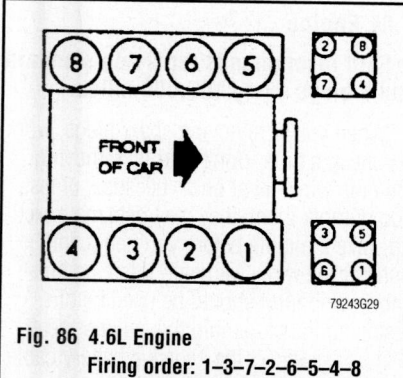

79243G29

Fig. 86 4.6L Engine
Firing order: 1–3–7–2–6–5–4–8
Distributorless ignition system

IGNITION COIL

REMOVAL & INSTALLATION

3.5L Engine

Left Side

See Figure 87.

➡ **Use compressed air to remove any foreign material from the ignition coil-on-plugs and surrounding area before removing the ignition coil-on-plugs.**

1. Disconnect the 3 Left Hand (LH) ignition coil-on-plug electrical connectors.
2. Remove the 3 Left Hand (LH) ignition coil-on-plug bolts.
3. Remove the 3 Left Hand (LH) ignition coil-on-plugs.

➡ **When removing the ignition coil-on-plugs, a slight twisting motion will break the seal and ease removal.**

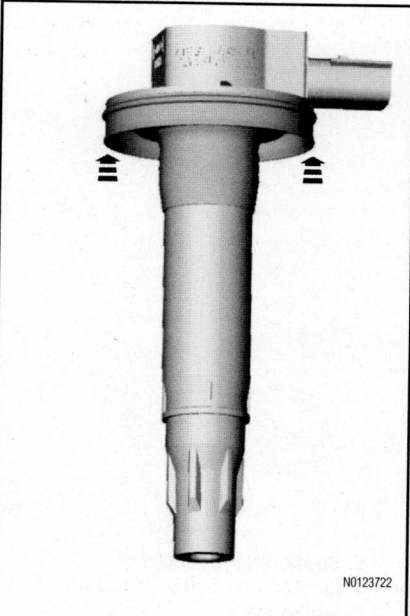

N0123722

Fig. 87 If damaged, install a new ignition coil-on-plug seat as shown

IGNITION SYSTEM

4. Remove the Left Hand (LH) ignition coil-on-plugs.

To install:

5. Inspect the ignition coil-on-plug seals for rips, nicks or tears. Remove and discard any damaged ignition coil-on-plug seals.
6. To install, slide the new ignition coil-on-plug seal onto the ignition coil-on-plug until it is fully seated at the top of the coil-on-plug.

➡ **Apply a small amount of silicone brake caliper grease and dielectric compound to the inside of the ignition coil-on-plug boots before installation.**

7. Install the Left Hand (LH) ignition coil-on-plugs.
8. Install the 3 Left Hand (LH) ignition coil-on-plugs.
9. Install the 3 Left Hand (LH) ignition coil-on-plug bolts. Tighten to 62 inch lbs. (7 Nm).
10. Connect the 3 Left Hand (LH) ignition coil-on-plug electrical connectors.

Right Side

See Figure 87.

➡ **The upper intake manifold must be removed to access the Right Hand (RH) ignition coil-on-plugs.**

1. Remove the upper intake manifold, as outlined in the Engine Mechanical Section.

➡ **Use compressed air to remove any foreign material from the ignition coil-on-plugs and surrounding area before removing the ignition coil-on-plugs.**

2. Disconnect the 3 Right Hand (RH) ignition coil-on-plug electrical connectors.
3. Remove the 3 Right Hand (RH) ignition coil-on-plug bolts.

➡ **When removing the ignition coil-on-plugs, a slight twisting motion will break the seal and ease removal.**

4. Remove the 3 Right Hand (RH) ignition coil-on-plugs.

To install:

5. Inspect the ignition coil-on-plug seals for rips, nicks or tears. Remove and discard any damaged ignition coil-on-plug seals.

6. To install, slide the new ignition coil-on-plug seal onto the ignition coil-on-plug until it is fully seated at the top of the coil-on-plug.

➡**Apply a small amount of silicone brake caliper grease and dielectric compound to the inside of the ignition coil-on-plug boots before installation.**

7. Install the 3 Right Hand (RH) ignition coil-on-plugs.

8. Install the 3 Right Hand (RH) ignition coil-on-plug bolts. Tighten to 62 inch lbs. (7 Nm).

9. Connect the 3 Right Hand (RH) ignition coil-on-plug electrical connectors.

10. Install the upper intake manifold. For

4.0L Engine

See Figure 88.

1. Disconnect the battery ground cable.
2. Disconnect the ignition coil electrical connector.
3. Disconnect the radio noise suppressor electrical connector, if equipped.

※※ WARNING

It is important to twist the spark plug wire boots while pulling upward to avoid possible damage to the spark plug wire.

➡**Spark plug wires must be connected to the correct ignition coil terminal. Mark the spark plug wires for installation reference.**

4. Squeeze the tabs and twist while pulling upward to disconnect the 6 spark plug wires.

5. Remove the 4 bolts and the ignition coil.

To install:

6. Apply silicone dielectric compound to the inside of the ignition coil boots.

7. Install the ignition coil; tighten the 4 bolts to 53 inch lbs. (6 Nm).

8. Install the spark plug wires to the correct spark plugs, as referenced during removal.

9. Connect the radio noise suppressor electrical connector, if equipped.

10. Connect the ignition coil connector.

11. Connect the battery ground cable.

4.6L Engine

See Figure 89.

1. Disconnect the battery ground cable.

2. Remove the bolts and the ignition coil-on-plugs.

To install:

3. Apply dielectric compound to the inside of the coil boots before installation.

4. Install the ignition coil-on-plugs and tighten the bolts to 53 inch lbs. (6 Nm).

5. Connect the battery ground cable.

IGNITION TIMING

INSPECTION

The ignition timing is preset to 10 degrees Before Top Dead Center (BTDC) and is not adjustable.

SPARK PLUGS

REMOVAL & INSTALLATION

3.5L Engine

See Figure 90.

1. Remove the 6 ignition coil-on-plugs, as outlined in this section.

➡**Only use hand tools when removing or installing the spark plugs or damage can occur to the cylinder head or spark plug.**

※※ WARNING

The spark plug procedure must be followed exactly or damage to the cylinder head and spark plug will result.

➡**Do not remove the spark plugs when the engine is hot or cold soaked. Spark plug thread or cylinder head damage can occur. Make sure the engine is warm (hand touch after cooling down) prior to spark plug removal.**

➡**Use compressed air to remove any foreign material in the spark plug well before removing the spark plugs.**

2. Remove the 6 spark plugs.

3. Inspect the spark plug and replace as necessary.

To install:

4. Adjust the spark plug gap as necessary: 0.0492–0.0531 in. (1.25–1.35mm).

5. Install the 6 spark plugs. Tighten to 11 ft. lbs. (15 Nm).

6. Install the 6 ignition coil-on-plugs, as outlined in this section.

4.0L Engine

➡**Ford recommends replacing standard spark plugs every 100,000 miles.**

When you're removing spark plugs, work on one at a time. Don't start by removing the plug wires all at once, because, unless you number them, they may become mixed up. Take a minute before you begin and number the wires with tape. Also, an anti-seize compound should be used before installing the plugs into the cylinder head.

1. Disconnect the negative battery cable, and if the vehicle has been run recently, allow the engine to thoroughly cool.

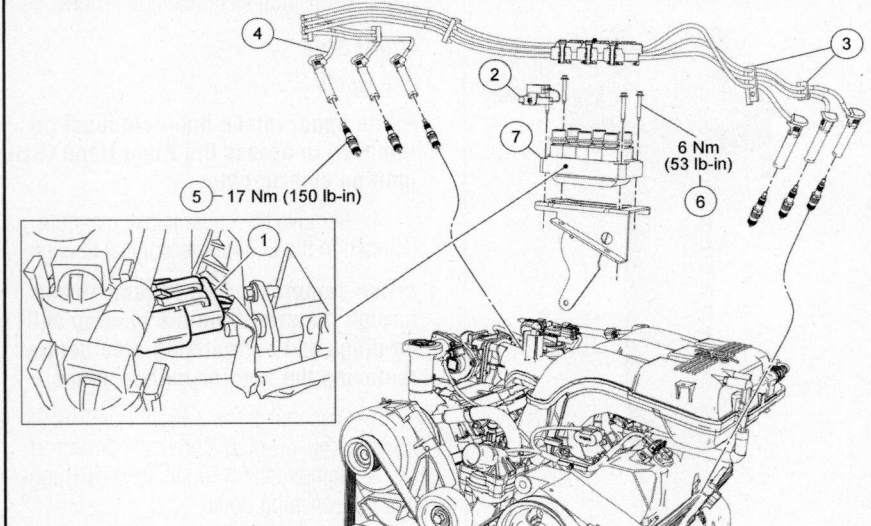

1. Ignition coil electrical connector
2. Radio noise suppressor electrical connector
3. Spark plug wire retainers
4. Spark plug wire (6 required)
5. Spark plug (6 required)
6. Ignition coil bolt (4 required)
7. Ignition coil

Fig. 88 Ignition system—4.0L Engine

36578_EXPL_G0139

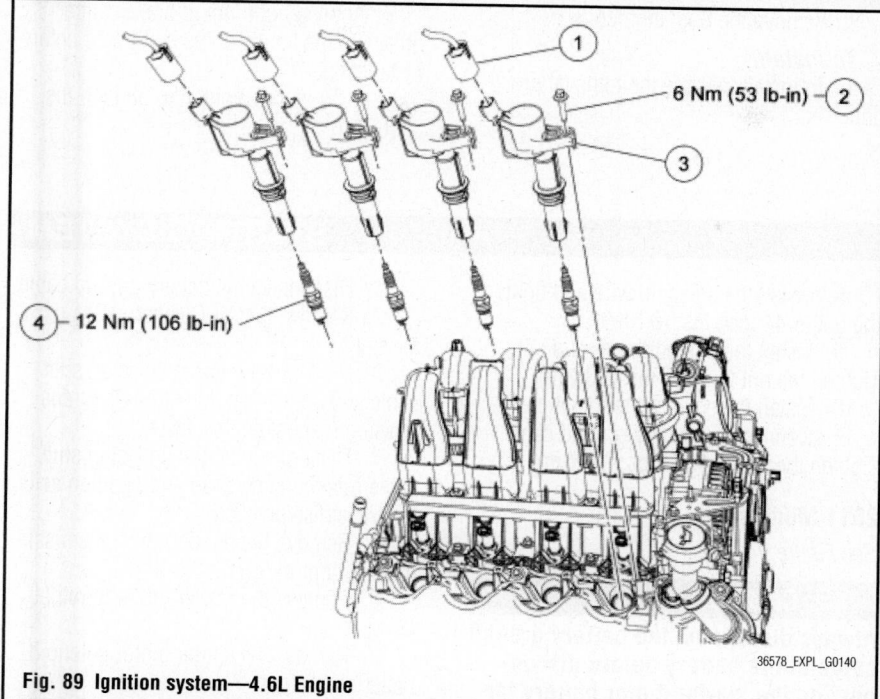

Fig. 89 Ignition system—4.6L Engine

2. Carefully twist the spark plug wire boot to loosen it, then pull upward and remove the boot from the plug. Be sure to pull on the boot and not on the wire, otherwise the connector located inside the boot may become separated.

3. Using compressed air, blow any water or debris from the spark plug well to assure that no harmful contaminants are allowed to enter the combustion chamber when the spark plug is removed.

➡**Remove the spark plugs when the engine is cold, if possible, to prevent damage to the threads. If removal of the plugs is difficult, apply penetrating oil or spray to the area around the base of the plug, and allow it a few minutes to work.**

4. Using a spark plug socket that is equipped with a rubber insert to properly hold the plug, turn the spark plug counter-

clockwise to loosen and remove the spark plug from the bore.

✳✳ WARNING

Be sure not to use a flexible extension on the socket. Use of a flexible extension may allow a shear force to be applied to the plug. A shear force could break the plug off in the cylinder head, leading to costly and frustrating repairs.

To install:

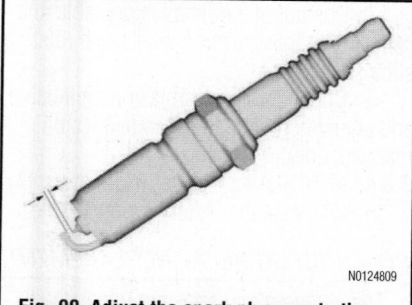

Fig. 90 Adjust the spark plug gap to the proper specification

5. Inspect the spark plug boot for tears or damage. If a damaged boot is found, the spark plug wire must be replaced.

➡**Coat the spark plug threads with an anti-seize compound before installing it into the cylinder head.**

6. Carefully thread the plug into the bore by hand. If resistance is felt before the plug is almost completely threaded, back the plug out and begin threading again. In small, hard to reach areas, an old spark plug wire and boot could be used as a threading tool. The boot will hold the plug while you twist the end of the wire and the wire is supple enough to twist before it would allow the plug to cross-thread.

✳✳ WARNING

Do not use the spark plug socket to thread the plugs. Always carefully thread the plug by hand or using an old plug wire to prevent the possibility of cross-threading and damaging the cylinder head bore.

7. Carefully tighten the spark plug to 13 ft. lbs. (17 Nm).

8. Apply a small amount of silicone dielectric compound to the end of the spark plug lead or inside the spark plug boot to prevent sticking, then install the boot to the spark plug and push until it clicks into place. The click may be felt or heard, then gently pull back on the boot to assure proper contact.

4.6 Engine

See Figure 91.

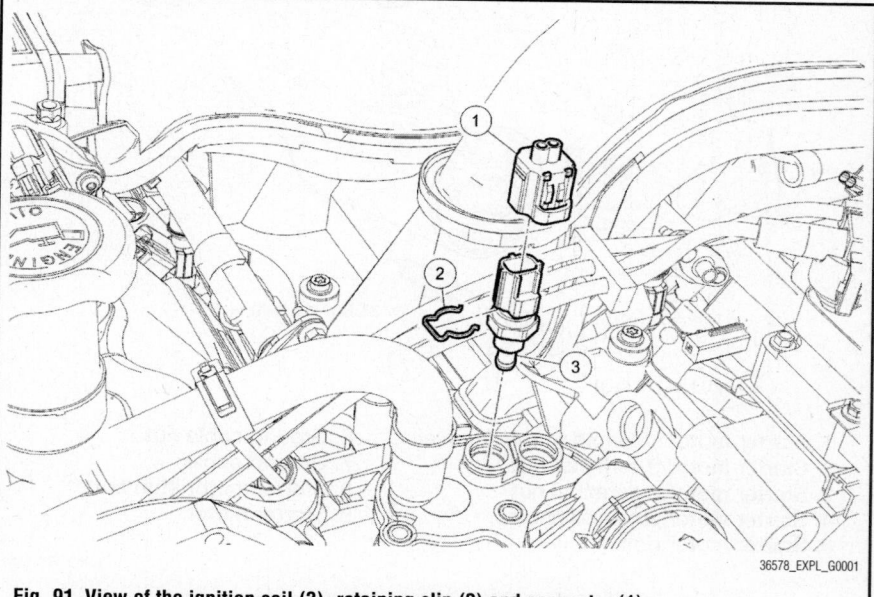

Fig. 91 View of the ignition coil (3), retaining clip (2) and connector (1)

1. Disconnect the 8 ignition coil electrical connectors.
2. Remove the 8 ignition coil bolts.

➡ **When removing the ignition coils, a slight twisting motion will break the seal and ease removal.**

3. Remove the 8 ignition coils.

To install:
4. To install, reverse the removal procedure.

5. Apply a light film of brake caliper grease to the inside of the coil boots before installation.
   a. To install, tighten to 53 inch lbs. (6 Nm).

ENGINE ELECTRICAL

STARTER

REMOVAL & INSTALLATION

2010 Models

See Figures 92 and 93.

1. With the vehicle in NEUTRAL, raise vehicle on hoist.
2. Disconnect the battery ground cable.
3. Remove the starter solenoid terminal cover.
4. Remove the nut and disconnect the starter solenoid battery cable.
5. Remove the nut and disconnect the starter solenoid wire.
6. Remove the 3 starter motor bolts and the starter motor.

To install:
7. Position the starter and install and tighten the starter motor bolts to 18 ft. lbs. (25 Nm).

8. Install the solenoid wire and tighten the nut to 44 inch lbs. (6 Nm).
9. Install the solenoid wire and nut. Tighten the nut to 10 ft. lbs. (13 Nm).
10. Install the solenoid terminal cover.
11. Connect the battery ground cable. Tighten the nut to 15 ft. lbs. (20 Nm).

2011 Models

See Figure 94.

> ❋❋ **CAUTION**
>
> **Always disconnect the battery ground cable at the battery before disconnecting the starter motor battery terminal lead. If a tool is shorted at the starter motor battery terminal, the tool can quickly heat enough to cause a skin burn. Failure to follow this instruction may result in serious personal injury.**

STARTING SYSTEM

1. Disconnect the battery ground cable.
2. Remove the Air Cleaner (ACL) assembly.
3. Disconnect the transmission shift cable and adjustment lock from the transmission manual control lever.
4. Disconnect the transmission shift cable rotating slide snap and position aside the transmission cable.
5. Remove the nut and the transmission manual control lever.
6. Remove the starter motor terminal cover.
7. Remove the starter motor solenoid battery cable nut.
8. Remove the starter motor solenoid wire nut.
9. Detach the wiring harness retainer from the starter motor stud bolt and position the wiring harness aside.
10. Remove the 2 starter motor stud bolts and the starter motor.

To install:
11. Position the starter motor and install the 2 stud bolts. Tighten to 20 ft. lbs. (27 Nm).
12. Position the wiring harness and attach the wiring harness retainer to the starter motor stud bolt.
13. Install the starter motor solenoid wire terminal and the nut. Tighten to 44 inch lbs. (5 Nm).
14. Install the starter motor solenoid battery cable terminal and the nut. Tighten to 106 inch lbs. (12 Nm).
15. Install the starter motor terminal cover.
16. Position the transmission manual control lever and install the nut. Tighten to 13 ft. lbs. (18 Nm).
17. Position the transmission cable and connect the transmission shift cable rotating slide snap.
18. Connect the transmission shift cable and adjustment lock to the transmission manual control lever.
19. Install the Air Cleaner (ACL) assembly.
20. Connect the battery ground cable.

SOLENOID OR RELAY REPLACEMENT

The solenoid and relay are integral with the starter.

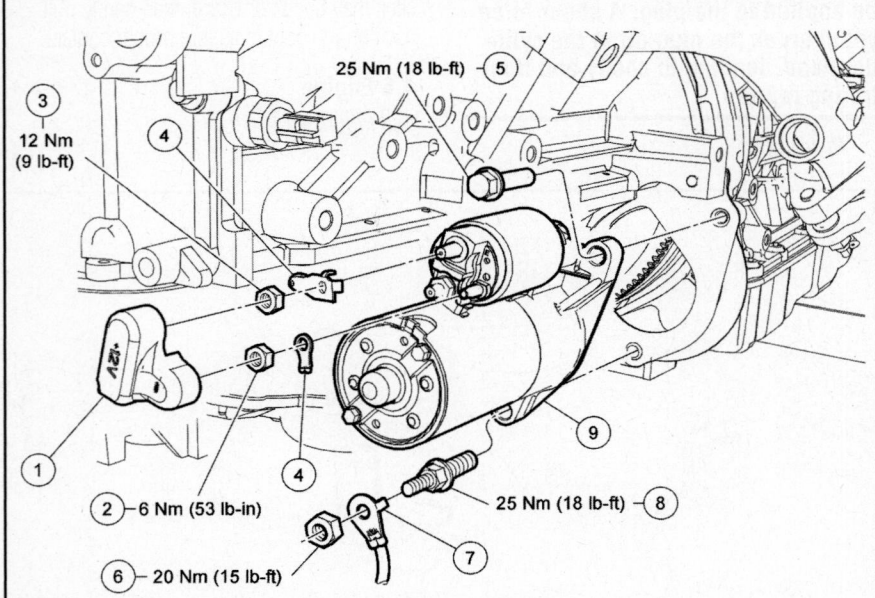

25 Nm (18 lb-ft) — ⑤
③
12 Nm (9 lb-ft)
④
④
①
② — 6 Nm (53 lb-in)
④
⑥ — 20 Nm (15 lb-ft)
⑦
25 Nm (18 lb-ft) — ⑧
⑨

1. Starter motor solenoid terminal cover
2. Starter motor S-terminal nut
3. Starter motor B-terminal nut
4. Starter motor solenoid cables
5. Starter motor bolt
6. Ground cable nut
7. Ground cable
8. Starter motor stud bolt
9. Starter motor

22086_EXPL_G0008

Fig. 92 Starter assembly shown in mounting position—4.0L engine

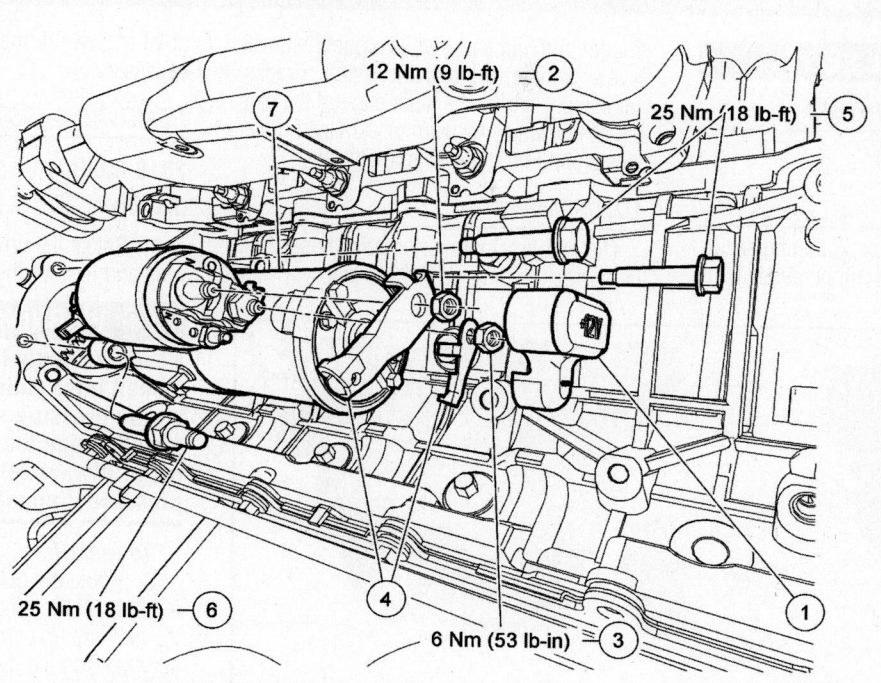

12 Nm (9 lb-ft) — (2)

25 Nm (18 lb-ft) — (5)

(7)

25 Nm (18 lb-ft) — (6)

6 Nm (53 lb-in) — (3)

(4)   (1)

1. Starter motor solenoid
terminal cover
2. B-terminal nut
3. S-terminal nut

4. Starter motor solenoid cables
5. Starter motor bolts (2 required)
6. Starter motor stud bolt
7. Starter motor

22086_EXPL_G0009

Fig. 93 Starter assembly shown in mounting position—4.6L engine

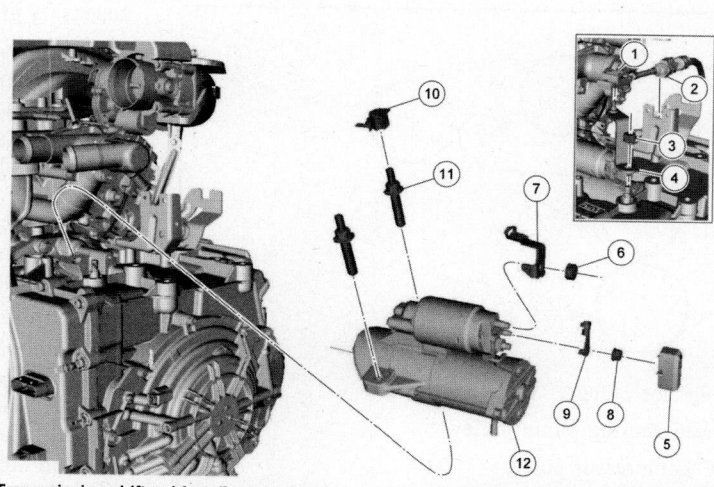

1. Transmission shift cable adjustment lock
2. Transmission shift cable rotating slide snap
3. Transmission manual control lever nut
4. Transmission manual control lever
5. Starter motor solenoid battery cable terminal cover
6. Starter motor solenoid battery cable nut

7. Starter motor solenoid battery cable terminal
8. Starter motor solenoid wire nut
9. Starter motor solenoid wire terminal
10. Wiring harness retainer
11. Starter motor stud bolt (2 required)
12. Starter motor

N0126511

Fig. 94 Exploded view of the starter motor mounting—3.5L engine

ENGINE MECHANICAL

ACCESSORY DRIVE BELTS

ACCESSORY BELT ROUTING

See Figures 95 through 97.

INSPECTION

Inspect the drive belt for signs of glazing or cracking. A glazed belt will be perfectly smooth from slippage, while a good belt will have a slight texture of fabric visible. Cracks will usually start at the inner edge of the belt and run outward. All worn or damaged drive belts should be replaced immediately.

ADJUSTMENT

The belt tensioner automatically set the correct tension on the accessory drive belt. No further adjustment is necessary.

REMOVAL & INSTALLATION

2010 Models

See Figure 98.

1. Rotate the drive belt tensioner clockwise and remove the drive belt.

☀☀ WARNING

Never suddenly let go of the tensioned idler pulley. The force of the spring pressure suddenly released may damage the idler pulley mechanism. Always release the spring pressure gradually.

To install:

2. Route the belt over the pulleys making sure all the grooves in the pulleys and the belt line up correctly. Refer to the accessory belt routing diagrams above.

3. Rotate belt tensioner clockwise and slip drive belt over idler pulley on tensioner.

2011 Models

➡**Under no circumstances should the accessory drive belt, tensioner or pulleys be lubricated as potential damage to the belt material and tensioner damping mechanism will occur. Do not apply any fluids or belt dressing to the accessory drive belt or pulleys.**

1. With the vehicle in NEUTRAL, position it on a hoist.

2. Working from the top of the vehicle, rotate the accessory drive belt tensioner clockwise and remove the accessory drive belt from the generator pulley.

3. Remove the 7 pin-type retainers and the RH splash shield.

4. Working from under the vehicle, remove the accessory drive belt.

To install:

☀☀ CAUTION

Working from under the vehicle, position the accessory drive belt on all pulleys, with the exception of the generator pulley.

➡**After installation, make sure the accessory drive belt is correctly seated on all pulleys.**

5. Working from the top of the vehicle, rotate the accessory drive belt

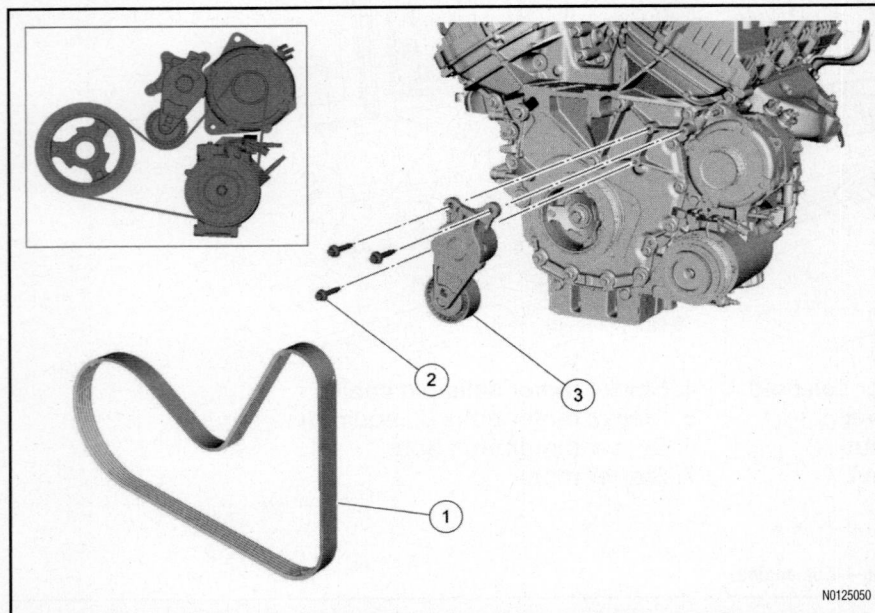

Fig. 95 View of the accessory drive belt (1), tensioner bolt (2) and tensioner (3)—3.5L engine

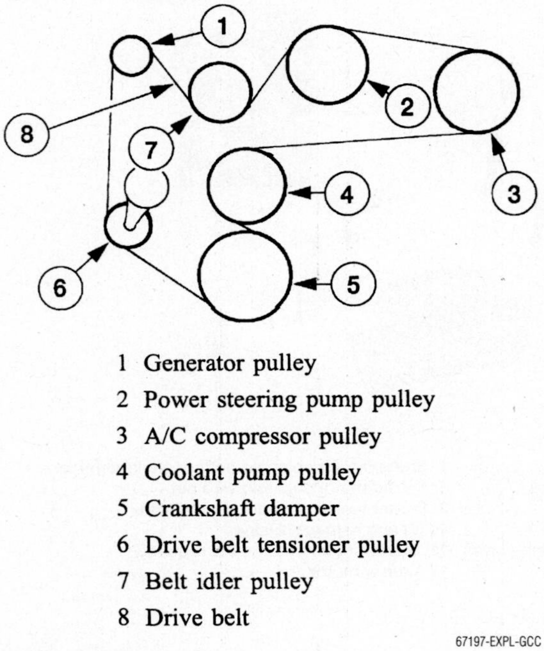

N0125050

1 Generator pulley
2 Power steering pump pulley
3 A/C compressor pulley
4 Coolant pump pulley
5 Crankshaft damper
6 Drive belt tensioner pulley
7 Belt idler pulley
8 Drive belt

Fig. 96 Accessory drive belt routing—4.0L Engine

67197-EXPL-GCC

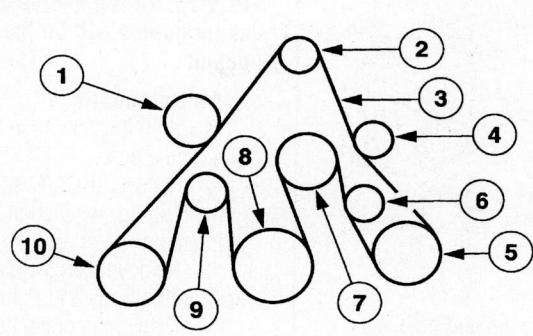

1 Belt idler pulley
2 Generator pulley
3 Drive belt
4 Belt idler pulley
5 Power steering pump pulley
6 Belt idler pulley
7 Coolant pump pulley
8 Crankshaft pulley
9 Drive belt tensioner pulley
10 A/C compressor pulley

67197-EXPL-GBB

Fig. 97 Accessory drive belt routing—4.6L Engine

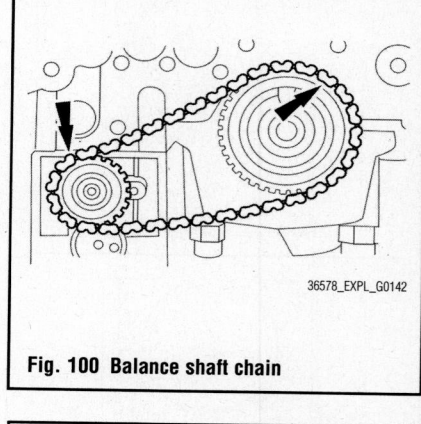

36578_EXPL_G0142

Fig. 100 Balance shaft chain

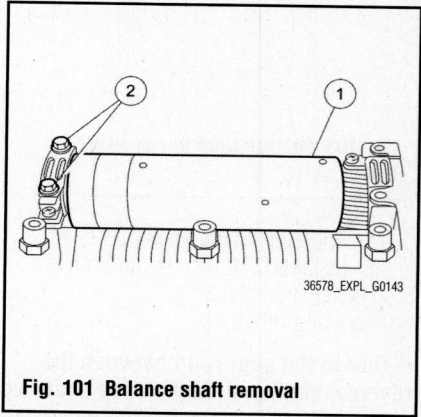

36578_EXPL_G0143

Fig. 101 Balance shaft removal

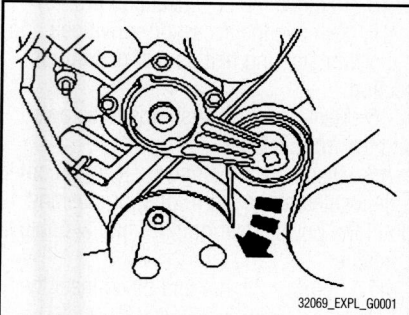

32069_EXPL_G0001

Fig. 98 Rotate the belt tensioner to relieve tension on the belt—4.6L engine shown, others similar

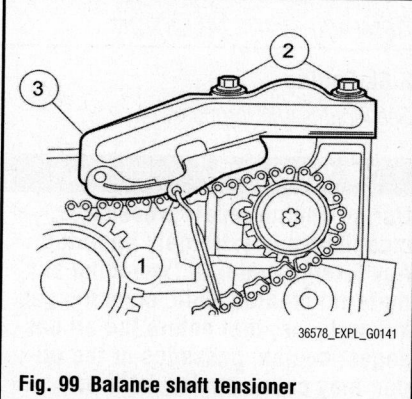

36578_EXPL_G0141

Fig. 99 Balance shaft tensioner

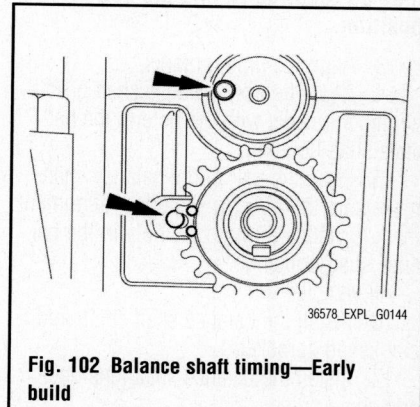

36578_EXPL_G0144

Fig. 102 Balance shaft timing—Early build

tensioner clockwise and install the accessory drive belt on the generator pulley.

6. Install the RH splash shield and the 7 pin-type retainers.

BALANCE SHAFT

REMOVAL & INSTALLATION

2010 Models

See Figures 99 through 105.

1. Remove timing chain and tensioner. Refer to Timing Chain and Tensioners.

2. Remove the balance shaft tensioner.
  a. Install a pin in the balance shaft tensioner.
  b. Remove the 2 bolts.
  c. Remove the balance shaft tensioner.
3. Remove the 2 bolts and the balance shaft chain guide.

➡**DO NOT remove the balance shaft sprocket bolt.**

4. Remove the balance shaft chain and crankshaft sprocket.
5. Remove the balance shaft.

6. Remove the 2 bolts.
7. Remove the balance shaft.

To install:

8. Install the balance shaft.
9. Install the balance shaft assembly.
10. Install the 2 bolts and tighten to 21 ft. lbs. (29 Nm).
Early build vehicles.

➡**Due to the gear ratio between the reversal shaft and the balance shaft, up to 7 complete turns of the balance shaft may be required to find the correct position.**

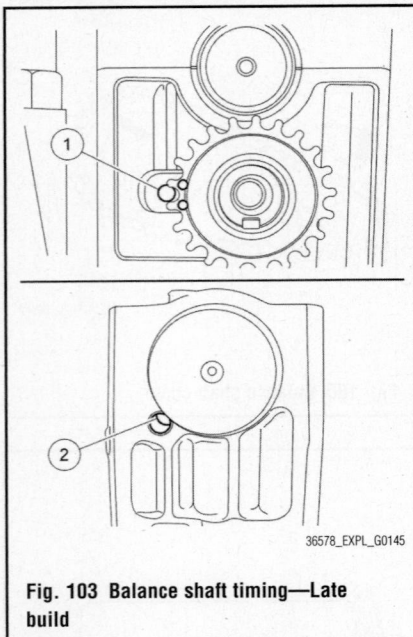

Fig. 103 Balance shaft timing—Late build

11. Align the timing marks.
12. Install a 0.16 inch (4 mm) pin to hold the shaft in place.
Late build vehicles.

➡**Due to the gear ratio between the reversal shaft and the balance shaft, up to 7 complete turns of the balance shaft may be required to find the correct position.**

13. Align the timing marks.
14. Align the front balance shaft gear alignment marks with the hole in the balance shaft housing.
15. From the rear of the balance shaft, make sure the balance shaft gear alignment mark is visible through the hole in the balance shaft housing.
All vehicles
16. Install the balance shaft chain and crankshaft sprocket.
17. Install the balance shaft tensioner and chain guide.

Fig. 104 Balance shaft chain and crankshaft sprocket

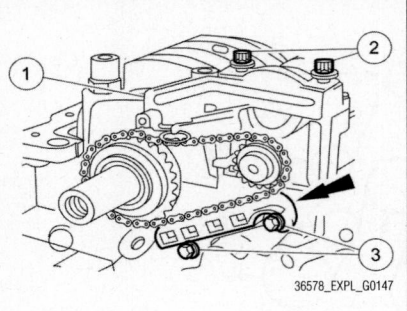

Fig. 105 Balance shaft tensioner and chain guide

a. Install the balance shaft tensioner.
b. Install the 2 bolts and tighten to 21 ft. lbs. (29 Nm).
c. Position the balance shaft chain guide, install the 2 bolts and tighten to 89 inch lbs. (10 Nm).
• Remove the pins from the tensioner and, if installed, the sprocket.
• Install the crankshaft key.
18. Install timing chain and tensioner. Refer to Timing Chain and Tensioners.

CAMSHAFT AND VALVE LIFTERS

REMOVAL & INSTALLATION

3.5L Engine

See Figures 106 through 114.

❊❊ WARNING

During engine repair procedures, cleanliness is extremely important. Any foreign material, including any material created while cleaning gasket surfaces, that enters the oil passages, coolant passages or the oil pan may cause engine failure.

❊❊ WARNING

Early build engines have 11 fastener valve covers, late build engines have 9 fastener valve covers. Do not attempt to install bolts in the 2 empty late build valve cover holes or damage to the valve cover will occur.

➡**On early build engines, the timing chain rides on the inner side of the RH timing chain guide. Late build engines are equipped with a different design RH timing chain guide that requires the timing chain to ride on the outer**

side of the RH timing chain guide. For service, all replacement RH timing chain guides will be the late build design.

All Camshafts

1. With the vehicle in NEUTRAL, position it on a hoist.
2. Recover the A/C system as outlined in the Heating, Ventilation & Air Conditioning Section.
3. Remove the cowl panel grille as outlined in the Body and Paint Section.
4. Detach the brake booster vacuum hose retainer from the strut tower brace.
5. Remove the 4 nuts and the strut tower brace.
6. Release the fuel system pressure as outlined in the Fuel System Section.
7. Remove the engine Air Cleaner (ACL) and ACL outlet pipe as outlined in this section.
8. Remove the battery tray.
9. Disconnect the engine wiring harness electrical connector.
10. Remove the nut and disconnect the 2 power feed wires from the positive battery terminal.
11. Remove the nut and disconnect the ground cable from the negative battery terminal.
12. Drain the cooling system as outlined in the Engine Cooling Section.
13. Remove the LF wheel and tire.
14. Remove the accessory drive belt and the power steering belt as outlined in this section.
15. Remove the 3 pushpins, 7 screws and the front valance.
16. Disconnect the power steering cooler tube located at the left front subframe and drain the power steering fluid into a suitable container.
17. Remove the nut and disconnect the A/C tube.
    a. Discard the O-ring seal and gasket seal.
18. Remove the nut and the A/C tube.
    a. Discard the O-ring seal and gasket seal.
19. Remove the degas bottle.
20. Disconnect the vacuum hose and the Evaporative Emission (EVAP) tube from the upper intake manifold.
21. Detach the EVAP tube pin-type retainer from the upper intake manifold.
22. Remove the EVAP canister purge valve as outlined in the Engine Performance & Emission Controls Section.
23. Disconnect the PCM and engine harness electrical connectors.
    a. Detach the wiring harness retainer.

24. Disconnect the 2 PCM electrical connectors.

25. Remove the engine wiring harness retainer from the bulkhead.

   a. Push the wiring harness retainer tab in.

   b. Slide the wiring harness up and out of the bulkhead.

26. Disconnect the upper radiator hose, lower radiator hose and 2 heater hoses from the thermostat housing.

27. Disconnect the transaxle control cable from the control lever.

28. Disconnect the transaxle control cable from the shift cable bracket and detach the wiring harness pin-type retainer.

29. If equipped, detach the engine block heater harness from the radiator support.

30. Disconnect the A/C pressure switch and remove the nut and disconnect the upper A/C tube from the condenser.

   a. Discard the O-ring seal.

31. Disconnect the fuel supply tube from the fuel rail as outlined in the Fuel System Section.

32. Detach the engine wiring harness retainer.

33. Detach the wire harness retainer from the RH valve cover stud bolt.

34. Remove the bolt and the ground cable from the engine.

35. Disconnect the hose from the power steering reservoir.

➡**Use a steering wheel holding device (such as Hunter® 28-75-1 or equivalent).**

36. Using a suitable holding device, hold the steering wheel in the straight-ahead position.

➡**Apply the brake to keep the halfshafts from rotating.**

37. Remove the RH and LH halfshaft nuts.

   a. Do not discard at this time.

38. Using the Front Wheel Hub Remover, separate the RH and LH halfshaft from the wheel hubs.

39. Remove the 2 lower scrivets from the rubber shield and position the shield aside.

40. Remove the bolt from the RH brake hose bracket.

❊❊ WARNING

Do not allow the intermediate shaft to rotate while it is disconnected from the gear or damage to the clockspring may occur. If there is evidence that the intermediate shaft has rotated, the clockspring must be

removed and recentered as outlined in the Chassis Electrical Section.

➡**Index-mark the steering column shaft position to the steering gear for reference during installation.**

41. Remove the bolt and disconnect the steering column shaft from the steering gear.

   a. Discard the bolt.

42. Remove the 4 Y-pipe-to-catalytic converter nuts.

   a. Discard the nuts.

43. Remove the 2 Y-pipe flange nuts.

   a. Detach the exhaust hanger and remove the Y-pipe.

   b. Discard the gaskets and nuts.

All-Wheel Drive (AWD) Vehicles

➡**Index-mark the driveshaft for installation.**

44. Remove and discard the 4 bolts and support the driveshaft with a length of mechanic's wire.

All Camshafts

45. Remove the drain plug and drain the engine oil.

   a. Install the drain plug and tighten to 20 ft. lbs. (27 Nm).

46. Remove and discard the engine oil filter.

47. Remove the Power Steering Pressure (PSP) tube bracket-to-steering gear bolt.

48. Remove the bolt, rotate the clamp plate clockwise and disconnect the PSP tube from the steering gear.

   a. Discard the O-ring seal.

49. Remove the 2 rear engine roll restrictor-to-transaxle bolts.

50. Remove the 2 front engine roll restrictor-to-transaxle bolts.

51. Remove and discard the upper stabilizer link nuts.

➡**The hex-holding feature can be used to prevent turning of the stud while removing the nuts.**

52. Remove and discard the tie-rod end nuts.

   a. Separate the tie-rod ends from the wheel knuckles.

❊❊ WARNING

Suspension fasteners are critical parts because they affect performance of vital components and systems and their failure may result in major service expense. New parts must be installed with the same part number or equivalent part, if replace-

ment is necessary. Do not use a replacement part of lesser quality or substitute design. Torque values must be used as specified during reassembly to make sure of correct retention of these parts.

❊❊ WARNING

Use care when releasing the lower arm and knuckle into the resting position or damage to the ball joint seal or Constant Velocity (CV) boot may occur.

➡**Use the hex-holding feature to prevent the stud from turning while removing the nut.**

53. Remove and discard the lower ball joint-to-wheel knuckle nuts.

   a. Separate the lower ball joints from the wheel knuckles.

54. Position the Powertrain Lift under the subframe assembly.

55. Remove the subframe bracket-to-body bolts.

56. Remove the rear subframe bolts and the subframe brackets.

57. Remove the front subframe bolts.

58. Lower the subframe assembly from the vehicle.

59. Pull the RH wheel knuckle outward and rotate it toward the rear of the vehicle.

   a. Secure the RH wheel knuckle assembly.

60. Remove the 2 intermediate shaft bracket nuts.

61. Remove the intermediate and half-shaft assembly.

❊❊ WARNING

The sharp edges on the stub shaft splines can slice or puncture the oil seal. Use care when inserting the stub shaft into the transmission or damage to the component may occur.

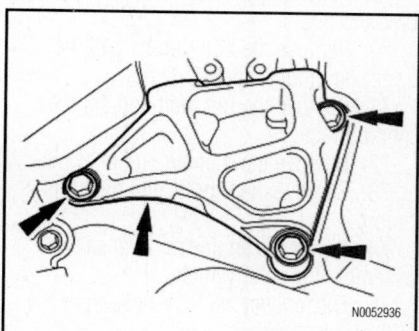

Fig. 106 Removal of the engine mount bracket bolts

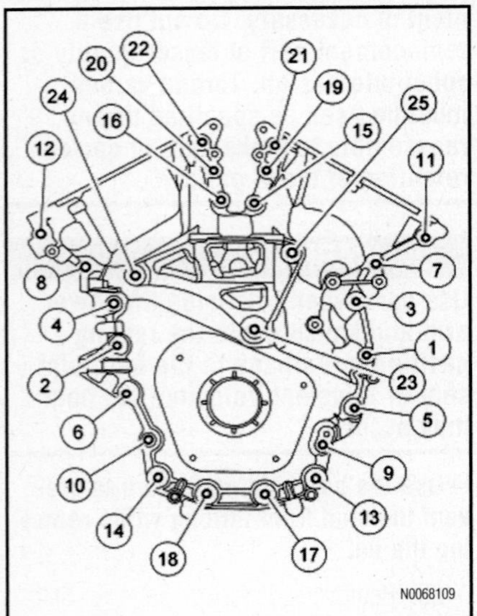

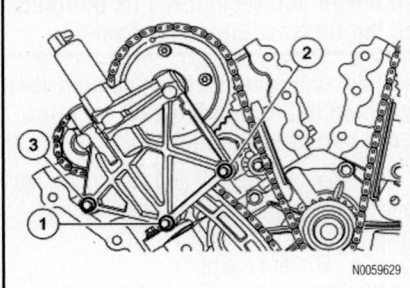

Fig. 107 Removal & installation of the 22 engine front cover bolts and the 3 engine mount bolts

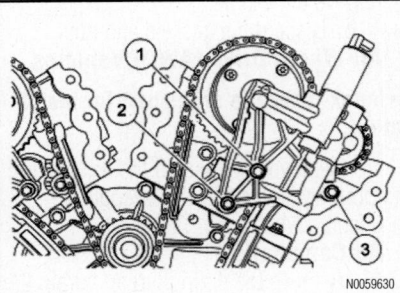

Fig. 108 Removal & installation of the RH VCT housing, and 3 bolts. Tighten in the sequence shown

Fig. 109 Removal & installation of the LH VCT housing, and 3 bolts. Tighten in the sequence shown

62. Using the Slide Hammer and Half-shaft Remover, remove the halfshaft from the transmission.

63. Remove and discard the circlip from the stub shaft.

64. Remove the 2 RH halfshaft support bracket studs.

65. Remove the 4 bolts and the RH half-shaft support bracket.

66. Remove the 2 secondary latches from the transmission fluid cooler tubes at the transmission fluid cooler thermal bypass valve.

67. Using the Transmission Cooler Tube Disconnect Tool, disconnect the transmission fluid cooler tubes from the transmission fluid cooler thermal bypass valve.

➡**Position a block of wood under the transaxle.**

68. Install the Powertrain Lift and Universal Adapter Brackets.

69. Remove the transaxle mount through bolt and nut.

70. Remove the bolt, 3 nuts and the transaxle mount bracket.

71. Remove the nut, bolt and engine mount brace.

72. Remove the 4 engine mount nuts.

73. Remove the 3 bolts and the engine mount.

74. Lower the engine and transaxle assembly from the vehicle.

75. Disconnect the PCV hose from the PCV valve.

76. Disconnect the Throttle Body (TB) electrical connector.

77. Detach the wiring harness retainers from the upper intake manifold.

78. Remove the upper intake manifold support bracket bolt.

79. Remove the wire harness pin-type retainer and the fuel tube bracket bolt from the upper intake manifold.

✳✳ WARNING

If the engine is repaired or replaced because of upper engine failure, typically including valve or piston damage, check the intake manifold for metal debris. If metal debris is found, install a new intake manifold. Failure to follow these instructions can result in engine damage.

80. Remove the 6 bolts and the upper intake manifold.
    a. Discard the gaskets.

81. Disconnect the RH catalyst monitor electrical connector.

82. Disconnect the RH Variable Camshaft Timing (VCT) solenoid electrical connector.

83. Disconnect the 3RH coil-on-plug electrical connectors.

84. Detach all of the wiring harness retainers from the RH valve cover and stud bolts.

85. Disconnect the LH VCT solenoid electrical connector.

86. Disconnect the 3 LH coil-on-plug electrical connectors.

87. Detach all of the wiring harness retainers from the LH valve cover and stud bolts.

88. Remove the 6 bolts and the 6 coil-on-plug assemblies.

89. Disconnect the PSP switch electrical connector.

90. Remove the PSP tube bracket-to-power steering pump bolt.

91. Remove the nut and the PSP tube bracket from the RH valve cover stud bolt.

92. Remove the 3 bolts and position aside the power steering pump.

93. Remove the 3 bolts and the accessory drive belt tensioner.

Early Build Vehicles

94. Loosen the 11 stud bolts and remove the LH valve cover. Discard the gasket.

95. Loosen the bolt, the 10 stud bolts and remove the RH valve cover. Discard the gasket.

Late Build Vehicles

96. Loosen the 9 stud bolts and remove the LH valve cover. Discard the gasket.

97. Loosen the 9 stud bolts and remove the RH valve cover. Discard the gasket.

All Vehicles

➡**VCT solenoid seal removal shown, spark plug tube seal removal similar.**

98. Inspect the VCT solenoid seals and the spark plug tube seals. Install new seals if damaged.
    a. Using the VCT Spark Plug Tube Seal Remover and Handle, remove the seal(s).

99. Using the Strap Wrench, remove the crankshaft pulley bolt and washer.
    a. Discard the bolt.

100. Using the 3 Jaw Puller, remove the crankshaft pulley.

101. Using the Oil Seal Remover, remove and discard the crankshaft front seal.

102. Remove the 2 bolts and the engine mount bracket.

➡**Only use hand tools to remove the studs.**

103. Remove the 2 engine mount studs.

104. Remove the 3 bolts and the engine mount bracket.

105. Remove the 22 engine front cover bolts.

106. Install 6 of the engine front cover bolts (finger tight) into the 6 threaded holes in the engine front cover.

a. Tighten the bolts one turn at a time in a crisscross pattern until the engine front cover-to-cylinder block seal is released.

b. Remove the engine front cover.

✳✳ WARNING

Only use a 3M(tm) Roloc® Bristle Disk (2-in white, part number 07528) to clean the engine front cover. Do not use metal scrapers, wire brushes or any other power abrasive disk to clean the engine front cover. These tools cause scratches and gouges that make leak paths.

107. Clean the engine front cover using a 3M(tm) Roloc® Bristle Disk (2-in white, part number 07528) in a suitable tool turning at the recommended speed of 15,000 rpm.

a. Thoroughly wash the engine front cover to remove any foreign material, including any abrasive particles created during the cleaning process.

✳✳ WARNING

Place clean, lint-free shop towels over exposed engine cavities. Carefully remove the towels so foreign material is not dropped into the engine. Any foreign material (including any material created while cleaning gasket surfaces) that enters the oil passages or the oil pan, may cause engine failure.

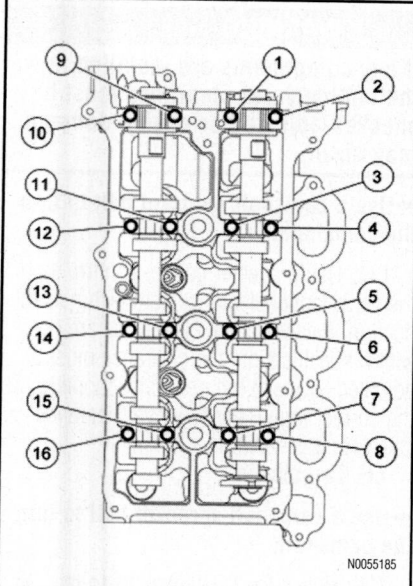

Fig. 110 Removal & installation of the LH camshaft bearing caps (8), and the bolts (16)

✳✳ WARNING

Do not use wire brushes, power abrasive discs or 3M(tm) Roloc® Bristle Disk (2-in white, part number 07528) to clean the sealing surfaces. These tools cause scratches and gouges that make leak paths. They also cause contamination that will cause premature engine failure. Remove all traces of sealant, including any sealant from the inner surface of the cylinder block and cylinder head.

108. Clean the sealing surfaces of the cylinder heads, the cylinder block and the oil pan in the following sequence.

a. Remove any large deposits of silicone or gasket material.

b. Apply silicone gasket remover and allow to set for several minutes.

c. Remove the silicone gasket remover. A second application of silicone gasket remover may be required if residual traces of silicone or gasket material remain.

d. Apply metal surface prep, to remove any remaining traces of oil or coolant and to prepare the surfaces to bond. Do not attempt to make the metal shiny. Some staining of the metal surfaces is normal.

e. Make sure the 2 locating dowel pins are seated correctly in the cylinder block.

Engines Equipped With Early Build RH Timing Chain Guides

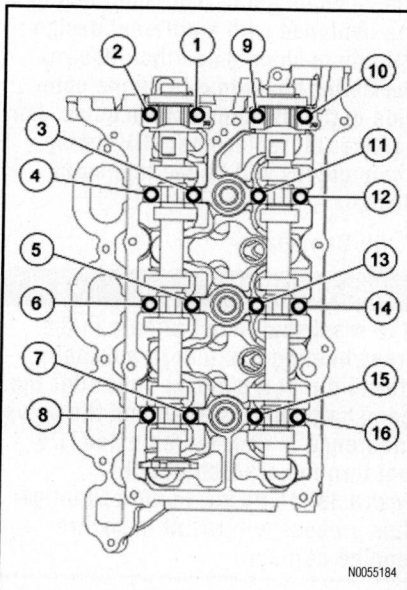

Fig. 111 Removal & installation of the RH camshaft bearing caps (8), and the bolts (16)

109. Rotate the crankshaft clockwise and align the timing marks on the VCT assemblies.

Engines Equipped With Late Build/Replacement RH Timing Chain Guides

110. Rotate the crankshaft clockwise and align the timing marks on the VCT assemblies as shown.

All Camshafts

➡ **The Camshaft Holding Tool will hold the camshafts in the Top Dead Center (TDC) position.**

111. Install the Camshaft Holding Tool onto the flats of the LH camshafts.

➡ **The Camshaft Holding Tool will hold the camshafts in the TDC position.**

112. Install the Camshaft Holding Tool onto the flats of the RH camshafts.

113. Remove the 3 bolts and the RH VCT housing.

114. Remove the 3 bolts and the LH VCT housing.

115. Remove the 2 bolts and the primary timing chain tensioner.

116. Remove the primary timing chain tensioner arm.

117. Remove the 2 bolts and the lower LH primary timing chain guide.

118. Remove the primary timing chain.

LH Camshafts

119. Compress the LH secondary timing chain tensioner and install a suitable lock-pin to retain the tensioner in the collapsed position.

➡ **The VCT bolt and the exhaust camshaft bolt must be discarded and new ones installed. However, the exhaust camshaft washer is reusable.**

120. Remove and discard the LH VCT assembly bolt and the LH exhaust camshaft sprocket bolt.

a. Remove the LH VCT assembly, secondary timing chain and the LH exhaust camshaft sprocket as an assembly.

➡ **When the Camshaft Holding Tool is removed, valve spring pressure will rotate the LH camshafts approximately 3 degrees to a neutral position.**

121. Remove the Camshaft Holding Tool from the LH camshafts.

✳✳ WARNING

The camshafts must remain in the neutral position during removal or engine damage may occur.

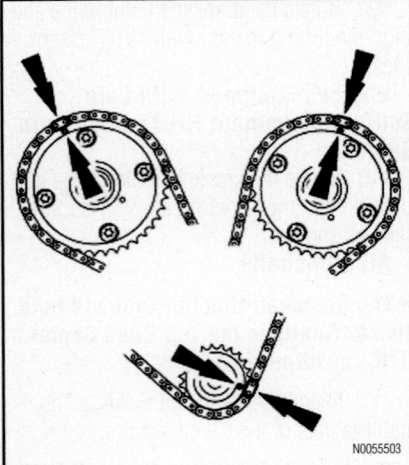

Fig. 112 Installation of the primary timing chain with the colored links aligned with the timing marks on the VCT assemblies

122. Verify the LH camshafts are in the neutral position.

➡**Cylinder head camshaft bearing caps are numbered to verify that they are assembled in their original positions.**

123. Remove the bolts and the LH camshaft bearing caps.

　a. Remove the LH camshafts.

RH Camshafts

124. Compress the RH secondary timing chain tensioner and install a suitable lockpin to retain the tensioner in the collapsed position.

➡**The VCT bolt and the exhaust camshaft bolt must be discarded and new ones installed. However, the exhaust camshaft washer is reusable.**

125. Remove and discard the RH VCT assembly bolt and the RH exhaust camshaft sprocket bolt.

　a. Remove the RH VCT assembly, secondary timing chain and the RH exhaust camshaft sprocket as an assembly.

126. Remove the Camshaft Holding Tool from the RH camshafts.

✳✳ WARNING

The camshafts must remain in the neutral position during removal or engine damage may occur.

127. Rotate the RH camshafts counterclockwise to the neutral position.

➡**Cylinder head camshaft bearing caps are numbered to verify that they are assembled in their original positions.**

128. Remove the bolts and the RH camshaft bearing caps.

　a. Remove the RH camshafts.

To install:

✳✳ CAUTION

Do not smoke, carry lighted tobacco or have an open flame of any type when working on or near any fuel-related component. Highly flammable mixtures are always present and may be ignited. Failure to follow these instructions may result in serious personal injury.

✳✳ WARNING

During engine repair procedures, cleanliness is extremely important. Any foreign material, including any material created while cleaning gasket surfaces that enters the oil passages, coolant passages or the oil pan, may cause engine failure.

✳✳ WARNING

Early build engines have 11 fastener valve covers, late build engines have 9 fastener valve covers. Do not attempt to install bolts in the 2 empty late build valve cover holes or damage to the valve cover will occur.

➡**On early build engines, the timing chain rides on the inner side of the RH timing chain guide. Late built engines are equipped with a different design RH timing chain guide that requires the timing chain to ride on the outer side of the RH timing chain guide. For service, all replacement RH timing chain guides will be the late build design.**

All Camshafts

✳✳ WARNING

The crankshaft must remain in the freewheeling position (crankshaft dowel pin at 9 o'clock) until after the camshafts are installed and the valve clearance is checked/adjusted. Do not turn the crankshaft until instructed to do so. Failure to follow this process will result in severe engine damage.

129. Rotate the crankshaft counterclockwise until the crankshaft dowel pin is in the 9 o'clock position.

LH Camshafts

✳✳ WARNING

The camshafts must remain in the neutral position during removal or engine damage may occur.

➡**Coat the camshafts with clean engine oil prior to installation.**

130. Position the camshafts onto the LH cylinder head in the neutral position.

➡**Cylinder head camshaft bearing caps are numbered to verify that they are assembled in their original positions.**

131. Install the 8 camshaft caps and the 16 bolts. Tighten the bolts to 89 inch lbs. (10 Nm).

RH Camshafts

✳✳ WARNING

The camshafts must remain in the neutral position during removal or engine damage may occur.

➡**Coat the camshafts with clean engine oil prior to installation.**

132. Position the camshafts onto the RH cylinder head in the neutral position as shown.

➡**Cylinder head camshaft bearing caps are numbered to verify that they are assembled in their original positions.**

133. Install the 8 camshaft caps and the 16 bolts. Tighten the bolts to 89 inch lbs. (10 Nm).

All Camshafts

✳✳ WARNING

If any components are installed new, the engine valve clearance must be checked/adjusted or engine damage may occur.

➡**Use a camshaft sprocket bolt to turn the camshafts.**

134. Using a feeler gauge, confirm that the valve tappet clearances are within specification. If valve tappet clearances are not within specification, the clearance must be adjusted by installing new valve tappet(s) of the correct size. Refer to Valve Clearance Check in this section.

LH Camshafts

➡**Use a camshaft sprocket bolt to turn the camshafts.**

135. Rotate the LH camshafts to the Top Dead Center (TDC) position and install the Camshaft Holding Tool on the flats of the camshafts.

136. Assemble the LH Variable Camshaft Timing (VCT) assembly, the LH exhaust camshaft sprocket and the LH secondary timing chain.

a. Align the colored links with the timing marks.

137. Position the LH secondary timing assembly onto the camshafts.

138. Install the new VCT bolt and new exhaust camshaft bolt and the original washer. Tighten in 4 stages.

a. Stage 1: Tighten to 30 ft. lbs. (40 Nm).

b. Stage 2: Loosen one full turn.

c. Stage 3: Tighten to 89 inch lbs. (10 Nm).

d. Stage 4: Tighten 90 degrees.

139. Remove the lockpin from the LH secondary timing chain tensioner.

RH Camshafts

➡**Use a camshaft sprocket bolt to turn the camshafts.**

140. Rotate the RH camshafts to the TDC position and install the Camshaft Holding Tool on the flats of the camshafts.

141. Assemble the RH VCT assembly, the RH exhaust camshaft sprocket and the RH secondary timing chain.

a. Align the colored links with the timing marks.

142. Position the RH secondary timing assembly onto the camshafts.

143. Install the new VCT bolt and new exhaust camshaft bolt and the original washer. Tighten in 4 stages.

a. Stage 1: Tighten to 30 ft. lbs. (40 Nm).

b. Stage 2: Loosen one full turn.

c. Stage 3: Tighten to 89 inch lbs. (10 Nm).

d. Stage 4: Tighten 90 degrees.

144. Remove the lockpin from the RH secondary timing chain tensioner.

All Camshafts

145. Rotate the crankshaft clockwise 60 degrees to the TDC position (crankshaft dowel pin at 11 o'clock).

146. Install the primary timing chain with the colored links aligned with the timing marks on the VCT assemblies and the crankshaft sprocket.

147. Install the lower LH primary timing chain guide and the 2 bolts. Tighten the bolts to 89 inch lbs. (10 Nm).

148. Install the primary timing chain tensioner arm.

149. Reset the primary timing chain tensioner.

a. Rotate the lever counterclockwise.

b. Using a soft-jawed vise, compress the plunger.

c. Align the hole in the lever with the hole in the tensioner housing.

d. Install a suitable lockpin.

➡**It may be necessary to rotate the crankshaft slightly to remove slack from the timing chain and install the tensioner.**

150. Install the primary tensioner and the 2 bolts. Tighten the bolts to 89 inch lbs. (10 Nm).

a. Remove the lockpin.

151. As a post-check, verify correct alignment of all timing marks.

152. Inspect the VCT housing seals for damage and replace as necessary.

⁑ WARNING

Make sure the dowels on the Variable Camshaft Timing (VCT) housing are fully engaged in the cylinder head prior to tightening the bolts. Failure to follow this process will result in severe engine damage.

153. Install the LH VCT housing and the 3 bolts. Tighten the bolts to 89 inch lbs. (10 Nm).

⁑ WARNING

Make sure the dowels on the Variable Camshaft Timing (VCT) housing are fully engaged in the cylinder head prior to tightening the bolts. Failure to follow this process will result in severe engine damage.

154. Install the RH VCT housing and the 3 bolts. Tighten the bolts to 89 inch lbs. (10 Nm).

155. Install the Alignment Pins.

⁑ WARNING

Failure to use Motorcraft® High Performance Engine RTV Silicone may cause the engine oil to foam excessively and result in serious engine damage.

➡**The engine front cover and bolts 17, 18, 19 and 20 must be installed within 4 minutes of the initial sealant application. The remainder of the engine front cover bolts and the engine mount bracket bolts must be installed and tighten within 35 minutes of the initial sealant application. If the time limits are exceeded, the sealant must be removed, the sealing area cleaned and sealant reapplied. To clean the sealing area, use silicone gasket remover and metal surface prep. Failure to follow this procedure can cause future oil leakage.**

156. Apply a 0.11 inch (3.0 mm) bead of Motorcraft® High Performance Engine RTV Silicone to the engine front cover sealing surfaces including the 3 engine mount bracket bosses.

a. Apply a 5.5 mm (0.21 in) bead of Motorcraft® High Performance Engine RTV Silicone to the oil pan-to-cylinder block joint and the cylinder head-to-cylinder block joint areas of the engine front cover in 5 places as indicated.

➡**Make sure the 2 locating dowel pins are seated correctly in the cylinder block.**

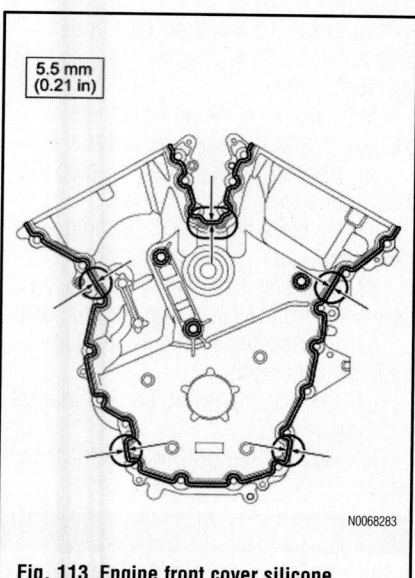

Fig. 113 Engine front cover silicone bead placement

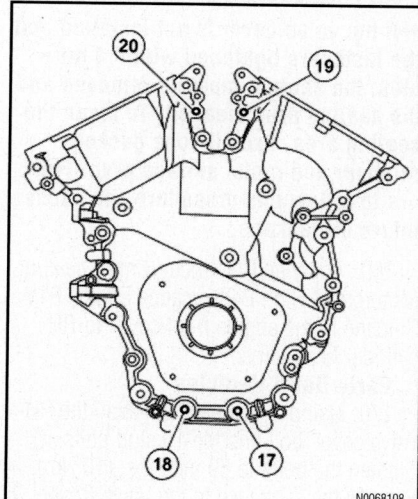

Fig. 114 Install the engine front cover and bolts 17, 18, 19 and 20. Tighten in sequence shown

157. Install the engine front cover and bolts 17, 18, 19 and 20. Tighten the bolts to 27 inch lbs. (3 Nm).

158. Remove the Alignment Pins.

➡**Do not tighten the bolts at this time.**

159. Install the engine mount bracket and the 3 bolts.

※※ **WARNING**

Do not expose the Motorcraft® High Performance Engine RTV Silicone to engine oil for at least 90 minutes after installing the engine front cover. Failure to follow this instruction may cause oil leakage.

160. Install the remaining engine front cover bolts. Tighten all of the engine front cover bolts and engine mount bracket bolts in the sequence shown in 2 stages:

a. Stage 1: Tighten bolts 1 thru 22 to 89 inch lbs. (10 Nm) and bolts 23, 24 and 25 to 133 inch lbs. (15 Nm).

b. Stage 2: Tighten bolts 1 thru 22 to 18 ft. lbs. (24 Nm) and bolts 23, 24 and 25 to 55 ft. lbs. (75 Nm).

※※ **WARNING**

The thread sealer on the engine mount studs (including new engine mount studs if applicable) must be cleaned off with a wire brush and new Threadlock and Sealer applied prior to installing the engine mount studs. Failure to follow this procedure may result in damage to the engine mount studs or engine.

161. Install the engine mount studs in the following sequence.

a. Clean the front cover engine mount stud holes with pressurized air to remove any foreign material.

b. Clean all the thread sealer from the engine mount studs (old and new studs).

c. Apply new Threadlock and Sealer to the engine mount stud threads.

d. Install the 2 engine mount studs. Tighten the stud mounts to 177 inch lbs. (20 Nm).

162. Install the engine mount bracket and the 2 bolts. Tighten the bolts to 18 ft. lbs. (24 Nm).

➡**Apply clean engine oil to the crankshaft front seal bore in the engine front cover.**

163. Using the Crankshaft Vibration Damper Installer and Front Crankshaft Seal Installer, install a new crankshaft front seal.

➡**Lubricate the outside diameter sealing surfaces with clean engine oil.**

164. Using the Crankshaft Vibration Damper Installer and Front Cover Oil Seal Installer, install the crankshaft pulley.

165. Using the Strap Wrench, install the crankshaft pulley washer and new bolt and tighten in 4 stages.

a. Stage 1: Tighten to 89 ft. lbs. (120 Nm).

b. Stage 2: Loosen one full turn.

c. Stage 3: Tighten to 37 ft. lbs. (50 Nm).

d. Stage 4: Tighten an additional 90 degrees.

166. Install the accessory drive belt tensioner and the 3 bolts. Tighten the bolts to 97 inch lbs. (11 Nm).

167. Install the power steering pump and the 3 bolts. Tighten the bolts to 18 ft. lbs. (25 Nm).

➡**Installation of new seals is only required if damaged seals were removed during disassembly of the engine.**

➡**Spark plug tube seal installation shown, VCT seal solenoid installation similar.**

168. Using the VCT Spark Plug Tube Seal Installer and Handle, install new VCT solenoid and/or spark plug tube seals.

※※ **WARNING**

Failure to use Motorcraft® High Performance Engine RTV Silicone may cause the engine oil to foam excessively and result in serious engine damage.

➡**If the valve cover is not installed and the fasteners tightened within 4 minutes, the sealant must be removed and the sealing area cleaned. To clean the sealing area, use silicone gasket remover and metal surface prep. Failure to follow this procedure can cause future oil leakage.**

169. Apply an 0.31 inch (8 mm) bead of Motorcraft® High Performance Engine RTV Silicone to the engine front cover-to-RH cylinder head joints.

Early Build Vehicles

170. Using a new gasket, install the RH valve cover, bolt and the 10 stud bolts. Tighten the bolts to 89 inch lbs. (10 Nm). Refer to the sequence in the Valve Cover procedure.

Late Build Vehicles

171. Using a new gasket, install the RH valve cover and tighten the 9 stud bolts.

Tighten the bolts to 89 inch lbs. (10 Nm). Refer to the sequence in the Valve Cover procedure.

All Vehicles

※※ **WARNING**

Failure to use Motorcraft® High Performance Engine RTV Silicone may cause the engine oil to foam excessively and result in serious engine damage.

➡**If the valve cover is not installed and the fasteners tightened within 4 minutes, the sealant must be removed and the sealing area cleaned. To clean the sealing area, use silicone gasket remover and metal surface prep. Failure to follow this procedure can cause future oil leakage.**

172. Apply an 0.31 inch (8 mm) bead of Motorcraft® High Performance Engine RTV Silicone to the engine front cover-to-LH cylinder head joints.

Early Build Vehicles

173. Using a new gasket, install the LH valve cover and 11 stud bolts. Tighten the bolts to 89 inch lbs. (10 Nm).

Late Build Vehicles

174. Using a new gasket, install the LH valve cover tighten the 9 stud bolts. Tighten the bolts to 89 inch lbs. (10 Nm).

All Vehicles

175. Install the PSP tube bracket and nut to the RH valve cover stud bolt. Tighten the bolt to 62 inch lbs. (7 Nm).

176. Install the PSP tube bracket bolt. Tighten the bolt to 89 inch lbs. (10 Nm).

177. Connect the PSP switch electrical connector.

178. Install the 6 coil-on-plug assemblies and the 6 bolts. Tighten the bolts to 62 inch lbs. (7 Nm).

179. Attach all of the wiring harness retainers to the LH valve cover and stud bolts.

180. Connect the 3 LH coil-on-plug electrical connectors.

181. Connect the LH VCT solenoid electrical connector.

182. Attach all of the wiring harness retainers to the RH valve cover and stud bolts.

183. Connect the 3 RH coil-on-plug electrical connectors.

184. Connect the RH VCT solenoid electrical connector.

185. Connect the RH CMS electrical connector.

※※ **WARNING**

If the engine is repaired or replaced because of upper engine failure, typi-

cally including valve or piston damage, check the intake manifold for metal debris. If metal debris is found, install a new intake manifold. Failure to follow these instructions can result in engine damage.

186. Using a new gasket, install the upper intake manifold and the 6 bolts. Tighten the bolts to 89 inch lbs. (10 Nm). Refer to the Intake Manifold procedure for the tightening sequence.

187. Install the fuel tube bracket bolt to the upper intake manifold and install the wiring harness pin-type retainer. Tighten the bolt to 53 inch lbs. (6 Nm).

188. Install the upper intake manifold support bracket bolt. Tighten the bolt to 89 inch lbs. (10 Nm).

189. Attach the wiring harness retainers to the upper intake manifold.

190. Connect the Throttle Body (TB) electrical connector.

191. Connect the PCV hose to the PCV valve.

192. Raise the engine and transaxle assembly into the vehicle.

193. Install the engine mount and the 3 bolts. Tighten the bolts to 66 ft. lbs. (90 Nm).

194. Install the 4 engine mount nuts. Tighten the nuts to 46 ft. lbs. (63 Nm).

195. Install the engine mount brace, the nut and the bolt. Tighten the nut and bolt to 177 inch lbs. (20 Nm).

196. Install the transaxle support insulator bracket, 3 nuts and the bolt. Tighten the nuts to 46 ft. lbs. (63 Nm), and the bolt to 41 ft. lbs. (55 Nm).

197. Install the transaxle support insulator through bolt and nut. Tighten the bolt to 129 ft. lbs. (175 Nm).

All-Wheel Drive (AWD)

➡A new Power Transfer Unit (PTU) seal must be installed whenever the intermediate shaft is removed.

198. Install a new PTU seal as outlined in the Drive Train Section.

All Camshafts

199. Connect the transaxle cooler tubes and install the 2 secondary latches.

200. Install the RH halfshaft support bracket and the 4 bolts.

   a. Tighten the halfshaft support-to-cylinder block bolts to 30 ft. lbs. (40 Nm).

   b. Tighten the catalytic converter-to-halfshaft support bolts to 177 inch lbs. (20 Nm).

201. Install the 2 halfshaft support bracket studs. Tighten the studs to 89 inch lbs. (10 Nm).

✱✱ WARNING

The circlips are unique in size and shape for each shaft. Make sure to use the specified circlip for the application or vehicle damage may occur.

202. Install the correct new circlip on the inboard stub shaft.

➡After insertion, pull the halfshaft inner end to make sure the circlip is locked.

203. Push the stub shaft into the transmission so the circlip locks into the differential side gear.

204. Rotate the LH wheel knuckle into position and insert the LH halfshaft into the wheel hub.

205. Install the intermediate and halfshaft assembly and the 2 bolts. Tighten the bolts to 18 ft. lbs. (25 Nm).

206. Rotate the RH wheel knuckle into position and insert the RH halfshaft into the wheel hub.

207. Using the Powertrain Lift, raise the subframe into the installed position.

208. Install the 2 front subframe bolts. Tighten the bolts to 148 ft. lbs. (200 Nm).

209. Position the subframe brackets and install the 4 bolts finger-tight.

210. Install the 2 rear subframe bolts. Tighten the bolts to 111 ft. lbs. (150 Nm).

211. Install the 4 subframe bracket-to-body bolts. Tighten the bolts to 41 ft. lbs. (55 Nm).

212. Position the ball joints into the wheel knuckles. Install the new ball joint nuts. Tighten the nuts to 148 ft. lbs. (200 Nm).

➡The hex-holding feature can be used to prevent turning of the stud while removing the nuts.

213. Install new tie-rod end nuts. Tighten the nuts to 111 ft. lbs. (150 Nm).

214. Install new upper stabilizer bar link nuts. Tighten the nuts to 111 ft. lbs. (150 Nm).

215. Install the 2 front engine roll restrictor-to-transaxle bolts. Tighten the bolts to 66 ft. lbs. (90 Nm).

216. Install the 2 rear engine roll restrictor-to-transaxle bolts. Tighten the bolts to 66 ft. lbs. (90 Nm).

217. Using a new O-ring seal, install the PSP tube onto the steering gear, rotate the clamp plate and install the bolt. Tighten the bolt to 18 ft. lbs. (25 Nm).

218. Install the PSP tube bracket-to-steering gear bolt. Tighten the bolt to 89 inch lbs. (10 Nm).

➡Lubricate the engine oil filter gasket with clean engine oil prior to installing the oil filter.

219. Install a new engine oil filter. Tighten the oil filter to 44 inch lbs. (5 Nm), and then rotate an additional 180 degrees.

AWD Vehicles

220. Line up the index marks on the rear driveshaft to the index marks on the PTU flange made during removal and install the 4 bolts. Tighten the bolts to 52 ft. lbs. (70 Nm).

All Camshafts

221. Using a new gasket, install the Y-pipe and install the 2 new nuts. Tighten the nuts to 30 ft. lbs. (40 Nm).

   a. Attach the exhaust hanger.

222. Install the Y-pipe assembly and 4 new nuts. Tighten the nuts to 30 ft. lbs. (40 Nm).

✱✱ WARNING

Do not allow the intermediate shaft to rotate while it is disconnected from the gear or damage to the clockspring may occur. If there is evidence that the intermediate shaft has rotated, the clockspring must be removed and recentered. Refer to the Chassis Electrical Section.

➡Align the index marks made during removal.

223. Install the steering intermediate shaft onto the steering gear and install a new bolt. Tighten the bolt to 17 ft. lbs. (23 Nm).

224. Position the RH brake hose bracket and install the bolt. Tighten the bolt to 22 ft. lbs. (30 Nm).

225. Position the rubber shield and install the 2 lower scrivets.

✱✱ WARNING

Do not tighten the wheel hub nut with the vehicle on the ground. The nut must be tightened to specification before the vehicle is lowered onto the wheels. Wheel bearing damage will occur if the wheel bearing is loaded with the weight of the vehicle applied.

➡Apply the brake to keep the halfshaft from rotating.

226. Using the previously removed RH and LH wheel hub nuts, seat the halfshaft. Tighten the nuts to 258 ft. lbs. (350 Nm).

   a. Remove and discard the wheel hub nuts.

✳✳ WARNING

The wheel hub nut contains a one-time locking chemical that is activated by the heat created when it is tightened. Install and tighten the new wheel hub nut to specification within 5 minutes of starting it on the threads. Always install a new wheel hub nut after loosening or when not tightened within the specified time or damage to the components can occur.

➡ **Apply the brake to keep the halfshaft from rotating.**

227. Install a new RH and LH wheel hub nut. Tighten the nut to 258 ft. lbs. (350 Nm).

228. Connect the hose to the power steering reservoir.

229. Install the oil level indicator.

230. Install the ground cable and bolt. Tighten the bolt to 106 inch lbs. (12 Nm).

231. Attach the wire harness retainer to the RH valve cover stud bolt.

232. Attach the engine wiring harness retainer.

233. Connect the fuel supply tube to the fuel rail.

234. Using a new O-ring seal, connect the upper A/C tube to the condenser and install the nut and connect the A/C pressure switch electrical connector. Tighten the nut to 133 inch lbs. (15 Nm).

235. If equipped, attach the block heater wiring harness retainer to the radiator and power steering tube.

236. Connect the transaxle control cable to the shift cable bracket.

237. Connect the transaxle control cable to the control lever.

238. Connect the upper radiator hose, lower radiator hose and heater hose to the thermostat housing.

239. Install the engine wiring harness retainer to the bulkhead.

   a. Slide the wiring harness in the bulkhead.

   b. Make sure the wiring harness retainer tab is below the bulkhead lip.

240. Connect the 2 PCM electrical connectors.

241. Connect the PCM and engine harness electrical connectors.

   a. Attach the wiring harness retainer.

242. Install the Evaporative Emission (EVAP) canister purge valve as outlined in the Engine Performance & Emission Controls Section.

243. Attach the EVAP tube pin-type retainer to the upper intake manifold.

244. Connect the vacuum hose and the EVAP tube to the upper intake manifold.

245. Install the degas bottle.

246. Using a new O-ring seal and gasket seal, install the A/C tube and the nut. Tighten the nut to 133 inch lbs. (15 Nm).

247. Using a new O-ring seal and gasket seal, connect the A/C tube and install the nut. Tighten the nut to 133 inch lbs. (15 Nm).

248. Connect the power steering cooler tube.

249. Install the front valance, 3 pushpins and 7 screws.

250. Install the accessory drive belt and the power steering belt as outlined in this section.

251. Install the LF wheel and tire.

252. Connect the ground cable to the negative battery terminal and install the nut. Tighten the nut to 53 inch lbs. (6 Nm).

253. Connect the power feed wire to the positive battery terminal and install the nut. Tighten the nut to 53 inch lbs. (6 Nm).

254. Connect the engine wiring harness electrical connector.

255. Install the battery tray.

256. Install the engine Air Cleaner (ACL) and ACL outlet pipe as outlined in this section.

257. Install the strut tower brace and the 4 nuts. Tighten the nuts to 26 ft. lbs. (35 Nm).

258. Attach the brake booster vacuum hose retainers to the strut tower brace.

259. Install the cowl panel grille as outlined in the Body and Paint Section.

✳✳ WARNING

Do not expose the Motorcraft® High Performance Engine RTV Silicone to engine oil for at least 90 minutes after installing the engine front cover. Failure to follow this instruction may cause oil leakage.

260. Fill the engine with clean engine oil.

261. Fill and bleed the cooling system as outlined in the Engine Cooling Section.

262. Fill the power steering system as outlined in the Steering Section.

263. Recharge the A/C system as outlined in the Heating, Ventilation & Air Conditioning Section.

4.0L Engine

See Figures 115 through 119.

➡ **You must carry out the RH and LH camshaft timing procedure when either camshaft is serviced. See "Timing Chain and Sprockets" section.**

1. Before servicing the vehicle, refer to Precautions.

2. Remove or disconnect the following:
- Negative battery cable for safety
- Cooling fan
- Camshaft roller followers; see "Rocker Arms/Shafts (Camshaft Roller Followers)"
- A/C tube bracket (position tube aside)

3. Rotate the crankshaft clockwise to position the number one cylinder at TDC.

✳✳ WARNING

Do not rotate the engine counterclockwise. Rotating the engine counterclockwise will result in incorrect timing of the engine.

4. Install the special clamping tool, 303-573, onto the crankshaft damper.

5. Install the special tools on the rear of the RH cylinder head and tighten the top 2 clamp bolts to 89 inch lbs. (10 Nm).

✳✳ WARNING

The RH camshaft sprocket is a LH threaded bolt.

6. Using the special tool and the Camshaft Sprocket Nut Socket, loosen the camshaft sprocket bolt.

Fig. 115 Install the special tool on the crankshaft pulley—4.0L Engine

Fig. 116 Using the special tool with the Camshaft Sprocket Nut Socket 303-565, loosen the RH camshaft sprocket bolt—4.0L Engine

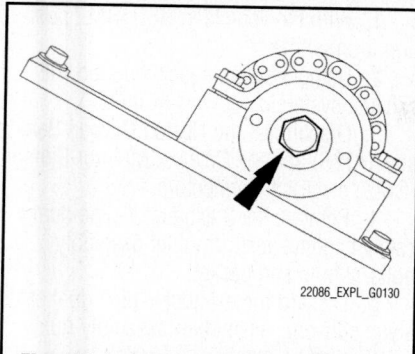

Fig. 117 Install the LH camshaft sprocket special holding tools—4.0L Engine

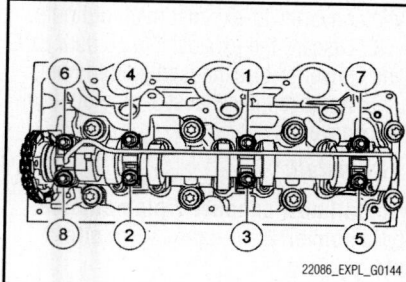

Fig. 118 Remove the bolts in the sequence shown and remove the camshaft bearing caps and the oil supply tube—4.0L Engine

7. Remove the RH sprocket bolt and position the camshaft sprocket and chain aside.

8. Install the special tools on the front of the LH camshaft and tighten the 2 top clamp bolts to 89 inch lbs. (10 Nm)

9. Remove the LH camshaft sprocket bolt and position the sprocket and chain aside.

10. On both sides, remove the bolts in the sequence shown and remove the camshaft bearing caps and the oil supply tube.

11. Remove the camshaft.

To install:

12. Lubricate all of the moving parts with clean engine oil.

13. Install camshaft onto the cylinder head.

14. Install the camshaft bearing caps, in their original locations, and torque the bolts in 2 steps:
   a. Step 1—53.5 inch lbs. (6 Nm).
   b. Step 2—12 ft. lbs. (16 Nm).

15. Install the camshaft oil supply tube.

16. Reposition the camshaft sprocket and chain, for each side, and loosely install the sprocket bolt.

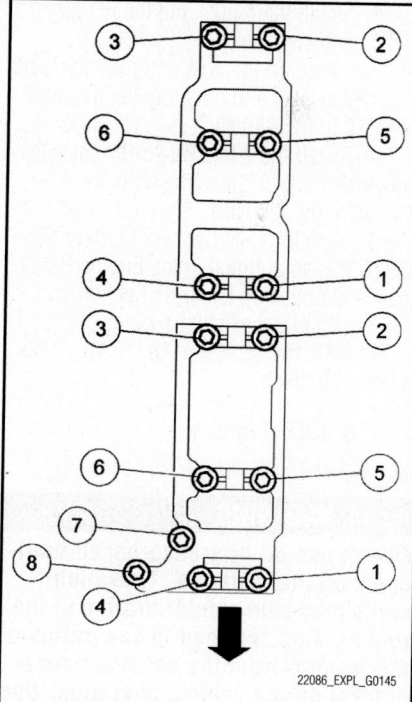

Fig. 119 Camshaft bearing cap torque sequence—4.0L Engine

❊❊ WARNING

The camshaft gear must turn freely on the camshaft. DO NOT tighten the bolt at this time.

17. Retime the camshafts. See the procedure in "Timing Chain and Sprocket" section.

18. Install or connect the following:
   • Camshaft roller followers
   • A/C tube and bracket
   • Valve covers
   • Cooling fan
   • Negative battery cable

19. Start the engine check for proper operation and leaks. Repair if necessary.

4.6L Engine

See Figure 120.

1. Before servicing the vehicle, refer to Precautions.

2. Remove or disconnect the following:

❊❊ WARNING

At no time, when the timing chains are removed and the cylinder heads are installed may the crankshaft or camshaft be rotated. Severe piston and valve damage will occur.

   • Timing chains, refer to Timing Chain and Sprockets.
   • Camshaft roller followers

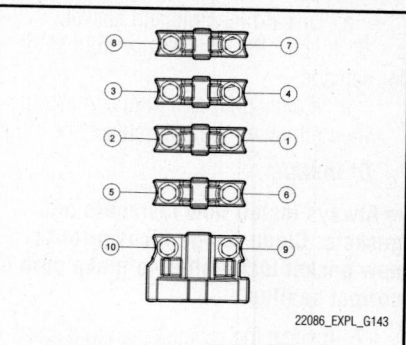

Fig. 120 Camshaft bearing bolt torque sequence—4.6L Engine

   • Camshaft sprocket
   • Camshaft bearing cap bolts (keeping them marked for reinstallation to original locations)
   • Camshaft from the cylinder head

To install:

3. Lubricate the camshaft journals with clean engine oil.

4. Install the camshaft onto the cylinder head.

5. Lubricate the camshaft bearing caps with clean engine oil.

6. Install the camshaft bearing caps and loosely install the bolts.

7. Tighten the bolts in the sequence shown.

8. Install the camshaft sprocket. Tighten the sprocket bolt in two stages.
   • Step 1: Tighten to 30 ft. lbs. (40 Nm)
   • Step 2: Tighten an additional 90 degrees.

9. Install the roller followers

10. Install the timing chains

CATALYTIC CONVERTER

REMOVAL & INSTALLATION

3.5L Engine

Left-Hand

➡**Always install new fasteners and gaskets. Clean flange faces prior to new gasket installation to make sure of correct sealing.**

1. With the vehicle in NEUTRAL, position it on a hoist.

2. Disconnect the LH Catalyst Monitor Sensor (CMS) electrical connector.

3. Remove the exhaust Y-pipe.

4. Remove the 2 catalytic converter support bracket-to-transmission bolts.

5. Remove the 4 nuts and the LH catalytic converter.

a. Discard the nuts and gasket.
6. Inspect the exhaust manifold studs for damage.
 a. If damaged, or if stud comes out when removing the nut, replace the stud.

To install:

➡️**Always install new fasteners and gaskets. Clean flange faces prior to new gasket installation to make sure of correct sealing.**

7. Inspect the exhaust manifold studs for damage.
 a. If damaged, or if stud comes out when removing the nut, replace the stud. Tighten the nut to 18 ft. lbs. (25 Nm).
8. Install the 4 nuts and the LH catalytic converter.
 a. Discard the nuts and gasket. Using a new gasket and nuts, tighten the nuts to 30 ft. lbs. (40 Nm).
9. Install the 2 catalytic converter support bracket-to-transmission bolts. Tighten the bolts to 35 ft. lbs. (48 Nm).
10. Install the exhaust Y-pipe.
11. Connect the LH Catalyst Monitor Sensor (CMS) electrical connector.
12. With the vehicle in NEUTRAL, lower it from the hoist.

Right-Hand

➡️**Always install new fasteners and gaskets. Clean flange faces prior to new gasket installation to make sure of correct sealing.**

1. With the vehicle in NEUTRAL, position it on a hoist.
2. Remove the exhaust Y-pipe.
3. Remove the RH Catalyst Monitor Sensor (CMS) as outlined in the Engine Performance & Emission Controls Section.
4. Remove the 2 bracket-to-RH catalytic converter bolts.
5. Remove the 4 nuts and the RH catalytic converter.
 a. Discard the nuts and gasket.
6. Inspect the exhaust manifold studs for damage.
 a. If damaged or if stud comes out when removing the nut, replace the stud.

To install:

➡️**Always install new fasteners and gaskets. Clean flange faces prior to new gasket installation to make sure of correct sealing.**

7. Inspect the exhaust manifold studs for damage.
 a. If damaged or if stud comes out when removing the nut, replace the stud. Tighten the nut to 18 ft. lbs. (25 Nm).

8. Install the 4 nuts and the RH catalytic converter.
 a. Discard the nuts and gasket. Using a new gasket and nuts, tighten the nuts to 30 ft. lbs. (40 Nm).
9. Install the 2 bracket-to-RH catalytic converter bolts. Tighten the bolts to 177 inch lbs. (20 Nm).
10. Install the RH Catalyst Monitor Sensor (CMS) as outlined in the Engine Performance & Emission Controls Section.
11. Install the exhaust Y-pipe.
12. With the vehicle in NEUTRAL, lower it from the hoist.

4.0L & 4.6L Engines

See Figures 121 and 122.

✸✸ WARNING

Do not use oil or grease-based lubricants on the isolators. These lubricants may cause deterioration of the rubber. This can lead to separation of the isolator from the exhaust hanger bracket during vehicle operation. Use only water-based lubricants on the isolators.

➡️**Exhaust fasteners are of a prevailing torque design. Use only new fasteners with the same part number as the original. Torque values must be used as specified during reassembly to make sure of correct retention of exhaust components.**

1. With the vehicle in NEUTRAL, position it on a hoist.
2. Using a suitable jack, support the exhaust system.
3. Disconnect the Heated Oxygen Sensor (HO2S) and the Catalyst Monitor Sensor (CMS) electrical connectors.
4. Remove the 2 exhaust Y-pipe dual catalytic converter-to-muffler assembly bolts, 2 nuts and gasket.
5. Discard the exhaust Y-pipe dual catalytic converter-to-muffler assembly nuts and gasket.
6. Remove the transmission support crossmember.
7. Remove the exhaust Y-pipe dual catalytic converter-to-exhaust manifold nuts.
8. Discard the exhaust Y-pipe dual catalytic converter-to-exhaust manifold nuts.
9. Remove the exhaust Y-pipe dual catalytic converter.

To install:

➡️**Install new exhaust Y-pipe dual catalytic converter-to-exhaust manifold nuts.**

➡️**Do not fully tighten the exhaust Y-pipe dual catalytic converter-to-exhaust manifold joint.**

10. Position the exhaust Y-pipe dual catalytic converter to the exhaust manifold and loosely tighten all 4 new nuts to stiffen the joint enough to maintain position. Tighten to 71 inch lbs. (8 Nm) then add additional torque if needed to stiffen the joint.

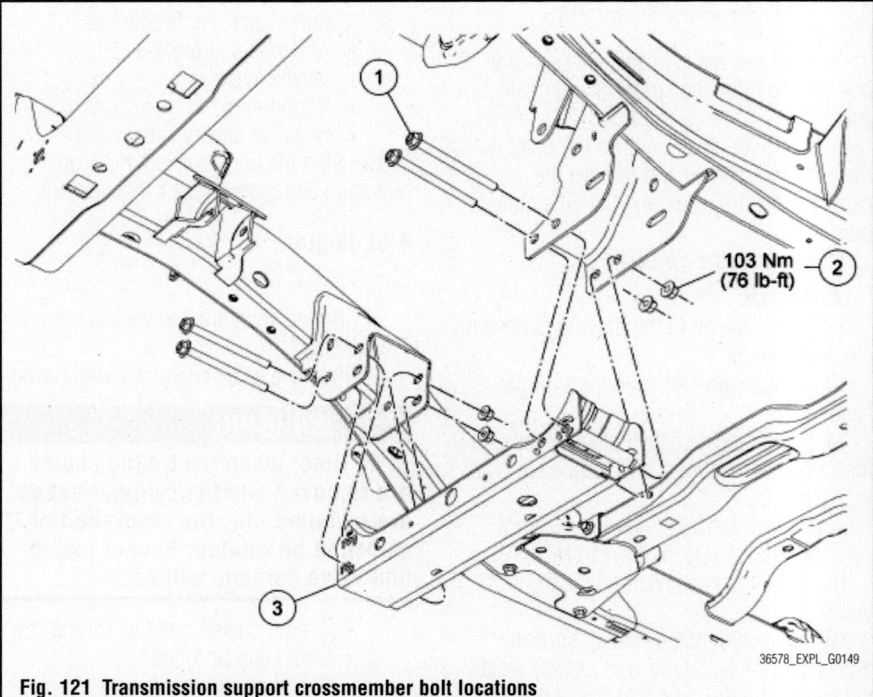

103 Nm (76 lb-ft)

36578_EXPL_G0149

Fig. 121 Transmission support crossmember bolt locations

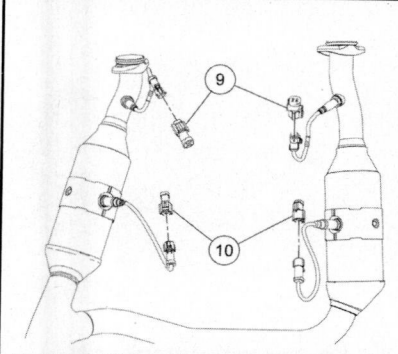

9. Heated Oxygen Sensor (HO2S) electrical connectors
10. Catalyst Monitor Sensor (CMS) electrical connectors

36578_EXPL_G0148

Fig. 122 Catalytic Converter locations

➡**Install new exhaust Y-pipe dual catalytic converter-to-muffler assembly gasket and nuts.**

11. Install the exhaust Y-pipe-dual catalytic converter-to-muffler assembly new gasket, 2 bolts and 2 new nuts and tighten to 30 ft. lbs. (40 Nm).

12. Tighten the 4 new exhaust Y-pipe dual catalytic converter-to-exhaust manifold nuts and tighten to 30 ft. lbs. (40 Nm).

13. Install the transmission support crossmember and tighten to 76 ft. lbs. (103 Nm).

14. Connect the HO2S and CMS electrical connectors.

15. Check to see if the exhaust system isolators are at zero load. If the exhaust system isolators are not at zero load, then carry out the exhaust system alignment procedure.

CRANKSHAFT DAMPER

REMOVAL & INSTALLATION

3.5L Engine

See Figures 123 through 125.

1. Raise and safely support the vehicle.
2. Remove the Right Hand (RH) splash shield.
3. Remove the accessory drive belt.
4. Using the Strap Wrench (SST 303-D055) or equivalent tool, remove the crankshaft pulley bolt and washer. Discard the bolt.
5. Using the 3 Jaw Puller (SST 303-D121) or equivalent tool, remove the crankshaft pulley.

To install:

6. Lubricate the crankshaft front seal inner lip with clean engine oil.

➡**Lubrication the outside diameter sealing surfaces with clean engine oil.**

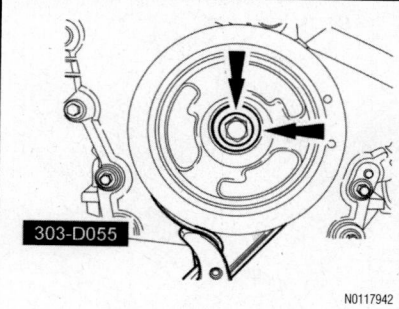

N0117942

Fig. 123 Using the Strap Wrench (SST 303-D055) or equivalent tool, remove the crankshaft pulley bolt and washer—3.5L engine

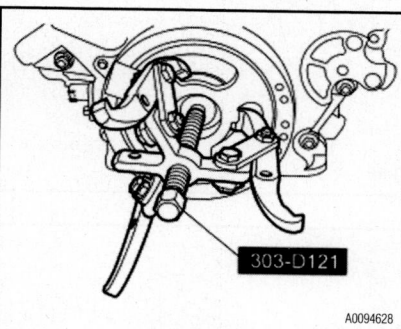

303-D121

A0094628

Fig. 124 Using the 3 Jaw Puller (SST 303-D121) or equivalent tool, remove the crankshaft pulley—3.5L engine

7. Using the Crankshaft Vibration Damper Replacer and Front Cover Oil Seal Installer (SST 303-102, 303-335) or equivalent tools, install the crankshaft pulley.

8. Using the Strap Wrench or equivalent tool, install the crankshaft pulley washer and new bolt and tighten in 4 stages:
   • Stage 1: Tighten to 89 ft. lbs. (120 Nm)
   • Stage 2: Loosen one full turn

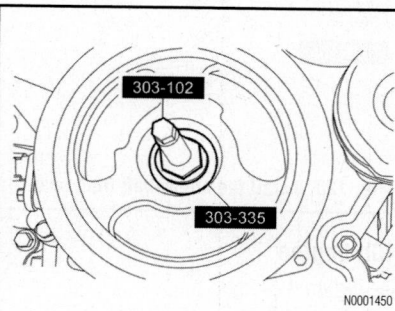

303-102

303-335

N0001450

Fig. 125 Using the Crankshaft Vibration Damper Replacer and Front Cover Oil Seal Installer (SST 303-102, 303-335) or equivalent tools, install the crankshaft pulley—3.5L engine

   • Stage 3: Tighten to 37 ft. lbs. (50 Nm)
   • Stage 4: Tighten an additional 90 degrees
9. Install the accessory drive belt.
10. Install the RH splash shield.
11. Lower the vehicle.

4.0L Engine

See Figure 126.

1. Remove the engine fan/clutch assembly and shroud.
2. Remove the accessory drive belt.
3. Unbolt and position the power steering cooler aside for clearance, if equipped.
4. Holding the pulley from turning, remove the crankshaft pulley bolt.
5. Use a puller and remove the crankshaft pulley.

To install:

6. Use a crankshaft pulley installation tool, press the pulley onto the crankshaft.

➡**Always use a new damper-to-crankshaft bolt. Do not attempt to re-use the old bolt.**

7. Install the damper-to-crankshaft snout and tighten to:
   a. Step 1: 41 ft. lbs. (55 Nm)
   b. Step 2: additional 85 degrees
8. Reposition the power steering oil cooler, if equipped.
9. Install the accessory drive belt.
10. Install the fan shroud.
11. Run the engine and check for oil leaks.

4.6L Engine

1. Remove the engine fan/clutch assembly and shroud.
2. Remove the accessory drive belt.
3. Holding the pulley from turning, remove the crankshaft pulley bolt.
4. Use a puller and remove the crankshaft pulley.

To install:

➡**If the crankshaft pulley is not installed within 4 minutes, the sealant must be removed and the sealing area cleaned.**

5. Apply silicone gasket and sealant to the Woodruff key slot.
6. Use a crankshaft pulley installation tool, press the pulley onto the crankshaft.

➡**Always use a new damper-to-crankshaft bolt. Do not attempt to re-use the old bolt.**

7. Install the crankshaft pulley and tighten the bolt as follows:
   a. Step 1: 89 ft. lbs. (120 Nm)

Fig. 126 Crankshaft damper bolt location—4.0L Engine

36578_EXPL_G0019

b. Step 2: LOOSEN the bolt one full turn

c. Step 3: 37 ft. lbs. (50 Nm)

d. Step 4: additional 90 degrees (do not exceed 148 ft. lbs. or 200 Nm of torque)

8. Install the accessory drive belt.

9. Install the fan shroud.

10. Run the engine and check for oil leaks.

CRANKSHAFT FRONT SEAL

REMOVAL & INSTALLATION

3.5L Engine

See Figures 127 and 128.

1. With the vehicle in NEUTRAL, position it on a hoist.

2. Remove the crankshaft pulley.

3. Using the Oil Seal Remover (SST 303-409) or equivalent tool, remove and discard the crankshaft front seal.

4. Inspect the crankshaft seal bore in the front cover for any damage or casting imperfections that may affect the crank seal outer diameter sealing. Repair/replace as necessary.

5. Clean all sealing surfaces with metal surface prep.

To install:

6. Apply clean engine oil to the crankshaft front seal bore in the engine front cover.

7. Using the Front Crankshaft Seal Installer and Crankshaft Vibration Damper Installer (SST 303-1251, 303-102) or equivalent tools, install a new crankshaft front seal.

8. Install the crankshaft pulley.

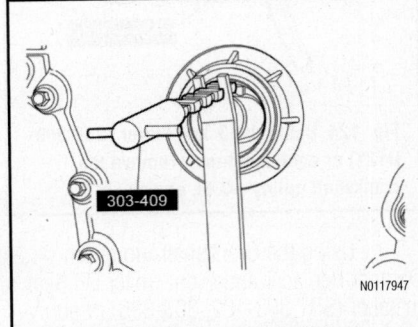

Fig. 127 Remove the crankshaft front seal

N0117947

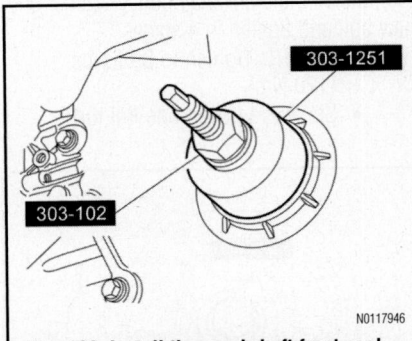

Fig. 128 Install the crankshaft front seal

N0117946

4.0L Engine

See Figure 129.

1. Before servicing the vehicle, refer to Precautions.

2. Remove the crankshaft pulley. Refer to Crankshaft Damper.

3. Using a proper seal remover, remove the front crankshaft seal.

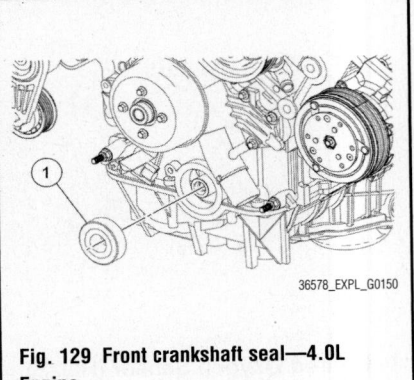

Fig. 129 Front crankshaft seal—4.0L Engine

36578_EXPL_G0150

To install:

4. Installation is the reverse of the removal procedure.

5. Lubricate the new seal lip before installation.

4.6L Engine

See Figure 130.

1. Before servicing the vehicle, refer to Precautions.

2. Remove the crankshaft pulley. Refer to Crankshaft Damper.

3. Using a proper seal remover, remove the front crankshaft seal.

To install:

4. Installation is the reverse of the removal procedure.

5. Lubricate the new seal lip before installation.

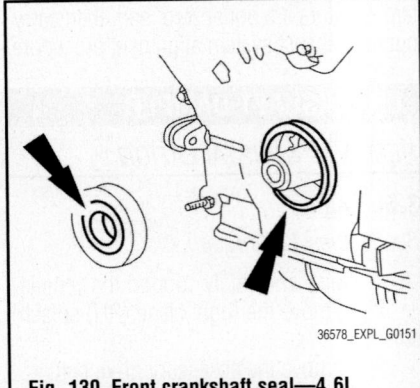

Fig. 130 Front crankshaft seal—4.6L Engine

36578_EXPL_G0151

CYLINDER HEAD

REMOVAL & INSTALLATION

3.5L Engine

Left-Hand

See Figures 131 and 132.

⁂⁂ WARNING

During engine repair procedures, cleanliness is extremely important. Any foreign material, including any material created while cleaning gasket surfaces, that enters the oil passages, coolant passages or the oil pan, may cause engine failure.

1. Remove the LH camshafts.
2. If equipped, remove the heat shield, and detach the block heater electrical connector. Remove the block heater wiring harness from the engine.
3. Disconnect the 6 fuel injector electrical connectors.
4. Disconnect the 2 LH Camshaft Position (CMP) sensor electrical connectors.
5. Remove the bolts and the LH CMP sensors.
6. Disconnect the LH Heated Oxygen Sensor (HO2S) electrical connector.
7. Disconnect the LH Catalyst Monitor Sensor (CMS) electrical connector.
8. Detach the wiring harness retainer from the rear of the LH cylinder head.
9. Detach the A/C compressor electrical connector.
10. Remove the nut and disconnect the generator B+ cable.

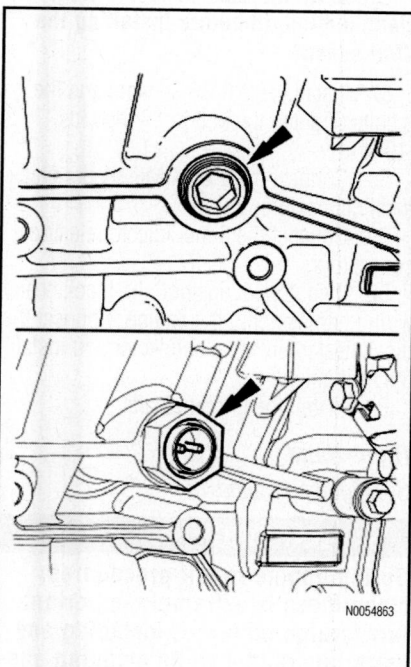

Fig. 131 Engine coolant drain plug location

11. Disconnect the generator electrical connector.
12. Detach the wiring harness from the generator.
13. Disconnect the Cylinder Head Temperature (CHT) sensor electrical connector.
14. Disconnect the Engine Oil Pressure (EOP) switch electrical connector and the wiring harness pin-type retainer.
15. Remove the nut, 2 bolts and A/C compressor.
16. Remove the nut, bolt and the generator.
17. Remove the LH HO2S. If necessary, use a penetrating lubricant to aid in sensor removal.
18. Remove the 3 bolts and the LH exhaust manifold heat shield.
19. Remove the 6 nuts and the LH catalytic converter. Discard the nuts and gasket. Clean & inspect the catalytic converter flange.
20. Remove and discard the 6 LH exhaust manifold studs.
21. Remove the LH cylinder block drain plug.
    a. Allow coolant to drain from the cylinder block.
22. Remove the 4 nuts and the RH catalytic converter.
    a. Discard the nuts and gasket.
    b. Remove the block heater wiring harness from the engine.
23. Remove the RH cylinder block drain plug or, if equipped, the block heater.
24. Disconnect the fuel supply tube-to-fuel rail connect coupling.
25. Remove the 2 thermostat housing-to-lower intake manifold bolts.

⁂⁂ WARNING

If the engine is repaired or replaced because of upper engine failure, typically including valve or piston damage, check the intake manifold for metal debris. If metal debris is found, install a new intake manifold. Failure to follow these instructions can result in engine damage.

26. Remove the 10 bolts and the lower intake manifold.
    a. Discard the gaskets.
    b. Clean and inspect all sealing surfaces.
27. Remove the bolt and the LH primary timing chain guide.

➡️**If the components are to be reinstalled, they must be installed in the** same positions. Mark the components for installation into their original locations.

28. Remove the valve tappets from the cylinder head.
29. Inspect the valve tappets.
30. Remove and discard the M6 bolt.

⁂⁂ WARNING

Place clean, lint-free shop towels over exposed engine cavities. Carefully remove the towels so foreign material is not dropped into the engine. Any foreign material (including any material created while cleaning gasket surfaces) that enters the oil passages or the oil pan, may cause engine failure.

⁂⁂ WARNING

Aluminum surfaces are soft and may be scratched easily. Never place the cylinder head gasket surface, unprotected, on a bench surface.

➡️**The cylinder head bolts must be discarded and new bolts must be installed. They are a tighten-to-yield design and cannot be reused.**

31. Remove and discard the 8 bolts from the cylinder head.
    a. Remove the cylinder head.
    b. Discard the cylinder head gasket.

⁂⁂ WARNING

Do not use metal scrapers, wire brushes, power abrasive discs or other abrasive means to clean the sealing surfaces. These tools cause scratches and gouges that make leak paths. Use a plastic scraping tool to remove all traces of the head gasket.

➡️**Observe all warnings or cautions and follow all application directions contained on the packaging of the silicone gasket remover and the metal surface prep.**

➡️**If there is no residual gasket material present, metal surface prep can be used to clean and prepare the surfaces.**

32. Clean the cylinder head-to-cylinder block mating surfaces of both the cylinder heads and the cylinder block in the following sequence.

a. Remove any large deposits of silicone or gasket material with a plastic scraper.

b. Apply silicone gasket remover, following package directions, and allow to set for several minutes.

c. Remove the silicone gasket remover with a plastic scraper. A second application of silicone gasket remover may be required if residual traces of silicone or gasket material remain.

d. Apply metal surface prep, following package directions, to remove any remaining traces of oil or coolant and to prepare the surfaces to bond with the new gasket. Do not attempt to make the metal shiny. Some staining of the metal surfaces is normal.

33. Support the cylinder head on a bench with the head gasket side up. Check the cylinder head distortion and the cylinder block distortion.

To install:

> ✳✳ **WARNING**
>
> **During engine repair procedures, cleanliness is extremely important. Any foreign material, including any material created while cleaning gasket surfaces that enters the oil passages, coolant passages or the oil pan, may cause engine failure.**

34. Install a new gasket, the LH cylinder head and 8 new bolts. Tighten in the proper sequence in 5 stages:

a. Stage 1: Tighten to 177 inch lbs. (20 Nm).

b. Stage 2: Tighten to 26 ft. lbs. (35 Nm).

c. Stage 3: Tighten 90 degrees.

d. Stage 4: Tighten 90 degrees.

e. Stage 5: Tighten 45 degrees.

35. Install the M6 bolt. Tighten the bolt to 89 inch lbs. (10 Nm).

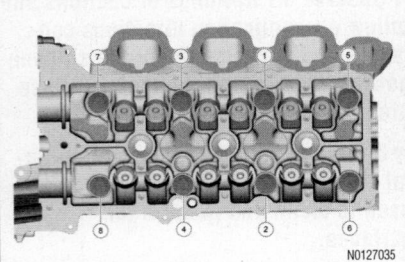

Fig. 132 LH cylinder head and tightening sequence

➡**The valve tappets must be installed in their original positions.**

➡**Coat the valve tappets with clean engine oil prior to installation.**

36. Install the valve tappets.

37. Install the LH upper primary timing chain guide and bolt. Tighten the bolts to 89 inch lbs. (10 Nm).

> ✳✳ **WARNING**
>
> **If the engine is repaired or replaced because of upper engine failure, typically including valve or piston damage, check the intake manifold for metal debris. If metal debris is found, install a new intake manifold. Failure to follow these instructions can result in engine damage.**

38. Using new intake manifold and thermostat housing gaskets, install the lower intake manifold and the 10 bolts.

a. Tighten in the proper sequence to 89 inch lbs. (10 Nm). Refer to the Intake Manifold procedure for the sequence.

39. Install the thermostat housing and the 2 bolts. Tighten the bolts to 89 inch lbs. (10 Nm).

40. Connect the fuel supply tube-to-fuel rail quick connect coupling.

41. If equipped, install the block heater wiring harness onto the engine:

a. Tighten the cylinder block drain plug to 89 inch lbs. (10 Nm), plus an additional 89 inch lbs. (10 Nm).

b. Tighten the block heater to 30 ft. lbs. (40 Nm).

42. Using a new gasket, install the RH catalytic converter and 4 new nuts. Tighten the nuts to 30 ft. lbs. (40 Nm).

43. Install the LH cylinder block drain plug. Tighten the drain plug to 177 inch lbs. (20 Nm), plus an additional 180°.

44. Install 6 new LH exhaust manifold studs. Tighten the studs to 106 inch lbs. (12 Nm).

> ✳✳ **WARNING**
>
> **Failure to tighten the exhaust manifold nuts to specification a second time will cause the exhaust manifold to develop an exhaust leak.**

45. Using a new gasket, install the LH catalytic converter and 3 new lower LH catalytic converter manifold-to-cylinder head nuts. Tighten in 2 stages in the proper sequence (refer to the Exhaust Manifold procedure):

a. Stage 1: Tighten the 2 lower LH

catalytic converter manifold-to-cylinder head nuts to 18 ft. lbs. (25 Nm).

b. Stage 2: Tighten the 2 new upper LH catalytic converter manifold-to-cylinder head nuts to 18 ft. lbs. (25 Nm).

46. Install the LH exhaust manifold heat shield and the 3 bolts. Tighten the bolts to 106 inch lbs. (12 Nm).

➡**Apply anti-seize to the threads of the HO2S before installing.**

47. Install the LH HO2S and tighten to 35 ft. lbs. (48 Nm).

48. Install the generator, bolt and nut. Tighten to 35 ft. lbs. (48 Nm).

49. Install the A/C compressor, the nut and 2 bolts. Tighten to 18 ft. lbs. (25 Nm).

50. Attach the Engine Oil Pressure (EOP) switch wiring harness pin-type retainer.

51. Attach the wiring harness retainer to the generator.

52. Connect the generator electrical connector.

53. Connect the generator B+ cable and install the nut. Tighten the nut to 62 inch lbs. (7 Nm).

54. Connect the A/C compressor electrical connector.

55. Connect the LH Catalyst Monitor Sensor (CMS) electrical connector. Install the wiring harness retainer to the rear of the LH cylinder head.

56. Connect the LH Heated Oxygen Sensor (HO2S) electrical connector.

➡**Lubricate the CMP sensor O-ring with clean engine oil before installing the CMP sensor.**

57. Install the 2 CMP sensors and the 2 bolts. Tighten the bolt to 89 inch lbs. (10 Nm).

58. Connect the 2 LH CMP sensor electrical connectors.

59. Connect the 6 fuel injector electrical connectors.

60. If equipped, position the block heater wiring harness onto the engine. Connect the block heater electrical connector and install the heat shield.

61. Install the LH camshafts.

Right-Hand

See Figures 133 and 134.

> ✳✳ **WARNING**
>
> **During engine repair procedures, cleanliness is extremely important. Any foreign material, including any material created while cleaning gasket surfaces, that enters the oil passages, coolant passages or the oil pan, may cause engine failure.**

➡On early build engines, the timing chain rides on the inner side of the RH timing chain guide. Late build engines are equipped with a different design RH timing chain guide that requires the timing chain to ride on the outer side of the RH timing chain guide. For service, all replacement RH timing chain guides will be the late build design.

All Vehicles

1. Remove the RH camshafts. For additional information, refer to Camshaft in this section.
2. If equipped, remove the heat shield and disconnect the block heater electrical connector. Remove the block heater wiring harness from the engine.
3. Disconnect the RH Heated Oxygen Sensor (HO2S) electrical connector.
4. Disconnect the 2 RH Camshaft Position (CMP) sensor electrical connectors.
5. Remove the 2 bolts and the RH CMP sensors.
6. Remove the bolt and the ground wire from the RH cylinder head.
7. Disconnect the 6 fuel injector electrical connectors.
8. Disconnect the Cylinder Head Temperature (CHT) sensor electrical connector.
9. Remove the LH cylinder block drain plug.
   a. Allow coolant to drain from the cylinder block.
10. Remove the 4 nuts and the RH catalytic converter.
   a. Discard the nuts and gasket.
11. Remove the RH cylinder block drain plug or, if equipped, the block heater.
   a. Allow coolant to drain from the cylinder block.
12. Remove the 6 nuts and the RH exhaust manifold.
   a. Discard the nuts and exhaust manifold gaskets.
13. Clean and inspect the RH exhaust manifold as outlined in this section.
14. Remove and discard the 6 RH exhaust manifold studs.

➡Do not use power tools to remove the bolt, or damage to the RH primary timing chain guide may occur.

15. Remove the bolt and the RH primary timing chain guide.
16. Remove the 2 bolts and the engine lifting eye.

➡Index-mark the location of the bracket on the cylinder head for installation.

17. Remove the bolt and the upper intake manifold support bracket.

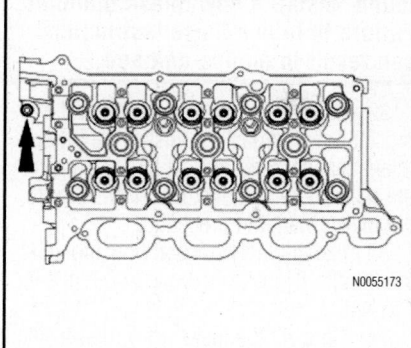

N0055173

Fig. 133 M6 bolt location

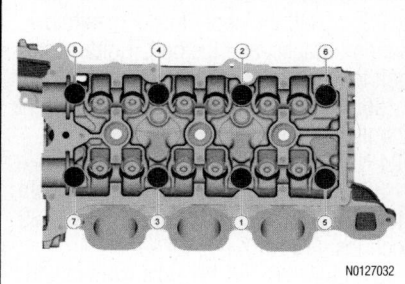

N0127032

Fig. 134 RH cylinder head installation and tightening sequence

18. Disconnect the fuel supply tube-to-fuel rail quick connect coupling.
19. Remove the 2 thermostat housing-to-lower intake manifold bolts.
   a. Remove the thermostat housing and discard the gasket and O-ring seal.

✳✳ WARNING

If the engine is repaired or replaced because of upper engine failure, typically including valve or piston damage, check the intake manifold for metal debris. If metal debris is found, install a new intake manifold. Failure to follow these instructions can result in engine damage.

20. Remove the 10 bolts and the lower intake manifold.
   a. Discard the gaskets.
21. Disconnect and remove the CHT sensor jumper harness.

➡If the components are to be reinstalled, they must be installed in the same positions. Mark the components for installation into their original locations.

22. Remove the valve tappets from the cylinder head.

23. Inspect the valve tappets.
24. Remove and discard the M6 bolt.

✳✳ WARNING

Place clean, lint-free shop towels over exposed engine cavities. Carefully remove the towels so foreign material is not dropped into the engine. Any foreign material (including any material created while cleaning gasket surfaces) that enters the oil passages or the oil pan, may cause engine failure.

✳✳ WARNING

Aluminum surfaces are soft and may be scratched easily. Never place the cylinder head gasket surface, unprotected, on a bench surface.

➡The cylinder head bolts must be discarded and new bolts must be installed. They are a tighten-to-yield design and cannot be reused.

25. Remove and discard the 8 bolts from the cylinder head.
   a. Remove the cylinder head.
   b. Discard the cylinder head gasket.

➡Do not use metal scrapers, wire brushes, power abrasive discs or other abrasive means to clean the sealing surfaces. These tools cause scratches and gouges that make leak paths. Use a plastic scraping tool to remove all traces of the head gasket.

➡Observe all warnings or cautions and follow all application directions contained on the packaging of the silicone gasket remover and the metal surface prep.

➡If there is no residual gasket material present, metal surface prep can be used to clean and prepare the surfaces.

26. Clean the cylinder head-to-cylinder block mating surfaces of both the cylinder heads and the cylinder block in the following sequence.
   a. Remove any large deposits of silicone or gasket material with a plastic scraper.
   b. Apply silicone gasket remover, following package directions, and allow to set for several minutes.
   c. Remove the silicone gasket remover with a plastic scraper. A second application of silicone gasket remover may be required if residual traces of silicone or gasket material remain.

d. Apply metal surface prep, following package directions, to remove any remaining traces of oil or coolant and to prepare the surfaces to bond with the new gasket. Do not attempt to make the metal shiny. Some staining of the metal surfaces is normal.

27. Support the cylinder head on a bench with the head gasket side up. Check the cylinder head distortion and the cylinder block distortion.

To install:

❋❋ WARNING

During engine repair procedures, cleanliness is extremely important. Any foreign material, including any material created while cleaning gasket surfaces that enters the oil passages, coolant passages or the oil pan, may cause engine failure.

➡On early build engines, the timing chain rides on the inner side of the RH timing chain guide. Late built engines are equipped with a different design RH timing chain guide that requires the timing chain to ride on the outer side of the RH timing chain guide. For service, all replacement RH timing chain guides will be the late build design.

All Vehicles

28. Install a new gasket, the RH cylinder head and 8 new bolts. Tighten in the sequence shown in 5 stages:
   a. Stage 1: Tighten to 177 inch lbs. (20 Nm).
   b. Stage 2: Tighten to 26 ft. lbs. (35 Nm).
   c. Stage 3: Tighten 90 degrees.
   d. Stage 4: Tighten 90 degrees.
   e. Stage 5: Tighten 45 degrees.
29. Install the M6 bolt. Tighten the bolt to 89 inch lbs. (10 Nm).

➡The valve tappets must be installed in their original positions.

➡Coat the valve tappets with clean engine oil prior to installation.

30. Install the valve tappets.
31. Install and connect the Cylinder Head Temperature (CHT) sensor jumper harness.

❋❋ WARNING

If the engine is repaired or replaced because of upper engine failure, typically including valve or piston damage, check the intake manifold for metal debris. If metal debris is found, install a new intake manifold. Failure to follow these instructions can result in engine damage.

32. Using new intake manifold and thermostat housing gaskets, install the lower intake manifold and the 10 bolts. Tighten the bolts to 89 inch lbs. (10 Nm). Refer to the Intake Manifold procedure.
33. Install the thermostat housing and the 2 bolts. Tighten the bolts to 89 inch lbs. (10 Nm).
34. Connect the fuel supply tube-to-fuel rail quick connect coupling.

➡Align the bracket with the index mark made during removal.

35. Install the upper intake manifold support bracket and the bolt. Tighten the bolt to 89 inch lbs. (10 Nm).
36. Install the engine lifting eye and the 2 bolts. Tighten the bolts to 18 ft. lbs. (24 Nm).
37. Install the RH primary timing chain guide and the bolt. Tighten the bolts to 89 inch lbs. (10 Nm).
38. Install 6 new RH exhaust manifold studs. Tighten the studs to 106 inch lbs. (12 Nm).

❋❋ WARNING

Failure to tighten the exhaust manifold nuts to specification a second time will cause the exhaust manifold to develop an exhaust leak.

39. Using a new gasket, install the RH exhaust manifold and 6 new nuts. Tighten in 2 stages in the sequence given in the Exhaust Manifold procedure:
   a. Stage 1: Tighten to 177 inch lbs. (20 Nm).
   b. Stage 2: Tighten to 18 ft. lbs. (25 Nm).
40. If equipped, install the block heater wiring harness onto the engine. Tighten the cylinder block drain plug to 89 inch lbs. (10 Nm), plus an additional 720 degrees. Tighten the block heater to 30 ft. lbs. (40 Nm).
41. Using a new gasket, install the RH catalytic converter and 4 new nuts. Tighten to 30 ft. lbs. (40 Nm).
42. Install the LH cylinder block drain plug. Tighten the drain plug to 142 inch lbs. (16 Nm) plus an additional 180 degrees.
43. Connect the Cylinder Head Temperature (CHT) sensor electrical connector.
44. Connect the 6 fuel injector electrical connectors.
45. Install the ground cable and the bolt to the RH cylinder head. Tighten the bolt to 89 inch lbs. (10 Nm).
46. Install the 2 CMP sensors and 2 bolts. Tighten to 89 inch lbs. (10 Nm).
47. Connect the 2 RH CMP sensor electrical connectors.
48. Connect the RH Heated Oxygen Sensor (HO2S) electrical connector.
49. If equipped, position the block heater wiring harness onto the engine. Connect the block heater electrical connector and install the heat shield.
50. Install the RH camshafts as outlined in this section.

4.0L Engine

See Figures 135 through 139.

1. Before servicing the vehicle, refer to Precautions.
2. Drain the cooling system.
3. Remove the camshaft roller followers. Refer to Rocker Arms/Shafts.
4. Remove the accessory drive belt.
5. On RH side cylinder head, remove or disconnect the following:
   • Heater hose tube bracket (position aside)
   • Battery ground cable
   • Alternator electrical connections and disconnect the pushpin
   • Accessory drive belt tensioner
   • Alternator mounting bracket assembly
   • Heater hose from the thermostat housing
   • ECT sensor electrical connector
   • Upper radiator hose
   • Coolant bypass hose
   • Thermostat housing
   • Position the engine wiring harness aside
   • Engine ground strap
   • Spark plug wires
   • Catalytic converter-to-RH exhaust manifold nuts
   • RH exhaust manifold and the gasket
   • 6 RH exhaust manifold studs
   • RH side hydraulic chain tensioner bolt on side of cylinder head
   • Holding tool onto RH camshaft
   • RH camshaft sprocket nut
   • RH camshaft cassette bolt
   • RH camshaft sprocket

➡Use a rubber band around the chain and cassette to hold the chain from falling.

6. On the LH side cylinder head, remove or disconnect the following:
   • Heater hose tube bracket (position aside)

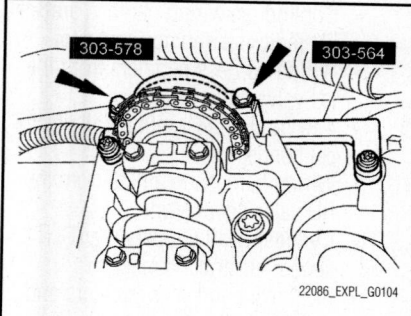

Fig. 135 Install a holding tool onto camshaft RH shown—4.0L Engine

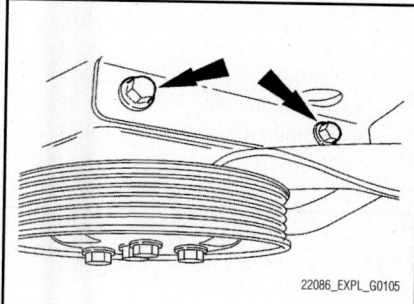

Fig. 136 Remove the 2 bolts as shown—4.0L Engine

- LH radio interference capacitor connector
- 2 bolts as shown
- Power steering pump bracket (position aside without disconnecting the pump lines)
- Ignition coil bracket
- Oil level indicator tube
- Exhaust pipe from LH exhaust manifold (discard nuts and gasket)
- LH exhaust manifold (discard nuts and gasket)
- 6 LH exhaust manifold studs
- LH camshaft chain tensioner bolt from side of head

7. Install a camshaft sprocket holding tool and remove the sprocket bolt.

8. Remove the LH camshaft cassette bolt in the front of the head.

9. Wrap a rubber band around the camshaft chain to the cassette to prevent it from falling during removal.

10. Remove the LH camshaft sprocket

❄❄ WARNING

To avoid damage to the camshaft cassette, an assistant will be required to lift the cylinder head from the vehicle. Watch the A/C tube on the RH side when lifting the head.

11. For either cylinder head, using the sequence shown, remove and discard the cylinder head bolts.

12. Lift the cylinder head(s) from the vehicle. Discard the gaskets.

To install:

➡ **The installation procedure that follows is for either cylinder head, unless otherwise specified.**

13. Clean all mating surfaces. Clean the bolt holes.

14. Position the new cylinder head gasket on the block mating surface.

15. Carefully set the cylinder head into position, watching for any possible interference with engine components.

16. Install the new 12mm bolts and tighten in 2 stages, in the sequence shown:
  a. Stage 1: 9 ft. lbs. (12 Nm)
  b. Stage 2: 18 ft. lbs. (25 Nm)

17. Install the 2 8mm bolts near the front of the cylinder head. Tighten the bolts to 24 ft. lbs. (32 Nm).

18. Now, retighten the 8 12mm cylinder head bolts, in the same sequence as above, to the following:
  a. Stage 1: 90 degrees additional
  b. Stage 2: 90 degrees additional

19. Install or connect the following:

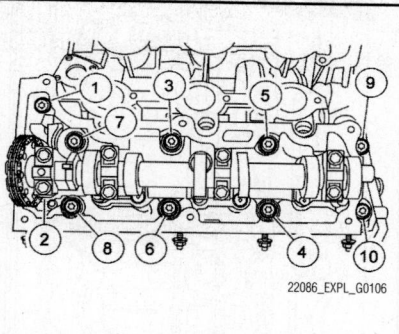

Fig. 137 Remove the cylinder head bolts in the sequence shown—4.0L Engine

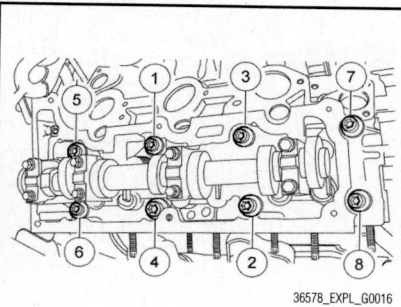

Fig. 138 Cylinder head 12mm bolt tightening sequence—4.0L Engine

- Camshaft chain and sprocket
- Camshaft cassette bolt; tighten to 9 ft. lbs. (12 Nm)
- New exhaust manifold studs; tighten to 9 ft. lbs. (12 Nm)
- Exhaust manifold; tighten the new nuts to 16 ft. lbs. (22 Nm)
- Exhaust pipe to the manifold; tighten the new nuts to 30 ft. lbs. (40 Nm)
- Spark plug wires to spark plugs (apply dielectric grease inside boots before installation)
- Engine ground strap (RH side)
- Engine wiring harness retaining bolt to side of engine; tighten bolt to 35 ft. lbs. (47 Nm) (RH side)
- Thermostat housing; torque the bolts to 8 ft. lbs. (11 Nm)
- Coolant hose to thermostat housing
- Upper radiator hose
- ECT sensor connector
- Heater hose to thermostat housing
- Oil level indicator tube (LH side)

20. Time the camshafts. See "Camshaft and Valve Lifters" section.

21. Install or connect the following:
- Alternator bracket; tighten the bolts to 31 ft. lbs. (42 Nm)
- Accessory drive belt tensioner; tighten the bolt to 35 ft. lbs. (47 Nm)
- Alternator electrical connections; tighten to 71 inch lbs. (8 Nm)
- Heater hose tube bracket; rear bolt to 17 ft. lbs. (25 Nm) and front bolt to 25 ft. lbs. (34 Nm)
- Ignition coil bracket; tighten the bolts to 89 inch lbs. (10 Nm)
- A/C compressor and power steering pump; tighten mounting bolts to 31 ft. lbs. (42 Nm)
- Ignition coil bracket to accessory drive bracket; tighten bolts to 89 inch lbs. (10 Nm)

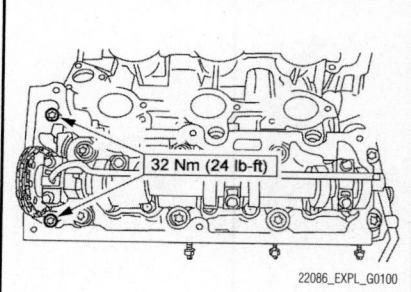

Fig. 139 Installing the 2 8mm cylinder head bolts—4.0L Engine

- Radio interference capacitor electrical connector
- Accessory drive belt
22. Fill and bleed the cooling system.

4.6L Engine

See Figures 140 through 149.

1. Before servicing the vehicle, refer to Precautions.

➥**Clean all mating surfaces as components are removed during this procedure.**

2. Remove the engine.

3. Transfer the engine to a proper workstand.

4. Remove or disconnect the following for access to the cylinder heads:
- Wiring harness retainers from the RH oil pan bolts
- Crankshaft position sensor electrical connector and detach the wiring harness retainer
- RH and LH camshaft position (CMP) sensor electrical connectors
- RH and LH variable camshaft timing (VCT) solenoid electrical connectors
- Wiring harness retainers from the front end of the engine

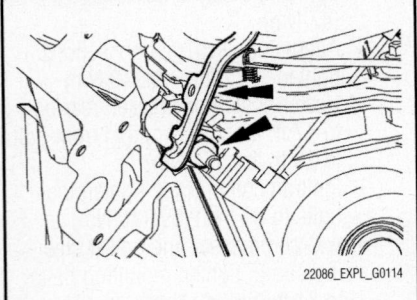

Fig. 140 Remove the cooling fan wiring harness bracket and the LH radio interference capacitor—4.6L Engine

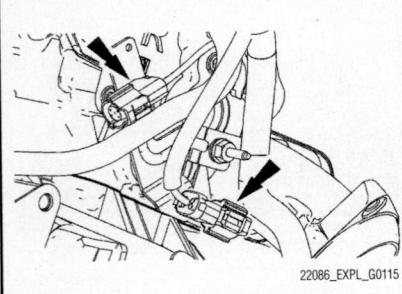

Fig. 141 Remove the electrical connector retainers and remove the engine wiring harness—4.6L Engine

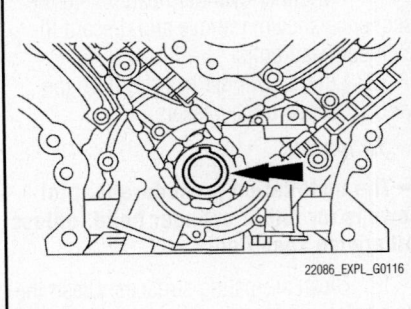

Fig. 142 Position the crankshaft keyway at the 12 o'clock position—4.6L Engine

- RH radio ignition interference capacitor
- Oil pressure sensor electrical connector
- LH CMP sensor electrical connector and detach the wiring harness retainers

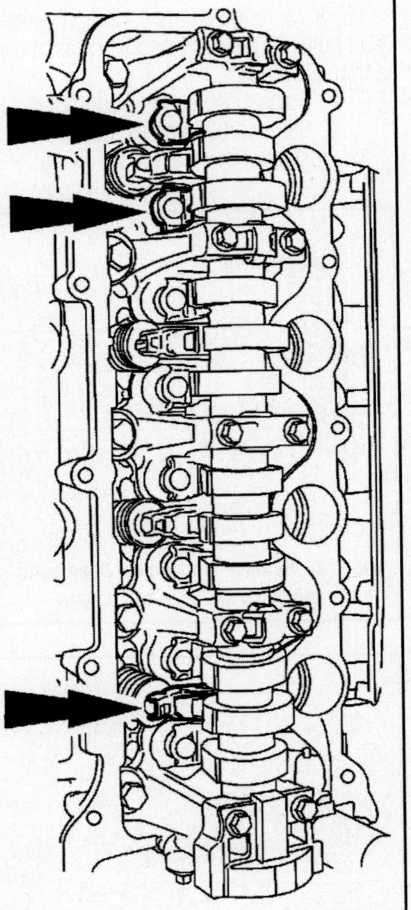

Fig. 143 Remove only the 3 roller followers, as indicated, from the RH cylinder head—4.6L Engine

- Cooling fan wiring harness bracket
- LH radio interference capacitor
- Wiring harness retainers from the LH valve cover studs
- 4 RH and 4 LH ignition coil electrical connectors
- Wiring harness retainers from the RH valve cover studs
- Cylinder head temperature (CHT) sensor electrical connector
- Electrical connector retainers and remove the engine wiring harness
- Breather tube from the RH valve cover
- Positive crankcase ventilation (PCV) tube from the LH valve cover
- Oil filter
- 8 ignition coils
- Position the oil level indicator aside

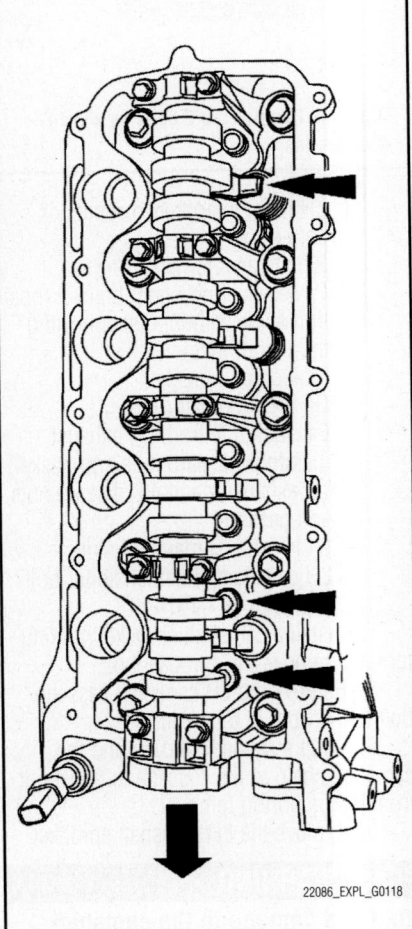

Fig. 144 Remove only the 3 roller followers, as indicated, from the LH cylinder head—4.6L Engine

- Valve covers
- Coolant pump pulley and the RH side accessory drive belt idler pulley
- Crankshaft pulley (discard pulley bolt)
- Front crankshaft seal

- 4 oil pan-to-engine front cover bolts
- Engine front cover
- Crankshaft sensor ring from the crankshaft
5. Position the crankshaft keyway at the 12 o'clock position.

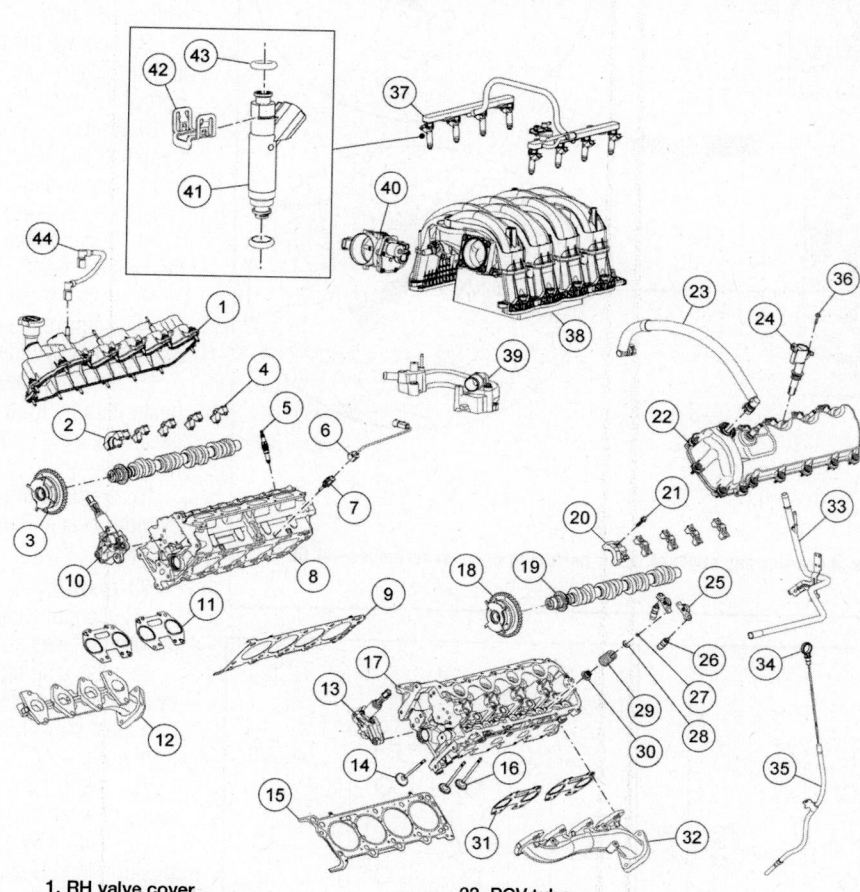

1. RH valve cover
2. RH camshaft thrust bearing cap
3. RH camshaft phaser sprocket
4. Camshaft bearing cap (8 required)
5. Spark plug (8 required)
6. Cylinder Head Temperature (CHT) sensor jumper harness
7. CHT sensor
8. RH cylinder head
9. RH cylinder head gasket
10. RH Variable Camshaft Timing (VCT) oil control solenoid assembly
11. Exhaust manifold gasket (2 required)
12. Exhaust manifold — RH
13. LH VCT oil control solenoid assembly
14. Exhaust valve (8 required)
15. LH cylinder head gasket
16. Intake valve (16 required)
17. LH cylinder head
18. LH camshaft phaser sprocket
19. LH camshaft
20. LH camshaft thrust bearing cap
21. Camshaft bearing cap bolt (20 required)
22. LH valve cover

23. PCV tube
24. Ignition coil (8 required)
25. Roller follower (24 required)
26. Hydraulic lash adjuster (24 required)
27. Valve spring retainer key (48 required)
28. Valve spring retainer (24 required)
29. Valve spring (24 required)
30. Valve stem seal (24 required)
31. Exhaust manifold gasket (2 required)
32. LH exhaust manifold
33. Coolant tube
34. Oil level indicator
35. Oil level indicator tube
36. Ignition coil bolt (8 required)
37. Fuel rail assembly
38. Intake manifold assembly
39. Engine coolant crossover
40. Electronic throttle body
41. Fuel injector (8 required)
42. Fuel injector clip (8 required)
43. O-ring seal (16 required)
44. PCV breather hose

36578_EXPL_G0018

Fig. 145 Cylinder head exploded view

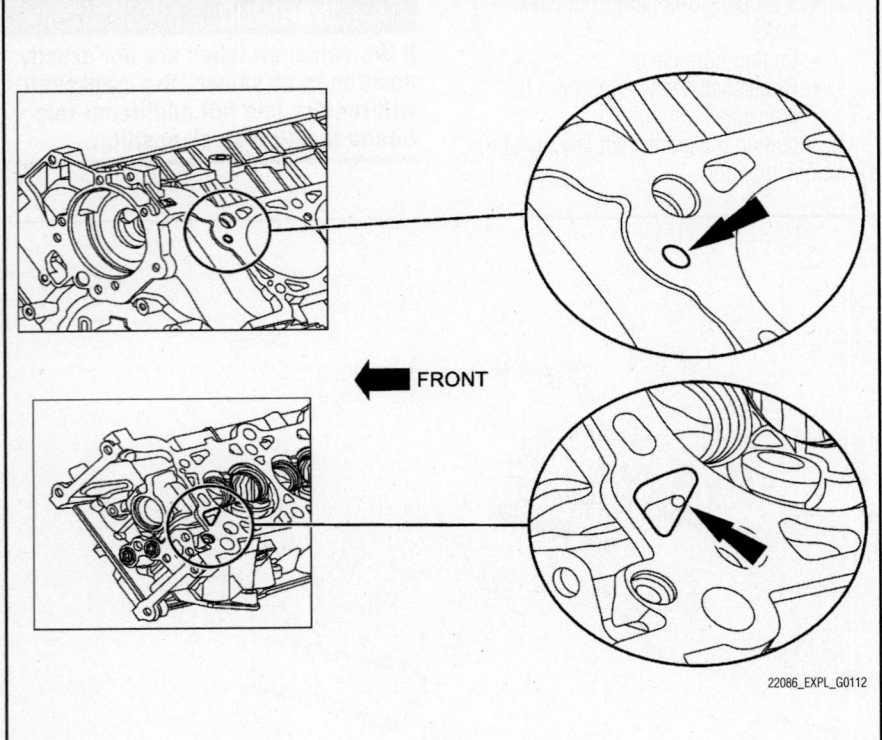

Fig. 146 Inspect the areas shown for any signs of wear, corrosion or deep scratches—4.6L Engine

6. The No. 1 cylinder camshaft exhaust lobe must be coming up on the exhaust stroke. Verify by noting the position of the 2 intake lobes and the exhaust lobe on the No. 1 cylinder.

7. Remove only the 3 roller followers shown from the RH and LH cylinder heads.

8. Rotate the crankshaft clockwise and position the crankshaft keyway at the 6 o'clock position.

9. Remove the timing chains, guides and sprockets. See "Timing Chain and Sprockets" section.

10. Remove the camshafts. Refer to Camshaft and Valve Lifter.

11. Remove all of the camshaft roller followers and lash adjusters.

12. Install lifting handles on each end of the cylinder heads.

13. Remove the exhaust manifolds.

14. Remove the nut and ground strap from the RH cylinder head.

15. Remove the stud bolt and the heater supply tube and hoses as an assembly from between the cylinder heads.

16. Remove the bolts and lift off the cylinder heads. Remove and discard the gaskets.

To install:

17. Carefully clean all cylinder head mating surfaces and bolt holes.

18. Use a straightedge to check the cylinder head surface flatness. Any distortion must be within 0.0004 in. (0.010 mm) from end to end.

19. Inspect the areas shown for any signs of wear, corrosion or deep scratches.

20. With new gaskets in place, carefully position the LH cylinder head into position. Use locator dowels, if necessary.

21. Install and tighten the cylinder head bolts, in the sequence shown.

22. Tighten the LH cylinder head bolts in 3 steps:

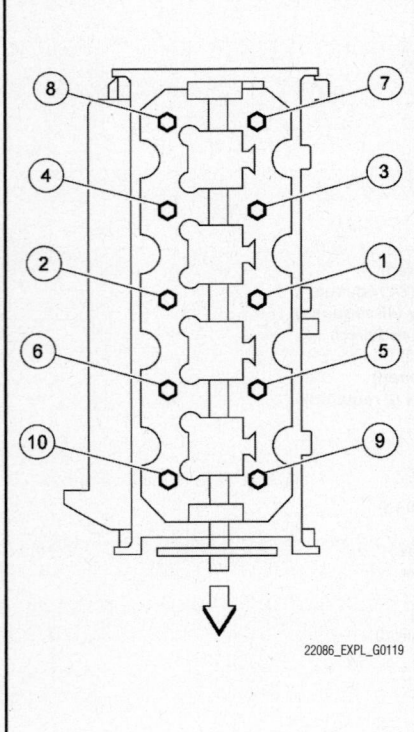

Fig. 147 Tighten the LH cylinder head bolts in the sequence shown—4.6L Engine

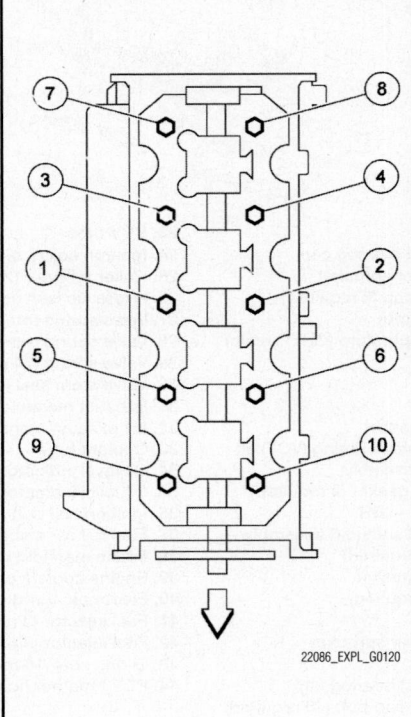

Fig. 148 Tighten the RH cylinder head bolts in the sequence shown—4.6L Engine

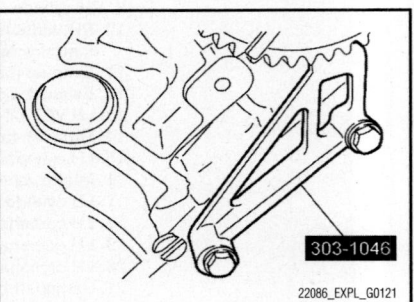

Fig. 149 Using the special tool, as shown, tighten the LH and RH camshaft phaser sprocket bolts—4.6L Engine

a. Step 1: 30 ft. lbs. (40 Nm)
b. Step 2: additional 90 degrees
c. Step 3: additional 90 degrees

23. Remove the cylinder head lifting handles from the end of the cylinder head.

24. Lubricate and install the LH cylinder head lash adjusters in their original positions.

25. With a new O-ring seal, loosely install the oil level indicator tube.

26. With a new gasket, install the LH exhaust manifold. Refer to Exhaust Manifold for tightening sequence and specifications.

27. With new gaskets in place, carefully position the RH cylinder head into position. Use locator dowels, if necessary.

28. Install and tighten the cylinder head bolts, in the sequence shown.

29. Tighten the RH cylinder head bolts in 3 steps:

a. Step 1: 30 ft. lbs. (40 Nm)
b. Step 2: additional 90 degrees
c. Step 3: additional 90 degrees

30. Remove the cylinder head lifting handles from the end of the cylinder head.

31. Lubricate and install the RH cylinder head lash adjusters in their original positions.

32. With a new gasket, install the RH exhaust manifold. Refer to Exhaust Manifold for tightening sequence and specifications.

33. Install or connect the following:
- Heater supply tube and the hoses as an assembly
- Ground strap
- LH and RH camshafts; refer to Camshafts and Valve Lifters.

34. Install the camshaft phaser sprockets and new camshaft phaser bolts finger-tight.

35. Using the special tool, as shown, tighten the LH and RH camshaft phaser sprocket bolts in 2 stages:

a. Stage 1: 30 ft. lbs. (40 Nm)
b. Stage 2: additional 90 degrees

36. Install the crankshaft sprocket, making sure the flange faces forward.

37. Rotate the crankshaft to position the crankshaft sprocket timing mark in the 6 o'clock position.

38. Install the camshaft sprockets and timing chains. Refer to Timing Chain and Sprockets.

39. Install the crankshaft sensor ring on the crankshaft.

40. Lubricate and install all of the camshaft roller followers.

41. Install the front cover. Refer to Timing Chain and Sprockets.

42. Install the 4 bolts to the front of the oil pan. Tighten the bolts to 15 ft. lbs. (20 Nm), then an additional 60 degrees.

43. Install a new front crankshaft oil seal. Refer to Crankshaft Front Seal.

44. Install the crankshaft pulley. Apply silicone to the keyway prior to installation.

45. Tighten the new crankshaft pulley bolt in 4 steps:

a. Step 1: 89 ft. lbs. (120 Nm)
b. Step 2: LOOSEN 1 full turn (360 degrees)
c. Step 3: 37 ft. lbs. (50 Nm)
d. Step 4: additional 90 degrees

46. Install or connect the following:
- RH side accessory drive belt idler pulley, the coolant pump pulley and the 5 bolts; tighten the bolts to 18 ft. lbs. (25 Nm)
- Valve covers; refer to Valve Covers.
- Tighten the oil level indicator tube bolt to 89 inch lbs. (10 Nm)
- 8 ignition coils
- New oil filter
- Positive crankcase ventilation (PCV) hose to the LH valve cover
- Breather tube to the RH valve cover
- Engine wiring harness and attach the electrical connectors to the heater supply tube bracket
- Cylinder head temperature (CHT) sensor electrical connector
- Wiring harness retainers to the RH valve cover studs
- RH and LH ignition coil electrical connectors
- Wiring harness retainers to the LH valve cover studs
- LH radio interference capacitor; tighten the nut to 18 ft. lbs. (25 Nm)
- Cooling fan wiring harness; tighten the nut to 18 ft. lbs. (25 Nm)
- LH camshaft position sensor and attach the wiring harness retainers
- Oil pressure sensor electrical connector
- RH radio interference capacitor; tighten the nut to 18 ft. lbs. (25 Nm)
- Wiring harness retainers
- RH and LH variable camshaft timing (VCT) solenoid electrical connectors
- RH and LH camshaft position (CMP) sensor electrical connectors
- Crankshaft position sensor electrical connector and attach the wiring harness retainer
- Wiring harness retainers to the RH oil pan bolts

47. Install the engine.
48. Refill all fluids. Check for leaks.

EXHAUST MANIFOLD

REMOVAL & INSTALLATION

3.5L Engine

Left Side

On the 3.5L engine, the exhaust manifold and catalytic converter are a single assembly. Please refer to Catalytic Converter for more information.

Right Side

See Figure 150.

1. Remove the RH catalytic converter as outlined in this section.
2. Disconnect the RH Heated Oxygen Sensor (HO2S) electrical connector.
3. Remove the 6 nuts and the RH exhaust manifold.

a. Discard the nuts and gasket.

4. Clean and inspect the RH exhaust manifold as outlined in this section.
5. Remove and discard the 6 RH exhaust manifold studs.

✻✻ WARNING

Do not use metal scrapers, wire brushes, power abrasive discs or other abrasive means to clean the sealing surfaces. These may cause scratches and gouges resulting in leak paths. Use a plastic scraper to clean the sealing surfaces.

6. Clean the exhaust manifold mating surface of the cylinder head with metal surface prep. Follow the directions on the packaging.

To install:

7. Install 6 new RH exhaust manifold studs. Tighten to 106 inch lbs. (12 Nm).

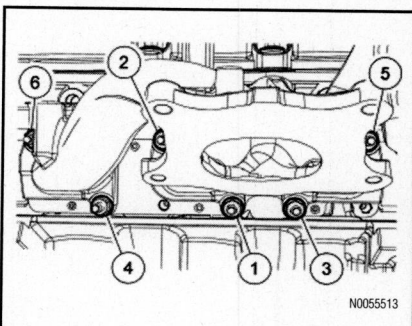

Fig. 150 RH exhaust manifold—3.5L engine

⁕⁕⁕ WARNING

Failure to tighten the exhaust manifold nuts to specification a second time will cause the exhaust manifold to develop an exhaust leak.

8. Using a new gasket, install the RH exhaust manifold and 6 new nuts. Tighten in 2 stages in the proper sequence.
   a. Stage 1: Tighten to 177 inch lbs. (20 Nm).
   b. Stage 2: Tighten to 18 ft. lbs. (25 Nm).
9. Connect the RH HO2S electrical connector.
10. Install the RH catalytic converter as outlined in this section.

4.0L Engine

See Figures 151 and 152.

1. Before servicing the vehicle, refer to Precautions.
2. Remove or disconnect the following:
   • Negative battery cable
   • EGR tube (RH manifold)
   • Exhaust pipe attaching bolts

• Exhaust manifold and discard the gasket

To install:

3. Clean the gasket mating surfaces.
4. Install or connect the following:
   • New gasket and the exhaust manifold. Torque the bolts to 16 ft. lbs. (22 Nm).
   • Exhaust pipe-to-manifold attaching bolts. Torque the bolts to 30 ft. lbs. (40 Nm).
   • EGR tube to the manifold. Torque the fastener to 30 ft. lbs. (40 Nm) (RH manifold)
   • Negative battery cable
5. Start the vehicle and check for leaks, repair if necessary.

4.6L Engine

Right Side

See Figure 153.

1. With the vehicle in NEUTRAL, position it on a hoist.
2. Remove the 4 nuts and disconnect the dual converter Y-pipe from the exhaust manifolds.

3. Remove the 3 bolts and the RH exhaust manifold heat shield.
4. Remove the 5 pushpins and the RH splash shield.
5. Remove the 8 nuts, the RH exhaust manifold and the 2 gaskets.
6. Discard the nuts and the gaskets.
7. Remove and discard the 8 RH exhaust manifold studs.

To install:

8. Installation is the reverse of the removal procedure, noting the following:
   a. Tighten the nuts in the sequence shown as follows:
   • Studs: 9 ft. lbs. (12 Nm); nuts: 18 ft. lbs. (25 Nm)
9. Tighten the Y-pipe new nuts as follows: (RL-BS0)
   • 30 ft. lbs. (40 Nm)
10. Tighten the intermediate shaft pinch bolt to 35 ft. lbs. (48 Nm).

Left Side

See Figure 154.

1. With the vehicle in NEUTRAL, position it on a hoist.

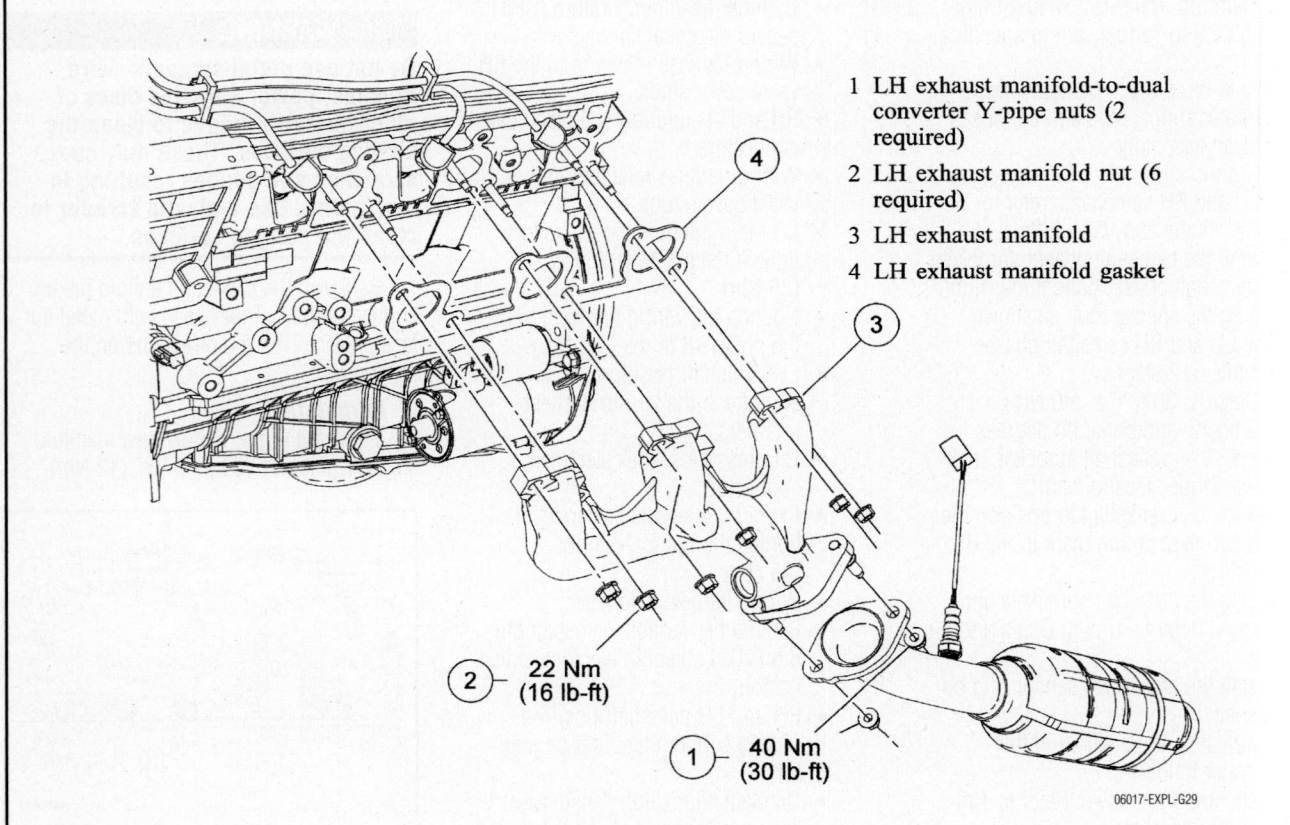

1 LH exhaust manifold-to-dual converter Y-pipe nuts (2 required)
2 LH exhaust manifold nut (6 required)
3 LH exhaust manifold
4 LH exhaust manifold gasket

22 Nm (16 lb-ft)
40 Nm (30 lb-ft)

06017-EXPL-G29

Fig. 151 Left side exhaust manifold—4.0L engine

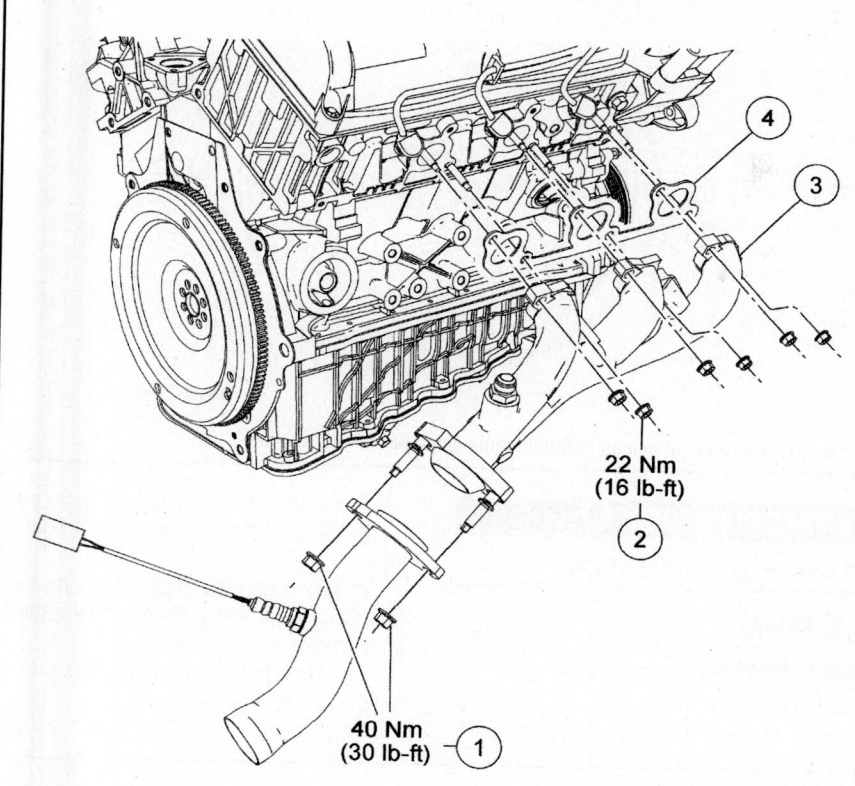

1 RH exhaust manifold-to-dual converter Y-pipe nuts (2 required)

2 RH exhaust manifold nuts (6 required)

3 RH exhaust manifold

4 RH exhaust manifold gasket

06017-EXPL-G30

Fig. 152 Right side exhaust manifold—4.0L engine

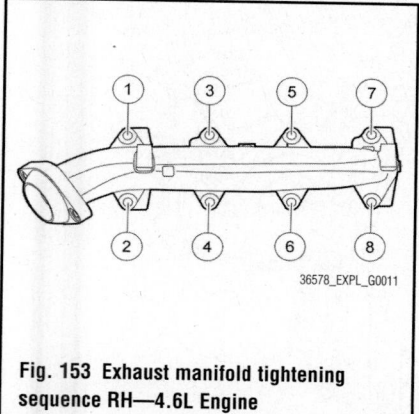

36578_EXPL_G0011

Fig. 153 Exhaust manifold tightening sequence RH—4.6L Engine

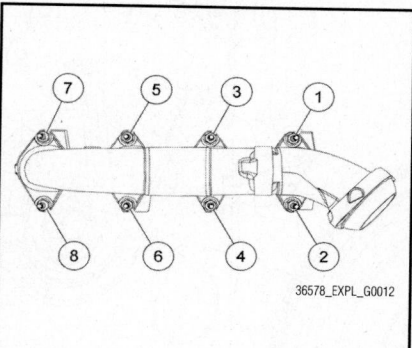

36578_EXPL_G0012

Fig. 154 Exhaust manifold tightening sequence LH—4.6L Engine

2. Detach the Evaporative Emission (EVAP) canister purge valve from the bracket and position the valve aside.

➡**Do not allow the lower steering column shaft to rotate while it is disconnected from the gear or the clockspring may be damaged. If there is**

evidence that the lower steering column shaft has rotated, the clockspring must be removed and re-centered.

3. Remove the intermediate steering shaft pinch bolt and disconnect the intermediate steering shaft from the lower steering column shaft.

4. Remove the 4 nuts and disconnect the dual converter Y-pipe from the exhaust manifolds.

5. Remove the 2 nuts and position the battery cable bracket aside.

6. Remove the 3 bolts and the LH exhaust manifold heat shield.

7. Remove and discard the pushpin.

8. Remove the 8 nuts, the LH exhaust manifold and the 2 gaskets.

9. Deflect the inner fender splash shield and remove the manifold between the splash shield and the frame rail.

10. Discard the nuts and the gaskets.

11. Remove and discard the 8 LH exhaust manifold studs.

To install:

12. Installation is the reverse of the removal procedure, noting the following:

a. Tighten the nuts in the sequence shown as follows:

• Studs: 9 ft. lbs. (12 Nm); nuts: 18 ft. lbs. (25 Nm)

13. Tighten the Y-pipe new nuts as follows:

(RL-BS0)

• 30 ft. lbs. (40 Nm)

14. Tighten the intermediate shaft pinch bolt to 35 ft. lbs. (48 Nm).

FLEXPLATE

REMOVAL & INSTALLATION

3.5L Engine

See Figure 155.

1. With the vehicle in NEUTRAL, position it on a hoist

2. Remove the transaxle..

3. Remove the 8 bolts and the flexplate.

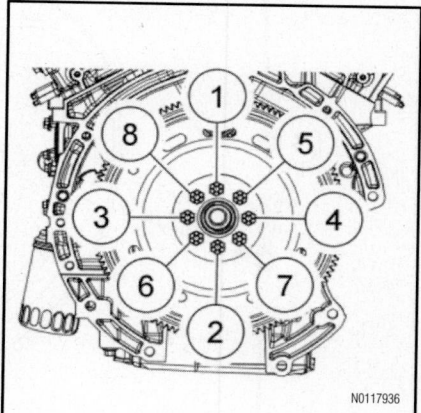

N0117936

Fig. 155 Flexplate tightening sequence—3.5L engine

To install:

➡One of the 8 flexplate holes are off-set so the flexplate can only be installed in one position.

4. Install the flexplate and the 8 bolts.
5. Tighten in the sequence shown to 59 ft. lbs. (80 Nm).
6. Install the transaxle.

4.0L & 4.6L Engines

See Figures 156 through 158.

1. Remove the transmission or transaxle.
2. Remove the flexplate attaching bolts and remove the flexplate.

To install:

3. Position the flexplate into position.
4. Select only the appropriate new bolts designed for flexplate application.
5. Install and tighten the bolts in sequence as shown:
   4.0L Engine:
   a. Stage 1: 37 ft. lbs. (51 Nm)
   b. Stage 2: Plus 90 degrees
   4.6L Engine: 59 ft. lbs. (80 Nm)
6. Install the transmission.

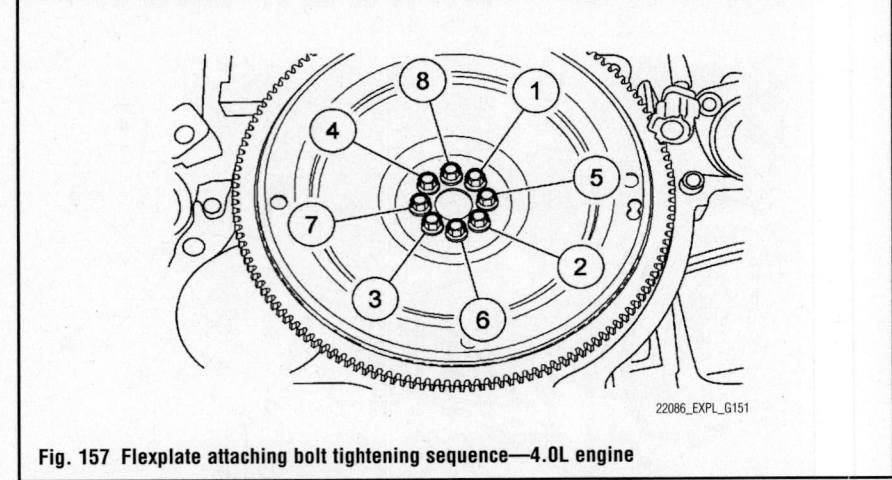

Fig. 157 Flexplate attaching bolt tightening sequence—4.0L engine

INTAKE MANIFOLD

REMOVAL & INSTALLATION

3.5L Engine

Upper Manifold

See Figure 159.

1. Remove the engine appearance cover.
2. Remove the Air Cleaner (ACL) outlet pipe.
3. Disconnect the Evaporative Emission (EVAP) canister vent solenoid and throttle body electrical connectors:
   a. Detach the 2 wiring harness pin-type retainers.

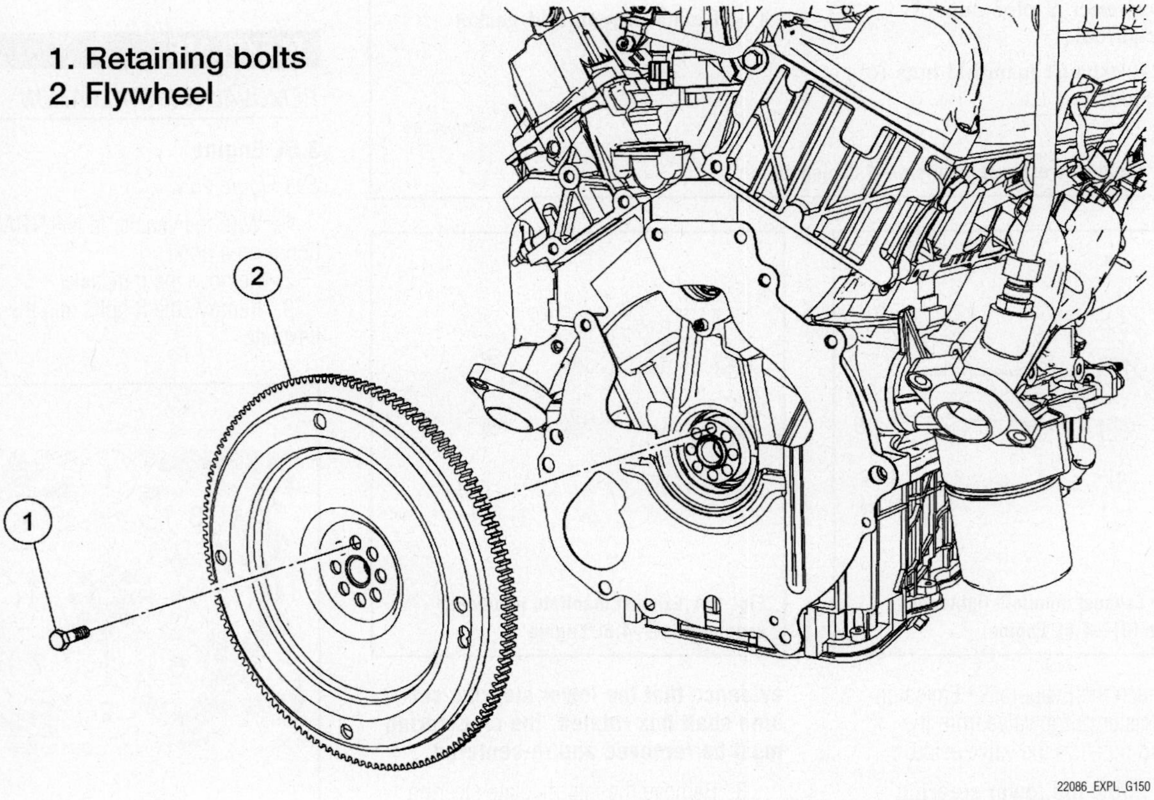

1. Retaining bolts
2. Flywheel

Fig. 156 Remove the flexplate attaching bolts (1) and remove the flexplate (2)—4.0L & 4.6L engine

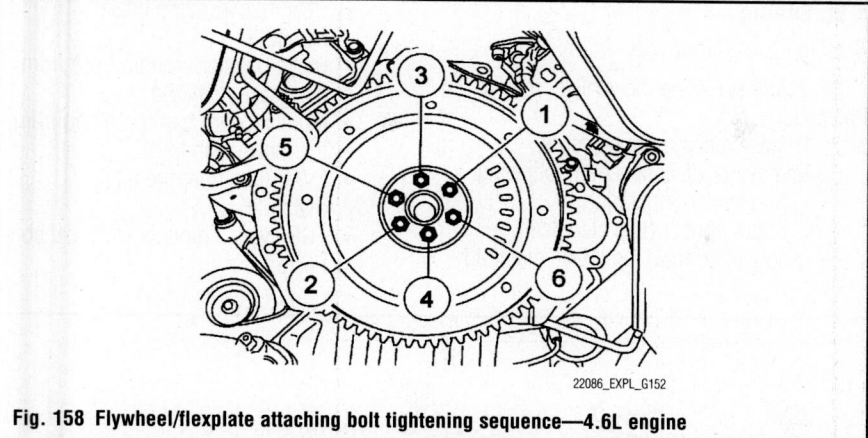

Fig. 158 Flywheel/flexplate attaching bolt tightening sequence—4.6L engine

4. Disconnect the EVAP vapor tube from the EVAP canister vent solenoid and position aside.

5. Release the clamp and disconnect the brake booster vacuum supply hose from the intake manifold.

6. Disconnect the 2 wiring harness/coolant tube retainers from the upper intake manifold.

7. Disconnect the crankcase ventilation hose from the PCV valve.

8. Remove the upper intake manifold support bracket bolt.

9. Remove the 7 bolts and the upper intake manifold.

　　a. Remove and discard the gaskets.

　　b. Clean and inspect all of the sealing surfaces of the upper and lower intake manifold.

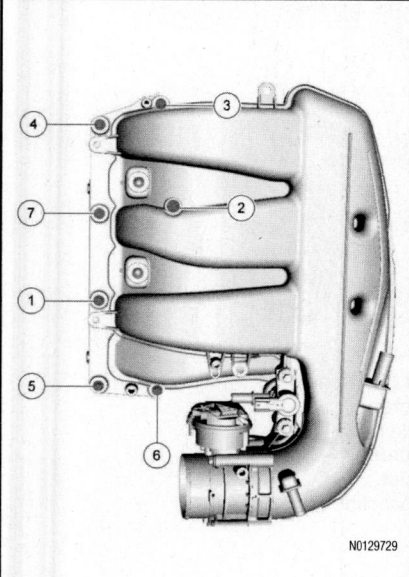

Fig. 159 Upper intake manifold tightening sequence—3.5L engine

To install:

> **⁂ WARNING**
>
> **If the engine is repaired or replaced because of upper engine failure, typically including valve or piston damage, check the intake manifold for metal debris. If metal debris is found, install a new intake manifold. Failure to follow these instructions can result in engine damage.**

10. Using new gaskets, install the upper intake manifold and the 7 bolts. Tighten the bolts in the proper sequence, as follows:

　　a. Stage 1: 89 inch lbs. (10 Nm)

　　b. Stage 2: Tighten an additional 45 degrees.

11. Install the upper intake manifold support bracket bolt. Tighten the bolt to 89 inch lbs. (10 Nm).

12. Connect the crankcase ventilation hose to the PCV valve.

13. Attach the 2 wiring harness/coolant tube retainers to the upper intake manifold.

14. Connect the brake booster vacuum hose and clamp to the intake manifold.

15. Connect the EVAP tube to the EVAP canister vent solenoid.

16. Connect the EVAP canister vent solenoid and throttle body electrical connectors.

17. Attach the 2 EVAP tube pin-type retainers to the upper intake manifold.

18. Install the ACL outlet pipe.

19. Install the engine appearance cover.

Lower Manifold

See Figure 160.

1. With the vehicle in NEUTRAL, position it on a hoist.

2. Release the fuel system pressure, as outlined in the Fuel System Section.

3. Disconnect the battery ground cable.

4. Drain the cooling system.

5. Remove the upper intake manifold, as outlined in this section.

6. Disconnect the 6 fuel injector electrical connectors.

7. Remove the bolt from the fuel supply tube-to-rail bracket.

8. Disconnect the fuel supply tube-to-fuel rail quick connect coupling.

9. Remove the 2 thermostat housing-to-lower intake manifold bolts.

10. Remove the 10 bolts and the lower intake manifold.

　　a. Remove and discard the intake manifold and thermostat housing gaskets.

　　b. Clean and inspect all sealing surfaces.

To install:

➡**If the engine is repaired or replaced because of upper engine failure, typically including valve or piston damage, check the intake manifold for metal debris. If metal debris is found, install a new intake manifold. Failure to follow these instructions can result in engine damage.**

11. Using new intake manifold and thermostat housing gaskets, install the lower intake manifold and the 10 bolts. Tighten in the sequence shown to 89 inch lbs. (10 Nm).

12. Install the 2 thermostat housing-to-lower intake manifold bolts. Tighten to 89 inch lbs. (10 Nm).

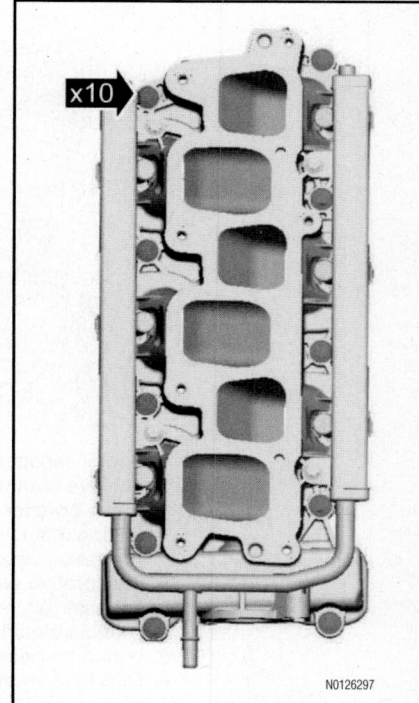

Fig. 160 Lower intake manifold bolt tightening sequence—3.5L engine

13. Connect the fuel supply tube-to-fuel rail quick connect coupling.

14. Install the bolt to the fuel supply tube-to-rail bracket. Tighten to 89 inch lbs. (10 Nm).

15. Connect the 6 fuel injector electrical connectors.

16. Install the upper intake manifold, as outlined in this section.

17. Connect the battery ground cable.

18. Fill and bleed the cooling system.

4.0L Engine

See Figures 161 and 162.

1. Before servicing the vehicle, refer to Precautions.

2. Release fuel system pressure.

3. Remove or disconnect the following:
   - Air cleaner outlet pipe
   - Knock sensor (KS) electrical connector from the intake manifold
   - PCV tube from the intake manifold
   - Brake booster vacuum hose from the intake manifold
   - Main vacuum harness fitting from the intake manifold
   - EVAP tube from the intake manifold
   - EGR system module electrical connector

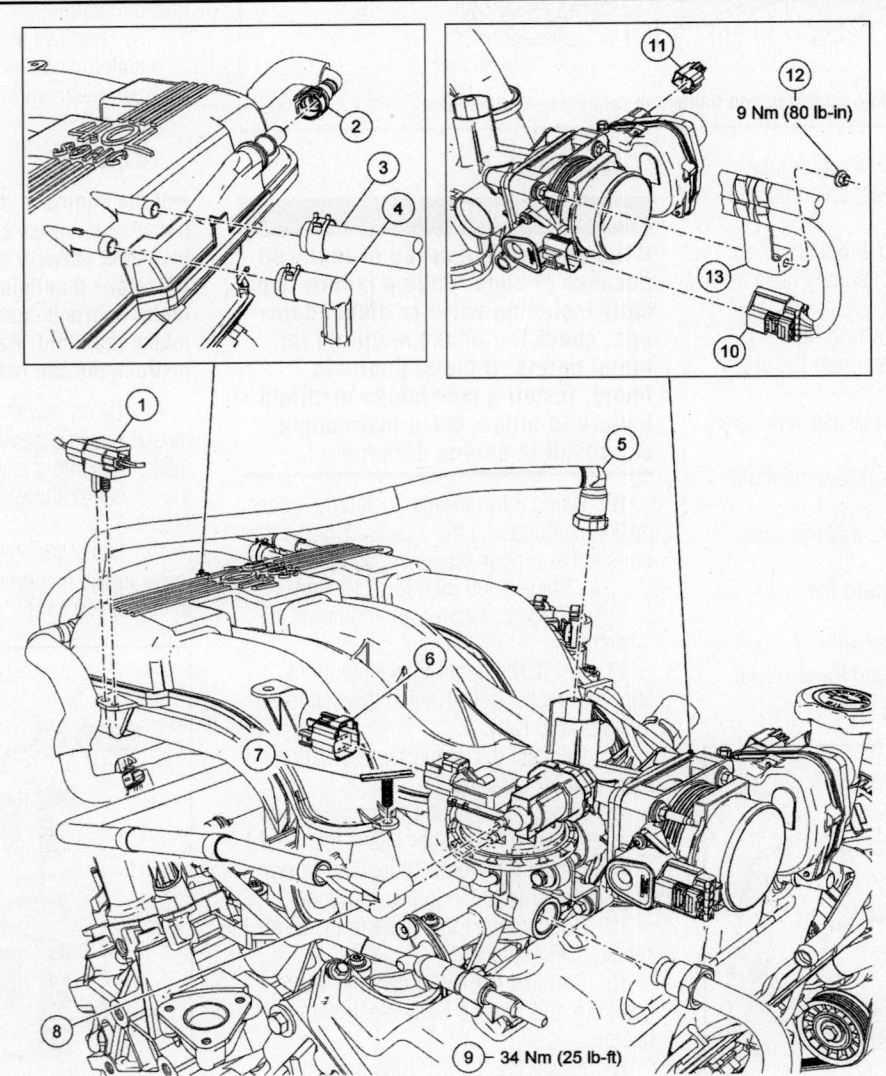

1. Knock sensor (KS) electrical connector
2. Positive crankcase ventilation (PCV) tube
3. Brake booster vacuum supply hose
4. Engine main vacuum harness-to-intake manifold fitting
5. Evaporative emissions (EVAP) tube
6. Exhaust gas recirculation (EGR) system module electrical connector
7. Wiring harness pin-type retainer
8. EGR system module vacuum fitting
9. EGR tube fitting
10. Throttle position (TP) sensor electrical connector
11. Electronic throttle body (TB) electrical connector
12. Wiring harness nut
13. Wiring harness bracket

22086_EXPL_G0081

Fig. 161 Exploded view of the external engine component to remove for intake manifold removal—4.0L engine

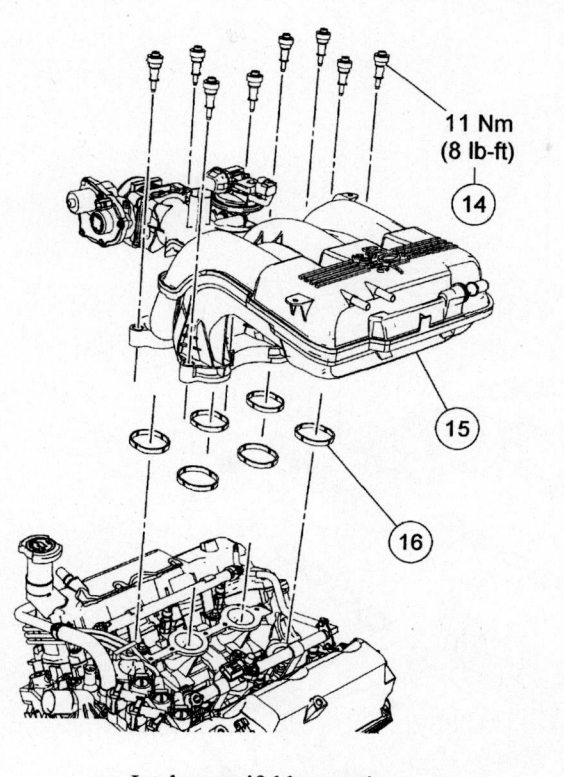

14 Intake manifold mounting bolts (8 required)

15 Intake manifold

16 Intake manifold gaskets

06017-EXPL-G27

Fig. 162 Intake manifold removal—4.0L engine

- Wiring harness retainer
- EGR system module vacuum fitting
- Exhaust manifold-to-EGR system module tube from the EGR system module
- TP sensor electrical connector
- Electronic Throttle Body (TB) electrical connector
- Wiring harness bracket from the electronic TB
- Intake manifold and the gaskets

To install:

4. Clean the sealing surfaces and inspect the gaskets. Install new gaskets if necessary.

5. Position the intake manifold and tighten the bolts to 8 ft. lbs. (11 Nm).

6. Install or connect the following:
- Wiring harness bracket to the electronic TB
- Electronic TB electrical connector
- TP sensor electrical connector
- Exhaust manifold-to-EGR system

module tube to the EGR system module
- EGR system module vacuum fitting
- Wiring harness retainer
- EGR system module electrical connector
- EVAP tube to the intake manifold
- Main vacuum harness fitting to the intake manifold
- Brake booster vacuum hose to the intake manifold
- PCV tube to the intake manifold
- Knock sensor (KS) electrical connector to the intake manifold
- Air cleaner outlet pipe

4.6L Engine

See Figures 163 and 164.

1. Before servicing the vehicle, refer to Precautions.

2. Relieve the fuel system pressure.

3. Remove or disconnect the following:
- Negative battery cable
- Air cleaner outlet pipe

- Fuel rail and injectors
- Electronic Throttle Body (TB) electrical connector
- EVAP tube from the intake manifold
- TP sensor electrical connector
- PCV hose from the heated PCV fitting on the intake manifold
- Position the heated PCV fitting aside
- Wiring harness retainers from the intake manifold
- Charge motion control valve (CMCV) electrical connector
- Intake manifold bolts and position the intake manifold forward
- Brake booster vacuum hose from the rear of the intake manifold
- Vacuum hose from the rear of the intake manifold

4. Remove the intake manifold and gaskets.

To install:

5. Clean and inspect the sealing surfaces.

> #### ☀ WARNING
>
> **Electrical and vacuum harnesses must not restrict movement of the CMCV control rods at the rear of the intake manifold. Use extreme care during the installation of the intake manifold to prevent any pinching of electrical and vacuum harnesses.**

6. Using new intake manifold gaskets, position the intake manifold.

7. Connect the vacuum hose to the rear of the intake manifold.

8. Connect the brake booster hose to the rear of the intake manifold.

9. Install the intake manifold bolts and tighten the bolts in the sequence shown in 2 stages:
   a. Stage 1: 18 inch lbs. (2 Nm)
   b. State 2: 89 inch lbs. (10 Nm)

10. Install or connect the following:
- CMCV electrical connector
- Wiring harness retainers to the intake manifold
- New O-ring seal, position the heated PCV fitting and install the bolts
- PCV hose to the heated PCV fitting on the intake manifold
- TP sensor electrical connector
- EVAP hose to the intake manifold
- Electronic TB electrical connector
- Fuel rail and injectors
- Air cleaner outlet pipe
- Negative battery cable

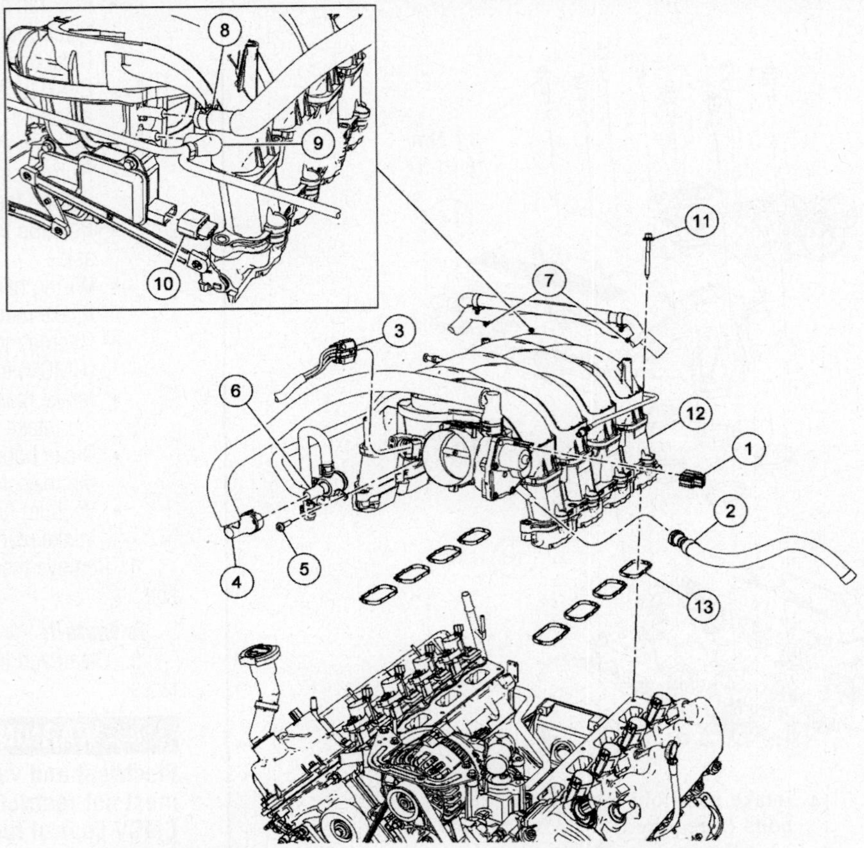

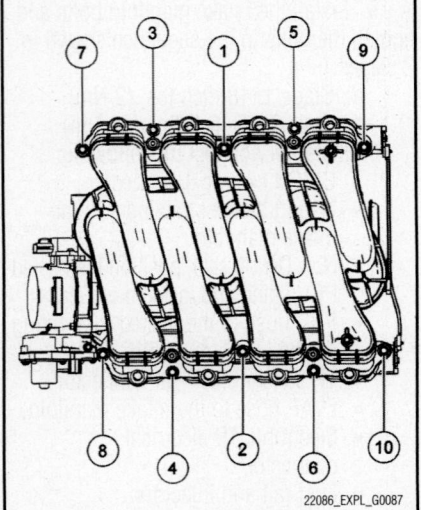

1. Electronic throttle body (TB) electrical connector
2. Evaporative emissions (EVAP) hose
3. Throttle position (TP) sensor electrical connector
4. Positive crankcase ventilation (PCV) hose
5. Heated PCV fitting bolt (2 required)
6. Heated PCV fitting
7. Wiring harness retainers
8. Brake booster vacuum hose
9. Vacuum hose
10. Charge motion control valve (CMCV) electrical connector
11. Intake manifold bolt (10 required)
12. Intake manifold
13. Intake manifold gasket

22086_EXPL_G0086

Fig. 163 Intake manifold and related components—4.6L engine

22086_EXPL_G0087

Fig. 164 Intake manifold bolt tightening sequence—4.6L engine

OIL PAN

REMOVAL & INSTALLATION

4.0L Engine

See Figure 165.

1. Before servicing the vehicle, refer to Precautions.
2. Raise the vehicle on a hoist.
3. Drain the engine oil.
4. Remove the oil pan bolts, oil pan and discard the gasket

To install:

➡**Do not use metal scrapers, wire brushes, power abrasive discs or other abrasive means to clean sealing surfaces. These tools cause scratches and gouges which make leak paths. Use a plastic scraping tool to remove all traces of the old oil pan gasket.**

5. Clean the pan and block mating surfaces.
6. Install a new gasket.
7. Position the oil pan. Torque the bolts, in an alternating pattern, to 97 inch lbs. (11 Nm).

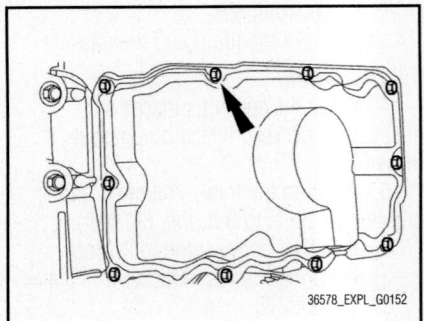

36578_EXPL_G0152

Fig. 165 Oil pan bolt location—4.0L engine

8. Torque the pan drain bolt to 19 ft. lbs. (26 Nm).

9. Fill the engine with clean oil.

10. Start the vehicle and check for leaks, repair if necessary.

4.6L Engine

See Figure 166.

1. Before servicing the vehicle, refer to Precautions.

2. With the vehicle in NEUTRAL position on a hoist.

3. Lower the front axle (4WD). Refer to Front Suspension in Suspension.

4. Remove the front stabilizer bar. Refer to Stabilizer Bar in Suspension.

5. Drain the engine oil.

6. Remove the nut and position the power steering pressure (PSP) hose bracket aside.

7. Remove the nut and position the battery cable bracket aside.

8. Disconnect the oil temperature sensor electrical connector.

9. Remove the bolts and the oil drain splash shield.

10. If equipped with a block heater, detach the block heater wiring harness retainer from the LH side oil pan bolt.

11. Remove the 16 bolts, the oil pan and the gasket.

To install:

❊❊ WARNING

Do not use metal scrapers, wire brushes, power abrasive discs, or other abrasive means to clean the sealing surfaces. These can cause scratches and gouges resulting in leak paths. Use a plastic scraper to clean the sealing surfaces.

12. Clean the sealing surfaces with metal surface cleaner.

➡**If the oil pan and gasket are not secured within four minutes of sealer application, the sealant must be removed and the sealing surfaces cleaned with metal surface cleaner.**

13. Apply silicone gasket and sealant at the front corners and rear corners of the pan-to-block mating surface.

14. Install a new oil pan gasket, position the oil pan and tighten the pan bolts, in the sequence shown, in 3 steps:
    a. Step 1: 18 inch lbs. (2 Nm)
    b. Step 2: 15 ft. lbs. (20 Nm)
    c. Step 3: additional 60 degrees of turn

15. If equipped with a block heater, attach the block heater wiring harness retainer to the LH oil pan bolt.

16. Position the oil drain splash shield and install the bolts.

17. Attach the wiring harness retainers to the RH oil pan bolts.

18. Connect the oil temperature sensor electrical connector.

19. Attach the battery cable bracket and install the nut to 89 inch lbs. (10 Nm).

20. Attach the PSP hose bracket and install the nut to 89 inch lbs. (10 Nm).

21. Install the stabilizer bar. Tighten the stabilizer bar end nut to 26 ft. lbs. (35 Nm) and the clamp bolts to 41 ft. lbs. (55 Nm).

22. Install the front axle. Tighten the axle mounting insulator bolts to 74 ft. lbs. (100 Nm).

23. Refill the engine with new oil.

OIL PUMP

REMOVAL & INSTALLATION

3.5L Engine

See Figures 167 through 173.

❊❊ WARNING

During engine repair procedures, cleanliness is extremely important. Any foreign material, including any material created while cleaning gasket surfaces, that enters the oil passages, coolant passages or the oil pan may cause engine failure.

➡**On early build engines, the timing chain rides on the inner side of the RH timing chain guide. Late build engines are equipped with a different design RH timing chain guide that requires the timing chain to ride on the outer side of the RH timing chain guide. For service, all replacement RH timing chain guides will be the late build design.**

All Vehicles

1. Remove the engine front cover as outlined in this section.

Engines Equipped With Early Build RH Timing Chain Guides

2. Rotate the crankshaft clockwise and align the timing marks on the Variable Camshaft Timing (VCT) assemblies.

Engines Equipped With Late Build/Replacement RH Timing Chain Guides

3. Rotate the crankshaft clockwise and align the timing marks on the VCT assemblies.

All Vehicles

➡**The Camshaft Holding Tool will hold the camshafts in the Top Dead Center (TDC) position.**

4. Install the Camshaft Holding Tool onto the flats of the LH camshafts.

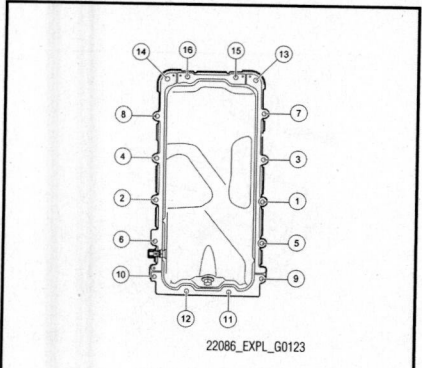

Fig. 166 Oil pan bolt tightening sequence—4.6L Engine

22086_EXPL_G0123

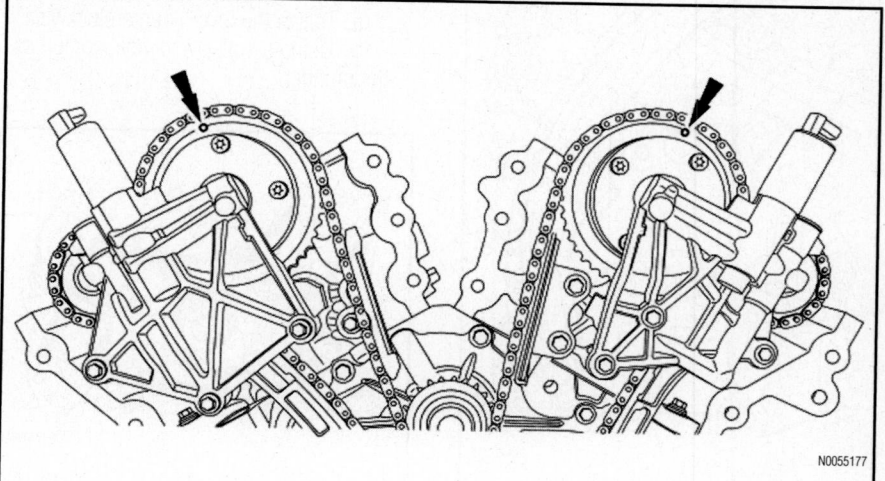

N0055177

Fig. 167 Early Build RH Timing Chain Guides

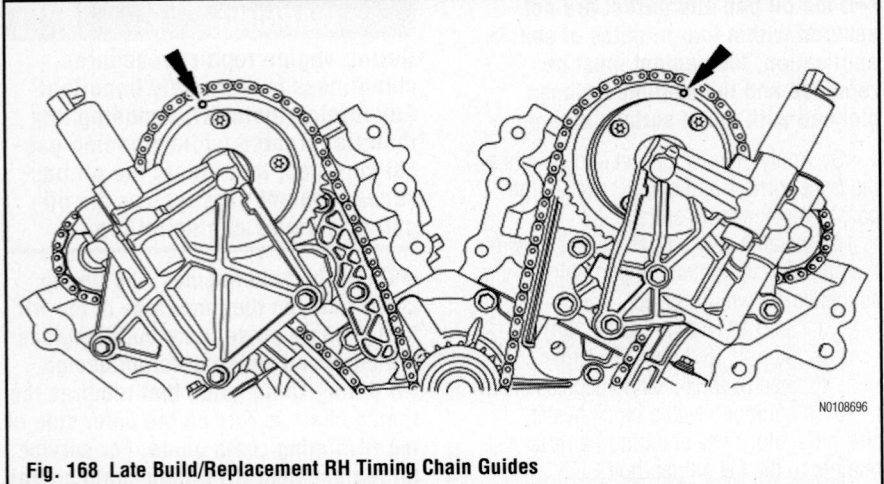

Fig. 168 Late Build/Replacement RH Timing Chain Guides

➤**The Camshaft Holding Tool will hold the camshafts in the TDC position.**

5. Install the Camshaft Holding Tool onto the flats of the RH camshafts.

6. Remove the 3 bolts and the RH VCT housing.

7. Remove the 3 bolts and the LH VCT housing.

8. Remove the 2 bolts and the primary timing chain tensioner.

9. Remove the primary timing chain tensioner arm.

10. Remove the 2 bolts and the lower LH primary timing chain guide.

11. Remove the primary timing chain.

12. Remove the crankshaft timing chain sprocket.

13. Remove the 2 bolts and the oil pump screen and pickup tube.
   a. Discard the O-ring seal.

14. Remove the 3 bolts and the oil pump.

To install:

15. Install the oil pump and the 3 bolts. Tighten the bolts to 89 inch lbs. (10 Nm).

16. Using a new O-ring seal, install the oil pump screen and pickup tube and the 2 bolts. Tighten the bolts to 89 inch lbs. (10 Nm).

17. Install the crankshaft timing chain sprocket.

18. Install the primary timing chain with the colored links aligned with the timing marks on the VCT assemblies and the crankshaft sprocket.

19. Install the LH primary timing chain guide and the 2 bolts. Tighten the bolts to 89 inch lbs. (10 Nm).

20. Install the primary timing chain tensioner arm.

21. Reset the primary timing chain tensioner.
   a. Rotate the lever counterclockwise.
   b. Using a soft-jawed vise, compress the plunger.

Fig. 171 Install the primary timing chain with the colored links aligned with the timing marks on the VCT assemblies and the crankshaft sprocket

   c. Align the hole in the lever with the hole in the tensioner housing.
   d. Install a suitable lockpin.

➤**It may be necessary to rotate the crankshaft slightly to remove slack from the timing chain and install the tensioner.**

22. Install the primary tensioner and the 2 bolts. Tighten the bolts to 89 inch lbs. (10 Nm).
   a. Remove the lockpin.

23. As a post-check, verify correct alignment of all timing marks.

24. Inspect the VCT housing seals for damage and replace as necessary.

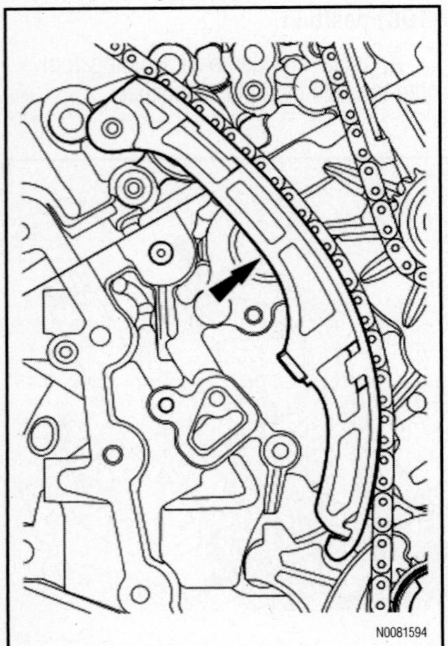

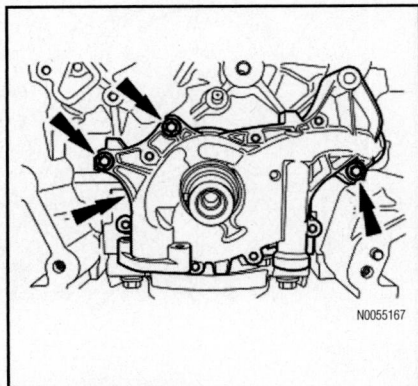

Fig. 169 Primary timing chain tensioner arm

Fig. 170 Oil Pump

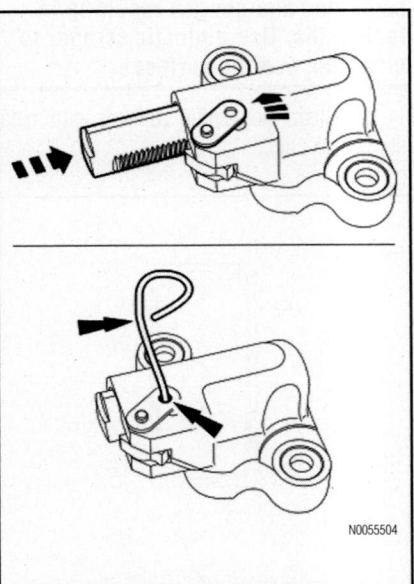

Fig. 172 Reset the primary timing chain tensioner

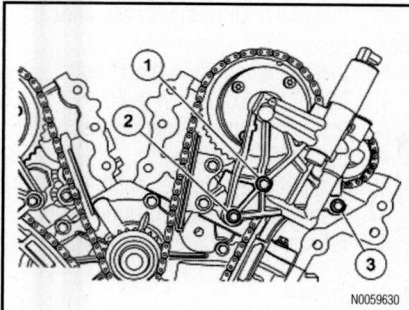

Fig. 173 Install the LH VCT housing and the 3 bolts

> ❊❊ **WARNING**
>
> **Make sure the dowels on the Variable Camshaft Timing (VCT) housing are fully engaged in the cylinder head prior to tightening the bolts. Failure to follow this process will result in severe engine damage.**

25. Install the LH VCT housing and the 3 bolts. Tighten the bolts to 89 inch lbs. (10 Nm) in the proper sequence.

> ❊❊ **WARNING**
>
> **Make sure the dowels on the Variable Camshaft Timing (VCT) housing are fully engaged in the cylinder head prior to tightening the bolts. Failure to follow this process will result in severe engine damage.**

26. Install the RH VCT housing and the 3 bolts. Tighten the bolts to 89 inch lbs. (10 Nm) in the proper sequence.

27. Install the engine front cover as outlined in this section.

4.0L Engine

See Figures 174 through 177.

1. Before servicing the vehicle, refer to Precautions.

2. With the vehicle in NEUTRAL, position it on a hoist.

3. Remove or disconnect the following:
   - Negative battery cable
   - Air cleaner outlet tube
   - Starter
   - Oil pan
   - Weatherstrip across front of engine compartment

4. Remove the bolt and position the power steering fluid reservoir aside.

5. Disconnect the coolant overflow hose. Remove the bolts and the coolant expansion tank.

6. On all models, remove the fan shroud.

7. Remove the heater hose bracket bolt as shown, then install a RH lifting eye, using the previously removed bolt.

➡**This is not a typical setup. Only the right side of the engine will be raised.**

8. Install the engine lifting tools.

9. On AWD models, remove the front stabilizer bar brackets (if equipped) and the crossmember.

10. On AWD models, remove the 4 bolts and the crossmember.

11. Remove the RH motor mount insulator nut.

12. Remove the LH motor mount insulator through-bolt.

13. Raise the engine.

14. Remove the 2 bell housing-to-cylinder block cradle bolts.

15. Remove the 2 Torx® bolts at the rear of the block cradle.

16. Remove the 20 bolts and 2 nuts along the outside of the cylinder block cradle. Mark the location of the 2 silver-colored bolts, with washer seals; these must be

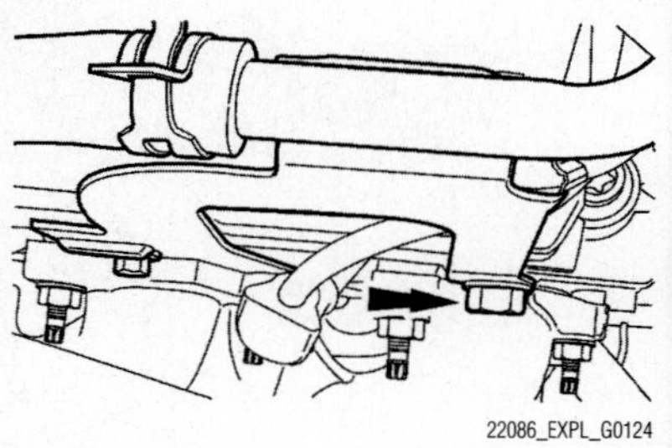

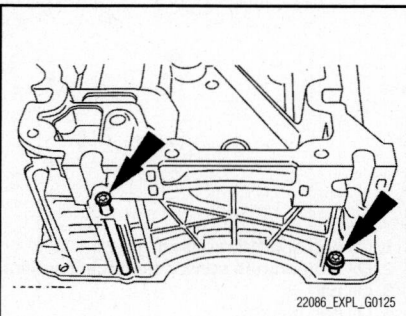

Fig. 174 Remove the heater hose bracket bolt as shown, then install a RH lifting eye, using the previously removed bolt— 4.0L

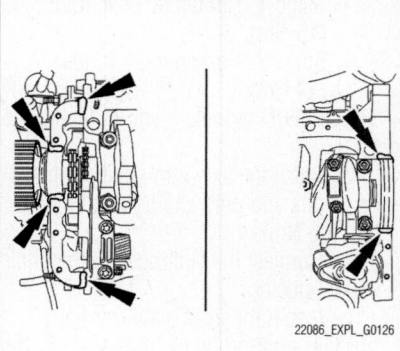

Fig. 175 Remove the 2 Torx® bolts at the rear of the block cradle—4.0L (shown with block cradle removed for clarity of location)

installed the same position, with new washer seals.

17. Remove the 8 cylinder block cradle inner bolts and 2 washer seals.

18. With the lifting device, raise the engine.

> ❊❊ **CAUTION**
>
> **Secure the assembly to the jack. Avoid any obstructions while lowering and raising the jack. Contact with obstructions may cause the assembly to fall off the jack, which may result in serious personal injury.**

19. On AWD models, perform the following:
   - a. Support the front axle with a suitable jack stand and secure with a safety strap or chain.
   - b. Disconnect the vent hose from the differential housing vent tube.
   - c. Remove and discard the axle housing bolts and nuts. Lower the axle.

20. Remove the cylinder block cradle.

21. Remove the oil pump bolts.

22. Remove the oil pump.

To install:

23. Lubricate the oil pump with clean engine oil.

24. Install the oil pump and tighten the bolts to 14 ft. lbs. (19 Nm).

25. Thoroughly clean all mating surfaces.

> ❊❊ **WARNING**
>
> **Do not use metal scrapers, wire brushes, power abrasive discs or other abrasive means to clean the sealing surfaces. These tools cause scratches and gouges which make leak paths. Use a plastic scraping tool to remove all traces of old sealant.**

Fig. 176 Apply silicone in the 6 places shown—4.0L Engine

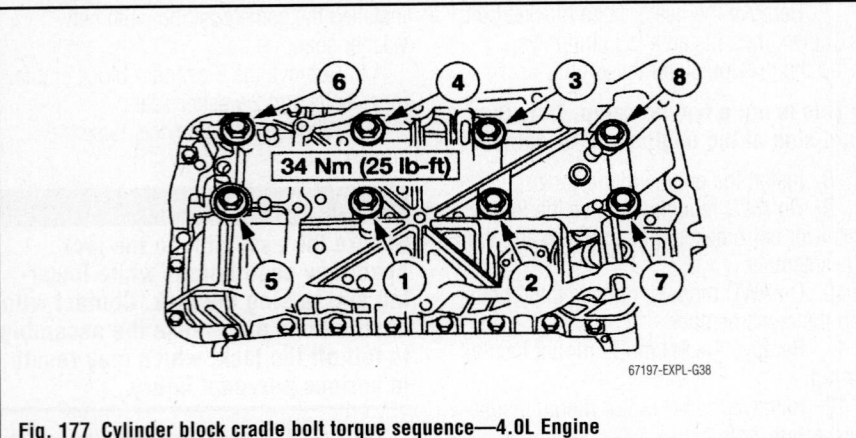

Fig. 177 Cylinder block cradle bolt torque sequence—4.0L Engine

➡**Failure to back off the set screws may result in damage to the cylinder block cradle.**

26. Back the set screws off until they are below the cylinder block cradle boss.

➡**If not secured within 4 minutes, the sealant must be removed and the sealing area cleaned.**

27. Apply silicone in the 6 places shown.
28. Position a new gasket and the cylinder block cradle.
29. Install and hand-tighten the 2 rear Torx® bolts.
30. Install the 2 bell housing-to-cylinder block cradle bolts. Tighten the bolts to 35 ft. lbs. (47 Nm).
31. Tighten the outer 20 bolts and 2 nuts to 89 inch lbs. (10 Nm).
32. Tighten the eight cradle inserts to 27 inch lbs. (3 Nm).
33. Install the two silver-covered bolts and new washer seals. Hand-tighten them at this time.
34. Install and hand-tighten the six remaining inner bolts.
35. Tighten the lower block cradle bolts in two stages:
   - Stage 1: Tighten to 11 ft. lbs. (15 Nm).
   - Stage 2: Tighten to 25 ft. lbs. (34 Nm).
36. On AWD models, perform the following:
   a. Raise the axle into position. Install new bolts and nuts and tighten to 49 ft. lbs. (66 Nm).
   b. Connect the vent hose to the differential housing.
   c. Install the front stabilizer bar brackets and torque the nuts to 41 ft. lbs. (55 Nm).
37. On all models, lower the engine and remove the lifting tools.

38. Install the LH engine support through-bolt and nut. Tighten to 76 ft. lbs. (103 Nm).
39. Install the RH engine support nut and tighten to 66 ft. lbs. (90 Nm).
40. Install the crossmember (AWD models). Tighten the retaining bolts to 76 ft. lbs. (103 Nm).

41. Install the oil pump screen and pickup tube.
42. Install the fan shroud and bolts.
43. Install the expansion tank.
44. Install the power steering reservoir.
45. Install the weatherstrip.
46. Install the air cleaner outlet pipe.
47. Connect the battery ground cable.
48. Fill the engine with clean engine oil.

4.6L Engine

See Figure 178.

1. Before servicing the vehicle, refer to Precautions.
2. Drain the engine oil.
3. Remove or disconnect the following:
   - Negative battery cable
   - Oil pan; refer to Oil Pan.
   - Three bolts and the oil pump screen cover and tube
   - Timing chains and sprockets; see "Timing Chain and Sprocket" section
   - Oil pump

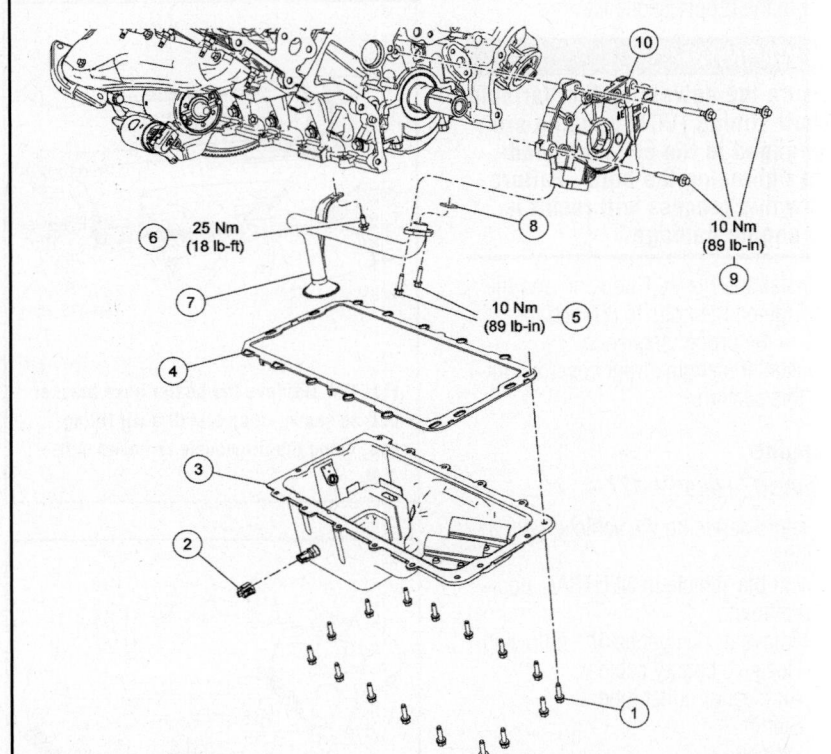

1. Oil pan bolt (16 required)
2. Oil temperature sensor electrical connector
3. Oil pan
4. Oil pan gasket
5. Oil pump screen and pickup tube-to-oil pump bolts (2 required)
6. Oil pump screen and pickup tube support bracket bolt
7. Oil pump screen and pickup tube
8. Oil pump screen and pickup tube O-ring seal
9. Oil pump bolts (3 required)
10. Oil pump

Fig. 178 Exploded view of the oil pan, oil pickup screen and tube, and the oil pump—4.6L Engine

To install:

➡**Lubricate the new O-ring seal with clean engine oil.**

4. Clean and inspect the mating surfaces. Install a new O-ring seal.
5. Position the oil pump.
6. Loosely install the bolts.
7. Tighten the bolts to 89 inch lbs. (10 Nm).
8. Install the timing chains and sprockets; see "Timing Chain and Sprocket" section.
9. Install the three oil pump screen and cover bolts.
  a. Tighten the oil pump screen and pickup tube-to-oil pump bolts to 89 inch lbs. (10 Nm).
  b. Tighten the oil pump screen and pickup tube-to-spacer bolt to 18 ft. lbs. (25 Nm).
10. Install the oil pan.

PISTON AND RING

POSITIONING

See Figure 179.

REAR MAIN SEAL

REMOVAL & INSTALLATION

3.5L Engine

See Figures 180 through 182.

1. With the vehicle in NEUTRAL, position it on a hoist.

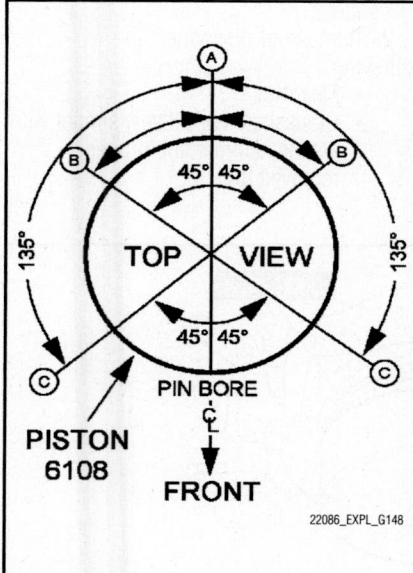

Fig. 179 Piston ring positioning—4.0L & 4.6L Engine

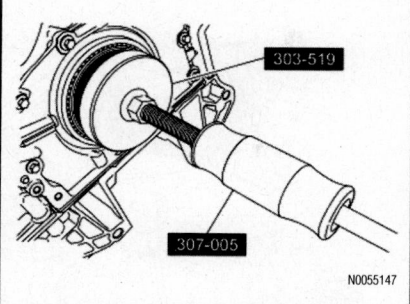

Fig. 180 Using the special tools to remove the rear main seal

2. Remove the flexplate.
3. Remove the crankshaft sensor ring.
4. Using the Crankshaft Rear Oil Seal Remover and Slide Hammer, remove and discard the crankshaft rear seal.
5. Clean all sealing surfaces with metal surface prep.

To install:

➡**Lubricate the seal lips and bore with clean engine oil prior to installation.**

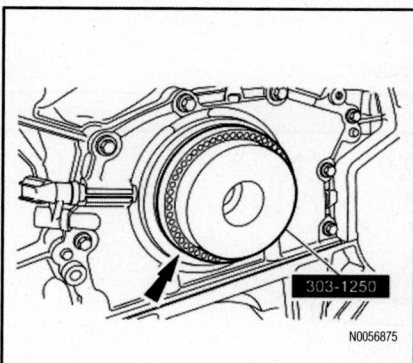

Fig. 181 Position the Rear Main Seal Installer onto the end of the crankshaft and slide a new crankshaft rear seal onto the tool

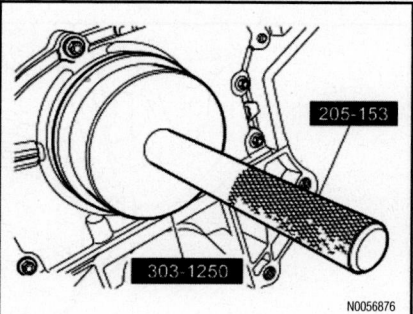

Fig. 182 Using the Rear Main Seal Installer and Handle, install the new crankshaft rear seal

6. Position the Rear Main Seal Installer onto the end of the crankshaft and slide a new crankshaft rear seal onto the tool.
7. Using the Rear Main Seal Installer and Handle, install the new crankshaft rear seal.
8. Install the crankshaft sensor ring.
9. Install the flexplate.

4.0L Engine

See Figures 183 through 187.

1. Before servicing the vehicle, refer to Precautions.
2. Remove the flexplate.
3. Remove the spacer plate and the flexplate-to-crankshaft spacer.

➡**The crankshaft rear seal may have a metal speedy sleeve. This sleeve must be removed before attempting to remove the seal.**

4. If necessary, remove the speedy sleeve using 2 screwdrivers or small pry bars.

✳✳ WARNING

Avoid scratching or damaging the oil crankshaft seal running surface during removal of the crankshaft rear oil seal.

5. Using special tool, 303-514, remove the oil slinger.
6. Using special tool, 303-519, remove the crankshaft rear oil seal.

To install:

➡**Be sure the crankshaft rear sealing surface is clean and free of any rust or corrosion. To clean the crankshaft rear sealing surface, use extra-fine emery cloth or extra-fine 0000 steel wool with metal surface cleaner.**

7. Lubricate the crankshaft rear oil seal with clean engine oil and install on the special tool.

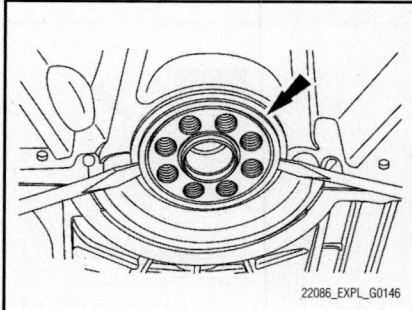

Fig. 183 If necessary, remove the speedy sleeve using 2 screwdrivers or small pry bars—4.0L Engine

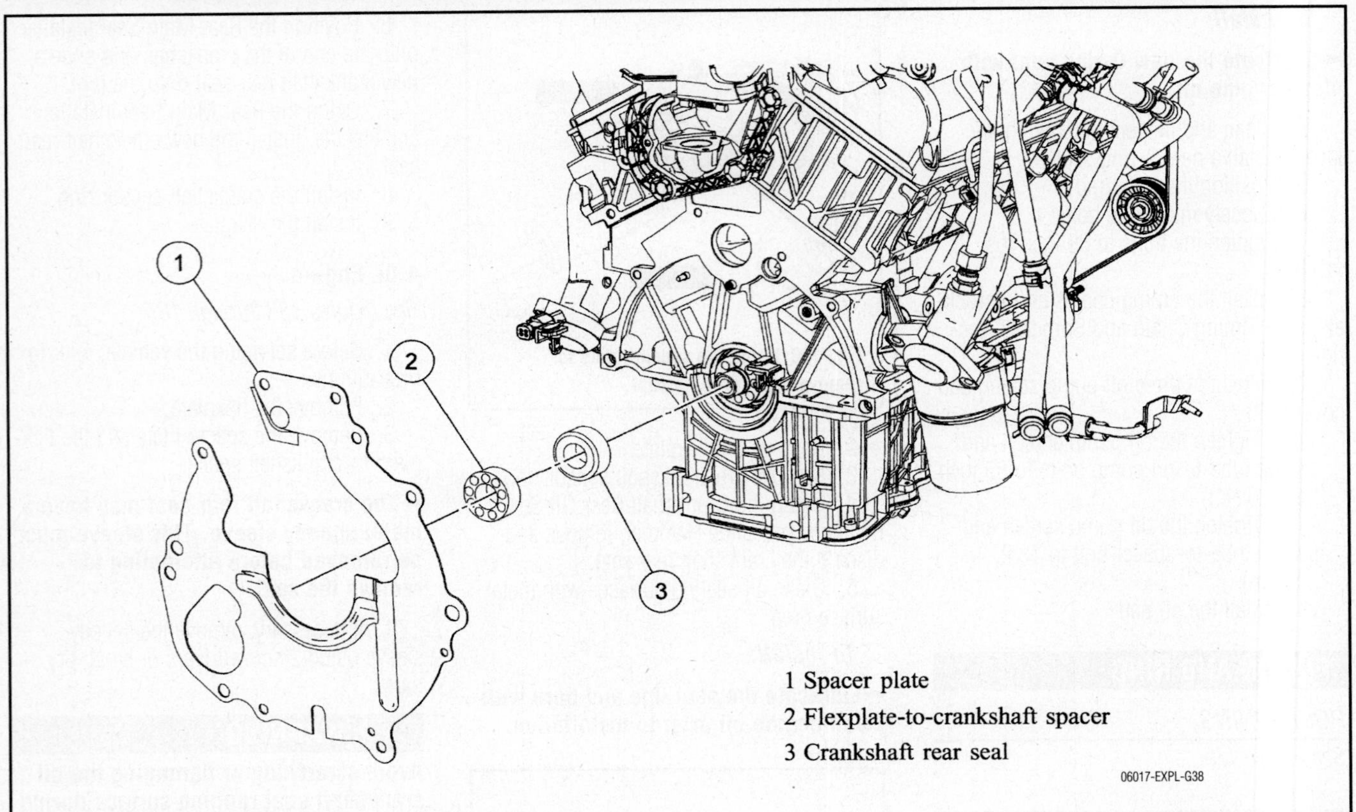

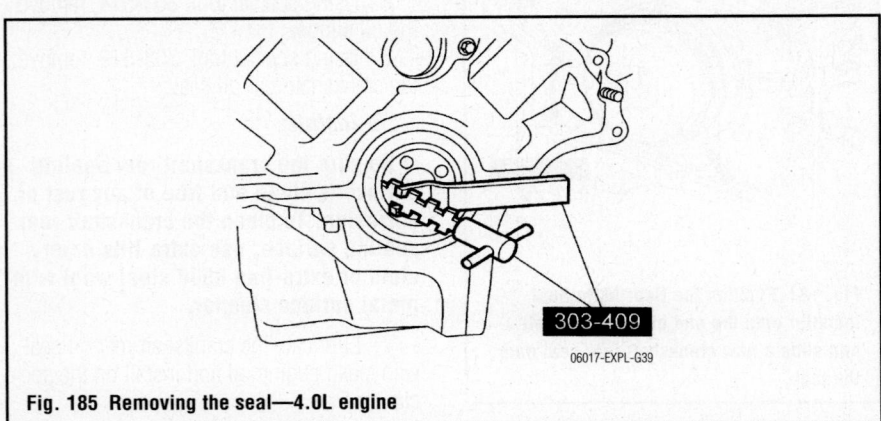

1 Spacer plate
2 Flexplate-to-crankshaft spacer
3 Crankshaft rear seal

06017-EXPL-G38

Fig. 184 Rear main seal and related parts—4.0L engine

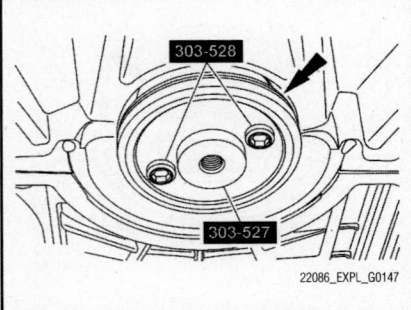

303-409

06017-EXPL-G39

Fig. 185 Removing the seal—4.0L engine

8. Using special tool 303-527 and 303-528, position the crankshaft rear oil seal.

9. Install the flexplate or flexplate.

4.6L Engine

See Figures 188 through 190.

1. Before servicing the vehicle, refer to Precautions.

2. Remove or disconnect the following:

- Flexplate
- Crankshaft rear oil seal slinger with a slide hammer and proper removed tool

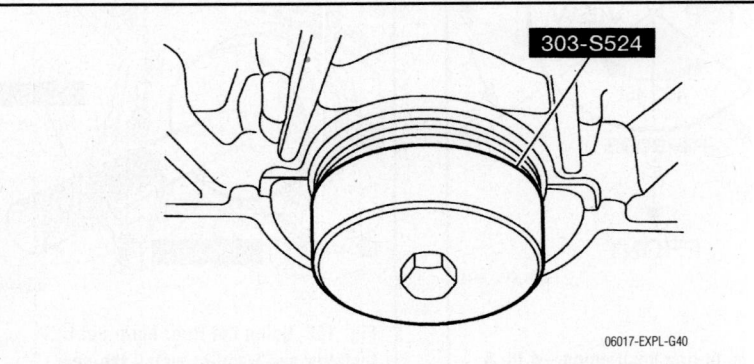

303-S524

06017-EXPL-G40

Fig. 187 Using special tool, 303-529, install the crankshaft rear oil seal

303-528

303-527

22086_EXPL_G0147

Fig. 186 Using special tool 303-527 and 303-528, position the crankshaft rear oil seal—4.0L Engine

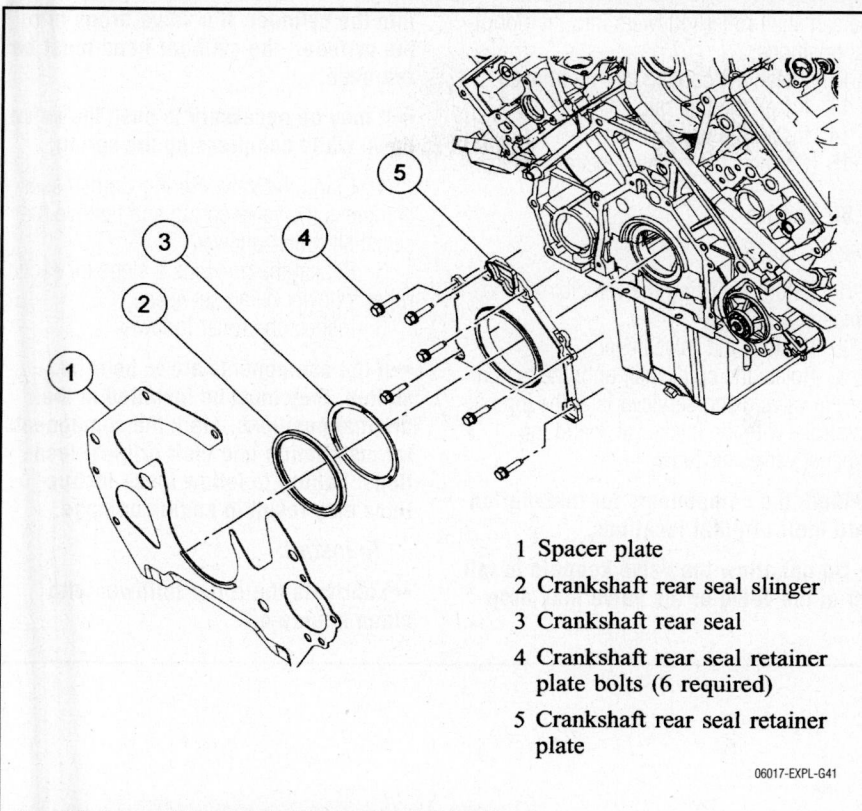

1 Spacer plate
2 Crankshaft rear seal slinger
3 Crankshaft rear seal
4 Crankshaft rear seal retainer plate bolts (6 required)
5 Crankshaft rear seal retainer plate

06017-EXPL-G41

Fig. 188 Rear main seal and related parts—4.6L engine

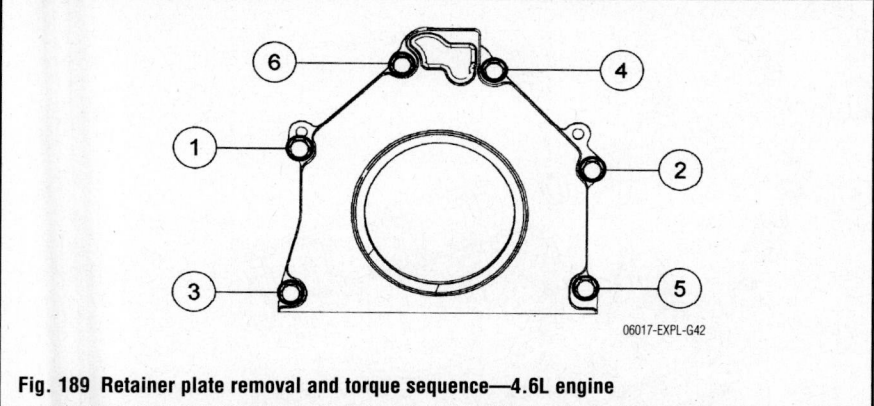

06017-EXPL-G42

Fig. 189 Retainer plate removal and torque sequence—4.6L engine

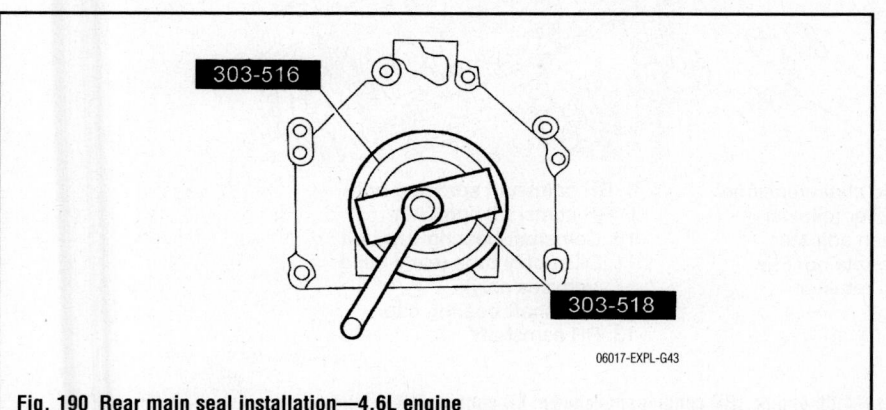

06017-EXPL-G43

Fig. 190 Rear main seal installation—4.6L engine

- Rear oil seal with a slide hammer and proper remover tool

To install:

3. Installation is the reverse of the removal procedure. Note the following:
- Lubricate the inner lip of the rear crankshaft seal with clean engine oil.
- Use the two Crankshaft Rear Oil Seal Installers to install the rear oil seal.
- Using the two Crankshaft Rear Oil Seal Installers and the Crankshaft Rear Oil Slinger Installer, install the crankshaft rear oil slinger.

ROCKER ARMS/SHAFTS

REMOVAL & INSTALLATION

This procedure covers the removal and installation of the Camshaft Roller Follower and Hydraulic Lash Adjusters.

4.0L Engine

See Figures 191 through 193.

1. Before servicing the vehicle, refer to Precautions.
2. Disconnect the negative battery cable.

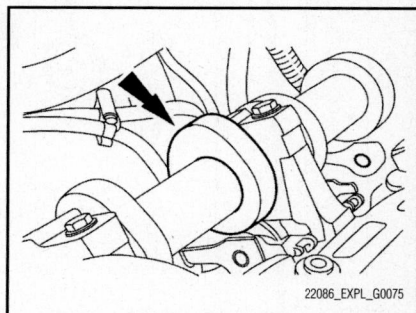

22086_EXPL_G0075

Fig. 191 Rotate the crankshaft until the camshaft for the cylinder being serviced is at base circle—4.0L engine

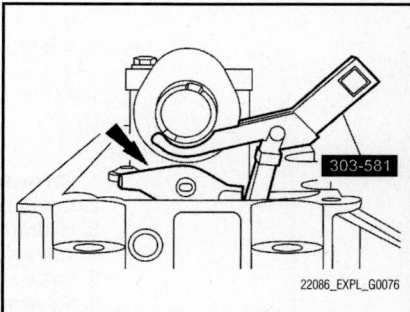

22086_EXPL_G0076

Fig. 192 Using special tool 303-581, remove the camshaft roller follower—4.0L engine

3. Remove the valve cover.

4. Remove the fuel rail.

5. Remove the cooling fan.

6. Rotate the crankshaft until the camshaft for the cylinder being serviced is at base circle.

➡**If removing more than one cam follower, label them so they can be returned to their original position.**

7. Using special tool 303-581, remove the camshaft roller followers.

8. Mark each lash adjuster before removal; remove each lash adjuster, as necessary.

To install:

9. Lubricate the lash adjusters and camshaft roller followers with clean engine oil.

10. Install each lash adjuster.

11. Using special tool 303-581, remove the camshaft roller followers into their original positions.

12. Install the cooling fan, if removed.

13. Install the fuel rail.

14. Install the valve cover.

15. Connect the negative battery cable.

4.6L Engine

See Figure 194.

1. Before servicing the vehicle, refer to Precautions.

2. Remove the valve covers.

3. Rotate the crankshaft until the piston for the valve being serviced is at the top of its stroke with the intake valve and the exhaust valves closed.

➡**Mark the components for installation into their original locations.**

➡**Do not allow the valve keepers to fall off of the valve or the valve may drop into the cylinder. If a valve drops into the cylinder, the cylinder head must be removed.**

➡**It may be necessary to push the valve down while compressing the spring.**

4. Using the Valve Spring Compressor, compress the valve spring and remove the camshaft roller follower.

5. Repeat the previous 2 steps for each roller follower being serviced.

6. Inspect the roller follower.

➡**If the components are to be reinstalled, they must be installed in their original positions. Mark the components for installation into their original locations. Failure to follow these instructions may result in engine damage.**

To install:

➡**Lubricate the roller follower with clean engine oil.**

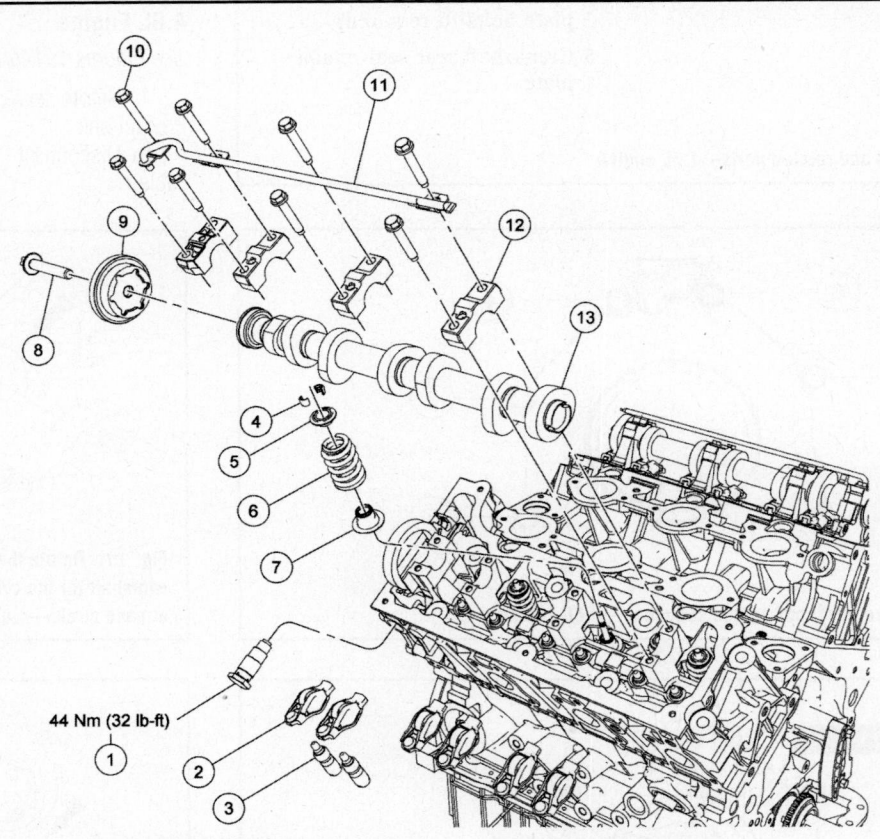

1. RH hydraulic chain tensioner
2. Camshaft roller follower
3. Hydraulic lash adjuster
4. Valve spring retainer key
5. Valve spring retainer
6. Valve spring
7. Valve seals
8. RH camshaft sprocket bolt
9. RH camshaft sprocket
10. Camshaft bearing cap bolt
11. Oil supply tube (early build vehicles only)
12. Camshaft bearing cap
13. RH camshaft

44 Nm (32 lb-ft)

22086_EXPL_G0070

Fig. 193 Exploded view of valve train components—4.0L engine (RH components shown; LH components similar)

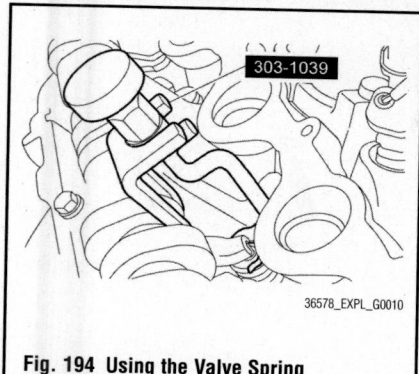

Fig. 194 Using the Valve Spring Compressor

7. Using the Valve Spring Compressor, compress the valve spring and install the camshaft roller follower.

8. Repeat the previous step for each roller follower being serviced.

9. Depending on the valve being serviced, install the LH or RH valve cover.

TIMING CHAIN COVER AND SEAL

REMOVAL & INSTALLATION

4.0L Engine

See Figures 195 through 198.

1. Disconnect the battery ground cable.

2. Drain the cooling system.

3. Remove the crankshaft front seal. Refer to Crankshaft Front Seal.

4. Remove the nut and detach the wiring harness bracket from the front cover.

5. Remove the 5 oil pan-to-front cover bolts.

6. Disconnect the lower radiator hose.

7. Remove the bolt and the drive belt tensioner.

8. Disconnect the heater hose from the coolant pump.

9. Disconnect the Crankshaft Position (CKP) sensor electrical connector.

10. Remove the nut and disconnect the generator B+ terminal.

11. Disconnect the generator electrical connector and detach the wiring harness retainer.

12. Remove the 3 generator bracket bolts and the generator bracket.

13. Remove the coil bracket-to-A/C compressor and power steering pump bracket bolt.

14. Remove the 4 bolts and the A/C compressor and power steering pump bracket.

15. Remove and discard the CKP sensor wiring harness retainers.

16. Disconnect the Engine Coolant Temperature (ECT) sensor electrical connector.

17. Disconnect the upper radiator hose from the thermostat housing.

18. Disconnect the heater hose from the thermostat housing.

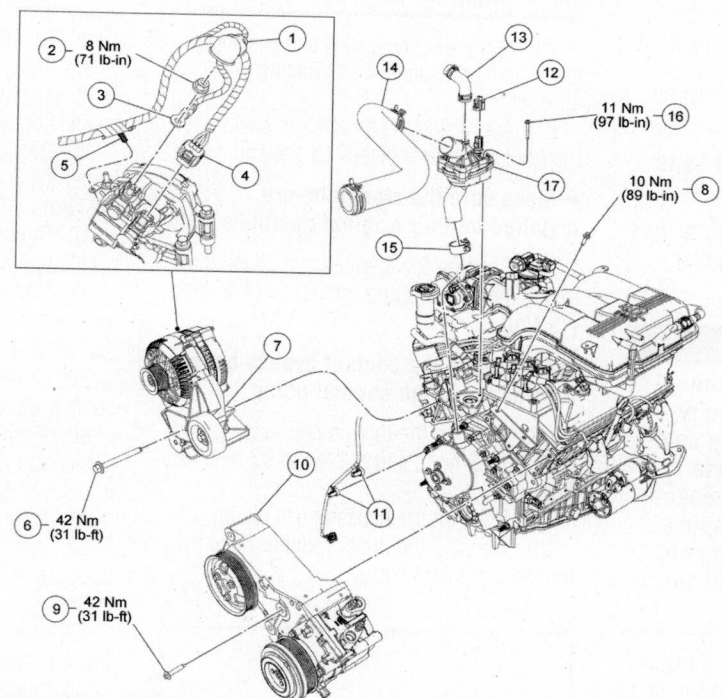

1. Generator B+ terminal cover
2. Generator B+ terminal nut
3. Generator B+ terminal
4. Generator electrical connector
5. Wiring harness retainer
6. Generator bracket bolt (3 required)
7. Generator bracket
8. Ignition coil bracket-to-A/C compressor and power steering pump bracket bolt
9. A/C compressor and power steering pump bracket bolt (4 required)
10. A/C compressor and power steering pump bracket
11. Wiring harness routing clips
12. Engine Coolant Temperature (ECT) sensor electrical connector
13. Heater hose
14. Upper radiator hose
15. Bypass hose clamp
16. Thermostat housing bolt (3 required)
17. Thermostat housing

Fig. 195 Front engine component locations—4.0L Engine

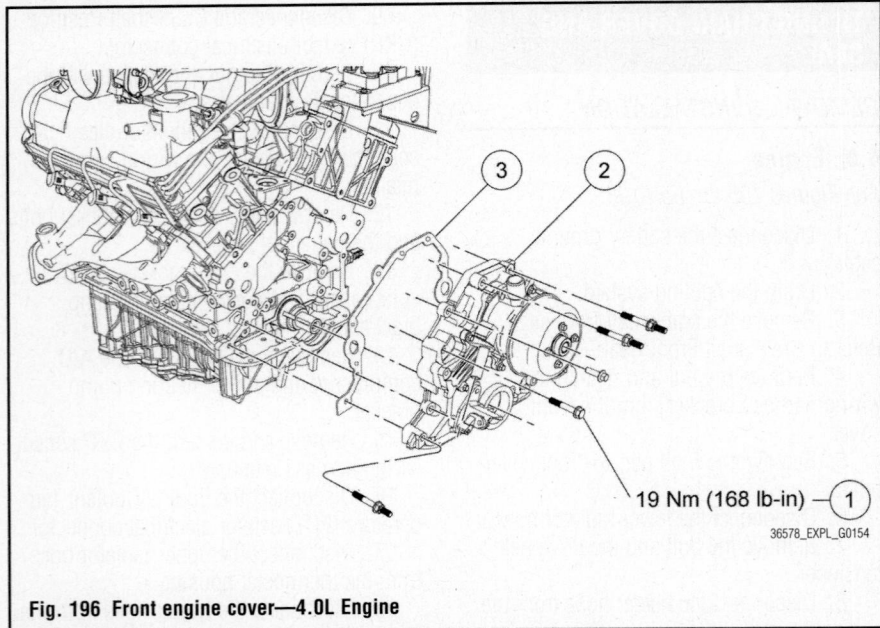

19 Nm (168 lb-in) — 1

36578_EXPL_G0154

Fig. 196 Front engine cover—4.0L Engine

→ **The bypass hose will be removed with the thermostat housing.**

19. Release the bypass hose clamp from the coolant pump end.

20. Remove the 3 bolts and the thermostat housing.

→ **Note the positions of the stud bolts for installation reference.**

21. Remove the 10 bolts, the engine front cover and the gasket. Discard the gasket

To install:

⁜⁜ **WARNING**

Do not use metal scrapers, wire brushes, power abrasive discs or other abrasive means to clean sealing surfaces. These tools cause scratches and gouges which make leak paths. Use a plastic scraping tool to remove all traces of the old front cover gasket and the silicone sealer.

22. Clean and inspect the gasket mating surfaces. Use silicone gasket remover and metal surface prep and a plastic scraping tool. Follow the directions on the packaging.

23. Position the front cover gasket.

⁜⁜ **WARNING**

If not secured within 4 minutes, the sealant must be removed and the sealing area cleaned. To clean the sealing area, use silicone gasket remover and metal surface prep. Follow the directions on the packaging.

Failure to follow this procedure can cause future oil leakage.

24. Apply silicone gasket and sealant to the oil pan and engine block mating surfaces.

25. Apply silicone gasket and sealant to the front cover in 2 places as shown.

→ **Make sure the stud bolts are installed in their original positions.**

26. Position the engine front cover and install the 10 bolts and tighten to 14 ft. lbs. (19 Nm).

→ **Make sure the coolant bypass hose is attached to the coolant pump.**

27. Position the thermostat housing and install the 3 bolts and tighten to 97 inch lbs. (11 Nm).

28. Position the bypass hose clamp.

29. Connect the upper radiator hose to the thermostat housing.

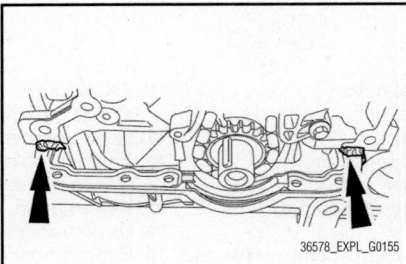

36578_EXPL_G0155

Fig. 197 Silicone application locations, oil pan —4.0L Engine

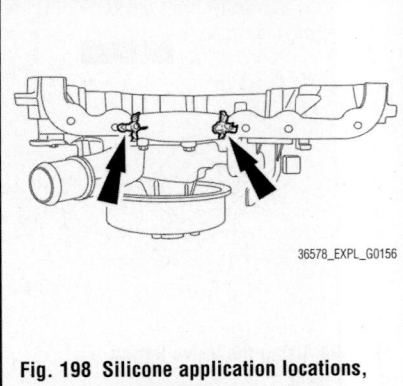

36578_EXPL_G0156

Fig. 198 Silicone application locations, front cover—4.0L Engine

30. Connect the heater hose to the thermostat housing.

31. Connect the ECT sensor electrical connector.

32. Install new wiring harness retainers and position the CKP sensor wiring.

33. Connect the CKP sensor electrical connector.

34. Position the A/C compressor and power steering pump bracket and install the 4 bolts and tighten to 31 ft. lbs. (42 Nm).

35. Install the ignition coil bracket-to-A/C compressor and power steering pump bracket bolt and tighten to 89 inch lbs. (10 Nm).

36. Position the generator bracket and install the 3 bolts tighten to 31 ft. lbs. (42 Nm).

37. Connect the generator electrical connector and attach the wiring harness retainer.

38. Connect the generator B+ terminal and install the nut and tighten to 71 inch lbs. (8 Nm).

39. Connect the heater hose to the coolant pump.

40. Position the accessory drive belt tensioner and install the bolt and tighten to 35 ft. lbs. (47 Nm).

41. Connect the lower radiator hose.

42. Install the 5 cylinder block cradle-to-front cover bolts and tighten to 10 ft. lbs. (14 Nm).

43. Position the wiring harness bracket and install the nut and tighten to 15 ft. lbs. (20 Nm).

44. Install the crankshaft front seal. Refer to Crankshaft Front Seal.

45. Connect the battery ground cable.

46. Fill the engine cooling system.

4.6L Engine

See Figures 199 through 203.

1. With the vehicle in NEUTRAL, position it on a hoist.

2. Remove the drain plug and drain the engine oil. To install, tighten to 17 ft. lbs. (23 Nm).

3. Remove the cooling fan shroud. Refer to Cooling Fan in Engine Cooling.

4. Remove the RH side idler pulley.

5. Remove the RH valve cover. Refer to Valve Covers.

6. Remove the LH valve cover. Refer to Valve Covers.

7. Remove the nut and position the RH radio interference capacitor aside.

8. Disconnect the RH Camshaft Position (CMP) sensor electrical connector.

9. Remove the nut and the cooling fan wiring harness bracket.

10. Remove the nut and position the LH radio interference capacitor aside.

11. Disconnect the LH CMP sensor electrical connector.

12. Remove the 4 bolts and the coolant pump pulley.

13. Remove the 2 nuts and detach the battery cable bracket from the power steering pump stud bolts.

14. Detach the wiring harness retainer from the power steering pump stud bolt.

15. Remove the 3 stud bolts and position the power steering pump aside.

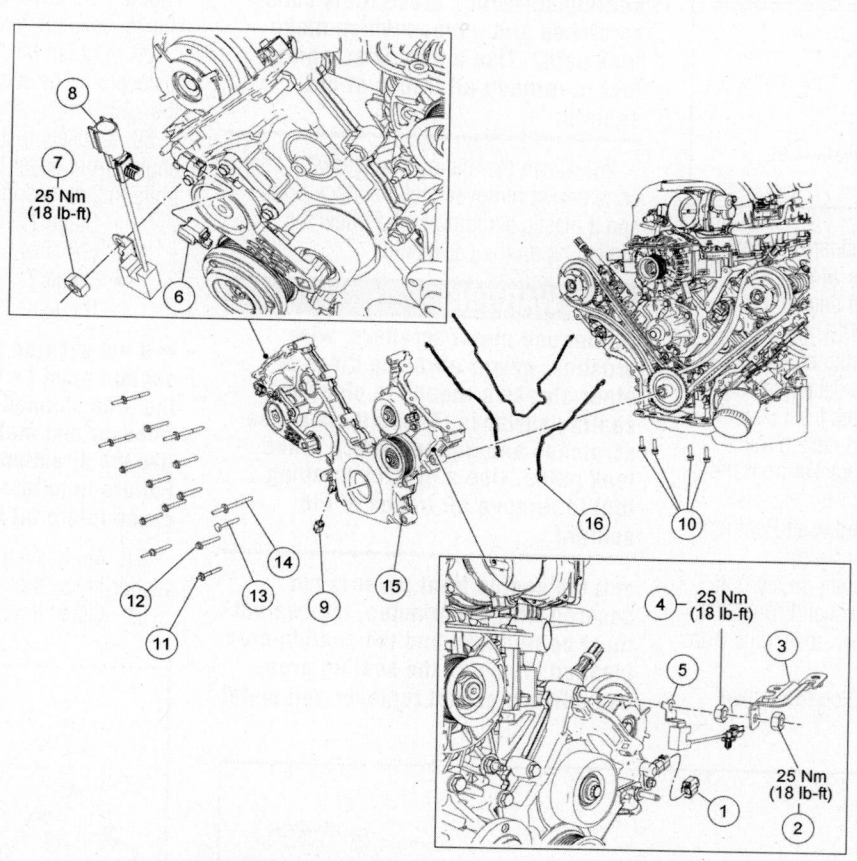

1. LH Camshaft Position (CMP) sensor electrical connector
2. Cooling fan wiring harness bracket nut
3. Cooling fan wiring harness bracket
4. LH radio interference capacitor nut
5. LH radio interference capacitor
6. RH CMP sensor electrical connector
7. RH radio interference capacitor nut
8. RH radio interference capacitor
9. Crankshaft Position (CKP) sensor electrical connector
10. Oil pan-to-engine front cover bolts (4 required)
11. Engine front cover stud bolt
12. Engine front cover bolt (8 required)
13. Engine front cover bolt
14. Engine front cover stud bolt (5 required)
15. Engine front cover
16. Engine front cover gasket (3 required

36578_EXPL_G0157

Fig. 199 Front cover bolt locations—4.6L Engine

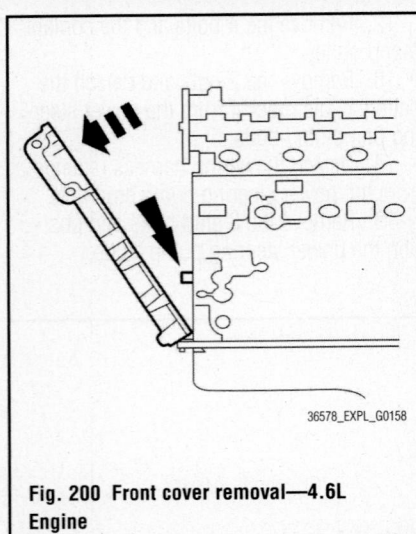

Fig. 200 Front cover removal—4.6L Engine

16. Support the power steering pump with a length of mechanic's wire.

17. Remove the nut and detach the Power Steering Pressure (PSP) hose bracket from the battery cable bracket.

18. Remove the nut and detach the battery cable bracket from the engine front cover.

19. Remove the nut and detach the transmission cooler tube bracket from the engine front cover.

20. Disconnect the Crankshaft Position (CKP) sensor electrical connector.

21. Remove the crankshaft pulley bolt and washer. Refer to Crankshaft Front Seal.

22. Remove the 4 oil pan-to-engine front cover bolts.

23. Remove the 15 engine front cover bolts and stud bolts.

24. Remove the engine front cover from the engine front cover-to-cylinder block dowel.

25. Remove and discard the engine front cover gaskets

To install:

✳✳ WARNING

Do not use metal scrapers, wire brushes, power abrasive discs or other abrasive means to clean the sealing surfaces. These tools cause scratches and gouges which make leak paths. Use a plastic scraping tool to remove all traces of old sealant.

26. Clean the mating surfaces with silicone gasket remover, metal surface prep and a plastic scraping tool. Follow the directions on the packaging.

✳✳ WARNING

Do not use metal scrapers, wire brushes, power abrasive discs or other abrasive means to clean the sealing surfaces. These tools cause scratches and gouges which make leak paths. Use a plastic scraping tool to remove all traces of old sealant.

➡**If the engine front cover is not secured within 4 minutes, the sealant must be removed and the sealing area cleaned. To clean the sealing area, use silicone gasket remover and metal surface prep. Follow the directions on the packaging. Failure to follow this procedure can cause future oil leakage.**

27. Apply a bead of silicone gasket and sealant along the cylinder head-to-cylinder block mating surface and the oil pan-to-cylinder block mating surface at the locations shown.

28. Install new engine front cover gaskets on the engine front cover. Position the engine front cover onto the dowels. Install the 15 fasteners finger-tight.

29. Tighten the 15 engine front cover fasteners in the sequence shown to 18 ft. lbs. (25 Nm).

30. Loosely install the 4 oil pan-to-engine front cover bolts, then tighten the bolts in 2 stages in the sequence shown.
- Stage 1: Tighten to 15 ft. lbs. (20 Nm).
- Stage 2: Tighten an additional 60 degrees.

➡**If not secured within 4 minutes, the sealant must be removed and the sealing area cleaned with silicone gasket remover and metal surface prep. Follow the directions on the packaging. Failure to follow this procedure can cause future oil leakage.**

31. Apply silicone gasket sealant to the Woodruff key slot in the crankshaft pulley.

32. Install the crankshaft front oil seal

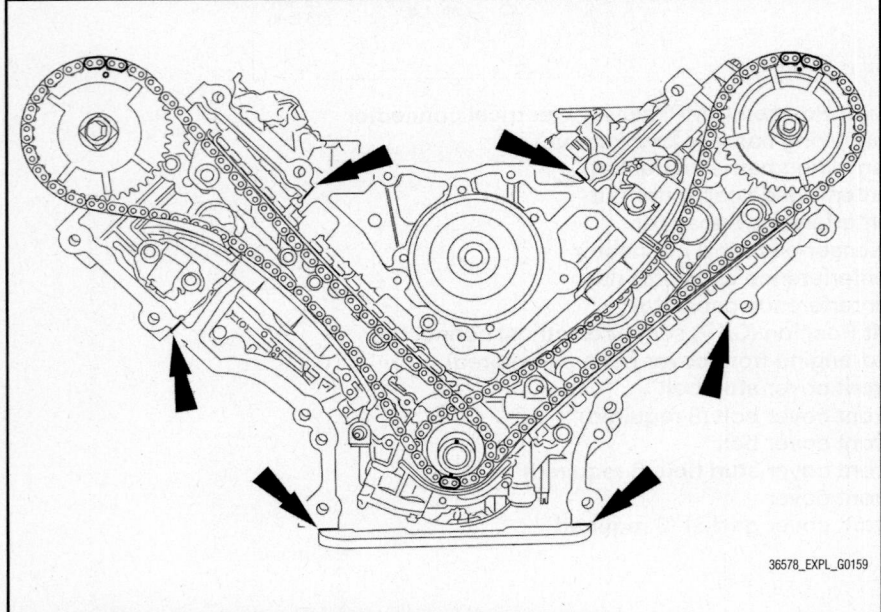

Fig. 201 Silicone application locations, front cover—4.6L Engine

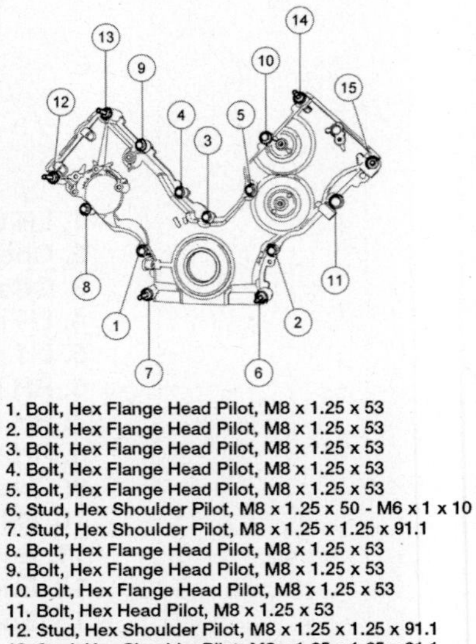

1. Bolt, Hex Flange Head Pilot, M8 x 1.25 x 53
2. Bolt, Hex Flange Head Pilot, M8 x 1.25 x 53
3. Bolt, Hex Flange Head Pilot, M8 x 1.25 x 53
4. Bolt, Hex Flange Head Pilot, M8 x 1.25 x 53
5. Bolt, Hex Flange Head Pilot, M8 x 1.25 x 53
6. Stud, Hex Shoulder Pilot, M8 x 1.25 x 50 - M6 x 1 x 10
7. Stud, Hex Shoulder Pilot, M8 x 1.25 x 1.25 x 91.1
8. Bolt, Hex Flange Head Pilot, M8 x 1.25 x 53
9. Bolt, Hex Flange Head Pilot, M8 x 1.25 x 53
10. Bolt, Hex Flange Head Pilot, M8 x 1.25 x 53
11. Bolt, Hex Head Pilot, M8 x 1.25 x 53
12. Stud, Hex Shoulder Pilot, M8 x 1.25 x 1.25 x 91.1
13. Stud, Hex Shoulder Pilot, M8 x 1.25 x 1.25 x 91.1
14. Stud, Hex Shoulder Pilot, M8 x 1.25 x 1.25 x 91.1
15. Stud, Hex Shoulder Pilot, M8 x 1.25 x 1.25 x 91.1

Fig. 202 Front cover bolt tightening sequence—4.6L Engine

and pulley. Refer to Crankshaft Front Oil Seal.

33. Connect the CKP sensor electrical connector.

34. Attach the transmission cooler tube bracket to the engine front cover and install the nut and tighten to 106 inch lbs. (12 Nm).

35. Attach the battery cable bracket to the front cover and install the nut and tighten to 89 inch lbs. (10 Nm).

36. Attach the PSP hose bracket to the battery cable bracket and install the nut and tighten to 89 inch lbs.(10 Nm).

37. Position the power steering pump and install the stud bolts and tighten to 18 ft. lbs. (25 Nm).

38. Attach the wiring harness retainer to the power steering pump stud bolt.

39. Position the battery cable bracket on the power steering pump stud bolts and install the nuts and tighten to 89 inch lbs. (10 Nm)

40. Position the coolant pump pulley and install the bolts and tighten the bolts to 18 ft. lbs. (25 Nm).

41. Connect the LH CMP sensor electrical connector.

42. Position the LH radio interference capacitor and install the nut and tighten to 18 ft. lbs. (25 Nm).

43. Position the cooling fan wiring harness bracket and install the nut.

44. Connect the RH CMP sensor electrical connector.

45. Position the RH radio interference capacitor and install the nut and tighten to 18 ft. lbs. (25 Nm).

46. Install the LH valve cover. Refer to Valve Covers.

47. Install the RH valve cover. Refer to Valve Covers.

48. Install the RH side idler pulley.

49. Install the cooling fan shroud.

50. Fill the engine with clean engine oil.

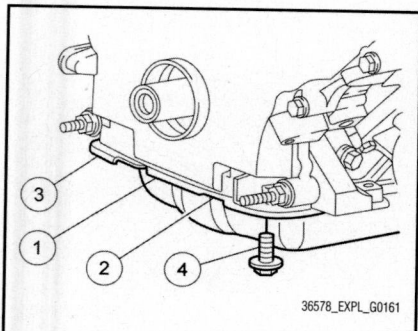

Fig. 203 Oil pan-to-engine front cover bolts—4.6L Engine

TIMING CHAIN AND SPROCKETS

REMOVAL & INSTALLATION

4.0L Engine

See Figures 204 through 208.

1. Before servicing the vehicle, refer to Precautions.
2. Remove the valve covers. Refer to Valve Covers.
3. Remove the fuel rail. Refer to Fuel System.
4. Remove the engine front cover. Refer to Front Cover and Seal.
5. Remove the thermostat housing.
6. Remove all of the roller followers.
   a. Rotate the crankshaft until the camshaft for the cylinder being serviced is at base circle.

➡**Mark each camshaft roller follower to make sure it is returned to its original position.**

   b. Using the Valve Spring Compressor, remove the camshaft roller followers.

➡**The camshaft roller followers must be installed in their original positions.**

➡**Lubricate the camshaft roller followers with clean engine oil**

➡**The LH and RH camshafts must be retimed when either camshaft is disturbed.**

7. Turn the crankshaft clockwise to position the No. 1 cylinder at Top Dead Center (TDC).
8. Remove the LH hydraulic chain tensioner.
   a. Discard the washer.
9. Remove the LH camshaft sprocket bolt.
   a. Install the Camshaft Sprocket Holding Tool and the Adapter for 303-564 and tighten the bolts to 89 inch lbs. (10 Nm).
   b. Remove the LH camshaft sprocket bolt.
10. Using the Crankshaft Holding Tool to prevent the crankshaft from turning, remove the jackshaft sprocket bolt.
11. Remove the 2 bolts and the primary chain tensioner.
12. Remove the primary chain and sprockets as an assembly.
13. Remove the LH cassette upper bolt.
14. Remove the LH cassette lower bolt and the LH cassette.

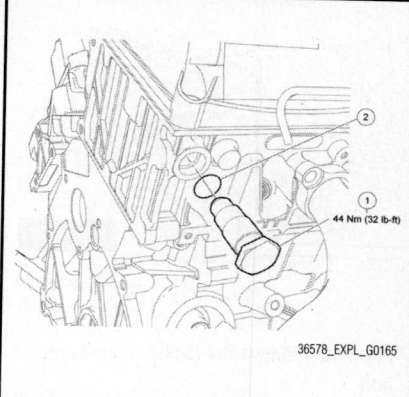

Fig. 204 LH hydraulic chain tensioner—RH similar

➡**RH side is similar.**

To install:

➡**The camshaft chain sprockets must be oriented correctly.**

15. Position the LH cassette.
16. Install the LH cassette lower bolt.
    a. Tighten to 14 ft. lbs. (19 Nm).
17. Install the LH cassette upper bolt.
    a. Tighten to 106 inch lbs. (12 Nm).
18. Install the jackshaft chain and sprockets as an assembly.
19. Install the jackshaft chain tensioner and the 2 bolts.
    a. Tighten to 80 inch lbs. (9 Nm).
20. Using the Crankshaft Holding Tool to prevent the crankshaft from turning, tighten the jackshaft sprocket bolt in 2 stages.
    a. Stage 1: Tighten to 33 ft. lbs. (45 Nm).
    b. Stage 2: Tighten an additional 90 degrees.

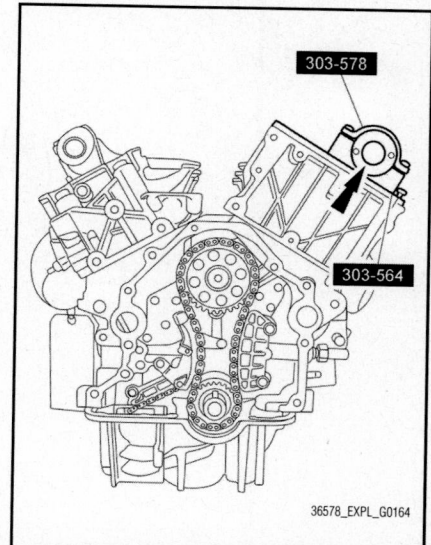

Fig. 205 Camshaft Sprocket Holding Tool

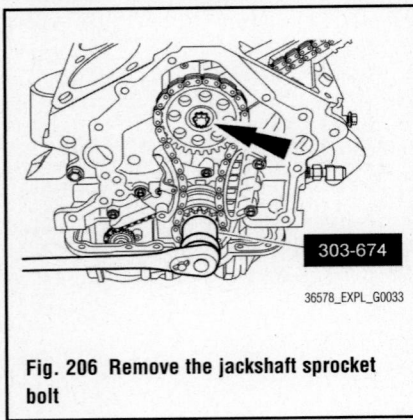

Fig. 206 Remove the jackshaft sprocket bolt

21. Loosely install the camshaft sprocket bolt.

22. Install the engine front cover.

➡**The LH and RH camshafts must be retimed when either camshaft is disturbed.**

➡**Install the LH hydraulic chain tensioner during camshaft timing.**

23. Retime the LH and RH camshafts. For additional information, refer to Camshaft Timing Procedure.

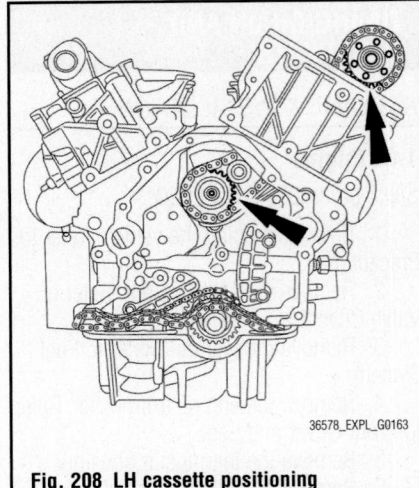

Fig. 208 LH cassette positioning

24. Install the camshaft roller followers. Reversed removal procedure.

25. Install the fuel rail.

26. Install the valve covers.

27. Fill and bleed the engine cooling system.

4.6L Engine

See Figures 209 through 221.

1. Remove the engine front cover. Refer to Timing Chain Cover and Seal.

2. Remove the crankshaft sensor ring from the crankshaft.

3. Position the crankshaft keyway at the 12 o'clock position.

➡**If the camshaft lobes are not exactly positioned as shown, the crankshaft will require one full additional rotation to 12 o'clock.**

4. The No. 1 cylinder must be coming up on the exhaust stroke with the crankshaft keyway at the 12 o'clock position. Verify by noting the position of the 2 intake lobes and the exhaust lobe on the No. 1 cylinder.

➡**If the components are to be reinstalled, they must be installed in their original positions. Mark the components for installation into their original locations. Failure to follow these instructions may result in engine damage.**

5. Remove only the 3 roller followers from the RH cylinder head. For additional information, refer to Cylinder Head.

➡**Do not allow the valve keepers to fall off the valve or the valve may drop into the cylinder. If a valve drops into the cylinder, the cylinder head must be removed.**

➡**It may be necessary to push the valve down while compressing the spring.**

6. Using the Valve Spring Compressor, remove the 3 roller followers designated in the previous step from the RH cylinder head. For additional information, refer to Cylinder Head.

➡**If the components are to be reinstalled, they must be installed in their original positions. Mark the compo-**

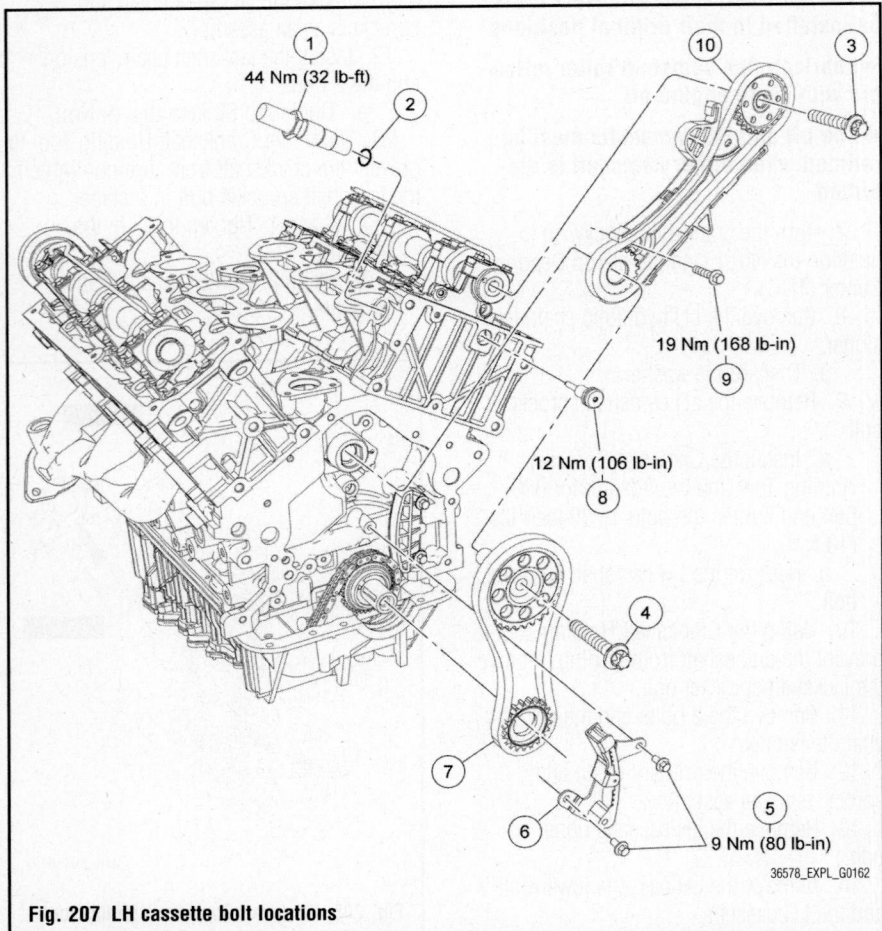

Fig. 207 LH cassette bolt locations

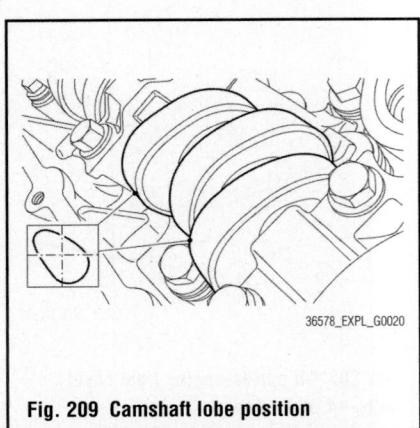

Fig. 209 Camshaft lobe position

nents for installation into their original locations. **Failure to follow these instructions may result in engine damage.**

7. Remove only the 3 roller followers shown in the illustration from the LH cylinder head. For additional information, refer to Cylinder Head.

➡ **Do not allow the valve keepers to fall off the valve or the valve may drop into the cylinder. If a valve drops into the cylinder, the cylinder head must be removed. For additional information, refer to Cylinder Head in this section.**

➡ **It may be necessary to push the valve down while compressing the spring.**

8. Using the Valve Spring Compressor, remove the 3 roller followers designated in the previous step from the LH cylinder head.

➡ **The crankshaft cannot be moved past the 6 o'clock position once set or engine damage may occur.**

9. Rotate the crankshaft clockwise and position the crankshaft keyway at the 6 o'clock position.

10. Remove the bolts, the LH timing chain tensioner and tensioner arm.

11. Remove the bolts, the RH timing chain tensioner and tensioner arm.

12. Remove the RH and LH timing chains and the crankshaft sprocket.

13. Remove the RH timing chain from the camshaft sprocket.

14. Remove the RH timing chain from the crankshaft sprocket.

15. Remove the LH timing chain from the camshaft sprocket.

16. Remove the LH timing chain and crankshaft sprocket.

17. Remove the LH and RH timing chain guides.

➡ **RH shown, LH similar.**

18. Remove the bolts.

19. Remove both timing chain guides.

➡ **Damage to the camshaft phaser sprocket assembly will occur if mishandled or used as a lifting or leveraging device.**

➡ **Only use hand tools to remove the camshaft phaser sprocket assembly or damage may occur to the camshaft or camshaft phaser unit.**

20. Using the Camshaft Phaser Locking Tool, remove the bolt and the RH camshaft phaser sprocket assembly.

21. Discard the camshaft phaser sprocket bolt.

➡ **Damage to the camshaft phaser sprocket assembly will occur if mishandled or used as a lifting or leveraging device.**

➡ **Only use hand tools to remove the camshaft phaser sprocket assembly or damage may occur to the camshaft or camshaft phaser unit.**

22. Using the Camshaft Phaser Locking Tool, remove the bolt and the LH camshaft phaser sprocket assembly.

23. Discard the camshaft phaser sprocket bolt.

24. Remove the front thrust camshaft bearing cap straight upward from the bearing towers or the bearing cap may be damaged from side loading.

25. Remove the 2 bolts and the RH cylinder head camshaft front bearing cap.

26. The camshaft bearing caps must be installed in their original locations. Record camshaft bearing cap locations. Failure to follow these instructions may result in engine damage.

27. Remove the remaining bolts in the sequence shown and remove the RH cylinder head camshaft bearing caps.

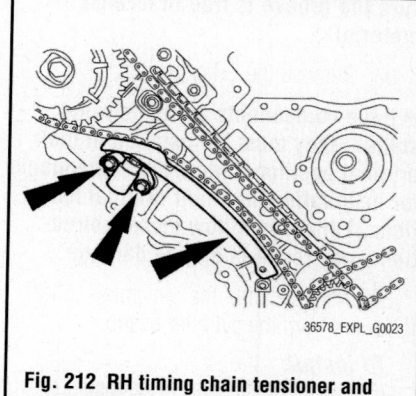

Fig. 212 RH timing chain tensioner and tensioner arm

28. Clean and inspect the RH camshaft bearing caps.

➡ **The camshaft front thrust bearing cap contains an oil metering groove. Make sure the groove is free of foreign material.**

29. Remove the RH camshaft.

➡ **Remove the front thrust camshaft bearing cap straight upward from the bearing towers or the bearing cap may be damaged from side loading.**

30. Remove the 2 bolts and the LH cylinder head camshaft front bearing cap.

➡ **The camshaft bearing caps must be installed in their original locations. Record camshaft bearing cap locations. Failure to follow these instructions may result in engine damage.**

31. Remove the remaining bolts in the sequence shown and remove the LH cylinder head camshaft bearing caps.

32. Clean and inspect the LH camshaft bearing caps.

➡ **The camshaft front thrust bearing cap contains an oil metering groove. Make**

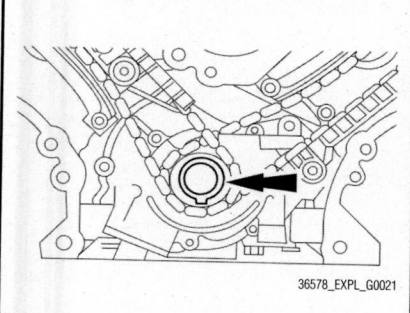

Fig. 210 Position the crankshaft keyway at the 6 o'clock position

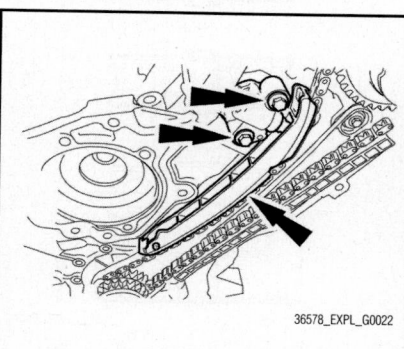

Fig. 211 LH timing chain tensioner and tensioner arm

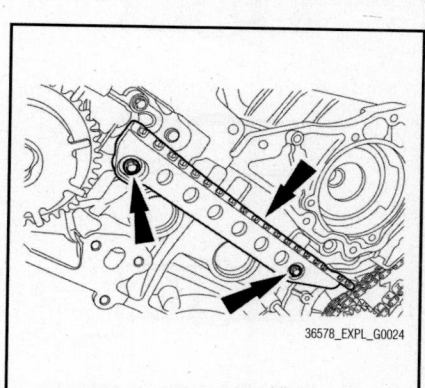

Fig. 213 LH and RH timing chain guides

sure the groove is free of foreign material.

33. Remove the LH camshaft.

➡If the components are to be reinstalled, they must be installed in their original positions. Mark the components for installation into their original locations. Failure to follow these instructions may result in engine damage.

34. Remove all of the remaining roller followers from the cylinder heads.

To install:

35. Install the LH and RH camshafts.

36. Lubricate the camshaft and camshaft journals with clean engine oil prior to installation.

➡LH shown, RH similar.

37. Install the LH and RH camshaft bearing caps in their original locations.

38. Lubricate the camshaft bearing caps with clean engine oil.

39. Position the front camshaft bearing cap.

40. Position the remaining camshaft bearing caps.

41. Install the bolts loosely.

42. Tighten to 89 inch lbs. (10 Nm) in the sequence shown.

➡Damage to the camshaft phaser sprocket assembly will occur if mishandled or used as a lifting or leveraging device.

➡LH shown, RH similar.

43. Install the camshaft phaser sprockets and new camshaft phaser bolts finger-tight.

➡Damage to the camshaft phaser sprocket assembly will occur if mishandled or used as a lifting or leveraging device.

➡Only use hand tools to remove the camshaft phaser sprocket assembly or damage may occur to the camshaft or camshaft phaser unit.

➡ LH shown, RH similar.

44. Using the Camshaft Phaser Locking Tool, tighten the LH and RH camshaft phaser sprocket bolts in 2 stages.
   a. Stage 1: Tighten to 30 ft. lbs. (40 Nm).
   b. Stage 2: Tighten an additional 90 degrees.

45. Install the crankshaft sprocket, making sure the flange faces forward.

46. Rotate the crankshaft to position the crankshaft sprocket timing mark in the 6 o'clock position.

➡If one or both of the tensioner mounting bolts are loosened or removed, the tensioner-sealing bead must be inspected for seal integrity. If cracks, tears, separation from the tensioner body or permanent compression of the seal bead is observed, install a new tensioner or engine damage may occur.

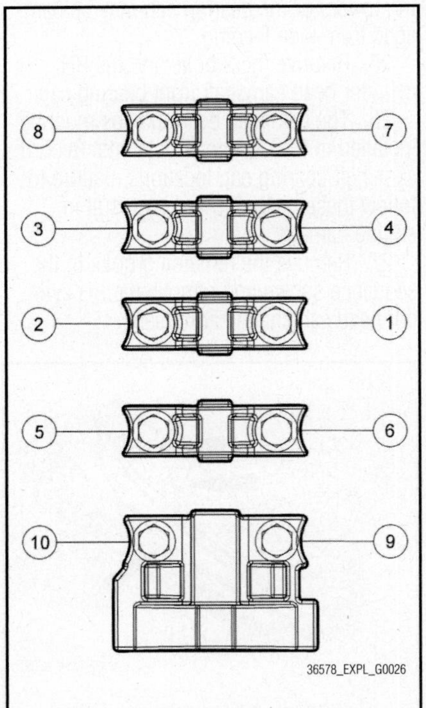

47. Inspect the RH and LH timing chain tensioners.

48. Install new tensioners as necessary.

➡Timing chain procedures must be followed exactly or damage to valves and pistons will result.

49. Compress the tensioner plunger, using a vise.

50. Install a retaining clip on the tensioner to hold the plunger in during installation.

51. Remove the tensioner from the vise.

52. If the colored links are not visible, mark one link on one end and one link on the other end and use as timing marks.

53. Install the 4 bolts and the LH and RH timing chain guides and tighten to 89 inch lbs. (10 Nm).

54. Position the lower end of the LH (inner) timing chain on the crankshaft sprocket, aligning the timing mark on the outer flange of the crankshaft sprocket with the single colored (marked) link on the chain.

➡Make sure the upper half of the timing chain is below the tensioner arm dowel.

55. Position the LH timing chain on camshaft sprocket. Make sure the camshaft sprocket timing mark is aligned with the colored (marked) chain link.

➡The LH timing chain tensioner arm has a bump near the dowel hole for identification.

56. Position the LH timing chain tensioner arm on the dowel pin and install the LH timing chain tensioner and bolts and tighten to 89 inch lbs. (10 Nm).

57. Remove the retaining clip from the LH timing chain tensioner.

58. Position the lower end of the RH (outer) timing chain on the crankshaft sprocket, aligning the timing mark on the

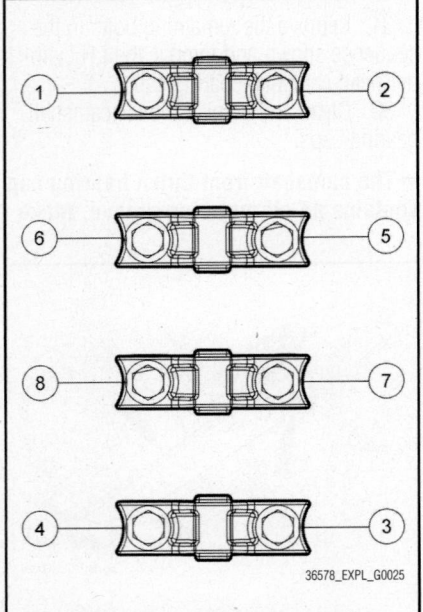

Fig. 214 Camshaft bearing cap removal sequence

36578_EXPL_G0025

36578_EXPL_G0026

Fig. 215 Camshaft bearing cap tightening sequence

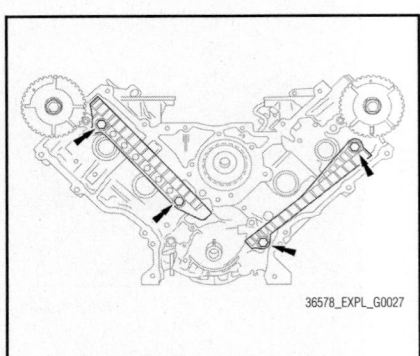

36578_EXPL_G0027

Fig. 216 LH and RH timing chain guide locations

sprocket with the single colored (marked) chain link.

➡The camshaft phaser and sprocket will be stamped with one of the illustrated timing marks for the RH camshaft.

➡The lower half of the timing chain must be positioned above the tensioner arm dowel.

59. Position the RH timing chain on the camshaft sprocket. Make sure the camshaft sprocket timing mark is aligned with the colored (marked) chain link.

60. Position the RH timing chain tensioner arm on the dowel pin and install the RH timing chain tensioner and bolts and tighten to 89 inch lbs. (10 Nm).

61. Remove the retaining clip from the RH timing chain tensioner.

➡The RH and LH camshaft phaser sprockets are similar. Refer to the single timing mark to identify the RH camshaft phaser sprocket and the L timing mark to identify the LH camshaft phaser sprocket.

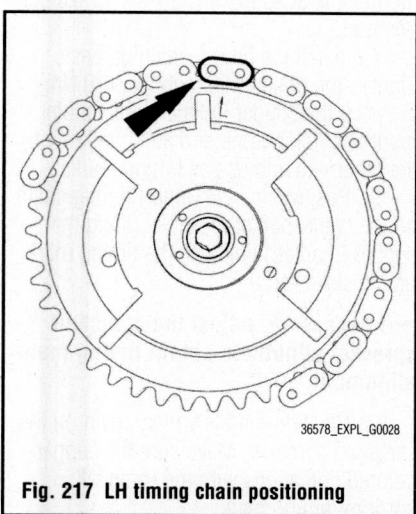

Fig. 217 LH timing chain positioning

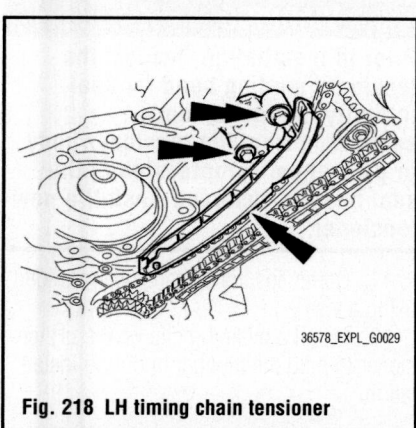

Fig. 218 LH timing chain tensioner

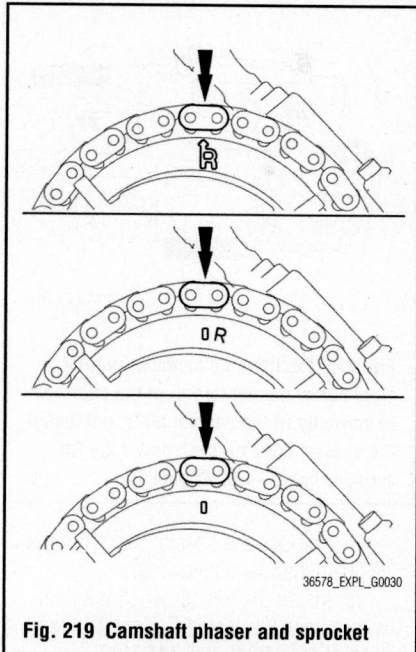

Fig. 219 Camshaft phaser and sprocket

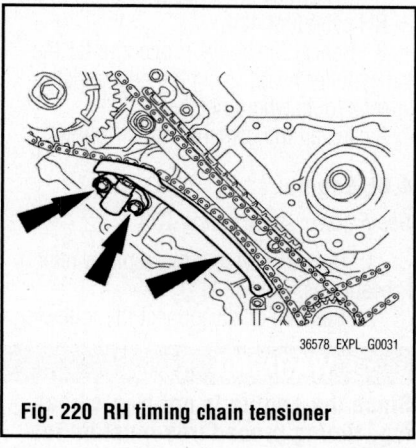

Fig. 220 RH timing chain tensioner

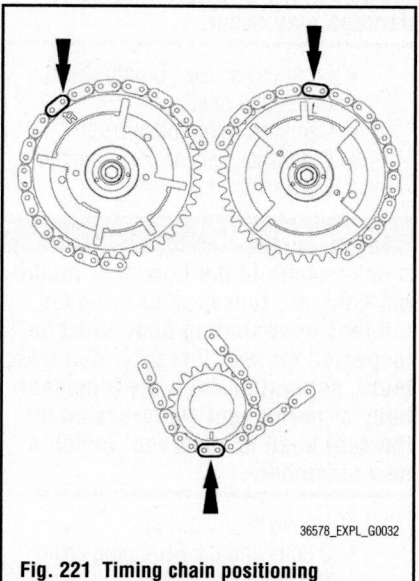

Fig. 221 Timing chain positioning

62. As a post-check, verify correct alignment of all timing marks. Make sure the timing marks on the sprockets correspond to the above note.

63. Install the crankshaft sensor ring on the crankshaft.

➡It is necessary to rotate the engine to position the camshaft lobes at base circle to install the roller followers.

64. Using the Valve Spring Compressor, install all of the camshaft roller followers.

65. Lubricate the roller followers with clean engine oil prior to installation.

66. Install the engine front cover.

CAMSHAFT TIMING PROCEDURE

4.0L Engine

See Figures 222 through 225.

➡You must retime both camshafts when either camshaft is disturbed.

1. If installed, remove the camshaft roller followers.

2. On the RH side, perform the following:

    a. Turn the crankshaft clockwise to position the number one cylinder at top dead center (TDC).

    b. Remove the retainer and position the A/C manifold tube aside.

✳✳ WARNING

Do not rotate the engine counterclockwise. Rotating the engine counterclockwise will result in incorrect timing of the engine.

➡The special tool must be installed on the damper and should contact the engine block, this positions the engine at TDC.

    c. Install the special tool on the crankshaft pulley.

    d. Install the special tools to the RH cylinder head and tighten the 2 top clamp bolts to 89 inch lbs. (10 Nm).

    e. Using the special tool with the Camshaft Sprocket Nut Socket 303-565, loosen the RH camshaft sprocket bolt.

    f. Loosen the top 2 special tool sprocket clamp bolts.

➡The camshaft timing slots are off-center.

    g. Position the camshaft timing slots below the centerline of the camshaft to correctly fit the special tools and install the special tools on the front of the RH cylinder head.

    h. Remove the RH camshaft tensioner.

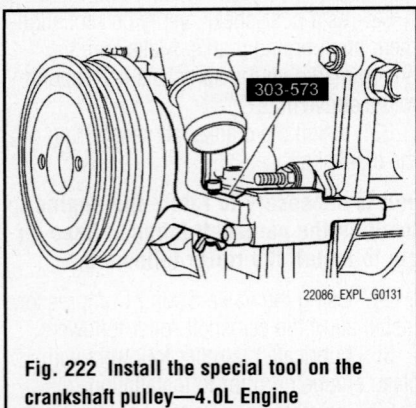

Fig. 222 Install the special tool on the crankshaft pulley—4.0L Engine

i. Install the special tool, 303-571, in place of the RH camshaft tensioner.

> ※※ **WARNING**
>
> **The RH camshaft sprocket bolt is a LH-threaded bolt.**

j. Tighten the sprocket special tool top 2 clamp bolts to 89 inch lbs. (10 Nm).

k. Using the special tool with the Camshaft Sprocket Nut Socket 303-565, tighten the camshaft bolt to 45 ft. lbs. (61 Nm).

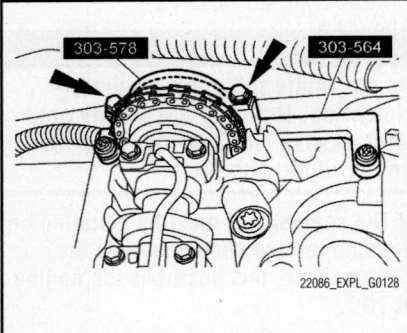

Fig. 223 Install the RH camshaft sprocket special holding tools—4.0L Engine

Fig. 224 Using the special tool with the Camshaft Sprocket Nut Socket 303-565, loosen the RH camshaft sprocket bolt—4.0L Engine

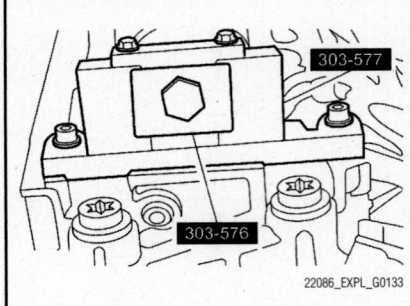

Fig. 225 Position the camshaft timing slots below the centerline of the camshaft to correctly fit the special tools and install the special tools on the front of the RH cylinder head—4.0L Engine

l. Remove the special tool from the RH camshaft tensioner hole.

m. Install the RH camshaft tensioner, with a new, lubricated O-ring. Tighten the tensioner to 32 ft. lbs. (44 Nm).

n. Remove the special tools from the RH cylinder head.

3. Repeat the above procedure for the LH cylinder head, using the appropriate special tools where needed.

4. Install the camshaft roller followers.

4.6L Engine
See Figures 226 through 234.

1. Before servicing the vehicle, refer to Precautions.

2. Remove or disconnect the following:

> ※※ **WARNING**
>
> **Since the engine is not free-wheeling, timing procedures must be followed exactly or piston and valve damage may occur.**

- Front cover; see "Timing Chain Cover and Seal"
- Camshaft roller followers
- Crankshaft sensor ring from the crankshaft

> ※※ **WARNING**
>
> **If one or both of the tensioner mounting bolts are loosened or removed, the tensioner-sealing bead must be inspected for seal integrity. If cracks, tears, separation from the tensioner body or permanent compression of the seal bead is observed, install a new tensioner.**

3. Remove the following:
- 2 bolts and the RH timing chain tensioner

- RH timing chain tensioner arm
- 2 bolts and the LH timing chain tensioner
- LH timing chain tensioner arm
- 2 bolts and the RH timing chain guide
- RH timing chain
- 2 bolts and the LH timing chain guide
- LH timing chain
- Crankshaft sprocket

To install:

> ※※ **WARNING**
>
> **Rotate the crankshaft counterclockwise only. Do not rotate past the position shown or severe piston and/or valve damage will occur.**

4. Using the special tool, position the crankshaft.

5. Install the crankshaft sprocket with the flange facing forward.

6. Rotate the LH camshaft timing sprocket until the timing mark is approximately at the 12 o'clock position. Rotate the RH camshaft timing sprocket until the timing mark is at approximately the 11 o'clock position.

7. Install the timing chain guides. Tighten the bolts to 89 inch lbs. (10 Nm).

8. If the copper links are not visible, mark one link on one end and one link on the other end and use as timing marks.

9. Position the LH (inner) timing chain on the crankshaft sprocket, aligning the copper (marked) link with the timing mark on the sprocket.

➡**If necessary, adjust the camshaft sprocket slightly to obtain timing mark alignment.**

10. Position the LH timing chain on the camshaft sprocket. Make sure the copper-colored link aligns with the camshaft sprocket timing mark.

> ※※ **WARNING**
>
> **Prior to installation, inspect the tensioner-sealing bead for seal integrity. If cracks, tears, separation from the tensioner body or permanent compression of the seal bead is observed, install a new tensioner.**

11. Compress the LH tensioner plunger, using a vise.

12. Install a retaining clip on the LH tensioner to hold the plunger in during installation.

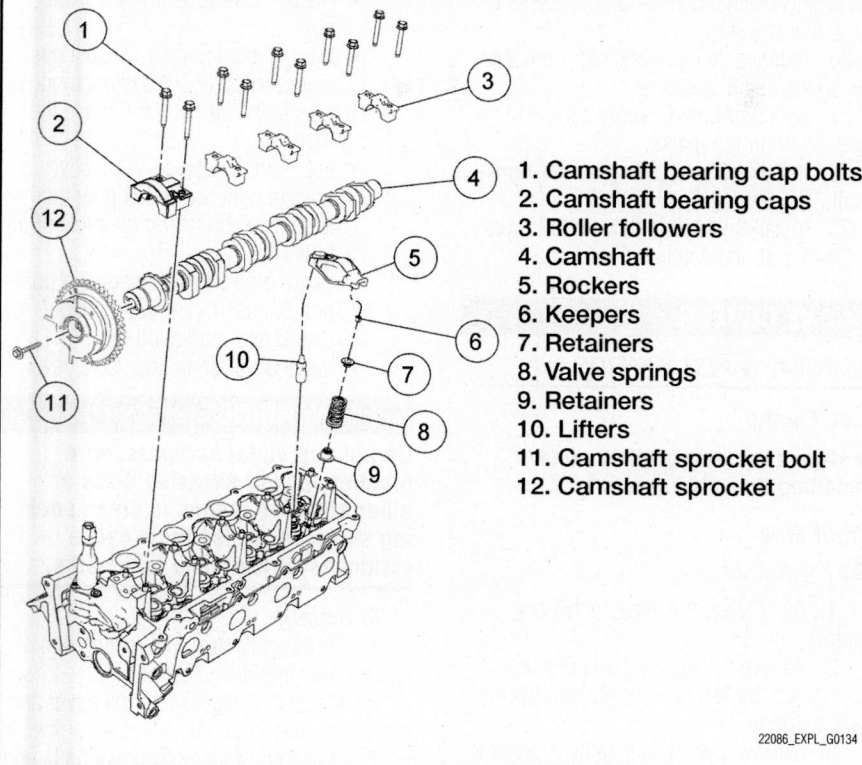

1. Camshaft bearing cap bolts
2. Camshaft bearing caps
3. Roller followers
4. Camshaft
5. Rockers
6. Keepers
7. Retainers
8. Valve springs
9. Retainers
10. Lifters
11. Camshaft sprocket bolt
12. Camshaft sprocket

22086_EXPL_G0134

Fig. 226 Exploded view of the timing components—4.6L Engine (LH head shown; RH head similar)

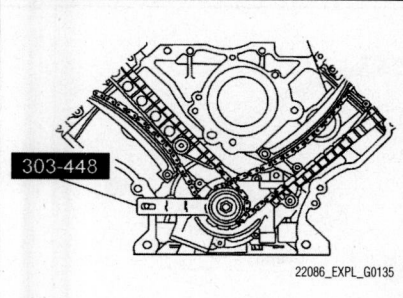

303-448

22086_EXPL_G0135

Fig. 227 Using the special tool, position the crankshaft—4.6L Engine

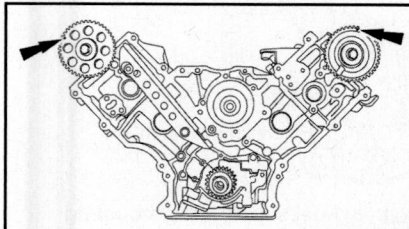

22086_EXPL_G0136

Fig. 228 Rotate the LH camshaft timing sprocket until the timing mark is approximately at the 12 o'clock position. Rotate the RH camshaft timing sprocket until the timing mark is at approximately the 11 o'clock position—4.6L Engine

➡The LH timing chain tensioner arm has a bump near the dowel hole for identification.

13. Position the LH timing chain tensioner arm on the dowel pin and install the LH timing chain tensioner and the bolts to 18 ft. lbs. (25 Nm).

14. Remove the retaining clip from the LH timing chain tensioner.

15. Position the RH (outer) timing chain on the crankshaft sprocket, aligning the copper (marked) link with the timing mark on the sprocket.

➡If necessary, adjust the camshaft sprocket slightly to obtain timing mark alignment.

16. Position the RH timing chain on the camshaft sprocket. Make sure the copper-colored link aligns with the camshaft sprocket timing mark.

❊❊ WARNING

Prior to installation, inspect the tensioner-sealing bead for seal integrity. If cracks, tears, separation from the tensioner body or permanent compression of the seal bead is observed, install a new tensioner.

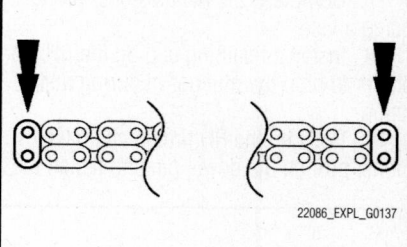

22086_EXPL_G0137

Fig. 229 If the copper links are not visible, mark one link on one end and one link on the other end and use as timing marks—4.6L Engine

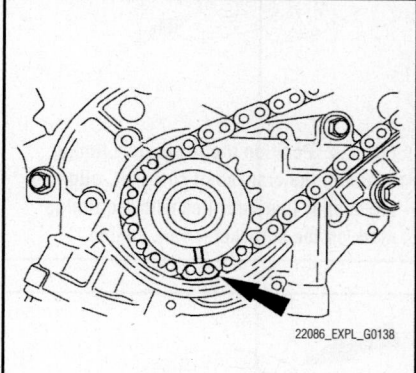

22086_EXPL_G0138

Fig. 230 Position the LH (inner) timing chain on the crankshaft sprocket, aligning the copper (marked) link with the timing mark on the sprocket—4.6L Engine

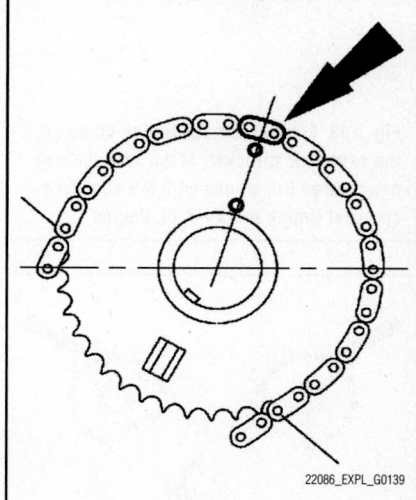

22086_EXPL_G0139

Fig. 231 Position the LH timing chain on the camshaft sprocket. Make sure the copper-colored link aligns with the camshaft sprocket timing mark—4.6L Engine

17. Compress the RH tensioner plunger, using a vise.

18. Install a retaining clip on the RH tensioner to hold the plunger in during installation.

19. Position the RH timing chain tensioner arm on the dowel pin and install the

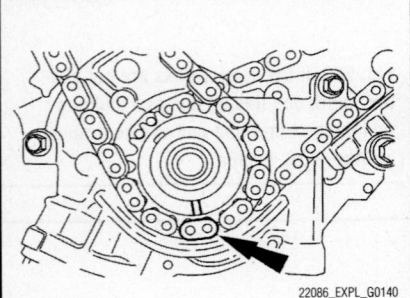

Fig. 232 Position the RH (outer) timing chain on the crankshaft sprocket, aligning the copper (marked) link with the timing mark on the sprocket—4.6L Engine

22086_EXPL_G0140

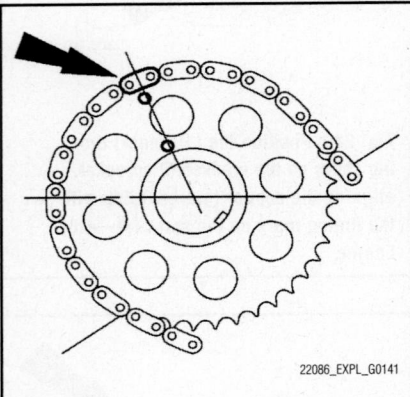

Fig. 233 Position the RH timing chain on the camshaft sprocket. Make sure the copper-colored link aligns with the camshaft sprocket timing mark—4.6L Engine

22086_EXPL_G0141

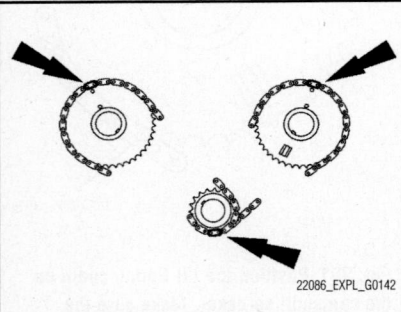

Fig. 234 As a post-check, verify correct alignment of all timing marks—4.6L Engine

22086_EXPL_G0142

RH timing chain tensioner and the bolts to 18 ft. lbs. (25 Nm).

20. Remove the retaining clip from the RH timing chain tensioner.

21. As a post-check, verify correct alignment of all timing marks.

22. Install the sensor ring on the crankshaft.

23. Install the camshaft roller followers.

24. Install the engine front cover.

VALVE COVERS

REMOVAL & INSTALLATION

4.0L Engine

➡ **Always use new gaskets when installing the valve covers.**

Right Side

See Figure 235.

1. Disconnect the negative battery cable.

2. Relieve the fuel system pressure and disconnect the fuel line supply tube springlock coupling.

3. Remove the intake manifold. Refer to Intake Manifold.

4. Remove or disconnect the following:
   • Heater hose tube bracket rear bolt

   • Heater hose tube bracket front bolt
   • Exhaust manifold-to-exhaust gas recirculation (EGR) system module tube lower fitting and remove the tube
   • Fuel supply tube-to-valve cover bracket bolt, the fuel supply tube-to-fuel rail bolts and the fuel supply tube
   • Spark plug wire retainers and position the spark plug wires aside
   • Crankcase ventilation tube
   • Valve cover bolts and valve cover

✳✳ WARNING

Do not use metal scrapers, wire brushes, power abrasive discs or other abrasive means to clean sealing surfaces. These tools cause scratches which make leak paths.

To install:

5. Thoroughly clean the mating surfaces of the engine and cover.

6. Install a new gasket to the cover and place the cover in position on the engine.

7. Install all of the hold-down bolts and tighten to 89 inch lbs. (10 Nm).

8. Install or connect the following:

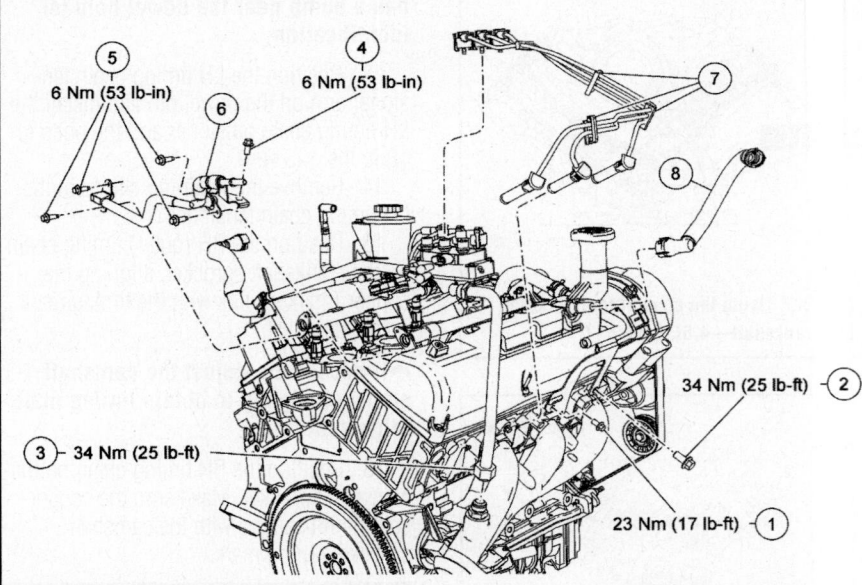

1. Heater hose tube bracket rear mounting bolt
2. Heater hose tube bracket front bolts (4 required)
3. Exhaust gas recirculation (EGR) system module tube
4. Fuel manifold-to-valve cover
5. Fuel supply tube mounting
6. Fuel supply tube
7. Spark plug wire retainers fitting
8. Crankcase ventilation tube

22086_EXPL_G0064

Fig. 235 Showing components for removal of the RH valve cover—4.0L engine

- Crankcase vent tube
- Spark plug cables to their wire looms and plugs
- Fuel supply tube-to-valve cover; use new O-ring seals
- EGR module tube; tighten the fasteners to 25 ft. lbs. (34 Nm)
- Coolant tube bracket front bolt to 25 ft. lbs. (34 Nm) and rear bolt to 17 ft. lbs. (23 Nm)

9. Install the intake manifold. See "Intake Manifold" in this section.

10. Reconnect the fuel supply line spring-lock coupling.

11. Refill the cooling system and run the engine.

12. Connect the negative battery cable.

13. Allow the engine to reach normal operating temperature (upper radiator hose hot) and check for leaks.

Left Side

1. Disconnect the negative battery cable.

2. Remove the intake manifold.

3. Remove or disconnect the following:
- Camshaft Position (CMP) sensor electrical connection
- Ignition coil electrical connector and harness retainer
- Fuel injector electrical connectors and harness retainer
- PCV tube
- PCV valve electrical connector
- Spark plug wire retainers
- Valve cover

※※ WARNING

Never pry between the valve cover and the cylinder head. Damage to the machined sealing surface, or distortion to the valve cover could occur, resulting in an oil leak.

To install:

4. Thoroughly clean the mating surfaces of the engine and cover.

5. Install a new gasket to the cover and place the cover in position on the engine.

6. Install or connect the following:
- Valve cover bolts to 89 inch lbs. (10 Nm)
- Spark plug wire retainers
- PCV valve electrical connector
- PCV tube
- Fuel injector wiring and connectors
- Ignition coil wiring and connector
- CMP sensor electrical connector
- Intake manifold; refer to Intake Manifold

4.6L Engine

Right Side

See Figures 236 and 237.

1. Remove or disconnect the following:
- Air cleaner and the air cleaner outlet pipe
- RH ignition coils
- Wiring harness from the powertrain control module
- RH variable camshaft timing (VCT) oil control solenoid electrical connector
- 2 wiring harness retainers from the RH valve cover studs
- Wiring harness pin-type retainer from the front of the RH valve cover
- Heater hose retainer from the RH valve cover
- Crankcase breather tube from the RH valve cover
- RH valve cover bolts and remove the RH valve cover and the RH valve cover gasket

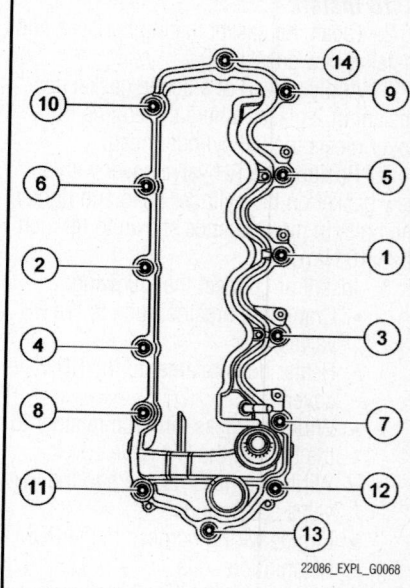

Fig. 237 Showing RH valve cover bolt tightening sequence—4.6L engine

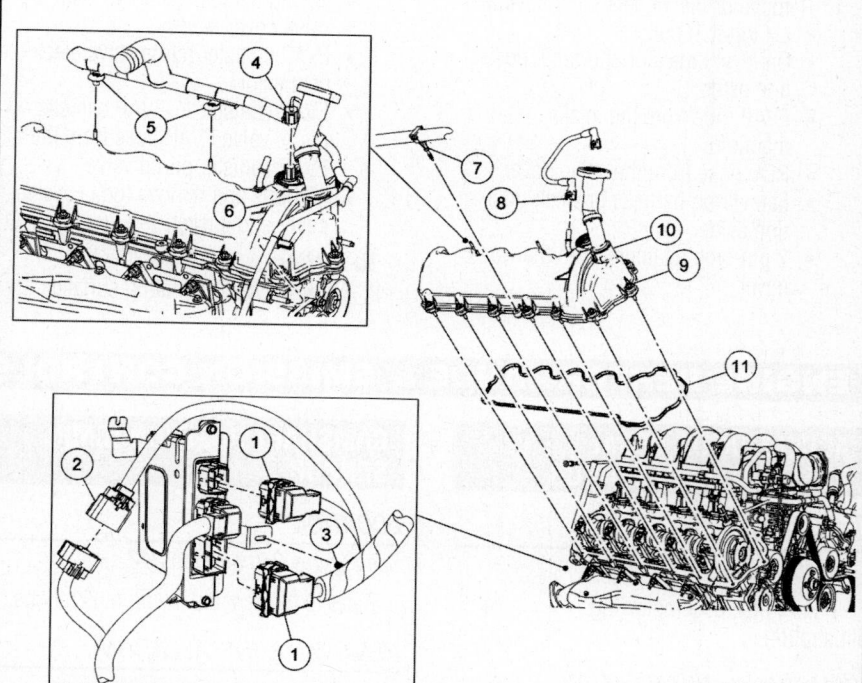

1. Engine wiring (VCT) oil control solenoid harness-to-powertrain control electrical connector
2. Engine wiring harness in-line electrical connector retainer
3. Wiring harness pin-type retainer
4. RH variable camshaft timing
5. Wiring harness retainers
6. *(image)*
7. Heater hose retainer retainer
8. Crankcase breather tube
9. RH valve cover bolts
10. RH valve cover
11. RH valve cover gasket

Fig. 236 Showing components to remove/install for valve cover—4.6L engine

To install:

2. Clean the gasket mating surfaces and install a new gasket.

3. Apply a bead of silicone gasket and sealant in 2 places where the engine front cover meets the RH cylinder head.

4. Position the RH valve cover with a new gasket on the cylinder head and tighten the bolts in the sequence shown to 89 inch lbs. (10 Nm).

5. Install or connect the following:
- Crankcase breather tube to the RH valve cover
- Heater hose retainer to the RH valve cover
- Wiring harness pin-type retainer to the front of the RH valve cover
- Wiring harness retainers to the RH valve cover studs
- Engine wiring harness to the PCM
- RH ignition coils
- Air cleaner and the air cleaner outlet pipe

Left Side

See Figure 238.

1. Remove or disconnect the following:
- LH ignition coils
- Oil level indicator and tube; position aside
- EVAP tube from the intake manifold
- PCV hose from the valve cover
- Fan wiring harness bracket; position aside
- 2 pin-type retainers from the valve cover

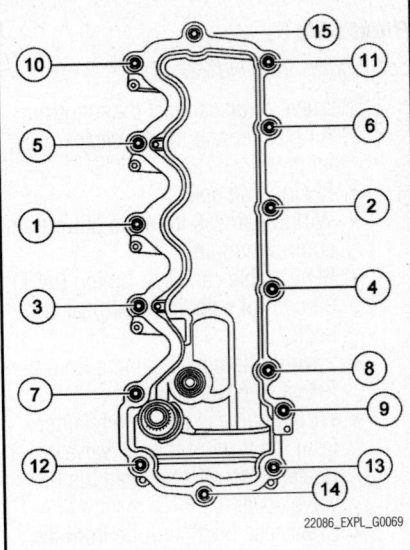

Fig. 238 Showing the LH valve cover bolt tightening sequence—4.6L engine

22086_EXPL_G0069

- Variable camshaft timing (VCT) solenoid electrical connector
- Wiring harness retainers from the valve cover studs
- EVAP canister purge valve electrical connector
- EVAP canister-to-EVAP canister purge valve EVAP hose from the EVAP canister purge valve
- 15 bolts and remove the LH valve cover and gasket

To install:

2. Clean the gasket mating surfaces.

3. Form a new silicone gasket on the valve cover.

4. Install the LH valve cover.

5. Apply a bead of silicone gasket and sealant in 2 places where the engine front cover meets the cylinder head.

6. Install the valve cover bolts and tighten, in sequence, to 89 inch lbs. (10 Nm).

7. Install or connect the following:
- EVAP canister-to-EVAP canister purge valve EVAP hose to the EVAP canister purge valve
- EVAP canister purge valve electrical connector
- Wiring harness retainers to the valve cover studs
- Variable camshaft timing (VCT) solenoid electrical connector
- 2 pin-type retainers to the valve cover
- Fan wiring harness bracket
- PCV hose to the valve cover
- EVAP tube to the intake manifold
- Oil level indicator and tube
- LH ignition coils

VALVE LASH

ADJUSTMENT

The 4.0L and 4.6L engine are equipped with hydraulic lash adjusters. Valve lash is maintained by the hydraulic lifter or hydraulic lash adjuster eliminating the need for any additional manual adjustment. No further adjustment is possible.

ENGINE PERFORMANCE & EMISSION CONTROLS

ACCELERATOR PEDAL POSITION (APP) SENSOR

LOCATION

See Figure 239.

Refer to the accompanying illustration.

REMOVAL & INSTALLATION

See Figure 239.

1. From atop the accelerator pedal, disconnect the pedal electrical connector.

2. Remove the attaching screws.

3. Remove the accelerator pedal position sensor.

To install:

4. To install, reverse removal.

CAMSHAFT POSITION (CMP) SENSOR

LOCATION

See Figures 240 through 242.

Refer to the accompanying illustrations.

REMOVAL & INSTALLATION

4.0L Engine

See Figure 241.

1. Disconnect the Camshaft Position (CMP) sensor electrical connector.

2. Remove the bolt and the CMP sensor.

To install:

3. To install, reverse the removal procedure and tighten bolt to 53 inch lbs. (6 Nm).

4.6L Engine

See Figure 242.

➡For RH side remove the Air Cleaner (ACL) outlet pipe.

1. Disconnect the Camshaft Position (CMP) sensor electrical connector.

2. Remove the bolt and the CMP sensor.

To install:

3. To install, reverse the removal procedure and tighten bolts to 89 inch lbs. (10 Nm).

CRANKSHAFT POSITION (CKP) SENSOR

LOCATION

See Figures 243 and 244.

Refer to the accompanying illustrations.

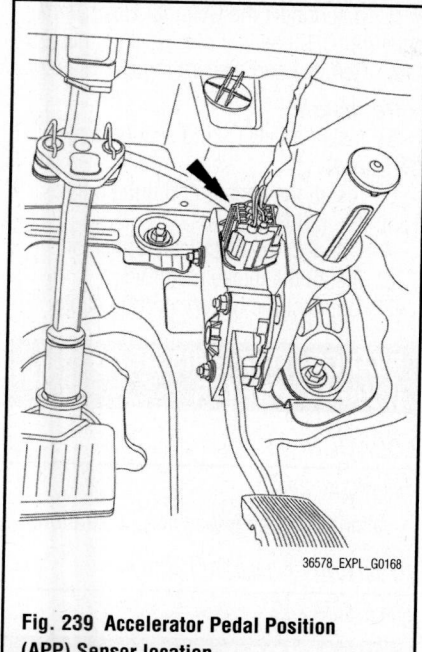

Fig. 239 Accelerator Pedal Position (APP) Sensor location

REMOVAL & INSTALLATION

4.0L Engine

See Figure 243.

1. With the vehicle in NEUTRAL, position it on a hoist.

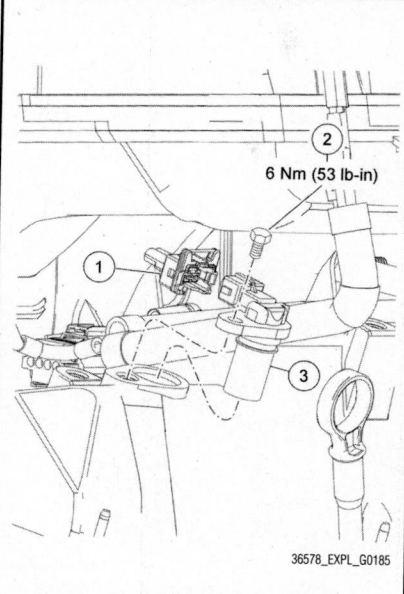

Fig. 241 Camshaft Position (CMP) Sensor location—4.0L Engine

2. Disconnect the Crankshaft Position (CKP) sensor electrical connector.
3. Remove the 2 bolts and the CKP sensor.

To install:

4. To install, reverse the removal

procedure and tighten to 89 inch lbs. (10 Nm).

➡**Be sure the sensor wiring is routed away from the battery cable.**

4.6L Engine

See Figure 244.

1. With the vehicle in NEUTRAL, position it on a hoist.
2. Remove the accessory drive belt. Refer to Accessory Drive Belt in Engine Mechanical.
3. Disconnect the A/C compressor coil electrical connector.
4. Detach the battery cable retainer from the A/C compressor stud bolts.
5. Remove the nut and detach the A/C tube bracket.
6. Remove the stud bolts and position the A/C compressor aside. Refer to Compressor in Heating & Air Conditioning.
7. Disconnect the Crankshaft Position (CKP) sensor electrical connector.
8. Remove the bolt and the CKP sensor.

To install:

9. To install, reverse the removal procedure and tighten bolt to 89 inch lbs. (10 Nm).

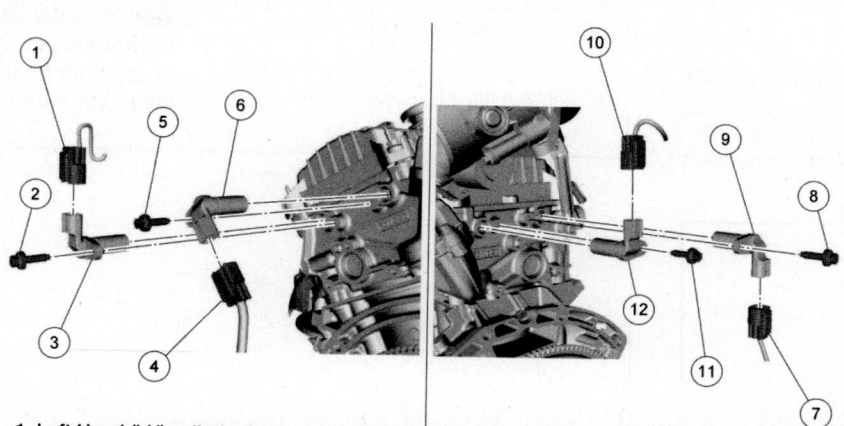

1. Left Hand (LH) cylinder head exhaust Camshaft Position (CMP) sensor electrical connector
2. LH cylinder head exhaust CMP sensor bolt
3. LH cylinder head exhaust CMP sensor
4. LH cylinder head intake CMP sensor electrical connector
5. LH cylinder head intake CMP sensor bolt
6. LH cylinder head intake CMP sensor
7. RH cylinder head exhaust CMP sensor electrical connector
8. RH cylinder head exhaust CMP sensor bolt
9. RH cylinder head exhaust CMP sensor
10. RH cylinder head intake CMP sensor electrical connector
11. RH cylinder head intake CMP sensor bolt
12. RH cylinder head intake CMP sensor

Fig. 240 Location of the Camshaft Position (CMP) sensors—3.5L engine

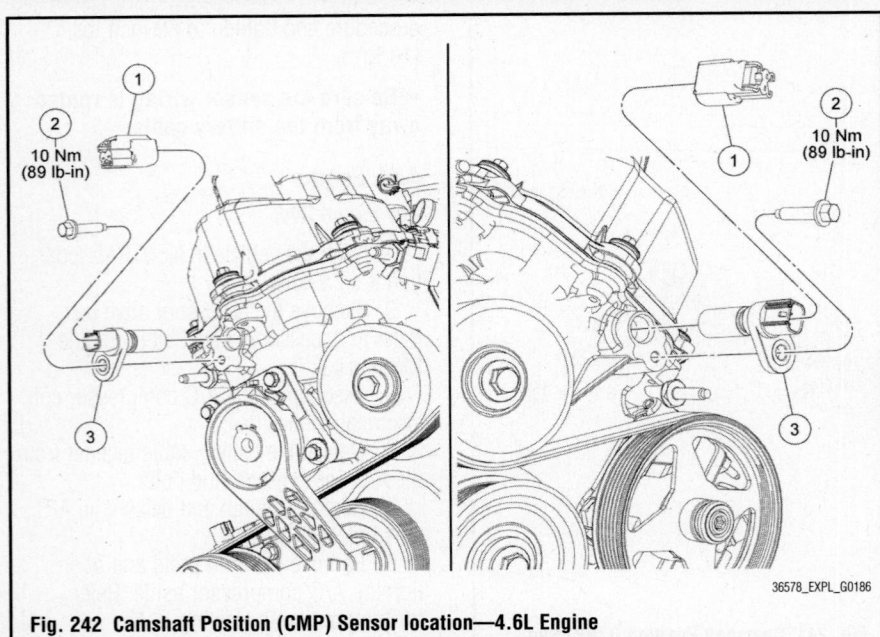

Fig. 242 Camshaft Position (CMP) Sensor location—4.6L Engine

ENGINE COOLANT TEMPERATURE (ECT) SENSOR

LOCATION

See Figures 245 and 246.

Refer to the accompanying illustrations.

REMOVAL & INSTALLATION

4.0L Engine

See Figure 91.

1. Disconnect the negative battery cable.
2. Drain the cooling system.
3. Disconnect the Engine Coolant Temperature (ECT) sensor electrical connector.

4. Remove the clip and the ECT sensor.

To install:

5. Installation is the reverse of the removal procedure.

4.6L Engine

See Figure 246.

➡Ford refers to the coolant temperature sensor described below as a Cylinder Head Temperature (CHT) sensor.

1. Disconnect the battery ground cable.
2. Remove the intake manifold.

3. Disconnect the Cylinder Head Temperature (CHT) sensor electrical connector.
4. Remove and discard the CHT sensor.

To install:

5. Install a new O-ring seal on a new CHT sensor.
6. Install the sensor and tighten it to 19 ft. lbs. (26 Nm).
7. Connect the electrical connector.
8. Install the intake manifold.
9. Connect the battery ground cable.

EVAPORATIVE EMISSIONS (EVAP) CANISTER

LOCATION

See Figure 247.

Refer to the accompanying illustration.

REMOVAL & INSTALLATION

See Figure 249.

❊❊ CAUTION

Always disconnect the battery ground cable at the battery when working on an evaporative emission (EVAP) system or fuel-related component. Highly flammable mixtures are always present and may be ignited. Failure to follow these instructions may result in serious personal injury.

❊❊ CAUTION

Do not smoke, carry lighted tobacco or have an open flame of any type when working on or near any

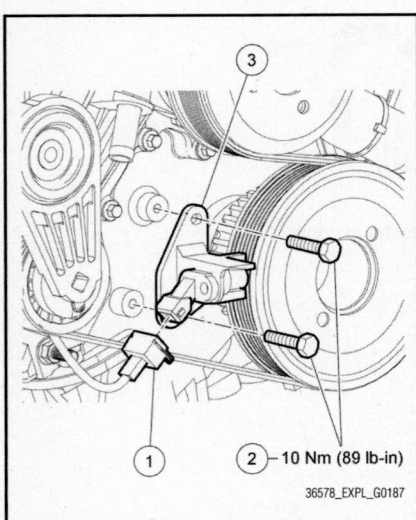

Fig. 243 Crankshaft Position (CMP) Sensor location—4.0L Engine

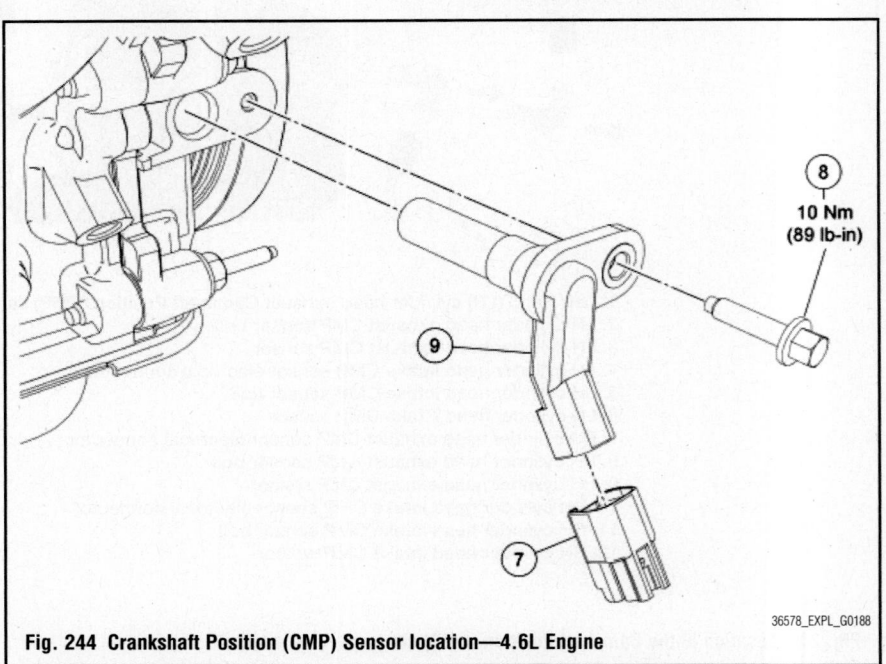

Fig. 244 Crankshaft Position (CMP) Sensor location—4.6L Engine

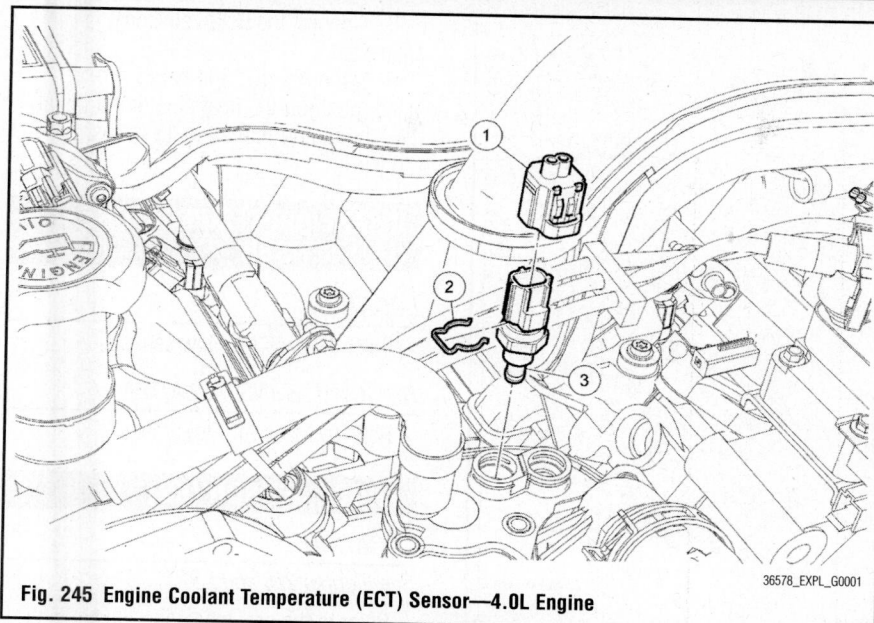

Fig. 245 Engine Coolant Temperature (ECT) Sensor—4.0L Engine

36578_EXPL_G0001

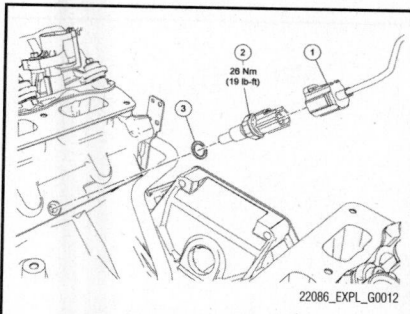

Fig. 246 Showing the location of the Cylinder Head Temperature (CHT) sensor connector (1), sensor (2), and the O-ring seal (3)—4.6L engine

22086_EXPL_G0012

fuel-related component. Highly flammable mixtures are always present and may be ignited. Failure to follow these instructions may result in serious personal injury.

→Use only water-based lubricants on the vapor hoses.

1. With the vehicle in NEUTRAL, position it on a hoist.
2. Disconnect the battery ground cable.
3. Remove the fuel tank. Refer to Fuel Tank in Fuel Systems.
4. Detach the Evaporative Emission (EVAP) canister from the fuel tank to gain access to the quick connect coupling.

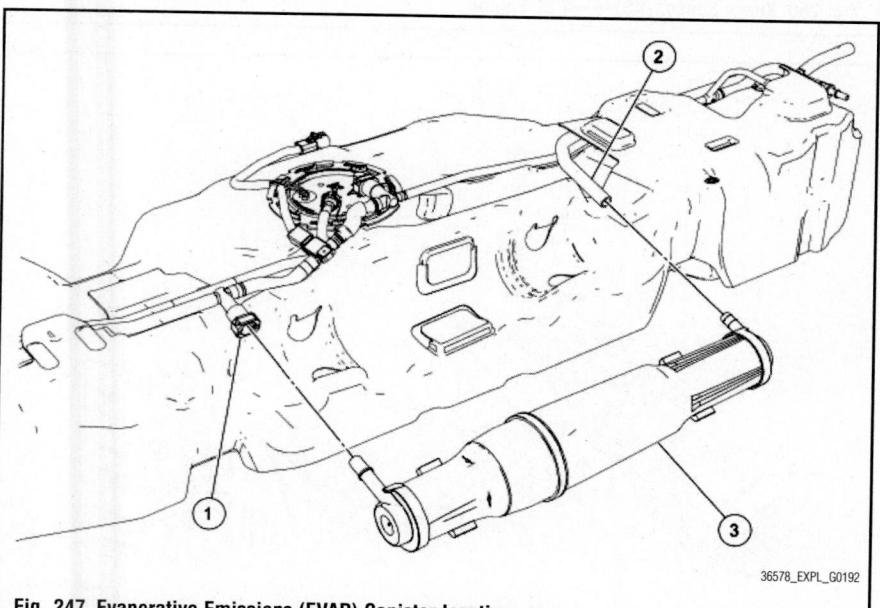

Fig. 247 Evaporative Emissions (EVAP) Canister location

36578_EXPL_G0192

5. Disconnect the Fuel Tank Pressure (FTP) sensor and vapor tube assembly quick connect coupling from the EVAP canister.
6. Disconnect the vapor hose from the EVAP canister.
7. Remove the EVAP canister.

To install:

8. To install, reverse the removal procedure.
9. Lubricate the vapor hoses with a water-based lubricant to ease installation.
10. Using a can tool, carry out the Evaporative Emission System Leak Test.

EXHAUST GAS RECIRCULATION (EGR) VALVE

LOCATION
See Figure 248.

Refer to the accompanying illustration.

REMOVAL & INSTALLATION
See Figure 248.

1. Disconnect the EGR system module electrical and vacuum connectors.
2. Disconnect the EGR system module-to-exhaust manifold tube upper fitting.

→**When installing the new EGR module gasket, install with the side with the raised circle facing the intake manifold.**

3. Remove the 2 bolts, the EGR system module and the gasket. Discard the gasket.

→**The EGR system module sealing surfaces are soft metals.**

4. Carefully clean the EGR system module sealing surfaces.

To install:

5. To install, reverse the removal procedure.
6. Install a new EGR system module gasket.
7. Install and tighten the module-to-exhaust manifold tube to 30 ft. lbs. (40 Nm).
8. Install and tighten the EGR system module to 18 ft. lbs. (25 Nm).

HEATED OXYGEN SENSOR (HO2S)

LOCATION
See Figure 249.

Refer to the accompanying illustration.

REMOVAL & INSTALLATION
See Figure 249.

1. With the vehicle in NEUTRAL, position it on a hoist.

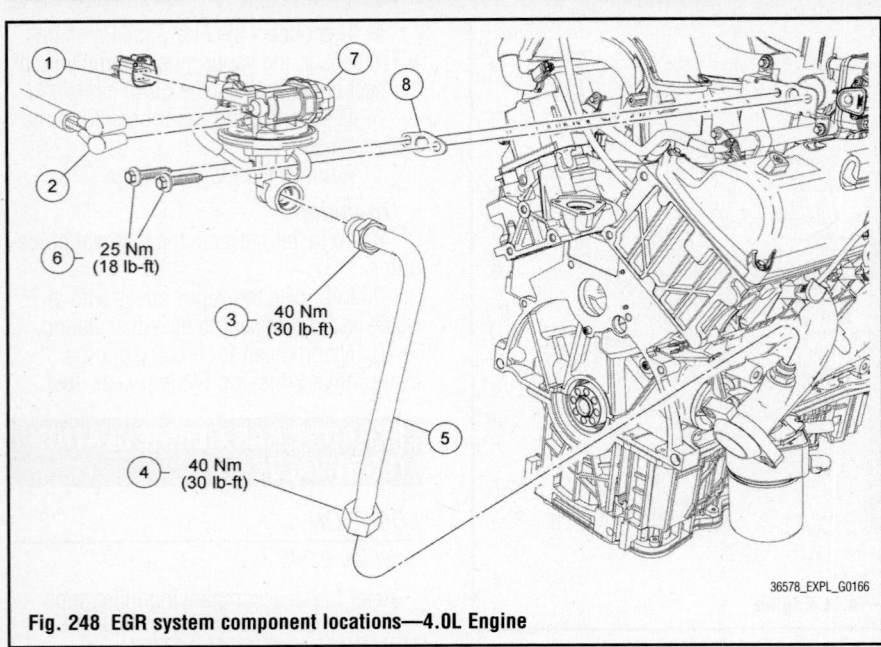

25 Nm
(18 lb-ft)

40 Nm
(30 lb-ft)

40 Nm
(30 lb-ft)

36578_EXPL_G0166

Fig. 248 EGR system component locations—4.0L Engine

2. If the RH Heated Oxygen Sensor (HO2S) is being serviced, remove the 2 bolts and position the heat shield aside.

3. Disconnect the HO2S electrical connector.

➡**If necessary, lubricate the HO2S with penetrating and lock lubricant to ease removal.**

4. Using the Exhaust Gas Oxygen Sensor Socket, remove the HO2S.

To install:

5. Apply a light coat of nickel anti-seize lubricant to the threads of the HO2S.

6. Using the Exhaust Gas Oxygen Sensor Socket, install the HO2S.

7. Using the Exhaust Gas Oxygen Sensor Socket, tighten to 30 ft. lbs. (41 Nm).

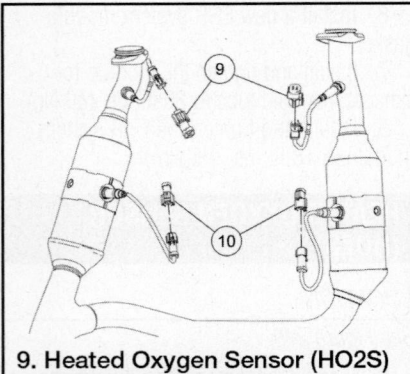

9. Heated Oxygen Sensor (HO2S) electrical connectors
10. Catalyst Monitor Sensor (CMS) electrical connectors

36578_EXPL_G0148

Fig. 249 Heated Oxygen Sensor (HO2S) locations

8. Connect the HO2S electrical connector.

9. If the RH HO2S is being serviced, position the heat shield and install the 2 bolts and tighten to 15 ft. lbs. (20 Nm).

INTAKE AIR TEMPERATURE (IAT) SENSOR

LOCATION

Refer to Mass Air Flow sensor.

REMOVAL & INSTALLATION

Refer to Mass Air Flow sensor.

KNOCK SENSOR (KS)

LOCATION

See Figures 250 and 251.

Refer to the accompanying illustrations.

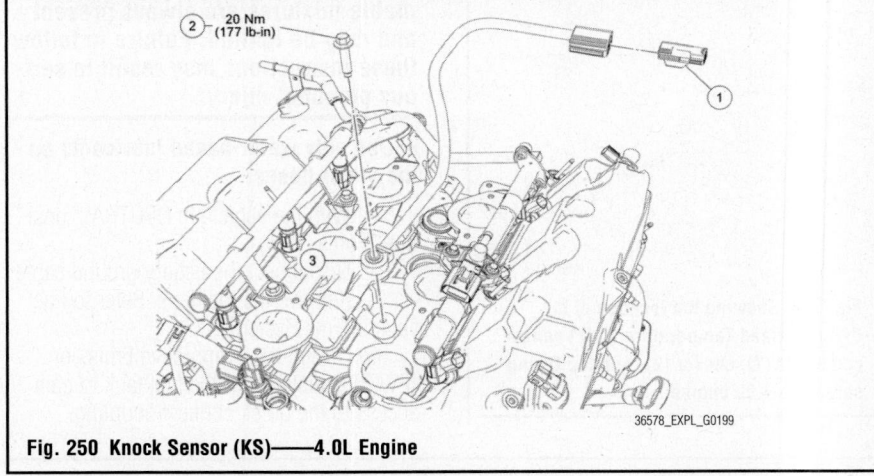

20 Nm
(177 lb-in)

36578_EXPL_G0199

Fig. 250 Knock Sensor (KS)——4.0L Engine

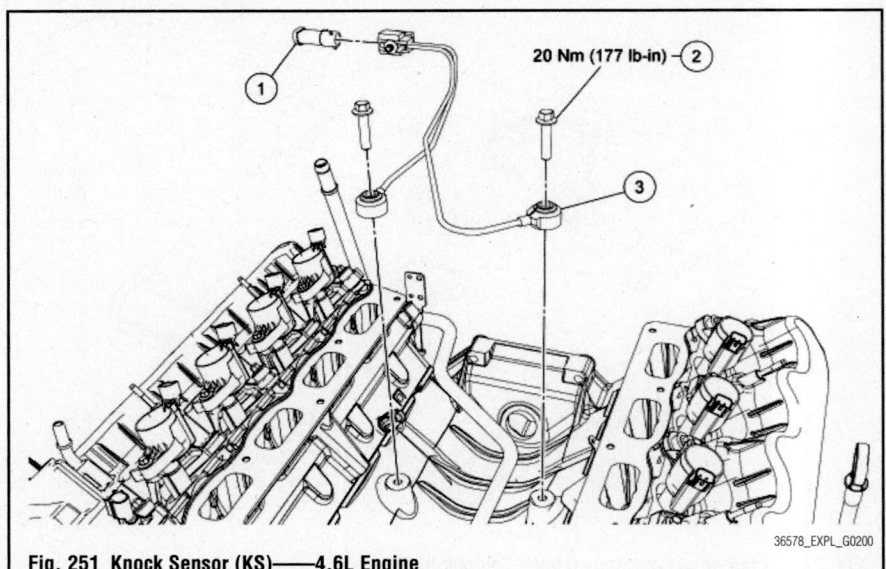

20 Nm (177 lb-in)

36578_EXPL_G0200

Fig. 251 Knock Sensor (KS)——4.6L Engine

REMOVAL & INSTALLATION

See Figures 250 and 251.

1. Remove the intake manifold. Refer to Intake Manifold in Engine Mechanical.
2. Disconnect the Knock Sensor (KS) electrical connector.
3. Remove the bolt and the KS.

To install:

4. To install, reverse the removal procedure and tighten to 15 ft. lbs. (20 Nm).

MALFUNCTION INDICATOR LIGHT (MIL)

RESET PROCEDURE

Clearing Diagnostic Trouble Codes, resets MIL.

MASS AIR FLOW (MAF) SENSOR

LOCATION

See Figures 252 and 253.

Refer to the accompanying illustrations.

REMOVAL & INSTALLATION

See Figures 252 through 253.

1. Disconnect the Mass Air Flow (MAF) sensor electrical connector.
2. Remove the 2 bolts and the MAF sensor.

To install:

3. To install, reverse the removal procedure and tighten bolts to 18 inch lbs. (2 Nm).

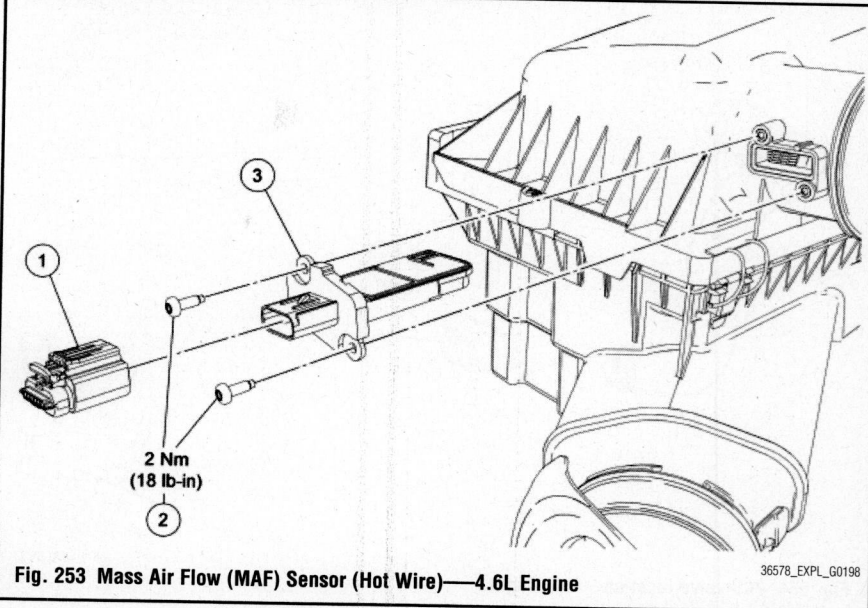

Fig. 253 Mass Air Flow (MAF) Sensor (Hot Wire)—4.6L Engine   36578_EXPL_G0198

POSITIVE CRANKCASE VENTILATION (PCV) VALVE

LOCATION

See Figure 254.

Refer to the accompanying illustrations. For 4.6L engine, the PCV valve is located on the LH valve cover.

REMOVAL & INSTALLATION

See Figure 254.

1. Disconnect the PCV valve electrical connector (if necessary).

2. Disconnect the PCV valve hose.

➡**If the PCV valve is removed from the valve cover, a new PCV valve must be installed.**

3. Rotate the PCV valve counterclockwise and remove it from the valve cover.

To install:

4. To install, reverse the removal procedure

POWERTRAIN CONTROL MODULE (PCM)

LOCATION

Passenger side, near side cowl, behind the glove compartment.

REMOVAL & INSTALLATION

All vehicles

➡**PCM installation DOES NOT require new keys.**

1. Retrieve the module configuration. Carry out the module configuration retrieval steps of the Programmable Module Installation (PMI) procedure:

a. Connect the IDS and identify the vehicle as normal.

b. From the Toolbox icon, select Module Programming and press the check mark.

c. Select Programmable Module Installation.

d. Select the module that is being replaced.

e. Follow the on-screen instructions, turn the ignition key to the OFF position, and press the check mark.

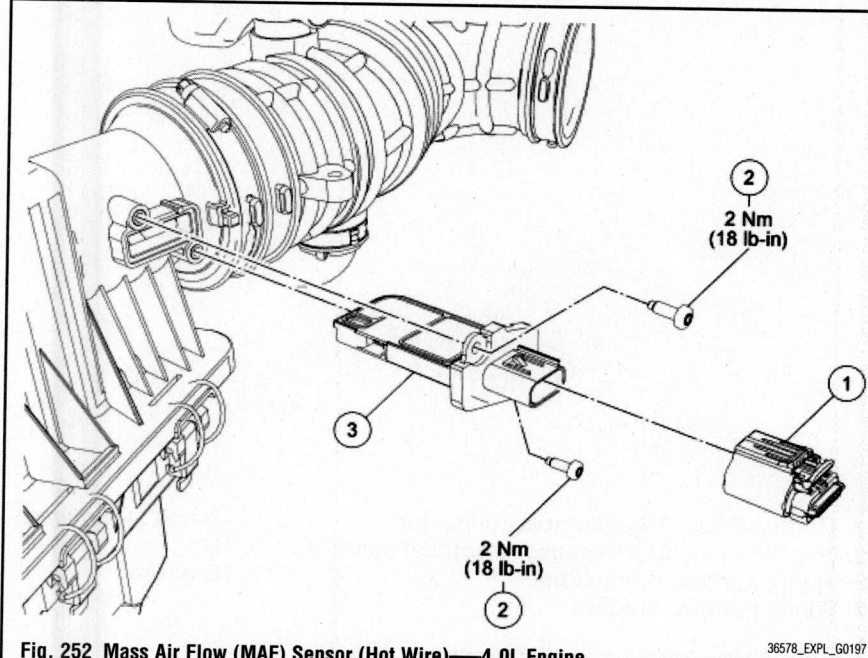

Fig. 252 Mass Air Flow (MAF) Sensor (Hot Wire)—4.0L Engine   36578_EXPL_G0197

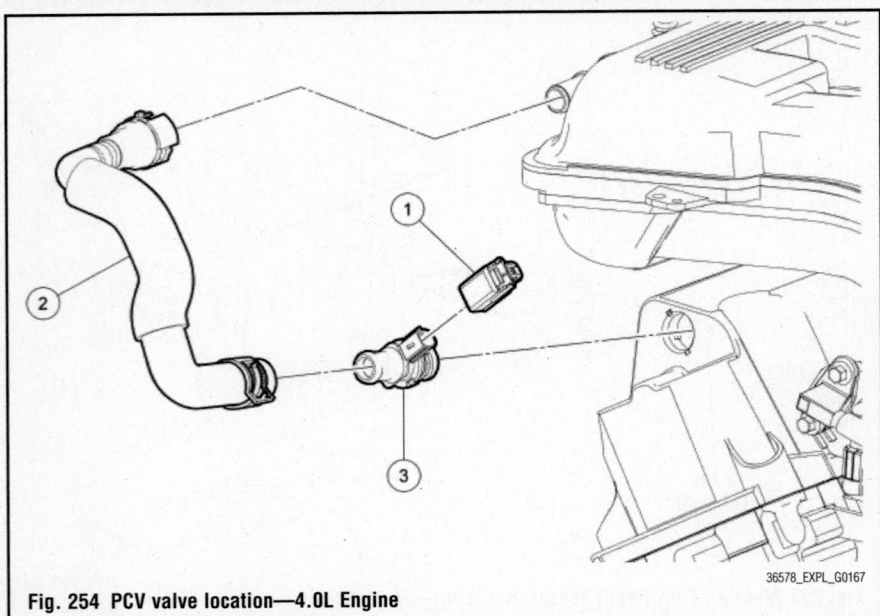

Fig. 254 PCV valve location—4.0L Engine

36578_EXPL_G0167

f. Install the new module and press the check mark.

g. Follow the on-screen instructions, turn the ignition key to the ON position, and press the check mark.

h. The IDS downloads the data into the new module and displays Module Configuration Complete.

i. Test module for correct operation.

Vehicles equipped with a 4.6L (3V) engine

2. Remove the Air Cleaner (ACL). Disconnect the RH front wheel speed sensor electrical connector.

3. Remove the nut(s) and position the A/C tube bracket(s) and wiring harness aside.

4. Disconnect the PCM connectors.

5. Remove the 2 bolts and the PCM.

To install:

6. Install the PCM and the 2 bolts and tighten to 89 inch lbs. (10 Nm).

7. Connect the PCM electrical connectors.

8. Position the wiring harness and the A/C tube bracket(s) and install the nut(s). Connect the RH front wheel speed sensor electrical connector and tighten to 62 inch lbs. (7 Nm).

Vehicles equipped with a 4.6L (3V) engine

9. Install the air cleaner assembly

All vehicles

10. Restore the module configuration. Carry out the module configuration restore steps of the Programmable Module Installation (PMI) procedure.

11. Using scan tool, reprogram the Passive Anti-Theft System (PATS). Carry out the Parameter Reset procedure.

RESET PROCEDURE

a. Connect the IDS and identify the vehicle as normal.

b. From the Toolbox icon, select Module Programming and press the check mark.

c. Select Programmable Module Installation.

d. Select the module that is being replaced.

e. Follow the on-screen instructions, turn the ignition key to the OFF position, and press the check mark.

f. Install the new module and press the check mark.

g. Follow the on-screen instructions, turn the ignition key to the ON position, and press the check mark.

h. The IDS downloads the data into the new module and displays Module Configuration Complete.

i. Test module for correct operation.

THROTTLE CONTROL ACTUATOR (TAC)

LOCATION

See Figures 255 and 256.

Refer to the accompanying illustrations.

REMOVAL & INSTALLATION

4.0L Engine

See Figure 255.

✸✸ CAUTION

Do not smoke, carry lighted tobacco or have an open flame of any type when working on or near any fuel-related component. Highly flammable mixtures are always present and may be ignited. Failure to follow these instructions may result in serious personal injury.

1. Remove the Air Cleaner (ACL) outlet tube.

2. Disconnect the Throttle Body (TB) electrical connector.

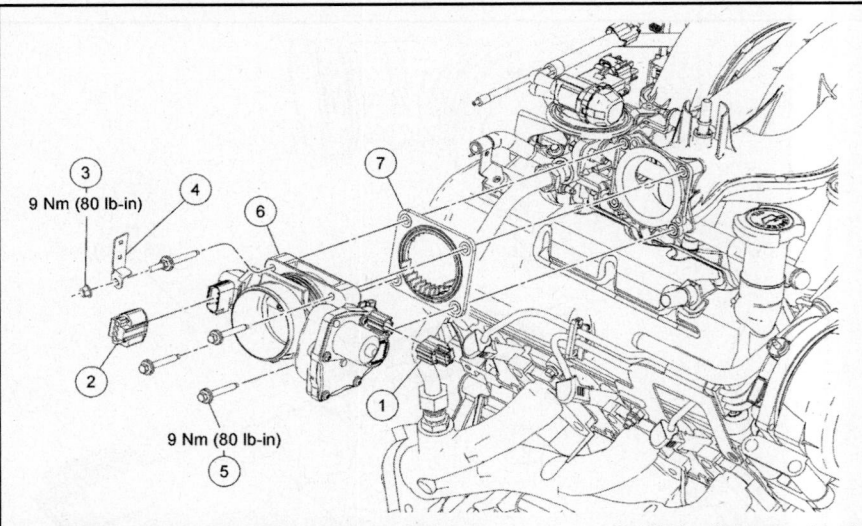

1. Throttle Body (TB) electrical connector
2. Throttle Position (TP) sensor electrical connector
3. Wiring harness bracket nut
4. Wiring harness bracket
5. TB bolt (4 required)
6. TB
7. TB gasket

36578_EXPL_G0204

Fig. 255 Throttle Control Actuator (TAC) location—4.0L Engine

3. Disconnect the Throttle Position (TP) sensor electrical connector.

4. Remove the nut and position the wiring harness bracket aside.

5. Remove the 4 bolts, the TB and the gasket. Discard the gasket.

To install:

6. To install, reverse the removal procedure.

7. Install a new TB gasket.

8. Tighten wiring harness bracket to 80 inch lbs. (9 Nm).

9. Tighten throttle body bolts to 80 inch lbs. (9 Nm).

4.6L Engine

See Figure 256.

1. Remove the Air Cleaner (ACL) outlet pipe.

2. Disconnect the electronic throttle control electrical connector.

3. Disconnect the Throttle Position (TP) sensor electrical connector.

4. Remove the 4 bolts, the Throttle Body (TB) and the TB gasket. Discard the gasket.

To install:

5. To install, reverse the removal procedure.

6. To install, tighten throttle body bolts to 89 inch lbs. (10 Nm).

THROTTLE POSITION SENSOR (TPS)

LOCATION

See Figure 257.

Refer to the accompanying illustration.

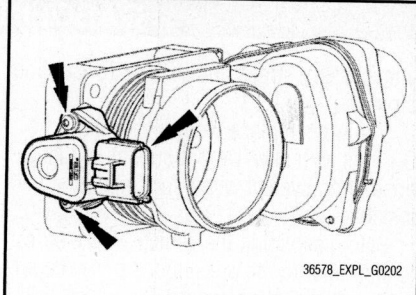

Fig. 257 Throttle Position Sensor (TPS) location

REMOVAL & INSTALLATION

See Figure 258.

All vehicles

1. Remove the Air Cleaner (ACL) outlet pipe.

2. Disconnect the Throttle Position (TP) sensor electrical connector.

Vehicles equipped with a 4.6L (3V) engine

3. Disconnect the PCV hose from the heated PCV fitting.

4. Disconnect the heated PCV fitting electrical connector.

5. Remove the 2 bolts and the heated PCV fitting.

6. Remove and discard the heated PCV fitting O-ring seal.

All vehicles

❊❊❊ **WARNING**

Do not put direct heat on the Throttle Position (TP) sensor or any other plastic parts because heat damage

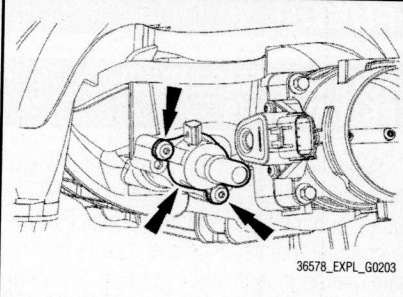

Fig. 258 2 bolts and the heated PCV fitting location—4.6L Engine

may occur. Damage may also occur if Electronic Throttle Body (ETB) temperature exceeds 248°F (120°C)

❊❊❊ **WARNING**

Do not use power tools.

7. Remove the TP sensor.

8. Using a suitable heat gun, apply heat to the top of the Electronic Throttle Body (ETB) until the top TP sensor bolt ear reaches approximately 130°F (55°C), this should take no more than 3 minutes using a 1100-watt heat gun. The heat gun should be about an 25.4 mm (1 in) away from the ETB. Monitor the temperature of the top TP sensor bolt ear on the ETB with a suitable temperature measuring device, such as a digital temperature laser or infrared thermometer, while heating the ETB.

9. Using hand tools, quickly remove the bolt farthest from the heat source first and discard.

10. Using hand tools, remove the remaining bolt and discard.

11. Remove and discard the TP sensor.

To install:
All vehicles

❊❊❊ **WARNING**

Do not use power tools.

12. Install the new TP sensor.

13. Using hand tools, install the 2 new bolts and tighten to 27 inch lbs. (3 Nm).

Vehicles equipped with a 4.6L (3V) engine

14. Install a new O-ring seal and position the heated PCV fitting and install the 2 bolts.

15. Connect the heated PCV fitting electrical connector.

16. Connect the PCV hose to the heated PCV fitting.

All vehicles

17. Connect the TP sensor electrical connector.

18. Install the ACL outlet pipe.

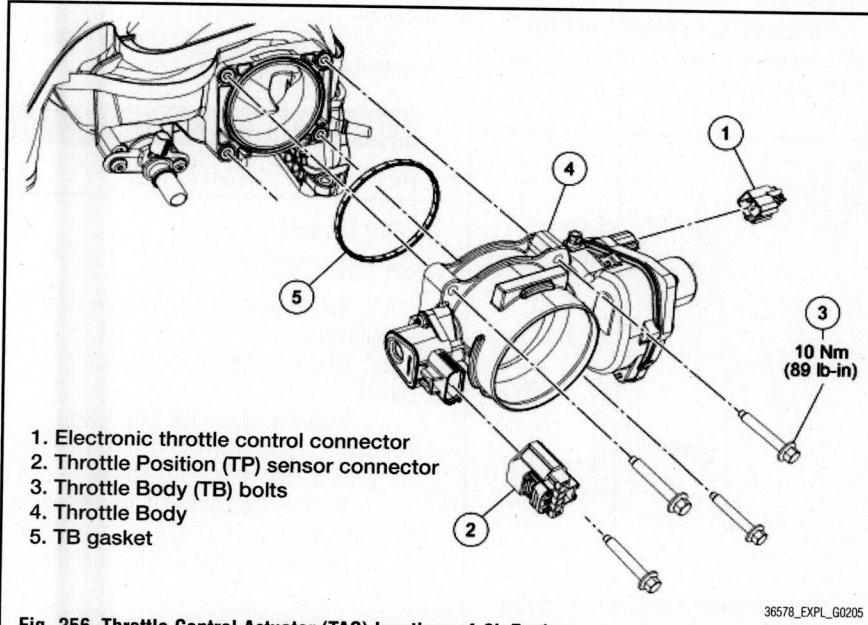

1. Electronic throttle control connector
2. Throttle Position (TP) sensor connector
3. Throttle Body (TB) bolts
4. Throttle Body
5. TB gasket

10 Nm
(89 lb-in)

Fig. 256 Throttle Control Actuator (TAC) location—4.6L Engine

FUEL GASOLINE FUEL INJECTION SYSTEM

FUEL SYSTEM SERVICE PRECAUTIONS

Safety is the most important factor when performing not only fuel system maintenance but any type of maintenance. Failure to conduct maintenance and repairs in a safe manner may result in serious personal injury or death. Maintenance and testing of the vehicle's fuel system components can be accomplished safely and effectively by adhering to the following rules and guidelines.

• To avoid the possibility of fire and personal injury, always disconnect the negative battery cable unless the repair or test procedure requires that battery voltage be applied.

• Always relieve the fuel system pressure prior to disconnecting any fuel system component (injector, fuel rail, pressure regulator, etc.), fitting or fuel line connection. Exercise extreme caution whenever relieving fuel system pressure to avoid exposing skin, face and eyes to fuel spray. Please be advised that fuel under pressure may penetrate the skin or any part of the body that it contacts.

• Immediately cap all open fittings to prevent contaminants from entering the fuel system during service.

• Fuel injection equipment is manufactured to very precise tolerances and fine clearances. It is therefore essential that absolute cleanliness is observed when working with these components. Always install blanking plugs to any open orifices or tubes.

• When reusing liquid or vapor tube connectors, make sure to use compressed air to remove any foreign material from the connector retaining clip area before separating from the tube.

• Always place a shop towel or cloth around the fitting or connection prior to loosening to absorb any excess fuel due to spillage. Ensure that all fuel spillage (should it occur) is quickly removed from engine surfaces. Ensure that all fuel soaked cloths or towels are deposited into a suitable waste container.

• Always keep a dry chemical (Class B) fire extinguisher near the work area.

• Do not allow fuel spray or fuel vapors to come into contact with a spark or open flame.

• Always use a back–up wrench when loosening and tightening fuel line connection fittings. This will prevent unnecessary stress and torsion to fuel line piping.

• Always replace worn fuel fitting O–rings with new. Do not substitute fuel hose or equivalent where fuel pipe is installed.

Before servicing the vehicle, make sure to also refer to the precautions in the beginning of this section as well.

RELIEVING FUEL SYSTEM PRESSURE

2010 Models

See Figure 259.

1. Before servicing the vehicle, refer to Precautions.
2. Remove the front passenger door frame scuff plate (retained by internal metal clips).
3. Remove the front passenger side interior kick panel.

➡️**It may be necessary to reposition the lower end of the door jam weather stripping to remove the front passenger door side interior kick panel.**

4. Disconnect the Inertia Fuel Shutoff (IFS) switch electrical connector.
5. Start the engine and let it idle until it stalls.
6. After the engine stalls, crank it for 5 seconds to ensure all system pressure is relieved.
7. Turn the ignition switch to the OFF position.
8. When the fuel system maintenance and/or repair is complete, reconnect the IFS electrical connector.

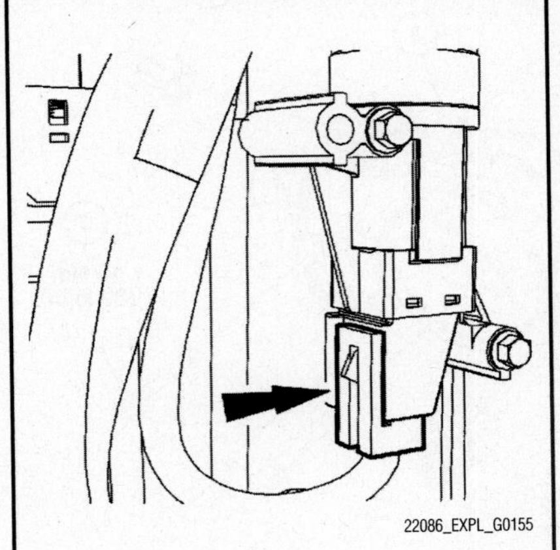

Fig. 259 Disconnect the Inertia Fuel Shutoff (IFS) switch electrical connector

22086_EXPL_G0155

2011 Models

1. Before servicing the vehicle, refer to Precautions.

✳️ CAUTION

Before working on or disconnecting any of the fuel tubes or fuel system components, relieve the fuel system pressure to prevent accidental spraying of fuel. Fuel in the fuel system remains under high pressure, even when the engine is not running. Failure to follow this instruction may result in serious personal injury.

➡️**The Fuel Pump (FP) relay is located in the Battery Junction Box (BJB), location F15.**

2. Remove the Fuel Pump (FP) relay.

➡️**The engine will crank and not start.**

3. Crank the engine for approximately 20 seconds.
4. Crank the engine an additional 20 seconds to make sure the fuel system pressure has been released.
5. Turn the ignition switch to the OFF position.
6. When fuel system service is complete, install the Fuel Pump (FP) relay.

➡️**It may take more than one key cycle to pressurize the fuel system. Cycle the ignition key and wait 3 seconds to pressurize the fuel system.**

7. Check for leaks prior to starting the engine.
8. Start the vehicle and check the fuel system for leaks

FUEL FILTER

REMOVAL & INSTALLATION

2010 Models

See Figure 260.

1. Before servicing the vehicle, refer to Precautions.
2. Disconnect the battery ground cable.
3. Properly relieve the fuel system pressure.
4. Raise the vehicle on a hoist.
5. Remove the bolts and the fuel filter heat shield.
6. Remove the nuts and the fuel filter shield.
7. Disconnect the quick release and

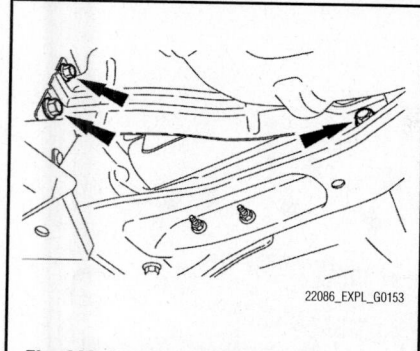

Fig. 260 Removing the fuel filter heat shield—4.0L & 4.6L engines

spring lock couplings and remove the fuel filter.

To install:

8. Remove any fuel line caps.

9. Install the new fuel filter, connecting the quick-release and spring-lock couplings.

10. Install the fuel filter shield.

11. Install the fuel filter heat shield. Torque the bolts to 15 ft. lbs. (20 Nm).

12. Reconnect the battery ground cable.

13. Lower the vehicle.

14. Start the vehicle, check for leaks and repair if necessary.

2011 Models

A lifetime fuel filter is used and serviced as part of the Fuel Pump (FP) module.

FUEL PUMP/ FUEL PUMP MODULE/FUEL TANK MODULE

REMOVAL & INSTALLATION

2010 Models

See Figure 261.

1. Before servicing the vehicle, refer to the Fuel System Precautions.

2. With the vehicle in NEUTRAL, position it on a hoist.

3. Release the fuel system pressure.

4. Remove the fuel tank. Refer to Fuel Tank.

5. Remove the EVAP canister.

6. Remove the fuel tank shield.

7. Disconnect the fuel pressure sensor and vapor tube assembly-to-fuel pump and the fuel tank vapor valves quick connect couplings.

8. Disconnect the vapor tube fitting.

9. Disconnect the fuel supply tube-to-fuel pump quick connect coupling.

10. Remove the fuel supply tube.

11. Using the special tool, remove the fuel pump locking ring.

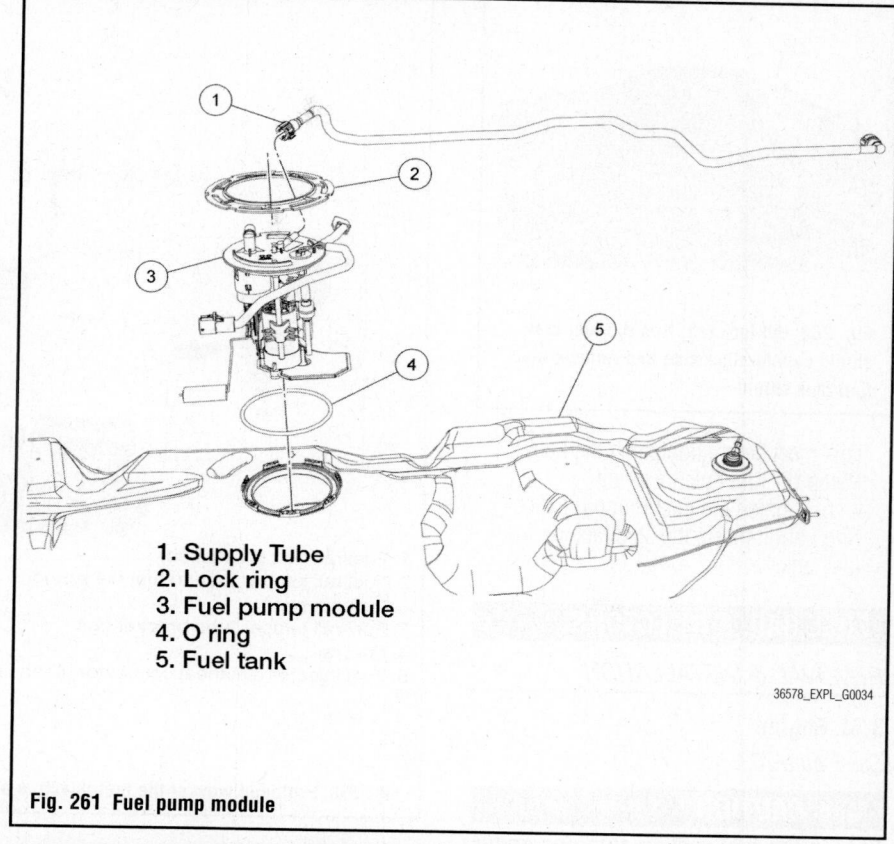

1. Supply Tube
2. Lock ring
3. Fuel pump module
4. O ring
5. Fuel tank

Fig. 261 Fuel pump module

⁂ WARNING

The fuel pump module must be handled carefully to avoid damage to the float arm and filter.

12. Remove the fuel pump module and the O-ring seal. Discard the O-ring seal.

To install:

13. Installation is the reverse of the removal procedure.

2011 Models

See Figure 262.

1. Before servicing the vehicle, refer to the Fuel System Precautions.

2. Remove the Fuel tank, as outlined in this section.

3. Lift lock tab, turn the fuel tank shield counterclockwise and remove the fuel tank shield.

➡**Place absorbent toweling in the immediate surrounding area in case of fuel spillage.**

⁂ WARNING

Carefully install the Fuel Tank Sender Unit Wrench to avoid damaging the fuel level sensor when removing the lock ring.

4. Using the Fuel Tank Sender Unit Wrench, remove the Fuel Pump (FP) module lock ring.

5. Carefully lift the Fuel Pump (FP) module out of the fuel tank enough to access and release the internal fuel tube-to-Fuel Pump (FP) module quick connect coupling.

➡**Some residual fuel may remain in the Fuel Pump (FP) module. Carefully drain into a suitable container.**

6. Completely remove the Fuel Pump (FP) module from the fuel tank.

➡**Inspect the surfaces of the Fuel Pump (FP) module flange and fuel tank O-ring seal contact surfaces. Do not polish or adjust the O-ring seal contact area of the fuel tank flange or the fuel tank. Install a new Fuel Pump (FP) module or fuel tank if the O-ring seal contact area is bent, scratched or corroded.**

7. Remove and discard the Fuel Pump (FP) module O-ring seal.

To install:

8. To install, reverse the removal procedure and note the following:

   a. Make sure the alignment arrows on the Fuel Pump (FP) module and the fuel

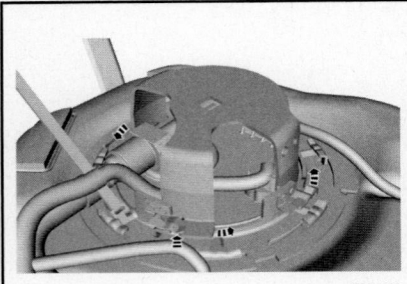

Fig. 262 Lift lock tab, turn the fuel tank shield counterclockwise and remove the fuel tank shield

tank meet before tightening the Fuel Pump (FP) module lock ring.

    b. Tighten the Fuel Pump (FP) lock ring until it meets the stop tabs on the fuel tank.

FUEL RAIL & INJECTORS

REMOVAL & INSTALLATION

3.5L Engine

See Figure 263.

> #### ☼ CAUTION
>
> **Fuel in the fuel system remains under high pressure even when the engine is not running. Before working on or disconnecting any of the fuel lines or fuel system components, the fuel system pressure must be relieved. Failure to follow these instructions may result in personal injury.**

> #### ☼ WARNING
>
> **If used as a leverage device, the fuel rail may be damaged. Care must be taken when working around the fuel rail.**

  1. Before servicing the vehicle, refer to the Fuel System Precautions.
  2. Release the fuel system pressure.
  3. Disconnect the battery ground cable.
  4. Remove the upper intake manifold, as outlined in the Engine Mechanical Section.
  5. Remove the fuel rail jumper tube bracket bolt.
  6. Disconnect the fuel rail jumper tube to fuel rail spring lock coupling and position the tube assembly aside.
  7. Disconnect the 6 fuel injector electrical connectors.
  8. Remove the 4 fuel rail bolts.
  9. Remove the fuel rail and injectors as an assembly.

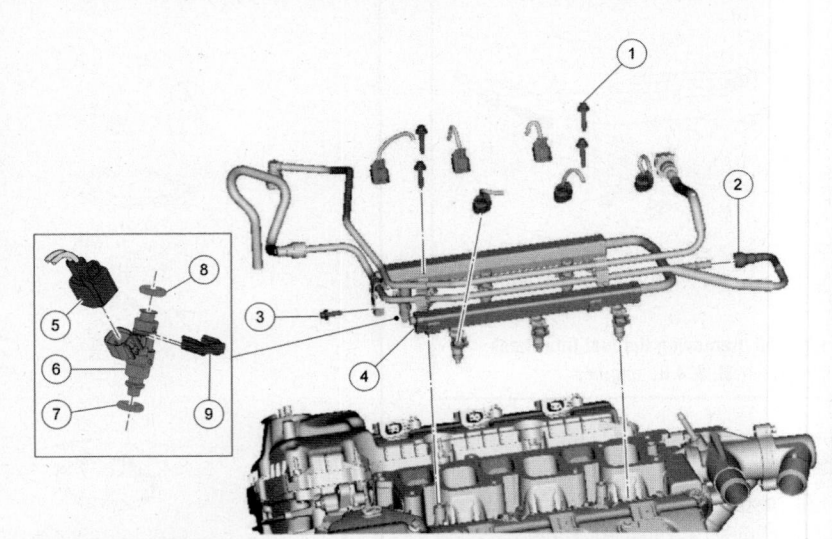

1. Fuel rail bolt (4 required)
2. Fuel rail jumper tube to fuel rail spring lock coupling
3. Fuel rail jumper tube bracket bolt
4. Fuel rail
5. Fuel injector electrical connector (6 required)
6. Fuel injector (6 required)
7. Lower fuel injector O-ring seal (6 required)
8. Upper fuel injector O-ring seal (6 required)
9. Fuel injector clip (6 required)

Fig. 263 Exploded view of the fuel injectors and fuel rail—3.5L engine

  10. Remove the 6 fuel injector clips and the 6 fuel injectors.

To install:

➡ **Use O-ring seals that are made of special fuel-resistant material. The use of ordinary O-rings seals can cause the fuel system to leak. Do not reuse the O-ring seals.**

➡ **The upper and lower fuel injector O-ring seals are similar in appearance but are not interchangeable.**

➡ **Install the new fuel injector O-ring seals and lubricate them with clean engine oil.**

  11. Replace the 12 fuel injector O-ring seals and lubricate them with clean engine oil.
  12. Install the 6 fuel injectors and the 6 fuel injector clips into the fuel rail.
  13. Install the fuel rail and fuel injectors as an assembly.
  14. Install the 4 fuel rail bolts. Tighten to 89 inch lbs. (10 Nm).
  15. Connect the 6 fuel injector electrical connectors.
  16. Position the tube assembly and connect the fuel rail jumper tube to fuel rail spring lock coupling.
  17. Install fuel rail jumper tube bracket bolt. Tighten to 89 inch lbs. (10 Nm).

  18. Install the upper intake manifold, as outlined in the Engine Mechanical.
  19. Connect the battery ground cable.
  20. Pressurize the fuel system

4.0L Engine

See Figure 264.

> #### ☼ CAUTION
>
> **Fuel in the fuel system remains under high pressure even when the engine is not running. Before working on or disconnecting any of the fuel lines or fuel system components, the fuel system pressure must be relieved. Failure to follow these instructions may result in personal injury.**

> #### ☼ WARNING
>
> **If used as a leverage device, the fuel rail may be damaged. Care must be taken when working around the fuel rail.**

  1. Before servicing the vehicle, refer to the Fuel System Precautions.
  2. Remove the intake manifold. Refer to Intake Manifold in Engine Mechanical.

3. Disconnect the spring lock coupling.

4. Remove the fuel supply tube bracket bolt.

5. Disconnect the fuel injector electrical connectors.

6. Disconnect the fuel pressure and temperature sensor electrical and vacuum connectors.

7. Remove the bolts and the fuel rail and injectors as an assembly.

✳✳ WARNING

O-ring seals are made of special fuel-resistant material. Use of ordinary O-ring seals can cause the fuel system to leak. Do not reuse O-ring seals.

➡ **Install new fuel injector-to-intake manifold O-ring seals and lubricate them with clean engine oil.**

8. Remove the fuel injectors and the fuel injector O-ring seals.

✳✳ WARNING

O-ring seals are made of special fuel-resistant material. Use of

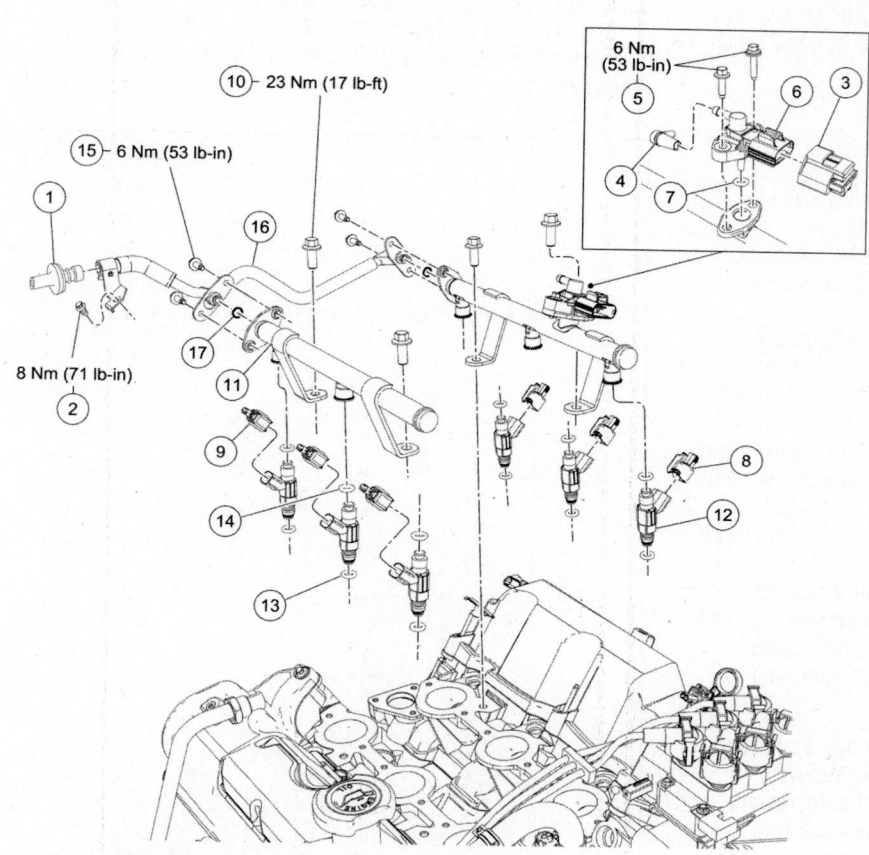

1. Fuel tube spring lock coupling
2. Fuel supply tube bracket bolt
3. Fuel pressure and temperature sensor electrical connector
4. Fuel pressure and temperature sensor vacuum hose
5. Fuel rail pressure and temperature sensor bolts (2 required)
6. Fuel rail pressure and temperature sensor
7. Fuel rail pressure and temperature sensor O-ring seal
8. Fuel injector electrical connector (LH side) (3 required)
9. Fuel injector electrical connector (RH side) (3 required)
10. Fuel rail bolt (4 required)
11. Fuel rail
12. Fuel injector (6 required)
13. Fuel injector-to-cylinder head O-ring seal (6 required)
14. Fuel injector-to-fuel rail O-ring seal (6 required)
15. Fuel supply tube bolt (4 required)
16. Fuel supply tube
17. Fuel supply tube O-ring seal (2 required)

36578_EXPL_G0036

Fig. 264 Fuel rail, injectors and related parts—4.0L engine

ordinary O-ring seals can cause the fuel system to leak. Do not reuse O-ring seals.

➡**Install new fuel injector-to-fuel rail O-ring seals and lubricate them with clean engine oil.**

To install:

9. Installation is the reverse of the removal procedure. Observe the following tightening specifications:
- Fuel rail bolts to 17 ft. lbs. (23 Nm).
- Fuel supply bracket bolt to 71 inch lbs. (8 Nm).

4.6L Engine

See Figure 265.

1. Before servicing the vehicle, refer to the Fuel System Precautions.
2. Release the fuel system pressure.
3. Disconnect the fuel supply tube spring lock coupling.
4. Detach the 2 Positive Crankcase Ventilation (PCV) coolant hose retainers from the fuel rail stud bolts and position the hose aside.
5. Disconnect the fuel rail pressure and temperature sensor electrical connector and vacuum hose.
6. Disconnect the 8 fuel injector electrical connectors.
7. Remove the fuel rail stud bolts.
8. Remove the fuel rail and fuel injectors as an assembly from the intake manifold.
9. Remove the retaining clips and fuel injectors from the fuel rail.

➡**The fuel injector clip can be reused if it is not damaged during removal. If the clip is reused, the 2 sides of the clip should be squeezed back into shape by placing it between index finger and thumb.**

10. Remove and discard the fuel injector O-ring seals.

To install:

11. Installation is the reverse of the removal procedure, noting the following:
   a. Use new O-ring seals.
   b. Use new fuel injector retaining clips, if needed.
   c. Tighten the fuel rail stud bolts to 89 inch lbs. (10 Nm).

FUEL TANK

REMOVAL & INSTALLATION

2010 Models

See Figure 266.

1. Before servicing the vehicle, refer to the Fuel System Precautions.
2. Release the fuel system pressure.
3. Disconnect negative battery cable.
4. Remove the driveshaft. For additional information, refer to Driveshaft in Drivetrain.
5. Drain the fuel tank.
6. If equipped, remove the 4 bolts and the transfer case skid plate.
7. Disconnect the filler pipe vapor tube-to-Fuel Tank Pressure (FTP) sensor and vapor tube assembly quick connect coupling.
8. Disconnect the fuel vapor hose from the Evaporative Emission (EVAP) canister vent valve.

9. Remove the 3 bolts and the fuel filter heat shield.
10. Remove the 2 nuts and the fuel filter shield.
11. Disconnect the fuel filter outlet quick connect coupling.
12. Disconnect the FTP and tube assembly-to-vapor tube quick connect coupling.
13. If equipped, remove the 4 bolts, 1 nut and the fuel tank skid plate.
14. Using a suitable jack, support the fuel tank.
15. Remove the bolt and the fuel tank rear support strap.

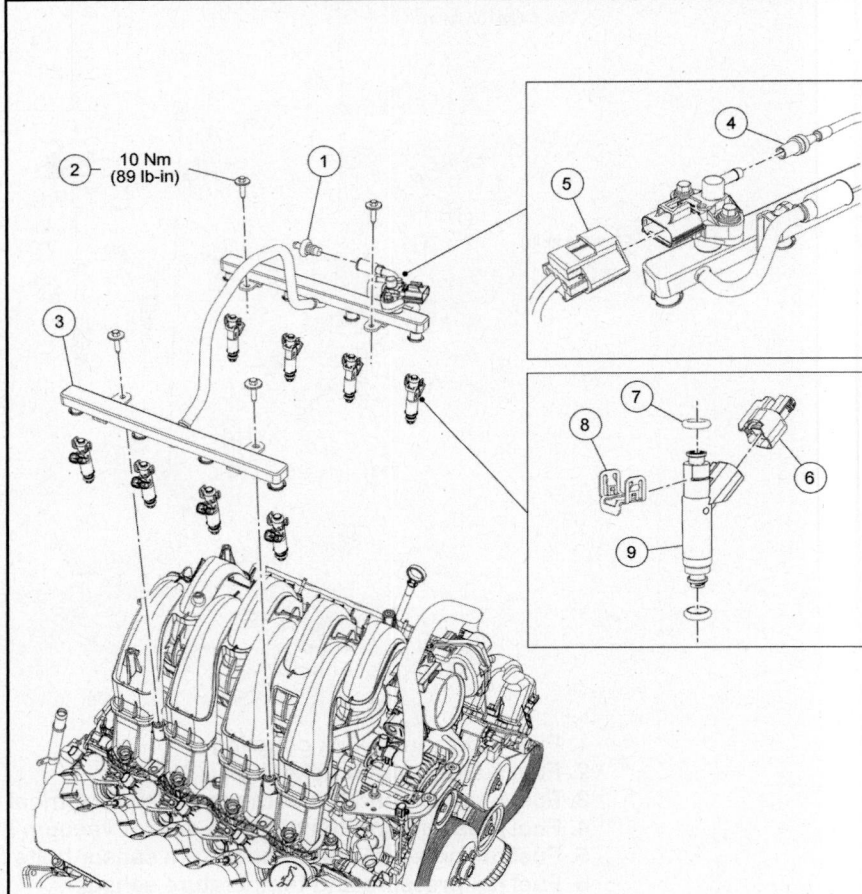

1. Fuel supply tube spring lock coupling
2. Fuel rail bolt (4 required)
3. Fuel rail
4. Vacuum hose
5. Fuel rail pressure and temperature sensor electrical connector
6. Fuel injector electrical connector (8 required)
7. O-ring seal (16 required)
8. Fuel injector retaining clip (8 required)
9. Fuel injector

36578_EXPL_G0037

Fig. 265 Exploded view of the fuel rail and injector components—4.6L engine

16. Remove the nut and the fuel tank front support strap.

17. Lower the fuel tank far enough to access the Fuel Pump (FP) electrical connector and disconnect the connector.

18. Remove the fuel tank from the vehicle.

➡**Make sure the fuel and vapor tubes are correctly routed prior to installing the fuel tank.**

To install:

19. To install, reverse the removal procedure and note the following:

   a. Tighten transfer case skid plate to 30 ft. lbs. (40 Nm).

   b. Tighten fuel filter heat shield to 15 ft. lbs. (20 Nm).

   c. Tighten fuel filter shield to 53 inch lbs. (6 Nm).

   d. Tighten fuel tank skid plate to 30 ft. lbs. (40 Nm).

   e. Tighten fuel tank support straps to 35 ft. lbs. (48 Nm).

2011 Models

1. Before servicing the vehicle, refer to the Fuel System Precautions.

2. With the vehicle in NEUTRAL, position it on a hoist.

3. Remove the muffler and tail pipe.

4. Drain the fuel tank.

5. If equipped, remove the driveshaft.

6. Remove the Evaporative Emission (EVAP) canister.

7. Disconnect the fuel vapor tube assembly-to-fuel tank filler pipe recirculation quick connect coupling.

8. Disconnect the fuel tank jumper tube-to-Fuel Pump (FP) assembly quick connect coupling.

9. Position the Powertrain Lift under the fuel tank.

10. Loosen the 2 rear fuel tank strap bolts.

11. Remove the 2 front fuel tank strap bolts. Calculate the correct torque wrench setting for the following torque.

➡**Do not bend or distort the fuel tank straps.**

12. Release the 2 straps from the fuel tank and carefully position aside.

13. Partially lower the fuel tank enough to allow access to the fuel tank wire to the main body wiring harness electrical connector.

14. Release the 2 wire harness retainers and disconnect the fuel tank wire to the main body wire harness electrical connector.

15. Release the fresh air hose vent cap and pin-type retainer from the body.

16. Carefully lower and remove the fuel tank from the vehicle.

To install:

17. Installation is the reverse of the removal procedure, noting the following:

   a. Tighten the front fuel tank strap bolts to 26 ft. lbs. (35 Nm).

   b. Tighten the rear fuel tank strap bolts to 26 ft. lbs. (35 Nm).

IDLE SPEED

ADJUSTMENT

The idle speed is controlled by the Electronic Control Module and is not adjustable.

THROTTLE BODY

REMOVAL & INSTALLATION

3.5L Engine

See Figure 267.

1. Remove the Air Cleaner (ACL) outlet pipe.

2. Disconnect the Throttle Body (TB) electrical connector.

3. Remove the 4 bolts and the Throttle Body (TB).

4. Remove and discard the Throttle Body (TB) gasket.

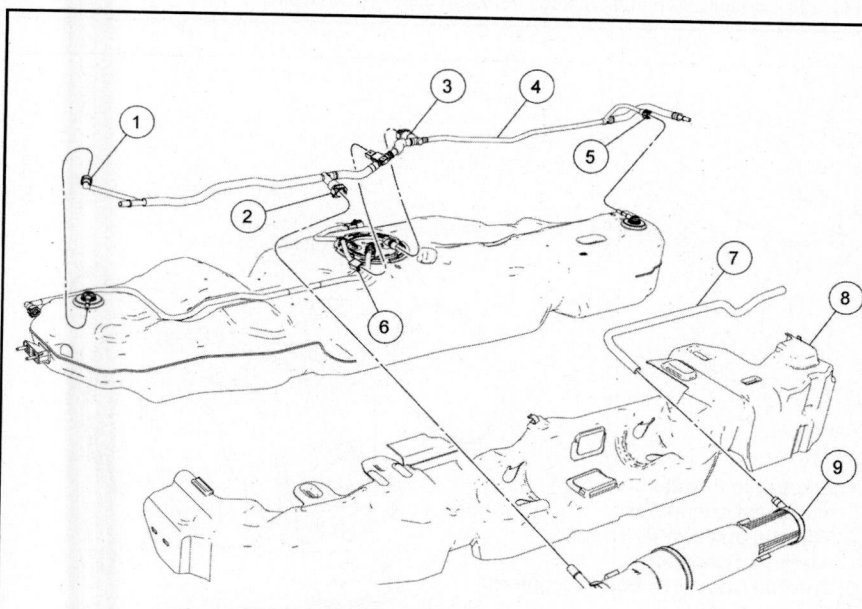

1. Fuel Tank Pressure (FTP) sensor and vapor tube assembly quick connect coupling
2. FTP sensor and vapor tube assembly quick connect coupling
3. FTP sensor and vapor tube assembly quick connect coupling
4. FTP sensor and vapor tube assembly
5. FTP sensor and vapor tube assembly quick connect coupling
6. FTP sensor electrical connector
7. Vapor hose
8. Fuel tank shield
9. Evaporative Emission (EVAP) canister

36578_EXPL_G0169

Fig. 266 Evaporative Emission (EVAP) canister vent valve location

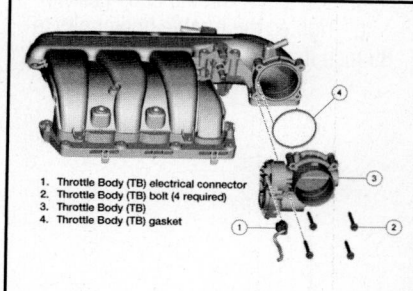

1. Throttle Body (TB) electrical connector
2. Throttle Body (TB) bolt (4 required)
3. Throttle Body (TB)
4. Throttle Body (TB) gasket

N0124807

Fig. 267 Exploded view of the throttle body—3.5L engine

To install:

5. Install a new Throttle Body (TB) gasket.

6. Install the Throttle Body (TB) and the 4 bolts. Tighten to 89 inch lbs. (10 Nm).

7. Connect the Throttle Body (TB) electrical connector.

8. Install the Air Cleaner (ACL) outlet pipe.

4.0L Engine

See Figure 268.

1. Before servicing the vehicle, refer to Precautions.

2. Disconnect the battery ground cable.

3. Remove the air cleaner outlet tube.

4. Disconnect the electronic throttle body (TB) electrical connector.

5. Disconnect the throttle position (TP) sensor electrical connector.

6. Remove the nut and position the wiring harness bracket aside (if needed for clearance).

7. Remove the bolts, the electronic TB and the gasket. Discard the gasket.

To install:

8. Installation is the reverse of the removal procedure.

9. Note the following:

a. Use a new throttle body gasket

b. Tighten the throttle body screws to 80 inch lbs. (9 Nm).

4.6L Engine

See Figure 269.

1. Before servicing the vehicle, refer to Precautions.

2. Disconnect the battery ground cable.

3. Remove the air cleaner outlet tube.

4. Disconnect the electronic throttle body (TB) electrical connectors.

5. Disconnect the throttle position (TP) sensor electrical connector.

6. Remove the bolts, the electronic TB and the gasket. Discard the gasket.

To install:

7. Installation is the reverse of the removal procedure, noting the following:

a. Use a new throttle body gasket.

b. Tighten the throttle body bolts to 89 inch lbs. (10 Nm).

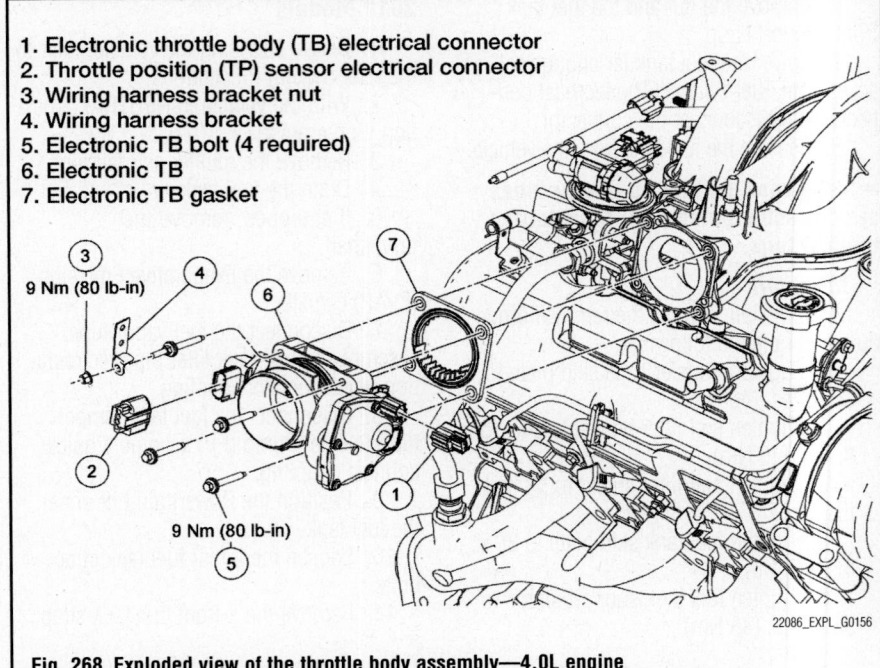

1. Electronic throttle body (TB) electrical connector
2. Throttle position (TP) sensor electrical connector
3. Wiring harness bracket nut
4. Wiring harness bracket
5. Electronic TB bolt (4 required)
6. Electronic TB
7. Electronic TB gasket

9 Nm (80 lb-in)

9 Nm (80 lb-in)

22086_EXPL_G0156

Fig. 268 Exploded view of the throttle body assembly—4.0L engine

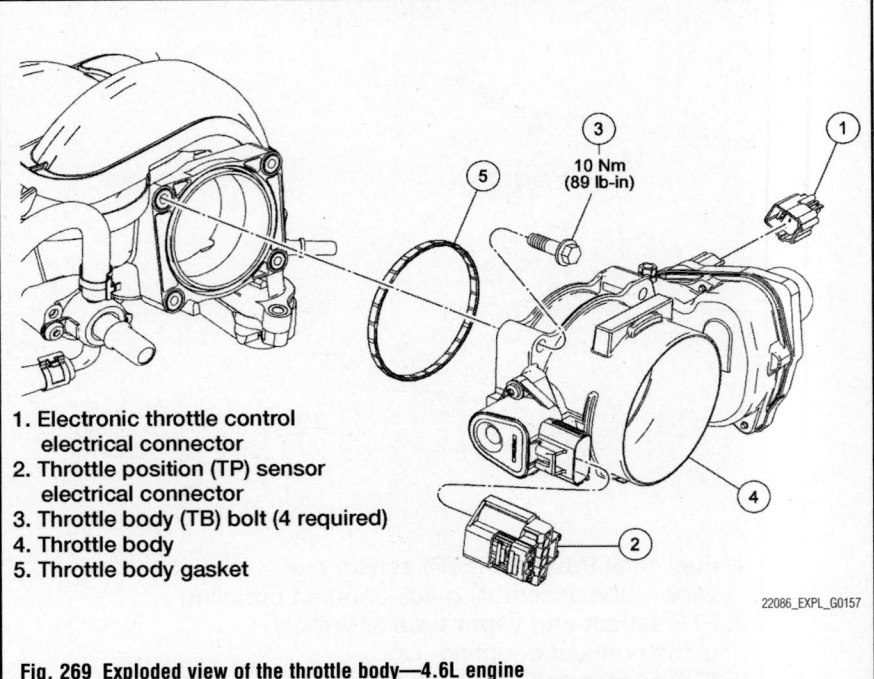

10 Nm (89 lb-in)

1. Electronic throttle control electrical connector
2. Throttle position (TP) sensor electrical connector
3. Throttle body (TB) bolt (4 required)
4. Throttle body
5. Throttle body gasket

22086_EXPL_G0157

Fig. 269 Exploded view of the throttle body—4.6L engine

HEATING & AIR CONDITIONING SYSTEM

BLOWER MOTOR

REMOVAL & INSTALLATION

2010 Models

See Figures 270 through 272.

1. Remove the screw and position aside the vacuum tank.
2. Disconnect the electrical connector.
3. Remove the screws.

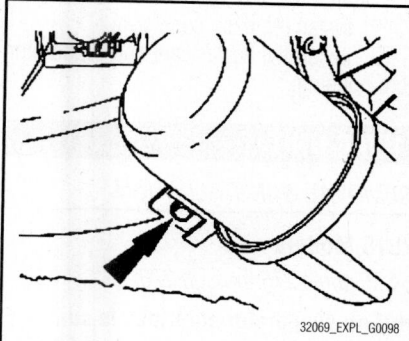

Fig. 270 Remove screw (arrow) from vacuum tank and position it aside

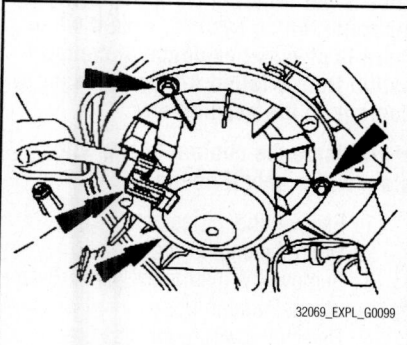

Fig. 271 Blower motor screws and electrical connector

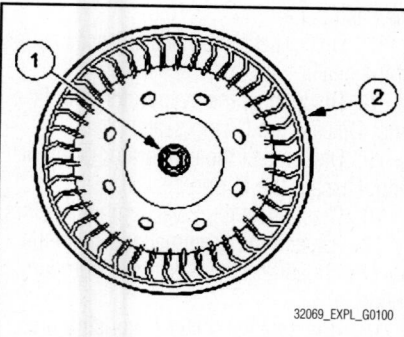

Fig. 272 Push clip (1) and blower motor wheel (2)

4. Remove the blower motor.
5. To remove the blower motor wheel from the blower motor:
   a. Remove the push clip.
   b. Remove the blower motor wheel.

To install:

6. Installation is the reverse of the removal procedure.

2011 Models

See Figure 273.

1. Remove the 3Right Hand (RH) lower instrument panel insulator retainers and the Right Hand (RH) lower instrument panel insulator.
2. Disconnect the blower motor electrical connector.
3. Depressor the 2 retaining tabs and detach the blower motor vent tube from the heater core and evaporator core housing.

➡**The blower motor vent tube must be completely detached from the heater core and evaporator core housing to allow the blower motor to be rotated.**

4. Rotate the blower motor counterclockwise to detach it from the heater core and evaporator core housing and remove the blower motor.

To install:

5. Install the blower motor and rotate clockwise to attach it to the heater core and evaporator core housing.
6. Install the blower motor vent tube to the heater core and evaporator core housing.
7. Connect the blower motor electrical connector.
8. Install the Right Hand (RH) lower

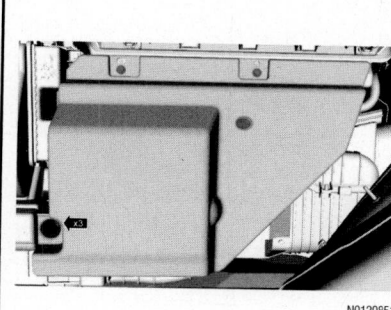

Fig. 273 Remove the 3Right Hand (RH) lower instrument panel insulator retainers and the Right Hand (RH) lower instrument panel insulator

instrument panel insulator and the 3 Right Hand (RH) lower instrument panel insulator retainers.

HEATER CORE

REMOVAL & INSTALLATION

2010 Models

See Figure 274.

➡**If a heater core leak is suspected, the heater core must be pressure leak tested before it is removed from the vehicle.**

1. Remove the heater core and evaporator core housing (HVAC housing). Refer to HVAC Unit.
2. Remove the following:
   • 2 LH floor duct screws
   • LH floor duct
   • 2 RH floor duct screws
   • RH floor duct
   • 3 housing brace screws
   • Housing brace
   • 3 heater tube cover screws
   • Heater tube cover
   • Heater tube seal
   • 4 heater core cover screws
   • Heater core cover
   • Heater core

To install:

3. Install the following:
   • Heater core
   • Heater core cover
   • 4 heater core cover screws
   • Heater tube seal
   • Heater tube cover
   • 3 heater tube cover screws
   • Housing brace
   • 3 housing brace screws
   • RH floor duct
   • 2 RH floor duct screws
   • LH floor duct
   • 2 LH floor duct screws

4. Install the heater core and evaporator core housing (HVAC housing). Refer to HVAC Unit.

2011 Models

See Figure 275.

➡**If a heater core leak is suspected, the heater core must be pressure leak tested before it is removed from the vehicle.**

1. Remove the heater core and evaporator core housing, as outlined in this section.
2. Remove the dash panel seal.

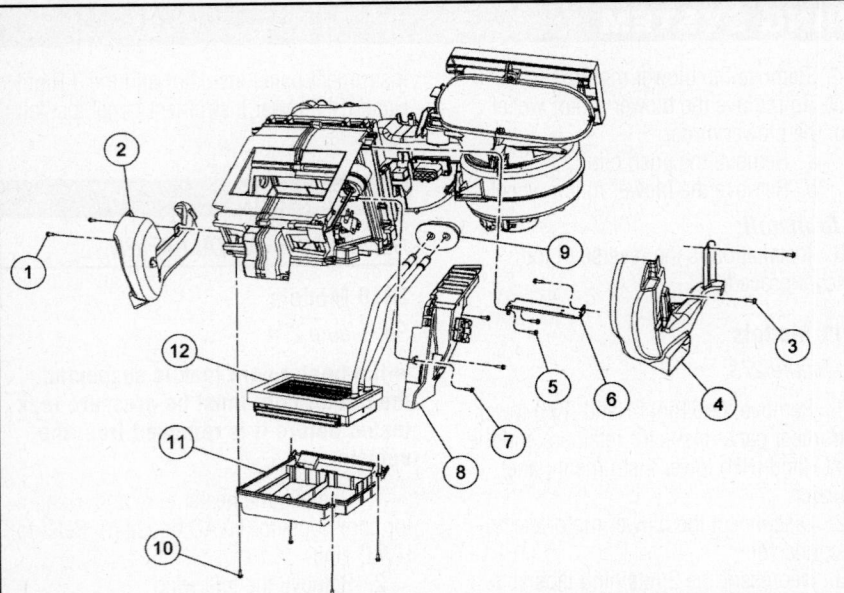

1. LH floor duct screw (2 required)
2. LH floor duct
3. RH floor duct screw (2 required)
4. RH floor duct
5. Housing brace screw (3 required)
6. Housing brace
7. Heater tube cover screw (3 required)
8. Heater tube cover
9. Heater tube seal
10. Heater core cover screw (4 required)
11. Heater core cover
12. Heater core

22086_EXPL_G0227

Fig. 274 Exploded view of the HVAC housing showing the heater core—2010 Models

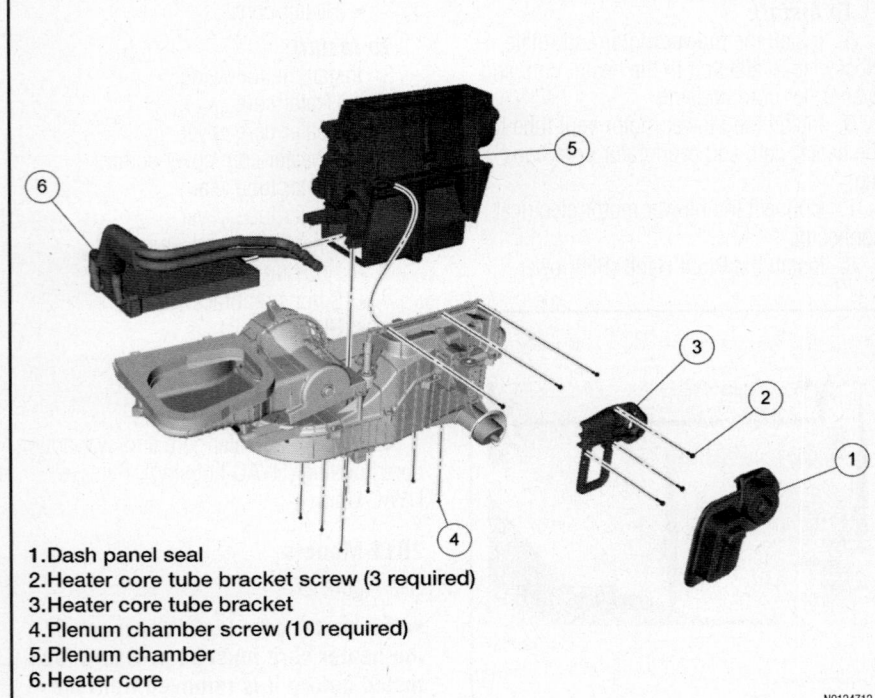

1. Dash panel seal
2. Heater core tube bracket screw (3 required)
3. Heater core tube bracket
4. Plenum chamber screw (10 required)
5. Plenum chamber
6. Heater core

N0124712

Fig. 275 Exploded view of the heater core and related components—2011 Models

3. Remove the 3 heater core tube support bracket screws and heater core tube support bracket.

4. Remove the 10 plenum chamber screws and separate the heater core and evaporator core housing.

5. Remove the heater core.

To install:

6. Install the heater core.

7. Connect the heater core and evaporator core housing and install the 10 plenum chamber screws.

8. Install the heater core tube support bracket and the 3 support bracket screws.

9. Install the dash panel seal.

10. Install the heater core and evaporator core housing.

HVAC UNIT

REMOVAL & INSTALLATION

2010 Models

See Figures 276 through 278.

➡️**If an evaporator core leak is suspected, the evaporator core must be vacuum leak tested before it is removed from the vehicle.**

➡️**Installation of a new suction accumulator is not required when repairing the air conditioning system, except when there is physical evidence of contamination from a failed A/C compressor or damage to the accumulator.**

➡️**Lubricate the coolant hoses with plain water only if needed.**

1. Recover the refrigerant.
2. Drain the engine coolant.
3. Remove the instrument panel. Refer to Instrument Panel in Body
4. Detach the wiring harness bracket (above the heater tube bracket) and position the harness aside.
5. Remove the heater tube bracket nut.
6. Remove the A/C line bracket nut at the dash panel.
7. Disconnect the 2 heater hose clamps at the heater core.
8. Disconnect the evaporator inlet fitting. Discard the O-ring seals.
9. Disconnect the evaporator outlet fitting. Discard the O-ring seals.
10. Disconnect the 2 vacuum connectors.
11. Detach the grommet and push the vacuum lines into the passenger compartment.
12. Remove the 4 HVAC housing nuts.
13. Disconnect the ground terminal bolt.
14. Remove the HVAC housing.

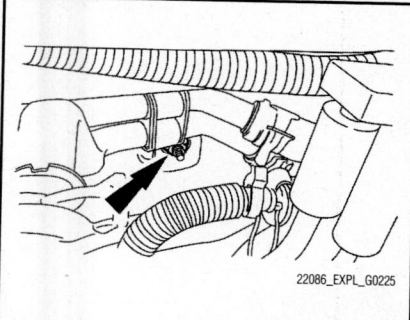

Fig. 276 Remove the heater tube bracket nut

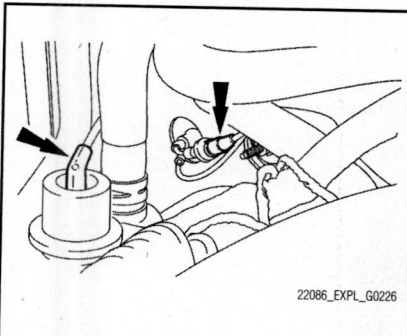

Fig. 277 Disconnect the 2 vacuum connectors

To install:

15. Position the HVAC housing into the vehicle.

16. Disconnect the ground terminal bolt.

17. Install the HVAC housing nuts. Tighten the nuts to 80 inch lbs. (9 Nm).

18. Position the grommet and vacuum lines back into the dash panel.

19. Connect the 2 vacuum connectors.

20. Install new O-ring seals and connect the evaporator inlet and outlet fittings.

21. Connect the heater hoses.

22. Install the A/C line bracket nut at the dash panel.

23. Install the heater tube bracket nut.

24. Attach the wiring harness bracket (above the heater tube bracket)

25. Install the instrument panel. Refer to Instrument Panel in Body.

26. Evacuate and recharge the A/C system. Refer to Charging the System.

27. Refill the cooling system.

28. Perform an A/C system leak test.

HEATER CORE & EVAPORATOR CORE HOUSING

REMOVAL & INSTALLATION

2011 Models

See Figure 279.

➡ **If a heater core leak is suspected, the heater core must be pressure leak tested before it is removed from the vehicle.**

1. Remove the instrument panel assembly.

2. Position the instrument panel with the passenger side supported as shown.

3. Remove the 3 instrument panel insulator screws and remove instrument panel insulator.

4. Remove the 2 Remote Function Actuator (RFA) module nuts and remove the Remote Function Actuator (RFA) module.

5. Remove the 2 floor duct screws and remove the floor duct.

6. Detach the in-vehicle temperature sensor aspirator from the heater core and evaporator core housing.

7. Remove the 6 heater core and evaporator core housing bolts.

8. Disconnect the 3 electrical connectors and detach the wire harness pin-type retainer.

9. Detach the 4 wire harness pin-type retainers and disconnect the electrical connector.

10. Disconnect the 3 electrical connectors, detach the wire harness pin-type retainer and detach the instrument panel wire harness from the heater core and evaporator core housing.

11. Remove the heater core and evaporator core housing.

To install:

12. Install the heater core and evaporator core housing.

13. Attach the instrument panel wire harness to the heater core and evaporator, attach the wire harness pin-type retainers and connect the 3 electrical connectors.

14. Connect the electrical connector and attach the 3 wire harness pin-type retainers.

15. Attach the wire harness pin-type retainer and connect the 3 electrical connectors.

16. Install the 6 heater core and evaporator core housing bolts. Tighten to 62 inch lbs. (7 Nm).

17. Attach the in-vehicle temperature sensor aspirator to the heater core and evaporator core housing.

18. Install the floor duct and the 2 floor duct screws.

19. Install the Remote Function Actuator (RFA) module and install the 2 Remote Function Actuator (RFA) module nuts.

20. Install the instrument panel insulator and the 3 instrument panel insulator screws. Tighten to 27 inch lbs. (3 Nm).

21. Install the instrument panel

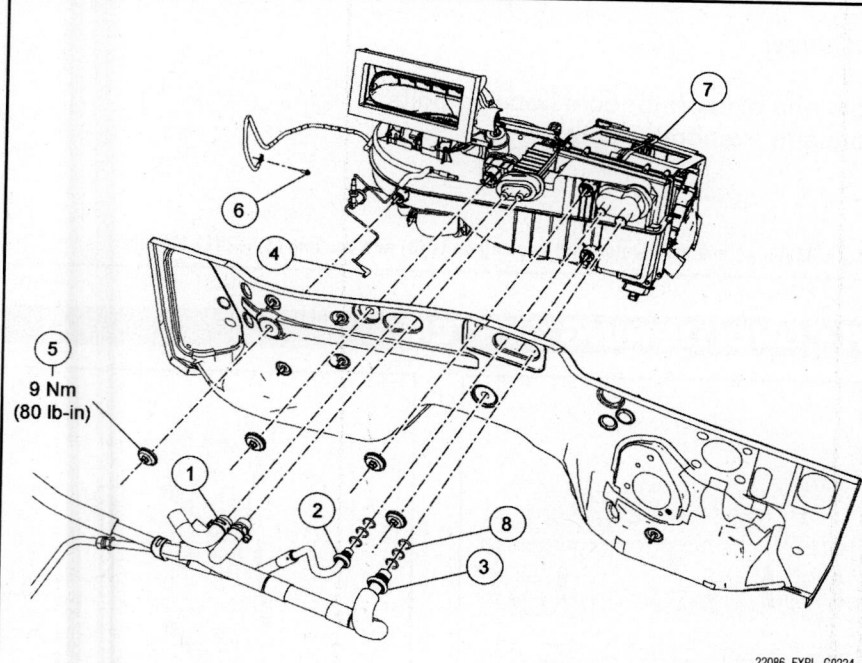

Fig. 278 Exploded view of the HVAC housing assembly: heater hoses (1), pressure hose (2), suction hose (3), vacuum connector (4), retaining nuts (5), screw (6), HVAC housing assembly (7), and O-ring seals (8)—2010 Models

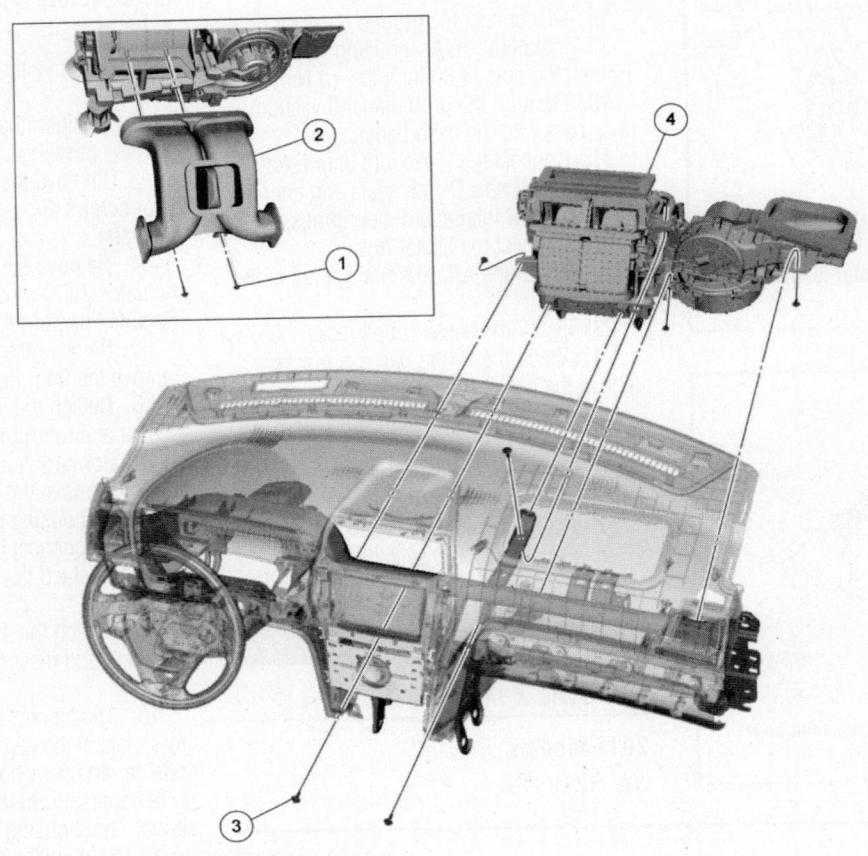

1. Floor duct screw
2. Floor duct
3. Heater core and evaporator core housing bolts
4. Heater core and evaporator core

N0124391

Fig. 279 View of the floor duct screws (1), floor duct (2), heater core & evaporator core housing bolts (3) and housing (4)—2011 Models

AUXILIARY HEATING & AIR CONDITIONING SYSTEM

BLOWER MOTOR

REMOVAL & INSTALLATION

2010 Models

See Figures 280 through 282.

1. Remove the bolts and the rear cargo management cover.

2. Remove the screw and pin-type retainer and remove the rear cargo management system.

3. Remove the access panel.

4. Remove the vent tube.

5. Disconnect the blower motor electrical connector.

6. Remove the 3 blower motor screws.

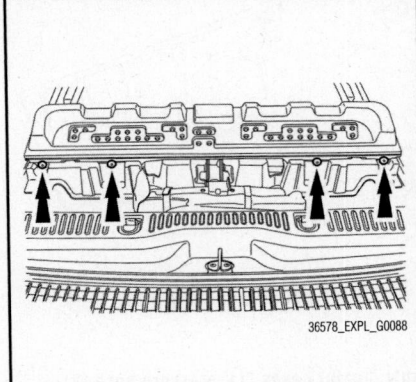

36578_EXPL_G0088

Fig. 280 Rear cargo management cover attachment locations

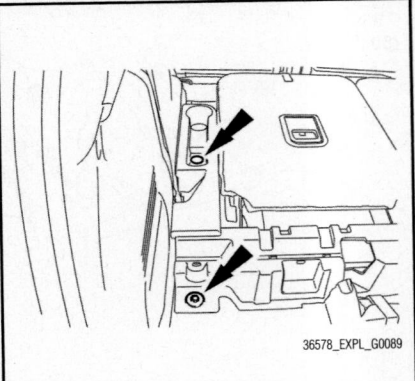

36578_EXPL_G0089

Fig. 281 Rear cargo management system attachment locations

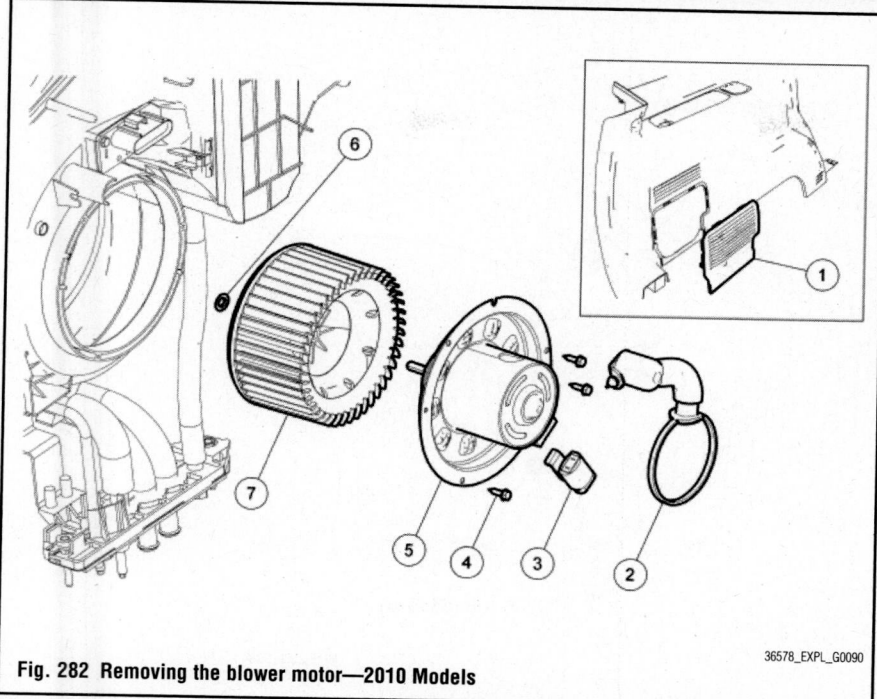

Fig. 282 Removing the blower motor—2010 Models

36578_EXPL_G0090

7. Remove the blower motor.
8. Remove the blower motor retainer.
9. Remove the blower motor wheel.

To install:

10. To install, reverse the removal procedure.

2011 Models

See Figure 283.

1. Remove the LH quarter trim panel.
2. Disconnect the auxiliary blower motor electrical connector.
3. Detach the 2 auxiliary wire harness clips from the auxiliary heater core and evaporator core housing and position the wire harness away from the blower motor.

4. Remove the 3 auxiliary blower motor screws.
5. Remove the auxiliary blower motor.
6. Installation is the reverse of the removal procedure.

HEATER CORE

REMOVAL & INSTALLATION

2010 Models

See Figures 284 through 286.

➡**Lubricate the coolant hoses with plain water only if needed.**

1. Position the vehicle on a hoist with the gear selector in NEUTRAL.
2. Using suitable tools, clamp-off the underbody heater hoses at the floor pan bracket.
3. Remove the parts in the order indicated in the following illustrations.
- (1) Clamp
- (2) Clamp
- (3) Auxiliary line floor pan bracket nut (2 req'd)
- (4) Line bracket screw (4 req'd)
- (5) Line bracket

➡**Item (4), the screw and line bracket are located inside the vehicle above the floor pan line bracket.**

- (6) Auxiliary harness electrical connector
- (7) Auxiliary housing bolt
- (8) Auxiliary housing bolt
- (9) Auxiliary housing nut
- (10) Blend door actuator electrical connector
- (11) Blend door actuator screw (3 req'd)
- (12) Auxiliary blend door actuator
- (13) Temperature blend door actuator screw (3 req'd)
- (14) Auxiliary temperature blend door actuator
- (15) Heater core cover screw (4 req'd)
- (16) Heater core cover
- (17) Clamp
- (18) Clamp
- (19) Auxiliary heater core

To install:

4. Installation is the reverse of the removal procedure.
5. Fill the engine cooling system.
6. Observe the following tightening specifications:
- Auxiliary housing bolts, 53 inch lbs. (6 Nm)
- Auxiliary housing nut, 53 inch lbs. (6 Nm)

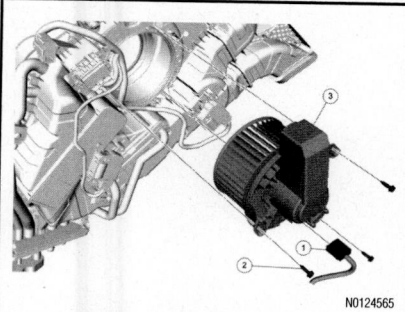

N0124565

Fig. 283 Exploded view of the auxiliary blower motor electrical connector (1), screw (2) and blower motor (3)—2011 Models

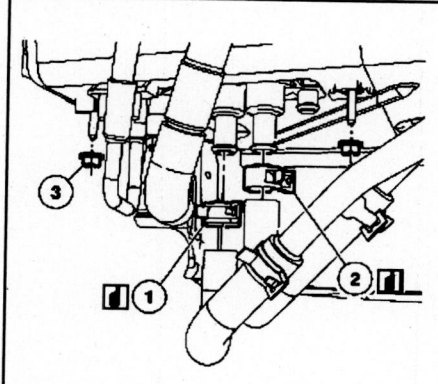

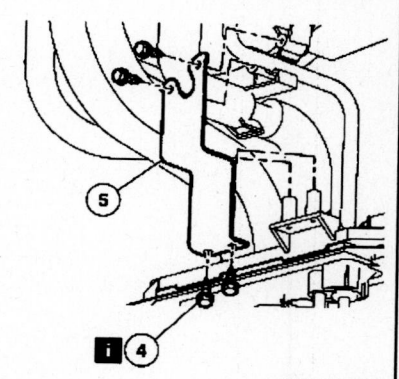

Fig. 284 Auxiliary heater core hose connections

32069_EXPL_G0147

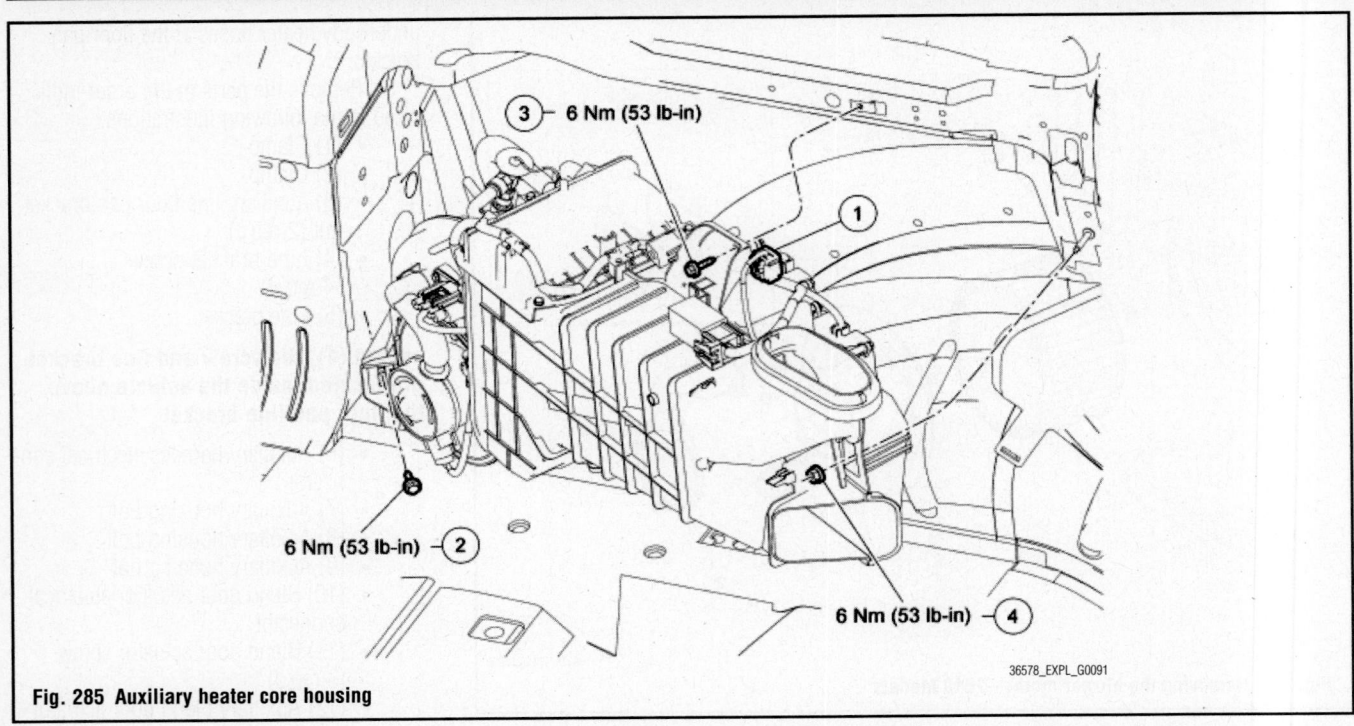

Fig. 285 Auxiliary heater core housing

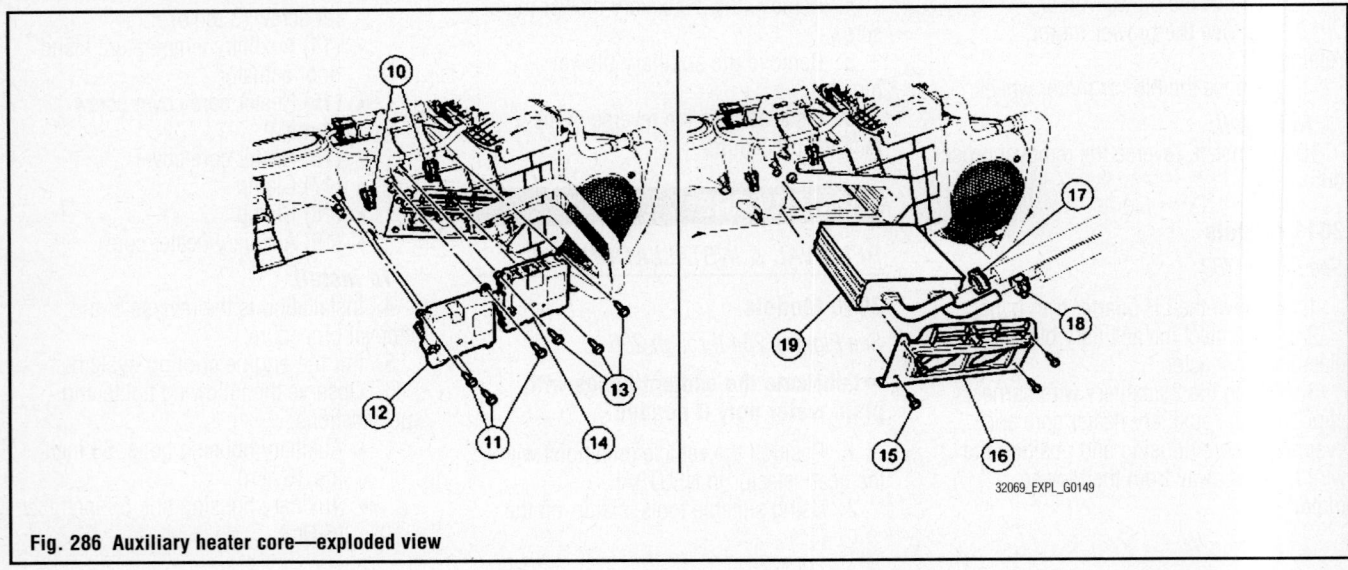

Fig. 286 Auxiliary heater core—exploded view

STEERING

POWER RACK & PINION STEERING GEAR

REMOVAL & INSTALLATION

2010 Models

See Figures 287 through 289.

1. Before servicing the vehicle, refer to Precautions.

All vehicles

⁂ **WARNING**

While repairing the power steering system, care should be taken to prevent the entry of contaminants or premature failure of the power steering components can result.

2. With the vehicle in NEUTRAL, position it on a hoist.

⁂ **WARNING**

Do not allow the steering wheel to rotate while the lower shaft is disconnected or damage to the clockspring can result. If there is evidence that the lower shaft has rotated, the clockspring must be removed and re-centered.

3. Hold the steering wheel in the straight-ahead position using a suitable device.

4. Using a suitable suction device, drain the power steering fluid reservoir.

5. Remove the 2 bolts and the oil drip shield.

➡**Install a new lower shaft-to-steering gear bolt.**

6. Remove and discard the lower shaft-to-steering gear bolt.

7. Disconnect the lower shaft from the steering gear.

8. Remove the steering line clamp plate nut.

9. Rotate the steering line clamp plate and disconnect the power steering lines.

➡**New O-rings must be installed whenever the power steering lines are disconnected.**

10. Remove and discard the 2 O-rings.

➡**New cotter pins must be installed.**

11. Remove and discard the 2 cotter pins.

➡**New tie rod end nuts must be installed.**

12. Remove and discard the 2 tie rod end nuts.

⁂ **WARNING**

Do not damage the tie rod end boot when installing the special tool.

13. Using the special tool, separate the 2 tie rod ends from the wheel knuckle.

14. Remove the 2 steering gear-to-crossmember nuts and bolts.

15. Remove the 2 bolts and remove the steering gear bracket.

4WD vehicles

➡On 4WD vehicles, the following steps (left lower arm only) must be carried out to provide clearance to remove the steering gear.

⁂ **WARNING**

Do not tighten the left lower arm inboard mounting nuts until the installation procedure is complete and the weight of the vehicle is resting on the wheel and tire assemblies. Make sure to tighten the lower arm forward nut before tightening the lower arm-to-frame nuts.

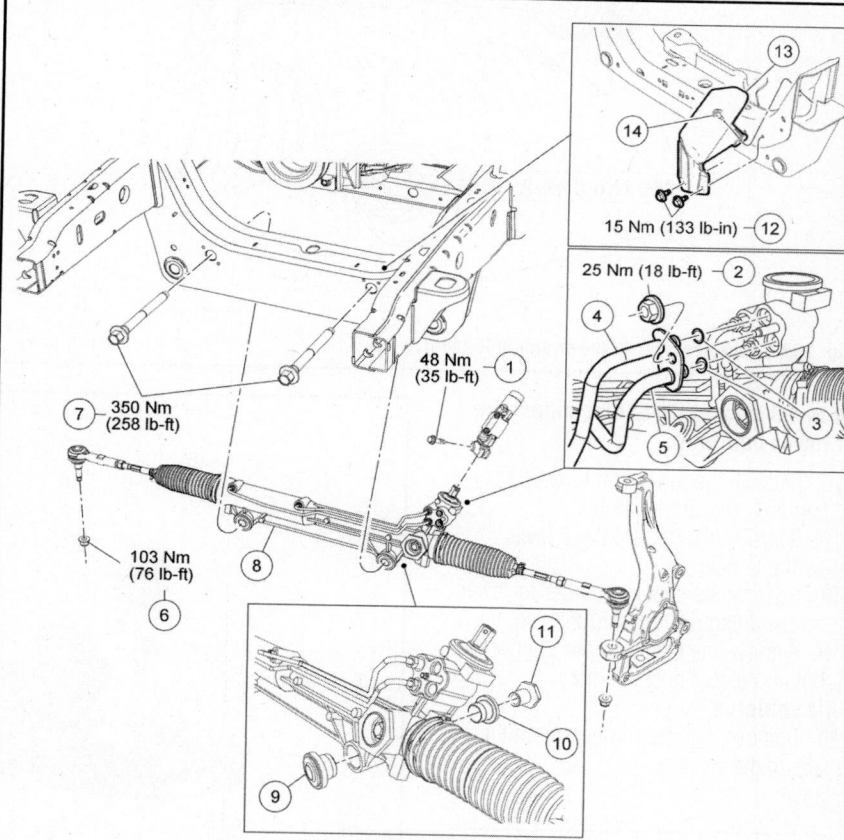

1. Lower steering column shaft-to-steering gear bolt
2. Steering line clamp plate nut
3. O-ring seals (2 required)
4. Power steering fluid cooler
5. Power steering pressure line
6. Tie-rod end nut (2 required)
7. Steering gear-to-crossmember bolts (2 required)
8. Steering gear
9. Forward steering gear bushing (2 required)
10. Rearward steering gear bushing (2 required)
11. Steering gear-to-crossmember nut (2 required)
12. Oil shield-to-crossmember bolts (2 required)
13. Oil shield
14. Oil shield pin-type retainer

36578_EXPL_G0079

Fig. 287 Steering gear and related parts

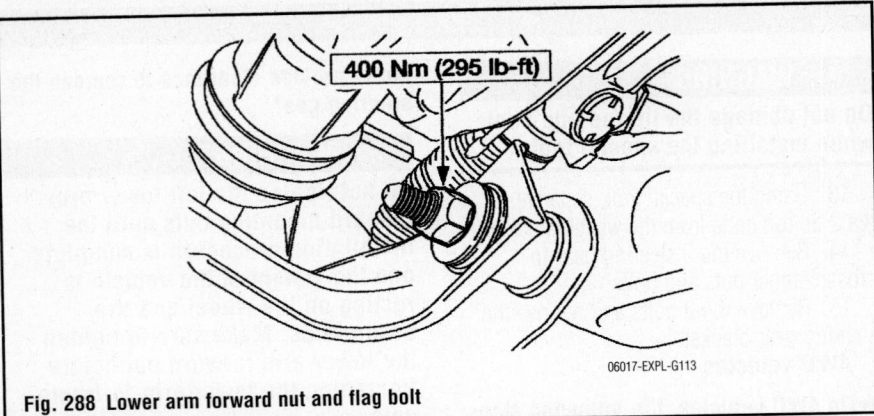

Fig. 288 Lower arm forward nut and flag bolt

400 Nm (295 lb-ft)

06017-EXPL-G113

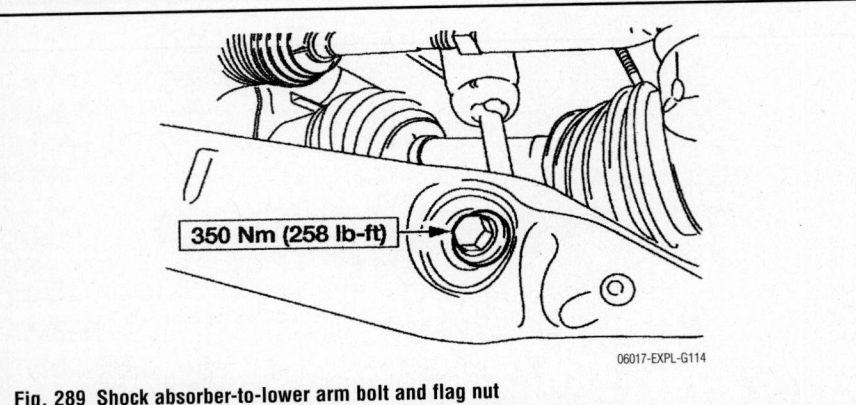

Fig. 289 Shock absorber-to-lower arm bolt and flag nut

350 Nm (258 lb-ft)

06017-EXPL-G114

➡ **It is not necessary to disconnect the left lower ball joint.**

16. Remove the lower arm forward nut and flag bolt. Discard the nut.

17. Remove and discard the 2 lower arm-to-frame nuts.

18. Remove the shock absorber-to-lower arm bolt and flag nut. Discard the flag nut.

19. Remove the stabilizer bar connecting link nut and disconnect the link.

All vehicles

20. Remove the steering gear from the left side of the vehicle.

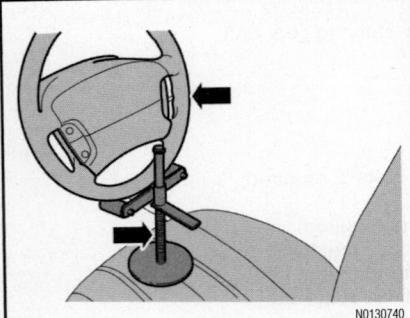

Fig. 290 Using a suitable holding device, hold the steering wheel in the straight-ahead position

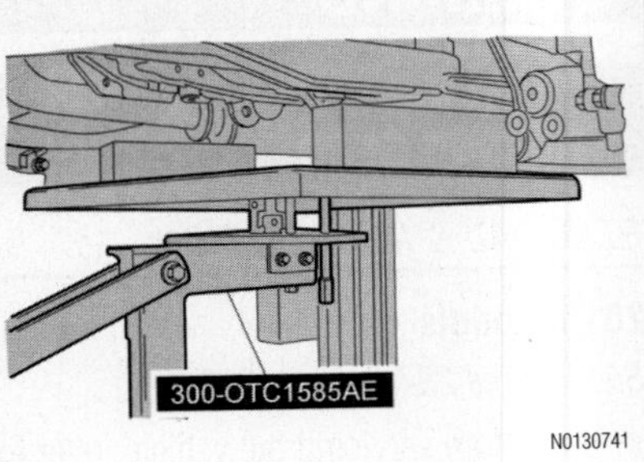

N0130740

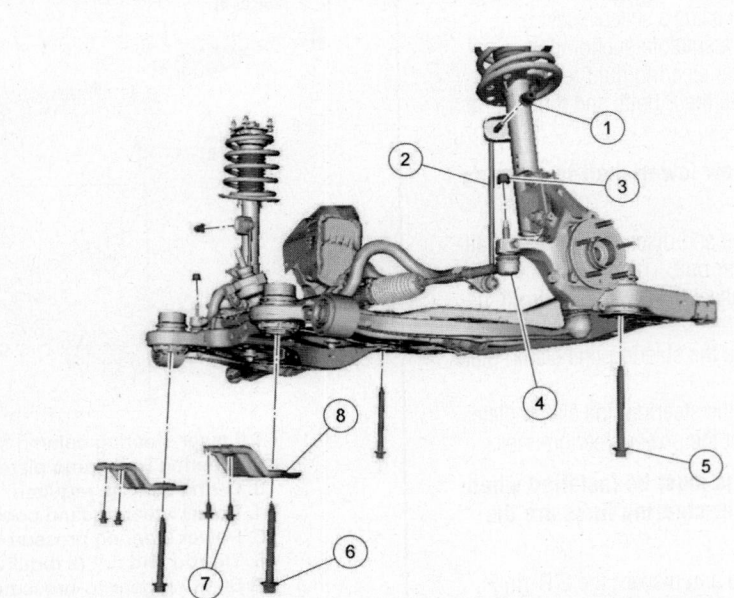

Fig. 291 Position 300-OTC1585AE, or equivalent powertrain lift, under the sub-frame

300-OTC1585AE

N0130741

To install:

21. Installation is the reverse of the removal procedure.

22. Install 2 new O-rings. Fill the power steering system

23. Observe the following torque specifications:

- Oil drip shield: 11 ft. lbs. (15 Nm)
- Lower shaft-to-steering gear bolt: 35 ft. lbs. (48 Nm)
- Fluid line clamp bolt: 18 ft. lbs. (25 Nm)
- Tie rod end nuts: 76 ft. lbs. (103 Nm)

1. Stabilizer bar link upper nut (2 required)
2. Stabilizer bar link
3. Outer tie rod-end nut (2 required)
4. Outer tie rod-end (2 required)
5. Subframe forward bolts (2 required)
6. Subframe rearward bolts (2 required)
7. Subframe support bracket bolt (4 required)
8. Subframe support bracket

N0124445

Fig. 292 Exploded view of the steering gear (1 of 2)—2011 Models

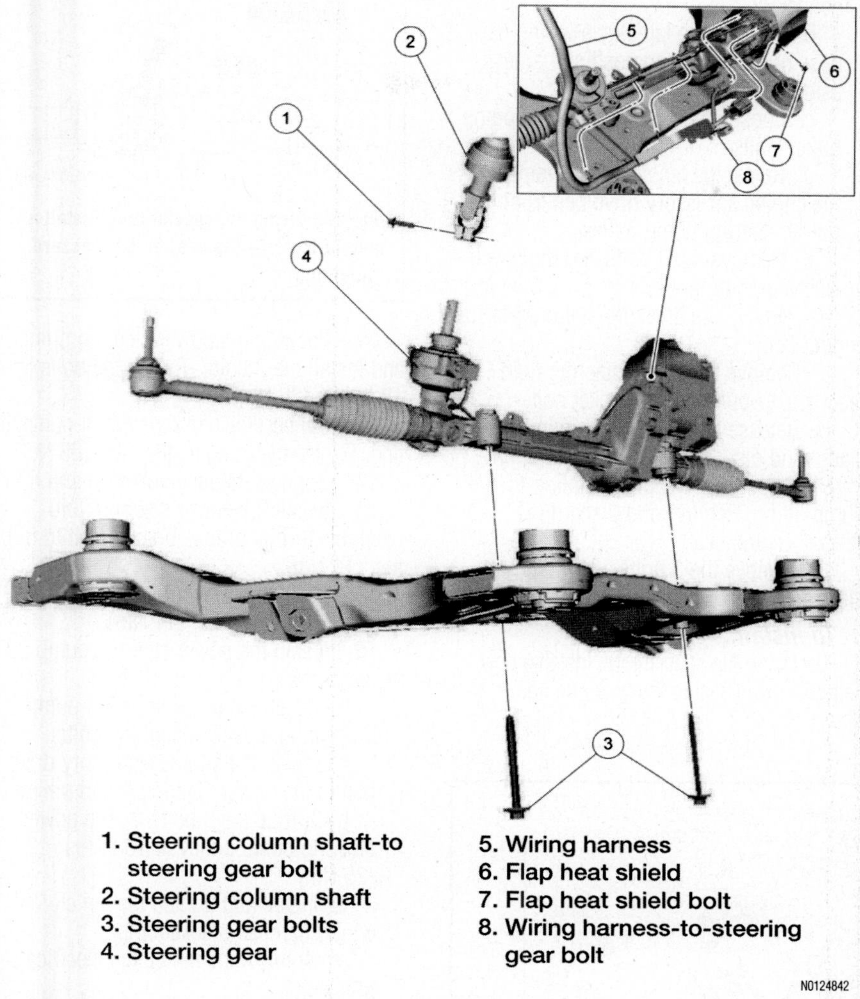

1. Steering column shaft-to steering gear bolt
2. Steering column shaft
3. Steering gear bolts
4. Steering gear
5. Wiring harness
6. Flap heat shield
7. Flap heat shield bolt
8. Wiring harness-to-steering gear bolt

N0124842

Fig. 293 Exploded view of the steering gear (1 of 2)—2011 Models

- Steering gear-to-crossmember nuts and bolts: 258 ft. lbs. (350 Nm)
- Steering gear bracket bolts: 52 ft. lbs. (70 Nm)
- Lower arm forward nut and flag bolt: 296 ft. lbs. (400 Nm)
- Lower arm rearward nut and flag bolt: 148 ft. lbs. (200 Nm)
- Shock absorber-to-lower arm bolt and flag nut: 258 ft. lbs. (350 Nm)
- Stabilizer bar connecting link nut: 26 ft. lbs. (35 Nm)

2011 Models

See Figures 290 through 293.

➡ **If installing a new steering gear, this procedure requires you to connect a suitable scan tool and upload the module configuration information from the Power Steering Control Module (PSCM).**

1. Using a suitable holding device, hold the steering wheel in the straight-ahead position.
2. Remove the front wheels and tires.
3. Remove and discard the steering column shaft-to-steering gear bolt and disconnect the steering column shaft from the steering gear.
4. Remove and discard the 2 stabilizer bar link upper nuts.
5. Remove the 2 outer tie-rod end nuts and separate the tie-rod ends from the wheel knuckle.
6. Remove the 4 retainers and the underbody shield.
7. Remove the exhaust Y-pipe.
8. Remove the roll restrictor-to-subframe bolt.
9. Remove the flap heat shield bolt and position the flap heat shield to access the Electronic Power Assist Steering (EPAS) electrical connectors.

10. Remove the wiring harness-to-steering gear bolt.
11. Disconnect the 2 Electronic Power Assist Steering (EPAS) electrical connectors and detach the 2 wiring pin-type retainers from the steering gear.
12. Remove the 2 RH inner fender shield-to-subframe pin-type retainers.
13. Position 300-OTC1585AE, or equivalent powertrain lift, under the subframe.
14. Remove the 2 subframe rearward bolts, the 4 support bracket bolts and the 2 subframe support brackets.
15. Loosen the 2 subframe forward bolts.
16. Lower the subframe to gain access to the steering gear.
17. Position the stabilizer bar to the full up position.
18. Remove and discard the 2 steering gear bolts and remove the steering gear from the Right Hand (RH) side of the vehicle.

To install:

19. Position the steering gear and install the 2 new steering gear bolts. Tighten to 122 ft. lbs. (165 Nm).
20. Raise the subframe.
21. Position the 2 subframe support brackets and install the 4 subframe support bracket bolts finger-tight.
22. Install the 2 subframe rearward bolts. Tighten the subframe rearward and forward bolts to 148 ft. lbs. (200 Nm).
23. Tighten the 4 subframe support bracket bolts. Tighten to 41 ft. lbs. (55 Nm).
24. Install the 2 RH inner fender shield-to-subframe pin-type retainers.
25. Connect the 2 Electronic Power Assist Steering (EPAS) electrical connectors and attach the wiring harness pin-type retainers to the steering gear.
26. Install the wiring harness-to-steering gear bolt. Tighten to 97 inch lbs. (11 Nm).
27. Position the flap heat shield and install the flap heat shield bolt. Tighten to 97 inch lbs. (11 Nm).
28. Install the roll restrictor-to-subframe bolt. Tighten to 66 ft. lbs. (90 Nm).
29. Install the exhaust Y-pipe.
30. Position the underbody shield and install the 4 retainers.
31. Position the 2 outer tie-rod ends and install the outer tie-rod end nuts. Tighten to 111 ft. lbs. (150 Nm).
32. Connect the stabilizer bar links and install the 2 new stabilizer bar link upper nuts. Tighten to 111 ft. lbs. (150 Nm).
33. Connect the steering column shaft to the steering gear and install the new steering column shaft-to-steering gear bolt. Tighten to 19 ft. lbs. (26 Nm).

34. Install the front wheels and tires.

35. When installing a new steering gear, it must be configured (using vehicle as-built data or module configuration information retrieved earlier in this procedure). Refer to the scan tool instructions to carry out Programmable Module Installation (PMI).

POWER STEERING PUMP

REMOVAL & INSTALLATION

4.0L Engine

See Figures 294 and 295.

✸✸ WARNING

While repairing the power steering system, care should be taken to prevent the entry of contaminants or premature failure of the power steering components can result.

1. Using a suitable suction device, drain the power steering fluid reservoir.

2. With the vehicle in NEUTRAL, position it on a hoist.

3. Remove the power steering pump pulley as follows:

a. Disconnect the fan clutch electrical connector.

b. Remove the fan clutch wiring harness bracket bolt and position harness aside.

c. Loosen the 3 power steering pump pulley bolts.

d. Rotate the tensioner and remove the engine accessory drive belt from the power steering pump pulley.

e. Remove the 3 bolts and the power steering pump pulley.

4. Remove the pressure line bracket-to-engine bolt.

5. Remove the power steering fluid reservoir-to-pump hose bracket bolt.

6. Release the reservoir-to-pump hose clamp and disconnect the hose.

7. Disconnect the pressure line-to-pump fitting. Remove and discard the Teflon® O-ring seal.

8. Remove the 3 bolts and the power steering pump.

To install:

9. Using the special tool, install a new Teflon® O-ring seal to the pressure line fitting.

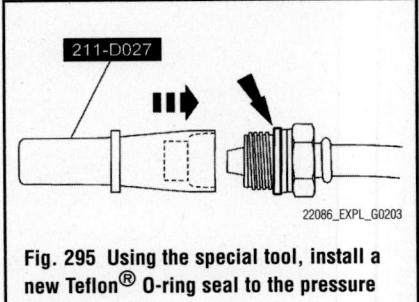

Fig. 295 Using the special tool, install a new Teflon® O-ring seal to the pressure line fitting

10. Position the power steering pump and install the 3 bolts. Torque the bolts to 18 ft. lbs. (25 Nm).

11. Connect the pressure line-to-pump fitting. Tighten the fitting to 48 ft. lbs. (65 Nm).

12. Connect the reservoir-to-pump hose.

13. Install the power steering fluid reservoir-to-pump hose bracket bolt to 8 ft. lbs. (11 Nm).

14. Install the pressure line bracket-to-engine bolt to 8 ft. lbs. (11 Nm).

15. Install the power steering pump pulley as follows:

a. Install the power steering pump pulley and loosely install the bolts.

b. Install the engine accessory drive belt to the power steering pump pulley.

c. Torque the 3 bolts for the power steering pump pulley to 18 ft. lbs. (25 Nm).

d. Install and tighten the fan clutch wiring harness bracket bolt.

e. Connect the fan clutch electrical connector.

16. Fill and bleed the power steering system. Refer to Bleeding.

4.6L Engine

See Figure 296.

1. Using a suitable suction device, drain the power steering fluid reservoir.

2. With the vehicle in NEUTRAL, position it on a hoist.

3. Remove the power steering pump pulley.

4. Remove the pressure line bracket-to-engine nut.

5. Compress the clamp and disconnect the reservoir-to-pump hose.

6. Disconnect the pressure line-to-pump fitting.

7. Remove and discard the Teflon® O-ring seal.

8. Remove the 2 engine wiring bracket nuts and position the wiring harness and ground cable aside.

9. Remove the 3 bolts and the power steering pump.

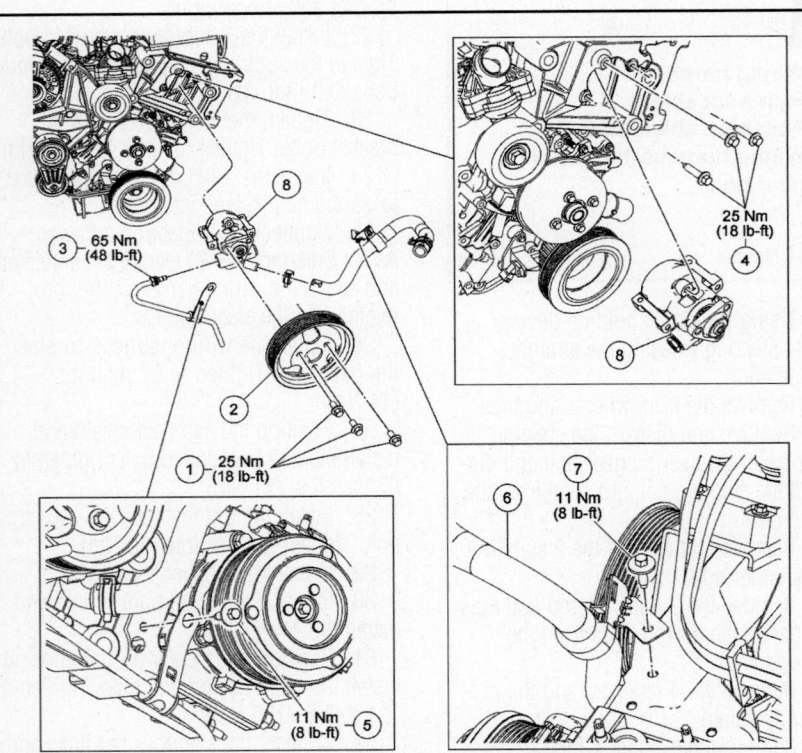

1. Power steering pump pulley bolts (3 required)
2. Power steering pump pulley
3. Pressure line-to-pump fitting
4. Power steering pump bolts (3 required)

5. Pressure line bracket-to-engine bolt
6. Power steering fluid reservoir-to-pump hose
7. Power steering fluid reservoir-to-pump hose bracket bolt
8. Power steering pump

Fig. 294 Showing the power steering pump, reservoir and related components—4.0L Engine

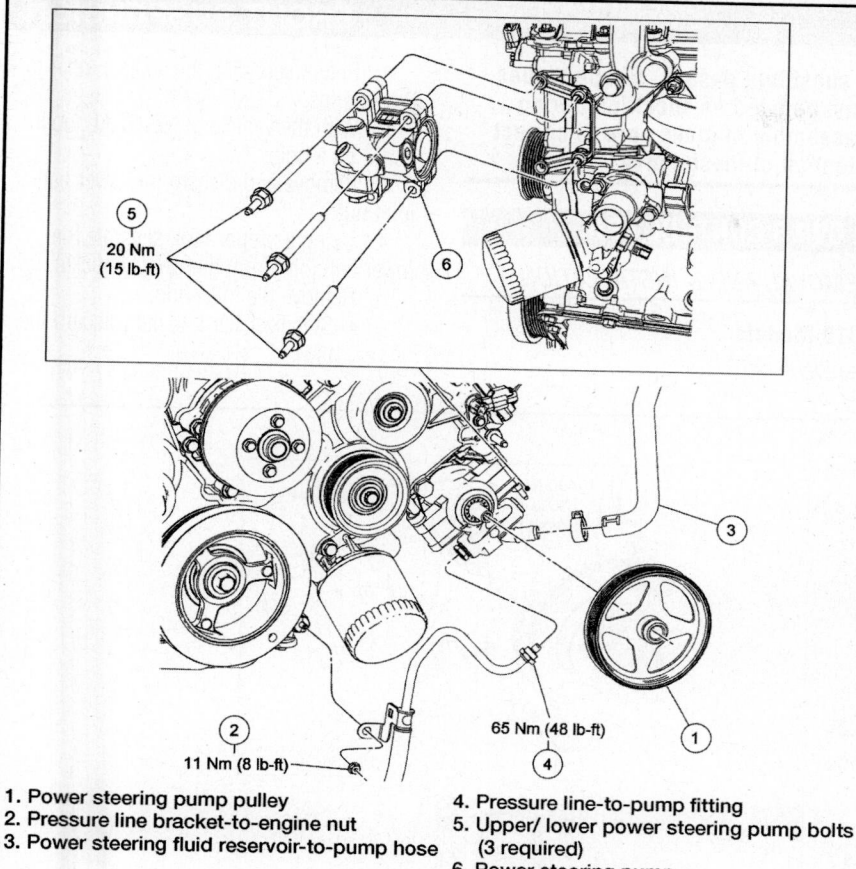

1. Power steering pump pulley
2. Pressure line bracket-to-engine nut
3. Power steering fluid reservoir-to-pump hose
4. Pressure line-to-pump fitting
5. Upper/ lower power steering pump bolts (3 required)
6. Power steering pump

22086_EXPL_G0256

Fig. 296 Showing the power steering pump, hoses and reservoir mounting—4.6L Engine

To install:

10. Using the special tool, install a new Teflon® O-ring seal on the pressure line-to-pump fitting.

11. Position the power steering pump and install the 3 bolts. Tighten to 15 ft. lbs. (20 Nm).

12. Position the ground cable and engine wiring bracket. Install the 2 nuts. Tighten to 15 ft. lbs. (20 Nm).

13. Connect the pressure line-to-pump fitting. Tighten to 48 ft. lbs. (65 Nm).

14. Connect the reservoir-to-pump hose.

15. Install the pressure line bracket-to-engine nut. Tighten to 97 inch lbs. (11 Nm).

16. Install the power steering pump pulley.

17. Fill the power steering system. Refer to Bleeding.

BLEEDING

Special tools:
• Vacuum Pump Kit 416-D002 (D95L-7559-A) or equivalent

• Evacuation Cap, Power Steering 211-265 or equivalent

❄❄ WARNING

If the air is not purged from the power steering system correctly, premature power steering pump failure can result. The condition can occur on pre-delivery vehicles with evidence of aerated fluid or on vehicles that have had steering component repairs.

➡**A whine heard from the power steering pump can be caused by air in the system. The power steering purge procedure must be carried out prior to any component repair for which power steering noise complaints are accompanied by evidence of aerated fluid.**

1. Remove the power steering pump reservoir cap. Check the fluid.

2. Raise the front wheels off the ground.

3. Tightly insert the stopper of the vacuum pump into the reservoir.

4. Start the engine.

5. Install the vacuum pump, apply vacuum, and maintain the maximum vacuum of 20–25 in-Hg (68–85 kPa).

6. If equipped with Hydro-Boost®, apply the brake pedal twice.

❄❄ WARNING

Do not hold the steering wheel against the stops for more than 3 to 5 seconds at a time. Damage to the power steering pump can occur.

7. Cycle the steering wheel fully from stop-to-stop 10 times.

8. Stop the engine.

9. Release the vacuum and remove the vacuum pump.

❄❄ WARNING

Do not overfill the reservoir.

10. Fill the reservoir.
   a. Use approved transmission fluid.

11. Start the engine.

12. Install the vacuum pump. Apply and maintain the maximum vacuum of 20–25 in-Hg (68–85 kPa).

❄❄ WARNING

Do not hold the steering wheel against the stops for more than 3 to 5 seconds at a time. Damage to the power steering pump can occur.

13. Cycle the steering wheel fully from stop-to-stop 10 times.

14. Stop the engine, release the vacuum and remove the vacuum pump.

❄❄ WARNING

Do not overfill the reservoir.

15. Fill the reservoir as needed and install the reservoir cap.

16. Visually inspect the power steering system for leaks.

❄❄ WARNING

Do not overfill the reservoir.

17. Fill the reservoir as needed and visually inspect the power steering system for leaks.

18. Install the reservoir cap.

SUSPENSION

※※ WARNING

Suspension fasteners are critical parts because they affect performance of vital components and systems and their failure may result in major service expense. New parts must be installed with the same part numbers or equivalent part, if replacement is necessary. Do not use a replacement part of lesser quality or substitute design. Torque values must be used as specified during reassembly to make sure of correct retention of these parts.

LOWER CONTROL ARM

REMOVAL AND & INSTALLATION

2010 Models

See Figure 297.

1. Before servicing the vehicle, refer to Precautions.
2. With the vehicle in NEUTRAL, position it on a hoist.
3. Remove and discard the lower ball joint nut.
4. Using a proper tool, separate the lower ball joint from the wheel knuckle.
5. Remove the following:
   - Stabilizer bar link nut (discard the nut)

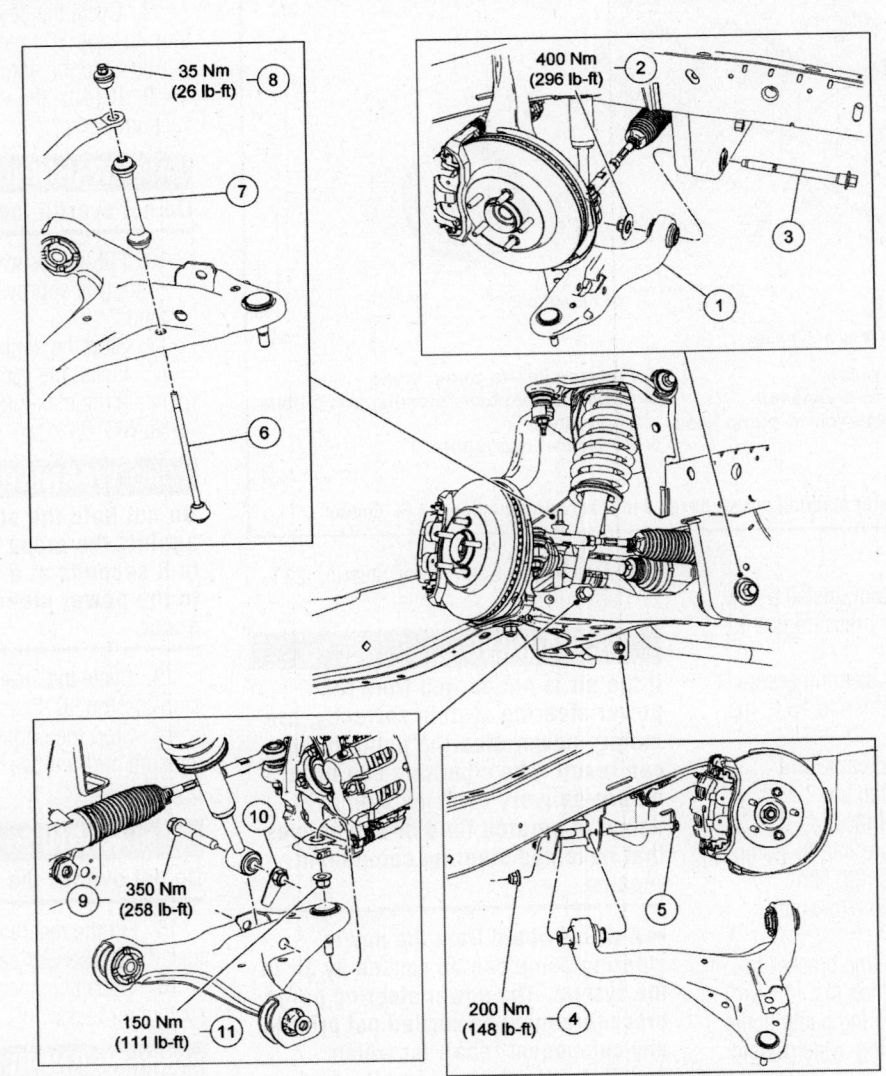

1. LH Lower arm
2. Lower arm forward nut
3. Lower arm forward bolt
4. Lower arm rearward nut
5. Lower arm rearward bolt
6. Stabilizer bar link stud
7. Stabilizer bar link assembly
8. Stabilizer bar link nut
9. Shock absorber lower bolt
10. Shock absorber lower flag nut
11. Lower ball joint nut

22086_EXPL_G0183

Fig. 297 Exploded view of the front suspension, showing the lower control arm and components

- Stabilizer bar link assembly
- Shock absorber lower bolt and flag nut (discard the fasteners)
- Lower arm forward nut and bolt (discard the fasteners)
- Lower arm rearward nut and bolt and the lower control arm

To install:

> **✻✻ WARNING**
>
> **Before tightening any suspension bushing fasteners, use a suitable jack to raise the suspension until the distance between the center of the hub and the lip of the fender is equal to the measurement taken in Step 1 (curb height).**

6. Installation is the reverse of the removal procedure, using new fasteners.

7. Note the following tightening specifications:

- Lower control arm rearward nut and bolt: 148 ft. lbs. (200 Nm)
- Lower arm forward nut and bolt: 296 ft. lbs. (400 Nm)
- Shock absorber lower bolt and flag nut: 258 ft. lbs. (350 Nm)
- Stabilizer bar link nut: 26 ft. lbs. (35 Nm)
- Lower ball joint nut: 111 ft. lbs. (150 Nm)

2011 Models

1. Remove the wheel and tire.

➡ **Use the hex-holding feature to prevent the stud from turning while removing the nut.**

2. Using a crowfoot wrench, remove and discard the lower ball joint nut.

> **✻✻ WARNING**
>
> **Use care when releasing the lower arm and knuckle into the resting position or damage to the ball joint seal may occur.**

3. Push the lower arm downward until the ball joint is clear of the wheel knuckle.

4. Remove and discard the lower arm forward bolt.

5. Remove and discard the lower arm rearward nuts and bolts.

   a. Install the new lower arm rearward bolts from the bottom of the lower arm bushing with the nuts on top.

6. If necessary, remove the lower arm rearward bushing. For additional information, refer to Lower Arm Bushing in this section.

> **✻✻ WARNING**
>
> **The lower arm forward bolt must be tightened with the weight of the vehicle on the wheels and tires or damage to the bushings may occur.**

To install:

> **✻✻ WARNING**
>
> **Suspension fasteners are critical parts because they affect performance of vital components and systems and their failure may result in major service expense. New parts must be installed with the same part numbers or equivalent part, if replacement is necessary. Do not use a replacement part of lesser quality or substitute design. Torque values must be used as specified during reassembly to make sure of correct retention of these parts.**

> **✻✻ WARNING**
>
> **The lower arm forward bolt must be tightened with the weight of the vehicle on the wheels and tires or damage to the bushings may occur.**

7. If necessary, install the lower arm rearward bushing.

8. Install and use a new lower arm rearward nuts and bolts. Tighten the new nuts to 73 ft. lbs. (99 Nm).

   a. Install the new lower arm rearward bolts from the bottom of the lower arm bushing with the nuts on top.

9. Install and use a new lower arm forward bolt. Tighten the new bolt to 136 ft. lbs. (185 Nm).

> **✻✻ WARNING**
>
> **Use care when releasing the lower arm and knuckle into the resting position or damage to the ball joint seal may occur.**

10. Push the lower arm upward until the ball joint is in the wheel knuckle.

➡ **Use the hex-holding feature to prevent the stud from turning while removing the nut.**

11. Using a crowfoot wrench, install and use a new lower ball joint nut. Tighten the nut to 148 ft. lbs. (200 Nm).

12. Install the wheel and tire.

LOWER CONTROL ARM BUSHING REPLACEMENT

2011 Models

See Figures 298 and 299.

1. Remove the lower arm as outlined above.

2. Index-mark the bushing-to-lower arm position for reference during the installation procedure.

➡ **The Drive Pinion Bearing Cone Remover is used to secure the lower arm bushing while separating the bushing from the lower arm.**

3. Using the Drive Pinion Bearing Cone Remover, a suitable press and adapters, remove the lower arm bushing.

To install:

➡ **The Drive Pinion Bearing Cone Remover is used to clamp and hold the lower arm while installing the bushing.**

4. Install the Drive Pinion Bearing Cone Remover onto the lower arm.

5. Transfer the index mark to the new lower arm bushing.

➡ **The Drive Pinion Bearing Cone Remover is used to clamp and hold the lower arm while installing the bushing.**

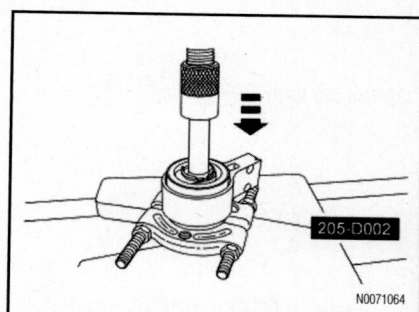

Fig. 298 Using the Drive Pinion Bearing Cone Remover, a suitable press and adapters, remove the lower arm bushing

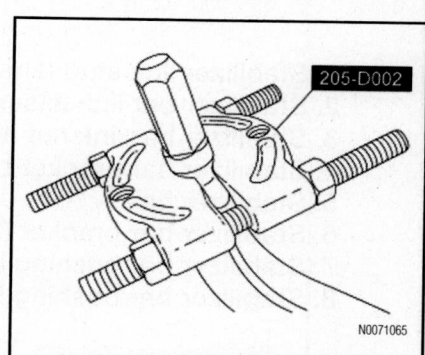

Fig. 299 Install the Drive Pinion Bearing Cone Remover onto the lower arm

6. Align the index marks and using the Drive Pinion Bearing Cone Remover, a suitable press and adapters, install a new lower arm bushing.

7. Install the lower arm.

STABILIZER BAR

REMOVAL & INSTALLATION

2010 Models

See Figure 300.

1. Before servicing the vehicle, refer to Precautions.

2. Remove and discard the 2 stabilizer bar nut and grommets.

3. Remove the 2 stabilizer bar studs.

4. Remove the 2 stabilizer bar links.

→**Inspect and clean the mating surfaces and the internal threads. Make sure all mating surfaces are free of foreign material and remove any thread locking compound from the internal threads.**

5. Remove and discard the 4 stabilizer bar-to-frame bolts.

6. Remove the 2 stabilizer bar brackets.

7. Remove the stabilizer bar.

→**Inspect the bushings for wear or damage. Install new bushings as necessary.**

8. Remove the 2 stabilizer bar bushings.

To install:

9. Installation is the reverse of the removal procedure

10. Always install new stabilizer bar-to-frame bolts and stabilizer bar nut and grommets.

11. Tighten the stabilizer bar bracket bolts to 41 ft. lbs. (55 Nm), with the vehicle at curb weight.

2011 Models

See Figures 301 through 303.

→**Make sure the steering wheel is in the unlocked position.**

→**The stabilizer bushing and bracket are part of the stabilizer bar assembly. The stabilizer bar will not turn easily in the bushing.**

All Vehicles

1. With the vehicle in NEUTRAL, position it on a hoist.

2. Disconnect the Heated Oxygen Sensor (HO2S) electrical connector and unclip the connector from the subframe.

All-Wheel Drive (AWD) Vehicles

3. Remove the exhaust Y-pipe as outlined in the Engine Mechanical Section.

All Vehicles

❋❋ WARNING

Do not use power tools to remove the stabilizer bar link nut. Damage to the stabilizer link ball joint or boot may occur.

→**To remove the stabilizer bar link nut, first loosen the nut, then use the hex-**

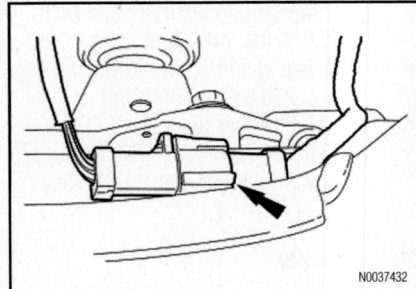

Fig. 301 Disconnect the Heated Oxygen Sensor (HO2S) electrical connector and unclip the connector from the subframe

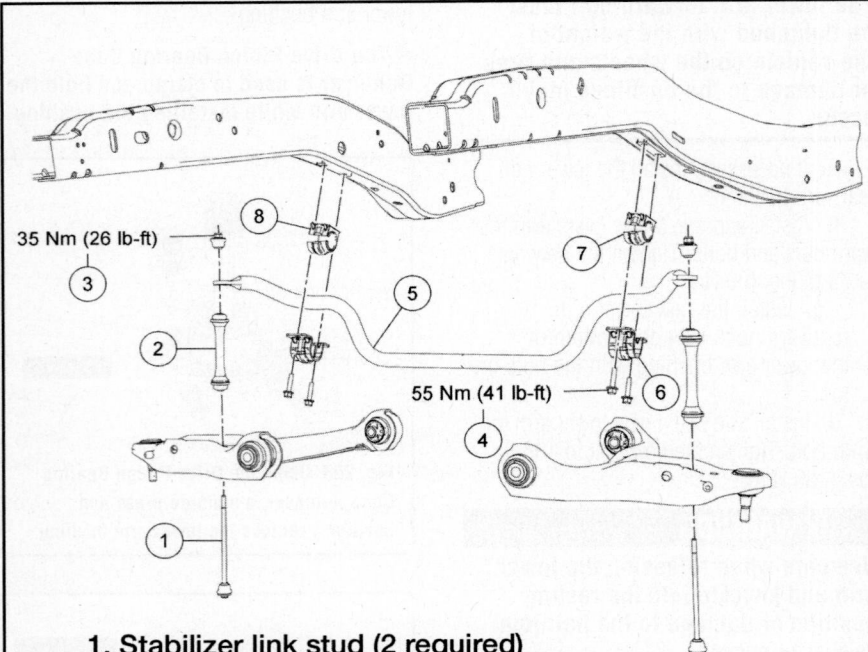

1. Stabilizer link stud (2 required)
2. Stabilizer bar link assembly (2 required)
3. Stabilizer bar link nut and grommet (2 required)
4. Stabilizer bar bracket bolt (4 required)
5. Stabilizer bar
6. Stabilizer bar bracket (2 required)
7. Stabilizer bar bushing LH
8. Stabilizer bar bushing RH

35 Nm (26 lb-ft)

55 Nm (41 lb-ft)

36578_EXPL_G0182

Fig. 300 Stabilizer bar and control links

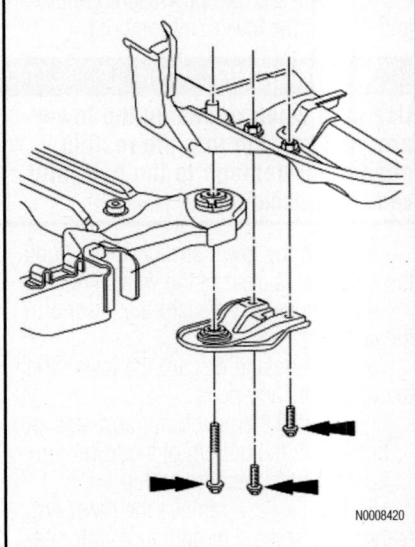

N0008420

Fig. 302 Remove and discard the subframe rearward bolts

holding feature to prevent the ball joint from turning while removing the stabilizer bar link nut.

4. Remove and discard the stabilizer bar link lower nuts.

→No special tools are necessary to separate the tie rod from the front knuckle; use a mallet to loosen the joint.

5. Remove and discard both tie-rod end nuts and separate the tie-rod ends from the knuckles.

→Install the new lower arm rearward bolts from the bottom of the lower arm bushing with the nuts on top.

6. Remove and discard the 4 lower arm rearward nuts and bolts.

7. Remove and discard the 2 lower arm forward bolts. Position both lower arms aside.

8. Using a suitable screw-type jackstand, support the rear of the subframe.

9. Remove the 2 steering gear nuts and bolts.
   a. Vehicles with Electronic Power Assist Steering (EPAS)
   b. Vehicles with Hydraulic Power Assist Steering (HPAS)

10. Remove and discard the 4 subframe bracket bolts.

11. Remove and discard the subframe forward bolts.

12. Remove and discard the subframe rearward bolts.
   a. Vehicles with EPAS
   b. Vehicle with HPAS

13. Lower the rear of the subframe approximately 21 inch (51 mm).

14. Remove and discard the LH and RH stabilizer bar bracket bolts.

15. Remove the stabilizer bar by guiding it between the subframe and the steering gear toward the RH side of the vehicle.

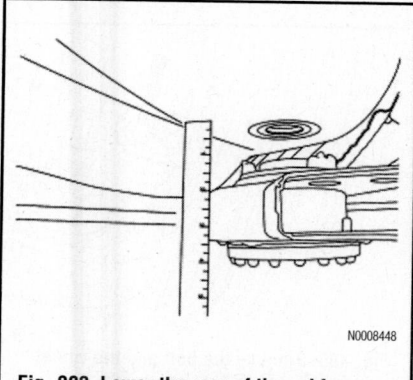

Fig. 303 Lower the rear of the subframe approximately 21 inch (51 mm)

N0008448

To install:

→Make sure the steering wheel is in the unlocked position.

→The stabilizer bushing and bracket are part of the stabilizer bar assembly. The stabilizer bar will not turn easily in the bushing.

16. Install the stabilizer bar by guiding it between the subframe and the steering gear away from the RH side of the vehicle.

All Vehicles

17. Install and use new LH and RH stabilizer bar bracket bolts. Tighten the new bolts to 41 ft. lbs. (55 Nm).

18. Raise the rear of the subframe approximately 21 inch (51 mm).

19. Install and use new subframe rearward bolts.
   a. Vehicles with EPAS tighten the new bolts to 111 ft. lbs. (150 Nm).
   b. Vehicle with HPAS, tighten the new bolts to 130 ft. lbs. (175 Nm).

20. Install and use new subframe forward bolts. Tighten the new bolts to 148 ft. lbs. (200 Nm).

21. Install and use 4 new subframe bracket bolts. Tighten the new bolts to 41 ft. lbs. (55 Nm).

22. Install the 2 steering gear nuts and bolts.
   a. Vehicles with Electronic Power Assist Steering (EPAS), tighten the nuts to 122 ft. lbs. (65 Nm).
   b. Vehicles with Hydraulic Power Assist Steering (HPAS), tighten the new nuts to 86 ft. lbs. (117 Nm).

23. Using a suitable screw-type jackstand, support the rear of the subframe.

24. Install and use 2 new 2 lower arm forward bolts. Reposition both lower arms. Tighten the new bolts to 136 ft. lbs. (185 Nm).

→Install the new lower arm rearward bolts from the bottom of the lower arm bushing with the nuts on top.

25. Install and use 4 new 4 lower arm rearward nuts and bolts. Tighten the new bolts to 73 ft. lbs. (99 Nm).

→No special tools are necessary to separate the tie rod from the front knuckle; use a mallet to loosen the joint.

26. Install and new tie-rod end nuts and separate the tie-rod ends to the knuckles. Tighten the new nuts to 111 ft. lbs. (150 Nm).

Do not use power tools to install the stabilizer bar link nut. Damage to the stabilizer link ball joint or boot may occur.

→To install the stabilizer bar link nut, use the hex-holding feature to prevent the ball joint from turning while installing the stabilizer bar link nut, then tighten the nut.

27. Install and use new stabilizer bar link lower nuts. Tighten the new nuts to 111 ft. lbs. (150 Nm).

All-Wheel Drive (AWD) Vehicles

28. Install the exhaust Y-pipe as outlined in the Engine Mechanical Section.

All Vehicles

29. Connect the Heated Oxygen Sensor (HO2S) electrical connector and clip the connector to the subframe.

30. With the vehicle in NEUTRAL, lower from the hoist.

STABILIZER BAR LINK

REMOVAL & INSTALLATION

2011 Models

1. With the vehicle in NEUTRAL, position it on a hoist. For additional information, refer to Jacking and Lifting.

Do not use power tools to remove the stabilizer bar link nuts. Damage to the stabilizer bar link ball joints or boots may occur.

→To remove the stabilizer bar link nuts, first loosen the nuts, then use the hex-holding feature to prevent the stabilizer bar link ball joints from turning while removing the stabilizer bar link nuts.

2. Remove and discard the stabilizer bar link lower nut.

3. Remove and discard the stabilizer bar link upper nut.

4. Remove the stabilizer bar link.

→To install the nuts, use the hex-holding feature to prevent the stabilizer link ball joints from turning while installing the nuts until snug. Finally, tighten the nuts using a socket and a torque wrench.

To install:

→To install the nuts, use the hex-holding feature to prevent the stabilizer link ball joints from turning while installing the nuts until snug. Finally, tighten the nuts using a socket and a torque wrench.

5. Install the stabilizer bar link.
6. Install and use a new stabilizer bar link upper nut. Tighten the new nut to 111 ft. lbs. (150 Nm).
7. Install and a new stabilizer bar link lower nut. Tighten the new nut to 111 ft. lbs. (150 Nm).

※ WARNING

Do not use power tools to remove the stabilizer bar link nuts. Damage to the stabilizer bar link ball joints or boots may occur.

➥To install the stabilizer bar link nuts, use the hex-holding feature to prevent the stabilizer bar link ball joints from turning while removing the stabilizer bar link nuts, and then tighten the nuts.

※ WARNING

Suspension fasteners are critical parts because they affect performance of vital components and systems and their failure may result in major service expense. New parts must be installed with the same part numbers or equivalent part, if replacement is necessary. Do not use a replacement part of lesser quality or substitute design. Torque values must be used as specified during reassembly to make sure of correct retention of these parts.

8. With the vehicle in NEUTRAL, lower from the hoist.

STEERING KNUCKLE

REMOVAL & INSTALLATION

2010 Models

See Figure 304.

1. Before servicing the vehicle, refer to the precautions in the beginning of this section.
2. Remove the wheel bearing and hub assembly. Refer to Wheel Hub and Bearing.
3. Remove the wheel speed sensor harness bracket bolt from the wheel knuckle.
4. Remove and discard the tie rod end nut.
5. Using a proper tool, separate the tie rod end from the wheel knuckle.
6. Remove and discard the lower ball joint nut.

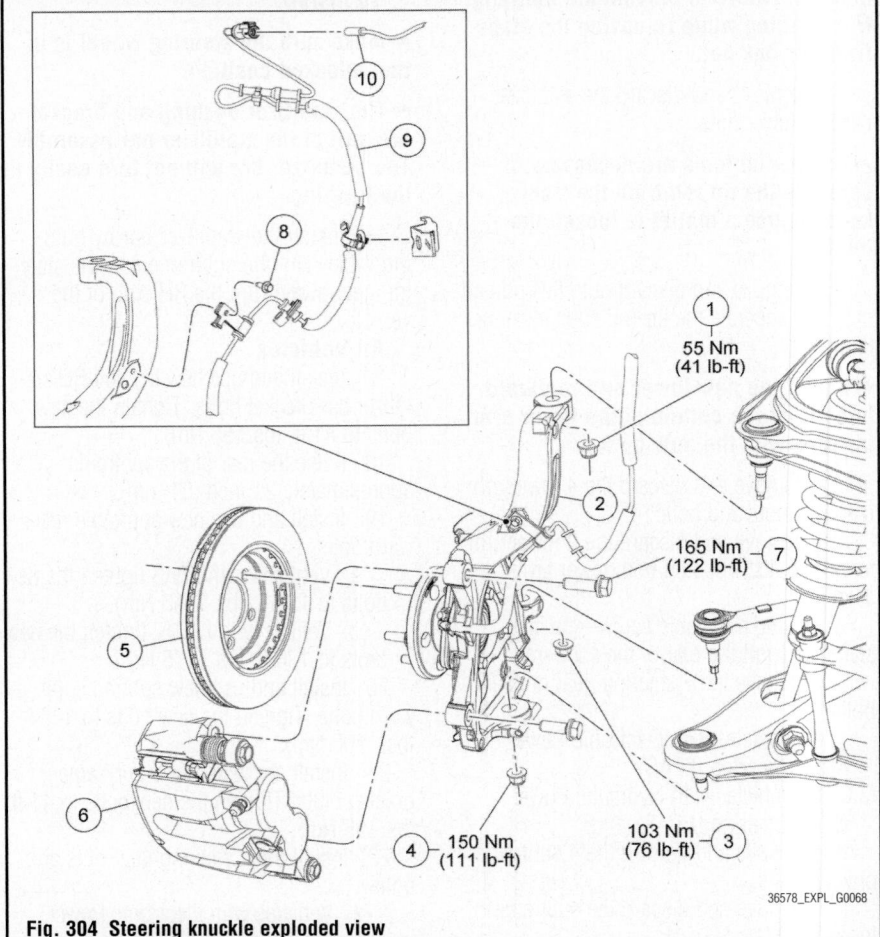

Fig. 304 Steering knuckle exploded view

36578_EXPL_G0068

7. Using a proper tool, separate the lower arm ball joint from the wheel knuckle.
8. Remove and discard the upper ball joint nut.
9. Using a proper tool, separate the upper arm ball joint from the wheel knuckle.
10. Remove the wheel knuckle.

To install:

11. Installation is the reverse of the removal procedure.
12. Use new fasteners where indicated.
13. Note the following tightening specifications:

- Wheel speed sensor: 71 inch lbs. (8 Nm)
- Upper ball joint nut: 41 ft. lbs. (55 Nm)
- Lower ball joint nut: 111 ft. lbs. (150 Nm)
- Tie rod end nut: 76 ft. lbs. (103 Nm)

14. Check and, if necessary, align the front end.

2011 Models

See Figures 305 and 306.

1. Remove the wheel and tire.

➥Do not discard the wheel hub nut at this time.

2. Remove the wheel hub nut.
3. Remove the brake disc.

➥No special tools are necessary to separate the tie rod from the front

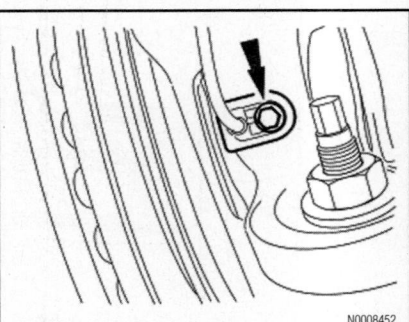

Fig. 305 Remove the bolt and the wheel speed sensor from the wheel knuckle. Position the wheel speed sensor aside

N0008452

knuckle; use a mallet to loosen the joint.

4. Remove and discard the tie-rod end nut, then separate the tie rod from the wheel knuckle.

5. Remove the bolt and the wheel speed sensor from the wheel knuckle. Position the wheel speed sensor aside.

➡Use the hex-holding feature to prevent the stud from turning while removing the nut.

6. Using a crowfoot wrench, remove and discard the lower ball joint nut.

7. Push the lower arm downward until the ball joint is clear of the wheel knuckle.

✳✳ WARNING

Do not allow the halfshaft to move outboard. Overextension of the tripod Constant Velocity (CV) joint may result in separation of internal parts, causing failure of the halfshaft.

8. Using the Front Wheel Hub Remover, press the halfshaft from the wheel bearing and hub. Support the halfshaft in a level position.

9. Remove and discard the strut-to-wheel knuckle nut and flagbolt.

10. Remove the wheel knuckle.

   a. If necessary, remove the wheel hub and bearing.

To install:

11. Position the wheel knuckle and install a new strut-to-wheel knuckle nut and flagbolt. Tighten the nut and flagbolt to 184 ft. lbs. (250 Nm).

12. While supporting the halfshaft in a level position, install the halfshaft into the wheel bearing and hub.

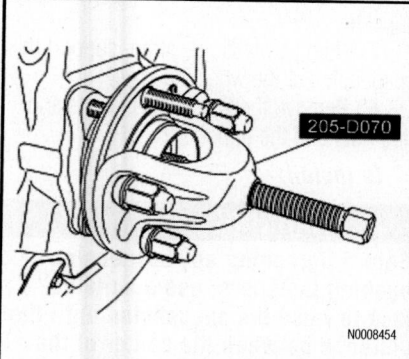

205-D070

N0008454

Fig. 306 Using the Front Wheel Hub Remover, press the halfshaft from the wheel bearing and hub

✳✳ WARNING

Use care not to damage the ball joint seal while installing the ball joint stud into the wheel knuckle.

13. Push the lower arm downward and install the ball joint stud into the wheel knuckle.

➡Use the hex-holding feature to prevent the stud from turning while installing the nut.

14. Using a crowfoot wrench, install the new lower ball joint nut. Tighten the nut to 148 ft. lbs. (200 Nm).

15. Position the wheel speed sensor and install the bolt. Tighten the bolt to 133 inch lbs. (15 Nm).

16. Position the tie-rod end stud into the wheel knuckle and install a new tie-rod end nut. Tighten the nut to 111 ft. lbs. (150 Nm).

17. Install the brake disc.

✳✳ WARNING

Do not tighten the front wheel hub nut with the vehicle on the ground. The nut must be tightened to specification before the vehicle is lowered onto the wheels. Wheel bearing damage will occur if the wheel bearing is loaded with the weight of the vehicle applied.

➡Apply the brake to keep the halfshaft from rotating.

18. Using the previously removed hub nut, seat the halfshaft. Tighten the nut to 258 ft. lbs. (350 Nm).

   a. Remove and discard the hub nut.

✳✳ WARNING

The wheel hub nut contains a one-time locking chemical that is activated by the heat created when it is tightened. Install and tighten the new wheel hub nut to specification within 5 minutes of starting it on the threads. Always install a new wheel hub nut after loosening or when not tightened within the specified time or damage to the components can occur.

➡Apply the brake to keep the halfshaft from rotating.

19. Install a new hub nut. Tighten the nut to 258 ft. lbs. (350 Nm).

20. Install the wheel and tire.

STRUT & SPRING ASSEMBLY

REMOVAL & INSTALLATION

2010 Models

See Figures 307 and 308.

✳✳ WARNING

All vehicles are equipped with gas-pressurized shock absorbers which will extend unassisted. Do not apply heat or flame to the shock absorbers during removal or component servicing. Failure to follow these instructions may result in personal injury.

1. Before servicing the vehicle, refer to Precautions.

2. Measure the distance from the center of the hub to the lip of the fender with the vehicle in a level, static ground position (curb height).

3. Remove and discard the 3 shock absorber upper mount nuts.

4. With the vehicle in NEUTRAL, position it on a hoist.

5. Using a suitable jack, support the lower control arm near the lower ball joint.

6. Remove and discard the stabilizer bar link nut and grommet and then remove the stabilizer bar link assembly.

7. Remove the shock absorber lower bolt and flag nut.

8. Remove and discard the upper ball joint nut.

✳✳ WARNING

Do not use a hammer to separate the ball joint from the wheel knuckle or damage to the wheel knuckle can result.

9. Using the proper separator tool, separate the upper ball joint from the wheel knuckle.

10. While lowering the suspension, remove the shock and spring assembly.

To install:

➡Before tightening any suspension bushing fasteners, use a suitable jack to raise the suspension until the distance between the center of the hub and the lip of the fender is equal to the measurement taken in Step 1 (curb height).

11. Position the shock absorber and spring assembly and raise the suspension into normal position.

12. Install a new upper ball joint nut. Torque to 41 ft. lbs. (55 Nm).

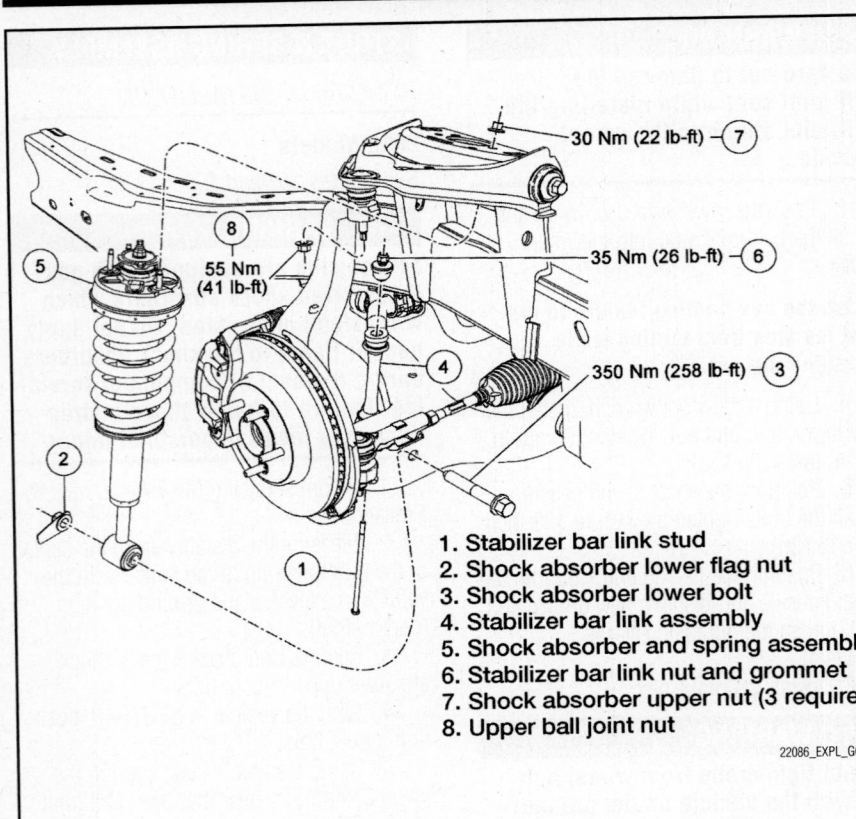

1. Stabilizer bar link stud
2. Shock absorber lower flag nut
3. Shock absorber lower bolt
4. Stabilizer bar link assembly
5. Shock absorber and spring assembly
6. Stabilizer bar link nut and grommet
7. Shock absorber upper nut (3 required)
8. Upper ball joint nut

22086_EXPL_G0178

Fig. 307 Shock absorber and spring assembly and related mounting components

Callouts on figure:
- 30 Nm (22 lb-ft) — 7
- 35 Nm (26 lb-ft) — 6
- 350 Nm (258 lb-ft) — 3
- 55 Nm (41 lb-ft)

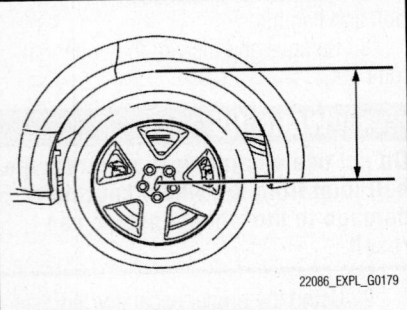

22086_EXPL_G0179

Fig. 308 Measure the distance from the center of the hub to the lip of the fender with the vehicle in a level, static ground position (curb height)

13. Install the lower shock absorber bolt and flag nut. Torque to 258 ft. lbs. (350 Nm).

14. Install a new stabilizer bar link nut and grommet. Torque to 26 ft. lbs. (35 Nm).

15. Install 3 new upper shock mounting nuts. Torque to 22 ft. lbs. (30 Nm).

16. Lower the vehicle.

2011 Models

✳✳ **CAUTION**

Do not apply heat or flame to the shock absorber or strut tube. The shock absorber and strut tube are gas pressurized and could explode if heated. Failure to follow this instruction may result in serious personal injury.

✳✳ **CAUTION**

Keep all body parts clear of shock absorbers or strut rods. Shock absorbers or struts can extend unassisted. Failure to follow this instruction may result in serious personal injury.

1. Loosen the upper strut mount nuts.
2. Raise and safely support the vehicle.
3. Remove the wheel and tire.
4. Remove and discard the stabilizer bar link upper nut.
5. Detach the wheel speed sensor harness from the strut.
6. Using a suitable jackstand, support the lower control arm.
7. Index-mark the 2 lower strut-to-wheel knuckle bolts.
8. Remove and discard the 2 lower strut-to-wheel knuckle nuts and bolts.

➡ **Damage to the lower control arm bushings may occur if the lower control arm is not supported.**

9. Remove and discard the 4 upper strut mount nuts. Carefully lower the lower control arm and remove the strut and spring assembly.

To install:

10. Position the strut and spring assembly and loosely install the 4 new upper strut mount nuts.

11. Position the strut and spring assembly to the wheel knuckle and install the 2 new lower strut-to-wheel knuckle nuts and bolts. Tighten to 184 ft. lbs. (250 Nm).

12. Attach the wheel speed sensor harness to the strut.

13. Install the a stabilizer bar link upper nut. Tighten to 111 ft. lbs. (150 Nm).

14. Tighten the 4 new upper strut mount nuts. Tighten to 41 ft. lbs. (55 Nm).

15. Install the wheel and tire.

16. Check and, if necessary, adjust the front end alignment.

UPPER CONTROL ARM

REMOVAL & INSTALLATION

2010 Models

See Figures 308 and 309.

1. Before servicing the vehicle, refer to the precautions in the beginning of this section.

2. Measure the distance from the center of the hub to the lip of the fender with the vehicle in a level, static ground position (curb height).

3. With the vehicle in NEUTRAL, position it on a hoist.

4. Using a suitable jack support the lower control arm near the lower ball joint.

5. Remove and discard the upper ball joint nut.

6. Using the proper separator tool, separate the upper ball joint from the wheel knuckle.

7. Using a plastic tie strap, support the suspension at the wheel knuckle.

8. Remove the 2 upper arm bolts and flag nuts and the upper arm.

To install:

✳✳ **WARNING**

Before tightening any suspension bushing fasteners, use a suitable jack to raise the suspension until the distance between the center of the hub and the lip of the fender is equal to the measurement taken for curb height.

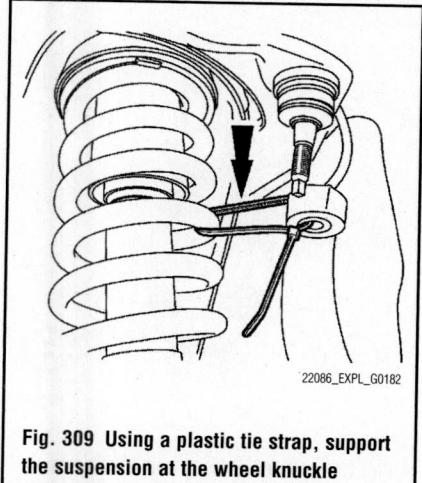

Fig. 309 Using a plastic tie strap, support the suspension at the wheel knuckle

9. Position the upper arm and install the bolts and flag nuts. Torque to 111 ft. lbs. (150 Nm).

10. With the jack still under the lower arm, remove the plastic tie strap.

11. Insert the upper ball joint stud into the wheel knuckle. Install a new nut and torque to 41 ft. lbs. (55 Nm).

12. Check and, if necessary, align the front end.

WHEEL HUB & BEARING

REMOVAL & INSTALLATION

2010 Models

2WD Models

See Figure 310.

1. With the vehicle in NEUTRAL, position it on a hoist.

2. Remove the bolts and position the caliper, pads and anchor plate assembly aside. Discard the bolts. Support the caliper and anchor plate assembly using mechanic's wire.

3. Remove the brake disc.

4. Remove the wheel speed sensor bolt and disconnect the wheel speed sensor from the wheel bearing and hub assembly.

5. Remove the 3 bolts and the wheel bearing and hub assembly.

To install:

6. Install the wheel bearing and hub assembly. Tighten the 3 bolts to 90 ft. lbs. (122 Nm).

7. Install the wheel speed sensor to the wheel bearing and hub assembly. Connect the electrical connector and install the bolt. Tighten bolt to 159 inch lbs. (18 Nm).

8. Install the brake disc.

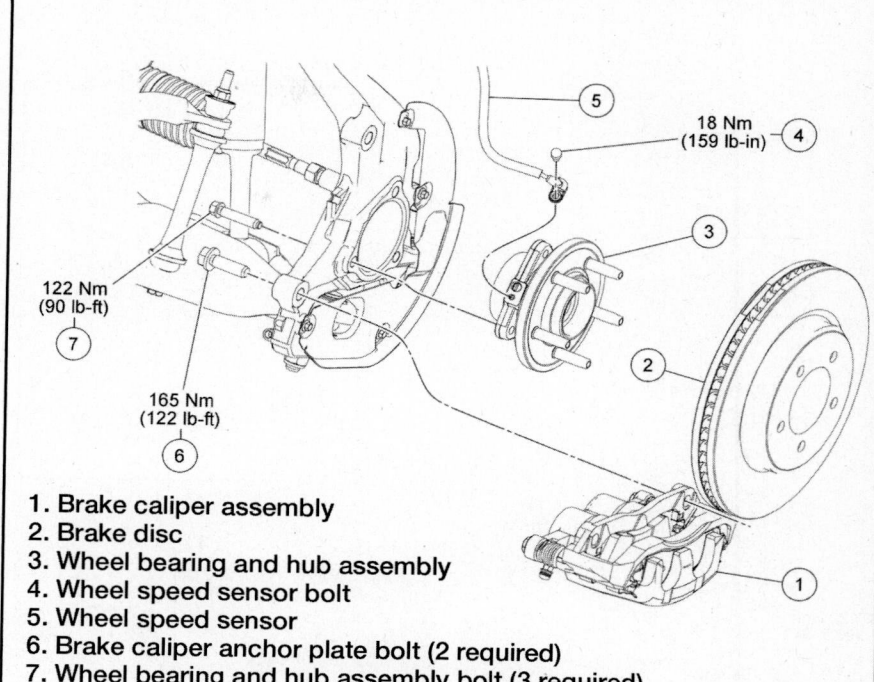

1. Brake caliper assembly
2. Brake disc
3. Wheel bearing and hub assembly
4. Wheel speed sensor bolt
5. Wheel speed sensor
6. Brake caliper anchor plate bolt (2 required)
7. Wheel bearing and hub assembly bolt (3 required)

Fig. 310 Wheel hub and bearing with torques—Front, 2WD

9. Install the caliper and anchor plate assembly. Tighten the bolts to 122 ft. lbs. (165 Nm).

4WD Models

See Figure 311.

1. With the vehicle in NEUTRAL, position it on a hoist.

2. Remove and discard the halfshaft nut and washer.

3. separate the outboard CV joint from the wheel hub.

4. Remove the bolts and position the caliper, pads and anchor plate assembly aside. Discard the bolts. Support the caliper and anchor plate assembly using mechanic's wire.

5. Remove the brake disc.

6. Remove the wheel speed sensor bolt and disconnect the wheel speed sensor from the wheel bearing and hub assembly.

7. Remove the 3 bolts and the wheel bearing and hub assembly.

To install:

8. Install the wheel bearing and hub assembly. Tighten the 3 bolts to 90 ft. lbs. (122 Nm).

9. Install the wheel speed sensor to the wheel bearing and hub assembly. Connect the electrical connector and install the bolt.

10. Install the brake disc.

11. Install the caliper and anchor plate assembly. Tighten the bolts to 122 ft. lbs. (165 Nm).

12. Install the outboard CV joint to the wheel hub.

13. Install a new nut and washer to the halfshaft. Tight the nut to 184 ft. lbs. (250 Nm).

14. Lower the vehicle.

2011 Models

See Figure 312.

1. Remove the wheel knuckle.

2. Remove and discard the 4 wheel bearing and wheel hub bolts, then separate the wheel bearing and wheel hub from the wheel knuckle.

❋❋ WARNING

The wheel knuckle bore must be clean enough to allow the wheel bearing and wheel hub to seat completely by hand. Do not press or draw the wheel hub and bearing into place or damage to the bearing may occur.

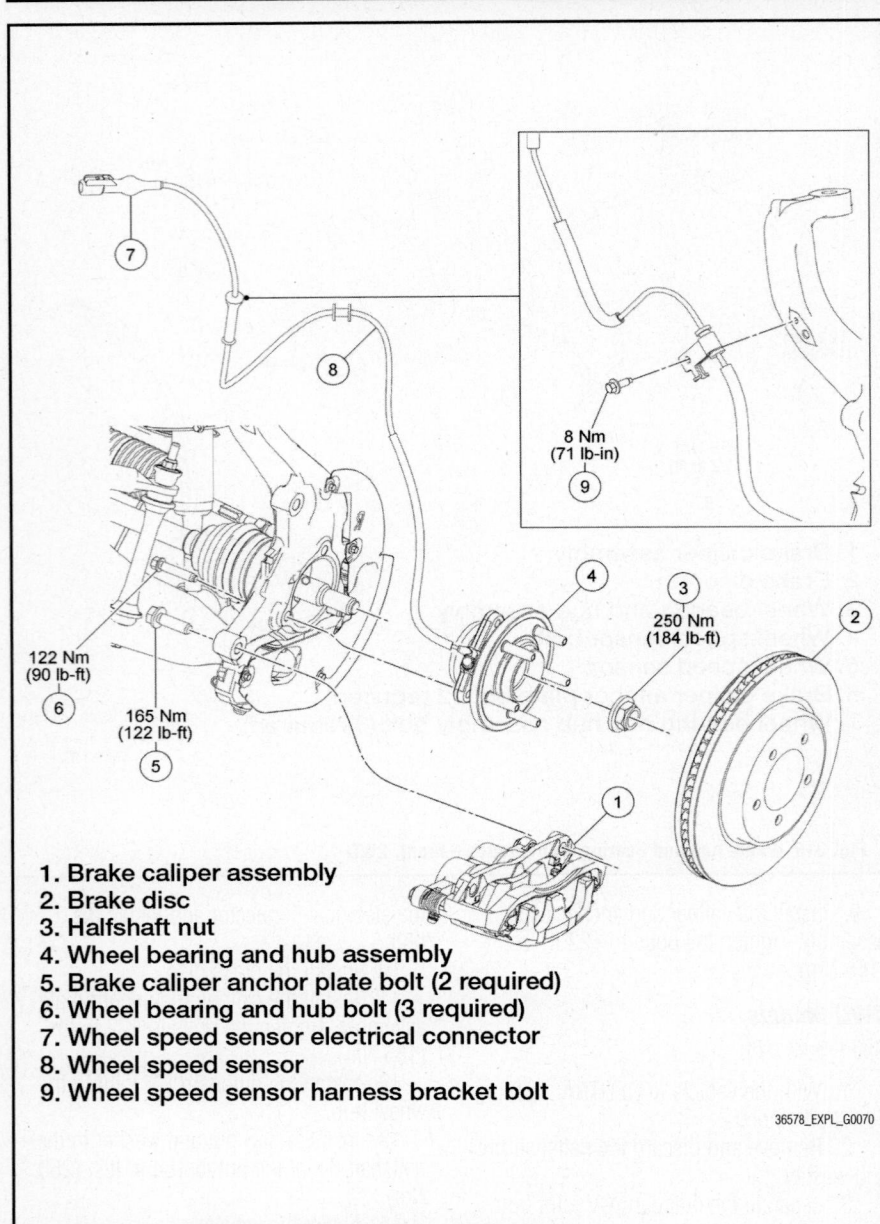

8 Nm
(71 lb-in)
9

250 Nm
(184 lb-ft)

122 Nm
(90 lb-ft)
6

165 Nm
(122 lb-ft)
5

1. Brake caliper assembly
2. Brake disc
3. Halfshaft nut
4. Wheel bearing and hub assembly
5. Brake caliper anchor plate bolt (2 required)
6. Wheel bearing and hub bolt (3 required)
7. Wheel speed sensor electrical connector
8. Wheel speed sensor
9. Wheel speed sensor harness bracket bolt

36578_EXPL_G0070

Fig. 311 Wheel hub and bearing with torques—Front, 4WD

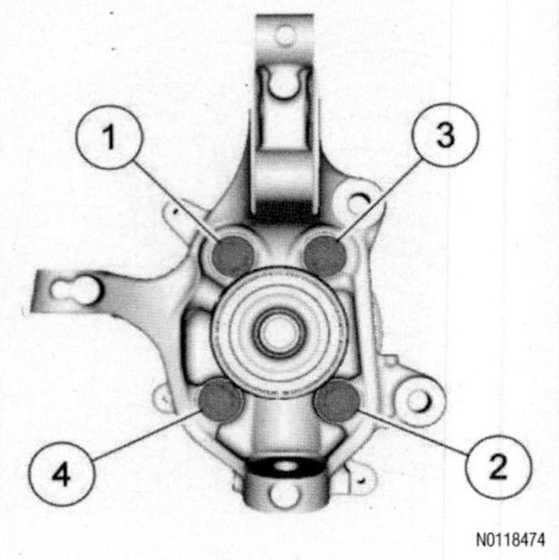

N0118474

Fig. 312 Wheel bearing and wheel hub bolt tightening sequence—2011 Models

3. Clean and inspect the knuckle bearing bore. If the wheel knuckle is cracked, install a new wheel knuckle.

→**Make sure the wheel hub-to-wheel knuckle mating surfaces are clean and free of any adhesive. Failure to clean the adhesive from both surfaces may cause bearing damage.**

4. Using a clean shop towel, clean the wheel hub-to-knuckle mating surfaces.

To install:

5. Lubricate the wheel hub-to-brake disc surface with anti-seize lubricant before installing the brake disc.

6. Position the wheel bearing and wheel hub assembly to the wheel knuckle and install 4 new wheel bearing and wheel hub bolts. Tighten to 122 ft. lbs. (165 Nm) in the sequence shown.

7. Install the wheel knuckle.

ADJUSTMENT

No adjustments are possible or necessary

SUSPENSION

REAR SUSPENSION

✳✳ WARNING

Suspension fasteners are critical parts because they affect performance of vital components and systems and their failure may result in major service expense. New parts must be installed with the same part numbers or equivalent part, if replacement is necessary. Do not use a replacement part of lesser quality or substitute design. Torque values must be used as specified during reassembly to make sure of correct retention of these parts.

KNUCKLE

REMOVAL & INSTALLATION

2010 Models

See Figures 313 through 316.

1. Before servicing the vehicle, refer to Precautions.

2. Measure the distance from the center of the hub to the lip of the fender with the vehicle in a level, static ground position (curb height).

3. If equipped, remove the wheel speed sensor bolt and position the sensor aside.

✳✳ WARNING

Do not loosen the halfshaft nut and washer until the wheel and tire are removed from the vehicle, as wheel bearing damage will occur if the wheel bearing is unloaded with the weight of the vehicle applied.

4. Remove the rear wheels.

5. Apply the brake to keep the halfshaft from rotating. Remove and discard the front wheel hub nut.

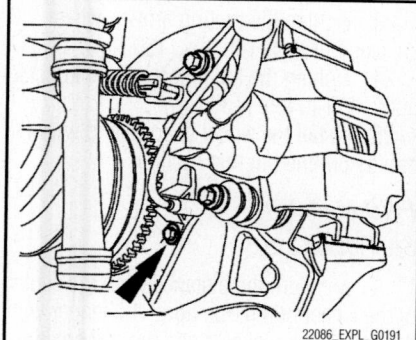

Fig. 313 Showing the location of the wheel speed sensor bolt

22086_EXPL_G0191

6. Remove the parking brake shoes.

7. Using a proper tool, press the halfshaft from the hub.

8. Position a suitable jack under the wheel knuckle and raise the suspension until the distance between the center of the hub and the lip of the fender is equal to the curb height measurement.

9. Remove and discard the following:
- toe link outboard nut and bolt
- upper arm outboard nut and bolt
- lower arm outboard nut and bolt
- 3 wheel knuckle bolts

10. Remove the wheel knuckle.

11. If a new wheel knuckle is being installed, remove the wheel bearing and wheel hub.

To install:

12. Position a suitable jack under the wheel knuckle and raise the suspension until the distance between the center of the hub and the lip of the fender is equal to the curb height measurement.

13. Position the wheel knuckle and install 3 new wheel knuckle bolts. Torque the bolts to 203 ft. lbs. (275 Nm).

14. Install a new lower arm outboard bolt and flag nut. Torque the nut to 203 ft. lbs. (275 Nm).

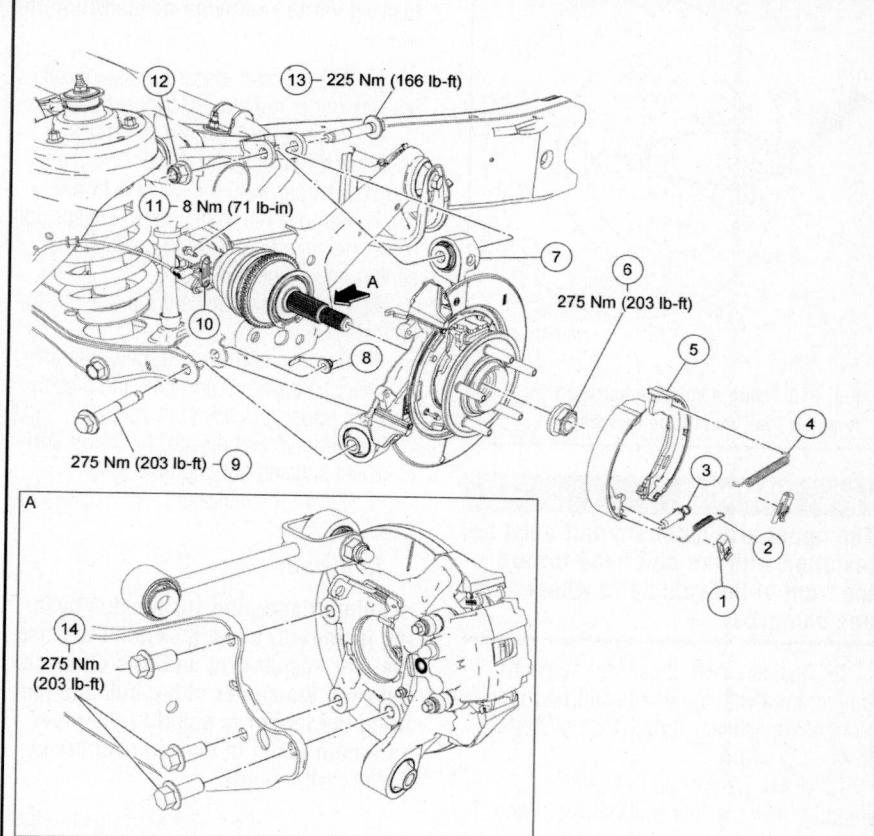

1. Parking brake shoe clip (2 required)
2. Parking brake shoe adjuster spring
3. Parking brake shoe adjuster
4. Parking brake shoe retracting spring
5. Parking brake shoe (2 required)
6. Halfshaft nut
7. Wheel knuckle
8. Lower arm outboard flagnut
9. Lower arm outboard bolt
10. Wheel speed sensor
11. Wheel speed sensor bolt
12. Upper arm outboard nut
13. Upper arm outboard bolt
14. Wheel knuckle bolts (3 required)

36578_EXPL_G0076

Fig. 314 Exploded view of the wheel knuckle, spindle, and related mounting components—2010 Models

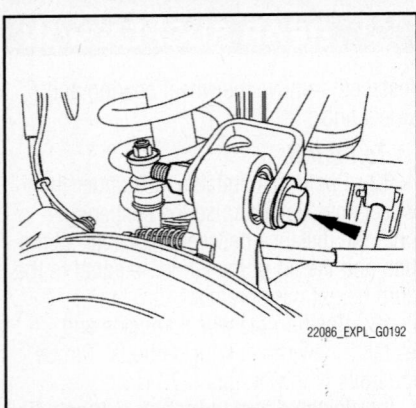

Fig. 315 Showing the proper direction for the upper arm outboard bolt

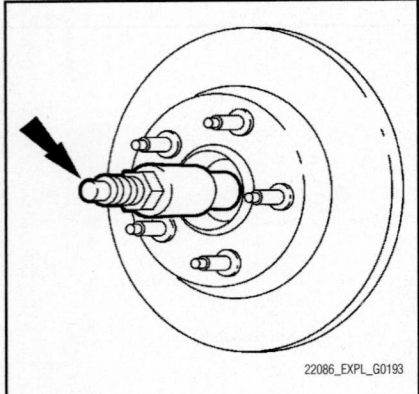

Fig. 316 Using a suitable halfshaft installer tool, install the halfshaft

☀☀ WARNING

The upper arm outboard bolt must be installed with the bolt head toward the front of the vehicle or wheel damage can occur.

15. Install a new upper arm outboard bolt and nut with the bolt head toward the front of the vehicle. Torque the bolt to 166 ft. lbs. (225 Nm).

16. Position the toe link and install a new toe link outboard bolt and nut.

17. Lower the suspension and remove the jack.

18. Install the parking brake shoes. See "Parking Brake" section.

19. Position the wheel speed sensor and install the bolt.

20. Using a suitable halfshaft installer tool, install the halfshaft.

21. Have an assistant press the brake pedal to keep the axle from turning, then install a new halfshaft nut and washer. Torque the nut to 203 ft. lbs. (275 Nm).

2011 Models

AWD Models

See Figures 317 and 318.

1. Measure the distance from the center of the wheel hub to the lip of the fender with the vehicle in a level, static ground position (curb height).

2. Remove the wheel bearing and wheel hub. For additional information, refer to Wheel Bearing and Wheel Hub in this section.

3. Using a suitable jackstand, support the lower arm.

4. Remove and discard the trailing arm-to-wheel knuckle nut and bolt.

➡**Use the hex-holding feature to prevent the stabilizer bar link stud from turning while removing or installing the nut.**

5. Remove and discard the stabilizer bar link upper nut and disconnect the link.

6. Remove and discard the shock absorber lower bolt and disconnect the shock absorber from the knuckle bracket.

7. Remove the wheel speed sensor bolt, disconnect the harness and position the sensor and harness aside.

8. Remove and discard the toe link-to-knuckle nut.

9. Remove and discard the upper arm-to-wheel knuckle nut and bolt and disconnect the upper arm from the knuckle.

10. Remove and discard the lower arm-to-wheel knuckle nut and bolt.

11. Lower the jackstand, and remove the knuckle.

To install:

➡**Before tightening suspension bushing fasteners, use a jackstand to raise the rear suspension until the distance between the center of the hub and the lip of the fender is equal to the measurement taken in the removal procedure (curb height).**

12. Position the wheel knuckle onto the toe link and loosely install a new lower arm-to-wheel knuckle nut and bolt.

13. Loosely install a new toe link-to-knuckle nut.

14. Position the wheel speed sensor harness and install the wheel speed sensor and bolt.

15. Connect the shock absorber to the knuckle and loosely install a new shock absorber lower bolt.

➡**Use the hex-holding feature to prevent the stabilizer bar link stud from turning while removing or installing the nut.**

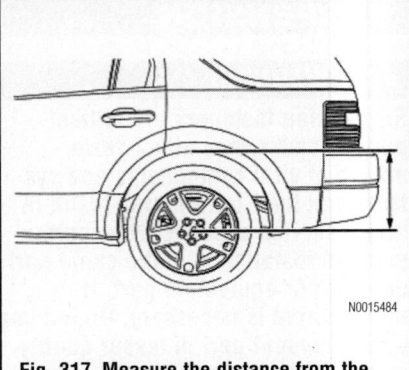

Fig. 317 Measure the distance from the center of the wheel hub to the lip of the fender with the vehicle in a level, static ground position (curb height)

16. Connect the stabilizer bar link and install a new stabilizer bar link upper nut. Tighten the nut to 41 ft. lbs. (55 Nm).

17. Loosely install a new trailing arm-to-wheel knuckle nut and bolt.

18. Raise the jackstand and loosely install a new upper arm-to-wheel knuckle nut and bolt.

19. Position a suitable jackstand under the lower control arm at the shock and spring assembly attachment point and raise the rear suspension until the distance between the center of the hub and the lip of the fender is equal to the measurement taken in Step 1 of the procedure (curb height).

➡**A slotted upper arm allows for the rear suspension camber to be adjusted by pushing inward or pulling outward on the wheel knuckle while tightening the upper arm-to-wheel knuckle nut.**

20. With the wheel knuckle pushed inward for maximum negative camber, tighten the upper arm-to-wheel knuckle nut to 148 ft. lbs. (200 Nm).

21. Tighten the lower arm-to-wheel knuckle bolt to 194 ft. lbs. (265 Nm).

22. Tighten the shock absorber bolt to 129 ft. lbs. (175 Nm).

23. Tighten the trailing arm-to-wheel knuckle nut to 111 ft. lbs. (150 Nm).

24. Tighten the toe link-to-wheel knuckle nut to 111 ft. lbs. (150 Nm).

25. Install the wheel bearing and wheel hub as outlined in this section.

FWD Models

See Figures 319.

1. Measure the distance from the center of the wheel hub to the lip of the fender with the vehicle in a level, static ground position (curb height).

2. Remove the wheel and tire.

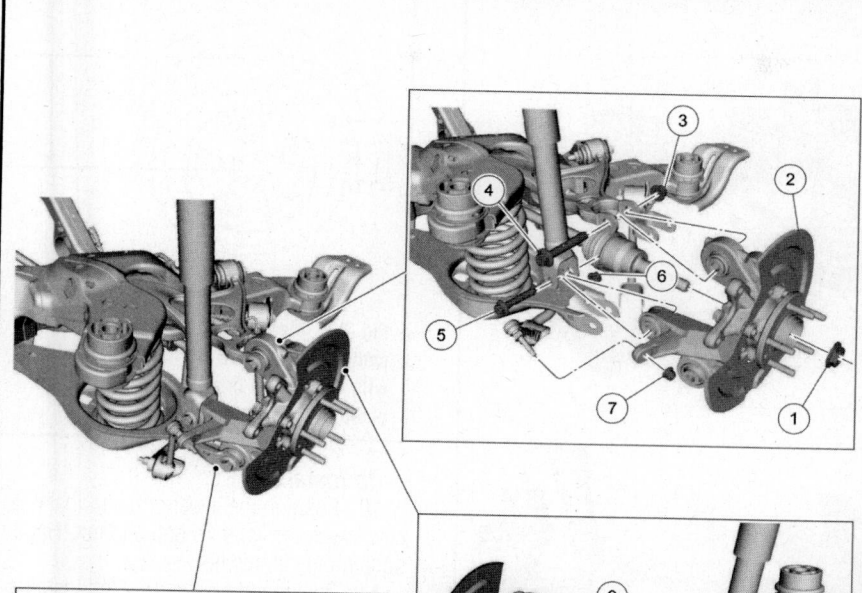

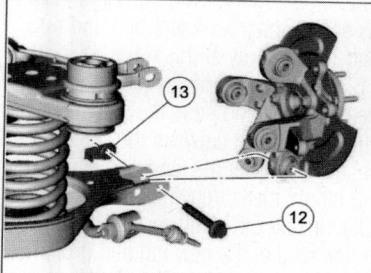

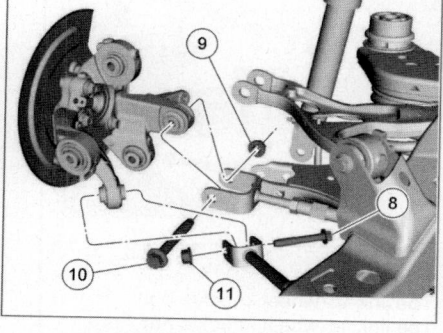

1. Wheel hub nut
2. RH Wheel knuckle
3. Upper arm-to-wheel knuckle nut
4. Upper arm-to-wheel knuckle bolt
5. Shock absorber lower bolt
6. Shock absorber lower nut
7. Stabilizer bar link upper nut
8. Trailing arm-to-wheel knuckle bolt
9. Toe link-to-wheel knuckle nut
10. Toe link-to-wheel knuckle bolt
11. Trailing arm-to-wheel knuckle nut
12. Lower arm-to-wheel knuckle bolt
13. Lower arm-to-wheel knuckle nut

N0118484

Fig. 318 Wheel knuckle—2011 AWD vehicles

3. Remove the brake disc.

4. Using a suitable jackstand, support the lower arm.

5. Remove and discard the trailing arm-to-wheel knuckle nut and bolt.

➡️**Use the hex-holding feature to prevent the stabilizer bar link stud from turning while removing the nut.**

6. Remove and discard the stabilizer bar link upper nut and disconnect the link.

7. Remove and discard the shock absorber lower bolt and disconnect the shock absorber.

8. Remove the wheel speed sensor bolt, disconnect the harness and position the sensor and harness assembly aside.

9. Remove and discard the toe link-to-knuckle nut.

10. Remove and discard the upper arm-to-wheel knuckle nut and bolt and disconnect the upper arm from the knuckle.

11. Remove and discard the lower arm-to-wheel knuckle nut and bolt.

12. Lower the jackstand, and remove the knuckle.

To install:

➡️**Before tightening any suspension bushing fasteners, use a jackstand to raise the rear suspension until the dis-**

tance between the center of the hub and the lip of the fender is equal to the measurement taken in the removal procedure (curb height).

13. Position the wheel knuckle onto the toe link and loosely install a new lower arm-to-wheel knuckle nut and bolt.

14. Loosely install a new toe link-to-knuckle nut.

15. Position the wheel speed sensor harness and install the wheel speed sensor and bolt. Tighten the bolt to 133 inch lbs. (15 Nm).

16. Connect the shock absorber to the knuckle and loosely install a new shock absorber lower bolt.

17. Connect the stabilizer bar link and install a new stabilizer bar link upper nut. Tighten the nut to 41 ft. lbs. (55 Nm).

➡️**Use the hex-holding feature to prevent the stabilizer bar link stud from turning while removing or installing the nut.**

18. Loosely install a new trailing arm-to-wheel knuckle nut and bolt.

19. Loosely install a new upper arm-to-wheel knuckle nut and bolt.

20. Position a suitable jackstand under the lower control arm at the shock and spring assembly attachment point and raise the rear suspension until the distance between the center of the hub and the lip of the fender is equal to the measurement taken in Step 1 of the procedure (curb height).

➡️**A slotted upper arm allows for the rear suspension camber to be adjusted by pushing inward or pulling outward on the wheel knuckle while tightening the upper arm-to-wheel knuckle nut.**

21. With the wheel knuckle pushed inward for maximum negative camber, tighten the upper arm-to-wheel knuckle nut to 148 ft. lbs. (200 Nm).

22. Tighten the lower arm-to-wheel knuckle bolt to 195 ft. lbs. (265 Nm).

23. Tighten the shock absorber bolt to 129 ft. lbs. (175 Nm).

24. Tighten the trailing arm-to-wheel knuckle nut to 111 ft. lbs. (150 Nm).

25. Tighten the toe link-to-knuckle nut to 111 ft. lbs. (150 Nm).

26. Install the brake disc.

27. Install the wheel and tire.

28. Check and if necessary, adjust the rear toe.

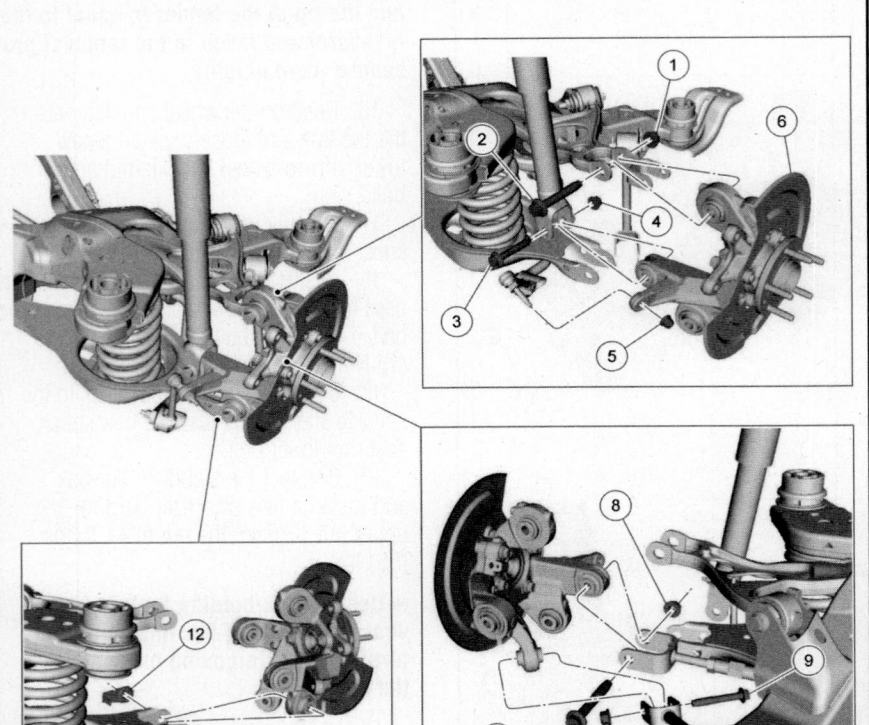

1. Upper arm-to-wheel knuckle nut
2. Upper arm-to-wheel knuckle bolt
3. Shock absorber lower bolt
4. Shock absorber lower nut
5. Stabilizer bar link upper nut
6. Wheel knuckle
7. Toe link-to-wheel knuckle bolt
8. Toe link-to-wheel knuckle nut
9. Trailing arm-to-wheel knuckle bolt
10. Trailing arm-to-wheel knuckle nut
11. Lower arm-to-wheel knuckle bolt
12. Lower arm-to-wheel knuckle nut

N0118482

Fig. 319 Wheel knuckle—2011 FWD vehicles

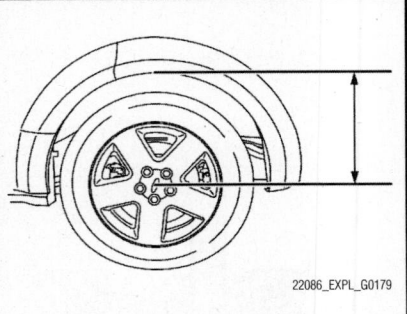

22086_EXPL_G0179

Fig. 320 Measure the distance from the center of the hub to the lip of the fender with the vehicle in a level, static ground position (curb height)

LOWER CONTROL ARM

REMOVAL & INSTALLATION

2010 Models

See Figures 320 and 321.

1. Before servicing the vehicle, refer to Precautions.

❊❊ WARNING

Orientation of the suspension fasteners is important. Make sure the fasteners are installed in the same direction as they were in when removed.

2. Measure the distance from the center of the hub to the lip of the fender with the vehicle in a level, static ground position (curb height).

3. With the vehicle in NEUTRAL, position it on a hoist.

4. Position a suitable jack under the wheel knuckle and raise the suspension until the distance between the center of the hub and the lip of the fender is equal to the curb height measurement.

5. Remove and discard the lower arm outboard bolt and flag nut.

6. Remove the stabilizer bar link nut and grommet, stud and link assembly. Discard the nut and grommet.

7. Lower the suspension and remove the jack.

8. Remove and discard the shock absorber lower nut and bolt.

9. Remove and discard the lower arm inboard nut and bolt and remove the lower arm.

To install:

10. Position the lower arm and install a new lower arm inboard bolt and nut. Hand-tighten only at this time.

11. Position the lower arm and install a new shock absorber lower bolt and nut. Hand-tighten only at this time.

12. Position a suitable jack under the wheel knuckle and raise the suspension until the distance between the center of the hub and the lip of the fender is equal to the curb height measurement.

13. Install the stabilizer link assembly, the link stud and a new nut and grommet. Torque the nut to 22 ft. lbs. (30 Nm).

14. Install a new lower arm outboard bolt and flag nut. Torque the nut to 203 ft. lbs. (275 Nm).

15. Tighten the lower arm inboard bolt to 185 ft. lbs. (250 Nm).

16. Tighten the shock absorber lower bolt to 203 ft. lbs. (275 Nm).

17. Lower the suspension and remove the jack.

2011 Models

See Figures 317 and 322.

1. Measure the distance from the center of the wheel hub to the lip of the fender with the vehicle in a level, static ground position (curb height).

2. Remove the rear wheel and tire.

➡Use the hex-holding feature to prevent the stabilizer bar link stud from turning while removing the nut.

3. Remove both stabilizer bar link upper nuts and disconnect the links from the wheel knuckle.
   a. Discard the nuts.

4. Position a screw-type jackstand under the lower arm.

5. Remove and discard the lower arm-to-knuckle bolt and nut.

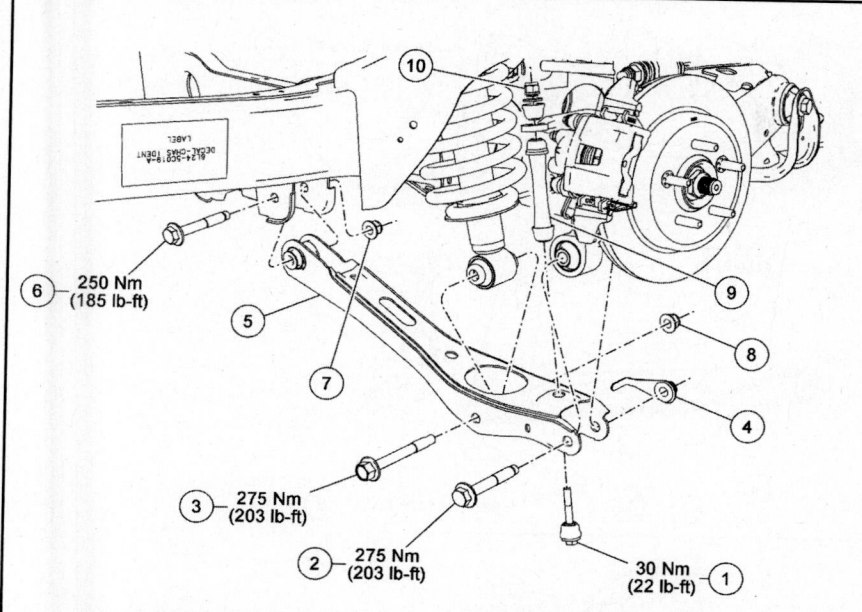

1. Stabilizer bar link stud
2. Lower arm outboard bolt
3. Shock absorber lower bolt
4. Lower arm outboard flag nut
5. Lower arm
6. Lower arm inboard bolt
7. Lower arm inboard nut
8. Shock absorber lower nut
9. Stabilizer bar link assembly
10. Stabilizer bar link nut and grommet

22086_EXPL_G0185

Fig. 321 Showing the lower arm and mounting components—2010 Models

➡Do not remove the lower arm inner bolt at this time.

6. Loosen the lower arm inner bolt.

7. Lower the jackstand and remove the spring.

8. Remove the lower arm inner bolt and lower arm.

  a. Discard the bolt.

To install:

➡Before tightening the lower arm bolts, use a jackstand to raise the rear suspension until the distance between the center of the hub and the lip of the fender is equal to the measurement taken in the Removal procedure (curb height).

9. Position the lower arm and loosely install the new lower arm inner bolt.

➡Make sure the lower spring seat is properly positioned in the lower arm.

10. Install the spring and position the screw-type jackstand under the lower arm.

➡Do not tighten the lower arm nut at this time.

11. Raise the jackstand and loosely install the new lower arm-to-knuckle bolt and nut.

12. Using the jackstand, raise the rear suspension until the distance between the center of the hub and the lip of the fender is equal to the measurement taken in the Removal procedure (curb height).

13. Tighten the lower arm-to-subframe bolt to 159 ft. lbs. (215 Nm).

14. Tighten the lower arm-to-knuckle bolt to 196 ft. lbs. (265 Nm).

➡Use the hex-holding feature to prevent the stabilizer bar link stud from turning while removing the nut.

15. Position the stabilizer bar links and install 2 new stabilizer bar link upper nuts. Tighten the nuts to 41 ft. lbs. (55 Nm).

16. Install the wheel and tire assembly.

SHOCK ABSORBER

REMOVAL & INSTALLATION

2011 Models

See Figure 323.

➡Use the hex-holding feature on the stock rod nut to prevent the shock rod from rotating when removing or installing the shock rod nut.

1. Remove the quarter trim panel.

2. Remove and discard the shock absorber upper mount nut.

3. Remove the wheel and tire.

➡Use the hex-holding feature to prevent the stabilizer bar link stud from turning while removing or installing the nut.

4. Remove and discard the stabilizer bar link upper nut and disconnect the link from the wheel knuckle.

5. Remove and discard the shock absorber lower bolt and remove the shock absorber.

To install:

6. Position the shock absorber and install a new shock absorber lower bolt. Tighten to 129 ft. lbs. (175 Nm).

➡Use the hex-holding feature to prevent the stabilizer bar link stud from turning while installing the nut.

7. Position the stabilizer bar link to the bar and install a new stabilizer bar link upper nut. Tighten to 41 ft. lbs. (55 Nm).

8. Install the wheel and tire.

9. Install a new shock absorber upper insulator and nut. Tighten to 41 ft. lbs. (55 Nm).

10. Install the quarter trim panel.

SPRING

REMOVAL & INSTALLTION

2011 Models

See Figures 317 and 324.

1. Measure the distance from the center of the wheel hub to the lip of the fender with the vehicle in a level, static ground position (curb height).

2. Remove the wheel and tire.

➡Use the hex-holding feature to prevent the stabilizer bar link studs from turning while removing the nuts.

3. Remove and discard the 2 stabilizer bar link upper nuts.

  a. Position the stabilizer bar away from the lower arm.

4. Using a suitable jackstand, support the lower arm.

5. Loosen the lower arm-to-subframe bolt.

6. Remove and discard the lower arm-to wheel knuckle bolt.

7. Lower the jackstand and remove the spring.

To install:

➡Make sure the lower spring seat is properly positioned in the lower arm.

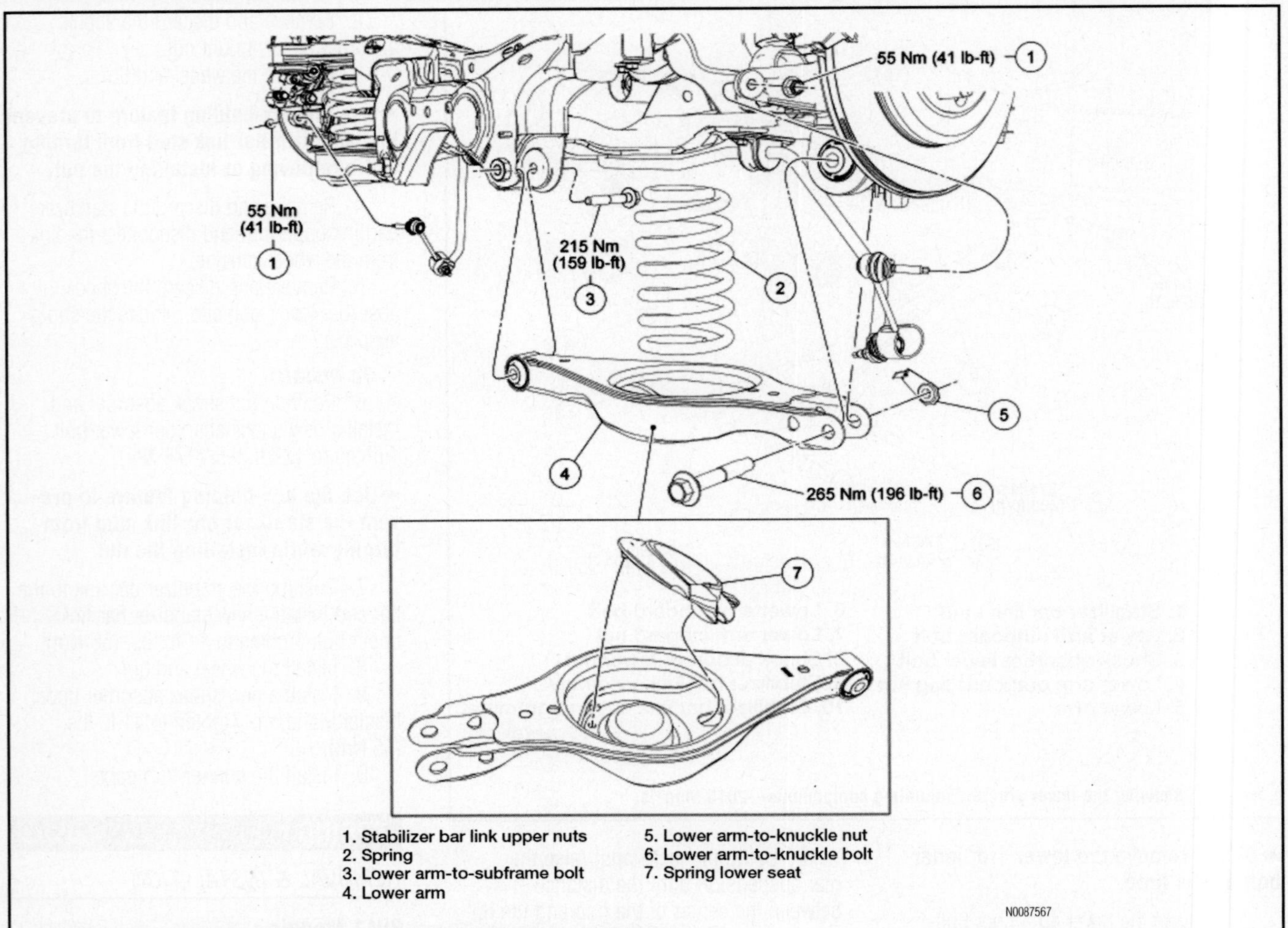

55 Nm (41 lb-ft) — ①

55 Nm
(41 lb-ft)
①

215 Nm
(159 lb-ft)
③

②

⑤

④

265 Nm (196 lb-ft) — ⑥

⑦

1. Stabilizer bar link upper nuts
2. Spring
3. Lower arm-to-subframe bolt
4. Lower arm
5. Lower arm-to-knuckle nut
6. Lower arm-to-knuckle bolt
7. Spring lower seat

N0087567

Fig. 322 Lower arm (FWD vehicle shown, AWD vehicle similar)—2011 Models

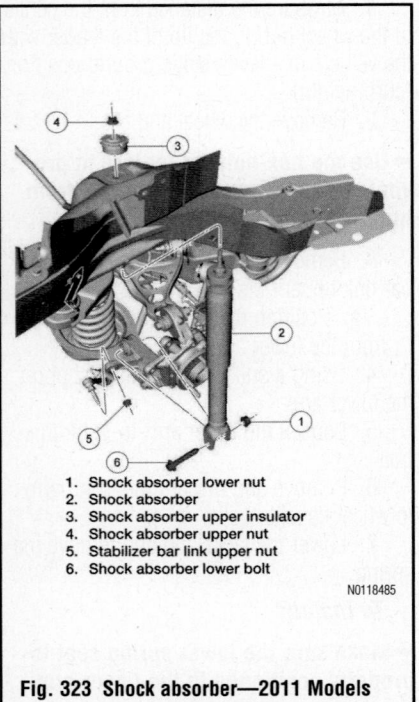

1. Shock absorber lower nut
2. Shock absorber
3. Shock absorber upper insulator
4. Shock absorber upper nut
5. Stabilizer bar link upper nut
6. Shock absorber lower bolt

N0118485

Fig. 323 Shock absorber—2011 Models

8. Inspect the upper and lower spring seats for damage and, if necessary, install new spring seats.

➡**Before tightening the lower arm bolts, use a jackstand to raise the rear suspension until the distance between the center of the hub and the lip of the fender is equal to the measurement taken in the Removal procedure (curb height).**

9. Install the spring and position the jackstand under the lower arm.

10. Raise the jackstand and loosely install a new lower arm-to-wheel knuckle bolt.

➡**Use the hex-holding feature to prevent the stabilizer bar link studs from turning while installing the nuts.**

11. Position the stabilizer bar and links and install 2 new stabilizer bar link upper nuts. Tighten the nuts to 41 ft. lbs. (55 Nm).

12. Using the jackstand, raise the rear suspension until the distance between the center of the hub and the lip of the fender is equal to the measurement taken in the Removal procedure (curb height).

13. Tighten the lower arm-to-wheel knuckle bolt to 196 ft. lbs. (265 Nm).

14. Tighten the lower arm-to-subframe bolt to 159 ft. lbs. (215 Nm).

15. Install the wheel and tire.

STABILIZER BAR

REMOVAL & INSTALLATION

2010 Explorer & Mountaineer

See Figures 308 and 325.

1. Before servicing the vehicle, refer to Precautions.

2. Measure the distance from the center of the hub to the lip of the fender with the vehicle in a level, static ground position (curb height).

3. Remove the wheel and tire assemblies.

4. Remove and discard the outboard nut and bolt from both upper arms.

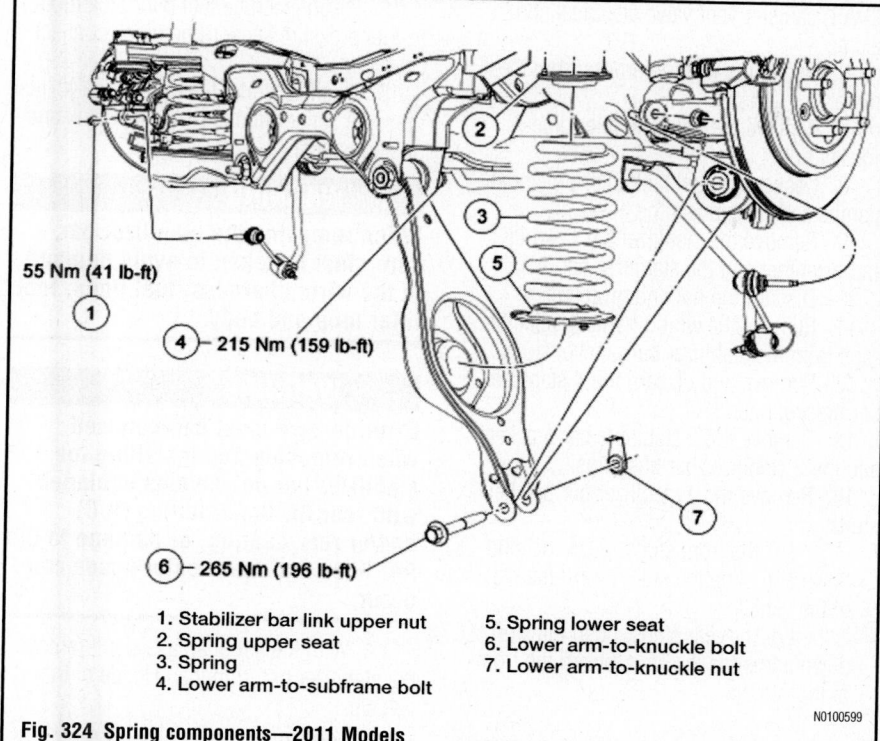

55 Nm (41 lb-ft) ①

④ 215 Nm (159 lb-ft)

⑥ 265 Nm (196 lb-ft)

1. Stabilizer bar link upper nut
2. Spring upper seat
3. Spring
4. Lower arm-to-subframe bolt
5. Spring lower seat
6. Lower arm-to-knuckle bolt
7. Lower arm-to-knuckle nut

N0100599

Fig. 324 Spring components—2011 Models

5. Remove the stabilizer bar link nut and grommet and the stabilizer bar link.

6. Discard the nut and grommet.

7. Remove and discard the 4 stabilizer bar bracket nuts.

8. Remove the 2 stabilizer bar brackets and the 2 stabilizer bar bushings.

9. Remove the 4 stabilizer bar bracket studs.

　a. For the front studs, push the stud down and slide the stud toward the rear of the vehicle.

　b. For the rear studs, push the stud down and slide the stud toward the front of the vehicle.

10. Disconnect the fuel filler pipe tube-to-fuel pressure sensor line quick connect coupling.

11. Unclip the fuel filler pipe tube-to-fuel pressure sensor line from the fuel tank and position aside.

❋❋ WARNING

Extreme care must be exercised when removing and installing the stabilizer bar on vehicles equipped with rear Air Conditioning (A/C) and/or rear heating or damage to the A/C lines and rear heater hoses can occur.

12. With the aid of an assistant, remove the stabilizer bar from the LH side of the vehicle.

To install:

13. With the aid of an assistant, install the stabilizer bar into the LH side of the vehicle.

14. Connect the fuel filler pipe tube-to-fuel sensor line.

15. Connect the fuel filler pipe tube-to-fuel pressure sensor line quick connect coupling.

16. Install the 4 stabilizer bar bracket studs.

17. Install the 2 stabilizer bar bushings and the 2 stabilizer bar brackets.

18. Install the 4 new stabilizer bar bracket nuts and tighten to 35 ft. lbs. (48 Nm).

19. Using the jack, raise the suspension until the distance between the center of the hub and the lip of the fender is equal to the measurement taken in Step 1 (curb height) in Removal.

20. Install the stabilizer bar link and new link nut and grommet and tighten the nut to 22 ft. lbs. (30 Nm).

❋❋ WARNING

The upper arm outboard bolts must be installed with the bolt head toward the front of the vehicle or wheel damage may occur.

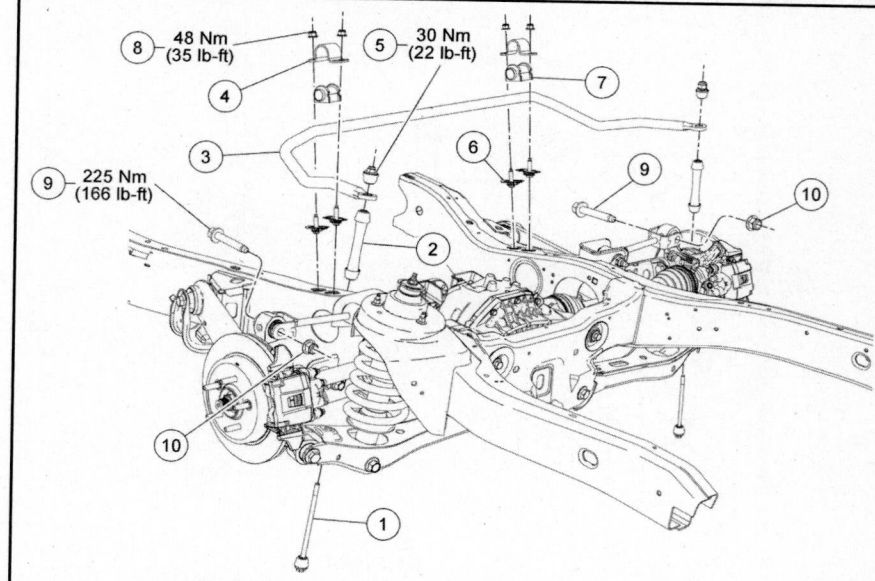

⑧ 48 Nm (35 lb-ft)　⑤ 30 Nm (22 lb-ft)

⑨ 225 Nm (166 lb-ft)

1. Stabilizer bar link stud (2 required)
2. Stabilizer bar link assembly (2 required)
3. Stabilizer bar
4. Stabilizer bar bracket (2 required)
5. Stabilizer bar link nut and grommet (2 required)
6. Stabilizer bar bracket stud (4 required)
7. Stabilizer bar bushing (2 required)
8. Stabilizer bar bracket nut (4 required)
9. Upper arm outboard bolts
10. Upper arm outboard nuts

36578_EXPL_G0073

Fig. 325 Rear suspension components with torques—2010 Explorer and Mountaineer

21. Install the 2 new upper arm outboard bolts and the 2 new upper arm outboard nuts and tighten to 166 ft. lbs. (225 Nm).

22. Remove the jack.

23. Install the wheel and tire.

2010 Explorer Sport-Trac

See Figures 308 and 326.

1. Before servicing the vehicle, refer to Precautions.

2. Measure the distance from the center of the hub to the lip of the fender with the vehicle in a level, static ground position (curb height).

3. Remove both upper arms. For additional information, refer to Upper Control Arm.

➡**Removal of the LH shock absorber lower bolt will allow more movement of the wheel knuckle when installing the stabilizer bar.**

4. Remove the LH shock absorber lower bolt.

5. Disconnect the Evaporative Emission (EVAP) canister vent valve electrical connector.

6. Unclip the wiring harness from the frame.

7. Remove the fuel tank filler pipe bracket bolt.

8. Loosen the fuel tank filler pipe hose clamps and disconnect the hose.

9. Remove the stabilizer bar link nut and grommet and the stabilizer bar link.

10. Discard the nut and grommet.

11. Remove the wiring harness retainer caps from the stabilizer bar bracket studs.

12. Remove and discard the 4 stabilizer bar bracket nuts.

13. Remove the 2 stabilizer bar brackets and the 2 stabilizer bar bushings.

14. Remove the 4 stabilizer bar bracket studs.

   a. For the front studs, push the stud down and slide the stud toward the rear of the vehicle.

   b. For the rear studs, push the stud down and slide the stud toward the front of the vehicle.

15. Disconnect the fuel filler pipe tube-to-fuel pressure sensor line quick connect coupling.

16. Unclip the fuel filler pipe tube-to-fuel pressure sensor line from the fuel tank and position aside.

✳✳ WARNING

When removing the stabilizer bar, care must be taken to avoid damage to the wiring harness, fuel lines, fuel filler tube and body.

✳✳ WARNING

Extreme care must be exercised when removing and installing the stabilizer bar on vehicles equipped with rear Air Conditioning (A/C) and/or rear heating, or damage to the A/C lines and rear heater hoses can occur.

17. With the aid of an assistant, remove the stabilizer bar from the LH side of the vehicle.

To install:

✳✳ WARNING

When installing the stabilizer bar, care must be taken to avoid damage to the wiring harness, fuel lines, fuel filler tube and body.

✳✳ WARNING

Extreme care must be exercised when removing and installing the stabilizer bar on vehicles equipped with rear Air Conditioning (A/C) and/or rear heating, or damage to the A/C lines and rear heater hose may occur.

18. With the aid of an assistant, install the stabilizer bar into the LH side of the vehicle.

19. Connect the fuel filler pipe tube-to-fuel sensor line.

20. Connect the fuel filler pipe tube-to-fuel pressure sensor line quick connect coupling.

21. Install the 4 stabilizer bar bracket studs.

22. Install the 2 stabilizer bar bushings and the 2 stabilizer bar brackets.

23. Install the 4 new stabilizer bar bracket nuts and tighten to 35 ft. lbs. (48 Nm).

24. Install the wiring harness retaining caps onto the stabilizer bar studs.

25. Use the jack to raise the suspension until the distance between the center of the

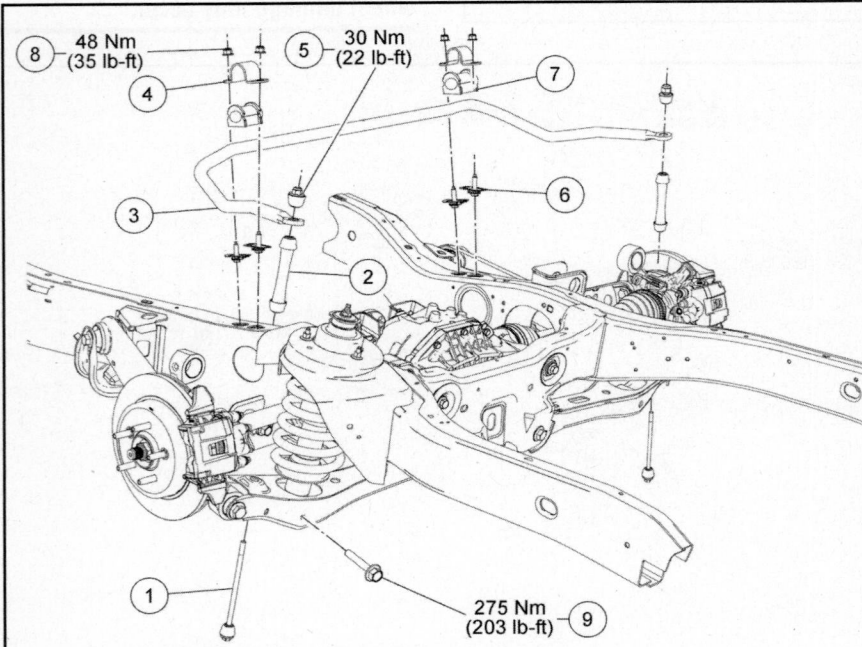

1. **Stabilizer bar link stud (2 required)**
2. **Stabilizer bar link assembly (2 required)**
3. **Stabilizer bar**
4. **Stabilizer bar bracket (2 required)**
5. **Stabilizer bar link nut and grommet (2 required)**
6. **Stabilizer bar bracket stud (4 required)**
7. **Stabilizer bar bushing (2 required)**
8. **Stabilizer bar bracket nut (4 required)**
9. **Shock absorber lower bolt**

36578_EXPL_G0074

Fig. 326 Rear suspension components with torques—2010 Sport-Trac

hub and the lip of the fender is equal to the measurement taken in Step 1 of the Upper Control Arm procedure in this section.

26. Install the stabilizer bar link, the new link nut and the grommet and tighten to 22 ft. lbs. (30 Nm).

27. Connect the fuel tank filler hose and tighten the 2 filler pipe hose clamps to 27 inch (3 Nm).

28. Install the fuel tank filler pipe bracket bolt and tighten to 133 inch lbs. (15 Nm).

29. Connect the wiring harness clip to the frame.

30. Connect the EVAP canister vent electrical connector.

31. Install the new LH shock absorber lower bolt and tighten to 203 ft. lbs. (275 Nm).

32. Install both upper arms.

2011 Models

See Figures 327 and 328.

➡ **Use the hex-holding feature to prevent the stabilizer bar link stud from turning while removing or installing the nut.**

1. With the vehicle in NEUTRAL, position it on a hoist.

2. Support the exhaust system with a suitable jackstand, disconnect the 2 muffler and tail pipe isolators and lower the exhaust approximately 2 inch (50.8 mm).

3. Remove and discard the 2 stabilizer bar link lower nuts.

4. Remove and discard the 4 stabilizer bar bracket bolts.

5. Remove the stabilizer bar.

To install:

6. Install the stabilizer bar.

7. Install the 4 new stabilizer bar bracket bolts. Tighten the new bolts to 41 ft. lbs. (55 Nm).

➡ **Use the hex-holding feature to prevent the stabilizer bar link stud from turning while installing the nut.**

8. Install the 2 new stabilizer bar link lower nuts. Tighten to 41 ft. lbs. (55 Nm).

9. Using a suitable jackstand, raise the exhaust system and connect the 2 muffler and tail pipe isolators.

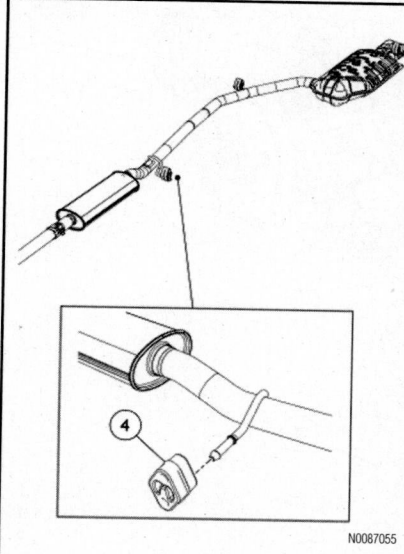

Fig. 328 View of the muffler and tail pipe isolator (4)—2011 Models

N0087055

STABILIZER BAR LINK

REMOVAL & INSTALLATION

2011 Models

➡ **Use the hex-holding feature to prevent the stabilizer bar link stud from turning while removing or installing the nut.**

1. Remove and discard the stabilizer bar link lower nut.

2. Remove the stabilizer bar link upper nut and stabilizer bar link. Discard the nut.

To install:

3. Position the stabilizer bar link and install the new stabilizer bar link upper nut. Tighten to 41 ft. lbs. (55 Nm).

4. Install the new stabilizer bar link lower nut. Tighten to 41 ft. lbs. (55 Nm).

STRUTS

REMOVAL & INSTALLATION

2010 Models

See Figure 329.

1. Before servicing the vehicle, refer to Precautions.

2. Remove the lower arm. Refer to Control Arms/Links.

3. Remove and discard the 3 shock absorber upper mount nuts and remove the shock absorber and spring assembly.

To install:

4. Install the shock absorber and torque the upper mount nuts to 22 ft. lbs. (30 Nm).

5. Install the lower arm. See "Control Arms/Links" section.

TOE LINK

REMOVAL & INSTALLATION

2010 Models

See Figures 308 and 330.

1. Before servicing the vehicle, refer to Precautions.

✳✳ WARNING

Orientation of the suspension fasteners is important. Make sure the fasteners are installed in the same direction as they were in when removed.

2. Measure the distance from the center of the hub to the lip of the fender with the vehicle in a level, static ground position (curb height).

63 Nm
(46 lb-ft)
②

55 Nm
(41 lb-ft)
③

1. Stabilizer bar
2. Stabilizer bar link lower nut
3. Stabilizer bar bracket bolts

N0100517

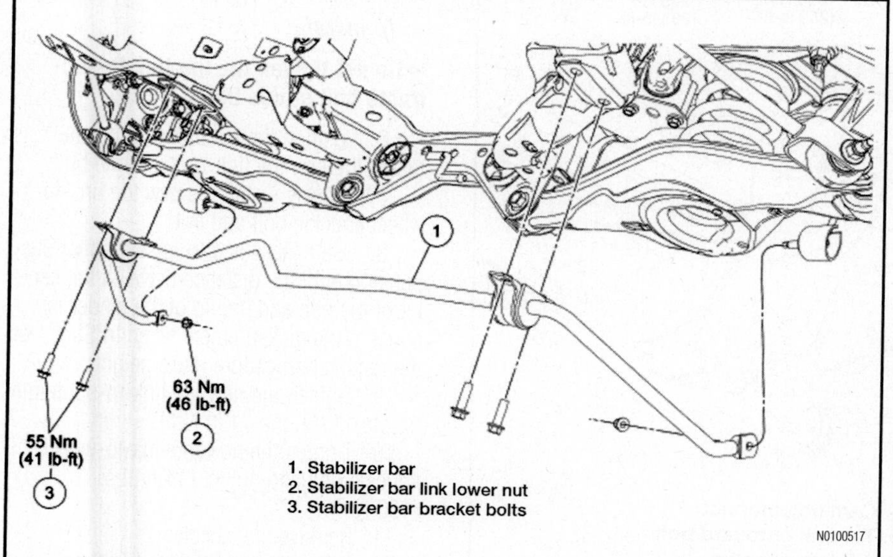

Fig. 327 Exploded view of the stabilizer bar (1), link lower nut (2) and bracket bolts (3)—2011 Models

3. With the vehicle in NEUTRAL, position it on a hoist.

4. Position a suitable jack under the wheel knuckle and raise the suspension until the distance between the center of the hub and the lip of the fender is equal to the curb height measurement.

5. Index-mark the toe link cam bolt to the subframe.

6. Remove the toe link cam adjuster nut, cam adjuster and cam bolt. Discard the nut.

7. Remove and discard the toe link outboard nut and bolt and remove the toe link.

To install:

8. If removed, install and raise the jack under the suspension to equal the curb height measurement.

9. Position the toe link and install a new outboard bolt and nut. Hand-tighten only at this time.

10. Install the toe link cam bolt, cam adjuster and a new nut. Hand-tighten only at this time.

11. If removed, install and raise the jack under the suspension to equal the curb height measurement.

12. Make sure the cam bolt and the adjustment cam are seated between the offsets before tightening the nut.

13. Align the index mark on the cam bolt with the index mark on the subframe and tighten the nut to 203 ft. lbs. (275 Nm).

14. Torque the toe link outboard bolt and nut to 240 ft. lbs. (325 Nm).

15. Lower the suspension and remove the jack.

16. Check and, if necessary, adjust the rear toe.

2011 Models

See Figures 317 and 331.

1. Measure the distance from the center of the wheel hub to the lip of the fender with the vehicle in a level, static ground position (curb height).

2. Remove the wheel and tire.

3. Use a jackstand to raise the rear suspension until the distance between the center of the hub and the lip of the fender is equal to the measurement taken in Step 1 of the procedure (curb height).

4. Remove and discard the toe link-to-wheel knuckle nut.

5. Remove and discard the toe link-to-subframe bolt.

To install:

→Do not tighten the toe link-to-subframe bolt at this time.

6. Position the toe link and loosely install the new toe link-to-subframe bolt.

7. Loosely install the new toe link-to-wheel knuckle bolt and nut.

8. Use a jackstand to raise the rear suspension until the distance between the center of the hub and the lip of the fender is equal to the measurement taken in Step 1 of the removal procedure (curb height).

9. Tighten the new toe link-to-subframe bolt to 111 ft. lbs. (150 Nm).

10. Tighten the new toe link-to-wheel knuckle bolt and nut to 111 ft. lbs. (150 Nm).

11. Remove the jackstand.

12. Install the rear wheels and tires.

13. Check and, if necessary, adjust the rear toe.

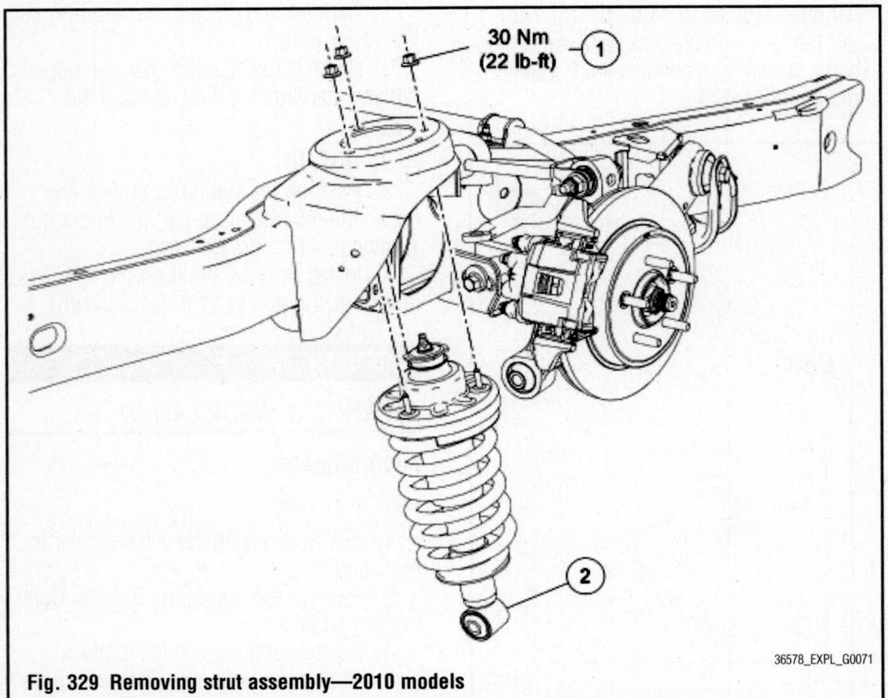

Fig. 329 Removing strut assembly—2010 models

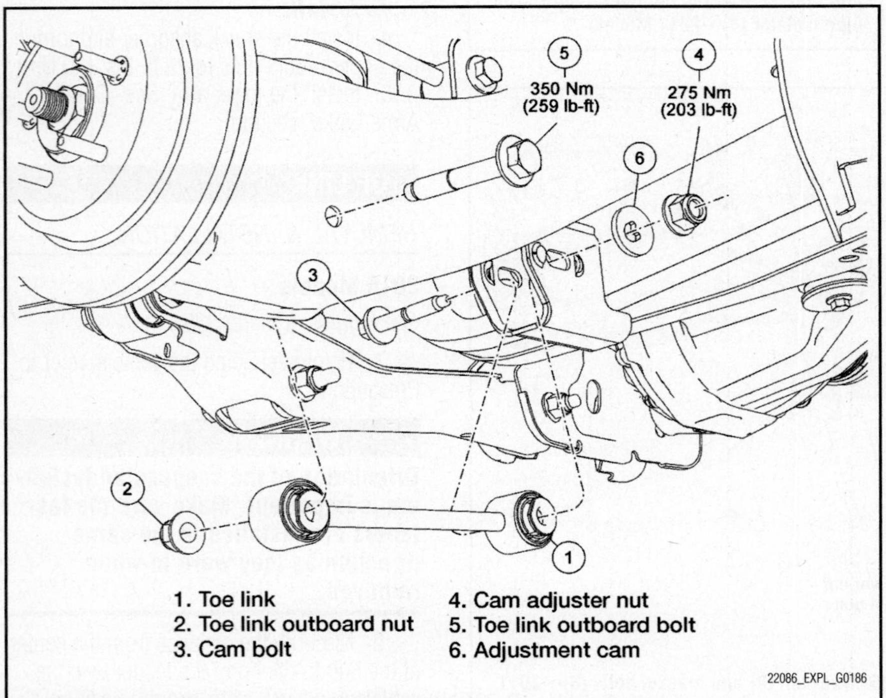

36578_EXPL_G0071

1. Toe link
2. Toe link outboard nut
3. Cam bolt
4. Cam adjuster nut
5. Toe link outboard bolt
6. Adjustment cam

22086_EXPL_G0186

Fig. 330 Showing the toe link and mounting components—2010 Models

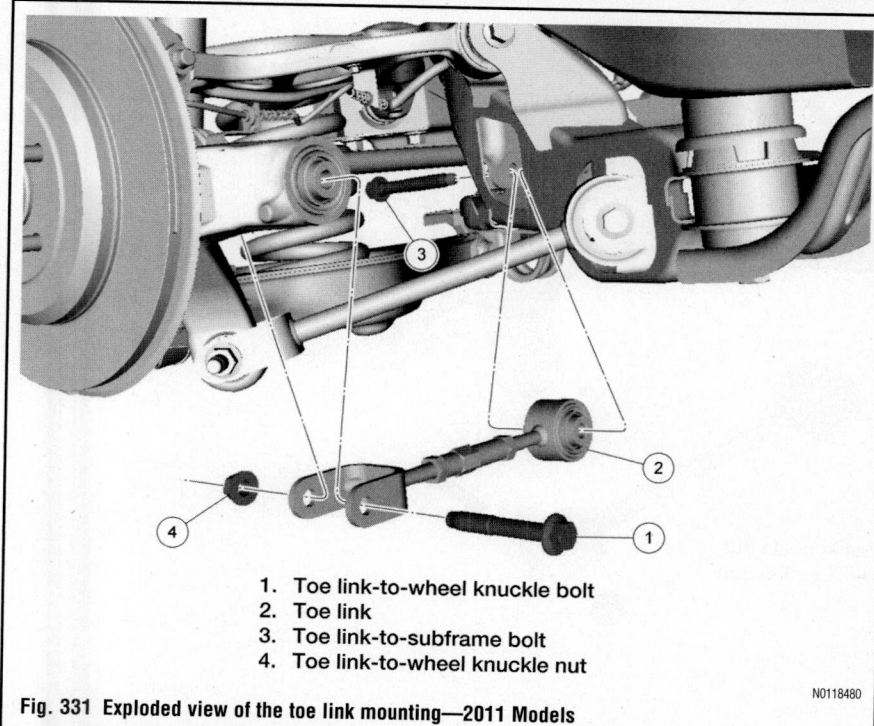

1. Toe link-to-wheel knuckle bolt
2. Toe link
3. Toe link-to-subframe bolt
4. Toe link-to-wheel knuckle nut

Fig. 331 Exploded view of the toe link mounting—2011 Models

N0118480

TRAILING ARM

REMOVAL & INSTALLATION

2010 Models

See Figure 332.

1. Remove the toe link. refer to Toe Link.
2. Remove the parking brake cable bracket bolt.
3. Remove and discard the trailing arm bolt.
4. Remove the 3 wheel knuckle bolts to the trailing arm bolts and discard the bolts.

To install:

5. To install, reverse the removal procedure.
6. Tighten parking brake cable bracket bolt to 89 inch lbs. (10 Nm).
7. Tighten new trailing arm bolt to 222 ft. lbs. (300 Nm) at curb height.
8. Tighten 3 new wheel knuckle bolts to 203 ft. lbs. (275 Nm).

2011 Models

See Figures 317 and 333.

1. Measure the distance from the center of the wheel hub to the lip of the fender with the vehicle in a level, static ground position (curb height).
2. Remove the wheel and tire.
3. Use a jackstand to raise the rear suspension until the distance between the center of the hub and the lip of the fender is equal to the measurement taken in Step 1 of the procedure (curb height).
4. Remove and discard the trailing arm-to-knuckle nut and bolt.
5. Remove and discard the trailing arm-to-subframe bolt.

To install:

➡ **Do not tighten the trailing arm-to-subframe bolt at this time.**

6. Position the trailing arm and loosely install the new trailing arm-to-subframe bolt.
7. Loosely install the new trailing arm-to-wheel knuckle bolt and nut.
8. Use a jackstand to raise the rear suspension until the distance between the center of the hub and the lip of the fender is equal to the measurement taken in Step 1 of the removal procedure (curb height).
9. Tighten the new trailing arm-to-subframe bolt to 122 ft. lbs. (165 Nm).
10. Tighten the new trailing arm-to-wheel knuckle bolt and nut to 111 ft. lbs. (150 Nm).
11. Remove the jackstand.
12. Install the rear wheels and tires.

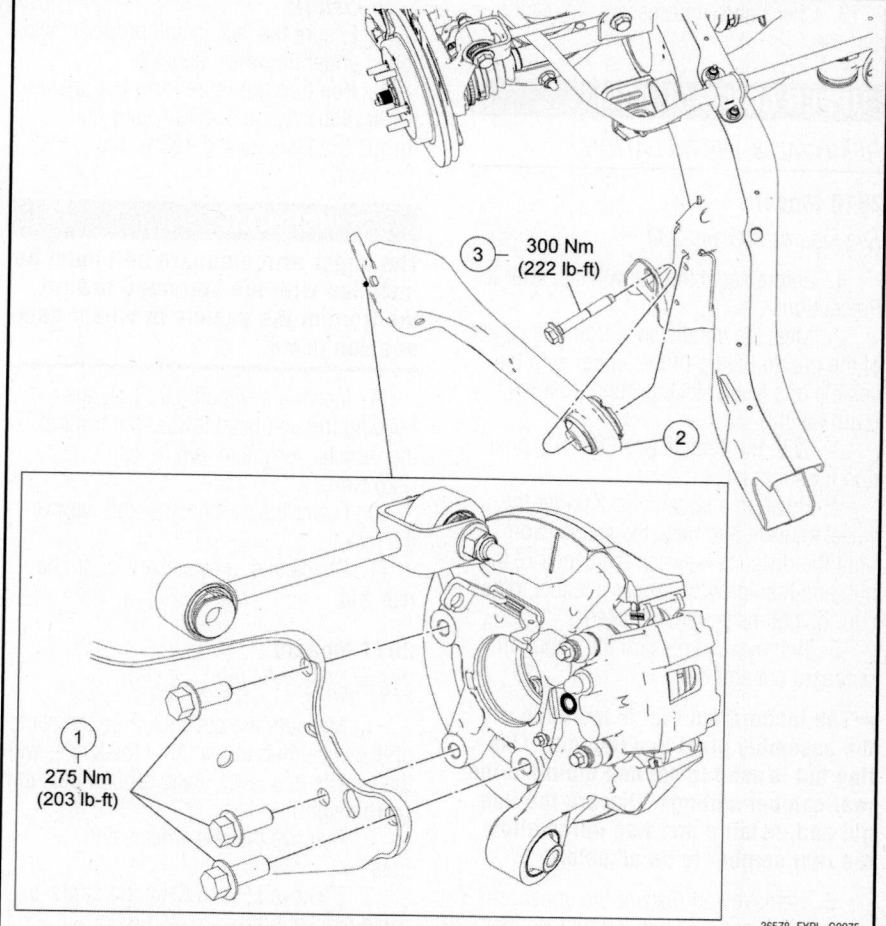

3 — 300 Nm (222 lb-ft)

1 — 275 Nm (203 lb-ft)

Fig. 332 Trailing arm mounting components—2010 Models

36578_EXPL_G0075

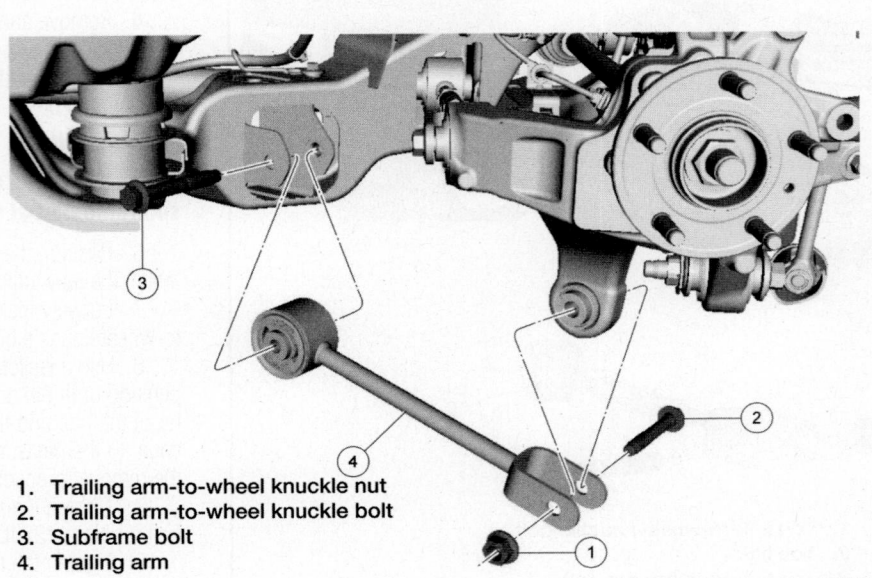

1. Trailing arm-to-wheel knuckle nut
2. Trailing arm-to-wheel knuckle bolt
3. Subframe bolt
4. Trailing arm

N0118481

Fig. 333 Exploded view of the trailing arm—2011 Models

13. Check and, if necessary, adjust the rear toe.

UPPER CONTROL ARM

REMOVAL & INSTALLATION

2010 Models

See Figures 308 and 334.

1. Before servicing the vehicle, refer to Precautions.

2. Measure the distance from the center of the hub to the lip of the fender with the vehicle in a level, static ground position (curb height).

3. With the vehicle in NEUTRAL, position it on a hoist.

4. Position a suitable jack under the wheel knuckle and raise the suspension until the distance between the center of the hub and the lip of the fender is equal to the curb height measurement taken.

5. Remove and discard the upper arm outboard nut and bolt.

➡**The inboard nut that is installed at the assembly plant is a flag nut. This flag nut is used to set and maintain the rear camber settings. Discard the flag nut and install a non-flag nut to allow the rear camber to be adjusted.**

6. Remove and discard the upper arm inboard bolt and flag nut and remove the upper arm.

To install:

7. Ensure the jack is still properly positioned under the wheel knuckle.

8. Position the upper arm and install a new inboard bolt and non-flag nut. Torque the fasteners to 185 ft. lbs. (250 Nm).

✳ **WARNING**

The upper arm outboard bolt must be installed with the bolt head toward the front of the vehicle or wheel damage can occur.

9. Install a new outboard bolt and nut with the bolt head toward the front of the vehicle. Torque to 166 ft. lbs. (225 Nm).

10. Lower the suspension and remove the jack.

11. Check and, if necessary, align the rear end.

2011 Models

See Figures 317, 335 and 336.

1. Measure the distance from the center of the wheel hub to the lip of the fender with the vehicle in a level, static ground position (curb height).

2. Remove the rear wheels and tires.

3. Remove LH and RH parking brake cable bracket bolts.

✳ **WARNING**

Do not allow the brake caliper to hang from the brake flexible hose or damage to the hose may occur.

4. Remove the 4 brake caliper anchor plate bolts and position the LH and RH brake caliper and anchor plate assemblies aside.

   a. Support the brake caliper and anchor plate assemblies using mechanic's wire.

5. Position screw-type jackstands under the LH and RH wheel knuckles.

6. Remove and discard the upper arm-to-knuckle bolt and nut.

7. Remove and discard the 2 upper arm-to-subframe rearward bolts.

➡**Use the hex-holding feature to prevent the stabilizer bar link stud from turning while removing or installing the nut.**

8. Remove and discard the LH and RH stabilizer bar link upper nuts and disconnect the links from the stabilizer bar.

9. Remove and discard the LH and RH lower shock bolts.

10. Remove and discard the 4 subframe bracket bolts.

11. Remove and discard the 2 subframe forward bolts and remove the 2 subframe brackets.

12. Remove and discard the 2 subframe rearward bolts and lower the subframe

1. Upper arm outboard bolt
2. Upper arm
3. Upper arm outboard nut
4. Upper arm inboard nut
5. Upper arm inboard bolt

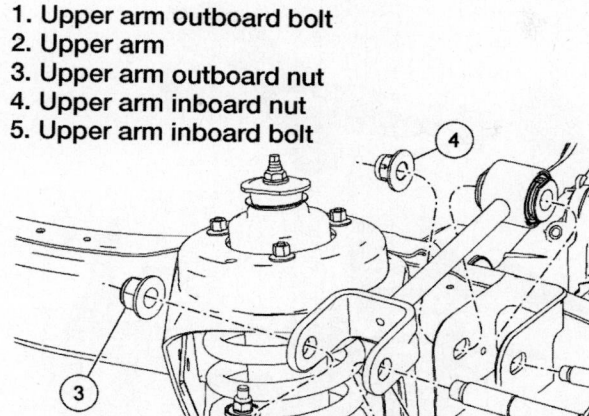

250 Nm
(185 lb-ft)

275 Nm
(203 lb-ft)

22086_EXPL_G0184

Fig. 334 Showing the upper arm and mounting components—2010 Models

enough to allow removal of the upper arm forward bolt.

13. Remove and discard the upper arm-to-subframe forward bolt and nut.

    a. Remove the upper arm.

14. If service to the upper arm rearward bushing is required, remove the upper arm bushing bolt and remove the upper arm bushing. Discard the bolt.

To install:

➡ **Before tightening the shock absorber lower bolts and upper arm nut and bolts, use a jackstand to raise the rear suspension until the distance between the center of the hub and the lip of the fender is equal to the measurement taken in the Removal procedure (curb height).**

15. If removed, install the upper arm bushing onto the upper arm in the following sequence.

    a. With the upper arm positioned so the top side is facing up and the upper arm bushing is positioned with the TOP OF PART facing up and the ARM TO THIS

SIDE arrow is pointing toward the upper arm. Install the upper arm bushing.

    b. Install a new upper arm rearward bushing bolt and tighten to 148 ft. lbs. (200 Nm).

16. Position the upper arm and loosely install the new upper arm-to-subframe forward bolt and nut.

17. Raise the subframe and install 2 new subframe rearward bolts. Tighten the bolts to 148 ft. lbs. (200 Nm).

18. Position the 2 subframe brackets and install 4 new subframe bracket bolts. Tighten the bolts to 41 ft. lbs. (55 Nm).

19. Install 2 new subframe forward bolts. Tighten the bolts to 148 ft. lbs. (200 Nm).

20. Loosely install new LH and RH shock absorber lower bolts.

➡ **Use the hex-holding feature to prevent the stabilizer bar link stud from turning while removing or installing the nut.**

21. Connect the LH and RH stabilizer bar links to the stabilizer bar and install the new nuts. Tighten the nuts to 41 ft. lbs. (55 Nm).

22. Loosely install 2 new upper arm-to-subframe rearward bolts.

23. Loosely install a new upper arm-to-knuckle bolt and nut.

24. Position the LH and RH brake caliper and anchor plate assemblies and install the 4 anchor plate bolts. Tighten the bolts to 76 ft. lbs. (103).

25. Install LH and RH parking brake cable bracket bolts. Tighten the bolts to 133 inch lbs. (15 Nm).

26. Using the screw-type jackstand, raise the rear suspension until the distance between the center of the hub and the lip of the fender is equal to the measurement taken in the removal procedure (curb height).

27. Tighten the upper arm-to-subframe forward bolt to 111 ft. lbs. (150 Nm).

28. Tighten the LH and RH shock absorber lower bolts to 129 ft. lbs. (175 Nm).

29. Tighten the 2 upper arm-to-subframe rearward bolts to 111 ft. lbs. (150 Nm).

➡ **A slotted upper arm allows for the rear suspension camber to be adjusted by pushing inward or pulling outward**

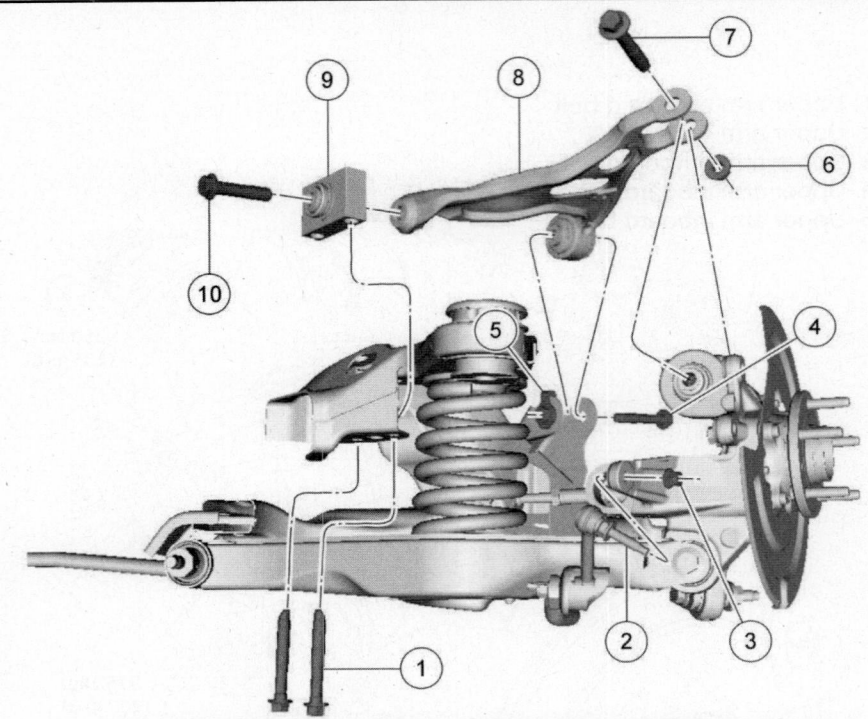

1. Upper arm-to-subframe rearward bolt (2 required)
2. Stabilizer bar link
3. Stabilizer bar link nut
4. Upper arm-to-subframe forward bolt
5. Upper arm-to-subframe forward flag nut
6. Upper arm-to-wheel knuckle nut
7. Upper arm-to-wheel knuckle bolt
8. Upper arm
9. Upper arm rearward bushing
10. Upper arm rearward bushing bolt

N0118478

Fig. 335 Exploded view of the upper control arm—2011 Models

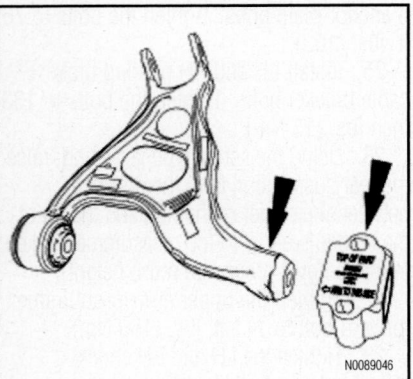

N0089046

Fig. 336 With the upper arm positioned so the top side is facing up and the upper arm bushing is positioned with the TOP OF PART facing up and the ARM TO THIS SIDE arrow is pointing toward the upper arm. Install the upper arm bushing

on the wheel knuckle while tightening the upper arm-to-wheel knuckle nut.

30. With the wheel knuckle pushed inward for maximum negative camber, tighten the upper arm-to-wheel knuckle nut to 148 ft. lbs. (200 Nm).

31. Remove the 2 jackstands.

32. Install the rear wheels and tires.

33. Check and, if necessary, adjust the rear camber.

WHEEL HUB & BEARING

REMOVAL & INSTALLATION

2010 Models

See Figure 337.

1. Remove the wheel knuckle. Refer to Knuckle.

2. Remove the 3 brake disc shield bolts.

3. Using the special tool and a suitable press, remove the wheel hub.

4. Remove the snap ring.

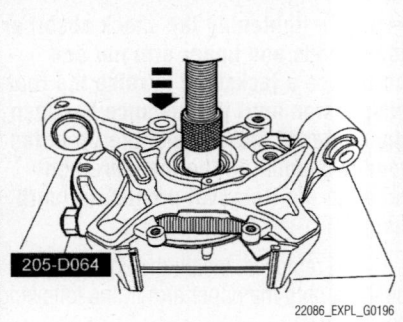

205-D064

22086_EXPL_G0196

Fig. 337 Using the special tool and a suitable press, remove the wheel hub—2011 Models

5. Using a suitable press and adapters, remove the wheel bearing.

To install:

6. Installation is the reverse of the removal procedure.

7. Tighten 3 brake disc shield bolts to 71 inch lbs. (8 Nm).

2011 Models
See Figure 338.

All Vehicles

1. Remove the brake disc.

2. Remove the wheel speed sensor bolt and position the sensor aside.

All-Wheel Drive (AWD) Vehicles

➥**Do not discard the nut at this time.**

3. Remove the wheel hub nut.

4. Using the Front Wheel Hub Remover, separate the halfshaft from the wheel hub.

All Vehicles

5. Remove the 4 bolts and the wheel bearing and wheel hub.
   a. Discard the bolts.

✳✳ WARNING

The wheel knuckle bore must be clean enough to allow the wheel bearing and wheel hub to seat completely by hand. Do not press or draw the wheel hub and bearing into place or damage to the bearing may occur.

✳✳ WARNING

Make sure the wheel hub-to-knuckle mating surfaces are clean and free of any adhesive. Failure to clean adhesive from both surfaces may cause bearing damage.

6. Using a clean shop towel, clean the wheel knuckle-to-mating surfaces and inspect the knuckle bearing bore.
   a. If the wheel knuckle is cracked, install a new wheel knuckle.

To install:
All Vehicles

7. Install the wheel bearing and wheel hub assembly.

8. Install the 4 new wheel bearing and wheel hub bolts. Tighten the bolts to 122 ft. lbs. (165 Nm) in a cross-pattern.

9. Install the brake disc.

10. Position the wheel speed sensor and install the bolt. Tighten the bolt to 133 inch lbs. (15 Nm).

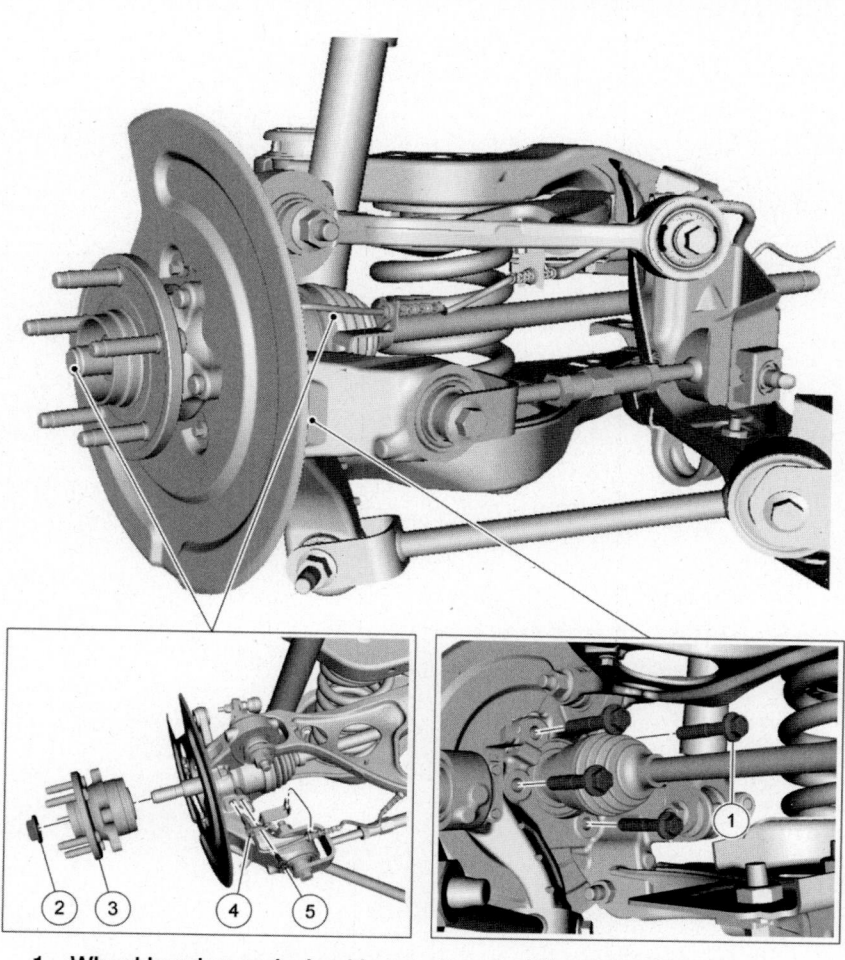

1. Wheel bearing and wheel hub bolt
2. Wheel hub nut
3. Wheel bearing and wheel hub
4. Wheel speed sensor
5. Wheel speed sensor bolt

N0118477

Fig. 338 Wheel bearing and wheel hub components—2011 AWD shown, FWD similar

AWD Vehicles

✳✳ WARNING

Do not tighten the rear wheel hub nut with the vehicle on the ground. The nut must be tightened to specification before the vehicle is lowered to the ground. Wheel bearing damage will occur if the wheel bearing is loaded with the weight of the vehicle applied.

➡**Apply the brake to keep the halfshaft from rotating.**

11. Position the halfshaft in the hub and use the previously removed wheel hub nut to seat the halfshaft. Tighten the nut to 258 ft. lbs. (350 Nm).

   a. Remove and discard the nut.

✳✳ WARNING

Install and tighten the new wheel hub nut to specification within 5 minutes of starting it on the threads. Always install a new wheel hub nut after loosening or when not tightening within the specified time or damage to the components may occur.

12. Install a new wheel hub nut. Tighten the nut to 258 ft. lbs. (350 Nm).

FORD

F-150 • SVT Raptor

7

BRAKES 7-14

**ANTI-LOCK BRAKE
SYSTEM (ABS) 7-14**
General Information..................7-14
  Precautions...........................7-14
Speed Sensors 7-14
  Removal & Installation...........7-14
**BLEEDING THE BRAKE
SYSTEM.......................7-17**
Bleeding Procedure..................7-17
  Bleeding Procedure 7-17
  Master Cylinder Bleeding 7-18
FRONT DISC BRAKES 7-18
Brake Caliper...........................7-18
  Removal & Installation...........7-18
Disc Brake Pads 7-18
  Removal & Installation...........7-18
PARKING BRAKE 7-19
Parking Brake Shoes 7-19
  Removal & Installation...........7-19
REAR DISC BRAKES 7-19
Brake Caliper...........................7-19
  Removal & Installation...........7-19
Disc Brake Pads 7-19
  Removal & Installation...........7-19

CHASSIS ELECTRICAL 7-21

**AIR BAG (SUPPLEMENTAL
RESTRAINT SYSTEM)........7-21**
General Information...................7-21
  Clockspring Centering..........7-24
  Deactivation & Reactivation...7-21
  Depowering & Repowering ...7-23
  Service Precautions 7-21

DRIVE TRAIN 7-26

Automatic Transmission Fluid...7-26
  Drain and Refill.....................7-26
  Filter Replacement 7-26
Front Driveshaft.......................7-32
  Removal & Installation...........7-32
Front Halfshaft.........................7-32
  Removal & Installation...........7-32
Front Pinion Seal......................7-33
  Removal & Installation..........7-33

Rear Axle Housing....................7-34
  Removal & Installation..........7-34
Rear Axle Shaft Bearing &
  Seal....................................7-37
  Removal & Installation..........7-37
Rear Axle Shaft, Bearing &
  Seal....................................7-35
  Removal & Installation..........7-35
Rear Driveshaft........................7-38
  Removal & Installation..........7-38
Rear Pinion Seal.......................7-39
  Removal & Installation..........7-39
Transfer Case Assembly 7-29
  Removal & Installation..........7-29

ENGINE COOLING 7-42

Engine Coolant.........................7-42
  Bleeding 7-46
  Drain & Refill Procedure........7-42
  Flushing...............................7-46
Engine Fan 7-46
  Removal & Installation..........7-46
Radiator...................................7-47
  Removal & Installation..........7-47
Thermostat 7-51
  Removal & Installation..........7-51
Water Pump 7-53
  Removal & Installation..........7-53

ENGINE ELECTRICAL........:.7-57

BATTERY SYSTEM 7-68
Battery....................................7-68
  Battery Reconnect/Relearn
    Procedure 7-68
  Removal & Installation..........7-68
CHARGING SYSTEM 7-57
Alternator 7-57
  Removal & Installation..........7-57
IGNITION SYSTEM 7-60
Firing Order.............................7-61
Ignition Coil 7-61
  Removal & Installation..........7-61
Ignition Timing 7-61
  Adjustment 7-61
Spark Plugs.............................7-61
  Removal & Installation..........7-61

STARTING SYSTEM 7-68
Starter 7-68
  Removal & Installation..........7-68

ENGINE MECHANICAL 7-71

Accessory Drive Belts 7-71
  Accessory Belt Routing........7-71
  Adjustment 7-71
  Inspection 7-71
  Removal & Installation..........7-71
Air Cleaner 7-73
  Filter/element
    Replacement 7-73
Camshaft and Valve Lifters........7-73
  Removal & Installation..........7-73
Catalytic Converter 7-98
  Removal & Installation..........7-98
Crankshaft Front Seal..............7-100
  Removal & Installation........7-100
Cylinder Head 7-101
  Removal & Installation........7-101
Exhaust Manifold 7-105
  Removal & Installation........7-105
Intake Manifold 7-112
  Removal & Installation........7-112
Oil Pan 7-118
  Removal & Installation........7-118
Oil Pump.................................7-125
  Removal & Installation........7-125
Rear Main Seal........................7-127
  Removal & Installation........7-127
Timing Chain & Sprockets......7-137
  Removal & Installation........7-137
Timing Chain Front Cover.......7-129
  Removal & Installation........7-129
Turbocharger 7-150
  Removal & Installation........7-150
Valve Covers 7-152
  Removal & Installation........7-152
Valve Lash...............................7-160
  Adjustment 7-160

**ENGINE PERFORMANCE &
EMISSION CONTROLS 7-160**

Camshaft Position (CMP)
  Sensor 7-160

Location..............................7-160
  Removal & Installation........7-160
Crankshaft Position (CKP)
Sensor...............................7-161
  Location..............................7-161
  Removal & Installation........7-162
Heated Oxygen (HO2S)
Sensor...............................7-164
  Location..............................7-164
  Removal & Installation........7-164
Intake Air Temperature (IAT)
Sensor...............................7-165
  Location..............................7-165
  Removal & Installation........7-165
Knock Sensor (KS).................7-167
  Location..............................7-167
  Removal & Installation........7-169
Manifold Absolute Pressure
(MAP) Sensor.......................7-169
  Location..............................7-169
  Removal & Installation........7-169
Mass Air Flow (MAF) Sensor ...7-170
  Location..............................7-170
  Removal & Installation........7-170
Powertrain Control Module
(PCM)................................7-163
  Location..............................7-163
  Programmable Module
  Installation (PMI)
  Procedure.........................7-164
  Removal & Installation........7-163
  Reprogram the Passive
  Anti-Theft System (PATS)..7-164

FUEL 7-171

**GASOLINE FUEL INJECTION
SYSTEM 7-171**
Fuel Filter...............................7-172
  Removal & Installation........7-172
Fuel Injectors 7-172
  Removal & Installation........7-172

Fuel Pump Module.................7-179
  Removal & Installation........7-179
Fuel System Service
Precautions..........................7-171
Fuel Tank..............................7-180
  Draining..............................7-180
  Removal & Installation........7-180
Idle Speed 7-181
  Adjustment 7-181
Relieving Fuel System
Pressure..............................7-171
Throttle Body (TB)..................7-181
  Removal & Installation........7-181

**HEATING & AIR
CONDITIONING SYSTEM...7-185**

Blower Motor 7-185
  Removal & Installation........7-185
Heater Core 7-185
  Removal & Installation........7-185

PRECAUTIONS 7-14

**SPECIFICATIONS AND
MAINTENANCE CHARTS 7-3**

Brake Specifications...................7-9
Camshaft Specifications..............7-6
Capacities 7-4
Crankshaft and Connecting
  Rod Specifications 7-6
Engine and Vehicle
  Identification 7-3
Engine Tune-Up Specifications.....7-4
Fluid Specifications....................7-5
General Engine
  Specifications 7-3
Piston and Ring
  Specifications 7-7
Scheduled Maintenance
  Intervals 7-10

Tire, Wheel and Ball Joint
  Specifications 7-9
Torque Specifications.................7-8
Valve Specifications 7-5
Wheel Alignment.......................7-9

STEERING 7-186

Power Steering Gear................7-186
  Removal & Installation........7-186
Power Steering Pump..............7-188
  Bleeding 7-190
  Fluid Fill Procedure 7-191
  Removal & Installation........7-188

SUSPENSION 7-192

FRONT SUSPENSION 7-192
Lower Ball Joint 7-192
  Removal & Installation........7-192
Lower Control Arm..................7-193
  Removal & Installation........7-193
Stabilizer Bar and Link 7-195
  Removal & Installation........7-195
Steering Knuckle 7-197
  Removal & Installation........7-197
Strut & Spring Assembly 7-200
  Removal & Installation........7-200
Upper Control Arm..................7-203
  Removal & Installation........7-203
Wheel Bearings 7-204
  Adjustment 7-205
  Removal & Installation........7-204
REAR SUSPENSION 7-206
Leaf Spring............................7-206
  Removal & Installation........7-206
Shock Absorber......................7-207
  Removal & Installation........7-207
Wheel Bearings 7-208
  Adjustment 7-208
  Removal & Installation........7-208

SPECIFICATIONS AND MAINTENANCE CHARTS

ENGINE AND VEHICLE IDENTIFICATION

Engine								Model Year	
Code ①	Liters (cc)	Cu. In.	Cyl.	Fuel Sys.	Engine Type	Eng. Mfg.		Code ②	Year
T	3.5	214	6	GTDI	DOHC	Ford		A	2010
M	3.7	226	6	EFI	DOHC Flex Fuel	Ford		B	2011
8	4.6 (3V)	281	8	EFI	SOHC	Ford			
W	4.6 (2V)	281	8	EFI	SOHC	Ford			
F	5.0	302	8	EFI	DOHC	Ford			
V	5.4	330	8	EFI	SOHC Flex-Fuel	Ford			
6	6.2	379	8	EFI	DOHC	Ford			

① 8th position of VIN

② 10th position of VIN

25759_F150_C0001

GENERAL ENGINE SPECIFICATIONS

All measurements are given in inches.

Year	Model	Engine Displacement Liters	Engine ID/VIN	Fuel System Type	Net Horsepower @ rpm	Net Torque @ rpm (ft. lbs.)	Bore x Stroke (in.)	Compression Ratio	Oil Pressure @ rpm
2010	F-150	4.6 (3V)	8	EFI	292@5700	320@4000	3.55x3.54	9.8:1	75@2000
		4.6 (2V)	W	EFI	248@4750	294@4000	3.55x3.54	9.4:1	40-75@2000
		5.4	V	EFI	320@5200	390@3500	3.55x4.16	9.8:1	40-75@2000
		6.2	6	EFI	411@5500	434@4500	4.02x3.74	9.8:1	NA
2011	F-150	3.5	T	GTDI	NA	NA	3.64x3.41	10.0:1	30@1500
		3.7	M	EFI	302@6500	278@4000	3.76x3.41	10.5:1	30@1500
		5.0	F	EFI	NA	NA	3.63x3.65	10.5:1	NA
		6.2	6	EFI	411@5500	434@4500	4.02x3.74	9.8:1	NA

NA: Not Available

25759_F150_C0002

ENGINE TUNE-UP SPECIFICATIONS

Year	Engine Displacement Liters	Engine ID/VIN	Spark Plug Gap (in.)	Ignition Timing (deg.) MT	Ignition Timing (deg.) AT	Fuel Pump (psi)	Idle Speed (rpm) MT	Idle Speed (rpm) AT	Valve Clearance Intake	Valve Clearance Exhaust
2010	4.6 (3V)	8	0.039-0.043	NA	10 BTDC	55-60	①	①	Hydraulic Lifters	Hydraulic Lifters
	4.6 (2V)	W	0.039-0.043	NA	10 BTDC	55-60	①	①	Hydraulic Lifters	Hydraulic Lifters
	5.4	V	0.039-0.043	NA	10 BTDC	55-60	①	①	Hydraulic Lifters	Hydraulic Lifters
	6.2	6	0.042-0.046	NA	10 BTDC	51-62	①	①	NA	NA
2011	3.5	T	0.035	NA	NA	62-73	①	①	0.006-0.01	0.0142-0.0181
	3.7	M	0.051-0.055	NA	NA	51-62	①	①	0.006-0.01	0.0142-0.0181
	5.0	F	0.049-0.053	NA	NA	51-62	①	①	Hydraulic Lifters	Hydraulic Lifters
	6.2	6	0.042-0.046	NA	10 BTDC	51-62	①	①	NA	NA

NA: Not Available

① Idle speed is electronically controlled and cannot be adjusted.

25759_F150_C0003

CAPACITIES

Year	Model	Engine Displacement Liters	Engine ID/VIN	Engine Oil with Filter	Transmission/axle (pts.) Auto.	Transmission/axle (pts.) Manual	Drive Axle (pts.) Front	Drive Axle (pts.) Rear	Transfer Case (pts.)	Fuel Tank (gal.)	Cooling System (qts.)
2010	F-150	4.6 (3V)	8	6.0	①	NA	3.5	5.5	3.2	②	15.8
		4.6 (2V)	W	6.0	①	NA	3.5	5.5	3.2	②	16.4
		5.4	V	7.0	①	NA	3.6	5.5	3.2	②	16.9
		6.2	6	7.0	③	NA	3.5	5.5	3.2	②	19.5
2011	F-150	3.5	T	6.0	③	NA	3.5	5.5	3.2	②	16.5
		3.7	M	6.0	③	NA	3.5	5.5	3.2	②	16.0
		5.0	F	7.7	③	NA	3.5	5.5	3.2	②	17.0
		6.2	6	7.0	③	NA	3.5	5.5	3.2	②	19.5

NOTE: All capacities are approximate. Add fluid gradually and ensure a proper fluid level is obtained.

NA: Not Applicable

① Specification is for dry fill:

  4R75E: 27.8 pts (4.6L 2V engine)

  6R80: 24.2 pts (4.6L 3V engine)

  6R80: 26.2 pts (5.4L engine)

② Standard fuel tank: 26 gals. Optional fuel tank: 36 gals.

③ Specification is for dry fill:

  3.5L engine: 26.2 pts.

  3.7L engine: 24.2 pts.

  5.0L engine: 26.2 pts.

  6.2L engine: 26.2 pts.

25759_F150_C0004

FLUID SPECIFICATIONS

Year	Model	Engine Disp. Liters	Engine Oil	Auto. Trans.	Drive Axle		Transfer Case	Power Steering Fluid	Brake Master Cylinder	Cooling System
					Front	Rear				
2010	F-150	4.6 (3V)	①	②	80W-90	③	④	Mercon® V ATF	DOT 3	⑤
		4.6 (2V)	①	②	80W-90	③	④	Mercon® V ATF	DOT 3	⑤
		5.4	①	②	80W-90	③	④	Mercon® V ATF	DOT 3	⑤
		6.2	①	②	80W-90	③	④	Mercon® V ATF	DOT 3	⑤
2011	F-150	3.5	⑦	②	80W-90	③	④	Mercon® V ATF	DOT 3	⑥
		3.7	①	②	80W-90	③	④	Mercon® V ATF	DOT 3	⑥
		5.0	①	②	80W-90	③	④	Mercon® V ATF	DOT 3	⑥
		6.2	①	②	80W-90	③	④	Mercon® V ATF	DOT 3	⑥

DOT: Department Of Transportation

① Motorcraft® SAE 5W-20 Premium Synthetic Blend or Full Synthetic Motor Oil

② MERCON® LV ATF

③ MERCON® 75W-140 Synthetic Rear Axle Lubricant

④ Motorcraft® Transfer Case Fluid

⑤ Motorcraft® Premium Gold Engine Coolant with Bittering Agent (yellow-colored) - or-
   Motorcraft® Specialty Orange Engine Coolant with Bittering Agent

⑥ Motorcraft® Specialty Orange Engine Coolant with Bittering Agent

⑦ Motorcraft® SAE 5W-30 Premium Synthetic Blend or Full Synthetic Motor Oil

25759_F150_C0005

VALVE SPECIFICATIONS

Year	Engine Displacement Liters	Engine ID/VIN	Seat Angle (deg.)	Face Angle (deg.)	Spring Test Pressure (lbs. @ in.)	Spring Free-Length (in.)	Spring Installed Height (in.)	Stem-to-Guide Clearance (in.)		Stem Diameter (in.)	
								Intake	Exhaust	Intake	Exhaust
2010	4.6 (3V)	8	44.5-45.0	45.5	171@1.22	2.220	1.660	0.0010-0.0030	0.0020-0.0040	0.2350-0.2360	0.2340-0.2350
	4.6 (2V)	W	45.5	45.25-45.75	132@1.1032	1.951	1.5630-1.587	0.0008-0.0027	0.0018-0.0037	0.2754-0.2746	0.2744-0.2736
	5.4	V	44.5-45.0	45.5	79@1.66	2.190	1.660	0.0010-0.0020	0.0030-0.0040	0.2350-0.2360	0.2340-0.2350
	6.2	6	44.5-45.0	45.5	303@1.637	2.562	2.154	0.0008-0.0028	0.0013-0.0033	0.3123-0.3131	0.3118-0.3126
2011	3.5	T	44.5-45.5	44.5-45.5	105@1.10	2.170	1.450	0.0008-0.0027	0.0013-0.0320	0.2157-0.2164	0.2151-0.2159
	3.7	M	44.5-45.5	45.25-45.75	115@1.06	1.889	1.450	0.0008-0.0027	0.0013-0.0320	0.2157-0.2164	0.2151-0.2159
	5.0	F				2.020	1.575	0.0008-0.0027	0.0018-0.0037	0.2368-0.2379	0.2368-0.2379
	6.2	6	44.5-45.0	45.5	303@1.637	2.562	2.154	0.0008-0.0028	0.0013-0.0033	0.3123-0.3131	0.3118-0.3126

25759_F150_C0006

CAMSHAFT SPECIFICATIONS

All measurements in inches unless noted

Year	Engine Displacement Liters	Engine Code/VIN	Journal Diameter	Brg. Oil Clearance	Shaft End-play	Runout	Journal Bore	Lobe Lift Intake	Lobe Lift Exhaust
2010	4.6 (3V)	8.0	1.126-1.127	0.001-0.003	0.001-0.007	0.001	1.126-1.127	0.217	0.217
	4.6 (2V)	W	1.0605-1.0615	0.001-0.003	0.001-0.007	0.002	1.0625-1.0635	0.2560	0.2560
	5.4	V	1.126-1.127	0.001-0.003	0.001-0.007	0.001	1.128-1.129	0.2170	0.2170
	6.2	6	1.125-1.126	0.0017-0.0037	0.0009-0.0059	0.0009	1.128-1.129	0.315	0.3090
2011	3.5	T	①	0.0029 Max.	0.0012-0.0066	0.00748	②	0.373	0.373
	3.7	M	③	0.0029 Max.	0.0012-0.0066	0.0015	④	0.3900	0.3800
	5.0	F	1.1267	0.001-0.002	0.0059	0.0016	1.1282-1.1292	0.2348	0.2160
	6.2	6	1.125-1.126	0.0017-0.0037	0.0009-0.0059	0.0009	1.128-1.129	0.315	0.3090

① 1st Journal: 1.2202-1.2209

Intermediate Journals: 1.021-1.022

② 1st Journal: 1.537-1.538

Intermediate Journals: 1.535-1.536

③ 1st Journal: 1.5350-1.5358

Intermediate Journals: 1.021-1.022

④ 1st Journal: 1.536-1.537

Intermediate Journals: 1.023-1.024

25759_F150_C0007

CRANKSHAFT AND CONNECTING ROD SPECIFICATIONS

All measurements are given in inches.

Year	Engine Displacement Liters	Engine ID/VIN	Crankshaft Main Brg. Journal Dia.	Crankshaft Main Brg. Oil Clearance	Crankshaft Shaft End-play	Connecting Rod Journal Diameter	Connecting Rod Oil Clearance	Connecting Rod Side Clearance
2010	4.6 (3V)	8	2.6567-2.6576	0.0009-0.0019	0.0030-0.0148	2.0859-2.0867	0.0004-0.0009	0.0020-0.0060
	4.6 (2V)	W	2.6500	0.0011-0.0026	0.0051-0.0120	2.0859-2.0867	0.0010-0.0027	0.0020 Max.
	5.4	V	2.6568-2.6576	0.0009-0.0019	0.0030-0.0148	2.0867-2.0859	0.0010-0.0025	0.0049-0.0187
	6.2	6	2.6568-2.6576	0.0009-0.0019	0.0050-0.0100	2.0761-2.0768	0.0009-0.0025	0.0390
2011	3.5	T	2.6570	0.0010-0.0016	0.0039-0.0114	2.2040-2.2050	0.0007-0.0021	0.0068-0.0167
	3.7	M	2.6570	0.0010-0.0016	0.0020-0.0114	2.204-2.2050	0.0007-0.0021	0.0068-0.0167
	5.0	F	2.657-2.6580	0.0009-0.0018	0.0110	2.0860-2.0870	0.0011-0.0027	0.0128
	6.2	6	2.6568-2.6576	0.0009-0.0019	0.0050-0.0100	2.0761-2.0768	0.0009-0.0025	0.0390

25759_F150_C0008

PISTON AND RING SPECIFICATIONS

All measurements are given in inches.

Year	Engine Displacement Liters	Engine ID/VIN	Piston Clearance	Ring Gap			Ring Side Clearance		
				Top Compression	Bottom Compression	Oil Control	Top Compression	Bottom Compression	Oil Control
2010	4.6 (3V)	8	0.0007-0.0019	0.0060-0.0120	0.0098-0.0197	0.0059-0.0256	0.0008-0.0020	0.0008-0.0020	NA
	4.6 (2V)	W	0.0007-0.0019	0.0100-0.0200	0.0100-0.0200	0.0060-0.0260	0.0012-0.0028	0.0012-0.0028	0.0018-0.0077
	5.4	V	0.0010-0.0018	0.0060-0.0120	0.0098-0.0197	0.0059-0.0256	0.0008-0.0031	0.0012-0.0028	NA
	6.2	6	0.0003-0.0015	0.0137-0.0196	0.0137-0.0196	0.0050-0.0250	0.0578-0.0590	0.0578-0.0590	NA
2011	3.5	T	0.0003-0.0017	0.0067-0.0106	0.0118-0.0216	0.0059-0.0177	0.0014-0.0031	0.0014-0.0031	NA
	3.7	M	0.0003-0.0017	0.0067-0.0106	0.0118-0.0216	0.0059-0.0177	0.0015-0.0031	0.0015-0.0031	NA
	5.0	F	0.0009-0.0023	0.0059-0.0098	0.0118-0.0216	0.0059-0.0177	0.0019-0.0031	0.0019-0.0028	NA
	6.2	6	0.0003-0.0015	0.0137-0.0196	0.0137-0.0196	0.0050-0.0250	0.0578-0.0590	0.0578-0.0590	NA

NA: Not Available

25759_F150_C0009

TORQUE SPECIFICATIONS
All readings in ft. lbs.

Year	Engine Disp. Liters	Engine ID/VIN	Cylinder Head Bolts	Main Bearing Bolts	Rod Bearing Bolts	Crankshaft Damper Bolts	Flywheel Bolts	Manifold Intake	Manifold Exhaust	Spark Plugs	Oil Pan Drain Plug
2010	4.6 (3V)	8	①	②	③	④	59	⑤	18	⑥	17
	4.6 (2V)	W	⑦	②	③	⑧	59	⑨	⑩	13	17
	5.4	V	⑪	⑫	⑬	④	59	⑭	18	⑥	17
	6.2	6	⑮	⑯	⑰	⑱	⑲	⑳	㉑	13	17
2011	3.5	T	㉒	NA	NA	㉓	59	⑨	㉔	10	20
	3.7	M	㉒	NA	NA	㉓	59	㉕	㉔	10	20
	5.0	F	㉖	NA	NA	㉗	㉘	㉙	㉚	10	19
	6.2	6	⑮	⑯	⑰	⑱	⑲	⑳	㉑	13	17

NA: Not Available

① Step 1: 30 ft. lbs.
Step 2: Additional 90 degrees
Step 3: Loosen 360 degrees
Step 4: 30 ft. lbs.
Step 5: Additional 90 degrees
Step 6: Additional 90 degrees

② Main bearing cap bolts:
Step 1: 30 ft. lbs.
Step 2: Additional 90 degrees
Jackscrews:
Step 3: 44 inch lbs.
Step 4: 89 inch lbs.
Side bolts:
Step 5: 15 ft. lbs.

③ Step 1: 17 ft. lbs.
Step 2: 32 ft. lbs.
Step 3: Additional 105 degrees

④ Step 1: 66 ft. lbs.
Step 2: Loosen 360 degrees
Step 3: 37 ft. lbs.
Step 4: Additional 90 degrees

⑤ Step 1: Finger tight
Step 2: 89 inch lbs.
Step 3: Additional 60 degrees
Step 4: Loosen 360 degrees
Step 5: 89 inch lbs.
Step 6: Additional 60 degrees

⑥ 106 inch lbs.

⑦ Step 1: 30 ft. lbs.
Step 2: Additional 90 degrees
Step 3: Additional 90 degrees

⑧ Step 1: 89 ft. lbs.
Step 2: Loosen 360 degrees
Step 3: 37 ft. lbs.
Step 4: Additional 90 degrees

⑨ 89 inch lbs.

⑩ Step 1: 13 ft. lbs.
Step 2: 20 ft. lbs.

⑪ Step 1: 30 ft. lbs.
Step 2: Additional 90 degrees
Step 3: Additional 90 degrees

⑫ Main bearing cap bolts:
Step 1: 30 ft. lbs.
Step 2: Additional 90 degrees
Side bolts:
Step 3: 22 ft. lbs.
Step 4: Additional 90 degrees

⑬ Step 1: 62 ft. lbs.
Step 2: Additional 105 degrees

⑭ Step 1: 18 inch lbs.
Step 2: 89 inch lbs.

⑮ M12 bolts:
Step 1: 18 ft. lbs.
Step 2: 44 ft. lbs.
Step 3: Additional 90 degrees
Step 4: Additional 90 degrees
M8 bolts: (LH cylinder head only)
Step 5: 15 ft. lbs.
Step 6: Additional 45 degrees

⑯ Outer main bearing cap bolts:
Step 1: 26 ft. lbs.
Step 2: 37 ft. lbs.
Step 3: Additional 90 degrees
Inner main bearing cap bolts:
Step 4: 26 ft. lbs.
Step 5: 65 ft. lbs.
Step 6: Additional 90 degrees
Side bolts:
Step 7: 15 ft. lbs.
Step 8: Additional 60 degrees

⑰ Step 1: 15 ft. lbs.
Step 2: 32 ft. lbs.

⑱ Step 1: 129 ft. lbs.
Step 2: Additional 90 degrees

⑲ Every other bolt: (1 through 4)
Step 1: 15 ft. lbs.
Step 2: 26 ft. lbs.
Step 3: Additional 60 degrees
Remaining 4 bolts: (5 through 8)
Step 4: 15 ft. lbs.
Step 5: 26 ft. lbs.
Step 6: Additional 60 degrees

⑳ Intake manifold bolts:
Step 1: 89 inch lbs.
Step 2: Additional 45 degrees
Fuel rail bolts:
Step 3: 89 inch lbs.
Step 4: Additional 90 degrees

㉑ Step 1: 18 ft. lbs.
Step 2: 24 ft. lbs.

㉒ Step 1: 15 ft. lbs.
Step 2: 26 ft. lbs.
Step 3: Additional 90 degrees
Step 4: Additional 90 degrees
Step 5: Additional 45 degrees

㉓ Step 1: 89 ft. lbs.
Step 2: Loosen 360 degrees
Step 3: 37 ft. lbs.
Step 4: Additional 90 degrees

㉔ Step 1: 14 ft. lbs.
Step 2: 18 ft. lbs.

㉕ Lower intake manifold: 89 inch lbs.
Upper intake manifold:
Step 1: 89 inch lbs.
Step 2: Additional 45 degrees

㉖ Step 1: 18 ft. lbs.
Step 2: 30 ft. lbs.
Step 3: Additional 90 degrees
Step 4: Additional 90 degrees

㉗ Step 1: 103 ft. lbs.
Step 2: Loosen 360 degrees
Step 3: 74 ft. lbs.
Step 4: Additional 90 degrees

㉘ Step 1: 15 ft. lbs.
Step 2: Additional 60 degrees

㉙ Step 1: 89 inch lbs.
Step 2: Additional 45 degrees

㉚ Step 1: 18 ft. lbs.
Step 2: 24 ft. lbs.

25759_F150_C0010

WHEEL ALIGNMENT

Year	Model		Caster Range (+/-Deg.)	Caster Preferred Setting (Deg.)	Camber Range (+/-Deg.)	Camber Preferred Setting (Deg.)	Toe-in (in.)
2010	F-150 RWD	LF	1.0	3.9	0.75	-0.2	0.20+/-0.20
		RF	1.0	4.3	0.75	-0.4	0.20+/-0.20
	F-150 4WD Except SVT Raptor	LF	1.0	3.8	0.75	-02	0.20+/-0.20
		RF	1.0	4.2	0.75	-0.4	0.20+/-0.20
	F-150 4WD SVT Raptor	LF	1.0	3.7	0.75	-0.45	0.20+/-0.20
		RF	1.0	3.7	0.75	-0.45	0.20+/-0.20
2011	F-150 RWD	LF	1.0	3.9	0.75	-0.2	0.20+/-0.20
		RF	1.0	4.3	0.75	-0.4	0.20+/-0.20
	F-150 4WD Except SVT Raptor	LF	1.0	3.8	0.75	-02	0.20+/-0.20
		RF	1.0	4.2	0.75	-0.4	0.20+/-0.20
	F-150 4WD SVT Raptor	LF	1.0	3.7	0.75	-0.45	0.20+/-0.20
		RF	1.0	3.7	0.75	-0.45	0.20+/-0.20

25759_F150_C0011

TIRE, WHEEL AND BALL JOINT SPECIFICATIONS

Year	Model	OEM Tires Standard	OEM Tires Optional	Tire Pressures (psi) Front	Tire Pressures (psi) Rear	Wheel Size	Ball Joint Inspection	Lug Nut (ft. lbs.)
2010	F-150	P235/75R17	NA	①	①	17	NA	150
2011	F-150	P235/75R17	NA	①	①	17	NA	150

OEM: Original Equipment Manufacturer

PSI: Pounds Per Square Inch

NA: Information not available

① Check label on driver's door jamb for proper inflation psi.

25759_F150_C0012

BRAKE SPECIFICATIONS

All measurements in inches unless noted

Year	Model		Brake Disc Original Thickness	Brake Disc Minimum Thickness	Brake Disc Max. Runout	Brake Drum Diameter Original Inside Diameter	Brake Drum Diameter Max. Wear Limit	Brake Drum Diameter Maximum Machine Diamter	Minimum Pad/Lining Thickness Front	Minimum Pad/Lining Thickness Rear	Brake Caliper Guide Pin (ft. lbs.)	Brake Caliper Caliper Bracket (ft. lbs.)
2010	F-150	F	NA	1.259	NA	NA	NA	NA	0.118	—	27	184
		R	NA	0.728	NA	NA	NA	NA	—	0.118	22	122
2011	F-150	F	NA	1.259	NA	NA	NA	NA	0.118	—	27	184
		R	NA	0.728	NA	NA	NA	NA	—	0.118	27	184

F: Front

R: Rear

NA: Information not available

25759_F150_C0013

SCHEDULED MAINTENANCE INTERVALS
2010 Ford F-150 - Normal

TO BE SERVICED	TYPE OF SERVICE	VEHICLE MILEAGE INTERVAL (x1000)												
		7.5	15	22.5	30	37.5	45	52.5	60	67.5	75	82.5	90	97.5
Manual transmission fluid	Replace	Every 150,000 miles												
Front differential fluid	Replace	Every 150,000 miles												
Engine coolant	Replace	At 6 years or 105,000 miles; then every 3 years or 45,000 miles												
Windshield for cracks, chips and pitting	Inspect	✓	✓	✓	✓	✓	✓	✓	✓	✓	✓	✓	✓	✓
Windshield wiper spray and wiper operation	Inspect	✓	✓	✓	✓	✓	✓	✓	✓	✓	✓	✓	✓	✓
Oil and fluid leaks	Inspect	✓	✓	✓	✓	✓	✓	✓	✓	✓	✓	✓	✓	✓
Radiator, coolers, heater and air conditioning hoses	Inspect	✓	✓	✓	✓	✓	✓	✓	✓	✓	✓	✓	✓	✓
Shocks struts and other suspension components for leaks and damage	Inspect	✓	✓	✓	✓	✓	✓	✓	✓	✓	✓	✓	✓	✓
Battery performance	Inspect	✓	✓	✓	✓	✓	✓	✓	✓	✓	✓	✓	✓	✓
Fluid levels (all)	Top off	✓	✓	✓	✓	✓	✓	✓	✓	✓	✓	✓	✓	✓
Drive belt	Replace													
Drive belt	Inspect	✓	✓	✓	✓	✓	✓	✓	✓	✓	✓	✓	✓	✓
Transfer case oil (4x4)	Replace	Every 150,000 miles												
Rear differential fluid	Replace	Every 150,000 miles												
Spark plugs	Replace												✓	
Engine air filter	Replace				✓				✓				✓	
Engine air filter	Inspect	✓	✓	✓	✓	✓	✓	✓	✓	✓	✓	✓	✓	✓
Exhaust system (Leaks, damage, loose parts and foreign material)	Inspect		✓			✓		✓			✓		✓	
Brake system (Pads/shoes/rotors/drums, brake lines and hoses, and parking brake system)	Inspect		✓			✓		✓			✓		✓	
Cooling system, hoses, clamps & coolant strength	Inspect		✓			✓		✓			✓		✓	
Steering linkage, ball joints, suspension, tie-rod ends, driveshaft and u-joints: lubricate if equipped with grease fittings	Inspect/Lubricate	✓	✓	✓	✓	✓	✓	✓	✓	✓	✓	✓	✓	✓
Inspect and related components for abnormal wear, noise looseness or drag	Inspect	✓	✓	✓	✓	✓	✓	✓	✓	✓	✓	✓	✓	✓
Rotate tires, inspect tread wear, measure tread depth and check pressure	Rotate	✓	✓	✓	✓	✓	✓	✓	✓	✓	✓	✓	✓	✓
Engine oil & filter	Replace	✓	✓	✓	✓	✓	✓	✓	✓	✓	✓	✓	✓	✓

Use of E85 50% of the time or greater, change engine oil and filter every 5,000 miles or 6 months.

25759_F150_C0014

SCHEDULED MAINTENANCE INTERVALS
2010 Ford F-150 - Severe

TO BE SERVICED	TYPE OF SERVICE	VEHICLE MILEAGE INTERVAL (x1000)											
		5	10	15	20	25	30	35	40	45	50	55	60
Engine oil & filter	Replace	✓	✓	✓	✓	✓	✓	✓	✓	✓	✓	✓	✓
Rotate tires, inspect tread wear, measure tread depth and check pressure	Rotate	✓	✓	✓	✓	✓	✓	✓	✓	✓	✓	✓	✓
Inspect and related components for abnormal wear, noise looseness or drag	Inspect	✓	✓	✓	✓	✓	✓	✓	✓	✓	✓	✓	✓
Steering linkage, ball joints, suspension, tie-rod ends, driveshaft and u-joints: lubricate if equipped with grease fittings	Inspect and Lubricate	✓	✓	✓	✓	✓	✓	✓	✓	✓	✓	✓	✓
Cooling system, hoses, clamps & coolant strength	Inspect		✓		✓		✓		✓		✓		✓
Brake system (Pads/shoes/rotors/drums, brake lines and hoses, and parking brake system)	Inspect		✓		✓		✓		✓		✓		✓
Exhaust system (Leaks, damage, loose parts and foreign material)	Inspect		✓		✓		✓		✓		✓		✓
Engine air filter	Inspect	✓	✓	✓	✓	✓	✓	✓	✓	✓	✓	✓	✓
Engine air filter	Replace				✓				✓				✓
Spark plugs	Replace												✓
Rear differential fluid	Replace	every 150,000 miles											
Transfer case oil (4x4)	Replace	every 150,000 miles											
Drive belt	Inspect	✓	✓	✓	✓	✓	✓	✓	✓	✓	✓	✓	✓
Drive belt	Replace	every 150,000 miles											
Fluid levels (all)	Top off	✓	✓	✓	✓	✓	✓	✓	✓	✓	✓	✓	✓
Battery performance	Inspect	✓	✓	✓	✓	✓	✓	✓	✓	✓	✓	✓	✓
Shocks struts and other suspension components for leaks and damage	Inspect	✓	✓	✓	✓	✓	✓	✓	✓	✓	✓	✓	✓
Radiator, coolers, heater and air conditioning hoses	Inspect	✓	✓	✓	✓	✓	✓	✓	✓	✓	✓	✓	✓
Oil and fluid leaks	Inspect	✓	✓	✓	✓	✓	✓	✓	✓	✓	✓	✓	✓
Windshield wiper spray and wiper operation	Inspect	✓	✓	✓	✓	✓	✓	✓	✓	✓	✓	✓	✓
Windshield for cracks, chips and pitting	Inspect	✓	✓	✓	✓	✓	✓	✓	✓	✓	✓	✓	✓
Engine coolant	Replace	At 6 years or 105,000 miles; then every 3 years or 45,000 miles											
Front differential fluid	Replace	every 150,000 miles											
Manual transmission fluid	Replace	every 105,000 miles											

Use of E85 50% of the time or greater, change engine oil and filter every 5,000 miles or 6 months.

25759_F150_C0015

SCHEDULED MAINTENANCE INTERVALS
2011 Ford F-150 - Normal

Service Item	Service Action	1	2	3	4	5	6	7	8	9	10	11	12	13	14	15
Engine oil & filter	Replace	✓	✓	✓	✓	✓	✓	✓	✓	✓	✓	✓	✓	✓	✓	✓
Spark plugs	Replace										✓					
Engine coolant	Replace										✓					✓
Halfshaft boots	Inspect	✓	✓	✓	✓	✓	✓	✓	✓	✓	✓	✓	✓	✓	✓	✓
Drive belt(s)	Inspect	✓	✓	✓	✓	✓	✓	✓	✓	✓	✓	✓	✓	✓	✓	✓
Drive belt(s)	Replace															✓
Auto transmisison fluid	Replace															✓
Engine air filter	Replace			✓			✓			✓			✓			✓
Engine air filter	Inspect	✓	✓	✓	✓	✓	✓	✓	✓	✓	✓	✓	✓	✓	✓	✓
Cooling system, hoses, clamps & coolant strength	Inspect	✓	✓	✓	✓	✓	✓	✓	✓	✓	✓	✓	✓	✓	✓	✓
Battery performance	Inspect	✓	✓	✓	✓	✓	✓	✓	✓	✓	✓	✓	✓	✓	✓	✓
Climate-controlled seat filter (if equipped)	Replace			✓			✓			✓			✓			✓
Exhaust system (Leaks, damage, loose parts and foreign material)	Inspect	✓	✓	✓	✓	✓	✓	✓	✓	✓	✓	✓	✓	✓	✓	✓
Horn, exterior lamps, turn signals and hazard warning light operation	Inspect	✓	✓	✓	✓	✓	✓	✓	✓	✓	✓	✓	✓	✓	✓	✓
Windshield for cracks, chips and pitting	Inspect	✓	✓	✓	✓	✓	✓	✓	✓	✓	✓	✓	✓	✓	✓	✓
Windshield wiper spray and wiper operation	Inspect	✓	✓	✓	✓	✓	✓	✓	✓	✓	✓	✓	✓	✓	✓	✓
Fluid levels (all)	Top off	✓	✓	✓	✓	✓	✓	✓	✓	✓	✓	✓	✓	✓	✓	✓
Brake system (Pads/shoes/rotors/drums, brake lines and hoses, and parking brake system)	Inspect	✓	✓	✓	✓	✓	✓	✓	✓	✓	✓	✓	✓	✓	✓	✓
Inspect wheels and related components for abnomal noise, wear, looseness or drag	Inspect	✓	✓	✓	✓	✓	✓	✓	✓	✓	✓	✓	✓	✓	✓	✓
Steering linkage, ball joints, suspension, tie-rod ends, driveshaft and u-joints: lubricate if equipped with grease fittings	Inspect/ Lubricate	✓	✓	✓	✓	✓	✓	✓	✓	✓	✓	✓	✓	✓	✓	✓
Radiator, coolers, heater and air conditioning hoses	Inspect	✓	✓	✓	✓	✓	✓	✓	✓	✓	✓	✓	✓	✓	✓	✓
Rotate tires, inspect tread wear, measure tread depth and check pressure	Inspect/ Rotate	✓	✓	✓	✓	✓	✓	✓	✓	✓	✓	✓	✓	✓	✓	✓
Suspension components for leaks and damage	Inspect	✓	✓	✓	✓	✓	✓	✓	✓	✓	✓	✓	✓	✓	✓	✓
Transfer case fluid	Replace															✓
Front differential fluid	Replace															✓
Rear differential fluid	Replace															✓

Oil change service intervals should be completed as indicated by the message center (Can be up to 1 year or 10,000 miles) If the message center is prematurely reset or is inoperative, perform the oil change interval at 6 months or 5,000 miles from your last oil change.

For extensive idling and or low speed driving, change engine oil and filter every 5,000 miles, 6 months or 200 hours of engine operation.

25759_F150_C0016

SCHEDULED MAINTENANCE INTERVALS
2011 Ford F-150 - Severe

Service Item	Service Action	1	2	3	4	5	6	7	8	9	10	11	12	13	14	15
Engine oil & filter	Replace	✓	✓	✓	✓	✓	✓	✓	✓	✓	✓	✓	✓	✓	✓	✓
Spark plugs	Replace						✓						✓			
Engine coolant	Replace										✓					
Rear differential fluid	Replace															✓
Drive belt(s)	Inspect	✓	✓	✓	✓	✓	✓	✓	✓	✓	✓	✓	✓	✓	✓	✓
Drive belt(s)	Replace															✓
Transfer case fluid	Replace															✓
Auto transmision fluid	Replace			✓			✓			✓			✓			✓
Engine air filter	Inspect/ Service	✓	✓	✓	✓	✓	✓	✓	✓	✓	✓	✓	✓	✓	✓	✓
Cooling system, hoses, clamps & coolant strength	Inspect	✓	✓	✓	✓	✓	✓	✓	✓	✓	✓	✓	✓	✓	✓	✓
Battery performance	Inspect	✓	✓	✓	✓	✓	✓	✓	✓	✓	✓	✓	✓	✓	✓	✓
Climate-controlled seat filter (if equipped)	Replace			✓			✓			✓			✓			✓
Exhaust system	Inspect	✓	✓	✓	✓	✓	✓	✓	✓	✓	✓	✓	✓	✓	✓	✓
Horn, exterior lamps, turn signals and hazard warning light operation	Inspect	✓	✓	✓	✓	✓	✓	✓	✓	✓	✓	✓	✓	✓	✓	✓
Oil and fluid leaks	Inspect	✓	✓	✓	✓	✓	✓	✓	✓	✓	✓	✓	✓	✓	✓	✓
Shocks struts and other suspension components for leaks and damage	Inspect	✓	✓	✓	✓	✓	✓	✓	✓	✓	✓	✓	✓	✓	✓	✓
Windshield for cracks, chips and pitting	Inspect	✓	✓	✓	✓	✓	✓	✓	✓	✓	✓	✓	✓	✓	✓	✓
Windshield wiper spray and wiper operation	Inspect	✓	✓	✓	✓	✓	✓	✓	✓	✓	✓	✓	✓	✓	✓	✓
Halfshaft & U-joints	Inspect	✓	✓	✓	✓	✓	✓	✓	✓	✓	✓	✓	✓	✓	✓	✓
Fluid levels (all)	Top off	✓	✓	✓	✓	✓	✓	✓	✓	✓	✓	✓	✓	✓	✓	✓
Brake system (Pads/shoes/rotors/drums, brake lines and hoses, and parking brake system)	Inspect	✓	✓	✓	✓	✓	✓	✓	✓	✓	✓	✓	✓	✓	✓	✓
Inspect wheels and related components for abnomal noise, wear, looseness or drag	Inspect	✓	✓	✓	✓	✓	✓	✓	✓	✓	✓	✓	✓	✓	✓	✓
Cabin air filter (If equipped)	Inspect/ Service	✓	✓	✓	✓	✓	✓	✓	✓	✓	✓	✓	✓	✓	✓	✓
Radiator, coolers, heater and air conditioning hoses	Inspect	✓	✓	✓	✓	✓	✓	✓	✓	✓	✓	✓	✓	✓	✓	✓
Rotate tires, inspect tread wear, measure tread depth and check pressure	Inspect/ Rotate	✓	✓	✓	✓	✓	✓	✓	✓	✓	✓	✓	✓	✓	✓	✓
Steering linkage, ball joints, suspension and tie-rod ends, lubricate if equipped with greases fittings	Inspect/ Lubricate	✓	✓	✓	✓	✓	✓	✓	✓	✓	✓	✓	✓	✓	✓	✓
Front differential fluid	Replace															✓

Oil change service intervals should be completed as indicated by the message center (Can be up to 1 year or 10,000 miles) If the message center is prematurely reset or is inoperative, perform the oil change interval at 6 months or 5,000 miles from your last oil change.

For extensive idling and or low speed driving, change engine oil and filter every 5,000 miles, 6 months or 200 hours of engine operation.

PRECAUTIONS

Before servicing any vehicle, please be sure to read all of the following precautions, which deal with personal safety, prevention of component damage, and important points to take into consideration when servicing a motor vehicle:

• Never open, service or drain the radiator or cooling system when the engine is hot; serious burns can occur from the steam and hot coolant.

• Observe all applicable safety precautions when working around fuel. Whenever servicing the fuel system, always work in a well-ventilated area. Do not allow fuel spray or vapors to come in contact with a spark, open flame, or excessive heat (a hot drop light, for example). Keep a dry chemical fire extinguisher near the work area. Always keep fuel in a container specifically designed for fuel storage; also, always properly seal fuel containers to avoid the possibility of fire or explosion. Refer to the additional fuel system precautions later in this section.

• Fuel injection systems often remain pressurized, even after the engine has been turned **OFF**. The fuel system pressure must be relieved before disconnecting any fuel lines. Failure to do so may result in fire and/or personal injury.

• Brake fluid often contains polyglycol ethers and polyglycols. Avoid contact with the eyes and wash your hands thoroughly after handling brake fluid. If you do get brake fluid in your eyes, flush your eyes with clean, running water for 15 minutes. If eye irritation persists, or if you have taken

brake fluid internally, IMMEDIATELY seek medical assistance.

• The EPA warns that prolonged contact with used engine oil may cause a number of skin disorders, including cancer. You should make every effort to minimize your exposure to used engine oil. Protective gloves should be worn when changing oil. Wash your hands and any other exposed skin areas as soon as possible after exposure to used engine oil. Soap and water, or waterless hand cleaner should be used.

• All new vehicles are now equipped with an air bag system, often referred to as a Supplemental Restraint System (SRS) or Supplemental Inflatable Restraint (SIR) system. The system must be disabled before performing service on or around system components, steering column, instrument panel components, wiring and sensors. Failure to follow safety and disabling procedures could result in accidental air bag deployment, possible personal injury and unnecessary system repairs.

• Always wear safety goggles when working with, or around, the air bag system. When carrying a non-deployed air bag, be sure the bag and trim cover are pointed away from your body. When placing a non-deployed air bag on a work surface, always face the bag and trim cover upward, away from the surface. This will reduce the motion of the module if it is accidentally deployed. Refer to the additional air bag system precautions later in this section.

• Clean, high quality brake fluid from a sealed container is essential to the safe and

proper operation of the brake system. You should always buy the correct type of brake fluid for your vehicle. If the brake fluid becomes contaminated, completely flush the system with new fluid. Never reuse any brake fluid. Any brake fluid that is removed from the system should be discarded. Also, do not allow any brake fluid to come in contact with a painted surface; it will damage the paint.

• Never operate the engine without the proper amount and type of engine oil; doing so WILL result in severe engine damage.

• Timing belt maintenance is extremely important. Many models utilize an interference-type, non-freewheeling engine. If the timing belt breaks, the valves in the cylinder head may strike the pistons, causing potentially serious (also time-consuming and expensive) engine damage. Refer to the maintenance interval charts for the recommended replacement interval for the timing belt, and to the timing belt section for belt replacement and inspection.

• Disconnecting the negative battery cable on some vehicles may interfere with the functions of the on-board computer system(s) and may require the computer to undergo a relearning process once the negative battery cable is reconnected.

• When servicing drum brakes, only disassemble and assemble one side at a time, leaving the remaining side intact for reference.

• Only an MVAC-trained, EPA-certified automotive technician should service the air conditioning system or its components.

BRAKES

ANTI-LOCK BRAKE SYSTEM (ABS)

GENERAL INFORMATION

PRECAUTIONS

• Certain components within the ABS system are not intended to be serviced or repaired individually.

• Do not use rubber hoses or other parts not specifically specified for and ABS system. When using repair kits, replace all parts included in the kit. Partial or incorrect repair may lead to functional problems and require the replacement of components.

• Lubricate rubber parts with clean, fresh brake fluid to ease assembly. Do not use shop air to clean parts; damage to rubber components may result.

• Use only DOT 3 brake fluid from an unopened container.

• If any hydraulic component or line is removed or replaced, it may be necessary to bleed the entire system.

• A clean repair area is essential. Always clean the reservoir and cap thoroughly before removing the cap. The slightest amount of dirt in the fluid may plug an orifice and impair the system function. Perform repairs after components have been thoroughly cleaned; use only denatured alcohol to clean components. Do not allow ABS components to come into contact with any substance containing mineral oil; this includes used shop rags.

• The Anti-Lock control unit is a microprocessor similar to other computer units in the vehicle. Ensure that the ignition switch is **OFF** before removing or installing con-

troller harnesses. Avoid static electricity discharge at or near the controller.

• If any arc welding is to be done on the vehicle, the control unit should be unplugged before welding operations begin.

SPEED SENSORS

REMOVAL & INSTALLATION

Front

See Figures 1 and 2.

1. Remove the brake disc.

➡**The harness connector is located in the engine compartment secured to the fender apron.**

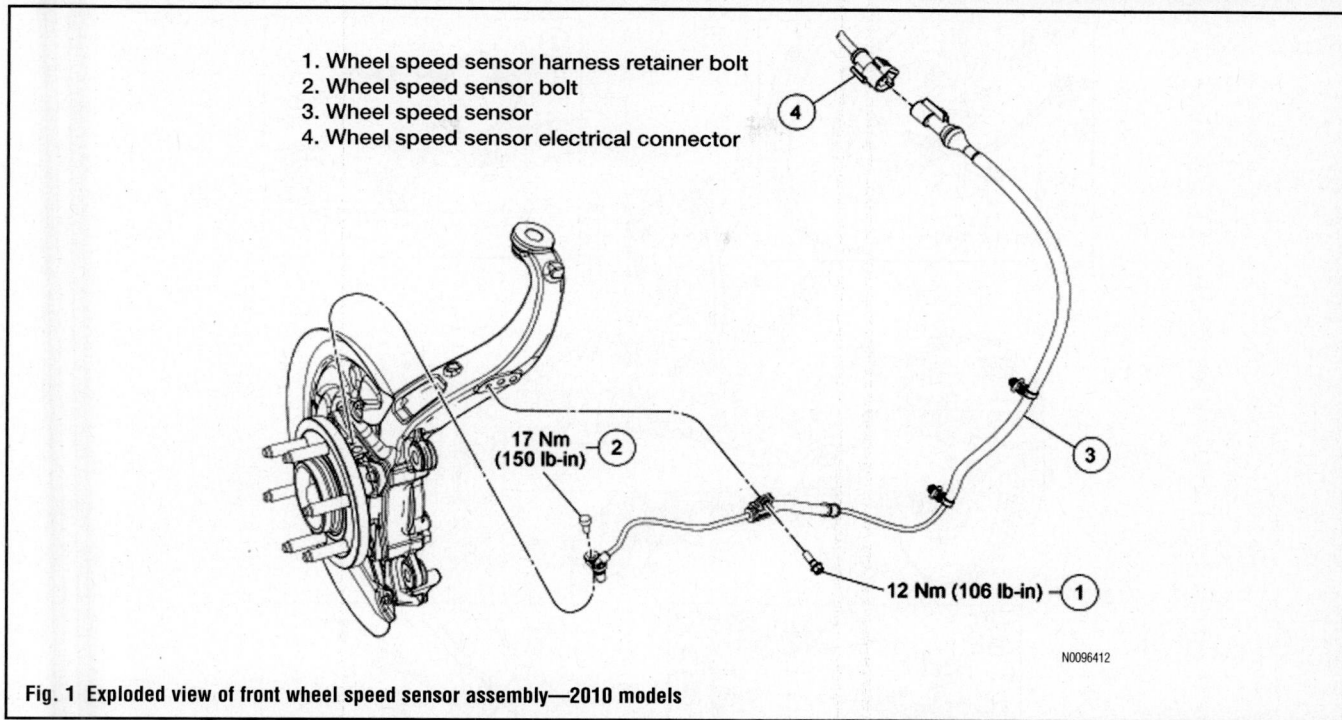

1. Wheel speed sensor harness retainer bolt
2. Wheel speed sensor bolt
3. Wheel speed sensor
4. Wheel speed sensor electrical connector

Fig. 1 Exploded view of front wheel speed sensor assembly—2010 models

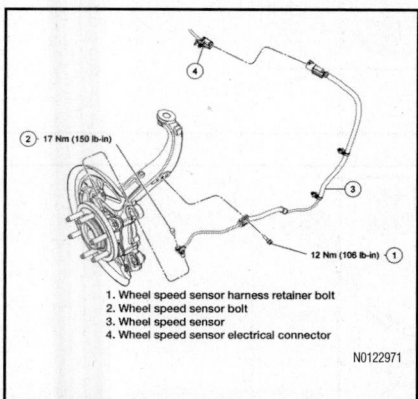

1. Wheel speed sensor harness retainer bolt
2. Wheel speed sensor bolt
3. Wheel speed sensor
4. Wheel speed sensor electrical connector

Fig. 2 Exploded view of front wheel speed sensor assembly—2011 models

2. Disconnect the wheel speed sensor electrical connector.

3. Detach the 2 wheel speed sensor harness pushpin retainers.

4. Detach the wheel speed sensor harness retainer from the brake hose.

5. Remove the wheel speed sensor harness retainer bolt.

6. Remove the bolt and the wheel speed sensor.

7. To install, reverse the removal procedure.

a. Tighten the wheel speed sensor retainer bolt to 106 inch lbs. (12 Nm).

b. Tighten the wheel speed sensor bolt to 13 ft. lbs. (17 Nm).

Rear

See Figures 3 through 5.

1. With the vehicle in NEUTRAL, position it on a hoist.

2. Disconnect the wheel speed sensor electrical connector.

3. Detach the wheel speed

sensor harness retainers and pushpin retainers.

4. Remove the wheel speed sensor bolt and the wheel speed sensor.

5. To install, reverse the removal procedure

a. Tighten the wheel speed sensor bolt to 11 ft. lbs. (15 Nm).

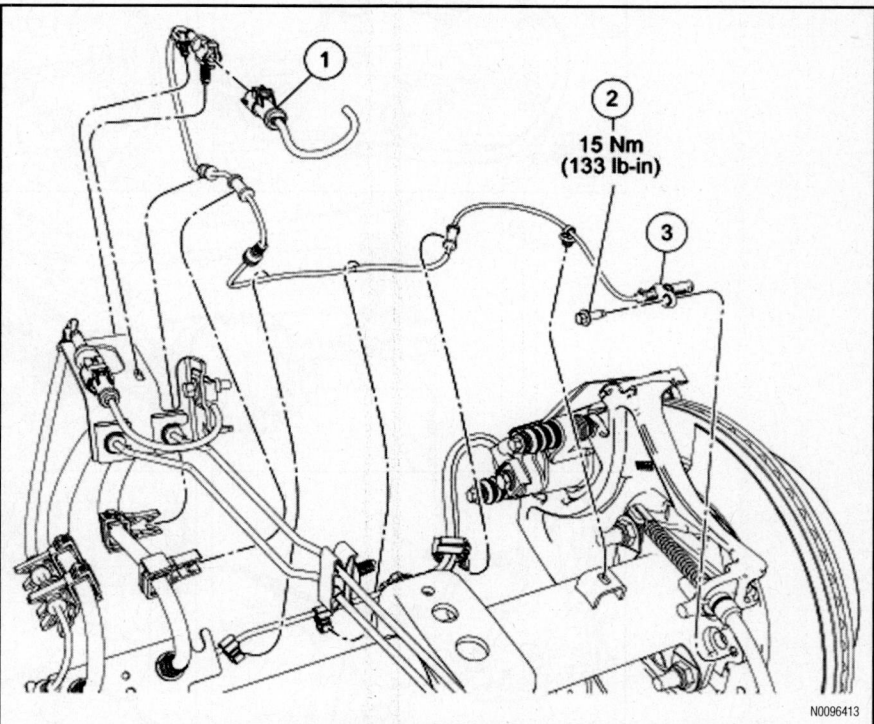

Fig. 3 Rear wheel speed sensor (3), bolt (2), and electrical connector (3)—2010 model

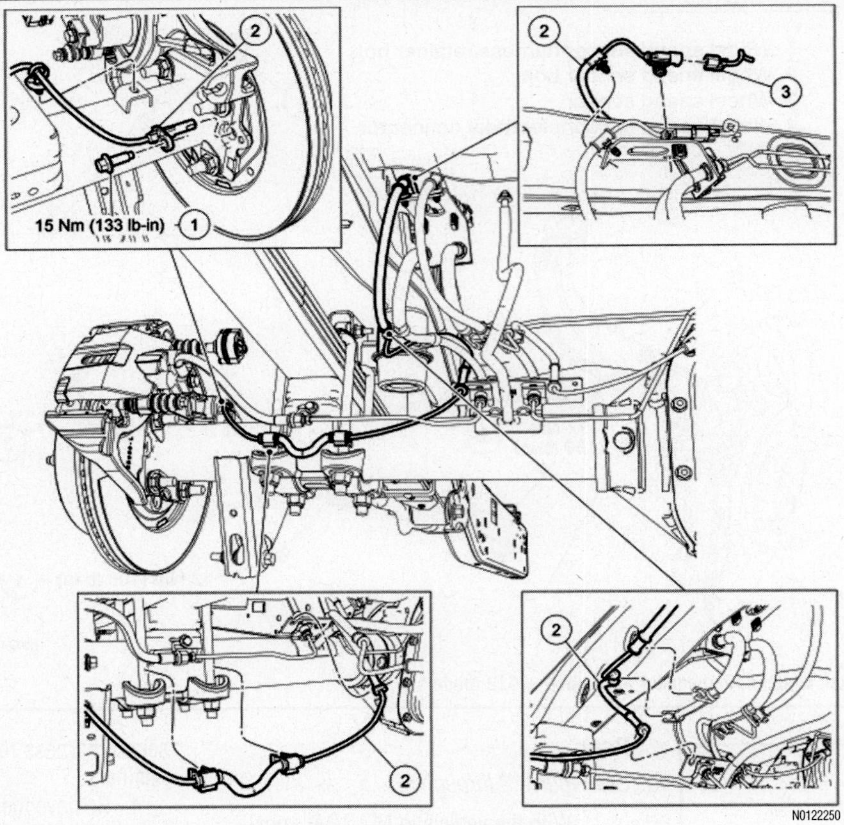

Fig. 4 Left rear wheel speed sensor (3), bolt (2), and electrical connector (3)—2011 model

15 Nm (133 lb-in)

N0122250

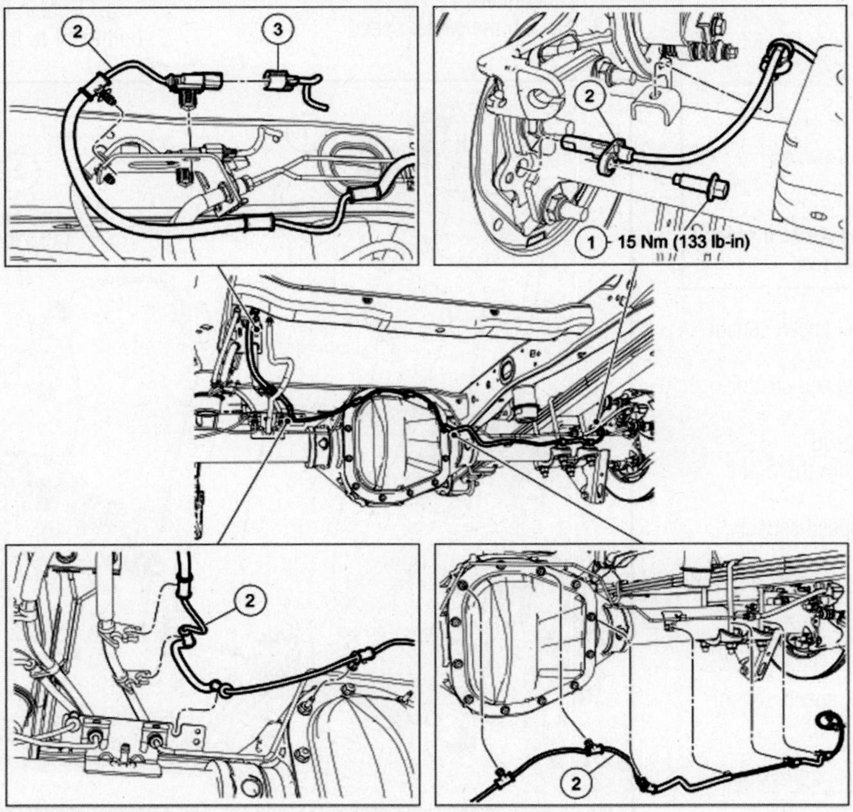

Fig. 5 Right rear wheel speed sensor (3), bolt (2), and electrical connector (3)—2011 model

15 Nm (133 lb-in)

N0122972

BRAKES

BLEEDING PROCEDURE

BLEEDING PROCEDURE

Pressure Bleeding

> ❋❋ **CAUTION**
>
> Do not use any fluid other than clean brake fluid meeting manufacturer's specification. Additionally, do not use brake fluid that has been previously drained. Following these instructions will help prevent system contamination, brake component damage and the risk of serious personal injury.

> ❋❋ **CAUTION**
>
> Carefully read cautionary information on product label. For additional information, consult the product Material Safety Data Sheet (MSDS) if available. Failure to follow these instructions may result in serious personal injury.

> ❋❋ **CAUTION**
>
> Do not allow the brake master cylinder to run dry during the bleeding operation. Master cylinder may be damaged if operated without fluid, resulting in degraded braking performance. Failure to follow this instruction may result in serious personal injury.

> ❋❋ **WARNING**
>
> Do not spill brake fluid on painted or plastic surfaces or damage to the surface may occur. If brake fluid is spilled onto a painted or plastic surface, immediately wash the surface with water.

➡ The Hydraulic Control Unit (HCU) bleeding procedure must be carried out if the HCU or any components upstream of the HCU are installed new.

➡ Pressure bleeding the brake system is preferred to manual bleeding.

1. Clean all dirt from the brake master cylinder filler cap and remove the filler cap.
2. Fill the brake master cylinder with clean specified brake fluid.

➡ Master cylinder pressure bleeder adapter tools are available from various manufacturers of pressure bleeding equipment. Follow the instructions of the equipment manufacturer when installing the adapter.

3. Install the bleeder adapter to the brake master cylinder reservoir and attach the bleeder tank hose to the fitting on the adapter.

➡ Make sure the bleeder tank contains enough clean, specified brake fluid to complete the bleeding operation.

4. Open the valve on the bleeder tank.
5. Apply 30–50 psi (207–345 kPa) to the brake system.
6. Remove the RH rear bleeder cap and place a box-end wrench on the bleeder screw. Attach a rubber drain tube to the RH rear bleeder screw and submerge the free end of the tube in a container partially filled with clean, specified brake fluid.
7. Loosen the RH rear bleeder screw. Leave open until clear, bubble-free brake fluid flows, then tighten the RH rear bleeder screw and remove the rubber hose.
8. Install the bleeder screw cap.
9. Continue bleeding the system, going in order from the LH rear bleeder screw to the RH front bleeder screw ending with the LH front bleeder screw.
10. Release the bleeder tank pressure and close the bleeder tank valve. Remove the tank hose from the adapter and remove the adapter from the brake fluid reservoir.

Manual Bleeding

> ❋❋ **CAUTION**
>
> Do not use any fluid other than clean brake fluid meeting manufacturer's specification. Additionally, do not use brake fluid that has been previously drained. Following these instructions will help prevent system contamination, brake component damage and the risk of serious personal injury.

> ❋❋ **CAUTION**
>
> Carefully read cautionary information on product label. For additional information, consult the product Material Safety Data Sheet (MSDS) if available. Failure to follow these instructions may result in serious personal injury.

> ❋❋ **CAUTION**
>
> Do not allow the brake master cylinder to run dry during the bleeding operation. Master cylinder may be damaged if operated without fluid, resulting in degraded braking performance. Failure to follow this instruction may result in serious personal injury.

> ❋❋ **WARNING**
>
> Do not spill brake fluid on painted or plastic surfaces or damage to the surface may occur. If brake fluid is spilled onto a painted or plastic surface, immediately wash the surface with water.

➡ The HCU bleeding procedure must be carried out if the HCU or any components upstream of the HCU are installed new.

➡ Pressure bleeding the brake system is preferred to manual bleeding.

1. Clean all dirt from the brake master cylinder filler cap and remove the filler cap.
2. Fill the brake master cylinder with clean specified brake fluid.
3. Remove the bleeder screw cap and place a box-end wrench on the RH rear bleeder screw. Attach a rubber drain hose to the RH rear bleeder screw and submerge the free end of the hose in a container partially filled with clean, specified brake fluid.
4. Have an assistant pump the brake pedal at least 3 times and then hold firm pressure on the brake pedal.
5. Loosen the RH rear bleeder screw until a stream of brake fluid comes out. While the assistant maintains pressure on the brake pedal, tighten the RH rear bleeder screw.
6. Repeat until clear, bubble-free fluid comes out.
7. Refill the brake master cylinder reservoir as necessary.
8. Remove the rubber hose and tighten the bleeder screw.
9. Install the bleeder screw cap.
10. Repeat Steps 2 through 5 for the LH rear, RH front and LH front bleeder screws in this order.

Hydraulic Control Unit (HCU)

➡ The HCU bleeding procedure must be carried out if the HCU or any components upstream of the HCU are installed new.

➡ Pressure bleeding the brake system is preferred to manual bleeding.

1. Follow the Pressure Bleeding or Manual Bleeding procedure steps to bleed the system.

2. Connect the scan tool and follow the ABS Service Bleed instructions.

3. Repeat the Pressure Bleeding or Manual Bleeding procedure steps to bleed the system.

MASTER CYLINDER BLEEDING

See Figures 6 and 7.

✻ CAUTION

Do not use any fluid other than clean brake fluid meeting manufacturer's specification. Additionally, do not use brake fluid that has been previously drained. Following these instructions will help prevent system contamination, brake component damage and the risk of serious personal injury.

✻ CAUTION

Carefully read cautionary information on product label. For additional information, consult the product Material Safety Data Sheet (MSDS) if available. Failure to follow these instructions may result in serious personal injury.

✻ CAUTION

Do not allow the brake master cylinder to run dry during the bleeding operation. Master cylinder may be

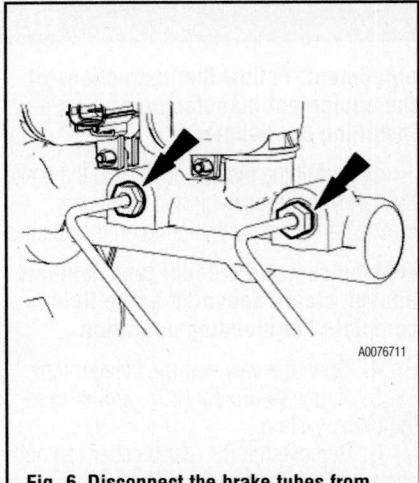

Fig. 6 Disconnect the brake tubes from the master cylinder

damaged if operated without fluid, resulting in degraded braking performance. Failure to follow this instruction may result in serious personal injury.

✻ WARNING

Do not spill brake fluid on painted or plastic surfaces or damage to the surface may occur. If brake fluid is spilled onto a painted or plastic surface, immediately wash the surface with water.

➡ When a new brake master cylinder has been installed, or the system is emptied or partially emptied, it should

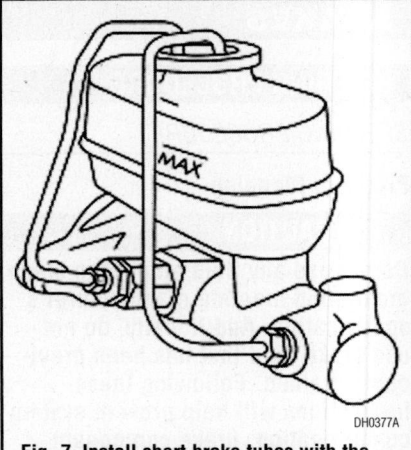

Fig. 7 Install short brake tubes with the ends submerged in the brake master cylinder reservoir

be primed to prevent air from entering the system.

1. Disconnect the brake tubes from the master cylinder.

2. Install short brake tubes with the ends submerged in the brake master cylinder reservoir.

3. Fill the brake master cylinder reservoir with clean, specified brake fluid.

4. Have an assistant pump the brake pedal until clear fluid flows from both brake tubes, without air bubbles.

5. Remove the short brake tubes and install the brake outlet tubes.

6. Bleed the brake system.

BRAKES

✻ WARNING

Dust and dirt accumulating on brake parts during normal use may contain asbestos fibers from production or aftermarket brake linings. Breathing excessive concentrations of asbestos fibers can cause serious bodily harm. Exercise care when servicing brake parts. Do not sand or grind brake lining unless equipment used is designed to contain the dust residue. Do not clean brake parts with compressed air or by dry brushing. Cleaning should be done by dampening the brake components with a fine mist of water, then wiping the brake components clean with a dampened cloth. Dispose of cloth and all residue containing asbestos fibers in

an impermeable container with the appropriate label. Follow practices prescribed by the Occupational Safety and Health Administration (OSHA) and the Environmental Protection Agency (EPA) for the handling, processing, and disposing of dust or debris that may contain asbestos fibers.

BRAKE CALIPER

REMOVAL & INSTALLATION

✻ CAUTION

Do not use any fluid other than clean brake fluid meeting manufacturer's specification. Additionally, do not use brake fluid that has been previ-

FRONT DISC BRAKES

ously drained. Following these instructions will help prevent system contamination, brake component damage and the risk of serious personal injury.

✻ CAUTION

Carefully read cautionary information on product label. For additional information, consult the product Material Safety Data Sheet (MSDS) if available. Failure to follow these instructions may result in serious personal injury.

✻ WARNING

Do not spill brake fluid on painted or plastic surfaces or damage to the surface may occur. If brake fluid is spilled onto a painted or plastic surface, immediately wash the surface with water.

1. Remove the wheel and tire.
2. Remove the brake caliper flow bolt and discard the 2 copper washers.
3. Remove the 2 brake caliper guide pin bolts and the brake caliper.

To install:

4. Using 2 new copper washers, position the brake flexible hose on the brake caliper and install the brake caliper flow bolt. Tighten to 30 ft. lbs. (40 Nm).

➡️**Tighten the lower caliper guide pin bolt first.**

5. Position the brake caliper on the brake caliper anchor plate and install the 2 guide pin bolts. Tighten to 27 ft. lbs. (37 Nm).
6. Bleed the brake caliper.
7. Install the wheel and tire.

DISC BRAKE PADS

REMOVAL & INSTALLATION

※ CAUTION

Do not use any fluid other than clean brake fluid meeting manufacturer's specification. Additionally, do not use brake fluid that has been previously drained. Following these instructions will help prevent system contamination, brake component damage and the risk of serious personal injury.

※ CAUTION

Carefully read cautionary information on product label. For additional information, consult the product Material Safety Data Sheet (MSDS) if available. Failure to follow these instructions may result in serious personal injury.

※ CAUTION

Always install new brake shoes or pads at both ends of an axle to reduce the possibility of brakes pulling vehicle to one side. Failure to follow this instruction may result in uneven braking and serious personal injury.

※ WARNING

Do not spill brake fluid on painted or plastic surfaces or damage to the surface may occur. If brake fluid is spilled onto a painted or plastic surface, immediately wash the surface with water.

1. Check the brake fluid level in the brake master cylinder reservoir.
2. If necessary, remove fluid until the brake master cylinder reservoir is half full.

3. Remove the wheel and tire.

➡️**Do not allow the caliper to hang from the brake hose or damage to the hose can occur.**

4. Remove the 2 brake caliper guide pin bolts and position the caliper aside.
   a. Support the caliper using mechanic's wire.
   b. Remove the brake pads and the 4 spring clips. Discard the spring clips.

To install:

➡️**Protect the pistons and boots when compressing the piston into its bore.**

5. Using a C-clamp and a worn brake pad, compress the disc brake caliper pistons into the brake caliper bore.

➡️**One brake disc pad kit contains the pads required for both the RH and LH side.**

6. Install the new spring clips and brake pads.

➡️**Tighten the lower caliper guide pin bolt first.**

7. Position the brake caliper on the brake caliper anchor plate and install the 2 guide pin bolts. Tighten to 27 ft. lbs. (37 Nm).
8. Install the wheel and tire.
9. Apply brakes several times to verify correct brake operation.
10. Fill the master cylinder with clean, specified brake fluid.

BRAKES

※ WARNING

Dust and dirt accumulating on brake parts during normal use may contain asbestos fibers from production or aftermarket brake linings. Breathing excessive concentrations of asbestos fibers can cause serious bodily harm. Exercise care when servicing brake parts. Do not sand or grind brake lining unless equipment used is designed to contain the dust residue. Do not clean brake parts with compressed air or by dry brushing. Cleaning should be done by dampening the brake components with a fine mist of water, then wiping the brake components clean with a dampened cloth. Dispose of cloth and all residue containing asbestos fibers in an impermeable container with the appropriate label.

Follow practices prescribed by the Occupational Safety and Health Administration (OSHA) and the Environmental Protection Agency (EPA) for the handling, processing, and disposing of dust or debris that may contain asbestos fibers.

BRAKE CALIPER

REMOVAL & INSTALLATION

※ CAUTION

Do not use any fluid other than clean brake fluid meeting manufacturer's specification. Additionally, do not use brake fluid that has been previously drained. Following these instructions will help prevent system contamination, brake component damage and the risk of serious personal injury.

REAR DISC BRAKES

※ CAUTION

Carefully read cautionary information on product label. For additional information, consult the product Material Safety Data Sheet (MSDS) if available. Failure to follow these instructions may result in serious personal injury.

※ WARNING

Do not spill brake fluid on painted or plastic surfaces or damage to the surface may occur. If brake fluid is spilled onto a painted or plastic surface, immediately wash the surface with water.

1. Remove the wheel and tire.
2. Remove the brake caliper flow bolt and discard the 2 copper washers.

➡Do not remove the guide pin stud bolt by twisting on the noise damper or damage to the damper may occur.

3. Remove the guide pin bolt, the guide pin stud bolt and the brake caliper.

To install:

4. Position the brake caliper and install the 2 guide pin bolts.

   a. Apply equal amounts of specified lubricant to the brake caliper-to-brake pad contact points. Tighten to 22 ft. lbs. (30 Nm).

   b. Using 2 new copper washers, position the brake hose on the brake caliper and install the flow bolt. Tighten to 30 ft. lbs. (40 Nm).

5. Bleed the brake caliper.

6. Install the wheel and tire.

DISC BRAKE PADS

REMOVAL & INSTALLATION

✳✳ CAUTION

Do not use any fluid other than clean brake fluid meeting manufacturer's specification. Additionally, do not use brake fluid that has been previously drained. Following these instructions will help prevent system contamination, brake component damage and the risk of serious personal injury.

✳✳ CAUTION

Carefully read cautionary information on product label. For additional information, consult the product Material Safety Data Sheet (MSDS) if available. Failure to follow these instructions may result in serious personal injury.

✳✳ CAUTION

Always install new brake shoes or pads at both ends of an axle to reduce the possibility of brakes pulling vehicle to one side. Failure to follow this instruction may result in uneven braking and serious personal injury.

✳✳ WARNING

Do not spill brake fluid on painted or plastic surfaces or damage to the surface may occur. If brake fluid is spilled onto a painted or plastic surface, immediately wash the surface with water.

1. Check the brake fluid level in the brake master cylinder reservoir. If required, remove fluid until the brake master cylinder reservoir is half full.

2. Remove the wheel and tire.

➡Do not allow the brake caliper to hang from the brake hose or damage to the hose can result.

✳✳ WARNING

Do not remove the guide pin stud bolt by twisting on the noise damper or damage to the damper may occur.

3. Remove the brake caliper guide pin bolt, the guide pin stud bolt and position the brake caliper aside. Support the caliper using mechanic's wire.

4. Measure the brake disc thickness and install a new brake disc if it is not within specification.

5. Remove the brake pads and the 2 slippers. Discard the slippers.

To install:

✳✳ WARNING

Protect the caliper pistons and boots when pushing the caliper piston into the caliper piston bores or damage to components may occur.

6. Using a C-clamp and a worn brake pad, compress the caliper piston into the caliper.

✳✳ WARNING

Do not allow grease, oil, brake fluid or other contaminants to contact the pad lining material or damage to components may occur. Do not install contaminated pads.

➡Install all new hardware supplied with the pad kit.

7. Install the 2 new slippers and brake pads.

8. Position the brake caliper and install the 2 guide pin bolts.

   a. Apply equal amounts of specified lubricant to the brake caliper-to-brake pad contact points.

   b. Tighten to 22 ft. lbs. (30 Nm).

9. Fill the master cylinder with clean specified brake fluid.

10. Install the wheel and tire.

11. Apply brakes several times to verify correct brake operation.

BRAKES

PARKING BRAKE

PARKING BRAKE SHOES

REMOVAL & INSTALLATION

See Figure 8.

➡One parking brake shoe kit contains the linings required for both the LH and RH side.

1. Release the parking brake cable tension.

   a. Release the parking brake.

   b. With the vehicle in NEUTRAL, position it on a hoist.

   c. With an assistant, release the parking brake cable tension by pulling down on the intermediate cable at the cable-to-cable union until the parking brake control sector rotates to its stop and a 0.15 inches (4 mm) x 5.9 inches (150 mm) retainer pin can be inserted.

   d. Disconnect the cable at the cable-to-cable union.

   e. To reload the tension on the parking brake cable, follow the release procedure in reverse.

2. Remove the rear brake disc.

3. Remove the brake shoe adjuster screw.

4. Remove the brake shoe adjuster screw spring.

5. Remove the 2 brake shoe hold-down springs and 2 pins.

6. Remove the brake shoe retracting spring and the parking brake shoes.

To install:

➡Using specified grease, lubricate the parking brake shoes where the shoe contacts the actuator lever and the support bracket.

7. Position the parking brake shoes and attach the retracting spring.

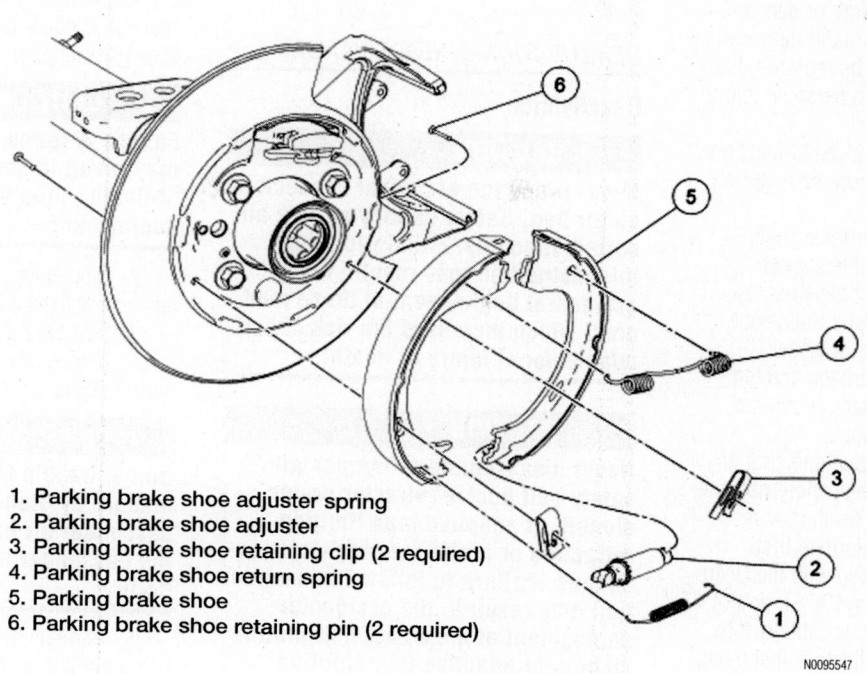

1. Parking brake shoe adjuster spring
2. Parking brake shoe adjuster
3. Parking brake shoe retaining clip (2 required)
4. Parking brake shoe return spring
5. Parking brake shoe
6. Parking brake shoe retaining pin (2 required)

N0095547

Fig. 8 Exploded view of parking brake shoes assembly

8. Install the 2 brake shoe hold-down pins and springs.
9. Install the brake shoe adjusting screw spring.

➡**Completely retract the parking brake adjusting screw before installation.**

10. Install the brake shoe adjusting screw.

11. Adjust the parking brake shoe.
12. Reload the tension on the parking brake cable.

CHASSIS ELECTRICAL — AIR BAG (SUPPLEMENTAL RESTRAINT SYSTEM)

GENERAL INFORMATION

✳✳ WARNING

These vehicles are equipped with an air bag system. The system must be disarmed before performing service on, or around, system components, the steering column, instrument panel components, wiring and sensors. Failure to follow the safety precautions and the disarming procedure could result in accidental air bag deployment, possible injury and unnecessary system repairs.

SERVICE PRECAUTIONS

Disconnect and isolate the battery negative cable before beginning any airbag system component diagnosis, testing, removal, or installation procedures. Allow system capacitor to discharge for two minutes before beginning any component service. This will disable the airbag system. Failure to disable the airbag system may result in accidental airbag deployment, personal injury, or death.

Do not place an intact undeployed airbag face down on a solid surface. The airbag will propel into the air if accidentally deployed and may result in personal injury or death.

When carrying or handling an undeployed airbag, the trim side (face) of the airbag should be pointing away from the body to minimize possibility of injury if accidental deployment occurs. Failure to do this may result in personal injury or death.

Replace airbag system components with OEM replacement parts. Substitute parts may appear interchangeable, but internal differences may result in inferior occupant protection. Failure to do so may result in occupant personal injury or death.

Wear safety glasses, rubber gloves, and long sleeved clothing when cleaning powder residue from vehicle after an airbag deployment. Powder residue emitted from a deployed airbag can cause skin irritation. Flush affected area with cool water if irritation is experienced. If nasal or throat irritation is experienced, exit the vehicle for fresh air until the irritation ceases. If irritation continues, see a physician.

Do not use a replacement airbag that is not in the original packaging. This may result in improper deployment, personal injury, or death.

The factory installed fasteners, screws and bolts used to fasten airbag components have a special coating and are specifically designed for the airbag system. Do not use substitute fasteners. Use only original equipment fasteners listed in the parts catalog when fastener replacement is required.

During, and following, any child restraint anchor service, due to impact event or vehicle repair, carefully inspect all mounting hardware, tether straps, and anchors for proper installation, operation, or damage. If a child restraint anchor is found damaged in any way, the anchor must be replaced. Failure to do this may result in personal injury or death.

Deployed and non-deployed airbags may or may not have live pyrotechnic material within the airbag inflator.

Do not dispose of driver/passenger/curtain airbags or seat belt tensioners unless you are sure of complete deployment. Refer to the Hazardous Substance Control System for proper disposal.

Dispose of deployed airbags and tensioners consistent with state, provincial, local, and federal regulations.

After any airbag component testing or service, do not connect the battery negative cable. Personal injury or death may result if the system test is not performed first.

If the vehicle is equipped with the Occupant Classification System (OCS), do not connect the battery negative cable before performing the OCS Verification Test using the scan tool and the appropriate diagnostic information. Personal injury or death may result if the system test is not performed properly.

Never replace both the Occupant Restraint Controller (ORC) and the Occupant Classification Module (OCM) at the same time. If both require replacement, replace one, then perform the Airbag System test before replacing the other.

Both the ORC and the OCM store Occupant Classification System (OCS) calibration data, which they transfer to one another when one of them is replaced. If both are replaced at the same time, an irreversible fault will be set in both modules and the OCS may malfunction and cause personal injury or death.

If equipped with OCS, the Seat Weight Sensor is a sensitive, calibrated unit and must be handled carefully. Do not drop or handle roughly. If dropped or damaged, replace with another sensor. Failure to do so may result in occupant injury or death.

If equipped with OCS, the front passenger seat must be handled carefully as well. When removing the seat, be careful when setting on floor not to drop. If dropped, the sensor may be inoperative, could result in occupant injury, or possibly death.

If equipped with OCS, when the passenger front seat is on the floor, no one should sit in the front passenger seat. This uneven force may damage the sensing ability of the seat weight sensors. If sat on and damaged, the sensor may be inoperative, could result in occupant injury, or possibly death.

DEACTIVATION & REACTIVATION

Deactivation

> ✳✳ **CAUTION**
> Never probe the electrical connectors on air bag, Safety Canopy or side air curtain modules. Failure to follow this instruction may result in the accidental deployment of these modules, which increases the risk of serious personal injury or death.

> ✳✳ **CAUTION**
> Never disassemble or tamper with safety belt buckle/retractor pretensioners or adaptive load limiting retractors or probe the electrical connectors. Failure to follow this instruction may result in the accidental deployment of the safety belt pretensioners or adaptive load limiting retractors which increases the risk of serious personal injury or death.

> ✳✳ **CAUTION**
> Do not handle, move or change the original horizontal mounting position of the Restraints Control Module (RCM) while the RCM is connected and the ignition switch is ON. Failure to follow this instruction may result in the accidental deployment of the Safety Canopy and cause serious personal injury or death.

➡ **The Supplemental Restraint System (SRS) must be fully operational and free of faults before releasing the vehicle to the customer.**

1. Depower the SRS.

> ✳✳ **CAUTION**
> Always deplete the backup power supply before repairing or installing any new front or side air bag Supplemental Restraint System (SRS) component and before servicing, removing, installing, adjusting or striking components near the front or side impact sensors or the restraints control module (RCM). Nearby components include doors, instrument panel, console, door latches, strikers, seats and hood latches.

To deplete the backup power supply energy, disconnect the battery ground cable and wait at least 1 minute. Be sure to disconnect auxiliary batteries and power supplies (if equipped).

> ✳✳ **CAUTION**
> Failure to follow these instructions may result in serious personal injury or death in the event of an accidental deployment.

2. Disconnect the battery ground cable and wait at least one minute.
3. Remove the driver air bag module.
4. Remove the 3 passenger air bag module bolts.

> ✳✳ **WARNING**
> Do not handle the passenger air bag module by grabbing the edges of the passenger air bag cover. Damage to the passenger air bag module may occur.

5. Partially remove the passenger air bag module from the instrument panel.
6. Disconnect the 2 passenger air bag module electrical connectors.
7. Under the passenger seat, slide and disengage the locking clip, release the tab and disconnect inline electrical connector.
8. Under the driver seat, slide and disengage the locking clip, release the tab and disconnect inline electrical connector.
9. Disconnect the LH side safety canopy module electrical connector.
   a. For regular cab, remove the LH side B-pillar trim panel.
   b. For SuperCab and SuperCrew, remove the LH side C-pillar trim panel.
10. Disconnect the RH side safety canopy module electrical connector.
   a. For regular cab, remove the RH side B-pillar trim panel.
   b. For SuperCab and SuperCrew, remove the RH side C-pillar trim panel.
11. Install the RCM fuse 31 (10A) in the SJB.
12. Connect the battery ground cable.

Reactivation
See Figure 9.

1. Remove RCM fuse 31 (10A) from the SJB.
2. Disconnect the battery ground cable and wait at least one minute.
3. Connect the LH side safety canopy module electrical connector.
   a. For regular cab, install the LH side B-pillar trim panel.

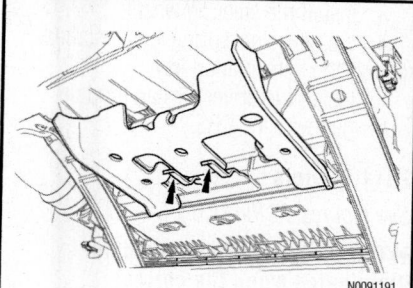

N0091191

Fig. 9 Position the passenger air bag module so that the tabs are oriented as shown

b. For SuperCab and Super-Crew, install the LH side C-pillar trim panel.

4. Connect the RH side safety canopy module electrical connector.

a. For regular cab, install the RH side B-pillar trim panel.

b. For SuperCab and SuperCrew, install the RH side C-pillar trim panel.

5. Under the driver seat, connect inline electrical connector, slide and engage the locking clip.

6. Under the driver seat, connect inline electrical connector, slide and engage the locking clip.

7. Connect the 2 passenger air bag module electrical connectors.

8. Position the passenger air bag module so that the tabs are oriented as shown.

9. Install the 3 passenger air bag module bolts.

10. Install the driver air bag module.

11. Repower the SRS.

DEPOWERING & REPOWERING

Depowering Procedure

> ✳✳ **CAUTION**
>
> **Always wear eye protection when servicing a vehicle. Failure to follow this instruction may result in serious personal injury.**

> ✳✳ **CAUTION**
>
> **Never probe the electrical connectors on air bag, Safety Canopy or side air curtain modules. Failure to follow this instruction may result in the accidental deployment of these modules, which increases the risk of serious personal injury or death.**

> ✳✳ **CAUTION**
>
> **Do not handle, move or change the original horizontal mounting position of the Restraints Control Module (RCM) while the RCM is connected and the ignition switch is ON. Failure to follow this instruction may result in the accidental deployment of the Safety Canopy and cause serious personal injury or death.**

> ✳✳ **CAUTION**
>
> **To reduce the risk of accidental deployment, do not use any memory saver devices. Failure to follow this instruction may result in serious personal injury or death.**

➡The air bag warning indicator illuminates when the correct Restraints Control Module (RCM) fuse is removed and the ignition is ON.

➡The Supplemental Restraint System (SRS) must be fully operational and free of faults before releasing the vehicle to the customer.

1. Turn all vehicle accessories OFF.
2. Turn the ignition OFF.
3. For 2010 models, at the Smart Junction Box (SJB), located below the RH side of the instrument panel, remove the cover and RCM fuse 31 (10A) from the SJB.
4. For 2011 models, at the Body Control Module (BCM), located below the RH side of the instrument panel, remove the cover and RCM fuse 36 (10A) from the BCM. For additional information, refer to the Wiring Diagrams manual.
5. Turn the ignition ON and monitor the air bag warning indicator for at least 30 seconds. The air bag warning indicator will remain lit continuously (no flashing) if the correct RCM fuse has been removed. If the air bag warning indicator does not remain illuminated continuously, remove the correct RCM fuse before proceeding.
6. Turn the ignition OFF.

> ✳✳ **CAUTION**
>
> **Always deplete the backup power supply before repairing or installing any new front or side air bag supplemental restraint system (SRS) component and before servicing, removing, installing, adjusting or striking components near the front or side impact sensors or the restraints control module (RCM). Nearby components include doors, instrument panel, console, door latches, strikers, seats and hood latches.**

To deplete the backup power supply energy, disconnect the battery ground cable and wait at least 1 minute. Be sure to disconnect auxiliary batteries and power supplies (if equipped).

> ✳✳ **CAUTION**
>
> **Failure to follow these instructions may result in serious personal injury or death in the event of an accidental deployment.**

7. Disconnect the battery ground cable and wait at least one minute.

Repowering Procedure

1. Turn the ignition from OFF to ON.
2. For 2010 models, install RCM fuse 31 (10A) to the SJB and close the cover.
3. For 2011 models, install RCM fuse 36 (10A) to the BCM and close the cover.

> ✳✳ **CAUTION**
>
> **Make sure no one is in the vehicle and there is nothing blocking or placed in front of any air bag module when the battery is connected. Failure to follow these instructions may result in serious personal injury in the event of an accidental deployment.**

4. Connect the battery ground cable.
5. Prove out the SRS as follows: Turn the ignition from ON to OFF. Wait 10 seconds, then turn the ignition back to ON and monitor the air bag warning indicator with the air bag modules installed. The air bag warning indicator will light continuously for approximately 6 seconds and then turn off. If an air bag SRS fault is present, the air bag warning indicator will: - fail to light. - remain lit continuously. - flash at a 5 Hz rate (RCM not configured). The air bag warning indicator may not illuminate until approximately 30 seconds after the ignition has been turned from the OFF to the ON position. This is the time required for the RCM to complete the testing of the SRS. If the air bag warning indicator is inoperative and a SRS fault exists, a chime will sound in a pattern of 5 sets of 5 beeps. If this occurs, the air bag warning indicator and any SRS fault discovered must be diagnosed and repaired. Clear all continuous DTCs from the RCM and Occupant Classification System Module (OCSM) using a scan tool.

CLOCKSPRING CENTERING

2010 Models

See Figure 10.

> ✳✳ **CAUTION**
>
> **If the clockspring is not correctly centralized, it may fail prematurely. If in doubt, repeat the centralizing procedure. Failure to follow these instructions may increase the risk of serious personal injury or death in a crash.**

> ✳✳ **WARNING**
>
> **Do not over-rotate the clockspring inner rotor. The internal ribbon wire is connected to the clockspring rotor. The internal ribbon wire acts as a stop and can be broken from its internal connection. Failure to follow this instruction may result in component damage and/or system failure.**

1. If a new clockspring was installed and the anti-rotation key has not been removed, proceed to the next step. If a new clockspring was installed and the anti-rotation key has been removed before the steering wheel is installed or the same clockspring is being installed, rotate the clockspring inner rotor counterclockwise and carefully feel for the ribbon wire to run out of length with slight resistance. Stop rotating the clockspring inner rotor at this point.

2. Starting with the clockspring inner rotor, wiring and electrical connector in the 12 o'clock position, rotate the inner rotor clockwise through 4 revolutions to center the clockspring. Verify that the clockspring is correctly centered by observing that after 4 revolutions:

    a. the clockspring rotor window is in the 4 o'clock position and the yellow indicator shows in the window.

    b. the 2 arrows located on the clockspring inner and outer rotor line up in the 6 o'clock position.

    c. the clockspring inner rotor, wiring and electrical connector are in the 12 o'clock position.

> ✳✳ **WARNING**
>
> **Before installing the steering wheel, make sure the road wheels are in the straight-ahead position. Damage to the clockspring may occur.**

3. Install the steering wheel.

4. If a new clockspring was installed, remove the anti-rotation key.

5. Install the driver air bag module.

6. Repower the SRS.

2011 Models

See Figures 11 through 14.

➡ **The air bag warning indicator illuminates when the correct Restraints Control Module (RCM) fuse is removed and the ignition is ON.**

➡ **The Supplemental Restraint System (SRS) must be fully operational and free of faults before releasing the vehicle to the customer.**

1. Remove the driver air bag module.

2. Remove the steering wheel.

3. Remove the upper and lower steering column shrouds.

    a. Remove the 3 screws.

    b. Unclip the lower steering column shroud from the upper steering column shroud and remove.

    c. If equipped, position the selector lever boot aside.

4. Disconnect the clockspring electrical connector.

5. Remove the 3 screws and clockspring.

To install:

> ✳✳ **CAUTION**
>
> **If the clockspring is not correctly centralized, it may fail prematurely. If in doubt, repeat the centralizing procedure. Failure to follow these instructions may increase the risk of serious personal injury or death in a crash.**

➡ **Typical clockspring shown.**

6. Position the clockspring onto the steering column.

    a. Align the electrical connector ends and the 2 clockspring pins on the back of the clockspring to the 2 steering wheel rotation sensor pin holes.

7. With the clockspring pins aligned to the steering wheel rotation sensor pin holes, push the clockspring in, seating the electrical connector.

> ✳✳ **WARNING**
>
> **If installing a new clockspring, do not remove the clockspring anti-rotation key until the steering wheel is installed. If the anti-rotation**

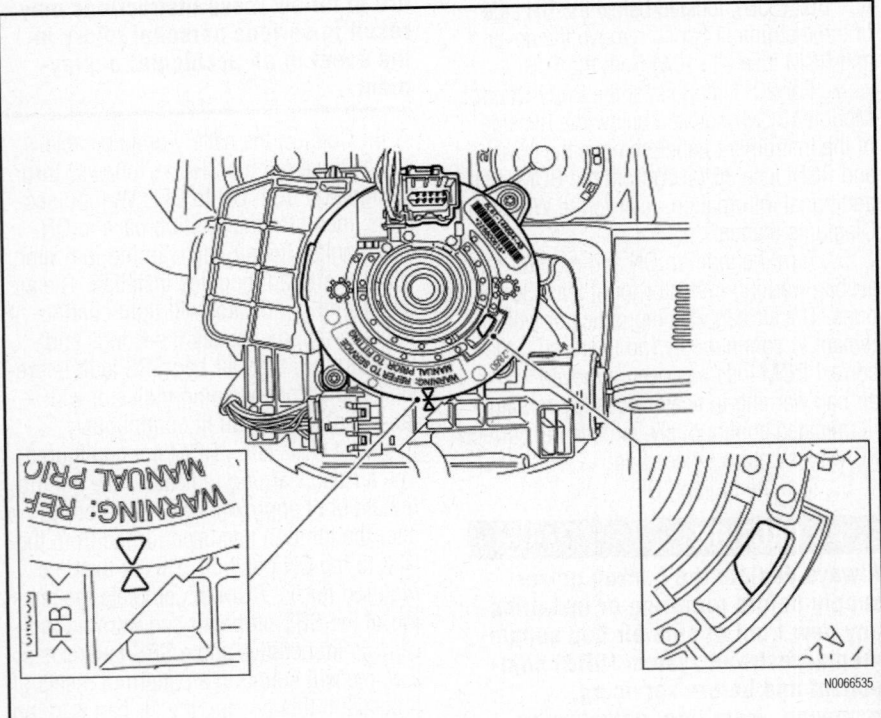

Fig. 10 Start with the clockspring inner rotor, wiring and electrical connector in the 12 o'clock position

N0066535

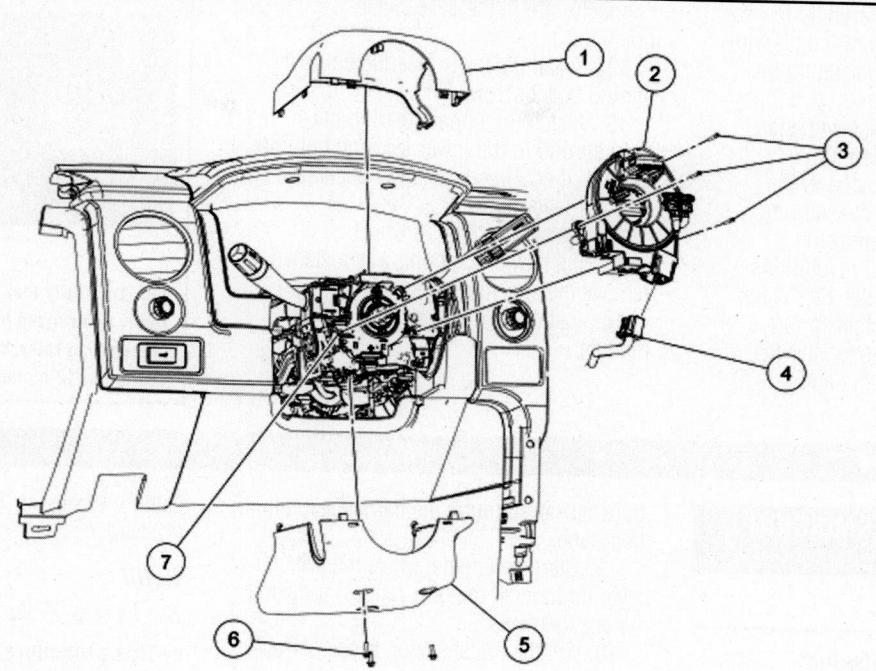

1. Upper steering column shroud
2. Clockspring
3. Clockspring screws (3 required)
4. Clockspring electrical connector
5. Lower steering column shroud
6. Lower steering column shroud screw (3 required)
7. Steering Column Control Module (SCCM)

N0121915

Fig. 11 Exploded view of the clockspring assembly

key has been removed before installing the steering wheel, the clockspring must be centered. Failure to follow this instruction may result in component damage and/or system failure.

8. Install the 3 clockspring screws.

N0112711

Fig. 12 Position the clockspring onto the steering column

9. Connect the clockspring electrical connector.

❊❊ CAUTION

If the clockspring is not correctly centralized, it may fail prematurely. If in doubt, repeat the centralizing procedure. Failure to follow these

N0112713

Fig. 13 With the clockspring pins aligned to the steering wheel rotation sensor pin holes, push the clockspring in, seating the electrical connector

instructions may increase the risk of serious personal injury or death in a crash.

❊❊ WARNING

Do not over-rotate the clockspring inner rotor. The internal ribbon wire is connected to the clockspring rotor. The internal ribbon wire acts as a stop and can be broken from its internal connection. Failure to follow this instruction may result in component damage and/or system failure.

10. If a new clockspring was installed and the anti-rotation key has not been removed proceed to Step 7. If a new clockspring was installed and the anti-rotation key has been removed before the steering wheel is installed, or the same clockspring is being installed, rotate the clockspring inner

rotor counterclockwise. Carefully feel for the ribbon wire to run out of length with slight resistance and stop rotating the clockspring inner rotor.

11. To center the clockspring, start with the clockspring rotated fully counterclockwise as indicated in the previous step. Rotate the clockspring inner rotor, wiring and connector clockwise through 3.5 full revolutions with the connector up in the 12 o'clock position. Verify that the clockspring is correctly centralized by observing that the clockspring rotor, wiring and

connector are in the 12 o'clock position.

12. Install the lower steering column shroud and 3 screws.

13. Attach the upper steering column shroud to the lower steering column shroud. If equipped, position back the selector lever boot.

14. Install the steering wheel.

15. If a new clockspring was installed, remove the anti-rotation key.

16. Install the driver air bag module.

N0121964

Fig. 14 Verify that the clockspring is correctly centralized by observing that the clockspring rotor, wiring and connector are in the 12 o'clock position

DRIVE TRAIN

AUTOMATIC TRANSMISSION FLUID

DRAIN AND REFILL

4R70E/4R75E Transmission

1. With the vehicle in NEUTRAL, position it on a hoist.

2. Loosen the transmission fluid pan bolts and allow the transmission fluid to drain.

3. After the transmission fluid has drained, remove the transmission fluid pan.

4. Do not remove the transmission fluid filter. It is not necessary to change the transmission fluid filter during a normal maintenance transmission fluid change.

5. Clean and inspect the transmission fluid pan, transmission fluid pan gasket and magnet.

To install:

6. Position the magnet into the transmission fluid pan.

➡**The transmission fluid pan gasket is reusable, clean and inspect for damage. If not damaged, the transmission fluid pan gasket should be reused.**

7. Install the transmission fluid pan and transmission fluid pan gasket.

   a. Position the transmission fluid pan with the transmission fluid pan gasket in place.

   b. Install the bolts. Tighten to 10 ft. lbs. (14 Nm).

✲✲ WARNING

The use of any other transmission fluid can result in the transmission failing to operate in a normal manner or transmission failure.

8. Fill the transmission. Add 5 qt. (4.7L) of clean transmission fluid to the

transmission through the transmission fluid filler tube.

9. Start the engine. Move the selector lever through all the gear ranges, checking for engagements.

10. Fill the transmission to the correct level.

11. Using the scan tool, start and run the engine until the transmission is at normal operating temperature 150–170°F (66–77°C), check and adjust the transmission fluid level and check for any leaks. If transmission fluid is needed, add transmission fluid in increments of 0.5 pt. (0.24L) until the correct level is achieved (transmission fluid should be in the cross-hatched area of the transmission fluid level indicator).

6R80 Transmission

1. With the vehicle in NEUTRAL, position it on a hoist.

➡**Some transmission fluid leakage may occur when removing the transmission fluid fill plug.**

2. Remove the transmission fluid fill plug fluid level indicator assembly located on the passenger side front portion of the transmission case. Removal of the transmission fluid fill plug will relieve any vacuum that might have built up in the transmission. This will aid in allowing the transmission fluid pan to be easily removed when the bolts are removed.

3. Remove the transmission fluid pan and allow the transmission fluid to drain.

➡**The transmission fluid pan gasket can be reused if not damaged.**

4. Install a new transmission fluid pan gasket, if required.

5. Install the transmission fluid pan and tighten the bolts in a crisscross

pattern. Tighten to 106 inch lbs. (12 Nm).

Refill
See Figures 15 through 17.

➡**This procedure contains the air purge steps required to purge air from the transmission fluid cooling system. This procedure is NOT intended for use with the Transmission Fluid Level Check.**

✲✲ WARNING

The vehicle should not be driven if the transmission fluid level is low as internal failure could result.

➡**The transmission fluid fill plug is located near the exhaust system. The exhaust will be extremely hot during this procedure.**

✲✲ WARNING

The use of any other transmission fluid than specified can result in the transmission failing to operate in a normal manner or transmission failure.

➡**If the transmission starts to slip, shifts slowly or shows signs of transmission fluid leaking, the transmission fluid level should be checked.**

➡**Here is an overview of the Transmission Fluid Drain and Refill procedure:**

- Adding 3.5 qt. (3.3L) of transmission fluid to the transmission is an initial fill enabling the engine to be started.
- The cold level range shown in the procedure allows the vehicle to be driven.
- The vehicle should be driven to allow the Transmission Fluid

Temperature (TFT) to reach 185–190°F (85–88°C) in order to purge the air from the transmission fluid cooling system.

- Fill the transmission fluid to the fill range on the transmission fluid level indicator at the normal operating range 176–185°F (80–85°C).

➡**The transmission will need 3.5 qt. (3.3L) of transmission fluid added to the transmission as an initial fill if:**

- the transmission has been overhauled.
- a new mechatronic assembly has been installed.
- the transmission fluid pan or transmission fluid filter have been removed.

1. Using the Transmission Fluid Fill Tube, add 3.5 qt. (3.3Lt) of transmission fluid to the transmission through the transmission fluid fill hole. For additional information, refer to Adding Additional Transmission Fluid in this procedure.

2. Check the transmission fluid level cold.

   a. The vehicle is safe to drive if the transmission fluid is in the cold level range 90–110°F (32–43°C).

   b. Using the scan tool and with the engine running, place the selector lever in each gear position and hold approximately 5 seconds. Place the selector lever in PARK, with the engine at idle (600-750 rpm).

3. Separate the transmission fluid level indicator from the transmission fluid fill plug.

4. Wipe the transmission fluid level indicator clean. Reinstall the transmission fluid level indicator only back into the transmission fluid fill plug hole to check the transmission fluid level. Repeat this until a consistent reading is established.

5. Add transmission fluid to the cold level location.

6. Install the transmission fluid fill plug. Tighten to 26 ft. lbs. (35 Nm).

7. While driving the vehicle, use the scan tool to verify that the TFT has

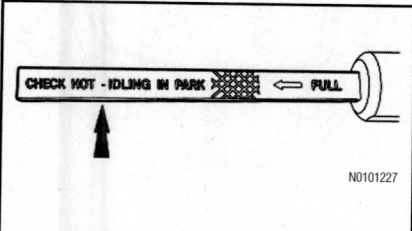

Fig. 15 Add transmission fluid to the cold level location

reached a temperature of 190°F (88°C). This will circulate the transmission fluid through the torque converter and the transmission fluid cooling system, eliminating any trapped air in the transmission fluid cooling system.

8. With the engine idling (600-750 rpm) in PARK, verify that the TFT is between 176–185°F (80–85°C).

9. Remove the transmission fluid fill plug transmission fluid level indicator assembly located on the passenger side front portion of the transmission case.

10. Separate the transmission fluid level indicator from the transmission fluid fill plug.

11. Wipe the transmission fluid level indicator clean. Reinstall the transmission fluid level indicator only back into the transmission fluid fill plug hole to check the transmission fluid level. Repeat this until a consistent reading is established.

12. Using the scan tool verify that the TFT is between 176–185°F (80–85°C). The transmission fluid level must be at the upper level of the crosshatch mark.

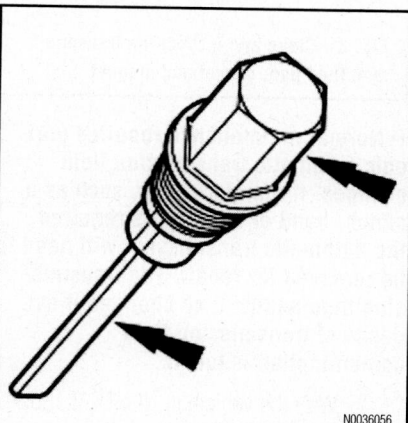

Fig. 16 Separate the transmission fluid level indicator from the transmission fluid fill plug

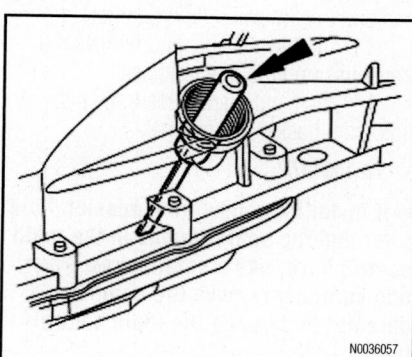

Fig. 17 Reinstall the transmission fluid level indicator only

➡**If the transmission fluid is not at the correct level, follow the steps for Adding Additional Transmission Fluid or Removing Transmission Fluid in this procedure.**

13. Install the transmission fluid fill plug. Tighten to 26 ft. lbs. (35 Nm).

Adding Additional Transmission Fluid
See Figure 18.

➡**To get an accurate transmission fluid level reading the engine should be idling (600-750 rpm) in PARK.**

1. Install the Transmission Fluid Fill Tube into the transmission fluid fill hole.

2. Fill the Transporter Fluid Evacuator/Injector with approximately 1 pt. (0.47L) of transmission fluid.

3. Hang the Transporter Fluid Evacuator/Injector under the vehicle, upright and close to the transmission.

4. Connect the open end of the fluid hose from the Transporter Fluid Evacuator/Injector onto the Transmission Fluid Fill Tube from the transmission case.

5. Use a Rubber Tip Air Nozzle to apply a maximum of 30 psi (206.85 kPa) to the open end of the vacuum/pressure hose from the Transporter Fluid Evacuator/Injector. Transmission fluid will immediately start flowing out of the Transporter Fluid Evacuator/Injector into the transmission.

➡**Do not overfill the transmission. The transmission fluid level must be at the upper level of the crosshatch mark.**

6. Reinstall the transmission fluid level indicator only back into the transmission fluid fill plug hole to check the transmission fluid level. Repeat this until a consistent reading is established.

7. Using the scan tool, verify that the TFT is between 176–185°F (80–85°C). The transmission fluid level must be at the upper level of the crosshatch mark.

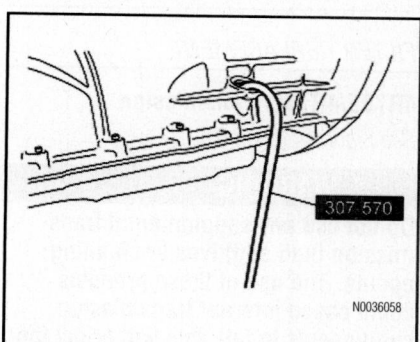

Fig. 18 Install the Transmission Fluid Fill Tube into the transmission fluid fill hole

➤If the transmission fluid is over full, follow the steps for Removing Transmission Fluid in this procedure.

8. Install the transmission fluid fill plug. Tighten to 26 ft. lbs. (35 Nm).

Removing Transmission Fluid

See Figure 19.

➤To get an accurate transmission fluid level reading the engine should be idling (600-750 rpm) in PARK.

1. If the transmission is overfilled, transmission fluid must be removed to the correct level. Use the Transporter Fluid Evacuator/Injector and the Vacuum Pump Kit to extract any excessive transmission fluid.

2. Using the scan tool, verify that the TFT is between 176–185°F (80–85°C). The transmission fluid level must be at the upper level of the crosshatch mark. Reinstall the transmission fluid level indicator only back into the transmission fluid fill plug hole to check the transmission fluid level. Repeat this until a consistent reading is established.

3. Install the transmission fluid fill plug. Tighten to 26 ft. lbs. (35 Nm).

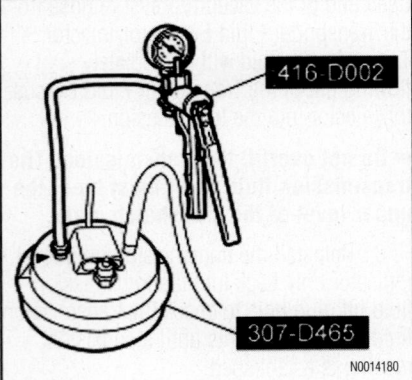

Fig. 19 Use the Transporter Fluid Evacuator/Injector and the Vacuum Pump Kit to extract any excessive transmission fluid

FILTER REPLACEMENT

4R70E/4R75E Transmission

See Figures 20 and 21.

✳✳ **WARNING**

Do not use any supplemental transmission fluid additives or cleaning agents. The use of these products could cause internal transmission components to fail; this will affect the operation of the transmission. Use of a transmission fluid other than specified could result in transmission failure.

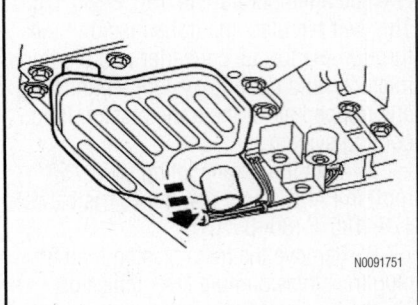

Fig. 20 Pull down evenly and remove the transmission fluid filter and seal

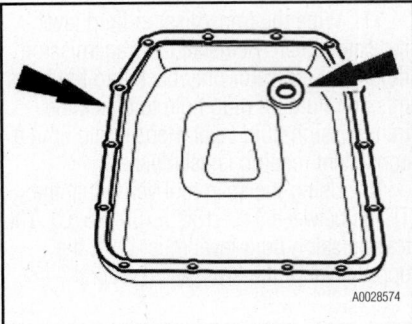

Fig. 21 Clean and inspect the transmission fluid pan, gasket and magnet

➤Normal maintenance requires periodic automatic transmission fluid changes. If a major repair, such as a clutch, band or bearing, is required, the automatic transmission will need to be removed for repair. The transmission fluid needs to be changed if evidence of transmission fluid contamination is found.

1. With the vehicle in NEUTRAL, position it on a hoist.

2. Loosen the transmission fluid pan bolts and allow transmission fluid to drain. After transmission fluid is drained, remove the bolts. Remove the transmission fluid pan and transmission fluid pan gasket.

3. Pull down evenly and remove the transmission fluid filter and seal.

4. Clean and inspect the transmission fluid pan, gasket and magnet.

To install:

➤If installing a new transmission fluid filter and the seal remains in the main control bore, use a small screwdriver and carefully remove the seal. Use care not to damage the main control bore.

➤If transmission is being repaired for a contamination-related failure, use a new transmission fluid filter and seal. The transmission fluid filter may be reused if no excessive contamination is present.

5. Install a new transmission fluid filter and seal as required.

6. Position the pan magnet into the transmission fluid pan.

➤The transmission fluid pan gasket is reusable. Clean and inspect for damage; if not damaged, the transmission fluid pan gasket should be reused.

7. Install the transmission fluid pan and gasket.

   a. Position the transmission fluid pan and gasket.

   b. Install the transmission fluid pan bolts. Tighten to 10 ft. lbs. (14 Nm).

➤When filling a dry transmission and converter, start with a minimum of 5 qt. (4.7L).

8. Fill the transmission to the correct level, using approved transmission fluid.

9. Verify for correct operation.

10. Check for leaks.

6R80 Transmission

See Figures 22 through 24.

✳✳ **WARNING**

The use of any transmission fluid other than specified can result in the transmission failing to operate in a normal manner or transmission failure.

1. With the vehicle in NEUTRAL, position it on a hoist.

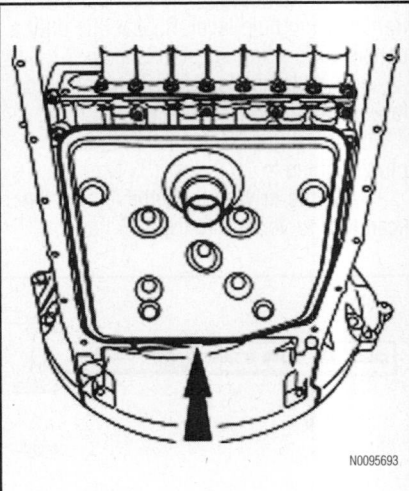

Fig. 22 Remove and discard the transmission fluid filter

2. Remove the transmission fluid fill plug transmission fluid level indicator assembly located on the passenger side front portion of the transmission case. Removal of the transmission fluid fill plug will relieve any vacuum that might have built up in the transmission. This will aid in allowing the transmission fluid pan to be easily removed when the bolts are removed.

3. Remove the transmission fluid pan and allow the transmission fluid to drain.

4. Remove the transmission fluid pan gasket.

➡**The transmission fluid filter may be reused if no excessive contamination is indicated.**

5. Remove and discard the transmission fluid filter.

6. Clean and inspect the transmission fluid pan and magnet.

To install:

➡**If the transmission is being repaired for a contamination-related failure, install a new transmission fluid filter and seal assembly. The transmission**

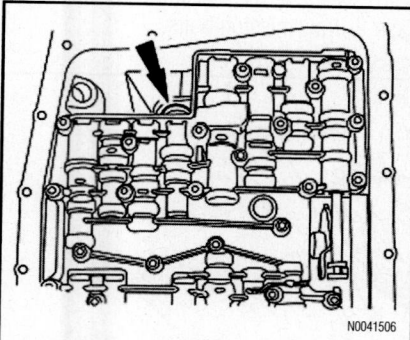

Fig. 23 If the seal is in the case, carefully remove the seal without scratching the case

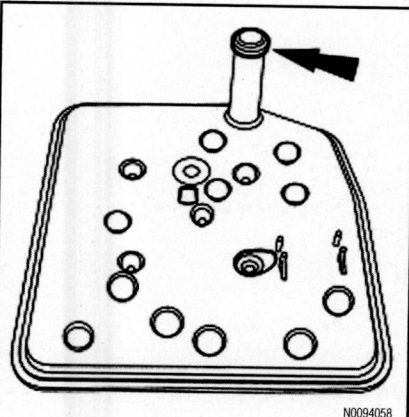

Fig. 24 Make sure that the seal is on the transmission fluid filter and lubricate the seal with automatic transmission fluid

fluid filter may be reused if no excessive contamination is indicated.

7. Inspect the transmission case for the transmission fluid filter seal. If the seal is in the case, carefully remove the seal without scratching the case.

8. Make sure that the seal is on the transmission fluid filter and lubricate the seal with automatic transmission fluid.

➡**The transmission fluid filter may be reused if no excessive contamination is indicated.**

9. If required, install a new transmission fluid filter.

10. Position the magnet in the transmission fluid pan.

➡**The transmission fluid pan gasket can be reused if not damaged.**

11. Install a new transmission fluid pan gasket if required.

12. Install the transmission fluid pan and tighten the bolts in a crisscross pattern. Tighten to 106 inch lbs. (12 Nm).

13. Using the Adding Additional Transmission Fluid procedure, fill and check the transmission fluid.

TRANSFER CASE ASSEMBLY

REMOVAL & INSTALLATION

See Figures 25 through 38.

1. With the vehicle in NEUTRAL, position it on a hoist.

2. If equipped, remove the 4 skid plate bolts and remove the skid plate.

3. Drain the fluid if the transfer case is to be disassembled.

4. Install the drain plug when finished draining. Tighten to 10 ft. lbs. (15 Nm).

5. Remove the front driveshaft.

6. Remove the rear driveshaft.

7. For vehicles with Electronic Shift-On-the-Fly (ESOF), disconnect the shift

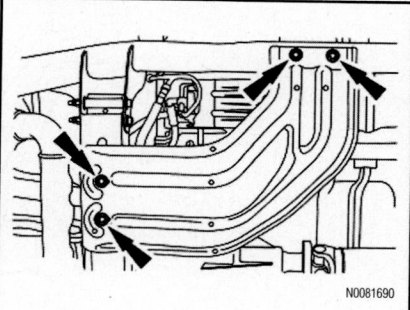

Fig. 25 If equipped, remove the 4 skid plate bolts and remove the skid plate

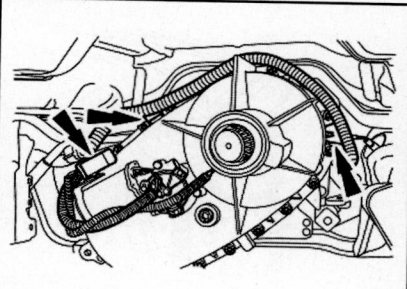

Fig. 26 Disconnect the shift motor electrical connector and detach the 2 harness retainer clips from the transfer case

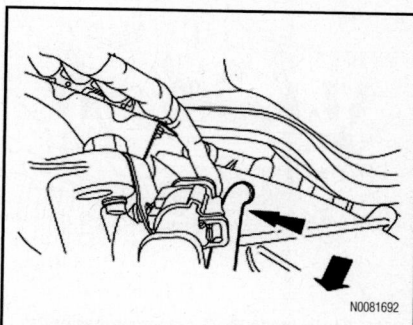

Fig. 27 Disconnect the vent hose from the transfer case

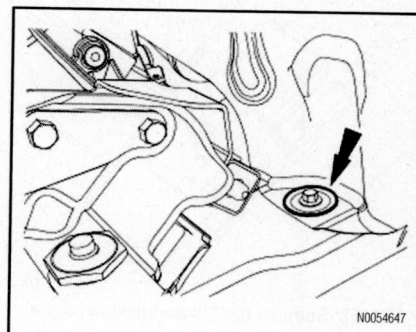

Fig. 28 Remove the RH exhaust heat shield bolt from the crossmember

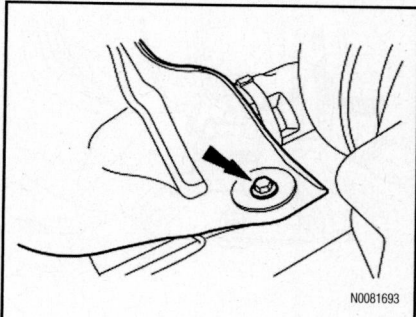

Fig. 29 Remove the LH exhaust heat shield bolt from the crossmember

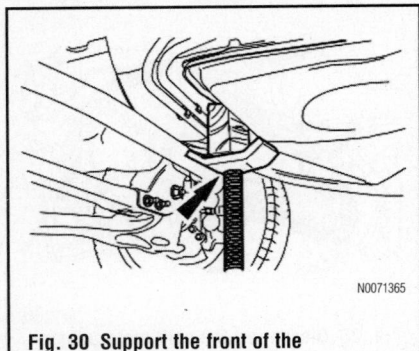

Fig. 30 Support the front of the transmission

Fig. 31 Remove the 4 crossmember bolts and nuts

Fig. 32 Remove the 2 transmission mount nuts and the crossmember

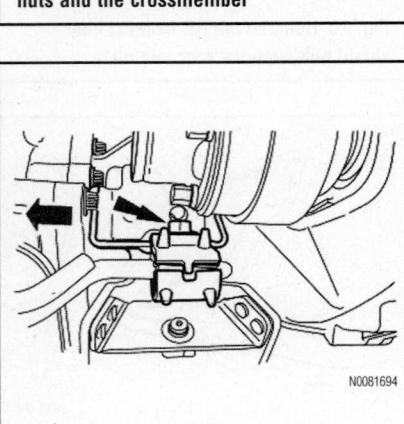

Fig. 33 Remove the bolt from the LH exhaust support bracket

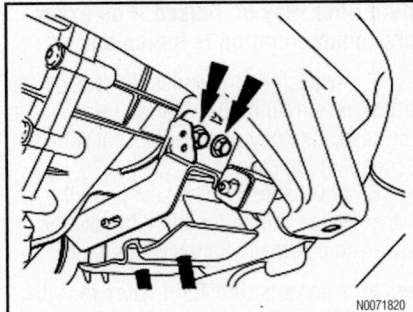

Fig. 34 Remove the 4 transmission mount bolts and the transmission mount

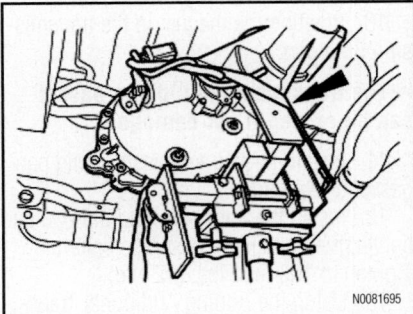

Fig. 35 Using a transmission jack, position it to the transfer case

motor electrical connector and detach the 2 harness retainer clips from the transfer case.

8. For vehicles with Mechanical Shift-On-The-Fly (MSOF):

  a. Disconnect the cable end from the shift lever.

  b. Remove the 2 shift cable mounting bracket nuts and the bracket.

9. Disconnect the vent hose from the transfer case.

10. Remove the RH exhaust heat shield bolt from the crossmember.

11. Remove the LH exhaust heat shield bolt from the crossmember.

12. Support the front of the transmission.

13. Remove the 4 crossmember bolts and nuts.

14. Remove the 2 transmission mount nuts and the crossmember.

15. Remove the bolt from the LH exhaust support bracket.

16. Remove the 4 transmission mount bolts and the transmission mount.

17. Using a transmission jack, position it to the transfer case. Secure the transfer case to the jack with a safety strap.

18. Remove and discard the 9 transfer case-to-transmission bolts.

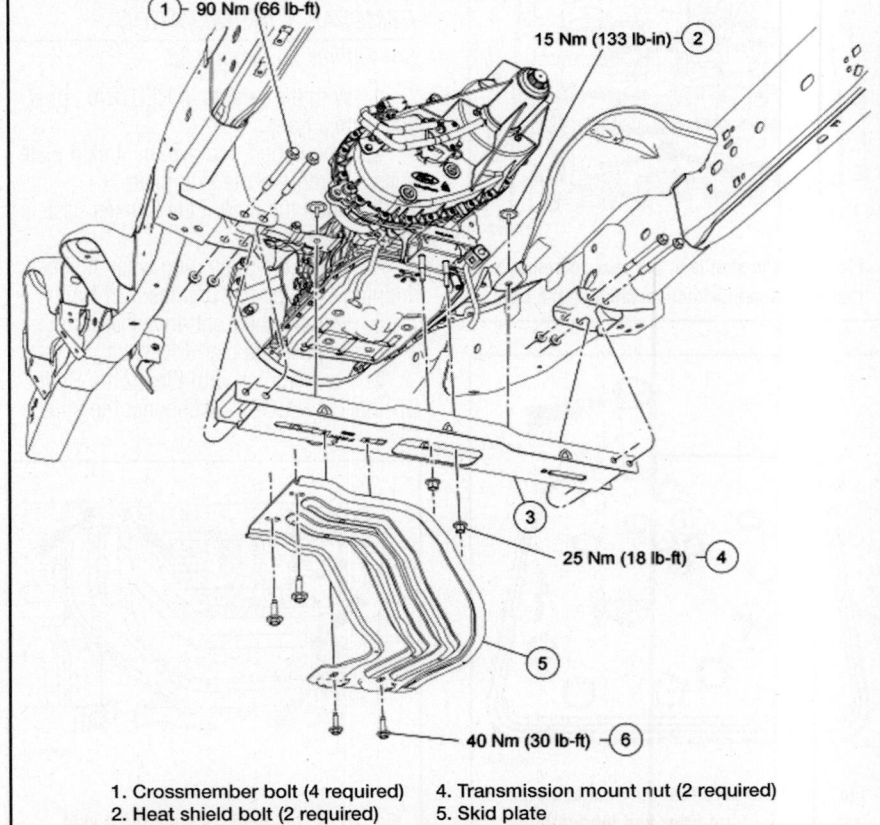

1. Crossmember bolt (4 required)
2. Heat shield bolt (2 required)
3. Crossmember
4. Transmission mount nut (2 required)
5. Skid plate
6. Skid plate bolt (4 required)

Fig. 36 Exploded view of Transfer Case - Left side

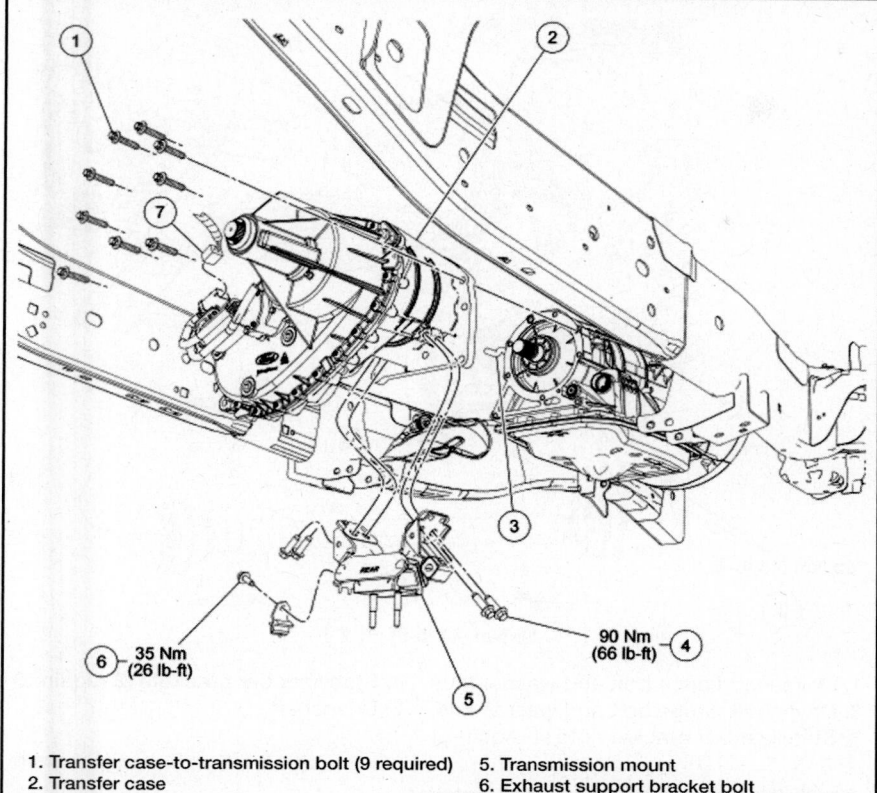

1. Transfer case-to-transmission bolt (9 required)
2. Transfer case
3. Vent tube
4. Transmission mount bolt (4 required)
5. Transmission mount
6. Exhaust support bracket bolt
7. Shift motor electrical connector - Electronic Shift-On-The-Fly (ESOF)

N0093053

Fig. 37 Exploded view of Transfer Case - Right side

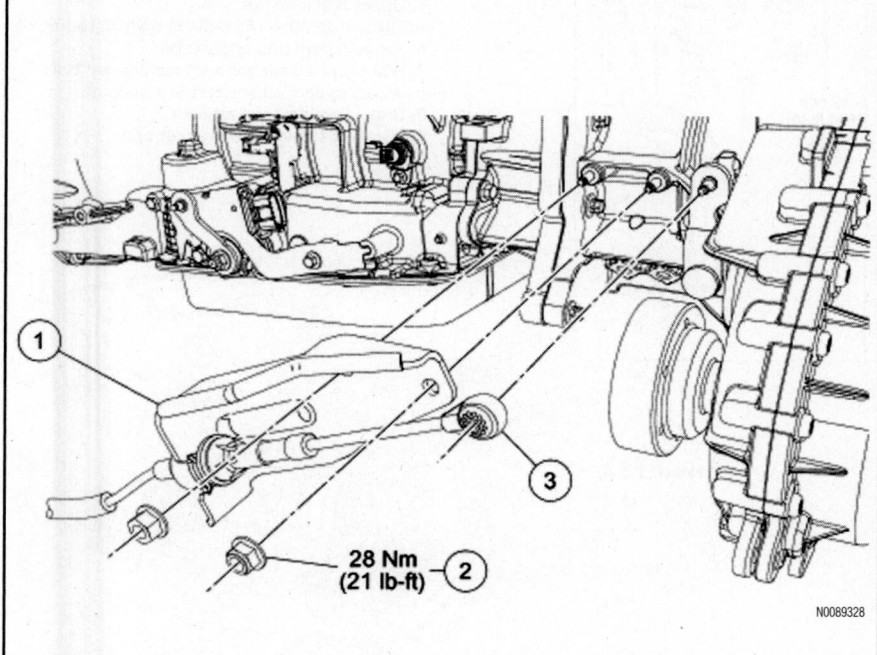

N0089328

Fig. 38 Exploded view of MSOF linkage showing shift cable mounting bracket (1), mounting bracket nut (2), and shift cable (3)

19. Separate the transfer case from the transmission and move the transfer case rearward 1 inch (25.4 mm). Move the transfer case rearward off the output shaft and lower it from the vehicle.

To install:

20. Position the transfer case to the transmission and onto the output shaft. With the transfer case 1 inch (25.4 mm) from the transmission, push the transfer case to the transmission.

➡**Do not reuse the old transfer case-to-transmission bolts.**

21. Install 9 new transfer case-to-transmission bolts. Tighten the bolts evenly in a cross pattern to 12.5 ft. lbs. (17 Nm).

22. Install the transmission mount and the 4 transmission mount bolts. Tighten to 66 ft. lbs. (90 Nm).

23. Install the LH exhaust support bracket and bolt. Tighten to 26 ft. lbs. (35 Nm).

24. Position the crossmember and the 2 transmission mount nuts. Do not tighten at this time.

25. Install the 4 crossmember bolts and nuts. Tighten the crossmember bolts to 66 ft. lbs. (90 Nm).

26. Tighten the transmission mount nuts to 18 ft. lbs. (25 Nm).

27. Install the LH exhaust heat shield bolt to the crossmember. Tighten to 11 ft. lbs. (15 Nm).

28. Install the RH exhaust heat shield bolt to the crossmember. Tighten to 11 ft. lbs. (15 Nm).

29. Connect the vent hose to the transfer case.

30. For vehicles with Electronic Shift-On-The-Fly (ESOF), connect the shift motor electrical connector and attach the 2 harness retainer clips to the transfer case.

31. For vehicles with Mechanical Shift-On-The-Fly (MSOF):

  a. Install the shift cable mounting bracket and the 2 nuts. Tighten to 21 ft. lbs. (28 Nm).

  b. Connect the cable end to the shift lever.

➡**Align the index marks made during removal.**

32. Install the rear driveshaft.

➡**Align the index marks made during removal.**

33. Install the front driveshaft.
34. If drained, fill the transfer case.
35. If equipped, position the skid plate and install the 4 skid plate bolts. Tighten to 30 ft. lbs. (40 Nm).

FRONT DRIVESHAFT

REMOVAL & INSTALLATION

See Figure 39.

1. With the vehicle in NEUTRAL, position the vehicle on a hoist.

2. If equipped, remove the 10 bolts and the forward and rearward skid plates.

3. Index-mark the front flange to the pinion flange.

4. Index-mark the rear flange to the transfer case flange.

5. Remove and discard the 6 rear flange-to-transfer case flange bolts and 3 washers.

6. Remove and discard the 6 front flange-to-pinion flange bolts and 2 washers.

7. Remove and discard the 4 stabilizer bar bracket nuts and allow the stabilizer bar to swing downward.

8. Remove the front driveshaft.

To install:

9. To install, reverse the removal procedure.

 a. Tighten the stabilizer bar bracket nuts to 41 ft. lbs. (55 Nm).

 b. Tighten the front flange-to-pinion flange bolts to 41 ft. lbs. (55 Nm).

 c. Tighten the flange-to-transfer case flange bolts to 41 ft. lbs. (55 Nm).

 d. Tighten the skid plate bolts to 35 ft. lbs. (48 Nm), if equipped.

FRONT HALFSHAFT

REMOVAL & INSTALLATION

See Figures 40 through 44.

❊❊ WARNING

Whenever a halfshaft is removed, a new circlip and stub shaft pilot bearing seal must be installed or damage to the component may occur.

1. With the vehicle in NEUTRAL, position it on a hoist.

2. Remove the dust cap.

3. Remove and discard the wheel hub nut.

4. Remove the wheel speed sensor harness bracket bolt and position the harness aside.

5. Detach the flexible hose retainer from the speed sensor harness.

6. Remove the brake flexible hose bracket bolt and disconnect the bracket from the wheel knuckle.

7. Remove the vacuum/vent tube at the vacuum/vent port of the Integrated Wheel End (IWE) disconnect.

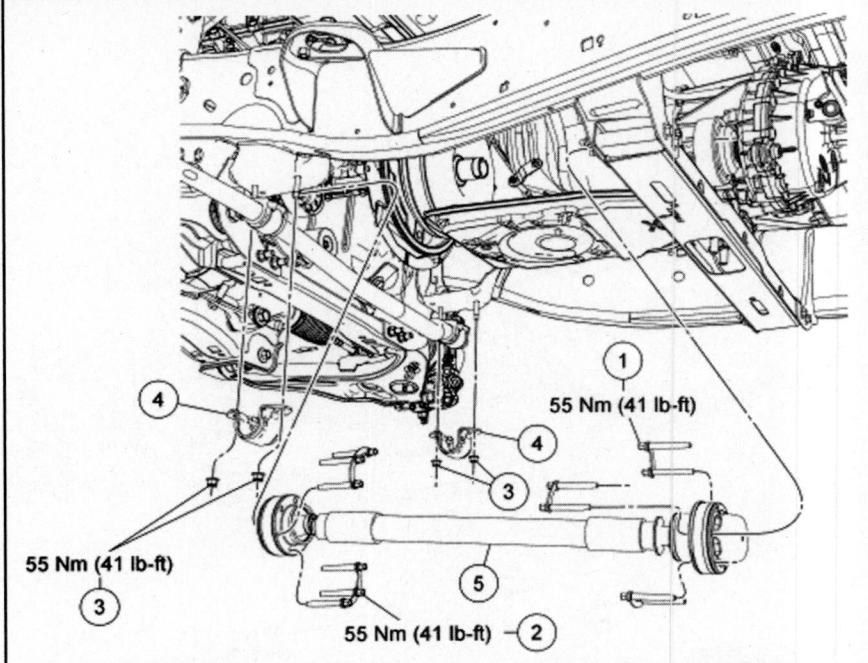

55 Nm (41 lb-ft)
55 Nm (41 lb-ft)
55 Nm (41 lb-ft)

1. Driveshaft flange bolt and washer kits
2. Driveshaft flange bolt and washer kits
3. Stabilizer bar bracket nuts (4 required)
4. Stabilizer bar brackets (2 required)
5. Driveshaft

N0071918

Fig. 39 Exploded view of front driveshaft assembly

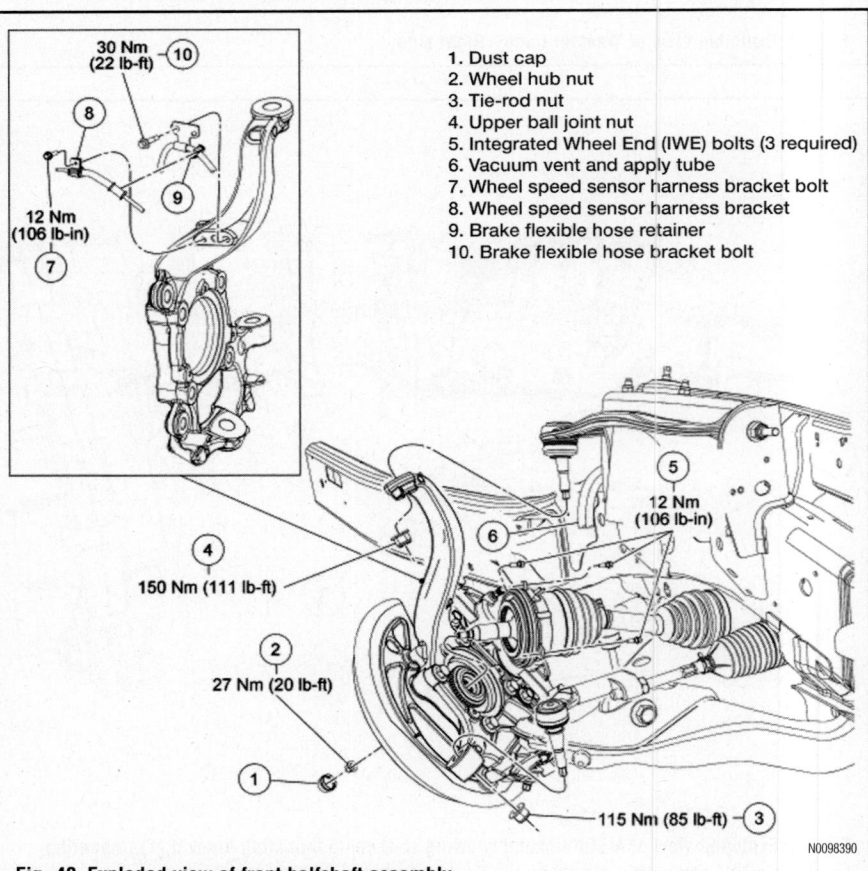

30 Nm (22 lb-ft)
12 Nm (106 lb-in)
150 Nm (111 lb-ft)
27 Nm (20 lb-ft)
115 Nm (85 lb-ft)
12 Nm (106 lb-in)

1. Dust cap
2. Wheel hub nut
3. Tie-rod nut
4. Upper ball joint nut
5. Integrated Wheel End (IWE) bolts (3 required)
6. Vacuum vent and apply tube
7. Wheel speed sensor harness bracket bolt
8. Wheel speed sensor harness bracket
9. Brake flexible hose retainer
10. Brake flexible hose bracket bolt

N0098390

Fig. 40 Exploded view of front halfshaft assembly

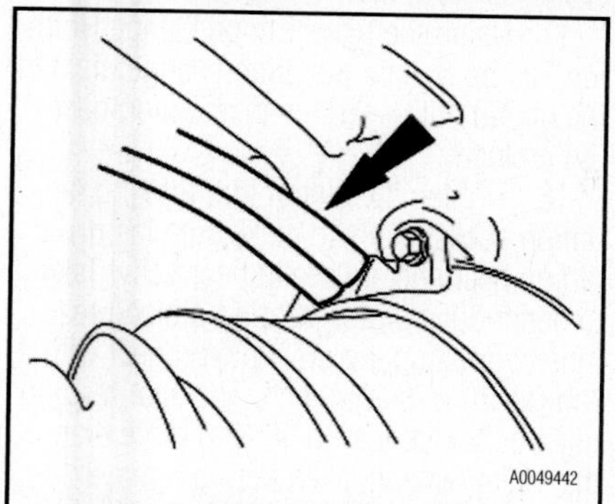

Fig. 41 Remove the vacuum/vent tube at the vacuum/vent port of the IWE disconnect

8. Remove the 3 IWE bolts.
9. Remove and discard the tie-rod end nut.

Disconnect the tie-rod end from the wheel knuckle.

Remove and discard the upper ball joint nut.

10. Disconnect the upper ball joint from the wheel knuckle.

⁂ WARNING

Do not damage the hub seal.

➡Allow the steering knuckle to swing outboard while keeping the CV shaft pushed inboard.

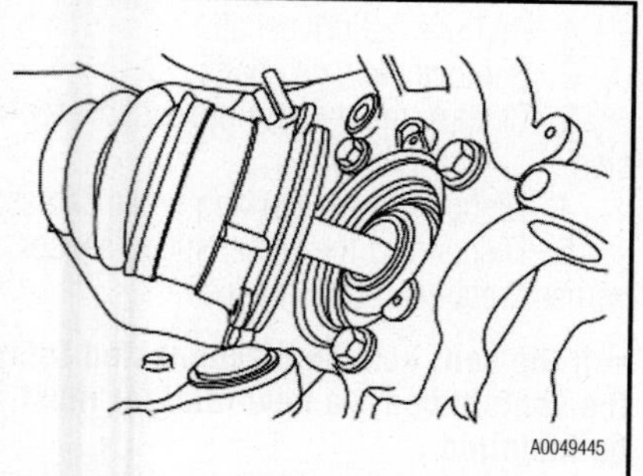

Fig. 42 Remove the CV shaft joint outboard end and IWE disconnect from the steering knuckle hub bearing

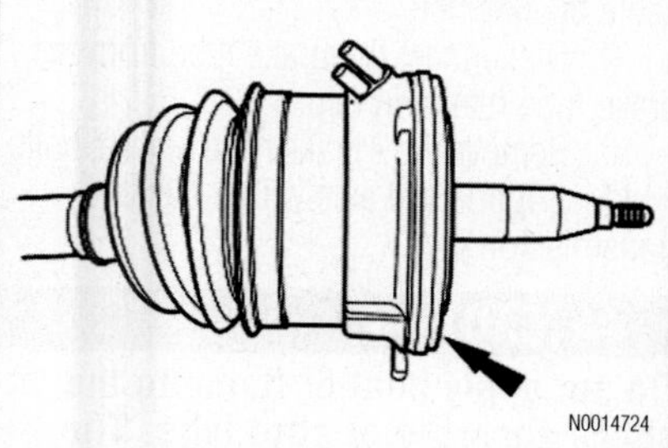

Fig. 43 Remove the IWE disconnect from the outboard CV joint housing

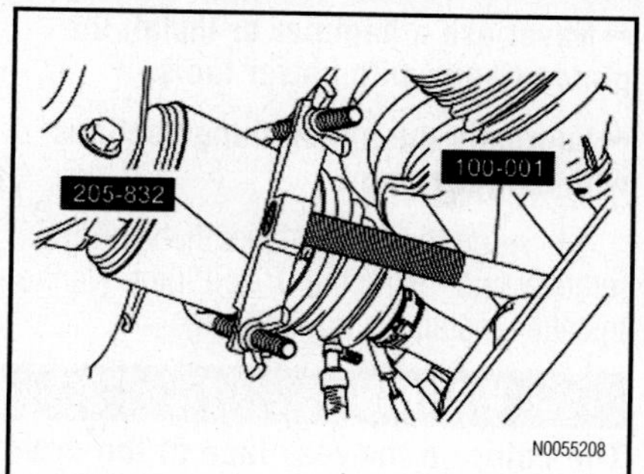

Fig. 44 Remove the halfshaft from the differential and the intermediate shaft

11. Once clearance is available, remove the CV shaft joint outboard end and IWE disconnect from the steering knuckle hub bearing.
12. Remove the IWE disconnect from the outboard CV joint housing.
13. Using the Halfshaft Remover and Slide Hammer, remove the halfshaft from the differential and the intermediate shaft.
14. Remove and discard the circlip and the stub shaft seal.

To install:

15. To install, reverse the removal procedure.

⁂ WARNING

Verify the spline engagement by checking for spline lash before installing the halfshaft nut or component damage may occur.

a. Tighten the new upper ball joint nut to 111 ft. lbs. (150 Nm).
b. Tighten the new tie-rod end nut to 85 ft. lbs. (115 Nm).
c. Tighten the IWE bolts to 106 inch lbs. (12 Nm).
d. Tighten the brake hose bracket bolt to 22 ft. lbs. (30 Nm).
e. Tighten the wheel speed sensor harness bracket to 106 inch lbs. (12 Nm).
f. Tighten the new wheel hub nut to 20 ft. lbs. (27 Nm).

FRONT PINION SEAL

REMOVAL & INSTALLATION

See Figures 45 through 49.

⁂ WARNING

The color on the rear face of the drive pinion nut is critical to this repair. Use the same color new drive pinion nut for installation as the original. If a new collapsible spacer must be installed for pinion bearing preload reduction, install the nut supplied with the new spacer or damage to the component may occur.

➡This operation disturbs the pinion bearing preload. Carefully reset the pinion bearing preload during assembly.

1. With the vehicle in NEUTRAL, position it on a hoist.
2. Remove the front disc brake pads.
3. Remove the front driveshaft.
4. Measure and record the pinion bearing preload.
5. Using an inch lbs. (Nm) torque wrench, rotate the pinion gear. Measure the torque required to maintain pinion gear rotation.
6. Index-mark the pinion flange and the drive pinion gear.
7. Using the Drive Pinion Flange Holding Fixture to hold the pinion flange, remove and discard the pinion nut and washer.
8. Using the 2 Jaw Puller, remove the pinion flange.
9. Inspect the pinion flange for burrs and damage. Inspect the end of the pinion flange that contacts the pinion bearing cone,

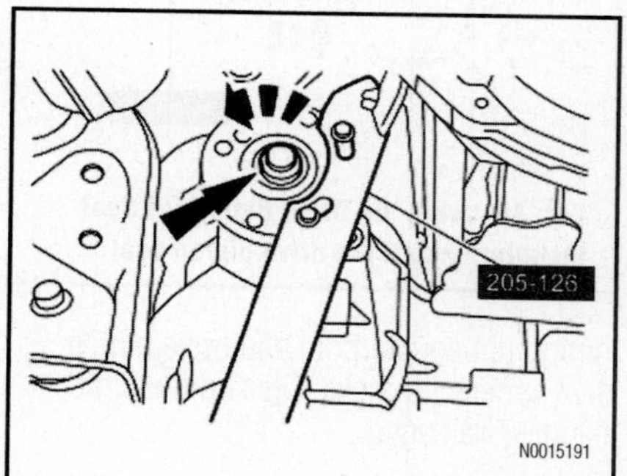

Fig. 45 Using the Drive Pinion Flange Holding Fixture to hold the pinion flange, remove and discard the pinion nut and washer

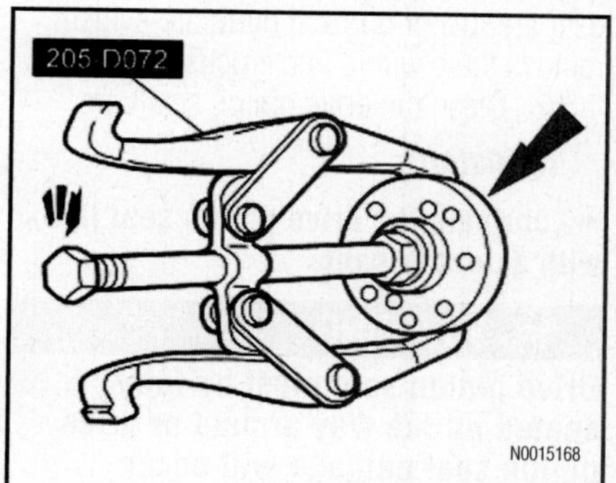

Fig. 46 Using the 2 Jaw Puller, remove the pinion flange

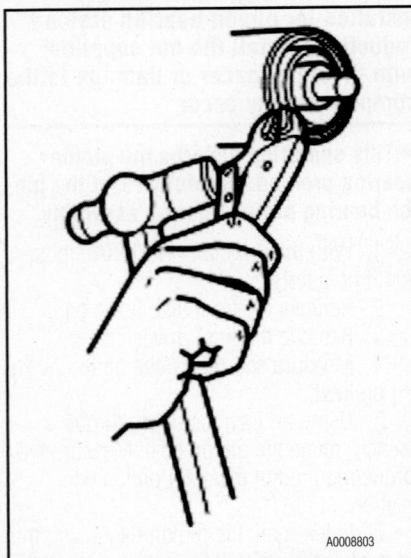

Fig. 47 Install gripping pliers and strike with a hammer to remove the drive pinion seal

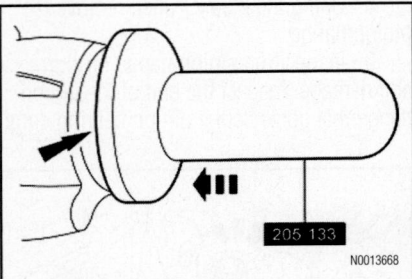

Fig. 48 Using the Drive Pinion Oil Seal Installer, install the drive pinion seal

pinion nut counterbore and drive pinion seal surface for nicks. Discard the pinion flange if damaged.

➥**Do not damage the axle housing.**

10. Force up on the metal flange of the drive pinion seal. Install gripping pliers and strike with a hammer to remove the drive pinion seal.

11. Verify the splines on the drive pinion gear are free of burrs. If burrs are evident, remove them with a fine crocus cloth.

12. Clean the drive pinion seal bore.

To install:

➥**Lubricate the drive pinion seal lips with axle lubricant.**

❊❊ WARNING

Drive pinion seal must be fully seated all the way around or drive pinion seal damage will occur.

13. Using the Drive Pinion Oil Seal Installer, install the drive pinion seal.

➥**Never use a hammer or install the pinion flange with power tools.**

➥**Lubricate the pinion flange splines with axle lubricant.**

14. Align the index marks made during removal and, using the Drive Pinion Flange Installer, install the pinion flange.

❊❊ WARNING

The color on the rear face of the drive pinion nut is critical to this repair. Use the same color new drive pinion nut for installation as the original. If a new collapsible spacer must be installed for pinion bearing preload reduction, install the nut supplied with the new spacer or damage to the component may occur.

15. Select the correct pinion nut for installation.

❊❊ WARNING

Install a new pinion nut with the same color as the original if not replacing the collapsible spacer or damage to the component may occur.

16. Install the new washer and pinion nut. Only hand-tighten the pinion nut at this time.

❊❊ WARNING

Do not loosen the pinion nut to reduce drive pinion bearing preload. Install a new drive pinion collapsible spacer and pinion nut if drive pinion bearing preload reduction is necessary. If a new collapsible spacer must be installed for pinion bearing preload reduction, install the nut supplied with the new spacer or damage to the component may occur.

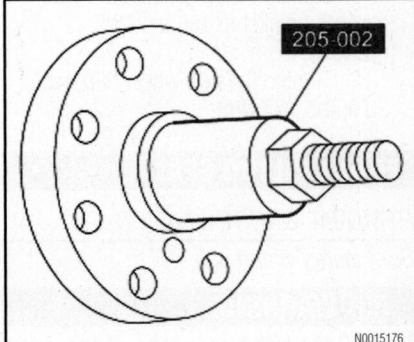

Fig. 49 Align the index marks made during removal and, using the Drive Pinion Flange Installer, install the pinion flange

17. Using the Drive Pinion Flange Holding Fixture to hold the pinion flange, tighten the pinion nut to set the drive pinion bearing preload.

18. Tighten the pinion nut, rotating the pinion occasionally to make sure the drive pinion bearings are seating correctly. Take frequent drive pinion bearing preload readings by rotating the drive pinion gear with a Nm (lb-in) torque wrench. The final reading must be 5 inch lbs. (0.56 Nm) more than the initial reading taken during removal.

19. Install the front driveshaft.

20. Install the front disc brake pads.

REAR AXLE HOUSING

REMOVAL & INSTALLATION

See Figures 50 and 51.

➥**Suspension fasteners are critical components because they affect performance of vital components and systems and their failure can result in major service expense. Install new components with the same component number or an equivalent component if installation is necessary. Do not use an installation component of lesser quality or substitute design. Torque values must be used as specified during reassembly to make sure of correct retention of these components.**

1. Remove the driveshaft.

2. Remove the axle shafts.

3. Release the parking brake cable tension.

4. Disconnect the parking brake cables.

5. Disconnect the wheel speed sensor harness retainers from the axle.

➥**If the vent hose is disconnected from the vehicle body, a new retainer must be installed.**

6. Disconnect the vent hose and remove the brake tube junction bracket bolt.

7. Remove the RH parking brake cable bracket bolt.

8. Remove the brake tube/parking brake cable bracket bolt.

9. Disconnect the brake tube from the brake tube retaining clip.

10. Remove the 2 brake hose bracket bolts.

11. Support the axle with a suitable transmission jack.

❊❊ CAUTION

Do not apply heat or flame to the shock absorber or strut tube. The shock absorber and strut tube are gas pressurized and could explode if heated. Failure to follow this

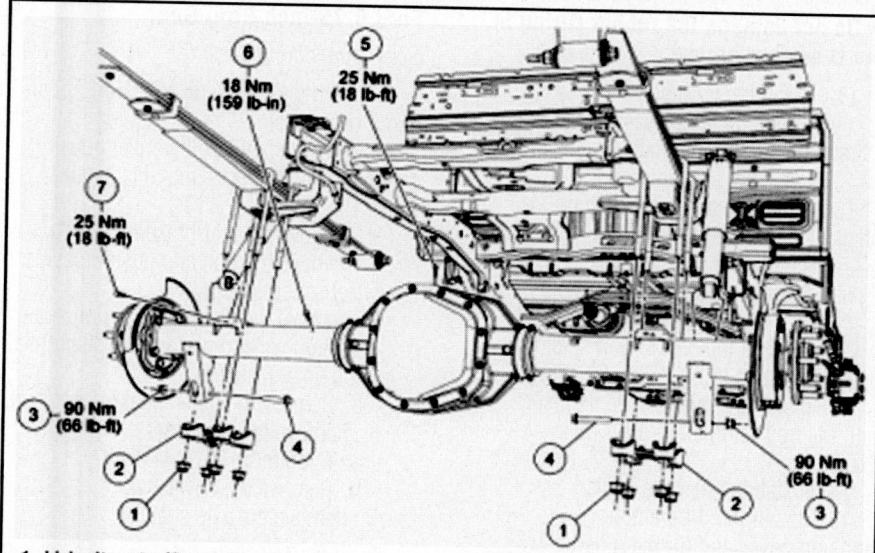

1. U-bolt nuts (8 required)
2. U-bolt plates (2 required)
3. Lower shock absorber nuts (2 required)
4. Lower shock absorber bolts (2 required)
5. Parking brake cable hold down bolt
6. Axle vent
7. Brake hose bracket bolt

Fig. 50 Exploded view of the rear axle/differential assembly

instruction may result in serious personal injury.

12. Remove and discard the 2 lower shock absorber nuts and 2 bolts.
13. Remove and discard the 8 U-bolt nuts and the 4 U-bolts.

✷✷ CAUTION

Secure the assembly to the jack. Avoid any obstructions while lowering and raising the jack. Contact with obstructions may cause the assembly to fall off the jack, which may result in serious personal injury.

14. Lower and remove the axle assembly.

To install:

15. To install the original assembly, reverse the removal procedure.

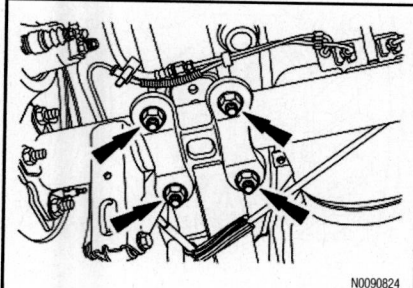

Fig. 51 Remove and discard the 8 U-bolt nuts and the 4 U-bolts

✷✷ WARNING

Final tightening of the U-bolt nuts must be done with the suspension at curb height or incorrect clamp load may occur.

16. With the suspension at curb height, tighten the new U-bolt nuts evenly in a cross-type pattern in 4 stages.

a. Stage 1: Tighten to 26 ft. lbs. (35 Nm).
b. Stage 2: Tighten to 52 ft. lbs. (70 Nm).
c. Stage 3: Tighten to 74 ft. lbs. (100 Nm).
d. Stage 4: Tighten to 98 ft. lbs. (133Nm).

17. Tighten the new lower shock absorber nuts to 66 ft. lbs. (90 Nm).
18. Tighten the brake hose bracket bolts to 18 ft. lbs. (25 Nm).
19. Tighten the brake tube/parking brake cable bracket bolt to 18 ft. lbs. (25 Nm).
20. Tighten the RH parking brake cable bracket bolt to 18 ft. lbs. (25 Nm).
21. Tighten the brake tube junction bracket bolt to 13 ft. lbs. (18 Nm).
22. Check the rear axle fluid level after installation.

REAR AXLE SHAFT, BEARING & SEAL

REMOVAL & INSTALLATION

Ford 8.8-inch Ring Gear
See Figures 52 through 55.

1. With the vehicle in NEUTRAL, position it on a hoist.
2. Remove the rear wheel and tire.
3. Remove the rear brake disc.
4. Remove the bolt and position aside the wheel speed sensor.
5. Remove the differential housing cover and drain the lubricant.

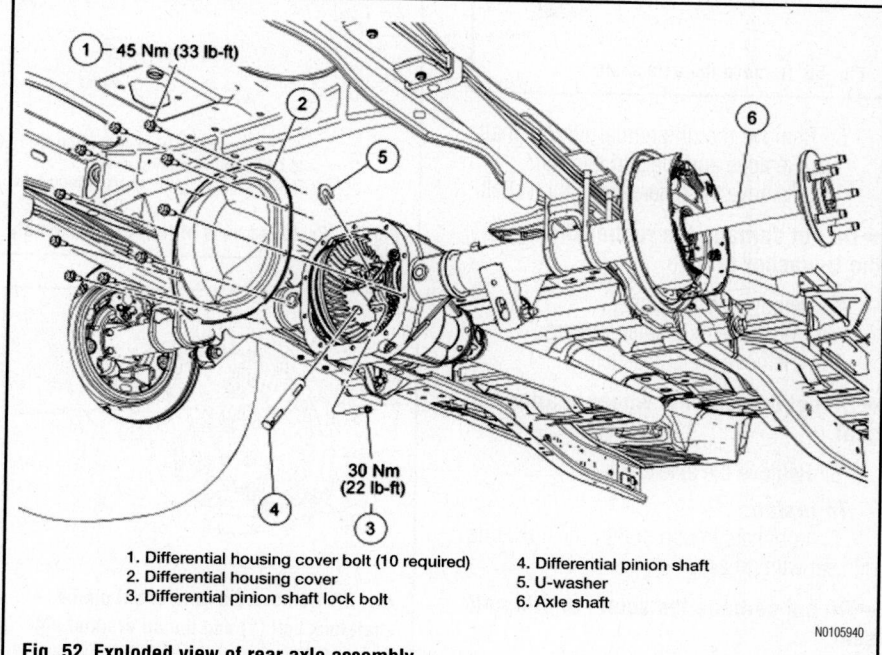

1. Differential housing cover bolt (10 required)
2. Differential housing cover
3. Differential pinion shaft lock bolt
4. Differential pinion shaft
5. U-washer
6. Axle shaft

Fig. 52 Exploded view of rear axle assembly

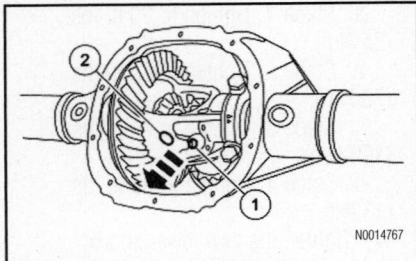

Fig. 53 Remove the bolt (1) and the differential pinion shaft (2)

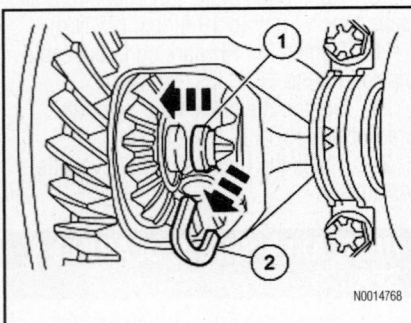

Fig. 54 Push the axle shaft (1) inboard and remove the U-washer (2)

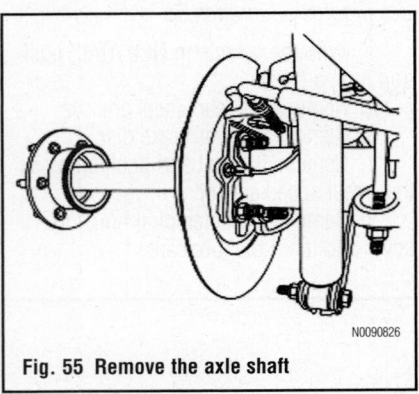

Fig. 55 Remove the axle shaft

6. Remove the differential pinion shaft.
   a. Remove and discard the bolt.
   b. Remove the differential pinion shaft.

➡**Do not damage the rubber O-ring in the U-washer groove.**

7. Remove the U-washer.
   a. Push the axle shaft inboard.
   b. Remove the U-washer.

➡**Do not damage the wheel bearing oil seal.**

8. Remove the axle shaft.

To install:

9. Lubricate the lip of the wheel bearing oil seal with grease.

➡**Do not damage the wheel bearing oil seal.**

10. Install the axle shaft.

➡**Do not damage the rubber O-ring in the U-washer groove.**

11. Install the U-washer.
    a. Position the U-washer on the button end of the axle shaft.
    b. Pull the axle shaft outward.
12. Install the differential pinion shaft.
    a. Align the bolt hole in the differential pinion shaft with the bolt hole in the case.
    b. Install the new pinion shaft lock bolt. Tighten to 22 ft. lbs. (30 Nm).
13. Install the wheel speed sensor and the bolt. Tighten to 10 ft. lbs. (15 Nm).
14. Install the rear brake disc.
15. Install the differential housing cover and fill the differential housing with the specified lubricant.
16. Install the rear wheel and tire.

Ford 9.75-inch Ring Gear

See Figures 56 through 60.

1. With the vehicle in NEUTRAL, position it on a hoist.
2. Remove the 12 differential housing cover bolts and remove the differential cover.
3. Remove the rear brake disc.
4. Remove the bolt and position aside the wheel speed sensor.
5. Remove the differential pinion shaft.
   a. Remove and discard the differential pinion shaft lock bolt.
   b. Remove the differential pinion shaft.
6. Remove the U-washer.
   a. Push in on the axle shaft.
   b. Remove the U-washer.
7. Remove the axle shaft.

To install:

8. Lubricate the lip of the axle shaft oil seal with grease.
   a. Install the axle shaft.

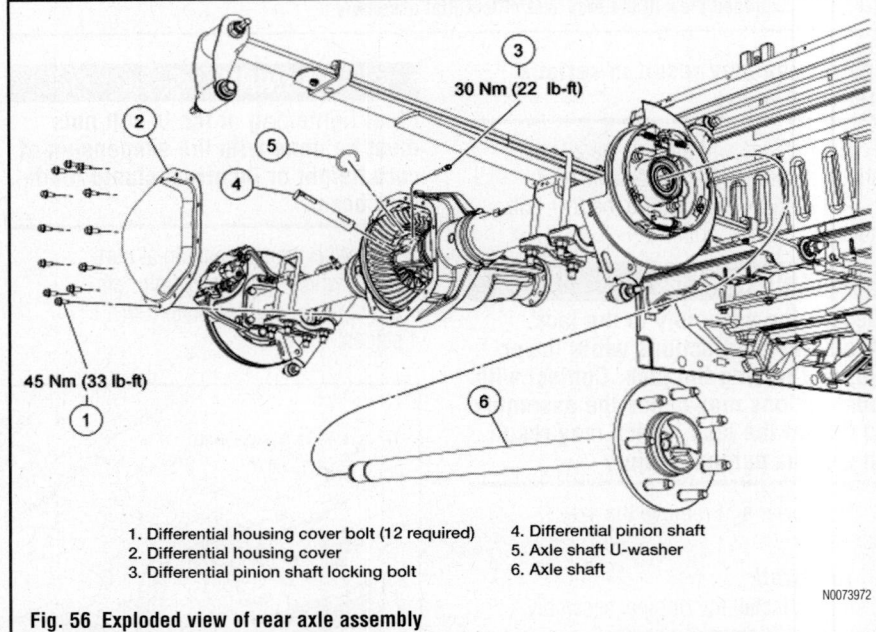

30 Nm (22 lb-ft)

45 Nm (33 lb-ft)

1. Differential housing cover bolt (12 required)
2. Differential housing cover
3. Differential pinion shaft locking bolt
4. Differential pinion shaft
5. Axle shaft U-washer
6. Axle shaft

Fig. 56 Exploded view of rear axle assembly

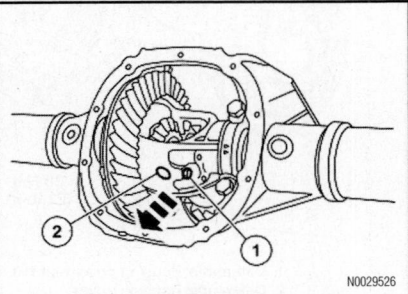

Fig. 57 Remove the differential pinion shaft lock bolt (1) and the differential pinion shaft (2)

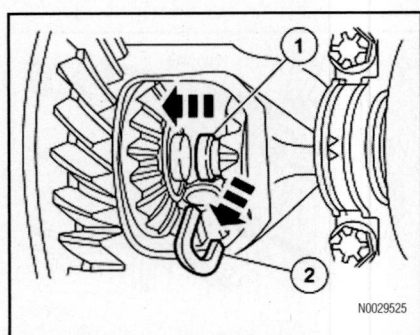

Fig. 58 Push in on the axle shaft (1) and remove the U-washer (2)

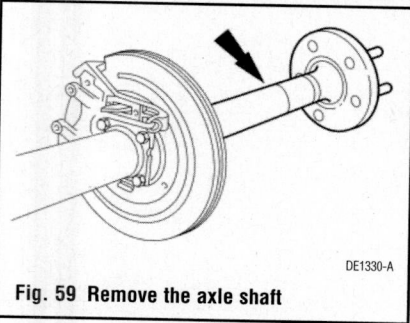

Fig. 59 Remove the axle shaft

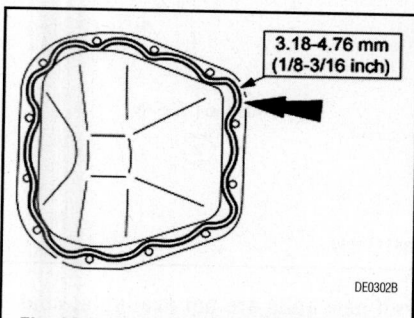

3.18–4.76 mm
(1/8–3/16 inch)

Fig. 60 Apply a new, continuous bead of sealant to the differential housing cover

➡Do not damage the rubber O-rings in the U-washer grooves.

9. Install the U-washer.
   a. Position the U-washer on the button end of the axle shaft.
   b. Pull the axle shaft outward.

➡If a new differential pinion shaft lock bolt is unavailable coat the threads of the original differential pinion shaft lock bolt with threadlock prior to installation.

10. Install the differential pinion shaft.
   a. Align the hole in the differential pinion shaft with the differential case lock bolt hole.
   b. Install a new differential pinion shaft lock bolt. Tighten to 22 ft. lbs. (30 Nm).
11. Install the wheel speed sensor and the bolt. Tighten to 10 ft. lbs. (15 Nm).
12. Install the rear brake disc.

➡Remove all of the silicone gasket and make sure the surfaces are free of oil before applying the new silicone gasket.

13. Clean the gasket mating surface of the axle and the differential housing cover.
14. Apply a new, continuous bead of sealant to the differential housing cover as shown.

➡The differential housing cover must be installed within 15 minutes of application of the silicone, or new sealant must be applied. If possible, allow one hour before filling with lubricant to ensure the silicone sealant has correctly cured.

15. Install the differential housing cover and the differential housing cover bolts. Tighten to 33 ft. lbs. (45 Nm).

➡For non SVT Traction-Lok axles, first fill the axle with 4 oz (118 ml) of friction modifier. No friction modifier should be used on SVT axles.

16. Remove the fill plug and fill the axle with the specified amount of lubricant. Install the filler plug. Tighten to 22 ft. lbs. (30 Nm).

REAR AXLE SHAFT BEARING AND SEAL

REMOVAL & INSTALLATION

Ford 8.8-inch Ring Gear
See Figures 61 through 63.

1. Remove the axle shaft.

➡If the axle shaft oil seal is leaking, the axle housing vent may be plugged with foreign material.

➡Use care to avoid damaging the axle shaft oil seal bore.

2. Using a suitable seal remover, remove and discard the axle shaft oil seal.
3. Inspect the rear wheel bearing and axle shaft for wear or damage.
4. If necessary, using the Axle Bearing

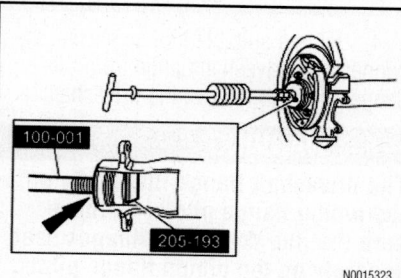

Fig. 61 If necessary, using the Axle Bearing Remover and Slide Hammer, remove the rear wheel bearing

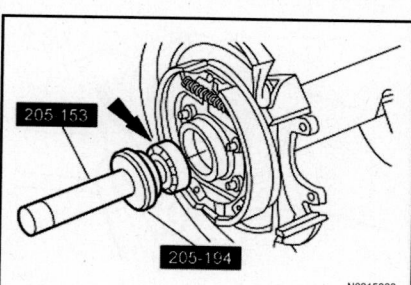

Fig. 62 If removed, use the Axle Bearing Installer and Handle to install the rear wheel bearing

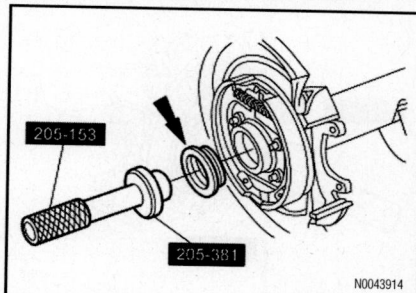

Fig. 63 Using the Axle Oil Seal Installer and Handle, install the new axle shaft oil seal

Remover and Slide Hammer, remove the rear wheel bearing.

To install:

5. If removed, lubricate the new rear wheel bearing with axle lubricant.
6. If removed, use the Axle Bearing Installer and Handle to install the rear wheel bearing.
7. Lubricate the lip of the new axle shaft oil seal with grease.
8. Using the Axle Oil Seal Installer and Handle, install the new axle shaft oil seal.
9. Install the axle shaft.

Ford 9.75-inch Ring Gear
See Figures 64 through 66.

1. Remove the axle shaft.

➡If only a new axle shaft oil seal needs to be installed, use care to avoid damaging the axle shaft oil seal bore.

2. Using a suitable seal remover, remove and discard the axle shaft oil seal.
3. Inspect the rear wheel bearing and axle shaft for wear or damage.
4. Using the Axle Bearing Remover and Slide Hammer, remove the rear wheel bearing.

To install:

5. Lubricate the new rear wheel bearing with axle lubricant.

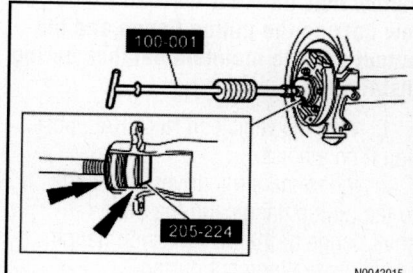

Fig. 64 Using the Axle Bearing Remover and Slide Hammer, remove the rear wheel bearing

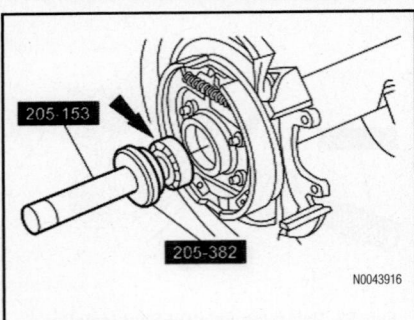

Fig. 65 Using the Axle Bearing Installer and Handle, install the rear wheel bearing

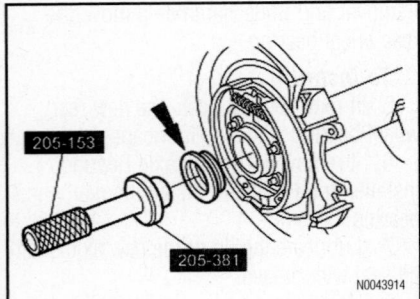

Fig. 66 Using the Axle Oil Seal Installer and Handle, install the new axle shaft oil seal

6. Using the Axle Bearing Installer and Handle, install the rear wheel bearing.

7. Lubricate the lip of the new axle shaft oil seal with grease.

8. Using the Axle Oil Seal Installer and Handle, install the new axle shaft oil seal.

9. Install the axle shaft.

REAR DRIVESHAFT

REMOVAL & INSTALLATION

One-Piece Driveshaft

See Figures 67 and 68.

➡For automatic transmissions, when installing a new driveshaft, match the yellow dots on the driveshaft to the yellow dots on the pinion flange and the output shaft to maintain balance during installation.

1. With the vehicle in NEUTRAL, position it on a hoist.

2. Index-mark the driveshaft flange to the pinion flange and the driveshaft flange to the transmission flange to maintain alignment during installation.

3. Remove and discard the 4 driveshaft flange bolts.

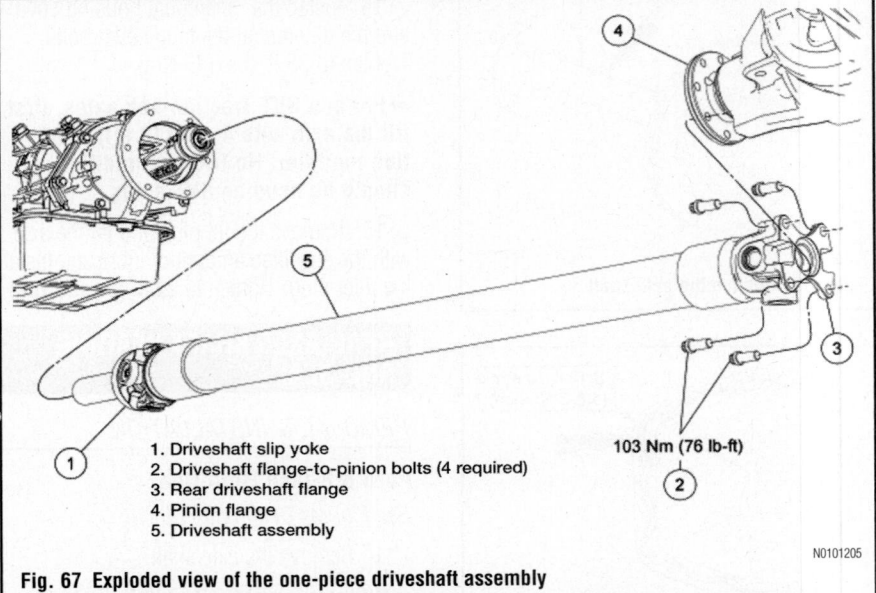

1. Driveshaft slip yoke
2. Driveshaft flange-to-pinion bolts (4 required)
3. Rear driveshaft flange
4. Pinion flange
5. Driveshaft assembly

103 Nm (76 lb-ft)

Fig. 67 Exploded view of the one-piece driveshaft assembly

> ✳✳ **WARNING**
>
> The driveshaft flange fits tightly on the flange pilot. Never hammer on the driveshaft or any of its components to disconnect the driveshaft flange from the flange pilot. Pry only in the area shown with a suitable tool to disconnect the driveshaft flange from the flange pilot or damage to the driveshaft flange can occur.

4. Using a suitable tool as shown, disconnect the driveshaft flange from the flange pilot and remove the driveshaft.

> ✳✳ **WARNING**
>
> The driveshaft flange fits tightly on the pinion flange pilots. To make sure that the driveshaft flanges seat squarely on the pinion flange pilots, tighten the driveshaft flange bolts evenly in a cross pattern or damage to the flanges can occur.

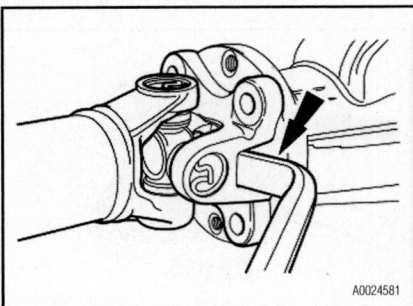

Fig. 68 Using a suitable tool as shown, disconnect the driveshaft flange from the flange pilot and remove the driveshaft

➡If new bolts are not available, coat the threads of the original driveshaft flange bolts with threadlock and sealer.

➡Align the index marks made during removal.

To install:

5. To install, reverse the removal procedure.

6. Tighten the 4 new driveshaft flange bolts to 76 ft. lbs. (103 Nm).

Two-Piece Driveshaft

See Figures 68 and 69.

➡For automatic transmissions, when installing a new driveshaft, match the yellow dots on the driveshaft to the yellow dots on the pinion flange and the output shaft to maintain balance during installation.

1. With the vehicle in NEUTRAL, position it on a hoist.

2. Index-mark the driveshaft flange to the pinion flange to maintain alignment during installation.

3. Index-mark the driveshaft to the extension housing to maintain alignment during installation.

4. Remove and discard the 4 driveshaft flange bolts.

> ✳✳ **WARNING**
>
> The driveshaft flange fits tightly on the flange pilot. Never hammer on the driveshaft or any of its components to disconnect the driveshaft flange from the flange pilot. Pry only in the area

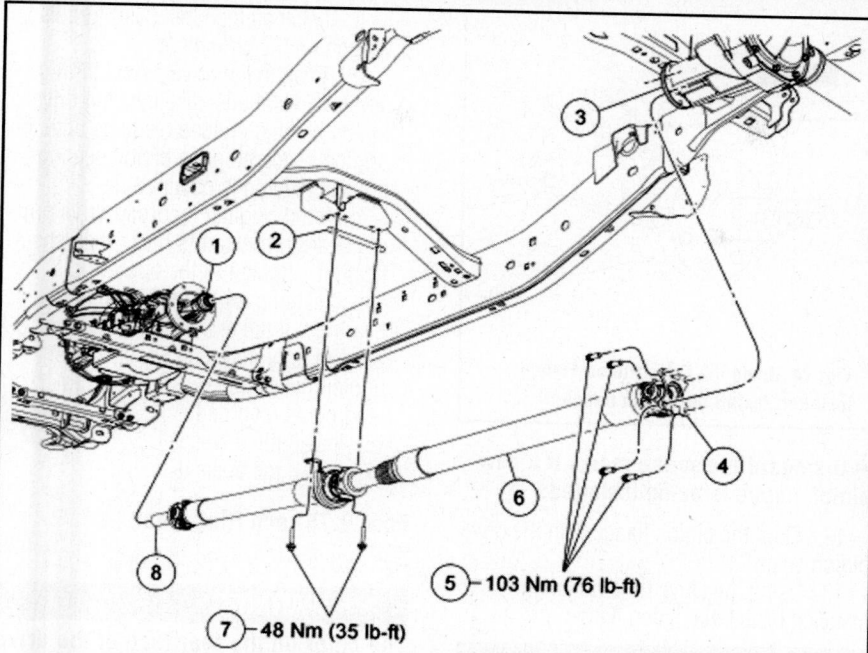

1. Transmission extension housing
2. Center bearing shim (if equipped)
3. Pinion flange
4. Driveshaft flange
5. Driveshaft flange-to-pinion bolts (4 required) (front fixed flange [8 required])
6. Driveshaft assembly
7. Driveshaft center bearing bolts (2 required)
8. Driveshaft slip yoke

5—103 Nm (76 lb-ft)
7—48 Nm (35 lb-ft)

N0105924

Fig. 69 Exploded view of the two-piece driveshaft assembly

shown with a suitable tool, to disconnect the driveshaft flange from the flange pilot or damage to the driveshaft flange can occur.

5. Using a suitable tool as shown, disconnect the driveshaft flange from the flange pilot.
6. Remove the driveshaft in the following sequence.
   a. Remove the 2 driveshaft center bearing bolts.
   b. Lower the driveshaft and slide the driveshaft slip yoke rearward off of the output shaft.
7. Plug the extension housing to prevent fluid loss.

❋❋ WARNING

The driveshaft flange fits tightly on the pinion flange pilots. To make sure that the driveshaft flanges seat squarely on the pinion flange pilots, tighten the driveshaft flange bolts evenly in a cross pattern or damage to the driveshaft flange can occur.

➡ If new bolts are not available, coat the threads of the original driveshaft flange bolts with threadlock and sealer.

➡ Align the index marks made during removal.

To install:

8. To install, reverse the removal procedure.
   a. Tighten the 2 driveshaft center bearing bolts to 35 ft. lbs. (48 Nm).
   b. Tighten the 4 new driveshaft flange bolts to 76 ft. lbs. (103 Nm).

REAR PINION SEAL

REMOVAL & INSTALLATION

Ford 8.8-inch Ring Gear
See Figures 47, 70 through 74.

❋❋ WARNING

The color on the rear face of the drive pinion nut is critical to this repair. Use the same color new drive pinion nut for installation. If a new collapsible spacer must be installed for pinion bearing preload reduction, install the nut supplied with the new spacer or damage to the component may occur.

1. With the vehicle in NEUTRAL, position it on a hoist.
2. Remove the brake disc.
3. Remove the driveshaft.
4. Using an Inch lbs. (Nm) torque wrench on the pinion nut, record the torque required to maintain rotation of the pinion gear through several revolutions.
5. Using the Drive Pinion Flange Holding Fixture to hold the pinion flange, remove and discard the pinion nut.
6. Index-mark the pinion flange in relation to the drive pinion stem to make sure of correct alignment during installation.
7. Using the 2 Jaw Puller, remove the pinion flange.
8. Force up on the metal flange of the drive pinion seal. Install gripping pliers and

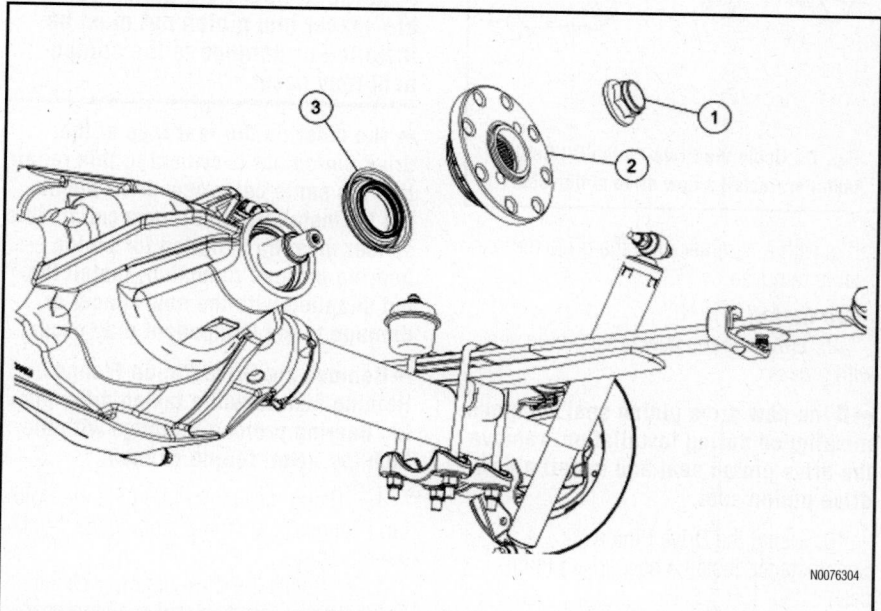

N0076304

Fig. 70 Exploded view showing pinion nut (1), pinion flange (2), and pinion seal (3)

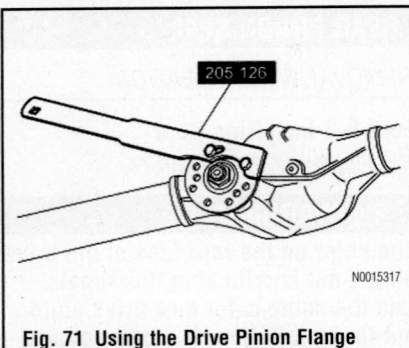

Fig. 71 Using the Drive Pinion Flange Holding Fixture to hold the pinion flange, remove and discard the pinion nut

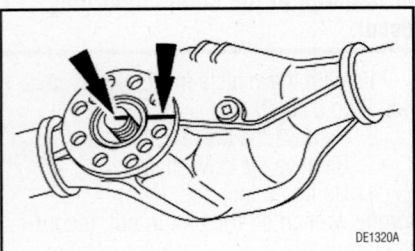

Fig. 72 Index-mark the pinion flange in relation to the drive pinion stem to make sure of correct alignment during installation

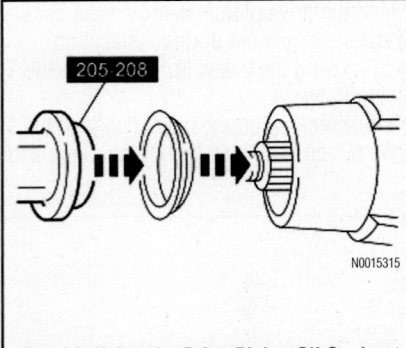

Fig. 73 Using the Drive Pinion Oil Seal Installer, install a new drive pinion seal

strike with a hammer until the drive pinion seal is removed.

To install:

9. Lubricate the new drive pinion seal with grease.

➡ **If the new drive pinion seal becomes misaligned during installation, remove the drive pinion seal and install a new drive pinion seal.**

10. Using the Drive Pinion Oil Seal Installer, install a new drive pinion seal.

11. Lubricate the pinion flange splines with axle lubricant.

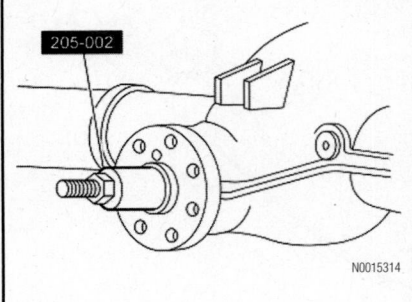

Fig. 74 Using the Drive Pinion Flange Installer, install the pinion flange

➡ **Disregard the scribe marks if a new pinion flange is being installed.**

12. Align the pinion flange with the drive pinion shaft.

13. Using the Drive Pinion Flange Installer, install the pinion flange.

☀ WARNING

Install a new pinion nut with the same color as the original if not replacing the collapsible spacer. If a new collapsible spacer is installed, install the nut in the kit or damage to the component may occur.

14. Position the new pinion nut.

☀ WARNING

Under no circumstances is the pinion nut to be backed off to reduce drive pinion bearing preload. If reduced drive pinion bearing preload is required, a new drive pinion collapsible spacer and pinion nut must be installed or damage to the component may occur.

➡ **The color on the rear face of the drive pinion nut is critical to this repair. Use the same color new drive pinion nut for installation. If a new collapsible spacer must be installed for pinion bearing preload reduction, install the nut supplied with the new spacer or damage to the component may occur.**

➡ **Remove the Drive Pinion Flange Holding Fixture while taking drive pinion bearing preload readings with the Inch lbs. (Nm) torque wrench.**

15. Using the Drive Pinion Flange Holding Fixture to hold the pinion flange, tighten the pinion nut.

　a. Rotate the drive pinion occasionally to make sure the drive pinion bearings are seating correctly.

　b. Install an Inch lbs. (Nm) torque wrench on the pinion nut.

　c. Rotating the drive pinion through several revolutions, take frequent drive pinion bearing preload readings until the original recorded drive pinion bearing preload reading is obtained.

　d. If the original recorded drive pinion bearing preload is lower than specifications, tighten to the appropriate specifications for used drive pinion bearings. If the drive pinion bearing preload is higher than specification, tighten the pinion nut to the original reading as recorded.

16. Install the driveshaft.

17. Install the brake disc.

Ford 9.75-inch Ring Gear

See Figures 47, 75 through 80.

☀ WARNING

The color on the rear face of the drive pinion nut is critical to this repair. Use the same color new drive pinion nut for installation. If a new collapsible spacer must be installed for pinion bearing preload reduction, install the nut supplied with the new spacer or damage to the component may occur.

1. With the vehicle in NEUTRAL, position it on a hoist.

2. Remove the brake disc.

3. Index-mark the driveshaft flange and pinion flange for correct alignment during installation.

4. Remove and discard the 4 driveshaft flange bolts.

➡ **The driveshaft centering socket yoke fits tightly on the pinion flange pilot. Never hammer on the driveshaft or any of its components to disconnect the driveshaft centering socket yoke from the pinion flange. Pry only in the area shown with a suitable tool to disconnect the driveshaft centering socket yoke from the pinion flange.**

5. Using a suitable tool as shown, disconnect the driveshaft centering socket yoke from the pinion flange.

6. Using mechanic's wire, position the driveshaft aside.

7. Using an Inch lbs. (Nm) torque wrench on the pinion nut, record the torque required to maintain rotation of the pinion gear through several revolutions.

8. Using the Drive Pinion Flange Holding Fixture to hold the pinion flange, remove and discard the pinion nut.

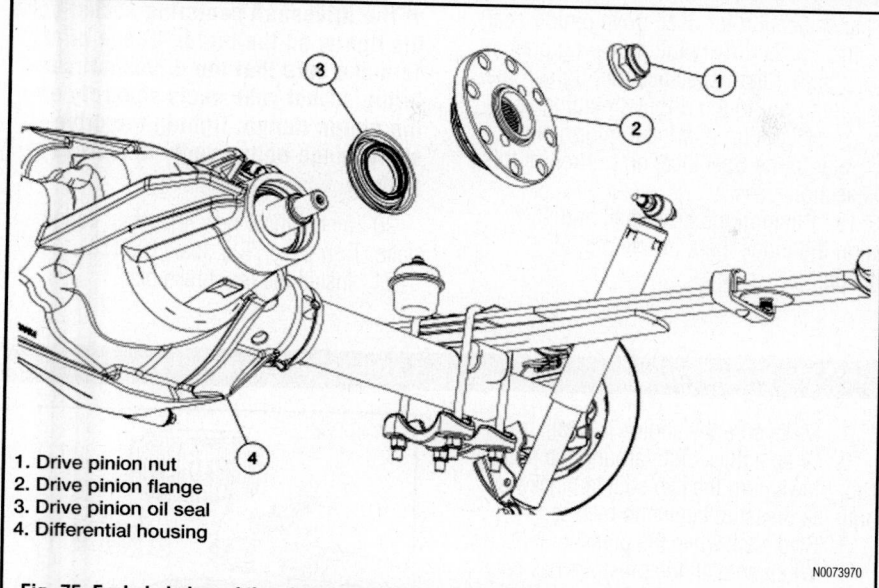

1. Drive pinion nut
2. Drive pinion flange
3. Drive pinion oil seal
4. Differential housing

N0073970

Fig. 75 Exploded view of the pinion flange and seal assembly

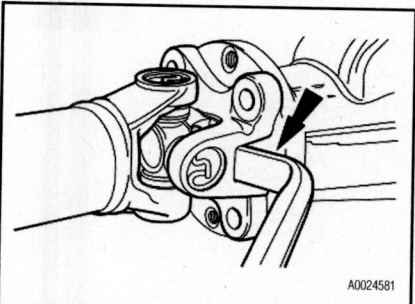

A0024581

Fig. 76 Using a suitable tool as shown, disconnect the driveshaft centering socket yoke from the pinion flange

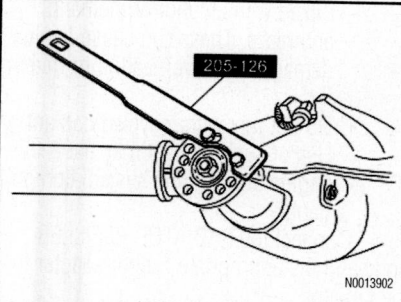

N0013902

Fig. 77 Using the Drive Pinion Flange Holding Fixture to hold the pinion flange, remove and discard the pinion nut

9. Index-mark the pinion flange in relation to the drive pinion stem to make sure of correct alignment during installation.

10. Using the 2 Jaw Puller, remove the pinion flange.

11. Force up on the metal flange of the drive pinion seal. Install gripping pliers and

strike with a hammer until the drive pinion seal is removed.

To install:

12. Lubricate the new drive pinion seal with grease.

13. Using the Drive Pinion Oil Seal Installer, install a new drive pinion seal.

14. Lubricate the pinion flange splines with axle lubricant.

➥**Disregard the scribe marks if a new pinion flange is being installed.**

15. Align the pinion flange with the drive pinion shaft.

16. Using the Drive Pinion Flange Installer, install the pinion flange.

✳✳ WARNING

Install a new pinion nut with the same color as the original if not

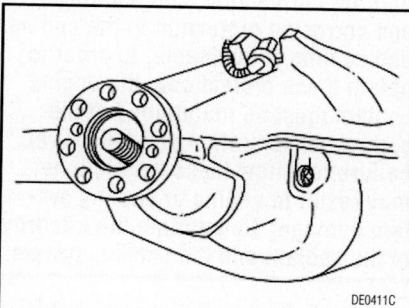

DE0411C

Fig. 78 Index-mark the pinion flange in relation to the drive pinion stem to make sure of correct alignment during installation

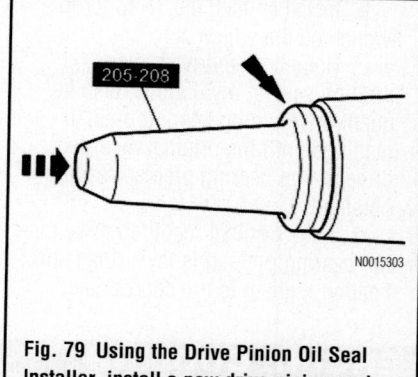

N0015303

Fig. 79 Using the Drive Pinion Oil Seal Installer, install a new drive pinion seal

replacing the collapsible spacer. If a new collapsible spacer is installed, install the nut in the kit, as indicated in the chart below, or damage to the component may occur.

17. Position the new pinion nut.

✳✳ WARNING

Under no circumstances is the pinion nut to be backed off to reduce drive pinion bearing preload. If reduced drive pinion bearing preload is required, a new drive pinion collapsible spacer and pinion nut must be installed or damage to the component may occur.

➥**Remove the Drive Pinion Flange Holding Fixture while taking drive pinion bearing preload readings with the Inch lbs. (Nm) torque wrench.**

18. Using the Drive Pinion Flange Holding Fixture to hold the pinion flange, tighten the pinion nut.

   a. Rotate the drive pinion occasionally to make sure the drive pinion bearings are seating correctly.

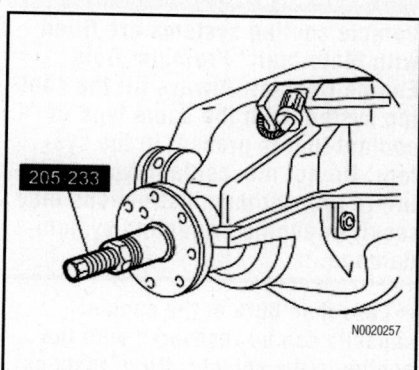

N0020257

Fig. 80 Using the Drive Pinion Flange Installer, install the pinion flange

b. Install an Inch lbs. (Nm) torque wrench on the pinion nut.

c. Rotating the drive pinion through several revolutions, take frequent drive pinion bearing preload readings until the original recorded drive pinion bearing preload reading is obtained.

d. If the original recorded drive pinion bearing preload is lower than specification, tighten to the appropriate specification for used drive pinion bearings. If the drive pinion bearing preload is higher than specification, tighten the pinion nut to the original reading as recorded. For additional information, refer to the Specification portion of this section.

19. Position the driveshaft and align the index mark on the pinion flange.

➡**The driveshaft centering socket yoke fits tightly on the pinion flange pilot. To make sure that the driveshaft centering socket yoke seats squarely on the pinion flange, tighten the driveshaft flange bolts evenly in a cross pattern.**

20. Install the 4 new driveshaft flange bolts. Tighten to 76 ft. lbs. (103 Nm).

21. Install the rear brake disc.

ENGINE COOLING

ENGINE COOLANT

DRAIN & REFILL PROCEDURE

2010 Models

> ❊❊ **CAUTION**
>
> **Always allow the engine to cool before opening the cooling system. Do not unscrew the coolant pressure relief cap when the engine is operating or the cooling system is hot. The cooling system is under pressure; steam and hot liquid can come out forcefully when the cap is loosened slightly. Failure to follow these instructions may result in serious personal injury.**

> ❊❊ **WARNING**
>
> **The coolant must be recovered in a suitable, clean container for reuse. If the coolant is contaminated it must be recycled or disposed of correctly. Failure to follow these instructions may result in engine or cooling system damage.**

> ❊❊ **WARNING**
>
> **Vehicle cooling systems are filled with Motorcraft® Premium Gold Engine Coolant. Always fill the cooling system with the same type of coolant that is present in the system. Do not mix coolant types. Failure to follow these instructions may result in engine or cooling system damage.**

➡**Less than 80% of the coolant capacity can be recovered with the engine in the vehicle. Dirty, rusty or contaminated coolant requires replacement.**

1. Make sure the engine is cool.

2. Wrap a thick cloth around the radiator cap. Slowly turn the cap counterclockwise until the pressure begins to release.

3. Step back while the pressure releases.

4. When sure all the pressure has been released, use the cloth to turn and remove the cap.

5. Place a suitable container below the radiator draincock. Drain the coolant.

6. Tighten the radiator draincock when finished.

Filling And Bleeding With Radiator Refiller

See Figures 81 and 82.

> ❊❊ **WARNING**
>
> **Vehicle cooling systems are filled with Motorcraft® Premium Gold Engine Coolant. Always fill the cooling system with the same type of coolant that is present in the system. Do not mix coolant types. Failure to follow these instructions may result in engine or cooling system damage.**

> ❊❊ **WARNING**
>
> **Engine coolant provides freeze protection, boil protection, cooling efficiency and corrosion protection to the engine and cooling components. In order to obtain these protections, the engine coolant must be maintained at the correct concentration and fluid level. Failure to follow these instructions may result in engine or cooling system damage. To maintain the integrity of the coolant and the cooling system:**
>
> - Do not mix coolant types. Mixing coolants may degrade the coolant's corrosion protection.
> - Do not add alcohol, methanol or brine, or any engine coolants

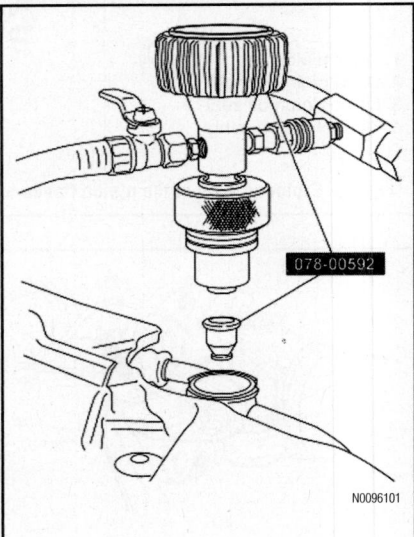

Fig. 81 Connect the radiator refiller body and the appropriate rubber adapter to the radiator

mixed with alcohol or methanol antifreeze. These can cause engine damage from overheating or freezing.

- Do not mix with recycled coolant. Use of such coolant may harm the engine and cooling system components.

1. Connect the RADIATOR REFILLER body and the appropriate rubber adapter to the radiator.

2. Clamp the radiator-to-coolant expansion tank hose near the radiator.

3. Follow the RADIATOR REFILLER manufacturer's instructions to fill and bleed the cooling system.

4. Recommended coolant concentration is 50/50 ethylene glycol to distilled water.

a. Maximum coolant concentration is 60/40 for cold weather areas.

b. Minimum coolant concentration is 40/60 for warm weather areas.

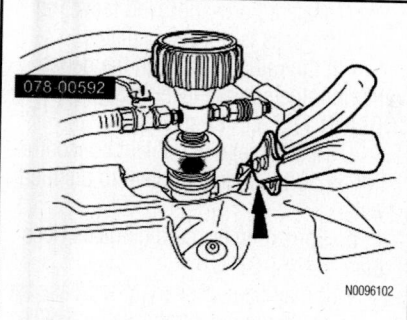

Fig. 82 Clamp the radiator-to-coolant expansion tank hose near the radiator

Filling And Bleeding Without Radiator Refiller

※ WARNING

Vehicle cooling systems are filled with Motorcraft® Premium Gold Engine Coolant. Always fill the cooling system with the same type of coolant that is present in the system. Do not mix coolant types. Failure to follow these instructions may result in engine or cooling system damage.

※ WARNING

Engine coolant provides freeze protection, boil protection, cooling efficiency and corrosion protection to the engine and cooling components. In order to obtain these protections, the engine coolant must be maintained at the correct concentration and fluid level. Failure to follow these instructions may result in engine or cooling system damage. To maintain the integrity of the coolant and the cooling system:

- Do not mix coolant types. Mixing coolants may degrade the coolant's corrosion protection.
- Do not add alcohol, methanol or brine, or any engine coolants mixed with alcohol or methanol antifreeze. These can cause engine damage from overheating or freezing.
- Do not mix with recycled coolant. Use of such coolant may harm the engine and cooling system components.

1. Fill the radiator through the radiator fill neck until the coolant level is at the bottom of the filler neck.

2. Recommended coolant concentration is 50/50 ethylene glycol to distilled water.

a. Maximum coolant concentration is 60/40 for cold weather areas.

b. Minimum coolant concentration is 40/60 for warm weather areas.

3. Install the radiator cap.

4. Fill the coolant expansion tank until the coolant reaches the COLD FILL mark.

5. On the Electronic Manual Temperature Control (EMTC), move the temperature blend selector to the full WARM position. On the Electronic Automatic Temperature Control (EATC), set the temperature to 90°F (32°C).

※ WARNING

If the air discharge remains cool and the engine coolant temperature gauge does not move, the engine coolant level is low in the engine and must be filled. Stop the engine, allow it to cool and fill the cooling system. Failure to follow this instructions may result in damage to the engine.

6. Run the engine at idle until it reaches normal operating temperature.

7. Add more correct coolant mixture to the coolant expansion tank until the coolant level is at the COLD FILL mark.

8. Turn the engine off and allow it to cool.

9. Start the engine and allow it to idle until it reaches normal operating temperature. While the engine is idling, feel for hot air from the A/C vents.

➡Hot air should discharge from the A/C vents. The engine coolant temperature gauge should maintain a stabilized reading in the middle of the NORMAL range and the upper radiator hose should feel hot to the touch.

10. Check the engine coolant level in the coolant expansion tank and fill it as necessary.

11. Repeat the previous 5 steps as necessary.

2011 Models

※ CAUTION

Always allow the engine to cool before opening the cooling system. Do not unscrew the coolant pressure relief cap when the engine is operating or the cooling system is hot. The cooling system is under pressure; steam and hot liquid can come out forcefully when the cap is loosened slightly. Failure to follow these instructions may result in serious personal injury.

※ WARNING

The coolant must be recovered in a suitable, clean container for reuse. If the coolant is contaminated it must be recycled or disposed of correctly. Failure to follow these instructions may result in engine or cooling system damage.

➡Less than 80% of the coolant capacity can be recovered with the engine in the vehicle. Dirty, rusty or contaminated coolant requires replacement.

➡During normal vehicle operation, Motorcraft® Specialty Orange Engine Coolant may change color from orange to pink or light red. As long as the engine coolant is clear and uncontaminated, this color change does not indicate the engine coolant has degraded nor does it require the engine coolant to be drained, the system to be flushed, or the engine coolant to be replaced.

1. With the vehicle in NEUTRAL, position it on a hoist.

2. Make sure the engine is cool.

3. Wrap a thick cloth around the pressure relief cap. Slowly turn the cap counterclockwise until the pressure begins to release.

4. Step back while the pressure releases.

5. When sure all the pressure has been released, use the cloth to turn and remove the cap.

6. Place a suitable container below the radiator draincock. Drain the coolant.

7. Tighten the radiator draincock when finished.

Filling And Bleeding With A Vacuum Cooling System Filler—Degas Bottle Systems

※ WARNING

The engine cooling system is filled with Motorcraft® Specialty Orange Engine Coolant. Always fill the cooling system with the manufacturer's specified coolant. If a non-specified coolant has been used the cooling system must be chemically flushed. Failure to follow these instructions may damage the engine or cooling system.

⁕⁕ WARNING

Engine coolant provides boil protection, corrosion protection, freeze protection, and cooling efficiency to the engine and cooling components. In order to obtain these protections, maintain the engine coolant at the correct concentration and fluid level in the degas bottle. To maintain the integrity of the coolant and the cooling system:

- Add Motorcraft® Specialty Orange Engine Coolant or equivalent meeting Ford specification WSS-M97B44-D (orange color). Do not mix coolant types.
- Do not add or mix with any other type of engine coolant. Mixing coolants may degrade the coolant's corrosion protection.
- Do not add alcohol, methanol, or brine, or any engine coolants mixed with alcohol or methanol antifreeze. These can cause engine damage from overheating or freezing.
- Ford Motor Company does NOT recommend the use of recycled engine coolant in vehicles originally equipped with Motorcraft® Specialty Orange Engine Coolant since a Ford-approved recycling process is not yet available.

1. Install the vacuum cooling system filler and follow the manufacturer's instructions to fill and bleed the cooling system.

  a. Recommended coolant concentration is 50/50 engine coolant to distilled water.

  b. For extremely cold climates (less than -34°F [-37°C]):

- It may be necessary to increase the coolant concentration above 50%.
- NEVER increase the coolant concentration above 60%.
- Maximum coolant concentration is 60/40 for cold weather areas.
- A coolant concentration of 60% will provide freeze point protection down to -58°F (-50°C).
- Engine coolant concentration above 60% will decrease the overheat protection characteristics of the engine coolant and may damage the engine.

  c. For extremely hot climates:

- It is still necessary to maintain the coolant concentration above 40%.
- NEVER decrease the coolant concentration below 40%.
- Minimum coolant concentration is 40/60 for warm weather areas.

- A coolant concentration of 40% will provide freeze point protection down to -15°F (-26°C).
- Engine coolant concentration below 40% will decrease the corrosion and freeze protection characteristics of the engine coolant and may damage the engine.

  d. Vehicles driven year-round in non-extreme climates should use a 50/50 mixture of engine coolant and distilled water for optimum cooling system and engine protection.

Filling And Bleeding Without A Vacuum Cooling System Filler— Degas Bottle Systems

⁕⁕ WARNING

The engine cooling system is filled with Motorcraft® Specialty Orange Engine Coolant. Always fill the cooling system with the manufacturer's specified coolant. If a non-specified coolant has been used the cooling system must be chemically flushed. Failure to follow these instructions may damage the engine or cooling system.

⁕⁕ WARNING

Engine coolant provides boil protection, corrosion protection, freeze protection and cooling efficiency to the engine and cooling components. In order to obtain these protections, maintain the engine coolant at the correct concentration and fluid level in the degas bottle. To maintain the integrity of the coolant and the cooling system:

- Add Motorcraft® Specialty Orange Engine Coolant or equivalent meeting Ford specification WSS-M97B44-D (orange color). Do not mix coolant types.
- Do not add or mix with any other type of engine coolant. Mixing coolants may degrade the coolant's corrosion protection.
- Do not add alcohol, methanol, or brine, or any engine coolants mixed with alcohol or methanol antifreeze. These can cause engine damage from overheating or freezing.
- Ford Motor Company does NOT recommend the use of recycled engine coolant in vehicles originally equipped with Motorcraft® Specialty Orange Engine Coolant

since a Ford-approved recycling process is not yet available.

1. Fill the radiator through the degas bottle until the coolant level is between the COOLANT FILL LEVEL marks.

  a. Recommended coolant concentration is 50/50 engine coolant to distilled water.

  b. For extremely cold climates (less than -34°F [-37°C]):

- It may be necessary to increase the coolant concentration above 50%.
- NEVER increase the coolant concentration above 60%.
- Maximum coolant concentration is 60/40 for cold weather areas.
- A coolant concentration of 60% will provide freeze point protection down to -58°F (-50°C).
- Engine coolant concentration above 60% will decrease the overheat protection characteristics of the engine coolant and may damage the engine.

  c. For extremely hot climates:

- It is still necessary to maintain the coolant concentration above 40%.
- NEVER decrease the coolant concentration below 40%.
- Minimum coolant concentration is 40/60 for warm weather areas.
- A coolant concentration of 40% will provide freeze point protection down to -15°F (-26°C).
- Engine coolant concentration below 40% will decrease the corrosion and freeze protection characteristics of the engine coolant and may damage the engine.

  d. Vehicles driven year-round in non-extreme climates should use a 50/50 mixture of engine coolant and distilled water for optimum cooling system and engine protection.

2. Select the maximum heater temperature and blower motor speed settings. Position the control to discharge air at A/C vents in instrument panel.

3. Start the engine and allow to idle. While engine is idling, feel for hot air at A/C vents.

⁕⁕ WARNING

If the air discharge remains cool and the Engine Coolant Temperature (ECT) gauge does not move, the engine coolant level is low and must be filled. Stop the engine, allow the engine to cool and fill cooling system. Failure to follow these instructions may result in damage to the engine.

4. Start the engine and allow it to idle until normal operating temperature is reached. Hot air should discharge from A/C vents. The Engine Coolant Temperature (ECT) gauge should maintain a stabilized reading in the middle of the NORMAL range. The upper radiator hose should feel hot to the touch.

5. Shut the engine off and allow the engine to cool.

6. Check the engine coolant level in the degas bottle and fill as necessary.

7. Repeat the previous 4 steps as necessary.

Filling And Bleeding With A Vacuum Cooling System Filler—Coolant Expansion Tank System

❋❋ WARNING

Vehicle cooling systems are filled with Motorcraft® Specialty Orange Engine Coolant. Always fill the cooling system with the manufacturer's specified coolant. If a non-specified coolant has been used the cooling system must be chemically flushed. Failure to follow these instructions may damage the engine or cooling system.

❋❋ WARNING

Engine coolant provides freeze protection, boil protection, cooling efficiency and corrosion protection to the engine and cooling components. In order to obtain these protections, the engine coolant must be maintained at the correct concentration and fluid level. Failure to follow these instructions may damage the engine or cooling system. To maintain the integrity of the coolant and the cooling system:

- Add Motorcraft® Specialty Orange Engine Coolant or equivalent meeting Ford specification WSS-M97B44-D (orange color). Do not mix coolant types.
- Do not add or mix with any other type of engine coolant. Mixing coolants may degrade the coolant's corrosion protection.
- Do not add alcohol, methanol or brine, or any engine coolants mixed with alcohol or methanol antifreeze. These can cause engine damage from overheating or freezing.

- Ford Motor Company does NOT recommend the use of recycled engine coolant in vehicles originally equipped with Motorcraft® Specialty Orange Engine Coolant since a Ford-approved recycling process is not yet available.

1. Connect the vacuum cooling system filler and the appropriate rubber adapter to the radiator.

2. Clamp the radiator-to-coolant expansion tank hose near the radiator.

3. Follow the vacuum cooling system filler manufacturer's instructions to fill and bleed the cooling system.

   a. Recommended coolant concentration is 50/50 engine coolant to distilled water.

   b. For extremely cold climates (less than -34°F [-37°C]):

   - It may be necessary to increase the coolant concentration above 50%.
   - NEVER increase the coolant concentration above 60%.
   - Maximum coolant concentration is 60/40 for cold weather areas.
   - A coolant concentration of 60% will provide freeze point protection down to -58°F (-50°C).
   - Engine coolant concentration above 60% will decrease the overheat protection characteristics of the engine coolant and may damage the engine.

   c. For extremely hot climates:

   - It is still necessary to maintain the coolant concentration above 40%.
   - NEVER decrease the coolant concentration below 40%.
   - Minimum coolant concentration is 40/60 for warm weather areas.
   - A coolant concentration of 40% will provide freeze point protection down to -15°F (-26°C).
   - Engine coolant concentration below 40% will decrease the corrosion and freeze protection characteristics of the engine coolant and may damage the engine.

   d. Vehicles driven year-round in non-extreme climates should use a 50/50 mixture of engine coolant and distilled water for optimum cooling system and engine protection.

Filling And Bleeding Without A Vacuum Cooling System Filler—Coolant Expansion Tank Systems

❋❋ WARNING

Vehicle cooling systems are filled with Motorcraft® Specialty Orange Engine

Coolant. Always fill the cooling system with the manufacturer's specified coolant. If a non-specified coolant has been used the cooling system must be chemically flushed. Failure to follow these instructions may damage the engine or cooling system.

❋❋ WARNING

Engine coolant provides freeze protection, boil protection, cooling efficiency and corrosion protection to the engine and cooling components. In order to obtain these protections, the engine coolant must be maintained at the correct concentration and fluid level. Failure to follow these instructions may damage the engine or cooling system. To maintain the integrity of the coolant and the cooling system:

- Add Motorcraft® Specialty Orange Engine Coolant or equivalent meeting Ford specification WSS-M97B44-D (orange color). Do not mix coolant types.
- Do not add or mix with any other type of engine coolant. Mixing coolants may degrade the coolant's corrosion protection.
- Do not add alcohol, methanol or brine, or any engine coolants mixed with alcohol or methanol antifreeze. These can cause engine damage from overheating or freezing.
- Ford Motor Company does NOT recommend the use of recycled engine coolant in vehicles originally equipped with Motorcraft® Specialty Orange Engine Coolant since a Ford-approved recycling process is not yet available.

Vehicles Equipped With 6.2L Engine

1. Release the clamp and disconnect the heater inlet hose from the heater inlet tube.

2. Fill the radiator through the radiator fill neck until engine coolant flows from the heater inlet tube.

   a. Recommended coolant concentration is 50/50 engine coolant to distilled water.

   b. For extremely cold climates (less than -34°F [-37°C]):

   - It may be necessary to increase the coolant concentration above 50%.
   - NEVER increase the coolant concentration above 60%.
   - Maximum coolant concentration is 60/40 for cold weather areas.

- A coolant concentration of 60% will provide freeze point protection down to -58°F (-50°C).
- Engine coolant concentration above 60% will decrease the overheat protection characteristics of the engine coolant and may damage the engine.

c. For extremely hot climates:

- It is still necessary to maintain the coolant concentration above 40%.
- NEVER decrease the coolant concentration below 40%.
- Minimum coolant concentration is 40/60 for warm weather areas.
- A coolant concentration of 40% will provide freeze point protection down to -15°F (-26°C).
- Engine coolant concentration below 40% will decrease the corrosion and freeze protection characteristics of the engine coolant and may damage the engine.

d. Vehicles driven year-round in non-extreme climates should use a 50/50 mixture of engine coolant and distilled water for optimum cooling system and engine protection.

3. Connect the heater inlet hose to the heater inlet tube and position the clamp.

All Vehicles

1. Fill the radiator through the radiator fill neck until the coolant level is at the bottom of the filler neck.

a. Recommended coolant concentration is 50/50 engine coolant to distilled water.

b. For extremely cold climates (less than -34°F [-37°C]):

- It may be necessary to increase the coolant concentration above 50%.
- NEVER increase the coolant concentration above 60%.
- Maximum coolant concentration is 60/40 for cold weather areas.
- A coolant concentration of 60% will provide freeze point protection down to -58°F (-50°C).
- Engine coolant concentration above 60% will decrease the overheat protection characteristics of the engine coolant and may damage the engine.

c. For extremely hot climates:

- It is still necessary to maintain the coolant concentration above 40%.
- NEVER decrease the coolant concentration below 40%.
- Minimum coolant concentration is 40/60 for warm weather areas.
- A coolant concentration of 40% will provide freeze point protection down to -15°F (-26°C).

- Engine coolant concentration below 40% will decrease the corrosion and freeze protection characteristics of the engine coolant and may damage the engine.

d. Vehicles driven year-round in non-extreme climates should use a 50/50 mixture of engine coolant and distilled water for optimum cooling system and engine protection.

2. Install the radiator cap.

3. Fill the coolant expansion tank until the coolant reaches the COLD FILL mark.

4. Select the maximum heater temperature and blower motor speed settings. Position the control to discharge air at A/C vents in instrument panel.

✳✳ WARNING

If the air discharge remains cool and the engine coolant temperature gauge does not move, the engine coolant level is low in the engine and must be filled. Stop the engine, allow it to cool and fill the cooling system. Failure to follow this instruction may result in damage to the engine.

5. Run the engine at idle until it reaches normal operating temperature.

6. Turn the engine off and allow it to cool.

7. Add the correct coolant mixture to the coolant expansion tank until the coolant level is at the COLD FILL mark.

8. Start the engine and allow it to idle until it reaches normal operating temperature. While the engine is idling, feel for hot air from the A/C vents.

➡Hot air should discharge from the A/C vents. The engine coolant temperature gauge should maintain a stabilized reading in the middle of the NORMAL range and the upper radiator hose should feel hot to the touch.

9. Check the engine coolant level in the coolant expansion tank and fill it as necessary.

10. Repeat the previous 5 steps as necessary.

BLEEDING

See above procedures.

FLUSHING

2010 Models

✳✳ CAUTION

Always allow the engine to cool before opening the cooling system. Do not

unscrew the coolant pressure relief cap when the engine is operating or the cooling system is hot. The cooling system is under pressure; steam and hot liquid can come out forcefully when the cap is loosened slightly. Failure to follow these instructions may result in serious personal injury.

1. Drain the engine cooling system.
2. Remove the thermostat.
3. Install the thermostat housing without the thermostat.

➡Refer to the cooling system flusher manufacturer's operating instructions for specific vehicle hook-up.

4. Use a cooling system flusher to flush the engine and radiator. Use premium cooling system flush.
5. Install the thermostat.
6. Fill and bleed the cooling system.

2011 Models

✳✳ CAUTION

Always allow the engine to cool before opening the cooling system. Do not unscrew the coolant pressure relief cap when the engine is operating or the cooling system is hot. The cooling system is under pressure; steam and hot liquid can come out forcefully when the cap is loosened slightly. Failure to follow these instructions may result in serious personal injury.

1. Drain the engine cooling system.
2. Remove the thermostat.
3. Install the coolant inlet connection (3.5L GTDI, 3.7L or 5.0L engines) or the coolant outlet connection (6.2L engines) without the thermostat.

➡Refer to the cooling system flusher manufacturer's operating instructions for specific vehicle hook-up.

4. Use a cooling system flusher to flush the engine and radiator.
5. Use Motorcraft® Premium Cooling System Flush and follow the directions on the packaging.
6. Install the thermostat.
7. Fill and bleed the cooling system.

ENGINE FAN

REMOVAL & INSTALLATION

See Figures 83 through 85.

1. Disconnect the battery cables.
2. Remove the Air Cleaner (ACL) outlet tube.

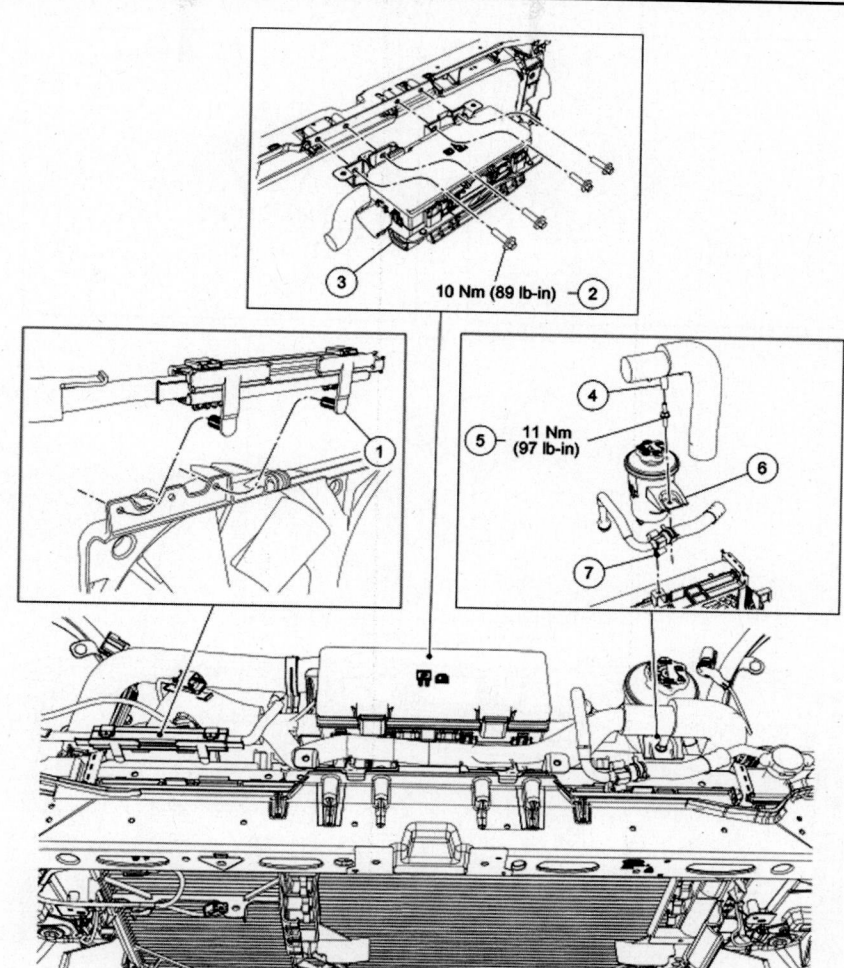

1. Alternator battery positive cable retainer
2. Battery Junction Box (BJB) bracket bolt (4 required)
3. BJB bracket
4. Wiring harness retainer
5. Power steering fluid reservoir stud bolt
6. Power steering fluid reservoir
7. Power steering fluid cooler hose retainer

N0103106

Fig. 83 Exploded view from top of fan/radiator assembly

3. Detach the power steering fluid cooler hose retainer from the cooling fan motor and shroud.

4. Detach the wiring harness retainer from the power steering fluid reservoir stud bolt.

5. Detach the wiring harness retainer from the LH side of the cooling fan motor and shroud.

6. Detach the 2 alternator B+ wire retainers from the top of the cooling fan motor and shroud.

7. Detach the wiring harness retainer from the RH side of the cooling fan motor and shroud.

8. Detach the upper radiator hose retainer from the cooling fan motor and shroud.

9. Detach the 3 wiring harness retainers from the RH side of the cooling fan motor and shroud.

10. Disconnect the 2 cooling fan electrical connectors.

11. Detach the 3 cooling fan wiring harness retainers.

12. Remove the 4 Battery Junction Box (BJB) bracket bolts.

13. Remove the power steering fluid reservoir stud bolt and position the power steering fluid reservoir and the wiring harness aside.

14. Remove the 2 bolts and the cooling fan motor and shroud.

To install:

15. To install, reverse the removal procedure.

a. Tighten the power steering fluid reservoir stud bolt to 97 inch lbs. (11 Nm).

b. Tighten the 4 BJB bracket bolts to 89 inch lbs. (10 Nm).

RADIATOR

REMOVAL & INSTALLATION

2010 Models

See Figures 86 through 93.

1. Recover the A/C system.
2. Drain the cooling system.
3. Remove the cooling fan motor and shroud.
4. Release the clamp and disconnect the upper radiator hose from the radiator.

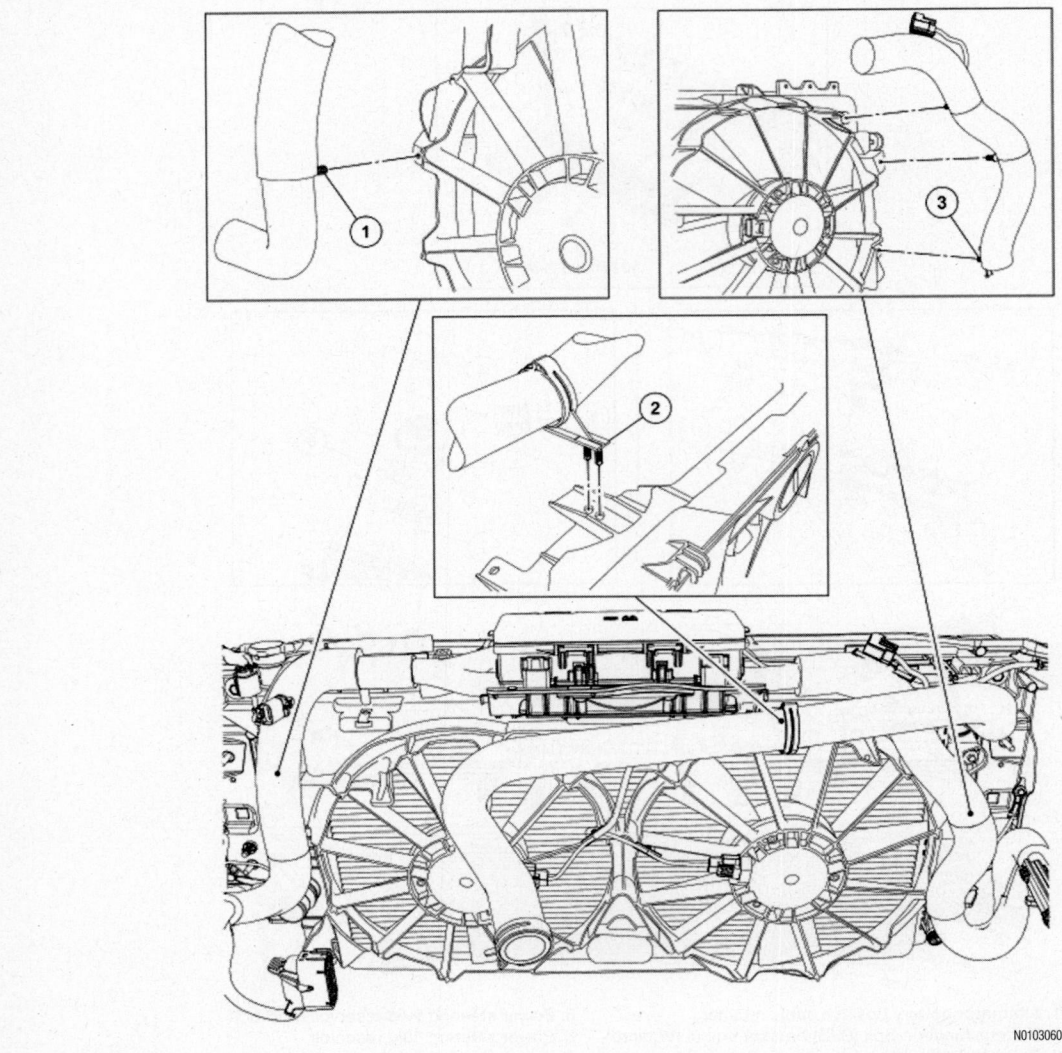

Fig. 84 Exploded view showing wiring harness retainer (1), upper radiator hose retainer (2), and wiring harness retainer (3)

5. Disconnect the overflow hose at the radiator.

6. Remove the spring clip and disconnect the lower radiator hose from the radiator.

7. Release the clamp and disconnect the power steering cooler hose from the power steering cooler.

8. Disconnect the Mass Air Flow (MAF) sensor electrical connector.

9. Release the clips and remove the Air Cleaner (ACL) cover.

10. Remove the ACL element.

11. Remove the 2 bolts and the coolant expansion tank/lower ACL half.

12. Remove the bolt and the nut and disconnect the A/C condenser fittings.

13. Discard the gasket seals and the O-ring seals.

➡**Lower air deflector pushpins shown, RH and LH pushpin retainers similar.**

14. Disconnect the 3 RH and 2 LH air deflector-to-condenser pushpin retainers and the 3 lower air deflector-to-bumper pushpin retainers.

15. Disconnect the 2 RH air deflector-to-frame pushpin retainers.

16. Disconnect the 2 LH air deflector-to-frame pushpin retainers.

17. Remove the transmission cooler tube secondary latches.

18. Using the Transmission Cooler Line Disconnect Tool, disconnect the transmission fluid cooler tubes.

19. Disconnect the horn electrical connector and detach the wiring harness and ambient temperature sensor retainers. Position the wiring harness aside.

20. Remove the 2 bolts and the radiator/condenser core as an assembly.

21. Disconnect the 2 transmission fluid cooler hoses from the radiator.

22. Release the lock tabs and separate the radiator from the condenser core.

To install:

23. Position the condenser core into the radiator locking tabs.

24. Connect the transmission fluid cooler hoses to the radiator.

25. Position the radiator/condenser core assembly into the vehicle and onto the radiator insulators.

26. Install the 2 radiator bolts. Tighten to 10 ft. lbs. (15 Nm).

27. Position the wiring harness into place and connect the horn electrical connector and attach ambient temperature sensors pushpin retainer.

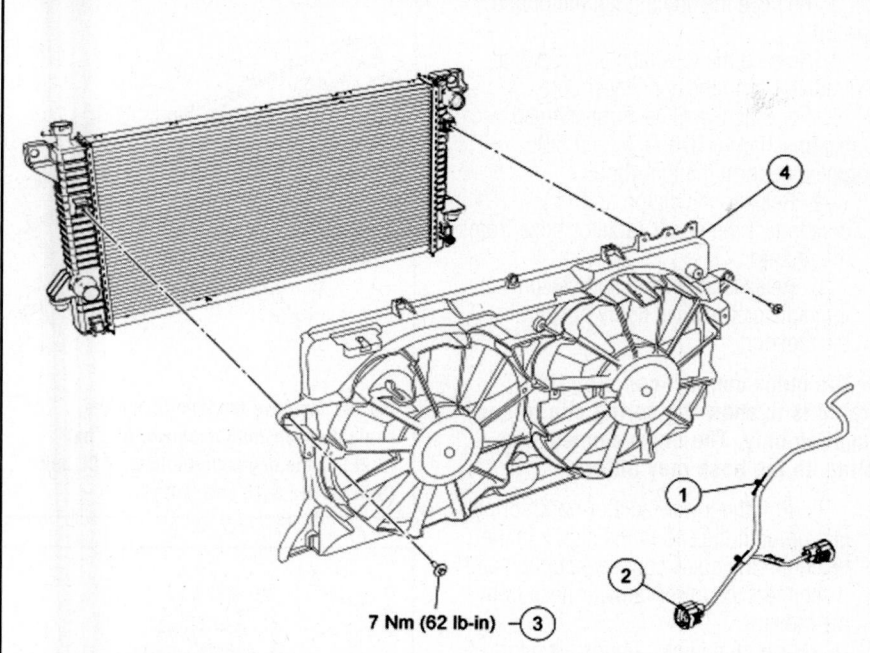

7 Nm (62 lb-in) — 3

1. Cooling fan wiring harness retainer (3 required)
2. Cooling fan electrical connector (2 required)
3. Cooling fan motor and shroud bolts
4. Cooling fan motor and shroud

N0103107

Fig. 85 Exploded view of cooling fan assembly

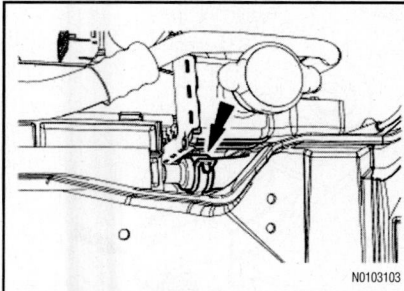

N0103103

Fig. 86 Release the clamp and disconnect the power steering cooler hose from the power steering cooler

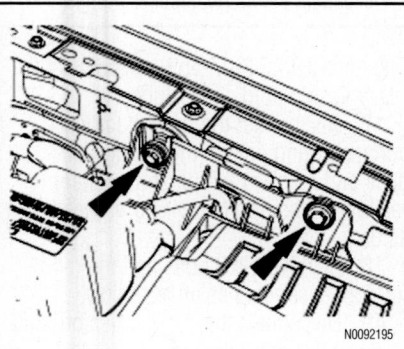

N0092195

Fig. 87 Remove the 2 bolts and the coolant expansion tank/lower ACL half

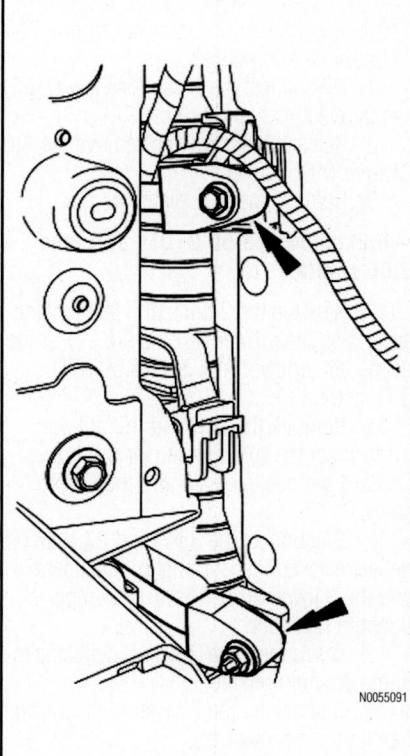

N0055091

Fig. 88 Remove the bolt and the nut and disconnect the A/C condenser fittings

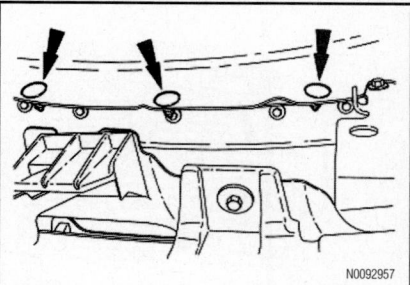

N0092957

Fig. 89 Disconnect the 3 RH and 2 LH air deflector-to-condenser pushpin retainers and the 3 lower air deflector-to-bumper pushpin retainers

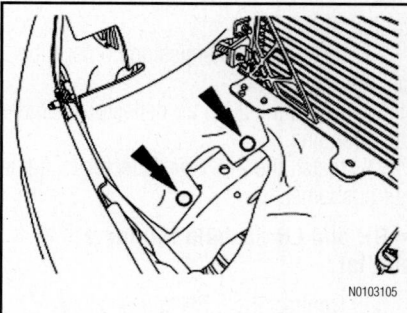

N0103105

Fig. 90 Disconnect the 2 RH air deflector-to-frame pushpin retainers

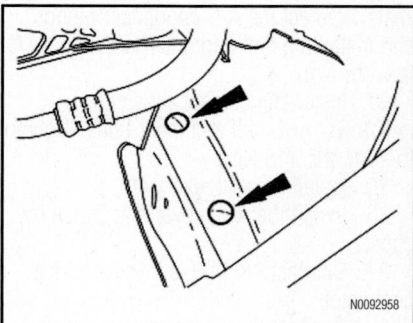

N0092958

Fig. 91 Disconnect the 2 LH air deflector-to-frame pushpin retainers

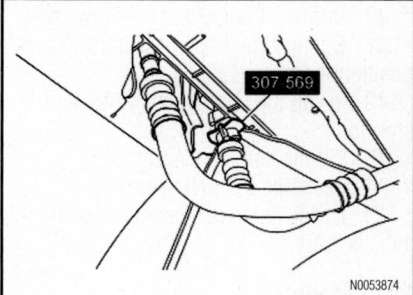

307 569

N0053874

Fig. 92 Using the Transmission Cooler Line Disconnect Tool, disconnect the transmission fluid cooler tubes

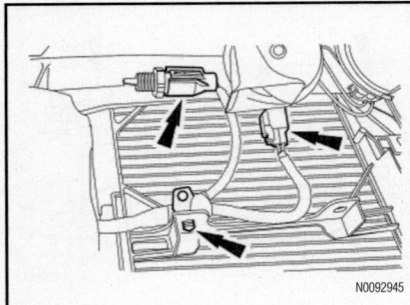

Fig. 93 Disconnect the horn electrical connector and detach the wiring harness and ambient temperature sensor retainers

28. Connect the transmission fluid cooler tubes.

29. Install the transmission cooler tube secondary latches.

30. Install the 2 LH air deflector-to-frame rail pushpins.

31. Install the 2 RH air deflector-to-frame rail pushpins.

➡**RH and LH pushpin retainers similar.**

32. Connect the 3 RH and 2 LH air deflector-to-condenser pushpin retainers and the 3 lower air deflector-to-bumper pushpin retainers.

33. Using new gasket seals and O-ring seals, connect the A/C condenser fittings and install the bolt and nut. Tighten to 10 ft. lbs. (15 Nm).

34. Install the coolant expansion tank/lower ACL half and the 2 bolts. Tighten to 10 ft. lbs. (15 Nm).

35. Install the ACL element.

36. Install the ACL cover and fasten the clips.

37. Connect the MAF sensor electrical connector.

38. Connect the power steering cooler hose to the power steering cooler and position the clamp.

39. Install lower radiator hose and the spring clip.

40. Connect the radiator overflow hose.

41. Connect the upper radiator hose and position the clamp.

42. Install the cooling fan motor and shroud.

43. Fill the cooling system.

44. Recharge the A/C system.

45. Check the transmission fluid and fill as necessary.

2011 Models

See Figures 93 through 96.

1. Recover the A/C system.

2. Drain the cooling system.

3. Remove the cooling fan motor and shroud.

4. Release the lock tabs and separate the radiator from the condenser core.

5. For 3.5L Gasoline Turbocharged Direct Injection (GTDI), 3.7L and 5.0L engines, perform the following:

   a. Release the clamp and disconnect the upper radiator hose from the radiator.

   b. Release the clamp and disconnect the radiator-to-degas bottle hose from the radiator.

➡**The quick connect coupling illustrated is to show the spring clip release location only. The quick connect coupling on the hose may differ.**

   c. Pull the lower radiator hose spring clip up until the end of the clip is in the detent on the quick connect coupling and disconnect the lower radiator hose from the radiator.

6. For 6.2L engines, perform the following:

   a. Release the clamp and disconnect the upper radiator hose from the radiator.

   b. Disconnect the overflow hose from the radiator.

   c. Remove the spring clip and disconnect the lower radiator hose from the radiator.

   d. Release the clamp and disconnect the power steering cooler hose from the power steering cooler.

7. Disconnect the Mass Air Flow (MAF) sensor electrical connector.

8. Release the clips and remove the Air Cleaner (ACL) cover.

9. Remove the ACL element.

➡**6.2L shown, 3.5L GTDI , 3.7L and 5.0L similar.**

10. Remove the 2 bolts and the coolant expansion tank/lower ACL half (6.2L) or the degas bottle/lower ACL half (3.5L GTDI , 3.7L and 5.0L).

11. Remove the bolt and the nut and disconnect the A/C condenser fittings. Discard the gasket seals and the O-ring seals.

12. Disconnect the 3 RH and 2 LH air deflector-to-condenser pushpin retainers and the 3 lower air deflector-to-bumper pushpin retainers.

13. Disconnect the 2 RH air deflector-to-frame pushpin retainers.

14. Disconnect the 2 LH air deflector-to-frame pushpin retainers.

15. Remove the transmission cooler tube secondary latches.

16. Using the Transmission Cooler Line

Fig. 94 Remove the 2 bolts and the coolant expansion tank/lower ACL half (6.2L) or the degas bottle/lower ACL half (3.5L GTDI , 3.7L and 5.0L)

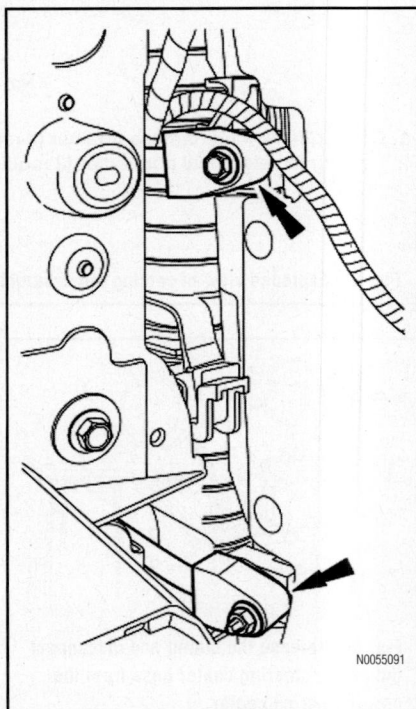

Fig. 95 Remove the bolt and the nut and disconnect the A/C condenser fittings

Disconnect Tool (307-569), disconnect the transmission fluid cooler tubes.

17. Disconnect the horn electrical connector and detach the wiring harness and ambient temperature sensor retainers. Position the wiring harness aside.

18. Remove the 2 bolts and the radiator/condenser core as an assembly.

19. Disconnect the 2 transmission fluid cooler hoses from the radiator.

20. Release the lock tabs and separate the radiator from the condenser core.

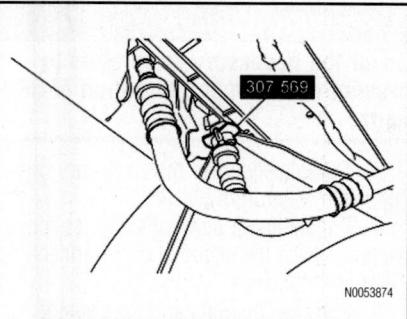

Fig. 96 Using the Transmission Cooler Line Disconnect Tool, disconnect the transmission fluid cooler tubes

To install:

21. Position the condenser core into the radiator locking tabs.

22. Connect the transmission fluid cooler hoses to the radiator.

23. Position the radiator/condenser core assembly into the vehicle and onto the radiator insulators.

24. Install the 2 radiator bolts. Tighten to 10 ft. lbs. (15 Nm).

25. Position the wiring harness into place and connect the horn electrical connector and attach ambient temperature sensors pushpin retainer.

26. Connect the transmission fluid cooler tubes.

27. Install the transmission cooler tube secondary latches.

28. Install the 2 LH air deflector-to-frame rail pushpins.

29. Install the 2 RH air deflector-to-frame rail pushpins.

30. Connect the 3 RH and 2 LH air deflector-to-condenser pushpin retainers and the 3 lower air deflector-to-bumper pushpin retainers.

31. Using new gasket seals and O-ring seals, connect the A/C condenser fittings and install the bolt and nut. Tighten to 10 ft. lbs. (15 Nm).

32. Install the coolant expansion tank/lower ACL half (6.2L) or degas bottle/lower ACL half (3.5L GTDI, 3.7L and 5.0L) and the 2 bolts.

a. Tighten the coolant expansion tank/lower ACL half bolts to 10 ft. lbs. (15 Nm).

b. Tighten the degas bottle/lower ACL half bolts to 13 ft. lbs. (17 Nm).

33. Install the ACL element.

34. Install the ACL cover and fasten the clips.

35. Connect the MAF sensor electrical connector.

36. For 3.5L gasoline turbocharged direct injection (GTDI), 3.7L and 5.0L engines, perform the following:

a. Push the spring clip in place and connect the lower radiator hose quick connect coupling to the radiator, making sure the coupling is secure.

b. Connect the radiator-to-degas bottle hose to the radiator and position the clamp.

c. Connect the upper radiator hose to the radiator and position the clamp.

37. For 6.2L engines, perform the following:

a. Connect the power steering cooler hose to the power steering cooler and position the clamp.

b. Install lower radiator hose and the spring clip.

c. Connect the radiator overflow hose.

d. Connect the upper radiator hose and position the clamp.

38. Install the cooling fan motor and shroud.

39. Filling the cooling system.

40. Recharge the A/C system.

41. Check the transmission fluid and fill as necessary.

THERMOSTAT

REMOVAL & INSTALLATION

3.5L GTDI Engine
See Figure 97.

➡**The manufacturer does not provide a specific Removal and Installation pro-**

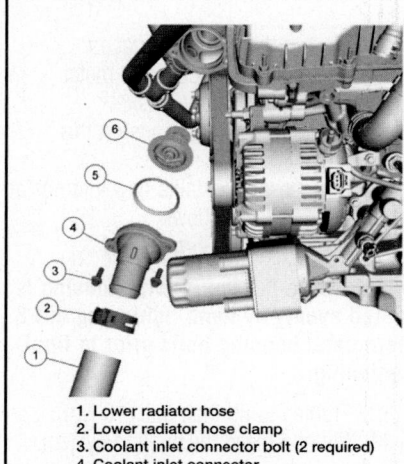

1. Lower radiator hose
2. Lower radiator hose clamp
3. Coolant inlet connector bolt (2 required)
4. Coolant inlet connector
5. Thermostat O-ring seal
6. Thermostat

Fig. 97 Exploded view of the thermostat assembly

cedure for this component. Refer to the graphic(s) when servicing this component.

3.7L Engine
See Figure 98.

1. Drain the cooling system.
2. Remove the air cleaner outlet pipe.

✳✳ WARNING

Cover the accessory drive belts to prevent coolant contamination of the belts.

3. Completely cover the accessory drive belts with waterproof plastic.

4. If installing a new coolant inlet connector, release the clamp and disconnect the lower radiator hose.

5. Remove the bolts and the coolant inlet connector.

6. Remove the thermostat and the thermostat O-ring seal. Discard the O-ring seal.

To install:

7. To install, reverse the removal procedure.

a. Use a new O-ring seal and lubricate it with clean engine coolant.

b. Tighten the coolant inlet connector bolts to 89 inch lbs. (10 Nm).

8. Fill and bleed the cooling system.

4.6L (2V) Engine
See Figure 99.

1. Drain the engine cooling system.
2. Remove the Air Cleaner (ACL) outlet pipe.

3. If servicing the thermostat housing, release the upper radiator hose clamp and disconnect the radiator hose from the thermostat housing.

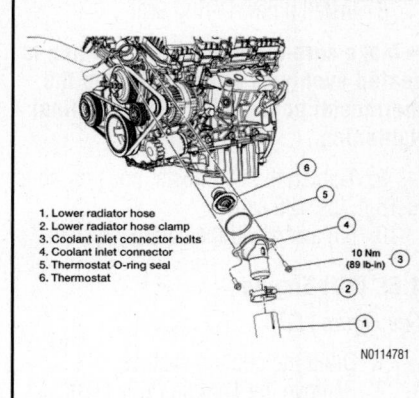

1. Lower radiator hose
2. Lower radiator hose clamp
3. Coolant inlet connector bolts
4. Coolant inlet connector
5. Thermostat O-ring seal
6. Thermostat

Fig. 98 Exploded view of the thermostat assembly

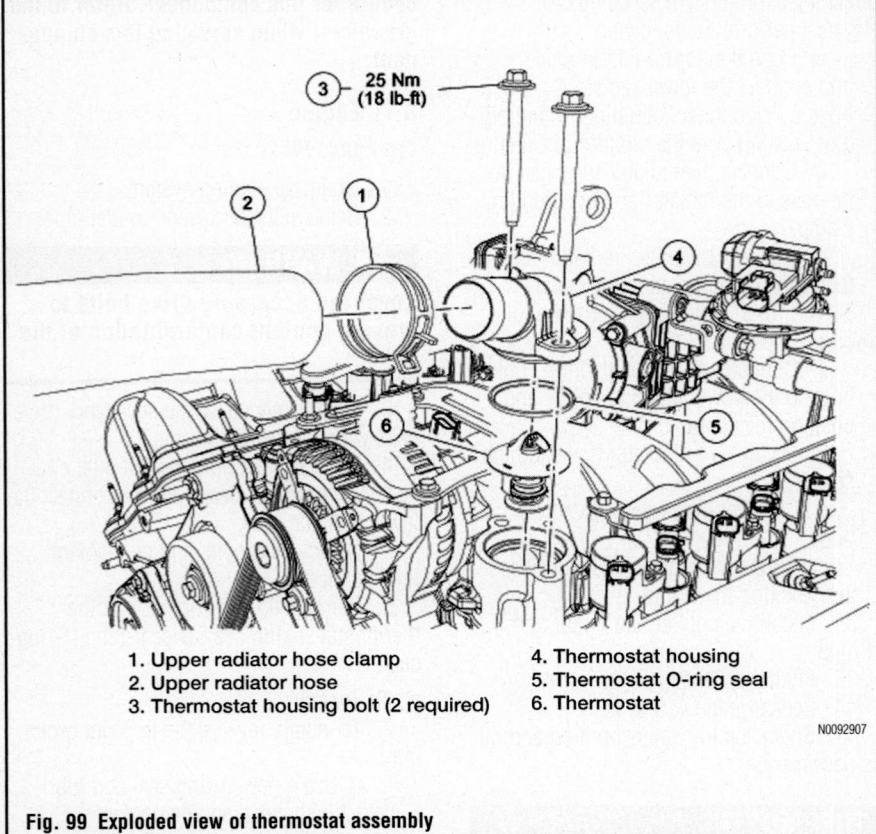

1. Upper radiator hose clamp
2. Upper radiator hose
3. Thermostat housing bolt (2 required)
4. Thermostat housing
5. Thermostat O-ring seal
6. Thermostat

N0092907

Fig. 99 Exploded view of thermostat assembly

4. Remove the 2 bolts, the thermostat housing and the thermostat. Discard the O-ring seal.

To install:

5. To install, reverse the removal procedure.

6. Inspect the mating surfaces. Clean the sealing surfaces with metal surface prep and silicone gasket remover. Follow the directions on the packaging.

7. If necessary, install a new thermostat with the spring facing down.

8. Install a new O-ring seal.

➡**Make sure the thermostat housing is seated evenly by hand tightening the thermostat housing bolts prior to final tightening.**

9. Tighten the thermostat housing bolts to 18 ft. lbs. (25 Nm).

10. Fill and bleed the cooling system.

4.6L (3V) Engine

See Figure 100.

1. Drain the cooling system.
2. Remove the Throttle Body (TB).
3. Disconnect the Evaporative Emission (EVAP) canister purge valve hose.
4. If servicing the thermostat housing,

release the upper radiator hose clamp and disconnect the radiator hose from the thermostat housing.

5. Remove the 2 bolts, the thermostat housing and the thermostat. Discard the O-ring seal.

To install:

6. To install, reverse the removal procedure.

7. Inspect the mating surfaces. Clean the sealing surfaces with metal surface prep and silicone gasket remover. Follow the directions on the packaging.

8. If necessary, install a new thermostat with the spring facing down.

9. Install a new O-ring seal.

➡**Make sure the thermostat housing is seated evenly by hand tightening the 2 thermostat housing bolts prior to final tightening.**

10. Tighten to 89 inch lbs. (10 Nm).
11. Fill and bleed the cooling system.

5.0L Engine

See Figure 101.

1. Drain the cooling system.
2. Remove the air cleaner outlet pipe.

Cover the accessory drive belts to prevent coolant contamination of the belts.

3. Completely cover the accessory drive belts with waterproof plastic.

4. If installing a new coolant inlet connector, release the clamp and disconnect the lower radiator hose.

5. Remove the bolts and the coolant inlet connector.

6. Remove the thermostat and the thermostat O-ring seal. Discard the O-ring seal.

To install:

7. To install, reverse the removal procedure.

a. Use a new O-ring seal and lubricate it with clean engine coolant.

b. Tighten the coolant inlet connector bolts to 89 inch lbs. (10 Nm).

8. Fill and bleed the cooling system.

5.4L (3V) Engine

See Figure 102.

1. Drain the engine cooling system.
2. Remove the Air Cleaner (ACL) intake pipe.

3. If servicing the thermostat housing, release the clamp and disconnect the upper radiator hose from the thermostat housing.

4. Remove the 2 bolts, the thermostat housing and the thermostat. Discard the O-ring seal.

To install:

5. To install, reverse the removal procedure.

6. Inspect the mating surfaces. Clean the sealing surfaces with metal surface prep and silicone gasket remover. Follow the directions on the packaging.

7. If necessary, install a new thermostat with the spring facing down.

8. Install a new O-ring seal.

➡**Make sure the thermostat housing is seated evenly by hand tightening the 2 thermostat housing bolts prior to final tightening.**

9. Tighten to 89 inch lbs. (10 Nm).
10. Fill and bleed the cooling system.

6.2L (2V) Engine

See Figure 103.

1. Drain the cooling system.
2. Remove the air cleaner outlet tube.
3. If a new coolant outlet connector is being installed, release the clamp and disconnect the upper radiator hose.

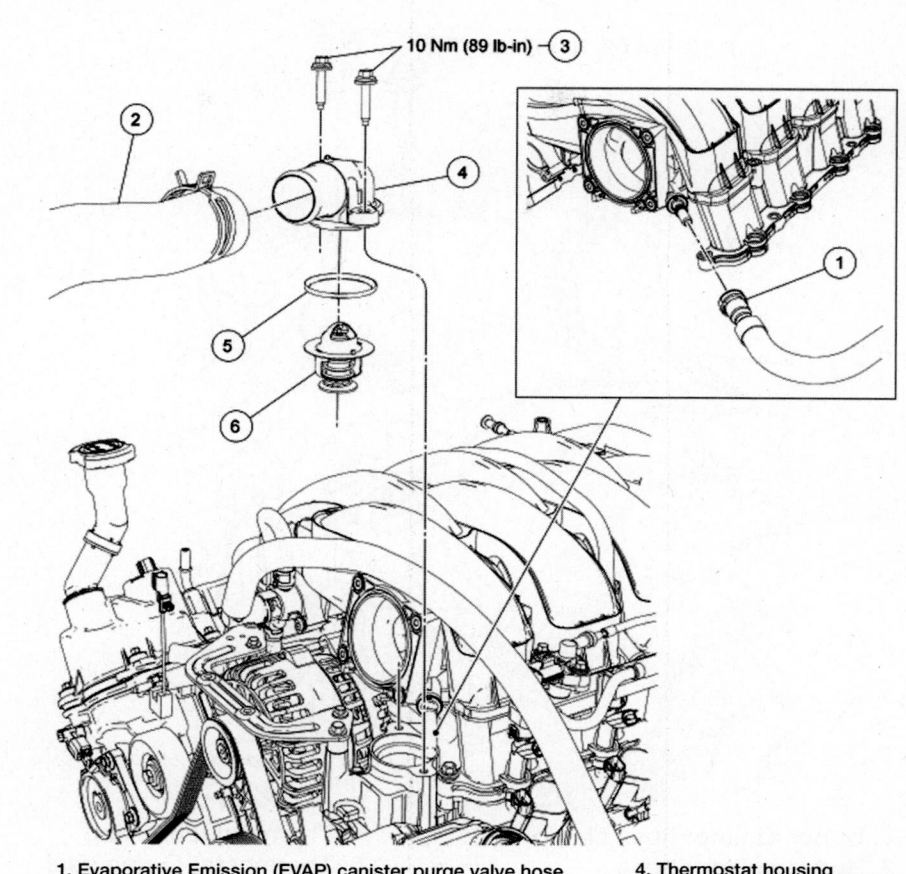

1. Evaporative Emission (EVAP) canister purge valve hose
2. Upper radiator hose
3. Thermostat housing bolts (2 required)
4. Thermostat housing
5. Thermostat O-ring seal
6. Thermostat

N0073567

Fig. 100 Exploded view of thermostat assembly

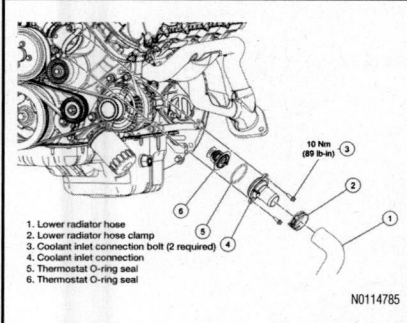

1. Lower radiator hose
2. Lower radiator hose clamp
3. Coolant inlet connection bolt (2 required)
4. Coolant inlet connection
5. Thermostat O-ring seal
6. Thermostat O-ring seal

N0114785

Fig. 101 Exploded view of the thermostat assembly

4. Remove the 2 bolts, the thermostat housing and the thermostat. Discard the O-ring seal.

To install:

5. To install, reverse the removal procedure.

6. Inspect the mating surfaces. Clean the sealing surfaces with metal surface prep

and silicone gasket remover. Follow the directions on the packaging.

7. If necessary, install a new thermostat with the spring facing down.

8. Install a new O-ring seal.

➡**Make sure the thermostat housing is seated evenly by hand tightening the 2 thermostat housing bolts prior to final tightening.**

9. Tighten to 89 inch lbs. (10 Nm).

10. Fill and bleed the cooling system.

WATER PUMP

REMOVAL & INSTALLATION

2010 Models

See Figures 104 and 105.

1. Drain the cooling system.

2. Remove the Air Cleaner (ACL) outlet tube.

3. Loosen the 4 coolant pump pulley bolts.

➡ **5.4L (3V) shown, 4.6L (2V) and 4.6L (3V) similar.**

4. Remove the accessory drive belt.

5. Remove the 4 bolts and the coolant pump pulley.

6. Remove the 4 bolts and the coolant pump. Discard the O-ring seal.

7. Inspect the sealing surfaces and clean with metal surface prep. Follow the directions on the packaging.

To install:

8. For 4.6L (2V), 4.6L (3V) and 5.4L (3V) engine, perform the following:

❋❋ CAUTION

Align the bolt holes with the bosses prior to insertion of the coolant pump and insert the pump straight into the coolant pump cavity. Do not rotate the coolant pump once installed in the coolant pump cavity or damage to the O-ring seal can occur, causing the coolant pump to leak.

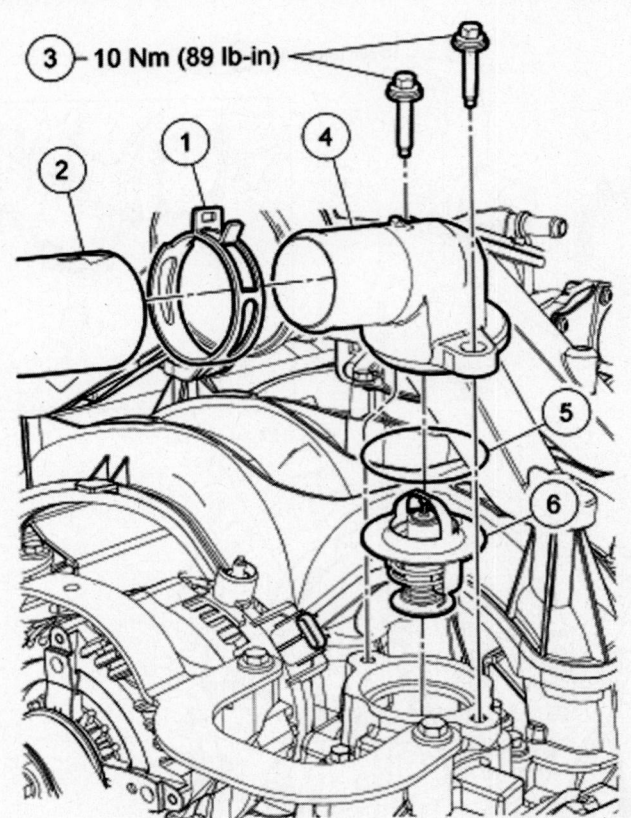

3 — 10 Nm (89 lb-in)

1. Upper radiator hose clamp
2. Upper radiator hose
3. Thermostat housing bolts (2 required)
4. Thermostat housing
5. Thermostat O-ring seal
6. Thermostat

N0054969

Fig. 102 Exploded view of thermostat assembly

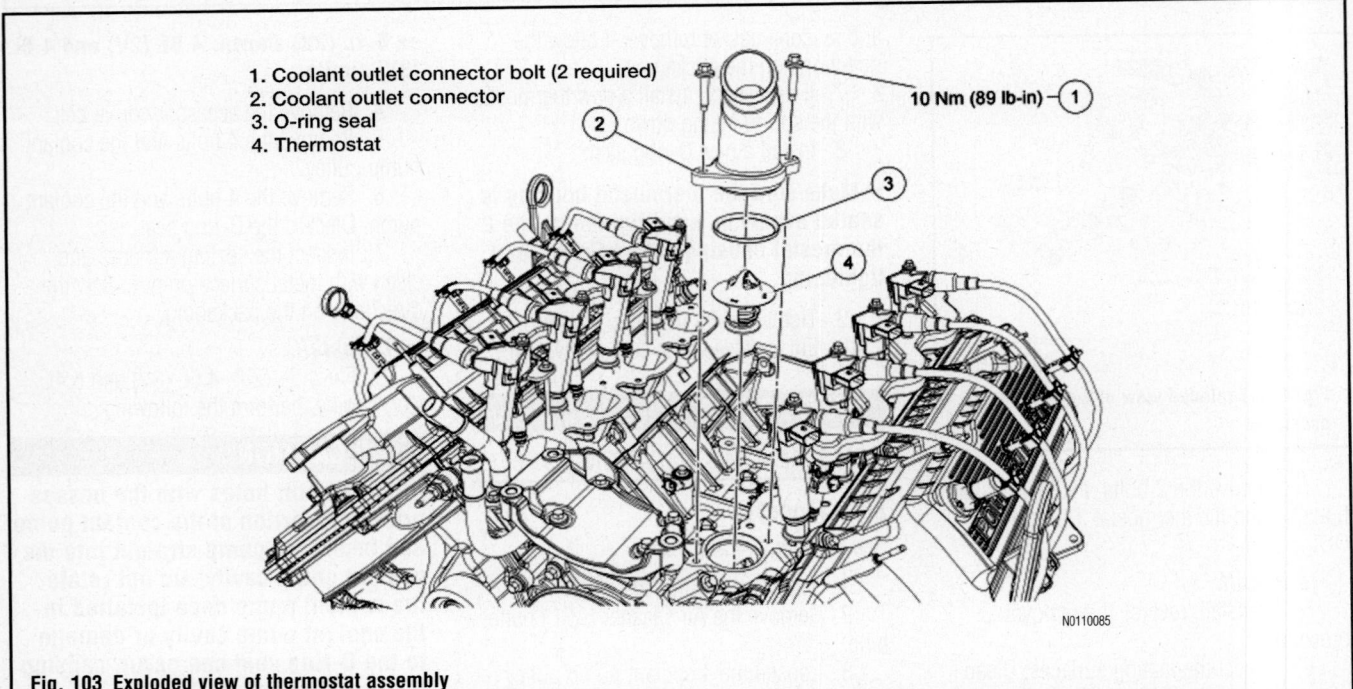

1. Coolant outlet connector bolt (2 required)
2. Coolant outlet connector
3. O-ring seal
4. Thermostat

10 Nm (89 lb-in) — 1

N0110085

Fig. 103 Exploded view of thermostat assembly

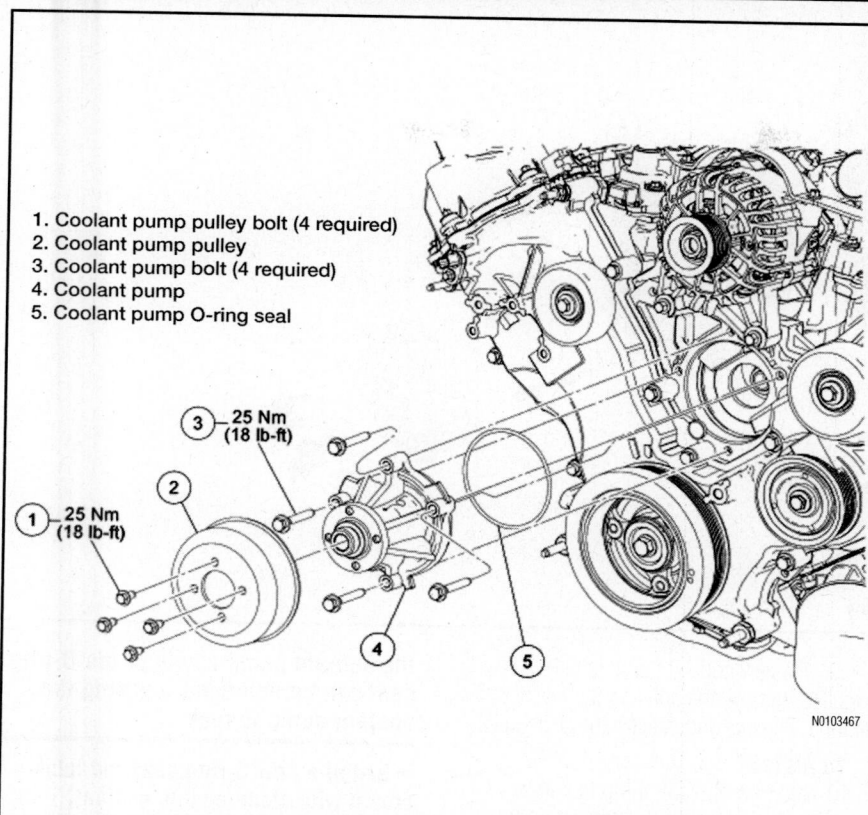

1. Coolant pump pulley bolt (4 required)
2. Coolant pump pulley
3. Coolant pump bolt (4 required)
4. Coolant pump
5. Coolant pump O-ring seal

3 — 25 Nm (18 lb-ft)

1 — 25 Nm (18 lb-ft)

N0103467

Fig. 104 Exploded view of coolant pump assembly—All engines except 6.2L (2V) engine

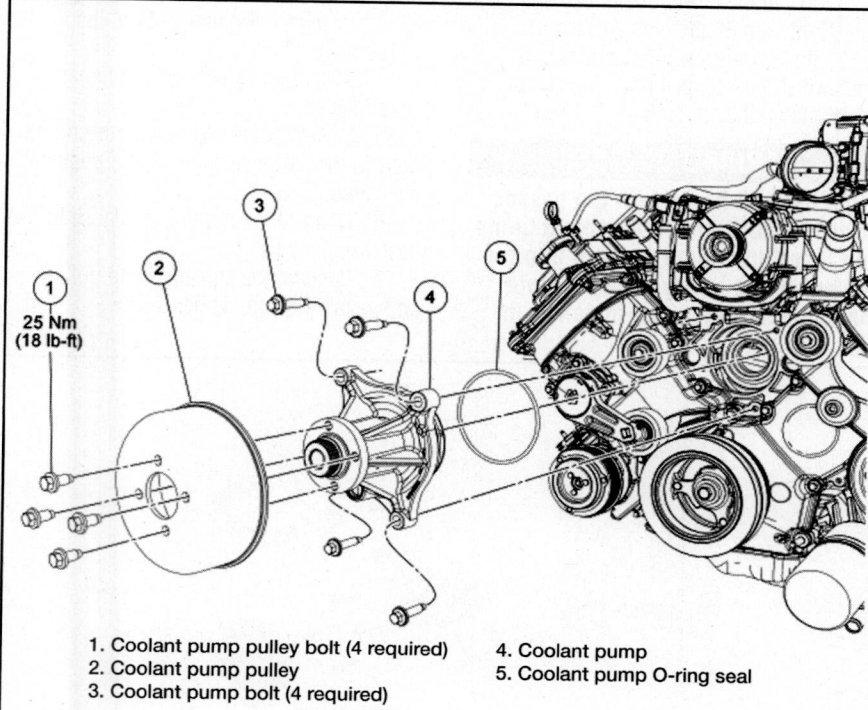

1 — 25 Nm (18 lb-ft)

1. Coolant pump pulley bolt (4 required)
2. Coolant pump pulley
3. Coolant pump bolt (4 required)

4. Coolant pump
5. Coolant pump O-ring seal

N0110078

Fig. 105 Exploded view of coolant pump assembly—6.2L (2V) engine

➡Install a new O-ring seal and lubricate with clean engine coolant.

   a. Install the coolant pump and 4 bolts. Tighten to 18 ft. lbs. (25 Nm).

   9. For 6.2L (2V) engines, perform the following:

✳✳ WARNING

Align the bolt holes with the bosses prior to insertion of the coolant pump and insert the pump straight into the coolant pump cavity. Do not rotate the coolant pump once installed in the coolant pump cavity or damage to the O-ring seal can occur, causing the coolant pump to leak.

➡Install a new O-ring seal and lubricate with clean engine coolant.

   a. Install the coolant pump and 4 bolts. Tighten the 4 bolts in a criss-cross pattern in 3 stages.
- Stage 1: Finger-tighten the bolts.
- Stage 2: Tighten the bolts to 15 ft. lbs. (20 Nm).
- Stage 3: Tighten the bolts an additional 45 degrees.

   10. Install the coolant pump pulley and loosely install the 4 bolts.

   11. Install the accessory drive belt.

   12. Tighten the 4 coolant pump pulley bolts to 18 ft. lbs. (25 Nm).

   13. Install the ACL outlet pipe.

   14. Fill the engine cooling system.

2011 Models

3.5L GTDI & 3.5L Engines

See Figures 106 and 107.

➡The manufacturer does not provide a specific Removal and Installation procedure for this component. Refer to the graphic(s) when servicing this component.

➡Install a new gasket and a new O-ring seal. Lubricate the O-ring seal with clean engine coolant.

   1. Tighten the coolant pump bolts in the sequence shown in 2 stages.

     a. Stage 1: Tighten to 89 inch lbs. (10 Nm).

     b. Stage 2: Tighten an additional 45 degrees.

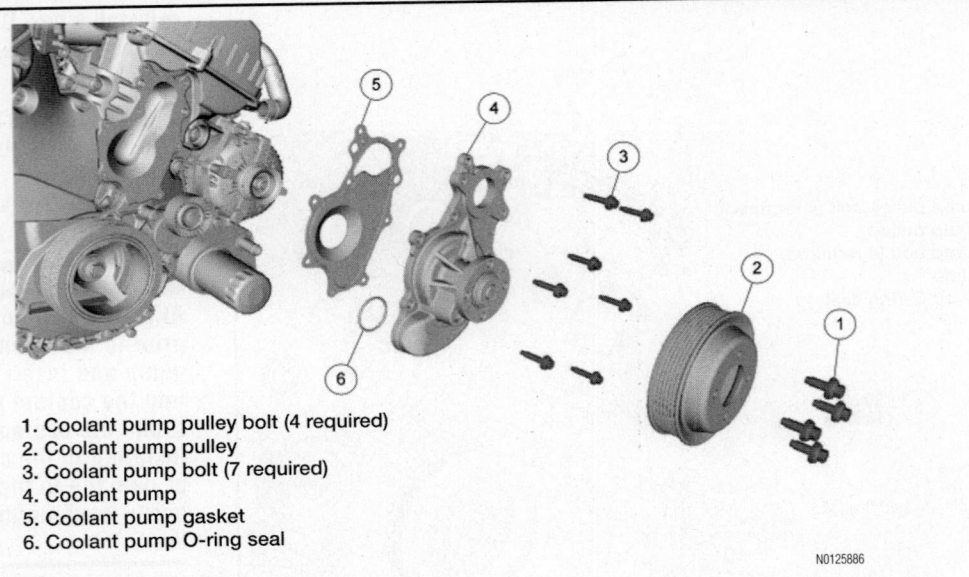

1. Coolant pump pulley bolt (4 required)
2. Coolant pump pulley
3. Coolant pump bolt (7 required)
4. Coolant pump
5. Coolant pump gasket
6. Coolant pump O-ring seal

N0125886

Fig. 106 Exploded view of the coolant pump assembly

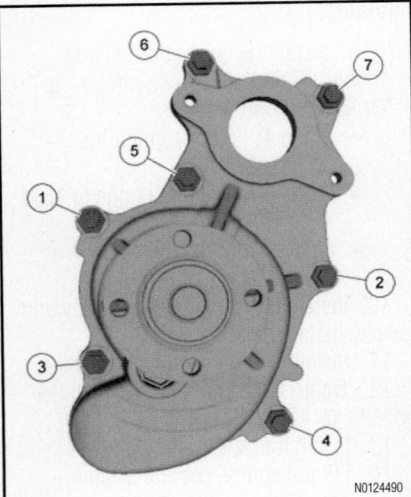

N0124490

Fig. 107 Tighten the coolant pump bolts in the sequence shown

5.0L Engine

See Figure 108.

1. Drain the cooling system.
2. Remove the air cleaner outlet pipe.
3. Loosen the 4 coolant pump pulley bolts.
4. Remove the thermostat housing.
5. Remove the bolts and the coolant pump pulley.
6. Disconnect the heater outlet hose from the heater outlet tube.
7. Release the clamp and disconnect the degas bottle-to-engine hose from the heater outlet tube.
8. Remove the 4 bolts and the coolant pump.

9. If a new coolant pump is being installed, remove the bolt and the heater outlet tube. Remove and discard the O-ring seal.

To install:

10. If a new coolant pump is being installed, install a new O-ring seal on the heater outlet tube and lubricate it with clean engine coolant.
11. Install the heater outlet tube and the bolt. Tighten to 89 inch lbs. (10 Nm).
12. Inspect the sealing surfaces and clean with metal surface prep. Follow the directions on the packaging.

✳✳ WARNING

Align the bolt holes with the bosses prior to insertion of the coolant pump and insert the pump straight into the coolant pump cavity. Do not rotate the coolant pump once installed in the coolant pump cavity or the O-ring seal can be damaged, causing the coolant pump to leak.

➡**Install a new O-ring seal and lubricate it with clean engine coolant.**

13. Install the coolant pump and the bolts
14. Tighten the coolant pump bolts in 2 stages
   a. Stage 1: Tighten to 15 ft. lbs. (20 Nm).
   b. Stage 2: Tighten an additional 60 degrees.
15. Connect the degas bottle-to-engine hose to the heater outlet tube and position the clamp.
16. Connect the heater outlet hose to the heater outlet tube.
17. Position the coolant pump pulley and install the bolts finger-tight.

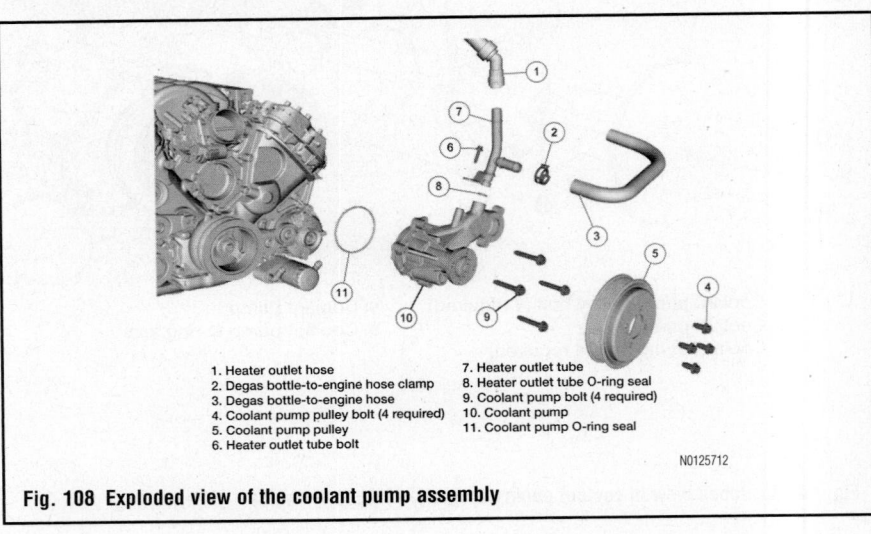

1. Heater outlet hose
2. Degas bottle-to-engine hose clamp
3. Degas bottle-to-engine hose
4. Coolant pump pulley bolt (4 required)
5. Coolant pump pulley
6. Heater outlet tube bolt
7. Heater outlet tube
8. Heater outlet tube O-ring seal
9. Coolant pump bolt (4 required)
10. Coolant pump
11. Coolant pump O-ring seal

N0125712

Fig. 108 Exploded view of the coolant pump assembly

18. Install the thermostat housing.

19. Tighten the coolant pump pulley bolts in a criss-cross pattern. Tighten to 18 ft. lbs. (25 Nm).

20. Install the air cleaner outlet tube.

21. Fill and bleed the cooling system.

6.2L Engine

See Figure 109.

1. Drain the cooling system.

2. Remove the Air Cleaner (ACL) outlet tube.

3. Loosen the 4 coolant pump pulley bolts.

4. Remove the accessory drive belt.

5. Remove the 4 bolts and the coolant pump pulley.

6. Remove the 4 bolts and the coolant pump. Discard the O-ring seal.

7. Inspect the sealing surfaces and clean with metal surface prep. Follow the directions on the packaging.

To install:

❄❄ WARNING

Align the bolt holes with the bosses prior to insertion of the coolant pump and insert the pump straight into the coolant pump cavity. Do not rotate the coolant pump once installed in the coolant pump cavity or the O-ring seal can be damaged, causing the coolant pump to leak.

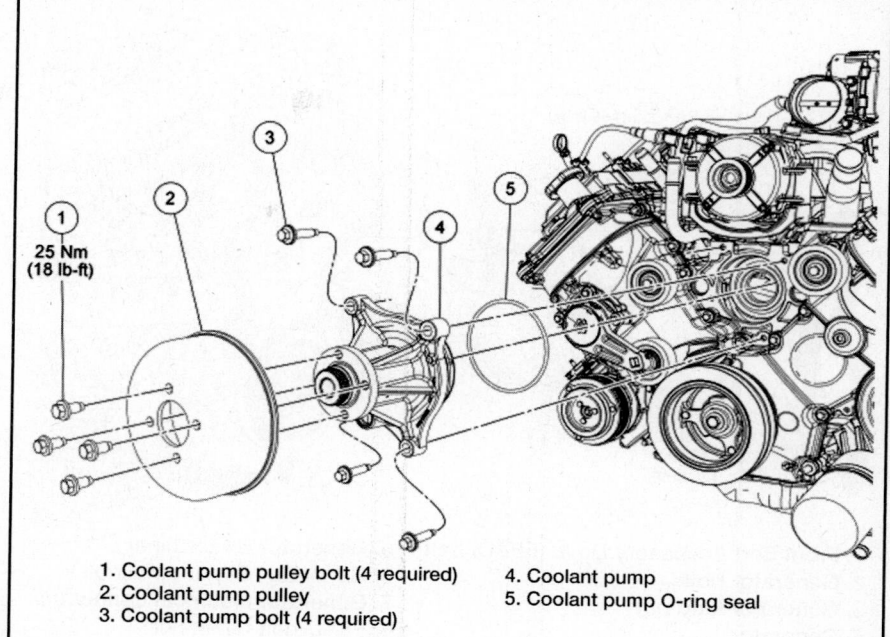

1. Coolant pump pulley bolt (4 required)
2. Coolant pump pulley
3. Coolant pump bolt (4 required)
4. Coolant pump
5. Coolant pump O-ring seal

N0110078

Fig. 109 Exploded view of the coolant pump assembly

➡ Install a new O-ring seal and lubricate with clean engine coolant.

8. Install the coolant pump and the 4 bolts. Tighten the 4 bolts in a criss-cross pattern in 3 stages.

    a. Stage 1: Finger-tighten the bolts.

    b. Stage 2: Tighten the bolts to 15 ft. lbs. (20 Nm).

    c. Stage 3: Tighten the bolts an additional 45 degrees.

9. Install the coolant pump pulley and loosely install the 4 bolts.

10. Install the accessory drive belt.

11. Tighten the 4 coolant pump pulley bolts. Tighten to 18 ft. lbs. (25 Nm).

12. Install the ACL outlet pipe.

13. Fill the engine cooling system.

ENGINE ELECTRICAL

CHARGING SYSTEM

ALTERNATOR

REMOVAL & INSTALLATION

3.5L GTDI Engine

See Figure 110.

1. Disconnect the battery.

2. Loosen clamp and position aside CAC inlet tube.

3. Remove the alternator stud nut.

4. Remove the ACL cover and Air Cleaner (ACL) outlet tube.

5. Rotate the accessory drive belt tensioner and remove the accessory drive belt from the alternator.

6. Position the alternator B+ protective boot aside, remove the B+ terminal nut and position the B+ terminal aside.

7. Disconnect the alternator electrical connector and position the harness aside.

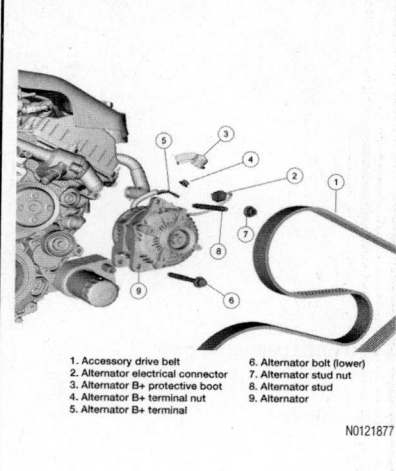

1. Accessory drive belt
2. Alternator electrical connector
3. Alternator B+ protective boot
4. Alternator B+ terminal nut
5. Alternator B+ terminal
6. Alternator bolt (lower)
7. Alternator stud nut
8. Alternator stud
9. Alternator

N0121877

Fig. 110 Exploded view of the alternator assembly—3.5L GTDI engine

8. Remove the lower alternator bolt.

9. Remove the alternator stud and the alternator.

To install:

10. To install, reverse the removal procedure.

    a. Tighten the lower alternator bolt to 35 ft. lbs. (47 Nm).

    b. Tighten the B+ terminal nut to 13 ft. lbs. (17 Nm).

    c. Tighten the alternator stud nut to 35 ft. lbs. (47 Nm).

3.7L Engine

See Figure 111.

1. Disconnect the battery.

2. Remove the Air Cleaner (ACL) outlet pipe.

3. Rotate the Front End Accessory Drive (FEAD) belt tensioner counterclockwise and position the FEAD belt aside.

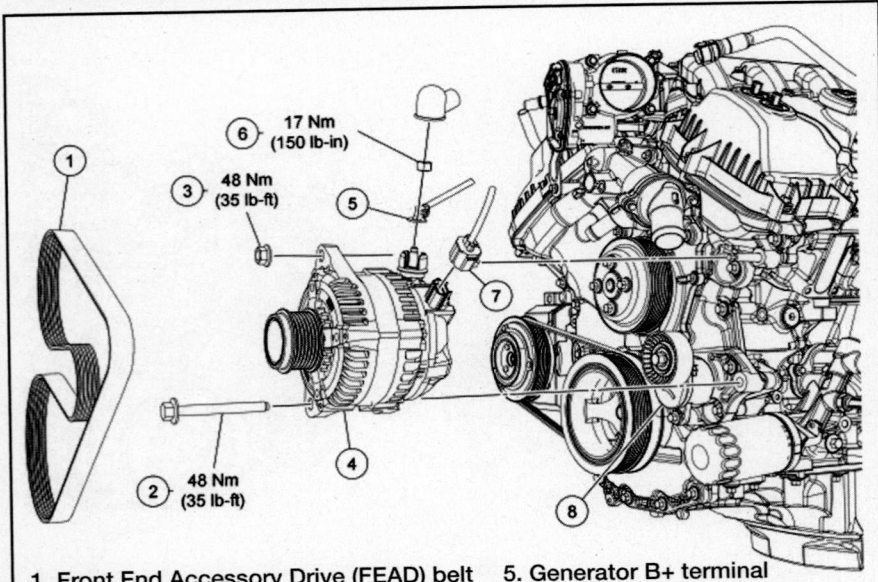

1. Front End Accessory Drive (FEAD) belt
2. Generator bolt
3. Generator stud nut
4. Generator
5. Generator B+ terminal
6. Generator B+ terminal nut
7. Generator electrical connector
8. FEAD belt tensioner

N0116435

Fig. 111 Exploded view of the alternator assembly—3.7L engine

4. Disconnect the alternator electrical connector.

5. Position the alternator B+ protective boot aside, remove the B+ nut and position the B+ terminal aside.

6. Remove the alternator stud nut.

7. Remove the alternator bolt and the alternator.

To install:

8. To install, reverse the removal procedure.

   a. Tighten the alternator bolt to 35 ft. lbs. (48 Nm).

   b. Tighten the alternator stud nut to 35 ft. lbs. (48 Nm).

   c. Tighten the B+ nut to 13 ft. lbs. (17 Nm).

4.6L (2V) and 5.4L (3V) Engines

See Figure 112.

1. Disconnect the battery.

2. Remove the Air Cleaner (ACL) outlet pipe.

3. Rotate the Front End Accessory Drive (FEAD) belt tensioner clockwise

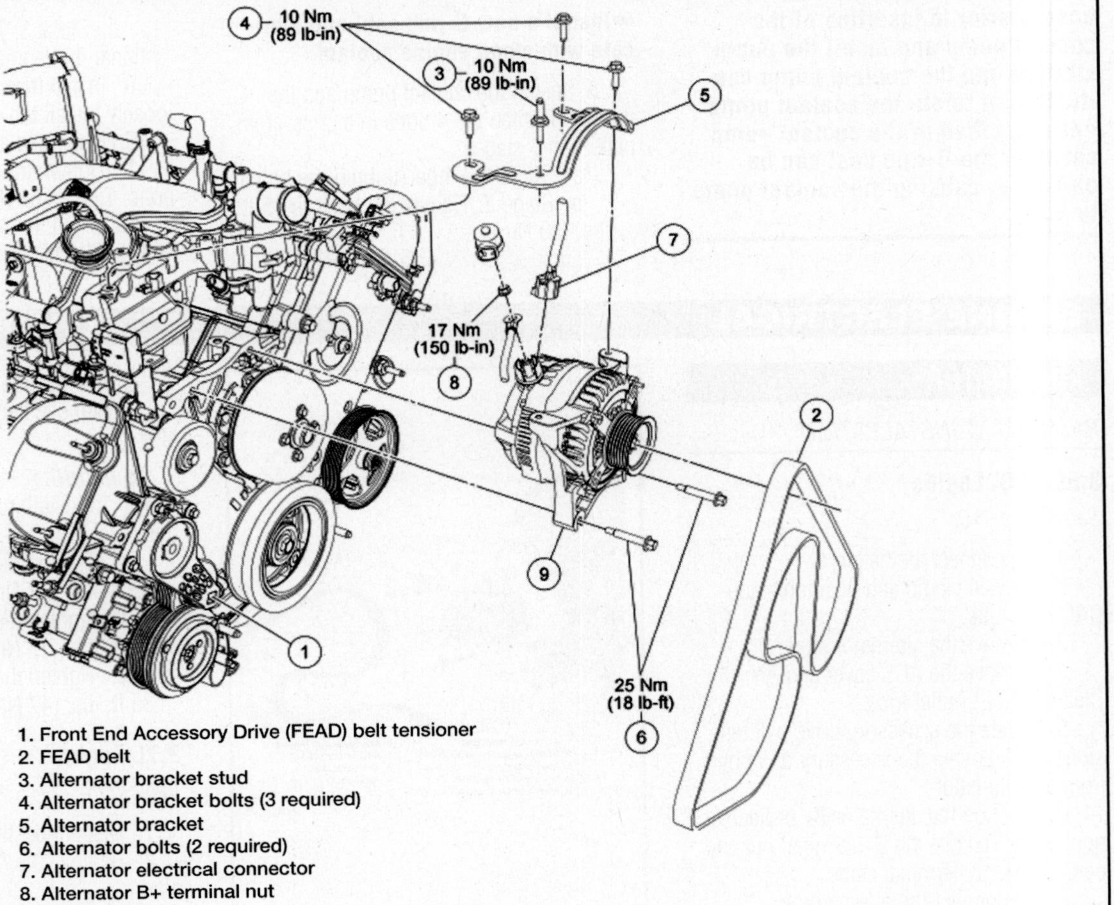

1. Front End Accessory Drive (FEAD) belt tensioner
2. FEAD belt
3. Alternator bracket stud
4. Alternator bracket bolts (3 required)
5. Alternator bracket
6. Alternator bolts (2 required)
7. Alternator electrical connector
8. Alternator B+ terminal nut
9. Alternator

N0110922

Fig. 112 Exploded view of alternator assembly—4.6L (2V) and 5.4L (3V) Engines

and position the FEAD belt aside.

4. Release the alternator harness locator from the alternator bracket.

5. Disconnect the alternator electrical connector.

6. Position the alternator B+ protective boot aside and remove the alternator B+ nut and terminal.

7. Remove the 4 bolts and the alternator bracket.

8. Loosen the 2 alternator bolts and remove the alternator.

To install:

9. To install, reverse the removal procedure.

    a. Tighten the 2 alternator bolts to 18 ft. lbs. (25 Nm).

    b. Tighten the 4 alternator bracket bolts to 89 inch lbs. (10 Nm).

    c. Tighten the alternator B+ nut to 13 ft. lbs. (17 Nm).

4.6L (3V) Engine

See Figure 113.

1. Disconnect the battery.

2. Remove the Air Cleaner (ACL) outlet pipe.

3. Rotate the Front End Accessory Drive (FEAD) belt tensioner clockwise and position the FEAD belt aside.

4. Release the alternator harness locator from the alternator bracket.

5. Remove the 4 bolts and the alternator bracket.

6. Loosen the 2 alternator bolts and position the alternator aside to access the electrical connections.

7. Disconnect the alternator electrical connector.

8. Position the alternator B+ protective boot aside, remove the alternator B+ nut and terminal and remove the alternator.

To install:

9. To install, reverse the removal procedure.

    a. Tighten the alternator B+ nut to 13 ft. lbs. (17 Nm).

    b. Tighten the 2 alternator bolts to 18 ft. lbs. (25 Nm).

    c. Tighten the 4 alternator bracket bolts to 89 inch lbs. (10 Nm).

5.0L Engine

See Figure 114.

1. Disconnect the battery.

2. Remove the Air Cleaner (ACL) outlet pipe.

3. Rotate the Front End Accessory Drive (FEAD) belt tensioner counter counterclockwise and position the FEAD belt aside.

4. Position the alternator B+ protective boot aside, remove the B+ terminal nut and position the B+ terminal aside.

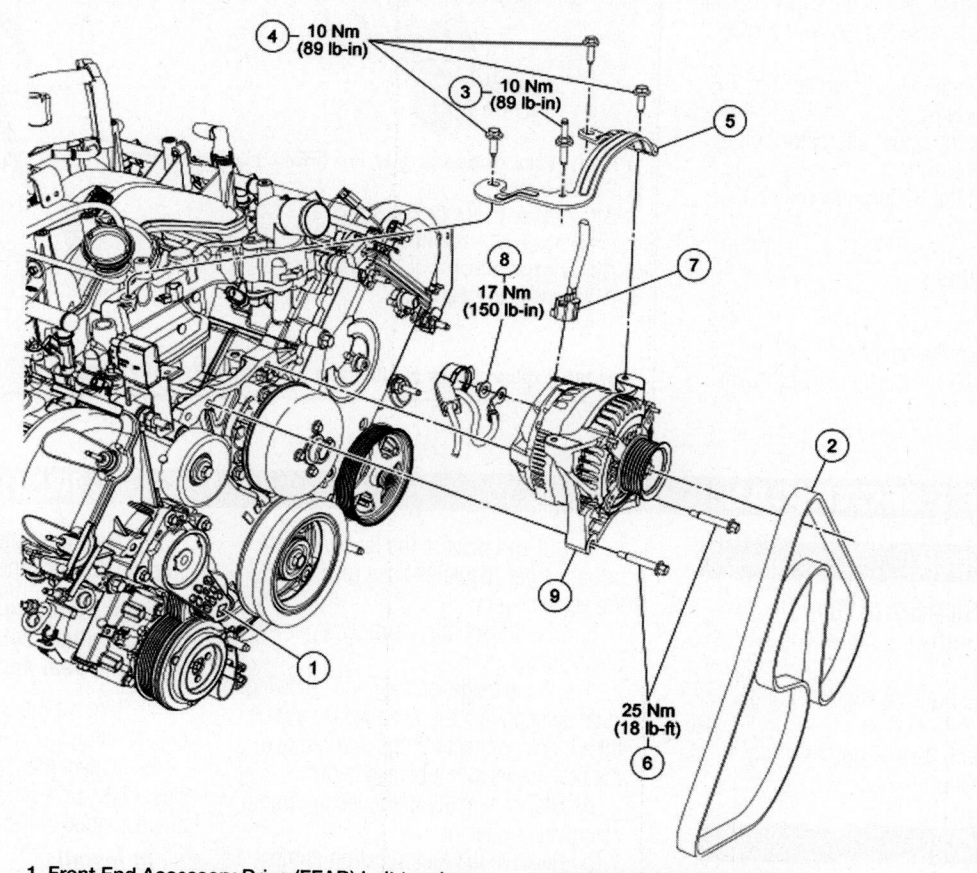

1. Front End Accessory Drive (FEAD) belt tensioner
2. FEAD belt
3. Alternator bracket stud
4. Alternator bracket bolts (3 required)
5. Alternator bracket
6. Alternator bolts (2 required)
7. Alternator electrical connector
8. Alternator B+ terminal nut
9. Alternator

N0105838

Fig. 113 Exploded view of the alternator assembly—4.6L (3V) engine

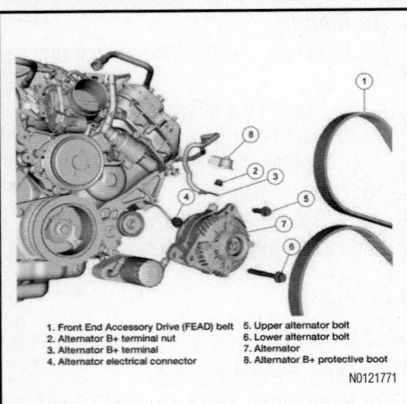

Fig. 114 Exploded view of the alternator assembly—5.0L engine

1. Front End Accessory Drive (FEAD) belt
2. Alternator B+ terminal nut
3. Alternator B+ terminal
4. Alternator electrical connector
5. Upper alternator bolt
6. Lower alternator bolt
7. Alternator
8. Alternator B+ protective boot

N0121771

5. Disconnect the alternator electrical connector.

6. Remove the upper alternator bolt.

7. Remove the lower alternator bolt and the alternator.

To install:

8. To install, reverse the removal procedure.

   a. Tighten the lower alternator bolt to 35 ft. lbs. (48 Nm).

   b. Tighten the upper alternator bolt to 35 ft. lbs. (48 Nm).

   c. Tighten the B+ terminal nut to 13 ft. lbs. (17 Nm).

6.2L (2V) Engine

See Figure 115.

1. Disconnect the battery.

2. Remove the Air Cleaner (ACL) outlet pipe.

3. Rotate the Front End Accessory Drive (FEAD) belt tensioner clockwise and position the FEAD belt aside.

4. Disconnect the alternator electrical connector.

5. Position the alternator B+ protective boot aside, remove the alternator B+ nut and terminal and remove the alternator.

6. Remove the 3 bolts and the alternator.

To install:

7. To install, reverse the removal procedure.

   a. Tighten the 3 alternator bolts to 35 ft. lbs. (47 Nm).

   b. Tighten the alternator B+ nut to 13 ft. lbs. (17 Nm).

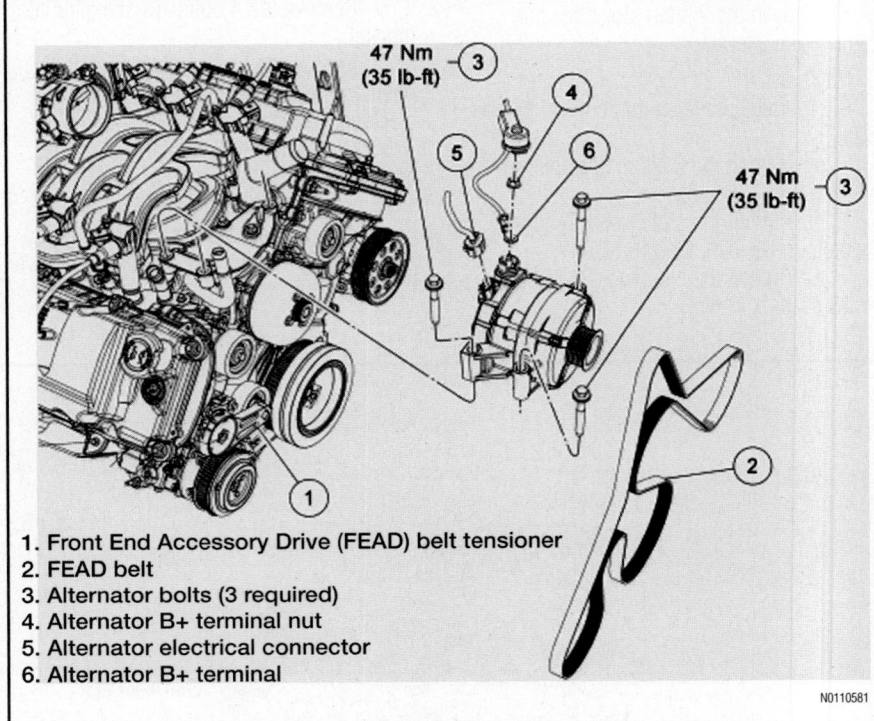

1. Front End Accessory Drive (FEAD) belt tensioner
2. FEAD belt
3. Alternator bolts (3 required)
4. Alternator B+ terminal nut
5. Alternator electrical connector
6. Alternator B+ terminal

N0110581

Fig. 115 Exploded view of alternator assembly—6.2L (2V) engine

ENGINE ELECTRICAL

FIRING ORDER

The 3.5L GTDI and 3.7L V6 engines firing order:
1–4–2–5–3–6.

The 4.6L and 5.4L V8 engines firing order: 1–3–7–2–6–5–4–8.

The 5.0L and 6.2L V8 engines firing order: 1–5–4–8–6–3–7–2.

IGNITION COIL

REMOVAL & INSTALLATION

3.5L GTDI Engine

See Figures 116 and 117.

1. For the right side, perform the following:

   a. Cut and discard the tie strap from turbocharger regulator hose retainer at the valve cover.

   b. Disconnect the 2 turbocharger regulator hoses.

2. For the left side, perform the following:

   a. Disconnect the 2 crankcase vent tube quick connect fittings and remove the crankcase vent tube assembly.

   b. Disconnect the fuel injection pump electrical connector.

   c. Remove the fuel injection pump noise insulator shield.

➡**Use compressed air to remove any foreign material from the ignition coil-on-plugs and surrounding area before removing the ignition coil-on-plugs.**

IGNITION SYSTEM

3. Disconnect the 6 ignition coil-on-plug electrical connectors.

➡**When removing the ignition coil-on-plugs, a slight twisting motion will break the seal and ease removal.**

4. Remove the 6 bolts and the 6 ignition coil-on-plugs.

5. Inspect the coil-on-plug seals for rips, nicks or tears. Remove and discard any damaged coil-on-plug seals.

To install:

6. To install, reverse the removal procedure.

7. Apply a small amount of dielectric grease to the inside of the ignition coil-on-plug boots before attaching to the spark plugs.

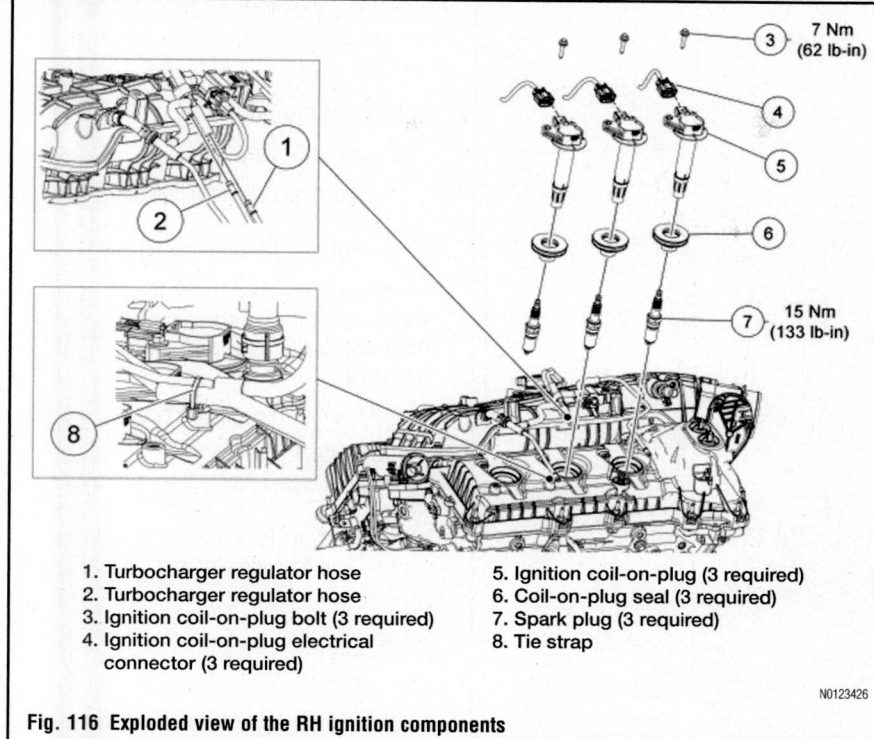

Fig. 116 Exploded view of the RH ignition components

1. Turbocharger regulator hose
2. Turbocharger regulator hose
3. Ignition coil-on-plug bolt (3 required)
4. Ignition coil-on-plug electrical connector (3 required)
5. Ignition coil-on-plug (3 required)
6. Coil-on-plug seal (3 required)
7. Spark plug (3 required)
8. Tie strap

N0123426

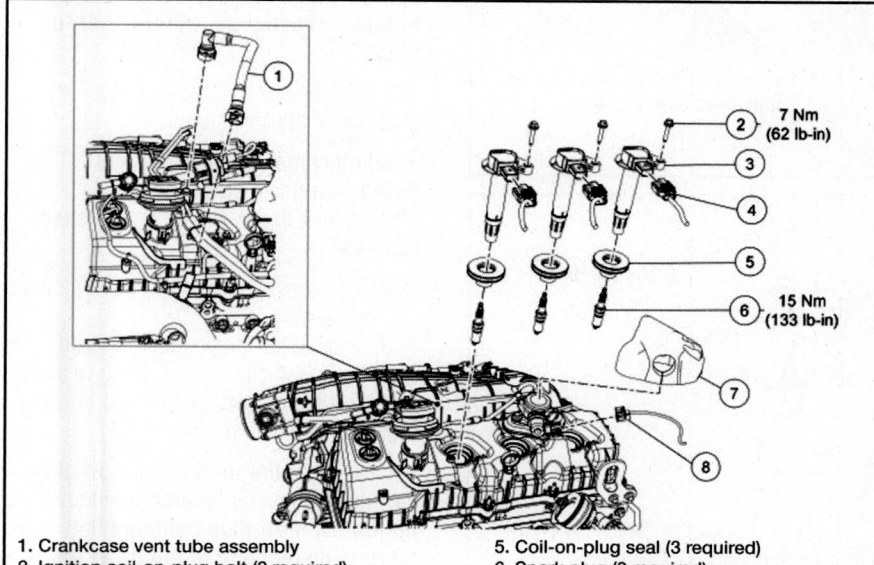

Fig. 117 Exploded view of the LH ignition components

1. Crankcase vent tube assembly
2. Ignition coil-on-plug bolt (3 required)
3. Ignition coil-on-plug (3 required)
4. Ignition coil-on-plug electrical connector (3 required)
5. Coil-on-plug seal (3 required)
6. Spark plug (3 required)
7. Fuel injection pump noise insulator shield
8. Fuel injection pump electrical connector

N0123427

8. Slide the new coil-on-plug seal onto the coil until it is fully seated at the top of the coil-on-plug.

3.7L Engine

See Figure 118.

1. For the right side, perform the following:

➡**The upper intake manifold must be removed to access the RH ignition coil-on-plugs.**

　a. Remove the upper intake manifold.

➡**LH side shown, RH side similar.**

➡**Use compressed air to remove any foreign material from the ignition coil-**

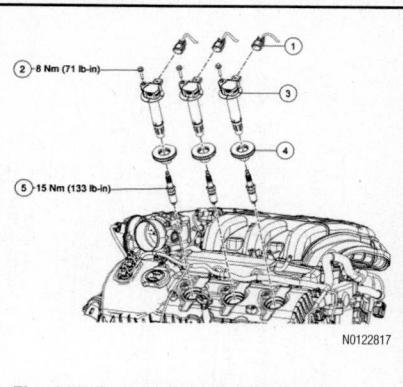

Fig. 118 Exploded view of the ignition components

N0122817

on-plugs and surrounding area before removing the ignition coil-on-plugs.

2. Disconnect the 6 ignition coil-on-plug electrical connectors.

➡**When removing the ignition coil-on-plugs, a slight twisting motion will break the seal and ease removal.**

3. Remove the 6 ignition coil-on-plug bolts and the 6 ignition coil-on-plugs.

4. Inspect the ignition coil-on-plug seals for rips, nicks or tears. Remove and discard any damaged ignition coil-on-plug seals.

➡**Verify that the ignition coil-on-plug spring is correctly located inside the ignition coil-on-plug boot and that there is no damage to the tip of the boot.**

To install:

5. To install, reverse the removal procedure.

6. Apply a small amount of dielectric grease to the inside of the ignition coil-on-plug boots before attaching to the spark plugs.

7. Slide the new ignition coil-on-plug seal onto the ignition coil-on-plug until it is fully seated at the top of the ignition coil-on-plug.

4.6L (2V) Engine

See Figure 119.

1. Disconnect the ignition coil electrical connector.

2. Remove the ignition coil retaining bolt.

3. Use a twisting motion while pulling up on the ignition coil and remove.

➡**Verify that the ignition coil spring is correctly located inside the ignition coil boot and that there is no damage to the tip of the boot.**

To install:

4. To install, reverse the removal procedure.

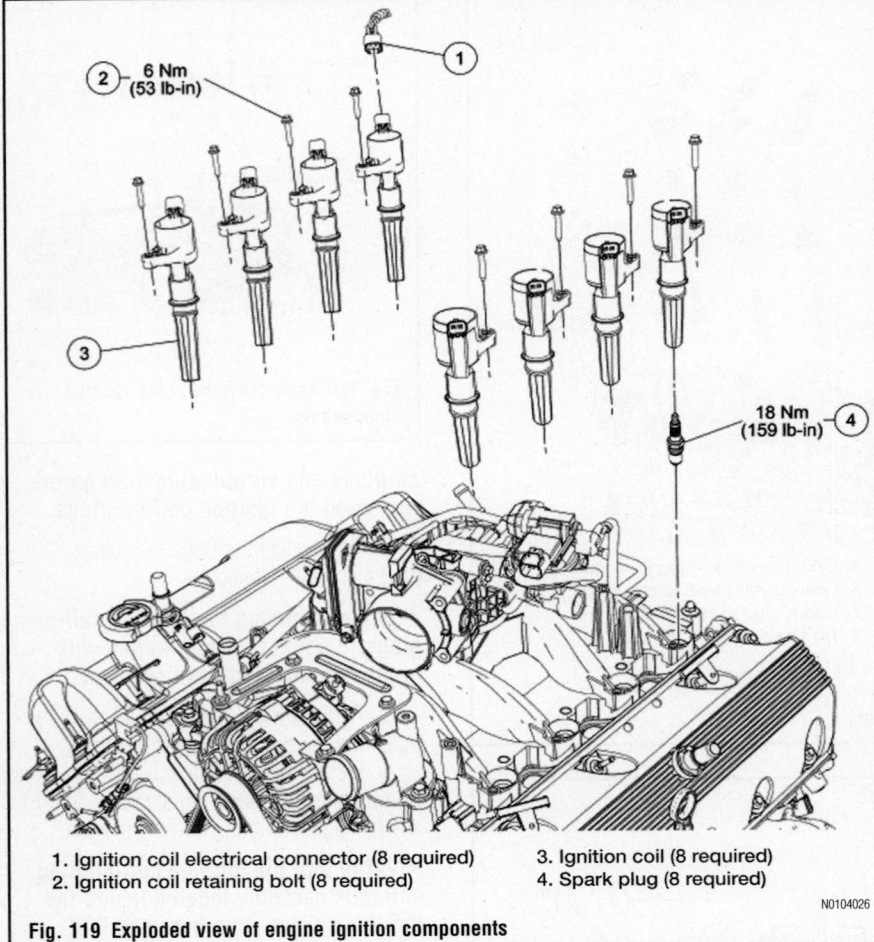

1. Ignition coil electrical connector (8 required)
2. Ignition coil retaining bolt (8 required)
3. Ignition coil (8 required)
4. Spark plug (8 required)

N0104026

Fig. 119 Exploded view of engine ignition components

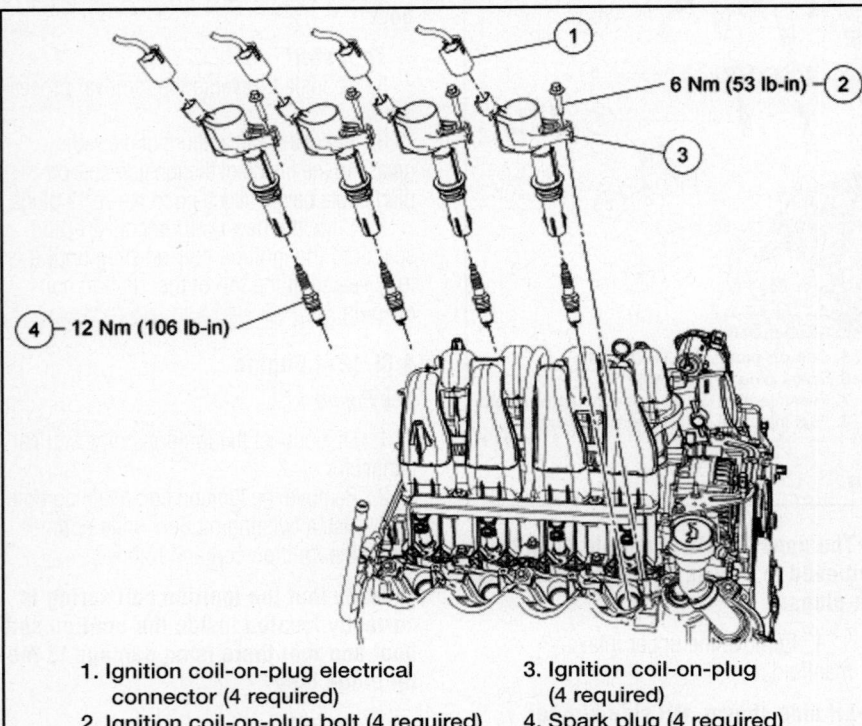

1. Ignition coil-on-plug electrical
   connector (4 required)
2. Ignition coil-on-plug bolt (4 required)
3. Ignition coil-on-plug
   (4 required)
4. Spark plug (4 required)

N0088949

Fig. 120 Exploded view of engine ignition components—Right side

5. Apply dielectric compound to the inside of the coil boots prior to installation.

4.6L (3V) Engine

See Figures 120 and 121.

1. Disconnect the ignition coil electrical connector.
2. Remove the ignition coil bolt.

➡ **When removing the ignition coils, a slight twisting motion will break the seal and ease removal.**

3. Remove the ignition coil.

To install:

4. To install, reverse the removal procedure.

5. Apply a light film of brake caliper grease to the inside of the coil boots before installation.

5.0L Engine

See Figure 122.

➡ **Use compressed air to remove any foreign material from the ignition coil-on-plugs and surrounding area before removing the ignition coil-on-plugs.**

1. Disconnect the 8 ignition coil-on-plug electrical connectors.

➡ **When removing the ignition coil-on-plugs, a slight twisting motion will break the seal and ease removal.**

2. Remove the 8 bolts and the 8 ignition coil-on-plugs.

3. Inspect the ignition coil-on-plug seals for rips, nicks or tears. Remove and discard any damaged ignition coil-on-plug seals.

➡ **Verify that the ignition coil-on-plug spring is correctly located inside the ignition coil-on-plug boot and that there is no damage to the tip of the boot.**

➡ **RH side shown, LH side similar.**

To install:

4. To install, reverse the removal procedure.

5. Apply a small amount of dielectric grease to the inside of the ignition coil-on-plug boots before attaching to the spark plugs.

6. Slide the new ignition coil-on-plug seal onto the ignition coil-on-plug until it is fully seated at the top of the ignition coil-on-plug.

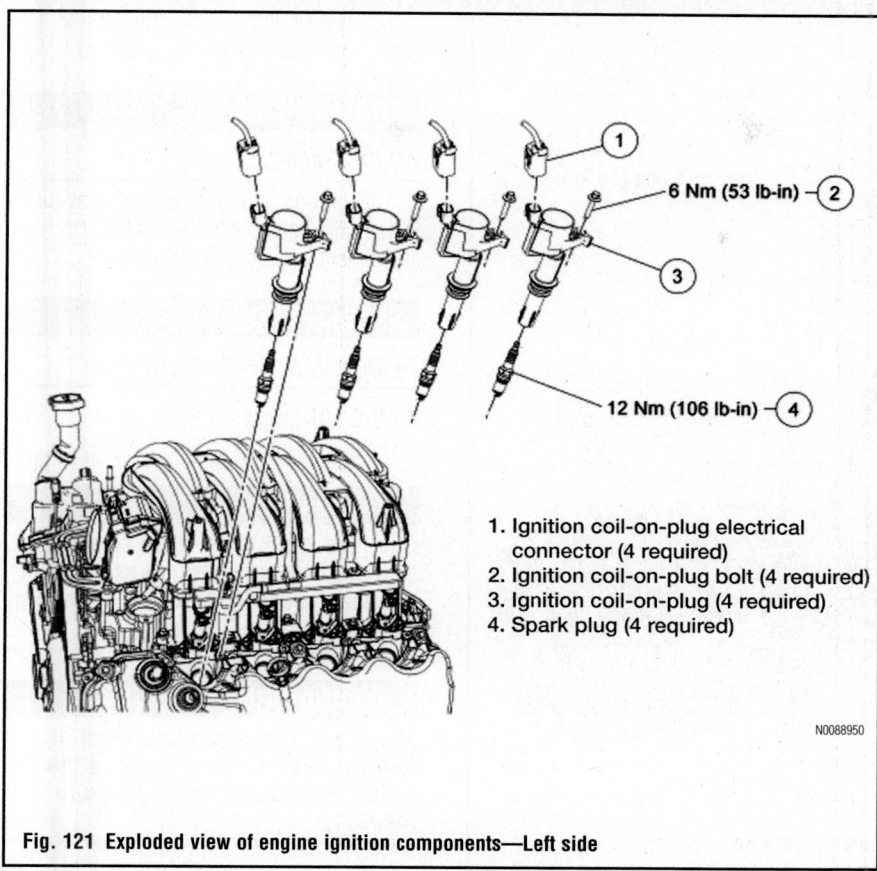

1. Ignition coil-on-plug electrical connector (4 required)
2. Ignition coil-on-plug bolt (4 required)
3. Ignition coil-on-plug (4 required)
4. Spark plug (4 required)

N0088950

Fig. 121 Exploded view of engine ignition components—Left side

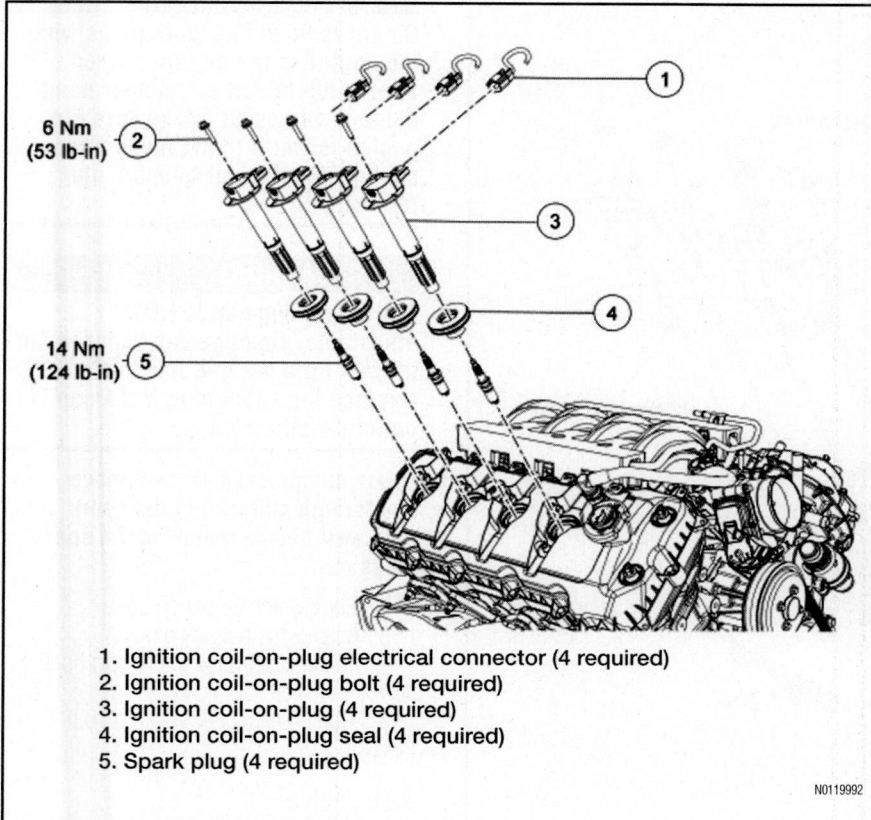

1. Ignition coil-on-plug electrical connector (4 required)
2. Ignition coil-on-plug bolt (4 required)
3. Ignition coil-on-plug (4 required)
4. Ignition coil-on-plug seal (4 required)
5. Spark plug (4 required)

N0119992

Fig. 122 Exploded view the ignition components

5.4L (3V) Engine

See Figures 123 and 124.

1. Disconnect the ignition coil-on-plug electrical connector.
2. Remove the ignition coil-on-plug bolt.

➡**When removing the ignition coil-on-plug, a slight twisting motion will break the seal and ease removal.**

3. Remove the ignition coil-on-plug.

➡**Verify that the ignition coil spring is correctly located inside the ignition coil-on-plug boot and that there is no damage to the tip of the boot.**

4. To install, reverse the removal procedure.
5. Apply a light coat of dielectric compound to the inside of the ignition coil boots.

6.2L (2V) Engine

See Figures 125 through 127.

1. Remove the Air Cleaner (ACL) outlet pipe.
2. Disconnect the heater coolant hose retainer from the ACL outlet pipe-to-Throttle Body (TB) adapter.
3. Disconnect the crankcase ventilation tube quick connect fitting from ACL outlet pipe-to-TB adapter.
4. Disconnect the brake booster vacuum hose from the ACL outlet pipe-to-TB adapter.
5. Remove the 2 bolts and the ACL outlet pipe-to-TB adapter.
6. Loosen the clamp and disconnect the TB adapter from the TB.
7. Disconnect the ignition wire.
8. Disconnect the ignition coil-on-plug electrical connector.
9. Remove the ignition coil-on-plug bolt.

➡**When removing the ignition coil-on-plug, a slight twisting motion will break the seal and ease removal.**

10. Remove the ignition coil-on-plug.

➡**Verify that the ignition coil spring is correctly located inside the ignition coil-on-plug boot and that there is no damage to the tip of the boot.**

11. To install, reverse the removal procedure.
12. Apply a light coat of dielectric compound to the inside of the ignition coil boots.
13. Tighten the ignition coil-on-plug bolt to 89 inch lbs. (10 Nm).

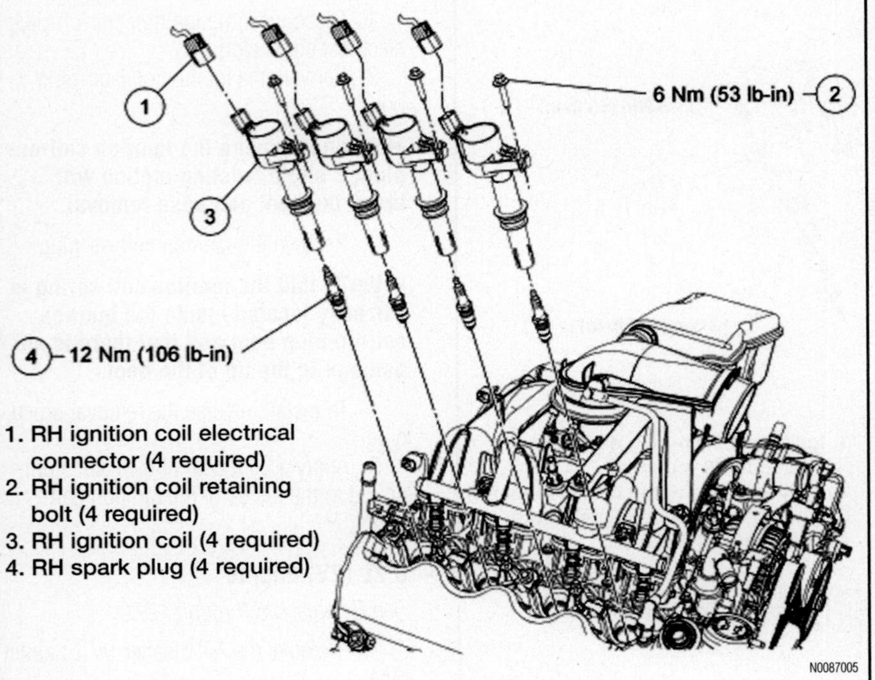

4. 12 Nm (106 lb-in)

1. RH ignition coil electrical connector (4 required)
2. RH ignition coil retaining bolt (4 required)
3. RH ignition coil (4 required)
4. RH spark plug (4 required)

N0087005

Fig. 123 Exploded view of engine ignition components—Right side

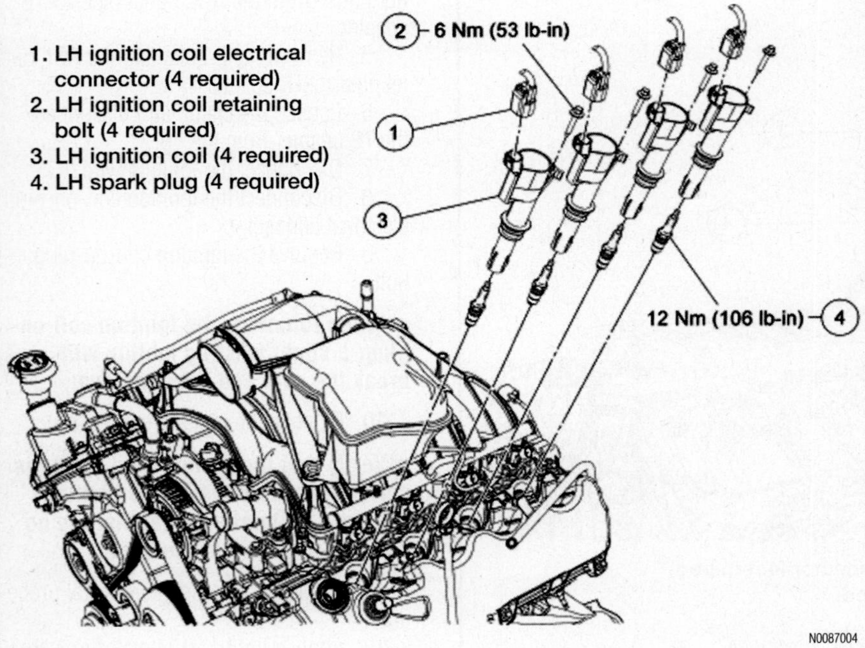

1. LH ignition coil electrical connector (4 required)
2. LH ignition coil retaining bolt (4 required)
3. LH ignition coil (4 required)
4. LH spark plug (4 required)

N0087004

Fig. 124 Exploded view of engine ignition components—Left side

14. Tighten the 2 ACL outlet pipe-to-TB adapter bolts to 89 inch lbs. (10 Nm).

IGNITION TIMING

ADJUSTMENT

The ignition timing is controlled by the Powertrain Control Module (PCM). No adjustment is necessary or possible.

SPARK PLUGS

REMOVAL & INSTALLATION

3.5L GTDI Engine

1. Remove the 6 ignition coil-on-plugs.

✳✳ WARNING

Only use hand tools when removing or installing the spark plugs, or damage may occur to the cylinder head or spark plug.

✳✳ WARNING

The spark plug procedure must be followed exactly or damage to the cylinder head and spark plug will result.

✳✳ WARNING

Do not remove the spark plugs when the engine is hot or cold soaked. Spark plug thread or cylinder head damage can occur. Make sure the engine is warm (hand touch after cooling down) prior to spark plug removal.

✳✳ WARNING

The spark plug gap is NOT adjustable. Damage can occur to the iridium tip if the gap is adjusted. Replace the spark plug if the gap is out of specification.

➡Use compressed air to remove any foreign material in the spark plug well before removing the spark plugs.

2. Remove the 6 spark plugs.
3. Inspect the 6 spark plugs.
4. To install, reverse the removal procedure.
5. Tighten the spark plugs to 10 ft. lbs. (15 Nm).

3.7L Engine

1. Remove the ignition coil-on-plugs.

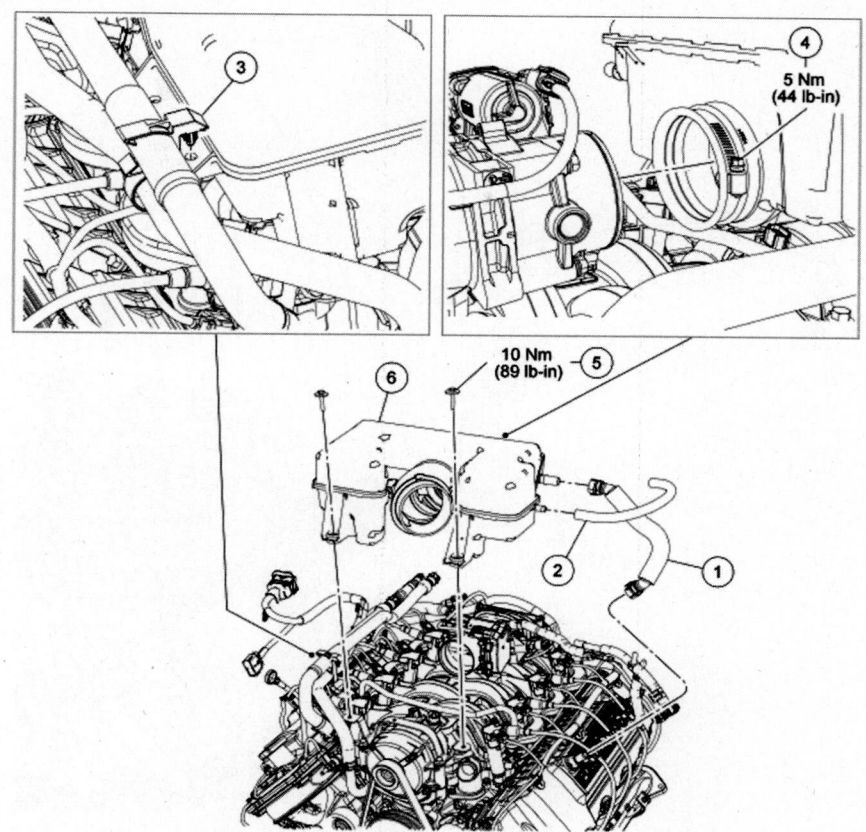

1. Crankcase ventilation tube
2. Brake booster vacuum hose
3. Heater coolant hose position retainer
4. Throttle Body (TB) adapter-to- TB clamp
5. ACL outlet pipe-to- TB adapter bolt (2 required)
6. ACL outlet pipe-to- TB adapter

N0110075

Fig. 125 Air Cleaner (ACL) Outlet Pipe-to-Throttle Body (TB) Adapter components

---

❊❊ WARNING

Only use hand tools when removing or installing the spark plugs, or damage may occur to the cylinder head or spark plug.

➡**Use compressed air to remove any foreign material from the spark plug well before removing the spark plugs.**

➡**If an original spark plug is used, make sure it is installed in the same cylinder from which it was taken. New spark plugs can be used in any cylinder.**

  2. Remove the 6 spark plugs.
  3. Inspect the spark plugs. Install new spark plugs as necessary.
  4. Adjust the spark plug gap as necessary.
  5. To install, reverse the removal procedure.
  6. Tighten the spark plugs to 10 ft. lbs. (15 Nm).

4.6L (2V) Engine

❊❊ WARNING

Do not remove the spark plugs when the engine is hot or cold soaked. Spark plug thread or cylinder head damage can occur. Make sure the engine is warm (hand touch after cooling down) prior to spark plug removal.

  1. Remove the ignition coil-on-plug.

❊❊ WARNING

Only use hand tools when removing or installing the spark plugs or damage can occur to the cylinder head or spark plug.

➡**Use compressed air to remove any foreign material from the spark plug well before removing the spark plugs.**

➡**If an original spark plug is used, make sure it is installed in the same cylinder from which it was taken. New spark plugs can be used in any cylinder.**

  2. Remove the spark plugs.
  3. Inspect the spark plugs. Install new spark plugs as necessary.
  4. To install, reverse the removal procedure.
  5. Tighten the spark plugs to 159 inch lbs. (18 Nm).

4.6L (3V) and 5.4L (3V) Engines

❊❊ WARNING

The spark plug procedure must be followed exactly or damage to the cylinder head and spark plug will result.

❊❊ WARNING

Do not remove the spark plugs when the engine is hot or cold soaked. Spark plug thread or cylinder head damage can occur. Make sure the engine is warm (hand touch after cooling down) prior to spark plug removal.

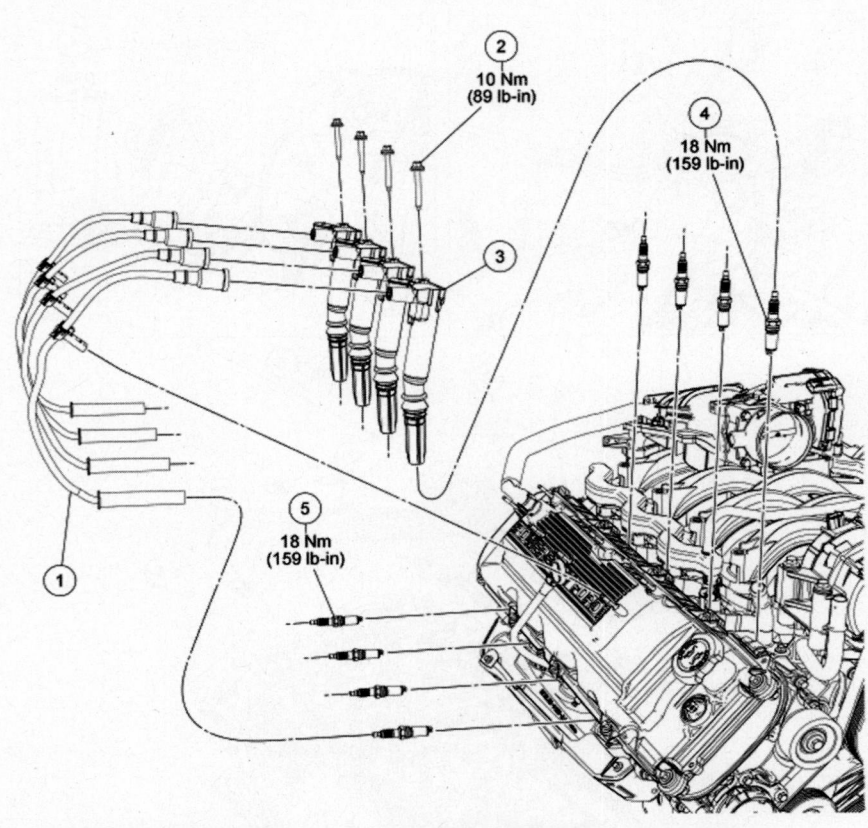

1. RH ignition wire (4 required)
2. RH ignition coil retaining bolt (4 required)
3. RH ignition coil (4 required)
4. RH upper spark plug (4 required)
5. RH lower spark plug (4 required)

N0110005

Fig. 126 Exploded view of the ignition components—Right side

1. Remove the ignition coil-on-plug.

⁂ **WARNING**

Only use hand tools when removing or installing the spark plugs or damage can occur to the cylinder head or spark plug.

➡ Use compressed air to remove any foreign material from the spark plug well before removing the spark plugs.

2. Remove the spark plug.
3. Inspect the spark plug.

To install:

4. Adjust the spark plug gap as necessary.

⁂ **WARNING**

Only use hand tools when removing or installing the spark plugs or damage can occur to the cylinder head or spark plug.

5. Install the spark plug. Tighten to 106 inch lbs. (12 Nm).
6. Install the ignition coil-on-plug.

5.0L Engine

1. Remove the ignition coil-on-plugs.

⁂ **WARNING**

Only use hand tools when removing or installing the spark plugs, or damage may occur to the cylinder head or spark plug.

➡ Use compressed air to remove any foreign material from the spark plug well before removing the spark plugs.

➡ If an original spark plug is used, make sure it is installed in the same cylinder from which it was taken. New spark plugs can be used in any cylinder.

2. Remove the 8 spark plugs.
3. Inspect the spark plugs. Install new spark plugs as necessary.

4. Adjust the spark plug gap as necessary.
5. To install, reverse the removal procedure.
6. Tighten the spark plugs to 10 ft. lbs. (15 Nm).

6.2L (2V) Engine

⁂ **WARNING**

The spark plug procedure must be followed exactly or damage to the cylinder head and spark plug will result.

⁂ **WARNING**

Do not remove the spark plugs when the engine is hot or cold soaked. Spark plug thread or cylinder head damage can occur. Make sure the engine is warm (hand touch after cooling down) prior to spark plug removal.

1. For the upper spark plugs, remove the ignition coil-on-plug.

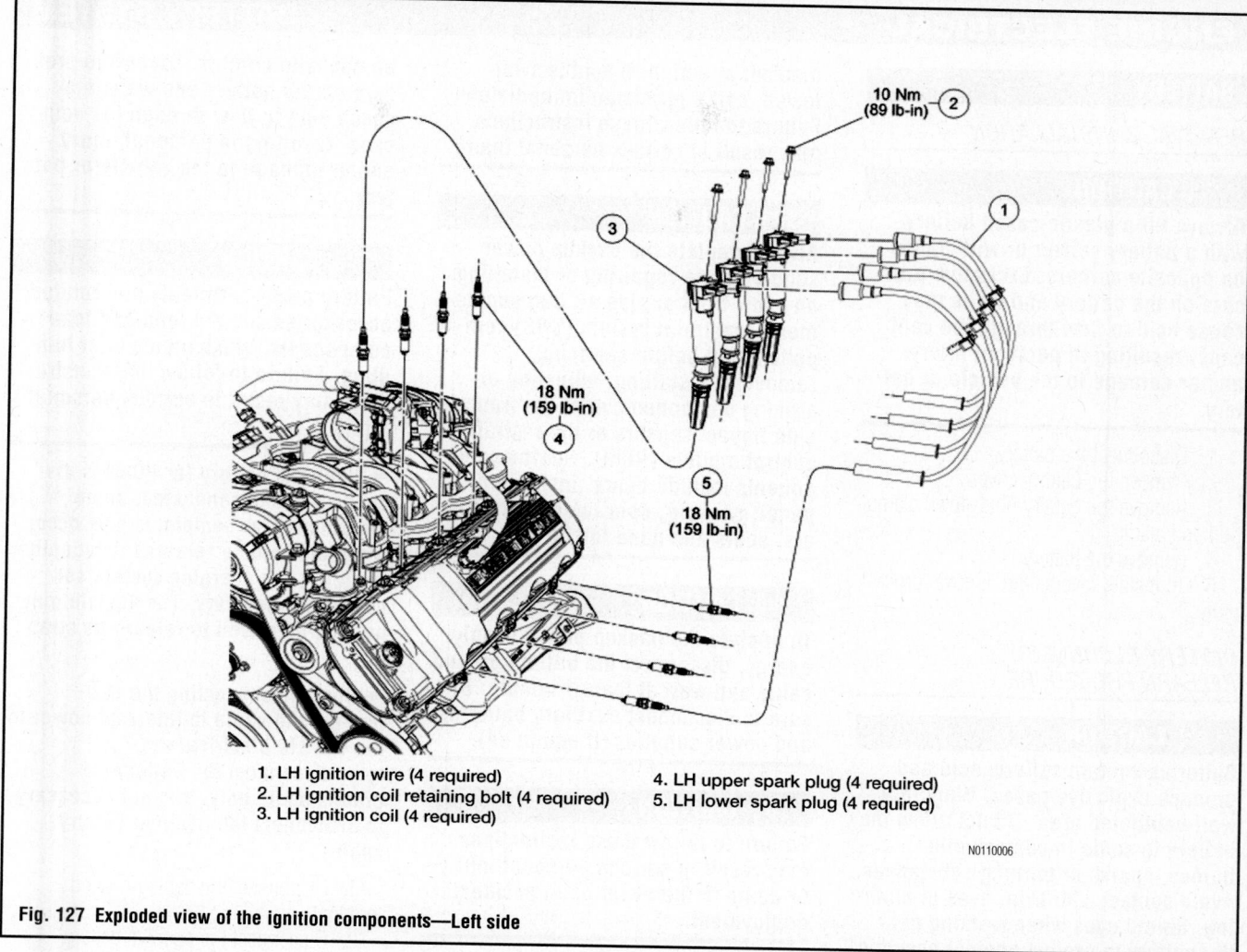

1. LH ignition wire (4 required)
2. LH ignition coil retaining bolt (4 required)
3. LH ignition coil (4 required)
4. LH upper spark plug (4 required)
5. LH lower spark plug (4 required)

N0110006

Fig. 127 Exploded view of the ignition components—Left side

2. For the lower spark plugs, disconnect the ignition wire from the lower spark plug.

✳✳ CAUTION

Only use hand tools when removing or installing the spark plugs or damage can occur to the cylinder head or spark plug.

➡ Use compressed air to remove any foreign material from the spark plug well before removing the spark plugs.

3. Remove the spark plug.
4. Inspect the spark plug.

To install:

5. Adjust the spark plug gap as necessary.

✳✳ WARNING

Only use hand tools when removing or installing the spark plugs or damage can occur to the cylinder head or spark plug.

6. Install the spark plug. Tighten to 159 inch lbs. (18 Nm).
7. For the lower spark plugs, connect the ignition wire from the lower spark plug.
8. For the upper spark plugs, install the ignition coil-on-plug.

ENGINE ELECTRICAL

BATTERY

REMOVAL & INSTALLATION

✳✳ CAUTION

Always lift a plastic-cased battery with a battery carrier or with hands on opposite corners. Excessive pressure on the battery end walls may cause acid to flow through the vent caps, resulting in personal injury and/or damage to the vehicle or battery.

1. Disconnect the battery.
2. Remove the battery cover.
3. Remove the battery hold-down clamp bolt and clamp.
4. Remove the battery.
5. To install, reverse the removal procedure.

BATTERY RECONNECT/ RELEARN PROCEDURE

✳✳ CAUTION

Batteries contain sulfuric acid and produce explosive gases. Work in a well-ventilated area. Do not allow the battery to come in contact with flames, sparks or burning substances. Avoid contact with skin, eyes or clothing. Shield eyes when working near the battery to protect against possible splashing of acid solution. In case of acid contact with skin or eyes, flush immediately with water for a minimum of 15 minutes, then get prompt

medical attention. If acid is swallowed, call a physician immediately. Failure to follow these instructions may result in serious personal injury.

✳✳ CAUTION

Always deplete the backup power supply before repairing or installing any new front or side air bag supplemental restraint system (SRS) component and before servicing, removing, installing, adjusting or striking components near the front or side impact sensors or the restraints control module (RCM). Nearby components include doors, instrument panel, console, door latches, strikers, seats and hood latches.

✳✳ CAUTION

To deplete the backup power supply energy, disconnect the battery ground cable and wait at least 1 minute. Be sure to disconnect auxiliary batteries and power supplies (if equipped).

✳✳ CAUTION

Failure to follow these instructions may result in serious personal injury or death in the event of an accidental deployment.

✳✳ CAUTION

Always lift a plastic-cased battery with a battery carrier or with hands

BATTERY SYSTEM

on opposite corners. Excessive pressure on the battery end walls may cause acid to flow through the vent caps, resulting in personal injury and/or damage to the vehicle or battery.

✳✳ CAUTION

Battery posts, terminals and related accessories contain lead and lead components. Wash hands after handling. Failure to follow these instructions may result in serious personal injury.

➡When the battery (or PCM) is disconnected and connected, some abnormal drive symptoms may occur while the vehicle relearns its adaptive strategy. The charging system set point may also vary. The vehicle may need to be driven to relearn its strategy.

➡When disconnecting the battery ground cable to interrupt power to the vehicle electrical system, disconnect the battery ground cable only. It is not necessary to disconnect the positive battery cable.

1. Disconnect the battery ground terminal.
2. Disconnect the positive battery terminal.
3. To connect, reverse the disconnect procedure.

ENGINE ELECTRICAL

STARTER

REMOVAL & INSTALLATION

2010 Models

See Figures 128 through 131.

✳✳ CAUTION

Always disconnect the battery ground cable at the battery before disconnecting the starter motor battery terminal lead. If a tool is shorted at the starter motor battery terminal, the tool can quickly heat enough to cause a skin burn. Failure to follow this instruction may result in serious personal injury.

1. With the vehicle in NEUTRAL, position it on a hoist.
2. Disconnect the battery ground cable.
3. Remove the terminal cover.
4. Remove the nut and disconnect the starter solenoid S-terminal eyelet.
5. Remove the nut and disconnect the starter solenoid B-terminal eyelet.
6. Remove the nut and disconnect the starter motor ground cable eyelet.
7. For vehicles with a 4.6L (2V) or 4.6L (3V) engine, perform the following:

➡Be sure to install the transmission cooler tube bracket on the bolt before installing the nut.

STARTING SYSTEM

a. Remove the wiring harness nut and bolt.

b. Remove the wiring harness bolt and position the wiring harness aside.

➡Tighten the upper bolt before tightening the lower fasteners.

c. Remove the stud bolt, the 2 bolts and position the starter motor aside.

d. Remove the bolt and the wiring harness bracket.
8. Remove the starter motor.
9. For vehicles equipped with a 5.4L (3V) or 6.2L (2V) engine, remove the stud bolt, the 2 bolts and the starter motor.

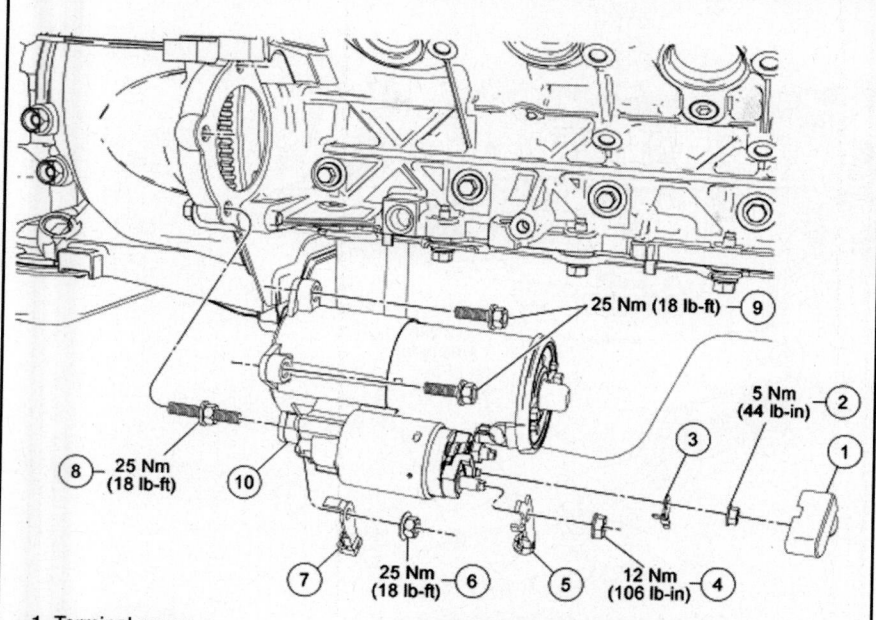

25 Nm (18 lb-ft) — 9

5 Nm (44 lb-in) — 2

8 — 25 Nm (18 lb-ft)

3

1

7

25 Nm (18 lb-ft) — 6

5

12 Nm (106 lb-in) — 4

1. Terminal cover
2. Starter solenoid S-terminal nut
3. Starter solenoid S-terminal eyelet
4. Starter solenoid B-terminal nut
5. Starter solenoid B-terminal eyelet
6. Starter motor ground cable nut
7. Starter motor ground cable eyelet
8. Starter motor mounting stud bolt
9. Starter motor mounting bolts (2 required)
10. Starter motor

N0096026

Fig. 128 Exploded view of starter motor assembly

To install:

10. To install, reverse the removal procedure.

➡**Tighten the upper bolt before tightening the lower fasteners.**

 a. Tighten the 2 starter motor bolts to 18 ft. lbs. (25 Nm).

 b. Tighten the wiring harness bracket bolt to 89 inch lbs. (10 Nm).

 c. Tighten the wiring harness nut and bolt to 89 inch lbs. (10 Nm).

 d. Tighten the nut for the starter motor ground cable eyelet to 18 ft. lbs. (25 Nm).

 e. Tighten the nut for the starter solenoid B-terminal eyelet to 106 inch lbs. (12 Nm).

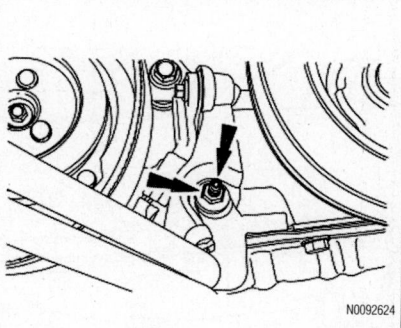

N0092624

Fig. 129 Remove the wiring harness nut and bolt

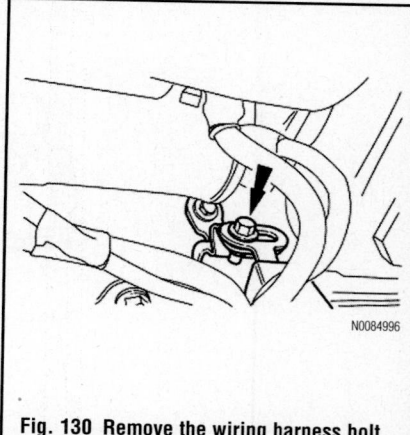

N0084996

Fig. 130 Remove the wiring harness bolt and position the wiring harness aside

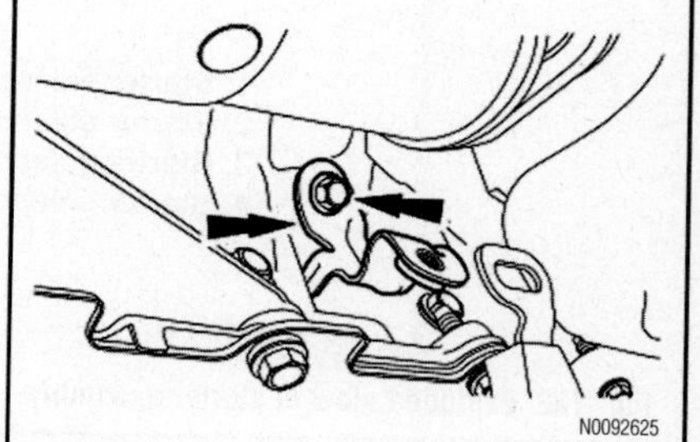

N0092625

Fig. 131 Remove the bolt and the wiring harness bracket

2011 Models

See Figures 132 and 133.

At the time of publication, procedures are still in development. For the 6.2L engine, you may refer to the 2010 model procedures. For the other engines, the manufacturer does not provide a specific Removal and Installation procedure for this component. Refer to the graphic(s) when servicing this component.

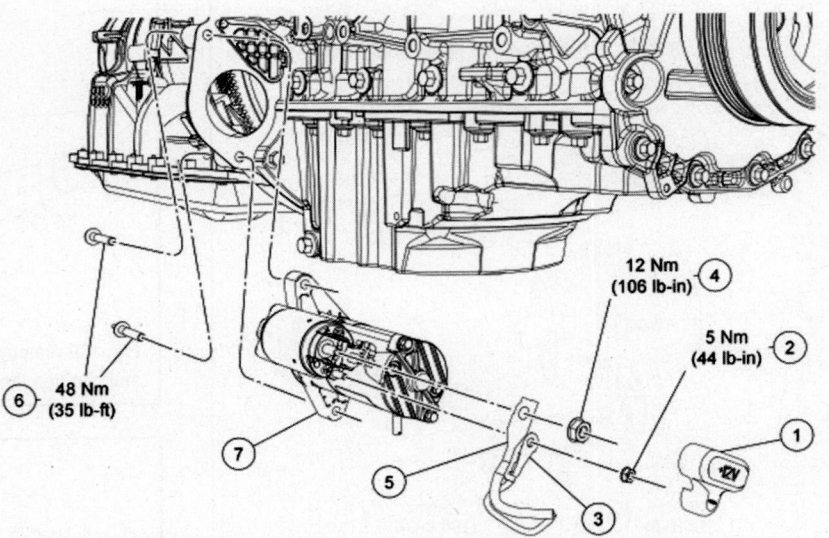

1. Starter solenoid terminal cover
2. Starter solenoid S-terminal nut
3. Starter solenoid S-terminal eyelet
4. Starter solenoid B+ terminal nut
5. Starter solenoid B+ terminal eyelet
6. Starter motor mounting stud bolts (2 required)
7. Starter motor

N0124700

Fig. 132 Exploded view of starter assembly—3.5L GTDI and 3.7L engines

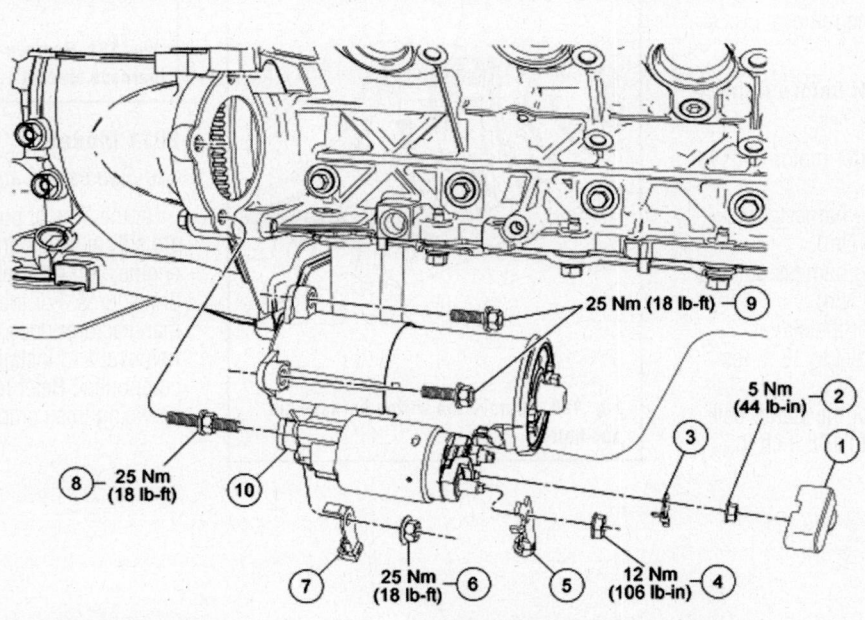

1. Terminal cover
2. Starter solenoid S-terminal nut
3. Starter solenoid S-terminal eyelet
4. Starter solenoid B-terminal nut
5. Starter solenoid B-terminal eyelet
6. Starter motor ground cable nut
7. Starter motor ground cable eyelet
8. Starter motor mounting stud bolt
9. Starter motor mounting bolts (2 required)
10. Starter motor

N0096026

Fig. 133 Exploded view of the starter assembly—5.0L and 6.2L engines

ENGINE MECHANICAL

➡Disconnecting the negative battery cable may interfere with the functions of the on board computer systems and may require the computer to undergo a relearning process, once the negative battery cable is reconnected.

ACCESSORY DRIVE BELTS

ACCESSORY BELT ROUTING

See Figures 134 through 137.

INSPECTION

1. Inspect the serpentine belt for the following:
- Cracks
- Tears
- Fraying
- Missing ribs

ADJUSTMENT

Accessory drive tension is accomplished by an automatic belt tensioner. No adjustment is necessary.

REMOVAL & INSTALLATION

Accessory Drive Belt—All Engines

See Figure 138.

1. Rotate the drive belt tensioner clockwise and remove the accessory drive belt.
2. To install, reverse the removal procedure.

3.5l GTDI, 3.7L And 5.0L Engines A/C Compressor Belt

See Figures 139 through 143.

✳✳ WARNING

Under no circumstances should the A/C compressor belt, accessory drive belt, tensioner or pulleys be lubricated as potential damage to the belt material and tensioner damping mechanism will occur. Do not apply any fluids or belt dressing to the A/C compressor belt, accessory drive belt or pulleys.

1. With the vehicle in NEUTRAL, position it on a hoist.
2. Remove the accessory drive belt.

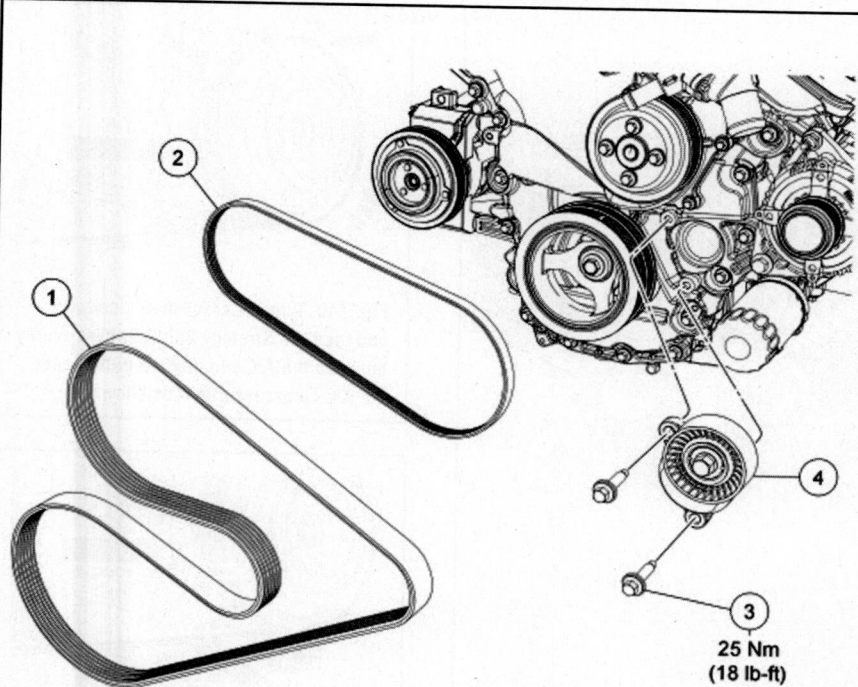

1. Belt idler pulley
2. Alternator pulley
3. Drive belt
4. Belt idler pulley
5. Power steering pump pulley
6. Belt idler pulley
7. Coolant pump pulley
8. Crankshaft pulley
9. Drive belt tensioner
10. A/C compressor pulley

N0053824

Fig. 135 Accessory drive belt routing—4.6L (3V) engine shown, 4.6L (2V) and 5.4L (3V) engines similar

3. For 3.5L and 3.7L engines, perform the following:
   a. Position the Stretchy Belt Remover (303-1419) on the A/C compressor belt as shown.

➡**Feed the Stretchy Belt Remover on to the A/C compressor pulley approximately 180 degrees.**

   b. Turn the crankshaft clockwise and feed the Stretchy Belt Remover evenly between the A/C compressor pulley and the A/C compressor belt as shown.
   c. Remove the A/C compressor belt.
   d. Fold the Stretchy Belt Remover around the inside of the A/C compressor belt as shown.
   e. In one quick motion, firmly pull the Stretchy Belt Remover from below the vehicle and remove the A/C compressor belt.
4. For the 5.0L engine, cut the A/C compressor belt and discard the belt.

To install:

➡**All installation graphics, 5.0L engine shown, 3.5L and 3.7L engines similar.**

5. Position the A/C compressor belt in 3 stages.
   a. Stage 1: Slide the A/C compressor belt between the crankshaft pulley and the accessory drive belt tensioner.
   b. Stage 2: Position the A/C compressor belt behind the crankshaft pulley with the accessory drive belt ribs facing towards the front of the vehicle.

➡**Make sure the A/C compressor belt is correctly seated on the A/C compressor pulley.**

   c. Stage 3: Position the A/C compressor belt onto the A/C compressor pulley with the lower portion of the accessory drive belt ribs facing towards

25 Nm
(18 lb-ft)

1. Accessory drive belt
2. A/C compressor drive belt
3. Accessory drive belt tensioner bolts
4. Accessory drive belt tensioner

N0117711

Fig. 134 Accessory drive belt routing—3.7L engine shown, 3.5L engine similar

1. Accessory drive belt
2. A/C compressor drive belt
3. Accessory drive belt tensioner bolt
4. Accessory drive belt tensioner

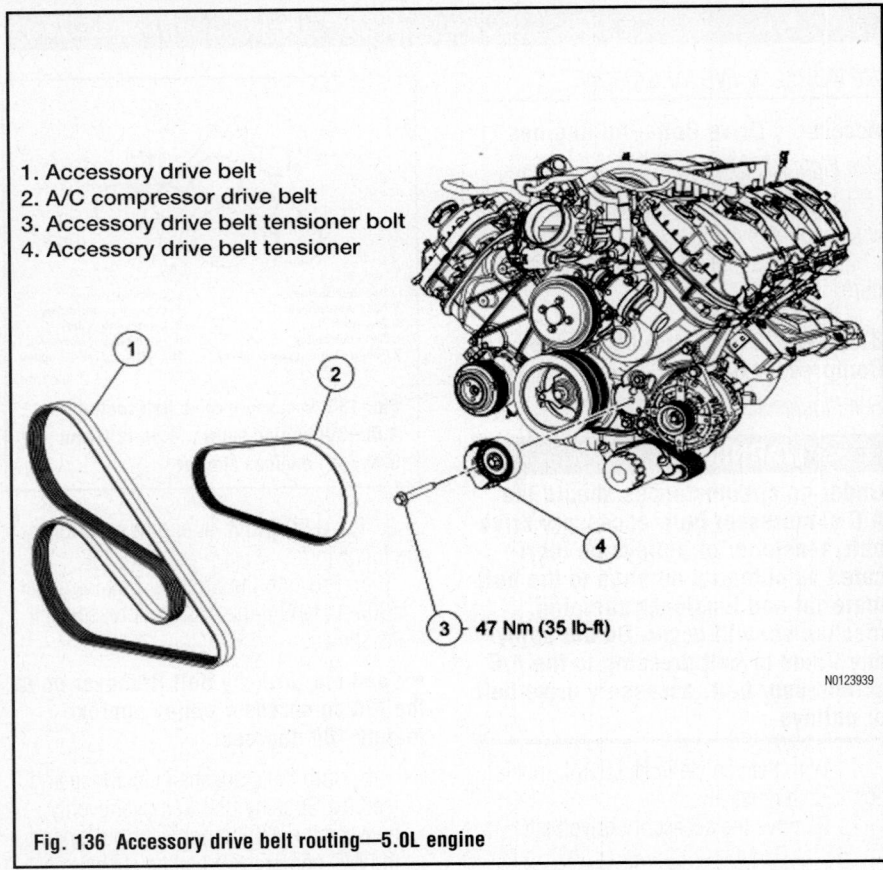

3 - 47 Nm (35 lb-ft)

N0123939

Fig. 136 Accessory drive belt routing—5.0L engine

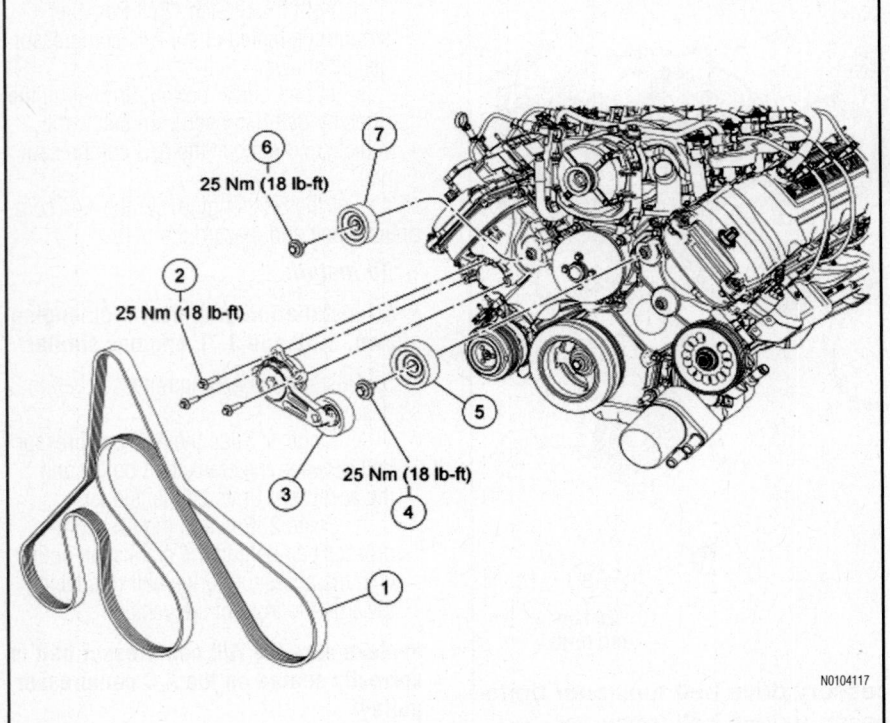

6 - 25 Nm (18 lb-ft)
2 - 25 Nm (18 lb-ft)
25 Nm (18 lb-ft)

N0104117

Fig. 137 Accessory drive belt (1) routing—6.2L (2V) engine

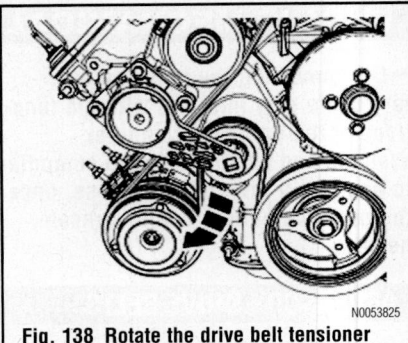

N0053825

Fig. 138 Rotate the drive belt tensioner clockwise and remove the accessory drive belt

303-1419

N0115832

Fig. 139 Position the Stretchy Belt Remover on the A/C compressor belt as shown

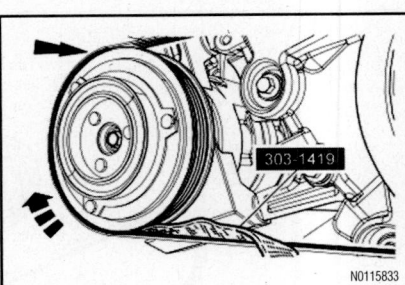

303-1419

N0115833

Fig. 140 Turn the crankshaft clockwise and feed the Stretchy Belt Remover evenly between the A/C compressor pulley and the A/C compressor belt as shown

303-1419

N0115836

Fig. 141 In one quick motion, firmly pull the Stretchy Belt Remover from below the vehicle and remove the A/C compressor belt

Fig. 142 Position the A/C compressor belt onto the A/C compressor pulley with the lower portion of the accessory drive belt ribs facing towards the front of the vehicle and above the oil pan as shown

the front of the vehicle and above the oil pan as shown.

➡️**After installation, make sure the A/C compressor belt is correctly seated on the crankshaft and A/C compressor pulleys.**

6. Position the A/C compressor belt onto the top of the crankshaft pulley and feed a tie strap with a minimum width of 0.12 inches (3 mm) through the crankshaft pulley spokes, up and over the A/C compressor belt and tighten the tie strap.

✳️✳️ **WARNING**

The A/C compressor belt must be above the oil pan flange or damage to the A/C compressor belt and engine can occur.

7. With the A/C compressor belt positioned above the oil pan flange, rotate the crankshaft by hand clockwise until the tie strap is at the 6 o'clock position.

➡️**After installation, make sure the A/C compressor belt is correctly seated on**

Fig. 143 Position the A/C compressor belt onto the top of the crankshaft pulley and feed a tie strap through the crankshaft pulley spokes, up and over the A/C compressor belt and tighten the tie strap

the crankshaft and A/C compressor pulleys.

8. Remove the tie strap and rotate the crankshaft clockwise 1 full rotation to verify the A/C compressor belt has correctly seated onto the crankshaft and A/C compressor pulleys.

9. Install the accessory drive belt.

AIR CLEANER

FILTER/ELEMENT REPLACEMENT

1. Loosen the clamp and detach the Air Cleaner (ACL) outlet pipe from the ACL cover.

2. Disconnect the Mass Air Flow (MAF) sensor electrical connector.

3. Release the retaining clamps and remove the ACL cover.

4. If servicing the ACL cover, remove the 2 screws and the MAF sensor.

5. Remove the ACL element.

✳️✳️ **WARNING**

The Air Cleaner (ACL) element must be fully seated into the ACL housing. Failure to do so will result in unusual engine noise.

6. To install, reverse the removal procedure.

CAMSHAFT AND VALVE LIFTERS

REMOVAL & INSTALLATION

3.5L GTDI Engine

Left Side

See Figures 144 through 146.

1. Remove the engine front cover. Refer to Timing Chain Front Cover.

2. Remove the 15 camshaft cap bolts, the 5 camshaft caps, and the mega cap.

3. Remove the LH camshafts.

To install:

➡️**Cylinder head camshaft bearing caps are numbered to verify that they are assembled in their original positions.**

4. Install the 5 camshaft caps, mega cap, valve train oil tube and the 15 bolts in the sequence shown.

5. Tighten to 71 inch lbs. (8 Nm) then additional 45 degrees.

6. Loosen the 4 camshaft caps bolts.

7. Tighten the 4 camshaft caps bolts in the sequence shown.

8. Tighten bolts 8, 9, 10 and 11 to 71 inch lbs. (8 Nm) then additional 45 degrees.

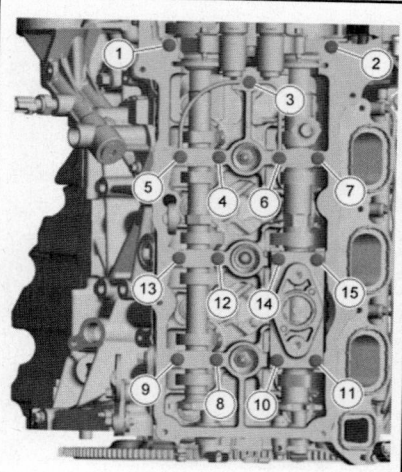

Fig. 144 Install the 5 camshaft caps, mega cap, valve train oil tube and the 15 bolts in the sequence shown

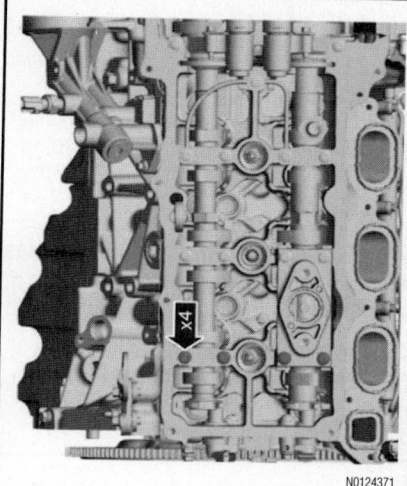

Fig. 145 Loosen the 4 camshaft caps bolts

✳️✳️ **WARNING**

If any components are installed new, the engine valve clearance must be checked/adjusted or engine damage may occur.

➡️**Use a camshaft sprocket bolt to turn the camshafts.**

9. Using a feeler gauge, confirm that the valve tappet clearances are within specification. If valve tappet clearances are not within specification, the clearance must be adjusted by installing new valve tappet(s) of the correct size.

10. Install the engine front cover.

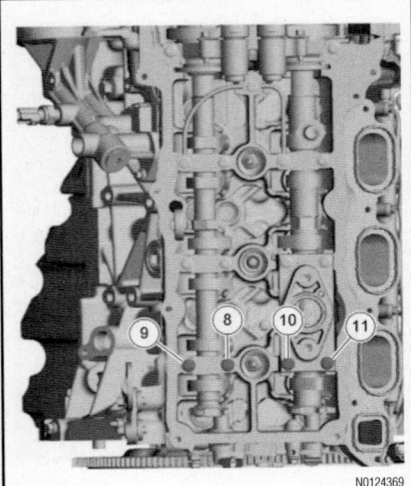

Fig. 146 Tighten the 4 camshaft caps bolts in the sequence shown

Right Side

See Figures 147 through 149.

1. Remove the engine front cover. Refer to Timing Chain Front Cover.

2. Remove the 15 camshaft cap bolts, the 5 camshaft caps, and the mega cap.

3. Remove the RH camshafts.

To install:

➡**Cylinder head camshaft bearing caps are numbered to verify that they are assembled in their original positions.**

4. Install the 6 camshaft caps, mega cap, valve train oil tube and the 15 bolts in the sequence shown.

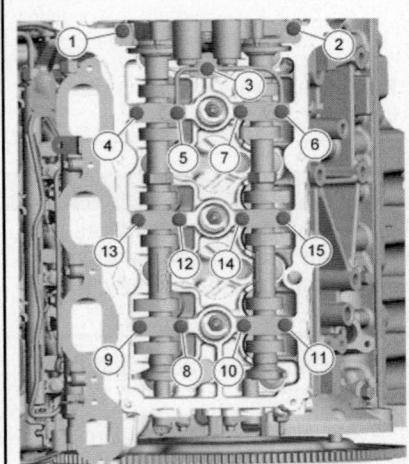

Fig. 147 Install the 6 camshaft caps, mega cap, valve train oil tube and the 15 bolts in the sequence shown

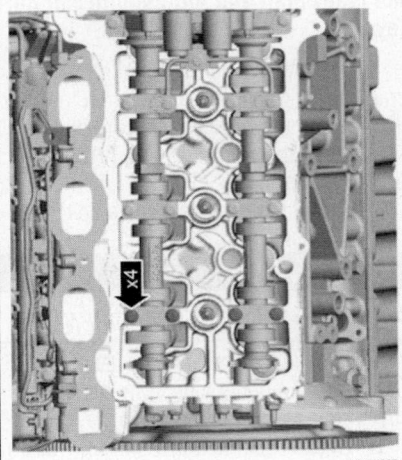

Fig. 148 Loosen the 4 camshaft caps bolts

5. Tighten to 71 inch lbs. (8 Nm) then additional 45 degrees.

6. Loosen the 4 camshaft caps bolts.

7. Tighten the 4 camshaft caps bolts in the sequence shown.

8. Tighten bolts 8, 9, 10 and 11 to 71 inch lbs. (8 Nm) then additional 45 degrees.

✳✳ WARNING

If any components are installed new, the engine valve clearance must be checked/adjusted or engine damage may occur.

➡**Use a camshaft sprocket bolt to turn the camshafts.**

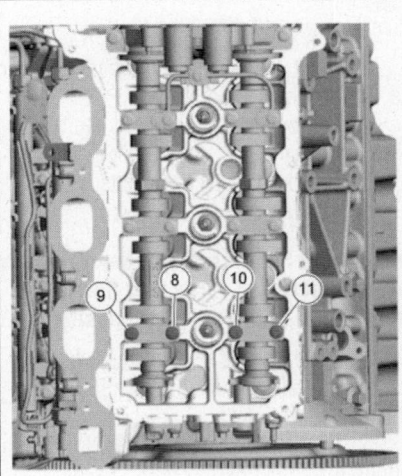

Fig. 149 Tighten the 4 camshaft caps bolts in the sequence shown

9. Using a feeler gauge, confirm that the valve tappet clearances are within specification. If valve tappet clearances are not within specification, the clearance must be adjusted by installing new valve tappet(s) of the correct size.

10. Install the engine front cover.

3.7L Engine

Left Side

See Figures 150 through 168.

✳✳ WARNING

During engine repair procedures, cleanliness is extremely important. Any foreign material, including any material created while cleaning gasket surfaces that enters the oil passages, coolant passages or the oil pan, may cause engine failure.

1. Remove the engine front cover. Refer to Timing Chain Front Cover.

2. Rotate the crankshaft clockwise and align the timing marks on the intake Variable Camshaft Timing (VCT) assemblies as shown.

3. Remove the 3 bolts and the LH valve train oil tube.

Fig. 150 Rotate the crankshaft clockwise and align the timing marks on the intake Variable Camshaft Timing (VCT) assemblies as shown

Fig. 151 Install the Camshaft Holding Tool onto the flats of the LH camshafts

Fig. 152 Mark the timing chain link that aligns with the timing mark on the LH intake VCT assembly as shown

Fig. 153 Mark the timing chain link that aligns with the timing mark on the RH intake VCT assembly as shown

➡ **The Camshaft Holding Tool will hold the camshafts in the Top Dead Center (TDC) position.**

4. Install the Camshaft Holding Tool (303-1248) onto the flats of the LH camshafts.

5. Remove the 3 bolts and the RH valve train oil tube.

➡ **The Camshaft Holding Tool will hold the camshafts in the TDC position.**

6. Install the Camshaft Holding Tool onto the flats of the RH camshafts.

➡ **The following 3 steps are for primary timing chains when the colored links are not visible.**

7. Mark the timing chain link that aligns with the timing mark on the LH intake VCT assembly as shown.

8. Mark the timing chain link that aligns with the timing mark on the RH intake VCT assembly as shown.

➡ **The crankshaft sprocket timing mark should be between the 2 colored links.**

9. Mark the 2 timing chain links that aligns with the timing mark on the crankshaft sprocket as shown.

10. Remove the 2 bolts and the primary timing chain tensioner.

11. Remove the primary timing chain tensioner arm.

12. Remove the 2 bolts and the lower LH primary timing chain guide.

➡ **Removal of the VCT oil control solenoid will aid in the removal of the primary timing chain.**

➡ **A slight twisting motion will aid in the removal of the VCT oil control solenoid.**

➡ **Keep the VCT oil control solenoid clean of dirt and debris.**

13. Remove the bolt and the LH intake VCT oil control solenoid.

➡ **Removal of the VCT oil control solenoid will aid in the removal of the primary timing chain.**

➡ **A slight twisting motion will aid in the removal of the VCT oil control solenoid.**

➡ **Keep the VCT oil control solenoid clean of dirt and debris.**

14. Remove the bolt and the RH intake VCT oil control solenoid.

15. Remove the primary timing chain.

Fig. 154 Mark the 2 timing chain links that aligns with the timing mark on the crankshaft sprocket as shown

Fig. 155 Remove the bolt and the LH intake VCT oil control solenoid

➡ **The 2 VCT oil control solenoids are removed for clarity.**

➡ **The Secondary Chain Hold Down is inserted through a hole in the top of the mega cap.**

16. Compress the LH secondary timing chain tensioner and install the Secondary Chain Hold Down (303-1530) in the hole on the rear of the secondary timing chain tensioner guide and let it hold against the mega cap to retain the tensioner in the collapsed position.

17. Remove and discard the 2 LH VCT assembly bolts.

18. Remove the 2 LH VCT assemblies and secondary timing chain.

19. Remove the Secondary Chain Hold Down.

➡ **When the Camshaft Holding Tool is removed, valve spring pressure may rotate the LH camshafts approximately 3 degrees to a neutral position.**

20. Remove the Camshaft Holding Tool from the LH camshafts.

➡ **Cylinder head camshaft bearing caps are numbered to verify that they are assembled in their original positions.**

Fig. 156 Compress the LH secondary timing chain tensioner and install the Secondary Chain Hold Down

Fig. 157 Remove and discard the 2 LH VCT assembly bolts

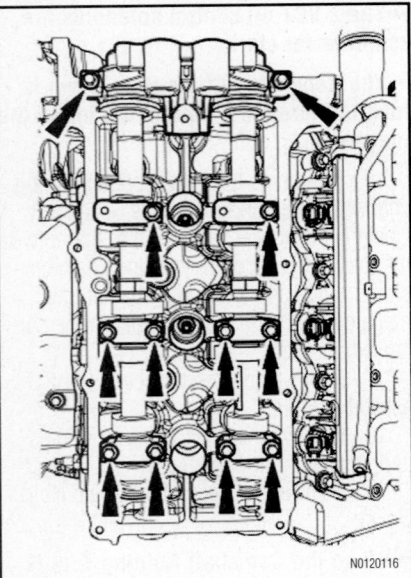

Fig. 158 Remove the 12 bolts, 6 camshaft caps, mega cap and the LH camshafts

➡Mark the exhaust and intake camshafts for installation into their original locations.

21. Remove the 12 bolts, 6 camshaft caps, mega cap and the LH camshafts.

To install:

➡Coat the camshafts with clean engine oil prior to installation.

22. Position the camshafts onto the LH cylinder head in the neutral position as shown.

❋❋ WARNING

The crankshaft must remain in the freewheeling position (crankshaft dowel pin at 9 o'clock) until after the camshafts are installed and the valve clearance is checked/adjusted. Do not turn the crankshaft until

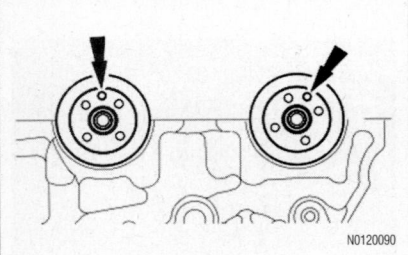

Fig. 159 Position the camshafts onto the LH cylinder head in the neutral position as shown

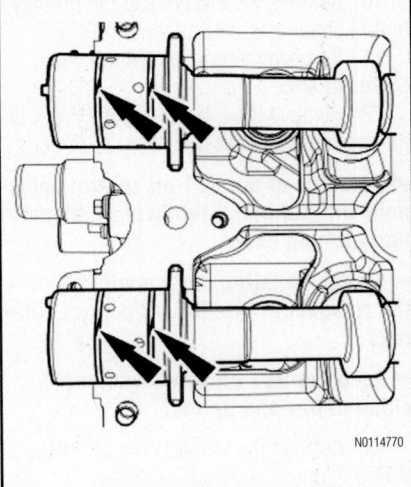

Fig. 160 Position the 4 camshaft seals gaps as shown

instructed to do so. Failure to follow this process will result in severe engine damage.

23. Rotate the crankshaft counterclockwise until the crankshaft dowel pin is in the 9 o'clock position.

❋❋ WARNING

The camshaft seal gaps must be at the 12 o'clock position or damage to the engine may occur.

24. Position the 4 camshaft seals gaps as shown.

➡Cylinder head camshaft bearing caps are numbered to verify that they are assembled in their original positions.

25. Install the 6 camshaft caps, mega cap, valve train oil tube and the 15 bolts in the sequence shown.
26. Tighten to 71 inch lbs. (8 Nm) then additional 45 degrees.
27. Loosen the 4 camshaft caps bolts.
28. Tighten the 4 camshaft caps bolts in the sequence shown.
29. Tighten bolts 8, 9, 10 and 11 to 71 inch lbs. (8 Nm) then additional 45 degrees.

❋❋ WARNING

If any components are installed new, the engine valve clearance must be checked/adjusted or engine damage may occur.

➡Use a camshaft sprocket bolt to turn the camshafts.

30. Using a feeler gauge, confirm that the valve tappet clearances are within speci-

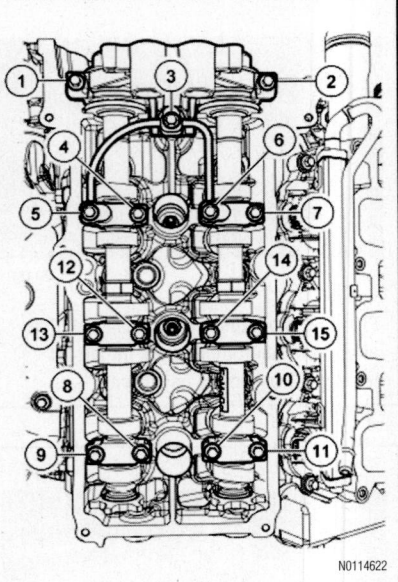

Fig. 161 Install the 6 camshaft caps, mega cap, valve train oil tube and the 15 bolts in the sequence shown

fication. If valve tappet clearances are not within specification, the clearance must be adjusted by installing new valve tappet(s) of the correct size.

31. Remove the 3 bolts and the LH valve train oil tube.
32. Rotate the LH camshafts to the TDC position as shown.

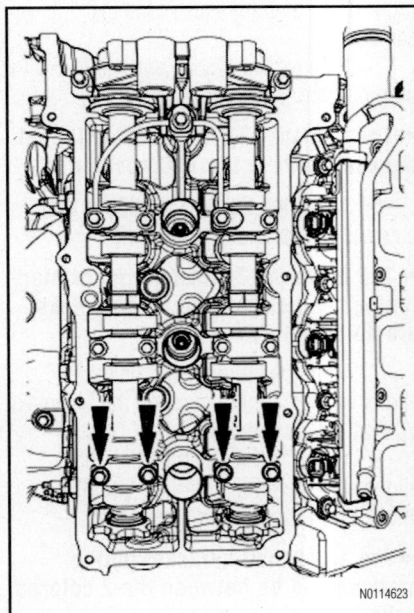

Fig. 162 Loosen the 4 camshaft caps bolts

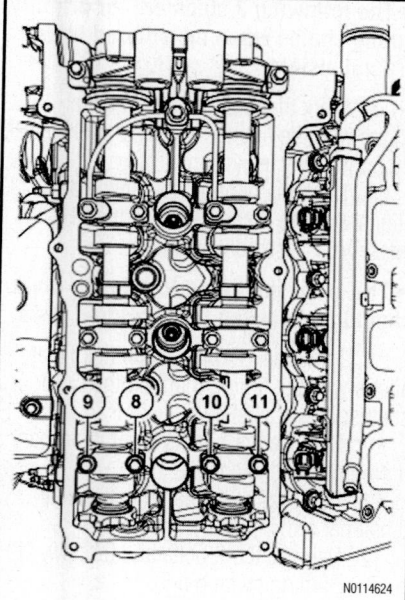

Fig. 163 Tighten the 4 camshaft caps bolts in the sequence shown

➡**The Camshaft Holding Tool will hold the camshafts in the Top Dead Center (TDC) position.**

33. Install the Camshaft Holding Tool onto the flats of the LH camshafts.

34. Compress the LH secondary timing chain tensioner and install the Secondary Chain Hold Down to retain the tensioner in the collapsed position.

35. Assemble the 2 LH VCT assemblies and the LH secondary timing chain.

36. Align the colored links with the timing marks.

➡**It may be necessary to rotate the camshafts slightly, to install the LH secondary timing assembly.**

37. Position the 2 LH VCT assemblies and secondary timing chain onto the camshafts by

Fig. 164 Rotate the LH camshafts to the TDC position as shown

Fig. 165 Align the colored links with the timing marks

aligning the holes in the VCT assemblies with the dowel pins in the camshafts.

38. Install the 2 new LH VCT bolts and tighten in 4 stages.

   a. Stage 1: Tighten to 30 ft. lbs. (40 Nm).

   b. Stage 2: Loosen one full turn.

   c. Stage 3: Tighten to 18 ft. lbs. (25 Nm).

   d. Stage 4: Tighten an additional 180 degrees.

➡**The 2 VCT oil control solenoids are removed for clarity.**

39. Compress the LH secondary timing chain tensioner and remove the Secondary Chain Hold Down.

40. Make sure the secondary timing chain is centered on the timing chain tensioner guides.

41. Rotate the crankshaft clockwise 60 degrees to the TDC position (crankshaft dowel pin at 11 o'clock).

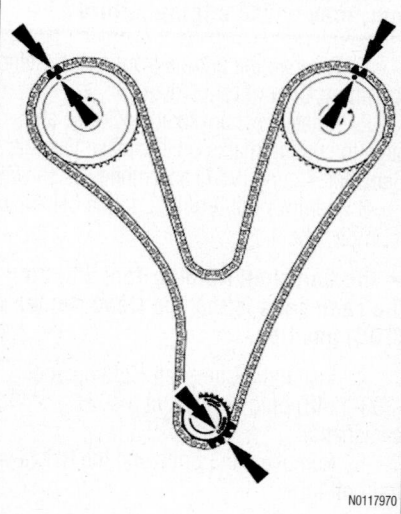

Fig. 166 Install the primary timing chain with the colored links aligned with the timing marks on the VCT assemblies and the crankshaft sprocket

➡**It may be necessary to rotate the camshafts slightly, to align the timing marks.**

42. Install the primary timing chain with the colored links aligned with the timing marks on the VCT assemblies and the crankshaft sprocket.

43. Install the lower LH primary timing chain guide and the 2 bolts. Tighten to 89 inch lbs. (10 Nm).

44. Install the primary timing chain tensioner arm.

45. Reset the primary timing chain tensioner.

   a. Release the ratchet detent.

   b. Using a soft-jawed vise, compress the ratchet plunger.

   c. Align the hole in the ratchet plunger with the hole in the tensioner housing.

   d. Install a suitable lockpin.

➡**It may be necessary to rotate the camshafts slightly to remove slack from the timing chain to install the tensioner.**

46. Install the primary tensioner and the 2 bolts. Tighten to 89 inch lbs. (10 Nm).

47. Remove the lockpin.

48. As a post-check, verify correct alignment of all timing marks.

   a. There are 48 links in between the RH intake VCT assembly colored link and the LH intake VCT assembly colored link.

   b. There are 35 links in between LH intake VCT assembly colored link and the 2 crankshaft sprocket links.

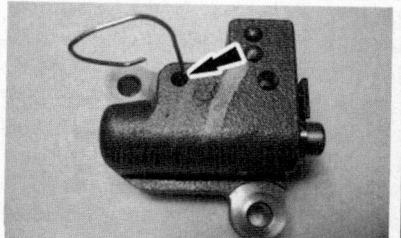

Fig. 167 Reset the primary timing chain tensioner

Fig. 168 RH intake VCT assembly colored link (1), the LH intake VCT assembly colored link (2), and the 2 crankshaft sprocket links (3)

N0120884

✳✳ WARNING

Do not use excessive force when installing the Variable Camshaft Timing (VCT) oil control solenoid. Damage to the mega cap could cause the cylinder head to be inoperable. If difficult to install the VCT oil control solenoid, inspect the bore and VCT oil control solenoid to ensure there are no burrs, sharp edges or contaminants present on the mating surface. Only clean the external surfaces as necessary.

➡A slight twisting motion will aid in the installation of the VCT oil control solenoid.

➡Keep the VCT oil control solenoid clean of dirt and debris.

49. Install the LH intake VCT oil control solenoid and the bolt.
50. Tighten to 71 inch lbs. (8 Nm) then an additional 20 degrees.

✳✳ WARNING

Do not use excessive force when installing the Variable Camshaft Timing (VCT) oil control solenoid. Damage to the mega cap could cause the cylinder head to be inoperable. If difficult to install the VCT oil control solenoid, inspect the bore and VCT oil control solenoid to ensure there are no burrs, sharp edges or contaminants present on the mating surface. Only clean the external surfaces as necessary.

➡A slight twisting motion will aid in the installation of the VCT oil control solenoid.

➡Keep the VCT oil control solenoid clean of dirt and debris.

51. Install the RH intake VCT oil control solenoid and the bolt.
52. Tighten to 71 inch lbs. (8 Nm) then an additional 20 degrees.
53. Remove the RH Camshaft Holding Tool.
54. Install the RH valve train oil tube and the 3 bolts and tighten in 2 stages.
   a. Stage 1: Tighten to 71 inch lbs. (8 Nm).
   b. Stage 2: Tighten an additional 45 degrees.
55. Remove the LH Camshaft Holding Tool.
56. Install the LH valve train oil tube and the 3 bolts and tighten in 2 stages.
   a. Stage 1: Tighten to 71 inch lbs. (8 Nm).
   b. Stage 2: Tighten an additional 45 degrees.
57. Install the engine front cover.

Right Side

See Figures 150 through 155, 166 through 180.

✳✳ WARNING

During engine repair procedures, cleanliness is extremely important. Any foreign material, including any material created while cleaning gasket surfaces that enters the oil passages, coolant passages or the oil pan, may cause engine failure.

1. Remove the engine front cover. Refer to Timing Chain Front Cover.
2. Rotate the crankshaft clockwise and align the timing marks on the intake Variable Camshaft Timing (VCT) assemblies as shown.
3. Remove the 3 bolts and the LH valve train oil tube.

➡The Camshaft Holding Tool will hold the camshafts in the Top Dead Center (TDC) position.

4. Install the Camshaft Holding Tool (303-1248) onto the flats of the LH camshafts.
5. Remove the 3 bolts and the RH valve train oil tube.

➡The Camshaft Holding Tool will hold the camshafts in the TDC position.

6. Install the Camshaft Holding Tool onto the flats of the RH camshafts.

➡The following 3 steps are for primary timing chains when the colored links are not visible.

7. Mark the timing chain link that aligns with the timing mark on the LH intake VCT assembly as shown.
8. Mark the timing chain link that aligns with the timing mark on the RH intake VCT assembly as shown.

➡The crankshaft sprocket timing mark should be between the 2 colored links.

9. Mark the 2 timing chain links that aligns with the timing mark on the crankshaft sprocket as shown.
10. Remove the 2 bolts and the primary timing chain tensioner.
11. Remove the primary timing chain tensioner arm.
12. Remove the 2 bolts and the lower LH primary timing chain guide.

➡Removal of the VCT oil control solenoid will aid in the removal of the primary timing chain.

➡A slight twisting motion will aid in the removal of the VCT oil control solenoid.

➡Keep the VCT oil control solenoid clean of dirt and debris.

13. Remove the bolt and the LH intake VCT oil control solenoid.

➡Removal of the VCT oil control solenoid will aid in the removal of the primary timing chain.

➡A slight twisting motion will aid in the removal of the VCT oil control solenoid.

➡Keep the VCT oil control solenoid clean of dirt and debris.

14. Remove the bolt and the RH intake VCT oil control solenoid.
15. Remove the primary timing chain.

N0118137

Fig. 169 Remove the bolt and the RH intake VCT oil control solenoid

➥The 2 VCT oil control solenoids are removed for clarity.

➥The Secondary Chain Hold Down is inserted through a hole in the top of the mega cap.

16. Compress the RH secondary timing chain tensioner and install the Secondary Chain Hold Down (303-1530) in the hole on the rear of the secondary timing chain tensioner guide and let it hold against the mega cap to retain the tensioner in the collapsed position.

17. Remove and discard the 2 RH VCT assembly bolts.

18. Remove the 2 RH VCT assemblies and secondary timing chain.

19. Remove the Secondary Chain Hold Down.

➥When the Camshaft Holding Tool is removed, valve spring pressure may rotate the RH camshafts approximately 3 degrees to a neutral position.

20. Remove the Camshaft Holding Tool from the RH camshafts.

➥Cylinder head camshaft bearing caps are numbered to verify that they are assembled in their original positions.

Fig. 170 Compress the RH secondary timing chain tensioner and install the Secondary Chain Hold Down

Fig. 171 Remove and discard the 2 RH VCT assembly bolts

➥Mark the exhaust and intake camshafts for installation into their original locations.

21. Remove the 12 bolts, 6 camshaft caps, mega cap and the RH camshafts.

To install:

➥Coat the camshafts with clean engine oil prior to installation.

22. Position the camshafts onto the RH cylinder head in the neutral position as shown.

❋❋ **WARNING**

The crankshaft must remain in the freewheeling position (crankshaft dowel pin at 9 o'clock) until after the camshafts are installed and the valve clearance is checked/adjusted. Do not turn the crankshaft until instructed to do so. Failure to follow this process will result in severe engine damage.

23. Rotate the crankshaft counterclockwise until the crankshaft dowel pin is in the 9 o'clock position.

❋❋ **WARNING**

The camshaft seal gaps must be at the 12 o'clock position or damage to the engine may occur.

24. Position the 4 camshaft seals gaps as shown.

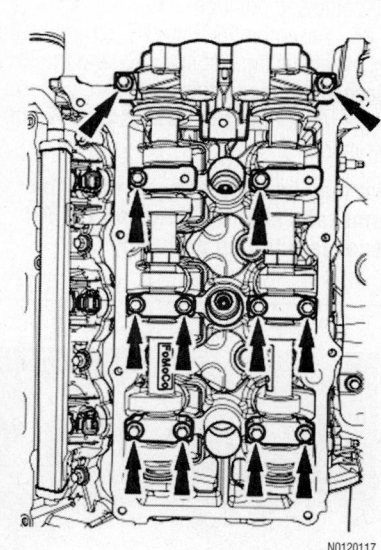

Fig. 172 Remove the 12 bolts, 6 camshaft caps, mega cap and the RH camshafts

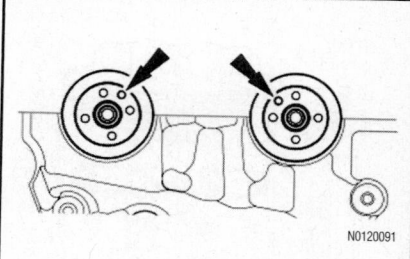

Fig. 173 Position the camshafts onto the RH cylinder head in the neutral position as shown

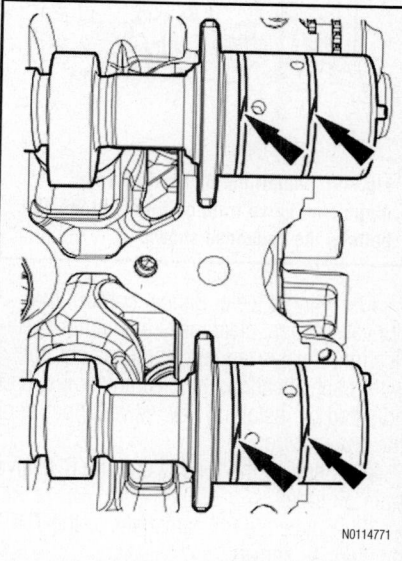

Fig. 174 Position the 4 camshaft seals gaps as shown

➥Cylinder head camshaft bearing caps are numbered to verify that they are assembled in their original positions.

25. Install the 6 camshaft caps, mega cap, valve train oil tube and the 15 bolts in the sequence shown.

26. Tighten to 71 inch lbs. (8 Nm) then additional 45 degrees.

27. Loosen the 4 camshaft caps bolts.

28. Tighten the 4 camshaft caps bolts in the sequence shown.

29. Tighten bolts 8, 9, 10 and 11 to 71 inch lbs. (8 Nm) then additional 45 degrees.

❋❋ **WARNING**

If any components are installed new, the engine valve clearance must be checked/adjusted or engine damage may occur.

➥Use a camshaft sprocket bolt to turn the camshafts.

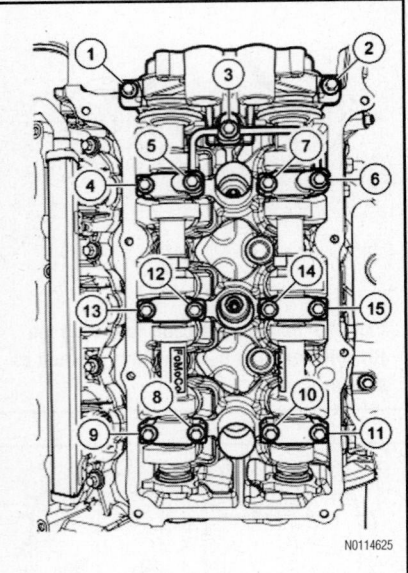

Fig. 175 Install the 6 camshaft caps, mega cap, valve train oil tube and the 15 bolts in the sequence shown

30. Using a feeler gauge, confirm that the valve tappet clearances are within specification. If valve tappet clearances are not within specification, the clearance must be adjusted by installing new valve tappet(s) of the correct size.

31. Remove the 3 bolts and the RH valve train oil tube.

32. Rotate the RH camshafts to the TDC position as shown.

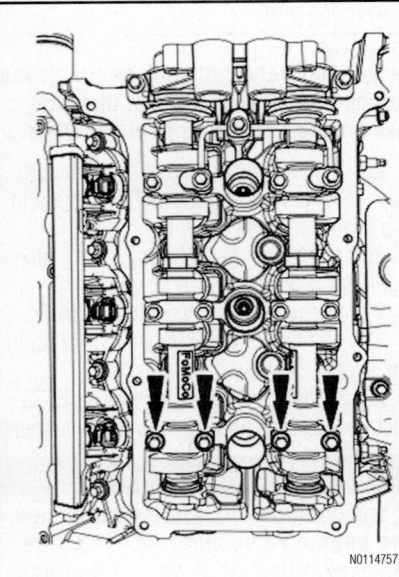

Fig. 176 Loosen the 4 camshaft caps bolts

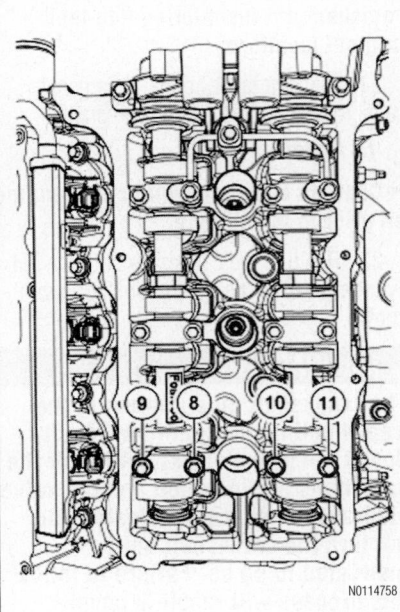

Fig. 177 Tighten the 4 camshaft caps bolts in the sequence shown

➡ **The Camshaft Holding Tool will hold the camshafts in the TDC position.**

33. Install the Camshaft Holding Tool onto the flats of the RH camshafts.

34. Compress the RH secondary timing chain tensioner and install the Secondary Chain Hold Down to retain the tensioner in the collapsed position.

35. Assemble the RH VCT assembly, the RH exhaust camshaft sprocket and the RH secondary timing chain.

36. Align the colored links with the timing marks.

➡ **It may be necessary to rotate the camshafts slightly, to install the RH secondary timing assembly.**

Fig. 178 Rotate the RH camshafts to the TDC position as shown

Fig. 179 Align the colored links with the timing marks

37. Position the 2 RH VCT assemblies and secondary timing chain onto the camshafts by aligning the holes in the VCT assemblies with the dowel pins in the camshafts.

38. Install the 2 new RH VCT bolts and tighten in 4 stages.
   a. Stage 1: Tighten to 30 ft. lbs. (40 Nm).
   b. Stage 2: Loosen one full turn.
   c. Stage 3: Tighten to 18 ft. lbs. (25 Nm).
   d. Stage 4: Tighten an additional 180 degrees.

➡ **The 2 VCT oil control solenoids are removed for clarity.**

39. Compress the RH secondary timing chain tensioner and remove the Secondary Chain Hold Down.

40. Make sure the secondary timing chain is centered on the timing chain tensioner guides.

41. Rotate the crankshaft clockwise 60 degrees to the TDC position (crankshaft dowel pin at 11 o'clock).

➡ **It may be necessary to rotate the camshafts slightly, to align the timing marks.**

Fig. 180 Position the 2 RH VCT assemblies and secondary timing chain onto the camshafts by aligning the holes in the VCT assemblies with the dowel pins in the camshafts

42. Install the primary timing chain with the colored links aligned with the timing marks on the VCT assemblies and the crankshaft sprocket.

43. Install the lower LH primary timing chain guide and the 2 bolts. Tighten to 89 inch lbs. (10 Nm).

44. Install the primary timing chain tensioner arm.

45. Reset the primary timing chain tensioner.

    a. Release the ratchet detent.

    b. Using a soft-jawed vise, compress the ratchet plunger.

    c. Align the hole in the ratchet plunger with the hole in the tensioner housing.

    d. Install a suitable lockpin.

➡ **It may be necessary to rotate the camshafts slightly to remove slack from the timing chain to install the tensioner.**

46. Install the primary tensioner and the 2 bolts.

    a. Tighten to 89 inch lbs. (10 Nm).

    b. Remove the lockpin.

47. As a post-check, verify correct alignment of all timing marks.

    a. There are 48 links in between the RH intake VCT assembly colored link and the LH intake VCT assembly colored link.

    b. There are 35 links in between LH intake VCT assembly colored link and the 2 crankshaft sprocket links.

✳✳ WARNING

Do not use excessive force when installing the Variable Camshaft Timing (VCT) oil control solenoid. Damage to the mega cap could cause the cylinder head to be inoperable. If difficult to install the VCT oil control solenoid, inspect the bore and VCT oil control solenoid to ensure there are no burrs, sharp edges or contaminants present on the mating surface. Only clean the external surfaces as necessary.

➡ **A slight twisting motion will aid in the installation of the VCT oil control solenoid.**

➡ **Keep the VCT oil control solenoid clean of dirt and debris.**

48. Install the LH intake VCT oil control solenoid and the bolt.

49. Tighten to 71 inch lbs. (8 Nm) then an additional 20 degrees.

✳✳ WARNING

Do not use excessive force when installing the Variable Camshaft Timing (VCT) oil control solenoid. Damage to the mega cap could cause the cylinder head to be inoperable. If difficult to install the VCT oil control solenoid, inspect the bore and VCT oil control solenoid to ensure there are no burrs, sharp edges or contaminants present on the mating surface. Only clean the external surfaces as necessary.

➡ **A slight twisting motion will aid in the installation of the VCT oil control solenoid.**

➡ **Keep the VCT oil control solenoid clean of dirt and debris.**

50. Install the RH intake VCT oil control solenoid and the bolt.

51. Tighten to 71 inch lbs. (8 Nm) then an additional 20 degrees.

52. Remove the RH Camshaft Holding Tool.

53. Install the RH valve train oil tube and the 3 bolts and tighten in 2 stages.

    a. Stage 1: Tighten to 71 inch lbs. (8 Nm).

    b. Stage 2: Tighten an additional 45 degrees.

54. Remove the LH Camshaft Holding Tool.

55. Install the LH valve train oil tube and the 3 bolts and tighten in 2 stages.

    a. Stage 1: Tighten to 71 inch lbs. (8 Nm).

    b. Stage 2: Tighten an additional 45 degrees.

56. Install the engine front cover.

5.0L Engine

Left Side

See Figures 181 through 195.

✳✳ WARNING

During engine repair procedures, cleanliness is extremely important. Any foreign material, including any material created while cleaning gasket surfaces, that enters the oil passages, coolant passages or the oil pan, can cause engine failure.

➡ **If the RH camshafts are being serviced at the same time as the LH camshafts, remove the RH camshafts first.**

➡ **If the components are to be reinstalled, they must be installed in their**

Fig. 181 Verify the data matrix on the camshafts is facing up, if not, rotate the crankshaft clockwise one revolution

original location. Mark the components for installation into their original location.

1. Remove the engine front cover. Refer to Timing Chain Front Cover.

2. Remove the LH intake and exhaust Camshaft Position (CMP) sensors.

3. Using the crankshaft holding tool, rotate the crankshaft clockwise until the keyway is at the 12 o'clock position.

4. Verify the data matrix on the camshafts is facing up, if not, rotate the crankshaft clockwise one revolution.

5. Remove the 2 bolts and the RH primary timing chain tensioner.

➡ **It may be necessary to rotate the crankshaft slightly to provide enough slack in the chain to remove the RH timing chain tensioner arm. Return the crankshaft keyway to the 12 o'clock position after removing the RH timing chain tensioner arm.**

6. Remove the RH timing chain tensioner arm.

➡ **It may be necessary to rotate the crankshaft slightly to provide enough slack in the chain to remove the RH timing chain guide. Return the crankshaft keyway to the 12 o'clock position after removing the RH timing chain guide.**

7. Remove the bolt and the RH timing chain guide.

8. Remove the RH primary timing chain.

9. Using the crankshaft holding tool, rotate the crankshaft counterclockwise until the crankshaft keyway is at the 9 o'clock position.

10. Remove the 2 bolts and the LH primary timing chain tensioner.

➡ **It may be necessary to rotate the crankshaft slightly to provide enough**

slack in the chain to remove the LH timing chain tensioner arm. Return the crankshaft keyway to the 9 o'clock position after removing the LH timing chain tensioner arm.

11. Remove the LH timing chain tensioner arm.

➡**It may be necessary to rotate the crankshaft slightly to provide enough slack in the chain to remove the LH timing chain guide. Return the crankshaft keyway to the 9 o'clock position after removing the LH timing chain guide.**

12. Remove the bolt and the LH timing chain guide.

13. Remove the LH primary timing chain.

14. Remove the 3 LH intake Variable Camshaft Timing (VCT) assembly bolts and the 3 LH exhaust VCT assembly bolts.

15. Slide the LH VCT assemblies and secondary timing chain forward 0.078 inches (2 mm).

16. Depress the LH secondary timing chain tensioner and turn the tensioner 90 degrees.

17. Remove the LH VCT assemblies and the LH secondary timing chain.

Fig. 182 Remove the 3 LH intake Variable Camshaft Timing (VCT) assembly bolts and the 3 LH exhaust VCT assembly bolts

Fig. 183 Slide the LH VCT assemblies and secondary timing chain forward

Fig. 184 Depress the LH secondary timing chain tensioner and turn the tensioner 90 degrees

Fig. 185 Remove the LH VCT assemblies and the LH secondary timing chain

Fig. 186 Remove the 4 bolts and the LH front camshaft bearing mega cap

➡**Intake camshaft shown, exhaust camshaft similar.**

18. Remove the VCT system oil filter from the intake and exhaust camshafts.

> ✴✴ **WARNING**
>
> **The front camshaft bearing mega cap must be removed first and then the remaining camshaft bearing caps. Failure to follow this direction may result in damage to the engine.**

19. Remove the 4 bolts and the LH front camshaft bearing mega cap.

Fig. 187 Install the LH intake and exhaust camshafts in the neutral position. Align the D-slots as shown

20. Remove the 16 bolts and the 8 camshaft bearing caps.

21. Remove the LH intake and exhaust camshafts.

To install:

➡**Lubricate the camshafts with clean engine oil prior to installation.**

22. Install the LH intake and exhaust camshafts in the neutral position. Align the D-slots as shown.

23. Install the 8 camshaft bearing caps and the 16 bolts. Do not tighten the bolts at this time.

24. Install the LH front camshaft bearing mega cap and the 4 bolts. Do not tighten the bolts at this time

25. Tighten the bolts in the sequence shown in 2 stages.

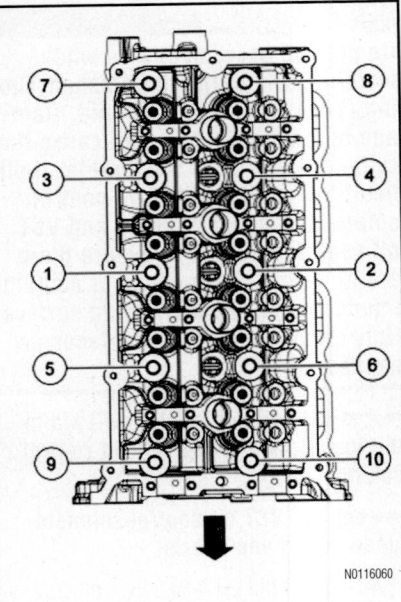

Fig. 188 Tighten the bolts in the sequence shown in 2 stages

a. Stage 1: Tighten to 53 inch lbs. (6 Nm).

b. Stage 2: Tighten an additional 45 degrees.

➡**Intake camshaft shown, exhaust camshaft similar.**

26. Install the VCT system oil filter in the intake and exhaust camshafts.

27. Install the secondary timing chain onto the LH VCT assemblies. Align the colored links on the secondary timing chain with the timing marks on the VCT assemblies as shown.

a. The timing mark on the intake VCT assembly should align between the 2 consecutive colored links.

b. The timing mark on the exhaust VCT assembly should align with the single colored link.

28. Install the LH VCT assemblies and the secondary timing chain onto the LH camshafts to a position 0.078 inches (2 mm) from fully seated. The timing mark on the exhaust VCT assembly should be in the 11 o'clock position.

➡**It may be necessary to rotate the exhaust camshaft slightly (using a wrench on the flats of the camshaft) to seat the VCT assemblies onto the camshafts.**

29. Rotate the secondary timing chain tensioner 90 degrees so the ramped area is facing forward and fully seat the VCT assemblies onto the camshafts.

30. If the secondary timing chain is not centered over the tensioner, reposition the VCT assemblies until they are fully seated on the camshafts.

➡**Use a wrench on the flats of the camshaft to hold the camshafts while tightening the VCT assembly bolts.**

31. Install the 3 LH intake VCT assembly bolts and the 3 LH exhaust VCT assembly bolts.

32. Tighten to 10 ft. lbs. (15 Nm) plus an additional 90 degrees.

33. Install the LH primary timing chain.

34. Align the colored link on the timing chain with the timing mark on the LH VCT assembly.

35. Align the remaining colored link on the timing chain with the timing mark on the crankshaft sprocket.

➡**It may be necessary to rotate the crankshaft slightly to provide enough slack in the chain to install the LH timing chain guide. Return the crankshaft keyway to the 9 o'clock position after installing the LH timing chain guide.**

36. Install the LH timing chain guide and bolt. Tighten to 89 inch lbs. (10 Nm).

➡**It may be necessary to rotate the crankshaft slightly to provide enough slack in the chain to install the LH timing chain tensioner arm. Return the crankshaft keyway to the 9 o'clock position after installing the LH timing chain tensioner arm.**

37. Install the LH timing chain tensioner arm.

➡**Complete the following 3 steps on both the LH and RH primary timing chain tensioners.**

❊❊ **WARNING**

Do not compress the ratchet assembly or damage to the tensioner will occur.

38. Compress the primary timing chain tensioner plunger, using an edge of a vise.

39. Using a small screwdriver or pick, push back and hold the ratchet mechanism, then push the ratchet arm back into the tensioner housing.

40. Install a suitable pin into the hole of the tensioner housing to hold the ratchet assembly and plunger in place during installation.

Fig. 189 Align the colored links on the secondary timing chain with the timing marks on the VCT assemblies as shown

Fig. 191 Align the colored link on the timing chain with the timing mark on the LH VCT assembly

Fig. 193 Align the colored link on the timing chain with the timing mark on the RH VCT assembly

Fig. 190 The timing mark on the exhaust VCT assembly should be in the 11 o'clock position

Fig. 192 Align the remaining colored link on the timing chain with the timing mark on the crankshaft sprocket

Fig. 194 Align the remaining colored link on the timing chain with the timing mark on the crankshaft sprocket

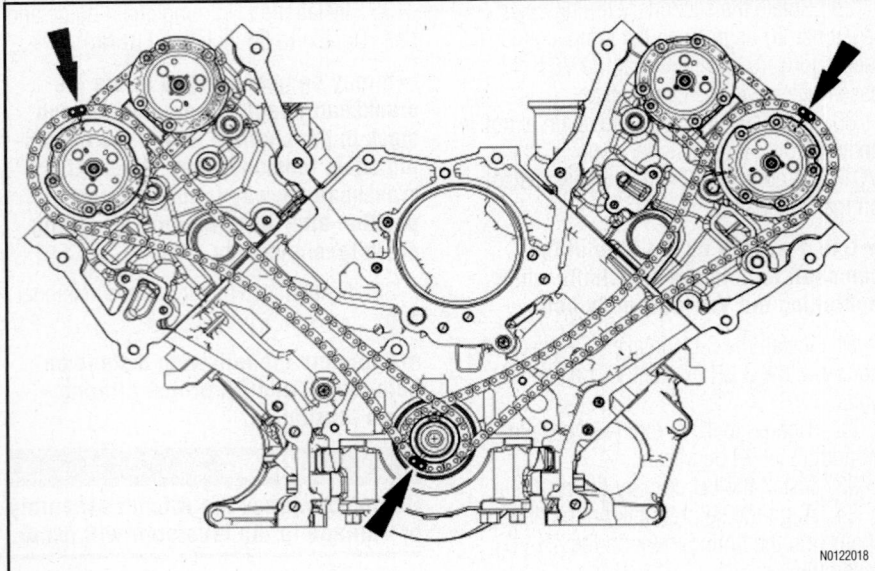

Fig. 195 With the crankshaft keyway still at the 12 o'clock position, verify the timing mark alignment is correct

41. Install the LH primary timing chain tensioner and 2 bolts.
   a. Tighten to 89 inch lbs. (10 Nm).
   b. Remove the holding pin from the tensioner.
42. Using the crankshaft holding tool, rotate the crankshaft clockwise until the crankshaft keyway is at the 12 o'clock position.
43. Install the RH primary timing chain.
44. Align the colored link on the timing chain with the timing mark on the RH VCT assembly.
45. Align the remaining colored link on the timing chain with the timing mark on the crankshaft sprocket.

➡It may be necessary to rotate the crankshaft slightly to provide enough slack in the chain to install the RH timing chain guide. Return the crankshaft keyway to the 12 o'clock position after installing the RH timing chain guide.

46. Install the RH timing chain guide and bolt. Tighten to 89 inch lbs. (10 Nm).

➡It may be necessary to rotate the crankshaft slightly to provide enough slack in the chain to install the RH timing chain tensioner arm. Return the crankshaft keyway to the 12 o'clock position after installing the RH timing chain tensioner arm.

47. Install the RH timing chain tensioner arm.
48. Install the RH primary timing chain tensioner and 2 bolts.

   a. Tighten to 89 inch lbs. (10 Nm).
   b. Remove the holding pin from the tensioner.
49. With the crankshaft keyway still at the 12 o'clock position, verify the timing mark alignment is correct.
50. Install the LH intake and exhaust CMP sensors.
51. Install the engine front cover.

Right Side
See Figures 181, 193, 194, 196 through 205.

✳✳ WARNING

During engine repair procedures, cleanliness is extremely important. Any foreign material, including any material created while cleaning gasket surfaces, that enters the oil passages, coolant passages or the oil pan, can cause engine failure.

➡If the components are to be reinstalled, they must be installed in their original location. Mark the components for installation into their original location.

1. Remove the engine front cover. Refer to Timing Chain Front Cover.
2. Remove the RH intake and exhaust Camshaft Position (CMP) sensors.
3. Using the crankshaft holding tool, rotate the crankshaft clockwise until the crankshaft keyway is at the 12 o'clock position.

4. Verify the data matrix on the camshafts is facing up, if not, rotate the crankshaft clockwise one revolution.
5. Remove the 2 bolts and the RH primary timing chain tensioner.

➡It may be necessary to rotate the crankshaft slightly to provide enough slack in the chain to remove the RH timing chain tensioner arm. Return the crankshaft keyway to the 12 o'clock position after removing the RH timing chain tensioner arm.

6. Remove the RH timing chain tensioner arm.

➡It may be necessary to rotate the crankshaft slightly to provide enough slack in the chain to remove the RH timing chain guide. Return the crankshaft keyway to the 12 o'clock position after removing the RH timing chain guide.

7. Remove the bolt and the RH timing chain guide.
8. Remove the RH primary timing chain.
9. Remove the 3 RH intake Variable Camshaft Timing (VCT) assembly bolts and the 3 RH exhaust VCT assembly bolts.

Fig. 196 Remove the 3 RH intake Variable Camshaft Timing (VCT) assembly bolts and the 3 RH exhaust VCT assembly bolts

Fig. 197 Slide the RH VCT assemblies and secondary timing chain forward

10. Slide the RH VCT assemblies and secondary timing chain forward 0.078 inches (2 mm).

11. Depress the RH secondary timing chain tensioner and turn the tensioner 90 degrees.

12. Remove the RH VCT assemblies and the RH secondary timing chain.

➡**Intake camshaft shown, exhaust camshaft similar.**

13. Remove the VCT system oil filter from the intake and exhaust camshafts.

✳✳ WARNING

The front camshaft bearing mega cap must be removed first and then the remaining camshaft bearing caps. Failure to follow this direction may result in damage to the engine.

14. Remove the 4 bolts and the RH front camshaft bearing mega cap.

15. Remove the 16 bolts and the 8 camshaft bearing caps.

16. Remove the RH intake and exhaust camshafts.

Fig. 198 Depress the RH secondary timing chain tensioner and turn the tensioner 90 degrees

Fig. 199 Remove the RH VCT assemblies and the RH secondary timing chain

Fig. 200 Remove the VCT system oil filter from the intake and exhaust camshafts

Fig. 201 Remove the 4 bolts and the RH front camshaft bearing mega cap

To install:

➡**Lubricate the camshafts with clean engine oil prior to installation.**

17. Install the RH intake and exhaust camshafts in the neutral position. Align the D-slots as shown.

18. Install the 8 camshaft bearing caps and the 16 bolts. Do not tighten the bolts at this time.

19. Install the RH front camshaft bearing mega cap and the 4 bolts. Do not tighten at this time

20. Tighten the bolts in the sequence shown in 2 stages.

Fig. 202 Install the RH intake and exhaust camshafts in the neutral position. Align the D-slots as shown

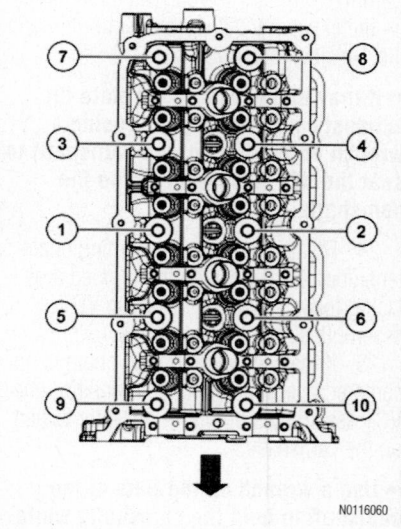

Fig. 203 Tighten the bolts in the sequence shown in 2 stages

a. Stage 1: Tighten to 53 inch lbs. (6 Nm).

b. Stage 2: Tighten an additional 45 degrees.

➡**Intake camshaft shown, exhaust camshaft similar.**

21. Install the VCT system oil filter in the intake and exhaust camshafts.

22. Install the secondary timing chain onto the RH VCT assemblies. Align the colored links on the secondary timing chain with the timing marks on the VCT assemblies as shown.

a. The timing mark on the intake VCT assembly should align between the 2 consecutive colored links.

b. The timing mark on the exhaust VCT assembly should align with the single colored link.

23. Install the RH VCT assemblies and the secondary timing chain onto the RH camshafts to a position 0.078 inches

Fig. 204 Align the colored links on the secondary timing chain with the timing marks on the VCT assemblies as shown

(2 mm) from fully seated. The timing mark on the exhaust VCT assembly should be in the 1 o'clock position.

➡ **It may be necessary to rotate the exhaust camshaft slightly (using a wrench on the flats of the camshaft) to seat the VCT assemblies onto the camshafts.**

24. Rotate the secondary timing chain tensioner 90 degrees so the ramped area is facing forward and fully seat the VCT assemblies onto the camshafts.

25. If the secondary timing chain is not centered over the tensioner, reposition the VCT assemblies until they are fully seated on the camshafts.

➡ **Use a wrench on the flats of the camshaft to hold the camshafts while tightening the VCT assembly bolts.**

26. Install the 3 RH intake VCT assembly bolts and the 3 RH exhaust VCT assembly bolts.

27. Tighten to 10 ft. lbs. (15 Nm) plus an additional 90 degrees.

28. Install the RH primary timing chain.

29. Align the colored link on the timing chain with the timing mark on the RH VCT assembly.

30. Align the remaining colored link on the timing chain with the timing mark on the crankshaft sprocket.

➡ **It may be necessary to rotate the crankshaft slightly to provide enough slack in the chain to install the RH timing chain guide. Return the crankshaft keyway to the 12 o'clock position after installing the RH timing chain guide.**

31. Install the RH timing chain guide and bolt. Tighten to 89 inch lbs. (10 Nm).

➡ **It may be necessary to rotate the crankshaft slightly to provide enough slack in the chain to install the RH timing chain tensioner arm. Return the**

crankshaft keyway to the 12 o'clock position after installing the RH timing chain tensioner arm.

32. Install the RH timing chain tensioner arm.

☼ WARNING

Do not compress the ratchet assembly or damage to the tensioner will occur.

33. Compress the primary timing chain tensioner plunger, using an edge of a vise.

34. Using a small screwdriver or pick, push back and hold the ratchet mechanism, then push the ratchet arm back into the tensioner housing.

35. Install a suitable pin into the hole of the tensioner housing to hold the ratchet assembly and plunger in place during installation.

36. Install the RH primary timing chain tensioner and 2 bolts.
   a. Tighten to 89 inch lbs. (10 Nm).
   b. Remove the holding pin from the tensioner.

37. Install the RH intake and exhaust CMP sensors.

38. Install the engine front cover.

4.6L (2V) Engine
See Figures 206 through 211.

1. Remove the timing drive components.

2. Install the Valve Spring Compressor Spacer between the valve spring coils to protect the valve stem seal from damage.

☼☼ WARNING

The camshaft roller followers must be installed in their original locations. Record the camshaft roller follower locations. Failure to follow these instructions may result in engine damage.

➡ **The 3 rearmost camshaft roller followers on the RH side must use Valve Spring Compressor 303-567 in the same manner.**

➡ **Do not allow the valve keepers to fall off the valve or the valve may drop into the cylinder. If a valve drops into the cylinder, the cylinder head must be removed.**

➡ **It may be necessary to push the valve down while compressing the spring.**

3. Using the Valve Spring Compressor (303-452), compress the valve spring and remove the camshaft roller follower.

4. Remove the bolt, camshaft sprocket and camshaft sprocket spacer from the camshaft being serviced.

5. Remove the Camshaft Aligner (303-380), and Camshaft Pulley Aligner (303-413) from the camshaft being serviced.

6. Remove the 13 bolts, 2 camshaft bearing caps and the camshaft.

7. Clean and inspect the camshaft bearing caps. One of the bearing caps contains an oil flow restriction groove.

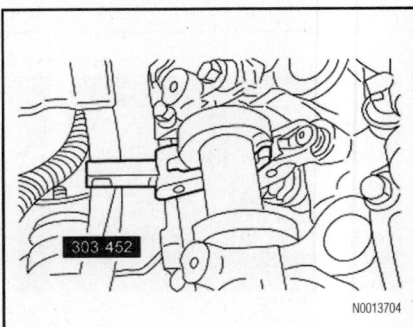

Fig. 207 Using the Valve Spring Compressor, compress the valve spring and remove the camshaft roller follower

Fig. 205 The timing mark on the exhaust VCT assembly should be in the 1 o'clock position

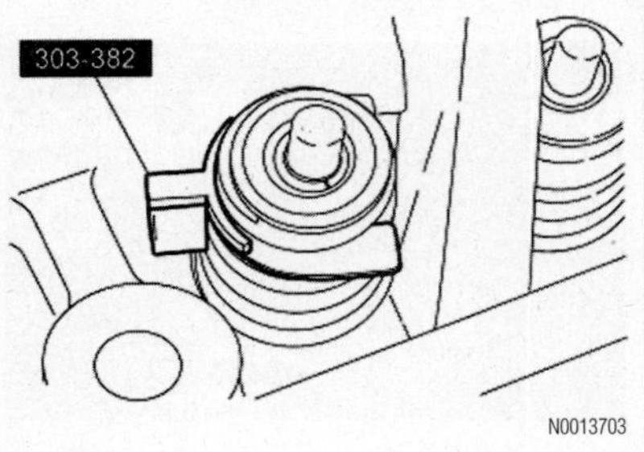

Fig. 206 Install the Valve Spring Compressor Spacer between the valve spring coils to protect the valve stem seal from damage

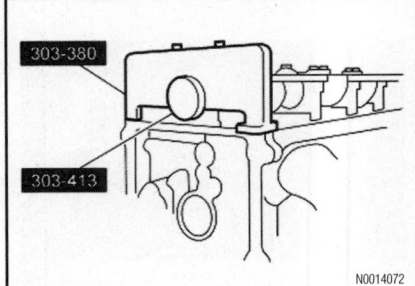

Fig. 208 Remove the Camshaft Aligner and Camshaft Pulley Aligner from the camshaft being serviced

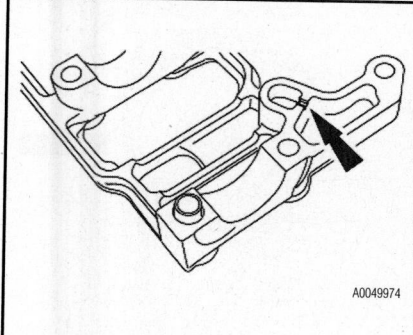

Fig. 209 Clean and inspect the camshaft bearing caps

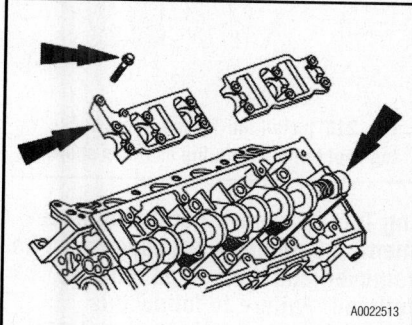

Fig. 210 Install the camshaft and the camshaft bearing caps in their original locations

Make sure the groove is free of foreign material.

To install:

8. Install the camshaft and the camshaft bearing caps in their original locations.

   a. Lubricate the camshaft with clean engine oil.

   b. Position the camshaft.

   c. Lubricate the camshaft bearing caps with clean engine oil.

   d. Position the 2 camshaft bearing caps.

   e. Install the 13 bolts loosely.

9. Tighten the 13 bolts in the sequence shown. Tighten to 89 inch lbs. (10 Nm).

10. Install the Camshaft Aligner and Camshaft Pulley Aligner on the camshaft being serviced.

11. Install the camshaft sprocket spacer, camshaft sprocket, washer and bolt onto the camshaft being serviced. Tighten the camshaft sprocket bolt in 2 stages:

   a. Stage 1: Tighten to 30 ft. lbs. (40 Nm).

   b. Stage 2: Tighten an additional 90 degrees.

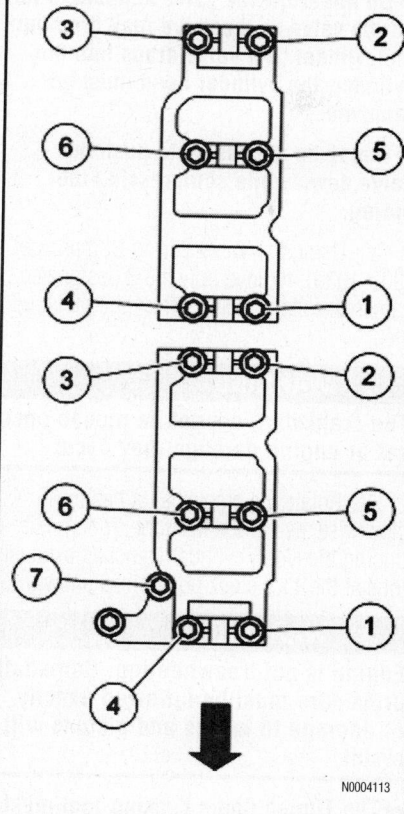

Fig. 211 Tighten the 13 bolts in the sequence shown

12. Install the Valve Spring Compressor Spacer between the valve spring coils to protect the valve stem seal from damage.

✳✳ WARNING

The camshaft roller followers must be installed in their original locations. Failure to follow this instruction may result in engine damage.

➡ The 3 rearmost camshaft roller followers on the RH side must use Valve Spring Compressor 303-567 in the same manner.

➡ Do not allow the valve keepers to fall off the valve or the valve may drop into the cylinder. If a valve drops into the cylinder, the cylinder head must be removed.

➡ It may be necessary to push the valve down while compressing the spring.

➡ Lubricate the camshaft roller followers with clean engine oil prior to installation.

13. Using the Valve Spring Compressor, compress the valve springs and install the camshaft roller followers.

14. Install the timing drive components.

4.6L (3V) Engine

Left Side

See Figures 212 through 222.

✳✳ WARNING

The camshaft procedure must be followed exactly or damage to the valves and pistons will result.

1. Remove the LH valve cover.

✳✳ WARNING

Damage to the camshaft phaser and sprocket assembly will occur if mishandled or used as a lifting or leveraging device.

2. Loosen and back off the LH camshaft phaser and sprocket bolt one full turn.

3. Disconnect the LH Camshaft Position (CMP) sensor electrical connector.

4. Remove the LH CMP sensor and the bolt.

5. Rotate the crankshaft clockwise until the No. 5 cylinder camshaft exhaust lobe opens the valve and the 2 intake lobes are in the 3 o'clock position as shown.

6. Remove only the 3 camshaft roller followers shown.

✳✳ WARNING

The camshaft roller followers must be installed in their original locations. Record camshaft roller follower locations. Failure to follow these instructions may result in engine damage.

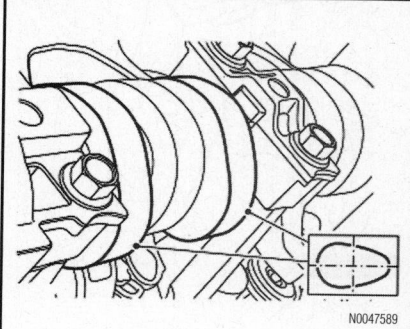

Fig. 212 Rotate the crankshaft clockwise until the No. 5 cylinder camshaft exhaust lobe opens the valve and the 2 intake lobes are in the 3 o'clock position as shown

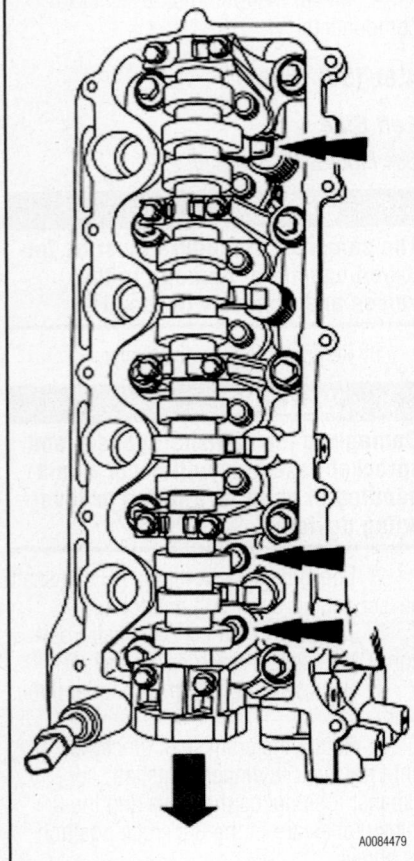

Fig. 213 Remove only the 3 camshaft roller followers shown

Fig. 214 Using the Valve Spring Compressor, remove only the 3 designated camshaft roller followers from the previous step

➡ Do not allow the valve keepers to fall off the valve or the valve may drop into the cylinder. If a valve drops into the cylinder, the cylinder head must be removed.

➡ It may be necessary to push the valve down while compressing the spring.

7. Using the Valve Spring Compressor (303-1039), remove only the 3 designated camshaft roller followers from the previous step.

❋❋ WARNING

The crankshaft cannot be moved once set or engine damage may occur.

8. Rotate the crankshaft a half turn clockwise, as viewed from the front, positioning the No. 5 cylinder camshaft exhaust lobe at the 11 o'clock position as shown.

❋❋ WARNING

Engine is not freewheeling. Camshaft procedure must be followed exactly or damage to valves and pistons will result.

➡ The Timing Chain Locking Tool must be installed square to the timing chain and the engine block.

➡ Engine front cover removed from art for clarity.

9. Install the Timing Chain Locking Tool (303-1175) in the LH timing chain as shown.

❋❋ WARNING

Do not remove the Timing Chain Locking Tool at any time during assembly. If the Timing Chain Lock-

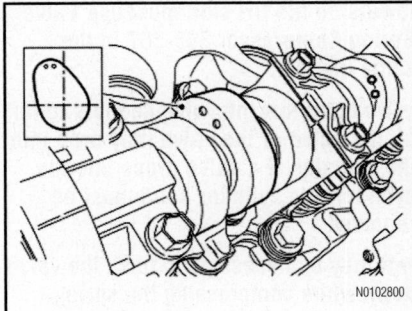

Fig. 215 Rotate the crankshaft a half turn clockwise, as viewed from the front, positioning the No. 5 cylinder camshaft exhaust lobe at the 11 o'clock position as shown

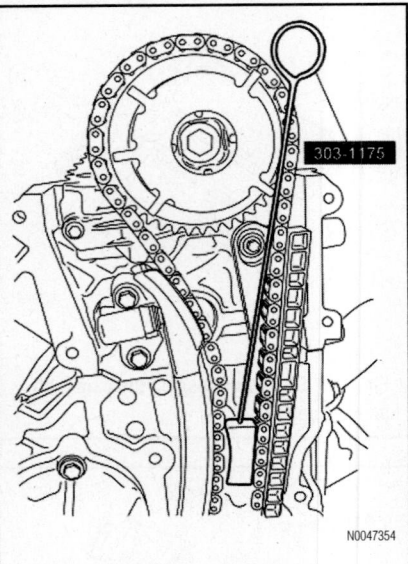

Fig. 216 Install the Timing Chain Locking Tool in the LH timing chain as shown

ing Tool is removed or out of placement, the engine front cover must be removed and the engine must be retimed. Failure to follow this instruction can result in damage to the valves and pistons.

❋❋ WARNING

The timing chain must be installed in its original position onto the camshaft phaser and sprocket using the scribed marks, or damage to valves and pistons will result.

10. Scribe a location mark on the timing chain and the camshaft phaser and sprocket assembly.

❋❋ WARNING

Remove the front thrust camshaft bearing cap straight upward from

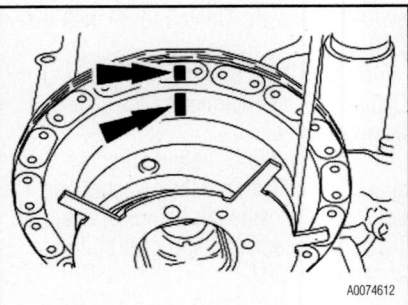

Fig. 217 Scribe a location mark on the timing chain and the camshaft phaser and sprocket assembly

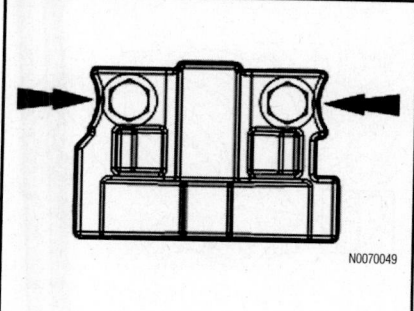

Fig. 218 Remove the 2 bolts and the LH cylinder head camshaft front bearing cap

the bearing towers or the bearing cap may be damaged from side loading.

11. Remove the 2 bolts and the LH cylinder head camshaft front bearing cap.

✳✳ WARNING

The camshaft bearing caps must be installed in their original locations. Record camshaft bearing cap locations. Failure to follow these instructions may result in engine damage.

12. Remove the remaining bolts in the sequence shown and remove the LH cylinder head camshaft bearing caps.

13. Clean and inspect the LH camshaft bearing caps. The camshaft front thrust bearing cap contains an oil metering groove. Make sure the groove is free of foreign material.

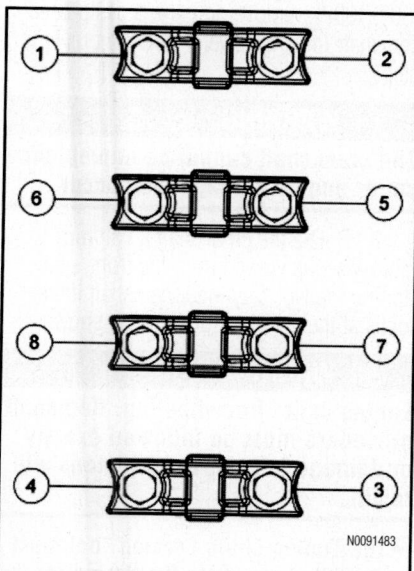

Fig. 219 Remove the remaining bolts in the sequence shown

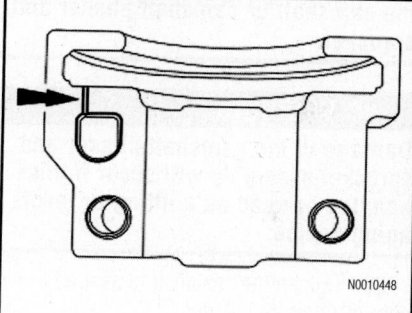

Fig. 220 Make sure the groove is free of foreign material

✳✳ WARNING

Damage to the camshaft phaser and sprocket assembly will occur if mishandled or used as a lifting or leveraging device.

✳✳ WARNING

Only use hand tools to remove the camshaft phaser and sprocket bolt or damage may occur to the camshaft or camshaft phaser and sprocket.

✳✳ WARNING

Do not remove the Timing Chain Locking Tool at any time during assembly. If the Timing Chain Locking Tool is removed or out of placement, the engine front cover must be removed and the engine must be retimed. Failure to follow this instruction can result in damage to the valves and pistons.

14. Remove the bolt and the camshaft phaser and sprocket assembly from the camshaft.

15. Discard the bolt and washer.

16. Remove the camshaft.

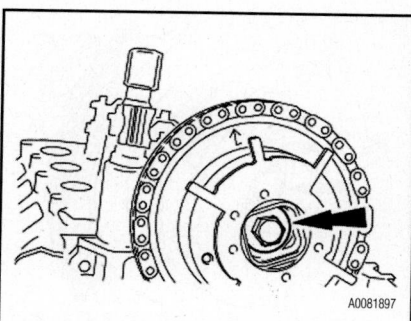

Fig. 221 Remove the bolt and the camshaft phaser and sprocket assembly from the camshaft

17. Remove and inspect the camshaft phaser and sprocket for damage.

To install:

➡ **Do not allow the camshaft roller followers to move out of position when installing the camshaft.**

18. Lubricate the camshaft and camshaft journals with clean engine oil and install the camshaft.

✳✳ WARNING

Do not remove the Timing Chain Locking Tool at any time during assembly. If the Timing Chain Locking Tool is removed or out of placement, the engine front cover must be removed and the engine must be retimed. Failure to follow this instruction can result in damage to the valves and pistons.

✳✳ WARNING

The timing chain must be installed in its original position onto the camshaft phaser and sprocket using the scribed marks, or damage to valves and pistons will result.

➡ **If replacement of the camshaft phaser and sprocket is necessary, transfer the scribe mark to the new camshaft phaser and sprocket.**

19. Position the camshaft phaser and sprocket into the timing chain with the timing chain scribe marks in alignment.

✳✳ WARNING

Do not remove the Timing Chain Locking Tool at any time during assembly. If the Timing Chain Locking Tool is removed or out of placement, the engine front cover must be removed and the engine must be retimed.

✳✳ WARNING

Damage to the camshaft phaser and sprocket assembly will occur if mishandled or used as a lifting or leveraging device.

20. Install the camshaft phaser and sprocket assembly onto the camshaft and install a new camshaft phaser and sprocket bolt finger-tight.

21. Install the camshaft bearing caps in their original locations.

a. Lubricate the camshaft bearing caps with clean engine oil.

b. Position the front camshaft bearing cap.

c. Position the remaining camshaft bearing caps.

d. Install the bolts loosely.

22. Tighten the bolts in the sequence shown. Tighten to 89 inch lbs. (10 Nm).

➡**Engine front cover removed from art for clarity.**

23. Remove the Timing Chain Locking Tool.

24. Rotate the crankshaft a half turn counterclockwise until the No. 5 cylinder camshaft exhaust lobe opens the valve and the 2 intake lobes are in the 3 o'clock position.

➡**Do not allow the valve keepers to fall off of the valve or the valve may drop into the cylinder. If a valve drops into the cylinder, the cylinder head must be removed.**

➡**It may be necessary to push the valve down while compressing the spring.**

25. Using the Valve Spring Compressor, install the 3 originally removed camshaft roller followers.

26. Install the CMP sensor and the bolt. Tighten to 89 inch lbs. (10 Nm).

27. Connect the CMP electrical connector.

❊❊ WARNING

Only use hand tools to install the camshaft phaser and sprocket assembly or damage may occur to

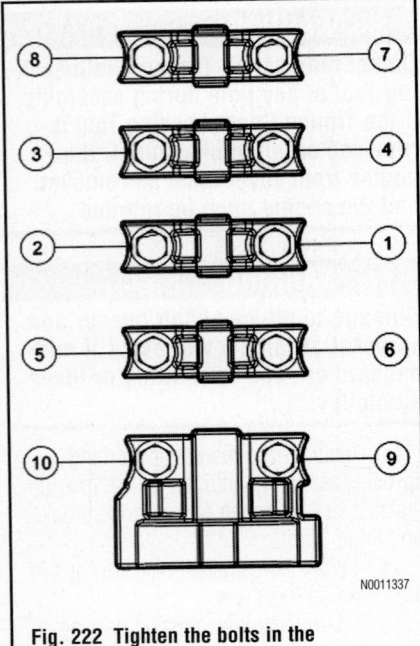

Fig. 222 Tighten the bolts in the sequence shown

the camshaft or camshaft phaser and sprocket.

❊❊ WARNING

Damage to the camshaft phaser and sprocket assembly will occur if mishandled or used as a lifting or leveraging device.

28. Tighten the camshaft phaser and sprocket bolt in 2 stages:

a. Stage 1: Tighten to 30 ft. lbs. (40 Nm).

b. Stage 2: Tighten an additional 90 degrees.

29. Install the LH valve cover.

Right Side

See Figures 222 through 233.

❊❊ WARNING

The camshaft procedure must be followed exactly or damage to the valves and pistons will result.

1. Remove the RH valve cover.

❊❊ WARNING

Damage to the camshaft phaser and sprocket assembly will occur if mishandled or used as a lifting or leveraging device.

2. Loosen and back off the RH camshaft phaser and sprocket bolt one full turn.

3. Disconnect the RH Camshaft Position (CMP) sensor electrical connector.

4. Remove the bolt and the RH CMP sensor.

5. Rotate the crankshaft clockwise until the No. 1 cylinder camshaft exhaust lobe is coming up on the exhaust stroke and the 2 intake lobes are positioned between 10 and 11 o'clock as shown.

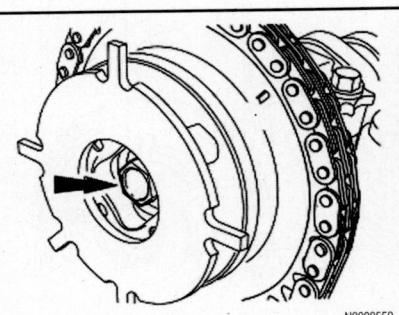

Fig. 223 Loosen and back off the RH camshaft phaser and sprocket bolt one full turn

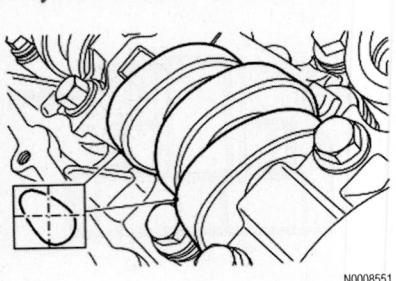

Fig. 224 Rotate the crankshaft clockwise until the No. 1 cylinder camshaft exhaust lobe is coming up on the exhaust stroke and the 2 intake lobes are positioned between 10 and 11 o'clock as shown

6. Remove only the 3 camshaft roller followers shown.

❊❊ WARNING

The camshaft roller followers must be installed in their original locations. Record camshaft roller follower locations. Failure to follow these instructions may result in engine damage.

➡**Do not allow the valve keepers to fall off the valve or the valve may drop into the cylinder. If a valve drops into the cylinder, the cylinder head must be removed.**

➡**It may be necessary to push the valve down while compressing the spring.**

7. Using the Valve Spring Compressor (303-1039), remove only the 3 designated camshaft roller followers from the previous step.

❊❊ WARNING

The crankshaft cannot be moved once set or engine damage may occur.

8. Rotate the crankshaft a half turn clockwise, as viewed from the front, positioning the No. 1 cylinder camshaft intake lobes at the 1 o'clock position as shown.

❊❊ WARNING

Engine is not freewheeling. Camshaft procedure must be followed exactly or damage to valves and pistons will result.

➡**The Timing Chain Locking Tool must be installed square to the timing chain and the engine block.**

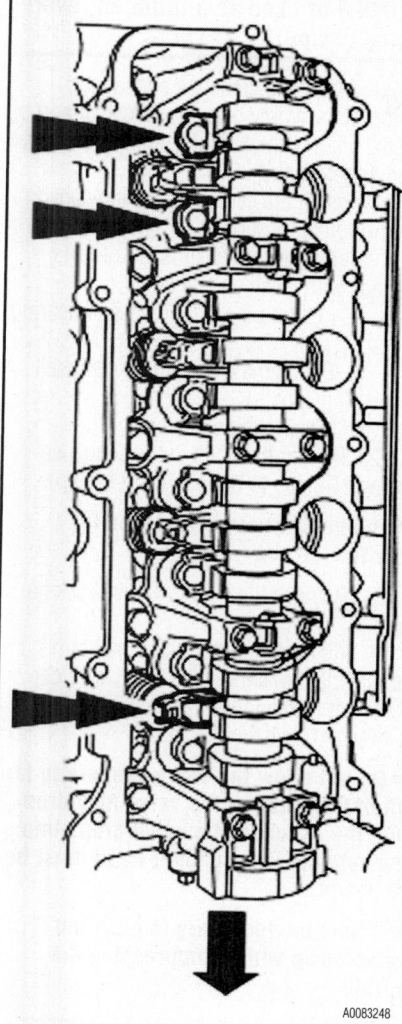

Fig. 225 Remove only the 3 camshaft roller followers shown

➡ **Engine front cover removed for clarity.**

9. Install the Timing Chain Locking Tool (303-1175) in the RH timing chain as shown.

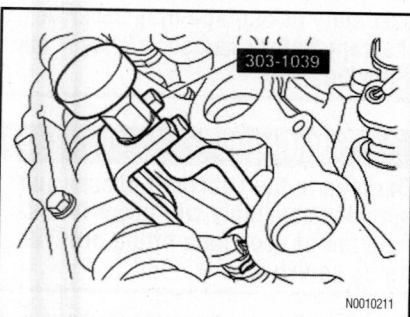

Fig. 226 Using the Valve Spring Compressor, remove only the 3 designated camshaft roller followers from the previous step

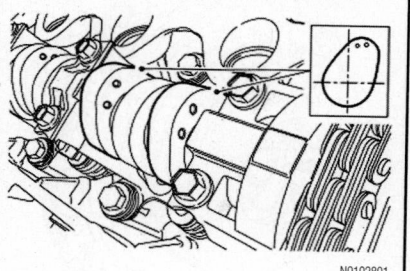

Fig. 227 Rotate the crankshaft a half turn clockwise, as viewed from the front, positioning the No. 1 cylinder camshaft intake lobes at the 1 o'clock position as shown

※※ **WARNING**

Do not remove the Timing Chain Locking Tool at any time during assembly. If the Timing Chain Locking Tool is removed or out of placement, the engine front cover must be removed and the engine must be retimed.

※※ **WARNING**

The timing chain must be installed in its original position onto the camshaft phaser and sprocket using the scribed marks, or damage to valves and pistons will result.

10. Scribe a location mark on the timing chain and the camshaft phaser and sprocket assembly.

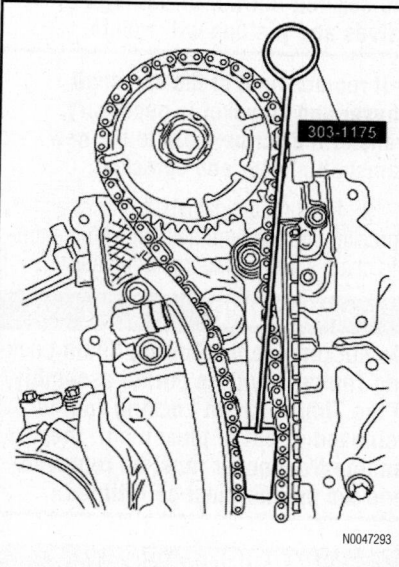

Fig. 228 Install the Timing Chain Locking Tool in the RH timing chain as shown

Fig. 229 Scribe a location mark on the timing chain and the camshaft phaser and sprocket assembly

※※ **WARNING**

Remove the front thrust camshaft bearing cap straight upward from the bearing towers or the bearing cap may be damaged from side loading.

11. Remove the 2 bolts and the RH cylinder head camshaft front bearing cap.

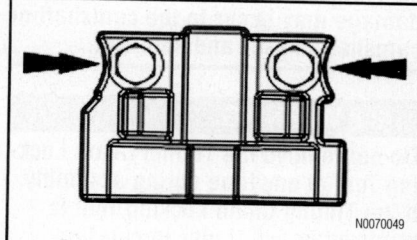

Fig. 230 Remove the 2 bolts and the RH cylinder head camshaft front bearing cap

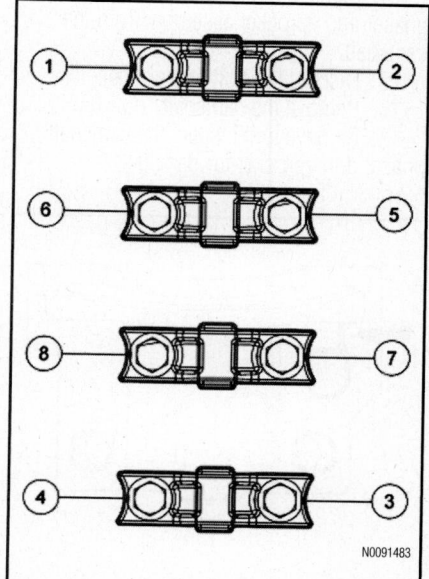

Fig. 231 Remove the remaining bolts in the sequence shown

> ※※ **WARNING**
>
> The camshaft bearing caps must be installed in their original locations. Record camshaft bearing cap locations. Failure to follow these instructions may result in engine damage.

12. Remove the remaining bolts in the sequence shown and remove the RH cylinder head camshaft bearing caps.

13. Clean and inspect the RH camshaft bearing caps. The camshaft front thrust bearing cap contains an oil metering groove. Make sure the groove is free of foreign material.

> ※※ **WARNING**
>
> Damage to the camshaft phaser and sprocket assembly will occur if mishandled or used as a lifting or leveraging device.

> ※※ **WARNING**
>
> Only use hand tools to remove the camshaft phaser and sprocket bolt or damage may occur to the camshaft or camshaft phaser and sprocket.

> ※※ **WARNING**
>
> Do not remove the Timing Chain Locking Tool at any time during assembly. If the Timing Chain Locking Tool is removed or out of placement, the engine front cover must be removed and the engine must be retimed.

14. Remove the bolt and the camshaft phaser and sprocket assembly from the camshaft.

15. Discard the bolt and washer.

16. Remove the camshaft.

17. Remove and inspect the camshaft phaser and sprocket for damage.

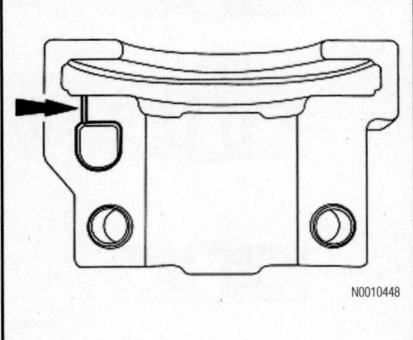

Fig. 232 Make sure the groove is free of foreign material

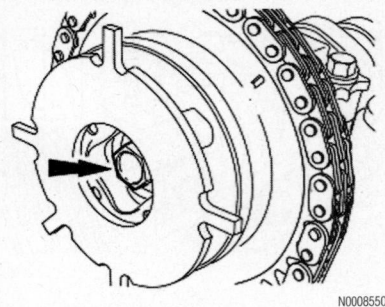

Fig. 233 Remove the bolt and the camshaft phaser and sprocket assembly from the camshaft

To install:

➡ Do not allow the camshaft roller followers to move out of position when installing the camshaft.

18. Lubricate the camshaft and camshaft journals with clean engine oil and install the camshaft.

> ※※ **WARNING**
>
> Do not remove the Timing Chain Locking Tool at any time during assembly. If the Timing Chain Locking Tool is removed or out of placement, the engine front cover must be removed and the engine must be retimed.

> ※※ **WARNING**
>
> The timing chain must be installed in its original position onto the camshaft phaser and sprocket using the scribed marks, or damage to valves and pistons will result.

➡ If replacement of the camshaft phaser and sprocket is necessary, transfer the scribe mark to the new camshaft phaser and sprocket.

19. Position the camshaft phaser and sprocket into the timing chain with the timing chain scribe marks in alignment.

> ※※ **WARNING**
>
> Do not remove the Timing Chain Locking Tool at any time during assembly. If the Timing Chain Locking Tool is removed or out of placement, the engine front cover must be removed and the engine must be retimed.

> ※※ **WARNING**
>
> Damage to the camshaft phaser and sprocket assembly will occur if mis-

handled or used as a lifting or leveraging device.

20. Install the camshaft phaser and sprocket assembly onto the camshaft and install a new camshaft phaser and sprocket bolt finger-tight.

21. Install the camshaft bearing caps in their original locations.

  a. Lubricate the camshaft bearing caps with clean engine oil.

  b. Position the front camshaft bearing cap.

  c. Position the remaining camshaft bearing caps.

  d. Install the bolts loosely.

22. Tighten the bolts in the sequence shown. Tighten to 89 inch lbs. (10 Nm).

➡ Engine front cover removed for clarity.

23. Remove the Timing Chain Locking Tool.

24. Rotate the crankshaft a half turn counterclockwise until the No. 1 cylinder camshaft intake lobes are positioned between 10 and 11 o'clock.

➡ Do not allow the valve keepers to fall off of the valve or the valve may drop into the cylinder. If a valve drops into the cylinder, the cylinder head must be removed.

➡ It may be necessary to push the valve down while compressing the spring.

25. Using the Valve Spring Compressor, install the 3 originally removed camshaft roller followers.

26. Install the CMP sensor and the bolt. Tighten to 89 inch lbs. (10 Nm).

27. Connect the CMP electrical connector.

> ※※ **WARNING**
>
> Only use hand tools to install the camshaft phaser and sprocket assembly or damage may occur to the camshaft or camshaft phaser and sprocket.

> ※※ **WARNING**
>
> Damage to the camshaft phaser and sprocket assembly will occur if mishandled or used as a lifting or leveraging device.

28. Tighten the new camshaft phaser and sprocket bolt in 2 stages:

  a. Stage 1: Tighten to 30 ft. lbs. (40 Nm).

b. Stage 2: Tighten an additional 90 degrees.

29. Install the RH valve cover.

5.4L (3V) Engine

Left Side

See Figures 234 through 244.

> ✳✳ **WARNING**
>
> **The camshaft procedure must be followed exactly or damage to the valves and pistons will result.**

1. Position the crankshaft damper spoke at the 12 o'clock position and the timing mark indentation at the 1 o'clock position.

2. Remove the LH valve cover.

> ✳✳ **WARNING**
>
> **Damage to the camshaft phaser and sprocket assembly will occur if mishandled or used as a lifting or leveraging device.**

> ✳✳ **WARNING**
>
> **Only use hand tools to remove the camshaft phaser and sprocket assembly or damage may occur to the camshaft or camshaft phaser and sprocket.**

3. Loosen and back off the LH camshaft phaser and sprocket bolt one full turn.

4. Disconnect the LH Camshaft Position (CMP) sensor electrical connector.

5. Remove the bolt and the LH CMP sensor.

➡ **If the camshaft lobes are not exactly positioned as shown, the crankshaft keyway will require one full additional rotation to 12 o'clock.**

6. The No. 5 cylinder camshaft lobe must be coming up on the exhaust stroke.

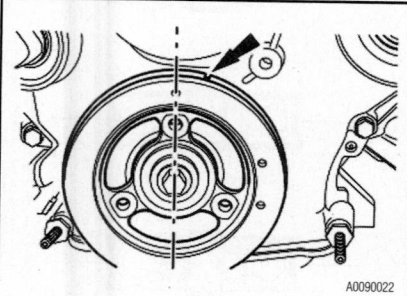

Fig. 234 Position the crankshaft damper spoke at the 12 o'clock position and the timing mark indentation at the 1 o'clock position

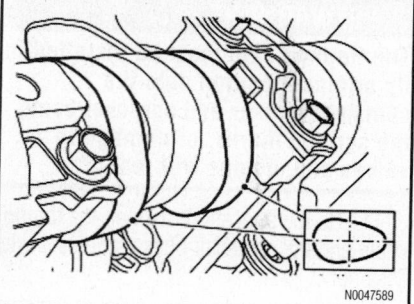

Fig. 235 Verify by noting the position of the 2 intake camshaft lobes and the exhaust lobe on the No. 5 cylinder

Verify by noting the position of the 2 intake camshaft lobes and the exhaust lobe on the No. 5 cylinder.

7. Remove only the 3 camshaft roller followers shown.

> ✳✳ **WARNING**
>
> **The camshaft roller followers must be installed in their original loca-**

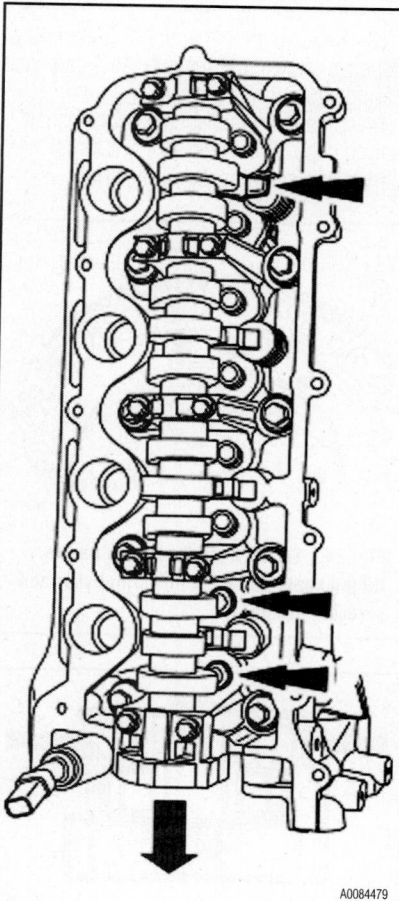

Fig. 236 Remove only the 3 camshaft roller followers shown

tions. Record camshaft roller follower locations. Failure to follow these instructions may result in engine damage.

➡ **Do not allow the valve keepers to fall off of the valve or the valve may drop into the cylinder. If a valve drops into the cylinder, the cylinder head must be removed.**

➡ **It may be necessary to push the valve down while compressing the spring.**

8. Using the Valve Spring Compressor (303-1039), remove only the 3 designated camshaft roller followers from the previous step.

> ✳✳ **WARNING**
>
> **The crankshaft cannot be moved past the 6 o'clock position once set or engine damage may occur.**

9. Rotate the crankshaft clockwise, as viewed from the front, positioning the crankshaft damper spoke at the 6 o'clock position and the timing mark indentation at the 7 o'clock position.

> ✳✳ **WARNING**
>
> **Engine is not freewheeling. Camshaft procedure must be followed exactly or damage to valves and pistons will result.**

Fig. 237 Using the Valve Spring Compressor, remove only the 3 designated camshaft roller followers from the previous step

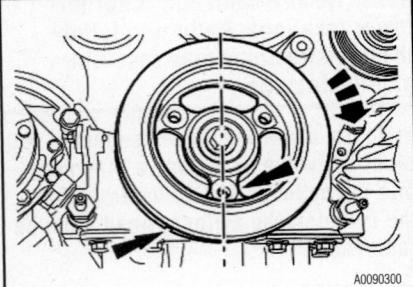

Fig. 238 Rotate the crankshaft clockwise, as viewed from the front, positioning the crankshaft damper spoke at the 6 o'clock position and the timing mark indentation at the 7 o'clock position

➡The Timing Chain Locking Tool must be installed square to the timing chain and the engine block.

➡Engine front cover removed for clarity.

10. Install the Timing Chain Locking Tool (303-1175) in the LH timing chain as shown.

⁕⁕ WARNING

Do not remove the Timing Chain Locking Tool at any time during assembly. If the Timing Chain Locking Tool is removed or out of placement, the engine front cover must be removed and the engine must be retimed.

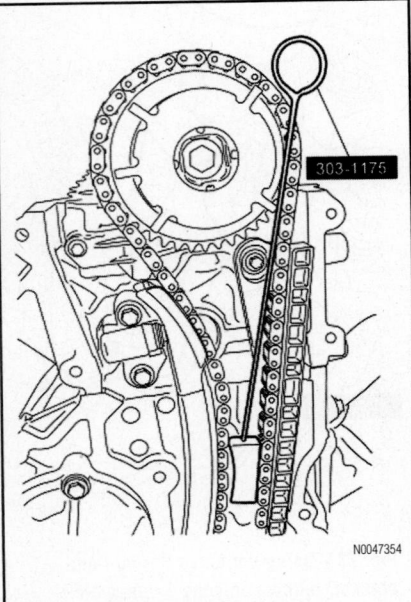

Fig. 239 Install the Timing Chain Locking Tool in the LH timing chain as shown

⁕⁕ WARNING

The timing chain must be installed in its original position onto the camshaft phaser and sprocket using the scribed marks, or damage to valves and pistons will result.

11. Scribe a location mark on the timing chain and the camshaft phaser and sprocket assembly.

⁕⁕ WARNING

Remove the front thrust camshaft bearing cap straight upward from the bearing towers or the bearing cap may be damaged from side loading.

12. Remove the 2 bolts and the LH camshaft front bearing cap.

⁕⁕ WARNING

The camshaft bearing caps must be installed in their original locations. Record camshaft bearing cap locations. Failure to follow these instructions may result in engine damage.

13. Remove the remaining 8 bolts in the sequence shown and remove the 4 camshaft bearing caps.

14. Clean and inspect the LH camshaft bearing caps. The camshaft front thrust bearing cap contains an oil metering

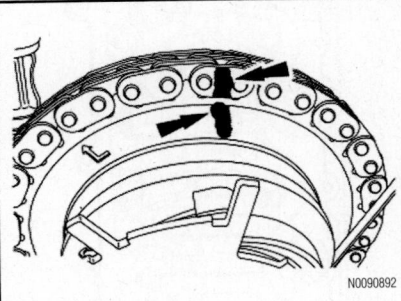

Fig. 240 Scribe a location mark on the timing chain and the camshaft phaser and sprocket assembly

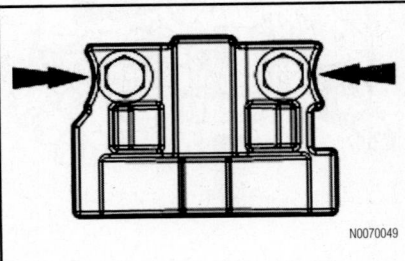

Fig. 241 Remove the 2 bolts and the LH camshaft front bearing cap

groove. Make sure the groove is free of foreign material.

⁕⁕ WARNING

Damage to the camshaft phaser and sprocket assembly will occur if mishandled or used as a lifting or leveraging device.

⁕⁕ WARNING

Only use hand tools to remove the camshaft phaser and sprocket bolt or damage may occur to the camshaft or camshaft phaser and sprocket.

⁕⁕ WARNING

Do not remove the Timing Chain Locking Tool at any time during assembly. If the Timing Chain Locking Tool is removed or out of placement, the engine front cover must be removed and the engine must be retimed.

15. Remove the bolt and the camshaft phaser and sprocket assembly from the camshaft.
16. Discard the bolt and washer.
17. Remove the camshaft.
18. Remove and inspect the camshaft phaser and sprocket for damage.

To install:

➡Do not allow the camshaft roller followers to move out of position when installing the camshaft.

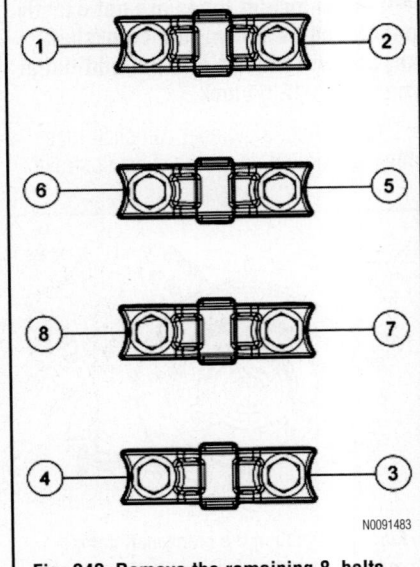

Fig. 242 Remove the remaining 8 bolts in the sequence shown and remove the 4 camshaft bearing caps

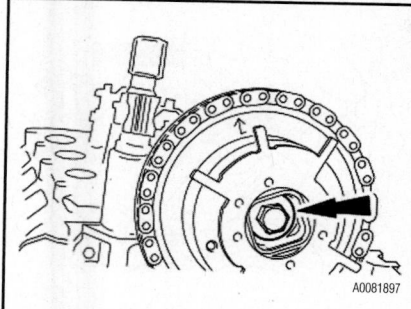

Fig. 243 Remove the bolt and the camshaft phaser and sprocket assembly from the camshaft

19. Lubricate the camshaft and camshaft journals with clean engine oil and install the camshaft.

※※ **WARNING**

Do not remove the Timing Chain Locking Tool at any time during assembly. If the Timing Chain Locking Tool is removed or out of placement, the engine front cover must be removed and the engine must be retimed.

※※ **WARNING**

The timing chain must be installed in its original position onto the camshaft phaser and sprocket using the scribed marks, or damage to valves and pistons will result.

➡ **If replacement of the camshaft phaser and sprocket is necessary, transfer the scribe mark to the new camshaft phaser and sprocket.**

20. Position the camshaft phaser and sprocket into the timing chain with the timing chain scribe marks in alignment.

※※ **WARNING**

Do not remove the Timing Chain Locking Tool at any time during assembly. If the Timing Chain Locking Tool is removed or out of placement, the engine front cover must be removed and the engine must be retimed.

※※ **WARNING**

Damage to the camshaft phaser and sprocket assembly will occur if mishandled or used as a lifting or leveraging device.

※※ **WARNING**

Only use hand tools to install the camshaft phaser and sprocket bolt or damage may occur to the camshaft or camshaft phaser and sprocket.

21. Install the camshaft phaser and sprocket assembly onto the camshaft and install a new camshaft phaser and sprocket bolt finger-tight.

➡ **Do not allow the camshaft roller followers to move out of position when installing the camshaft.**

22. Install the 5 camshaft bearing caps in their original locations.
   a. Lubricate the camshaft bearing caps with clean engine oil.
   b. Position the 2 front camshaft bearing cap.
   c. Position the remaining 8 camshaft bearing caps.
   d. Install the 10 bolts loosely.
   e. Tighten the bolts in the sequence shown. Tighten to 89 inch lbs. (10 Nm).

➡ **Engine front cover removed for clarity.**

23. Remove the Timing Chain Locking Tool.
24. Rotate the crankshaft a half turn counterclockwise and position the crankshaft damper spoke at the 12 o'clock position and the timing mark indentation at the 1 o'clock position.

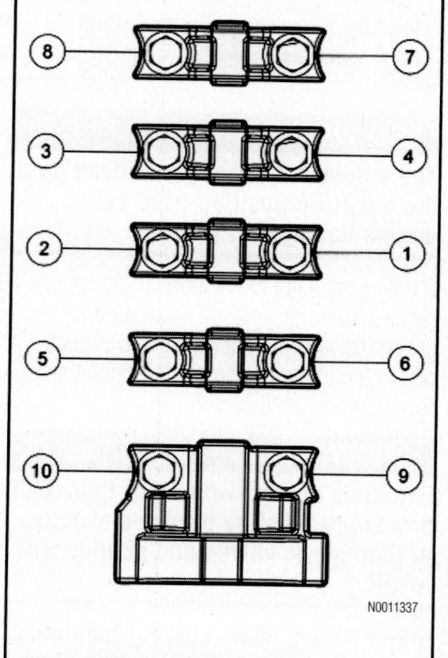

Fig. 244 Tighten the bolts in the sequence shown

25. Verify correct camshaft position by noting the position of the No. 5 cylinder intake and exhaust camshaft lobes.

➡ **Do not allow the valve keepers to fall off of the valve or the valve may drop into the cylinder. If a valve drops into the cylinder, the cylinder head must be removed.**

➡ **It may be necessary to push the valve down while compressing the spring.**

26. Using the Valve Spring Compressor, install the 3 originally removed camshaft roller followers.
27. Install the CMP sensor and the bolt. Tighten to 89 inch lbs. (10 Nm).
28. Connect the CMP electrical connector.

※※ **WARNING**

Only use hand tools to install the camshaft phaser and sprocket assembly or damage may occur to the camshaft or camshaft phaser and sprocket.

※※ **WARNING**

Damage to the camshaft phaser and sprocket assembly will occur if mishandled or used as a lifting or leveraging device.

29. Tighten the camshaft phaser and sprocket bolt in 2 stages:
   a. Stage 1: Tighten to 30 ft. lbs. (40 Nm).
   b. Stage 2: Tighten an additional 90 degrees.
30. Install the LH valve cover.

Right Side

See Figures 222, 234, 245 through 253.

※※ **WARNING**

The camshaft procedure must be followed exactly or damage to the valves and pistons will result.

1. Position the crankshaft damper spoke at the 12 o'clock position and the timing mark indentation at the 1 o'clock position.
2. Remove the RH valve cover.

※※ **WARNING**

Damage to the camshaft phaser and sprocket assembly will occur if mishandled or used as a lifting or leveraging device.

✳✳ WARNING

Only use hand tools to remove the camshaft phaser and sprocket assembly or damage may occur to the camshaft or camshaft phaser and sprocket.

3. Loosen and back off the RH camshaft phaser and sprocket bolt one full turn.

4. Disconnect the RH Camshaft Position (CMP) sensor electrical connector.

5. Remove the bolt and the RH CMP sensor.

➡If the camshaft lobes are not exactly positioned as shown, the crankshaft will require one full additional rotation to 12 o'clock.

6. The No. 1 cylinder camshaft exhaust lobe must be coming up on the exhaust stroke. Verify by noting the position of the 2 intake camshaft lobes and the exhaust lobe on the No. 1 cylinder.

7. Remove only the 3 camshaft roller followers shown.

✳✳ WARNING

The camshaft roller followers must be installed in their original locations. Record camshaft roller follower locations. Failure to follow these instructions may result in engine damage.

➡Do not allow the valve keepers to fall off of the valve or the valve may drop into the cylinder. If a valve drops into the cylinder, the cylinder head must be removed.

➡It may be necessary to push the valve down while compressing the spring.

8. Using the Valve Spring Compressor (303-1039), remove only the 3 designated camshaft roller followers from the previous step.

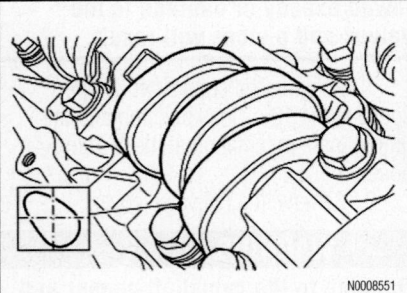

Fig. 245 Verify by noting the position of the 2 intake camshaft lobes and the exhaust lobe on the No. 1 cylinder

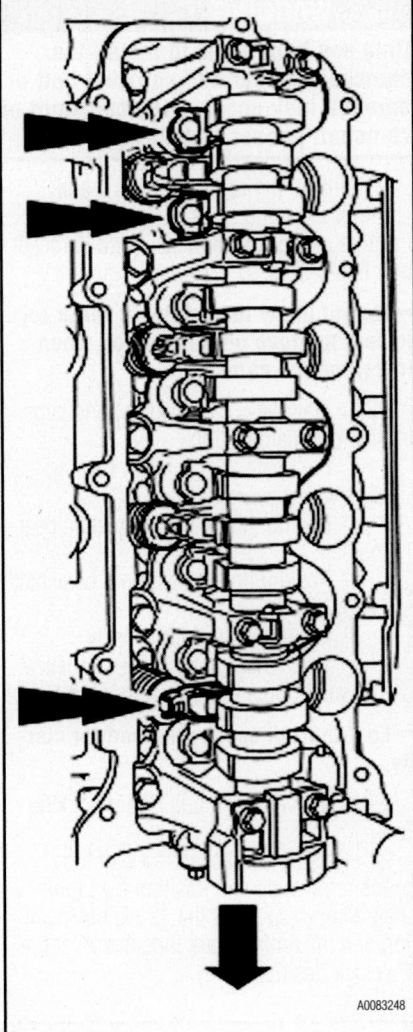

Fig. 246 Remove only the 3 camshaft roller followers shown

✳✳ WARNING

The crankshaft cannot be moved past the 6 o'clock position once set or engine damage may occur.

9. Rotate the crankshaft clockwise, as viewed from the front, positioning the crankshaft damper spoke at the 6 o'clock position and the timing mark indentation at the 7 o'clock position.

✳✳ WARNING

Engine is not freewheeling. Camshaft procedure must be followed exactly or damage to valves and pistons will result.

➡The Timing Chain Locking Tool must be installed square to the timing chain and the engine block.

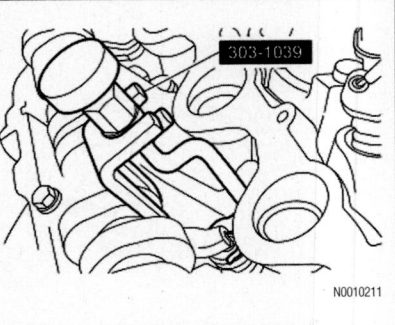

Fig. 247 Using the Valve Spring Compressor, remove only the 3 designated camshaft roller followers from the previous step

Fig. 248 Rotate the crankshaft clockwise, as viewed from the front, positioning the crankshaft damper spoke at the 6 o'clock position and the timing mark indentation at the 7 o'clock position

➡Engine front cover removed for clarity.

10. Install the Timing Chain Locking Tool (303-1175) in the RH timing chain as shown.

✳✳ WARNING

Do not remove the Timing Chain Locking Tool at any time during assembly. If the Timing Chain Locking Tool is removed or out of placement, the engine front cover must be removed and the engine must be retimed.

✳✳ WARNING

The timing chain must be installed in its original position onto the camshaft phaser and sprocket using the scribed marks, or damage to valves and pistons will result.

11. Scribe a location mark on the timing chain and the camshaft phaser and sprocket assembly.

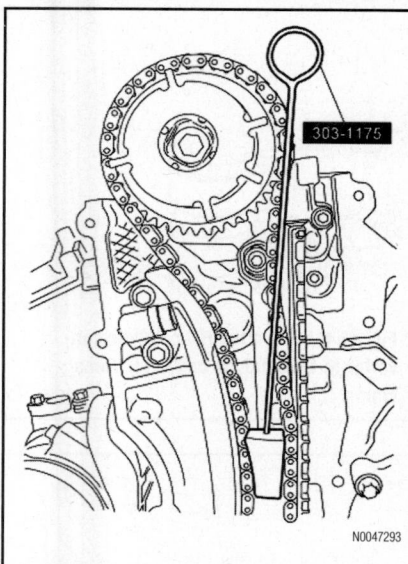

Fig. 249 Install the Timing Chain Locking Tool in the RH timing chain as shown

✳✳ WARNING

Remove the front thrust camshaft bearing cap straight upward from the bearing towers or the bearing cap may be damaged from side loading.

12. Remove the 2 bolts and the front camshaft bearing cap.

✳✳ WARNING

The camshaft bearing caps must be installed in their original locations. Record camshaft bearing cap locations. Failure to follow these instructions may result in engine damage.

13. Remove the remaining bolts in the sequence shown and remove the remaining camshaft bearing caps.

14. Clean and inspect the RH camshaft bearing caps. The camshaft front thrust bearing cap contains an oil metering

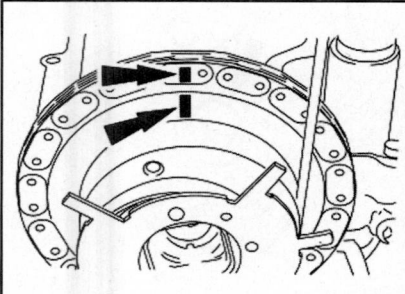

Fig. 250 Scribe a location mark on the timing chain and the camshaft phaser and sprocket assembly

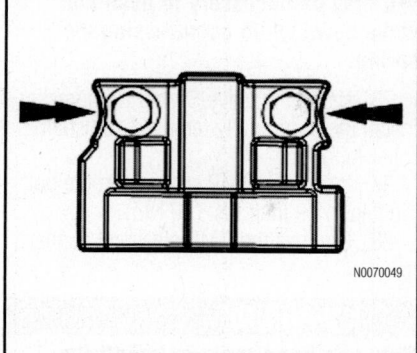

Fig. 251 Remove the 2 bolts and the front camshaft bearing cap

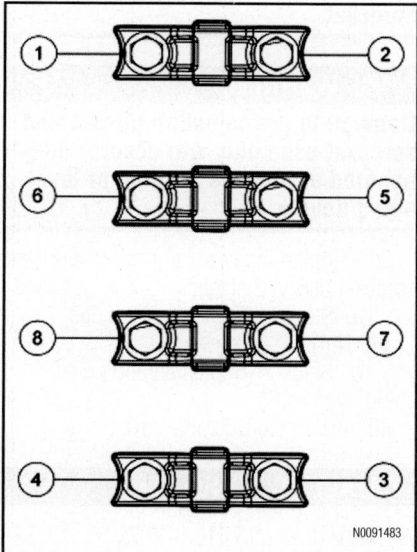

Fig. 252 Remove the remaining bolts in the sequence shown and remove the remaining camshaft bearing caps

groove. Make sure the groove is free of foreign material.

✳✳ WARNING

Damage to the camshaft phaser and sprocket assembly will occur if mishandled or used as a lifting or leveraging device.

✳✳ WARNING

Only use hand tools to remove the camshaft phaser and sprocket bolt or damage may occur to the camshaft or camshaft phaser and sprocket.

✳✳ WARNING

Do not remove the Timing Chain Locking Tool at any time during assembly. If the Timing Chain Lock-

ing Tool is removed or out of placement, the engine front cover must be removed and the engine must be retimed.

15. Remove the bolt and the camshaft phaser and sprocket assembly from the camshaft.

16. Discard the bolt and washer.

17. Remove the camshaft.

18. Remove and inspect the camshaft phaser and sprocket for damage.

To install:

➡ **Do not allow the camshaft roller followers to move out of position when installing the camshaft.**

19. Lubricate the camshaft and camshaft journals with clean engine oil and install the camshaft.

✳✳ WARNING

Do not remove the Timing Chain Locking Tool at any time during assembly.. If the Timing Chain Locking Tool is removed or out of placement, the engine front cover must be removed and the engine must be retimed.

✳✳ WARNING

The timing chain must be installed in its original position onto the camshaft phaser and sprocket using the scribed marks, or damage to valves and pistons will result.

➡ **If replacement of the camshaft phaser and sprocket is necessary, transfer the scribe mark to the new camshaft phaser and sprocket.**

20. Position the camshaft phaser and sprocket into the timing chain with the timing chain scribe marks in alignment.

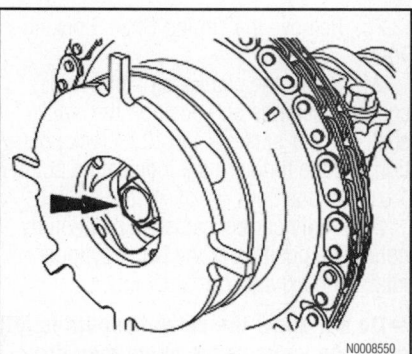

Fig. 253 Remove the bolt and the camshaft phaser and sprocket assembly from the camshaft

❊❊ **WARNING**

Do not remove the Timing Chain Locking Tool at any time during assembly. If the Timing Chain Locking Tool is removed or out of placement, the engine front cover must be removed and the engine must be retimed.

❊❊ **WARNING**

Damage to the camshaft phaser and sprocket assembly will occur if mishandled or used as a lifting or leveraging device.

❊❊ **WARNING**

Only use hand tools to install the camshaft phaser and sprocket bolt or damage may occur to the camshaft or camshaft phaser and sprocket.

21. Install the camshaft phaser and sprocket assembly onto the camshaft and install a new camshaft phaser and sprocket bolt finger-tight.

➡Do not allow the camshaft roller followers to move out of position when installing the camshaft.

22. Install the 5 camshaft bearing caps in their original locations.
　　a. Lubricate the camshaft bearing caps with clean engine oil.
　　b. Position the front camshaft bearing cap.
　　c. Position the remaining camshaft bearing caps.
　　d. Install the 10 bolts loosely.
　　e. Tighten the 10 bolts in the sequence shown. Tighten to 89 inch lbs. (10 Nm).

➡Engine front cover removed for clarity.

23. Remove the Timing Chain Locking Tool.
24. Rotate the crankshaft a half turn counterclockwise and position the crankshaft damper spoke at the 12 o'clock position and the timing mark indentation at the 1 o'clock position.
25. Verify correct camshaft position by noting the position of the No. 1 cylinder intake and exhaust camshaft lobes.

➡Do not allow the valve keepers to fall off of the valve or the valve may drop into the cylinder. If a valve drops into the cylinder, the cylinder head must be removed.

➡It may be necessary to push the valve down while compressing the spring.

26. Using the Valve Spring Compressor, install the 3 originally removed camshaft roller followers.
27. Install the CMP sensor and the bolt. Tighten to 89 inch lbs. (10 Nm).
28. Connect the CMP electrical connector.

❊❊ **WARNING**

Only use hand tools to install the camshaft phaser and sprocket assembly or damage may occur to the camshaft or camshaft phaser and sprocket.

❊❊ **WARNING**

Damage to the camshaft phaser and sprocket assembly will occur if mishandled or used as a lifting or leveraging device.

29. Tighten the new camshaft phaser and sprocket bolt in 2 stages:
　　a. Stage 1: Tighten to 30 ft. lbs. (40 Nm).
　　b. Stage 2: Tighten an additional 90 degrees.
30. Install the RH valve cover.

CATALYTIC CONVERTER

REMOVAL & INSTALLATION
See Figures 254 through 260.

❊❊ **WARNING**

Do not use oil or grease-based lubricants on the isolators. These lubricants may cause deterioration of the rubber. This can lead to separation of the isolator from the exhaust hanger bracket during vehicle operation.

➡The exhaust Y-pipe dual catalytic converter is a 2-piece assembly. The RH and LH converters can be serviced separately as needed.

1. With the vehicle in NEUTRAL, position it on a hoist.
2. Disconnect the 2 Catalyst Monitor Sensor (CMS) electrical connectors.
3. Disconnect the 2 Heated Oxygen Sensor (HO2S) pushpins and electrical connectors.
4. Loosen the RH catalytic converter-to-LH catalytic converter Torca clamp.
5. Remove the 2 nuts on the LH catalytic converter-to-exhaust manifold joint.

Fig. 254 Loosen the RH catalytic converter-to-LH catalytic converter Torca clamp

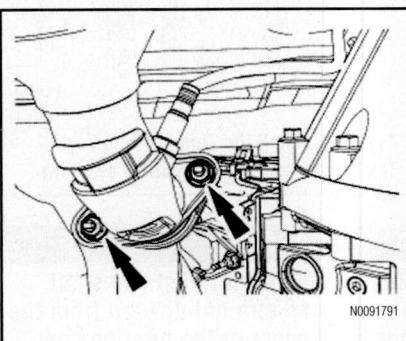
Fig. 255 Remove the 2 nuts on the LH catalytic converter-to-exhaust manifold joint

6. Discard the nuts.
7. Remove the LH catalytic converter from the vehicle.
8. For 4WD models, remove the transfer case skid plate and 4 bolts, if equipped.
9. Using an appropriate tool, support the transmission.
10. Remove the 2 heat shield bolts from the transmission crossmember.
11. Remove the 2 transmission insulator and retainer/exhaust support bracket assembly nuts.

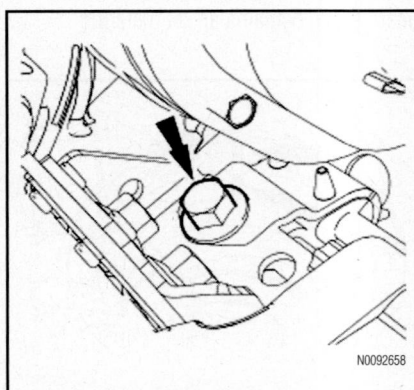
Fig. 256 Remove the LH isolator cap from the transmission insulator and retainer/exhaust support bracket assembly

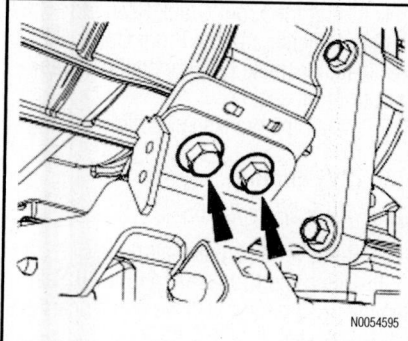

Fig. 257 Remove the 4 transmission insulator and retainer/exhaust support bracket assembly bolts

12. Remove the 4 transmission crossmember nuts and 4 bolts and remove the transmission crossmember from the vehicle.

13. Remove the LH isolator cap from the transmission insulator and retainer/exhaust support bracket assembly.

14. For 4WD models, remove the 4 transmission insulator and retainer/exhaust support bracket assembly bolts and remove the transmission insulator and retainer/exhaust support bracket assembly from the vehicle.

15. For RWD models, perform the following:

a. If equipped with a 6R80 transmission, remove the 3 transmission insulator and retainer/exhaust support bracket assembly bolts and remove the transmission insulator and retainer/exhaust support bracket assembly from the vehicle.

b. If equipped with a 4R70E or 4R75E transmission, remove the 4 transmission insulator and retainer/exhaust support bracket assembly bolts and remove the transmission insulator and retainer/exhaust support bracket assembly from the vehicle.

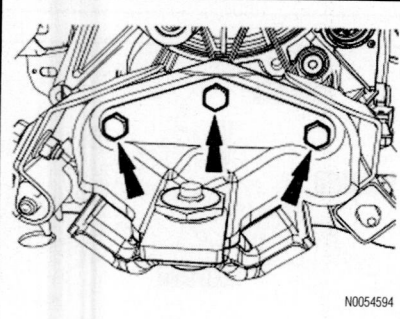

Fig. 258 If equipped with a 6R80 transmission, remove the 3 transmission insulator and retainer/exhaust support bracket assembly bolts

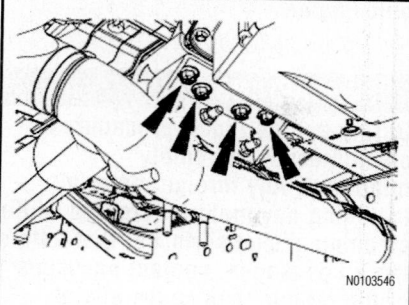

Fig. 259 If equipped with a 4R70E or 4R75E transmission, remove the 4 transmission insulator and retainer/exhaust support bracket assembly bolts

16. Remove the 2 RH catalytic converter-to-exhaust intermediate pipe bolts.

17. With help of an assistant, remove the 2 nuts on the RH catalytic converter-to-exhaust manifold joint and remove the RH catalytic converter from the vehicle.

18. Discard the nuts.

To install:

➡**Clean the mating surfaces of the manifold outlet flare and the catalytic converter inlet flare.**

19. With the help of an assistant, position the RH catalytic converter into the vehicle and loosely install 2 new RH catalytic converter-to-exhaust manifold nuts.

20. Loosely install the 2 RH catalytic converter-to-intermediate pipe bolts.

21. For RWD models, if equipped with a 6R80 transmission, install the transmission insulator and retainer/exhaust bracket assembly and 3 bolts. Tighten to 66 ft. lbs. (90 Nm).

22. For RWD models, if equipped with a 4R70E or 4R75E transmission, install the transmission insulator and retainer/exhaust bracket assembly and the 4 bolts. Tighten to 59 ft. lbs. (80 Nm).

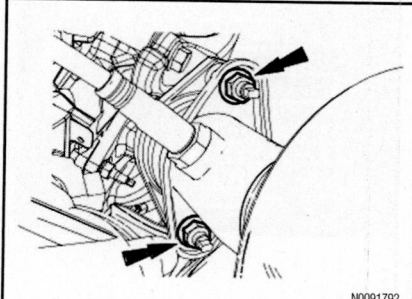

Fig. 260 With help of an assistant, remove the 2 nuts on the RH catalytic converter-to-exhaust manifold joint

23. For 4WD vehicles, Install the transmission insulator and retainer/exhaust support bracket assembly and 4 bolts. Tighten to 66 ft. lbs. (90 Nm).

24. Loosely install the LH isolator cap and bolt onto the transmission insulator and retainer/exhaust support bracket assembly.

25. Install the transmission crossmember, 4 bolts and 4 nuts. Tighten to 66 ft. lbs. (90 Nm).

26. Install the 2 transmission insulator and retainer/exhaust support bracket assembly nuts. Tighten to 76 ft. lbs. (103 Nm).

27. Install the 2 heat shield bolts into the transmission crossmember. Tighten to 10 ft. lbs. (15 Nm).

28. For 4WD models, install the transfer case skid plate and 4 bolts, if equipped. Tighten to 18 ft. lbs. (24 Nm).

29. Slide the LH catalytic converter into the RH catalytic converter up to the stop on the LH catalytic converter and position the LH catalytic converter into place.

30. Loosely install the 2 new LH converter-to-exhaust manifold nuts.

31. Tighten the 2 new RH catalytic converter-to-exhaust manifold nuts in the following sequence:

a. Tighten the RH lower catalytic converter-to-exhaust manifold nut to 30 ft. lbs. (40 Nm).

b. Tighten the RH upper catalytic converter-to-exhaust manifold nut to 30 ft. lbs. (40 Nm).

c. Tighten the LH isolator cap bolt. Tighten to 26 ft. lbs. (35 Nm).

d. Tighten the RH catalytic converter-to-LH catalytic converter Torca clamp. Tighten to 41 ft. lbs. (55 Nm).

32. Tighten the 2 new LH catalytic converter-to-exhaust manifold nuts in the following sequence:

a. Snug the LH inner catalytic converter-to-exhaust manifold nut.

b. Tighten the LH outer catalytic converter-to-exhaust manifold nut to 30 ft. lbs. (40 Nm).

c. Tighten the LH inner catalytic converter-to-exhaust manifold nut to 30 ft. lbs. (40 Nm).

33. Tighten the exhaust Y-pipe dual catalytic converter-to-exhaust intermediate pipe bolts in the following sequence:

a. Snug the outer exhaust Y-pipe dual catalytic converter-to-exhaust intermediate pipe bolt.

b. Tighten the inner exhaust Y-pipe dual catalytic converter-to-exhaust intermediate pipe bolt to 46 ft. lbs. (63 Nm).

c. Tighten the outer exhaust Y-pipe dual catalytic converter-to-exhaust intermediate pipe bolt to 46 ft. lbs. (63 Nm).

34. Connect the 2 HO2S pushpins and electrical connectors.

35. Connect the 2 CMS electrical connectors.

CRANKSHAFT FRONT SEAL

REMOVAL & INSTALLATION

3.5L GTDI and 3.7L Engines

See Figures 261 and 262.

1. With the vehicle in NEUTRAL, position it on a hoist.
2. Remove the crankshaft pulley.
3. Using the Oil Seal Remover (303-409), remove and discard the crankshaft front seal.
4. Clean all sealing surfaces with metal surface prep.

To install:

➡ **Apply clean engine oil to the crankshaft front seal bore in the engine front cover.**

5. Using the Front Crankshaft Seal Installer (303-1251) and Crankshaft Vibration Damper Installer (303-102), install a new crankshaft front seal.
6. Install the crankshaft pulley.

5.0L Engine

See Figures 263 and 264.

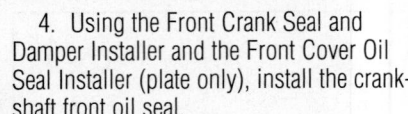

※※ **WARNING**

During engine repair procedures, cleanliness is extremely important. Any foreign material, including any material created while cleaning gasket surfaces, that enters the oil passages, coolant passages or the oil pan, can cause engine failure.

1. With the vehicle in NEUTRAL, position it on a hoist.
2. Remove the crankshaft pulley.

※※ **WARNING**

Use care not to damage the engine front cover or the crankshaft when removing the seal.

3. Using the Oil Seal Remover (303-409), remove the crankshaft front oil seal.

To install:

➡ **Lubricate the engine front cover bore and the crankshaft front oil seal inner lip with clean engine oil.**

4. Using the Front Crank Seal and Damper Installer and the Front Cover Oil Seal Installer (plate only), install the crankshaft front oil seal.
5. Install the crankshaft pulley.

4.6L (2V) Engine

See Figures 265 and 266.

1. Remove the crankshaft pulley.
2. Using the Crankshaft Front Oil Seal Remover (303-107), remove and discard the crankshaft seal.

To install:

3. Lubricate the engine front cover and the crankshaft front seal inner lip with clean engine oil.
4. Using the Crankshaft Front Oil Seal Installer (303-635), the Crankshaft Vibration Damper Installer (303-102) and the Front Cover Oil Seal Installer (303-335), install the new crankshaft front seal into the engine front cover.
5. Install the crankshaft pulley.

4.6L (3V) Engine

See Figures 267 and 268.

1. Remove the crankshaft pulley.
2. Using the Crankshaft Front Seal

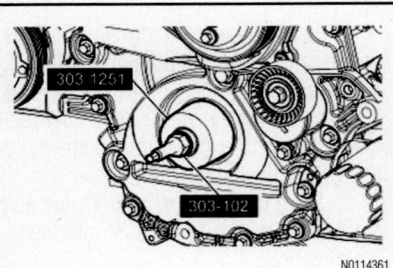

Fig. 261 Using the Oil Seal Remover, remove and discard the crankshaft front seal

Fig. 263 Using the Oil Seal Remover, remove the crankshaft front oil seal

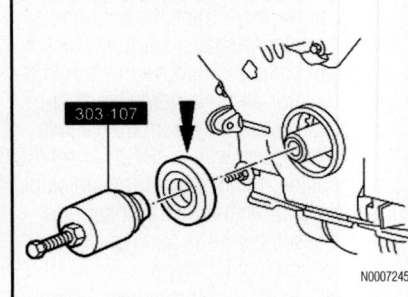

Fig. 265 Using the Crankshaft Front Oil Seal Remover, remove and discard the crankshaft seal

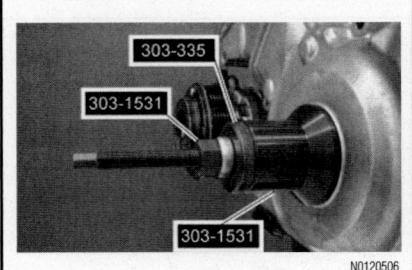

Fig. 262 Using the Front Crankshaft Seal Installer and Crankshaft Vibration Damper Installer, install a new crankshaft front seal

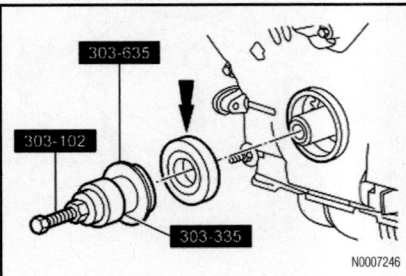

Fig. 264 Using the Front Crank Seal and Damper Installer and the Front Cover Oil Seal Installer (plate only), install the crankshaft front oil seal

Fig. 266 Using the Crankshaft Front Oil Seal Installer, the Crankshaft Vibration Damper Installer and the Front Cover Oil Seal Installer, install the new crankshaft front seal into the engine front cover

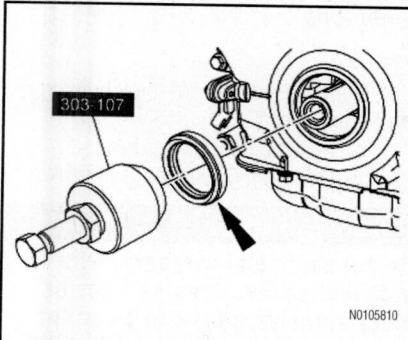

Fig. 267 Using the Crankshaft Front Seal Remover, remove the crankshaft front seal

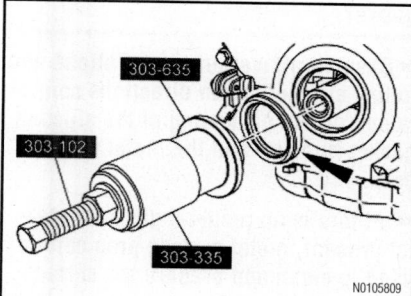

Fig. 268 Using the Crankshaft Vibration Damper Installer, the Front Cover Seal Installer and the Crankshaft Front Seal Installer, install the crankshaft front seal

Remover (303-107), remove the crankshaft front seal.

To install:

3. Lubricate the engine front cover and the crankshaft front seal inner lip with clean engine oil.

4. Using the Crankshaft Front Oil Seal Installer (303-635), the Crankshaft Vibration Damper Installer (303-102) and the Front Cover Oil Seal Installer (303-335), install the new crankshaft front seal into the engine front cover.

5. Install the crankshaft pulley.

5.4L (3V) Engine

See Figures 265 through 269.

1. With the vehicle in NEUTRAL, position it on a hoist.

2. Rotate the tensioner clockwise and remove the accessory drive belt from the crankshaft pulley.

3. Remove the crankshaft pulley bolt and washer. Discard the crankshaft pulley bolt.

4. Using the 3 Jaw Puller, remove the crankshaft pulley.

---

5. Using the Crankshaft Front Oil Seal Remover (303-107), remove and discard the crankshaft seal.

To install:

6. Lubricate the engine front cover and the new crankshaft seal inner lip with clean engine oil.

7. Using the Crankshaft Front Oil Seal Installer (303-635), the Crankshaft Vibration Damper Installer (303-102) and the Front Cover Oil Seal Installer (303-335), install the new crankshaft front seal into the engine front cover.

➡ If not secured within 4 minutes, the sealant must be removed and the sealing area cleaned with metal surface prep and silicone gasket remover. Allow to dry until there is no sign of wetness, or 4 minutes, whichever is longer. Failure to follow this procedure can cause future oil leakage.

8. Apply silicone gasket and sealant to the Woodruff key slot in the crankshaft pulley.

9. Using the Crankshaft Vibration Damper Installer (303-102), install the crankshaft pulley.

10. Using a new crankshaft pulley bolt, install the bolt and washer and tighten the bolt in 4 stages.

a. Stage 1: Tighten to 66 ft. lbs. (90 Nm).
b. Stage 2: Loosen 360 degrees.
c. Stage 3: Tighten to 37 ft. lbs. (50 Nm).
d. Stage 4: Tighten an additional 90 degrees.

11. Rotate the tensioner clockwise and install the accessory drive belt onto the crankshaft pulley.

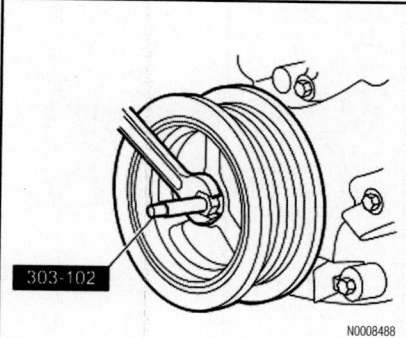

Fig. 269 Using the Crankshaft Vibration Damper Installer, install the crankshaft pulley

---

CYLINDER HEAD

REMOVAL & INSTALLATION

3.5L GTDI Engine

✳✳ CAUTION

Do not smoke, carry lighted tobacco or have an open flame of any type when working on or near any fuel-related component. Highly flammable mixtures are always present and may be ignited. Failure to follow these instructions may result in serious personal injury.

✳✳ CAUTION

Before working on or disconnecting any of the fuel tubes or fuel system components, relieve the fuel system pressure to prevent accidental spraying of fuel. Fuel in the fuel system remains under high pressure, even when the engine is not running. Failure to follow this instruction may result in serious personal injury.

✳✳ CAUTION

Do not carry personal electronic devices such as cell phones, pagers or audio equipment of any type when working on or near any fuel-related component. Highly flammable mixtures are always present and may be ignited. Failure to follow these instructions may result in serious personal injury.

✳✳ CAUTION

Always disconnect the battery ground cable at the battery when working on an evaporative emission (EVAP) system or fuel-related component. Highly flammable mixtures are always present and may be ignited. Failure to follow these instructions may result in serious personal injury.

✳✳ CAUTION

Clean all fuel residue from the engine compartment. If not removed, fuel residue may ignite when the engine is returned to operation. Failure to follow this instruction may result in serious personal injury.

※※ WARNING

During engine repair procedures, cleanliness is extremely important. Any foreign material, including any material created while cleaning gasket surfaces that enters the oil passages, coolant passages or the oil pan, may cause engine failure.

➡If the cylinder head is replaced, a new secondary timing chain tensioner will need to be installed.

※※ WARNING

Place clean, lint-free shop towels over exposed engine cavities. Carefully remove the towels so foreign material is not dropped into the engine. Any foreign material (including any material created while cleaning gasket surfaces) that enters the oil passages or the oil pan, may cause engine failure

※※ WARNING

Aluminum surfaces are soft and may be scratched easily. Never place the cylinder head gasket surface, unprotected, on a bench surface.

➡The cylinder head bolts must be discarded and new bolts must be installed. They are a tighten-to-yield design and cannot be reused.

Left Side

See Figure 270.

1. Remove and discard the 8 bolts from the cylinder head.
   a. Remove the cylinder head.
   b. Discard the cylinder head gasket.

※※ WARNING

Do not use metal scrapers, wire brushes, power abrasive discs or other abrasive means to clean the sealing surfaces. These tools cause scratches and gouges that make leak paths. Use a plastic scraping tool to remove all traces of the head gasket.

➡Observe all warnings or cautions and follow all application directions contained on the packaging of the silicone gasket remover and the metal surface prep.

➡If there is no residual gasket material present, metal surface prep can be used to clean and prepare the surfaces.

2. Clean the cylinder head-to-cylinder block mating surfaces of both the cylinder heads and the cylinder block in the following sequence.
   a. Remove any large deposits of silicone or gasket material with a plastic scraper.
   b. Apply silicone gasket remover, following package directions, and allow to set for several minutes.
   c. Remove the silicone gasket remover with a plastic scraper. A second application of silicone gasket remover may be required if residual traces of silicone or gasket material remain.

   Apply metal surface prep, following package directions, to remove any remaining traces of oil or coolant and to prepare the surfaces to bond with the new gasket. Do not attempt to make the metal shiny. Some staining of the metal surfaces is normal

3. Support the cylinder head on a bench with the head gasket side up. Check the cylinder head distortion and the cylinder block distortion.

To install:

➡If the cylinder head is replaced, a new secondary timing chain tensioner will need to be installed.

4. Install a new gasket, the LH cylinder head and 8 new bolts. Tighten in the sequence shown in 5 stages:
   a. Stage 1: Tighten to 15 ft. lbs. (20 Nm).
   b. Stage 2: Tighten to 26 ft. lbs. (35 Nm).
   c. Stage 3: Tighten 90 degrees.
   d. Stage 4: Tighten 90 degrees
   e. Stage 5: Tighten 45 degrees.

Right Side

See Figure 271.

1. Remove and discard the 8 bolts from the cylinder head.
   a. Remove the cylinder head.
   b. Discard the cylinder head gasket.

※※ WARNING

Do not use metal scrapers, wire brushes, power abrasive discs or other abrasive means to clean the sealing surfaces. These tools cause scratches and gouges that make leak paths. Use a plastic scraping tool to remove all traces of the head gasket.

➡Observe all warnings or cautions and follow all application directions contained on the packaging of the silicone gasket remover and the metal surface prep.

➡If there is no residual gasket material present, metal surface prep can be used to clean and prepare the surfaces.

2. Clean the cylinder head-to-cylinder block mating surfaces of both the cylinder heads and the cylinder block in the following sequence.
   a. Remove any large deposits of silicone or gasket material with a plastic scraper.
   b. Apply silicone gasket remover, following package directions, and allow to set for several minutes.
   c. Remove the silicone gasket remover with a plastic scraper. A second application of silicone gasket remover may be required if residual traces of silicone or gasket material remain.

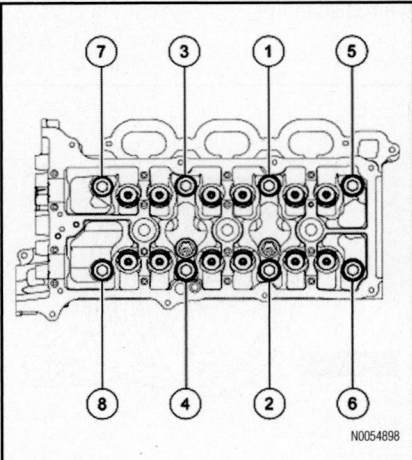

Fig. 270 Tighten in the sequence shown in 5 stages

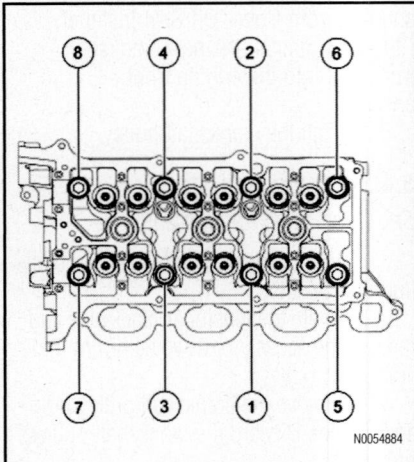

Fig. 271 Tighten in the sequence shown in 5 stages

Apply metal surface prep, following package directions, to remove any remaining traces of oil or coolant and to prepare the surfaces to bond with the new gasket. Do not attempt to make the metal shiny. Some staining of the metal surfaces is normal

3. Support the cylinder head on a bench with the head gasket side up. Check the cylinder head distortion and the cylinder block distortion.

To install:

➡️If the cylinder head is replaced, a new secondary timing chain tensioner will need to be installed.

4. Install a new gasket, the RH cylinder head and 8 new bolts. Tighten in the sequence shown in 5 stages:
   a. Stage 1: Tighten to 15 ft. lbs. (20 Nm).
   b. Stage 2: Tighten to 26 ft. lbs. (35 Nm).
   c. Stage 3: Tighten 90 degrees.
   d. Stage 4: Tighten 90 degrees.
   e. Stage 5: Tighten 45 degrees.

3.7L Engine

> ※ **CAUTION**
>
> **Do not smoke, carry lighted tobacco or have an open flame of any type when working on or near any fuel-related component. Highly flammable mixtures are always present and may be ignited. Failure to follow these instructions may result in serious personal injury.**

> ※ **CAUTION**
>
> **Before working on or disconnecting any of the fuel tubes or fuel system components, relieve the fuel system pressure to prevent accidental spraying of fuel. Fuel in the fuel system remains under high pressure, even when the engine is not running. Failure to follow this instruction may result in serious personal injury.**

> ※ **CAUTION**
>
> **Do not carry personal electronic devices such as cell phones, pagers or audio equipment of any type when working on or near any fuel-related component. Highly flammable mixtures are always present and may be ignited. Failure to follow these instructions**

may result in serious personal injury.

> ※ **CAUTION**
>
> **Always disconnect the battery ground cable at the battery when working on an evaporative emission (EVAP) system or fuel-related component. Highly flammable mixtures are always present and may be ignited. Failure to follow these instructions may result in serious personal injury.**

> ※ **CAUTION**
>
> **Clean all fuel residue from the engine compartment. If not removed, fuel residue may ignite when the engine is returned to operation. Failure to follow this instruction may result in serious personal injury.**

> ※ **WARNING**
>
> **During engine repair procedures, cleanliness is extremely important. Any foreign material, including any material created while cleaning gasket surfaces that enters the oil passages, coolant passages or the oil pan, may cause engine failure.**

➡️If the cylinder head is replaced, a new secondary timing chain tensioner will need to be installed.

> ※ **WARNING**
>
> **During engine repair procedures, cleanliness is extremely important. Any foreign material, including any material created while cleaning gasket surfaces that enters the oil passages, coolant passages or the oil pan, may cause engine failure.**

➡️If the cylinder head is replaced, a new secondary timing chain tensioner will need to be installed.

Left Side

See Figures 272 through 274.

1. Release the fuel system pressure.
2. Disconnect the battery ground cable.
3. Detach and disconnect the RH and LH Heated Oxygen Sensor (HO2S) electrical connectors.
4. Remove and discard the LH and RH catalytic converter-to-exhaust manifold nuts and lower the catalytic converter assembly.
5. Remove the LH camshafts.
6. Remove the lower intake manifold.

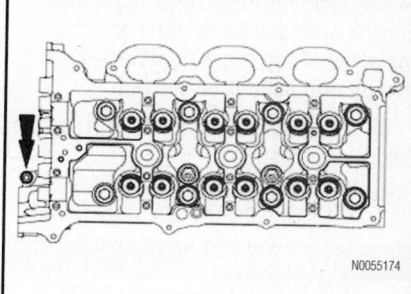

Fig. 272 Remove and discard the M6 bolt

> ※ **WARNING**
>
> **Do not use power tools to remove the bolt or damage to the LH primary timing chain guide may occur.**

7. Remove the bolt and the LH upper primary timing chain guide.
8. Disconnect the 2 LH Camshaft Position (CMP) sensors electrical connectors.
9. Remove the 2 bolts and the 2 LH CMP sensors.
10. Inspect the valve tappets.
11. Remove and discard the M6 bolt.

> ※ **WARNING**
>
> **Place clean, lint-free shop towels over exposed engine cavities. Carefully remove the towels so foreign material is not dropped into the engine. Any foreign material (including any material created while cleaning gasket surfaces) that enters the oil passages or the oil pan, may cause engine failure**

> ※ **WARNING**
>
> **Aluminum surfaces are soft and may be scratched easily. Never place the cylinder head gasket surface, unprotected, on a bench surface.**

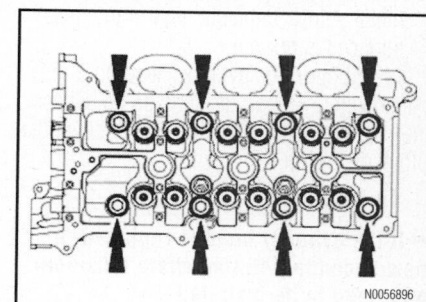

Fig. 273 Remove and discard the 8 bolts from the cylinder head

➡The cylinder head bolts must be discarded and new bolts must be installed. They are a tighten-to-yield design and cannot be reused.

12. Remove and discard the 8 bolts from the cylinder head.
   a. Remove the cylinder head.
   b. Discard the cylinder head gasket.

✳✳ WARNING

Do not use metal scrapers, wire brushes, power abrasive discs or other abrasive means to clean the sealing surfaces. These tools cause scratches and gouges that make leak paths. Use a plastic scraping tool to remove all traces of the head gasket.

➡Observe all warnings or cautions and follow all application directions contained on the packaging of the silicone gasket remover and the metal surface prep.

➡If there is no residual gasket material present, metal surface prep can be used to clean and prepare the surfaces.

13. Clean the cylinder head-to-cylinder block mating surfaces of both the cylinder heads and the cylinder block in the following sequence.
   a. Remove any large deposits of silicone or gasket material with a plastic scraper.
   b. Apply silicone gasket remover, following package directions, and allow to set for several minutes.
   c. Remove the silicone gasket remover with a plastic scraper. A second application of silicone gasket remover may be required if residual traces of silicone or gasket material remain.
   d. Apply metal surface prep, following package directions, to remove any remaining traces of oil or coolant and to prepare the surfaces to bond with the new gasket. Do not attempt to make the metal shiny. Some staining of the metal surfaces is normal

14. Support the cylinder head on a bench with the head gasket side up. Check the cylinder head distortion and the cylinder block distortion.

To install:

➡If the cylinder head is replaced, a new secondary timing chain tensioner will need to be installed.

15. Install a new gasket, the LH cylinder head and 8 new bolts. Tighten in the sequence shown in 5 stages:

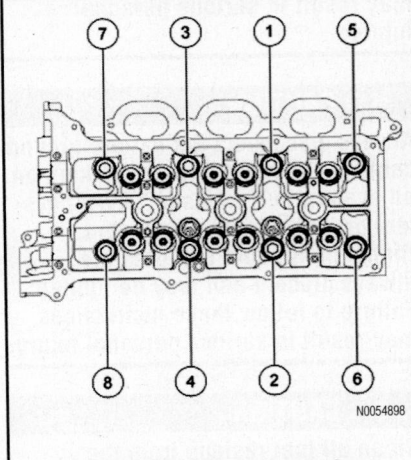

Fig. 274 Tighten in the sequence shown in 5 stages

   a. Stage 1: Tighten to 15 ft. lbs. (20 Nm).
   b. Stage 2: Tighten to 26 ft. lbs. (35 Nm).
   c. Stage 3: Tighten 90 degrees.
   d. Stage 4: Tighten 90 degrees.
   e. Stage 5: Tighten 45 degrees.
16. Install the M6 bolt. Tighten to 89 inch lbs. (10 Nm).

➡The valve tappets must be installed in their original positions.

➡Coat the valve tappets with clean engine oil prior to installation.

17. Install the valve tappets.

➡Lubricate the 2 CMP sensor O-ring seals with clean engine oil.

18. Install the 2 LH CMP sensors and the 2 bolts. Tighten to 89 inch lbs. (10 Nm).
19. Connect the 2 LH CMP sensors electrical connectors.
20. Install the LH upper primary timing chain guide and the bolt. Tighten to 89 inch lbs. (10 Nm).
21. Install the lower intake manifold.
22. Install the LH camshafts.
23. Raise the catalytic converter and install the new LH and RH catalytic converter-to-exhaust manifold nuts. Tighten to 35 ft. lbs. (45 Nm).
24. Connect and attach the RH and LH HO2S electrical connectors.
25. Connect the battery ground cable.

Right Side

See Figures 275 through 277.

1. Release the fuel system pressure.
2. Disconnect the battery ground cable.

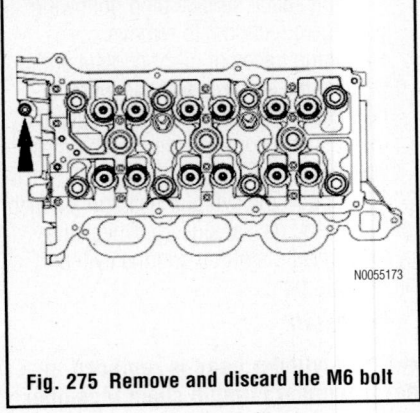

Fig. 275 Remove and discard the M6 bolt

3. Detach and disconnect the RH and LH Heated Oxygen Sensor (HO2S) electrical connectors.
4. Remove and discard the LH and RH catalytic converter-to-exhaust manifold nuts and lower the catalytic converter assembly.
5. Remove the RH camshafts.
6. Remove the lower intake manifold.
7. Disconnect the Cylinder Head Temperature (CHT) sensor electrical connector.

✳✳ WARNING

Do not use power tools to remove the bolt or damage to the RH primary timing chain guide may occur.

8. Remove the bolt and the RH primary timing chain guide.
9. Disconnect the 2 RH Camshaft Position (CMP) sensors electrical connectors.
10. Remove the 2 bolts and the 2 RH CMP sensors.
11. Remove the bolt and ground wire from the rear of the RH cylinder head.
12. Detach the wiring harness retainer from the rear of the RH cylinder head.
13. Inspect the valve tappets.
14. Remove and discard the M6 bolt.

✳✳ WARNING

Place clean, lint-free shop towels over exposed engine cavities. Carefully remove the towels so foreign material is not dropped into the engine. Any foreign material (including any material created while cleaning gasket surfaces) that enters the oil passages or the oil pan, may cause engine failure

✳✳ WARNING

Aluminum surfaces are soft and may be scratched easily. Never place the cylinder head gasket surface, unprotected, on a bench surface.

➡The cylinder head bolts must be discarded and new bolts must be installed. They are a tighten-to-yield design and cannot be reused.

15. Remove and discard the 8 bolts from the cylinder head.
   a. Remove the cylinder head.
   b. Discard the cylinder head gasket.

✳✳ WARNING

Do not use metal scrapers, wire brushes, power abrasive discs or other abrasive means to clean the sealing surfaces. These tools cause scratches and gouges that make leak paths. Use a plastic scraping tool to remove all traces of the head gasket.

➡Observe all warnings or cautions and follow all application directions contained on the packaging of the silicone gasket remover and the metal surface prep.

➡If there is no residual gasket material present, metal surface prep can be used to clean and prepare the surfaces.

16. Clean the cylinder head-to-cylinder block mating surfaces of both the cylinder heads and the cylinder block in the following sequence.
   a. Remove any large deposits of silicone or gasket material with a plastic scraper.
   b. Apply silicone gasket remover, following package directions, and allow to set for several minutes.
   c. Remove the silicone gasket remover with a plastic scraper. A second application of silicone gasket remover may be required if residual traces of silicone or gasket material remain.
   d. Apply metal surface prep, following package directions, to remove any remaining traces of oil or coolant and to prepare the surfaces to bond with the

new gasket. Do not attempt to make the metal shiny. Some staining of the metal surfaces is normal

17. Support the cylinder head on a bench with the head gasket side up. Check the cylinder head distortion and the cylinder block distortion.

To install:

➡If the cylinder head is replaced, a new secondary timing chain tensioner will need to be installed.

18. Install a new gasket, the RH cylinder head and 8 new bolts. Tighten in the sequence shown in 5 stages:
   a. Stage 1: Tighten to 15 ft. lbs. (20 Nm).
   b. Stage 2: Tighten to 26 ft. lbs. (35 Nm).
   c. Stage 3: Tighten 90 degrees.
   d. Stage 4: Tighten 90 degrees
   e. Stage 5: Tighten 45 degrees.
19. Install the M6 bolt. Tighten to 89 inch lbs. (10 Nm).

➡The valve tappets must be installed in their original positions.

➡Coat the valve tappets with clean engine oil prior to installation.

20. Install the valve tappets.
21. Attach the wiring harness retainer to the rear of the RH cylinder head.
22. Install the ground wire and bolt to the rear of the RH cylinder head. Tighten to 89 inch lbs. (10 Nm).

➡Lubricate the 2 CMP sensor O-ring seals with clean engine oil.

23. Install the 2 RH CMP sensors and the 2 bolts. Tighten to 89 inch lbs. (10 Nm).

24. Connect the 2 RH CMP sensors electrical connectors.
25. Install the RH primary timing chain guide and the bolt. Tighten to 89 inch lbs. (10 Nm).
26. Connect the CHT sensor electrical connector.
27. Install the lower intake manifold.
28. Install the RH camshafts.
29. Raise the catalytic converter and install the new LH and RH catalytic converter-to-exhaust manifold nuts. Tighten to 35 ft. lbs. (45 Nm).
30. Connect and attach the RH and LH HO2S electrical connectors.
31. Connect the battery ground cable.

5.0L Engine
See Figures 278 and 279.

➡The manufacturer does not provide a specific Removal and Installation procedure for this component. Refer to the graphic(s) when servicing this component.

1. Tighten the new cylinder head bolts in 4 stages in the sequence shown.
   a. Stage 1: Tighten to 18 ft. lbs. (25 Nm).
   b. Stage 2: Tighten to 30 ft. lbs. (40 Nm).
   c. Stage 3: Tighten an additional 90 degrees.
   d. Stage 4: Tighten an additional 90 degrees.

EXHAUST MANIFOLD

REMOVAL & INSTALLATION

3.5L GTDI Engine

Left Side
See Figures 280 and 281.

1. Remove the LH turbocharger.
2. Remove the 8 exhaust manifold nuts and the LH exhaust manifold. Discard the nuts and gasket.
3. Clean and inspect the LH exhaust manifold.
4. Remove and discard the 8 LH exhaust manifold studs.

✳✳ WARNING

Do not use metal scrapers, wire brushes, power abrasive discs or other abrasive means to clean the sealing surfaces. These may cause scratches and gouges resulting in leak paths. Use a plastic scraper to clean the sealing surfaces.

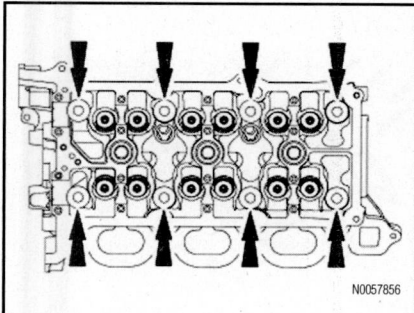
Fig. 286 Remove and discard the 8 bolts from the cylinder head

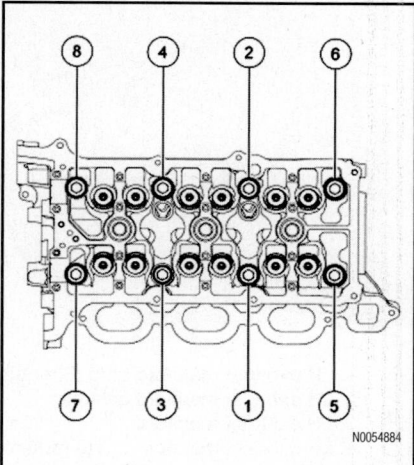
Fig. 287 Tighten in the sequence shown in 5 stages

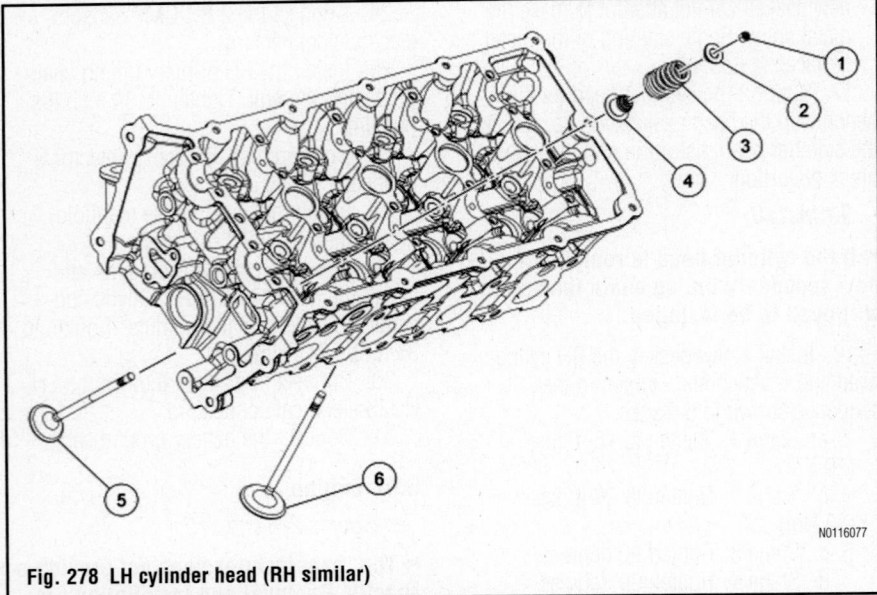

Fig. 278 LH cylinder head (RH similar)

5. Clean the exhaust manifold mating surface of the cylinder head with metal surface prep. Follow the directions on the packaging.

To install:

6. Install 8 new LH exhaust manifold studs. Tighten to 106 inch lbs. (12 Nm).

✳✳ WARNING

Failure to tighten the exhaust manifold nuts to specification a second time will cause the exhaust manifold to develop an exhaust leak.

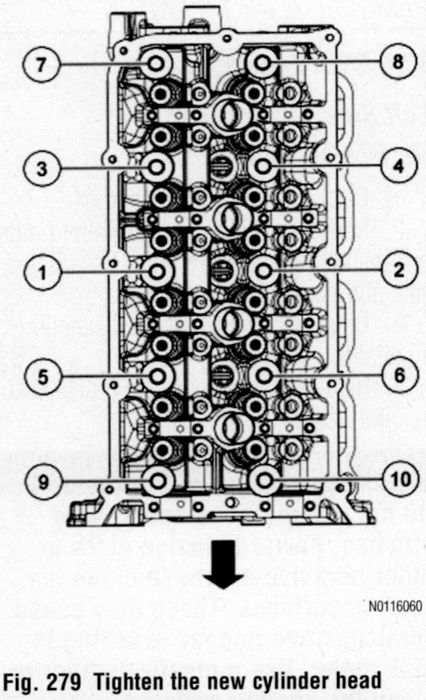

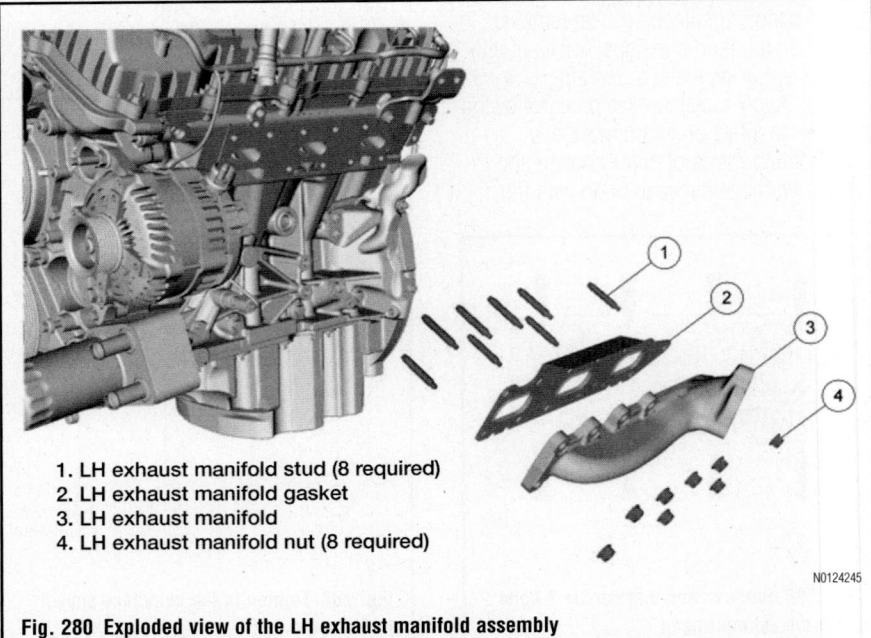

7. Using a new gasket, install the LH exhaust manifold and 8 new nuts. Tighten in 2 stages in the sequence shown:

    a. Stage 1: Tighten to 14 ft. lbs. (19 Nm).

    b. Stage 2: Tighten to 18 ft. lbs. (25 Nm).

Right Side

See Figures 282 and 283.

1. Remove the RH turbocharger.

2. Remove the 8 exhaust manifold nuts and the RH exhaust manifold. Discard the nuts and gasket.

3. Clean and inspect the RH exhaust manifold.

4. Remove and discard the 8 RH exhaust manifold studs.

✳✳ WARNING

Do not use metal scrapers, wire brushes, power abrasive discs or other abrasive means to clean the sealing surfaces. These may cause scratches and gouges resulting in leak paths. Use a plastic scraper to clean the sealing surfaces.

5. Clean the exhaust manifold mating surface of the cylinder head with metal surface prep. Follow the directions on the packaging.

To install:

6. Install 8 new RH exhaust manifold studs. Tighten to 106 inch lbs. (12 Nm).

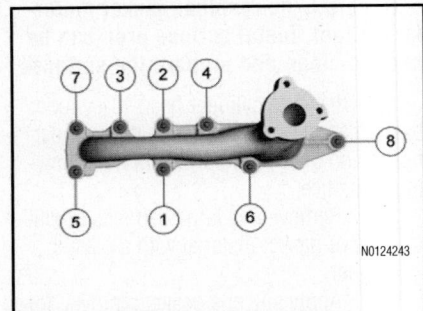

Fig. 281 Tighten in 2 stages in the sequence shown

1. LH exhaust manifold stud (8 required)
2. LH exhaust manifold gasket
3. LH exhaust manifold
4. LH exhaust manifold nut (8 required)

Fig. 280 Exploded view of the LH exhaust manifold assembly

Fig. 279 Tighten the new cylinder head bolts in 4 stages in the sequence shown

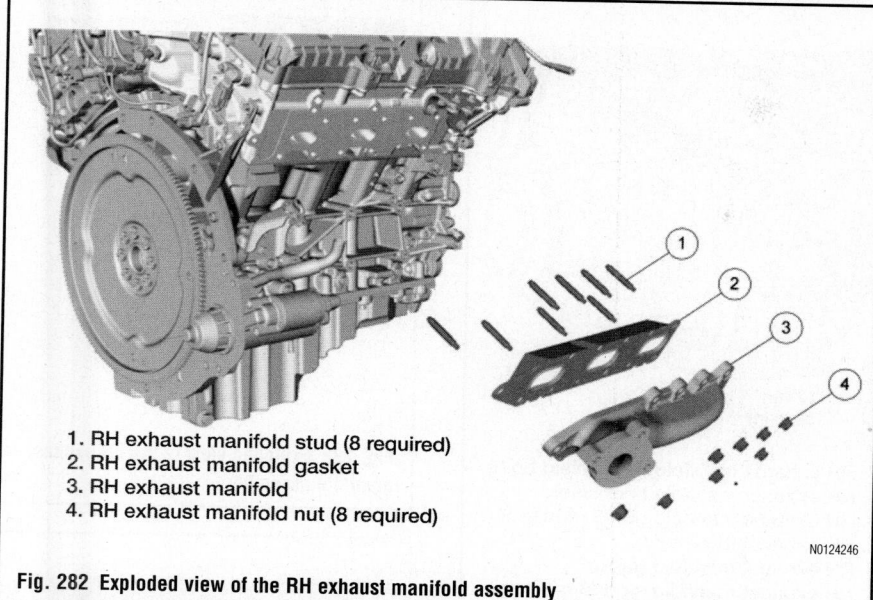

1. RH exhaust manifold stud (8 required)
2. RH exhaust manifold gasket
3. RH exhaust manifold
4. RH exhaust manifold nut (8 required)

N0124246

Fig. 282 Exploded view of the RH exhaust manifold assembly

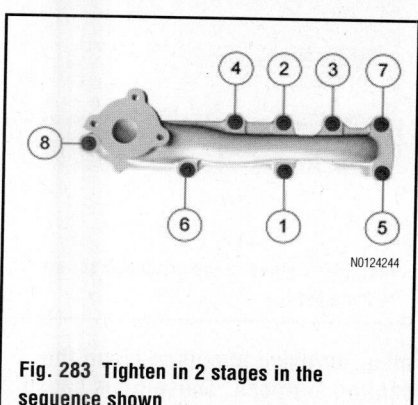

N0124244

Fig. 283 Tighten in 2 stages in the sequence shown

☀ WARNING

Failure to tighten the exhaust manifold nuts to specification a second time will cause the exhaust manifold to develop an exhaust leak.

7. Using a new gasket, install the RH exhaust manifold and 8 new nuts. Tighten in 2 stages in the sequence shown:
   a. Stage 1: Tighten to 14 ft. lbs. (19 Nm).
   b. Stage 2: Tighten to 18 ft. lbs. (25 Nm).

3.7L Engine

Left Side

See Figures 284 and 285.

1. With the vehicle in NEUTRAL, position it on a hoist.
2. Detach and disconnect the RH and LH Heated Oxygen Sensor (HO2S) electrical connectors.

3. Remove and discard the LH and RH catalytic convertor-to-exhaust manifold nuts and lower the catalytic convertor assembly.
4. Remove the 2 bolts and the LH exhaust manifold heat shield.
5. Remove the 6 nuts and the LH manifold. Discard the nuts and gasket.
6. Clean and inspect the LH exhaust manifold.
7. Remove and discard the 6 LH exhaust manifold studs.

☀ WARNING

Do not use metal scrapers, wire brushes, power abrasive discs or other abrasive means to clean the sealing surfaces. These may cause scratches and gouges resulting in leak paths. Use a plastic scraper to clean the sealing surfaces.

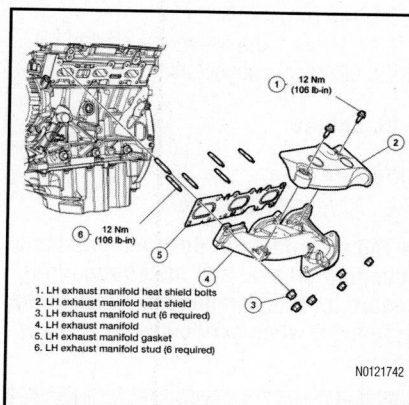

1. LH exhaust manifold heat shield bolts
2. LH exhaust manifold heat shield
3. LH exhaust manifold nut (6 required)
4. LH exhaust manifold
5. LH exhaust manifold gasket
6. LH exhaust manifold stud (6 required)

N0121742

Fig. 284 Exploded view of the LH exhaust manifold assembly

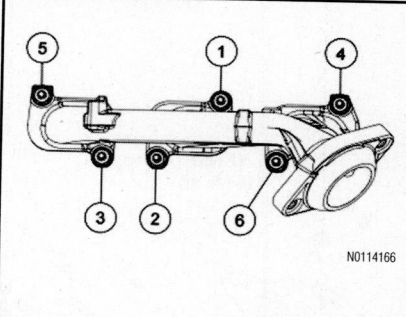

N0114166

Fig. 285 Tighten in 2 stages in the sequence shown

8. Clean the exhaust manifold mating surface of the cylinder head with metal surface prep. Follow the directions on the packaging.

To install:

9. Install 6 new LH exhaust manifold studs. Tighten to 106 inch lbs. (12 Nm).

☀ WARNING

Failure to tighten the exhaust manifold nuts to specification a second time will cause the exhaust manifold to develop an exhaust leak.

10. Using a new gasket, install the LH exhaust manifold and 6 new nuts. Tighten in 2 stages in the sequence shown:
    a. Stage 1: Tighten to 14 ft. lbs. (19 Nm).
    b. Stage 2: Tighten to 18 ft. lbs. (25 Nm).
11. Install the LH exhaust manifold heat shield and the 2 bolts. Tighten to 106 inch lbs. (12 Nm).
12. Raise the catalytic convertor and install the new LH and RH catalytic convertor-to-exhaust manifold nuts. Tighten to 35 ft. lbs. (45 Nm).
13. Connect and attach the RH and LH HO2S electrical connectors.

Right Side

See Figures 286 and 287.

1. With the vehicle in NEUTRAL, position it on a hoist.
2. Detach and disconnect the RH and LH Heated Oxygen Sensor (HO2S) electrical connectors.
3. Remove and discard the LH and RH catalytic convertor-to-exhaust manifold nuts and lower the catalytic convertor assembly.
4. Remove the 2 bolts and the RH exhaust manifold heat shield.
5. Remove the 6 nuts and the RH exhaust manifold. Discard the nuts and gasket.

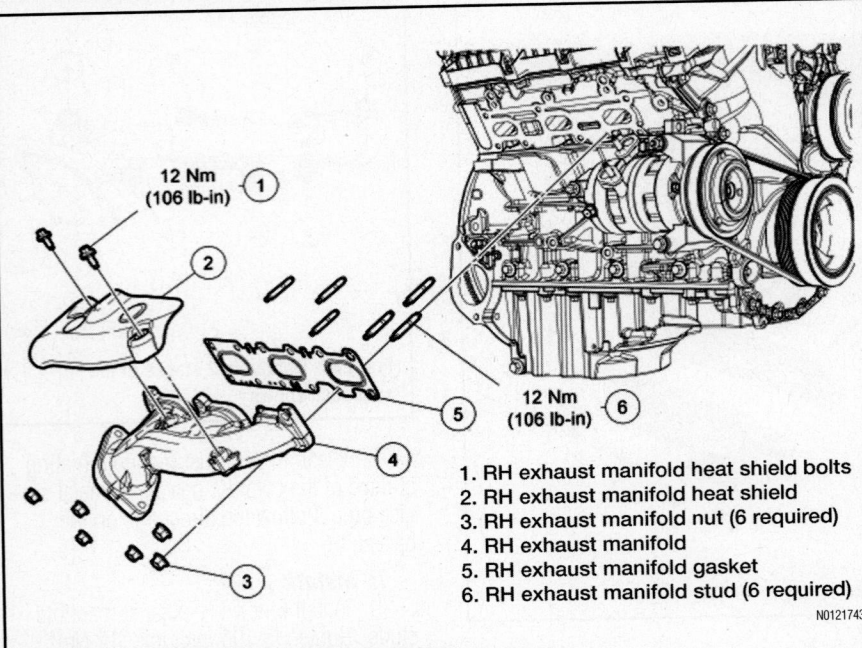

1. RH exhaust manifold heat shield bolts
2. RH exhaust manifold heat shield
3. RH exhaust manifold nut (6 required)
4. RH exhaust manifold
5. RH exhaust manifold gasket
6. RH exhaust manifold stud (6 required)

N0121743

Fig. 286 Exploded view of the RH exhaust manifold assembly

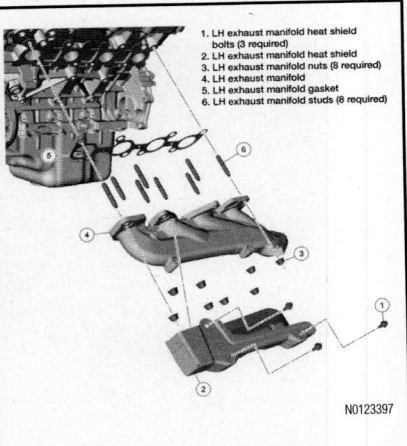

1. LH exhaust manifold heat shield bolts (3 required)
2. LH exhaust manifold heat shield
3. LH exhaust manifold nuts (8 required)
4. LH exhaust manifold
5. LH exhaust manifold gasket
6. LH exhaust manifold studs (8 required)

N0123397

Fig. 288 Exploded view of the LH exhaust manifold assembly

6. Clean and inspect the RH exhaust manifold.

7. Remove and discard the 6 RH exhaust manifold studs.

❋❋ WARNING

Do not use metal scrapers, wire brushes, power abrasive discs or other abrasive means to clean the sealing surfaces. These may cause scratches and gouges resulting in leak paths. Use a plastic scraper to clean the sealing surfaces.

8. Clean the exhaust manifold mating surface of the cylinder head with metal surface prep. Follow the directions on the packaging.

To install:

9. Install 6 new RH exhaust manifold studs. Tighten to 106 inch lbs. (12 Nm).

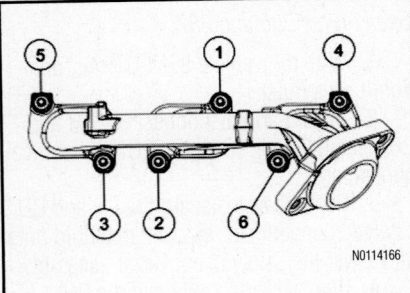

N0114166

Fig. 287 Tighten in 2 stages in the sequence shown

❋❋ WARNING

Failure to tighten the exhaust manifold nuts to specification a second time will cause the exhaust manifold to develop an exhaust leak.

10. Using a new gasket, install the RH exhaust manifold and 6 new nuts. Tighten in 2 stages in the sequence shown:
 a. Stage 1: Tighten to 14 ft. lbs. (19 Nm).
 b. Stage 2: Tighten to 18 ft. lbs. (25 Nm).

11. Install the RH exhaust manifold heat shield and the 2 bolts. Tighten to 106 ft. lbs. (12 Nm).

12. Raise the catalytic convertor and install the new LH and RH catalytic convertor-to-exhaust manifold nuts. Tighten to 35 ft. lbs. (45 Nm).

13. Connect and attach the RH and LH HO2S electrical connectors.

5.0L Engine

Left Side

See Figures 288 and 289.

➡The manufacturer does not provide a specific Removal and Installation procedure for this component. Refer to the graphic(s) when servicing this component.

❋❋ WARNING

Do not use metal scrapers, wire brushes, power abrasive discs or

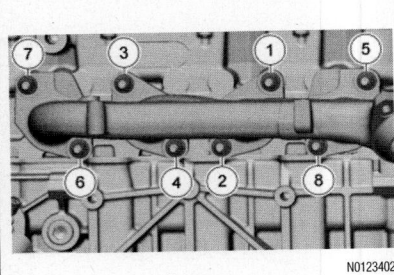

N0123402

Fig. 289 Tighten in the sequence shown in 2 stages

other abrasive means to clean the sealing surfaces. These tools cause scratches and gouges which make leak paths. Use a plastic scraper to clean the sealing surfaces.

1. Clean the exhaust manifold mating surface of the cylinder head with metal surface prep. Follow the directions on the packaging.

2. Install 8 new LH exhaust manifold studs. Tighten to 18 ft. lbs. (24 Nm).

3. Install new gaskets, the LH exhaust manifold and 8 new nuts. Tighten in the sequence shown in 2 stages.
 a. Stage 1: Tighten to 18 ft. lbs. (24 Nm).
 b. Stage 2: Tighten to 24 ft. lbs. (32 Nm).

Right Side

See Figures 290 and 291.

➡The manufacturer does not provide a specific Removal and Installation procedure for this component. Refer to the graphic(s) when servicing this component.

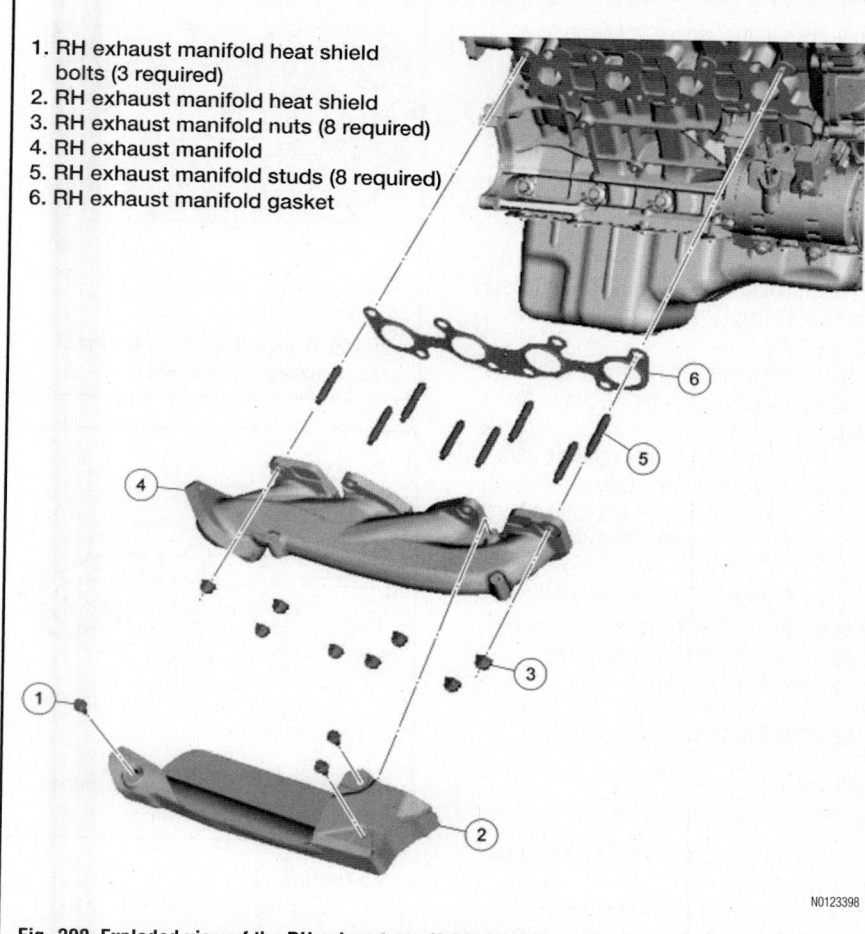

1. RH exhaust manifold heat shield bolts (3 required)
2. RH exhaust manifold heat shield
3. RH exhaust manifold nuts (8 required)
4. RH exhaust manifold
5. RH exhaust manifold studs (8 required)
6. RH exhaust manifold gasket

Fig. 290 Exploded view of the RH exhaust manifold assembly

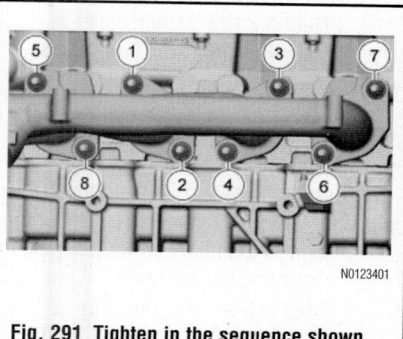

Fig. 291 Tighten in the sequence shown in 2 stages

✳✳ WARNING

Do not use metal scrapers, wire brushes, power abrasive discs or other abrasive means to clean the sealing surfaces. These tools cause scratches and gouges which make leak paths. Use a plastic scraper to clean the sealing surfaces.

1. Clean the exhaust manifold mating surface of the cylinder head with metal surface prep. Follow the directions on the packaging.

2. Install 8 new RH exhaust manifold studs. Tighten to 18 ft. lbs. (24 Nm).

3. Install new gaskets, the RH exhaust manifold and 8 new nuts. Tighten in the sequence shown in 2 stages.

   a. Stage 1: Tighten to 18 ft. lbs. (24 Nm).

   b. Stage 2: Tighten to 24 ft. lbs. (32 Nm).

4.6L (2V) Engine

Left Side

See Figure 292

1. With the vehicle in NEUTRAL, position it on a hoist.

2. Remove the LH inner fenderwell.

3. Remove the 4 exhaust Y-pipe flange nuts (2 RH and 2 LH) and position the exhaust Y-pipe flange aside.

4. Remove the EGR system module-to-exhaust manifold tube.

5. Remove and discard the 8 exhaust manifold nuts.

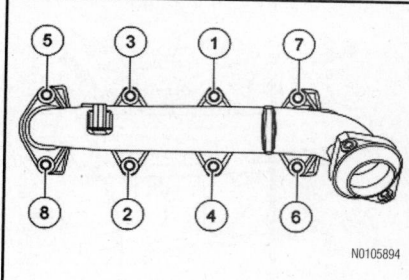

Fig. 292 Tighten in the sequence shown in 2 stages

6. Remove and discard the 8 exhaust manifold-to-cylinder head studs.

7. Remove the LH exhaust manifold and discard the gasket.

8. Inspect the exhaust manifold for flatness.

To install:

✳✳ WARNING

Do not use metal scrapers, wire brushes, power abrasive discs or other abrasive means to clean the sealing surfaces. These may cause scratches and gouges resulting in leak paths. Use a plastic scraper to clean the sealing surfaces.

9. Clean the sealing surfaces with metal surface prep.

10. Position the new exhaust manifold gaskets, the LH exhaust manifold and install 8 new exhaust manifold-to-cylinder head studs. Tighten to 106 inch lbs. (12 Nm).

11. Install 8 new exhaust manifold nuts and tighten in the sequence shown in 2 stages.

   a. Stage 1: Tighten to 13 ft. lbs. (18 Nm).

   b. Stage 2: Tighten to 15 ft. lbs. (20 Nm).

12. Install the EGR system module-to-exhaust manifold tube. Tighten to 30 ft. lbs. (40 Nm).

13. Position the Y-pipe flange and install the 4 nuts (2 RH and 2 LH). Tighten to 30 ft. lbs. (40 Nm).

14. Install the LH inner fenderwell.

Right Side

See Figures 293 and 294.

1. With the vehicle in NEUTRAL, position it on a hoist.

2. Remove the starter.

3. Remove the RH inner fenderwell.

4. Remove the 4 exhaust Y-pipe flange nuts (2 RH and 2 LH) and position the exhaust Y-pipe flange aside.

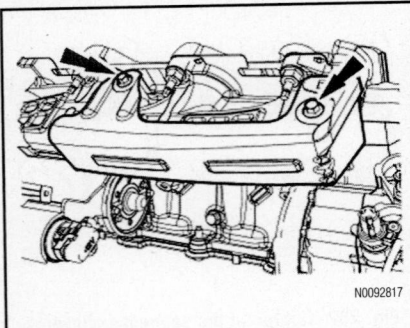

Fig. 293 Remove the 2 bolts and the exhaust manifold heat shield

5. Loosen the 2 RH catalytic converter-to-exhaust intermediate pipe bolts.

6. Remove the 2 bolts and the exhaust manifold heat shield.

7. Remove and discard the 8 exhaust manifold nuts.

8. Remove the RH exhaust manifold and discard the 2 gaskets.

9. Remove and discard the 8 exhaust manifold-to-cylinder head studs.

10. Inspect the exhaust manifold for flatness.

To install:

❋❋ WARNING

Do not use metal scrapers, wire brushes, power abrasive discs, or other abrasive means to clean the sealing surfaces. These may cause scratches and gouges resulting in leak paths. Use a plastic scraper to clean the sealing surfaces.

11. Clean the sealing surfaces with metal surface prep.

12. Install 8 new exhaust manifold-to-cylinder head studs and then, using 2 new exhaust manifold gaskets, position the 2 gaskets and exhaust manifold onto the cylinder head. Tighten to 106 inch lbs. (12 Nm).

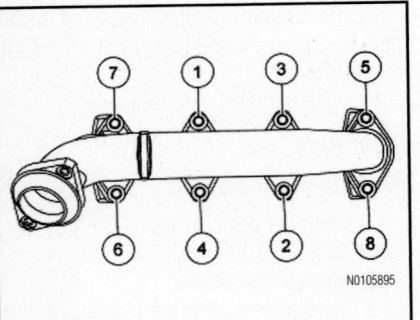

Fig. 294 Tighten in the sequence shown in 2 stages

13. Install 8 new exhaust manifold nuts and tighten in the sequence shown in 2 stages.

   a. Stage 1: Tighten to 18 Nm (159 lb-in).

   b. Stage 2: Tighten to 20 Nm (177 lb-in).

14. Install the exhaust manifold heat shield and the 2 bolts. Tighten to 89 inch lbs. (10 Nm).

15. Position the Y-pipe flange and install 4 nuts (2 RH and 2 LH). Tighten to 30 ft. lbs. (40 Nm).

16. Tighten the 2 RH catalytic converter-to-exhaust intermediate pipe bolts in the following sequence.

   a. Snug the outer RH catalytic converter-to-exhaust intermediate pipe bolt.

   b. Tighten the inner RH catalytic converter-to-exhaust intermediate pipe bolt.

   c. Tighten the outer RH catalytic converter-to-exhaust intermediate pipe bolt.

17. Install the RH inner fenderwell.

18. Install the starter.

4.6L (3V) Engine

Left Side

See Figures 295 through 297.

1. With the vehicle in NEUTRAL, position it on a hoist.

2. Remove the LH inner fenderwell.

3. Remove and discard the 4 exhaust manifold-to-dual converter Y-pipe flange nuts.

4. Remove the 2 dual converter Y-pipe-to-exhaust pipe flange bolts.

5. Remove the 3 bolts and the LH exhaust manifold heat shield.

6. Remove the 8 nuts, the LH exhaust manifold and the 2 gaskets. Discard the nuts and the gaskets.

7. Remove and discard the 8 LH exhaust manifold studs.

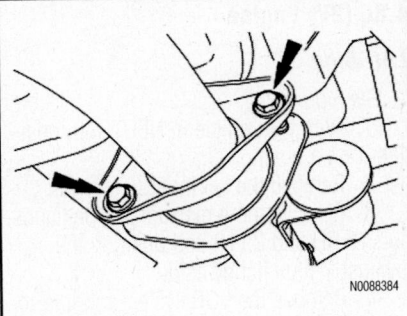

Fig. 295 Remove the 2 dual converter Y-pipe-to-exhaust pipe flange bolts

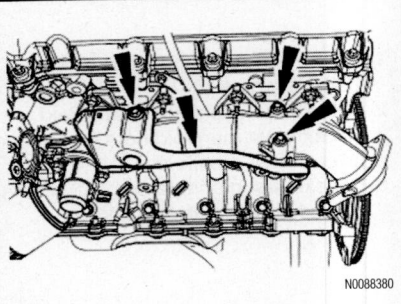

Fig. 296 Remove the 3 bolts and the LH exhaust manifold heat shield

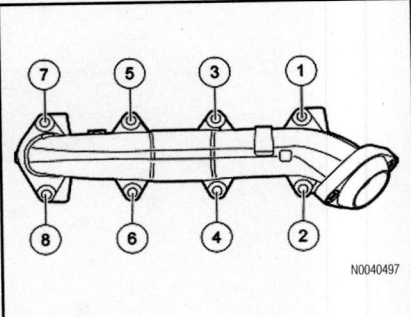

Fig. 297 Tighten the 8 exhaust manifold nuts in the sequence shown

To install:

8. Clean and inspect the LH exhaust manifold.

9. Install 8 new LH exhaust manifold studs. Tighten to 106 inch lbs. (12 Nm).

10. Position 2 new gaskets, the LH exhaust manifold and install 8 new nuts finger-tight.

11. Tighten the 8 exhaust manifold nuts in the sequence shown. Tighten to 18 ft. lbs. (25 Nm).

12. Install the heat shield and the 3 bolts. Tighten to 89 inch lbs. (10 Nm).

13. Connect the dual converter Y-pipe to the exhaust manifolds and install 4 new nuts. Tighten to 30 ft. lbs. (40 Nm).

14. Install the 2 dual converter Y-pipe-to-exhaust pipe flange bolts. Tighten to 35 ft. lbs. (47 Nm).

15. Install the LH inner fenderwell.

Right Side

See Figures 295 and 298.

1. With the vehicle in NEUTRAL, position it on a hoist.

2. Remove the starter.

3. Remove the RH inner fenderwell.

4. Remove and discard the 4 exhaust manifold-to-dual converter Y-pipe flange nuts.

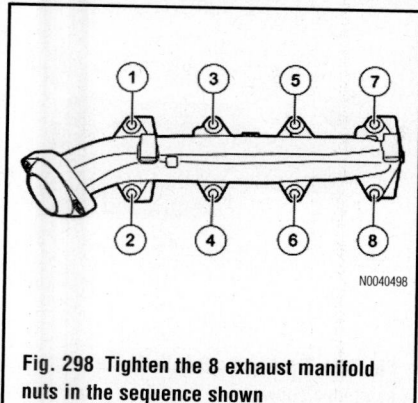

Fig. 298 Tighten the 8 exhaust manifold nuts in the sequence shown

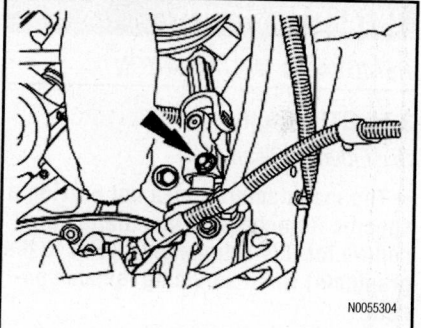

Fig. 299 Remove the bolt and disconnect the steering shaft and position aside

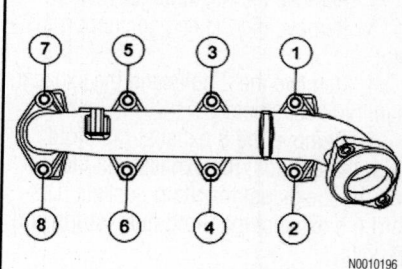

Fig. 301 Tighten to 18 ft. lbs. (25 Nm) in the sequence shown

5. Remove the 2 dual converter Y-pipe-to-exhaust pipe bolts.

6. Rotate the accessory drive belt tensioner clockwise and detach the accessory drive belt from the A/C compressor.

7. Remove the 3 bolts and position the A/C compressor aside.

8. Remove and discard the 8 exhaust manifold nuts.

9. Remove and discard the 8 exhaust manifold studs.

10. Remove the RH exhaust manifold and the gaskets. Discard the gaskets.

To install:

11. Clean and inspect the exhaust manifold.

12. Position the new gaskets and the RH exhaust manifold.

13. Install 8 new RH exhaust manifold studs. Tighten to 106 inch lbs. (12 Nm).

14. Install 8 new exhaust manifold nuts finger-tight.

15. Tighten the 8 exhaust manifold nuts in the sequence shown. Tighten to 18 ft. lbs. (25 Nm).

16. Position the A/C compressor and install the 3 bolts. Tighten to 18 ft. lbs. (25 Nm).

17. Rotate the accessory drive belt tensioner clockwise and install the accessory drive belt on the A/C compressor.

18. Connect the dual converter Y-pipe to the exhaust manifolds and install 4 new nuts. Tighten to 30 ft. lbs. (40 Nm).

19. Install the 2 dual converter Y-pipe-to-exhaust pipe flange bolts. Tighten to 35 ft. lbs. (47 Nm).

20. Install the RH inner fenderwell.

21. Install the starter.

5.4L (3V) Engine

Left Side

See Figures 299 through 301.

1. With the vehicle in NEUTRAL, position it on a hoist.

2. Remove the Air Cleaner (ACL) outlet pipe.

3. Remove the coolant expansion bottle.

> ※※ **WARNING**
>
> **Do not allow the steering column shaft to rotate while the intermediate shaft is disconnected or damage to the clockspring can result. If there is evidence that the shaft has rotated, the clockspring must be removed and re-centered.**

4. Remove the bolt and disconnect the steering shaft and position aside.

5. Remove the 4 (2 LH and 2 RH) exhaust manifold-to-catalytic converter nuts.

6. For 4WD vehicles, remove the front driveshaft.

7. Remove the 8 exhaust manifold nuts, the 8 studs, the exhaust manifold and the 2 exhaust manifold gaskets. Discard the exhaust manifold nuts, studs and gaskets.

> ※※ **WARNING**
>
> **Do not use metal scrapers, wire brushes, power abrasive discs or other abrasive means to clean the**

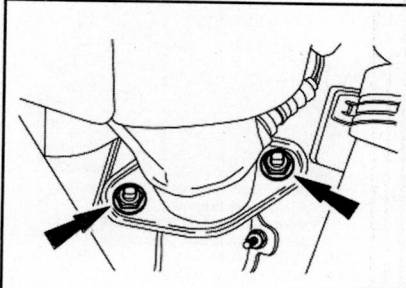

Fig. 300 Remove the 4 (2 LH and 2 RH) exhaust manifold-to-catalytic converter nuts

sealing surfaces. These may cause scratches and gouges resulting in leak paths. Use a plastic scraper to clean the sealing surfaces.

► Clean the sealing surfaces with metal surface prep. Follow the directions on the packaging.

8. Remove and discard the 2 exhaust manifold gaskets. Clean the sealing surfaces with metal surface prep.

9. Inspect the exhaust manifold.

To install:

10. Using 2 new exhaust manifold gaskets and 8 new studs, position the 2 gaskets and exhaust manifold and install the 8 studs. Tighten to 106 inch lbs. (12 Nm).

11. Using new exhaust manifold nuts, install the 8 nuts. Tighten to 18 ft. lbs. (25 Nm) in the sequence shown.

12. For 4WD vehicles, install the front driveshaft.

> ※※ **WARNING**
>
> **Do not allow the steering column shaft to rotate while the intermediate shaft is disconnected or damage to the clockspring can result. If there is evidence that the shaft has rotated, the clockspring must be removed and re-centered.**

13. Connect the steering shaft and install the bolt. To install, tighten to 22 ft. lbs. (30 Nm).

14. Install the 4 exhaust manifold-to-catalytic converter nuts.

15. Install the coolant expansion tank.

16. Install the ACL outlet tube.

Right Side

See Figure 302.

1. With the vehicle in NEUTRAL, position it on a hoist.

2. Remove the RH inner fenderwell.

3. Remove the RH engine support insulator.

4. Remove the 2 bolts and the exhaust manifold heat shield.

5. Remove the 8 exhaust manifold nuts, the 8 studs, the exhaust manifold and the 2 exhaust manifold gaskets. Discard the exhaust manifold nuts, studs and gaskets.

☀ WARNING

Do not use metal scrapers, wire brushes, power abrasive discs or other abrasive means to clean the sealing surfaces. These may cause scratches and gouges resulting in leak paths. Use a plastic scraper to clean the sealing surfaces.

➡ Clean the sealing surfaces with metal surface prep. Follow the directions on the packaging.

6. Remove and discard the 2 exhaust manifold gaskets. Clean the sealing surfaces with metal surface prep.

7. Inspect the exhaust manifold.

To install:

8. Using 2 new exhaust manifold gaskets and 8 new studs, position the 2 gaskets and exhaust manifold and install the 8 studs. Tighten to 106 inch lbs. (12 Nm).

9. Using 8 new exhaust manifold nuts, install the 8 nuts. Tighten to 18 ft. lbs. (25 Nm) in the sequence shown.

10. Position the exhaust manifold heat shield and install the 2 bolts. Tighten to 89 inch lbs. (10 Nm).

11. Install the RH engine support insulator.

12. Install the RH inner fenderwell.

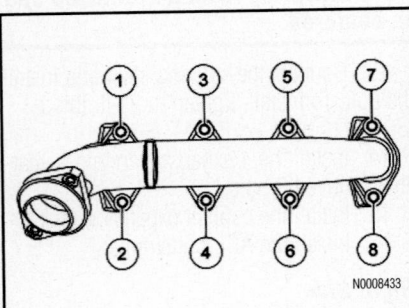

Fig. 302 Tighten to 18 ft. lbs. (25 Nm) in the sequence shown

INTAKE MANIFOLD

REMOVAL & INSTALLATION

3.5L GTDI Engine

See Figures 303 and 304.

➡ The manufacturer does not provide a specific Removal and Installation procedure for this component. Refer to the graphic(s) when servicing this component.

1. Loosen the 8 bolts and remove the intake manifold.

   a. Remove and discard the gaskets.

   b. Clean and inspect all of the sealing surfaces of the cylinder heads and the intake manifold.

To install:

☀ WARNING

If the engine is repaired or replaced because of upper engine failure, typically including valve or piston damage, check the intake manifold for metal debris. If metal debris is found, install a new intake manifold. Failure to follow these instructions can result in engine damage.

2. Using new gaskets, install the intake manifold and tighten the 8 bolts in the

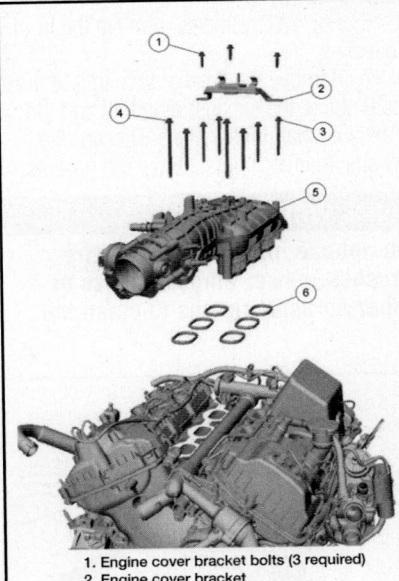

1. Engine cover bracket bolts (3 required)
2. Engine cover bracket
3. Intake manifold bolt (6 required)
4. Intake manifold bolt (2 required)
5. Intake manifold
6. Intake manifold gasket

Fig. 303 Exploded view of the intake manifold assembly

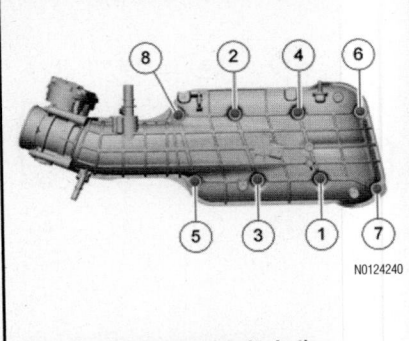

Fig. 304 Tighten the 8 bolts in the sequence shown

sequence shown. Tighten to 89 inch lbs. (10 Nm).

3.7L Engine

Upper Intake Manifold

See Figures 305 through 307.

1. Remove the Air Cleaner (ACL) outlet pipe.

2. Disconnect the PCV tube quick connect coupling from the intake manifold.

3. Disconnect the Throttle Body (TB) electrical connector.

4. Detach the TB electrical connector wiring harness pin-type retainer from the TB.

5. Disconnect Evaporative Emission (EVAP) tube from the EVAP canister purge valve.

6. Detach the EVAP hose retainer from the intake manifold.

7. Disconnect the EVAP canister purge valve electrical connector.

8. Detach the EVAP canister purge valve electrical connector wiring harness pin-type retainer.

9. Disconnect the brake booster vacuum hose from the engine.

10. Detach the wiring harness pin-type retainer from the rear of the upper intake manifold.

11. Remove the upper intake manifold support bracket bolt from the front of the RH cylinder head.

12. Loosen the 7 bolts and remove the upper intake manifold.

   a. Remove and discard the gaskets.

   b. Clean and inspect all of the sealing surfaces of the upper and lower intake manifold.

To install:

☀ WARNING

If the engine is repaired or replaced because of upper engine failure, typically including valve or piston damage, check the intake manifold for

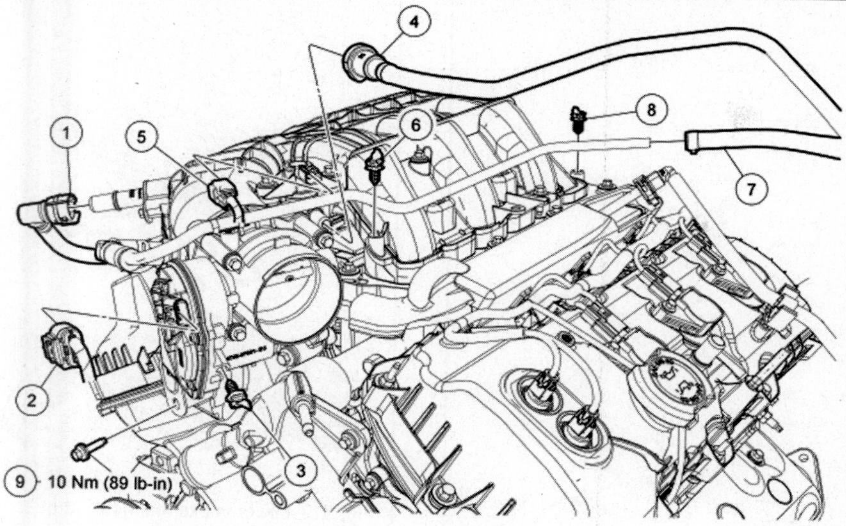

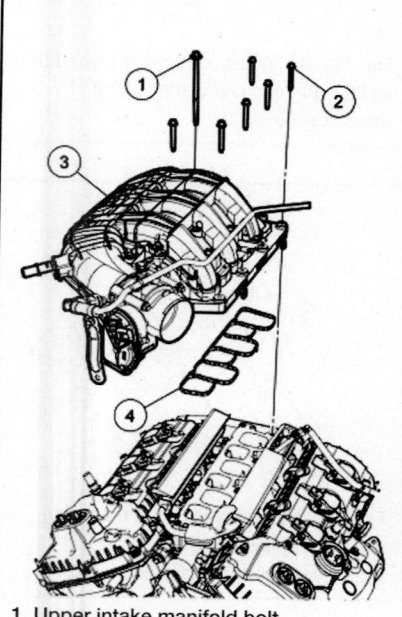

1. PCV tube quick connect coupling
2. Throttle Body (TB) electrical connector
3. TB electrical connector wiring harness pin-type retainer
4. Evaporative Emission (EVAP) tube
5. EVAP canister purge valve electrical connector
6. EVAP canister purge valve electrical connector wiring harness pin-type retainer
7. Brake booster vacuum hose
8. Wiring harness pin-type retainer
9. Upper intake manifold support bracket bolt

N0121773

Fig. 305 Upper intake manifold—1 of 2

1. Upper intake manifold bolt
2. Upper intake manifold bolt (6 required)
3. Upper intake manifold
4. Upper intake manifold gasket

N0114102

Fig. 306 Upper intake manifold—2 of 2

metal debris. If metal debris is found, install a new intake manifold. Failure to follow these instructions can result in engine damage.**

13. Using new gaskets, install the upper intake manifold and tighten the 7 bolts in the sequence shown in 2 stages.

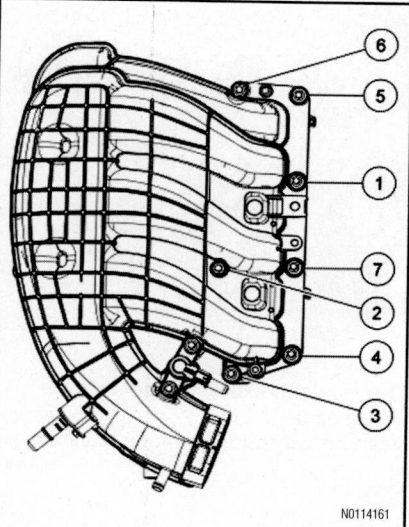

N0114161

Fig. 307 Tighten the 7 bolts in the sequence shown in 2 stages

a. Stage 1: Tighten to 89 inch lbs. (10 Nm).
b. Stage 2: Tighten an additional 45 degrees.

14. Install the upper intake manifold support bracket bolt to the RH cylinder head. Tighten to 89 inch lbs. (10 Nm).

15. Attach the wiring harness pin-type retainer to the rear of the upper intake manifold.

16. Connect the brake booster vacuum hose to the engine.

17. Connect the EVAP canister purge valve electrical connector.

18. Attach the EVAP canister purge valve electrical connector wiring harness pin-type retainer.

19. Connect EVAP tube to the EVAP canister purge valve.

20. Attach the EVAP hose retainer to the intake manifold.

21. Connect the TB electrical connector.

22. Attach the TB electrical connector wiring harness pin-type retainer to the TB.

23. Connect the PCV tube quick connect coupling to the intake manifold.

24. Install the ACL outlet pipe.

Lower Intake Manifold

See Figures 308 through 312.

➡ **The manufacturer does not provide a specific Removal and Installation procedure for this component. Refer to the graphic(s) when servicing this component.**

To install:

❋❋ WARNING

If the engine is repaired or replaced because of upper engine failure, typically including valve or piston damage, check the intake manifold for metal debris. If metal debris if found, install a new intake manifold. Failure to follow these instructions can result in engine damage.

1. Using new lower intake manifold gaskets, install the lower intake manifold and the 10 bolts and tighten in the sequence shown. Tighten to 89 inch lbs. (10 Nm).

2. Using new thermostat housing gasket and coolant tube O-ring seal, install the thermostat housing and the 4 bolts and tighten in the sequence shown in 2 stages.

a. Stage 1: Tighten to 71 inch lbs. (8 Nm).
b. Stage 2: Tighten an additional 45 degrees.

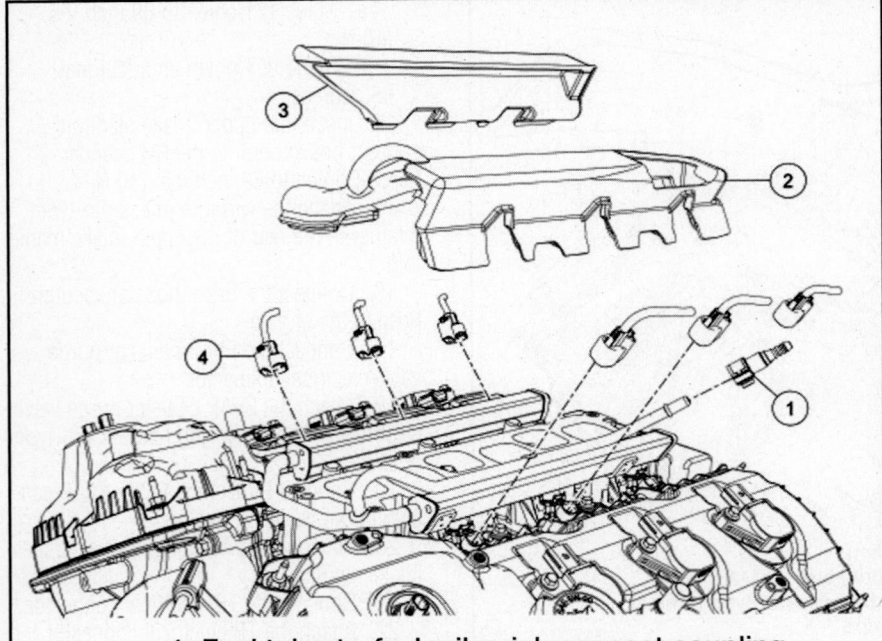

1. Fuel tube-to-fuel rail quick connect coupling
2. LH fuel rail noise insulator shield
3. RH fuel rail noise insulator shield
4. Fuel injector electrical connector (6 required)

N0119405

Fig. 308 Lower intake manifold—1 of 3

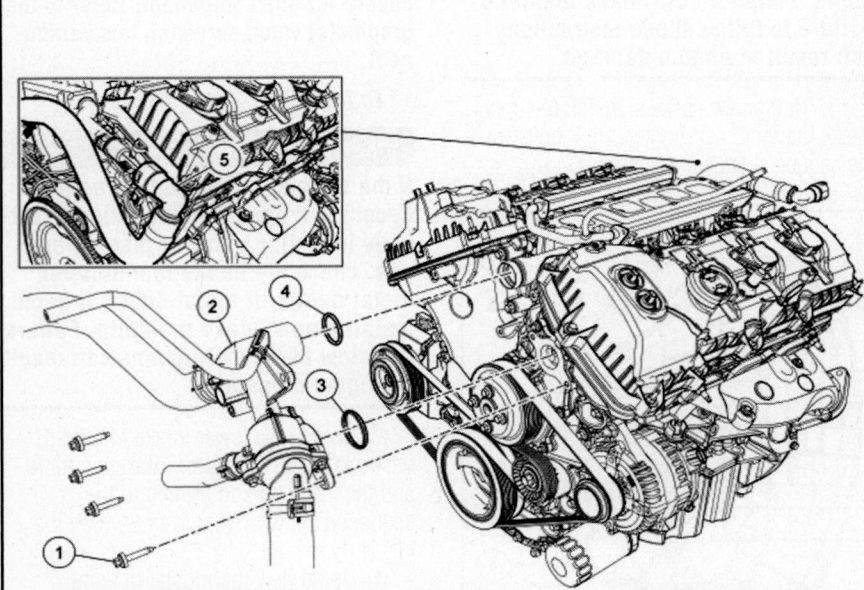

1. Thermostat housing bolt (4 required)
2. Thermostat housing
3. Thermostat housing gasket
4. Thermostat housing-to-coolant tube O-ring seal
5. Heater hose-to-lower intake manifold

N0119406

Fig. 309 Lower intake manifold—2 of 3

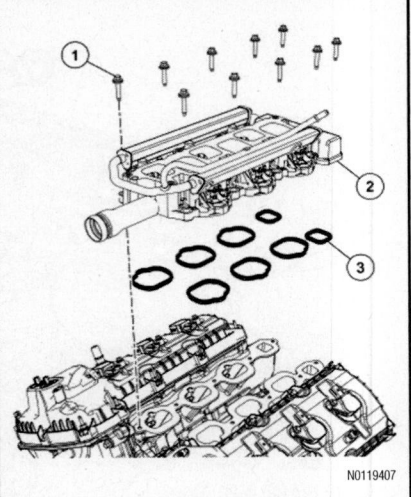

N0119407

Fig. 310 Lower intake manifold—3 of 3: showing bolts (1), manifold (2), and gaskets (3)

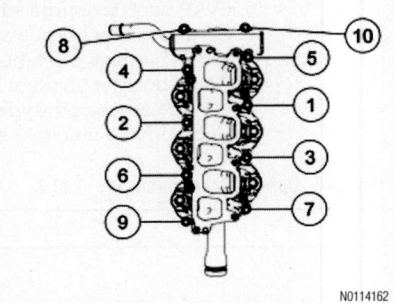

N0114162

Fig. 311 Install the lower intake manifold and the 10 bolts and tighten in the sequence shown

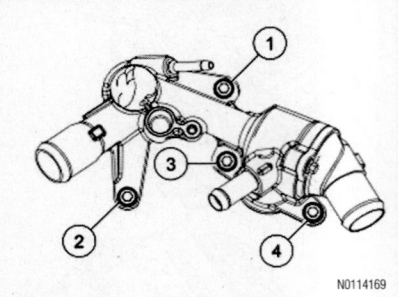

N0114169

Fig. 312 Install the thermostat housing and the 4 bolts and tighten in the sequence shown in 2 stages

5.0L Engine

See Figures 313 through 315.

➡The manufacturer does not provide a specific Removal and Installation procedure for this component. Refer to the graphic(s) when servicing this component.

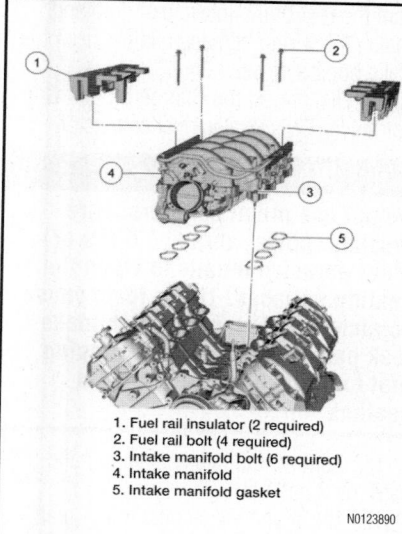

1. Fuel rail insulator (2 required)
2. Fuel rail bolt (4 required)
3. Intake manifold bolt (6 required)
4. Intake manifold
5. Intake manifold gasket

N0123890

Fig. 313 Exploded view of the intake manifold assembly

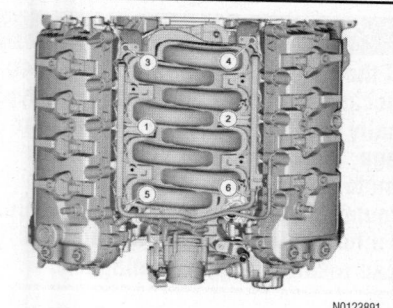

N0123891

Fig. 314 Tighten the 6 intake manifold bolts in the sequence shown in 2 stages

N0123892

Fig. 315 Tighten in the sequence shown in 3 stages

To install:

❊❊ WARNING

If the engine is repaired or replaced because of upper engine failure, typically including valve or piston damage, check the intake manifold for

metal debris. If metal debris if found, install a new intake manifold. Failure to follow these instructions can result in engine damage.

➡ Clean the sealing surfaces with metal surface prep. Follow the directions on the packaging. Inspect the mating surfaces.

1. Using new gaskets, install the intake manifold.
2. Tighten the 6 intake manifold bolts in the sequence shown in 2 stages.
   a. Stage 1: Tighten to 89 inch lbs. (10 Nm).
   b. Stage 2: Tighten an additional 45 degrees.
3. Install the 4 fuel rail bolts. Tighten in the sequence shown in 3 stages.
   a. Stage 1: Hand-tighten.
   b. Stage 2: Tighten to 89 inch lbs. (10 Nm).
   c. Stage 2: Tighten an additional 90 degrees.

4.6L (2V) Engine

See Figure 316.

❊❊ CAUTION

Do not smoke, carry lighted tobacco or have an open flame of any type when working on or near any fuel-related component. Highly flammable mixtures are always present and may be ignited. Failure to follow these instructions may result in serious personal injury.

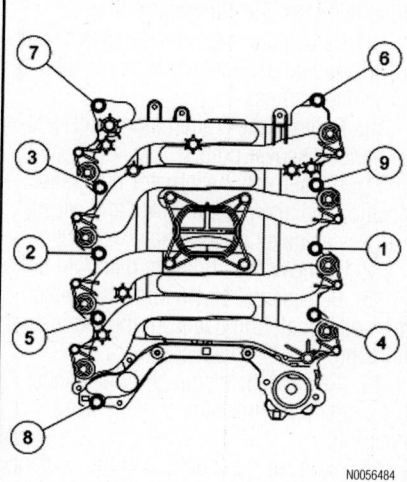

N0056484

Fig. 316 Tighten the 9 intake manifold bolts in the sequence shown

❊❊ CAUTION

Before working on or disconnecting any of the fuel tubes or fuel system components, relieve the fuel system pressure to prevent accidental spraying of fuel. Fuel in the fuel system remains under high pressure, even when the engine is not running. Failure to follow this instruction may result in serious personal injury.

1. Disconnect the battery ground cable.
2. Disconnect the fuel supply tube quick connect coupling.
3. Drain the cooling system.
4. Remove the 8 ignition coils.
5. Remove the alternator.
6. Remove the EGR system module-to-exhaust manifold tube.
7. Disconnect the EGR system module electrical connector.
8. Disconnect the quick connect couplings and remove the PCV tube.
9. Disconnect the Electronic Throttle Control (ETC) and the wiring harness retainer.
10. Disconnect the heater coolant hose and position aside.
11. Disconnect the 8 fuel injector electrical connectors.
12. Disconnect the Evaporative Emission (EVAP) canister purge valve electrical connector and EVAP tube quick connect fitting.
13. Disconnect the Knock Sensor (KS) electrical connector, electrical connector retainer and the 2 engine wiring harness retainers to the rear of the intake manifold.
14. Disconnect the brake booster vacuum hose.
15. Disconnect the upper radiator coolant hose and position aside.
16. Remove the 2 thermostat housing bolts and the thermostat housing and discard the O-ring seal.
17. Remove the thermostat.
18. Remove the 9 intake manifold bolts.
19. Remove the intake manifold and discard the RH and LH intake manifold gaskets.

To install:

❊❊ WARNING

Do not use metal scrapers, wire brushes, power abrasive discs or other abrasive means to clean the sealing surfaces. These tools cause scratches and gouges which make leak paths. Use a plastic scraping tool to remove all traces of old sealant.

20. Clean the mating surfaces of the cylinder head and the intake manifold with metal surface prep and silicone gasket remover. Follow the directions on the packaging.

✳✳ WARNING

If the engine is repaired or replaced because of upper engine failure, typically including valve or piston damage, check the intake manifold for metal debris. If metal debris is found, install a new intake manifold. Failure to follow these instructions can result in engine damage.

21. Install the intake manifold in the following sequence.
   a. Position the new intake manifold gaskets.
   b. Position the intake manifold.
   c. Loosely install the 9 intake manifold bolts.
22. Tighten the 9 intake manifold bolts in the sequence shown. Tighten to 89 inch lbs. (10 Nm).
23. Install the thermostat, a new thermostat housing O-ring seal, the thermostat housing and the 2 bolts. Tighten to 18 ft. lbs. (25 Nm).
24. Connect the upper radiator coolant hose.
25. Connect the fuel supply tube quick connect coupling.
26. Connect the brake booster vacuum hose.
27. Connect the KS electrical connector, electrical connector retainer and the 2 engine wiring harness retainers to the rear of the intake manifold.
28. Connect the EVAP canister purge valve electrical connector and the EVAP tube quick connect fitting.
29. Connect the 8 fuel injector electrical connectors.
30. Connect the heater coolant hose.
31. Connect the ETC and the wiring harness retainer.
32. Position the PCV tube and connect the quick connect couplings.
33. Connect the EGR system module electrical connector.
34. Install the EGR system module-to-exhaust manifold tube. Tighten to 30 ft. lbs. (40 Nm).
35. Install the 8 ignition coils.
36. Install the alternator.
37. Connect the battery ground cable.
38. Fill and bleed the engine cooling system.

4.6L (3V) Engine
See Figure 317.

✳✳ CAUTION

Do not smoke, carry lighted tobacco or have an open flame of any type when working on or near any fuel-related component. Highly flammable mixtures are always present and may be ignited. Failure to follow these instructions may result in serious personal injury.

✳✳ CAUTION

Before working on or disconnecting any of the fuel tubes or fuel system components, relieve the fuel system pressure to prevent accidental spraying of fuel. Fuel in the fuel system remains under high pressure, even when the engine is not running. Failure to follow this instruction may result in serious personal injury.

1. Disconnect the battery ground cable.
2. Remove the Air Cleaner (ACL) outlet pipe.
3. Drain the cooling system.
4. Remove the fuel rail and injectors.
5. Disconnect the quick connect couplings and remove the PCV tube.
6. Disconnect the heated PCV element electrical connector.

→**Four-Wheel Drive (4WD) shown, Rear Wheel Drive (RWD) similar.**

7. Disconnect the brake booster vacuum hose from the vacuum tee.
8. Rotate the accessory drive belt tensioner clockwise and detach the accessory drive belt from the alternator pulley.
9. Detach the radio interference capacitor wiring harness retainer from the alternator wiring harness.
10. Remove the 2 alternator bracket-to-coolant crossover bolts.
11. Loosen the 2 alternator nuts, and position the alternator, bracket and wiring harness aside as an assembly.
12. Remove the 10 intake manifold bolts.
13. Release the clamp and disconnect the upper radiator hose from the thermostat housing.
14. Release the clamp and disconnect the heater hose from the coolant crossover manifold.
15. Remove the 2 bolts and the coolant crossover manifold and discard the 2 gaskets.
16. Position the intake manifold forward and detach the 3 wiring harness retainers

from the rear of the intake manifold and detach the wiring harness retainer from the brake booster hose.
17. Disconnect the Charge Motion Control Valve (CMCV) electrical connector.

✳✳ WARNING

Do not use metal scrapers, wire brushes, power abrasive discs or other abrasive means to clean the sealing surfaces. These tools cause scratches and gouges which make leak paths. Use a plastic scraping tool to remove all traces of old sealant.

18. Remove the intake manifold and discard the 2 gaskets.
19. Clean and inspect the intake manifold and coolant crossover manifold sealing surfaces with metal surface prep. Follow the directions on the packaging.

To install:

✳✳ WARNING

If the engine is repaired or replaced because of upper engine failure, typically including valve or piston damage, check the intake manifold for metal debris. If metal debris is found, install a new intake manifold. Failure to follow these instructions can result in engine damage.

20. Using 2 new intake manifold gaskets, position the intake manifold.
21. Connect the CMCV electrical connector.

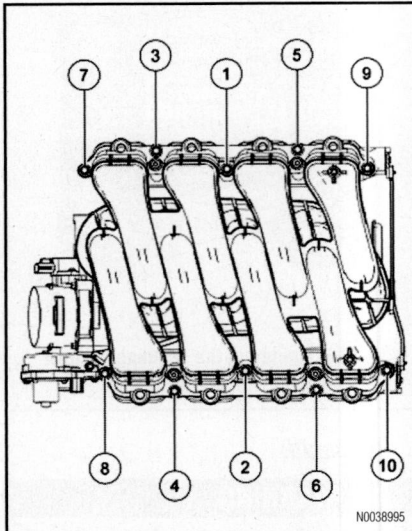

Fig. 317 Install the 10 intake manifold bolts and tighten the bolts in the sequence shown in 6 stages

22. Attach the wiring harness retainers to the rear of the intake manifold and attach the brake booster vacuum hose to the wiring harness retainer.

23. Using 2 new gaskets, position the coolant crossover manifold assembly and install the 2 bolts. Tighten to 89 inch lbs. (10 Nm).

24. Position the heater hose on the coolant crossover and install the clamp.

25. Position the upper radiator hose on the thermostat housing and install the clamp.

26. Install the 10 intake manifold bolts and tighten the bolts in the sequence shown in 6 stages.

    a. Stage 1: Tighten finger-tight.

    b. Stage 2: Tighten to 89 inch lbs. (10 Nm).

    c. Stage 3: Tighten an additional 60 degrees.

    d. Stage 4: Loosen all 10 bolts a minimum of one full turn (360 degrees).

    e. Stage 5: Tighten to 89 inch lbs. (10 Nm).

    f. Stage 6: Tighten an additional 60 degrees.

27. Position the alternator and tighten the 2 nuts. Tighten to 18 ft. lbs. (25 Nm).

28. Install the 2 alternator bracket-to-coolant crossover bolts. Tighten to 89 inch lbs. (10 Nm).

29. Attach the radio interference capacitor wiring harness retainer to the alternator wiring harness.

30. Rotate the accessory drive belt tensioner clockwise and install the accessory drive belt on the alternator pulley.

31. Connect the brake booster vacuum hose to the vacuum tee.

32. Connect the heated PCV element electrical connector.

33. Install the PCV tube.

34. Install the fuel rail.

35. Install the ACL outlet pipe.

36. Connect the battery ground cable.

37. Fill the cooling system.

5.4L (3V) Engine

See Figure 318.

❉❉ CAUTION

Do not smoke, carry lighted tobacco or have an open flame of any type when working on or near any fuel-related component. Highly flammable mixtures are always present and may be ignited. Failure to follow these instructions may result in serious personal injury.

❉❉ CAUTION

Before working on or disconnecting any of the fuel tubes or fuel system components, relieve the fuel system pressure to prevent accidental spraying of fuel. Fuel in the fuel system remains under high pressure, even when the engine is not running. Failure to follow this instruction may result in serious personal injury.

1. Drain the cooling system.

2. Remove the alternator.

3. Disconnect the quick connect couplings and remove the crankcase ventilation tube.

4. Remove the bolt, loosen the clamp and remove the air intake resonator assembly.

5. Remove the 3 bolts and the Throttle Body (TB)-to-Air Cleaner (ACL) outlet tube adapter.

6. Disconnect the quick connect couplings and remove the PCV tube.

7. Disconnect the fuel supply tube quick connect coupling.

8. Disconnect the electrical connector and the Evaporative Emission (EVAP) tube quick connect coupling from the EVAP canister purge valve.

9. Disconnect the upper radiator hose from the thermostat housing.

10. Disconnect the heater coolant hose from the coolant crossover manifold assembly.

11. Disconnect the 8 fuel injector electrical connectors.

12. Disconnect the Throttle Position (TP) sensor and Electronic Throttle Control (ETC) electrical connectors.

13. Disconnect the 4 LH ignition coil and the LH Variable Camshaft Timing (VCT) solenoid electrical connectors and detach the 2 engine wiring harness retainers from the LH valve cover studs.

14. Disconnect the intake manifold vacuum tube from the brake booster vacuum hose.

➡**The intake manifold vacuum tube must be removed with the intake manifold as an assembly.**

15. Disconnect the intake manifold vacuum tube from the LH valve cover stud bolt and the support bracket at the rear of the LH cylinder head.

16. Remove the 10 intake manifold bolts.

❉❉ WARNING

Do not use metal scrapers, wire brushes, power abrasive discs or other abrasive means to clean the sealing surfaces. These tools cause scratches and gouges which make leak paths. Use a plastic scraping tool to remove all traces of old sealant.

17. Remove the 3 bolts, the coolant crossover manifold assembly and discard the gaskets.

18. Clean and inspect the sealing surfaces with silicone gasket remover and metal surface prep. Follow the directions on the packaging.

➡**The intake manifold vacuum tube must be positioned under the engine wiring harness and removed with the intake manifold as an assembly.**

19. Position the intake forward to gain access to the wiring harness retainers.

20. Disconnect the 2 engine wiring harness retainers from the rear of the intake manifold.

21. Disconnect the Cylinder Head Temperature (CHT) sensor jumper harness electrical connector retainer.

❉❉ WARNING

Do not use metal scrapers, wire brushes, power abrasive discs or other abrasive means to clean the sealing surfaces. These tools cause scratches and gouges which make leak paths. Use a plastic scraping tool to remove all traces of old sealant.

➡**The intake manifold vacuum tube must be positioned under the engine wiring harness and removed with the intake manifold as an assembly.**

22. Remove the intake manifold and discard the gaskets.

23. Clean and inspect the sealing surfaces with silicone gasket remover and metal surface prep. Follow the directions on the packaging.

To install:

❉❉ WARNING

If the engine is repaired or replaced because of upper engine failure, typically including valve or piston damage, check the intake manifold for metal debris. If metal debris is found, install a new intake manifold. Failure to follow these instructions can result in engine damage.

➡**The intake manifold vacuum tube must be positioned under the engine**

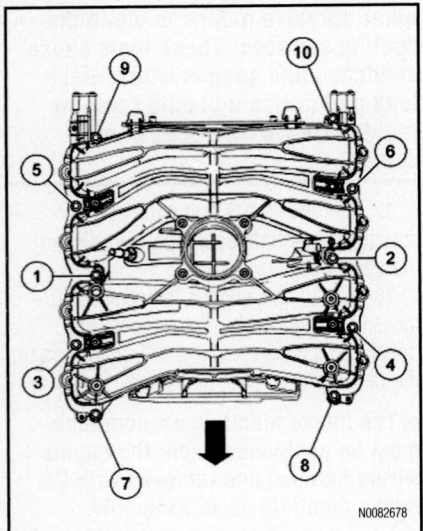

Fig. 318 Install the 10 intake manifold bolts and tighten in 2 stages in the sequence shown

wiring harness during installation of the intake manifold.

24. Using new intake manifold gaskets, position the intake manifold.

25. Position the intake manifold forward and connect the CHT sensor jumper harness electrical connector retainer.

26. Connect the 2 engine wiring harness retainers to the rear of the intake manifold and position back the intake manifold assembly.

27. Using new gaskets, position the coolant crossover manifold assembly and install the 3 bolts. Tighten to 89 inch lbs. (10 Nm).

28. Install the 10 intake manifold bolts and tighten in 2 stages in the sequence shown.

    a. Stage 1: Tighten to 18 inch lbs. (2 Nm).

    b. Stage 2: Tighten to 89 inch lbs. (10 Nm).

29. Connect the intake manifold vacuum tube to the support bracket and the valve cover stud.

30. Connect the brake booster vacuum hose to the intake manifold vacuum tube and position the clamp.

31. Connect the 4 LH ignition coil and the LH VCT solenoid electrical connectors and attach the 2 engine wiring harness retainers to the LH valve cover studs.

32. Connect the TP sensor and electronic throttle control electrical connectors.

33. Connect the 8 fuel injector electrical connectors.

34. Connect the heater coolant hose to the coolant crossover manifold assembly.

35. Connect the upper radiator hose to the thermostat housing.

36. Connect the electrical connector and the EVAP tube quick connect coupling to the EVAP canister purge valve.

37. Connect the fuel supply tube quick connect coupling.

38. Position the PCV tube and connect the quick connect couplings.

39. Position the TB -to-ACL outlet tube adapter and install the 3 bolts. Tighten the bolt to 89 inch lbs. (10 Nm).

40. Position the air intake resonator assembly, install the bolt and the clamp. Tighten the bolt to 89 inch lbs. (10 Nm).

41. Position the crankcase ventilation tube and connect the quick connect couplings.

42. Install the alternator.

43. Fill and bleed the engine cooling system.

OIL PAN

REMOVAL & INSTALLATION

3.5L GTDI & 3.7L Engines

See Figures 319 through 328.

❋❋ WARNING

During engine repair procedures, cleanliness is extremely important. Any foreign material, including any material created while cleaning gasket surfaces, that enters the oil passages, coolant passages or the oil pan, may cause engine failure.

1. With the vehicle in NEUTRAL, position it on a hoist.

2. Disconnect the battery ground cable.

➡**Only one wire harness retainer and one electrical connector shown, others similar.**

3. Disconnect the 2 HO2S electrical connectors.

    a. Disconnect the 2 HO2S electrical connector retainers.

    b. If equipped, disconnect the 5 transmission wire harness retainers from the transfer case wire harness.

4. Disconnect the HO2S electrical connector at the LH rear of the transmission.

5. Disconnect the electrical connector retainer from the bracket at the rear of the transmission.

❋❋ WARNING

Do not pull on the wire harness to disconnect the connector or damage to the connector will occur.

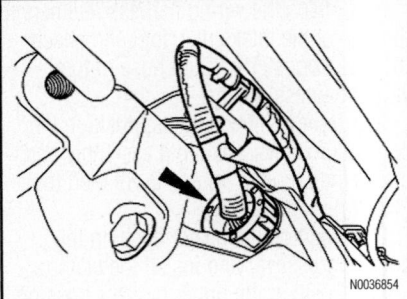

Fig. 319 Disconnect the transmission vehicle harness connector by twisting the outer shell and pulling back on the connector

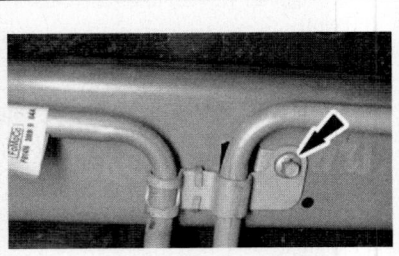

Fig. 320 Remove the bolt for the transmission cooler tube bracket from the radiator support

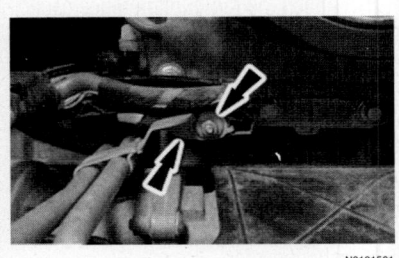

Fig. 321 Remove the nut and the transmission cooler line bracket from the engine front cover stud bolt

6. Disconnect the transmission vehicle harness connector by twisting the outer shell and pulling back on the connector.

7. Loosen the 4 upper bellhousing-to-engine bolts 5 mm (0.19 in).

8. Remove the oil level indicator.

9. If equipped, remove the 4 front bolts and the skid plate.

10. Remove the front air dam.

11. Remove the bolt for the transmission cooler tube bracket from the radiator support.

12. Remove the drain plug and drain the engine oil. Install the drain plug and tighten to 20 ft. lbs. (27 Nm).

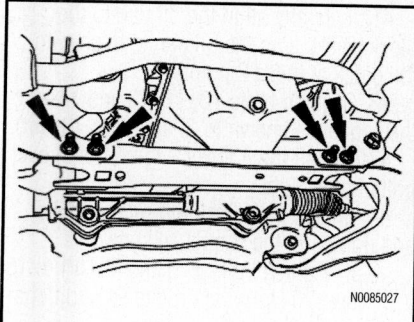

Fig. 312 Remove the 4 nuts and bolts and the crossmember

13. Remove and discard the engine oil filter.

14. Remove the nut and the transmission cooler line bracket from the engine front cover stud bolt.

15. Detach the alternator wiring harness from the engine front cover.

16. Remove the starter motor.

17. Detach the starter motor wiring harness retainer from the oil pan.

18. Remove the 4 nuts and bolts and the crossmember.

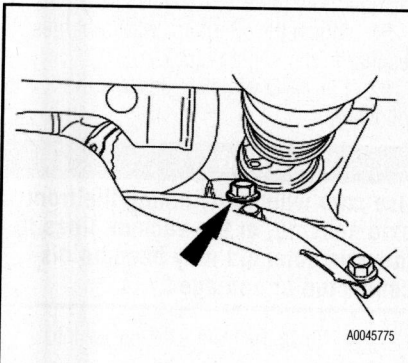

Fig. 323 Remove the upper front axle carrier mounting bushing bolt

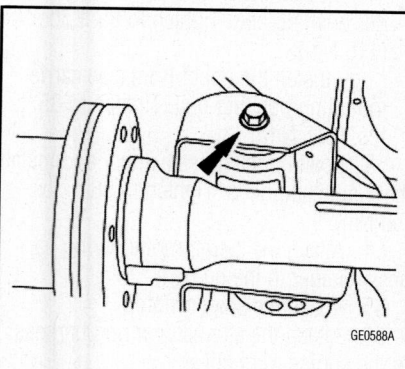

Fig. 324 Remove the axle shaft housing carrier bushing bolt

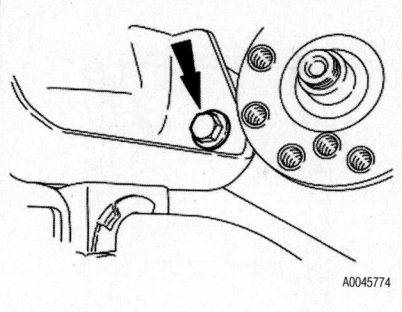

Fig. 325 Remove the lower front axle carrier mounting bushing bolt

19. For 4WD vehicles, perform the following:

   a. Position a suitable hydraulic jack under the front axle. Securely strap the jack to the axle.

   b. Remove the upper front axle carrier mounting bushing bolt.

   c. Remove the axle shaft housing carrier bushing bolt.

➡ **Front driveshaft removed for clarity only.**

   d. Remove the lower front axle carrier mounting bushing bolt.

✳✳ WARNING

Use care when lowering the front axle housing, or the vacuum lines to the axle solenoid may become disconnected or damaged.

   e. Lower the axle to allow clearance for the oil pan to be removed.

20. Loosen the engine-to-bellhousing bolt above the starter motor 0.19 inches (5 mm).

21. Remove the oil pan-to-bellhousing bolt from below the starter motor.

22. Loosen the 2 LH bellhousing-to-engine bolts 0.19 inches (5 mm).

23. Remove the 2 LH bellhousing-to-oil pan bolts.

24. Loosen the 2 transmission crossmember nuts.

25. Slide the transmission rearward 0.19 inches (5 mm).

26. Remove the 4 lower engine front cover bolts.

27. Remove the 16 oil pan bolts.

28. Using a suitable pry tool, locate the 2 pry pads at the LH and RH sides of the oil pan and pry the oil pan loose and remove.

➡ **The alternator wiring harness retainer is being removed for clearance to install the oil pan.**

29. Detach the alternator wiring harness retainer from the engine block.

✳✳ WARNING

Only use a 3M Roloc Bristle Disk (2-inch white) to clean the oil pan. Do not use metal scrapers, wire brushes or any other power abrasive disk to clean. These tools cause scratches and gouges that make leak paths.

30. Clean the engine oil pan using a 3M Roloc Bristle Disk (2-inch white) in a suitable tool turning at the recommended speed of 15,000 rpm.

31. Thoroughly wash the oil pan to remove any foreign material, including any abrasive particles created during the cleaning process.

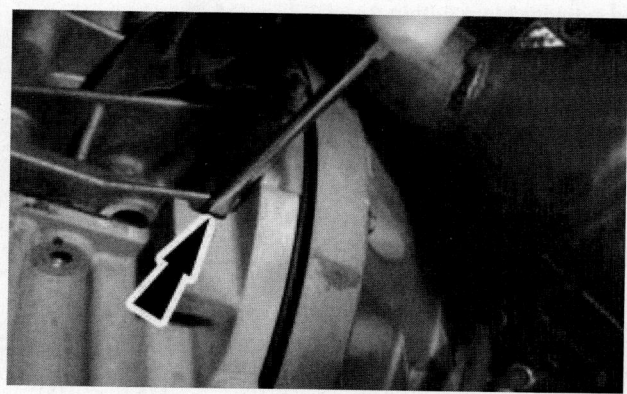

Fig. 326 Using a suitable pry tool, locate the 2 pry pads at the LH and RH sides of the oil pan and pry the oil pan loose and remove

Do not use wire brushes, power abrasive discs or 3M Roloc Bristle Disk (2-inch white) to clean the cylinder block and engine front cover sealing surfaces. These tools cause scratches and gouges that make leak paths. They also cause contamination that causes premature engine failure. Remove all traces of the gasket.

32. Clean the sealing surfaces of the cylinder block and engine front cover in the following sequence.

a. Remove any large deposits of silicone or gasket material.

b. Apply silicone gasket remover and allow to set for several minutes.

c. Remove the silicone gasket remover. A second application of silicone gasket remover may be required if residual traces of silicone or gasket material remain.

d. Apply metal surface prep to remove any remaining traces of oil and to prepare the surfaces to bond. Do not attempt to make the metal shiny. Some staining of the metal surfaces is normal.

To install:

33. Apply a bead of Motorcraft® High Performance Engine RTV Silicone to the 2 engine front cover-to-cylinder block joint areas on the sealing surface of the oil pan.

Failure to use Motorcraft® High Performance Engine RTV Silicone may cause the engine oil to foam excessively and result in serious engine damage.

➡**The oil pan and the 4 specified bolts must be installed and the oil pan aligned to the cylinder block within 4 minutes of sealant application. Final tightening of the oil pan bolts must be carried out within 60 minutes of sealant application.**

34. Apply a bead of Motorcraft® High Performance Engine RTV Silicone to the sealing surface of the oil pan-to-engine block and to the oil pan-to-engine front cover mating surface.

35. Apply a bead of Motorcraft® High Performance Engine RTV Silicone to the 2 crankshaft seal retainer plate-to-cylinder block joint areas on the sealing surface of the oil pan.

➡**The oil pan and the 4 specified bolts must be installed within 4 minutes of the start of sealant application.**

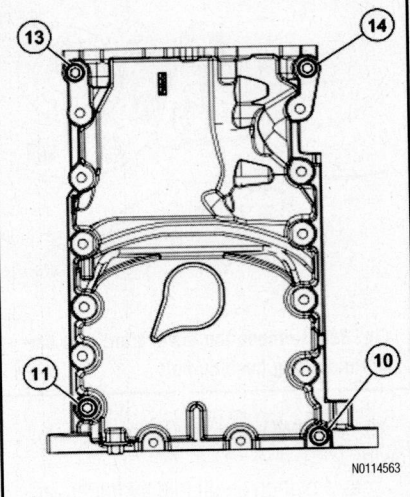

Fig. 327 Install the oil pan and bolts 10, 11, 13 and 14 finger-tight

➡**Keep the oil pan as close as possible to the transmission while installing, then slide forward towards the engine front cover to prevent wiping off of the sealant.**

36. Install the oil pan and bolts 10, 11, 13 and 14 finger-tight.

37. Tighten the 2 LH bellhousing-to-engine bolts. Do not torque at this time.

38. Tighten the RH engine-to-bellhousing bolt. Do not torque at this time.

39. Install and tighten the 2 LH bellhousing-to-oil pan bolts. Do not torque at this time.

40. Install and tighten the RH oil pan-to-bellhousing bolt. Do not torque at this time.

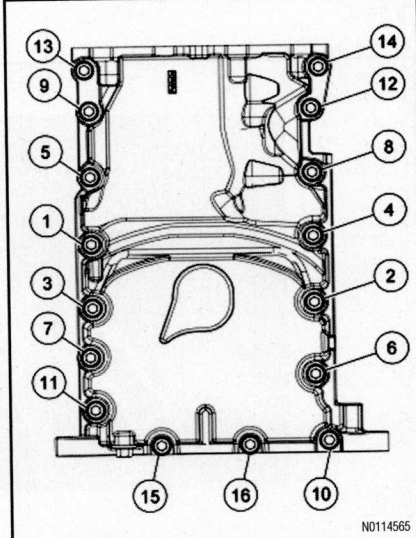

Fig. 328 Install the remaining oil pan bolts and tighten in the sequence shown

41. Laterally align the oil pan to the block. Make sure the oil pan is flush with the block at these 2 points.

42. Tighten bolts 10, 11, 13 and 14 in the sequence shown to 27 inch lbs. (3 Nm).

43. Install the 4 lower engine front cover bolts finger-tight.

44. Install the remaining oil pan bolts and tighten in the sequence shown.

a. Tighten bolts 1–9 and 11–14 to 15 ft. lbs. (20 Nm), then rotate an additional 45 degrees.

b. Tighten bolts 15 and 16 to 89 inch lbs. (10 Nm), then rotate an additional 45 degrees.

c. Tighten bolt 10 to 15 ft. lbs. (20 Nm), then rotate an additional 90 degrees.

45. Tighten the 4 lower engine front cover bolts to 18 ft. lbs. (24 Nm).

46. Tighten the 2 LH bellhousing-to-engine bolts to 35 ft. lbs. (48 Nm).

47. Tighten the RH engine-to-bellhousing bolt to 35 ft. lbs. (48 Nm).

48. Tighten the 2 LH bellhousing-to-oil pan bolts to 35 ft. lbs. (48 Nm).

49. Tighten the RH oil pan-to-bellhousing bolt to 35 ft. lbs. (48 Nm).

50. Tighten the 2 transmission crossmember nuts to 75 ft. lbs. (103 Nm).

51. Attach the alternator wiring harness retainer to the engine block.

52. For 4WD vehicles, perform the following:

Use care when positioning the front axle housing, or the vacuum lines to the axle solenoid may become disconnected or damaged.

a. Raise the front axle carrier into position.

b. Install the lower front axle carrier mounting bushing bolt. Tighten to 85 ft. lbs. (115 Nm).

c. Install the axle shaft housing carrier bushing bolt. Tighten to 85 ft. lbs. (115 Nm).

d. Install the upper front axle carrier mounting bushing bolt. Tighten to 85 ft. lbs. (115 Nm).

53. Position the crossmember and install the 4 nuts and bolts. Tighten to 66 ft. lbs. (90 Nm).

54. Attach the starter motor wiring harness retainer to the oil pan.

55. Install the starter motor.

56. Attach the alternator wiring harness to the engine front cover.

57. Install the transmission cooler line bracket and nut to the engine front cover stud bolt. Tighten to 106 inch lbs. (12 Nm).

➥Do not lubricate the engine oil filter gasket.

58. Install a new engine oil filter.
59. Position the transmission cooler tube bracket to the radiator support and install the bolt. Tighten to 106 inch lbs. (12 Nm).
Install the front air dam.
60. If equipped, install the skid plate and the 4 bolts. Tighten to 35 ft. lbs. (48 Nm).
61. Install the oil level indicator.
62. Tighten the 4 upper bellhousing-to-engine bolts to 35 ft. lbs. (48 Nm).
63. Connect the transmission vehicle harness connector by pushing the connector into the transmission and twisting the outer shell.
64. Connect the electrical connector retainer to the bracket at the rear of the transmission.
65. Connect the Heated Oxygen Sensor (HO2S) electrical connector.

➥Only one wire harness retainer and one electrical connector shown, others similar.

66. If equipped, connect the 5 transmission wire harness retainers to the transfer case wire harness.
   a. Connect the 2 HO2S electrical connector retainers.
   b. Connect the 2 HO2S electrical connectors.
67. Fill the engine with clean engine oil.
68. Connect the battery ground cable.

5.0L Engine

See Figure 329.

➥The manufacturer does not provide a specific Removal and Installation procedure for this component. Refer to the graphic(s) when servicing this component.

To install:

✳✳ WARNING

Do not use metal scrapers, wire brushes, power abrasive discs or other abrasive means to clean the sealing surfaces. These tools cause scratches and gouges, which make leak paths. Use a plastic scraping tool to remove all traces of old sealant.

1. Inspect the oil pan and engine sealing surfaces. Clean the mating surfaces of the engine and oil pan with silicone gasket remover and metal surface prep. Follow the directions on the packaging.

➥If the oil pan is not installed and the fasteners tightened within 5 minutes, the sealant must be removed and the sealing area cleaned. To clean the sealing area, use silicone gasket remover and metal surface prep. Failure to follow this procedure can cause future oil leakage. If this timing cannot be met, tighten fasteners 7, 8, 9 and 10 to 71 inch lbs. (8 Nm) within 5 minutes of applying the sealer and final torque all of the fasteners within 1 hour of applying the sealer.

➥If the engine front cover has been removed, it is only necessary to apply sealant to the crankshaft rear seal retainer plate-to-cylinder block sealing surfaces.

2. Apply a bead of silicone sealant to the crankshaft rear seal retainer plate-to-cylinder block sealing surfaces and the engine front cover-to-cylinder block sealing surfaces.

➥Fastener locations 7, 13 and 16 are stud bolts.

3. Using a new gasket, install the oil pan and tighten the fasteners in sequence in 3 stages.
   a. Stage 1: Tighten to 18 inch lbs. (2 Nm)
   b. Stage 2: Tighten to 89 inch lbs. (10 Nm).
   c. Stage 3: Tighten an additional 45 degrees.

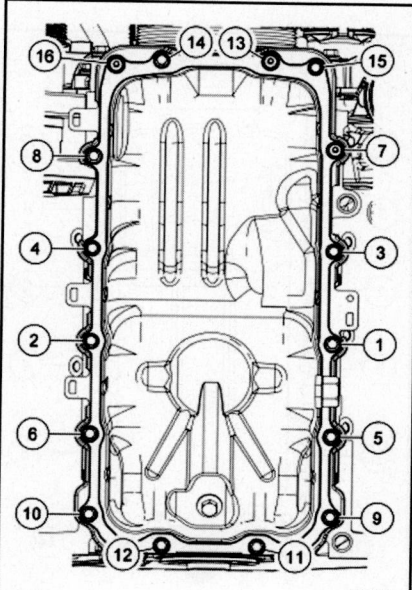

Fig. 329 Using a new gasket, install the oil pan and tighten the fasteners in sequence in 3 stages

4.6L (2V) Engine

See Figures 330 through 336.

1. With the vehicle in NEUTRAL, position it on a hoist.
2. Drain the engine oil.
3. If equipped, remove the 4 skid plate bolts and the skid plate.
4. Remove the bolt and position the starter electrical harness and support bracket aside.
5. Remove the nut and position aside the transmission cooler tube support bracket and the starter wiring harness support bracket.
6. Remove the 4 bolts and the cross-member.
7. For 4WD vehicles, perform the following:
   a. Position a suitable hydraulic jack under the front axle. Securely strap the jack to the axle.

➥Rotate the steering column so the pinch bolt for the steering column coupling allows clearance for the isolator bolt.

   b. Remove the upper front axle carrier mounting bushing bolt.

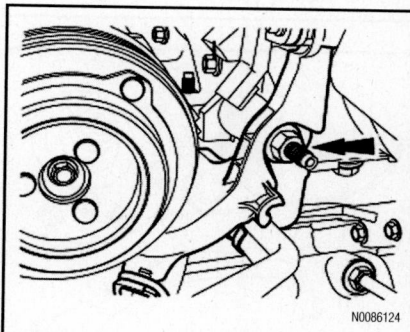

Fig. 330 Remove the nut and position aside the transmission cooler tube support bracket and the starter wiring harness support bracket

Fig. 331 Remove the 4 bolts and the crossmember

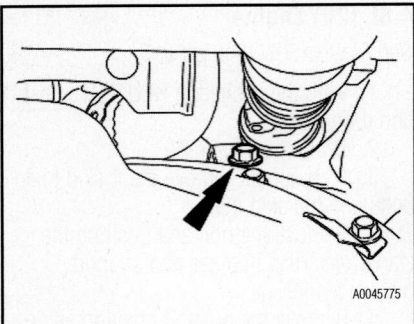

Fig. 332 Remove the upper front axle carrier mounting bushing bolt

Fig. 333 Remove the axle shaft housing carrier bushing bolt

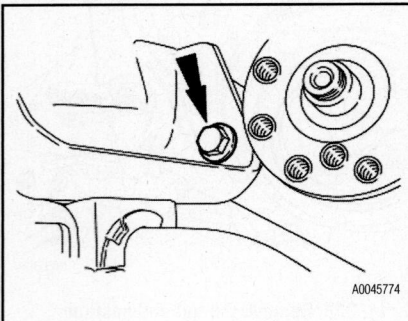

Fig. 334 Remove the lower front axle carrier mounting bushing bolt

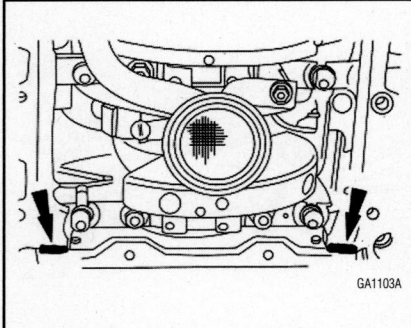

Fig. 335 Apply silicone gasket and sealant in the locations shown

c. Remove the axle shaft housing carrier bushing bolt.

d. Remove the lower front axle carrier mounting bushing bolt.

e. Partially lower the front axle assembly.

✻✻ WARNING

Do not use metal scrapers, wire brushes, power abrasive discs or other abrasive means to clean the sealing surfaces. These may cause scratches and gouges resulting in leak paths. Use a plastic scraper to clean the sealing surfaces.

8. Remove the 16 oil pan bolts, the oil pan and discard the oil pan gasket. Clean the sealing surfaces with silicone gasket remover and metal surface prep. Follow the directions on the packaging. Inspect the mating surfaces.

To install:

➡️**If the oil pan is not secured within 4 minutes, the sealant must be removed and the sealing area cleaned with silicone gasket remover and metal surface prep. Follow the directions on the packaging. Allow to dry until there is no sign of wetness, or 4 minutes, whichever is longer. Failure to follow this procedure can cause future oil leakage.**

9. Apply the silicone gasket and sealant at the engine front cover-to-cylinder block mating surface.

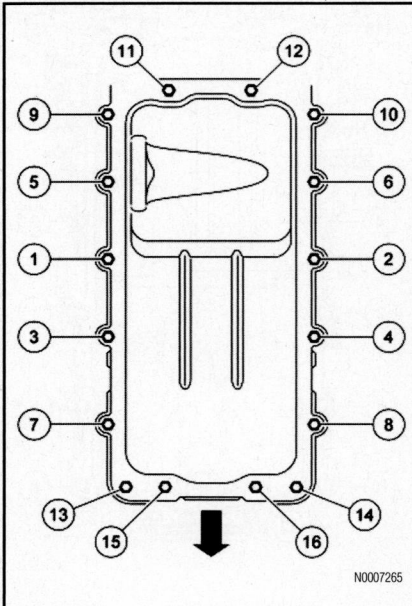

Fig. 336 Tighten the bolts in 3 stages in the sequence shown

➡️**If the oil pan is not secured within 4 minutes, the sealant must be removed and the sealing area cleaned with silicone gasket remover and metal surface prep. Follow the directions on the packaging. Allow to dry until there is no sign of wetness, or 4 minutes, whichever is longer. Failure to follow this procedure can cause future oil leakage.**

10. Apply silicone gasket and sealant in the locations shown.

11. Position the new oil pan gasket and the oil pan and loosely install the 16 bolts.

12. Tighten the bolts in 3 stages in the sequence shown.

a. Stage 1: Tighten to 18 inch lbs. (2 Nm).

b. Stage 2: Tighten to 15 ft. lbs. (20 Nm).

c. Stage 3: Tighten an additional 60 degrees.

13. For 4WD vehicles, perform the following:

a. Position the front axle.

➡️**Rotate the steering column so the pinch bolt for the steering column coupling allows clearance for the isolator bolt.**

b. Install the upper front axle carrier mounting bushing bolt. Tighten to 66 ft. lbs. (90 Nm).

c. Install the axle shaft housing carrier bushing nut and bolt. Tighten to 66 ft. lbs. (90 Nm).

d. Install the lower front axle carrier mounting bushing bolt. Tighten to 66 ft. lbs. (90 Nm).

14. Install the crossmember and the 4 bolts. Tighten to 85 ft. lbs. (115 Nm).

15. Position the transmission cooler tube support bracket and the starter wiring harness support bracket and install the nut. Tighten to 89 inch lbs. (10 Nm).

16. Position the starter electrical harness and support bracket and install the bolt. Tighten to 89 inch lbs. (10 Nm).

17. If equipped, install the skid plate and the 4 bolts. Tighten to 18 ft. lbs. (25 Nm).

18. Install the engine oil pan drain plug and fill the engine with clean engine oil. Tighten to 17 ft. lbs. (23 Nm).

4.6L (3V) Engine

See Figures 337 through 343.

1. With the vehicle in NEUTRAL, position it on a hoist.

2. Remove the oil drain plug and drain the engine oil. Install the drain plug when finished. Tighten to 17 ft. lbs. (23 Nm).

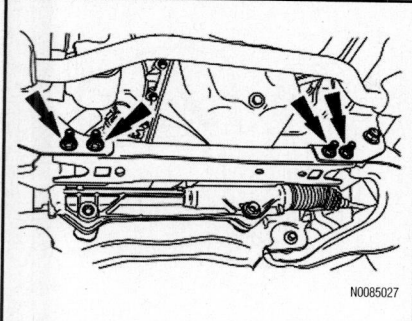

Fig. 337 Remove the 4 nuts, the 4 bolts and the crossmember

3. If equipped, remove the 4 bolts and the skid plate.
4. Remove the 4 nuts, the 4 bolts and the crossmember.
5. For 4WD vehicles, perform the following:

a. Position a suitable hydraulic jack under the front axle housing. Securely strap the jack to the axle.

➡Rotate the steering column so the pinch bolt for the steering column coupling allows clearance for the mounting bushing bolt.

b. Remove the upper front axle housing mounting bushing bolt.

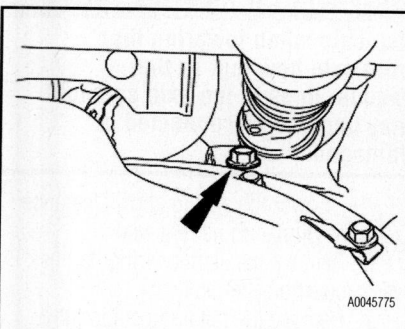

Fig. 338 Remove the upper front axle housing mounting bushing bolt

Fig. 339 Remove the front axle housing mounting bushing bolt

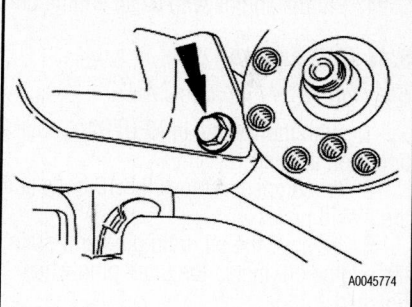

Fig. 340 Remove the lower front axle housing mounting bushing bolt

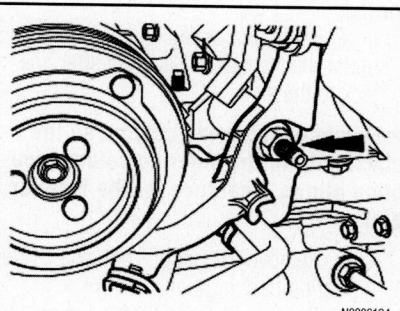

Fig. 341 Remove the nut and position the starter wiring harness and the transmission fluid cooler tubes aside

c. Remove the front axle housing mounting bushing bolt.
d. Remove the lower front axle housing mounting bushing bolt.

✳✳ WARNING
Use care when lowering the front axle housing, or the vacuum lines to the axle solenoid may become disconnected or damaged.

6. Lower the front axle housing to allow clearance for the oil pan to be removed.
7. Remove the transmission fluid cooling tubes bracket bolt.

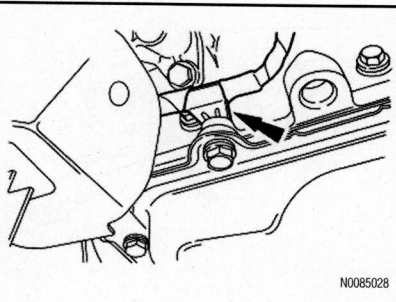

Fig. 342 Detach the oil pressure switch wiring harness from the oil pan bolt

8. Remove the starter wiring harness bolt.
9. Remove the nut and position the starter wiring harness and the transmission fluid cooler tubes aside.
10. Detach the oil pressure switch wiring harness from the oil pan bolt.
11. Remove the 16 bolts, the oil pan and the gasket. Discard the gasket.

✳✳ WARNING
Do not use metal scrapers, wire brushes, power abrasive discs or other abrasive means to clean the sealing surfaces. These tools cause scratches and gouges, which make leak paths. Use a plastic scraping tool to remove all traces of old sealant.

12. Inspect the oil pan. Clean the gasket mating surfaces of the oil pan and engine block with silicone gasket remover and metal surface prep. Follow the directions on the packaging.

To install:

➡If not secured within 4 minutes, the sealant must be removed and the sealing area cleaned with silicone gasket remover and metal surface prep. Follow the directions on the packaging. Allow to dry until there is no sign of wetness, or 4 minutes, whichever is longer. Failure to follow this procedure can cause future oil leakage.

13. Apply silicone gasket and sealant at the crankshaft rear seal retainer plate-to-cylinder block sealing surface.

➡If not secured within 4 minutes, the sealant must be removed and the sealing area cleaned with silicone gasket remover and metal surface prep. Follow the directions on the packaging. Allow to dry until there is no sign of wetness, or 4 minutes, whichever is longer. Failure to follow this procedure can cause future oil leakage.

14. Apply silicone gasket and sealant at the engine front cover-to-cylinder block sealing surface.
15. Position a new gasket and the oil pan and install the 16 bolts.
16. Tighten the bolts in the sequence shown in 3 stages.

a. Stage 1: Tighten to 18 inch lbs. (2 Nm).
b. Stage 2: Tighten to 15 ft. lbs. (20 Nm).
c. Stage 3: Tighten an additional 60 degrees.

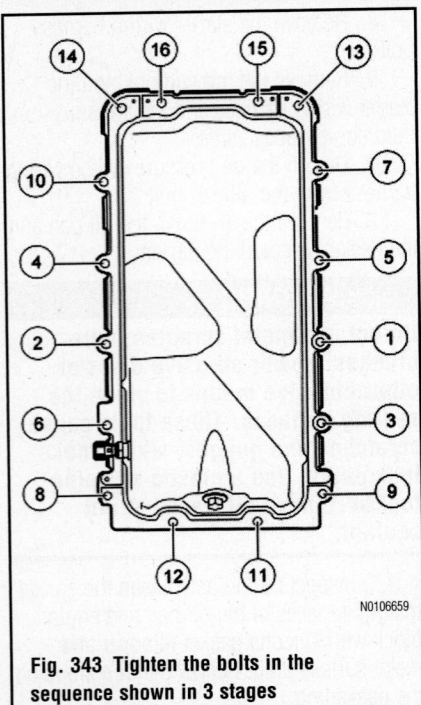

Fig. 343 Tighten the bolts in the sequence shown in 3 stages

17. Attach the oil pressure switch wiring harness to the oil pan bolt.

18. Position the starter wiring harness and the transmission fluid cooler tubes and install the nut. Tighten to 89 inch lbs. (10 Nm).

19. Install the starter wiring harness bolt. Tighten to 89 inch lbs. (10 Nm).

20. Install the transmission fluid cooling tubes bracket bolt. Tighten to 35 ft. lbs. (48 Nm).

⁂ WARNING

Use care when positioning the front axle housing, or the vacuum lines to the axle solenoid may become disconnected or damaged.

21. For 4WD vehicles, perform the following:

a. Raise the front axle into position.

b. Install the lower front axle housing mounting bushing bolt. Tighten to 66 ft. lbs. (90 Nm).

c. Install the front axle housing mounting bushing bolt. Tighten to 66 ft. lbs. (90 Nm).

d. Install the upper front axle housing mounting bushing bolt. Tighten to 66 ft. lbs. (90 Nm).

22. Position the crossmember and install the 4 bolts and the 4 nuts. Tighten to 85 ft. lbs. (115 Nm).

23. If equipped, position the skid plate and install the 4 bolts. Tighten to 18 ft. lbs. (25 Nm).

24. Fill the engine with clean engine oil.

5.4L (3V) Engine

See Figures 344 through 348.

1. With the vehicle in NEUTRAL, position it on a hoist.

2. If equipped, remove the 10 bolts and the 2 skid plates.

3. Remove the oil drain plug and drain the engine oil. Install the drain plug when finished.
Tighten to 17 ft. lbs. (23 Nm).

4. Remove the 4 nuts, the 4 bolts and the crossmember.

5. For 4WD vehicles, perform the following:

a. Position a suitable hydraulic jack under the front axle. Securely strap the jack to the axle.

➡ **Rotate the steering column so the pinch bolt for the steering column coupling allows clearance for the isolator bolt.**

b. Remove the upper front axle carrier mounting bushing bolt.

c. Remove the axle shaft housing carrier bushing bolt.

d. Remove the lower front axle carrier mounting bushing bolt.

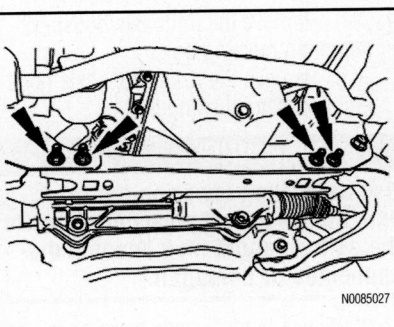

Fig. 344 Remove the 4 nuts, the 4 bolts and the crossmember

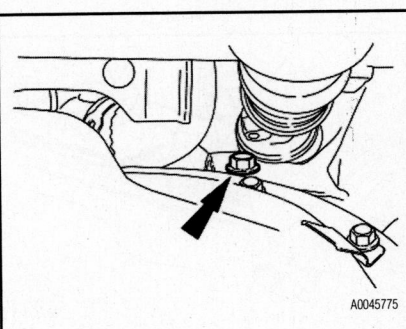

Fig. 345 Remove the upper front axle carrier mounting bushing bolt

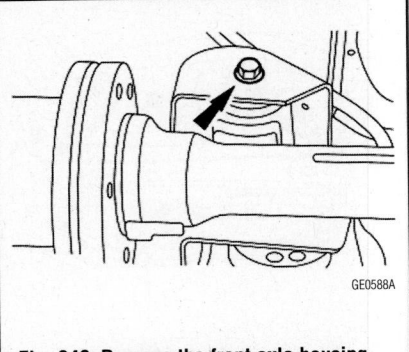

Fig. 346 Remove the front axle housing mounting bushing bolt

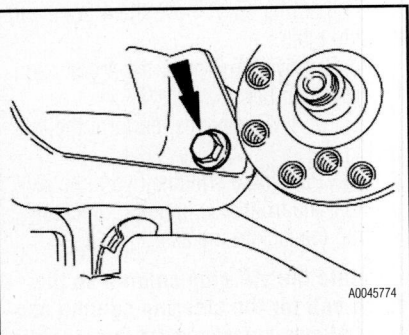

Fig. 347 Remove the lower front axle housing mounting bushing bolt

⁂ WARNING

Use care when lowering the front axle housing, or the vacuum lines to the axle solenoid may become disconnected or damaged.

e. Lower the axle to allow clearance for the oil pan to be removed.

6. Remove the starter wiring harness rear support bracket bolt.

7. Remove the nut and position the starter wiring harness and the transmission fluid cooler tubes aside.

8. Detach the oil pressure switch wiring harness from the oil pan bolt.

9. Remove the 16 bolts, the oil pan and the gasket. Discard the gasket.

⁂ WARNING

Do not use metal scrapers, wire brushes, power abrasive discs or other abrasive means to clean the sealing surfaces. These tools cause scratches and gouges, which make leak paths. Use a plastic scraping tool to remove all traces of old sealant.

10. Inspect the oil pan. Clean the gasket mating surfaces of the oil pan and engine block with silicone gasket remover and metal surface prep. Follow the directions on the packaging.

To install:

➡ **If not secured within 4 minutes, the sealant must be removed and the sealing area cleaned with silicone gasket remover and metal surface prep. Follow the directions on the packaging. Allow to dry until there is no sign of wetness, or 4 minutes, whichever is longer. Failure to follow this procedure can cause future oil leakage.**

11. Apply silicone gasket and sealant at the crankshaft rear seal retainer plate-to-cylinder block sealing surface.

➡ **If not secured within 4 minutes, the sealant must be removed and the sealing area cleaned with silicone gasket remover and metal surface prep. Follow the directions on the packaging. Allow to dry until there is no sign of wetness, or 4 minutes, whichever is longer. Failure to follow this procedure can cause future oil leakage.**

12. Apply silicone gasket and sealant at the engine front cover-to-cylinder block sealing surface.

13. Position a new gasket and the oil pan and install the 16 bolts.

14. Tighten the bolts in the sequence shown in 3 stages.

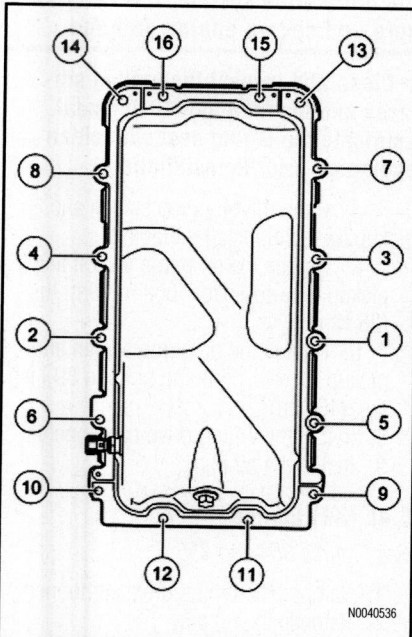

Fig. 348 Tighten the bolts in the sequence shown in 3 stages

a. Stage 1: Tighten to 18 inch lbs. (2 Nm).

b. Stage 2: Tighten to 15 ft. lbs. (20 Nm).

c. Stage 3: Tighten an additional 60 degrees.

15. Attach the oil pressure switch wiring harness to the oil pan bolt.

16. Position the transmission fluid cooler tube support bracket, the starter wiring harness support bracket and install the nut. Tighten to 89 inch lbs. (10 Nm).

17. Position the starter wiring harness and install the starter wiring harness rear support bracket bolt. Tighten to 89 inch lbs. (10 Nm).

18. Install the transmission fluid cooling tubes rear support bracket bolt. Tighten to 35 ft. lbs. (48 Nm).

19. For 4WD vehicles, perform the following:

❊❊❊ WARNING

Use care when positioning the front axle housing, or the vacuum lines to the axle solenoid may become disconnected or damaged.

a. Raise the front axle carrier into position.

b. Install the lower front axle carrier mounting bushing bolt. Tighten to 85 ft. lbs. (115 Nm).

c. Install the axle shaft housing carrier bushing bolt. Tighten to 85 ft. lbs. (115 Nm).

d. Install the upper front axle carrier mounting bushing bolt. Tighten to 85 ft. lbs. (115 Nm).

20. For all vehicles, position the crossmember and install the 4 bolts and the 4 nuts. Tighten to 66 ft. lbs. (90 Nm).

21. For 4WD vehicles, install the 2 skid plates and the 10 bolts. Tighten to 35 ft. lbs. (48 Nm).

22. Fill the engine with clean engine oil.

OIL PUMP

REMOVAL & INSTALLATION

3.5L GTDI and 3.7L Engines

See Figure 349.

➡ **The manufacturer does not provide a specific Removal and Installation procedure for this component. Refer to the graphic(s) when servicing this component.**

1. Install the oil pump and the 3 bolts. Tighten to 89 inch lbs. (10 Nm).

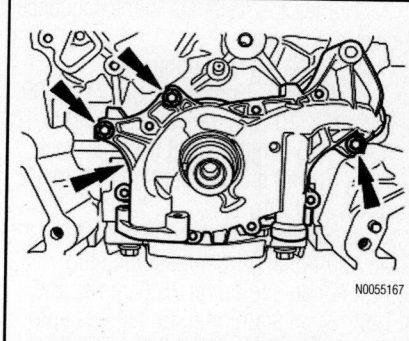

Fig. 349 Install the oil pump and the 3 bolts

5.0L Engine

See Figure 350.

❊❊❊ WARNING

During engine repair procedures, cleanliness is extremely important. Any foreign material, including any material created while cleaning gasket surfaces, that enters the oil passages, coolant passages or the oil pan, can cause engine failure.

1. With the vehicle in NEUTRAL, position it on a hoist.

2. Remove the engine front cover. Refer to Timing Chain Front Cover.

3. Remove the oil pan.

4. Remove the 2 bolts, the 2 stud bolts and the oil pump.

To install:

5. Rotate the inner rotor of the oil pump assembly to align the flats on the crankshaft and slip the oil pump over the crankshaft until seated against the block.

6. Rotate the oil pump until the bolt holes are aligned to the block and install the fasteners.

➡ **Oil pump must be held against the cylinder block until all bolts are tightened.**

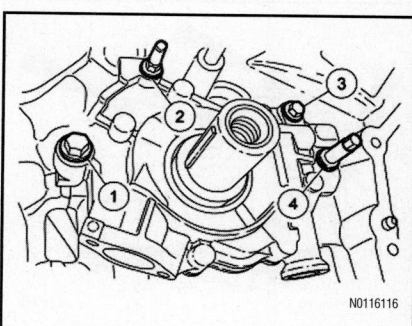

Fig. 350 Tighten the fasteners in the sequence shown in 3 stages

7. Tighten the fasteners in the sequence shown in 3 stages:

    a. Stage 1: Hand tighten.

    b. Stage 2: Tighten the bolt (1) to 89 inch lbs. (10 Nm), the stud bolt (2) to 18 ft. lbs. (25 Nm), the bolt (3) to 89 inch lbs. (10 Nm) and the stud bolt (4) to 15 ft. lbs. (20 Nm).

    c. Stage 3: Tighten the bolt (1) an additional 45 degrees, the stud bolt (2) an additional 75 degrees, the bolt (3) an additional 45 degrees and the stud bolt (4) an additional 60 degrees.

8. Install the oil pan.

9. Install the engine front cover.

4.6L (2V) Engine

See Figures 351 and 352.

1. With the vehicle in NEUTRAL, position it on a hoist.

2. Remove the timing drive components.

3. Remove the oil pan.

4. Remove the 3 bolts and the oil pump screen and pickup tube. Discard the O-ring seal.

5. Remove the 3 bolts and the oil pump.

Fig. 351 Remove the 3 bolts and the oil pump screen and pickup tube

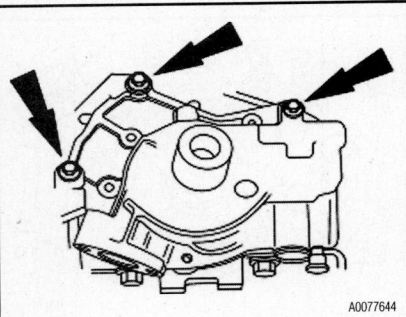

Fig. 352 Remove the 3 bolts and the oil pump

To install:

✲✲ WARNING

Do not use metal scrapers, wire brushes, power abrasive discs or other abrasive means to clean the sealing surfaces. These tools cause scratches and gouges which make leak paths. Use a plastic scraping tool to remove all traces of old sealant.

6. Clean the sealing surfaces with metal surface prep. Follow the directions on the packaging.

7. Install the oil pump and the 3 bolts. Tighten to 89 inch lbs. (10 Nm).

✲✲ WARNING

Make sure the O-ring is in place and not damaged. A missing or damaged O-ring can cause foam in the lubrication system, low oil pressure and severe engine damage.

➡ **Install a new O-ring seal and lubricate with clean engine oil.**

8. Install the oil pump screen and pickup tube and the 3 bolts.

    a. Tighten the oil pump screen bracket bolt to 18 ft. lbs. (25 Nm).

    b. Tighten the pickup tube bolts to 89 inch lbs. (10 Nm).

9. Install the oil pan.

10. Install the timing drive components.

4.6L (3V) Engine

See Figures 353 and 354.

1. Remove the oil pan.

2. Remove the timing drive components.

3. Remove the bolts and the oil pump screen and pickup tube.

4. Remove the 3 bolts and the oil pump.

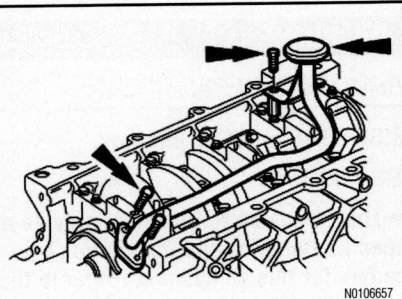

Fig. 353 Remove the bolts and the oil pump screen and pickup tube

Fig. 354 Remove the 3 bolts and the oil pump

To install:

✲✲ WARNING

Do not use metal scrapers, wire brushes, power abrasive discs or other abrasive means to clean the sealing surfaces. These tools cause scratches and gouges which make leak paths. Use a plastic scraping tool to remove all traces of old sealant.

5. Clean the sealing surfaces with metal surface prep. Follow the directions on the packaging. Inspect the mating surfaces.

6. Position the oil pump and install the bolts. Tighten to 89 inch lbs. (10 Nm).

✲✲ WARNING

Make sure the O-ring seal is in place and not damaged. A missing or damaged O-ring seal can cause foam in the lubrication system, low oil pressure and severe engine damage.

➡ **Clean and inspect the mating surfaces and install a new O-ring seal. Lubricate the O-ring seal with clean engine oil prior to installation.**

7. Position the oil pump screen and pickup tube and install the bolts.

    a. Tighten the oil pump screen and pickup tube-to-spacer bolt to 18 ft. lbs. (25 Nm).

    b. Tighten the oil pump screen and pickup tube-to-oil pump bolts to 89 inch lbs. (10 Nm).

8. Install the timing drive components.

9. Install the oil pan.

5.4L (3V) Engine

See Figures 354 and 355.

1. Remove the timing drive components.

2. Remove the oil pan.

3. Remove the 3 bolts and the oil pump screen and pickup tube.

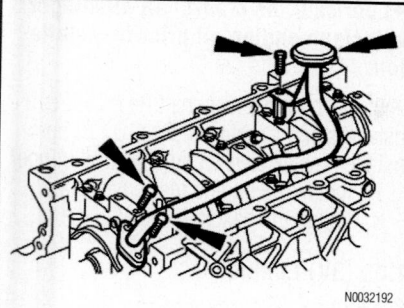

Fig. 355 Remove the 3 bolts and the oil pump screen and pickup tube

4. Remove the 3 bolts and the oil pump.

To install:

✷✷ WARNING

Do not use metal scrapers, wire brushes, power abrasive discs or other abrasive means to clean the sealing surfaces. These tools cause scratches and gouges which make leak paths. Use a plastic scraping tool to remove all traces of old sealant.

5. Clean the sealing surfaces with metal surface prep. Follow the directions on the packaging. Inspect the mating surfaces.

6. Position the oil pump and install the 3 bolts. Tighten to 89 inch lbs. (10 Nm).

✷✷ WARNING

Make sure the O-ring is in place and not damaged. A missing or damaged O-ring can cause foam in the lubrication system, low oil pressure and severe engine damage.

➡**Clean and inspect the mating surfaces and install a new O-ring. Lubricate the O-ring with clean engine oil prior to installation.**

7. Position the oil pump screen and pickup tube and install the 3 bolts.
   a. Tighten the 2 oil pump screen and pickup tube-to-oil pump bolts to 89 inch lbs. (10 Nm).
   b. Tighten the oil pump screen and pickup tube-to-spacer bolt to 18 ft. lbs. (25 Nm).

8. Install the oil pan.
9. Install the timing drive components.

REAR MAIN SEAL

REMOVAL & INSTALLATION

3.5L GTDI and 3.7L Engines
See Figures 356 through 358.

1. With the vehicle in NEUTRAL, position it on a hoist.
2. Remove the flexplate.
3. Remove the crankshaft sensor ring.
4. Using the Crankshaft Rear Oil Seal Remover (303-519) and Slide Hammer (307-005), remove and discard the crankshaft rear seal.
5. Clean all sealing surfaces with metal surface prep.

To install:

➡**Lubricate the seal lips and bore with clean engine oil prior to installation.**

6. Position the Rear Main Seal Installer (303-1250) onto the end of the crankshaft and slide a new crankshaft rear seal onto the tool.
7. Using the Rear Main Seal Installer (303-1250) and Handle (205-153), install the new crankshaft rear seal.
8. Install the crankshaft sensor ring.
9. Install the flexplate.

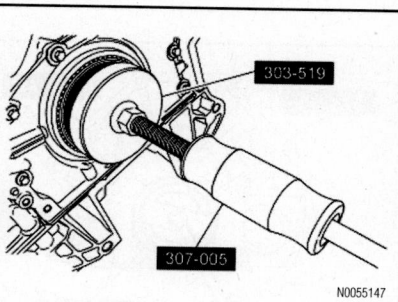

Fig. 356 Using the Crankshaft Rear Oil Seal Remover and Slide Hammer, remove the crankshaft rear seal

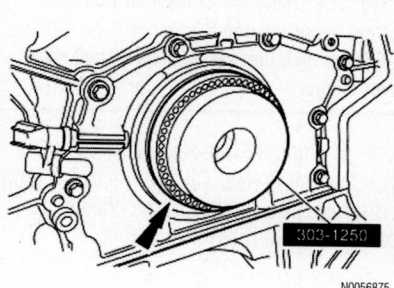

Fig. 357 Position the Rear Main Seal Installer onto the end of the crankshaft and slide a new crankshaft rear seal onto the tool

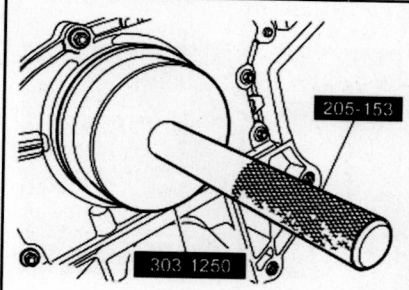

Fig. 358 Using the Rear Main Seal Installer and Handle, install the new crankshaft rear seal

5.0L Engine
See Figures 359 through 361.

1. With the vehicle in NEUTRAL, position it on a hoist.
2. Remove the flexplate.
3. Remove the engine separator plate.

➡**Inspect the crankshaft sensor ring for damage. If the crankshaft sensor ring has been dropped or has any visual damage, it must be discarded.**

4. Remove the crankshaft sensor ring.
5. Using the Crankshaft Rear Oil Seal

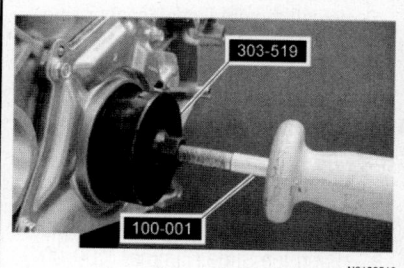

Fig. 359 Using the Crankshaft Rear Oil Seal Remover and Slide Hammer, remove the crankshaft rear seal

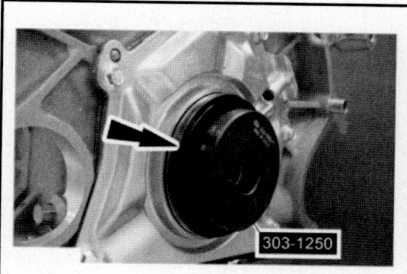

Fig. 360 Position the Rear Main Seal Installer onto the end of the crankshaft and slide a new crankshaft rear seal onto the tool

Fig. 361 Using the Rear Main Seal Installer and Handle, install the new crankshaft rear seal

Remover (303-519) and Slide Hammer (100-001), remove and discard the crankshaft rear seal.

6. Clean all sealing surfaces with metal surface prep.

To install:

➡ Lubricate the seal lips and bore with clean engine oil prior to installation.

7. Position the Rear Main Seal Installer (303-1250) onto the end of the crankshaft and slide a new crankshaft rear seal onto the tool.

8. Using the Rear Main Seal Installer (303-1250) and Handle (205-153), install the new crankshaft rear seal.

9. Install the crankshaft sensor ring.
10. Install the engine separator plate.
11. Install the flexplate.

4.6L (2V) Engine

See Figures 362 through 365.

1. Remove the flexplate.
2. Remove the engine rear cover plate.
3. Using the Slide Hammer (100-001) and Crankshaft Rear Oil Slinger Remover (303-514), remove and discard the crankshaft oil slinger.

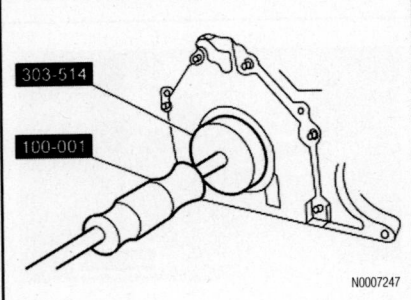

Fig. 362 Using the Slide Hammer and Crankshaft Rear Oil Slinger Remover, remove and discard the crankshaft oil slinger

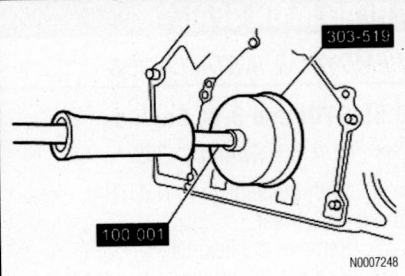

Fig. 363 Using the Slide Hammer and Crankshaft Rear Oil Seal Remover, remove and discard the crankshaft rear seal

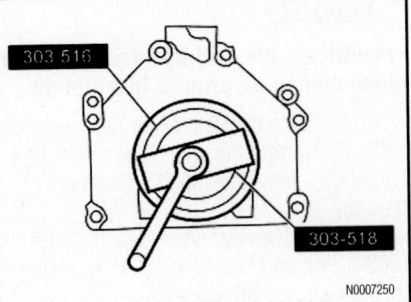

Fig. 364 Using the Crankshaft Rear Oil Seal Installers, install a new crankshaft rear seal

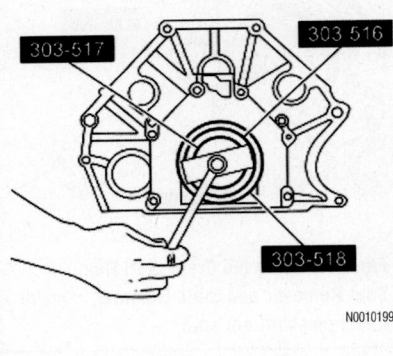

Fig. 365 Using the Crankshaft Rear Oil Seal Installers and Crankshaft Rear Oil Slinger Installer, install a new crankshaft oil slinger

4. Using the Slide Hammer (100-001) and Crankshaft Rear Oil Seal Remover (303-519), remove and discard the crankshaft rear seal.

To install:

➡ Lubricate the crankshaft rear seal with clean engine oil prior to installation.

5. Using the Crankshaft Rear Oil Seal Installers, install a new crankshaft rear seal.

➡ Lubricate the crankshaft oil slinger with clean engine oil prior to installation.

6. Using the Crankshaft Rear Oil Seal Installers and Crankshaft Rear Oil Slinger Installer, install a new crankshaft oil slinger.

7. Install the engine rear cover plate.
8. Install the flexplate.

4.6L (3V) Engine

See Figures 362 through 365.

1. Remove the flexplate.
2. Remove the engine-to-transmission spacer plate.
3. Using the Slide Hammer (100-001) and Crankshaft Rear Oil Slinger Remover (303-514), remove and discard the crankshaft oil slinger.
4. Using the Slide Hammer (100-001) and Crankshaft Rear Oil Seal Remover (303-519), remove and discard the crankshaft rear seal.

To install:

➡ Lubricate the inner lip of the crankshaft rear seal with clean engine oil.

5. Using the Crankshaft Rear Oil Seal Installers, install a new crankshaft rear seal.
6. Using the Crankshaft Rear Oil Seal Installers and Crankshaft Rear Oil Slinger Installer, install a new crankshaft oil slinger.
7. Install the engine-to-transmission spacer plate.
8. Install the flexplate.

5.4L (3V) Engine

See Figures 362 through 366.

1. Remove the transmission.
2. Remove the 8 bolts and the flexplate.
3. Remove the engine rear cover plate.
4. Using the Slide Hammer (100-001) and Crankshaft Rear Oil Slinger Remover (303-514), remove and discard the crankshaft oil slinger.
5. Using the Slide Hammer (100-001) and Crankshaft Rear Oil Seal Remover (303-519), remove and discard the crankshaft rear seal.

To install:

➡ Lubricate the crankshaft rear seal with clean engine oil prior to installation.

6. Using the Crankshaft Rear Oil Seal Installers, install a new crankshaft rear seal.

➡ Lubricate the crankshaft oil slinger with clean engine oil prior to installation.

7. Using the Crankshaft Rear Oil Seal Installers and Crankshaft Rear Oil Slinger Installer, install a new crankshaft oil slinger.

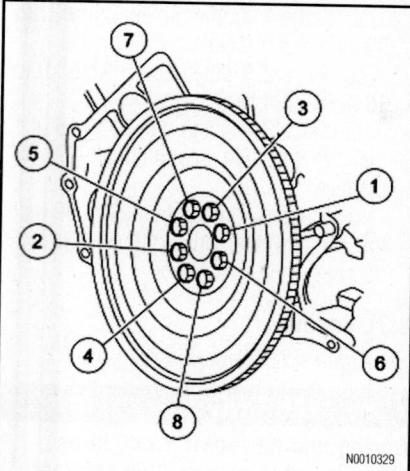

Fig. 366 Install the flexplate and tighten the 8 bolts in the sequence shown

8. Install the engine rear cover plate.
9. Install the flexplate and tighten the 8 bolts in the sequence shown. Tighten to 59 ft. lbs. (80 Nm).
10. Install the transmission.

TIMING CHAIN FRONT COVER

REMOVAL & INSTALLATION

3.5L GTDI Engine
See Figures 367 through 371.

> ✳✳ **WARNING**
>
> **During engine repair procedures, cleanliness is extremely important. Any foreign material, including any material created while cleaning gasket surfaces that enters the oil passages, coolant passages or the oil pan, may cause engine failure.**

> ✳✳ **WARNING**
>
> **Only use a 3M Roloc Bristle Disk (2-inch white) to clean the engine front cover. Do not use metal scrapers, wire brushes or any other power abrasive disk to clean the engine front cover.**

> ✳✳ **WARNING**
>
> **Place clean, lint-free shop towels over exposed engine cavities. Carefully remove the towels so foreign material is not dropped into the engine. Any foreign material (including any material created while cleaning gasket surfaces) that enters the oil passages or the oil pan may cause engine failure.**

> ✳✳ **WARNING**
>
> **Do not use wire brushes, power abrasive discs or 3M Roloc Bristle Disk (2-inch white) to clean the sealing surfaces of the engine block, cylinder heads, and oil pan. These tools cause contamination that can cause premature engine failure. Remove all traces of sealant, including any sealant from the inner surface of the cylinder block and cylinder head.**

> ✳✳ **WARNING**
>
> **Failure to use Motorcraft® High Performance Engine RTV Silicone may cause the engine oil to foam excessively and result in serious engine damage.**

➡ **Use the Spindle Bearing Installer to remove and install the front cover radial seal.**

➡ **The manufacturer does not provide a specific Removal and Installation procedure for this component. Refer to the graphic(s) when servicing this component.**

1. Using a suitable pry tool, locate the 7 pry pads shown and pry the engine front cover loose and remove.

➡ **The front cover radial seal must be replaced.**

2. Using the Spindle Bearing Installer and Handle, remove the front cover radial seal from the rear side of the front cover.

To install:

3. Using the Spindle Bearing Installer, install a new front cover radial seal from the rear side of the front cover.

> ✳✳ **WARNING**
>
> **Failure to use Motorcraft® High Performance Engine RTV Silicone may cause the engine oil to foam excessively and result in serious engine damage.**

➡ **The engine front cover and bolts 1, 2, 7, 8, 16, 17, 18, 19, 20 and 21 must be installed within 4 minutes of the initial sealant application. The remainder of the engine front cover bolts and the engine mount bracket bolts must be installed and tightened within 35 minutes of the initial sealant application. If the time limits are exceeded, the**

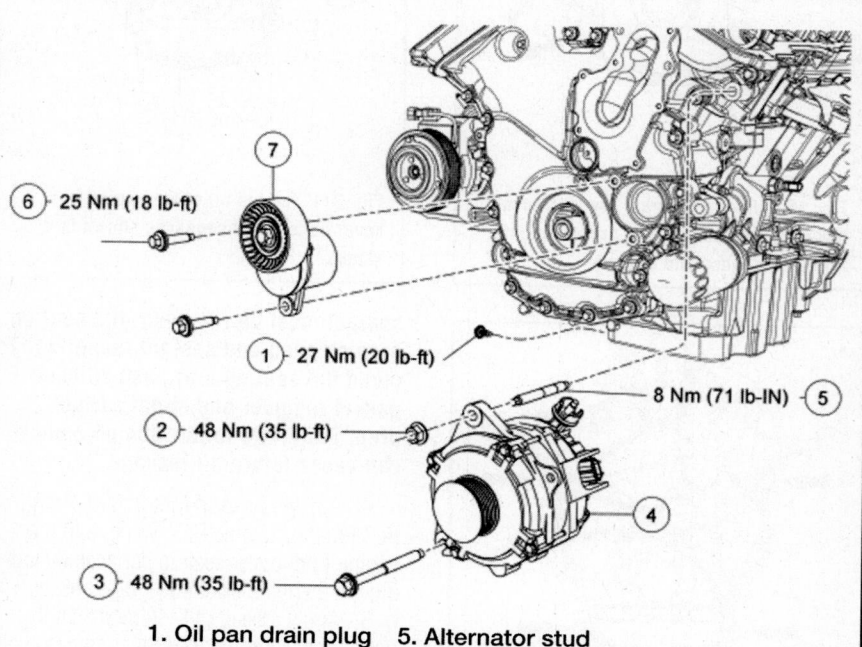

1. Oil pan drain plug
2. Alternator nut
3. Alternator bolt
4. Alternator
5. Alternator stud
6. Accessory drive belt tensioner bolt (2 required)
7. Accessory drive belt tensioner

Fig. 367 Exploded view of the components that must be removed for access to the engine front cover

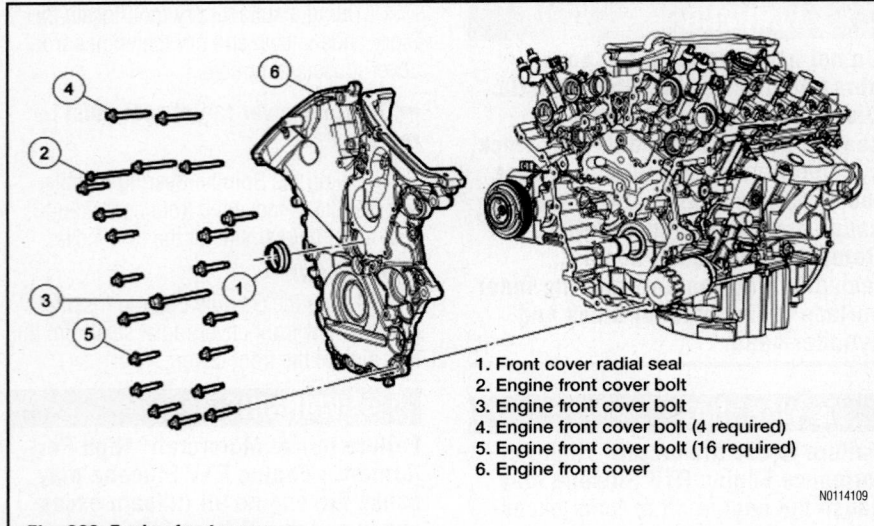

1. Front cover radial seal
2. Engine front cover bolt
3. Engine front cover bolt
4. Engine front cover bolt (4 required)
5. Engine front cover bolt (16 required)
6. Engine front cover

N0114109

Fig. 368 Engine front cover

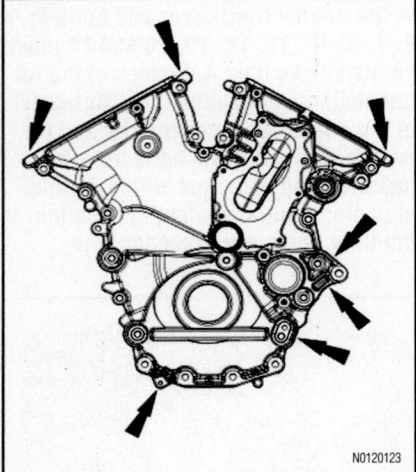

N0120123

Fig. 369 Using a suitable pry tool, locate the 7 pry pads shown and pry the engine front cover loose and remove

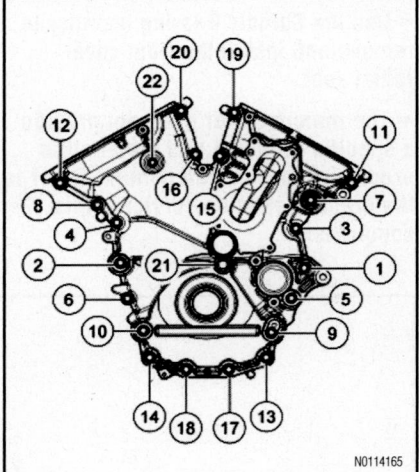

N0114165

Fig. 371 Tighten all of the engine front cover bolts in the sequence shown in 4 stages

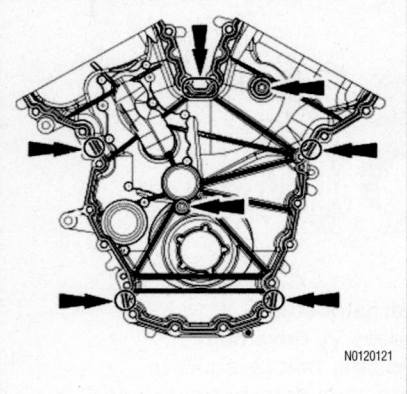

N0120121

Fig. 370 Apply a bead of Motorcraft® High Performance Engine RTV Silicone to the engine front cover

a. Stage 1: Tighten bolts 1 thru 21 to 89 inch lbs. (10 Nm).
b. Stage 2: Tighten bolts 1 thru 20 to 18 ft. lbs. (24 Nm).
c. Stage 3: Tighten bolt 21 to 15 ft. lbs. (20 Nm) then an additional 90 degrees.
d. Stage 4: Tighten bolt 22 to 89 inch lbs. (10 Nm) then an additional 45 degrees.

3.7L Engine

See Figures 372 through 376.

> **✳✳ WARNING**
>
> During engine repair procedures, cleanliness is extremely important. Any foreign material, including any material created while cleaning gasket surfaces that enters the oil passages, coolant passages or the oil pan, may cause engine failure.

> **✳✳ WARNING**
>
> Only use a 3M Roloc Bristle Disk (2-inch white) to clean the engine front cover. Do not use metal scrapers, wire brushes or any other power abrasive disk to clean the engine front cover.

> **✳✳ WARNING**
>
> Place clean, lint-free shop towels over exposed engine cavities. Carefully remove the towels so foreign material is not dropped into the engine. Any foreign material (including any material created while cleaning gasket surfaces) that enters the oil passages or the oil pan may cause engine failure.

> **✳✳ WARNING**
>
> Do not use wire brushes, power abrasive discs or 3M Roloc Bristle Disk (2-inch white) to clean the sealing surfaces of the engine block, cylinder heads, and oil pan. These tools cause contamination that can cause premature engine failure. Remove all traces of sealant, including any sealant from the inner surface of the cylinder block and cylinder head.

> **✳✳ WARNING**
>
> Failure to use Motorcraft® High Performance Engine RTV Silicone may cause the engine oil to foam exces-

sealant must be removed, the sealing area cleaned and sealant reapplied. To clean the sealing area, use silicone gasket remover and metal surface prep. Failure to follow this procedure can cause future oil leakage.

4. Apply a bead of Motorcraft® High Performance Engine RTV Silicone to the engine front cover sealing surfaces including the 2 engine front cover bolt bosses.

5. Apply a bead of Motorcraft® High Performance Engine RTV Silicone to the oil pan-to-cylinder block joint and the cylinder head-to-cylinder block joint areas of the engine front cover in 5 places as indicated.

6. Install the engine front cover bolts. Tighten all of the engine front cover bolts in the sequence shown in 4 stages:

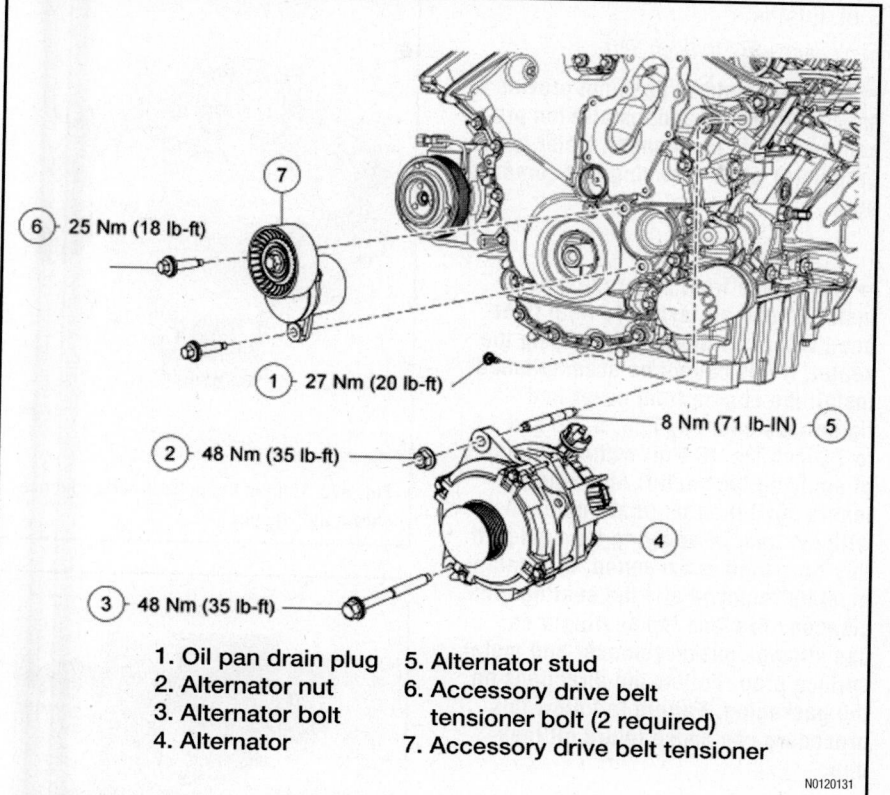

1. Oil pan drain plug
2. Alternator nut
3. Alternator bolt
4. Alternator
5. Alternator stud
6. Accessory drive belt tensioner bolt (2 required)
7. Accessory drive belt tensioner

N0120131

Fig. 372 Exploded view of the components you must remove to access the engine front cover

sively and result in serious engine damage.

➡Use the Spindle Bearing Installer to remove and install the front cover radial seal.

➡The manufacturer does not provide a specific Removal and Installation procedure for this component. Refer to the graphic(s) when servicing this component.

1. Using a suitable pry tool, locate the 7 pry pads shown and pry the engine front cover loose and remove.

➡The front cover radial seal must be replaced.

2. Using the Spindle Bearing Installer and Handle, remove the front cover radial seal from the rear side of the front cover.

To install:

3. Using the Spindle Bearing Installer, install a new front cover radial seal from the rear side of the front cover.

✳✳ WARNING

Failure to use Motorcraft® High Performance Engine RTV Silicone may cause the engine oil to foam exces-

sively and result in serious engine damage.

➡The engine front cover and bolts 1, 2, 7, 8, 16, 17, 18, 19, 20 and 21 must be installed within 4 minutes of the initial sealant application. The remainder of the engine front cover bolts and the engine mount bracket bolts must be installed and tightened

within 35 minutes of the initial sealant application. If the time limits are exceeded, the sealant must be removed, the sealing area cleaned and sealant reapplied. To clean the sealing area, use silicone gasket remover and metal surface prep. Failure to follow this procedure can cause future oil leakage.

4. Apply a bead of Motorcraft® High Performance Engine RTV Silicone to the engine front cover sealing surfaces including the 2 engine front cover bolt bosses.

5. Apply a bead of Motorcraft® High Performance Engine RTV Silicone to the oil pan-to-cylinder block joint and the cylinder head-to-cylinder block joint areas of the engine front cover in 5 places as indicated.

➡Make sure the 2 locating dowel pins are seated correctly in the cylinder block.

6. Install the engine front cover and bolts 1, 2, 7, 8, 16, 17, 18, 19, 20 and 21. Tighten in sequence to 27 inch lbs. (3 Nm).

7. Install the engine front cover bolts. Tighten all of the engine front cover bolts in the sequence shown in 4 stages:

a. Stage 1: Tighten bolts 1 thru 21 to 89 inch lbs. (10 Nm).

b. Stage 2: Tighten bolts 1 thru 20 to 18 ft. lbs. (24 Nm).

c. Stage 3: Tighten bolt 21 to 15 ft. lbs. (20 Nm) then an additional 90 degrees.

d. Stage 4: Tighten bolt 22 to 89 inch lbs. (10 Nm) then an additional 45 degrees.

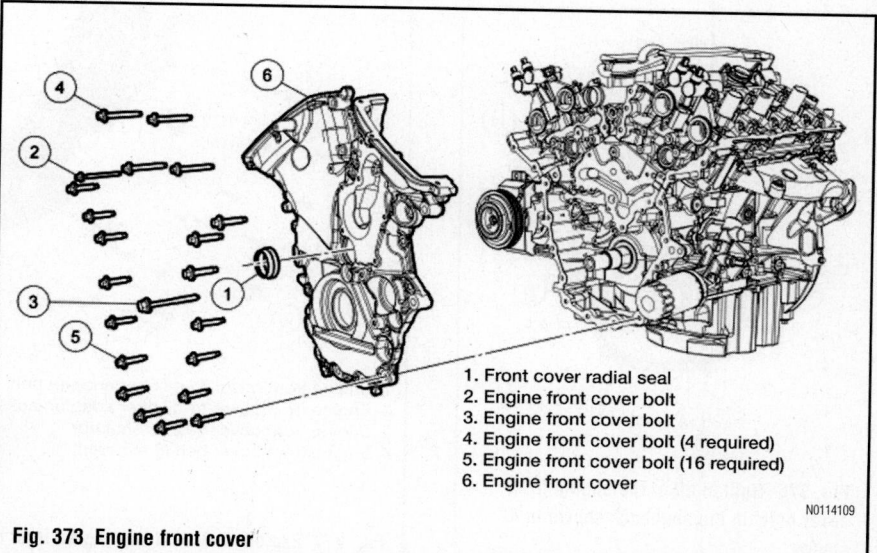

1. Front cover radial seal
2. Engine front cover bolt
3. Engine front cover bolt
4. Engine front cover bolt (4 required)
5. Engine front cover bolt (16 required)
6. Engine front cover

N0114109

Fig. 373 Engine front cover

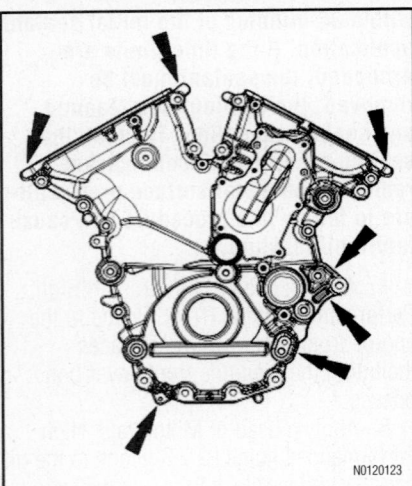

Fig. 374 Using a suitable pry tool, locate the 7 pry pads shown and pry the engine front cover loose and remove

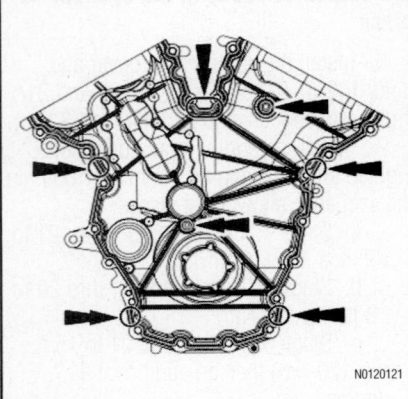

Fig. 375 Apply a bead of Motorcraft® High Performance Engine RTV Silicone to the engine front cover

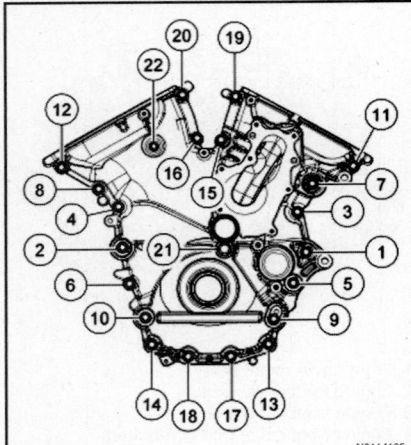

Fig. 376 Tighten all of the engine front cover bolts in the sequence shown in 4 stages

5.0L Engine

See Figures 377 through 380.

➡The manufacturer does not provide a specific Removal and Installation procedure for this component. Refer to the graphic(s) when servicing this component.

To install:

➡The engine front cover must be installed and all fasteners final tightened within 5 minutes of applying the sealer. If this cannot be accomplished, install the engine front cover and tighten fasteners 6, 7, 8, 9, 10 and 11 to 71 inch lbs. (8 Nm) within 5 minutes of applying the sealer. All of the fasteners must then be final tightened within 1 hour of applying the sealer. If this time limit is exceeded, all sealant must be removed and the sealing area cleaned. To clean the sealing area, use silicone gasket remover and metal surface prep. Follow the directions on the packaging. Failure to follow this procedure can cause future oil leakage.

1. Tighten the bolts in the sequence shown in 2 stages.
   a. Stage 1: Tighten bolts 1–15 to 18 ft. lbs. (25 Nm) and bolts 16–19 to 89 inch lbs. (10 Nm).
   b. Stage 2: Tighten bolts 1-15 an additional 60 degrees and bolts 16-19 an additional 45 degrees.

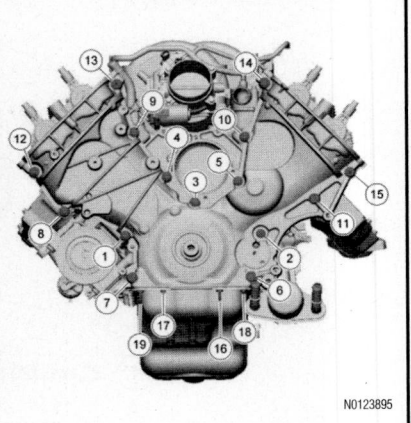

Fig. 378 Tighten the bolts in the sequence shown in 2 stages

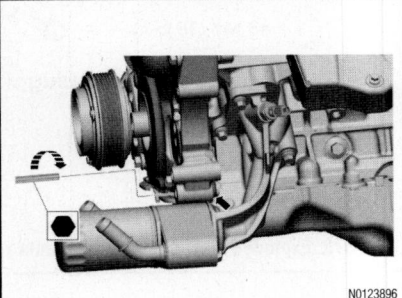

Fig. 379 Using a 10 mm Hex Bit, rotate the engine front cover jackscrew into contact with the oil filter adapter

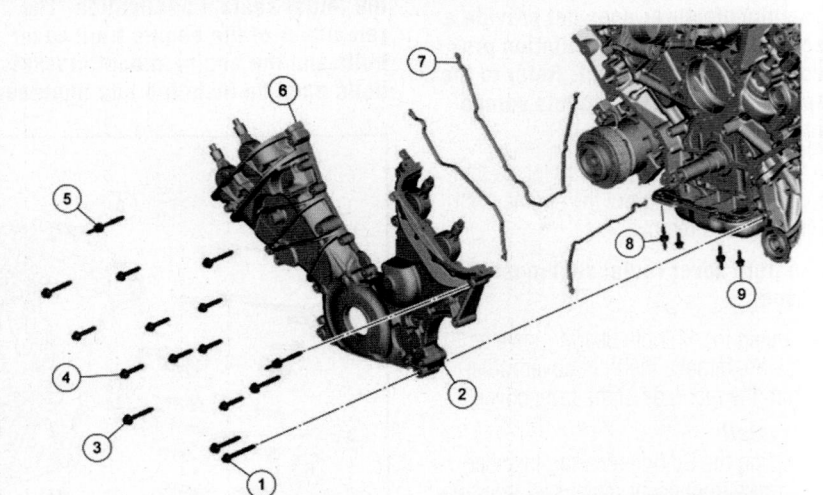

1. Engine front cover-to-oil filter adapter bolt
2. Engine front cover-to-oil filter adapter jackscrew
3. Engine front cover bolt (5 required)
4. Engine front cover bolt (8 required)
5. Engine front cover stud bolt (2 required)
6. Engine front cover
7. Engine front cover gasket (3 required)
8. Oil pan stud bolt (2 required)
9. Oil pan bolt (2 required)

Fig. 377 Exploded view of the engine front cover assembly

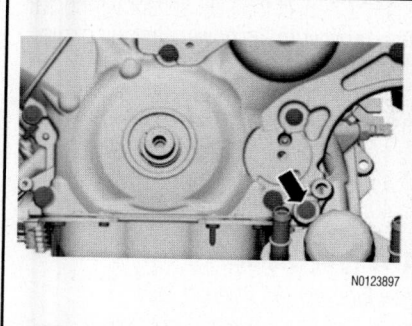

Fig. 380 Tighten the engine front cover-to-oil filter adapter bolt

2. Using a 10 mm Hex Bit, rotate the engine front cover jackscrew into contact with the oil filter adapter to 44 inch lbs. (5 Nm).

3. Tighten the engine front cover-to-oil filter adapter bolt to 18 ft. lbs. (25 Nm) plus an additional 60 degrees.

4.6L (2V) Engine

See Figures 381 through 384.

1. With the vehicle in NEUTRAL, position it on a hoist.

2. Remove the LH valve cover.

3. Remove the RH valve cover.

4. Rotate the tensioner clockwise and remove the drive belt.

5. Disconnect the Engine Oil Pressure (EOP) sensor wiring harness retainer from the power steering pump stud bolt.

6. Remove the 2 bolts, the stud bolt and position the power steering pump assembly aside.

7. Disconnect the Camshaft Position (CMP) sensor electrical connector.

8. Remove the nut and position the LH radio interference capacitor aside.

9. Remove the nut and position the RH radio interference capacitor aside.

10. Remove the oil drain plug and drain the engine oil. Install the drain plug when finished. Tighten to 17 ft. lbs. (23 Nm).

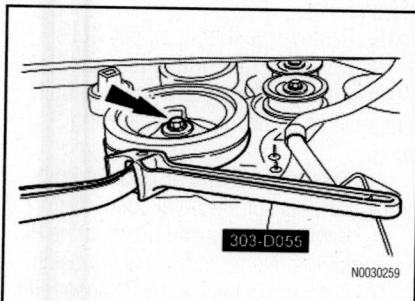

Fig. 381 Using the Strap Wrench, remove the bolt and washer and discard the bolt

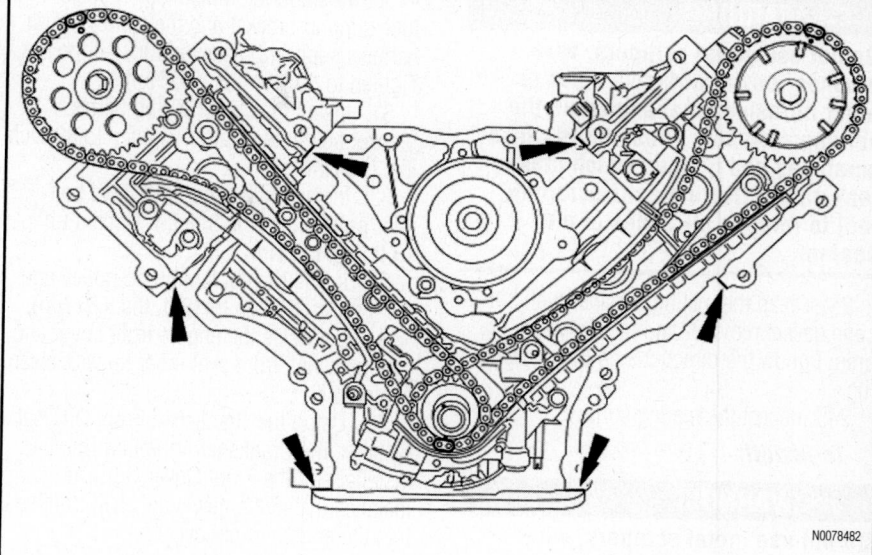

Fig. 382 Apply a bead of silicone gasket and sealant along the cylinder head-to-cylinder block surface and the oil pan-to-cylinder block surface

✳✳ WARNING

This bolt is a torque-to-yield design and cannot be reused. Failure to follow this instruction may result in engine damage.

11. Using the Strap Wrench (303-D055), remove the bolt and washer and discard the bolt.

12. Using the Crankshaft Vibration Damper Remover, remove the crankshaft pulley.

13. Using the Crankshaft Front Oil Seal Remover, remove and discard the crankshaft seal.

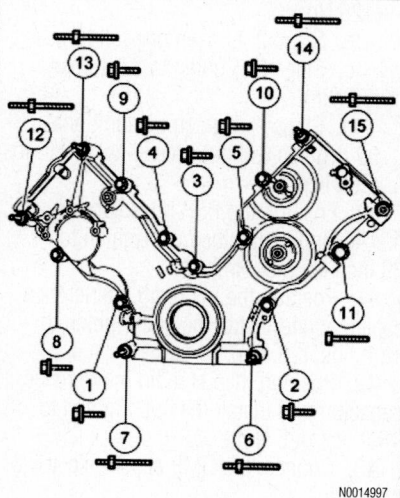

Fig. 383 Tighten the 15 engine front cover fasteners in the sequence shown

14. Remove the 4 coolant pump pulley bolts and the coolant pump pulley.

15. Remove the 3 bolts and the 3 accessory drive belt idler pulleys.

16. Remove the starter wiring harness bracket bolt at the starter.

17. Remove the nut and position aside the transmission cooler tube support bracket and the starter wiring harness support bracket.

18. Disconnect the Crankshaft Position (CKP) sensor electrical connector.

19. Remove the nut and position aside the Power Steering Pressure (PSP) hose support bracket.

20. Remove the 4 oil pan bolts.

21. Remove the 9 bolts and the 6 stud bolts from the front cover.

22. Remove the engine front cover from the front cover-to-cylinder block dowel. Remove and discard the engine front cover gaskets.

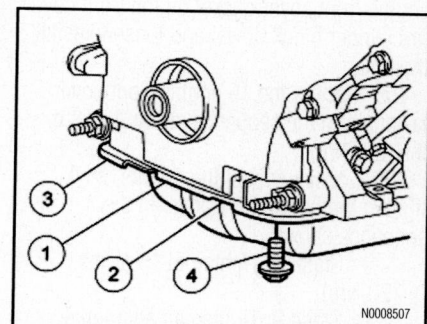

Fig. 384 Loosely install the 4 bolts, then tighten the bolts in 2 stages, in the sequence shown

❊❊ WARNING

Do not use metal scrapers, wire brushes, power abrasive discs or other abrasive means to clean the sealing surfaces. These tools cause scratches and gouges which make leak paths. Use a plastic scraping tool to remove all traces of old sealant.

23. Clean the mating surfaces with silicone gasket remover and metal surface prep. Follow the directions on the packaging.

24. Inspect the mating surfaces.

To install:

❊❊ WARNING

Do not use metal scrapers, wire brushes, power abrasive discs or other abrasive means to clean the sealing surfaces. These tools cause scratches and gouges which make leak paths. Use a plastic scraping tool to remove all traces of old sealant.

➡ **If the engine front cover is not secured within 4 minutes, the sealant must be removed and the sealing area cleaned with silicone gasket remover and metal surface prep. Follow the directions on the packaging. Allow to dry until there is no sign of wetness, or 4 minutes, whichever is longer. Failure to follow this procedure can cause future oil leakage.**

➡ **Make sure that the engine front cover gasket is in place on the engine front cover before installation.**

25. Apply a bead of silicone gasket and sealant along the cylinder head-to-cylinder block surface and the oil pan-to-cylinder block surface, at the locations shown.

26. Install the engine front cover with the engine front cover gasket on the front cover-to-cylinder block dowel and loosely install the bolts.

27. Tighten the 15 engine front cover fasteners in the sequence shown to 18 ft. lbs. (25 Nm).

28. Loosely install the 4 bolts, then tighten the bolts in 2 stages, in the sequence shown.

   a. Stage 1: Tighten to 15 ft. lbs. (20 Nm).

   b. Stage 2: Tighten an additional 60 degrees.

29. Connect the CKP sensor electrical connector.

30. Position the transmission cooler tube support bracket and the starter wiring harness support bracket and install the nut. Tighten to 89 inch lbs. (10 Nm).

31. Install the starter wiring harness bracket bolt at the starter. Tighten to 89 inch lbs. (10 Nm).

32. Install the 3 accessory drive belt idler pulleys and the 3 bolts. Tighten to 18 ft. lbs. (25 Nm).

33. Install the coolant pump pulley and the 4 bolts. Tighten to 18 ft. lbs. (25 Nm).

34. Lubricate the engine front cover and the crankshaft front seal inner lip with clean engine oil.

35. Using the Crankshaft Front Oil Seal Installer, the Crankshaft Vibration Damper Installer and the Front Cover Oil Seal Installer, install the new crankshaft front seal into the engine front cover.

➡ **If not secured within 4 minutes, the sealant must be removed and the sealing area cleaned with metal surface prep and silicone gasket remover. Allow to dry until there is no sign of wetness, or 4 minutes, whichever is longer. Failure to follow this procedure can cause future oil leakage.**

36. Apply silicone gasket and sealant to the Woodruff key slot in the crankshaft pulley.

37. Lubricate the crankshaft pulley sealing area with clean engine oil prior to installation.

38. Using the Crankshaft Vibration Damper Installer, install the crankshaft pulley.

39. Using a new crankshaft pulley bolt, install the crankshaft pulley bolt and washer. Using the Strap Wrench to hold the crankshaft pulley, tighten the bolt in 4 stages:

   a. Stage 1: Tighten to 89 ft. lbs. (120 Nm).

   b. Stage 2: Loosen one full turn.

   c. Stage 3: Tighten to 37 ft. lbs. (50 Nm).

   d. Stage 4: Tighten an additional 90 degrees without exceeding 148 ft. lbs. (200 Nm).

40. Position the PSP hose support bracket and install the nut. Tighten to 89 inch lbs. (10 Nm).

41. Position the RH radio interference capacitor and install the nut. Tighten to 18 ft. lbs. (25 Nm).

42. Position the LH radio interference capacitor and install the nut. Tighten to 18 ft. lbs. (25 Nm).

43. Connect the CMP sensor electrical connector.

44. Position the power steering pump assembly and install the 2 bolts and the stud bolt. Tighten to 18 ft. lbs. (25 Nm).

45. Connect the EOP sensor wiring harness retainer to the power steering pump stud bolt.

46. Rotate the tensioner clockwise and install the drive belt.

47. Install the RH valve cover.

48. Install the LH valve cover.

49. Fill the engine with clean engine oil.

4.6L (3V) Engine

See Figures 385 through 387.

1. With the vehicle in NEUTRAL, position it on a hoist.

2. Remove the RH valve cover.

3. Remove the LH valve cover.

4. Loosen the 4 coolant pump pulley bolts.

5. Rotate the tensioner clockwise and remove the accessory drive belt.

6. Remove the 4 bolts and the coolant pump pulley.

7. Remove the drain plug and drain the engine oil. Install the drain plug when finished. Tighten to 17 ft. lbs. (23 Nm).

8. Remove the starter wiring harness bracket bolt at the starter.

9. Remove the nut and position the transmission cooler tube support bracket and the starter wiring harness support bracket aside.

10. Disconnect the Crankshaft Position (CKP) sensor electrical connector.

11. Remove the nut and position aside the Power Steering Pressure (PSP) hose support bracket.

12. Remove the crankshaft pulley bolt and washer. Discard the crankshaft pulley bolt.

13. Using the 3 Jaw Puller, remove the crankshaft pulley.

14. Using the Crankshaft Front Seal Remover, remove and discard the crankshaft front seal.

15. Remove the 3 bolts and the 3 accessory drive idler pulleys.

16. Remove the 3 bolts and the accessory drive belt tensioner.

17. If equipped, remove the 4 bolts and the skid plate.

18. Remove the 4 front oil pan bolts.

19. Disconnect the wiring harness retainer, remove the 2 bolts, the stud bolt and position aside the power steering pump.

20. Disconnect the RH Camshaft Position (CMP) sensor electrical connector.

21. Remove the nut and position the RH radio ignition interference capacitor aside.

22. Disconnect the LH CMP sensor electrical connector.

23. Remove the nut and position the LH radio ignition interference capacitor aside.

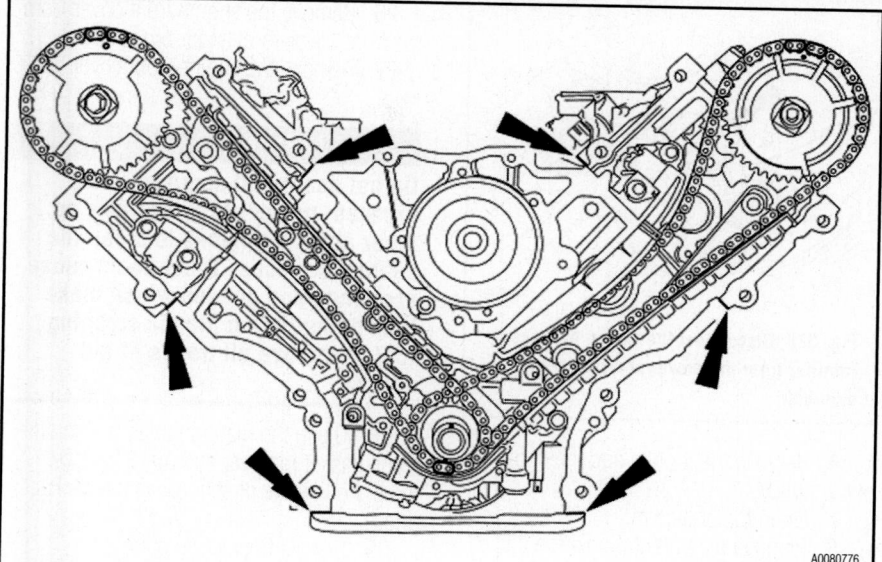

Fig. 385 Apply a bead of silicone gasket and sealant along the cylinder head-to-cylinder block surface and the oil pan-to-cylinder block surface

24. Remove the 9 bolts and the 6 stud bolts.

25. Remove the engine front cover from the front cover-to-cylinder block dowel. Remove and discard the 3 engine front cover gaskets.

✳✳ WARNING

Do not use metal scrapers, wire brushes, power abrasive discs or other abrasive means to clean the sealing surfaces. These tools cause scratches and gouges which make leak paths. Use a plastic scraping tool to remove all traces of old sealant.

26. Clean the mating surfaces with silicone gasket remover and metal surface prep. Follow the directions on the packaging.

27. Inspect the mating surfaces.

To install:

✳✳ WARNING

Do not use metal scrapers, wire brushes, power abrasive discs or other abrasive means to clean the sealing surfaces. These tools cause scratches and gouges which make leak paths. Use a plastic scraping tool to remove all traces of old sealant.

➡**If the engine front cover is not secured within 4 minutes, the sealant must be removed and the sealing area cleaned.**

To clean the sealing area, use silicone gasket remover and metal surface prep. Allow to dry until there is no sign of wetness, or 4 minutes, whichever is longer. Follow the directions on the packaging. Failure to follow this procedure can cause future oil leakage.

➡**Make sure that the engine front cover gaskets are in place on the engine front cover before installation.**

28. Apply a bead of silicone gasket and sealant along the cylinder head-to-cylinder block surface and the oil pan-to-cylinder block surface, at the locations shown.

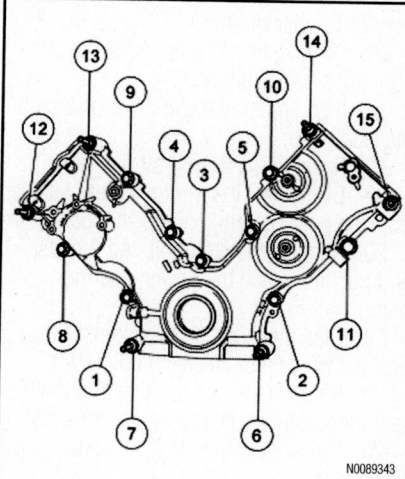

Fig. 386 Tighten the 15 engine front cover fasteners in the sequence shown in 2 stages

29. Install 3 new engine front cover gaskets on the engine front cover. Position the engine front cover onto the dowels. Install the 15 fasteners finger-tight.

30. Tighten the 15 engine front cover fasteners in the sequence shown in 2 stages.

   a. Stage 1: Tighten fasteners 1 through 15 to 18 ft. lbs. (25 Nm).

   b. Stage 2: Tighten fasteners 6 and 7 to 35 ft. lbs. (48 Nm).

31. Loosely install the 4 bolts, then tighten the bolts in 2 stages, in the sequence shown.

   a. Stage 1: Tighten to 15 ft. lbs. (20 Nm).

   b. Stage 2: Tighten an additional 60 degrees.

32. Connect the CKP sensor electrical connector.

33. Position the starter wiring harness support bracket and the transmission cooler tube support bracket and tighten the nut. Tighten to 89 inch lbs. (10 Nm).

34. Install the starter wiring harness bracket bolt at the starter. Tighten to 89 inch lbs. (10 Nm).

35. Lubricate the engine front cover and the new crankshaft seal inner lip with clean engine oil.

36. Using the Front Cover Oil Seal Installer, the Crankshaft Front Seal Installer and the Crankshaft Vibration Damper Installer, install a new crankshaft front seal into the engine front cover.

➡**If not secured within 4 minutes, the sealant must be removed and the sealing area cleaned with metal surface prep and silicone gasket remover. Follow the directions on the packaging. Allow to dry until there is no sign of wetness, or 4 minutes, whichever is longer. Failure to follow this procedure can cause future oil leakage.**

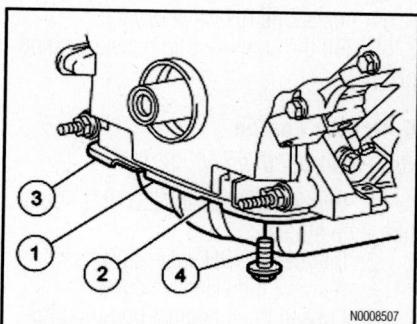

Fig. 387 Loosely install the 4 bolts, then tighten the bolts in 2 stages, in the sequence shown

37. Apply silicone gasket and sealant to the Woodruff key slot on the crankshaft pulley.

38. Use the Crankshaft Vibration Damper Installer to install the crankshaft pulley.

39. Position the washer on the new crankshaft pulley bolt and install the new crankshaft pulley bolt finger-tight. Tighten the new crankshaft pulley bolt in 4 stages.

    a. Stage 1: Tighten to 89 ft. lbs. (120 Nm).

    b. Stage 2: Loosen 360 degrees.

    c. Stage 3: Tighten to 37 ft. lbs. (50 Nm).

    d. Stage 4: Tighten an additional 90 degrees.

40. Install the accessory drive belt tensioner and the 3 bolts. Tighten to 18 ft. lbs. (25 Nm).

41. Install the 3 accessory drive idler pulleys and the 3 bolts. Tighten to 18 ft. lbs. (25 Nm).

42. Position the coolant pump pulley and install the 4 bolts finger-tight.

43. If equipped, install the skid plate and the 4 bolts. Tighten to 18 ft. lbs. (25 Nm).

44. Position the power steering pump and install the 2 bolts and the stud bolt. Tighten to 18 ft. lbs. (25 Nm).

45. Attach the engine wiring harness to the power steering pump stud bolt.

46. Position the PSP hose support bracket and install the nut. Tighten to 30 ft. lbs. (40 Nm).

47. Connect the RH CMP sensor electrical connector.

48. Install the RH radio ignition interference capacitor and the nut. Tighten to 18 ft. lbs. (25 Nm).

49. Connect the LH CMP sensor electrical connector.

50. Install the LH radio ignition interference capacitor and the nut. Tighten to 18 ft. lbs. (25 Nm).

51. Install the accessory drive belt.

52. Tighten the 4 coolant pump pulley bolts. Tighten to 18 ft. lbs. (25 Nm).

53. Install the LH valve cover.

54. Install the RH valve cover.

55. Fill the crankcase with clean engine oil.

5.4L (3V) Engine

See Figures 388 through 391.

1. With the vehicle in NEUTRAL, position it on a hoist.

2. Remove the RH valve cover.

3. Remove the LH valve cover.

4. Loosen the 4 coolant pump pulley bolts.

5. Rotate the tensioner clockwise and remove the accessory drive belt.

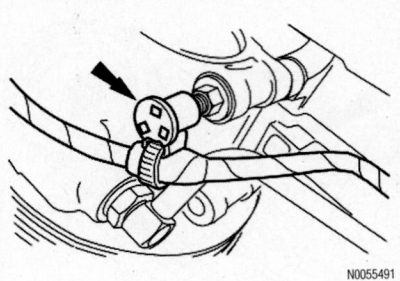

Fig. 388 Disconnect the wiring harness retainer from the power steering pump stud bolt

6. Remove the 4 bolts and the coolant pump pulley.

7. Drain the engine oil.

8. Remove the bolt and position the starter wiring harness and starter wiring harness rear support bracket aside.

9. Remove the nut and position aside the transmission cooler tube support bracket and the starter wiring harness support bracket.

10. Disconnect the Crankshaft Position (CKP) sensor electrical connector.

11. Remove the nut and position aside the Power Steering Pressure (PSP) hose support bracket.

12. Remove the crankshaft pulley bolt and washer. Discard the crankshaft pulley bolt.

13. Remove and discard the crankshaft pulley bolt. Using the 3 Jaw Puller, remove the crankshaft pulley.

14. Using the Crankshaft Front Oil Seal Remover, remove and discard the crankshaft front seal.

15. Remove the 3 bolts and the 3 accessory drive idler pulleys.

16. Remove the 3 bolts and the accessory drive belt tensioner.

17. If equipped, remove the 4 bolts and the skid plate.

18. Remove the 4 front oil pan bolts.

19. Disconnect the wiring harness retainer from the power steering pump stud bolt.

20. Remove the stud bolt, the 2 bolts, and position aside the power steering pump.

21. Disconnect the RH Camshaft Position (CMP) sensor electrical connector.

22. Remove the nut and position the RH radio ignition interference capacitor aside.

23. Disconnect the LH CMP sensor electrical connector.

24. Remove the nut and position the LH radio ignition interference capacitor aside.

25. Remove the 10 bolts and the 5 studs from the front cover.

26. Remove the engine front cover from the front cover-to-cylinder block dowel.

27. Remove the engine front cover gaskets.

⁂ WARNING

Do not use metal scrapers, wire brushes, power abrasive discs or other abrasive means to clean the sealing surfaces. These tools cause scratches and gouges which make leak paths. Use a plastic scraping tool to remove all traces of old sealant.

28. Clean the mating surfaces with silicone gasket remover and metal surface prep. Follow the directions on the packaging.

29. Inspect the mating surfaces.

To install:

⁂ WARNING

Do not use metal scrapers, wire brushes, power abrasive discs or other abrasive means to clean the sealing surfaces. These tools cause scratches and gouges which make leak paths. Use a plastic scraping tool to remove all traces of old sealant.

➡️If the engine front cover is not secured within 4 minutes, the sealant must be removed and the sealing area cleaned. To clean the sealing area, use silicone gasket remover and metal surface prep. Allow to dry until there is no sign of wetness, or 4 minutes, whichever is longer. Follow the directions on the packaging. Failure to follow this procedure can cause future oil leakage.

➡️Make sure that the engine front cover gasket is in place on the engine front cover before installation.

30. Apply a bead of silicone gasket and sealant along the cylinder head-to-cylinder block surface and the oil pan-to-cylinder block surface, at the locations shown.

31. Install a new engine front cover gasket on the engine front cover. Position the engine front cover onto the dowels. Install the fasteners finger-tight.

32. Tighten the 15 engine front cover fasteners in the sequence shown in 2 stages.

    a. Stage 1: Tighten fasteners 1 through 15 to 18 ft. lbs. (25 Nm).

    b. Stage 2: Tighten fasteners 6 and 7 to 35 ft. lbs. (48 Nm).

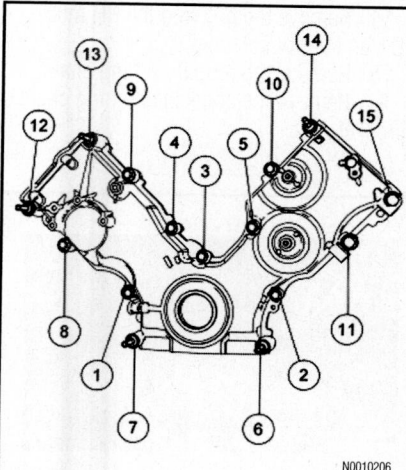

Fig. 389 Apply a bead of silicone gasket and sealant along the cylinder head-to-cylinder block surface and the oil pan-to-cylinder block surface

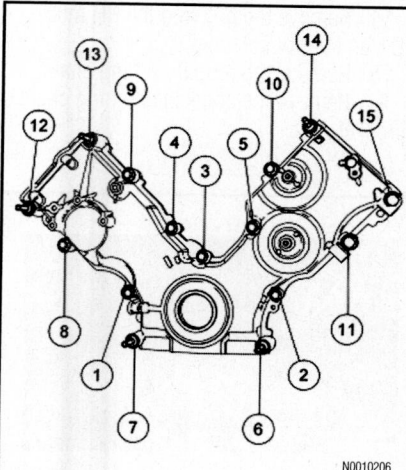

Fig. 390 Tighten the 15 engine front cover fasteners in the sequence shown in 2 stages

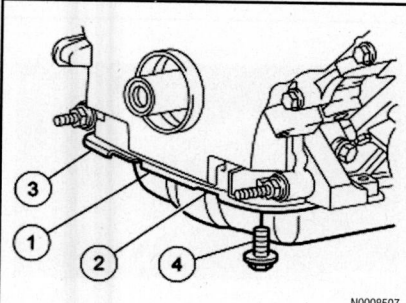

Fig. 391 Loosely install the 4 oil pan bolts, then tighten in 2 stages, in the sequence shown

33. Loosely install the 4 oil pan bolts, then tighten in 2 stages, in the sequence shown.

   a. Stage 1: Tighten to 15 ft. lbs. (20 Nm).

   b. Stage 2: Tighten an additional 60 degrees.

34. Connect the CKP sensor electrical connector.

35. Position the starter wiring harness support bracket and the transmission cooler tube support bracket and tighten the nut. Tighten to 89 inch lbs. (10 Nm).

36. Position the starter wiring harness and starter wiring harness rear support bracket and install the bolt. Tighten to 89 inch lbs. (10 Nm).

37. Lubricate the engine front cover and the crankshaft seal inner lip with clean engine oil.

38. Using the Crankshaft Vibration Damper Installer, Front Cover Oil Seal Installer and the Crankshaft Front Oil Seal Installer, install a new crankshaft front seal into the engine front cover.

➡ If not secured within 4 minutes, the sealant must be removed and the sealing area cleaned with metal surface prep and silicone gasket remover. Allow to dry until there is no sign of wetness, or 4 minutes, whichever is longer. Failure to follow this procedure can cause future oil leakage.

39. Apply silicone gasket and sealant to the Woodruff key slot in the crankshaft pulley.

40. Use the Crankshaft Vibration Damper Installer to install the crankshaft pulley.

41. Tighten the new crankshaft pulley bolt in 4 stages.

   a. Stage 1: Tighten to 66 ft. lbs. (90 Nm).

   b. Stage 2: Loosen 360 degrees.

   c. Stage 3: Tighten to 37 ft. lbs. (50 Nm).

   d. Stage 4: Tighten an additional 90 degrees.

42. Install the accessory drive belt tensioner and the 3 bolts. Tighten to 18 ft. lbs. (25 Nm).

43. Install the 3 accessory drive idler pulleys and the 3 bolts. Tighten to 18 ft. lbs. (25 Nm).

44. Position the coolant pump pulley and install the 4 bolts finger-tight.

45. If equipped, install the skid plate and the 4 bolts. Tighten to 35 ft. lbs. (48 Nm).

46. Position the power steering pump and install the stud bolt and the 2 bolts. Tighten to 18 ft. lbs. (25 Nm).

47. Attach the engine wiring harness to the power steering pump stud bolt.

48. Position the PSP hose support bracket and install the nut. Tighten to 89 inch lbs. (10 Nm).

49. Connect the RH CMP sensor electrical connector.

50. Install the LH radio ignition interference capacitor and the nut. Tighten to 18 ft. lbs. (25 Nm).

51. Connect the LH CMP sensor electrical connector.

52. Install the RH radio ignition interference capacitor and the nut. Tighten to 18 ft. lbs. (25 Nm).

53. Rotate the tensioner clockwise and install the accessory drive belt.

54. Tighten the 4 coolant pump pulley bolts. Tighten to 18 ft. lbs. (25 Nm).

55. Install the LH valve cover.

56. Install the RH valve cover.

57. Fill the crankcase with clean engine oil.

TIMING CHAIN & SPROCKETS

REMOVAL & INSTALLATION

⚹⚹ WARNING

During engine repair procedures, cleanliness is extremely important. Any foreign material, including any material created while cleaning gasket surfaces, that enters the oil passages, coolant passages or the oil pan may cause engine failure.

3.5L GTDI and 3.7L Engines

See Figures 392 through 410.

1. Remove the engine front cover. Refer to Timing Chain Front Cover.

2. Rotate the crankshaft clockwise and align the timing marks on the intake Variable Camshaft Timing (VCT) assemblies as shown.

3. Remove the 3 bolts and the LH valve train oil tube.

➡ **The Camshaft Holding Tool will hold the camshafts in the Top Dead Center (TDC) position.**

4. Install the Camshaft Holding Tool (303-1248) onto the flats of the LH camshafts.

5. Remove the 3 bolts and the RH valve train oil tube.

➡ **The Camshaft Holding Tool will hold the camshafts in the TDC position.**

6. Install the Camshaft Holding Tool onto the flats of the RH camshafts.

➡ **The following 3 steps are for primary timing chains that the colored links are not visible.**

Fig. 392 Rotate the crankshaft clockwise and align the timing marks on the intake Variable Camshaft Timing (VCT) assemblies as shown

Fig. 393 Install the Camshaft Holding Tool onto the flats of the LH camshafts

Fig. 394 Mark the timing chain link that aligns with the timing mark on the LH intake VCT assembly as shown

7. Mark the timing chain link that aligns with the timing mark on the LH intake VCT assembly as shown.

8. Mark the timing chain link that aligns with the timing mark on the RH intake VCT assembly as shown.

➡ **The crankshaft sprocket timing mark should be between the 2 colored links.**

9. Mark the 2 timing chain links that align with the timing mark on the crankshaft sprocket as shown.

10. Remove the 2 bolts and the primary timing chain tensioner.

Fig. 395 Mark the timing chain link that aligns with the timing mark on the RH intake VCT assembly as shown

Fig. 396 Mark the 2 timing chain links that align with the timing mark on the crankshaft sprocket as shown

11. Remove the primary timing chain tensioner arm.

12. Remove the 2 bolts and the lower LH primary timing chain guide.

➡ **Removal of the VCT oil control solenoid will aid in the removal of the primary timing chain.**

➡ **A slight twisting motion will aid in the removal of the VCT oil control solenoid.**

➡ **Keep the VCT oil control solenoid clean of dirt and debris.**

13. Remove the bolt and the LH intake VCT oil control solenoid.

➡ **Removal of the VCT oil control solenoid will aid in the removal of the primary timing chain.**

➡ **A slight twisting motion will aid in the removal of the VCT oil control solenoid.**

➡ **Keep the VCT oil control solenoid clean of dirt and debris.**

14. Remove the bolt and the RH intake VCT oil control solenoid.

15. Remove the primary timing chain.

16. Remove the crankshaft timing chain sprocket.

Fig. 397 Remove the 2 bolts and the lower LH primary timing chain guide

Fig. 398 Remove the bolt and the LH intake VCT oil control solenoid

※※ **WARNING**

Do not use power tools to remove the bolt or damage to the LH primary timing chain guide may occur.

17. Remove the bolt and the upper LH primary timing chain guide.

➡ **The 2 VCT oil control solenoids are removed for clarity.**

➡ **The Secondary Chain Hold Down is inserted through a hole in the top of the mega cap.**

18. Compress the LH secondary timing chain tensioner and install the Secondary Chain Hold Down in the hole on the rear of the secondary timing chain tensioner guide and let it hold against the mega cap to retain the tensioner in the collapsed position.

19. Remove and discard the 2 LH VCT assembly bolts.

20. Remove the 2 LH VCT assemblies and secondary timing chain.

➡ **The 2 VCT oil control solenoids are removed for clarity.**

➡ **The Secondary Chain Hold Down is inserted through a hole in the top of the mega cap.**

21. Compress the RH secondary timing chain tensioner and install the Secondary Chain Hold Down in the hole on the rear of the secondary timing chain tensioner guide and let it hold against the mega cap to retain the tensioner in the collapsed position.

22. Remove and discard the 2 RH VCT assembly bolts.

23. Remove the 2 RH VCT assemblies and secondary timing chain.

※※ **WARNING**

Do not use power tools to remove the bolt or damage to the RH primary timing chain guide may occur.

24. Remove the bolt and the RH primary timing chain guide.

25. Remove the 9 bolts and the timing chain gear. Discard the gasket.

※※ **WARNING**

The following steps are only for the replacement of the secondary timing chain tensioners. Do not reuse the secondary timing chain tensioners if removed, or damage to the engine may occur.

➡ **A slight twisting motion will aid in the removal of the VCT oil control solenoid.**

➡ **Keep the VCT oil control solenoid clean of dirt and debris.**

26. Remove the LH exhaust VCT oil control solenoid.

27. Remove the LH secondary timing chain tensioner shoe.

28. Remove the LH secondary timing chain tensioner by pushing up from the bottom and remove.

➡ **A slight twisting motion will aid in the removal of the VCT oil control solenoid.**

➡ **Keep the VCT oil control solenoid clean of dirt and debris.**

29. Remove the RH exhaust VCT oil control solenoid.

30. Remove the RH secondary timing chain tensioner shoe.

31. Remove the RH secondary timing chain tensioner by pushing up from the bottom and remove.

To install:

32. Using a new gasket, install the timing chain gear and the 9 bolts. Tighten in the sequence shown in 2 stages:

Fig. 399 Remove the bolt and the upper LH primary timing chain guide

Fig. 401 Remove and discard the 2 LH VCT assembly bolts

Fig. 403 Remove the LH exhaust VCT oil control solenoid

Fig. 400 Compress the LH secondary timing chain tensioner and install the Secondary Chain Hold Down

Fig. 402 Remove the 9 bolts and the timing chain gear

Fig. 404 Remove the LH secondary timing chain tensioner shoe

Fig. 405 Tighten in the sequence shown in 2 stages

Fig. 406 Install the RH secondary timing chain tensioner by pushing it down all the way until a snap is heard and the tensioner is seated all the way down the mega cap bore

a. Stage 1: Tighten to 89 inch lbs. (10 Nm).

b. Stage 2: Tighten an additional 45 degrees.

33. Install the RH primary timing chain guide and the bolt. Tighten to 89 inch lbs. (10 Nm).

❋❋ WARNING

The following steps are only for the replacement of the secondary timing chain tensioners. Do not reuse the secondary timing chain tensioners if removed or damage to the engine may occur.

➡️**Apply clean engine oil to the secondary timing chain tensioner O-ring seals and mega cap bore.**

➡️**Do not remove the secondary timing chain tensioner shipping clip, until instructed to do so.**

34. Install the RH secondary timing chain tensioner by pushing it down all the way until a snap is heard and the tensioner is seated all the way down the mega cap bore.

35. Install the RH secondary timing chain tensioner shoe.

36. Remove and discard the RH secondary timing chain tensioner shipping clip.

37. Assemble the RH Variable Camshaft Timing (VCT) assembly, the RH exhaust camshaft sprocket and the RH secondary timing chain.

38. Align the colored links with the timing marks.

➡️**It may be necessary to rotate the camshafts slightly, to install the RH secondary timing assembly.**

39. Position the 2 RH VCT assemblies and secondary timing chain onto the camshafts by aligning the holes in the VCT assemblies with the dowel pins in the camshafts.

40. Install the 2 new RH VCT bolts and tighten in 4 stages.

a. Stage 1: Tighten to 30 ft. lbs. (40 Nm).

b. Stage 2: Loosen one full turn.

c. Stage 3: Tighten to 18 ft. lbs. (25 Nm).

d. Stage 4: Tighten an additional 180 degrees.

41. Activate the RH secondary timing chain tensioner by pressing down on the secondary tensioner shoe until it bottoms out, let go of the tensioner and it will spring up putting tension on the chain.

❋❋ WARNING

Do not use excessive force when installing the Variable Camshaft Timing (VCT) oil control solenoid. Damage to the mega cap could cause the cylinder head to be inoperable. If difficult to install the VCT oil control solenoid, inspect the bore and VCT oil control solenoid to ensure there are no burrs, sharp edges or contaminants present on the mating surface. Only clean the external surfaces as necessary.

➡️**A slight twisting motion will aid in the installation of the VCT oil control solenoid.**

➡️**Keep the VCT oil control solenoid clean of dirt and debris.**

42. Install the RH exhaust VCT oil control solenoid. Tighten to 71 inch lbs. (8 Nm) then an additional 20 degrees.

➡️**Apply clean engine oil to the secondary timing chain tensioner O-ring seals and mega cap bore.**

➡️**Do not remove the secondary timing chain tensioner shipping clip, until instructed to do so.**

43. Install the LH secondary timing chain tensioner by pushing it down all the way

Fig. 407 Remove and discard the RH secondary timing chain tensioner shipping clip

Fig. 408 Align the colored links with the timing marks

until a snap is heard and the tensioner is seated all the way down the mega cap bore.

44. Install the LH secondary timing chain tensioner shoe.

45. Remove and discard the LH secondary timing chain tensioner shipping clip.

46. Assemble the 2 LH VCT assemblies and the LH secondary timing chain.

47. Align the colored links with the timing marks.

➡️**It may be necessary to rotate the camshafts slightly, to install the LH secondary timing assembly.**

48. Position the 2 LH VCT assemblies and secondary timing chain onto the camshafts by aligning the holes in the VCT assemblies with the dowel pins in the camshafts.

49. Install the 2 new LH VCT bolts and tighten in 4 stages.

a. Stage 1: Tighten to 30 ft. lbs. (40 Nm).

b. Stage 2: Loosen one full turn.

c. Stage 3: Tighten to 18 ft. lbs. (25 Nm).

d. Stage 4: Tighten an additional 180 degrees.

50. Activate the LH secondary timing chain tensioner by pressing down on the

secondary tensioner shoe until it bottoms out, let go of the tensioner and it will spring up putting tension on the chain.

✲✲ WARNING

Do not use excessive force when installing the Variable Camshaft Timing (VCT) oil control solenoid. Damage to the mega cap could cause the cylinder head to be inoperable. If difficult to install the VCT oil control solenoid, inspect the bore and VCT oil control solenoid to ensure there are no burrs, sharp edges or contaminants present on the mating surface. Only clean the external surfaces as necessary.

➡**A slight twisting motion will aid in the installation of the VCT oil control solenoid.**

➡**Keep the VCT oil control solenoid clean of dirt and debris.**

51. Install the LH exhaust VCT control solenoid. Tighten to 71 inch lbs. (8 Nm) then an additional 20 degrees.

➡**The following steps are for engines with the secondary timing chain tensioner not removed.**

52. Compress the RH secondary timing chain tensioner and install the Secondary Chain Hold Down to retain the tensioner in the collapsed position.

53. Assemble the RH VCT assembly, the RH exhaust camshaft sprocket and the RH secondary timing chain.

54. Align the colored links with the timing marks.

➡**It may be necessary to rotate the camshafts slightly, to install the RH secondary timing assembly.**

55. Position the 2 RH VCT assemblies and secondary timing chain onto the camshafts by aligning the holes in the VCT assemblies with the dowel pins in the camshafts.

56. Install the 2 new RH VCT bolts and tighten in 4 stages.
    a. Stage 1: Tighten to 30 ft. lbs. (40 Nm).
    b. Stage 2: Loosen one full turn.
    c. Stage 3: Tighten to 18 ft. lbs. (25 Nm).
    d. Stage 4: Tighten an additional 180 degrees.

➡**The 2 VCT oil control solenoids are removed for clarity.**

57. Compress the RH secondary timing chain tensioner and remove the Secondary Chain Hold Down.

58. Make sure the secondary timing chain is centered on the timing chain tensioner guides.

59. Compress the LH secondary timing chain tensioner and install the Secondary Chain Hold Down to retain the tensioner in the collapsed position.

60. Assemble the 2 LH VCT assemblies and the LH secondary timing chain.

61. Align the colored links with the timing marks.

➡**It may be necessary to rotate the camshafts slightly, to install the LH secondary timing assembly.**

62. Position the 2 LH VCT assemblies and secondary timing chain onto the camshafts by aligning the holes in the VCT assemblies with the dowel pins in the camshafts.

63. Install the 2 new LH VCT bolts and tighten in 4 stages.
    a. Stage 1: Tighten to 30 ft. lbs. (40 Nm).
    b. Stage 2: Loosen one full turn.
    c. Stage 3: Tighten to 18 ft. lbs. (25 Nm).
    d. Stage 4: Tighten an additional 180 degrees.

➡**The 2 VCT oil control solenoids are removed for clarity.**

64. Compress the LH secondary timing chain tensioner and remove the Secondary Chain Hold Down.

65. Make sure the secondary timing chain is centered on the timing chain tensioner guides.

➡**The following steps are for all engines.**

66. Install the upper LH primary timing chain guide and the bolt. Tighten to 89 inch lbs. (10 Nm).

67. Install the crankshaft timing chain sprocket with timing dot mark out.

➡**It may be necessary to rotate the camshafts slightly, to align the timing marks.**

68. Install the primary timing chain with the colored links aligned with the timing marks on the VCT assemblies and the crankshaft sprocket.

69. Install the lower LH primary timing chain guide and the 2 bolts. Tighten to 89 inch lbs. (10 Nm).

70. Install the primary timing chain tensioner arm.

71. Reset the primary timing chain tensioner.
    a. Release the ratchet detent.

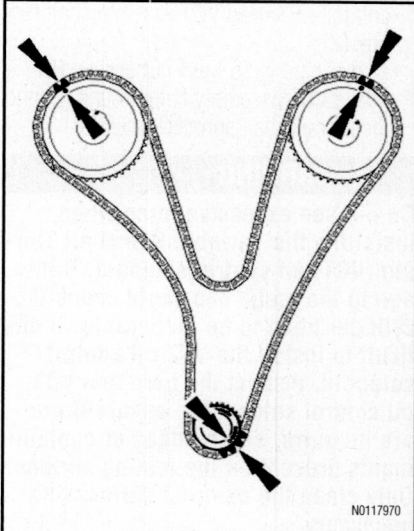

Fig. 409 Install the primary timing chain with the colored links aligned with the timing marks on the VCT assemblies and the crankshaft sprocket

    b. Using a soft-jawed vise, compress the ratchet plunger.
    c. Align the hole in the ratchet plunger with the hole in the tensioner housing.
    d. Install a suitable lockpin.

➡**It may be necessary to rotate the camshafts slightly to remove slack from the timing chain to install the tensioner.**

72. Install the primary tensioner and the 2 bolts.
    a. Tighten to 89 inch lbs. (10 Nm).
    b. Remove the lockpin.

73. As a post-check, verify correct alignment of all timing marks.
    a. There is 48 links in between the RH intake VCT assembly colored link (1)

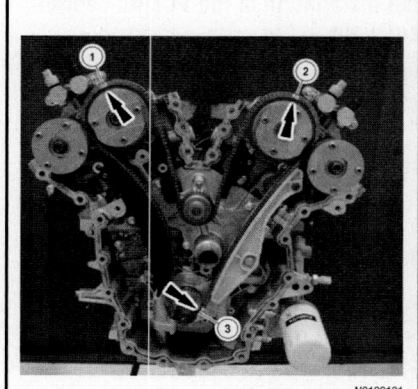

Fig. 410 As a post-check, verify correct alignment of all timing marks

and the LH intake VCT assembly colored link (2).

　b. There is 35 links in between RH intake VCT assembly colored link (2) and the 2 crankshaft sprocket links (3).

✻✻ WARNING

Do not use excessive force when installing the Variable Camshaft Timing (VCT) oil control solenoid. Damage to the mega cap could cause the cylinder head to be inoperable. If difficult to install the VCT oil control solenoid, inspect the bore and VCT oil control solenoid to ensure there are no burrs, sharp edges or contaminants present on the mating surface. Only clean the external surfaces as necessary.

➡ **A slight twisting motion will aid in the installation of the VCT oil control solenoid.**

➡ **Keep the VCT oil control solenoid clean of dirt and debris.**

　74. Install the LH intake VCT oil control solenoid and the bolt. Tighten to 71 inch lbs. (8 Nm). then an additional 20 degrees.

✻✻ WARNING

Do not use excessive force when installing the Variable Camshaft Timing (VCT) oil control solenoid. Damage to the mega cap could cause the cylinder head to be inoperable. If difficult to install the VCT oil control solenoid, inspect the bore and VCT oil control solenoid to ensure there are no burrs, sharp edges or contaminants present on the mating surface. Only clean the external surfaces as necessary.

➡ **A slight twisting motion will aid in the installation of the VCT oil control solenoid.**

➡ **Keep the VCT oil control solenoid clean of dirt and debris.**

　75. Install the RH intake VCT oil control solenoid and the bolt. Tighten to 71 inch lbs. (8 Nm) then an additional 20 degrees.
　76. Remove the RH Camshaft Holding Tool.
　77. Install the RH valve train oil tube and the 3 bolts and tighten in 2 stages.
　　a. Stage 1: Tighten to 71 inch lbs. (8 Nm).
　　b. Stage 2: Tighten an additional 45 degrees.
　78. Remove the LH Camshaft Holding Tool.

　79. Install the LH valve train oil tube and the 3 bolts and tighten in 2 stages.
　　a. Stage 1: Tighten to 71 inch lbs. (8 Nm).
　　b. Stage 2: Tighten an additional 45 degrees.
　80. Install the engine front cover.

5.0L Engine

See Figures 411 through 424.

✻✻ WARNING

During engine repair procedures, cleanliness is extremely important. Any foreign material, including any material created while cleaning gasket surfaces, that enters the oil passages, coolant passages or the oil pan, can cause engine failure.

　1. Remove the engine front cover. Refer to Timing Chain Front Cover.
　2. Using the crankshaft holding tool, rotate the crankshaft clockwise until the keyway is at the 12 o'clock position.
　3. Verify the data matrix on the camshafts is facing up, if not, rotate the crankshaft clockwise one revolution.
　4. Remove the 2 bolts and the RH primary timing chain tensioner.

Fig. 411 Verify the data matrix on the camshafts is facing up, if not, rotate the crankshaft clockwise one revolution

Fig. 412 Remove the 2 bolts and the RH primary timing chain tensioner

➡ **It may be necessary to rotate the crankshaft slightly to provide enough slack in the chain to remove the RH timing chain tensioner arm. Return the crankshaft keyway to the 12 o'clock position after removing the RH timing chain tensioner arm.**

　5. Remove the RH timing chain tensioner arm.

➡ **It may be necessary to rotate the crankshaft slightly to provide enough slack in the chain to remove the RH timing chain guide. Return the crankshaft keyway to the 12 o'clock position after removing the RH timing chain guide.**

　6. Remove the bolt and the RH timing chain guide.
　7. Remove the RH primary timing chain.
　8. Remove the 3 RH intake Variable Camshaft Timing (VCT) assembly bolts and the 3 RH exhaust VCT assembly bolts.
　9. Slide the RH VCT assemblies and secondary timing chain forward 2 mm (0.078 in).
　10. Depress the RH secondary timing chain tensioner and turn the tensioner 90 degrees.

Fig. 413 Remove the 3 RH intake Variable Camshaft Timing (VCT) assembly bolts and the 3 RH exhaust VCT assembly bolts

Fig. 414 Slide the RH VCT assemblies and secondary timing chain forward

11. Remove the RH VCT assemblies and the RH secondary timing chain.

12. Using the crankshaft holding tool, rotate the crankshaft counterclockwise until the crankshaft keyway is at the 9 o'clock position.

13. Remove the 2 bolts and the LH primary timing chain tensioner.

➡️**It may be necessary to rotate the crankshaft slightly to provide enough slack in the chain to remove the LH timing chain tensioner arm. Return the crankshaft keyway to the 9 o'clock position after removing the LH timing chain tensioner arm.**

14. Remove the LH timing chain tensioner arm.

➡️**It may be necessary to rotate the crankshaft slightly to provide enough slack in the chain to remove the LH timing chain guide. Return the crankshaft keyway to the 9 o'clock position after removing the LH timing chain guide.**

15. Remove the bolt and the LH timing chain guide.

16. Remove the LH primary timing chain.

17. Remove the 3 LH intake Variable Camshaft Timing (VCT) assembly bolts and the 3 LH exhaust VCT assembly bolts.

18. Slide the LH VCT assemblies and secondary timing chain forward 2 mm (0.078 in).

19. Depress the LH secondary timing chain tensioner and turn the tensioner 90 degrees.

20. Remove the LH VCT assemblies and the LH secondary timing chain.

21. Remove the crankshaft sprocket.

To install:

22. Install the crankshaft sprocket with the flange facing forward.

23. Install the secondary timing chain onto the LH VCT assemblies. Align the colored links on the secondary timing chain with the timing marks on the VCT assemblies as shown.

 a. The timing mark on the intake VCT assembly should align between the 2 consecutive colored links.

 b. The timing mark on the exhaust VCT assembly should align with the single colored link.

24. Install the LH VCT assemblies and the secondary timing chain onto the LH camshafts to a position 0.078 inches (2 mm) from fully seated. The timing mark

on the exhaust VCT assembly should be in the 11 o'clock position.

➡️**It may be necessary to rotate the exhaust camshaft slightly (using a wrench on the flats of the camshaft) to seat the VCT assemblies onto the camshafts.**

25. Rotate the secondary timing chain tensioner 90 degrees so the ramped area is facing forward and fully seat the VCT assemblies onto the camshafts.

26. If the secondary timing chain is not centered over the tensioner, reposition the VCT assemblies until they are fully seated on the camshafts.

➡️**Use a wrench on the flats of the camshaft to hold the camshafts while tightening the VCT assembly bolts.**

27. Install the 3 LH intake VCT assembly bolts and the 3 LH exhaust VCT assembly bolts. Tighten to 10 ft. lbs. (15 Nm) plus an additional 90 degrees.

28. Install the LH primary timing chain.

29. Align the colored link on the timing chain with the timing mark on the LH VCT assembly.

30. Align the remaining colored link on the timing chain with the timing mark on the crankshaft sprocket.

➡️**It may be necessary to rotate the crankshaft slightly to provide enough slack in the chain to install the LH timing chain guide. Return the crankshaft keyway to the 9 o'clock position after installing the LH timing chain guide.**

31. Install the LH timing chain guide and bolt. Tighten to 89 inch lbs. (10 Nm).

➡️**It may be necessary to rotate the crankshaft slightly to provide enough slack in the chain to install the LH timing chain tensioner arm. Return the crankshaft keyway to the 9 o'clock**

Fig. 415 Depress the RH secondary timing chain tensioner and turn the tensioner 90 degrees

Fig. 417 The timing mark on the exhaust VCT assembly should be in the 11 o'clock position

Fig. 416 Align the colored links on the secondary timing chain with the timing marks on the VCT assemblies as shown

Fig. 418 Align the colored link on the timing chain with the timing mark on the LH VCT assembly

Fig. 419 Align the remaining colored link on the timing chain with the timing mark on the crankshaft sprocket

position after installing the LH timing chain tensioner arm.

32. Install the LH timing chain tensioner arm.

➡**Complete the following 3 steps on both the LH and RH primary timing chain tensioners.**

✳✳ WARNING

Do not compress the ratchet assembly or damage to the tensioner will occur.

33. Compress the primary timing chain tensioner plunger, using an edge of a vise.

34. Using a small screwdriver or pick, push back and hold the ratchet mechanism, then push the ratchet arm back into the tensioner housing.

35. Install a suitable pin into the hole of the tensioner housing to hold the ratchet assembly and plunger in place during installation.

36. Install the LH primary timing chain tensioner and 2 bolts.
   a. Tighten to 89 inch lbs. (10 Nm).
   b. Remove the holding pin from the tensioner.

37. Using the crankshaft holding tool, rotate the crankshaft clockwise until the

Fig. 420 Align the colored links on the secondary timing chain with the timing marks on the VCT assemblies as shown

Fig. 421 The timing mark on the exhaust VCT assembly should be in the 12 o'clock position

crankshaft keyway is at the 12 o'clock position.

38. Install the secondary timing chain onto the RH VCT assemblies. Align the colored links on the secondary timing chain with the timing marks on the VCT assemblies as shown.
   a. The timing mark on the intake VCT assembly should align between the 2 consecutive colored links.
   b. The timing mark on the exhaust VCT assembly should align with the single colored link.

39. Install the RH VCT assemblies and the secondary timing chain onto the RH camshafts to a position 0.078 inches (2 mm) from fully seated. The timing mark on the exhaust VCT assembly should be in the 12 o'clock position.

➡**It may be necessary to rotate the exhaust camshaft slightly (using a wrench on the flats of the camshaft) to seat the VCT assemblies onto the camshafts.**

40. Rotate the secondary timing chain tensioner 90 degrees so the ramped area is facing forward and fully seat the VCT assemblies onto the camshafts.

41. If the secondary timing chain is not centered over the tensioner, reposition the VCT assemblies until they are fully seated on the camshafts.

➡**Use a wrench on the flats of the camshaft to hold the camshafts while tightening the VCT assembly bolts.**

Fig. 422 Align the colored link on the timing chain with the timing mark on the RH VCT assembly

Fig. 423 Align the remaining colored link on the timing chain with the timing mark on the crankshaft sprocket

42. Install the 3 RH intake VCT assembly bolts and the 3 RH exhaust VCT assembly bolts. Tighten to 10 ft. lbs. (15 Nm) plus an additional 90 degrees.

43. Install the RH primary timing chain.

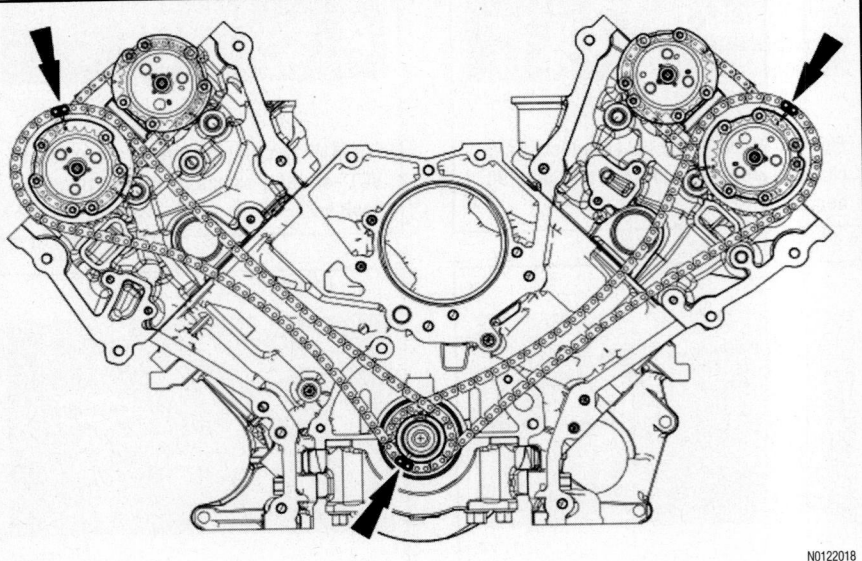

Fig. 424 With the crankshaft keyway still at the 12 o'clock position, verify the timing mark alignment is correct

44. Align the colored link on the timing chain with the timing mark on the RH VCT assembly.

45. Align the remaining colored link on the timing chain with the timing mark on the crankshaft sprocket.

➡It may be necessary to rotate the crankshaft slightly to provide enough slack in the chain to install the RH timing chain guide. Return the crankshaft keyway to the 12 o'clock position after installing the RH timing chain guide.

46. Install the RH timing chain guide and bolt. Tighten to 89 inch lbs. (10 Nm).

➡It may be necessary to rotate the crankshaft slightly to provide enough slack in the chain to install the RH timing chain tensioner arm. Return the crankshaft keyway to the 12 o'clock position after installing the RH timing chain tensioner arm.

47. Install the RH timing chain tensioner arm.

48. Install the RH primary timing chain tensioner and 2 bolts.
   a. Tighten to 89 inch lbs. (10 Nm).
   b. Remove the holding pin from the tensioner.

49. With the crankshaft keyway still at the 12 o'clock position, verify the timing mark alignment is correct.

50. Install the engine front cover.

4.6L (2V) Engine

See Figures 425 through 437.

❊❊ WARNING

Since the engine is not free-wheeling, the timing procedures must be followed exactly or piston and valve damage can occur.

1. Remove the engine front cover. Refer to Timing Chain Front Cover.

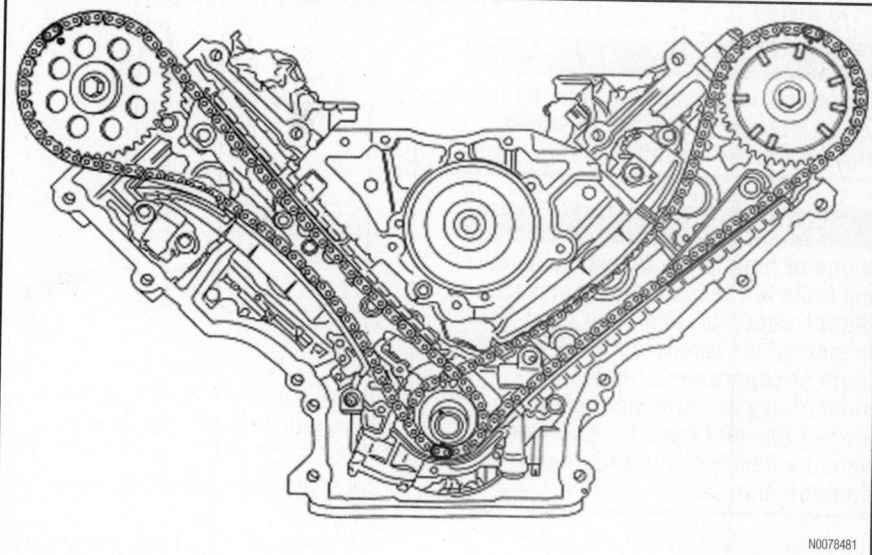

Fig. 426 Rotate the crankshaft until the timing mark on the RH camshaft sprocket is approximately at the 11 o'clock position and the timing mark on the LH camshaft sprocket is approximately at the 12 o'clock position

2. Remove the crankshaft sensor ring from the crankshaft.

3. Rotate the crankshaft until the timing mark on the RH camshaft sprocket is approximately at the 11 o'clock position and the timing mark on the LH camshaft sprocket is approximately at the 12 o'clock position.

4. Install the Camshaft Aligner (303-380) and Camshaft Pulley Aligner (303-413) on the camshaft.

❊❊ WARNING

If one or both of the tensioner mounting bolts are loosened or removed, the tensioner-sealing bead must be inspected for seat integrity. If cracks, tears or separation from the tensioner body or permanent compression of the seal bead is observed, install a new tensioner or engine damage may occur.

5. Remove the timing chain tensioning system from both timing chains.
   a. Remove the 4 bolts.
   b. Remove the 2 timing chain tensioners.
   c. Remove the 2 timing chain tensioner arms.

6. Remove the 2 timing chains and the crankshaft sprocket.

7. Remove the timing chain guides.
   a. Remove the 2 bolts.
   b. Remove the LH timing chain guide.
   c. Remove the 2 bolts.
   d. Remove the RH timing chain guide.

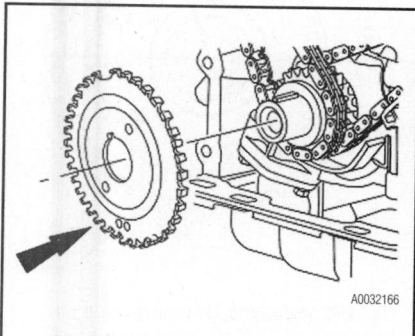

Fig. 425 Remove the crankshaft sensor ring from the crankshaft

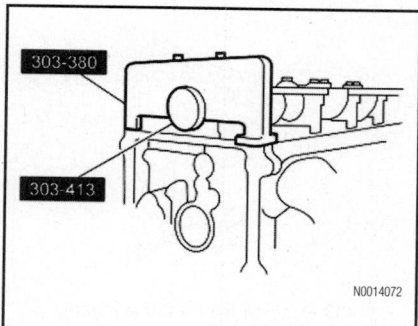

Fig. 427 Install the Camshaft Aligner and Camshaft Pulley Aligner on the camshaft

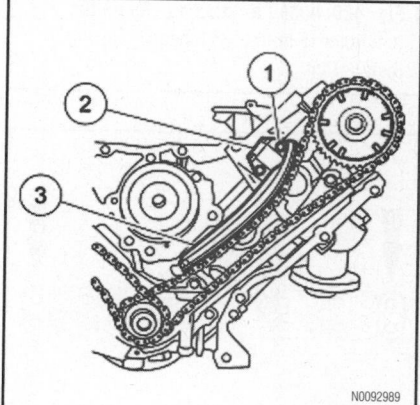

Fig. 428 Remove the bolts (1), the timing chain tensioners (2) and the timing chain tensioner arms (3)

To install:

⁂ WARNING

Timing chain procedures must be followed exactly or damage to valves and pistons will result.

⁂ WARNING

If one or both of the tensioner mounting bolts are loosened or removed, the tensioner-sealing bead must be inspected for seat integrity. If cracks, tears or separation from the tensioner body or permanent compression of the seal bead is observed, install a new tensioner or engine damage may occur.

8. Compress the tensioner plunger, using a vise.

9. Install a retaining clip on the tensioner to hold the plunger in during installation.

10. If the copper links are not visible, mark one link on one end and one link on the other end, and use as timing marks.

11. Install the crankshaft sprocket, making sure the flange faces forward.

12. Install the timing chain guides.

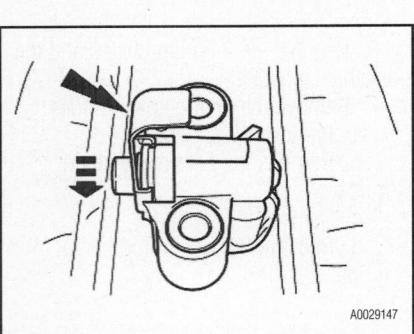

Fig. 429 Install a retaining clip on the tensioner to hold the plunger in during installation

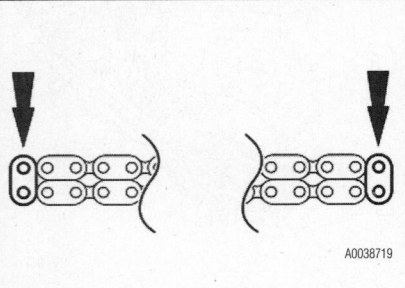

Fig. 430 If the copper links are not visible, mark one link on one end and one link on the other end, and use as timing marks

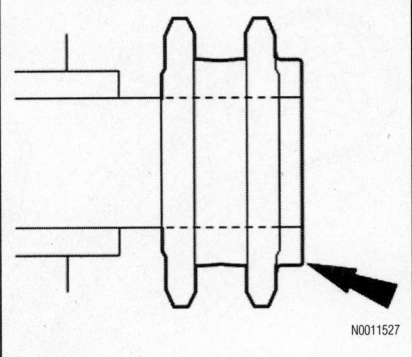

Fig. 431 Install the crankshaft sprocket, making sure the flange faces forward

a. Position the LH timing chain guide.

b. Install the 2 LH bolts. Tighten to 89 inch lbs. (10 Nm).

c. Position the RH timing chain guide.

d. Install the 2 RH bolts. Tighten to 89 inch lbs. (10 Nm).

⁂ WARNING

Unless otherwise instructed, do not rotate either the crankshaft or the camshafts, when the timing chains

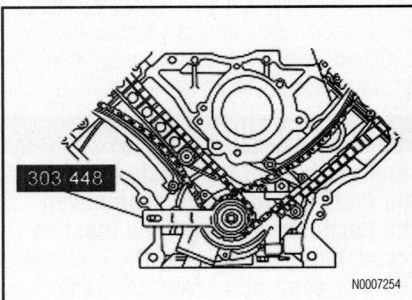

Fig. 432 Using the Crankshaft Holding Tool, position the crankshaft so the No. 1 cylinder is at TDC

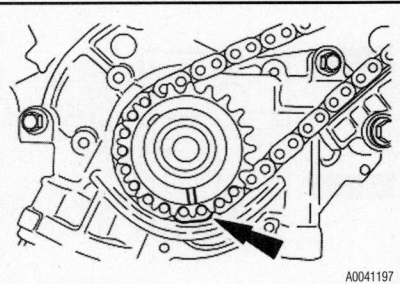

Fig. 433 Position the LH (inner) timing chain on the crankshaft sprocket, aligning the copper (marked) link with the timing mark on the sprocket

are removed and the cylinder heads are installed. Severe piston and valve damage will occur.

➡ The No. 1 cylinder is at Top Dead Center (TDC) when the stud on the engine block fits into the slot in the handle of the special tool.

13. Using the Crankshaft Holding Tool (303-448), position the crankshaft so the No. 1 cylinder is at TDC.

14. Remove the Crankshaft Holding Tool.

15. Position the LH (inner) timing chain on the crankshaft sprocket, aligning the copper (marked) link with the timing mark on the sprocket.

16. Install the LH timing chain on the camshaft sprocket, aligning the copper (marked) link with the timing marks on the sprocket.

➡ The LH timing chain tensioner arm has a bump near the dowel hole for identification.

17. Position the LH timing chain tensioner arm on the dowel pin and install the LH timing chain tensioner and the 2 bolts. Tighten to 18 ft. lbs. (25 Nm).

18. Remove the retaining clip from the LH timing chain tensioner.

19. Position the RH (outer) timing chain on the crankshaft sprocket, aligning the copper (marked) link with the timing mark on the sprocket.

20. Install the RH timing chain on the camshaft sprocket, aligning the copper (marked) link with the timing marks on the sprocket.

21. Position the RH timing chain tensioner arm on the dowel pin and install the

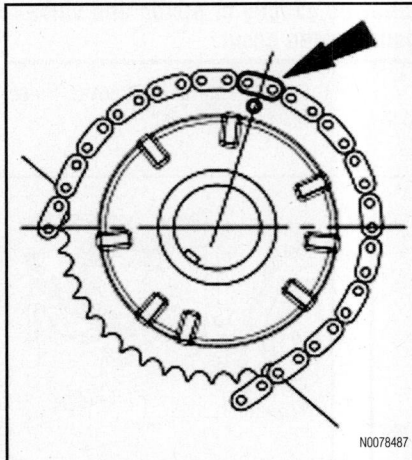

Fig. 434 Install the LH timing chain on the camshaft sprocket, aligning the copper (marked) link with the timing marks on the sprocket

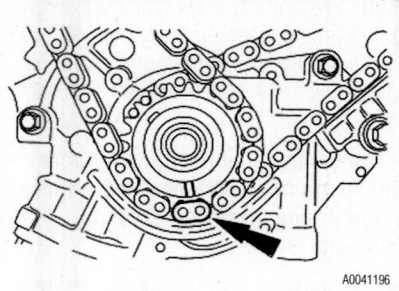

Fig. 435 Position the RH (outer) timing chain on the crankshaft sprocket, aligning the copper (marked) link with the timing mark on the sprocket

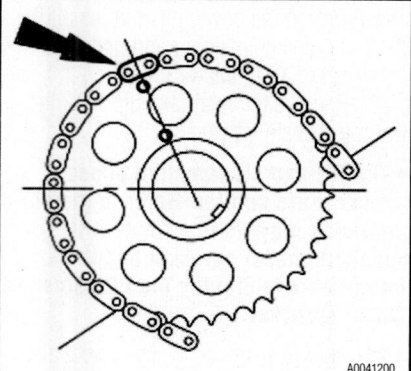

Fig. 436 Install the RH timing chain on the camshaft sprocket, aligning the copper (marked) link with the timing marks on the sprocket

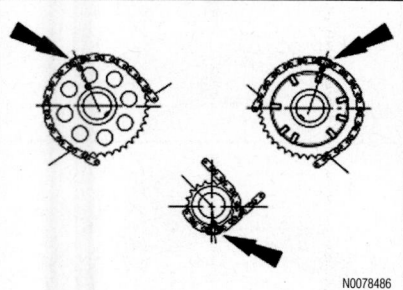

Fig. 437 Make sure that the copper (marked) chain links are lined up with the dots on the crankshaft sprockets and the camshaft sprocket

RH timing chain tensioner and the 2 bolts. Tighten to 18 ft. lbs. (25 Nm).

22. Remove the retaining clip from the RH timing chain tensioner.

23. Make sure that the copper (marked) chain links are lined up with the dots on the crankshaft sprockets and the camshaft sprocket.

24. Remove the Camshaft Aligner and Camshaft Pulley Aligner from the camshaft.

25. Install the crankshaft sensor ring on the crankshaft.

26. Install the engine front cover.

4.6L (3V) Engine

See Figures 438 through 448.

1. Remove the engine front cover. Refer to Timing Chain Front Cover.

2. Remove the crankshaft sensor ring from the crankshaft.

3. Rotate the crankshaft clockwise and position the crankshaft keyway at the 6 o'clock position.

4. Remove the bolts, the LH timing chain tensioner and tensioner arm.

5. Remove the bolts, the RH timing chain tensioner and tensioner arm.

6. Remove the RH and LH timing chains and the crankshaft sprocket.

   a. Remove the RH timing chain from the camshaft sprocket.

   b. Remove the RH timing chain from the crankshaft sprocket.

   c. Remove the LH timing chain from the camshaft sprocket.

   d. Remove the LH timing chain and crankshaft sprocket.

7. Remove the LH and RH timing chain guides.

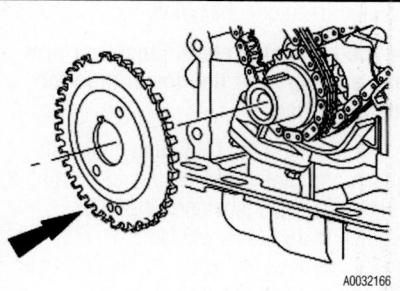

Fig. 438 Remove the crankshaft sensor ring from the crankshaft

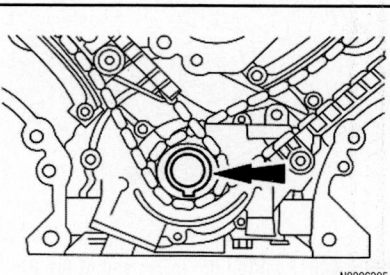

Fig. 439 Rotate the crankshaft clockwise and position the crankshaft keyway at the 6 o'clock position

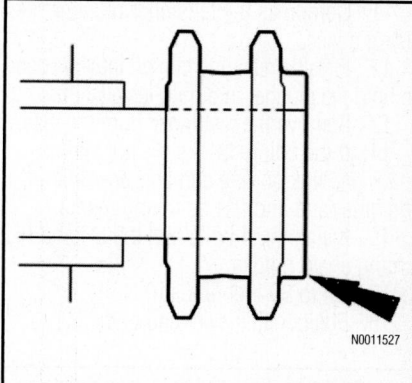

Fig. 440 Install the crankshaft sprocket, making sure the flange faces forward

Fig. 441 Rotate the crankshaft to position the crankshaft sprocket timing mark in the 6 o'clock position

   a. Remove the bolts.

   b. Remove both timing chain guides.

To install:

8. Install the crankshaft sprocket, making sure the flange faces forward.

9. Rotate the crankshaft to position the crankshaft sprocket timing mark in the 6 o'clock position.

❊❊ WARNING

If one or both of the tensioner mounting bolts are loosened or removed, the tensioner-sealing bead must be inspected for seal integrity. If cracks, tears, separation from the tensioner body or permanent compression of the seal bead is observed, install a new tensioner or engine damage may occur.

10. Inspect the RH and LH timing chain tensioners. Install new tensioners as necessary.

❊❊ WARNING

Timing chain procedures must be followed exactly or damage to valves and pistons will result.

11. Compress the tensioner plunger, using a vise.

12. Install a retaining clip on the tensioner to hold the plunger in during installation.

13. Remove the tensioner from the vise.

14. If the colored links are not visible, mark one link on one end and one link on the other end and use as timing marks.

15. Install the 4 bolts and the LH and RH timing chain guides.

Tighten to 89 inch lbs. (10 Nm).

16. Position the lower end of the LH

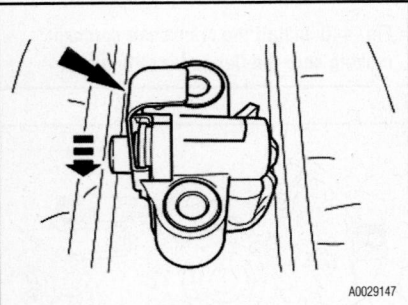

Fig. 442 Install a retaining clip on the tensioner to hold the plunger in during installation

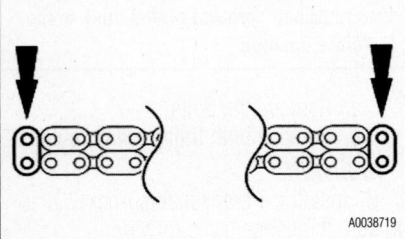

Fig. 443 If the colored links are not visible, mark one link on one end and one link on the other end and use as timing marks

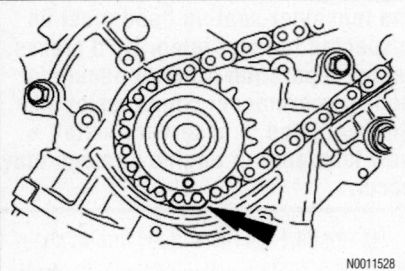

Fig. 444 Position the lower end of the LH (inner) timing chain on the crankshaft sprocket, aligning the timing mark on the outer flange of the crankshaft sprocket with the single colored (marked) link on the chain

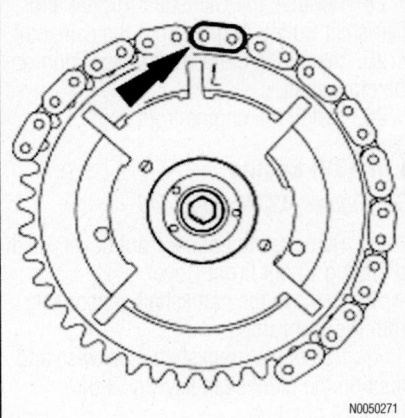

Fig. 445 Position the LH timing chain on the camshaft sprocket. Make sure the camshaft sprocket timing mark is aligned with the colored (marked) chain link

(inner) timing chain on the crankshaft sprocket, aligning the timing mark on the outer flange of the crankshaft sprocket with the single colored (marked) link on the chain.

➡ **Make sure the upper half of the timing chain is below the tensioner arm dowel.**

17. Position the LH timing chain on the camshaft sprocket. Make sure the camshaft sprocket timing mark is aligned with the colored (marked) chain link.

➡ **The LH timing chain tensioner arm has a bump near the dowel hole for identification.**

18. Position the LH timing chain tensioner arm on the dowel pin and install the LH timing chain tensioner and bolts. Tighten to 18 ft. lbs. (25 Nm).

19. Remove the retaining clip from the LH timing chain tensioner.

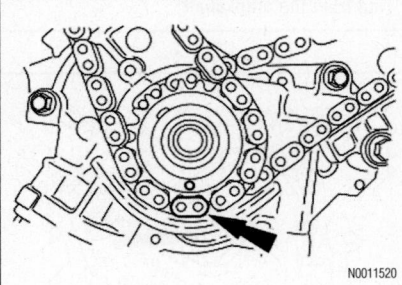

Fig. 446 Position the lower end of the RH (outer) timing chain on the crankshaft sprocket, aligning the timing mark on the sprocket with the single colored (marked) chain link

20. Position the lower end of the RH (outer) timing chain on the crankshaft sprocket, aligning the timing mark on the sprocket with the single colored (marked) chain link.

➡ **The camshaft phaser and sprocket will be stamped with one of the illustrated timing marks for the RH camshaft.**

➡ **The lower half of the timing chain must be positioned above the tensioner arm dowel.**

21. Position the RH timing chain on the camshaft sprocket. Make sure the camshaft sprocket timing mark is aligned with the colored (marked) chain link.

22. Position the RH timing chain tensioner arm on the dowel pin and install the RH timing chain tensioner and bolts.

Tighten to 18 ft. lbs. (25 Nm).

23. Remove the retaining clip from the RH timing chain tensioner.

➡ **The RH and LH camshaft phaser sprockets are similar. Refer to the single timing mark to identify the RH camshaft phaser sprocket and the L timing mark to identify the LH camshaft phaser sprocket.**

24. As a post-check, verify correct alignment of all timing marks. Make sure the timing marks on the sprockets correspond to the above note.

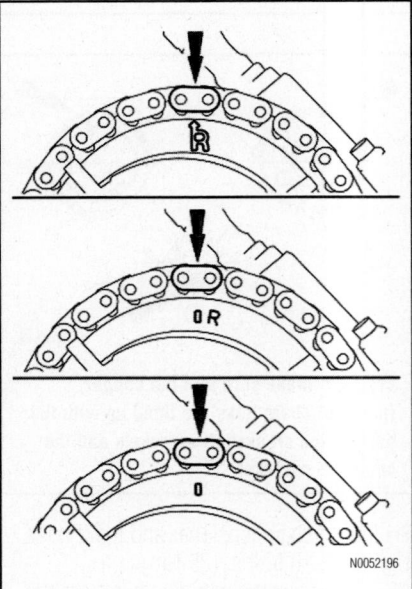

Fig. 447 Position the RH timing chain on the camshaft sprocket. Make sure the camshaft sprocket timing mark is aligned with the colored (marked) chain link

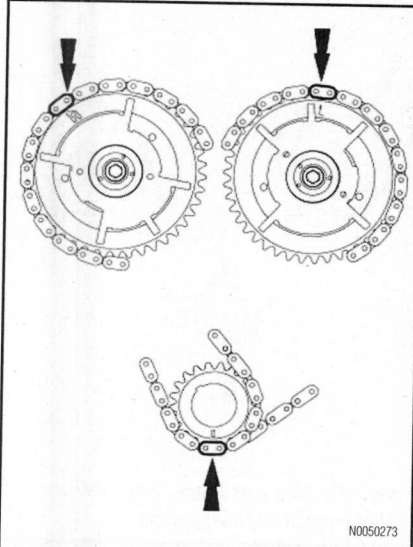

Fig. 448 As a post-check, verify correct alignment of all timing marks

25. Install the crankshaft sensor ring on the crankshaft.
26. Install the engine front cover.

5.4L (3V) Engine

See Figures 449 through 458.

1. Remove the engine front cover. Refer to Timing Chain Front Cover.
2. Remove the crankshaft sensor ring from the crankshaft.

✳✳ WARNING

The crankshaft cannot be moved past the 6 o'clock position once set or engine damage may occur.

3. Rotate the crankshaft clockwise and position the crankshaft keyway at the 6 o'clock position.

✳✳ WARNING

If one or both tensioner mounting bolts are loosened or removed, the

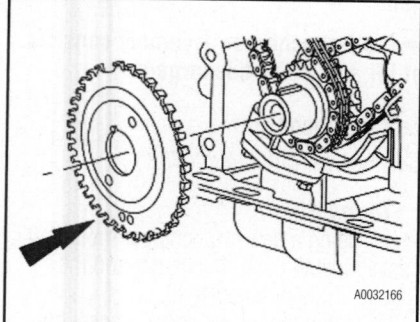

Fig. 449 Remove the crankshaft sensor ring from the crankshaft

tensioner-sealing bead must be inspected for seal integrity. If cracks, tears, separation from the tensioner body or permanent compression of the seal bead is observed, install a new tensioner or engine damage may occur.

4. Remove the 2 bolts, the LH timing chain tensioner and tensioner arm.

✳✳ WARNING

If one or both tensioner mounting bolts are loosened or removed, the tensioner-sealing bead must be inspected for seal integrity. If cracks, tears, separation from the tensioner body or permanent compression of the seal bead is observed, install a new tensioner or engine damage may occur.

5. Remove the 2 bolts, the RH timing chain tensioner and tensioner arm.
6. Remove the RH and LH timing chains and the crankshaft sprocket.
   a. Remove the RH timing chain from the camshaft sprocket.
   b. Remove the RH timing chain from the crankshaft sprocket.
   c. Remove the LH timing chain from the camshaft sprocket.
   d. Remove the LH timing chain and crankshaft sprocket.
7. Remove the LH and RH timing chain guides.
   a. Remove the 4 bolts.
   b. Remove both timing chain guides.

To install:

✳✳ WARNING

Timing chain procedures must be followed exactly or damage to valves and pistons will result.

✳✳ WARNING

Prior to installation, inspect the tensioner-sealing bead for seal integrity. If cracks, tears, separation from the tensioner body or permanent compression of the seal bead is observed, install a new tensioner or engine damage may occur.

8. Compress the tensioner plunger, using a vise.
9. Install a retaining clip on the tensioner to hold the plunger in during installation.
10. Remove the tensioner from the vise.
11. If the copper links are not visible, mark 2 links on one end and 1 link on the other end, and use as timing marks.

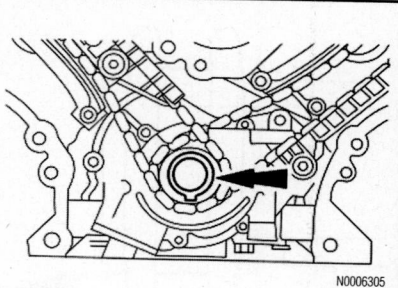

Fig. 450 Rotate the crankshaft clockwise and position the crankshaft keyway at the 6 o'clock position

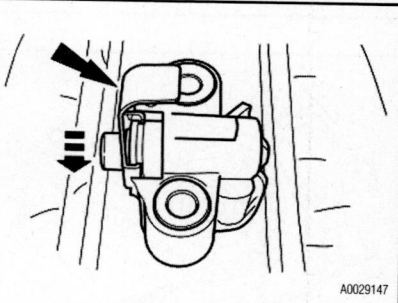

Fig. 451 Install a retaining clip on the tensioner to hold the plunger in during installation

12. Install the crankshaft sprocket, making sure the flange faces forward.
13. Install the 4 bolts and the LH and RH timing chain guides. Tighten to 89 inch lbs. (10 Nm).
14. Position the lower end of the LH (inner) timing chain on the crankshaft sprocket, aligning the timing mark on the outer flange of the crankshaft sprocket with the single copper (marked) link on the chain.

➡Make sure the upper half of the timing chain is below the tensioner arm dowel.

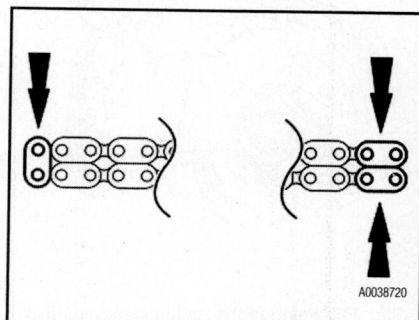

Fig. 452 If the copper links are not visible, mark 2 links on one end and 1 link on the other end, and use as timing marks

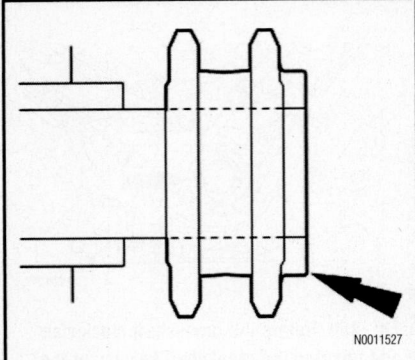

Fig. 453 Install the crankshaft sprocket, making sure the flange faces forward

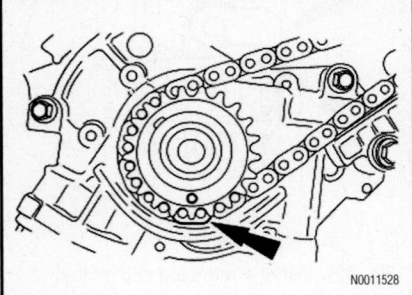

Fig. 454 Position the lower end of the LH (inner) timing chain on the crankshaft sprocket, aligning the timing mark on the outer flange of the crankshaft sprocket with the single copper (marked) link on the chain

15. Position the timing chain on the camshaft phaser and sprocket with the timing mark positioned between the 2 copper (marked) chain links.

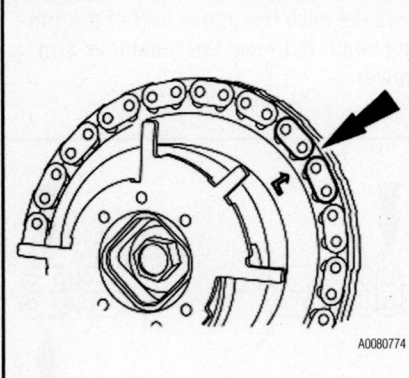

Fig. 455 Position the timing chain on the camshaft phaser and sprocket with the timing mark positioned between the 2 copper (marked) chain links

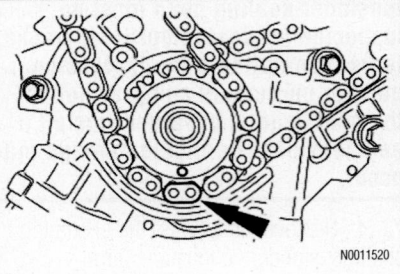

Fig. 456 Position the lower end of the RH (outer) timing chain on the crankshaft sprocket, aligning the timing mark on the sprocket with the single copper (marked) chain link

➡The LH timing chain tensioner arm has a bump near the dowel hole for identification.

16. Position the LH timing chain tensioner arm on the dowel pin and install the LH timing chain tensioner and the 2 bolts. Tighten to 18 ft. lbs. (25 Nm).
17. Remove the retaining clip from the LH timing chain tensioner.
18. Position the lower end of the RH (outer) timing chain on the crankshaft sprocket, aligning the timing mark on the sprocket with the single copper (marked) chain link.

➡The lower half of the timing chain must be positioned above the tensioner arm dowel.

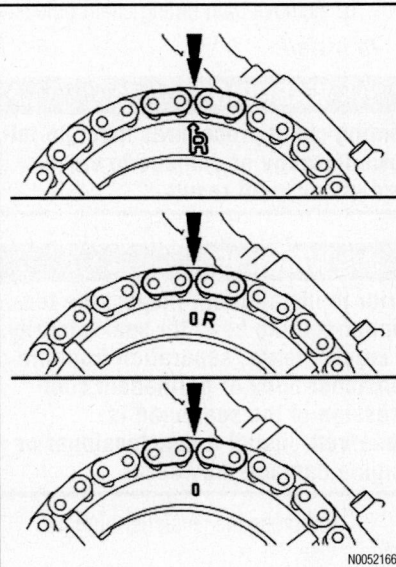

Fig. 457 Position the RH timing chain on the camshaft phaser and sprocket. Make sure the timing mark is positioned between the 2 copper (marked) chain links

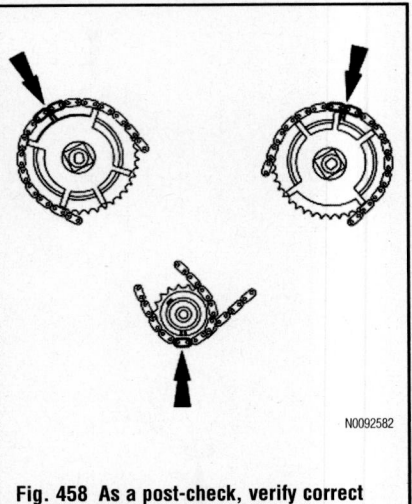

Fig. 458 As a post-check, verify correct alignment of all timing marks

➡The camshaft phaser and sprocket will be stamped with one of the illustrated timing marks for the RH camshaft.

19. Position the RH timing chain on the camshaft phaser and sprocket. Make sure the timing mark is positioned between the 2 copper (marked) chain links.
20. Position the RH timing chain tensioner arm on the dowel pin and install the RH timing chain tensioner and the 2 bolts. Tighten to 18 ft. lbs. (25 Nm).
21. Remove the retaining clip from the RH timing chain tensioner.
22. As a post-check, verify correct alignment of all timing marks.
23. Install the crankshaft sensor ring on the crankshaft.
24. Install the engine front cover.

TURBOCHARGER

REMOVAL & INSTALLATION

➡The manufacturer does not provide a specific Removal and Installation procedure for this component. Refer to the graphic(s) when servicing this component.

➡The turbocharger assembly consists of LH and RH turbochargers.

Left Turbocharger
See Figures 459 through 462.

To install:
1. Using a new turbocharger mounting gasket, install the turbocharger and the 3 bolts. Tighten finger-tight.
2. Install the turbocharger bracket bolt. Tighten finger-tight.
3. Tighten the turbocharger mounting bolts. Tighten to 24 ft. lbs. (32 Nm).

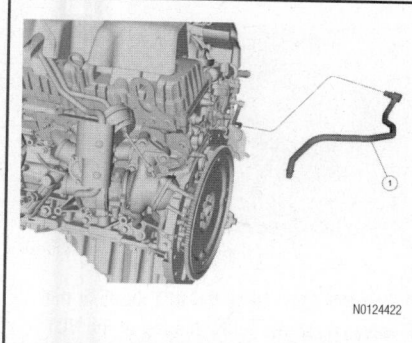

Fig. 459 LH turbocharger coolant supply hose

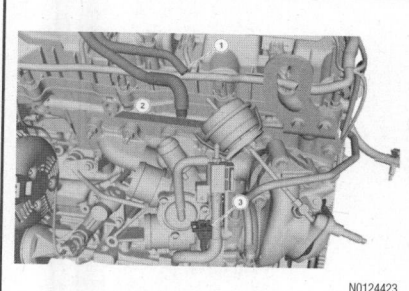

Fig. 460 LH turbocharger wastegate hose (1), bypass vacuum hose (2), and the pressure regulator solenoid electrical connector (3)

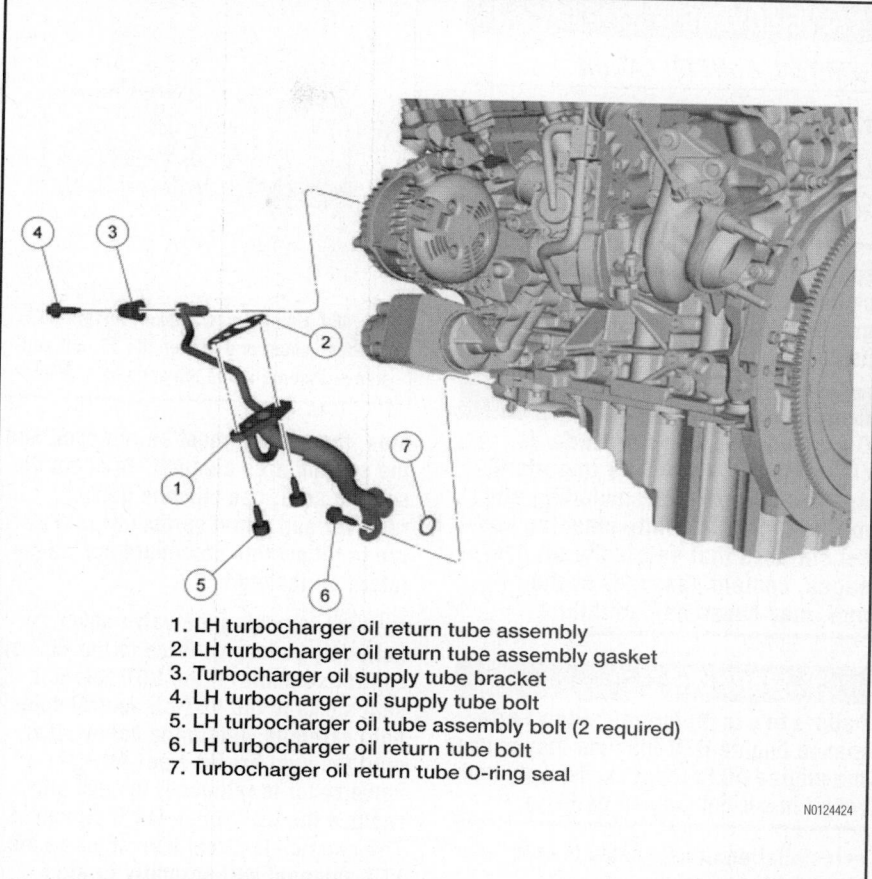

1. LH turbocharger oil return tube assembly
2. LH turbocharger oil return tube assembly gasket
3. Turbocharger oil supply tube bracket
4. Turbocharger oil supply tube bolt
5. LH turbocharger oil tube assembly bolt (2 required)
6. LH turbocharger oil return tube bolt
7. Turbocharger oil return tube O-ring seal

Fig. 461 Exploded view of LH turbocharger—1 of 2

4. Tighten the turbocharger bracket bolt. Tighten to 13 ft. lbs. (18 Nm).

➡Lubricate the cylinder block bore with clean engine oil.

➡Apply clean engine oil to the O-ring seal.

➡Make sure the turbocharger oil supply tube in positioned in the cylinder block during the installation of the turbocharger oil return tube.

5. Using a new turbocharger oil return tube gasket and O-ring seal, install the turbocharger oil tube assembly and the 2 bolts at the turbocharger. Tighten in the following stages:

a. Stage 1: Install the bolt for the oil pressure tube side halfway.

b. Stage 2: Install the bolt for the oil drain tube side and tighten to 71 inch lbs. (8 Nm).

c. Stage 3: Tighten the bolt for the oil drain tube side an additional 30 degrees.

d. Stage 4: Tighten the bolt for the oil pressure tube side to 71 inch lbs. (8 Nm).

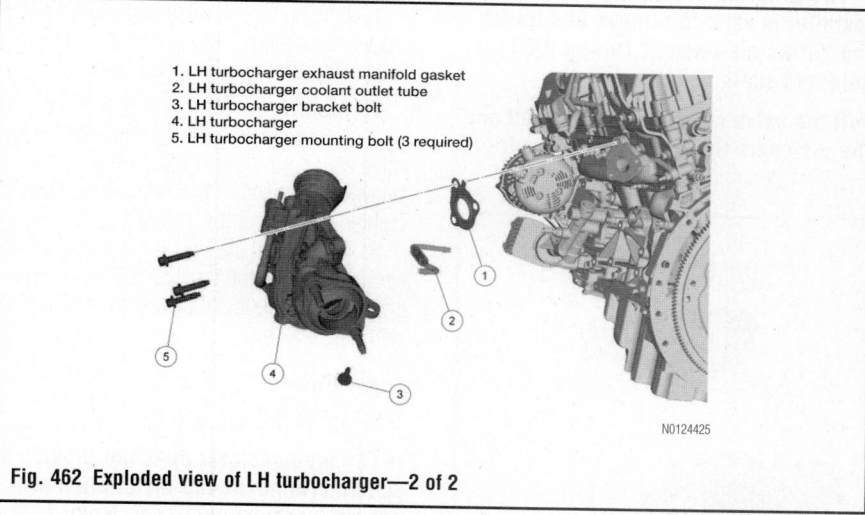

1. LH turbocharger exhaust manifold gasket
2. LH turbocharger coolant outlet tube
3. LH turbocharger bracket bolt
4. LH turbocharger
5. LH turbocharger mounting bolt (3 required)

Fig. 462 Exploded view of LH turbocharger—2 of 2

e. Stage 5: Tighten the bolt for the oil pressure tube side an additional 30 degrees.

6. Install the turbocharger oil return tube bolt at the cylinder block. Tighten in the following stages:

a. Stage 1: Tighten to 89 inch lbs. (10 Nm).

b. Stage 2: Tighten an additional 45 degrees.

7. Install the turbocharger oil supply tube bracket and bolt. Tighten in the following stages:

a. Stage 1: Tighten to 89 inch lbs. (10 Nm).

b. Stage 2: Tighten an additional 45 degrees.

VALVE COVERS

REMOVAL & INSTALLATION

3.5L GTDI Engine

Left Side

See Figures 463 through 465.

➡The manufacturer does not provide a specific Removal and Installation procedure for this component. Refer to the graphic(s) when servicing this component.

✳✳ WARNING

During engine repair procedures, cleanliness is extremely important. Any foreign material, including any material created while cleaning gasket surfaces that enters the oil passages, coolant passages or the oil pan, may cause engine failure.

✳✳ WARNING

Failure to use Motorcraft® High Performance Engine RTV Silicone may cause the engine oil to foam excessively and result in serious engine damage.

➡Installation of new seals is only required if damaged seals were removed.

➡The Differential Bearing Cone Installer is used to remove and install the Variable Camshaft Timing (VCT) solenoid seals.

➡If the valve cover is not installed and the fasteners tightened within 4 min-

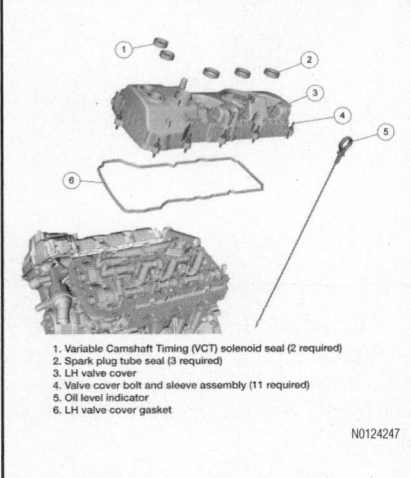

1. Variable Camshaft Timing (VCT) solenoid seal (2 required)
2. Spark plug tube seal (3 required)
3. LH valve cover
4. Valve cover bolt and sleeve assembly (11 required)
5. Oil level indicator
6. LH valve cover gasket

N0124247

Fig. 463 Exploded view of the LH valve cover assembly

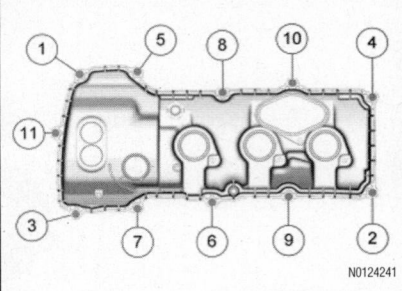

Fig. 464 Using a new gasket, install the LH valve cover and tighten the 11 bolt and sleeve assemblies in the sequence shown

utes, the sealant must be removed and the sealing area cleaned. To clean the sealing area, use silicone gasket remover and metal surface prep. Failure to follow this procedure can cause future oil leakage.

➡When removing the valve cover do not apply excessive force to the VCT oil control solenoid. If the VCT solenoid seal sticks to the VCT oil control solenoid carefully wiggle the valve cover until the seal breaks free. After the valve cover is removed, inspect and replace the VCT solenoids if damaged. The plastic electrical connector on the VCT solenoid will normally rotate approximately 12 degrees inside the steel housing.

　1. Loosen the 11 valve cover bolts and sleeve assemblies and remove the valve cover. Discard the valve cover gasket.

To install:

　2. Using a new gasket, install the LH valve cover and tighten the 11 bolt and sleeve assemblies in the sequence shown. Tighten to 89 inch lbs. (10 Nm).

　3. Make sure the VCT seals in the valve cover are below the top of the VCT oil control solenoid electrical connector or the VCT seal may leak oil.

Right Side

See Figures 465 through 467.

➡The manufacturer does not provide a specific Removal and Installation procedure for this component. Refer to the graphic(s) when servicing this component.

✳✳ WARNING

During engine repair procedures, cleanliness is extremely important. Any foreign material, including any material created while cleaning

Fig. 465 Make sure the VCT seals in the valve cover are below the top of the VCT oil control solenoid electrical connector or the VCT seal may leak oil

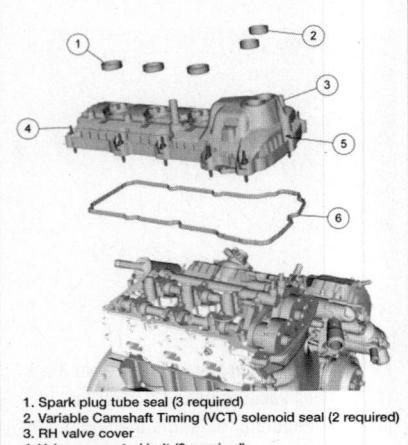

1. Spark plug tube seal (3 required)
2. Variable Camshaft Timing (VCT) solenoid seal (2 required)
3. RH valve cover
4. Valve cover stud bolt (8 required)
5. Valve cover bolt (3 required)
6. RH valve cover gasket

N0124248

Fig. 466 Exploded view of the RH valve cover assembly

gasket surfaces that enters the oil passages, coolant passages or the oil pan, may cause engine failure.

✳✳ WARNING

Failure to use Motorcraft® High Performance Engine RTV Silicone may cause the engine oil to foam excessively and result in serious engine damage.

➡Installation of new seals is only required if damaged seals were removed.

➡The Differential Bearing Cone Installer is used to remove and install the Variable Camshaft Timing (VCT) solenoid seals.

➡If the valve cover is not installed and the fasteners tightened within 4 min-

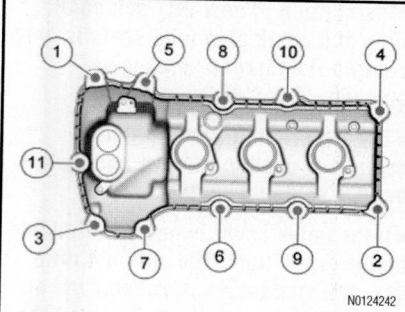

Fig. 467 Using a new gasket, install the RH valve cover and tighten the 3 valve cover bolts and the 8 valve cover std bolts in the sequence shown

utes, the sealant must be removed and the sealing area cleaned. To clean the sealing area, use silicone gasket remover and metal surface prep. Failure to follow this procedure can cause future oil leakage.

➡When removing the valve cover do not apply excessive force to the VCT oil control solenoid. If the VCT solenoid seal sticks to the VCT oil control solenoid carefully wiggle the valve cover until the seal breaks free. After the valve cover is removed, inspect and replace the VCT solenoids if damaged. The plastic electrical connector on the VCT solenoid will normally rotate approximately 12 degrees inside the steel housing.

1. Loosen the 3 valve cover bolts and, the 8 valve cover stud bolts, and remove the valve cover. Discard the valve cover gasket.

To install:

2. Using a new gasket, install the RH valve cover and tighten the 3 valve cover bolts and the 8 valve cover std bolts in the sequence shown. Tighten to 89 inch lbs. (10 Nm).

3. Make sure the VCT seals in the valve cover are below the top of the VCT oil control solenoid electrical connector or the VCT seal may leak oil.

3.7L Engine

Left Side

See Figures 465, 468 through 470.

➡The manufacturer does not provide a specific Removal and Installation procedure for this component. Refer to the graphic(s) when servicing this component.

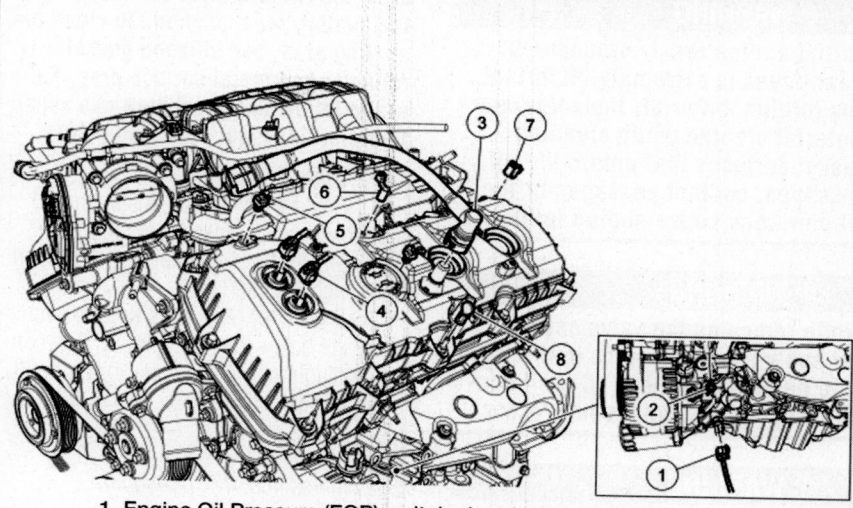

1. Engine Oil Pressure (EOP) switch electrical connector
2. EOP switch electrical connector wiring harness pin-type retainer
3. Crankcase ventilation tube
4. LH Variable Camshaft Timing (VCT) electrical connector (2 required)
5. LH valve cover wiring harness pin-type retainer (2 required)
6. LH valve cover stud bolt wiring harness retainer
7. LH valve cover stud bolt wiring harness retainer
8. LH valve cover stud bolt wiring harness retainer

Fig. 468 LH valve cover assembly—1 of 2

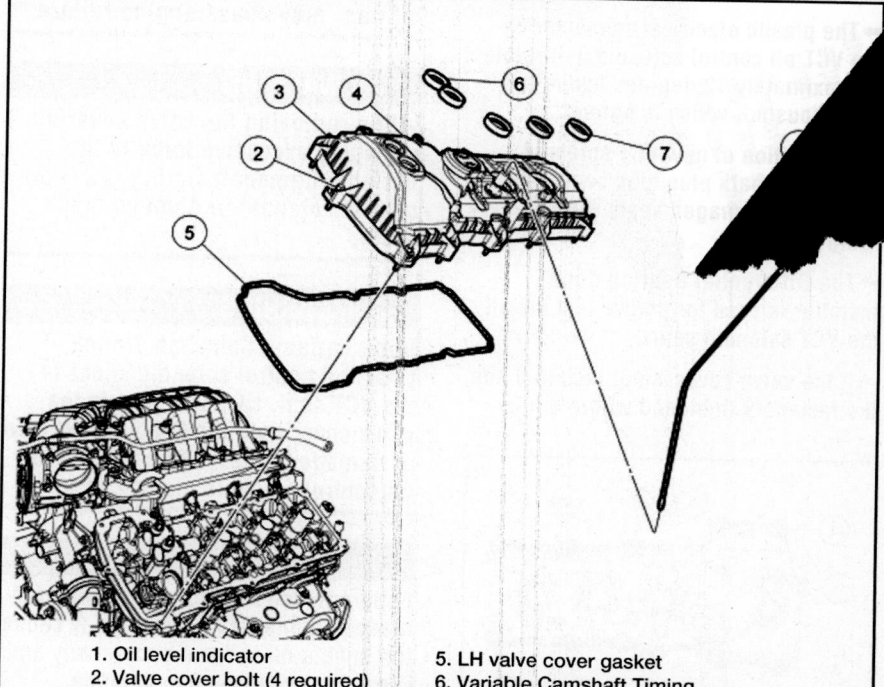

1. Oil level indicator
2. Valve cover bolt (4 required)
3. Valve cover stud bolt (7 required)
4. LH valve cover
5. LH valve cover gasket
6. Variable Camshaft Timing (VCT) solenoid seal (2 required)
7. Spark plug tube seal (3 required)

Fig. 469 LH valve cover assembly—2 of 2

※ WARNING

During engine repair procedures, cleanliness is extremely important. Any foreign material, including any material created while cleaning gasket surfaces that enters the oil passages, coolant passages or the oil pan, may cause engine failure.

※ WARNING

While removing the valve cover do not apply excessive force to the Variable Camshaft Timing (VCT) oil control solenoid or damage may occur.

※ WARNING

If the Variable Camshaft Timing (VCT) oil control solenoid sticks to the VCT seal, carefully wiggle the valve cover until the bond breaks free or damage to the VCT seal and VCT oil control solenoid may occur.

※ WARNING

Failure to use Motorcraft® High Performance Engine RTV Silicone may cause ~~engine oil to foam excessively and~~ ~~engine damage.~~

~~ical connector on~~
~~solenoid will rotate~~
~~grees inside the~~
~~is normal.~~

~~VCT solenoid~~
~~tube seals is only~~
~~seals were~~

➡The Differential Bearing Cone Installer is used to remove and install the VCT solenoid seals.

➡If the valve cover is not installed and the fasteners tightened within 4 min-

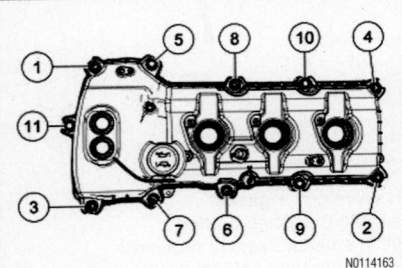

Fig. 470 Using a new gasket, install the LH valve cover and tighten the 4 bolts and 7 stud bolts in the sequence shown

N0114163

---

utes, the sealant must be removed and the sealing area cleaned. To clean the sealing area, use silicone gasket remover and metal surface prep. Failure to follow this procedure can cause future oil leakage.

To install:

1. Using a new gasket, install the LH valve cover and tighten the 4 bolts and 7 stud bolts in the sequence shown. Tighten to 89 inch lbs. (10 Nm).
2. Ensure the VCT seals in the valve cover are below the top of the VCT oil control solenoid electrical connector or the VCT seal may leak oil.

Right Side

See Figures 465, 471 through 473.

➡The manufacturer does not provide a specific Removal and Installation procedure for this component. Refer to the graphic(s) when servicing this component.

※ WARNING

During engine repair procedures, cleanliness is extremely important. Any foreign material, including any material created while cleaning gasket surfaces that enters the oil passages, coolant passages or the oil pan, may cause engine failure.

※ WARNING

While removing the valve cover do not apply excessive force to the Variable Camshaft Timing (VCT) oil control solenoid or damage may occur.

※ WARNING

If the Variable Camshaft Timing (VCT) oil control solenoid sticks to the VCT seal, carefully wiggle the valve cover until the bond breaks free or damage to the VCT seal and VCT oil control solenoid may occur.

※ WARNING

Failure to use Motorcraft® High Performance Engine RTV Silicone may cause the engine oil to foam excessively and result in serious engine damage.

➡The plastic electrical connector on the VCT oil control solenoid will rotate approximately 12 degrees inside the steel housing, which is normal.

➡Installation of new VCT solenoid seals and spark plug tube seals is only required if damaged seals were removed.

➡The Differential Bearing Cone Installer is used to remove and install the VCT solenoid seals.

➡If the valve cover is not installed and the fasteners tightened within 4 minutes, the sealant must be removed and the sealing area cleaned. To clean the sealing area, use silicone gasket remover and metal surface prep. Failure to follow this procedure can cause future oil leakage.

To install:

1. Using a new gasket, install the RH valve cover and tighten the 3 bolts and 8 stud bolts in the sequence shown. Tighten to 89 inch lbs. (10 Nm).
2. Ensure the VCT seals in the valve cover are below the top of the VCT oil control solenoid electrical connector or the VCT seal may leak oil.

5.0L Engine

Left Side

See Figures 474 and 475.

➡The manufacturer does not provide a specific Removal and Installation procedure for this component. Refer to the graphic(s) when servicing this component.

※ WARNING

During engine repair procedures, cleanliness is extremely important. Any foreign material, including any material created while cleaning gasket surfaces, that enters the oil passages, coolant passages or the oil pan, can cause engine failure.

1. Inspect the 2 VCT solenoid seals. Remove any damaged seals.
2. Using the Differential Bearing Cone Installer (205-142) and Handle (205-153), remove the seal(s).
3. Inspect the spark plug tube seals. Remove any damaged seals.
4. Using the VCT Spark Plug Tube Seal Remover (303-1247/1) and Handle (205-153), remove the seal(s).

To install:

➡Installation of new seals is only required if damaged seals were removed.

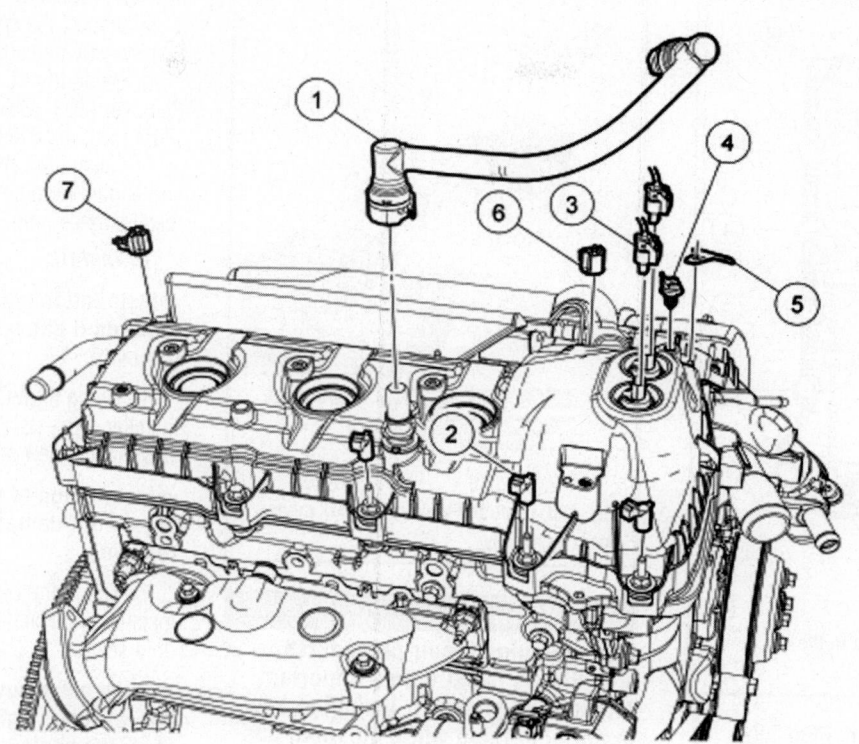

1. PCV tube
2. RH valve cover stud bolt wiring harness retainer (3 required)
3. RH Variable Camshaft Timing (VCT) electrical connector (2 required)
4. RH valve cover wiring harness pin-type retainer
5. RH valve cover stud bolt wiring harness retainer
6. RH valve cover stud bolt wiring harness retainer
7. RH valve cover stud bolt wiring harness retainer

N0114107

Fig. 471 RH valve cover assembly—1 of 2

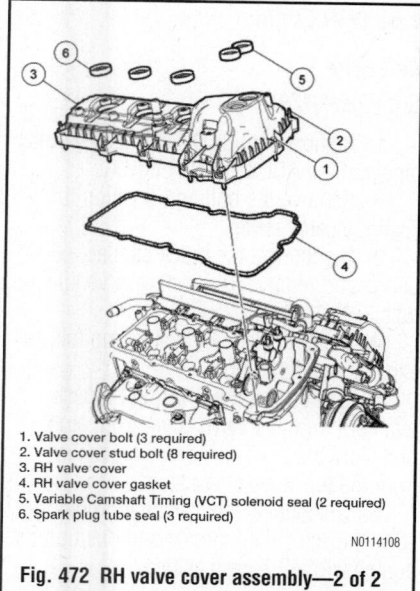

1. Valve cover bolt (3 required)
2. Valve cover stud bolt (8 required)
3. RH valve cover
4. RH valve cover gasket
5. Variable Camshaft Timing (VCT) solenoid seal (2 required)
6. Spark plug tube seal (3 required)

N0114108

Fig. 472 RH valve cover assembly—2 of 2

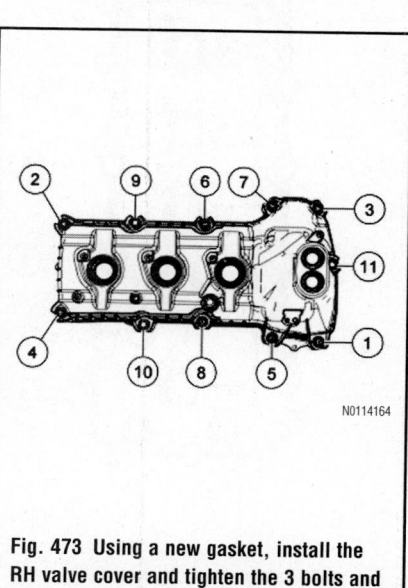

N0114164

Fig. 473 Using a new gasket, install the RH valve cover and tighten the 3 bolts and 8 stud bolts in the sequence shown

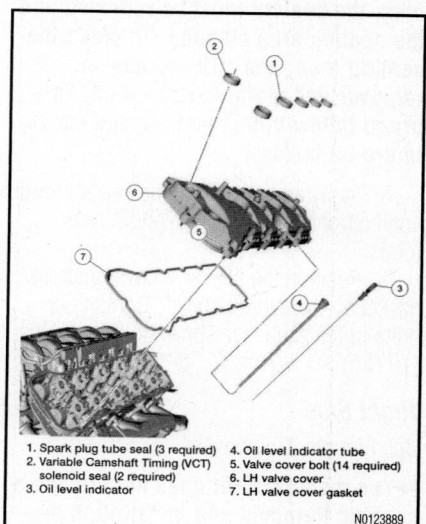

1. Spark plug tube seal (3 required)
2. Variable Camshaft Timing (VCT) solenoid seal (2 required)
3. Oil level indicator
4. Oil level indicator tube
5. Valve cover bolt (14 required)
6. LH valve cover
7. LH valve cover gasket

N0123889

Fig. 474 Exploded view of the LH valve cover assembly

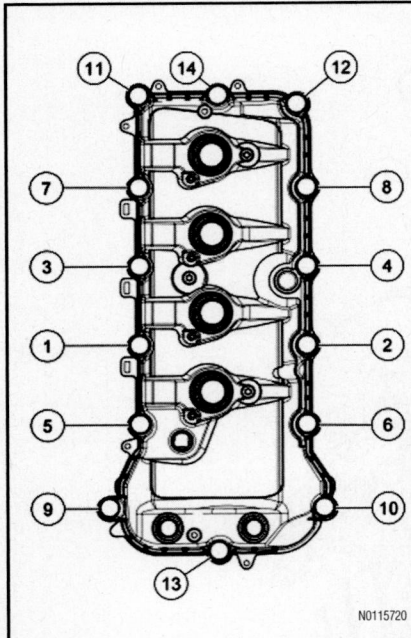

Fig. 475 Tighten the bolts in the sequence shown

5. Using the VCT Spark Plug Tube Seal Installer (303-1247/2) and Handle (205-153), install new spark plug tube seals.

➡**Installation of new seals is only required if damaged seals were removed.**

6. Using the Differential Bearing Cone Installer and Handle, install new VCT solenoid seal(s).

➡**If the valve cover is not installed and the fasteners tightened within 5 minutes, the sealant must be removed and the sealing area cleaned. To clean the sealing area, use silicone gasket remover and metal surface prep. Failure to follow this procedure can cause future oil leakage.**

7. Apply a bead of silicone sealant to the engine front cover-to-LH cylinder head joints.

8. Position the LH valve cover and new gasket on the cylinder head. Tighten the bolts in the sequence shown to 89 inch lbs. (10 Nm).

Right Side

See Figures 476 and 477.

➡**The manufacturer does not provide a specific Removal and Installation procedure for this component. Refer to the graphic(s) when servicing this component.**

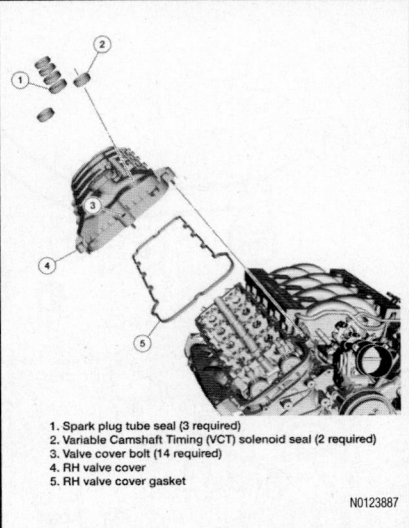

1. Spark plug tube seal (3 required)
2. Variable Camshaft Timing (VCT) solenoid seal (2 required)
3. Valve cover bolt (14 required)
4. RH valve cover
5. RH valve cover gasket

Fig. 476 Exploded view of the RH valve cover assembly

✳✳ **WARNING**

During engine repair procedures, cleanliness is extremely important. Any foreign material, including any material created while cleaning gasket surfaces, that enters the oil passages, coolant passages or the oil pan, can cause engine failure.

---

1. Inspect the 2 VCT solenoid seals. Remove any damaged seals.

2. Using the Differential Bearing Cone

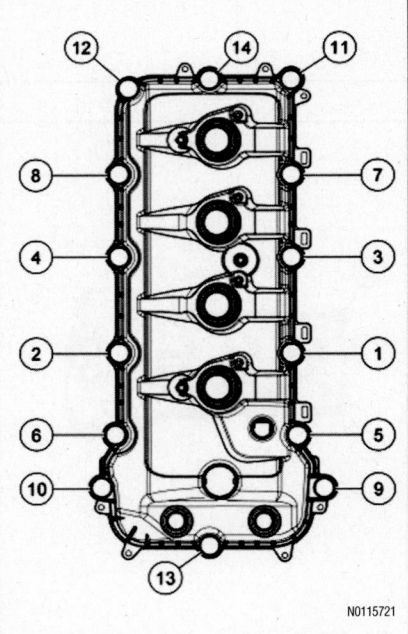

Fig. 477 Tighten the bolts in the sequence shown

Installer (205-142) and Handle (205-153), remove the seal(s).

3. Inspect the spark plug tube seals. Remove any damaged seals.

4. Using the VCT Spark Plug Tube Seal Remover (303-1247/1) and Handle (205-153), remove the seal(s).

5. Clean the valve cover, cylinder head and engine front cover sealing surfaces with metal surface prep.

To install:

➡**Installation of new seals is only required if damaged seals were removed.**

6. Using the VCT Spark Plug Tube Seal Installer (303-1247/2) and Handle (205-153), install new spark plug tube seals.

➡**Installation of new seals is only required if damaged seals were removed.**

7. Using the Differential Bearing Cone Installer and Handle, install new VCT solenoid seal(s).

➡**If the valve cover is not installed and the fasteners tightened within 5 minutes, the sealant must be removed and the sealing area cleaned. To clean the sealing area, use silicone gasket remover and metal surface prep. Failure to follow this procedure can cause future oil leakage.**

8. Apply a bead of silicone sealant to the engine front cover-to-RH cylinder head joints.

9. Position the RH valve cover and new gasket on the cylinder head. Tighten the bolts in the sequence shown to 89 inch lbs. (10 Nm).

4.6L (2V) Engine

Left Side

See Figure 478.

1. Remove the Air Cleaner (ACL) outlet pipe and the ACL assembly cover.

2. Remove the bolt and position the oil level indicator aside.

3. Disconnect the quick connect couplings and remove the crankcase ventilation tube.

4. Remove the EGR system module-to-exhaust manifold tube.

5. Disconnect the 2 wiring harness retainers from the valve cover front stud bolts and the 2 wiring harness retainers from the top valve cover studs.

6. Disconnect the Camshaft Position (CMP) electrical connector and position the engine wiring harness aside.

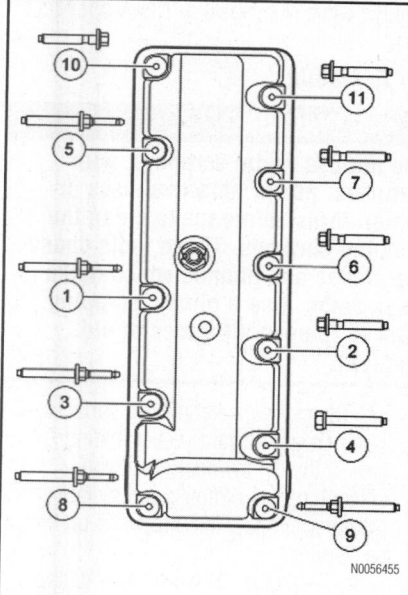

Fig. 478 Position the valve cover and tighten the 11 fasteners in the sequence shown

⚹⚹ WARNING

Do not use metal scrapers, wire brushes, power abrasive discs or other abrasive means to clean the sealing surfaces. These tools cause scratches and gouges which make leak paths. Use a plastic scraping tool to remove all traces of old sealant.

7. Remove the 6 bolts, the 5 stud bolts and the LH valve cover.

    a. Clean the valve cover mating surface of the cylinder head with silicone gasket remover and metal surface prep. Follow the directions on the packaging.

    b. Discard the valve cover gasket. Clean the valve cover gasket groove with soap and water or a suitable solvent.

To install:

8. Apply instant gel adhesive completely around the gasket groove in the valve cover and install the new valve cover gasket.

➡If the valve cover is not secured within 4 minutes, the sealant must be removed and the sealing area cleaned with silicone gasket remover and metal surface prep. Follow the directions on the packaging. Allow to dry until there is no sign of wetness, or 4 minutes, whichever is longer. Failure to follow this procedure can cause future oil leakage.

9. Apply a bead of silicone gasket and sealant in 2 places where the engine front cover meets the cylinder head.

10. Position the valve cover and tighten the 11 fasteners in the sequence shown to 10 Nm (89 lb-in).

11. Position the engine wiring harness and connect the CMP electrical connector.

12. Connect the 2 wiring harness retainers to the valve cover front stud bolts and the 2 wiring harness retainers to the top valve cover stud bolts.

13. Install the EGR system module-to-exhaust manifold tube.

14. Position the oil level indicator and install the bolt. Tighten to 89 inch lbs. (10 Nm).

15. Position the crankcase ventilation tube and connect the quick connect coupling.

16. Install the ACL outlet pipe and the ACL assembly cover.

Right Side

See Figures 479 and 480.

1. Disconnect the quick connect couplings and remove the PCV tube.

2. Disconnect the wiring harness retainers from the engine front cover stud bolt, the front valve cover stud bolt and the top valve cover stud bolts.

3. Disconnect the PCM electrical connector and position the transmission wiring harness aside.

⚹⚹ WARNING

Do not use metal scrapers, wire brushes, power abrasive discs or other abrasive means to clean the sealing surfaces. These tools cause scratches and gouges which make leak paths. Use a plastic scraping tool to remove all traces of old sealant.

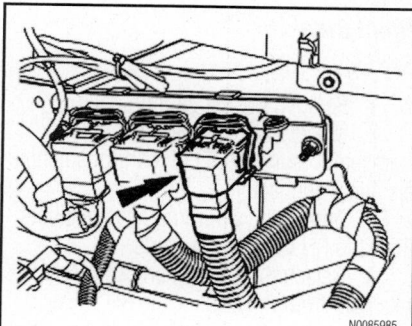

Fig. 479 Disconnect the PCM electrical connector and position the transmission wiring harness aside

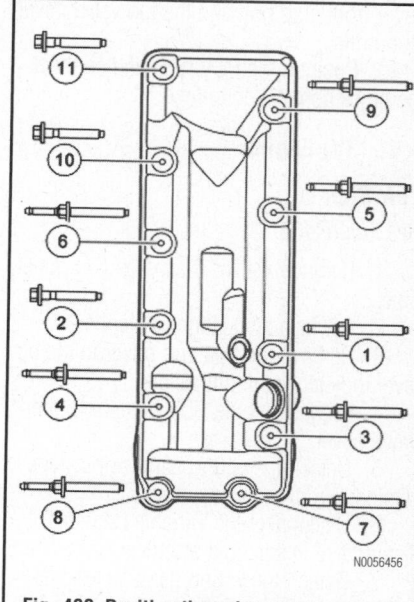

Fig. 480 Position the valve cover and install the 11 fasteners in the sequence shown

4. Remove the 11 fasteners and remove the RH valve cover.

    a. Clean the valve cover mating surface of the cylinder head with silicone gasket remover and metal surface prep. Follow the directions on the packaging.

    b. Discard the valve cover gasket. Clean the valve cover gasket groove with soap and water or a suitable solvent.

To install:

5. Apply instant gel adhesive completely around the gasket groove in the valve cover and install the new valve cover gasket.

➡If the valve cover is not secured within 4 minutes, the sealant must be removed and the sealing area cleaned with silicone gasket remover and metal surface prep. Follow the directions on the packaging. Allow to dry until there is no sign of wetness, or 4 minutes, whichever is longer. Failure to follow this procedure can cause future oil leakage.

6. Apply the silicone gasket and sealant in 2 places where the engine front cover meets the cylinder head.

7. Position the valve cover and install the 11 fasteners in the sequence shown to 89 inch lbs. (10 Nm).

8. Position the transmission wiring harness and connect the PCM electrical connector.

9. Connect the wiring harness retainers to the engine front cover stud bolt, the valve

cover front stud bolt and the top valve cover stud bolts.

10. Position the PCV tube and connect the quick connect couplings.

4.6L (3V) Engine

Left Side

See Figure 481.

1. Remove the Air Cleaner (ACL) outlet pipe.
2. Remove the LH ignition coils.
3. Remove the bolt and position the oil level indicator and tube aside.
4. Disconnect the PCV hose from the valve cover.
5. Detach the wiring harness pin-type retainers from the valve cover.
6. Disconnect the Variable Camshaft Timing (VCT) solenoid electrical connector.
7. Detach the wiring harness retainers from the valve cover studs.
8. Loosen the 10 bolts and remove the LH valve cover and gasket. Discard the gasket.

To install:

❊❊ WARNING

Do not use metal scrapers, wire brushes, power abrasive discs or

other abrasive means to clean the sealing surfaces. These tools cause scratches and gouges which make leak paths. Use a plastic scraping tool to remove all traces of old sealant.

9. Clean the gasket mating surfaces.
   a. Clean the valve cover mating surface of the cylinder head with silicone gasket remover and metal surface prep. Follow the directions on the packaging.
   b. Clean the valve cover gasket groove in the valve cover with soap and water or a suitable solvent.
10. Install a new gasket on the LH valve cover.

➡**If the valve cover is not secured within 4 minutes, the sealant must be removed and the sealing area cleaned with metal surface prep. Failure to follow this procedure may cause future oil leakage.**

11. Apply a bead of silicone gasket and sealant in 2 places where the engine front cover meets the cylinder head.
12. Position the LH valve cover with a new gasket and tighten the 10 bolts in the sequence shown. Tighten to 89 inch lbs. (10 Nm).
13. Attach the wiring harness retainers to the valve cover studs.
14. Connect the VCT solenoid electrical connector.
15. Connect the wiring harness pin-type retainers to the valve cover.
16. Connect the PCV hose to the valve cover.
17. Position the oil level indicator tube and install the bolt. Tighten to 89 inch lbs. (10 Nm).
18. Install the LH ignition coils.
19. Install the Air Cleaner (ACL) outlet pipe.

Right Side

See Figure 482.

1. Remove the RH ignition coils.
2. Disconnect the RH Variable Camshaft Timing (VCT) oil control solenoid electrical connector.
3. Detach the wiring harness retainers from the RH valve cover studs.
4. Detach the wiring harness pin-type retainers from the front of the RH valve cover.
5. Disconnect the crankcase breather tube from the RH valve cover.
6. Loosen the 9 RH valve cover bolts and remove the RH valve cover and

the RH valve cover gasket. Discard the gasket.

To install:

❊❊ WARNING

Do not use metal scrapers, wire brushes, power abrasive discs or other abrasive means to clean the sealing surfaces. These tools cause scratches and gouges which make leak paths. Use a plastic scraping tool to remove all traces of old sealant.

7. Clean the gasket mating surfaces.
   a. Clean the valve cover mating surface of the RH cylinder head with silicone gasket remover and metal surface prep. Follow the directions on the packaging.
   b. Clean the RH valve cover gasket groove with soap and water or a suitable solvent.
8. Install a new gasket on the RH valve cover.

➡**If the RH valve cover is not secured within 4 minutes, the sealant must be removed and the sealing area cleaned**

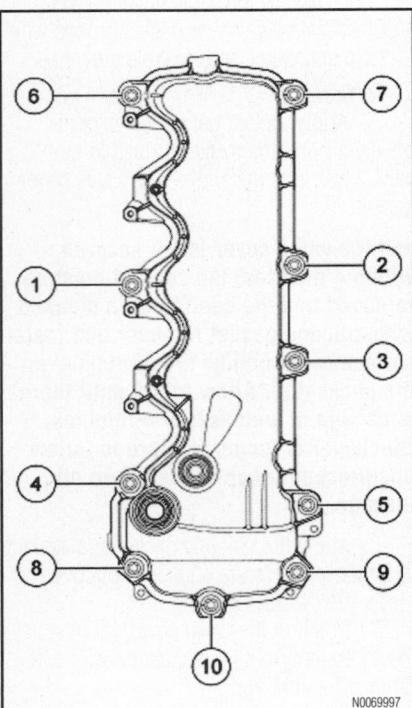

Fig. 481 Position the LH valve cover with a new gasket and tighten the 10 bolts in the sequence shown

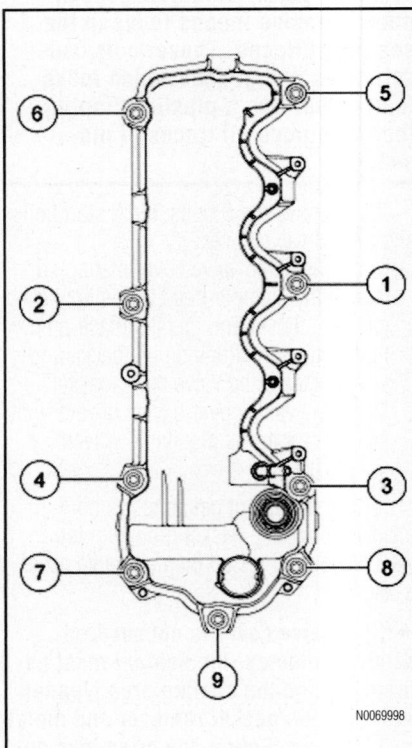

Fig. 482 Position the RH valve cover with a new gasket on the cylinder head and tighten the 9 bolts in the sequence shown

with metal surface prep. Failure to follow this procedure may cause future oil leakage.

9. Apply a bead of silicone gasket and sealant in 2 places where the engine front cover meets the RH cylinder head.

10. Position the RH valve cover with a new gasket on the cylinder head and tighten the 9 bolts in the sequence shown. Tighten to 89 inch lbs. (10 Nm).

11. Connect the crankcase breather tube to the RH valve cover.

12. Attach the wiring harness pin-type retainers to the front of the RH valve cover.

13. Attach the wiring harness retainers to the RH valve cover studs.

14. Connect the RH VCT oil control solenoid electrical connector.

15. Install the RH ignition coils.

5.4L (3V) Engine

Left Side

See Figure 481.

1. Remove the Air Cleaner (ACL) outlet pipe.

2. Remove the bolt and position the oil level indicator and tube aside.

3. Disconnect the quick connect couplings and remove the PCV tube.

4. Disconnect the intake manifold vacuum tube hose from the brake booster.

5. Disconnect the intake manifold vacuum tube from the support bracket and the valve cover stud.

6. Disconnect the Variable Camshaft Timing (VCT) solenoid electrical connector.

7. Disconnect the 3 wiring harness retainers from the front of the LH valve cover and the 2 wiring harness retainers from the LH valve cover studs.

8. Remove the 4 LH ignition coils.

> ### ✳✳ WARNING
> Do not use metal scrapers, wire brushes, power abrasive discs or other abrasive means to clean the sealing surfaces. These tools cause scratches and gouges which make leak paths. Use a plastic scraping tool to remove all traces of old sealant.

> ### ✳✳ WARNING
> When removing the valve cover, make sure to avoid damaging the Variable Camshaft Timing (VCT) solenoid.

➡ The fasteners are part of the valve cover and should not be removed.

9. Loosen the 10 fasteners and remove the LH valve cover and gasket.

   a. Clean the valve cover mating surface of the cylinder head with silicone gasket remover and metal surface prep. Follow the directions on the packaging.

   b. Discard the valve cover gasket. Clean the valve cover gasket groove with soap and water or a suitable solvent.

To install:

➡ If the valve cover is not secured within 4 minutes, the sealant must be removed and the sealing area cleaned with silicone gasket remover and metal surface prep. Follow the directions on the packaging. Allow to dry until there is no sign of wetness, or 4 minutes, whichever is longer. Failure to follow this procedure can cause future oil leakage.

10. Apply a bead of silicone gasket and sealant in 2 places where the engine front cover meets the cylinder head.

> ### ✳✳ WARNING
> When installing the valve cover, make sure to avoid damaging the Variable Camshaft Timing (VCT) solenoid.

11. Position the LH valve cover and new gasket on the cylinder head and tighten the 10 fasteners in the sequence shown. Tighten to 89 inch lbs. (10 Nm).

12. Position the intake manifold vacuum tube assembly onto the support bracket and the valve cover stud.

13. Connect the intake manifold vacuum tube hose to the brake booster.

14. Install the 4 LH ignition coils.

15. Connect the 3 wiring harness retainers to the front of the RH valve cover and the 2 wiring harness retainers to the RH valve cover studs.

16. Connect the VCT solenoid electrical connector.

17. Position the PCV tube and connect the quick connect couplings.

18. Position the oil level indicator and tube and install the bolt. Tighten to 89 inch lbs. (10 Nm).

19. Install the ACL outlet pipe.

Right Side

See Figures 482 and 483.

1. Disconnect the battery ground cable.

2. Disconnect the quick connect couplings and remove the crankcase ventilation tube.

3. Disconnect the Variable Camshaft Timing (VCT) solenoid electrical connector.

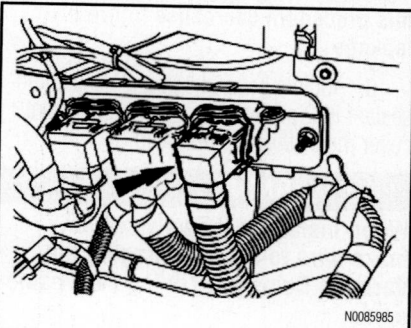

Fig. 483 Disconnect the PCM electrical connector and position aside

4. Disconnect the 2 wiring harness retainers from the front of the RH valve cover and the 2 wiring harness retainers from the RH valve cover studs.

5. Remove the 4 RH ignition coils.

6. Disconnect the PCM electrical connector and position aside.

> ### ✳✳ WARNING
> Do not use metal scrapers, wire brushes, power abrasive discs or other abrasive means to clean the sealing surfaces. These tools cause scratches and gouges which make leak paths. Use a plastic scraping tool to remove all traces of old sealant.

> ### ✳✳ WARNING
> When removing the valve cover, make sure to avoid damaging the Variable Camshaft Timing (VCT) solenoid.

➡ The fasteners are part of the valve cover and should not be removed.

7. Loosen the 9 fasteners and remove the RH valve cover and gasket.

   a. Clean the valve cover mating surface of the cylinder head with silicone gasket remover and metal surface prep. Follow the directions on the packaging.

   b. Discard the valve cover gasket. Clean the valve cover gasket groove with soap and water or a suitable solvent.

To install:

➡ If the valve cover is not secured within 4 minutes, the sealant must be removed and the sealing area cleaned with silicone gasket remover and metal surface prep. Follow the directions on the packaging. Allow to dry until there is no sign of wetness, or 4 minutes, whichever is longer. Failure to follow this procedure can cause future oil leakage.

8. Apply a bead of silicone gasket and sealant in 2 places where the engine front cover meets the cylinder head.

✳✳ WARNING

When installing the valve cover, make sure to avoid damaging the Variable Camshaft Timing (VCT) solenoid.

9. Position the RH valve cover and new gasket on the cylinder head and tighten the 9 fasteners in the sequence shown. Tighten to 89 inch lbs. (10 Nm).

10. Connect the PCM electrical connector.

11. Install the 4 RH ignition coils.

12. Connect the 2 wiring harness retainers to the front of the RH valve cover and the 2 wiring harness retainers to the RH valve cover studs.

13. Connect the VCT solenoid electrical connector.

14. Position the crankcase ventilation tube and connect the quick connect couplings.

15. Connect the battery ground cable.

VALVE LASH

ADJUSTMENT

All engines use hydraulic lash adjusters. No adjustment is necessary.

ENGINE PERFORMANCE & EMISSION CONTROLS

CAMSHAFT POSITION (CMP) SENSOR

LOCATION

4.6L (2V) Engine
See Figure 484.

Refer to the accompanying illustration.

4.6L (3V) and 5.4L (3V) Engines
See Figures 485 and 486.

Refer to the accompanying illustrations.

6.2L (2V) Engine
See Figure 487.

Refer to the accompanying illustration.

REMOVAL & INSTALLATION

4.6L (2V) Engine

1. Disconnect the Camshaft Position (CMP) sensor electrical connector.

2. Remove the bolt and the CMP sensor.

3. To install, reverse the removal procedure.

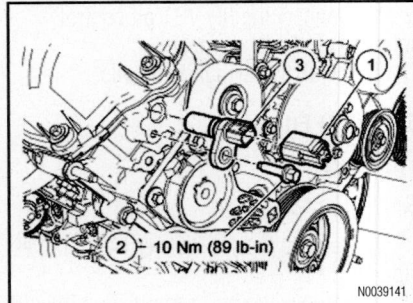

Fig. 485 Exploded view of CMP sensor assembly showing electrical connector (1), bolt (2) and CMP sensor (3)—Right side

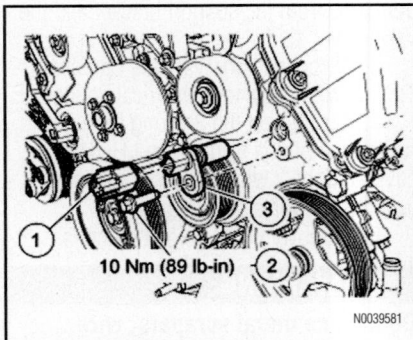

Fig. 486 Exploded view of CMP sensor assembly showing electrical connector (1), bolt (2) and CMP sensor (3)—Left side

4. Lubricate the CMP sensor O-ring seal with clean engine oil prior to installation.

5. To install, tighten to 89 inch lbs. (10 Nm).

4.6L (3V) and 5.4L (3V) Engines

1. For the left side, remove the Air Cleaner (ACL) outlet pipe and resonator.

2. Disconnect the Camshaft Position (CMP) sensor electrical connector.

Fig. 484 Exploded view of CMP sensor assembly showing electrical connector (1), bolt (2) and CMP sensor (3)

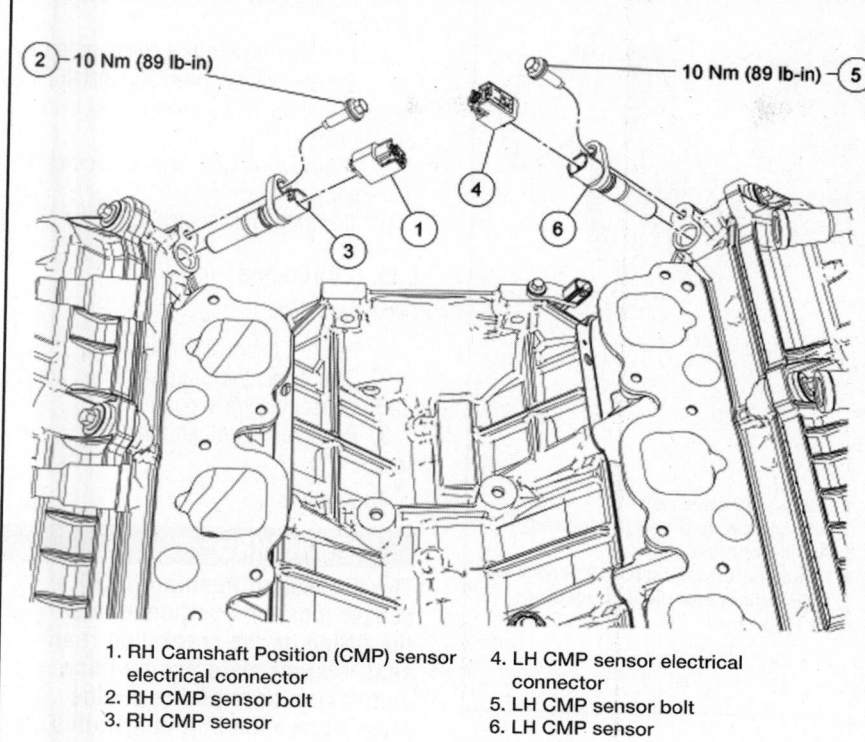

1. RH Camshaft Position (CMP) sensor electrical connector
2. RH CMP sensor bolt
3. RH CMP sensor
4. LH CMP sensor electrical connector
5. LH CMP sensor bolt
6. LH CMP sensor

N0110678

Fig. 487 Exploded view of CMP sensor assemblies

3. Remove the bolt and the CMP sensor.
4. To install, reverse the removal procedure.
5. Lubricate the CMP sensor O-ring seal with clean engine oil prior to installation.
6. To install, tighten to 89 inch lbs. (10 Nm).

5.0L Engine

See Figure 488.

1. For both RH & LH Intake Camshaft Position (CMP) sensors, and RH Exhaust CMP Sensor:
   a. Disconnect the Camshaft Position (CMP) sensor electrical connector.
   b. Remove the bolt and the CMP sensor.

➡**If removing the LH exhaust CMP sensor, perform the following steps:**

2. Position the vehicle on a hoist.
3. If equipped with 4 wheel drive, index-mark the front flange to the pinion flange.
4. If equipped with 4 wheel drive, remove the 6 front flange-to-pinion flange bolts and 2 washers and position the driveshaft aside. Discard the 6 bolts and 2 washers
5. Remove the 2 bolts and the LH heat

shield from the rear of the LH cylinder head.
6. Disconnect the CMP sensor electrical connector.
7. Remove the 2 transmission support insulator nuts.
8. Remove the CMP bolt.

➡**Make sure the transmission jack contacts the outer ribs of the transmission fluid pan.**

9. Position a suitable high-lift transmission jack under the transmission. Raise the transmission until the CMP sensor can be removed.

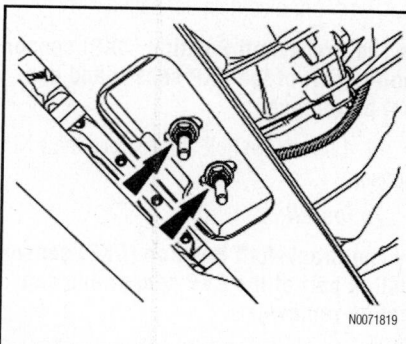

N0071819

Fig. 488 Remove the 2 transmission support insulator nuts

10. Remove the CMP sensor.

To install:

➡**If installing the LH exhaust CMP sensor, perform the following steps:**

➡**The bolt must be torqued while the transmission is raised**

11. Position the Camshaft Position (CMP) sensor and install the bolt. Tighten to 89 inch lbs. (10 Nm).
12. Using the suitable high-lift transmission jack, lower the transmission and install the 2 transmission support insulator nuts. Tighten to 75 ft. lbs. (103 Nm).
13. Connect the CMP sensor electrical connector.
14. Position the LH heat shield onto the rear of the LH cylinder head and install the 2 bolts. Tighten to 89 inch lbs. (10 Nm).
15. If equipped with 4 wheel drive, position back the driveshaft, align the index mark and install 2 washers and 6 new bolts. Tighten to 41 ft. lbs. (55 Nm).
16. For both RH & LH Intake Camshaft Position (CMP) sensors, and RH Exhaust CMP Sensor:
   a. Position the CMP sensor and install the bolt. Tighten to 89 inch lbs. (10 Nm).
   b. Connect the CMP sensor electrical connector.

6.2L (2V) Engine

1. Disconnect the Camshaft Position (CMP) sensor electrical connector.
2. Remove the bolt and the CMP sensor.
3. To install, reverse the removal procedure.
4. Lubricate the CMP sensor O-ring seal with clean engine oil prior to installation.
5. To install, tighten to 89 inch lbs. (10 Nm).

CRANKSHAFT POSITION (CKP) SENSOR

LOCATION

4.6L (2V), 4.6L (3V), and 5.4L (3V) Engines

See Figure 489.

Refer to the accompanying illustration.

6.2L (2V) Engine

See Figure 490.

Refer to the accompanying illustration.

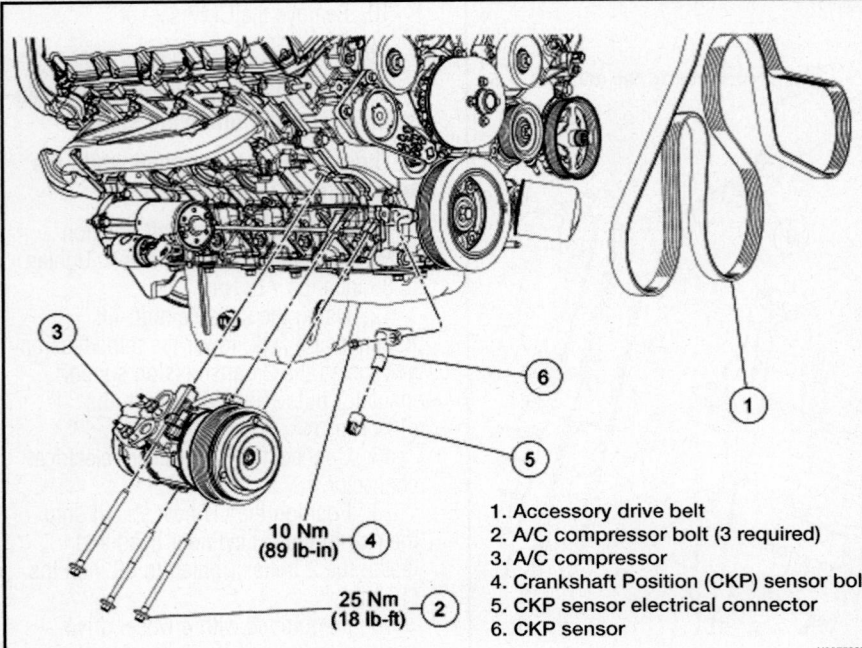

1. Accessory drive belt
2. A/C compressor bolt (3 required)
3. A/C compressor
4. Crankshaft Position (CKP) sensor bolt
5. CKP sensor electrical connector
6. CKP sensor

N0075097

Fig. 489 Exploded view showing CKP sensor location

REMOVAL & INSTALLATION

4.6L (2V), 4.6L (3V), and 5.4L (3V) Engines

1. With the vehicle in NEUTRAL, position it on a hoist.
2. Rotate the accessory drive belt clockwise and detach the accessory drive belt from the A/C compressor pulley.
3. Loosen the A/C compressor bolts enough to slide the A/C compressor down approximately 1 inch (25 mm), to allow access to the Crankshaft Position (CKP) sensor.
4. Disconnect the CKP sensor electrical connector.

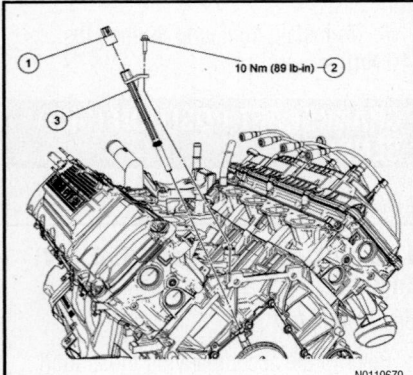

N0110679

Fig. 490 Exploded view of the CKP sensor assembly showing electrical connector (1), bolt (2), and CKP sensor (3)

5. Remove the bolt and the CKP sensor.
6. To install, reverse the removal procedure.

    a. Lubricate the O-ring seal with clean engine oil prior to installation.
    b. To install, tighten the CKP sensor bolt to 89 inch lbs. (10 Nm).
    c. To install, tighten the A/C compressor bolts to 18 ft. lbs. (25 Nm).

5.0L Engine

1. Remove the intake manifold.
2. Disconnect the Cylinder Head Temperature (CHT) sensor electrical connector.
3. Remove the stud bolt, the bolt and the RH heat shield from the rear of the RH cylinder head.
4. Disconnect the Crankshaft Position (CKP) sensor electrical connector.

➡The Crankshaft Position (CKP) sensor bolt is part of the CKP sensor and cannot be removed.

5. Loosen the bolt and remove the CKP sensor.

To install:

➡The Crankshaft Position (CKP) sensor bolt is part of the CKP sensor and cannot be removed.

6. Position the CKP sensor and tighten the bolt. Tighten to 89 inch lbs. (10 Nm).

7. Connect the CKP sensor electrical connector.
8. Position the RH heat shield onto the rear of the RH cylinder head and install the stud bolt and the bolt. Tighten to 89 inch lbs. (10 Nm).
9. Connect the CHT sensor electrical connector.
10. Install the intake manifold.

6.2L (2V) Engine

See Figure 491.

1. Remove the intake manifold.
2. Disconnect the Crankshaft Position (CKP) sensor electrical connector.
3. Remove the bolt and the CKP sensor.

To install:

❊❊ WARNING

The Crankshaft Position (CKP) sensor must be positioned into the fitting on the crankshaft rear seal retainer plate and be flush against the boss on the engine block before the bolt is installed. If the CKP sensor is installed incorrectly, the CKP sensor can be damaged.

4. Position the CKP sensor and install the bolt. Tighten to 89 inch lbs. (10 Nm).
5. Connect the CKP sensor electrical connector.
6. Install the intake manifold

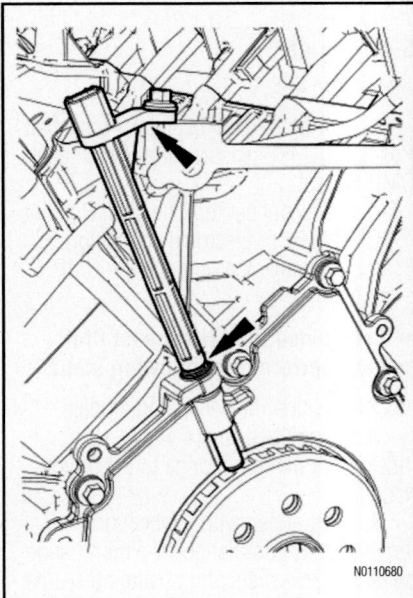

N0110680

Fig. 491 Position the CKP sensor and install the bolt

POWERTRAIN CONTROL MODULE (PCM)

LOCATION

See Figure 492.

Refer to the accompanying illustration.

REMOVAL & INSTALLATION

2010 Models

➡**Any PCM replacement will require that ALL customer keys are available to be reprogrammed at the time of installation. PCM replacement DOES NOT require new keys.**

1. Retrieve the module configuration. Carry out the module configuration retrieval steps of the Programmable Module Installation (PMI) procedure.
2. Disconnect the PCM electrical connectors.
3. Remove the bolts, the PCM and the gasket.

To install:

4. Install the gasket, the PCM and the bolts. Tighten to 80 inch lbs. (9 Nm).
5. Connect the PCM electrical connectors.
6. Restore the module configuration. Carry out the module configuration restore steps of the Programmable Module Installation (PMI) procedure.
7. Reprogram the Passive Anti-Theft System (PATS). Carry out the Key Programming Using Two Programmed Keys procedure.

8. Using the scan tool, perform the Misfire Monitor Neutral Profile Correction procedure, following the on-screen instructions.

2011 Models

See Figures 493 and 494.

➡**Any Powertrain Control Module (PCM) replacement will require that ALL customer keys are available to be reprogrammed at the time of installation. PCM replacement DOES NOT require new keys.**

1. Retrieve the module configuration. Carry out the module configuration retrieval steps of the Programmable Module Installation (PMI) procedure.
2. For vehicles equipped with a 3.5L Gasoline Turbocharged Direct Injection (GTDI) Engine:
   a. Disconnect the 2 Powertrain Control Module (PCM) electrical connectors.
   b. Disengage and remove the PCM cover.
   c. If the PCM support bracket is damaged, remove the nut and position the ground cable aside and remove the 2 PCM stud bolts and slide the PCM support bracket out of the bulkhead.
3. For vehicles equipped with a 3.7L, 5.0L (4V) or 6.2L (2V) engine:
   a. Disconnect the Powertrain Control Module (PCM) electrical connectors.
   b. Remove the 2 PCM-to-PCM support bracket bolts and the PCM.

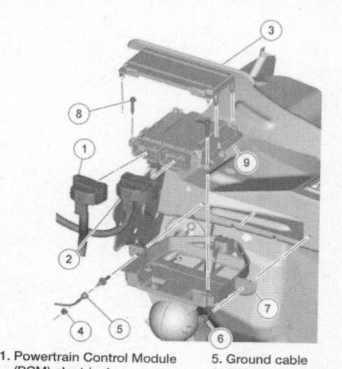

1. Powertrain Control Module (PCM) electrical connector
2. PCM electrical connector
3. PCM cover
4. Ground cable nut
5. Ground cable
6. PCM stud bolt (2 required)
7. PCM support bracket
8. PCM-to-PCM support bracket bolt (2 required)
9. PCM

N0124436

Fig. 493 Exploded view of the 3.5L GTDI engine PCM assembly

   c. Remove the stud bolts, the PCM and the gasket.

To install:

4. For vehicles equipped with a 3.7L, 5.0L (4V) or 6.2L (2V) engine:
   a. Install the gasket, the PCM and the 2 stud bolts.
   b. Connect the PCM electrical connectors.
5. For vehicles equipped with a 3.5L Gasoline Turbocharged Direct Injection (GTDI) Engine:
   a. If the PCM support bracket was removed, position the support bracket assembly into the bulkhead and install the 2 stud bolts.
   b. If the PCM support bracket was removed, position the ground cable and install the nut.
   c. Position the PCM onto the support bracket and install the 2 bolts.
   d. Install the PCM cover.
   e. Connect the 2 PCM electrical connectors.

➡**The following steps are for all engines.**

6. Restore the module configuration. Carry out the module configuration restore steps of the Programmable Module Installation (PMI) procedure.
7. Reprogram the Passive Anti-Theft System (PATS). Carry out the Key Programming Using Two Programmed Keys procedure.
8. Using the scan tool, perform the Misfire Monitor Neutral Profile Correction procedure, following the on-screen instructions.
9. Carry out he transmission solenoid body strategy identification.

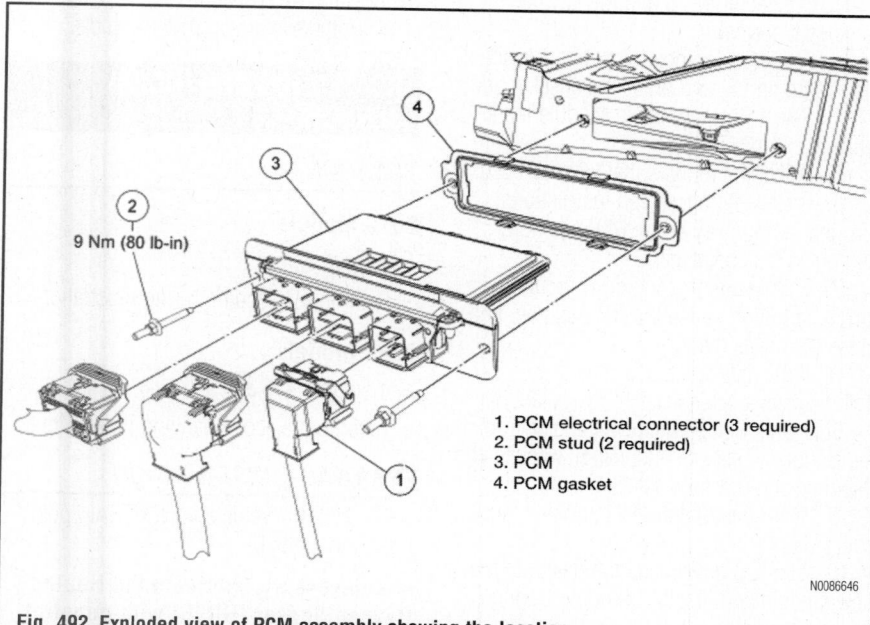

9 Nm (80 lb-in)

1. PCM electrical connector (3 required)
2. PCM stud (2 required)
3. PCM
4. PCM gasket

N0086646

Fig. 492 Exploded view of PCM assembly showing the location

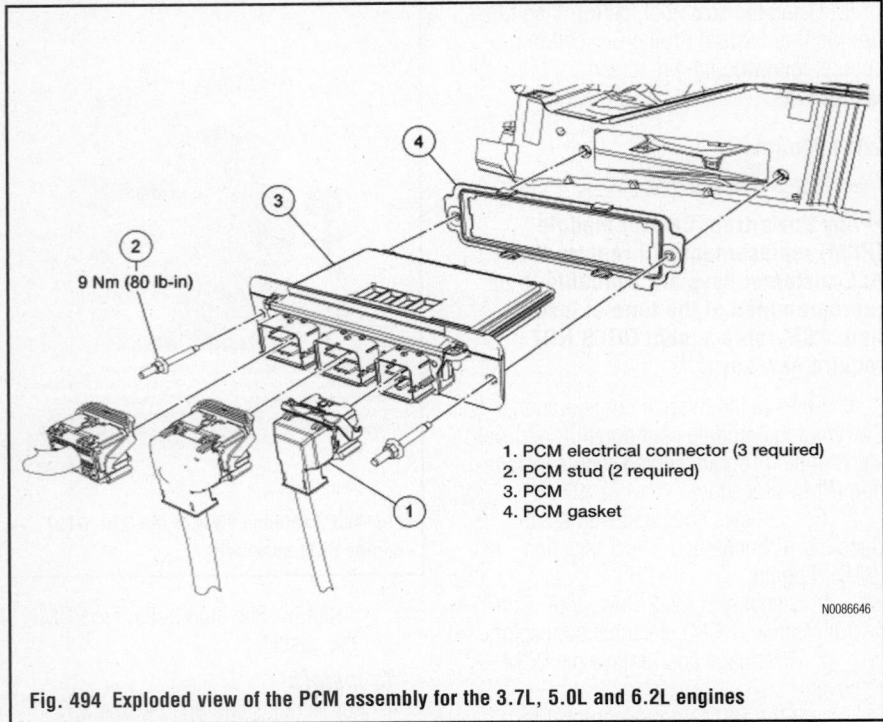

Fig. 494 Exploded view of the PCM assembly for the 3.7L, 5.0L and 6.2L engines

1. PCM electrical connector (3 required)
2. PCM stud (2 required)
3. PCM
4. PCM gasket

9 Nm (80 lb-in)

N0086646

PROGRAMMABLE MODULE INSTALLATION (PMI) PROCEDURE

Programmable Module Installation (PMI) Using the Integrated Diagnostic System (IDS) When the Original Module is Available

➡Following module installation, some modules require a separate learning procedure be carried out. For adaptive learning and calibration instructions, refer to the specific module removal and installation procedures.

1. Connect the IDS and identify the vehicle as normal.
2. From the Toolbox icon, select Module Programming and press the check mark.
3. Select Programmable Module Installation.
4. Select the module that is being replaced.
5. Follow the on-screen instructions, turn the ignition key to the OFF position, and press the check mark.
6. Install the new module and press the check mark.
7. Follow the on-screen instructions, turn the ignition key to the ON position, and press the check mark.
8. The IDS downloads the data into the new module and displays Module Configuration Complete.
9. Test module for correct operation.

Programmable Module Installation (PMI) Using the Integrated Diagnostic System (IDS) When the Original Module is NOT Available

➡Following module installation, some modules require a separate learning procedure be carried out. For adaptive learning and calibration instructions, refer to the specific module removal and installation procedures.

1. Install the new module.
2. Connect the IDS and identify the vehicle as normal.
3. From the Toolbox icon, select Module Programming and press the check mark.
4. Select Programmable Module Installation.
5. Select the module that was replaced.
6. Follow the on-screen instructions, turn the ignition key to the OFF position, and press the check mark.
7. Follow the on-screen instructions, turn the ignition key to the ON position, and press the check mark.
8. If the data is not available, the IDS displays a screen stating to contact the As-Built Data Center. Retrieve the data from the technician service publication website at this time and press the check mark.
9. Enter the module data and press the check mark.
10. The IDS downloads the data into the new module and displays Module Configuration Complete.

11. Test module for correct operation.

REPROGRAM THE PASSIVE ANTI-THEFT SYSTEM (PATS)

➡A minimum of 2 Passive Anti-Theft System (PATS) keys must be programmed into the Instrument Cluster (IC) to complete this procedure and allow the vehicle to start.

1. Turn the key from the OFF position to the ON position.
2. From the scan tool, follow the on-screen instructions to ENTER SECURITY ACCESS.
3. From the scan tool, select: Parameter Reset and follow the on-screen instructions.

➡If the IC or the IC and the PCM were replaced, updated or reconfigured, follow Steps 4-9. All vehicle keys are erased during the parameter reset procedure. Verify at least 2 vehicle keys are available prior to carrying out the PATS parameter reset. If only the PCM was replaced, go to Step 9.

4. From the scan tool, select: Ignition Key Code Erase and follow the on-screen instructions.
5. Turn the key to the OFF position and disconnect the scan tool.
6. Turn the key to the ON position for 6 seconds.
7. Turn the key to the OFF position and remove the key.
8. Insert the second PATS key into the ignition lock cylinder and turn the key to the ON position for 6 seconds.
9. Both keys now start the vehicle.

HEATED OXYGEN (HO2S) SENSOR

LOCATION

2010 Models
See Figure 495.

Refer to the accompanying illustration.

2011 Models
See Figures 496 and 497.

Refer to the accompanying illustrations.

REMOVAL & INSTALLATION

1. With the vehicle in NEUTRAL, position it on a hoist.

➡If necessary, lubricate the Heated Oxygen Sensor (HO2S) with penetrat-

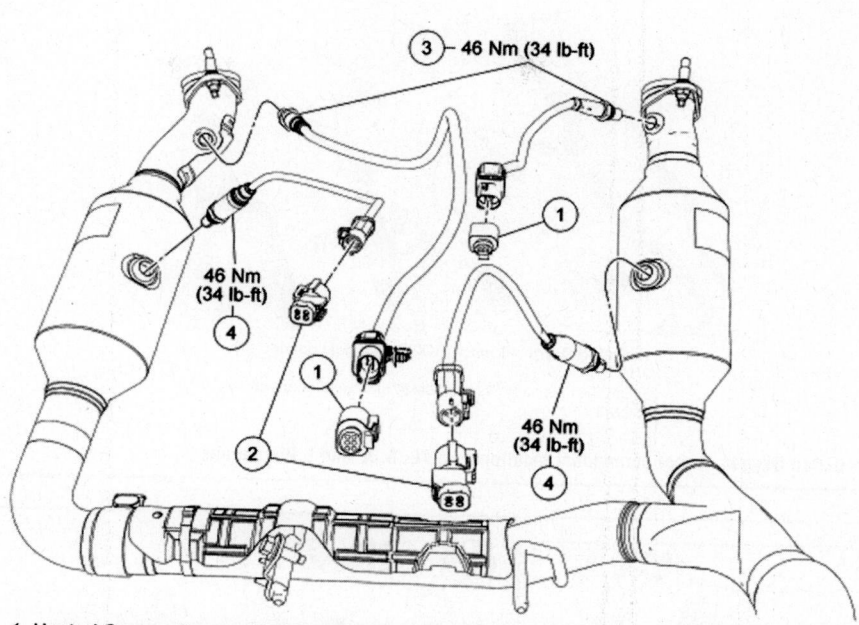

1. Heated Oxygen Sensor (HO2S) electrical connectors (2 required)
2. Catalyst Monitor Sensor (CMS) electrical connectors (2 required)
3. HO2S (2 required)
4. CMS (2 required)

N0086648

Fig. 495 Exploded view showing typical locations of HO2S

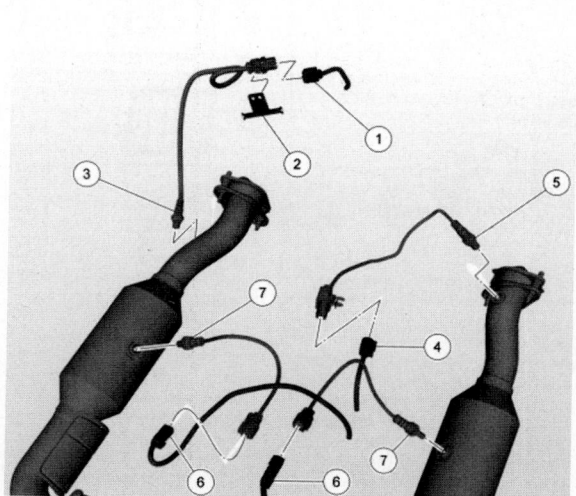

1. Heated Oxygen Sensor (HO2S) electrical connector
2. HO2S wiring harness electrical connector retainer
3. HO2S
4. HO2S electrical connector
5. HO2S
6. Catalyst Monitor Sensor (CMS) electrical connectors
7. CMS

N0125709

Fig. 496 Exploded view of Heated Oxygen sensor component locations—3.5L GTDI engine

ing and lock lubricant to assist in removal.

2. Using the Exhaust Gas Oxygen Sensor Socket, remove the HO2S.

3. To install, reverse the removal procedure.

   a. Apply anti-seize to the threads of the HO2S.

   b. Calculate the correct torque wrench setting for the following torque.

   c. To install, tighten to 34 ft. lbs. (46 Nm).

INTAKE AIR TEMPERATURE (IAT) SENSOR

LOCATION

2010 Models

See Figure 498.

The Intake Air Temperature (IAT) sensor provides the Sequential Multi-Port Fuel Injection (SFI) system mixture temperature information. The IAT sensor is used both as a density corrector for air flow calculation and to proportion cold enrichment fuel flow. The IAT sensor is installed in the air cleaner inlet tube.

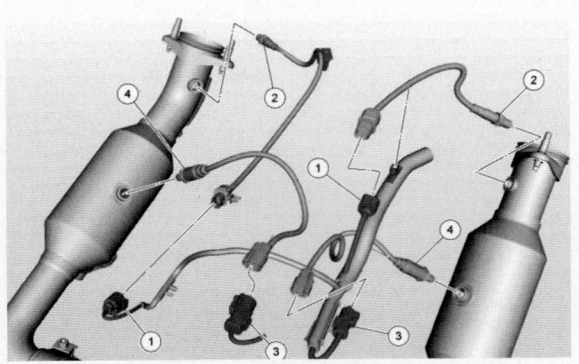

1. Heated Oxygen Sensor (HO2S) electrical connectors
2. HO2S
3. Catalyst Monitor Sensor (CMS) electrical connectors
4. CMS

N0125711

Fig. 497 Exploded view of Heated Oxygen sensor component locations—3.7L, 5.0L and 6.2L engines

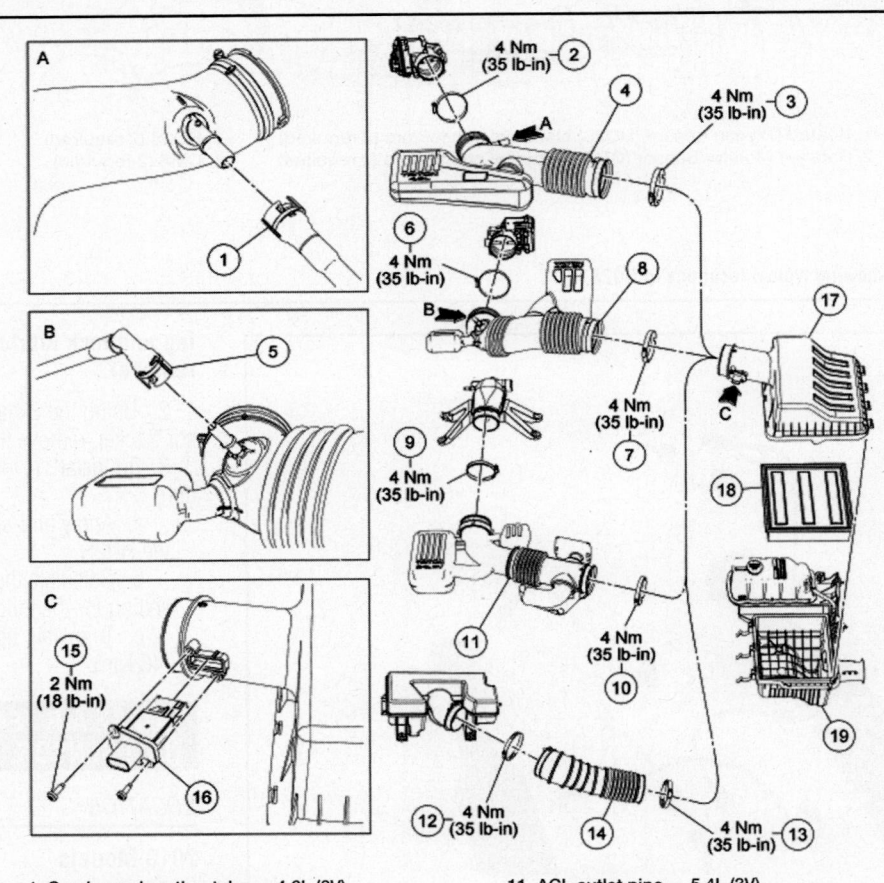

1. Crankcase breather tube — 4.6L (2V)
2. Air Cleaner (ACL) outlet pipe-to-throttle body clamp — 4.6L (2V)
3. ACL outlet pipe-to- ACL cover clamp — 4.6L (2V)
4. ACL outlet pipe — 4.6L (2V)
5. Crankcase breather tube — 4.6L (3V)
6. ACL outlet pipe-to-throttle body clamp — 4.6L (3V)
7. ACL outlet pipe-to- ACL cover clamp — 4.6L (3V)
8. ACL outlet pipe — 4.6L (3V)
9. ACL outlet pipe-to-throttle body adapter clamp — 5.4L (3V)
10. ACL outlet pipe-to- ACL cover clamp — 5.4L (3V)
11. ACL outlet pipe — 5.4L (3V)
12. ACL outlet pipe-to-throttle body adapter clamp — 6.2L (2V)
13. ACL outlet pipe-to- ACL cover clamp — 6.2L (2V)
14. ACL outlet pipe — 6.2L (2V)
15. Mass Air Flow (MAF) sensor screw (2 required)
16. MAF sensor
17. ACL cover
18. ACL element
19. Coolant expansion tank assembly

N0101946

Fig. 498 Exploded view of intake air system components

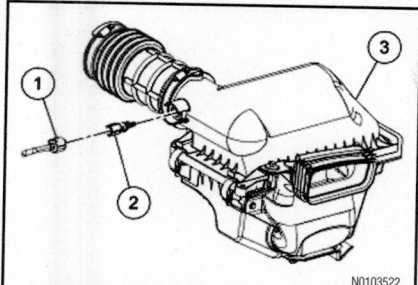

Fig. 499 Disconnect the IAT sensor electrical connector (1), and remove the IAT sensor (2) from the air cleaner (3)

REMOVAL & INSTALLATION

2010 Models

➡The manufacturer does not provide a specific Removal and Installation procedure for this component. Refer to the graphic(s) when servicing this component.

2011 3.5L GTDI Engine

See Figure 499.

1. Disconnect the Intake Air Temperature (IAT) sensor electrical connector.
2. Remove the IAT sensor.
3. Lift the tab and turn the IAT sensor counterclockwise to remove.
4. To install, reverse the removal procedure.
5. Make sure the IAT sensor tab is fully seated during installation.

KNOCK SENSOR (KS)

LOCATION

See Figures 500 through 505.

Refer to the accompanying illustrations.

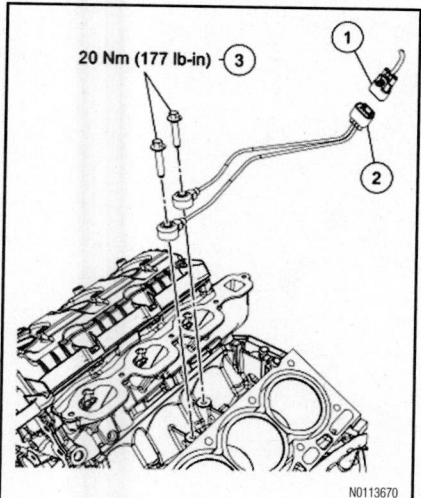

Fig. 500 Knock Sensor (KS) electrical connector (1), KS (2), and KS bolt (3)—3.5L GTDI and 3.7L Engines

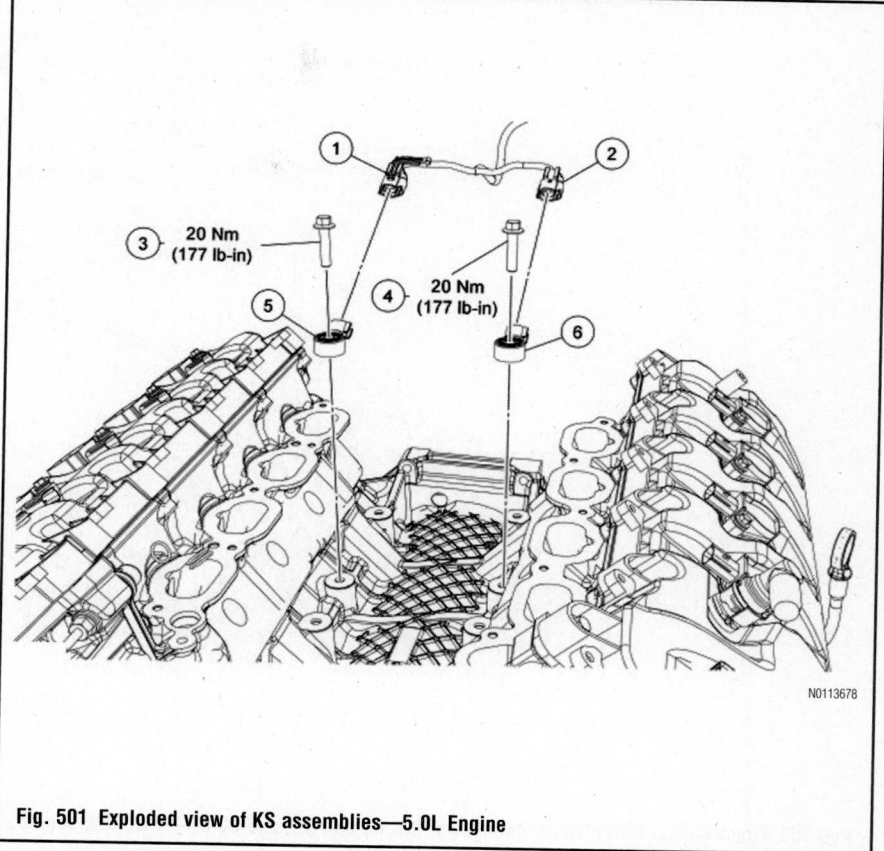

Fig. 501 Exploded view of KS assemblies—5.0L Engine

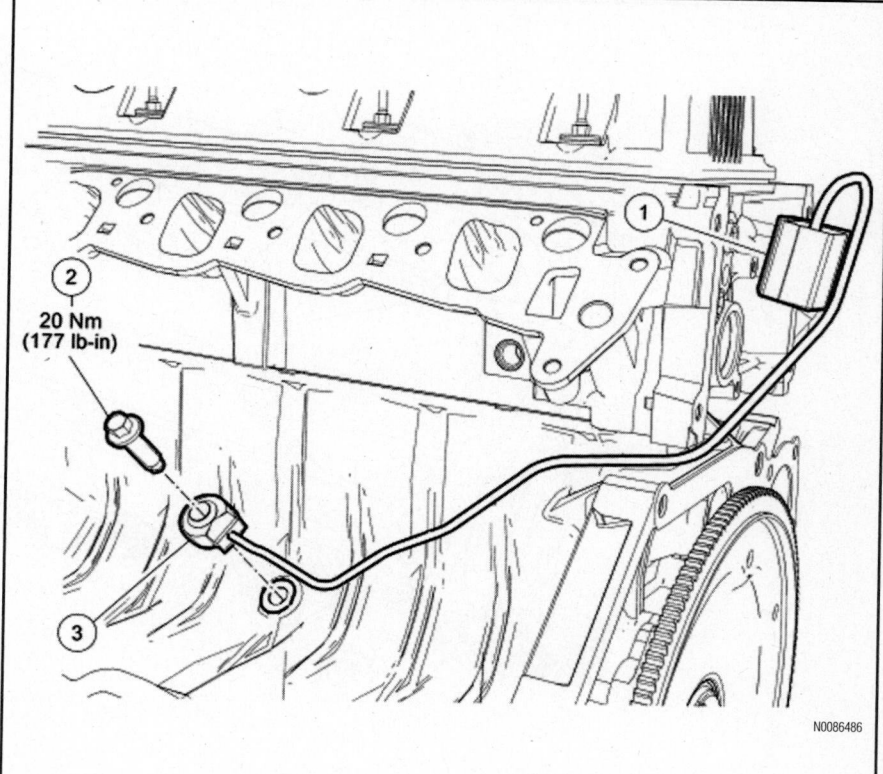

Fig. 502 Knock Sensor (KS) electrical connector (1), KS bolt (2), and KS (3)—4.6L (2V) engine

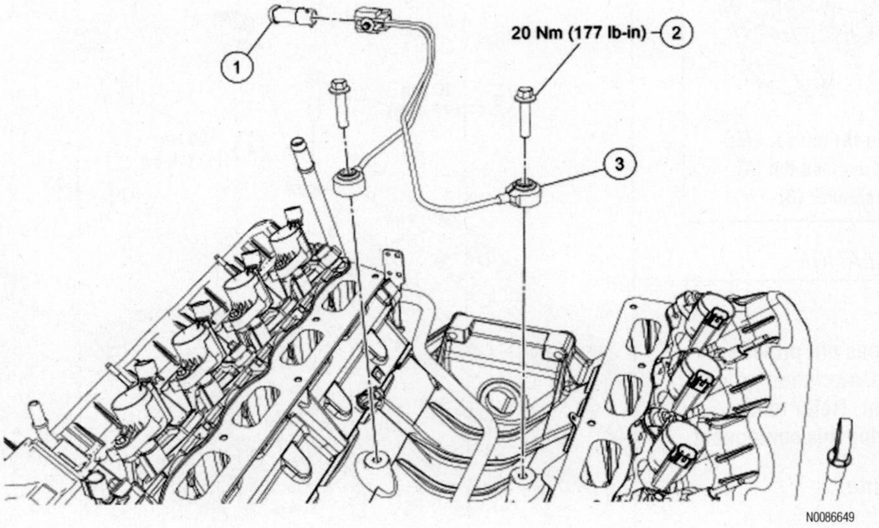

Fig. 503 Knock Sensor (KS) electrical connector (1), KS bolt (2), and KS (3)—4.6L (3V) engine

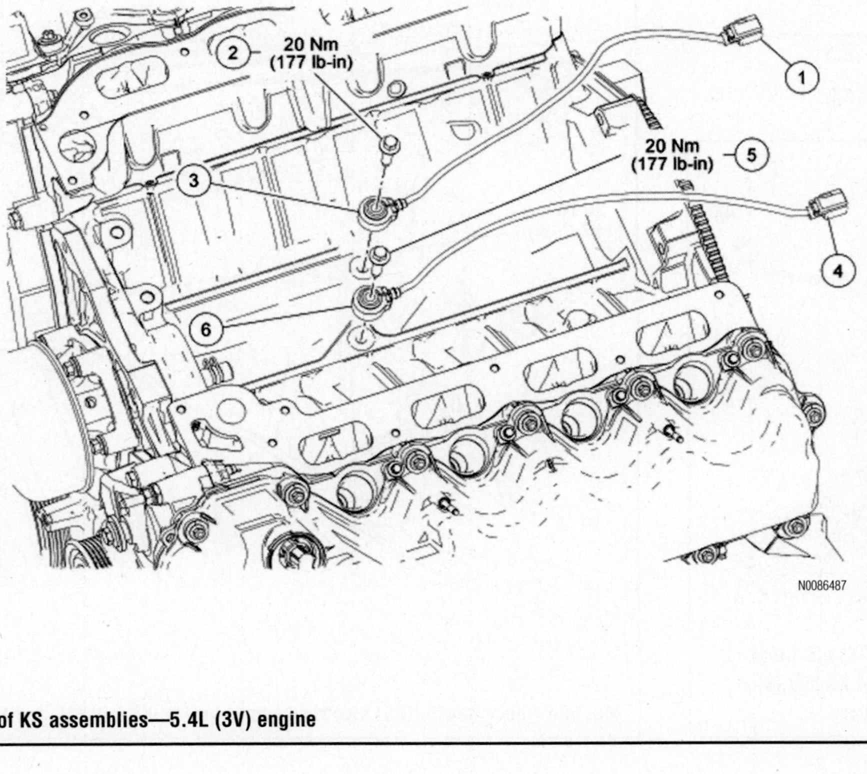

Fig. 504 Exploded view of KS assemblies—5.4L (3V) engine

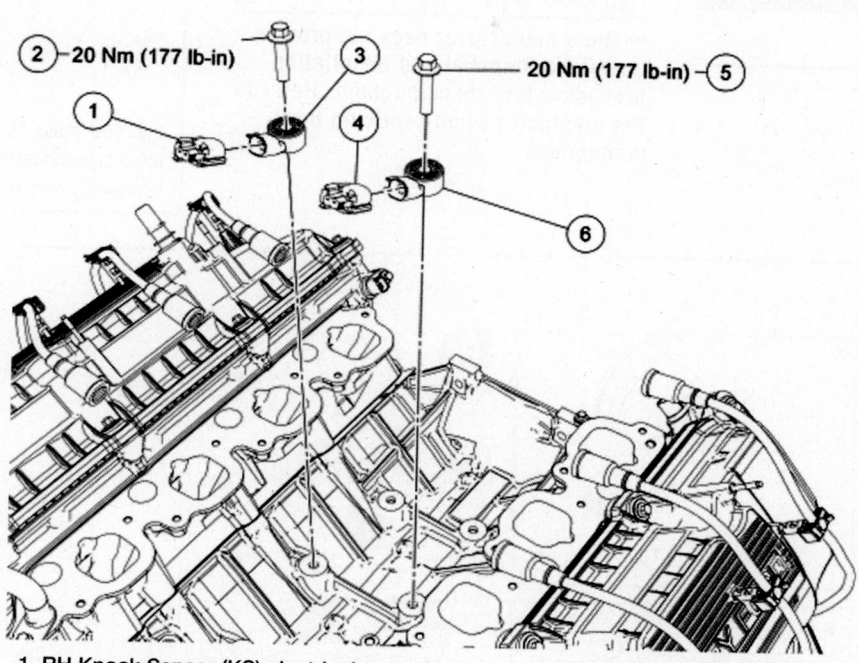

Fig. 505 Exploded view of KS assemblies—6.2L (2V) engine

1. RH Knock Sensor (KS) electrical connector
2. RH KS bolt
3. RH KS
4. LH KS electrical connector
5. LH KS bolt
6. LH KS

N0110682

REMOVAL & INSTALLATION

1. Remove the intake manifold.
2. Disconnect the Knock Sensor (KS) electrical connector.
3. Remove the bolt and the KS.
4. To install, reverse the removal procedure.
5. To install, tighten to 15 ft. lbs. (20 Nm).

MANIFOLD ABSOLUTE PRESSURE (MAP) SENSOR

LOCATION

See Figure 506.

Refer to the accompanying illustration.

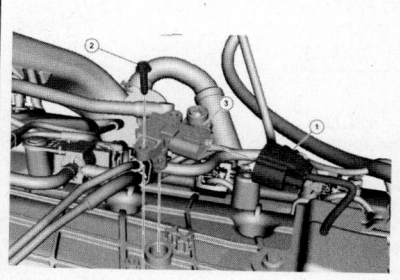

Fig. 506 Manifold Absolute Pressure (MAP)/Intake Air Temperature 2 (IAT2) sensor electrical connector (1), MAP/IAT2 sensor bolt (2), and MAP/IAT2 sensor (3)—3.5L GTDI engine

N0124479

REMOVAL & INSTALLATION

3.5L GTDI Engine

➡The Turbocharger Boost Pressure (TCBP)/Charge Air Cooler Temperature (CACT) sensor and the Manifold Absolute Pressure (MAP)/ Intake Air Temperature 2 (IAT2) sensor are not interchangeable.

1. Disconnect the MAP / IAT2 sensor electrical connector.
2. Remove the bolt and the MAP / IAT2 sensor.

To install:

3. Lubricate the MAP/IAT2 sensor O-ring seal with clean engine oil.

4. Install the MAP/IAT2 sensor and the bolt.

5. Connect the MAP/IAT2 sensor electrical connector.

MASS AIR FLOW (MAF) SENSOR

LOCATION

2010 Models

See Figure 507.

Refer to the accompanying illustration.

2011 Models (except 3.5L GTDI Engine)

See Figure 508.

Refer to the accompanying illustration.

REMOVAL & INSTALLATION

➡**The manufacturer does not provide a specific Removal and Installation procedure for this component. Refer to the graphic(s) when servicing this component.**

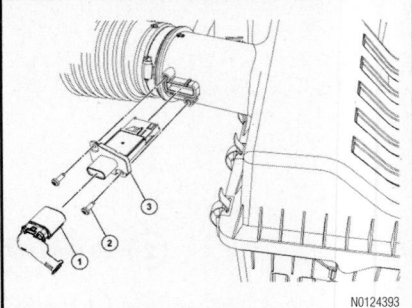

Fig. 508 Mass Air Flow (MAF) sensor electrical connector (1), MAF sensor screws (2), and MAF sensor (3)

N0124393

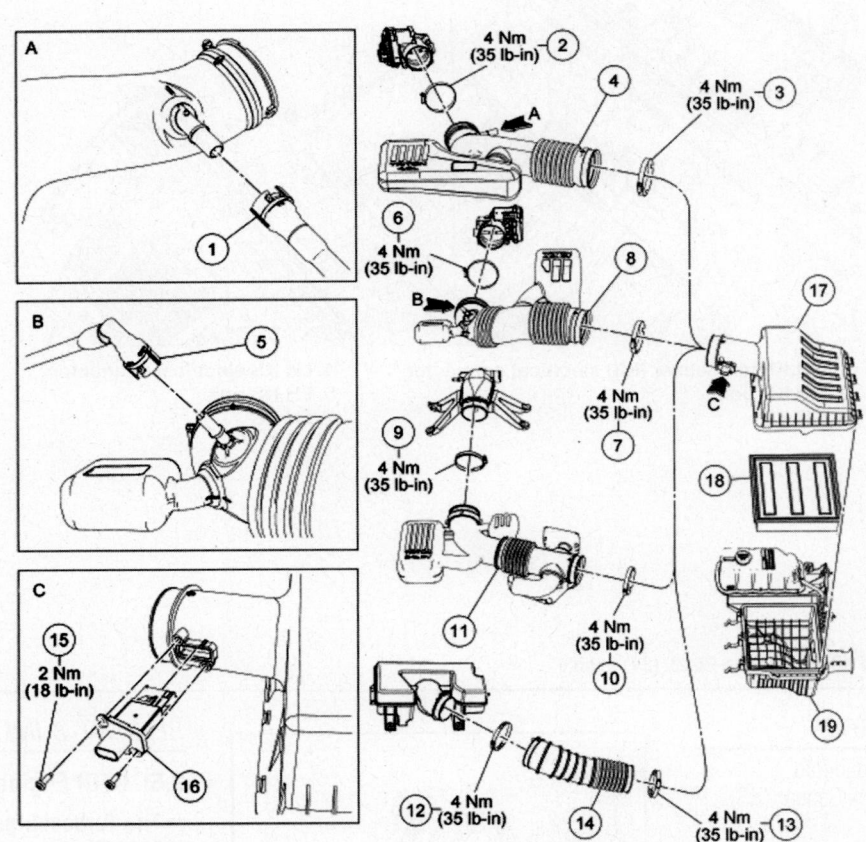

1. Crankcase breather tube — 4.6L (2V)
2. Air Cleaner (ACL) outlet pipe-to-throttle body clamp — 4.6L (2V)
3. ACL outlet pipe-to- ACL cover clamp — 4.6L (2V)
4. ACL outlet pipe — 4.6L (2V)
5. Crankcase breather tube — 4.6L (3V)
6. ACL outlet pipe-to-throttle body clamp — 4.6L (3V)
7. ACL outlet pipe-to- ACL cover clamp — 4.6L (3V)
8. ACL outlet pipe — 4.6L (3V)
9. ACL outlet pipe-to-throttle body adapter clamp — 5.4L (3V)
10. ACL outlet pipe-to- ACL cover clamp — 5.4L (3V)
11. ACL outlet pipe — 5.4L (3V)
12. ACL outlet pipe-to-throttle body adapter clamp — 6.2L (2V)
13. ACL outlet pipe-to- ACL cover clamp — 6.2L (2V)
14. ACL outlet pipe — 6.2L (2V)
15. Mass Air Flow (MAF) sensor screw (2 required)
16. MAF sensor
17. ACL cover
18. ACL element
19. Coolant expansion tank assembly

N0101946

Fig. 507 Exploded view of intake air system components

FUEL   **GASOLINE FUEL INJECTION SYSTEM**

FUEL SYSTEM SERVICE PRECAUTIONS

Safety is the most important factor when performing not only fuel system maintenance but any type of maintenance. Failure to conduct maintenance and repairs in a safe manner may result in serious personal injury or death. Maintenance and testing of the vehicle's fuel system components can be accomplished safely and effectively by adhering to the following rules and guidelines.

• To avoid the possibility of fire and personal injury, always disconnect the negative battery cable unless the repair or test procedure requires that battery voltage be applied.

• Always relieve the fuel system pressure prior to disconnecting any fuel system component (injector, fuel rail, pressure regulator, etc.), fitting or fuel line connection. Exercise extreme caution whenever relieving fuel system pressure to avoid exposing skin, face and eyes to fuel spray. Please be advised that fuel under pressure may penetrate the skin or any part of the body that it contacts.

• Always place a shop towel or cloth around the fitting or connection prior to loosening to absorb any excess fuel due to spillage. Ensure that all fuel spillage (should it occur) is quickly removed from engine surfaces. Ensure that all fuel soaked cloths or towels are deposited into a suitable waste container.

• Always keep a dry chemical (Class B) fire extinguisher near the work area.

• Do not allow fuel spray or fuel vapors to come into contact with a spark or open flame.

• Always use a back-up wrench when loosening and tightening fuel line connection fittings. This will prevent unnecessary stress and torsion to fuel line piping.

• Always replace worn fuel fitting O-rings with new Do not substitute fuel hose or equivalent where fuel pipe is installed.

✳✳ CAUTION

Do not smoke, carry lighted tobacco or have an open flame of any type when working on or near any fuel-related component. Highly flammable mixtures are always present and may be ignited. Failure to follow these instructions may result in serious personal injury.

✳✳ CAUTION

Before working on or disconnecting any of the fuel tubes or fuel system components, relieve the fuel system pressure to prevent accidental spraying of fuel. Fuel in the fuel system remains under high pressure, even when the engine is not running. Failure to follow this instruction may result in serious personal injury.

✳✳ CAUTION

Do not carry personal electronic devices such as cell phones, pagers or audio equipment of any type when working on or near any fuel-related component. Highly flammable mixtures are always present and may be ignited. Failure to follow these instructions may result in serious personal injury.

✳✳ CAUTION

When handling fuel, always observe fuel handling precautions and be prepared in the event of fuel spillage. Spilled fuel may be ignited by hot vehicle components or other ignition sources. Failure to follow these instructions may result in serious personal injury.

Before servicing the vehicle, make sure to also refer to the precautions in the beginning of this section as well.

RELIEVING FUEL SYSTEM PRESSURE

2010 Models

See Figures 509 through 513.

1. Refer to the fuel system precautions at the beginning of this section.
2. Disconnect the battery ground cable.
3. For the 5.4L (3V) engine, remove the air intake resonator assembly bolt and loosen the clamp. Rotate the air intake resonator assembly upward until it stops.
4. For the 4.6L (3V) engine, remove the Evaporative Emission (EVAP) purge valve bracket bolt and position the bracket aside.

➡**4.6L (2V) shown, 4.6L (3V) and 5.4L (3V) similar.**

5. Remove the fuel pressure relief valve cap.

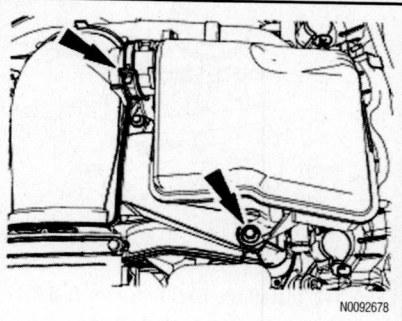

Fig. 509 Remove the air intake resonator assembly bolt and loosen the clamp

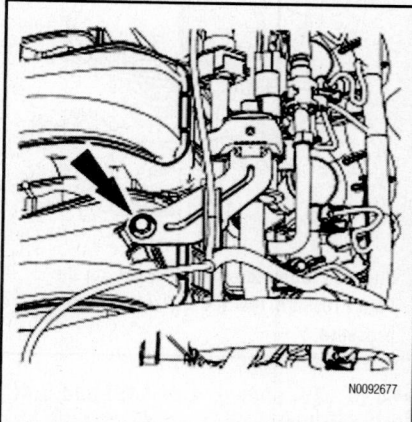

Fig. 510 Remove the Evaporative Emission (EVAP) purge valve bracket bolt and position the bracket aside

➡**4.6L (2V) shown, 4.6L (3V) and 5.4L (3V) similar.**

6. Install the Fuel Pressure Test Kit onto the fuel pressure relief valve.

➡**Open the manual valve slowly to relieve the system pressure. This may drain fuel from the fuel system. Place fuel in a suitable container.**

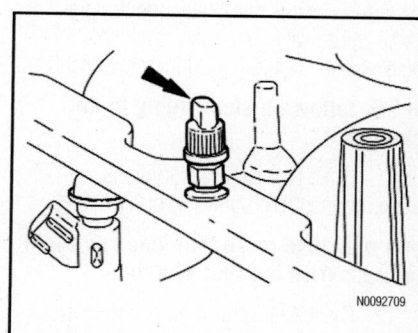

Fig. 511 Remove the fuel pressure relief valve cap

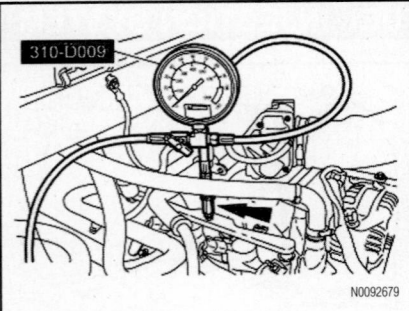

Fig. 512 Install the Fuel Pressure Test Kit onto the fuel pressure relief valve

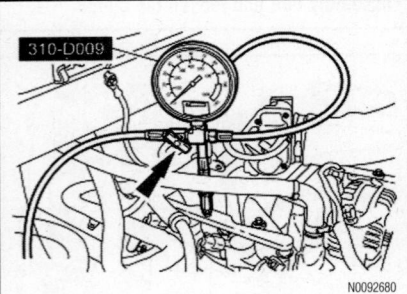

Fig. 513 Open the manual valve on the Fuel Pressure Test Kit and relieve the pressure

➡**4.6L (2V) shown, 4.6L (3V) and 5.4L (3V) similar.**

7. Open the manual valve on the Fuel Pressure Test Kit and relieve the pressure.

➡**4.6L (2V) shown, 4.6L (3V) and 5.4L (3V) similar.**

8. Install the fuel pressure relief valve cap.

9. For the 5.4L (3V) engine, once fuel system service is complete, loosen the clamp and rotate the air intake resonator assembly into position and install the bolt. Tighten to 89 inch lbs. (10 Nm).

10. For the 4.6L (3V) engine, once fuel system service is complete, position the EVAP purge valve into place and install the bracket bolt. Tighten to 89 inch lbs. (10 Nm).

➡**The following steps apply to all engines.**

11. Once fuel system service is complete, connect the battery ground cable.

➡**It may take more than one key cycle to pressurize the fuel system.**

12. Cycle the ignition key to the ON position and wait 3 seconds to pressurize the fuel system. Check for leaks before starting the engine.

2011 Models

See Figure 514.

1. Refer to the fuel system precautions at the beginning of this section.

2. With the vehicle in NEUTRAL, position it on a hoist.

➡**The Fuel Pump Control Module (FPCM) is located on the frame rail above the spare tire.**

3. Disconnect the Fuel Pump Control Module (FPCM) electrical connector.

4. Start the engine and allow it to idle until it stalls.

5. After the engine stalls, crank the engine for approximately 5 seconds to make sure the fuel rail pressure has been released.

6. Turn the ignition switch to the OFF position.

➡**The following steps are for Gasoline Turbocharged Direct Injection (GTDI) equipped vehicles**

➡**On vehicles equipped with Gasoline Turbocharged Direct Injection (GTDI), it is necessary to release the high pressure fuel system prior to disconnecting a low pressure fuel tube quick connect coupling.**

➡**To release the fuel pressure in the high pressure fuel tube, wrap the flare nut with a shop towel to absorb any residual fuel pressure during the loosening of the flare nut.**

7. Disconnect the high pressure fuel tube-to-fuel injection pump flare nut to release the fuel pressure.

8. Connect the high pressure fuel tube-to-fuel injection pump flare nut. Tighten to 22 ft. lbs. (30 Nm).

➡**The following steps are for all vehicles.**

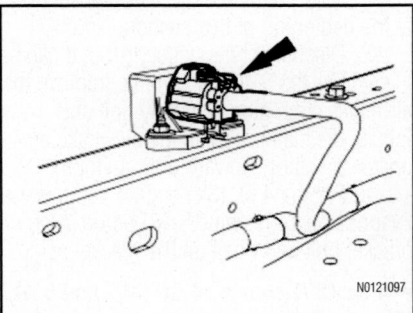

Fig. 514 Disconnect the Fuel Pump Control Module (FPCM) electrical connector

9. When fuel system service is complete, reconnect the FPCM electrical connector.

➡**It may take more than one key cycle to pressurize the fuel system.**

10. Cycle the ignition key and wait 3 seconds to pressurize the fuel system. Check for leaks before starting the engine.

11. Start the vehicle and check the fuel system for leaks.

FUEL FILTER

REMOVAL & INSTALLATION

The fuel filter is serviced as a part of the fuel pump module.

FUEL INJECTORS

REMOVAL & INSTALLATION

3.5L GTDI Engine

See Figures 515 through 525.

➡**A clean working environment is essential to prevent dirt or foreign material contamination.**

1. Refer to the fuel system precautions at the beginning of this section.

2. Release the fuel system pressure.

3. Disconnect the battery ground cable.

4. Remove the intake manifold.

5. Remove the fuel injection pump noise insulator shield.

➡**To release the fuel pressure in the high pressure fuel tube, wrap the fuel injection pump flare nut with a shop towel to absorb any residual fuel pressure during the loosening of the fuel injection pump flare nut.**

6. Loosen the high pressure fuel tube-to-fuel injection pump flare nut.

   a. Loosen the high pressure fuel tube-to-LH fuel rail flare nut.

   b. Loosen the high pressure fuel tube-to-RH fuel rail flare nut.

   c. Remove and discard the high pressure fuel tube.

7. Remove and discard the high pressure fuel tube bracket nut and bolt.

8. If necessary, disconnect the Fuel Rail Pressure (FRP) sensor electrical connector.

⁂ WARNING

Pull out the fuel rails in the direction of the fuel injector axis or damage may occur to the fuel injectors.

➡**Use compressed air and remove any dirt or foreign material from the cylin-**

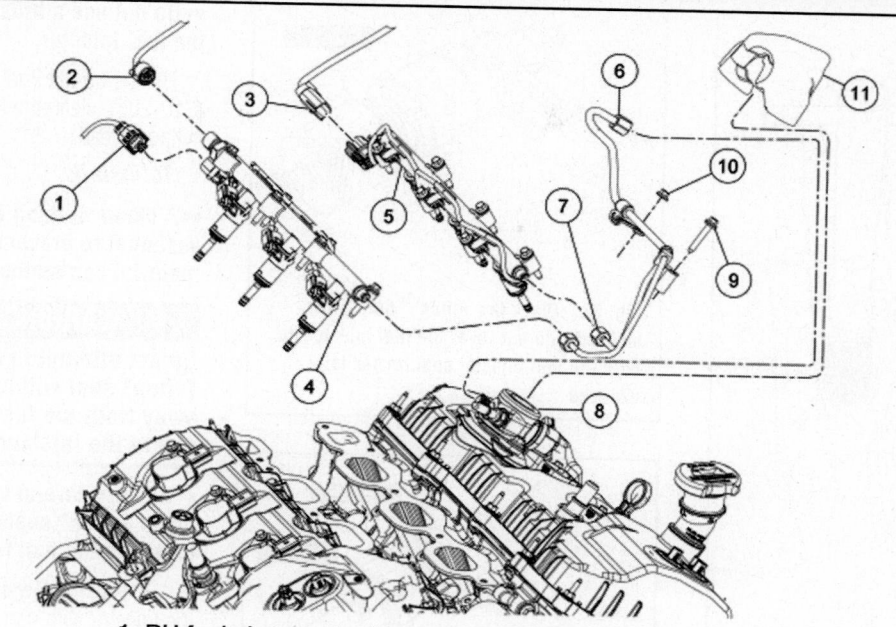

1. RH fuel charge wire harness electrical connector
2. Fuel Rail Pressure (FRP) sensor electrical connector
3. LH fuel charge wire harness electrical connector
4. RH fuel rail
5. LH fuel rail
6. High pressure fuel tube-to-fuel injection pump flare nut
7. High pressure fuel tube-to-fuel rail flare nut
8. Fuel injection pump
9. High pressure fuel tube bracket bolt
10. High pressure fuel tube bracket nut
11. Fuel injection pump noise insulator shield

Fig. 515 Exploded view of the fuel rail assembly

N0119479

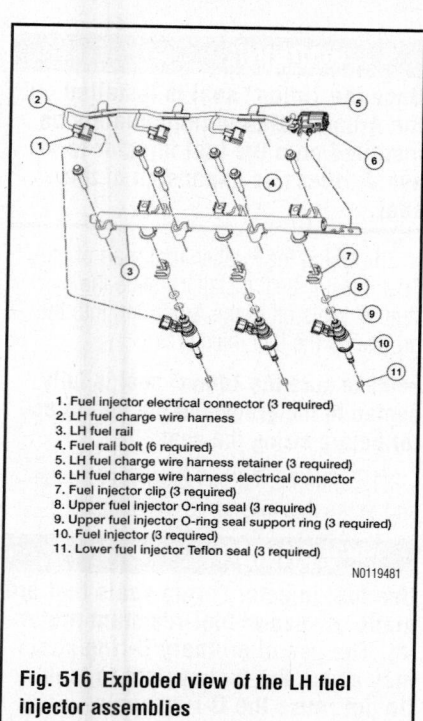

1. Fuel injector electrical connector (3 required)
2. LH fuel charge wire harness
3. LH fuel rail
4. Fuel rail bolt (6 required)
5. LH fuel charge wire harness retainer (3 required)
6. LH fuel charge wire harness electrical connector
7. Fuel injector clip (3 required)
8. Upper fuel injector O-ring seal (3 required)
9. Upper fuel injector O-ring seal support ring (3 required)
10. Fuel injector (3 required)
11. Lower fuel injector Teflon seal (3 required)

N0119481

Fig. 516 Exploded view of the LH fuel injector assemblies

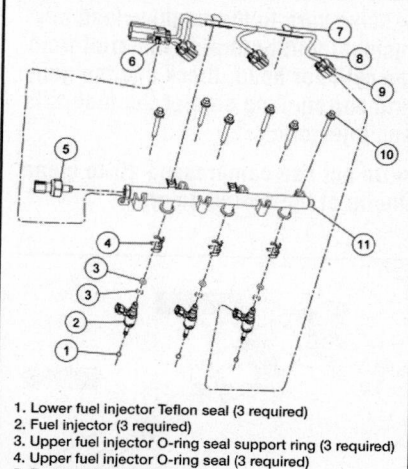

1. Lower fuel injector Teflon seal (3 required)
2. Fuel injector (3 required)
3. Upper fuel injector O-ring seal support ring (3 required)
4. Upper fuel injector O-ring seal (3 required)
5. Fuel injector clip (3 required)
6. FRP sensor
7. RH fuel charge wire harness electrical connector
8. RH fuel charge wire harness retainer (2 required)
9. RH fuel charge wire harness
10. Fuel injector electrical connector (3 required)
11. Fuel rail bolt (6 required)
12. RH fuel rail

N0119480

Fig. 517 Exploded view of the RH fuel injector assemblies

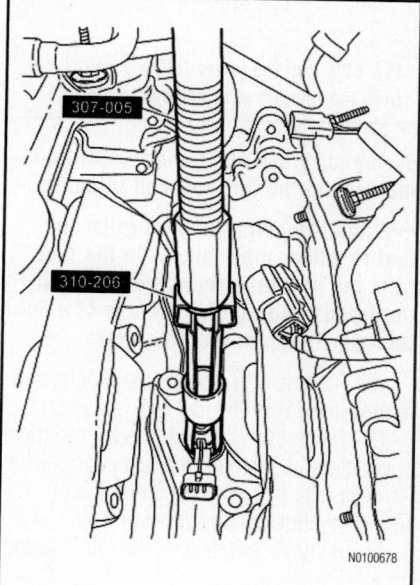

N0100678

Fig. 518 Using the Slide Hammer and the Fuel Injector Remover, remove the fuel injectors

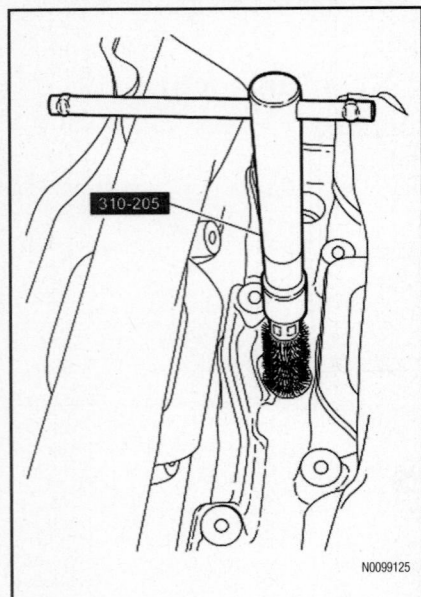

Fig. 519 Using the Fuel Injector Brush, clean the fuel injector bore in the cylinder head

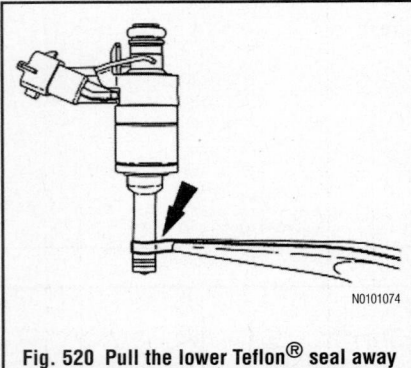

Fig. 520 Pull the lower Teflon® seal away from the injector with narrow tip pliers

der head, block and general surrounding area of the fuel rail and injectors.

➡**When removing the fuel rails, the fuel injectors may remain in the fuel rails but normally remain in the cylinder heads and require the use of a Fuel Injector Remover tool to extract.**

9. Remove and discard the 6 bolts and remove the LH or RH fuel rail.

10. Disconnect the fuel injector electrical connectors, disconnect the fuel charge wire harness retainers from the fuel rail and remove the fuel charge wire harness.

11. Remove and discard the fuel injector clips.

12. Remove and discard the upper fuel injector O-ring seals.

13. Remove and discard the upper fuel injector O-ring seal support rings.

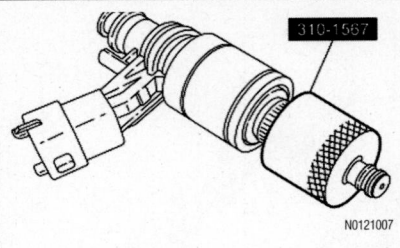

Fig. 521 Place the Teflon® Seal Sizer, knurled side out, over the fuel injector tip until the fuel injector seal recess is exposed

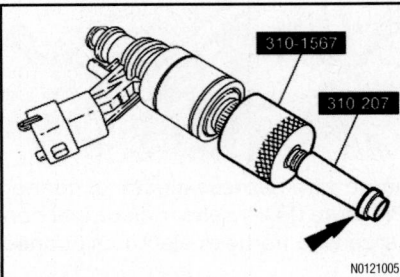

Fig. 522 Install the new lower Teflon® seals on the narrow end of the Arbor (310-207) (part of the Fuel Injector Seal Installer), then install the Arbor on the fuel injector tips

14. Using the Slide Hammer (307-005) and the Fuel Injector Remover (310-206), remove the fuel injectors.

➡**Make sure to thoroughly clean any residual fuel or foreign material from the cylinder head, block and the general surrounding area of the fuel rails and injectors.**

➡**Do not use compressed air to clean the tip of the fuel injector.**

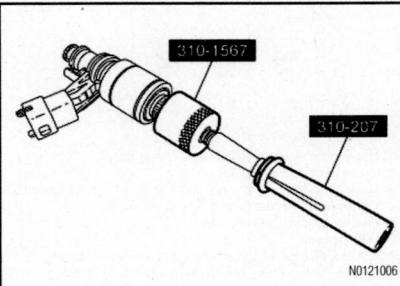

Fig. 523 Using the Pusher Tool (part of the Fuel Injector Seal Installer), slide the Teflon® seals off of the Arbor and into the groove on the fuel injectors

➡**Do not use a brush to clean the tip of the fuel injector.**

15. Using the Fuel Injector Brush (310-205), clean the fuel injector bore in the cylinder head.

To install:

➡**A clean working environment is essential to prevent dirt or foreign material contamination.**

✳✳ **WARNING**

Do not attempt to cut the lower Teflon® seal without first pulling it away from the fuel injector or damage to the injector may occur.

➡**Be very careful when removing the lower Teflon® seals, not to scratch, nick or gouge the fuel injectors.**

16. Pull the lower Teflon® seal away from the injector with narrow tip pliers.

17. Carefully cut and discard the lower fuel injector Teflon® seals.

18. Place the Teflon® Seal Sizer (310-1567), knurled side out, over the fuel injector tip until the fuel injector seal recess is exposed.

➡**Do not lubricate the new lower Teflon® fuel injector seals.**

19. Install the new lower Teflon® seals on the narrow end of the Arbor (part of the Fuel Injector Seal Installer), then install the Arbor on the fuel injector tips.

✳✳ **WARNING**

Once the Teflon® seal is installed on the Arbor, it should immediately be installed onto the fuel injector to avoid excessive expansion of the seal.

20. Using the Pusher Tool (part of the Fuel Injector Seal Installer), slide the Teflon® seals off of the Arbor and into the groove on the fuel injectors.

➡**Make sure the Teflon® seal is fully seated in the groove on the fuel injector before sizing the seal.**

21. Slide the Teflon® Seal Sizer off the end of the fuel injector to size the seal.

✳✳ **WARNING**

Use fuel injector O-ring seals that are made of special fuel-resistant material. The use of ordinary O-ring seals may cause the fuel system to leak. Do not reuse the O-ring seals.

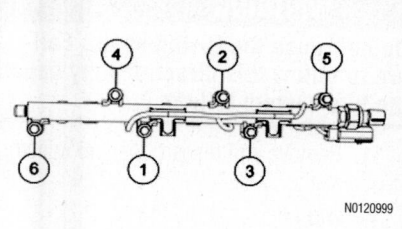

Fig. 524 Push down on the fuel rail face above the injectors and tighten in the sequence shown

➡**Do not lubricate any fuel injector seals.**

➡**Install the fuel injectors into the cylinder head within 15 minutes due to Teflon® seal expansion.**

22. Install the new upper fuel injector O-ring seals.

23. Install the new fuel injector clips.

➡**The anti-rotation finger of the fuel injector clip must slip into the groove of the fuel rail cup.**

➡**The fuel rail pressure sensor must be replaced if it is removed from the RH fuel rail.**

24. Install the fuel injectors into the fuel rails.

　　a. Install the fuel charge wire harness to the fuel rail and connect the harness retainers.

　　b. Connect the electrical connectors.

⁂ **WARNING**

It is very important to visually inspect the routing of the fuel charge wire harness to make sure that they will not be pinched or damaged between the fuel rail and the cylinder head during installation.

➡**Tighten the bolts using a method that draws the fuel rail evenly to the head, preventing a rocking motion.**

25. If necessary, install the 6 new bolts and the RH fuel rail assembly.

　　a. Push down on the fuel rail face above the injectors and tighten in the sequence shown.

　　b. Tighten to 89 inch lbs. (10 Nm).

　　c. Tighten an additional 45 degrees.

⁂ **WARNING**

It is very important to visually inspect the routing of the fuel charge wire

harness to make sure that they will not be pinched or damaged between the fuel rail and the cylinder head during installation.

➡**Tighten the bolts using a method that draws the fuel rail evenly to the head, preventing a rocking motion.**

26. If necessary, install the 6 new bolts and the LH fuel rail assembly:

　　a. Push down on the fuel rail face above the injectors and tighten in the sequence shown.

　　b. Tighten to 89 inch lbs. (10 Nm).

　　c. Tighten an additional 45 degrees.

27. If necessary, Connect the FRP sensor electrical connector.

➡**To install, apply clean engine oil to the threads of the 3 high-pressure fuel tube flare nuts.**

28. Position a new high-pressure fuel tube and hand start the 3 flare nuts in the following order:

　　a. Hand tighten the high pressure fuel tube-to-RH fuel rail flare nut.

　　b. Hand tighten the high pressure fuel tube-to-LH fuel rail flare nut.

　　c. Hand tighten the high pressure fuel tube-to-fuel injection pump flare nut.

29. Loosely install a new high pressure fuel tube bracket nut.

30. Loosely install a new high pressure fuel tube bracket bolt.

31. Tighten the 3 high-pressure fuel tube flare nuts in the following order.

　　a. Tighten the high pressure fuel tube-to-RH fuel rail flare nut.

　　b. Tighten to 10 ft. lbs. (15 Nm).

　　c. Tighten an additional 30 degrees.

　　d. Tighten to 24 ft. lbs. (32 Nm).

　　e. Tighten the high pressure fuel tube-to-LH fuel rail flare nut.

　　f. Tighten to 10 ft. lbs. (15 Nm).

　　g. Tighten an additional 30 degrees.

　　h. Tighten to 24 ft. lbs. (32 Nm).

　　i. Tighten the high pressure fuel tube-to-fuel injection pump flare nut.

　　j. Tighten to 10 ft. lbs. (15 Nm).

　　k. Tighten an additional 30 degrees.

　　l. Tighten to 24 ft. lbs. (32 Nm).

32. Tighten the high-pressure fuel tube bracket bolt.

　　a. Tighten to 89 inch lbs. (10 Nm).

　　b. Tighten and additional 45 degrees.

33. Tighten the high-pressure fuel tube bracket nut. Tighten to 71 inch lbs. (8 Nm).

34. Install the fuel injection pump noise insulator shield.

35. Install the intake manifold.

36. Connect the battery ground cable.

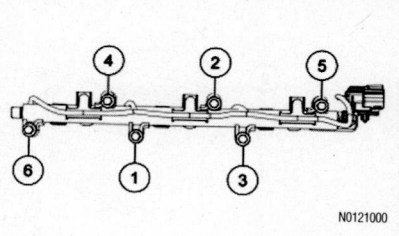

Fig. 525 Push down on the fuel rail face above the injectors and tighten in the sequence shown

3.7L Engine

See Figure 526.

1. Refer to the fuel system precautions at the beginning of this section.

2. Release the fuel system pressure.

3. Disconnect the battery ground cable.

4. Remove the upper intake manifold.

5. Disconnect the fuel tube-to-fuel rail quick connect coupling.

6. Remove the LH and RH fuel rail noise insulator shields.

7. Disconnect the 6 fuel injector electrical connectors.

8. Remove the 4 fuel rail bolts.

9. Remove the fuel rail and injectors as an assembly.

10. Remove the 6 fuel injector clips and the 6 fuel injectors.

11. Remove and discard the 12 fuel injector O-ring seals.

To install:

⁂ **WARNING**

Use O-ring seals that are made of special fuel-resistant material. The use of ordinary O-rings may cause the fuel system to leak. Do not reuse the O-ring seals.

➡**The upper and lower fuel injector O-ring seals are similar in appearance, but are not interchangeable.**

12. Install the new O-ring seals onto the fuel injectors and lubricate them with clean engine oil.

13. Install the 6 fuel injectors and the 6 fuel injector clips into the fuel rail.

14. Install the fuel rail and fuel injectors as an assembly.

15. Install the 4 fuel rail bolts. Tighten to 89 inch lbs. (10 Nm).

16. Connect the 6 fuel injector electrical connectors.

17. Install the LH and RH fuel rail noise insulator shields.

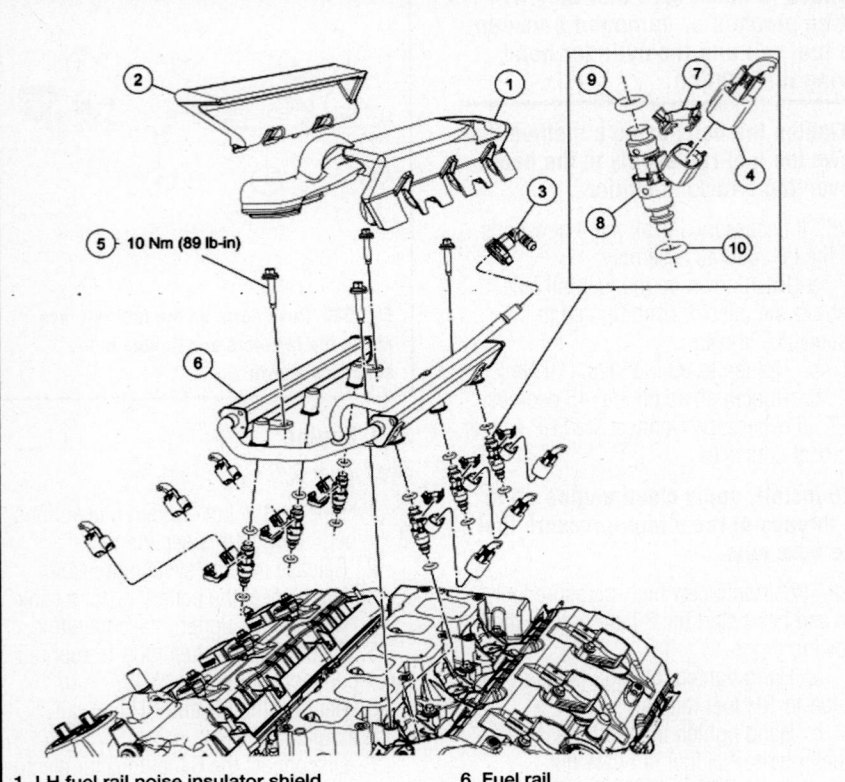

1. LH fuel rail noise insulator shield
2. RH fuel rail noise insulator shield
3. Fuel tube-to-fuel rail quick connect coupling
4. Fuel injector electrical connector (6 required)
5. Fuel rail bolt (4 required)
6. Fuel rail
7. Fuel injector clip (6 required)
8. Fuel injector (6 required)
9. Upper fuel injector O-ring seal (6 required)
10. Lower fuel injector O-ring seal (6 required)

N0114067

Fig. 526 Exploded view of the fuel rail and fuel injector assemblies

18. Connect the fuel tube-to-fuel rail quick connect coupling.
19. Install the upper intake manifold.
20. Connect the battery ground cable.

5.0L Engine

See Figures 527 and 528.

1. Refer to the fuel system precautions at the beginning of this section.
2. Release the fuel system pressure.
3. Disconnect the battery ground cable.
4. Disconnect the 2 Evaporative Emission (EVAP) tube retaining clips from the fuel rail.
5. Remove the LH and RH fuel rail insulators.
6. Disconnect the 8 fuel injector electrical connectors.
7. Disconnect the fuel supply tube.
8. Remove the 4 fuel rail bolts.
9. Remove the fuel rail and fuel injectors as an assembly from the intake manifold.
10. Remove the retaining clips and fuel injectors from the fuel rail.

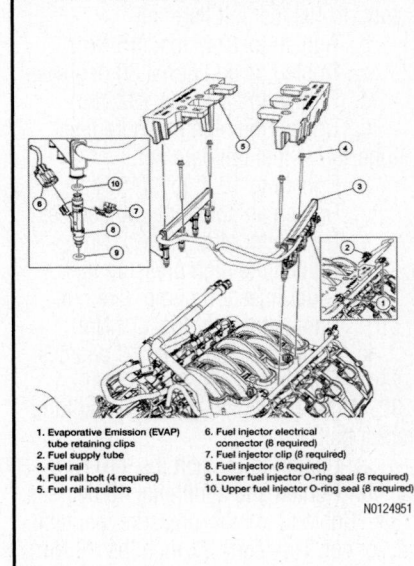

1. Evaporative Emission (EVAP) tube retaining clips
2. Fuel supply tube
3. Fuel rail
4. Fuel rail bolt (4 required)
5. Fuel rail insulators
6. Fuel injector electrical connector (8 required)
7. Fuel injector clip (8 required)
8. Fuel injector (8 required)
9. Lower fuel injector O-ring seal (8 required)
10. Upper fuel injector O-ring seal (8 required)

N0124951

Fig. 527 Exploded view of the fuel rail and fuel injector assemblies

❊❊ WARNING

Do not reuse the O-ring seals. Failure to follow this direction may cause the fuel system to leak.

11. Remove and discard the fuel injector O-ring seals.

To install:

❊❊ WARNING

Use O-ring seals that are made of special fuel-resistant material. Use of ordinary O-ring seals may cause the fuel system to leak.

12. Install new O-ring seals on the fuel injectors.

➡ **The fuel injector clip can be reused if it is not damaged during removal. If the clip is reused, the 2 sides of the clip should be squeezed back into shape by placing it between index finger and thumb.**

➡ **Lubricate the upper and lower fuel injector O-ring seals with clean engine oil prior to installation.**

13. Install the fuel injectors and retaining clips onto the fuel rail.
14. Install the fuel rail and fuel injectors as an assembly onto the intake manifold.
15. Install the 4 bolts and tighten in the sequence shown in 3 stages.
   a. Stage 1: Hand tighten.
   b. Stage 2: Tighten to 89 inch lbs. (10 Nm).

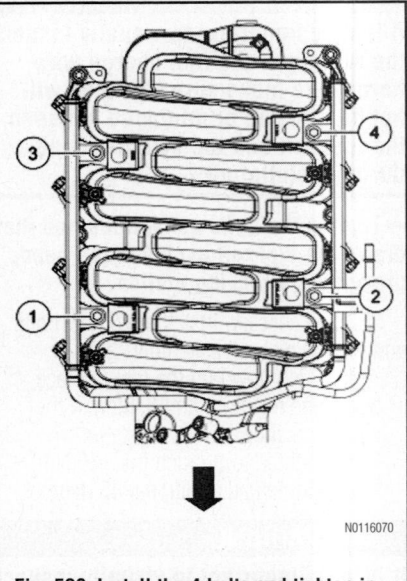

N0116070

Fig. 528 Install the 4 bolts and tighten in the sequence shown in 3 stages

c. Stage 3: Tighten an additional 90 degrees.

16. Connect the fuel supply tube.

17. Connect the 8 fuel injector electrical connectors.

18. Install the LH and RH fuel rail insulators.

19. Connect the 2 EVAP tube retaining clips to the fuel rail.

20. Connect the battery ground cable.

➡**For the following engines, the manufacturer does not provide a specific Removal and Installation procedure for this component. Refer to the graphic(s) when servicing this component.**

4.6L (2V) Engine

See Figure 529.

The manufacturer does not provide a procedure for this engine. Refer to the accompanying illustration when servicing this component.

4.6L (3V) Engine

See Figure 530.

The manufacturer does not provide a procedure for this engine. Refer to the accompanying illustration when servicing this component.

5.4L (3V) Engine

See Figure 531.

The manufacturer does not provide a procedure for this engine. Refer to the

accompanying illustration when servicing this component.

6.2L (2V) Engine

See Figure 532.

> **✳✳ WARNING**
>
> **Fuel injection equipment is manufactured to very precise tolerances and fine clearances. It is therefore essential that absolute cleanliness is observed when working with these components. Always install blanking plugs to any open orifices or tubes.**

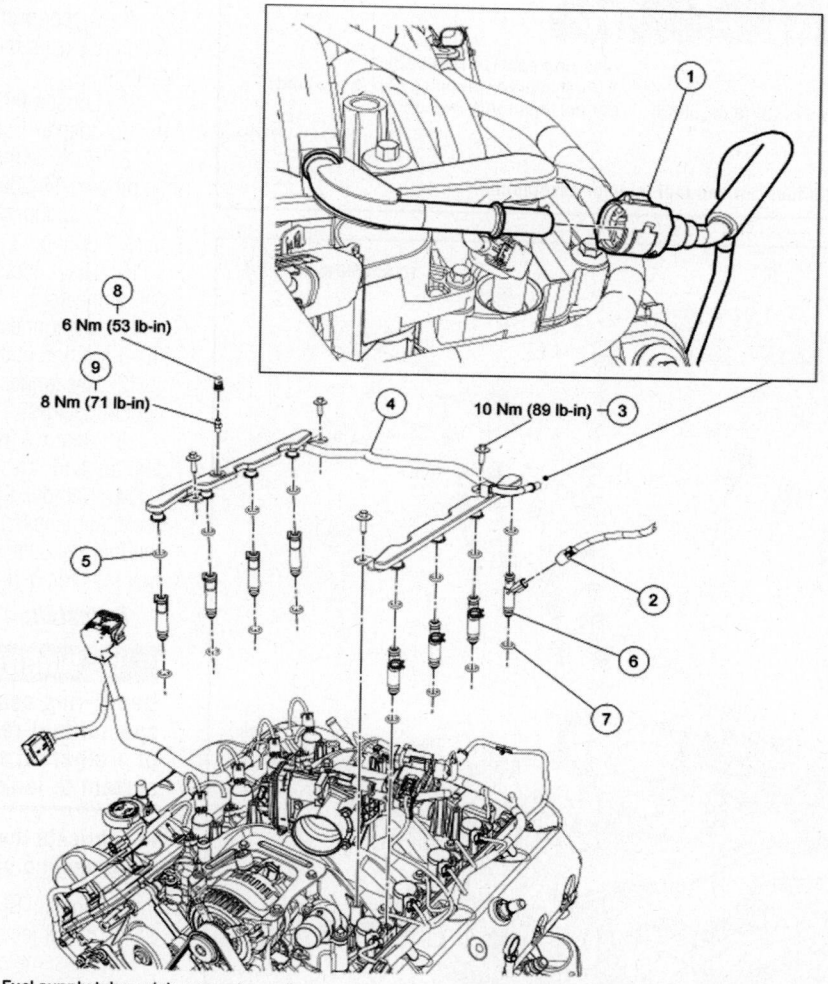

1. Fuel supply tube quick connect coupling
2. Fuel injector electrical connector (8 required)
3. Fuel rail bolt (4 required)
4. Fuel rail
5. Fuel injector-to-fuel rail O-ring seal (8 required)
6. Fuel injector (8 required)
7. Fuel injector-to-intake manifold O-ring seal (8 required)
8. Fuel pressure relief valve cap
9. Fuel pressure relief valve

N0101542

Fig. 529 Exploded view of the fuel rail and fuel injector assemblies

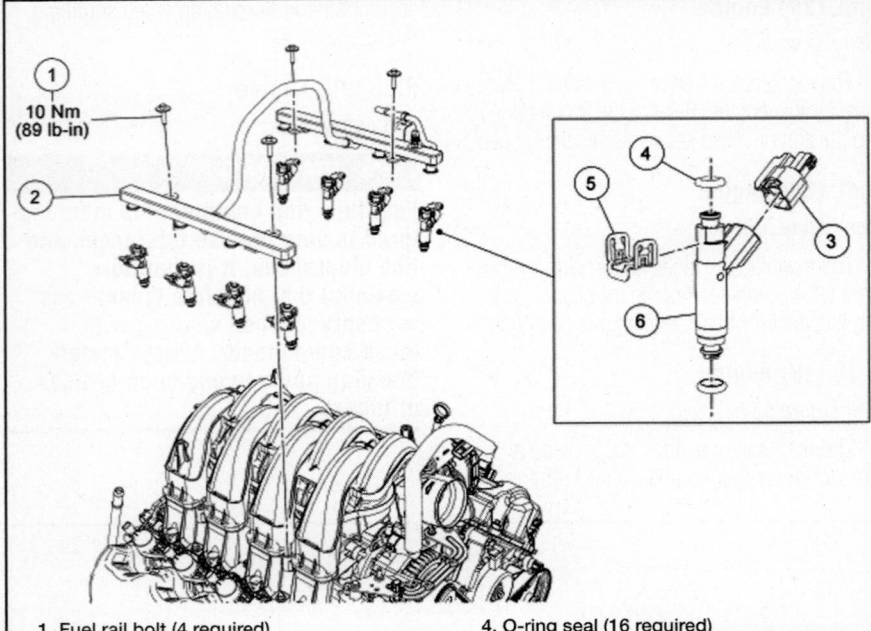

1. Fuel rail bolt (4 required)
2. Fuel rail
3. Fuel injector electrical connector (8 required)
4. O-ring seal (16 required)
5. Fuel injector retaining clip (8 required)
6. Fuel injector (8 required)

N0091133

Fig. 530 Exploded view of the fuel rail and fuel injector assemblies

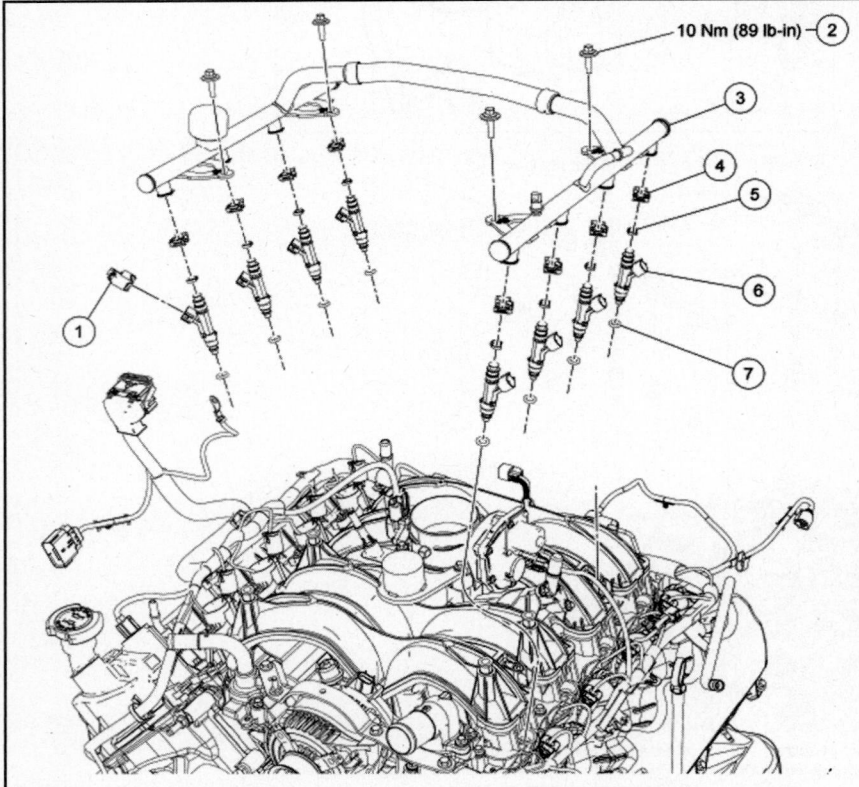

1. Fuel injector electrical connector (8 required)
2. Fuel rail bolt (4 required)
3. Fuel rail
4. Fuel injector-to-fuel rail locking clip (8 required)
5. Fuel injector-to-fuel rail O-ring (8 required)
6. Fuel injector (8 required)
7. Fuel injector-to-intake manifold O-ring (8 required)

N0101540

Fig. 531 Exploded view of the fuel rail and fuel injector assemblies

✴✴ WARNING

When reusing liquid or vapor tube connectors, make sure to use compressed air to remove any foreign material from the connector retaining clip area before separating from the tube.

1. Refer to the fuel system precautions at the beginning of this section.
2. Disconnect the battery ground cable.
3. Remove the Air Cleaner (ACL) outlet tube.
4. Disconnect the heater coolant hose retainer from the ACL outlet pipe-to-Throttle Body (TB) adapter.
5. Disconnect the crankcase ventilation tube quick connect fitting from the ACL outlet pipe-to-TB adapter.
6. Disconnect the brake booster vacuum hose from the ACL outlet pipe-to-TB adapter.
7. Loosen the clamp and disconnect the TB adapter from the TB.
8. Remove the 2 bolts and the ACL outlet pipe-to-TB adapter.
9. Disconnect the fuel tube quick connect coupling.
10. Disconnect the 8 ignition coil electrical connectors.
11. Disconnect the 8 ignition wires from the 8 ignition coils.
12. Disconnect the 8 fuel injector electrical connectors.
13. Remove the 4 fuel rail bolts and the fuel rail and injectors as an assembly.
14. Remove the fuel injector-to-fuel rail locks and separate the 8 fuel injectors from the fuel rail. Discard the upper and lower fuel injector O-ring seals.

To install:

✴✴ WARNING

Use O-ring seals that are made of special fuel-resistant material. Use of ordinary O-rings can cause the fuel system to leak.

➡**Lubricate the new O-ring seals with clean engine oil prior to installation.**

15. Install 16 new O-ring seals on each of the fuel injectors.
16. Assemble the 8 fuel injectors onto the fuel rail and install the 8 fuel injector retaining clips.
17. Install the fuel rail and fuel injectors as an assembly onto the intake manifold.
18. Install the 4 fuel rail bolts in 2 stages.

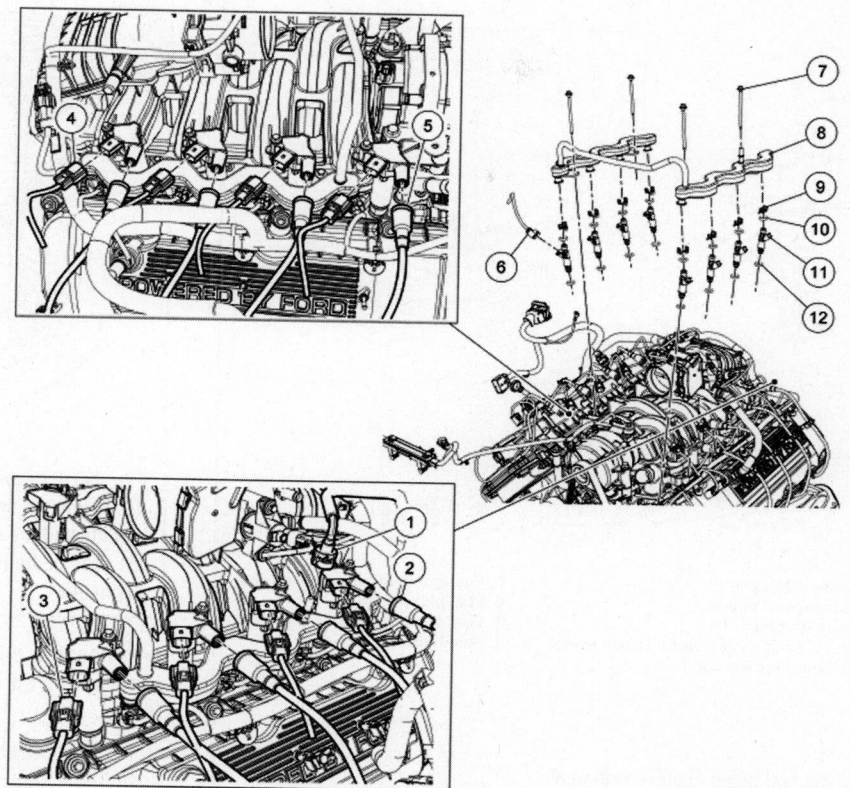

1. Fuel supply tube quick connect coupling
2. LH ignition wire (4 required)
3. LH ignition coil electrical connector (4 required)
4. RH ignition coil electrical connector (4 required)
5. RH ignition wire (4 required)
6. Fuel injector electrical connector (8 required)
7. Fuel rail bolt (4 required)
8. Fuel rail
9. Fuel injector-to-fuel rail locking clip (8 required)
10. Fuel injector-to-fuel rail O-ring (8 required)
11. Fuel injector (8 required)
12. Fuel injector-to-intake manifold O-ring (8 required)

N0110026

Fig. 532 Exploded view of the fuel rail and fuel injector assemblies

a. Stage 1: Tighten to 89 inch lbs. (10 Nm).

b. Stage 2: Tighten an additional 90 degrees.

19. Connect the 8 fuel injector electrical connectors.

20. Connect the 8 ignition wires to the 8 ignition coils.

21. Connect the 8 ignition coil electrical connectors.

22. Connect the fuel tube quick connect coupling.

23. Position the ACL outlet pipe-to-TB adapter and install the 2 bolts. Tighten to 89 inch lbs. (10 Nm).

24. Tighten the TB adapter-to-TB clamp.

25. Connect the brake booster vacuum hose from the ACL outlet pipe-to-TB adapter.

26. Connect the crankcase ventilation tube quick connect fitting to the ACL outlet pipe-to-TB adapter.

27. Connect the heater coolant hose retainer to the ACL outlet pipe-to-TB adapter.

28. Install the ACL outlet tube.

29. Connect the battery ground cable.

FUEL PUMP MODULE

REMOVAL & INSTALLATION

See Figures 533 through 536.

1. Refer to the fuel system precautions at the beginning of this section.

2. With the vehicle in NEUTRAL, position it on a hoist.

3. Remove the fuel tank.

4. Using soapy water, clean a minimum of 3 inches (76 mm) surface area around the Fuel Pump (FP) module.

5. If equipped, remove the 4 fuel pump module cover nuts and remove the fuel pump module cover.

6. Disconnect the fuel supply tube and Fuel Tank Pressure (FTP) sensor and vapor tube assembly quick connect couplings at the FP module.

7. Using the Fuel Tank Sending Unit Wrench (310-123), remove the FP module locking ring.

※※ WARNING

The Fuel Pump (FP) module must be handled carefully to avoid damage to the float arm and the filter.

➡ **If the FP does not clear the FP mounting flange on the fuel tank, the use of a screwdriver may be necessary.**

8. Remove the FP module.

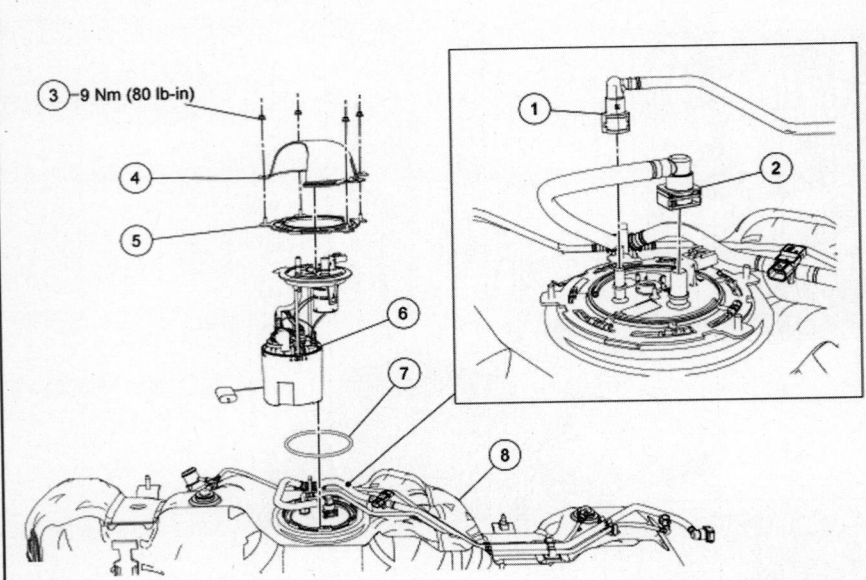

1. Fuel supply tube quick connect coupling
2. Fuel Tank Pressure (FTP) sensor and vapor tube assembly quick connect coupling
3. Fuel pump module cover nuts (4 required) (Raptor models only)
4. Fuel pump module cover (Raptor models only)
5. Fuel pump module locking ring
6. Fuel pump module
7. Fuel pump module O-ring seal
8. Fuel tank

N0105352

Fig. 533 Exploded view of the fuel pump module assembly

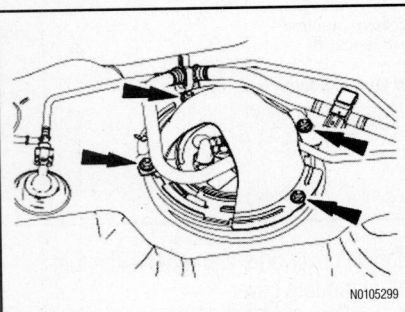

N0105299

Fig. 534 If equipped, remove the 4 fuel pump module cover nuts and remove the fuel pump module cover

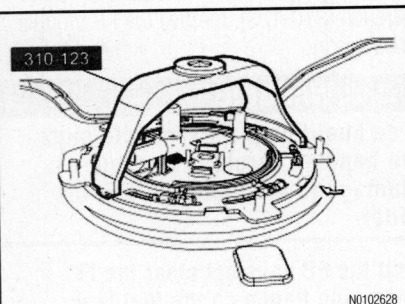

N0102628

Fig. 535 Using the Fuel Tank Sending Unit Wrench, remove the FP module locking ring

a. If necessary, insert a screwdriver into the empty FP rod hole and slightly pull the screwdriver inboard until the base of the FP clears the FP mounting flange.

b. Remove and discard the FP module O-ring seal.

To install:

9. To install, reverse the removal procedure.

10. Install a new FP module O-ring seal and lubricate with clean engine oil.

FUEL TANK

DRAINING

See Figure 537.

1. Refer to the fuel system precautions at the beginning of this section.

2. With the vehicle in NEUTRAL, position it on a hoist.

3. Relieve the fuel system pressure.

4. Disconnect the battery ground cable.

5. Remove the driveshaft.

6. Disconnect the fuel tank filler pipe from the fuel tank.

➡**Do not use a hose larger than 0.5inches (13 mm) diameter.**

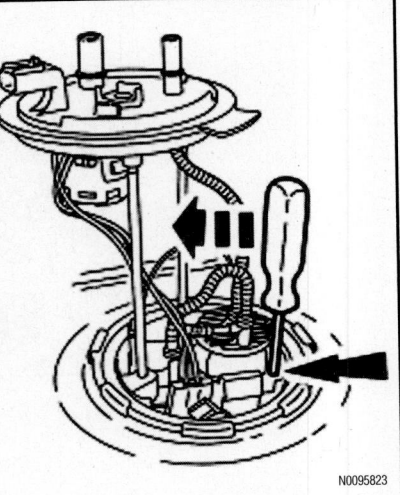

N0095823

Fig. 536 If necessary, insert a screwdriver into the empty FP rod hole and slightly pull the screwdriver inboard until the base of the FP clears the FP mounting flange

➡**Follow the operating instructions supplied by the equipment manufacturer.**

7. Attach the semi-flexible fuel draining hose to the 100 Gallon Gasoline Hand Pump Storage Tanker and insert the hose through the disconnected filler pipe hose at least 21 inches (53 cm) into the fuel tank.

8. Pump the fuel into the fuel storage tank.

REMOVAL & INSTALLATION

1. Refer to the fuel system precautions at the beginning of this section.

2. Drain the fuel tank.

3. Disconnect the fuel tank fuel supply tube-to-center fuel supply tube quick connect coupling.

4. Disconnect the Fuel Tank Pressure (FTP) sensor and vapor tube assembly-to-

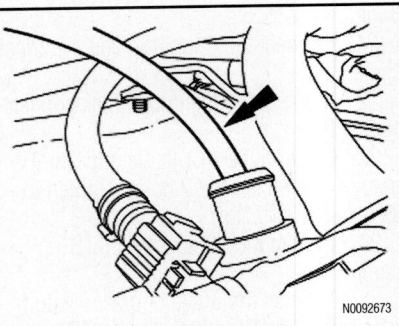

N0092673

Fig. 537 Insert the hose through the disconnected filler pipe hose into the fuel tank

Evaporative Emission (EVAP) canister assembly vapor tube quick connect coupling.

5. Disconnect the FTP sensor and Fuel Pump (FP) module electrical connectors, and if equipped, retainer(s).

6. Disconnect the fuel tank filler pipe-to-FTP sensor and vapor tube assembly quick connect coupling.

7. If equipped, remove the 4 fuel tank skid plate nuts and the skid plate.

8. Use a suitable jack to support the fuel tank.

9. Remove the 2 fuel tank support strap-to-frame bolts and remove the fuel tank support straps.

10. Lower the fuel tank out of the vehicle.

To install:

11. To install, reverse the removal procedure.

   a. Tighten the 2 fuel tank support strap-to-frame bolts to 35 ft. lbs. (47 Nm).

   b. Tighten the 4 fuel tank skid plate nuts to 15 ft. lbs. (20 Nm).

IDLE SPEED

ADJUSTMENT

The idle speed is controlled by the PCM. No adjustment is necessary.

THROTTLE BODY (TB)

REMOVAL & INSTALLATION

3.5L GTDI Engine

See Figure 538.

1. Remove the Air Cleaner (ACL) outlet pipe.

2. Disconnect the Throttle Body (TB) electrical connector.

3. Loosen the clamp and disconnect the Charge Air Cooler (CAC) outlet pipe-to-TB.

4. Remove the 4 bolts and the TB. Discard the TB gasket.

To install:

5. To install, reverse the removal procedure.

➡ **Install a new TB gasket.**

6. Tighten the 4 TB bolts to 89 inch lbs. (10 Nm).

3.7L Engine

See Figure 539.

1. Remove the engine Air Cleaner (ACL) outlet pipe.

2. Disconnect the electronic throttle control electrical connector.

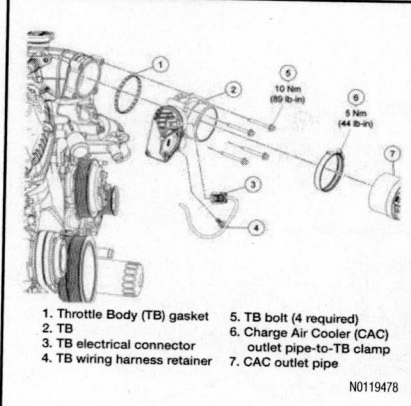

1. Throttle Body (TB) gasket
2. TB
3. TB electrical connector
4. TB wiring harness retainer
5. TB bolt (4 required)
6. Charge Air Cooler (CAC) outlet pipe-to-TB clamp
7. CAC outlet pipe

N0119478

Fig. 538 Exploded view of the throttle body assembly

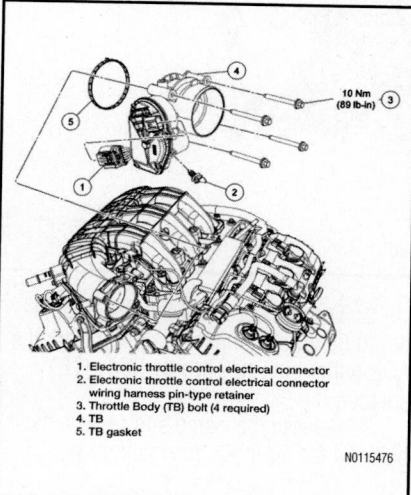

1. Electronic throttle control electrical connector
2. Electronic throttle control electrical connector wiring harness pin-type retainer
3. Throttle Body (TB) bolt (4 required)
4. TB
5. TB gasket

N0115476

Fig. 539 Exploded view of the throttle body assembly

3. Detach the electronic throttle control electrical connector wiring harness pin-type retainer.

4. Remove the 4 bolts and the Throttle Body (TB). Discard the TB gasket.

To install:

5. To install, reverse the removal procedure.

6. Install a new TB gasket.

7. Tighten the 4 TB bolts to 89 inch lbs. (10 Nm).

5.0L Engine

See Figure 540.

1. Remove the Air Cleaner (ACL) outlet pipe.

2. Disconnect the Electronic Throttle Control (ETC) electrical connector.

3. Remove the 4 bolts and the Throttle Body (TB) Discard the gasket.

To install:

4. Using a new gasket, position the TB and install the 4 bolts loosely.

5. While holding the TB in the most upward position tighten the 4 bolts in 2 stages.

   a. Stage 1: Tighten to 89 inch lbs. (10 Nm).

   b. Stage 2: Tighten an additional 45 degrees.

6. Connect the ETC electrical connector.

7. Install the ACL outlet pipe.

4.6L (2V) Engine

See Figure 541.

1. Remove the Air Cleaner (ACL) outlet pipe.

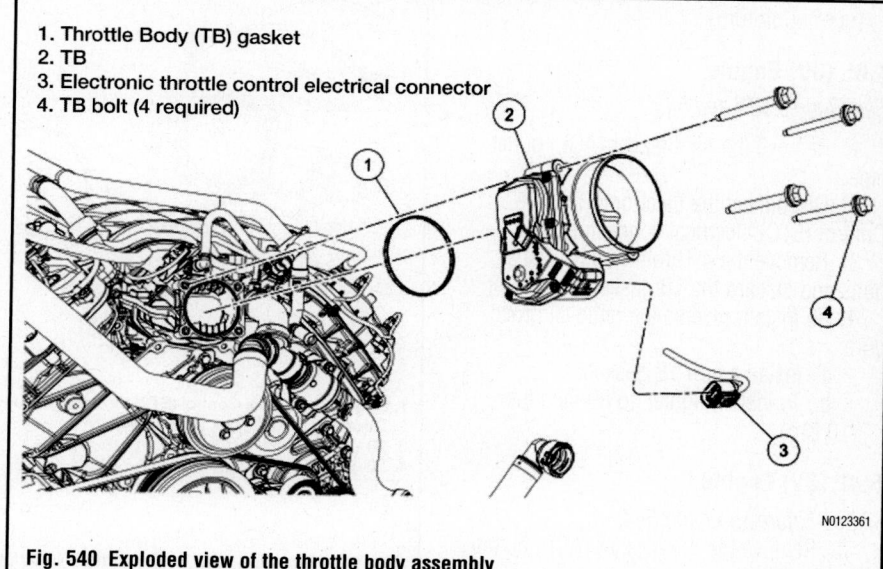

1. **Throttle Body (TB) gasket**
2. **TB**
3. **Electronic throttle control electrical connector**
4. **TB bolt (4 required)**

N0123361

Fig. 540 Exploded view of the throttle body assembly

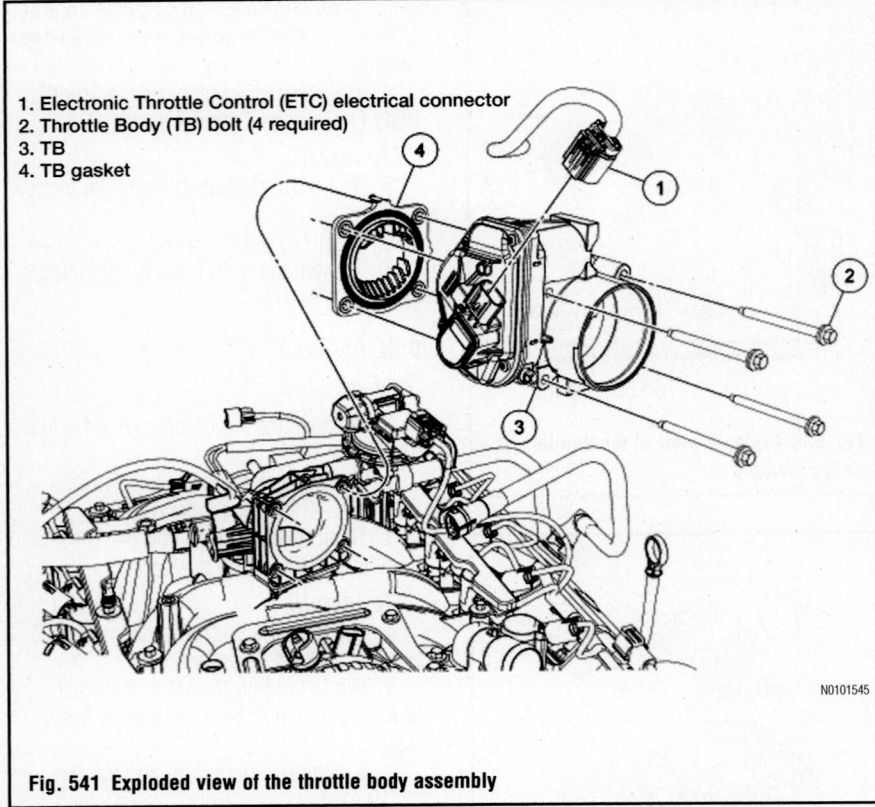

1. Electronic Throttle Control (ETC) electrical connector
2. Throttle Body (TB) bolt (4 required)
3. TB
4. TB gasket

N0101545

Fig. 541 Exploded view of the throttle body assembly

2. Disconnect the Electronic Throttle Control (ETC) electrical connector.

3. Remove the 4 Throttle Body (TB) bolts and discard the TB gasket.

To install:

4. To install, reverse the removal procedure.

   a. Install a new TB gasket.

   b. Tighten the 4 TB bolts to 89 inch lbs. (10 Nm).

   c. Tighten an additional 90 degrees (one-fourth turn).

4.6L (3V) Engine

See Figures 542 and 543.

1. Remove the Air Cleaner (ACL) outlet pipe.

2. Disconnect the Electronic Throttle Control (ETC) electrical connector.

3. Remove the 4 Throttle Body (TB) bolts and discard the TB gasket.

4. To install, reverse the removal procedure.

   a. Install a new TB gasket.

   b. To install, tighten to 89 inch lbs. (10 Nm).

5.4L (3V) Engine

See Figures 543 and 544.

1. Remove the Air Cleaner (ACL) outlet pipe.

2. Disconnect the crankcase ventilation tube quick connect coupling from the ACL outlet pipe-to-Throttle Body (TB) adapter.

3. Release the clamp and remove the bolt and the air intake resonator assembly.

4. Remove the 3 ACL outlet pipe-to-TB adapter bolts.

5. Remove the ACL outlet pipe-to-TB adapter.

6. Disconnect the Electronic Throttle Control (ETC) electrical connector.

7. Disconnect the Throttle Position (TP) sensor electrical connector.

8. Remove the 4 bolts, the vibration damper and the TB assembly.

9. Discard the TB O-ring seal.

To install:

10. Using a new O-ring seal, position the TB , the vibration damper and tighten the 4 bolts in 2 stages.

   a. Stage 1: Tighten to 80 inch lbs. (9 Nm).

   b. Stage 2: Tighten an additional 90 degrees (one-fourth turn).

11. Connect the TP sensor electrical connector.

12. Connect the ETC electrical connector.

13. Position the ACL outlet pipe-to-TB adapter.

   a. Install the 3 ACL outlet pipe-to-TB adapter bolts. Tighten to 89 inch lbs. (10 Nm).

   b. Position the air intake resonator assembly, install the bolt and the clamp. Tighten to 89 inch lbs. (10 Nm).

14. Connect the crankcase ventilation tube quick connect coupling to the ACL outlet pipe-to-TB adapter.

15. Install the ACL outlet pipe.

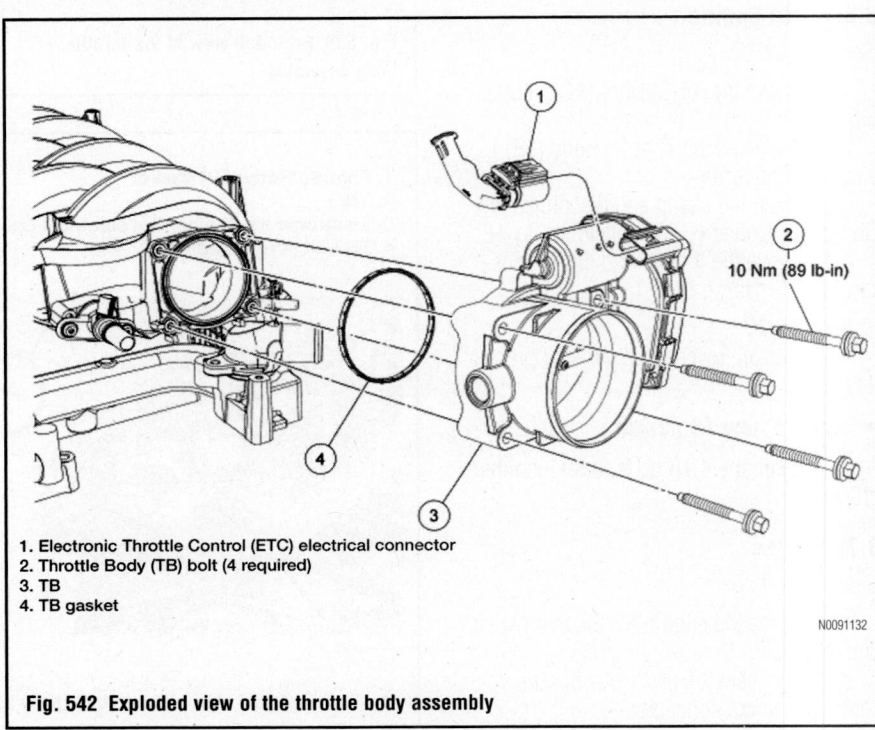

1. Electronic Throttle Control (ETC) electrical connector
2. Throttle Body (TB) bolt (4 required)
3. TB
4. TB gasket

10 Nm (89 lb-in)

N0091132

Fig. 542 Exploded view of the throttle body assembly

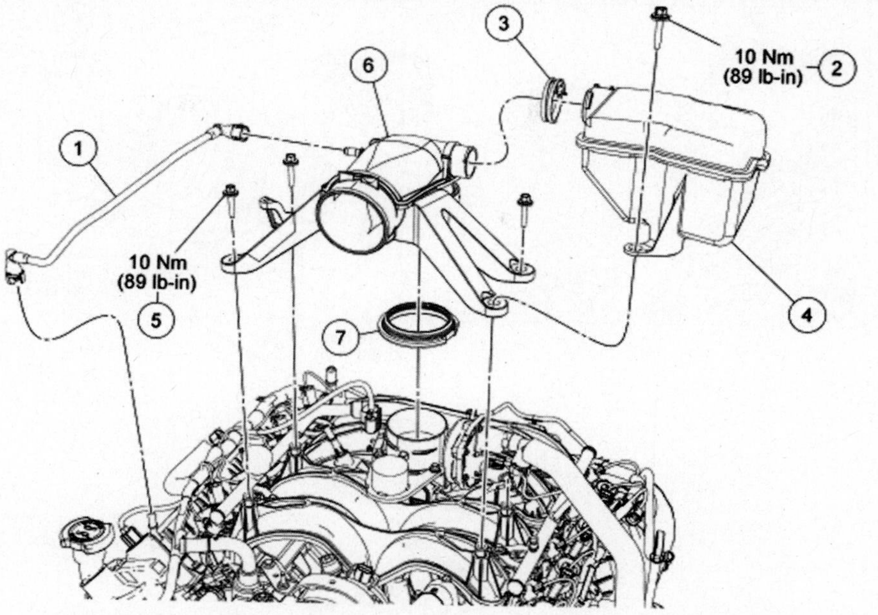

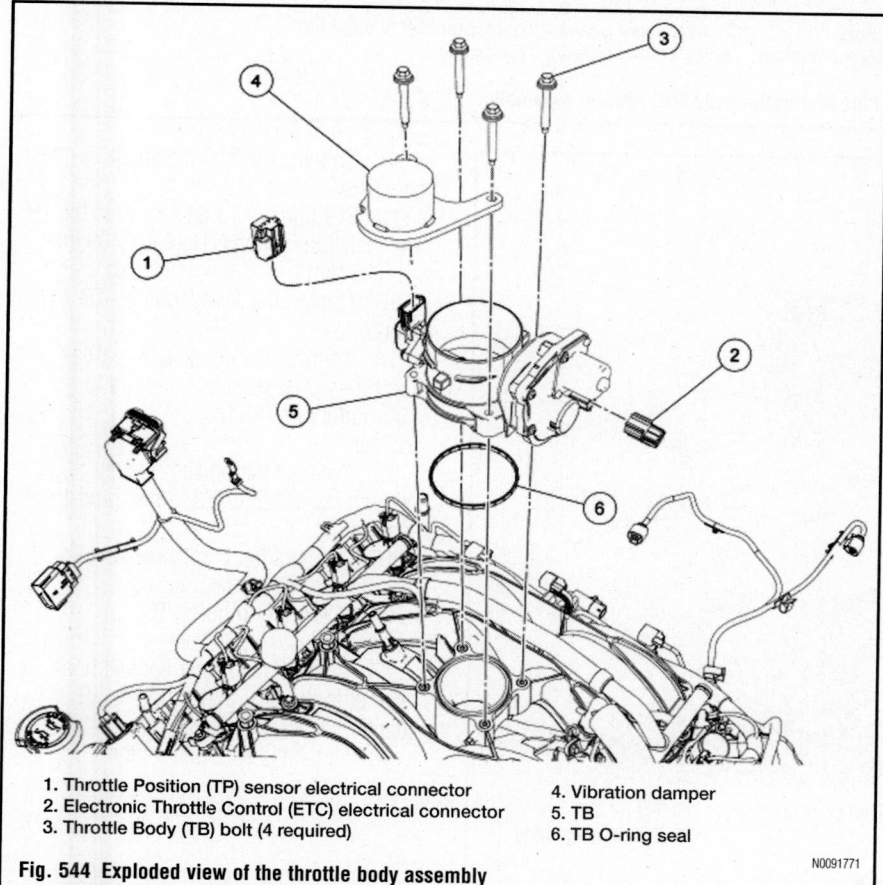

1. Crankcase ventilation tube
2. Air intake resonator assembly bolt
3. Throttle Body (TB) adapter-to-air intake resonator clamp
4. Air intake resonator
5. Air Cleaner (ACL) outlet pipe-to-TB adapter bolt (3 required)
6. ACL outlet pipe-to- TB adapter
7. ACL outlet pipe-to- TB adapter seal

N0091770

Fig. 543 Exploded view of Air Cleaner (ACL) Outlet Pipe-to-Throttle Body (TB) Adapter and Air Intake Resonator assembly

1. Throttle Position (TP) sensor electrical connector
2. Electronic Throttle Control (ETC) electrical connector
3. Throttle Body (TB) bolt (4 required)
4. Vibration damper
5. TB
6. TB O-ring seal

N0091771

Fig. 544 Exploded view of the throttle body assembly

6.2L (2V) Engine

See Figures 545 and 556.

1. Remove the Air Cleaner (ACL) outlet tube.

2. Disconnect the heater coolant hose retainer from the ACL outlet pipe-to-Throttle Body (TB) adapter.

3. Disconnect the crankcase ventilation tube quick connect fitting from ACL outlet pipe-to-TB adapter.

4. Disconnect the brake booster vacuum hose from the ACL outlet pipe-to-TB adapter.

5. Remove the 2 bolts and the ACL outlet pipe-to-TB adapter.

6. Loosen the clamp and disconnect the TB adapter from the TB.

7. Disconnect the Electronic Throttle Control (ETC) electrical connector.

8. Remove the 4 bolts and the TB assembly.

9. Discard the TB O-ring seal.

To install:

10. Using a new O-ring seal, position the TB and tighten the 4 bolts in 2 stages.

a. Stage 1: Tighten to 106 inch lbs. (12 Nm).

b. Stage 2: Tighten an additional 60 degrees.

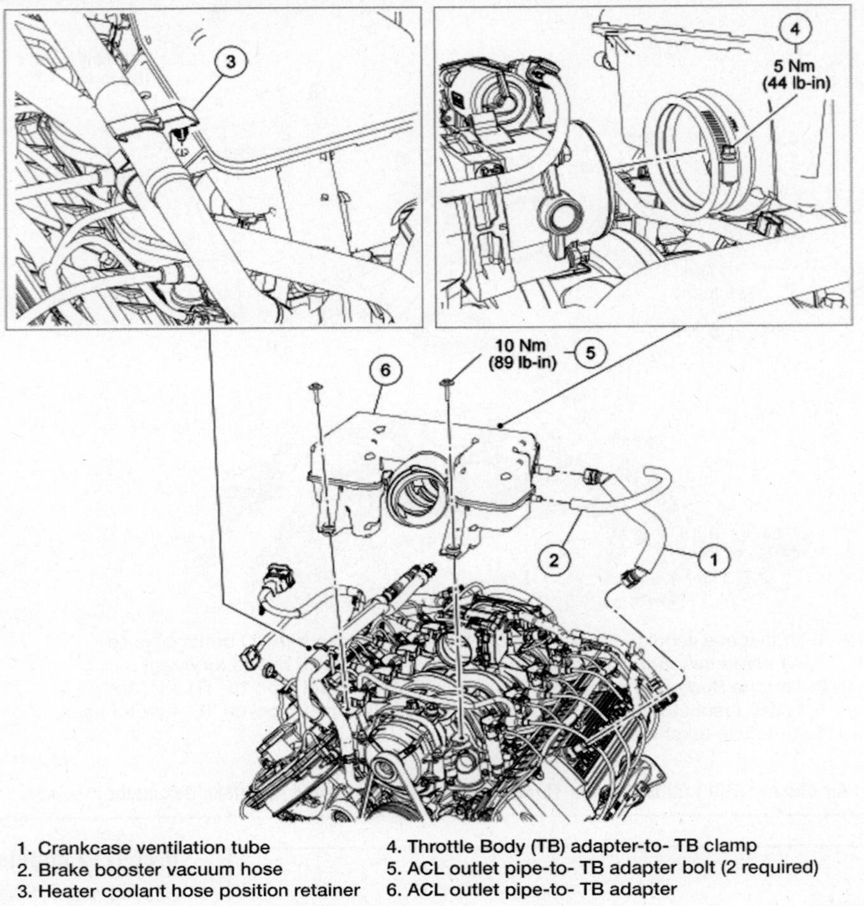

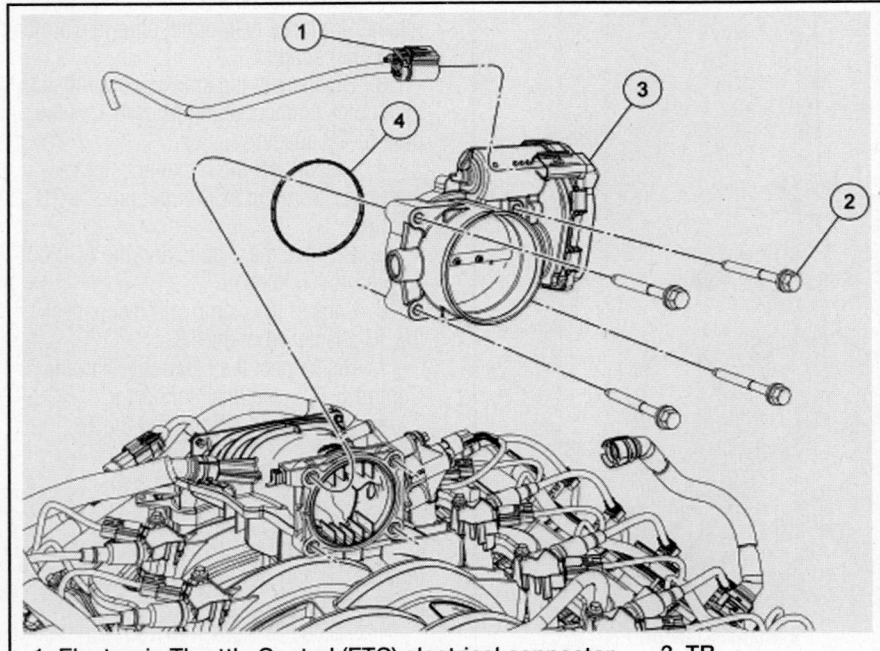

1. Crankcase ventilation tube
2. Brake booster vacuum hose
3. Heater coolant hose position retainer
4. Throttle Body (TB) adapter-to- TB clamp
5. ACL outlet pipe-to- TB adapter bolt (2 required)
6. ACL outlet pipe-to- TB adapter

N0110075

Fig. 545 Exploded view of Air Cleaner (ACL) Outlet Pipe-to-Throttle Body (TB) Adapter assembly

1. Electronic Throttle Control (ETC) electrical connector
2. Throttle Body (TB) bolt (4 required)
3. TB
4. TB O-ring seal

N0110027

Fig. 546 Exploded view of the throttle body assembly

11. Connect the ETC electrical connector.

12. Position the TB adapter onto the TB and install the 2 bolts. Tighten to 89 inch lbs. (10 Nm).

13. Tighten the TB adapter-to-TB clamp.

14. Connect the crankcase ventilation tube quick connect coupling to the ACL outlet pipe-to-TB adapter.

15. Connect the brake booster vacuum hose to the ACL outlet pipe-to-TB adapter.

16. Connect the crankcase ventilation tube quick connect fitting to the ACL outlet pipe-to-TB adapter.

17. Connect the heater coolant hose retainer to the ACL outlet pipe-to-TB adapter.

18. Install the ACL outlet tube.

HEATING & AIR CONDITIONING SYSTEM

BLOWER MOTOR

REMOVAL & INSTALLATION

See Figure 547.

❋❋ WARNING

The blower motors for vehicles equipped with dual-zone Electronic Automatic Temperature Control (EATC) and vehicles equipped with Electronic Manual Temperature Control (EMTC) are not interchangeable. If the wrong blower motor is installed for the specific vehicle application, the blower motor circuit components will be damaged. Use only the correct blower motor listed for the specific vehicle application in the Ford Catalog Advantage or equivalent.

1. Remove the junction box cover.
2. Disconnect the blower motor electrical connector.
3. Remove the 3 blower motor screws.
4. Remove the blower motor.
5. To install, reverse the removal procedure.

HEATER CORE

REMOVAL & INSTALLATION

See Figures 548 and 549.

➡ If a heater core leak is suspected, the heater core must be leak tested before it is removed from the vehicle.

1. Remove the heater core and evaporator core housing.
   a. Drain the engine coolant.
   b. Recover the refrigerant.
   c. Remove the instrument panel.
   d. Disconnect the 2 heater core quick disconnect fittings at the heater core.
   e. Remove the Thermostatic Expansion Valve (TXV) manifold and tube bracket bolt.
   f. Remove the TXV fitting nut and disconnect the fitting. Discard the gasket seals.
   g. Remove the 3 heater core and evaporator core housing nuts.
   h. Detach the 3 harness electrical connectors from the heater

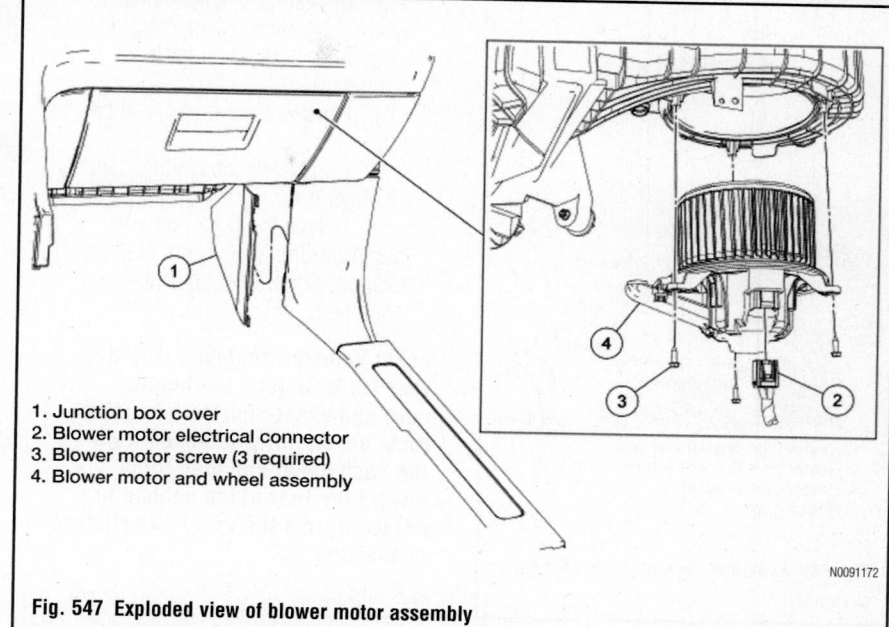

1. Junction box cover
2. Blower motor electrical connector
3. Blower motor screw (3 required)
4. Blower motor and wheel assembly

N0091172

Fig. 547 Exploded view of blower motor assembly

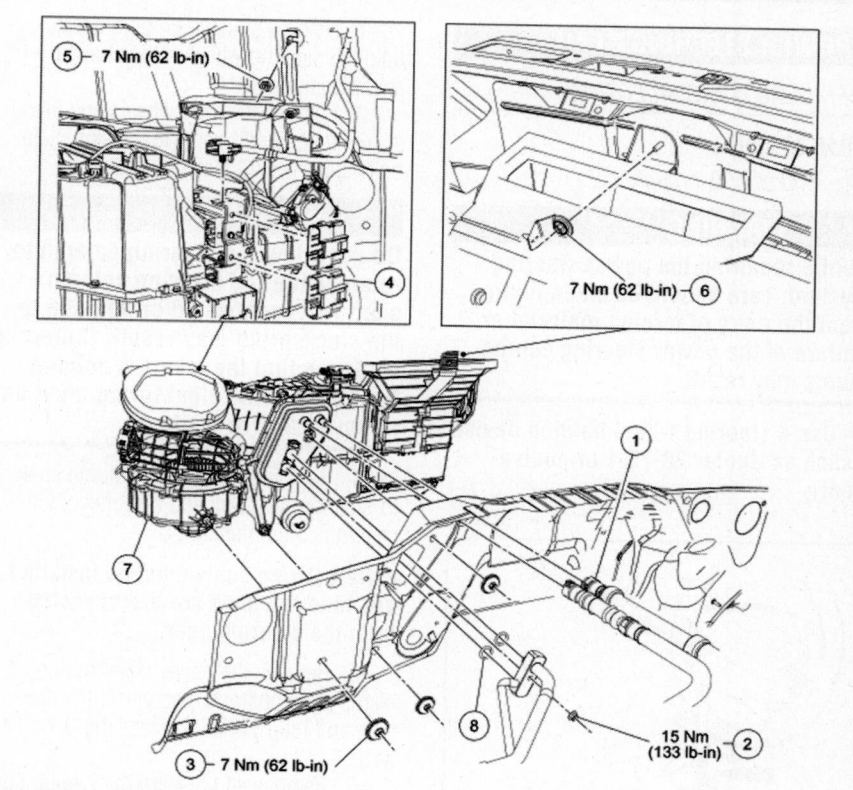

1. Heater hose quick disconnect fitting (2 required)
2. Thermostatic Expansion Valve (TXV) fitting nut
3. Heater core and evaporator core housing nut (3 required)
4. Body harness electrical connector (3 required)
5. Air inlet duct bracket nut
6. Plenum chamber nut
7. Heater core and evaporator core housing
8. Gasket seal (2 pieces from kit required)

N0087379

Fig. 548 Exploded view of the heater core and evaporator core housing assembly

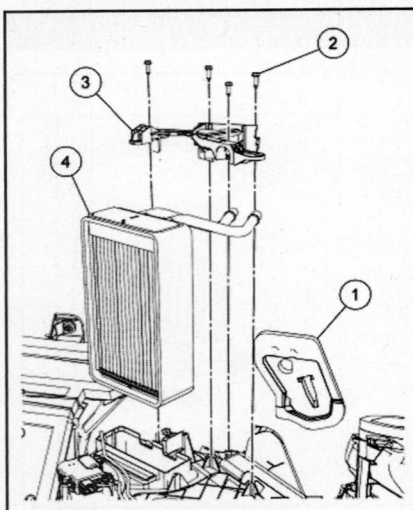

1. Heater tube dash panel seal
2. Heater core bracket screw (4 required)
3. Heater core bracket
4. Heater core

N0091139

Fig. 549 Exploded view of the heater core assembly

core and evaporator core housing bracket.

i. Detach the 2 antenna cable retainers from the heater core and evaporator core housing (if equipped).

j. Remove the air inlet duct bracket nut.

k. Completely loosen the plenum chamber nut.

l. Detach the floor console duct from the heater core and evaporator core housing (if equipped).

➡**For vehicles equipped with a rear footwell duct, the heater core and evaporator core housing must be carefully detached from the dash panel and then tilted toward the rear of the vehicle to detach it from the rear footwell duct connection.**

m. Remove the heater core and evaporator core housing.

2. Remove the heater hose quick disconnect clips from the heater core.

3. Remove the heater tube dash panel seal.

4. Remove the 4 heater core bracket screws and the bracket.

5. Remove the heater core.

To install:

➡**The heater core seal must be correctly installed to prevent airflow from bypassing the heater core.**

6. To install, reverse the removal procedure.

a. Install new O-ring seals.

b. Tighten the TXV fitting nut to 10 ft. lbs. (15 Nm).

c. Fill the engine cooling system.

d. Add the correct amount of clean PAG oil to the refrigerant system.

STEERING

POWER STEERING GEAR

REMOVAL & INSTALLATION

2010 Models
See Figures 550 through 552.

✳✳ WARNING

While repairing the power steering system, care should be taken to prevent the entry of foreign material or failure of the power steering components may result.

➡**Use a steering wheel holding device (such as Hunter 28-75-1 or equivalent).**

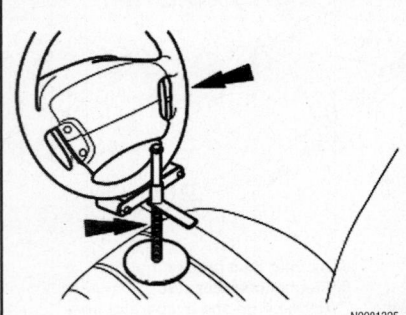

N0081325

Fig. 550 Using a suitable holding device, hold the steering wheel in the straight-ahead position

1. Using a suitable holding device, hold the steering wheel in the straight-ahead position.

2. Remove the front wheels and tires.

3. If equipped, remove the skid plate bolts and the skid plate.

✳✳ WARNING

Do not allow the steering column to rotate while the steering column shaft is disconnected or damage to the clockspring may result. If there is evidence that the steering column has rotated, the clockspring must be removed and re-centered.

4. Remove the steering column shaft-to-steering gear bolt and disconnect the steering column shaft.

➡**New O-ring seals must be installed any time the lines are disconnected from the steering gear.**

5. Remove the power steering line clamp plate bolt and disconnect the pressure and return lines. Discard the O-ring seals.

6. Remove and discard the 2 outer tie-rod end nuts.

✳✳ WARNING

Use care when installing the Ball Joint Tool Separator or damage to the tie-rod end boot may occur.

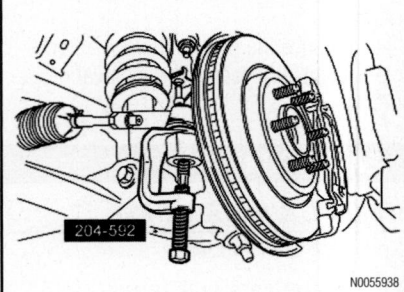

204-592

N0055938

Fig. 551 Using the Ball Joint Tool Separator, separate the outer tie-rod ends from the wheel knuckles

7. Using the Ball Joint Tool Separator (204-592), separate the outer tie-rod ends from the wheel knuckles.

8. Remove the 2 steering gear bolts and nuts.

9. Remove the steering gear through the LH wheel opening.

To install:

10. Install new O-ring seals on the pressure and return lines.

✳✳ WARNING

Make sure the LH steering gear bushing is seated correctly or failure of the steering gear may occur. The RH side bushing does not have locking tabs.

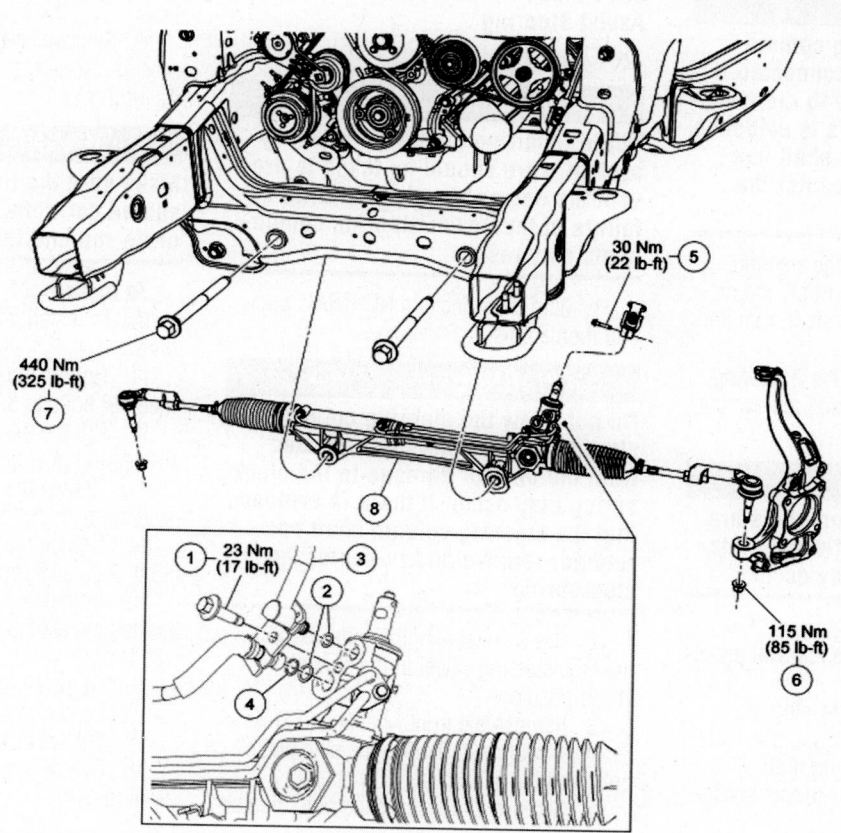

1. Power steering line clamp plate bolt
2. Power steering line O-ring seals (2 required)
3. Power steering return line
4. O-ring seal
5. Steering column shaft-to-steering gear bolt
6. Outer tie-rod end nut (2 required)
7. Steering gear-to-crossmember bolt (2 required)
8. Steering gear

N0096177

Fig. 552 Exploded view of the steering gear assembly

11. Install the steering gear through the LH wheel opening.

12. Install the 2 steering gear bolts and nuts. Tighten to 325 ft. lbs. (440 Nm).

13. Position the 2 outer tie-rod ends and install the nuts. Tighten the new nuts to 85 ft. lbs. (115 Nm).

14. Connect the pressure and return line and install the steering line clamp plate bolt. Tighten to 17 ft. lbs. (23 Nm).

15. Connect the steering column shaft to the steering gear and install the bolt. Tighten to 22 ft. lbs. (30 Nm).

16. If equipped, install the skid plate and the bolts.

    a. For all except SVT Raptor, tighten to 18 ft. lbs. (25 Nm).

    b. For SVT Raptor, tighten to 35 ft. lbs. (48 Nm).

17. Fill the power steering system.

18. Check and, if necessary, adjust the front toe.

2011 Models with Electronic Power Assist Steering

See Figure 553.

1. If installing a new steering gear, connect the scan tool and upload the module configuration information from the Power Steering Control Module (PSCM).

❊❊ WARNING

Disconnect the negative battery cable anytime the steering gear is being serviced or damage to the steering gear internal power relay may occur resulting in steering gear replacement.

2. Disconnect the battery ground cable.

3. With the vehicle in NEUTRAL, position it on a hoist.

❊❊ WARNING

Do not allow the steering column shaft to rotate while disconnected

from the gear or damage to the clock-spring may occur. If there is evidence that the steering column shaft has rotated, remove and re-center the clockspring.

4. Use a suitable holding device to hold the steering wheel in the straight-ahead position.

5. Remove the front wheels and tires.

6. If equipped, remove the skid plate bolts and the skid plate.

7. Remove and discard the outer tie-rod end nuts.

❊❊ WARNING

Use care when installing the Ball Joint Tool Separator or damage to the tie-rod end boot may occur.

8. Using the Ball Joint Tool Separator, disconnect the tie-rod ends from the wheel knuckles.

> ❊❊ **WARNING**
>
> **Do not allow the steering column shaft to rotate while disconnected from the gear or damage to the clockspring may occur. If there is evidence that the steering column shaft has rotated, remove and re-center the clockspring.**

9. Remove and discard the steering column shaft-to-steering gear bolt and disconnect the steering column shaft from the steering gear.

10. Remove and discard the 2 steering gear-to-crossmember bolts and remove the steering gear.

> ❊❊ **WARNING**
>
> **Make sure the tie-rod end boots are seated correctly on the tie-rod ends or tie-rod end failure may occur.**

To install:

11. To install, reverse the removal procedure.

12. When installing a new steering gear, it must be configured (using vehicle as-built data or module configuration information retrieved earlier in this procedure).

13. Tighten the 2 steering gear-to-crossmember bolts to 325 ft. lbs. (440 Nm).

14. Tighten the steering column shaft-to-steering gear bolt to 22 ft. lbs. (30 Nm).

15. Tighten the outer tie-rod end nuts to 85 ft. lbs. (115 Nm).

16. To install (all except SVT Raptor), tighten the skid plate bolts to 18 ft. lbs. (25 Nm).

17. To install (SVT Raptor), tighten the skid plate bolts to 35 ft. lbs. (48 Nm).

18. Check and, if necessary, adjust the front toe.

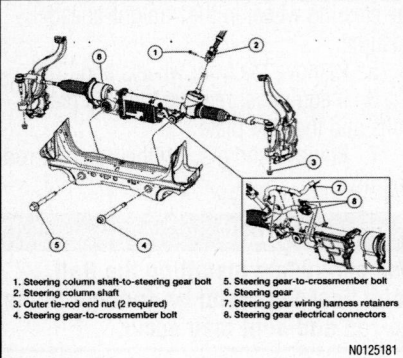

1. Steering column shaft-to-steering gear bolt
2. Steering column shaft
3. Outer tie-rod end nut (2 required)
4. Steering gear-to-crossmember bolt
5. Steering gear-to-crossmember bolt
6. Steering gear
7. Steering gear wiring harness retainers
8. Steering gear electrical connectors

N0125181

Fig. 553 Exploded view of the Electronic Power Assist steering gear assembly

2011 Models with Hydraulic Power Assist Steering

See Figure 554.

> ❊❊ **WARNING**
>
> **While repairing the power steering system, care should be taken to prevent the entry of foreign material or failure of the power steering components may result.**

1. With the vehicle in NEUTRAL, position it on a hoist.

> ❊❊ **WARNING**
>
> **Do not allow the steering column shaft to rotate while disconnected from the gear or damage to the clockspring may occur. If there is evidence that the steering column shaft has rotated, remove and re-center the clockspring.**

2. Use a suitable holding device and hold the steering wheel in the straight-ahead position.

3. Remove the front wheels and tires.

4. If equipped, remove the skid plate bolts and the skid plate.

5. Remove and discard the outer tie-rod end nuts.

> ❊❊ **WARNING**
>
> **Use care when installing the Ball Joint Tool Separator or damage to the tie-rod end boot may occur.**

6. Using the Ball Joint Tool Separator, disconnect the tie-rod ends from the wheel knuckles.

> ❊❊ **WARNING**
>
> **Do not allow the steering column shaft to rotate while disconnected from the gear or damage to the clockspring may occur. If there is evidence that the steering column shaft has rotated, remove and re-center the clockspring.**

7. Remove and discard the steering column shaft-to-steering gear bolt and disconnect the steering column shaft from the steering gear.

> ❊❊ **WARNING**
>
> **Install new O-ring seals any time the lines are disconnected from the steering gear or a fluid leak may occur.**

8. Remove the steering line clamp plate-to-steering gear bolt, and disconnect the power steering lines. Discard the O-ring seals.

9. Remove and discard the 2 steering gear-to-crossmember bolts and remove the steering gear.

> ❊❊ **WARNING**
>
> **Make sure the tie-rod end boots are seated correctly on the tie-rod ends or tie-rod end failure may occur.**

To install:

10. To install, reverse the removal procedure.

11. Tighten the 2 steering gear-to-crossmember bolts to 325 ft. lbs. (440 Nm).

12. Tighten the steering line clamp plate-to-steering gear bolt to 17 ft. lbs. (23 Nm).

13. Tighten the steering column shaft-to-steering gear bolt to 22 ft. lbs. (30 Nm).

14. Tighten the outer tie-rod end nuts to 85 ft. lbs. (115 Nm).

15. To install (all except SVT Raptor), tighten the skid plate bolts to 18 ft. lbs. (25 Nm).

16. To install (SVT Raptor), tighten the skid plate bolts to 35 ft. lbs. (48 Nm).

17. Fill the power steering system.

18. Check and, if necessary, adjust the front toe.

POWER STEERING PUMP

REMOVAL & INSTALLATION

2010 Models

See Figure 555.

> ❊❊ **WARNING**
>
> **While repairing the power steering system, care should be taken to prevent the entry of foreign material or failure of the power steering components may result.**

1. Remove the power steering pump pulley.

2. Using a suitable suction device, remove the power steering fluid from the fluid reservoir.

3. Release the clamp and disconnect the power steering pump supply hose.

4. Remove the pressure line bracket-to-engine nut.

5. Disconnect the pressure line-to-pump fitting and position it aside. Discard the Teflon® seal.

6. Disconnect the oil pressure sending unit wire harness retainer from the power steering pump stud.

7. Remove the power steering pump stud bolt.

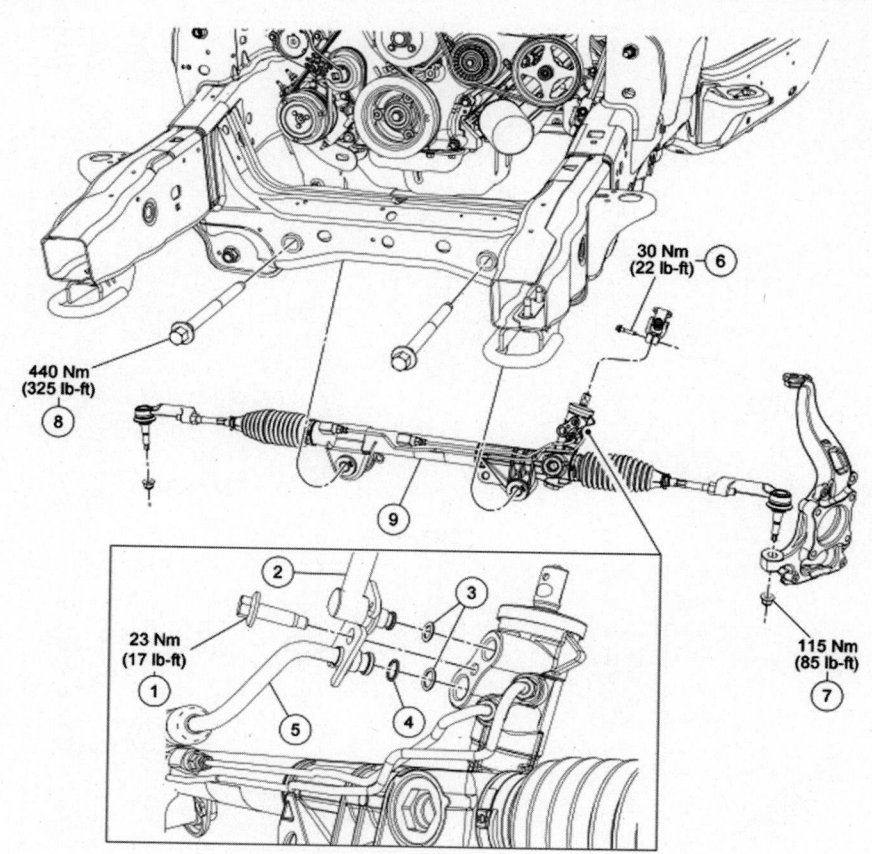

1. Steering line clamp plate-to-steering gear bolt
2. Return line
3. O-ring seals (2 required)
4. Back-up O-ring seal
5. Pressure line
6. Steering column shaft-to-steering gear bolt
7. Outer tie-rod end nut (2 required)
8. Steering gear-to-crossmember bolt (2 required)
9. Steering gear

N0121116

Fig. 554 Exploded view of the Hydraulic Power Assist Steering gear assembly

8. From under the hood, remove the 2 power steering pump bolts and the pump.

➡**A new Teflon® seal must be installed any time the line is disconnected from the power steering pump.**

To install:

9. To install, reverse the removal procedure.

10. Tighten the 2 power steering pump bolts to 18 ft. lbs. (25 Nm).

11. Tighten the power steering pump stud bolt to 18 ft. lbs. (25 Nm).

12. Using the Teflon® Seal Installer Set, install a new Teflon® seal on the pressure line-to-pump fitting.

13. Tighten the pressure line-to-pump fitting to 55 ft. lbs. (75 Nm).

14. Install the pressure line bracket-to-engine nut.

   a. On the 5.4L engine, tighten to 30 ft. lbs. (40 Nm).

   b. On the 4.6L engine, tighten to 106 inch lbs. (12 Nm).

15. Fill the power steering system.

2011 Models

✳✳ WARNING

While repairing the power steering system, care should be taken to prevent the entry of foreign material or failure of the power steering components may result.

1. With the vehicle in NEUTRAL, position it on a hoist.

2. Using a suitable suction device, remove the power steering fluid from the fluid reservoir.

3. Release the clamp and disconnect the supply hose.

4. Remove and discard the pressure line clamp plate-to-pump bolt.

5. Disconnect the pressure line from the pump.

6. Remove the 3 power steering pump bolts and the power steering pump.

To install:

7. To install, reverse the removal procedure.

8. Tighten the 3 power steering pump bolts to 18 ft. lbs. (25 Nm).

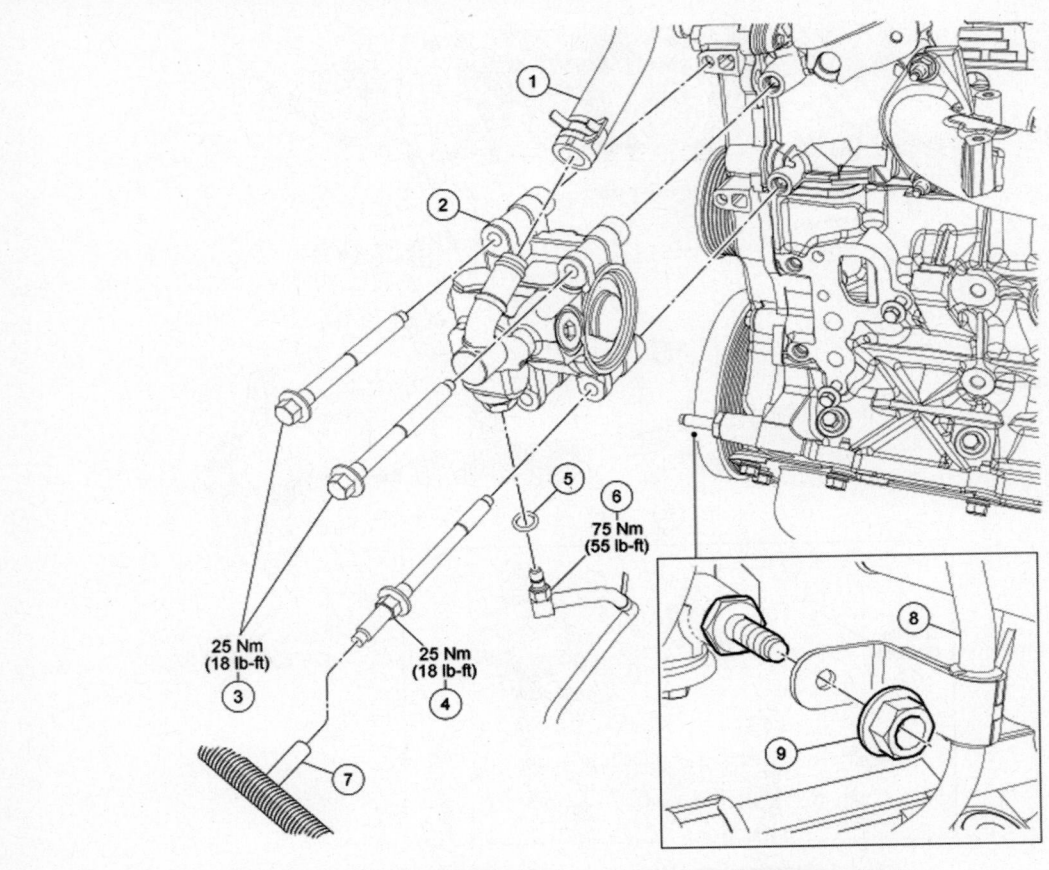

1. Power steering pump supply hose
2. Power steering pump
3. Power steering pump bolts (2 required)
4. Power steering pump stud bolt
5. Teflon seal
6. Pressure line-to-pump fitting
7. Wiring harness retainer
8. Power steering pressure line
9. Pressure line bracket-to-engine nut

25 Nm (18 lb-ft)
25 Nm (18 lb-ft)
75 Nm (55 lb-ft)

N0105547

Fig. 555 Exploded view of the power steering pump assembly—2010 Models

9. Tighten the pressure line clamp plate-to-pump bolt to 18 ft. lbs. (25 Nm).
10. Fill the power steering system.

BLEEDING
See Figure 556.

✳✳ WARNING
If the air is not purged from the power steering system correctly, premature power steering pump failure may result. The condition may occur on pre-delivery vehicles with evidence of aerated fluid or on vehicles that have had steering component repairs.

➡A whine heard from the power steering pump can be caused by air in the system. The power steering purge procedure must be carried out prior to any component repair for which power steering noise complaints are accompanied by evidence of aerated fluid.

1. Remove the power steering reservoir cap. Check the fluid.
2. Raise the front wheels off the floor.
3. Tightly insert the Power Steering Evac-

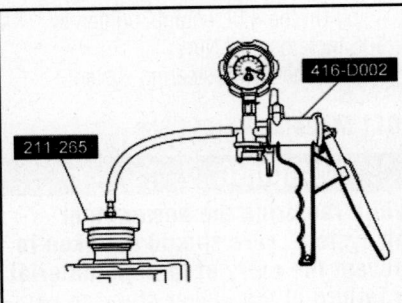

211 265

416-D002

N0081477

Fig. 556 Tightly insert the Power Steering Evacuation Cap into the reservoir and connect the Vacuum Pump Kit

uation Cap (211-265) into the reservoir and connect the Vacuum Pump Kit (416-D002).
4. Start the engine.
5. Using the Vacuum Pump Kit, apply vacuum and maintain the maximum vacuum of 20–25 in-Hg (68–85 kPa).
6. If the Vacuum Pump Kit does not maintain vacuum, check the power steering system for leaks before proceeding.
7. If equipped with Hydro-Boost, apply the brake pedal 4 times.

✳✳ WARNING
Do not hold the steering wheel against the stops for an extended amount of time. Damage to the power steering pump may occur.

8. Cycle the steering wheel fully from stop-to-stop 10 times.
9. Stop the engine.

10. Release the vacuum and remove the Vacuum Pump Kit and the Power Steering Evacuation Cap.

➡ **Do not overfill the reservoir.**

11. Fill the reservoir as needed with the specified fluid.
12. Start the engine.
13. Install the Power Steering Evacuation Cap and the Vacuum Pump Kit. Apply and maintain the maximum vacuum of 20–25 in-Hg (68–85 kPa).

✳✳ WARNING

Do not hold the steering wheel against the stops for an extended amount of time. Damage to the power steering pump may occur.

14. Cycle the steering wheel fully from stop-to-stop 10 times.
15. Stop the engine, release the vacuum and remove the Vacuum Pump Kit and the Power Steering Evacuation Cap.

➡ **Do not overfill the reservoir.**

16. Fill the reservoir as needed with the specified fluid and install the reservoir cap.
17. Visually inspect the power steering system for leaks.

FLUID FILL PROCEDURE

See Figure 557.

✳✳ WARNING

If the air is not purged from the power steering system correctly, premature power steering pump failure may result. The condition can occur on pre-delivery vehicles with evidence of aerated fluid or on vehicles that have had steering component repairs.

1. Remove the power steering fluid reservoir cap.
2. Install the Power Steering Evacuation Cap, Power Steering Fill Adapter Manifold and Vacuum Pump Kit as shown.

➡ **The Power Steering Fill Adapter Manifold control valves are in the OPEN position when the points of the handles face the center of the Power Steering Fill Adapter Manifold.**

3. Close the Power Steering Fill Adapter Manifold control valve (fluid side).

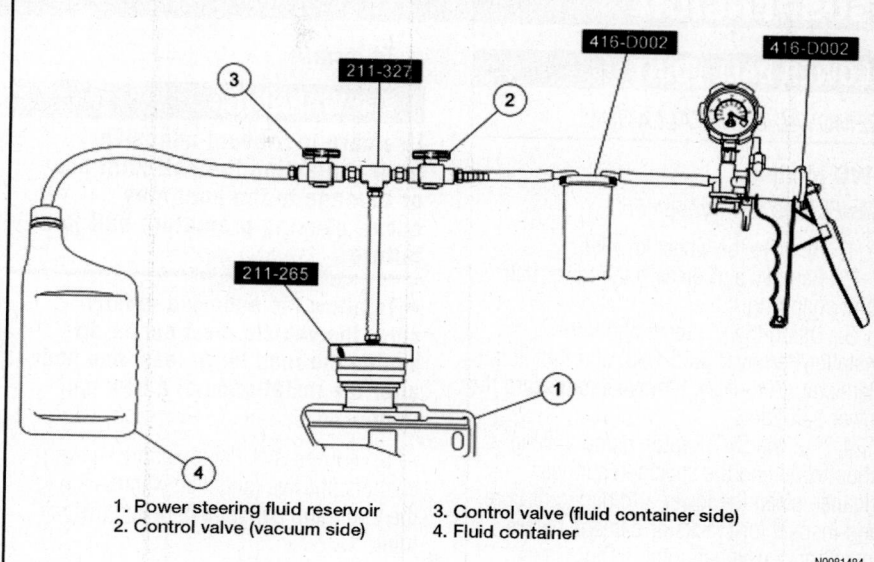

1. Power steering fluid reservoir
2. Control valve (vacuum side)
3. Control valve (fluid container side)
4. Fluid container

Fig. 557 Install the Power Steering Evacuation Cap, Power Steering Fill Adapter Manifold and Vacuum Pump Kit as shown

4. Open the Power Steering Fill Adapter Manifold control valve (vacuum side).
5. Using the Vacuum Pump Kit, apply 20–25 in-Hg (68–85 kPa) of vacuum to the power steering system.
6. Observe the Vacuum Pump Kit gauge for 30 seconds.
7. If the Vacuum Pump Kit gauge reading drops more than 0.88 in-Hg (3 kPa), correct any leaks in the power steering system or the Power Steering Evacuation Cap, Power Steering Fill Adapter Manifold and Vacuum Pump Kit before proceeding.

➡ **The Vacuum Pump Kit gauge reading will drop slightly during this step.**

8. Slowly open the Power Steering Fill Adapter Manifold control valve (fluid side) until power steering fluid completely fills the hose and then close the control valve.
9. Using the Vacuum Pump Kit, apply 20–25 in-Hg (68–85 kPa) of vacuum to the power steering system.
10. Close the Power Steering Fill Adapter Manifold control valve (vacuum side).
11. Slowly open the Power Steering Fill Adapter Manifold control valve (fluid side).

12. Once power steering fluid enters the fluid reservoir and reaches the minimum fluid level indicator line on the reservoir, close the Power Steering Fill Adapter Manifold control valve (fluid side).
13. Remove the Power Steering Evacuation Cap, Power Steering Fill Adapter Manifold and Vacuum Pump Kit.
14. Install the reservoir cap.

✳✳ WARNING

Do not hold the steering wheel against the stops for an extended amount of time. Damage to the power steering pump may occur.

➡ **There will be a slight drop in the power steering fluid level in the reservoir when the engine is started.**

15. Start the engine and turn the steering wheel from stop-to-stop.
16. Turn the ignition switch to the OFF position.

➡ **Do not overfill the reservoir.**

17. Remove the reservoir cap and fill the reservoir with the specified fluid.
18. Install the reservoir cap.

LOWER BALL JOINT

REMOVAL & INSTALLATION

4WD Models

See Figures 558 through 560.

1. Remove the wheel knuckle.
2. Remove and discard the lower ball joint snap ring.
3. Using the C-Frame and Screw Installer/Remover (205-086) and Ball Joint Remover (204-182), remove and discard the lower ball joint.
4. For the SVT Raptor, using a clean shop towel and the specified surface cleaner, clean the lower arm ball joint bore and inspect for cracks or damage before installing a new ball joint. If there is evidence of cracks or damage, a new lower arm must be installed.

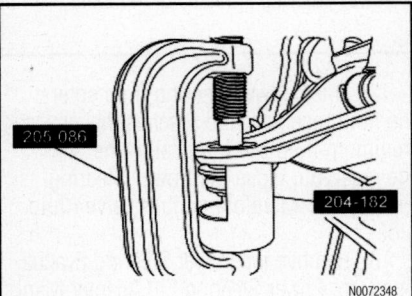

Fig. 558 Using the C-Frame and Screw Installer/Remover and Ball Joint Remover, remove and discard the lower ball joint

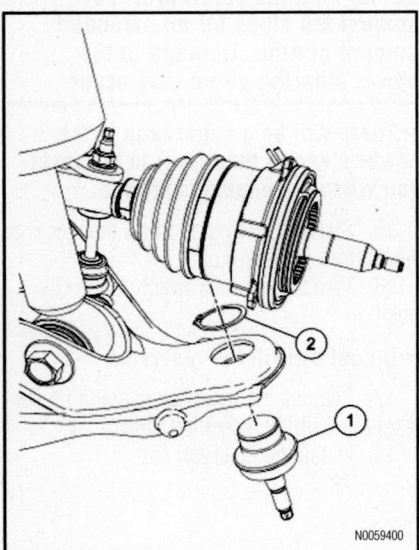

Fig. 559 Exploded view of lower ball joint assembly (1) and snap ring (2)

To install:

> ☀☀ **WARNING**
>
> **Use care to prevent adhesive from contacting the ball joint boot or damage to the boot may occur, causing premature ball joint failure.**

➡ To allow the adhesive to fully cure, the vehicle must not be driven on the road for at least one hour after the installation of a new ball joint.

5. For the SVT Raptor, apply an even coat of adhesive (supplied with the kit) to the lower arm ball joint bore and the ball joint.

> ☀☀ **WARNING**
>
> **Do not damage the lower ball joint boot when installing the C-Frame and Screw Installer/Remover and Ball Joint Installer/Remover or premature failure of the ball joint may occur.**

➡ Make sure the lower ball joint snap ring is fully seated.

6. Using the C-Frame and Screw Installer/Remover (205-086) and Ball Joint Installer/Remover (204-358), install the new lower ball joint.
7. Install the new lower ball joint snap ring.
8. For the SVT Raptor, using a clean shop towel and the specified surface cleaner, wipe any excess adhesive from the ball joint and lower arm.
9. Install the wheel knuckle.

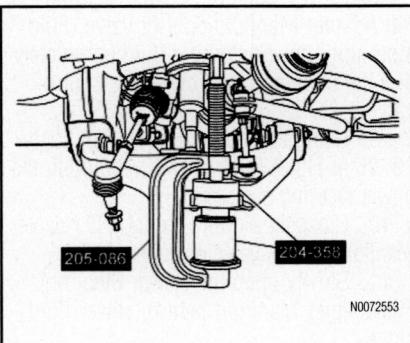

Fig. 560 Using the C-Frame and Screw Installer/Remover and Ball Joint Installer/Remover, install the new lower ball joint

RWD Models

See Figure 561.

1. Remove the wheel knuckle.
2. Remove and discard the lower ball joint snap ring.
3. Using the C-Frame and Screw Installer/Remover and Ball Joint Remover, remove the lower ball joint.

To install:

> ☀☀ **WARNING**
>
> **Do not damage the lower ball joint boot when installing the C-Frame and Screw Installer/Remover and Ball Joint Installer/Remover or premature failure of the ball joint may occur.**

➡ Make sure the ball joint snap ring is fully seated.

4. Using the C-Frame and Screw Installer/Remover and Ball Joint Installer/Remover, install the lower ball joint.
5. Install the new ball joint snap ring.
6. Install the wheel knuckle

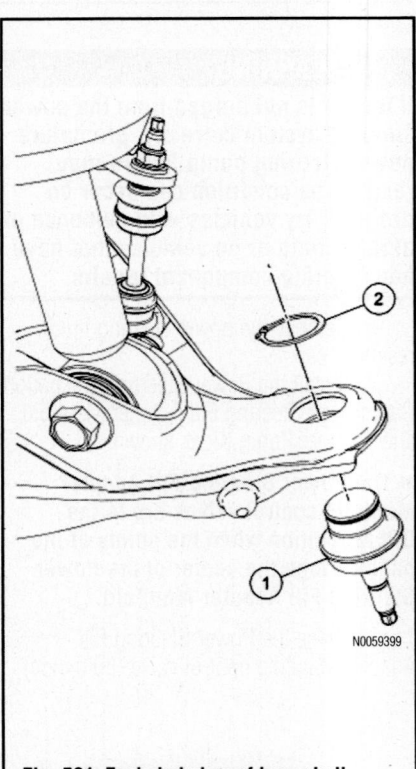

Fig. 561 Exploded view of lower ball joint (1) and snap ring (2)

LOWER CONTROL ARM

REMOVAL & INSTALLATION

4WD Models

See Figures 562 through 564.

✳✳ WARNING

Suspension fasteners are critical parts because they affect performance of vital components and systems and their failure may result in major service expense. New parts must be installed with the same part numbers or equivalent parts, if replacement is necessary. Do not use a replacement part of lesser quality or substitute design. Torque values must be used as specified during reassembly to make sure of correct retention of these parts.

1. Measure the distance from the center of the hub to the lip of the fender with the vehicle in a level, static ground position (curb height).
2. Remove the wheel knuckle.

➡ **Use the hex-holding feature to prevent the stud from turning while removing the nut.**

3. Remove and discard the stabilizer bar link lower nut.
4. Remove and discard the lower arm rearward nut and bolt.
5. Remove and discard the lower arm forward nut and bolt.
6. Remove the shock absorber lower nut, bolt and the lower arm.
7. Discard the shock absorber lower nut and bolt.

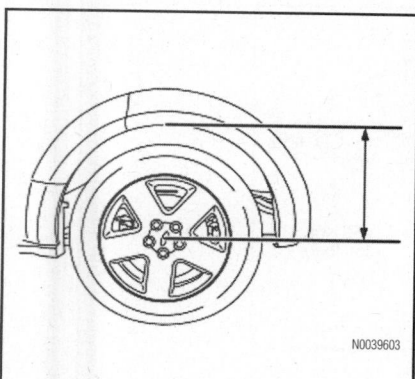

Fig. 562 Measure the distance from the center of the hub to the lip of the fender with the vehicle in a level, static ground position (curb height)

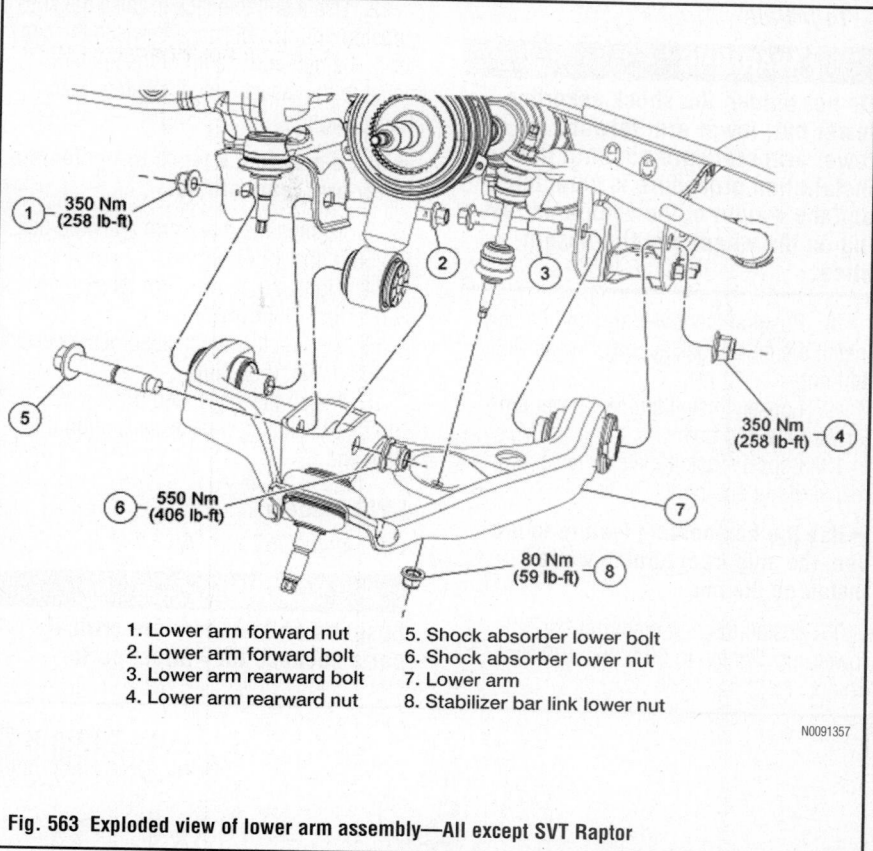

1. Lower arm forward nut
2. Lower arm forward bolt
3. Lower arm rearward bolt
4. Lower arm rearward nut
5. Shock absorber lower bolt
6. Shock absorber lower nut
7. Lower arm
8. Stabilizer bar link lower nut

Fig. 563 Exploded view of lower arm assembly—All except SVT Raptor

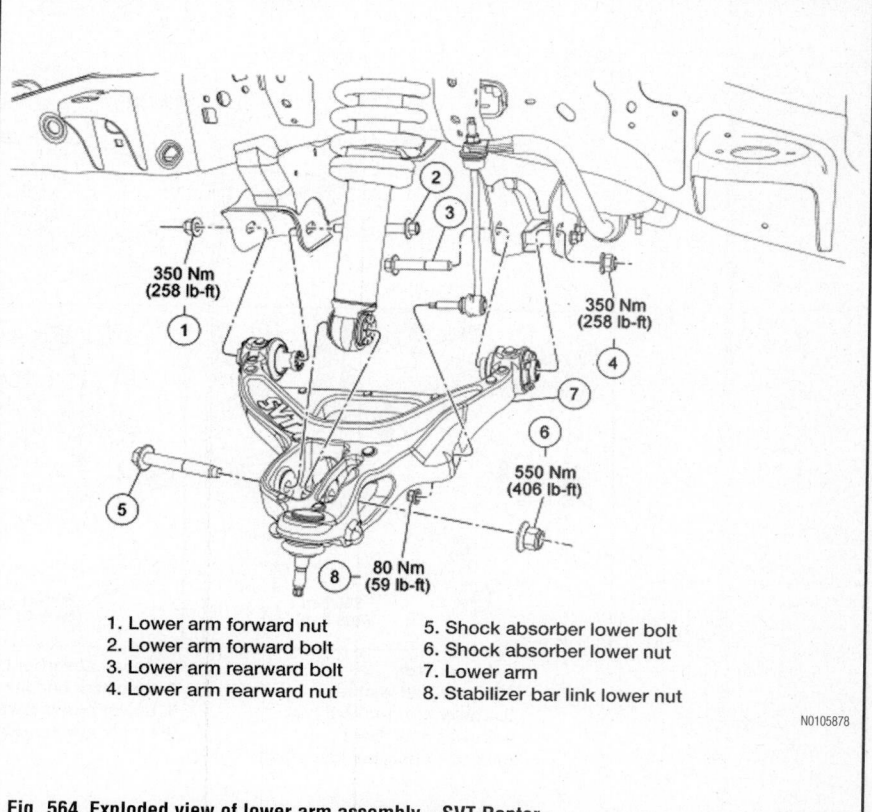

1. Lower arm forward nut
2. Lower arm forward bolt
3. Lower arm rearward bolt
4. Lower arm rearward nut
5. Shock absorber lower bolt
6. Shock absorber lower nut
7. Lower arm
8. Stabilizer bar link lower nut

Fig. 564 Exploded view of lower arm assembly—SVT Raptor

To install:

※※ WARNING

Do not tighten the shock absorber lower nut, lower arm forward nut or lower arm rearward nut until the installation procedure is complete and the weight of the vehicle is resting on the wheel and tire assemblies.

8. Position the lower arm and loosely install the new shock absorber lower bolt and nut.

9. Loosely install the new lower arm forward nut and bolt.

10. Loosely install the new lower arm rearward nut and bolt.

➡ Use the hex-holding feature to prevent the stud from turning while installing the nut.

11. Install the new stabilizer bar link lower nut. Tighten to 59 ft. lbs. (80 Nm).

12. Use a suitable jack to raise the suspension until the distance between the center of the hub and the lip of the fender is equal to the measurement taken in Step 1 (curb height).

➡ Use a crowfoot wrench to tighten the lower arm rearward nut.

13. Tighten the lower arm rearward nut to 258 ft. lbs. (350 Nm).

14. Tighten the lower arm forward nut to 258 ft. lbs. (350 Nm).

15. Tighten the shock absorber lower nut to 406 ft. lbs. (550 Nm).

16. Install the wheel and tire.

17. Check and, if necessary, align the front end.

RWD Models

See Figures 565 and 566.

※※ WARNING

Suspension fasteners are critical parts because they affect performance of vital components and systems and their failure may result in major service expense. New parts must be installed with the same part numbers or equivalent parts, if

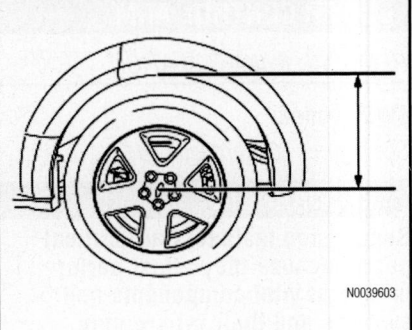

Fig. 565 Measure the distance from the center of the hub to the lip of the fender with the vehicle in a level, static ground position (curb height)

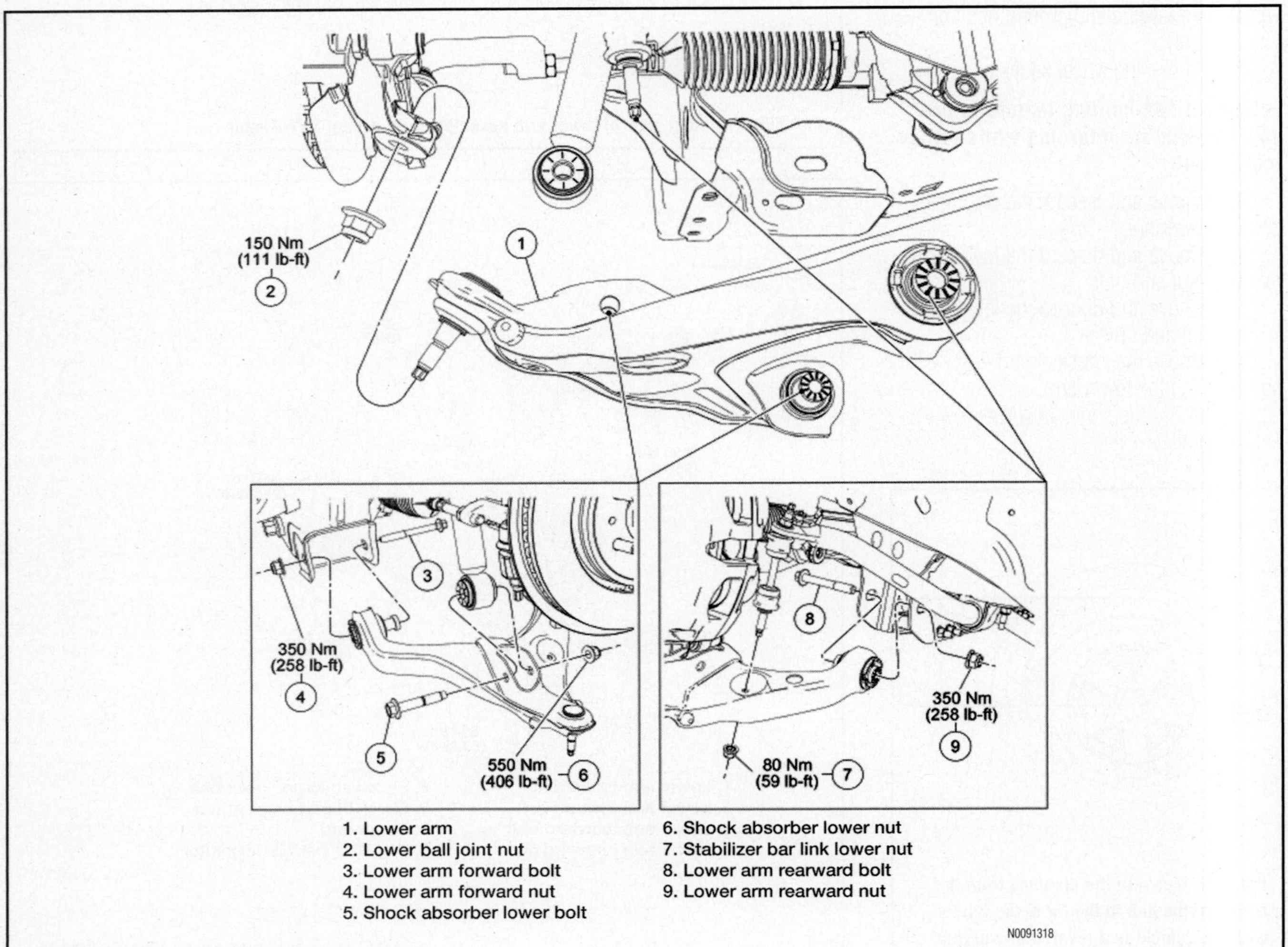

150 Nm (111 lb-ft) ②

350 Nm (258 lb-ft) ④

550 Nm (406 lb-ft) ⑥

350 Nm (258 lb-ft) ⑨

80 Nm (59 lb-ft) ⑦

1. Lower arm
2. Lower ball joint nut
3. Lower arm forward bolt
4. Lower arm forward nut
5. Shock absorber lower bolt
6. Shock absorber lower nut
7. Stabilizer bar link lower nut
8. Lower arm rearward bolt
9. Lower arm rearward nut

Fig. 566 Exploded view of lower arm assembly

replacement is necessary. Do not use a replacement part of lesser quality or substitute design. Torque values must be used as specified during reassembly to make sure of correct retention of these parts.

1. Measure the distance from the center of the hub to the lip of the fender with the vehicle in a level, static ground position (curb height).

2. Remove the wheel and tire.

➡ **Use the hex-holding feature to prevent the stud from turning while removing the nut.**

3. Remove and discard the stabilizer bar link lower nut.

4. Remove and discard the lower ball joint nut.

✳✳ **WARNING**

Make sure to use the Ball Joint Separator when separating the lower ball joint from the knuckle to prevent damage to the ball joint boot.

5. Using the Ball Joint Separator, separate the ball joint from the knuckle.

6. Remove and discard the lower arm rearward nut and bolt.

7. Remove and discard the lower arm forward nut and bolt.

8. Remove the shock absorber lower nut, bolt and the lower arm.

9. Discard the shock absorber lower nut and bolt.

To install:

10. Position the lower arm and loosely install the new shock absorber lower bolt and nut.

11. Loosely install the new lower arm forward nut and bolt.

12. Loosely install the new lower arm rearward nut and bolt.

13. Position the lower ball joint into the wheel knuckle and install the new lower ball joint nut. Tighten to 111 ft. lbs. (150 Nm).

14. Install the new stabilizer bar link lower nut. Tighten to 59 ft. lbs. (80 Nm).

15. Use a suitable jack to raise the suspension until the distance between the center of the hub and the lip of the fender is equal to the measurement taken in Step 1 (curb height).

➡ **Use a crowfoot wrench to tighten the lower arm rearward nut.**

16. Tighten the lower arm rearward nut to 258 ft. lbs. (350 Nm).

17. Tighten the lower arm forward nut to 258 ft. lbs. (350 Nm).

18. Tighten the shock absorber lower nut to 406 ft. lbs. (550 Nm).

19. Install the wheel and tire.

20. Check and, if necessary, align the front end.

STABILIZER BAR AND LINK

REMOVAL & INSTALLATION

4WD Models

See Figures 567 and 568.

✳✳ **WARNING**

Suspension fasteners are critical parts because they affect performance of vital components and systems and their failure may result in major service expense. New parts must be installed with the same part numbers or equivalent parts, if replacement is necessary. Do not use a replacement part of lesser quality or substitute design. Torque values must be used as specified during reassembly to make sure of correct retention of these parts.

1. With the vehicle in NEUTRAL, position it on a hoist.

➡ **LH side shown, RH side similar.**

➡ **Use the hex-holding feature to prevent the stud from turning while removing the nut.**

2. Remove and discard the 2 stabilizer bar link upper nuts.

✳✳ **WARNING**

Do not hold the stabilizer link boot with any tool, as damage to the boot will occur.

➡ **Use the hex-holding feature to prevent the stud from turning while removing the nut.**

3. Remove and discard the 2 stabilizer bar link lower nuts and remove the 2 stabilizer bar links.

4. If equipped, remove the 10 bolts and the forward and rearward skid plates.

5. Remove the 4 stabilizer bar bracket nuts, brackets and the stabilizer bar. Discard the nuts.

6. Remove and discard the stabilizer bar bracket bolt plates.

➡ **Make sure the stabilizer bar bushings raised center lip is installed into the bracket groove.**

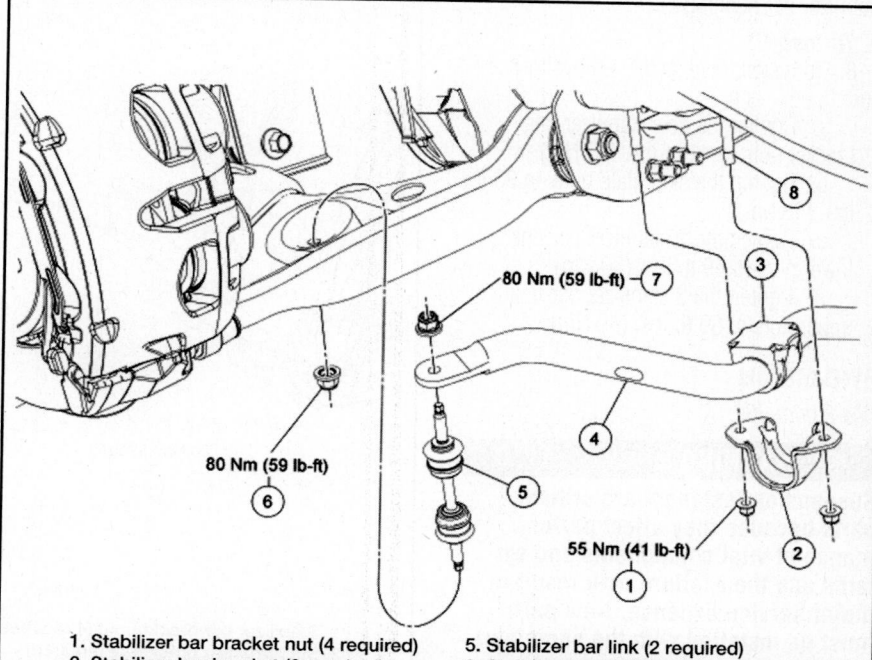

1. Stabilizer bar bracket nut (4 required)
2. Stabilizer bar bracket (2 required)
3. Stabilizer bar bushing (2 required)
4. Stabilizer bar
5. Stabilizer bar link (2 required)
6. Stabilizer bar link lower nut (2 required)
7. Stabilizer bar link upper nut (2 required)
8. Stabilizer bar bracket bolt plate

N0055535

Fig. 567 Exploded view of the stabilizer bar and link assembly—All except SVT Raptor

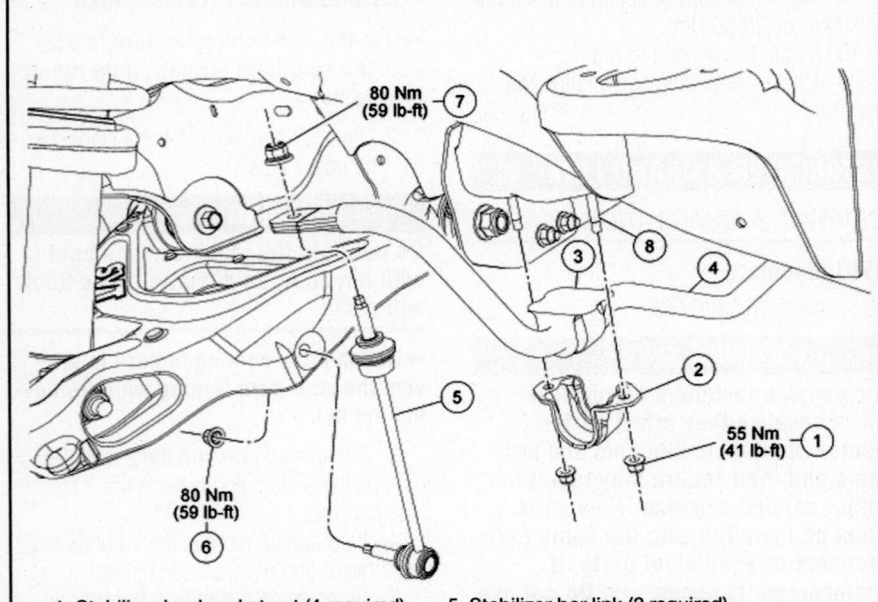

Fig. 568 Exploded view of the stabilizer bar and link assembly—SVT Raptor

1. Stabilizer bar bracket nut (4 required)
2. Stabilizer bar bracket (2 required)
3. Stabilizer bar bushing (2 required)
4. Stabilizer bar
5. Stabilizer bar link (2 required)
6. Stabilizer bar link lower nut (2 required)
7. Stabilizer bar link upper nut (2 required)
8. Stabilizer bar bracket bolt plate

N0105879

➡ **LH side shown, RH side similar.**

1. With the vehicle in NEUTRAL, position it on a hoist.

➡ **Use the hex-holding feature to prevent the stud from turning while removing the nut.**

2. Remove and discard the 2 stabilizer bar link upper nuts.

✳✳ WARNING

Do not hold the stabilizer link boot with any tool, as damage to the boot will occur.

➡ **Use the hex-holding feature to prevent the stud from turning while removing the nut.**

3. Remove and discard the 2 stabilizer bar link lower nuts and remove the 2 stabilizer bar links.

4. Remove the 4 stabilizer bar bracket nuts, brackets and the stabilizer bar. Discard the nuts.

5. Remove and discard the stabilizer bracket bolt plates.

➡ **Make sure the stabilizer bar bushings raised center lip is installed into the bracket groove.**

7. Inspect and, if necessary, install new stabilizer bar bushings.

To install:

8. To install, reverse the removal procedure.

  a. Tighten the new stabilizer bar bracket nuts to 41 ft. lbs. (55 Nm).

  b. Tighten the skid plate bolts to 35 ft. lbs. (48 Nm).

  c. Tighten the 2 stabilizer bar link lower nuts to 59 ft. lbs. (80 Nm).

  d. Tighten the 2 stabilizer bar link upper nuts to 59 ft. lbs. (80 Nm).

RWD Models

See Figure 569.

✳✳ WARNING

Suspension fasteners are critical parts because they affect performance of vital components and systems and their failure may result in major service expense. New parts must be installed with the same part numbers or equivalent parts, if replacement is necessary. Do not use a replacement part of lesser quality or substitute design. Torque values must be used as specified during reassembly to make sure of correct retention of these parts.

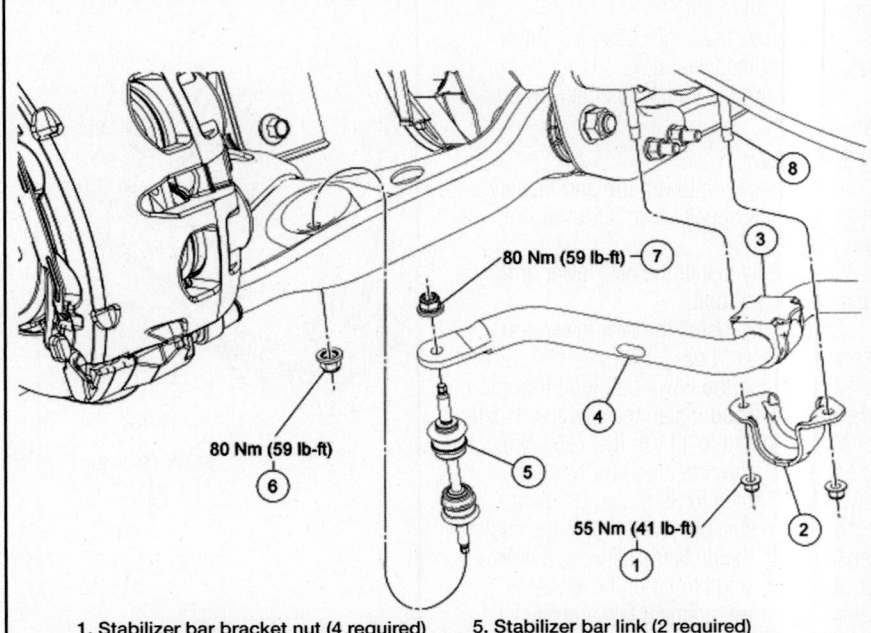

Fig. 569 Exploded view of stabilizer bar assembly

1. Stabilizer bar bracket nut (4 required)
2. Stabilizer bar bracket (2 required)
3. Stabilizer bar bushing (2 required)
4. Stabilizer bar
5. Stabilizer bar link (2 required)
6. Stabilizer bar link lower nut (2 required)
7. Stabilizer bar link upper nut (2 required)
8. Stabilizer bar bracket bolt plate

N0055535

6. Inspect and, if necessary, install new stabilizer bar bushings.

7. To install, reverse the removal procedure.

   a. Tighten the new stabilizer bar bracket nuts to 41 ft. lbs. (55 Nm).

   b. Tighten the new stabilizer bar link lower nuts to 59 ft. lbs. (80 Nm).

   c. Tighten the new stabilizer bar link upper nuts to 59 ft. lbs. (80 Nm).

STEERING KNUCKLE

REMOVAL & INSTALLATION

4WD Models

See Figures 570 through 574.

❊❊ WARNING

Suspension fasteners are critical parts because they affect performance of vital components and systems and their failure may result in major service expense. New parts must be installed with the same part numbers or equivalent part, if replacement is necessary. Do not use a replacement part of lesser quality or substitute design. Torque values must be used as specified during reassembly to make sure of correct retention of these parts.

1. Remove the wheel bearing and wheel hub.

2. Remove and discard the tie-rod end nut.

3. Using the Ball Joint Separator (204-592), separate the tie-rod end from the wheel knuckle.

4. Remove the wheel speed sensor harness bracket bolt and position the harness aside.

5. Remove the brake hose bracket bolt and position aside.

➡**Use the hex-holding feature to prevent the stud from turning while removing the nut.**

6. Remove and discard the stabilizer bar link lower nut.

7. Remove and discard the shock absorber lower nut and bolt.

8. Remove the 3 Integrated Wheel End (IWE) bolts.

9. Remove and discard the upper ball joint nut.

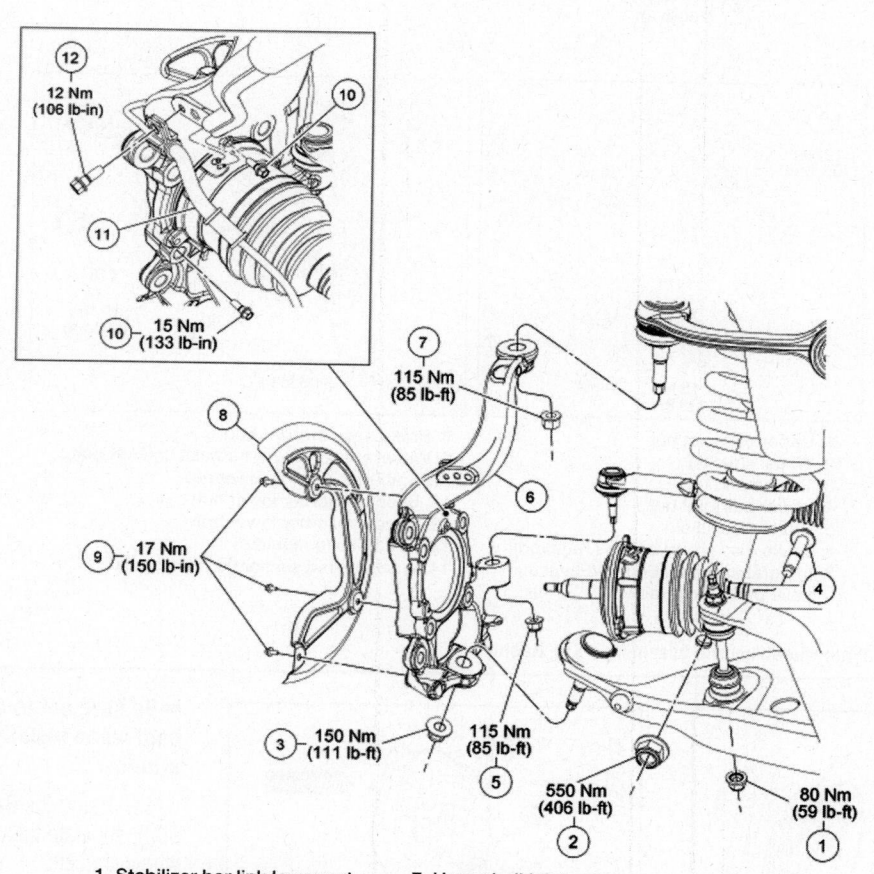

1. Stabilizer bar link lower nut
2. Shock absorber lower nut
3. Lower ball joint nut
4. Shock absorber lower bolt
5. Tie-rod end nut
6. Wheel knuckle
7. Upper ball joint nut
8. Brake disc shield
9. Brake disc shield bolts (3 required)
10. Integrated Wheel End (IWE) bolts (3 required)
11. Wheel speed sensor harness bracket
12. Wheel speed sensor harness bracket bolt

N0091358

Fig. 570 Exploded view of the wheel knuckle assembly—All except SVT Raptor

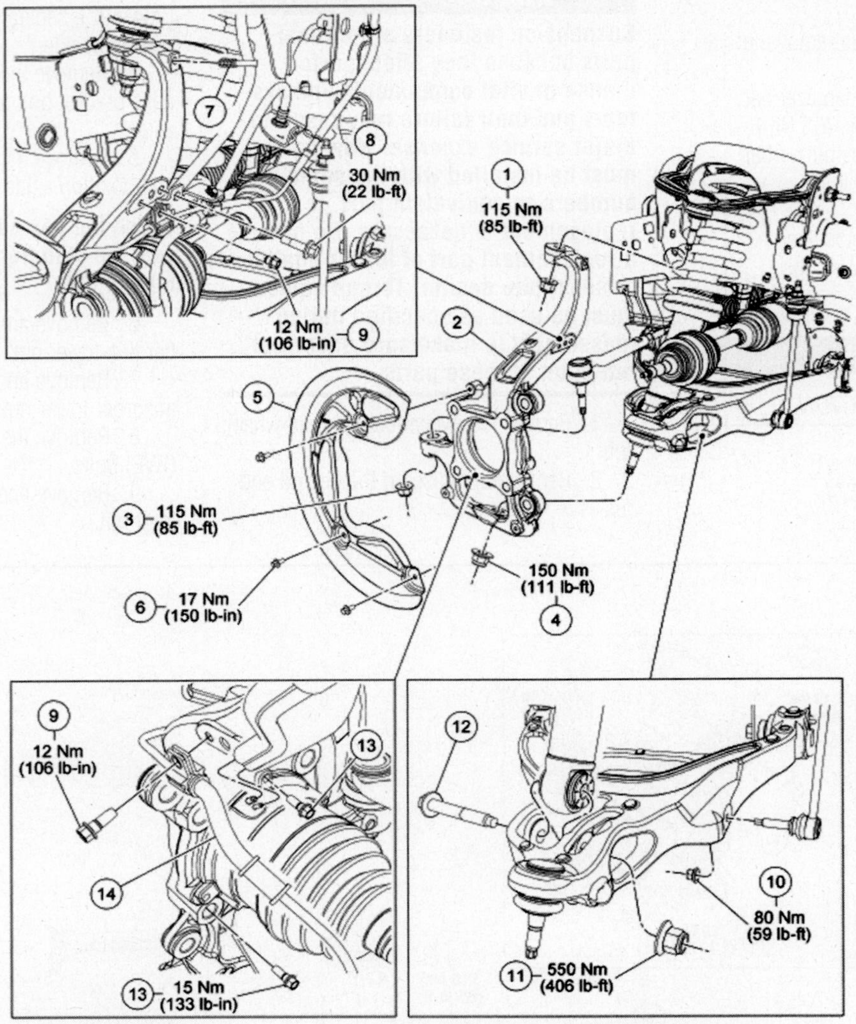

30 Nm
(22 lb-ft)

115 Nm
(85 lb-ft)

12 Nm
(106 lb-in)

115 Nm
(85 lb-ft)

17 Nm
(150 lb-in)

150 Nm
(111 lb-ft)

12 Nm
(106 lb-in)

15 Nm
(133 lb-in)

80 Nm
(59 lb-ft)

550 Nm
(406 lb-ft)

1. Upper ball joint nut
2. Wheel knuckle
3. Tie-rod end nut
4. Lower ball joint nut
5. Brake disc shield
6. Brake disc shield bolts (3 required)
7. Integrated Wheel End (IWE) vacuum hose push-pin retainer
8. Brake hose bracket bolt
9. Wheel speed sensor harness bracket bolt
10. Stabilizer bar link lower nut
11. Shock absorber lower nut
12. Shock absorber lower bolt
13. IWE bolts (3 required)
14. Wheel speed sensor harness bracket

N0105877

Fig. 571 Exploded view of the wheel knuckle assembly—SVT Raptor

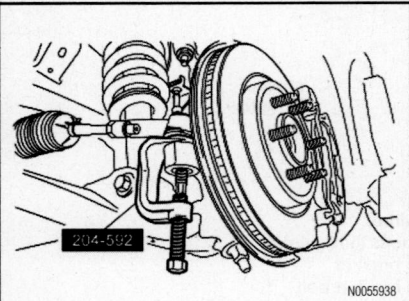

204-592

N0055938

Fig. 572 Using the Ball Joint Separator, separate the tie-rod end from the wheel knuckle

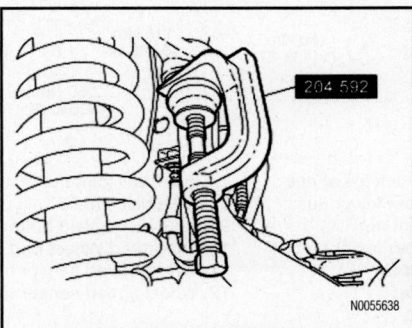

204-592

N0055638

Fig. 573 Using the Ball Joint Separator, separate the upper ball joint from the wheel knuckle

➡ **Be sure not to damage the ball joint boot when installing the Ball Joint Separator.**

10. Using the Ball Joint Separator (204-592), separate the upper ball joint from the wheel knuckle.

11. Remove and discard the lower ball joint nut.

✲ WARNING

Make sure to use the Ball Joint Separator when separating the lower ball joint from the knuckle to prevent damage to the ball joint boot.

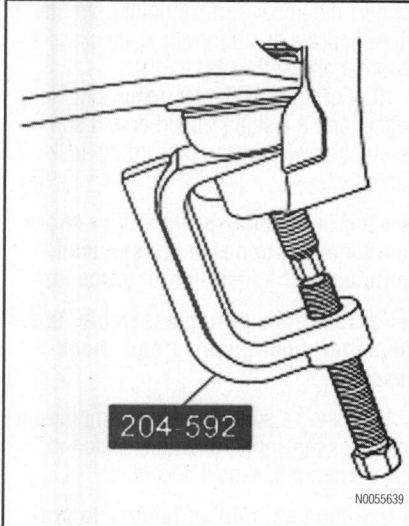

Fig. 574 Using the Ball Joint Separator, separate the lower ball joint from the wheel knuckle and remove the wheel knuckle

12. Using the Ball Joint Separator (204-592), separate the lower ball joint from the wheel knuckle and remove the wheel knuckle.

13. If necessary, remove the 3 brake disc shield bolts and remove the brake disc shield.

To install:

❊❊ WARNING

Do not tighten the lower shock nut until the installation procedure is complete and the weight of the vehicle is resting on the wheel and tire assemblies or incorrect clamp load and bushing damage may occur.

➡ **When servicing the shock absorber lower nut, take care not to damage the stabilizer link.**

14. If necessary, install the brake disc shield and 3 brake disc shield bolts. Tighten to 13 ft. lbs. (17 Nm).

15. Position the lower ball joint into the wheel knuckle and install the new nut. Tighten to 111 ft. lbs. (150 Nm).

16. Position the upper ball joint and install the new nut. Tighten to 85 ft. lbs. (115 Nm).

17. Position the IWE and install the 3 IWE bolts. Tighten to 10 ft. lbs. (15 Nm).

➡ **Do not tighten the nut at this time.**

18. Loosely install the new shock absorber lower nut and bolt.

➡ **Use the hex-holding feature to prevent the stud from turning while installing the nut.**

19. Install the new stabilizer bar link lower nut. Tighten to 59 ft. lbs. (80 Nm).

20. Position the wheel speed sensor harness bracket and install the bolt. Tighten to 106 inch lbs. (12 Nm).

21. Position the brake hose bracket and install the bolt. Tighten to 22 ft. lbs. (30 Nm).

22. Install the new tie-rod end nut. Tighten to 85 ft. lbs. (115 Nm).

23. Install the wheel bearing and wheel hub.

24. With the weight of the vehicle on the wheel and tire, tighten the shock absorber lower nut to 406 ft. lbs. (550 Nm).

25. Check and, if necessary, align the front end.

RWD Models

See Figures 575 and 576.

❊❊ WARNING

Suspension fasteners are critical parts because they affect performance of vital components and systems and their failure may result in

major service expense. New parts must be installed with the same part numbers or equivalent parts, if replacement is necessary. Do not use a replacement part of lesser quality or substitute design. Torque values must be used as specified during reassembly to make sure of correct retention of these parts.

1. Remove the wheel bearing and wheel hub.

2. Remove and discard the tie-rod end nut.

3. Using the Ball Joint Separator, separate the tie-rod end from the wheel knuckle.

4. Remove the wheel speed sensor harness bracket bolt and position the harness aside.

➡ **Use the hex-holding feature to prevent the stud from turning while removing the nut.**

5. Remove and discard the stabilizer bar link lower nut.

6. Remove and discard the shock absorber lower nut and bolt.

7. Remove and discard the upper ball joint nut.

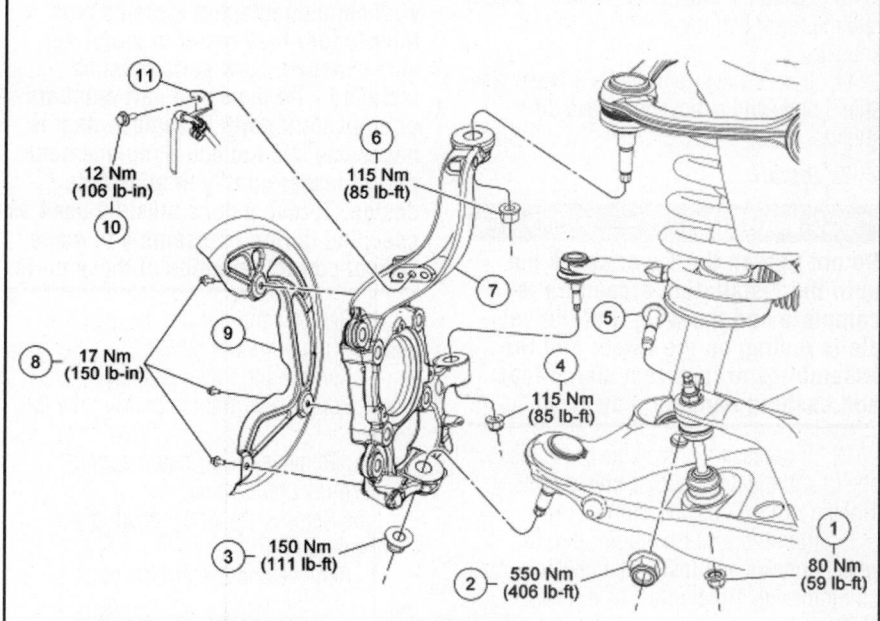

1. Stabilizer bar link lower nut
2. Shock absorber lower nut
3. Lower ball joint nut
4. Tie-rod end nut
5. Shock absorber lower bolt
6. Upper ball joint nut
7. Wheel knuckle
8. Brake disc shield bolts (3 required)
9. Brake disc shield
10. Wheel speed sensor harness bracket bolt
11. Wheel speed sensor harness bracket

Fig. 575 Exploded view of the wheel knuckle assembly

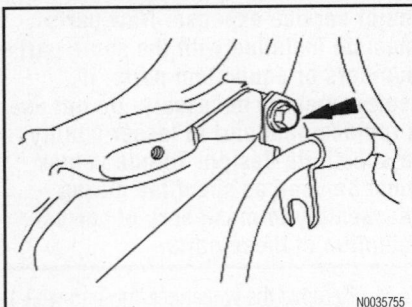

Fig. 576 Remove the wheel speed sensor harness bracket bolt and position the harness aside

➡Be sure not to damage the ball joint boot when installing the Ball Joint Separator.

8. Using the Ball Joint Separator, separate the upper ball joint from the wheel knuckle.

9. Remove and discard the lower ball joint nut.

✳✳ WARNING

Make sure to use the Ball Joint Separator when separating the lower ball joint from the knuckle to prevent damage to the ball joint boot.

10. Using the Ball Joint Separator, separate the lower ball joint from the wheel knuckle.

11. If necessary, remove the 3 brake disc shield bolts and remove the brake disc shield.

To install:

✳✳ WARNING

Do not tighten the lower shock nut until the installation procedure is complete and the weight of the vehicle is resting on the wheel and tire assemblies or incorrect clamp load and bushing damage may occur.

12. If necessary, install the brake disc shield and the 3 brake disc shield bolts. Tighten to 13 ft. lbs. (17 Nm).

Position the lower ball joint into the wheel knuckle and install the new lower ball joint nut. Tighten to 111 ft. lbs. (150 Nm).

13. Position the upper ball joint into the wheel knuckle and install the new upper ball joint nut. Tighten to 85 ft. lbs. (115 Nm).

➡Do not tighten the nut at this time.

14. Loosely install the new shock absorber lower nut and bolt.

➡Use the hex-holding feature to prevent the stud from turning while installing the nut.

15. Position the stabilizer bar link and install the new stabilizer bar link lower nut. Tighten to 59 ft. lbs. (80 Nm).

16. Position the wheel speed sensor harness bracket and install the wheel speed sensor harness bracket bolt. Tighten to 106 inch lbs. (12 Nm).

17. Position the tie-rod end and install the new tie-rod end nut. Tighten to 85 ft. lbs. (115 Nm).

18. Install the wheel bearing and wheel hub.

19. With the weight of the vehicle on the wheel and tire, tighten the shock absorber lower nut to 406 ft. lbs. (550 Nm).

20. Check and, if necessary, align the front end.

STRUT & SPRING ASSEMBLY

REMOVAL & INSTALLATION

4WD Models

See Figures 577 through 580.

✳✳ WARNING

Suspension fasteners are critical parts because they affect performance of vital components and systems and their failure may result in major service expense. New parts must be installed with the same part numbers or equivalent parts, if replacement is necessary. Do not use a replacement part of lesser quality or substitute design. Torque values must be used as specified during reassembly to make sure of correct retention of these parts.

1. Remove and discard the shock absorber upper mount nuts.

2. Remove the wheel and tire.

3. For the SVT Raptor, perform the following:

   a. Remove the strut and spring assembly upper spacer.

   b. Remove the wheel bearing and wheel hub.

4. Remove and discard the tie-rod end nut.

5. Using the Ball Joint Separator, separate the tie-rod end from the wheel knuckle.

6. Remove and discard the upper ball joint nut.

7. Remove and discard the shock absorber lower nut and bolt.

8. Using the Ball Joint Separator, dis-

connect the upper arm ball joint from the wheel knuckle and remove the shock absorber and spring assembly.

9. For the SVT Raptor, remove the lock washer and the shock absorber and spring assembly lower spacer. Discard the lock washer.

➡If the individual spring and/or shock components are not being serviced, continue to the installation procedure.

➡For reference during assembly, index the upper mount, spring and shock absorber.

10. Using a suitable spring compressor, compress the spring until the tension is released from the shock absorber.

➡Use the hex-holding feature to prevent the shock rod from turning while removing the nut.

11. While holding the shock rod, remove the nut and the shock absorber. Discard the nut.

12. Remove the upper mount, dust boot and insulator.

To install:

✳✳ WARNING

Do not tighten the lower shock nut until the installation procedure is complete and the weight of the vehicle is resting on the wheel and tire assemblies or incorrect clamp load and bushing damage may occur.

13. Position the shock absorber and spring and install the dust boot (if equipped), insulator and the upper mount.

➡Align the index marks made during disassembly.

14. Using a suitable spring compressor, compress the spring until the tension is released from the shock absorber.

➡Use the hex-holding feature to prevent the shock rod from turning while installing the nut.

15. While holding the shock rod, install the new shock absorber and the shock rod nut. Tighten to 41 ft. lbs. (55 Nm).

16. For the SVT Raptor, install the shock absorber and spring assembly lower spacer and a new lock washer.

➡Do not tighten the nut at this time.

17. Position the shock absorber and loosely install the new shock absorber lower nut and bolt.

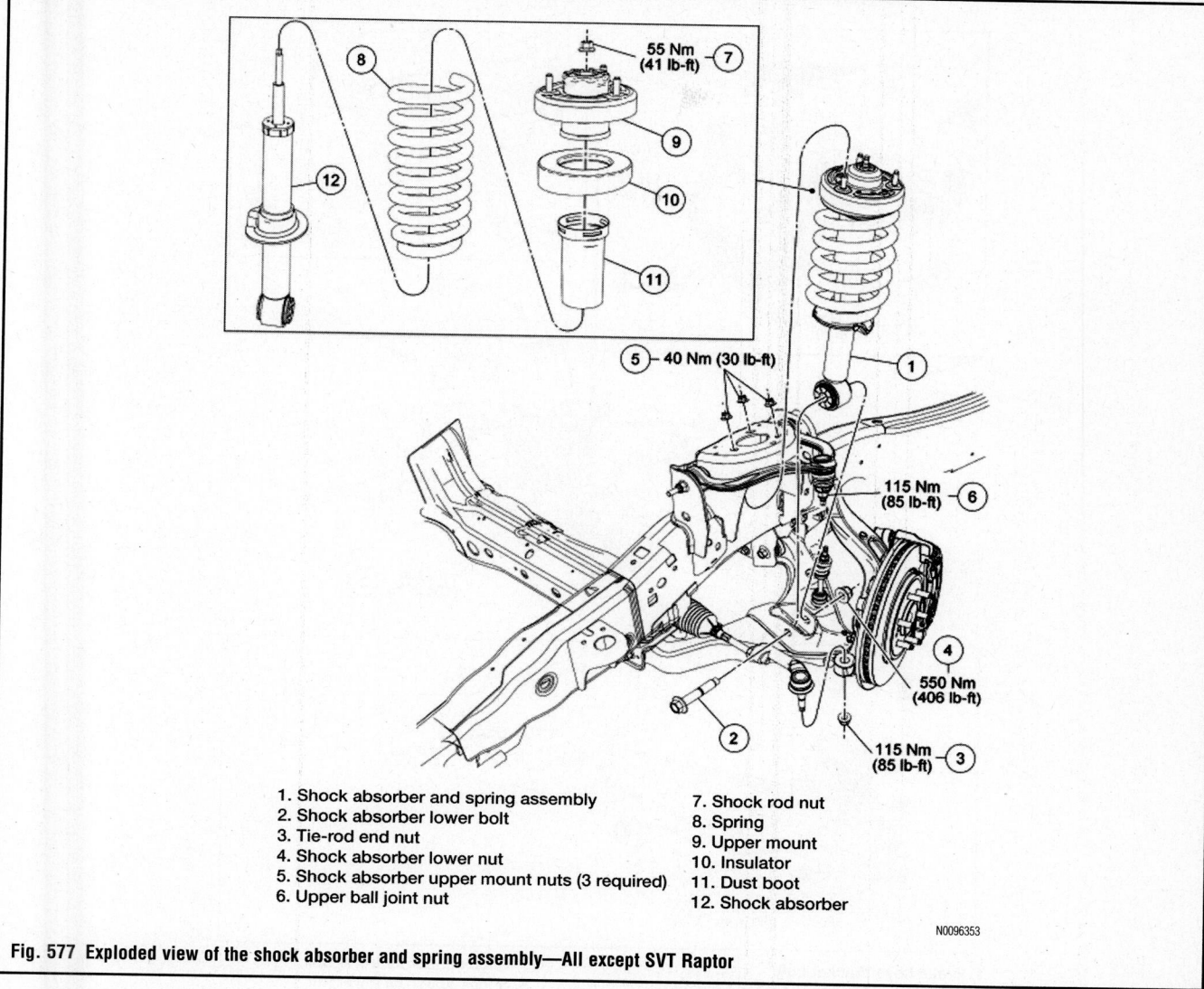

1. Shock absorber and spring assembly
2. Shock absorber lower bolt
3. Tie-rod end nut
4. Shock absorber lower nut
5. Shock absorber upper mount nuts (3 required)
6. Upper ball joint nut
7. Shock rod nut
8. Spring
9. Upper mount
10. Insulator
11. Dust boot
12. Shock absorber

Fig. 577 Exploded view of the shock absorber and spring assembly—All except SVT Raptor

18. Connect the upper arm ball joint to the wheel knuckle and install the new nut. Tighten to 85 ft. lbs. (115 Nm).

19. Install the new tie-rod end nut. Tighten to 85 ft. lbs. (115 Nm).

20. For the SVT Raptor, install the wheel bearing and wheel hub.

21. Install the wheel and tire.

22. Install the new shock absorber upper mount nuts. Tighten to 30 ft. lbs. (40 Nm).

23. With the weight of the vehicle on the wheel and tire, tighten the shock absorber lower nut to 406 ft. lbs. (550 Nm).

RWD Models

See Figures 579 through 581.

✴✴ WARNING

Suspension fasteners are critical parts because they affect performance of vital components and systems and their failure may result in major service expense. New parts must be installed with the same part numbers or equivalent parts, if replacement is necessary. Do not use a replacement part of lesser quality or substitute design. Torque values must be used as specified during reassembly to make sure of correct retention of these parts.

1. Remove and discard the shock absorber upper mount nuts.

2. Remove the wheel and tire.

3. Remove and discard the tie-rod end nut.

4. Using the Ball Joint Separator, separate the tie-rod end from the wheel knuckle.

5. Remove and discard the upper ball joint nut.

6. Remove and discard the stabilizer bar link upper nut.

7. Remove and discard the shock absorber lower nut and bolt.

8. Using the Ball Joint Separator, disconnect the upper arm ball joint from the wheel knuckle and remove the shock absorber and spring assembly.

➡️ If the individual spring and/or shock components are not being serviced, continue to the installation procedure.

➡️ For reference during assembly, index the upper mount, spring and shock absorber.

9. Using a suitable spring compressor, compress the spring until the tension is released from the shock absorber.

➡️ Use the hex-holding feature to prevent the shock rod from turning while removing the nut.

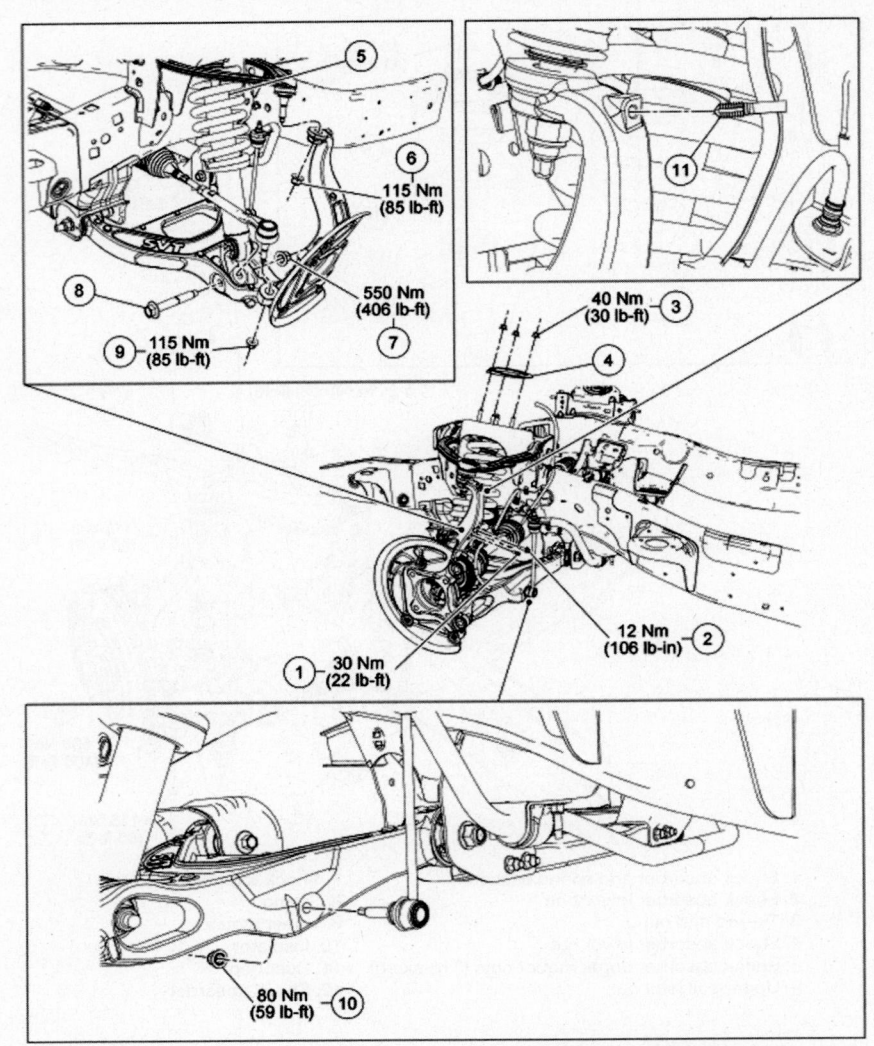

1. Brake hose bracket bolt
2. Wheel speed sensor harness bracket bolt
3. Shock absorber upper mount nuts (3 required)
4. Shock absorber and spring assembly upper spacer
5. Shock absorber and spring assembly
6. Upper ball joint nut
7. Shock absorber lower bolt
8. Shock absorber lower nut
9. Tie-rod end nut
10. Stabilizer bar link lower nut
11. Integrated Wheel End (IWE) vacuum hose pushpin retainer

N0105876

Fig. 578 Exploded view of the shock absorber and spring assembly—SVT Raptor

10. While holding the shock rod, remove the nut and the shock absorber. Discard the nut.

11. Remove the upper mount, dust boot and insulator.

To install:

❋❋ WARNING

Do not tighten the lower shock nut until the installation procedure is complete and the weight of the vehicle is resting on the wheel and tire assemblies or incorrect clamp load and bushing damage may occur. Position the shock absorber and

spring and install the dust boot, insulator and the upper mount.

➤**Align the index marks made during disassembly.**

12. Using a suitable spring compressor, compress the spring until the tension is released from the shock absorber.

➤**Use the hex-holding feature to prevent the shock rod from turning while installing the nut.**

13. While holding the shock rod, install the new shock absorber and the shock rod nut. Tighten to 41 ft. lbs. (55 Nm).

➤**Do not tighten the nut at this time.**

14. Position the shock absorber and loosely install the new shock absorber lower nut and bolt.

15. Connect the upper arm ball joint to the wheel knuckle and install the new nut. Tighten to 85 ft. lbs. (115 Nm).

16. Install a new stabilizer bar link upper nut. Tighten to 59 ft. lbs. (80 Nm).

17. Install the new tie-rod end nut. Tighten to 85 ft. lbs. (115 Nm).

18. Install the wheel and tire.

19. Install the new shock absorber upper mount nuts. Tighten to 30 ft. lbs. (40 Nm).

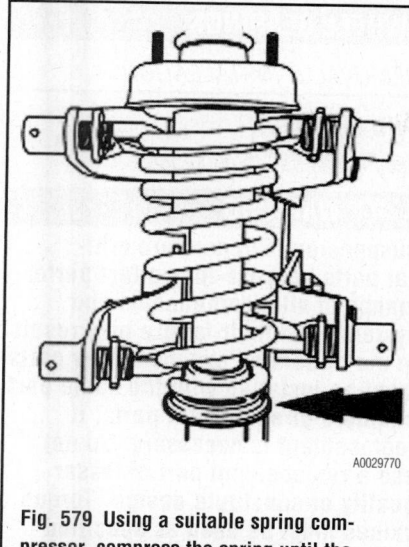

Fig. 579 Using a suitable spring compressor, compress the spring until the tension is released from the shock absorber

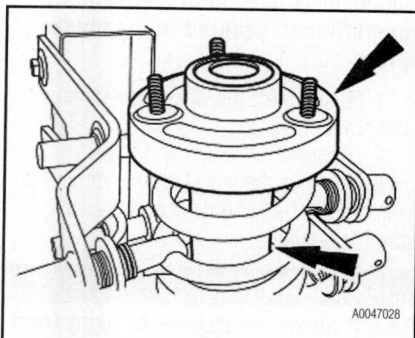

Fig. 580 Remove the upper mount, dust boot and insulator

20. With the weight of the vehicle on the wheel and tire, tighten the shock absorber lower nut to 406 ft. lbs. (550 Nm).

UPPER CONTROL ARM

REMOVAL & INSTALLATION

4WD Models

See Figures 582 and 583.

✳✳ WARNING

Suspension fasteners are critical parts because they affect performance of vital components and systems and their failure may result in major service expense. New parts must be installed with the same part numbers or equivalent parts, if replacement is necessary. Do not use a replacement part of lesser quality or substitute design. Torque values

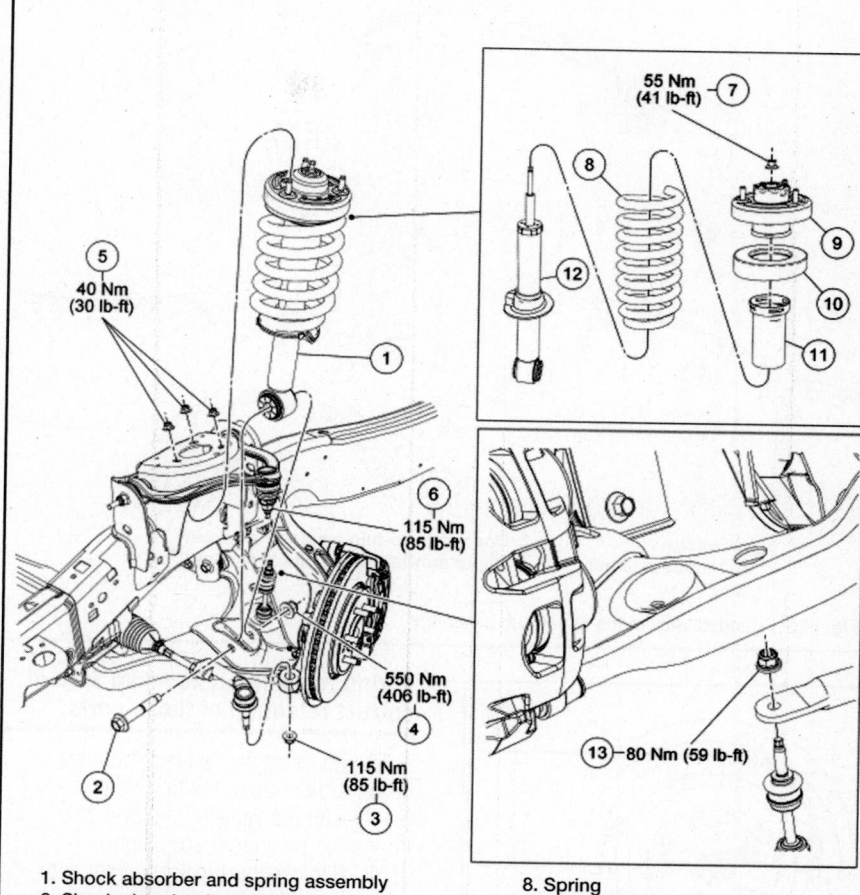

1. Shock absorber and spring assembly
2. Shock absorber lower bolt
3. Tie-rod end nut
4. Shock absorber lower nut
5. Shock absorber upper mount nuts (3 required)
6. Upper ball joint nut
7. Shock rod nut
8. Spring
9. Upper mount
10. Insulator
11. Dust boot
12. Shock absorber
13. Stabilizer bar link upper nut

Fig. 581 Exploded view of the shock absorber and spring assembly

must be used as specified during reassembly to make sure of correct retention of these parts.

1. Measure the distance from the center of the hub to the lip of the fender with the vehicle in a level, static ground position (curb height).
2. Remove the shock absorber and spring assembly.
3. Remove and discard the upper ball joint nut.
4. Using the Ball Joint Separator, separate the upper ball joint from the wheel knuckle.
5. Remove the upper arm-to-frame nuts and bolts and the upper arm. Discard the nuts and bolts.

To install:

➡**Do not tighten the nuts at this time.**

6. Position the upper arm and loosely install the new upper arm-to-frame bolts and nuts.
7. Install the shock absorber and spring assembly.
8. Position the ball joint into the wheel knuckle and install the new upper ball joint nut. Tighten to 85 ft. lbs. (115 Nm).
9. Use a suitable jack to raise the suspension until the distance between the center of the hub and the lip of the fender is equal to the measurement taken in Step 1 (curb height).
10. Tighten the upper arm-to-frame nuts to 111 ft. lbs. (150 Nm).

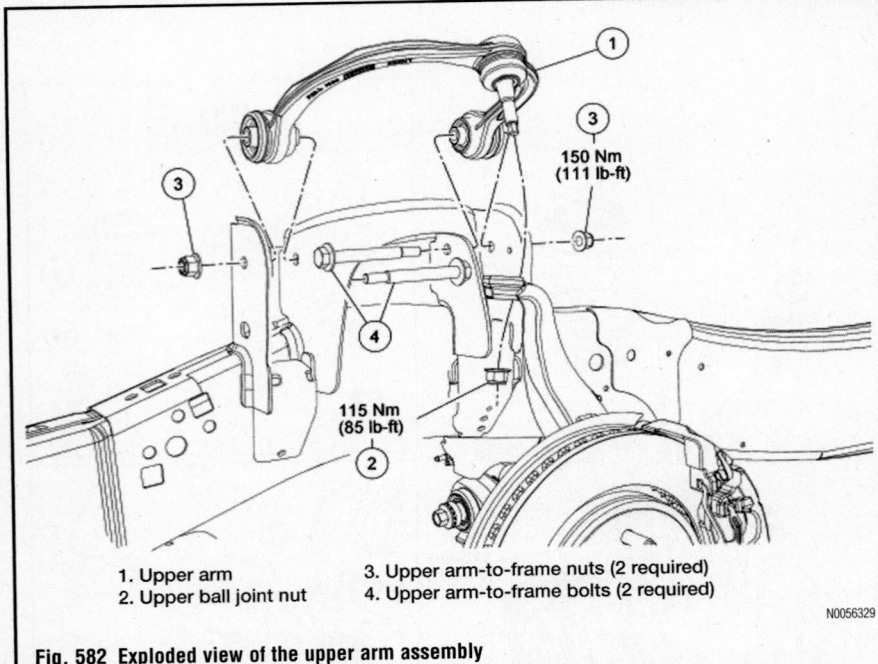

1. Upper arm
2. Upper ball joint nut
3. Upper arm-to-frame nuts (2 required)
4. Upper arm-to-frame bolts (2 required)

N0056329

Fig. 582 Exploded view of the upper arm assembly

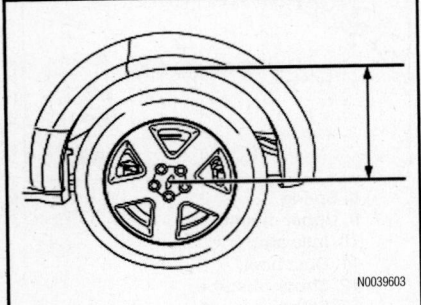

N0039603

Fig. 583 Measure the distance from the center of the hub to the lip of the fender with the vehicle in a level, static ground position (curb height)

11. Check and, if necessary, align the front end.

RWD Models

See Figure 582.

❊❊❊ WARNING

Suspension fasteners are critical parts because they affect performance of vital components and systems and their failure may result in major service expense. New parts must be installed with the same part numbers or equivalent parts, if replacement is necessary. Do not use a replacement part of lesser quality or substitute design. Torque values must be used as specified

during reassembly to make sure of correct retention of these parts.

1. Measure the distance from the center of the hub to the lip of the fender with the vehicle in a level, static ground position (curb height).
2. Remove the shock absorber and spring assembly.
3. Remove and discard the upper ball joint nut.
4. Using the Ball Joint Separator, separate the upper ball joint from the wheel knuckle.
5. Remove the upper arm-to-frame nuts and bolts and the upper arm. Discard the nuts and bolts.

To install:

➡ **Do not tighten the nuts at this time.**

6. Position the upper arm and loosely install the new upper arm-to-frame bolts and nuts.
7. Install the shock absorber and spring assembly.
8. Position the ball joint into the wheel knuckle and install the new upper ball joint nut. Tighten to 85 ft. lbs. (115 Nm).
9. Use a suitable jack to raise the suspension until the distance between the center of the hub and the lip of the fender is equal to the measurement taken in Step 1 (curb height).
10. Tighten the upper arm-to-frame nuts to 111 ft. lbs. (150 Nm).
11. Check and, if necessary, align the front end.

WHEEL BEARINGS

REMOVAL & INSTALLATION

4WD Models

See Figures 584 through 586.

❊❊❊ WARNING

Suspension fasteners are critical parts because they affect performance of vital components and systems and their failure may result in major service expense. New parts must be installed with the same part numbers or equivalent parts, if replacement is necessary. Do not use a replacement part of lesser quality or substitute design. Torque values must be used as specified during reassembly to make sure of correct retention of these parts.

➡ **The wheel speed sensor electrical connector is located in the engine compartment, secured to the fender apron.**

1. Disconnect the wheel speed sensor electrical connector.
2. Remove the wheel and tire.
3. Remove the wheel speed sensor harness bracket bolt and detach the harness from the retainers.

❊❊❊ WARNING

Do not allow the caliper to hang from the brake hose or damage to the hose may result.

4. Remove the 2 bolts and position the brake caliper and anchor plate assembly aside. Discard the bolts.
5. Support the brake caliper and anchor plate assembly using mechanic's wire.
6. Remove the brake disc.
7. Remove the halfshaft nut dust cap.
8. Remove and discard the halfshaft nut.
9. Remove the 4 bolts and the wheel bearing and hub. Discard the bolts.
10. If installing a new wheel bearing and wheel hub, remove the wheel speed sensor bolt and the wheel speed sensor.

❊❊❊ WARNING

If the original wheel bearing and wheel hub is being installed, install a new wheel hub O-ring seal or damage to the wheel bearing may occur.

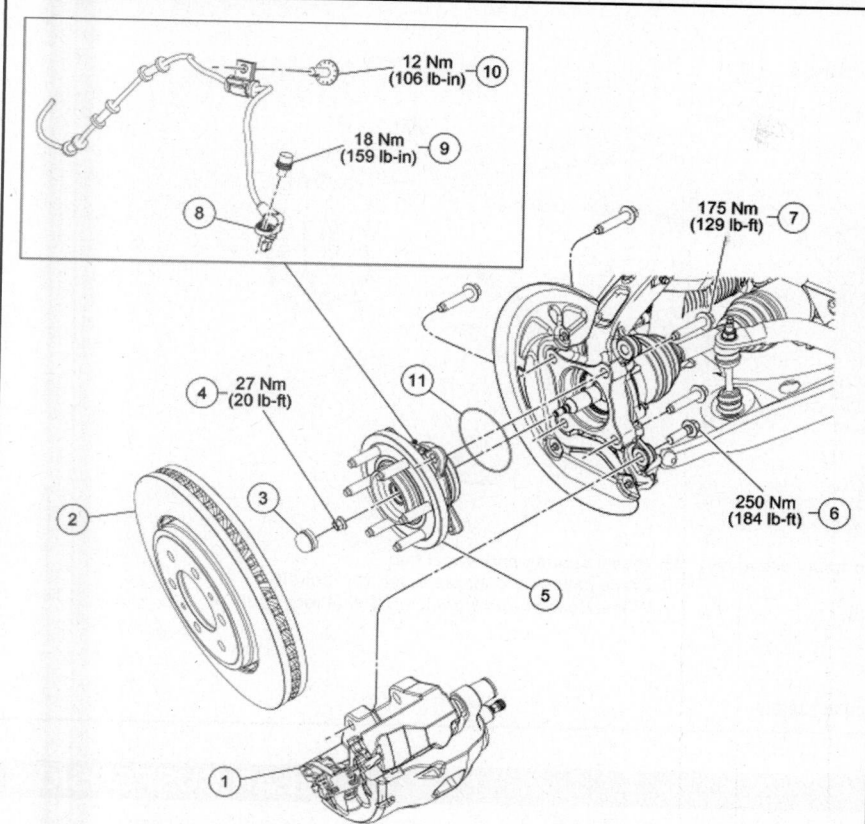

Fig. 584 Exploded view of wheel hub and bearing assembly

1. Brake caliper and anchor plate assembly
2. Brake disc
3. Dust cap
4. Halfshaft nut
5. Wheel bearing and wheel hub
6. Brake caliper anchor plate bolt (2 required)
7. Wheel bearing and wheel hub bolt (4 required)
8. Wheel speed sensor
9. Wheel speed sensor bolt
10. Wheel speed sensor harness bracket bolt
11. O-ring seal

N0102737

⁕⁕ WARNING

Verify the spline engagement by checking for spline lash before installing the halfshaft nut or damage to the halfshaft and wheel bearing and hub may occur.

11. To install, reverse the removal procedure.

    a. Tighten the wheel speed sensor bolt to 13 ft. lbs. (18 Nm).

    b. Tighten the new hub bolts to 129 ft. lbs. (175 Nm).

    c. Tighten the new halfshaft nut to 20 ft. lbs. (27 Nm).

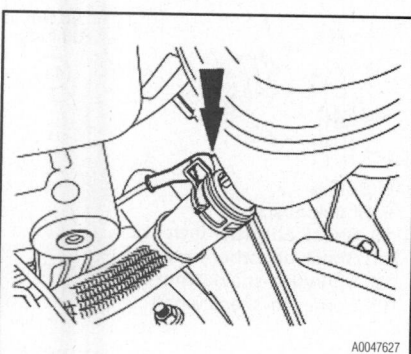

Fig. 585 Disconnect the wheel speed sensor electrical connector

A0047627

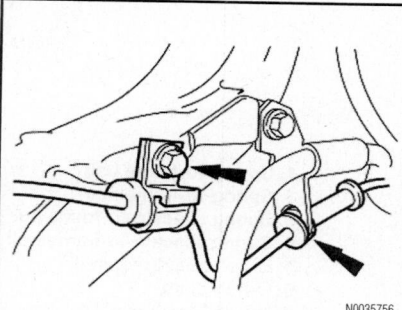

Fig. 586 Remove the wheel speed sensor harness bracket bolt and detach the harness from the retainers

N0035756

    d. Tighten the new brake caliper bolts to 184 ft. lbs. (250 Nm).

    e. Tighten the wheel speed sensor harness bracket bolt to 106 inch lbs. (12 Nm).

RWD Models

See Figure 587.

⁕⁕ WARNING

Suspension fasteners are critical parts because they affect performance of vital components and systems and their failure may result in major service expense. New parts must be installed with the same part numbers or equivalent parts, if replacement is necessary. Do not use a replacement part of lesser quality or substitute design. Torque values must be used as specified during reassembly to make sure of correct retention of these parts.

➡ **The wheel speed electrical connector is located in the engine compartment secured to the fender apron.**

1. Disconnect the wheel speed sensor electrical connector.

2. Remove the wheel and tire.

3. Remove the wheel speed sensor harness bracket bolt and detach the harness from the retainers.

⁕⁕ WARNING

Do not allow the caliper to hang from the brake hose or damage to the hose may result.

4. Remove the 2 bolts and position the brake caliper and anchor plate assembly aside. Discard the bolts.

5. Support the brake caliper and anchor plate assembly using mechanic's wire.

6. Remove the brake disc.

7. Remove the 4 bolts and the wheel bearing and wheel hub. Discard the 4 bolts.

8. If installing a new wheel bearing and wheel hub, remove the bolt and the wheel speed sensor.

9. To install, reverse the removal procedure.

    a. Tighten the wheel speed sensor bolt to 13 ft. lbs. (18 Nm).

    b. Tighten the new wheel hub bolts to 129 ft. lbs. (175 Nm).

    c. Tighten the brake caliper bolts to 184 ft. lbs. (250 Nm).

ADJUSTMENT

No adjustment is possible. If there is damage, wear, or excess play, replace the bearing.

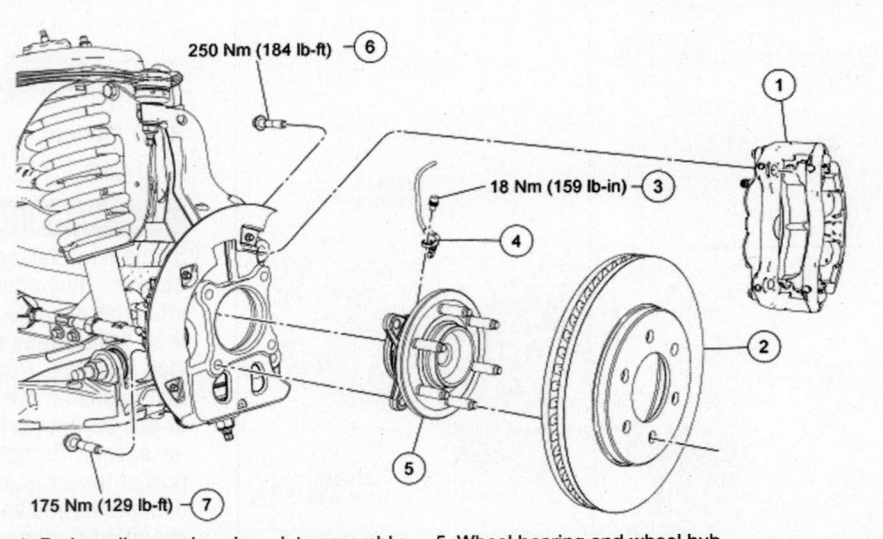

250 Nm (184 lb-ft) — ⑥

18 Nm (159 lb-in) — ③

175 Nm (129 lb-ft) — ⑦

1. Brake caliper and anchor plate assembly
2. Brake disc
3. Wheel speed sensor bolt
4. Wheel speed sensor
5. Wheel bearing and wheel hub
6. Brake caliper anchor plate bolt (2 required)
7. Wheel bearing and wheel hub bolt (4 required)

N0102888

Fig. 587 Exploded view of the wheel hub and bearing assembly

SUSPENSION   REAR SUSPENSION

LEAF SPRING

REMOVAL & INSTALLATION

See Figure 588.

✳✳ CAUTION

Do not apply heat or flame to the shock absorber or strut tube. The shock absorber and strut tube are gas pressurized and could explode if heated. Failure to follow this instruction may result in serious personal injury.

✳✳ CAUTION

Keep all body parts clear of shock absorbers or strut rods. Shock absorbers or struts can extend unassisted. Failure to follow this instruction may result in serious personal injury.

✳✳ WARNING

Suspension fasteners are critical parts because they affect performance of vital components and systems and their failure may result in major service expense. New parts must be installed with the same part numbers or equivalent part, if

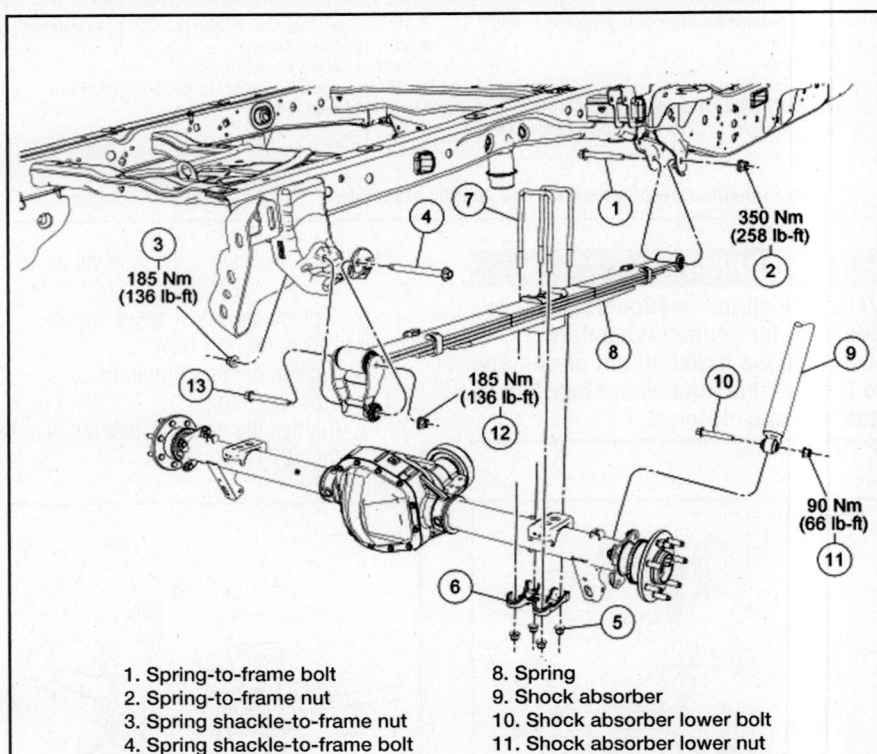

185 Nm (136 lb-ft)

185 Nm (136 lb-ft)

350 Nm (258 lb-ft)

90 Nm (66 lb-ft)

1. Spring-to-frame bolt
2. Spring-to-frame nut
3. Spring shackle-to-frame nut
4. Spring shackle-to-frame bolt
5. U-bolt nut (4 required)
6. U-bolt plate
7. U-bolt (2 required)
8. Spring
9. Shock absorber
10. Shock absorber lower bolt
11. Shock absorber lower nut
12. Spring-to-shackle nut
13. Spring-to-shackle bolt

N0106006

Fig. 588 Exploded view of rear leaf spring assembly

replacement is necessary. Do not use a replacement part of lesser quality or substitute design. Torque values must be used as specified during reassembly to make sure of correct retention of these parts.

1. Remove the wheel and tire.
2. Using a suitable jack, support the axle.
3. Remove the shock absorber lower nut and bolt. Discard the nut and bolt.
4. Remove the 4 U-bolt nuts, the U-bolt plate and the 2 U-bolts. Discard the nuts and the U-bolts.
5. For the LH spring, lower the fuel tank to gain access to the spring shackle-to-frame bolt.
6. For the RH spring, remove the muffler to gain access to the spring-to-frame bolt.
7. Remove and discard the spring-to-frame nut and bolt.
8. Remove and discard the spring shackle-to-frame nut and bolt.

➡ **Only lower the axle enough to gain access to remove the spring.**

9. Lower the jack and remove the spring and shackle assembly.
10. If necessary, remove the spring-to-shackle nut, bolt and spring shackle. Discard the nut and bolt.
11. For 4WD vehicles, remove the Four-Wheel Drive (4WD) spring spacer.

To install:

➡ **The SVT Raptor spring spacer must be positioned with the jounce bumper pad inboard and the arrow facing the front of the vehicle.**

12. For 4WD vehicles, position the spring spacer and make sure that it is correctly seated between the axle and spring with the nose pointed to the front of the vehicle.
13. If necessary, install a new shackle-to-spring bolt and nut. Tighten until snug.
14. Position the spring and install a new spring shackle-to-frame bolt and nut. Tighten until snug.
15. Position the U-bolt plate and install the new U-bolts and nuts. Tighten until snug.
16. Install a new spring-to-frame bolt and nut. Tighten until snug.
17. Install a new shock absorber lower bolt and nut. Tighten until snug.
18. Install the wheel and tire.
19. Lower the vehicle until the weight of the vehicle is resting on the wheels and tires (curb height).

20. Tighten the spring shackle-to-frame nut to 136 ft. lbs. (185 Nm).
21. Tighten the spring-to-frame nut to 258 ft. lbs. (350 Nm).
22. If necessary, tighten the spring-to-shackle nut to 136 ft. lbs. (185 Nm).
23. For the LH spring, raise the fuel tank.
24. For the RH spring, install the muffler.
25. Tighten the U-bolt nuts in 4 stages.
   a. Stage 1: Tighten in a cross pattern to 26 ft. lbs. (35 Nm).
   b. Stage 2: Tighten in a cross pattern to 52 ft. lbs. (70 Nm).
   c. Stage 3: Tighten in a cross pattern to 74 ft. lbs. (100 Nm).
   d. Stage 4: Tighten in a cross pattern to 98 ft. lbs. (133 Nm).
26. Tighten the shock absorber lower nut to 66 ft. lbs. (90 Nm).

SHOCK ABSORBER

REMOVAL & INSTALLATION
See Figures 589 and 590.

❋❋ CAUTION

Do not apply heat or flame to the shock absorber or strut tube. The shock absorber and strut tube are gas pressurized and could explode if heated. Failure to follow this instruction may result in serious personal injury.

❋❋ CAUTION

Keep all body parts clear of shock absorbers or strut rods. Shock absorbers or struts can extend unassisted. Failure to follow this instruction may result in serious personal injury.

❋❋ WARNING

Suspension fasteners are critical parts because they affect performance of vital components and systems and their failure may result in major service expense. New parts must be installed with the same part numbers or equivalent part, if replacement is necessary. Do not use a replacement part of lesser quality or substitute design. Torque values must be used as specified during reassembly to make sure of correct retention of these parts.

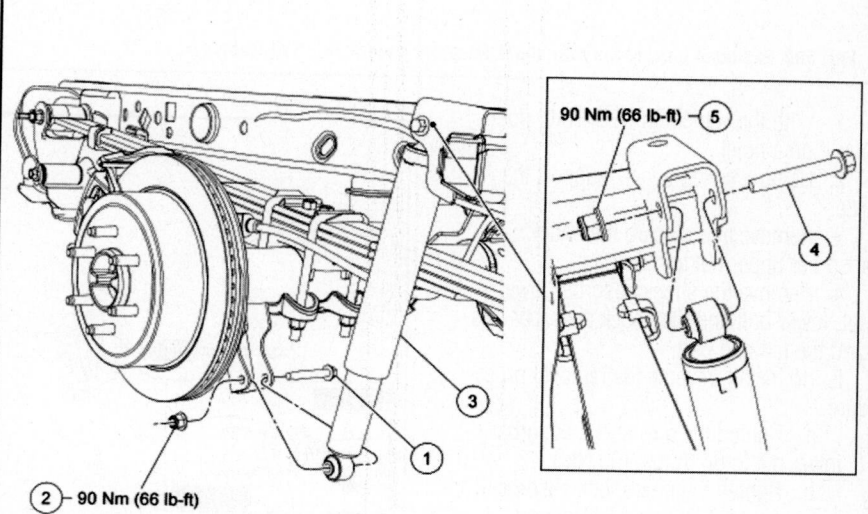

2 — 90 Nm (66 lb-ft)

90 Nm (66 lb-ft) — 5

1. Shock absorber lower bolt
2. Shock absorber lower nut
3. Shock absorber
4. Shock absorber upper bolt
5. Shock absorber upper nut

N0074806

Fig. 589 Exploded view of the rear shock absorber assembly—All except SVT Raptor

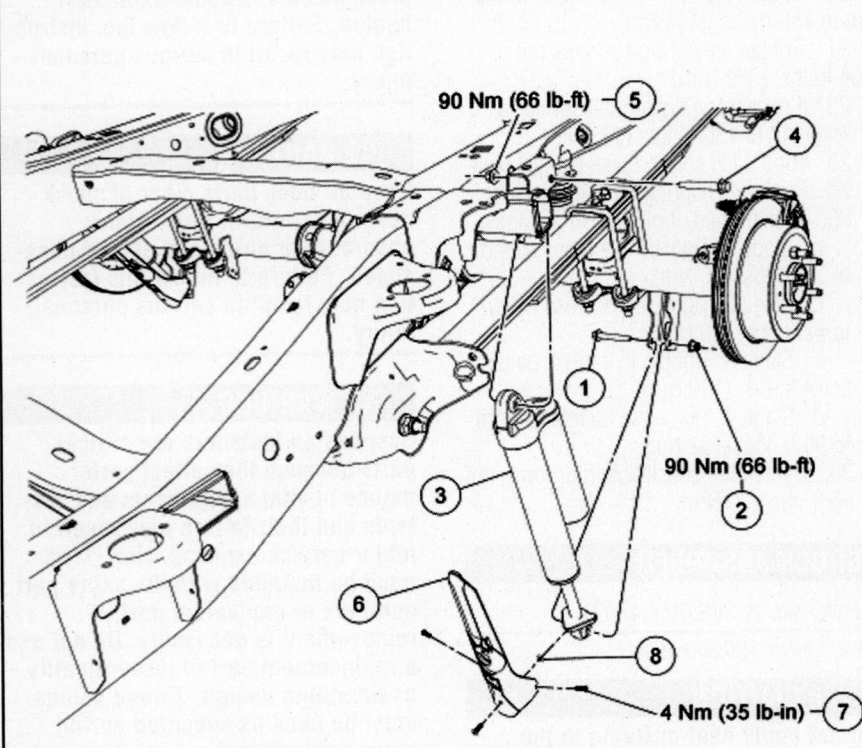

Fig. 590 Exploded view of the rear shock absorber assembly—SVT Raptor

90 Nm (66 lb-ft) — 5
4
90 Nm (66 lb-ft)
2
1
3
6
8
4 Nm (35 lb-in) — 7

1. Shock absorber lower bolt
2. Shock absorber lower nut
3. Shock absorber
4. Shock absorber upper bolt
5. Shock absorber upper nut
6. Shock absorber shield
7. Shock absorber shield bolt (3 required)
8. Shock absorber shield washer

N0105991

1. With the vehicle in NEUTRAL, position it on a hoist.

2. Using a suitable jack, support the axle.

3. Remove and discard the shock absorber upper nut and bolt.

4. Remove the shock absorber lower nut, lower bolt and the shock absorber. Discard the nut and bolt.

5. To install, reverse the removal procedure.

   a. Tighten the new shock absorber lower nut to 66 ft. lbs. (90 Nm).

   b. Tighten the new shock absorber upper nut to 66 ft. lbs. (90 Nm).

WHEEL BEARINGS

REMOVAL & INSTALLATION

8.8-inch Ring Gear Rear Axle

See Figures 591 through 593.

1. Remove the axle shaft.

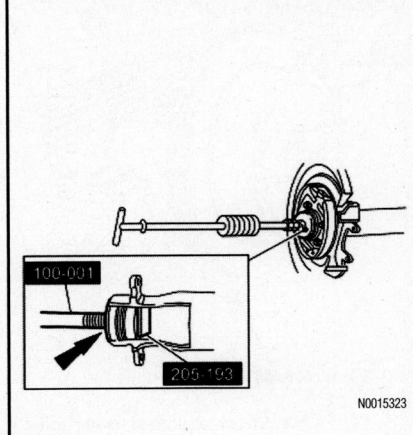

Fig. 591 Using the Axle Bearing Remover and Slide Hammer, remove the rear wheel bearing

N0015323

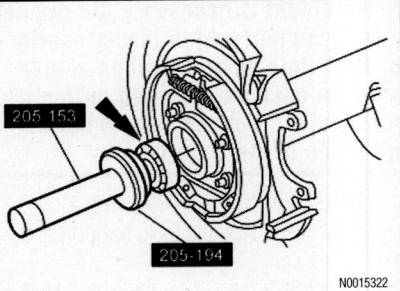

Fig. 592 Use the Axle Bearing Installer and Handle to install the rear wheel bearing

N0015322

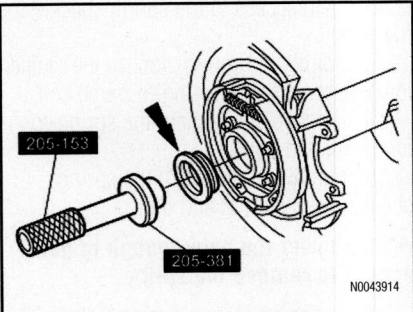

Fig. 593 Using the Axle Oil Seal Installer and Handle, install the new axle shaft oil seal

N0043914

➡ If the axle shaft oil seal is leaking, the axle housing vent may be plugged with foreign material.

➡ Use care to avoid damaging the axle shaft oil seal bore.

2. Using a suitable seal remover, remove and discard the axle shaft oil seal.

3. Inspect the rear wheel bearing and axle shaft for wear or damage.

4. Using the Axle Bearing Remover (205-193) and Slide Hammer (100-001), remove the rear wheel bearing.

To install:

5. Lubricate the new rear wheel bearing with axle lubricant.

6. Using the Axle Bearing Installer (205-194) and Handle (205-153), install the rear wheel bearing.

7. Lubricate the lip of the new axle shaft oil seal with grease.

8. Using the Axle Oil Seal Installer (205-381) and Handle (205-153), install the new axle shaft oil seal.

9. Install the axle shaft.

ADJUSTMENT

No adjustment is possible. If there is damage, wear, or excess play, replace the bearing and seal.

FORD

F-250 • F-350

8

BRAKES 8-15

ANTI-LOCK BRAKE SYSTEM (ABS) 8-15
General Information..................8-15
  Precautions.........................8-15
Speed Sensors 8-15
  Removal & Installation..........8-15
BLEEDING THE BRAKE SYSTEM 8-19
Bleeding Procedure.................8-19
  Bleeding Procedure 8-19
  Bleeding the ABS System 8-20
  Master Cylinder Bleeding 8-20
FRONT DISC BRAKES 8-21
Brake Caliper........................8-21
  Removal & Installation..........8-21
Disc Brake Pads 8-22
  Removal & Installation..........8-22
PARKING BRAKE 8-24
Parking Brake Shoes 8-24
  Parking Brake Shoe
  Adjustment 8-25
  Removal & Installation..........8-24
REAR DISC BRAKES 8-23
Brake Caliper........................8-23
  Removal & Installation..........8-23
Disc Brake Pads 8-23
  Removal & Installation..........8-23

CHASSIS ELECTRICAL 8-25

AIR BAG (SUPPLEMENTAL RESTRAINT SYSTEM) 8-25
General Information..................8-25
  Clockspring Centering..........8-30
  Deactivation and Reactivation
   of System 8-26
  Depowering and Repowering
   the System......................8-29
  Service Precautions 8-25

DRIVE TRAIN 8-32

Automatic Transmission
  Fluid................................8-32
  Drain and Refill..................8-32
  Filter Replacement 8-33
Clutch..................................8-39

Bleeding 8-40
  Removal & Installation..........8-39
Front Driveshaft....................8-42
  Removal & Installation..........8-42
Front Pinion Seal 8-42
  Removal & Installation..........8-42
Manual Transmission Assembly...8-34
  Removal & Installation..........8-34
Manual Transmission Fluid......8-39
  Drain and Refill 8-39
Rear Axle Shaft......................8-43
  Removal & Installation..........8-43
Rear Axle Wheel Bearing and
  Hub Seal 8-46
  Removal & Installation..........8-46
Rear Axle Wheel Hub 8-44
  Removal & Installation..........8-44
Rear Driveshaft......................8-48
  Removal & Installation..........8-48
Rear Pinion Seal....................8-51
  Removal & Installation..........8-51
Transfer Case Assembly 8-40
  Removal & Installation..........8-41

ENGINE COOLING 8-53

Engine Coolant.........................8-53
  Bleeding 8-56
  Drain & Refill Procedure.......8-53
  Flushing...........................8-56
Engine Fan 8-57
  Removal & Installation..........8-57
Radiator..................................8-58
  Removal & Installation..........8-58
Thermostat 8-60
  Removal & Installation..........8-60
Water Pump (Coolant Pump) 8-62
  Removal & Installation..........8-62

ENGINE ELECTRICAL 8-65

BATTERY SYSTEM 8-69
Battery 8-69
  Battery Reconnect/Relearn
   Procedure 8-69
  Removal & Installation..........8-69
CHARGING SYSTEM 8-65
Alternator 8-65
  Removal & Installation..........8-65

IGNITION SYSTEM 8-68
Firing Order............................8-68
Ignition Coil 8-68
  Removal & Installation..........8-68
Ignition Timing......................8-68
  Adjustment 8-68
Spark Plugs............................8-68
  Removal & Installation..........8-68
STARTING SYSTEM 8-69
Starter 8-69
  Removal & Installation..........8-69

ENGINE MECHANICAL 8-71

Accessory Drive Belts 8-71
  Accessory Belt Routing.........8-71
  Adjustment 8-71
  Inspection 8-71
  Removal & Installation..........8-71
Air Cleaner 8-72
  Filter/Element Replacement ..8-72
  Removal & Installation..........8-72
Camshaft and Valve Lifters........8-73
  Removal & Installation..........8-73
Catalytic Converter 8-87
  Removal & Installation..........8-87
Crankshaft Front Seal...............8-87
  Removal & Installation..........8-87
Cylinder Head 8-90
  Removal & Installation..........8-90
Diesel Particulate Filter 8-87
  Removal & Installation..........8-87
Exhaust Manifold 8-91
  Removal & Installation..........8-91
Intake Manifold 8-100
  Removal & Installation.........8-100
Oil Pan 8-115
  Removal & Installation.........8-115
Oil Pump 8-124
  Removal & Installation.........8-124
Piston and Ring.......................8-125
  Positioning 8-125
Rear Main Seal........................8-125
  Removal & Installation.......8-125
Timing Chain & Sprockets 8-135
  Removal & Installation........8-135
Timing Chain Front Cover.......8-128
  Removal & Installation.......8-128

Turbocharger 8-147
   Removal & Installation........8-147
Valve Covers 8-151
   Removal & Installation........8-151
Valve Lash..............................8-161
   Adjustment 8-161

ENGINE PERFORMANCE & EMISSION CONTROLS 8-161

Camshaft Position (CMP)
  Sensor 8-161
   Location.............................8-161
   Removal & Installation........8-161
Crankshaft Position (CKP)
  Sensor 8-162
   Location.............................8-162
   Removal & Installation........8-162
Engine Coolant Temperature
  (ECT) Sensor 8-165
   Location.............................8-165
   Removal & Installation........8-165
Heated Oxygen Sensor
  (HO2S)................................8-168
   Location.............................8-168
   Removal & Installation........8-168
Intake Air Temperature
  Sensor 2 (IAT2)..................8-169
   Location.............................8-169
   Removal & Installation........8-169
Knock Sensor (KS)..................8-169
   Location.............................8-169
   Removal & Installation........8-169
Manifold Absolute Pressure
  (MAP) Sensor 8-170
   Location.............................8-170
   Removal & Installation........8-170
Mass Air Flow (MAF)
  Sensor 8-172
   Location.............................8-172
   Removal & Installation........8-170
Powertrain Control Module
  (PCM) 8-172
  Extended Idle Shutdown
   Initialization 8-175
   Location.............................8-172
  Passive Anti-Theft System
   (PATS) Parameter
   Reset 8-174
  Programmable Module
   Installation (PMI)
   Procedure 8-174
   Removal & Installation........8-172
Throttle Position (TP)
  Sensor 8-175
   Location.............................8-175
   Removal & Installation........8-175

FUEL 8-177

DIESEL FUEL INJECTION SYSTEM 8-188

Fuel Filter..............................8-188
  Draining Water from the
   System 8-190
   Removal & Installation........8-188
Fuel Supply Pump...................8-199
   Removal & Installation........8-199
Fuel System Purging..............8-191
   Bleeding 8-191
Fuel System Service
  Precautions 8-188
Glow Plugs............................8-204
   Removal & Installation........8-204
Injection Lines.......................8-193
   Removal & Installation........8-193
Injection Pump.......................8-201
   Removal & Installation........8-201
Injectors 8-195
   Removal & Installation........8-195
Relieving Fuel System
  Pressure.............................8-188

GASOLINE FUEL INJECTION SYSTEM 8-177

Fuel Filter..............................8-177
   Removal & Installation........8-177
Fuel Injectors 8-177
   Removal & Installation........8-177
Fuel Pump.............................8-181
   Removal & Installation........8-181
Fuel System Service
  Precautions 8-177
Fuel Tank...............................8-183
  Draining..............................8-183
   Removal & Installation........8-184
Idle Speed 8-184
  Adjustment 8-184
Relieving Fuel System
  Pressure.............................8-177
Throttle Body.........................8-184
  Removal &
   Installation.......................8-184

HEATING & AIR CONDITIONING SYSTEM...8-205

Blower Motor 8-205
  Removal &
   Installation.......................8-205
Heater Core 8-206
  Removal &
   Installation.......................8-206

PRECAUTIONS 8-15

SPECIFICATIONS AND MAINTENANCE CHARTS 8-3

Brake Specifications.................8-10
Camshaft Specifications.............8-6
Capacities 8-4
Crankshaft and Connecting
  Rod Specifications 8-6
Engine and Vehicle
  Identification 8-3
Engine Tune-Up Specifications ...8-3
Fluid Specifications...................8-5
General Engine Specifications.....8-3
Piston and Ring Specifications ...8-7
Scheduled Maintenance
  Intervals........................8-11-14
Tire, Wheel and Ball Joint
  Specifications 8-9
Torque Specifications................8-8
Valve Specifications 8-5
Wheel Alignment......................8-9

STEERING 8-207

Power Steering Gear...............8-207
   Removal & Installation........8-207
Power Steering Pump.............8-210
  Bleeding 8-211
  Fluid Fill Procedure 8-212
   Removal & Installation........8-210

SUSPENSION 8-213

FRONT SUSPENSION 8-213

Coil Spring............................8-213
   Removal & Installation........8-213
Control Links 8-215
   Removal & Installation........8-215
Lower Ball Joint 8-218
   Removal & Installation........8-218
Stabilizer Bar.........................8-220
   Removal & Installation........8-220
Steering Knuckle 8-221
   Removal & Installation........8-221
Upper Ball Joint 8-223
   Removal & Installation........8-223
Wheel Bearings & Wheel Hub...8-225
  Adjustment 8-227
   Removal & Installation........8-225

REAR SUSPENSION 8-228

Leaf Spring............................8-228
   Removal & Installation........8-228
Shock Absorber......................8-230
   Removal & Installation........8-230
Stabilizer Bar & Link 8-230
   Removal & Installation........8-230
Wheel Bearings 8-231
   Removal & Installation........8-231

SPECIFICATIONS AND MAINTENANCE CHARTS

ENGINE AND VEHICLE IDENTIFICATION

			Engine					Model Year	
Code ①	Liters (cc)	Cu. In.	Cyl.	Fuel Sys.	Engine Type	Eng. Mfg.		Code ②	Year
5	5.4 (5400)	330	8	EFI	Gasoline	Ford		A	2010
R	6.4 (6400)	390	8	Turbocharge	Diesel	Ford		B	2011
Y	6.8 (6800)	415	10	EFI	Gasoline	Ford			
6	6.2 (6200)	379	8	EFI	Gasoline	Ford			
T	6.7 (6700)	409	8	Turbocharge	Diesel	Ford			

① 8th position of VIN

② 10th position of VIN

25759_F250_C0001

GENERAL ENGINE SPECIFICATIONS

All measurements are given in inches.

Year	Model	Engine Displacement Liters (cc)	Engine ID/VIN	Fuel System Type	Net Horsepower @ rpm	Net Torque @ rpm (ft. lbs.)	Bore x Stroke (in.)	Com-pression Ratio	Oil Pressure @ rpm
2010	F-250/F-350	5.4 (5400)	5	SFI	310@5500	365@3500	3.55x4.17	9.8:1	40-75@2000
		6.4 (6400)	R	Turbo	350@3000	650@2000	3.87x4.13	17.2:1	45@1800
		6.8 (6800)	Y	EFI	305@4250	410@2750	3.55x4.17	9.0:1	40-75@2000
2011	F-250/F-350	6.2 (6200)	6	EFI	385@5500	405@4500	4.02x3.74	9.8:1	NA
		6.7 (6700)	T	Turbo	390@2800	735@1600	3.90x4.25	16.2:1	35@1800
		6.8 (6800)	Y	EFI	305@4250	410@2750	3.55x4.17	9.0:1	40-75@2000

SFI: Sequential Multi-Port Fuel Injection

EFI: Electronic Fuel Injection

25759_F250_C0002

ENGINE TUNE-UP SPECIFICATIONS

Year	Engine Displacement Liters	Engine ID/VIN	Spark Plug Gap (in.)	Ignition Timing (deg.)		Idle Speed (rpm)		Valve Clearance	
				MT	AT	MT	AT	Intake	Exhaust
2010	5.4	5	0.039-0.043	10 BTDC	10 BTDC	①	①	HYD	HYD
	6.4 Diesel	R	NA	NA	NA	①	①	HYD	HYD
	6.8	Y	0.039-0.003	10 BTDC	10 BTDC	①	①	HYD	HYD
2011	6.2	6	0.039-0.043	10 BTDC	10 BTDC	①	①	HYD	HYD
	6.7 Diesel	T	NA	NA	NA	①	①	HYD	HYD
	6.8	Y	0.039-0.043	10 BTDC	10 BTDC	①	①	HYD	HYD

HYD: Hydraulic Lash Adjusters

① Idle speed is electronically controlled and cannot be adjusted.

25759_F250_C0003

CAPACITIES

Year	Model	Engine Displacement Liters	Engine ID/VIN	Engine Oil with Filter	Transmission (pts.)		Drive Axle (pts.)		Transfer Case (pts.)	Fuel Tank (gal.)	Cooling System (qts.)
					Auto.*	Manual	Front	Rear			
2010	F-250/F-350	5.4	5	7.0	14.2	11.6	5.8	①	4.0	②	25.7
		6.4	R	15.0	14.2	11.6	5.8	①	4.0	②	29.6
		6.8	Y	7.0	14.2	11.6	5.8	①	4.0	②	26.7
2011	F-250/F-350	6.2	6	7.0	③	N/A	5.8	④	4.0	⑤	21.3
		6.7	T	13.0	③	N/A	5.8	④	4.0	⑤	29.4
		6.8	Y	7.0	③	N/A	5.8	④	4.0	⑤	26.7

NOTE: All capacities are approximate. Add fluid gradually and ensure a proper fluid level is obtained.

* Drain & refill

① 10.5 inch: 6.9 pts.

 Dana 80: 8.9 pts.

② Aft-of-axle steel fuel tank: 40 gal.

 Auxiliary steel fuel tank (midship mounted): 19 gal.

 Midship plastic fuel tank: 30 or 38 gal.

③ Torqeshift transmission: 14.2 pts.

 Torqeshift6 transmission - EARLY build:

 If only the transmission fluid drain plug or pan was removed: 20 pts.

 If the main control was removed: 24 pts.

 If the transmission was removed and disassembled: 36 pts.

 Torqeshift6 transmission - LATE build:

 If only the transmission fluid drain plug or pan was removed: 16.4 pts.

 If the main control was removed: 20.4 pts.

 If the transmission was removed and disassembled: 32.4 pts.

④ 10.5 inch: 6.9 pts.

 Dana 80: 8.5 pts.

⑤ Aft-of-axle steel fuel tank: 40 gal.

 Mid-ship fuel tank: 28 gal.

 Plastic fuel tank: 40 gal.

25759_F250_C0004

FLUID SPECIFICATIONS

Year	Model	Engine Disp. Liters	Engine Oil	Manual Trans.	Auto. Trans.	Drive Axle Front	Rear	Transfer Case	Power Steering Fluid	Brake Master Cylinder	Cooling System
2010	F250/F350	5.4	5W-20	①	②	80W-90	③	④	⑤	DOT 3	⑥
		6.4	⑦	①	②	80W-90	③	④	⑤	DOT 3	⑥
		6.8	5W-20	①	②	80W-90	③	④	⑤	DOT 3	⑥
2011	F250/F350	6.2	5W-20	NA	②	80W-90	⑧	④	⑤	DOT 3	⑥
		6.7	⑨	NA	②	80W-90	⑧	④	⑤	DOT 3	⑥
		6.8	5W-20	NA	②	80W-90	⑧	④	⑤	DOT 3	⑥

DOT: Department Of Transpotation

NA Not Available

① Motorcraft Trasnsfer Case Fluid

② Mercon LV Automatic Transmission Fluid (ATF)

③ Dana 80: 75W-90 Synthetic Axle Lubricant

  Dana S110 & S130: 75W-90 Synthetic Axle Lubricant

  Ford 10.50-inch Ring Gear: 75W-90 Synthetic Axle Lubricant

④ Motorcraft Transfer Case Fluid

⑤ Mercon V ATF

⑥ Motorcraft Premium Gold Engine Coolant with Bittering Agent

⑦ 15W-40 Super Duty Diesel Motor Oil

⑧ Dana 80: 75W-90 Synthetic Axle Lubricant

  Ford 10.50-inch Ring Gear: 75W-90 Synthetic Axle Lubricant

⑨ 10W-30 Super Duty Diesel Motor Oil

25759_F250_C0005

VALVE SPECIFICATIONS

Year	Engine Displacement Liters	Engine ID/VIN	Seat Angle (deg.)	Face Angle (deg.)	Spring Test Pressure (lbs. @ in.)	Spring Free-Length (in.)	Spring Installed Height (in.)	Stem-to-Guide Clearance (in.) Intake	Exhaust	Stem Diameter (in.) Intake	Exhaust
2010	5.4	5	44.5-45	45.5	79.0@1.66	2.190	1.660	0.0010-0.0020	0.0030-0.0040	0.2350-0.2360	0.2340-0.2350
	6.4 Diesel	R	①	②	NA	2.045	1.830	0.0040 max.	0.0040 max.	0.2735-0.2742	0.2735-0.2742
	6.8	Y	44.5-45	45.5	79.0@1.66	2.220	1.660	0.0010-0.0030	0.0020-0.0040	0.2350-0.2360	0.2340-0.2350
2011	6.2	6	44.5-45	45.5	45.0@2.154	2.562	2.154	0.0008-0.0028	0.0013-0.0033	0.3123-0.3131	0.3118-0.3126
	6.7 Diesel	T	③	④	NA	1.956	1.338	0.0030	0.0030	0.2740-0.2750	0.2740-0.2750
	6.8	Y	44.5-45	45.5	79.0@1.66	2.220	1.660	0.0010-0.0030	0.0020-0.0040	0.2350-0.2360	0.2340-0.2350

NA Not Available

① Intake: 37.5 degrees

  Exhaust: 40.0 degrees

② Intake: 37.0 degrees

  Exhaust: 39.5 degrees

③ Intake: 30.25 degrees from deck face

  Exhaust: 45.25 degrees from deck face

④ Intake: 29.5 +/- 0.25 degrees from stem axis

  Exhaust: 44.5 +/- 0.25 degrees from stem axis

25759_F250_C0006

CAMSHAFT SPECIFICATIONS

All measurements in inches unless noted

Year	Engine Displacement Liters	Engine Code/VIN	Journal Diameter	Brg. Oil Clearance	Shaft End-play	Runout	Journal Bore	Lobe Lift Intake	Lobe Lift Exhaust
2010	5.4	5	1.126-1.127	0.001-0.003	0.001-0.007	0.001	1.128-1.129	0.217	0.217
	6.4 Diesel	R	2.440-2.441	0.0015-0.006	0.002-0.008	0.002	2.443-2.446	0.2290	0.2326
	6.8	Y	1.126-1.127	0.0009-0.0029	0.001-0.007	0.004	1.128-1.129	0.216	0.2170
2011	6.2	6	1.125-1.126	0.0017-0.0037	0.0009-0.0059	0.0009	1.128-1.129	0.315	0.309
	6.7 Diesel	T	2.363-2.364	0.0009-0.002	0.002-0.006	0.002	2.363-2.364	0.2240	0.2320
	6.8	Y	1.126-1.127	0.0009-0.0029	0.001-0.007	0.004	1.128-1.129	0.216	0.2170

25759_F250_C0007

CRANKSHAFT AND CONNECTING ROD SPECIFICATIONS

All measurements are given in inches.

Year	Engine Displacement Liters	Engine ID/VIN	Crankshaft Main Brg. Journal Dia.	Crankshaft Main Brg. Oil Clearance	Crankshaft Shaft End-play	Crankshaft Thrust on No.	Connecting Rod Journal Diameter	Connecting Rod Oil Clearance	Connecting Rod Side Clearance
2010	5.4	5	2.6568-2.6576	0.0009-0.0019	0.0030-0.0148	NA	2.0877-2.0885	0.0010-0.0025	0.0049-0.0187
	6.4 Diesel	R	3.178-3.179 ①	0.0006-0.0035	0.0200 max.	NA	2.834-2.835 ①	NA	0.009-0.0420
	6.8	Y	2.6568-2.6576	0.0009-0.0019	0.0030-0.0148	NA	2.0877-2.0885	0.0009-0.0025	0.0049-0.0187
2011	6.2	6	2.6568-2.6576	0.0009-0.0019	0.005-0.0100	NA	2.0761-2.0768	0.0009-0.0025	0.0390 max.
	6.7 Diesel	T	3.188-3.189 ②	0.001-0.0030	0.0120 max.	NA	2.834 +/- 0.0004	0.001-0.0040	0.004-0.0180
	6.8	Y	2.6568-2.6576	0.0009-0.0019	0.0030-0.0148	NA	2.0877-2.0885	0.0009-0.0025	0.0049-0.0187

NA: Not Available

① Standard size shown. There are undersizes for this engine @ 0.010, 0.020, and 0.030 inches.

② Standard size shown. There is a 0.009 inches undersize also for this engine.

25759_F250_C0008

PISTON AND RING SPECIFICATIONS

All measurements are given in inches.

Year	Engine Displacement Liters	Engine ID/VIN	Piston Clearance	Ring Gap			Ring-To-Groove Clearance		
				Top Compression	Bottom Compression	Oil Control	Top Compression	Bottom Compression	Oil Control
2010	5.4	5	0.0010-0.0018	0.0060-0.0120	0.0098-0.0197	0.0059-0.0256	0.0008-0.0031	0.0012-0.0028	NA
	6.4 Diesel	R	0.0018-0.0037	0.0110-0.0310	0.0560-0.0760	0.0090-0.0290	NA	0.0020-0.0038	0.0015-0.0037
	6.8	Y	0.0010-0.0018	0.0059-0.0118	0.0098-0.0196	0.0059-0.0256	0.0012-0.0020	0.0012-0.0031	NA
2011	6.2	6	0.0003-0.0015	0.0137-0.0196	0.0137-0.0196	0.0050-0.0250	0.0578-0.0590	0.0578-0.0590	NA
	6.7 Diesel	T	0.0010-0.0030	0.0090-0.0150	0.0150-0.0230	0.0090-0.0190	NA	0.0020	0.001
	6.8	Y	0.0010-0.0018	0.0059-0.0118	0.0098-0.0196	0.0059-0.0256	0.0012-0.0020	0.0012-0.0031	NA

NA: Not Available

25759_F250_C0009

TORQUE SPECIFICATIONS
All readings in ft. lbs.

Year	Engine Disp. Liters	Engine ID/VIN	Cylinder Head Bolts	Main Bearing Bolts	Rod Bearing Bolts	Crankshaft Damper Bolts	Flywheel Bolts	Manifold Intake	Manifold Exhaust	Spark Plugs	Oil Pan Drain Plug
2010	5.4	5	①	②	③	④	59	⑤	⑥	⑦	10
	6.4 Diesel	R	①	⑧	⑨	⑩	⑪	⑫	⑬	NA	32
	6.8	Y	⑭	⑮	⑯	⑰	59	⑤	18	⑦	10
2011	6.2	6	⑱	NA	NA	⑲	⑳	㉑	㉒	13	10
	6.7 Diesel	T	㉓	NA	NA	㉔	㉕	㉖	㉗	NA	㉘
	6.8	Y	⑭	⑮	⑯	⑰	59	⑤	18	⑦	10

NA Not Available or Not Applicable

① Step 1: Bolts 1-10: 70 ft. lbs.

Step 2: Loosen bolts 1-10

Step 3: Bolts 1-10: 115 ft. lbs.

Step 4: Bolts 1-10: Additional 90 degrees

Step 5: Bolts 1-10: An additional 90 degrees

Step 6: Bolts 11-15: 18 ft. lbs.

Step 7: Bolts 11-15: 23 ft. lbs.

② 10 vertical main cap bolts:

Step 1: 30 ft. lbs.

Step 2: Additional 90 degrees

10 side bolts:

Step 1: 22 ft. lbs.

Step 2: Additional 90 degrees

③ Step 1: 32 ft. lbs.

Step 2: Additional 105 degrees

④ Step 1: 66 ft. lbs.

Step 2: Loosen 360 degrees

Step 3: 37 ft. lbs.

Step 4: Additional 90 degrees

⑤ Step 1: 18 inch lbs.

Step 2: 89 inch lbs.

⑥ Exh. manifold-to-cylinder head studs: 106 inch lbs.

Exh. manifold nuts: 18 ft. lbs.

⑦ 106 inch lbs.

⑧ Step 1: 110 ft. lbs.

Step 2: 130 ft. lbs.

Step 3: 170 ft. lbs.

⑨ Step 1: 33 ft. lbs.

Step 2: 50 ft. lbs.

⑩ Step 1: 50 ft. lbs.

Step 2: Additional 90 degrees

⑪ Step 1: 44 inch lbs.

Step 2: 69 ft. lbs.

⑫ 97 inch lbs.

⑬ Step 1: 18 ft. lbs.

Step 2: 18 ft. lbs. (2nd time)

⑭ Step 1: 30 ft. lbs.

Step 2: Additional 90 degrees

Step 3: Additional 90 degrees (2nd time)

⑮ Step 1: Bolts 1-12: 30 ft. lbs.

Step 2: Additional 90 degrees

Step 3: Bolts 13-24: 22 ft. lbs.

Step 4: Additional 90 degrees

⑯ Step 1: 32 ft. lbs.

Step 2: Additional 105 degrees

⑰ Step 1: 66 ft. lbs.

Step 2: Loosen 360 degrees

Step 3: 37 ft. lbs.

Step 4: Additional 90 degrees

⑱ Step 1: 80 inch lbs.

Step 2: Additional 45 degrees

⑲ Step 1: 129 ft. lbs.

Step 2: Additional 90 degrees

⑳ Step 1: Bolts 1-4: 177 inch lbs.

Step 2: 26 ft. lbs.

Step 3: Additional 60 degrees

Step 4: Bolts 5-8: 177 inch lbs.

Step 5: 26 ft. lbs.

Step 6: Additional 60 degrees

㉑ Step 1: 89 inch lbs.

Step 2: Additional 90 degrees

㉒ Step 1: 18 ft. lbs.

Step 2: 24 ft. lbs.

㉓ Step 1: Bolts 1-18: 177 inch lbs.

Step 2: 36 ft. lbs.

Step 3: 36 ft. lbs. (second time)

Step 4: 36 ft. lbs. (third time)

Step 5: Additional 90 degrees

Step 6: Adt'l 90 degrees (2nd time)

Step 7: Adt'l 90 degrees (3rd time)

Step 8: Bolts 19-23: 22 ft. lbs.

㉔ Step 1: 22 ft. lbs.

Step 2: Additional 90 degrees

㉕ Step 1: 44 inch lbs.

Step 2: 74 ft. lbs.

㉖ Upper intake manifold: 89 inch lbs.

Lower intake manifold: 18 ft. lbs.

㉗ Step 1: 177 inch lbs.

Step 2: 22 ft. lbs.

Step 3: 22 ft. lbs. (second time)

㉘ Engine oil drain plug is a quarter turn design

25759_F250_C0010

WHEEL ALIGNMENT

Year	Model		Caster Range (+/-Deg.)	Caster Preferred Setting (Deg.)	Camber Range (+/-Deg.)	Camber Preferred Setting (Deg.)	Toe-in (in.)
2010	F250/350 RWD	F/LH	①	②	1.0	0.62	0.1+/-0.75
	Pickup	F/RH	①	②	1.0	0.62	0.1+/-0.75
	F250 4WD	F/LH	①	③	0.75	0.15	0.1+/-0.25
	Pickup	F/RH	①	③	0.75	0.15	0.1+/-0.25
	F350 RWD Chassis	F/LH	①	④	1.0	0.62	0.1+/-0.25
	Cab SRW	F/RH	①	④	1.0	0.62	0.1+/-0.25
	F350 RWD Chassis	F/LH	①	⑤	1.0	0.62	0.1+/-0.25
	Cab DRW	F/RH	①	⑤	1.0	0.62	0.1+/-0.25
	F350 4WD	F/LH	①	⑥	0.75	0.15	0.1+/-0.25
	Pickup SRW	F/RH	①	⑥	0.75	0.15	0.1+/-0.25
	F350 4WD	F/LH	①	⑦	0.75	0.15	0.1+/-0.25
	Pickup DRW	F/RH	①	⑦	0.75	0.15	0.1+/-0.25
2011			Information NA				

NA Not Available

SRW Single Rear Wheel

DRW Dual Rear Wheel

F/LF: Front left side

F/RF: Front right side

① Heavy duty suspension: 1.3

  Standard Suspension: 1.2

② Heavy duty suspension: 3.6

  Standard suspension: 4.0

③ Heavy duty suspension: 2.8

  Standard suspension: 3.5

④ Heavy duty suspension: 3.2

  Standard suspension: 3.5

⑤ Heavy duty suspension: 2.5

  Standard suspension: 2.9

⑥ Heavy duty suspension: 2.1

  Standard suspension: 2.7

⑦ Heavy duty suspension: 2.6

  Standard suspension: 3.3

25759_F250_C0011

TIRE, WHEEL AND BALL JOINT SPECIFICATIONS

Year	Model	OEM Tires Standard	OEM Tires Optional	Tire Pressures (psi) Front	Tire Pressures (psi) Rear	Wheel Size	Ball Joint Inspection	Lug Nut (ft. lbs.)
2010	F-250	NA	①	②	②	NA	③	165
	F-350	NA	①	②	②	NA	③	165
2011	F-250	NA	①	②	②	NA	③	165
	F-350	NA	①	②	②	NA	③	165

NA: Information not available

OEM: Original Equipment Manufacturer

PSI: Pounds Per Square Inch

① Multiple optional tires available; consult tire dealer.

② See placard on vehicle

③ Upper: 0.0.024 in.; Lower: 0.004 in.

25759_F250_C0012

BRAKE SPECIFICATIONS

All measurements in inches unless noted

Year	Model		Brake Disc			Brake Drum Diameter			Minimum Pad/Lining Thickness		Brake Caliper	
			Original Thickness	Minimum Thickness	Max. Runout	Original Inside Diameter	Max. Wear Limit	Maximum Machine Diamter	Front	Rear	Caliper Bolts (ft. lbs.)	Anchor Plate (ft. lbs.)
2010	F250	F	NA	1.433	0.002	NA	NA	NA	0.118	—	56	166
		R	NA	1.275	NA	NA	NA	NA	—	0.118	①	203
	F350	F	NA	1.433	0.002	NA	NA	NA	0.118	—	56	166
		R	NA	1.275	NA	NA	NA	NA	—	0.118	①	203
2011	F250	F	NA	1.433	0.002	NA	NA	NA	0.118	—	56	166
		R	NA	1.275	NA	NA	NA	NA	—	0.118	①	203
	F350	F	NA	1.433	0.002	NA	NA	NA	0.118	—	56	166
		R	NA	1.275	NA	NA	NA	NA	—	0.118	①	203

F: Front

R: Rear

NA: Not Available

① Single Rear Wheel (SRW): 26 ft. lbs.

   Dual Rear Wheel (DRW): 56 ft. lbs.

25759_F250_C0013

SCHEDULED MAINTENANCE INTERVALS
2010-11 Ford F-250/F-350 (except 2011 Diesel Engines) - Normal

TO BE SERVICED	TYPE OF SERVICE	VEHICLE MILEAGE INTERVAL (x1000)												
		7.5	15	22.5	30	37.5	45	52.5	60	67.5	75	82.5	90	97.5
Manual transmission fluid	Replace	Every 150,000 miles												
Front differential fluid	Replace	Every 150,000 miles												
Engine coolant	Replace	At 6 years or 105,000 miles; then every 3 years or 45,000 miles												
Windshield for cracks, chips and pitting	Inspect	✓	✓	✓	✓	✓	✓	✓	✓	✓	✓	✓	✓	✓
Windshield wiper spray and wiper operation	Inspect	✓	✓	✓	✓	✓	✓	✓	✓	✓	✓	✓	✓	✓
Oil and fluid leaks	Inspect	✓	✓	✓	✓	✓	✓	✓	✓	✓	✓	✓	✓	✓
Radiator, coolers, heater and air conditioning hoses	Inspect	✓	✓	✓	✓	✓	✓	✓	✓	✓	✓	✓	✓	✓
Shocks struts and other suspension components for leaks and damage	Inspect	✓	✓	✓	✓	✓	✓	✓	✓	✓	✓	✓	✓	✓
Battery performance	Inspect	✓	✓	✓	✓	✓	✓	✓	✓	✓	✓	✓	✓	✓
Fluid levels (all)	Top off	✓	✓	✓	✓	✓	✓	✓	✓	✓	✓	✓	✓	✓
Drive belt	Replace													
Drive belt	Inspect	✓	✓	✓	✓	✓	✓	✓	✓	✓	✓	✓	✓	✓
Transfer case oil (4x4)	Replace	Every 150,000 miles												
Rear differential fluid	Replace	Every 150,000 miles												
Spark plugs	Replace												✓	
Engine air filter	Replace				✓				✓				✓	
Engine air filter	Inspect	✓	✓	✓	✓	✓	✓	✓	✓	✓	✓	✓	✓	✓
Exhaust system (Leaks, damage, loose parts and foreign material)	Inspect		✓		✓		✓		✓		✓	✓		
Brake system (Pads/shoes/rotors/drums, brake lines and hoses, and parking brake system)	Inspect		✓		✓		✓		✓		✓	✓		
Cooling system, hoses, clamps & coolant strength	Inspect		✓		✓		✓		✓		✓	✓		
Steering linkage, ball joints, suspension, tie-rod ends, driveshaft and u-joints: lubricate if equipped with grease fittings	Inspect/ Lubricate	✓	✓	✓	✓	✓	✓	✓	✓	✓	✓	✓	✓	✓
Inspect and related components for abnormal wear, noise looseness or drag	Inspect	✓	✓	✓	✓	✓	✓	✓	✓	✓	✓	✓	✓	✓
Rotate tires, inspect tread wear, measure tread depth and check pressure	Rotate	✓	✓	✓	✓	✓	✓	✓	✓	✓	✓	✓	✓	✓
Engine oil & filter	Replace	✓	✓	✓	✓	✓	✓	✓	✓	✓	✓	✓	✓	✓

Use of E85 50% of the time or greater, change engine oil and filter every 5,000 miles or 6 months.

SCHEDULED MAINTENANCE INTERVALS
2010-11 Ford F-250/F-350 (except 2011 Diesel Engines) - Severe

TO BE SERVICED	TYPE OF SERVICE	VEHICLE MILEAGE INTERVAL (x1000)											
		5	10	15	20	25	30	35	40	45	50	55	60
Engine oil & filter	Replace	✓	✓	✓	✓	✓	✓	✓	✓	✓	✓	✓	✓
Rotate tires, inspect tread wear, measure tread depth and check pressure	Rotate	✓	✓	✓	✓	✓	✓	✓	✓	✓	✓	✓	✓
Inspect and related components for abnormal wear, noise looseness or drag	Inspect	✓	✓	✓	✓	✓	✓	✓	✓	✓	✓	✓	✓
Steering linkage, ball joints, suspension, tie-rod ends, driveshaft and u-joints: lubricate if equipped with grease fittings	Inspect and Lubricate	✓	✓	✓	✓	✓	✓	✓	✓	✓	✓	✓	✓
Cooling system, hoses, clamps & coolant strength	Inspect		✓		✓		✓		✓		✓		✓
Brake system (Pads/shoes/rotors/drums, brake lines and hoses, and parking brake system)	Inspect		✓		✓		✓		✓		✓		✓
Exhaust system (Leaks, damage, loose parts and foreign material)	Inspect		✓		✓		✓		✓		✓		✓
Engine air filter	Inspect	✓	✓	✓	✓	✓	✓	✓	✓	✓	✓	✓	✓
Engine air filter	Replace				✓				✓				✓
Spark plugs	Replace												✓
Rear differential fluid	Replace	every 150,000 miles											
Transfer case oil (4x4)	Replace	every 150,000 miles											
Drive belt	Inspect	✓	✓	✓	✓	✓	✓	✓	✓	✓	✓	✓	✓
Drive belt	Replace	every 150,000 miles											
Fluid levels (all)	Top off	✓	✓	✓	✓	✓	✓	✓	✓	✓	✓	✓	✓
Battery performance	Inspect	✓	✓	✓	✓	✓	✓	✓	✓	✓	✓	✓	✓
Shocks struts and other suspension components for leaks and damage	Inspect	✓	✓	✓	✓	✓	✓	✓	✓	✓	✓	✓	✓
Radiator, coolers, heater and air conditioning hoses	Inspect	✓	✓	✓	✓	✓	✓	✓	✓	✓	✓	✓	✓
Oil and fluid leaks	Inspect	✓	✓	✓	✓	✓	✓	✓	✓	✓	✓	✓	✓
Windshield wiper spray and wiper operation	Inspect	✓	✓	✓	✓	✓	✓	✓	✓	✓	✓	✓	✓
Windshield for cracks, chips and pitting	Inspect	✓	✓	✓	✓	✓	✓	✓	✓	✓	✓	✓	✓
Engine coolant	Replace	At 6 years or 105,000 miles; then every 3 years or 45,000 miles											
Front differential fluid	Replace	every 150,000 miles											
Manual transmission fluid	Replace	every 105,000 miles											

Use of E85 50% of the time or greater, change engine oil and filter every 5,000 miles or 6 months.

25759_F250_C0015

SCHEDULED MAINTENANCE INTERVALS
2011 Ford F-250/F-350 Diesel Engines - Normal

Service Item	Service Action	1	2	3	4	5	6	7	8	9	10	11	12	13	14	15
Engine coolant strength hoses & clamps	Inspect	✓	✓	✓	✓	✓	✓	✓	✓	✓	✓	✓	✓	✓	✓	✓
Rear differential fluid	Replace															✓
Front differential fluid	Replace															✓
Transfer case fluid	Replace															✓
Drive belt	Inspect	✓	✓	✓	✓	✓	✓	✓	✓	✓	✓	✓	✓	✓	✓	✓
Drive belt	Replace															✓
Automatic transmision fluid & filter	Replace															✓
Battery performance	Inspect	✓	✓	✓	✓	✓	✓	✓	✓	✓	✓	✓	✓	✓	✓	✓
Brake system	Inspect	✓	✓	✓	✓	✓	✓	✓	✓	✓	✓	✓	✓	✓	✓	✓
Climate-controlled seat filter (if equipped)	Replace		✓			✓				✓			✓			✓
Engine oil and filter	Replace	✓	✓	✓	✓	✓	✓	✓	✓	✓	✓	✓	✓	✓	✓	✓
Exhaust system	Inspect	✓	✓	✓	✓	✓	✓	✓	✓	✓	✓	✓	✓	✓	✓	✓
Horn, exterior lamps, turn signals and hazard warning light operation	Inspect	✓	✓	✓	✓	✓	✓	✓	✓	✓	✓	✓	✓	✓	✓	✓
Shocks struts and other suspension components for leaks and damage	Inspect	✓	✓	✓	✓	✓	✓	✓	✓	✓	✓	✓	✓	✓	✓	✓
Windshield for cracks, chips and pitting	Inspect	✓	✓	✓	✓	✓	✓	✓	✓	✓	✓	✓	✓	✓	✓	✓
Windshield wiper spray and wiper operation	Inspect	✓	✓	✓	✓	✓	✓	✓	✓	✓	✓	✓	✓	✓	✓	✓
Fluid leaks	Inspect	✓	✓	✓	✓	✓	✓	✓	✓	✓	✓	✓	✓	✓	✓	✓
Fluid levels (all)	Top off	✓	✓	✓	✓	✓	✓	✓	✓	✓	✓	✓	✓	✓	✓	✓
Fuel filters (frame & engine mounted)	Replace		✓		✓		✓		✓		✓		✓			✓
Inspect wheels and related components for abnomal noise, wear, looseness or drag	Inspect	✓	✓	✓	✓	✓	✓	✓	✓	✓	✓	✓	✓	✓	✓	✓
Steering linkage, ball joints, suspension, tie-rod ends, driveshaft and u-joints: lubricate if equipped with grease fittings	Inspect/Lubricate	✓	✓	✓	✓	✓	✓	✓	✓	✓	✓	✓	✓	✓	✓	✓
Radiator, coolers, heater and air conditioning hoses	Inspect	✓	✓	✓	✓	✓	✓	✓	✓	✓	✓	✓	✓	✓	✓	✓
Rotate tires, inspect tread wear, measure tread depth and check pressure	Rotate/Inspect	✓	✓	✓	✓	✓	✓	✓	✓	✓	✓	✓	✓	✓	✓	✓
Air filter restriction gauge, replace filter as required	Inspect/Service	✓	✓	✓	✓	✓	✓	✓	✓	✓	✓	✓	✓	✓	✓	✓
Refill diesel exhaust fluid tank	Check/Refill	✓	✓	✓	✓	✓	✓	✓	✓	✓	✓	✓	✓	✓	✓	✓
Air inlet foam filter	Replace			✓					✓				✓			✓
Engine coolant and secondary coolant	Replace										✓					✓

Oil change service intervals should be completed as indicated by the message center (Can be up to 1 year or 10,000 miles) If the message center is prematurely reset or is inoperative, perform the oil change interval at 6 months or 5,000 miles from your last oil change.

Engine coolant and secondary coolant change every 6 years or 105,000 miles; after initial change, every 3 years or 45,000 miles.

SCHEDULED MAINTENANCE INTERVALS
2011 Ford F-250/F-350 Diesel Engines - Severe

Service Item	Service Action	1	2	3	4	5	6	7	8	9	10	11	12	13	14	15
Engine coolant strength hoses & clamps	Inspect	✓	✓	✓	✓	✓	✓	✓	✓	✓	✓	✓	✓	✓	✓	✓
Rear differential fluid	Replace					✓					✓					✓
Front differential fluid	Replace															✓
Transfer case fluid	Replace						✓						✓			
Drive belt	Inspect	✓	✓	✓	✓	✓	✓	✓	✓	✓	✓	✓	✓	✓	✓	✓
Drive belt	Replace															✓
Automatic transmission fluid & filter	Replace															✓
Battery performance	Inspect	✓	✓	✓	✓	✓	✓	✓	✓	✓	✓	✓	✓	✓	✓	✓
Brake system (adjust parking brake if required).	Inspect	✓	✓	✓	✓	✓	✓	✓	✓	✓	✓	✓	✓	✓	✓	✓
Climate-controlled seat filter (if equipped)	Replace			✓			✓			✓			✓			✓
Engine oil and filter	Replace	✓	✓	✓	✓	✓	✓	✓	✓	✓	✓	✓	✓	✓	✓	✓
Exhaust system	Inspect	✓	✓	✓	✓	✓	✓	✓	✓	✓	✓	✓	✓	✓	✓	✓
Horn, exterior lamps, turn signals and hazard warning light operation	Inspect	✓	✓	✓	✓	✓	✓	✓	✓	✓	✓	✓	✓	✓	✓	✓
Shocks struts and other suspension components for leaks and damage	Inspect	✓	✓	✓	✓	✓	✓	✓	✓	✓	✓	✓	✓	✓	✓	✓
Windshield for cracks, chips and pitting	Inspect	✓	✓	✓	✓	✓	✓	✓	✓	✓	✓	✓	✓	✓	✓	✓
Windshield wiper spray and wiper operation	Inspect	✓	✓	✓	✓	✓	✓	✓	✓	✓	✓	✓	✓	✓	✓	✓
Fluid leaks	Inspect	✓	✓	✓	✓	✓	✓	✓	✓	✓	✓	✓	✓	✓	✓	✓
Fluid levels (all)	Top off	✓	✓	✓	✓	✓	✓	✓	✓	✓	✓	✓	✓	✓	✓	✓
Fuel filters (frame & engine mounted)	Replace		✓		✓		✓		✓		✓		✓		✓	
Inspect wheels & related comp. for abnomal noise, wear, looseness or drag	Inspect	✓	✓	✓	✓	✓	✓	✓	✓	✓	✓	✓	✓	✓	✓	✓
Steering linkage, ball joints, suspension, tie-rod ends, driveshaft and u-joints: lubricate grease fittings	Inspect/ Lubricate	✓	✓	✓	✓	✓	✓	✓	✓	✓	✓	✓	✓	✓	✓	✓
Radiator, coolers, heater and air conditioning hoses	Inspect	✓	✓	✓	✓	✓	✓	✓	✓	✓	✓	✓	✓	✓	✓	✓
Rotate tires, inspect tread wear, measure tread depth and check pressure	Rotate/ Inspect	✓	✓	✓	✓	✓	✓	✓	✓	✓	✓	✓	✓	✓	✓	✓
Air filter restriction gauge, replace filter as required	Inspect/ Service	✓	✓	✓	✓	✓	✓	✓	✓	✓	✓	✓	✓	✓	✓	✓
Refill diesel exhaust fluid tank	Check/ Refill	✓	✓	✓	✓	✓	✓	✓	✓	✓	✓	✓	✓	✓	✓	✓
Air inlet foam filter	Replace					✓				✓			✓			✓
Engine coolant and secondary coolant	Replace						✓						✓			

Oil change service intervals should be completed as indicated by the message center (Can be up to 1 year or 10,000 miles) If the message center is prematurely reset or is inoperative, perform the oil change interval at 6 months or 5,000 miles from your last oil change.

For off-road and dusty driving conditions, change the engine oil and filter every 7,500 miles or 300 engine hours.

For towing a camper or trailer change engine coolant every 60,000 mile or 2,400 engine hours.

PRECAUTIONS

Before servicing any vehicle, please be sure to read all of the following precautions, which deal with personal safety, prevention of component damage, and important points to take into consideration when servicing a motor vehicle:

• Never open, service or drain the radiator or cooling system when the engine is hot; serious burns can occur from the steam and hot coolant.

• Observe all applicable safety precautions when working around fuel. Whenever servicing the fuel system, always work in a well-ventilated area. Do not allow fuel spray or vapors to come in contact with a spark, open flame, or excessive heat (a hot drop light, for example). Keep a dry chemical fire extinguisher near the work area. Always keep fuel in a container specifically designed for fuel storage; also, always properly seal fuel containers to avoid the possibility of fire or explosion. Refer to the additional fuel system precautions later in this section.

• Fuel injection systems often remain pressurized, even after the engine has been turned **OFF**. The fuel system pressure must be relieved before disconnecting any fuel lines. Failure to do so may result in fire and/or personal injury.

• Brake fluid often contains polyglycol ethers and polyglycols. Avoid contact with the eyes and wash your hands thoroughly after handling brake fluid. If you do get brake fluid in your eyes, flush your eyes with clean, running water for 15 minutes. If eye irritation persists, or if you have taken brake fluid internally, IMMEDIATELY seek medical assistance.

• The EPA warns that prolonged contact with used engine oil may cause a number of skin disorders, including cancer. You should make every effort to minimize your exposure to used engine oil. Protective gloves should be worn when changing oil. Wash your hands and any other exposed skin areas as soon as possible after exposure to used engine oil. Soap and water, or waterless hand cleaner should be used.

• All new vehicles are now equipped with an air bag system, often referred to as a Supplemental Restraint System (SRS) or Supplemental Inflatable Restraint (SIR) system. The system must be disabled before performing service on or around system components, steering column, instrument panel components, wiring and sensors. Failure to follow safety and disabling procedures could result in accidental air bag deployment, possible personal injury and unnecessary system repairs.

• Always wear safety goggles when working with, or around, the air bag system. When carrying a non-deployed air bag, be sure the bag and trim cover are pointed away from your body. When placing a non-deployed air bag on a work surface, always face the bag and trim cover upward, away from the surface. This will reduce the motion of the module if it is accidentally deployed. Refer to the additional air bag system precautions later in this section.

• Clean, high quality brake fluid from a sealed container is essential to the safe and proper operation of the brake system. You should always buy the correct type of brake fluid for your vehicle. If the brake fluid becomes contaminated, completely flush the system with new fluid. Never reuse any brake fluid. Any brake fluid that is removed from the system should be discarded. Also, do not allow any brake fluid to come in contact with a painted surface; it will damage the paint.

• Never operate the engine without the proper amount and type of engine oil; doing so WILL result in severe engine damage.

• Timing belt maintenance is extremely important. Many models utilize an interference-type, non-freewheeling engine. If the timing belt breaks, the valves in the cylinder head may strike the pistons, causing potentially serious (also time-consuming and expensive) engine damage. Refer to the maintenance interval charts for the recommended replacement interval for the timing belt, and to the timing belt section for belt replacement and inspection.

• Disconnecting the negative battery cable on some vehicles may interfere with the functions of the on-board computer system(s) and may require the computer to undergo a relearning process once the negative battery cable is reconnected.

• When servicing drum brakes, only disassemble and assemble one side at a time, leaving the remaining side intact for reference.

• Only an MVAC-trained, EPA-certified automotive technician should service the air conditioning system or its components.

BRAKES

ANTI-LOCK BRAKE SYSTEM (ABS)

GENERAL INFORMATION

PRECAUTIONS

• Certain components within the ABS system are not intended to be serviced or repaired individually.

• Do not use rubber hoses or other parts not specifically specified for and ABS system. When using repair kits, replace all parts included in the kit. Partial or incorrect repair may lead to functional problems and require the replacement of components.

• Lubricate rubber parts with clean, fresh brake fluid to ease assembly. Do not use shop air to clean parts; damage to rubber components may result.

• Use only DOT 3 brake fluid from an unopened container.

• If any hydraulic component or line is removed or replaced, it may be necessary to bleed the entire system.

• A clean repair area is essential. Always clean the reservoir and cap thoroughly before removing the cap. The slightest amount of dirt in the fluid may plug an orifice and impair the system function. Perform repairs after components have been thoroughly cleaned; use only denatured alcohol to clean components. Do not allow ABS components to come into contact with any substance containing mineral oil; this includes used shop rags.

• The Anti-Lock control unit is a microprocessor similar to other computer units in the vehicle. Ensure that the ignition switch is **OFF** before removing or installing controller harnesses. Avoid static electricity discharge at or near the controller.

• If any arc welding is to be done on the vehicle, the control unit should be unplugged before welding operations begin.

SPEED SENSORS

REMOVAL & INSTALLATION

Front

2010 4WD F250/F350

See Figure 1.

1. Remove the disc brake shield.
2. Disconnect the wheel speed sensor electrical connector.

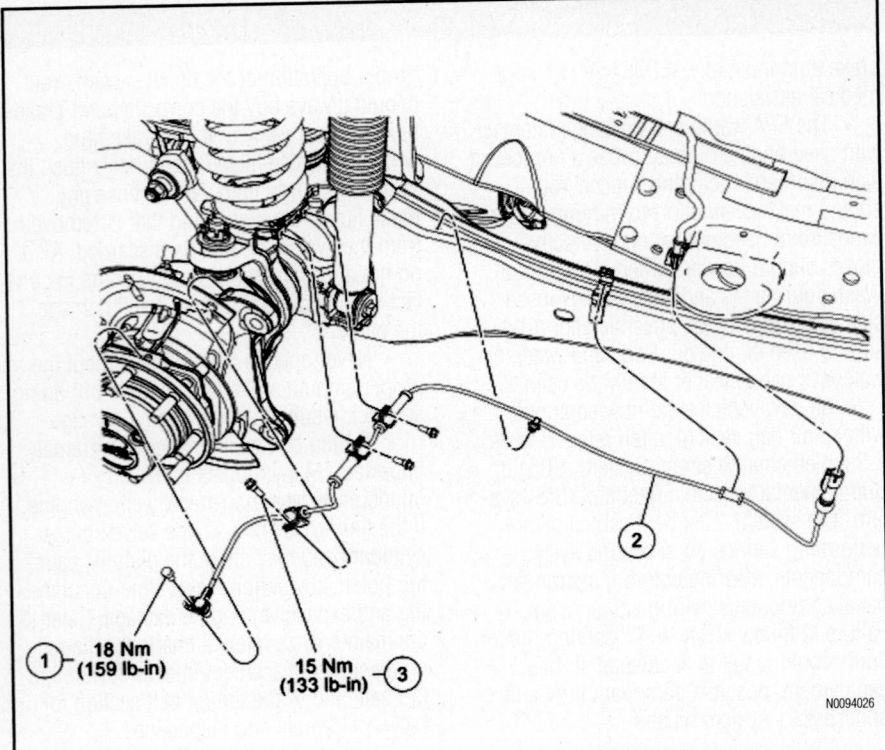

**18 Nm
(159 lb-in)**

**15 Nm
(133 lb-in)**

N0094026

Fig. 1 Remove the wheel speed sensor harness bolts (3), the wheel speed sensor bolt (1), and the wheel speed sensor (2)

3. Detach the wheel speed sensor harness from the radius arm.
4. Remove the 3 wheel speed sensor harness bolts.
5. Remove the wheel speed sensor bolt and the sensor.

❊❊ WARNING

Make sure the wheel speed sensor harness is correctly routed to prevent the brake disc from damaging the harness.

6. To install, reverse the removal procedure.
    a. Tighten the wheel speed sensor bolt to 13 ft. lbs. (18 Nm).
    b. Tighten the 3 wheel speed sensor harness bolts to 10 ft. lbs. (15 Nm).

2011 4WD F250/F350

See Figure 2.

1. Remove the disc brake shield.
2. Disconnect the wheel speed sensor electrical connector.
3. Detach the wheel speed sensor harness from the radius arm.
4. Remove the 3 wheel speed sensor harness bolts.

5. Remove the wheel speed sensor bolt and the sensor.

❊❊ WARNING

Make sure the wheel speed sensor harness is correctly routed to prevent the brake disc from damaging the harness.

6. To install, reverse the removal procedure.
    a. Tighten the wheel speed sensor bolt to 13 ft. lbs. (18 Nm).
    b. Tighten the 3 wheel speed sensor harness bolts to 106 inch lbs. (12 Nm).

2010 RWD F250/F350

See Figure 3.

1. Remove the wheel and tire.
2. Disconnect the wheel speed sensor electrical connector.
3. Remove the wheel speed sensor harness bolts and detach the harness from the radius arm.
4. Remove the wheel speed sensor bolt and the sensor.

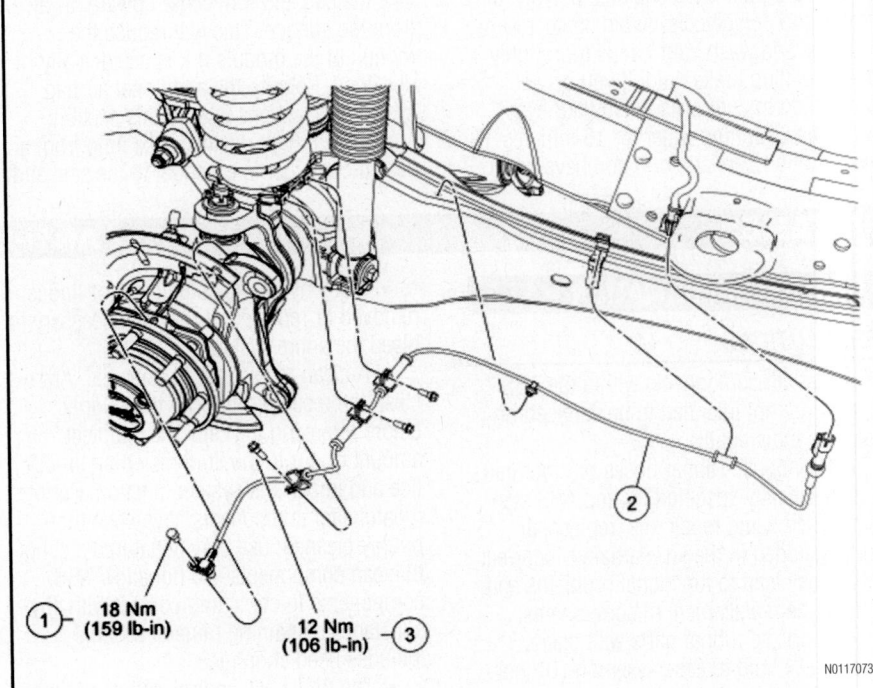

**18 Nm
(159 lb-in)**

**12 Nm
(106 lb-in)**

N0117073

Fig. 2 Remove the wheel speed sensor bolts (1), the wheel speed sensors (2), and the wheel speed sensor harness bolts

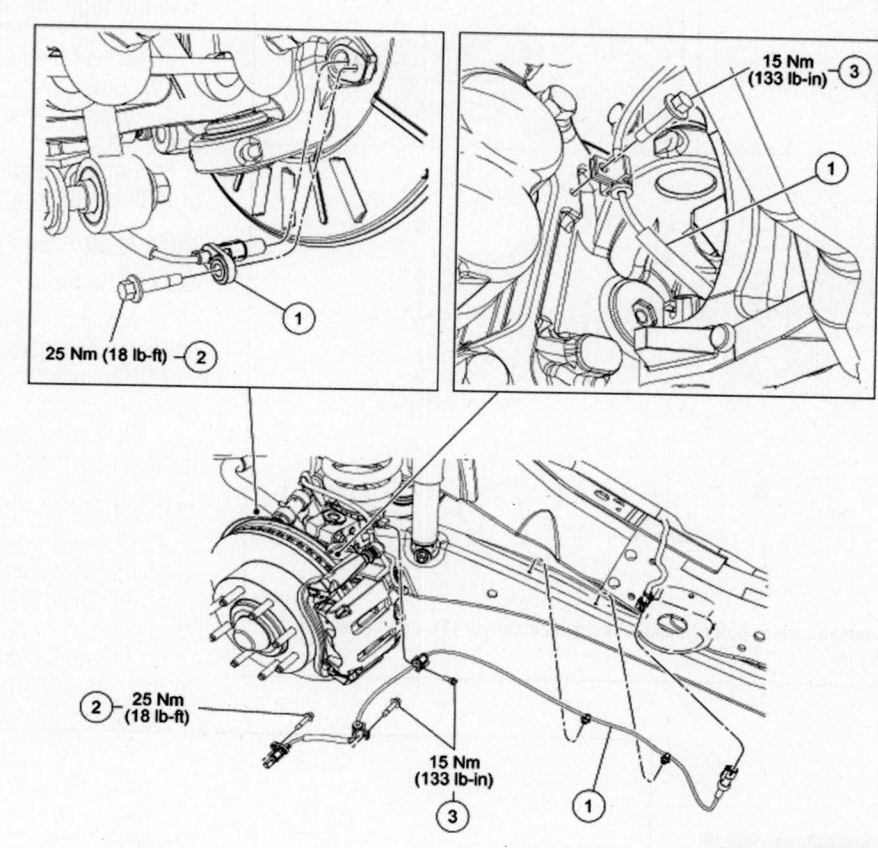

Fig. 3 Remove the wheel speed sensor harness bolts (3), the wheel speed sensor bolt (2), and the wheel sped sensor (1)

Make sure the wheel speed sensor harness is correctly routed to prevent the brake disc from damaging the harness.

5. To install, reverse the removal procedure.
   a. Tighten the wheel speed sensor bolt to 18 ft. lbs. (25 Nm).
   b. Tighten the wheel speed sensor harness bolts to 10 ft. lbs. (15 Nm).

2011 RWD F250/F350

See Figure 4.

1. Remove the wheel and tire.
2. Disconnect the wheel speed sensor electrical connector.
3. Remove the wheel speed sensor harness bolts and detach the harness from the radius arm.
4. Remove the wheel speed sensor bolt and the sensor.

Make sure the wheel speed sensor harness is correctly routed to prevent the brake disc from damaging the harness.

5. To install, reverse the removal procedure.
   a. Tighten the wheel speed sensor bolt to 18 ft. lbs. (25 Nm).
   b. Tighten the wheel speed sensor harness bolts to 106 inch lbs. (12 Nm).

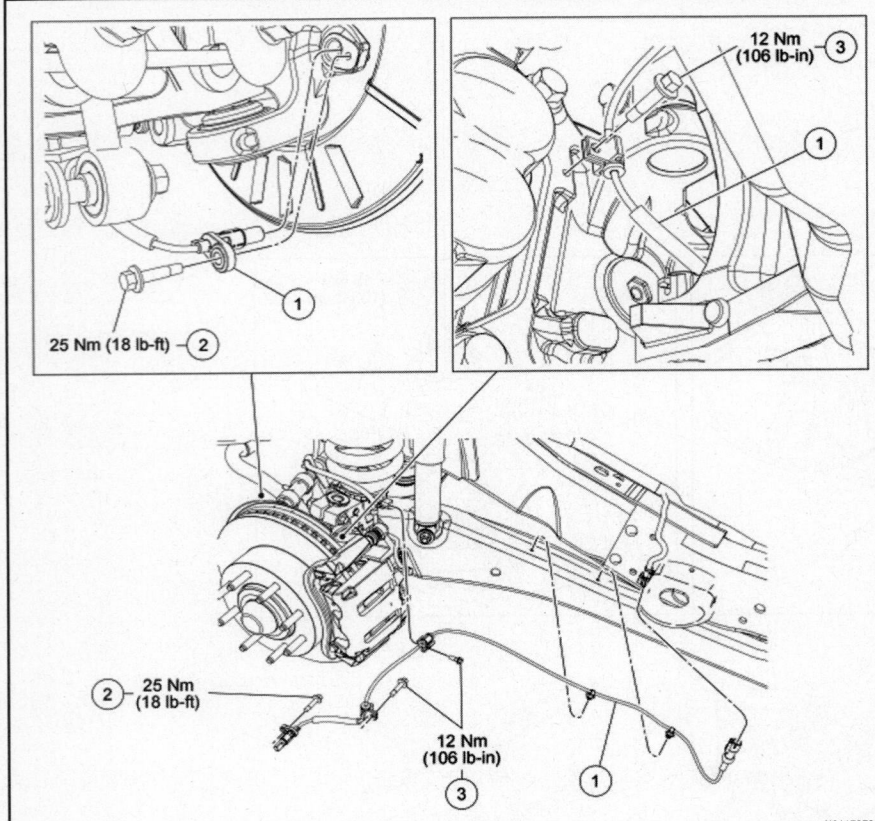

Fig. 4 Remove the wheel speed sensor bolt (2), the wheel speed sensor (1), and the wheel speed sensor harness bolts (3)

1. With the vehicle in NEUTRAL, position it on a hoist.
2. Disconnect the wheel speed sensor electrical connector.

⁂ WARNING

The wheel speed sensor is constructed from plastic, excessive force may damage the wheel speed sensor.

3. Remove the wheel speed sensor bolt and the sensor.
4. To install, reverse the removal procedure.
5. Tighten the wheel speed sensor bolt to 15 ft. lbs. (20 Nm).

2011 F250/F350 Four Channel

See Figures 6 and 7.

1. With the vehicle in NEUTRAL, position it on a hoist.
2. Disconnect the wheel speed sensor electrical connector.
3. Detach the wheel speed sensor harness from the rear axle.

➡ **F-350 shown, F-250 similar.**

4. Remove the wheel speed sensor bolt and the wheel speed sensor.
5. To install, reverse the removal procedure.
6. Tighten the wheel speed sensor bolt to 15 ft. lbs. (20 Nm).

Rear

2010 F250/F350

See Figure 5.

⁂ WARNING

Clean off any dirt or foreign material that may have collected around the wheel speed sensor before removal to prevent contamination of the axle lubricant. Failure to follow this instruction may result in damage to the rear axle.

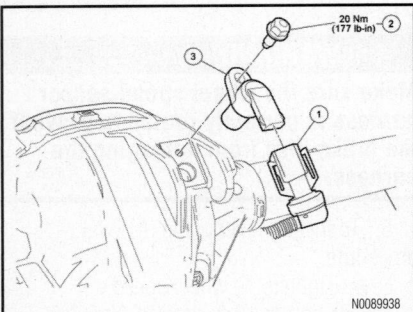

Fig. 5 Disconnect the wheel speed sensor electrical connector (1), and remove the wheel speed sensor bolt (2) and the wheel speed sensor (3)

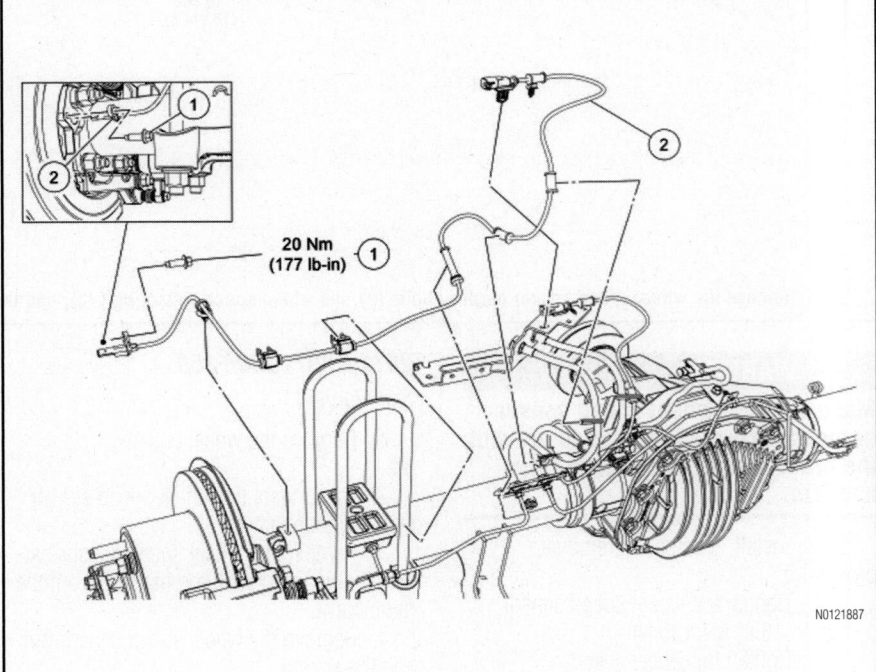

Fig. 6 Remove the wheel speed sensor bolt (1) and the wheel speed sensor (2) (Left side)

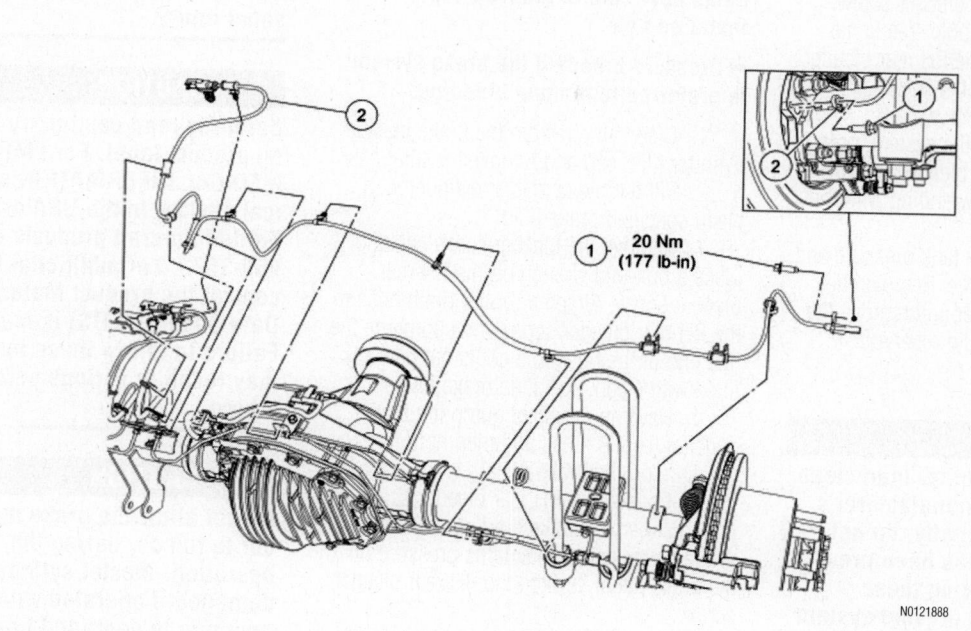

Fig. 7 Remove the wheel speed sensor bolt (1) and the wheel speed sensor (2) (Right side)

N0121888

20 Nm
(177 lb-in)

BRAKES

BLEEDING THE BRAKE SYSTEM

BLEEDING PROCEDURE

BLEEDING PROCEDURE

Pressure Bleeding

※ CAUTION

Do not use any fluid other than clean brake fluid meeting manufacturer's specification. Additionally, do not use brake fluid that has been previously drained. Following these instructions will help prevent system contamination, brake component damage and the risk of serious personal injury.

※ CAUTION

Carefully read cautionary information on product label. For additional information, consult the product Material Safety Data Sheet (MSDS) if available. Failure to follow these instructions may result in serious personal injury.

※ CAUTION

Do not allow the brake master cylinder to run dry during the bleeding operation. Master cylinder may be damaged if operated without fluid, resulting in degraded braking performance. Failure to follow this instruction may result in serious personal injury.

※ WARNING

Do not spill brake fluid on painted or plastic surfaces or damage to the surface may occur. If brake fluid is spilled onto a painted or plastic surface, immediately wash the surface with water.

→The Hydraulic Control Unit (HCU) bleeding procedure must be carried out if the HCU or any components upstream of the HCU are installed new.

→Pressure bleeding the brake system is preferred to manual bleeding.

1. Clean all dirt from the brake master cylinder filler cap and remove the filler cap.
2. Fill the brake master cylinder with clean specified brake fluid.

→Master cylinder pressure bleeder adapter tools are available from various manufacturers of pressure bleeding equipment. Follow the instructions of the equipment manufacturer when installing the adapter.

Install the bleeder adapter to the brake master cylinder reservoir and attach the bleeder tank hose to the fitting on the adapter.

→Make sure the bleeder tank contains enough clean, specified brake fluid to complete the bleeding operation.

3. Open the valve on the bleeder tank.
4. Apply 30–50 psi (207–345 kPa) to the brake system.
5. Remove the RH rear bleeder cap and place a box-end wrench on the bleeder screw. Attach a rubber drain tube to the RH rear bleeder screw and submerge the free

end of the tube in a container partially filled with clean, specified brake fluid.

6. Loosen the RH rear bleeder screw. Leave open until clear, bubble-free brake fluid flows, then tighten the RH rear bleeder screw and remove the rubber hose.

7. Install the bleeder screw cap.

8. Continue bleeding the system, going in order from the LH rear bleeder screw to the RH front bleeder screw ending with the LH front bleeder screw.

9. Release the bleeder tank pressure and close the bleeder tank valve. Remove the tank hose from the adapter and remove the adapter from the brake fluid reservoir.

Manual Bleeding

✱✱ CAUTION

Do not use any fluid other than clean brake fluid meeting manufacturer's specification. Additionally, do not use brake fluid that has been previously drained. Following these instructions will help prevent system contamination, brake component damage and the risk of serious personal injury.

✱✱ CAUTION

Carefully read cautionary information on product label. For EMERGENCY MEDICAL INFORMATION seek medical advice. In the USA or Canada on Ford/Motorcraft products call: 1-800-959-3673. For additional information, consult the product Material Safety Data Sheet (MSDS) if available. Failure to follow these instructions may result in serious personal injury.

✱✱ CAUTION

Do not allow the brake master cylinder to run dry during the bleeding operation. Master cylinder may be damaged if operated without fluid, resulting in degraded braking performance. Failure to follow this instruction may result in serious personal injury.

✱✱ WARNING

Do not spill brake fluid on painted or plastic surfaces or damage to the surface may occur. If brake fluid is spilled onto a painted or plastic surface, immediately wash the surface with water.

➡The HCU bleeding procedure must be carried out if the HCU or any components upstream of the HCU are installed new.

➡Pressure bleeding the brake system is preferred to manual bleeding.

1. Clean all dirt from the brake master cylinder filler cap and remove the filler cap.

2. Fill the brake master cylinder with clean specified brake fluid.

3. Remove the bleeder screw cap and place a box-end wrench on the RH rear bleeder screw. Attach a rubber drain hose to the RH rear bleeder screw and submerge the free end of the hose in a container partially filled with clean, specified brake fluid.

4. Have an assistant pump the brake pedal at least 3 times and then hold firm pressure on the brake pedal.

5. Loosen the RH rear bleeder screw until a stream of brake fluid comes out. While the assistant maintains pressure on the brake pedal, tighten the RH rear bleeder screw.

6. Repeat until clear, bubble-free fluid comes out.

7. Refill the brake master cylinder reservoir as necessary.

8. Remove the rubber hose and tighten the bleeder screw.

9. Install the bleeder screw cap.

10. Repeat Steps 2 through 5 for the LH rear, RH front and LH front bleeder screws in this order.

Hydraulic Control Unit (HCU)

➡The HCU bleeding procedure must be carried out if the HCU or any components upstream of the HCU are installed new.

➡Pressure bleeding the brake system is preferred to manual bleeding.

1. Follow the Pressure Bleeding or Manual Bleeding procedure steps to bleed the system.

2. Connect the scan tool and follow the ABS Service Bleed instructions.

3. Repeat the Pressure Bleeding or Manual Bleeding procedure steps to bleed the system.

MASTER CYLINDER BLEEDING

✱✱ CAUTION

Do not use any fluid other than clean brake fluid meeting manufacturer's specification. Additionally, do not use brake fluid that has been previously drained. Following these

instructions will help prevent system contamination, brake component damage and the risk of serious personal injury.

✱✱ CAUTION

Carefully read cautionary information on product label. For EMERGENCY MEDICAL INFORMATION seek medical advice. In the USA or Canada on Ford/Motorcraft products call: 1-800-959-3673. For additional information, consult the product Material Safety Data Sheet (MSDS) if available. Failure to follow these instructions may result in serious personal injury.

✱✱ CAUTION

Do not allow the brake master cylinder to run dry during the bleeding operation. Master cylinder may be damaged if operated without fluid, resulting in degraded braking performance. Failure to follow this instruction may result in serious personal injury.

✱✱ WARNING

Do not spill brake fluid on painted or plastic surfaces or damage to the surface may occur. If brake fluid is spilled onto a painted or plastic surface, immediately wash the surface with water.

➡When a new brake master cylinder has been installed, or the system is emptied or partially emptied, it should be primed to prevent air from entering the system.

1. Disconnect the brake tubes from the master cylinder.

2. Install short brake tubes with the ends submerged in the brake master cylinder reservoir.

3. Fill the brake master cylinder reservoir with clean, specified brake fluid.

4. Have an assistant pump the brake pedal until clear fluid flows from both brake tubes, without air bubbles.

5. Remove the short brake tubes and install the brake outlet tubes.

6. Bleed the brake system.

BLEEDING THE ABS SYSTEM

See Bleeding Procedure above.

BRAKES

FRONT DISC BRAKES

❊❊ WARNING

Dust and dirt accumulating on brake parts during normal use may contain asbestos fibers from production or aftermarket brake linings. Breathing excessive concentrations of asbestos fibers can cause serious bodily harm. Exercise care when servicing brake parts. Do not sand or grind brake lining unless equipment used is designed to contain the dust residue. Do not clean brake parts with compressed air or by dry brushing. Cleaning should be done by dampening the brake components with a fine mist of water, then wiping the brake components clean with a dampened cloth. Dispose of cloth and all residue containing asbestos fibers in an impermeable container with the appropriate label. Follow practices prescribed by the Occupational Safety and Health Administration (OSHA) and the Environmental Protection Agency (EPA) for the handling, processing, and disposing of dust or debris that may contain asbestos fibers.

❊❊ CAUTION

Do not use any fluid other than clean brake fluid meeting manufacturer's specification. Additionally, do not use brake fluid that has been previously drained. Following these instructions will help prevent system contamination, brake component damage and the risk of serious personal injury.

❊❊ CAUTION

Carefully read cautionary information on product label. For EMERGENCY MEDICAL INFORMATION seek medical advice. In the USA or Canada on Ford/Motorcraft products call: 1-800-959-3673. For additional information, consult the product Material Safety Data Sheet (MSDS) if available. Failure to follow these instructions may result in serious personal injury.

❊❊ WARNING

Do not spill brake fluid on painted or plastic surfaces or damage to the surface may occur. If brake fluid is spilled onto a painted or plastic

surface, immediately wash the surface with water.

BRAKE CALIPER

REMOVAL & INSTALLATION

See Figure 8.

1. Remove the wheel and tire.
2. Remove the brake caliper flow bolt and position the brake flexible hose aside.
3. Discard the 2 copper washers.
4. Remove the 2 brake caliper bolts and the brake caliper.

To install:

❊❊ WARNING

Tighten the bottom caliper bolt before tightening the top caliper bolt or damage to guide pins may occur.

❊❊ WARNING

Make sure the caliper pin boots are correctly seated to prevent damage to guide pins.

5. Position the brake caliper and install the 2 brake caliper bolts. Tighten to 56 ft. lbs. (76 Nm).

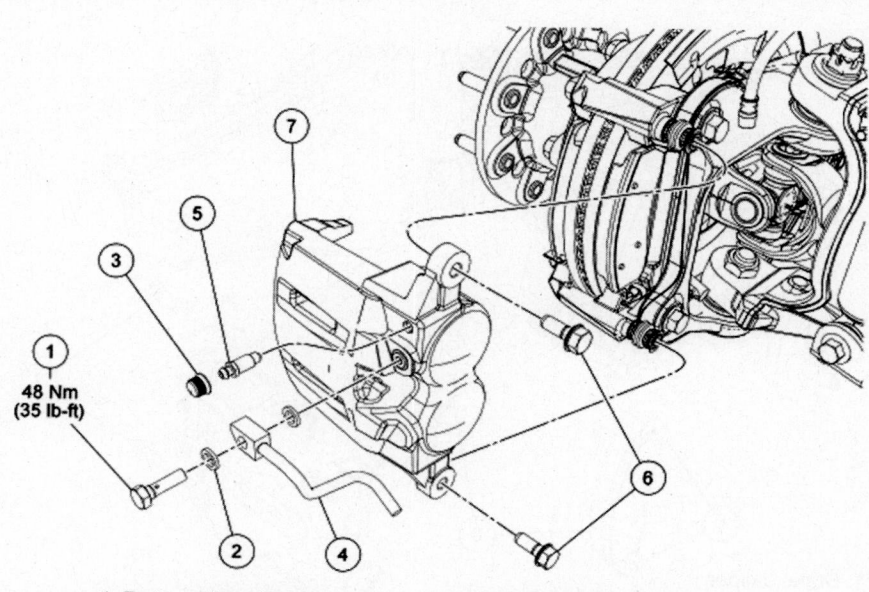

1. Brake caliper flow bolt
2. Copper washer (2 required)
3. Bleeder screw cap
4. Brake flexible hose
5. Brake bleeder screw
6. Brake caliper bolts (2 required)
7. Brake caliper

48 Nm
(35 lb-ft)

N0093073

Fig. 8 Exploded view of front disc caliper assembly

6. Using 2 new copper washers, position the brake flexible hose and install the brake caliper flow bolt. Tighten to 35 ft. lbs. (48 Nm).

7. Bleed the brake caliper.

8. Install the wheel and tire.

DISC BRAKE PADS

REMOVAL & INSTALLATION

See Figure 9.

1. Check the brake fluid level in the brake master cylinder reservoir.

2. If required, remove the fluid until the brake master cylinder reservoir is half full.

3. Remove the wheel and tire.

> ※ **WARNING**
>
> **Do not pry in the caliper sight hole to retract the pistons, as this can damage the pistons and boots.**

> ※ **WARNING**
>
> **Do not allow the brake caliper to hang from the brake hose or damage to the hose can occur.**

4. Remove the 2 brake caliper bolts and position the caliper aside. Support the caliper using mechanic's wire.

> ※ **CAUTION**
>
> **Always install new brake shoes or pads at both ends of an axle to reduce the possibility of brakes pulling vehicle to one side. Failure to follow this instruction may result in uneven braking and serious personal injury.**

5. Remove the 2 brake pads and the retraction clips. Discard the retraction clips.

6. Measure the brake disc thickness, machine if necessary. Install a new brake disc if it is not within specification.

To install:

> ※ **WARNING**
>
> **Do not allow grease, oil, brake fluid or other contaminants to contact the pad lining material. Do not install contaminated pads or damage to components may occur.**

➡ **If installing new brake pads, install all new hardware as supplied with the brake pad kit.**

7. Install the new retracting clips and the 2 brake pads.

> ※ **WARNING**
>
> **Protect the piston and boots when pushing the caliper piston into the caliper piston bores or damage to components may occur.**

8. If installing new brake pads, using a suitable tool and a worn brake pad, compress the disc brake caliper pistons into the caliper.

> ※ **WARNING**
>
> **Tighten the bottom caliper bolt before tightening the top caliper bolt or damage to guide pins may occur.**

> ※ **WARNING**
>
> **Make sure the caliper pin boots are correctly seated to prevent damage to the guide pins.**

9. Position the brake caliper and install the 2 bolts. Tighten to 56 ft. lbs. (76 Nm).

10. Install the wheel and tire.

11. Fill the brake master cylinder reservoir with clean brake fluid.

12. Apply brakes several times to verify correct brake operation.

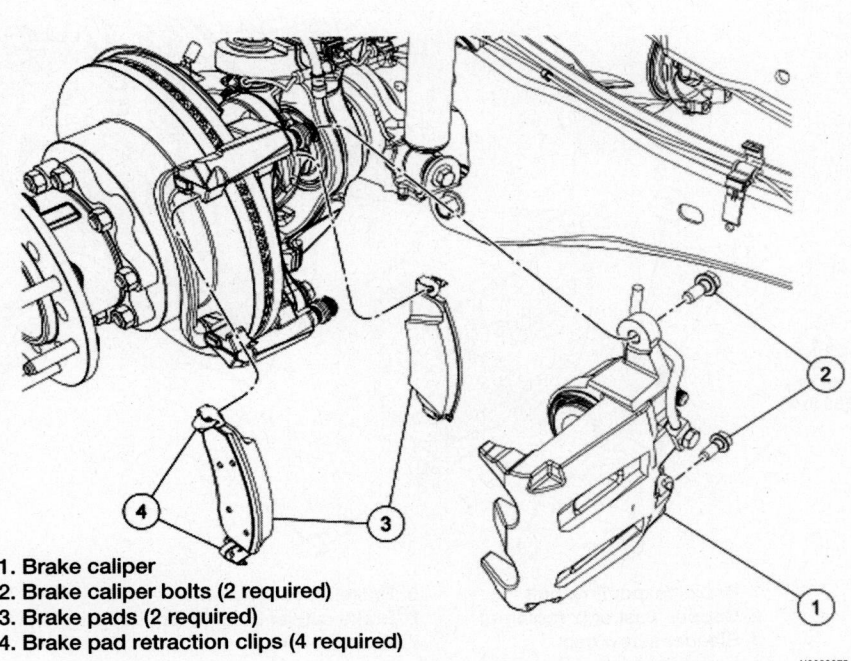

1. Brake caliper
2. Brake caliper bolts (2 required)
3. Brake pads (2 required)
4. Brake pad retraction clips (4 required)

N0093075

Fig. 9 Exploded view of front brake and pad assembly

BRAKES

REAR DISC BRAKES

❋❋ WARNING

Dust and dirt accumulating on brake parts during normal use may contain asbestos fibers from production or aftermarket brake linings. Breathing excessive concentrations of asbestos fibers can cause serious bodily harm. Exercise care when servicing brake parts. Do not sand or grind brake lining unless equipment used is designed to contain the dust residue. Do not clean brake parts with compressed air or by dry brushing. Cleaning should be done by dampening the brake components with a fine mist of water, then wiping the brake components clean with a dampened cloth. Dispose of cloth and all residue containing asbestos fibers in an impermeable container with the appropriate label. Follow practices prescribed by the Occupational Safety and Health Administration (OSHA) and the Environmental Protection Agency (EPA) for the handling, processing, and disposing of dust or debris that may contain asbestos fibers.

❋❋ CAUTION

Do not use any fluid other than clean brake fluid meeting manufacturer's specification. Additionally, do not use brake fluid that has been previously drained. Following these instructions will help prevent system contamination, brake component damage and the risk of serious personal injury.

❋❋ CAUTION

Carefully read cautionary information on product label. For EMERGENCY MEDICAL INFORMATION seek medical advice. In the USA or Canada on Ford/Motorcraft products call: 1-800-959-3673. For additional information, consult the product Material Safety Data Sheet (MSDS) if available. Failure to follow these instructions may result in serious personal injury.

❋❋ WARNING

Do not spill brake fluid on painted or plastic surfaces or damage to the surface may occur. If brake fluid is spilled onto a painted or plastic surface, immediately wash the surface with water.

BRAKE CALIPER

REMOVAL & INSTALLATION
See Figure 10.

1. Remove the wheel and tire.
2. Remove the brake caliper flow bolt and discard the 2 copper washers.

❋❋ WARNING

Do not pry in the caliper sight hole to retract the pistons, as this can damage the pistons and boots.

3. Remove the 2 brake caliper bolts and the caliper.

To install:
4. To install, reverse the removal procedure.
   a. For F-250/350 Single Rear Wheel (SRW), tighten the brake caliper bolts to 26 ft. lbs. (35 Nm).
   b. For F-350 Dual Rear Wheels (DRW), tighten the brake caliper bolts to 56 ft. lbs. (76 Nm).
   c. Install new copper washers.
   d. Tighten the brake caliper flow bolt to 26 ft. lbs. (35 Nm).
   e. Bleed the brake caliper.

DISC BRAKE PADS

REMOVAL & INSTALLATION
See Figure 11.

❋❋ CAUTION

Always install new brake shoes or pads at both ends of an axle to reduce the possibility of brakes pulling vehicle to one side. Failure to follow this instruction may result in uneven braking and serious personal injury.

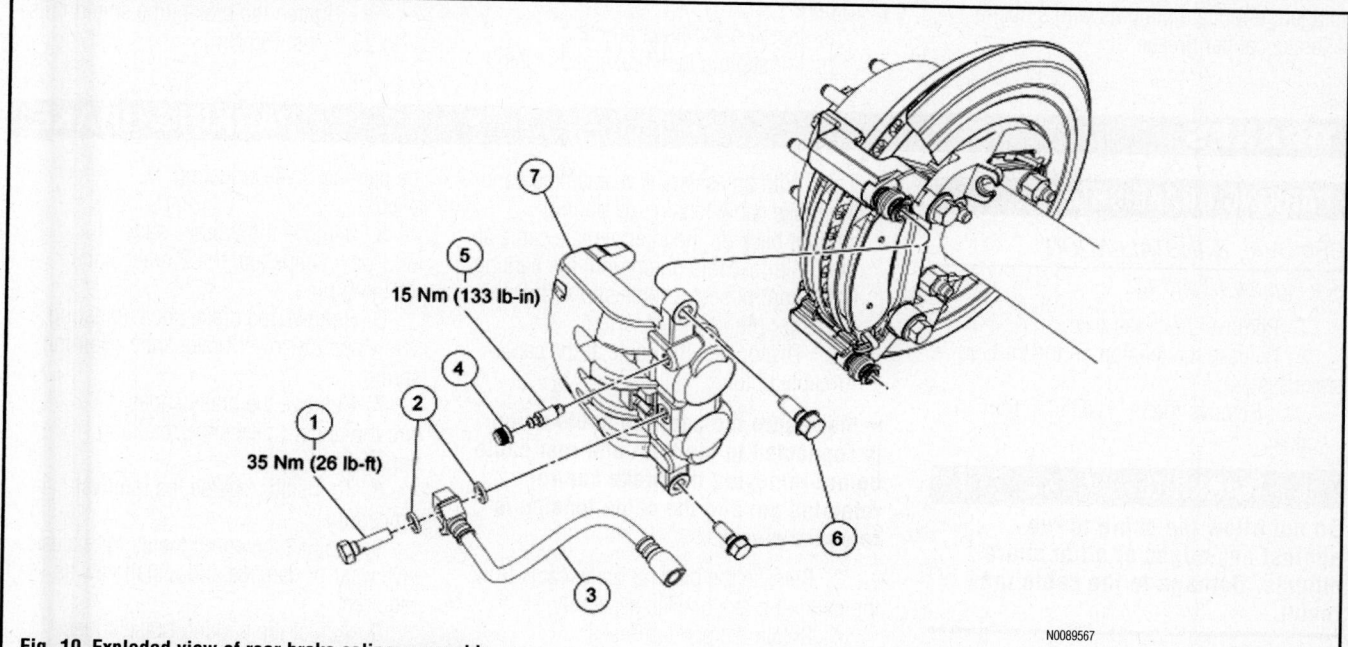

Fig. 10 Exploded view of rear brake caliper assembly

15 Nm (133 lb-in)

35 Nm (26 lb-ft)

N0089567

1. If necessary, remove the brake fluid until the brake master cylinder reservoir is half full.

2. Remove the wheel and tire.

3. If equipped, remove the 2 brake tube shield nuts and the brake tube shield.

> **❋❋ WARNING**
>
> **Do not pry in caliper sight hole to retract pistons as this can damage the pistons and boots.**

> **❋❋ WARNING**
>
> **Do not allow the brake caliper to hang from the brake hose or damage to the hose can occur.**

4. Remove the 2 brake caliper bolts and position the caliper aside. Support the caliper using mechanic's wire.

5. Remove the 2 brake pads and inspect for wear or contamination. Remove the 4 retraction clips.

   a. Discard the retraction clips.

   b. Inspect the disc brake caliper for leaks.

6. Measure the brake disc thickness. Install a new brake disc if not within specification.

7. Inspect the disc brake anchor plate assembly.

   a. Check the guide pin boots for damage.

   b. Check the guide pins for binding and damage.

   c. Install new pins if worn or damaged. Lubricate the pins with silicone brake caliper grease.

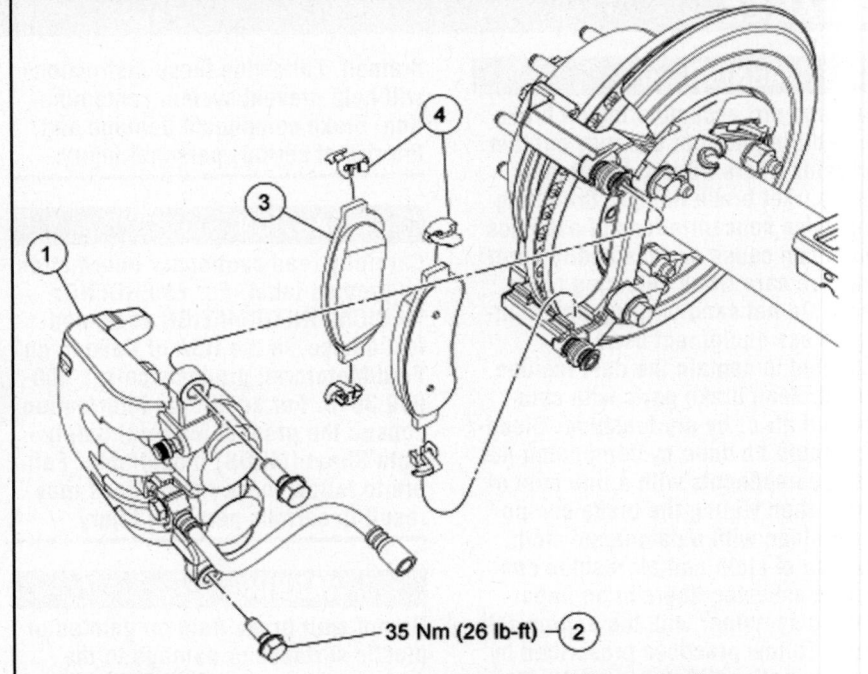

35 Nm (26 lb-ft) – ②

1. Brake caliper
2. Brake caliper bolt (2 required)
3. Brake pad (2 required)
4. Brake pad retraction clips (4 required)

N0063074

Fig. 11 Exploded view of rear brake and pad assembly

> **❋❋ WARNING**
>
> **Protect the piston and boots when pushing the caliper piston into the caliper bore or damage to the piston and/or boots may occur.**

To install:

8. To install, reverse the removal procedure.

   a. Install new retraction clips.

   b. If installing new brake pads, using a suitable tool and a worn brake pad, compress the disc brake caliper pistons into the caliper.

   c. For F-250/350 Single Rear Wheel (SRW), tighten the brake caliper bolts to 26 ft. lbs. (35 Nm).

   d. For F-350 Dual Rear Wheels (DRW), tighten the brake caliper bolts to 56 ft. lbs. (76 Nm).

   e. Tighten the brake tube shield nuts to 26 ft. lbs. (35 Nm).

BRAKES   PARKING BRAKE

PARKING BRAKE SHOES

REMOVAL & INSTALLATION

See Figures 12 and 13.

1. Remove the brake disc.

2. Release the tension on the parking brake system.

   a. Remove the LH cowl side trim panel.

> **❋❋ WARNING**
>
> **Do not allow the cable to rub against any edges or other sharp objects. Damage to the cable may result.**

   b. With an assistant, release the parking brake cable tension by pulling straight back on the intermediate cable at the cable-to-cable union until the parking brake control sector rotates to a stop and a retainer pin can be inserted.

   c. Disconnect the cable at the cable-to-cable union.

➡**Make sure the cable-to-cable union is connected to the front and rear cable before removing the brake control retaining pin and the cable tension is reloaded slowly.**

3. Release the parking brake cable from the parking brake bracket assembly.

4. Rotate the parking brake cable 90 degrees to release it from the parking brake actuating lever.

5. Remove the 2 brake shoe hold-down clips and the 2 brake shoe retaining pins.

6. Remove the brake shoe adjusting screw and the lower brake shoe retaining spring.

7. Remove the brake shoes and the upper brake shoe retaining spring.

8. To install, reverse the removal procedure.

9. Inspect the components for excessive wear or damage and install new as required.

10. Adjust the parking brake shoes.

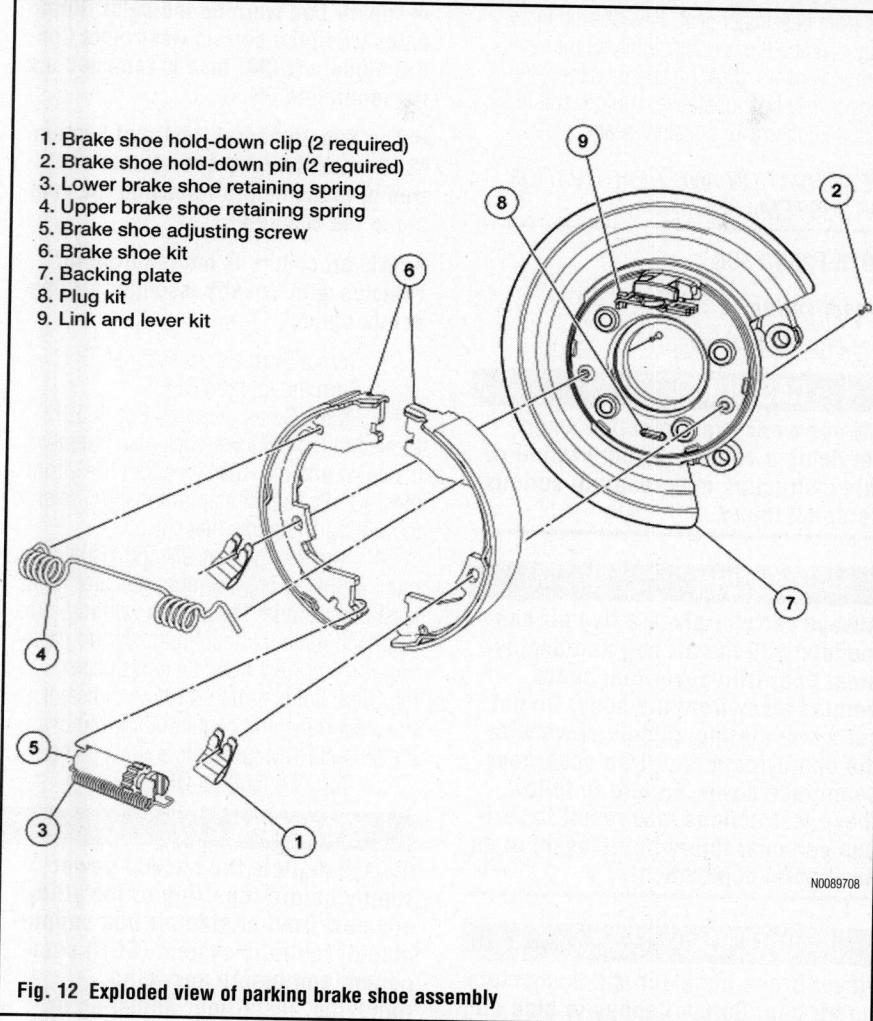

1. Brake shoe hold-down clip (2 required)
2. Brake shoe hold-down pin (2 required)
3. Lower brake shoe retaining spring
4. Upper brake shoe retaining spring
5. Brake shoe adjusting screw
6. Brake shoe kit
7. Backing plate
8. Plug kit
9. Link and lever kit

N0089708

Fig. 12 Exploded view of parking brake shoe assembly

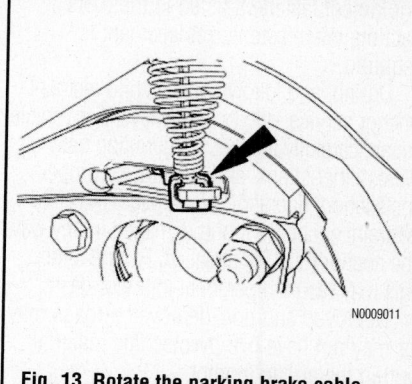

N0009011

Fig. 13 Rotate the parking brake cable 90 degrees to release it from the parking brake actuating lever

PARKING BRAKE SHOE ADJUSTMENT

➡**Make sure that the parking brake is fully released.**

1. With the vehicle in NEUTRAL, position it on a hoist.
2. Remove the brake adjusting hole cover from the backing plate.
3. Turn the brake adjuster screw to expand the parking brake shoe and linings until they drag against the drum-in-hat brake disc.
4. Back off the brake adjuster screw until no drag is evident.
5. Install the brake adjusting hole cover into the backing plate.

CHASSIS ELECTRICAL   AIR BAG (SUPPLEMENTAL RESTRAINT SYSTEM)

GENERAL INFORMATION

✳✳ WARNING

These vehicles are equipped with an air bag system. The system must be disarmed before performing service on, or around, system components, the steering column, instrument panel components, wiring and sensors. Failure to follow the safety precautions and the disarming procedure could result in accidental air bag deployment, possible injury and unnecessary system repairs.

SERVICE PRECAUTIONS

Disconnect and isolate the battery negative cable before beginning any airbag system component diagnosis, testing, removal, or installation procedures. Allow system capacitor to discharge for two minutes before beginning any component service. This will disable the airbag system. Failure to disable the airbag system may result in accidental airbag deployment, personal injury, or death.

Do not place an intact undeployed airbag face down on a solid surface. The airbag will propel into the air if accidentally deployed and may result in personal injury or death.

When carrying or handling an undeployed airbag, the trim side (face) of the airbag should be pointing away from the body to minimize possibility of injury if accidental deployment occurs. Failure to do this may result in personal injury or death.

Replace airbag system components with OEM replacement parts. Substitute parts may appear interchangeable, but internal differences may result in inferior occupant protection. Failure to do so may result in occupant personal injury or death.

Wear safety glasses, rubber gloves, and long sleeved clothing when cleaning powder residue from vehicle after an airbag deployment. Powder residue emitted from a deployed airbag can cause skin irritation. Flush affected area with cool water if irritation is experienced. If nasal or throat irritation is experienced, exit the vehicle for fresh air until the irritation ceases. If irritation continues, see a physician.

Do not use a replacement airbag that is not in the original packaging. This may result in improper deployment, personal injury, or death.

The factory installed fasteners, screws and bolts used to fasten airbag components have a special coating and are specifically designed for the airbag system. Do not use substitute fasteners. Use only original equipment fasteners listed in the parts catalog when fastener replacement is required.

During, and following, any child restraint anchor service, due to impact event or vehicle repair, carefully inspect all mounting hardware, tether straps, and anchors for proper installation, operation, or damage. If a child restraint anchor is found damaged in any way, the anchor must be replaced. Failure to do this may result in personal injury or death.

Deployed and non-deployed airbags may or may not have live pyrotechnic material within the airbag inflator.

Do not dispose of driver/passenger/curtain airbags or seat belt tensioners unless you are sure of complete deployment. Refer to the Hazardous Substance Control System for proper disposal.

Dispose of deployed airbags and tensioners consistent with state, provincial, local, and federal regulations.

After any airbag component testing or service, do not connect the battery negative cable. Personal injury or death may result if the system test is not performed first.

If the vehicle is equipped with the Occupant Classification System (OCS), do not connect the battery negative cable before performing the OCS Verification Test using the scan tool and the appropriate diagnostic information. Personal injury or death may result if the system test is not performed properly.

Never replace both the Occupant Restraint Controller (ORC) and the Occupant Classification Module (OCM) at the same time. If both require replacement, replace one, then perform the Airbag System test before replacing the other.

Both the ORC and the OCM store Occupant Classification System (OCS) calibration data, which they transfer to one another when one of them is replaced. If both are replaced at the same time, an irreversible fault will be set in both modules and the OCS may malfunction and cause personal injury or death.

If equipped with OCS, the Seat Weight Sensor is a sensitive, calibrated unit and must be handled carefully. Do not drop or handle roughly. If dropped or damaged, replace with another sensor. Failure to do so may result in occupant injury or death.

If equipped with OCS, the front passenger seat must be handled carefully as well. When removing the seat, be careful when setting on floor not to drop. If dropped, the sensor may be inoperative, could result in occupant injury, or possibly death.

If equipped with OCS, when the passenger front seat is on the floor, no one should sit in the front passenger seat. This uneven force may damage the sensing ability of the seat weight sensors. If sat on and damaged, the sensor may be inoperative, could result in occupant injury, or possibly death.

DEACTIVATION AND REACTIVATION OF SYSTEM

2010 F250/F350

Deactivation

See Figures 14 through 17.

> ❋❋ **CAUTION**
>
> **Always wear eye protection when servicing a vehicle. Failure to follow this instruction may result in serious personal injury.**

> ❋❋ **CAUTION**
>
> **Always carry or place a live air bag module with the air bag and deployment door/trim cover/tear seam pointed away from the body. Do not set a live air bag module down with the deployment door/trim cover/tear seam face down. Failure to follow these instructions may result in serious personal injury in the event of an accidental deployment.**

> ❋❋ **CAUTION**
>
> **Never probe the electrical connectors on air bag, Safety Canopy or side air curtain modules. Failure to follow this instruction may result in the accidental deployment of these modules, which increases the risk of serious personal injury or death.**

> ❋❋ **CAUTION**
>
> **Never disassemble or tamper with safety belt buckle/retractor pretensioners or adaptive load limiting retractors or probe the electrical connectors. Failure to follow this instruction may result in the accidental deployment of the safety belt pretensioners or adaptive load limiting retractors which increases the risk of serious personal injury or death.**

> ❋❋ **CAUTION**
>
> **To reduce the risk of accidental deployment, do not use any memory saver devices. Failure to follow this instruction may result in serious personal injury or death.**

➡ **The air bag warning indicator illuminates when the correct Restraints Control Module (RCM) fuse is removed and the ignition is ON.**

➡ **The Supplemental Restraint System (SRS) must be fully operational and free of faults before releasing the vehicle to the customer.**

➡ **This procedure is not required for vehicles with driver/passenger air bag delete option.**

1. Turn all vehicle accessories OFF.
2. Turn the ignition OFF.
3. At the Smart Junction Box (SJB), located in the RH lower kick panel, remove the cover and the RCM fuse 32 (10A) from the SJB . For additional information, refer to the Wiring Diagrams manual.
4. Turn the ignition ON and visually monitor the air bag warning indicator for at least 30 seconds. The air bag warning indicator will remain lit continuously (no flashing) if the correct RCM fuse has been removed. If the air bag warning indicator does not remain lit continuously, remove the correct RCM fuse before proceeding.
5. Turn the ignition OFF.

> ❋❋ **CAUTION**
>
> **Always deplete the backup power supply before repairing or installing any new front or side air bag supplemental restraint system (SRS) component and before servicing, removing, installing, adjusting or striking components near the front or side impact sensors or the restraints control module (RCM). Nearby components include doors, instrument panel, console, door latches, strikers, seats and hood latches.**

To deplete the backup power supply energy, disconnect the battery ground cable and wait at least 1 minute. Be sure to disconnect auxiliary batteries and power supplies (if equipped).

Failure to follow these instructions may result in serious personal injury or death in the event of an accidental deployment.

6. Disconnect the battery ground cable and wait at least one minute.
7. Position the road wheels in the straight-ahead position.
8. If equipped, center the tilt steering column.

> ❋❋ **WARNING**
>
> **Turn the steering wheel so that the top is at 90 degrees (at the 9 o'clock position) to the left from the straight-**

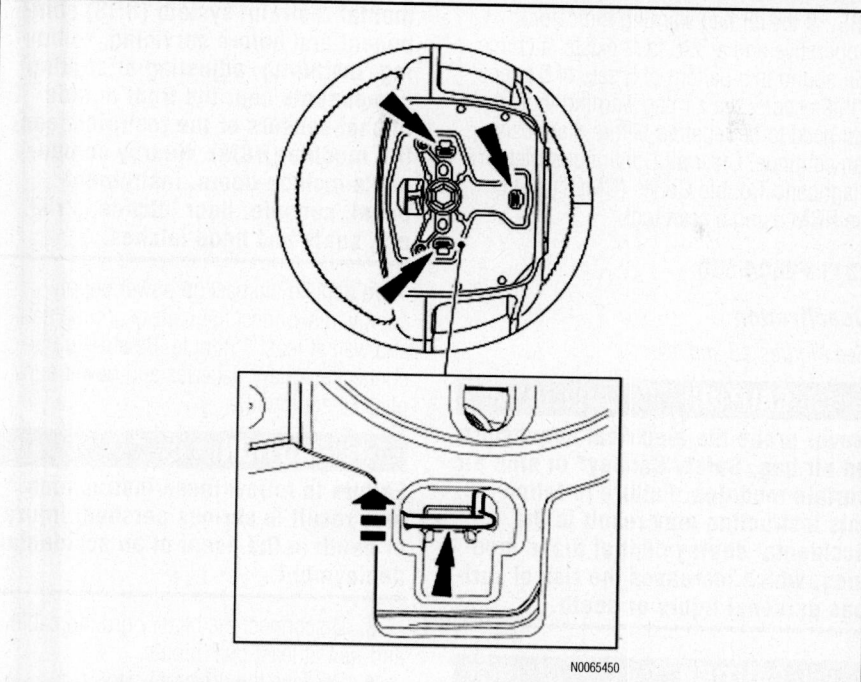

Fig. 14 Access the 3 driver air bag module wire clips through the back of the steering wheel cover

N0065450

ahead position to access the driver air bag module wire clips and to prevent damage to the steering column multifunction switch. Failure to follow this instruction may result in component damage.

9. Turn the steering wheel so the top of the wheel is 90 degrees to the left (at the 9 o'clock position).

10. If equipped, remove the screw and steering column manual tilt lever.

11. Remove the 3 screws and steering column lower shroud.

12. Remove the steering column upper shroud.

➡ Use a mirror to view the rear of the steering wheel to locate the 3 driver air bag module wire clips.

13. Using a screwdriver or suitable tool, release the wire clips from the steering wheel hooks.

14. Access the 3 driver air bag module wire clips through the back of the steering wheel cover and push each wire clip toward the center of the steering wheel to release.

15. Disconnect the driver air bag module and horn switch electrical connectors and remove the driver air bag module from the steering wheel.

16. Turn the steering wheel so the road wheels are in the straight-ahead position.

Fig. 15 Remove and discard the 4 passenger air bag trim cover screws

N0060584

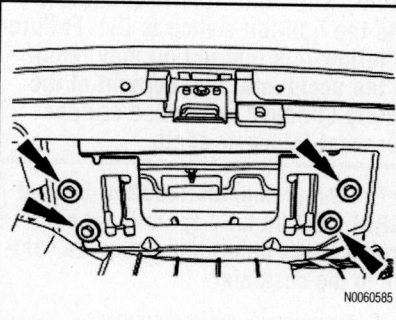

Fig. 16 Remove and discard the 4 nuts and move the passenger air bag module from the instrument panel

N0060585

17. Open and lower the glove compartment door.

18. Remove and discard the 4 passenger air bag trim cover screws.

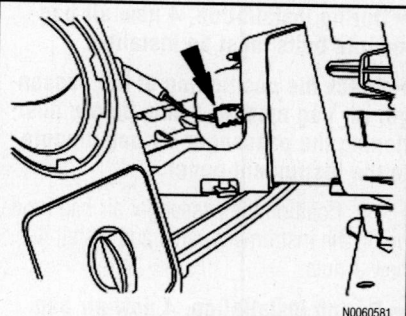

Fig. 17 Disconnect the electrical connector and remove the passenger air bag module

N0060581

✳✳ WARNING

Do not handle the passenger air bag module by grabbing the edges of the air bag trim cover. Failure to follow this instruction may result in component damage and/or system failure.

19. Remove and discard the 4 nuts and move the passenger air bag module from the instrument panel.

20. Disconnect the electrical connector and remove the passenger air bag module.

21. Install the RCM fuse 32 (10A) to the SJB.

22. Connect the battery ground cable.

Reactivation

1. Remove the RCM fuse 32 (10A) from the SJB.

2. Disconnect the battery ground cable and wait at least one minute.

✳✳ WARNING

Match the electrical connector key to the keyway in the passenger air bag module. The passenger air bag module electrical connector is unique and cannot be reversed when connected to the passenger air bag module. Do not force the electrical connector into the passenger air bag module. Failure to follow these instructions may result in component damage and/or system failure.

3. Connect the electrical connector to the passenger air bag module.

✳✳ WARNING

Do not handle the passenger air bag module by grabbing the edges of the air bag trim cover. Failure to follow this instruction may result in component damage and/or system failure.

➡During installation, 4 new air bag module bolts must be installed.

➡Check the positioning of the passenger air bag module J-nuts before positioning the passenger air bag module to the instrument panel.

4. Position the passenger air bag module in the instrument panel and install 4 new J-nuts.

➡During installation, 4 new air bag module deployment door screws must be installed.

5. Install the 4 new passenger air bag module deployment door screws.
6. Connect the horn switch and driver air bag module electrical connectors.
7. Position the driver air bag module to the steering wheel, lining up the locator pins.
8. Firmly press the driver air bag module to engage the 3 driver air bag module wire clips to the steering wheel.
9. Install the steering column lower shroud.
10. Install the steering column upper shroud.
11. Install the 3 steering column lower shroud screws.
12. If equipped, install the steering column manual tilt lever and screw.
13. Turn the ignition from OFF to ON.
14. Install the RCM fuse 32 (10A) to the SJB and install the cover.

⁂ CAUTION

Make sure no one is in the vehicle and there is nothing blocking or placed in front of any air bag module when the battery is connected. Failure to follow these instructions may result in serious personal injury in the event of an accidental deployment.

15. Connect the battery ground cable.
16. Prove out the SRS as follows: Turn the ignition from ON to OFF. Wait 10 seconds, then turn it back to ON and visually monitor the air bag warning indicator with the air bag modules installed. The air bag warning indicator will light continuously for approximately 6 seconds and then turn off. If an air bag SRS fault is present, the air bag warning indicator will either:—fail to light.—remain lit continuously.—flash. The air bag warning indicator may not illuminate until approximately 30 seconds after the ignition has been turned from the OFF to the ON position. This is the time required for the RCM to complete the testing of the

SRS . If the air bag warning indicator is inoperative and a SRS fault exists, a chime will sound in a pattern of 5 sets of 5 beeps. If this occurs, the air bag warning indicator will need to be repaired before diagnosis can continue. Clear all Continuous Memory Diagnostic Trouble Codes (CMDTCs) from the RCM using a scan tool.

2011 F250/F350

Deactivation
See Figures 18 and 19.

⁂ CAUTION

Never probe the electrical connectors on air bag, Safety Canopy® or side air curtain modules. Failure to follow this instruction may result in the accidental deployment of these modules, which increases the risk of serious personal injury or death.

⁂ CAUTION

Never disassemble or tamper with safety belt buckle/retractor pretensioners or adaptive load limiting retractors or probe the electrical connectors. Failure to follow this instruction may result in the accidental deployment of the safety belt pretensioners or adaptive load limiting retractors which increases the risk of serious personal injury or death.

⁂ CAUTION

Do not handle, move or change the original horizontal mounting position of the restraints control module (RCM) while the RCM is connected and the ignition switch is ON. Failure to follow this instruction may result in the accidental deployment of the Safety Canopy® and cause serious personal injury or death.

➡The Supplemental Restraint System (SRS) must be fully operational and free of faults before releasing the vehicle to the customer.

1. If equipped with side impact protection, position both front seats all the way up and the seat track to the middle of travel.
2. Depower the SRS.

⁂ CAUTION

Always deplete the backup power supply before repairing or installing any new front or side air bag supple-

mental restraint system (SRS) component and before servicing, removing, installing, adjusting or striking components near the front or side impact sensors or the restraints control module (RCM). Nearby components include doors, instrument panel, console, door latches, strikers, seats and hood latches.

To deplete the backup power supply energy, disconnect the battery ground cable and wait at least 1 minute. Be sure to disconnect auxiliary batteries and power supplies (if equipped).

⁂ CAUTION

Failure to follow these instructions may result in serious personal injury or death in the event of an accidental deployment.

3. Disconnect the battery ground cable and wait at least one minute.
4. Remove the driver air bag.
5. For vehicles with a passenger air bag, remove the passenger air bag.
6. For vehicles with side impact protection, perform the following:
   a. Remove the RH A-pillar trim panel.
   b. Remove the RH sun visor.
   c. Remove the screws and disconnect the electrical connector.
   d. Remove the screw and the RH sun visor retaining clip.
   e. From between the headliner and the roof sheet metal, locate the RH Safety Canopy module electrical connector just to the rear of the A-pillar.
   f. Disconnect the RH Safety Canopy module electrical connector.
   g. Slide the electrical connector lock up and wiggle the electrical connector out of the Safety Canopy module.
   h. From under the rear of the RH front seat, slide and disengage the locking

Fig. 18 Locate the RH Safety Canopy module electrical connector just to the rear of the A-pillar

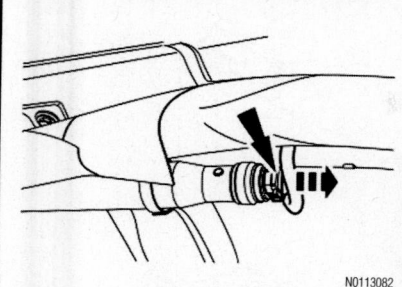

Fig. 19 Slide the electrical connector lock up and wiggle the electrical connector out of the Safety Canopy module

clip, release the tab and disconnect side air bag module electrical connector.

i. Remove the LH A-pillar trim panel.

j. Remove the LH sun visor.

k. Remove the screws and disconnect the electrical connector.

l. Remove the screw and the LH sun visor retaining clip.

m. From between the headliner and the roof sheet metal, locate the LH Safety Canopy module electrical connector just to the rear of the A-pillar.

n. Disconnect the LH Safety Canopy module electrical connector.

o. Slide the electrical connector lock up and wiggle the electrical connector out of the Safety Canopy module.

p. From under the rear of the LH front seat, slide and disengage the locking clip, release the tab and disconnect side air bag module electrical connector.

7. Install RCM fuse 33 (10A) to the Body Control Module (BCM).

8. Connect the battery ground cable.

Reactivation

1. Remove RCM fuse 33 (10A) from the BCM .

2. Disconnect the battery ground cable and wait at least one minute.

3. For vehicles with side impact protection, perform the following:

a. From under the rear of the LH front seat, connect side air bag module electrical connector, slide and engage the locking clip.

b. Connect the LH Safety Canopy module electrical connector.

c. After the electrical connector is connected, push the lock back into the electrical connector.

d. Position the LH sun visor retaining clip and install the screw.

e. Install the LH sun visor.

f. Connect the electrical connector and install the screws.

g. Install the LH A-pillar trim panel.

h. From under the rear of the RH front seat, connect side air bag module electrical connector, slide and engage the locking clip.

i. Connect the RH Safety Canopy module electrical connector.

j. After the electrical connector is connected, push the lock back into the electrical connector.

k. Position the RH sun visor retaining clip and install the screw.

l. Install the RH sun visor.

m. Connect the electrical connector and install the screws.

n. Install the RH A-pillar trim panel.

4. If equipped, install the passenger air bag.

5. Install the driver air bag.

6. Repower the SRS.

DEPOWERING AND REPOWERING THE SYSTEM

Depowering Procedure

> ⁂ **CAUTION**
>
> **Never probe the electrical connectors on air bag, Safety Canopy or side air curtain modules. Failure to follow this instruction may result in the accidental deployment of these modules, which increases the risk of serious personal injury or death.**

> ⁂ **CAUTION**
>
> **Never disassemble or tamper with safety belt buckle/retractor pretensioners or adaptive load limiting retractors or probe the electrical connectors. Failure to follow this instruction may result in the accidental deployment of the safety belt pretensioners or adaptive load limiting retractors which increases the risk of serious personal injury or death.**

> ⁂ **CAUTION**
>
> **To reduce the risk of accidental deployment, do not use any memory saver devices. Failure to follow this instruction may result in serious personal injury or death.**

➡ **The air bag warning indicator illuminates when the correct Restraints Control Module (RCM) fuse is removed and the ignition is ON.**

➡ **The Supplemental Restraint System**

(SRS) must be fully operational and free of faults before releasing the vehicle to the customer.

➡ **This procedure is not required for vehicles with driver/passenger air bag delete option.**

1. Turn all vehicle accessories OFF.

2. Turn the ignition to OFF.

3. For 2010 models, at the Smart Junction Box (SJB), located in the RH lower kick panel, remove the lower kick panel fuse cover and the RCM fuse 32 (10A) from the SJB.

4. For 2011 models, at the Body Control Module (BCM), located in the RH lower kick panel, remove the lower kick panel fuse cover and the RCM fuse 33 (10A) from the BCM.

5. Turn the ignition ON and visually monitor the air bag warning indicator for at least 30 seconds. The air bag warning indicator will remain lit continuously (no flashing) if the correct RCM fuse has been removed. If the air bag warning indicator does not remain lit continuously, remove the correct RCM fuse before proceeding.

6. Turn the ignition to OFF.

> ⁂ **CAUTION**
>
> **Always deplete the backup power supply before repairing or installing any new front or side air bag supplemental restraint system (SRS) component and before servicing, removing, installing, adjusting or striking components near the front or side impact sensors or the restraints control module (RCM). Nearby components include doors, instrument panel, console, door latches, strikers, seats and hood latches.**

To deplete the backup power supply energy, disconnect the battery ground cable and wait at least 1 minute. Be sure to disconnect auxiliary batteries and power supplies (if equipped).

Failure to follow these instructions may result in serious personal injury or death in the event of an accidental deployment.

7. Disconnect the battery ground cable and wait at least one minute.

Repowering Procedure

1. Turn the ignition from OFF to ON.

2. For 2010 models, install RCM fuse 32 (10A) to the SJB and install the lower kick panel fuse cover.

3. For 2011 models, install RCM fuse 33 (10A) to the BCM and install the lower kick panel fuse cover.

✳✳ CAUTION

Make sure no one is in the vehicle and there is nothing blocking or placed in front of any air bag module when the battery is connected. Failure to follow these instructions may result in serious personal injury in the event of an accidental deployment.

4. Connect the battery ground cable.
5. Prove out the RCM as follows: Turn the ignition from ON to OFF. Wait 10 seconds, then turn the ignition back to ON and visually monitor the air bag warning indicator with the air bag modules installed. The air bag warning indicator will light continuously for approximately 6 seconds and then turn OFF. If an air bag SRS fault is present, the air bag warning indicator will: —fail to light. —remain lit continuously. —flash at a 5 Hz rate (RCM not configured). The air bag warning indicator might not light until approximately 30 seconds after the ignition has been turned from the OFF to the ON position. This is the time required for the RCM to complete the testing of the SRS . If the air bag warning indicator is inoperative and a SRS fault exists, a chime will sound in a pattern of 5 sets of 5 beeps. If this occurs, the air bag warning indicator and any SRS fault discovered must be diagnosed and repaired. Clear all Continuous Memory Diagnostic Trouble Codes (CMDTCs) from the RCM using a scan tool.

CLOCKSPRING CENTERING

2010 Models

See Figures 20 through 22.

➡The air bag warning indicator illuminates when the correct Restraints Control Module (RCM) fuse is removed and the ignition is ON.

➡The Supplemental Restraint System (SRS) must be fully operational and free of faults before releasing the vehicle to the customer.

1. If equipped, tilt the steering wheel in the downward position and lock the tilt handle.
2. Remove the driver air bag module.

✳✳ WARNING

To prevent damage to the clockspring make sure the road wheels are in the straight-ahead position.

3. Remove the steering wheel.

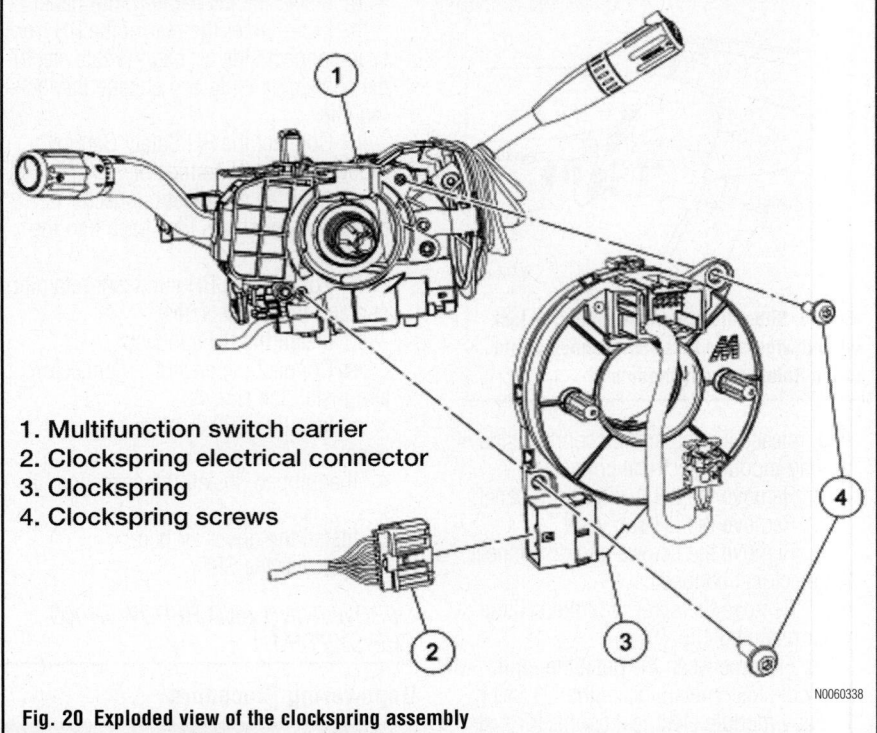

1. Multifunction switch carrier
2. Clockspring electrical connector
3. Clockspring
4. Clockspring screws

Fig. 20 Exploded view of the clockspring assembly

4. Disconnect the clockspring electrical connector.
5. Remove the 2 screws and clockspring.

To install:

✳✳ WARNING

If installing a new clockspring, do not remove the clockspring anti-rotation key until the steering wheel is installed. If the anti-rotation key has been removed before installing the steering wheel, the clockspring must be centered. Failure to follow this instruction may result in component damage and/or system failure.

6. Install the clockspring and 2 screws.
7. Connect the clockspring electrical connector.

✳✳ CAUTION

If the clockspring is not correctly centralized, it may fail prematurely. If in doubt, repeat the centralizing procedure. Failure to follow these instructions may increase the risk of serious personal injury or death in a crash.

✳✳ WARNING

Do not over-rotate the clockspring inner rotor. The internal ribbon wire is connected to the clockspring rotor. The internal ribbon wire acts as a

stop and can be broken from its internal connection. Failure to follow this instruction may result in component damage and/or system failure.

8. If a new clockspring was installed and the anti-rotation key has not been removed proceed to Step 5. If a new clockspring was installed and the anti-rotation key has been removed before the steering wheel is installed or the same clockspring is being installed, rotate the clockspring inner rotor counterclockwise and carefully feel for the ribbon wire to run out of length with slight resistance. Stop rotating the clockspring inner rotor at this point.

9. Starting with the clockspring rotated fully counterclockwise as indicated in Step 3, rotate the clockspring inner rotor, wiring and connector clockwise through 3 full

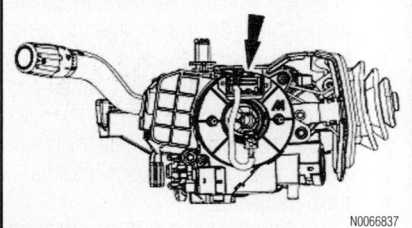

Fig. 21 Verify that the clockspring is correctly centralized by observing that the clockspring rotor, wiring and connector are in the 12 o'clock position

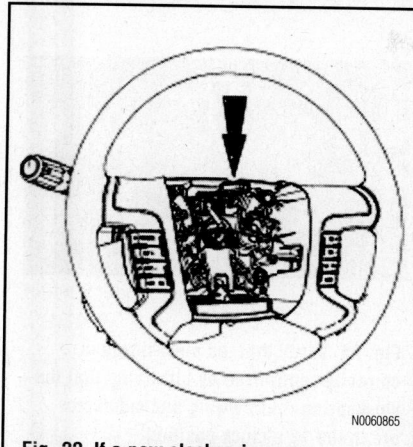

Fig. 22 If a new clockspring was installed, remove the anti-rotation key

revolutions to center the clockspring with the connector ending up in the 12 o'clock position. The clockspring is now centered. Verify that the clockspring is correctly centralized by observing that the clockspring rotor, wiring and connector are in the 12 o'clock position.

10. Install the steering wheel.

11. If a new clockspring was installed, remove the anti-rotation key.

12. Install the driver air bag module.

2011 Models

See Figures 23 through 26.

➡The air bag warning indicator illuminates when the correct Restraints Control Module (RCM) fuse is removed and the ignition is ON.

➡The Supplemental Restraint System (SRS) must be fully operational and free of faults before releasing the vehicle to the customer.

1. Remove the driver air bag module.

2. Remove the steering wheel.

3. Disconnect the clockspring electrical connector.

4. Remove the 3 clockspring screws.

5. Remove the clockspring.

6. Pull the clockspring straight off the steering column to disconnect it from the SCCM and disengage the clockspring pins from the steering wheel rotation sensor pin holes.

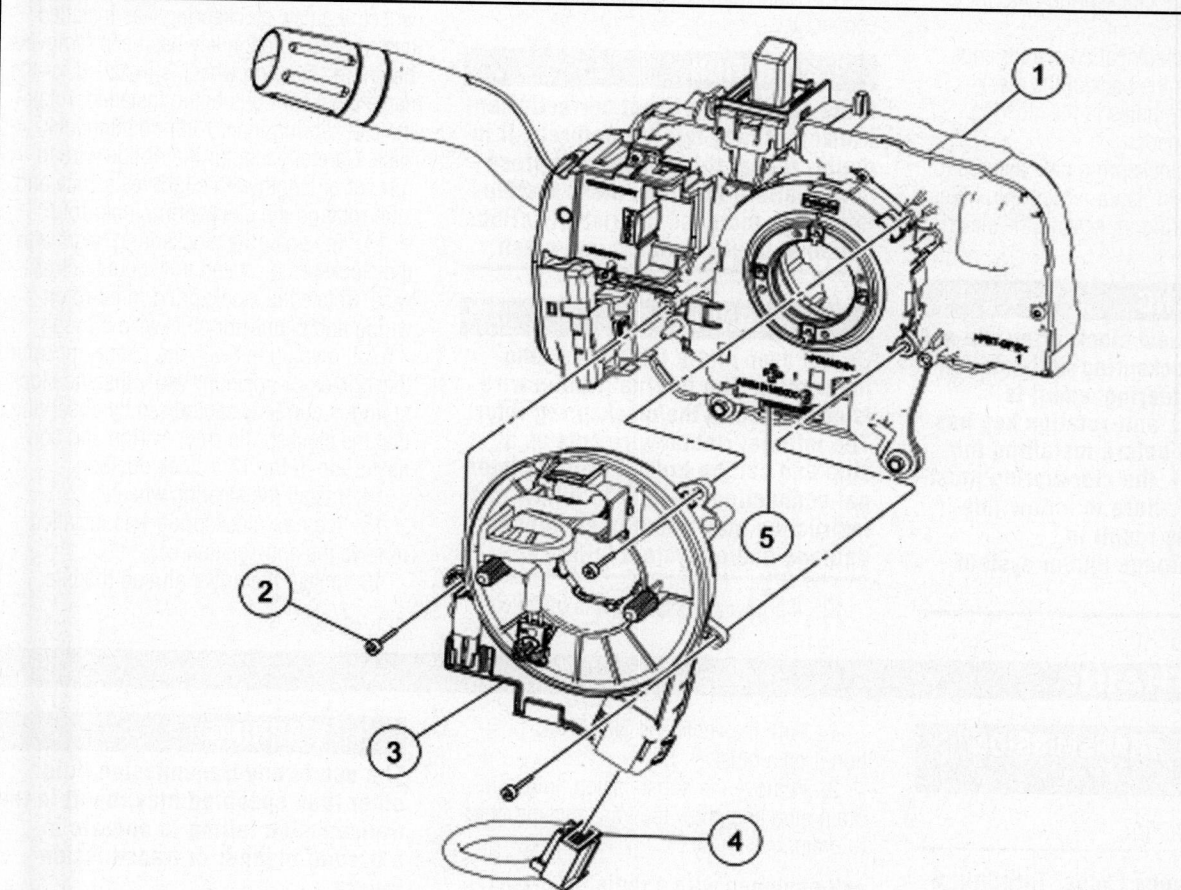

1. **Steering Column Control Module (SCCM)**
2. **Clockspring screws (3 required)**
3. **Clockspring**
4. **Clockspring electrical connector**
5. **SCCM electrical connector**

Fig. 23 Exploded view of the clockspring assembly

N0112711

Fig. 24 Align the electrical connector ends and the 2 pins on the back of the clockspring to the 2 pin holes in the steering wheel rotation sensor

N0112713

Fig. 25 With the clockspring pins aligned to the steering wheel rotation sensor pin holes, push the clockspring in, seating the electrical connector

N0112714

Fig. 26 Verify that the clockspring is correctly centralized by observing that the clockspring rotor, wiring and connector are in the 12 o'clock position

To install:

7. Position the clockspring onto the steering column.

8. Align the electrical connector ends and the 2 pins on the back of the clockspring to the 2 pin holes in the steering wheel rotation sensor.

9. With the clockspring pins aligned to the steering wheel rotation sensor pin holes, push the clockspring in, seating the electrical connector.

> ✳ **WARNING**
>
> **If installing a new clockspring, do not remove the clockspring anti-rotation key until the steering wheel is installed. If the anti-rotation key has been removed before installing the steering wheel, the clockspring must be centered. Failure to follow this instruction may result in component damage and/or system failure.**

10. Install the 3 clockspring screws.

11. Connect the clockspring electrical connector.

> ✳ **CAUTION**
>
> **If the clockspring is not correctly centralized, it may fail prematurely. If in doubt, repeat the centralizing procedure. Failure to follow these instructions may increase the risk of serious personal injury or death in a crash.**

> ✳ **WARNING**
>
> **Do not over-rotate the clockspring inner rotor. The internal ribbon wire is connected to the clockspring rotor. The internal ribbon wire acts as a stop and can be broken from its internal connection. Failure to follow this instruction may result in component damage and/or system failure.**

12. If a new clockspring was installed

and the anti-rotation key has not been removed proceed with installing the steering wheel. If a new clockspring was installed and the anti-rotation key has been removed before the steering wheel is installed, or the same clockspring is being installed, rotate the clockspring inner rotor counterclockwise. Carefully feel for the ribbon wire to run out of length with slight resistance and stop rotating the clockspring inner rotor.

13. To center the clockspring, start with the clockspring rotated fully counterclockwise. Rotate the clockspring inner rotor, wiring and connector clockwise through 3.5 full revolutions with the connector up in the 12 o'clock position. Verify that the clockspring is correctly centralized by observing that the clockspring rotor, wiring and connector are in the 12 o'clock position.

14. Install the steering wheel.

15. If a new clockspring was installed, remove the anti-rotation key.

16. Install the driver air bag module.

DRIVE TRAIN

AUTOMATIC TRANSMISSION FLUID

DRAIN AND REFILL

All Transmissions Except TorqShift 6

> ✳ **WARNING**
>
> **Use transmission fluid specific for this transmission. Do not use any supplemental transmission fluid additives or cleaning agents. The use of these products can cause internal transmission components to fail, which will affect the operation of the transmission.**

1. With the vehicle in NEUTRAL, position it on a hoist.

2. Remove the transmission fluid pan drain plug and allow the transmission fluid to drain.

➡ **If equipped with a radiator in-tank transmission fluid cooler or an Oil-To-Air (OTA) cooler, the coolers will need to be flushed.**

3. Only flush the cooler tubes and radiator in-tank transmission fluid cooler if carrying out a transmission overhaul or when installing a remanufactured transmission.

To refill:

4. Install the transmission fluid pan drain plug. Tighten to 13 ft. lbs. (18 Nm).

> ✳ **WARNING**
>
> **The use of any transmission fluid other than specified may result in the transmission failing to operate in a normal manner or transmission failure.**

5. Fill the transmission. Add 7.5 qt (7.1L) of transmission fluid to the transmission through the transmission fluid filler tube.

6. Start the engine. Move the selector lever through all the gear ranges, checking for engagements.

7. Using the scan tool with the engine running, check and make sure the transmission is at normal operating temperature

150–170°F (66–77°C). Check and adjust the transmission fluid level and check for any leaks. If transmission fluid is needed, add transmission fluid in increments of 0.5 pt (0.24L) until the correct level is achieved.

TorqShift 6 Transmission

See Figure 27.

⁑ WARNING

Use transmission fluid specific for this transmission. Do not use any supplemental transmission fluid additives or cleaning agents. The use of these products can cause internal transmission components to fail, which will affect the operation of the transmission.

1. With the vehicle in NEUTRAL, position it on a hoist.
2. Remove the transmission fluid pan drain plug and allow the transmission fluid to drain.
   To refill:
3. Install the transmission fluid pan drain plug. Tighten to 13 ft. lbs. (18 Nm).

⁑ WARNING

The use of any transmission fluid other than specified may result in the transmission failing to operate in a normal manner or transmission failure.

4. Fill the transmission through the transmission fluid filler tube.
   a. If ONLY the transmission fluid drain plug or pan was removed, 10.0 qt (add 9.5 L) of transmission fluid.
   b. If the main control was removed, add 12.0 qt (11.4 L) of transmission fluid.

c. If the transmission was removed and disassembled, add 18.0 pt (17.0 L) of transmission fluid.
5. Start the engine. Move the selector lever through all gear ranges while checking for engagements to allow the main control hydraulic circuits to fill with transmission fluid.
6. Using the scan tool with the engine running, check and make sure the transmission is at normal operating temperature 180–200°F (82–93°C). Check and adjust the transmission fluid level and check for any leaks. If transmission fluid is needed, add transmission fluid in increments of 0.5 pt (0.24L) until the correct level is achieved.

FILTER REPLACEMENT

All Transmissions Except TorqShift Transmissions

See Figures 28 through 31.

⁑ WARNING

The use of any other in-line transmission fluid filter other than listed will cause damage to the transmission.

➡**Use the following guidelines for the in-line transmission fluid filter:**

- If the transmission was overhauled and the vehicle was equipped with an in-line transmission fluid filter, install a new in-line transmission fluid filter.
- If the transmission was overhauled and the vehicle was not equipped with an in-line transmission fluid filter, install a new in-line transmission fluid filter kit.
- If the transmission is being installed for a non-internal repair, do not install an in-line transmission filter or filter kit.

- If installing a new or a Ford-authorized remanufactured transmission, install an in-line transmission fluid filter.
1. With the vehicle in NEUTRAL, position it on a hoist.
2. Cut a section of return tube, as shown.
3. Install the tubing ferrule hose assembly connector into the end of the cut, cleaned and de-burred tubing end. Finger-tighten the ferrule nut. Once finger-tight, then tighten an additional one and one-half turns to seat the ferrule in the connector.

⁑ WARNING

The in-line transmission fluid filter has a bypass valve in it. The arrow on the in-line transmission fluid filter indicates the direction of the transmission fluid flow through the in-line transmission fluid filter. The filter must be installed in the transmission fluid cooler return tube with the arrow pointing away from the transmission fluid cooler and toward the transmission (the return tube has transmission fluid coming out of the transmission fluid cooler going to the transmission). If the in-line transmission fluid filter is not installed correctly, it will cause internal transmission damage.

⁑ WARNING

Do not install any rubber hoses or steel tubing with a bend entering the filter greater than 60 degrees.

4. Using a suitable length of hose, install the in-line transmission fluid filter. Tighten the clamps.

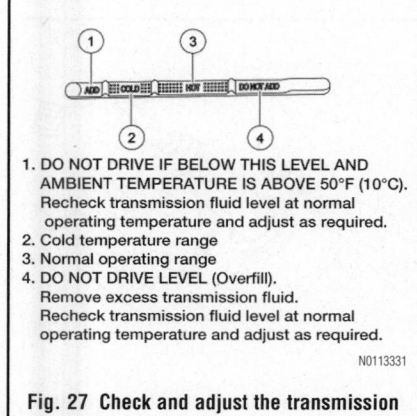

1. DO NOT DRIVE IF BELOW THIS LEVEL AND AMBIENT TEMPERATURE IS ABOVE 50°F (10°C). Recheck transmission fluid level at normal operating temperature and adjust as required.
2. Cold temperature range
3. Normal operating range
4. DO NOT DRIVE LEVEL (Overfill). Remove excess transmission fluid. Recheck transmission fluid level at normal operating temperature and adjust as required.

N0113331

Fig. 27 Check and adjust the transmission fluid level

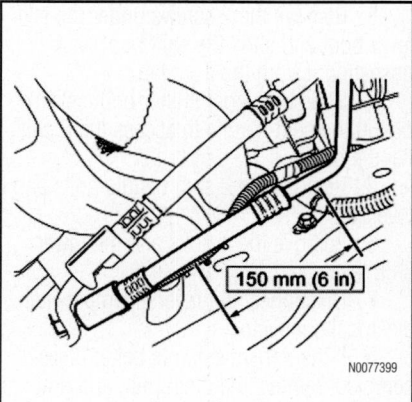

N0077399

Fig. 28 Cut a section of return tube

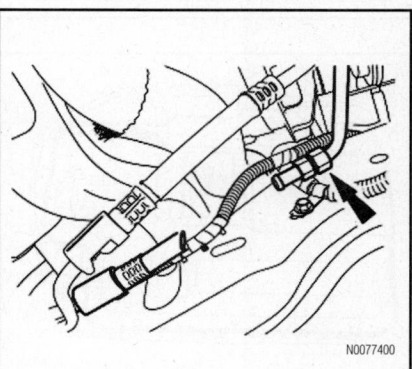

N0077400

Fig. 29 Install the tubing ferrule hose assembly connector into the end of the cut, cleaned and de-burred tubing end

5. Clean a visible section of the transmission fluid pan and install the sticker.

6. Fill the transmission with transmission fluid to the specified level.

7. Verify correct operation.

8. Check the in-line transmission fluid filter for leaks.

TorqShift Transmission

1. With the vehicle in NEUTRAL, position it on a hoist.

2. Remove the transmission fluid drain plug and allow the transmission fluid to drain.

3. Remove the transmission fluid pan and transmission fluid pan gasket.

4. Remove the transmission fluid filter.

❊❊ WARNING

Carefully remove the transmission fluid filter seal. Damage to the seal bore will cause transmission failure.

5. Inspect the transmission fluid bore for the transmission fluid seal. If the seal is in the bore, carefully remove the seal.

To install:

➡**Prior to installing the transmission filter, make sure that the old transmission fluid filter seal has been removed.**

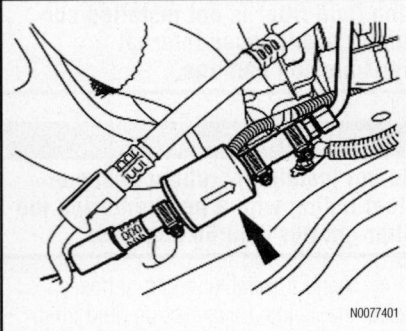

Fig. 30 Using a suitable length of hose, install the in-line transmission fluid filter

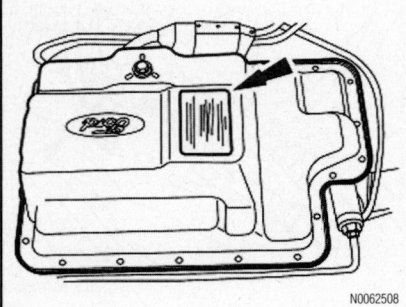

Fig. 31 Clean a visible section of the transmission fluid pan and install the sticker

6. Install a new transmission fluid filter and seal assembly.

➡**Tighten all the transmission fluid pan bolts in a crisscross pattern.**

7. Install the transmission fluid pan gasket and transmission fluid pan. Tighten to 15 ft. lbs. (20 Nm).

8. Install the transmission fluid pan drain plug. Tighten to 13 ft. lbs. (18 Nm).

❊❊ WARNING

The use of any other transmission fluid than specified can result in the transmission failing to operate in a normal manner or transmission failure.

9. Fill the transmission. Add 7.5 qt (7.0L) of transmission fluid to the transmission through the transmission fluid filler tube.

10. Start the engine. Move the selector lever through all the gear ranges, checking for engagements.

11. Using the scan tool with the engine running, check and make sure the transmission is at normal operating temperature 150–170°F (66–77°C). Check and adjust the transmission fluid level and check for any leaks. If transmission fluid is needed, add transmission fluid in increments of 0.5 pt (0.24L) until the correct level is achieved.

MANUAL TRANSMISSION ASSEMBLY

REMOVAL & INSTALLATION

2010 Tremec 5-Speed Transmission with Diesel Engine

See Figures 32 through 37.

1. With the vehicle in NEUTRAL, position it on a hoist.

2. Disconnect the battery ground cable.

3. Remove the 2 screws under the shift lever boot and slide the shift boot back, unseating it from the front tab.

4. Slide the upper shifter boot assembly up the shift handle to access the 2 shift handle bolts.

5. Remove the 2 shift handle bolts and lever.

6. Remove the 4 bolts and the lower shift lever.

7. Disconnect the reverse lamp switch electrical connector.

8. If the transmission is being disassembled, remove the drain plug and drain the transmission fluid.

9. Remove the starter.

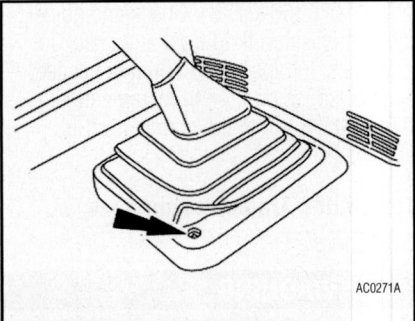

Fig. 32 Remove the 2 screws under the shift lever boot and slide the shift boot back, unseating it from the front tab

10. Remove the driveshaft.

11. Disconnect the wiring harness retainers from the transmission and crossmember and position the harness aside.

➡**Slide the heat shield back and rotate counterclockwise 45 degrees while pushing inward.**

12. Remove the clutch slave cylinder and position aside.

13. Disconnect the fuel tubes from the fuel tube clip on the transmission case and position aside.

14. Using the High Lift Transmission Jack, support the transmission.

❊❊ WARNING

Securely strap the High Lift Transmission Jack to the transmission.

15. Remove the 2 transmission mount nuts from the crossmember.

16. Loosen the top 2 RH crossmember bracket nuts.

17. Remove the 4 lower RH crossmember nuts.

18. Remove the 3 LH crossmember bolts and remove the crossmember.

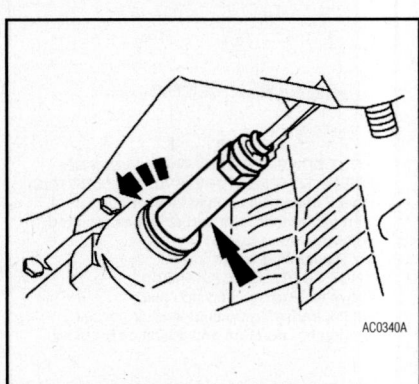

Fig. 33 Remove the clutch slave cylinder and position aside

Fig. 34 Remove the 2 transmission mount nuts from the crossmember

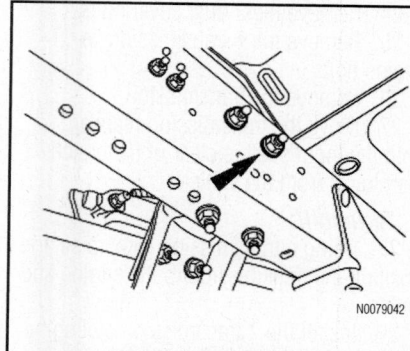

Fig. 35 Loosen the top 2 RH crossmember bracket nuts

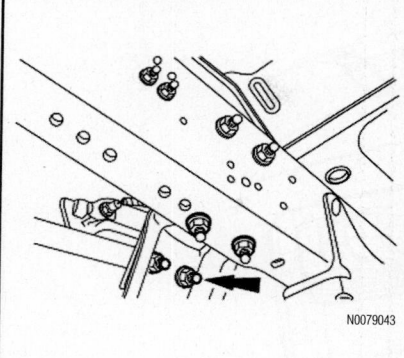

Fig. 36 Remove the 4 lower RH crossmember nuts

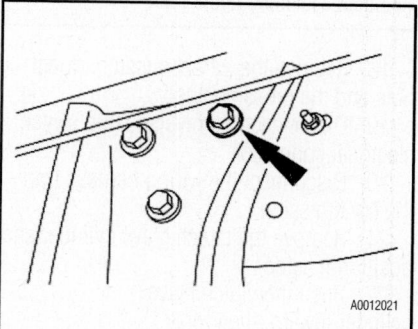

Fig. 37 Remove the 3 LH crossmember bolts and remove the crossmember

19. Remove 2 engine-to-transmission spacer plate bolts.
20. Remove the 7 transmission-to-engine bolts.
21. Remove the transmission by moving the transmission rearward until the input shaft is clear of the clutch, then lower from the vehicle.

To install:
22. Using the High Lift Transmission Jack, raise and position the transmission to the engine and clutch.
23. Install the 7 transmission-to-engine bolts. Tighten to 46 ft. lbs. (63 Nm).
24. Position the crossmember and install the 3 LH crossmember bolts. Tighten to 66 ft. lbs. (90 Nm).
25. Install the 4 RH crossmember nuts and tighten the upper 2 crossmember bracket nuts. Tighten to 52 ft. lbs. (70 Nm).
26. Install the 2 transmission mount nuts. Tighten to 60 ft. lbs. (81 Nm).
27. Install the 2 engine-to-transmission spacer plate bolts. Tighten to 21 ft. lbs. (28 Nm).
28. Remove the transmission jack.
29. Position the clutch slave cylinder.

➡**Push in and rotate the clutch slave cylinder clockwise 45 degrees to the lock position.**

30. Install the starter.
31. Install the rear driveshaft.
32. Connect the reverse lamp switch electrical connector then attach the wiring harness retainers to the transmission and crossmember.
33. Install the fuel tubes into the plastic clip on the transmission case.

➡**Refill the transmission with clean, specified lubricant.**

34. If drained, install the drain plug and refill the transmission. Tighten to 15 ft. lbs. (20 Nm).

➡**When installing, a slight wiggle may be necessary to seat the shifter lever between the detents.**

➡**Apply threadlock to the threads of the bolts.**

35. Install the lower gear shift lever and the 4 bolts. Tighten to 8 ft. lbs. (11 Nm).

➡**Apply threadlock to the threads of the bolts.**

36. Slide the upper shifter boot assembly up the handle shift and install the shift handle and bolts. Tighten to 21 ft. lbs. (28 Nm).
37. Install the front tab of the upper and lower shifter boot assembly under the floor pan. Install the 2 rear shifter boot screws.
38. Connect the battery ground cable.

2010 ZF 6-Speed Transmission with Gasoline Engine
See Figures 38 through 48.

1. Pull the shift lever boot upward to access the shift housing.
2. Loosen the upper gearshift lever bolt, then remove the upper gearshift lever.
3. Remove the 2 screws and the lower shift lever boot.
4. Remove the 4 shift housing bolts and the shift housing.
5. For vehicles with a manual shift transfer case:
   a. Shift the transfer case into 4H.
   b. Remove the 2 screws that attach the bezel and boot assembly to the floor.
   c. Slide the bezel and boot up the shift lever. Remove the bolt that attaches the shift lever to the transfer case control lever assembly, and remove the shift lever and the bezel and boot assembly.
6. With the vehicle in NEUTRAL, position it on a hoist.
7. If the transmission is being disassembled, drain the transmission fluid.
8. Remove the exhaust Y-pipe.
9. Remove the starter.
10. Remove the skid plate, if equipped.
11. Remove the transfer case, if equipped.

➡**Index-mark the driveshaft to the flange. Remove and discard the driveshaft bolts.**

12. Disconnect the rear driveshaft and position it aside.
13. Disconnect the fuel tubes from the transmission.

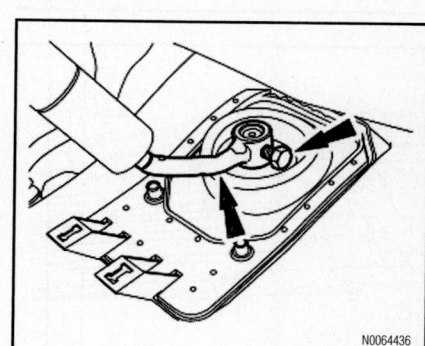

Fig. 38 Loosen the upper gearshift lever bolt, then remove the upper gearshift lever

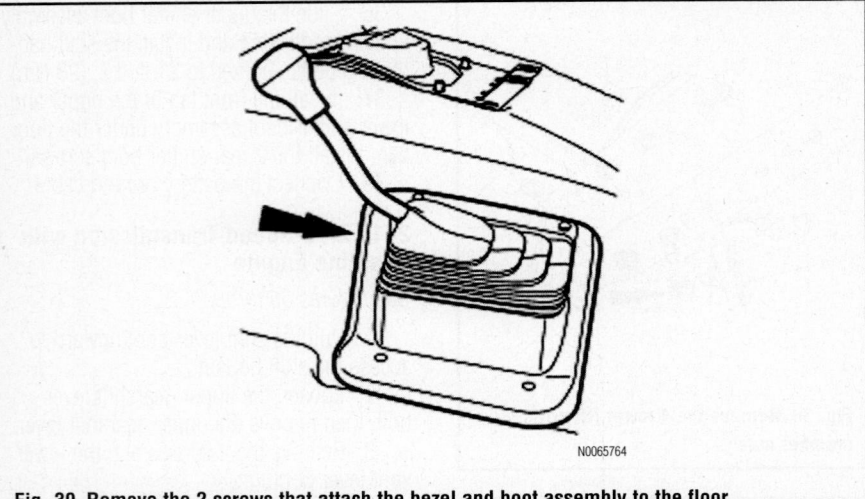

Fig. 39 Remove the 2 screws that attach the bezel and boot assembly to the floor

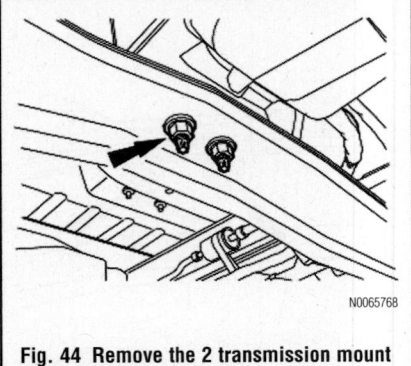

Fig. 44 Remove the 2 transmission mount nuts and the crossmember

14. Remove any Power Take-Off (PTO) equipment, if equipped.

15. Using the Transmission Jack, support the transmission.

⁕⁕ WARNING

Securely strap the Transmission Jack to the transmission.

16. Remove the 4 RH crossmember nuts.

17. Remove the 3 LH crossmember bolts.

18. Remove the 2 transmission mount nuts and the crossmember.

19. Disconnect the reverse lamp switch electrical connector.

20. Disconnect the wiring harness from the transmission.

21. Remove the clutch slave cylinder and position it aside.

22. Push the clutch slave cylinder inward, then rotate counterclockwise 45 degrees to remove.

23. Disconnect the transmission fluid cooler tubes.

24. Remove the 2 dust cover bolts.

25. Remove the 7 transmission-to-engine bolts.

26. Remove the transmission.

27. Move the transmission rearward until the input shaft is clear of the clutch, then lower from the vehicle.

To install:

28. Using a transmission jack, raise and position the transmission to the engine and clutch.

29. Install the 7 transmission-to-engine bolts. Tighten to 46 ft. lbs. (63 Nm).

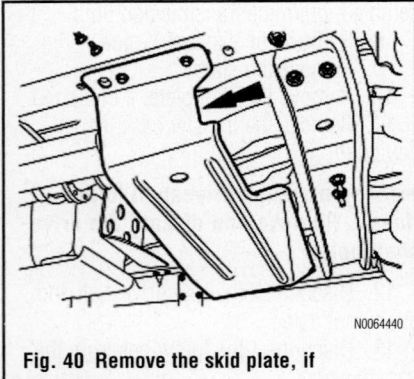

Fig. 40 Remove the skid plate, if equipped

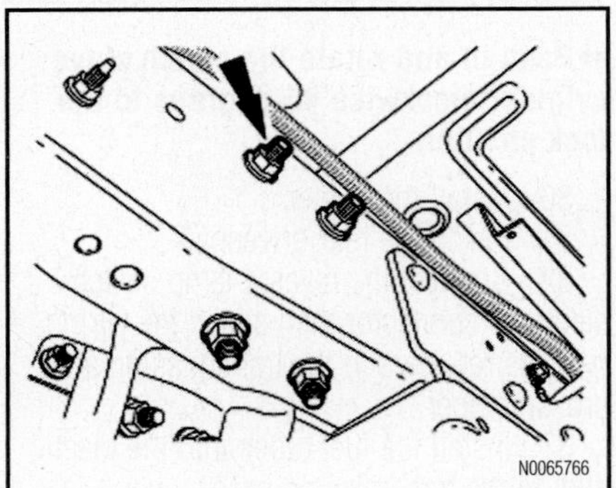

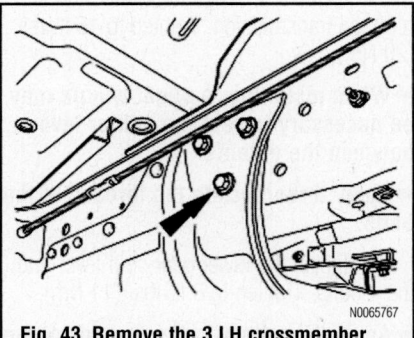

Fig. 42 Remove the 4 RH crossmember nuts

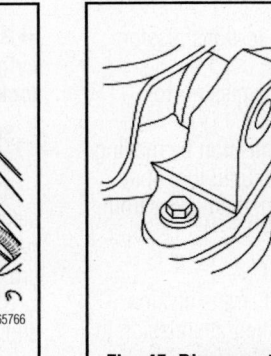

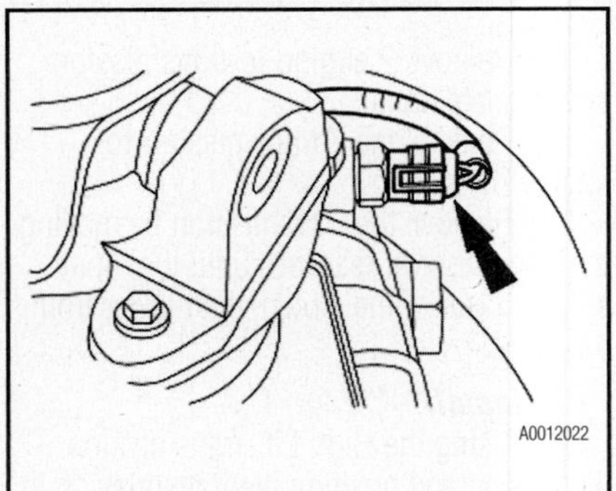

Fig. 45 Disconnect the reverse lamp switch electrical connector

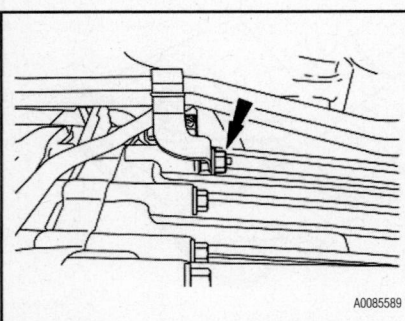

Fig. 41 Disconnect the fuel tubes from the transmission

Fig. 43 Remove the 3 LH crossmember bolts

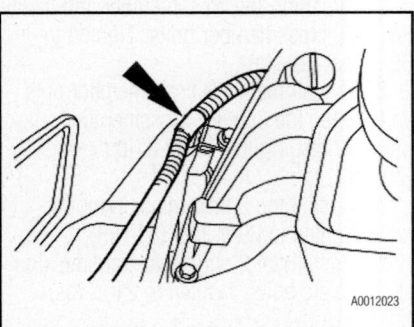

Fig. 46 Disconnect the wiring harness from the transmission

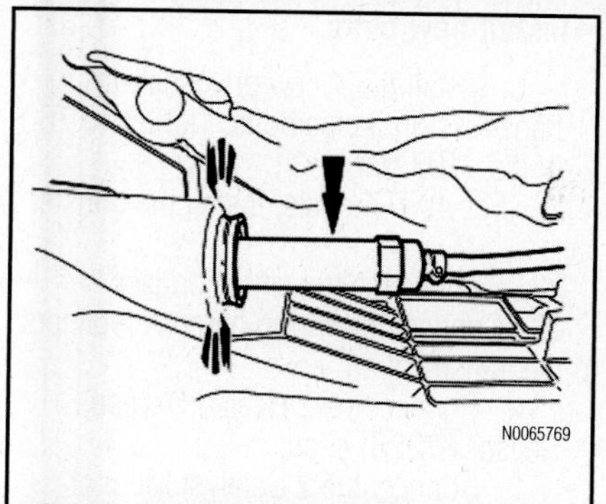

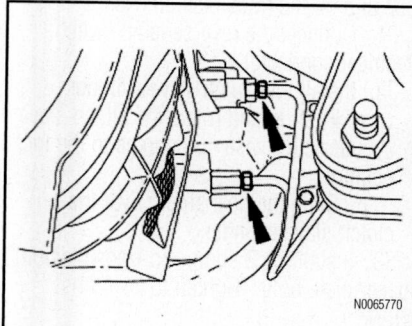

Fig. 47 Remove the clutch slave cylinder and position it aside

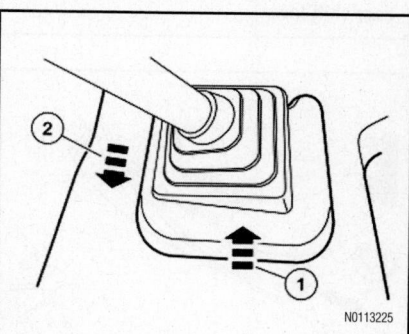

Fig. 48 Disconnect the transmission fluid cooler tubes

30. Position the crossmember in the vehicle. Install the 3 LH transmission support crossmember bolts. Tighten to 52 ft. lbs. (70 Nm).

31. Install the 4 RH transmission support crossmember nuts. Tighten to 52 ft. lbs. (70 Nm).

➡The transmission mount studs may have come out of the insulator when the nuts were removed. Install new insulator studs if they came out during removal.

32. Install the transmission mount studs or nuts.

　　a. Tighten the studs to 55 ft. lbs. (75 Nm).

　　b. Tighten the nuts to 60 ft. lbs. (81 Nm).

33. Install the 2 dust cover bolts. Tighten to 21 ft. lbs. (28 Nm).

34. Remove the Transmission Jack.

35. Connect the transmission fluid cooler tubes. Tighten to 20 ft. lbs. (27 Nm).

36. Install the clutch slave cylinder.

37. Rotate the clutch slave cylinder clockwise 45 degrees to lock in position.

38. Install the starter.

39. Install the exhaust Y-pipe.

40. Install the transfer case, if equipped.

41. If the transfer case control lever assembly was removed from the transmission, it must be correctly aligned.

➡**Make sure the index marks made during removal are aligned.**

42. Connect the driveshaft. Install 4 new driveshaft flange bolts. Tighten to 75 ft. lbs. (102 Nm).

43. Install any Power Take-Off (PTO) equipment, if equipped.

44. Connect the fuel tubes to the transmission.

45. Connect the reverse lamp switch electrical connector.

46. Connect the wiring harness to the transmission.

47. Refill the transmission to specification. Refill the transmission with clean transmission fluid.

✷✷ WARNING

Do not use a silicone sealing compound or damage to the components can occur.

➡**Do not wait longer than 10 minutes to tighten the 4 bolts due to the rapid cure time of the sealant.**

48. Install the gearshift lever and shift housing assembly.

　　a. Tighten to 17 ft. lbs. (23 Nm).

　　b. Apply gasket maker to the shift housing and the main case.

49. Install the lower shift lever boot and the 2 screws.

50. Apply threadlock and sealer to the gearshift lever bolt. Install the upper gearshift lever. Tighten to 26 ft. lbs. (35 Nm).

51. Install the shift lever boot.

52. For vehicles with a manual shift transfer case:

　　a. Position the transfer case shift lever with the bezel and boot assembly and install the bolt. Tighten to 20 ft. lbs. (27 Nm).

　　b. Position the bezel and boot assembly and install the 2 screws.

　　c. Verify the shift sequence from 2H to 4L to 2H.

2011 Tremec 5-Speed Transmission
See Figures 49 through 53.

✷✷ CAUTION

Do not breathe dust or use compressed air to blow dust from storage containers or friction components. Remove dust using government-approved techniques. Friction component dust may be a cancer and lung disease hazard. Exposure to potentially hazardous components may occur if dusts are created during repair of friction components, such as brake pads and clutch discs. Exposure may also cause irritation to skin, eyes and respiratory tract, and may cause allergic reactions and/or may lead to other chronic health effects. If irritation persists, seek medical attention or advice. Failure to follow these instructions may result in serious personal injury.

1. With the vehicle in NEUTRAL, position it on a hoist.

2. Disconnect the battery ground cable.

3. Remove the upper gear shift lever boot.

　　a. Pull up the rear of the upper gear shift lever boot.

　　b. Slide the upper gear shift lever boot back, to unseat it from the front tabs.

4. Slide the upper gear shift lever boot up the upper gear shift lever to access the 2 bolts.

5. Remove the 2 bolts and remove the upper gear shift lever.

6. Remove the 4 screws and the lower gear shift lever boot.

7. Remove the 4 bolts and the lower gear shift lever.

8. Remove the starter.

9. Remove 2 engine-to-transmission spacer plate bolts.

10. Remove the exhaust Y-pipe with dual catalytic converters.

11. If the transmission is being disassembled, remove the drain plug and drain the transmission fluid.

12. Remove the clutch slave cylinder and position aside.

Fig. 49 Pull up the rear of the upper gear shift lever boot (1) and slide the upper gear shift lever boot back (2), to unseat it from the front tabs

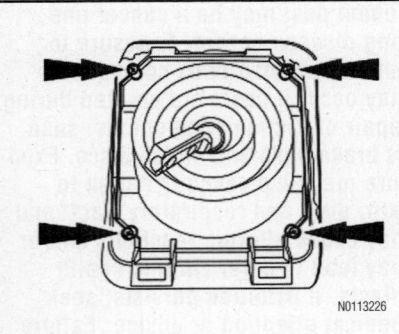

Fig. 50 Remove the 4 screws and the lower gear shift lever boot

13. Slide the heat shield back and rotate counterclockwise 45 degrees while pushing inward.

14. Disconnect the reverse lamp switch electrical connector.

15. Disconnect the fuel tubes from the fuel tube clip on the transmission case and position aside.

16. Disconnect the wiring harness retainers from the transmission and position the harness aside.

   a. Disconnect the 2 Heated Oxygen Sensor (HO2S) clips.

   b. Disconnect the 2 Catalyst Monitor Sensor (CMS) clips.

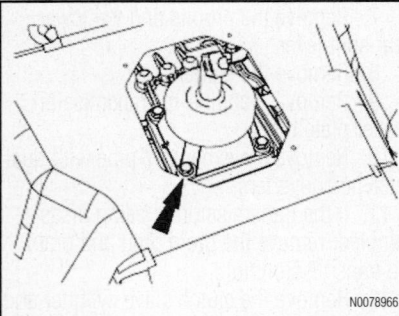

Fig. 51 Remove the 4 bolts and the lower gear shift lever

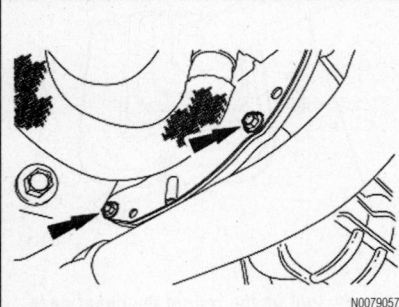

Fig. 52 Remove 2 engine-to-transmission spacer plate bolts

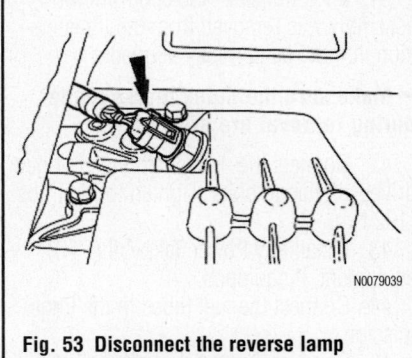

Fig. 53 Disconnect the reverse lamp switch electrical connector

   c. Disconnect the wiring harness clips.

17. Using the High Lift Transmission Jack, support the transmission.

18. Securely strap the High Lift Transmission Jack to the transmission.

19. For 4WD models, remove the transfer case.

➡**The following steps are for RWD models only.**

➡**If a pry area is not available on the driveshaft side, it may be necessary to tap the driveshaft yoke with a plastic or rubber soft-faced hammer.**

➡**Index-mark the driveshaft flange.**

20. Remove and discard the 4 driveshaft-to-transmission flange bolts. Disconnect the driveshaft from the transmission. Using mechanic's wire, support the driveshaft.

21. Remove the transmission support crossmember.

➡**The following steps are for all vehicles.**

22. Remove the 7 transmission-to-engine bolts.

23. Remove the transmission by moving the transmission rearward until the input shaft is clear of the clutch, then lower from the vehicle.

To install:

24. Using the High Lift Transmission Jack, raise and position the transmission to the engine and clutch.

25. Install the 7 transmission-to-engine bolts. Tighten to 46 ft. lbs. (63 Nm).

26. For RWD models, perform the following:

   a. Install the transmission support crossmember.

➡**Align the index marks made during removal.**

➡**Install new bolts.**

   b. Install the 4 new driveshaft-to-transmission flange bolts. Tighten to 76 ft. lbs. (103 Nm).

27. For 4WD models, install the transfer case.

28. Remove the transmission jack.

29. Connect the wiring harness retainers to the transmission:

   a. Connect the 2 Heated Oxygen Sensor (HO2S) clips.

   b. Connect the 2 Catalyst Monitor Sensor (CMS) clips.

   c. Connect the wiring harness clips.

30. Install the fuel tubes into the fuel tube clip on the transmission case.

31. Connect the reverse lamp switch electrical connector.

32. Install the clutch slave cylinder.

   a. Push in and rotate the clutch slave cylinder clockwise 45 degrees to the lock position.

   b. Slide the heat shield over the clutch slave cylinder.

33. Install the 2 engine-to-transmission spacer plate bolts. Tighten to 21 ft. lbs. (28 Nm).

34. Install the starter.

35. Install the exhaust Y-pipe with dual catalytic converters.

➡**Refill the transmission with clean, specified lubricant.**

36. If drained, install the drain plug and refill the transmission. Tighten to 15 ft. lbs. (20 Nm).

➡**When installing, a slight wiggle may be necessary to seat the lower gear shift lever between the detents.**

➡**Apply threadlock to the threads of the bolts.**

37. Install the lower gear shift lever and the 4 bolts. Tighten to 97 inch lbs. (11 Nm).

38. Install the lower gear shift lever boot and 4 screws.

➡**Apply threadlock to the threads of the bolts.**

39. Slide the upper gear shift lever boot up the upper gear shift lever. Install the upper gear shift lever and the 2 bolts. Tighten to 21 ft. lbs. (28 Nm).

40. Install the upper gear shift lever boot.

   a. Slide the upper gear shift lever boot forward to clip the front tabs.

   b. Push down the rear of the upper gear shift lever boot to attach the clips.

41. Connect the battery ground cable.

MANUAL TRANSMISSION FLUID

DRAIN AND REFILL

➡ **Transmission fluid usage:**

- Gas engines use MERCON® V Fluid.
- Diesel engines use Motorcraft Full Synthetic Fluid.

1. With the vehicle in NEUTRAL, position it on a hoist.

➡ **Drain the transmission while the transmission fluid is warm.**

2. Position a drain pan under the transmission and remove the drain plug.
3. Drain the transmission fluid.
4. Apply threadlock and sealer and install the drain plug. Tighten to 26 ft. lbs. (35 Nm).

➡ **Prior to removal, clean the area around the fill plug.**

5. Remove the fill plug.

➡ **Do not overfill the transmission. This will cause transmission fluid to be forced out of the case.**

6. Using an Oil Suction Gun, fill the transmission with the recommended fluid.
7. Apply threadlock and sealer and install the fill plug. Tighten to 26 ft. lbs. (35 Nm).

CLUTCH

REMOVAL & INSTALLATION

See Figures 54 and 55.

1. Remove the transmission.
2. Index–mark the clutch pressure plate and the flywheel, if reinstalling these parts.
3. Remove the clutch pressure plate bolts, the clutch pressure plate and the clutch disc.
4. Inspect the transmission input shaft pilot bearing:
   - For misalignment and looseness in the crankshaft (gasoline engine) or flywheel (diesel engine).
   - Needle rollers for scoring, discoloration, wear and broken rollers.
   - Seal for damage and lubricant leakage.
5. Install a new transmission input shaft pilot bearing if any of these conditions are present.

➡ **Use emery cloth to remove minor imperfections in the clutch disc friction surface.**

6. Inspect the clutch disc for the following:

- oil and grease saturation.
- worn and loose rivets at the hub.
- broken springs.
- wear and rust on the splines.

7. Install a new clutch disc if any of these conditions are present.

➡ **If necessary, use a suitable cleaning solution to remove any oil film from the clutch pressure plate friction surface.**

8. Inspect the clutch pressure plate levers for heavy wear associated with binding. Also, inspect for substantial difference in lever wear. Inspect the clutch pressure plate friction surface for scoring, burning, heat checking, distortion, warping and dishing.

9. Install a new clutch pressure plate if any of these conditions are present.

➡ **If necessary, use a suitable cleaning solution to clean the flywheel clutch surface.**

10. Inspect the flywheel for the following:

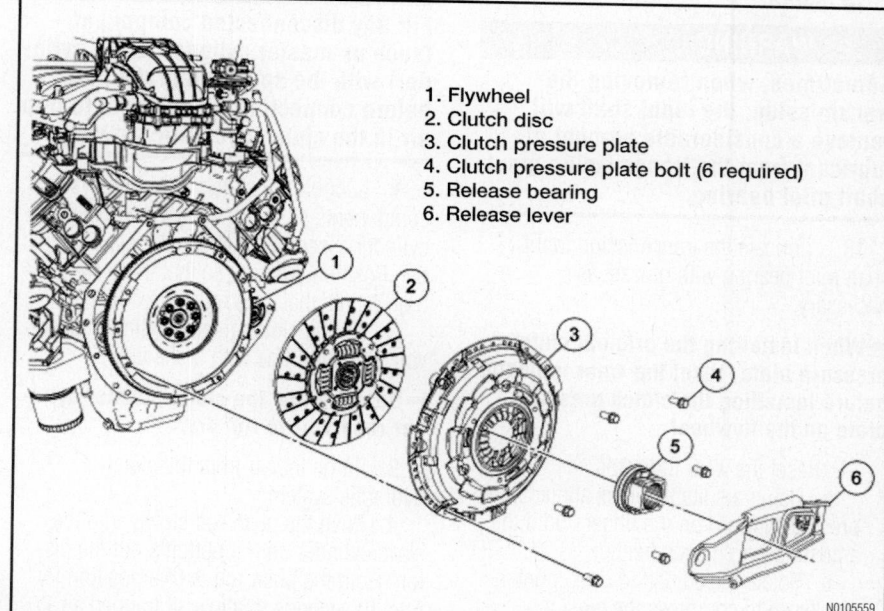

1. Flywheel
2. Clutch disc
3. Clutch pressure plate
4. Clutch pressure plate bolt (6 required)
5. Release bearing
6. Release lever

N0105559

Fig. 54 Exploded view of the clutch disc and pressure plate assembly—5.4L and 6.8L Engines

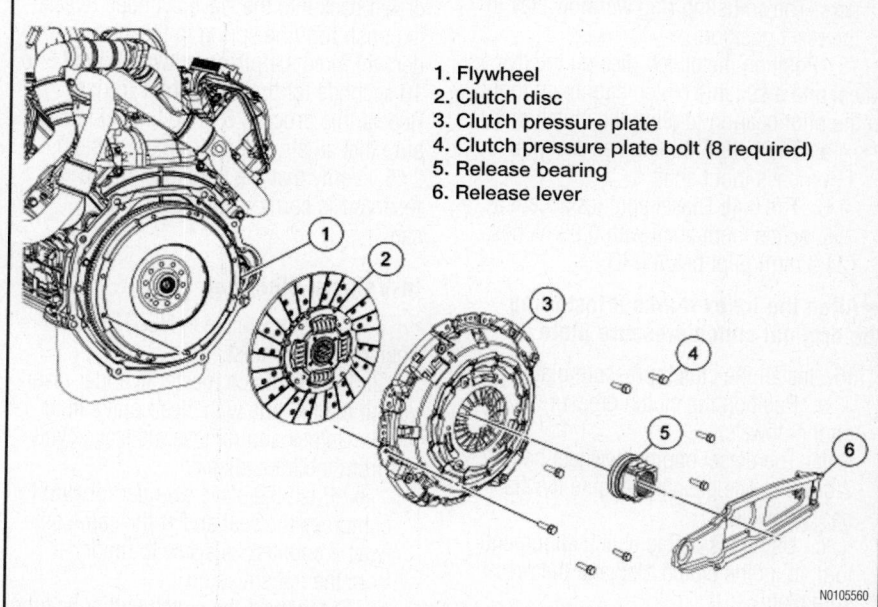

1. Flywheel
2. Clutch disc
3. Clutch pressure plate
4. Clutch pressure plate bolt (8 required)
5. Release bearing
6. Release lever

N0105560

Fig. 55 Exploded view of the clutch disc and pressure plate assembly—6.4L Diesel Engine

- surface cracks
- heat check
- glazing
- scoring
- scratches or grooves

11. For minor damage, finish the flywheel surface with coarse emery cloth or with a fine grade (400 grit) sandpaper. To polish the surface, stroke parallel to the machine lines.

12. Inspect the ring gear for worn, chopped or broken teeth.

To install:

✷✷ WARNING

Sometimes, when removing the transmission, the input shaft will remove a considerable amount of lubricant from the transmission input shaft pilot bearing.

13. Lubricate the transmission input shaft pilot bearing with grease, as necessary.

➡**When installing the original clutch pressure plate, reset the wear indicator before installing the clutch pressure plate on the flywheel.**

14. Reset the wear indicator.

a. Using a suitable press and adapter, press downward on the fingers until the adjusting ring moves freely.

b. Rotate the adjusting ring counter-clockwise to compress the tension springs. Hold the adjusting ring in this position.

c. Release the pressure on the fingers. The adjusting ring will now stay in the reset position.

15. Position the clutch disc on the flywheel and a suitable clutch alignment tool in the pilot bearing to align the clutch disc.

a. The 5.4L/6.8L engines accept a 1¼ inches input shaft.

b. The 6.4L Diesel engines accept a 1⅜ inches input shaft with 0.98 inches (24.9 mm) pilot bearing ID.

➡**Align the index marks if installing the original clutch pressure plate.**

16. Install the clutch pressure plate.

a. Position the clutch pressure plate on the dowels.

b. The diesel engine flywheel has 2 dowels. The gasoline engine flywheel has 3 dowels.

c. Using a suitable clutch alignment tool, align the clutch disc and the pressure plate.

17. Install the clutch pressure plate bolts and tighten in a star pattern sequence.

a. For the 5.4L and 6.8L engines, tighten to 33 ft. lbs. (45 Nm).

b. For the 6.4L Diesel engine, tighten to 21 ft. lbs. (28 Nm).

18. Remove the clutch alignment tool.

19. Install the transmission.

20. Test the system for normal operation.

BLEEDING

Bench Bleeding

✷✷ WARNING

Fill any disconnected component (such as master cylinder, slave cylinder) with the specified brake fluid before connecting it, so as not to trap air in the clutch hydraulic system.

1. Support the clutch hydraulic system components so that the reservoir/master cylinder assembly is above the slave cylinder. Position the tube so that there are no high points that could trap air.

2. Fill the clutch master cylinder reservoir to the full line with brake fluid.

➡**Do not allow the clutch master cylinder reservoir to run dry.**

3. Purge the air from the clutch hydraulic system.

4. Push the push rod slowly into the slave cylinder until it bottoms out the piston. Hold the push rod in this position for 5 to 10 seconds to allow all trapped air to rise through the system. Look for air bubbles in the fluid in the clutch hydraulic reservoir. Very slowly, so that air is not drawn back into the slave cylinder, release the push rod (the spring in the slave cylinder will force the piston outward). Wait 5 to 10 seconds for the air bubbles to rise. Repeat this process 5 to 10 times to make sure that all air purged from the system.

5. Verify that the fluid level in the reservoir is correct and install the cap.

In-Vehicle Bleeding

1. With the vehicle in NEUTRAL, position it on a hoist.

2. Fill the clutch master cylinder reservoir to the full line with clean brake fluid.

3. Unlock and remove the slave cylinder from the transmission.

a. Push the slave cylinder forward to compress the seal and at the same time twist it counterclockwise to unlock it from the transmission.

4. Disconnect the clutch hydraulic tube from the floor pan clip.

5. Position the slave cylinder and the hydraulic tube so that there are no high points that could trap air in the system.

a. Position the slave cylinder push rod downward. Route the hydraulic tube upward as straight as possible toward the master cylinder so that the air can flow freely to the fluid reservoir.

➡**Do not allow the clutch master cylinder reservoir to run dry.**

6. Purge the air from the clutch hydraulic system.

7. Push the push rod slowly into the slave cylinder until it bottoms out the piston. Hold the push rod in this position for 5 to 10 seconds to allow all trapped air to rise through the system. Very slowly, so that air is not drawn back into the slave cylinder, release the push rod (the spring in the slave cylinder will force the piston outward). Wait 5 to 10 seconds for the air bubbles to rise. Tap the lines to assist in releasing air bubbles, which may be trapped in the line bends. Repeat this process until all air purged from the system. Verify that the fluid in the reservoir is free of air bubbles.

8. Install the slave cylinder.

a. Compress and twist the slave cylinder clockwise to lock it onto the transmission.

9. Connect the clutch hydraulic tube to the floor pan clip.

10. Slowly depress and release the clutch pedal 20 to 25 times to bleed any air still trapped in the system. Verify that the fluid in the reservoir is free of air bubbles.

11. Verify that the fluid level in the reservoir is correct and install the cap.

TRANSFER CASE ASSEMBLY

The New Venture Gear transfer cases are either manual or electric shift.

When the Four-Wheel Drive (4WD) is engaged, power is supplied to all 4 wheels through the transfer case. The transfer cases are either Manual Shift-On-Stop (MSOS) 4x4 system or Electronic Shift-On-The-Fly (ESOF) 4x4 system.

The MSOS 4WD system is engaged or disengaged by rotating the control for both front wheel hub locks from the FREE or LOCK position, then manually engaging or disengaging the transfer case with the floor-mounted shifter.

The ESOF 4WD system is engaged or disengaged by a rotary control located on the instrument panel that allows selection of 2WD, 4x4 high or 4x4 low operations.

When the vehicle is in 2WD operation,

the sprocket that drives the drive chain is freewheeling.

When in the 4x4 mode of operation, torque is transferred from the main input shaft through the drive chain to the transfer case front output shaft. The front output driveshaft then transfers this torque to the front differential.

REMOVAL & INSTALLATION

See Figures 56 through 60.

➡ **Shift the transfer case to 2H.**

1. With the vehicle in NEUTRAL, position it on a hoist.

2. If equipped, remove the 4 bolts and the skid plate.

3. For vehicles equipped with a flange, perform the following:

➡ **Index-mark the front driveshaft to the transfer case flange.**

a. Remove and discard the 4 front driveshaft bolts and position the front driveshaft aside.

➡ **Index-mark the rear driveshaft to the transfer case flange.**

b. Remove and discard the 4 rear driveshaft bolts and position the rear driveshaft aside.

Fig. 56 If equipped, remove the 4 bolts and the skid plate

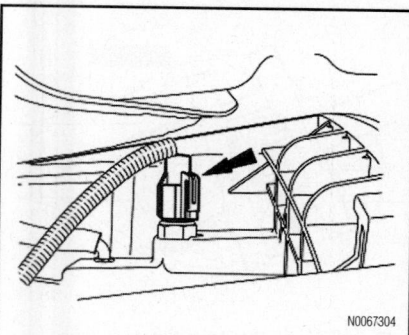

Fig. 57 Disconnect the 3-position mode switch electrical connector

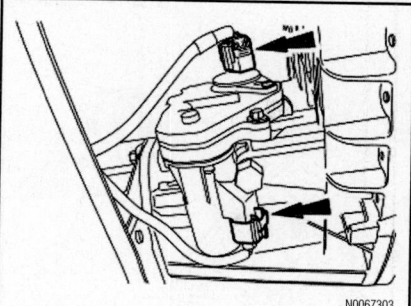

Fig. 58 Disconnect the gear motor encoder electrical connector and the gear motor electrical connector

4. For vehicles equipped with a slip yoke, remove the driveshaft.

5. For vehicles with manual shift, perform the following:

a. Disconnect the manual shift linkage from the transmission.

b. Disconnect the 3-position mode switch electrical connector.

6. For vehicles with electric shift, perform the following:

a. Disconnect the gear motor encoder electrical connector and the gear motor electrical connector.

7. Disconnect the vent hose.

8. If disassembly is necessary, drain the fluid. Install the drain plug when finished. Tighten to 20 ft. lbs. (27 Nm).

9. Position a suitable high-lift jack to the transfer case and secure it with safety straps.

10. Remove the 6 transfer case-to-transmission bolts.

11. Separate the transfer case from the extension housing. Pull the transfer case rearward, then lower the transfer case from the vehicle.

To install:

12. Secure the transfer case to the high-lift jack with a safety strap. Position the transfer case to the extension housing.

13. Install the 6 transfer case-to-transmission bolts. Tighten to 37 ft. lbs. (50 Nm).

14. For vehicles with electric shift, connect the gear motor encoder electrical connector and the gear motor electrical connector.

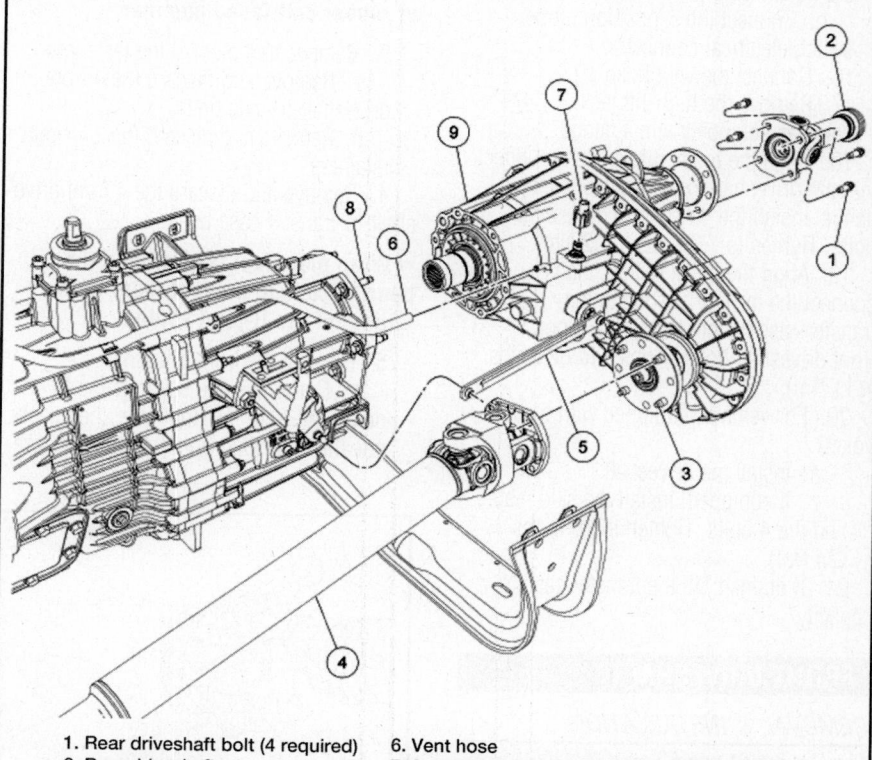

1. Rear driveshaft bolt (4 required)
2. Rear driveshaft
3. Front driveshaft bolt (4 required)
4. Front driveshaft
5. Transfer case shift linkage
6. Vent hose
7. 3-position mode switch electrical connector
8. Transfer case-to-transmission bolt (6 required)
9. Transfer case

Fig. 59 Exploded view of the transfer case assembly—Manual Shift

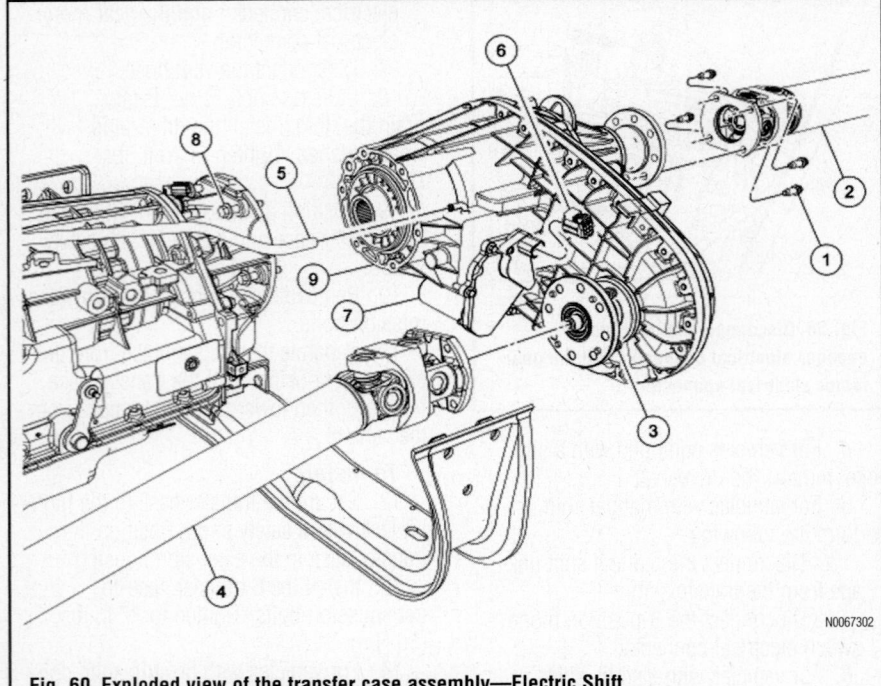

Fig. 60 Exploded view of the transfer case assembly—Electric Shift

15. For vehicles with manual shift:
a. Connect the manual shift linkage to the transmission.
b. Connect the 3-position mode switch electrical connector.
16. Connect the vent hose.
17. Remove the high-lift jack.
Vehicles equipped with a flange
18. Align the index marks, then connect the rear driveshaft to the transfer case flange. Install the 4 new rear driveshaft bolts. Tighten to 75 ft. lbs. (102 Nm).
19. Align the index marks, then connect the front driveshaft to the transfer case flange. Install the 4 new front driveshaft bolts. Tighten to 82 ft. lbs. (111 Nm).
20. For vehicles equipped with a slip yoke:
a. Install the driveshaft.
b. If equipped, install the skid plate and the 4 bolts. Tighten to 18 ft. lbs. (24 Nm).
21. If drained, fill the transfer case to capacity.

FRONT DRIVESHAFT

REMOVAL & INSTALLATION

See Figures 61 and 62.

1. With the vehicle in NEUTRAL, position it on a hoist.
2. Index-mark the front driveshaft to the front axle and the transfer case.

➡ **It may be necessary to unseat the bearing cup assemblies by tapping on the yoke or bearing cup with a plastic or rubber soft-faced hammer.**

3. Remove and discard the fasteners.
a. Remove and discard the 4 front driveshaft-to-axle bolts.
b. Remove and discard the 2 U-joint retainers.
4. Remove and discard the 4 front driveshaft-to-transfer case bolts.

➡ **Wrap electrical tape around the bearing cups to prevent them from falling off the U-joint spider.**

5. Remove the front driveshaft.
a. Compress and separate the front driveshaft from the front axle, then separate the driveshaft from the transfer case.

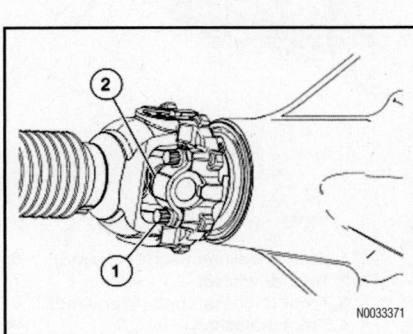

Fig. 61 Remove the 4 front driveshaft-to-axle bolts (1) and the 2 U-joint retainers (2)

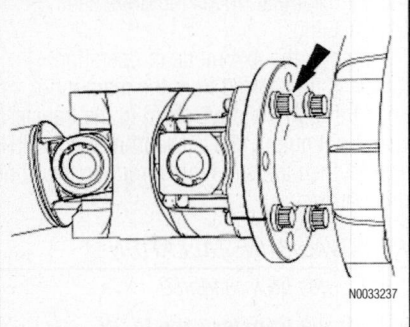

Fig. 62 Remove and discard the 4 front driveshaft-to-transfer case bolts

To install:

➡ **Install the front driveshaft with the index marks aligned.**

➡ **Install new bolts and retainers.**

6. To install, reverse the removal procedure.
a. Tighten the 4 front driveshaft-to-transfer case bolts to 74 ft. lbs. (100 Nm).
b. Tighten the 2 U-joint retainers to 26 ft. lbs. (35 Nm).

FRONT PINION SEAL

REMOVAL & INSTALLATION

See Figures 63 through 65.

1. With the vehicle in NEUTRAL, position it on a hoist.
2. Remove the front wheels and tires.

✳✳ WARNING

Do not allow the brake caliper to hang from the brake hose or damage to the hose can occur.

3. Remove the 2 brake caliper bolts from the LH and RH brake calipers and position the calipers aside.

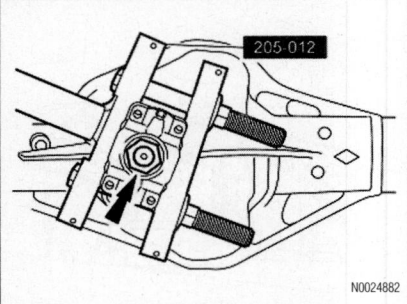

Fig. 63 Using the Drive Pinion Flange Holding Fixture, remove and discard the pinion nut and washer

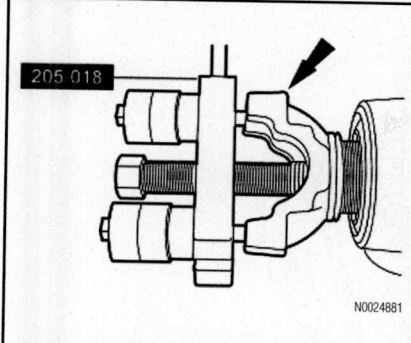

Fig. 64 Using the Drive Pinion Flange Remover, remove the flange

Support the calipers using mechanic's wire.

4. Index-mark the front driveshaft and the front axle flange to maintain driveline balance.

5. Disconnect the front driveshaft from the front axle flange and position it aside.

   a. Remove and discard the 4 bolts and 2 retainers.

   b. Disconnect the front driveshaft from the front axle flange.

   c. Tape the bearing cups to the spider to prevent them from falling off the spider.

   d. Position the driveshaft aside.

6. Measure the pinion bearing torque preload. Record the reading.

   a. Rotate the pinion with an Inch lb. (Nm) torque wrench. Record the torque necessary to maintain rotation of the pinion through several revolutions.

7. Using the Drive Pinion Flange Holding Fixture (205-012), remove and discard the pinion nut and washer.

➡ **Index-mark the flange and the pinion shaft.**

8. Using the Drive Pinion Flange Remover (205-018), remove the flange.

9. Using the Slide Hammer (100-001) and Bushing Remover (307-001), remove the pinion seal. Discard the seal.

10. Clean and inspect the following:

• The seal mounting surface.

• The flange lugs and the flange end that contacts the bearing cone.

• Verify that the flange nut counterbore and the seal contact surfaces are smooth and free of nicks.

To install:

11. Using a suitable driver, install the pinion seal.

➡ **Lightly coat the pinion seal lip with lubricant.**

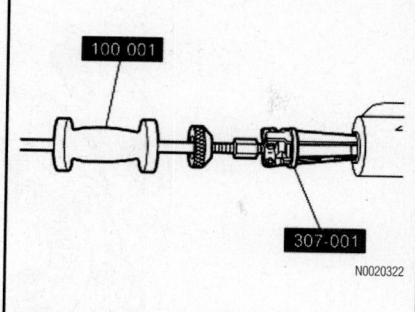

Fig. 65 Using the Slide Hammer and Bushing Remover, remove the pinion seal

➡ **Never use a metal hammer on the pinion flange or install the flange with power tools. If necessary, use a plastic hammer to tap on a tight fitting flange.**

➡ **Align the index marks.**

12. Lightly coat the flange splines and seal mating area with lubricant, then install the flange and a new washer and pinion nut.

➡ **Never back off the pinion nut to reduce preload. If preload reduction is necessary, install a new collapsible spacer and pinion nut.**

13. Tighten the nut.

   a. Use the Drive Pinion Flange Holding Fixture to prevent the flange from turning while tightening the nut. Remove the Drive Pinion Flange Holding Fixture when taking pinion bearing torque preload readings.

   b. Take frequent pinion bearing torque preload readings.

   c. The final reading must be 5 inch lbs. (0.56 Nm) more than the initial reading taken during removal.

➡ **Align the index-marks on the front driveshaft and the front axle flange to maintain driveline balance.**

14. Connect the front driveshaft to the front axle flange.

   a. Remove the tape from the bearing cups.

   b. Connect the front driveshaft to the front axle flange.

   c. Install the 2 new retainers and 4 new bolts. Tighten to 26 ft. lbs. (35 Nm).

15. Install the LH and RH brake calipers and the brake caliper bolts. Tighten to 56 ft. lbs. (76 Nm).

16. Install the front wheels and tires.

REAR AXLE SHAFT

REMOVAL & INSTALLATION

Dana

See Figure 66.

1. Set the parking brake.
2. Remove the 8 axle shaft bolts.
3. Remove the axle shaft.
4. Inspect the following components:

   a. The O-ring for damage. Install a new O-ring as necessary.

   b. The axle shaft for cracked material around the holes or oversized holes. Install new components as necessary.

➡ **Lubricate the O-ring with premium long-life grease.**

5. To install, reverse the removal procedure.

6. Tighten the 8 axle shaft bolts to 98 ft. lbs. (133 Nm).

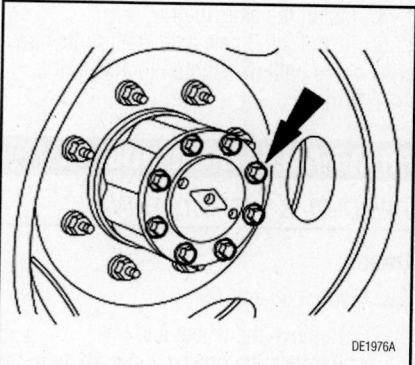

Fig. 66 Remove the 8 axle shaft bolts

Ford

See Figure 67.

➡ **The wheels and tires do not have to be removed in order to remove the axle shafts.**

1. Remove and discard the 8 axle shaft bolts.

2. Remove the axle shaft.

3. Inspect the axle shaft O-ring seal for cracks, nicks or wear and install a new seal, if required.

To install:

✳✳ WARNING

The hub and the axle shaft flange mating interface must be clean and free from oil, grease or any other contaminates before the axle shaft is completely pressed into the hub or damage to the components can occur.

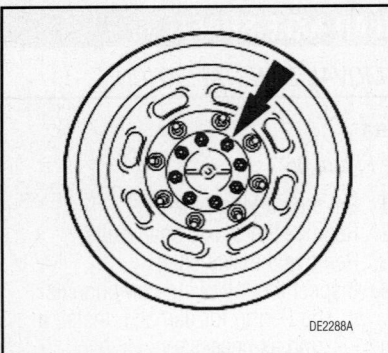

Fig. 67 Remove and discard the 8 axle shaft bolts

➡To ease the axle shaft installation into the hub, lightly lubricate the O-ring seal with grease prior to installing it on the axle shaft.

➡Verify that the O-ring seal is fully seated in the axle shaft O-ring gland after installation.

4. Install the axle shaft.
5. Install the 8 new axle shaft bolts in a criss cross pattern. Tighten to 108 ft. lbs. (147 Nm).

REAR AXLE WHEEL HUB

REMOVAL & INSTALLATION

Dana

See Figures 68 and 69.

1. Remove the wheel and tire.
2. Remove the brake caliper anchor plate.
3. Remove the axle shaft.

➡Make sure that the drive tangs on the Wheel Hub Nut Socket engage the 4 slots of the hub nut.

4. Using the Wheel Hub Nut Socket (205-282), remove the hub nut.
5. Remove the outer rear wheel bearing.
6. Remove the rear hub and brake disc assembly.
7. Remove the 8 bolts and separate the rear hub from the rear brake disc.
8. Inspect the rear hub for the following:
   - Cracks and damage around the bolt holes.
   - Oversized holes.

To install:

✳✳ WARNING

Install a new rear hub seal after removing the rear hub from the axle. A damaged or worn seal can permit

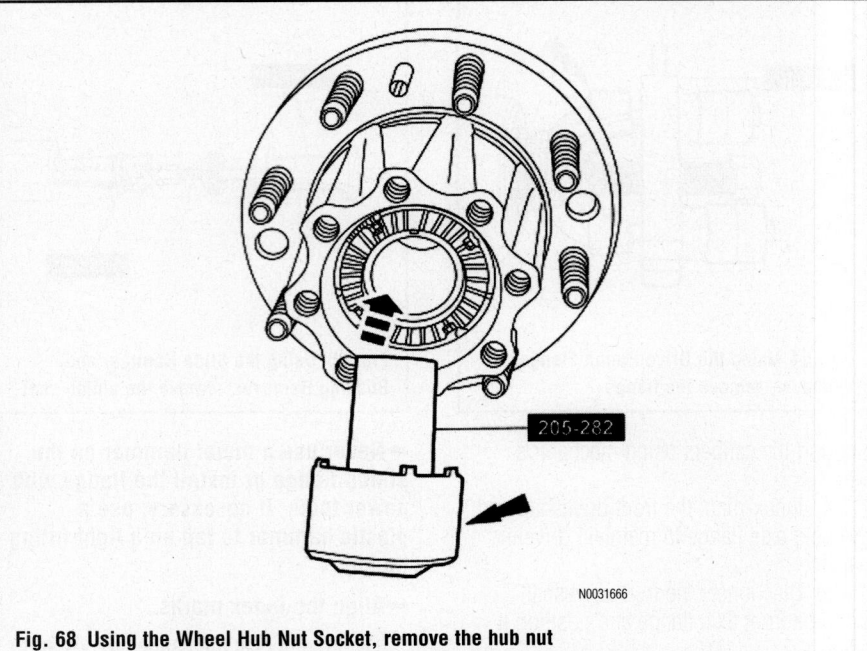

Fig. 68 Using the Wheel Hub Nut Socket, remove the hub nut

bearing lubricant to reach the brake linings, resulting in ineffective brake operation.

✳✳ WARNING

Clean and remove any dirt or foreign material in the rear hub bolt holes or damage to components may occur.

9. Install a new rear hub seal.
10. Position the rear brake disc on the rear hub and install the 8 bolts. Tighten to 114 ft. lbs. (155 Nm).
11. Wrap the spindle threads with electrician's tape to prevent damage while installing the rear hub and brake disc assembly.
12. Lightly coat the spindle and pack each rear wheel bearing with premium long-life grease.
13. Slide the rear hub and brake disc assembly over the axle housing spindle. Remove the electrician's tape.
14. Install the outer rear wheel bearing.
15. Start the hub nut making sure that the tab aligns correctly in the keyway prior to thread engagement.

➡The following hub nut tightening sequence will prevent side-to-side end play of the hub and brake disc assembly.

➡Apply inward pressure to the socket to separate the ratcheting components of the hub nut.

16. To adjust the bearings, tighten the hub nut. Tighten to 70 ft. lbs. (95 Nm).
17. Back off the hub nut 90 degrees.
18. Tighten the hub nut. Tighten to 18 ft. lbs. (24 Nm).
19. To verify that there is no side-to-side end play, attach a magnetically mounted dial indicator to the spindle end and place the dial indicator tip on the outboard surface of the hub. Check for side-to-side end play.

➡Final bearing adjustment has zero end play. The maximum torque to rotate the hub is 20 inch lbs. (2.3 Nm) when end play is zero.

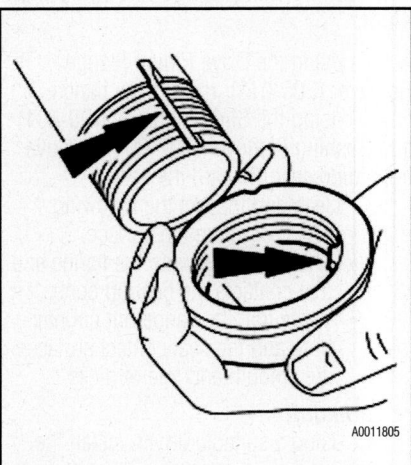

Fig. 69 Start the hub nut making sure that the tab aligns correctly in the keyway prior to thread engagement

20. Install the axle shaft.
21. Install the brake caliper and anchor plate.
22. Install the wheel and tire.

Ford

See Figures 70 through 73.

1. Loosen the 8 axle shaft bolts.
2. Remove the wheel(s) and tire(s).
3. For Single Rear Wheel (SRW) vehicles, remove the brake caliper and brake disc.
4. Remove and discard the 8 axle shaft bolts. Remove the axle shaft.

➡ **The wheel hub nuts are RH thread (right hub) and LH thread (left hub). Each wheel hub nut is stamped RH or LH.**

5. Install the Ford Axle Locknut Socket (205-282) so that the drive tangs of the tool engage the 4 slots in the wheel hub nut.

✳✳ WARNING

Under no circumstances are power tools to be used when carrying out these operations or damage to the component may occur.

✳✳ WARNING

The wheel hub nut should not ratchet during this operation. If it does, check the Ford Axle Locknut Socket tabs for wear. They should be a

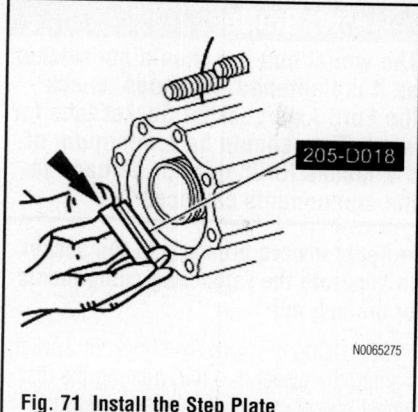

Fig. 71 Install the Step Plate

minimum of 0.2 inches (5.08 mm) or damage to the components can occur.

➡ **Discard the wheel hub nut if the wheel hub nut comes apart during removal.**

➡ **Apply inward pressure to the socket to separate the ratcheting components of the hub nut.**

6. Using the Ford Axle Locknut Socket, remove the hub nut (counterclockwise for RH thread; clockwise for LH thread).
7. Install the Step Plate (205-D018).
8. Using the Step Plate (205-D018) and 2 Jaw Puller (205-D026), loosen the rear wheel hub to the point of removal.

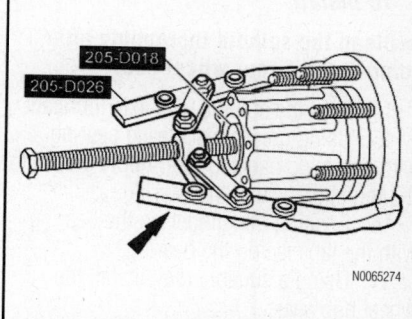

Fig. 72 Using the Step Plate and 2 Jaw Puller, loosen the rear wheel hub to the point of removal

✳✳ WARNING

Do not drop the outer hub bearing when removing the hub or damage to the component may occur.

9. Remove the rear wheel hub assembly.

➡ **Install a new wheel hub seal each time the hub assembly is removed.**

➡ **The inner bearing is located behind the wheel hub seal.**

10. Remove the wheel hub seal, slinger and inner bearing.

✳✳ WARNING

Use extreme care not to scratch or gouge the seal or bearing surfaces or damage to the component may occur.

11. If after wheel hub removal, the wheel hub seal or seal inner sleeve remains on the spindle, remove it using the Step Plate (205-D018) and 2 Jaw Puller (205-D026).
12. Inspect the seal surface and inner shoulder for scratches and damage.
13. Remove all scratches, gouges or galling damage with crocus cloth.

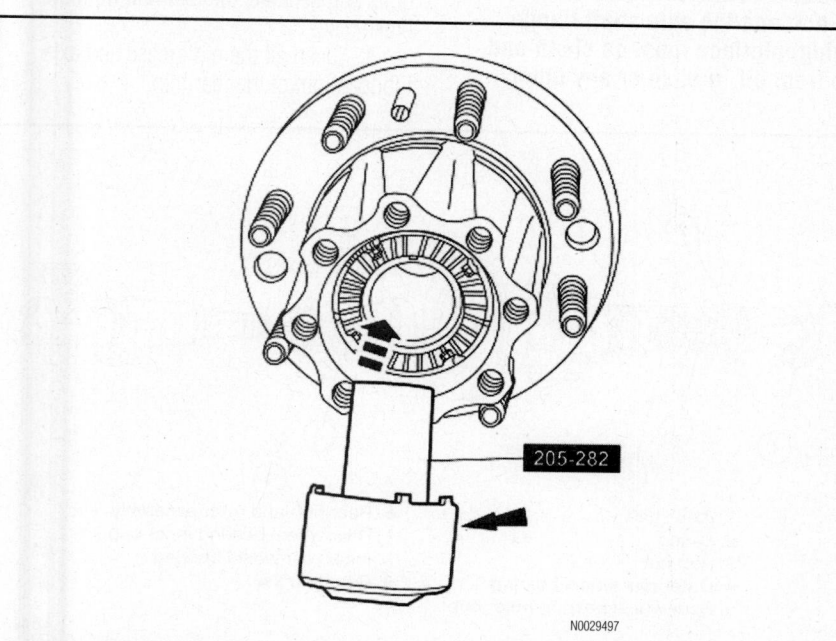

Fig. 70 Install the Ford Axle Locknut Socket so that the drive tangs of the tool engage the 4 slots in the wheel hub nut

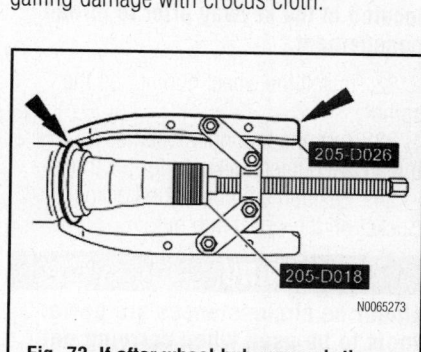

Fig. 73 If after wheel hub removal, the wheel hub seal or seal inner sleeve remains on the spindle, remove it using the Step Plate and 2 Jaw Puller

To install:

➡ Clean the spindle thoroughly after removing the rear wheel hub.

14. Coat the spindle with axle lubricant.

15. Using grease, pack each bearing with a bearing packing tool. Apply grease to the thrust surface of the bearing.

16. Position the slinger on the bearing with the tabs facing the bearing.

17. Using a suitable tool, install the wheel hub seals.

18. Verify the slinger is correctly centered in the bore.

➡ The wheel hub bearings must be pre-lubricated prior to installation.

19. Fill the wheel hub cavity with 1 oz (29.6 ml) of axle lubricant.

✷✷ WARNING

Use extreme care not to damage the hub seal by allowing it to contact the spindle during installation or damage to the component may occur.

➡ Coat the spindle and wheel hub seal inside diameter with axle lubricant.

➡ Installing the rear wheel hub in this manner causes the outer bearing to act as a pilot, making the installation easier.

20. Push the rear wheel hub and outer bearing onto the spindle as an assembly.

21. Hold the outer bearing seated and use the bearing as a pilot.

✷✷ WARNING

Install a new hub nut if the hub nut comes apart during installation or damage to the component may occur.

➡ Make sure the wheel hub nut tab is located in the keyway prior to thread engagement.

22. Install the wheel hub nut on the spindle.

23. Turn the hub nut clockwise for RH thread or counterclockwise for LH thread.

24. Position the Ford Axle Locknut Socket on the wheel hub nut.

✷✷ WARNING

Under no circumstances are power tools to be used when carrying out these operations or damage to the component may occur.

✷✷ WARNING

The wheel hub nut should not ratchet as it is tightened. If it does, check the Ford Axle Locknut Socket tabs for wear. They should be a minimum of 0.2 inches (5.08 mm) or damage to the components can occur.

➡ Apply inward pressure to the socket to separate the ratcheting components of the hub nut.

25. Using the Ford Axle Locknut Socket, tighten the wheel hub nut, rotating the rear wheel hub occasionally while tightening. Tighten to 70 ft. lbs. (95 Nm).

26. Using the Ford Axle Locknut Socket, back off the hub nut 180 degrees.

➡ Apply inward pressure to the socket to separate the ratcheting components of the hub nut.

27. Tighten the hub nut to 15 ft. lbs. (20 Nm).

28. To verify that there is no side-to-side end play, attach a magnetically mounted dial indicator to the spindle end and place the dial indicator tip on the outboard surface of the wheel hub. Check for side-to-side end play.

➡ Final bearing adjustment has zero end play.

29. Inspect the axle shaft O-ring seal for cracks, nicks or wear and replace it if required.

✷✷ WARNING

The hub and the axle shaft flange mating interface must be clean and free from oil, grease or any other contaminates before the axle shaft is completely pressed into the hub or damage to the components can occur.

➡ To ease the axle shaft installation into the hub, lightly lubricate the O-ring seal with grease prior to installing it on the axle shaft.

➡ Verify that the O-ring seal is fully seated in the axle shaft O-ring gland after installation.

30. Install the axle shaft.

31. Install and tighten the 8 new axle shaft bolts until they seat.

32. For SRW vehicles, install the brake disc and caliper.

33. Check the axle lubricant level.

34. Install the wheel(s) and tire(s).

35. Tighten the 8 new axle shaft bolts. Tighten to 108 ft. lbs. (147 Nm).

REAR AXLE WHEEL BEARING AND HUB SEAL

REMOVAL & INSTALLATION

Dana

See Figure 74.

1. Remove the rear wheel hub.

2. Remove the rear hub seal and the inner rear wheel bearing. Discard the rear hub seal.

3. If not done previously, remove the 8 bolts and separate the rear hub from the brake disc.

4. Clean all the old grease and axle lubricant out of the rear hub.

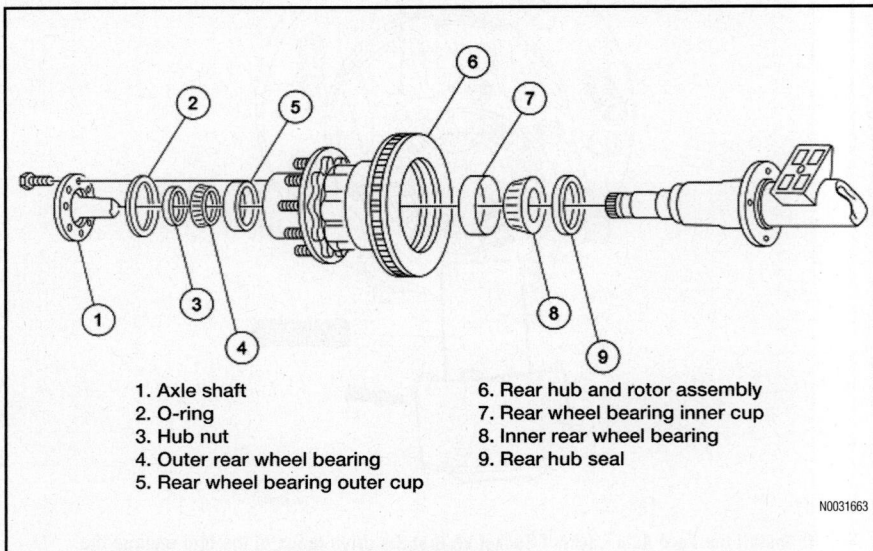

1. Axle shaft
2. O-ring
3. Hub nut
4. Outer rear wheel bearing
5. Rear wheel bearing outer cup
6. Rear hub and rotor assembly
7. Rear wheel bearing inner cup
8. Inner rear wheel bearing
9. Rear hub seal

N0031663

Fig. 74 Exploded view of wheel bearing assembly—F350

5. Remove the inner and outer bearing cups.

   a. For model 80, use Rear Wheel Hub Bearing Cup Remover 205-277 and Adapter 205-153 to remove the inner bearing cup. For model S110 or S130, use a suitable brass drift.

   b. For model 80, use Rear Wheel Hub Bearing Cup Remover 205-275 and Adapter 205-153 to remove the outer bearing cup. For model S110 or S130, use a suitable brass drift.

6. Clean the following components:
- The rear axle housing spindle.
- All the old grease and axle lubricant from the rear hub.
- The rear wheel bearings and cups.

7. Inspect the bearing races and rollers for pitting, galling or erratic wear patterns. Check the rollers for end wear. Discard the bearings, if necessary.

To install:

8. For model 80, using the Rear Axle Drawbar and the Rear Wheel Hub Bearing Cup Installers 205-100 and 205-278, install the inner and outer bearing cups. For model S110 or S130, use a suitable driver.

9. Check to see if a 0.0015 inches (0.038 mm) feeler gauge can be inserted between the cups and the rear hub at any point around each cup. Reseat the bearing cups, if necessary.

10. Install the inner rear wheel bearing in the rear hub.

11. Install a new rear hub seal.

   a. For model 80, use a suitable seal installer.

   b. For model S110 or S130, use the Wheel Hub Inner Wheel Installer and Adapter.

12. Position the rear brake disc on the rear hub and install the 8 bolts. Tighten to 114 ft. lbs. (155 Nm).

13. Install the rear wheel hub.

Ford

See Figures 75 through 81.

➡The Single Rear Wheel (SRW) wheel hub and the Dual Rear Wheels (DRW) wheel hub are different in appearance, however, the tools and procedures are the same with one exception: the brake disc can remain attached to the DRW hub if the longer driver handle is used to remove and install the bearing cups and seals.

➡A SRW wheel hub cutaway is shown for clarity in this procedure. However, the procedure is the same for the DRW wheel hub.

1. Remove the wheel hub.

2. Position the Handle (205-153) and Differential Bearing Cup Installer (308-163) on the inner bearing.

3. Using the Handle and Differential Bearing Cup Installer and holding the Handle straight, drive the inner bearing, slinger and wheel hub seal out of the wheel hub as a unit.

4. Remove and discard the bearing, slinger and wheel hub seal.

5. Position the Wheel Hub Inner Bearing Cup Remover (205-421) into the wheel hub cavity and onto the inner bearing cup.

6. Using the Handle and Wheel Hub Inner Bearing Cup Remover, drive the inner bearing cup from the wheel hub and discard the cup.

7. Reposition the wheel hub facing downward. Position the Handle and Wheel Hub Outer Bearing Cup Remover on the outer bearing cup.

8. Using the Handle and Wheel Hub Outer Bearing Cup Remover, drive the outer bearing cup from the wheel hub and discard the cup.

To install:

9. With the wheel hub facing upward, position the new outer bearing cup in the wheel hub bore and place the Handle (205-153) and Axle Bearing Installer (205-099) on the bearing cup.

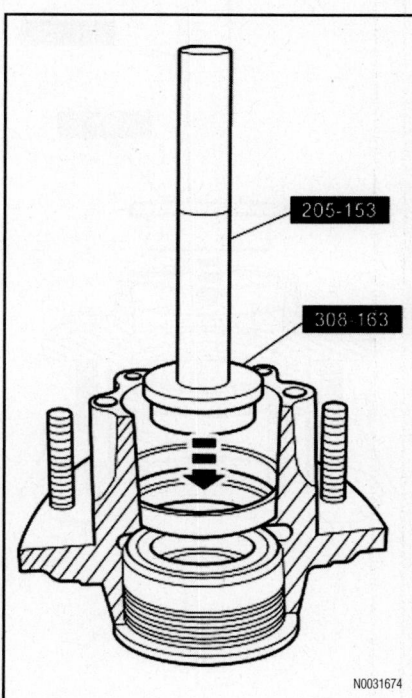

Fig. 75 Position the Handle and Differential Bearing Cup Installer on the inner bearing

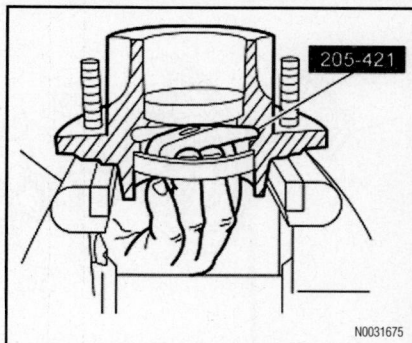

Fig. 76 Position the Wheel Hub Inner Bearing Cup Remover into the wheel hub cavity and onto the inner bearing cup

10. Using the Handle and Axle Bearing Installer, drive the outer bearing cup into the fully seated position.

11. Reposition the wheel hub facing downward. Position the inner bearing cup in the wheel hub bore and place the Handle (205-153) and Axle Bearing Installer (205-100) on the bearing cup.

12. Using the Handle and Axle Bearing Installer, drive the inner bearing cup into the fully seated position.

➡The wheel hub bearings must be pre-lubricated with grease prior to installation. Pack each bearing with a bearing packing tool. Also apply grease to the thrust surface of the bearing.

13. Position the greased inner bearing in the inner bearing cup.

✳✳ WARNING

The slinger must be correctly centered on the bearing or damage to the components can occur.

➡The grease on the bearing and slinger holds the slinger in position during seal installation.

14. Position the slinger on the greased bearing with the tangs facing the bearing.

15. With the slinger in place, position the wheel hub seal in the wheel hub bore and place the Handle (205-153) and Wheel Hub Oil Seal Installer (205-422) on the wheel hub seal.

16. Using the Handle and Wheel Hub Oil Seal Installer and holding the Handle straight, drive the wheel hub seal into position so that the seal flange bottoms out in the wheel hub.

17. Verify that the slinger is correctly centered in the bore.

18. Install the wheel hub.

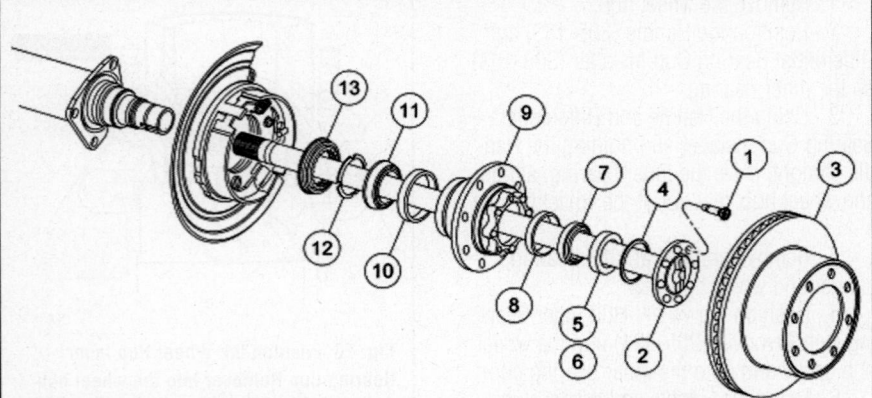

1. Axle shaft bolt (8 required)
2. Axle shaft
3. Brake disc rotor (Single Rear Wheel (SRW))
3. Wheel hub and brake disc
   (Dual Rear Wheels (DRW))
4. O-ring
5. Wheel hub nut (RH)
6. Wheel hub nut (LH)
7. Outer bearing cone and roller
8. Outer bearing cup
9. Rear wheel hub
10. Inner bearing cup
11. Inner bearing cone and roller
12. Slinger
13. Wheel hub seal

N0103011

Fig. 77 Exploded view of wheel bearing assembly

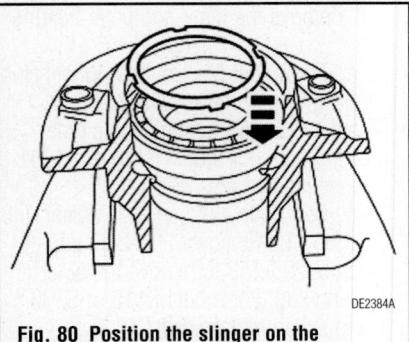

Fig. 80 Position the slinger on the greased bearing with the tangs facing the bearing

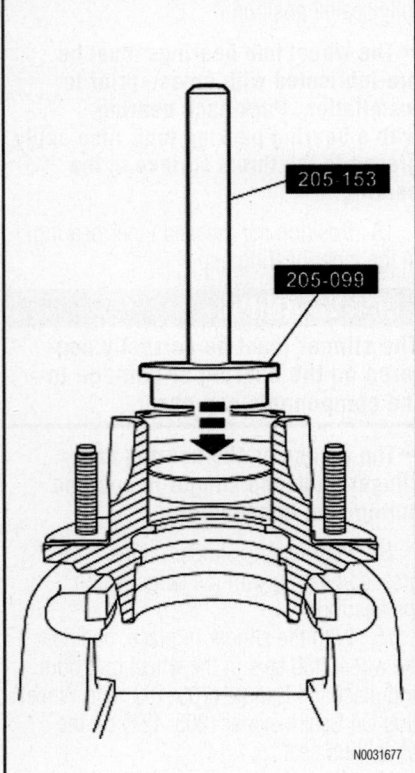

N0031677

Fig. 78 With the wheel hub facing upward, position the new outer bearing cup in the wheel hub bore and place the Handle and Axle Bearing Installer on the bearing cup

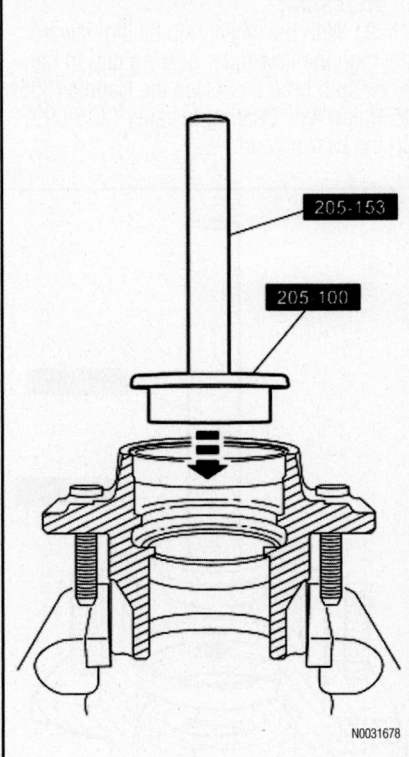

N0031678

Fig. 79 Position the inner bearing cup in the wheel hub bore and place the Handle and Axle Bearing Installer on the bearing cup

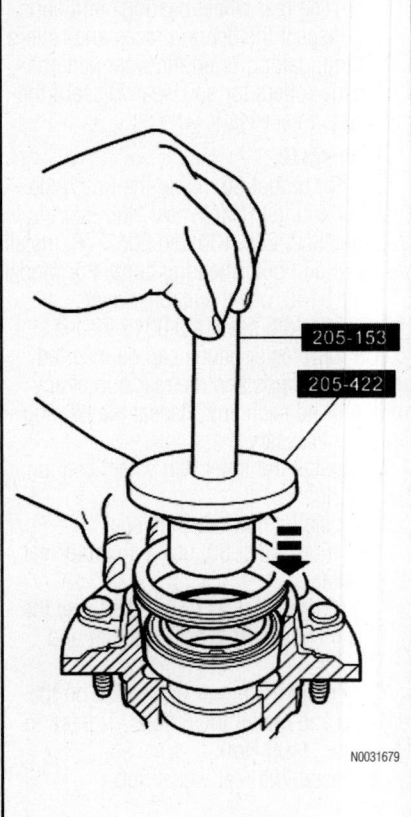

N0031679

Fig. 81 With the slinger in place, position the wheel hub seal in the wheel hub bore and place the Handle and Wheel Hub Oil Seal Installer on the wheel hub seal

REAR DRIVESHAFT

REMOVAL & INSTALLATION

Rear Driveshaft - One Piece 4WD

See Figures 82 and 83.

1. With vehicle in NEUTRAL, position it on a hoist.

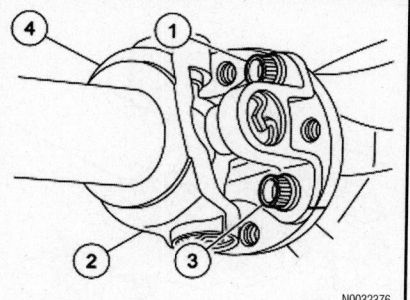

Fig. 82 Remove and discard the 4 rear driveshaft-to-transfer case bolts and the 2 U-joint retainers

2. Index-mark the driveshaft yokes and flanges to the attaching transmission, transfer case and axle flanges and yokes.
3. For vehicles with split pin yoke:
   a. Remove and discard the 4 rear driveshaft-to-transfer case bolts and the 2 U-joint retainers.

➡**It may be necessary to unseat the bearing cup assemblies by tapping on the yoke or bearing cup with a plastic or rubber soft-faced hammer.**

   b. Disconnect the driveshaft from the yoke.
4. For vehicles with circular flange:
   a. Remove and discard the 4 bolts.

➡**The driveshaft yoke fits tightly on the rear axle pinion flange pilot. Pry only in the slot on each side of the driveshaft yoke, with a suitable tool, to disconnect the yoke from the flange.**

➡**It may be necessary to tap the driveshaft yoke with a plastic or rubber soft-faced hammer if a pry area is not present on the driveshaft yoke.**

   b. Using a suitable tool, disconnect the driveshaft flange and remove the driveshaft from the vehicle.

To install:

➡**Align the index marks.**

5. Position the driveshaft yoke on the transfer case flange and loosely install the 4 new bolts.
6. For vehicles with split pin yoke:

➡**Align the index marks.**

   a. Position the bearing cups in the rear axle pinion flange.

✷✷ WARNING

Install new bolts and new retainers or damage can occur.

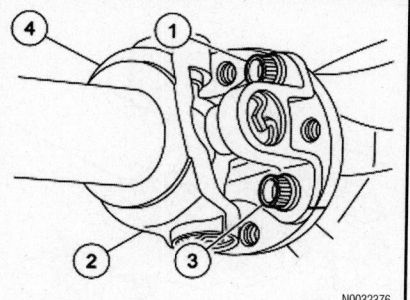

Fig. 83 Install the 4 new driveshaft-to-transfer case bolts and tighten in sequence

   b. Install the 2 new retainers and 4 new rear driveshaft-to-split pin yoke bolts. Tighten to 46 ft. lbs. (62 Nm).
7. For vehicles with circular flange:

➡**The driveshaft yoke fits tightly on the rear axle pinion flange pilot. To make sure that the yoke seats squarely on the flange, tighten the bolts evenly in a cross pattern.**

➡**Bolt direction is vehicle application dependent.**

   a. Install the 4 new driveshaft-to-transfer case bolts. Tighten in the sequence shown to 74 ft. lbs. (100 Nm).

Rear Driveshaft - One Piece RWD
See Figure 84.

1. With the vehicle in NEUTRAL, position it on a hoist.
2. Index-mark the driveshaft to the transmission and the rear axle.
3. For vehicles with circular flange:

➡**It may be necessary to tap the driveshaft yoke with a plastic or rubber soft-faced hammer if a pry area is not present on the driveshaft yoke.**

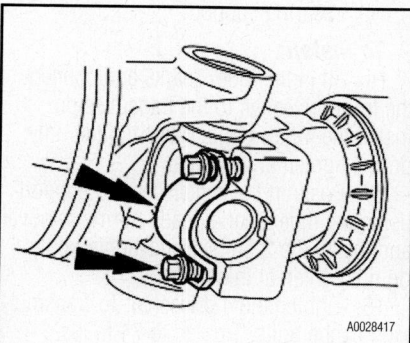

Fig. 84 Remove and discard the 4 split pin bolts and the 2 U-joint retainers

   a. Remove and discard the 4 flange bolts.
4. For vehicles with rear axle split pin yoke:

➡**It may be necessary to tap the driveshaft yoke with a plastic or rubber soft-faced hammer if a pry area is not present on the driveshaft yoke.**

   a. Remove and discard the 4 split pin bolts and the 2 U-joint retainers.
5. For vehicles with transmission slip yokes:

➡**Do not allow the output shaft to rotate while moving the driveshaft rearward.**

   a. Lower the driveshaft and slide it rearward off the transmission output shaft.

To install:
6. For vehicles with transmission slip yokes:

➡**Align the index marks.**

   a. Lubricate the slip-yoke spline with grease and position the slip yoke on the transmission output shaft.
7. For vehicles with circular flange:

➡**Align the index marks.**

➡**Bolt direction is vehicle application dependent.**

   a. Position the driveshaft flange and install 4 new bolts. Tighten to 74 ft. lbs. (100 Nm).
8. For vehicles with split pin yoke:

➡**Align the index marks.**

   a. Install the 2 new retainers and 4 new rear driveshaft-to-split pin yoke bolts. Tighten to 46 ft. lbs. (62 Nm).

Rear Driveshaft - Three Piece
See Figures 85 through 89.

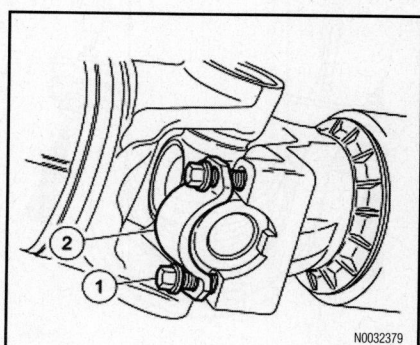

Fig. 85 Disconnect the driveshaft from the axle flange

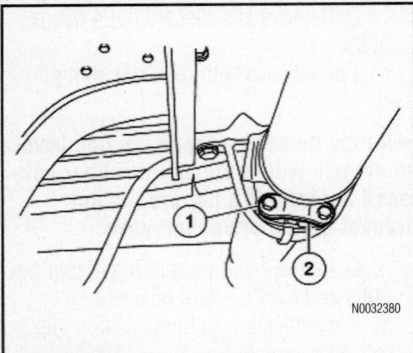

Fig. 86 Remove the 4 bolts (1) and the 2 U-joint retainers (2)

1. With the vehicle in NEUTRAL, position it on a hoist.
2. Index-mark the driveshaft flanges and slip joints.

➡It may be necessary to unseat the bearing cup assembly by tapping on the yoke or bearing cup with a plastic or rubber soft-faced hammer.

3. Disconnect the driveshaft from the axle flange.
   a. Remove and discard the 4 bolts.
   b. Remove and discard the 2 U-joint retainers.
   c. Using mechanic's wire, support the driveshaft.
4. Disconnect the driveshaft from the coupling shaft.
   a. Remove and discard the 4 bolts.
   b. Remove the 2 U-joint retainers.
   c. Using mechanic's wire, support the driveshaft.
5. Index-mark the center support bearing bracket for reference during installation.
6. Remove the 2 center bearing support bolts.
7. Remove the rear coupling shaft assembly.

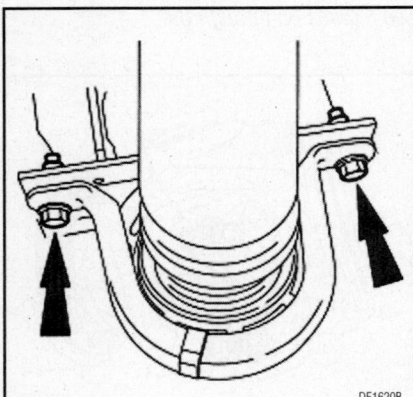

Fig. 87 Remove the 2 center bearing support bolts

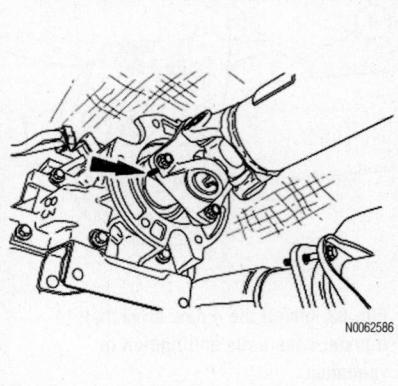

Fig. 88 Remove and discard the 4 flange bolts

➡It may be necessary to tap the driveshaft yoke with a plastic or rubber soft-faced hammer if a pry area is not available on the driveshaft yoke.

8. Remove and discard the 4 flange bolts.
9. Index-mark the center support bearing bracket for reference during installation.
10. Remove the 2 center bearing support bolts.
11. Remove the front driveshaft.
12. Clean grease deposits, dirt and rust from the following:
    • The driveshaft yoke areas.
    • All driveshaft components.
    • Wipe the bearing and rubber insulator of the driveshaft center bearing. Do not immerse in solvent.
13. Inspect the following:
    • The U-joint slip yoke boot for rips or holes. Install a new boot if necessary.
    • The driveshaft center bearing support for wear or rough action. If roughness or wear is evident, install a new driveshaft center bearing support.

To install:
14. Align the index marks and connect the front driveshaft to the transmission. Install the 4 new bolts. Hand-tighten only; do not tighten at this time.
15. Position the center bearing support using the index marks made during removal and install the 2 bolts. Hand-tighten only; do not tighten at this time.
16. Tighten the 4 driveshaft-to-transmission flange bolts. Tighten to 74 ft. lbs. (100 Nm).

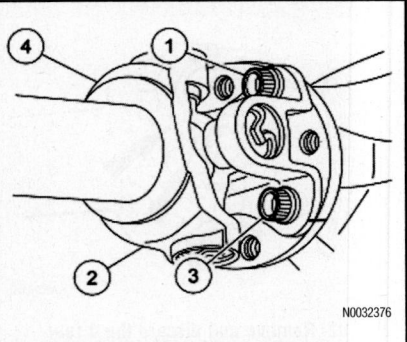

Fig. 89 Tighten the new bolts in the sequence shown

✳✳ WARNING
Make sure that the center bearing is correctly aligned when tightening fasteners or bearing failure and/or NVH issues may occur.

17. Tighten the 2 driveshaft center bearing support bolts. Tighten to 52 ft. lbs. (70 Nm).
18. Position the rear coupling shaft assembly using the index marks made during removal and install the 2 center support bearing bolts. Hand-tighten only; do not tighten at this time.
19. Connect the rear coupling shaft assembly to the front driveshaft. Install the 2 new retainers and 4 driveshaft-to-coupling shaft bolts. Tighten to 46 ft. lbs. (62 Nm).

➡The flange fits tightly on the rear axle pinion flange pilot. To make sure that the yoke seats squarely on the flange, tighten the bolts evenly in a cross pattern.

20. Connect the rear coupling shaft assembly to the rear axle. Install the 4 new bolts.
21. Tighten the new bolts in the sequence shown, to 74 ft. lbs. (100 Nm).

✳✳ WARNING
Make sure that the center bearing is correctly aligned when tightening fasteners or bearing failure and/or NVH issues may occur.

22. Tighten the 2 center bearing support bolts. Tighten to 52 ft. lbs. (70 Nm).

Rear Driveshaft - Two Piece
See Figure 90.

1. With the vehicle in NEUTRAL, position it on a hoist.
2. Index-mark the driveshaft flanges.

➡It may be necessary to tap the drive-shaft yoke with a plastic or rubber soft-faced hammer if a pry area is not present on the driveshaft yoke.

3. Remove and discard the 4 rear coupling shaft-to-rear axle bolts. Disconnect the driveshaft from the axle flange.

4. Using mechanic's wire, support the driveshaft.

➡It may be necessary to tap the drive-shaft yoke with a plastic or rubber soft-faced hammer if a pry area is not present on the driveshaft side.

5. Remove and discard the 4 drive-shaft-to-transmission flange bolts. Disconnect the driveshaft from the transmission.

6. Using mechanic's wire, support the driveshaft.

7. Index-mark the center support bearing bracket for reference during installation.

8. Remove the 2 center bearing support bolts.

9. Remove the driveshaft assembly.

To install:

10. To install, reverse the removal procedure.

11. Clean grease deposits, dirt and rust from the following:
- The driveshaft flange yoke areas.
- All driveshaft slip yoke areas.

✳✳ WARNING

Make sure that the center bearing is correctly aligned when tightening fasteners or bearing failure and/or NVH issues may occur.

➡**Align index marks made during removal.**

➡**Install new bolts and retainers.**

12. Tighten the 2 center bearing support bolts to 52 ft. lbs. (70 Nm).

13. Tighten the 4 driveshaft-to-transmission flange bolts to 74 ft. lbs. (100 Nm).

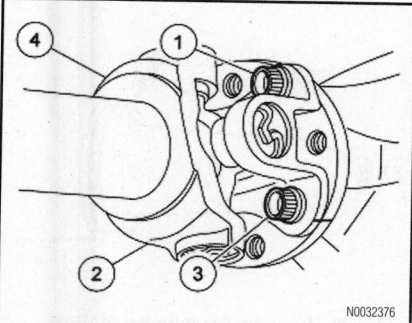

Fig. 90 Tighten the 4 rear coupling shaft-to-rear axle bolts in the sequence shown

14. Tighten the 4 rear coupling shaft-to-rear axle bolts in the sequence shown to 74 ft. lbs. (100 Nm).

REAR PINION SEAL

REMOVAL & INSTALLATION

Dana 80

See Figures 91 through 95.

1. With the vehicle in NEUTRAL, position it on a hoist.

2. To maintain driveline balance, index-mark the driveshaft flange and the pinion flange.

3. Remove and discard the 4 driveshaft flange bolts.

✳✳ WARNING

The driveshaft flange fits tightly on the rear axle flange pilot. Using a suitable tool, pry to disconnect the driveshaft flange or damage to the driveshaft may occur.

➡It may be necessary to tap the drive-shaft flange with a plastic or rubber soft-faced hammer if a pry area is not available on the driveshaft flange.

➡**Do not allow the driveshaft to hang unsupported.**

4. Using a suitable tool as shown, disconnect the driveshaft flange from the pinion flange and support the driveshaft using mechanic's wire.

➡**Index-mark the flange to the pinion shaft.**

5. Using the Drive Pinion Flange Holding Fixture (205-126) to prevent the flange from turning, remove and discard the pinion shaft locknut and washer.

6. Using the 2 Jaw Puller, remove the pinion flange.

7. Using the Slide Hammer (100-001)

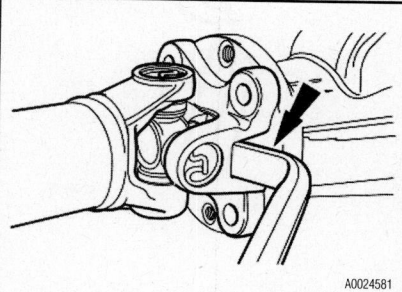

Fig. 91 Using a suitable tool as shown, disconnect the driveshaft flange from the pinion flange

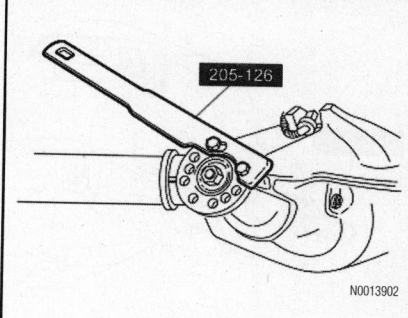

Fig. 92 Using the Drive Pinion Flange Holding Fixture to prevent the flange from turning, remove and discard the pinion shaft locknut and washer

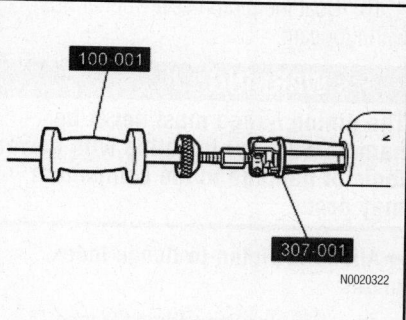

Fig. 93 Using the Slide Hammer and Bushing Remover, remove the pinion seal

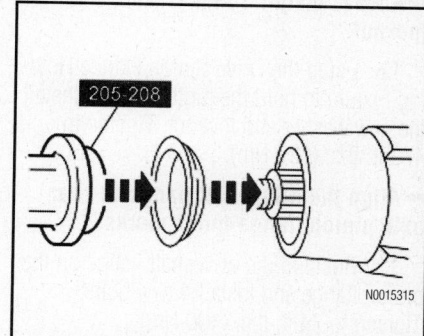

Fig. 94 Using the Drive Pinion Oil Seal Installer, install the pinion seal

and Bushing Remover (307-001), remove the pinion seal.

8. Clean the rear axle pinion seal seat.

To install:

✳✳ WARNING

If the pinion seal becomes cocked during installation, remove the seal and install a new one. Make sure the garter spring remains in place during assembly. If the spring is dislodged, a new pinion seal must be installed or damage to the component may occur.

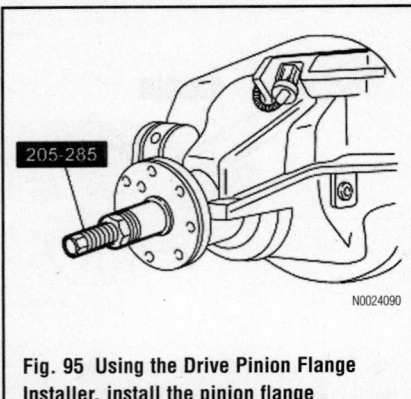

Fig. 95 Using the Drive Pinion Flange Installer, install the pinion flange

9. Using the Drive Pinion Oil Seal Installer (205-208), install the pinion seal.

10. Coat the pinion seal (rubber lips) with lubricant.

❊❊ WARNING

The pinion flange must never be hammered on or installed with power tools or damage to the component may occur.

➡**Align the pinion-to-flange index marks.**

11. Using the Drive Pinion Flange Installer (205-285), install the pinion flange.

➡**Always install a new washer and locknut.**

12. Using the Drive Pinion Flange Holding Fixture to hold the pinion flange, install the new washer and locknut. Tighten to 470 ft. lbs. (637 Nm).

➡**Align the driveshaft flange-to-rear axle pinion flange index marks.**

13. Position the driveshaft flange on the pinion flange and install 4 new bolts. Tighten to 74 ft. lbs. (100 Nm).

Ford 10.50 Inch Ring Gear

See Figures 96 through 98.

❊❊ WARNING

The color on the rear face of the drive pinion nut is critical to this repair. Use the same color new drive pinion nut for installation. If a new collapsible spacer must be installed for pinion bearing preload reduction, install the nut supplied with the new spacer kit or damage to the component may occur.

1. Remove the axle shafts.
2. Remove the driveshaft.

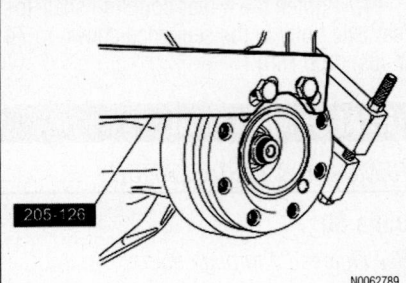

Fig. 96 Using the Drive Pinion Flange Holding Fixture to hold the pinion flange, remove the pinion nut

3. Install a Nm torque wrench on the pinion nut and record the rotational torque required to maintain rotation of the pinion through several revolutions.

4. Using the Drive Pinion Flange Holding Fixture (205-126) to hold the pinion flange, remove the pinion nut. Discard the pinion nut.

5. Mark the pinion flange in relation to the drive pinion stem to make sure alignment is correct during installation.

6. Using the 2 Jaw Puller, remove the pinion flange.

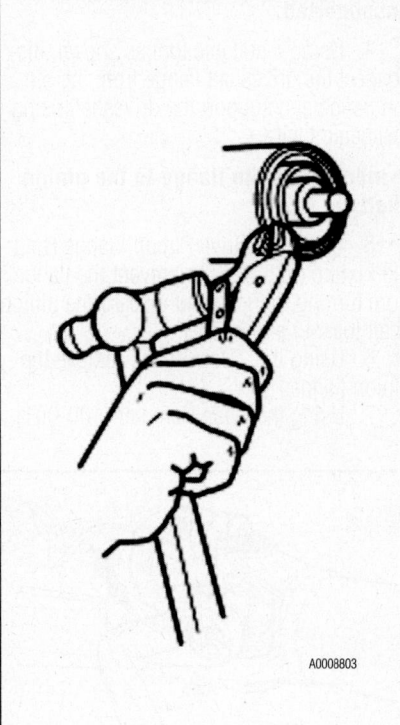

Fig. 97 Install gripping pliers to the seal flange and strike with a hammer until the rear axle drive pinion seal is removed

7. Force up on the metal flange of the rear axle drive pinion seal. Install gripping pliers to the seal flange and strike with a hammer until the rear axle drive pinion seal is removed.

To install:

8. Lubricate the new pinion seal with clean long-life grease.

❊❊ WARNING

If the rear axle drive pinion seal becomes misaligned during installation, remove it and install a new seal. Failure to install a new seal will result in a fluid leak and possible component damage.

9. Using the Drive Pinion Oil Seal Installer (205-208), install a new rear axle drive pinion seal.

10. Lubricate the pinion flange splines with clean synthetic rear axle lubricant.

➡**Disregard the scribe marks if a new pinion flange is being installed.**

11. Align the pinion flange with the drive pinion shaft.

12. Using the Drive Pinion Flange Holding Fixture and Drive Pinion Flange Installer, install the pinion flange.

❊❊ WARNING

Install a new pinion nut with the same color as the original if not replacing the collapsible spacer or damage to the component may occur.

13. Install the new washer and pinion nut. Only hand-tighten the pinion nut at this time.

❊❊ WARNING

Do not loosen the pinion nut to reduce drive pinion bearing preload. Install a new drive pinion collapsible

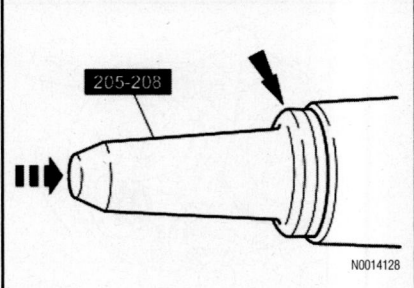

Fig. 98 Using the Drive Pinion Oil Seal Installer, install a new rear axle drive pinion seal

spacer and pinion nut if drive pinion bearing preload reduction is necessary. If a new collapsible spacer must be installed for pinion bearing preload reduction, install the nut supplied with the new spacer kit or damage to the component may occur.

14. Using the Drive Pinion Flange Holding Fixture to hold the pinion flange, tighten the pinion nut to set the drive pinion bearing preload.

15. Tighten the pinion nut, rotating the pinion occasionally to make sure the drive pinion bearings are seating correctly. Take frequent drive pinion bearing preload read-

ings by rotating the drive pinion gear with a Nm (lb-in) torque wrench. The final readings must be 5 inch lbs. (0.56 Nm) more than the initial reading taken during removal.

16. Install the driveshaft.
17. Install the axle shafts.

ENGINE COOLING

ENGINE COOLANT

DRAIN & REFILL PROCEDURE

2010 Models

✳ CAUTION

Always allow the engine to cool before opening the cooling system. Do not unscrew the coolant pressure relief cap when the engine is operating or the cooling system is hot. The cooling system is under pressure; steam and hot liquid can come out forcefully when the cap is loosened slightly. Failure to follow these instructions may result in serious personal injury.

✳ WARNING

Always fill the cooling system with the same type of coolant that was drained from the system. Do not mix coolant types. Failure to follow these instructions may result in damage to the cooling system.

✳ WARNING

The coolant must be recovered in a suitable, clean container for reuse. If the coolant is contaminated, it must be recycled or disposed of correctly and the system filled with new coolant. Failure to follow these instructions may result in damage to the cooling system.

➡ Less than 80% of coolant capacity can be recovered with the engine in the vehicle. Dirty, rusty or contaminated coolant requires replacement.

1. Place a suitable container below the radiator draincock. If equipped, disconnect the coolant return hose at the fluid cooler.
2. Remove the pressure relief cap from the degas bottle.
3. Open the radiator draincock and drain the coolant into a suitable container.

4. Close the radiator draincock when finished.

Filling And Bleeding With Radiator Refiller

✳ WARNING

With the engine cold, fill vehicles to within the cold fill range on the degas bottle. This fill level will allow for coolant expansion. Overfilling the degas bottle may result in damage to the pressure cap, which can cause the engine to overheat.

✳ WARNING

For diesel engine, do not add Motorcraft Diesel Cooling System Additive when refilling the cooling system with new coolant. An excessive amount of additive may cause formation of gels that may cause coolant flow restriction, plugging of passages and overheating.

✳ WARNING

For diesel engine, when refilling the cooling system with new coolant, verify that the specified coolant is used. Not all coolants contain a nitrite additive package. Failure to have nitrite in the cooling system may result in major corrosive damage to the engine cooling system components.

➡ For diesel engine, when reusing the coolant that was drained from the cooling system, check the antifreeze and anticorrosion level of the coolant.

1. Install the RADIATOR REFILLER and follow the manufacturer's instructions to fill and bleed the cooling system.

➡ Recommended coolant concentration is 50/50 ethylene glycol to distilled water.

- Maximum coolant concentration is 60/40 for cold weather areas.
- Minimum coolant concentration is 40/60 for warm weather areas.

Filling And Bleeding Without Radiator Refiller

✳ WARNING

Engine coolant provides freeze protection, boil protection, cooling efficiency and corrosion protection to the engine and cooling components. In order to obtain these protections, the engine coolant must be maintained at the correct concentration and fluid level in the degas bottle. Failure to follow these instructions may result in damage to the cooling system. To maintain the integrity of the coolant and the cooling system:

- Add Motorcraft Premium Gold Engine Coolant with Bittering Agent. Always fill the cooling system with the same type of coolant that was drained from the system. Do not mix coolant types.
- Do not add orange-colored Motorcraft Specialty Orange Engine Coolant with Bittering Agent (US). Mixing coolants may degrade the coolant's corrosion protection.
- Do not add alcohol, methanol, brine or any engine coolants mixed with alcohol or methanol antifreeze. These can cause engine damage from overheating or freezing.

✳ WARNING

For diesel engine, do not add Motorcraft Diesel Cooling System Additive when refilling the cooling system with new coolant. An excessive amount of additive may cause formation of gels that may cause coolant flow restriction, plugging of passages and overheating.

✳✳ WARNING

For diesel engine, when refilling the cooling system with new coolant, verify that the specified coolant is used. Not all coolants contain a nitrite additive package. Failure to have nitrite in the cooling system may result in major corrosive damage to the engine cooling system components.

➡**For diesel engine, when reusing the coolant that was drained from the cooling system, check the antifreeze and anticorrosion level of the coolant.**

➡**Failure to block the radiator off will require more time before the thermostat will open.**

1. Position a piece of cardboard on the driver's side half of the radiator.

➡**The degas bottle cap must be loose so that the cooling system does not get pressurized.**

2. Fill the degas bottle to the maximum fill line.

➡**Recommended coolant concentration is 50/50 ethylene glycol to distilled water.**

- Maximum coolant concentration is 60/40 for cold weather areas.
- Minimum coolant concentration is 40/60 for warm weather areas.

3. Install the degas bottle cap until it starts to ratchet. Back the degas bottle cap off one-half turn.
4. Start and idle the engine until the coolant level stabilizes.
5. Refill the degas bottle to the maximum fill line.
6. Install the degas bottle cap until it starts to ratchet. Back the degas bottle cap off one-half turn.
7. Run the engine at 3,000 rpm for 2 minutes.
8. Bring the engine to an idle.
9. Determine if the thermostat has opened by feeling the temperature of the radiator tubes on the passenger side of the radiator. If the tubes are cool then the thermostat has not opened. If the tubes are warm or hot then the thermostat has opened.
10. If the coolant level has dropped below the minimum fill line then refill the degas bottle to the maximum fill line.
11. Install the degas bottle cap until it starts to ratchet. Back the degas bottle cap off one-half turn.

12. Repeat Steps 5 through 7 until the thermostat opens.

➡**The coolant level will rise before the thermostat opens due to thermal expansion. The coolant level will drop after the thermostat opens due to air exiting the radiator.**

13. Repeat Steps 5 and 7 until the coolant level stabilizes.
14. Stop the engine and remove the cardboard from the radiator.
15. Restart and idle the engine for 5 minutes to stabilize the coolant temperature.
16. Fill the degas bottle to 0.787 inches (20 mm) above the maximum fill line.
17. Install the degas bottle cap.
18. Verify that the cardboard has been removed from the radiator.

2011 Models

Draining

✳✳ CAUTION

Always allow the engine to cool before opening the cooling system. Do not unscrew the coolant pressure relief cap when the engine is operating or the cooling system is hot. The cooling system is under pressure; steam and hot liquid can come out forcefully when the cap is loosened slightly. Failure to follow these instructions may result in serious personal injury.

✳✳ WARNING

Always fill the cooling system with the manufacturer's specified coolant. If a non-specified coolant has been used the cooling system must be chemically flushed. Failure to follow these instructions may damage the engine or cooling system.

✳✳ WARNING

The coolant must be recovered in a suitable, clean container for reuse. If the coolant is contaminated, it must be recycled or disposed of correctly, the cooling system must be chemically flushed and filled with new coolant. Failure to follow these instructions may damage the cooling system.

➡**Less than 80% of coolant capacity can be recovered with the engine in the vehicle. Dirty, rusty or contaminated coolant requires replacement.**

1. Place a suitable container below the radiator draincock.
2. Remove the pressure relief cap from the degas bottle.
3. Open the radiator draincock and drain the coolant into a suitable container.
4. Close the radiator draincock when finished.

Filling And Bleeding With A Vacuum Cooling System Filler

✳✳ WARNING

Vehicle cooling systems are filled with Motorcraft Specialty Orange Engine Coolant. Always fill the cooling system with the manufacturer's specified coolant. Mixing coolant types degrades the corrosion protection of Motorcraft Specialty Orange Engine Coolant. Failure to follow these instructions may damage the engine or cooling system.

✳✳ WARNING

Engine coolant provides freeze protection, boil protection, corrosion protection and cooling efficiency to the engine and cooling components. In order to obtain these protections, maintain the engine coolant at the correct concentration and fluid level. Failure to follow these instructions may damage the engine or cooling system. To maintain the integrity of the coolant and the cooling system:

- Do not mix coolant types. Mixing coolants may degrade the coolant's corrosion protection.
- Do not add alcohol, methanol or brine, or any engine coolants mixed with alcohol or methanol antifreeze. These can cause engine damage from overheating or freezing.
- Do not mix with recycled coolant. Use of such coolant may harm the engine and cooling system components.

✳✳ WARNING

With the engine cold, fill vehicles to within the cold fill range shown on the degas bottle. This fill level will allow for coolant expansion. Overfilling the degas bottle may damage the pressure cap, which can cause the engine to overheat.

1. Install the Airlift Cooling System Tester and follow the manufacturer's instructions to fill and bleed the cooling system.

a. Recommended coolant concentration is 50/50 ethylene glycol to distilled water.

b. For extremely cold climates (less than -34°F (-37°C):

• It may be necessary to increase the coolant concentration above 50%.

• NEVER increase the coolant concentration above 60%.

• Maximum coolant concentration is 60/40 for cold weather areas.

• A coolant concentration of 60% will provide freeze point protection down to -58°F (-50°C).

• Engine coolant concentration above 60% will decrease the overheat protection characteristics of the engine coolant and may damage the engine.

c. For extremely hot climates:

• It is still necessary to maintain the coolant concentration above 40%.

• NEVER decrease the coolant concentration below 40%.

• Minimum coolant concentration is 40/60 for warm weather areas.

• A coolant concentration of 40% will provide freeze point protection down to -15°F (-26°C).

• Engine coolant concentration below 40% will decrease the corrosion and freeze protection characteristics of the engine coolant and may damage the engine.

d. Vehicles driven year-round in non-extreme climates should use a 50/50 mixture of engine coolant and distilled water for optimum cooling system and engine protection.

Filling And Bleeding Without A Vacuum Cooling System Tester

❄❄ WARNING

Vehicle cooling systems are filled with Motorcraft® Specialty Orange Engine Coolant. Always fill the cooling system with the same type of coolant that is present in the system. Do not mix coolant types. Mixing coolant types degrades the corrosion protection of Motorcraft® Specialty Orange Engine Coolant. Failure to follow these instructions may damage the engine or cooling system.

❄❄ WARNING

Engine coolant provides freeze protection, boil protection, corrosion protection and cooling efficiency to the engine and cooling components. In order to obtain these protections, maintained the engine coolant at the correct concentration and fluid level. Failure to follow these instructions may damage the engine or cooling system. To maintain the integrity of the coolant and the cooling system:

• Do not mix coolant types. Mixing coolants may degrade the coolant's corrosion protection.

• Do not add alcohol, methanol or brine, or any engine coolants mixed with alcohol or methanol antifreeze. These can cause engine damage from overheating or freezing.

• Do not mix with recycled coolant. Use of such coolant may harm the engine and cooling system components.

➡ **Failure to block the radiator off will require more time before the thermostat will open.**

1. Position a piece of cardboard on the driver's side half of the radiator.

2. For 6.2L engines:

a. Release the clamp and disconnect the heater inlet hose from the heater inlet tube.

b. Fill the degas bottle until engine coolant flows from the heater inlet tube.

c. Connect the heater inlet hose to the heater inlet tube and position the clamp.

➡ **The degas bottle cap must be loose so that the cooling system does not get pressurized.**

3. Fill the degas bottle to the maximum fill line.

a. Recommended coolant concentration is 50/50 ethylene glycol to distilled water.

b. For extremely cold climates (less than -34°F [-37°C]):

• It may be necessary to increase the coolant concentration above 50%.

• NEVER increase the coolant concentration above 60%.

• Maximum coolant concentration is 60/40 for cold weather areas.

• A coolant concentration of 60% will provide freeze point protection down to -58°F (-50°C).

• Engine coolant concentration above 60% will decrease the overheat protection characteristics of the engine coolant and may damage the engine.

c. For extremely hot climates:

• It is still necessary to maintain the coolant concentration above 40%.

• NEVER decrease the coolant concentration below 40%.

• Minimum coolant concentration is 40/60 for warm weather areas.

• A coolant concentration of 40% will provide freeze point protection down to -15°F (-26°C).

• Engine coolant concentration below 40% will decrease the corrosion and freeze protection characteristics of the engine coolant and may damage the engine.

d. Vehicles driven year-round in non-extreme climates should use a 50/50 mixture of engine coolant and distilled water for optimum cooling system and engine protection.

4. Install the degas bottle cap until it starts to ratchet. Back the degas bottle cap off one-half turn.

5. Start and idle the engine until the coolant level stabilizes.

6. Refill the degas bottle to the maximum fill line.

7. Install the degas bottle cap until it starts to ratchet. Back the degas bottle cap off one-half turn.

8. Run the engine at 3,000 rpm for 2 minutes.

9. Bring the engine to an idle.

10. Determine if the thermostat has opened by feeling the temperature of the radiator tubes on the passenger side of the radiator. If the tubes are cool then the thermostat has not opened. If the tubes are warm or hot then the thermostat has opened.

11. If the coolant level has dropped below the minimum fill line then refill the degas bottle to the maximum fill line.

12. Install the degas bottle cap until it starts to ratchet. Back the degas bottle cap off one-half turn.

13. Repeat Steps 5 through 7 until the thermostat opens.

14. The coolant level will rise before the thermostat opens due to thermal expansion. The coolant level will drop after the thermostat opens due to air exiting the radiator.

15. Repeat Steps 5 and 7 until coolant level stabilizes.

16. Stop the engine and remove the cardboard from the radiator.

17. Restart and idle the engine for 5 minutes to stabilize the coolant temperature.

18. Fill the degas bottle to 0.787 inches (20 mm) above the maximum fill line.

19. Install the degas bottle cap.

20. Verify that the cardboard has been removed from the radiator.

BLEEDING

See the above procedures.

FLUSHING

Diesel Engine

See Figures 99 and 100.

✳✳ WARNING

This procedure should be used to clean and flush the diesel cooling system to make sure that all rust is removed from the system. Failure to follow these instructions may result in engine damage.

✳✳ WARNING

If oil or fuel is present in the cooling system, refer to the appropriate Technical Service Bulletins (TSBs) that pertain to 6.0L diesel engine cooling system concerns and follow the procedure outlined. Failure to remove all contaminants from the cooling system may result in engine damage.

✳✳ CAUTION

Always allow the engine to cool before opening the cooling system. Do not unscrew the coolant pressure relief cap when the engine is operating or the cooling system is hot. The cooling system is under pressure; steam and hot liquid can come out forcefully when the cap is loosened slightly. Failure to follow these instructions may result in serious personal injury.

1. Once pressure is released, remove the pressure relief cap.

2. Drain the cooling system.

3. Remove the thermostat.

➡**Both thermostats must be removed from the housing assembly.**

4. Position the thermostat housing assembly in the vise. Press down on the thermostat crossbar and rotate the thermostats to remove them from the housing assembly.

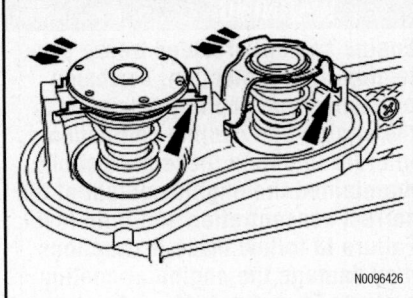

Fig. 99 Press down on the thermostat crossbar and rotate the thermostats to remove them from the housing assembly

➡**Do not fill cooling system at this time.**

➡**Use the old O-ring seal during the flushing procedure.**

5. Install the thermostat housing assembly without the thermostats.

➡**The RH cylinder block drain plug is not removed at this time.**

6. Remove the LH cylinder block drain plug and drain the cylinder block of coolant.

➡**Lightly lubricate the O-ring seal on the cylinder block drain plug with clean engine oil before installing.**

7. Install the LH cylinder block drain plug. Tighten to 15 ft. lbs. (20 Nm).

➡**For commercial vehicles with auxiliary heaters, use 2.83L (3 qt) of Motorcraft Engine Cooling System Iron Cleaner (VC-9).**

➡**The use of excessive Motorcraft Engine Cooling System Iron cleaner (VC-9) can cause gelling.**

8. Fill the cooling system with water and 2 qts (1.89L) of Motorcraft Engine Cooling System Iron Cleaner (VC-9).

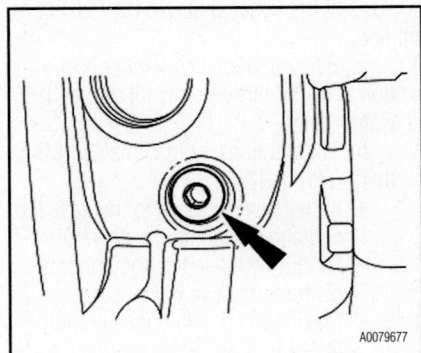

Fig. 100 Remove the LH cylinder block drain plug and drain the cylinder block of coolant

➡**Failure to allow the engine to run for one hour will result in insufficient cleaning of the cooling system.**

9. Using the scan tool, use the active command and set the engine rpm to 2,000. Run the engine for one hour.

✳✳ CAUTION

Always allow the engine to cool before opening the cooling system. Do not unscrew the coolant pressure relief cap when the engine is operating or the cooling system is hot. The cooling system is under pressure; steam and hot liquid can come out forcefully when the cap is loosened slightly. Failure to follow these instructions may result in serious personal injury.

10. Once pressure is released, remove the pressure relief cap.

11. Drain the cooling system.

12. Leave the radiator draincock open.

13. Remove the LH cylinder block drain plug.

14. Remove the starter.

15. Remove the RH cylinder block drain plug.

➡**Failure to flush all the Motorcraft Engine Cooling System Iron Cleaner (VC-9) from the cooling system will result in shortened coolant protection against corrosion.**

16. Flush the cooling system with clean water through the degas bottle to completely remove the Motorcraft Engine Cooling System Iron Cleaner (VC-9) from the cooling system.

17. Flush the cooling system with clean water until no foam or discoloration is draining from the cooling system.

18. Backflush the heater core.

➡**Failure to flush all the Motorcraft Engine Cooling System Iron Cleaner (VC-9) from the cooling system will result in shortened coolant protection against corrosion.**

19. Flush the cooling system with clean water through the degas bottle to completely remove the Motorcraft Engine Cooling System Iron Cleaner (VC-9) from the cooling system.

20. Flush the cooling system with clean water until no foam or discoloration is draining from the cooling system.

21. Close the radiator draincock.

➡**Do not fill the cooling system at this time.**

→**Replace the thermostat housing assembly O-ring seal.**

22. Install the thermostats.

→**Lightly lubricate the O-ring seal on the cylinder block drain plug with clean engine oil before installing.**

23. Install the RH cylinder block drain plug. Tighten to 15 ft. lbs. (20 Nm).
24. Install the starter.

→**Lightly lubricate the O-ring seal on the cylinder block drain plug with clean engine oil before installing.**

25. Install the LH cylinder block drain plug. Tighten to 15 ft. lbs. (20 Nm).
26. Fill the cooling system.

Gasoline Engine

✳✳ CAUTION

Always allow the engine to cool before opening the cooling system. Do not unscrew the coolant pressure relief cap when the engine is operating or the cooling system is hot. The cooling system is under pressure; steam and hot liquid can come out forcefully when the cap is loosened slightly. Failure to follow these instructions may result in serious personal injury.

1. Once pressure is released, remove the pressure relief cap. Drain the cooling system.
2. Remove the coolant thermostat.
3. Install the coolant hose connection without the coolant thermostat.

→**Refer to the cooling system flusher manufacturer's operating instructions for specific vehicle hook-up.**

4. Use a cooling system flusher to flush the engine and radiator. Use Premium Cooling System Flush or equivalent.
5. Install the coolant thermostat.
6. Backflush the heater core, if necessary.
7. Fill the cooling system.

ENGINE FAN

REMOVAL & INSTALLATION

6.4L Diesel Engine

1. Remove the upper cooling fan shroud.
2. Disconnect the cooling fan clutch electrical connector. Unclip and position the fan wiring aside.

→**The fan clutch has a LH thread.**

3. Using the Fan Clutch Nut Wrench and Fan Hub Nut Wrench, remove the cooling fan and clutch.
4. If necessary, remove the 6 bolts and separate the cooling fan and the clutch.
5. To install, reverse the removal procedure.
6. Tighten the fan hub nut to 111 ft. lbs. (150 Nm).

Gasoline Engines

1. For 5.4L engines:
   a. Remove the Air Cleaner (ACL) outlet pipe.

✳✳ WARNING

The large clutch assembly nut has a RH thread and must be rotated counterclockwise to remove it.

   b. Using the Fan Pulley Holding Wrench and the Fan Clutch Nut Wrench, remove the fan and fan clutch from the coolant pump pulley.
2. For 6.8L engines:
   a. With the vehicle in NEUTRAL, position it on a hoist.
3. Press the 5 position retaining tabs and rotate the lower cooling fan shroud upward until the position retainer tab locks into position.
   a. Disconnect the 2 lower radiator hose assembly position retainers and position the radiator hose assembly aside.
   b. Remove the 4 nuts and position the stabilizer bar downward.

✳✳ WARNING

The large clutch assembly nut has a RH thread and must be rotated counterclockwise to remove it.

   c. Using the Fan Pulley Holding Wrench and the Fan Clutch Nut Wrench, remove the fan and fan clutch from the coolant pump pulley.
4. If servicing the cooling fan or clutch, remove the 4 bolts and separate the cooling fan and cooling fan clutch.

To install:

5. To install, reverse the removal procedure.
6. For 6.8L engines:
   a. Tighten the fan clutch nut to 98 ft. lbs. (133 Nm).
   b. Tighten the 4 stabilizer bar nuts to 35 ft. lbs. (48 Nm).
7. for 5.4L engines, tighten the fan clutch nut to 41 ft. lbs. (55 Nm).

6.2L Engine

1. With the vehicle in NEUTRAL, position it on a hoist.
2. Remove the air cleaner outlet pipe.
3. Detach the radiator-to-degas bottle hose retainer from the cooling fan shroud.
4. Disconnect the cooling fan clutch electrical connector.
5. Remove the bolt and detach the cooling fan clutch wiring harness bracket from the cooling fan shroud.
6. For vehicles without Electronic Shift-On-The-Fly (ESOF):
   a. Disconnect the ESOF solenoid electrical connector from the blank.
   b. Detach the 6 wiring harness retainers from the RH side of the cooling fan shroud.
7. For vehicles with ESOF:
   a. Disconnect the vacuum reservoir-to-hubs vacuum connector from the vacuum reservoir.
   b. Disconnect the vacuum solenoid electrical connector.
   c. Disconnect the intake manifold-to-vacuum reservoir vacuum hose connector from the vacuum reservoir.
   d. Detach the 2 wiring harness retainers from the vacuum reservoir and the 4 wiring harness retainers from the RH side of the cooling fan shroud.
8. Remove the bolt and position the power steering fluid reservoir aside.
9. Detach the degas bottle-to-engine hose retainer from the cooling fan shroud.
10. Detach the 5 wiring harness retainers from the cooling fan shroud.
11. Detach the front impact severity sensor wiring harness retainer from the cooling fan shroud.
12. Press the 5 position retaining tabs and rotate the lower cooling fan shroud upward.
13. Remove the 2 lower cooling fan shroud bolts.
14. Using the Fan Pulley Holding Wrench and the Fan Clutch Nut Wrench, remove the cooling fan and cooling fan clutch from the coolant pump pulley and position the cooling fan and cooling fan clutch in the cooling fan shroud.
15. Remove the 2 upper cooling fan shroud bolts.
16. Remove the cooling fan, the cooling fan clutch and the cooling fan shroud.
17. If servicing the cooling fan or the cooling fan clutch, remove the 4 bolts and separate the cooling fan from the cooling fan clutch.
18. To install, reverse the removal procedure.

19. Tighten the fan clutch nut to 98 ft. lbs. (133 Nm)

RADIATOR

REMOVAL & INSTALLATION

6.4L Diesel Engine

See Figure 101.

1. Remove the upper fan shroud.
  a. Drain the cooling system.
  b. Remove the RH Charge Air Cooler (CAC) tube.
  c. If equipped with vacuum pump (electric), disconnect the vacuum solenoid electrical connector from the vacuum solenoid and disconnect the 2 pin-type retainers from the upper cooling fan shroud.
  d. If equipped with vacuum pump (electric), disconnect the vacuum hose at the RH battery box.
  e. If equipped with vacuum pump (electric), disconnect the vacuum hose at the degas bottle.
  f. Loosen the clamp and disconnect the LH CAC tube from the turbocharger.
  g. Remove the spring clip, disconnect the upper radiator hose from the radiator and position aside.
  h. Disconnect the coolant pump-to-fuel cooler hose from the power steering reservoir.
  i. Remove the 2 bolts and disconnect the power steering reservoir from the upper cooling fan shroud.
  j. Disconnect the coolant hose from the upper cooling fan shroud.
  k. Remove the 4 bolts and the upper cooling fan shroud.

2. When removing the upper cooling fan shroud, raise the RH side first to remove it from the vehicle.

3. Remove the 5 pushpins and the top air deflector.

4. Detach the battery cable from the radiator. Position the battery cable aside.

5. Remove the spring clip and disconnect the lower radiator hose from the radiator.

✳✳ WARNING

Failure to plug the openings for the transmission cooler hoses may result in siphoning of the transmission fluid. This may result in damage to the transmission, if the transmission fluid is not checked and topped-off after the repair is complete.

➡ Install plugs in the transmission cooler hoses.

6. Disconnect the transmission fluid cooler hoses and drain the fluid into a suitable container.

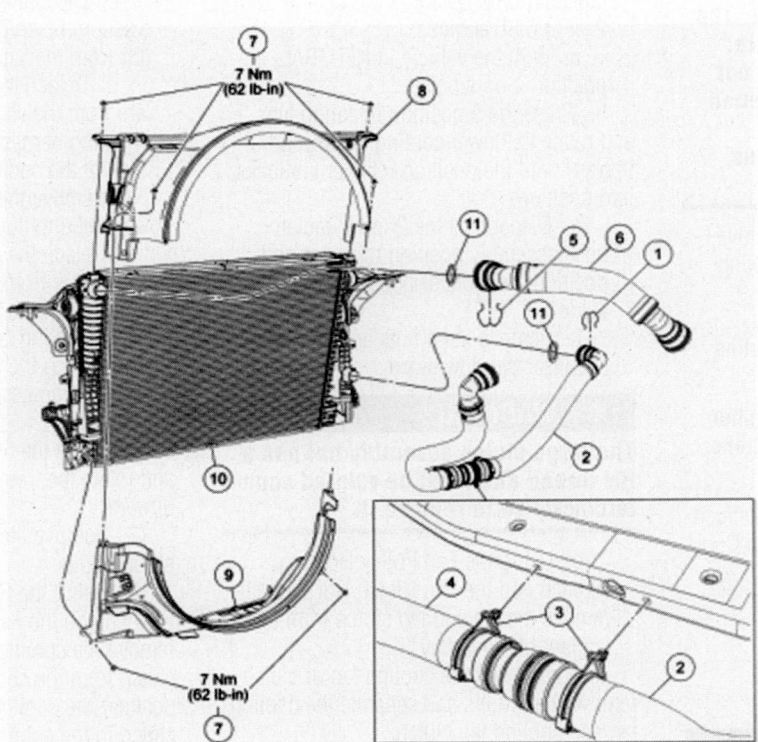

1. Lower radiator hose spring clip
2. Lower radiator hose
3. Lower radiator hose retainers (2 required)
4. Lower radiator hose-to-engine block hose
5. Upper radiator hose spring clip
6. Upper radiator hose
7. Cooling fan shroud bolts (6 required)
8. Upper cooling fan shroud
9. Lower cooling fan shroud
10. Radiator
11. Coolant hose quick connect coupling O-ring seals

N0069580

Fig. 101 Exploded view of cooling fan shroud assembly

7. Remove the 2 RH air deflector push-pins from the radiator.

8. Remove the bolt and position the fuel cooling system radiator aside.

9. Remove the 2 LH air deflector push-pins from the radiator.

10. Detach the power steering fluid hose retainer from the radiator.

11. Remove the 2 bolts and position the transmission fluid cooler aside.

12. Secure the transmission fluid cooler as needed.

13. Detach the A/C fitting from the RH battery tray.

14. Detach the A/C hose retainer from the RH inner fender splash shield.

15. Remove the 2 bolts and detach the A/C condenser from the radiator.

16. Secure the A/C condenser as needed.

17. Remove the 2 lower fan shroud bolts.

18. With the help of an assistant, remove the radiator.

19. To install, reverse the removal procedure.

20. Check the transmission fluid level and fill as necessary.

6.7L Diesel Engine

See Figure 102.

1. Drain the cooling system.
2. Drain the secondary cooling system.
3. Evacuate the A/C system.
4. Remove the upper cooling fan shroud.
5. Remove the grille.
6. Remove the air cleaner.
7. Remove the secondary battery.
8. Remove the 2 Charge Air Cooler (CAC) bolts.
9. Remove the top 2 secondary radiator bolts.
10. Remove the condenser inlet jumper line fitting nut and disconnect the compressor-to-condenser discharge line from the jumper line.

➡ **The quick connect coupling illustrated is to show the spring clip release location only. The quick connect coupling on the hose may differ.**

11. Pull the coolant pump-to-secondary radiator hose spring clip up until the end of the clip is in the detent on the quick connect coupling and disconnect the coolant pump-to-secondary radiator coolant pump-to-radiator T-connector from the T-connector.

12. Release the clamp and disconnect the secondary radiator-to-EGR cooler hose from the radiator.

➡ **The quick connect coupling illustrated is to show the spring clip release location only. The quick connect coupling on the hose may differ.**

13. Pull the upper radiator hose spring clip up until the end of the clip is in the detent on the quick connect coupling and disconnect the upper radiator hose from the radiator.

14. Detach the secondary radiator-to-Charge Air Cooler (CAC) and fuel cooler hose retainer from the radiator.

15. Detach the power steering hose retainer from the lower cooling fan shroud.

16. Squeeze the tabs, disconnect the secondary radiator-to-CAC quick connect coupling from the CAC and position the CAC and fuel cooler hoses under the CAC.

17. Release the clamp and disconnect the primary radiator overflow hose from the radiator.

18. Remove the 2 lower cooling fan shroud bolts.

➡ **The quick connect coupling illustrated is to show the spring clip release location only. The quick connect coupling on the hose may differ.**

19. Pull the lower radiator hose spring clip up until the end of the clip is in the detent on the quick connect coupling and disconnect the lower radiator hose from the radiator.

20. Remove the 3 lower air deflector pushpins from the front bumper.

21. Remove the bottom 2 secondary cooling system radiator bolts.

22. Secure the lower cooling fan shroud to the cooling fan stator.

23. Remove the four radiator bracket bolts and the 2 radiator brackets.

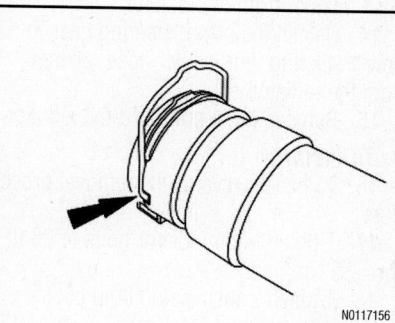

Fig. 102 To install, push the spring clip in place and connect the coolant pump-to-secondary radiator hose quick connect coupling, making sure the coupling is secure

N0117156

24. With the help of an assistant, remove the radiator.

To install:

25. To install, reverse the removal procedure.

26. Tighten the four radiator bracket bolts to 26 ft. lbs. (35 Nm).

27. To install, push the spring clip in place and connect the coolant pump-to-secondary radiator hose quick connect coupling, making sure the coupling is secure.

28. To install, push the spring clip in place and connect the upper radiator hose quick connect coupling, making sure the coupling is secure.

29. To install, push the spring clip in place and connect the lower radiator hose quick connect coupling, making sure the coupling is secure.

> ❋❋ **WARNING**
>
> **Evaluate the cooling system condition before filling the cooling system. Failure to follow these instructions can damage the engine.**

30. Evaluate the cooling system condition.

> ❋❋ **WARNING**
>
> **Evaluate the cooling system condition before filling the secondary cooling system. Failure to follow these instructions can damage the engine.**

31. Evaluate the secondary cooling system condition.

32. Evacuate, leak test and charge the refrigerant system.

5.4L & 6.8L Engines

See Figures 103 and 104.

1. With the vehicle in NEUTRAL, position it on a hoist.

2. Drain the engine cooling system.

3. Remove the cooling fan.

4. Remove the cooling fan shroud.
   a. Press the 5 position retaining tabs and rotate the lower cooling fan shroud upward until the position retainer tab locks into position.
   b. Remove the 4 bolts and the engine cooling fan shroud assembly.

5. Remove the 2 bolts and position the power steering fluid cooler aside.

6. Remove the 2 bolts and disconnect the A/C condenser from the radiator.

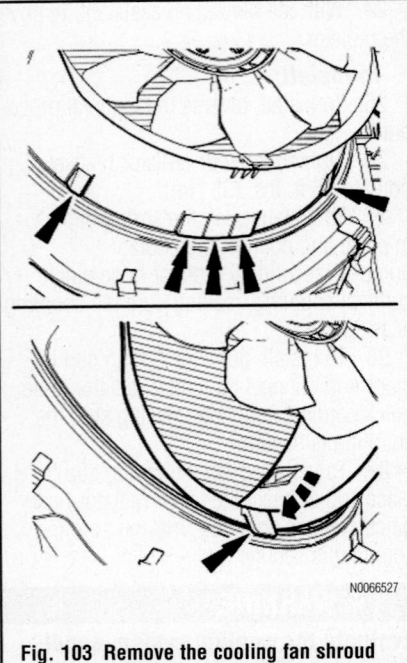

Fig. 103 Remove the cooling fan shroud

✷✷ WARNING

Failure to plug the openings for the transmission cooler hoses may result in siphoning of the transmission fluid. This may result in damage to the transmission, if the transmission fluid is not checked and topped-off after the repair is complete.

➡**Install plugs in the transmission cooler hoses.**

7. Remove the 2 bolts and disconnect the 2 hoses and the transmission auxiliary fluid cooler from the radiator.

8. Disconnect the 2 radiator air deflector retainers.

9. Remove the clip and disconnect the lower radiator hose quick connect coupling.

10. If equipped, disconnect the hood switch electrical connector and pushpin retainer.

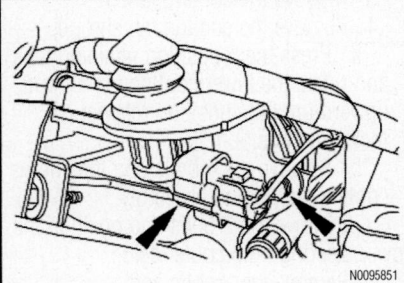

Fig. 104 If equipped, disconnect the hood switch electrical connector and pushpin retainer

11. Remove the 4 radiator-to-radiator support bolts, the 2 radiator-to-radiator support clamps and the radiator.

12. If servicing the radiator, remove the radiator support insulators.

13. To install, reverse the removal procedure.

6.2L Engine

1. Drain the cooling system.

2. Remove the 3 lower air deflector pushpins from the radiator.

3. Remove the cooling fan and the cooling fan shroud.

4. Remove the grille.

5. Remove the 2 bolts and position the A/C condenser aside.

6. Remove the 2 bolts and position the transmission fluid cooler aside.

7. Release the clamp and disconnect the radiator overflow hose from the radiator.

8. Remove the spring clip and disconnect lower radiator hose from the radiator.

9. Remove the 3 RH air deflector pushpins from the radiator.

✷✷ WARNING

Failure to plug the openings for the transmission cooler hoses may result in siphoning of the transmission fluid, and may damage the transmission if the transmission fluid is not checked and filled as required.

10. Release the clamps and disconnect the 2 transmission fluid cooler hoses from the radiator.

11. Remove the spring clip and disconnect the upper radiator hose.

12. Remove the LH air deflector pushpin from the radiator.

13. Detach the power steering fluid cooler-to-power steering fluid reservoir hose retainer from the radiator.

14. Detach the power steering gear-to-power steering fluid cooler hose retainer from the radiator.

15. Remove the 4 bolts and the radiator.

To install:

16. To install, reverse the removal procedure.

17. Tighten the 4 radiator bolts to 26 ft. lbs. (35 Nm).

18. Tighten transmission fluid cooler bolts to 97 inch lbs. (11 Nm).

19. To install, install the spring clip and connect the upper radiator hose to the radiator, making sure the upper radiator hose is secure.

20. To install, install the spring clip and connect the lower radiator hose to the radia-

tor, making sure the lower radiator hose is secure.

THERMOSTAT

REMOVAL & INSTALLATION

6.4L Diesel Engine
See Figure 105.

➡**Removal of the vertical EGR cooler is not required to service the thermostats.**

1. Remove the upper cooling fan shroud.

2. Remove the degas bottle.
   a. Drain the engine cooling system.
   b. Remove the LH battery.
   c. Loosen the clamp and disconnect the EGR cooler-to-degas bottle hose from the degas bottle.
   d. If equipped, disconnect the vacuum hose connector.
   e. Remove the 4 bolts and lift up the degas bottle in order to access the engine-to-degas bottle hose.
   f. Remove the spring clip and disconnect the engine-to-degas bottle hose from the degas bottle. Remove the degas bottle from the vehicle.

3. Using a mirror, find the end of the upper radiator hose spring clip. Remove the spring clip, disconnect the upper radiator hose from the thermostat housing and position the upper radiator hose aside.

4. Remove and discard the nut and the vertical EGR cooler lower clamp.

5. Remove the bolt and the vertical EGR cooler lower bracket.

➡**Vertical EGR cooler removed from art for clarity.**

6. Disconnect the wiring from the heater return tube.

7. Remove the 2 bolts and position out the LH heater return tube.

8. Remove and discard the O-ring seal.

➡**The 6.4L diesel engine uses 2 thermostats.**

9. Remove the 4 bolts, the collar and the thermostat housing.

10. Lift the bottom of the collar up and rotate toward the engine to remove.

✷✷ WARNING

If the thermostats are contaminated with engine oil, new thermostats must be installed. Reusing a thermostat that has been exposed to engine oil may result in engine overheating.

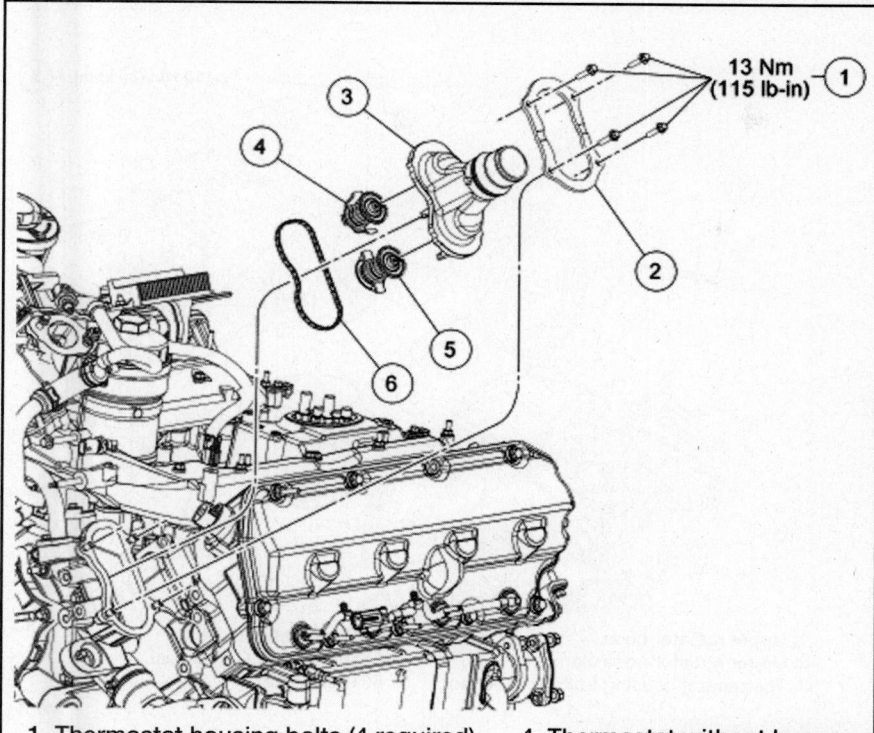

1. Thermostat housing bolts (4 required)
2. Thermostat housing collar
3. Thermostat housing
4. Thermostat without bypass
5. Thermostat with bypass
6. Thermostat housing gasket

N0089260

Fig. 105 Exploded view of thermostat assembly

11. Remove the thermostats and the gasket from the thermostat housing. Discard the gasket.

To install:

12. Install a new gasket and the thermostats into the thermostat housing.

13. Install the thermostat housing, the collar and the 4 bolts.

➡**Vertical EGR cooler removed from art for clarity.**

➡**Install a new O-ring seal.**

14. Install the LH heater return tube and the 2 bolts.

15. Connect the wiring to the heater return tube.

16. Position the lower vertical EGR cooler bracket and loosely install the bolt.

17. Install a new vertical EGR cooler lower clamp. Tighten the clamp nut in 3 stages.

    a. Stage 1: Tighten the nut to 89 inch lbs. (10 Nm).

    b. Stage 2: Loosen the nut 720 degrees (2 complete turns).

    c. Stage 3: Tighten the nut to 71 inch lbs. (8 Nm).

18. Tighten the lower EGR cooler bracket bolt. Tighten to 46 ft. lbs. (62 Nm).

19. Connect the upper radiator hose to the thermostat housing. Install the spring clip.

20. Verify the spring clip is correctly seated.

21. Install the degas bottle.

22. Install the upper cooling fan shroud.

6.7L Diesel Engine

See Figure 106.

1. Drain the cooling system.

➡**The quick connect coupling illustrated is to show the spring clip release location only. The quick connect coupling on the hose may differ.**

2. Pull the upper radiator hose spring clip up until the end of the clip is in the detent on the quick connect coupling. Disconnect the upper radiator hose from the coolant outlet connection.

3. Remove the three bolts and the coolant outlet connection.

➡**During installation, make sure the coolant outlet connection is fully seated on the coolant crossover manifold assembly before tightening the bolts.**

4. Remove the thermostat assembly.

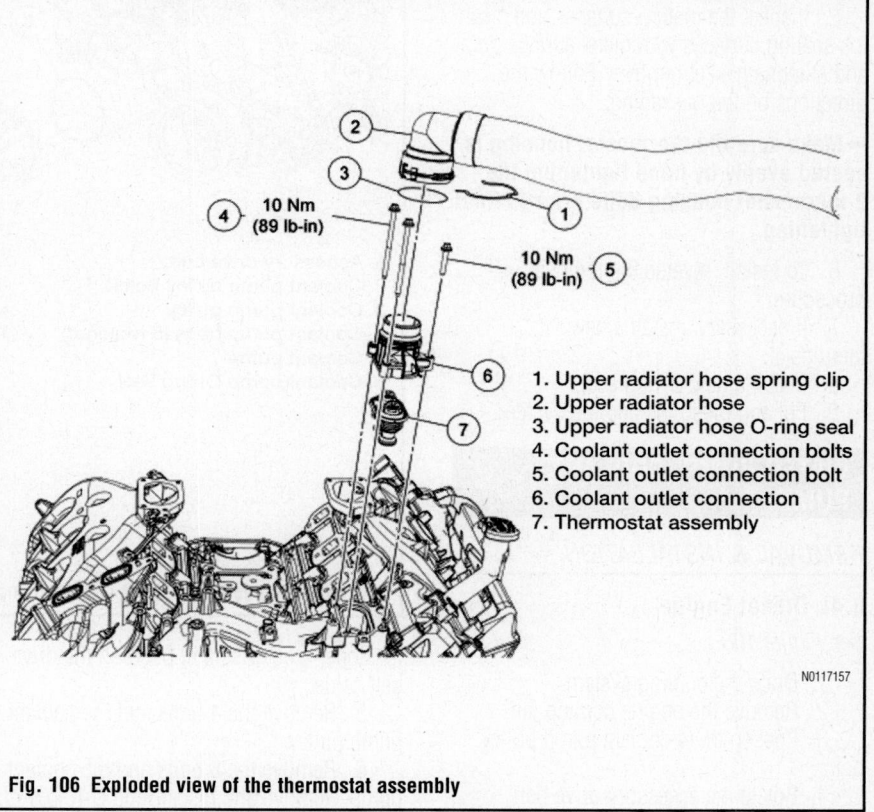

1. Upper radiator hose spring clip
2. Upper radiator hose
3. Upper radiator hose O-ring seal
4. Coolant outlet connection bolts
5. Coolant outlet connection bolt
6. Coolant outlet connection
7. Thermostat assembly

N0117157

Fig. 106 Exploded view of the thermostat assembly

To install:

5. To install, reverse the removal procedure.

6. To install, position the thermostat with the bleed hole toward the engine.

7. Tighten the coolant outlet bolts to 89 inch lbs. (10 Nm).

8. To install, push the spring clip in place and connect the upper radiator hose quick connect coupling, making sure the coupling is secure.

❊❊ WARNING

Evaluate the cooling system condition before filling the cooling system. Failure to follow these instructions can damage the engine

9. Evaluate the cooling system condition.

5.4L, 6.2L & 6.8L Engines

See Figure 107.

1. Drain the engine cooling system.

2. Remove the Air Cleaner (ACL) outlet pipe.

3. If servicing the thermostat housing, disconnect the upper radiator hose from the thermostat housing.

4. Remove the 2 bolts, position the thermostat housing aside and remove the thermostat. Discard the O-ring seal.

5. Inspect the mating surfaces and clean the sealing surfaces with metal surface prep and silicone gasket remover. Follow the directions on the packaging.

➡**Make sure the thermostat housing is seated evenly by hand tightening the 2 thermostat housing bolts prior to final tightening.**

6. To install, reverse the removal procedure.

7. If necessary, install a new thermostat.

8. Install a new O-ring seal.

9. Fill and bleed the cooling system.

WATER PUMP (COOLANT PUMP)

REMOVAL & INSTALLATION

6.4L Diesel Engine

See Figure 108.

1. Drain the cooling system.

2. Remove the engine cooling fan.

3. Loosen the 4 coolant pump pulley bolts.

4. Rotate the accessory drive belt

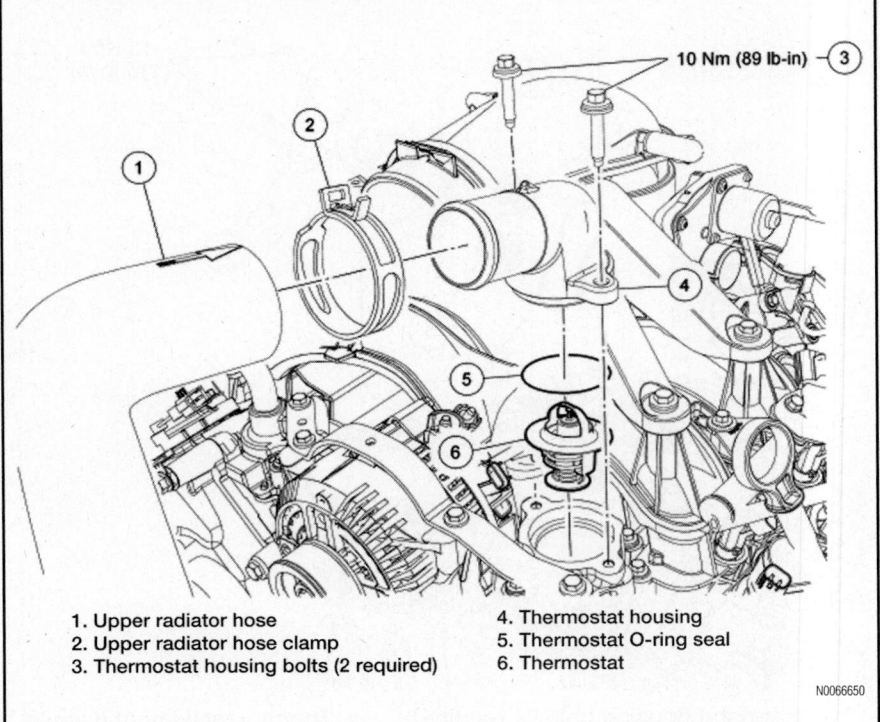

1. Upper radiator hose
2. Upper radiator hose clamp
3. Thermostat housing bolts (2 required)
4. Thermostat housing
5. Thermostat O-ring seal
6. Thermostat

N0066650

Fig. 107 Exploded view of thermostat assembly

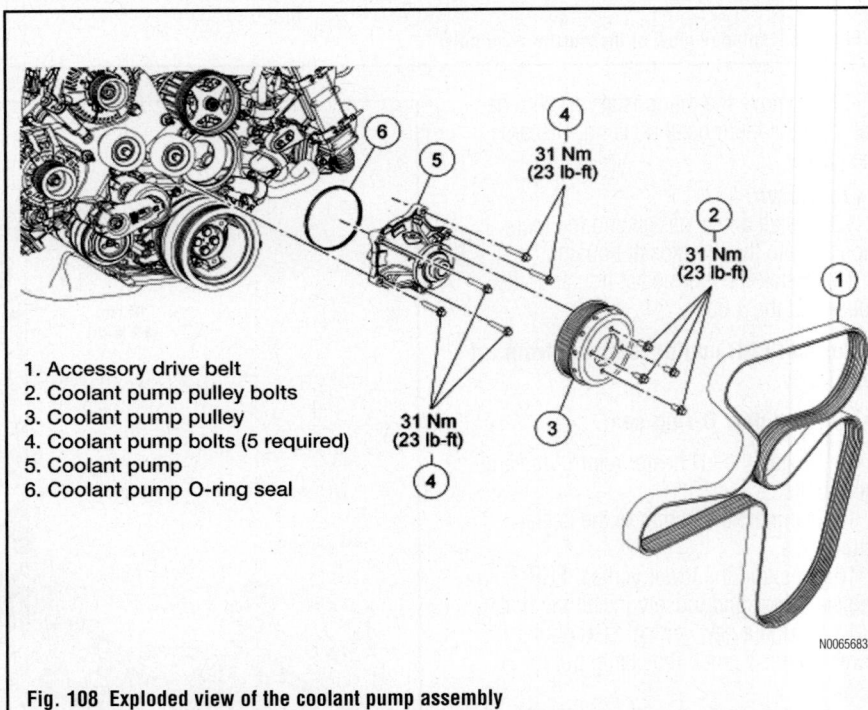

1. Accessory drive belt
2. Coolant pump pulley bolts
3. Coolant pump pulley
4. Coolant pump bolts (5 required)
5. Coolant pump
6. Coolant pump O-ring seal

N0065683

Fig. 108 Exploded view of the coolant pump assembly

tensioner clockwise and position the drive belt aside.

5. Remove the 4 bolts and the coolant pump pulley.

6. Remove the 5 bolts and the coolant pump. Remove and discard the O-ring seal.

To install:

7. To install, reverse the removal procedure.

8. Install a new O-ring seal.

9. Tighten the coolant pump mounting bolts to 23 ft. lbs. (31 Nm).

10. Tighten the coolant pump pulley bolts to 23 ft. lbs. (31 Nm).

6.7L Diesel Engine

See Figures 109 and 110.

1. Drain the cooling system.
2. Remove the cooling fan drive assembly.
3. Remove the 4 nuts and position the cooling fan stator aside.
4. Disconnect the Camshaft Position (CMP) sensor electrical connector and detach the 3 wiring harness retainers.
5. Remove the power steering pressure hose bracket screw.
6. Remove the 2 bolts and position the battery cable bracket aside.
7. Remove the 6 large and the 12 small bolts, the coolant pump and the gasket. Discard the gasket.

To install:

8. Install a new gasket on the coolant pump.
9. Position the coolant pump and install the 12 small bolts. Tighten the bolts evenly. Tighten to 89 inch lbs. (10 Nm)
10. Install the 6 large bolts. Tighten to 18 ft. lbs. (24 Nm).
11. Position the battery cable bracket and install the 2 bolts. Tighten to 106 inch lbs. (12 Nm).
12. Install the power steering pressure hose bracket screw.
13. Connect the Camshaft Position (CMP) sensor electrical connector and attach the 3 wiring harness retainers.
14. Position the cooling fan stator and install the 4 nuts. Tighten to 13.5 ft. lbs. (17 Nm).
15. Install the cooling fan drive assembly.

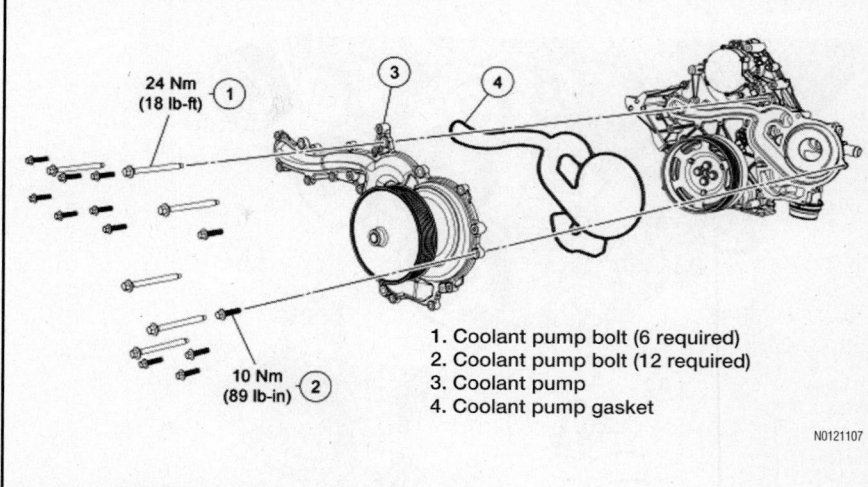

1. Coolant pump bolt (6 required)
2. Coolant pump bolt (12 required)
3. Coolant pump
4. Coolant pump gasket

N0121107

Fig. 110 Exploded view of the coolant pump assembly

❊❊ WARNING

Evaluate the cooling system condition before filling the cooling system. Failure to follow these instructions can damage the engine.

16. Evaluate the cooling system condition.

6.7L Diesel Engine Powertrain Secondary Cooling

See Figures 109 and 111 through 113.

➡**The coolant pump, pulley and housing are replaced as an assembly.**

1. Drain the secondary cooling system.
2. Remove the cooling fan.
3. Remove the 4 nuts and position the cooling fan stator aside.
4. Remove the cooling fan stator standoff from the secondary coolant pump.
5. Rotate the accessory drive belt tensioner clockwise and detach the accessory drive belt from the secondary coolant pump pulley.
6. Remove the bolt and the accessory drive belt tensioner.

➡**The quick connect coupling illustrated is to show the spring clip release location only. The quick connect coupling on the hose may differ.**

7. Pull the degas bottle-to-coolant pump hose spring clip up until the end of the clip is in the detent on the quick connect coupling. Disconnect the degas bottle-to-coolant pump hose from the secondary coolant pump.

➡**Single alternator shown, dual alternator similar**

8. Pull the coolant pump-to-radiator hose spring clip up until the end of the clip is in the detent on the quick connect coupling. Disconnect the coolant pump-to-radiator hose from the secondary coolant pump.

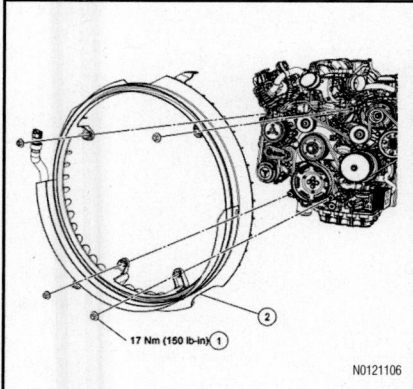

N0121106

Fig. 109 Remove the 4 nuts (1) and position the cooling fan stator (2) aside

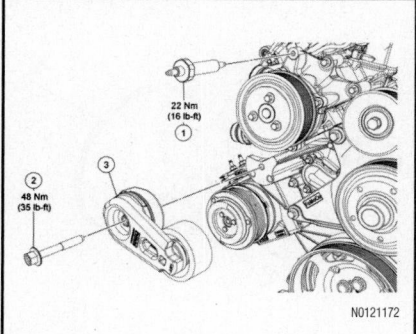

N0121172

Fig. 111 Remove the cooling fan stator standoff (1) from the secondary coolant pump; drive belt tensioner bolt (2) and drive belt tensioner (3)

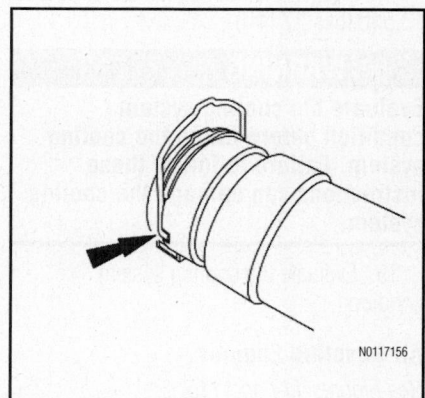

N0117156

Fig. 112 Quick coupling spring clip release

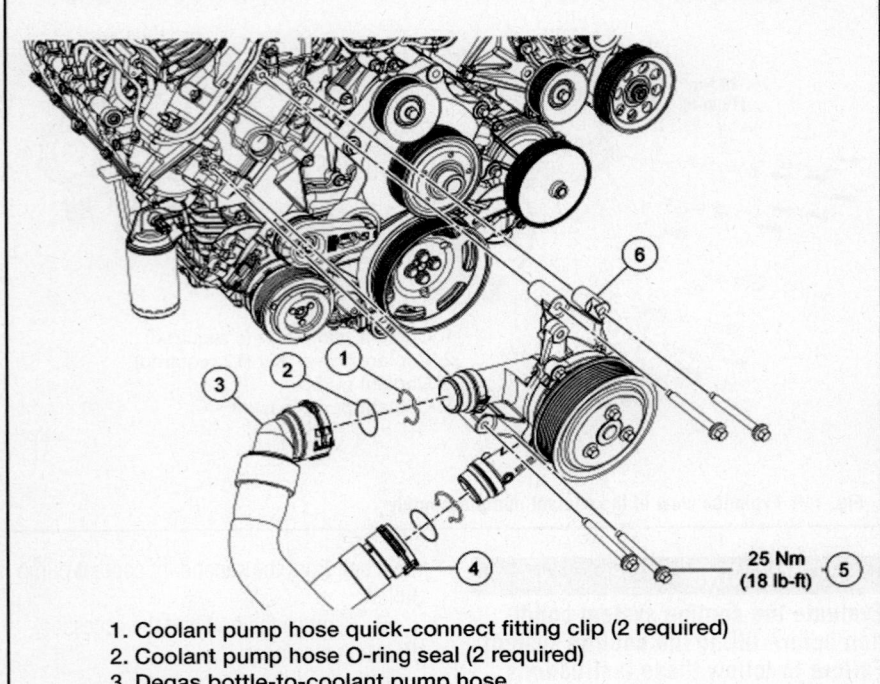

1. Coolant pump hose quick-connect fitting clip (2 required)
2. Coolant pump hose O-ring seal (2 required)
3. Degas bottle-to-coolant pump hose
4. Coolant pump-to-radiator hose
5. Coolant pump bolt (4 required)
6. Coolant pump

N0116516

Fig. 113 Exploded view of the secondary coolant pump assembly

2. Remove the cooling fan.

3. Loosen the 4 coolant pump pulley bolts.

4. Remove the accessory drive belt.

5. Remove the 4 bolts and the coolant pump pulley.

6. Remove the 4 bolts and the coolant pump. Discard the O-ring seal.

7. Inspect the sealing surfaces and clean with metal surface prep.

To install:

✳✳ WARNING

Align the bolt holes with the bosses prior to insertion of the coolant pump and insert the pump straight into the coolant pump cavity. Do not rotate the coolant pump once installed in the coolant pump cavity or damage to the O-ring seal can occur, causing the coolant pump to leak.

➥Install a new O-ring seal and lubricate with clean engine coolant.

9. Remove the 4 bolts and the secondary coolant pump, the pulley and the housing.

To install:

10. To install, reverse the removal procedure.

11. Tighten the 4 secondary coolant pump bolts to 18 ft. lbs. (25 Nm).

12. Tighten the accessory drive belt tensioner bolt to 35 ft. lbs. (48 Nm).

13. Tighten the cooling fan stator standoff to 16 ft. lbs. (22 Nm).

14. Tighten the cooling fan stator nuts to 13.5 ft. lbs. (17 Nm).

✳✳ WARNING

Evaluate the cooling system condition before filling the cooling system. Failure to follow these instructions can damage the cooling system.

15. Evaluate the cooling system condition.

All Gasoline Engines

See Figures 114 and 115.

1. Drain the engine cooling system.

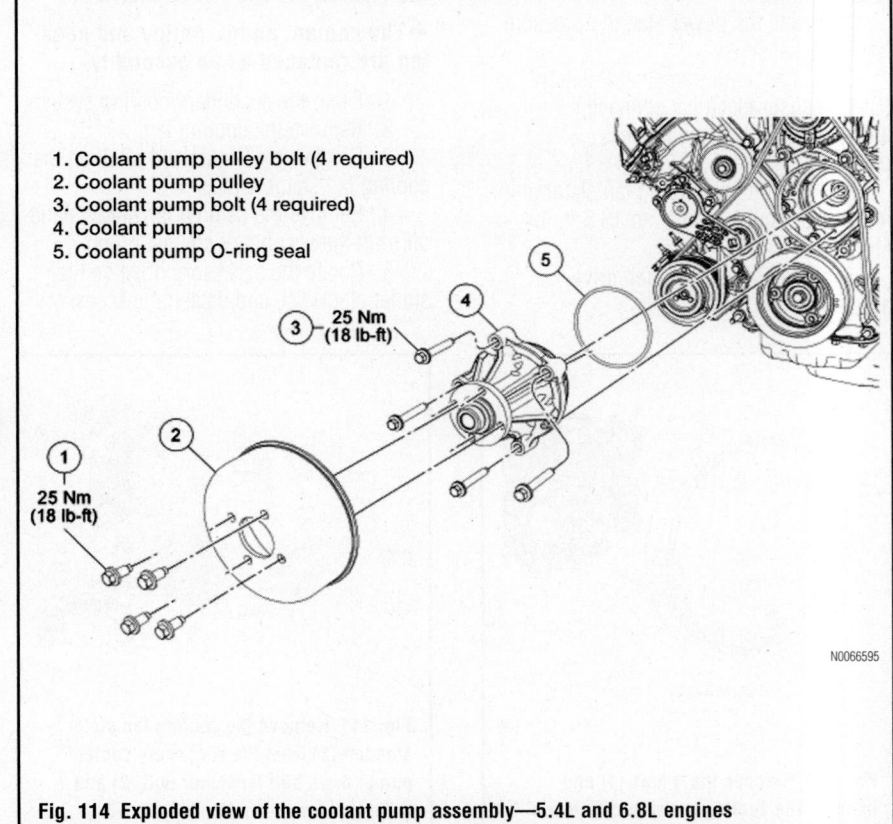

1. Coolant pump pulley bolt (4 required)
2. Coolant pump pulley
3. Coolant pump bolt (4 required)
4. Coolant pump
5. Coolant pump O-ring seal

25 Nm (18 lb-ft)

25 Nm (18 lb-ft)

N0066595

Fig. 114 Exploded view of the coolant pump assembly—5.4L and 6.8L engines

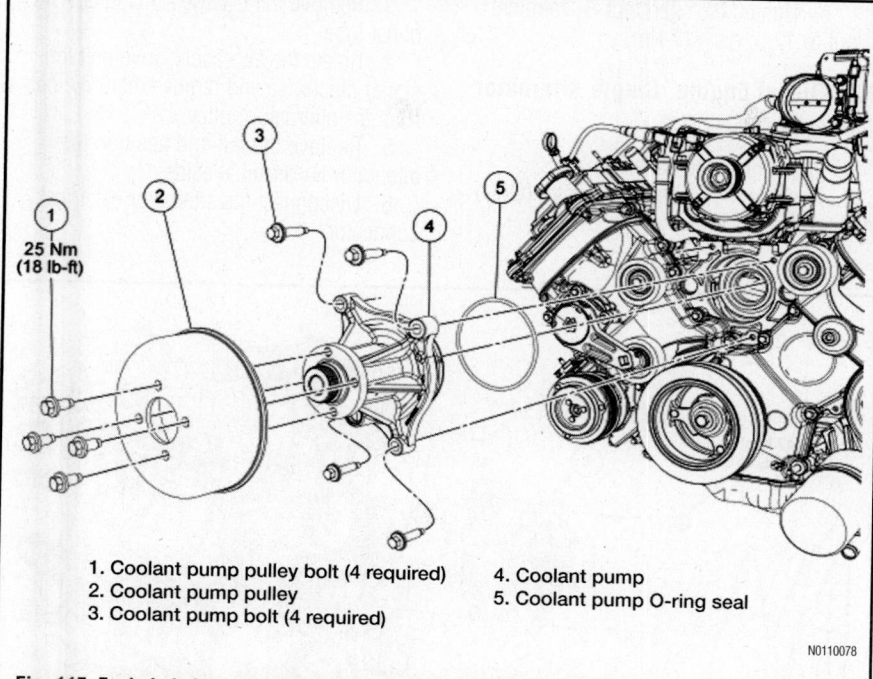

1. Coolant pump pulley bolt (4 required)
2. Coolant pump pulley
3. Coolant pump bolt (4 required)
4. Coolant pump
5. Coolant pump O-ring seal

N0110078

Fig. 115 Exploded view of the coolant pump assembly—6.2L engine

8. 5.4L and 6.8L engines, install the coolant pump and 4 bolts. Tighten to 18 ft. lbs. (25 Nm).

9. 6.2L engine, install the coolant pump and the 4 bolts. Tighten the 4 bolts in a criss-cross pattern in 3 stages

   a. Stage 1: Finger-tighten the bolts

   b. Stage 2: Tighten to 15 ft. lbs. (20 Nm).

   c. Stage 3: Tighten an additional 45 degrees.

10. Install the coolant pump pulley and 4 bolts.

11. Install the accessory drive belt.

12. Tighten the 4 bolts for the coolant pump pulley. Tighten to 18 ft. lbs. (25 Nm).

13. Install the cooling fan.

14. Fill the engine cooling system.

ENGINE ELECTRICAL

CHARGING SYSTEM

ALTERNATOR

REMOVAL & INSTALLATION

6.4L Diesel, Dual Alternators

See Figure 116.

➡This procedure applies to the primary (lower) and/or secondary (upper) alternator of the dual alternator system.

1. For both alternators:
   a. Disconnect the batteries.
   b. Remove the Air Cleaner (ACL) assembly.

2. For the primary alternator, remove the fender splash shield.

3. for the secondary alternator, loosen the RH Charge Air Cooler (CAC) tube clamp at the intake throttle adapter and position the CAC tube aside.

➡The following steps apply to both alternators.

4. Rotate the accessory drive belt tensioner clockwise and remove the drive belt from the alternator pulley.

5. Remove the nut(s) and position the alternator B+ terminal(s) aside.

6. Disconnect the alternator electrical connector.

7. Remove the 2 lower bolts to the alternator.

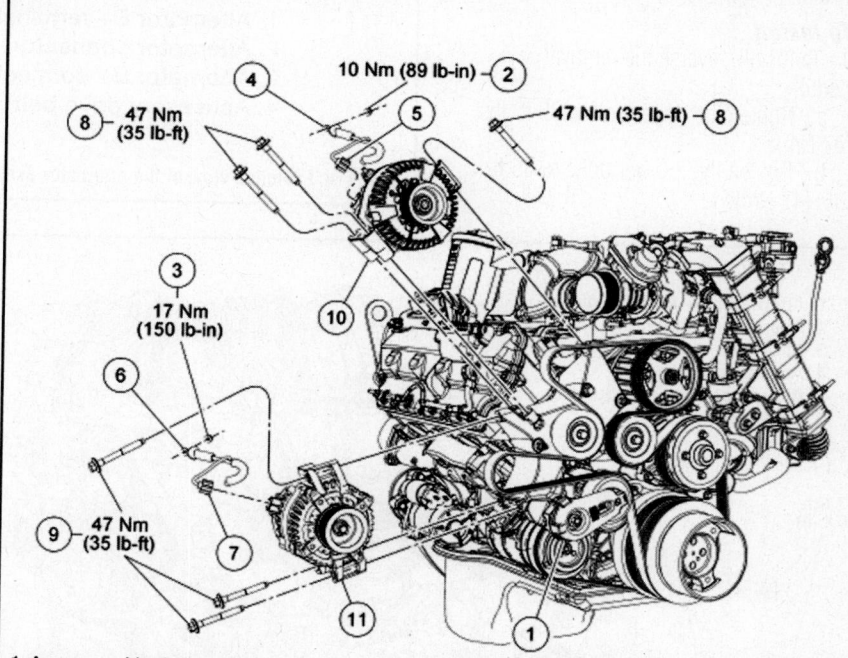

1. Accessory drive belt tensioner
2. Alternator B+ terminal nut — upper alternator
3. Alternator B+ terminal nut — lower alternator
4. Alternator B+ terminal — upper alternator
5. Alternator electrical connector — upper alternator
6. Alternator B+ terminal — lower alternator
7. Alternator electrical connector — upper alternator
8. Alternator bolts (3 required) — upper alternator
9. Alternator bolts (3 required) — lower alternator
10. Alternator — upper
11. Alternator — lower

N0089579

Fig. 116 Exploded view of the dual alternator assemblies

8. Remove the upper bolt and the alternator.

To install:

9. To install, reverse the removal procedure.

    a. Tighten the upper bolt to 35 ft. lbs. (47 Nm).

    b. Tighten the 2 lower bolts to 35 ft. lbs. (47 Nm).

    c. Tighten the alternator B+ terminal nut(s)to 12 ft. lbs. (17 Nm).

6.4L Diesel, Single Alternator

See Figure 117.

1. Disconnect the batteries.
2. Remove the Air Cleaner (ACL) assembly.
3. Remove the fender splash shield.
4. Rotate the accessory drive belt tensioner clockwise and remove the drive belt from the alternator pulley.
5. Remove the nut and position the alternator B+ terminal aside.
6. Disconnect the alternator electrical connector.
7. Remove the 2 lower bolts to the alternator.
8. Remove the upper bolt and the alternator.

To install:

9. To install, reverse the removal procedure.

    a. Tighten the upper bolt to 35 ft. lbs. (47 Nm).

    b. Tighten the 2 lower bolts to 35 ft. lbs. (47 Nm).

    c. Tighten the alternator B+ terminal nut to 12 ft. lbs. (17 Nm).

6.7L Diesel Engine, Single Alternator

See Figure 118.

1. Disconnect the batteries.
2. Remove the Charge Air Cooler (CAC) inlet tube.

3. Remove the Charge Air Cooler (CAC) outlet tube.
4. Rotate the accessory drive belt tensioner clockwise and remove the drive belt from the alternator pulley.
5. Remove the nut and position the alternator B+ terminal aside.
6. Disconnect the alternator electrical connector.

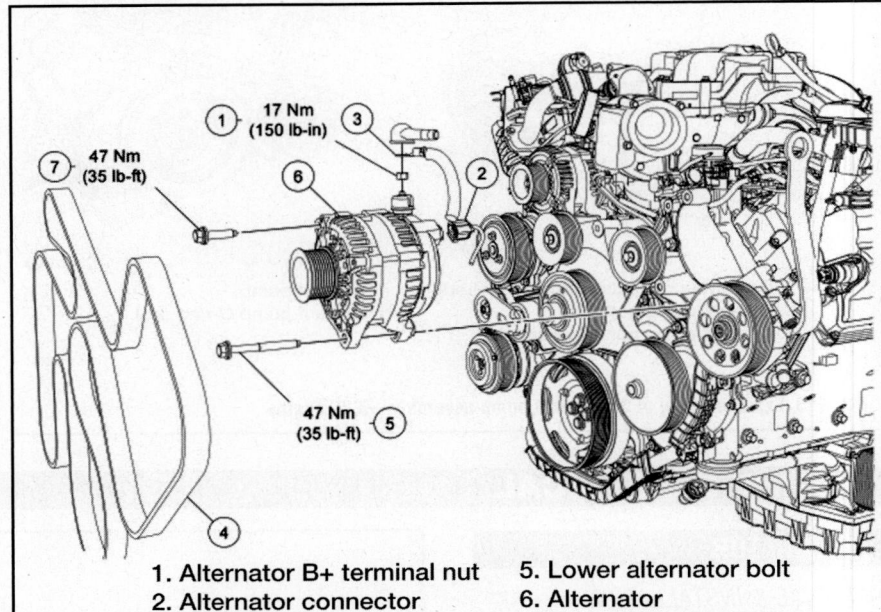

1. **Alternator B+ terminal nut**
2. **Alternator connector**
3. **Alternator B+ connector**
4. **Accessory drive belt**
5. **Lower alternator bolt**
6. **Alternator**
7. **Upper alternator bolt**

Fig. 118 Exploded view of the alternator assembly

N0115685

1. Alternator B+ terminal nut
2. Alternator connector
3. Alternator electrical connector
4. Accessory drive belt
5. Alternator bolts (3 required)
6. Alternator

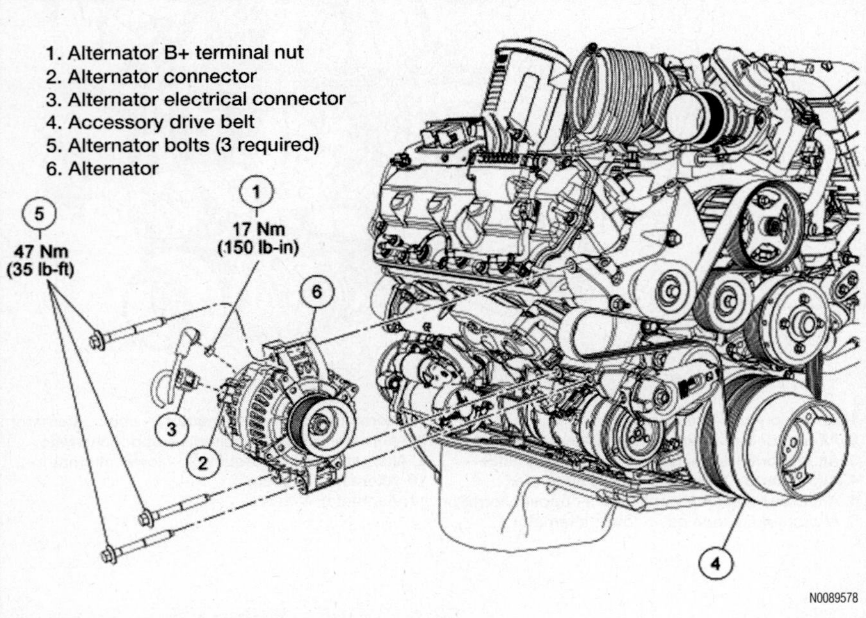

Fig. 117 Exploded view of the alternator assembly

N0089578

7. Remove the 2 alternator bolts and the alternator.
8. To install, reverse the removal procedure.

    a. Tighten the 2 alternator bolts to 35 ft. lbs. (47 Nm).

    b. Tighten the alternator B+ terminal nut to 13 ft. lbs. (17 Nm).

5.4L Engine

See Figure 119.

1. Disconnect the battery.
2. Remove the Air Cleaner (ACL) intake pipe.
3. Release the accessory drive belt tension and remove the drive belt from the alternator pulley.
4. Remove the 4 bolts and the alternator bracket.
5. Release the harness locator.
6. Remove the 2 bolts and position the alternator aside.

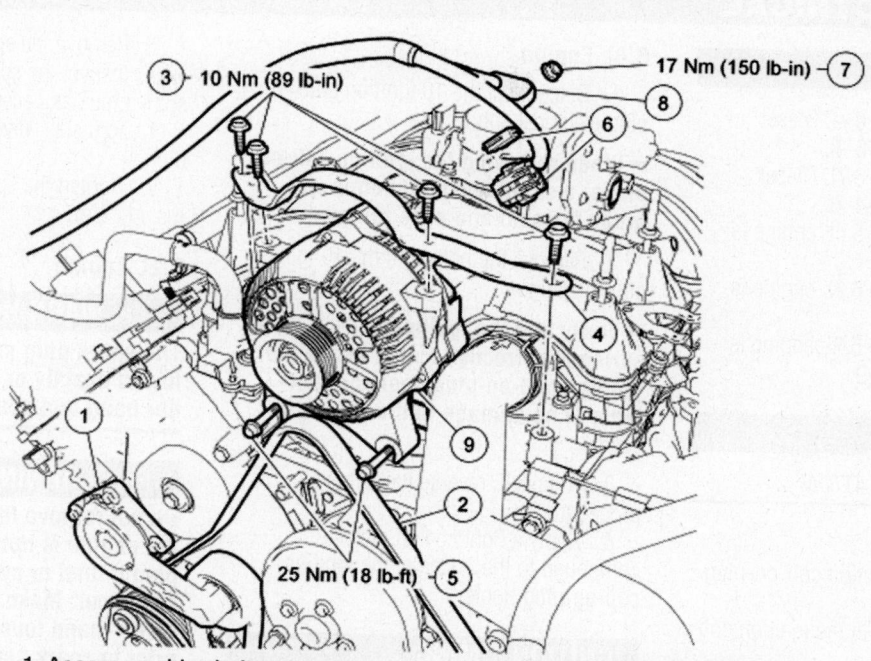

1. Accessory drive belt tensioner
2. Accessory drive belt
3. Alternator bracket bolts (4 required)
4. Alternator bracket
5. Alternator bolts (2 required)
6. Alternator electrical connectors
7. Alternator B+ terminal nut
8. Alternator B+ terminal
9. Alternator

N0089577

Fig. 119 Exploded view of the alternator assembly

7. Disconnect the 2 alternator electrical connectors.

※※ WARNING

When installing the alternator, make sure to hand-start the alternator B+ terminal nut to prevent cross-threading.

8. Remove the nut and position the alternator B+ terminal aside.
9. Remove the alternator.

To install:
10. To install, reverse the removal procedure.
  a. Tighten the alternator B+ terminal nut to 12 ft. lbs. (17 Nm).
  b. Tighten the 2 alternator bolts to 18 ft. lbs. (25 Nm).

  c. Tighten the 4 alternator bracket bolts to 89 inch lbs. (10 Nm).

6.2L and 6.8L Engines

1. Disconnect the battery.
2. For 6.8L engine, remove the Air Cleaner (ACL) outlet pipe.
3. For 6.2L engine, remove the air intake expansion resonator.
4. Release the accessory drive belt tension and remove the drive belt from the alternator pulley.
5. Disconnect the alternator electrical connector.
6. Remove the nut and position the alternator B+ terminal aside.
7. For 6.2L engine, remove the 3 bolts, the alternator bracket and the alternator.

8. For 6.8L engine:
  a. Remove the 4 bolts and the alternator bracket.
  b. Remove the 2 alternator bolts and the alternator.

To install:
9. To install, reverse the removal procedure.
10. For 6.8L engine:
  a. Tighten the 2 alternator bolts to 18 ft. lbs. (25 Nm).
  b. Tighten the 4 alternator bracket bolts to 89 inch lbs. (10 Nm).
11. For 6.2L engine, tighten the 3 alternator bolts to 35 ft. lbs. (47 Nm).
12. Tighten the alternator B+ terminal nut to 13 ft. lbs. (17 Nm).

FIRING ORDER

The firing order for the 6.4L Diesel engine is 1–2–7–3–4–5–6–8.

The firing order for the 6.7L Diesel engine is 1–3–7–2–6–5–4–8.

The firing order for the 5.4L engine is 1–3–7–2–6–5–4–8.

The firing order for the 6.2L engine is 1–5–4–8–6–3–7–2.

The firing order for the 6.8L engine is 1–6–5–10–2–7–3–8–4–9.

IGNITION COIL

REMOVAL & INSTALLATION

5.4L Engine

1. Disconnect the ignition coil-on-plug electrical connector.
2. Remove the bolt and the ignition coil-on-plug.
3. Remove the ignition coil-on-plug, using a twisting motion while pulling up on the ignition coil-on-plug.

➡**Verify that the ignition coil-on-plug spring is correctly located inside the ignition coil-on-plug boot and that there is no damage to the tip of the boot.**

4. To install, reverse the removal procedure.
5. Apply a light coat of dielectric compound to the inside of the ignition coil boots.

6.2L Engine

1. Remove the Air Cleaner (ACL) outlet pipe.
2. Remove the intake air resonator.
3. Disconnect the 8 ignition wires.
4. Disconnect the 8 ignition coil-on-plug electrical connectors.
5. Remove the 8 ignition coil-on-plug bolts.

➡**When removing the ignition coil-on-plugs, a slight twisting motion will break the seal and ease removal.**

6. Remove the 8 ignition coil-on-plugs.

➡**Verify that the ignition coil spring is correctly located inside the ignition coil-on-plug boot and that there is no damage to the tip of the boot.**

7. To install, reverse the removal procedure.
8. Apply a light coat of dielectric compound to the inside of the ignition coil boots.

6.8L Engine

1. Disconnect the 10 ignition coil-on-plug electrical connectors.

➡**When removing the ignition coil-on-plugs, a slight twisting motion will break the seal and ease removal.**

2. Remove the bolts and the 10 ignition coil-on-plugs.

➡**Verify that the ignition coil-on-plug spring is correctly located inside the ignition coil-on-plug boot and that there is no damage to the tip of the boot.**

3. To install, reverse the removal procedure.
4. Apply a light coat of dielectric compound to the inside of the ignition coil-on-plug boots.

IGNITION TIMING

ADJUSTMENT

Ignition timing is controlled by the Powertrain Control Module (PCM). No adjustment is necessary or possible.

SPARK PLUGS

REMOVAL & INSTALLATION

5.4L & 6.8L Engines

1. Remove the ignition coil-on-plug.

> ✳✳ **WARNING**
>
> **Do not remove the spark plugs when the engine is hot or cold soaked. Spark plug thread or cylinder head damage can occur. Make sure the engine is warm (hand touch after cooling down) prior to spark plug removal.**

> ✳✳ **WARNING**
>
> **Only use hand tools when removing or installing the spark plugs or damage can occur to the cylinder head or spark plug.**

➡**Use compressed air to remove any foreign material from the spark plug well before removing the spark plugs.**

➡**If an original spark plug is used, make sure it is installed in the same cylinder from which it was taken. New spark plugs can be used in any cylinder.**

2. Remove the spark plugs.
3. Inspect the spark plugs. Install new spark plugs as necessary.
4. To install, reverse the removal procedure
5. Tighten the spark plugs to 106 inch lbs. (12 Nm).

6.2L Engine

> ✳✳ **WARNING**
>
> **The spark plug procedure must be followed exactly or damage to the cylinder head and spark plug will result.**

> ✳✳ **WARNING**
>
> **Do not remove the spark plugs when the engine is hot or cold soaked. Spark plug thread or cylinder head damage can occur. Make sure the engine is warm (hand touch after cooling down) prior to spark plug removal.**

1. To remove the upper spark plugs, remove the ignition coil-on-plugs.
2. To remove the lower spark plugs, disconnect the ignition wire from the lower spark plugs.

> ✳✳ **WARNING**
>
> **Only use hand tools when removing or installing the spark plugs or damage can occur to the cylinder head or spark plug.**

➡**Use compressed air to remove any foreign material from the spark plug well before removing the spark plugs.**

3. Remove the spark plugs.
4. Inspect the spark plugs.

To install:

5. Adjust the spark plug gaps as necessary. For the correct spark plug gap specification, refer to Specifications in this section.

> ✳✳ **WARNING**
>
> **Only use hand tools when removing or installing the spark plugs or damage can occur to the cylinder head or spark plug.**

6. Install the spark plugs. Tighten to 13 ft. lbs. (18 Nm).
7. For the lower spark plugs, connect the ignition wire to the lower spark plugs.
8. For the upper spark plugs, install the ignition coil-on-plugs.

ENGINE ELECTRICAL

BATTERY

REMOVAL & INSTALLATION

❊❊ CAUTION

Batteries contain sulfuric acid and produce explosive gases. Work in a well-ventilated area. Do not allow the battery to come in contact with flames, sparks or burning substances. Avoid contact with skin, eyes or clothing. Shield eyes when working near the battery to protect against possible splashing of acid solution. In case of acid contact with skin or eyes, flush immediately with water for a minimum of 15 minutes, then get prompt medical attention. If acid is swallowed, call a physician immediately. Failure to follow these instructions may result in serious personal injury.

❊❊ CAUTION

Always deplete the backup power supply before repairing or installing any new front or side air bag Supplemental Restraint System (SRS) component and before servicing, removing, installing, adjusting or striking components near the front or side impact sensors or the Restraints Control Module (RCM). Nearby components include doors, instrument panel, console, door latches, strikers, seats and hood latches.

To deplete the backup power supply energy, disconnect the battery ground cable and wait at least 1 minute. Be sure to disconnect auxiliary batteries and power supplies (if equipped).

❊❊ WARNING

Failure to follow these instructions may result in serious personal injury or death in the event of an accidental deployment.

❊❊ CAUTION

Always lift a plastic-cased battery with a battery carrier or with hands on opposite corners. Excessive pressure on the battery end walls may cause acid to flow through the vent caps, resulting in personal injury and/or damage to the vehicle or battery.

❊❊ CAUTION

Do not get underneath the frame-mounted battery when disconnecting or connecting the auxiliary battery safety straps. The battery is heavy and could fall. Failure to follow this instruction may result in serious personal injury.

1. Disconnect the battery, negative cable first, then the positive cable.

❊❊ WARNING

Be sure the battery cover is reinstalled to avoid premature battery failure.

2. If equipped, remove the battery cover.
3. Release the cable from the battery cover.
4. Remove the battery hold-down clamp bolt.
5. Remove the battery.
6. To install, reverse the removal procedure.

BATTERY RECONNECT/RELEARN PROCEDURE

➡When the battery is disconnected and connected, some abnormal drive symptoms may occur while the vehicle relearns its adaptive strategy. The vehicle may need to be driven to relearn its strategy.

➡When the battery is disconnected and connected, the illumination display needs to be calibrated. After the battery is connected, rotate the dimmer switch from the lowest dim position to the full bright, dome ON position.

➡When disconnecting the battery ground cable to interrupt power to the vehicle electrical system, disconnect the battery ground cable only. It is not necessary to disconnect the positive battery cable.

ENGINE ELECTRICAL

STARTER

REMOVAL & INSTALLATION

Diesel Engines
See Figure 120.

❊❊ CAUTION

Always disconnect the battery ground cable at the battery before disconnecting the starter motor battery terminal lead. If a tool is shorted at the starter motor battery terminal, the tool can quickly heat enough to cause a skin burn. Failure to follow this instruction may result in serious personal injury.

➡A protective cap or boot is provided over the battery input terminal on all vehicle lines and must be installed after repairing.

1. Disconnect the battery ground cable.
2. Remove the nut and position aside the starter motor battery cable bracket.
3. Remove the starter solenoid protective cap.
4. Label and disconnect the starter motor electrical connections.
5. Remove the top starter bolt and stud bolt.
6. Remove the lower starter bolt and the starter.

To install:

7. Position the starter motor and install the 3 bolts in 3 stages.
   a. Stage 1: Install the 3 bolts finger-tight.
   b. Stage 2: Tighten the upper starter bolt to 18 ft. lbs. (25 Nm).
   c. Stage 3: Tighten the stud bolt and the lower starter bolt to 18 ft. lbs. (25 Nm).
8. Connect the starter wiring.
9. Install the starter solenoid protective cap.
10. Position back the starter motor battery cable bracket and install the nut. Tighten to 18 ft. lbs. (25 Nm).
11. Connect the battery ground cable.

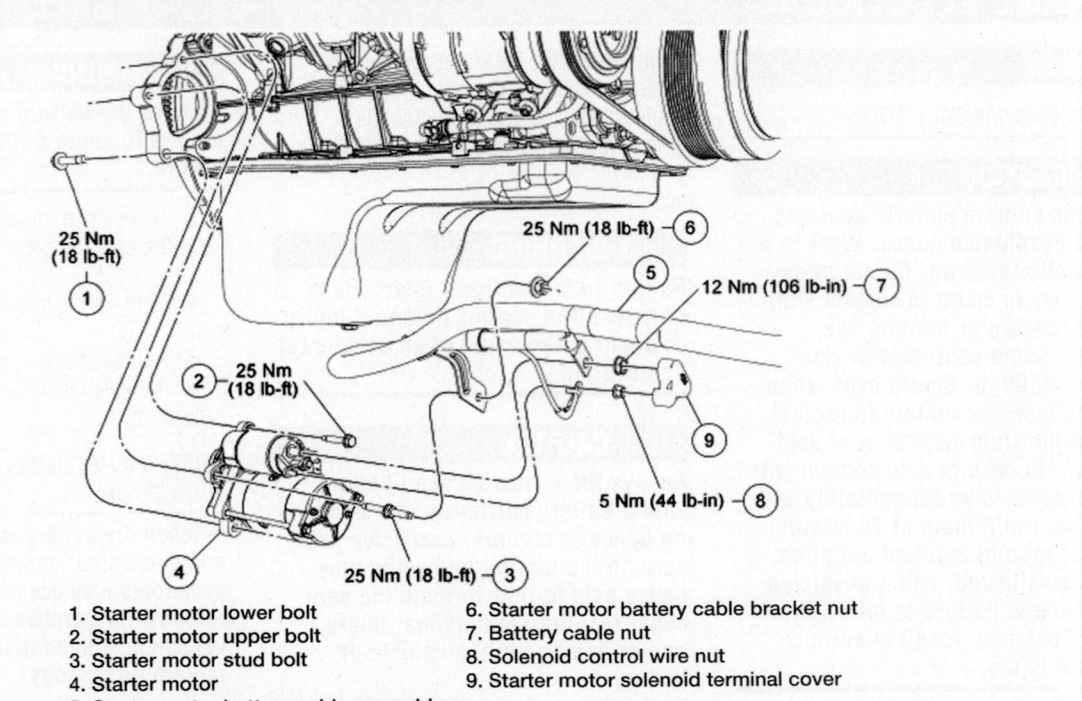

Fig. 120 Exploded view of starter motor assembly

1. Starter motor lower bolt
2. Starter motor upper bolt
3. Starter motor stud bolt
4. Starter motor
5. Starter motor battery cable assembly
6. Starter motor battery cable bracket nut
7. Battery cable nut
8. Solenoid control wire nut
9. Starter motor solenoid terminal cover

N0076376

Gasoline Engines

See Figure 121.

> ※ **CAUTION**
>
> **Always disconnect the battery ground cable at the battery before disconnecting the starter motor battery terminal lead. If a tool is shorted at the starter motor battery terminal, the tool can quickly heat enough to cause a skin burn. Failure to follow this instruction may result in serious personal injury.**

1. With the vehicle in NEUTRAL, position it on a hoist.
2. Disconnect the battery ground cable.
3. Remove the starter terminal cover and remove the nut and the solenoid S-terminal electrical connection.
4. Remove the nut and the solenoid B-terminal electrical connection.
5. Remove the 3 bolts and the starter motor.

To install:

6. To install, reverse the removal procedure.

   a. Loosely install the 3 starter motor bolts.

   b. Tighten the upper bolt to 18 ft. lbs. (25 Nm).

   c. Tighten the lower bolts to 18 ft. lbs. (25 Nm).

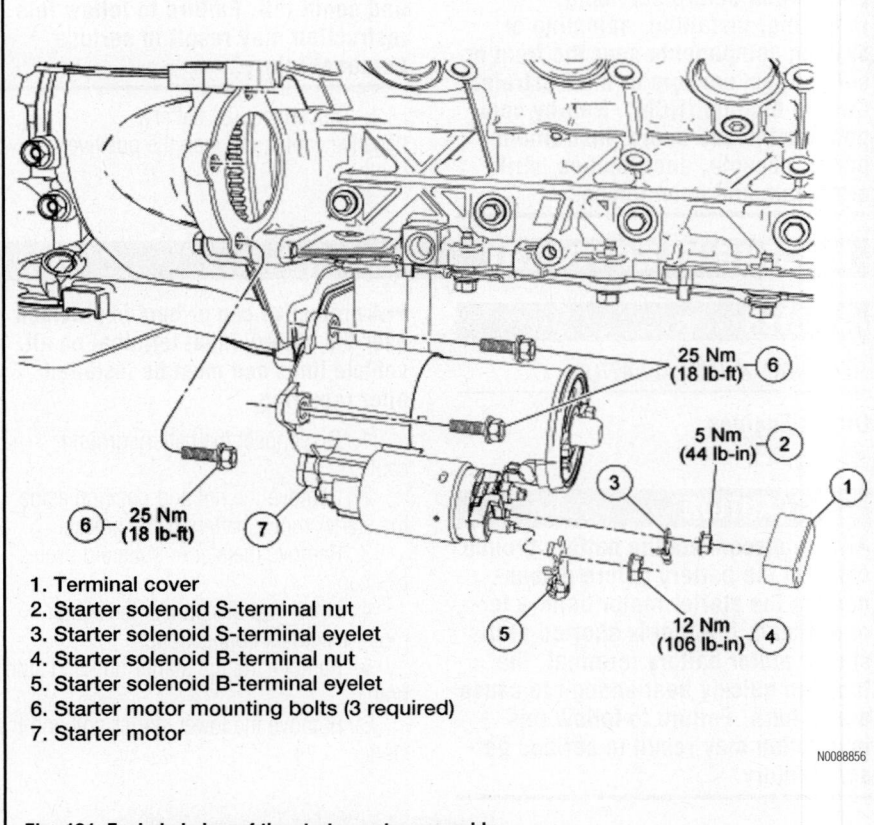

1. Terminal cover
2. Starter solenoid S-terminal nut
3. Starter solenoid S-terminal eyelet
4. Starter solenoid B-terminal nut
5. Starter solenoid B-terminal eyelet
6. Starter motor mounting bolts (3 required)
7. Starter motor

N0088856

Fig. 121 Exploded view of the starter motor assembly

ENGINE MECHANICAL

➡ Disconnecting the negative battery cable may interfere with the functions of the on board computer systems and may require the computer to undergo a relearning process, once the negative battery cable is reconnected.

ACCESSORY DRIVE BELTS

ACCESSORY BELT ROUTING

Gasoline Engines

See Figures 122 through 125.

Refer to the accompanying illustrations.

Diesel Engines

See Figures 126 through 130.

Refer to the accompanying illustrations.

INSPECTION

Inspect serpentine belts for cracks, tears, checking and/or fraying. Replace the belt if any of these are present.

ADJUSTMENT

The drive belt tension is created by automatic belt tensioners. No adjustment is necessary.

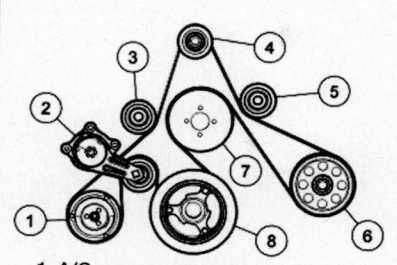

1. A/C compressor pulley
1. Accessory drive belt idler pulley and bracket assembly (without A/C)
2. Accessory drive belt tensioner
3. Belt idler pulley
4. Alternator pulley
5. Belt idler pulley
6. Power steering pump pulley
7. Coolant pump pulley
8. Crankshaft pulley

N0113324

Fig. 123 Front End Accessory Drive (FEAD) Exploded View—6.2L (2V) engine

REMOVAL & INSTALLATION

6.4L Diesel Engine

1. Remove the cooling fan upper shroud.

➡ The engine cooling fan has unevenly spaced blades. Position the fan to

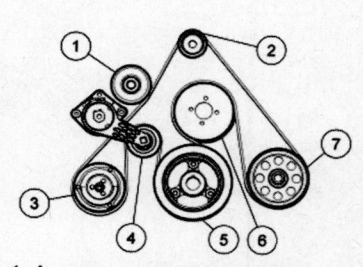

1. Accessory drive belt idler pulley
2. Alternator pulley
3. A/C clutch pulley
4. Accessory drive belt tensioner pulley
5. Crankshaft pulley
6. Coolant pump pulley
7. Power steering pump pulley

N0113269

Fig. 124 Front End Accessory Drive (FEAD) Exploded View—6.8L (3V) engine with A/C

access the accessory drive belt tensioner.

2. Rotate the accessory drive belt tensioner clockwise and remove the accessory drive belt.

3. Rotate the A/C compressor belt tensioner counterclockwise and remove the A/C compressor belt.

➡ First detach the drive belt from the bottom of the A/C compressor pulley, then remove it from the crankshaft pulley, and finally slide the belt out from between the tensioner bracket and the A/C compressor pulley.

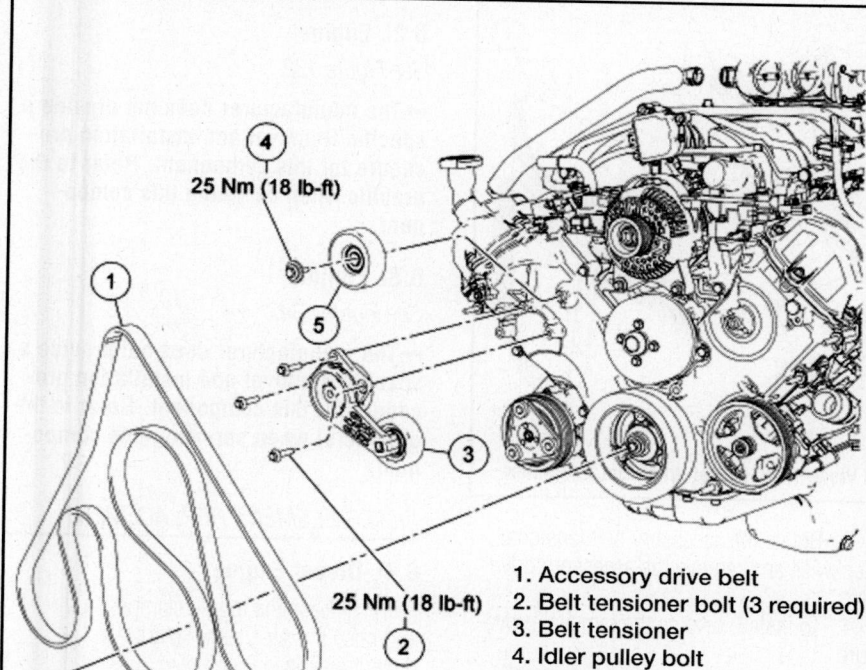

25 Nm (18 lb-ft)

25 Nm (18 lb-ft)

1. Accessory drive belt
2. Belt tensioner bolt (3 required)
3. Belt tensioner
4. Idler pulley bolt
5. Idler pulley

N0010006

Fig. 122 Front End Accessory Drive (FEAD) Exploded View—5.4L (3V) engine

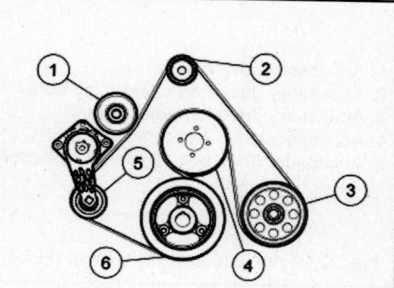

1. Accessory drive belt idler pulley
2. Alternator pulley
3. Power steering pump pulley
4. Coolant pump pulley
5. Accessory drive belt tensioner pulley
6. Crankshaft pulley

N0113270

Fig. 125 Front End Accessory Drive (FEAD) Exploded View—6.8L (3V) engine without A/C

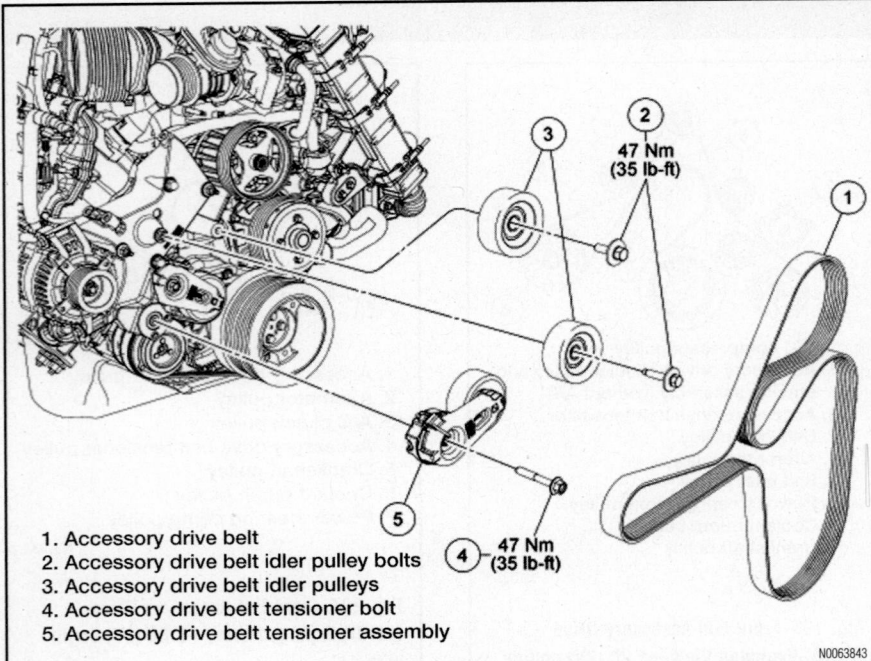

1. Accessory drive belt
2. Accessory drive belt idler pulley bolts
3. Accessory drive belt idler pulleys
4. Accessory drive belt tensioner bolt
5. Accessory drive belt tensioner assembly

N0063843

Fig. 126 Front End Accessory Drive (FEAD) Exploded View—6.4L Diesel With Single Alternator

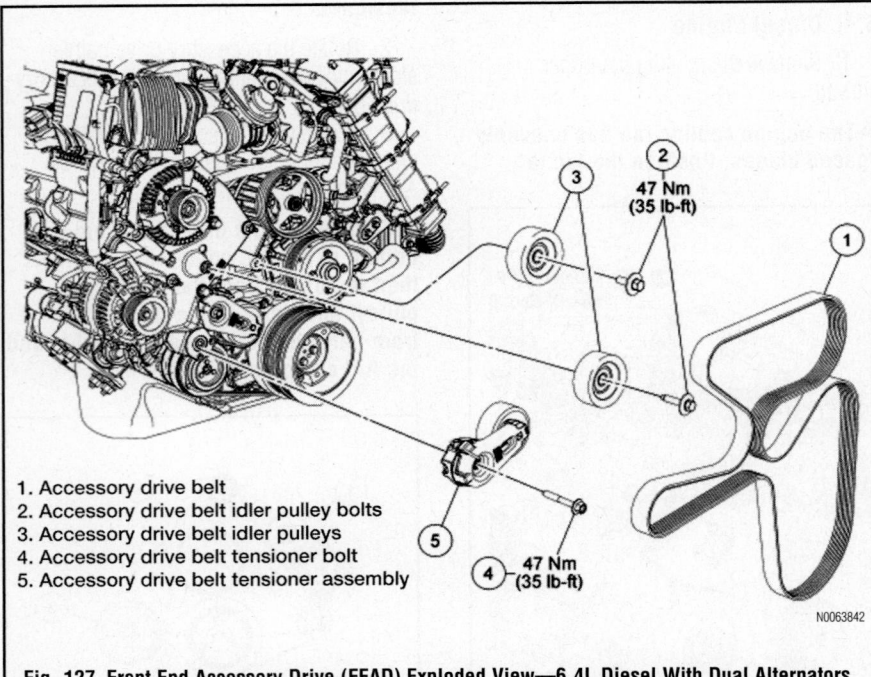

1. Accessory drive belt
2. Accessory drive belt idler pulley bolts
3. Accessory drive belt idler pulleys
4. Accessory drive belt tensioner bolt
5. Accessory drive belt tensioner assembly

N0063842

Fig. 127 Front End Accessory Drive (FEAD) Exploded View—6.4L Diesel With Dual Alternators

4. To install, reverse the removal procedure.

6.7L Diesel Engine

1. Remove the Air Cleaner (ACL) outlet pipe.
2. Disconnect the cooling fan clutch electrical connector and remove the bracket bolt.

3. Rotate the accessory belt tensioner clockwise and remove the accessory drive belt.
4. To install, reverse the removal procedure.

Gasoline Engines

1. Rotate the drive belt tensioner clockwise and remove the accessory drive belt.

2. To install, reverse the removal procedure.

AIR CLEANER

REMOVAL & INSTALLATION

6.4L Diesel Engine

1. Disconnect the restriction gauge and Mass Air Flow (MAF) sensor electrical connectors.
2. Loosen the clamp and disconnect the Air Cleaner (ACL) outlet pipe from the ACL .
3. Disconnect the secondary air intake hose from the ACL outlet housing.
4. Pull up on the ACL to remove it from the ACL support bracket.
5. To install, reverse the removal procedure.

6.7L Diesel Engine

See Figure 131.

➡The manufacturer does not provide a specific Removal and Installation procedure for this component. Refer to the graphic(s) when servicing this component.

5.4L Engine

The Air Cleaner (ACL) housing is an integral part of the degas bottle and cannot be serviced separately. Refer to the Engine Cooling section.

6.2L Engine

See Figure 132.

➡The manufacturer does not provide a specific Removal and Installation procedure for this component. Refer to the graphic when servicing this component.

6.8L Engine

See Figure 134.

➡The manufacturer does not provide a specific Removal and Installation procedure for this component. Refer to the graphic(s) when servicing this component.

FILTER/ELEMENT REPLACEMENT

6.4L Diesel Engine

1. Release the toggle clamps and raise the Air Cleaner (ACL) outlet housing.
2. Disconnect the secondary air intake hose from the ACL outlet housing and set the housing aside.

Fig. 128 A/C Compressor Drive Components—6.4L Diesel showing A/C compressor drive belt (1), A/C drive belt tensioner bolt (2), and A/C drive belt tensioner (3)

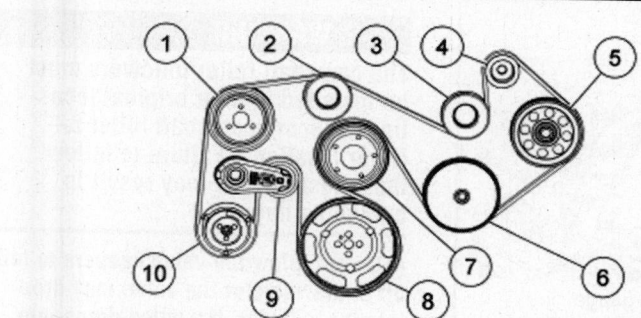

1. Water pump pulley
2. Accessory drive belt idler pulley
3. Accessory drive belt idler pulley
4. Alternator pulley
5. Power steering pump pulley
6. Coolant pump pulley
7. Cooling fan drive assembly
8. Crankshaft pulley
9. Accessory drive belt tensioner
10. A/C clutch pulley
10. Accessory drive belt idler pulley and bracket assembly (without A/C)

Fig. 129 Front End Accessory Drive (FEAD) Exploded View—6.7L Diesel With Single Alternator

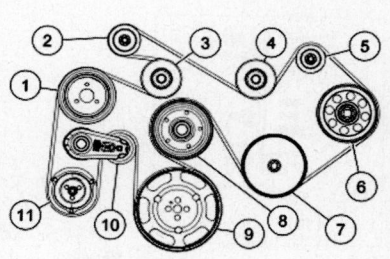

1. Water pump pulley
2. Alternator pulley
3. Accessory drive belt idler pulley
4. Accessory drive belt idler pulley
5. Alternator pulley
6. Power steering pump pulley
7. Coolant pump pulley
8. Cooling fan drive assembly
9. Crankshaft pulley
10. Accessory drive belt tensioner
11. A/C clutch pulley
11. Accessory drive belt idler pulley and bracket assembly (without A/C)

Fig. 130 Front End Accessory Drive (FEAD) Exploded View—6.7L Diesel With Dual Alternators

6. To install, reverse the removal procedure.

CAMSHAFT AND VALVE LIFTERS

REMOVAL & INSTALLATION

5.4L Engine

Left Side

See Figures 135 through 146.

✳✳ WARNING

The camshaft procedure must be followed exactly or damage to the valves and pistons will result.

1. Position the crankshaft damper spoke at the 12 o'clock position and the timing mark indentation at the 1 o'clock position.
2. Remove the LH valve cover.

✳✳ WARNING

Damage to the camshaft phaser and sprocket assembly will occur if mishandled or used as a lifting or leveraging device.

✳✳ WARNING

Only use hand tools to remove the camshaft phaser and sprocket assembly or damage may occur to the camshaft or camshaft phaser and sprocket.

✳✳ WARNING

Do not use a tool to pry the element from the Air Cleaner (ACL) housing. Failure to follow this instruction may result in ACL and engine damage.

3. Pull outboard on the top edge of the ACL element and remove the element.
4. Discard the ACL element.

To install:

➡Make sure the element is positioned inboard of the stop feature in the ACL housing.

5. Position a new ACL element into the air cleaner housing.
6. Push the element down and inboard to compress the seal into the ACL housing.

7. Connect the secondary air intake hose to the ACL outlet housing and position the cover on the ACL housing.
8. Secure the 2 toggle clamps.

Gasoline Engines

1. Disconnect the Air Cleaner (ACL) outlet pipe from the ACL cover.
2. Disconnect the Mass Air Flow (MAF) sensor electrical connector.
3. Release the retaining clips and position the ACL cover aside.
4. If servicing the ACL cover, remove the 2 bolts and the MAF sensor.
5. Remove the ACL element.

✳✳ WARNING

The Air Cleaner (ACL) element must be fully seated into the ACL housing. Failure to do so will result in unusual engine noise.

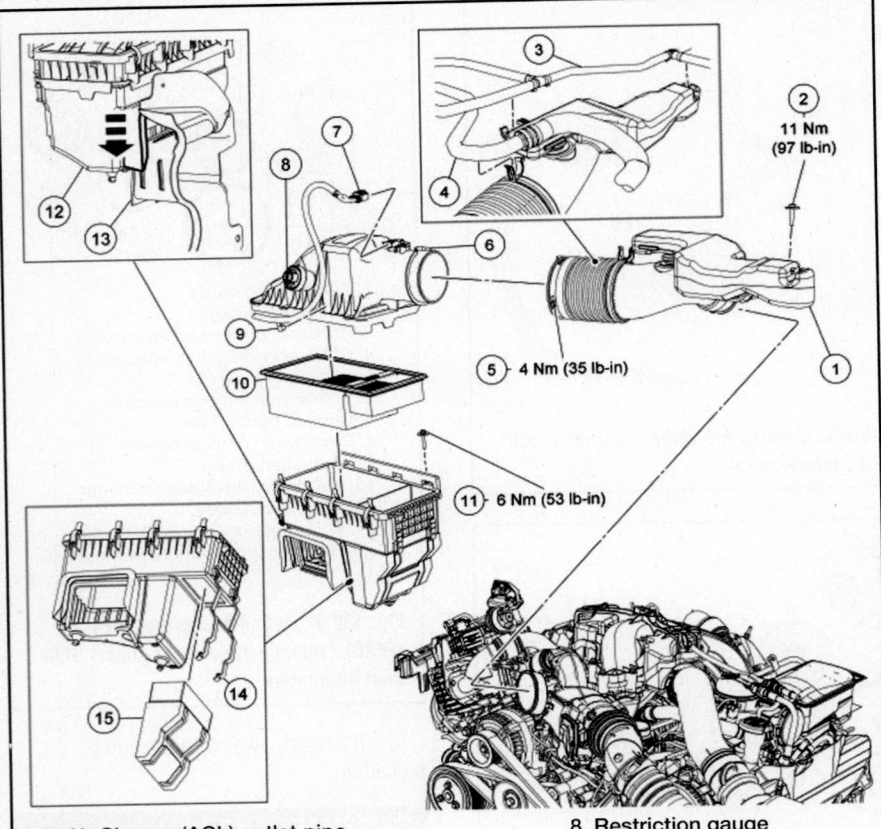

1. Air Cleaner (ACL) outlet pipe
2. ACL outlet pipe bolt
3. Degas bottle coolant hose
4. EGR cooler hose
5. Air Cleaner (ACL) outlet pipe clamp (2 required)
6. ACL cover
7. Mass Air Flow (MAF) sensor electrical connector
8. Restriction gauge
9. Wiring harness retainer
10. ACL element
11. ACL housing bolt
12. ACL housing
13. ACL inlet pipe
14. ACL filter element retainer
15. ACL filter element (foam)

N0116258

Fig. 131 Exploded view of the intake air system components

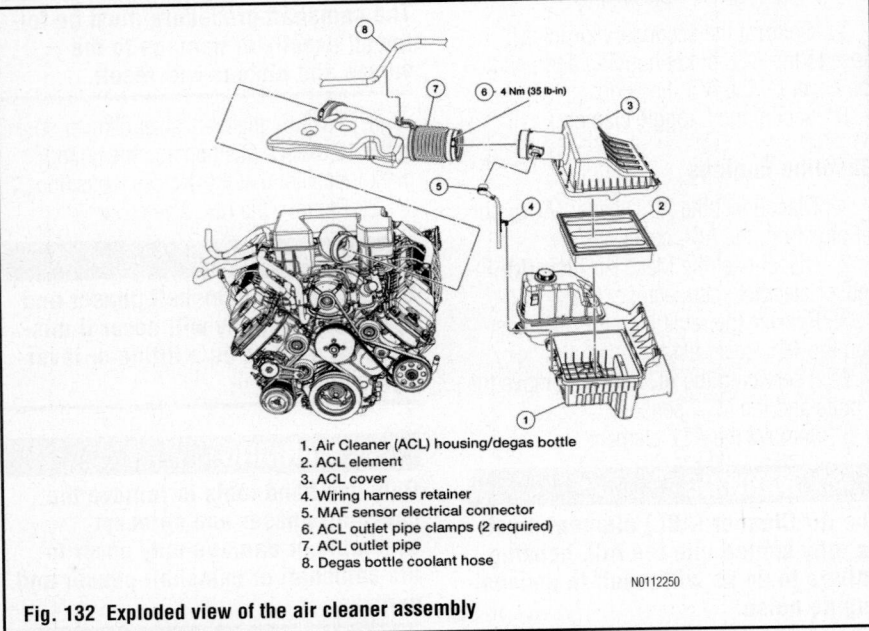

1. Air Cleaner (ACL) housing/degas bottle
2. ACL element
3. ACL cover
4. Wiring harness retainer
5. MAF sensor electrical connector
6. ACL outlet pipe clamps (2 required)
7. ACL outlet pipe
8. Degas bottle coolant hose

N0112250

Fig. 132 Exploded view of the air cleaner assembly

3. Loosen and back off the LH camshaft phaser and sprocket bolt one full turn.

4. Disconnect the LH Camshaft Position (CMP) sensor electrical connector.

5. Remove the bolt and the LH CMP sensor.

➡**If the camshaft lobes are not exactly positioned as shown, the crankshaft keyway will require one full additional rotation to 12 o'clock.**

6. The No. 5 cylinder camshaft lobe must be coming up on the exhaust stroke. Verify by noting the position of the 2 intake camshaft lobes and the exhaust lobe on the No. 5 cylinder.

7. Remove only the 3 camshaft roller followers shown.

✳✳ WARNING

The camshaft roller followers must be installed in their original locations. Record camshaft roller follower locations. Failure to follow these instructions may result in engine damage.

➡**Do not allow the valve keepers to fall off of the valve or the valve may drop into the cylinder. If a valve drops into the cylinder, the cylinder head must be removed.**

➡**It may be necessary to push the valve down while compressing the spring.**

8. Using the Valve Spring Compressor (303-1039), remove only the 3 designated camshaft roller followers from the previous step.

✳✳ WARNING

The crankshaft cannot be moved past the 6 o'clock position once set or engine damage may occur.

9. Rotate the crankshaft clockwise, as viewed from the front, positioning the crankshaft damper spoke at the 6 o'clock position and the timing mark indentation at the 7 o'clock position.

✳✳ WARNING

Engine is not freewheeling. Camshaft procedure must be followed exactly or damage to valves and pistons will result.

➡**The Timing Chain Locking Tool must be installed square to the timing chain and the engine block.**

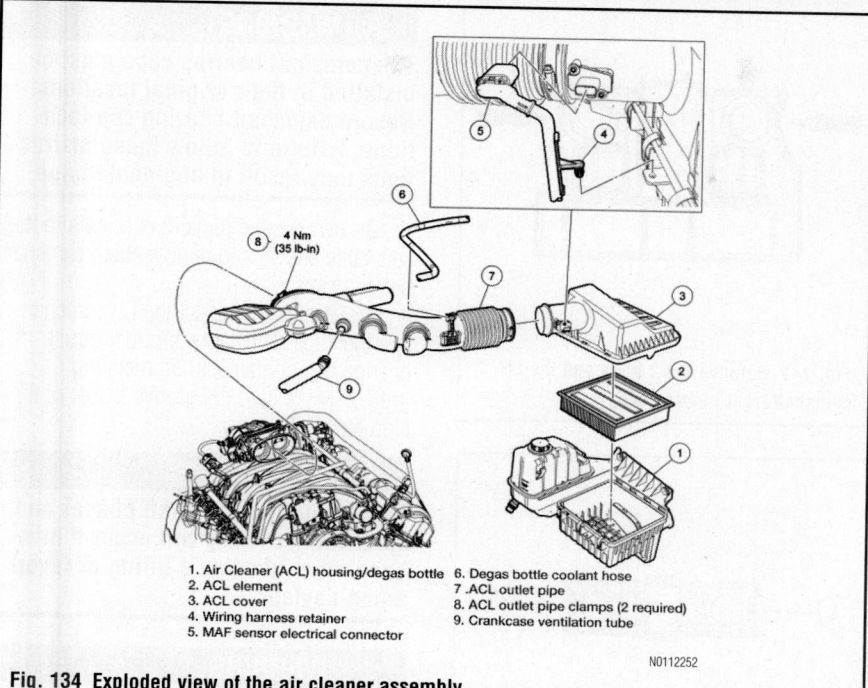

1. Air Cleaner (ACL) housing/degas bottle
2. ACL element
3. ACL cover
4. Wiring harness retainer
5. MAF sensor electrical connector
6. Degas bottle coolant hose
7. ACL outlet pipe
8. ACL outlet pipe clamps (2 required)
9. Crankcase ventilation tube

N0112252

Fig. 134 Exploded view of the air cleaner assembly

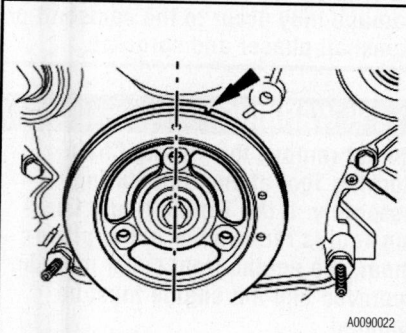

A0090022

Fig. 135 Position the crankshaft damper spoke at the 12 o'clock position and the timing mark indentation at the 1 o'clock position

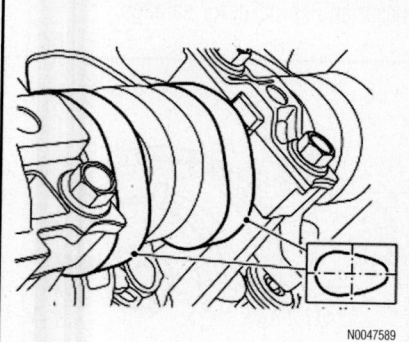

N0047589

Fig. 136 Verify by noting the position of the 2 intake camshaft lobes and the exhaust lobe on the No. 5 cylinder

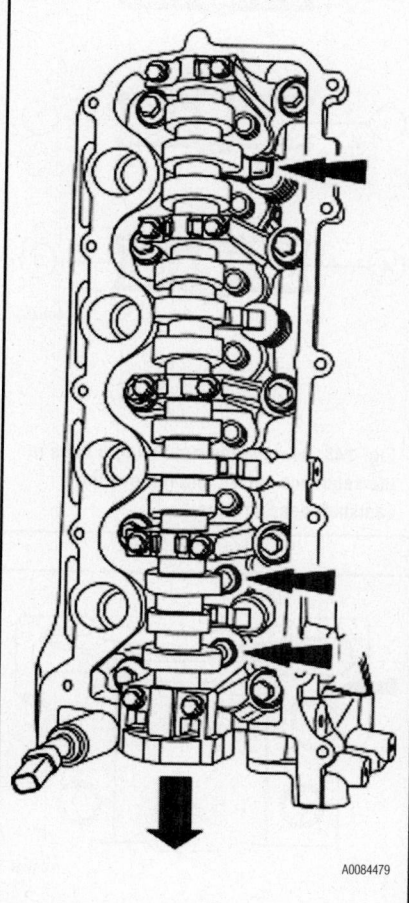

A0084479

Fig. 137 Remove only the 3 camshaft roller followers shown

➡ Engine front cover removed for clarity.

10. Install the Timing Chain Locking Tool (303-1175) in the LH timing chain as shown.

✳✳ WARNING

Do not remove the Timing Chain Locking Tool at any time during assembly. If the Timing Chain Locking Tool is removed or out of placement, the engine front cover must be removed and the engine must be retimed.

303-1039

N0010191

Fig. 138 Using the Valve Spring Compressor, remove only the 3 designated camshaft roller followers from the previous step

A0090300

Fig. 139 Rotate the crankshaft clockwise, as viewed from the front, positioning the crankshaft damper spoke at the 6 o'clock position and the timing mark indentation at the 7 o'clock position

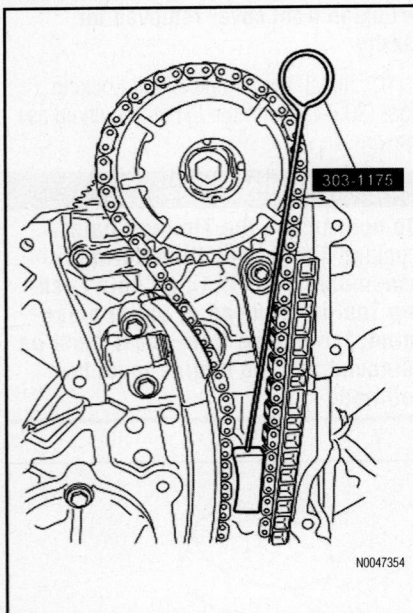

Fig. 140 Install the Timing Chain Locking Tool in the LH timing chain as shown

❋❋ WARNING

The timing chain must be installed in its original position onto the camshaft phaser and sprocket using the scribed marks, or damage to valves and pistons will result.

11. Scribe a location mark on the timing chain and the camshaft phaser and sprocket assembly.

❋❋ WARNING

Remove the front thrust camshaft bearing cap straight upward from the bearing towers or the bearing cap may be damaged from side loading.

12. Remove the 2 bolts and the LH camshaft front bearing cap.

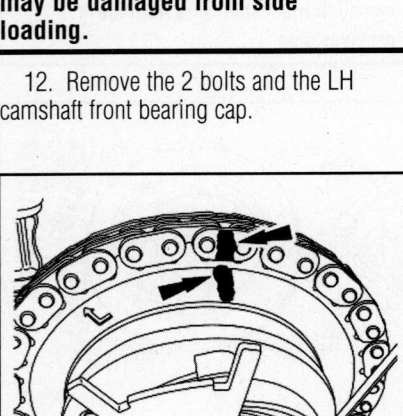

Fig. 141 Scribe a location mark on the timing chain and the camshaft phaser and sprocket assembly

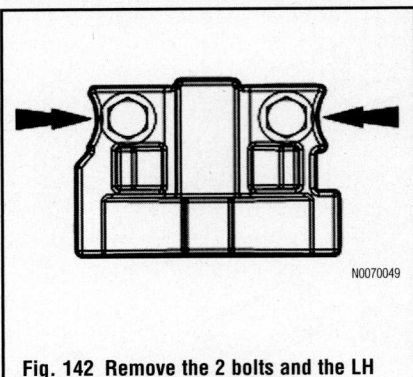

Fig. 142 Remove the 2 bolts and the LH camshaft front bearing cap

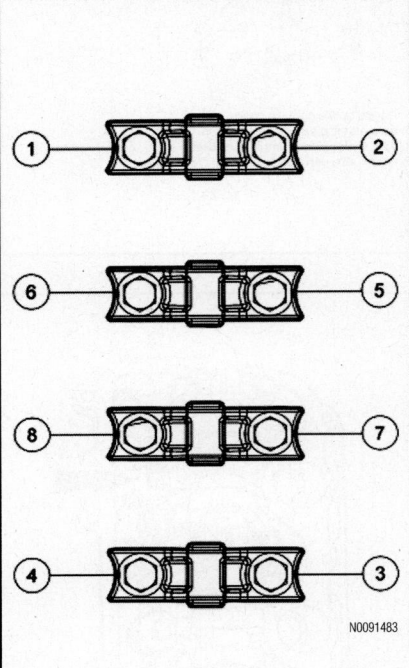

Fig. 143 Remove the remaining 8 bolts in the sequence shown and remove the 4 camshaft bearing caps

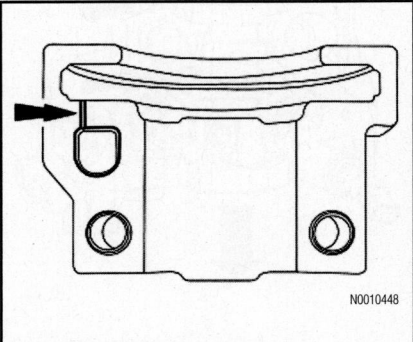

Fig. 144 Make sure the groove is free of foreign material

❋❋ WARNING

The camshaft bearing caps must be installed in their original locations. Record camshaft bearing cap locations. Failure to follow these instructions may result in engine damage.

13. Remove the remaining 8 bolts in the sequence shown and remove the 4 camshaft bearing caps.

14. Clean and inspect the LH camshaft bearing caps. The camshaft front thrust bearing cap contains an oil metering groove. Make sure the groove is free of foreign material.

❋❋ WARNING

Damage to the camshaft phaser and sprocket assembly will occur if mishandled or used as a lifting or leveraging device.

❋❋ WARNING

Only use hand tools to remove the camshaft phaser and sprocket bolt or damage may occur to the camshaft or camshaft phaser and sprocket.

❋❋ WARNING

Do not remove the Timing Chain Locking Tool at any time during assembly. If the Timing Chain Locking Tool is removed or out of placement, the engine front cover must be removed and the engine must be retimed.

15. Remove the bolt and the camshaft phaser and sprocket assembly from the camshaft.

16. Discard the bolt and washer.

17. Remove the camshaft.

18. Remove and inspect the camshaft phaser and sprocket for damage.

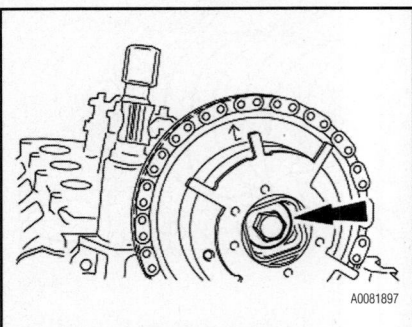

Fig. 145 Remove the bolt and the camshaft phaser and sprocket assembly from the camshaft

To install:

➡️ Do not allow the camshaft roller followers to move out of position when installing the camshaft.

19. Lubricate the camshaft and camshaft journals with clean engine oil and install the camshaft.

✳️✳️ WARNING

Do not remove the Timing Chain Locking Tool at any time during assembly. If the Timing Chain Locking Tool is removed or out of placement, the engine front cover must be removed and the engine must be retimed.

✳️✳️ WARNING

The timing chain must be installed in its original position onto the camshaft phaser and sprocket using the scribed marks, or damage to valves and pistons will result.

➡️ If replacement of the camshaft phaser and sprocket is necessary, transfer the scribe mark to the new camshaft phaser and sprocket.

20. Position the camshaft phaser and sprocket into the timing chain with the timing chain scribe marks in alignment.

✳️✳️ WARNING

Do not remove the Timing Chain Locking Tool at any time during assembly. If the Timing Chain Locking Tool is removed or out of placement, the engine front cover must be removed and the engine must be retimed.

✳️✳️ WARNING

Damage to the camshaft phaser and sprocket assembly will occur if mishandled or used as a lifting or leveraging device.

✳️✳️ WARNING

Only use hand tools to install the camshaft phaser and sprocket bolt or damage may occur to the camshaft or camshaft phaser and sprocket.

21. Install the camshaft phaser and sprocket assembly onto the camshaft and install a new camshaft phaser and sprocket bolt finger-tight.

➡️ Do not allow the camshaft roller followers to move out of position when installing the camshaft.

22. Install the 5 camshaft bearing caps in their original locations.
   a. Lubricate the camshaft bearing caps with clean engine oil.
   b. Position the 2 front camshaft bearing cap.
   c. Position the remaining 8 camshaft bearing caps.
   d. Install the 10 bolts loosely.
   e. Tighten the bolts in the sequence shown. Tighten to 89 inch lbs. (10 Nm).

➡️ Engine front cover removed for clarity.

23. Remove the Timing Chain Locking Tool.

24. Rotate the crankshaft a half turn counterclockwise and position the crankshaft damper spoke at the 12 o'clock position and the timing mark indentation at the 1 o'clock position.

25. Verify correct camshaft position by noting the position of the No. 5 cylinder intake and exhaust camshaft lobes.

➡️ Do not allow the valve keepers to fall off of the valve or the valve may drop into the cylinder. If a valve drops into the cylinder, the cylinder head must be removed.

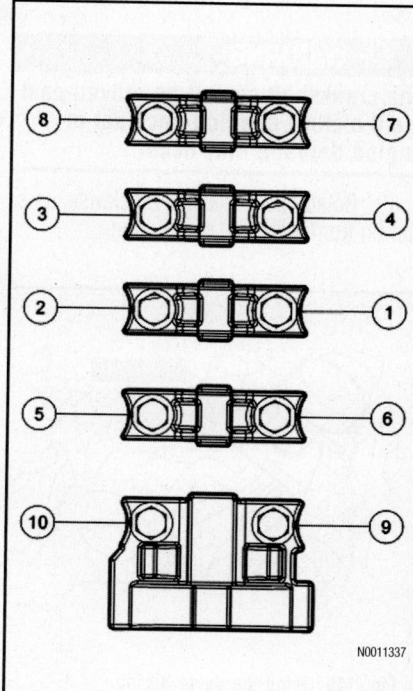

N0011337

Fig. 146 Tighten the bolts in the sequence shown

➡️ It may be necessary to push the valve down while compressing the spring.

26. Using the Valve Spring Compressor, install the 3 originally removed camshaft roller followers.

27. Install the CMP sensor and the bolt. Tighten to 89 inch lbs. (10 Nm).

28. Connect the CMP electrical connector.

✳️✳️ WARNING

Only use hand tools to install the camshaft phaser and sprocket assembly or damage may occur to the camshaft or camshaft phaser and sprocket.

✳️✳️ WARNING

Damage to the camshaft phaser and sprocket assembly will occur if mishandled or used as a lifting or leveraging device.

29. Tighten the camshaft phaser and sprocket bolt in 2 stages:
   a. Stage 1: Tighten to 30 ft. lbs. (40 Nm).
   b. Stage 2: Tighten an additional 90 degrees.

30. Install the LH valve cover.

Right Side

See Figures 135, 142 through 144, 146 through 153.

✳️✳️ WARNING

The camshaft procedure must be followed exactly or damage to the valves and pistons will result.

1. Position the crankshaft damper spoke at the 12 o'clock position and the timing mark indentation at the 1 o'clock position.

2. Remove the RH valve cover.

✳️✳️ WARNING

Damage to the camshaft phaser and sprocket assembly will occur if mishandled or used as a lifting or leveraging device.

✳️✳️ WARNING

Only use hand tools to remove the camshaft phaser and sprocket assembly or damage may occur to the camshaft or camshaft phaser and sprocket.

3. Loosen and back off the RH camshaft phaser and sprocket bolt one full turn.

4. Disconnect the RH Camshaft Position (CMP) sensor electrical connector.

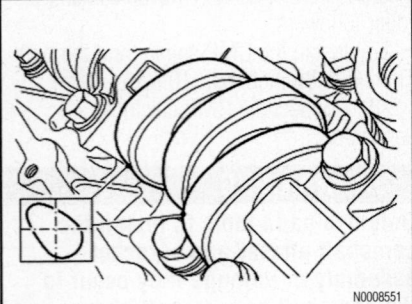

Fig. 147 Verify by noting the position of the 2 intake camshaft lobes and the exhaust lobe on the No. 1 cylinder

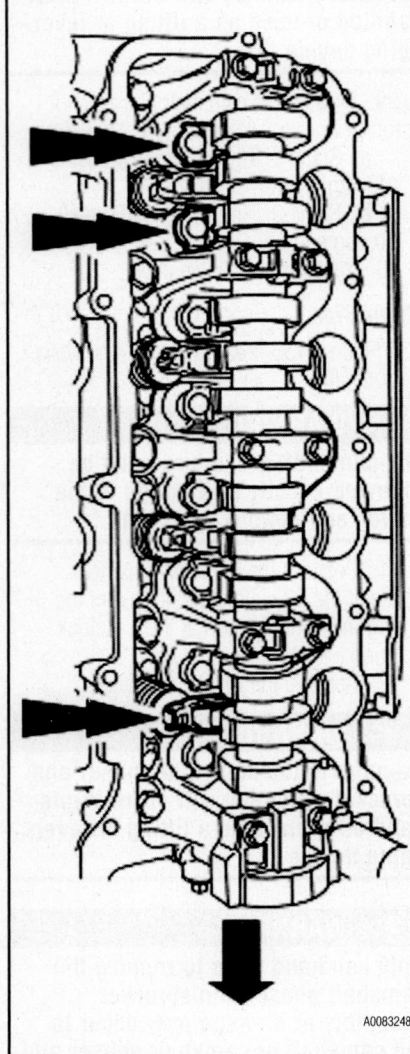

Fig. 148 Remove only the 3 camshaft roller followers shown

5. Remove the bolt and the RH CMP sensor.

➡ **If the camshaft lobes are not exactly positioned, the crankshaft will require one full additional rotation to 12 o'clock.**

6. The No. 1 cylinder camshaft exhaust lobe must be coming up on the exhaust stroke. Verify by noting the position of the 2 intake camshaft lobes and the exhaust lobe on the No. 1 cylinder.

7. Remove only the 3 camshaft roller followers shown.

❋❋ WARNING

The camshaft roller followers must be installed in their original locations. Record camshaft roller follower locations. Failure to follow these instructions may result in engine damage.

➡ **Do not allow the valve keepers to fall off of the valve or the valve may drop into the cylinder. If a valve drops into the cylinder, the cylinder head must be removed.**

➡ **It may be necessary to push the valve down while compressing the spring.**

8. Using the Valve Spring Compressor (303-1039), remove only the 3 designated camshaft roller followers from the previous step.

❋❋ WARNING

The crankshaft cannot be moved past the 6 o'clock position once set or engine damage may occur.

9. Rotate the crankshaft clockwise, as viewed from the front, positioning

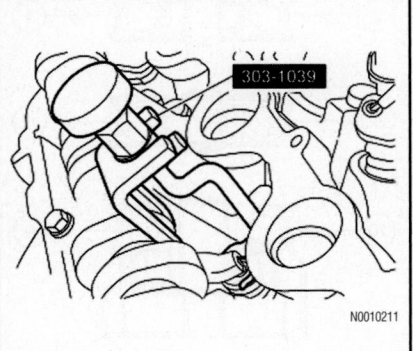

Fig. 149 Using the Valve Spring Compressor, remove only the 3 designated camshaft roller followers from the previous step

the crankshaft damper spoke at the 6 o'clock position and the timing mark indentation at the 7 o'clock position.

❋❋ WARNING

Engine is not freewheeling. Camshaft procedure must be followed exactly or damage to valves and pistons will result.

➡ **The Timing Chain Locking Tool must be installed square to the timing chain and the engine block.**

➡ **Engine front cover removed for clarity.**

10. Install the Timing Chain Locking Tool (303-1175) in the RH timing chain as shown.

❋❋ WARNING

Do not remove the Timing Chain Locking Tool at any time during assembly. If the Timing Chain Locking Tool is removed or out of placement, the engine front cover must be removed and the engine must be retimed.

❋❋ WARNING

The timing chain must be installed in its original position onto the camshaft phaser and sprocket using the scribed marks, or damage to valves and pistons will result.

11. Scribe a location mark on the timing chain and the camshaft phaser and sprocket assembly.

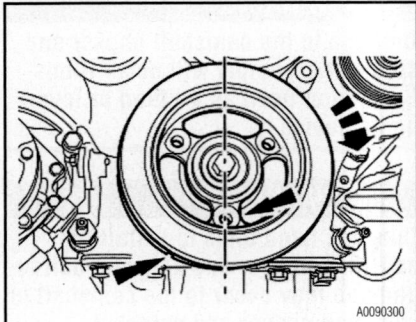

Fig. 150 Rotate the crankshaft clockwise, as viewed from the front, positioning the crankshaft damper spoke at the 6 o'clock position and the timing mark indentation at the 7 o'clock position

⁂ WARNING

Remove the front thrust camshaft bearing cap straight upward from the bearing towers or the bearing cap may be damaged from side loading.

12. Remove the 2 bolts and the front camshaft bearing cap.

⁂ WARNING

The camshaft bearing caps must be installed in their original locations. Record camshaft bearing cap locations. Failure to follow these instructions may result in engine damage.

13. Remove the remaining bolts in the sequence shown and remove the remaining camshaft bearing caps.
14. Clean and inspect the RH camshaft bearing caps. The camshaft front thrust bearing cap contains an oil metering groove. Make sure the groove is free of foreign material.

⁂ WARNING

Damage to the camshaft phaser and sprocket assembly will occur if mishandled or used as a lifting or leveraging device.

⁂ WARNING

Only use hand tools to remove the camshaft phaser and sprocket bolt or damage may occur to the camshaft or camshaft phaser and sprocket.

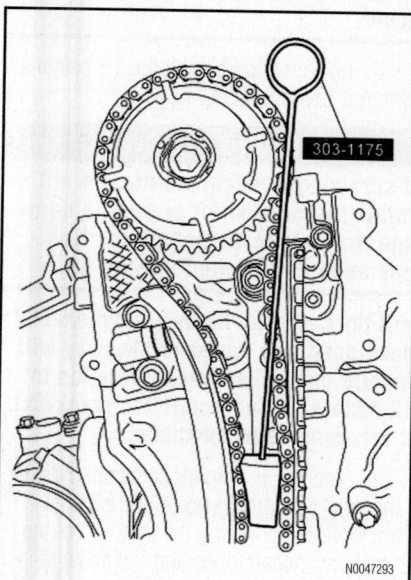

Fig. 151 Install the Timing Chain Locking Tool in the RH timing chain as shown

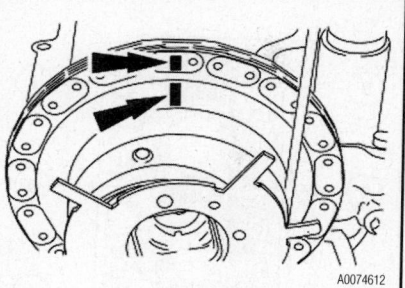

Fig. 152 Scribe a location mark on the timing chain and the camshaft phaser and sprocket assembly

⁂ WARNING

Do not remove the Timing Chain Locking Tool at any time during assembly. If the Timing Chain Locking Tool is removed or out of placement, the engine front cover must be removed and the engine must be retimed.

15. Remove the bolt and the camshaft phaser and sprocket assembly from the camshaft.
16. Discard the bolt and washer.
17. Remove the camshaft.
18. Remove and inspect the camshaft phaser and sprocket for damage.

To install:

➡ Do not allow the camshaft roller followers to move out of position when installing the camshaft.

19. Lubricate the camshaft and camshaft journals with clean engine oil and install the camshaft.

⁂ WARNING

Do not remove the Timing Chain Locking Tool at any time during

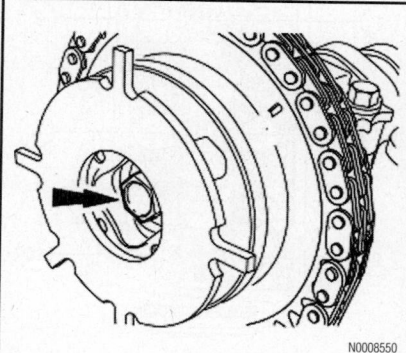

Fig. 153 Remove the bolt and the camshaft phaser and sprocket assembly from the camshaft

assembly. If the Timing Chain Locking Tool is removed or out of placement, the engine front cover must be removed and the engine must be retimed.

⁂ WARNING

The timing chain must be installed in its original position onto the camshaft phaser and sprocket using the scribed marks, or damage to valves and pistons will result.

➡ If replacement of the camshaft phaser and sprocket is necessary, transfer the scribe mark to the new camshaft phaser and sprocket.

20. Position the camshaft phaser and sprocket into the timing chain with the timing chain scribe marks in alignment.

⁂ WARNING

Do not remove the Timing Chain Locking Tool at any time during assembly. If the Timing Chain Locking Tool is removed or out of placement, the engine front cover must be removed and the engine must be retimed.

⁂ WARNING

Damage to the camshaft phaser and sprocket assembly will occur if mishandled or used as a lifting or leveraging device.

⁂ WARNING

Only use hand tools to install the camshaft phaser and sprocket bolt or damage may occur to the camshaft or camshaft phaser and sprocket.

21. Install the camshaft phaser and sprocket assembly onto the camshaft and install a new camshaft phaser and sprocket bolt finger-tight.

➡ Do not allow the camshaft roller followers to move out of position when installing the camshaft.

22. Install the 5 camshaft bearing caps in their original locations.
   a. Lubricate the camshaft bearing caps with clean engine oil.
   b. Position the front camshaft bearing cap.
   c. Position the remaining camshaft bearing caps.
   d. Install the 10 bolts loosely.

e. Tighten the 10 bolts in the sequence shown. Tighten to 89 inch lbs. (10 Nm).

➡**Engine front cover removed for clarity.**

23. Remove the Timing Chain Locking Tool.

24. Rotate the crankshaft a half turn counterclockwise and position the crankshaft damper spoke at the 12 o'clock position and the timing mark indentation at the 1 o'clock position.

25. Verify correct camshaft position by noting the position of the No. 1 cylinder intake and exhaust camshaft lobes.

➡**Do not allow the valve keepers to fall off of the valve or the valve may drop into the cylinder. If a valve drops into the cylinder, the cylinder head must be removed.**

➡**It may be necessary to push the valve down while compressing the spring.**

26. Using the Valve Spring Compressor, install the 3 originally removed camshaft roller followers.

27. Install the CMP sensor and the bolt. Tighten to 89 inch lbs. (10 Nm).

28. Connect the CMP electrical connector.

※※ **WARNING**

Only use hand tools to install the camshaft phaser and sprocket assembly or damage may occur to the camshaft or camshaft phaser and sprocket.

※※ **WARNING**

Damage to the camshaft phaser and sprocket assembly will occur if mishandled or used as a lifting or leveraging device.

29. Tighten the new camshaft phaser and sprocket bolt in 2 stages:
   a. Stage 1: Tighten to 30 ft. lbs. (40 Nm).
   b. Stage 2: Tighten an additional 90 degrees.

30. Install the RH valve cover.

6.2L Engine

See Figures 154 and 155.

➡**The manufacturer does not provide a specific Removal and Installation procedure for this component. Refer to the graphic(s) when servicing this component.**

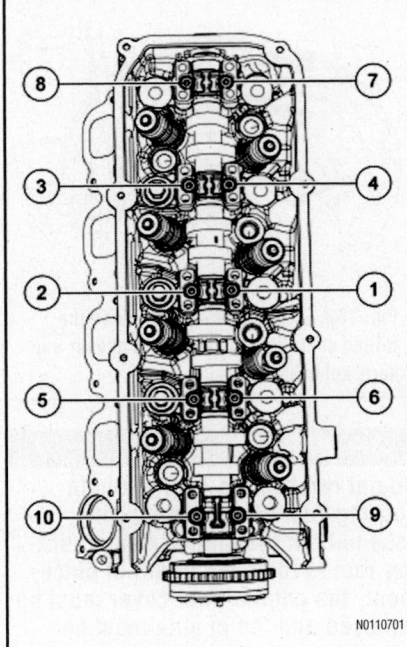

N0110701

Fig. 154 Left camshaft tightening sequence

※※ **WARNING**

The camshaft bearing caps must be installed in their original locations. Record camshaft bearing cap locations. Failure to follow these instructions may result in engine damage.

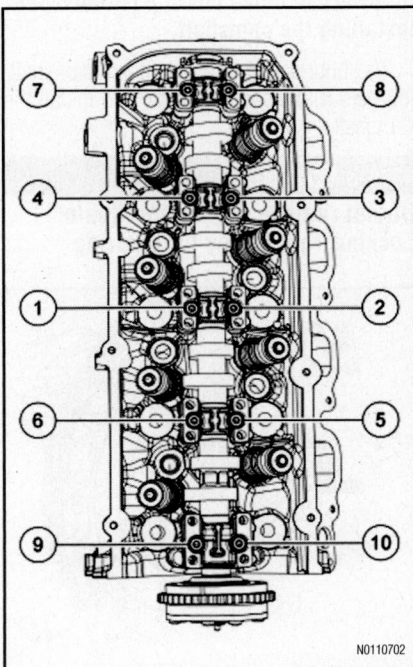

N0110702

Fig. 155 Right camshaft tightening sequence

1. Position the 5 camshaft bearing caps in their original locations and install the 10 bolts in the sequence shown, in 2 stages.
   a. Stage 1: Tighten to 53 inch lbs. (6 Nm).
   b. Stage 2: Tighten an additional 45 degrees.

6.8L Engine

Left Side

See Figures 135, 156 through 170.

※※ **WARNING**

The camshaft procedure must be followed exactly or damage to the valves and pistons will result.

1. Position the crankshaft damper spoke at the 12 o'clock position and the timing mark indentation at the 1 o'clock position.

2. Remove the LH valve cover.

※※ **WARNING**

The balance shaft bearing caps must be installed in their original locations or engine damage may occur. Record camshaft bearing cap locations.

3. Using the sequence shown, remove the 6 bolts, then the 3 balance shaft bearing caps and the balance shaft.

※※ **WARNING**

Only use hand tools to loosen the sprocket bolt or damage to the camshaft or camshaft sprocket may occur.

4. Loosen and back off the LH camshaft sprocket bolt one full turn.

※※ **WARNING**

If servicing both camshafts, do not rotate the crankshaft or engine damage may occur. Camshaft position has been established in Step 8.

➡**If the camshaft lobes are not exactly positioned, the crankshaft keyway will require one full additional rotation to 12 o'clock. Do not rotate the crankshaft if servicing both camshafts.**

5. The No. 6 cylinder camshaft exhaust lobe must be coming up on the exhaust stroke. Verify by noting the position of the 2 intake camshaft lobes and the exhaust lobe on the No. 6 cylinder.

6. Remove only the 4 camshaft roller followers shown.

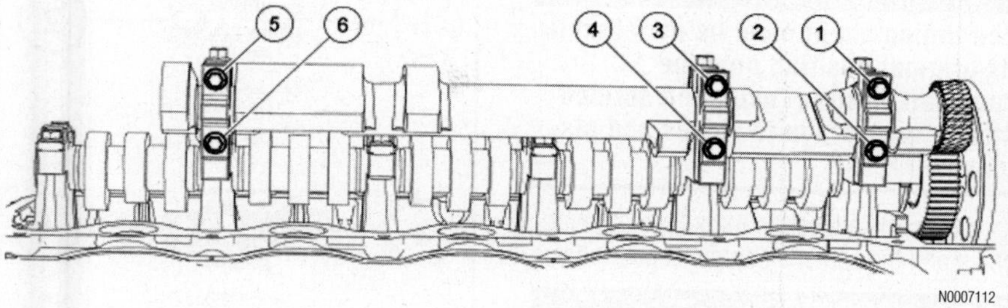

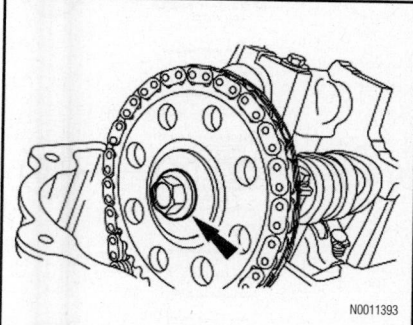

Fig. 156 Using the sequence shown, remove the 6 bolts, then the 3 balance shaft bearing caps and the balance shaft

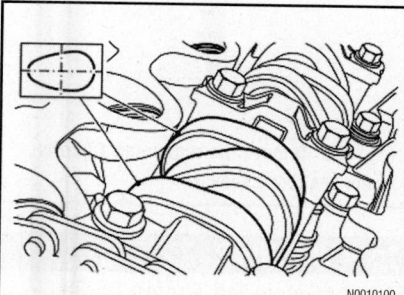

Fig. 157 Loosen and back off the LH camshaft sprocket bolt one full turn

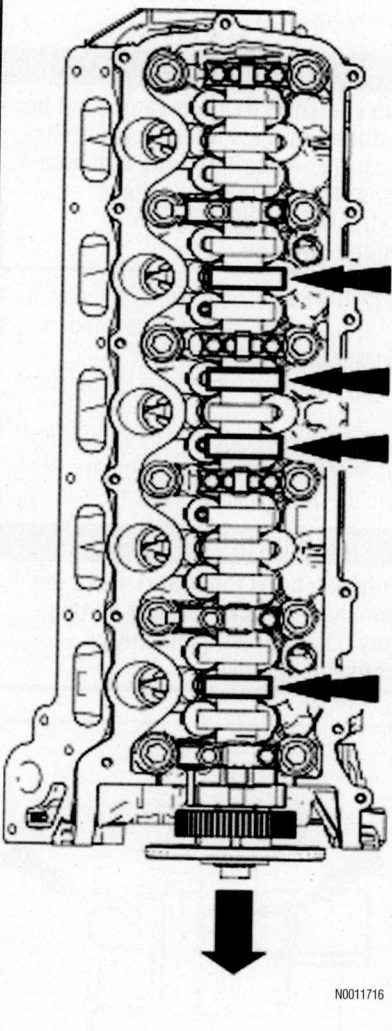

Fig. 158 The No. 6 cylinder camshaft exhaust lobe must be coming up on the exhaust stroke

✳✳ WARNING

The camshaft roller followers must be installed in their original locations or engine damage may occur. Record camshaft roller follower locations.

➡️Do not allow the valve keepers to fall off the valve or the valve may drop into the cylinder. If a valve drops into the cylinder, the cylinder head must be removed.

➡️It may be necessary to push the valve down while compressing the spring.

Fig. 159 Remove only the 4 camshaft roller followers shown

7. Using the Valve Spring Compressor (303-1039), remove only the 4 camshaft roller followers designated in the previous step.

Fig. 160 Using the Valve Spring Compressor, remove only the 4 camshaft roller followers designated

✳✳ WARNING

The crankshaft cannot be moved past the 6 o'clock position once set. Failure to follow this instruction may result in engine damage.

8. Rotate the crankshaft clockwise, as viewed from the front, positioning the crankshaft damper spoke at the 6 o'clock position and the timing mark indentation at the 7 o'clock position.

✳✳ WARNING

Engine is not freewheeling. Camshaft procedure must be followed exactly or damage to valves and pistons will result.

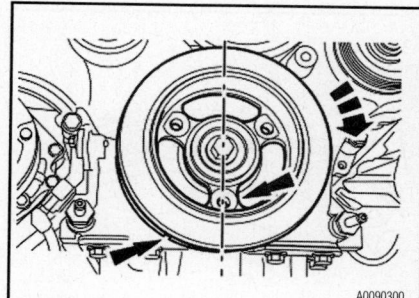

Fig. 161 Rotate the crankshaft clockwise, as viewed from the front, positioning the crankshaft damper spoke at the 6 o'clock position and the timing mark indentation at the 7 o'clock position

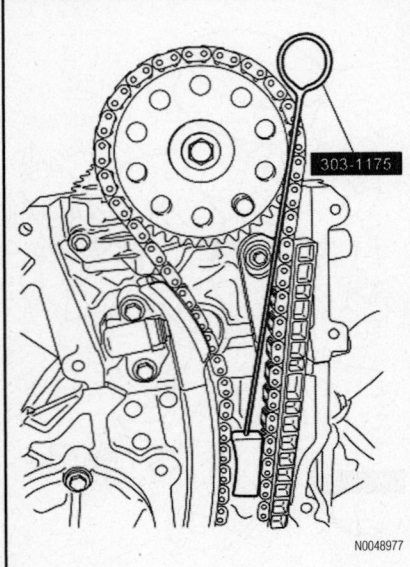

Fig. 162 Install the Timing Chain Locking Tool in the LH timing chain as shown

✳✳ WARNING

The Timing Chain Locking Tool must be installed square to the timing chain and the engine block or engine damage may occur.

➡ Front cover removed for clarity.

9. Install the Timing Chain Locking Tool in the LH timing chain as shown.

✳✳ WARNING

Do not remove the Timing Chain Locking Tool at any time during assembly. If the Timing Chain Locking Tool is removed or out of placement, the engine front cover must be removed and the engine must be retimed.

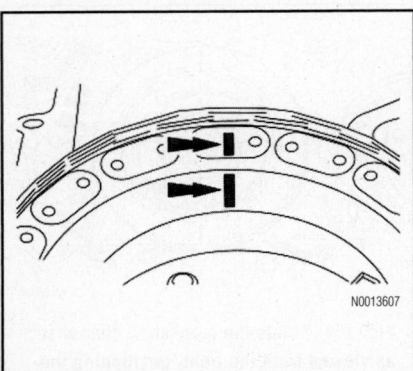

Fig. 163 Scribe a location mark on the timing chain and the camshaft sprocket assembly

✳✳ WARNING

The timing chain must be installed in its original position onto the camshaft sprocket using the scribed marks, or damage to valves and pistons will result.

10. Scribe a location mark on the timing chain and the camshaft sprocket assembly.

✳✳ WARNING

Remove the front thrust camshaft bearing cap straight upward from the bearing towers, or the bearing cap may be damaged from side loading.

11. Remove the 2 bolts and the camshaft front bearing cap.

✳✳ WARNING

The camshaft bearing caps must be installed in their original locations. Record camshaft bearing cap locations. Failure to follow these instructions may result in engine damage.

12. Remove the remaining 10 bolts in the sequence shown and remove the camshaft bearing caps.
13. Clean and inspect the LH camshaft bearing caps.
14. The camshaft front thrust bearing cap contains an oil metering groove. Make sure the groove is free of foreign material.

✳✳ WARNING

Only use hand tools to remove the camshaft sprocket bolt or damage may occur to the camshaft or camshaft sprocket.

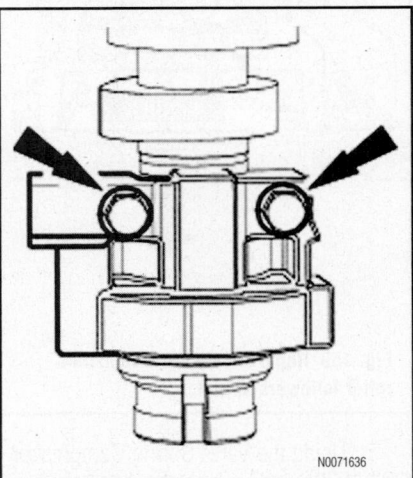

Fig. 164 Remove the 2 bolts and the camshaft front bearing cap

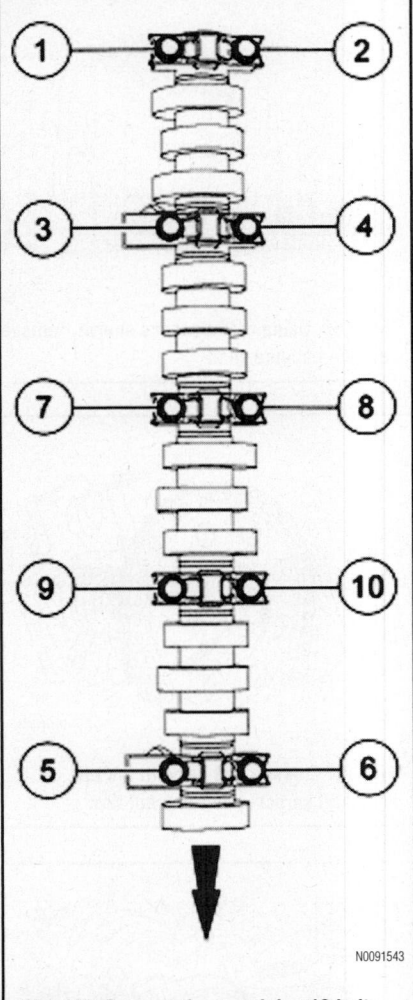

Fig. 165 Remove the remaining 10 bolts in the sequence shown

✳✳ WARNING

Do not remove the Timing Chain Locking Tool at any time during assembly. If the Timing Chain Locking Tool is removed or out of placement, the engine front cover must be removed and the engine must be retimed.

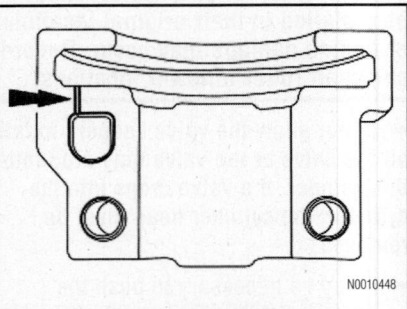

Fig. 166 Make sure the groove is free of foreign material

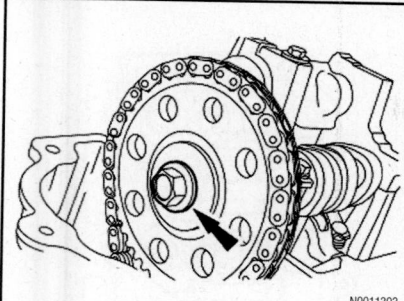

Fig. 167 Remove the bolt and withdraw the camshaft from the sprocket assembly leaving the sprocket assembly and timing chain in place

15. Remove the bolt and withdraw the camshaft from the sprocket assembly leaving the sprocket assembly and timing chain in place.

16. Discard the bolt and washer.

To install:

17. Lubricate the camshaft and camshaft journals with clean engine oil.

✳✳ WARNING

Do not remove the Timing Chain Locking Tool at any time during assembly. If the Timing Chain Locking Tool is removed or out of placement, the engine front cover must be removed and the engine must be retimed.

➡**Do not allow the roller followers to move out of position when installing the camshaft.**

18. Install the camshaft into the camshaft sprocket assembly and onto the head. Install a new camshaft sprocket bolt finger-tight.

✳✳ WARNING

Do not remove the Timing Chain Locking Tool at any time during assembly. If the Timing Chain Locking Tool is removed or out of placement, the engine front cover must be removed and the engine must be retimed.

✳✳ WARNING

The timing chain must be installed in its original position onto the camshaft sprocket using the scribed marks, or damage to valves and pistons will result.

19. Verify the camshaft sprocket and tim-

ing chain scribe marks are still in alignment.

➡**Do not allow the roller followers to move out of position when installing the camshaft.**

20. Install the camshaft bearing caps in their original locations.
   a. Lubricate the camshaft bearing caps with clean engine oil.
   b. Position the front camshaft bearing cap.
   c. Position the remaining camshaft bearing caps.
   d. Install the 12 bolts loosely.

21. Tighten the 12 LH camshaft bearing cap bolts in 2 stages:
   a. Stage 1: Tighten to 71 inch lbs. (8 Nm) in the sequence shown.
   b. Stage 2: Tighten an additional 45 degrees.

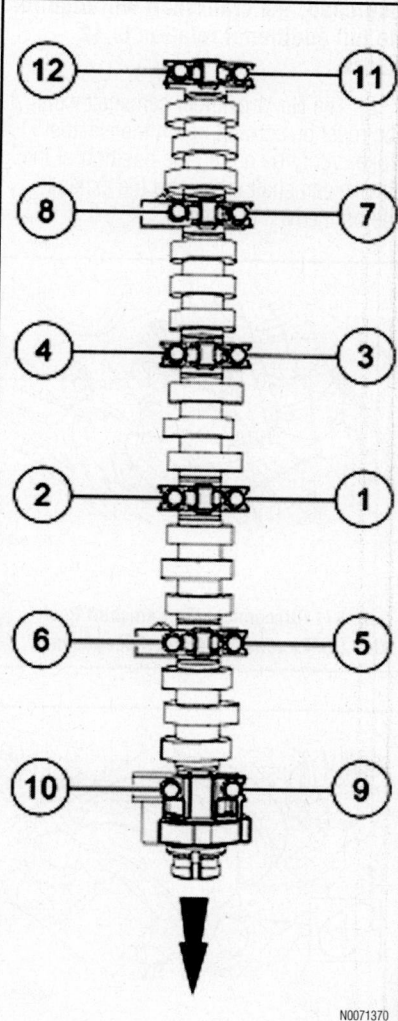

Fig. 168 Tighten the 12 LH camshaft bearing cap bolts in sequence

22. Remove the Timing Chain Locking Tool.

23. Rotate the crankshaft a half turn counterclockwise and position the crankshaft damper spoke at the 12 o'clock position and the timing mark indentation at the 1 o'clock position.

24. The No. 6 cylinder camshaft exhaust lobe must be coming up on the exhaust stroke. Verify by noting the position of the 2 intake camshaft lobes and the exhaust lobe on the No. 6 cylinder.

➡**Do not allow the valve keepers to fall off the valve or the valve may drop into the cylinder. If a valve drops into the cylinder, the cylinder head must be removed.**

➡**It may be necessary to push the valve down while compressing the spring.**

➡**Lubricate the camshaft roller followers prior to installation.**

25. Using the Valve Spring Compressor, install the 4 originally removed camshaft roller followers.

✳✳ WARNING

Only use hand tools to install the camshaft sprocket assembly or damage may occur to the camshaft or camshaft sprocket.

✳✳ WARNING

Damage to the camshaft sprocket assembly will occur if mishandled or used as a lifting or leveraging device.

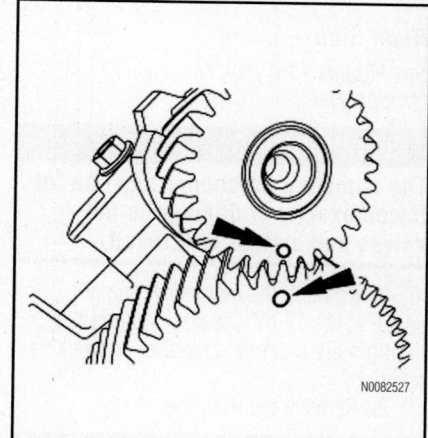

Fig. 169 Rotate the crankshaft clockwise until the camshaft balance shaft drive gear timing mark will align with the balance shaft timing mark

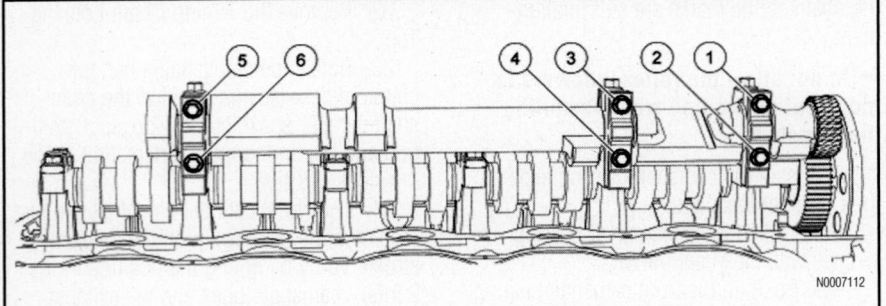

Fig. 170 Position the 3 balance shaft bearing caps and install the 6 bolts and tighten in the sequence shown

26. Tighten the camshaft sprocket bolt in 2 stages:

   a. Stage 1: Tighten to 30 ft. lbs. (40 Nm).

   b. Stage 2: Tighten an additional 90 degrees.

27. Lubricate the balance shaft journals with clean engine oil.

➡ Camshaft sprocket removed from art for clarity.

28. Rotate the crankshaft clockwise until the camshaft balance shaft drive gear timing mark will align with the balance shaft timing mark and position the balance shaft on the journals.

✳ WARNING

The balance shaft bearing caps must be installed into their original locations or engine damage may occur.

29. Position the 3 balance shaft bearing caps and install the 6 bolts and tighten in the sequence shown. Tighten to 89 inch lbs. (10 Nm).

30. Install the LH valve cover.

Right Side

See Figures 135, 139, 163 and 171 through 180.

✳ WARNING

The camshaft procedure must be followed exactly or damage to the valves and pistons will result.

1. Position the crankshaft damper spoke at the 12 o'clock position and the timing mark indentation at the 1 o'clock position.

2. Remove the RH valve cover.

✳ WARNING

Only use hand tools to loosen the camshaft sprocket bolt or damage may occur to the camshaft or camshaft sprocket.

3. Loosen and back off the RH camshaft sprocket bolt one full turn.

4. Disconnect the Camshaft Position (CMP) sensor electrical connector.

5. Remove the bolt and the CMP sensor.

➡ If the camshaft lobes are not exactly positioned, the crankshaft will require one full additional rotation to 12 o'clock.

6. The No. 1 cylinder camshaft exhaust lobe must be coming up on the exhaust stroke. Verify by noting the position of the 2 intake camshaft lobes and the exhaust lobe on the No. 1 cylinder.

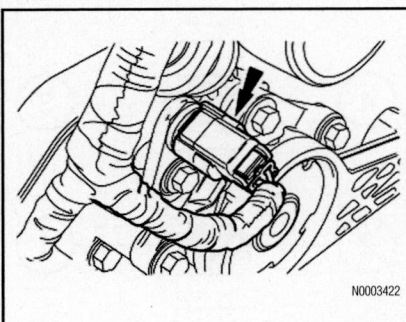

Fig. 171 Disconnect the Camshaft Position (CMP) sensor electrical connector

Fig. 172 Verify by noting the position of the 2 intake camshaft lobes and the exhaust lobe on the No. 1 cylinder

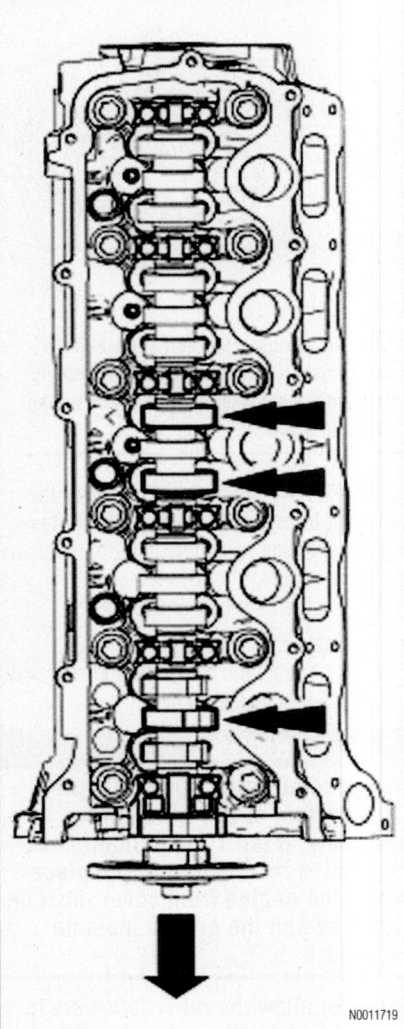

Fig. 173 Remove only the 3 camshaft roller followers shown from the RH cylinder head

✳ WARNING

If the components are to be reinstalled, they must be installed in the same positions. Mark the components for installation into the original locations. Failure to follow these instructions may result in engine damage.

7. Remove only the 3 camshaft roller followers shown from the RH cylinder head.

✳ WARNING

The camshaft roller followers must be installed in their original locations. Record camshaft roller follower locations. Failure to follow these instructions may result in engine damage.

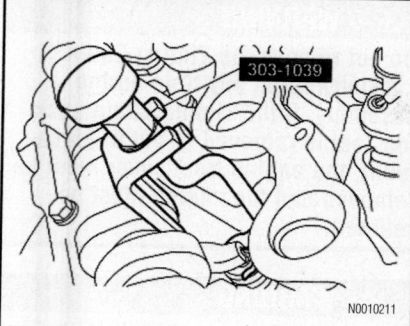

Fig. 174 Using the Valve Spring Compressor, remove only the 3 designated camshaft roller followers

➡Do not allow the valve keepers to fall off the valve or the valve may drop into the cylinder. If a valve drops into the cylinder, the cylinder head must be removed.

➡It may be necessary to push the valve down while compressing the spring.

8. Using the Valve Spring Compressor (303-1039), remove only the 3 designated camshaft roller followers from the previous step.

✳✳ WARNING

The crankshaft cannot be moved past the 6 o'clock position once set. Failure to follow this instruction may result in engine damage.

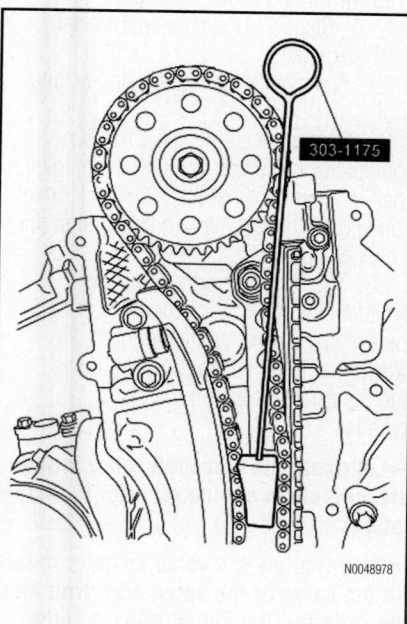

Fig. 175 Install the Timing Chain Locking Tool in the RH timing chain as shown

9. Rotate the crankshaft clockwise, as viewed from the front, positioning the crankshaft damper spoke at the 6 o'clock position and the timing mark indentation at the 7 o'clock position.

✳✳ WARNING

Engine is not freewheeling. Camshaft procedure must be followed exactly or damage to valves and pistons will result.

➡The Timing Chain Locking Tool must be installed square to the timing chain and the engine block.

➡Front cover removed for clarity.

10. Install the Timing Chain Locking Tool (303-1175) in the RH timing chain as shown.

✳✳ WARNING

Do not remove the timing chain wedge tool at any time during assembly. If the Timing Chain Locking Tool is removed or out of placement, the engine front cover must be removed and the engine must be retimed.

✳✳ WARNING

The timing chain must be installed in its original position onto the camshaft sprocket using the scribed marks, or damage to valves and pistons will result.

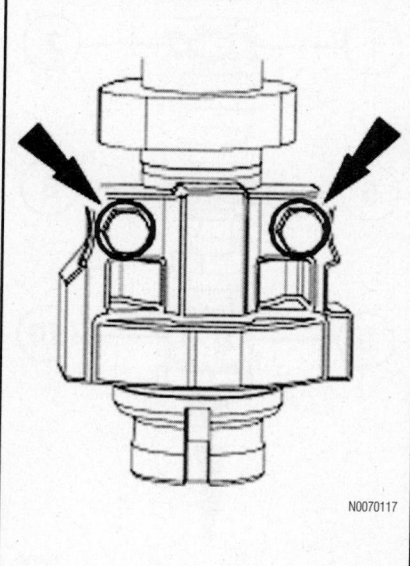

Fig. 176 Remove the 2 bolts and the camshaft front bearing cap

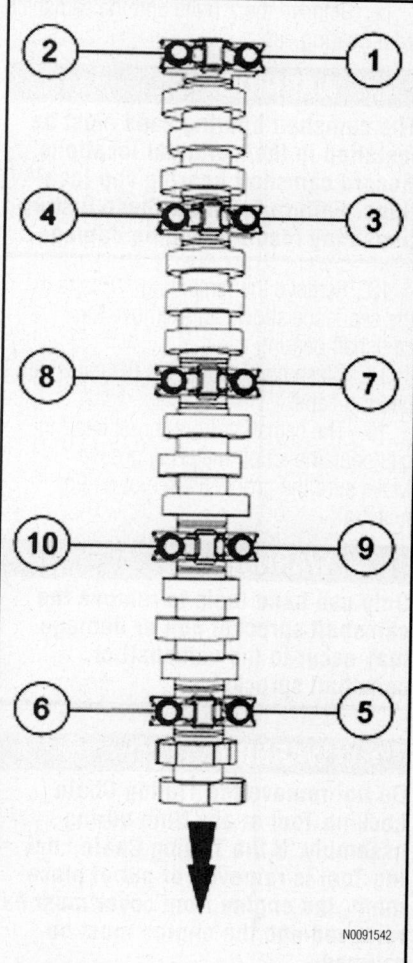

Fig. 177 Remove the remaining 10 bolts in the sequence shown

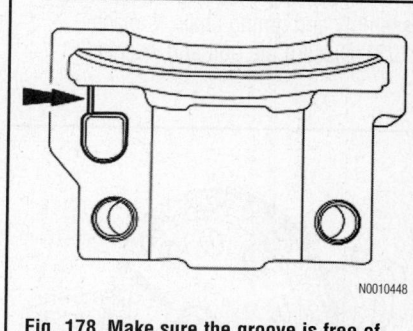

Fig. 178 Make sure the groove is free of foreign material

11. Scribe a location mark on the timing chain and the camshaft sprocket assembly.

✳✳ WARNING

Remove the front thrust camshaft bearing cap straight upward from the bearing towers or the bearing cap may be damaged from side loading.

12. Remove the 2 bolts and the camshaft front bearing cap.

✳ WARNING

The camshaft bearing caps must be installed in their original locations. Record camshaft bearing cap locations. Failure to follow these instructions may result in engine damage.

13. Remove the remaining 10 bolts in the sequence shown and remove the camshaft bearing caps.

14. Clean and inspect the RH camshaft bearing caps.

15. The camshaft front thrust bearing cap contains an oil metering groove. Make sure the groove is free of foreign material.

✳ WARNING

Only use hand tools to remove the camshaft sprocket bolt or damage may occur to the camshaft or camshaft sprocket.

✳ WARNING

Do not remove the Timing Chain Locking Tool at any time during assembly. If the Timing Chain Locking Tool is removed or out of placement, the engine front cover must be removed and the engine must be retimed.

16. Remove the bolt and withdraw the camshaft and balance shaft gear from the sprocket assembly leaving the sprocket assembly and timing chain in place.

17. Discard the bolt and washer.

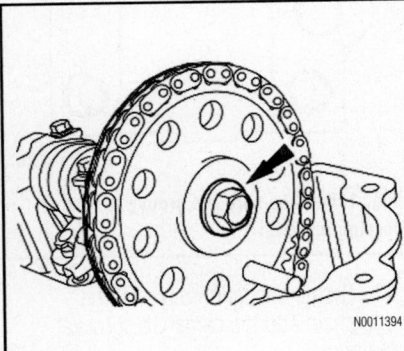

N0011394

Fig. 179 Remove the bolt and withdraw the camshaft and balance shaft gear from the sprocket assembly leaving the sprocket assembly and timing chain in place

To install:

18. Lubricate the camshaft and camshaft journals with clean engine oil.

✳ WARNING

Do not remove the Timing Chain Locking Tool at any time during assembly. If the Timing Chain Locking Tool is removed or out of placement, the engine front cover must be removed and the engine must be retimed.

➡ **Do not allow the roller followers to move out of position when installing the camshaft.**

19. Install the camshaft into the camshaft sprocket assembly and onto the head. Install a new camshaft sprocket bolt finger-tight.

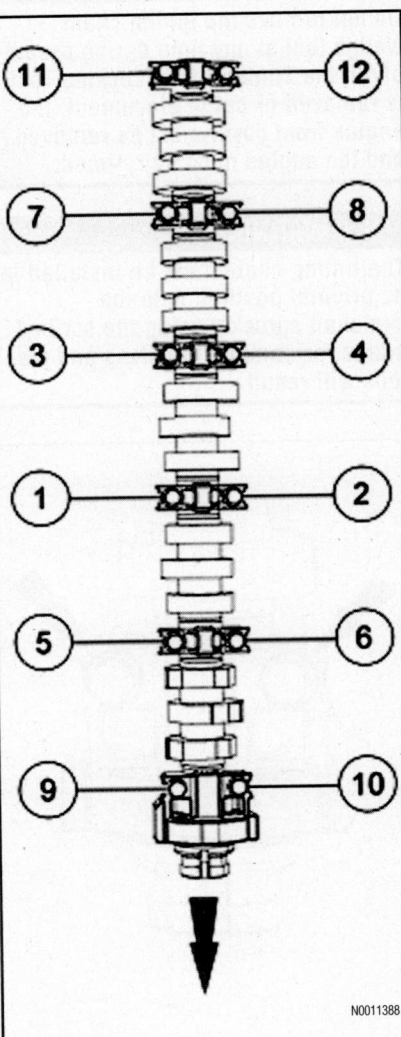

N0011388

Fig. 180 Tighten the 12 RH camshaft bearing cap bolts in sequence

✳ WARNING

Do not remove the Timing Chain Locking Tool at any time during assembly. If the Timing Chain Locking Tool is removed or out of placement, the engine front cover must be removed and the engine must be retimed.

✳ WARNING

The timing chain must be installed in its original position onto the camshaft sprocket using the scribed marks, or damage to valves and pistons will result.

20. Verify the camshaft sprocket and timing chain scribe marks are still in alignment.

➡ **Do not allow the roller followers to move out of position when installing the camshaft.**

21. Install the camshaft bearing caps in their original locations.

   a. Lubricate the camshaft bearing caps with clean engine oil.

   b. Position the front camshaft bearing cap.

   c. Position the remaining camshaft bearing caps.

   d. Install the 12 bolts loosely.

22. Tighten the 12 RH camshaft bearing cap bolts in 2 stages:

   a. Stage 1: Tighten to 71 inch lbs. (8 Nm) in the sequence shown.

   b. Stage 2: Tighten an additional 45 degrees.

23. Remove the Timing Chain Locking Tool.

24. Rotate the crankshaft a half turn counterclockwise and position the crankshaft damper spoke at the 12 o'clock position and the timing mark indentation at the 1 o'clock position.

25. The No. 1 cylinder camshaft exhaust lobe must be coming up on the exhaust stroke. Verify by noting the position of the 2 intake camshaft lobes and the exhaust lobe on the No. 1 cylinder.

➡ **Lubricate the camshaft roller followers with clean engine oil prior to installation.**

➡ **Do not allow the valve keepers to fall off the valve or the valve may drop into the cylinder. If a valve drops into the cylinder, the cylinder head must be removed.**

➡️It may be necessary to push the valve down while compressing the spring.

26. Using the Valve Spring Compressor, install the 3 originally removed camshaft roller followers.

27. Install the CMP sensor and the bolt.

28. Connect the CMP electrical connector.

✳️ WARNING

Only use hand tools to install the camshaft sprocket assembly or damage may occur to the camshaft or camshaft sprocket.

29. Tighten the camshaft sprocket bolt in 2 stages:

    a. Stage 1: Tighten to 30 ft. lbs. (40 Nm).

    b. Stage 2: Tighten an additional 90 degrees.

30. Install the RH valve cover.

CATALYTIC CONVERTER

REMOVAL & INSTALLATION

Gasoline Engines

➡️**Some applications are equipped with a catalytic converter delete pipe in place of the underbody catalytic converter. The catalytic converter delete pipe mounts in the exhaust system the same way as the underbody catalytic converter. The catalytic converter delete pipe does not have a Catalyst Monitor Sensor (CMS).**

1. With the vehicle in NEUTRAL, position it on a hoist.

2. If equipped, remove the skid plate.

3. Remove the 2 exhaust Y-pipe flange bolts.

4. Loosen the catalytic converter-to-muffler Torca clamp or, if equipped, the catalytic converter-to-exhaust intermediate pipe Torca clamp.

5. If equipped, disconnect the exhaust intermediate pipe isolator and the front muffler isolator.

6. Disconnect the catalytic converter from the isolator.

7. Remove the catalytic converter.

To install:

8. Position the catalytic converter into the muffler or, if equipped, the exhaust intermediate pipe.

9. If equipped, connect the exhaust intermediate pipe isolator, the front muffler isolator and the catalytic converter isolator.

10. Install the 2 exhaust Y-pipe flange bolts. Tighten to 30 ft. lbs. (40 Nm).

11. Make sure the button on the catalytic converter is fully inserted into the button slot on the muffler or, if equipped, the exhaust intermediate pipe and tighten the catalytic converter-to-muffler Torca clamp or, if equipped, the exhaust intermediate pipe Torca clamp. Tighten to 41 ft. lbs. (55 Nm).

➡️**The exhaust system alignment procedure only needs to be carried out if the exhaust system isolators are not at zero load.**

12. Check to see if the exhaust system isolators are at zero load. If the exhaust system isolators are not at zero load, carry out the exhaust system alignment procedure.

13. If equipped, install the skid plate.

DIESEL PARTICULATE FILTER

REMOVAL & INSTALLATION

1. With the vehicle in NEUTRAL, position it on a hoist.

2. Remove the tail pipe.

3. If equipped, remove the exhaust intermediate pipe.

4. Disconnect the Exhaust Gas Temperature (EGT) sensor electrical connector.

5. Using a suitable lifting device support the Diesel Particulate Filter (DPF).

6. Remove the DPF pressure sensor.

7. Remove the 7 DPF-to-Oxidation Catalytic Converter (OC) nuts. Discard the nuts.

8. Disconnect the isolators and lower the DPF from the vehicle.

9. Discard the DPF-to-OC gasket.

To install:

➡️**Make sure the DPF-to-OC gasket surface is clean.**

10. Install a new DPF-to-OC gasket.

11. Using a suitable lifting device, position the DPF in the vehicle and connect the isolator.

12. Install the 7 new DPF-to-OC nuts. Tighten to 30 ft. lbs. (40 Nm).

✳️ WARNING

Make sure all 7 Oxidation Catalytic Converter (OC)-to-Diesel Particulate Filter (DPF) filter nuts have been installed before installing the DPF pressure sensor or damage to the DPF or DPF pressure sensor may occur.

13. Install the DPF pressure sensor.

14. If equipped, install the exhaust intermediate pipe.

15. Install the tail pipe.

16. Connect the EGT sensor electrical connector.

➡️**The exhaust system alignment procedure only needs to be carried out if the exhaust system isolators are not at zero load.**

17. Check to see if the exhaust system isolators are at zero load. If the exhaust system isolators are not at zero load, carry out the exhaust system alignment procedure.

18. If a new DPF was installed, reset the DPF parameter.

CRANKSHAFT FRONT SEAL

REMOVAL & INSTALLATION

6.4L Diesel Engine

See Figures 181 through 184.

1. Remove the crankshaft pulley.

2. Punch 2 holes in the seal.

3. Using the Oil Seal Remover (303-D060), remove and discard the crankshaft seal.

➡️**Production seals will not have a wear sleeve. If a service part has been installed, it will have a wear sleeve.**

4. If equipped, using the Crankshaft Seal Remover (303-1260), remove and discard the crankshaft seal wear sleeve.

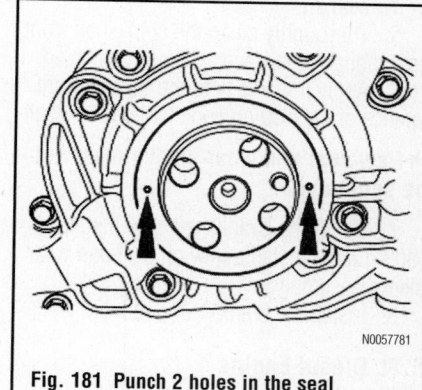

N0057781

Fig. 181 Punch 2 holes in the seal

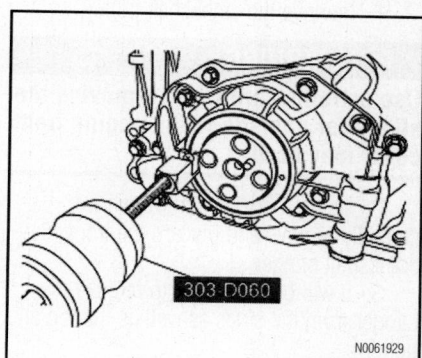

303-D060

N0061929

Fig. 182 Using the Oil Seal Remover, remove and discard the crankshaft seal

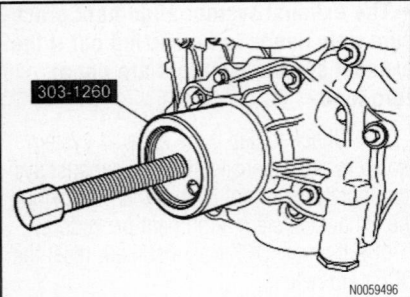

Fig. 183 If equipped, using the Crankshaft Seal Remover, remove and discard the crankshaft seal wear sleeve

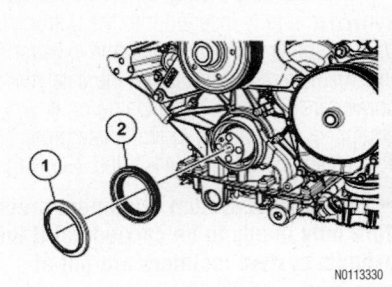

Fig. 185 Front crankshaft slinger (1) and crankshaft seal (2)

Fig. 188 Position the installation sleeve onto the crankshaft, slide the new front crankshaft seal over the installation sleeve onto the crankshaft

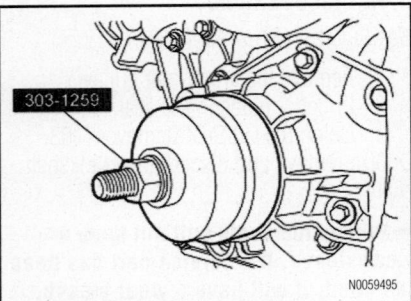

Fig. 184 Using the Crankshaft Seal Installer, install a new oil seal and wear sleeve assembly

Fig. 186 Using 2 pocket screwdrivers, carefully remove and discard the front crankshaft slinger

Fig. 189 Position the new front crankshaft slinger on the crankshaft

To install:

5. Thoroughly clean the crankshaft front seal mounting surface.

6. Apply threadlock to the outer circumference of the leading edge of the crankshaft.

➡**New seal and wear sleeve must not be separated.**

7. Using the Crankshaft Seal Installer (303-1259), install a new oil seal and wear sleeve assembly.

8. Install the crankshaft pulley.

6.7L Diesel Engine

See Figures 185 through 190.

1. Remove the crankshaft pulley.

▓▓ **WARNING**

Use extreme care when removing the slinger or damage to the engine front cover may occur.

2. Using 2 pocket screwdrivers, carefully remove and discard the front crankshaft slinger.

3. It will be necessary to remove the slinger from the sides as well as the top and bottom.

➡**Do not scratch or damage the crankshaft during removal or installation of the front crankshaft seal.**

4. Using the Front Crank Seal Remover (303-1510), remove and discard the front crankshaft seal from the engine front cover.

5. Clean and inspect the crankshaft sealing surface.

To install:

▓▓ **WARNING**

Failure to install the front crankshaft seal with the part numbers facing out may result in engine damage.

➡**Do not discard the installation sleeve provided with the front crankshaft seal. It is used for installation of the crankshaft seal.**

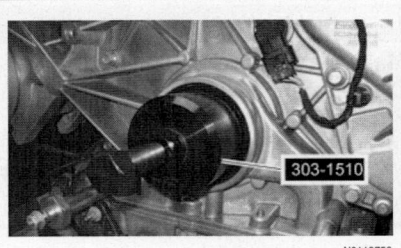

Fig. 187 Using the Front Crank Seal Remover, remove and discard the front crankshaft seal from the engine front cover

➡**Check for correct orientation of the installation sleeve prior to sliding the seal on the crankshaft.**

➡**Apply clean engine oil to the seal and crankshaft sealing surface.**

6. Position the installation sleeve onto the crankshaft, slide the new front crankshaft seal over the installation sleeve onto the crankshaft.

7. Remove the installation sleeve.

8. Position the new front crankshaft slinger on the crankshaft.

9. Using the Front Crank Seal Installer (303-1509), install a new front crankshaft seal and front crankshaft slinger.

Fig. 190 Using the Front Crank Seal Installer, install a new front crankshaft seal and front crankshaft slinger

10. Install the crankshaft pulley.

5.4L Engine

See Figures 191 through 193.

1. With the vehicle in NEUTRAL, position it on a hoist.

2. Press the position retaining tabs and rotate the lower cooling fan shroud upward until the position retainer tab locks into position.

3. Rotate the tensioner clockwise and remove the accessory drive belt from the crankshaft pulley.

4. Remove the crankshaft pulley bolt and washer. Discard the crankshaft pulley bolt.

5. Using the 3 Jaw Puller, remove the crankshaft pulley.

6. Using the Crankshaft Front Oil Seal Remover (303-107), remove and discard the crankshaft seal.

To install:

7. Lubricate the engine front cover and the new crankshaft seal inner lip with clean engine oil.

8. Using the Crankshaft Front Oil Seal

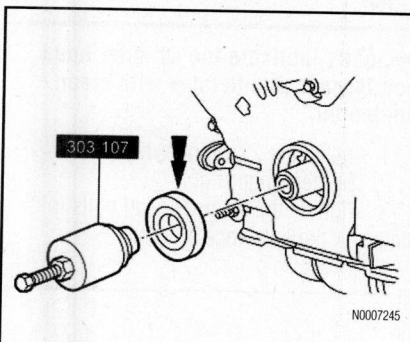

Fig. 191 Using the Crankshaft Front Oil Seal Remover, remove and discard the crankshaft seal

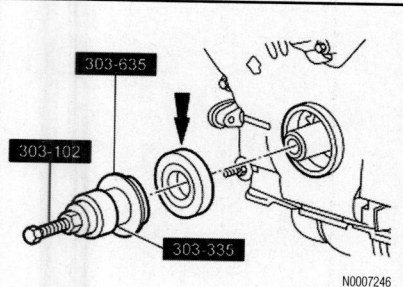

Fig. 192 Using the Crankshaft Front Oil Seal Installer, the Crankshaft Vibration Damper Installer and the Front Cover Oil Seal Installer, install the new crankshaft front seal into the engine front cover

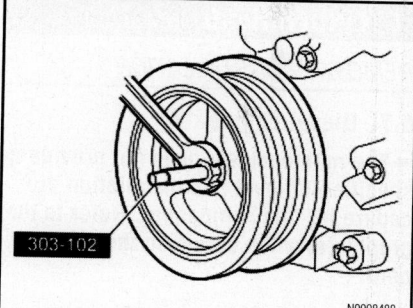

Fig. 193 Using the Crankshaft Vibration Damper Installer, install the crankshaft pulley

Installer (303-635), the Crankshaft Vibration Damper Installer (303-102) and the Front Cover Oil Seal Installer (303-335), install the new crankshaft front seal into the engine front cover.

➡**If not secured within 4 minutes, the sealant must be removed and the sealing area cleaned with metal surface prep and silicone gasket remover. Allow to dry until there is no sign of wetness, or 4 minutes, whichever is longer. Failure to follow this procedure can cause future oil leakage.**

9. Apply silicone gasket and sealant to the Woodruff key slot in the crankshaft pulley.

10. Using the Crankshaft Vibration Damper Installer (303-102), install the crankshaft pulley.

11. Using a new crankshaft pulley bolt, install the bolt and washer and tighten the bolt in 4 stages.

   a. Stage 1: Tighten to 66 ft. lbs. (90 Nm).

   b. Stage 2: Loosen 360 degrees.

   c. Stage 3: Tighten to 37 ft. lbs. (50 Nm).

   d. Stage 4: Tighten an additional 90 degrees.

12. Rotate the tensioner clockwise and install the accessory drive belt onto the crankshaft pulley.

13. Press the position retaining tab and rotate the lower cooling fan shroud downward until the position retainer tab locks into position.

6.8L Engine

See Figures 194 through 197.

1. With the vehicle in NEUTRAL, position it on a hoist.

2. Press the position retaining tabs and rotate the lower cooling fan shroud upward until the position retainer tab locks into position.

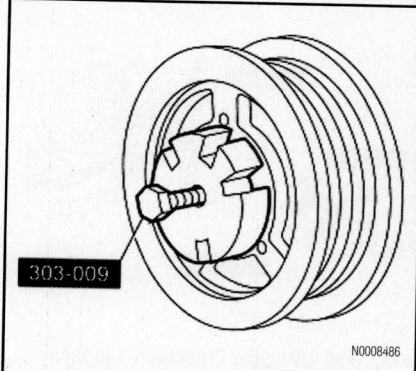

Fig. 194 Using the Crankshaft Vibration Damper Remover, remove the crankshaft pulley

3. Rotate the tensioner clockwise and remove the accessory drive belt.

4. Remove the crankshaft pulley bolt and washer. Discard the crankshaft pulley bolt.

5. Using the Crankshaft Vibration Damper Remover (303-009), remove the crankshaft pulley.

6. Using the Crankshaft Front Oil Seal Remover (303-107), remove and discard the crankshaft front seal.

To install:

7. Lubricate the engine front cover and the crankshaft front seal inner lip with clean engine oil.

8. Using the Crankshaft Vibration Damper Installer (303-102), Front Cover Oil Seal Installer (303-335) and Crankshaft Front Oil Seal Installer (303-635), install a new crankshaft front seal.

➡**If not secured within 4 minutes, the sealant must be removed and the sealing area cleaned with silicone gasket remover and metal surface prep. Follow the directions on the packaging. Allow to dry until there is no sign of wetness, or 4 minutes, whichever is longer. Failure to follow**

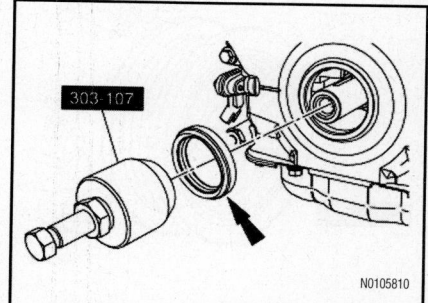

Fig. 195 Using the Crankshaft Front Oil Seal Remover, remove and discard the crankshaft front seal

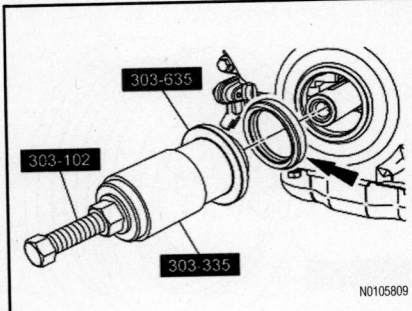

Fig. 196 Using the Crankshaft Vibration Damper Installer, Front Cover Oil Seal Installer and Crankshaft Front Oil Seal Installer, install a new crankshaft front seal

this procedure may cause future oil leakage.

9. Apply silicone gasket and sealant to the Woodruff key slot in the crankshaft pulley.

10. Using the Crankshaft Vibration Damper Installer (303-102), install the crankshaft pulley.

11. Using a new crankshaft pulley bolt, install the bolt and washer and tighten the bolt in 4 stages.

    a. Stage 1: Tighten to 66 ft. lbs. (90 Nm).

    b. Stage 2: Loosen 360 degrees.

    c. Stage 3: Tighten to 37 ft. lbs. (50 Nm).

    d. Stage 4: Tighten an additional 90 degrees.

12. Rotate the tensioner clockwise and install the accessory drive belt.

13. Press the position retaining tab and rotate the lower cooling fan shroud downward until the position retainer tab locks into position.

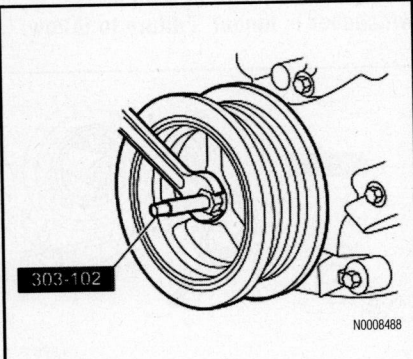

Fig. 197 Using the Crankshaft Vibration Damper Installer, install the crankshaft pulley

CYLINDER HEAD

REMOVAL & INSTALLATION

6.7L Diesel Engine

➡The manufacturer does not provide a specific Removal and Installation procedure for this component. Refer to the graphic(s) when servicing this component.

Left Cylinder Head

See Figure 198.

❊❊ WARNING

Using too much engine oil on the threads of the cylinder head bolts may cause damage to the threads and poor sealing. Using anti-seize compounds, grease or any other lubricants other than engine oil on the cylinder head bolt threads may affect the true torque value of the bolts.

➡Lightly lubricate the cylinder head bolt threads and flanges with clean engine oil.

1. Install the 23 cylinder head bolts.
2. Tighten finger-tight.
3. Tighten the cylinder head bolts in 8 stages in the sequence shown.

    a. Stage 1: Tighten bolts 1 through 18 to 15 ft. lbs. (20 Nm).

    b. Stage 2: Tighten bolts 1 through 18 to 36 ft. lbs. (49 Nm).

    c. Stage 3: Tighten bolts 1 through 18, a second time to 36 ft. lbs. (49 Nm).

    d. Stage 4: Tighten bolts 1 through 18, a third time to 36 ft. lbs. (49 Nm).

    e. Stage 5: Tighten bolts 1 through 18, an additional 90 degrees.

    f. Stage 6: Tighten bolts 1 through 18, a second time, an additional 90 degrees.

    g. Stage 7: Tighten bolts 1 through 18, a third time, an additional 90 degrees.

    h. Stage 8: Tighten bolts 19 through 23 to 22 ft. lbs. (30 Nm).

Right Cylinder Head

See Figure 199.

❊❊ WARNING

Using too much engine oil on the threads of the cylinder head bolts may cause damage to the threads and poor sealing. Using anti-seize compounds, grease or any other lubricants other than engine oil on the cylinder head bolt threads may affect the true torque value of the bolts.

➡Lightly lubricate the cylinder head bolt threads and flanges with clean engine oil.

1. Install the 22 cylinder head bolts.
2. Tighten finger-tight.
3. Tighten the cylinder head bolts in 8 stages in the sequence shown.

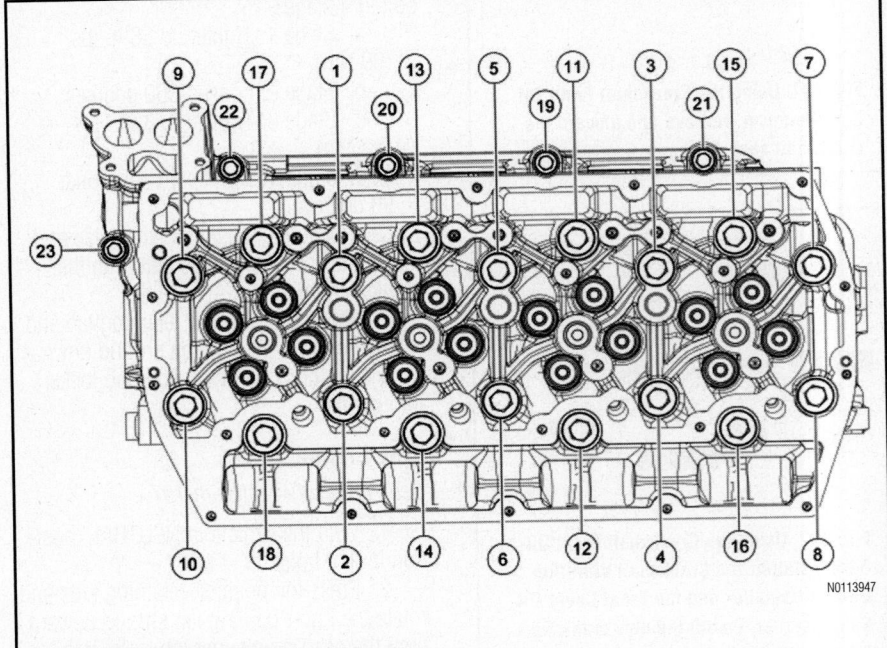

Fig. 198 Left cylinder tightening sequence

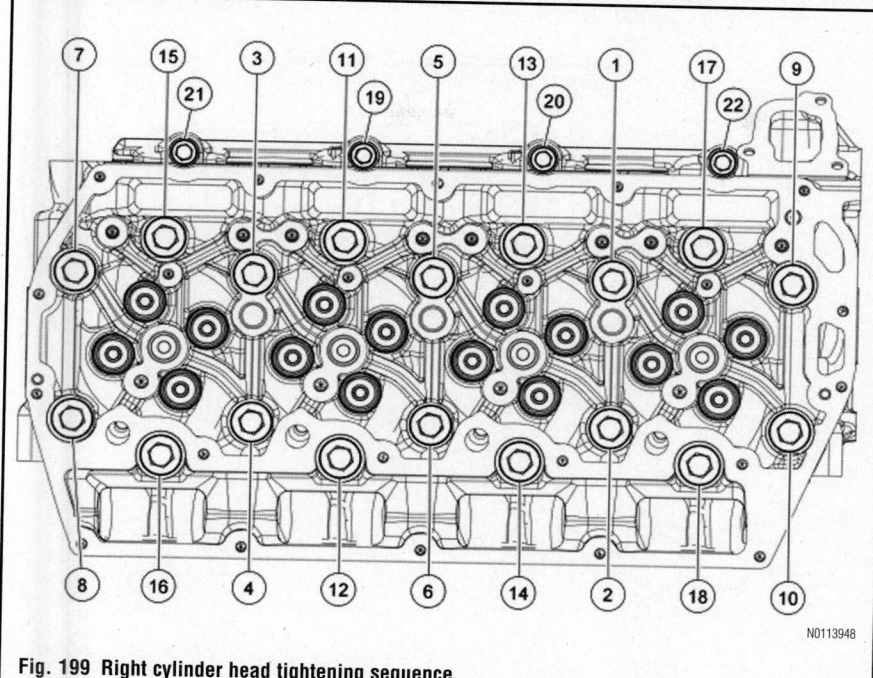

Fig. 199 Right cylinder head tightening sequence

a. Stage 1: Tighten bolts 1 through 18 to 15 ft. lbs. (20 Nm).

b. Stage 2: Tighten bolts 1 through 18 to 36 ft. lbs. (49 Nm).

c. Stage 3: Tighten bolts 1 through 18, a second time to 36 ft. lbs. (49 Nm).

d. Stage 4: Tighten bolts 1 through 18, a third time to 36 ft. lbs. (49 Nm).

e. Stage 5: Tighten bolts 1 through 18, an additional 90 degrees.

f. Stage 6: Tighten bolts 1 through 18, a second time, an additional 90 degrees.

g. Stage 7: Tighten bolts 1 through 18, a third time, an additional 90 degrees.

h. Stage 8: Tighten bolts 19 through 22 to 22 ft. lbs. (30 Nm).

6.2L Engine

➡The manufacturer does not provide a specific Removal and Installation procedure for this component. Refer to the graphic(s) when servicing this component.

❋❋ WARNING

Make sure all coolant residue and foreign material are cleaned from the block surface and cylinder bore. Failure to follow this instruction may result in engine damage.

➡The use of sealing aids (aviation cement, copper spray and glue) is not permitted. The gasket must be installed dry.

➡The cylinder head bolts must be discarded and new bolts installed. They are a tighten-to-yield design and cannot be reused.

Left Cylinder Head

See Figure 200.

1. Tighten the 11 bolts in 6 stages, in the sequence shown.

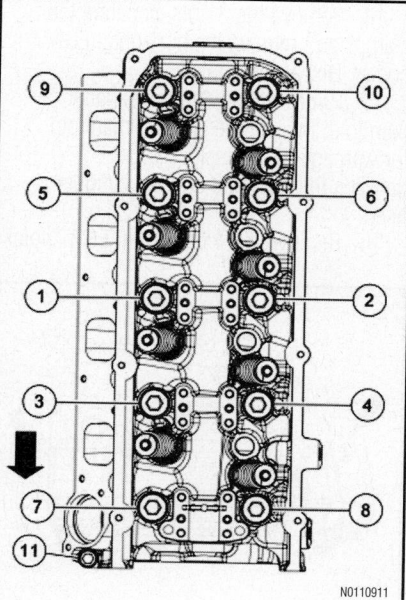

Fig. 200 Tighten the 11 bolts in 6 stages, in the sequence shown

a. Stage 1: Tighten the M12 fasteners to 18 ft. lbs. (25 Nm).

b. Stage 2: Tighten the M12 fasteners to 44 ft. lbs. (60 Nm).

c. Stage 3: Tighten the M12 fasteners an additional 90 degrees.

d. Stage 4: Tighten the M12 fasteners an additional 90 degrees.

e. Stage 5: Tighten the M8 fastener to 15 ft. lbs. (20 Nm).

f. Stage 6: Tighten the M8 fastener an additional 45 degrees.

Right Cylinder Head

See Figure 201.

1. Tighten the 10 bolts in 4 stages, in the sequence shown.

a. Stage 1: Tighten the M12 fasteners to 18 ft. lbs. (25 Nm).

b. Stage 2: Tighten the M12 fasteners to 44 ft. lbs. (60 Nm).

c. Stage 3: Tighten the M12 fasteners an additional 90 degrees.

d. Stage 4: Tighten the M12 fasteners an additional 90 degrees.

EXHAUST MANIFOLD

REMOVAL & INSTALLATION

6.4L Diesel Engine

Left Side

See Figures 202 through 205.

1. Remove the LH turbocharger inlet pipe.

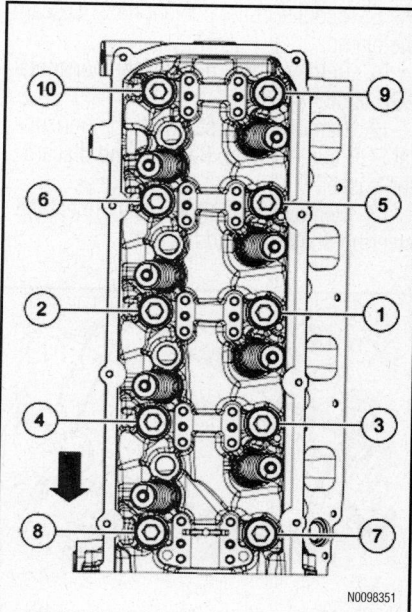

Fig. 201 Tighten the 10 bolts in 4 stages, in the sequence shown

2. Remove the degas bottle.

3. Remove the LH front wheel and tire.

4. Remove the LH fender splash shield.

5. Remove the oil level indicator. Remove the nut for the oil level indicator tube.

6. Remove the bolt and position the oil level indicator tube aside. Remove and discard the O-ring seal.

7. Disconnect the anti-lock module electrical connector and position aside.

8. Loosen the clamp for the EGR cooler coolant supply hose.

✳✳ WARNING

The coolant hose clamps used on this engine are constant tension worm gear clamps. Standard worm gear clamps cannot be used. Failure to use the correct coolant hose clamps may result in hose joint failure.

➡ **Position a drain pan prior to removing the EGR cooler coolant supply tube.**

9. Remove the bolts and the EGR cooler coolant supply tube. Discard the clamp on the hose and the O-ring seal on the tube.

✳✳ WARNING

The coolant hose clamps used on this engine are constant tension worm gear clamps. Standard worm gear clamps cannot be used. Failure to use the correct coolant hose clamps may result in hose joint failure.

10. Loosen the clamp and disconnect the EGR cooler outlet coolant hose. Discard the clamp.

11. Remove the 2 nuts for the horizontal EGR cooler outlet.

12. Remove the 2 studs for the horizontal EGR cooler outlet. Remove and discard the gasket.

13. Remove the bolt and disconnect the steering shaft. Discard the bolt.

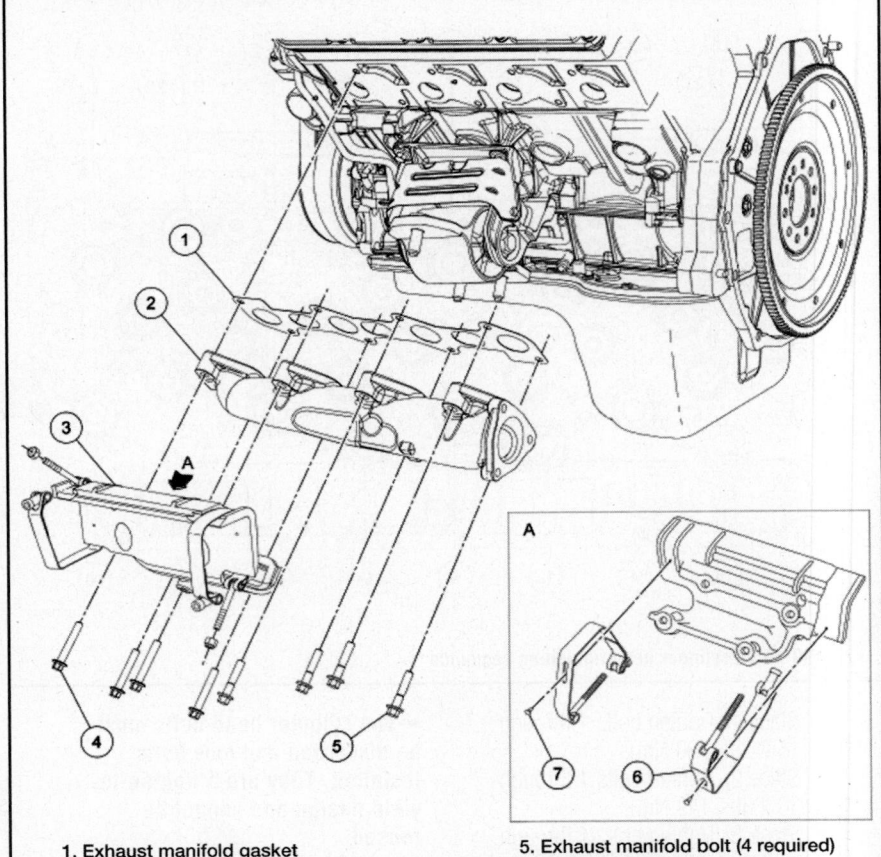

1. Exhaust manifold gasket
2. Exhaust manifold
3. Horizontal EGR cooler bracket
4. Horizontal EGR cooler bracket bolt (4 required)
5. Exhaust manifold bolt (4 required)
6. Clamp (2 required)
7. Pin (2 required)

N0086860

Fig. 203 Exploded view of the exhaust manifold LH

14. Remove the 2 nuts, separate the clamps and remove the horizontal EGR cooler. Discard the nuts.

15. Prior to removing the exhaust manifold, inspect the exhaust manifold for warpage with a feeler gauge between the manifold and the cylinder head.

16. Remove the 4 horizontal EGR cooler bracket bolts and the bracket. Discard the bolts.

17. Remove the 4 bolts, the exhaust manifold and the exhaust manifold gasket. Discard the bolts and gasket.

18. Remove the 2 pins from the back of the horizontal EGR cooler bracket. Remove and discard the EGR cooler clamps.

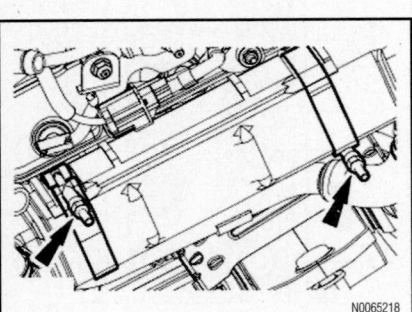

N0065218

Fig. 202 Remove the 2 nuts, separate the clamps and remove the horizontal EGR cooler

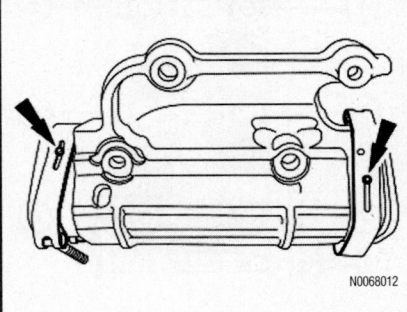

N0068012

Fig. 204 Remove the 2 pins from the back of the horizontal EGR cooler bracket

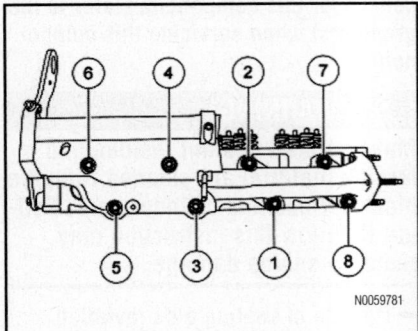

N0059781

Fig. 205 Tighten the exhaust manifold bolts in 2 stages in the sequence shown

To install:

19. Position the new horizontal EGR cooler clamps and install 2 new pins.

20. Position the new gasket and the LH exhaust manifold. Loosely install the 4 new exhaust manifold bolts.

21. Position the horizontal EGR cooler bracket and loosely install the 4 new bolts.

22. Tighten the exhaust manifold bolts in 2 stages in the sequence shown.

   a. Stage 1: Tighten to 18 ft. lbs. (25 Nm).

   b. Stage 2: Tighten again to 18 ft. lbs. (25 Nm).

23. Insert the horizontal EGR cooler locating pin into the slot in the horizontal EGR cooler bracket and install the 2 new clamp nuts. Tighten the clamps for the horizontal EGR cooler in 3 stages.

   a. Stage 1: Tighten to 89 ft. lbs. (10 Nm).

   b. Stage 2: Loosen the clamps 720 degrees.

   c. Stage 3: Tighten to 71 inch lbs. (8 Nm).

24. Position the steering shaft into the housing. Install the new steering shaft bolt. Tighten to 35 ft. lbs. (48 Nm).

25. Position a new horizontal EGR cooler outlet gasket and install the 2 studs. Tighten to 13 ft. lbs. (17 Nm).

❋❋ WARNING

Do not bend or twist the Exhaust Gas Recirculation (EGR) cooler bellows or damage to the EGR cooler may occur.

➡️Inspect the corrugation of the vertical EGR cooler inlet to make sure that the corrugation ribs are not touching and are not damaged.

26. Install the 2 horizontal EGR cooler outlet nuts. Tighten to 23 ft. lbs. (31 Nm).

❋❋ WARNING

The coolant hose clamps used on this engine are constant tension worm gear clamps. Standard worm gear clamps cannot be used. Failure to use the correct coolant hose clamps may result in hose joint failure.

27. Using a new clamp, connect the EGR cooler coolant outlet hose to the horizontal EGR cooler.

❋❋ WARNING

The coolant hose clamps used on this engine are constant tension worm gear clamps. Standard worm gear clamps cannot be used. Failure to

use the correct coolant hose clamps may result in hose joint failure.

➡️Install a new O-ring seal and clamp on the coolant supply tube.

➡️Position the flexible section of hose on the EGR cooler prior to installing the tube.

➡️Make sure the oil level indicator tube is positioned behind the EGR cooler coolant supply tube before installing the EGR cooler coolant supply tube.

28. Position a new clamp and install the EGR cooler coolant supply tube and bolts. Tighten to 10 ft. lbs. (13 Nm).

29. Tighten the clamp for the EGR cooler coolant supply hose.

Connect the anti-lock module electrical connector.

➡️Install a new O-ring seal on the oil level tube prior to installing.

30. Position the oil level indicator tube. Install the bolt. Tighten to 10 ft. lbs. (13 Nm).

31. Install the nut for the oil level indicator tube. Install the oil level indicator. Tighten to 23 ft. lbs. (31 Nm).

32. Install the LH fender splash shield.

33. Install the LH front wheel and tire.

34. Install the degas bottle.

35. Install the LH turbocharger inlet pipe.

Right Side

See Figures 206 through 220.

1. Remove the Air Cleaner (ACL) assembly.

2. Remove the auxiliary air intake tube.

3. If equipped, recover the A/C system.

❋❋ WARNING

Position a suitable material in front of the Charge Air Cooler (CAC) or damage to the CAC may occur.

4. Disconnect the battery ground cables.

5. With the vehicle in NEUTRAL, position it on a hoist.

6. Remove the 2 exhaust downpipe-to-Oxidation Catalytic Converter (OC) pipe bolts.

7. Remove and discard the exhaust downpipe clamp. Position aside the exhaust downpipe. Remove and discard the exhaust downpipe gasket.

8. Disconnect the Exhaust Pressure (EP) sensor tube from the EGR-OC pipe.

9. Remove the EGR-OC pipe bracket-to-bracket bolt and washer. Remove the

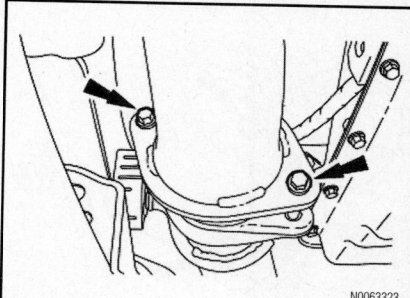

Fig. 206 Remove the 2 exhaust downpipe-to-Oxidation Catalytic Converter (OC) pipe bolts

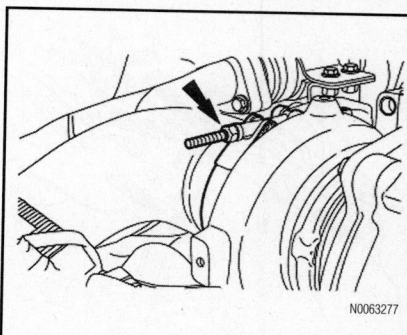

Fig. 207 Remove and discard the exhaust downpipe clamp

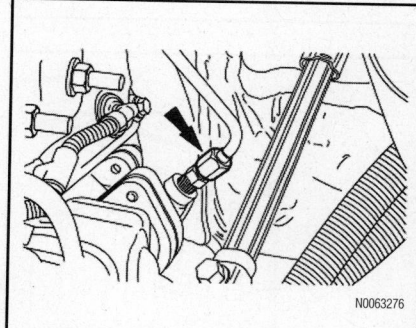

Fig. 208 Disconnect the Exhaust Pressure (EP) sensor tube from the EGR-OC pipe

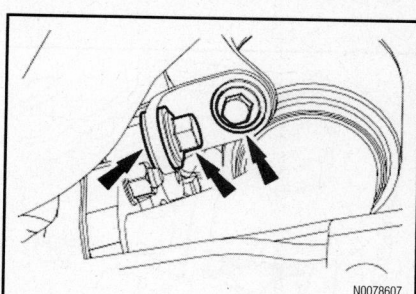

Fig. 209 Remove the EGR-OC pipe bracket-to-bracket bolt and washer. Remove the bracket-to-cylinder head bolt, washers and the bracket

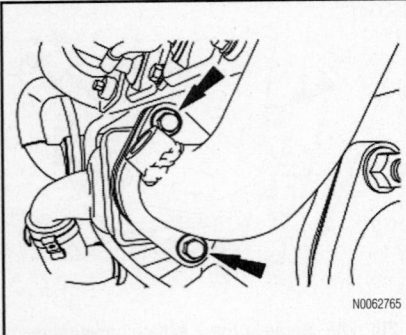

Fig. 210 Remove the 2 EGR-OC-to-EGR cooler bolts

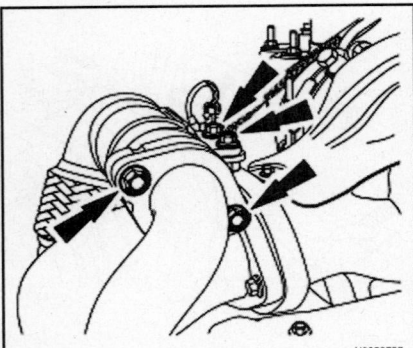

Fig. 211 Remove the 2 EGR-OC pipe bolts and the 2 EGR-OC-to-turbocharger bracket bolts

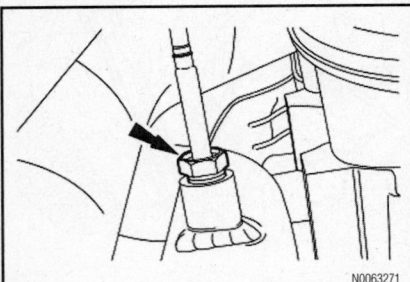

Fig. 212 Remove the Exhaust Gas Recirculation Temperature (EGRT) sensor from the RH turbocharger inlet pipe

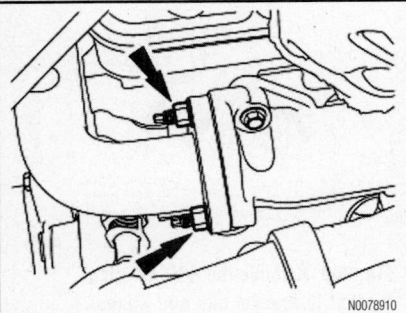

Fig. 213 Remove and discard the 3 RH turbocharger inlet pipe-to-exhaust manifold nuts

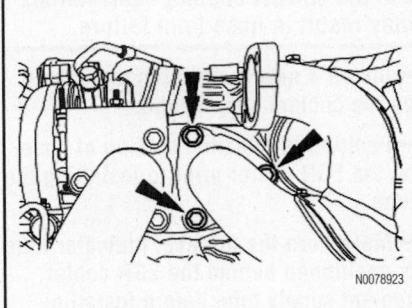

Fig. 214 Remove the 3 RH turbocharger inlet pipe bolts

bracket-to-cylinder head bolt, washers and the bracket. Discard the bolts.

10. Remove the 2 EGR-OC-to-EGR cooler bolts. Discard the bolts and gasket.

11. Remove the 2 EGR-OC pipe bolts and the 2 EGR-OC-to-turbocharger bracket bolts.

    a. Position the EGR-OC pipe aside.

    b. Discard the bolts and gasket.

12. Remove the RH front tire and wheel.

13. Remove the RH fender splash shield.

14. Remove the Exhaust Gas Recirculation Temperature (EGRT) sensor from the RH turbocharger inlet pipe.

15. Remove and discard the 3 RH turbocharger inlet pipe-to-exhaust manifold nuts.

16. Remove the 3 RH turbocharger inlet pipe-to-exhaust manifold studs. Discard the studs.

17. Remove the 3 RH turbocharger inlet pipe bolts.

    a. Position the RH turbocharger inlet pipe aside.

    b. Discard the bolts and gasket.

18. Remove the nut and position the battery cable bracket aside.

19. Remove the cover for the starter terminals.

20. Remove the 2 retaining nuts for the starter solenoid wiring. Position the starter wiring aside.

21. If equipped with A/C:

    a. Disconnect the A/C compressor wire retainer. Position the wiring aside.

    b. Remove the 2 nuts and position aside the A/C hoses.

    c. Discard the O-ring seal and gaskets.

    d. Plug or cap the openings.

22. If equipped with an automatic transmission, remove the retaining nut and position the transmission fluid indicator tube off the stud.

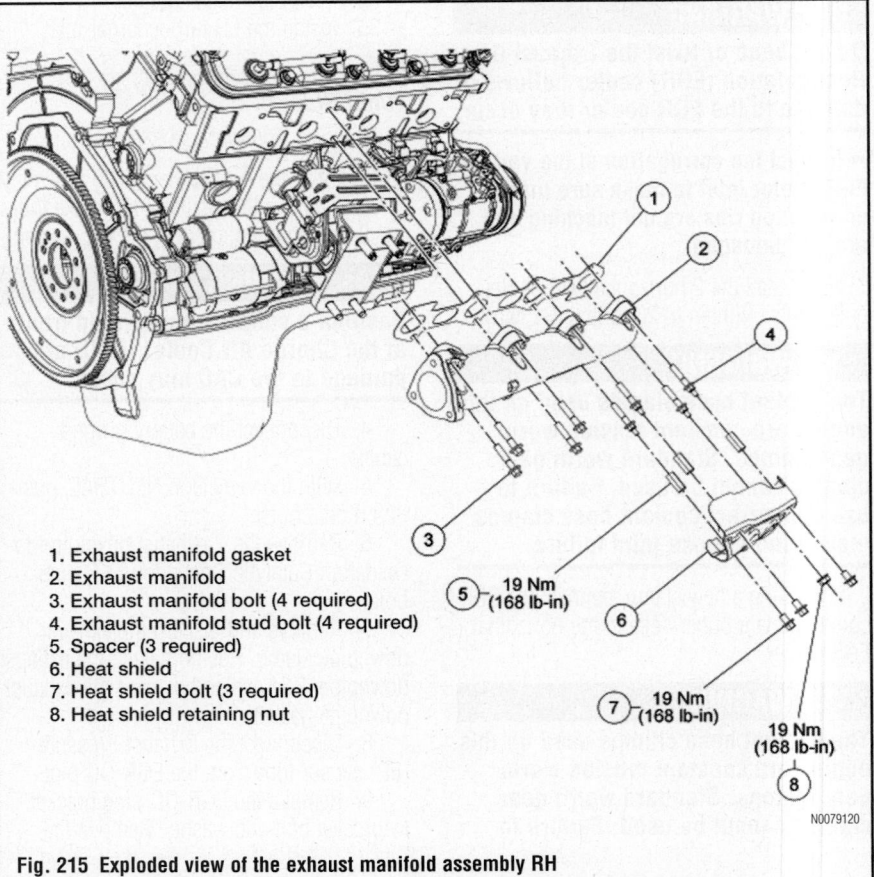

1. Exhaust manifold gasket
2. Exhaust manifold
3. Exhaust manifold bolt (4 required)
4. Exhaust manifold stud bolt (4 required)
5. Spacer (3 required)
6. Heat shield
7. Heat shield bolt (3 required)
8. Heat shield retaining nut

5 — 19 Nm (168 lb-in)

7 — 19 Nm (168 lb-in)

19 Nm (168 lb-in)

Fig. 215 Exploded view of the exhaust manifold assembly RH

23. Prior to removing the exhaust manifold, inspect the exhaust manifold for warpage with a feeler gauge between the manifold and the cylinder head.

24. Remove the 3 bolts and nut for the heat shield. Remove the heat shield.

25. Remove the 3 spacers from the exhaust manifold stud bolts.

➡**Mark the location of the fasteners prior to removing.**

26. Remove the 4 stud bolts and 4 bolts. Remove the exhaust manifold and exhaust manifold gasket. Discard the gasket, stud bolts and bolts.

To install:

27. Position a new exhaust manifold gasket and the exhaust manifold. Install the 4 new stud bolts and the 4 new bolts. Tighten in 2 stages in the sequence shown.

    a. Stage 1: Tighten to 18 ft. lbs. (25 Nm).

    b. Stage 2: Tighten again to 18 ft. lbs. (25 Nm).

28. Install the 3 spacers on the exhaust manifold stud bolts. Tighten to 14 ft. lbs. (19 Nm).

29. Position the exhaust manifold heat shield. Install the nut and 3 bolts. Tighten to 14 ft. lbs. (19 Nm).

30. If equipped with an automatic transmission, position back the transmission fluid level indicator tube and install the nut.

31. For vehicles with A/C:

➡**Install a new O-ring seal and gasket.**

    a. Install the A/C hoses and 2 nuts. Tighten to 11 ft. lbs. (15 Nm).

    b. Position back and connect the A/C compressor wire retainer.

32. Position back the starter wiring. Install the 2 retaining nuts for the starter solenoid wiring.

33. Install the cover for the starter terminals.

34. Position back the battery cable

bracket and install the nut. Tighten to 18 ft. lbs. (25 Nm).

35. Position back the RH turbocharger inlet pipe. Install a new gasket and the 3 new RH turbocharger inlet pipe-to-exhaust manifold studs. Tighten to 13 ft. lbs. (18 Nm).

36. Install a new turbocharger inlet pipe gasket and loosely install the 3 new RH turbocharger inlet pipe bolts. Tighten the top 2 bolts to 18 ft. lbs. (25 Nm).

※※ WARNING

Due to limited access, one of the specific Half-moon wrenches and other tools described must be used to correctly tighten the fasteners in this step. Failure to follow this instruction may result in engine failure.

➡**To complete this step, it will be necessary to use the following tools:**

- A ⅜-inch drive torque wrench that is 9.5 inches (241.3 mm) or 14.5 inches (368.3 mm) from center of the handle to the center of the square drive.
- One of the 10-mm/12-mm Half-moon wrenches listed in the following chart.
- A 12-mm Allen socket (to drive the Half-moon wrench).

➡**To obtain the required torque value of 18 ft. lbs. (25 Nm), it will be crucial to orient the Half-moon wrench in the direction shown and 180 degrees (straight out) from the torque wrench.**

37. Tighten the RH turbocharger inlet pipes-to-turbocharger bottom bolt.

38. Refer to the following chart for torque wrench setting, based on the specific Half-moon wrench and torque wrench length being used.

※※ WARNING

Make sure the correct bolts are installed in the bracket or damage to the bracket can occur.

39. Position the 2 EGR-OC pipe and loosely install the 2 new bracket bolts. Install a new gasket and loosely install the 2 new bolts.

40. Install the 3 new RH turbocharger inlet pipe-to-exhaust manifold nuts. Tighten to 23 ft. lbs. (31 Nm).

41. Install the EGRT sensor into the RH turbocharger inlet pipe. Tighten to 32 ft. lbs. (44 Nm).

42. Install the RH fender splash shield.

43. Install the RH front tire and wheel.

※※ WARNING

Failure to install and correctly tighten the Exhaust Gas Recirculation (EGR)-Oxidation Catalytic Converter (OC) pipe support bolts will result in damage to the horizontal EGR cooler and possible engine damage.

44. Install the bracket, washers and loosely install the 2 new bolts for the EGR-OC pipe bracket.

45. Install the new gasket and the 2 new bolts for the EGR cooler. Tighten to 23 ft. lbs. (31 Nm).

46. Tighten the 2 EGR-OC pipe bolts at the RH turbocharger inlet pipe. Tighten to 23 ft. lbs. (31 Nm).

47. Tighten the 2 bolts for the EGR-OC pipe bracket at the turbocharger. Tighten to 23 ft. lbs. (31 Nm).

48. Install a new gasket and loosely install the new clamp for the exhaust downpipe.

    a. Align the new exhaust downpipe-to-turbocharger clamp so that the exhaust downpipe clip and the opening in the exhaust downpipe-to-turbocharger clamp are aligned and tighten to maintain position.

    b. Align the downpipe so that the area just above the flat in the pipe is approximately 0.787 inches (20 mm) from the frame.

※※ WARNING

Failure to install and correctly tighten the Exhaust Gas Recirculation (EGR)-OC pipe support bolt will result in damage to the horizontal EGR cooler and possible engine damage.

49. Tighten the bolt for the EGR-OC pipe bracket. Tighten to 23 ft. lbs. (31 Nm).

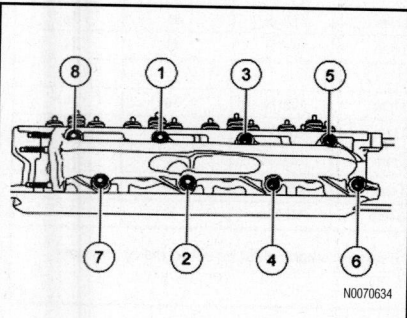

Fig. 216 Tighten in 2 stages in the sequence shown

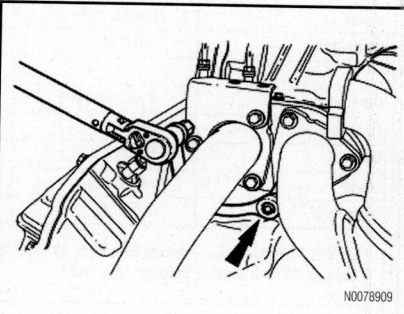

Fig. 217 Tighten the RH turbocharger inlet pipes-to-turbocharger bottom bolt

Torque Chart — Turbocharger Inlet Pipes-to-Turbocharger, Bottom 2 Bolts					
Half-Moon Wrench Brand	Wrench Part Number	Wrench Size	Torque Wrench Length	Torque Wrench Setting	
				Nm	lb-in
Cornwell®	BWM-1012MM	10/12 mm	9.5 in	20	177
Gear Wrench®	9851	10/12 mm	9.5 in	18	159
Matco®	MHM1012	10/12 mm	9.5 in	18	159
Mac®	HMM1012R	10/12 mm	9.5 in	15	133
Snap-On®	CXM1012	10/12 mm	9.5 in	18	159
Cornwell®	BWM-1012MM	10/12 mm	14.5 in	19	168
Gear Wrench®	9851	10/12 mm	14.5 in	18	159
Matco®	MHM1012	10/12 mm	14.5 in	18	159
Mac®	HMM1012R	10/12 mm	14.5 in	16	142
Snap-On®	CXM1012	10/12 mm	14.5 in	18	159

NOTE: To achive the required torque of 25 Nm (18 lb-ft), the torque wrench must be set to the appropriate Torque Wrench Setting listed in this chart.

N0091273

Fig. 218 Refer to the following chart for torque wrench setting

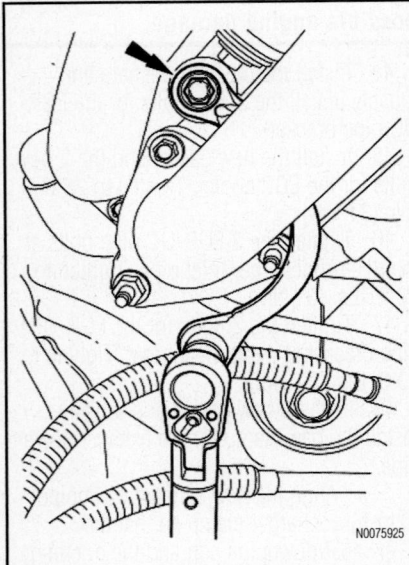

N0075925

Fig. 219 Tighten the EGR-OC pipe bracket-to-LH cylinder head bolt

❊❊ WARNING

Failure to install and correctly tighten the Exhaust Gas Recirculation (EGR)-Oxidation Catalytic Converter (OC) pipe support bolt will result in damage to the horizontal EGR cooler and possible engine damage.

❊❊ WARNING

Due to limited access, one of the specific Half-moon wrenches and other tools described must be used to correctly tighten the fasteners in this step. Failure to follow this instruction may result in engine failure.

➡**To complete this step, it will be necessary to use the following tools:**

- A ⅜-inch drive torque wrench that is 14.5 inches (368.3 mm) or 15.0 inches (381.0 mm) from the center of the handle to the center of the square drive.

- One of the 11-mm/13-mm Half-moon wrenches listed in the following chart.
- A 11-mm Allen socket (to drive the Half-moon wrench).

➡**To obtain the required torque value of 46 ft. lbs. (63 Nm), it will be crucial to orient the Half-moon wrench in the direction shown and 180 degrees (straight out) from the torque wrench. The torque wrench must be set to the value specified in the following chart, for the Half-moon wrench and torque wrench length being used.**

50. Tighten the EGR-OC pipe bracket-to-LH cylinder head bolt.

51. Refer to the following chart for torque wrench setting, based on the specific Half-moon wrench and torque wrench length being used.

52. Connect the EP sensor tube to the EGR-OC pipe. Tighten to 15 ft. lbs. (20 Nm).

53. Install the 2 exhaust downpipe-to-OC pipe bolts. Tighten to 30 ft. lbs. (40 Nm).

54. Tighten the clamp for the exhaust downpipe. Tighten to 11 ft. lbs. (15 Nm).

55. Connect the battery ground cables.

56. If equipped, evacuate and charge the A/C system.

57. Position the auxiliary air intake hose in the vehicle.

58. Install the ACL assembly.

Torque Chart—OC- EGR Pipe Bracket-to-LH Cylinder Head Bolt					
Half-Moon Wrench Brand	Wrench Part Number	Wrench Size	Torque Wrench Length	Torque Wrench Setting	
				Nm	lb-ft
Cornwell®	BWM-1113MM	11/13 mm	14.5 in	48	35
Gear Wrench®	9852	11/13 mm	14.5 in	46	34
Matco®	MHM1113	11/13 mm	14.5 in	46	34
Mac®	HMM1113R	11/13 mm	14.5 in	46	34
Snap-On®	CXM1113	11/13 mm	14.5 in	46	34
Cornwell®	BWM-1113MM	11/13 mm	15.0 in	49	36
Gear Wrench®	9852	11/13 mm	15.0 in	49	36
Matco®	MHM1113	11/13 mm	15.0 in	48	35
Mac®	HMM1113R	11/13 mm	15.0 in	48	35
Snap-On®	CXM1113	11/13 mm	15.0 in	48	35

NOTE: To achive the required torque of 63 Nm (46 lb-ft), the torque wrench must be set to the appropriate Torque Wrench Setting listed in this chart.

N0076311

Fig. 220 Refer to the following chart for torque wrench setting

6.7L Diesel Engine

Left Side

See Figures 221 and 222.

➡**The manufacturer does not provide a specific Removal and Installation procedure for this component. Refer to the graphic(s) when servicing this component.**

1. Using a new gasket, install the LH exhaust manifold and 8 new nuts. Tighten the nuts in 3 stages in the sequence shown.
   a. Stage 1: Tighten to 15 ft. lbs. (20 Nm).
   b. Stage 2: Tighten to 22 ft. lbs. (30 Nm).
   c. Stage 3: Tighten a second time, to 22 ft. lbs. (30 Nm).

Right Side

See Figures 223 and 224.

➡**The manufacturer does not provide a specific Removal and Installation procedure for this component. Refer to the graphic(s) when servicing this component.**

1. Using a new gasket, install the RH exhaust manifold and 8 new nuts. Tighten

2. Remove the degas bottle assembly.
3. Remove the 4 exhaust Y-pipe flange nuts.
4. Remove the 3 bolts and the exhaust manifold heat shield.
5. Remove the 8 nuts, 8 exhaust manifold-to-cylinder head studs and the exhaust manifold. Discard the 8 nuts and the 8 studs.

✳✳ WARNING

Do not use metal scrapers, wire brushes, power abrasive discs or other abrasive means to clean the sealing surfaces. These may cause scratches and gouges resulting in leak paths. Use a plastic scraper to clean the sealing surfaces.

6. Remove and discard the exhaust manifold gaskets.
7. Clean the sealing surfaces with metal surface prep. Follow the directions on the packaging.
8. Inspect the exhaust manifold.

To install:

9. Install 8 new exhaust manifold-to-cylinder head studs. Tighten to 106 inch lbs. (12 Nm).
10. Using new exhaust manifold gaskets, position the 2 gaskets and the exhaust manifold and install 8 new exhaust manifold nuts.
11. Tighten the exhaust manifold nuts to 18 ft. lbs. (25 Nm) in the sequence shown.
12. Position the exhaust manifold heat shield and install the 3 bolts. Tighten to 10 ft. lbs. (14 Nm).
13. Install the 4 exhaust Y-pipe flange nuts. Tighten to 30 ft. lbs. (40 Nm).
14. Install the degas bottle assembly.
15. Install the LH fender splash shield.

Right Side

See Figure 226.

1. With the vehicle in NEUTRAL, position it on a hoist.
2. Remove the starter.
3. Remove the RH inner fenderwell.
4. Remove the 4 exhaust Y-pipe flange nuts.
5. Remove the 2 bolts and the exhaust manifold heat shield.
6. Remove the 8 nuts, 8 exhaust manifold-to-cylinder head studs and the exhaust manifold. Discard the 8 nuts and the 8 studs.

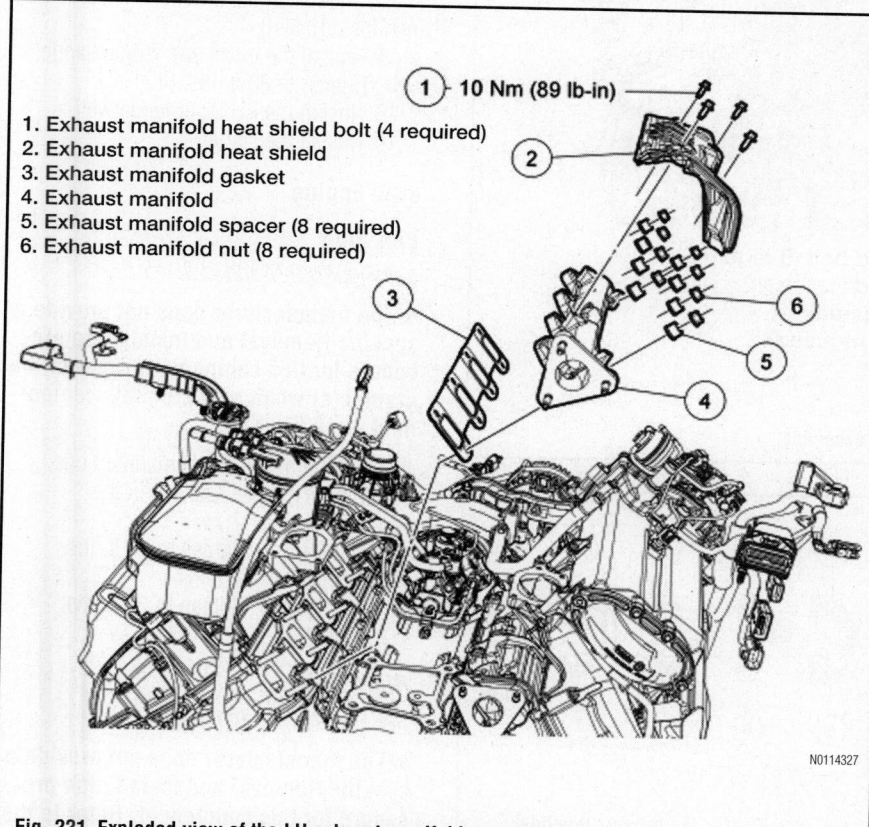

1. Exhaust manifold heat shield bolt (4 required)
2. Exhaust manifold heat shield
3. Exhaust manifold gasket
4. Exhaust manifold
5. Exhaust manifold spacer (8 required)
6. Exhaust manifold nut (8 required)

1 - 10 Nm (89 lb-in)

N0114327

Fig. 221 Exploded view of the LH exhaust manifold assembly

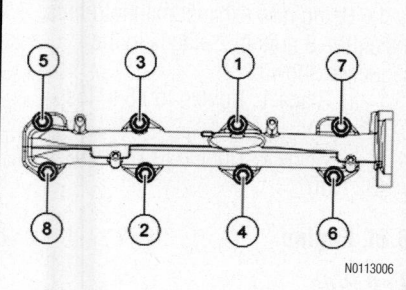

N0113006

Fig. 222 Tighten the exhaust manifold nuts in 3 stages in the sequence shown

the nuts in 3 stages in the sequence shown.
   a. Stage 1: Tighten to 15 ft. lbs. (20 Nm).
   b. Stage 2: Tighten to 22 ft. lbs. (30 Nm).
   c. Stage 3: Tighten a second time, to 22 ft. lbs. (30 Nm).

5.4L Engine

Left Side

See Figure 225.

1. Remove the LH fender splash shield.

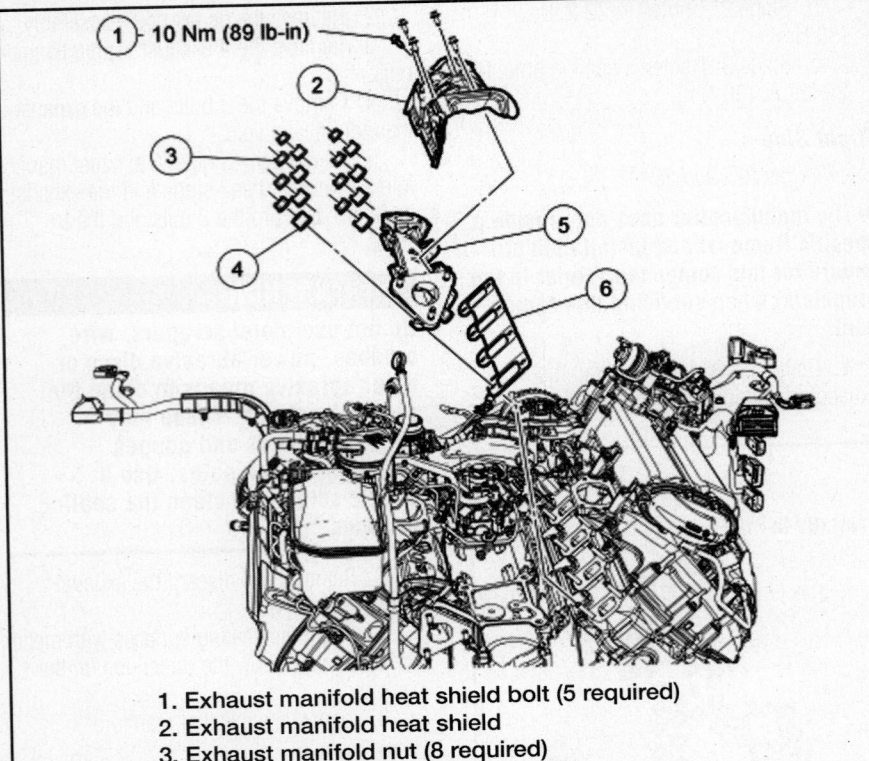

1. Exhaust manifold heat shield bolt (5 required)
2. Exhaust manifold heat shield
3. Exhaust manifold nut (8 required)
4. Exhaust manifold spacer (8 required)
5. Exhaust manifold
6. Exhaust manifold gasket

N0115853

Fig. 223 Exploded view of the RH exhaust manifold assembly

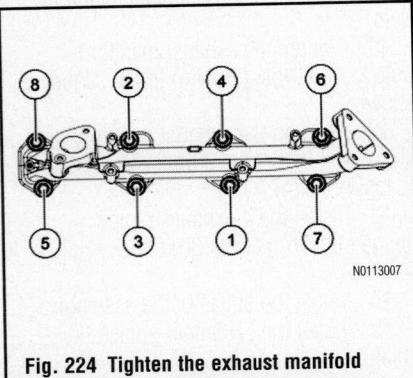

N0113007

Fig. 224 Tighten the exhaust manifold nuts in 3 stages in the sequence shown

❋❋ WARNING

Do not use metal scrapers, wire brushes, power abrasive discs or other abrasive means to clean the sealing surfaces. These may cause scratches and gouges resulting in leak paths. Use a plastic scraper to clean the sealing surfaces.

7. Remove and discard the exhaust manifold gaskets.
8. Clean the sealing surfaces with metal

N0010196

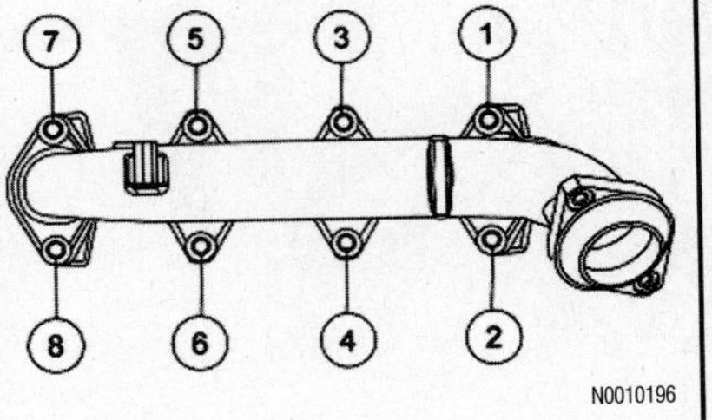

Fig. 225 Tighten the exhaust manifold nuts to 18 ft. lbs. (25 Nm) in the sequence shown

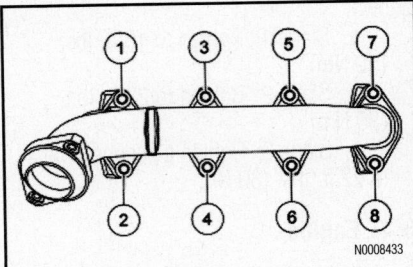

N0008433

Fig. 226 Tighten the 8 new exhaust manifold nuts to 18 ft. lbs. (25 Nm) in the sequence shown

surface prep. Follow the directions on the packaging.

9. Inspect the exhaust manifold.

To install:

10. Install 8 new exhaust manifold-to-cylinder head studs. Tighten to 106 inch lbs. (12 Nm).

11. Using new exhaust manifold gaskets, position the gaskets and the exhaust manifold and install 8 new exhaust manifold nuts.

12. Tighten the 8 new exhaust manifold nuts to 18 ft. lbs. (25 Nm) in the sequence shown.

13. Position the exhaust manifold heat shield and install the 2 bolts. Tighten to 89 inch lbs. (10 Nm).

14. Install the 4 exhaust Y-pipe flange nuts. Tighten to 30 ft. lbs. (40 Nm).

15. Install the RH inner fenderwell.

16. Install the starter.

6.2L Engine

Left Side

See Figures 227 and 228.

➡**The manufacturer does not provide a specific Removal and Installation procedure for this component. Refer to the graphic(s) when servicing this component.**

1. Using new exhaust manifold nuts, install the 8 nuts in 2 stages in the sequence shown.
   a. Stage 1: Tighten to 18 ft. lbs. (25 Nm).
   b. Stage 2: Tighten to 24 ft. lbs. (32 Nm).

Right Side

See Figures 229 and 230.

➡**The manufacturer does not provide a specific Removal and Installation procedure for this component. Refer to the graphic(s) when servicing this component.**

1. Using new exhaust manifold nuts, install the 8 nuts in 2 stages in the sequence shown.
   a. Stage 1: Tighten to 18 ft. lbs. (25 Nm).
   b. Stage 2: Tighten to 24 ft. lbs. (32 Nm).

6.8L Engine

Left Side

See Figures 231 and 232.

1. With the vehicle in NEUTRAL, position it on a hoist.

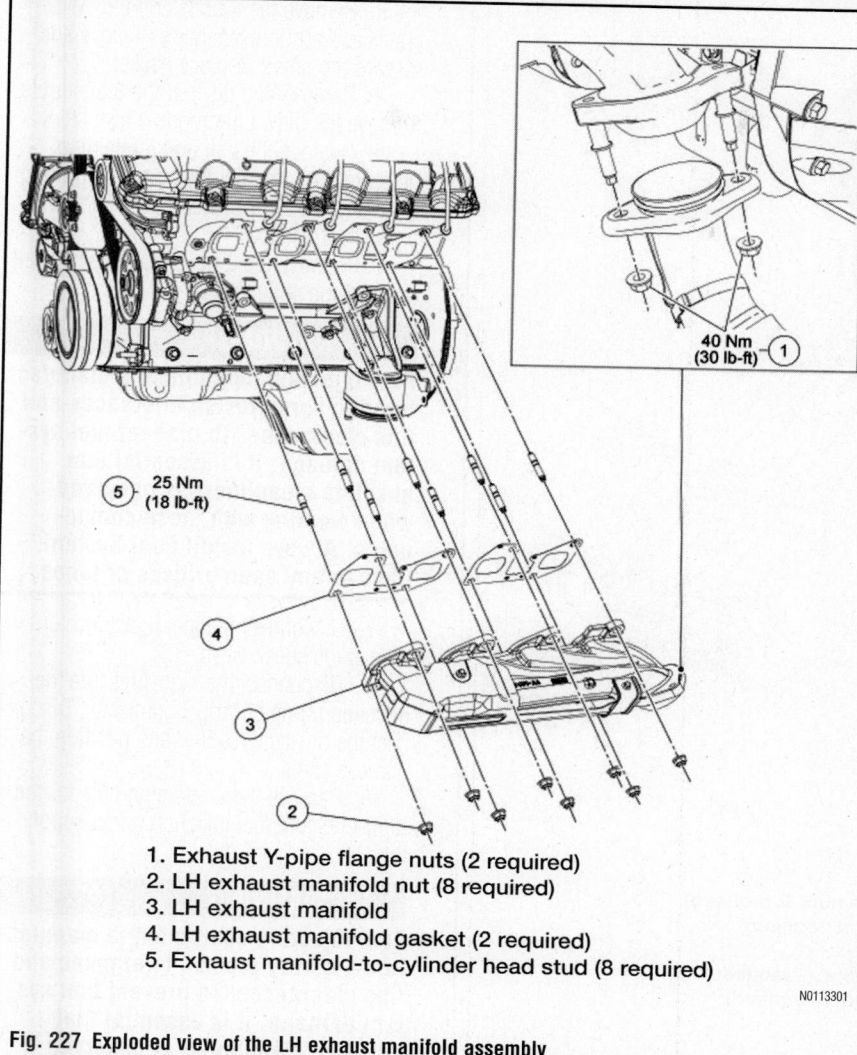

1. Exhaust Y-pipe flange nuts (2 required)
2. LH exhaust manifold nut (8 required)
3. LH exhaust manifold
4. LH exhaust manifold gasket (2 required)
5. Exhaust manifold-to-cylinder head stud (8 required)

N0113301

Fig. 227 Exploded view of the LH exhaust manifold assembly

2. Remove the 4 exhaust Y-pipe flange nuts.

3. Remove the 3 bolts and the exhaust manifold heat shield.

4. Remove the 10 nuts and the exhaust manifold. Discard the 10 nuts.

5. Inspect the exhaust manifold.

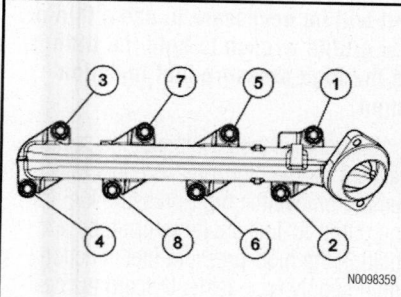

N0098359

Fig. 228 Using new exhaust manifold nuts, install the 8 nuts in 2 stages in the sequence shown

✳✳ WARNING

Do not use metal scrapers, wire brushes, power abrasive discs or other abrasive means to clean the sealing surfaces. These tools cause scratches and gouges which make leak paths. Use a plastic scraping tool to remove all traces of old sealant. Failure to follow this procedure may cause future oil leakage.

➡ Clean the sealing surfaces with metal surface prep. Follow the directions on the packaging.

6. Remove and discard the exhaust manifold gaskets. Clean the sealing surfaces with metal surface prep.

7. Remove and discard the 10 exhaust manifold-to-cylinder head studs.

To install:

8. Install 10 new exhaust manifold-to-cylinder head studs. Tighten to 106 inch lbs. (12 Nm).

9. Using new exhaust manifold gaskets, position the gaskets and the exhaust manifold and install 10 new exhaust manifold nuts.

10. Tighten the 10 new exhaust manifold nuts to 18 ft. lbs. (25 Nm) in the sequence shown.

11. Position the exhaust manifold heat shield and install the 3 bolts. Tighten to 10 ft. lbs. (14 Nm).

12. Install the 4 exhaust Y-pipe flange nuts. Tighten to 30 ft. lbs. (40 Nm).

Right Side

See Figures 233 and 234.

1. With the vehicle in NEUTRAL, position it on a hoist.

2. If equipped, remove the transmission filler tube.

3. Remove the starter.

4. Remove the RH inner fenderwell.

5. Remove the 4 exhaust Y-pipe flange nuts.

6. Remove the 2 bolts and the exhaust manifold heat shield.

7. Remove the 10 nuts and the exhaust manifold.

8. Inspect the exhaust manifold.

✳✳ WARNING

Do not use metal scrapers, wire brushes, power abrasive discs or other abrasive means to clean the sealing surfaces. These tools cause scratches and gouges which make leak paths. Use a plastic scraping tool to remove all traces of old sealant. Failure to follow this procedure may cause future oil leakage.

➡ Clean the sealing surfaces with metal surface prep. Follow the directions on the packaging.

9. Remove and discard the exhaust manifold gaskets. Clean the sealing surfaces with Motorcraft metal surface prep.

10. Remove and discard the 10 exhaust manifold-to-cylinder head studs.

To install:

11. Install 10 new exhaust manifold-to-cylinder head studs. Tighten to 106 inch lbs. (12 Nm).

12. Using new exhaust manifold gaskets, position the gaskets and the exhaust manifold and install 10 new exhaust manifold nuts.

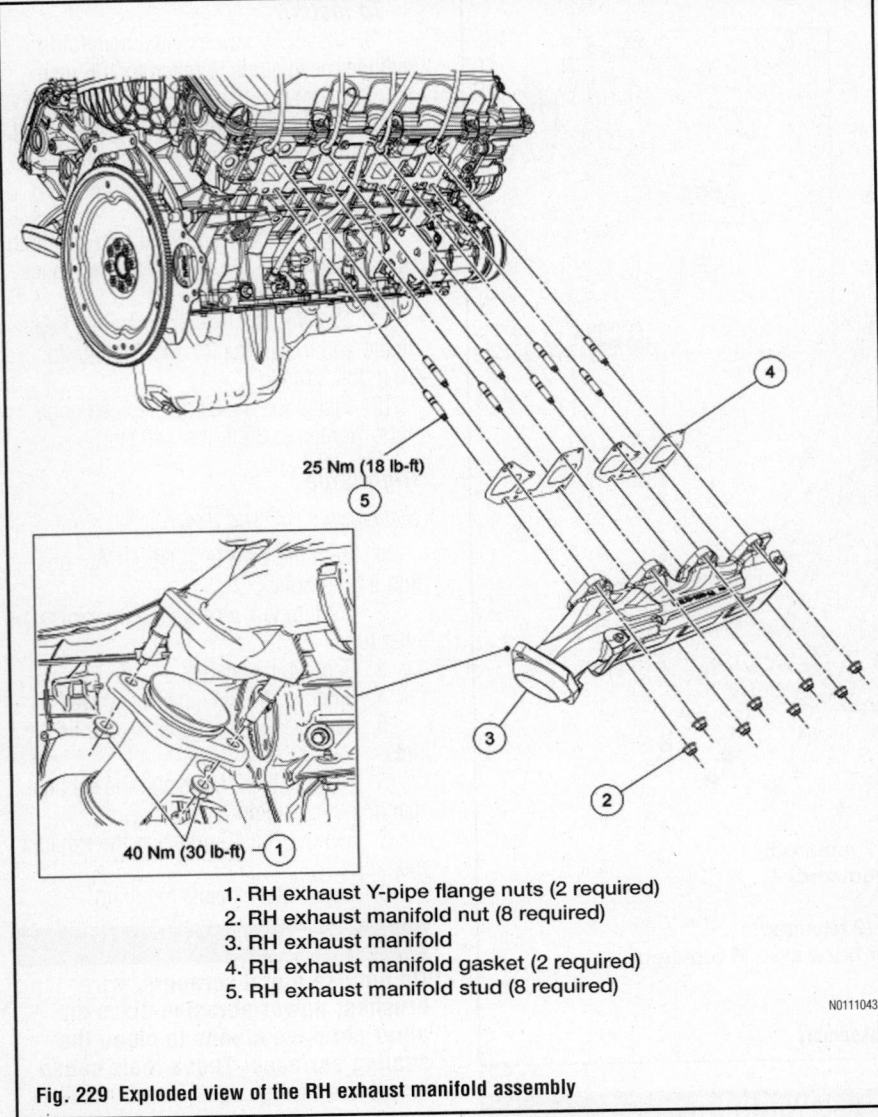

25 Nm (18 lb-ft)

40 Nm (30 lb-ft)

1. RH exhaust Y-pipe flange nuts (2 required)
2. RH exhaust manifold nut (8 required)
3. RH exhaust manifold
4. RH exhaust manifold gasket (2 required)
5. RH exhaust manifold stud (8 required)

N0111043

Fig. 229 Exploded view of the RH exhaust manifold assembly

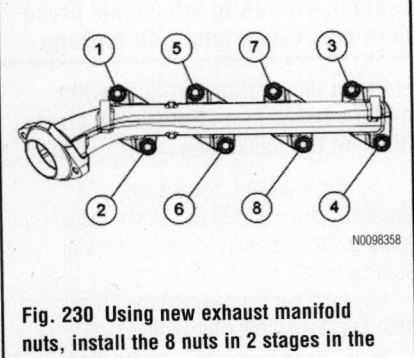

N0098358

Fig. 230 Using new exhaust manifold nuts, install the 8 nuts in 2 stages in the sequence shown

13. Tighten the 10 new exhaust manifold nuts to 18 ft. lbs. (25 Nm) in the sequence shown.

14. Position the exhaust manifold heat shield and install the 2 bolts. Tighten to 10 ft. lbs. (14 Nm).

15. Install the 4 exhaust manifold-to-catalytic converter nuts. Tighten to 30 ft. lbs. (40 Nm).

16. Install the RH inner fenderwell.

17. Install the starter.

18. If equipped, install the transmission filler tube.

INTAKE MANIFOLD

REMOVAL & INSTALLATION

6.4L Diesel Engine
See Figures 235 through 266.

➡**It is recommended that this component be serviced with the vehicle body removed.**

1. Remove the turbocharger.

2. Disconnect the crankcase vent oil separator tube from the crankcase vent oil separator.

3. Remove the 4 bolts and the crankcase vent oil separator. Remove and discard the press-in-place gasket.

4. Remove and discard the 3 pushnuts. Remove the glow plug module heat shield.

5. Remove the bolt and 5 retaining nuts. Remove the fuel tube bracket, ground strap and the high-pressure fuel injection pump heat shield.

6. Remove the 2 bolts from the fuel rail supply tube retainers.

✳✳ WARNING

Fuel injection equipment is manufactured to very precise tolerances and fine clearances. To prevent fuel system damage, it is essential that absolute cleanliness is observed when working with these components. Always install Fuel System Caps to any open orifices or tubes.

7. Disconnect the fuel injector return tube at the check valve.

8. Disconnect the high-pressure fuel injection pump electrical connector. Disconnect the pin-type retainer and position the harness aside.

9. Remove the 2 retaining nuts for the high-pressure fuel injection pump supply tube.

✳✳ WARNING

Fuel injection equipment is manufactured to very precise tolerances and fine clearances. To prevent fuel system damage, it is essential that absolute cleanliness is observed when working with these components. Always install Fuel System Caps to any open orifices or tubes.

➡**Use a back-up wrench to prevent the fittings in the high-pressure fuel injection pump from turning. If the fittings move, the high-pressure fuel injection pump fittings must be retightened.**

➡**It will be necessary to use a thin or low profile wrench to hold the fittings on the high-pressure fuel injection pump.**

10. Remove the 2 nuts and the sealing washers for the high-pressure fuel injection pump. Remove the high-pressure fuel injection pump-to-fuel cooler return tube and position the high-pressure fuel injection pump supply tube aside. Discard the sealing washers.

11. Disconnect the electrical connector for the engine cooling fan. Squeeze the tabs and remove the cooling fan electrical connector from the stator.

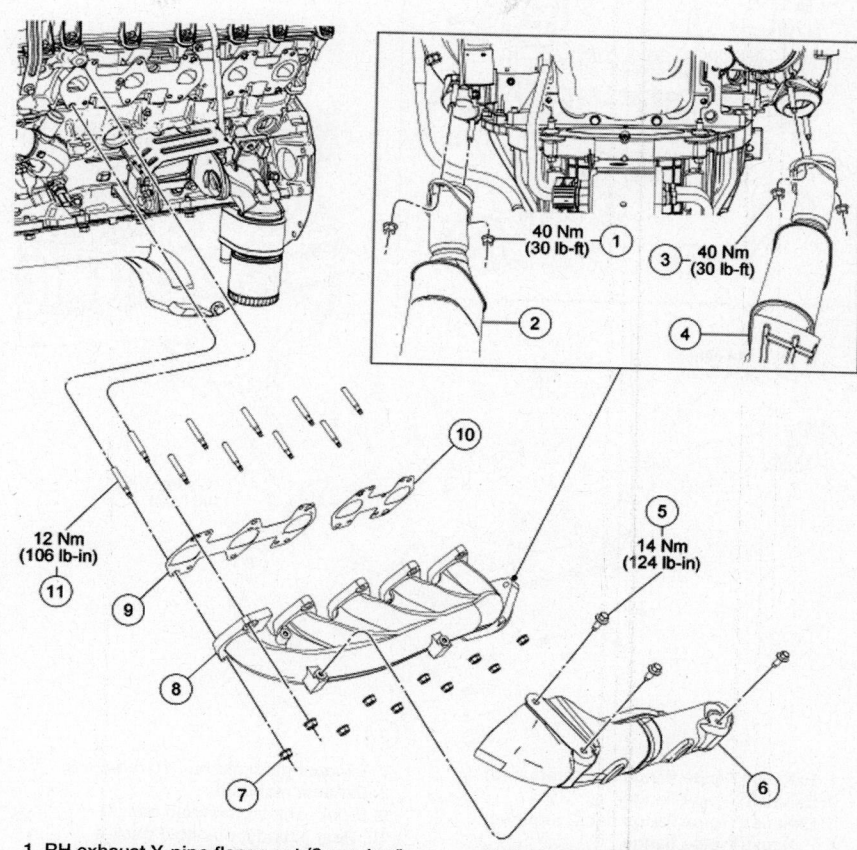

1. RH exhaust Y-pipe flange nut (2 required)
2. RH exhaust Y-pipe flange
3. LH exhaust Y-pipe flange nut (2 required)
4. LH exhaust Y-pipe flange
5. Exhaust manifold heat shield bolt (3 required)
6. Exhaust manifold heat shield
7. Exhaust manifold nut (10 required)
8. Exhaust manifold
9. Front exhaust manifold gasket
10. Rear exhaust manifold gasket
11. Exhaust manifold-to-cylinder head
   stud (10 required)

N0105862

Fig. 231 Exploded view of the exhaust manifold LH

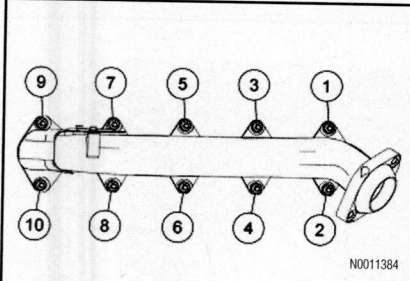

N0011384

Fig. 232 Tighten the 10 new exhaust manifold nuts to 18 ft. lbs. (25 Nm) in the sequence shown

➡**The cooling fan has a LH thread.**

12. Using the Fan Clutch Nut Wrench and Fan Hub Nut Wrench, remove the engine cooling fan.

13. Remove the 2 nuts, 2 bolts and engine cooling fan stator.

14. Remove the accessory drive belt.

15. If equipped, remove the A/C drive belt. Remove the belt from the bottom of the A/C clutch pulley, then remove it from the crankshaft pulley.

16. Remove the retaining nut for the power steering hoses.

➡**Raise the supply tube up to clear the Engine Coolant Temperature (ECT) sensor connector when positioning the power steering pump aside.**

17. Remove the 3 bolts and position the power steering pump aside.

➡**The Front End Accessory Drive (FEAD) is not removed, it is positioned forward to access the front banjo bolt.**

➡**It may be necessary to position the accessory drive tensioner to access the lower bolt. Remove the bottom bolt first.**

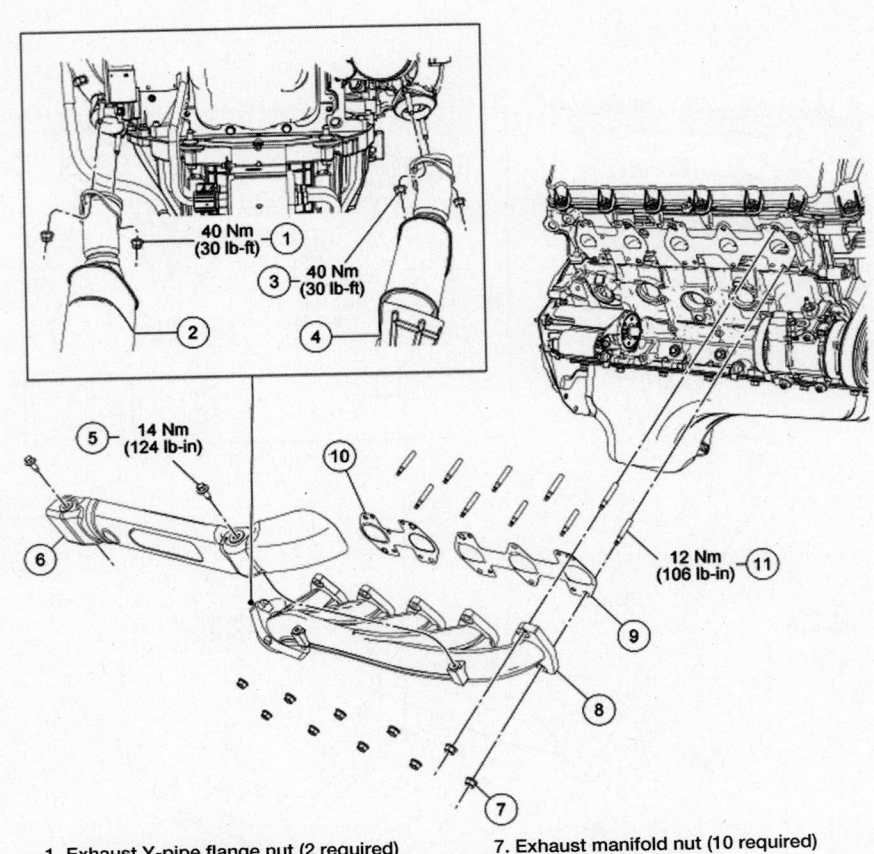

1. Exhaust Y-pipe flange nut (2 required)
2. Exhaust Y-pipe flange
3. Exhaust Y-pipe flange nut (2 required)
4. Exhaust Y-pipe flange
5. Exhaust manifold heat shield bolt (2 required)
6. Exhaust manifold heat shield
7. Exhaust manifold nut (10 required)
8. Exhaust manifold
9. Front exhaust manifold gasket
10. Rear exhaust manifold gasket
11. Exhaust manifold-to-cylinder head stud (10 required)

Fig. 233 Exploded view of the exhaust manifold RH

18. Remove the 2 nuts, 2 bolts and slide the FEAD assembly forward.

19. Remove the bolt and the EGR cooler coolant tube. Remove and discard the O-ring seal.

❊❊ WARNING

The coolant hose clamps used on this engine are constant tension worm gear clamps. Standard worm gear clamps cannot be used. Failure to use the correct coolant hose clamps may result in hose joint failure.

20. Loosen the clamp and disconnect the EGR cooler hose. Discard the EGR cooler clamp.

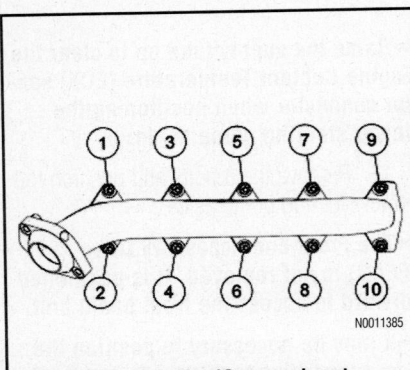

Fig. 234 Tighten the 10 new exhaust manifold nuts to 18 ft. lbs. (25 Nm) in the sequence shown

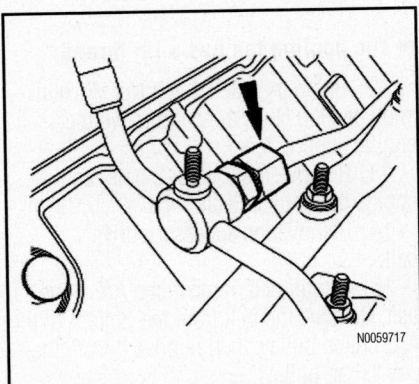

Fig. 235 Disconnect the fuel injector return tube at the check valve

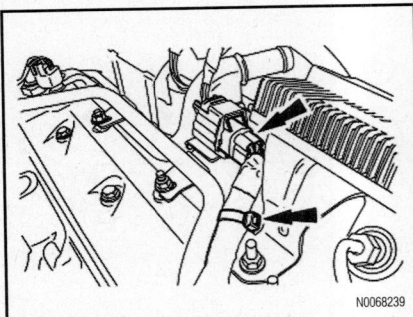

Fig. 236 Disconnect the high-pressure fuel injection pump electrical connector

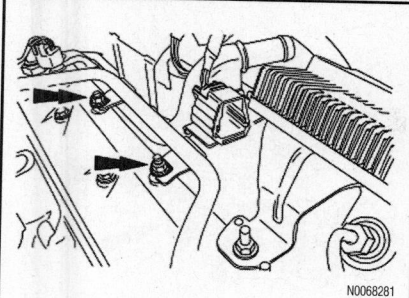

Fig. 237 Remove the 2 retaining nuts for the high-pressure fuel injection pump supply tube

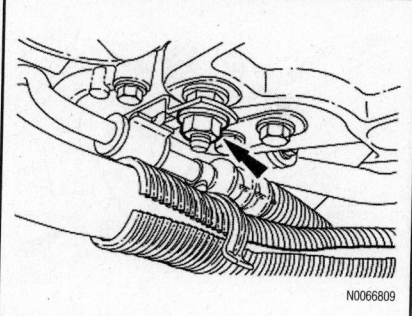

Fig. 241 Remove the retaining nut for the power steering hoses

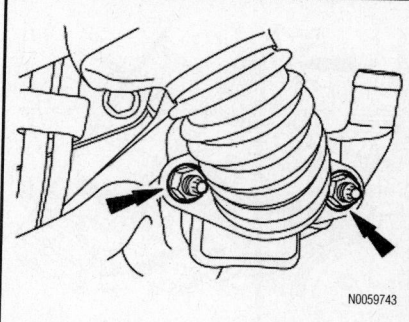

Fig. 245 Remove the 2 retaining nuts for the vertical EGR cooler

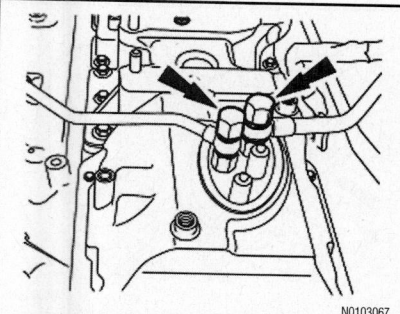

Fig. 238 Remove the 2 nuts and the sealing washers for the high-pressure fuel injection pump

Fig. 242 Remove the 2 nuts, 2 bolts and slide the FEAD assembly forward

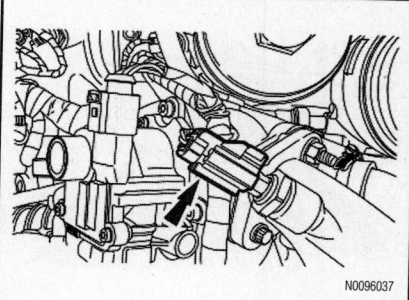

Fig. 246 Disconnect the Exhaust Gas Recirculation Temperature (EGRT) sensor electrical connector

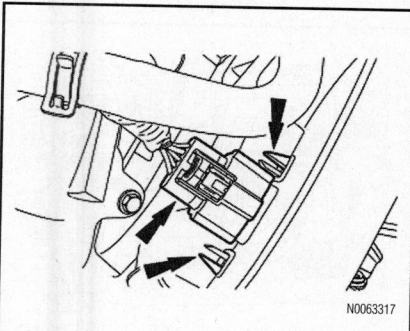

Fig. 239 Disconnect the electrical connector for the engine cooling fan

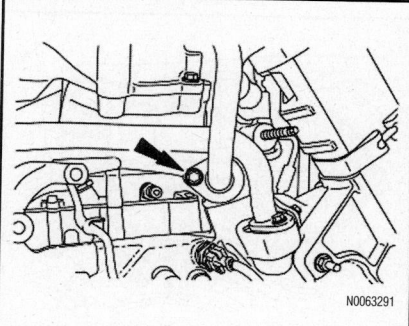

Fig. 243 Remove the bolt and the EGR cooler coolant tube

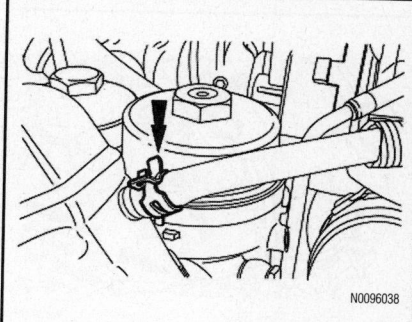

Fig. 247 Disconnect the coolant hose from the vertical EGR cooler

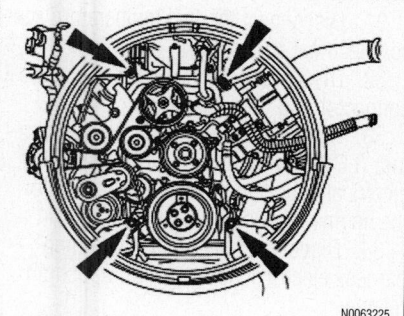

Fig. 240 Remove the 2 nuts, 2 bolts and engine cooling fan stator

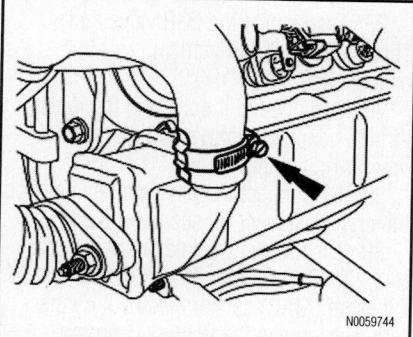

Fig. 244 Loosen the clamp and disconnect the EGR cooler hose

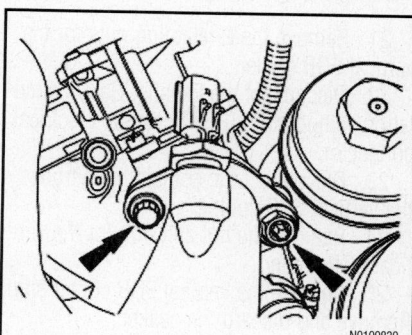

Fig. 248 Remove the nut and bolt for the vertical EGR cooler

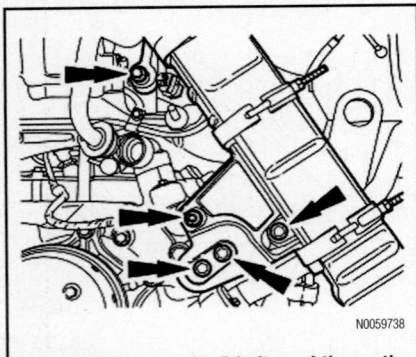

Fig. 249 Remove the 5 bolts and the vertical EGR cooler assembly

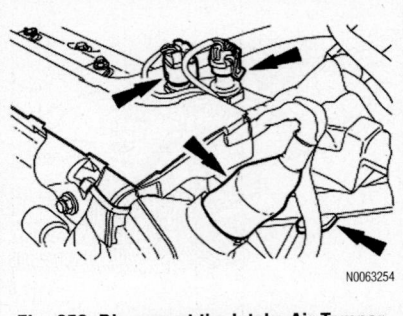

Fig. 252 Disconnect the Intake Air Temperature 2 (IAT2) and Manifold Absolute Pressure (MAP) sensor electrical connectors

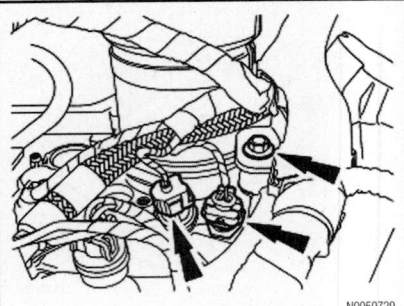

Fig. 255 Disconnect the Engine Oil Temperature (EOT) and Engine Oil Pressure (EOP) electrical connectors

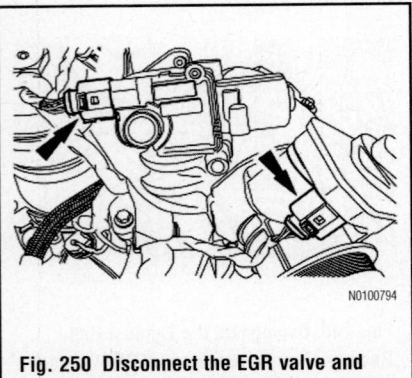

Fig. 250 Disconnect the EGR valve and Throttle Body (TB) electrical connectors

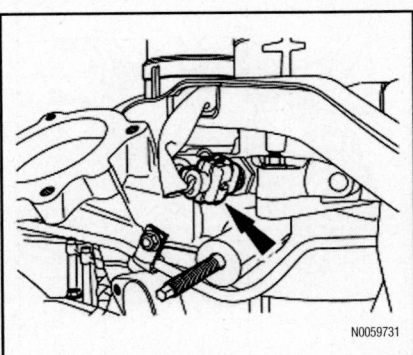

Fig. 253 Disconnect the fuel temperature sensor electrical connector

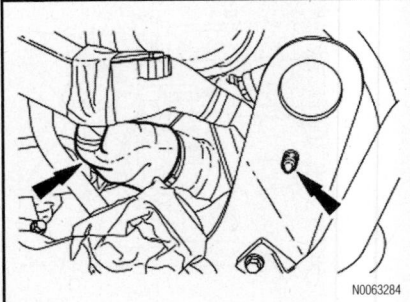

Fig. 256 Disconnect the LH fuel charging harness electrical connector and pushpin retainer

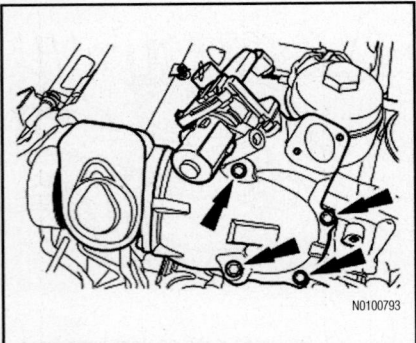

Fig. 251 Remove the 4 bolts and the intake throttle adapter

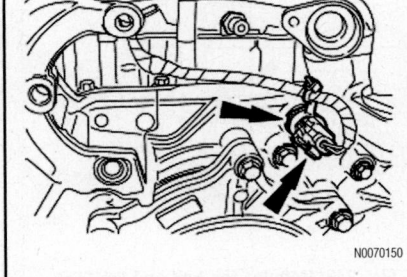

Fig. 254 Disconnect the ECT sensor electrical connector and wire retainer

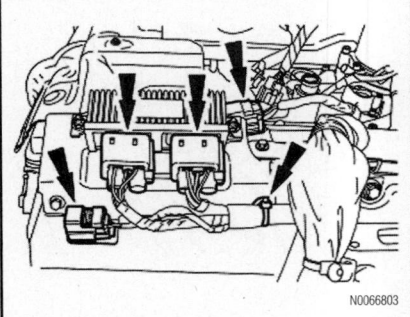

Fig. 257 Disconnect the glow plug module electrical connectors

21. Remove the 2 retaining nuts for the vertical EGR cooler.

22. Disconnect the Exhaust Gas Recirculation Temperature (EGRT) sensor electrical connector.

23. Disconnect the coolant hose from the vertical EGR cooler.

24. Remove the nut and bolt for the vertical EGR cooler.

25. Remove the vertical EGR cooler stud. Remove and discard the gasket.

26. Remove the 5 bolts and the vertical EGR cooler assembly. Remove and discard the gasket.

27. Disconnect the EGR valve and Throttle Body (TB) electrical connectors.

28. Remove the 4 bolts and the intake throttle adapter. Remove and discard the press-in-place gasket.

29. Disconnect the pin-type retainer from the crankcase vent oil separator tube.

30. Disconnect the Intake Air Temperature 2 (IAT2) and Manifold Absolute Pressure (MAP) sensor electrical connectors. Disconnect the RH fuel charging wiring harness electrical connector and wire retainer.

31. Disconnect the fuel temperature sensor electrical connector.

32. Disconnect the ECT sensor electrical connector and wire retainer.

33. Disconnect the Engine Oil Temperature (EOT) and Engine Oil Pressure (EOP) electrical connectors. Remove the bolt for the engine harness.

34. Disconnect the LH fuel charging harness electrical connector and pushpin retainer.

35. Disconnect the glow plug module electrical connectors. Disconnect the pin-type retainers.

Fig. 258 Remove the heater supply tube bolt and position the engine wiring harness aside

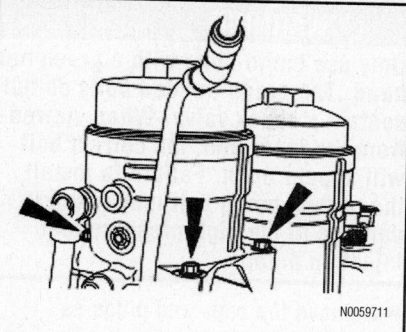

Fig. 262 Remove the 3 bolts and the fuel filter module

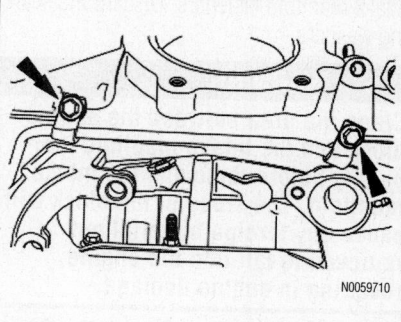

Fig. 264 Remove the 2 bolts for the fuel injector return tube retainer

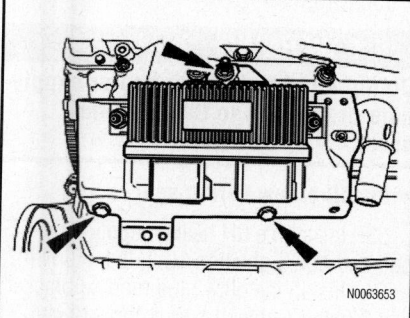

Fig. 259 Remove the 3 bolts and the glow plug module bracket

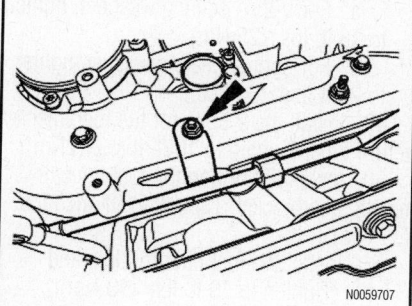

Fig. 263 Remove the nut for the fuel injector return tube bracket

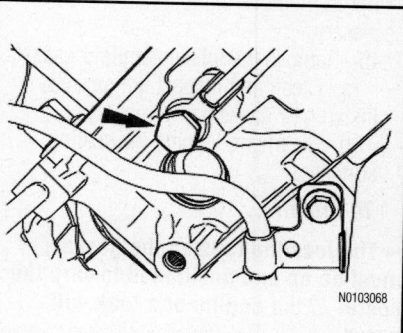

Fig. 265 Remove the LH and RH banjo bolts and sealing washers

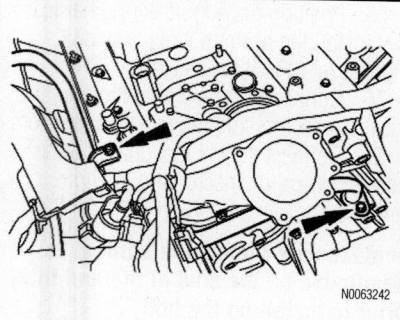

Fig. 260 Remove the nut, bolt and the RH heater supply tube

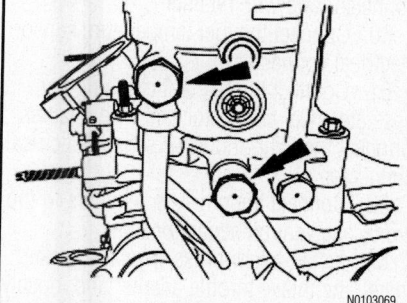

Fig. 261 Remove the banjo bolts for the fuel supply and return tubes at the fuel filter module

36. Remove the heater supply tube bolt and position the engine wiring harness aside.

37. Remove the 3 bolts and the glow plug module bracket.

❈❈ WARNING

Do not bend or flex the heater supply tube or damage to the tube may occur.

38. Remove the nut, bolt and the RH heater supply tube. Remove and discard the O-ring seal.

❈❈ WARNING

Fuel injection equipment is manufactured to very precise tolerances and fine clearances. To prevent fuel system damage, it is essential that absolute cleanliness is observed when working with these components. Always install Fuel System Caps to any open orifices or tubes.

39. Remove the banjo bolts for the fuel supply and return tubes at the fuel filter module. Remove and discard the sealing washers.

❈❈ WARNING

Fuel injection equipment is manufactured to very precise tolerances and fine clearances. To prevent fuel system damage, it is essential that absolute cleanliness is observed when working with these components. Always install Fuel System Caps to any open orifices or tubes.

40. Remove the 3 bolts and the fuel filter module.

41. Remove the nut for the fuel injector return tube bracket.

42. Remove the 2 bolts for the fuel injector return tube retainer.

❈❈ WARNING

Fuel injection equipment is manufactured to very precise tolerances and fine clearances. To prevent fuel system damage, it is essential that absolute cleanliness is observed when working with these components. Always install Fuel System Caps to any open orifices or tubes.

43. Remove the LH and RH banjo bolts and sealing washers. Position the fuel injector return tube as needed to access the

intake manifold fasteners. Discard the sealing washers.

✳✳ WARNING

Clean the area between the engine block and the intake manifold thoroughly before removing the intake manifold. The slope of the block will cause any foreign material not removed to fall into the engine, resulting in engine damage.

➡**Mark the location of the fasteners prior to removing.**

44. Remove the 16 bolts and the intake manifold. Remove the fuel return tube, if necessary.
45. Remove the intake manifold gaskets.
    a. Clean and inspect the gaskets. Install new gaskets if necessary.
    b. Clean and inspect the sealing surfaces.

To install:

➡**The locating tabs on the gaskets must be up and positioned toward the center of the engine or a leak will occur.**

46. Install the intake manifold gaskets.
47. Position the fuel return tube, if removed. Install the intake manifold and 16 bolts and tighten in 2 stages, in the sequence shown.
    a. Stage 1: Loosely assemble all bolts in the sequence shown.
    b. Stage 2: Tighten to 97 inch lbs. (11 Nm).

✳✳ WARNING

Only use banjo bolts with a green hex head. The green-headed bolts do not contain a check valve. When viewed from the inner end, the correct bolt will appear open. Failure to install the correct banjo bolt may result in damage to the high-pressure fuel injection pump.

➡**Remove the caps and plugs as needed.**

48. Position the fuel injector return tube. Install new sealing washers and the 2 banjo bolts at the cylinder heads.
    a. For Viton® sealing washers, tighten to 18 ft. lbs. (25 Nm).
    b. For copper sealing washer, tighten to 28 ft. lbs. (38 Nm).
49. Install the 2 bolts for the fuel injector return tube. Tighten to 10 ft. lbs. (13 Nm).
50. Install the nut on the fuel injector return tube bracket. Tighten to 97 inch lbs. (11 Nm).
51. Install the fuel filter module and 3 bolts. Tighten to 10 ft. lbs. (13 Nm).

✳✳ WARNING

Only use banjo bolts with a green hex head. The green-headed bolts do not contain a check valve. When viewed from the inner end, the correct bolt will appear open. Failure to install the correct banjo bolt may result in damage to the high-pressure fuel injection pump.

➡**Remove the Fuel System Caps as needed.**

52. Install new sealing washers and the banjo bolts at the fuel filter module.
    a. For M14 banjo bolt with Viton® sealing washers, tighten to 21 ft. lbs. (28 Nm).
    b. For M14 banjo bolt with copper sealing washer, tighten to 35 ft. lbs. (47 Nm).
    c. For M12 banjo bolt with Viton® sealing washers, tighten to 18 ft. lbs. (25 Nm).
    d. For M12 banjo bolt with copper sealing washer, tighten to 28 ft. lbs. (38 Nm).

✳✳ WARNING

Do not bend or flex the heater supply tube or damage to the tube may occur.

➡**Install a new O-ring seal.**

53. Install the RH heater supply tube, bolt and nut. Tighten to 10 ft. lbs. (13 Nm).
54. Install the glow plug module bracket and 3 bolts. Tighten to 10 ft. lbs. (13 Nm).

➡**The engine harness must be positioned between the glow plug module bracket and the heater supply tube.**

55. Position the engine wiring harness and install the heater supply tube bolt. Tighten to 10 ft. lbs. (13 Nm).
56. Connect the glow plug module electrical connectors and the pin-type retainers.
57. Connect the LH fuel charging harness electrical connector and pushpin retainer.

➡**Make sure the engine harness is positioned on the stud at the fuel filter prior to installing the bolt.**

58. Install the bolt for the engine wire harness. Connect the EOP and EOT sensor electrical connectors.
59. Connect the ECT sensor electrical connector and wire retainer.
60. Connect the fuel temperature sensor electrical connector.
61. Connect the RH fuel charging harness electrical connector and wire retainer. Connect the IAT2 and MAP sensor electrical connector.
62. Connect the pin-type retainers to the crankcase vent oil separator tube.
63. Install a new press-in-place gasket. Install the intake throttle adapter and loosely install the 4 bolts.
64. Connect the EGR valve and TB electrical connectors.

N0059777

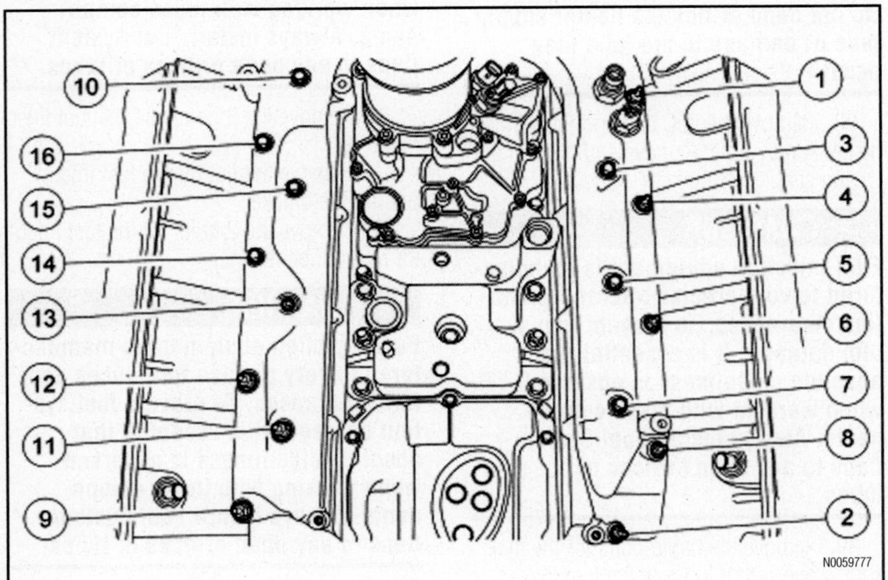

Fig. 266 Install the intake manifold and 16 bolts and tighten in 2 stages, in the sequence shown

➡️**Install a new horizontal EGR cooler gasket prior to installing the vertical EGR cooler.**

65. Position the vertical EGR cooler assembly and loosely install the 5 bolts.

66. Install a new vertical EGR cooler gasket and the stud. Tighten to 13 ft. lbs. (17 Nm).

67. Install the nut and bolt for the vertical EGR cooler. Tighten to 23 ft. lbs. (31 Nm).

68. Connect the EGRT sensor electrical connector.

69. Connect the coolant hose to the vertical EGR cooler.

⁂ WARNING

Do not bend or twist the Exhaust Gas Recirculation (EGR) cooler bellows or damage to the EGR cooler may occur.

➡️**Inspect the corrugation of the vertical EGR cooler inlet to make sure that the corrugation ribs are not touching and are not damaged.**

70. Install the 2 nuts for the vertical EGR cooler. Tighten to 23 ft. lbs. (31 Nm).

⁂ WARNING

The coolant hose clamps used on this engine are constant tension worm gear clamps. Standard worm gear clamps cannot be used. Failure to use the correct coolant hose clamps may result in hose joint failure.

➡️**Install a new clamp on the EGR cooler hose.**

71. Connect the EGR cooler hose and tighten the clamp.

72. Tighten the 5 vertical EGR cooler mounting bracket bolts.

    a. Tighten the M8 bolts to 23 ft. lbs. (31 Nm).

    b. Tighten the M10 bolt to 46 ft. lbs. (62 Nm).

➡️**Vertical EGR cooler removed from art for clarity.**

73. Tighten the 4 bolts for the intake throttle adapter. Tighten to 89 inch lbs. (10 Nm).

➡️**Install a new O-ring seal.**

74. Install the EGR cooler coolant tube and bolt. Tighten to 89 inch lbs. (10 Nm).

➡️**It may be necessary to position the tensioner to install the lower bolt. Install the lower bolt last.**

75. Position back the FEAD assembly.

Install the 2 nuts and 2 bolts. Tighten to 35 ft. lbs. (47 Nm).

➡️**Raise the supply tube up to clear the ECT sensor connector when repositioning the power steering pump.**

➡️**Make sure the power steering pressure tube retainer is on the retaining stud prior to tightening the bolts for the power steering pump.**

76. Install the power steering pump and 3 bolts. Tighten to 18 ft. lbs. (25 Nm).

77. Install the retaining nut for the power steering hose and tube. Tighten to 18 ft. lbs. (25 Nm).

78. If equipped, install the A/C drive belt.

79. Install the accessory drive belt.

80. Install the engine cooling fan stator, 2 nuts and 2 bolts. Tighten to 18 ft. lbs. (25 Nm).

➡️**The cooling fan has a LH thread.**

81. Using the Fan Clutch Nut Wrench and Fan Hub Nut Wrench, install the engine cooling fan. Tighten to 111 ft. lbs. (150 Nm).

82. Install the cooling fan electrical connector into the stator. Connect the electrical connector for the engine cooling fan.

➡️**Use a back-up wrench to prevent the fittings in the high-pressure fuel injection pump from turning. If the fittings move, the high-pressure fuel injection pump fittings must be retightened.**

➡️**It will be necessary to use a thin or low profile wrench to hold the fittings on the high-pressure fuel injection pump.**

83. Install new sealing washers, high-pressure fuel injection pump supply tube, high-pressure fuel injection pump-to-fuel cooler return tube and nuts at the high-pressure fuel injection pump.

    a. For Viton® sealing washers, tighten to 18 ft. lbs. (25 Nm).

    b. For copper sealing washer, tighten to 28 ft. lbs. (38 Nm).

84. Install the 2 retaining nuts for the fuel injection pump supply tube. Tighten to 97 inch lbs. (11 Nm).

85. Position back and connect the pin-type retainer. Connect the high-pressure fuel injection pump electrical connector.

➡️**Use a crowfoot wrench to aid in tightening the fitting.**

86. Connect the fuel injector return tube at the check valve. Tighten to 21 ft. lbs. (28 Nm).

87. Install the 2 bolts for the fuel rail supply tube retainers. Tighten to 10 ft. lbs. (13 Nm).

⁂ WARNING

Failure to correctly install the fuel pump heat shield may result in engine damage.

➡️**Make sure the ground strap is mounted on the stud closest to the glow plug module.**

88. Position the high-pressure fuel injection pump heat shield, ground strap and fuel tube bracket. Install the bolt and 5 retaining nuts.

    a. Tighten the fuel line bracket nuts to 62 inch lbs. (7 Nm).

    b. Tighten the remaining fasteners to 10 ft. lbs. (13 Nm).

➡️**Use a socket to aid in installing the pushnuts.**

89. Position the glow plug module cover and install the 3 new pushnuts.

➡️**Install a new press-in-place gasket.**

90. Install the crankcase vent oil separator and 4 bolts. Tighten to 10 ft. lbs. (13 Nm).

91. Connect the crankcase vent oil separator tube.

92. Install the turbocharger.

6.7L Diesel Engine

Upper Intake Manifold

See Figures 267 through 269.

1. Disconnect the Manifold Absolute Pressure (MAP) sensor electrical connector and wire harness retainers.

2. Disconnect the coolant hose retainer from the upper intake manifold.

3. Remove the transmission oil level indicator tube bolt and the engine oil level indicator tube bolt .

4. If equipped, disconnect the vacuum hose retainer from the upper intake manifold.

5. Remove the 15 bolts and the upper intake manifold.

    a. Cover or tape the opening on the valve covers and lower intake manifold.

    b. Remove and discard the gaskets.

To install:

⁂ WARNING

Failure to install the upper intake manifold heat shield may result in upper intake manifold damage.

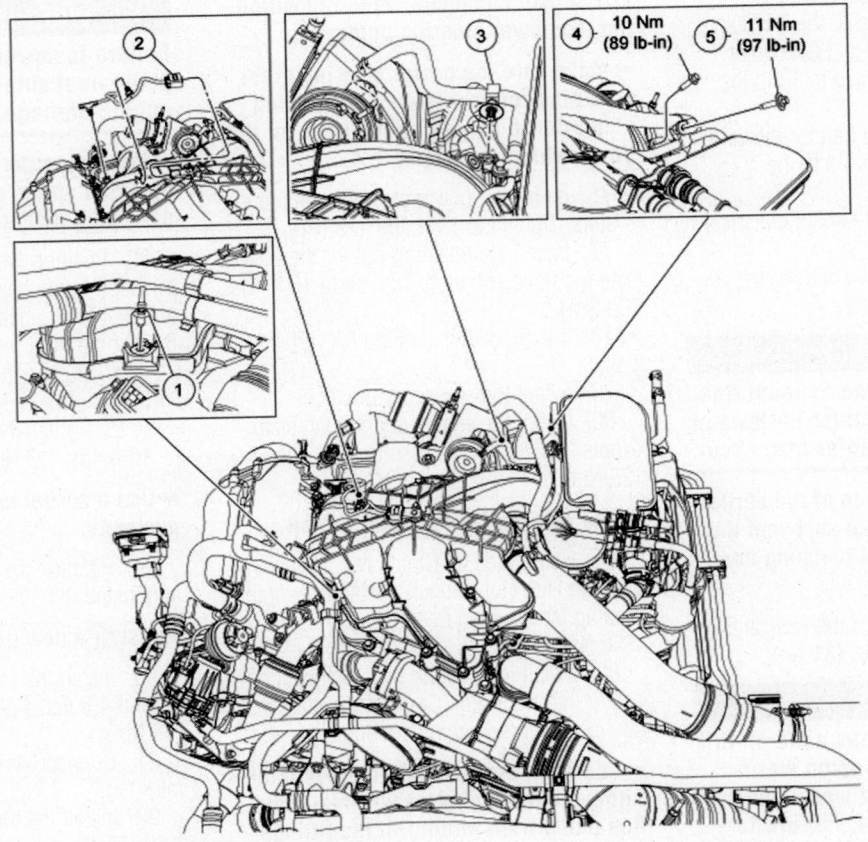

1. Coolant hose retainer
2. Manifold Absolute Pressure (MAP) sensor electrical connector
3. Vacuum hose retainer
4. Transmission oil level indicator tube bolt
5. Engine oil level indicator tube bolt

N0116376

Fig. 267 Disconnect the Manifold Absolute Pressure (MAP) sensor electrical connector and wire harness retainers

6. If installing a new upper intake manifold:

    a. Install the upper intake manifold heat shield:

- Align the tab on the front side of the heat shield to tuck under the weld flange.
- Wrap the ears of the heat shield around the boss.
- Tuck the rear ear of the heat shield under the weld flange. (If 1 and 2 are done correctly, this falls into place)

➡**Remove the cover or tape from the valve covers and lower intake manifold prior to installing the upper intake manifold.**

7. Using new gaskets, install the upper intake manifold and the 15 bolts. Tighten in the sequence shown. Tighten to 89 inch lbs. (10 Nm).

8. If equipped, connect the vacuum hose retainer to the upper intake manifold.

9. Install the engine oil level indicator tube bolt and the transmission oil level indicator tube bolt.

    a. Tighten the engine oil level indicator tube bolt to 89 inch lbs. (10 Nm).

    b. Tighten the transmission oil level indicator tube bolt to 97 inch lbs. (11 Nm).

10. Connect the coolant hose retainer to the upper intake manifold.

11. Connect the MAP sensor electrical connector and wire harness retainers.

Lower Intake Manifold

See Figures 270 and 271.

1. Remove the upper intake manifold.

2. Remove the air cleaner Air Cleaner (ACL) outlet tube.

3. Release the clip and disconnect the Charge Air Cooler (CAC) outlet tube from the Throttle Body (TB).

4. Disconnect the TB electrical connector.

5. Disconnect the Exhaust Gas Recirculation Temperature (EGRT) sensor electrical connector and the wire harness retainer.

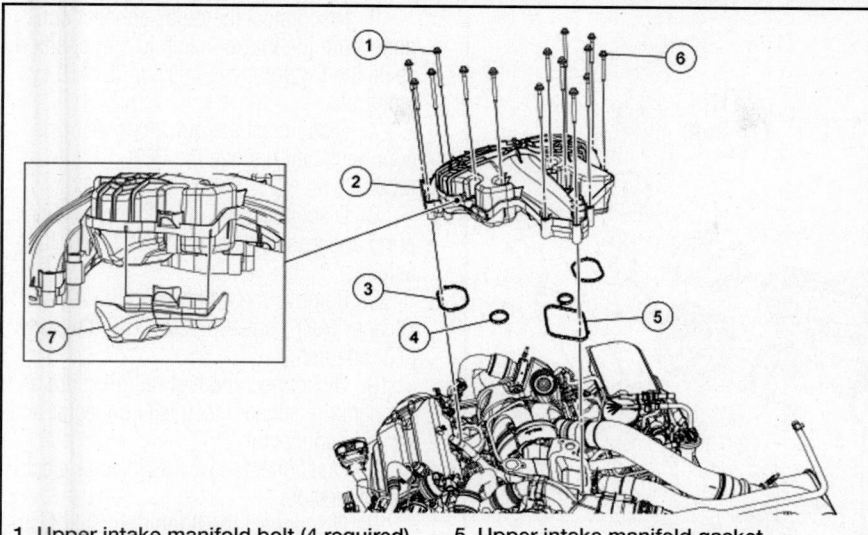

1. Upper intake manifold bolt (4 required)
2. Upper intake manifold
3. Upper intake manifold gasket (2 required)
4. Upper intake manifold gasket
5. Upper intake manifold gasket
6. Upper intake manifold bolt (11 required)
7. Upper intake manifold shield

N0116108

Fig. 268 Exploded view of the upper intake manifold assembly

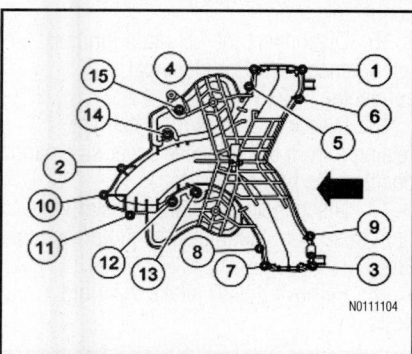

N0111104

Fig. 269 Tighten the upper intake manifold bolts in the sequence shown

6. Remove the 4 bolts and the EGR cooler outlet pipe. Discard the gaskets.

7. Release the clip and disconnect the CAC inlet tube from the turbocharger.

➡**Vehicles with over 14,000 pounds Gross Vehicle Weight Rating (GVWR), will only have the lower turbocharger inlet boot.**

8. Loosen the turbocharger inlet hose clamps.

a. Loosen the 2 lower turbocharger inlet hose clamps.

b. If equipped, loosen the 2 upper turbocharger inlet hose clamps.

9. Disconnect the crankcase ventilation hose from the lower intake manifold.

10. Remove the 3 bolts and the lower intake manifold.

11. Remove the turbocharger inlet hose(s) as needed.

To install:

➡**Position the turbocharger inlet hose(s) as needed.**

12. Install the lower intake manifold and the 3 bolts. Tighten to 18 ft. lbs. (24 Nm).

13. Connect the crankcase ventilation hose to the lower intake manifold.

➡**Vehicles with over 14,000 pounds GVWR, will only have the lower turbocharger inlet boot.**

14. Tighten the turbocharger inlet hose clamps.

a. Tighten the 2 lower turbocharger inlet hose clamps.

b. If equipped, tighten the 2 upper turbocharger inlet hose clamps.

15. Connect the CAC inlet tube to the turbocharger and install the clip

16. Using new gaskets, install the EGR cooler outlet pipe and 4 bolts. Tighten to 89 inch lbs. (10 Nm).

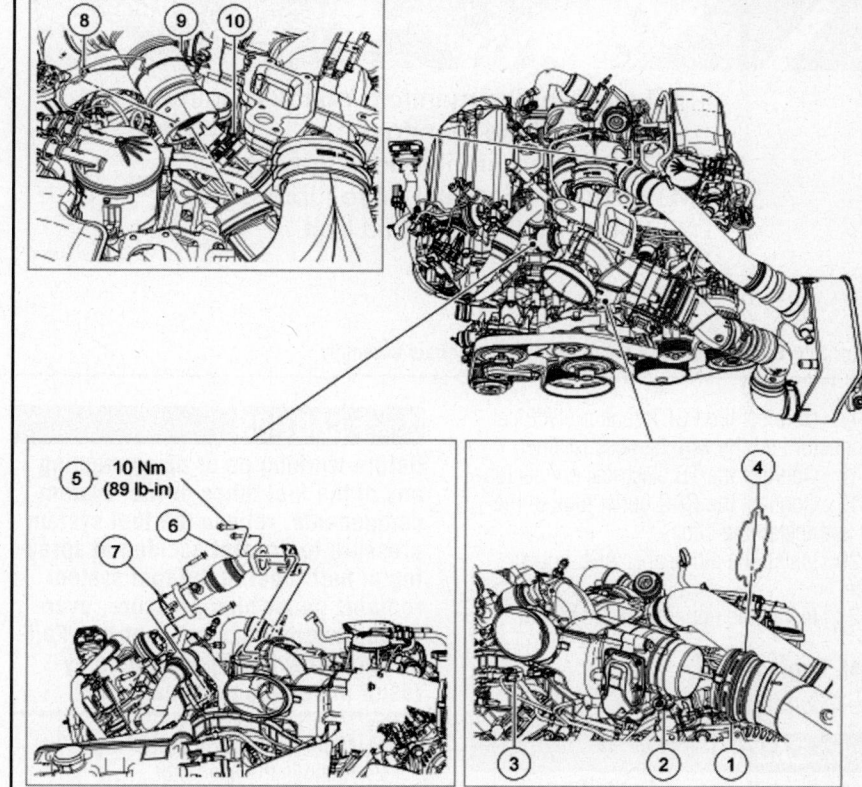

1. Charge Air Cooler (CAC) outlet tube
2. Throttle Body (TB) electrical connector
3. EGRT sensor electrical connector
4. CAC outlet hose clip
5. EGR outlet pipe bolt (4 required)
6. EGR outlet pipe
7. EGR outlet pipe gaskets
8. CAC inlet hose clip
9. CAC inlet tube
10. Crankcase vent hose

N0113230

Fig. 270 Release the clip and disconnect the Charge Air Cooler (CAC) outlet tube from the Throttle Body (TB)

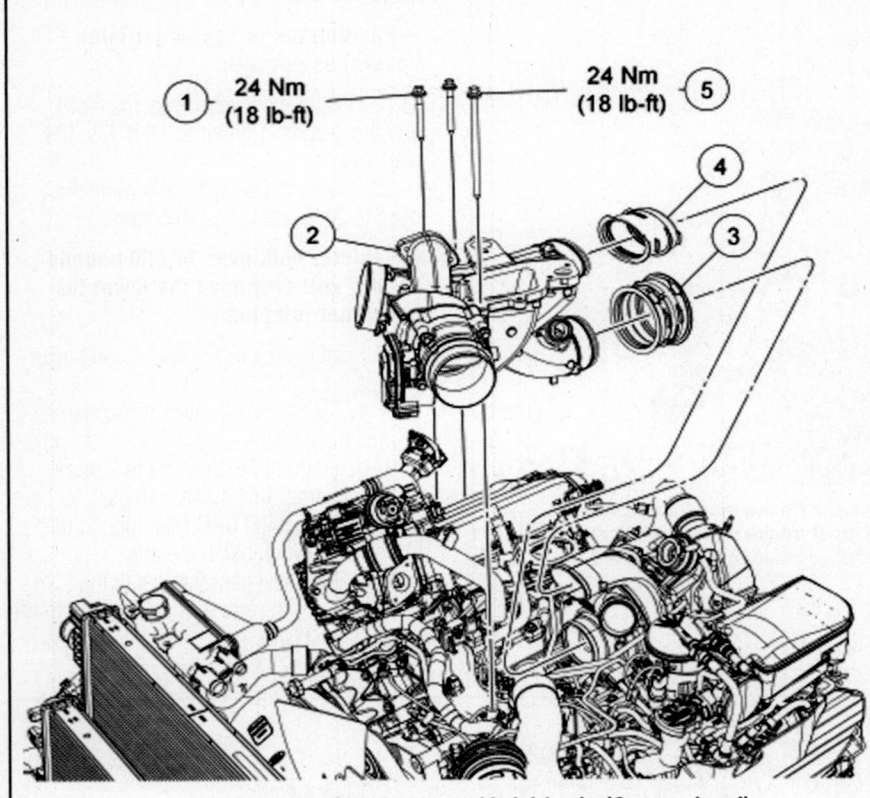

1. Lower intake manifold bolt (2 required)
2. Lower intake manifold
3. Turbocharger inlet hose (lower)
4. Turbocharger inlet hose (upper)
5. Lower intake manifold bolt

N0113231

Fig. 271 Exploded view of the lower intake manifold assembly

17. Connect the EGRT sensor electrical connector and the wire harness retainer.
18. Connect the TB electrical connector.
19. Connect the CAC outlet tube to the TB and install the clip
20. Install the air cleaner ACL outlet tube.
21. Install the upper intake manifold.

5.4L Engine

See Figures 272 and 273.

✳✳ CAUTION

Do not smoke, carry lighted tobacco or have an open flame of any type when working on or near any fuel-related component. Highly flammable mixtures are always present and may be ignited. Failure to follow these instructions may result in serious personal injury.

✳✳ CAUTION

Before working on or disconnecting any of the fuel tubes or fuel system components, relieve the fuel system pressure to prevent accidental spraying of fuel. Fuel in the fuel system remains under high pressure, even when the engine is not running. Failure to follow this instruction may result in serious personal injury.

1. Drain the cooling system.
2. Remove the alternator.
3. Disconnect the fuel supply spring lock coupling from the fuel rail.
4. Disconnect the upper radiator hose from the thermostat housing.
5. Disconnect the heater coolant hose from the engine coolant crossover manifold assembly.

6. Disconnect the quick connect coupling from the intake manifold and position aside the Evaporative Emission (EVAP) system tube.
7. Disconnect the quick connect couplings and remove the PCV tube.
8. Disconnect the quick connect coupling and position the crank case vent tube aside.
9. Remove the 4 bolts and the Air Cleaner (ACL) outlet pipe-to-Throttle Body (TB) adapter.
10. Disconnect the fuel rail pressure and temperature sensor electrical connector and vacuum connector.
11. Disconnect the 8 fuel injector electrical connectors.
12. Disconnect the 8 ignition coil electrical connectors.
13. Disconnect the Throttle Position (TP) sensor and Electronic Throttle Control (ETC) electrical connectors.
14. Disconnect the LH Variable Camshaft Timing (VCT) solenoid electrical connector.
15. Disconnect the LH radio ignition interference capacitor electrical connector.
16. Disconnect the wiring harness retainers from the LH valve cover studs and position the harness aside.
17. Disconnect the brake booster vacuum hose from the intake manifold vacuum tube.
18. Remove the 10 intake manifold bolts.

✳✳ WARNING

Do not use metal scrapers, wire brushes, power abrasive discs or other abrasive means to clean the sealing surfaces. These tools cause scratches and gouges which make leak paths. Use a plastic scraping tool to remove all traces of old sealant.

19. Remove the 3 bolts, the engine coolant crossover manifold assembly and discard the gaskets.
20. Clean and inspect the sealing surfaces with silicone gasket remover and metal surface prep. Follow the directions on the packaging.
21. Disconnect the intake manifold vacuum tube from the valve cover stud and the support bracket.
22. Disconnect the engine wiring harness retainer from the rear of the intake manifold.

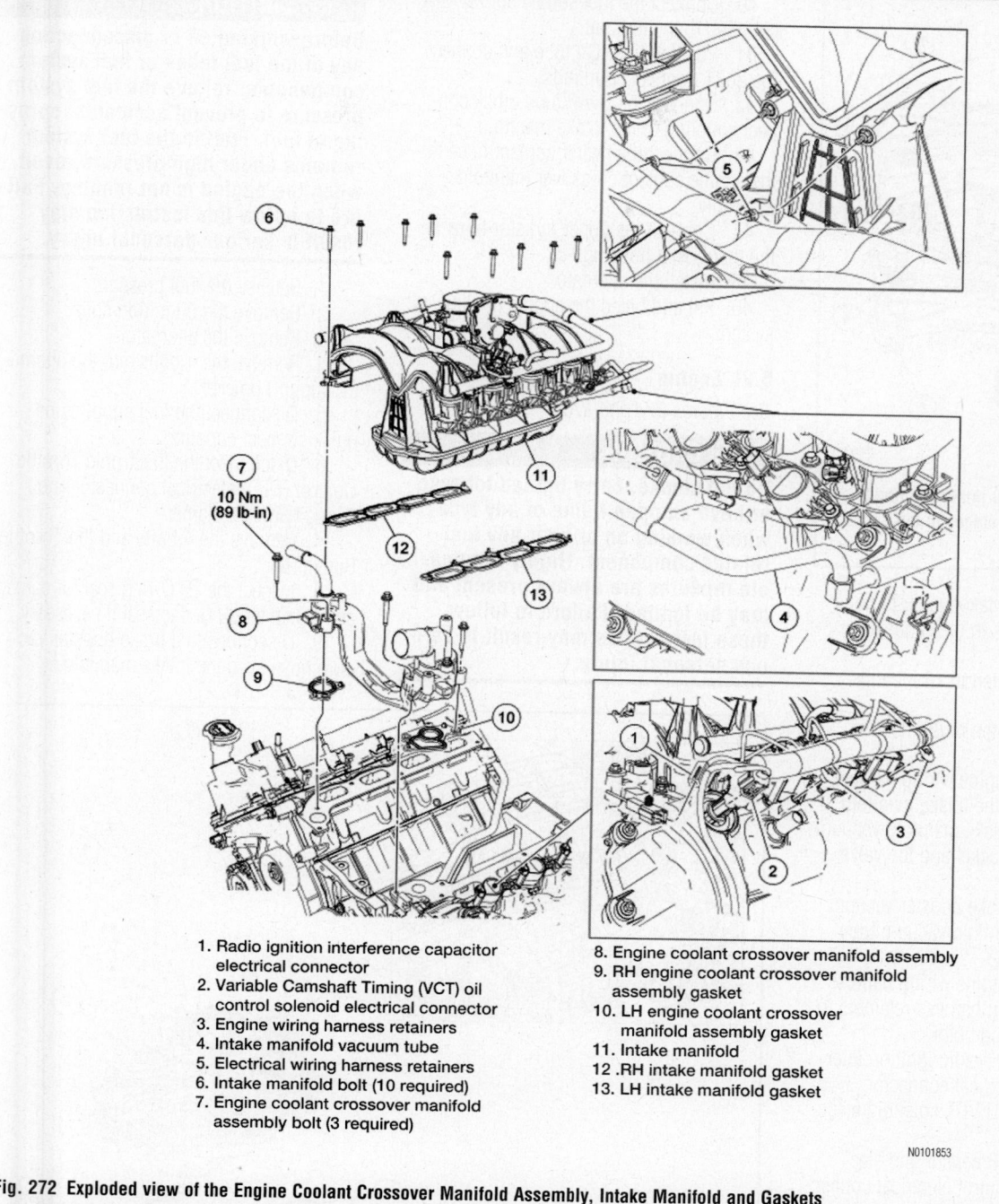

1. Radio ignition interference capacitor electrical connector
2. Variable Camshaft Timing (VCT) oil control solenoid electrical connector
3. Engine wiring harness retainers
4. Intake manifold vacuum tube
5. Electrical wiring harness retainers
6. Intake manifold bolt (10 required)
7. Engine coolant crossover manifold assembly bolt (3 required)
8. Engine coolant crossover manifold assembly
9. RH engine coolant crossover manifold assembly gasket
10. LH engine coolant crossover manifold assembly gasket
11. Intake manifold
12. RH intake manifold gasket
13. LH intake manifold gasket

N0101853

Fig. 272 Exploded view of the Engine Coolant Crossover Manifold Assembly, Intake Manifold and Gaskets

---

❋❋ WARNING

Do not use metal scrapers, wire brushes, power abrasive discs or other abrasive means to clean the sealing surfaces. These tools cause scratches and gouges which make leak paths. Use a plastic scraping tool to remove all traces of old sealant.

23. Remove the intake manifold and intake manifold vacuum tube as an assembly. Discard the intake manifold gaskets.

24. Clean and inspect the sealing surfaces with metal surface prep and silicone gasket remover. Follow the directions on the packaging.

To install:

❋❋ WARNING

If the engine is repaired or replaced because of upper engine failure, typically including valve or piston damage, check the intake manifold for metal debris. If metal debris is found, install a new intake manifold. Failure to follow these instructions can result in engine damage.

25. Using new intake manifold gaskets, position the intake manifold and intake manifold vacuum tube as an assembly.

26. Using new gaskets, position the engine coolant crossover manifold assembly and install the 3 bolts. Tighten to 89 inch lbs. (10 Nm).

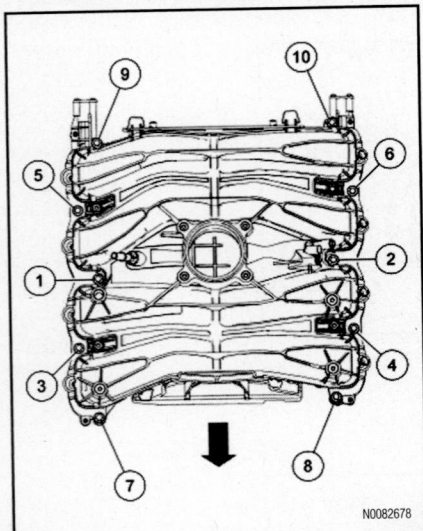

Fig. 273 Install the 10 intake manifold bolts and tighten in 2 stages in the sequence shown

27. Install the 10 intake manifold bolts and tighten in 2 stages in the sequence shown.

　a. Stage 1: Tighten to 18 inch lbs. (2 Nm).

　b. Stage 2: Tighten to 89 inch lbs. (10 Nm).

28. Connect the engine wiring harness retainer to the rear of the intake manifold.

29. Connect the intake manifold vacuum tube to the support bracket and the valve cover stud.

30. Connect the brake booster vacuum hose to the intake manifold vacuum tube and position the clamp.

31. Position the engine wiring harness and connect the wiring harness retainers to the LH valve cover stud bolts.

32. Connect the LH radio ignition interference capacitor electrical connector.

33. Connect the LH VCT solenoid electrical connector.

34. Connect the TP sensor and electronic acceleration control electrical connectors.

35. Connect the 8 fuel injector electrical connectors.

36. Connect the 8 ignition coil electrical connectors.

37. Connect the fuel rail pressure and temperature sensor electrical connector and vacuum connector.

38. Position the ACL outlet pipe-to-TB adapter and install the 4 bolts. Tighten to 89 inch lbs. (10 Nm).

39. Connect the crankcase vent tube quick connect coupling to the ACL outlet pipe-to-TB adapter.

40. Connect the fuel supply spring lock coupling to the fuel rail.

41. Position the PCV tube and connect the quick connect couplings.

42. Connect the EVAP tube quick connect coupling to the intake manifold.

43. Connect the heater coolant hose to the engine coolant crossover manifold assembly.

44. Connect the upper radiator hose to the thermostat housing.

45. Install the alternator.

46. Fill and bleed the engine cooling system.

6.2L Engine

See Figures 274 and 275.

✳✳ CAUTION

Do not smoke, carry lighted tobacco or have an open flame of any type when working on or near any fuel-related component. Highly flammable mixtures are always present and may be ignited. Failure to follow these instructions may result in serious personal injury.

✳✳ CAUTION

Before working on or disconnecting any of the fuel tubes or fuel system components, relieve the fuel system pressure to prevent accidental spraying of fuel. Fuel in the fuel system remains under high pressure, even when the engine is not running. Failure to follow this instruction may result in serious personal injury.

1. Release the fuel pressure.

2. Remove the 8 ignition coils.

3. Remove the alternator.

4. Remove the 4 bolts and the alternator support bracket.

5. Disconnect the fuel supply tube quick connect coupling.

6. Disconnect the Electronic Throttle Control (ETC) electrical connector and wiring harness retainer.

7. Remove the 4 bolts and the Throttle Body (TB).

8. Inspect the TB O-ring seal for damage and install a new O-ring seal if necessary.

9. Disconnect the brake booster vacuum hose from the intake manifold.

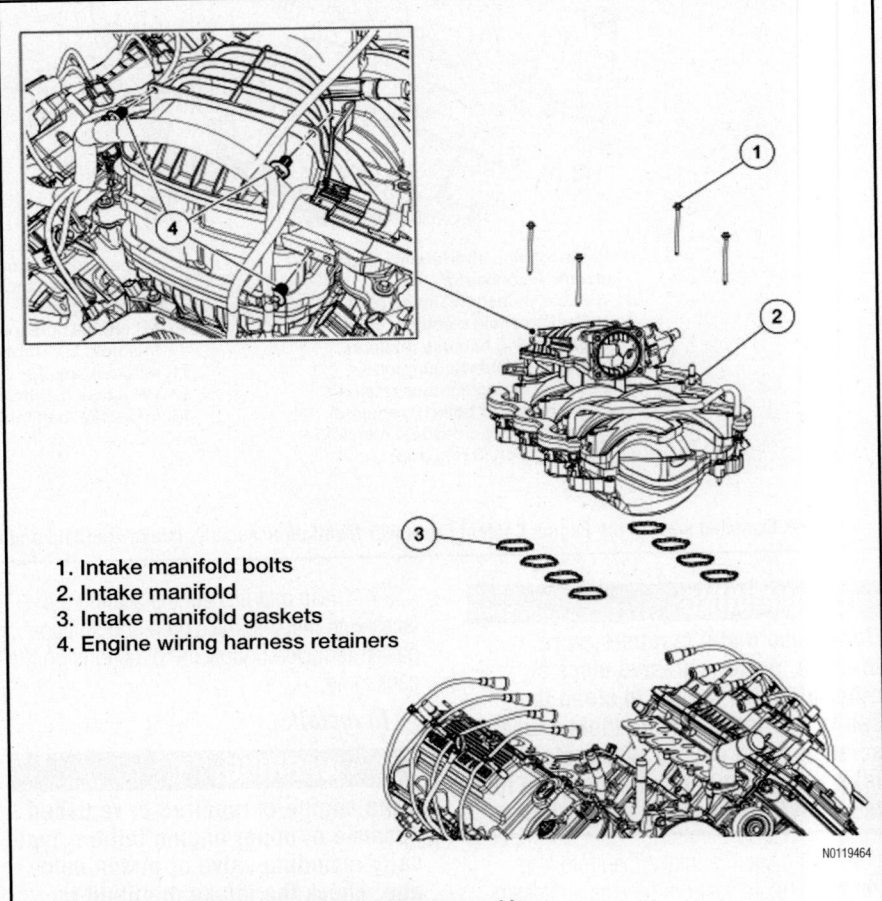

1. Intake manifold bolts
2. Intake manifold
3. Intake manifold gaskets
4. Engine wiring harness retainers

Fig. 274 Exploded view of the intake manifold assembly

10. Disconnect the Evaporative Emission (EVAP) tube quick connect coupling from the EVAP canister purge valve.

11. Disconnect the EVAP canister purge valve electrical connector.

12. Disconnect the quick connect couplings and remove the PCV tube.

13. Disconnect the 8 fuel injector electrical connectors.

➡**The fuel rail is removed with the intake manifold as an assembly.**

14. Remove the 4 fuel rail bolts.

15. Disconnect the 4 wiring harness retainers from the rear of the intake manifold.

16. Loosen the 12 intake manifold bolts.

⁕⁕ WARNING

Do not use metal scrapers, wire brushes, power abrasive discs or other abrasive means to clean the sealing surfaces. These tools cause scratches and gouges which make leak paths. Use a plastic scraping tool to remove all traces of old sealant.

17. Remove the intake manifold.

   a. Clean and inspect the cylinder head sealing surfaces with silicone gasket remover and metal surface prep. Follow the directions on the packaging.

   b. Inspect the 8 intake manifold gaskets for damage and install new gaskets if necessary.

To install:

⁕⁕ WARNING

If the engine is repaired or replaced because of upper engine failure, typically including valve or piston damage, check the intake manifold for metal debris. If metal debris is found, install a new intake manifold.

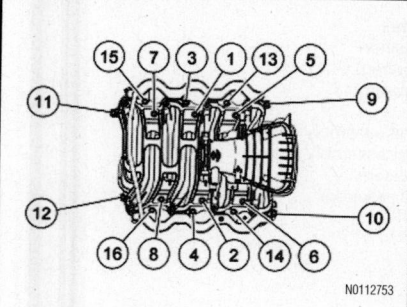

Fig. 275 Tighten the 12 intake manifold bolts and the 4 fuel rail bolts in 2 stages in the sequence shown

N0112753

Failure to follow these instructions can result in engine damage.

18. Position the intake manifold onto the engine.

19. Loosely install the 4 fuel rail bolts.

20. Tighten the 12 intake manifold bolts and the 4 fuel rail bolts in 2 stages in the sequence shown.

   a. Stage 1: Tighten to 89 inch lbs. (10 Nm).

   b. Stage 2: Tighten an additional 90 degrees.

21. Connect the 4 wiring harness retainers to the rear of the intake manifold.

22. Connect the 8 fuel injector electrical connectors.

23. Position the PCV tube and connect the quick connect couplings.

24. Connect the electrical connector and the EVAP tube quick connect coupling to the EVAP canister purge valve.

25. Position the TB and tighten the 4 bolts in 2 stages.

   a. Stage 1: Tighten to 106 inch lbs. (12 Nm).

   b. Stage 2: Tighten an additional 60 degrees.

26. Connect the Electronic Throttle Control (ETC) electrical connector and wiring harness retainer.

27. Connect the brake booster vacuum hose to the intake manifold.

28. Connect the fuel supply tube quick connect coupling.

29. Position the alternator support bracket and install the 4 bolts.

   a. Stage 1: Tighten to 15 ft. lbs. (20 Nm).

   b. Stage 2: Tighten an addition 45 degrees.

30. Install the alternator.

31. Install the 8 ignition coils.

6.8L Engine

See Figures 276 and 277.

⁕⁕ CAUTION

Do not smoke, carry lighted tobacco or have an open flame of any type when working on or near any fuel-related component. Highly flammable mixtures are always present and may be ignited. Failure to follow these instructions may result in serious personal injury.

⁕⁕ CAUTION

Before working on or disconnecting any of the fuel tubes or fuel system components, relieve the fuel system pressure to prevent accidental spraying of fuel. Fuel in the fuel system remains under high pressure, even when the engine is not running. Failure to follow this instruction may result in serious personal injury.

1. Disconnect the fuel supply spring lock coupling from the fuel rail.

2. Drain the cooling system.

3. Remove the alternator.

4. Remove the Air Cleaner (ACL) outlet pipe.

5. Disconnect the upper radiator hose from the thermostat housing.

6. Disconnect the heater coolant hose and PCV coolant hose from the engine coolant crossover assembly.

7. Disconnect the Intake Manifold Runner Control (IMRC) actuator electrical connector.

8. Disconnect the fuel rail pressure and temperature sensor electrical connector and vacuum connector.

9. Disconnect the 10 fuel injector electrical connectors.

10. Disconnect the PCV tube quick connect coupling from the intake manifold.

11. Disconnect the Evaporative Emission (EVAP) tube quick connect coupling from the intake manifold.

12. Disconnect the quick connect coupling and remove the crankcase ventilation tube.

13. Disconnect the wiring harness and vacuum harness retainers from the rear of the intake manifold.

14. Disconnect the engine vacuum hose connections from the rear of the intake manifold and position aside.

15. Disconnect the 2 heated PCV coolant hoses from the intake manifold.

16. Disconnect the Throttle Position (TP) sensor and Electronic Throttle Control (ETC) electrical connectors.

17. Disconnect the engine wiring harness position retainers from the intake manifold.

18. Remove the 12 intake manifold bolts.

⁕⁕ WARNING

Do not use metal scrapers, wire brushes, power abrasive discs or other abrasive means to clean the sealing surfaces. These tools cause scratches and gouges which make leak paths. Use a plastic scraping tool to remove all traces of old sealant.

19. Remove the 3 bolts, the engine coolant crossover manifold assembly and discard the 2 gaskets.

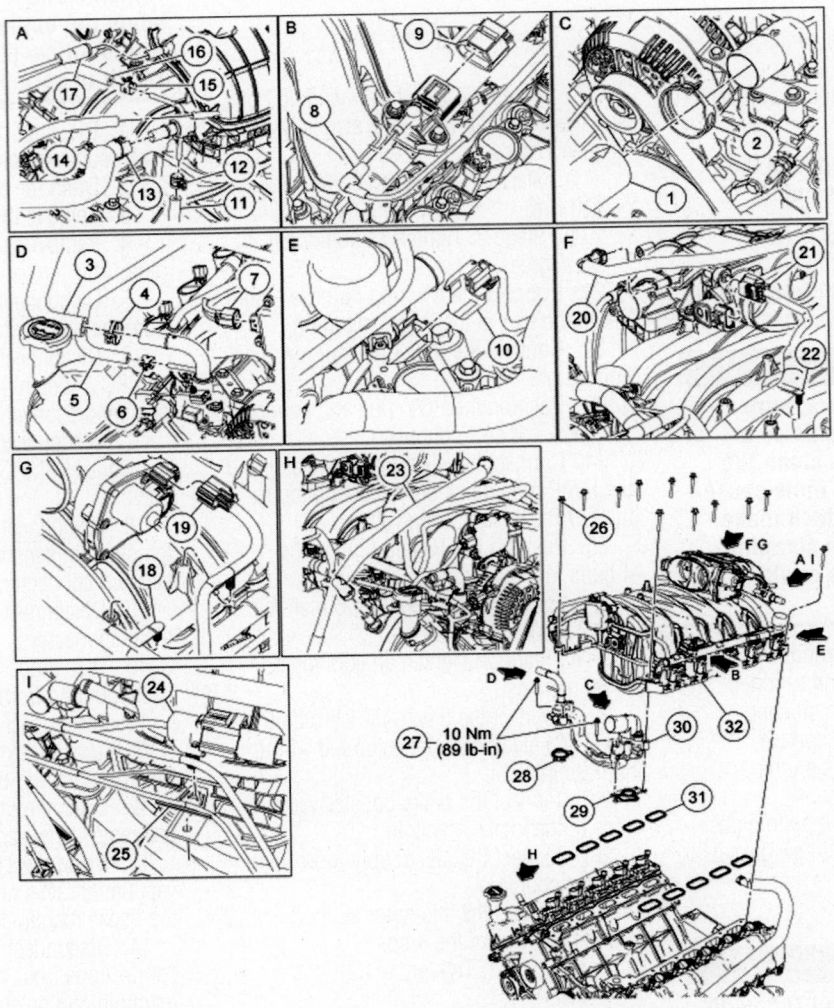

1. Radiator hose
2. Radiator hose clamp
3. Heater hose
4. Heater hose clamp
5. PCV coolant hose
6. PCV coolant hose clamp
7. Intake Manifold Runner Control (IMRC) actuator electrical connector
8. Fuel rail pressure and temperature sensor vacuum hose
9. Fuel rail pressure and temperature sensor electrical connector
10. Fuel injector electrical connector (10 required)
11. PCV coolant hose
12. PCV coolant hose clamp
13. PCV tube
14. Engine vacuum hose
15. PCV coolant hose clamp
16. PCV coolant hose
17. Intake manifold vacuum hose
18. Engine wiring harness retainer
19. Electronic Throttle Control (ETC) electrical connector
20. Evaporative Emission (EVAP) tube quick connect coupling
21. Throttle Position (TP) sensor electrical connector
22. Engine wiring harness retainer
23. Crankcase ventilation tube
24. Engine wiring harness retainer
25. Engine vacuum harness retainer
26. Intake manifold bolt (12 required)
27. Engine coolant crossover assembly bolts (3 required)
28. RH engine coolant crossover assembly gasket
29. LH engine coolant crossover assembly gasket
30. Engine coolant crossover assembly
31. Intake manifold gaskets (10 required)
32. Intake manifold assembly

N0105858

Fig. 276 Exploded view of the intake manifold assembly

20. Clean and inspect the sealing surfaces with silicone gasket remover and metal surface prep. Follow the directions on the packaging.

✳✳ WARNING

Do not use metal scrapers, wire brushes, power abrasive discs or other abrasive means to clean the sealing surfaces. These tools cause scratches and gouges which make leak paths. Use a plastic scraping tool to remove all traces of old sealant.

21. Remove the intake manifold and discard the 10 gaskets.

22. Clean and inspect the sealing surfaces with silicone gasket remover and metal surface prep. Follow the directions on the packaging.

To install:

✳✳ WARNING

If the engine is repaired or replaced because of upper engine failure, typically including valve or piston damage, check the intake manifold for metal debris. If metal debris is found, install a new intake manifold. Failure to follow these instructions can result in engine damage.

23. Using 10 new intake manifold gaskets, position the intake manifold.

24. Using 2 new gaskets, position the engine coolant crossover manifold assembly and install the 3 bolts. Tighten to 89 inch lbs. (10 Nm).

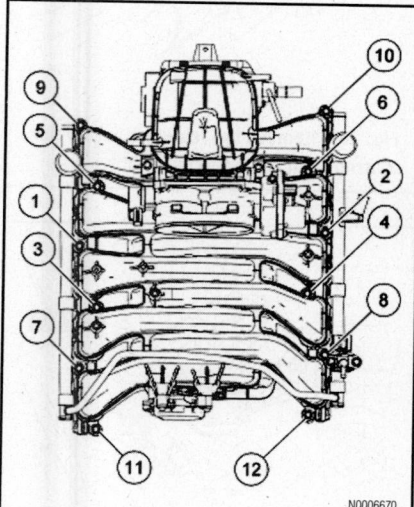

Fig. 277 Install the intake manifold bolts and tighten in 2 stages in the sequence shown

25. Install the intake manifold bolts and tighten in 2 stages in the sequence shown.
   a. Stage 1: Tighten to 18 inch lbs. (2 Nm).
   b. Stage 2: Tighten to 89 inch lbs. (10 Nm).

26. Connect the TP sensor and ETC electrical connectors.

27. Connect the engine wiring harness position retainers to the intake manifold.

28. Connect the engine vacuum hose connections to the rear of the intake manifold.

29. Connect the wiring harness and vacuum harness retainers to the rear of the intake manifold.

30. Connect the PCV tube quick connect coupling to the intake manifold.

31. Position the EVAP tube and connect the quick connect coupling to the intake manifold.

32. Connect the 2 heated PCV coolant hoses to the intake manifold.

33. Connect the 10 fuel injector electrical connectors.

34. Connect the fuel rail pressure and temperature sensor electrical connector and vacuum connector.

35. Connect the IMRC actuator electrical connector.

36. Connect the fuel supply spring lock coupling to the fuel rail.

37. Connect the heater coolant hose to the coolant crossover assembly.

38. Connect the heated PCV coolant hose to the coolant crossover assembly.

39. Connect the upper radiator hose to the thermostat housing.

40. Position the crankcase ventilation tube and connect the quick connect coupling.

41. Install the alternator.

42. Install the ACL outlet pipe.

43. Fill and bleed the engine cooling system.

OIL PAN

REMOVAL & INSTALLATION

6.4L Diesel Engine—Lower Oil Pan
See Figures 278 through 289.

✳✳ WARNING

Position a suitable protective material in front of the Charge Air Cooler (CAC) or damage to the CAC may occur.

➡ It is recommended that this component be serviced with the vehicle body partially lifted.

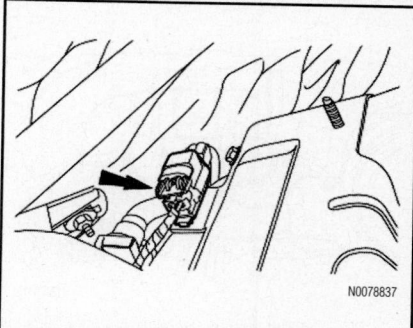

Fig. 278 Disconnect the Exhaust Gas Recirculation Temperature (EGRT) sensor electrical connector from the glow plug bracket

1. Disconnect the battery ground cables.

2. Remove the turbocharger.

3. Remove the upper cooling fan shroud.

4. If equipped, remove the secondary alternator.

5. Disconnect the windshield washer hose.

6. Disconnect the underhood light electrical connector and pin-type retainers. Position the wiring aside.

➡ **Mark the location of the hinges prior to removing the hood.**

7. With the help of an assistant, disconnect the hood lift rods. Remove the 4 bolts and the hood.

8. Disconnect the crankcase vent oil separator drain tube.

9. Remove the 4 bolts and the crankcase vent oil separator. Remove and discard the press-in-place gasket.

10. Disconnect the PCM electrical connector and wire retainer.

11. Remove the 3 pushnuts and glow plug module heat shield. Discard the pushnuts.

12. Disconnect the glow plug module electrical connectors.

13. Position the glow plug electrical connectors out from under the cowl.

14. Remove the 2 nuts and glow plug module.

15. Disconnect the Exhaust Gas Recirculation Temperature (EGRT) sensor electrical connector from the glow plug bracket.

16. Remove the EGR-Oxidation Catalytic Converter (OC) pipe from the vehicle.

➡ **Engine removed from the vehicle for clarity.**

17. Remove the bolt and the 5 retaining nuts for the high-pressure fuel injection pump heat shield.

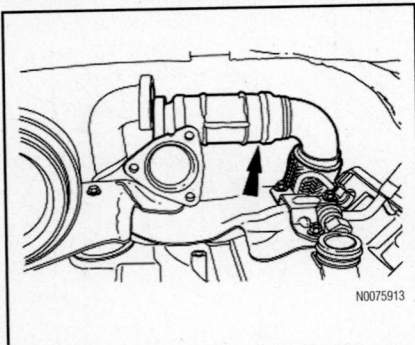

Fig. 279 Remove the EGR-Oxidation Catalytic Converter (OC) pipe from the vehicle

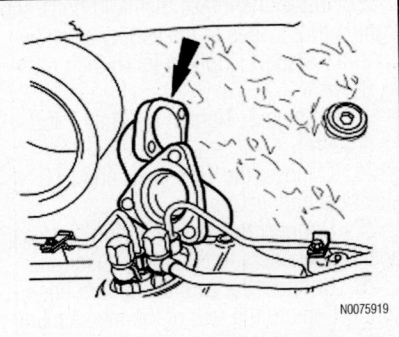

Fig. 282 Remove the RH turbocharger inlet pipe

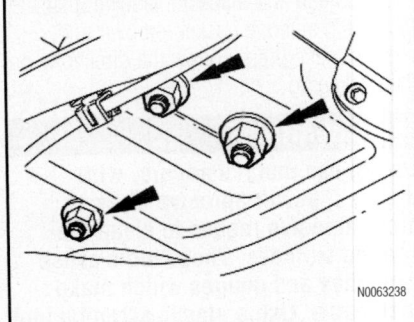

Fig. 285 Remove and discard the 3 LH engine mount retaining nuts

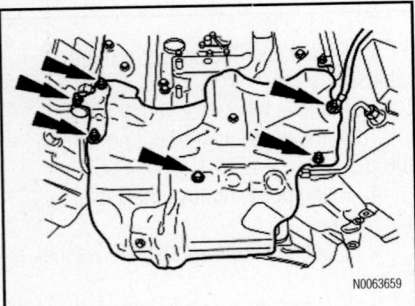

Fig. 280 Remove the bolt and the 5 retaining nuts for the high-pressure fuel injection pump heat shield

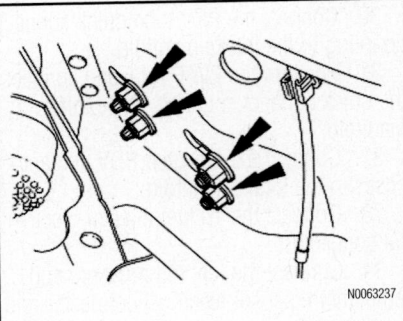

Fig. 283 Remove and discard the 4 RH engine mount retaining nuts

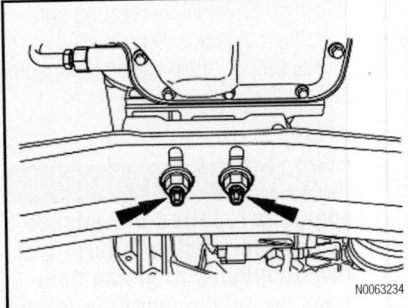

Fig. 286 Loosen the 2 transmission mount retaining nuts

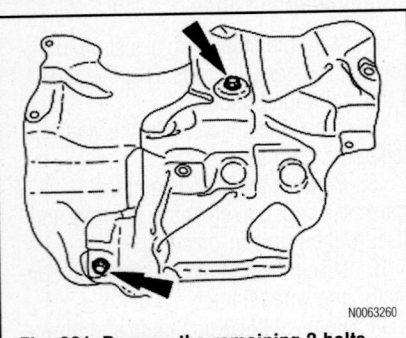

Fig. 281 Remove the remaining 2 bolts and the high-pressure fuel injection pump heat shield

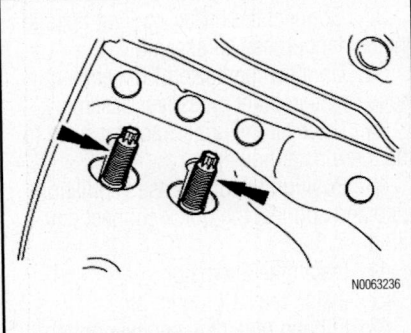

Fig. 284 Remove and discard the 2 upper studs for the RH motor mount

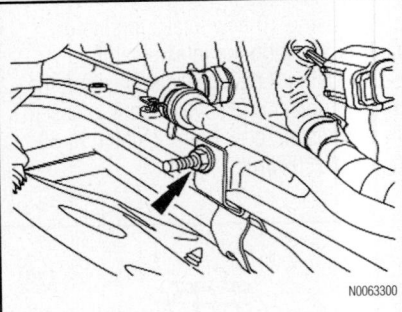

Fig. 287 Remove the retaining nut for the transmission cooler tubes

18. Remove the fuel tube bracket and position the ground strap.

➡**High-pressure fuel injection pump heat shield removed for clarity.**

19. Remove the remaining 2 bolts and the high-pressure fuel injection pump heat shield.
20. Remove the RH turbocharger inlet pipe.
21. Remove the oil pan drain plug and drain the oil.
22. Install the drain plug. Tighten to 32 ft. lbs. (44 Nm).
23. Remove and discard the 4 RH engine mount retaining nuts.

24. Remove and discard the 2 upper studs for the RH motor mount.
25. Remove and discard the 3 LH engine mount retaining nuts.
26. Loosen the 2 transmission mount retaining nuts.
27. Remove the 2 exhaust downpipe bolts.
28. Remove the bolt and position aside the ground cable.
29. Remove the retaining nut for the transmission cooler tubes. Disconnect the transmission cooler tubes from the stud.

➡**Mark the location of the 5 longer bolts.**

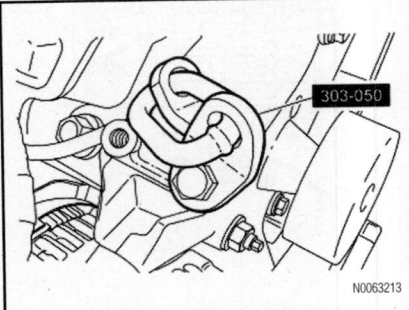

Fig. 288 Install the Engine Lifting Bracket on the Front End Accessory Drive (FEAD) bracket

30. Remove as many of the oil pan bolts as possible.

31. Install the Engine Lifting Bracket (303-050) on the Front End Accessory Drive (FEAD) bracket.

✳ WARNING

Use a Heavy Duty Floor Crane and load leveler rated at a minimum of 2,000 lbs. (907 kg) or damage to the vehicle may occur.

➡ **It will be necessary to position the exhaust downpipe aside to get the lift that is required to remove the oil pan.**

32. Position the Heavy Duty Floor Crane with a commercially available load leveler and attach the chains to the front of the engine.

✳ WARNING

Make sure the exhaust downpipe is loose during the raising of the engine or damage to the vehicle may occur.

➡ **The engine will need kept level in order to remove the oil pan.**

33. Raise the Heavy Duty Floor Crane as needed to get the required lift to remove the oil pan.

34. Support the engine with jackstands or other suitable support devices.

35. Remove the remaining oil pan bolts and position the oil pan to access the oil pickup tube bolts.

36. Remove the bolts for the oil pickup tube and place the tube in the oil pan. Remove the oil pan.

37. Remove and discard the oil pickup tube O-ring seal.

38. Remove and discard the press-in-place gasket.

To install:

39. Install a new press-in-place gasket for the oil pan.

➡ **Install a new O-ring seal on the oil pickup tube and place the tube in the oil pan.**

40. Position the oil pan and install the pickup tube and 2 bolts. Tighten to 10 ft. lbs. (13 Nm).

41. Install the oil pan and the 22 bolts.
   a. Install the 5 longer oil pan bolts.
   b. Install the 17 remaining oil pan bolts.
   c. Tighten the bolts to 10 ft. lbs. (13 Nm).

42. Lower the engine.

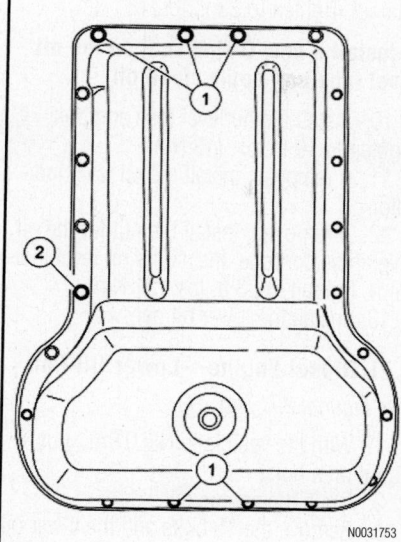

Fig. 289 Install the 5 longer oil pan bolts (1) and the remaining bolts (2)

43. Position back the transmission cooler tubes on the stud and install the nut.

44. Position back the ground cable and install the bolt. Tighten to 35 ft. lbs. (47 Nm).

45. Loosely install the 2 exhaust downpipe bolts.

✳ WARNING

Only use hand tools when installing the transmission mount retaining nuts or damage to the transmission mount may occur.

46. Remove and discard the 2 transmission mount retaining nuts. Install the 2 new transmission mount retaining nuts. Tighten to 85 ft. lbs. (115 Nm).

✳ WARNING

Only use hand tools when installing the engine mount retaining nuts or damage to the engine mount may occur.

47. Install the 3 new LH engine mount retaining nuts. Tighten to 148 ft. lbs. (200 Nm).

48. Install the 2 new upper studs for the RH engine mount. Tighten to 59 ft. lbs. (80 Nm).

✳ WARNING

Only use hand tools when installing the engine mount retaining nuts or damage to the engine mount may occur.

49. Install the 4 new RH engine mount retaining nuts. Tighten to 85 ft. lbs. (115 Nm).

50. Position the RH turbocharger inlet pipe in the vehicle.

✳ WARNING

Failure to correctly install the high-pressure fuel injection pump heat shield may result in engine damage.

➡ **High-pressure fuel injection pump heat shield removed for clarity.**

51. Install the high-pressure fuel injection pump heat shield in the vehicle and install the 2 center bolts. Tighten to 10 ft. lbs. (13 Nm).

➡ **Engine removed from the vehicle for clarity.**

52. Position the fuel tube bracket and ground strap. Install the 5 retaining nuts and bolt for the high-pressure fuel injection pump heat shield.
   a. Tighten the fuel line bracket nuts to 62 inch lbs. (7 Nm).
   b. Tighten the remaining fasteners to 10 ft. lbs. (13 Nm).

53. Position the EGR-OC pipe in the vehicle.

54. Connect the EGRT sensor electrical connector to the glow plug module bracket.

55. Install the glow plug module and 2 retaining nuts. Tighten to 10 ft. lbs. (13 Nm).

56. Connect the glow plug module electrical connectors.

➡ **Use a socket to aid on installing the pushnuts.**

57. Install the glow plug module heat shield and 3 new pushnuts.

58. Connect the PCM electrical connector and wire retainer.

➡ **Install a new press-in-place gasket.**

59. Install the crankcase vent oil separator and 4 bolts. Tighten to 10 ft. lbs. (13 Nm).

60. Connect the crankcase vent oil separator drain tube.

61. With the help of an assistant, install the hood and 4 bolts. Connect the hood lift rods. Tighten to 10 ft. lbs. (13 Nm).

62. Connect the underhood light electrical connector and pin-type retainers.

63. Connect the windshield washer hose.

64. If equipped, install the secondary alternator.

65. Install the upper cooling fan shroud.

66. Install the turbocharger.

67. Connect the battery ground cables.

68. Fill the engine with the correct motor oil for the climate.

6.4L Diesel Engine—Upper Oil Pan

See Figure 290.

1. Remove the lower oil pan.

2. With a partial body lift, remove the oil level indicator. Remove the retaining nut for the oil level indicator tube.

3. If the body is on, remove the oil level indicator.

4. Remove the bolt. Remove the oil level indicator tube and position it aside. Remove and discard the O-ring seal.

5. Remove the bolt for the fuel tube retainer.

6. Remove the 9 bolts and the upper oil pan.

7. Remove and discard the press-in-place gasket. Clean and inspect the sealing surfaces.

To install:

8. Position a new press-in-place gasket, the upper oil pan and install the 9 bolts. Tighten to 10 ft. lbs. (13 Nm).

9. Install the bolt for the fuel tube retainer. Tighten to 23 ft. lbs. (31 Nm).

➡ **Install a new O-ring seal on the oil level tube and apply clean oil.**

10. Install the oil level tube and bolt. Tighten to 10 ft. lbs. (13 Nm).

11. If removed, install the oil level indicator.

12. If removed, install the nut for the oil level indicator tube. Install the oil level indicator. Tighten to 23 ft. lbs. (31 Nm).

13. Install the lower oil pan.

6.7L Diesel Engine—Lower Oil Pan

See Figures 291 and 292.

1. With the vehicle in NEUTRAL, position it on a hoist.

2. Drain the engine oil.

3. Remove the 15 bolts and the lower oil pan. Remove and discard the gasket.

To install:

4. Using a new gasket, install the lower oil pan and the 15 bolts. Tighten in the sequence shown. Tighten to 89 inch lbs. (10 Nm).

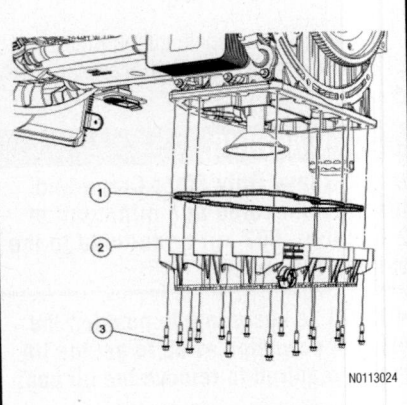

Fig. 291 Exploded view of the lower oil pan assembly showing the oil pan gasket (1), the lower oil pan (2) and the mounting bolts (3)

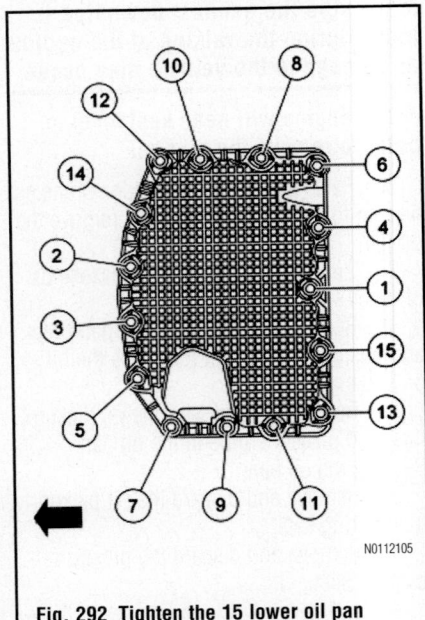

Fig. 292 Tighten the 15 lower oil pan bolts in the sequence shown

5. Fill the engine with the correct engine oil for the climate.

6.7L Diesel Engine—Upper Oil Pan

See Figures 293 through 294.

1. Remove the oil level indicator.

2. Remove the flexplate.

3. Remove the oil cooler.

4. Remove and discard the oil filter.

5. Disconnect the Engine Oil Temperature (EOT) sensor and Engine Oil Pressure (EOP) switch electrical connectors.

6. Remove the nut from the oil filter header and position aside the engine wire harness.

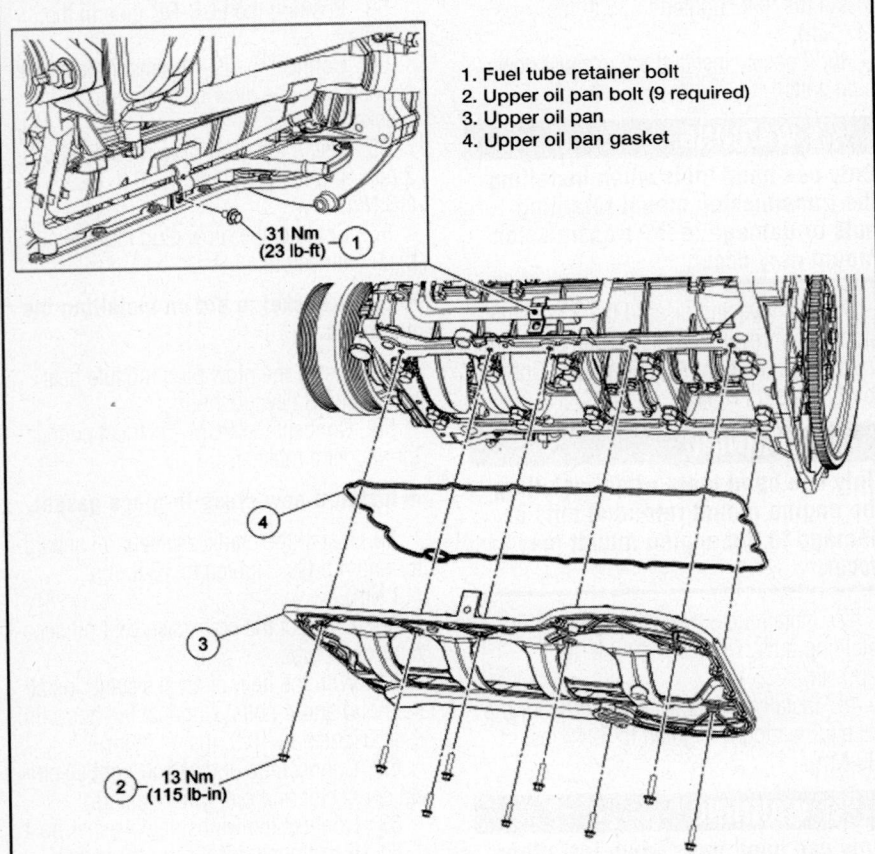

1. Fuel tube retainer bolt
2. Upper oil pan bolt (9 required)
3. Upper oil pan
4. Upper oil pan gasket

31 Nm (23 lb-ft)

13 Nm (115 lb-in)

Fig. 290 Exploded view of the upper oil pan assembly

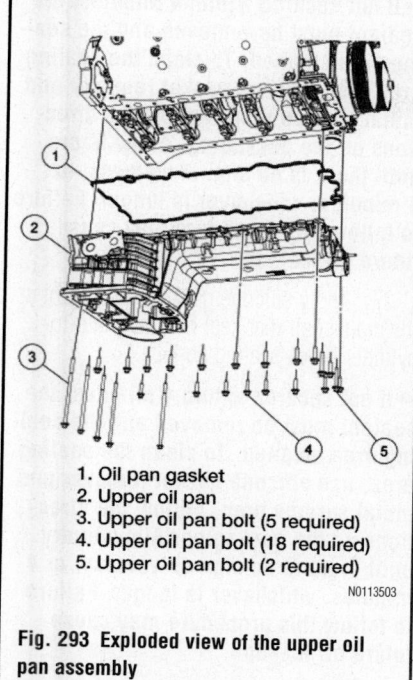

1. Oil pan gasket
2. Upper oil pan
3. Upper oil pan bolt (5 required)
4. Upper oil pan bolt (18 required)
5. Upper oil pan bolt (2 required)

N0113503

Fig. 293 Exploded view of the upper oil pan assembly

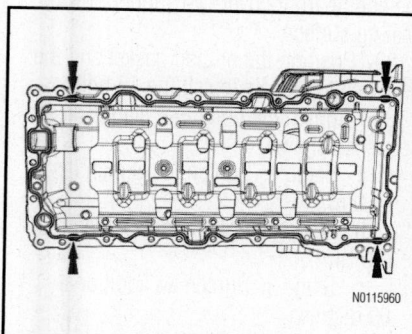

N0115960

Fig. 294 Apply a dime-sized bead of sealant at the 4 cover joints

7. Remove the nut and position aside the transmission cooler tubes.

8. Remove the nut and position aside the side engine wire harness.

9. Remove the 2 nuts from the front of the engine and position the engine wire harness aside.

➡**Do not remove the zero leak plug from the oil pan.**

10. Remove the 25 bolts and the upper oil pan.

   a. Remove and discard the gasket.
   b. Clean and inspect the sealing surfaces.

To install:

11. Install a new gasket in the upper oil pan.

12. Apply a dime-sized bead of sealant at the 4 cover joints.

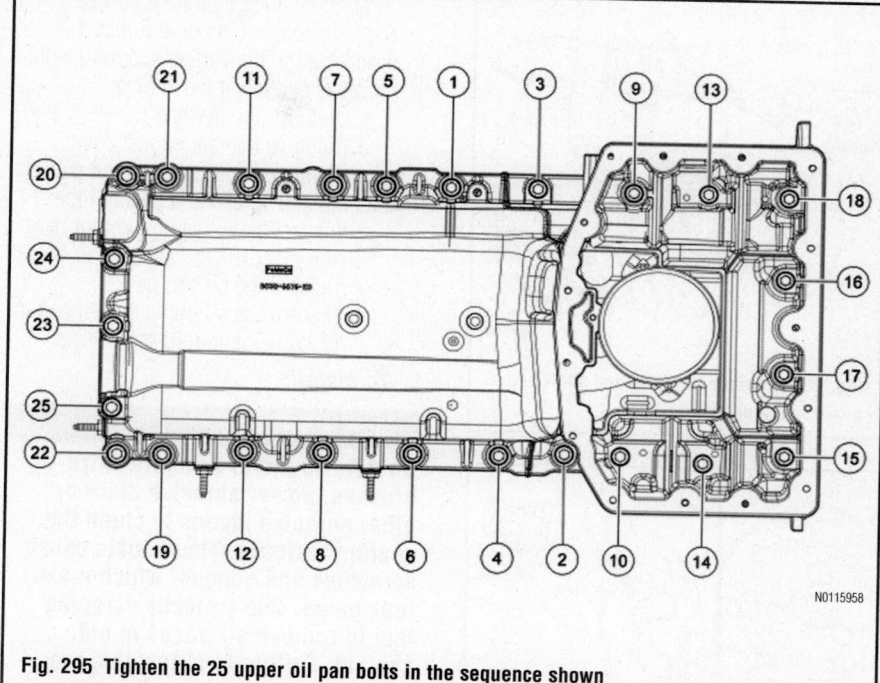

N0115958

Fig. 295 Tighten the 25 upper oil pan bolts in the sequence shown

➡**Final torque must be reached within 30 minutes of sealant application.**

➡**Do not remove the zero leak plug from the oil pan.**

13. With the help of an assistant, install the upper oil pan and 25 bolts. Tighten in 2 stages in the sequence shown.

   a. Stage 1: Tighten to 18 inch lbs. (2 Nm).
   b. Stage 2: Tighten to 18 ft. lbs. (24 Nm).

14. Position the front wire harness and install the 2 nuts. Tighten to 106 inch lbs. (12 Nm).

15. Position the side wire harness and install the nut. Tighten to 106 inch lbs. (12 Nm).

16. Position the transmission cooler tubes and install the nut. Tighten to 106 inch lbs. (12 Nm).

17. Position the engine wire harness at the oil filter header and install the nut. Tighten to 106 inch lbs. (12 Nm).

18. Connect the EOP switch and EOT sensor electrical connectors.

19. Install a new oil filter.
20. Install the oil cooler.
21. Install the flexplate.
22. Install the oil level indicator.

5.4L Engine

See Figures 296 through 300.

1. With the vehicle in NEUTRAL, position it on a hoist.

2. Remove the alternator.
3. Remove the engine cooling fan.
4. Disconnect the crankcase vent tube quick connect coupling from the Air Cleaner (ACL) outlet pipe-to-Throttle Body (TB) adapter.

5. Disconnect the vacuum hose from the ACL outlet pipe-to-TB adapter.

6. Disconnect the wiring harness retainer from the ACL outlet pipe-to-TB adapter.

7. Remove the 4 ACL outlet pipe-to-TB adapter bolts.

8. Remove the ACL outlet pipe-to-TB adapter.

9. Install the Engine Support Bar, Support Hook and Engine Support Bracket.

10. Drain the engine oil.

11. Remove and discard the engine oil filter.

✲✲ WARNING

If metal foreign material is present in the oil cooler, mechanical concerns exist.

12. Remove the threaded shaft and position the oil cooler aside. Inspect the engine oil cooler.

13. Press the position retaining tabs and rotate the lower cooling fan shroud upward until the position retainer tab locks into position.

14. Remove the nut, the transmission auxiliary fluid cooler tube support bracket and the starter wiring harness support

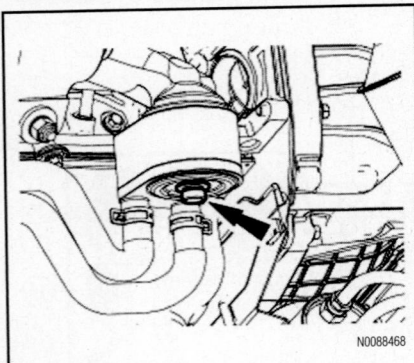

Fig. 296 Remove the threaded shaft and position the oil cooler aside

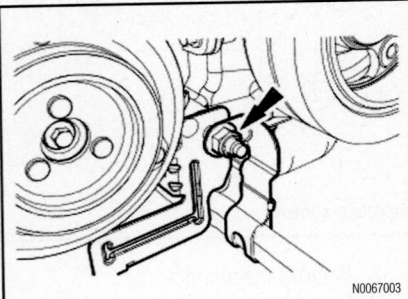

Fig. 297 Remove the nut, the transmission auxiliary fluid cooler tube support bracket and the starter wiring harness support bracket from the engine front cover stud bolt

bracket from the engine front cover stud bolt.

15. Remove and discard the 7 engine support insulator-to-crossmember nuts.

16. Using the Engine Support Bar, Support Hook and Engine Support Bracket, raise the engine assembly.

17. If equipped with an A/T, remove the 2 bolts and the flexplate inspection cover.

18. Remove 16 oil pan bolts and position the oil pan onto the crossmember.

19. Remove the 3 bolts and position the oil pump screen and pickup tube into the oil pan.

20. If equipped with an A/T, remove the oil pan and the oil pump screen and pick tube:

    a. Inspect the oil pan gasket for damage.

    b. Discard the oil pan gasket.

    c. Discard the oil pump screen and pickup tube O-ring seal.

21. If equipped with a M/T:

    a. Position the oil pan onto the engine and install one bolt at the front and one bolt at the rear of the oil pan to hold it in position.

b. Using the Engine Support Bar, Support Hook and Engine Support Bracket, align the engine support insulator studs and lower the engine.

    c. Remove the flywheel.

    d. Remove the rear engine cover.

    e. Remove the 2 bolts, the oil pan and the oil pump screen and pickup tube:

- Inspect the oil pan gasket for damage.
- Discard the oil pan gasket.
- Discard the oil pump screen and pickup tube O-ring seal.

To install:

> ❊❊ **WARNING**
>
> **Do not use metal scrapers, wire brushes, power abrasive discs or other abrasive means to clean the sealing surfaces. These tools cause scratches and gouges, which make leak paths. Use a plastic scraping tool to remove all traces of old sealant. Failure to follow this procedure may cause future oil leakage.**

22. Inspect the oil pan. Clean the mating surface for the oil pan with silicone gasket remover and metal surface prep. Follow the directions on the packaging.

23. Install a new O-ring seal onto the oil pump screen and pickup tube.

24. Position the oil pump screen and pickup tube in the oil pan and position the oil pan and new gasket into the vehicle.

25. If equipped with a M/T:

    a. Install the rear engine cover.

    b. Install the flywheel.

    c. Using the Engine Support Bar, Support Hook and Engine Support Bracket, raise the engine.

> ❊❊ **WARNING**
>
> **Make sure to install a new O-ring seal. A missing or damaged O-ring seal can cause foam in the lubrication system and low oil pressure. Failure to follow this instruction may result in engine damage.**

➡Clean and inspect the mating surfaces and install a new O-ring seal. Lubricate the O-ring seal with clean engine oil prior to installation.

26. Position the oil pump screen and pickup tube and install the bolts.

    a. Tighten the oil pump screen and pickup tube-to-oil pump bolts to 89 inch lbs. (10 Nm).

    b. Tighten the oil pump screen and pickup tube-to-spacer bolt to 18 ft. lbs. (25 Nm).

➡If not secured within 4 minutes, the sealant must be removed and the sealing area cleaned. To clean the sealing area, use silicone gasket remover and metal surface prep. Follow the directions on the packaging. Allow to dry until there is no sign of wetness, or 4 minutes, whichever is longer. Failure to follow this procedure may cause future oil leakage.

27. Apply silicone gasket and sealant at the crankshaft rear seal retainer plate-to-cylinder block sealing surface.

➡If not secured within 4 minutes, the sealant must be removed and the sealing area cleaned. To clean the sealing area, use silicone gasket remover and metal surface prep. Follow the directions on the packaging. Allow to dry until there is no sign of wetness, or 4 minutes, whichever is longer. Failure to follow this procedure may cause future oil leakage.

28. Apply silicone gasket and sealant at the engine front cover-to-cylinder block sealing surface.

29. Position the oil pan gasket and the oil pan and loosely install the 16 bolts.

30. Tighten the bolts in 3 stages, in the sequence shown.

    a. Stage 1: Tighten to 18 inch lbs. (2 Nm).

    b. Stage 2: Tighten to 177 inch lbs. (20 Nm).

    c. Stage 3: Tighten an additional 60 degrees.

31. If equipped with an A/T, position the flexplate inspection cover and install the 2 bolts. Tighten to 25 ft. lbs. (34 Nm).

32. Using the Engine Support Bar, Support Hook and Engine Support Bracket, align the engine support insulator studs and lower the engine.

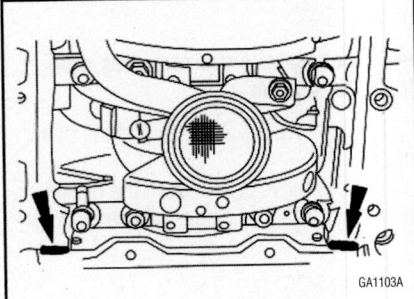

Fig. 298 Apply silicone gasket and sealant at the crankshaft rear seal retainer plate-to-cylinder block sealing surface

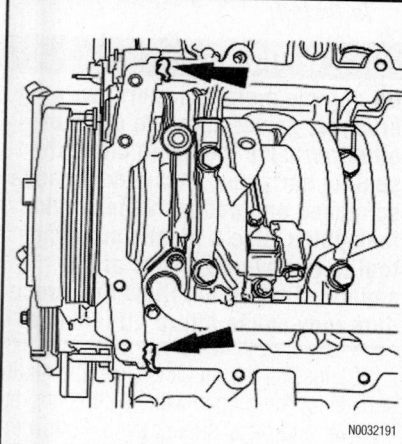

Fig. 299 Apply silicone gasket and sealant at the engine front cover-to-cylinder block sealing surface

❊❊ WARNING

Only use hand tools when installing the engine support insulator nuts or damage to the engine support insulator may occur.

33. Install 4 new RH engine support insulator nuts. Tighten to 85 ft. lbs. (115 Nm).

34. Only use hand tools when installing the engine support insulator nuts or damage to the engine support insulator may occur.

35. Install 3 new LH engine support insulator nuts. Tighten to 148 ft. lbs. (200 Nm).

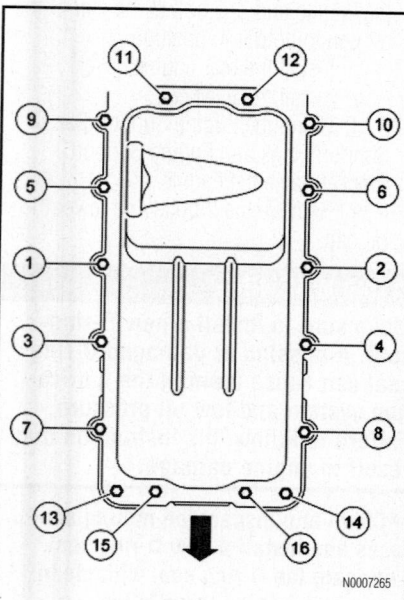

Fig. 300 Tighten the bolts in 3 stages, in the sequence shown

36. Position the transmission auxiliary fluid cooler tube support bracket and the starter wiring harness support bracket onto the engine front cover stud bolt and install the nut. Tighten to 18 ft. lbs. (25 Nm).

37. Press the position retaining tab and rotate the lower cooling fan downward until the position retainer tab locks into position.

38. Position the oil cooler and install the threaded shaft. Tighten to 43 ft. lbs. (58 Nm).

39. Install a new engine oil filter. Tighten to 12 ft. lbs. (16 Nm).

40. Install the ACL outlet pipe-to-TB adapter.

41. Install the 4 ACL outlet pipe-to-TB adapter bolts. Tighten to 89 inch lbs. (10 Nm).

42. Connect the wiring harness retainer to the ACL outlet pipe-to-TB adapter.

43. Connect the vacuum hose to the ACL outlet pipe-to-TB adapter.

44. Connect the crankcase vent tube quick connect coupling to the ACL outlet pipe-to-TB adapter.

45. Install the engine cooling fan.

46. Install the alternator.

47. Fill the crankcase with clean engine oil.

6.2L Engine

See Figure 301.

➡ **The manufacturer does not provide a specific Removal and Installation procedure for this component. Refer to the graphic(s) when servicing this component.**

1. Position a new gasket and the oil pan and install the 20 bolts.

2. Tighten the bolts in the sequence shown in 3 stages.

   a. Stage 1: Tighten to 18 inch lbs. (2 Nm).

   b. Stage 2: Tighten to 89 inch lbs. (10 Nm).

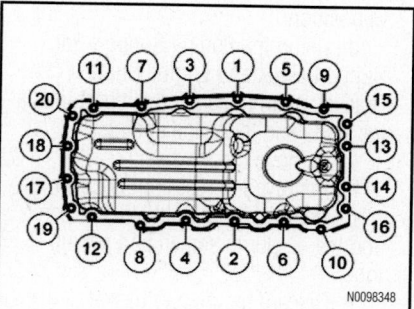

Fig. 301 Tighten the bolts in the sequence shown in 3 stages

   c. Stage 3: Tighten an additional 45 degrees.

6.8L Engine

See Figures 302 through 309.

1. With the vehicle in NEUTRAL, position it on a hoist.

2. Remove the alternator.

3. Remove the engine cooling fan.

4. Remove the Throttle Body (TB) spacer.

5. Install the Engine Support Bar, Support Hook and Engine Support Bracket.

6. Remove and discard the oil filter.

7. Drain the engine oil.

8. If equipped, remove the threaded insert and position the engine oil cooler aside.

9. Remove the nut, the transmission auxiliary fluid cooler tube support bracket and the starter wiring harness support bracket from the engine front cover stud bolt.

10. If equipped with an A/T:

11. Remove the nut and disconnect the fuel tube bracket.

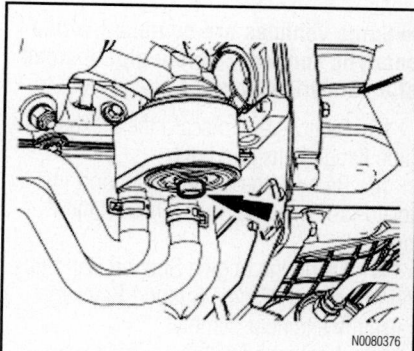

Fig. 302 If equipped, remove the threaded insert and position the engine oil cooler aside

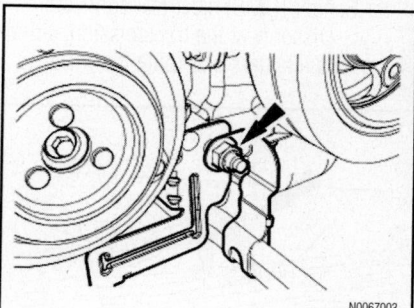

Fig. 303 Remove the nut, the transmission auxiliary fluid cooler tube support bracket and the starter wiring harness support bracket from the engine front cover stud bolt

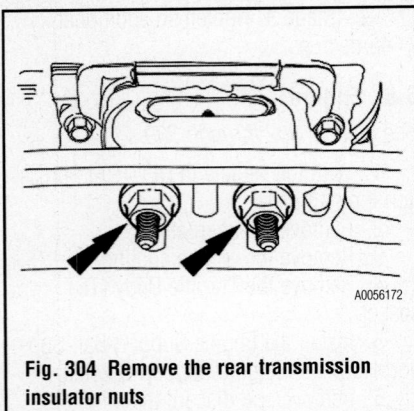

Fig. 304 Remove the rear transmission insulator nuts

12. Detach the fuel supply tube and the fuel vapor tube from the position retainer at the rear of the engine.

➡The transmission insulator studs may come out of the insulator while removing the nuts. Install the studs if the studs come out of the insulator.

13. Remove the rear transmission insulator nuts.

14. If equipped, remove the bolts and the skid plate.

➡Some vehicles are equipped with a catalytic converter delete pipe instead of a catalytic converter.

15. Remove and discard the 2 exhaust Y-pipe flange bolts and nuts.

16. Remove the 7 engine support insulator-to-crossmember nuts. Discard the 7 nuts.

17. Using the Engine Support Bar, Support Hook and Engine Support Bracket, raise the engine assembly.

18. If equipped with an A/T:
a. Disconnect the Turbine Shaft Speed (TSS) sensor electrical connector.
b. Disconnect the LH Catalyst Monitor Sensor (CMS) electrical connector.
c. Disconnect the transmission wiring harness retainers and route the wiring

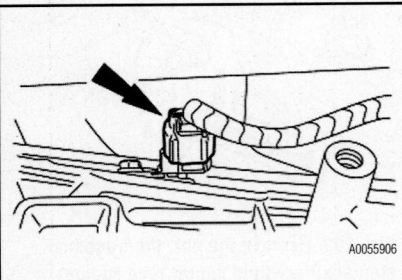

Fig. 305 Disconnect the Turbine Shaft Speed (TSS) sensor electrical connector

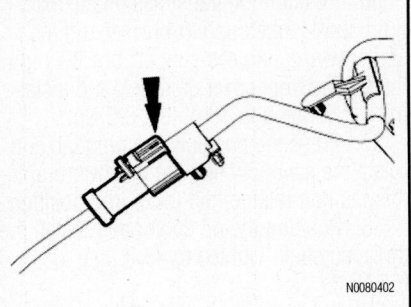

Fig. 306 Disconnect the LH Catalyst Monitor Sensor (CMS) electrical connector

harness over the top of the transmission and out of the way.
d. Remove the 2 flexplate inspection cover bolts, then remove the cover.

⁘ WARNING
Support the transmission on the oil pan rails only or internal transmission damage can occur.

e. Install a Transmission Jack and raise the transmission.
f. Remove the 18 bolts and partially lower the oil pan.
g. Remove the 3 bolts and position the oil pump screen and pickup tube into the oil pan.
h. Remove the oil pan and the oil pump screen and pickup tube;
• Discard the oil pan gasket.
• Discard the oil pump screen and pickup tube O-ring seal.

19. If equipped with a M/T:
a. Remove 18 oil pan bolts and position the oil pan onto the crossmember.
b. Remove the 3 bolts and position the oil pump screen and pickup tube into the oil pan.
c. Position the oil pan onto the engine and install 1 bolt at the front and 1 bolt at the rear of the oil pan to hold it in position.
d. Using the Engine Support Bar, Support Hook and Engine Support Bracket, align the engine support insulator studs and lower the engine.
e. Remove the flywheel.
f. Remove the rear engine cover.
g. Remove the 2 bolts, the oil pan and the oil pump screen and pickup tube:
• Discard the oil pan gasket.
• Discard the oil pump screen and pickup tube O-ring seal.

To install:

⁘ WARNING
Do not use metal scrapers, wire brushes, power abrasive discs or other abrasive means to clean the sealing surfaces. These tools cause scratches and gouges which make leak paths. Use a plastic scraping tool to remove all traces of old sealant. Failure to follow this procedure may cause future oil leakage.

20. Inspect the oil pan. Clean the mating surface for the oil pan with silicone gasket remover and metal surface prep. Follow the directions on the packaging.

⁘ WARNING
Make sure to install a new O-ring seal. A missing or damaged O-ring seal can cause foam in the lubrication system and low oil pressure. Failure to follow this instruction may result in engine damage.

➡Clean and inspect the mating surfaces and install a new O-ring seal. Lubricate the O-ring seal with clean engine oil.

21. Install a new O-ring seal onto the oil pump screen and pickup tube.

22. Position the oil pump screen and pickup tube in the oil pan and position the oil pan and new gasket into the vehicle.

23. If equipped with a M/T:
a. Position the oil pan onto the engine and install one bolt at the front of the engine and one bolt at the rear of the oil pan to hold it in position.
b. Install the rear engine cover.
c. Install the flywheel.
d. Using the Engine Support Bar, Support Hook and Engine Support Bracket, raise the engine.
e. Remove the 2 bolts and lower the oil pan.

⁘ WARNING
Make sure to install a new O-ring seal. A missing or damaged O-ring seal can cause foam in the lubrication system and low oil pressure. Failure to follow this instruction may result in engine damage.

➡Clean and inspect the mating surfaces and install a new O-ring seal. Lubricate the O-ring seal with clean engine oil prior to installation.

24. Position the oil pump screen and pickup tube and install the bolts.

a. Tighten the oil pump screen and pickup tube-to-oil pump bolts to 89 inch lbs. (10 Nm).

b. Tighten the oil pump screen and pickup tube-to-spacer bolt to 18 ft. lbs. (25 Nm).

➡ **If the oil pan is not secured within 4 minutes, the sealant must be removed and the sealing area cleaned with silicone gasket remover and metal surface prep. Follow the directions on the packaging. Allow to dry until there is no sign of wetness, or 4 minutes, whichever is longer. Failure to follow this procedure may cause future oil leakage.**

25. Apply silicone gasket and sealant at the crankshaft rear seal retainer plate-to-cylinder block sealing surface.

➡ **If the oil pan is not secured within 4 minutes, the sealant must be removed and the sealing area cleaned with silicone gasket remover and metal surface prep. Follow the directions on the packaging. Allow to dry until there is no sign of wetness, or 4 minutes, whichever is longer. Failure to follow this procedure may cause future oil leakage.**

26. Apply silicone gasket and sealant at the engine front cover-to-cylinder block sealing surface.
27. Position the oil pan gasket and the oil pan and loosely install the 18 bolts.
28. Tighten the 18 bolts in 3 stages, in the sequence shown.

a. Stage 1: Tighten to 18 inch lbs. (2 Nm).

b. Stage 2: Tighten to 15 ft. lbs. (20 Nm).

c. Stage 3: Tighten an additional 60 degrees.
29. If equipped with an A/T:

a. Lower the transmission and remove the jack.

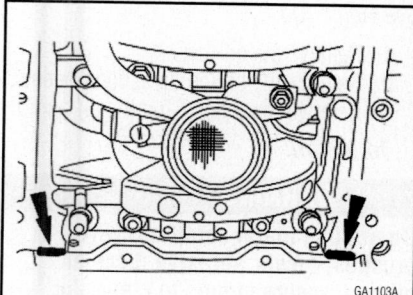

Fig. 307 Apply silicone gasket and sealant at the crankshaft rear seal retainer plate-to-cylinder block sealing surface

b. Position the flexplate inspection cover, then install the 2 bolts. Tighten to 25 ft. lbs. (34 Nm).
30. Using the Engine Support Bar, Support Hook and Engine Support Bracket, align the engine support insulator studs and lower the engine.

✳✳ WARNING
Only use hand tools when installing the engine support insulator nuts or damage to the engine support insulator may occur.

31. Install 4 new RH engine support insulator nuts. Tighten to 85 ft. lbs. (115 Nm).

✳✳ WARNING
Only use hand tools when installing the engine support insulator nuts or damage to the engine support insulator may occur.

32. Install 3 new LH engine support insulator nuts. Tighten to 148 ft. lbs. (200 Nm).
33. If equipped with an A/T:

a. Route the wiring harness over the top of the transmission and connect the wiring harness retainers.

b. Connect the CMS electrical connector.

c. Connect the TSS sensor electrical connector.

➡ **Some vehicles are equipped with a catalytic converter delete pipe instead of a catalytic converter.**

d. Install 2 new exhaust Y-pipe flange bolts and nuts. Tighten to 30 ft. lbs. (40 Nm).

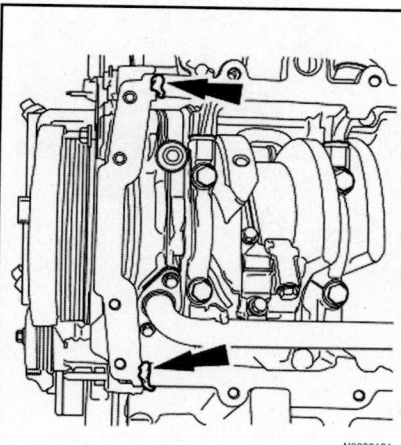

Fig. 308 Apply silicone gasket and sealant at the engine front cover-to-cylinder block sealing surface

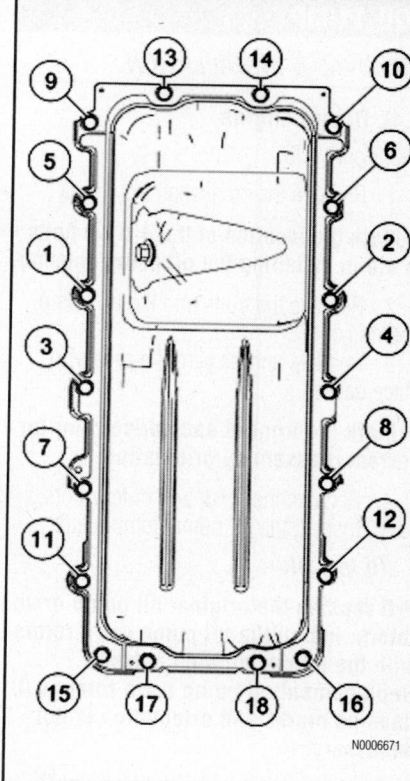

Fig. 309 Tighten the 18 bolts in 3 stages, in the sequence shown

e. If equipped, position the skid plate and install the 4 bolts. Tighten to 18 ft. lbs. (24 Nm).

f. Attach the fuel supply tube and the fuel vapor tube to the position retainer at the rear of the engine.

g. Connect the fuel tube bracket and install the nut. Tighten to 106 inch lbs. (12 Nm).

h. Install the 2 rear transmission insulator nuts. Tighten to 85 ft. lbs. (115 Nm).
34. Position the transmission auxiliary fluid cooler tube support bracket and the starter wiring harness support bracket onto the engine front cover stud bolt and install the nut. Tighten to 18 ft. lbs. (25 Nm).
35. If equipped, position the engine oil cooler and install the threaded insert. Tighten to 43 ft. lbs. (58 Nm).
36. Install a new oil filter. Tighten to 12 ft. lbs. (16 Nm).
37. Install the TB spacer.
38. Install the engine cooling fan.
39. Install the alternator.
40. Fill the crankcase with clean engine oil.

OIL PUMP

REMOVAL & INSTALLATION

6.4L Diesel Engine

See Figure 310.

1. Remove the crankshaft front seal.

➡**Mark the location of the 4 short bolts to aid in installing the oil pump housing.**

2. Remove the bolts and the oil pump housing.

3. Remove and discard the press-in-place gasket.

➡**Mark the front of each drive rotor for correct reassembly orientation.**

4. Remove the inner and outer rotors.
5. Inspect the oil pump components.

To install:

➡**If reusing the original oil pump drive rotors, install the oil pump drive rotors with the marks pointing outward. Replacement oil pump drive rotors will have no marks and orientation is not necessary.**

6. Lubricate the inner drive rotor with clean engine oil and install onto the crankshaft. Lubricate the outer drive rotor with clean engine oil and mesh with the inner drive gear rotor.

➡**Install a new press-in-place gasket.**

7. Install the oil pump housing and the bolts.

   a. Tighten the 7 long bolts to 23 ft. lbs. (31 Nm).

   b. Tighten the 4 short bolts to 16 ft. lbs. (22 Nm).

8. Install the crankshaft front seal.

5.4L Engine

See Figure 311.

1. Remove the timing drive components.
2. Remove the oil pan.
3. Remove the 3 bolts and the oil pump.

To install:

✳✳ WARNING

Do not use metal scrapers, wire brushes, power abrasive discs or other abrasive means to clean the sealing surfaces. These tools cause scratches and gouges which make leak paths. Use a plastic scraping tool to remove all traces of old sealant.

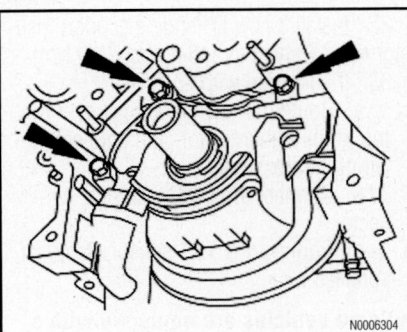

Fig. 311 Remove the 3 bolts and the oil pump

4. Clean the sealing surfaces with metal surface prep. Follow the directions on the packaging. Inspect the mating surfaces.

5. Position the oil pump and install the 3 bolts. Tighten to 89 inch lbs. (10 Nm).

6. Install the oil pan.
7. Install the timing drive components.

6.2L Engine

See Figure 312.

➡**The manufacturer does not provide a specific Removal and Installation procedure for this component. Refer to the graphic(s) when servicing this component.**

1. Position the oil pump and install the 2 upper bolts and the 2 lower stud bolts in 5 stages.

   a. Stage 1: Tighten all fasteners to 18 inch lbs. (2 Nm).

   b. Stage 2: Tighten the 2 upper bolts to 89 inch lbs. (10 Nm).

   c. Stage 3: Tighten the 2 lower stud bolts to 15 ft. lbs. (20 Nm).

   d. Stage 4: Tighten the 2 upper bolts an additional 45 degrees.

   e. Stage 5: Tighten the 2 lower stud bolts an additional 60 degrees.

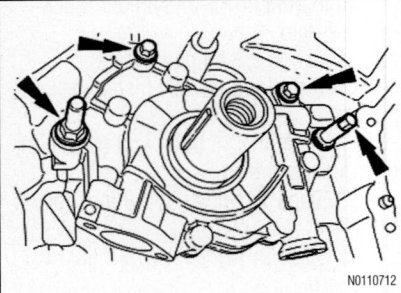

Fig. 312 Position the oil pump and install the 2 upper bolts and the 2 lower stud bolts in 5 stages

6.8L Engine

See Figure 311.

1. Remove the oil pan.
2. Remove the timing drive components.
3. Remove the 3 bolts and the oil pump.

To install:

✳✳ WARNING

Do not use metal scrapers, wire brushes, power abrasive discs or other abrasive means to clean the sealing surfaces. These tools cause scratches and gouges which make leak paths. Use a plastic scraping tool to remove all traces of old sealant.

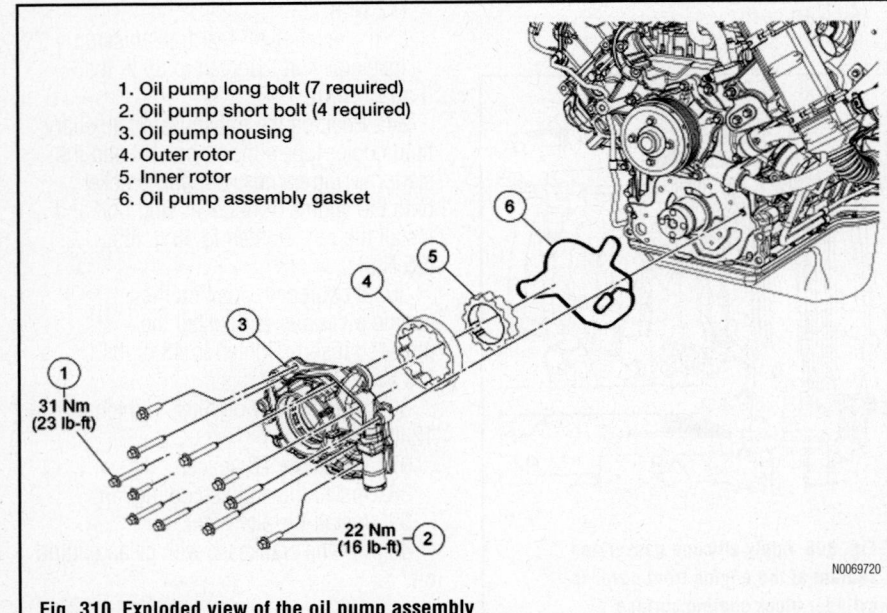

1. Oil pump long bolt (7 required)
2. Oil pump short bolt (4 required)
3. Oil pump housing
4. Outer rotor
5. Inner rotor
6. Oil pump assembly gasket

31 Nm (23 lb-ft)

22 Nm (16 lb-ft)

Fig. 310 Exploded view of the oil pump assembly

4. Clean the sealing surfaces with metal surface prep. Follow the directions on the packaging. Inspect the mating surfaces.

5. Position the oil pump and install the 3 bolts. Tighten to 89 inch lbs. (10 Nm).

6. Install the timing drive components.

7. Install the oil pan.

PISTON AND RING

POSITIONING

6.4L Diesel Engine

See Figure 313.

> ☀ **WARNING**
>
> **Make sure the ring openings are 120 degrees from each other or engine damage may occur.**

1. Install new piston rings.

a. The top compression ring is identified with one indentation mark and a 15-degree keystone cross section. The ring must be installed with the indentation mark facing towards the piston crown (top).

b. The intermediate ring is identified with 2 indentation marks and a rectangular profile. The ring must be installed with the indentation marks facing towards the piston crown (top).

c. Install the oil control ring. Make sure the oil ring gap is 180-degrees from the spring wire latch.

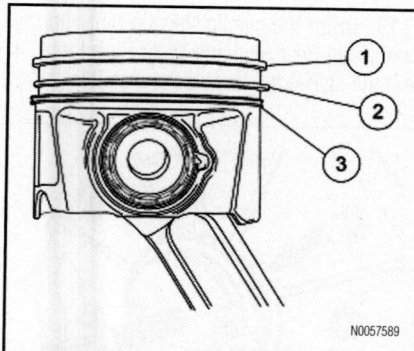

Fig. 313 Piston rings placement; top compression ring (1), intermediate ring (2), and oil control ring (3)

6.2L Engine

See Figure 314.

5.4L & 6.8L Engines

See Figure 315.

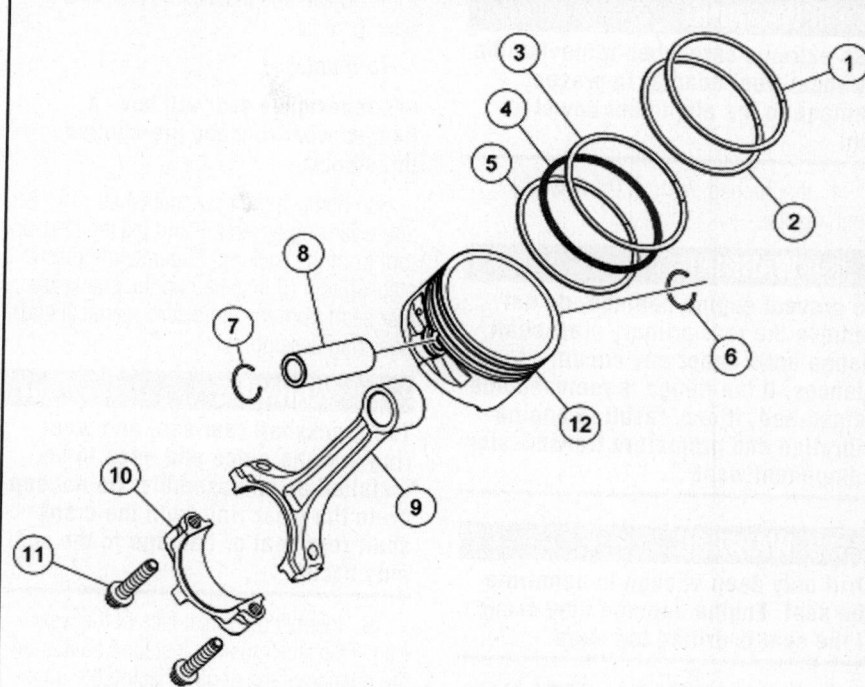

1. Piston compression upper ring
2. Piston compression lower ring
3. Piston oil control upper segment ring
4. Piston oil control spacer
5. Piston oil control lower segment ring
6. Piston pin retainer
7. Piston pin retainer
8. Piston pin
9. Connecting rod
10. Connecting rod bearing cap
11. Connecting rod bearing cap bolt (2 required)
12. Piston

N0105892

Fig. 314 Exploded view of the piston assembly showing the order of the piston rings

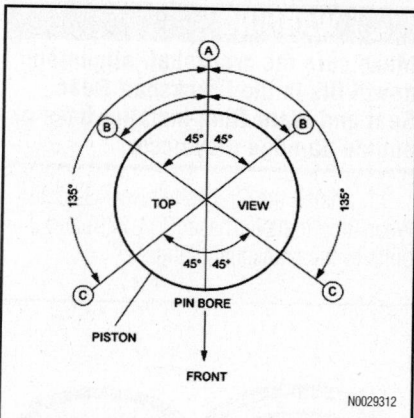

Fig. 315 Make sure the ring gaps for oil spacer (A), oil ring (B), compression ring (C) are correctly spaced around the circumference of the piston.

REAR MAIN SEAL

REMOVAL & INSTALLATION

6.4L Diesel Engine

See Figures 316 through 323.

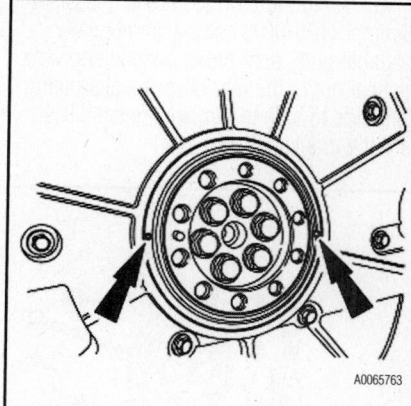

Fig. 316 Using a center punch, mark a location for 2 holes 180 degrees apart

1. Remove the transmission.

2. If equipped with a M/T, remove the clutch disc and pressure plate.

3. Remove the 10 bolts and the flexplate or flywheel. Discard the bolts.

⁂ WARNING

Use extreme care when removing the flywheel front adapter to prevent damage to the alignment dowel pin.

4. If equipped, remove the flywheel front adapter.

⁂ WARNING

To prevent engine damage, do not remove the rear primary crankshaft flange bolts under any circumstances. If the flange is removed and reinstalled, it may result in engine vibration and premature transmission component wear.

⁂ WARNING

Drill only deep enough to penetrate the seal. Engine damage may occur if the seal is drilled too deep.

5. Using a center punch, mark a location for 2 holes 180 degrees apart, 0.37 inches (9.53 mm) from the outer diameter of the crankshaft flange. Using a drill bit of the appropriate size for the slide hammer dent puller attachment being used, drill a hole on each side of the crankshaft rear seal as shown. Drill the holes to a depth of 0.34 inches (8.76 mm) to capture the metal case of the crankshaft seal as well as the wear ring.

6. Using the 2 drilled holes, the Slide Hammer (100-001) and a commercially available body dent puller attachment, walk the seal out of the rear cover by alternating from side to side to remove the seal. Discard the crankshaft rear seal.

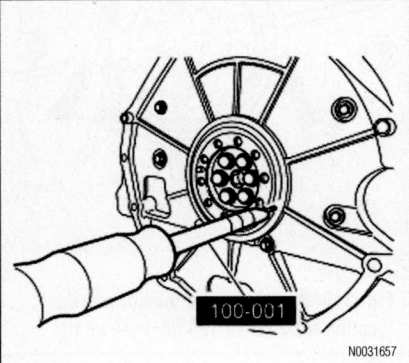

Fig. 317 Using the 2 drilled holes, the Slide Hammer and a commercially available body dent puller attachment, walk the seal out of the rear cover by alternating from side to side to remove the seal

7. Clean and inspect the crankshaft sealing surface.

To install:

➡ **A redesigned seal will have a flanged wear ring and pre-applied threadlock.**

8. Remove the new crankshaft rear seal and wear ring assembly and plastic step-up tool from the packing. Separate the plastic step-up tool (if installed on the crankcase rear seal) from the crankcase rear seal and wear ring assembly.

⁂ WARNING

The crankshaft rear seal and wear ring are one-piece and need to be installed as an assembly. Do not separate the wear ring from the crankshaft rear seal or damage to the seal may occur.

9. Identify the metal face of the wear ring. This face must be installed so it is on the outside of the engine (facing the transmission).

➡ **Lubricate the outer diameter of the rubber seal with a solution of dish soap and water (approximately 50/50 mix) prior to assembly. Do not use any other type of lubricant.**

10. Lubricate the outer diameter of the rubber seal with a solution of dish soap and water.

⁂ WARNING

Make sure the crankshaft alignment dowel fits in the Crankshaft Rear Seal and Wear Ring Installer base or engine damage may occur.

11. Install the Crankshaft Rear Seal and Wear Ring Installer base (303-770) and 2 bolts to the crankshaft flange.

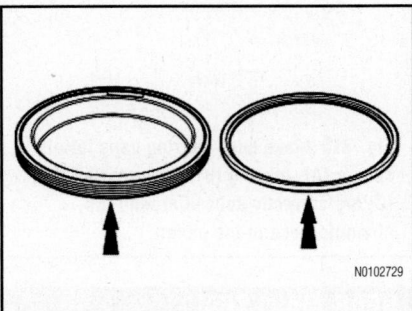

Fig. 318 Separate the plastic step-up tool (if installed on the crankcase rear seal) from the crankcase rear seal and wear ring assembly

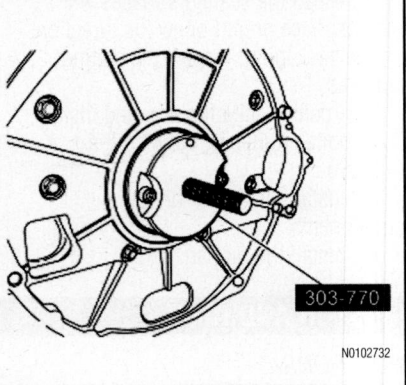

Fig. 319 Install the Crankshaft Rear Seal and Wear Ring Installer base and 2 bolts to the crankshaft flange

➡ **When positioning the crankshaft rear seal and wear ring assembly on the Crankshaft Rear Seal and Wear Ring Installer base, align it to the opening on the engine rear cover and manually start the crankcase rear seal installation.**

12. Position the crankshaft rear seal and wear ring assembly on the Crankshaft Rear Seal and Wear Ring Installer base.

⁂ WARNING

The plastic step-up tool increases the flat surface area of the Crankshaft Rear Seal and Wear Ring Installer. Failure to use the plastic step-up tool during installation will result in damage to the crankshaft rear seal and wear ring assembly.

13. Insert the plastic step-up tool into the Crankshaft Rear Seal and Wear Ring Installer with the step-edge toward the installer.

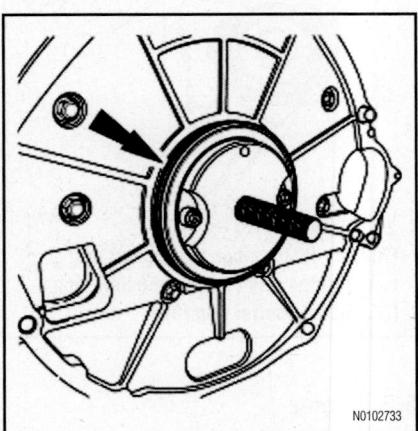

Fig. 320 Position the crankshaft rear seal and wear ring assembly on the Crankshaft Rear Seal and Wear Ring Installer base

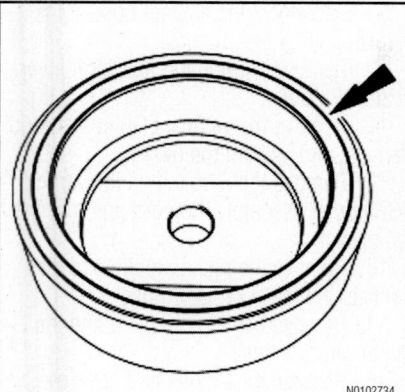

Fig. 321 Insert the plastic step-up tool into the Crankshaft Rear Seal and Wear Ring Installer with the step-edge toward the installer

✳✳ WARNING

The crankshaft rear seal face and the wear ring must be flush with the rear engine cover or damage to the crankshaft rear seal or wear ring may occur.

✳✳ WARNING

Do not allow the engine to rotate during the installation of the crankshaft rear seal and wear ring assembly or damage to the crankshaft rear seal or wear ring may occur.

14. Using the Crankshaft Rear Seal and Wear Ring Installer, install the new crankshaft rear seal and wear ring assembly until the installation tool contacts the rear engine cover.

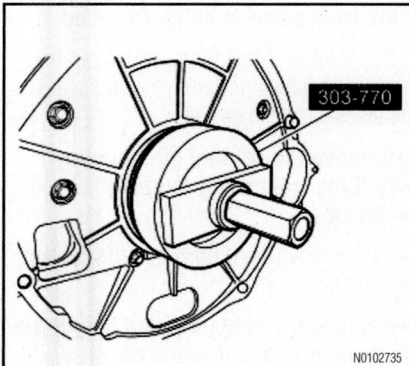

Fig. 322 Using the Crankshaft Rear Seal and Wear Ring Installer, install the new crankshaft rear seal and wear ring assembly until the installation tool contacts the rear engine cover

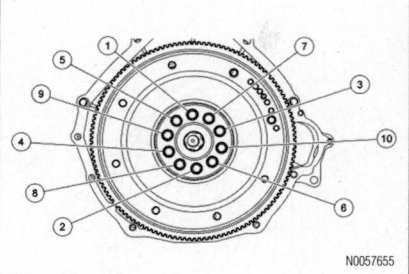

Fig. 323 Tighten the bolts in 2 stages, in the sequence shown

15. If equipped, install the flywheel front adapter.
16. Install the flexplate or flywheel and 10 new bolts. Tighten the bolts in 2 stages, in the sequence shown.
   a. Stage 1: Tighten to 44 inch lbs. (5 Nm).
   b. Stage 2: Tighten to 69 ft. lbs. (94 Nm).
17. If equipped, install the clutch disc and pressure plate.
18. Install the transmission.

6.7L Diesel Engine

See Figure 324.

1. Remove the flexplate.
2. Remove the ignition pulse crankshaft sensor ring.

➡Do not scratch or damage the crankshaft during removal or installation of the rear crankshaft seal.

3. Using the Rear Crank Seal Remover, remove and discard the rear crankshaft seal.
4. Clean and inspect the crankshaft sealing surface.

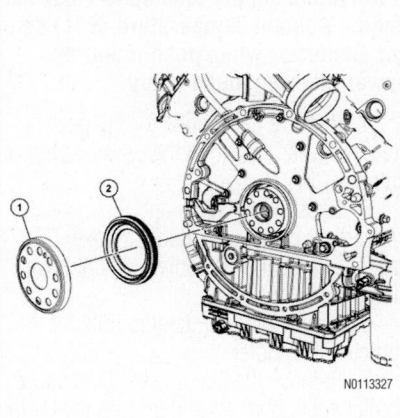

Fig. 324 Remove the ignition pulse crankshaft sensor ring (1) and the rear crankshaft seal (2)

To install:

✳✳ WARNING

Failure to install the rear crankshaft seal with the part numbers facing out may result in engine damage.

➡Do not discard the installation sleeve provided with the rear crankshaft seal. It is used for installation of the crankshaft seal.

➡Check for correct orientation of the installation sleeve prior to sliding the seal on the crankshaft.

➡Apply clean engine oil to the seal and crankshaft sealing surface.

5. Position the installation sleeve onto the crankshaft, slide the new rear crankshaft seal over the installation sleeve onto the crankshaft.
6. Remove the installation sleeve.
7. Using the Rear Crank Seal Installer, install the new rear crankshaft seal.
8. Install the ignition pulse crankshaft sensor ring.
9. Install the flexplate.

5.4L & 6.8L Engines

See Figures 325 through 329.

1. Remove the transmission.
2. Remove the 8 bolts and the flexplate.
3. Remove the engine rear cover plate.
4. Using the Slide Hammer (100-001) and Crankshaft Rear Oil Slinger Remover (303-514), remove and discard the crankshaft oil slinger.
5. Using the Slide Hammer (100-001) and Crankshaft Rear Oil Seal Remover (303-519), remove and discard the crankshaft rear seal.

To install:

➡Lubricate the crankshaft rear seal with clean engine oil prior to installation.

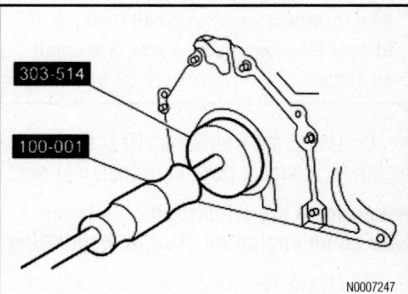

Fig. 325 Using the Slide Hammer and Crankshaft Rear Oil Slinger Remover, remove and discard the crankshaft oil slinger

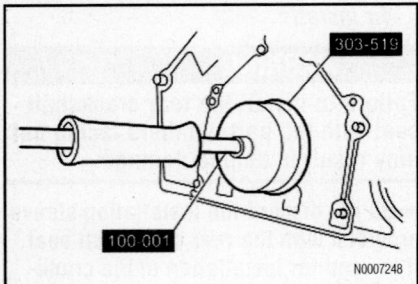

Fig. 326 Using the Slide Hammer and Crankshaft Rear Oil Seal Remover, remove and discard the crankshaft rear seal

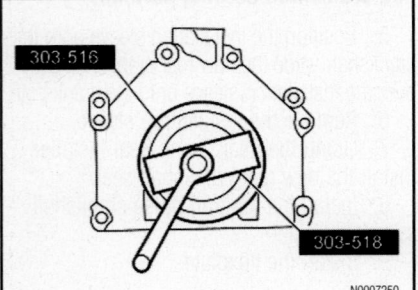

Fig. 327 Using the Crankshaft Rear Oil Seal Installers, install a new crankshaft rear seal

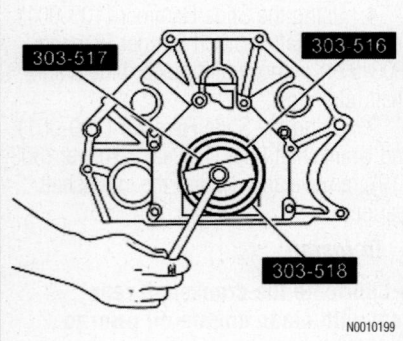

Fig. 328 Using the Crankshaft Rear Oil Seal Installers and Crankshaft Rear Oil Slinger Installer, install a new crankshaft oil slinger

6. Using the Crankshaft Rear Oil Seal Installers, install a new crankshaft rear seal.

➡**Lubricate the crankshaft oil slinger with clean engine oil prior to installation.**

7. Using the Crankshaft Rear Oil Seal Installers and Crankshaft Rear Oil Slinger Installer, install a new crankshaft oil slinger.

8. Install the engine rear cover plate.

9. Install the flexplate and tighten the 8

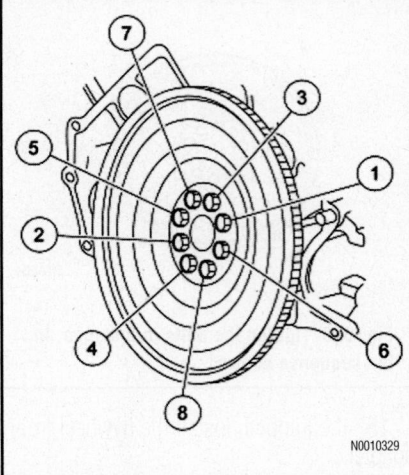

Fig. 329 Install the flexplate and tighten the 8 bolts in the sequence shown

bolts in the sequence shown. Tighten to 59 ft. lbs. (80 Nm).

10. Install the transmission.

TIMING CHAIN FRONT COVER

REMOVAL & INSTALLATION

6.4L Diesel Engine

See Figures 330 through 332.

✳✳ WARNING

Position a suitable protective material in front of the Charge Air Cooler (CAC) or damage to the CAC may occur.

1. Remove the Air Cleaner (ACL) outlet pipe.

2. Remove the crankshaft front seal.

3. Remove the retaining nut for the power steering hose and tube.

➡**Raise the supply tube up to clear the Engine Coolant Temperature (ECT) sensor connector when positioning the power steering pump aside.**

4. Remove the 3 bolts for the power steering pump. Position the power steering pump aside.

5. Loosen the clamp and disconnect the vertical EGR cooler coolant hose. Discard the vertical EGR cooler coolant hose clamp.

6. Remove the 2 retaining nuts for the vertical EGR cooler.

7. Remove the bolt and the EGR cooler coolant tube. Remove and discard the O-ring seal.

8. Disconnect the Exhaust Gas Recirculation Temperature (EGRT) sensor electrical connector.

9. Disconnect the coolant hose at the vertical EGR cooler.

10. Remove the nut and bolt for the vertical EGR cooler.

11. Remove the vertical EGR cooler stud. Remove and discard the gasket.

12. Remove the 5 bolts and the vertical EGR cooler assembly. Remove and discard the gasket.

13. Remove the retaining clip and disconnect the lower radiator hose.

14. Remove the retaining clip and the upper radiator hose.

15. Remove the 2 bolts and position aside the heater return tube. Remove and discard the O-ring seal.

16. Remove the 2 bolts and disconnect the EGR cooler coolant supply tube from the front cover. Remove and discard the O-ring seal and the clamp.

17. Remove the bolt and the accessory drive belt tensioner.

18. If equipped, remove the bolt and the A/C belt tensioner.

19. Remove the bolt and the accessory drive belt idler pulley.

20. Disconnect the ECT sensor electrical connector and wire retainer.

21. Remove the nut and 2 bolts for the heater supply tube and engine wiring harness.

✳✳ WARNING

Do not bend or flex the heater supply tube or damage to the tube may occur.

22. Position the heater supply tube as needed so that it will not interfere with the removal of the front cover. Secure the tube as needed. Remove and discard the O-ring seal.

➡**Remove the thermostat housing only if the front cover is being replaced.**

23. Remove the 4 bolts, collar and the thermostat housing. Remove and discard the press-in-place gasket.

➡**Remove the coolant pump pulley only if the front cover is being replaced.**

24. Remove the 4 bolts and the coolant pump pulley.

➡**Remove the coolant pump only if the front cover is being replaced.**

25. Remove the 5 bolts and the coolant pump. Discard the O-ring seal.

➡**Mark the location of the 4 short bolts to aid in installing the oil pump housing.**

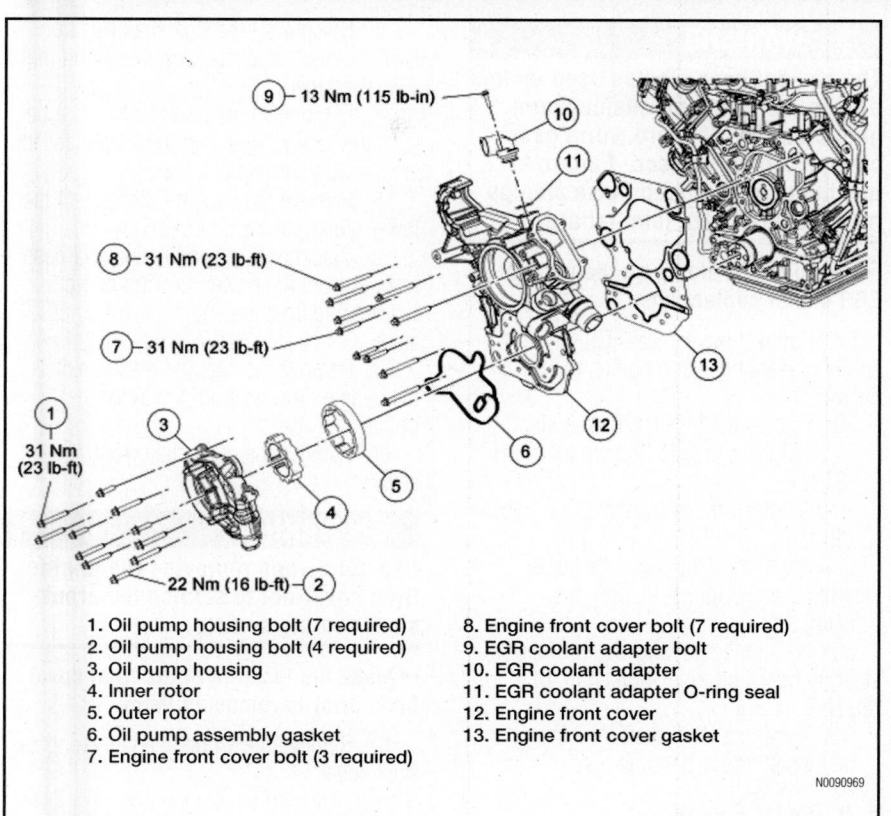

Fig. 330 Exploded view of front cover assembly

1. Oil pump housing bolt (7 required)
2. Oil pump housing bolt (4 required)
3. Oil pump housing
4. Inner rotor
5. Outer rotor
6. Oil pump assembly gasket
7. Engine front cover bolt (3 required)
8. Engine front cover bolt (7 required)
9. EGR coolant adapter bolt
10. EGR coolant adapter
11. EGR coolant adapter O-ring seal
12. Engine front cover
13. Engine front cover gasket

26. Remove the 11 bolts and the oil pump housing. Remove and discard the press-in-place gasket.

➡ **Mark the front of each drive rotor for correct reassembly orientation.**

27. Remove the inner and outer oil pump drive rotors.

➡ **Make the location of the front cover fasteners prior to removing them.**

28. Remove the 10 bolts and the engine front cover.

✳✳ **WARNING**

Sealant is used where the upper and lower crankcase meet. Failure to cut the sealant may result in pulling the lower crankcase seal out while removing the front cover gasket.

➡ **Engine removed for clarity.**

29. Use a thin-blade scraper to cut the sealant where the upper and lower crankcase meet. Remove and discard the front cover gasket.

30. Remove the bolt and the EGR coolant adapter. Remove and discard the O-ring seal.

To install:

➡ **Install a new O-ring seal.**

31. Install the EGR coolant adapter and bolt. Tighten to 10 ft. lbs. (13 Nm).

32. Apply a dime-sized bead of sealant at the front joint of the upper and lower crankcase.

✳✳ **WARNING**

Failure to use guide pins to position the front cover gasket may lead to oil in the coolant.

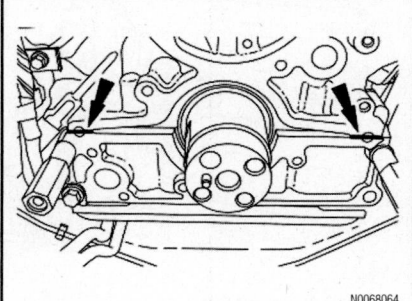

Fig. 331 Apply a dime-sized bead of sealant at the front joint of the upper and lower crankcase

➡ **Use guide studs to aid in installation. Studs must be fabricated locally.**

33. Position the new front cover gasket on the engine and install guide pins.

34. Position the engine front cover and loosely install the 10 bolts.

➡ **Install oil pump drive rotors with marks pointing outward.**

35. Lubricate the inner drive rotor with clean engine oil and install onto the crankshaft. Lubricate the outer drive rotor with clean engine oil and mesh with the inner drive rotor.

36. Install a new press-in-place gasket, the oil pump housing and the 11 bolts.

  a. Tighten the 7 long bolts to 23 ft. lbs. (31 Nm).

  b. Tighten the 4 short bolts to 16 ft. lbs. (22 Nm).

37. Tighten the 10 engine front cover bolts. Tighten to 23 ft. lbs. (31 Nm).

➡ **Install a new O-ring seal on the coolant pump.**

38. If removed, install the coolant pump and the 5 bolts. Tighten to 23 ft. lbs. (31 Nm).

39. If removed, install the coolant pump pulley and the 4 bolts. Tighten to 23 ft. lbs. (31 Nm).

40. If removed, install a new press-in-place gasket. Install the thermostat housing, collar and 4 bolts. Tighten to 10 ft. lbs. (13 Nm).

✳✳ **WARNING**

Do not bend or flex the heater supply tube or damage to the tube may occur.

➡ **Install a new O-ring seal.**

41. Position back the heater supply tube.

42. Install the nut and 2 bolts for the heater supply tube and engine wiring harness. Tighten to 10 ft. lbs. (13 Nm).

Fig. 332 Position the new front cover gasket on the engine and install guide pins

43. Connect the ECT sensor electrical connector and wire retainer.

44. Install the accessory drive belt idler pulley and bolt. Tighten to 35 ft. lbs. (47 Nm).

45. If equipped, install the A/C belt tensioner and bolt. Tighten to 35 ft. lbs. (47 Nm).

46. Install the accessory drive belt tensioner and bolt. Tighten to 35 ft. lbs. (47 Nm).

➡️**Install a new O-ring seal on the tube.**

➡️**Hand start both bolts prior to tightening the bolts.**

47. Position back the EGR cooler coolant supply tube and install the 2 bolts. Tighten to 10 ft. lbs. (13 Nm).

➡️**Install a new O-ring seal.**

48. Position back the heater return tube and install the 2 bolts. Tighten to 10 ft. lbs. (13 Nm).

49. Install the upper radiator hose and retaining clip.

50. Position back the lower radiator hose and install the retaining clip.

➡️**Install a new horizontal EGR cooler gasket prior to installing the vertical EGR cooler.**

51. Position the vertical EGR cooler assembly and loosely install the 5 bolts.

52. Install a new vertical EGR cooler gasket and the stud. Tighten to 13 ft. lbs. (17 Nm).

53. Install the nut and bolt for the vertical EGR cooler. Tighten to 23 ft. lbs. (31 Nm).

54. Connect the EGRT sensor electrical connector. Connect the coolant hose to the vertical EGR cooler.

➡️**Install a new O-ring seal.**

55. Install the vertical EGR cooler tube and bolt. Tighten to 89 inch lbs. (10 Nm).

✳✳ WARNING
Do not bend or twist the EGR cooler bellows or damage to the EGR cooler may occur.

➡️**Inspect the corrugation of the vertical EGR cooler inlet to make sure that the corrugation ribs are not touching and are not damaged.**

56. Install the 2 nuts for the vertical EGR cooler. Tighten to 23 ft. lbs. (31 Nm).

✳✳ WARNING
The coolant hose clamps used on this engine are constant tension worm gear clamps. Standard worm gear clamps cannot be used. Failure to use the correct coolant hose clamps may result in hose joint failure.

➡️**Install a new clamp on the vertical EGR cooler coolant hose.**

57. Connect the vertical EGR cooler coolant hose and tighten the clamp.

58. Tighten the 5 EGR cooler bolts.
  a. Tighten the M8 bolts to 23 ft. lbs. (31 Nm).
  b. Tighten the M10 bolt to 46 ft. lbs. (62 Nm).

59. Install the 3 bolts for the power steering pump. Tighten to 18 ft. lbs. (25 Nm).

60. Install the retaining nut for the power steering hose and tube. Tighten to 18 ft. lbs. (25 Nm).

61. Install the crankshaft front seal.

62. Install the ACL outlet pipe.

6.7L Diesel Engine
See Figures 333 and 334.

1. Remove the upper oil pan.

2. Remove the cooling module, cooling fan stator and cooling fan.

3. Remove the accessory drive belt , accessory drive belt tensioner and cooling fan drive assembly.

4. Remove the A/C compressor.

5. Remove the vacuum pump.

6. Disconnect the Camshaft Position (CMP) sensor electrical connector and the 3 wire retainers.

7. Disconnect the power steering tube from the retainer. Remove the 2 bolts for the engine wire harness.

8. Remove the clip and disconnect the lower radiator hose.

9. Disconnect the engine wire harness retainer from the power steering pump bracket and position engine wire harness aside.

10. Remove the clip and disconnect the engine fill hose from the degas bottle.

11. Remove the crankshaft front seal.

✳✳ WARNING
Use care when removing the engine front cover not to scratch the crankshaft sealing surface.

➡️**Make the location of the front cover bolts prior to removing them.**

12. Remove the 14 bolts and the engine front cover.
  a. Discard the engine front cover.
  b. Clean and inspect the sealing surfaces.

To install:

✳✳ WARNING
Failure to properly align the engine front cover to the oil pan rail may result in engine damage.

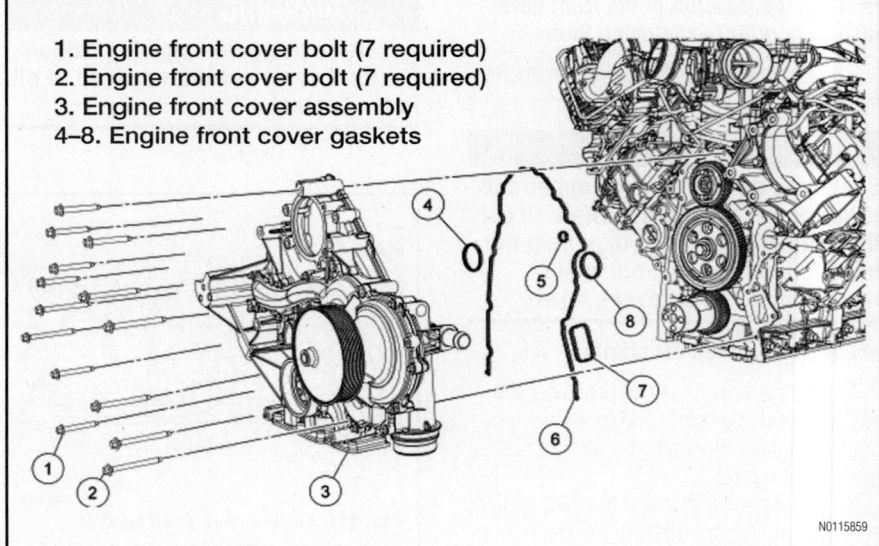

1. Engine front cover bolt (7 required)
2. Engine front cover bolt (7 required)
3. Engine front cover assembly
4–8. Engine front cover gaskets

N0115859

Fig. 333 Exploded view of the engine front cover

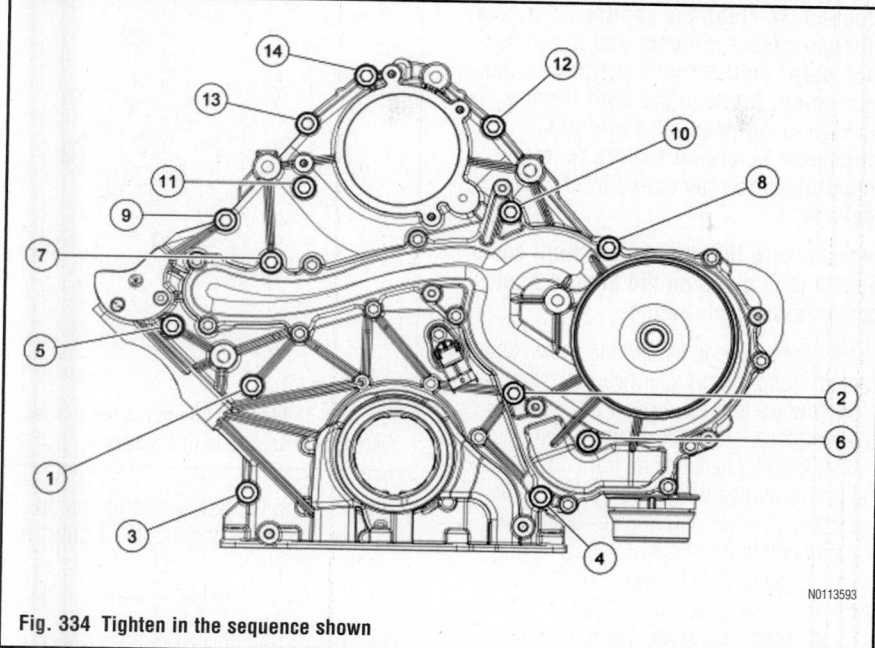

Fig. 334 Tighten in the sequence shown

> ✴✴ **WARNING**
>
> **Use care when installing the engine front cover not to scratch the crankshaft sealing surface.**

➡**Use the Gauge Bar to align the bottom of the engine front cover to the oil pan rail prior to torquing the engine front cover.**

13. Using new gaskets, install the new engine front cover and 14 bolts.

　a. Support the oil pump gerotor assembly in the engine front cover bore.

　b. Position the engine front cover assembly over the crankshaft without contacting the front sealing surface.

　c. Align the oil pump gerotor assembly with the crankshaft drive flats.

　d. Align the engine front cover assembly locating pin.

14. Slide the front cover assembly over the crankshaft post to the cylinder block sealing surface.

　a. Hand start bolt number 1 and 2.

　b. Using the Gauge Bar, align the bottom of the engine front cover to the oil pan rail.

　c. Install the remaining engine front cover bolts. Tighten in the sequence shown.

　d. Tighten to 18 ft. lbs. (24 Nm).

15. As a post-check, using the Gauge Bar and Feeler Gauge Set, verify alignment of the engine front cover to the oil pan rail is within 0.009 inches (0.25 mm).

➡**If the engine front cover alignment is not within specification, loosen the bolts and repeat step 1.**

16. Install the crankshaft front seal.

17. Connect the engine fill hose to the degas bottle and install the clip.

18. Position back the engine wire harness and connect the engine wire harness retainer to the power steering pump bracket.

19. Connect the lower radiator hose and install the clip

20. Install the 2 bolts for the engine wire harness. Connect the power steering tube to the retainer. Tighten to 89 inch lbs. (10 Nm).

21. Connect the CMP sensor electrical connector and the 3 wire retainers.

22. Install the vacuum pump.

23. Install the A/C compressor.

24. Install the cooling fan drive assembly, accessory drive belt tensioner and accessory drive belt.

25. Install the cooling fan, cooling fan stator and cooling module.

26. Install the upper oil pan.

5.4L Engine

See Figures 335 through 337.

1. With the vehicle in NEUTRAL, position it on a hoist.

2. Drain the engine oil.

3. Remove the engine cooling fan shroud.

4. Remove the engine cooling fan.

5. Remove the RH valve cover.

6. Remove the LH valve cover.

7. Loosen the 4 coolant pump pulley bolts.

8. Rotate the tensioner clockwise and remove the accessory drive belt.

9. Remove the bolt and the accessory drive idler pulley.

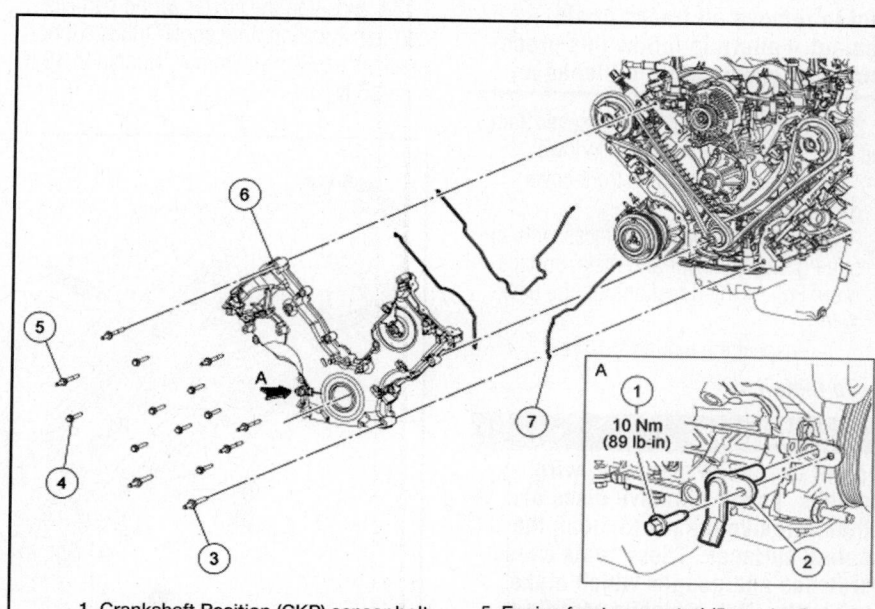

1. Crankshaft Position (CKP) sensor bolt
2. CKP sensor
3. Engine front cover stud (2 required)
4. Engine front cover bolt (8 required)
5. Engine front cover stud (5 required)
6. Engine front cover
7. Engine front cover gasket (3 required)

Fig. 335 Exploded view of engine front cover assembly

10. Remove the 3 bolts and the accessory drive belt tensioner.

11. Remove the crankshaft pulley bolt and washer. Discard the crankshaft pulley bolt.

12. Using the 3 Jaw Puller, remove the crankshaft pulley.

13. Using the Crankshaft Front Oil Seal Remover, remove the crankshaft seal.

14. Remove the 3 bolts and position the power steering pump assembly aside.

15. Remove the 2 nuts and the RH and LH radio ignition interference capacitors.

16. Disconnect the RH Camshaft Position (CMP) sensor electrical connector.

17. Disconnect the LH CMP sensor electrical connector.

18. Remove the 4 bolts and the coolant pump pulley.

19. Disconnect the Crankshaft Position (CKP) sensor electrical connector.

20. Remove the nut and the starter wiring harness and transmission cooler tube support brackets from the stud bolt.

21. Remove the 4 front oil pan bolts.

22. Remove the 8 bolts and the 7 studs.

✳✳ WARNING

Do not use metal scrapers, wire brushes, power abrasive discs or other abrasive means to clean the sealing surfaces. These tools cause scratches and gouges which make leak paths. Use a plastic scraping tool to remove all traces of old sealant. Failure to follow this procedure may cause future oil leakage.

23. Remove the engine front cover from the front cover to cylinder block dowel.

   a. Remove the engine front cover gaskets.

   b. Clean the mating surfaces with silicone gasket remover and metal surface prep. Follow the directions on the packaging.

   c. Inspect the mating surfaces.

To install:

✳✳ WARNING

Do not use metal scrapers, wire brushes, power abrasive discs or other abrasive means to clean the sealing surfaces. These tools cause scratches and gouges which make leak paths. Use a plastic scraping tool to remove all traces of old sealant.

➡If the engine front cover is not secured within 4 minutes, the sealant must be removed and the sealing area

cleaned. To clean the sealing area, use silicone gasket remover and metal surface prep. Follow the directions on the packaging. Allow to dry until there is no sign of wetness, or 4 minutes, whichever is longer. Failure to follow this procedure may cause future oil leakage.

➡Make sure that the engine front cover gasket is in place on the engine front cover before installation.

24. Apply a bead of silicone gasket and sealant along the cylinder head-to-cylinder block surface and the oil pan-to-cylinder block surface, at the locations shown.

25. Install a new engine front cover gasket on the engine front cover. Position the engine front cover onto the dowels. Install the fasteners finger-tight.

26. Tighten the 15 engine front cover fasteners in sequence in 2 stages.

   a. Stage 1: Tighten fasteners 1 through 15 to 18 ft. lbs. (25 Nm).

   b. Stage 2: Tighten fasteners 6 and 7 to 35 ft. lbs. (48 Nm).

27. Loosely install the bolts, then tighten the bolts in 2 stages.

   a. Stage 1: Tighten to 15 ft. lbs. (20 Nm).

   b. Stage 2: Tighten an additional 60 degrees.

28. Connect the CKP sensor electrical connector.

29. Position the starter wiring harness and transmission fluid cooler tubes support brackets and install the nut. Tighten to 18 ft. lbs. (25 Nm).

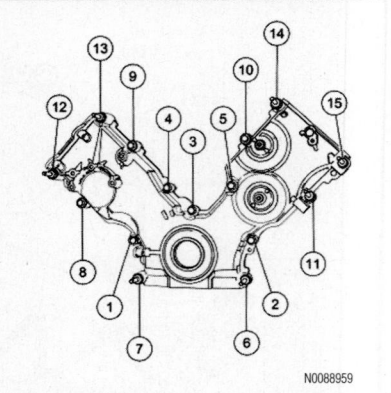

Fig. 337 Tighten the 15 engine front cover fasteners in sequence in 2 stages

30. Position the power steering pump assembly and install the 3 bolts. Tighten to 18 ft. lbs. (25 Nm).

31. Connect the RH CMP sensor electrical connector.

32. Connect the LH CMP sensor electrical connector.

33. Install the RH and LH radio ignition interference capacitors and the 2 nuts. Tighten to 89 inch lbs. (10 Nm).

34. Install the accessory drive belt tensioner and the 3 bolts. Tighten to 18 ft. lbs. (25 Nm).

35. Install the coolant pump pulley and the 4 bolts finger-tight.

36. Install the accessory drive idler pulley and the bolt. Tighten to 18 ft. lbs. (25 Nm).

37. Lubricate the engine front cover and the crankshaft front seal inner lip with clean engine oil.

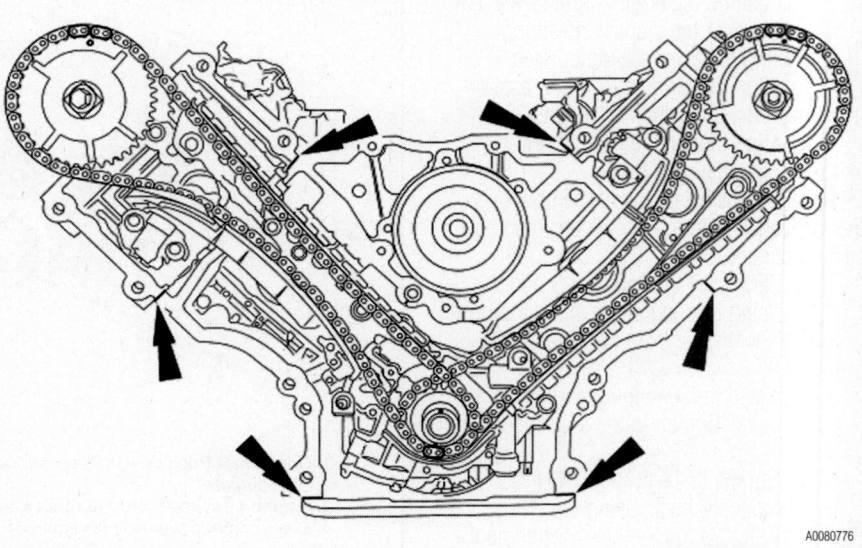

Fig. 336 Apply a bead of silicone gasket and sealant along the cylinder head-to-cylinder block surface and the oil pan-to-cylinder block surface, at the locations shown

38. Using the Crankshaft Front Oil Seal Installer, the Crankshaft Vibration Damper Installer and the Front Cover Oil Seal Installer, install the new crankshaft front seal into the engine front cover.

➡**If not secured within 4 minutes, the sealant must be removed and the sealing area cleaned with metal surface prep and silicone gasket remover. Allow to dry until there is no sign of wetness, or 4 minutes, whichever is longer. Failure to follow this procedure can cause future oil leakage.**

39. Apply silicone gasket and sealant to the Woodruff key slot in the crankshaft pulley.

40. Using the Crankshaft Vibration Damper Installer, install the crankshaft pulley.

41. Using a new crankshaft pulley bolt, install the bolt and washer and tighten the bolt in 4 stages.
   a. Stage 1: Tighten to 66 ft. lbs. (90 Nm).
   b. Stage 2: Loosen 360 degrees.
   c. Stage 3: Tighten to 37 ft. lbs. (50 Nm).
   d. Stage 4: Tighten an additional 90 degrees.

42. Rotate the tensioner clockwise and install the accessory drive belt.

43. Tighten the 4 coolant pump pulley bolts. Tighten to 18 ft. lbs. (25 Nm).

44. Install the RH valve cover.

45. Install the LH valve cover.

46. Install the engine cooling fan.

47. Install the engine cooling fan shroud.

48. Fill the crankcase with clean engine oil.

6.2L Engine

See Figures 338 through 340.

➡**The manufacturer does not provide a specific Removal and Installation procedure for this component. Refer to the graphic(s) when servicing this component.**

☀☀ WARNING

Do not use metal scrapers, wire brushes, power abrasive discs or other abrasive means to clean the sealing surfaces. These tools cause scratches and gouges which make leak paths. Use a plastic scraping tool to remove all traces of old sealant.

➡**If the engine front cover is not secured within 4 minutes, the sealant**

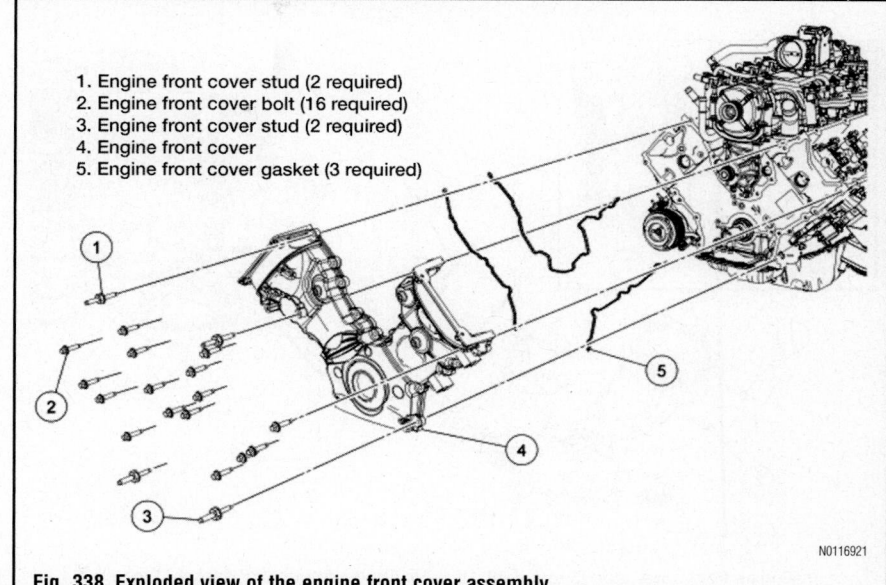

1. Engine front cover stud (2 required)
2. Engine front cover bolt (16 required)
3. Engine front cover stud (2 required)
4. Engine front cover
5. Engine front cover gasket (3 required)

N0116921

Fig. 338 Exploded view of the engine front cover assembly

must be removed and the sealing area cleaned. To clean the sealing area, use silicone gasket remover and metal surface prep. Allow to dry until there is no sign of wetness, or 4 minutes, whichever is longer. Failure to follow this procedure can cause future oil leakage.

➡**Make sure that the engine front cover gasket is in place on the engine front cover before installation.**

1. Tighten the 20 engine front cover fasteners in the sequence shown in 3 stages.
   a. Stage 1: Tighten all fasteners to 89 inch lbs. (10 Nm).
   b. Stage 2: Tighten all fasteners to 15 ft. lbs. (20 Nm).
   c. Stage 3: Tighten all fasteners an additional 45 degrees.

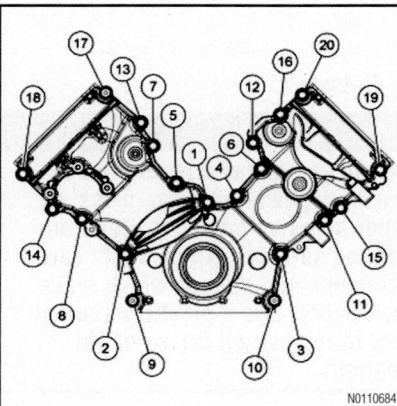

N0110684

Fig. 339 Tighten the 20 engine front cover fasteners in the sequence shown in 3 stages

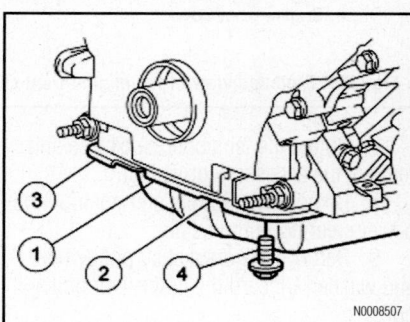

N0008507

Fig. 340 Loosely install the 4 bolts, then tighten in 2 stages, in the sequence shown

2. Loosely install the 4 bolts, then tighten in 2 stages, in the sequence shown.
   a. Stage 1: Tighten to 89 inch lbs. (10 Nm).
   b. Stage 2: Tighten an additional 45 degrees.

3. Tighten the new crankshaft pulley bolt in 2 stages.
   a. Stage 1: Tighten to 129 ft. lbs. (175 Nm).
   b. Stage 2: Tighten an additional 90 degrees.

6.8L Engine

See Figures 341 through 343.

1. With the vehicle in NEUTRAL, position it on a hoist.

2. Drain the engine oil.

3. Remove the engine cooling fan shroud.

4. Remove the engine cooling fan.

5. Remove the RH valve cover.

6. Remove the LH valve cover.

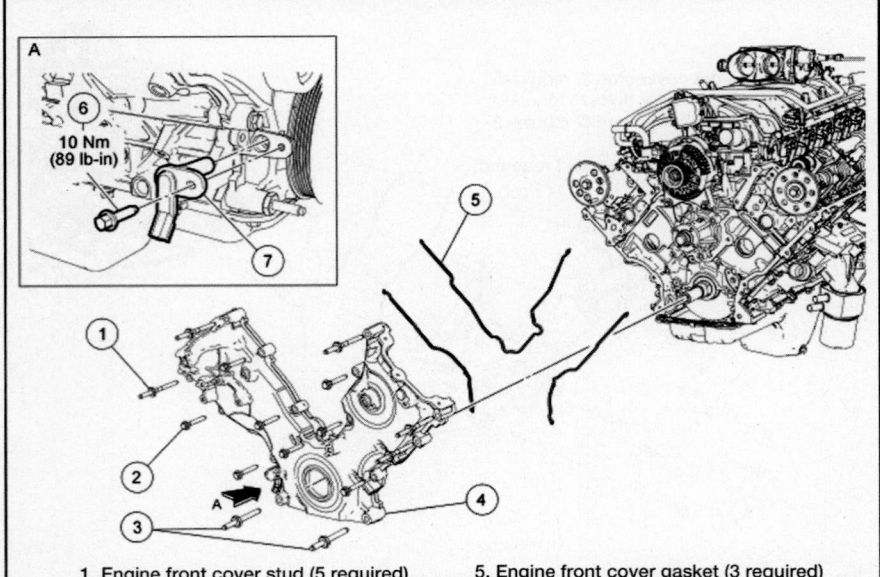

1. Engine front cover stud (5 required)
2. Engine front cover bolt (8 required)
3. Engine front cover studs (2 required)
4. Engine front cover
5. Engine front cover gasket (3 required)
6. Crankshaft Position (CKP) sensor bolt
7. CKP sensor

N0087829

Fig. 341 Exploded view of the engine front cover assembly

7. Rotate the tensioner clockwise and remove the accessory drive belt.

8. Remove the 3 bolts and position the power steering pump aside.

9. Remove the crankshaft pulley bolt and washer. Discard the crankshaft pulley bolt.

10. Using the Crankshaft Vibration Damper Remover, remove the crankshaft pulley.

11. Using the Crankshaft Front Oil Seal Remover, remove and discard the crankshaft front seal.

12. Remove the bolt and the accessory drive idler pulley.

13. Remove the 4 bolts and the coolant pump pulley.

14. Remove the 3 bolts and the accessory drive belt tensioner.

15. Disconnect the Crankshaft Position (CKP) sensor electrical connector.

16. Remove the nut and the starter wiring harness and transmission cooler tube support brackets from the stud bolt.

17. Disconnect the RH and LH radio ignition interference capacitor electrical connectors.

18. Disconnect the Camshaft Position (CMP) sensor electrical connector.

19. Remove the 2 nuts and the RH and LH radio ignition interference capacitors.

20. Remove the 4 front oil pan bolts.

21. Remove the 8 bolts and the 7 studs.

✳✳ WARNING

Do not use metal scrapers, wire brushes, power abrasive discs or other abrasive means to clean the sealing surfaces. These tools cause scratches and gouges which make leak paths. Use a plastic scraping tool to remove all traces of old sealant.

22. Remove the engine front cover from the front cover to cylinder block dowel.

a. Remove the engine front cover gaskets.

b. Clean the mating surfaces with silicone gasket remover and metal surface prep.

c. Inspect the mating surfaces.

To install:

✳✳ WARNING

Do not use metal scrapers, wire brushes, power abrasive discs or other abrasive means to clean the sealing surfaces. These tools cause scratches and gouges which make leak paths. Use a plastic scraping tool to remove all traces of old sealant.

➡If the engine front cover is not secured within 4 minutes, the sealant must be removed and the sealing area cleaned. To clean the sealing area, use

silicone gasket remover and metal surface prep. Allow to dry until there is no sign of wetness, or 4 minutes, whichever is longer. Follow the directions on the packaging. Failure to follow this procedure may cause future oil leakage.

➡Make sure that the engine front cover gasket is in place on the engine front cover before installation.

23. Apply a bead of silicone gasket and sealant along the cylinder head-to-cylinder block surface and the oil pan-to-cylinder block surface, at the locations shown.

24. Install a new engine front cover gasket on the engine front cover. Position the engine front cover onto the dowels. Install the 15 fasteners finger-tight.

25. Tighten the engine front cover fasteners in sequence in 3 stages.

a. Stage 1: Tighten fasteners 1 through 5 to 18 ft. lbs. (25 Nm).

b. Stage 2: Tighten fasteners 6 and 7 to 35 ft. lbs. (48 Nm).

c. Stage 3: Tighten fasteners 8 through 15 to 18 ft. lbs. (25 Nm).

26. Loosely install the bolts, then tighten the bolts in 2 stages.

a. Stage 1: Tighten to 15 ft. lbs. (20 Nm).

b. Stage 2: Tighten an additional 60 degrees.

27. Connect the CKP sensor electrical connector.

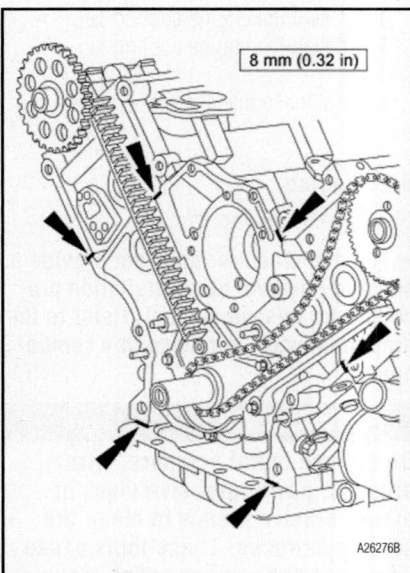

8 mm (0.32 in)

A26276B

Fig. 342 Apply a bead of silicone gasket and sealant along the cylinder head-to-cylinder block surface and the oil pan-to-cylinder block surface, at the locations shown

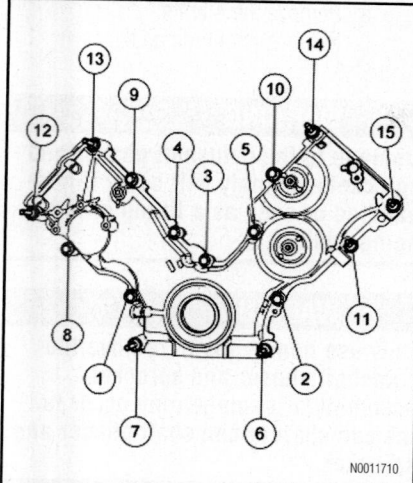

Fig. 343 Tighten the engine front cover fasteners in sequence in 3 stages

28. Position the power steering pump and install the 3 bolts. Tighten to 18 ft. lbs. (25 Nm).

29. Position the transmission cooler tube and starter electrical harness support brackets and install the nut. Tighten to 18 ft. lbs. (25 Nm).

30. Connect the CMP sensor electrical connector.

31. Install the LH radio ignition interference capacitor and the nut. Tighten to 18 ft. lbs. (25 Nm).

32. Install the RH radio ignition interference capacitor and the nut. Tighten to 18 ft. lbs. (25 Nm).

33. Connect the radio ignition interference capacitor electrical connectors.

34. Install the accessory drive belt tensioner and the 3 bolts. Tighten to 18 ft. lbs. (25 Nm).

35. Install the coolant pump pulley and the 4 bolts. Tighten to 18 ft. lbs. (25 Nm).

36. Install the accessory drive idler pulley and the 3 bolts. Tighten to 18 ft. lbs. (25 Nm).

37. Lubricate the engine front cover and the crankshaft seal inner lip with clean engine oil.

38. Using the Crankshaft Vibration Damper Installer, Front Cover Oil Seal Installer and Crankshaft Front Oil Seal Installer, install a new crankshaft front seal.

➡If not secured within 4 minutes, the sealant must be removed and the sealing area cleaned. To clean the sealing area, use silicone gasket remover and metal surface prep. Follow the directions on the packaging. Allow to dry until there is no sign of wetness, or 4

minutes, whichever is longer. Failure to follow this procedure may cause future oil leakage.

39. Apply silicone gasket and sealant to the Woodruff key slot on the crankshaft pulley.

40. Using the Crankshaft Vibration Damper Installer, install the crankshaft pulley.

41. Tighten the new crankshaft pulley bolt in 4 stages.
   a. Stage 1: Tighten to 66 ft. lbs. (90 Nm).
   b. Stage 2: Loosen 360 degrees.
   c. Stage 3: Tighten to 37 ft. lbs. (50 Nm).
   d. Stage 4: Tighten an additional 90 degrees.

42. Rotate the tensioner clockwise and install the accessory drive belt.

43. Install the RH valve cover.

44. Install the LH valve cover.

45. Install the engine cooling fan.

46. Install the engine cooling fan shroud.

47. Fill the crankcase with clean engine oil.

TIMING CHAIN & SPROCKETS

REMOVAL & INSTALLATION

5.4L Engine

See Figures 344 through 357.

1. Remove the engine front cover.
2. Remove the crankshaft sensor ring from the crankshaft.
3. Position the crankshaft keyway at the 12 o'clock position.

➡If the camshaft lobes are not exactly positioned, the crankshaft will require one full additional rotation to 12 o'clock.

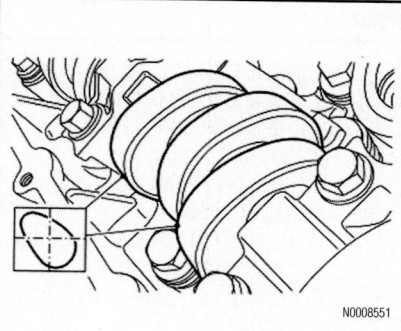

Fig. 344 Verify by noting the position of the 2 intake camshaft lobes and the exhaust lobe on the No. 1 cylinder

4. The No. 1 cylinder camshaft exhaust lobe must be coming up on the exhaust stroke. Verify by noting the position of the 2 intake camshaft lobes and the exhaust lobe on the No. 1 cylinder.

✳ WARNING

If the components are to be reinstalled, they must be installed in the same positions. Mark the components for installation into the original locations. Failure to follow these instructions may result in engine damage.

5. Remove only the 3 camshaft roller followers shown from the RH cylinder head.

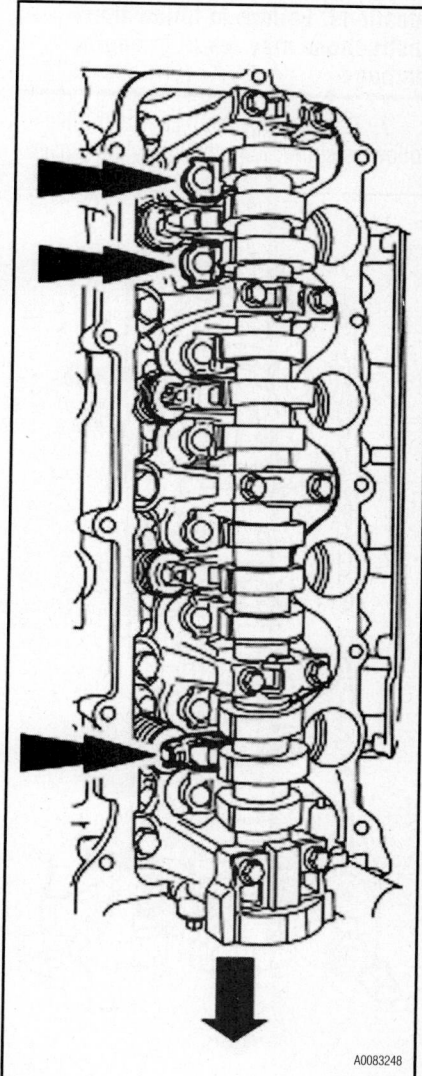

Fig. 345 Remove only the 3 camshaft roller followers shown from the RH cylinder head

➡**Do not allow the valve keepers to fall off of the valve or the valve may drop into the cylinder. If a valve drops into the cylinder, the cylinder head must be removed.**

➡**It may be necessary to push the valve down while compressing the spring.**

6. Using the Valve Spring Compressor, remove the 3 designated camshaft roller followers in the previous step from the RH cylinder head.

❊❊ **WARNING**

If the components are to be reinstalled, they must be installed in the same positions. Mark the components for installation into the original locations. Failure to follow these instructions may result in engine damage.

7. Remove only the 3 camshaft roller followers shown from the LH cylinder head.

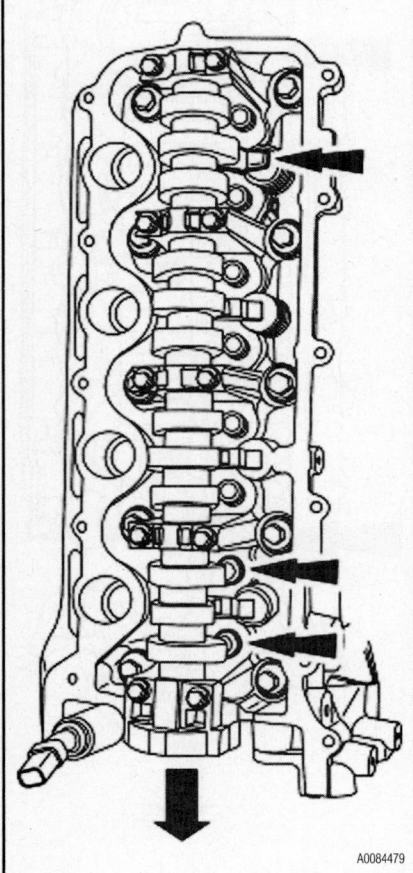

Fig. 346 Remove only the 3 camshaft roller followers shown from the LH cylinder head

➡**Do not allow the valve keepers to fall off of the valve or the valve may drop into the cylinder. If a valve drops into the cylinder, the cylinder head must be removed.**

➡**It may be necessary to push the valve down while compressing the spring.**

8. Using the Valve Spring Compressor, remove the 3 designated camshaft roller followers in the previous step from the LH cylinder head.

❊❊ **WARNING**

The crankshaft cannot be moved past the 6 o'clock position once set or engine damage may occur.

9. Rotate the crankshaft clockwise and position the crankshaft keyway at the 6 o'clock position.

❊❊ **WARNING**

If one or both tensioner mounting bolts are loosened or removed, the tensioner-sealing bead must be inspected for seal integrity. If cracks, tears, separation from the tensioner body or permanent compression of the seal bead is observed, install a new tensioner or engine damage may occur.

10. Remove the 2 bolts, the LH timing chain tensioner and tensioner arm.

❊❊ **WARNING**

If one or both tensioner mounting bolts are loosened or removed, the tensioner-sealing bead must be inspected for seal integrity. If cracks, tears, separation from the tensioner body or permanent compression of the seal bead is observed, install a new tensioner or engine damage may occur.

11. Remove the 2 bolts, the RH timing chain tensioner and tensioner arm.
12. Remove the RH and LH timing chains and the crankshaft sprocket.
   a. Remove the RH timing chain from the camshaft sprocket.
   b. Remove the RH timing chain from the crankshaft sprocket.
   c. Remove the LH timing chain from the camshaft sprocket.
   d. Remove the LH timing chain and crankshaft sprocket.
13. Remove the LH and RH timing chain guides.

   a. Remove the 4 bolts.
   b. Remove both timing chain guides.

❊❊ **WARNING**

Damage to the camshaft phaser and sprocket assembly will occur if mishandled or used as a lifting or leveraging device.

❊❊ **WARNING**

Only use hand tools to remove the camshaft phaser and sprocket assembly or damage may occur to the camshaft or camshaft phaser and sprocket.

14. Using the Cam Phaser Locking Tool, remove the bolt and the RH camshaft phaser and sprocket assembly. Discard the camshaft phaser and sprocket bolt.

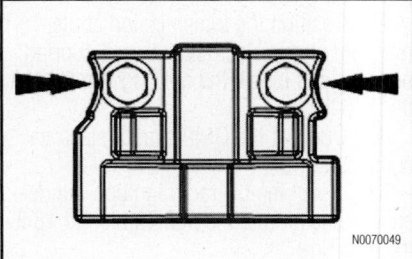

Fig. 347 Remove the 2 bolts and the RH cylinder head camshaft front bearing cap

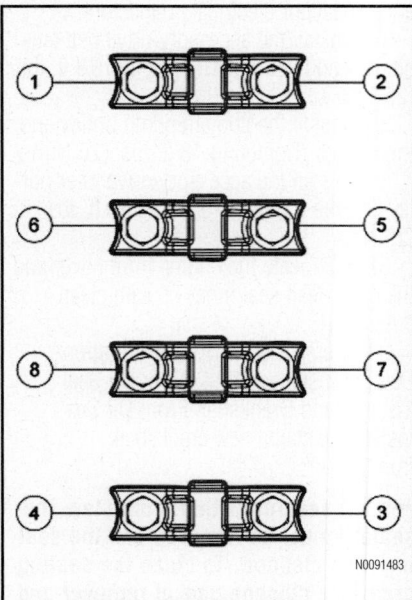

Fig. 348 Remove the remaining 8 bolts in the sequence shown and remove the RH cylinder head camshaft bearing caps

Damage to the camshaft phaser and sprocket assembly will occur if mishandled or used as a lifting or leveraging device.

Only use hand tools to remove the camshaft phaser and sprocket assembly or damage may occur to the camshaft or camshaft phaser and sprocket.

15. Using the Cam Phaser Locking Tool, remove the bolt and the LH camshaft phaser and sprocket assembly. Discard the camshaft phaser and sprocket bolt.

Remove the front thrust camshaft bearing cap straight upward from the bearing towers or the bearing cap may be damaged from side loading.

16. Remove the 2 bolts and the RH cylinder head camshaft front bearing cap.

The camshaft bearing caps must be installed in their original locations. Record camshaft bearing cap locations. Failure to follow these instructions may result in engine damage.

17. Remove the remaining 8 bolts in the sequence shown and remove the RH cylinder head camshaft bearing caps.
18. Clean and inspect the RH camshaft bearing caps.
19. The camshaft front thrust bearing cap contains an oil metering groove. Make sure the groove is free of foreign material.
20. Remove the RH camshaft.

Remove the front thrust camshaft bearing cap straight upward from the bearing towers or the bearing cap may be damaged from side loading.

21. Remove the 2 bolts and the LH cylinder camshaft front bearing cap.

The camshaft bearing caps must be installed in their original locations. Record camshaft bearing cap locations. Failure to follow these instructions may result in engine damage.

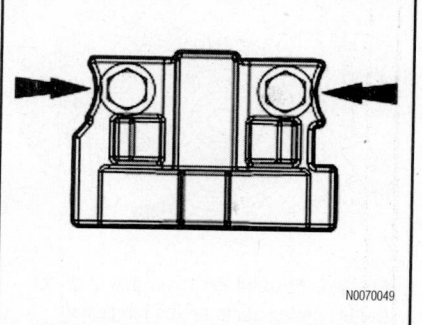

Fig. 349 Remove the 2 bolts and the LH cylinder camshaft front bearing cap

22. Remove the remaining 8 bolts in the sequence shown and remove the LH cylinder head camshaft bearing caps.
23. Clean and inspect the LH camshaft bearing caps.
24. The camshaft front thrust bearing cap contains an oil metering groove. Make sure the groove is free of foreign material.
25. Remove the LH camshaft.

If the components are to be reinstalled, they must be installed in the same positions. Mark the components for installation into their original locations. Failure to follow these instructions may result in engine damage.

26. Remove all of the remaining camshaft roller followers from the cylinder heads.

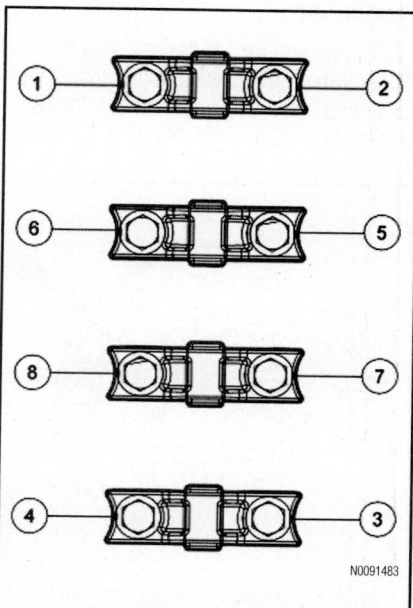

Fig. 350 Remove the remaining 8 bolts in the sequence shown and remove the LH cylinder head camshaft bearing caps

To install:
27. Install the LH and RH camshafts.
28. Lubricate the camshaft and camshaft journals with clean engine oil prior to installation.
29. Install the 5 LH and 5 RH camshaft bearing caps in their original locations.
   a. Lubricate the camshaft bearing caps with clean engine oil.
   b. Position the front camshaft bearing cap.
   c. Position the remaining camshaft bearing caps.
   d. Install the 20 bolts loosely.
   e. Tighten to 89 inch lbs. (10 Nm) in the sequence shown.

Damage to the camshaft phaser and sprocket assembly will occur if mishandled or used as a lifting or leveraging device.

30. Position the camshaft phaser and sprockets and install 2 new camshaft phaser and sprocket bolts finger-tight.

Damage to the camshaft phaser and sprocket assembly will occur if mishandled or used as a lifting or leveraging device.

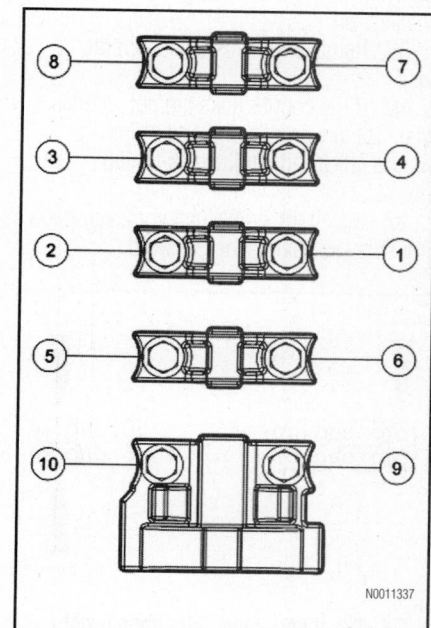

Fig. 351 Tighten to 89 inch lbs. (10 Nm) in the sequence shown

✳✳ WARNING

Only use hand tools to remove the camshaft phaser and sprocket assembly or damage may occur to the camshaft or camshaft phaser and sprocket.

31. Using the Cam Phaser Locking Tool, tighten the LH and RH camshaft phaser and sprocket bolts in 2 stages.

    a. Stage 1: Tighten to 30 ft. lbs. (40 Nm).

    b. Stage 2: Tighten an additional 90 degrees.

32. Position the crankshaft with the Crankshaft Holding Tool, then remove the tool.

✳✳ WARNING

Timing chain procedures must be followed exactly or damage to valves and pistons will result.

✳✳ WARNING

Prior to installation, inspect the tensioner-sealing bead for seal integrity. If cracks, tears, separation from the tensioner body or permanent compression of the seal bead is observed, install a new tensioner or engine damage may occur.

33. Compress the tensioner plunger, using a vise.

34. Install a retaining clip on the tensioner to hold the plunger in during installation.

35. Remove the tensioner from the vise.

36. If the copper links are not visible, mark 2 links on one end and 1 link on the other end, and use as timing marks.

37. Install the crankshaft sprocket, making sure the flange faces forward.

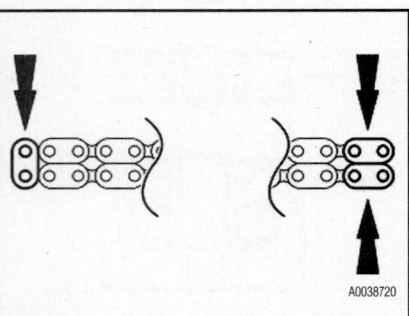

Fig. 352 If the copper links are not visible, mark 2 links on one end and 1 link on the other end, and use as timing marks

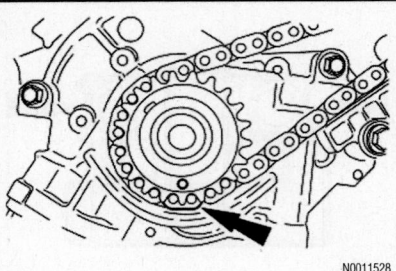

Fig. 353 Position the lower end of the LH (inner) timing chain on the crankshaft sprocket, aligning the timing mark on the outer flange of the crankshaft sprocket with the single copper (marked) link on the chain

38. Position the LH and RH timing chain guides and install the 4 bolts. Tighten to 89 inch lbs. (10 Nm).

39. Position the lower end of the LH (inner) timing chain on the crankshaft sprocket, aligning the timing mark on the outer flange of the crankshaft sprocket with the single copper (marked) link on the chain.

➡**Make sure the upper half of the timing chain is below the tensioner arm dowel.**

40. Position the timing chain on the camshaft phaser and sprocket with the timing mark positioned between the 2 copper (marked) chain links.

➡**The LH timing chain tensioner arm has a bump near the dowel hole for identification.**

41. Position the LH timing chain tensioner arm on the dowel pin and install the LH timing chain tensioner and the 2 bolts. Tighten to 18 ft. lbs. (25 Nm).

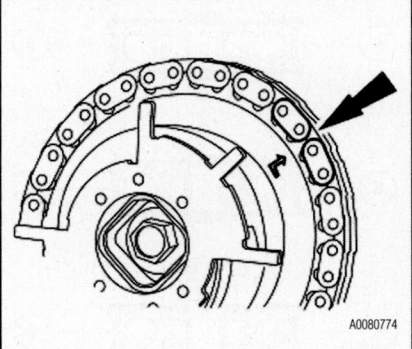

Fig. 354 Position the timing chain on the camshaft phaser and sprocket with the timing mark positioned between the 2 copper (marked) chain links

42. Remove the retaining clip from the LH timing chain tensioner.

43. Position the lower end of the RH (outer) timing chain on the crankshaft sprocket, aligning the timing mark on the sprocket with the single copper (marked) chain link.

➡**The lower half of the timing chain must be positioned above the tensioner arm dowel.**

➡**The camshaft phaser and sprocket will be stamped with one of the illustrated timing marks for the RH camshaft.**

44. Position the RH timing chain on the camshaft phaser and sprocket. Make sure the timing mark is positioned between the 2 copper (marked) chain links.

45. Position the RH timing chain tensioner arm on the dowel pin and install the RH timing chain tensioner and the 2 bolts. Tighten to 18 ft. lbs. (25 Nm).

46. Remove the retaining clip from the RH timing chain tensioner.

47. As a post-check, verify correct alignment of all timing marks.

48. Install the crankshaft sensor ring on the crankshaft.

✳✳ WARNING

If the components are to be reinstalled, they must be installed into their original locations. Failure to follow these instructions may result in engine damage.

➡**Do not allow the valve keepers to fall off of the valve or the valve may drop into the cylinder. If a valve drops into the cylinder, the cylinder head must be removed.**

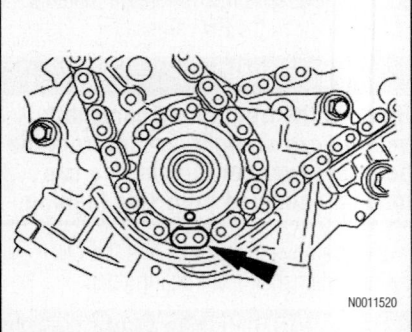

Fig. 355 Position the lower end of the RH (outer) timing chain on the crankshaft sprocket, aligning the timing mark on the sprocket with the single copper (marked) chain link

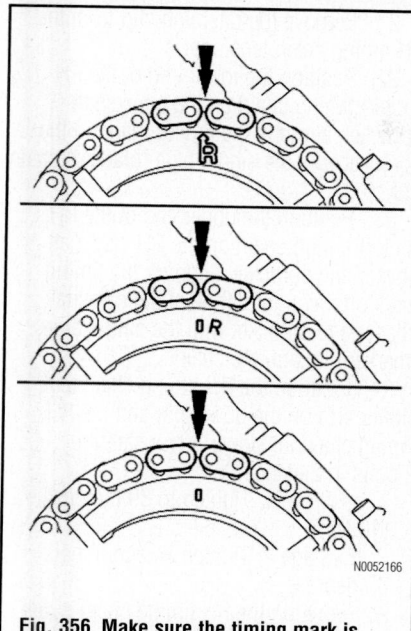

Fig. 356 Make sure the timing mark is positioned between the 2 copper (marked) chain links

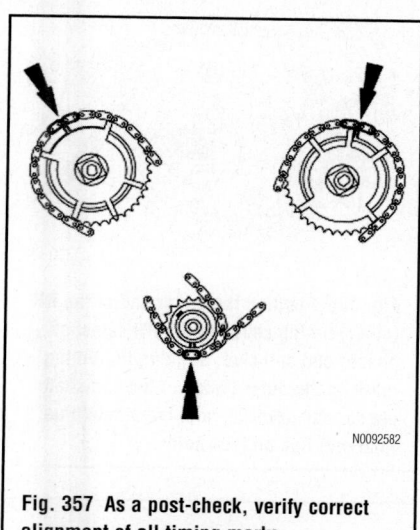

Fig. 357 As a post-check, verify correct alignment of all timing marks

➡ It may be necessary to push the valve down while compressing the spring.

49. Using the Valve Spring Compressor, install all of the camshaft roller followers.
50. Lubricate the camshaft roller followers with clean engine oil prior to installation.
51. Install the engine front cover.

6.2L Engine

See Figures 358 through 366.

1. Remove the engine front cover.
2. Position the crankshaft keyway at the 11 o'clock position.

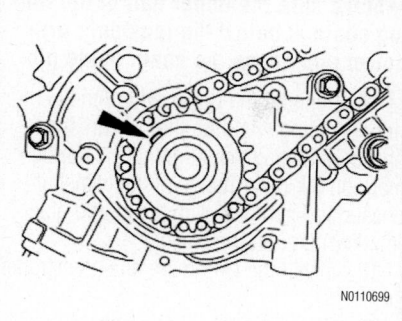

Fig. 358 Position the crankshaft keyway at the 11 o'clock position

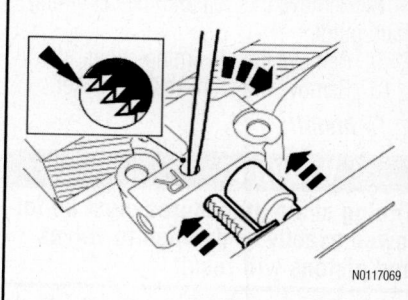

Fig. 360 Using a small pick, carefully push the tensioner rack pawl retainer away from the rack pawl

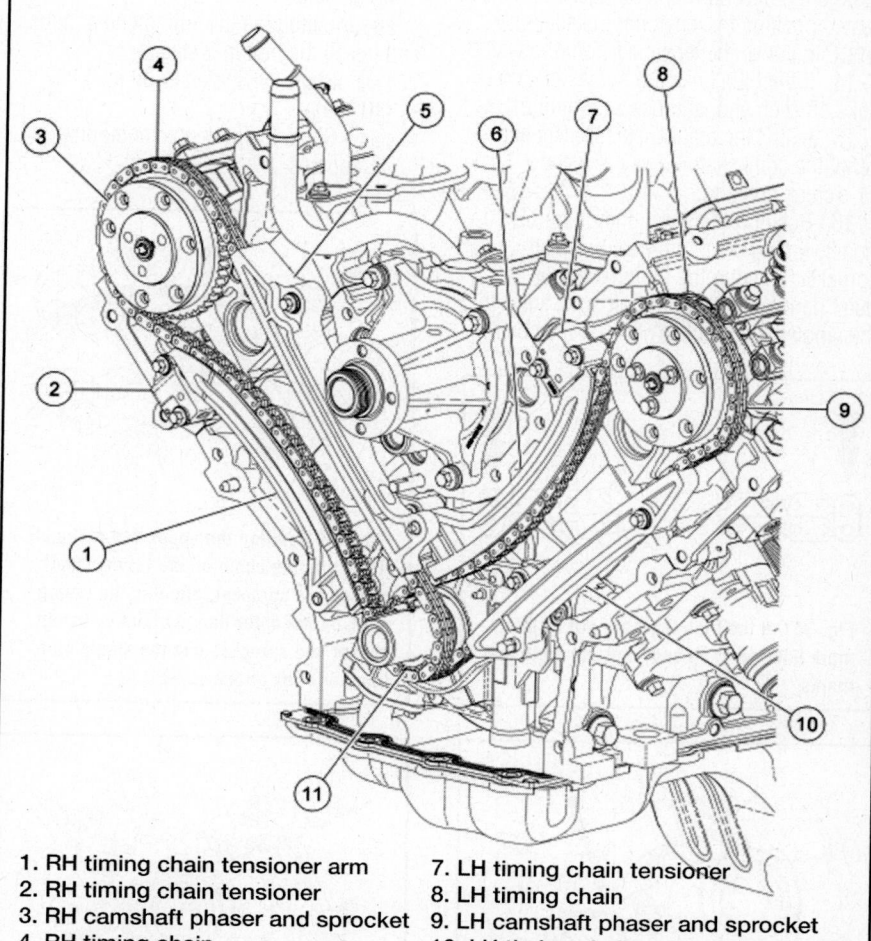

1. RH timing chain tensioner arm
2. RH timing chain tensioner
3. RH camshaft phaser and sprocket
4. RH timing chain
5. RH timing chain guide
6. LH timing chain tensioner arm
7. LH timing chain tensioner
8. LH timing chain
9. LH camshaft phaser and sprocket
10. LH timing chain guide
11. Crankshaft sprocket

Fig. 359 Timing chain assembly

3. Remove the 2 bolts, the RH timing chain tensioner and tensioner arm.
4. Remove the bolt and the RH timing chain guide.
5. Remove the RH timing chain.

6. Remove the 2 bolts and the LH timing chain tensioner.
7. Remove the LH timing chain tensioner arm.

8. Remove the bolt and the LH timing chain guide.

9. Remove the LH timing chain.

10. Remove the crankshaft sprocket.

To install:

> ❊❊ **WARNING**
>
> **Timing chain procedures must be followed exactly or damage to valves and pistons will result.**

11. Using a small pick, carefully push the tensioner rack pawl retainer away from the rack pawl and compress the tensioner plunger and rack using a vise.

12. Install a small pick into the tensioner to hold the rack pawl and plunger in the seated position for tensioner installation.

13. Remove the tensioner from the vise.

14. If the blue links are not visible, mark links on each end, and use as timing marks.

15. Install the crankshaft sprocket and verify the crankshaft keyway is at the 11 o'clock position.

16. Position the lower end of the LH (inner) timing chain on the crankshaft sprocket, aligning the timing mark on the outer flange of the crankshaft sprocket with the single blue (marked) link on the chain.

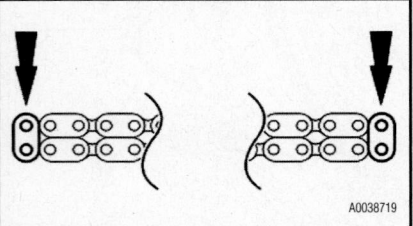

Fig. 361 If the blue links are not visible, mark links on each end, and use as timing marks

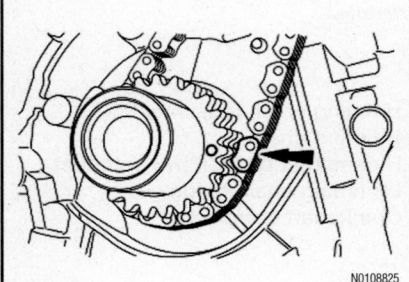

Fig. 362 Position the lower end of the LH (inner) timing chain on the crankshaft sprocket, aligning the timing mark on the outer flange of the crankshaft sprocket with the single blue (marked) link on the chain

➡**Make sure the upper half of the timing chain is below the tensioner arm dowel and above the chain guide pin.**

17. Position the upper end of the LH (inner) timing chain on the LH camshaft phaser and sprocket, aligning the timing mark on the outer flange of the camshaft phaser and sprocket with the single blue (marked) link on the chain.

18. Install the LH timing chain tensioner arm.

19. Position the LH timing chain tensioner and install the 2 bolts in 2 stages.

    a. Stage 1: Tighten to 89 inch lbs. (10 Nm).

    b. Stage 2: Tighten an additional 45 degrees.

20. Position the LH timing chain guide and install the bolt in 2 stages.

    a. Stage 1: Tighten to 89 inch lbs. (10 Nm).

    b. Stage 2: Tighten an additional 45 degrees.

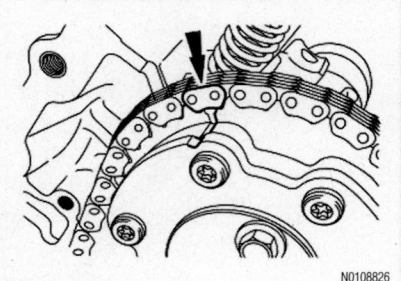

Fig. 363 Position the upper end of the LH (inner) timing chain on the LH camshaft phaser and sprocket, aligning the timing mark on the outer flange of the camshaft phaser and sprocket with the single blue (marked) link on the chain

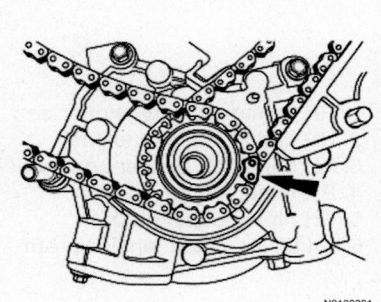

Fig. 364 Position the lower end of the RH (outer) timing chain on the crankshaft sprocket, aligning the timing mark on the sprocket with the single blue (marked) chain link

21. Remove the retaining clip from the LH timing chain tensioner.

22. Position the lower end of the RH (outer) timing chain on the crankshaft sprocket, aligning the timing mark on the sprocket with the single blue (marked) chain link.

23. Position the upper end of the RH (outer) timing chain on the RH camshaft phaser and sprocket, aligning the timing mark on the outer flange of the camshaft phaser and sprocket with the single blue (marked) link on the chain.

24. Position the RH timing chain tensioner arm on the dowel pin and the RH timing chain tensioner and install the 2 bolts in 2 stages.

    a. Stage 1: Tighten to 89 inch lbs. (10 Nm).

    b. Stage 2: Tighten an additional 45 degrees.

25. Position the RH timing chain guide and install the bolt in 2 stages.

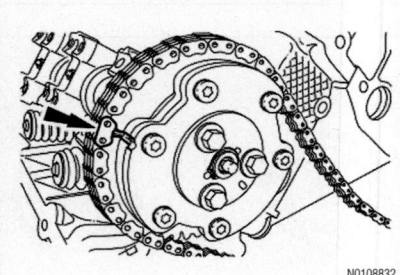

Fig. 365 Position the upper end of the RH (outer) timing chain on the RH camshaft phaser and sprocket, aligning the timing mark on the outer flange of the camshaft phaser and sprocket with the single blue (marked) link on the chain

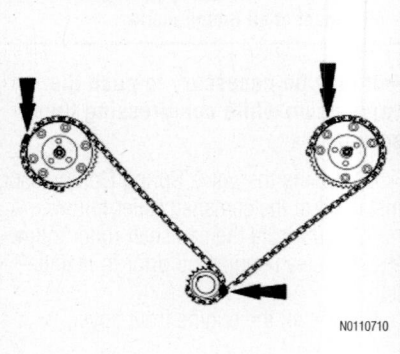

Fig. 366 As a post-check, verify correct alignment of all timing marks

a. Stage 1: Tighten to 89 inch lbs. (10 Nm).

b. Stage 2: Tighten an additional 45 degrees.

26. Remove the retaining clip from the RH timing chain tensioner.

27. As a post-check, verify correct alignment of all timing marks.

28. Install the engine front cover.

6.8L Engine

See Figures 367 through 390.

1. Remove the engine front cover.

> ❉❉ **WARNING**
>
> **Only use hand tools to loosen the sprocket bolt or damage to the camshaft or camshaft sprocket may occur.**

2. Loosen and back off the RH camshaft sprocket bolt one full turn.

> ❉❉ **WARNING**
>
> **Only use hand tools to loosen the sprocket bolt or damage to the camshaft or camshaft sprocket may occur.**

3. Loosen the LH camshaft sprocket bolt.

> ❉❉ **WARNING**
>
> **The balance shaft bearing caps must be installed in their original locations or engine damage may occur. Record camshaft bearing cap locations.**

4. Using the sequence shown, remove the 6 bolts, then the 3 balance shaft bearing caps and the balance shaft.

5. Remove the crankshaft sensor ring from the crankshaft.

6. Position the crankshaft keyway at the 12 o'clock position.

➡ **If the camshaft lobes are not exactly positioned, the crankshaft will require**

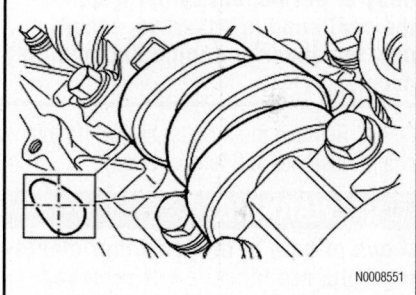

Fig. 368 Verify by noting the position of the 2 intake camshaft lobes and the exhaust lobe on the No. 1 cylinder

one full additional rotation to 12 o'clock.

7. The No. 1 cylinder camshaft exhaust lobe must be coming up on the exhaust stroke. Verify by noting the position of the 2 intake camshaft lobes and the exhaust lobe on the No. 1 cylinder.

> ❉❉ **WARNING**
>
> **If the components are to be reinstalled, they must be installed in the same positions or engine damage may occur. Mark the components for installation into their original locations.**

8. Remove only the 3 camshaft roller followers shown from the RH cylinder head.

➡ **Do not allow the valve keepers to fall off the valve or the valve may drop into the cylinder. If a valve drops into the cylinder, the cylinder head must be removed.**

➡ **It may be necessary to push the valve down while compressing the spring.**

9. Using the Valve Spring Compressor, remove the 3 designated camshaft roller followers in the previous step from the RH cylinder head.

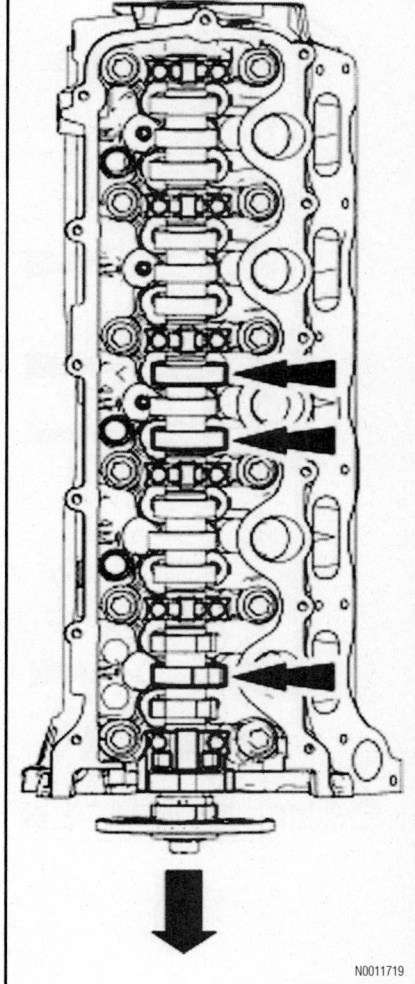

Fig. 369 Remove only the 3 camshaft roller followers shown from the RH cylinder head

> ❉❉ **WARNING**
>
> **If the components are to be reinstalled, they must be installed in the same positions or engine damage may occur. Mark the components for installation into their original locations.**

10. Remove only the 4 camshaft roller followers shown from the LH cylinder head.

➡ **Do not allow the valve keepers to fall off the valve or the valve may drop into the cylinder. If a valve drops into the cylinder, the cylinder head must be removed.**

➡ **It may be necessary to push the valve down while compressing the spring.**

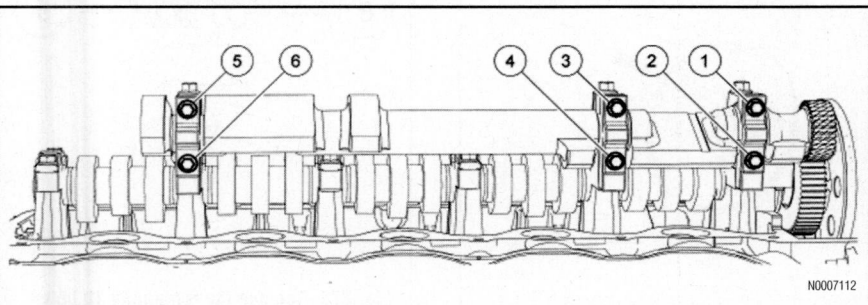

Fig. 367 Using the sequence shown, remove the 6 bolts, then the 3 balance shaft bearing caps and the balance shaft

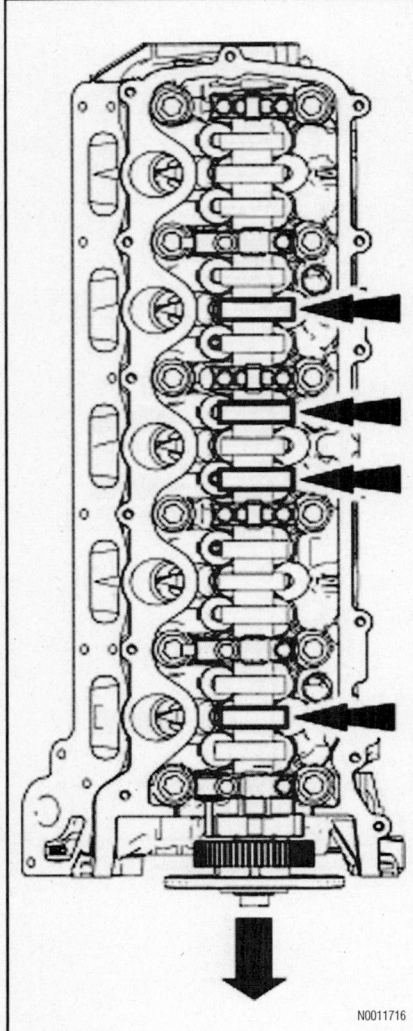

Fig. 370 Remove only the 4 camshaft roller followers shown from the LH cylinder head

11. Using the Valve Spring Compressor, remove the 4 designated camshaft roller followers in the previous step from the LH cylinder head.

※※ WARNING

The crankshaft cannot be moved past the 6 o'clock position once set or engine damage may occur.

12. Rotate the crankshaft clockwise and position the crankshaft keyway at the 6 o'clock position.

※※ WARNING

If one or both of the tensioner mounting bolts are loosened or removed, the tensioner-sealing bead must be inspected for seal integrity. If cracks, tears, separation from the tensioner

body or permanent compression of the seal bead is observed, install a new tensioner or engine damage may occur.

13. Remove the 2 bolts, the LH timing chain tensioner and tensioner arm.

※※ WARNING

If one or both of the tensioner mounting bolts are loosened or removed, the tensioner-sealing bead must be inspected for seal integrity. If cracks, tears, separation from the tensioner body or permanent compression of the seal bead is observed, install a new tensioner or engine damage may occur.

14. Remove the 2 bolts, the RH timing chain tensioner and tensioner arm.
15. Remove the LH and RH timing chain and the crankshaft sprockets.
   a. Remove the RH timing chain from the camshaft sprocket.
   b. Remove the RH timing chain from the crankshaft sprocket.
   c. Remove the LH timing chain from the camshaft sprocket.
   d. Remove the LH timing chain and the crankshaft sprocket.
16. Remove the 4 bolts and the timing chain guides.
   a. Remove the bolts.
   b. Remove the timing chain guides.
17. Remove the bolts and the RH and LH camshaft sprockets.
18. Remove the balance shaft drive gear from the LH camshaft.

※※ WARNING

Remove the front thrust camshaft bearing cap straight upward from the bearing towers, or the bearing cap may be damaged from side loading.

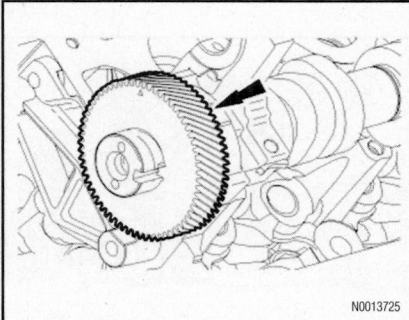

Fig. 371 Remove the balance shaft drive gear from the LH camshaft

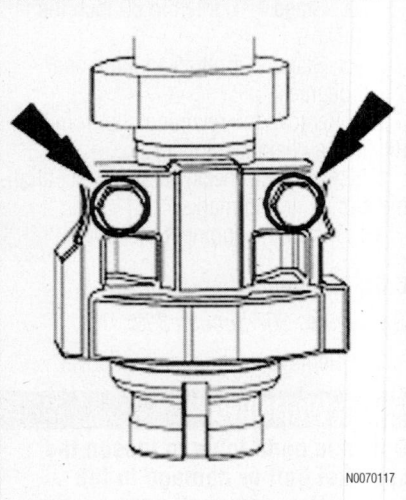

Fig. 372 Remove the 2 bolts and the RH camshaft front bearing cap

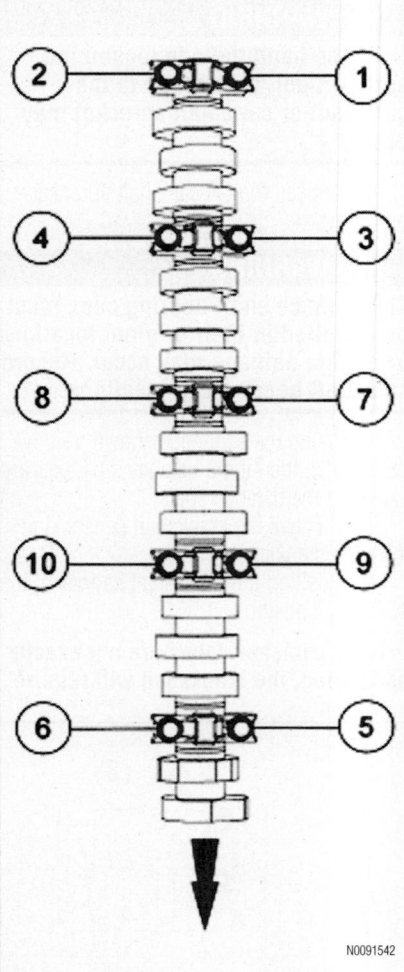

Fig. 373 Remove the remaining 10 bolts in the sequence shown and remove the RH cylinder head camshaft bearing caps

19. Remove the 2 bolts and the RH camshaft front bearing cap.

✳✳ WARNING

The camshaft bearing caps must be installed in their original locations. Record camshaft bearing cap locations. Failure to follow these instructions may result in engine damage.

20. Remove the remaining 10 bolts in the sequence shown and remove the RH cylinder head camshaft bearing caps.
21. Clean and inspect the RH camshaft bearing caps.
22. The camshaft front thrust bearing cap contains an oil metering groove. Make sure the groove is free of foreign material.
23. Remove the RH camshaft.

✳✳ WARNING

Remove the front thrust camshaft bearing cap straight upward from the bearing towers, or the bearing cap may be damaged from side loading.

24. Remove the 2 bolts and the LH camshaft front bearing cap.

✳✳ WARNING

The camshaft bearing caps must be installed in their original locations. Record camshaft bearing cap locations. Failure to follow these instructions may result in engine damage.

25. Remove the remaining 10 bolts in the sequence shown and remove the LH

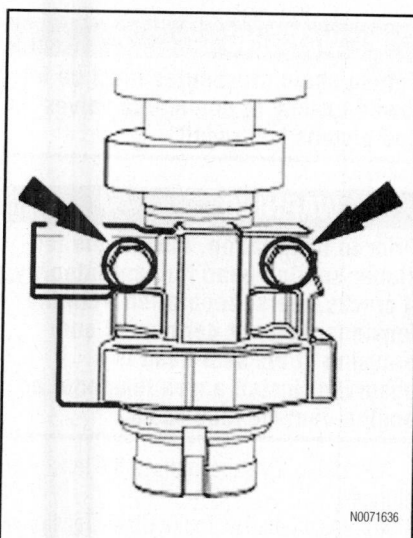

Fig. 374 Remove the 2 bolts and the LH camshaft front bearing cap

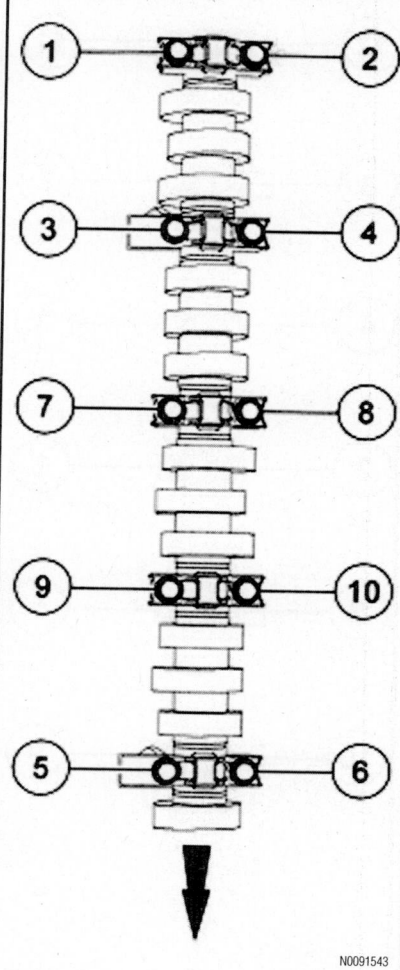

Fig. 375 Remove the remaining 10 bolts in the sequence shown and remove the LH cylinder head camshaft bearing caps

cylinder head camshaft bearing caps.
26. Clean and inspect the LH camshaft bearing caps.
27. The camshaft front thrust bearing cap contains an oil metering groove. Make sure the groove is free of foreign material.
28. Remove the LH camshaft.

✳✳ WARNING

If the components are to be reinstalled, they must be installed in the same positions or engine damage may occur. Mark the components for installation into their original locations.

29. Remove all of the remaining camshaft roller followers from the cylinder heads.

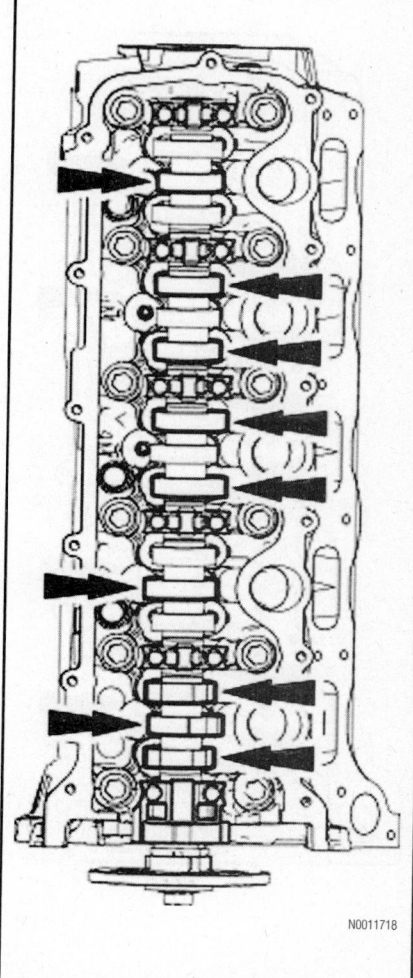

Fig. 376 Install only the identified camshaft roller followers onto the RH cylinder head

To install:

✳✳ WARNING

Timing chain procedures must be followed exactly or damage to valves and pistons will result.

✳✳ WARNING

If the components are to be reinstalled, they must be installed into their original locations or engine damage may occur.

➡Camshaft shown installed to clarify camshaft roller follower position.

➡Lubricate the camshaft roller followers with clean engine oil prior to installation.

30. Install only the identified camshaft roller followers onto the RH cylinder head.

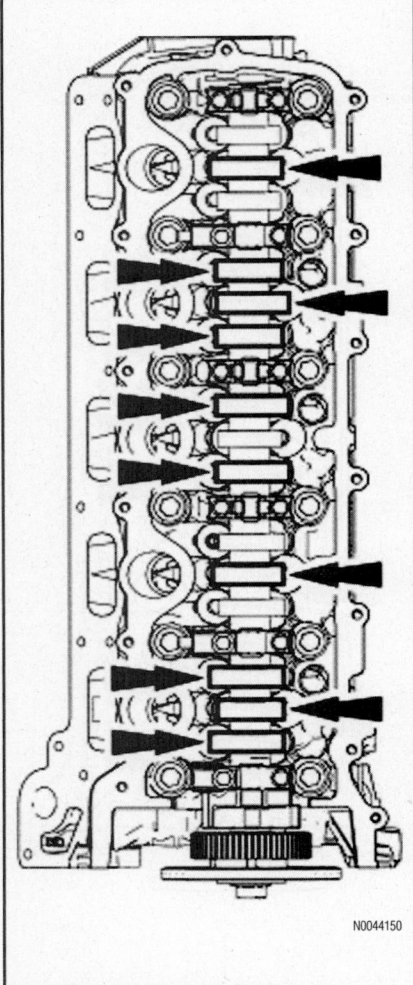

Fig. 377 Install only the identified camshaft roller followers onto the LH cylinder head

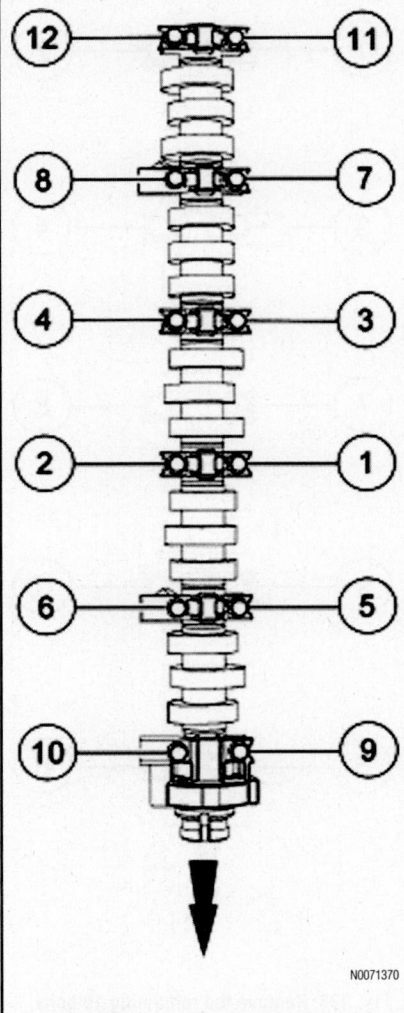

Fig. 378 Tighten the 12 LH camshaft bearing cap bolts in 2 stages

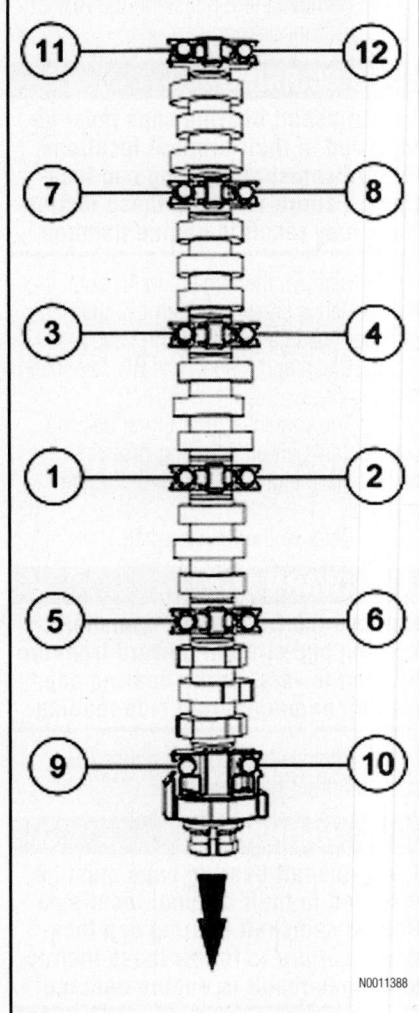

Fig. 379 Tighten the 12 RH camshaft bearing cap bolts in 2 stages

✳✳ WARNING

If the components are to be reinstalled, they must be installed into their original locations or engine damage may occur.

➥Camshaft shown installed to clarify camshaft roller follower position.

➥Lubricate the camshaft roller followers prior to installation.

31. Install only the identified camshaft roller followers onto the LH cylinder head.

32. Install the LH and RH camshafts.

33. Lubricate the camshaft and camshaft journals with clean engine oil prior to installation.

34. Install the LH and RH camshaft bearing caps in their original locations.

a. Lubricate the camshaft bearing caps with clean engine oil.

b. Position the front camshaft bearing cap.

c. Position the remaining camshaft bearing caps.

d. Install the 24 bolts loosely.

35. Tighten the 12 LH camshaft bearing cap bolts in 2 stages:

a. Stage 1: Tighten to 71 inch lbs. (8 Nm) in the sequence shown.

b. Stage 2: Tighten an additional 45 degrees.

36. Tighten the 12 RH camshaft bearing cap bolts in 2 stages:

a. Stage 1: Tighten to 71 inch lbs. (8 Nm) in the sequence shown.

b. Stage 2: Tighten an additional 45 degrees.

37. Install the balance shaft drive gear onto the LH camshaft.

38. Install both camshaft sprockets and camshaft sprocket bolts finger-tight.

✳✳ WARNING

Timing chain procedures must be followed exactly or damage to valves and pistons will result.

✳✳ WARNING

Prior to installation, inspect the tensioner-sealing bead for seal integrity. If cracks, tears, separation from the tensioner body or permanent compression of the seal bead is observed, install a new tensioner or engine damage may occur.

39. Using a vise, compress the tensioner plunger.

40. Install the Hydraulic Chain Tensioner Retaining Clip on the tensioner to hold the plunger in during installation.

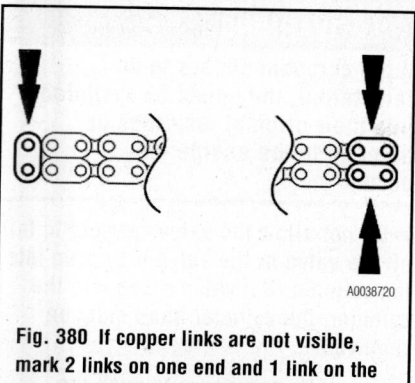

Fig. 380 If copper links are not visible, mark 2 links on one end and 1 link on the other end, and use as timing marks

➡ **There are 61 links in each timing chain.**

41. If copper links are not visible, mark 2 links on one end and 1 link on the other end, and use as timing marks.

42. Install the timing chain guides and the 4 bolts. Tighten to 89 inch lbs. (10 Nm).

43. Preposition the camshafts in the following sequence.
   a. Rotate the LH camshaft until the timing mark is approximately at 12 o'clock.
   b. Rotate the RH camshaft until the timing mark is approximately at 11 o'clock.

✳✳ WARNING

Rotate the crankshaft counterclockwise only. Do not rotate past the position shown or severe piston and/or valve damage can occur.

44. Position the crankshaft with the Crankshaft Holding Tool, then remove the tool.

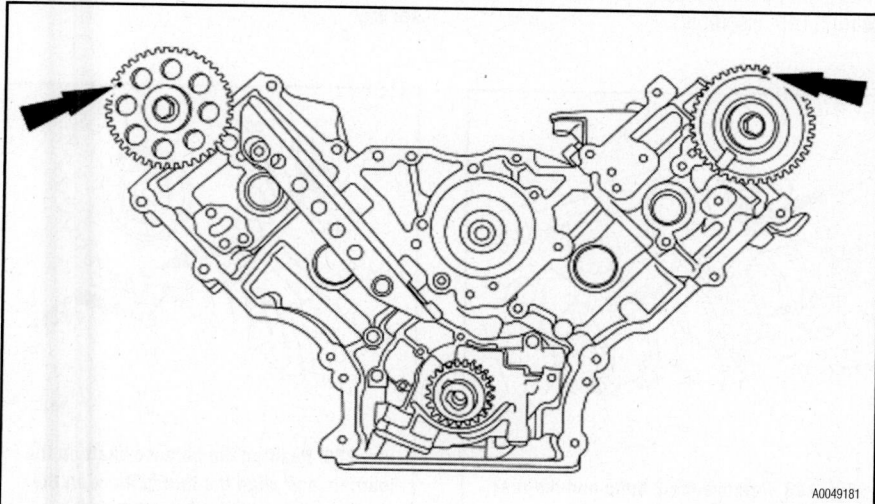

Fig. 381 Preposition the camshafts in the following sequence

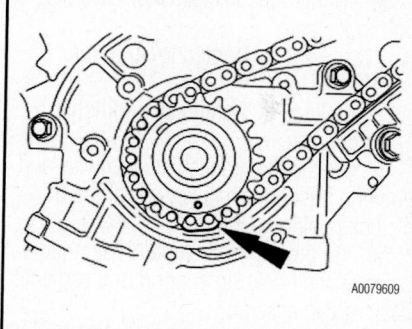

Fig. 382 Install the lower end of the LH timing chain, aligning the timing marks

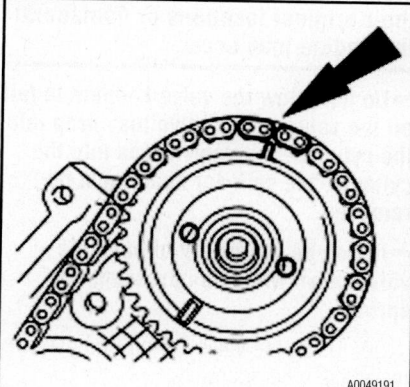

Fig. 383 Install the LH timing chain on the camshaft sprocket with the 2 chain (marked) links and the timing marks aligned

45. Install the crankshaft sprocket, making sure the flange faces forward.

46. Install the lower end of the LH timing chain, aligning the timing marks.

➡ **Be sure the upper half of the timing chain is below the tensioner guide dowel.**

47. Install the LH timing chain on the camshaft sprocket with the 2 chain (marked) links and the timing marks aligned.

➡ **The LH timing chain tensioner arm has a bump near the dowel hole for identification.**

48. Position the LH timing chain tensioner arm on the dowel pin and install the LH timing chain tensioner and the 2 bolts. Tighten to 18 ft. lbs. (25 Nm).

➡ **Be sure the chain link and crankshaft sprocket timing marks are aligned.**

➡ **The lower half of the timing chain must be positioned above the dowel.**

49. Install the RH (outer) timing chain on the crankshaft sprocket.

50. Position the timing chain on the camshaft sprocket. Make sure the 2 copper-colored (marked) links align with the camshaft sprocket timing mark.

51. Position the RH timing chain tensioner arm on the dowel pin and install the

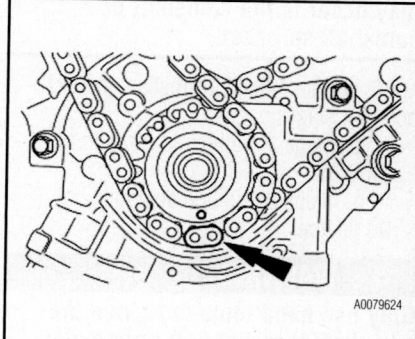

Fig. 384 Install the RH (outer) timing chain on the crankshaft sprocket

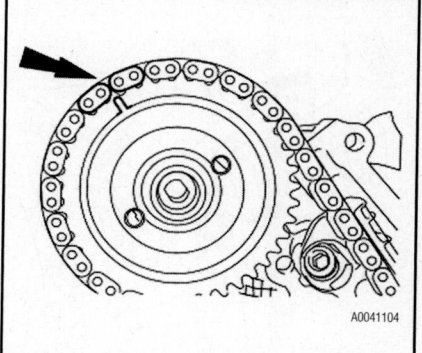

Fig. 385 Make sure the 2 copper-colored (marked) links align with the camshaft sprocket timing mark

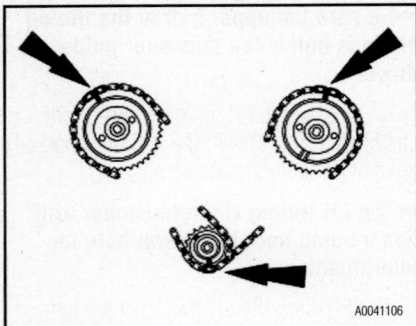

Fig. 386 Check for correct alignment of all timing marks

RH timing chain tensioner and the 2 bolts. Tighten to 18 ft. lbs. (25 Nm).

52. Remove the Hydraulic Chain Tensioner Retaining Clips from the RH and LH timing chain tensioners.

53. Check for correct alignment of all timing marks.

54. Install the crankshaft sensor ring on the crankshaft.

✷✷ WARNING

Only use hand tools to tighten the camshaft sprocket bolt or damage may occur to the camshaft or camshaft sprocket.

55. Tighten the RH camshaft sprocket bolt in 2 stages:
   a. Stage 1: Tighten to 30 ft. lbs. (40 Nm).
   b. Stage 2: Tighten an additional 90 degrees.

✷✷ WARNING

Only use hand tools to tighten the camshaft sprocket bolt or damage may occur to the camshaft or camshaft sprocket.

56. Tighten the LH camshaft sprocket bolt in 2 stages:
   a. Stage 1: Tighten to 30 ft. lbs. (40 Nm).
   b. Stage 2: Tighten an additional 90 degrees.

57. Rotate the crankshaft clockwise and position the crankshaft keyway at the 6 o'clock position.

58. Remove the 2 bolts and the middle balance shaft bearing support and camshaft bearing cap assembly.

✷✷ WARNING

If the components are to be reinstalled, they must be installed into their original locations or damage to the engine may occur.

➥ Do not allow the valve keepers to fall off the valve or the valve may drop into the cylinder. If a valve drops into the cylinder, the cylinder head must be removed.

➥ It may be necessary to push the valve down while compressing the spring.

59. Using the Valve Spring Compressor, install the roller follower.

60. Lubricate the camshaft roller follower with clean engine oil prior to installation.

61. Position the camshaft bearing cap and install the bolts in 2 stages:
   a. Stage 1: Tighten to 71 inch lbs. (8 Nm).
   b. Stage 2: Tighten an additional 45 degrees.

62. Remove the 2 bolts and the rear balance shaft bearing support and camshaft bearing cap assembly.

✷✷ WARNING

If the components are to be reinstalled, they must be installed into their original locations or damage to the engine may occur.

➥ Do not allow the valve keepers to fall off the valve or the valve may drop into the cylinder. If a valve drops into the cylinder, the cylinder head must be removed.

➥ It may be necessary to push the valve down while compressing the spring.

63. Using the Valve Spring Compressor, install the roller follower.

64. Lubricate the camshaft roller follower with clean engine oil prior to installation.

65. Position the camshaft bearing cap and install the bolts in 2 stages:
   a. Stage 1: Tighten to 71 inch lbs. (8 Nm).
   b. Stage 2: Tighten an additional 45 degrees.

✷✷ WARNING

If the components are to be reinstalled, they must be installed into their original locations or engine damage may occur.

➥ Do not allow the valve keepers to fall off the valve or the valve may drop into the cylinder. If a valve drops into the cylinder, the cylinder head must be removed.

➥ It may be necessary to push the valve down while compressing the spring.

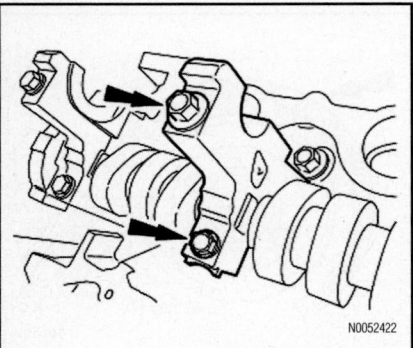

Fig. 387 Remove the 2 bolts and the middle balance shaft bearing support and camshaft bearing cap assembly

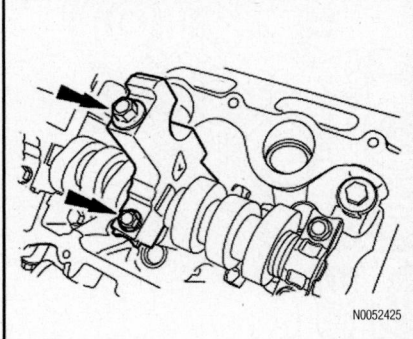

Fig. 388 Remove the 2 bolts and the rear balance shaft bearing support and camshaft bearing cap assembly

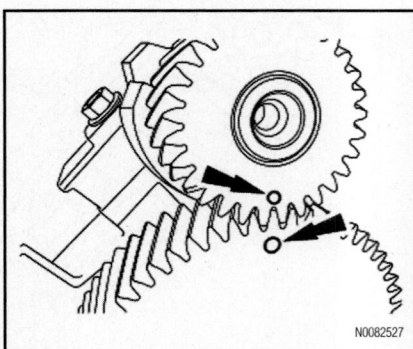

Fig. 389 Position the balance shaft on the journals and align the timing mark on the balance shaft with the camshaft timing mark as shown

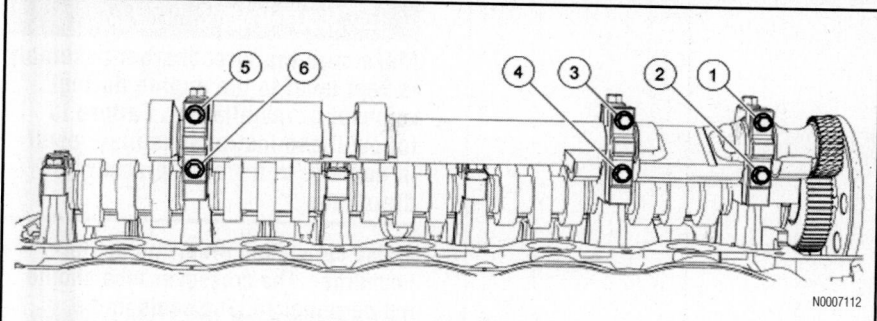

Fig. 390 Position the 3 balance shaft bearing caps and install the 6 bolts and tighten in the sequence shown

66. Using the Valve Spring Compressor, install all of the remaining camshaft roller followers.

67. Lubricate the camshaft roller followers with clean engine oil prior to installation.

68. Rotate the crankshaft counterclockwise and position the crankshaft keyway at the 11 o'clock position.

69. Lubricate the balance shaft journals with clean engine oil.

➡**Camshaft sprocket removed from art for clarity.**

70. Position the balance shaft on the journals and align the timing mark on the balance shaft with the camshaft timing mark as shown.

✳✳ WARNING

The balance shaft bearing caps must be installed into their original locations or engine damage may occur.

71. Position the 3 balance shaft bearing caps and install the 6 bolts and tighten in the sequence shown. Tighten to 89 inch lbs. (10 Nm).

72. Install engine front cover.

TURBOCHARGER

REMOVAL & INSTALLATION

6.4L Diesel Engine

See Figures 391 through 394.

➡**It is recommended that this component be serviced with the vehicle body removed.**

1. Remove the body.

2. Remove the turbocharger inlet pipes. Carry out the Exhaust Gas Recirculation (EGR) Oxidation Catalytic Converter (OC) and Turbocharger Inlet Pipes—6.4L Diesel, Body Off procedure.

3. Remove the clamp and disconnect the Air Cleaner (ACL) outlet tube-to-

crankcase vent oil separator hose at the vent oil separator.

4. Loosen the clamp and remove the ACL outlet tube.

✳✳ WARNING

Do not lean on, pull on or use the turbocharger oil supply tube as a handle or damage to the turbocharger oil supply tube may occur.

➡**Use a back-up wrench to prevent the fittings from turning.**

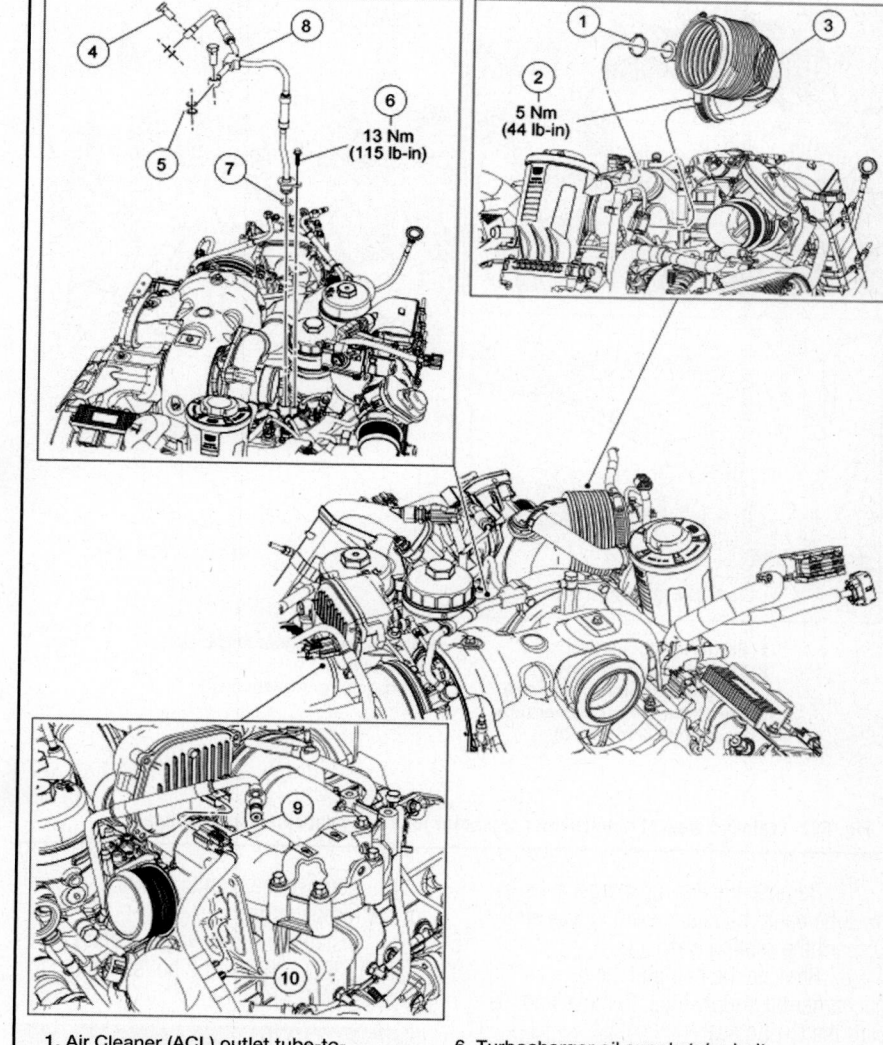

1. Air Cleaner (ACL) outlet tube-to-crankcase vent oil separator hose clamp
2. ACL outlet tube clamp
3. ACL outlet tube
4. Turbocharger oil supply tube banjo bolt (2 required)
5. Sealing washer (4 required)
6. Turbocharger oil supply tube bolt
7. O-ring seal
8. Turbocharger oil supply tube
9. Turbocharger actuator electrical connector
10. Pin-type retainer

Fig. 391 Exploded view of the turbocharger oil, air and electrical connections

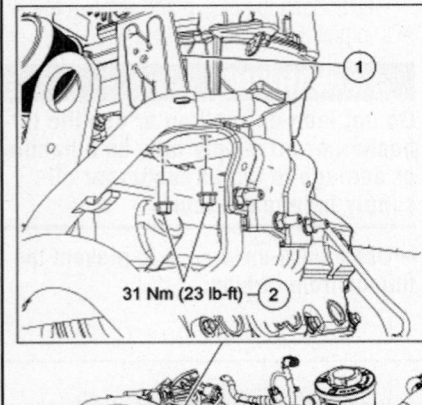

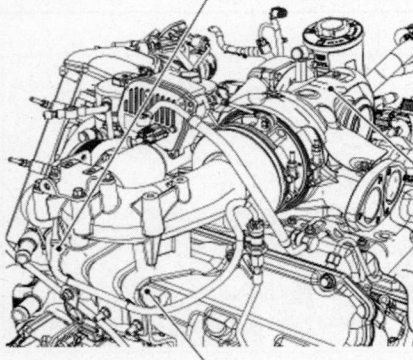

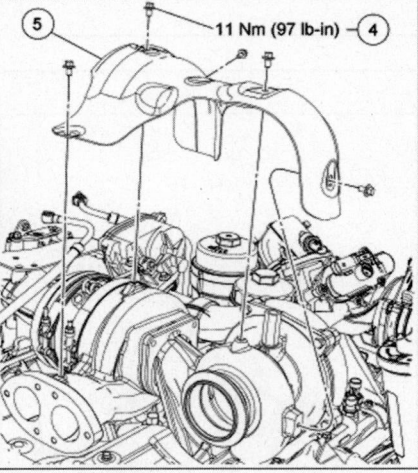

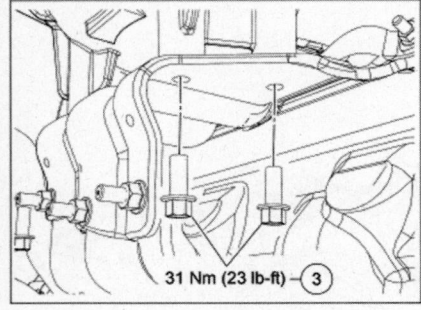

1. Front fuel cooler bracket
2. Turbocharger crossover tube front bolts (2 required)
3. Turbocharger crossover tube rear bolts (2 required)
4. Turbocharger heat shield bolt (5 required)
5. Turbocharger heat shield

N0103087

Fig. 392 Exploded view of turbocharger crossover tube and heat shield assemblies

5. Remove the 2 turbocharger oil supply tube banjo bolts and sealing washers. Discard the sealing washers.

6. Remove the bolt and the turbocharger oil supply tube. Remove and discard the O-ring seal.

7. Disconnect the turbocharger actuator electrical connector and pin-type retainer.

8. Remove the 4 bolts for the turbocharger crossover tube and the front fuel cooler bracket.

9. Remove the 5 bolts and the turbocharger heat shield.

10. Remove the 2 bolts and hold downs for the turbocharger.

11. Install the Turbocharger Lifting Bracket (303-1266) and 2 bolts. Tighten to 15 ft. lbs. (20 Nm).

✳✳ WARNING
Failure to use the Turbocharger Lifting Bracket during removal, handling or installation of the turbocharger could result in a low-pressure to high-pressure turbocharger seal failure.

✳✳ WARNING
Make sure the turbocharger assembly is kept level to the engine during removal or installation. Failure to follow these instructions may result in damage to the high-pressure oil drain tube.

➡ **Use care when removing the turbocharger. The crossover tube should not be removed. The seals in the crossover tube are one-time-use seals and must be installed new.**

12. Using the Heavy Duty Floor Crane, remove the turbocharger assembly.

13. Remove the turbocharger oil drain tubes.
   a. Remove and discard the low-pressure drain tube.
   b. Remove the high-pressure oil drain tube.
   c. Remove and discard the 2 O-ring seals.

To install:
14. If removed, install the Turbocharger Lifting Bracket and 2 bolts. Tighten to 15 ft. lbs. (20 Nm).

➡ **Lubricate the low-pressure oil drain tube with clean engine oil prior to installing.**

➡ **Install the low-pressure drain tube with the taper side down.**

15. Install the new low-pressure turbocharger oil drain tube in the turbocharger.

➡ **Install 2 new O-ring seals and lubricate with clean engine oil prior to installing the tube.**

16. Install the turbocharger high-pressure oil drain tube.

✳✳ WARNING
Failure to use the Turbocharger Lifting Bracket during removal, handling or installation of the turbocharger could result in a low-pressure to high-pressure turbocharger seal failure.

✳✳ WARNING
Make sure the turbocharger assembly is kept level to the engine during removal or installation. Failure to follow these instructions may result in damage to the high-pressure oil drain tube.

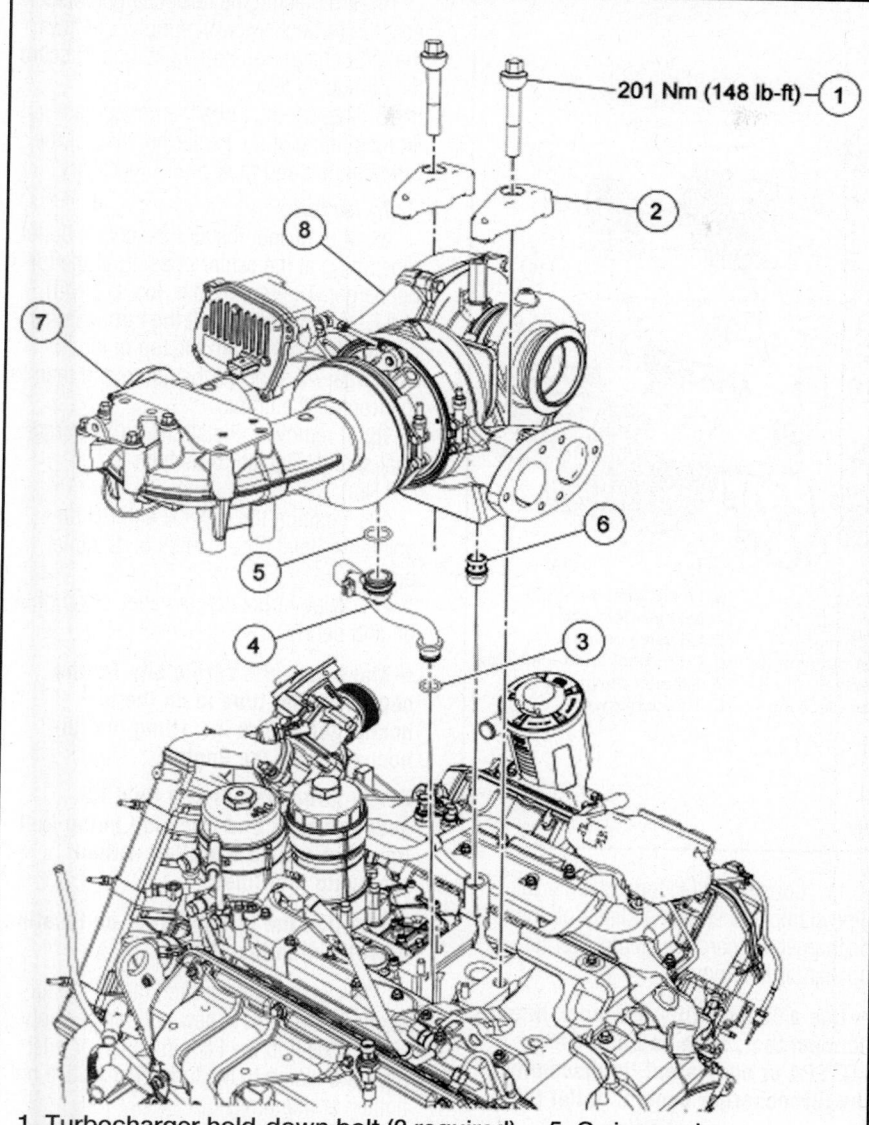

1. Turbocharger hold-down bolt (2 required)
2. Turbocharger hold down (2 required)
3. O-ring seal
4. High-pressure drain tube
5. O-ring seal
6. Low-pressure drain tube
7. Fuel cooler bracket
8. Turbocharger assembly

N0103088

Fig. 393 Exploded view of the turbocharger assembly

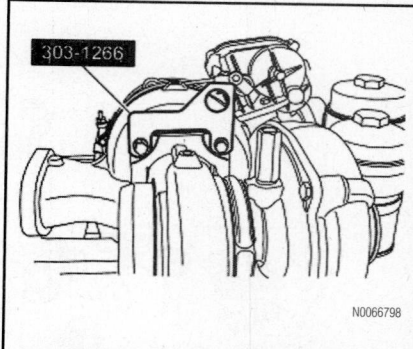

Fig. 394 Install the Turbocharger Lifting Bracket

17. Using the Heavy Duty Floor Crane, install the turbocharger assembly.

➡**After removing the Turbocharger Lifting Bracket, the 2 bolt holes remain open on the turbocharger.**

18. Remove the 2 bolts and the Turbocharger Lifting Bracket.

19. Install the 2 turbocharger hold downs and the bolts. Tighten to 148 ft. lbs. (201 Nm).

20. Position the turbocharger heat shield and install the 5 bolts. Tighten to 97 inch lbs. (11 Nm).

21. Position the front fuel cooler bracket. Install the 4 bolts for the turbocharger crossover tube. Tighten to 23 ft. lbs. (31 Nm).

22. Connect the turbocharger actuator electrical connector and pin-type retainer.

➡**Install a new O-ring seal and apply clean engine oil.**

23. Position the turbocharger oil supply tube and install the bolt. Tighten to 10 ft. lbs. (13 Nm).

24. Pre-lubricate the oil inlet holes of the turbocharger assembly with clean oil and spin the compressor wheel several times to coat the bearings with oil.

✳✳ WARNING

Only use banjo bolts with a green hex head. The green-headed bolts do not contain a check valve. When viewed from the inner end, the correct bolt will appear open. Failure to install the correct banjo bolt may result in damage to the turbochargers.

➡**Use a back-up wrench to prevent the fittings from turning.**

25. Install new sealing washers and the 2 oil supply tube banjo bolts on the turbocharger oil supply fittings.
   a. For Viton® sealing washers, tighten to 18 ft. lbs. (25 Nm).
   b. For copper sealing washer, tighten to 28 ft. lbs. (38 Nm).
   c. Verify that the turbocharger oil supply tube does not contact the turbocharger actuator linkage.

26. Install the ACL outlet tube and tighten the clamp.

➡**Install a new clamp prior to connecting the hose.**

27. Connect the ACL outlet tube-to-crankcase vent oil separator hose to the vent oil separator and tighten the clamp.

28. Install the turbocharger inlet pipes. Carry out the Exhaust Gas Recirculation (EGR) Oxidation Catalytic Converter (OC) and Turbocharger Inlet Pipes—6.4L Diesel, Body Off procedure.

29. Install the body.

6.7L Diesel Engine

See Figures 395 and 396.

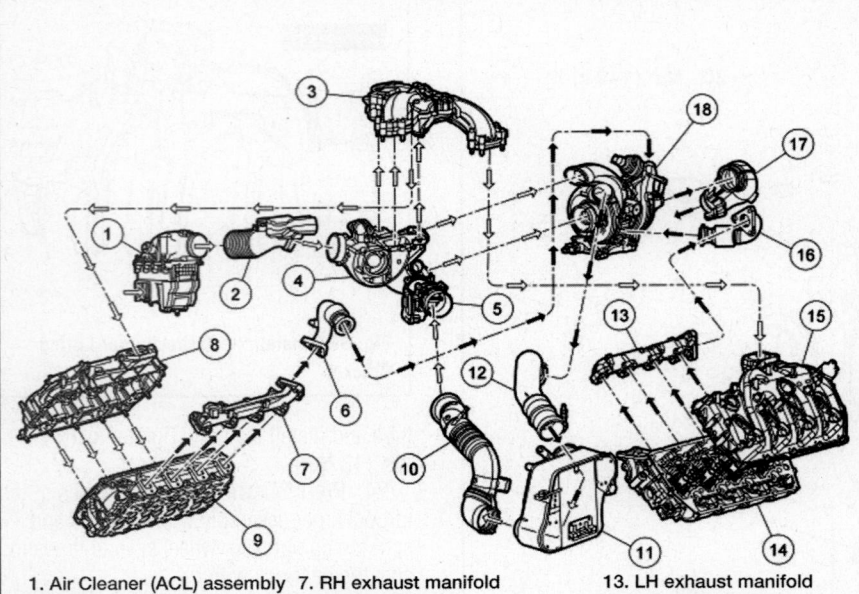

1. Air Cleaner (ACL) assembly
2. ACL outlet pipe
3. Upper intake manifold
4. Lower intake manifold
5. Throttle Body (TB)
6. RH turbocharger inlet pipe
7. RH exhaust manifold
8. RH valve cover
9. RH cylinder head
10. Charge Air Cooler outlet tube
11. Charge Air Cooler
12. Charge Air Cooler inlet tube
13. LH exhaust manifold
14. LH cylinder head
15. LH valve cover
16. LH turbocharger inlet pipe
17. Exhaust downpipe
18. Turbocharger

N0113524

Fig. 395 Exploded view of the turbocharger assembly

✳✳ WARNING

The engine oil must be changed any time the turbocharger is removed from the engine. The passages in the block underneath the turbocharger are direct passages to the lubrication system. Debris and or coolant may enter lubrication system and engine damage may occur.

1. Disconnect the battery ground cable.
2. Drain the primary engine cooling system.
3. Remove the lower intake manifold.
4. Disconnect the heater core inlet hose from the heater inlet tube.
5. Remove 2 bolts and the heater core inlet tube.
6. Inspect O-ring seal for damage, replace if necessary.
7. Disconnect the turbocharger actuator electrical connector.
8. If equipped, disconnect the turbocharger wastegate actuator vacuum hose.
9. Remove the upper exhaust downpipe.
10. Loosen the RH turbocharger inlet pipe clamp and slide the clamp off the turbocharger. Discard the clamp after turbocharger is removed.

11. Loosen the LH turbocharger inlet pipe clamp and slide the clamp off the turbocharger. Discard the clamp after turbocharger is removed.

➡**Use a ⅜ inch Jiffy-tite quick line disconnect tool, such as Snap-On® LDTSP4 or equivalent, to disconnect the turbocharger coolant outlet tube.**

➡**If necessary, remove the turbocharger heat shield and discard the bolts.**

12. Disconnect the turbocharger coolant outlet tube from the turbocharger.

➡**Lift the turbocharger off locating dowels before positioning forward for removal.**

➡**The turbocharger is a tight fit between cowl and injection pump fuel lines but comes out without removing fuel lines.**

13. Remove the 4 bolts and the turbocharger. Discard the turbocharger gasket and bolts.

➡**Use a ⅜ inch Jiffy-tite quick line disconnect tool, such as Snap-On® LDTSP4 or equivalent, to disconnect the turbocharger coolant outlet tube.**

14. If replacing the turbocharger, disconnect the turbocharger oil supply tube from the turbocharger oil supply fittings. Discard the oil supply tube.
15. Inspect the turbocharger coolant outlet tube fitting at the center housing of the turbocharger and replace, as necessary.

To install:

16. If removed, install the coolant outlet tube fitting at the center housing of the turbocharger. Tighten to 16 ft. lbs. (22 Nm).
17. If removed, install the turbocharger oil supply tube, first to the top of the turbocharger oil supply tube fitting and then to the front of the fitting.
18. If removed, install the turbocharger heat shield. Tighten to 89 inch lbs. (10 Nm).
19. Position the new LH and RH turbocharger inlet pipe clamps on the inlet pipes.
20. Wipe turbocharger valley clean of all oil and debris.

➡**Make sure the spring clip for the coolant outlet tube is on the turbocharger before installing the turbocharger on the engine.**

➡**The turbocharger is a tight fit between cowl and injection pump fuel lines but can be installed without removing fuel lines.**

➡**Position the turbocharger on locating dowels when installing.**

21. Using a new gasket, install the turbocharger and the 4 new bolts finger tight.
22. Position the LH turbocharger inlet pipe and clamp to the turbocharger. Do not tighten at this time.
23. Position the RH turbocharger inlet pipe and clamp to the turbocharger. Do not tighten at this time.
24. Tighten the turbocharger bolts to 41 ft. lbs. (55 Nm) in sequence shown.

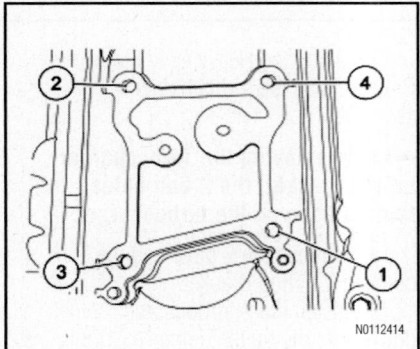

N0112414

Fig. 396 Tighten the turbocharger bolts in sequence shown

➡The LH turbocharger inlet pipe clamp nut should be in vertical position.

25. Tighten the LH turbocharger inlet pipe and clamp to 10 ft. lbs. (15 Nm).

➡The RH turbocharger inlet pipe clamp nut should be in vertical position.

26. Tighten the RH turbocharger inlet pipe and clamp to 10 ft. lbs. (15 Nm).
27. Install the upper exhaust downpipe.
28. Position the coolant outlet tube and install it into the turbocharger spring clip fitting.
29. If equipped, connect the turbocharger wastegate actuator vacuum hose.
30. Connect the turbocharger actuator electrical connector.

➡Lubricate the O-ring seal with engine coolant.

31. Install the heater core inlet tube and the 2 bolts. Tighten to 89 inch lbs. (10 Nm).
32. Connect the heater core inlet hose to the heater inlet tube.
33. Install the lower intake manifold.
34. Remove and discard the engine oil filter.
35. Drain the engine oil by turning the oil pan drain plug one quarter turn Counterclockwise (CCW).
36. Install the engine oil pan drain plug and tighten one quarter turn Clockwise (CW).

➡Lubricate the engine oil filter seal with clean engine oil.

37. Install a new engine oil filter.
38. Fill the engine with the correct motor oil for the climate.
39. Connect the battery ground cable.
40. Evaluate the primary cooling system.
41. Perform the cooling system pressure test.

VALVE COVERS

REMOVAL & INSTALLATION

6.4L Diesel Engine

Left Side

See Figure 397.

✳✳ WARNING

Position a suitable protective material in front of the Charge Air Cooler (CAC) or damage to the CAC may occur.

1. Remove the degas bottle.

2. Loosen the clamp and remove the degas bottle-to-engine hose.
3. Loosen the clamp, disconnect the heater hose and position it aside.
4. Disconnect the Exhaust Pressure (EP) sensor electrical connector and retainer.
5. Disconnect the wiring harness retainers from the LH valve cover bracket. Disconnect the glow plug electrical connector.
6. Disconnect the wiring harness retainer and position the engine wiring aside.
7. Remove the oil level indicator and tube nut.
8. Remove the oil level indicator and tube bolt, detach the tube from the engine block and position the tube aside. Remove and discard the O-ring seal.

✳✳ WARNING

Do not disconnect the glow plug electrical connector before dislodging the seal from the valve cover or the wiring harness may be damaged.

9. Using an appropriate tool, dislodge the glow plug wiring harness seals from the valve cover.
10. Disconnect the glow plug electrical connectors by pulling on the glow plug wiring harness tee above the seal. Remove the glow plug wiring harness.
11. Remove the 4 turbocharger crossover tube bolts.
12. Disconnect the EP sensor tube fitting from the EGR oxidation pipe.
13. Remove the nut and the EP sensor and tube assembly.
14. Remove the 4 LH valve cover bracket nuts.
15. Remove the 3 LH valve cover bracket assembly nuts. Separate and remove the upper and lower LH valve cover brackets.
16. Remove the 6 bolts, the 4 stud bolts and the LH valve cover. Remove the discard the valve cover gasket.

To install:

17. To install, reverse the removal procedure.
   a. Install a new valve cover gasket.
   b. Alternate tightening the valve cover bolts to tighten evenly.
   c. Make sure that the turbocharger crossover tube is square to the turbocharger when the valve cover bracket is installed.
   d. Tighten the 6 bolts and the 4 stud bolts to 80 inch lbs. (9 Nm).

   e. Tighten the 3 LH valve cover bracket assembly nuts to 23 ft. lbs. (31 Nm).
   f. Tighten the 4 LH valve cover bracket nuts to 80 inch lbs. (9 Nm).
   g. Tighten the nut for the EP sensor and tube assembly to 80 inch lbs. (9 Nm).
   h. Tighten the EP sensor tube fitting to the EGR oxidation pipe to 15 ft. lbs. (20 Nm).
   i. Tighten the 4 turbocharger crossover tube bolts to 23 ft. lbs. (31 Nm).
   j. Tighten the oil level indicator tube to the engine block to 10 ft. lbs. (13 Nm).
   k. Tighten the oil level indicator tube nut to 23 ft. lbs. (31 Nm).

Right Side

See Figure 398.

✳✳ WARNING

Position a suitable protective material in front of the Charge Air Cooler (CAC) or damage to the CAC may occur.

1. Position the vehicle on a hoist.
2. Disconnect the battery ground cable(s).
3. Remove the Air Cleaner (ACL) assembly.
4. Disconnect the crankcase vent oil separator tube from the crankcase vent oil separator.
5. Loosen the ACL outlet tube clamp and detach the ACL outlet tube from the turbocharger.
6. Remove the 4 bolts, the crankcase vent oil separator and the ACL outlet pipe as an assembly. Remove and discard the crankcase vent oil separator press-in-place gasket.
7. Disconnect the PCM electrical connector and retainer. Disconnect the in-line electrical connector and position the engine wiring harness on the engine.
8. Remove the 3 pushnuts and the glow plug module heat shield. Discard the 3 pushnuts.
9. Disconnect the high-pressure fuel injection pump electrical connector and detach the retainer from the glow plug module bracket.
10. Disconnect the glow plug module and the EGRT sensor electrical connectors, detach the wiring retainer and position the wiring harnesses aside.
11. Remove the nut and position the ground strap aside.
12. Remove the engine wiring harness bolt.

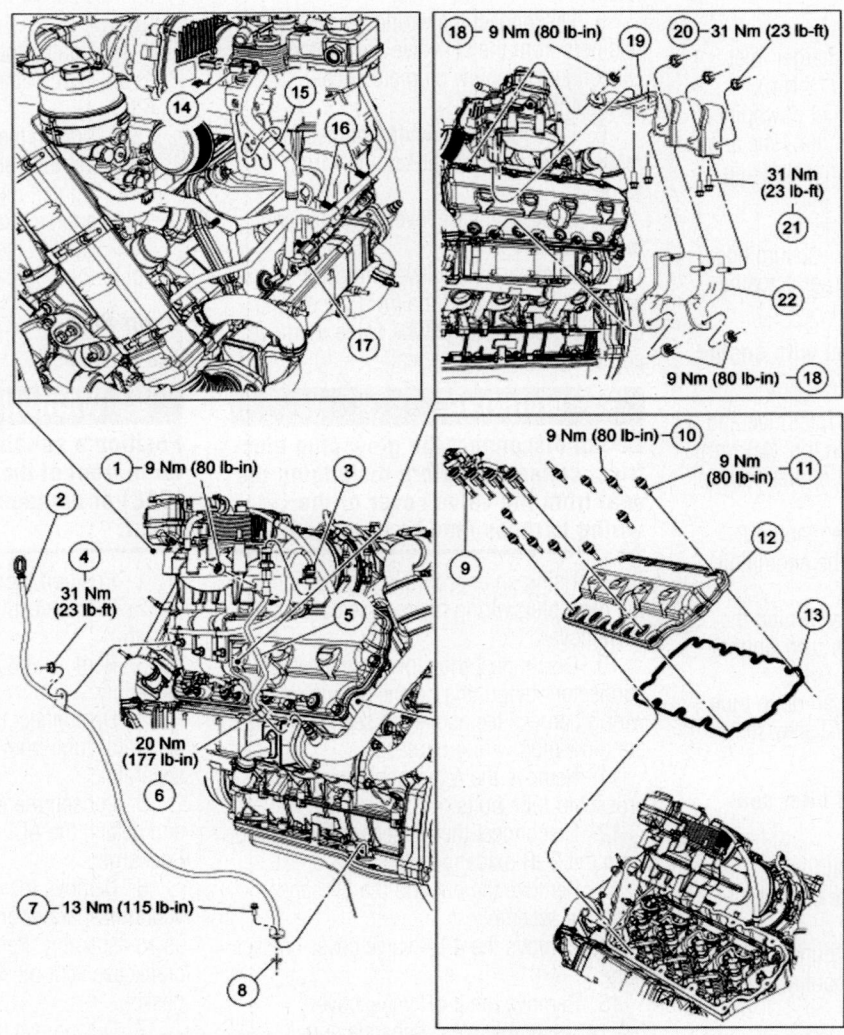

1. Exhaust Pressure (EP) sensor tube assembly nut
2. Oil level indicator and tube
3. EP sensor electrical connector and retaining clip
4. Oil level indicator and tube nut
5. EP sensor tube assembly
6. EP sensor tube assembly fitting
7. Oil level indicator and tube bolt
8. Oil level indicator and tube O-ring seal
9. LH glow plug harness and retaining clip
10. LH valve cover stud bolt (4 required)
11. LH valve cover bolt (6 required)
12. LH valve cover
13. LH valve cover gasket
14. Turbocharger actuator electrical connector
15. Turbocharger actuator wiring retainer
16. EP sensor wiring retainers (2 required)
17. LH glow plug harness electrical connector
18. LH valve cover bracket nuts (3 required)
19. LH valve cover upper bracket
20. LH valve cover bracket assembly nut (3 required)
21. Turbocharger crossover tube bolt (4 required)
22. LH valve cover lower bracket

N0101546

Fig. 397 Exploded view of the left valve cover assembly

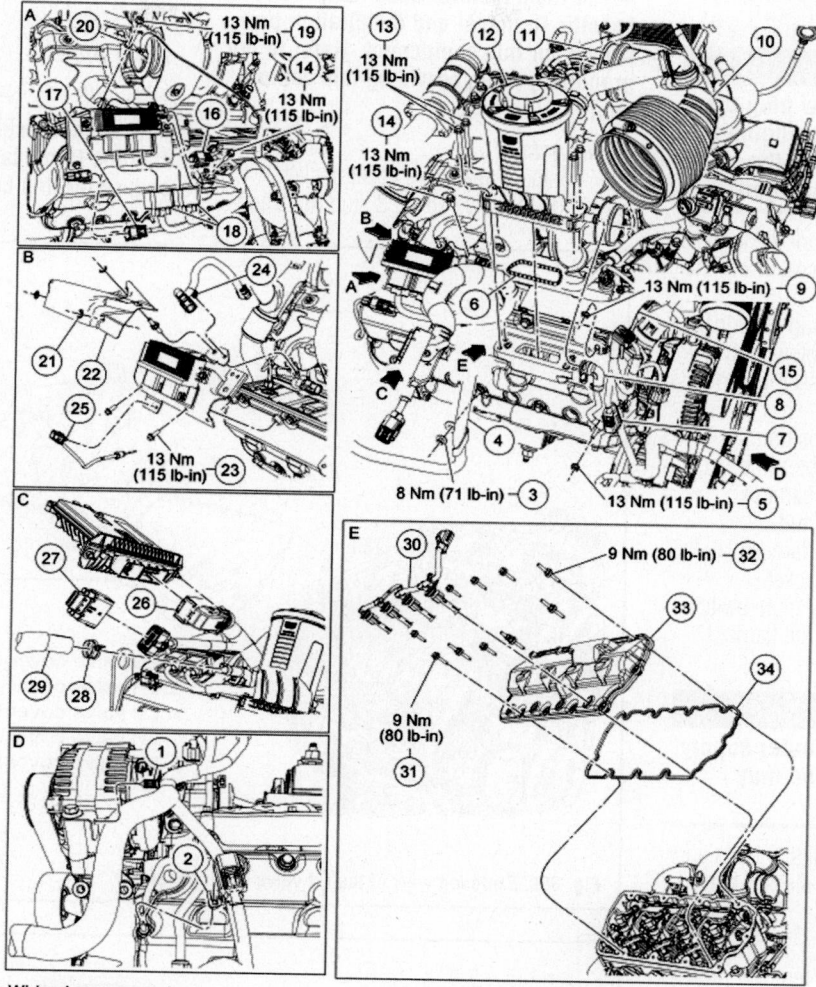

1. Wiring harness retainer
2. Wiring harness retainer
3. Transmission fluid tube and indicator nut (if equipped)
4. Transmission fluid tube and indicator (if equipped)
5. Crankcase vent oil separator tube nut
6. Crankcase vent oil separator gasket
7. Glow plug electrical connector and retainer
8. Crankcase vent oil separator drain tube
9. Heater supply tube nut
10. Air Cleaner (ACL) outlet pipe
11. ACL outlet pipe clamp
12. Crankcase vent oil separator
13. Crankcase vent oil separator bolts (4 required)
14. Engine wiring harness bolt
15. Engine wiring harness
16. High-pressure fuel injection pump electrical connector
17. Exhaust Gas Recirculation Temperature (EGRT) sensor electrical connector

18. Glow plug module electrical connectors (2 required)
19. Ground wire nut
20. Ground wire
21. Glow plug module heat shield pushnut (3 required)
22. Glow plug module heat shield
23. Glow plug module bracket bolt (3 required)
24. High-pressure fuel injection pump electrical connector retainer
25. EGRT sensor electrical connector retainer
26. PCM electrical connector
27. In-line electrical connector
28. Heater inlet hose clamp
29. Heater inlet hose
30. RH glow plug wiring harness
31. RH valve cover bolt (6 required)
32. RH valve cover stud bolt (6 required)
33. RH valve cover
34. RH valve cover gasket

Fig. 398 Exploded view of the right side valve cover

13. Remove the heater supply tube nut.

14. Remove the 3 bolts and the glow plug module bracket.

15. If equipped with an A/T, remove the nut and position the transmission fluid indicator tube aside.

✳✳ WARNING

Do not disconnect the glow plug electrical connector before dislodging the seal from the valve cover or the wiring harness may be damaged.

16. Using an appropriate tool, dislodge the glow plug wiring harness seals from the valve cover.

17. Disconnect the glow plug electrical connectors by pulling on the glow plug wiring harness tee above the seal. Remove the glow plug wiring harness.

18. Remove the nut and position the crankcase ventilation drain tube aside.

19. Disconnect the wiring harness retainer from the valve cover stud.

20. Disconnect the wiring harness retainer from the alternator bracket.

21. Disconnect the A/C pressure switch electrical connector. Position the harness aside.

✳✳ WARNING

Do not bend or flex the heater supply tube or damage to the tube may occur.

22. Remove the 4 stud bolts, 6 bolts and the valve cover. Remove and discard the valve cover gasket.

To install:

23. To install, reverse the removal procedure.

    a. Install a new valve cover gasket.

    b. Alternate tightening the valve cover bolts to tighten evenly.

    c. Install a new crankcase vent oil separator press-in-place gasket.

    d. Tighten the 4 stud bolts and 6 bolts for the valve cover to 80 inch lbs. (9 Nm).

    e. Tighten the 3 bolts for the glow plug module bracket to 10 ft. lbs. (13 Nm).

    f. Tighten the heater supply tube nut to 10 ft. lbs. (13 Nm).

    g. Tighten the engine wiring harness bolt to 10 ft. lbs. (13 Nm).

    h. Tighten the ground strap nut to 10 ft. lbs. (13 Nm).

    i. Tighten the 4 crankcase vent oil separator and the ACL outlet pipe bolts to 10 ft. lbs. (13 Nm).

6.7L Diesel Engine

Left Side

See Figures 399 and 400.

➡**The manufacturer does not provide a specific Removal and Installation procedure for this component. Refer to the graphic(s) when servicing this component.**

To install:

1. Using a new valve cover gasket, install the LH valve cover, 3 stud bolts and 15 bolts. Tighten in 2 stages in the sequence shown.

    a. Stage 1: Tighten to 106 inch lbs. (12 Nm).

    b. Stage 2: Tighten a second time, to 106 inch lbs. (12 Nm).

Right Side

See Figures 401 and 402.

➡**The manufacturer does not provide a specific Removal and Installation procedure for this component. Refer to the**

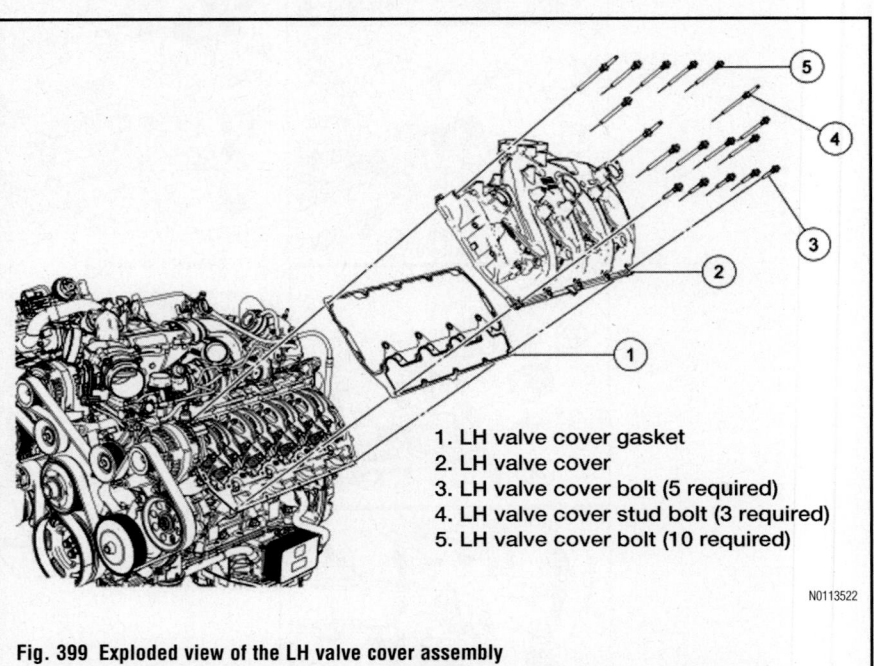

1. LH valve cover gasket
2. LH valve cover
3. LH valve cover bolt (5 required)
4. LH valve cover stud bolt (3 required)
5. LH valve cover bolt (10 required)

N0113522

Fig. 399 Exploded view of the LH valve cover assembly

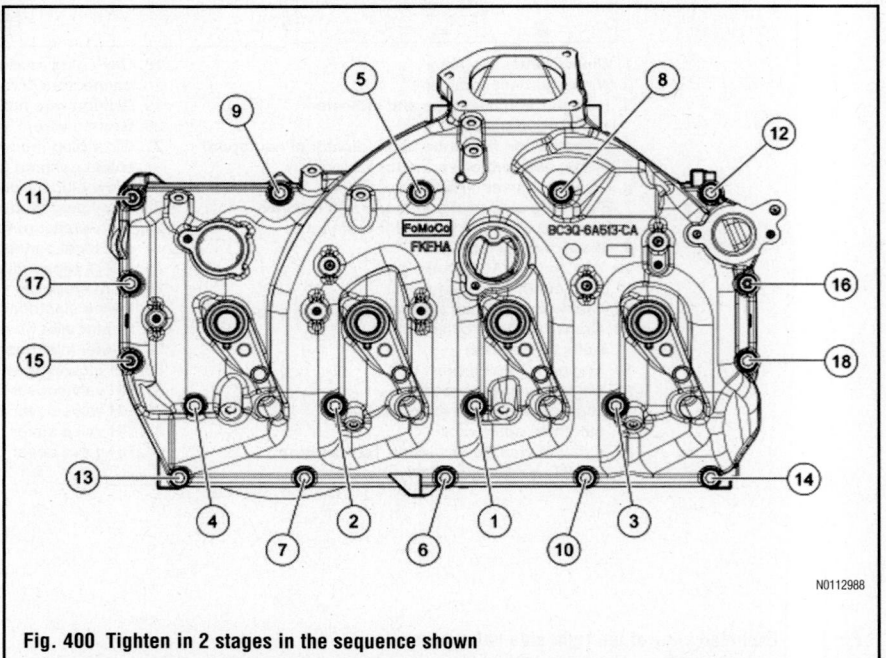

N0112988

Fig. 400 Tighten in 2 stages in the sequence shown

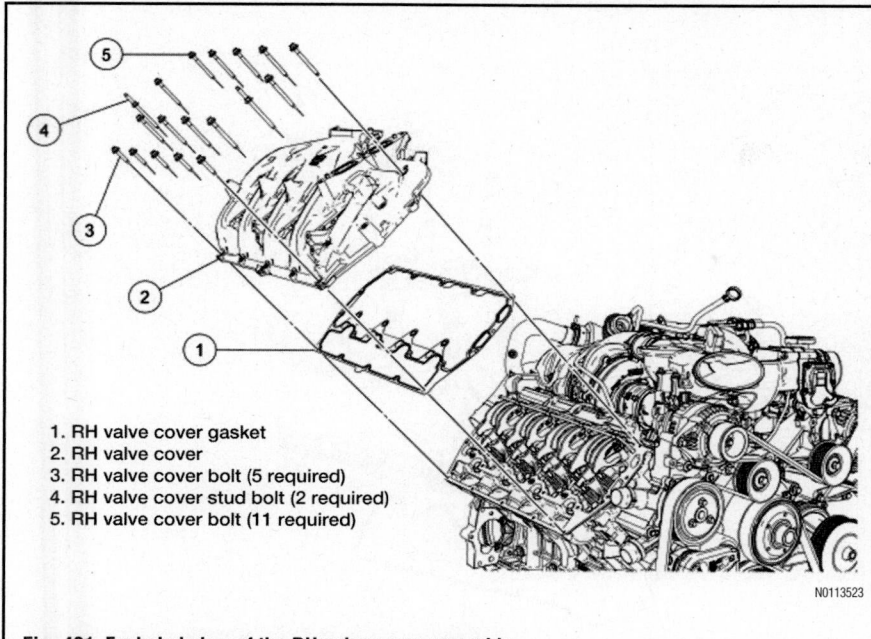

1. RH valve cover gasket
2. RH valve cover
3. RH valve cover bolt (5 required)
4. RH valve cover stud bolt (2 required)
5. RH valve cover bolt (11 required)

N0113523

Fig. 401 Exploded view of the RH valve cover assembly

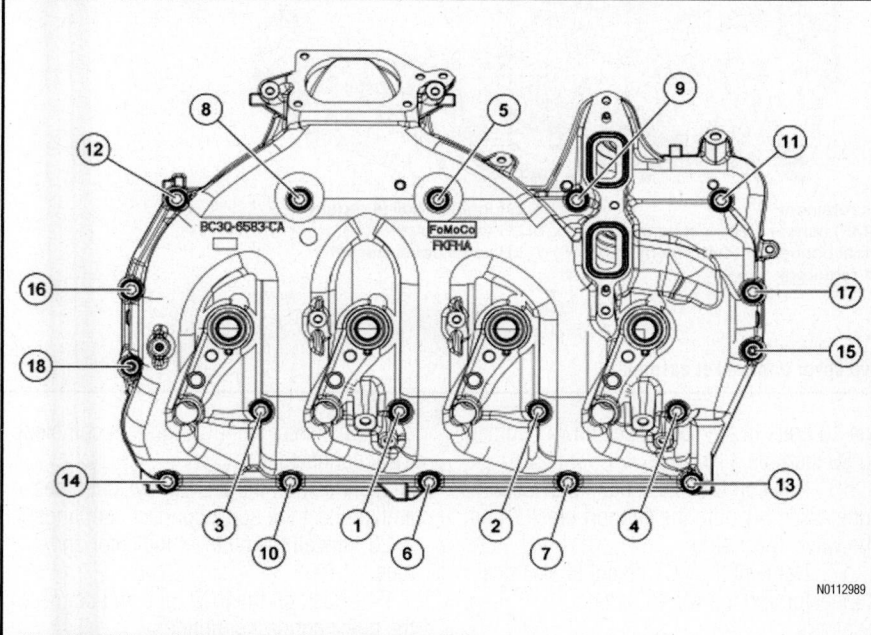

N0112989

Fig. 402 Tighten in 2 stages in the sequence shown

graphic(s) when servicing this component.

To install:

1. Using a new valve cover gasket, install the LH valve cover, 2 stud bolts and 16 bolts. Tighten in 2 stages in the sequence shown.

  a. Stage 1: Tighten to 106 inch lbs. (12 Nm).

  b. Stage 2: Tighten a second time, to 106 inch lbs. (12 Nm).

5.4L Engine

Left Side

See Figures 403 through 405.

1. Remove the Air Cleaner (ACL) outlet pipe.

2. Remove the degas bottle assembly.

3. Remove the oil level indicator and tube.

4. Disconnect the degas bottle coolant outlet hose.

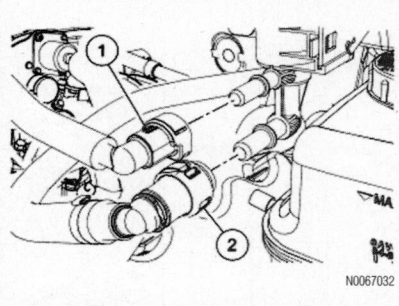

N0067032

Fig. 403 Disconnect the 2 Evaporative Emission (EVAP) system tube quick connect couplings (1, 2)

5. Disconnect the 2 Evaporative Emission (EVAP) system tube quick connect couplings and position the tubes aside.

6. Disconnect the quick connect couplings and remove the PCV tube.

7. Disconnect the 4 LH ignition coil electrical connectors.

8. Remove the 4 bolts and the 4 LH ignition coils. Remove the ignition coil, using a twisting motion while pulling up on the ignition coil.

9. Disconnect the intake manifold vacuum tube hose from the brake booster.

10. Disconnect the radio ignition interference capacitor electrical connector.

11. Disconnect the Variable Camshaft Timing (VCT) solenoid electrical connector and the wiring harness retainers.

12. Disconnect the intake manifold vacuum tube from the support bracket and the valve cover stud.

✳✳ WARNING

Do not use metal scrapers, wire brushes, power abrasive discs or other abrasive means to clean the sealing surfaces. These tools cause scratches and gouges which make leak paths. Use a plastic scraping tool to remove all traces of old sealant. Failure to follow this procedure may cause future oil leakage.

✳✳ WARNING

When removing the valve cover, make sure to avoid damaging the Variable Camshaft Timing (VCT) solenoid.

➡**The fasteners are part of the valve cover and should not be removed.**

13. Fully loosen the 10 fasteners and remove the LH valve cover and gasket.

  a. Clean the valve cover mating surface of the cylinder head with silicone

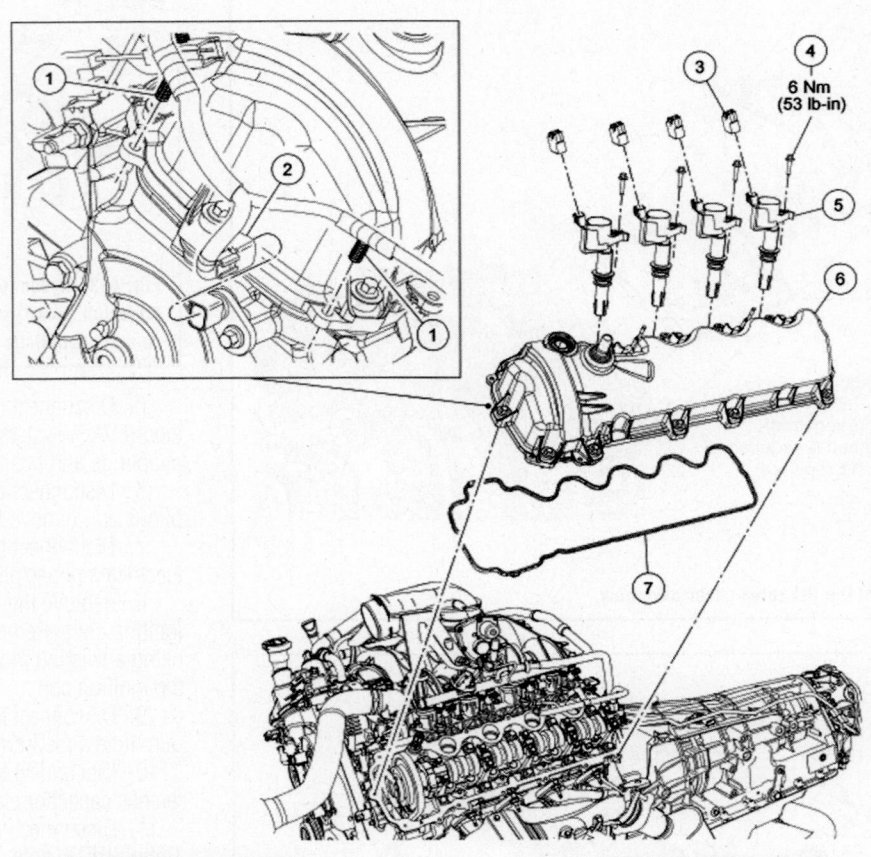

1. Engine wiring harness retainers
2. Camshaft Position (CMP) sensor electrical connector
3. LH ignition coil electrical connector (4 required)
4. LH ignition coil bolt (4 required)
5. LH ignition coil (4 required)
6. LH valve cover
7. LH valve cover gasket

N0087771

Fig. 404 Exploded view of the LH ignition coils, valve cover and gasket assembly

gasket remover and metal surface prep. Follow the directions on the packaging.

b. Discard the valve cover gasket. Clean the valve cover gasket groove with soap and water or a suitable solvent.

To install:

➡ If the valve cover is not secured within 4 minutes, the sealant must be removed and the sealing area cleaned with silicone gasket remover and metal surface prep. Follow the directions on the packaging. Allow to dry until there is no sign of wetness, or 4 minutes, whichever is longer. Failure to follow this procedure may cause future oil leakage.

14. Apply a bead of silicone gasket and sealant in 2 places where the engine front cover meets the cylinder head.

15. Position the LH valve cover and a new gasket on the cylinder head and tighten the 10 bolts in the sequence shown. Tighten to 89 inch lbs. (10 Nm).

16. Position the intake manifold vacuum tube assembly onto the support bracket and the valve cover stud.

17. Connect the VCT solenoid electrical connector and the wiring harness retainers.

18. Connect the radio ignition interference capacitor electrical connector.

19. Connect the intake manifold vacuum tube hose to the brake booster.

➡ Verify that the ignition coil spring is correctly located inside the ignition coil boot and that there is no damage to the tip of the boot.

20. Install the 4 LH ignition coils and the 4 bolts.

a. Apply a light coat of dielectric compound to the inside of the ignition coil boots prior to installation.

21. Connect the 4 LH ignition coil electrical connectors.

22. Position the 2 EVAP system tubes and connect the quick connect couplings.

23. Install the oil level indicator and tube.

24. Position the PCV tube and connect the quick connect couplings.

25. Connect the degas bottle coolant outlet hose.

26. Install the degas bottle assembly.

27. Install the ACL outlet pipe.

Right Side

See Figures 406 and 407.

1. Drain the engine cooling system.

2. If equipped, remove the bolt and position the transmission filler tube aside.

3. Disconnect the quick connect coupling and position the crankcase vent tube aside.

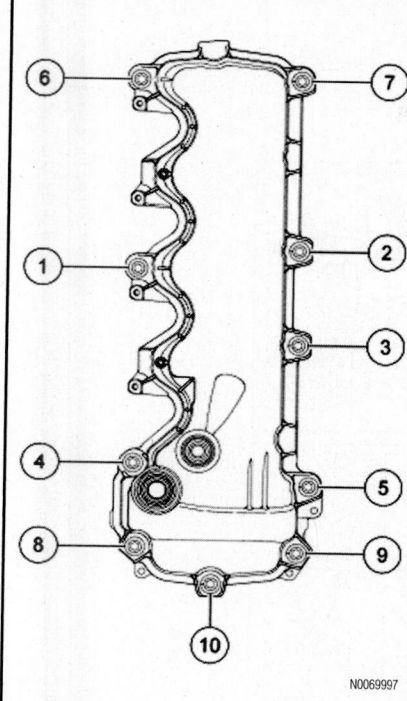

Fig. 405 Position the LH valve cover and a new gasket on the cylinder head and tighten the 10 bolts in the sequence shown

4. Disconnect the heater coolant hose from the engine coolant crossover manifold assembly.

5. Disconnect the 2 PCM electrical connectors and the wiring harness retainers from the support bracket and position aside.

6. Disconnect the 4 RH ignition coil electrical connectors.

7. Remove the 4 RH bolts and the 4 RH ignition coils.

8. Remove the ignition coil, using a twisting motion while pulling up on the ignition coil.

9. Disconnect the Variable Camshaft Timing (VCT) solenoid electrical connector.

10. Disconnect the 4 wiring harness retainers from the valve cover and position the wiring harness aside.

✳✳ WARNING

Do not use metal scrapers, wire brushes, power abrasive discs or other abrasive means to clean the sealing surfaces. These tools cause scratches and gouges which make leak paths. Use a plastic scraping tool to remove all traces of old sealant. Failure to follow this procedure may cause future oil leakage.

✳✳ WARNING

When removing the valve cover, make sure to avoid damaging the Variable Camshaft Timing (VCT) solenoid.

➡The fasteners are part of the valve cover and should not be removed.

11. Fully loosen the 9 fasteners and remove the RH valve cover and gasket.
   a. Clean the valve cover mating surface of the cylinder head with silicone gasket remover and metal surface prep. Follow the directions on the packaging.
   b. Discard the valve cover gasket. Clean the valve cover gasket groove with soap and water or a suitable solvent.

To install:

➡If the valve cover is not secured within 4 minutes, the sealant must be removed and the sealing area cleaned with silicone gasket remover and metal surface prep. Follow the directions on the packaging. Allow to dry until there is no sign of wetness, or 4 minutes, whichever is longer. Failure to follow this procedure may cause future oil leakage.

12. Apply a bead of silicone gasket and sealant in 2 places where the engine front cover meets the cylinder head.

✳✳ WARNING

When installing the valve cover, make sure to avoid damaging the Variable Camshaft Timing (VCT) solenoid.

13. Position the RH valve cover and new gasket on the cylinder head and tighten the 9 bolts in the sequence shown. Tighten to 89 inch lbs. (10 Nm).

14. Connect the wiring harness retainers to the valve cover.

15. Connect the VCT solenoid electrical connector.

➡Verify that the ignition coil spring is correctly located inside the ignition coil boot and that there is no damage to the tip of the boot.

16. Install the 4 RH ignition coils and the 4 bolts.

17. Apply a light coat of dielectric compound to the inside of the ignition coil boots prior to installation.

18. Connect the 4 RH ignition coil electrical connectors.

19. Connect the 2 PCM electrical connectors and the wiring harness retainers to the support bracket.

20. Position the crankcase vent tube and connect the quick connect couplings.

21. Connect the heater coolant hose to the engine coolant crossover manifold assembly.

22. If equipped, position the transmission filler tube and install the bolt. Tighten to 89 inch lbs. (10 Nm).

23. Fill and bleed the engine cooling system.

6.8L Engine

Left Side

See Figures 408 through 410.

1. Remove the Air Cleaner (ACL) outlet pipe.

2. Remove the LH ignition coils.

3. Remove the oil level indicator and tube.

4. Disconnect the quick connect couplings and remove the PCV tube.

5. Disconnect the engine wiring harness retainers from the valve cover studs and position the wiring harness aside.

✳✳ WARNING

Do not use metal scrapers, wire brushes, power abrasive discs or other abrasive means to clean the sealing surfaces. These tools cause scratches and gouges which make leak paths. Use a plastic scraping tool to remove all traces of old sealant.

➡The bolts are part of the valve cover and should not be removed.

6. Loosen the 17 fasteners in the sequence shown and remove the LH valve cover and gasket.
   a. Clean and inspect the sealing surfaces with silicone gasket remover and metal surface prep. Follow the directions on the packaging.
   b. Discard the valve cover gasket. Clean the valve cover gasket groove with soap and water or a suitable solvent.

To install:

➡If the valve cover is not secured within 4 minutes, the sealant must be removed and the sealing area cleaned with silicone gasket remover and metal surface prep. Follow the directions on the packaging. Allow to dry until there is no sign of wetness, or 4 minutes, whichever is longer. Failure to follow this procedure may cause future oil leakage.

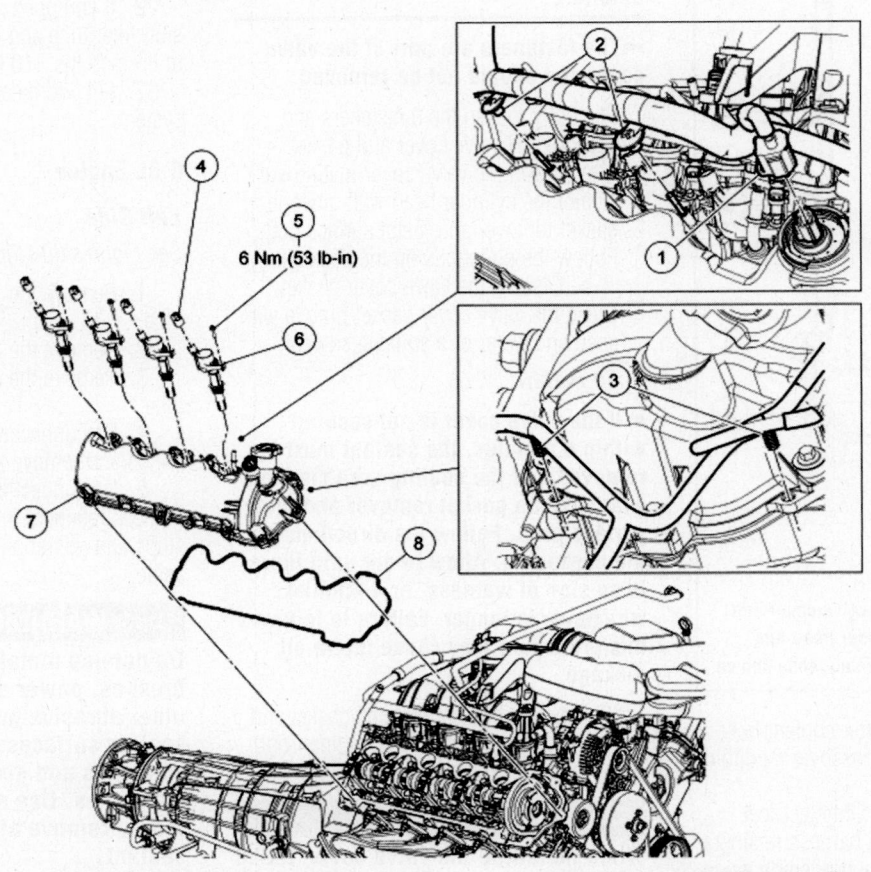

6 Nm (53 lb-in)

1. Variable Camshaft Timing (VCT) solenoid electrical connector
2. Engine wiring harness retainers
3. Engine wiring harness retainers
4. RH ignition coil electrical connector (4 required)
5. RH ignition coil bolt (4 required)
6. RH ignition coil (4 required)
7. RH valve cover
8. RH valve cover gasket

N0076926

Fig. 406 Exploded view of the RH ignition coils, valve cover and gasket assembly

7. Apply a bead of silicone gasket and sealant in 2 places where the engine front cover meets the cylinder head.

8. Position the LH valve cover and new gasket on the cylinder head and tighten the 17 fasteners in the sequence shown. Tighten to 89 inch lbs. (10 Nm).

9. Position the engine wiring harness and connect the harness retainers onto the valve cover studs.

10. Position the PCV tube and connect the quick connect couplings.

11. Install the LH ignition coils.

12. Install the oil level indicator and tube.

13. Install the ACL outlet pipe.

Right Side

See Figures 411 through 413.

1. Remove the RH ignition coils.

2. Remove the bolt and position the transmission filler tube aside.

3. Disconnect the quick connect coupling and position the crankcase vent tube aside.

4. Disconnect the 2 PCM electrical connectors and the wiring harness retainers from the support bracket and position aside.

5. Disconnect the Camshaft Position (CMP) sensor electrical connector.

6. Disconnect the 4 wiring harness retainers from the valve cover and position the wiring harness aside.

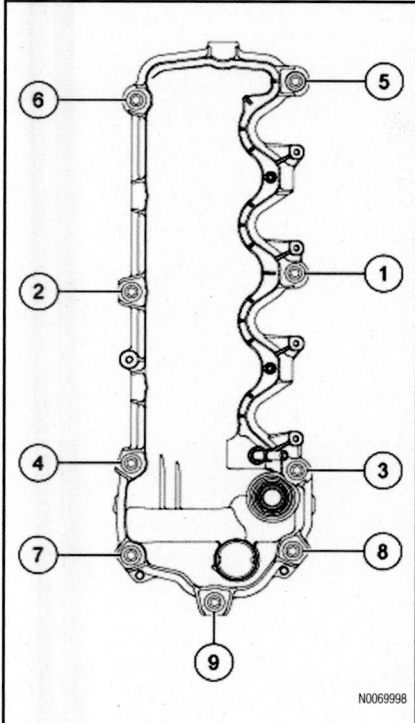

Fig. 407 Position the RH valve cover and new gasket on the cylinder head and tighten the 9 bolts in the sequence shown

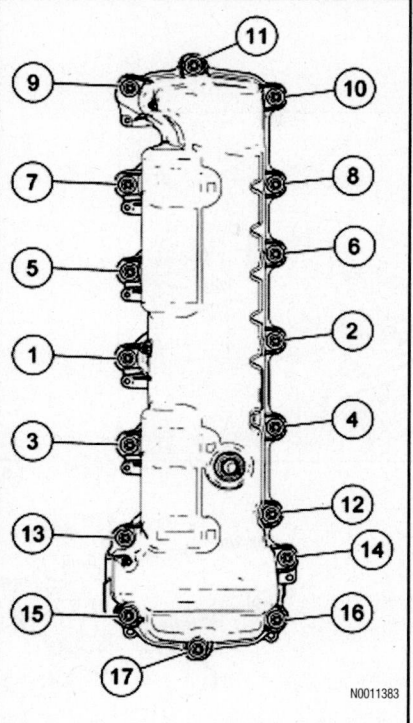

Fig. 408 Loosen the 17 fasteners in the sequence shown and remove the LH valve cover and gasket

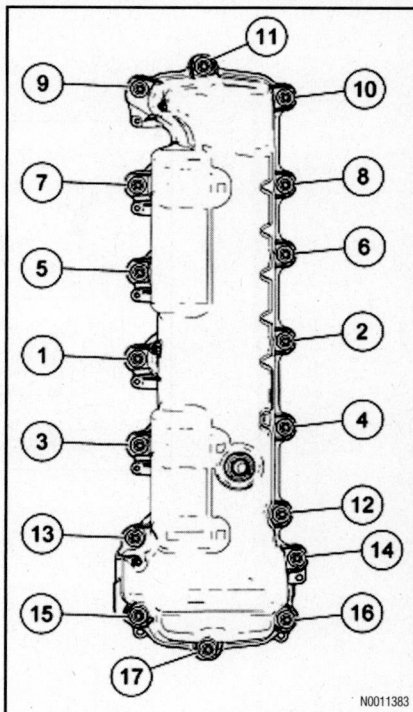

Fig. 410 Position the LH valve cover and new gasket on the cylinder head and tighten the 17 fasteners in the sequence shown

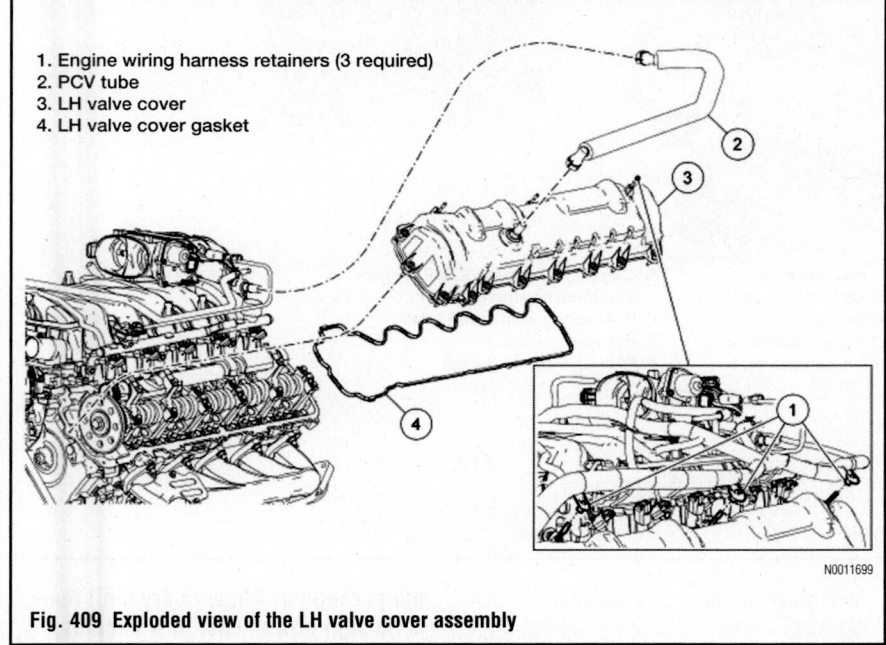

1. Engine wiring harness retainers (3 required)
2. PCV tube
3. LH valve cover
4. LH valve cover gasket

Fig. 409 Exploded view of the LH valve cover assembly

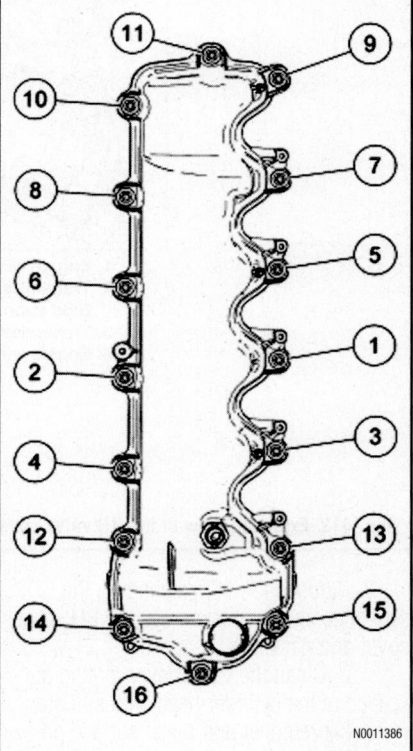

Fig. 411 Loosen the 16 fasteners in the sequence shown and remove the RH valve cover and gasket

❈❈ WARNING

Do not use metal scrapers, wire brushes, power abrasive discs or other abrasive means to clean the sealing surfaces. These tools cause scratches and gouges which make leak paths. Use a plastic scraping tool to remove all traces of old sealant. Failure to follow this procedure may cause future oil leakage.

➡The fasteners are part of the valve cover and should not be removed.

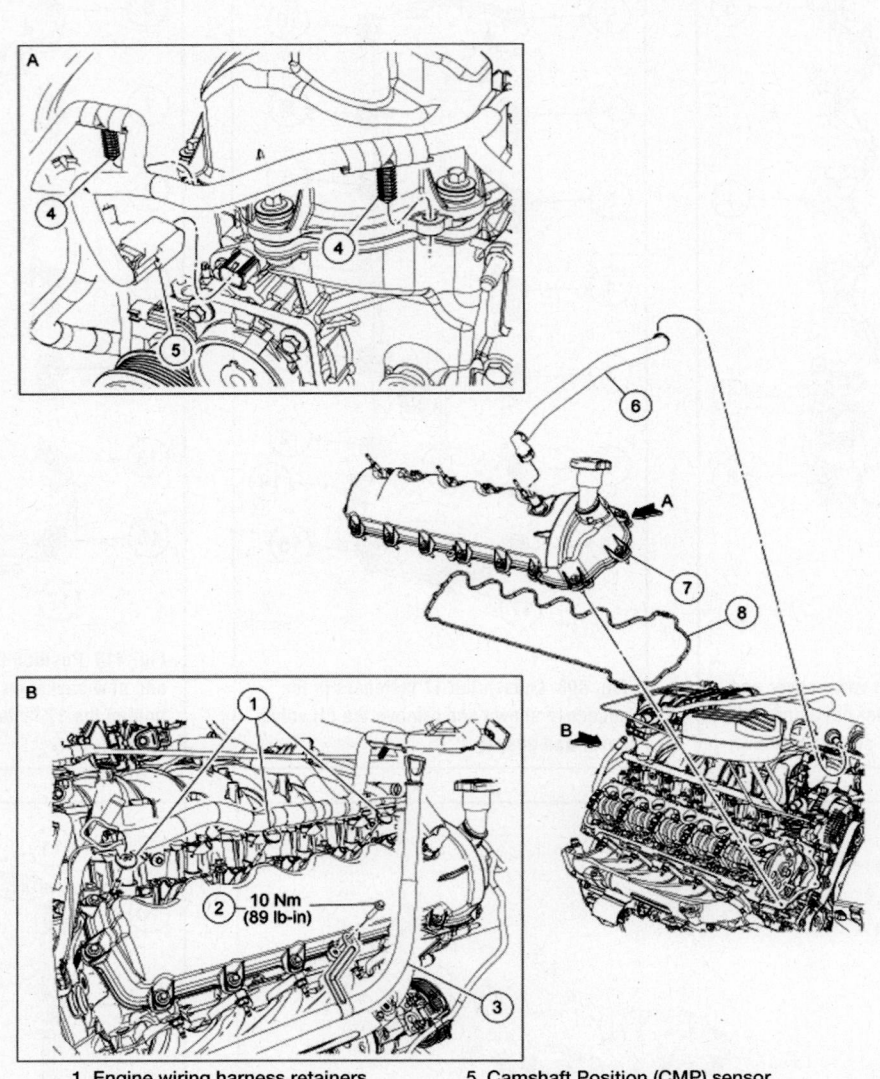

Fig. 412 Exploded view of the RH valve cover assembly

1. Engine wiring harness retainers
2. Transmission fluid level indicator tube support bracket bolt
3. Transmission fluid level indicator tube
4. Engine wiring harness retainers
5. Camshaft Position (CMP) sensor electrical connector
6. Crankcase ventilation tube
7. RH valve cover
8. RH valve cover gasket

N0087828

7. Loosen the 16 fasteners in the sequence shown and remove the RH valve cover and gasket.

  a. Clean the valve cover mating surface of the cylinder head with silicone gasket remover and metal surface prep. Follow the directions on the packaging.

  b. Discard the valve cover gasket. Clean the valve cover gasket groove with soap and water or a suitable solvent.

To install:

➡️ If the valve cover is not secured within 4 minutes, the sealant must be removed and the sealing area cleaned with silicone gasket remover and metal surface prep. Follow the directions on the packaging. Allow to dry until there is no sign of wetness, or 4 minutes, whichever is longer. Failure to follow this procedure may cause future oil leakage.

8. Apply a bead of silicone gasket and sealant in 2 places where the engine front cover meets the cylinder head.

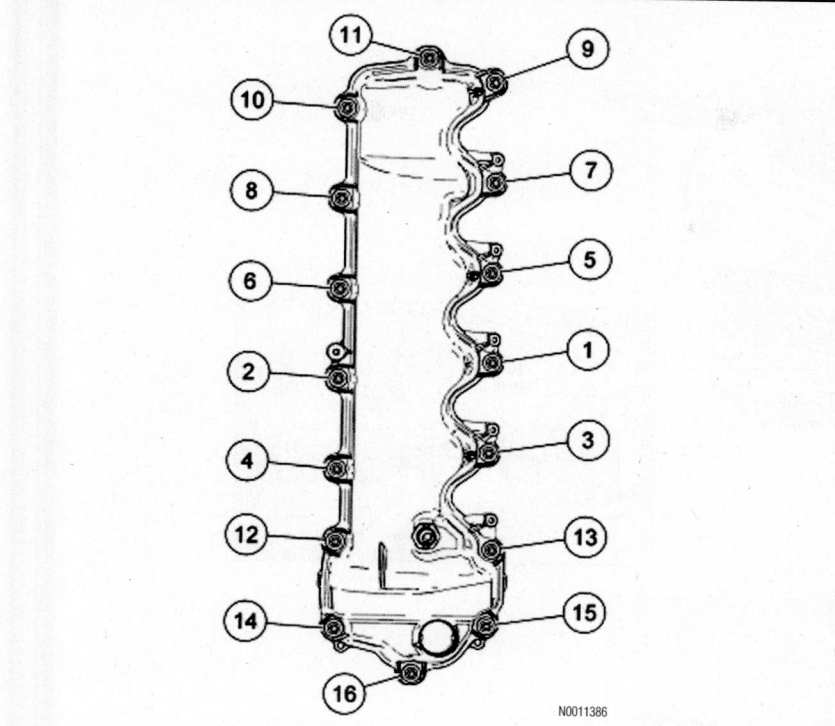

Fig. 413 Position the RH valve cover and new gasket on the cylinder head and tighten the 16 fasteners in the sequence shown

9. Position the RH valve cover and new gasket on the cylinder head and tighten the 16 fasteners in the sequence shown. Tighten to 89 inch lbs. (10 Nm).

10. Connect the wiring harness retainers to the valve cover.

11. Connect the CMP sensor electrical connector.

12. Connect the 2 PCM electrical connectors and the wiring harness retainers to the support bracket.

13. Position the crankcase vent tube and connect the quick connect couplings.

14. Position the transmission filler tube and install the bolt. Tighten to 89 inch lbs. (10 Nm).

15. Install the RH ignition coils.

VALVE LASH

ADJUSTMENT

All engines are equipped with hydraulic lash adjusters. No adjustment is necessary or possible.

ENGINE PERFORMANCE & EMISSION CONTROLS

CAMSHAFT POSITION (CMP) SENSOR

LOCATION

See Figures 414 through 418.

Refer to the accompanying illustrations.

REMOVAL & INSTALLATION

6.4L Diesel Engine

1. With the vehicle in NEUTRAL, position it on a hoist.

❊❊ WARNING

Make sure the ignition switch is in the OFF position prior to working on the electronic engine controls or the vehicle can be damaged.

2. Turn the ignition switch to the OFF position.

➡The Camshaft Position (CMP) sensor is located on the driver side of the engine.

3. Disconnect the CMP sensor electrical connector.

4. Remove the bolt, the CMP sensor and discard the O-ring seals.

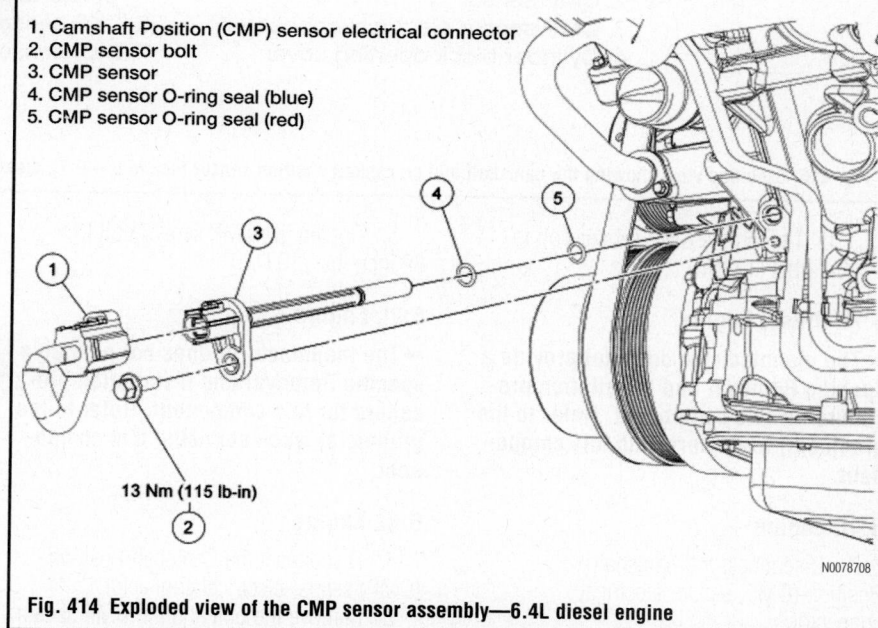

1. Camshaft Position (CMP) sensor electrical connector
2. CMP sensor bolt
3. CMP sensor
4. CMP sensor O-ring seal (blue)
5. CMP sensor O-ring seal (red)

13 Nm (115 lb-in)

Fig. 414 Exploded view of the CMP sensor assembly—6.4L diesel engine

➡Make sure the blue O-ring seal is installed first and seated near the flange. The red O-ring seal is installed second and is seated near the metal tip.

➡Apply clean engine oil to the new O-ring seals prior to installation.

5. To install, reverse the removal procedure.

a. Install new O-ring seals.

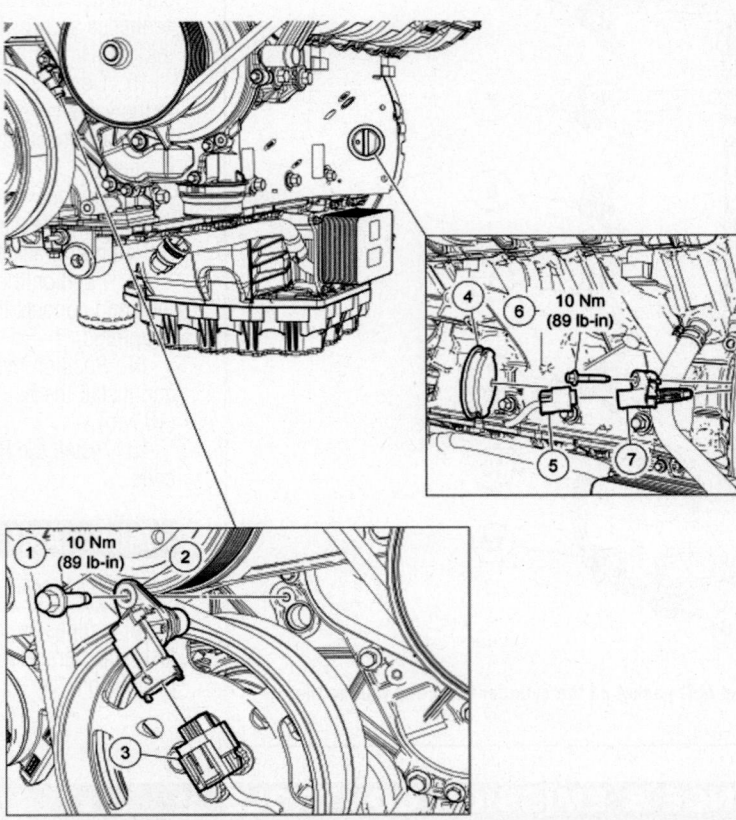

1. Camshaft Position (CMP) sensor bolt
2. CMP sensor
3. CMP sensor electrical connector
4. Cylinder block opening cover
5. Crankshaft Position (CKP) sensor electrical connector
6. CKP sensor bolt
7. CKP sensor

N0113134

Fig. 415 Exploded view showing the camshaft and crankshaft position sensor locations—6.7L diesel engine

b. Tighten the CMP sensor bolt to 10 ft. lbs. (13 Nm).

6.7L Diesel Engine

→The manufacturer does not provide a specific Removal and Installation procedure for this component. Refer to the graphic(s) when servicing this component.

5.4L Engine

1. Disconnect the Camshaft Position (CMP) sensor electrical connector.
2. Remove the bolt and the CMP sensor.
3. Lubricate the O-ring seal with clean engine oil prior to installation.
4. To install, reverse the removal procedure.

5. Tighten the CMP sensor bolt to 89 inch lbs. (10 Nm).

6.2L Engine

→The manufacturer does not provide a specific Removal and Installation procedure for this component. Refer to the graphic(s) when servicing this component.

6.8L Engine

1. Disconnect the Camshaft Position (CMP) sensor electrical connector.
2. Remove the bolt and the CMP sensor.
3. Lubricate the O-ring seal with clean engine oil prior to installation.
4. To install, reverse the removal procedure.
5. Tighten the CMP sensor bolt to 89 inch lbs. (10 Nm).

CRANKSHAFT POSITION (CKP) SENSOR

LOCATION

See Figures 419 through 422.

Refer to the accompanying illustrations.

REMOVAL & INSTALLATION

6.4L Diesel Engine

1. With the vehicle in NEUTRAL, position it on a hoist.

❊❊ WARNING

Make sure the ignition switch is in the OFF position prior to working on the electronic engine controls or the vehicle can be damaged.

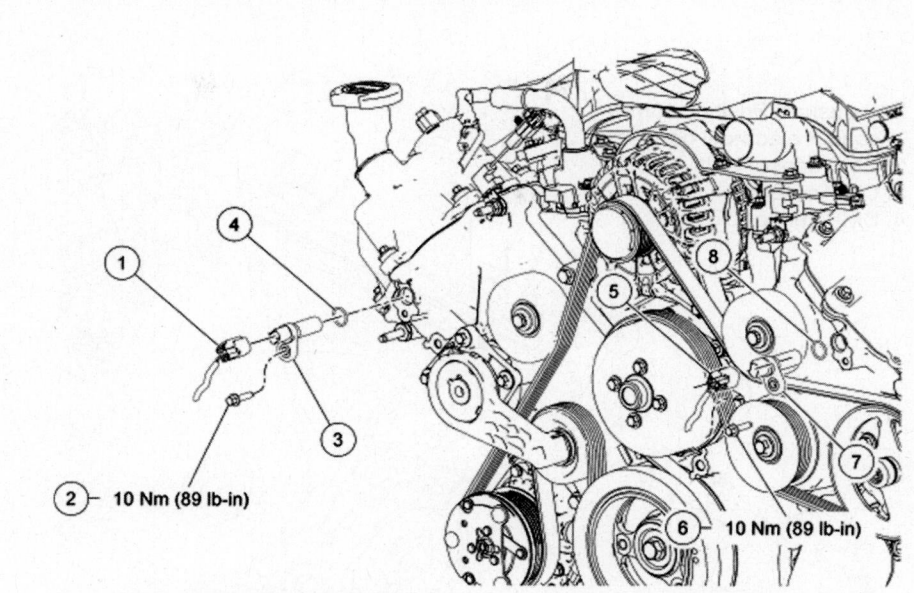

1. RH Camshaft Position (CMP) sensor
   electrical connector
2. RH CMP sensor bolt
3. RH CMP sensor
4. RH CMP sensor O-ring seal

5. LH CMP sensor electrical connector
6. LH CMP sensor bolt
7. LH CMP sensor
8. LH CMP sensor O-ring seal

N0004348

Fig. 416 Exploded view of the CMP sensor assembly—5.4L engine

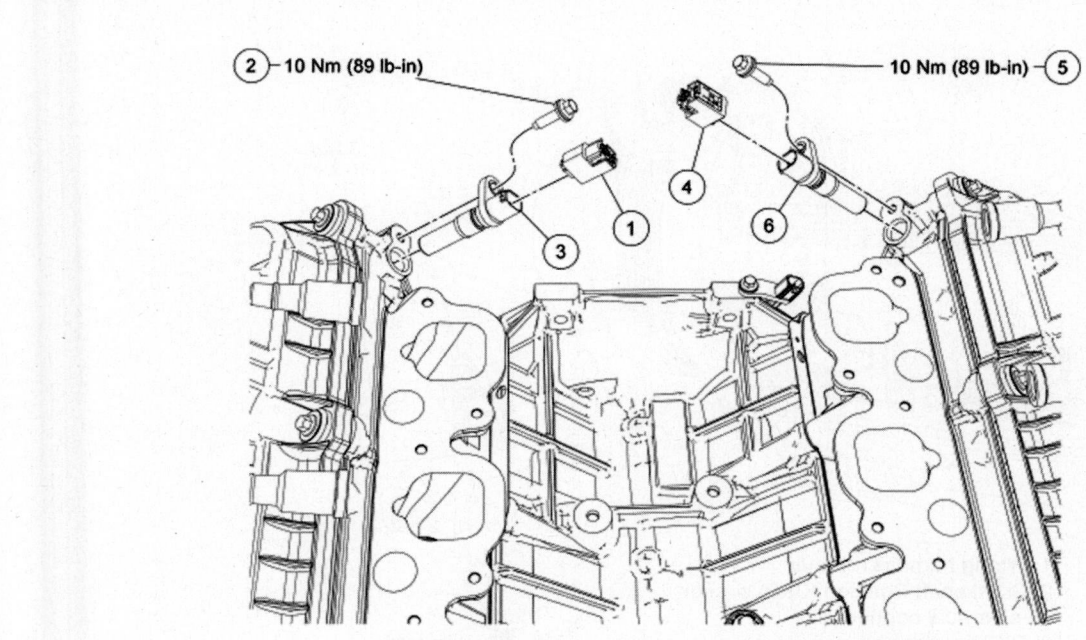

1. RH Camshaft Position (CMP) sensor
   electrical connector
2. RH CMP sensor bolt
3. RH CMP sensor

4. LH CMP sensor electrical
   connector
5. LH CMP sensor bolt
6. LH CMP sensor

N0110678

Fig. 417 Exploded view of the CMP sensor locations—6.2L engine

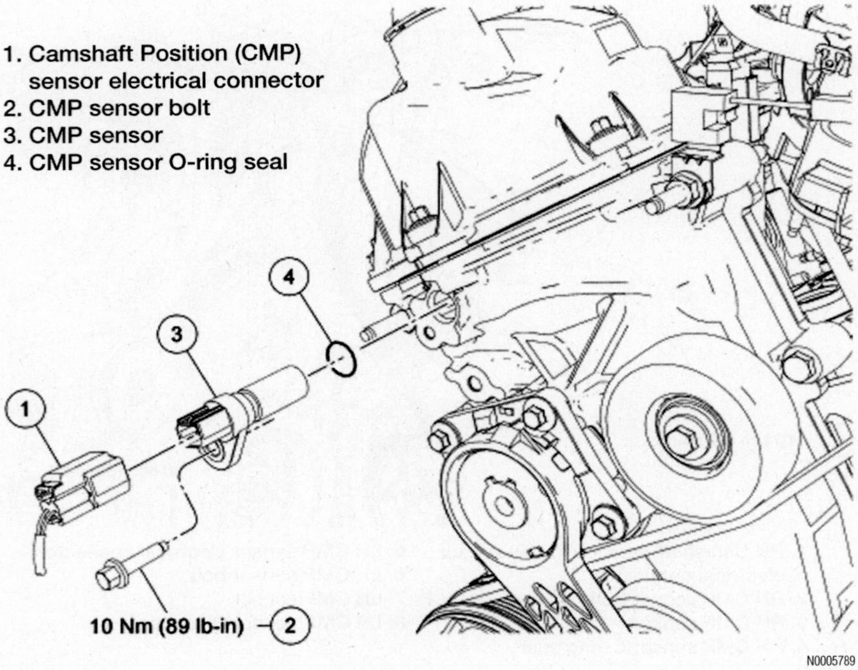

1. Camshaft Position (CMP) sensor electrical connector
2. CMP sensor bolt
3. CMP sensor
4. CMP sensor O-ring seal

10 Nm (89 lb-in)

N0005789

Fig. 418 Exploded view of the CMP sensor assembly—6.8L engine

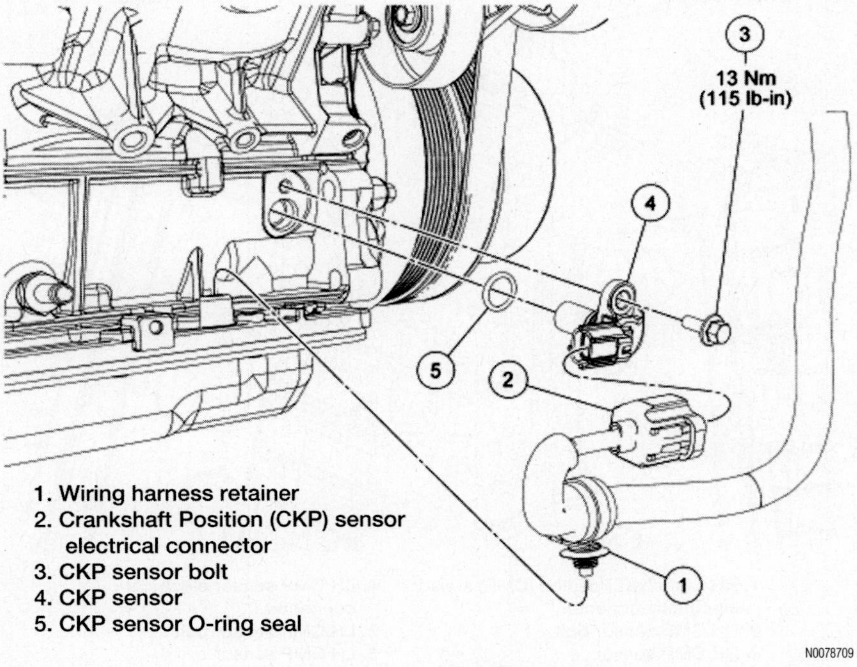

3
13 Nm (115 lb-in)

1. Wiring harness retainer
2. Crankshaft Position (CKP) sensor electrical connector
3. CKP sensor bolt
4. CKP sensor
5. CKP sensor O-ring seal

N0078709

Fig. 419 Exploded view of the CKP sensor assembly—6.4L diesel engine

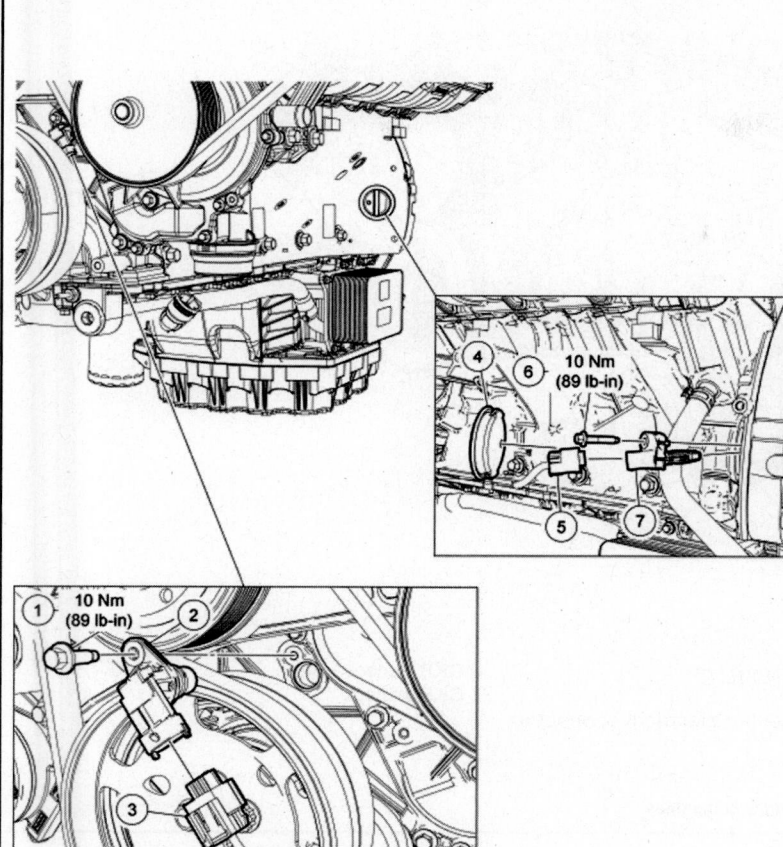

1. Camshaft Position (CMP) sensor bolt
2. CMP sensor
3. CMP sensor electrical connector
4. Cylinder block opening cover
5. Crankshaft Position (CKP) sensor electrical connector
6. CKP sensor bolt
7. CKP sensor

N0113134

Fig. 420 Exploded view showing the camshaft and crankshaft position sensor locations—6.7L diesel engine

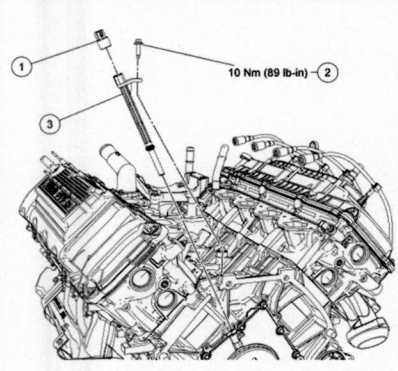

N0110679

Fig. 421 Crankshaft Position (CKP) sensor (3), CKP sensor bolt (2), and CKP sensor electrical connector (1)—6.2L engine

2. Turn the ignition switch to the OFF position.

3. Remove the bolt and position the battery ground cable aside.

4. If equipped, remove the bolt and flagnut, and position the steering linkage damper aside.

5. Detach the wiring harness retainer.

6. Disconnect the Crankshaft Position (CKP) sensor electrical connector.

7. Remove the bolt, the CKP sensor and discard the O-ring seal.

To install:

8. To install, reverse the removal procedure.

➡Apply clean engine oil to the O-ring seal prior to installation.

a. Install a new O-ring seal.

b. Tighten the CKP sensor bolt to 10 ft. lbs. (13 Nm).

c. Tighten the steering linkage bolt and flagnut to 76 ft. lbs. (103 Nm).

9. Tighten the battery ground cable bolt to 35 ft. lbs. (47 Nm).

6.7L Diesel Engine

➡The manufacturer does not provide a specific Removal and Installation procedure for this component. Refer to the graphic(s) when servicing this component.

6.2L Engine

➡The manufacturer does not provide a specific Removal and Installation procedure for this component. Refer to the graphic(s) when servicing this component.

5.4L & 6.8L Engines

1. With the vehicle in NEUTRAL, position it on a hoist.

2. Remove the accessory drive belt.

3. Remove the 3 bolts and position the A/C compressor aside.

4. Disconnect the Crankshaft Position (CKP) sensor electrical connector.

5. Remove the bolt and the CKP sensor.

To install:

6. To install, reverse the removal procedure.

a. Lubricate the O-ring seal with clean engine oil prior to installation.

b. Tighten the CKP sensor bolt to 89 inch lbs. (10 Nm).

c. Tighten the A/C compressor bolts to 18 ft. lbs. (25 Nm).

ENGINE COOLANT TEMPERATURE (ECT) SENSOR

LOCATION

See Figures 423 through 425.

Refer to the accompanying illustrations.

REMOVAL & INSTALLATION

6.4L Diesel Engine

✳✳ WARNING

Make sure the ignition switch is in the OFF position prior to working on the electronic engine controls or the vehicle may be damaged.

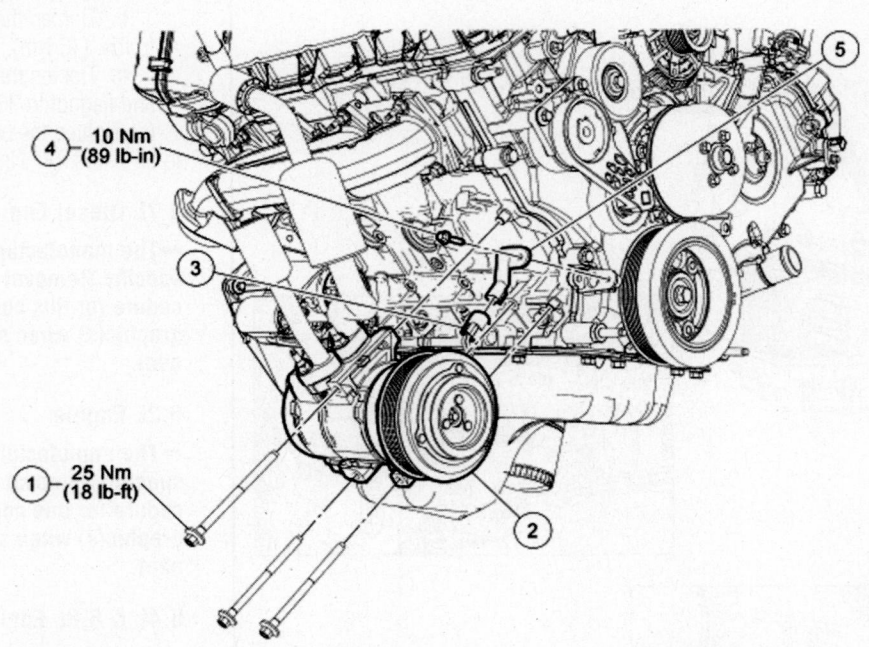

4. 10 Nm (89 lb-in)

1. 25 Nm (18 lb-ft)

1. A/C compressor bolt (3 required)
2. A/C compressor
3. Crankshaft Position (CKP) sensor electrical connector
4. CKP sensor bolt
5. CKP sensor

N0065047

Fig. 422 Exploded view of the CKP sensor assembly—5.4L and 6.8L engines

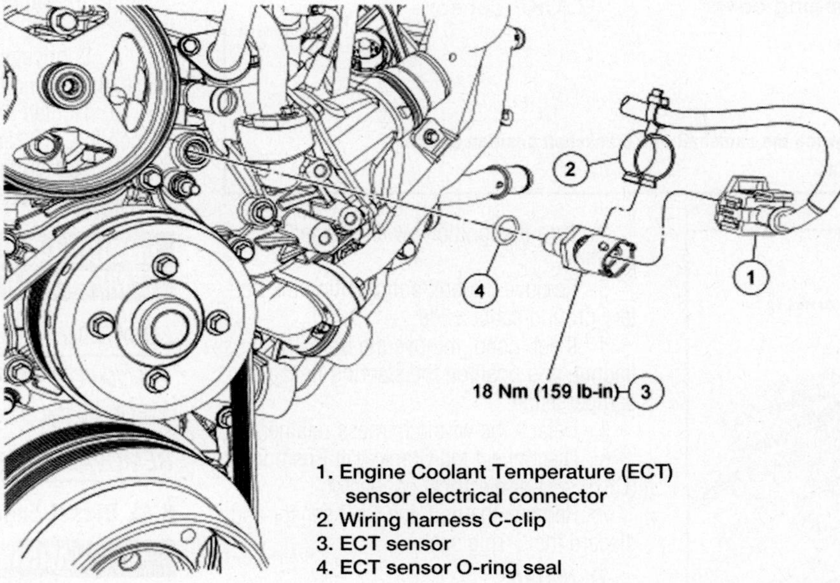

18 Nm (159 lb-in)

1. Engine Coolant Temperature (ECT) sensor electrical connector
2. Wiring harness C-clip
3. ECT sensor
4. ECT sensor O-ring seal

N0078710

Fig. 423 Exploded view of ECT assembly—6.4L diesel engine

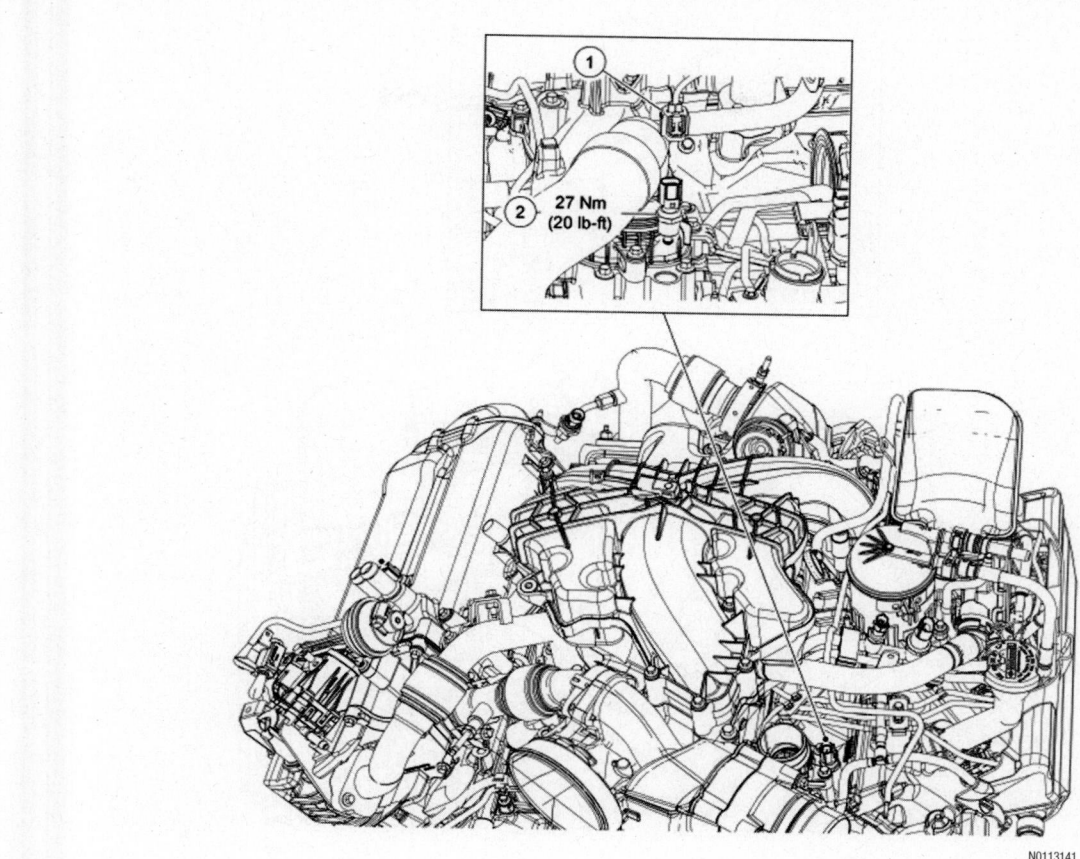

Fig. 424 ECT sensor (primary cooling system) electrical connector (1) and ECT sensor (2)—6.7L diesel engine

1. Turn the ignition switch to the OFF position.
2. Drain the engine cooling system.
3. Remove the engine cooling fan.
4. Detach the wiring harness C-clip from the Engine Coolant Temperature (ECT) sensor.
5. Disconnect the ECT electrical connector.
6. Remove the ECT sensor and discard the O-ring seal.

To install:

➡Apply clean engine oil to the new O-ring seal prior to installation.

7. Using a new O-ring seal, install the ECT sensor. Tighten to 13 ft. lbs. (18 Nm).
8. Connect the ECT sensor electrical connector.

✳✳ WARNING

Make sure the C-clip is correctly installed or the wiring harness can be damaged by the accessory drive belt.

9. Attach the wiring harness C-clip to the ECT sensor.
10. Fill and bleed the engine cooling system.
11. Install the engine cooling fan.

6.7L Diesel Engine

Primary Cooling System

✳✳ WARNING

Make sure the ignition switch is in the OFF position prior to working on the electronic engine controls or the vehicle may be damaged.

1. Turn the ignition switch to the OFF position.
2. Drain the engine primary cooling system.
3. Disconnect the Engine Coolant Temperature (ECT) electrical connector.

4. Remove the ECT sensor.

To install:

5. Install the ECT sensor. Tighten to 20 ft. lbs. (27 Nm).
6. Connect the ECT sensor electrical connector.
7. Fill and bleed the engine primary cooling system.

Secondary Cooling System

✳✳ WARNING

Make sure the ignition switch is in the OFF position prior to working on the electronic engine controls or the vehicle may be damaged.

1. Turn the ignition switch to the OFF position.
2. Drain the powertrain secondary cooling system.
3. Disconnect the Engine Coolant Temperature (ECT) 2 electrical connector.

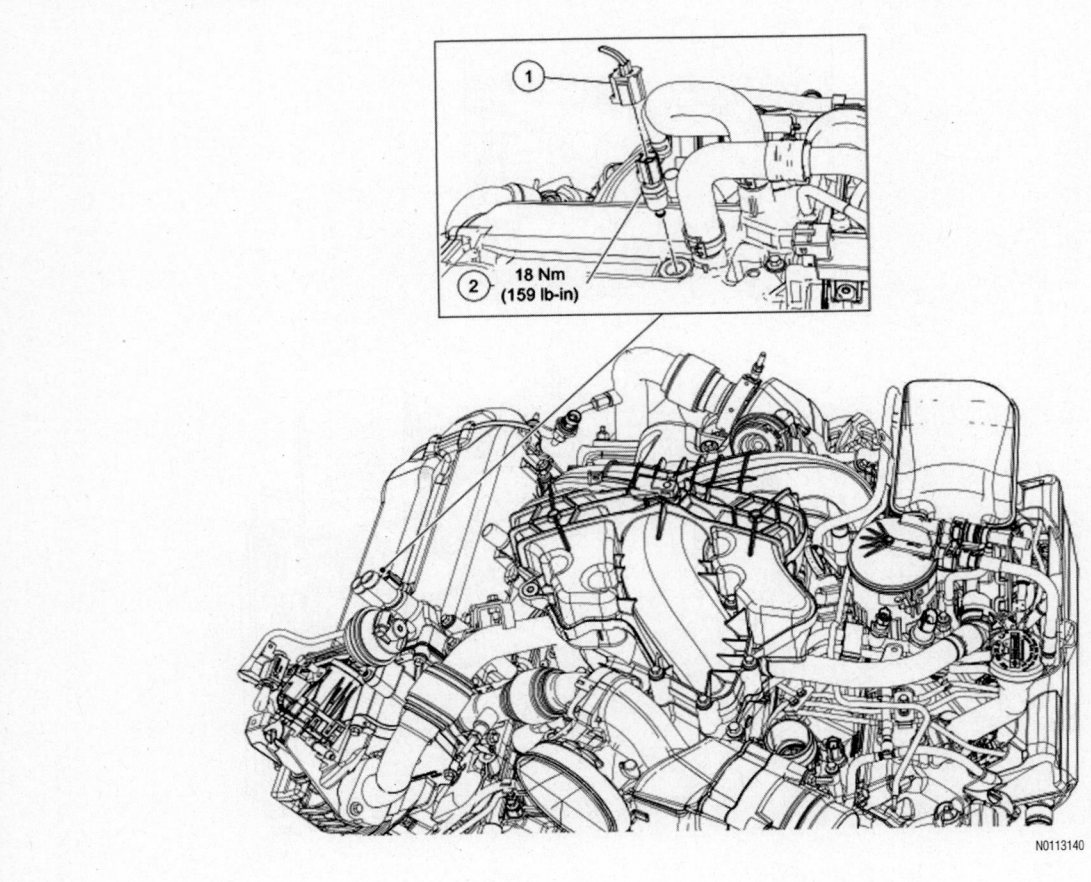

Fig. 425 ECT 2 sensor (secondary cooling system) electrical connector (1) and ECT sensor (2)—6.7L diesel engine

4. Remove the ECT 2 sensor.

To install:

5. Install the ECT 2 sensor. Tighten to 13 ft. lbs. (18 Nm).

6. Connect the ECT 2 sensor electrical connector.

7. Fill and bleed the powertrain secondary cooling system.

HEATED OXYGEN SENSOR (HO2S)

LOCATION

See Figures 426 and 427.

Refer to the accompanying illustrations.

REMOVAL & INSTALLATION

5.4L & 6.8L Engines

1. With the vehicle in NEUTRAL, position it on a hoist.

2. Disconnect the Heated Oxygen Sensor (HO2S) electrical connector.

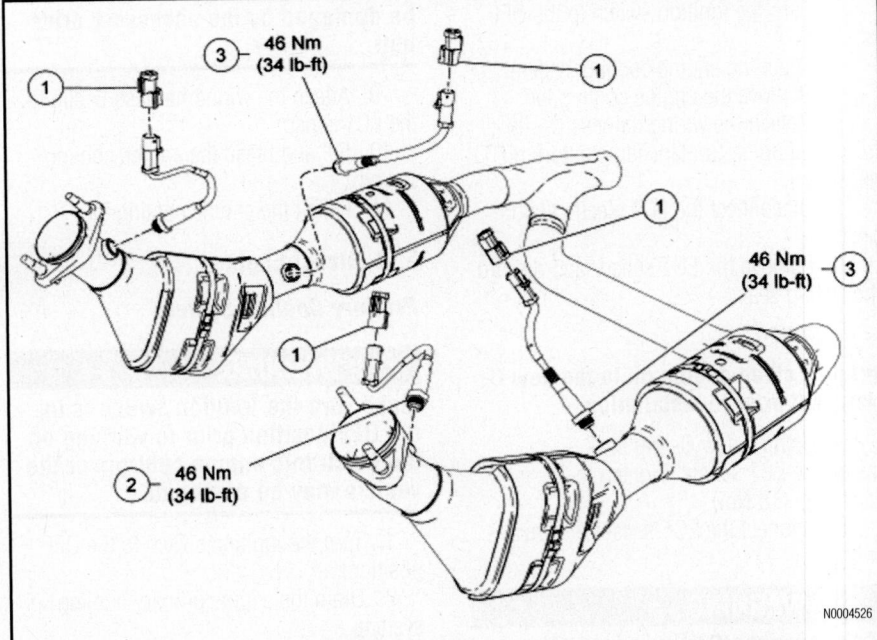

Fig. 426 Exploded view of Heated Oxygen Sensor (HO2S) and Catalyst Monitor Sensor (CMS) electrical connectors (1), HO2S (2) and CMS (3)—5.4L engine shown, 6.8L similar

3. Using the Exhaust Gas Oxygen Sensor Socket, remove the HO2S.

4. Apply penetrating lubricant to the HO2S to assist in removal.

To install:

5. Install the HO2S.

a. Apply a light coat of high temperature nickel anti-seize lubricant to the HO2S threads prior to installation.

b. Using the Exhaust Gas Oxygen Sensor Socket, tighten to 34 ft. lbs. (46 Nm).

6. Connect the HO2S electrical connector.

6.2L Engine

➡The manufacturer does not provide a specific Removal and Installation procedure for this component. Refer to the graphic(s) when servicing this component.

INTAKE AIR TEMPERATURE SENSOR 2 (IAT2)

LOCATION

6.4L Diesel Engine

See Figure 428.

Refer to the accompanying illustration.

REMOVAL & INSTALLATION

6.4L Diesel Engine

✳✳ WARNING

Make sure the ignition switch is in the OFF position prior to working on the electronic engine control or the vehicle may be damaged.

1. Turn the ignition switch to the OFF position.

2. Disconnect the Intake Air Temperature 2 (IAT2) electrical connector.

3. Remove the IAT2 sensor.

4. To install, reverse the removal procedure.

5. Tighten the IAT2 sensor bolt to 10 ft. lbs. (14 Nm).

KNOCK SENSOR (KS)

LOCATION

See Figures 429 through 431.

Refer to the accompanying illustrations.

REMOVAL & INSTALLATION

5.4L Engine

1. Remove the intake manifold.

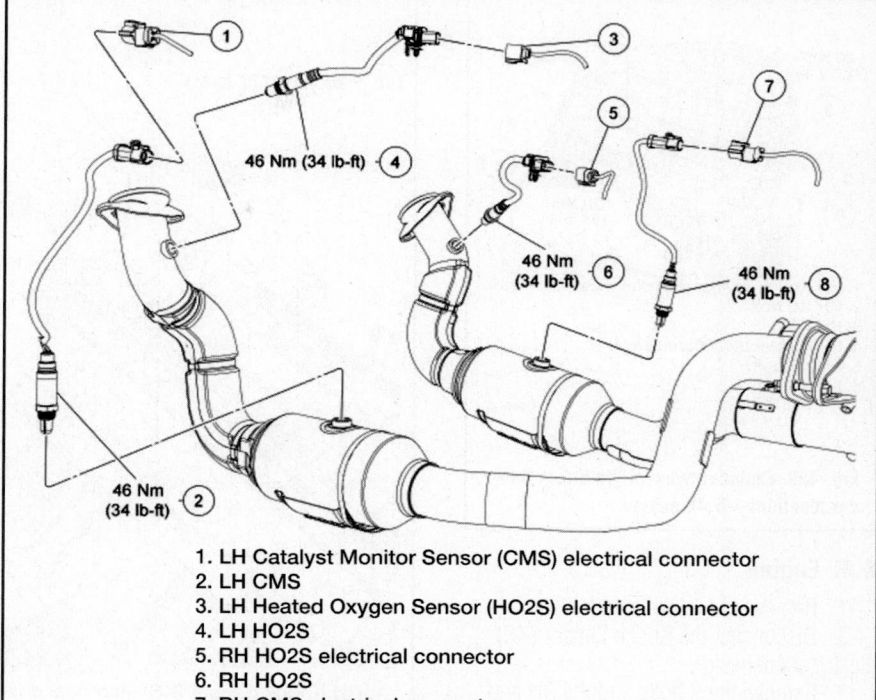

1. LH Catalyst Monitor Sensor (CMS) electrical connector
2. LH CMS
3. LH Heated Oxygen Sensor (HO2S) electrical connector
4. LH HO2S
5. RH HO2S electrical connector
6. RH HO2S
7. RH CMS electrical connector
8. RH CMS

N0113128

Fig. 427 Exploded view of Heated Oxygen Sensor (HO2S) and Catalyst Monitor Sensor (CMS) assemblies—6.2L engine

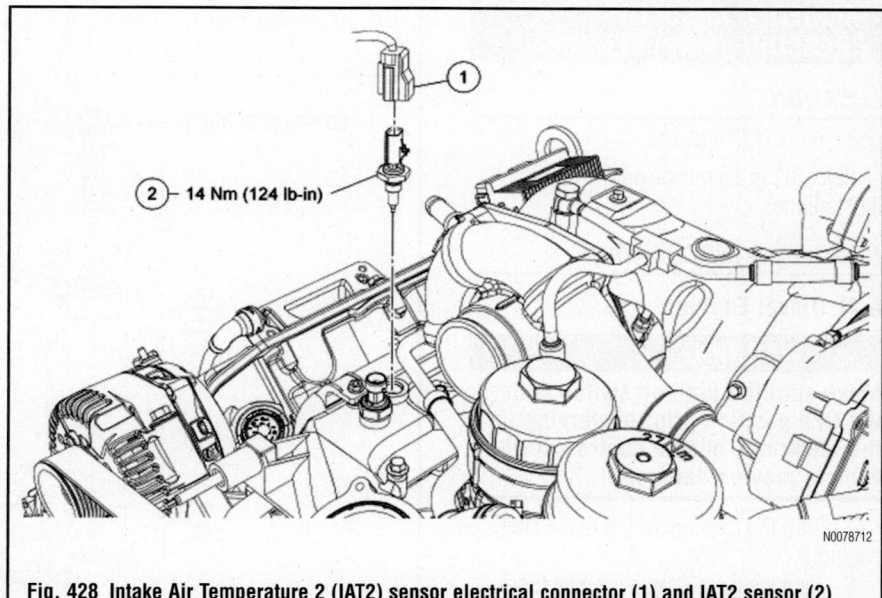

N0078712

Fig. 428 Intake Air Temperature 2 (IAT2) sensor electrical connector (1) and IAT2 sensor (2)

2. Disconnect the Knock Sensor (KS) electrical connectors.

3. Remove the 2 bolts and the 2 KS.

4. To install, reverse the removal procedure.

5. Tighten the KS bolts to 15 ft. lbs. (20 Nm).

6.2L Engine

➡The manufacturer does not provide a specific Removal and Installation procedure for this component. Refer to the graphic(s) when servicing this component.

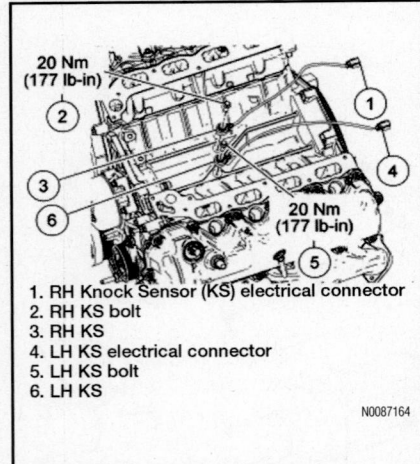

1. RH Knock Sensor (KS) electrical connector
2. RH KS bolt
3. RH KS
4. LH KS electrical connector
5. LH KS bolt
6. LH KS

N0087164

Fig. 429 Exploded view of the Knock Sensor locations—5.4L engine

6.8L Engine

1. Remove the intake manifold.
2. Disconnect the Knock Sensor (KS) electrical connector.
3. Remove the 2 bolts and the RH and LH KS .
4. To install, reverse the removal procedure.
5. Tighten the KS bolts to 15 ft. lbs. (20 Nm).

MANIFOLD ABSOLUTE PRESSURE (MAP) SENSOR

LOCATION

See Figures 432 and 433.

Refer to the accompanying illustrations.

REMOVAL & INSTALLATION

6.4L Diesel Engine

> ⁑ **WARNING**
>
> **Make sure the ignition switch is in the OFF position prior to working on the electronic engine controls or the vehicle may be damaged.**

1. Turn the ignition switch to the OFF position.
2. Remove the air cleaner outlet tube.
3. Disconnect the Manifold Absolute Pressure (MAP) sensor electrical connector.
4. Remove the MAP sensor.
5. To install, reverse the removal procedure.
6. Tighten the MAP sensor bolt to 106 inch lbs. (12 Nm).

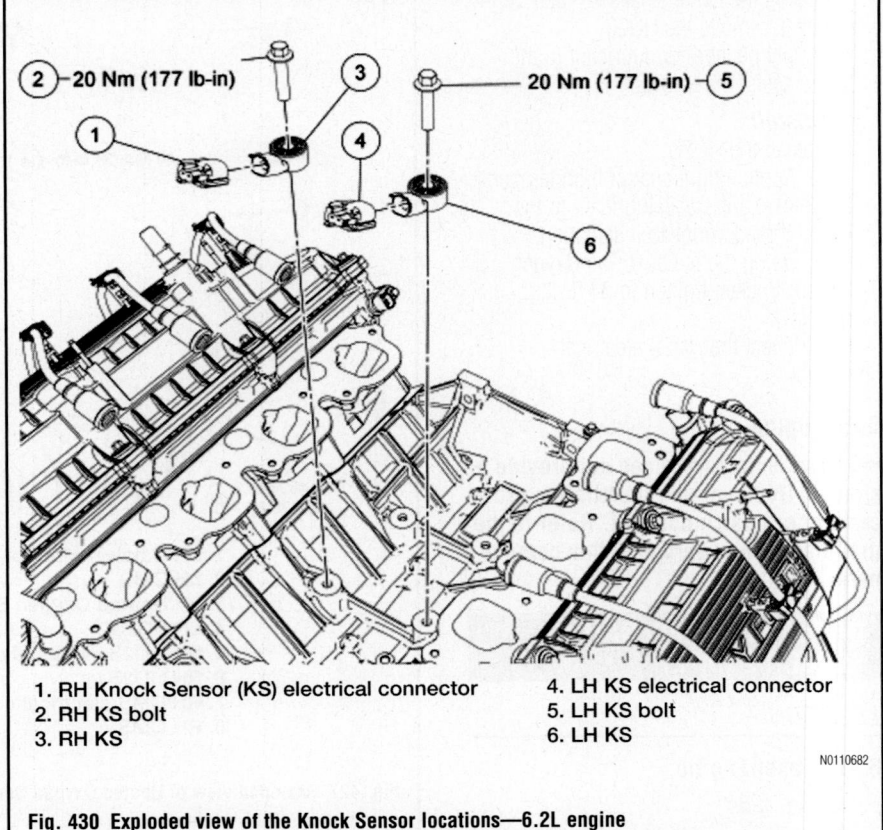

1. RH Knock Sensor (KS) electrical connector
2. RH KS bolt
3. RH KS
4. LH KS electrical connector
5. LH KS bolt
6. LH KS

N0110682

Fig. 430 Exploded view of the Knock Sensor locations—6.2L engine

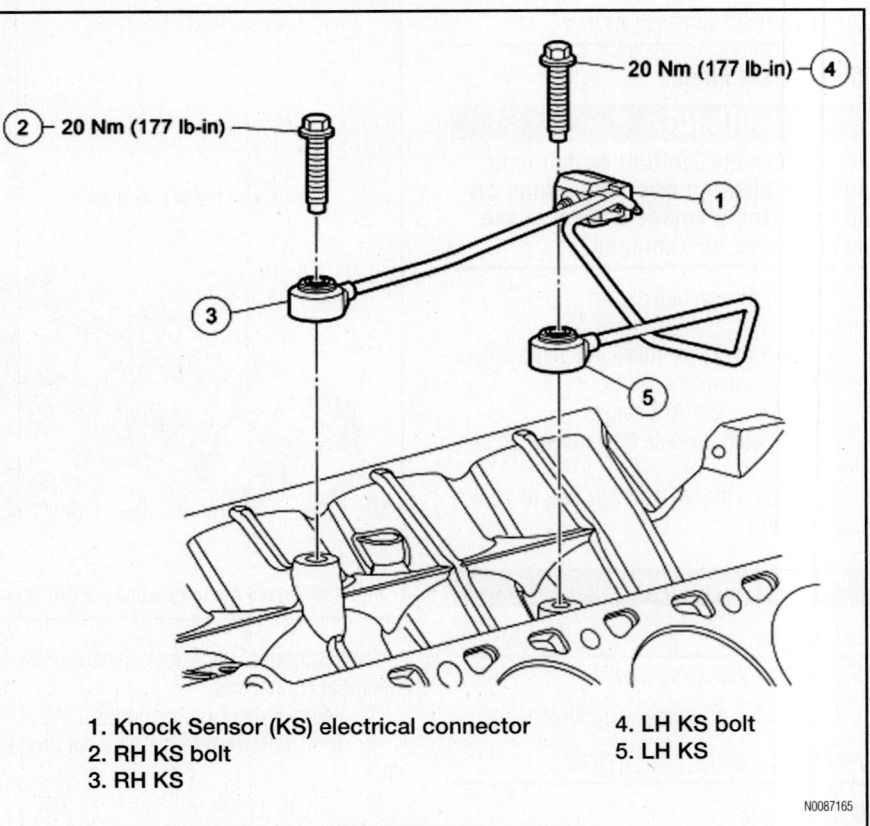

1. Knock Sensor (KS) electrical connector
2. RH KS bolt
3. RH KS
4. LH KS bolt
5. LH KS

N0087165

Fig. 431 Exploded view of the Knock Sensor locations—6.8L engine

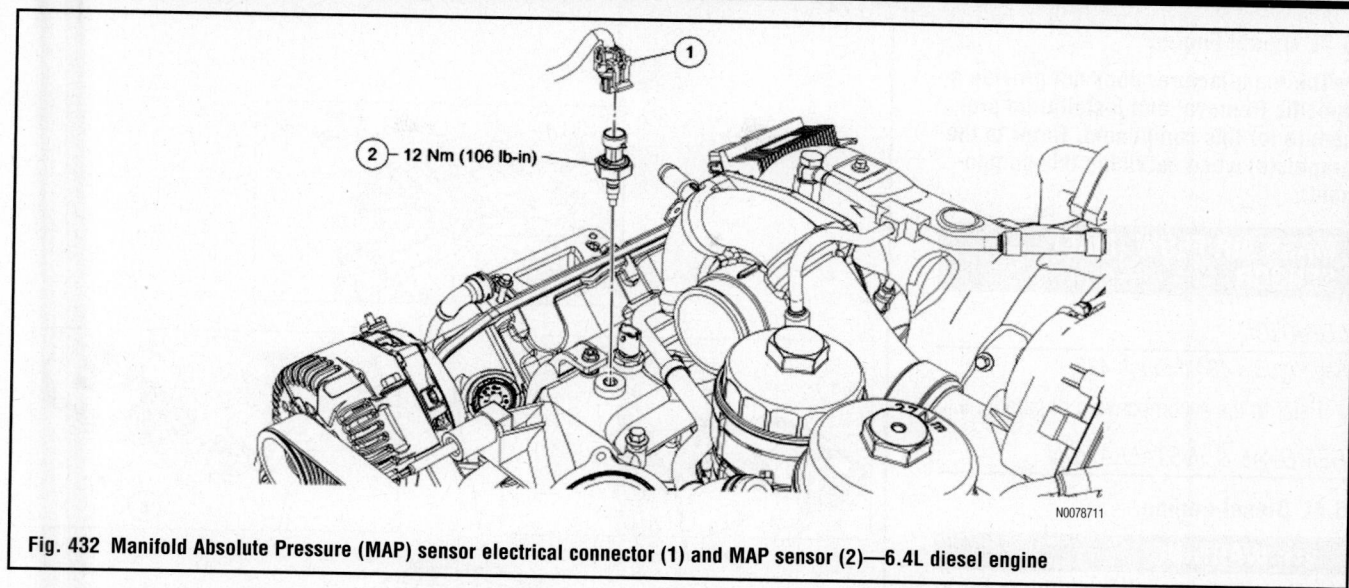

Fig. 432 Manifold Absolute Pressure (MAP) sensor electrical connector (1) and MAP sensor (2)—6.4L diesel engine

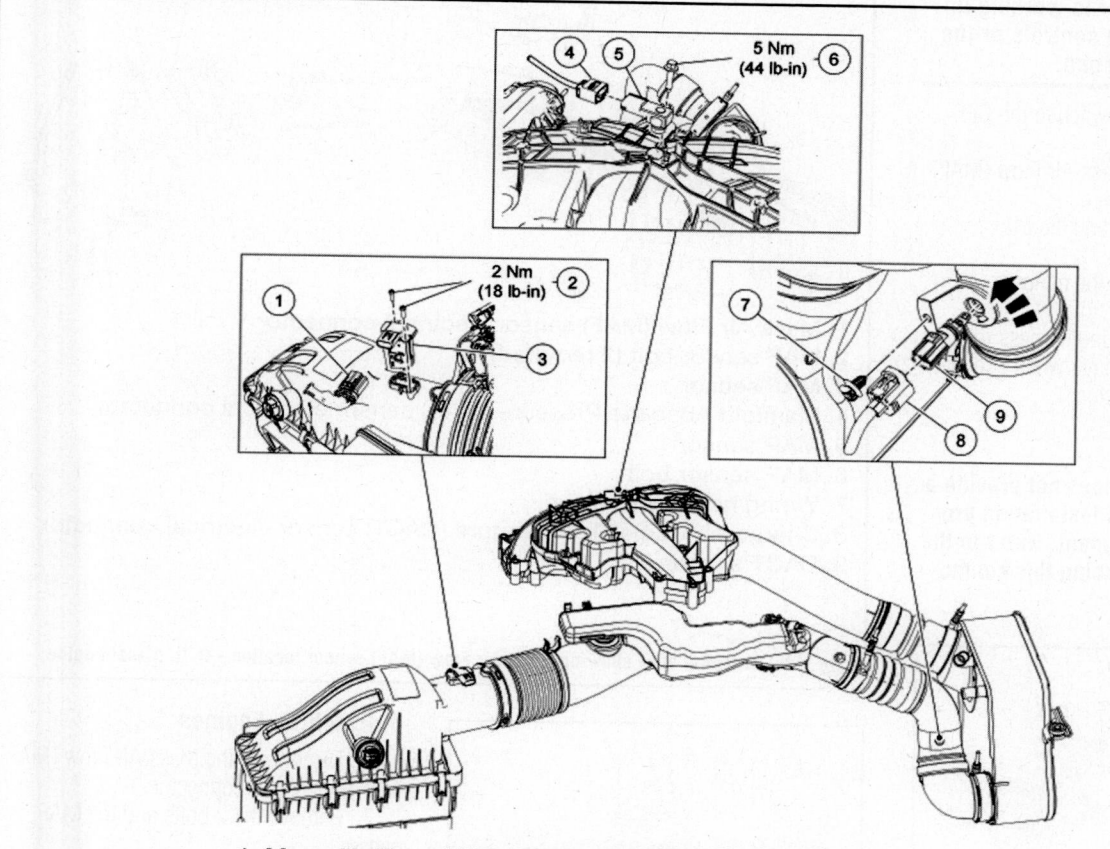

1. Mass Air Flow (MAF) sensor electrical connector
2. MAF sensor bolt (2 required)
3. MAF sensor
4. Manifold Absolute Pressure (MAP) sensor electrical connector
5. MAP sensor
6. MAP sensor bolt
7. Wiring harness retainer
8. Charge Air Cooler Temperature (CACT) sensor electrical connector
9. CACT sensor

Fig. 433 Exploded view showing Manifold Absolute Pressure (MAP) sensor location—6.7L diesel engine

6.7L Diesel Engine

➡The manufacturer does not provide a specific Removal and Installation procedure for this component. Refer to the graphic(s) when servicing this component.

MASS AIR FLOW (MAF) SENSOR

LOCATION

See Figures 434 through 436.

Refer to the accompanying illustrations.

REMOVAL & INSTALLATION

6.4L Diesel Engine

> ❋❋ **WARNING**

Make sure the ignition switch is in the OFF position prior to working on the electronic engine controls or the vehicle may be damaged.

1. Turn the ignition switch to the OFF position.
2. Disconnect the Mass Air Flow (MAF) sensor electrical connector.
3. Remove the bolts and the MAF sensor.
4. To install, reverse the removal procedure.
5. Make sure the wiring harness retainer is attached to the air cleaner when connecting the electrical connector.

6.7L Diesel Engine

➡The manufacturer does not provide a specific Removal and Installation procedure for this component. Refer to the graphic(s) when servicing this component.

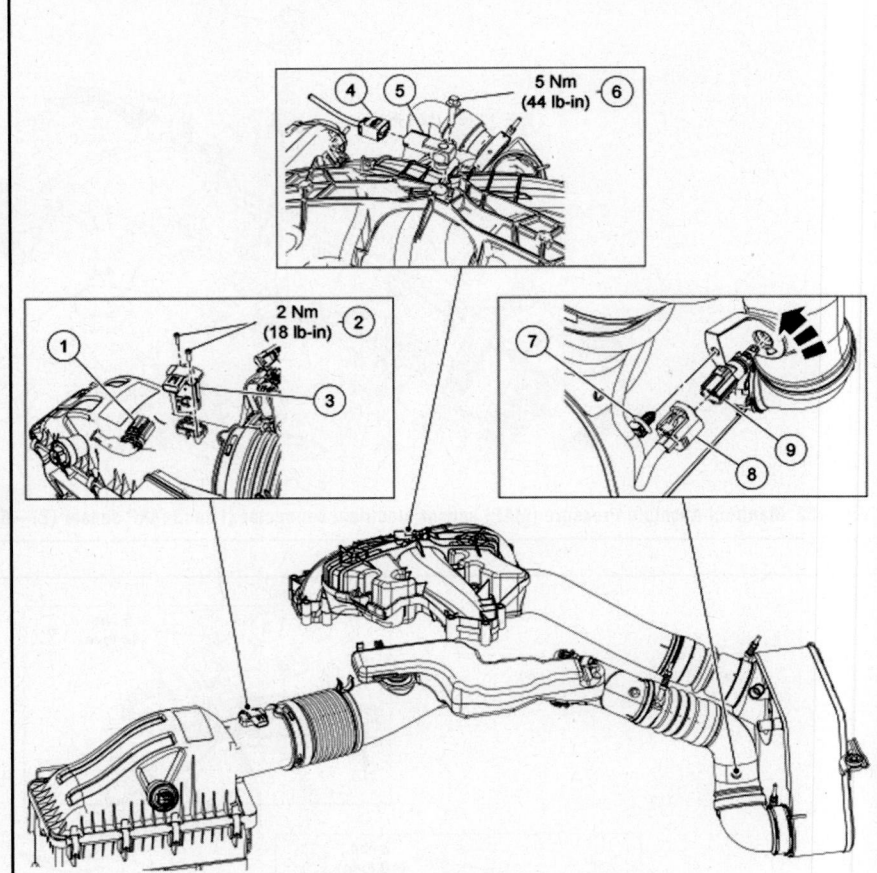

1. Mass Air Flow (MAF) sensor electrical connector
2. MAF sensor bolt (2 required)
3. MAF sensor
4. Manifold Absolute Pressure (MAP) sensor electrical connector
5. MAP sensor
6. MAP sensor bolt
7. Wiring harness retainer
8. Charge Air Cooler Temperature (CACT) sensor electrical connector
9. CACT sensor

N0113137

Fig. 435 Exploded view showing Mass Air Flow (MAF) sensor location—6.7L diesel engine

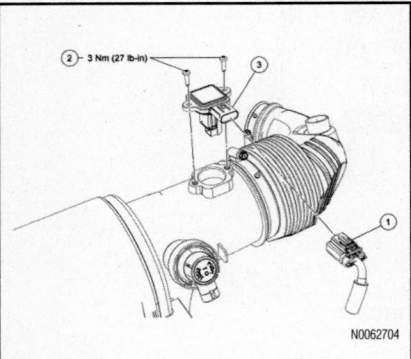

N0062704

Fig. 434 Mass Air Flow (MAF) sensor electrical connector (1), MAF sensor bolts (2) and MAF sensor (3)—6.4L diesel engine

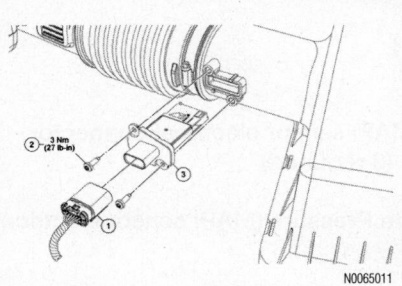

N0065011

Fig. 436 Mass Air Flow (MAF) sensor electrical connector (1), MAF sensor bolts (2) and MAF sensor (3)—5.4L and 6.8L engines

5.4L & 6.8L Engines

1. Disconnect the Mass Air Flow (MAF) sensor electrical connector.
2. Remove the 2 bolts and the MAF sensor.
3. To install, reverse the removal procedure.

POWERTRAIN CONTROL MODULE (PCM)

LOCATION

See Figures 437 through 439.

Refer to the accompanying illustrations.

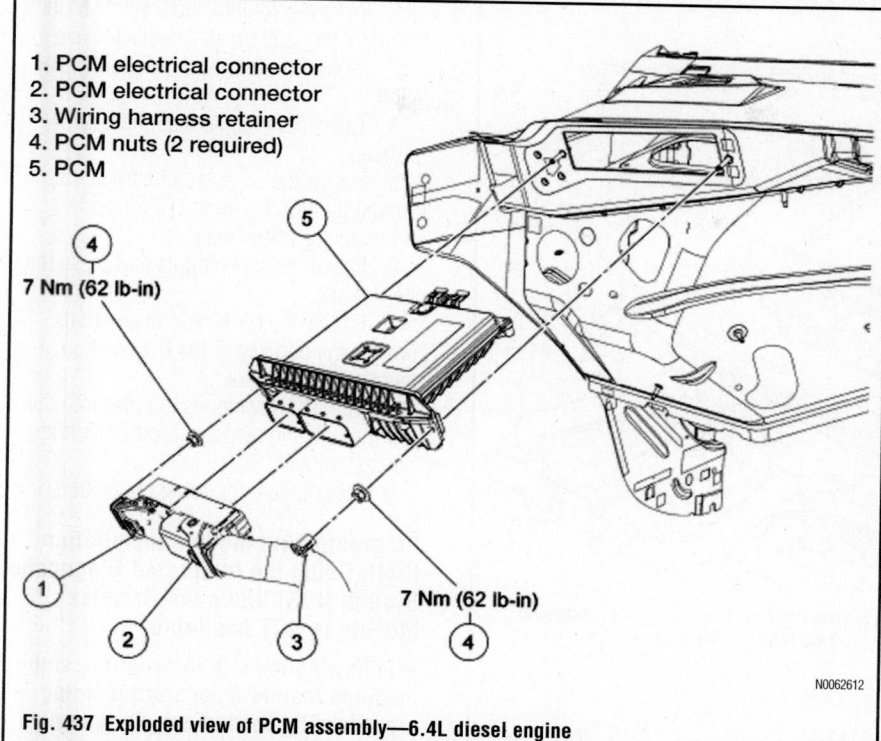

1. PCM electrical connector
2. PCM electrical connector
3. Wiring harness retainer
4. PCM nuts (2 required)
5. PCM

7 Nm (62 lb-in)

7 Nm (62 lb-in)

N0062612

Fig. 437 Exploded view of PCM assembly—6.4L diesel engine

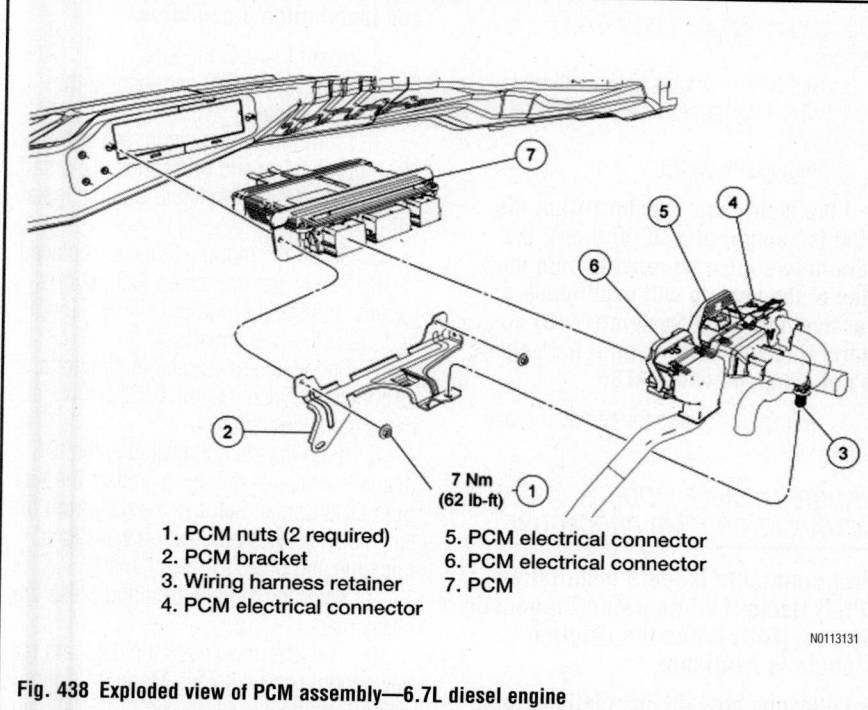

1. PCM nuts (2 required)
2. PCM bracket
3. Wiring harness retainer
4. PCM electrical connector
5. PCM electrical connector
6. PCM electrical connector
7. PCM

7 Nm (62 lb-ft)

N0113131

Fig. 438 Exploded view of PCM assembly—6.7L diesel engine

REMOVAL & INSTALLATION

6.4L Diesel Engine

✳✳ WARNING

Make sure the ignition switch is in the OFF position prior to working on the electronic engine controls or the vehicle may be damaged.

1. Turn the ignition switch to the OFF position.
2. Retrieve the module configuration. Carry out the module configuration retrieval steps of the Programmable Module Installation (PMI) procedure.
3. Remove the air cleaner element.
4. Remove the transmission fluid level indicator.
5. Disconnect the PCM electrical connectors.
6. Detach the wiring harness retainer.
7. Remove the 2 nuts and the PCM.

To install:

8. Position the PCM and install the 2 nuts
9. Attach the wiring harness retainer.
10. Connect the PCM electrical connectors. Make sure the wiring harness connector is attached.
11. Install the transmission fluid level indicator.
12. Install the air cleaner element.
13. Restore the module configuration. Carry out the module configuration restore steps of the Programmable Module Installation (PMI) procedure.

➡ **If the Instrument Cluster (IC) or the PCM (or both) is being replaced, the parameters must be reset in both modules or the vehicle will experience a Passive Anti-Theft System (PATS) no start. This will occur even if the vehicle is not equipped with PATS .**

14. Carry out the PATS Parameter Reset.
15. For vehicles with Circuit Deactivation Ignition Module (CDIM), carry out the extended idle shut down initialization procedure.

6.7L Diesel Engine

✳✳ WARNING

Make sure the ignition switch is in the OFF position prior to working on the electronic engine controls or the vehicle may be damaged.

1. Turn the ignition switch to the OFF position.
2. Retrieve the module configuration. Carry out the module configuration retrieval steps of the Programmable Module Installation (PMI) procedure.
3. Detach the wiring harness retainer.
4. Disconnect the PCM electrical connectors.
5. Remove the 2 nuts and the PCM bracket.
6. Remove the PCM.

To install:

7. Position the PCM and bracket.
8. Connect the PCM electrical connectors.

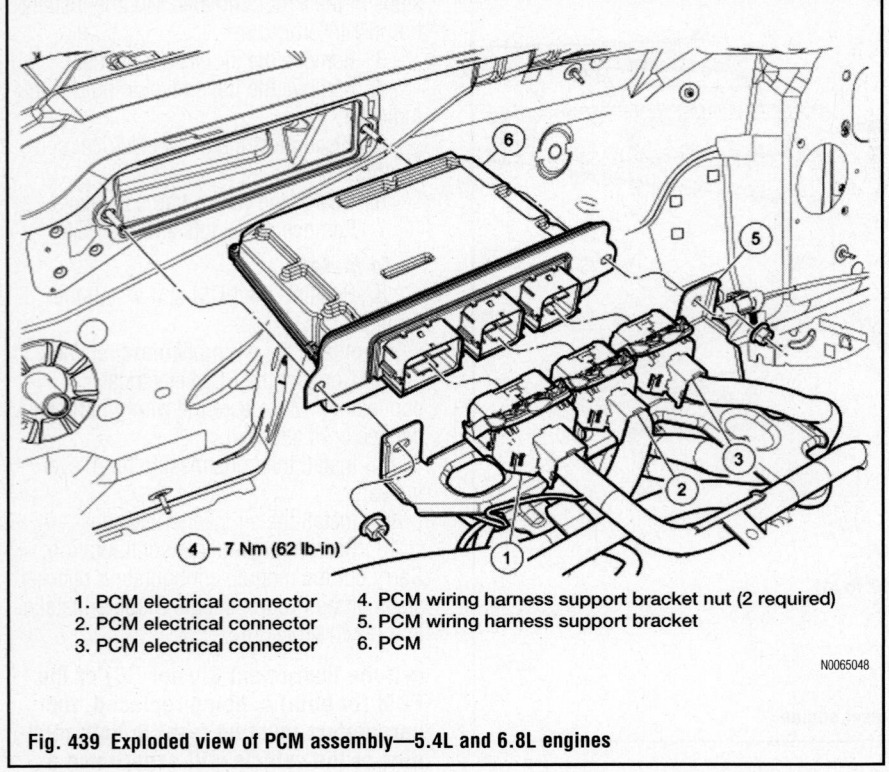

1. PCM electrical connector
2. PCM electrical connector
3. PCM electrical connector
4. PCM wiring harness support bracket nut (2 required)
5. PCM wiring harness support bracket
6. PCM

N0065048

Fig. 439 Exploded view of PCM assembly—5.4L and 6.8L engines

9. Attach the wiring harness retainer.
10. Restore the module configuration. Carry out the module configuration restore steps of the Programmable Module Installation (PMI) procedure.

➡**If the Instrument Cluster (IC) or the PCM (or both) is being replaced, the parameters must be reset in both modules or the vehicle will experience a Passive Anti-Theft System (PATS) no start. This will occur even if the vehicle is not equipped with PATS.**

11. Carry out the PATS Parameter Reset.
12. For vehicles with Circuit Deactivation Ignition Module (CDIM), carry out the extended idle shut down initialization procedure.

5.4L & 6.8L Engines

➡**Refer to the Powertrain Control/ Emissions Diagnosis (PC/ED) manual for correct Vehicle Communication Module (VCM) hook-up procedure.**

1. If servicing the PCM, connect the scan tool to the vehicle. Allow the scan tool to identify the vehicle and obtain configuration data.

➡**All programmable module information will automatically be retrieved by the VCM.**

2. Disconnect the 3 PCM electrical connectors.
3. Remove the 2 nuts and position the PCM wiring harness support bracket aside.
4. Remove the PCM.

➡**If the Instrument Cluster (IC) or the PCM is being replaced (or both), the parameters must be reset in both modules or the vehicle will experience a Passive Anti-Theft System (PATS) no-start. This will occur even if the vehicle is not equipped with PATS.**

5. To install, reverse the removal procedure.

PROGRAMMABLE MODULE INSTALLATION (PMI) PROCEDURE

Programmable Module Installation (PMI) Using the Integrated Diagnostic System (IDS) When the Original Module is Available

➡**Following module installation, some modules require a separate learning procedure be carried out. For adaptive learning and calibration instructions, refer to the specific module removal and installation procedures.**

1. Connect the IDS and identify the vehicle as normal.

2. From the Toolbox icon, select Module Programming and press the check mark.
3. Select Programmable Module Installation.
4. Select the module that is being replaced.
5. Follow the on-screen instructions, turn the ignition key to the OFF position, and press the check mark.
6. Install the new module and press the check mark.
7. Follow the on-screen instructions, turn the ignition key to the ON position, and press the check mark.
8. The IDS downloads the data into the new module and displays Module Configuration Complete.
9. Test module for correct operation.

Programmable Module Installation (PMI) Using the Integrated Diagnostic System (IDS) When the Original Module is NOT Available

➡**Following module installation, some modules require a separate learning procedure be carried out. For adaptive learning and calibration instructions, refer to the specific module removal and installation procedures.**

1. Install the new module.
2. Connect the IDS and identify the vehicle as normal.
3. From the Toolbox icon, select Module Programming and press the check mark.
4. Select Programmable Module Installation.
5. Select the module that was replaced.
6. Follow the on-screen instructions, turn the ignition key to the OFF position, and press the check mark.
7. Follow the on-screen instructions, turn the ignition key to the ON position, and press the check mark.
8. If the data is not available, the IDS displays a screen stating to contact the As-Built Data Center. Retrieve the data from the technician service publication website at this time and press the check mark.
9. Enter the module data and press the check mark.
10. The IDS downloads the data into the new module and displays Module Configuration Complete.
11. Test module for correct operation.

PASSIVE ANTI-THEFT SYSTEM (PATS) PARAMETER RESET

➡**A minimum of 2 Passive Anti-Theft System (PATS) keys must be programmed into the Instrument Cluster**

(IC) to complete this procedure and allow the vehicle to start.

1. Turn the key from the OFF position to the ON position.

2. From the scan tool, follow the on-screen instructions to ENTER SECURITY ACCESS.

3. From the scan tool, select: Parameter Reset and follow the on-screen instructions.

➡**If the IC or the IC and the PCM were replaced, updated or reconfigured, follow Steps 4-9. All vehicle keys are erased during the parameter reset procedure. Verify at least 2 vehicle keys are available prior to carrying out the PATS parameter reset. If only the PCM was replaced, go to Step 9.**

4. From the scan tool, select: Ignition Key Code Erase and follow the on-screen instructions.

5. Turn the key to the OFF position and disconnect the scan tool.

6. Turn the key to the ON position for 6 seconds.

7. Turn the key to the OFF position and remove the key.

8. Insert the second PATS key into the ignition lock cylinder and turn the key to the ON position for 6 seconds.

9. Both keys now start the vehicle.

EXTENDED IDLE SHUTDOWN INITIALIZATION

➡**Repair DTC P0602 (Powertrain Control Module Program Error) and all DTCs related to the parking brake, the base hydraulic brake system and accelerator pedal. These DTCs being present will prevent the Circuit Deactivation Ignition Module (CDIM) from being enabled.**

1. Apply the parking brake.

2. Turn the ignition key to the ON position (engine off).

3. Fully depress the brake and accelerator pedals.

➡**Do not change the pedal positions. Changing the pedal positions during the enabling procedure will reset the 240-second timer to zero.**

4. Keep both pedals depressed for 240 seconds (4 minutes).

 a. At the end of 240 seconds, the powertrain Malfunction Indicator Lamp (MIL) (wrench light) will flash for 20 seconds.

 b. Both pedals may be released once the MIL (wrench light) begins to flash.

 c. If the system is already enabled, the MIL (wrench light) will not turn on or flash.

5. Turn the ignition key to the OFF position.

THROTTLE POSITION (TP) SENSOR

LOCATION

5.4L & 6.8L Engines

The Throttle Position (TP) sensor is attached to the throttle body.

REMOVAL & INSTALLATION

5.4L Engine

See Figures 440 through 445.

1. Remove the Air Cleaner (ACL) outlet pipe.

2. Disconnect the crankcase vent tube quick connect coupling from the ACL outlet pipe-to-Throttle Body (TB) adapter.

3. Disconnect the vacuum hose and wire harness retainer from the ACL outlet pipe-to-TB adapter and position aside.

4. Remove the 4 bolts and the ACL outlet pipe-to-TB adapter.

5. Remove the TB O-ring seal.

6. Disconnect the Throttle Position (TP) sensor electrical connector.

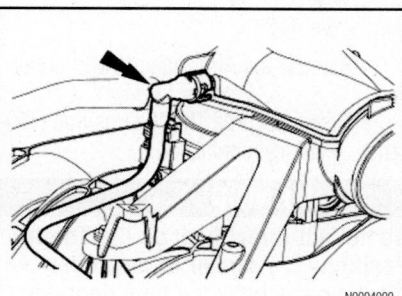

Fig. 440 Disconnect the crankcase vent tube quick connect coupling from the ACL outlet pipe-to-Throttle Body (TB) adapter

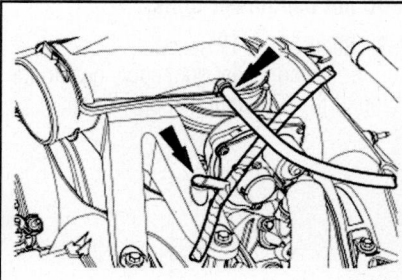

Fig. 441 Disconnect the vacuum hose and wire harness retainer from the ACL outlet pipe-to-TB adapter and position aside

Fig. 442 Remove the 4 bolts and the ACL outlet pipe-to-TB adapter

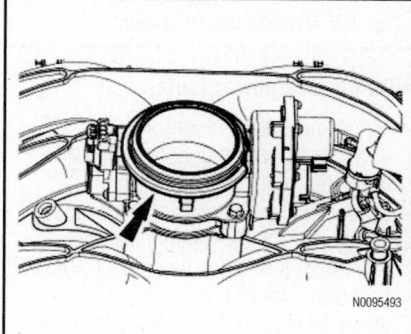

Fig. 443 Remove the TB O-ring seal

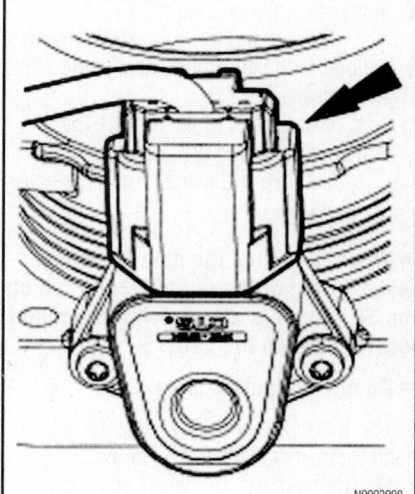

Fig. 444 Disconnect the Throttle Position (TP) sensor electrical connector

✻✻ WARNING

Do not put direct heat on the Throttle Position (TP) sensor or any other plastic parts because heat damage may occur. Damage may also occur if Electronic Throttle Body (ETB) temperature exceeds 248°F (120°C).

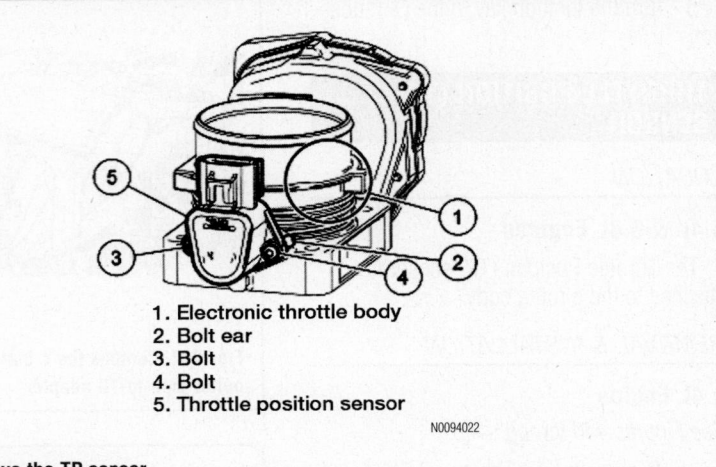

1. Electronic throttle body
2. Bolt ear
3. Bolt
4. Bolt
5. Throttle position sensor

N0094022

Fig. 445 Remove the TP sensor

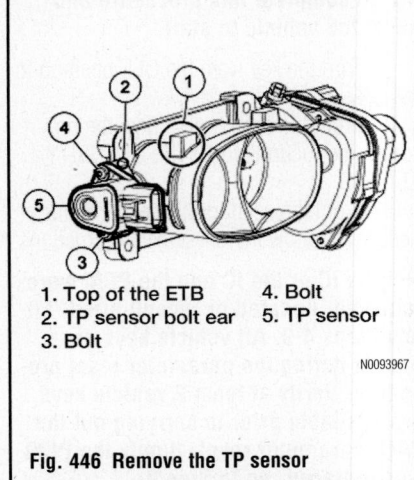

1. Top of the ETB   4. Bolt
2. TP sensor bolt ear   5. TP sensor
3. Bolt

N0093967

Fig. 446 Remove the TP sensor

➡**Do not use power tools.**

7. Remove the TP sensor.

a. Using a heat gun, apply heat to the top of the ETB until the top TP sensor bolt ear reaches approximately 130°F (55°C), this should take no more than 3 minutes using an 1,100-watt heat gun. The heat gun should be about 1 inch (25.4 mm) away from the ETB .

b. Monitor the temperature of the top TP sensor bolt ear on the ETB with a digital temperature laser or infrared thermometer, while heating the ETB .

c. Using hand tools, quickly remove the bolt farthest from the heat source first and discard.

d. Using hand tools, remove the remaining bolt and discard.

e. Remove and discard the TP sensor.

To install:

➡**When installing the new TP sensor, make sure that the radial locator tab on the TP sensor is aligned with the radial locator hole on the ETB.**

➡**Do not use power tools.**

8. Install the new TP sensor. Using hand tools, install the 2 new bolts.

9. Connect the TP sensor electrical connector.

10. Install the TB O-ring seal.

11. Install the ACL outlet pipe-to-TB adapter and the 4 bolts. Tighten to 89 inch lbs. (10 Nm).

12. Connect the wire harness retainer and vacuum hose to the ACL outlet pipe-to-TB adapter.

13. Connect the crankcase vent tube quick connect coupling to the ACL outlet pipe-to-TB adapter.

14. Install the ACL outlet pipe.

6.8L Engine

See Figure 446.

1. Remove the Air Cleaner (ACL) outlet pipe.

2. Disconnect the Throttle Position (TP) sensor electrical connector.

> ※※ **WARNING**
>
> **Do not put direct heat on the Throttle Position (TP) sensor or any other plastic parts because heat damage may occur. Damage may also occur if Electronic Throttle Body (ETB) temperature exceeds 248°F (120°C).**

➡**Do not use power tools.**

3. Remove the TP sensor.

a. Using a heat gun, apply heat to the top of the ETB until the top TP sensor

bolt ear reaches approximately 130°F (55°C), this should take no more than 3 minutes using an 1,100-watt heat gun. The heat gun should be about 1 inch (25.4 mm) away from the ETB .

b. Monitor the temperature of the top TP sensor bolt ear on the ETB with a digital temperature laser or infrared thermometer, while heating the ETB .

c. Using hand tools, quickly remove the bolt farthest from the heat source first and discard.

d. Using hand tools, remove the remaining bolt and discard.

e. Remove and discard the TP sensor.

To install:

➡**When installing the new TP sensor, make sure that the radial locator tab on the TP sensor is aligned with the radial locator hole on the ETB.**

➡**Do not use power tools.**

4. Install the new TP sensor.

5. Using hand tools, install the 2 new bolts.

6. Connect the TP sensor electrical connector.

7. Install the ACL outlet pipe.

FUEL

FUEL SYSTEM SERVICE PRECAUTIONS

Safety is the most important factor when performing not only fuel system maintenance but any type of maintenance. Failure to conduct maintenance and repairs in a safe manner may result in serious personal injury or death. Maintenance and testing of the vehicle's fuel system components can be accomplished safely and effectively by adhering to the following rules and guidelines.

• To avoid the possibility of fire and personal injury, always disconnect the negative battery cable unless the repair or test procedure requires that battery voltage be applied.

• Always relieve the fuel system pressure prior to disconnecting any fuel system component (injector, fuel rail, pressure regulator, etc.), fitting or fuel line connection. Exercise extreme caution whenever relieving fuel system pressure to avoid exposing skin, face and eyes to fuel spray. Please be advised that fuel under pressure may penetrate the skin or any part of the body that it contacts.

• Always place a shop towel or cloth around the fitting or connection prior to loosening to absorb any excess fuel due to spillage. Ensure that all fuel spillage (should it occur) is quickly removed from engine surfaces. Ensure that all fuel soaked cloths or towels are deposited into a suitable waste container.

• Always keep a dry chemical (Class B) fire extinguisher near the work area.

• Do not allow fuel spray or fuel vapors to come into contact with a spark or open flame.

• Always use a back-up wrench when loosening and tightening fuel line connection fittings. This will prevent unnecessary stress and torsion to fuel line piping.

• Always replace worn fuel fitting O-rings with new Do not substitute fuel hose or equivalent where fuel pipe is installed.

Before servicing the vehicle, make sure to also refer to the precautions in the beginning of this section as well.

RELIEVING FUEL SYSTEM PRESSURE

See Figure 447.

❊❊ CAUTION

Do not smoke, carry lighted tobacco or have an open flame of any type when working on or near any fuel-related component. Highly flammable mixtures are always present and may be ignited. Failure to follow these instructions may result in serious personal injury.

❊❊ CAUTION

Before working on or disconnecting any of the fuel tubes or fuel system components, relieve the fuel system pressure to prevent accidental spraying of fuel. Fuel in the fuel system remains under high pressure, even when the engine is not running. Failure to follow this instruction may result in serious personal injury.

1. With the vehicle in NEUTRAL, position it on a hoist.
2. Disconnect the Fuel Pump (FP) module electrical connector.
3. Start the engine and allow it to idle until it stalls.
4. After the engine stalls, crank the engine for approximately 5 seconds to make sure the fuel rail pressure has been released.
5. Turn the ignition switch to the OFF position.
6. When fuel system service is complete, connect the FP module electrical connector.

➡**It may take more than one key cycle to pressurize the fuel system.**

7. Cycle the ignition key and wait 3 seconds to pressurize the fuel system. Check for leaks before starting the engine.

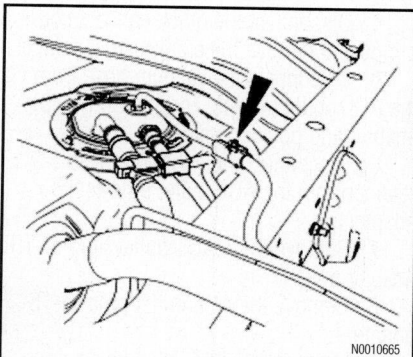

N0010665

Fig. 447 Disconnect the Fuel Pump (FP) module electrical connector

8. Install the scan tool. Turn the key ON with the engine OFF. Cycle the key OFF, then ON. Select the appropriate vehicle and engine qualifier. Clear all DTCs and carry out a PCM reset.
9. Start the vehicle and check the fuel system for leaks.

FUEL FILTER

REMOVAL & INSTALLATION

➡**Some residual fuel may remain in the fuel filter after releasing the fuel system pressure. Upon disconnecting or removing the fuel filter, carefully drain any residual fuel into a suitable container.**

1. With the vehicle in NEUTRAL, position it on a hoist.
2. Disconnect the fuel supply tube-to-fuel filter inlet quick connect coupling.
3. Disconnect the fuel supply tube-to-fuel filter outlet quick connect coupling.
4. Remove and discard the fuel filter.
5. To install, reverse the removal procedure.
6. Install a new fuel filter.

FUEL INJECTORS

REMOVAL & INSTALLATION

5.4L Engine
See Figure 448.

❊❊ CAUTION

Do not smoke, carry lighted tobacco or have an open flame of any type when working on or near any fuel-related component. Highly flammable mixtures are always present and may be ignited. Failure to follow these instructions may result in serious personal injury.

❊❊ CAUTION

Before working on or disconnecting any of the fuel tubes or fuel system components, relieve the fuel system pressure to prevent accidental spraying of fuel. Fuel in the fuel system remains under high pressure, even when the engine is not running. Failure to follow this instruction may result in serious personal injury.

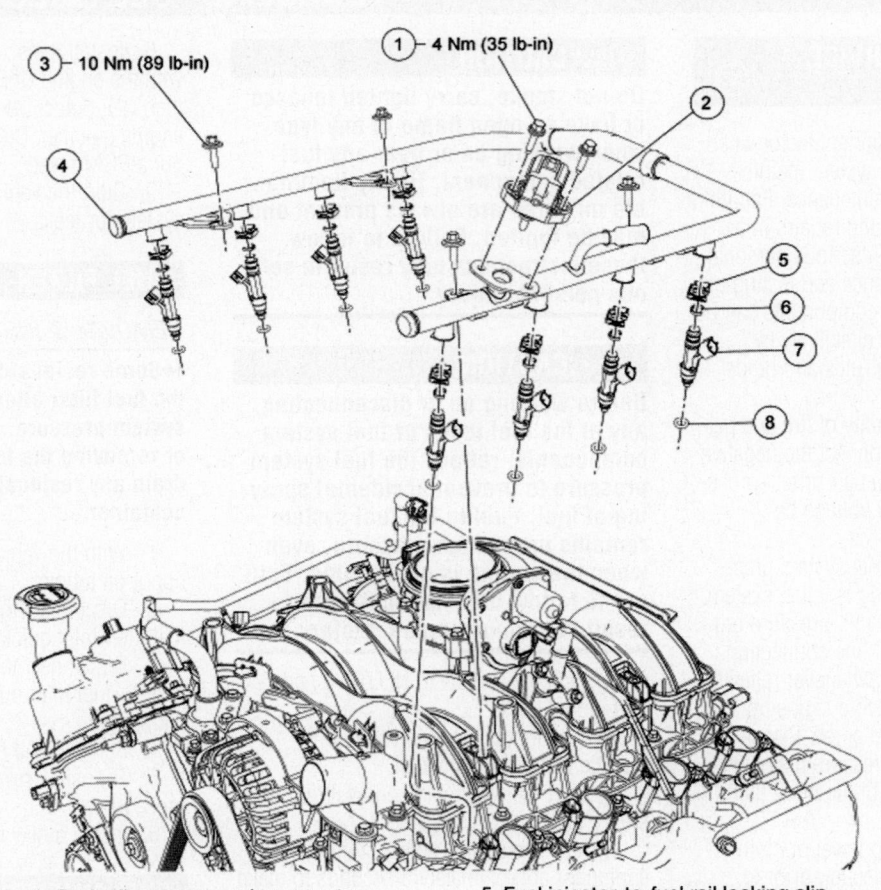

1. Fuel rail pressure and temperature sensor bolt (2 required)
2. Fuel rail pressure and temperature sensor
3. Fuel rail bolt (4 required)
4. Fuel rail
5. Fuel injector-to-fuel rail locking clip (8 required)
6. Fuel injector-to-fuel rail O-ring seal (8 required)
7. Fuel injector (8 required)
8. Fuel injector-to-intake manifold O-ring seal (8 required)

N0087577

Fig. 448 Exploded view of the fuel rail and fuel injector assemblies

※※ WARNING

Fuel injection equipment is manufactured to very precise tolerances and fine clearances. It is therefore essential that absolute cleanliness is observed when working with these components. Always install blanking plugs to any open orifices or tubes.

※※ WARNING

When reusing liquid or vapor tube connectors, make sure to use compressed air to remove any foreign material from the connector retaining clip area before separating from the tube.

1. Release the fuel system pressure.
2. Disconnect the battery ground cable.
3. Remove the Air Cleaner (ACL) outlet tube.
4. Disconnect the quick connect couplings and remove the crankcase vent tube.
5. Disconnect the vacuum hose from the ACL outlet pipe-to-Throttle Body (TB) adapter and position aside.
6. Disconnect the wiring harness retainer from the ACL outlet pipe-to-TB adapter.
7. Remove the 4 ACL outlet pipe-to-TB adapter bolts.
8. Remove the ACL outlet pipe-to-TB adapter.
9. Disconnect the quick connect couplings and remove the PCV tube.

10. Disconnect the Evaporative Emission (EVAP) tube quick connect coupling from the intake manifold and position aside.
11. Disconnect the fuel rail pressure and temperature sensor electrical and vacuum connectors.
12. Disconnect the 8 fuel injector electrical connectors.
13. Disconnect the Electronic Throttle Control (ETC) electrical connector.
14. Disconnect the Throttle Position (TP) sensor electrical connector.
15. Disconnect the fuel supply tube spring lock coupling.

➡**When removing the fuel rail, leave the fuel injectors in the intake manifold. This will make removal of the fuel rail easier.**

16. Remove the 4 fuel rail bolts and the fuel rail.

➡Lubricate the new O-ring seal with clean engine oil prior to installation.

17. If servicing the fuel rail, remove the 2 bolts and the fuel rail pressure and temperature sensor. Discard the O-ring seal.

✳✳ WARNING

Use O-ring seals that are made of special fuel-resistant material. Use of ordinary O-rings can cause the fuel system to leak.

➡Lubricate the new O-ring seals with clean engine oil prior to installation.

18. Remove the fuel injectors from the intake manifold and discard the upper and lower fuel injector O-ring seals.

To install:

19. To install, reverse the removal procedure.

20. Tighten the 4 fuel rail bolts to 89 inch lbs. (10 Nm).

21. Tighten the 4 ACL outlet pipe-to-TB adapter bolts to 89 inch lbs. (10 Nm).

6.2L Engine
See Figure 449.

➡The manufacturer does not provide a specific Removal and Installation procedure for this component. Refer to the graphic(s) when servicing this component.

6.8L Engine
See Figure 450.

✳✳ CAUTION

Do not smoke, carry lighted tobacco or have an open flame of any type when working on or near any fuel-related component. Highly flammable mixtures are always present and may be ignited. Failure to follow these instructions may result in serious personal injury.

✳✳ CAUTION

Before working on or disconnecting any of the fuel tubes or fuel system components, relieve the fuel system pressure to prevent accidental spraying of fuel. Fuel in the fuel system remains under high pressure, even when the engine is not running. Failure to follow this instruction may result in serious personal injury.

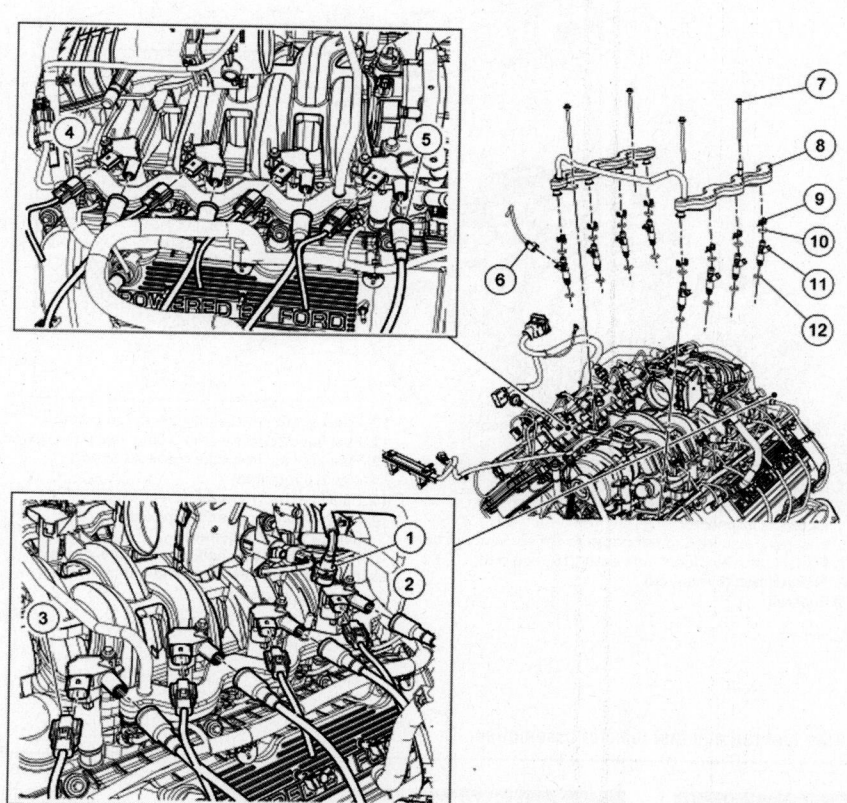

1. Fuel supply tube quick connect coupling
2. LH ignition wire (4 required)
3. LH ignition coil electrical connector (4 required)
4. RH ignition coil electrical connector (4 required)
5. RH ignition wire (4 required)
6. Fuel injector electrical connector (8 required)
7. Fuel rail bolt (4 required)
8. Fuel rail
9. Fuel injector-to-fuel rail locking clip (8 required)
10. Fuel injector-to-fuel rail O-ring (8 required)
11. Fuel injector (8 required)
12. Fuel injector-to-intake manifold O-ring (8 required)

N0110026

Fig. 449 Exploded views of the fuel rail and fuel injector assembly

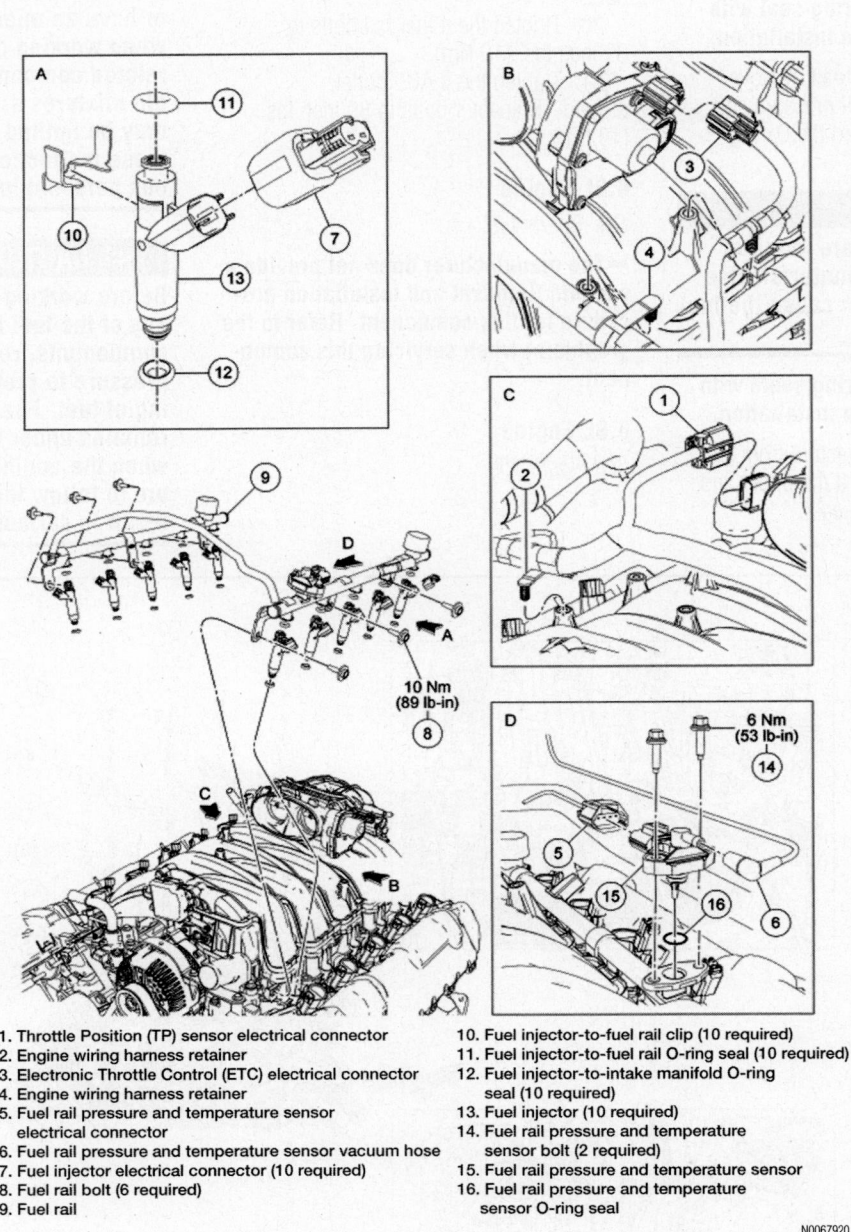

1. Throttle Position (TP) sensor electrical connector
2. Engine wiring harness retainer
3. Electronic Throttle Control (ETC) electrical connector
4. Engine wiring harness retainer
5. Fuel rail pressure and temperature sensor
    electrical connector
6. Fuel rail pressure and temperature sensor vacuum hose
7. Fuel injector electrical connector (10 required)
8. Fuel rail bolt (6 required)
9. Fuel rail
10. Fuel injector-to-fuel rail clip (10 required)
11. Fuel injector-to-fuel rail O-ring seal (10 required)
12. Fuel injector-to-intake manifold O-ring
    seal (10 required)
13. Fuel injector (10 required)
14. Fuel rail pressure and temperature
    sensor bolt (2 required)
15. Fuel rail pressure and temperature sensor
16. Fuel rail pressure and temperature
    sensor O-ring seal

N0067920

Fig. 450 Exploded view of the fuel rail and fuel injector assemblies

⁂ **WARNING**

Fuel injection equipment is manufactured to very precise tolerances and fine clearances. It is therefore essential that absolute cleanliness is observed when working with these components. Always install blanking plugs to any open orifices or tubes.

⁂ **WARNING**

When reusing liquid or vapor tube connectors, make sure to use compressed air to remove any foreign material from the connector retaining clip area before separating from the tube.

1. Release the fuel system pressure.
2. Disconnect the battery ground cable.
3. Remove the Air Cleaner (ACL) outlet pipe.
4. Disconnect the fuel supply tube spring lock coupling.
5. Disconnect the Electronic Throttle Control (ETC) electrical connector.

6. Disconnect the Throttle Position (TP) sensor electrical connector.

7. Disconnect the fuel rail pressure and temperature sensor electrical and vacuum connectors.

8. Disconnect the 10 fuel injector electrical connectors.

9. Detach the 2 main engine wiring harness retainers from the intake manifold and position the harness for access to remove the fuel rail.

➡When removing the fuel rail, leave the fuel injectors in the intake manifold. This will ease removal of the fuel rail.

10. Remove the 6 bolts, the 10 fuel injector-to-fuel rail clips and separate the fuel rail from the injectors and remove the fuel rail.

✳ WARNING

Use specified service O-ring seals that are made of special fuel-resistant material. Use of ordinary O-rings can cause the fuel system to leak.

➡Lubricate the new O-ring seals with clean engine oil prior to installation.

11. Remove the fuel injectors from the intake manifold and discard the upper and lower fuel injector O-ring seals.

12. If servicing the fuel rail, remove the 2 bolts and the fuel rail pressure and temperature sensor. Discard the O-ring seal.

13. To install, reverse the removal procedure.

14. Tighten the fuel rail bolts to 89 inch lbs. (10 Nm).

FUEL PUMP

REMOVAL & INSTALLATION

2010 Plastic Fuel Tank
See Figures 451 and 452.

✳ CAUTION

Do not smoke, carry lighted tobacco or have an open flame of any type when working on or near any fuel-related component. Highly flammable mixtures are always present and may be ignited. Failure to follow these instructions may result in serious personal injury.

✳ CAUTION

When handling fuel, always observe fuel handling precautions and be prepared in the event of fuel spillage.

Spilled fuel may be ignited by hot vehicle components or other ignition sources. Failure to follow these instructions may result in serious personal injury.

➡The fuel tank must be drained completely. Upon removal of the Fuel Pump (FP) module, the tank must be inspected for contamination.

1. Remove the fuel tank.

✳ WARNING

Clean the fuel tank of any dirt or foreign material before servicing the Fuel Pump (FP) module. In extreme dirt or dusty conditions it may be necessary to wash the fuel tank using a water hose. Before removing the FP module, make sure that there is no residual dirt or foreign material around the FP module flange. If dirt or foreign material enter the fuel tank, damage to the FP module or other fuel system components may occur.

2. Clean the area around the FP module mounting flange.

➡Mark the orientation of the FP module on the fuel tank to aid in installation.

3. Using the Lock Ring Wrench (310-123), remove the FP module lock ring.

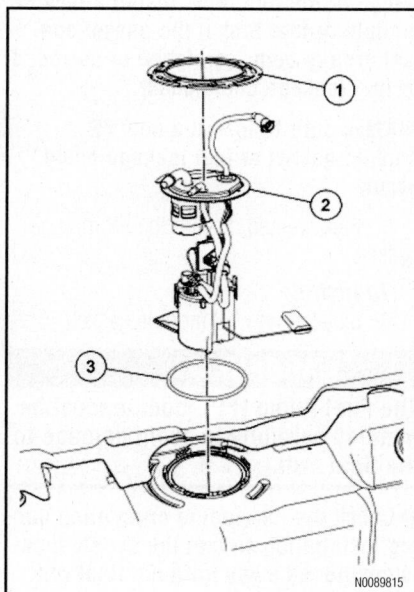

Fig. 451 Fuel Pump (FP) module lock ring (1), FP Module (2), and FP module O-ring seal (3)

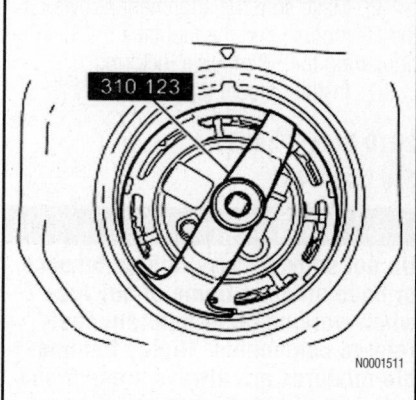

Fig. 452 Using the Lock Ring Wrench, remove the FP module lock ring

✳ WARNING

The Fuel Pump (FP) module must be handled carefully to avoid damage to the float arm.

4. Completely remove the FP module from the fuel tank.

➡Inspect the surfaces of the FP module flange and fuel tank O-ring seal contact surfaces. Do not polish or adjust the O-ring seal contact area of the fuel tank flange or the fuel tank. Install a new FP module or fuel tank if the O-ring seal contact area is bent, scratched or corroded or fuel leakage could occur.

➡Make sure to install a new FP module O-ring seal and lock ring or fuel leakage could occur.

➡Apply clean engine oil to the O-ring seal prior to installation.

5. Remove and discard the FP module O-ring seal.

To install:

➡Apply clean engine oil to the O-ring seal prior to installation.

6. Install a new FP module O-ring seal.

✳ WARNING

The Fuel Pump (FP) module must be handled carefully to avoid damage to the float arm.

7. Install the FP module into the fuel tank and rotate clockwise until the alignment arrows on the FP module and fuel tank meet.

8. Using the Lock Ring Wrench, install the new FP module lock ring.

9. Make sure the alignment arrows on the FP module and the fuel tank meet before tightening the FP module lock ring.

10. Install the fuel tank.

2010 Steel Fuel Tank

See Figure 453.

> ❋❋ **CAUTION**
>
> Do not smoke, carry lighted tobacco or have an open flame of any type when working on or near any fuel-related component. Highly flammable mixtures are always present and may be ignited. Failure to follow these instructions may result in serious personal injury.

> ❋❋ **CAUTION**
>
> When handling fuel, always observe fuel handling precautions and be prepared in the event of fuel spillage. Spilled fuel may be ignited by hot vehicle components or other ignition sources. Failure to follow these instructions may result in serious personal injury.

➡The fuel tank must be drained completely. Upon removal of the Fuel Pump (FP) module, the tank must be inspected for contamination.

1. Remove the fuel tank.

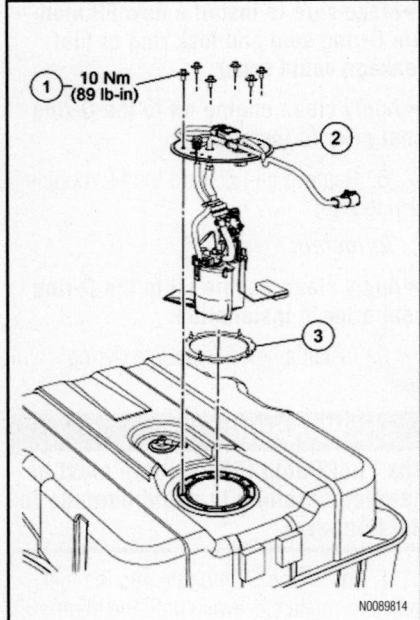

Fig. 453 Fuel Pump (FP) module bolts (1), FP Module (2), and FP module gasket (3)

> ❋❋ **WARNING**
>
> Clean the fuel tank of any dirt or foreign material before servicing the Fuel Pump (FP) module. In extreme dirt or dusty conditions it may be necessary to wash the fuel tank using a water hose. Before removing the FP module, make sure that there is no residual dirt or foreign material around the FP module flange. If dirt or foreign material enter the fuel tank, damage to the FP module or other fuel system components may occur.

2. Clean the area around the FP mounting flange.

➡Mark the orientation of the FP module on the fuel tank to aid in installation.

3. Remove the 6 bolts from the FP module.

> ❋❋ **WARNING**
>
> The Fuel Pump (FP) module must be handled carefully to avoid damage to the float arm.

4. Completely remove the FP module from the fuel tank.

➡Inspect the surfaces of the FP module flange and fuel tank gasket contact surfaces. Do not polish or adjust the gasket contact area of the fuel tank flange or the fuel tank. Install a new FP module or fuel tank if the gasket contact area is bent, scratched or corroded or fuel leakage could occur.

➡Make sure to install a new FP module gasket or fuel leakage could occur.

5. Remove and discard the FP module gasket.

To install:
6. Install a new FP module gasket.

> ❋❋ **WARNING**
>
> The Fuel Pump (FP) module must be handled carefully to avoid damage to the float arm.

➡Check the FP module orientation during installation so that the supply tube is positioned away from the float rod.

7. Install the FP module into the fuel tank.

8. Rotate the FP module clockwise until the alignment marks on the FP module and

fuel tank meet and then install the 6 bolts. Tighten to 89 inch lbs. (10 Nm).

9. Install the fuel tank.

2011 Models

See Figures 454 through 456.

> ❋❋ **CAUTION**
>
> Do not smoke, carry lighted tobacco or have an open flame of any type when working on or near any fuel-related component. Highly flammable mixtures are always present and may be ignited. Failure to follow these instructions may result in serious personal injury.

> ❋❋ **CAUTION**
>
> Before working on or disconnecting any of the fuel tubes or fuel system components, relieve the fuel system pressure to prevent accidental spraying of fuel. Fuel in the fuel system remains under high pressure, even when the engine is not running. Failure to follow this instruction may result in serious personal injury.

> ❋❋ **CAUTION**
>
> When handling fuel, always observe fuel handling precautions and be prepared in the event of fuel spillage.

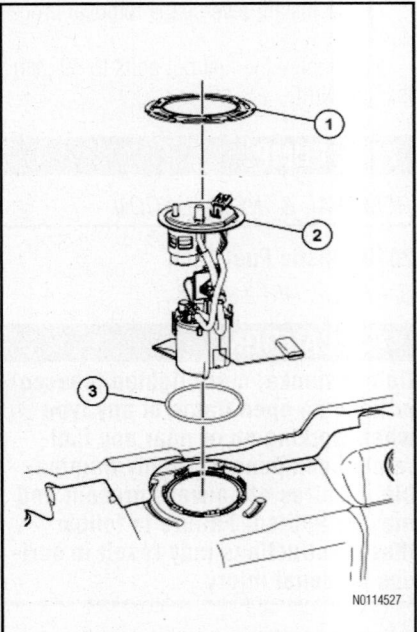

Fig. 454 Exploded view of the Fuel Pump (FP) module showing the lock ring (1), the FP module (2) and the O-ring (3)

Spilled fuel may be ignited by hot vehicle components or other ignition sources. Failure to follow these instructions may result in serious personal injury.

✱✱ CAUTION

Do not carry personal electronic devices such as cell phones, pagers or audio equipment of any type when working on or near any fuel-related component. Highly flammable mixtures are always present and may be ignited. Failure to follow these instructions may result in serious personal injury.

➡The Fuel Pump (FP) module has a serviceable fuel level sender.

➡To avoid introducing contamination into the fuel tank use water to clean the FP module connections, couplings, flange surface and the immediate surrounding area of any dirt or foreign material. Blow dry thoroughly with shop air after cleaning.

1. Remove the fuel tank.

✱✱ WARNING

Carefully install the lock ring wrench to avoid damaging the Fuel Pump (FP) module when removing the lock ring

2. Install the lock ring wrench and remove the FP module lock ring.

✱✱ WARNING

The Fuel Pump (FP) module must be removed and handled carefully to avoid damage to the float arm.

➡The FP module will have residual fuel remaining internally, drain into a suitable container.

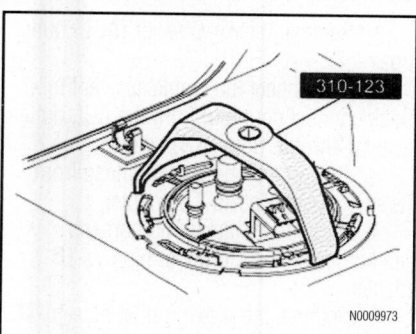

Fig. 455 Install the lock ring wrench and remove the FP module lock ring

➡If necessary, insert a screwdriver into the empty FP module rod hole and slightly pull the screwdriver inboard until the base of the FP module clears the tank opening.

3. Carefully remove the FP module from the fuel tank.
4. Remove and discard the FP module O-ring seal.
5. Inspect the FP module for missing or broken components. Remove any missing or broken components from the fuel tank

To install:

➡Inspect the mating surfaces of the FP module flange and the fuel tank O-ring seal contact surfaces. Wipe clean with a lint-free rag.

➡Manually sweep the float arm to ensure freedom of travel.

6. Install a new FP module O-ring seal.

✱✱ WARNING

The Fuel Pump (FP) module must be handled carefully to avoid damage to the float arm.

7. Install the FP module by inserting float rod through fuel tank opening first.

✱✱ WARNING

Carefully install the lock ring wrench to avoid damaging the Fuel Pump (FP) module when installing the lock ring

➡Install a new lock ring if it is bent, damaged or corroded

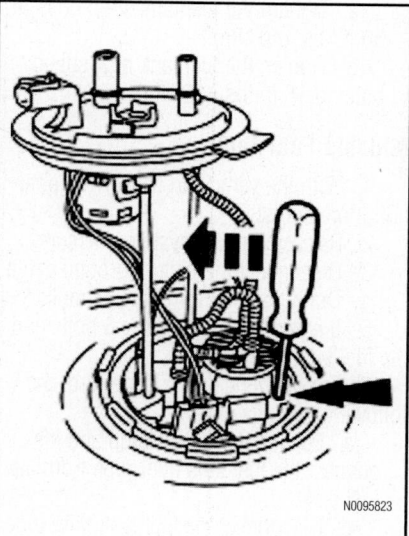

Fig. 456 Carefully remove the FP module from the fuel tank

➡Make sure the alignment tab on the FP module and the fuel tank meet before tightening the fuel tank lock ring.

8. Install the lock ring wrench and tighten the FP module lock ring.
9. Install the fuel tank.

FUEL TANK

DRAINING

See Figure 457.

✱✱ CAUTION

Do not smoke, carry lighted tobacco or have an open flame of any type when working on or near any fuel-related component. Highly flammable mixtures are always present and may be ignited. Failure to follow these instructions may result in serious personal injury.

✱✱ CAUTION

Do not carry personal electronic devices such as cell phones, pagers or audio equipment of any type when working on or near any fuel-related component. Highly flammable mixtures are always present and may be ignited. Failure to follow these instructions may result in serious personal injury.

✱✱ CAUTION

When handling fuel, always observe fuel handling precautions and be prepared in the event of fuel spillage. Spilled fuel may be ignited by hot vehicle components or other ignition sources. Failure to follow these instructions may result in serious personal injury.

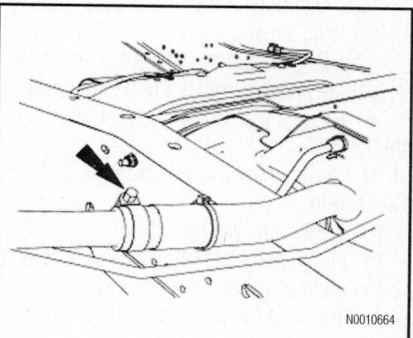

Fig. 457 Remove the filler pipe hose at the filler pipe hose connection

✳✳ CAUTION

Remove the fuel filler cap slowly. The fuel system may be under pressure. If the fuel filler cap is venting vapor or if you hear a hissing sound, wait until it stops before completely removing the fuel filler cap. Otherwise, fuel may spray out. Failure to follow these instructions may result in serious personal injury.

1. With the vehicle in NEUTRAL, position it on a hoist.
2. Disconnect the battery ground cable.
3. Remove the filler pipe hose at the filler pipe hose connection. Loosen the clamp and disconnect the hose.

➡**Follow the operating instructions supplied by the equipment manufacturer.**

4. Insert the hose from the 100 Gallon Manual Fuel Tanker and siphon the fuel through the fuel filler hose opening.

REMOVAL & INSTALLATION

Aft-Of-Axle Fuel Tank

1. With the vehicle in NEUTRAL, position it on a hoist.
2. Release the fuel system pressure.
3. Disconnect the battery ground cable.
4. Drain the fuel from the fuel tank.
5. Loosen the 2 hose clamps and disconnect the fuel tank filler pipe and fuel tank filler pipe vent hose from the fuel tank.
6. For gasoline engines, perform the following:

    a. Disconnect the fuel supply tube-to-Fuel Pump (FP) module quick connect coupling.

    b. Disconnect the fuel vapor tube-to-fuel tank grade vent valve quick connect coupling.

7. For diesel engines, perform the following:

    a. Disconnect the fuel supply tube-to-fuel level sensor quick connect coupling.

    b. Disconnect the fuel return tube-to-fuel level sensor quick connect coupling.

8. Place a jack under the fuel tank shield.
9. Remove the 4 bolts from the fuel tank shield.
10. Lower the fuel tank.
11. Remove the 2 nuts from the fuel tank straps and remove the fuel tank straps.
12. Remove the fuel tank from the fuel tank shield.
13. To install, reverse the removal procedure.

    a. Tighten the fuel tank straps to 59 ft. lbs. (80 Nm).

    b. Tighten the 4 bolts for the fuel tank shield to 66 ft. lbs. (90 Nm).

Auxiliary Fuel Tank

➡**Some auxiliary tanks are stand alone applications and some are dual tank applications.**

1. With the vehicle in NEUTRAL, position it on a hoist.
2. Release the fuel system pressure.
3. Disconnect the battery ground cable.
4. Drain the fuel from the fuel tank.
5. Loosen the 2 hose clamps and disconnect the fuel tank filler pipe and the fuel tank filler pipe vent hose from the fuel tank.
6. For gasoline engines, perform the following:

    a. Disconnect the fuel vapor tube-to-Fuel Pump (FP) module quick connect coupling and the fuel supply tube-to-FP module quick connect coupling.

    b. Disconnect the fuel vapor tube-to-fuel tank grade vent valve quick connect couplings.

    c. For diesel engines, disconnect the fuel return tube-to-fuel level sensor quick connect coupling and fuel supply tube-to-fuel level sensor quick connect coupling.

7. Remove the 4 bolts and fuel tank heat shield.
8. Place a jack under the fuel tank.
9. Remove 2 bolts and carefully position the 2 fuel tank straps aside.
10. Lower the fuel tank.
11. To install, reverse the removal procedure.

    a. Tighten the fuel tank strap bolts to 30 ft. lbs. (40 Nm).

    b. Tighten the fuel tank heat shield bolts to 16 ft. lbs. (22 Nm).

Midship Fuel Tank

1. With the vehicle in NEUTRAL, position it on a hoist.
2. Release the fuel system pressure.
3. Disconnect the battery ground cable.
4. Drain the fuel from the fuel tank.
5. If equipped, remove the 6 bolts and the fuel tank shield.
6. For gasoline engines, perform the following:

    a. Loosen the hose clamp and disconnect the fuel tank filler pipe from the fuel tank.

    b. Disconnect the fuel tank filler pipe vent tube quick connect coupling.

7. For diesel engines, loosen the 2 hose clamps and disconnect the fuel tank filler pipe and fuel tank filler pipe vent tube from the fuel tank.

8. Place a jack under the fuel tank.
9. Remove the 4 fuel tank strap bolts and remove the 2 fuel tank straps.
10. Slightly lower the fuel tank.
11. For gasoline engines, perform the following:

    a. Disconnect the fuel vapor tube-to-Fuel Pump (FP) module quick connect coupling and the fuel supply tube-to-FP module quick connect coupling.

    b. Disconnect the fuel vapor tube-to-fuel tank grade vent valve quick connect couplings.

12. For diesel engines, perform the following:

    a. Disconnect the fuel return tube-to-fuel level sensor quick connect coupling and the fuel supply tube-to-fuel level sensor quick connect coupling.

    b. Remove the fuel vapor hose from the fuel tank grade vent valves.

    c. Disconnect the fuel level sensor electrical connector.

13. Lower the fuel tank.
14. To install, reverse the removal procedure.

    a. Tighten the 4 fuel tank strap bolts to 30 ft. lbs. (40 Nm).

    b. Tighten the fuel tank shield bolts to 16 ft. lbs. (22 Nm).

IDLE SPEED

ADJUSTMENT

The idle speed is controlled by the Powertrain Control Module (PCM). No adjustment is necessary or possible.

THROTTLE BODY

REMOVAL & INSTALLATION

5.4L Engine

See Figures 458 and 459.

1. Remove the Air Cleaner (ACL) outlet tube.
2. Disconnect the crankcase vent tube quick connect coupling from the ACL outlet pipe-to-Throttle Body (TB) adapter.
3. Disconnect the vacuum hose from the ACL outlet pipe-to-TB adapter.
4. Disconnect the wiring harness retainer from the ACL outlet pipe-to-TB adapter.
5. Remove the 4 ACL outlet pipe-to-TB adapter bolts.
6. Remove the ACL outlet pipe-to-TB adapter.

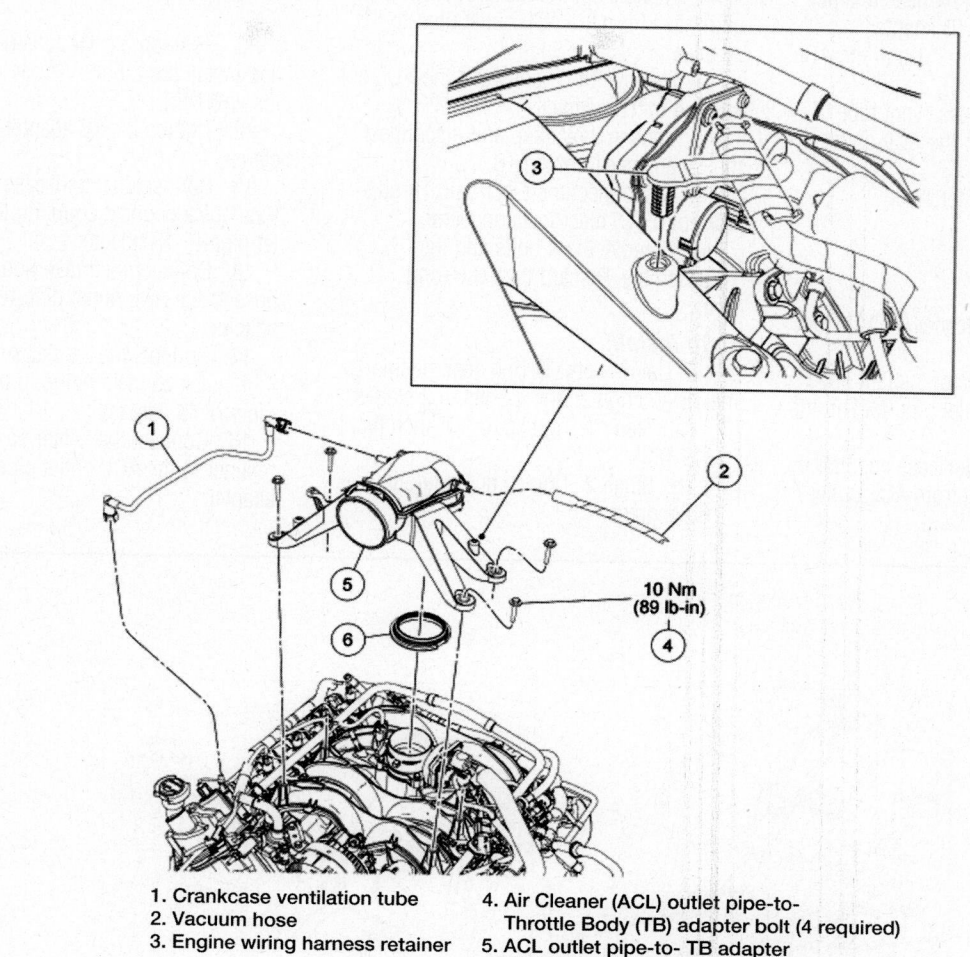

1. Crankcase ventilation tube
2. Vacuum hose
3. Engine wiring harness retainer
4. Air Cleaner (ACL) outlet pipe-to-Throttle Body (TB) adapter bolt (4 required)
5. ACL outlet pipe-to- TB adapter
6. ACL outlet pipe-to- TB adapter seal

10 Nm (89 lb-in)

N0063671

Fig. 458 Exploded view of the Air Cleaner (ACL) Outlet Pipe-to-Throttle Body (TB) Adapter

7. Disconnect the Electronic Throttle Control (ETC) electrical connector.

8. Disconnect the Throttle Position (TP) sensor electrical connector.

9. Remove the 4 bolts and the TB assembly. Discard the TB O-ring seal.

To install:

10. Using a new O-ring seal, install the TB and tighten the 4 bolts in 2 stages.

  a. Stage 1: Tighten to 80 inch lbs. (9 Nm).

  b. Stage 2: Tighten an additional 90 degrees (one-fourth turn).

11. Connect the TP sensor electrical connector.

12. Connect the ETC electrical connector.

13. Install the ACL outlet pipe-to-TB adapter.

14. Install the 4 ACL outlet pipe-to-TB adapter bolts. Tighten to 89 inch lbs. (10 Nm).

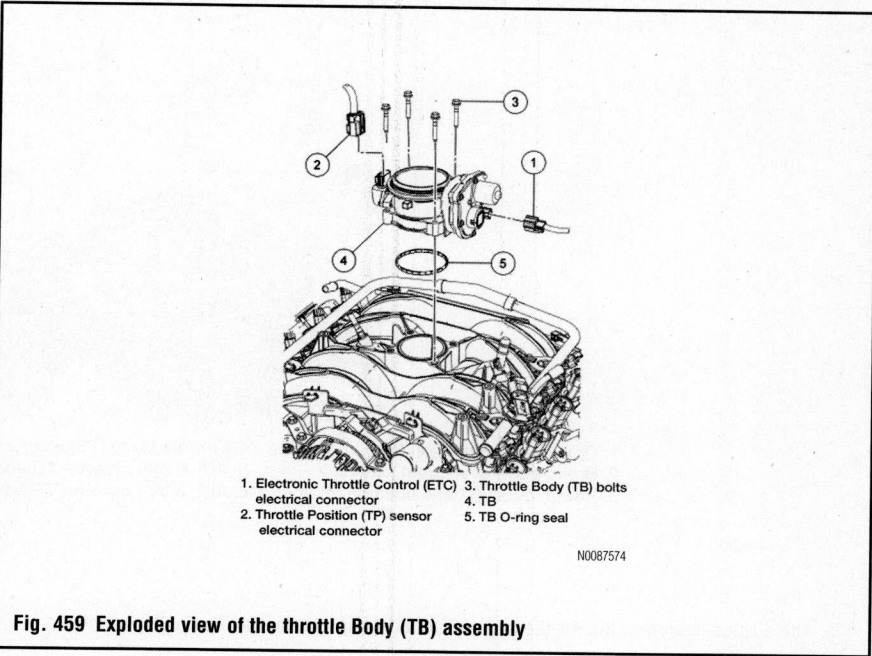

1. Electronic Throttle Control (ETC) electrical connector
2. Throttle Position (TP) sensor electrical connector
3. Throttle Body (TB) bolts
4. TB
5. TB O-ring seal

N0087574

Fig. 459 Exploded view of the throttle Body (TB) assembly

15. Connect the wiring harness retainer to the ACL outlet pipe-to-TB adapter.

16. Connect the vacuum hose to the ACL outlet pipe-to-TB adapter.

17. Connect the crankcase vent tube quick connect coupling to the ACL outlet pipe-to-TB adapter.

18. Install the ACL outlet tube.

6.2L Engine

See Figures 460 and 461.

1. Remove the Air Cleaner (ACL) outlet tube.

2. Disconnect the heater coolant hose retainer from the ACL outlet pipe-to-Throttle Body (TB) adapter.

3. Disconnect the crankcase ventilation tube quick connect fitting from ACL outlet pipe-to-TB adapter.

4. Disconnect the brake booster vacuum hose from the ACL outlet pipe-to-TB adapter.

5. Remove the 2 bolts and the ACL outlet pipe-to-TB adapter.

6. Loosen the clamp and disconnect the TB adapter from the TB.

7. Disconnect the Electronic Throttle Control (ETC) electrical connector.

8. Remove the 4 bolts and the TB assembly. Discard the TB O-ring seal.

To install:

9. Using a new O-ring seal, position the TB and tighten the 4 bolts in 2 stages.
   a. Stage 1: Tighten to 106 inch lbs. (12 Nm).
   b. Stage 2: Tighten an additional 60 degrees.

10. Connect the ETC electrical connector.

11. Position the TB adapter onto the TB and install the 2 bolts. Tighten to 89 inch lbs. (10 Nm).

12. Tighten the TB adapter-to-TB clamp.

13. Connect the crankcase ventilation tube quick connect coupling to the ACL outlet pipe-to-TB adapter.

14. Connect the brake booster vacuum hose to the ACL outlet pipe-to-TB adapter.

15. Connect the crankcase ventilation tube quick connect fitting to the ACL outlet pipe-to-TB adapter.

16. Connect the heater coolant hose retainer to the ACL outlet pipe-to-TB adapter.

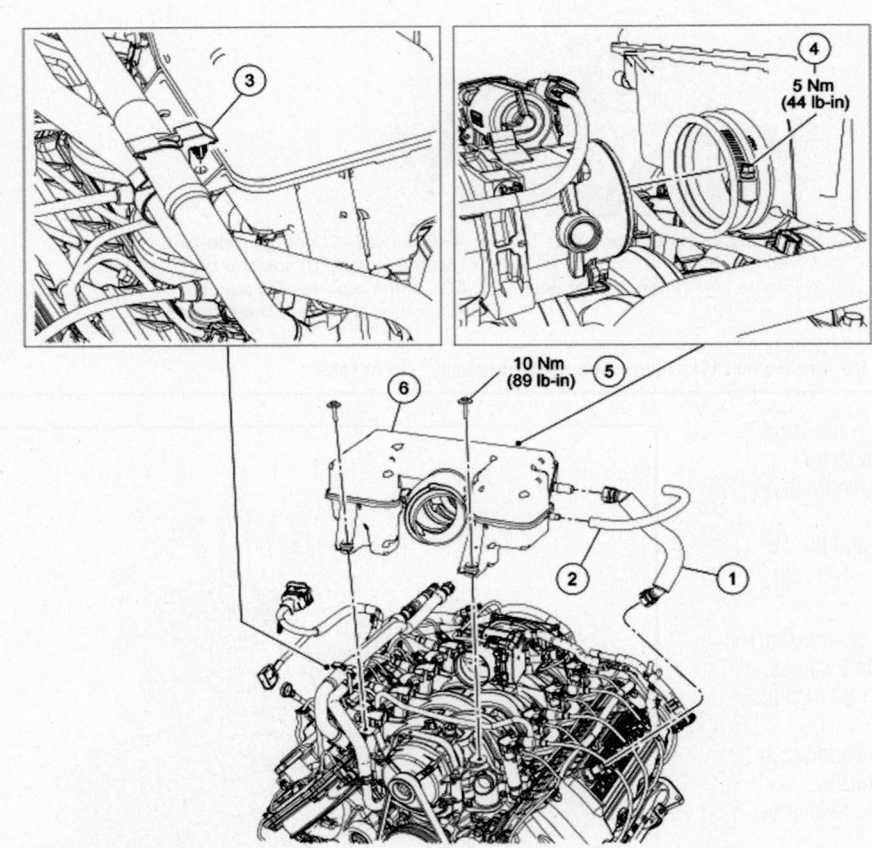

1. Crankcase ventilation tube
2. Brake booster vacuum hose
3. Heater coolant hose position retainer
4. Throttle Body (TB) adapter-to- TB clamp
5. ACL outlet pipe-to- TB adapter bolt (2 required)
6. ACL outlet pipe-to- TB adapter

N0110075

Fig. 460 Exploded view of the Air Cleaner (ACL) Outlet Pipe-to-Throttle Body (TB) adapter

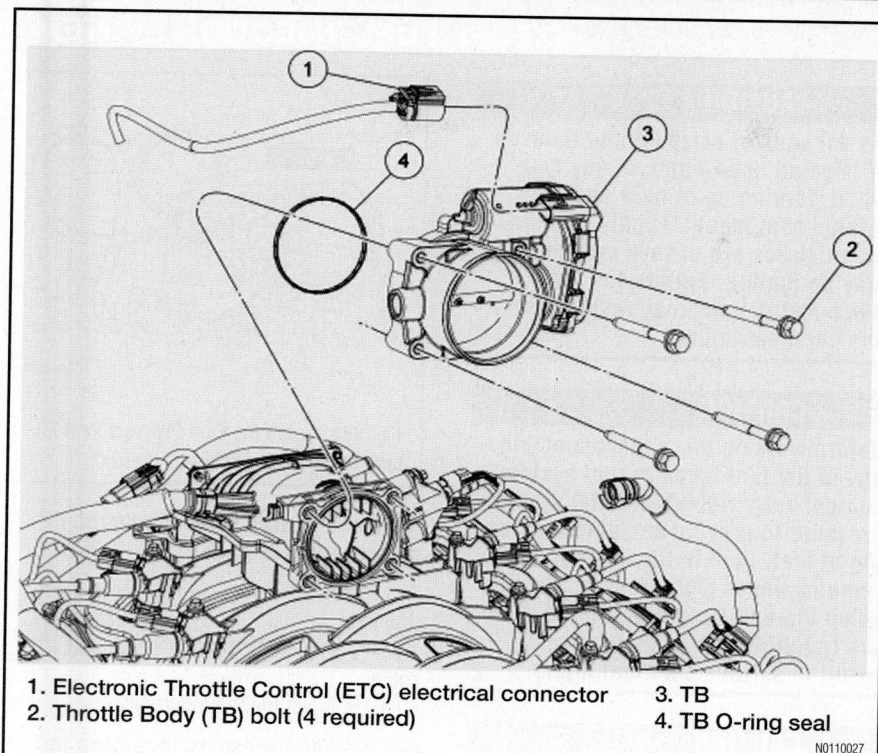

1. Electronic Throttle Control (ETC) electrical connector
2. Throttle Body (TB) bolt (4 required)
3. TB
4. TB O-ring seal

N0110027

Fig. 461 Exploded view of the Throttle Body (TB) assembly

17. Install the ACL outlet tube.

6.8L Engine

See Figure 462.

1. Remove the Air Cleaner (ACL) outlet tube.

2. Disconnect the Electronic Throttle Control (ETC) electrical connector.

3. Disconnect the Throttle Position (TP) sensor electrical connector.

4. Remove the 4 bolts and the TB assembly. Discard the TB O-ring seal.

To install:

5. Using a new O-ring seal, install the TB and tighten the 4 bolts in 2 stages.

a. Stage 1: Tighten to 80 inch lbs. (9 Nm).

b. Stage 2: Tighten an additional 90 degrees (1/4 turn).

6. Connect the TP sensor electrical connector.

7. Connect the ETC electrical connector.

8. Install the ACL outlet tube.

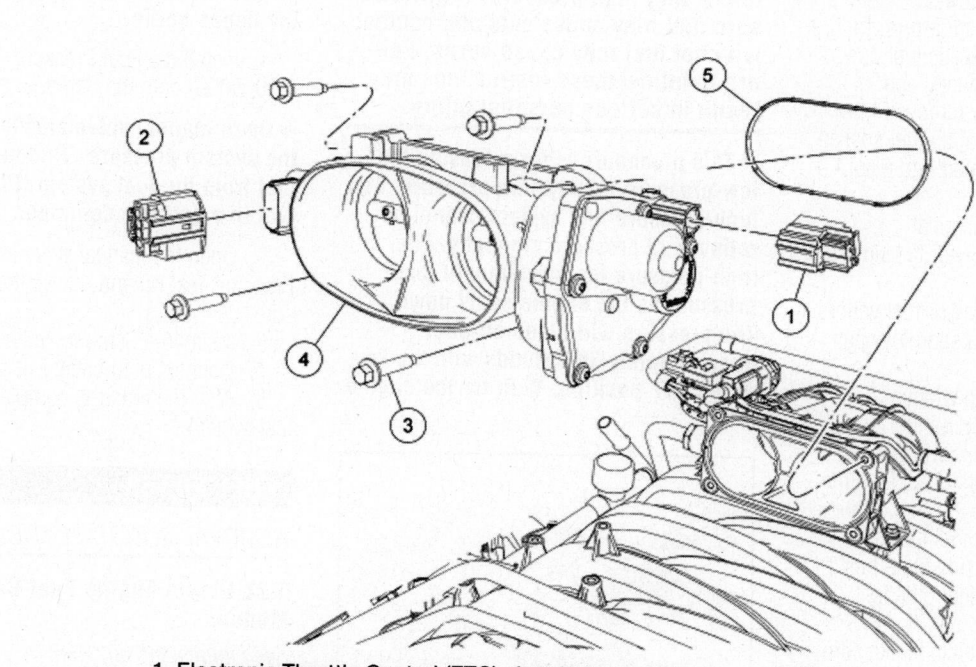

1. Electronic Throttle Control (ETC) electrical connector
2. Throttle Position (TP) sensor electrical connector
3. Throttle Body (TB) bolt (4 required)
4. TB
5. TB gasket

N0063676

Fig. 462 Exploded view of the Throttle Body (TB) assembly

FUEL SYSTEM SERVICE PRECAUTIONS

Safety is the most important factor when performing not only fuel system maintenance but any type of maintenance. Failure to conduct maintenance and repairs in a safe manner may result in serious personal injury or death. Maintenance and testing of the vehicle's fuel system components can be accomplished safely and effectively by adhering to the following rules and guidelines.

• To avoid the possibility of fire and personal injury, always disconnect the negative battery cable unless the repair or test procedure requires that battery voltage be applied.

• Always relieve the fuel system pressure prior to disconnecting any fuel system component (injector, fuel rail, pressure regulator, etc.), fitting or fuel line connection. Exercise extreme caution whenever relieving fuel system pressure to avoid exposing skin, face and eyes to fuel spray. Please be advised that fuel under pressure may penetrate the skin or any part of the body that it contacts.

• Always place a shop towel or cloth around the fitting or connection prior to loosening to absorb any excess fuel due to spillage. Ensure that all fuel spillage (should it occur) is quickly removed from engine surfaces. Ensure that all fuel soaked cloths or towels are deposited into a suitable waste container.

• Always keep a dry chemical (Class B) fire extinguisher near the work area.

• Do not allow fuel spray or fuel vapors to come into contact with a spark or open flame.

• Always use a back-up wrench when loosening and tightening fuel line connection fittings. This will prevent unnecessary stress and torsion to fuel line piping.

• Always replace worn fuel fitting O-rings with new. Do not substitute fuel hose or equivalent where fuel pipe is installed.

Before servicing the vehicle, make sure to also refer to the precautions in the beginning of this section as well.

RELIEVING FUEL SYSTEM PRESSURE

See Figures 463 and 464.

❊❊ CAUTION

Do not smoke, carry lighted tobacco or have an open flame of any type when working on or near any fuel-related component. Highly flammable mixtures are always present and may be ignited. Failure to follow these instructions may result in serious personal injury.

❊❊ CAUTION

Before working on or disconnecting any of the fuel tubes or fuel system components, relieve the fuel system pressure to prevent accidental spraying of fuel. Fuel in the fuel system remains under high pressure, even when the engine is not running. Failure to follow this instruction may result in serious personal injury.

❊❊ CAUTION

Do not work on the fuel system until the pressure has been released and the engine has cooled. Fuel in the high-pressure fuel system is hot and under very high pressure. High-pressure fuel may cause cuts and contact with hot fuel may cause burns. Failure to follow these instructions may result in serious personal injury.

➡This procedure is for releasing the low-pressure fuel system pressure. The high-pressure fuel system cannot be relieved of pressure manually. The high-pressure fuel system will lose pressure as the engine cools down. The pressure will bleed off after approximately 30 seconds with the key in the OFF position. Wait for the engine

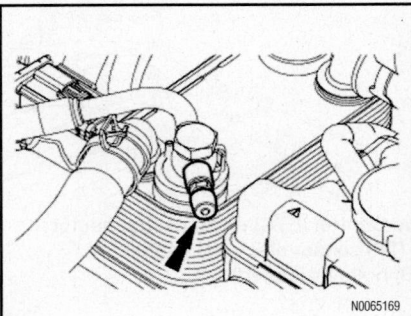

Fig. 463 Remove the Schrader valve cap

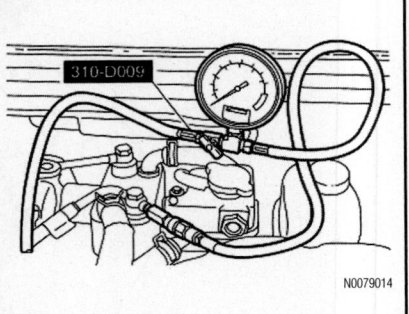

Fig. 464 Install the Fuel Pressure Test Kit onto the Schrader valve

to be cool before servicing the high-pressure fuel system.

1. With the vehicle in NEUTRAL, position it on a hoist.
2. Disconnect both battery ground cables.
3. Remove the Schrader valve cap.

➡It may be necessary to remove the degas bottle cap to install the Fuel Pressure Test Kit onto the Schrader valve. If the degas bottle cap is removed, cap off the degas bottle to prevent foreign material from entering the degas bottle.

4. Install the Fuel Pressure Test Kit (310-D009) onto the Schrader valve.

➡Open manual valve slowly to relieve the system pressure. This may drain fuel from the fuel system. Place the fuel in a suitable container.

5. Open the manual valve on the Fuel Pressure Test Kit and relieve the fuel pressure.
6. Install the Schrader valve cap.
7. Connect both battery ground cables.
8. After the repair is complete, bleed the fuel system.

FUEL FILTER

REMOVAL & INSTALLATION

6.2L Diesel Engine Fuel Conditioning Module

See Figures 465 and 466.

❊❊ CAUTION

When handling fuel, always observe fuel handling precautions and be prepared in the event of fuel spillage. Spilled fuel may be ignited by hot

vehicle components or other ignition sources. Failure to follow these instructions may result in serious personal injury.

1. Release the fuel system pressure.

➡Once the fuel conditioning module is drained and the fuel system service is completed, make sure the fuel/water separator drain valve is completely closed to prevent air from entering into the fuel system.

2. Open the fuel/water separator drain valve and drain the fuel into a suitable container.

3. Disconnect the Fuel Pump (FP) and the water in fuel sensor electrical connectors.

4. Disconnect the fuel tank-to-fuel conditioning module fuel supply tube and fuel conditioning module-to-fuel tank fuel return tube quick connect coupling.

5. Disconnect the fuel tank-to-fuel conditioning module-to-engine fuel supply tube and engine-to-fuel conditioning module fuel return tube spring lock coupling.

6. Remove the 3 mounting nuts and the fuel conditioning module.

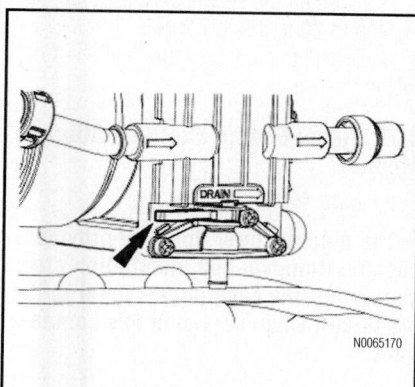

Fig. 465 Open the fuel/water separator drain valve

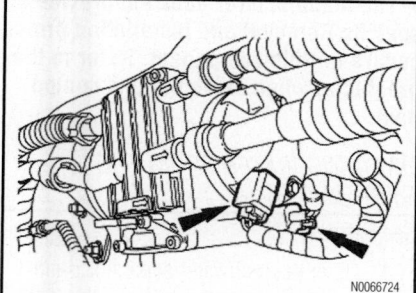

Fig. 466 Disconnect the Fuel Pump (FP) and the water in fuel sensor electrical connectors

✸✸ WARNING

Only use a fuel conditioning module that has a brown cover on the Fuel Pump (FP) (low-pressure FP). Installing a fuel conditioning module with a black cover on the FP (high-pressure FP) may result in damage to the high-pressure fuel system.

7. To install, reverse the removal procedure.

8. Tighten the fuel conditioning module mounting nuts to 15 ft. lbs. (20 Nm).

Disassembly
See Figure 467.

✸✸ WARNING

The fuel conditioning module that is used with the 6.4L diesel engine has a brown pump cover. Installing a fuel conditioning module with a black cover may result in damage to the high-pressure fuel system.

1. Remove the fuel filter cover and drain the fuel from the housing. Remove and discard the O-ring seal.

2. Remove the fuel filter and discard.

3. If necessary, remove the bolt and the drain valve cover.

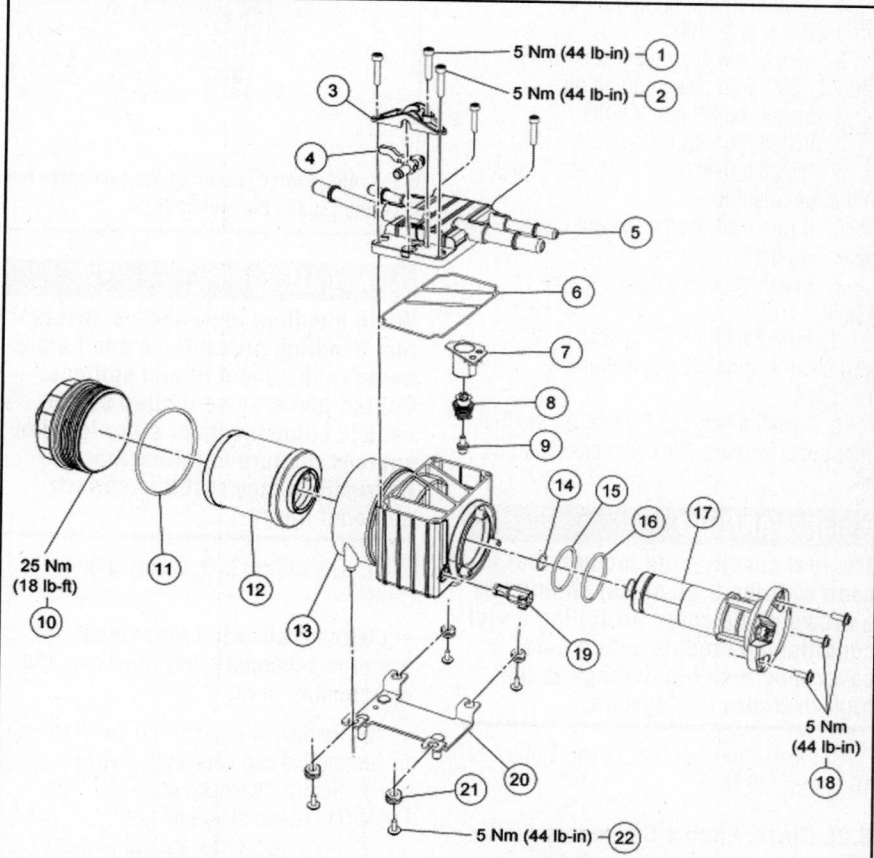

1. Drain valve cover bolt
2. Manifold cover bolt (4 required)
3. Drain valve cover
4. Drain valve
5. Manifold cover
6. Manifold cover gasket
7. Return valve retainer
8. Return valve
9. Return valve plunger
10. Fuel filter cover
11. Fuel filter cover O-ring seal
12. Fuel filter
13. Fuel conditioning module body
14. Fuel Pump (FP) O-ring seal
15. FP O-ring seal
16. FP O-ring seal
17. FP
18. FP bolts (3 required)
19. Water-in-fuel sensor
20. Fuel conditioning module mounting bracket
21. Fuel conditioning module mounting bracket rubber grommet
22. Fuel conditioning module mounting bracket bolts (4 required)

Fig. 467 Exploded view of the fuel conditioning module

4. Remove the 4 bolts and the manifold cover. Remove and discard the press-in-place gasket.

5. Remove the return valve assembly.

6. Remove the 3 bolts and the Fuel Pump (FP). Remove and discard the O-ring seals.

7. Remove the 4 bolts and the fuel conditioning module mounting bracket.

8. Inspect the fuel conditioning module mounting bracket rubber grommets for damage. If any fuel conditioning module mounting bracket rubber grommets are damaged, install a new grommet(s).

Assembly

1. Install the fuel conditioning mounting bracket and 4 bolts.

2. Install new O-ring seals on the FP and lubricate with clean engine oil.

3. Install the FP and 3 bolts.

4. Install the return valve assembly.

5. Install a new press-in-place gasket in the fuel manifold.

6. If removed, install the drain valve cover and bolt.

7. Install the manifold cover and 4 bolts.

8. Lubricate the O-ring seal with clean engine oil and install the fuel filter.

9. Install a new O-ring seal on the fuel filter cover and lubricate with clean engine oil.

✳✳ WARNING

The fuel conditioning module that is used with the 6.4L diesel engine has a brown pump cover. Installing a fuel conditioning module with a black cover may result in damage to the high-pressure fuel system.

10. Install the fuel filter cover. Tighten to 18 ft. lbs. (25 Nm).

6.2L Diesel Engine Secondary Fuel Filter

See Figure 468.

✳✳ CAUTION

Do not smoke, carry lighted tobacco or have an open flame of any type when working on or near any fuel-related component. Highly flammable mixtures are always present and may be ignited. Failure to follow these instructions may result in serious personal injury.

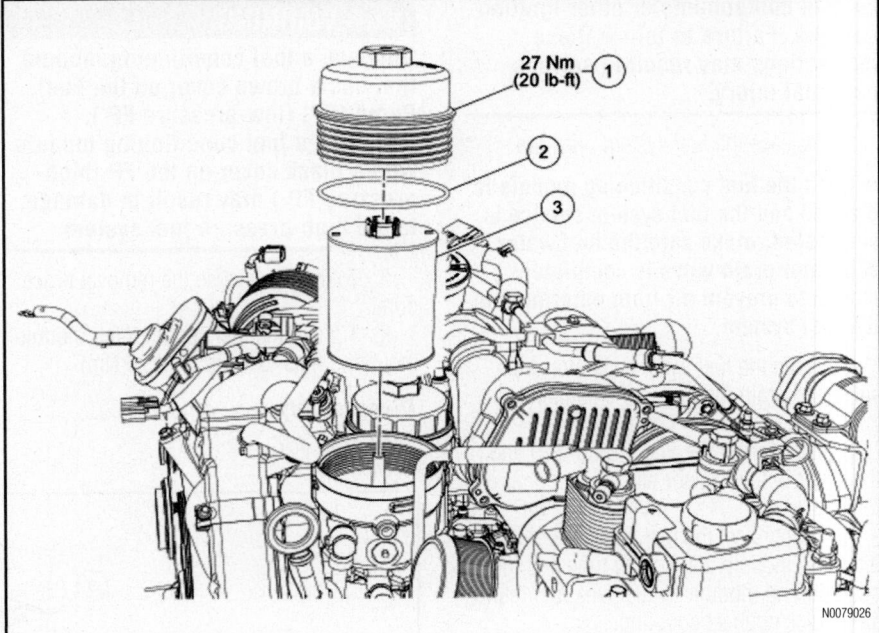

Fig. 468 Exploded view of the secondary fuel filter assembly showing the cap (1), the cap O-ring (2) and the fuel filter (3)

✳✳ CAUTION

When handling fuel, always observe fuel handling precautions and be prepared in the event of fuel spillage. Spilled fuel may be ignited by hot vehicle components or other ignition sources. Failure to follow these instructions may result in serious personal injury.

1. Disconnect both battery ground cables.

➡Clean all dirt and foreign material from the secondary fuel filter cap and surrounding area.

2. Remove the secondary fuel filter cap by turning the cap counterclockwise.

3. Remove the secondary fuel filter. Discard the secondary fuel filter.

4. Remove the O-ring seal from the secondary fuel filter cap. Discard the O-ring seal.

To install:

5. Carefully clean all mating surfaces.

6. Install a new O-ring seal onto the secondary fuel filter cap.

7. Install a new secondary fuel filter into the secondary fuel filter housing.

➡Apply clean engine oil to the O-ring seal.

8. Slowly install the secondary fuel filter cap allowing the fuel to soak into the secondary fuel filter until it contacts the secondary fuel filter housing.

9. Tighten the secondary fuel filter cap. Tighten to 20 ft. lbs. (27 Nm).

10. Bleed the low pressure fuel system.

6.7L Diesel Engine Fuel Conditioning Module

See Figure 469.

➡The manufacturer does not provide a specific Removal and Installation procedure for this component. Refer to the graphic(s) when servicing this component.

6.7L Diesel Engine Secondary Fuel Filter

See Figure 470.

➡The manufacturer does not provide a specific Removal and Installation procedure for this component. Refer to the graphic(s) when servicing this component.

DRAINING WATER FROM THE SYSTEM

See Figure 471.

1. Open the fuel/water separator drain valve and drain the fuel into a suitable container.

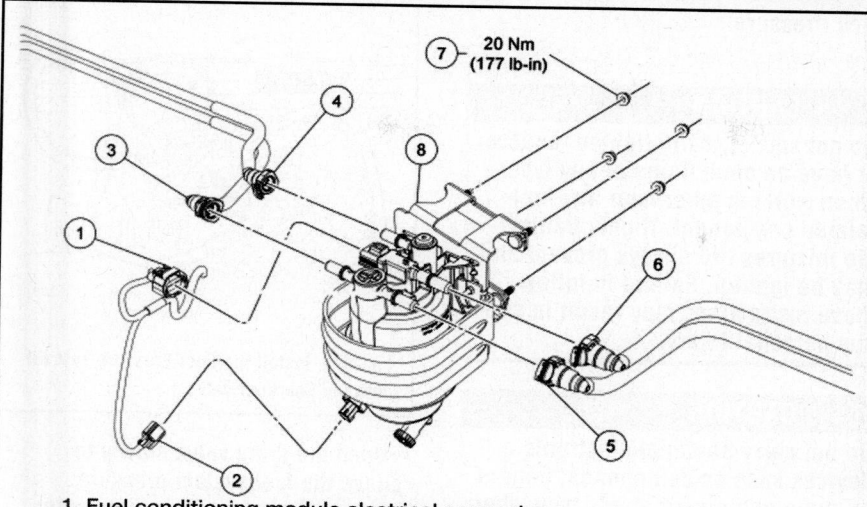

1. Fuel conditioning module electrical connector
2. Water-in-fuel sensor connector
3. Rear fuel return tube quick connect coupling-to-fuel conditioning module
4. Rear fuel supply tube quick connect coupling-to-fuel conditioning module
5. Rear fuel return tube quick connect coupling-to-fuel conditioning module
6. Rear fuel supply tube quick connect coupling-to-fuel conditioning module
7. Fuel conditioning module nut (4 required)
8. Fuel conditioning module

N0114555

Fig. 469 Exploded view of the Fuel Conditioning Module

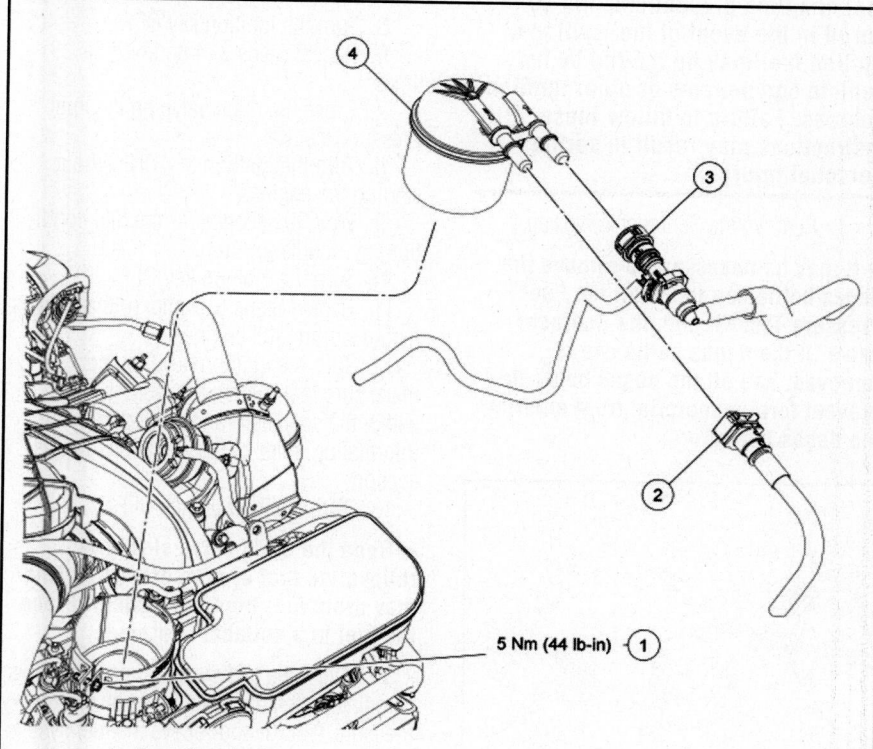

1. Bracket bolt
2. Fuel filter-to-fuel injection pump supply tube fitting
3. Fuel injector return hose-to-fuel filter fitting
4. Secondary fuel filter

N0114554

Fig. 470 Exploded view of the secondary fuel filter assembly

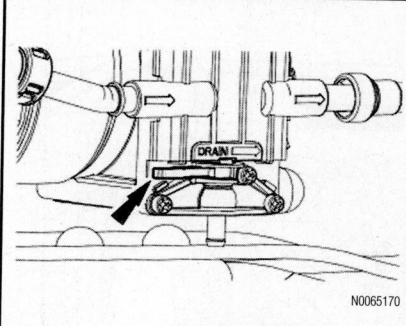

N0065170

Fig. 471 Open the fuel/water separator drain valve

FUEL SYSTEM PURGING

BLEEDING

High Pressure

See Figures 472 and 473.

❋❋ CAUTION

Do not smoke, carry lighted tobacco or have an open flame of any type when working on or near any fuel-related component. Highly flammable mixtures are always present and may be ignited. Failure to follow these instructions may result in serious personal injury.

❋❋ CAUTION

Do not carry personal electronic devices such as cell phones, pagers or audio equipment of any type when working on or near any fuel-related component. Highly flammable mixtures are always present and may be ignited. Failure to follow these instructions may result in serious personal injury.

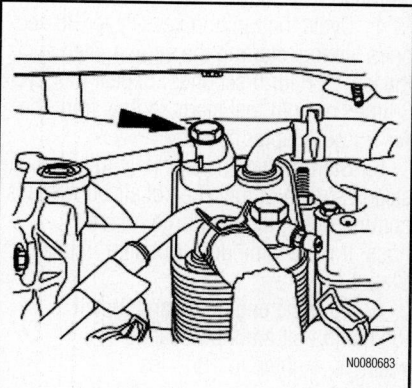

N0080683

Fig. 472 Remove the rear banjo bolt on the fuel cooler

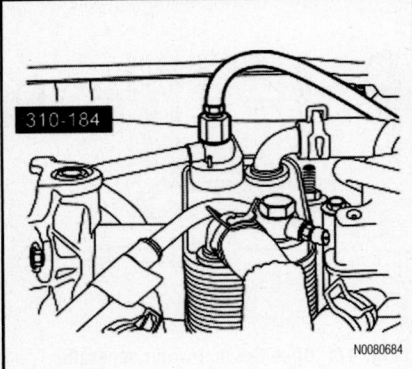

Fig. 473 Install the Air Purge Adapter in place of the rear banjo bolt

✳✳ CAUTION

When handling fuel, always observe fuel handling precautions and be prepared in the event of fuel spillage. Spilled fuel may be ignited by hot vehicle components or other ignition sources. Failure to follow these instructions may result in serious personal injury.

1. Bleed the low-pressure fuel system. For additional information, refer to Fuel System Bleeding—Low Pressure, Diesel Engine in this section.
2. Remove the rear banjo bolt on the fuel cooler.

➡**Use the old banjo bolt sealing washers when installing the Air Purge Adapter.**

➡**The Air Purge Adapter will drain fuel out of the fuel system. Install the open end of the Air Purge Adapter into a suitable fuel container.**

3. Install the Air Purge Adapter (310-184) in place of the rear banjo bolt.
4. Cycle the ignition key ON for 30 seconds without starting the engine, then cycle the key OFF for 5 seconds. Repeat this cycle 3 times or until fuel starts to flow from the Air Purge Adapter hose.
5. Start the engine and let it idle until a steady stream of fuel (free of air bubbles) is coming out of the Air Purge Adapter hose. If the engine does not start, repeat Step 4.
6. Turn the engine off and install the banjo bolt and new sealing washers. Tighten to 18 ft. lbs. (25 Nm).
7. Start the engine and let it idle for 5 minutes.

Low Pressure

See Figures 474 and 475.

✳✳ CAUTION

Do not smoke, carry lighted tobacco or have an open flame of any type when working on or near any fuel-related component. Highly flammable mixtures are always present and may be ignited. Failure to follow these instructions may result in serious personal injury.

✳✳ CAUTION

Do not carry personal electronic devices such as cell phones, pagers or audio equipment of any type when working on or near any fuel-related component. Highly flammable mixtures are always present and may be ignited. Failure to follow these instructions may result in serious personal injury.

✳✳ CAUTION

When handling fuel, always observe fuel handling precautions and be prepared in the event of fuel spillage. Spilled fuel may be ignited by hot vehicle components or other ignition sources. Failure to follow these instructions may result in serious personal injury.

1. Remove the Schrader valve cap.

➡**It may be necessary to remove the degas bottle cap to install the Fuel Pressure Test Kit onto the Schrader valve. If the degas bottle cap is removed, cap off the degas bottle to prevent foreign material from entering the degas bottle.**

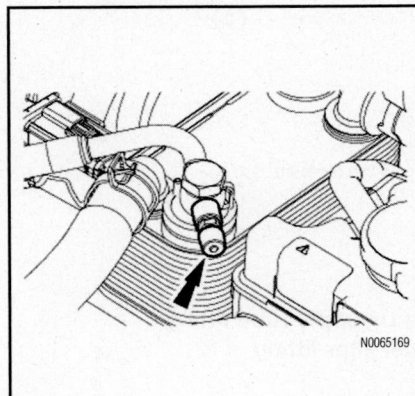

Fig. 474 Remove the Schrader valve cap

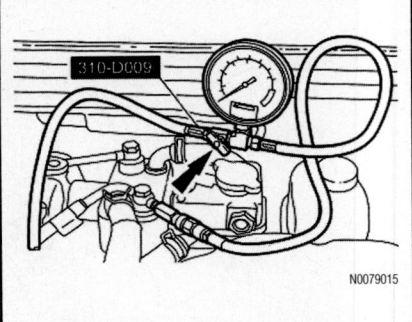

Fig. 475 Install the Fuel Pressure Test Kit onto the Schrader valve

➡**Open the drain valve slowly to relieve the fuel system pressure. This may drain fuel from the system. Place the fuel in a suitable container.**

2. Install the Fuel Pressure Test Kit (310-D009) onto the Schrader valve, and open the drain valve on the Fuel Pressure Test Kit.
3. Turn the ignition key ON without starting the engine.
4. Wait 30 seconds for the fuel conditioning module to run.
5. Turn the ignition key OFF.
6. Repeat Steps 3, 4 and 5 three times.
7. Close the drain valve on the Fuel Pressure Test Kit.
8. Turn the ignition key ON without starting the engine.
9. Wait 30 seconds for the fuel conditioning module to run.
10. Turn the ignition key OFF.
11. Repeat Steps 8, 9 and 10 three times before starting the engine.
12. Turn the ignition key ON and make sure fuel system pressure is within the specified range. For additional information, refer to Specifications in this section.
13. Turn the ignition key OFF.

➡**Open the drain valve slowly to relieve the fuel system pressure. This may drain fuel from the system. Place the fuel in a suitable container.**

14. Once the fuel system pressure test is complete, open the drain valve on the Fuel Pressure Test Kit and relieve the fuel system pressure.
15. If a no start condition still exists, perform the high-pressure fuel system bleed.
16. Install the Schrader valve cap.

INJECTION LINES

REMOVAL & INSTALLATION

Fuel Injection Pump Supply Tube

See Figures 476 and 477.

1. Shut the engine off and wait 5 minutes to allow fuel in the fuel filter module to partially drain.

2. Remove the turbocharger.

3. Remove the EGR-Oxidation Catalytic Converter (OC) pipe from the vehicle.

4. Remove the bolt and the 5 retaining nuts for the high-pressure fuel injection pump heat shield. Remove the fuel tube bracket and position the ground wire.

5. Remove the remaining 2 bolts and the high-pressure fuel injection pump heat shield.

6. Remove the 2 high-pressure fuel injection pump supply tube bracket nuts.

✳✳ WARNING

Fuel injection equipment is manufactured to very precise tolerances and fine clearances. To prevent fuel system damage, it is essential that absolute cleanliness is observed when working with these components. Always install Fuel System Caps to any open orifices or tubes.

➡**Use a back-up wrench to prevent the fittings in the high-pressure fuel injection pump from turning. If the fittings move, the high-pressure fuel injection pump fittings must be retightened.**

➡**It will be necessary to use a thin or low profile wrench to hold the fittings on the high-pressure fuel injection pump.**

7. Remove the high-pressure fuel injection pump supply tube-to-high-pressure fuel injection pump nut, sealing washers and the high-pressure fuel injection pump supply tube. Discard the sealing washers.

To install:

➡**Use a back-up wrench to prevent the fittings in the high-pressure fuel injection pump from turning. If the fittings move, the high-pressure fuel injection pump fittings must be retightened.**

➡**It will be necessary to use a thin or low profile wrench to hold the fittings on the high-pressure fuel injection pump.**

8. Install the new sealing washers and high-pressure fuel injection pump supply tube and nut to the high-pressure fuel injection pump.

    a. For Viton® sealing washers, tighten to 18 ft. lbs. (25 Nm).

    b. For copper sealing washer, tighten to 28 ft. lbs. (38 Nm).

9. Install the high-pressure fuel injection pump supply tube bracket nuts. Tighten to 97 inch lbs. (11 Nm).

✳✳ WARNING

Failure to correctly install the high-pressure fuel injection pump heat shield may result in engine damage.

10. Install the high-pressure fuel injection pump heat shield in the vehicle and install the 2 center bolts. Tighten to 10 ft. lbs. (13 Nm).

11. Position the fuel tube bracket and ground wire. Install the 5 retaining nuts and bolt for the high-pressure fuel pump shield.

    a. Tighten the fuel tube bracket nuts to 62 inch lbs. (7 Nm).

    b. Tighten the remaining fasteners to 10 ft. lbs. (13 Nm).

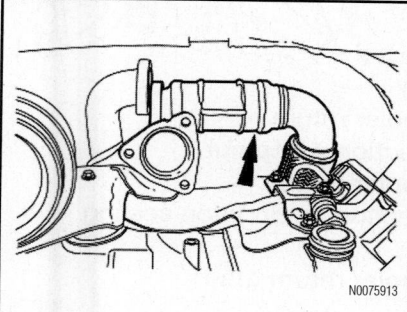

Fig. 476 Remove the EGR-Oxidation Catalytic Converter (OC) pipe from the vehicle

N0075913

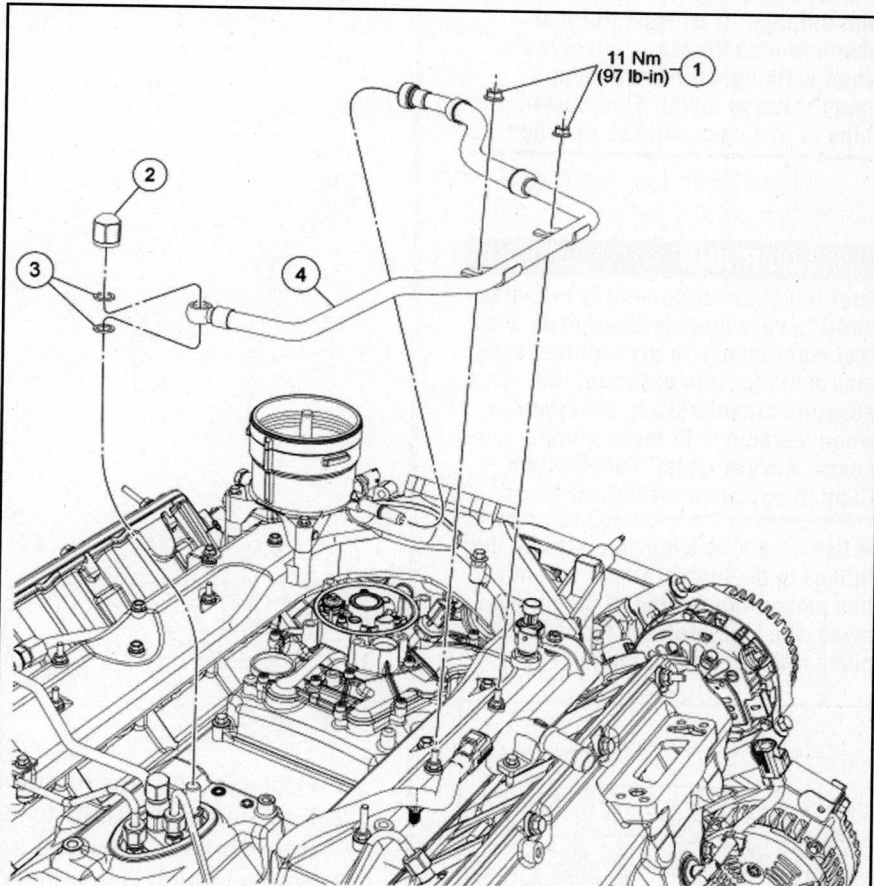

1. Fuel injection pump supply tube bracket nuts (2 required)
2. Fuel injection pump supply tube-to-high-pressure fuel injection pump nut
3. Fuel injection pump supply tube-to-high-pressure fuel injection pump Viton sealing washers (2 required)
4. Fuel injection pump supply tube

N0103075

Fig. 477 Exploded view of the fuel injection pump supply tube

12. Position the EGR-OC pipe in the vehicle.

13. Install the turbocharger.

Fuel Injection Pump-To-Fuel Cooler Return Tube

See Figures 478 and 479.

1. Remove the turbocharger.

2. Remove the EGR-Oxidation Catalytic Converter (OC) pipe from the vehicle.

3. Remove the bolt and the 5 retaining nuts for the high-pressure fuel injection pump heat shield. Remove the fuel tube bracket and position the ground wire.

4. Remove the remaining 2 bolts and the high-pressure fuel injection pump heat shield.

❈❈ WARNING

Fuel injection equipment is manufactured to very precise tolerances and fine clearances. To prevent fuel system damage, it is essential that absolute cleanliness is observed when working with these components. Always install Fuel System Caps to any open orifices or tubes.

5. Disconnect the fuel injector return tube fitting at the check valve.

❈❈ WARNING

Fuel injection equipment is manufactured to very precise tolerances and fine clearances. To prevent fuel system damage, it is essential that absolute cleanliness is observed when working with these components. Always install Fuel System Caps to any open orifices or tubes.

➡**Use a back-up wrench to prevent the fittings in the high-pressure fuel injection pump from turning. If the fittings move, the high-pressure fuel injection pump fittings must be retightened.**

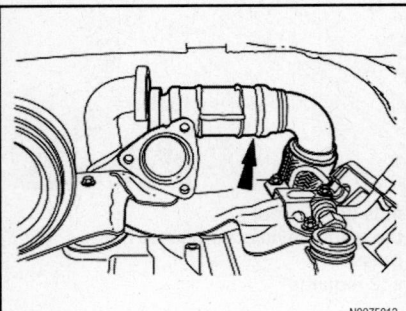

Fig. 478 Remove the EGR-Oxidation Catalytic Converter (OC) pipe from the vehicle

N0075913

➡**It will be necessary to use a thin or low profile wrench to hold the fittings on the high-pressure fuel injection pump.**

6. Remove the nut, sealing washers and fuel injection pump-to-fuel cooler return tube. Discard the sealing washers.

To install:

➡**Use a back-up wrench to prevent the fittings in the high-pressure fuel injection pump from turning. If the fittings move, the high-pressure fuel injection pump fittings must be retightened.**

➡**It will be necessary to use a thin or low profile wrench to hold the fittings on the high-pressure fuel injection pump.**

7. Install the fuel injection pump-to-fuel cooler return tube, new sealing washers and nut.

    a. For Viton® sealing washers, tighten to 18 ft. lbs. (25 Nm).

    b. For copper sealing washer, tighten to 28 ft. lbs. (38 Nm).

➡**Use a crowfoot wrench to aid in tightening the fitting.**

8. Connect the fuel injector return tube fitting at the check valve.

9. Using a torque adapter, tighten to 21 ft. lbs. (28 Nm).

❈❈ WARNING

Failure to correctly install the high-pressure fuel injection pump heat shield may result in engine damage.

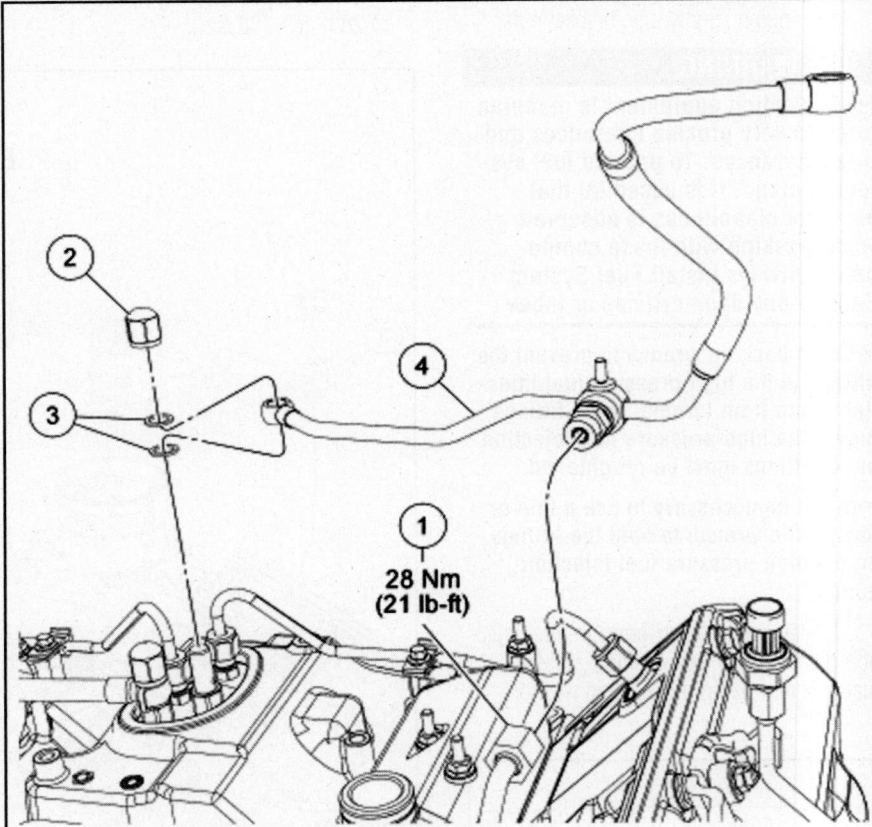

1. Fuel injector return tube fitting
2. Fuel injection pump-to-fuel cooler return tube-to-high-pressure fuel injection pump nut
3. Fuel injection pump-to-fuel cooler return tube-to-high-pressure fuel injection pump Viton sealing washers (2 required)
4. Fuel injection pump-to-fuel cooler return tube

Fig. 479 Exploded view of the fuel injection pump-to-fuel cooler return tube assembly

N0103076

10. Install the high-pressure fuel injection pump heat shield in the vehicle and install the 2 center bolts. Tighten to 10 ft. lbs. (13 Nm).

11. Position the fuel tube bracket and ground wire. Install the 5 retaining nuts and bolt for the high-pressure fuel pump shield.

   a. Tighten the fuel tube bracket nuts to 62 inch lbs. (7 Nm).

   b. Tighten the remaining fasteners to 10 ft. lbs. (13 Nm).

12. Position the EGR-OC pipe in the vehicle.

13. Install the turbocharger.

Fuel Injector Supply Tube

➡When installing a new fuel injector supply tube, the fuel injector must be removed and a new O-ring seal and sealing washer installed on it. Additionally, whenever a fuel injector supply tube fitting is loosened, a new fuel injector supply tube must be installed. Therefore, the steps required to remove and install a fuel injector supply tube are included in the fuel injector procedure

INJECTORS

REMOVAL & INSTALLATION

6.4L Diesel Engine

See Figures 480 through 482.

✳✳ CAUTION

Do not work on the fuel system until the pressure has been released and the engine has cooled. Fuel in the high-pressure fuel system is hot and under very high pressure. High-pressure fuel may cause cuts and contact with hot fuel may cause burns. Failure to follow these instructions may result in serious personal injury.

1. Shut the engine off and wait until the engine is cool or 5 minutes, whichever is longer, to allow the high-pressure fuel system pressure to bleed off and the fuel to cool.

2. Remove the LH or RH valve cover.

✳✳ CAUTION

Contact with exposed fuel injector wiring, if energized, may result in electric shock. Use care when working on or around energized fuel injector wiring. Fuel injector wiring supplies high voltage to operate the fuel injectors. Failure to follow this

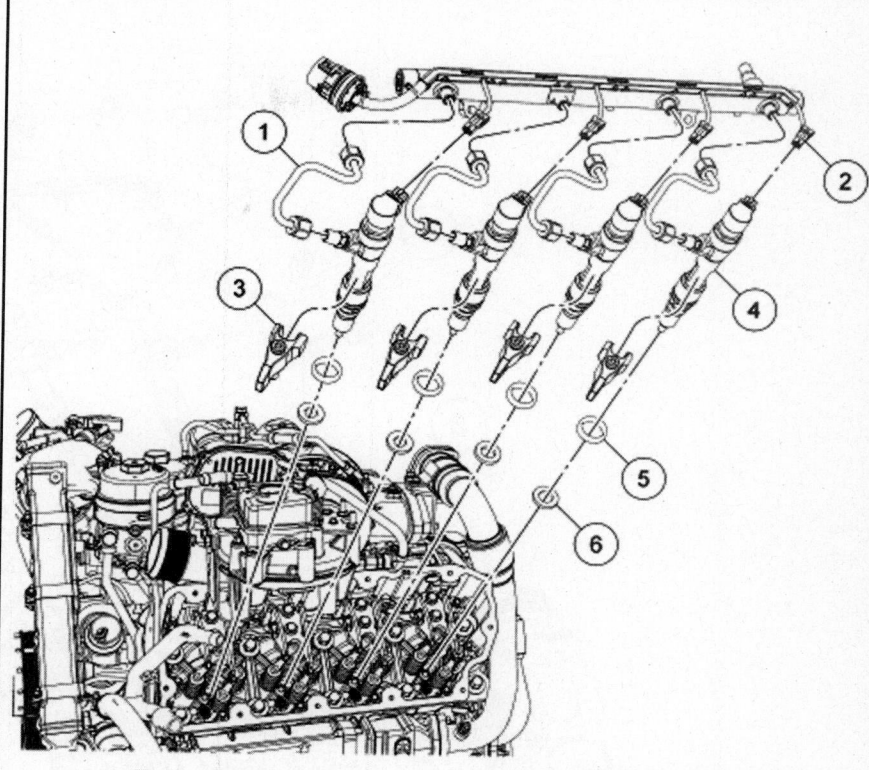

1. Fuel rail-to-fuel injector tube (4 required)
2. Fuel injector electrical connector (4 required)
3. Fuel injector hold-down clamp assembly (4 required)
4. Fuel injector (4 required)
5. Fuel injector O-ring seal (4 required)
6. Combustion gasket (4 required)

N0101521

Fig. 480 Exploded view of the LH fuel injectors assembly

instruction may result in serious personal injury.

3. Make sure the ignition switch is in the OFF position.

4. Using the Fuel Injector Connector Disconnect Tool, disconnect the fuel injector electrical connectors. Detach the fuel charging wiring harness from the fuel rail.

5. If necessary, disconnect the Fuel Rail Pressure (FRP) sensor electrical connector.

✳✳ WARNING

Fuel injection equipment is manufactured to very precise tolerances and fine clearances. To prevent fuel system damage, it is essential that absolute cleanliness is observed when working with these components. Always install Fuel System Caps on any open orifices or tubes.

➡Use a back-up wrench on the fuel injector fittings.

6. Remove and discard the fuel injector supply tube.

7. Prior to removing the injector assembly, insert clean shop towels in the oil drain holes adjacent to each glow plug.

✳✳ WARNING

Failure to account for all fuel injector hold-down clamp assembly bolt retainers or pieces of retainers prior to placing the vehicle back in service may cause engine damage. A missing retainer can be ingested into the lube oil system causing severe engine damage.

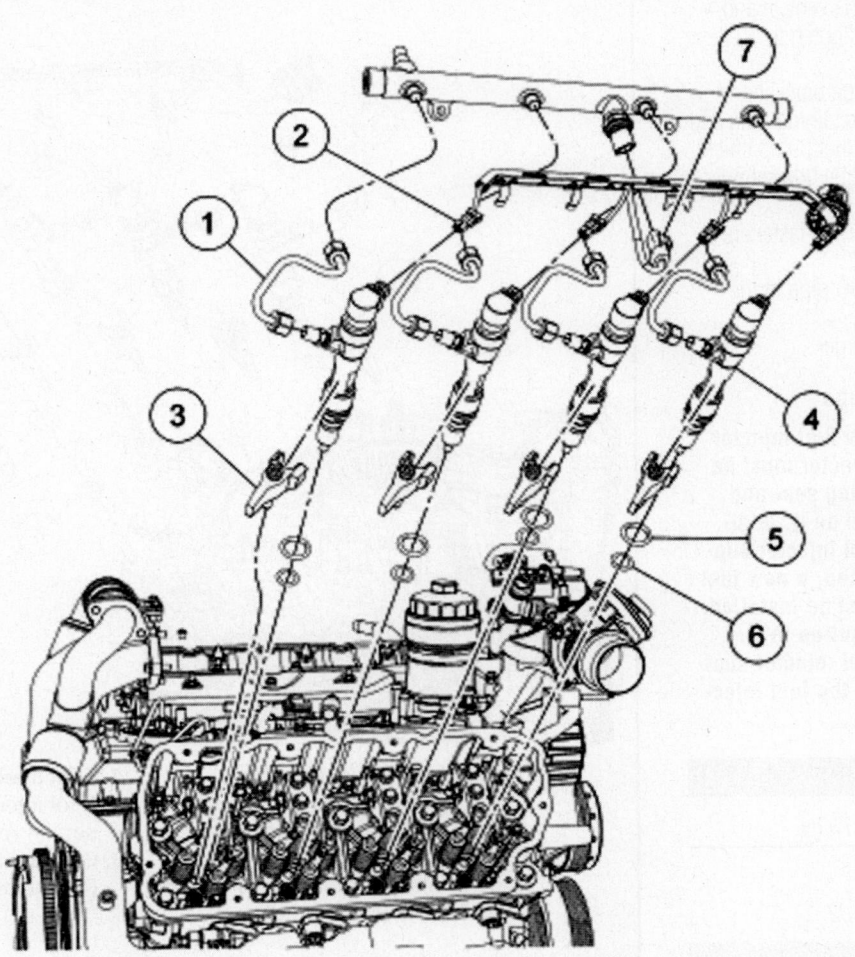

1. Fuel rail-to-fuel injector tube (4 required)
2. Fuel injector electrical connector (4 required)
3. Fuel injector hold-down clamp assembly (4 required)
4. Fuel injector (4 required)
5. Fuel injector O-ring seal (4 required)
6. Combustion gasket (4 required)
7. Fuel Rail Pressure (FRP) sensor electrical connector

N0101520

Fig. 481 Exploded view of the RH fuel injectors assembly

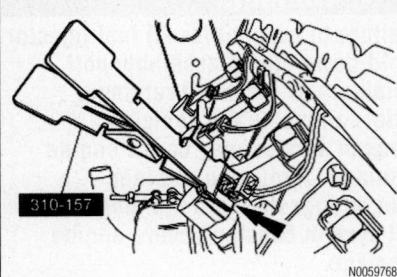

310-157

N0059768

Fig. 482 Using the Fuel Injector Connector Disconnect Tool, disconnect the fuel injector electrical connectors

✳✳ WARNING

To prevent engine damage, do not use air tools to remove the fuel injectors. The fuel injector hold-down clamp assembly bolt retainer that extracts the injector can dislodge and fall into the oil drain hole.

➡There is no need to drain the fuel rail.

➡If engine coolant is found in the combustion chambers, it may be

necessary to install a new injector sleeve.

8. Loosen the bolt, and remove the fuel injector hold-down clamp assembly and the fuel injector.

9. Remove and discard the O-ring seal and soft steel combustion gasket.

10. Install a Fuel Injector Cup on the fuel injector nozzle and store the fuel injector in the Fuel Injector Holding Rack.

➡If a fuel injector hold-down clamp assembly bolt retainer or piece of a retainer is missing from the fuel injector hold-down clamp assembly, it must be located prior to removing the shop towels.

11. Remove the shop towels.

To install:

➡Lubricate the fuel injector and O-ring seal with clean engine oil.

12. Install a new O-ring seal and a soft steel combustion gasket on the fuel injector.

13. Make sure the bead on the soft steel combustion gasket is facing the cylinder head.

✴✴ WARNING

Failure to tighten the injector correctly can lead to engine failure.

✴✴ WARNING

To prevent engine damage, do not use air tools to install the fuel injectors. The fuel injector hold-down clamp bolt retainer that extracts the injector can dislodge and fall into the oil drain hole.

✴✴ WARNING

If the fuel injector hold-down clamp assembly bolt retainer is damaged or missing, a new fuel injector hold-down clamp assembly must be installed, or the clamp assembly will not be able to remove the fuel injector.

14. Install the fuel injector, the fuel injector hold-down clamp assembly and the bolt. Tighten to 18 inch lbs. (2 Nm).

➡Use a back-up wrench on the fuel injector fittings.

➡Use a crowfoot wrench to aid in tightening the fuel injector supply tube.

15. Install the new fuel injector supply tube in the following sequence.

a. Remove the Fuel System Caps from the high-pressure fuel rail and the fuel injector one at a time prior to assembly of each tube.

b. Position the new fuel injector supply tube between the high-pressure fuel rail and fuel injectors and fully hand-start and seat the tube fittings onto the mating high-pressure fuel rail and fuel injector high-pressure connectors. Snug the fuel injector supply tube fittings using the inside-out step sequence (the 2 inside tubes then the 2 outside tubes).

c. Calculate the correct torque wrench

setting for the following torque. Using a torque adapter, tighten to 18 inch lbs. (2 Nm).

d. Tighten the fuel injector hold-down clamp bolt. Tighten to 28 ft. lbs. (38 Nm).

➡Pre-tighten the fuel injector fitting first, then the fuel rail fitting.

e. Pre-tighten the fuel injector supply tube fittings.

f. Calculate the correct torque wrench setting for the following torque. Using a torque adapter, tighten to 106 inch lbs. (12 Nm).

➡Place a visible mark with a permanent marker on the high-pressure fuel rail and fuel injector threaded connection. Turning the tube fittings one flat of the nut is equal to 60 degrees.

g. Final tighten the fuel injector supply tube fittings. Tighten the fittings 60 degrees.

16. If necessary, connect the FRP sensor electrical connector.

17. Connect the fuel injector electrical connector.

18. Install the LH or RH valve cover.

19. Bleed the high-pressure fuel system.

6.7L Diesel Engine

See Figures 483 through 486.

✴✴ CAUTION

Contact with exposed fuel injector wiring, if energized, may result in electric shock. Use care when working on or around energized fuel injector wiring. Fuel injector wiring supplies high voltage to operate the fuel injectors. Failure to follow this instruction may result in serious personal injury.

✴✴ CAUTION

Always disconnect the battery ground cable at the battery when working on an evaporative emission (EVAP) system or fuel-related component. Highly flammable mixtures are always present and may be ignited. Failure to follow these instructions may result in serious personal injury.

➡During the repair or installation of fuel-related components, cap, tape or otherwise appropriately protect all fuel openings to prevent the ingress of dirt or other contamination. Remove caps,

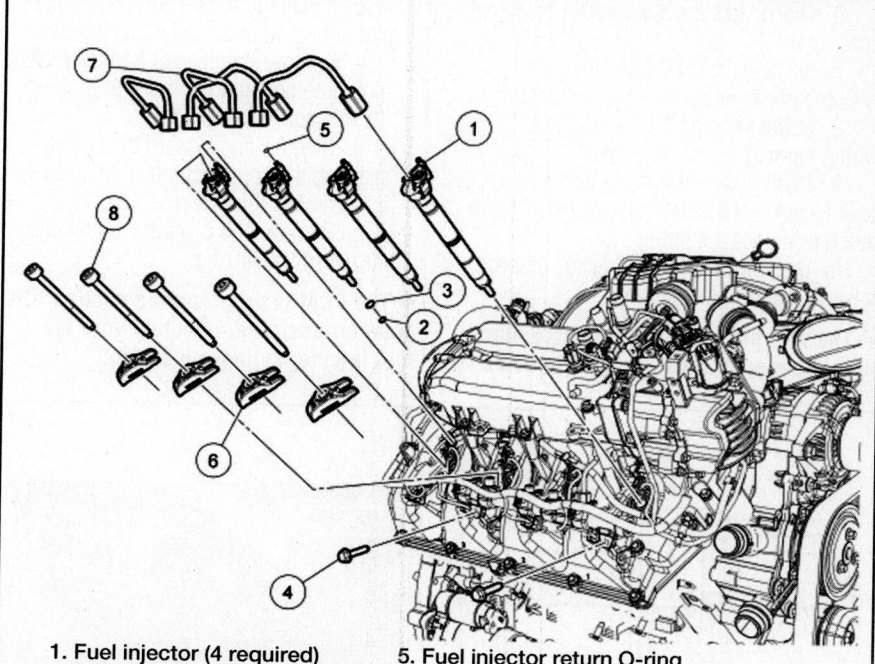

1. Fuel injector (4 required)
2. Copper combustion gasket
3. Fuel injector body O-ring seal
4. Fuel rail bolt (2 required)
5. Fuel injector return O-ring
6. Fuel injector hold-down clamp (4 required)
7. Fuel injector supply tube
8. Fuel injector hold-down clamp bolt

N0113041

Fig. 483 Exploded view of the RH fuel injector assembly (LH similar)

tape and other protective materials prior to installation.

Do not work on the fuel system until the pressure has been released and the engine has cooled. Fuel in the high-pressure fuel system is hot and under very high pressure. High-pressure fuel may cause cuts and contact with hot fuel may cause burns. Failure to follow these instructions may result in serious personal injury.

1. Release the fuel system pressure.
2. Disconnect the battery ground cables.
3. Remove the RH or LH fender splash shield.

➡The glow plug module must be removed if the RH fuel injectors are being removed.

4. If necessary, remove the glow plug module.

➡It may be necessary to unthread the engine sound shield retainers from the engine.

5. Remove the 5 RH or 5 LH engine sound shield retainers and the RH or LH engine sound shield.
6. Disconnect the fuel injector electrical connector.
7. Disconnect the 3 fuel charging wiring harness retainers from the fuel rail.
8. Position aside the fuel injector wiring harness.
9. Push down on the tabs and pull up on the center of the fuel injector return hose fitting to unlock the fitting.
10. Disconnect the fuel injector return hose fitting from the fuel injector.

➡The fuel pressure control valve electrical connector must be disconnected

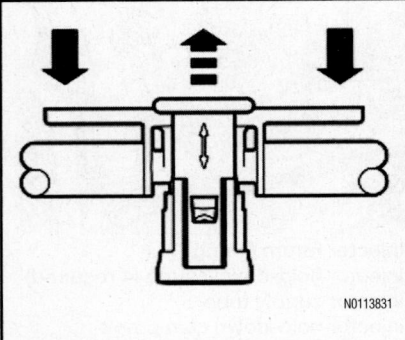

Fig. 484 Push down on the tabs and pull up on the center of the fuel injector return hose fitting to unlock the fitting

---

to remove the cylinder No. 8 fuel injector.

11. If necessary, disconnect the fuel pressure control valve electrical connector.

Fuel injection equipment is manufactured to very precise tolerances and fine clearances. To prevent fuel system damage, it is essential that absolute cleanliness is observed when working with these components.

➡The fuel injector supply tube cannot be reused.

12. Remove and discard the fuel injector supply tube.

➡The fuel injector hold-down clamp bolts are torque-to-yield and cannot be reused.

13. Remove and discard the fuel injector hold-down clamp bolt.
14. Remove the fuel injector hold-down clamp.
15. Install the Injector Removal Tool (310-230).
   a. Install the Injector Removal Tool to the fuel injector and fully hand-tighten the Injector Removal Tool mounting bolt.
   b. Install the Allen-head push bolt and tighten to remove the fuel injector.
   c. Remove the Injector Removal Tool mounting bolt and the lower portion of the Injector Removal Tool.
   d. Remove and discard the O-ring seal and the copper combustion gasket from the fuel injector.
   e. Remove and discard the fuel injector return fuel O-ring.

➡The PCM is programmed with an IQA code for each fuel injector. Note the fuel injector cylinder location.

Fig. 485 Install the Injector Removal Tool

---

16. Install the fuel injector into the Fuel Injector Cup and store the fuel injector in the corresponding cylinder location in the Fuel Injector Holding Rack.

To install:

17. Install a new fuel injector body O-ring seal and a new copper combustion gasket onto the fuel injector.
18. Install a new fuel injector return fuel O-ring.

➡If a fuel injector is being reused, make sure to install it in the original location.

19. Install the fuel injector, the fuel injector hold-down clamp and a new fuel injector hold-down clamp bolt.
   a. Lubricate the fuel injector hold-down clamp bolt mating surface of the fuel injector hold-down clamp with clean engine oil.
   b. Tighten the fuel injector hold-down clamp bolt to 22 ft. lbs. (30 Nm).
   c. Tighten the fuel injector hold-down clamp bolt an additional 90 degrees.

➡If more than one fuel injector supply tube has been removed from either cylinder head, the 2 fuel rail mounting bolts must be loosened before the new fuel injector supply tubes are installed.

20. If necessary, loosen the 2 fuel rail mounting bolts.

➡Use a deep-well crowfoot socket to tighten the fuel injector supply tube.

21. Install the new fuel injector supply tube in the following sequence.
   a. Position the new fuel injector supply tube between the fuel rail and the fuel injector. Fully hand-start and seat the fuel injector supply tube fittings onto the fuel rail and the fuel injector high-pressure connectors.
   b. If necessary, tighten the 2 fuel rail mounting bolts. Tighten to 18 ft. lbs. (24 Nm).
   c. Pre-tighten the fuel injector supply tube fittings.
   d. Tighten the fuel injector fitting to 15 ft. lbs. (20 Nm).
   e. Tighten the fuel rail fitting to 15 ft. lbs. (20 Nm).
   f. Final-tighten the fuel injector supply tube fittings.
   g. Tighten the fuel injector fitting to 26 ft. lbs. (35 Nm).
   h. Tighten the fuel rail fitting to 26 ft. lbs. (35 Nm).
22. If necessary, connect the fuel pressure control valve electrical connector.
23. Connect the fuel injector return hose fitting to the fuel injector.

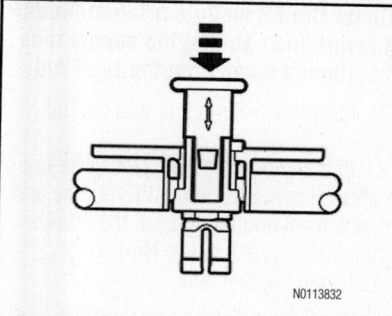

Fig. 486 Push down on the center of the fuel injector return hose fitting to lock the fitting

24. Push down on the center of the fuel injector return hose fitting to lock the fitting.

25. Connect the 3 fuel injector wiring harness retainers to the fuel rail.

26. Connect the fuel injector electrical connector.

27. Position the RH or LH engine sound shield and install the 5 RH or LH engine sound shield retainers.

28. If necessary, install the glow plug module.

29. Install the RH or LH fender splash shield.

30. Connect the battery ground cable(s).

➡A fuel injector replacement label must be installed for each fuel injector that was replaced.

31. Install the fuel injector replacement label to the top of the oil separator housing and circle the cylinder number for the fuel injector that has been replaced.

➡The PCM must be programmed with the proper fuel injector IQA codes.

32. Using the scan tool, program the PCM with the appropriate fuel injector IQA code for any fuel injector that was replaced. For additional information, refer to the Powertrain Control/Emissions Diagnosis (PC/ED) manual.

33. Prime the fuel system by cycling the ignition 3 times as follows:

   a. Turn the ignition key ON without cranking the engine.

   b. Wait 30 seconds for the fuel conditioning module to run.

   c. Turn the ignition key OFF.

FUEL SUPPLY PUMP

REMOVAL & INSTALLATION

Plastic Fuel Tank

See Figures 487 and 488.

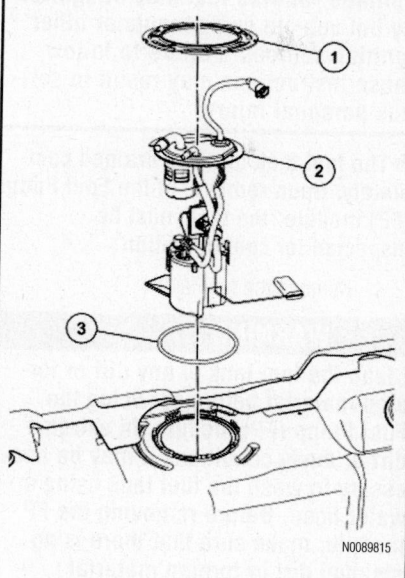

Fig. 487 Fuel Pump (FP) module lock ring (1), FP Module (2), and FP module O-ring seal (3)

✳✳ CAUTION

Do not smoke, carry lighted tobacco or have an open flame of any type when working on or near any fuel-related component. Highly flammable mixtures are always present and may be ignited. Failure to follow these instructions may result in serious personal injury.

✳✳ CAUTION

When handling fuel, always observe fuel handling precautions and be prepared in the event of fuel spillage. Spilled fuel may be ignited by hot vehicle components or other ignition sources. Failure to follow these instructions may result in serious personal injury.

➡The fuel tank must be drained completely. Upon removal of the Fuel Pump (FP) module, the tank must be inspected for contamination.

1. Remove the fuel tank.

✳✳ WARNING

Clean the fuel tank of any dirt or foreign material before servicing the Fuel Pump (FP) module. In extreme dirt or dusty conditions it may be necessary to wash the fuel tank using a water hose. Before removing the FP module, make sure that there is

no residual dirt or foreign material around the FP module flange. If dirt or foreign material enter the fuel tank, damage to the FP module or other fuel system components may occur.

2. Clean the area around the FP module mounting flange.

➡Mark the orientation of the FP module on the fuel tank to aid in installation.

3. Using the Lock Ring Wrench (310-123), remove the FP module lock ring.

✳✳ WARNING

The Fuel Pump (FP) module must be handled carefully to avoid damage to the float arm.

4. Completely remove the FP module from the fuel tank.

➡Inspect the surfaces of the FP module flange and fuel tank O-ring seal contact surfaces. Do not polish or adjust the O-ring seal contact area of the fuel tank flange or the fuel tank. Install a new FP module or fuel tank if the O-ring seal contact area is bent, scratched or corroded or fuel leakage could occur.

➡Make sure to install a new FP module O-ring seal and lock ring or fuel leakage could occur.

➡Apply clean engine oil to the O-ring seal prior to installation.

5. Remove and discard the FP module O-ring seal.

To install:

➡Apply clean engine oil to the O-ring seal prior to installation.

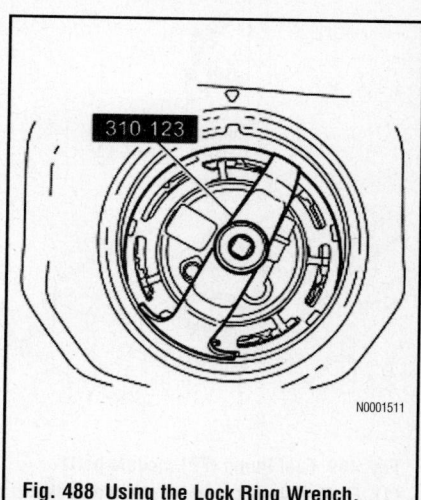

Fig. 488 Using the Lock Ring Wrench, remove the FP module lock ring

6. Install a new FP module O-ring seal.

The Fuel Pump (FP) module must be handled carefully to avoid damage to the float arm.

7. Install the FP module into the fuel tank and rotate clockwise until the alignment arrows on the FP module and fuel tank meet.

8. Using the Lock Ring Wrench, install the new FP module lock ring.

9. Make sure the alignment arrows on the FP module and the fuel tank meet before tightening the FP module lock ring.

10. Install the fuel tank.

Steel Fuel Tank

See Figure 489.

Do not smoke, carry lighted tobacco or have an open flame of any type when working on or near any fuel-related component. Highly flammable mixtures are always present and may be ignited. Failure to follow these instructions may result in serious personal injury.

When handling fuel, always observe fuel handling precautions and be prepared in the event of fuel

spillage. Spilled fuel may be ignited by hot vehicle components or other ignition sources. Failure to follow these instructions may result in serious personal injury.**

➡The fuel tank must be drained completely. Upon removal of the Fuel Pump (FP) module, the tank must be inspected for contamination.

1. Remove the fuel tank.

Clean the fuel tank of any dirt or foreign material before servicing the Fuel Pump (FP) module. In extreme dirt or dusty conditions it may be necessary to wash the fuel tank using a water hose. Before removing the FP module, make sure that there is no residual dirt or foreign material around the FP module flange. If dirt or foreign material enter the fuel tank, damage to the FP module or other fuel system components may occur.

2. Clean the area around the FP mounting flange.

➡Mark the orientation of the FP module on the fuel tank to aid in installation.

3. Remove the 6 bolts from the FP module.

The Fuel Pump (FP) module must be handled carefully to avoid damage to the float arm.

4. Completely remove the FP module from the fuel tank.

➡Inspect the surfaces of the FP module flange and fuel tank gasket contact surfaces. Do not polish or adjust the gasket contact area of the fuel tank flange or the fuel tank. Install a new FP module or fuel tank if the gasket contact area is bent, scratched or corroded or fuel leakage could occur.

➡Make sure to install a new FP module gasket or fuel leakage could occur.

5. Remove and discard the FP module gasket.

To install:

6. Install a new FP module gasket.

The Fuel Pump (FP) module must be handled carefully to avoid damage to the float arm.

➡Check the FP module orientation during installation so that the supply tube is positioned away from the float rod.

7. Install the FP module into the fuel tank.

8. Rotate the FP module clockwise until the alignment marks on the FP module and fuel tank meet and then install the 6 bolts. Tighten to 89 inch lbs. (10 Nm).

9. Install the fuel tank.

2011 Models

See Figures 490 through 492.

Do not smoke, carry lighted tobacco or have an open flame of any type when working on or near any fuel-related component. Highly flammable mixtures are always present and may be ignited. Failure to follow these instructions may result in serious personal injury.

Before working on or disconnecting any of the fuel tubes or fuel system components, relieve the fuel system pressure to prevent accidental spraying of fuel. Fuel in the fuel system remains under high pressure, even when the engine is not running. Failure to follow this instruction may result in serious personal injury.

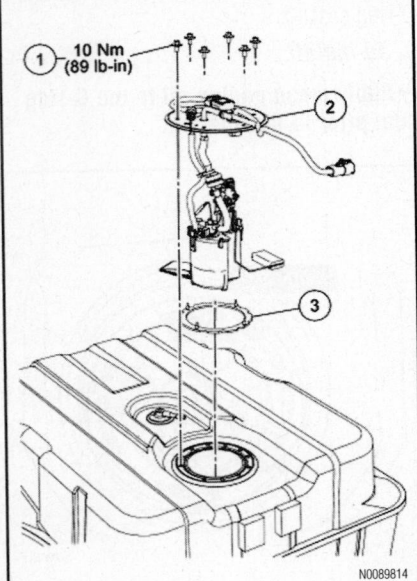

Fig. 489 Fuel Pump (FP) module bolts (1), FP Module (2), and FP module gasket (3)

N0089814

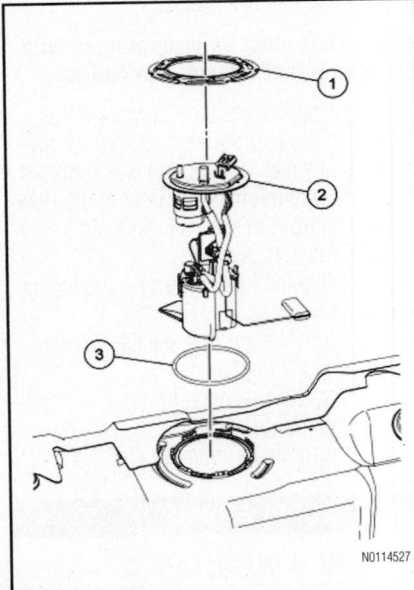

N0114527

Fig. 490 Exploded view of the Fuel Pump (FP) module showing the lock ring (1), the FP module (2) and the O-ring (3)

❋❋ CAUTION

When handling fuel, always observe fuel handling precautions and be prepared in the event of fuel spillage. Spilled fuel may be ignited by hot vehicle components or other ignition sources. Failure to follow these instructions may result in serious personal injury.

❋❋ CAUTION

Do not carry personal electronic devices such as cell phones, pagers or audio equipment of any type when working on or near any fuel-related component. Highly flammable mixtures are always present and may be ignited. Failure to follow these instructions may result in serious personal injury.

➡The Fuel Pump (FP) module has a serviceable fuel level sender.

➡To avoid introducing contamination into the fuel tank use water to clean the FP module connections, couplings, flange surface and the immediate surrounding area of any dirt or foreign material. Blow dry thoroughly with shop air after cleaning.

1. Remove the fuel tank.

❋❋ WARNING

Carefully install the lock ring wrench to avoid damaging the Fuel Pump (FP) module when removing the lock ring

2. Install the lock ring wrench and remove the FP module lock ring.

❋❋ WARNING

The Fuel Pump (FP) module must be removed and handled

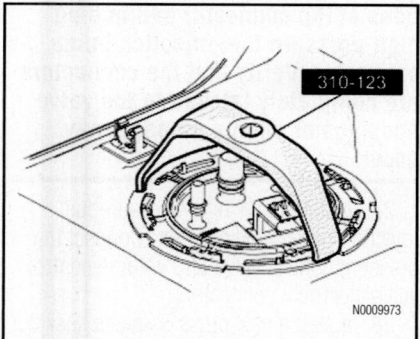

Fig. 491 Install the lock ring wrench and remove the FP module lock ring

carefully to avoid damage to the float arm.

➡The FP module will have residual fuel remaining internally, drain into a suitable container.

➡If necessary, insert a screwdriver into the empty FP module rod hole and slightly pull the screwdriver inboard until the base of the FP module clears the tank opening.

3. Carefully remove the FP module from the fuel tank.

4. Remove and discard the FP module O-ring seal.

5. Inspect the FP module for missing or broken components. Remove any missing or broken components from the fuel tank

To install:

➡Inspect the mating surfaces of the FP module flange and the fuel tank O-ring seal contact surfaces. Wipe clean with a lint-free rag.

➡Manually sweep the float arm to ensure freedom of travel.

6. Install a new FP module O-ring seal.

❋❋ WARNING

The Fuel Pump (FP) module must be handled carefully to avoid damage to the float arm.

7. Install the FP module by inserting float rod through fuel tank opening first.

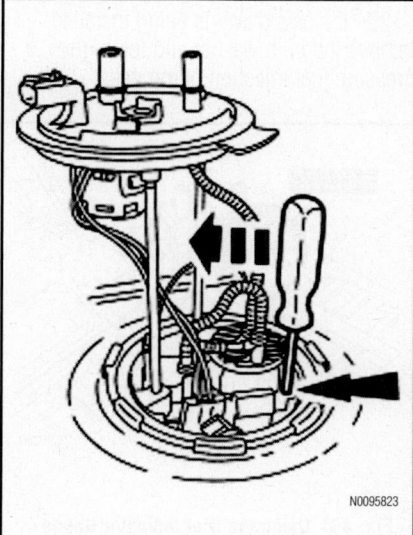

Fig. 492 Carefully remove the FP module from the fuel tank

❋❋ WARNING

Carefully install the lock ring wrench to avoid damaging the Fuel Pump (FP) module when installing the lock ring

➡Install a new lock ring if it is bent, damaged or corroded

➡Make sure the alignment tab on the FP module and the fuel tank meet before tightening the fuel tank lock ring.

8. Install the lock ring wrench and tighten the FP module lock ring.

9. Install the fuel tank.

INJECTION PUMP

REMOVAL & INSTALLATION

See Figures 493 through 496.

❋❋ CAUTION

Do not work on the fuel system until the pressure has been released and the engine has cooled. Fuel in the high-pressure fuel system is hot and under very high pressure. High-pressure fuel may cause cuts and contact with hot fuel may cause burns. Failure to follow these instructions may result in serious personal injury.

1. Shut the engine off and wait until the engine is cool or 5 minutes, whichever is longer, to allow the high-pressure fuel system to bleed off and the fuel to cool.

2. Remove the turbocharger.

3. Remove the EGR-Oxidation Catalytic Converter (OC) pipe from the vehicle.

4. Remove the bolt and the 5 retaining nuts for the high-pressure fuel injection pump heat shield. Remove the fuel tube bracket and position aside the ground wire.

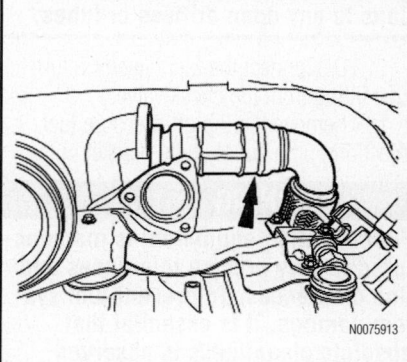

Fig. 493 Remove the EGR-Oxidation Catalytic Converter (OC) pipe from the vehicle

5. Remove the remaining 2 bolts and the high-pressure fuel injection pump heat shield.

6. Remove the RH turbocharger inlet pipe.

7. In order to remove the RH turbocharger inlet pipe, roll it to the left side of the vehicle and then remove the RH turbocharger inlet pipe.

8. Remove the 3 pushnuts and the glow plug module heat shield. Discard the pushnuts.

9. Remove the 2 fuel rail supply tube bracket bolts.

✳ WARNING

Fuel injection equipment is manufactured to very precise tolerances and fine clearances. To prevent fuel system damage, it is essential that absolute cleanliness is observed when working with these components. Always install Fuel System Caps to any open orifices or tubes.

➡ **Use a back-up wrench to prevent the fittings in the high-pressure fuel injection pump from turning. If the fittings move, the high-pressure fuel injection pump fittings must be retightened.**

➡ **It will be necessary to use a thin or low profile wrench to hold the fittings on the high-pressure fuel injection pump.**

10. Remove and discard the fuel rail supply tubes.

✳ WARNING

Fuel injection equipment is manufactured to very precise tolerances and fine clearances. To prevent fuel system damage, it is essential that absolute cleanliness is observed when working with these components. Always install Fuel System Caps to any open orifices or tubes.

11. Disconnect the fuel injector return tube fitting from the check valve.

12. Remove the 2 high-pressure fuel injection pump supply tube bracket nuts.

✳ WARNING

Fuel injection equipment is manufactured to very precise tolerances and fine clearances. To prevent fuel system damage, it is essential that absolute cleanliness is observed when working with these components. Always install Fuel System Caps to any open orifices or tubes.

➡ **Use a back-up wrench to prevent the fittings in the high-pressure fuel injection pump from turning. If the fittings move, the high-pressure fuel injection pump fittings must be retightened.**

➡ **It will be necessary to use a thin or low profile wrench to hold the fittings on the high-pressure fuel injection pump.**

13. Remove the nuts and the sealing washers for the high-pressure fuel injection pump. Remove the high-pressure fuel injection pump supply tube and fuel injection pump-to-cooler return tube. Discard the sealing washers.

14. Disconnect the high-pressure fuel injection pump electrical connector.

15. Remove the 5 bolts and the high-pressure fuel injection pump cover.

16. Remove and discard the press-in-place gasket from the high-pressure pump cover.

➡ **Use a thin gasket scraper to separate the gasket from the crankcase.**

17. Disconnect the pressure control valve and volume control valve electrical connectors. Remove and discard the high-pressure fuel injection pump cover gasket.

18. Using the Dial Indicator Gauge with Holding Fixture (100-002), check the high-pressure fuel injection pump drive gear backlash.

19. Remove the 3 bolts and the high-pressure fuel injection pump.

➡ **The high-pressure fuel injection pump drive gear bolt is a LH thread.**

20. If a new pump is being installed, remove the bolt, washer and the high-pressure fuel injection pump gear.

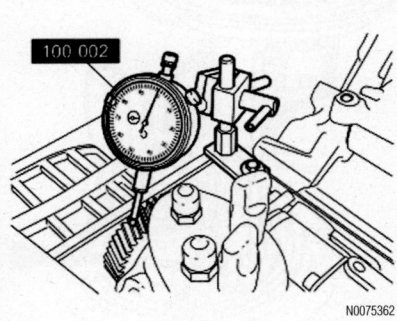

Fig. 494 Using the Dial Indicator Gauge with Holding Fixture, check the high-pressure fuel injection pump drive gear backlash

To install:

✳ WARNING

The protruding hub of the high-pressure fuel injection pump drive gear must be facing the high-pressure fuel injection pump. Failure to install the gear correctly will result in engine damage.

➡ **The high-pressure fuel injection pump drive gear bolt is a LH thread.**

➡ **The high-pressure fuel injection pump gear bolt will not be tightened at this time.**

21. If a new pump is being installed, install the high-pressure fuel injection pump drive gear, washer and bolt.

22. Install the high-pressure fuel injection pump and 3 bolts. Tighten to 45 ft. lbs. (61 Nm).

➡ **The high-pressure fuel injection pump gear bolt has a LH thread.**

➡ **Use a tool such as a Snap-On® FRDHM15 torque adapter, or equivalent, to tighten the bolt.**

23. If a new high-pressure fuel injection pump has been installed, tighten the gear bolt.

24. Using a torque adapter, tighten to 57 ft. lbs. (77 Nm).

25. Using the Dial Indicator Gauge with Holding Fixture, check the high-pressure fuel injection pump drive gear backlash. For additional information, refer to Specifications in this section.

26. Clean the cover mounting surface and apply a dime-sized bead of sealant at the seams.

✳ WARNING

Inspect the volume control valve and the pressure control valve electrical connectors for damage or obstructions at the connector and mating high-pressure fuel injection pump connector. Verify that the connectors are completely latched to the valve housings or engine damage may occur.

27. Install a new high-pressure fuel injection pump cover gasket. Connect the pressure control valve and volume control valve electrical connectors.

28. Install a new press-in-place gasket in the high-pressure fuel injection pump cover.

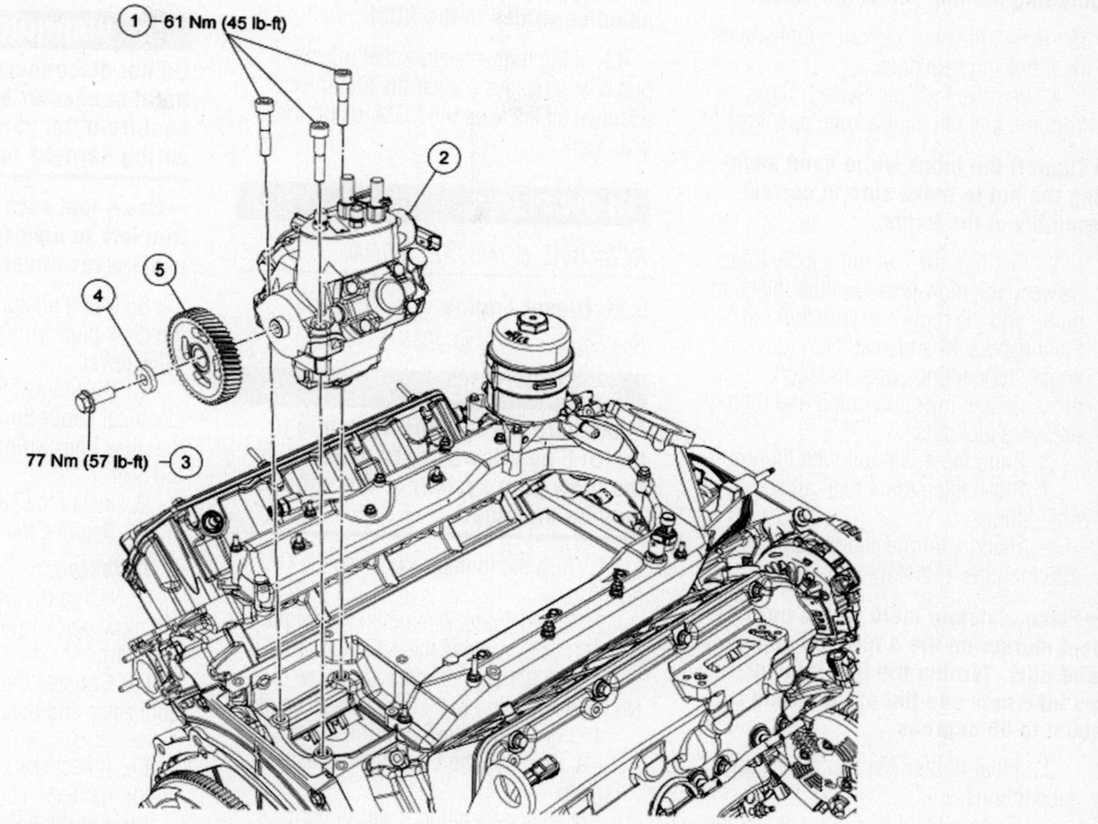

① — 61 Nm (45 lb-ft)

②

⑤

④

77 Nm (57 lb-ft) — ③

1. High-pressure fuel injection pump bolts (3 required)
2. High-pressure fuel injection pump
3. High-pressure fuel injection pump gear bolt (LH thread)
4. High-pressure fuel injection pump gear washer
5. High-pressure fuel injection pump gear

N0066938

Fig. 495 Exploded view of the fuel injection pump assembly

➡**Do not remove the Fuel System Caps from the high-pressure fuel injection pump until the fuel tubes are being installed.**

29. Install the high-pressure fuel injection pump cover and 5 bolts. Tighten to 10 ft. lbs. (13 Nm).

30. Connect the high-pressure fuel injection pump electrical connector.

➡**Use a back-up wrench to prevent the fittings in the high-pressure fuel injection pump from turning. If the fittings move, the high-pressure fuel injection pump fittings must be retightened.**

➡**It will be necessary to use a thin or low profile wrench to hold the fittings on the high-pressure fuel injection pump.**

31. Install new sealing washers, high-pressure fuel injection pump supply tube, fuel injection pump-to-cooler return tube and nuts at the high-pressure fuel injection pump.

a. For Viton® sealing washers, tighten to 18 ft. lbs. (25 Nm).

b. For copper sealing washer, tighten to 28 ft. lbs. (38 Nm).

32. Install the 2 fuel injection pump supply tube bracket nuts. Tighten to 97 inch lbs. (11 Nm).

➡**Use a crowfoot wrench to aid in tightening the fitting.**

33. Connect the fuel injector return tube fitting to the check valve.

34. Using a torque adapter, tighten to 21 ft. lbs. (28 Nm).

➡**Use a back-up wrench to prevent the fittings in the high-pressure fuel injection pump from turning. If the fittings move, the high-pressure fuel injection pump fittings must be retightened.**

➡**It will be necessary to use a thin or low profile wrench to hold the fittings on the high-pressure fuel injection pump.**

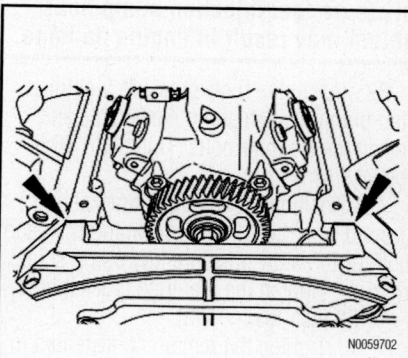

N0059702

Fig. 496 Clean the cover mounting surface and apply a dime-sized bead of sealant at the seams

➡**Use a crowfoot wrench to aid in tightening the fuel rail supply tube.**

35. Install the new fuel rail supply tubes in the following sequence.

   a. Remove the Fuel System Caps from the fuel rail supply tube openings.

➡**Support the tubes while hand snugging the nut to make sure of correct assembly of the joints.**

   b. Position the fuel rail supply tubes between the high-pressure fuel injection pump and the high-pressure fuel rail. Fully hand start and seat the 4 fuel rail supply tube fittings onto the high-pressure fuel injection pump and high-pressure fuel rails.

   c. Snug the 4 fuel rail tube fittings.

   d. Pre-tighten the 4 fuel rail supply tube fittings.

   e. Using a torque adapter, tighten to 106 inch lbs. (12 Nm).

➡**Place a visible mark with a permanent marker on the 4 fuel rail supply tube nuts. Turning the fuel injector supply tube nuts one flat of the fitting is equal to 60 degrees.**

   f. Final-tighten the fuel rail supply tube fittings.

   g. Tighten the 4 fuel rail supply tube fittings 60 degrees.

36. Install the 2 fuel rail supply tube bracket bolts. Tighten to 10 ft. lbs. (13 Nm).

➡**Use a socket to aid in installing the retainers.**

37. Install the glow plug module heat shield and 3 new pushnuts.

38. Position the RH turbocharger inlet pipe in the vehicle.

✳✳ WARNING

Failure to correctly install the high-pressure fuel injection pump heat shield may result in engine damage.

39. Install the high-pressure fuel injection pump heat shield in the vehicle and install the 2 center bolts. Tighten to 10 ft. lbs. (13 Nm).

40. Position the fuel tube bracket and ground wire. Install the 5 retaining nuts and bolt for the high-pressure fuel pump shield.

   a. Tighten the fuel tube bracket nuts to 62 inch lbs. (7 Nm).

   b. Tighten the remaining fasteners to 10 ft. lbs. (13 Nm).

41. Position the EGR-OC pipe in the vehicle.

42. Install the turbocharger.

➡**Clearing the DTCs or Keep Alive Memory (KAM) does not reset the adaptive values in the PCM.**

43. If the high-pressure fuel injection pump was replaced, clear the fuel injector adaptive tables from the PCM, using the scan tool.

GLOW PLUGS

REMOVAL & INSTALLATION

6.2L Diesel Engine

See Figures 497 and 498.

✳✳ WARNING

Make sure the ignition switch is in the OFF position prior to working on the glow plug system or the vehicle may be damaged.

1. Turn the ignition switch to the OFF position.

2. For RH side, if removing glow plug No. 1, 3 or 5, remove the Air Cleaner (ACL).

3. For RH side, if removing glow plug No. 7, remove the RH fender splash shield.

4. For LH side, perform the following:

   a. Remove the LH fender splash shield.

   b. Disconnect the 3 wiring harness in-line electrical connectors at the LH frame rail, detach the electrical connectors from the bracket and position the wiring harnesses aside.

5. If necessary, detach the glow plug wiring harness retainer.

✳✳ WARNING

Do not disconnect the glow plug electrical connector before dislodging the seal from the valve cover or the wiring harness may be damaged.

➡**Use a tool such as a body bone or trim fork to dislodge the seal. Do not use a screwdriver.**

6. Using an appropriate tool, dislodge the glow plug wiring harness seal from the valve cover.

7. Disconnect the glow plug electrical connector by pulling on the glow plug wiring harness tee above the seal.

8. Install the Glow Plug Sleeve.

9. Remove the glow plug.

To install:

10. Using the Glow Plug Sleeve, install the glow plug. Tighten to 10 ft. lbs. (14 Nm).

11. Connect the glow plug electrical connector and press the seal on the valve cover.

12. If necessary, attach the glow plug wiring harness retainer.

13. For the left side:

   a. Connect the 3 wiring harness in-line electrical connectors at the LH frame rail and attach the electrical connectors to the bracket.

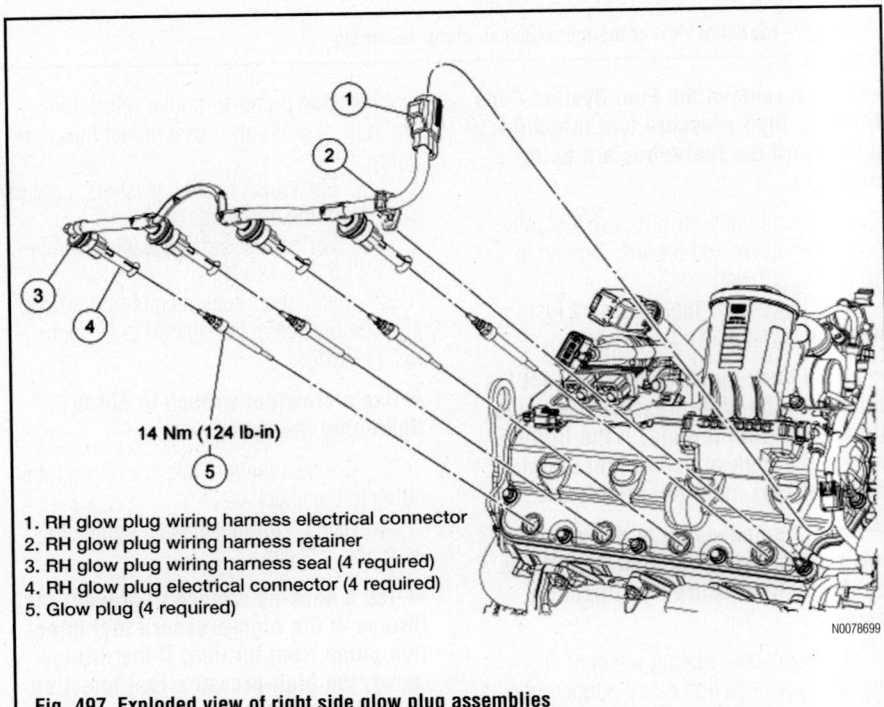

14 Nm (124 lb-in)

1. RH glow plug wiring harness electrical connector
2. RH glow plug wiring harness retainer
3. RH glow plug wiring harness seal (4 required)
4. RH glow plug electrical connector (4 required)
5. Glow plug (4 required)

N0078699

Fig. 497 Exploded view of right side glow plug assemblies

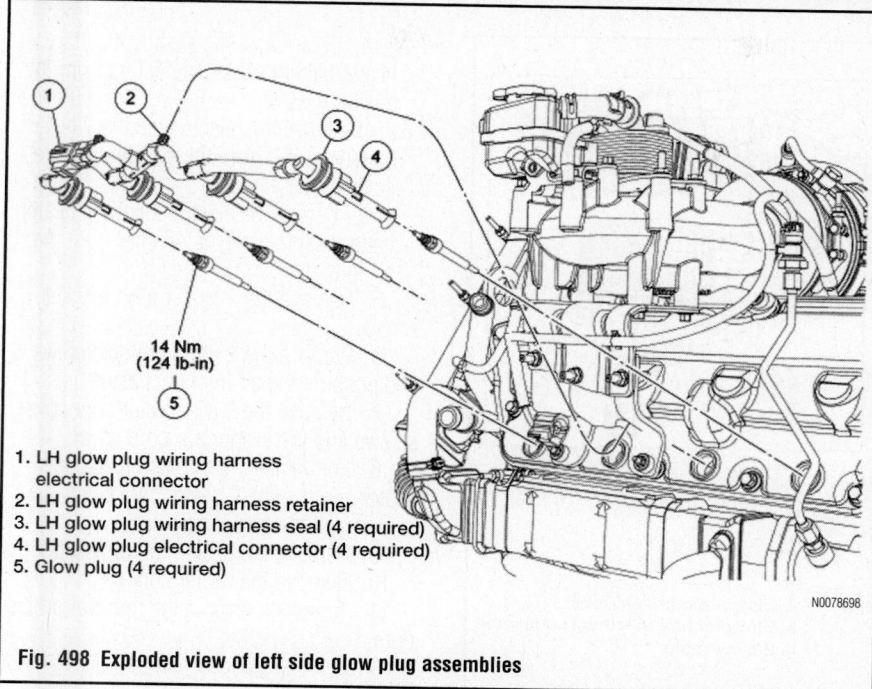

1. LH glow plug wiring harness electrical connector
2. LH glow plug wiring harness retainer
3. LH glow plug wiring harness seal (4 required)
4. LH glow plug electrical connector (4 required)
5. Glow plug (4 required)

Fig. 498 Exploded view of left side glow plug assemblies

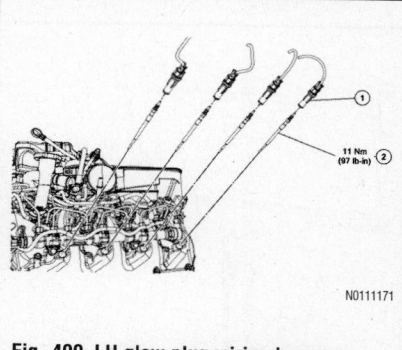

Fig. 499 LH glow plug wiring harness electrical connector (1) and glow plug (2)

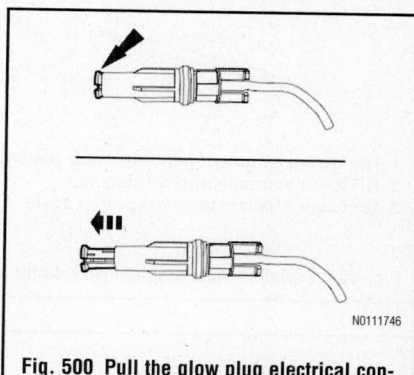

Fig. 500 Pull the glow plug electrical connector out of the outer sleeve

b. Install the LH fender splash shield.

14. For the RH side:

a. If removed, install the RH fender splash shield.

b. If removed, install the ACL.

6.7L Diesel Engine

See Figures 499 and 500.

1. Remove the LH or RH fender splash shield.

2. Using the tabs on the top of glow plug connector, pull the glow plug connector off the glow plug.

3. Remove the glow plug.

➥**RH similar.**

To install:

4. Install the glow plug. Tighten to 97 inch lbs. (11 Nm).

5. Pull the glow plug electrical connector out of the outer sleeve.

6. Connect the glow plug electrical connector to the glow plug and push the connector down to lock the connector on the glow plug.

7. Install the LH or RH fender splash shield.

HEATING & AIR CONDITIONING SYSTEM

BLOWER MOTOR

REMOVAL & INSTALLATION

2010 Models

See Figures 501 through 503.

➥**The blower motor vent tube must be completely removed from the blower motor before it can be rotated and disengaged from the heater core and evaporator core housing.**

1. Remove the RH lower instrument panel insulator.

2. Remove the RH lower A-pillar junction box trim cover.

➥**The carpet below the blower motor must be positioned aside to access the dash panel insulator.**

3. Position the dash panel insulator below the blower motor aside.

4. Detach the 2 blower motor vent tube clips and remove the vent tube.

5. Disconnect the blower motor electrical connector.

6. Rotate the blower motor counterclockwise to disengage it from the heater core and evaporator core housing.

7. Remove the blower motor.

❄❄ WARNING

If the wheel is to be reused, clean the corrosion from the shaft end prior to removing the wheel.

8. Remove the wheel from the blower motor.

a. Remove the push clip.

b. Remove the wheel from the blower motor.

9. To install, reverse the removal procedure.

2011 Models

See Figure 504.

1. Remove the Body Control Module (BCM).

2. Disconnect the blower motor electrical connector.

3. Remove the blower motor-to-blower motor housing extension screw.

4. Remove the 2 blower motor-to-heater core and evaporator core housing screws.

5. Remove the 2 blower motor housing extension screws.

6. Remove the blower motor and blower motor housing extension.

7. To install, reverse the removal procedure.

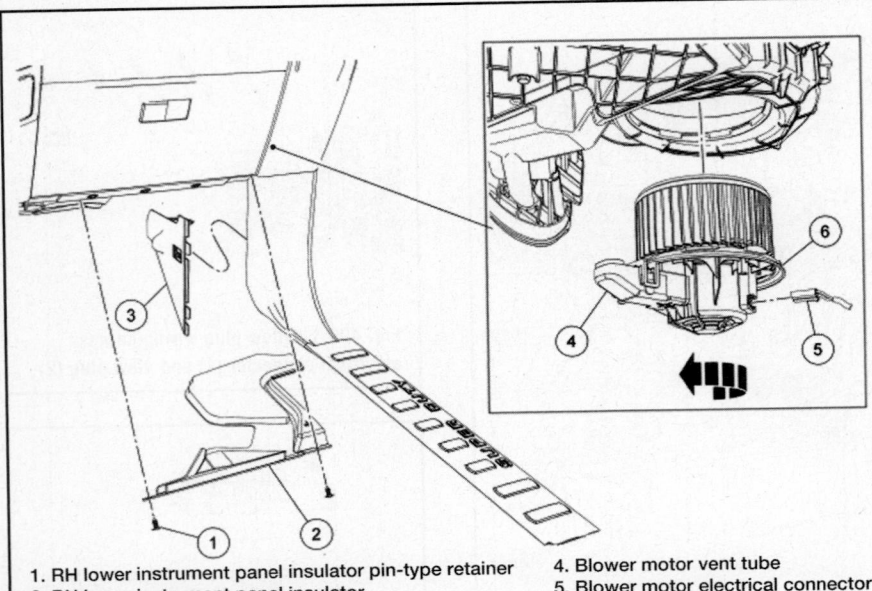

1. RH lower instrument panel insulator pin-type retainer
2. RH lower instrument panel insulator
3. RH lower A-pillar junction box trim cover
4. Blower motor vent tube
5. Blower motor electrical connector
6. Blower motor

N0064199

Fig. 501 Exploded view of the blower motor assembly

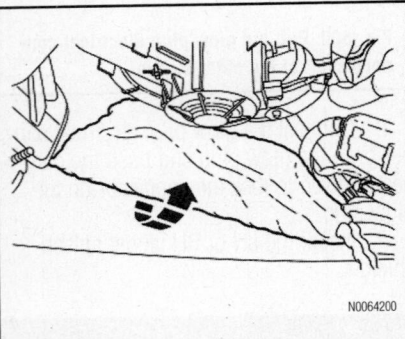

N0064200

Fig. 502 Position the dash panel insulator below the blower motor aside

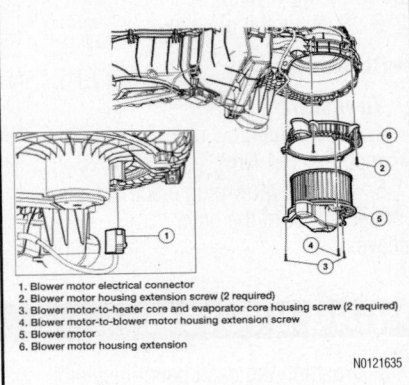

1. Blower motor electrical connector
2. Blower motor housing extension screw (2 required)
3. Blower motor-to-heater core and evaporator core housing screw (2 required)
4. Blower motor-to-blower motor housing extension screw
5. Blower motor
6. Blower motor housing extension

N0121635

Fig. 504 Exploded view of the blower motor assembly

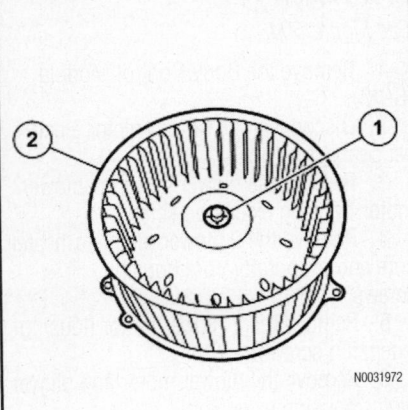

N0031972

Fig. 503 Remove the push clip (1) and the wheel (2)

HEATER CORE

REMOVAL & INSTALLATION

2010 Models

See Figure 505.

➡**If a heater core leak is suspected, the heater core must be leak tested before it is removed from the vehicle.**

1. Remove the heater core and evaporator core housing.
2. Remove the heater tube dash panel seal.
3. Remove the heater core bracket screw.
4. For vehicles with electric auxiliary heater:

a. Disconnect the electric auxiliary heater battery cable connectors from the auxiliary heater.

b. Detach the electric auxiliary heater battery cables from the evaporator core cover.

c. Detach the electric auxiliary heater battery cable pin-type retainer from the air inlet duct.

5. Remove the 2 heater tube bracket screws.
6. Remove the 3 air inlet duct screws and position the air inlet duct aside.
7. Remove the 6 evaporator core cover screws and the evaporator core cover.
8. For vehicles with electric auxiliary heater, remove the 2 heater core cover screws and the heater core cover.
9. Remove the heater core bracket.
10. Remove the heater core.
11. To install, reverse the removal procedure.

2011 Models

➡**If a heater core leak is suspected, the heater core must be leak tested before it is removed from the vehicle.**

1. For gasoline engines, drain the engine coolant.
2. For diesel engines, drain the engine primary cooling system.
3. Remove the instrument panel.
4. For diesel engines with electric heater:

a. Disconnect the Auxiliary Heater Control Module (AHCM) electrical connector.

b. Remove the 2 AHCM screws and position the AHCM aside.

5. Remove the 2 heater core cover screws and remove the cover.
6. Remove the 2 heater core tube clips at the heater core and disconnect the heater core tubes from the heater core. Discard the O-ring seals.
7. Remove the heater core.

To install:

8. To install, reverse the removal procedure.
9. Install new O-ring seals.

✳✳ WARNING

Evaluate the cooling system condition before filling the engine cooling system. Failure to follow these instructions can result in damage to the engine.

10. For diesel engines, evaluate the cooling system condition.
11. For gasoline engines, fill and bleed the cooling system.

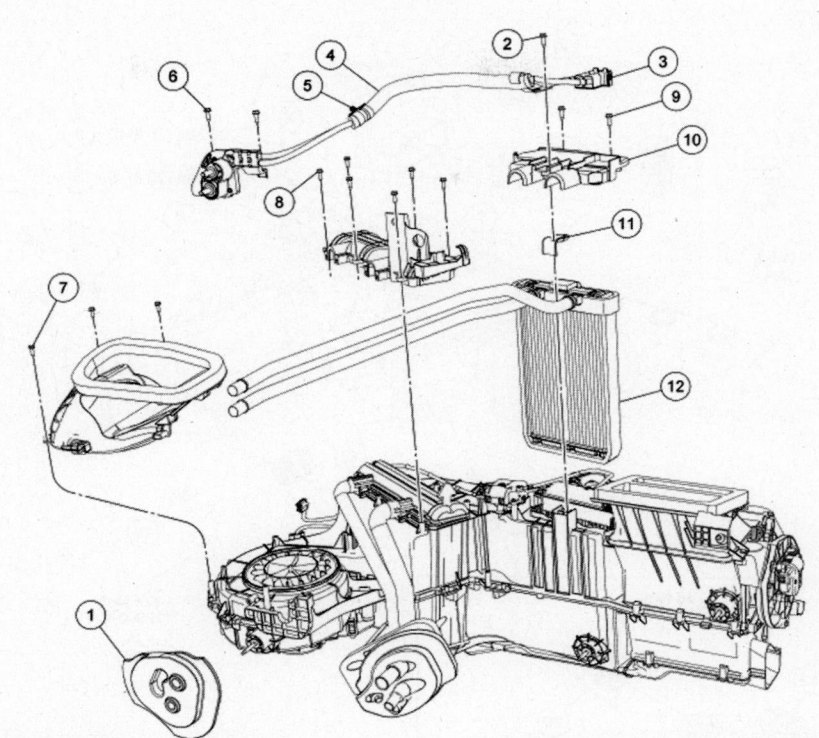

1. Heater tube dash panel seal
2. Heater core bracket screw
3. Electric auxiliary heater battery cable connector
4. Electric auxiliary heater battery cable
5. Electric auxiliary heater battery cable pin-type retainer
6. Heater tube bracket screw (2 required)
7. Air inlet duct screw (3 required)
8. Evaporator core cover screw (6 required)
9. Heater core cover screw (2 required)
10. Heater core cover
11. Heater core bracket
12. Heater core

N0068082

Fig. 505 Exploded view of the heater core assembly

STEERING

POWER STEERING GEAR

REMOVAL & INSTALLATION

2010 Models

See Figures 506 through 508.

✳✳ WARNING

While repairing the power steering system, care should be taken to prevent the entry of contaminants or failure of the power steering components may result.

✳✳ WARNING

The steering gear bolts must not be reused. The threads of the bolts are coated with a dry adhesive. When the bolts are removed, the dry adhesive is degraded. If the bolts are reused,

failure of the bolts and/or steering gear may occur.

1. With the vehicle in NEUTRAL, position it on a hoist.
2. Place the front wheels in the straight-ahead position.
3. Remove the ignition key.
4. Remove the fender splash shield.
5. Disconnect and position aside the ABS module electrical connector.
6. Disconnect the steering gear coupling shield from the line fitting and slide the shield upward on the intermediate shaft.

✳✳ WARNING

Do not allow the steering column shaft to rotate while the intermediate shaft is disconnected or damage to the clockspring can result. If there is evidence that the shaft has rotated,

the clockspring must be removed and re-centered.

7. Remove the lower steering column shaft-to-steering gear bolt.
8. Disconnect the lower steering column shaft from the steering gear.
9. Disconnect the pressure line-to-steering gear fitting. Discard the O-ring seal.
10. Disconnect the return hose-to-steering gear fitting. Discard the O-ring seal.
11. Remove the cotter pin, retainer cap and the inner drag link-to-sector shaft nut in the following sequence.
    a. Remove and discard the cotter pin.
    b. Remove the sector shaft retainer cap and nut.
12. Using the Steering Arm Remover (211-003), disconnect the inner drag link from the sector shaft arm.
13. Remove the 3 bolts and the steering gear. Discard the bolts.

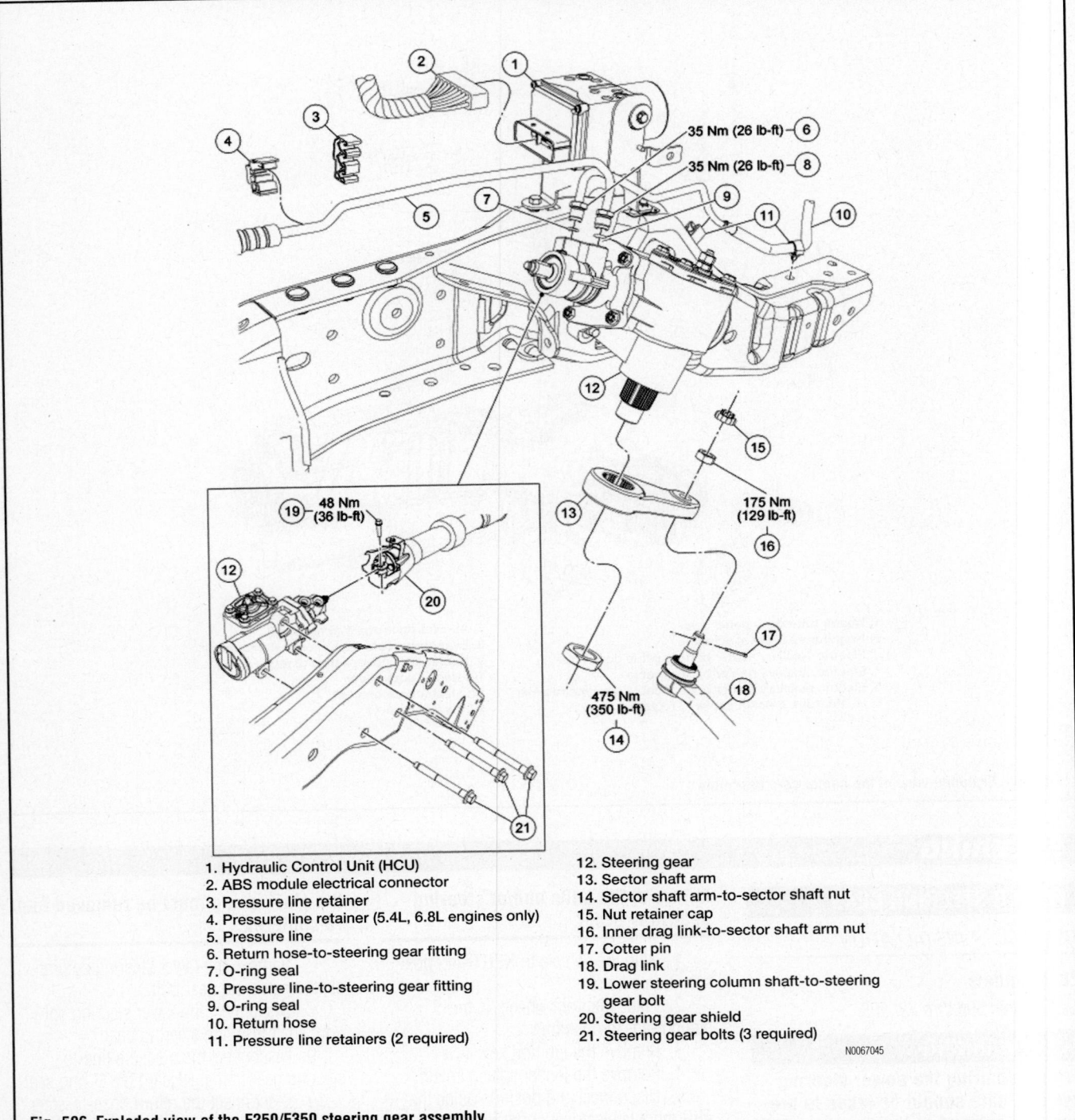

Fig. 506 Exploded view of the F250/F350 steering gear assembly

1. Hydraulic Control Unit (HCU)
2. ABS module electrical connector
3. Pressure line retainer
4. Pressure line retainer (5.4L, 6.8L engines only)
5. Pressure line
6. Return hose-to-steering gear fitting
7. O-ring seal
8. Pressure line-to-steering gear fitting
9. O-ring seal
10. Return hose
11. Pressure line retainers (2 required)
12. Steering gear
13. Sector shaft arm
14. Sector shaft arm-to-sector shaft nut
15. Nut retainer cap
16. Inner drag link-to-sector shaft arm nut
17. Cotter pin
18. Drag link
19. Lower steering column shaft-to-steering gear bolt
20. Steering gear shield
21. Steering gear bolts (3 required)

N0067045

⁕⁕ **WARNING**

The sector shaft arm-to-sector shaft nut must not be reused. The threads of the nut are coated with a dry adhesive. When the nut is removed, the dry adhesive is degraded. If the nut is reused, failure of the nut and/or sector shaft arm and shaft may occur.

14. Remove the sector shaft arm-to-sector shaft nut. Discard the nut.

15. Using the Steering Arm Remover, remove the sector shaft arm.

⁕⁕ **WARNING**

New O-ring seals must be installed on the pressure and return line/hose fittings or a fluid leak may occur.

16. To install, reverse the removal procedure.

a. Tighten the new sector shaft arm-to-sector shaft nut to 350 ft. lbs. (475 Nm).

b. Tighten the new steering gear bolts to 122 ft. lbs. (165 Nm).

c. Tighten the sector shaft retainer cap and nut to 129 ft. lbs. (175 Nm).

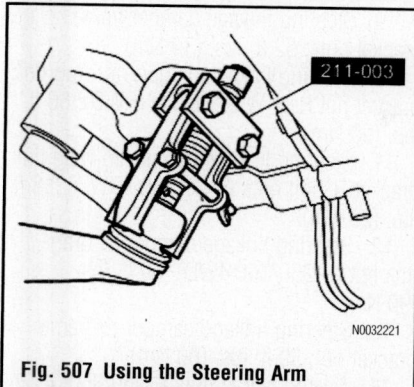

Fig. 507 Using the Steering Arm Remover, disconnect the inner drag link from the sector shaft arm

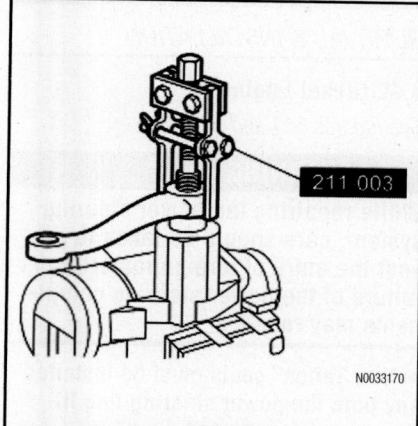

Fig. 508 Using the Steering Arm Remover, remove the sector shaft arm

d. Tighten the return hose-to-steering gear fitting to 26 ft. lbs. (35 Nm).

e. Tighten the pressure line-to-steering gear fitting to 26 ft. lbs. (35 Nm).

f. Tighten the lower steering column shaft-to-steering gear bolt to 36 ft. lbs. (48 Nm).

17. Use a new cotter pin.

18. Fill the power steering system.

2011 Models

See Figures 509 and 510.

✳✳ CAUTION

Never loosen, reposition or deform the tie-rod adjusting sleeve aligner bracket. Incorrect positioning of the tie-rod adjusting sleeve clamps may result in steering linkage binding and loss of vehicle control. Failure to follow this instruction may result in serious personal injury to the vehicle occupant(s).

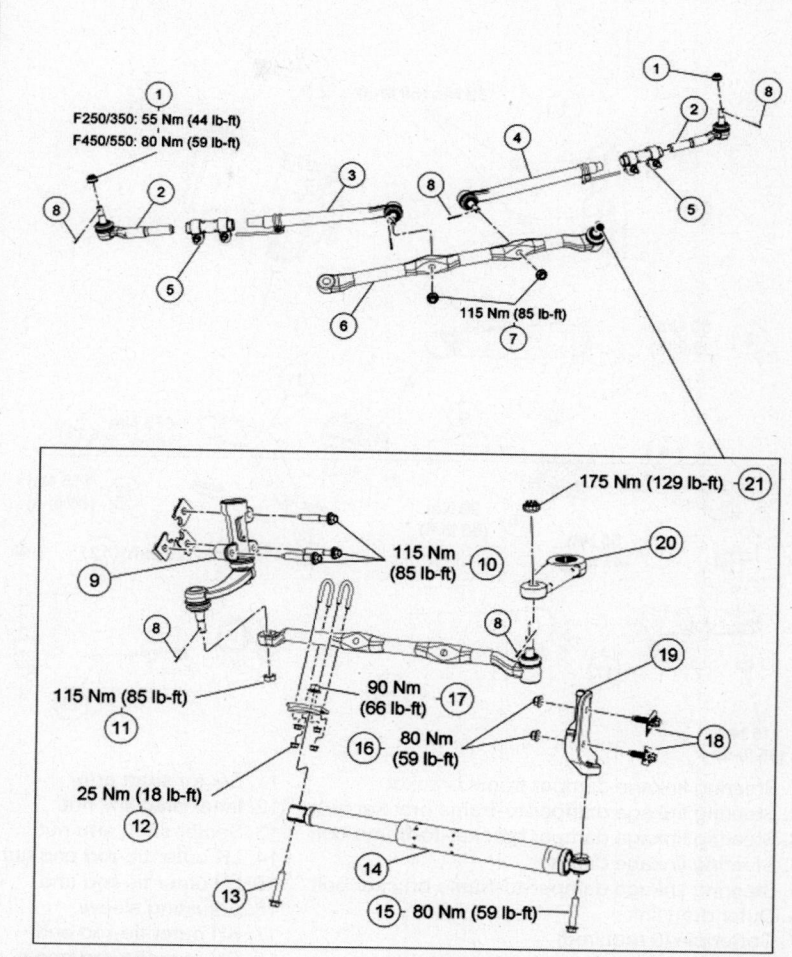

F250/350: 55 Nm (44 lb-ft)
F450/550: 80 Nm (59 lb-ft)

115 Nm (85 lb-ft)

175 Nm (129 lb-ft)

115 Nm (85 lb-ft)

115 Nm (85 lb-ft)

90 Nm (66 lb-ft)

80 Nm (59 lb-ft)

25 Nm (18 lb-ft)

80 Nm (59 lb-ft)

1. Tie-rod end nut
2. Outer tie-rod end
3. RH inner tie-rod
4. LH inner tie-rod
5. Adjusting sleeve
6. Center link
7. Center link nut (2 required)
8. Cotter pin (6 required)
9. Idler arm
10. Idler arm bracket-to-frame bolt (3 required)
11. Idler arm-to-center link nut
12. Steering linkage-to-center link bracket nut
13. Steering linkage damper-to-center link bracket bolt
14. Steering linkage damper
15. Steering linkage damper-to-frame bracket bolt (1 required)
16. Frame bracket-to-frame nut (2 required)
17. Steering linkage damper-to-center link bracket nut
18. Damper bracket-to-frame bolt (2 required)
19. Frame bracket
20. Sector shaft arm
21. Sector shaft nut

Fig. 509 Exploded view of steering gear linkage—1 of 2

✳✳ WARNING

Make sure the steering linkage nut retainers are correctly positioned on the nuts to allow for cotter pin installation. Do not tighten or loosen the nut to align the retainer slot with the cotter pin hole. Overtightening of the fasteners may result in premature failure of steering linkage components.

➡Position the outer drag link so it is parallel with the wheel knuckle before tightening the outer tie-rod end nut.

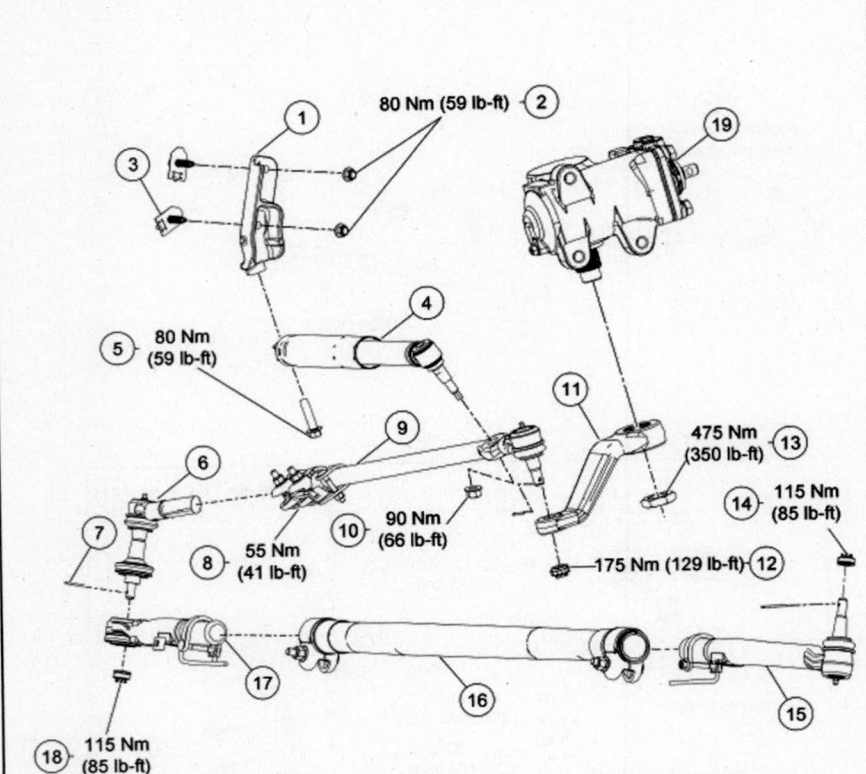

80 Nm (59 lb-ft)

80 Nm (59 lb-ft)

475 Nm (350 lb-ft)

90 Nm (66 lb-ft)

55 Nm (41 lb-ft)

175 Nm (129 lb-ft)

115 Nm (85 lb-ft)

115 Nm (85 lb-ft)

1. Steering linkage damper frame bracket
2. Steering linkage damper-to-frame bracket nuts
3. Steering linkage damper bracket-to-frame bolt
4. Steering linkage damper
5. Steering linkage damper-to-frame bracket bolt
6. Outer drag link
7. Cotter pin (3 required)
8. Adjusting sleeve
9. Inner drag link
10. Steering linkage damper-to-drag link nut

11. Sector shaft arm
12. Inner drag link nut
13. Sector shaft arm nut
14. LH outer tie-rod end nut
15. LH outer tie-rod end
16. Adjusting sleeve
17. RH outer tie-rod end
18. RH outer tie-rod end nut
19. Steering gear

N0116466

Fig. 510 Exploded view of steering gear linkage—2 of 2

→Count the number of turns required to remove the tie rods or drag links for reference during assembly.

→The sector shaft arm nut has a dry adhesive on the threads. Do not reuse the sector shaft arm nut.

→The manufacturer does not provide a specific Removal and Installation procedure for this component. Refer to the graphic(s) when servicing this component.

The following are torque specifications for installing the steering gear linkage:
1. Drag link clamp nut: 41 ft. lbs. (55 Nm)

2. Inner tie-rod to Center Link nut (F-250/350 Rear Wheel Drive (RWD)): 65 ft. lbs. (88 Nm)
3. Outer drag link nut: 85 ft. lbs. (115 Nm)
4. Outer tie-rod end nut: 85 ft. lbs. (115 Nm)
5. Sector shaft arm nut: 350 ft. lbs. (475 Nm)
6. Sector Shaft Arm to Draglink/Centerlink Nut: 129 ft. lbs. (175 Nm)
7. Steering Idler Arm to Frame Bolts: 85 ft. lbs. (115 Nm)
8. Steering Idler Arm to Centerlink Nut: 85 ft. lbs. (115 Nm)

9. Steering linkage damper frame bracket nuts: 52 ft. lbs. (70 Nm)
10. Steering linkage damper-to-drag link bracket nut Rear Wheel Drive (RWD): 66 ft. lbs. (90 Nm)
11. Steering linkage damper-to-drag link bracket U-bolt nuts (F-250/350 RWD): 18 ft. lbs. (25 Nm)
12. Steering linkage damper-to-drag link nut (F-250/350 4WD): 66 ft. lbs. (90 Nm)
13. Steering linkage damper-to-frame bracket nut: 59 ft. lbs. (80 Nm)
14. Tie-rod clamp nuts F-250/350: 41 ft. lbs. (55 Nm)

POWER STEERING PUMP

REMOVAL & INSTALLATION

6.4L Diesel Engine

See Figures 511 and 512.

✳✳ WARNING

While repairing the power steering system, care should be taken to prevent the entry of foreign material or failure of the power steering components may result.

→New Teflon® seals must be installed any time the power steering line fittings are disconnected.

1. Remove the power steering pump pulley.
2. Remove the pressure line/supply hose bracket nut.
3. Release the clamp and disconnect the power steering pump supply hose.
4. Disconnect the pressure line-to-pump fitting. Remove and discard the Teflon® seal.
5. Remove the 3 bolts and the power steering pump.

→Make sure that the power steering pump bolts are installed in their original positions.

→Thoroughly clean all foreign material from the pressure line-to-pump threads before installing the fitting.

To install:
6. To install, reverse the removal procedure.
7. Tighten the power steering pump bolts to 18 ft. lbs. (25 Nm).
8. Using the Teflon® Seal Installer Set (211-D027), install a new Teflon® seal on the pressure line fitting.
9. Tighten the pressure line-to-pump fitting to 55 ft. lbs. (75 Nm).

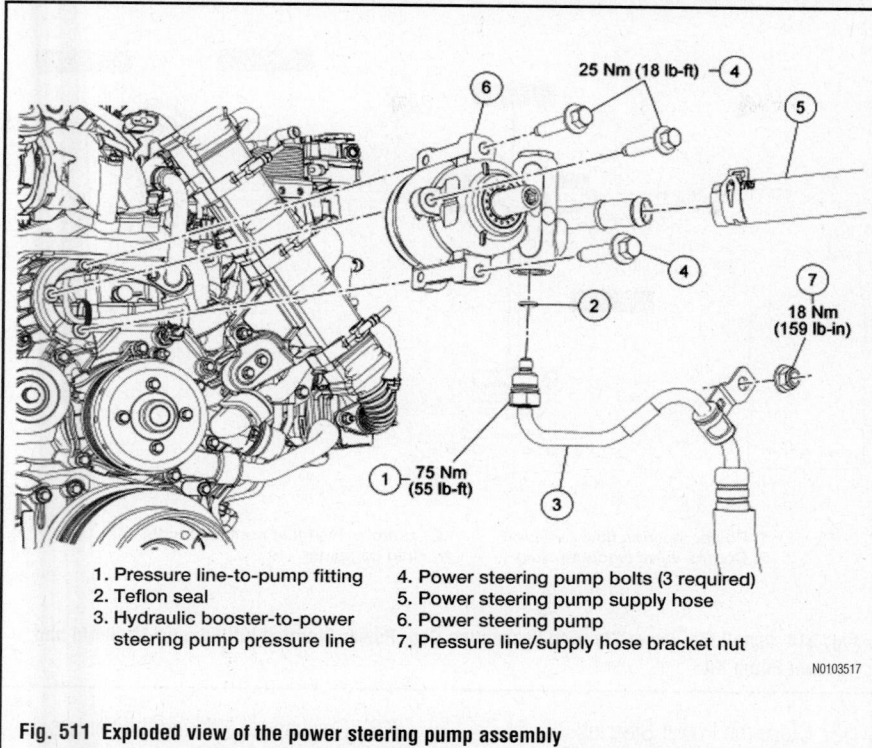

1. Pressure line-to-pump fitting
2. Teflon seal
3. Hydraulic booster-to-power steering pump pressure line
4. Power steering pump bolts (3 required)
5. Power steering pump supply hose
6. Power steering pump
7. Pressure line/supply hose bracket nut

Fig. 511 Exploded view of the power steering pump assembly

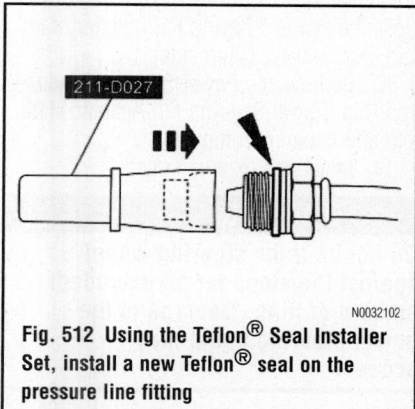

Fig. 512 Using the Teflon® Seal Installer Set, install a new Teflon® seal on the pressure line fitting

10. Tighten the pressure line/supply hose bracket nut to 13 ft. lbs. (18 Nm).
11. Fill the power steering system.

5.4L & 6.8L Engines

See Figure 512.

✳✳ WARNING

While repairing the power steering system, care should be taken to prevent the entry of foreign material or failure of the power steering components may result.

➡ **New Teflon® seals must be installed any time the power steering line fittings are disconnected.**

1. Remove the power steering pump pulley.
2. Release the clamp and disconnect the power steering pump supply hose.
3. Remove the pressure line bracket/pump bolt.
4. Disconnect the pressure line-to-pump fitting. Discard the Teflon® seal.
5. Remove the 2 bolts and the power steering pump.

➡ **Make sure that the power steering pump bolts are installed in their original positions.**

➡ **Thoroughly clean all foreign material from the pressure line-to-pump threads before installing the fitting.**

To install:

6. To install, reverse the removal procedure.
7. Tighten the power steering pump bolts to 18 ft. lbs. (25 Nm).
8. Using the Teflon® Seal Installer Set (211-D027), install a new Teflon® seal on the pressure line fitting.
9. Tighten the pressure line-to-pump fitting to 55 ft, lbs. (75 Nm).
10. Tighten the pressure line bracket/pump bolt to 18 ft. lbs. (25 Nm).
11. Fill the power steering system.

BLEEDING

See Figure 513.

✳✳ WARNING

If the air is not purged from the power steering system correctly, premature power steering pump failure may result. The condition may occur on pre-delivery vehicles with evidence of aerated fluid or on vehicles that have had steering component repairs.

➡ **A whine heard from the power steering pump can be caused by air in the system. The power steering purge procedure must be carried out prior to any component repair for which power steering noise complaints are accompanied by evidence of aerated fluid.**

1. Remove the power steering reservoir cap. Check the fluid.
2. Raise the front wheels off the floor.
3. Tightly insert the Power Steering Evacuation Cap (211-265) into the reservoir and connect the Vacuum Pump Kit (416-D002).
4. Start the engine.
5. Using the Vacuum Pump Kit, apply vacuum and maintain the maximum vacuum of 20–25 inches Hg (68–85 kPa).
6. If the Vacuum Pump Kit does not maintain vacuum, check the power steering system for leaks before proceeding.
7. If equipped with Hydro-Boost, apply the brake pedal 4 times.

✳✳ WARNING

Do not hold the steering wheel against the stops for an extended amount of time. Damage to the power steering pump may occur.

8. Cycle the steering wheel fully from stop-to-stop 10 times.

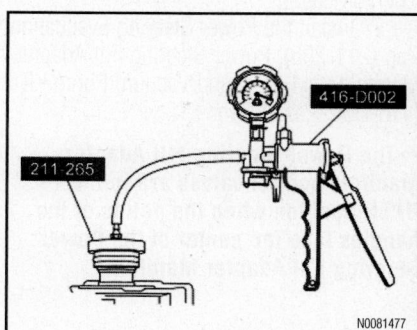

Fig. 513 Tightly insert the Power Steering Evacuation Cap into the reservoir and connect the Vacuum Pump Kit

9. Stop the engine.

10. Release the vacuum and remove the Vacuum Pump Kit and the Power Steering Evacuation Cap.

➡**Do not overfill the reservoir.**

11. Fill the reservoir as needed with the specified fluid.

12. Start the engine.

13. Install the Power Steering Evacuation Cap and the Vacuum Pump Kit. Apply and maintain the maximum vacuum of 20–25 inches Hg (68–85 kPa).

✳✳ WARNING

Do not hold the steering wheel against the stops for an extended amount of time. Damage to the power steering pump may occur.

14. Cycle the steering wheel fully from stop-to-stop 10 times.

15. Stop the engine, release the vacuum and remove the Vacuum Pump Kit and the Power Steering Evacuation Cap.

➡**Do not overfill the reservoir.**

16. Fill the reservoir as needed with the specified fluid and install the reservoir cap.

17. Visually inspect the power steering system for leaks.

FLUID FILL PROCEDURE

See Figure 514.

✳✳ WARNING

If the air is not purged from the power steering system correctly, premature power steering pump failure may result. The condition can occur on pre-delivery vehicles with evidence of aerated fluid or on vehicles that have had steering component repairs.

1. Remove the power steering fluid reservoir cap.

2. Install the Power Steering Evacuation Cap (211-265), Power Steering Fill Adapter Manifold (211-327) and Vacuum Pump Kit (416-D002) as shown.

➡**The Power Steering Fill Adapter Manifold control valves are in the OPEN position when the points of the handles face the center of the Power Steering Fill Adapter Manifold.**

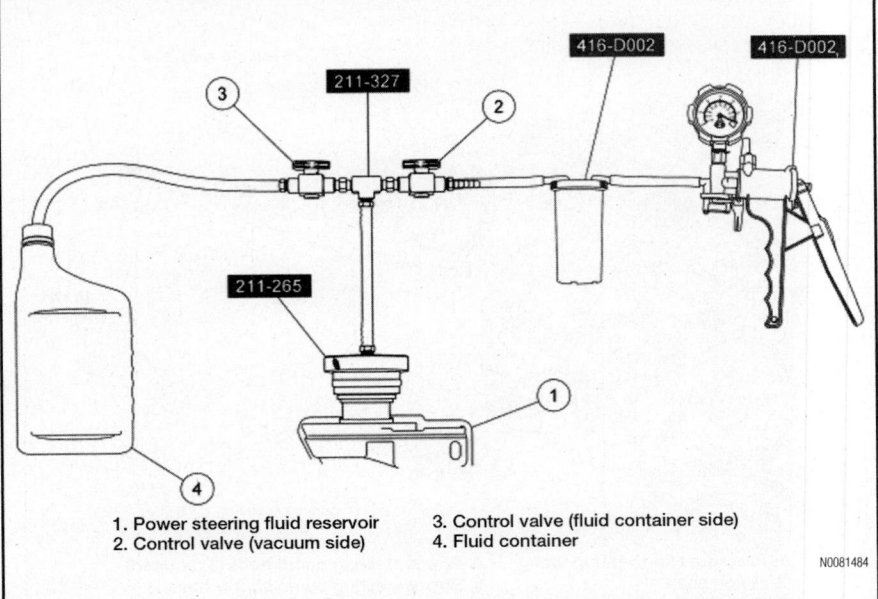

1. Power steering fluid reservoir
2. Control valve (vacuum side)
3. Control valve (fluid container side)
4. Fluid container

N0081484

Fig. 514 Install the Power Steering Evacuation Cap, Power Steering Fill Adapter Manifold and Vacuum Pump Kit

3. Close the Power Steering Fill Adapter Manifold control valve (fluid side).

4. Open the Power Steering Fill Adapter Manifold control valve (vacuum side).

5. Using the Vacuum Pump Kit, apply 20–25 inches Hg (68–85 kPa) of vacuum to the power steering system.

6. Observe the Vacuum Pump Kit gauge for 30 seconds.

7. If the Vacuum Pump Kit gauge reading drops more than 3 kPa (0.88 in-Hg), correct any leaks in the power steering system or the Power Steering Evacuation Cap, Power Steering Fill Adapter Manifold and Vacuum Pump Kit before proceeding.

➡**The Vacuum Pump Kit gauge reading will drop slightly during this step.**

8. Slowly open the Power Steering Fill Adapter Manifold control valve (fluid side) until power steering fluid completely fills the hose and then close the control valve.

9. Using the Vacuum Pump Kit, apply 20–25 inches Hg (68–85 kPa) of vacuum to the power steering system.

10. Close the Power Steering Fill Adapter Manifold control valve (vacuum side).

11. Slowly open the Power Steering Fill Adapter Manifold control valve (fluid side).

12. Once power steering fluid enters the fluid reservoir and reaches the minimum fluid level indicator line on the reservoir, close the Power Steering Fill Adapter Manifold control valve (fluid side).

13. Remove the Power Steering Evacuation Cap, Power Steering Fill Adapter Manifold and Vacuum Pump Kit.

14. Install the reservoir cap.

✳✳ WARNING

Do not hold the steering wheel against the stops for an extended amount of time. Damage to the power steering pump may occur.

➡**There will be a slight drop in the power steering fluid level in the reservoir when the engine is started.**

15. Start the engine and turn the steering wheel from stop-to-stop.

16. Turn the ignition switch to the OFF position.

➡**Do not overfill the reservoir.**

17. Remove the reservoir cap and fill the reservoir with the specified fluid.

18. Install the reservoir cap.

SUSPENSION

COIL SPRING

REMOVAL & INSTALLATION

2010 4WD Models

See Figures 515 and 516.

✳✳ CAUTION

Do not apply heat or flame to the shock absorber or strut tube. The shock absorber and strut tube are gas pressurized and could explode if heated. Failure to follow this instruction may result in serious personal injury.

✳✳ WARNING

Suspension fasteners are critical parts because they affect performance of vital components and systems and their failure can result in major service expense. They must be replaced with the same part number or an equivalent part if replacement is necessary. Do not use a replacement part of lesser quality or substitute design. Torque values must be used as specified during reassembly to make sure of correct retention of these parts.

1. Remove the wheel and tire.
2. Index-mark the spring and the spring upper insulator.
3. Using a suitable jack, support the front axle assembly.
4. Remove and discard the front shock absorber lower bolt and flag nut.
5. Remove and discard the stabilizer bar link lower bolt.
6. Lower the axle and remove the spring.

➡Inspect the spring upper and lower seats, install new as necessary.

7. To install, reverse the removal procedure.
8. Tighten the new stabilizer bar link lower bolt to 111 ft. lbs. (150 Nm).
9. Tighten the new front shock absorber lower bolt to 111 ft. lbs. (150 Nm).

2011 4WD Models

See Figures 517 and 518.

✳✳ CAUTION

Do not apply heat or flame to the shock absorber or strut tube. The shock absorber and strut tube are gas

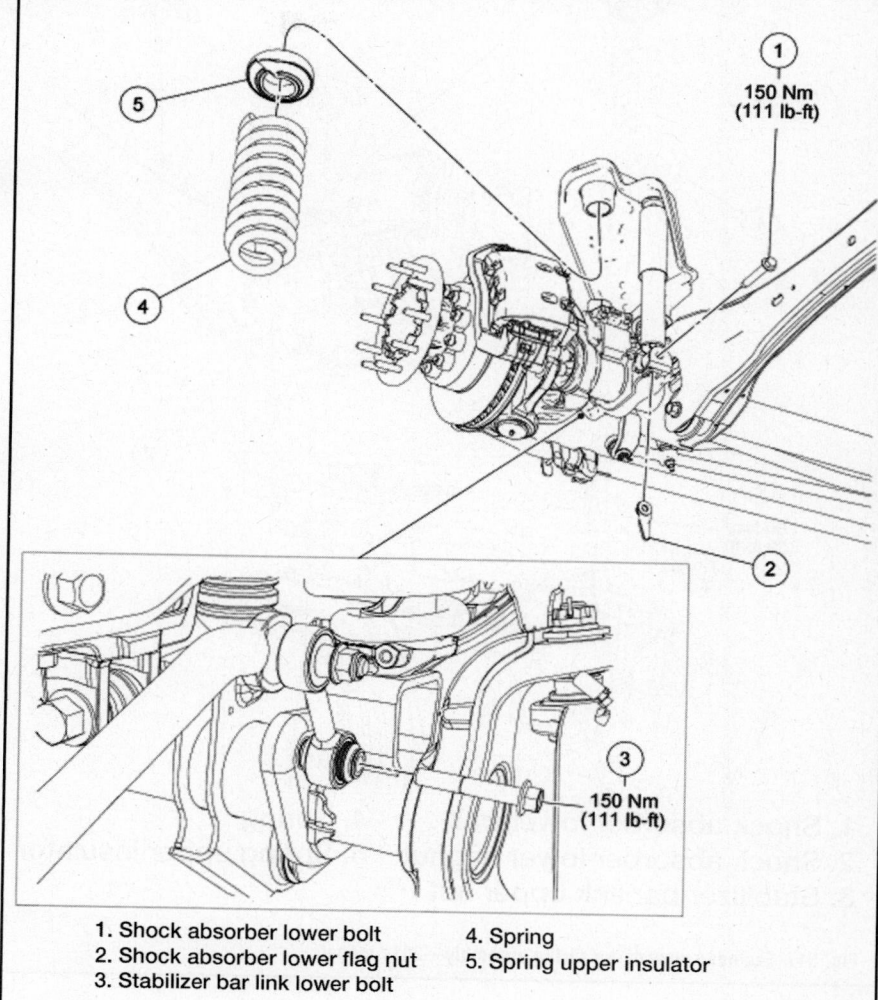

1. Shock absorber lower bolt
2. Shock absorber lower flag nut
3. Stabilizer bar link lower bolt
4. Spring
5. Spring upper insulator

N0067841

Fig. 515 Exploded view of the spring assembly—2010 models

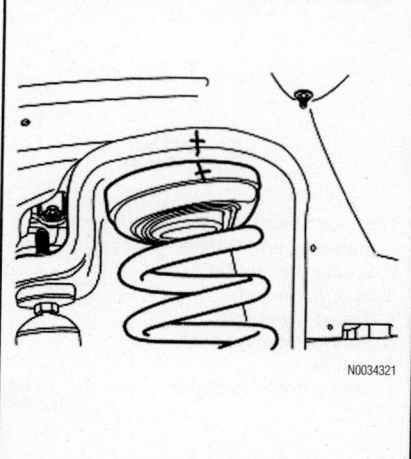

N0034321

Fig. 516 Index-mark the spring and the spring upper insulator

pressurized and could explode if heated. Failure to follow this instruction may result in serious personal injury.

✳✳ WARNING

Suspension fasteners are critical parts because they affect performance of vital components and systems and their failure can result in major service expense. They must be replaced with the same part number or an equivalent part if replacement is necessary. Do not use a replacement part of lesser quality or substitute design. Torque values must be used as specified during reassembly to make sure of correct retention of these parts.

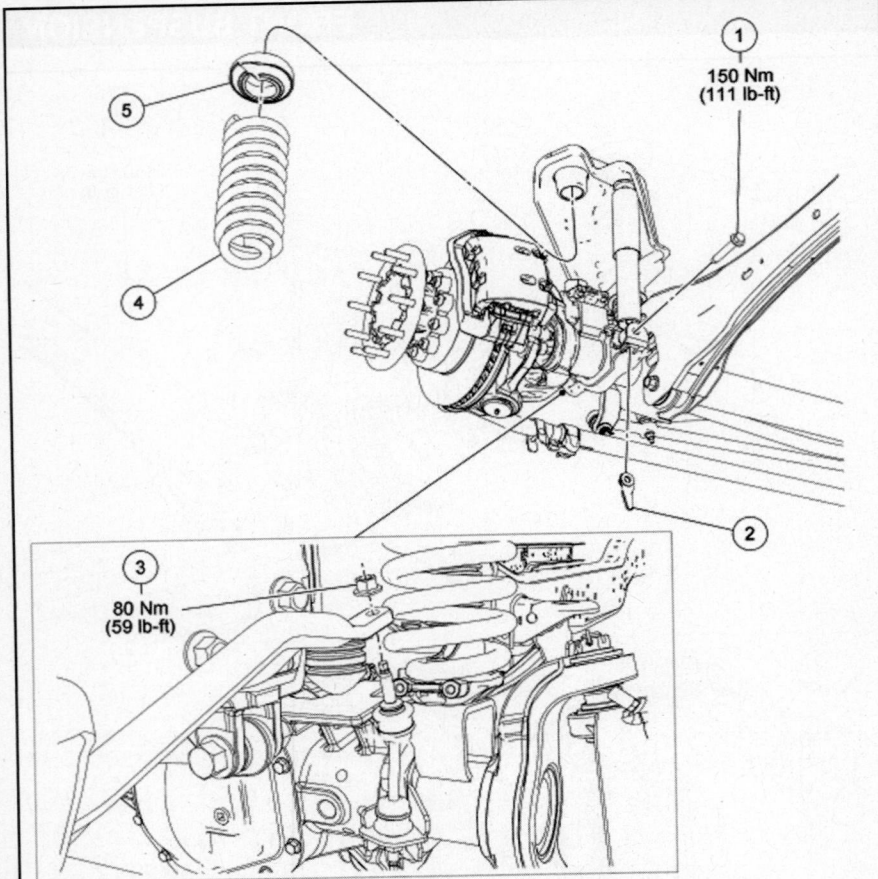

1. Shock absorber lower bolt
2. Shock absorber lower flagnut
3. Stabilizer bar link upper nut
4. Spring
5. Spring upper insulator

N0101483

Fig. 517 Exploded view of the spring assembly—2011 models

3. Using a suitable jack, support the front axle assembly.

4. Remove and discard the front shock absorber lower bolt and flagnut.

5. Remove and discard the stabilizer bar link upper nut.

6. Lower the axle and remove the spring.

➡**Inspect the spring upper and lower seats, install new as necessary.**

7. To install, reverse the removal procedure.

   a. Tighten the new stabilizer bar link upper nut to 59 ft. lbs. (80 Nm).

   b. Tighten the new front shock absorber lower bolt to 111 ft. lbs. (150 Nm).

2010 and 2011 RWD Models

See Figure 519.

✻✻ WARNING

Suspension fasteners are critical parts because they affect performance of vital components and systems and their failure can result in major service expense. They must be replaced with the same part number or an equivalent part if replacement is necessary. Do not use a replacement part of lesser quality or substitute design. Torque values must be used as specified during reassembly to make sure of correct retention of these parts.

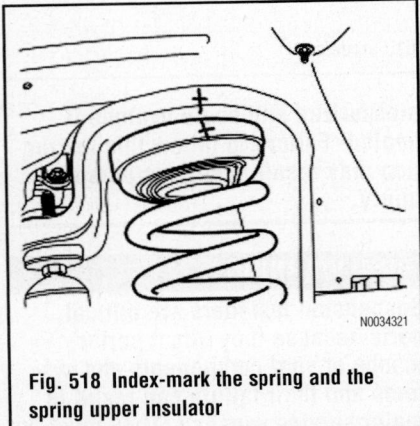

N0034321

Fig. 518 Index-mark the spring and the spring upper insulator

➡**Use the hex-holding feature to prevent the ball stud from turning while removing or installing the stabilizer link nut.**

1. Remove the wheel and tire.
2. Index-mark the spring and the spring upper insulator.

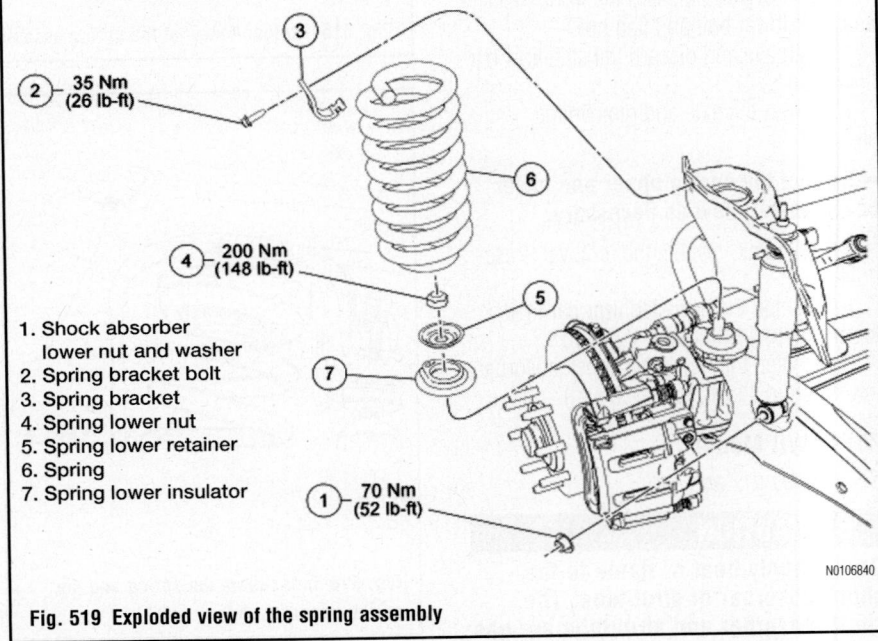

1. Shock absorber lower nut and washer
2. Spring bracket bolt
3. Spring bracket
4. Spring lower nut
5. Spring lower retainer
6. Spring
7. Spring lower insulator

N0106840

Fig. 519 Exploded view of the spring assembly

1. Remove the wheel and tire.

2. Using a suitable jack, support the front axle assembly.

3. Remove the shock absorber lower nut and washer, then detach the shock from the mounting stud. Discard the nut.

4. Remove the spring bracket bolt and bracket. Discard the bolt.

5. Lower the front axle until the spring is free of the spring upper seat.

6. Using an extension through the top of the spring, remove and discard the spring lower nut.

7. Remove the spring lower retainer and the spring.

➡️**Inspect the spring upper and lower insulators, install new as necessary.**

8. To install, reverse the removal procedure.

9. Tighten the new spring lower nut to 148 ft. lbs. (200 Nm).

10. Tighten the new spring bracket bolt to 26 ft. lbs. (35 Nm).

11. Tighten the new shock absorber lower nut to 52 ft. lbs. (70 Nm).

CONTROL LINKS

REMOVAL & INSTALLATION

4WD Radius Arm

See Figure 520.

✳️ WARNING

Suspension fasteners are critical parts because they affect performance of vital components and systems and their failure can result in major service expense. They must be replaced with the same part number or an equivalent part if replacement is necessary. Do not use a replacement part of lesser quality or substitute design. Torque values must be used as specified during reassembly to make sure of correct retention of these parts.

1. Remove the shock absorber.

✳️ WARNING

Tighten the radius arm front nuts with the suspension at curb height or damage to the bushings may occur.

2. Remove and discard the 2 radius arm front nuts and bolts.

3. Remove the wheel speed sensor harness bolt.

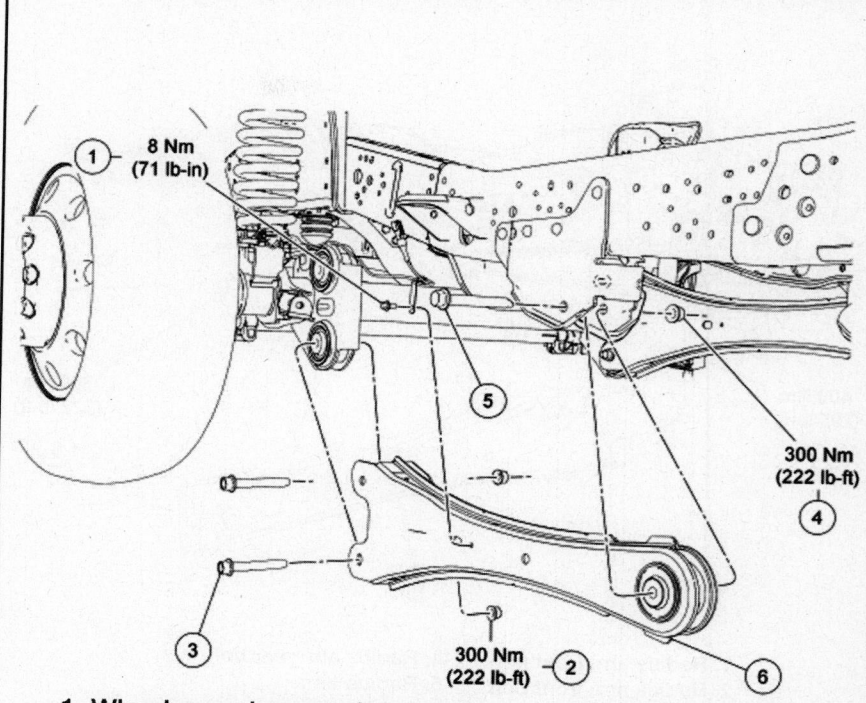

1. Wheel speed sensor harness bolt
2. Radius arm front nut (2 required)
3. Radius arm front bolt (2 required)
4. Radius arm rear nut
5. Radius arm rear bolt
6. Radius arm

8 Nm (71 lb-in)
300 Nm (222 lb-ft)
300 Nm (222 lb-ft)

N0034303

Fig. 520 Exploded view of the radius arm assembly

✳️ WARNING

Tighten the radius arm rear nut with the suspension at curb height or damage to the bushing may occur.

4. Remove and discard the radius arm rear nut and bolt.

5. Remove the radius arm.

6. To install, reverse the removal procedure.

   a. Tighten the new radius arm rear nut to 222 ft. lbs. (300 Nm).

   b. Tighten the new radius arm front nuts to 222 ft. lbs. (300 Nm).

RWD Radius Arm

See Figure 521.

✳️ WARNING

Suspension fasteners are critical parts because they affect performance of vital components and systems and their failure can result in major service expense. They must be replaced with the same part number

or an equivalent part if replacement is necessary. Do not use a replacement part of lesser quality or substitute design. Torque values must be used as specified during reassembly to make sure of correct retention of these parts.**

1. Remove the spring.

2. Remove and discard the radius arm front nut and bolt.

✳️ WARNING

Tighten the radius arm rear nut with the suspension at curb height or damage to the bushing may occur.

3. Remove and discard the radius arm rear nut and bolt.

4. Remove the radius arm.

5. To install, reverse the removal procedure.

6. Tighten the new radius arm rear nut to 222 ft. lbs. (300 Nm).

7. Tighten the new radius arm front nut to 295 ft. lbs. (400 Nm).

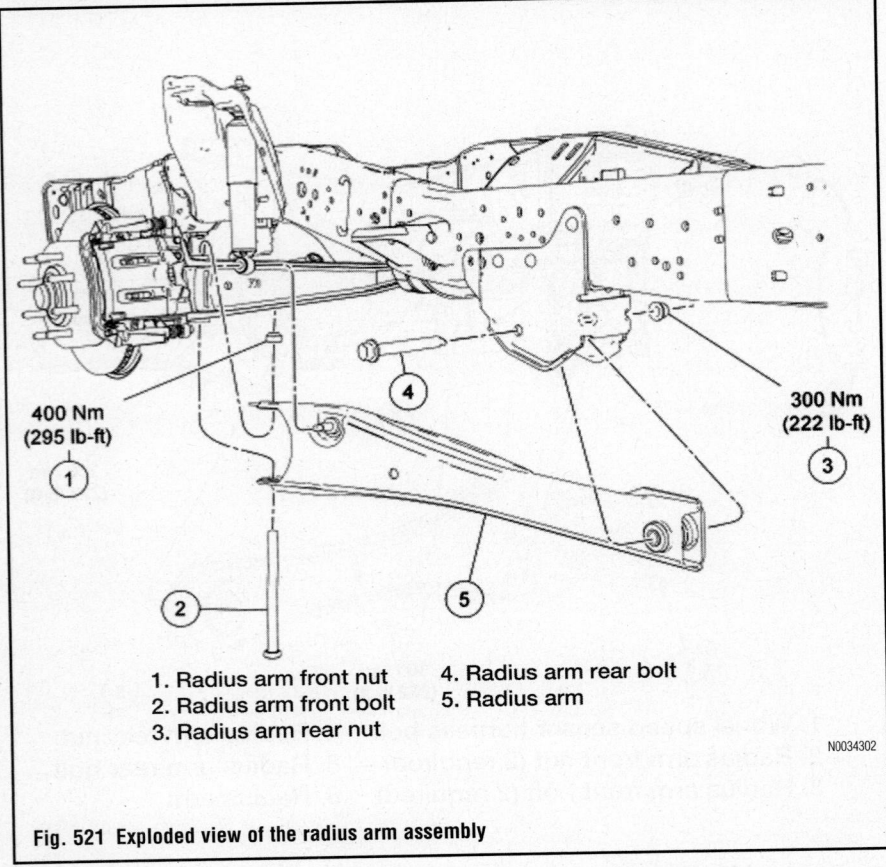

400 Nm
(295 lb-ft)
①

②

④

⑤

③

300 Nm
(222 lb-ft)

1. Radius arm front nut
2. Radius arm front bolt
3. Radius arm rear nut
4. Radius arm rear bolt
5. Radius arm

N0034302

Fig. 521 Exploded view of the radius arm assembly

3. Remove the track bar-to-frame nut and bolt and disconnect the track bar. Discard the nut and bolt.

➡First loosen the nut, then use the hex-holding feature to prevent the track bar ball joint from turning while removing the nut.

4. Remove and discard the track bar ball joint nut.

➡It may be necessary to rotate the track bar forward before installing the Steering Arm Remover.

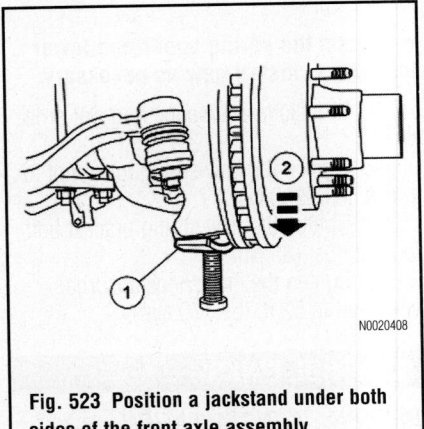

①

②

N0020408

Fig. 523 Position a jackstand under both sides of the front axle assembly

Track Bar

See Figures 522 through 524.

✳✳ WARNING

Suspension fasteners are critical parts because they affect performance of vital components and systems and their failure can result in major service expense. They must be replaced with the same part number or an equivalent part if replacement is necessary. Do not use a replacement part of lesser quality or substitute design. Torque values must be used as specified during reassembly to make sure of correct retention of these parts.

1. With the vehicle in NEUTRAL, position it on a hoist.

➡To prevent the front suspension from shifting when the track bar is removed, the front axle must be supporting the vehicle weight.

2. Load the front suspension with the vehicle weight.

a. Position a jackstand under both sides of the front axle assembly.

b. Lower the vehicle until the front axle is supporting the vehicle weight.

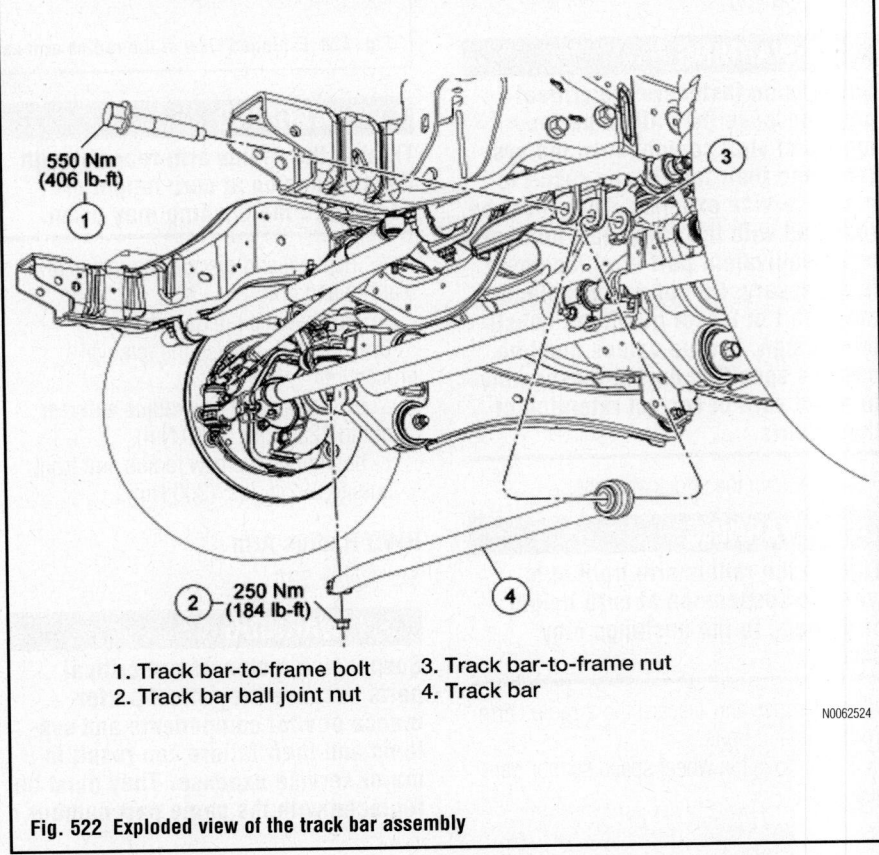

550 Nm
(406 lb-ft)
①

③

②
250 Nm
(184 lb-ft)

④

1. Track bar-to-frame bolt
2. Track bar ball joint nut
3. Track bar-to-frame nut
4. Track bar

N0062524

Fig. 522 Exploded view of the track bar assembly

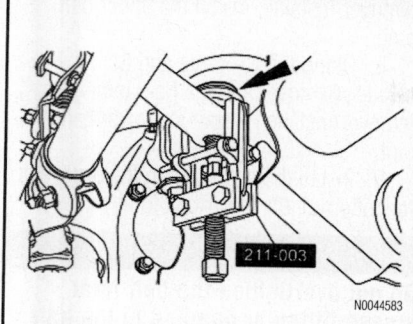

Fig. 524 Using the Steering Arm Remover (211-003), disconnect the track bar from the ball joint and remove the track bar

5. Using the Steering Arm Remover, disconnect the track bar from the ball joint and remove the track bar.

To install:

☀ WARNING

Tighten the track bar-to-frame bolt with the suspension at curb height or damage to the bushing may occur.

6. Position the track bar and install the bracket nut and bolt. Do not tighten the nut at this time.

☀ WARNING

Use the hex-holding feature to prevent the track bar ball joint from turning while installing the nut, tighten the nut until snug. Final tighten the nut with the suspension at curb height or damage to the ball joint may occur.

7. Position the track bar onto the ball joint and install the nut. Do not tighten the nut at this time.
8. With the vehicle weight still supported by the jackstands, tighten the new track bar ball joint nut to 184 ft. lbs. (250 Nm).
9. With the vehicle weight still supported by the jackstands, tighten the new track bar-to-frame bolt to 406 ft. lbs. (550 Nm).

2010 4WD Stabilizer Bar Link

See Figure 525.

☀ WARNING

Suspension fasteners are critical parts because they affect performance of vital components and systems and their failure can result in major service expense. They must be replaced with the same part number

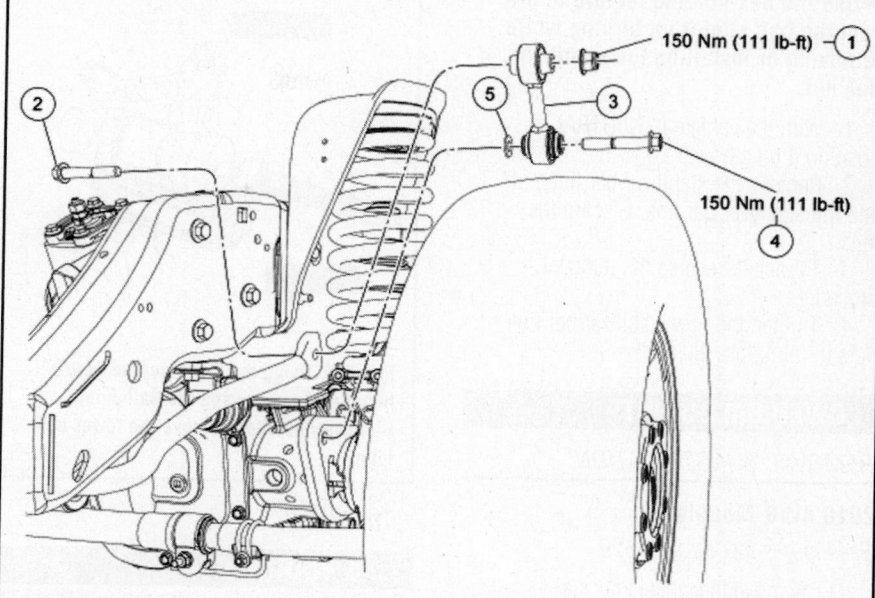

1. Stabilizer bar link upper nut (2 required)
2. Stabilizer bar link upper bolt (2 required)
3. Stabilizer bar link (2 required)
4. Stabilizer bar link lower bolt (2 required)
5. Washer

Fig. 525 Exploded view of the stabilizer bar link (4WD) assembly

or an equivalent part if replacement is necessary. Do not use a replacement part of lesser quality or substitute design. Torque values must be used as specified during reassembly to make sure of correct retention of these parts.

1. With the vehicle in NEUTRAL, position it on a hoist.
2. Remove the stabilizer bar link lower bolt and washer. Discard the bolt.

➡ **If the clinch nut in the axle is stripped or damaged, remove the clinch nut and install a new flagnut in place of the clinch nut.**

3. Remove and discard the stabilizer bar link upper nut, bolt and washer.
4. Remove the stabilizer bar link.
5. To install, reverse the removal procedure.
6. Tighten the new stabilizer bar link upper nut to 111 ft. lbs. (150 Nm).
7. Tighten the new stabilizer bar link lower bolt to 111 ft. lbs. (150 Nm).

2011 4WD Stabilizer Bar Link

See Figure 526.

☀ WARNING

Suspension fasteners are critical parts because they affect perfor-

mance of vital components and systems and their failure can result in major service expense. They must be replaced with the same part number or an equivalent part if replacement is necessary. Do not use a replacement part of lesser quality or substitute design. Torque values must be used as specified during reassembly to make sure of correct retention of these parts.

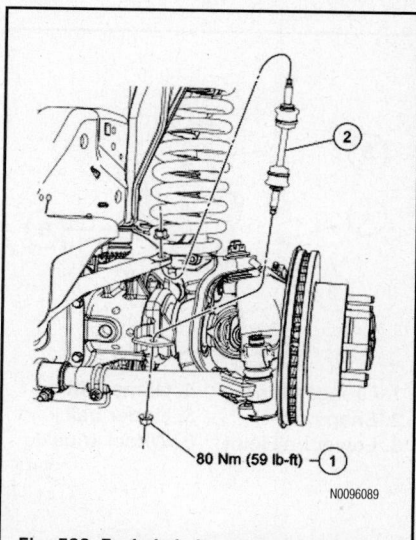

Fig. 526 Exploded view of the stabilizer bar link assembly

➥ **Use the hex-holding feature to prevent the ball stud from turning while removing or installing the stabilizer link nut.**

1. With the vehicle in NEUTRAL, position it on a hoist.
2. Remove the stabilizer bar link nuts and the stabilizer bar link. Discard the nuts.
3. To install, reverse the removal procedure.
4. Tighten the new stabilizer bar link nuts to 59 ft. lbs. (80 Nm).

LOWER BALL JOINT

REMOVAL & INSTALLATION

2010 4WD Models

See Figures 527 through 529.

1. Remove the wheel knuckle.
2. If equipped, remove the ball joint grease fitting.
3. Position the wheel knuckle in a vise and remove the snap ring from the lower ball joint.

✳✳ WARNING

To avoid damage to the components, do not use heat to aid ball joint removal.

4. Using the C-Frame and Screw Installer/Remover (205-086) and the Ball Joint Remover/Installer (204-358), remove the lower ball joint.
5. Using the C-Frame and Screw Installer/Remover (205-086) and the Ball Joint Remover/Installer (204-355), remove the upper ball joint.

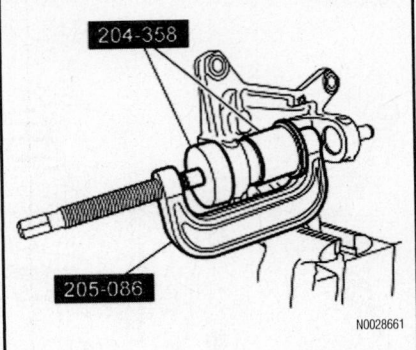

Fig. 528 Using the C-Frame and Screw Installer/Remover and the Ball Joint Remover/Installer, remove the lower ball joint

To install:

✳✳ WARNING

The grease fitting must be removed from the ball joint prior to installation or damage to the grease fitting can occur.

✳✳ WARNING

To avoid damage to components, do not use heat to aid installation.

➥ **Clean the wheel knuckle ball joint bore.**

6. Position the ball joint into the wheel knuckle.

➥ **The upper ball joint must be installed first.**

7. Using the C-Frame and Screw Installer/Remover and the Ball Joint

Remover/Installer, install the upper ball joint.
8. Using the C-Frame and Screw Installer/Remover and the Ball Joint Remover/Installer, install the lower ball joint.
9. Install the snap ring in the groove at the bottom of the lower ball joint.

✳✳ WARNING

Do not overtighten the ball joint grease fitting or damage to the ball joint may occur.

10. If removed, install the ball joint grease fitting.
11. Install the wheel knuckle.

2011 4WD Models

See Figures 530 through 532.

1. Remove the wheel knuckle.
2. If equipped, remove the ball joint grease fitting.
3. Position the wheel knuckle in a vise and remove the snap ring from the lower ball joint.

✳✳ WARNING

To avoid damage to the components, do not use heat to aid ball joint removal.

4. Using the C-Frame and Screw Installer/Remover (205-086) and the Ball Joint Remover/Installer (204-358), remove the lower ball joint.

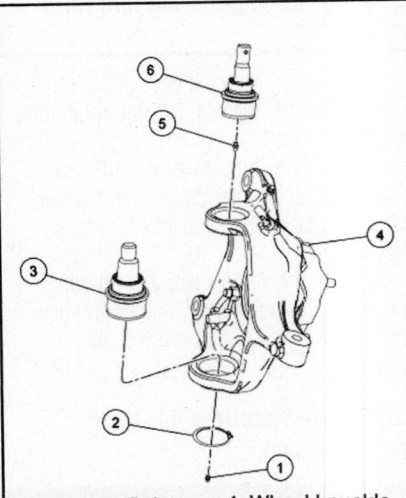

1. Grease fitting
2. Snap ring
3. Lower ball joint
4. Wheel knuckle
5. Grease fitting
6. Upper ball joint

Fig. 530 Exploded view of the wheel knuckle assembly

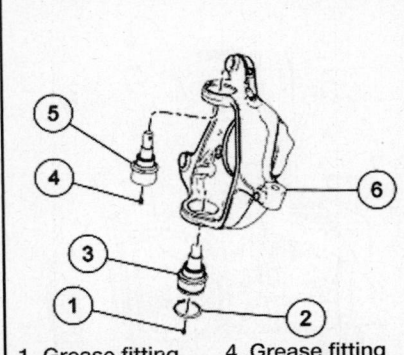

1. Grease fitting
2. Snap ring
3. Lower ball joint
4. Grease fitting
5. Upper ball joint
6. Wheel knuckle

Fig. 527 Exploded view of the wheel knuckle assembly

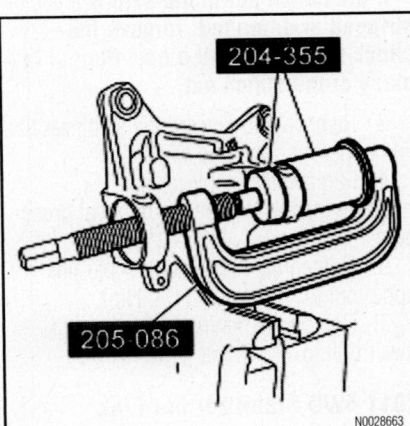

Fig. 529 Using the C-Frame and Screw Installer/Remover and the Ball Joint Remover/Installer, remove the upper ball joint

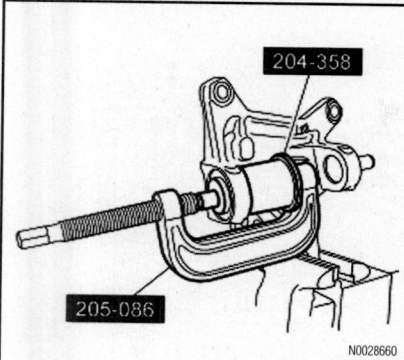

Fig. 531 Using the C-Frame and Screw Installer/Remover and the Ball Joint Remover/Installer, remove the lower ball joint

5. Using the C-Frame and Screw Installer/Remover (205-086) and the Ball Joint Remover/Installer (204-355), remove the upper ball joint.

To install:

✳✳ WARNING

The grease fitting must be removed from the ball joint prior to installation or damage to the grease fitting can occur.

✳✳ WARNING

To avoid damage to components, do not use heat to aid installation.

➡**Clean the wheel knuckle ball joint bore.**

6. Position the ball joint into the wheel knuckle.

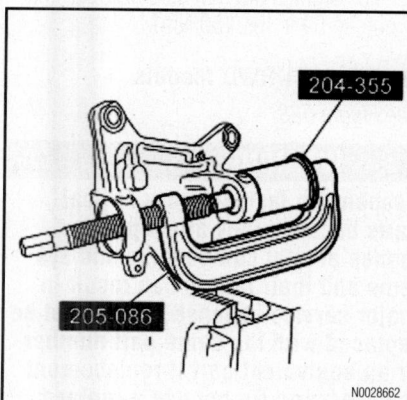

Fig. 532 Using the C-Frame and Screw Installer/Remover and the Ball Joint Remover/Installer, remove the upper ball joint

➡**The upper ball joint must be installed first.**

7. Using the C-Frame and Screw Installer/Remover and the Ball Joint Remover/Installer, install the upper ball joint.
8. Using the C-Frame and Screw Installer/Remover and the Ball Joint Remover/Installer, install the lower ball joint.
9. Install the snap ring in the groove at the bottom of the lower ball joint.

✳✳ WARNING

Do not overtighten the ball joint grease fitting or damage to the ball joint may occur.

10. If removed, install the ball joint grease fitting.
11. Install the wheel knuckle.

2010 and 2011 RWD Models

See Figures 533 through 535.

1. Remove the wheel spindle or wheel knuckle assembly.
2. Remove the lower ball joint grease plug.
3. Position the wheel spindle in a vise and remove the snap ring from the lower ball joint.

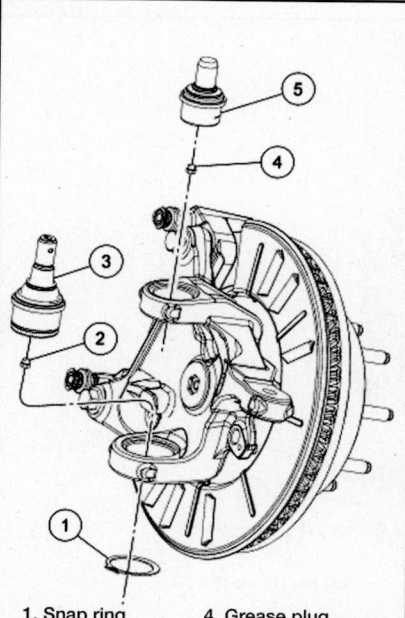

1. Snap ring
2. Grease fitting
3. Lower ball joint
4. Grease plug
5. Upper ball joint

Fig. 533 Exploded view of the wheel knuckle assembly

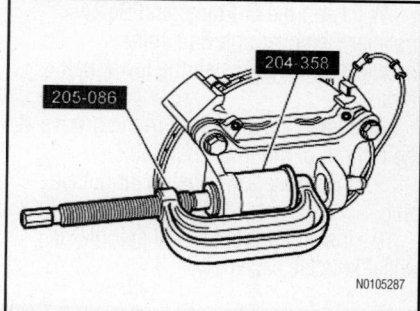

Fig. 534 Using the C-Frame and Screw Installer/Remover and Ball Joint Installer/Remover, remove the lower ball joint

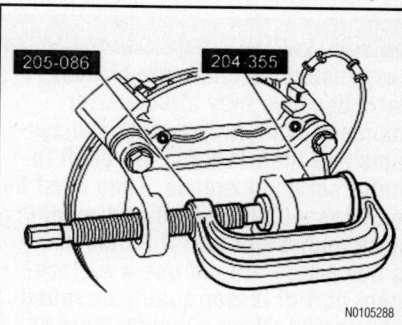

Fig. 535 Using the C-Frame and Screw Installer/Remover and Ball Joint Installer/Remover, remove the upper ball joint

✳✳ WARNING

To avoid damage to the components, do not use heat to aid ball joint removal.

4. Using the C-Frame and Screw Installer/Remover (205-086) and Ball Joint Installer/Remover (204-358), remove the lower ball joint.
5. Using the C-Frame and Screw Installer/Remover (205-086) and Ball Joint Installer/Remover(204-358), remove the upper ball joint.

To install:

✳✳ WARNING

To avoid damage to components, do not use heat to aid installation.

➡**Clean the wheel knuckle ball joint bores.**

➡**The upper ball joint must be installed first.**

6. Using the C-Frame and Screw Installer/Remover and Ball Joint Installer/Remover, install the upper ball joint.

7. Using the C-Frame and Screw Installer/Remover and Ball Joint Installer/Remover, install the lower ball joint.

8. Install the snap ring in the groove at the bottom of the lower ball joint.

9. Install the lower ball joint grease plug.

10. Install the front wheel spindle or wheel knuckle assembly.

STABILIZER BAR

REMOVAL & INSTALLATION

2010 4WD Models

See Figure 536.

> ❊❊ **WARNING**
>
> **Suspension fasteners are critical parts because they affect performance of vital components and systems and their failure can result in major service expense. They must be replaced with the same part number or an equivalent part if replacement is necessary. Do not use a replacement part of lesser quality or substitute design. Torque values must be used as specified during reassembly to make sure of correct retention of these parts.**

1. With the vehicle in NEUTRAL, position it on a hoist.

➡ **If the clinch nut in the axle is stripped or damaged, remove the clinch nut and install a new flagnut in place of the clinch nut.**

2. Remove and discard the stabilizer bar link upper nuts, bolts and washers.

3. Remove the stabilizer bar bracket nuts, brackets and the stabilizer bar. Discard the nuts.

4. To install, reverse the removal procedure.

5. Tighten the new stabilizer bar bracket nuts to 35 ft. lbs. (48 Nm).

6. Tighten the new stabilizer bar link upper nuts to 111 ft. lbs. (150 Nm).

2011 4WD Models

See Figure 537.

> ❊❊ **WARNING**
>
> **Suspension fasteners are critical parts because they affect performance of vital components and systems and their failure can result in major service expense. They must be replaced with the same part number or an equivalent part if replacement is necessary. Do not use a replacement part of lesser quality or substi-**

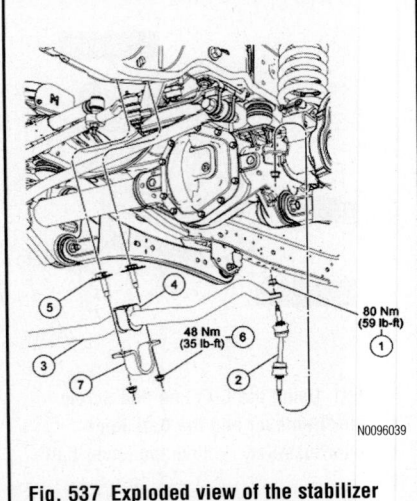

Fig. 537 Exploded view of the stabilizer bar assembly

tute design. Torque values must be used as specified during reassembly to make sure of correct retention of these parts.

➡ **Use the hex-holding feature to prevent the ball stud from turning while removing or installing the stabilizer link nut.**

1. With the vehicle in NEUTRAL, position it on a hoist.

2. Remove the stabilizer bar link nuts and stabilizer bar links. Discard the nuts.

3. Remove the stabilizer bar bracket nuts, brackets and the stabilizer bar. Discard the nuts.

4. To install, reverse the removal procedure.

  a. Tighten the new stabilizer bar bracket nuts to 35 ft. lbs. (48 Nm).

  b. Tighten the new stabilizer bar link nuts to 59 ft. lbs. (80 Nm).

2010 & 2011 RWD Models

See Figure 538.

> ❊❊ **WARNING**
>
> **Suspension fasteners are critical parts because they affect performance of vital components and systems and their failure can result in major service expense. They must be replaced with the same part number or an equivalent part if replacement is necessary. Do not use a replacement part of lesser quality or substitute design. Torque values must be used as specified during reassembly to make sure of correct retention of these parts.**

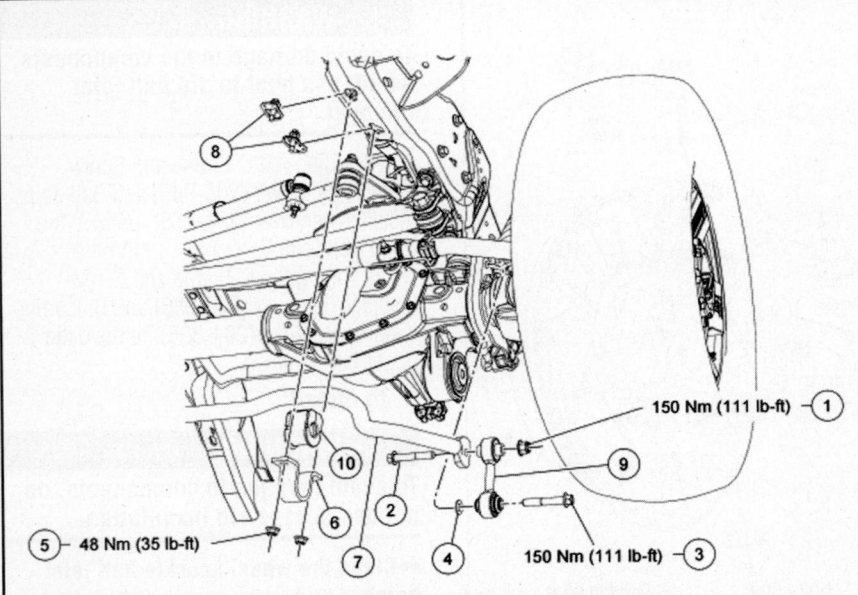

1. Stabilizer bar link upper nut (2 required)
2. Stabilizer bar link upper bolt (2 required)
3. Stabilizer bar link lower bolt (2 required)
4. Washer (2 required)
5. Stabilizer bar bracket nut (4 required)
6. Stabilizer bar bracket (2 required)
7. Stabilizer bar
8. Stabilizer bar bracket bolt and retainer (4 required)
9. Stabilizer bar link (2 required)
10. Stabilizer bar bushing (2 required)

N0063746

Fig. 536 Exploded view of the stabilizer bar (4WD) assembly

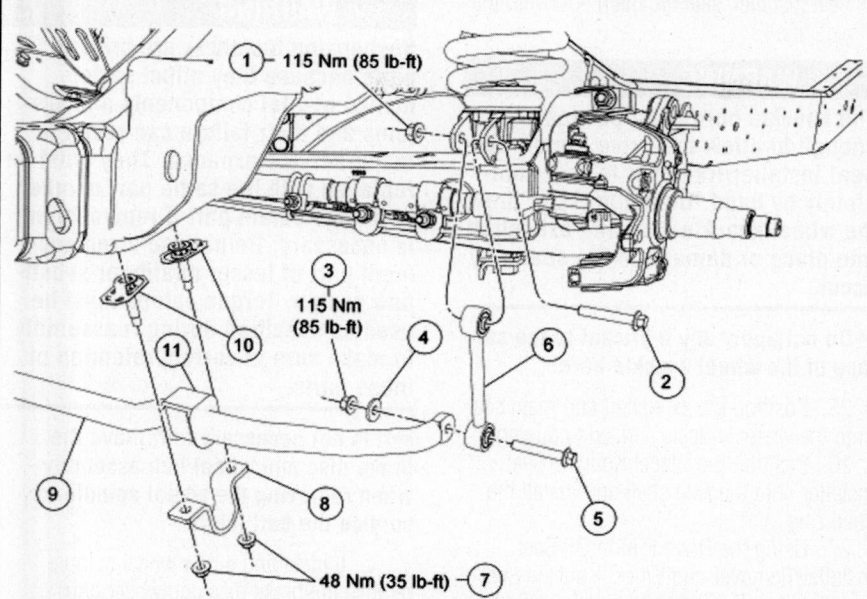

1. Stabilizer bar link upper nut (2 required)
2. Stabilizer bar link upper bolt (2 required)
3. Stabilizer bar link lower nut (2 required)
4. Washer (2 required)
5. Stabilizer bar link lower bolt (2 required)
6. Stabilizer bar link (2 required)
7. Stabilizer bar bracket nuts (4 required)
8. Stabilizer bar bracket
9. Stabilizer bar
10. Stabilizer bar bracket bolts and retainers (4 required)
11. Stabilizer bar bushing (2 required)

Fig. 538 Exploded view of the stabilizer bar and link (RWD) assembly

1. With the vehicle in NEUTRAL, position it on a hoist.
2. Remove and discard the stabilizer bar link upper nuts, washers and bolts.
3. Remove the stabilizer bar link lower nuts, washers, bolts and the stabilizer bar links. Discard the nuts, bolts and washers.
4. Remove the stabilizer bar bracket nuts, brackets and the stabilizer bar. Discard the nuts.
5. To install, reverse the removal procedure.
6. Tighten the new stabilizer bar bracket nuts to 35 ft. lbs. (48 Nm).
7. Tighten the new stabilizer bar link lower nuts, bolts and washers to 85 ft. lbs. (115 Nm).
8. Tighten the new stabilizer bar link upper nut to 85 ft. lbs. (115 Nm).

STEERING KNUCKLE

REMOVAL & INSTALLATION

4WD Models

See Figures 539 through 542.

1. Remove the wheel bearing and wheel hub.
2. Using a drift, drive the axle shaft main seal out of the wheel knuckle.

3. If equipped, disconnect the pulse vacuum hub hose.
4. Remove the axle shaft and main seal.
5. Remove the cotter pin and the tie-rod end nut. Discard the cotter pin.
6. If removing the RH wheel knuckle, using the C-Frame and Screw Assembly (211-023), disconnect the RH tie-rod end from the wheel knuckle.

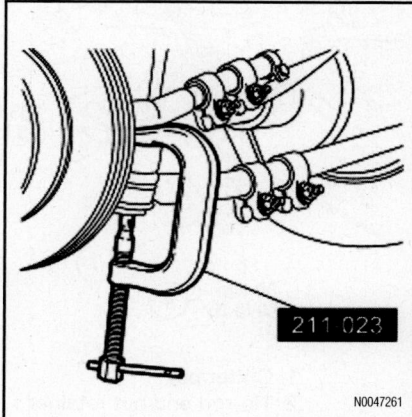

Fig. 539 If removing the RH wheel knuckle, using the C-Frame and Screw Assembly, disconnect the RH tie-rod end from the wheel knuckle

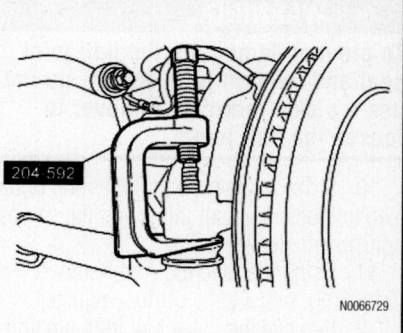

Fig. 540 If removing the LH wheel knuckle, using the Ball Joint Separator, disconnect the LH tie-rod end from the wheel knuckle

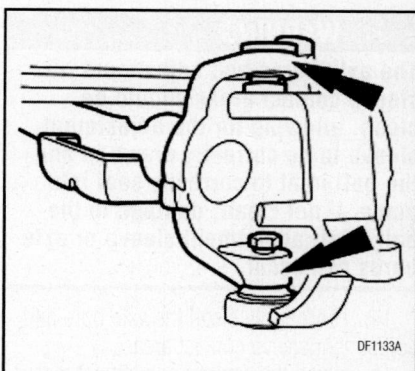

Fig. 541 Strike the lower and upper end of the axle to loosen the ball joints and the camber adjustment sleeve

7. If removing the LH wheel knuckle, using the Ball Joint Separator (204-592), disconnect the LH tie-rod end from the wheel knuckle.
8. Remove the upper ball joint cotter pin and nut. Discard the cotter pin.
9. Loosen, but do not remove, the lower ball joint nut.

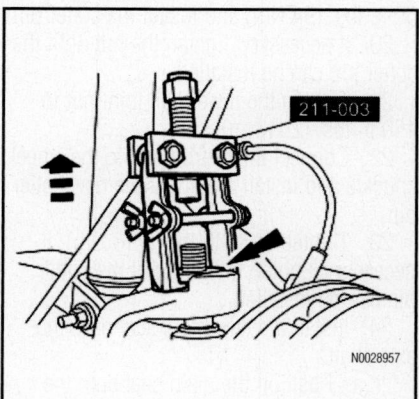

Fig. 542 Using the Steering Arm Remover, remove the camber adjuster

⁂ **WARNING**

To prevent damage to the ball joint seal and the ball joint socket, do not use a pickle fork-type remover to loosen the ball joints.

10. Strike the lower and upper end of the axle to loosen the ball joints and the camber adjustment sleeve.

11. Using the Steering Arm Remover (211-003), remove the camber adjuster.

12. Remove the lower ball joint nut and the wheel knuckle. Discard the nut.

13. Clean and inspect the wheel knuckle bore. If the wheel knuckle is cracked, a new one must be installed.

To install:

⁂ **WARNING**

The axle bores and adjustment sleeve contact areas should be clean, allowing for the adjustment sleeve to be correctly drawn in and the ball joint to correctly seat into place. If not clean, damage to the ball joint, adjustment sleeve or axle bores can occur.

14. Thoroughly clean the axle bore and adjustment sleeve contact areas.

15. Install the camber adjustment sleeve.

16. Position the wheel knuckle onto the axle and install the nut onto the upper ball joint. Do not tighten the nut at this time.

17. Apply threadlock and sealer to the threads of the lower ball joint and install the new nut onto the lower ball joint. Do not tighten the nut at this time.

18. Tighten the lower ball joint nut to 44 ft. lbs. (59 Nm).

➡ **Do not loosen the nut to install the cotter pin.**

19. Tighten the upper ball joint nut to 69 ft. lbs. (94 Nm) and install the cotter pin.

20. If necessary, tighten the nut until the cotter pin can be installed.

21. Tighten the lower ball joint nut to 150 ft. lbs. (204 Nm).

22. Connect the tie-rod end to the wheel knuckle and install the nut and a new cotter pin.

23. Tighten to 85 ft. lbs. (115 Nm). If necessary, tighten the nut until the cotter pin can be installed.

24. Install the new main seal onto the axle shaft.

   a. Position the main seal onto the axle shaft.

   b. Using the Drive Pinion Oil Seal Installer/Remover and Wheel Knuckle

Seal Installer, seat the main seal onto the axle shaft.

⁂ **WARNING**

The knuckle bore must be clean enough to allow the Drive Pinion Oil Seal Installer/Remover to seat completely by hand. Do not press or draw the wheel knuckle seal and axle shaft into place or damage to the seal may occur.

➡ **Do not apply any lubricant to the surface of the wheel knuckle bore.**

25. Position the axle shaft and main seal in to the wheel knuckle and axle housing.

26. Position the Wheel Knuckle Seal Installer onto the axle shaft and install the snap ring.

27. Using the Drive Pinion Oil Seal Installer/Remover and Wheel Knuckle Seal Installer, install the wheel knuckle seal and axle shaft.

28. Install the wheel bearing and wheel hub.

29. If equipped, connect the pulse vacuum hub hose.

RWD Models
See Figure 543.

⁂ **WARNING**

Suspension fasteners are critical parts because they affect performance of vital components and systems and their failure can result in major service expense. They must be replaced with the same part number or an equivalent part if replacement is necessary. Do not use a replacement part of lesser quality or substitute design. Torque values must be used as specified during reassembly to make sure of correct retention of these parts.

➡ **It is not necessary to remove the brake disc and wheel hub assembly when removing the wheel spindle to service the ball joints.**

1. If installing a new wheel spindle, remove the brake disc and wheel hub assembly. If the wheel spindle is being removed to service the ball joints, remove the brake pads.

2. Disconnect the wheel speed sensor electrical connector and detach the sensor harness from the brake hose.

3. Remove the cotter pin, nut retainer and the tie-rod end nut. Discard the cotter pin.

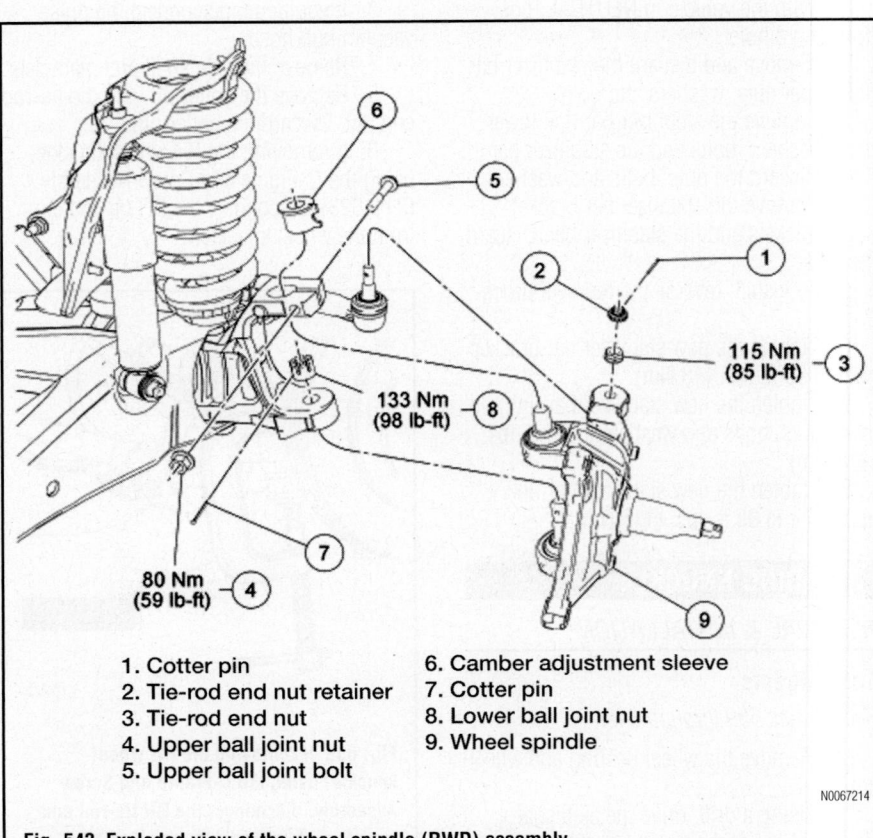

1. Cotter pin
2. Tie-rod end nut retainer
3. Tie-rod end nut
4. Upper ball joint nut
5. Upper ball joint bolt
6. Camber adjustment sleeve
7. Cotter pin
8. Lower ball joint nut
9. Wheel spindle

115 Nm (85 lb-ft)
133 Nm (98 lb-ft)
80 Nm (59 lb-ft)

N0067214

Fig. 543 Exploded view of the wheel spindle (RWD) assembly

4. Using the Pitman Arm Puller, disconnect the tie-rod end.

5. Remove and discard the upper ball joint nut and bolt.

✳✳ WARNING

Do not allow the camber adjustment sleeve to contact the ball joint seal when installing a sleeve, or damage to the ball joint seal may occur.

6. Remove the camber adjustment sleeve.

✳✳ WARNING

To prevent damage to the ball joint seal and the ball joint socket, do not use a pickle fork-type remover to loosen the ball joints.

7. Remove and discard the cotter pin, then loosen, but do not remove, the lower ball joint nut.

8. Strike the lower end of the front axle to free the lower ball joint from the axle.

➡ **Tighten the lower ball joint nut further, if necessary, in order to insert a new cotter pin.**

9. Remove the lower ball joint nut and the front wheel spindle. Discard the nut.

10. To install, reverse the removal procedure.

11. Tighten the new lower ball joint nut to 98 ft. lbs. (133 Nm).

12. Tighten the new upper ball joint nut to 59 ft. lbs. (80 Nm).

13. Tighten the tie-rod end nut to 85 ft. lbs. (115 Nm).

14. Check and, if necessary, align the front end.

UPPER BALL JOINT

REMOVAL & INSTALLATION

2010 4WD Models

See Figures 544 through 546.

1. Remove the wheel knuckle.

2. If equipped, remove the ball joint grease fitting.

3. Position the wheel knuckle in a vise and remove the snap ring from the lower ball joint.

✳✳ WARNING

To avoid damage to the components, do not use heat to aid ball joint removal.

4. Using the C-Frame and Screw Installer/Remover (205-086) and the Ball

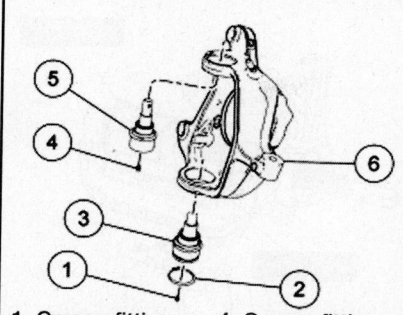

1. Grease fitting
2. Snap ring
3. Lower ball joint
4. Grease fitting
5. Upper ball joint
6. Wheel knuckle

N0034300

Fig. 544 Exploded view of the wheel knuckle assembly

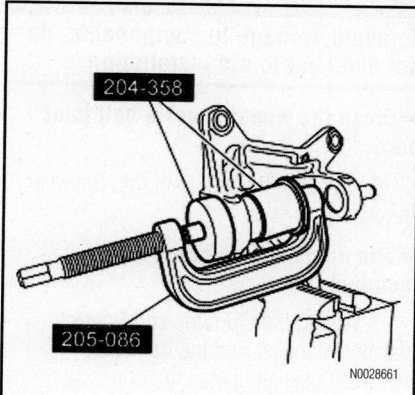

N0028661

Fig. 545 Using the C-Frame and Screw Installer/Remover and the Ball Joint Remover/Installer, remove the lower ball joint

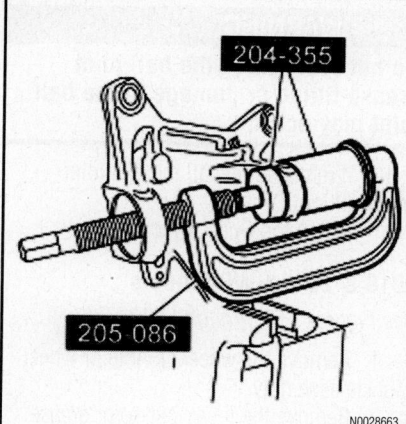

N0028663

Fig. 546 Using the C-Frame and Screw Installer/Remover and the Ball Joint Remover/Installer, remove the upper ball joint

Joint Remover/Installer (204-358), remove the lower ball joint.

5. Using the C-Frame and Screw Installer/Remover (205-086) and the Ball Joint Remover/Installer (204-355), remove the upper ball joint.

To install:

✳✳ WARNING

The grease fitting must be removed from the ball joint prior to installation or damage to the grease fitting can occur.

✳✳ WARNING

To avoid damage to components, do not use heat to aid installation.

➡ Clean the wheel knuckle ball joint bore.

6. Position the ball joint into the wheel knuckle.

➡ **The upper ball joint must be installed first.**

7. Using the C-Frame and Screw Installer/Remover and the Ball Joint Remover/Installer, install the upper ball joint.

8. Using the C-Frame and Screw Installer/Remover and the Ball Joint Remover/Installer, install the lower ball joint.

9. Install the snap ring in the groove at the bottom of the lower ball joint.

✳✳ WARNING

Do not overtighten the ball joint grease fitting or damage to the ball joint may occur.

10. If removed, install the ball joint grease fitting.

11. Install the wheel knuckle.

2011 4WD Models

See Figures 547 through 549.

1. Remove the wheel knuckle.

2. If equipped, remove the ball joint grease fitting.

3. Position the wheel knuckle in a vise and remove the snap ring from the lower ball joint.

✳✳ WARNING

To avoid damage to the components, do not use heat to aid ball joint removal.

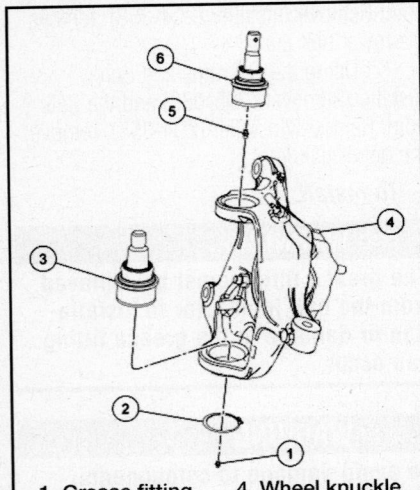

1. Grease fitting
2. Snap ring
3. Lower ball joint
4. Wheel knuckle
5. Grease fitting
6. Upper ball joint

N0111736

Fig. 547 Exploded view of the wheel knuckle assembly

4. Using the C-Frame and Screw Installer/Remover (205-086) and the Ball Joint Remover/Installer (204-358), remove the lower ball joint.

5. Using the C-Frame and Screw Installer/Remover (205-086) and the Ball Joint Remover/Installer (204-355), remove the upper ball joint.

To install:

❉❉ WARNING

The grease fitting must be removed from the ball joint prior to installation or damage to the grease fitting can occur.

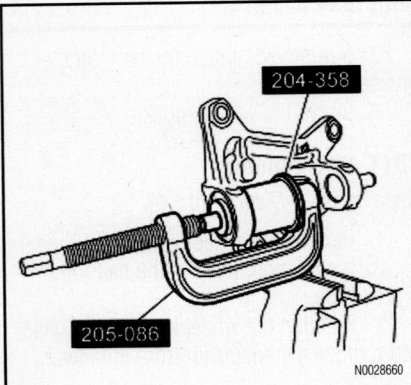

Fig. 548 Using the C-Frame and Screw Installer/Remover and the Ball Joint Remover/Installer, remove the lower ball joint

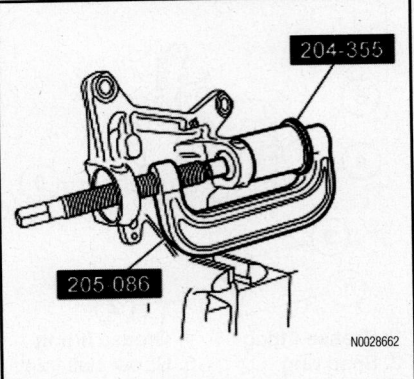

Fig. 549 Using the C-Frame and Screw Installer/Remover and the Ball Joint Remover/Installer, remove the upper ball joint

❉❉ WARNING

To avoid damage to components, do not use heat to aid installation.

➡ Clean the wheel knuckle ball joint bore.

6. Position the ball joint into the wheel knuckle.

➡ **The upper ball joint must be installed first.**

7. Using the C-Frame and Screw Installer/Remover and the Ball Joint Remover/Installer, install the upper ball joint.

8. Using the C-Frame and Screw Installer/Remover and the Ball Joint Remover/Installer, install the lower ball joint.

9. Install the snap ring in the groove at the bottom of the lower ball joint.

❉❉ WARNING

Do not overtighten the ball joint grease fitting or damage to the ball joint may occur.

10. If removed, install the ball joint grease fitting.

11. Install the wheel knuckle.

2010 & 2011 RWD Models

See Figures 550 through 552.

1. Remove the wheel spindle or wheel knuckle assembly.

2. Remove the lower ball joint grease plug.

3. Position the wheel spindle in a vise and remove the snap ring from the lower ball joint.

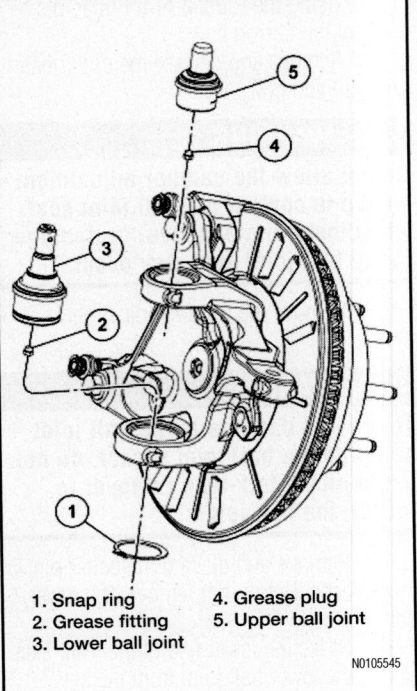

1. Snap ring
2. Grease fitting
3. Lower ball joint
4. Grease plug
5. Upper ball joint

N0105545

Fig. 550 Exploded view of the wheel knuckle assembly

❉❉ WARNING

To avoid damage to the components, do not use heat to aid ball joint removal.

4. Using the C-Frame and Screw Installer/Remover (205-086) and Ball Joint Installer/Remover (204-358), remove the lower ball joint.

5. Using the C-Frame and Screw Installer/Remover (205-086) and Ball Joint Installer/Remover (204-358), remove the upper ball joint.

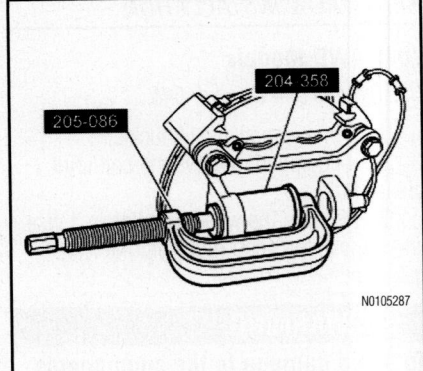

Fig. 551 Using the C-Frame and Screw Installer/Remover and Ball Joint Installer/Remover, remove the lower ball joint

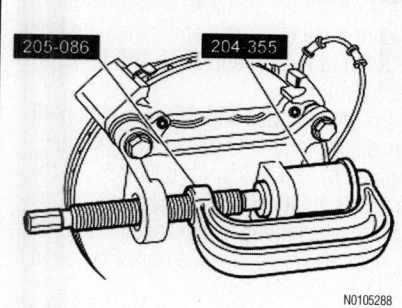

Fig. 552 Using the C-Frame and Screw Installer/Remover and Ball Joint Installer/Remover, remove the upper ball joint

To install:

✳✳ WARNING

To avoid damage to components, do not use heat to aid installation.

➡**Clean the wheel knuckle ball joint bores.**

➡**The upper ball joint must be installed first.**

6. Using the C-Frame and Screw Installer/Remover and Ball Joint Installer/Remover, install the upper ball joint.

7. Using the C-Frame and Screw Installer/Remover and Ball Joint Installer/Remover, install the lower ball joint.

8. Install the snap ring in the groove at the bottom of the lower ball joint.

9. Install the lower ball joint grease plug.

10. Install the front wheel spindle or wheel knuckle assembly.

WHEEL BEARINGS & WHEEL HUB

REMOVAL & INSTALLATION

4WD Models

See Figures 553 through 556.

1. Remove the wheel and tire.
2. If equipped with ABS:
    a. Unclip the wheel speed sensor harness from the frame.
    b. Remove the 2 wheel speed sensor harness bolts.
    c. Remove the wheel speed sensor harness-to-wheel knuckle bolt.
3. For vehicles with Dual Rear Wheels (DRW), remove and discard the 8 wheel extension nuts and the wheel extension.

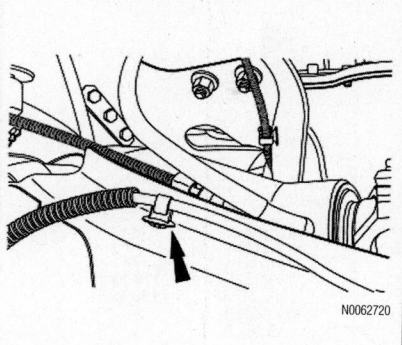

Fig. 553 Unclip the wheel speed sensor harness from the frame

✳✳ WARNING

Do not allow the caliper to hang from the brake hose or damage to the hose can occur.

4. Remove the 2 brake caliper anchor plate bolts and position the brake caliper aside.

5. Support the brake caliper using mechanic's wire.

6. Index-mark and remove the brake disc.

✳✳ WARNING

The service replacement kit includes 2 O-ring seals; one for testing the hub lock assembly and one for reassembly into the wheel hub. DO NOT REUSE O-RING SEALS or hub lock failure may occur.

➡**Due to the fit of the splines, the hub lock will be difficult to remove. Lifting or lightly prying (with a small bar) on the axle U-joint will ease removal. When prying on the cap/hub flange, work around the flange to uniformly withdraw the hub lock.**

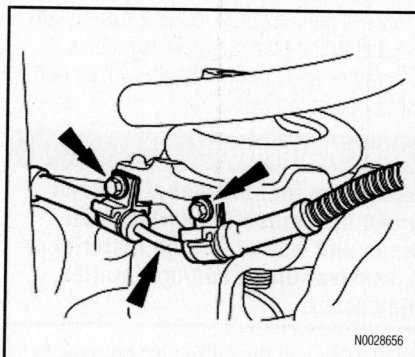

Fig. 554 Remove the 2 wheel speed sensor harness bolts

➡**Always check the vacuum leak rate of the wheel end assembly when repairing or diagnosing the axle, wheel end or hub lock performance.**

7. Remove the hub lock.
    a. Loosen each screw 1 to 2 turns.
    b. Gently pry on the hub lock cap edge to release gasket adhesion.
    c. Remove and discard the screws.
    d. While lifting/jiggling the axle U-joint, pull or uniformly pry the hub lock from the wheel bearing and wheel hub.
8. Remove the axle shaft snap ring.

➡**The wheel bearing and wheel hub assembly is a slip-fit design and should not require a puller to remove it.**

9. Remove the 4 wheel hub nuts and the wheel hub. Discard the nuts.

10. If necessary, remove the brake disc shield.

11. If equipped with ABS, remove the wheel speed sensor bolt and position the sensor aside.

12. Remove and discard the wheel bearing and wheel hub O-ring seal.

13. Position the wheel bearing and wheel hub in a vise with protective caps and remove the 4 studs using 2 mounting nuts.

To install:

14. Position the wheel bearing and wheel hub in a vise with protective caps and install the 4 studs using 2 mounting nuts.

➡**Any time the wheel bearing and wheel hub are removed for any reason, a new O-ring seal must be installed. Failure to do so can cause a vacuum leak and loss of Four-Wheel Drive (4WD) operations.**

15. Install a new wheel bearing and wheel hub O-ring seal.

16. If equipped with ABS, position the wheel speed sensor and install the bolt. Tighten to 13 ft. lbs. (18 Nm).

17. If removed, position the brake disc shield.

➡**Apply a coat of grease to the O-ring area of the wheel bearing and wheel hub before installation.**

18. Position the wheel bearing and wheel hub and install the 4 new nuts. Tighten to 133 ft. lbs. (180 Nm).

19. Install the axle shaft snap ring.

➡**Any time the hub lock is removed, a new O-ring seal must be installed. Failure to do so can cause a vacuum leak and loss of 4WD functions.**

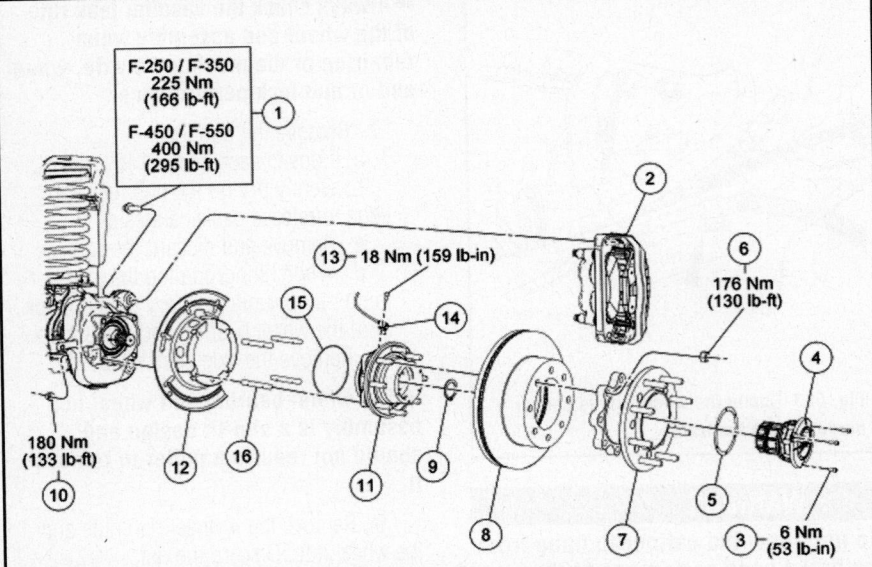

F-250 / F-350
225 Nm
(166 lb-ft)

F-450 / F-550
400 Nm
(295 lb-ft)

13 — 18 Nm (159 lb-in)

176 Nm
(130 lb-ft)

180 Nm
(133 lb-ft)

6 Nm
(53 lb-in)

1. Brake caliper anchor plate bolt (2 required)
2. Brake caliper
3. Hublock screw
4. Hublock
5. Hublock gasket
6. Wheel extension nut (8 required)
7. Wheel extension
8. Brake disc
9. Axle shaft snap ring
10. Wheel bearing and wheel hub nut (4 required)
11. Wheel bearing and wheel hub
12. Brake disc shield
13. Wheel speed sensor bolt
14. Wheel speed sensor
15. Wheel bearing and wheel hub O-ring
16. Wheel bearing and wheel hub stud

N0096279

Fig. 555 Exploded view of the wheel bearing and wheel hub assembly

20. Install a new hub lock O-ring seal.

> ※※ **WARNING**
>
> **The service replacement kit includes 2 O-ring seals; one for testing the hub lock assembly and one for reassembly into the wheel hub. DO NOT REUSE O-RING SEALS or hub lock failure may occur.**

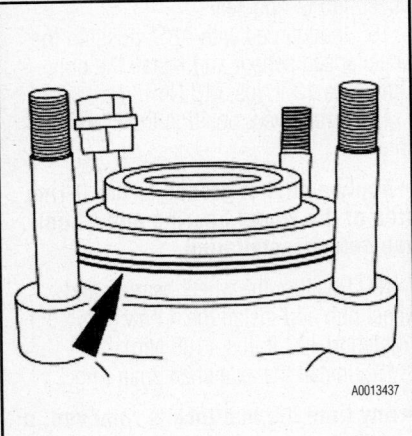

A0013437

Fig. 556 Remove and discard the wheel bearing and wheel hub O-ring seal

→**Always check the vacuum leak rate of the wheel end assembly when repairing or diagnosing the axle, wheel end or hub lock performance.**

21. Install a new hub lock gasket, then install the hub lock in the following sequence.

   a. Rotate the hub lock dial clockwise to the lock position. Apply the specified grease to the inner and outer splines.

   b. Insert the hub lock into the wheel hub while slowly turning the wheel hub to align the splines. Lift/jiggle the axle U-joint while pushing the hub lock into the wheel hub.

22. Install new hub lock screws. Rotate the dial to the counterclockwise position (free/auto) and confirm that the wheel hub turns free of the axle shaft.

> ※※ **WARNING**
>
> **Make sure that the wheel hub and brake disc mounting surfaces are clean and free of foreign material or excessive runout and/or vibration may occur.**

23. Position the brake disc onto the wheel hub noting the position of the index mark.

24. Position the brake caliper and anchor plate assembly and install the bolts. F-250 and F-350, tighten to 166 ft. lbs. (225 Nm).

25. If equipped with DRW, position the wheel extension and install the new nuts. Tighten to 130 ft. lbs. (176 Nm).

26. If equipped with ABS:

   a. Install the wheel speed sensor harness-to-wheel knuckle bolt. Tighten to 11 ft. lbs. (15 Nm).

   b. Install the 2 wheel speed sensor harness-to-axle bolts. Tighten to 11 ft. lbs. (15 Nm).

   c. Connect the wheel speed sensor harness to the frame.

RWD Models

See Figure 557.

1. Remove the wheel and tire.

> ※※ **WARNING**
>
> **Do not allow the brake caliper to hang from the brake hose or damage to the hose can occur.**

2. Remove the 2 brake caliper anchor plate bolts and position the brake caliper and anchor plate assembly aside.

3. Support the brake caliper and anchor plate assembly using mechanic's wire.

4. Remove the grease cap.

5. Remove the cotter pin, wheel spindle nut retainer, nut and flat washer. Discard the wheel spindle nut.

→**Inspect the condition of the wheel spindle and threads, clean or install new components as necessary.**

6. Remove the outer wheel bearing, then remove the brake disc and hub assembly.

> ※※ **WARNING**
>
> **Do not damage the wheel bearing cage while removing. A damaged wheel bearing cage may cause premature bearing failure.**

7. Using a suitable slide hammer and bearing seal remover, remove the inner wheel bearing seal and bearing.

To install:

> ※※ **WARNING**
>
> **Do not spin the bearing dry with compressed air or damage to the bearing may result.**

→**Remove all traces of lubricant from the bearings, hub and spindle. Inspect**

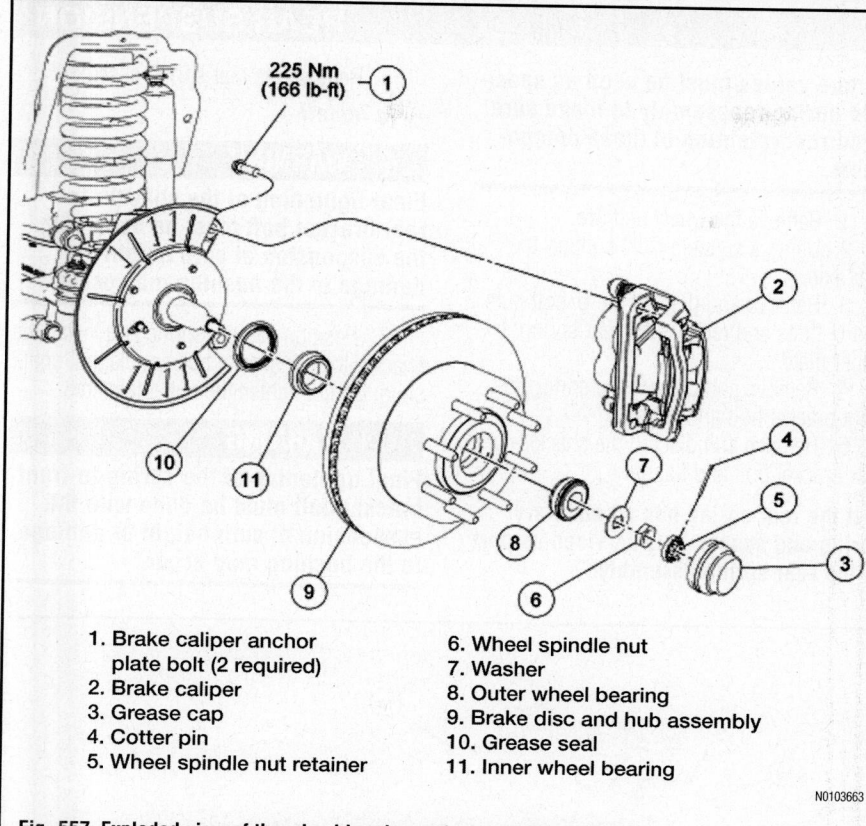

1. Brake caliper anchor plate bolt (2 required)
2. Brake caliper
3. Grease cap
4. Cotter pin
5. Wheel spindle nut retainer
6. Wheel spindle nut
7. Washer
8. Outer wheel bearing
9. Brake disc and hub assembly
10. Grease seal
11. Inner wheel bearing

N0103663

Fig. 557 Exploded view of the wheel bearing and wheel hub assembly

bearings and bearing cups for pitting, spalling or unusual wear. If either bearings or bearing cups are worn or damaged, both bearings and bearing cups should be installed new.

➡It is recommended that bearings and bearing cups be installed in sets. If cups are worn or damaged, install the inner and outer bearing cups in the hub with an appropriate bearing cup driver tool. Check for correct seating of the new bearing cups by trying to insert a 0.015 inches (0.38 mm) feeler gauge between the bottom face of the cup and wheel hub seat. It should not be possible to insert the feeler gauge.

8. Remove all burrs, nicks or scratches from the shoulder of the spindle and seal bore in the hub with emery cloth.

9. Pack the inside of the hub with wheel bearing grease. Fill the hub until the grease is flush with the inside diameters of both bearing cups.

10. Using a bearing packer, pack the wheel bearings with wheel bearing grease. If a packer is not available, work as much lubricant as possible between the rollers and cages.

11. Place the inner wheel bearing in the inner cup and, using a suitable seal installer, install the wheel bearing hub seal. Make sure the seal is fully seated and lubricated.

✳✳ WARNING

Keep the hub and brake disc assembly centered on the wheel spindle to prevent damage to the grease seal and spindle threads.

12. Position the brake disc and hub assembly onto the wheel spindle.

➡**Do not tighten the nut at this time.**

13. Position the outer wheel bearing cone and roller assembly and the flat washer on the spindle, then loosely install the wheel spindle nut.

14. Adjust the wheel bearing end play.

15. Position the brake caliper and anchor plate assembly and install the 2 bolts. Tighten the bolts to 166 ft. lbs. (225 Nm).

16. Install the wheel and tire.

ADJUSTMENT

RWD Models

✳✳ WARNING

If bearings are adjusted too tightly, they will overheat and wear rapidly. An adjustment that is excessively loose can cause pounding and contribute to uneven tire wear, steering difficulties and inefficient brakes. Check bearing adjustment at regular inspection intervals.

✳✳ WARNING

New wheel seals must be installed when the hub is removed. A damaged or worn seal can permit bearing lubricant to reach the brake linings, resulting in ineffective brake operation and necessitating premature replacement of the linings.

1. Remove the wheel and tire.

2. Remove the grease cap.

3. Remove the cotter pin and the wheel hub nut. Discard the cotter pin.

4. While rotating the wheel clockwise, tighten the wheel hub nut to 21 ft. lbs. (28 Nm) to seat the bearings.

5. Back off the wheel hub nut until loose (approximately 120 degrees to 180 degrees).

6. While rotating the wheel, tighten the wheel hub nut to 18 inch lbs. (2 Nm). Turning torque required to rotate the hub should be 18 inch lbs. (2 Nm).

7. Install a new cotter pin.

8. Install the grease cap.

9. Install the wheel and tire.

LEAF SPRING

REMOVAL & INSTALLATION

2010 Models
See Figure 558.

Torque values must be used as specified during reassembly to make sure of correct retention of these components.

1. Remove the wheel and tire.
2. Using a suitable jack, support the rear axle.
3. Remove and discard the U-bolt nuts and U-bolts and remove the rear spring upper plate.
4. Remove and discard the spring-to-front bracket bolt and flagnut.
5. Remove and discard the shackle-to-rear bracket bolt and flagnut.

➡ If the rear spring has an auxiliary spring and spacer, it is serviced as part of the rear spring assembly.

6. Remove the rear spring assembly.

To install:

7. Position the rear spring and install the shackle-to-rear bracket bolt and flagnut until snug. Do not tighten the nut at this time.

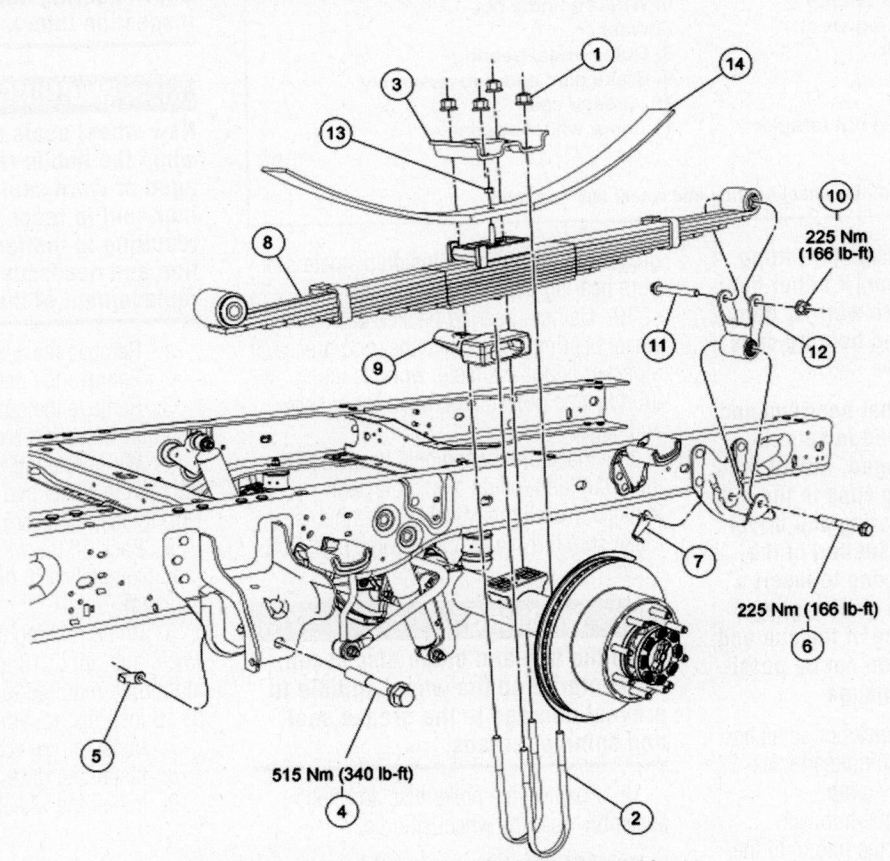

225 Nm (166 lb-ft)

225 Nm (166 lb-ft)

515 Nm (340 lb-ft)

1. U-bolt nut (4 required)
2. U-bolt (2 required)
3. Spring upper plate
4. Spring-to-front bracket bolt
5. Spring-to-front bracket flagnut
6. Shackle-to-rear bracket bolt
7. Shackle-to-rear bracket flagnut
8. Spring assembly
9. Spacer
10. Spring-to-shackle nut
11. Spring-to-shackle bolt
12. Spring shackle
13. Auxiliary spring nut
14. Auxiliary spring

N0101196

Fig. 558 Exploded view of the rear suspension leaf spring

8. Install the spring-to-front bracket bolt and flagnut until snug. Do not tighten the nut at this time.

❊❊ WARNING

Final tightening of the U-bolt nuts must be done with the suspension at curb height or incorrect clamp load may occur.

9. Position the spring upper plate and install the U-bolts and nuts, align the U-bolts so they are as vertical as possible, and tighten until snug. Do not fully tighten the nuts at this time.

10. With the suspension at curb height, tighten the new shackle-to-rear bracket bolt to 166 ft. lbs. (225 Nm).

11. With the suspension at curb height, tighten the new spring-to-front bracket bolt to 340 ft. lbs. (515 Nm).

12. With the suspension at curb height, tighten the new nuts evenly in a cross-type pattern in 4 stages.

    a. Stage 1: Tighten to 37 ft. lbs. (50 Nm).

    b. Stage 2: Tighten to 74 ft. lbs. (100 Nm).

    c. Stage 3: Tighten to 111 ft. lbs. (150 Nm).

    d. Stage 4: Tighten to 148 ft. lbs. (200 Nm).

13. Install the wheel and tire.

2011 Models

See Figure 559.

❊❊ WARNING

Suspension fasteners are critical components because they affect performance of vital components and systems and their failure can result in major service expense. Install new components with the same component number or an equivalent component if installation is necessary. Do not use an installation component of lesser quality or substitute design. Torque values must be used as specified during reassembly to make sure of correct retention of these components.

1. Remove the wheel and tire.
2. Using a suitable jack, support the rear axle.
3. Remove and discard the U-bolt nuts and U-bolts and remove the rear spring bottom cap.
4. Remove and discard the spring-to-front bracket bolt and nut.

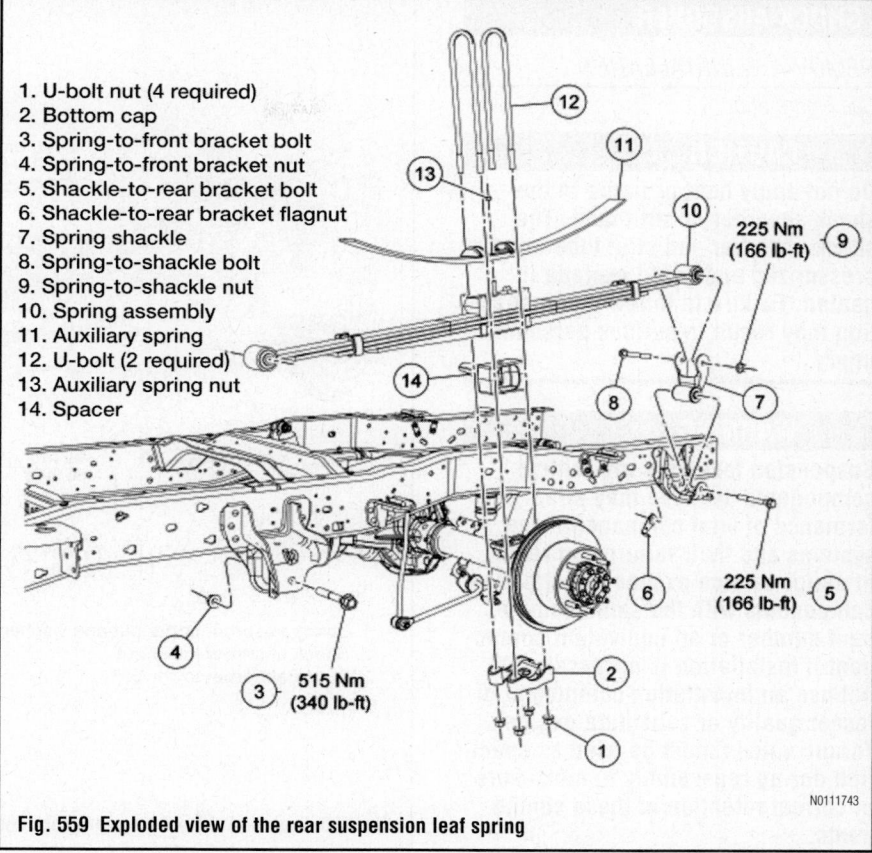

1. U-bolt nut (4 required)
2. Bottom cap
3. Spring-to-front bracket bolt
4. Spring-to-front bracket nut
5. Shackle-to-rear bracket bolt
6. Shackle-to-rear bracket flagnut
7. Spring shackle
8. Spring-to-shackle bolt
9. Spring-to-shackle nut
10. Spring assembly
11. Auxiliary spring
12. U-bolt (2 required)
13. Auxiliary spring nut
14. Spacer

225 Nm (166 lb-ft)

225 Nm (166 lb-ft)

515 Nm (340 lb-ft)

N0111743

Fig. 559 Exploded view of the rear suspension leaf spring

5. Remove and discard the shackle-to-rear bracket bolt and flagnut.

➡ **If the rear spring has an auxiliary spring and spacer, it is serviced as part of the rear spring assembly.**

6. Remove the rear spring assembly.

To install:

❊❊ WARNING

Final tightening of the shackle-to-rear bracket bolt must be done with the suspension at curb height or damage to the bushing may occur.

7. Position the rear spring and install the shackle-to-rear bracket bolt and flagnut until snug. Do not tighten the nut at this time.

❊❊ WARNING

Final tightening of the spring-to-front bracket bolt must be done with the suspension at curb height or damage to the bushing may occur.

8. Install the spring-to-front bracket bolt and nut until snug. Do not tighten the nut at this time.

❊❊ WARNING

Final tightening of the U-bolt nuts must be done with the suspension at curb height or incorrect clamp load may occur.

9. Position the bottom cap and install the U-bolts and nuts, align the U-bolts so they are as vertical as possible, and tighten until snug. Do not fully tighten the nuts at this time.

10. With the suspension at curb height, tighten the new shackle-to-rear bracket bolt to 166 ft. lbs. (225 Nm).

11. With the suspension at curb height, tighten the new spring-to-front bracket bolt to 340 ft. lbs. (515 Nm).

12. With the suspension at curb height, tighten the new nuts evenly in a cross-type pattern in 4 stages.

    a. Stage 1: Tighten to 48 ft. lbs. (65 Nm).

    b. Stage 2: Tighten to 96 ft. lbs. (130 Nm).

    c. Stage 3: Tighten to 148 ft. lbs. (200 Nm).

    d. Stage 4: Tighten to 195 ft. lbs. (265 Nm).

13. Install the wheel and tire.

SHOCK ABSORBER

REMOVAL & INSTALLATION

See Figure 560.

✳✳ CAUTION

Do not apply heat or flame to the shock absorber or strut tube. The shock absorber and strut tube are gas pressurized and could explode if heated. Failure to follow this instruction may result in serious personal injury.

✳✳ WARNING

Suspension fasteners are critical components because they affect performance of vital components and systems and their failure can result in major service expense. Install new components with the same component number or an equivalent component if installation is necessary. Do not use an installation component of lesser quality or substitute design. Torque values must be used as specified during reassembly to make sure of correct retention of these components.

1. With the vehicle in NEUTRAL, position it on a hoist.

2. Using a suitable jack, support the rear axle.

3. Remove and discard the shock absorber lower nut and bolt.

4. Remove and discard the shock absorber upper nut and remove the shock absorber.

5. To install, reverse the removal procedure.

   a. Tighten the new shock absorber upper nut to 52 ft. lbs. (70 Nm).

   b. Tighten the new shock absorber lower nut and bolt to 66 ft. lbs. (90 Nm).

STABILIZER BAR & LINK

REMOVAL & INSTALLATION

2010 Models

See Figures 561 and 562.

✳✳ WARNING

Suspension fasteners are critical components because they affect performance of vital components and systems and their failure can result in major service expense. Install new components with the same compo-

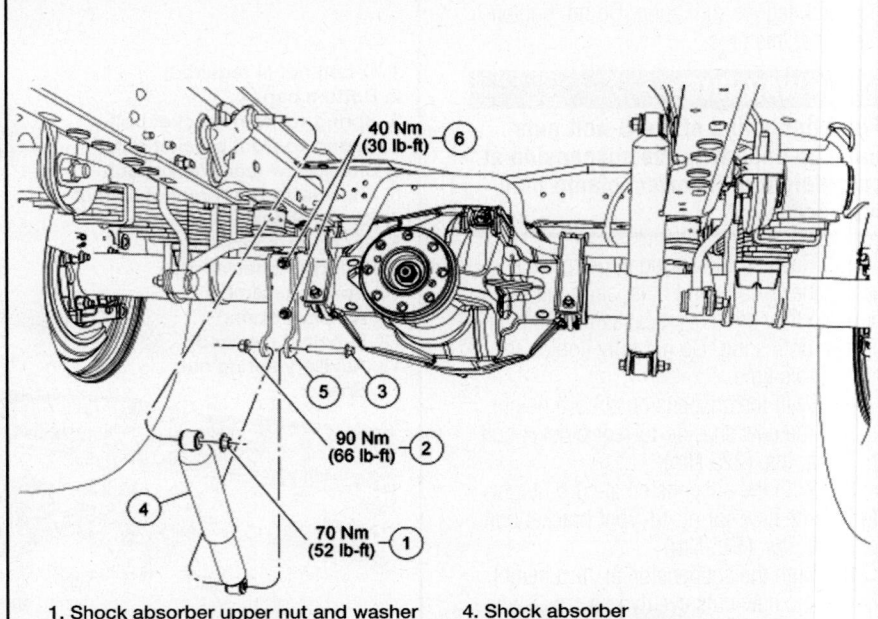

1. Shock absorber upper nut and washer
2. Shock absorber lower nut
3. Shock absorber lower bolt
4. Shock absorber
5. Shock absorber bracket
6. Shock absorber bracket nuts (2 required)

Fig. 560 Exploded view of the rear shock absorber assembly

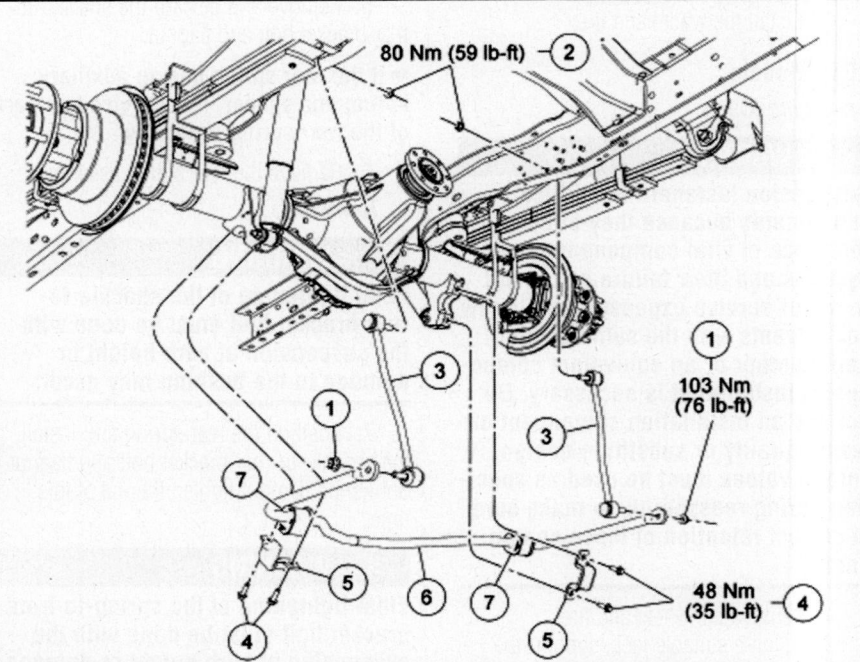

1. Stabilizer bar link lower nuts (2 required)
2. Stabilizer bar link upper nuts (2 required)
3. Stabilizer bar links (2 required)
4. Stabilizer bar bracket bolts (4 required)
5. Stabilizer bar brackets (2 required)
6. Stabilizer bar
7. Stabilizer bar bushings

Fig. 561 F-250 and F-350 Wide Frame Vehicles

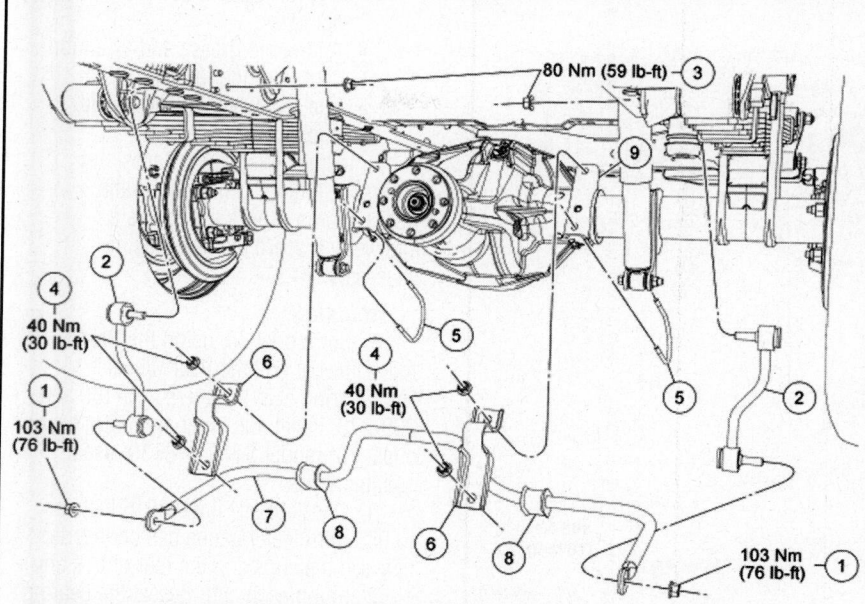

1. Stabilizer bar link lower nuts (2 required)
2. Stabilizer bar links (2 required)
3. Stabilizer bar link upper nuts (2 required)
4. Stabilizer bar bracket nuts (4 required)
5. Stabilizer bar bracket U-bolts (2 required)
6. Stabilizer bar brackets (2 required)
7. Stabilizer bar
8. Stabilizer bar bushings
9. Stabilizer bar mounting bracket (2 required)

Fig. 562 F-350 Single Rear Wheel (SRW), Narrow Frame Vehicles

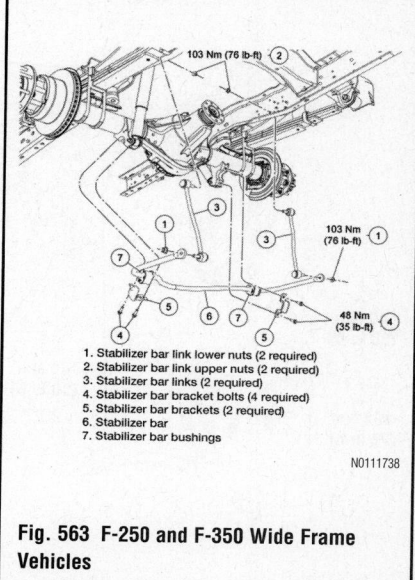

1. Stabilizer bar link lower nuts (2 required)
2. Stabilizer bar link upper nuts (2 required)
3. Stabilizer bar links (2 required)
4. Stabilizer bar bracket bolts (4 required)
5. Stabilizer bar brackets (2 required)
6. Stabilizer bar
7. Stabilizer bar bushings

Fig. 563 F-250 and F-350 Wide Frame Vehicles

nent number or an equivalent component if installation is necessary. Do not use an installation component of lesser quality or substitute design. Torque values must be used as specified during reassembly to make sure of correct retention of these components.

1. With the vehicle in NEUTRAL, position it on a hoist.
2. Remove and discard the stabilizer bar link lower nuts.
3. Remove and discard the stabilizer bar link upper nuts and remove the stabilizer bar links.
4. For F-350 Single Rear Wheel (SRW) narrow frame vehicles, remove the stabilizer bar bracket nuts, U-bolts, brackets and the stabilizer bar. Discard the nuts and U-bolts.
5. For F-250/F-350 wide frame vehicles, remove the stabilizer bar bracket bolts, brackets and the stabilizer bar. Discard the bolts.

To install:
6. To install, reverse the removal procedure.
7. For F-250/F-350 wide frame vehicles, tighten the new stabilizer bar bracket bolts to 35 ft. lbs. (48 Nm).

8. For F-350 Single Rear Wheel (SRW) narrow frame vehicles, tighten the new stabilizer bar bracket nuts to 30 ft. lbs. (40 Nm).
9. Tighten the new stabilizer bar link upper nuts to 59 ft. lbs. (80 Nm).
10. Tighten the new stabilizer bar link lower nuts to 76 ft. lbs. (103 Nm).

2011 Models
See Figures 563 through 565.

WARNING

Suspension fasteners are critical components because they affect performance of vital components and systems and their failure can result in major service expense. Install new components with the same component number or an equivalent component if installation is necessary. Do not use an installation component of lesser quality or substitute design. Use specified torque values during reassembly to make sure correct retention of these components.

1. With the vehicle in NEUTRAL, position it on a hoist.
2. Remove and discard the stabilizer bar link lower nuts.

3. For F-250/F-350 wide frame vehicles equipped with diesel engine and (inboard) reductant tank, lower the reductant tank assembly:
a. Support the reductant tank assembly with a suitable jackstand.
b. Remove the four cover bolts.
c. Lower the reductant tank assembly.
4. Remove and discard the stabilizer bar link upper nuts and remove the stabilizer bar links.
5. For F-350 Single Rear Wheel (SRW) narrow frame vehicles, remove the stabilizer bar bracket nuts, U-bolts, brackets and the stabilizer bar. Discard the nuts and U-bolts.
6. For F-250/F-350 wide frame vehicles, remove the stabilizer bar bracket bolts, brackets and the stabilizer bar. Discard the bolts.
7. To install, reverse the removal procedure.
a. Tighten the new stabilizer bar bracket bolts to 35 ft. lbs. (48 Nm).
b. Tighten the new stabilizer bar bracket nuts to 30 ft. lbs. (40 Nm).
c. Tighten the new stabilizer bar link upper nuts to 76 ft. lbs. (103 Nm).
d. Tighten the reductant tank cover bolts to 15 ft. lbs. (20 Nm).
e. Tighten the new nuts to 76 ft. lbs. (103 Nm).

WHEEL BEARINGS

REMOVAL & INSTALLATION

2010 and 2011 Dana Rear Axle
See Figure 566.

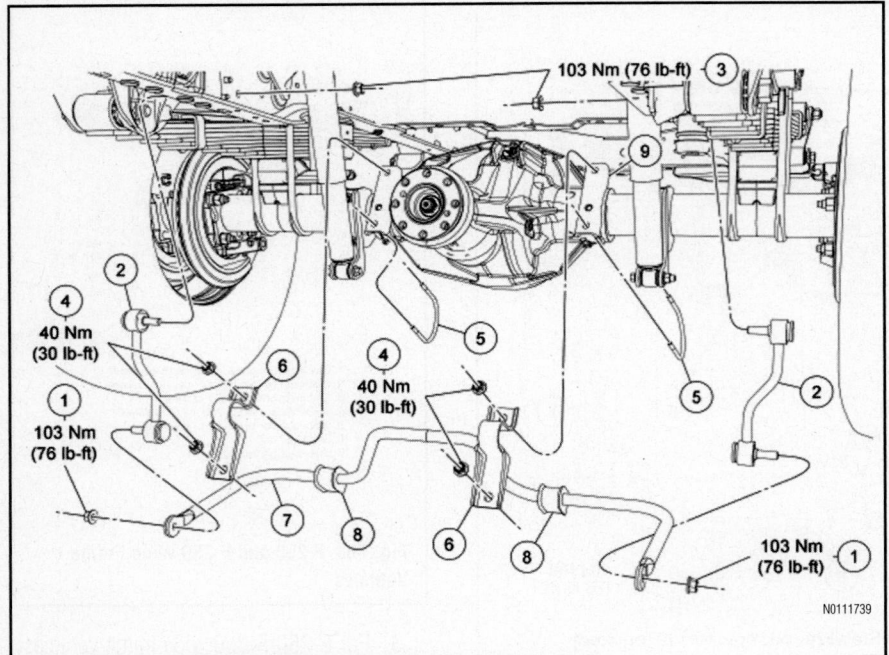

Fig. 564 F-350 Single Rear Wheel (SRW), Narrow Frame Vehicles

1. Remove the rear wheel hub.
2. Remove the rear hub seal and the inner rear wheel bearing. Discard the rear hub seal.
3. If not done previously, remove the 8 bolts and separate the rear hub from the brake disc.
4. Clean all the old grease and axle lubricant out of the rear hub.
5. Remove the inner and outer bearing cups.

  a. For model 80, use Rear Wheel Hub Bearing Cup Remover 205-277 and Adapter 205-153 to remove the inner bearing cup. For model S110 or S130, use a suitable brass drift.

  b. For model 80, use Rear Wheel Hub Bearing Cup Remover 205-275 and Adapter 205-153 to remove the outer bearing cup. For model S110 or S130, use a suitable brass drift.

6. Clean the following components:
- The rear axle housing spindle.
- All the old grease and axle lubricant from the rear hub.
- The rear wheel bearings and cups.

7. Inspect the bearing races and rollers for pitting, galling or erratic wear patterns. Check the rollers for end wear. Discard the bearings, if necessary.

To install:

8. For model 80, using the Rear Axle Drawbar and the Rear Wheel Hub Bearing Cup Installers 205-100 and 205-278, install the inner and outer bearing cups. For model S110 or S130, use a suitable driver.

9. Check to see if a 0.0015 inches (0.038 mm) feeler gauge can be inserted between the cups and the rear hub at any point around each cup. Reseat the bearing cups, if necessary.

10. Install the inner rear wheel bearing in the rear hub.

11. Install a new rear hub seal.

  a. For model 80, use a suitable seal installer.

  b. For model S110 or S130, use the Wheel Hub Inner Wheel Installer and Adapter.

12. Position the rear brake disc on the rear hub and install the 8 bolts. Tighten to 114 ft. lbs. (155 Nm).

13. Install the rear wheel hub.

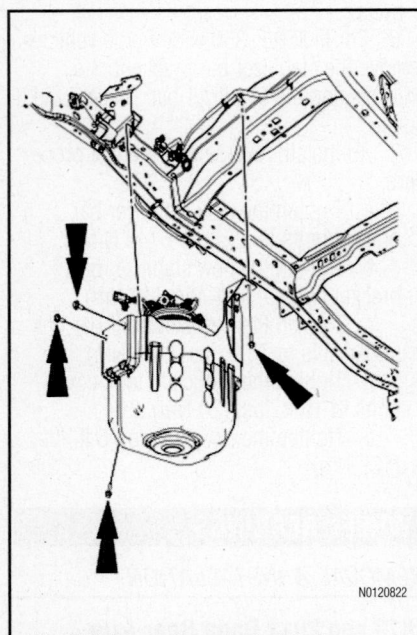

Fig. 565 Lower the reductant tank assembly

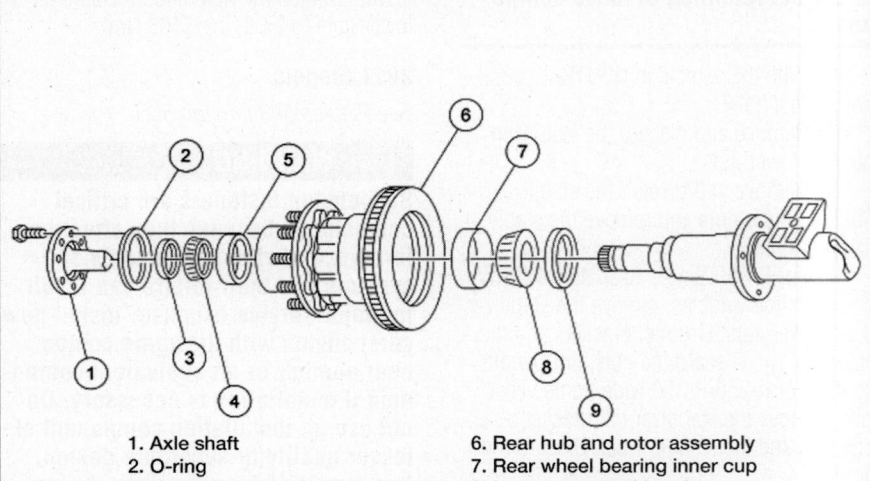

1. Axle shaft
2. O-ring
3. Hub nut
4. Outer rear wheel bearing
5. Rear wheel bearing outer cup
6. Rear hub and rotor assembly
7. Rear wheel bearing inner cup
8. Inner rear wheel bearing
9. Rear hub seal

Fig. 566 Exploded view of the rear wheel hub and bearing assembly

2010 and 2011 Ford Rear Axle

See Figures 567 through 571.

➥The Single Rear Wheel (SRW) wheel hub and the Dual Rear Wheels (DRW) wheel hub are different in appearance, however, the tools and procedures are the same with one exception: the brake disc can remain attached to the DRW hub if the longer driver handle is used to remove and install the bearing cups and seals.

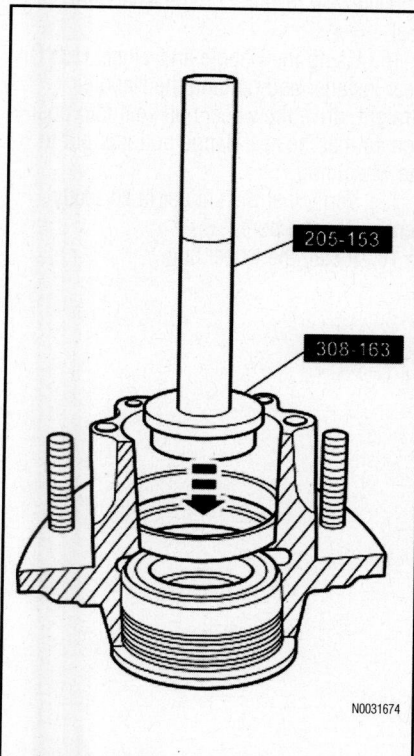

Fig. 567 Position the Handle and Differential Bearing Cup Installer on the inner bearing

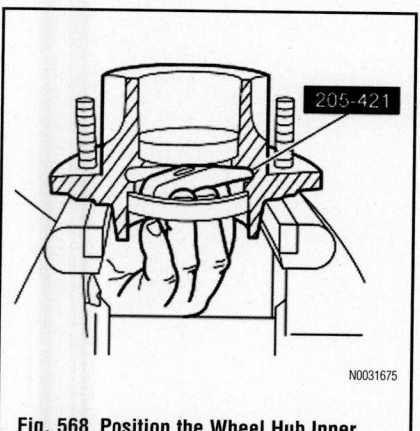

Fig. 568 Position the Wheel Hub Inner Bearing Cup Remover into the wheel hub cavity and onto the inner bearing cup

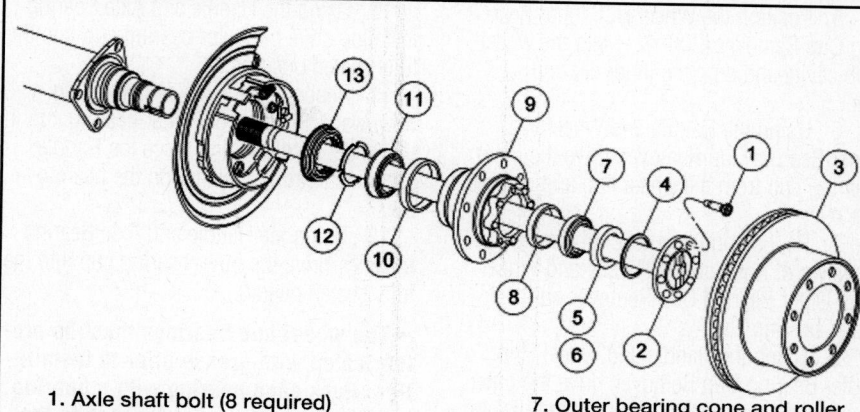

1. Axle shaft bolt (8 required)
2. Axle shaft
3. Brake disc rotor (Single Rear Wheel (SRW))
3. Wheel hub and brake disc (Dual Rear Wheels (DRW))
4. O-ring
5. Wheel hub nut (RH)
6. Wheel hub nut (LH)
7. Outer bearing cone and roller
8. Outer bearing cup
9. Rear wheel hub
10. Inner bearing cup
11. Inner bearing cone and roller
12. Slinger
13. Wheel hub seal

N0103011

Fig. 569 Exploded view of the wheel hub and wheel bearing assembly—2010 model

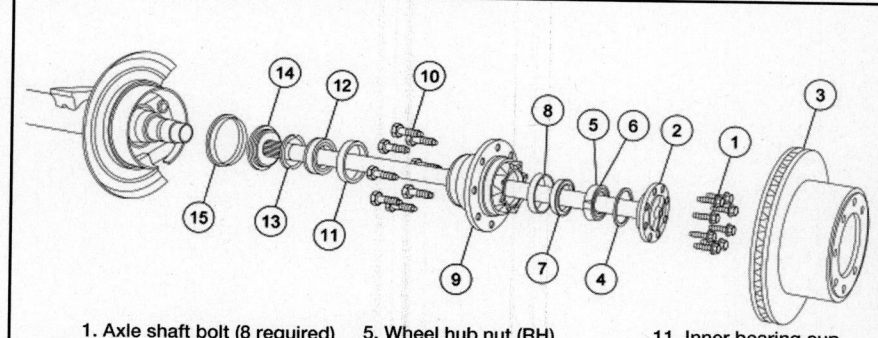

1. Axle shaft bolt (8 required)
2. Axle shaft
3. Brake disc rotor (Single Rear Wheel (SRW))
3. Wheel hub and brake disc (Dual Rear Wheels (DRW))
4. O-ring
5. Wheel hub nut (RH)
6. Wheel hub nut (LH)
7. Outer bearing cone and roller
8. Outer bearing cup
9. Rear wheel hub
10. Wheel studs
11. Inner bearing cup
12. Inner bearing cone and roller
13. Slinger
14. Wheel hub seal
15. Anti-lock speed sensor ring

N0112786

Fig. 570 Exploded view of the wheel hub and wheel bearing assembly—2011 model

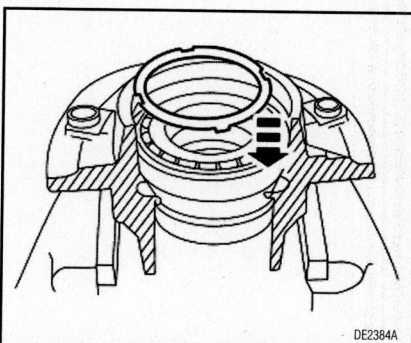

Fig. 571 Position the slinger on the greased bearing with the tangs facing the bearing

➥A SRW wheel hub cutaway is shown for clarity in this procedure. However, the procedure is the same for the DRW wheel hub.

1. Remove the wheel hub.
2. Position the Handle (205-153) and Differential Bearing Cup Installer (308-163) on the inner bearing.
3. Using the Handle and Differential Bearing Cup Installer and holding the Handle straight, drive the inner bearing, slinger and wheel hub seal out of the wheel hub as a unit.
4. Remove and discard the bearing, slinger and wheel hub seal.

5. Position the Wheel Hub Inner Bearing Cup Remover (205-421) into the wheel hub cavity and onto the inner bearing cup.

6. Using the Handle and Wheel Hub Inner Bearing Cup Remover, drive the inner bearing cup from the wheel hub and discard the cup.

7. Reposition the wheel hub facing downward. Position the Handle and Wheel Hub Outer Bearing Cup Remover on the outer bearing cup.

8. Using the Handle and Wheel Hub Outer Bearing Cup Remover, drive the outer bearing cup from the wheel hub and discard the cup.

To install:

9. With the wheel hub facing upward, position the new outer bearing cup in the wheel hub bore and place the Handle and Axle Bearing Installer on the bearing cup.

10. Using the Handle and Axle Bearing Installer, drive the outer bearing cup into the fully seated position.

11. Reposition the wheel hub facing downward. Position the inner bearing cup in the wheel hub bore and place the Handle and Axle Bearing Installer on the bearing cup.

12. Using the Handle and Axle Bearing Installer, drive the inner bearing cup into the fully seated position.

➡**The wheel hub bearings must be pre-lubricated with grease prior to installation. Pack each bearing with a bearing packing tool. Also apply grease to the thrust surface of the bearing.**

13. Position the greased inner bearing in the inner bearing cup.

❋❋ WARNING

The slinger must be correctly centered on the bearing or damage to the components can occur.

➡**The grease on the bearing and slinger holds the slinger in position during seal installation.**

14. Position the slinger on the greased bearing with the tangs facing the bearing.

15. With the slinger in place, position the wheel hub seal in the wheel hub bore and place the Handle and Wheel Hub Oil Seal Installer on the wheel hub seal.

16. Using the Handle and Wheel Hub Oil Seal Installer and holding the Handle straight, drive the wheel hub seal into position so that the seal flange bottoms out in the wheel hub.

17. Verify that the slinger is correctly centered in the bore.

18. Install the wheel hub.

FORD

Fiesta

BRAKES 9-9

ANTI-LOCK BRAKE SYSTEM (ABS).......................**9-9**
General Information.....................9-9
  Precautions.........................9-9
Hydraulic Control Unit (HCU) 9-10
  Removal & Installation.........9-10
Speed Sensors 9-9
  Removal & Installation.........9-9
BLEEDING THE BRAKE SYSTEM......................**9-12**
Bleeding Procedure...................9-12
  Bleeding Procedure 9-12
  Brake Caliper Bleeding 9-14
  Master Cylinder Bleeding 9-15
  Wheel Cylindder Bleeding 9-15
FRONT DISC BRAKES **9-16**
Brake Caliper...........................9-16
  Removal & Installation.........9-16
Disc Brake Pads 9-17
  Removal & Installation.........9-17
PARKING BRAKE **9-19**
Parking Brake Cables 9-19
  Adjustment 9-19
REAR DRUM BRAKES **9-17**
Brake Drum 9-17
  Removal & Installation.........9-17
Brake Shoes 9-18
  Adjustment 9-19
  Removal & Installation.........9-18

CHASSIS ELECTRICAL **000**

AIR BAG (SUPPLEMENTAL RESTRAINT SYSTEM)........**9-21**
Driver Air Bag Module 9-24
  Removal & Installation.........9-24
General Information...................9-21
  Arming the System 9-22
  Clockspring Centering.........9-22
  Disarming the System 9-21
  Service Precautions 9-21

DRIVE TRAIN.................**9-25**

Automatic Transaxle Case 9-25
  Removal & Installation.........9-25
Automatic Transaxle Fluid 9-25
  Drain and Refill...................9-25
Clutch.....................................9-26
  Bleeding 9-27
  Removal & Installation.........9-26
Front Halfshaft.........................9-27
  Removal & Installation.........9-27
Manual Transaxle Fluid 9-25
  Drain and Refill...................9-25
Manual Transaxle Support Insulator.................................9-25
  Removal & Installation.........9-25

ENGINE COOLING **9-29**

Block Heater 9-30
  Removal & Installation.........9-30
Coolant (Water) Pump...............9-31
  Removal & Installation.........9-31
Cooling Fan Motor and Shroud 9-33
  Removal & Installation.........9-33
Degas Bottle............................9-34
  Removal & Installation.........9-34
Engine Coolant.........................9-29
  Drain & Refill Procedure and Bleeding 9-29
  Flushing 9-30
Radiator..................................9-35
  Removal & Installation.........9-35
Thermostat 9-35
  Removal & Installation.........9-35

ENGINE ELECTRICAL.........**9-36**

CHARGING SYSTEM **9-36**
Alternator (Generator)...............9-36
  Removal & Installation.........9-36
IGNITION SYSTEM **9-36**
Firing Order.............................9-36
Ignition Coil 9-36
  Removal & Installation.........9-36
Ignition Timing.........................9-36
  Adjustment 9-36

Spark Plugs.............................9-36
  Removal & Installation.........9-36
STARTING SYSTEM **9-37**
Starter 9-37
  Removal & Installation.........9-37

ENGINE MECHANICAL **9-38**

Accessory Drive Belts 9-38
  Removal & Installation.........9-38
Air Cleaner 9-39
  Removal & Installation.........9-39
Camshaft and Valve Lifters 9-39
  Removal & Installation.........9-40
Camshaft Phaser and Sprocket 9-40
  Removal & Installation.........9-40
Catalytic Converter 9-42
  Removal & Installation.........9-42
Crankshaft Front Seal 9-43
  Removal & Installation.........9-43
Crankshaft Pulley 9-43
  Removal & Installation.........9-43
Cylinder Head 9-45
  Removal & Installation.........9-45
Intake Manifold 9-47
  Removal & Installation.........9-47
Oil Pan 9-48
  Removal & Installation.........9-48
Oil Pump 9-49
  Removal & Installation.........9-49
Timing Belt & Sprockets 9-49
  Removal & Installation.........9-49
Timing Belt Cover 9-50
  Removal & Installation.........9-50
Valve Covers 9-51
  Removal & Installation.........9-51

ENGINE PERFORMANCE & EMISSION CONTROLS **9-52**

Camshaft Position (CMP) Sensor 9-52
  Location.............................9-52
Catalyst Monitor Sensor (CMS) 9-52
  Location.............................9-52

Crankshaft Position (CKP)
   Sensor 9-52
     Location 9-52
Engine Coolant Temperature
   (ECT) Sensor 9-52
     Location 9-52
Heated Oxygen (HO2S)
   Sensor 9-53
     Location 9-53
Knock Sensor (KS)...................9-53
     Location 9-53
Mass Air Flow (MAF)
   Sensor 9-53
     Location 9-53
Variable Camshaft Timing
   (VCT) Oil Control
   Solenoid 9-53
     Location 9-53

FUEL............................9-54

GASOLINE FUEL INJECTION SYSTEM.......................9-54
Fuel Filter.................................9-55
   Removal & Installation..........9-55
Fuel Injectors 9-55
   Removal & Installation..........9-55
Fuel Pump (FP) Module............9-55
   Removal & Installation..........9-55
Fuel Rail 9-55
   Removal & Installation..........9-55
Fuel System Service
   Precautions 9-54
Fuel Tank..................................9-55
   Draining 9-55
   Removal & Installation..........9-55

Relieving Fuel System
   Pressure................................9-54
Throttle Body...........................9-57
   Removal & Installation..........9-57

HEATING & AIR CONDITIONING SYSTEM.......................9-57
Blower Motor 9-57
   Removal & Installation..........9-57
Heater Core 9-57
   Removal & Installation..........9-57

PRECAUTIONS.................9-9

SPECIFICATIONS AND MAINTENANCE CHARTS 9-3
Brake Specifications 9-7
Camshaft Specifications.............9-5
Capacities 9-4
Crankshaft and Connecting
   Rod Specifications 9-5
Engine and Vehicle
   Identification 9-3
Engine Tune-Up Specifications ...9-3
Fluid Specifications 9-4
General Engine Specifications.....9-3
Piston and Ring
   Specifications 9-5
Scheduled Maintenance
   Intervals 9-8
Tire, Wheel and Ball Joint
   Specifications 9-7
Torque Specifications 9-6

Valve Specifications 9-4
Wheel Alignment.......................9-6

STEERING 9-58
Power Steering Gear.................9-58
   Removal & Installation..........9-58

SUSPENSION..................9-59

FRONT SUSPENSION 9-59
Lower Control Arm...................9-59
   Removal & Installation..........9-59
Stabilizer Bar...........................9-59
   Removal & Installation..........9-59
Strut & Spring Assembly 9-59
   Removal & Installation..........9-59
Wheel Bearings 9-60
   Removal & Installation..........9-60
Wheel Knuckle 9-61
   Removal & Installation..........9-61
Wheel Studs 9-62
   Removal & Installation..........9-62

REAR SUSPENSION 9-63
Axle Assembly 9-63
   Removal & Installation..........9-63
Shock Absorber.........................9-64
   Removal & Installation..........9-64
Spring 9-64
   Removal & Installation..........9-64
Trailing Arm Bushing 9-64
   Removal & Installation..........9-64
Wheel Bearing & Hub 9-65
   Removal & Installation..........9-65
Wheel Studs.............................9-65
   Removal & Istallation..........9-65

SPECIFICATIONS AND MAINTENANCE CHARTS

ENGINE AND VEHICLE IDENTIFICATION

Engine							Model Year	
Code ①	Liters (cc)	Cu. In.	Cyl.	Fuel Sys.	Engine Type	Eng. Mfg.	Code ②	Year
J	1.6L	97.4	4	MRFS ③	DOHC	Ford	B	2011

① 8th position of VIN

② 10th position of VIN

③ 2-Speed Mechanical Returnless Fuel System (MRFS) with Sequential Multi-Port Fuel Injection (MFI)

25759_FIES_C0001

GENERAL ENGINE SPECIFICATIONS

All measurements are given in inches.

Year	Model	Engine Displacement Liters (cc)	Engine ID/VIN	Fuel System Type	Net Horsepower @ rpm	Net Torque @ rpm (ft. lbs.)	Bore x Stroke (in.)	Com-pression Ratio	Oil Pressure @ rpm
2011	Fiesta	1.6 (1596)	J	MRFS ①	120@6000	112@4050	3.11X3.20	11:01	29@2000

① 2-Speed Mechanical Returnless Fuel System (MRFS) with Sequential Multi-Port Fuel Injection (MFI)

25759_FIES_C0002

ENGINE TUNE-UP SPECIFICATIONS

Year	Engine Displacement Liters	Engine ID/VIN	Spark Plug Gap (in.)	Ignition Timing (deg.) MT	Ignition Timing (deg.) AT	Fuel Pump (psi)	Idle Speed (rpm) MT	Idle Speed (rpm) AT	Valve Clearance Intake	Valve Clearance Exhaust
2011	1.6 (1596)	J	0.027-0.032	①	①	65	N/A	N/A	0.0010-0.0027	0.0011-0.003

① Controlled by the Powertrain Control Module (PCM) and cannot be manually adjusted

25759_FIES_C0003

CAPACITIES

Year	Model	Engine Displacement Liters	Engine ID/VIN	Engine Oil with Filter (qts.)	Transaxle (pts.)		Drive Axle (pts.)		Transfer Case (pts.)	Fuel Tank (gal.)	Cooling System (qts.)
					Auto.	Manual	Front	Rear			
2011	Fiesta	1.6	J	4.3	1.6 ①	4.4	N/A	N/A	N/A	12.0	5.8

NOTE: All capacities are approximate. Add fluid gradually and ensure a proper fluid level is obtained.

N/A - Not applicable

① The six-speed automatic transmission in the Fiesta ia a "sealed for-life" system that Ford states is service-free for 150,000 miles.

 The transmission is not equipped with a dipstick.

25759_FIES_C0004

FLUID SPECIFICATIONS

Year	Model	Engine Displacement Liters	Engine Oil	Manual Transaxle	Auto. Transaxle	Power Steering Fluid	Brake Master Cylinder	Cooling System
2011	Fiesta	1.6	①	②	③	④	DOT 3	⑤

DOT: Department Of Transportation

N/A - Not Applicable

① 5W-20 Premium Synthetic Blend Motor Oil

② Motorcraft® Full Synthetic Manual Transmission Fluid

③ Motorcraft® Dual Clutch Transmission Fluid

④ The rack and pinion steering gear that is used with the Electronic Power Assist Steering (EPAS) system is a manual (non-hydraulic) steering gear that is

 contained within a 1-piece die cast aluminum housing.

⑤ Motorcraft® Specialty Orange Engine Coolant

25759_FIES_C0005

VALVE SPECIFICATIONS

Year	Engine Displacement Liters	Engine ID/VIN	Seat Angle (deg.)	Face Angle (deg.)	Spring Test Pressure (lbs. @ in.)	Spring Free-Length (in.)	Spring Installed Height (in.)	Stem-to-Guide Clearance (in.)		Stem Diameter (in.)	
								Intake	Exhaust	Intake	Exhaust
2011	1.6	J	45	44.5	40 @ 1.4	1.92	1.450	0.0010-0.0027	0.0011-0.0030	0.235-0.2353	0.234-0.2343

25759_FIES_C0006

CAMSHAFT SPECIFICATIONS
All measurements in inches unless noted

Year	Engine Displacement Liters	Engine Code/VIN	Journal Diameter	Brg. Oil Clearance	Shaft End-play	Runout	Journal Bore	Lobe Height Intake	Lobe Height Exhaust
2011	1.6	J	0.98-0.9804	0.009-0.0017	0.003-0.008	0.0008	0.0008-0.0027	0.350	0.351

25759_FIES_C0007

CRANKSHAFT AND CONNECTING ROD SPECIFICATIONS
All measurements are given in inches.

Year	Engine Displacement Liters	Engine ID/VIN	Crankshaft Main Brg. Journal Dia.	Crankshaft Main Brg. Oil Clearance	Crankshaft Shaft End-play	Crankshaft Thrust on No.	Connecting Rod Journal Diameter	Connecting Rod Oil Clearance	Connecting Rod Side Clearance
2011	1.6	J	1.888-1.8890	0.0009-0.0017	0.008-0.0170	3	1.731-1.7320	0.0007-0.0021	0.0068-0.0167

25759_FIES_C0008

PISTON AND RING SPECIFICATIONS
All measurements are given in inches.

Year	Engine Displacement Liters	Engine ID/VIN	Piston Clearance	Ring Gap Top Compression	Ring Gap Bottom Compression	Ring Gap Oil Control	Ring Side Clearance Top Compression	Ring Side Clearance Bottom Compression	Ring Side Clearance Oil Control
2011	1.6	J	0.0005-0.0008	0.0062-0.0102	0.0118-0.0216	0.0078-0.0295	0.048-0.0490	0.0590-0.0600	0.079-0.08

25759_FIES_C0009

TORQUE SPECIFICATIONS
All readings in ft. lbs.

Year	Engine Disp. Liters	Engine ID/VIN	Cylinder Head Bolts	Main Bearing Bolts	Rod Bearing Bolts	Crankshaft Damper Bolts	Flywheel/Flexplate Bolts	Manifold Intake	Manifold Exhaust	Spark Plugs	Oil Pan Drain Plug
2011	1.6 (1596)	J	①	②	③	④	⑤	13	N/A	11	21

N/A - Not Avaiable

① Stage 1: Tighten to 44 INCH lbs.
　Stage 2: Tighten to 133 INCH lbs.
　Stage 3: Tighten to 26 ft. lbs.
　Stage 4: Tighten an additional 75 degrees
② Stage 1: Tighten to 168 INCH lbs.
　Stage 2: Tighen an additional 60 degrees.
③ Stage 1: Tighten to 159 INCH lbs.
　Stage 2: Wait 2 seconds
　Stage 3: Tighten and additional 35 degrees.

④ Stage 1: Tighten to 74 ft. lbs.
　Stage 2: Tighten an additional 90 degrees, using a strap wrench
　Stage 3: Wait 10 seconds
　Stage 4: Tighten an additional 15 degrees, using a strap wrench
⑤ Stage 1: Tighten to 22 ft. lbs.
　Stage 2: Tighten an additional 80 degrees

25759_FIES_C0010

WHEEL ALIGNMENT

Year	Model		Caster ① Range	Caster ① Preferred Setting	Camber ① Range	Camber ① Preferred Setting	Toe-in
2011	Fiesta	F	0.75	+3.37	0.75	-0.70	0.15 +/- 0.35 ②
		R	—	—	0.75	-1.52	0.31 +/- 0.30 ③

① Nominal setting (reference only) no adjustment.
② Toe @ curb ride height (positive value is toe-in, negative value is toe-out).
② Only total toe defined.

25759_FIES_C0011

TIRE, WHEEL AND BALL JOINT SPECIFICATIONS

| Year | Model | OEM Tires | | Tire Pressures (psi) | | Wheel Size | Ball Joint Inspection | Lug Nut (ft. lbs.) ② |
		Standard	Optional	Front	Rear			
2011	Fiesta	P185/60HR15	①	40	40	15	NA	100

OEM: Original Equipment Manufacturer

PSI: Pounds Per Square Inch

NA: Information not available

① P195/50HR16 Standard on the SEL & SES models

② The Wheel Nut torque specification is for Clean, Dry Wheel Stud and Wheel Nut Threads

25759_FIES_C0012

BRAKE SPECIFICATIONS

All measurements in inches unless noted

| Year | Model | | Brake Disc | | | Brake Drum Diameter | | | Minimum Pad/Lining Thickness | | Brake Caliper | |
			Original Thickness	Minimum Thickness	Max. Runout	Original Inside Diameter	Max. Wear Limit	Maximum Machine Diamter	Front	Rear	Anchor Plate Bolt (ft. lbs.)	Guide Pin Bolts (ft. lbs.)
2011	Fiesta	F	NA	0.905	NA	—	—	—	0.118	—	50	21
		R	—	—	—	NA	8.030	NA	—	0.039	—	—

F: Front

R: Rear

NA: Information not available

25759_FIES_C0013

SCHEDULED MAINTENANCE INTERVALS
Fiesta

Service Item	Service Action	1	2	3	4	5	6	7	8	9	10
Accessory drive belt	Inspect	✓	✓	✓	✓	✓	✓	✓	✓	✓	✓
Accessory drive belt	Replace	Every 150,000 miles									
Automatic transmission fluid	Replace	Every 150,000 miles									
Battery performance	Inspect	✓	✓	✓	✓	✓	✓	✓	✓	✓	✓
Brake system (Pads/shoes/rotors/drums, brake lines and hoses, and parking brake	Inspect	✓	✓	✓	✓	✓	✓	✓	✓	✓	✓
Cabin air filter	Inspect/ Service	✓	✓	✓	✓	✓	✓	✓	✓	✓	✓
Clutch operation	Inspect	✓	✓	✓	✓	✓	✓	✓	✓	✓	✓
Cooling system, hoses, clamps & coolant strength	Inspect	✓	✓	✓	✓	✓	✓	✓	✓	✓	✓
Engine coolant	Replace										✓
Exhaust system (Leaks, damage, loose parts and foreign material)	Inspect	✓	✓	✓	✓	✓	✓	✓	✓	✓	✓
Engine oil & filter	Replace	✓	✓	✓	✓	✓	✓	✓	✓	✓	✓
Fluid levels (all)	Inspect	✓	✓	✓	✓	✓	✓	✓	✓	✓	✓
Halfshaft boots	Inspect	✓	✓	✓	✓	✓	✓	✓	✓	✓	✓
Horn, exterior lamps, turn signals and hazard warning light operation	Inspect	✓	✓	✓	✓	✓	✓	✓	✓	✓	✓
Inspect wheels and related components for abnormal noise,	Inspect	✓	✓	✓	✓	✓	✓	✓	✓	✓	✓
Oil and fluid leaks	Inspect	✓	✓	✓	✓	✓	✓	✓	✓	✓	✓
Radiator, coolers, heater and air conditioning hoses	Inspect	✓	✓	✓	✓	✓	✓	✓	✓	✓	✓
Rotate tires, inspect tread wear, measure tread depth and check	Rotate/ Inspect	✓	✓	✓	✓	✓	✓	✓	✓	✓	✓
Shocks struts and other suspension components for leaks and damage	Inspect	✓	✓	✓	✓	✓	✓	✓	✓	✓	✓
Engine air filter	Inspect/ Service	✓	✓	✓	✓	✓	✓	✓	✓	✓	✓
Spark plugs	Replace										✓
Steering linkage, ball joints, suspension and tie-rod ends, lubricate if equipped with greases	Inspect/ Lubricate	✓	✓	✓	✓	✓	✓	✓	✓	✓	✓
Windshield wiper spray and wiper operation	Inspect	✓	✓	✓	✓	✓	✓	✓	✓	✓	✓
Windshield for cracks, chips and pitting	Inspect	✓	✓	✓	✓	✓	✓	✓	✓	✓	✓
Manual transmission fluid	Replace					✓					✓
Timing belt	Replace	Every 150,000 miles									

Oil change service intervals should be completed as indicated by the message center. (Can be up to 1 year or 10,000 miles)

If the message center is prematurely reset or is inoperative, perform the oil change interval at 6 months or 5,000 miles from last oil change.

For extensive idling and or low speed driving, change the engine oil and filter every 5,000 miles, 6 months or 200 hours of engine operation.

For commercial use or extensive idling, change spark plugs at 60,000 miles.

25759_FIES_C0014

PRECAUTIONS

Before servicing any vehicle, please be sure to read all of the following precautions, which deal with personal safety, prevention of component damage, and important points to take into consideration when servicing a motor vehicle:

- Never open, service or drain the radiator or cooling system when the engine is hot; serious burns can occur from the steam and hot coolant.

- Observe all applicable safety precautions when working around fuel. Whenever servicing the fuel system, always work in a well-ventilated area. Do not allow fuel spray or vapors to come in contact with a spark, open flame, or excessive heat (a hot drop light, for example). Keep a dry chemical fire extinguisher near the work area. Always keep fuel in a container specifically designed for fuel storage; also, always properly seal fuel containers to avoid the possibility of fire or explosion. Refer to the additional fuel system precautions later in this section.

- Fuel injection systems often remain pressurized, even after the engine has been turned **OFF**. The fuel system pressure must be relieved before disconnecting any fuel lines. Failure to do so may result in fire and/or personal injury.

- Brake fluid often contains polyglycol ethers and polyglycols. Avoid contact with the eyes and wash your hands thoroughly after handling brake fluid. If you do get brake fluid in your eyes, flush your eyes with clean, running water for 15 minutes. If eye irritation persists, or if you have taken brake fluid internally, IMMEDIATELY seek medical assistance.

- The EPA warns that prolonged contact with used engine oil may cause a number of skin disorders, including cancer. You should make every effort to minimize your exposure to used engine oil. Protective gloves should be worn when changing oil. Wash your hands and any other exposed skin areas as soon as possible after exposure to used engine oil. Soap and water, or waterless hand cleaner should be used.

- All new vehicles are now equipped with an air bag system, often referred to as a Supplemental Restraint System (SRS) or Supplemental Inflatable Restraint (SIR) system. The system must be disabled before performing service on or around system components, steering column, instrument panel components, wiring and sensors. Failure to follow safety and disabling procedures could result in accidental air bag deployment, possible personal injury and unnecessary system repairs.

- Always wear safety goggles when working with, or around, the air bag system. When carrying a non-deployed air bag, be sure the bag and trim cover are pointed away from your body. When placing a non-deployed air bag on a work surface, always face the bag and trim cover upward, away from the surface. This will reduce the motion of the module if it is accidentally deployed. Refer to the additional air bag system precautions later in this section.

- Clean, high quality brake fluid from a sealed container is essential to the safe and proper operation of the brake system. You should always buy the correct type of brake fluid for your vehicle. If the brake fluid becomes contaminated, completely flush the system with new fluid. Never reuse any brake fluid. Any brake fluid that is removed from the system should be discarded. Also, do not allow any brake fluid to come in contact with a painted surface; it will damage the paint.

- Never operate the engine without the proper amount and type of engine oil; doing so WILL result in severe engine damage.

- Timing belt maintenance is extremely important. Many models utilize an interference-type, non-freewheeling engine. If the timing belt breaks, the valves in the cylinder head may strike the pistons, causing potentially serious (also time-consuming and expensive) engine damage. Refer to the maintenance interval charts for the recommended replacement interval for the timing belt, and to the timing belt section for belt replacement and inspection.

- Disconnecting the negative battery cable on some vehicles may interfere with the functions of the on-board computer system(s) and may require the computer to undergo a relearning process once the negative battery cable is reconnected.

- When servicing drum brakes, only disassemble and assemble one side at a time, leaving the remaining side intact for reference.

- Only an MVAC-trained, EPA-certified automotive technician should service the air conditioning system or its components.

BRAKES

GENERAL INFORMATION

PRECAUTIONS

- Certain components within the ABS system are not intended to be serviced or repaired individually.

- Do not use rubber hoses or other parts not specifically specified for and ABS system. When using repair kits, replace all parts included in the kit. Partial or incorrect repair may lead to functional problems and require the replacement of components.

- Lubricate rubber parts with clean, fresh brake fluid to ease assembly. Do not use shop air to clean parts; damage to rubber components may result.

- Use only DOT 3 brake fluid from an unopened container.

- If any hydraulic component or line is removed or replaced, it may be necessary to bleed the entire system.

- A clean repair area is essential. Always clean the reservoir and cap thoroughly before removing the cap. The slightest amount of dirt in the fluid may plug an orifice and impair the system function. Perform repairs after components have been thoroughly cleaned; use only denatured alcohol to clean components. Do not allow ABS components to come into contact with any substance containing mineral oil; this includes used shop rags.

- The Anti-Lock control unit is a microprocessor similar to other computer units in the vehicle. Ensure that the ignition switch is **OFF** before removing or installing controller harnesses. Avoid static electricity discharge at or near the controller.

- If any arc welding is to be done on the vehicle, the control unit should be unplugged before welding operations begin.

ANTI-LOCK BRAKE SYSTEM (ABS)

SPEED SENSORS

REMOVAL & INSTALLATION

Front

See Figures 1 and 2.

1. Remove the wheel and tire.
2. Position the rear portion of the splash shield aside.
   a. Remove the 3 pushpin retainers.
   b. Position the splash shield aside.

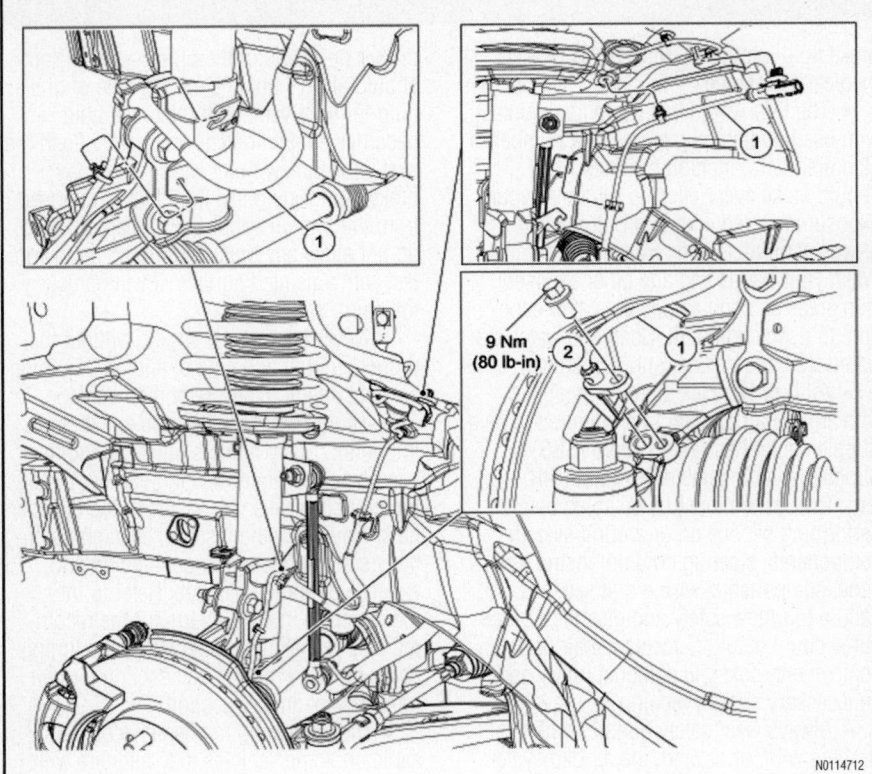

Fig. 1 Exploded view and location of the wheel speed sensor. Wheel speed sensor (1), Wheel speed sensor bolt (2)

3. Disconnect the wheel speed sensor electrical connector.

4. Detach the wheel speed sensor from the body and wheel knuckle.

5. Remove the wheel speed sensor bolt.

6. Remove the wheel speed sensor.

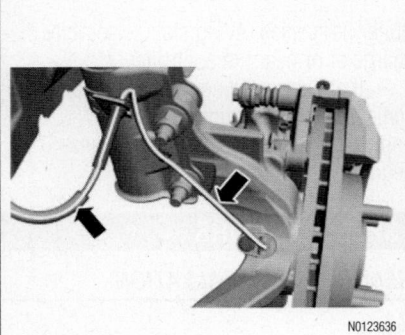

Fig. 2 The white stripe on the wheel speed sensor harness is used for orientation purposes. Correct routing of the wheel speed sensor and harness is essential to prevent contact damage to the harness

✳✳ CAUTION

The white stripe on the wheel speed sensor harness is used for orientation purposes. Correct routing of the wheel speed sensor and harness is essential to prevent contact damage to the harness.

To install:

✳✳ CAUTION

The white stripe on the wheel speed sensor harness is used for orientation purposes. Correct routing of the wheel speed sensor and harness is essential to prevent contact damage to the harness.

7. Install the wheel speed sensor.

8. Install the wheel speed sensor bolt. Tighten the bolt to 80 inch lbs. (9 Nm).

9. Attach the wheel speed sensor from the body and wheel knuckle.

10. Connect the wheel speed sensor electrical connector.

11. Position the rear portion of the splash shield aside.

   a. Position the splash shield aside.

   b. Install the 3 pushpin retainers.

12. Install the wheel and tire.

Rear

See Figure 3.

1. Refer to the accompanying illustration.

HYDRAULIC CONTROL UNIT (HCU)

REMOVAL & INSTALLATION

See Figures 4 through 7.

✳✳ WARNING

Do not use any fluid other than clean brake fluid meeting manufacturer's specification. Additionally, do not use brake fluid that has been previously drained. Following these instructions will help prevent system contamination, brake component damage and the risk of serious personal injury.

✳✳ WARNING

Carefully read cautionary information on product label. For EMERGENCY MEDICAL INFORMATION seek medical advice. In the USA or Canada on Ford/Motorcraft products call: 1-800-959-3673. For additional information, consult the product Material Safety Data Sheet (MSDS) if available. Failure to follow these instructions may result in serious personal injury.

✳✳ CAUTION

Do not spill brake fluid on painted or plastic surfaces or damage to the surface may occur. If brake fluid is spilled onto a painted or plastic surface, immediately wash the surface with water.

→The Hydraulic Control Unit (HCU) and ABS module are serviced as an assembly.

1. If installing a new HCU /ABS module, connect the scan tool and upload the module configuration information from the ABS module.

2. With the vehicle in NEUTRAL, position it on a hoist.

3. Remove the 2 HCU bracket-to-frame bolts.

4. Remove the nut and evaporator outlet tube bracket.

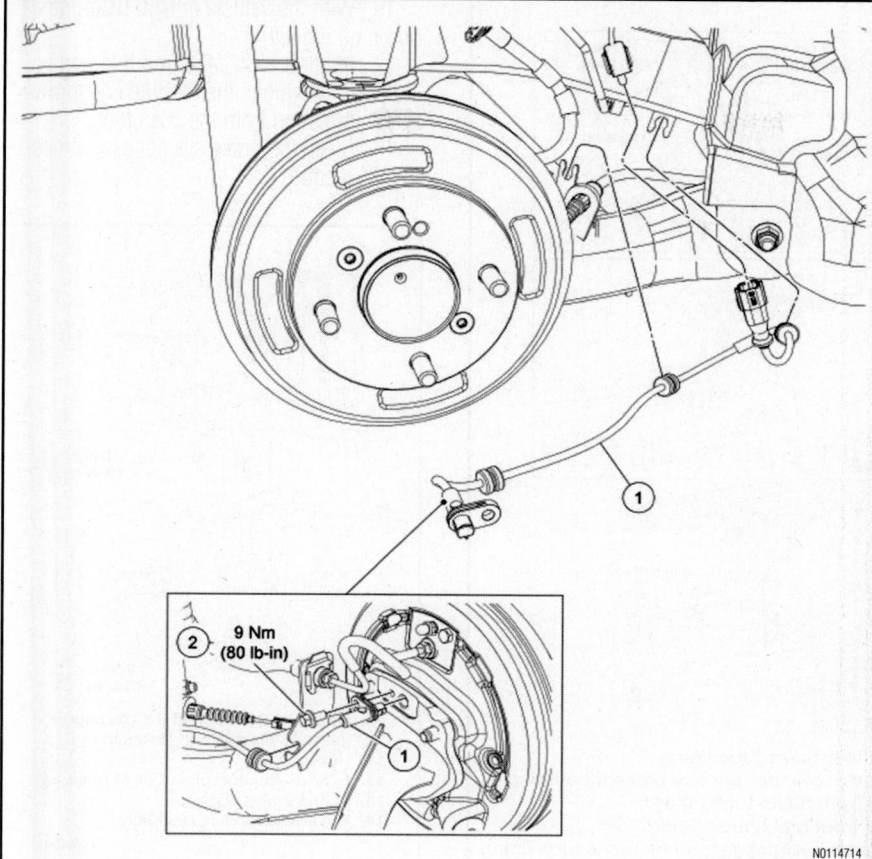

Fig. 3 Exploded view and location of the wheel speed sensor. Wheel speed sensor (1), Wheel speed sensor bolt (2)

5. Disconnect the exhaust camshaft Variable Camshaft Timing (VCT) oil control solenoid electrical connector.

➡Cap the brake tube connections to prevent fluid loss or dirt contamination.

6. Disconnect the 6 brake tubes from the HCU.

7. Disconnect the HCU /ABS module electrical connector.

8. Position the HCU to the center line of the vehicle and remove the HCU.

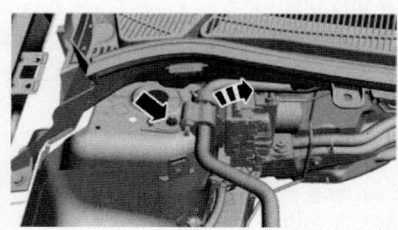

Fig. 4 Remove the nut and evaporator outlet tube bracket

To install:

✳✳ WARNING

Do not use any fluid other than clean brake fluid meeting manufacturer's specification. Additionally, do not use brake fluid that has been previously drained. Following these instructions will help prevent system contamination, brake component damage and the risk of serious personal injury.

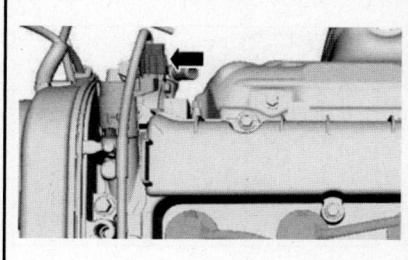

Fig. 5 Disconnect the exhaust camshaft Variable Camshaft Timing (VCT) oil control solenoid electrical connector

✳✳ WARNING

Carefully read cautionary information on product label. For EMERGENCY MEDICAL INFORMATION seek medical advice. In the USA or Canada on Ford/Motorcraft products call: 1-800-959-3673. For additional information, consult the product Material Safety Data Sheet (MSDS) if available. Failure to follow these instructions may result in serious personal injury.

✳✳ CAUTION

Do not spill brake fluid on painted or plastic surfaces or damage to the surface may occur. If brake fluid is spilled onto a painted or plastic surface, immediately wash the surface with water.

➡The Hydraulic Control Unit (HCU) and ABS module are serviced as an assembly.

9. Position the HCU to the center line of the vehicle and install the HCU.

10. Connect the HCU /ABS module electrical connector.

➡Cap the brake tube connections to prevent fluid loss or dirt contamination.

11. Connect the 6 brake tubes from the HCU. Tighten the brake tube fittings to 150 inch lbs. (17 Nm).

12. Connect the exhaust camshaft Variable Camshaft Timing (VCT) oil control solenoid electrical connector.

13. Install the nut and evaporator outlet tube bracket. Tighten the nut to 71 inch lbs. (8 Nm).

14. Install the 2 HCU bracket-to-frame bolts. Tighten the bolts to 18 ft. lbs. (24 Nm).

15. If installing a new HCU /ABS module, connect the scan tool and upload the module configuration information from the ABS module.

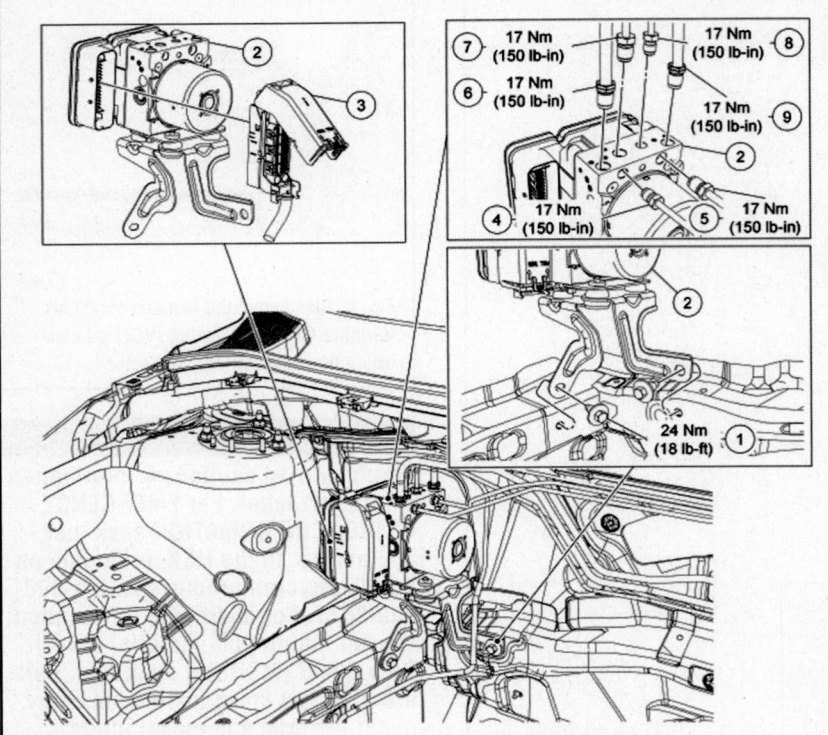

16. With the vehicle in NEUTRAL, position it on a hoist.

17. If a new HCU /ABS module was installed, download the module configuration information from the scan tool.

18. Bleed the brake system as outlined in this section.

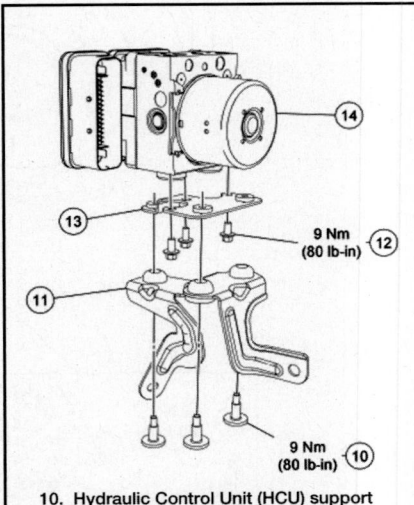

1. Hydraulic Control Unit (HCU) bracket-to-frame bolt (2 required)
2. HCU /ABS module assembly
3. HCU /ABS module electrical connector
4. RH rear brake tube fitting
5. LH rear brake tube fitting
6. Master cylinder primary brake tube fitting
7. LH front brake tube fitting
8. RH front brake tube fitting
9. Master cylinder secondary brake tube fitting

N0114713

Fig. 6 Hydraulic Control Unit (HCU), Brake Tubes, Electrical Connector and Bracket

10. Hydraulic Control Unit (HCU) support plate-to-bracket bolt (3 required)
11. HCU bracket
12. HCU -to-support plate bolt (3 required)
13. HCU support plate
14. HCU /ABS module assembly

N0114191

Fig. 7 Hydraulic Control Unit (HCU) and Brackets

BRAKES   BLEEDING THE BRAKE SYSTEM

BLEEDING PROCEDURE

BLEEDING PROCEDURE

Pressure Bleeding
See Figure 8.

❊ CAUTION

Do not use any fluid other than clean brake fluid meeting manufacturer's specification. Additionally, do not use brake fluid that has been previously drained. Following these instructions will help prevent system contamination, brake component damage and the risk of serious personal injury.

❊ CAUTION

Carefully read cautionary information on product label. For EMERGENCY MEDICAL INFORMATION seek medical advice. In the USA or Canada on Ford/Motorcraft products call: 1-800-

959-3673. For additional information, consult the product Material Safety Data Sheet (MSDS) if available. Failure to follow these instructions may result in serious personal injury.

❊ WARNING

Do not allow the brake master cylinder to run dry during the bleeding operation. Master cylinder may be damaged if operated without fluid, resulting in degraded braking performance. Failure to follow this instruction may result in serious personal injury.

➡Do not spill brake fluid on painted or plastic surfaces or damage to the surface may occur. If brake fluid is spilled onto a painted or plastic surface, immediately wash the surface with water.

➡The Hydraulic Control Unit (HCU) bleeding procedure must be carried out

if the HCU or any components upstream of the HCU are installed new.

➡Pressure bleeding the brake system is preferred to manual bleeding.

1. Clean all dirt from the brake master cylinder filler cap and remove the filler cap.

   a. Fill the brake master cylinder

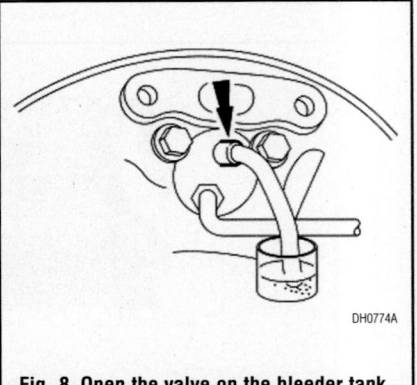

DH0774A

Fig. 8 Open the valve on the bleeder tank

reservoir with clean, specified brake fluid.

➡ **Master cylinder pressure bleeder adapter tools are available from various manufacturers of pressure bleeding equipment. Follow the instructions of the manufacturer when installing the adapter.**

2. Install the bleeder adapter to the brake master cylinder reservoir, and attach the bleeder tank hose to the fitting on the adapter.

➡ **Make sure the bleeder tank contains enough clean, specified brake fluid to complete the bleeding operation.**

3. Open the valve on the bleeder tank.
   a. Apply 30–50 psi to the brake system.
4. Remove the RR bleeder screw cap and place a box-end wrench on the bleeder screw. Attach a rubber drain hose to the RR bleeder screw and submerge the free end of the hose in a container partially filled with clean, specified brake fluid.
5. Loosen the RR bleeder screw. Leave open until clear, bubble-free brake fluid flows, then tighten the RR bleeder screw to specifications. Refer to Specifications in this section. Remove the rubber hose.
6. Continue bleeding the rest of the system, going in order from the LR bleeder screw to the RF bleeder screw, ending with the LF bleeder screw.
   a. Tighten the brake caliper and wheel cylinder bleeder screws to specifications. Refer to Specifications in this section.
7. Close the bleeder tank valve. Remove the tank hose from the adapter and remove the adapter. Fill the reservoir with clean, specified brake fluid and install the reservoir cap.
8. Bleeder Screws Specifications:
- Brake caliper bleeder screws 89 inch lbs. (10 Nm).
- Wheel cylinder bleeder screws 54 inch lbs. (6 Nm).
- Master cylinder brake tube fittings 155 inch lbs. (18 Nm).

Manual Bleeding

See Figures 9 and 10.

❈❈ CAUTION

Do not use any fluid other than clean brake fluid meeting manufacturer's specification. Additionally, do not use brake fluid that has been previously drained. Following these instructions will help prevent system contamination, brake component

damage and the risk of serious personal injury.

❈❈ CAUTION

Carefully read cautionary information on product label. For EMERGENCY MEDICAL INFORMATION seek medical advice. In the USA or Canada on Ford/Motorcraft products call: 1-800-959-3673. For additional information, consult the product Material Safety Data Sheet (MSDS) if available. Failure to follow these instructions may result in serious personal injury.

❈❈ WARNING

Do not allow the brake master cylinder to run dry during the bleeding operation. Master cylinder may be damaged if operated without fluid, resulting in degraded braking performance. Failure to follow this instruction may result in serious personal injury.

❈❈ WARNING

Do not spill brake fluid on painted or plastic surfaces or damage to the surface may occur. If brake fluid is spilled onto a painted or plastic surface, immediately wash the surface with water.

➡ **Pressure bleeding the brake system is preferred to manual bleeding.**

1. Clean all the dirt from around the brake fluid reservoir cap and remove the filler cap.
   a. Fill the brake master cylinder reservoir with clean, specified brake fluid.
2. Remove the RR bleeder screw cap and place a box-end wrench on the bleeder screw. Attach a rubber drain hose to the RR bleeder screw and submerge the free end of the hose in a container partially filled with clean, specified brake fluid.
3. Have an assistant pump and then hold firm pressure on the brake pedal.
4. Loosen the RR bleeder screw until a stream of brake fluid comes out. While an assistant maintains pressure on the brake pedal, tighten the RR bleeder screw.
   a. Repeat until clear, bubble-free fluid comes out.
   b. Refill the brake master cylinder reservoir as necessary.
5. Tighten the RR bleeder screw to specifications. Refer to Specifications in this

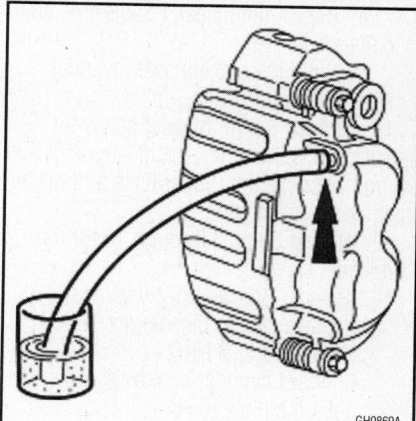

Fig. 9 Remove the RF bleeder cap and place a box-end wrench on the bleeder screw. Attach a rubber drain hose to the RF bleeder screw and submerge the free end of the hose in a container partially filled with clean, specified brake fluid

section. Remove the rubber hose and install the bleeder screw cap.
6. Repeat Steps 2 through 5 for the LR bleeder screw.
7. Remove the RF bleeder cap and place a box-end wrench on the bleeder screw. Attach a rubber drain hose to the RF bleeder screw and submerge the free end of the hose in a container partially filled with clean, specified brake fluid.
8. Have an assistant pump and then hold firm pressure on the brake pedal.
9. Loosen the RF bleeder screw until a stream of brake fluid comes out. While the assistant maintains pressure on the brake pedal, tighten the RF bleeder screw.

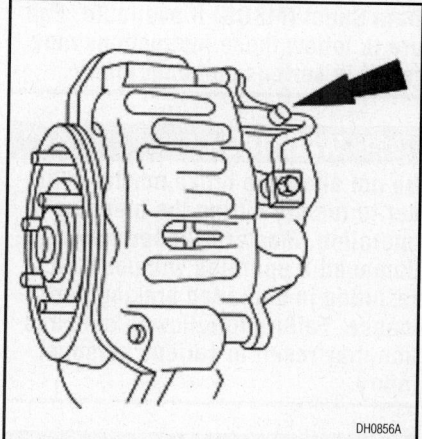

Fig. 10 Tighten the RF bleeder screw to specifications. Refer to Specifications in this section. Remove the rubber hose and install the bleeder screw cap

a. Repeat until clear, bubble-free fluid comes out.

b. Refill the brake master cylinder reservoir as necessary.

10. Tighten the RF bleeder screw to specifications. Refer to Specifications in this section. Remove the rubber hose and install the bleeder screw cap.

11. Repeat Steps 7 through 10 for the LF bleeder screw.

12. Bleeder Screws Specifications:
- Brake caliper bleeder screws 89 inch lbs. (10 Nm).
- Wheel cylinder bleeder screws 54 inch lbs. (6 Nm).
- Master cylinder brake tube fittings 155 inch lbs. (18 Nm).

Hydraulic Control Unit (HCU) Bleeding

❊❊ CAUTION

Do not use any fluid other than clean brake fluid meeting manufacturer's specification. Additionally, do not use brake fluid that has been previously drained. Following these instructions will help prevent system contamination, brake component damage and the risk of serious personal injury.

❊❊ CAUTION

Carefully read cautionary information on product label. For EMERGENCY MEDICAL INFORMATION seek medical advice. In the USA or Canada on Ford/Motorcraft products call: 1-800-959-3673. For additional information, consult the product Material Safety Data Sheet (MSDS) if available. Failure to follow these instructions may result in serious personal injury.

❊❊ WARNING

Do not allow the brake master cylinder to run dry during the bleeding operation. Master cylinder may be damaged if operated without fluid, resulting in degraded braking performance. Failure to follow this instruction may result in serious personal injury.

❊❊ WARNING

Do not spill brake fluid on painted or plastic surfaces or damage to the surface may occur. If brake fluid is spilled onto a painted or plastic surface, immediately wash the surface with water.

➡ Pressure bleeding the brake system is preferred to manual bleeding.

1. Follow the Pressure Bleeding or Manual Bleeding procedure steps to bleed the system.

2. Connect the scan tool and follow the ABS Service Bleed instructions.

3. Repeat the Pressure Bleeding or Manual Bleeding procedure steps to bleed the system.

BRAKE CALIPER BLEEDING

See Figures 11 and 12.

❊❊ CAUTION

Do not use any fluid other than clean brake fluid meeting manufacturer's specification. Additionally, do not use brake fluid that has been previously drained. Following these instructions will help prevent system contamination, brake component damage and the risk of serious personal injury.

❊❊ CAUTION

Carefully read cautionary information on product label. For EMERGENCY MEDICAL INFORMATION seek medical advice. In the USA or Canada on Ford/Motorcraft products call: 1-800-959-3673. For additional information, consult the product Material Safety

Data Sheet (MSDS) if available. Failure to follow these instructions may result in serious personal injury.

❊❊ WARNING

Do not allow the brake master cylinder to run dry during the bleeding operation. Master cylinder may be damaged if operated without fluid, resulting in degraded braking performance. Failure to follow this instruction may result in serious personal injury.

❊❊ WARNING

Do not spill brake fluid on painted or plastic surfaces or damage to the surface may occur. If brake fluid is spilled onto a painted or plastic surface, immediately wash the surface with water.

➡ It is not necessary to do a complete brake system bleed if only the brake caliper was disconnected or installed new.

1. Remove the bleeder screw cap and place a box-end wrench on the bleeder screw. Attach a rubber drain hose to the bleeder screw and submerge the free end of the hose in a container partially filled with clean, specified brake fluid.

2. Have an assistant pump the brake pedal at least 2 times and then hold firm pressure on the brake pedal.

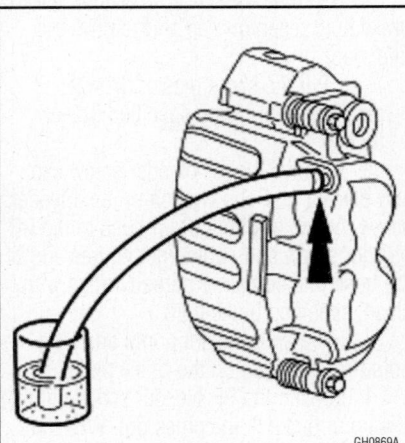

GH0869A

Fig. 11 Remove the bleeder screw cap and place a box-end wrench on the bleeder screw. Attach a rubber drain hose to the bleeder screw and submerge the free end of the hose in a container partially filled with clean, specified brake fluid.

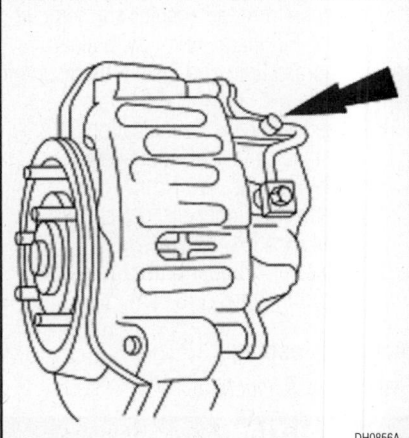

DH0856A

Fig. 12 Tighten the bleeder screw to specifications. Refer to Specifications in this section. Remove the rubber hose and install the bleeder screw cap

3. Loosen the bleeder screw until a stream of brake fluid comes out. While the assistant maintains pressure on the brake pedal, tighten the bleeder screw.

   a. Repeat until clear, bubble-free fluid comes out.

   b. Refill the brake master cylinder reservoir as necessary.

4. Tighten the bleeder screw to specifications. Refer to Specifications in this section. Remove the rubber hose and install the bleeder screw cap.

5. Bleeder Screws Specifications:
- Brake caliper bleeder screws 89 inch lbs. (10 Nm).
- Wheel cylinder bleeder screws 54 inch lbs. (6 Nm).
- Master cylinder brake tube fittings 155 inch lbs. (18 Nm).

MASTER CYLINDER BLEEDING

See Figure 13.

❊❊ CAUTION

Do not use any fluid other than clean brake fluid meeting manufacturer's specification. Additionally, do not use brake fluid that has been previously drained. Following these instructions will help prevent system contamination, brake component damage and the risk of serious personal injury.

❊❊ CAUTION

Carefully read cautionary information on product label. For EMERGENCY MEDICAL INFORMATION seek medical advice. In the USA or Canada on Ford/Motorcraft products call: 1-800-959-3673. For additional information, consult the product Material Safety Data Sheet (MSDS) if available. Failure to follow these instructions may result in serious personal injury.

❊❊ WARNING

Do not allow the brake master cylinder to run dry during the bleeding operation. Master cylinder may be damaged if operated without fluid, resulting in degraded braking performance. Failure to follow this instruction may result in serious personal injury.

❊❊ WARNING

Do not spill brake fluid on painted or plastic surfaces or damage to the

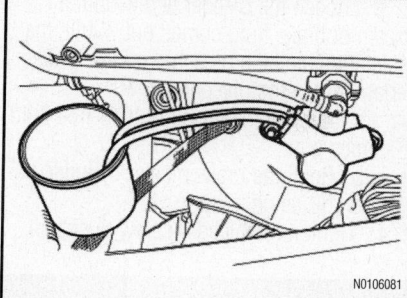

N0106081

Fig. 13 Install short brake tubes onto the primary and secondary ports with the ends submerged in a container partially filled with clean, specified brake fluid

surface may occur. If brake fluid is spilled onto a painted or plastic surface, immediately wash the surface with water.

➡When the brake master cylinder has been installed new or the system has been emptied or partially emptied, it must be primed to prevent air from entering the system.

1. Disconnect the brake outlet tubes from the master cylinder.

2. Install short brake tubes onto the primary and secondary ports with the ends submerged in a container partially filled with clean, specified brake fluid.

3. Have an assistant pump the brake pedal until clear fluid flows from the brake tubes without air bubbles.

4. Remove the short brake tubes, and install the master cylinder brake tubes.

   a. Tighten the brake tube fittings to specifications. Remove the rubber hose and install the bleeder screw cap.

5. Bleeder Screws Specifications:
- Brake caliper bleeder screws 89 inch lbs. (10 Nm).
- Wheel cylinder bleeder screws 54 inch lbs. (6 Nm).
- Master cylinder brake tube fittings 155 inch lbs. (18 Nm).

6. Bleed the brake system as outlined in this section.

WHEEL CYLINDDER BLEEDING

See Figure 14.

❊❊ CAUTION

Do not use any fluid other than clean brake fluid meeting manufacturer's specification. Additionally, do not use brake fluid that has been previously drained. Following these instructions will help prevent system

contamination, brake component damage and the risk of serious personal injury.

❊❊ CAUTION

Carefully read cautionary information on product label. For EMERGENCY MEDICAL INFORMATION seek medical advice. In the USA or Canada on Ford/Motorcraft products call: 1-800-959-3673. For additional information, consult the product Material Safety Data Sheet (MSDS) if available. Failure to follow these instructions may result in serious personal injury.

❊❊ WARNING

Do not allow the brake master cylinder to run dry during the bleeding operation. Master cylinder may be damaged if operated without fluid, resulting in degraded braking performance. Failure to follow this instruction may result in serious personal injury.

❊❊ WARNING

Do not spill brake fluid on painted or plastic surfaces or damage to the surface may occur. If brake fluid is spilled onto a painted or plastic surface, immediately wash the surface with water.

➡It is not necessary to do a complete brake system bleed if only the wheel cylinder was disconnected or installed new.

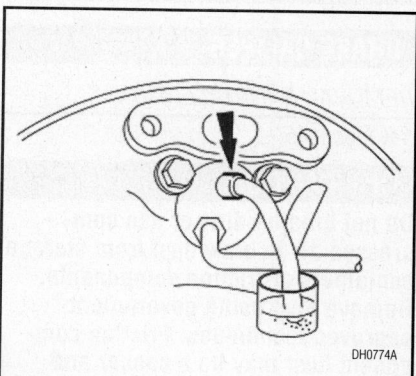

DH0774A

Fig. 14 Remove the bleeder screw cap and place a box-end wrench on the bleeder screw. Attach a rubber drain hose to the bleeder screw and submerge the free end of the hose in a container partially filled with clean, specified brake fluid

1. Remove the bleeder screw cap and place a box-end wrench on the bleeder screw. Attach a rubber drain hose to the bleeder screw and submerge the free end of the hose in a container partially filled with clean, specified brake fluid.

2. Have an assistant pump the brake pedal at least 2 times and then hold firm pressure on the brake pedal.

3. Loosen the bleeder screw until a stream of brake fluid comes out. While the assistant maintains pressure on the brake pedal, tighten the bleeder screw.

a. Repeat until clear, bubble-free fluid comes out.

b. Refill the brake master cylinder reservoir as necessary.

4. Tighten the bleeder screw to specifi- cations. Remove the rubber hose and install the bleeder screw cap.

5. Bleeder Screws Specifications:
- Brake caliper bleeder screws 89 inch lbs. (10 Nm).
- Wheel cylinder bleeder screws 54 inch lbs. (6 Nm).
- Master cylinder brake tube fittings 155 inch lbs. (18 Nm).

BRAKES

✳✳ CAUTION

Dust and dirt accumulating on brake parts during normal use may contain asbestos fibers from production or aftermarket brake linings. Breathing excessive concentrations of asbestos fibers can cause serious bodily harm. Exercise care when servicing brake parts. Do not sand or grind brake lining unless equipment used is designed to contain the dust residue. Do not clean brake parts with compressed air or by dry brushing. Cleaning should be done by dampening the brake components with a fine mist of water, then wiping the brake components clean with a dampened cloth. Dispose of cloth and all residue containing asbestos fibers in an impermeable container with the appropriate label. Follow practices prescribed by the Occupational Safety and Health Administration (OSHA) and the Environmental Protection Agency (EPA) for the handling, processing, and disposing of dust or debris that may contain asbestos fibers.

BRAKE CALIPER

REMOVAL & INSTALLATION
See Figure 15.

✳✳ CAUTION

Do not breathe dust or use compressed air to blow dust from storage containers or friction components. Remove dust using government-approved techniques. Friction component dust may be a cancer and lung disease hazard. Exposure to potentially hazardous components may occur if dusts are created during repair of friction components, such as brake pads and clutch discs. Exposure may also cause irritation to skin, eyes and respiratory tract, and

may cause allergic reactions and/or may lead to other chronic health effects. If irritation persists, seek medical attention or advice. Failure to follow these instructions may result in serious personal injury.

✳✳ CAUTION

Do not use any fluid other than clean brake fluid meeting manufacturer's specification. Additionally, do not use brake fluid that has been previously drained. Following these

FRONT DISC BRAKES

instructions will help prevent system contamination, brake component damage and the risk of serious personal injury.

✳✳ CAUTION

Carefully read cautionary information on product label. For EMERGENCY MEDICAL INFORMATION seek medical advice. In the USA or Canada on Ford/Motorcraft products call: 1-800-959-3673. For additional information, consult the product Material Safety

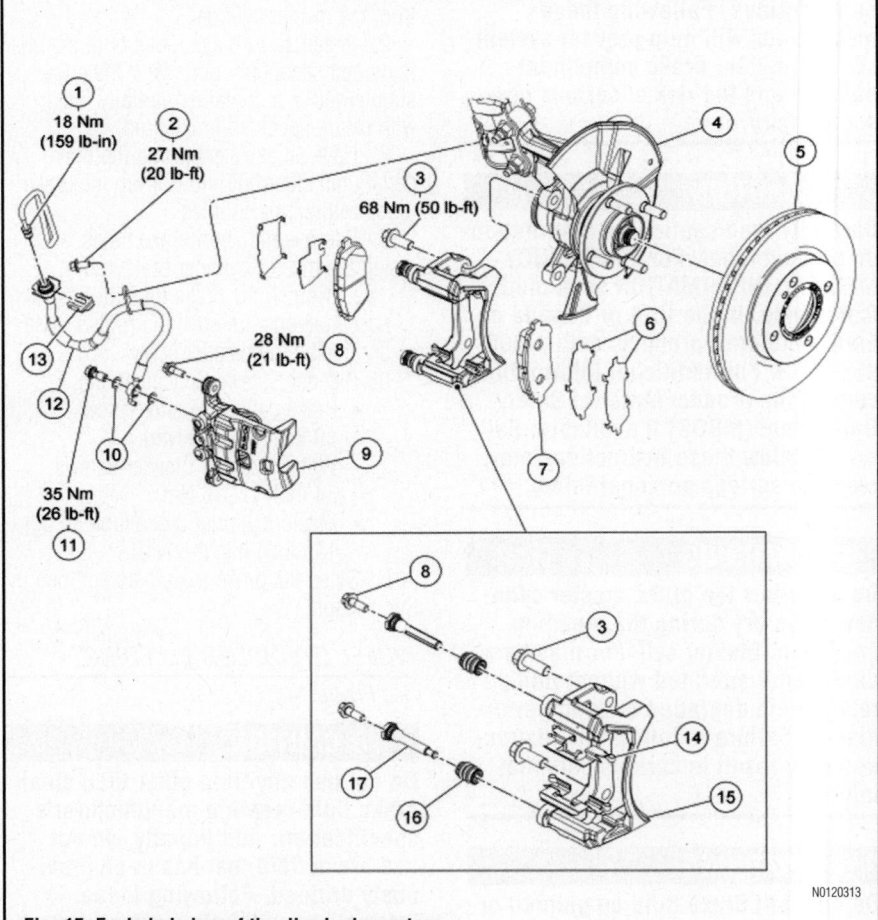

Fig. 15 Exploded view of the disc brake system

N0120313

Data Sheet (MSDS) if available. Failure to follow these instructions may result in serious personal injury.

✳✳ WARNING

Do not spill brake fluid on painted or plastic surfaces or damage to the surface may occur. If brake fluid is spilled onto a painted or plastic surface, immediately wash the surface with water.

At the time of publication, Ford does not provide a specific removal and installation procedure for brake pads or calipers. When servicing this component, please heed all notes, warnings and cautions, and refer to the accompanying illustration. Items in the exploded view may NOT be listed in order of removal.

DISC BRAKE PADS

REMOVAL & INSTALLATION
See Figure 15.

✳✳ CAUTION

Do not breathe dust or use compressed air to blow dust from storage

---

containers or friction components. Remove dust using government-approved techniques. Friction component dust may be a cancer and lung disease hazard. Exposure to potentially hazardous components may occur if dusts are created during repair of friction components, such as brake pads and clutch discs. Exposure may also cause irritation to skin, eyes and respiratory tract, and may cause allergic reactions and/or may lead to other chronic health effects. If irritation persists, seek medical attention or advice. Failure to follow these instructions may result in serious personal injury.

✳✳ CAUTION

Do not use any fluid other than clean brake fluid meeting manufacturer's specification. Additionally, do not use brake fluid that has been previously drained. Following these instructions will help prevent system contamination, brake component damage and the risk of serious personal injury.

✳✳ CAUTION

Carefully read cautionary information on product label. For EMERGENCY MEDICAL INFORMATION seek medical advice. In the USA or Canada on Ford/Motorcraft products call: 1-800-959-3673. For additional information, consult the product Material Safety Data Sheet (MSDS) if available. Failure to follow these instructions may result in serious personal injury.

✳✳ WARNING

Do not spill brake fluid on painted or plastic surfaces or damage to the surface may occur. If brake fluid is spilled onto a painted or plastic surface, immediately wash the surface with water.

At the time of publication, Ford does not provide a specific removal and installation procedure for brake pads or calipers. When servicing this component, please heed all notes, warnings and cautions, and refer to the accompanying illustration. Items in the exploded view may NOT be listed in order of removal.

BRAKES

✳✳ CAUTION

Dust and dirt accumulating on brake parts during normal use may contain asbestos fibers from production or aftermarket brake linings. Breathing excessive concentrations of asbestos fibers can cause serious bodily harm. Exercise care when servicing brake parts. Do not sand or grind brake lining unless equipment used is designed to contain the dust residue. Do not clean brake parts with compressed air or by dry brushing. Cleaning should be done by dampening the brake components with a fine mist of water, then wiping the brake components clean with a dampened cloth. Dispose of cloth and all residue containing asbestos fibers in an impermeable container with the appropriate label. Follow practices prescribed by the Occupational Safety and Health Administration (OSHA) and the Environmental Protection Agency (EPA) for the handling, processing, and disposing of

---

dust or debris that may contain asbestos fibers.

BRAKE DRUM

REMOVAL & INSTALLATION
See Figures 16 and 17.

✳✳ CAUTION

Do not breathe dust or use compressed air to blow dust from storage containers or friction components. Remove dust using government-approved techniques. Friction component dust may be a cancer and lung disease hazard. Exposure to potentially hazardous components may occur if dusts are created during repair of friction components, such as brake pads and clutch discs. Exposure may also cause irritation to skin, eyes and respiratory tract, and may cause allergic reactions and/or may lead to other chronic health effects. If irritation persists, seek medical attention or advice. Failure to follow these

---

REAR DRUM BRAKES

instructions may result in serious personal injury.

✳✳ CAUTION

Do not use any fluid other than clean brake fluid meeting manufacturer's specification. Additionally, do not use brake fluid that has been previously drained. Following these instructions will help prevent system contamination, brake component damage and the risk of serious personal injury.

✳✳ CAUTION

Carefully read cautionary information on product label. For EMERGENCY MEDICAL INFORMATION seek medical advice. In the USA or Canada on Ford/Motorcraft products call: 1-800-959-3673. For additional information, consult the product Material Safety Data Sheet (MSDS) if available. Failure to follow these instructions may result in serious personal injury.

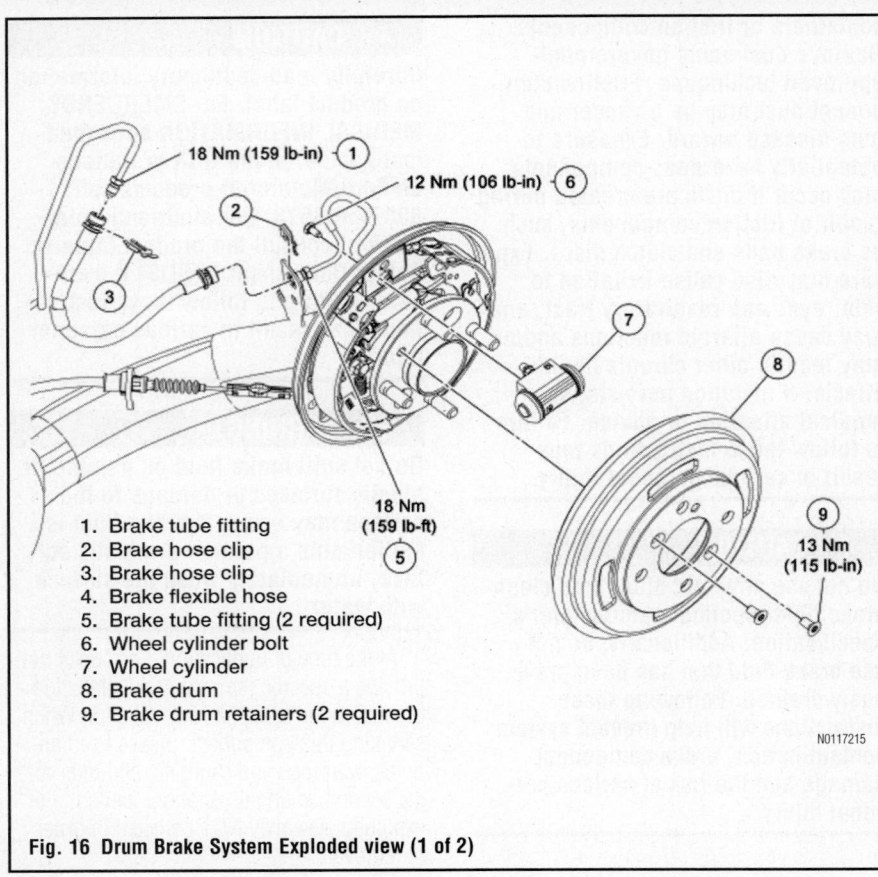

1. Brake tube fitting
2. Brake hose clip
3. Brake hose clip
4. Brake flexible hose
5. Brake tube fitting (2 required)
6. Wheel cylinder bolt
7. Wheel cylinder
8. Brake drum
9. Brake drum retainers (2 required)

18 Nm (159 lb-in) ①
12 Nm (106 lb-in) ⑥
18 Nm (159 lb-ft) ⑤
13 Nm (115 lb-in) ⑨

N0117215

Fig. 16 Drum Brake System Exploded view (1 of 2)

At the time of publication, Ford does not provide a specific removal and installation procedure for drum brake components. When servicing this component, please heed all notes, warnings and cautions, and refer to the accompanying illustration. Items in the exploded view may NOT be listed in order of removal.

BRAKE SHOES

REMOVAL & INSTALLATION

See Figures 16 and 17.

✳✳ CAUTION

Do not breathe dust or use compressed air to blow dust from storage containers or friction components. Remove dust using government-approved techniques. Friction component dust may be a cancer and lung disease hazard. Exposure to potentially hazardous components may occur if dusts are created during repair of friction components, such as brake pads and clutch discs. Exposure may also cause irritation to skin, eyes and respiratory tract, and may cause allergic reactions and/or may lead to other chronic health

✳✳ WARNING

Do not spill brake fluid on painted or plastic surfaces or damage to the surface may occur. If brake fluid is spilled onto a painted or plastic surface, immediately wash the surface with water.

✳✳ CAUTION

Always install new brake shoes or pads at both ends of an axle to reduce the possibility of brakes pulling vehicle to one side. Failure to follow this instruction may result in uneven braking and serious personal injury.

➡Make sure that all mating surfaces are free of foreign material and apply the specified silicone grease to the brake shoe contact points on the brake backing plate.

➡For brake system and component bleeding procedures see this section.

➡Removing the drum brake backing plate, the wheel hub and bearing must be removed as outlined in the Suspension Section.

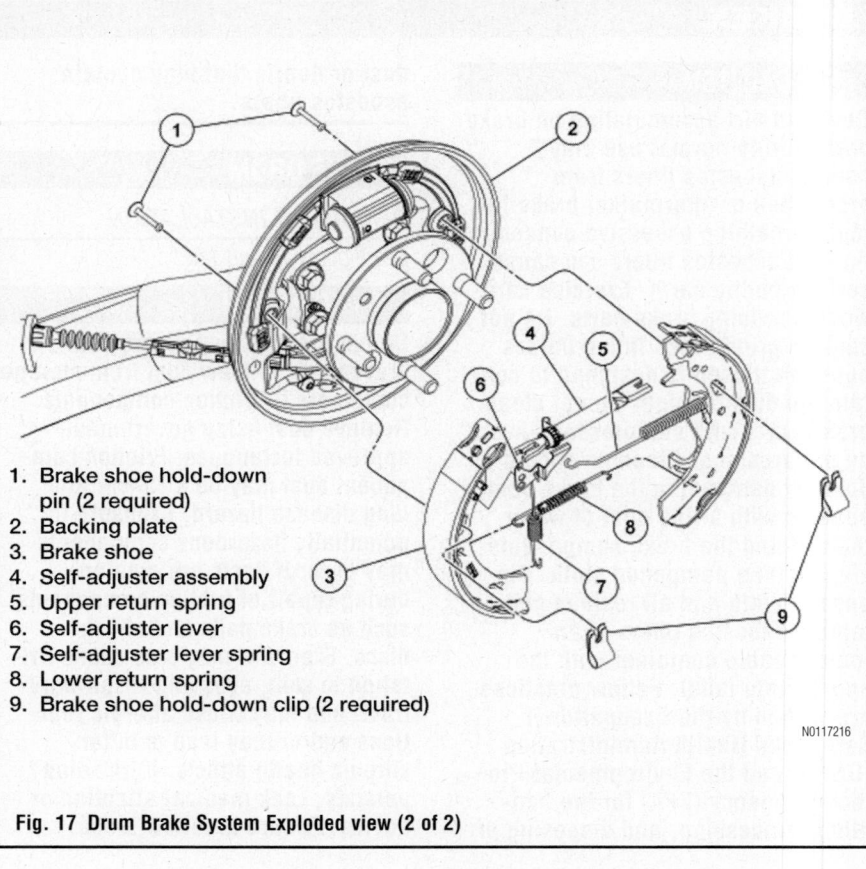

1. Brake shoe hold-down pin (2 required)
2. Backing plate
3. Brake shoe
4. Self-adjuster assembly
5. Upper return spring
6. Self-adjuster lever
7. Self-adjuster lever spring
8. Lower return spring
9. Brake shoe hold-down clip (2 required)

N0117216

Fig. 17 Drum Brake System Exploded view (2 of 2)

effects. If irritation persists, seek medical attention or advice. Failure to follow these instructions may result in serious personal injury.

✳✳ CAUTION

Do not use any fluid other than clean brake fluid meeting manufacturer's specification. Additionally, do not use brake fluid that has been previously drained. Following these instructions will help prevent system contamination, brake component damage and the risk of serious personal injury.

✳✳ CAUTION

Carefully read cautionary information on product label. For EMERGENCY MEDICAL INFORMATION seek medical advice. In the USA or Canada on Ford/Motorcraft products call: 1-800-959-3673. For additional information, consult the product Material Safety Data Sheet (MSDS) if available. Failure to follow these instructions may result in serious personal injury.

✳✳ WARNING

Do not spill brake fluid on painted or plastic surfaces or damage to the surface may occur. If brake fluid is spilled onto a painted or plastic surface, immediately wash the surface with water.

✳✳ CAUTION

Always install new brake shoes or pads at both ends of an axle to reduce the possibility of brakes pulling vehicle to one side. Failure to follow this instruction may result in uneven braking and serious personal injury.

➡Make sure that all mating surfaces are free of foreign material and apply the specified silicone grease to the brake shoe contact points on the brake backing plate.

➡For brake system and component bleeding procedures see this section.

➡When removing the drum brake backing plate, the wheel hub and bearing must be removed as outlined in the Suspension Section.

At the time of publication, Ford does not provide a specific removal and installation procedure for drum brake components. When servicing this component, please heed all notes, warnings and cautions, and refer to the accompanying illustration. Items in the exploded view may NOT be listed in order of removal.

ADJUSTMENT

See Figures 18 and 19.

1. Remove the brake drum. See the Rear Drum Brakes in this section.
2. Using the Brake Adjustment Gauge,

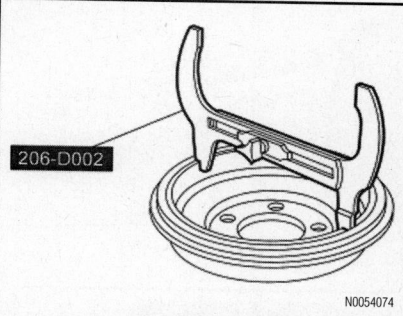

Fig. 18 Using the Brake Adjustment Gauge, measure the inside diameter of the brake drum

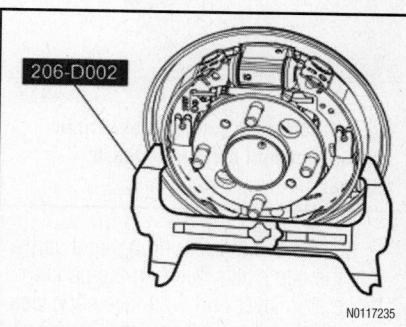

Fig. 19 Position the Brake Adjustment Gauge on the brake shoes and linings and adjust accordingly

measure the inside diameter of the brake drum.

3. Position the Brake Adjustment Gauge on the brake shoes and linings and adjust accordingly.
4. Install the brake drum.

BRAKES

PARKING BRAKE

PARKING BRAKE CABLES

ADJUSTMENT

See Figures 20 through 22.

1. Remove the floor console finish panel to access the parking brake cable adjuster nut as outlined in this section.
2. Make sure the parking brake control handle is in the fully released position.
3. Remove the brake drums.
   a. Inspect drum brake assembly. Install new components as necessary.
4. Loosen the self-adjuster one full turn on both axle ends.
5. Using a cable tie, secure the parking brake actuation lever to the brake shoe as shown on the passenger side rear.
6. Install a 4mm Allen wrench against the parking brake actuation lever on driver side rear only.

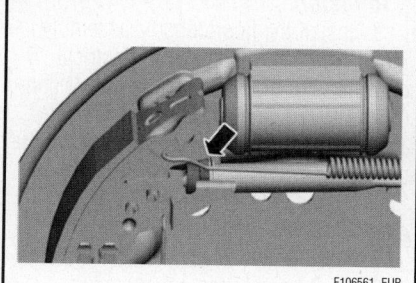

Fig. 20 Loosen the self-adjuster one full turn on both axle ends

7. Adjust the parking brake cable adjuster nut until the Allen wrench falls out.
8. Remove the cable tie.
9. Adjust the brake shoes.
10. If new rear cables have been

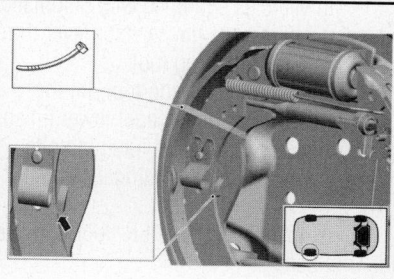

Fig. 21 Using a cable tie, secure the parking brake actuation lever to the brake shoe as shown on the passenger side rear

installed, carry out the following sub steps. If new rear cables have not been installed, proceed to step 11.

   a. Cycle parking brake control lever to the 10th notch 10 times to stretch the new cables.

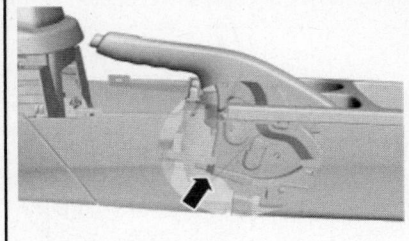

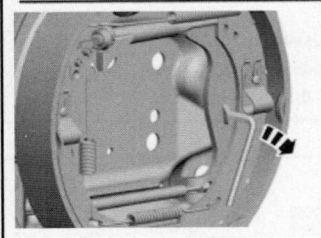

Fig. 22 Adjust the parking brake cable adjuster nut until the Allen wrench falls out

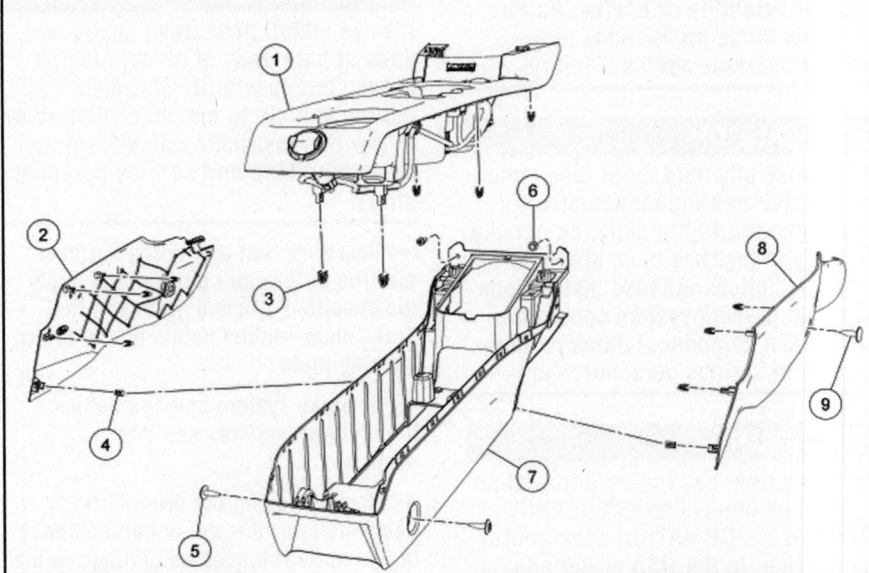

1. Floor console finish panel
2. RH floor console side panel
3. Floor console finish panel clips (6 required)
4. Floor console side panel clips (4 required)
5. Floor console rear screws (2 required)
6. Floor console front screws (2 required)
7. Floor console assembly
8. LH floor console side panel
9. Side panel push pin (2 required)

Fig. 23 Floor Console Exploded view

b. Remove the rear drums and verify that the gap exists between the parking brake stop lever and the brake shoe web.

c. If the gap is zero, repeat step 2 and steps 4 thru 9.

11. After assembling the wheel, verify the wheel turns freely to ensure there is no brake drag present.

12. Fully depress the brake pedal 10 times. Apply the parking brake to verify correct operation.

13. Install the floor console finish panel as outlined in this section.

Floor Console

See Figures 23 and 24.

1. On vehicles equipped with automatic transmission, remove the selector lever trim ring using a non-marring tool.

2. Using a non-marring tool, lift the corners of the instrument panel lower finish panel upward to release the retaining clips.

a. Disconnect the electrical connectors.

3. Remove the RH and LH floor console side trim panels.

a. Remove the side panel push pins.

b. Pull outward to release the floor console side panel clips.

4. Apply the parking brake handle in the full upright position.

5. Position the seats fully forward and remove the 2 floor console rear screws.

6. Remove the 2 floor console front screws.

7. Disconnect the 2 console electrical connectors on the right side and the 2 console electrical connectors on the left side. Separate the data cable pin type retainer from the console on the right side.

8. Remove the floor console assembly.

To install:

9. Install the floor console assembly.

10. Connect the 2 console electrical connectors on the right side and the 2 console electrical connectors on the left side. Attach the data cable pin type retainer to the console on the right side.

11. Install the 2 floor console front screws.

12. Position the seats fully forward and install the 2 floor console rear screws.

13. Apply the parking brake handle in the full upright position.

14. Install the RH and LH floor console side trim panels.

a. Push inward to engage the floor console side panel clips.

b. Install the side panel push pins.

15. Push the corners of the instrument panel lower finish panel downward to engage the retaining clips.

a. Connect the electrical connectors.

16. On vehicles equipped with automatic transmission, install the selector lever trim ring using a non-marring tool.

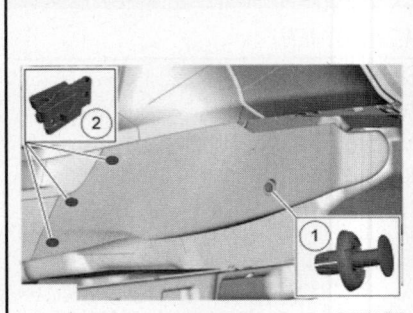

Fig. 24 Remove the RH and LH floor console side trim panels

CHASSIS ELECTRICAL — AIR BAG (SUPPLEMENTAL RESTRAINT SYSTEM)

GENERAL INFORMATION

✳✳ CAUTION

These vehicles are equipped with an air bag system. The system must be disarmed before performing service on, or around, system components, the steering column, instrument panel components, wiring and sensors. Failure to follow the safety precautions and the disarming procedure could result in accidental air bag deployment, possible injury and unnecessary system repairs.

SERVICE PRECAUTIONS

Disconnect and isolate the battery negative cable before beginning any airbag system component diagnosis, testing, removal, or installation procedures. Allow system capacitor to discharge for two minutes before beginning any component service. This will disable the airbag system. Failure to disable the airbag system may result in accidental airbag deployment, personal injury, or death.

Do not place an intact undeployed airbag face down on a solid surface. The airbag will propel into the air if accidentally deployed and may result in personal injury or death.

When carrying or handling an undeployed airbag, the trim side (face) of the airbag should be pointing towards the body to minimize possibility of injury if accidental deployment occurs. Failure to do this may result in personal injury or death.

Replace airbag system components with OEM replacement parts. Substitute parts may appear interchangeable, but internal differences may result in inferior occupant protection. Failure to do so may result in occupant personal injury or death.

Wear safety glasses, rubber gloves, and long sleeved clothing when cleaning powder residue from vehicle after an airbag deployment. Powder residue emitted from a deployed airbag can cause skin irritation. Flush affected area with cool water if irritation is experienced. If nasal or throat irritation is experienced, exit the vehicle for fresh air until the irritation ceases. If irritation continues, see a physician.

Do not use a replacement airbag that is not in the original packaging. This may result in improper deployment, personal injury, or death.

The factory installed fasteners, screws and bolts used to fasten airbag components have a special coating and are specifically designed for the airbag system. Do not use substitute fasteners. Use only original equipment fasteners listed in the parts catalog when fastener replacement is required.

During, and following, any child restraint anchor service, due to impact event or vehicle repair, carefully inspect all mounting hardware, tether straps, and anchors for proper installation, operation, or damage. If a child restraint anchor is found damaged in any way, the anchor must be replaced. Failure to do this may result in personal injury or death.

Deployed and non-deployed airbags may or may not have live pyrotechnic material within the airbag inflator.

Do not dispose of driver/passenger/curtain airbags or seat belt tensioners unless you are sure of complete deployment. Refer to the Hazardous Substance Control System for proper disposal.

Dispose of deployed airbags and tensioners consistent with state, provincial, local, and federal regulations.

After any airbag component testing or service, do not connect the battery negative cable. Personal injury or death may result if the system test is not performed first.

If the vehicle is equipped with the Occupant Classification System (OCS), do not connect the battery negative cable before performing the OCS Verification Test using the scan tool and the appropriate diagnostic information. Personal injury or death may result if the system test is not performed properly.

Never replace both the Occupant Restraint Controller (ORC) and the Occupant Classification Module (OCM) at the same time. If both require replacement, replace one, then perform the Airbag System test before replacing the other.

Both the ORC and the OCM store Occupant Classification System (OCS) calibration data, which they transfer to one another when one of them is replaced. If both are replaced at the same time, an irreversible fault will be set in both modules and the OCS may malfunction and cause personal injury or death.

If equipped with OCS, the Seat Weight Sensor is a sensitive, calibrated unit and must be handled carefully. Do not drop or handle roughly. If dropped or damaged, replace with another sensor. Failure to do so may result in occupant injury or death.

If equipped with OCS, the front passenger seat must be handled carefully as well. When removing the seat, be careful when setting on floor not to drop. If dropped, the sensor may be inoperative, could result in occupant injury, or possibly death.

If equipped with OCS, when the passenger front seat is on the floor, no one should sit in the front passenger seat. This uneven force may damage the sensing ability of the seat weight sensors. If sat on and damaged, the sensor may be inoperative, could result in occupant injury, or possibly death.

DISARMING THE SYSTEM

✳✳ CAUTION

Never probe the electrical connectors on air bag, Safety Canopy® or side air curtain modules. Failure to follow this instruction may result in the accidental deployment of these modules, which increases the risk of serious personal injury or death.

✳✳ CAUTION

Never disassemble or tamper with safety belt buckle/retractor pretensioners, adaptive load limiting retractors, safety belt inflators, or probe the electrical connectors. Failure to follow this instruction may result in the accidental deployment of the safety belt pretensioners, adaptive load limiting retractors, or safety belt inflators, which increases the risk of serious personal injury or death.

✳✳ CAUTION

To reduce the risk of accidental deployment, do not use any memory saver devices. Failure to follow this instruction may result in serious personal injury or death.

➡**The air bag warning indicator illuminates when the correct Restraints Control Module (RCM) fuse is removed and the ignition is ON.**

➡**The Supplemental Restraint System (SRS) must be fully operational and free of faults before releasing the vehicle to the customer.**

1. Turn all vehicle accessories OFF.
2. Turn the ignition OFF.

3. At the Central Junction Box (CJB), located behind the glove box, remove RCM fuse 20 (10A) from the CJB.

4. Turn the ignition ON and monitor the air bag warning indicator for at least 30 seconds. The air bag warning indicator flashes once, then remains illuminated continuously (no flashing) if the correct RCM fuse has been removed. If the air bag warning indicator does not remain illuminated continuously, remove the correct RCM fuse before proceeding.

5. Turn the ignition OFF.

※※ CAUTION

Always deplete the backup power supply before repairing or installing any new front or side air bag supplemental restraint system (SRS) component and before servicing, removing, installing, adjusting or striking components near the front or side impact sensors or the restraints control module (RCM). Nearby components include doors, instrument panel, console, door latches, strikers, seats and hood latches. Refer to the Description and Operation portion of Supplemental Restraint System for location of the RCM and impact sensor(s). To deplete the backup power supply energy, disconnect the battery ground cable and wait at least 1 minute. Be sure to disconnect auxiliary batteries and power supplies (if equipped). Failure to follow these instructions may result in serious personal injury or death in the event of an accidental deployment.

6. Disconnect the batter ground cable and wait at least one minute.

ARMING THE SYSTEM

See Figures 25 and 26.

Vehicles with keyed ignition (vehicles with ignition switch)

1. Turn the ignition from OFF to ON.

2. Install RCM fuse 20 (10A) to the CJB.

※※ CAUTION

Make sure no one is in the vehicle and there is nothing blocking or placed in front of any air bag module when the battery is connected. Failure to follow these instructions may result in serious personal injury in the event of an accidental deployment.

3. Connect the battery ground cable.

4. Prove out the SRS as follows: Turn the ignition from ON to OFF. Wait 10 seconds, then turn the ignition back to ON and monitor the air bag warning indicator with the air bag modules installed. The air bag warning indicator illuminates continuously for approximately 6 seconds and then turns off. If a SRS fault is present, the air bag warning indicator indicates the fault in one of the following ways: - fail to light. - remain lit continuously. - flash. The flashing might not occur until approximately 30 seconds after the ignition has been turned from OFF to ON. This is the time required for the RCM to complete the testing of the SRS. If the air bag warning indicator is inoperative and a SRS fault exists, a chime sounds in a pattern of 5 sets of 5 beeps. If this occurs, diagnose and repair the air bag warning indicator and any SRS fault discovered. Clear all continuous DTCs from the RCM and Occupant Classification System Module (OCSM) using a scan tool.

Vehicles with Intelligent Access (IA) (vehicles with push button start system)

5. Install RCM fuse 20 (10A) to the CJB and install the cover.

6. Remove the Smart Keyless Ignition Relay (CJB relay 7).

7. Install a fused (15A) jumper wire between Smart Keyless Entry Ignition Relay (CJB relay 7) socket pins 3 and 5.

※※ CAUTION

Make sure no one is in the vehicle and there is nothing blocking or

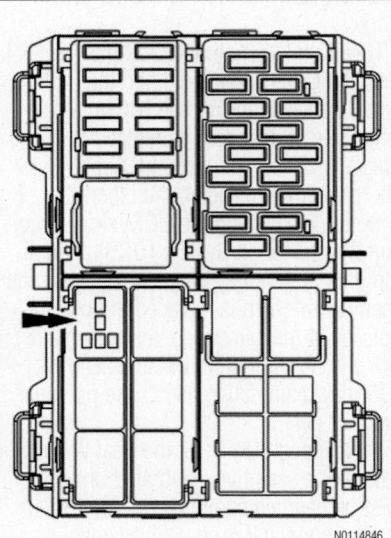

Fig. 25 Remove the Smart Keyless Ignition Relay (CJB relay 7).

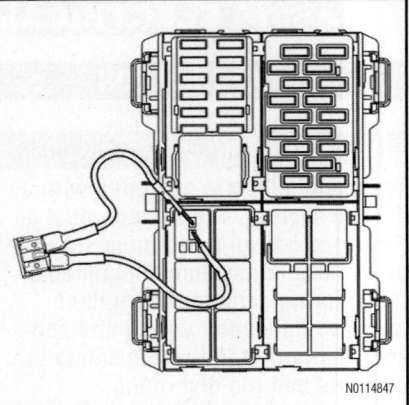

Fig. 26 Install a fused (15A) jumper wire between Smart Keyless Entry Ignition Relay (CJB relay 7) socket pins 3 and 5

placed in front of any air bag module when the battery is connected. Failure to follow these instructions may result in serious personal injury in the event of an accidental deployment.

8. Connect the battery ground cable.

9. Remove the fused jumper wire from the CJB.

10. Install the Smart Keyless Ignition Relay (CJB relay 7).

11. Prove out the SRS as follows: With the ignition OFF, wait 10 seconds, then turn the ignition ON and monitor the air bag warning indicator with the air bag modules installed. The air bag warning indicator illuminates continuously for approximately 6 seconds and then turns off. If an air bag SRS fault is detected, the air bag warning indicator indicates the fault in one of the following ways: - fail to light. - remain lit continuously. - flash. The flashing might not occur until approximately 30 seconds after the ignition has been turned from OFF to ON. This is the time required to complete testing of the SRS. If the air bag warning indicator is inoperative and a SRS fault exists, a chime will sound in a pattern of 5 sets of 5 beeps. If this occurs, diagnose and repair the air bag warning indicator and any SRS fault discovered. Clear all RCM and OCSM CMDTCs.

CLOCKSPRING CENTERING

See Figure 27.

➡The air bag warning indicator illuminates when the correct Restraints Control Module (RCM) fuse is removed and the ignition is ON.

➡The Supplemental Restraint System (SRS) must be fully operational and free of faults before releasing the vehicle to the customer.

⁂

Make sure the road wheels are in the straight-ahead position to prevent damage to the clockspring.

1. Remove the steering wheel as outlined in this section.
2. Remove the steering column shroud as outlined in this section.
3. Disconnect the clockspring electrical connectors, disengage the 3 retaining tabs and remove the clockspring.

To install:

⁂ ⁂

If installing a new clockspring, do not remove the clockspring anti-rotation key until the steering wheel is installed. If the anti-rotation key has been removed before installing the steering wheel, the clockspring must be centered. Failure to follow this instruction may result in component damage and/or system failure.

4. Position the clockspring onto the steering column and engage the retaining tabs to the multi-function switch.
5. Connect the clockspring electrical connectors.

⁂ ⁂

If the clockspring is not correctly centralized, it may fail prematurely. If in doubt, repeat the centralizing procedure. Failure to follow these instructions may increase the risk of serious personal injury or death in a crash.

⁂ ⁂

Do not over-rotate the clockspring inner rotor. The internal ribbon wire is connected to the clockspring rotor. The internal ribbon wire acts as a stop and can be broken from its internal connection. Failure to follow this instruction may result in component damage and/or system failure.

6. If a new clockspring was installed and the anti-rotation key has not been removed proceed to Step 5. If a new clock-

spring was installed and the anti-rotation key has been removed before the steering wheel is installed or the same clockspring is being installed, rotate the clockspring inner rotor counterclockwise and carefully feel for the ribbon wire to run out of length with slight resistance. Stop rotating the clockspring inner rotor at this point.

7. Starting with the clockspring rotated fully counterclockwise as indicated in Step 3, rotate the clockspring inner rotor, wiring and connector clockwise through 3.75 full revolutions with the connector ending up in the 12 o'clock position. Verify the clockspring is correctly centralized by observing that the clockspring rotor, wiring and connector are in the 12 o'clock position.

Install the steering column shroud as outlined in this section.

8. Install the steering wheel as outlined in this section.
9. If a new clockspring was installed, remove the anti-rotation key.
10. Install the driver air bag module as outlined in this section.

Steering Column Shroud

See Figures 28 and 29.

1. Pulling upward, detach the upper steering column shroud from the lower steering column shroud.
   a. Slide the upper steering column shroud out of the Instrument Cluster (IC) trim panel and remove the shroud.
2. Remove the 3 screws and the lower steering column shroud.

To install:

3. Install the 3 screws and the lower steering column shroud. Tighten the screws to 9 inch lbs. (1 Nm).
4. Pushing downward, attach the upper steering column shroud to the lower steering column shroud.

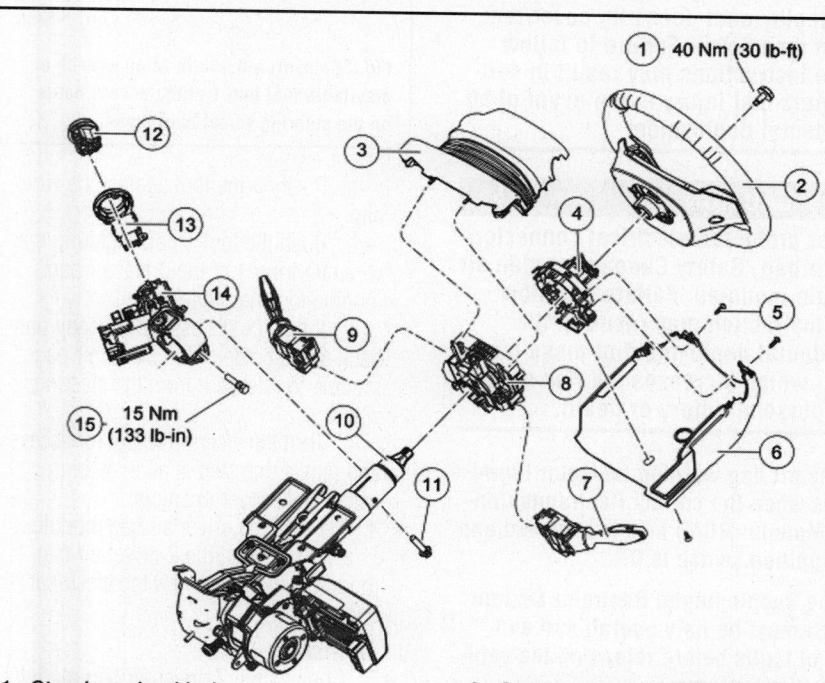

1. Steering wheel bolt
2. Steering wheel
3. Upper steering column shroud
4. Clockspring
5. Steering column shroud bolt (2 required)
6. Lower steering column shroud
7. Switch assembly
8. Steering column multifunction switch
9. Switch assembly wiper/washer
10. Steering column
11. Steering column lock bolt
12. Ignition switch cylinder
13. Passive Anti-Theft System (PATS) transceiver electrical connector
14. Ignition switch housing
15. Ignition switch housing bolt

Fig. 27 Clockspring exploded view

N0119131

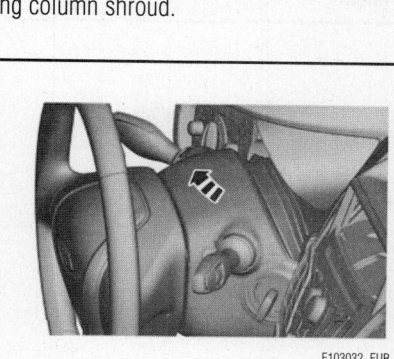

E103032_EUR

Fig. 28 Pulling upward, detach the upper steering column shroud from the lower steering column shroud

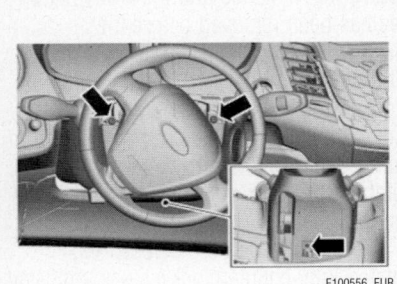

Fig. 29 Remove the 3 screws and the lower steering column shroud

a. Slide the upper steering column shroud into the Instrument Cluster (IC) trim panel and install the shroud.

Steering Wheel

See Figures 30 and 31.

1. Remove the driver air bag module as outlined in this section.
2. Turn the steering wheel to the straight-ahead position.
3. Remove the steering wheel as follows:
   a. Disconnect the electrical connector.
   b. Remove the bolt and the steering wheel.

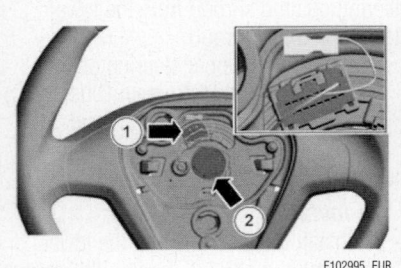

Fig. 30 Disconnect the electrical connector. Remove the bolt and the steering wheel

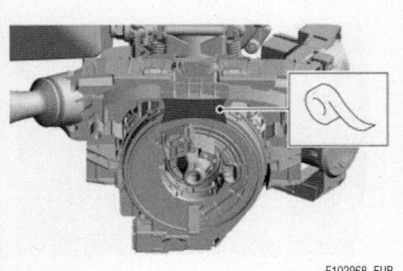

Fig. 31 Tape the clockspring center rotor to the outer housing to keep it from rotating

4. Tape the clockspring center rotor to the outer housing to keep it from rotating.

To install:

5. Tape the clockspring center rotor to the outer housing to keep it from rotating.
6. Install the steering wheel as follows:
   a. Install the bolt and the steering wheel. Tighten the bolt to 30 ft. lbs. (40 Nm).
   b. Connect the electrical connector.
7. Turn the steering wheel to the straight-ahead position.
8. Install the driver air bag module as outlined in this section.

DRIVER AIR BAG MODULE

REMOVAL & INSTALLATION

See Figure 32 and 33.

✷✷ CAUTION

Always carry or place a live air bag module with the air bag and deployment door/trim cover/tear seam pointed away from the body. Do not set a live air bag module down with the deployment door/trim cover/tear seam face down. Failure to follow these instructions may result in serious personal injury in the event of an accidental deployment.

✷✷ CAUTION

Never probe the electrical connectors on air bag, Safety Canopy® or side air curtain modules. Failure to follow this instruction may result in the accidental deployment of these modules, which increases the risk of serious personal injury or death.

➡The air bag warning indicator illuminates when the correct Restraints Control Module (RCM) fuse is removed and the ignition switch is ON.

➡The Supplemental Restraint System (SRS) must be fully operational and free of faults before releasing the vehicle to the customer.

1. Disarm the SRS, as outlined in this section.
2. Insert a 0.118 in Allen wrench or a suitable tool into 1 of the access holes on the steering wheel back cover.
3. Separate the driver air bag module from the steering wheel in the following sequence.

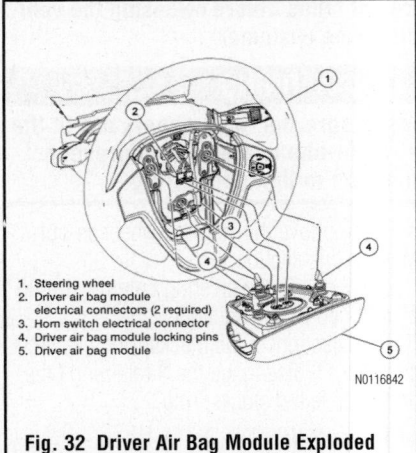

1. Steering wheel
2. Driver air bag module electrical connectors (2 required)
3. Horn switch electrical connector
4. Driver air bag module locking pins
5. Driver air bag module

Fig. 32 Driver Air Bag Module Exploded view

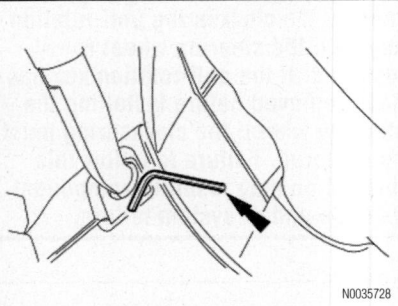

Fig. 33 Insert a 0.118 in Allen wrench or a suitable tool into 1 of the access holes on the steering wheel back cover

a. Position the tool against the wire clip.
b. Push the tool in, disengaging the wire clip from 1 of the driver air bag module locking pins.
c. It may be necessary to gently pull back on that side of the driver air bag module to release it from the steering wheel.
d. Turn the steering wheel for access and repeat this step at all 3 steering wheel back cover openings.
4. Remove the driver air bag module.
   a. Disconnect the 2 driver air bag module and the horn switch electrical connectors.

To install:

5. Connect the 2 driver air bag module and the horn switch electrical connectors.
6. Align the driver air bag module locking pins to the steering wheel and, while pushing inward, seat the 3 driver air bag module locking pins to the steering wheel wire clips.
7. Arm the SRS as outlined in this section.

DRIVE TRAIN

AUTOMATIC TRANSAXLE CASE

REMOVAL & INSTALLATION
See Figures 34 and 35.

Fig. 34 Remove and discard the halfshaft seal

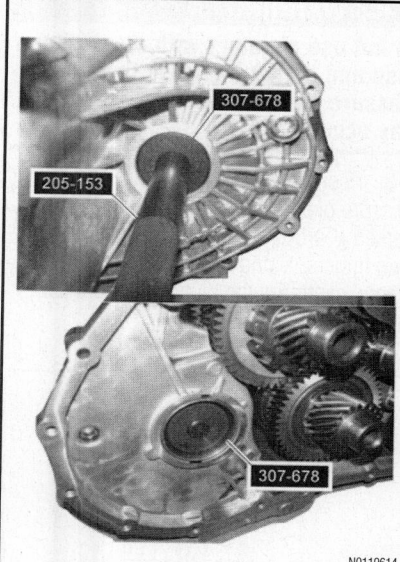

Fig. 35 Using the special tools, remove the differential case bearing cup

1. Remove and discard the halfshaft seal.
2. Using the special tools, remove the differential case bearing cup.

To install:

➡ **If a new differential gear bearing, transmission case, differential or clutch housing are installed, measure the differential shim for the correct size.**

3. Using the special tools, install the differential gear bearing cup.

4. Install the new halfshaft seal on the special tools.
5. Using the special tools, install the new halfshaft seal.

AUTOMATIC TRANSAXLE FLUID

DRAIN AND REFILL
See Figures 36 and 37.

1. With the vehicle in NEUTRAL, position it on a hoist.

➡ **Prior to removal, clean the area surrounding the fill plug.**

2. Remove the fill plug.
3. Remove the drain plug and drain the fluid.
4. Install the drain plug. Tighten the drain plug to 32 ft. lbs. (43 Nm).

➡ **Do not overfill the transaxle. This will cause transaxle fluid to be forced out of the case.**

Using a suitable oil suction gun, fill the transaxle to the correct level with the specified fluid. Add transmission fluid

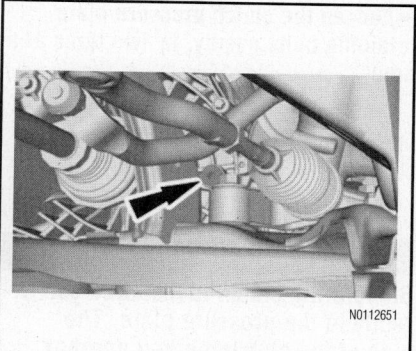

Fig. 36 Remove the fill plug

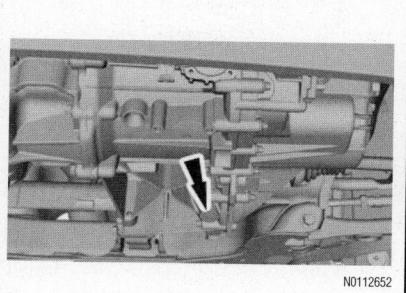

Fig. 37 Remove the drain plug and drain the fluid

until the oil runs out of the fill port in a continuous stream. The transaxle is full when the oil flow from the fill port has slowed to a broken stream or dripping.

➡ **Use a ball head hex socket to torque to specifications.**

5. Install the fill plug. Tighten the plug to 32 ft. lbs. (43 Nm).

MANUAL TRANSAXLE FLUID

DRAIN AND REFILL
See Figure 38.

1. With the vehicle in NEUTRAL, position it on a hoist.
2. Release the 7 retainers and remove the shift cable cover.

➡ **Before removing, clean the area around the filler plug.**

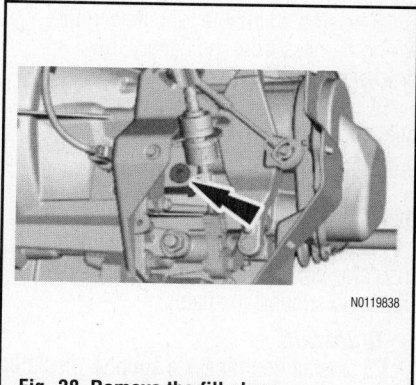

Fig. 38 Remove the fill plug

3. Remove the fill plug.
4. Using a suitable oil suction gun, fill the transaxle to the correct level with the specified fluid.
   a. Transaxle fluid level: 0.196–0.393 in. (5–10 mm) below the lower edge of the filler plug bore.
5. Install the fill plug. Tighten the fill plug to 26 ft. lbs. (35 Nm).
6. Install the shift cables cover.

MANUAL TRANSAXLE SUPPORT INSULATOR

REMOVAL & INSTALLATION
See Figure 39.

1. With the vehicle in NEUTRAL, position it on a hoist.
2. Remove the battery.

Fig. 39 Install the transaxle support insulator and install the 2 transaxle support insulator bolts and the 2 nuts.

3. Remove the cowl assembly as outlined in this section.

4. Remove the Air Cleaner (ACL) assembly and outlet pipe as outlined in the Engine Mechanical Section.

5. Remove the PCM cover bolt and the PCM cover.

6. Disconnect the 3 PCM electrical connectors.

7. Remove the 3 battery tray bolts and the battery tray.

8. Using a suitable tool, detach the wiring harness from the battery tray bracket.

9. Remove the 3 battery tray bracket nuts and remove the battery tray bracket.

10. Install the special tools and support the engine.

11. Remove the 2 transaxle support insulator bolts and nuts and remove the transaxle support insulator.

To install:

12. Install the transaxle support insulator and install the 2 transaxle support insulator bolts and the 2 nuts.

   a. Tighten the 2 bolts to 66 ft. lbs. (90 Nm).

   b. Tighten the 2 nuts to 92 ft. lbs. (125 Nm).

Install the battery tray bracket and the 3 battery tray bracket nuts. Tighten the nuts to 18 ft. lbs. (25 Nm).

13. Attach the wiring harness to the battery tray bracket.

14. Install the battery tray and 3 battery tray bolts. Tighten the bolts to 89 inch lbs. (10 Nm).

15. Connect the 3 PCM electrical connectors.

16. Install the PCM cover and the PCM cover bolt. Tighten the bolt to 53 inch lbs. (6 Nm).

17. Install the ACL and the outlet pipe as outlined in the Engine Mechanical Section.

18. Install the cowl assembly as outlined in this section.

19. Install the battery.

CLUTCH

REMOVAL & INSTALLATION

See Figures 40 through 43.

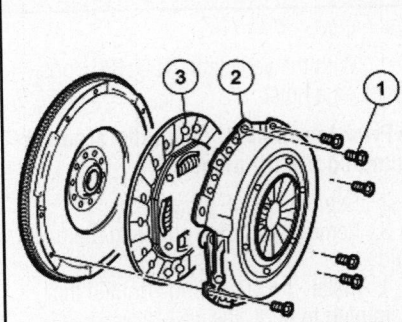

1. Clutch pressure plate-to-flywheel bolts
2. Clutch pressure plate
3. Clutch disc

N0106459

Fig. 40 Clutch Disc and Pressure Plate exploded view

1. Remove the transaxle.

➡**Loosen the clutch pressure plate retaining bolts evenly, by two turns at a time.**

2. Remove and discard the 6 clutch pressure plate retaining bolts, remove the clutch disc and pressure plate.

To install:

✳✳ WARNING

Be sure the clutch is installed correctly in the pressure plate. The side of the clutch marked gearbox side faces the pressure plate

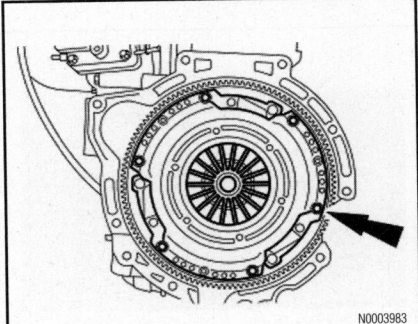

Fig. 41 Remove and discard the 6 clutch pressure plate retaining bolts, remove the clutch disc and pressure plate

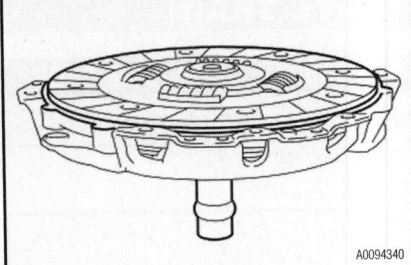

Fig. 42 Position the clutch disc on the clutch pressure plate with the side of the clutch marked gearbox side facing the pressure plate fingers. Using a suitable clutch aligner, centralize the clutch disc to the clutch pressure plate

fingers. **Failure to install the clutch plate will damage the clutch assembly during installation on the flywheel.**

✳✳ WARNING

Do not use cleaners with a petroleum base and do not immerse the clutch pressure plate in solvent or damage may occur.

3. Position the clutch disc on the clutch pressure plate with the side of the clutch marked gearbox side facing the pressure plate fingers. Using a suitable clutch aligner, centralize the clutch disc to the clutch pressure plate.

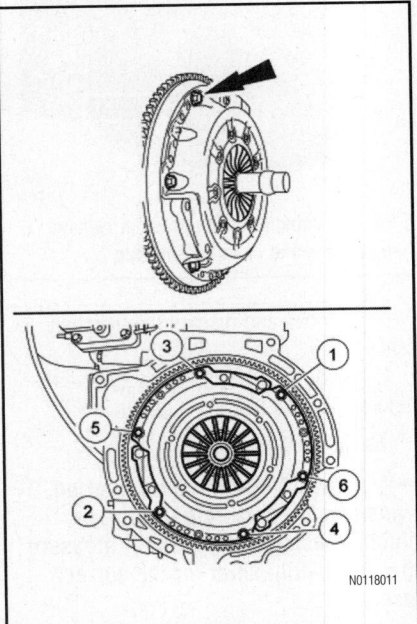

Fig. 43 Tighten the bolts evenly two turns at a time in the pattern shown

➡️Tighten the clutch pressure plate-to-flywheel bolts finger tight and then evenly by two turns at a time to the specified torque.

4. Using a suitable clutch aligner, position the clutch disc and clutch pressure plate on the flywheel. Install the 6 new clutch pressure plate-to-flywheel bolts.

5. Tighten the bolts evenly two turns at a time in the pattern shown in the figure below. Tighten the bolts to 21 ft. lbs. (29 Nm).

6. Install the transaxle.

BLEEDING

See Figures 44 and 45.

❈❈ CAUTION

Carefully read cautionary information on product label. For EMERGENCY MEDICAL INFORMATION seek medical advice. In the USA or Canada on Ford/Motorcraft products call: 1-800-959-3673. For additional information, consult the product Material Safety Data Sheet (MSDS) if available. Failure to follow these instructions may result in serious personal injury.

❈❈ WARNING

If brake fluid is spilled on the paint, immediately wash the affected area with cold water or damage can occur.

➡️**Do not reuse brake fluid.**

1. Remove the Air Cleaner (ACL) assembly and outlet pipe as outlined in the Engine Mechanical Section.

2. Remove the brake fluid reservoir cap.

3. Drain the brake fluid reservoir to the MIN mark.

4. Remove the clutch slave cylinder bleed fitting dust cap.

N0117098

Fig. 44 Remove the brake fluid reservoir cap

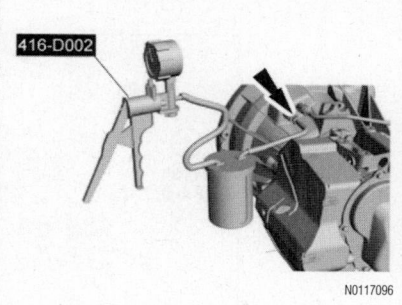

N0117096

Fig. 45 Install the special tool and loosen the clutch slave cylinder bleed fitting

5. Install the special tool and loosen the clutch slave cylinder bleed fitting.

6. Using the special tool, bleed the clutch system.

7. Fill the reservoir of the special tool with approximately 4.06 oz of brake fluid.

8. Loosen the clutch slave cylinder bleed fitting.

9. Pump approximately 3.38 oz of brake fluid into the clutch system.

10. Tighten the clutch slave cylinder bleed fitting.

11. Install the clutch slave cylinder bleed fitting dust cap.

12. Install the brake fluid reservoir cap.

13. Check the fluid level in the brake fluid reservoir and add as necessary.

➡️**Carefully move the gearshift lever into REVERSE.**

14. Test the operation of the clutch control system.

a. Start the engine, after 2 seconds press the clutch pedal and carefully move the gearshift lever into REVERSE. If there are abnormal noises, automatically bleed the clutch control system by pressing the clutch pedal 4 or 5 times. During bleeding, full travel of the clutch pedal must be reached.

b. Test the operation of the clutch control system again after 30 seconds. If there are still abnormal noises perform steps 2 to 10 again.

15. Install the ACL assembly and outlet pipe assembly as outlined in the Engine Mechanical Section.

FRONT HALFSHAFT

REMOVAL & INSTALLATION

See Figures 46 through 48.

At the time of publication, Ford does not provide a specific removal and installation procedure for the Front Halfshaft. When servicing this component, please heed all notes, warnings and cautions, and refer to the accompanying illustration. Items in the exploded view may NOT be listed in order of removal.

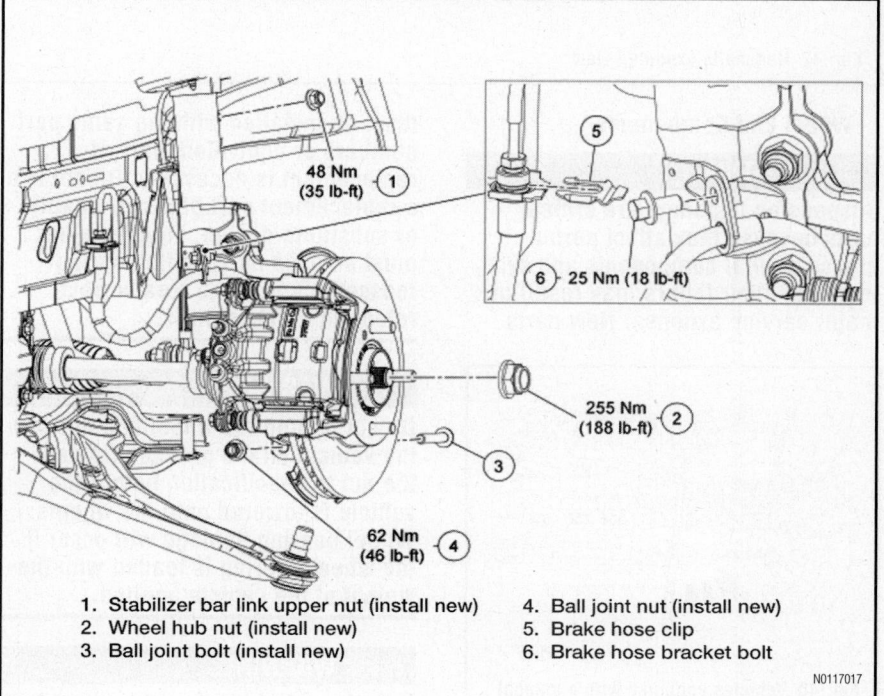

1. Stabilizer bar link upper nut (install new)
2. Wheel hub nut (install new)
3. Ball joint bolt (install new)
4. Ball joint nut (install new)
5. Brake hose clip
6. Brake hose bracket bolt

N0117017

Fig. 46 Wheel End Components exploded view

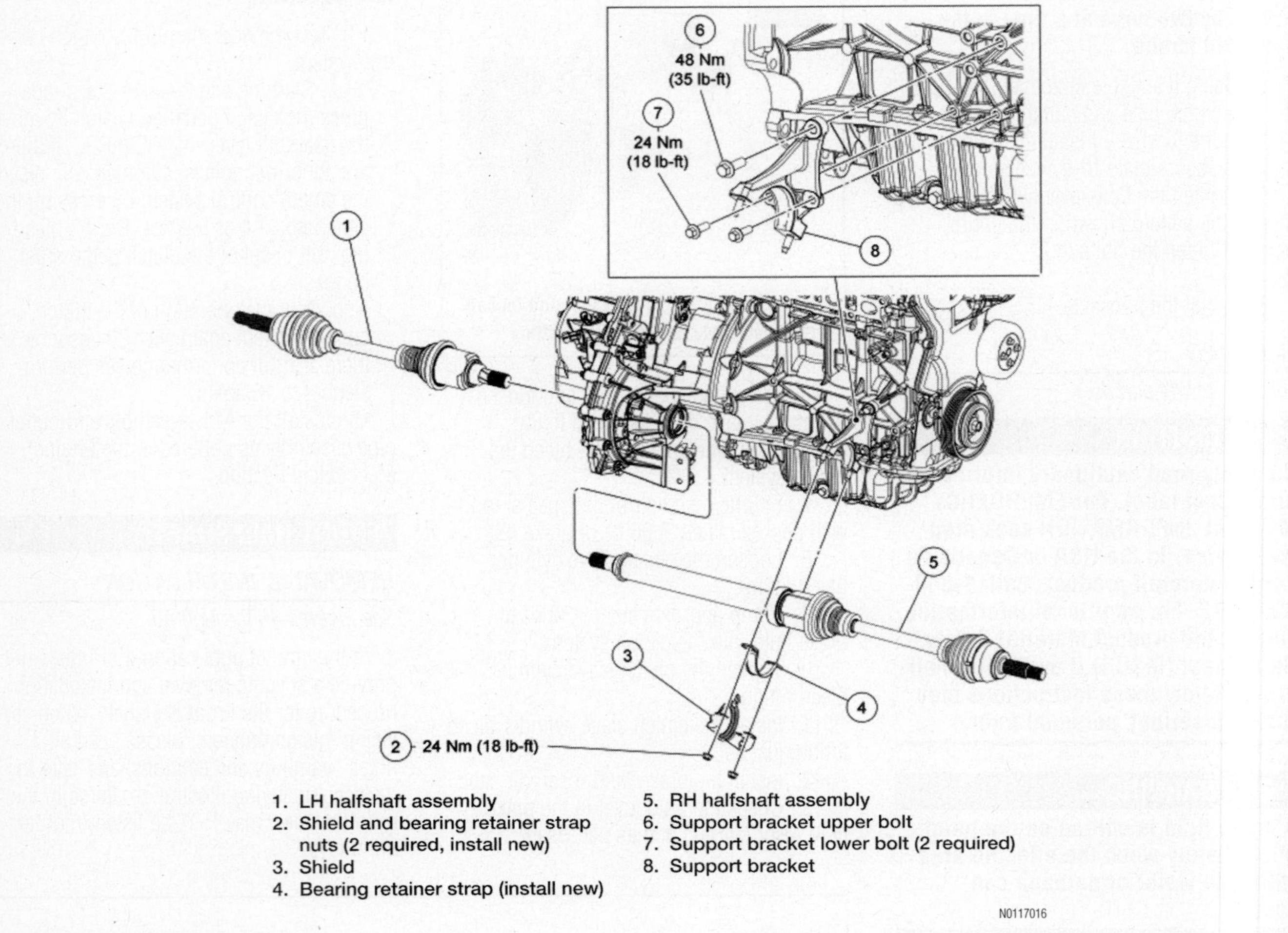

⑥
48 Nm
(35 lb-ft)
⑦
24 Nm
(18 lb-ft)
⑧

①

⑤

③

④

② 24 Nm (18 lb-ft)

1. LH halfshaft assembly
2. Shield and bearing retainer strap nuts (2 required, install new)
3. Shield
4. Bearing retainer strap (install new)

5. RH halfshaft assembly
6. Support bracket upper bolt
7. Support bracket lower bolt (2 required)
8. Support bracket

N0117016

Fig. 47 Halfshafts exploded view

Wheel End Components

❊❊ WARNING

Suspension fasteners are critical parts because they affect performance of vital components and systems and their failure may result in major service expense. New parts

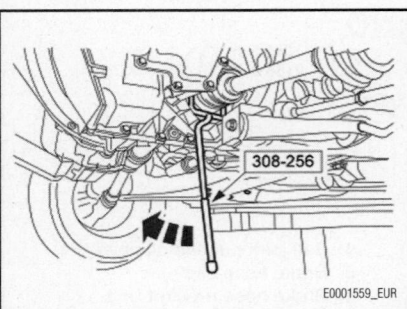

E0001559_EUR

Fig. 48 Vehicles equipped with a manual transmission, use special tool 308-256 to detach the LH halfshaft

must be installed with the same part numbers or equivalent part, if replacement is necessary. Do not use a replacement part of lesser quality or substitute design. Torque values must be used as specified during reassembly to make sure correct retention of these parts.

❊❊ WARNING

Do not tighten the wheel hub nut with the vehicle on the ground. Tighten the nut to specification before the vehicle is lowered onto the wheels. Wheel bearing damage will occur if the wheel bearing is loaded with the weight of the vehicle applied.

❊❊ WARNING

Install and tighten the new wheel hub nut to specification in a continuous rotation. Always install a new wheel

hub nut after loosening or when not tightened to specification in a continuous rotation or damage to the components may occur.

➥Apply the brake to keep the halfshaft from rotating while tightening the wheel hub nut.

Halfshafts

❊❊ WARNING

Install the bearing retainer strap (item 4) on the bracket studs before the shield (item 3) and tighten the nuts evenly in stages (alternating from top to bottom) or incorrect bearing clamp load may occur causing component damage.

❊❊ WARNING

The inner joint must not be bent more than 18 degrees. The outer joint must not be bent more than 45 degrees. Damage to the halfshaft will occur.

✳✳ WARNING

Install a new halfshaft seal any time the halfshaft is removed from the transmission/transaxle or a leak

may occur as outlined in this section.

➡Install the RH halfshaft shield so the clip is seated in the notch on the support bracket.

1. Refer to the procedures and/or exploded views in this section for any

Warnings, Notices, Notes, Materials, Specifications and Special Tools. Items in the exploded views may not be listed in order of removal.

2. With the vehicle in NEUTRAL, position it on a hoist.

3. Vehicles equipped with a manual transmission, use special tool 308-256 to detach the LH halfshaft.

ENGINE COOLING

ENGINE COOLANT

DRAIN & REFILL PROCEDURE AND BLEEDING

Draining

1. With the vehicle in NEUTRAL, position it on a hoist.

✳✳ CAUTION

Always allow the engine to cool before opening the cooling system. Do not unscrew the coolant pressure relief cap when the engine is operating or the cooling system is hot. The cooling system is under pressure; steam and hot liquid can come out forcefully when the cap is loosened slightly. Failure to follow these instructions may result in serious personal injury.

✳✳ WARNING

The coolant must be recovered in a suitable, clean container for reuse. If the coolant is contaminated, it must be recycled or disposed of correctly. Using contaminated coolant may damage the engine or cooling system components.

➡During normal vehicle operation, Motorcraft Specialty Orange Engine Coolant may change color from orange to pink or light red. As long as the engine coolant is clear and uncontaminated, this color change does not indicate the engine coolant has degraded nor does it require the engine coolant to be drained, the system to be flushed, or the engine coolant to be replaced.

➡Release the pressure in the cooling system by slowly turning the pressure relief cap one half turn counterclockwise. When the pressure has been released, remove the pressure relief cap.

2. Place a suitable container below the lower radiator hose.

a. Release the clamp, disconnect the lower radiator hose from the radiator and allow the coolant to drain.

Filling and Bleeding with a Vacuum Cooling System Filler

✳✳ WARNING

The engine cooling system is filled with Motorcraft® Specialty Orange Engine Coolant. Always fill the cooling system with the manufacturer's specified coolant. If a non-specified coolant has been used the cooling system must be chemically flushed. Refer to Flushing in this section. Failure to follow these instructions may damage the engine or cooling system.

✳✳ WARNING

Engine coolant provides freeze protection, boil protection, cooling efficiency and corrosion protection to the engine and cooling components. In order to obtain these protections, the engine coolant must be maintained at the correct concentration and fluid level in the coolant expansion tank. To maintain the integrity of the coolant and the cooling system:

- Add Motorcraft® Specialty Orange Engine Coolant or equivalent meeting Ford specification WSS-M97B44-D (orange color).
- Do not add or mix with any other type of engine coolants. Mixing coolants degrades the coolant's corrosion protection.
- Do not add alcohol, methanol or brine, or any engine coolants mixed with alcohol or methanol antifreeze. These can cause engine damage from overheating or freezing.
- Ford Motor Company does NOT recommend the use of recycled engine coolant in vehicles originally equipped with Motorcraft®

Specialty Orange Engine Coolant since a Ford-approved recycling process is not yet available.

3. Connect the lower radiator hose to the radiator and position the clamp.

4. Install the vacuum cooling system filler and follow the manufacturer's instructions to fill and bleed the cooling system.

a. Recommended coolant concentration is 50/50 ethylene glycol to distilled water.

b. For extremely cold climates (less than -34°F [-37°C]):
- It may be necessary to increase the coolant concentration above 50%.
- NEVER increase the coolant concentration above 60%.
- Maximum coolant concentration is 60/40 for cold weather areas.
- A coolant concentration of 60% will provide freeze point protection down to -58°F (-50°C).
- Engine coolant concentration above 60% will decrease the overheat protection characteristics of the engine coolant and may damage the engine.

c. For extremely hot climates:
- It is still necessary to maintain the coolant concentration above 40%.
- NEVER decrease the coolant concentration below 40%.
- Minimum coolant concentration is 40/60 for warm weather areas.
- A coolant concentration of 40% will provide freeze point protection down to -15°F (-26°C).
- Engine coolant concentration below 40% will decrease the corrosion and freeze protection characteristics of the engine coolant and may damage the engine.

d. Vehicles driven year-round in non-extreme climates should use a 50/50 mixture of engine coolant and distilled water for optimum cooling system and engine protection.

Filling and Bleeding without a Vacuum Cooling System Filler

✳✳ WARNING

The engine cooling system is filled with Motorcraft® Specialty Orange Engine Coolant. Always fill the cooling system with the manufacturer's specified coolant. If a non-specified coolant has been used the cooling system must be chemically flushed. Refer to Flushing in this section. Failure to follow these instructions may damage the engine or cooling system.

✳✳ WARNING

Engine coolant provides freeze protection, boil protection, cooling efficiency and corrosion protection to the engine and cooling components. In order to obtain these protections, the engine coolant must be maintained at the correct concentration and fluid level in the coolant expansion tank. To maintain the integrity of the coolant and the cooling system:

- Add Motorcraft® Specialty Orange Engine Coolant or equivalent meeting Ford specification WSS-M97B44-D (orange color).
- Do not add or mix with any other type of engine coolants. Mixing coolants degrades the coolant's corrosion protection.
- Do not add alcohol, methanol or brine, or any engine coolants mixed with alcohol or methanol antifreeze. These can cause engine damage from overheating or freezing.
- Ford Motor Company does NOT recommend the use of recycled engine coolant in vehicles originally equipped with Motorcraft® Specialty Orange Engine Coolant since a Ford-approved recycling process is not yet available.

5. Connect the lower radiator hose to the radiator and position the clamp.

6. Fill the radiator through the degas bottle until the coolant level is at the max fill line on the degas bottle.

   a. Recommended coolant concentration is 50/50 ethylene glycol to distilled water.

   b. For extremely cold climates (less than -34°F [-37°C]):
   - It may be necessary to increase the coolant concentration above 50%.
   - NEVER increase the coolant concentration above 60%.

- Maximum coolant concentration is 60/40 for cold weather areas.
- A coolant concentration of 60% will provide freeze point protection down to -58°F (-50°C).
- Engine coolant concentration above 60% will decrease the overheat protection characteristics of the engine coolant and may damage the engine.

   c. For extremely hot climates:
   - It is still necessary to maintain the coolant concentration above 40%.
   - NEVER decrease the coolant concentration below 40%.
   - Minimum coolant concentration is 40/60 for warm weather areas.
   - A coolant concentration of 40% will provide freeze point protection down to -15°F (-26°C).
   - Engine coolant concentration below 40% will decrease the corrosion and freeze protection characteristics of the engine coolant and may damage the engine.

   d. Vehicles driven year-round in non-extreme climates should use a 50/50 mixture of engine coolant and distilled water for optimum cooling system and engine protection.

7. Install the pressure relief cap.

✳✳ WARNING

If the engine overheats or the fluid level in the coolant expansion tank drops below the min fill line, allow the engine to cool. Once engine is cool, add coolant to the coolant expansion tank to the max fill line. Failure to follow these instructions may damage the engine.

8. Start the engine, run and hold at 2,500 rpm for 15 minutes.

✳✳ WARNING

If the engine overheats or the fluid level in the coolant expansion tank drops below the min fill line, allow the engine to cool. Once engine is cool, add coolant to the coolant expansion tank to the max fill line. Failure to follow these instructions may damage the engine.

9. Increase the engine speed to 5,000 rpm and then decrease to idle. Repeat six times.

✳✳ WARNING

If the engine overheats or the fluid level in the coolant expansion tank

drops below the min fill line, allow the engine to cool. Once engine is cool, add coolant to the coolant expansion tank to the max fill line. Failure to follow these instructions may damage the engine.

10. Increase the engine speed to 4,000 rpm for ten seconds, then return the engine speed to 2,500 rpm and hold for another ten minutes.

11. Decrease the engine speed to idle, shut the engine off and allow to cool.

12. Check the engine and cooling system for any leaks.

13. Check the coolant level in the degas bottle and fill as necessary.

FLUSHING

✳✳ WARNING

Always allow the engine to cool before opening the cooling system. Do not unscrew the coolant pressure relief cap when the engine is operating or the cooling system is hot. The cooling system is under pressure; steam and hot liquid can come out forcefully when the cap is loosened slightly. Failure to follow these instructions may result in serious personal injury.

1. Drain the cooling system as outlined in this section.

2. Remove the thermostat as outlined in this section.

3. Install the coolant hose connection without the thermostat. Tighten the bolts to 89 inch lbs. (10 Nm).

➡ Refer to the cooling system Pro Flush and Fill operating instructions for specific vehicle hook-up.

4. Use cooling system Pro Flush and Fill, Flush Kit and Drain Kit to flush the cooling system.

   a. Use Motorcraft® Premium Cooling System Flush. Follow the directions on the packaging.

5. Install the thermostat as outlined in this section.

6. Fill the cooling system as outlined in this section.

BLOCK HEATER

REMOVAL & INSTALLATION

See Figures 49 through 51.

1. Drain the cooling system as outlined in this section.

Fig. 49 Remove the block heater

2. Disconnect the block heater electrical connector.

Vehicles equipped with a split ring design block heater

➡Use a 1 1/4 in, 12-point flare nut crowfoot wrench (such as Snap-on® stock number AN850820B, or equivalent) to remove the block heater.

3. Remove the block heater.

Vehicles equipped with a V-lock design block heater

4. Remove the block heater retaining nut and the block heater, then remove the V-lock and the threaded rod.

To install:

➡Install only a V-lock design block heater.

5. Clean the engine block mating surface with Motorcraft® Metal Surface Prep. Follow the directions on the packaging.

6. Position the block heater and finger-tighten the nut, making sure the block heater electrical connector points to the 8 o'clock position.

7. Tighten the block heater nut. Tighten the nut to 27 inch lbs. (3 Nm).

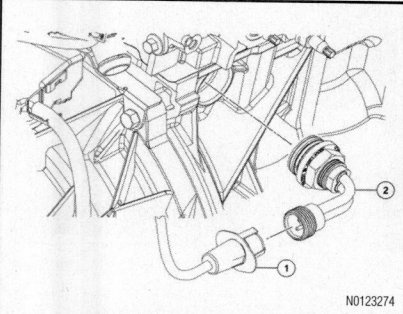

Fig. 50 Split Ring Design exploded view. Block heater wiring harness (1), Block heater (2)

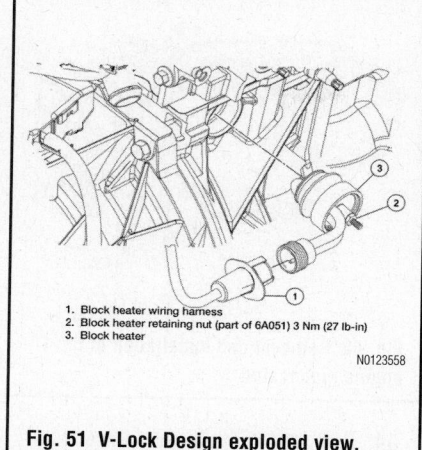

1. Block heater wiring harness
2. Block heater retaining nut (part of 6A051) 3 Nm (27 lb-in)
3. Block heater

Fig. 51 V-Lock Design exploded view.

✷✷ WARNING

Route the block heater power cable away from hot or rotating components, or the cable can be damaged.

8. Connect the electrical connector.

9. Fill and bleed the cooling system as outlined in this section.

COOLANT (WATER) PUMP

REMOVAL & INSTALLATION

See Figures 52 through 64.

All vehicles

1. Drain the cooling system as outlined in this section.

2. Loosen the 4 coolant pump pulley bolts.

3. Remove the accessory drive belt.

Vehicles with A/C

4. Remove the 2 bolts, the studbolt, and position the A/C compressor aside and support it with a length of mechanic's wire.

Vehicles without A/C

5. Remove the 3 bolts and the accessory drive belt idler pulley bracket.

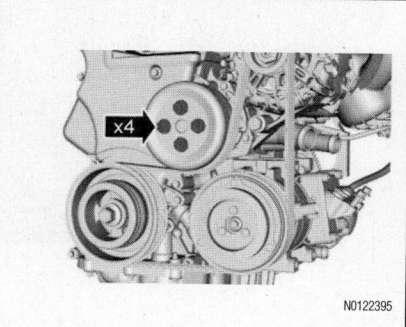

Fig. 52 Loosen the 4 coolant pump pulley bolts

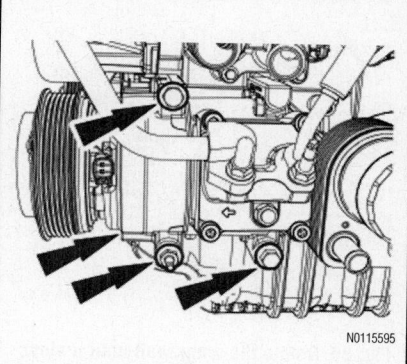

Fig. 53 Remove the 2 bolts, the studbolt, and position the A/C compressor aside and support it with a length of mechanic's wire

All vehicles

6. Remove the engine plug bolt.

➡The Crankshaft Top Dead Center (TDC) Pin will contact the crankshaft and prevent it from turning past TDC. However, the crankshaft can still be rotated in the counterclockwise direction. The crankshaft must remain at the TDC position during the coolant pump removal and installation.

7. Install the Crankshaft TDC Pin.

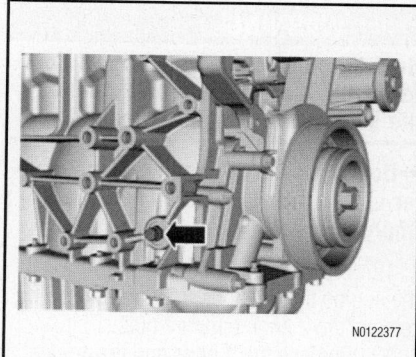

Fig. 54 Remove the engine plug bolt

Fig. 55 Install the Crankshaft TDC Pin

Fig. 56 Rotate the crankshaft until it stops against the Crankshaft TDC Pin

➡ **Only rotate the crankshaft in the clockwise direction.**

8. Rotate the crankshaft until it stops against the Crankshaft TDC Pin.

Vehicles with A/C

9. Remove the nut and position the A/C bracket aside.

All Vehicles

10. Release the 2 tabs and position the degas bottle aside.

➡ **Use a wooden block to protect the oil pan when supporting the engine**

11. Using a floor jack and a block of wood, support the engine.

✳✳ WARNING

Hold the engine mount studs while removing the engine mount nuts or the powertrain may be damaged.

➡ **Do not loosen the engine mount center bolt or the engine may become improperly positioned.**

12. Using the holding feature to prevent the engine mount studs from turning, remove the 2 engine mount nuts.

13. Remove the 3 bolts and the engine mount.

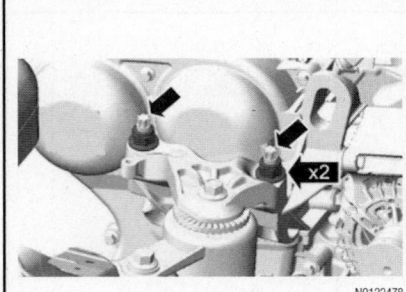

Fig. 57 Using the holding feature to prevent the engine mount studs from turning, remove the 2 engine mount nuts

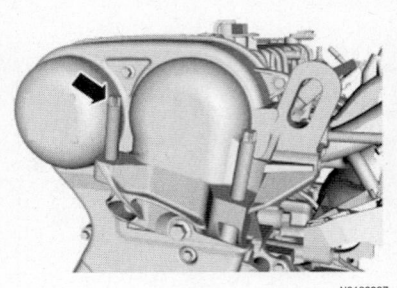

Fig. 58 Removal and installation of the 1 engine mount stud

14. Remove the 4 bolts and the coolant pump pulley.

15. Remove the 1 engine mount stud.

16. Remove the 9 bolts and the timing belt cover.

✳✳ WARNING

Do not rotate the crankshaft while installing the special tool or the engine may be damaged.

17. Hold the timing belt in position.

18. Install the Timing Belt Holding Tools in 3 places as shown.

19. Mark the position of the timing belt for assembly reference.

Fig. 60 Rotate the timing belt tensioner clockwise. Align the 2 holes on the tensioner and install a small screwdriver or holding pin

20. Release the timing belt tension.
   a. Rotate the timing belt tensioner clockwise.
   b. Align the 2 holes on the tensioner and install a small screwdriver or holding pin.

21. Remove the bolt and the timing belt tensioner. Discard the bolt.

22. Remove the 6 bolts, the coolant pump and the gasket. Discard the gasket.

To install:
All Vehicles

23. Clean the sealing surfaces with metal surface prep. Follow the directions on the packaging.

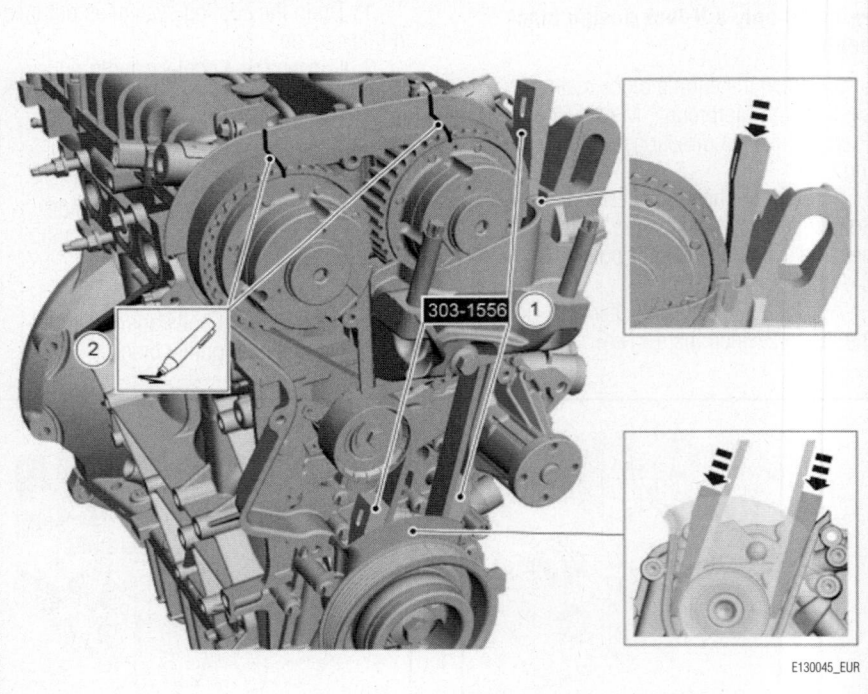

Fig. 59 Mark the position of the timing belt for assembly reference

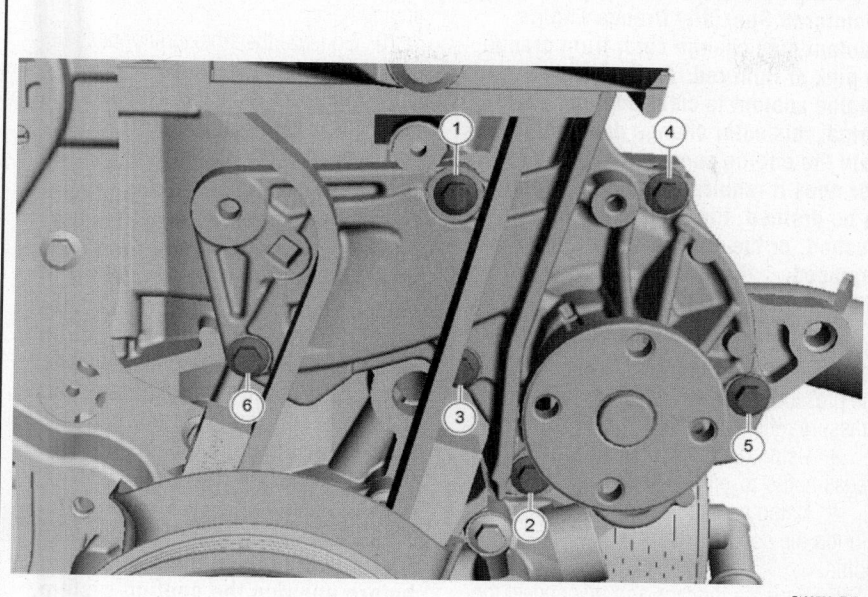

Fig. 61 Removal and installation of the 6 bolts, the coolant pump and the gasket

24. Install a new gasket, the coolant pump and the 6 bolts.

25. Tighten the bolts in the proper sequence to 89 inch lbs. (10 Nm).

26. Position the timing belt tensioner and install a new bolt. Tighten to 177 inch lbs. (20 Nm).

27. Make sure the timing belt is in the position noted during removal.

28. Remove the timing belt tensioner holding tool.

29. Remove the Timing Belt Holding Tools.

30. Make sure the timing belt is in the position noted during removal.

31. Remove the 3 Timing Belt Holding Tools.

32. Remove the Crankshaft TDC Pin.

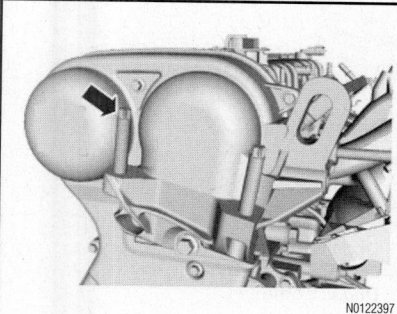

Fig. 62 Removal and installation of the 1 engine mount stud

33. Install the engine plug bolt. Tighten the bolt to 177 inch lbs. (20 Nm).

34. Position the timing belt cover and install the 9 bolts. Tighten the bolts to 80 inch lbs. (9 Nm).

35. Position the coolant pump pulley and install the 4 bolts finger tight.

36. Install the 1 engine mount stud finger tight.

✸✸ WARNING

The 2 engine mount studs must be tightened to specification or the powertrain may be damaged.

37. Tighten the 2 engine mount studs to specification before installing the engine mount nuts. Tighten the studs to 71 inch lbs. (8 Nm).

➡ **Do not loosen the engine mount center bolt or the engine may become improperly positioned.**

38. Position the engine mount and install the 2 nuts. Tighten the nuts to 59 ft. lbs. (80 Nm).

39. Install the 3 engine mount bolts finger tight.

40. Remove the jack and the wood block.

41. Tighten the 3 engine mount bolts. Tighten the bolts to 35 ft. lbs. (48 Nm).

42. Install the degas bottle.

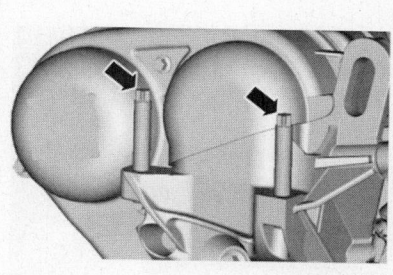

Fig. 63 Tighten the 2 engine mount studs to specification before installing the engine mount nuts

Fig. 64 Remove the 2 bolts, the studbolt, and position the A/C compressor aside and support it with a length of mechanic's wire

Vehicles with A/C

43. Position the A/C bracket and install the nut. Tighten the nut to 89 inch lbs. (10 Nm).

44. Position the A/C compressor and install the 2 bolts and the studbolt. Tighten the bolts to 18 ft. lbs. (24 Nm).

Vehicles without A/C

45. Position the accessory drive belt idler pulley bracket and install the 3 bolts. Tighten the bolts to 18 ft. lbs. (24 Nm).

All vehicles

46. Install the accessory drive belt. For additional information, refer to Accessory Drive.

47. Tighten the 4 coolant pump pulley bolts. Tighten the bolts to 177 inch lbs. (20 Nm).

48. Fill and bleed the cooling system as outlined in this section.

COOLING FAN MOTOR AND SHROUD

REMOVAL & INSTALLATION
See Figure 65.

1. Remove the air cleaner as outlined in the Engine Mechanical Section.

Fig. 65 Detach the transmission vent hose from the cooling fan and shroud

2. Detach the transmission vent hose from the cooling fan and shroud.

3. Detach the upper 2 wiring harness pushpins from the cooling fan shroud.

4. Release the 2 cooling fan shroud clips.

5. Detach the lower 2 wiring harness pushpins from the cooling fan shroud and disconnect the cooling fan electrical connector.

6. Remove the cooling fan and shroud.

To install:

7. Install the cooling fan and shroud.

8. Attach the lower 2 wiring harness pushpins to the cooling fan shroud and connect the cooling fan electrical connector.

9. Engage the 2 cooling fan shroud clips.

10. Attach the upper 2 wiring harness pushpins to the cooling fan shroud.

11. Attach the transmission vent hose to the cooling fan and shroud.

12. Install the air cleaner as outlined in the Engine Mechanical Section.

DEGAS BOTTLE

REMOVAL & INSTALLATION

See Figure 66.

1. Remove the A/C tube bracket nut and detach the bracket from the stud.

✴✴ CAUTION

Always allow the engine to cool before opening the cooling system. Do not unscrew the coolant pressure relief cap when the engine is operating or the cooling system is hot. The cooling system is under pressure; steam and hot liquid can come out forcefully when the cap is loosened slightly. Failure to follow these instructions may result in serious personal injury.

➡**During normal vehicle operation, Motorcraft Specialty Orange Engine Coolant may change color from orange to pink or light red. As long as the engine coolant is clear and uncontaminated, this color change does not indicate the engine coolant has degraded nor does it require the engine coolant to be drained, the system to be flushed, or the engine coolant to be replaced.**

2. Release the pressure in the cooling system by slowly turning the pressure relief cap one half turn counterclockwise. When the pressure has been released, remove the pressure relief cap.

3. Using hose pinch pliers, clamp the degas bottle-to-engine hose.

4. Using a suitable suction device, siphon the coolant from the degas bottle.

5. Squeeze the tabs and disconnect the engine-to-degas bottle hose.

6. Release the 2 clips and lift the degas bottle hose to access the degas bottle-to-engine hose.

7. Release the clamp, disconnect the degas bottle-to-engine hose and remove the degas bottle.

To install:

8. Engage the clamp, connect the degas bottle-to-engine hose and remove the degas bottle.

9. Engage the 2 clips and lift the degas

bottle hose to access the degas bottle-to-engine hose.

10. Squeeze the tabs and connect the engine-to-degas bottle hose.

11. Release the hose pinch pliers from the degas bottle-to-engine hose.

12. Replace the pressure relief cap.

➡**During normal vehicle operation, Motorcraft Specialty Orange Engine Coolant may change color from orange to pink or light red. As long as the engine coolant is clear and uncontaminated, this color change does not indicate the engine coolant has degraded nor does it require the engine coolant to be drained, the system to be flushed, or the engine coolant to be replaced.**

✴✴ CAUTION

Always allow the engine to cool before opening the cooling system. Do not unscrew the coolant pressure relief cap when the engine is operating or the cooling system is hot. The cooling system is under pressure; steam and hot liquid can come out forcefully when the cap is loosened slightly. Failure to follow these instructions may result in serious personal injury.

13. Install the A/C tube bracket nut and detach the bracket from the stud. Tighten the nut to 89 inch lbs. (10 Nm).

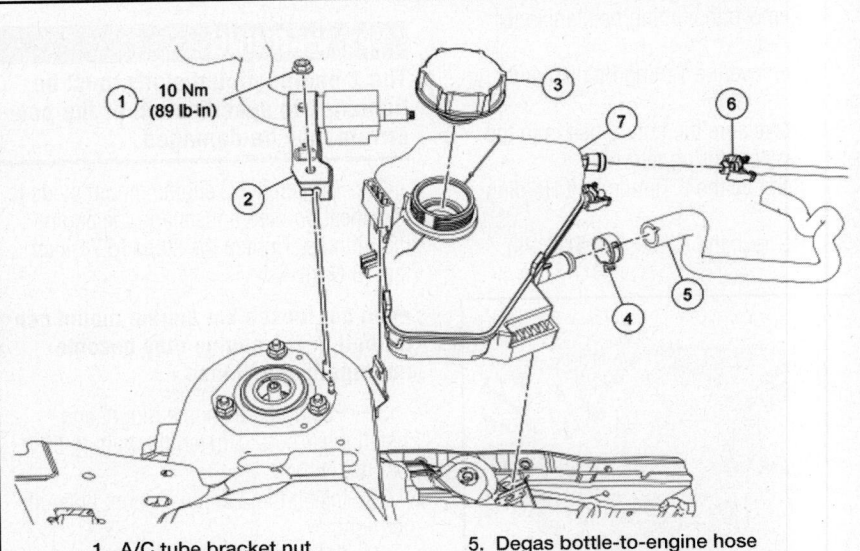

1. A/C tube bracket nut
2. A/C tube bracket
3. Pressure relief cap
4. Degas bottle-to-engine hose clamp
5. Degas bottle-to-engine hose
6. Engine-to-degas bottle hose
7. Degas bottle

Fig. 66 Degas bottle components exploded view

14. Fill the degas bottle with a 50/50 mixture of Motorcraft® Specialty Orange Engine Coolant and distilled water.

RADIATOR

REMOVAL & INSTALLATION

See Figure 67.

All Vehicles

1. Remove the cooling fan motor and shroud as outlined in this section.
2. Drain the cooling system as outlined in this section.
3. Release the clamp and disconnect the upper radiator hose from the radiator.
4. Remove the trim pushpin on the LH side of the grille.
5. Remove the 2 radiator clips and the 2 rubber grommets.

Vehicles with A/C

6. Release the 2 A/C condenser clips from the radiator and push the radiator up and the A/C condenser down to detach the condenser from the radiator.

All vehicles

7. Tilt the top of the radiator toward the engine, lift the radiator off the radiator supports and remove the radiator.

To install:

Vehicles with A/C

8. Position the radiator in the vehicle, slide the A/C condenser into the top slots on the radiator and clip the A/C condenser to the bottom of the radiator.
9. Position the radiator and A/C condenser assembly on the radiator supports.

Vehicles without A/C

10. Position the radiator on the radiator supports.

All Vehicles

11. Install the 2 rubber grommets and the 2 radiator clips.
12. Install the trim pushpin on the LH side of the grille.

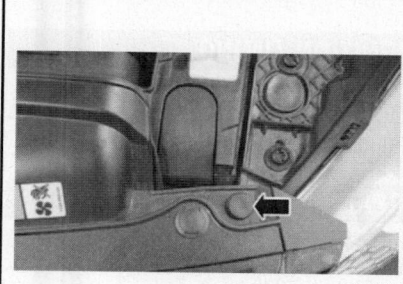

Fig. 67 Remove the trim pushpin on the LH side of the grille

13. Connect the upper radiator hose and position the clamp.
14. Install the cooling fan motor and shroud as outlined in this section.
15. Fill and bleed the cooling system as outlined in this section.

THERMOSTAT

REMOVAL & INSTALLATION

See Figures 68 through 70

1. Drain the cooling system as outlined in this section.
2. Remove the generator. For additional information, refer to Charging System.
3. Release the clamp and disconnect the lower radiator hose from the coolant connection.
4. Release the clamp and disconnect the oil cooler hose from the coolant connection.
5. Remove the 4 bolts, the coolant connection and the gasket.
   a. Discard the gasket.
6. Remove the thermostat and the O-ring seal.
   a. Discard the O-ring seal.

To install:

7. Position the thermostat and use new O-ring seal.
8. Position the thermostat with the weep hole at the 12 o'clock position.
9. Position a new gasket, the coolant connection and install the 4 bolts finger tight. Tighten the bolts in the proper sequence in 2 stages.
   a. Stage 1: Tighten to 18 inch lbs. 2 Nm).
   b. Stage 2: Tighten to 89 inch lbs. (10 Nm).

Fig. 69 Position the thermostat with the weep hole at the 12 o'clock position

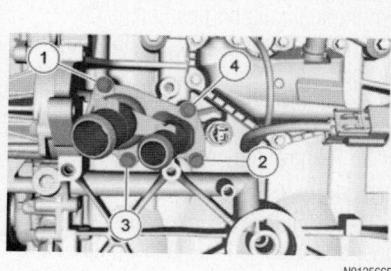

Fig. 70 Position a new gasket, the coolant connection and install the 4 bolts finger tight

10. Connect the oil cooler hose to the coolant connection and position the clamp.
11. Connect the lower radiator hose to the coolant connection and position the clamp.
12. Install the generator. For additional information, refer to Charging System.
13. Fill and bleed the cooling system as outlined in this section.

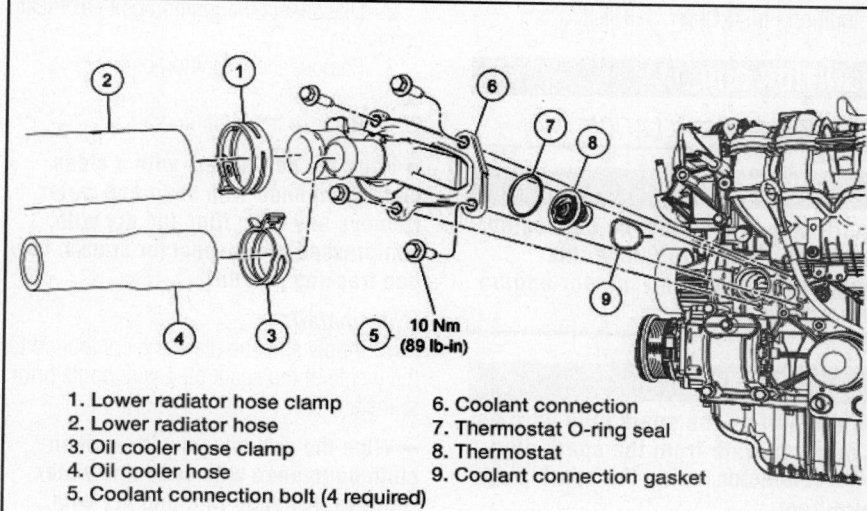

1. Lower radiator hose clamp
2. Lower radiator hose
3. Oil cooler hose clamp
4. Oil cooler hose
5. Coolant connection bolt (4 required)
6. Coolant connection
7. Thermostat O-ring seal
8. Thermostat
9. Coolant connection gasket

10 Nm (89 lb-in)

Fig. 68 Thermostat components exploded view

ENGINE ELECTRICAL

ALTERNATOR (GENERATOR)

REMOVAL & INSTALLATION

See Figure 71.

1. Disconnect the battery.
2. Remove the accessory drive belt as outlined in the Engine Mechanical Section.
3. Remove the generator B+ terminal protective cover and nut. Position the generator B+ terminal aside.
4. Disconnect the generator electrical connector.
5. Detach the upper degas bottle hose from the fuel rail and position aside.
6. Remove the generator nut and the stud bolt.
7. Remove the upper and lower generator bolts.
8. Remove the generator.

To install:

9. Install the generator and generator upper and lower bolts. Hand-tighten the bolts. Do not torque the bolt at this time.
10. Install the generator stud bolt. Tighten the bolt to 89 inch lbs. (10 Nm).
11. Install the generator nut. Tighten the nut to 35 ft. lbs. (48 Nm).
12. Tighten the generator upper and lower bolts. Tighten the bolts to 35 ft. lbs. (48 Nm).
13. Attach the upper degas bottle hose to the fuel rail.

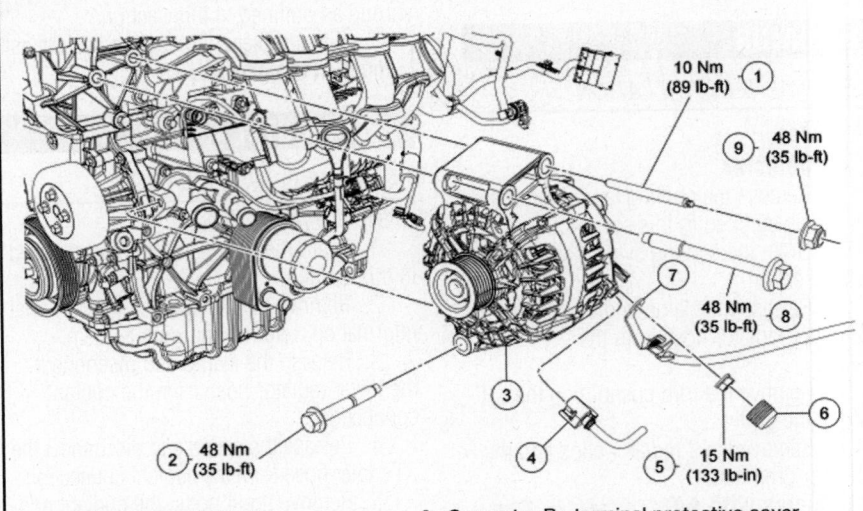

1. Generator stud bolt
2. Lower generator bolt
3. Generator
4. Generator electrical connector
5. Generator B+ terminal nut
6. Generator B+ terminal protective cover
7. Generator B+ terminal
8. Upper generator bolt
9. Generator nut

N0117160

Fig. 71 Alternator components exploded view

14. Connect the generator electrical connector.
15. Position the generator B+ terminal on the generator and install the nut. Tighten the nut to 133 inch lbs. (15 Nm).
16. Install the generator B+ terminal protective cover.
17. Install the accessory drive belt as outlined in the Engine Mechanical Section.
18. Connect the battery.

ENGINE ELECTRICAL

FIRING ORDER

Ignition Firing Order: 1-3-4-2.

IGNITION COIL

REMOVAL & INSTALLATION

✹✹ WARNING

Spark plug wires must be connected correctly. Failure to follow this instruction may result in poor engine performance.

✹✹ WARNING

Do not pull on the spark plug wire as it may separate from the spark plug wire connector inside the spark plug wire boot.

1. Disconnect the spark plug wires from the ignition coil by slightly twisting while pulling upwards.
2. Disconnect the ignition coil electrical connector.
3. Remove the 4 ignition coil bolts.
4. Remove the ignition coil.

➡ **Wipe the coil towers with a clean cloth dampened with soap and water. Remove any soap film and dry with compressed air. Inspect for cracks, carbon tracking and dirt.**

To install:

5. Apply silicone dielectric compound to the inside of the spark plug wire boots prior to installation.

➡ **Wipe the coil towers with a clean cloth dampened with soap and water. Remove any soap film and dry with compressed air. Inspect for cracks, carbon tracking and dirt.**

6. Install the ignition coil.
7. Install the 4 ignition coil bolts. Tighten the bolts to 53 inch lbs. (6 Nm).
8. Connect the ignition coil electrical connector.
9. Connect the spark plug wires from the ignition coil by slightly twisting while pulling upwards.

IGNITION TIMING

ADJUSTMENT

Ignition timing is not adjustable.

SPARK PLUGS

REMOVAL & INSTALLATION

See Figures 72 through 74.

1. Detach the spark plug wire if routed through another spark plug wire.

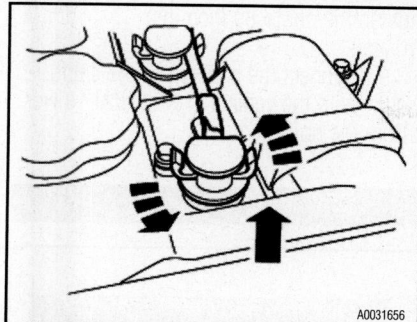

Fig. 72 Disconnect the spark plug wires from the spark plugs by slightly twisting while pulling upwards

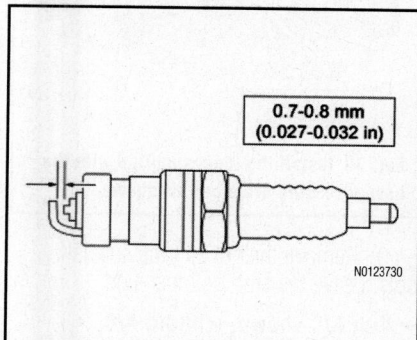

0.7-0.8 mm
(0.027-0.032 in)

Fig. 73 Check and adjust the spark plug gap

※※ **WARNING**

Spark plug wires must be connected correctly. Failure to follow this

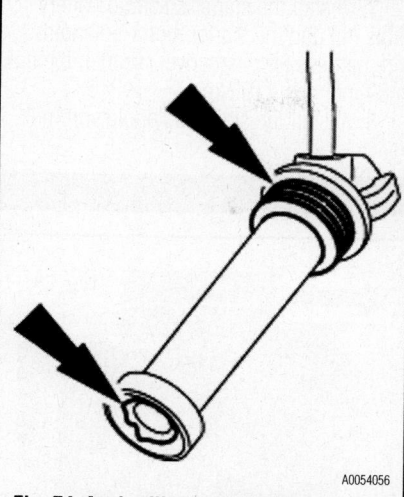

Fig. 74 Apply silicone dielectric compound

instruction may result in poor engine performance.

※※ **WARNING**

Do not pull on the spark plug wire as it may separate from the spark plug wire connector inside the spark plug wire boot.

2. Disconnect the spark plug wires from the spark plugs by slightly twisting while pulling upwards.

➡Remove any foreign material with compressed air.

3. Remove the spark plugs.
4. Inspect the spark plugs.
5. Check and adjust the spark plug gap as necessary.

To install:

6. Apply silicone dielectric compound.
7. Check and adjust the spark plug gap as necessary.
8. Inspect the spark plugs.

➡Remove any foreign material with compressed air.

9. Install the spark plugs. Tighten the plugs to 133 inch lbs. (15 Nm).

※※ **WARNING**

Spark plug wires must be connected correctly. Failure to follow this instruction may result in poor engine performance.

※※ **WARNING**

Do not pull on the spark plug wire as it may separate from the spark plug wire connector inside the spark plug wire boot.

10. Connect the spark plug wires to the spark plugs by slightly twisting while pushing downward..
11. Attach the spark plug wire if routed through another spark plug wire.

ENGINE ELECTRICAL

STARTER

REMOVAL & INSTALLATION
See Figure 75.

※※ **CAUTION**

Always disconnect the battery ground cable at the battery before disconnecting the starter motor battery terminal lead. If a tool is shorted at the starter motor battery terminal, the tool can quickly heat enough to cause a skin burn. Failure to follow this instruction may result in serious personal injury.

1. With the vehicle in NEUTRAL, position it on a hoist.
2. Disconnect the battery ground cable.
3. Remove the starter solenoid wire nut.
4. Remove the starter solenoid battery cable nut and the starter motor solenoid wire harness terminal cover.

STARTING SYSTEM

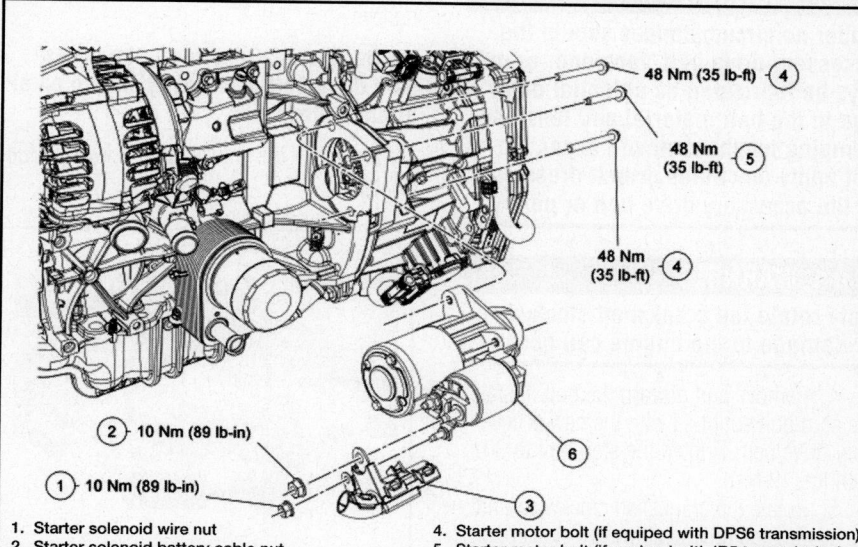

48 Nm (35 lb-ft) — ④

48 Nm (35 lb-ft) ⑤

48 Nm (35 lb-ft) ④

② 10 Nm (89 lb-in)

① 10 Nm (89 lb-in)

⑥

③

1. Starter solenoid wire nut
2. Starter solenoid battery cable nut
3. Starter motor solenoid wire harness terminal cover
4. Starter motor bolt (if equiped with IB5 transmission)
4. Starter motor bolt (if equiped with DPS6 transmission)
5. Starter motor bolt (if equiped with IB5 transmission)
5. Starter motor bolt (if equiped with DPS6 transmission)
6. Starter motor

Fig. 75 Starter motor exploded view

5. Remove the bolts and the starter motor.

To install:

6. Install the bolts and the starter motor. Tighten the bolts to 35 ft. lbs. (48 Nm).

7. Install the starter solenoid battery cable nut and the starter motor solenoid wire harness terminal cover. Tighten the nut to 89 inch lbs. (10 Nm).

8. Install the starter solenoid wire nut.

Tighten the nut to 89 inch lbs. (10 Nm).

9. Connect the battery ground cable.

10. With the vehicle in NEUTRAL, lower it from the hoist.

ENGINE MECHANICAL

→Disconnecting the negative battery cable may interfere with the functions of the on board computer systems and may require the computer to undergo a relearning process, once the negative battery cable is reconnected.

ACCESSORY DRIVE BELTS

REMOVAL & INSTALLATION

See Figures 76 through 80.

✳✳ WARNING

Under no circumstances should the accessory drive belt, tensioner or pulleys be lubricated as potential damage to the belt material and tensioner damping mechanism will occur. Do not apply any fluids or belt dressing to the accessory drive belt or pulleys.

1. With the vehicle in NEUTRAL, position it on a hoist.

2. Remove the 2 bolts and the accessory drive belt splash shield.

3. Cut and discard accessory drive belt.

To install:

✳✳ WARNING

Under no circumstances should the accessory drive belt, tensioner or pulleys be lubricated as potential damage to the belt material and tensioner damping mechanism will occur. Do not apply any fluids or belt dressing to the accessory drive belt or pulleys.

✳✳ WARNING

Only rotate the crankshaft clockwise or damage to the engine can occur.

4. Remove and discard the bolt. Install the stud bolt supplied with the new accessory drive belt. Tighten the stud bolt to 80 inch lbs. (9 Nm).

5. Rotate the crankshaft clockwise until the designated hole Is at the 5 o'clock position.

6. Install the tools supplied with the new accessory drive belt.

   a. Install the supplied nut finger tight.

E105355_EUR

Fig. 76 Remove and discard the bolt. Install the stud bolt supplied with the new accessory drive belt

→**Without A/C shown, with A/C similar.**

7. Position the accessory drive belt onto the coolant pump, generator and idler pulleys.

→**After installation, verify the accessory drive belt is correctly seated on all of the pulleys.**

8. Rotate the crankshaft clockwise 1 full rotation.

E105356_EUR

Fig. 77 Rotate the crankshaft clockwise until the designated hole Is at the 5 o'clock position

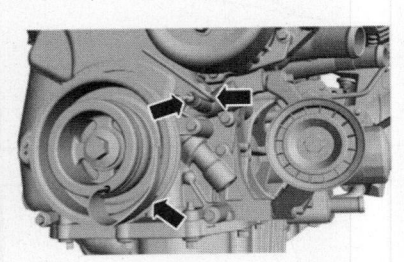

E101529_EUR

Fig. 78 Install the tools supplied with the new accessory drive belt as shown

9. Remove the nut and the special tools. Leave the stud bolt installed.

→**With A/C shown, without A/C similar.**

10. Verify the accessory drive belt is correctly seated on all of the pulleys.

11. Position the accessory drive belt splash shield and install the 2 bolts. Tighten the bolts to 80 inch lbs. (9 Nm).

E101530_EUR

Fig. 79 Position the accessory drive belt onto the coolant pump, generator and idler pulleys as shown

Fig. 80 Verify the accessory drive belt is correctly seated on all of the pulleys

AIR CLEANER

REMOVAL & INSTALLATION

See Figure 81.

At the time of publication, Ford does not provide a specific removal and installation procedure for the Front Half-shaft. When servicing this component, please heed all notes, warnings and cautions, and refer to the accompanying illustration. Items in the exploded view may NOT be listed in order of removal.

CAMSHAFT AND VALVE LIFTERS

REMOVAL & INSTALLATION

See Figures 82 through 87.

⁂ WARNING

During engine repair procedures, cleanliness is extremely important. Any foreign material (including any material created while cleaning gasket surfaces) that enters the oil passages, coolant passages or the oil pan can cause engine failure.

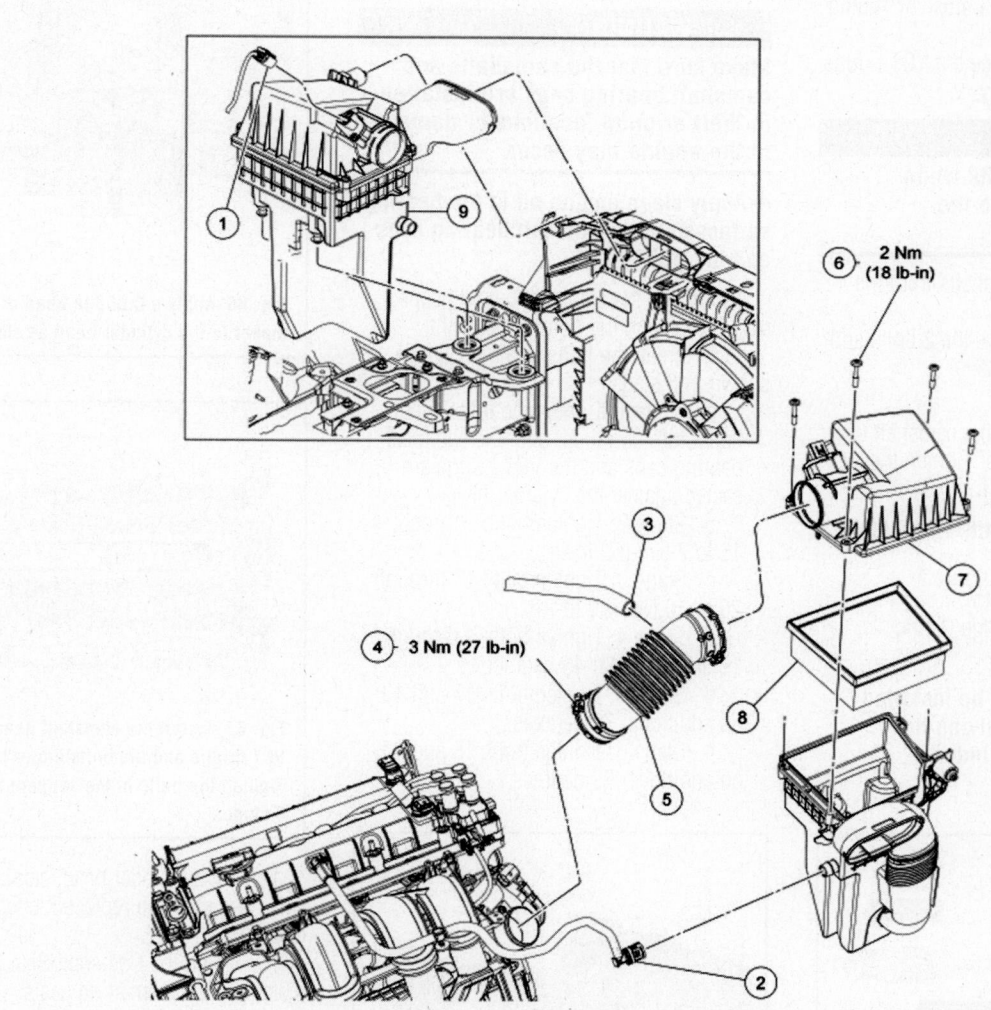

1. Mass Air Flow (MAF) sensor electrical connector
2. Crankcase ventilation tube
3. Brake booster vacuum tube assembly
4. Air Cleaner (ACL) outlet pipe clamp (2 required)
5. ACL outlet pipe
6. ACL cover screw (4 required)
7. ACL cover
8. ACL element
9. ACL assembly

Fig. 81 Intake Air System components exploded view

✳✳ WARNING

Do not rotate the camshafts unless instructed to in this procedure. Rotating the camshafts or crankshaft with timing components loosened or removed can cause serious damage to the valves and pistons.

1. Remove the camshaft phaser and sprockets.
2. Using the Input Shaft Oil Seal Remover and Slide Hammer, remove the 2 camshaft oil seals.

➡**Note the position of each component before removal.**

3. Remove the bolts for the camshaft bearing caps and Variable Camshaft Timing (VCT) bridge.
   a. Inspect and replace the VCT bridge O-ring seal, if necessary.

✳✳ WARNING

Do not pry on camshafts when removing or damage to the camshafts may occur.

4. Remove the 2 camshafts from the cylinder head.
5. If necessary, remove the 2 bolts and the camshaft trigger wheels.

To install:

6. If removed, install the camshaft trigger wheels and the 2 bolts. Tighten the bolts to 15 ft. lbs. (21 Nm).

➡**Lubricate the camshafts with clean engine oil.**

7. Install the camshafts.
8. Install the VCT bridge O-ring seal.

➡**The VCT bridge must be installed within 5 minutes of applying the gasket maker to the cylinder head.**

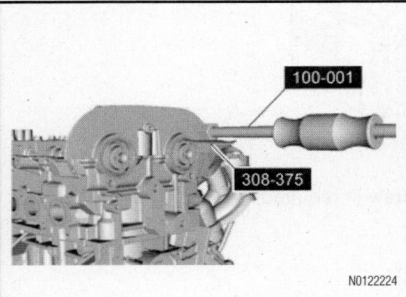

Fig. 82 Using the Input Shaft Oil Seal Remover and Slide Hammer, remove the 2 camshaft oil seals.

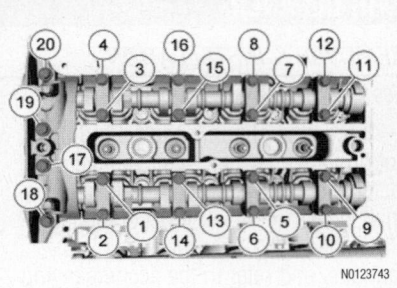

Fig. 83 Remove the bolts for the camshaft bearing caps and Variable Camshaft Timing (VCT) bridge in the sequence shown

9. Apply a 0.059 in bead of gasket maker to the cylinder head.

✳✳ WARNING

Make sure that the camshafts and camshaft bearing caps are installed in their original locations or damage to the engine may occur.

➡**Apply clean engine oil to the bearing surfaces of the camshaft bearing caps and the VCT bridge.**

10. Install the camshaft bearing caps, VCT bridge and the bolts finger tight.
11. Tighten the bolts in the sequence shown in 6 stages.
   a. Stage 1: Tighten the bolts evenly, half a turn at a time, until the camshaft bearing caps and the VCT bridge are seated against the cylinder head.
   b. Stage 2: Tighten bolts 1 through 16 to 7 Nm (62 lb-in).
   c. Stage 3: Tighten bolts 17 through 20 to 10 Nm (89 lb-in).
   d. Stage 4: Tighten bolts 1 through 16 an additional 45 degrees.
   e. Stage 5: Tighten bolts 17 and 19 an additional 70 degrees.
   f. Stage 6: Tighten bolts 18 and 20 an additional 53 degrees.

Fig. 84 If necessary, remove the 2 bolts and the camshaft trigger wheels.

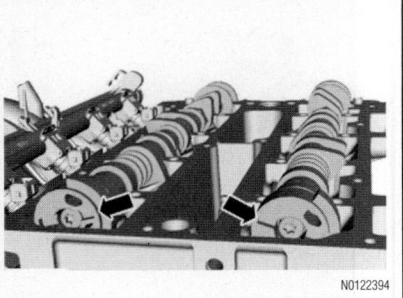

Fig. 85 Install the camshafts as shown

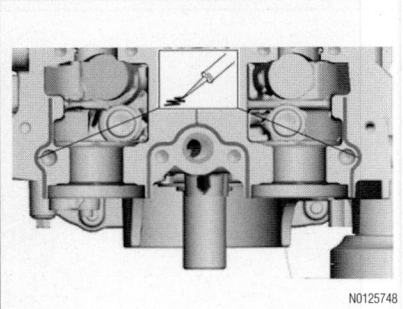

Fig. 86 Apply a 0.059 in bead of gasket maker to the cylinder head as shown

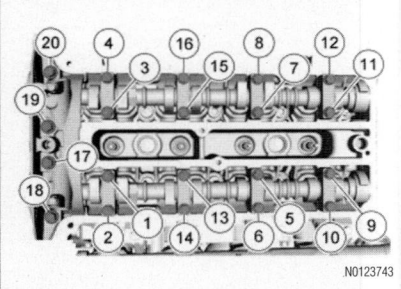

Fig. 87 Install the camshaft bearing caps, VCT bridge and the bolts finger tight. Tighten the bolts in the sequence shown in 6 stages

12. If the cylinder head, camshafts or valve tappets were replaced, check the valve clearance.
13. Using the Camshaft Seal Installer, install the 2 camshaft oil seals.
14. Install the camshaft phaser and sprocket.

CAMSHAFT PHASER AND SPROCKET

REMOVAL & INSTALLATION

See Figures 88 through 91.

⁂ **WARNING**

Do not loosen or remove the crankshaft pulley bolt without first installing the special tools. The crankshaft pulley and the crankshaft timing sprocket are not keyed to the crankshaft. Before any repair requiring loosening or removal of the crankshaft pulley bolt, the crankshaft and camshafts must be locked in place by the special service tools, otherwise severe engine damage can occur.

⁂ **WARNING**

During engine repair procedures, cleanliness is extremely important. Any foreign material, including any material created while cleaning gasket surfaces, that enters the oil passages, coolant passages or the oil pan can cause engine failure.

1. With the vehicle in NEUTRAL, position it on a hoist.
2. Remove the valve cover as outlined in this section.
3. Remove the timing belt as outlined in this section.
4. Remove the VCT Alignment Tool.

→Use an open-ended wrench to hold the camshafts by the hexagon to prevent the camshafts from turning.

5. Remove the 2 camshaft phaser and sprocket plugs.

→Use an open-ended wrench to hold the camshafts by the hexagon to prevent the camshafts from turning.

6. Remove the 2 bolts and the camshaft phaser and sprockets.

To install:
7. Loosen the 2 bolts for the LH engine lift eye.

→It may be necessary to use an open-ended wrench to turn the camshafts by the hexagon to align the camshafts.

8. Install the Camshaft Alignment Plate into the end of the camshafts.

→Use an open-ended wrench to hold the camshafts by the hexagon to prevent the camshafts from turning.

→The timing marks of the camshaft phaser and sprocket must be at the 12 o'clock position.

9. Install the 2 camshaft phaser and sprocket, bolts and the VCT Alignment

Fig. 89 Remove the 2 camshaft phaser and sprocket plugs

Fig. 90 Install the Camshaft Alignment Plate into the end of the camshafts.

Tool. Tighten the 2 bolts to 18 ft. lbs. (25 Nm).
10. Remove the VCT Alignment Tool.
11. Remove the Camshaft Alignment Plate.

→Use an open-ended wrench to hold the camshafts by the hexagon to prevent the camshafts from turning.

12. Tighten the 2 camshaft phaser and sprocket bolts an additional 75°.

⁂ **WARNING**

The special tool can only be installed if the valve timing is correct.

13. Install the Camshaft Alignment Plate into the end of the camshafts.

→The special tool can only be installed if the valve timing is correct.

14. Install the VCT Alignment Tool.
   a. If the special tools cannot be installed, repeat the adjustment according to the preceding steps.
15. Remove the VCT Alignment Tool.
16. Remove the Camshaft Alignment Plate.

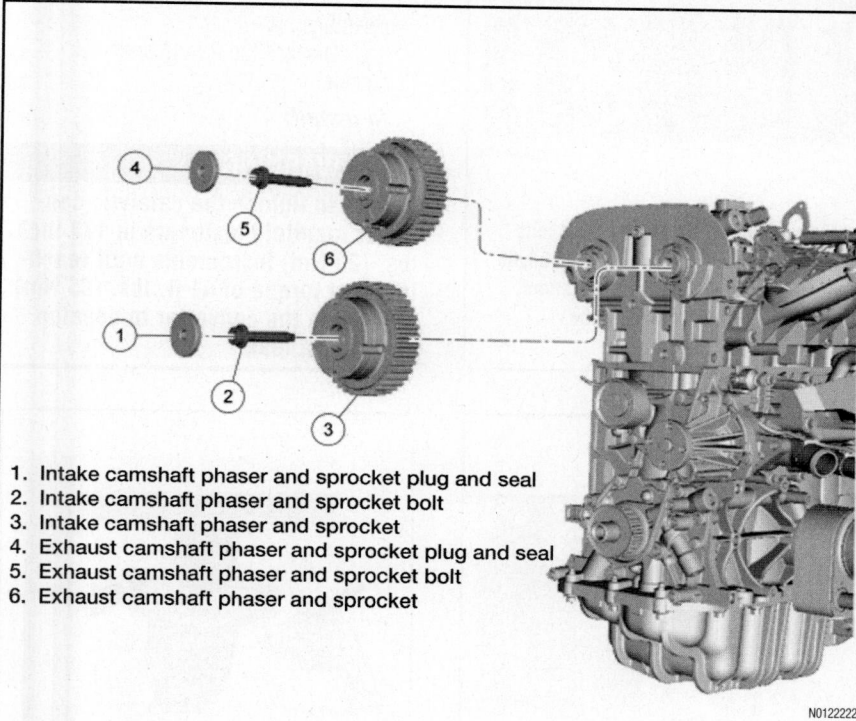

1. Intake camshaft phaser and sprocket plug and seal
2. Intake camshaft phaser and sprocket bolt
3. Intake camshaft phaser and sprocket
4. Exhaust camshaft phaser and sprocket plug and seal
5. Exhaust camshaft phaser and sprocket bolt
6. Exhaust camshaft phaser and sprocket

Fig. 88 Camshaft Phaser and sprocket components exploded view

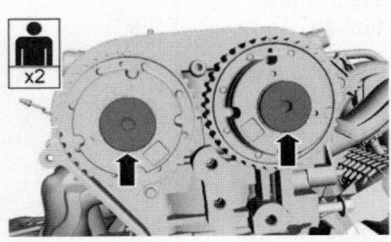

Fig. 91 Install the 2 camshaft phaser and sprocket plugs

→**Use an open-ended wrench to hold the camshafts by the hexagon to prevent the camshafts from turning.**

17. Install the 2 camshaft phaser and sprocket plugs. Tighten the plugs to 142 inch lbs. (16 Nm).

18. Install the VCT Alignment Tool.

19. Install the timing belt as outlined in this section.

20. Tighten the 2 bolts for the LH engine lift eye. Tighten the bolts to 168 inch lbs. (19 Nm).

21. Install the valve cover as outlined in this section.

CATALYTIC CONVERTER

REMOVAL & INSTALLATION

See Figures 92 through 96.

❉❉ **WARNING**

Exhaust fasteners are of a torque prevailing design. Use only new fasteners with the same part number as the original. Torque values must be used as specified during reassembly to make sure of correct retention of exhaust components.

1. With the vehicle in NEUTRAL, position it on a hoist.

2. Remove the Heated Oxygen Sensor (HO2S) as outlined in the Engine Performance & Emission Control Section.

3. Remove the 4 bolts and position aside the heat shield.

4. Remove and discard the 4 nuts and 1 bolt.

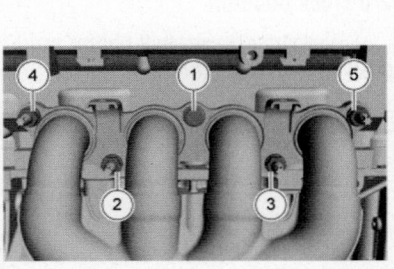

Fig. 93 Remove and discard the 4 nuts and 1 bolt. Install a new gasket, catalytic converter assembly and new fasteners. Tighten the bolt and 4 nuts in the sequence shown, in 3 stages

5. Remove the RH halfshaft as outlined in the Drive Train Section.

6. Remove the Catalyst Monitor Sensor (CMS) as outlined in the Engine Performance & Emission Controls Section.

7. Remove the 3 bolts and the halfshaft support bracket.

8. Remove the 4 bolts and the catalytic converter bracket.

❉❉ **WARNING**

Do not forcibly bend or twist the exhaust flexible pipe. Failure to follow these instructions may cause damage to the flexible pipe.

9. Using cable ties, support the exhaust flexible pipe with a support wrap or suitable splint.

❉❉ **WARNING**

Do not forcibly bend or twist the exhaust flexible pipe. Failure to follow these instructions may cause damage to the flexible pipe.

10. Detach the muffler and tailpipe assembly isolator and remove the 2 catalytic converter-to-muffler and tailpipe assembly nuts.

   a. Remove the catalytic converter assembly.

   b. Discard the 2 nuts and gaskets.

To install:

❉❉ **WARNING**

Failure to tighten the catalytic converter manifold fasteners in 177 inch lbs. (20 Nm) increments until reaching final torque of 41 ft. lbs. (55 Nm) will cause the converter to develop an exhaust leak.

Fig. 92 Remove the 4 bolts and position aside the heat shield

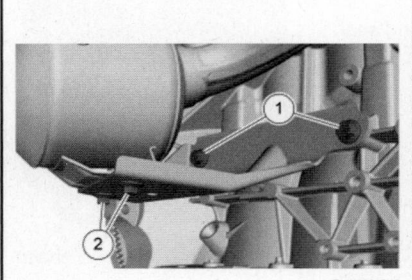

Fig. 94 Remove the 4 bolts and the catalytic converter bracket.

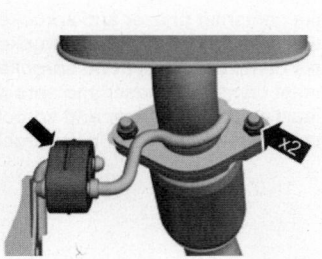

Fig. 95 Remove the catalytic converter assembly. Discard the 2 nuts and gaskets.

11. Install a new gasket, catalytic converter assembly and new fasteners. Tighten the bolt and 4 nuts in the proper sequence, in 3 stages.

    a. Stage 1: Tighten to 177 inch lbs. (20 Nm).

    b. Stage 2: Tighten to 30 ft. lbs. (40 Nm).

    c. Stage 3: Tighten to 41 ft. lbs. (55 Nm).

❋❋ WARNING

Do not forcibly bend or twist the exhaust flexible pipe. Failure to follow these instructions may cause damage to the flexible pipe.

12. Install a new gasket and 2 new catalytic converter-to-muffler and tailpipe assembly nuts.

    a. Attach the muffler and tailpipe assembly isolator. Tighten the nuts to 35 ft. lbs. (48 Nm).

13. Remove the cable ties, support wrap or suitable splint from the exhaust flexible pipe.

14. Install the catalytic converter bracket and the 4 bolts.

15. Tighten the 2 catalytic converter bracket-to-engine block bolts to 37 ft. lbs. (50 Nm).

16. Tighten the 2 catalytic converter bracket-to-catalytic converter bolts to 18 ft. lbs. (25 Nm).

17. Install the halfshaft support bracket and the 3 bolts.

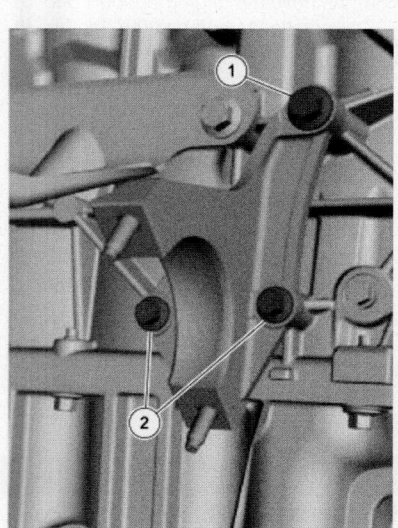

Fig. 96 Install the halfshaft support bracket and the 3 bolts. Tighten the upper bolt to 35 ft. lbs. (48 Nm). Tighten the 2 lower bolts to 18 ft. lbs. (24 Nm).

    a. Tighten the upper bolt to 35 ft. lbs. (48 Nm).

    b. Tighten the 2 lower bolts to 18 ft. lbs. (24 Nm).

18. Install the RH halfshaft as outlined in the Drive Train Section.

19. Install the Catalyst Monitor Sensor (CMS) as outlined in the Engine Performance & Emission Controls Section.

20. Install the 4 bolts and the heat shield. Tighten the bolts to 89 inch lbs. (10 Nm).

21. Install the Heated Oxygen Sensor (HO2S) as outlined in the Engine Performance & Emission Controls Section.

22. Fill the transmission/transaxle to the correct fluid level as outlined in the Drive Train Section.

CRANKSHAFT FRONT SEAL

REMOVAL & INSTALLATION

See Figures 97 through 99.

1. Remove the timing belt.
2. Remove the crankshaft sprocket gear.
3. Using the Input Shaft Oil Seal Remover and Slide Hammer, remove the crankshaft front oil seal.

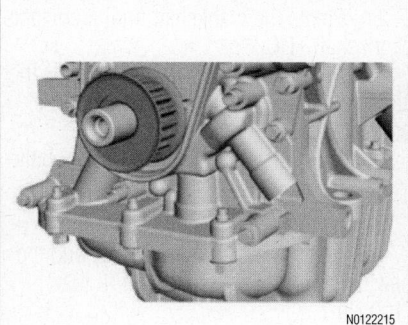

Fig. 97 Remove the crankshaft sprocket gear

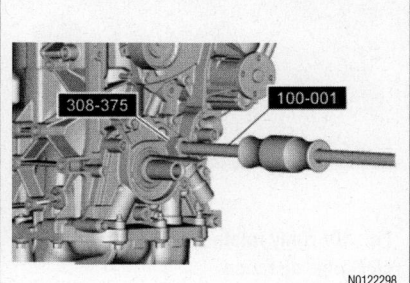

Fig. 98 Using the Input Shaft Oil Seal Remover and Slide Hammer, remove the crankshaft front oil seal

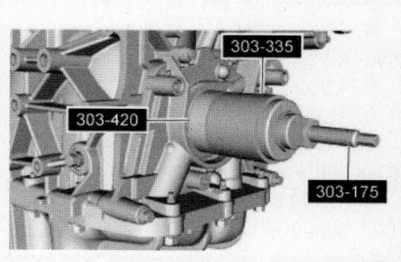

Fig. 99 Using the Crankshaft Vibration Damper Installer, Front Cover Oil Seal Installer and Front Crankshaft Seal Replacer, install the crankshaft front oil seal

To install:

➡**Lubricate the oil seal with clean engine oil.**

4. Using the Crankshaft Vibration Damper Installer, Front Cover Oil Seal Installer and Front Crankshaft Seal Replacer, install the crankshaft front oil seal.

5. Install the crankshaft sprocket gear.

6. Install the timing belt.

CRANKSHAFT PULLEY

REMOVAL & INSTALLATION

See Figures 100 through 103.

❋❋ WARNING

Do not loosen or remove the crankshaft pulley bolt without first installing the special tools. The crankshaft pulley and the crankshaft timing sprocket are not keyed to the crankshaft. Before any repair requiring loosening or removal of the crankshaft pulley bolt, the crankshaft and camshafts must be locked in place by the special service tools, otherwise severe engine damage can occur.

❋❋ WARNING

During engine repair procedures, cleanliness is extremely important. Any foreign material, including any material created while cleaning gasket surfaces, that enters the oil passages, coolant passages or the oil pan can cause engine failure.

1. With the vehicle in NEUTRAL, position it on a hoist.

2. Remove the upper and lower cowl panel grilles as outlined in the Body Section.

3. Remove the RH front wheel and tire.

4. Remove the 2 bolts and accessory drive belt splash shield.

5. Loosen the 4 coolant pump bolts.

6. Remove the generator.

7. Release the 2 tabs and position the degas bottle aside.

8. Using a floor jack and a block of wood, support the engine.

❊❊ WARNING

The engine mount studs must be held while removing the engine mount nuts or damage to the powertrain may occur.

❊❊ WARNING

Do not loosen the engine mount center bolt or the engine may become improperly positioned.

9. Use the holding feature to prevent the engine mount studs from turning, remove the 2 engine mount nuts.

10. Remove the 3 bolts and the engine mount.

11. Remove the 4 bolts and coolant pump pulley.

12. Remove the 1 engine mount stud.

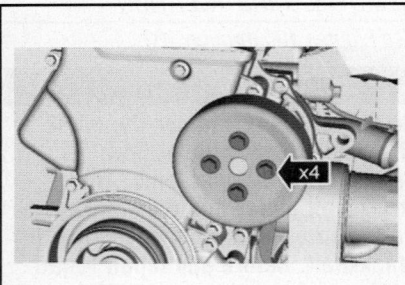

N0122176

Fig. 100 Remove the 4 bolts and coolant pump pulley

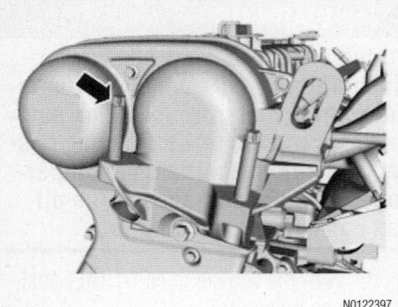

N0122397

Fig. 101 Remove the 1 engine mount stud

13. Remove the 9 bolts and the timing belt cover.

14. Remove the 3 bolts and the engine mount bracket.

15. Using an engine mount bracket bolt, install the Engine Lifting Bracket.

16. Install the Engine Support Bar and support the engine.

17. Remove the floor jack and block of wood.

➡ **Only rotate the crankshaft in a clockwise direction.**

18. Using the crankshaft pulley bolt, turn the crankshaft clockwise until the markings on the camshaft phaser and sprockets are at the 11 o'clock position.

19. Remove the engine plug bolt.

➡ **The Crankshaft Top Dead Center (TDC) Timing Pin will contact the crankshaft and prevent it from turning past TDC. However, the crankshaft can still be rotated in the counterclockwise direction. The crankshaft must remain at the TDC position during the crankshaft pulley removal and installation.**

20. Install the Crankshaft TDC Pin.

➡ **Only rotate the crankshaft clockwise direction.**

21. Rotate the crankshaft until it contacts Crankshaft TDC Pin.

22. Using the Strap Wrench, remove the crankshaft pulley bolt and the crankshaft pulley.

    a. Discard the crankshaft pulley bolt.

23. Install the VCT Alignment Tool.

To install:

24. Install the crankshaft pulley and the new bolt. Tighten the bolt to 74 ft. lbs. (100 Nm).

E86729_EUR

Fig. 102 Only rotate the crankshaft in a clockwise direction.

Using the crankshaft pulley bolt, turn the crankshaft clockwise until the markings on the camshaft phaser and sprockets are at the 11 o'clock position as shown

    a. The final torque of the crankshaft will be completed in following steps.

25. Remove the Crankshaft TDC Timing Pin.

26. Remove the VCT Alignment Tool.

27. Tighten the crankshaft bolt in the following 3 stages.

    a. Stage 1: Using the Strap wrench, tighten an additional 90 degrees.

    b. Stage 2: Wait for 10 seconds.

    c. Stage 3: Using the Strap wrench, tighten an additional 15 degrees.

➡ **Only rotate the crankshaft clockwise direction.**

28. Rotate the crankshaft about 1 3/4 turns.

29. Install the Crankshaft TDC Timing Pin.

➡ **Only rotate the crankshaft clockwise direction.**

30. Rotate the crankshaft until it stops against the Crankshaft TDC Timing Pin.

➡ **The special tool can only be installed if the valve timing is correct.**

31. Install the VCT Alignment Tool.

    a. If the special tool cannot be installed, repeat the adjustment according to the preceding steps.

32. Remove the VCT Alignment Tool.

33. Remove the Crankshaft TDC Timing Pin.

34. Install the engine plug bolt. Tighten the bolt to 177 inch lbs. (20 Nm).

35. Using a floor jack and a block of wood, support the engine.

36. Remove the Engine Support Bar.

37. Remove the bolt and the Engine Lifting Bracket.

38. Install the engine mount bracket and the 3 bolts finger tight.

    a. Tighten the 2 bolts to 41 ft. lbs. (55 Nm).

    b. Tighten the bolt to 41 ft. lbs. (55 Nm).

39. Install the timing belt cover and the 9 bolts. Tighten the bolts to 80 inch lbs. (9 Nm).

40. Install the coolant pump pulley and the 4 bolts finger tight.

41. Install the 1 engine mount stud finger tight.

❊❊ WARNING

The 2 engine mount studs must be torqued or damage to the powertrain may occur.

42. Torque the 2 engine mount studs before installing the engine mount nuts. Tighten the nuts to 71 inch lbs. (8 Nm).

Fig. 103 Install the engine mount bracket and the 3 bolts finger tight. Tighten the (1) bolt to 41 ft. lbs. (55 Nm). Tighten the (2) bolts to 41 ft. lbs. (55 Nm)

> ✷✷ **WARNING**
>
> **Do not loosen the engine mount center bolt or the engine may become improperly positioned.**

43. Install the engine mount and the 2 nuts. Tighten the 2 nuts to 59 ft. lbs. (80 Nm).
44. Install the 3 engine mount bolts. Tighten the bolts to 35 ft. lbs. (48 Nm).
45. Position the degas bottle on the 2 retainer tabs.
46. Install the generator as outlined in the Engine Electrical Section.
47. Tighten the 4 coolant pump bolts to 177 inch lbs. (20 Nm).
48. Install the accessory drive belt splash shield and the 2 bolts. Tighten the bolts to 80 inch lbs. (9 Nm).
49. Install the RH front wheel and tire.
50. Install the upper and lower cowl panel grilles.

CYLINDER HEAD

REMOVAL & INSTALLATION

See Figures 104 through 115.

1. With the vehicle in NEUTRAL, position it on a hoist.
2. Release the fuel system pressure as outlined in the Fuel System Section.
3. Disconnect the battery ground cable.
4. Remove the Air Cleaner (ACL) outlet tube as outlined in this section.
5. Remove the Heated Oxygen Sensor (HO2S) as outlined in the Engine Performance & Emission Controls Section.
6. Drain the engine cooling system as outlined in the Engine Cooling Section.
7. Drain the engine oil. Install the drain plug and tighten to 21 ft. lbs. (28 Nm).
8. Remove and discard the engine oil filter.

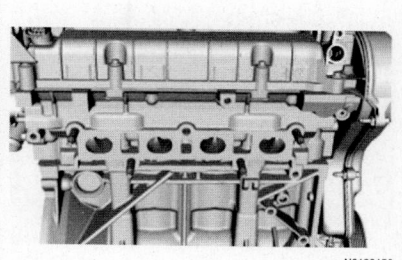

Fig. 104 Remove the 4 catalytic converter studs and discard

9. Remove the Catalyst Monitor Sensor (CMS) as outlined in the Engine Performance & Emission Controls Section.
10. Remove the 2 catalytic converter-to-muffler nuts and separate the catalytic converter from the muffler.
   a. Discard the gasket.

> ✷✷ **WARNING**
>
> **Do not excessively bend or twist the exhaust flexible pipe. Failure to follow these instructions may cause damage to the flexible pipe.**

Support the exhaust flexible pipe with a support wrap or suitable splint.

11. Remove the 4 bolts and the lower catalytic converter bracket.
12. Remove the 4 bolts and the catalytic converter heat shield.
13. Remove the 4 catalytic converter nuts and bolt.
   a. Discard the 4 nuts and bolt.
14. Position the catalytic converter back and secure with mechanic wire.
   a. Discard the catalytic converter gasket.
15. If equipped, disconnect the block heater electrical connector.
16. Remove the 4 catalytic converter studs and discard.
17. Disconnect the fuel tube spring lock couplings from the fuel rail as outlined in the Fuel System Section.
18. Disconnect the 4 fuel injector electrical connectors.
19. Disconnect the Throttle Body (TB) electrical connector.
   a. Detach the wiring harness retainer from the TB.
20. Remove the screw and the oil level indicator and tube.
   a. Inspect and replace the O-ring seal, if necessary.

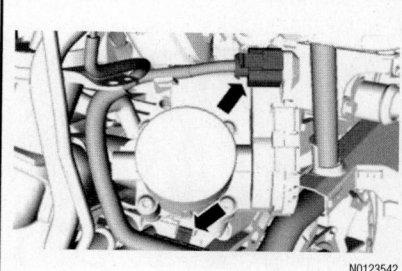

Fig. 105 Disconnect the Throttle Body (TB) electrical connector. Detach the wiring harness retainer from the TB

21. Disconnect the PCV hose from the intake manifold.
22. Remove the bolt for the Evaporative Emission (EVAP) canister purge valve.
23. Disconnect the brake booster vacuum tube from the intake manifold.
24. Disconnect the EVAP canister purge valve tube from the intake manifold and position the EVAP canister purge valve aside.
25. Detach the Knock Sensor (KS) electrical connector from the bottom of the intake manifold.

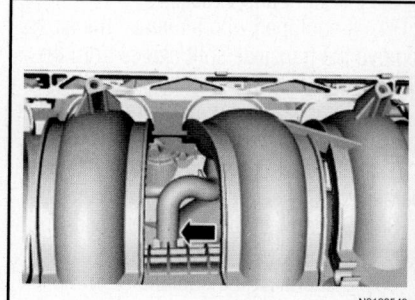

Fig. 106 Disconnect the PCV hose from the intake manifold

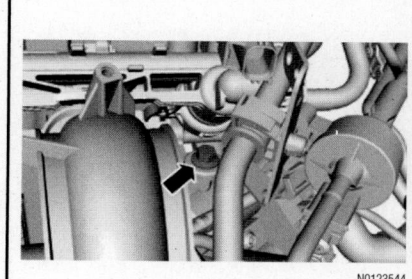

Fig. 107 Remove the bolt for the Evaporative Emission (EVAP) canister purge valve

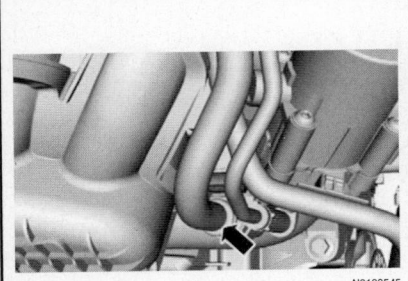

Fig. 108 Disconnect the brake booster vacuum tube from the intake manifold

a. Detach the 2 wiring harness retainers from the bottom of the intake manifold.

26. Remove the valve tappets.

27. Remove the 2 lower bolts for the intake manifold.

28. Remove the 4 bolts and the timing belt cover backplate.

29. Disconnect the ignition coil electrical connector and remove the 4 screws and the ignition coil.

30. Detach the fuel tube retainer from the coolant outlet bracket.

a. Detach the 2 wiring harness retainers and the coolant hose retainer from the coolant outlet bracket.

31. If equipped with a manual transaxle, remove the transaxle shift cables from the clip.

32. Remove the nut, bolt and the bracket from the coolant outlet.

33. Disconnect the Engine Coolant Temperature (ECT) sensor electrical connector.

34. Disconnect the 2 coolant hoses from the coolant outlet.

35. Disconnect the coolant return hose from the cylinder head.

36. Using a floor jack and a block of wood, support the engine.

37. Remove the Engine Support Bar.

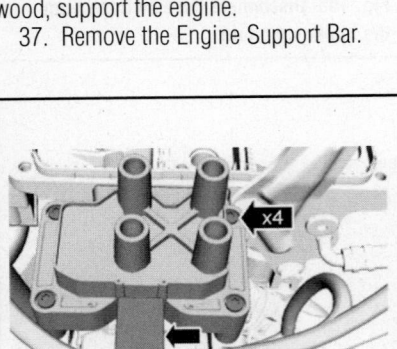

Fig. 109 Disconnect the ignition coil electrical connector and remove the 4 screws and the ignition coil

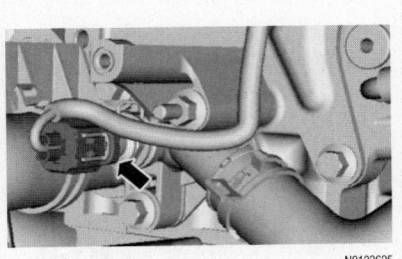

Fig. 110 Disconnect the Engine Coolant Temperature (ECT) sensor electrical connector

38. Remove the bolt and the Engine Lifting Bracket.

➡**Make sure that the cylinder head is at ambient air temperature before removing the cylinder head bolts.**

39. Remove the 10 cylinder head bolts in the proper sequence.

a. Remove the cylinder head.

b. Discard the cylinder head bolts and gasket.

40. Support the cylinder head on a bench with the head gasket side up. Check the cylinder head distortion and the cylinder block distortion.

To install:

➡**If there is no residual gasket material present, metal surface prep can be used to clean and prepare the surfaces.**

41. Clean the cylinder head-to-cylinder block mating surface of both the cylinder head and the cylinder block in the following sequence.

a. Remove any large deposits of gasket material with a plastic scraper.

b. Apply metal surface prep, following package directions, to remove any traces of oil or coolant, and to prepare the surfaces to bond with the new gasket. Do not attempt to make the metal shiny. Some staining of the metal surfaces is normal.

➡**Lubricate the bolts with clean engine oil prior to installation.**

42. Install the cylinder head gasket, cylinder head and 10 new bolts. Tighten the bolts in the proper sequence in 4 stages:

a. Stage 1: Tighten to 44 inch lbs. (5 Nm).

b. Stage 2: Tighten to 133 inch lbs. (15 Nm).

c. Stage 3: Tighten to 26 ft. lbs. (35 Nm).

d. Stage 4: Tighten an additional 75°.

43. Using an engine mount bracket bolt, install the Engine Lifting Bracket.

44. Install the Engine Support Bar and support the engine.

45. Remove the floor jack and block of wood.

46. Connect the coolant return hose to the cylinder head.

47. Connect the 2 coolant hoses to the coolant outlet.

48. Connect the ECT sensor electrical connector.

49. Install the coolant outlet bracket, nut and the bolt. Tighten the bolt to 53 inch lbs. (6 Nm).

50. If equipped with a manual transaxle, install the transaxle shift cables to the clip.

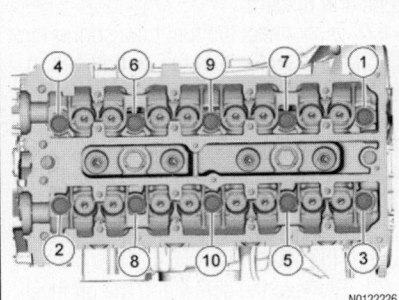

Fig. 111 Remove the 10 cylinder head bolts in the proper sequence

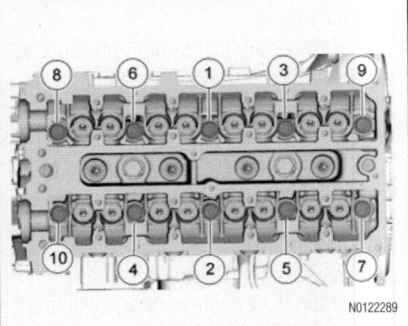

Fig. 112 Install the cylinder head gasket, cylinder head and 10 new bolts. Tighten the bolts in the proper sequence in 4 stages

51. Attach the fuel tube retainer to the coolant outlet bracket.

a. Attach the 2 wiring harness and coolant hose retainers to the coolant outlet bracket.

52. Install the ignition coil, 4 screws and connect the ignition coil electrical connector. Tighten the screws to 53 inch lbs. (6 Nm).

53. Install the timing belt cover backplate and the 4 bolts. Tighten the bolts to 80 inch lbs. (9 Nm).

54. Install the 2 lower bolts for the intake manifold. Tighten the bolts to 159 inch lbs. (18 Nm).

55. Install the valve tappets.

56. Attach the KS electrical connector to bottom of the intake manifold.

a. Attach the 2 wiring harness retainers to the bottom of the intake manifold.

57. Position and connect the EVAP canister purge valve tube to the intake manifold.

58. Connect the brake booster vacuum tube to the intake manifold.

59. Install the bolt for the EVAP canister purge valve. Tighten the bolt to 80 inch lbs. (9 Nm).

60. Connect the PCV hose to the intake manifold.

➡**Lubricate the O-ring seal with clean engine oil.**

61. Install the oil level indicator and tube and the screw. Tighten the screw to 35 inch lbs. (4 Nm).

62. Connect the TB electrical connector.

a. Attach the wiring harness retainer to the TB.

63. Connect the 4 fuel injector electrical connectors.

64. Connect the fuel tube spring lock couplings to the fuel rail as outlined in the Fuel System Section.

65. Install the 4 new catalytic converter studs. Tighten the studs to 150 inch lbs. (17 Nm).

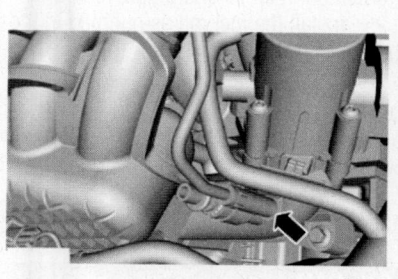

Fig. 113 Position and connect the EVAP canister purge valve tube to the intake manifold

66. If equipped, connect the block heater electrical connector.

67. Using a new gasket, position the catalytic converter and install the 4 new nuts and bolt finger tight.

✳✳ WARNING

Failure to tighten the catalytic converter manifold fasteners in 177 inch lbs. increments until reaching final torque of 41 ft. lbs. will cause the converter to develop an exhaust leak.

68. Tighten the bolt and 4 nuts in the proper sequence, in 3 stages.

a. Stage 1: Tighten all fasteners in sequence to 177 inch lbs. (20 Nm).

b. Stage 2: Tighten all fasteners in sequence to 30 ft. lbs. (40 Nm).

c. Stage 3: Tighten all fasteners in sequence to 41 ft. lbs. (55 Nm).

69. Install the catalytic converter heat shield and the 4 bolts. Tighten the bolts to 89 inch lb (10 Nm).

70. Install the lower catalytic converter bracket and the 4 bolts and tighten in the proper sequence.

a. Tighten the catalytic converter bracket-to-engine block bolts to 37 ft. lbs. (50 Nm).

b. Tighten the catalytic converter bracket-to-catalytic converter bolts to 18 ft. lbs. (25 Nm).

✳✳ WARNING

Do not excessively bend or twist the exhaust flexible pipe. Failure to follow these instructions may cause damage to the flexible pipe.

71. Remove the support for the exhaust flexible pipe.

72. Using a new gasket, position the catalytic converter to the muffler and install the

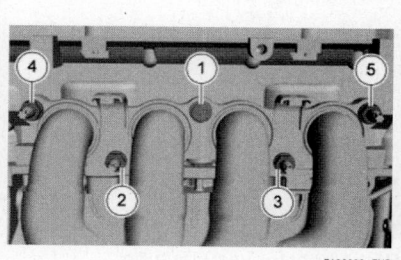

Fig. 114 Using a new gasket, position the catalytic converter and install the 4 new nuts and bolt finger tight. Tighten the bolt and 4 nuts in the proper sequence, in 3 stages

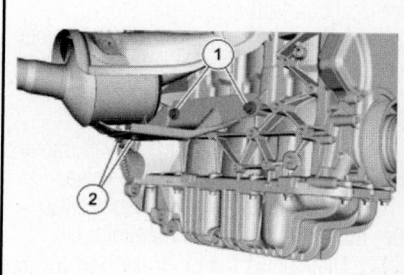

Fig. 115 Install the lower catalytic converter bracket and the 4 bolts and tighten in the proper sequence. Tighten the catalytic converter bracket-to-engine block bolts (1) to 37 ft. lbs. (50 Nm) and tighten the catalytic converter bracket-to-catalytic converter bolts to 18 ft. lbs. (25 Nm).

2 catalytic converter nuts. Tighten the nuts to 35 ft. lbs. (48 Nm).

73. Install the CMS as outlined in the Engine Performance & Emission Controls Section.

➡**Lubricate the engine oil filter gasket with clean engine oil prior to installing the oil filter.**

74. Install a new engine oil filter. Tighten the filter to 133 inch lbs. (15 Nm).

75. Install the HO2S as outlined in the Engine Performance & Emission Controls Section.

76. Install the ACL outlet tube as outlined in this section.

77. Connect the battery ground cable.

78. Fill the engine with clean engine oil.

79. Fill the engine cooling system as outlined in the Engine Cooling Section.

INTAKE MANIFOLD

REMOVAL & INSTALLATION

See Figures 116 and 117.

1. Remove the air cleaner outlet tube as outlined in this section.

2. Disconnect the crankcase vent tube from the valve cover.

a. Detach the 2 crankcase vent tube retainers.

3. Remove the fuel rail as outlined in the Fuel System Section.

4. Remove the generator as outlined in the Engine Electrical Section.

5. Remove the screw and the oil level indicator and tube.

6. Inspect and replace the O-ring seal, if necessary.

7. Disconnect the Throttle Body (TB) electrical connector.

   a. Detach the wiring harness retainer from the TB.

8. Disconnect the PCV hose from the intake manifold.

9. Remove the bolt for the Evaporative Emission (EVAP) canister purge valve.

10. Disconnect the brake booster vacuum tube from the intake manifold.

11. Disconnect the EVAP canister purge valve tube from the intake manifold and position the EVAP canister purge valve aside.

12. Detach the Knock Sensor (KS) electrical connector from the bottom of the intake manifold.

   a. Detach the 2 wiring harness retainers from the bottom of the intake manifold.

13. Remove the 7 bolts for the intake manifold.

To install:

✳✳ WARNING

If the engine is repaired or replaced because of upper engine failure, typically including valve or piston damage, check the intake manifold for metal debris. If metal debris is

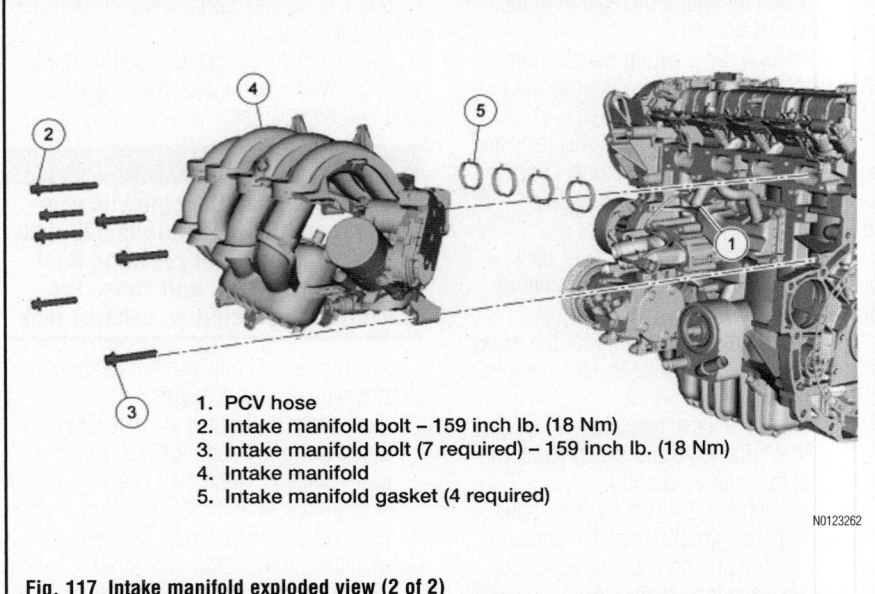

1. PCV hose
2. Intake manifold bolt – 159 inch lb. (18 Nm)
3. Intake manifold bolt (7 required) – 159 inch lb. (18 Nm)
4. Intake manifold
5. Intake manifold gasket (4 required)

N0123262

Fig. 117 Intake manifold exploded view (2 of 2)

found, install a new intake manifold. Failure to follow these instructions can result in engine damage.

14. Inspect and install new intake manifold gaskets, if necessary.

15. Install the intake manifold and the 7 bolts. Tighten the bolts to 13 ft. lbs. (18 Nm).

16. Attach the KS electrical connector to bottom of the intake manifold.

17. Attach the 2 wiring harness retainers to the bottom of the intake manifold.

18. Position and connect the EVAP canister purge valve tube to the intake manifold.

19. Connect the brake booster vacuum tube to the intake manifold.

20. Install the bolt for the EVAP canister purge valve. Tighten the bolt to 80 inch lbs. (9 Nm).

21. Connect the PCV hose to the intake manifold.

22. Connect the TB electrical connector.

   a. Attach the wiring harness retainer to the TB.

➡**Lubricate the O-ring seal with clean engine oil.**

23. Install the oil level indicator and tube and the screw. Tighten the screw to 35 inch lbs. (4 Nm).

24. Install the generator. For additional information, refer to Charging System.

25. Install the fuel rail as outlined in the Fuel System Section.

26. Connect the crankcase vent tube to the valve cover.

   a. Attach the 2 crankcase vent tube retainers.

27. Install the air cleaner outlet tube as outlined in this section.

OIL PAN

REMOVAL & INSTALLATION

See Figures 118 and 119.

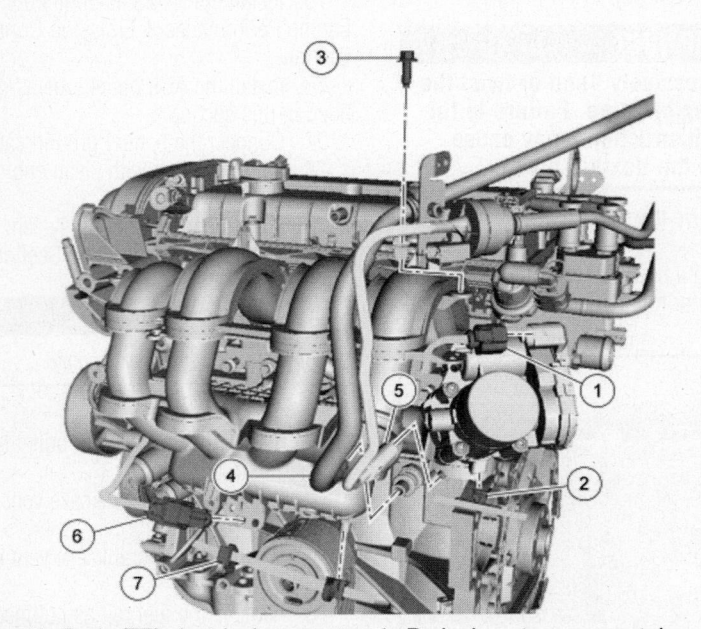

1. Throttle Body (TB) electrical connector
2. TB wiring harness retainer
3. Evaporative Emission (EVAP) canister purge valve bolt – 80 inch lb. (9 Nm)
4. Brake booster vacuum tube
5. EVAP canister purge valve tube
6. Knock Sensor (KS) electrical connector
7. Wiring harness retainer (2 required)

N0123261

Fig. 116 Intake manifold exploded view (1 of 2)

1. With the vehicle in NEUTRAL, position it on a hoist.

2. Remove the screw and the oil level indicator and tube.

   a. Inspect and replace the O-ring seal, if necessary.

3. Drain the engine oil. Install the drain plug and tighten to 21 ft. lbs. (28 Nm).

4. Remove and discard the engine oil filter.

5. Remove the 17 bolts from the oil pan.

6. Using the 3 pry pads, remove the oil pan.

To install:

❊❊ WARNING

Do not use metal scrapers, wire brushes, power abrasive discs or other abrasive means to clean the sealing surfaces. These tools cause scratches and gouges, which make leak paths. Use a plastic scraping tool to remove traces of sealant.

7. Clean and inspect all mating surfaces using silicone gasket remover.

8. Install 2 M8x20 studs for oil pan alignment.

➡**The oil pan must be installed within 5 minutes of applying the sealant.**

❊❊ WARNING

If the oil pan is not secured within 5 minutes of sealant application, the sealant must be removed and the sealing area cleaned with metal surface prep. Allow to dry until there is no sign of wetness, or 5 minutes, whichever is longer. Failure to follow this procedure can cause future oil leakage

9. Apply a 0.137 inch (3.5 mm) bead of sealant to the oil pan.

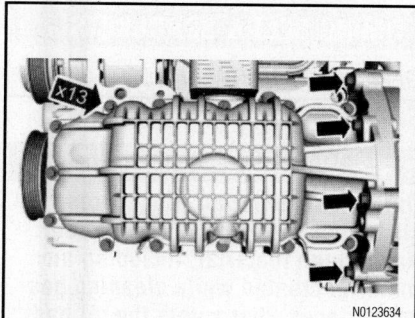

Fig. 118 Remove the 17 bolts from the oil pan

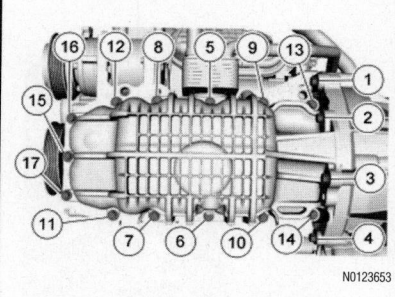

Fig. 119 Tighten the oil pan bolts in the following sequence in 3 stages

10. Install the oil pan using the 2 studs for alignment.

11. Install 15 bolts finger tight and remove the 2 alignment studs and install the remaining 2 bolts finger tight.

12. Tighten the oil pan bolts in the following sequence in 3 stages.

   a. Stage 1: Tighten bolts 1 through 4 to 35 ft. lbs. (48 Nm).

   b. Stage 2: Tighten bolts 5 through 17 to 89 inch lbs. (10 Nm).

   c. Stage 3: Tighten bolts 5 through 17 to 177 inch lbs. (20 Nm).

➡**Lubricate the engine oil filter gasket with clean engine oil prior to installing the oil filter.**

13. Install a new engine oil filter. Tighten the filter to 133 inch lbs. (15 Nm).

➡**Lubricate the O-ring seal with clean engine oil.**

14. Install the oil level indicator and tube and the screw. Tighten the screw to 35 inch lbs. (4 Nm).

15. Fill the engine with clean engine oil.

OIL PUMP

REMOVAL & INSTALLATION

See Figure 121.

1. Remove the crankshaft front seal as outlined in this section.

2. Remove the oil pan as outlined in this section.

3. Remove the 4 bolts and the timing belt cover backplate.

4. Remove the 3 bolts and the oil pump screen and pickup tube.

5. Inspect and replace the oil pump screen and pickup tube O-ring seal, if necessary.

6. Remove the 8 bolts and the oil pump.

7. Remove and discard the oil pump gasket.

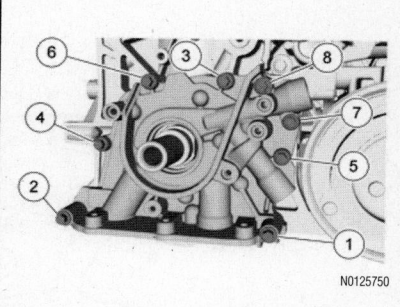

Fig. 120 Install a new gasket, the oil pump and the 8 bolts in their original position and tighten in sequence shown in 2 stages

To install:

8. Install a new gasket, the oil pump and the 8 bolts in their original position and tighten in sequence shown in 2 stages.

   a. Stage 1: Tighten to 53 inch lbs. (6 Nm).

   b. Stage 2: Tighten to 80 inch lbs. (9 Nm).

9. Install the oil pump screen and pickup tube and 3 bolts. Tighten the bolts to 80 inch lbs. (9 Nm).

10. Install the timing belt cover backplate and the 4 bolts. Tighten the bolts to 80 inch lbs. (9 Nm).

11. Install the oil pan as outlined in this section.

12. Install the crankshaft front seal as outlined in this section.

TIMING BELT COVER

REMOVAL & INSTALLATION

See Figures 121 through 123.

All Timing Belt Covers

1. With the vehicle in NEUTRAL, position it on a hoist.

Upper Timing Belt Cover

2. Loosen the 4 coolant pump pulley bolts.

3. Remove the accessory drive belt. For additional information, refer to Accessory Drive.

4. Remove the engine mount.

5. Remove the 4 bolts and coolant pump pulley.

6. Remove the 1 engine mount stud.

7. Remove the 9 bolts and the upper timing belt cover.

Lower Timing Belt Cover

8. Remove the crankshaft pulley as outlined in this section.

9. Remove the 3 bolts and the lower timing belt cover.

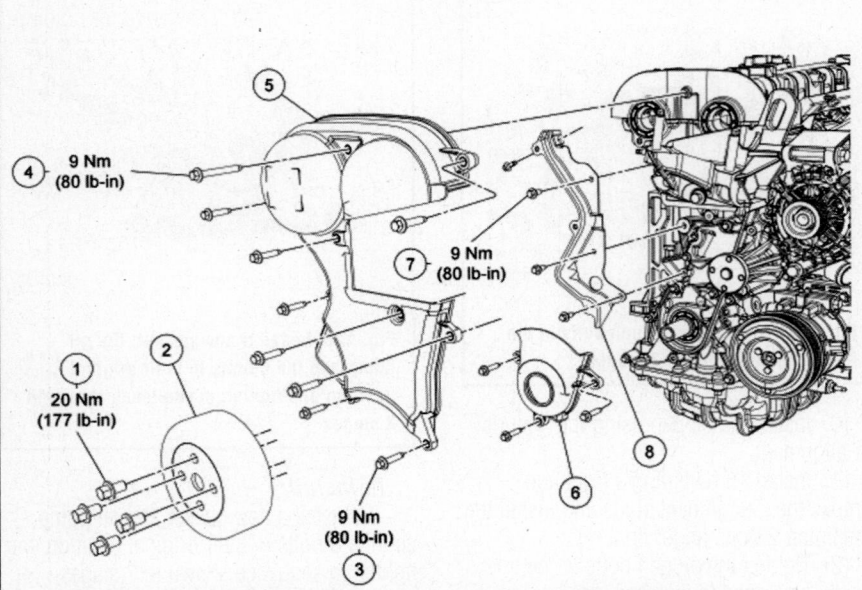

1. Coolant pump pulley bolt (3 required)
2. Coolant pump pulley
3. Upper and lower timing belt cover bolt (12 required)
4. Upper timing belt cover bolt
5. Upper timing belt cover
6. Lower timing belt cover
7. Timing belt cover backplate bolts
8. Timing belt cover backplate

N0116465

Fig. 121 Timing belt cover and components exploded view

Timing Belt Cover Backplate

10. Loosen the 4 coolant pump pulley bolts.

11. Remove the accessory drive belt. For additional information, refer to Accessory Drive.

12. Remove the engine mount.

13. Remove the 4 bolts and coolant pump pulley.

14. Remove the 1 engine mount stud.

15. Remove the 9 bolts and the upper timing belt cover.

16. Remove the 4 bolts and the timing belt cover backplate.

To install:
Timing Belt Cover Backplate

17. Install the timing belt cover backplate and the 4 bolts. Tighten the bolts to 80 inch lbs. (9 Nm).

18. Install the upper timing belt cover and the 9 bolts. Tighten the bolts to 80 inch lbs. (9 Nm).

19. Install the 1 engine mount stud finger tight.

✳✳ WARNING

The 2 engine mount studs must be torqued or damage to the powertrain may occur.

20. Torque the 2 engine mount studs before installing the engine mount nuts. Tighten the nuts to 71 inch lbs. (8 Nm).

21. Install the coolant pump pulley and the 4 bolts.

   a. Do not torque at this time.

22. Install the engine mount as outlined in this section.

23. Install the accessory drive belt as outlined in this section.

24. Tighten the 4 coolant pump pulley bolts to 177 inch lbs. (20 Nm).

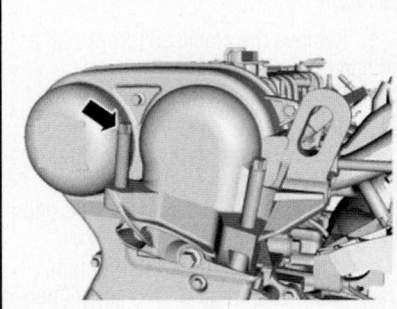

N0122397

Fig. 122 Install the 1 engine mount stud finger tight

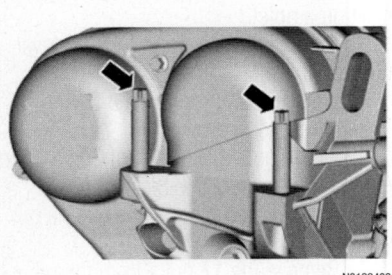

N0122480

Fig. 123 Torque the 2 engine mount studs before installing the engine mount nuts

Lower Timing Belt Cover

25. Install the lower timing belt cover and the 3 bolts. Tighten the bolts to 80 inch lbs. (9 Nm).

26. Install the crankshaft pulley as outlined in this section.

Upper Timing Belt Cover

27. Install the upper timing belt cover and the 9 bolts. Tighten the bolts to 80 inch lbs. (9 Nm).

28. Install the 1 engine mount stud finger tight.

✳✳ WARNING

The 2 engine mount studs must be torqued or damage to the powertrain may occur.

29. Torque the 2 engine mount studs before installing the engine mount nuts. Tighten the studs to 71 inch lbs. (8 Nm).

30. Install the coolant pump pulley and the 4 bolts.

   a. Do not torque at this time.

31. Install the engine mount.

32. Install the accessory drive belt. For additional information, refer to Accessory Drive.

33. Tighten the 4 coolant pump pulley bolts to 177 inch lbs. (20 Nm).

TIMING BELT & SPROCKETS

REMOVAL & INSTALLATION

See Figures 124, 125 and 126.

✳✳ WARNING

During engine repair procedures, cleanliness is extremely important. Any foreign material, including any material created while cleaning gasket surfaces, that enters the oil passages, coolant passages or the oil pan can cause engine failure.

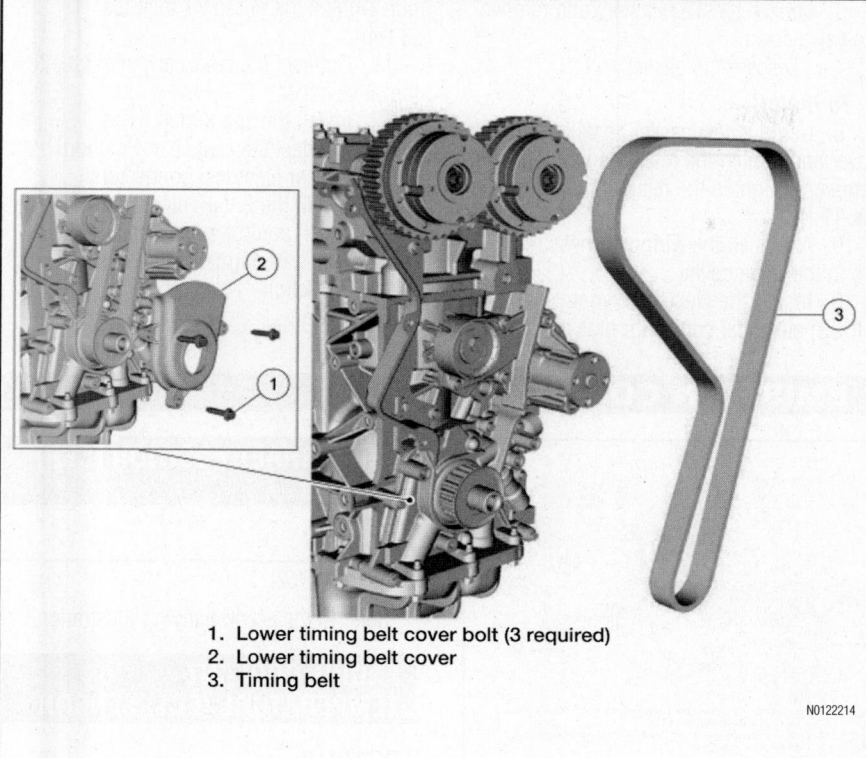

1. Lower timing belt cover bolt (3 required)
2. Lower timing belt cover
3. Timing belt

N0122214

Fig. 124 Timing Belt components exploded view

1. With the vehicle in NEUTRAL, position it on a hoist.
2. Remove the crankshaft pulley as outlined in this section.
3. Remove the 3 bolts and the lower timing belt cover.
4. Install the VCT Alignment Tool.

✳✳ WARNING

The timing belt tensioner spring is under load. Extra care must be taken

N0122213

Fig. 125 Remove the timing belt. Rotate the timing belt tensioner clockwise (1). Align the 2 holes on the tensioner and install a small screwdriver or holding pin. Remove the timing belt (2)

at all times when handling the tensioner. Failure to follow this instruction may result in personal injury.

5. Remove the timing belt.
   a. Rotate the timing belt tensioner clockwise.

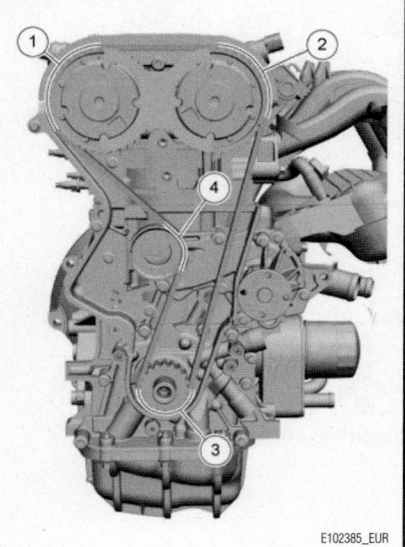

E102385_EUR

Fig. 126 Install the timing belt in the proper sequence

b. Align the 2 holes on the tensioner and install a small screwdriver or holding pin. Remove the timing belt.
   To install:
6. Install the timing belt in the proper sequence.

✳✳ CAUTION

The timing belt tensioner spring is under load. Extra care must be taken at all times when handling the tensioner. Failure to follow this instruction may result in personal injury.

7. Remove the timing belt tensioner holding tool.
8. Install the lower timing belt cover and the 3 bolts. Tighten the bolts to 80 inch lbs. (9 Nm).
9. Install the crankshaft pulley.

VALVE COVERS

REMOVAL & INSTALLATION
See Figure 127.

✳✳ WARNING

During engine repair procedures, cleanliness is extremely important. Any foreign material, including any material created while cleaning gasket surfaces, that enters the oil passages, coolant passages or the oil pan can cause engine failure.

✳✳ WARNING

Do not use metal scrapers, wire brushes, power abrasive discs or other abrasive means to clean the sealing surfaces. These tools cause scratches and gouges which make leak paths.

1. Remove the 2 Variable Camshaft Timing (VCT) oil control solenoids as out-

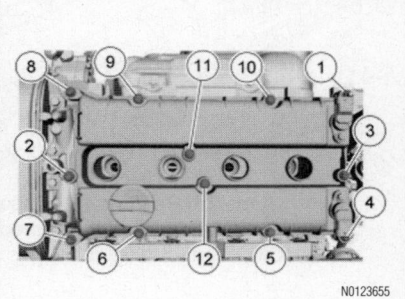

N0123655

Fig. 127 Removal & installation of the valve cover retainers

lined in the Engine Performance & Emission Controls Section.

2. Disconnect the 2 Camshaft Position (CMP) sensor electrical connectors.

3. Remove the spark plug wires.

4. Disconnect the crankcase vent tube from the valve cover.

5. Remove the nut and the Heated Oxygen Sensor (HO2S) electrical connector bracket.

6. Detach all the wiring harness retainers from the valve cover.

7. Loosen the 12 retainers and remove the valve cover.

   a. Discard the gasket.

To install:

8. Using a new gasket, install the valve cover and tighten the retainers in the proper sequence. Tighten the retainers to 80 inch lbs. (9 Nm).

9. Attach all the wiring harness retainers to the valve cover.

10. Install the Heated Oxygen Sensor (HO2S) electrical connector bracket and

nut. Tighten the nut to 71 inch lbs. (8 Nm).

11. Connect the crankcase vent tube to the valve cover.

12. Install the spark plug wires.

13. Connect the Camshaft Position (CMP) sensor electrical connectors.

14. Install the 2 Variable Camshaft Timing (VCT) oil control solenoids as outlined in the Engine Performance & Emission Controls Section.

ENGINE PERFORMANCE & EMISSION CONTROLS

CAMSHAFT POSITION (CMP) SENSOR

LOCATION

See Figure 128.

Refer to the accompanying illustration.

CATALYST MONITOR SENSOR (CMS)

LOCATION

See Figure 129.

Refer to the accompanying illustration.

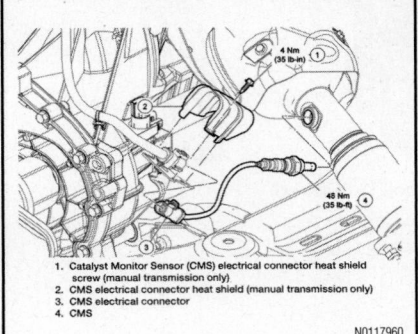

1. Catalyst Monitor Sensor (CMS) electrical connector heat shield screw (manual transmission only)
2. CMS electrical connector heat shield (manual transmission only)
3. CMS electrical connector
4. CMS

N0117960

Fig. 129 Catalyst Monitor Sensor (CMS)

CRANKSHAFT POSITION (CKP) SENSOR

LOCATION

See Figure 130.

Refer to the accompanying illustration.

ENGINE COOLANT TEMPERATURE (ECT) SENSOR

LOCATION

See Figure 131.

Refer to the accompanying illustration.

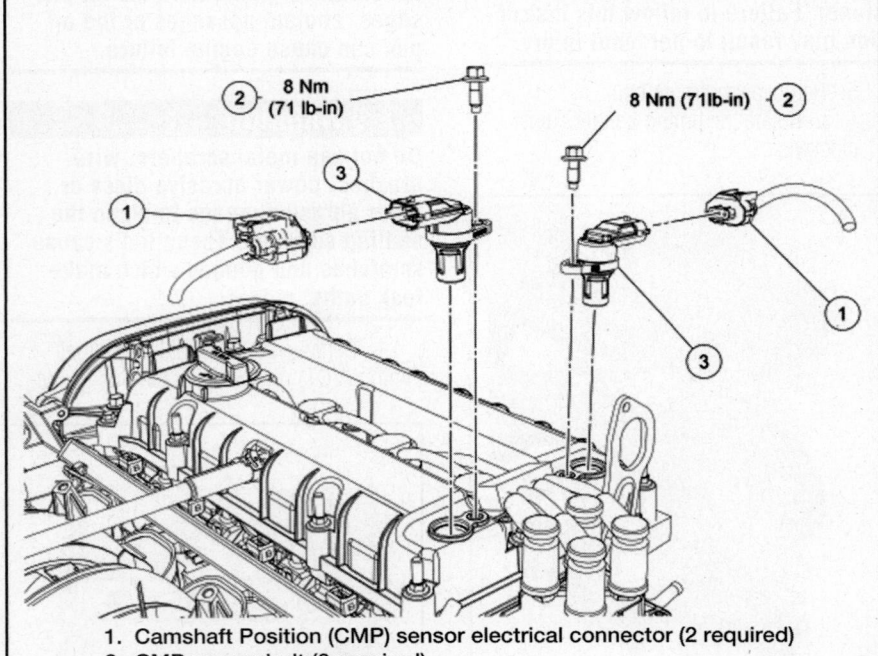

1. Camshaft Position (CMP) sensor electrical connector (2 required)
2. CMP sensor bolt (2 required)
3. CMP sensor (2 required)

N0117649

Fig. 128 Camshaft Position (CMP) Sensor

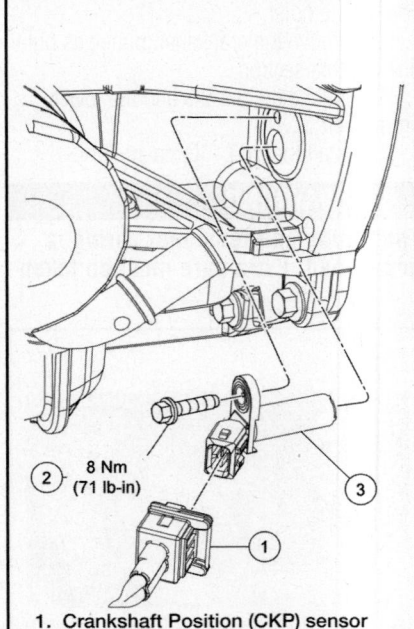

1. Crankshaft Position (CKP) sensor electrical connector (part of 12B581)
2. CKP sensor bolt
3. CKP sensor

N0119159

Fig. 130 Crankshaft Position (CKP) Sensor

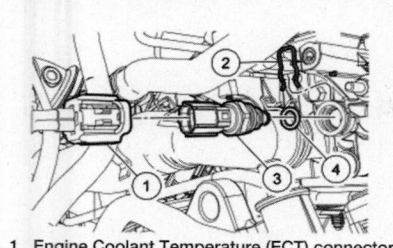

1. Engine Coolant Temperature (ECT) connector
2. ECT sensor retaining clip
3. ECT sensor
4. Sensor O-ring seal

N0117647

Fig. 131 Engine Coolant Temperature (ECT) Sensor

HEATED OXYGEN (HO2S) SENSOR

LOCATION

See Figure 132.

Refer to the accompanying illustration.

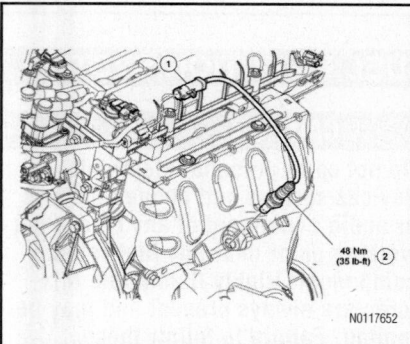

N0117652

Fig. 132 Heated Oxygen Sensor (HO2S) electrical connector (1), HO2S (2)

KNOCK SENSOR (KS)

LOCATION

See Figure 133.

Refer to the accompanying illustration.

MASS AIR FLOW (MAF) SENSOR

LOCATION

See Figure 134.

Refer to the accompanying illustration.

VARIABLE CAMSHAFT TIMING (VCT) OIL CONTROL SOLENOID

LOCATION

See Figure 135.

Refer to the accompanying illustration.

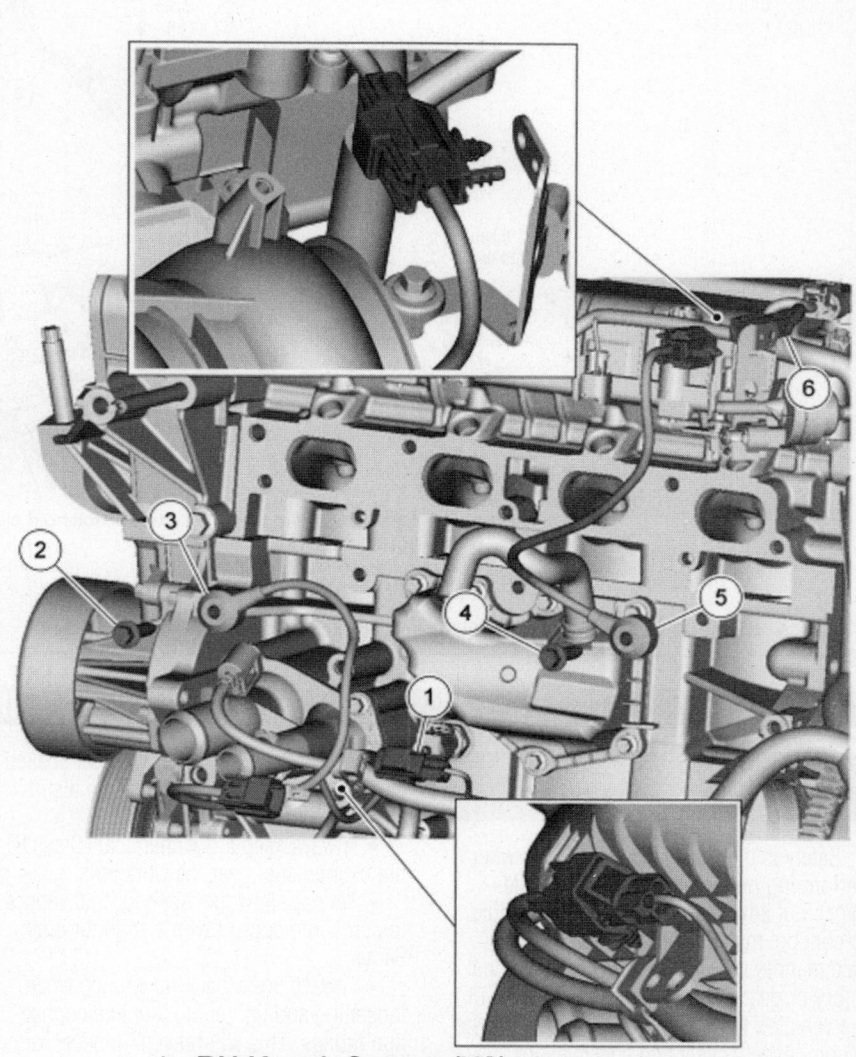

1. **RH Knock Sensor (KS) electrical connector**
2. **RH KS bolt – 177 inch lb. (20 Nm)**
3. **RH KS**
4. **LH KS bolt – 177 inch lb. (20 Nm)**

N0124080

Fig. 133 Knock Sensor (KS)

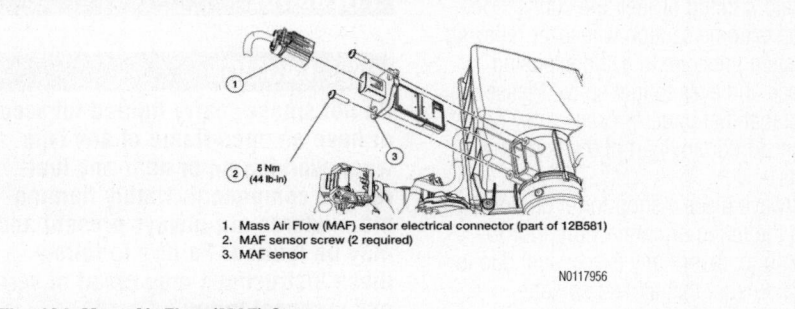

1. Mass Air Flow (MAF) sensor electrical connector (part of 12B581)
2. MAF sensor screw (2 required)
3. MAF sensor

N0117956

Fig. 134 Mass Air Flow (MAF) Sensor

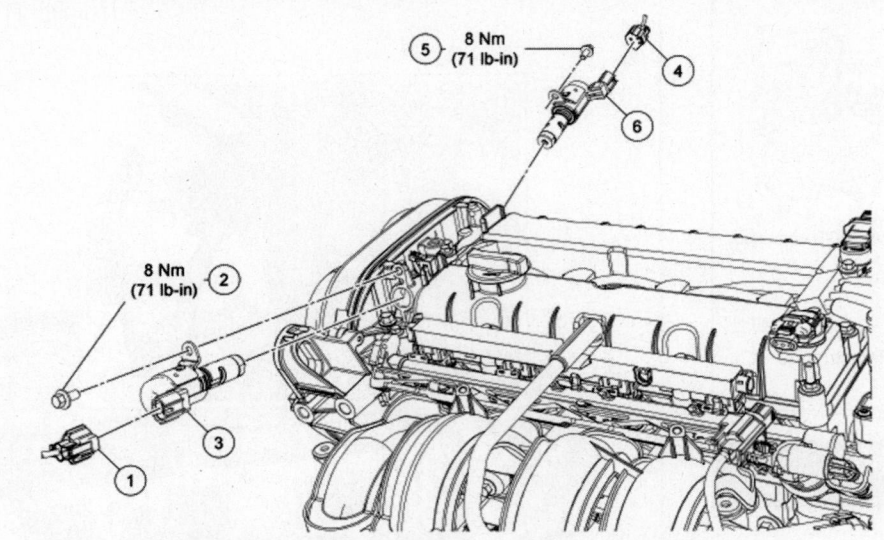

1. LH Variable Camshaft Timing (VCT) oil control solenoid electrical connector
2. VCT oil control solenoid bolt (2 required)
3. VCT oil control solenoid (2 required)

N0122870

Fig. 135 Variable Camshaft Timing (VCT) Oil Control Solenoid

FUEL   **GASOLINE FUEL INJECTION SYSTEM**

FUEL SYSTEM SERVICE PRECAUTIONS

Safety is the most important factor when performing not only fuel system maintenance but any type of maintenance. Failure to conduct maintenance and repairs in a safe manner may result in serious personal injury or death. Maintenance and testing of the vehicle's fuel system components can be accomplished safely and effectively by adhering to the following rules and guidelines.

• To avoid the possibility of fire and personal injury, always disconnect the negative battery cable unless the repair or test procedure requires that battery voltage be applied.

• Always relieve the fuel system pressure prior to disconnecting any fuel system component (injector, fuel rail, pressure regulator, etc.), fitting or fuel line connection. Exercise extreme caution whenever relieving fuel system pressure to avoid exposing skin, face and eyes to fuel spray. Please be advised that fuel under pressure may penetrate the skin or any part of the body that it contacts.

• Always place a shop towel or cloth around the fitting or connection prior to loosening to absorb any excess fuel due to spillage. Ensure that all fuel spillage (should it occur) is quickly removed from engine surfaces. Ensure that all fuel soaked cloths or towels are deposited into a suitable waste container.

• Always keep a dry chemical (Class B) fire extinguisher near the work area.

• Do not allow fuel spray or fuel vapors to come into contact with a spark or open flame.

• Always use a back-up wrench when loosening and tightening fuel line connection fittings. This will prevent unnecessary stress and torsion to fuel line piping.

• Always replace worn fuel fitting O-rings with new Do not substitute fuel hose or equivalent where fuel pipe is installed.

Before servicing the vehicle, make sure to also refer to the precautions in the beginning of this section as well.

RELIEVING FUEL SYSTEM PRESSURE

✳ CAUTION

Do not smoke, carry lighted tobacco or have an open flame of any type when working on or near any fuel-related component. Highly flammable mixtures are always present and may be ignited. Failure to follow these instructions may result in serious personal injury.

✳ CAUTION

Do not carry personal electronic devices such as cell phones, pagers or audio equipment of any type when working on or near any fuel-related component. Highly flammable mixtures are always present and may be ignited. Failure to follow these instructions may result in serious personal injury.

✳ CAUTION

Before working on or disconnecting any of the fuel tubes or fuel system components, relieve the fuel system pressure to prevent accidental spraying of fuel. Fuel in the fuel system remains under high pressure, even when the engine is not running. Failure to follow this instruction may result in serious personal injury.

✳ CAUTION

When handling fuel, always observe fuel handling precautions and be prepared in the event of fuel spillage. Spilled fuel may be ignited by hot vehicle components or other ignition sources. Failure to follow these instructions may result in serious personal injury.

➡ The Fuel Pump (FP) module fuse is located in the Battery Junction Box (BJB), location F8.

1. Remove the FP module fuse.

➡ **The engine will crank and not start.**

2. Crank the engine for approximately 20 seconds.

3. Crank the engine an additional 20 seconds to make sure the fuel system pressure has been released.

4. Turn the ignition switch to the OFF position.

5. When fuel system service is complete, install the FP module fuse.

➡ **It may take more than one key cycle to pressurize the fuel system. Cycle the ignition key and wait 3 seconds to pressurize the fuel system.**

6. Check for leaks prior to starting the engine.

7. Start the vehicle and check the fuel system for leaks.

FUEL FILTER

REMOVAL & INSTALLATION

A lifetime fuel filter is serviced as part of the FP module.

FUEL INJECTORS

REMOVAL & INSTALLATION

1. The fuel injectors are serviced with the fuel rail.

FUEL PUMP (FP) MODULE

REMOVAL & INSTALLATION

✳✳ CAUTION

Do not smoke, carry lighted tobacco or have an open flame of any type when working on or near any fuel-related component. Highly flammable mixtures are always present and may be ignited. Failure to follow these instructions may result in serious personal injury.

✳✳ CAUTION

Do not carry personal electronic devices such as cell phones, pagers or audio equipment of any type when working on or near any fuel-related component. Highly flammable mixtures are always present and may be ignited. Failure to follow these

instructions may result in serious personal injury.

✳✳ CAUTION

When handling fuel, always observe fuel handling precautions and be prepared in the event of fuel spillage. Spilled fuel may be ignited by hot vehicle components or other ignition sources. Failure to follow these instructions may result in serious personal injury.

✳✳ CAUTION

Before working on or disconnecting any of the fuel tubes or fuel system components, relieve the fuel system pressure to prevent accidental spraying of fuel. Fuel in the fuel system remains under high pressure, even when the engine is not running. Failure to follow this instruction may result in serious personal injury.

✳✳ CAUTION

Always disconnect the battery ground cable at the battery when working on an evaporative emission (EVAP) system or fuel-related component. Highly flammable mixtures are always present and may be ignited. Failure to follow these instructions may result in serious personal injury.

➡ The Fuel Pump (FP) module has a serviceable fuel level sender.

➡ To avoid introducing contamination into the fuel tank use water to clean the FP module connections, couplings, flange surface and the immediate surrounding area of any dirt or foreign material. Blow dry thoroughly with shop air after cleaning.

1. Remove the fuel tank.

➡ Carefully install the lock ring wrench to avoid damaging the Fuel Pump (FP) module when removing the lock ring.

2. Using the lock ring wrench, rotate the lock ring counterclockwise and remove the FP module lock ring.

➡ The Fuel Pump (FP) module must be handled carefully to avoid damage to the float arm.

➡ The FP module will have residual fuel remaining internally, drain into a suitable container.

3. Remove the FP module from the fuel tank.

➡ Inspect the mating surfaces of the FP module flange and the fuel tank O-ring seal contact surfaces. Do not polish or adjust the O-ring seal contact area of the fuel tank flange or the fuel tank. Install a new FP module or fuel tank if the O-ring seal contact area is bent, scratched or corroded.

➡ To install, apply clean engine oil to the new O-ring seal.

4. Remove and discard the FP module O-ring seal.

To install:

5. Install a new FP module O-ring seal.

➡ To install, apply clean engine oil to the new O-ring seal.

6. Install the FP module to the fuel tank.

7. Using the lock ring wrench, rotate the lock ring clockwise and install the FP module lock ring.

8. Install the fuel tank.

FUEL RAIL

REMOVAL & INSTALLATION

✳✳ CAUTION

Do not smoke, carry lighted tobacco or have an open flame of any type when working on or near any fuel-related component. Highly flammable mixtures are always present and may be ignited. Failure to follow these instructions may result in serious personal injury.

✳✳ CAUTION

Before working on or disconnecting any of the fuel tubes or fuel system components, relieve the fuel system pressure to prevent accidental spraying of fuel. Fuel in the fuel system remains under high pressure, even when the engine is not running. Failure to follow this instruction may result in serious personal injury.

✳✳ CAUTION

Clean all fuel residue from the engine compartment. If not removed, fuel residue may ignite when the engine is returned to operation. Failure to follow this instruction may result in serious personal injury.

❋❋ CAUTION

Do not carry personal electronic devices such as cell phones, pagers or audio equipment of any type when working on or near any fuel-related component. Highly flammable mixtures are always present and may be ignited. Failure to follow these instructions may result in serious personal injury.

❋❋ CAUTION

Always disconnect the battery ground cable at the battery when working on an evaporative emission (EVAP) system or fuel-related component. Highly flammable mixtures are always present and may be ignited. Failure to follow these instructions may result in serious personal injury.

1. Release the fuel system pressure.
2. Disconnect the battery ground cable.
3. Disconnect the valve cover vent hose from the valve cover and position the hose out of the way.
4. Disconnect the degas bottle vent hose from the two clips on the fuel rail.
5. Disconnect the fuel tube-to-fuel rail spring lock coupling.
6. Disconnect the 4 fuel injector electrical connectors.
7. Remove the 2 bolts, the fuel rail and the 4 injectors.

➡Use O-ring seals that are made of special fuel resistant material. Use of ordinary O-rings can cause the fuel system to leak. Do not reuse the O-ring seals.

8. Remove the fuel injector retaining clips and the fuel injectors.
9. Remove and discard the O-ring seals.

➡Install new O-ring seals and lubricate them with clean engine oil.

To install:

➡Install new O-ring seals and lubricate them with clean engine oil.

10. Install the O-ring seals.
11. Install the fuel injector retaining clips and the fuel injectors.

➡Use O-ring seals that are made of special fuel resistant material. Use of ordinary O-rings can cause the fuel system to leak. Do not reuse the O-ring seals.

12. Install the 2 bolts, the fuel rail and the 4 injectors. Tighten the bolts to 97 inch lbs. (11 Nm).
13. Connect the 4 fuel injector electrical connectors.
14. Connect the fuel tube-to-fuel rail spring lock coupling.
15. Connect the degas bottle vent hose from the two clips on the fuel rail.
16. Connect the valve cover vent hose from the valve cover and position the hose out of the way.
17. Connect the battery ground cable.

FUEL TANK

DRAINING

❋❋ CAUTION

Do not smoke, carry lighted tobacco or have an open flame of any type when working on or near any fuel-related component. Highly flammable mixtures are always present and may be ignited. Failure to follow these instructions may result in serious personal injury.

❋❋ CAUTION

Do not carry personal electronic devices such as cell phones, pagers or audio equipment of any type when working on or near any fuel-related component. Highly flammable mixtures are always present and may be ignited. Failure to follow these instructions may result in serious personal injury.

❋❋ CAUTION

When handling fuel, always observe fuel handling precautions and be prepared in the event of fuel spillage. Spilled fuel may be ignited by hot vehicle components or other ignition sources. Failure to follow these instructions may result in serious personal injury.

❋❋ CAUTION

Remove the fuel filler cap slowly. The fuel system may be under pressure. If the fuel filler cap is venting vapor or if you hear a hissing sound, wait until it stops before completely removing the fuel filler cap. Otherwise, fuel may spray out. Failure to follow these instructions may result in serious personal injury.

1. Disconnect the battery ground cable.

➡The supplemental refueling adapter is located in the luggage compartment.

2. Install the supplemental refueling adapter and a length of semi-rigid fuel drain tube into the Easy Fuel(tm) (capless) fuel tank filler pipe.
3. Attach the Fuel Storage Tanker to the fuel drain tube and drain as much fuel as possible from the Easy Fuel(tm) (capless) fuel tank filler pipe, lowering the fuel level below the fuel tank inlet spout.

➡Some residual fuel may remain in the fuel tank filler pipe. Carefully drain into a suitable container.

4. Release the clamp and position the fuel tank filler pipe hose aside. Tighten the clamp to 35 inch lbs. (4 Nm).
5. Secure the fuel tank filler pipe hose above the fuel level.
6. Insert the fuel drain tube into the fuel tank filler pipe hose, attach the Fuel Storage Tanker and drain as much fuel as possible from the fuel tank.

REMOVAL & INSTALLATION

See Figure 136.

❋❋ CAUTION

Do not smoke, carry lighted tobacco or have an open flame of any type when working on or near any fuel-related component. Highly flammable mixtures are always present and may be ignited. Failure to follow these instructions may result in serious personal injury.

❋❋ CAUTION

Do not carry personal electronic devices such as cell phones, pagers or audio equipment of any type when working on or near any fuel-related component. Highly flammable mixtures are always present and may be ignited. Failure to follow these instructions may result in serious personal injury.

❋❋ CAUTION

Before working on or disconnecting any of the fuel tubes or fuel system components, relieve the fuel system pressure to prevent accidental spraying of fuel. Fuel in the fuel system remains under high pressure, even when the engine is not running. Failure to follow this instruction may result in serious personal injury.

✳✳ CAUTION

When handling fuel, always observe fuel handling precautions and be prepared in the event of fuel spillage. Spilled fuel may be ignited by hot vehicle components or other ignition sources. Failure to follow these instructions may result in serious personal injury.

✳✳ CAUTION

Always disconnect the battery ground cable at the battery when working on an evaporative emission (EVAP) system or fuel-related component. Highly flammable mixtures are always present and may be ignited. Failure to follow these instructions may result in serious personal injury.

1. With the vehicle in NEUTRAL, position it on a hoist.
2. Release the fuel system pressure.
3. Disconnect the battery ground cable.
4. Drain the fuel tank.
5. Disconnect the muffler and tailpipe assembly from the insulators.
6. Remove the 5 nuts and fuel tank heat shield.
7. Disconnect the fuel vapor tube assembly-to-fuel tank quick connect coupling.
8. Loosen the hose clamp and disconnect the fuel tank filler pipe from the fuel tank.
9. Position the Powertrain Lift under the fuel tank.

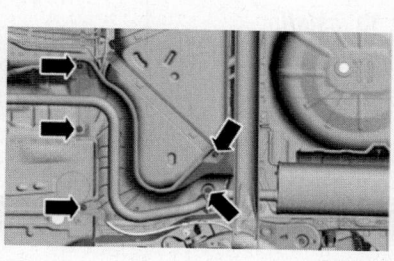

Fig. 136 Remove the 5 nuts and fuel tank heat shield

➡Some residual fuel may remain in the fuel tank filler pipe after draining the fuel tank. Carefully drain any residual fuel into a suitable container.

10. Release the clamp and disconnect the fuel tank filler pipe from the fuel tank.
11. Position the Powertrain Lift under the fuel tank.
12. Remove the 3 fuel tank strap bolts.
13. Partially lower the fuel tank for access.
14. Disconnect the fuel supply tube-to-Fuel Pump (FP) module quick connect coupling.
15. Disconnect the FP module electrical connector.
16. Lower the fuel tank.

To install:

17. Raise the fuel tank.
18. Connect the FP module electrical connector.
19. Connect the fuel supply tube-to-Fuel Pump (FP) module quick connect coupling.
20. Partially lower the fuel tank for access.
21. Install the 3 fuel tank strap bolts. Tighten the bolts to 18 ft. lbs. (25 Nm).

22. Position the Powertrain Lift under the fuel tank.
23. Connect the fuel tank filler pipe to the fuel tank, and tighten the clamp. Tighten the clamp to 35 inch lbs. (4 Nm).
24. Position the Powertrain Lift under the fuel tank.
25. Tighten the hose clamp and connect the fuel tank filler pipe to the fuel tank.
26. Connect the fuel vapor tube assembly-to-fuel tank quick connect coupling.
27. Install the 5 nuts and fuel tank heat shield.
28. Connect the muffler and tailpipe assembly to the insulators.
29. Fill the fuel tank.
30. Connect the battery ground cable.
31. With the vehicle in NEUTRAL, lower from the hoist.

THROTTLE BODY

REMOVAL & INSTALLATION

1. Remove the Air Cleaner (ACL) outlet pipe.
2. Disconnect the electronic throttle control electrical connector.
3. Remove the 4 bolts and the Throttle Body (TB).
   a. Remove and discard the TB gasket.

To install:

4. Install a new TB gasket.
5. Install the TB, and the 4 bolts. Tighten the bolts to 71 inch lbs. (8 Nm).
6. Connect the electronic throttle control electrical connector.
7. Install the Air Cleaner (ACL) outlet pipe.
8. If the TB was replaced, turn the key ON without cranking the engine for 1 minute to allow the PCM to learn the adaptive table values for the new TB.

HEATING & AIR CONDITIONING SYSTEM

BLOWER MOTOR

REMOVAL & INSTALLATION

1. With the ignition in the ON position, select the PANEL climate control mode. Switch the ignition to the OFF position.
2. Remove the brake pedal and bracket assembly.
3. Disconnect the blower motor electrical connector.
4. Remove the 3 blower motor screws.
5. Remove the blower motor.

To install:

6. Install the blower motor.
7. Install the 3 blower motor screws.

8. Connect the blower motor electrical connector.
9. Install the brake pedal and bracket assembly.
10. With the ignition in the ON position, select the PANEL climate control mode. Switch the ignition to the OFF position.

HEATER CORE

REMOVAL & INSTALLATION

See Figure 137.

1. Remove the heater core and evaporator core housing.
2. Remove the dash panel seal.

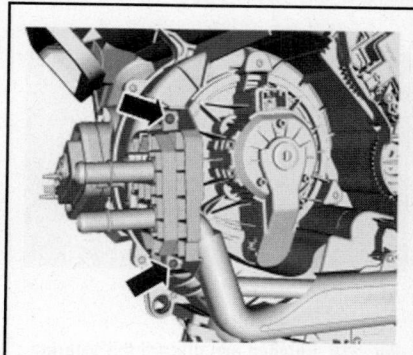

Fig. 137 Remove the 2 heater core tube bracket screws and remove the bracket

3. Remove the 2 heater core tube bracket screws and remove the bracket.

4. Remove the 3 heater tube cover screws and remove the heater tube cover.

5. Remove the heater core retainer screw and position the retainer aside.

6. Remove the heater core.

To install:

7. Install the heater core.

8. Install the heater core retainer screw and position the retainer aside.

9. Install the 3 heater tube cover

screws and remove the heater tube cover.

10. Install the 2 heater core tube bracket screws and remove the bracket.

11. Install the dash panel seal.

12. Install the heater core and evaporator core housing.

STEERING

POWER STEERING GEAR

REMOVAL & INSTALLATION

See Figures 138 through 141.

1. Using a suitable holding device, hold the steering wheel in the straight-ahead position.

✳✳ WARNING

Do not allow the steering column to rotate while the steering column shaft is disconnected or damage to the clockspring may result. If there is evidence that the steering column shaft has rotated, remove and re-center the clockspring as outlined in the Chassis Electrical Section.

2. Remove and discard the steering column shaft-to-steering gear bolt and disconnect the steering column shaft from the steering gear.

3. Remove the front wheels and tires.

4. Remove and discard the 2 outer tie rod nuts.

5. Using the Tie Rod End Remover, separate the outer tie rods from the wheel knuckles.

6. Remove and discard the 2 stabilizer bar link-to-strut nuts and disconnect the stabilizer bar links from the struts.

7. Remove the 2 subframe brace-to-body bolts.

Fig. 139 Using the Tie Rod End Remover, separate the outer tie rods from the wheel knuckles

8. Disconnect the exhaust isolator.

9. Remove the engine roll restrictor bolt.

10. Support the front subframe using a suitable transmission jack.

11. Mark the position of the subframe-to-frame mounting location at each mounting point on the vehicle frame rails to aide in installation.

12. Remove the 4 subframe bolts and discard the 2 rearward bolts.

13. Lower the front subframe approximately 6.102 inch (155 mm).

14. Remove the 3 steering gear bolts and the steering gear.

To install:

15. Position the steering gear and install

the 3 bolts. Tighten the bolts to 66 ft. lbs. (90 Nm).

16. Raise the subframe and loosely Install the 4 subframe bolts.

17. Align the subframe to the locating marks made during removal.

➡**RH and LH dimensions are identical. All measurements on center.**

18. Measure for correct positioning of the subframe to vehicle underbody.

   a. Location 1 - 10.236 inch (260 mm)

   b. Location 2 - 26.22 inch (666 mm)

19. Tighten the subframe bolts.

   a. Tighten the forward bolts to 44 ft. lbs. (60 Nm).

   b. Tighten the new rearward bolts to 74 ft. lbs. (100 Nm).

   c. Tighten the rearward bolts an additional 240°.

20. Position the engine roll restrictor and install the engine roll restrictor bolt. Tighten the bolt to 37 ft. lbs. (50 Nm).

21. Connect the exhaust isolator.

22. Install the 2 subframe brace-to-body bolts. Tighten the bolts to 37 ft. lbs. (50 Nm).

23. Position the stabilizer bar links and install the 2 new stabilizer bar link-to-strut nuts. Tighten the nuts to 35 ft. lbs. (48 Nm).

Fig. 138 Remove and discard the steering column shaft-to-steering gear bolt and disconnect the steering column shaft from the steering gear

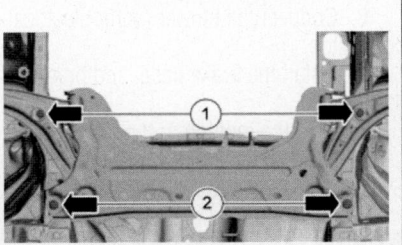

Fig. 140 Mark the position of the subframe-to-frame mounting location at each mounting point on the vehicle frame rails to aide in installation. Remove the 4 subframe bolts and discard the 2 rearward bolts

Fig. 141 Measure for correct positioning of the subframe to vehicle underbody

24. Position the outer tie rods and install the new 2 outer tie rod nuts. Tighten the nuts to 39 ft. lbs. (53 Nm).

✳✳ CAUTION

Do not reuse steering column shaft bolts. This may result in fastener failure and steering column shaft detachment or loss of steering control. Failure to follow this instruction may result in serious injury to vehicle occupant(s).

25. Connect the steering column shaft and install a new steering column shaft-to-steering gear bolt. Tighten the bolt to 24 ft. lbs. (32 Nm).

26. Check and, if necessary, adjust the front toe.

SUSPENSION

LOWER CONTROL ARM

REMOVAL AND & INSTALLATION

✳✳ WARNING

Suspension fasteners are critical parts that affect performance of vital components and systems. Failure of these fasteners may result in major service expense. Use the same or equivalent parts if replacement is necessary. Do not use a replacement part of lesser quality or substitute design. Tighten fasteners as specified. Remove the wheel and tire.

✳✳ WARNING

Use care when releasing the lower arm and wheel knuckle into the resting position or damage to the ball joint seal may occur.

✳✳ WARNING

Tighten suspension bushing fasteners with the weight of the vehicle resting on the wheel and tires or incorrect clamp load and bushing damage may occur.

✳✳ WARNING

Do not use a prying device or separator fork between the ball joint and the wheel knuckle. Damage to the ball joint or ball joint seal may result. Only use the pry bar by inserting it into the lower control arm body opening.

1. Remove and discard the ball joint nut and bolt. Using a pry bar, separate the ball joint stud from the wheel knuckle.

2. Remove and discard the forward and rear lower arm bolts and remove the lower arm.

To install:

➡ Do not tighten the forward and rear lower arm bolts at this time.

3. Position the lower arm and loosely install the new forward and rear bolts.

4. Insert the ball joint stud into the wheel knuckle and install the new ball joint bolt and nut. Tighten the bolt to 38 ft. lbs. (52 Nm).

5. Install the wheel and tire.

6. Lower the hoist so the weight of the vehicle is resting on the wheels and tires.

7. Tighten the new forward and rear lower arm bolts in 2 stages
   a. Stage 1: Tighten to 46 ft. lbs. (63 Nm).
   b. Stage 2: Tighten an additional 180 degrees.

8. Check and, if necessary, align the front end.

STABILIZER BAR

REMOVAL & INSTALLATION
See Figure 142.

✳✳ WARNING

Suspension fasteners are critical parts because they affect performance of vital components and systems and their failure may result in major service expense. New parts must be installed with the same part

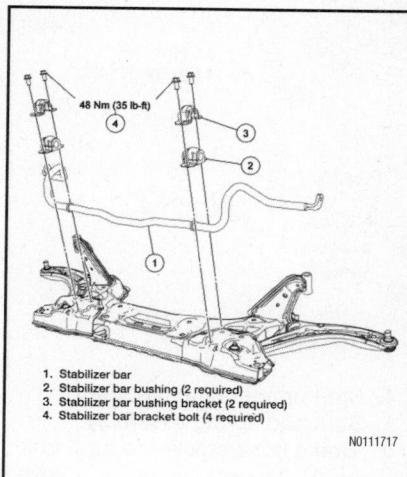

1. Stabilizer bar
2. Stabilizer bar bushing (2 required)
3. Stabilizer bar bushing bracket (2 required)
4. Stabilizer bar bracket bolt (4 required)

N0111717

Fig. 142 Stabilizer bar components exploded view

numbers or equivalent part, if replacement is necessary. Do not use a replacement part of lesser quality or substitute design. Torque values must be used as specified during reassembly to make sure correct retention of these parts.

1. Remove the front subframe.
2. Remove the stabilizer bar bracket bolts and brackets.
   a. Discard the bolts.
3. Remove the stabilizer bar bushings.
4. Remove the stabilizer bar.

To install:

✳✳ WARNING

The stabilizer bar bushings must be positioned correctly with the slit in the bushing toward the rear of the vehicle or damage to the bushings may occur.

5. Position the stabilizer bar with the bushings installed with the slit in the bushing toward the rear of the vehicle.

6. Position the stabilizer bar brackets and install the new bolts. Tighten the bolts to 35 ft. lbs. (48 Nm).

7. Install the front subframe.

STRUT & SPRING ASSEMBLY

REMOVAL & INSTALLATION
See Figure 143.

✳✳ WARNING

Suspension fasteners are critical parts because they affect performance of vital components and systems and their failure may result in major service expense. New parts must be installed with the same part numbers or equivalent part, if replacement is necessary. Do not use a replacement part of lesser quality or substitute design. Torque values must be used as specified during reassembly to make sure correct retention of these parts.

✳✳ WARNING

Support the strut and spring assembly to prevent damage.

1. Remove the wheel and tire.

➡ Drivers side only

2. Position aside the brake fluid reservoir (main container).

3. Position aside the air conditioner hose support bracket.

4. Remove and discard the 3 strut and spring assembly upper mount nuts.

5. Disconnect the wheel speed sensor harness from the strut and spring assembly bracket.

6. Remove the stabilizer bar link upper nut and detach the link from the strut.

   a. Discard the nut.

   b. To install, tighten the new nut to 41 ft. lbs. (55 Nm).

7. Remove the brake flexible hose bracket bolt and disconnect the hose from the strut and spring assembly.

8. Remove the wheel knuckle-to-strut nuts, bolts and the strut and spring assembly.

   a. Discard the wheel knuckle-to-strut nuts and bolts.

   b. To install, tighten the new wheel knuckle-to-strut nuts to 59 ft. lbs. (80

Nm) and then tighten an additional 90 degrees.

➡ Insert LH knuckle-to-strut bolts from the knuckle arm side.

9. Insert RH knuckle-to-strut bolts from the brake caliper side.

To install:

➡ Insert LH knuckle-to-strut bolts to the knuckle arm side.

10. Insert RH knuckle-to-strut bolts to the brake caliper side.

11. Install the wheel knuckle-to-strut nuts, bolts and the strut and spring assembly.

   a. To install, tighten the new wheel knuckle-to-strut nuts to 59 ft. lbs. (80 Nm) and then tighten an additional 90 degrees.

12. Install the brake flexible hose bracket bolt and disconnect the hose to the strut and spring assembly. Tighten the bolt to 19 ft. lbs. (26 Nm).

13. Install the stabilizer bar link upper nut and detach the link to the strut. Tighten the new nut to 41 ft. lbs. (55 Nm).

14. Connect the wheel speed sensor harness to the strut and spring assembly bracket.

15. Install and discard the 3 strut and spring assembly upper mount nuts. Tighten the new nuts to 22 ft. lbs. (30 Nm).

16. Reposition the air conditioner hose support bracket. Tighten the bracket to 62 inch lbs. (7 Nm).

17. Reposition the brake fluid reservoir (main container). Tighten the reservoir to 62 inch lbs. (7 Nm).

18. Check and, if necessary, align the front end.

WHEEL BEARINGS

REMOVAL & INSTALLATION

See Figure 144.

➡ When the wheel hub is pressed from the bearing, the bearing inner race will come out with the hub. Never try to install the race back into the bearing. Always install a new bearing.

✳✳ WARNING

Make sure to keep the knuckle level and supported during pressing operations, or damage to the knuckle can occur. Support the knuckle as close to the bearing bore as possible. Do not use knuckle extremities as supports.

➡ If removing the wheel hub, the wheel bearing must be replaced.

➡ The Anti-Lock Brake System (ABS) tone ring is part of the wheel bearing assembly.

1. Remove the wheel knuckle.

2. Using the Step Plate and a suitable press, remove the wheel hub from the wheel bearing.

➡ This step may not be necessary if the inner wheel bearing race remains in the wheel knuckle after removing the wheel hub.

3. Using the Pinion Bearing Cone Remover and a suitable press, remove the inner wheel bearing race from the wheel hub.

4. Remove the snap ring.

5. Using the Wheel Hub Cup Remover/Installer and a suitable press, remove the outer wheel bearing race from the wheel knuckle.

To install:

➡ Install the wheel bearing with the pink colored wheel speed sensor ring facing towards the transmission side.

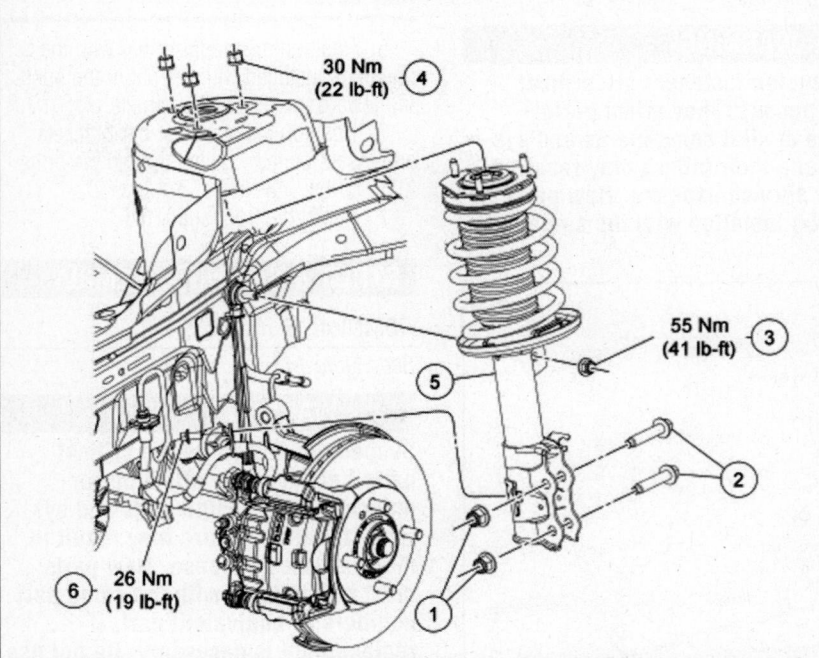

1. Wheel knuckle-to-strut nut (2 required)
2. Wheel knuckle-to-strut bolt (2 required)
3. Stabilizer bar link upper nut
4. Strut upper nut (3 required)
5. Strut and spring assembly
6. Brake hose bracket to strut bolt

N0118469

Fig. 143 Strut and Spring Assembly exploded view

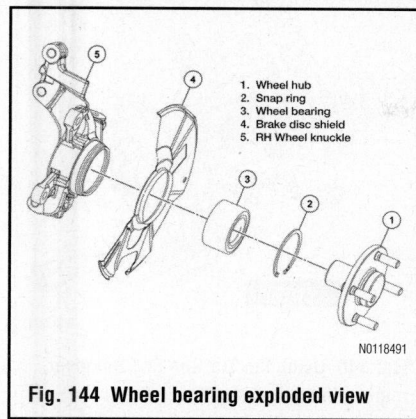

Fig. 144 Wheel bearing exploded view

1. Wheel hub
2. Snap ring
3. Wheel bearing
4. Brake disc shield
5. RH Wheel knuckle

6. Using the Wheel Hub Bearing Cup Installer and a suitable press, install the wheel bearing into the wheel knuckle.

7. Install the snap ring.

> ❋❋ **WARNING**
>
> **The wheel bearing inner race must be supported during hub installation. Failure to do so will damage the bearing.**

8. Using the Wheel Hub Bearing Cup Installer, Step Plate and a suitable press, install the wheel hub into the wheel bearing.

9. Install the wheel knuckle.

WHEEL KNUCKLE

REMOVAL & INSTALLATION

See Figure 146.

> ❋❋ **WARNING**
>
> **Suspension fasteners are critical parts that affect performance of vital components and systems. Failure of these fasteners may result in major service expense. Use the same or equivalent parts if replacement is necessary. Do not use a replacement part of lesser quality or substitute design. Tighten fasteners as specified.**

> ❋❋ **WARNING**
>
> **Do not tighten the wheel hub nut with the vehicle on the ground. Tighten the nut to specification before the vehicle is lowered onto the wheels. Wheel bearing damage will occur if the wheel bearing is loaded with the weight of the vehicle applied.**

> ❋❋ **WARNING**
>
> **Install and tighten the new wheel hub nut to specification in a continuous**

rotation. **Always install a new wheel hub nut after loosening or when not tightened to specification in a continuous rotation or damage to the component may occur.**

1. Remove the wheel and tire.

➡**Apply the brake to prevent the half-shaft from rotating while loosening the wheel hub nut.**

2. Remove and discard the wheel hub nut.

3. Remove the brake flexible hose bracket bolt and disconnect the brake flexible hose from the strut and spring assembly.

> ❋❋ **WARNING**
>
> **Do not allow the brake caliper to hang from the brake hose or damage to the brake hose can occur.**

4. Remove the 2 brake caliper anchor plate bolts and position the brake caliper assembly aside.

   a. Support the brake caliper assembly using mechanic's wire.

5. Remove the brake disc.

6. If equipped with Anti-Lock Brake System (ABS), remove the wheel speed sen-

sor bolt and position the wheel speed sensor aside.

> ❋❋ **WARNING**
>
> **Do not remove the tie-rod end nut or damage to the tie-rod end may occur.**

7. Loosen the tie-rod end nut.

8. Using the Tie-Rod End Remover, detach the tie-rod end from the wheel knuckle.

   a. Remove and discard the tie-rod end nut.

> ❋❋ **WARNING**
>
> **Do not use a prying device or separator fork between the ball joint and the wheel knuckle. Damage to the ball joint or ball joint seal may result. Only use the pry bar by inserting it into the lower arm body opening.**

> ❋❋ **WARNING**
>
> **Use care when releasing the lower arm and wheel knuckle into the resting position or damage to the ball joint seal may occur.**

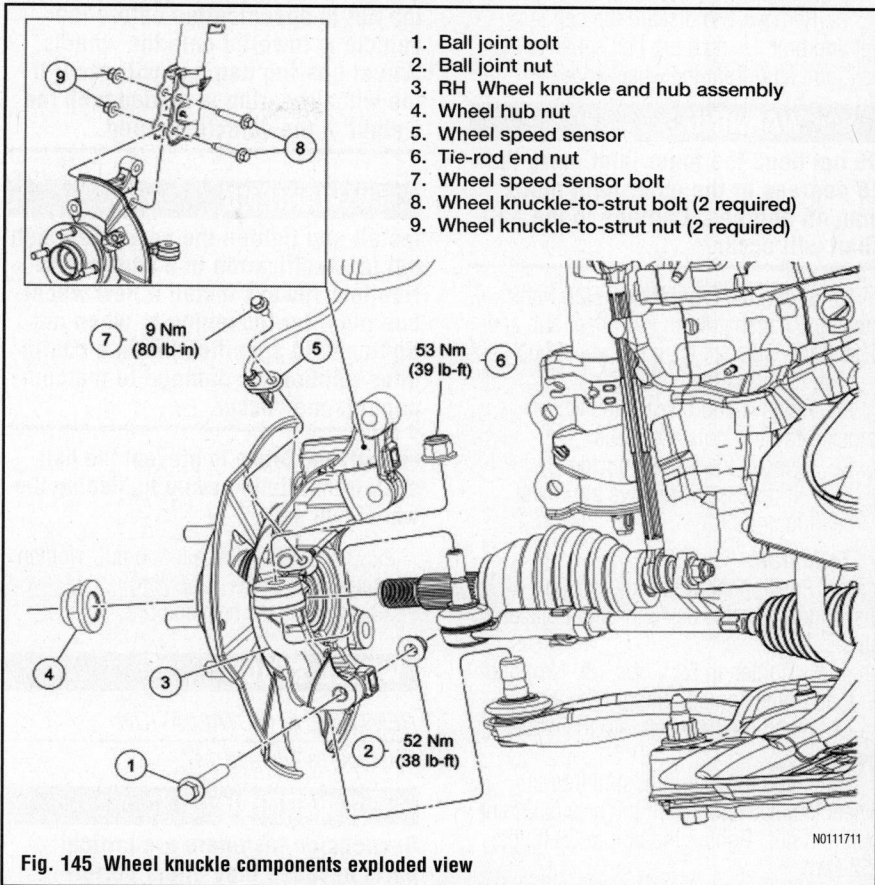

1. Ball joint bolt
2. Ball joint nut
3. RH Wheel knuckle and hub assembly
4. Wheel hub nut
5. Wheel speed sensor
6. Tie-rod end nut
7. Wheel speed sensor bolt
8. Wheel knuckle-to-strut bolt (2 required)
9. Wheel knuckle-to-strut nut (2 required)

9 Nm (80 lb-in)

53 Nm (39 lb-ft)

52 Nm (38 lb-ft)

Fig. 145 Wheel knuckle components exploded view

9. Remove and discard the ball joint nut and bolt. Using a pry bar, separate the ball joint stud from the wheel knuckle.

※※ WARNING

Do not bend the inner joint more than 18 degrees or the outer joint more than 45 degrees. Damage to the half-shaft will occur.

10. Using the Front Wheel Hub Remover, press the halfshaft from the wheel hub and detach the halfshaft from the wheel hub
    a. Support the halfshaft.
11. Remove and discard the wheel knuckle-to-strut nuts and bolts.
12. Remove the wheel knuckle.
    a. If necessary, remove the wheel bearing and hub.

To install:
13. Position the wheel knuckle and install new wheel knuckle-to-strut bolts and nuts.
    a. Tighten to 59 ft. lbs. (80 Nm) and then tighten an additional 90 degrees.
14. Insert the halfshaft into the wheel hub.
15. Insert the ball joint stud into the wheel knuckle and install the new ball joint bolt and nut. Tighten the bolt to 38 ft. lbs. (52 Nm).
16. Attach the tie-rod end to the wheel knuckle and install a new tie-rod end nut. Tighten the nut to 39 ft. lbs. (53 Nm).
17. If equipped with ABS, position the wheel speed sensor and install the wheel speed sensor bolt. Tighten the bolt to 80 inch lbs. (9 Nm).
18. Install the brake disc.
19. Position the brake caliper assembly and install the 2 brake caliper anchor plate bolts. Tighten the bolts to 50 ft. lbs. (68 Nm).
20. Using the Halfshaft Installer, install the halfshaft into the wheel hub.
21. Connect the brake flexible hose to the strut and spring assembly and install the brake flexible hose bracket bolt. Tighten the bolt to 19 ft. lbs. (26 Nm).

※※ WARNING

Do not tighten the wheel hub nut with the vehicle on the ground. Tighten

the nut to specification before the vehicle is lowered onto the wheels. Wheel bearing damage will occur if the wheel bearing is loaded with the weight of the vehicle applied.

※※ WARNING

Install and tighten the new wheel hub nut to specification in a continuous rotation. Always install a new wheel hub nut after loosening or when not tightened to specification in a continuous rotation, or damage to the components may occur.

➡ Apply the brake to prevent the half-shaft from rotating while tightening the wheel hub nut.

22. Install a new wheel hub nut. Tighten the nut to 188 ft. lbs. (255 Nm).
23. Install the wheel and tire.

WHEEL STUDS

REMOVAL & INSTALLATION
See Figures 146 and 147.

※※ WARNING

Suspension fasteners are critical parts because they affect performance of vital components and systems and their failure may result in major service expense. New parts must be installed with the same part numbers or equivalent part, if replacement is necessary. Do not use a replacement part of lesser quality or substitute design. Torque values must be used as specified during reassembly to make sure correct retention of these parts.

➡ Make sure the steering wheel is in the UNLOCKED position.

1. Remove the brake disc.
2. Using the Tie-Rod End Remover, remove the wheel stud.

To install:

➡ Make sure to use washers that have an ID that is larger than the OD of the wheel stud serrations. Use enough

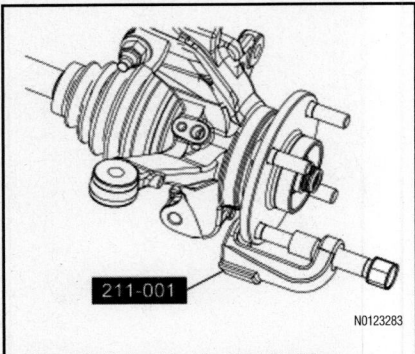

Fig. 146 Using the Tie-Rod End Remover, remove the wheel stud

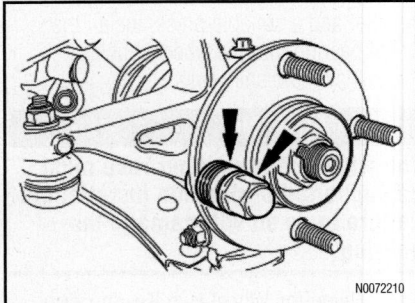

Fig. 147 Position the wheel stud in the flange, making sure the serrations on the stud line up with the serrations in the flange. Install the washers and a wheel nut

washers (approximately 4) to allow the wheel stud to fully seat against the hub flange.

3. Position the wheel stud in the flange, making sure the serrations on the stud line up with the serrations in the flange. Install the washers and a wheel nut.

※※ WARNING

Do not use power tools to install the wheel stud or damage to the flange may occur.

4. Tighten the wheel nut until the stud is seated against the hub flange.
5. Remove the wheel nut and the washers. Discard the wheel nut.
6. Install the brake disc.

AXLE ASSEMBLY

REMOVAL & INSTALLATION

See Figure 148.

➡Suspension fasteners are critical parts that affect performance of vital components and systems. Failure of these fasteners may result in major service expense. Use the same or equivalent parts if replacement is necessary. Do not use a replacement part of lesser quality or substitute design. Tighten fasteners as specified.

1. Remove the floor console.
2. Remove the parking brake adjustment nut retaining clip.
3. Loosen the parking brake adjustment nut 5 turns.
4. Remove the wheel and tire.
5. Disconnect both parking brake actuation lever cables.
6. Compress the clips and pull both parking brake cables through the mounting brackets.

➡Cap the brake tube connections to prevent fluid loss.

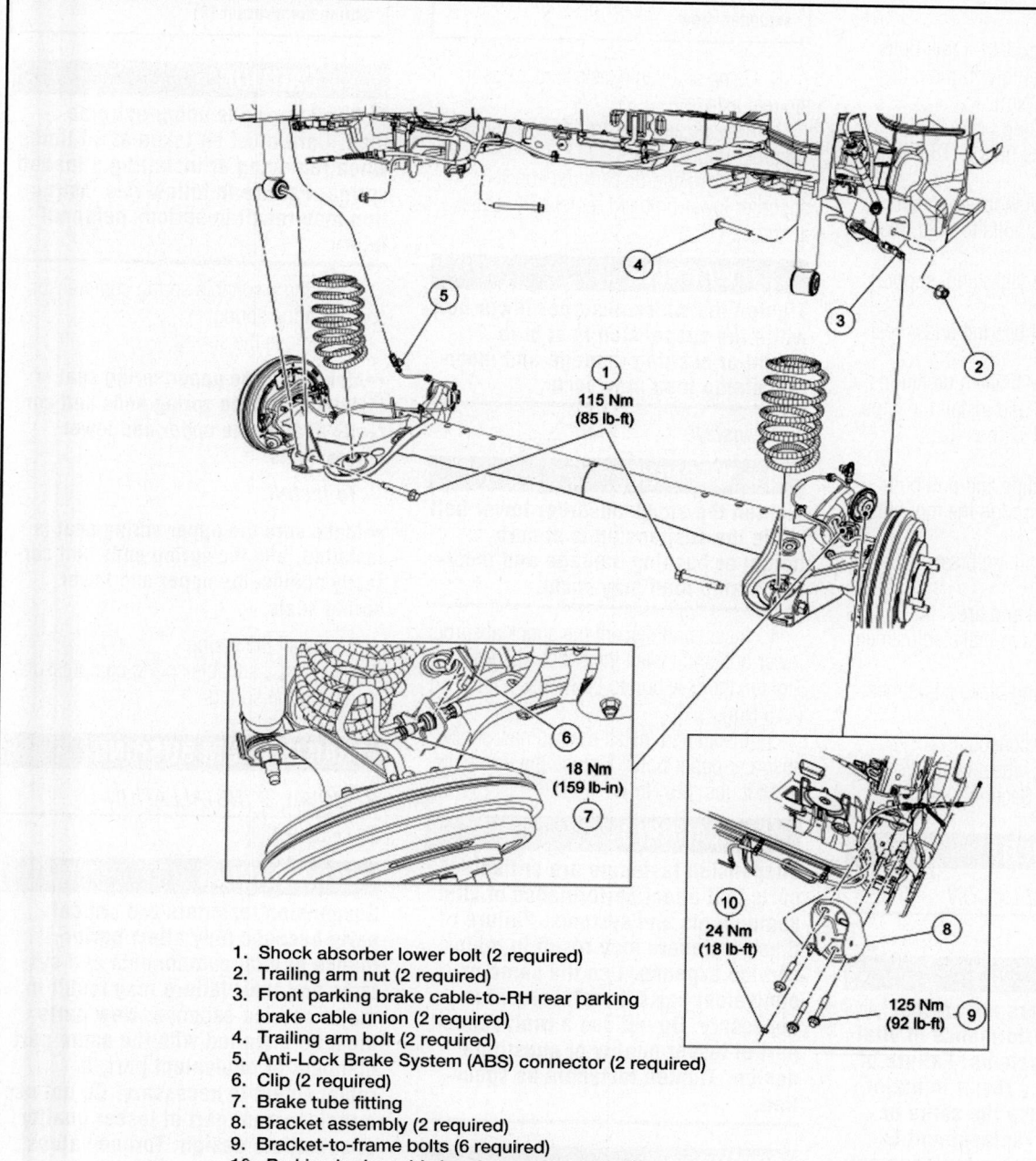

115 Nm
(85 lb-ft)

18 Nm
(159 lb-in)

24 Nm
(18 lb-ft)

125 Nm
(92 lb-ft)

1. Shock absorber lower bolt (2 required)
2. Trailing arm nut (2 required)
3. Front parking brake cable-to-RH rear parking brake cable union (2 required)
4. Trailing arm bolt (2 required)
5. Anti-Lock Brake System (ABS) connector (2 required)
6. Clip (2 required)
7. Brake tube fitting
8. Bracket assembly (2 required)
9. Bracket-to-frame bolts (6 required)
10. Parking brake cable bracket nut (2 required)

N0111733

Fig. 148 Axle components exploded view

7. Disconnect the rear brake tube fittings from the rear brake hoses and remove the clips.

8. Remove the wheel bearing and wheel hub assemblies.

9. Using a suitable jackstand, support the rear axle assembly.

10. Remove and discard the 2 shock absorber lower bolts.

11. Remove the 2 parking brake cable bracket nuts.

12. Remove the 6 bracket-to-frame bolts and remove the axle assembly

To install:

13. Install the 6 bracket-to-frame bolts and install the axle assembly. Tighten the bolts to 92 ft. lbs. (125 Nm).

14. Install the 2 parking brake cable bracket nuts. Tighten the nuts to 18 ft. lbs. (24 Nm).

15. Install the 2 new shock absorber lower bolts. Tighten the bolts to 85 ft. lbs. (115 Nm).

16. Using a suitable jackstand, support the rear axle assembly.

17. Install the wheel bearing and wheel hub assemblies.

18. Connect the rear brake tube fittings to the rear brake hoses and install the clips. Tighten the fittings to 159 inch lbs. (18 Nm)..

19. Compress the clips and pull both parking brake cables through the mounting brackets.

20. Connect both parking brake actuation lever cables.

21. Install the wheel and tire.

22. Tighten the parking brake adjustment nut 5 turns.

23. Install the parking brake adjustment nut retaining clip.

24. Install the floor console.

25. Bleed the brake wheel cylinders as outlined in the Brakes Section.

SHOCK ABSORBER

REMOVAL & INSTALLATION

See Figure 149.

❊❊ WARNING

Suspension fasteners are critical parts that affect performance of vital components and systems. Failure of these fasteners may result in major service expense. Use the same or equivalent parts if replacement is necessary. Do not use a replacement part of lesser quality or substitute design. Tighten fasteners as specified.

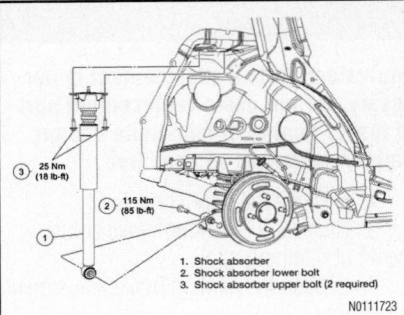

Fig. 149 Shock absorber components exploded view

1. Using a suitable jackstand, support the rear axle.

2. Remove and discard the two shock absorber upper bolts.

3. Remove and discard the shock absorber lower bolt and remove the shock absorber.

❊❊ WARNING

Tighten the shock absorber lower bolt while the suspension is at curb height or bushing damage and incorrect clamp load may occur.

To install:

❊❊ WARNING

Tighten the shock absorber lower bolt while the suspension is at curb height or bushing damage and incorrect clamp load may occur.

4. Install and discard the shock absorber lower bolt and install the shock absorber. Tighten the new bolt to 85 ft. lbs. (115 Nm).

5. Install and install the two new shock absorber upper bolts. Tighten the new bolts to 18 ft. lbs. (25 Nm).

❊❊ WARNING

Suspension fasteners are critical parts that affect performance of vital components and systems. Failure of these fasteners may result in major service expense. Use the same or equivalent parts if replacement is necessary. Do not use a replacement part of lesser quality or substitute design. Tighten fasteners as specified.

SPRING

REMOVAL & INSTALLATION

See Figure 150.

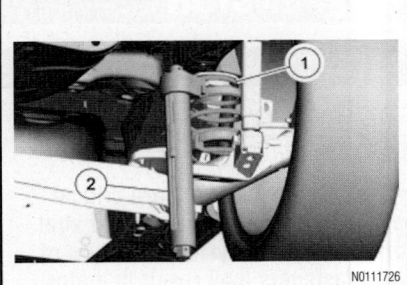

Fig. 150 Spring components. Spring (1), Spring compressor (2)

❊❊ CAUTION

The coil spring is under extreme load. Care must be taken at all times when removing or installing a loaded spring. Failure to follow this instruction may result in serious personal injury.

1. Using a suitable spring compressor, compress the spring.

2. Remove the spring.

➡Make sure the upper spring seat is installed, and the spring ends butt correctly against the upper and lower spring seats.

To install:

➡Make sure the upper spring seat is installed, and the spring ends butt correctly against the upper and lower spring seats.

3. Install the spring.

4. Using a suitable spring compressor, compress the spring.

TRAILING ARM BUSHING

REMOVAL & INSTALLATION

See Figure 151.

❊❊ WARNING

Suspension fasteners are critical parts because they affect performance of vital components and systems and their failure may result in major service expense. New parts must be installed with the same part numbers or equivalent part, if replacement is necessary. Do not use a replacement part of lesser quality or substitute design. Torque values must be used as specified during reassembly to make sure correct retention of these parts.

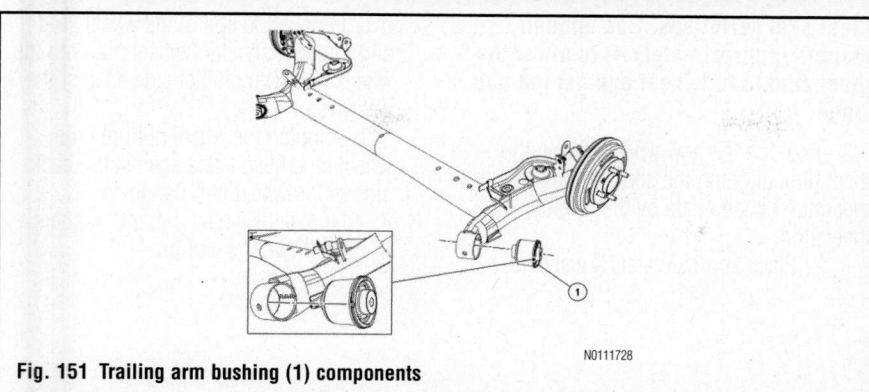

Fig. 151 Trailing arm bushing (1) components

1. Remove the wheel and tire.
2. Using a suitable jackstand, support the rear axle assembly.
3. Remove the 2 parking brake cable bracket bolts.
4. Remove the 6 axle bracket-to-frame bolts and remove the axle assembly
5. Lower the subframe and remove the 2 trailing arm bolts.
6. Using the special tools, remove the trailing arm bushing.

To install:

7. Using the special tool, Install the trailing arm bushing.
8. Lower the subframe and install the 2 trailing arm bolts. Tighten the bolts to 59 ft. lbs. (80 Nm) then tighten an additional 120 degrees.
9. Install the 6 axle bracket-to-frame bolts and install the axle assembly. Tighten the bolts to 92 ft. lbs. (125 Nm).
10. Install the 2 parking brake cable bracket bolts. Tighten bolts to 18 ft. lbs. (24 Nm).
11. Using a suitable jackstand, support the rear axle assembly.
12. Install the wheel and tire.

WHEEL BEARING & HUB

REMOVAL & INSTALLATION

See Figure 152.

✳✳ WARNING

Suspension fasteners are critical parts that affect performance of vital components and systems. Failure of these fasteners may result in major service expense. Use the same or equivalent parts if replacement is necessary. Do not use a replacement part of lesser quality or substitute design. Tighten fasteners as specified.

1. Remove the brake drum.
2. Remove the wheel speed sensor bolt and remove the wheel speed sensor.

3. Remove the wheel bearing and wheel hub assembly.
4. Remove and discard the 4 wheel bearing and wheel hub assembly bolts.
5. Remove the wheel bearing and wheel hub assembly.

To install:

6. Install the wheel bearing and wheel hub assembly with 4 new bolts in the proper sequence.
   a. Tighten all 4 bolts to 48 ft. lbs. (65 Nm).
   b. Loosen each bolt 90 degrees.

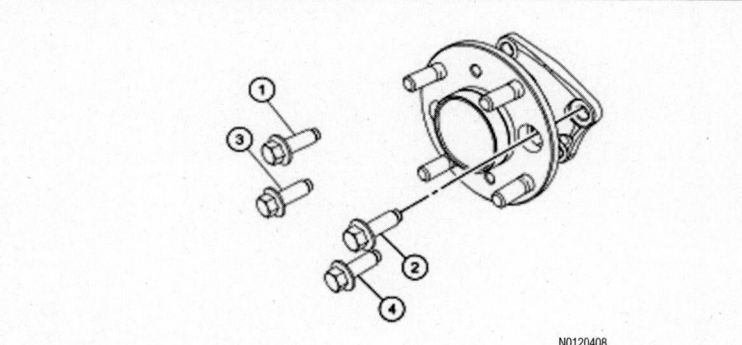

Fig. 152 Install the wheel bearing and wheel hub assembly with 4 new bolts in the proper sequence

c. Tighten each bolt to 48 ft. lbs. (65 Nm) using the sequence shown.
7. Install the wheel speed sensor and install the wheel speed sensor bolt. Tighten the bolt to 80 inch lbs. (9 Nm).
8. Install the brake drum.

WHEEL STUDS

REMOVAL & ISTALLATION

See Figure 153.

✳✳ WARNING

Suspension fasteners are critical parts because they affect performance of vital components and systems and their failure may result in major service expense. New parts must be installed with the same part numbers or equivalent part, if replacement is necessary. Do not use a replacement part of lesser quality or substitute design. Torque values must be used as specified during reassembly to make sure of correct retention of these parts.

1. Remove the brake drum.

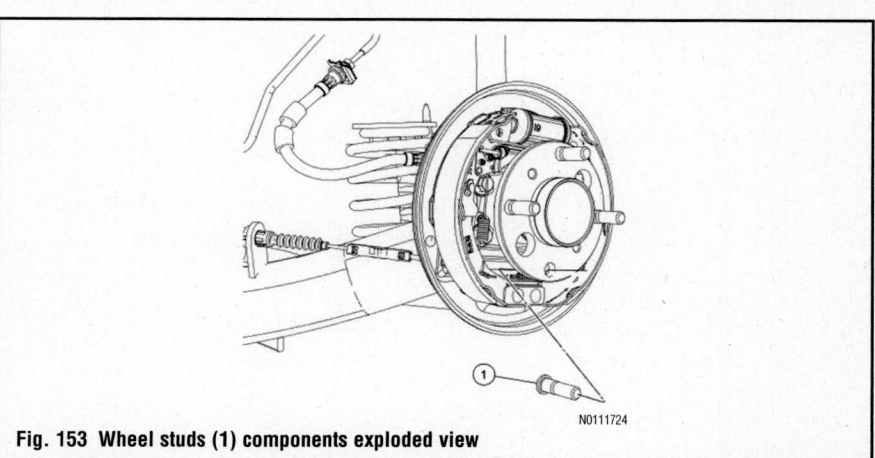

Fig. 153 Wheel studs (1) components exploded view

Never use a hammer to remove a wheel stud. Damage to the wheel hub may result.

2. Using the C-Frame and Screw Installer/Remover, remove the wheel stud.

➡**Make sure to use washers that have an ID that is larger than the OD of the** wheel stud serrations. Use enough washers (approximately 4) to allow the wheel stud to fully seat against the hub flange.

3. Position the new wheel stud in the wheel hub, aligning the serrations in the wheel hub flange made by the original wheel stud.

a. Place approximately 4 washers over the outside end of the wheel stud and thread a standard wheel nut onto the wheel stud with the flat side against the washers.

b. Tighten the wheel nut until the wheel stud head seats against the back side of the wheel hub flange.

4. Remove the wheel nut and washers.

5. Install the brake drum.

FORD, LINCOLN AND MERCURY

Diagnostic Trouble Codes

DIAGNOSTIC TROUBLE CODES... **DTC-1**

OBD II Trouble Code List (P0xxx Codes) DTC-2
OBD II Trouble Code List (P1xxx Codes) DTC-50
OBD II Trouble Code List (P2xxx Codes) DTC-68
OBD II Vehicle Applications DTC-1
   Ford DTC-1
   Lincoln..DTC-1
   Mercury DTC-1
Introduction DTC-1

DIAGNOSTIC TROUBLE CODES

OBD II VEHICLE APPLICATIONS

FORD

Crown Victoria
2010–2011
- 4.6L . . . . .VIN V
- 4.6L . . . . VIN W

Edge
2010–2011
- 3.5L . . . . .VIN C
- 3.7L . . . . .VIN K

Explorer, Explorer Sport Trac
2010–2011
- 3.5L . . . . VIN 8
- 4.0L . . . . VIN E
- 4.6L . . . . VIN 8

F-150, F-250, F-350
2010–2011
- 3.5L . . . . VIN T
- 3.7L . . . . VIN M
- 4.6L . . . . VIN 8
- 4.6L . . . . VIN W
- 5.4L . . . . VIN 5
- 5.4L . . . . VIN V
- 6.2L . . . . VIN 6
- 6.4L . . . . VIN R
- 6.7L . . . . VIN T
- 6.8L . . . . VIN S
- 6.8L . . . . VIN 6

E-150, E-250, E-350
2010–2011
- 4.6L . . . . VIN W
- 5.4L . . . . VIN L
- 6.0L . . . . VIN P
- 6.8L . . . . VIN S

Escape
2010–2011
- 2.5L . . . . VIN 7
- 3.0L . . . . VIN G

Escape Hybrid
2010–2011
- 2.5L . . . . VIN 3

Expedition
2010–2011
- 5.4L . . . . VIN 5

LINCOLN

MKX
2010–2011
- 3.5L . . . . .VIN C
- 3.7L . . . . .VIN K

Navigator
2010–2011
- 5.4L . . . . VIN 5

Town Car
2010–2011
- 4.6L . . . . .VIN V
- 4.6L . . . . VIN W

MERCURY

Grand Marquis
2010–2011
- 4.6L . . . . .VIN V
- 4.6L . . . . VIN W

Mariner
2010–2011
- 2.5L . . . . VIN 7
- 3.0L . . . . .VIN G

Mariner Hybrid
2010–2011
- 2.5L . . . . VIN 3

Mountaineer
2010
- 4.0L . . . . VIN E
- 4.6L . . . . VIN 8

INTRODUCTION

To use this information, first read and record all codes in memory along with any Freeze Frame data. *If the PCM reset function is done prior to recording any data, all codes and freeze frame data will be lost!* Look up the desired code by DTC number, Code Title and Conditions (enable criteria) that indicate why a code set, and how to drive the vehicle.

OBD II Trouble Code List (P0xxx Codes)

DTC	Trouble Code Title & Conditions
DTC: P0001	**Fuel Volume Regulator Control Circuit/Open:** The powertrain control module (PCM) monitors the fuel volume regulator (FVR) and fuel volume regulator return (FVRRTN) circuits to the PCM for high and low voltage.
DTC: P0002	**Fuel Volume Regulator Control Circuit Range/Performance**
DTC: P0003	**Fuel Volume Regulator Control Circuit Low:** The powertrain control module (PCM) monitors the fuel volume regulator (FVR) and fuel volume regulator return (FVRRTN) circuits to the PCM for high and low voltage.
DTC: P0004	**Fuel Volume Regulator Control Circuit High:** The powertrain control module (PCM) monitors the fuel volume regulator (FVR) and fuel volume regulator return (FVRRTN) circuits to the PCM for high and low voltage.
DTC: P000A	**Intake A Camshaft Position Slow Response Bank 1:** The powertrain control module (PCM) monitors and evaluates the response of the actual position on a target position change. The setpoint and camshaft position are saved at the beginning of a setpoint change. If this change over time is large enough (gradient), the camshaft phasing change is evaluated. If the change after the diagnostic time is smaller than a threshold, a slow response is detected, and if the value is greater, then there is no concern. By detecting a concern, an anti-bounce counter is incremented otherwise the counter is decremented. If the counter exceeds an adjustable limit, this DTC sets.
DTC: P000B	**Exhaust B Camshaft Position Slow Response Bank 1:** The powertrain control module (PCM) monitors and evaluates the response of the actual position on a target position change. The setpoint and camshaft position are saved at the beginning of a setpoint change. If this change over time is large enough (gradient), the camshaft phasing change is evaluated. If the change after the diagnostic time is smaller than a threshold, a slow response is detected, and if the value is greater, then there is no concern. By detecting a concern, an anti-bounce counter is incremented otherwise the counter is decremented. If the counter exceeds an adjustable limit, this DTC sets.
DTC: P000E	**Fuel Volume Regulator Control Exceeded Learning Limit:** The powertrain control module (PCM) monitors the operation of the fuel volume control valve and calculates parameters necessary for an ideal engine operation. These parameters are stored in the adaptive strategy table. The table is used as a correction factor when controlling engine operation and corrects for wear or aging of components. The DTC is set when the adaptive strategy has reached its minimum or maximum learning limits.
DTC: P0010	**Intake Camshaft Position Actuator Circuit/Open (Bank 1):** The powertrain control module (PCM) monitors the variable camshaft timing (VCT) circuit for high and low voltage. The test fails if the voltage exceeds or falls below a calibrated limit for a calibrated amount of time.
DTC: P0011	**Intake Camshaft Position Timing - Over-Advanced (Bank 1):** The powertrain control module (PCM) monitors the variable camshaft timing (VCT) position for an over-advanced camshaft timing. The test fails when the camshaft timing exceeds a maximum calibrated value or remains in an advanced position.
DTC: P0012	**Intake Camshaft Position Timing - Over-Retarded (Bank 1):** The powertrain control module (PCM) monitors the variable camshaft timing (VCT) position for over-retarded camshaft timing. The test fails when the camshaft timing exceeds a maximum calibrated value or remains in a retarded position.
DTC: P0013	**Exhaust Camshaft Position Actuator Circuit/Open (Bank 1):** The powertrain control module (PCM) monitors the variable camshaft timing (VCT) circuit for high and low voltage. The test fails if the voltage exceeds a calibrated limit for a calibrated amount of time.
DTC: P0014	**Exhaust Camshaft Position Timing - Over-Advanced (Bank 1):** The powertrain control module (PCM) monitors the variable camshaft timing (VCT) position for an over-advanced camshaft timing. The test fails when the camshaft timing exceeds a maximum calibrated value or remains in an advanced position.
DTC: P0015	**Exhaust Camshaft Position Timing - Over-Retarded (Bank 1):** The powertrain control module (PCM) monitors the variable camshaft timing (VCT) position for over-retarded camshaft timing. The test fails when the camshaft timing exceeds a maximum calibrated value or remains in a retarded position.
DTC: P0016	**Crankshaft Position - Camshaft Position Correlation - Bank 1 Sensor A:** The powertrain control module (PCM) monitors the variable camshaft timing (VCT) position for a misalignment between the camshaft and crankshaft. The test fails when the misalignment is one tooth or greater. This DTC can also set due to VCT system concerns (oil contamination or VCT solenoid stuck).
DTC: P0017	**Crankshaft Position - Camshaft Position Correlation - Bank 1 Sensor B:** The powertrain control module (PCM) monitors the variable camshaft timing (VCT) position for a misalignment between the camshaft and crankshaft. The test fails when the misalignment is 1 tooth or greater. This DTC can also set due to VCT system concerns (oil contamination or VCT solenoid stuck).

DTC	Trouble Code Title & Conditions
DTC: P0018	**Crankshaft Position - Camshaft Position Correlation - Bank 2 Sensor A:** The powertrain control module (PCM) monitors the variable camshaft timing (VCT) position for a misalignment between the camshaft and crankshaft. The test fails when the misalignment is 1 tooth or greater. This DTC can also be set due to VCT system concerns (oil contamination or VCT solenoid stuck).
DTC: P0019	**Crankshaft Position - Camshaft Position Correlation - Bank 2 Sensor B:** The powertrain control module (PCM) monitors the variable camshaft timing (VCT) position for a misalignment between the camshaft and crankshaft. The test fails when the misalignment is 1 tooth or greater. This DTC can also set due to VCT system concerns (oil contamination or VCT solenoid stuck).
DTC: P0020	**Intake Camshaft Position Actuator Circuit/Open (Bank 2):** The powertrain control module (PCM) monitors the variable camshaft timing (VCT) circuit for high and low voltage. The test fails if the voltage exceeds a calibrated limit for a calibrated amount of time.
DTC: P0021	**Intake Camshaft Position Timing - Over-Advanced (Bank 2):** The powertrain control module (PCM) monitors the variable camshaft timing (VCT) position for an over-advanced camshaft timing. The test fails when the camshaft timing exceeds a maximum calibrated value or remains in an advanced position.
DTC: P0022	**Intake Camshaft Position Timing - Over-Retarded (Bank 2):** The Powertrain Control Module (PCM) monitors the Variable Camshaft Timing (VCT) position for over-retarded camshaft timing. The test fails when the camshaft timing exceeds a maximum calibrated value or remains in a retarded position. **NOTE: This DTC may be accompanied by other DTCs. Diagnose all CMP sensor DTCs first. If no CMP sensor related DTCs are present, continue to follow diagnosis for this DTC.**
DTC: P0023	**Exhaust Camshaft Position Actuator Circuit/Open (Bank 2):** The powertrain control module (PCM) monitors the variable camshaft timing (VCT) circuit for high and low voltage. The test fails if the voltage exceeds a calibrated limit for a calibrated amount of time.
DTC: P0024	**Exhaust Camshaft Position Timing - Over-Advanced (Bank 2):** The powertrain control module (PCM) monitors the variable camshaft timing (VCT) position for an over-advanced camshaft timing. The test fails when the camshaft timing exceeds a maximum calibrated value or remains in an advanced position.
DTC: P0025	**Exhaust Camshaft Position Timing - Over-Retarded (Bank 2):** The powertrain control module (PCM) monitors the variable camshaft timing (VCT) position for over-retarded camshaft timing. The test fails when the camshaft timing exceeds a maximum calibrated value or remains in a retarded position.
DTC: P0030	**HO2S Heater Control Circuit (Bank 1, Sensor 1) (For Vehicles With HO2S (4-pin)):** The powertrain control module (PCM) monitors the heater in the heated oxygen sensor (HO2S) for correct operation. The PCM controls the heater on and off duty cycle to maintain a calibrated temperature. The test fails when the sensor does not warm up to the required temperature in a calibrated amount of time. The test also fails when the PCM is not able to maintain the required temperature after the sensor is warm.
DTC: P0031	**HO2S Heater Control Circuit Low (Bank 1, Sensor 1):** The powertrain control module (PCM) monitors the heater in the heated oxygen sensor (HO2S) for correct operation. The PCM controls the heater on and off duty cycle to maintain a calibrated temperature. The test fails when the sensor does not warm up to the required temperature in a calibrated amount of time. The test also fails when the PCM is not able to maintain the required temperature after the sensor is warm.
DTC: P0032	**HO2S Heater Control Circuit High (Bank 1, Sensor 1):** The powertrain control module (PCM) monitors the heater in the heated oxygen sensor (HO2S) for correct operation. The PCM controls the heater on and off duty cycle to maintain a calibrated temperature. The test fails when the sensor does not warm up to the required temperature in a calibrated amount of time. The test also fails when the PCM is not able to maintain the required temperature after the sensor is warm.
DTC: P0034	**Turbocharger/Supercharger Bypass Valve A Control Circuit Low:** The powertrain control module (PCM) continuously monitors the TCBY circuit for concerns. This DTC sets when the PCM detects a short to ground in the circuit.
DTC: P0035	**Turbocharger/Supercharger Bypass Valve A Control Circuit High:** The powertrain control module (PCM) continuously monitors the TCBY circuit for concerns. This DTC sets when the PCM detects an open circuit or high voltage in the circuit.
DTC: P0036	**HO2S Heater Control Circuit (Bank 1, Sensor 2):** The powertrain control module (PCM) monitors the heater in the heated oxygen sensor (HO2S) for correct operation. The PCM controls the heater on and off duty cycle to maintain a calibrated temperature. The test fails when the sensor does not warm up to the required temperature in a calibrated amount of time. The test also fails when the PCM is not able to maintain the required temperature after the sensor is warm.

DTC	Trouble Code Title & Conditions
DTC: P0037	**HO2S Heater Control Circuit Low (Bank 1, Sensor 2):** The powertrain control module (PCM) monitors the heater in the heated oxygen sensor (HO2S) for correct operation. The PCM controls the heater on and off duty cycle to maintain a calibrated temperature. The test fails when the sensor does not warm up to the required temperature in a calibrated amount of time. The test also fails when the PCM is not able to maintain the required temperature after the sensor is warm.
DTC: P0038	**HO2S Heater Control Circuit High (Bank 1, Sensor 2):** The powertrain control module (PCM) monitors the heater in the heated oxygen sensor (HO2S) for correct operation. The PCM controls the heater on and off duty cycle to maintain a calibrated temperature. The test fails when the sensor does not warm up to the required temperature in a calibrated amount of time. The test also fails when the PCM is not able to maintain the required temperature after the sensor is warm.
DTC: P0040	**Oxygen Sensor Signals Swapped Bank 1 Sensor 1/Bank 2 Sensor 1:** The heated oxygen sensor (HO2S) monitor determines if the HO2S signal response for a fuel shift corresponds to the correct engine bank. The test fails when there is no response from the HO2S being tested. **NOTE: Connect the HO2S connector to the correct bank.**
DTC: P0041	**Oxygen Sensor Signals Swapped Bank 1 Sensor 2/Bank 2 Sensor 2:** The Heated Oxygen Sensor (HO2S) monitor determines if the HO2S signal response for a fuel shift corresponds to the correct engine bank. The test fails when there is no response from the HO2S being tested. **NOTE: Connect the HO2S connector to the correct bank.**
DTC: P0046	**Turbo/Super Charger Boost Control Solenoid A Circuit Range/Performance:** The variable geometry turbine (VGT) solenoid driver circuit is monitored by the powertrain control module (PCM) and is not within the calibrated value.
DTC: P0050	**HO2S Heater Control Circuit (Bank 2, Sensor 1):** The Powertrain Control Module (PCM) monitors the heater in the Heated Oxygen Sensor (HO2S) for correct operation. The PCM controls the heater on/off duty cycle to maintain a temperature of 780°C (1,436°F). The test fails when the sensor does not warm up to the required temperature in a calibrated amount of time. The test also fails when the PCM is not able to maintain the required temperature after the sensor is warm. **NOTE: Inspect the connectors for signs of damage, water ingress, or corrosion.**
DTC: P0053	**HO2S Heater Resistance (Bank 1, Sensor 1):** Heater current requirements too low or high in the Heated Oxygen Sensor (HO2S) heater control circuit **NOTE: Inspect the connectors for signs of damage, water ingress, or corrosion.**
DTC: P0054	**HO2S Heater Resistance (Bank 1, Sensor 2):** Heater current requirements too low or high in the Heated Oxygen Sensor (HO2S) heater control circuit **NOTE: Inspect the connectors for signs of damage, water ingress, or corrosion.**
DTC: P0055	**HO2S Heater Resistance (Bank 1, Sensor 3):** Heater current requirements too low or high in the Heated Oxygen Sensor (HO2S) heater control circuit **NOTE: Inspect the connectors for signs of damage, water ingress, or corrosion.**
DTC: P0059	**HO2S Heater Resistance (Bank 2, Sensor 1):** Heater current requirements too low or high in the Heated Oxygen Sensor (HO2S) heater control circuit **NOTE: Inspect the connectors for signs of damage, water ingress, or corrosion.**
DTC: P0060	**HO2S Heater Resistance (Bank 2, Sensor 2):** Heater current requirements too low or high in the Heated Oxygen Sensor (HO2S) heater control circuit **NOTE: Inspect the connectors for signs of damage, water ingress, or corrosion.**
DTC: P0068	**Manifold Absolute Pressure (MAP)/Mass Air Flow (MAF) - Throttle Position Correlation:** The Powertrain Control Module (PCM) monitors a vehicle operation rationality check by comparing sensed throttle position to mass air flow readings. If during a Key On Engine Running (KOER) self-test, the comparison of the Throttle Position (TP) sensor and MAF sensor readings are not consistent with the calibrated load values, the test fails and a DTC is stored in continuous memory. **NOTE: Diagnose any MAF or TP circuit DTCs first. Drive the vehicle and exercise the throttle and the TP sensor in all gears. A TP PID less than 4.82% (0.24 volt) with a LOAD PID greater than 55%, or a TP PID greater than 49.05% (2.44 volts) with a LOAD PID less than 30% indicates a concern is present.**
DTC: P0069	**MAP - Barometric Pressure Correlation:** The difference between the manifold absolute pressure (MAP) and barometric pressure (BARO) sensors is monitored by the powertrain control module (PCM) and is greater than the maximum calibrated limit.
DTC: P006B	**MAP/Exhaust Pressure Correlation:** The difference between the MAP and EP sensors is monitored by the powertrain control module (PCM) and is greater than the maximum calibrated limit.

DTC	Trouble Code Title & Conditions
DTC: P0070	**Ambient Air Temperature Sensor Circuit:** The powertrain control module (PCM) continuously monitors this sensor for concerns. This DTC sets when the ambient air temperature (AAT) sensor reading is greater than 71.1°C (160°F).
DTC: P0072	**Ambient Air Temperature Sensor Circuit Low:** The DTC indicates the sensor signal is less than the self-test minimum.
DTC: P0073	**Ambient Air Temperature Sensor Circuit High:** The DTC indicates the sensor signal is greater than the self-test maximum.
DTC: P0074	**Ambient Air Temperature Sensor Circuit Intermittent/Erratic:** The powertrain control module (PCM) continuously monitors the AAT circuit for concerns. This DTC sets if the PCM detects a sudden change in the ambient air temperature (AAT) sensor signal that changes beyond the minimum or maximum calibrated limit.
DTC: P007B	**Charge Air Cooler Temperature Sensor Circuit Range/Performance (Bank 1):** The powertrain control module (PCM) continuously monitors this sensor for concerns. This DTC sets when the charge air cooler temperature (CAC_T) parameter identification (PID) does not correlate with the intake air temperature (IAT) or the intake air temperature 2 (IAT2) PIDs at ignition on. It will also set if the IAT PID reading is greater than a maximum calibrated value while driving.
DTC: P007C	**Charge Air Cooler Temperature Sensor Circuit Low (Bank 1):** The powertrain control module (PCM) continuously monitors the CACT circuit for concerns. The test fails when the temperature is greater than the calibrated value for the sensor or a short to ground is detected in the circuit.
DTC: P007D	**Charge Air Cooler Temperature Sensor Circuit High (Bank 1):** The powertrain control module (PCM) continuously monitors the CACT circuit for concerns. The test fails when the temperature is lower than the calibrated value for the sensor or an open or short to voltage is detected in the circuit.
DTC: P0087	**Fuel Rail/System Pressure - Too Low:** The powertrain control module (PCM) regulates the fuel rail pressure by controlling the fuel volume regulator. When the PCM is no longer capable of maintaining the fuel pressure within the calibrated parameters, the DTC is set.
DTC: P0088	**Fuel Rail/System Pressure - Too High:** The powertrain control module (PCM) regulates the fuel rail pressure by controlling the fuel volume regulator. When the PCM is no longer capable of maintaining the fuel pressure within the calibrated parameters, the DTC is set.
DTC: P0089	**Fuel Pressure Regulator Performance:** The powertrain control module (PCM) monitors the fuel pressure control valve (FPCV) circuit for an electrical concern. The test fails when the signal moves outside the minimum or maximum allowable calibrated parameters for a specified fuel pressure control valve duty cycle by the PCM command.
DTC: P008A	**Low Pressure Fuel System Pressure - Too Low:** The powertrain control module (PCM) monitors the fuel pressure sensor. This DTC sets when the low pressure fuel system pressure falls below an expected threshold.
DTC: P008B	**Low Pressure Fuel System Pressure - Too High:** The powertrain control module (PCM) monitors the fuel pressure sensor. This DTC sets when the low pressure fuel system pressure rises above an expected threshold.
DTC: P008C	**Fuel Cooler Pump Control Circuit/Open:** The powertrain control module (PCM) monitors the fuel cooling pump driver circuit for an electrical concern. This DTC is set when the PCM detects an open condition on the fuel cooler pump (FCP) circuit.
DTC: P008D	**Fuel Cooler Pump Control Circuit Low:** The powertrain control module (PCM) monitors the fuel cooling pump driver circuit for an electrical concern. This DTC is set when the PCM detects a short to ground condition on the fuel cooling pump (FCP) circuit.
DTC: P008E	**Fuel Cooler Pump Control Circuit High:** The powertrain control module (PCM) monitors the fuel cooling pump driver circuit for an electrical concern. This DTC is set when the PCM detects a short to voltage on the fuel cooler pump (FCP) circuit.
DTC: P008F	**Engine Coolant Temperature/Fuel Temperature Correlation:** The powertrain control module (PCM) monitors and compares the engine coolant temperature (ECT) and fuel rail temperature (FRT) during the initial key ON cycle. This DTC is set when the maximum difference between the ECT and FRT exceeds the calibrated threshold.
DTC: P0090	**Fuel Pressure Regulator Control Circuit:** The powertrain control module (PCM) monitors the fuel pressure control valve (FPCV) circuit for an electrical concern. The test fails when the signal moves outside the minimum or maximum allowable calibrated parameters for a specified fuel pressure control valve duty cycle by the PCM command.

DTC	Trouble Code Title & Conditions
DTC: P0091	**Fuel Pressure Regulator Control Circuit Low:** The powertrain control module (PCM) monitors the fuel pressure control valve (FPCV) circuit for an electrical concern. The test fails when the signal moves outside the minimum or maximum allowable calibrated parameters for a specified fuel pressure control valve duty cycle by the PCM command.
DTC: P0092	**Fuel Pressure Regulator Control Circuit High:** The powertrain control module (PCM) monitors the fuel pressure control valve (FPCV) circuit for an electrical concern. The test fails when the signal moves outside the minimum or maximum allowable calibrated parameters for a specified fuel pressure control valve duty cycle by the PCM command.
DTC: P0093	**Fuel System Leak Detected - Large Leak:** The powertrain control module (PCM) monitors the fuel volume control valve value necessary to maintain a desired fuel rail pressure and sets a DTC when the set point needed for the fuel volume control valve to maintain desired fuel rail pressure exceeds a calibrated limit.
DTC: P0096	**Intake Air Temperature Sensor 2 Circuit Range/Performance:** IAT2 sensor input to the powertrain control module (PCM) is monitored and is not within the calibrated value.
DTC: P0097	**Intake Air Temperature Sensor 2 Circuit Low:** Indicates the sensor signal is less than the self-test minimum. The Intake Air Temperature 2 (IAT2) sensor minimum is 0.2 volt **NOTE: Monitor the IAT2 PID value. A typical IAT2 temperature should be greater than the IAT1 temperature.**
DTC: P0098	**Intake Air Temperature Sensor 2 Circuit High:** Indicates the sensor signal is greater than the self-test maximum. The Intake Air Temperature 2 (IAT2) sensor maximum is 4.6 volts. **NOTE: Monitor the IAT2 PID value. A typical IAT2 temperature should be greater than the IAT1 temperature.**
DTC: P009A	**Intake Air Temperature /Ambient Air Temperature Correlation:** The DTC indicates that the intake air temperature (IAT) and ambient air temperature (AAT) sensor readings differ by more than a calibrated value.
DTC: P00BA	**Low Fuel Pressure Forced Limited Power:** This DTC sets when the fuel delivery volume is less than the requested fuel delivery volume and the PCM has reduced engine power as a result.
DTC: P00BB	**Fuel Injector Insufficient Flow - Forced Limited Power:** This DTC sets when the requested fuel delivery volume is greater than the fuel injectors maximum delivery volume.
DTC: P00C1	**Turbocharger/Supercharger Bypass Valve B Control Circuit Low:** The powertrain control module (PCM) continuously monitors the TCBY2 circuit for concerns. This DTC sets when the PCM detects a short to ground in the circuit.
DTC: P00C2	**Turbocharger/Supercharger Bypass Valve B Control Circuit High:** The powertrain control module (PCM) continuously monitors the TCBY2 circuit for concerns. This DTC sets when the PCM detects an open circuit or high voltage in the circuit.
DTC: P00C6	**Fuel Rail Pressure Too Low - Engine Cranking:** The high pressure fuel system must reach a minimum pressure threshold before the engine can be started. If the high pressure fuel system cannot achieve this threshold within certain time and crankshaft rotation limits, the PCM attempts to start the engine at fuel pump module pressure and sets DTC P00C6.
DTC: P00CE	**Intake Air Temperature Measurement System - Multiple Sensor Correlation:** The powertrain control module (PCM) monitors the intake air system for concerns at ignition start. The test fails when the intake air temperature (IAT), charge air cooler temperature (CAC_T) and the intake air temperature 2 (IAT2) parameter identifications (PIDs) are each more than 16.67° C (30° F) different from each other at start up. The DTC sets when the PCM detects that each sensor is out of the calibrated range at engine start up after a soak period of at least 6 hours when a block heater is not used.
DTC: P0100	**Mass Or Volume Air Flow A Circuit:** The powertrain control module (PCM) continuously monitors the mass air flow (MAF) sensor for concerns. The MAF sensor is monitored for a low sensor period. If the sensor period changes below a minimum calibrated limit for greater than 1.5 seconds, the DTC sets.
DTC: P0101	**Mass or Volume Air Flow A Circuit Range/Performance:** If the engine speed is below 1500 RPM a MAF PID reading greater than 4.0 volts indicates a concern, if the engine speed is above 1500 RPM a MAF PID reading greater than 4.9 Volts indicates a concern.
DTC: P0102	**Mass or Volume Air Flow A Circuit Low:** The mass air flow (MAF) sensor circuit is monitored by the powertrain control module (PCM) for low voltage input through the comprehensive component monitor (CCM). If during ignition on engine running the voltage changes below a minimum calibrated limit, the DTC is set.

DTC	Trouble Code Title & Conditions
DTC: P0103	**Mass or Volume Air Flow A Circuit High:** The mass airflow (MAF) sensor circuit is monitored by the powertrain control module (PCM). This DTC sets if during key ON engine running (KOER) the sensor output changes above a maximum calibrated limit.
DTC: P0104	**Mass or Volume Air Flow A Circuit Intermittent/Erratic:** A concern exists in the mass air flow (MAF) sensor A circuit, or the air tube containing the sensor, causing an incorrect sensor output reading.
DTC: P0106	**Manifold Absolute Pressure (MAP/BARO) Sensor Range/Performance (For All Others):** MAP sensor input to the powertrain control module (PCM) is monitored and is not within the calibrated value.
DTC: P0107	**Manifold Absolute Pressure (MAP)/Barometric Pressure (BARO) Sensor Low:** The MAP signal voltage is lower than a specified value indicating an open circuit or a short to ground.
DTC: P0108	**Manifold Absolute Pressure (MAP)/Barometric Pressure (BARO) Sensor High:** The MAP signal voltage is higher than a specified value indicating a short to power.
DTC: P0109	**Manifold Absolute Pressure (MAP)/Barometric Pressure (BARO) Sensor Intermittent:** The sensor signal to the powertrain control module (PCM) is failing intermittently.
DTC: P0111	**Intake Air Temperature (IAT) Sensor 1 Circuit Range/Performance:** Indicates the IAT rationality test has failed. This DTC indicates that the IAT value is higher than a calibrated value and could prevent one or more on-board diagnostic (OBD) monitors from completing. The powertrain control module (PCM) runs this logic after an engine off and a calibrated soak period (typically 6 hours). This soak period allows IAT and engine coolant temperature (ECT) or cylinder head temperature (CHT) to stabilize and not differ by more than a calibrated value. DTC P0111 sets when the IAT at engine start exceeds the ECT or CHT by more than a calibrated value, typically 17°C (30°F). **NOTE: Make sure the IAT and the CHT or ECT are similar when the engine is cold.**
DTC: P0112	**Intake Air Temperature (IAT) Sensor 1 Circuit Low:** The DTC indicates the sensor signal is less than the self-test minimum.
DTC: P0113	**Intake Air Temperature (IAT) Sensor 1 Circuit High:** The DTC indicates the sensor signal is greater than the self-test maximum.
DTC: P0114	**Intake Air Temperature (IAT) Sensor 1 Intermittent/Erratic:** Indicates the sensor signal was intermittent during the comprehensive component monitor (CCM).
DTC: P0115	**Engine Coolant Temperature Sensor 1 Circuit:** This DTC indicates that the engine coolant temperature (ECT) sensor signal is too high or too low during the key on engine running (KOER) self-test. This DTC sets if the ECT sensor signal falls below or exceeds the calibrated threshold at any time during the KOER self-test.
DTC: P0116	**Engine Coolant Temperature Sensor 1 Circuit Range/Performance:** Indicates the engine coolant temperature rationality test has failed. The powertrain control module (PCM) logic that sets this DTC indicates the ECT or cylinder head temperature (CHT) drifted higher than the nominal sensor calibration curve and could prevent one or more on-board diagnostic (OBD) monitors from executing. The PCM runs this logic after an engine off calibrated soak period (typically 6 hours). This soak period allows the intake air temperature (IAT) and engine coolant temperature to stabilize and not differ by more than a calibrated value.
DTC: P0117	**Engine Coolant Temperature Sensor 1 Circuit Low:** Indicates the sensor signal is less than the self-test minimum. The engine coolant temperature (ECT) sensor minimum is 0.2 volt or 121°C (250°F).
DTC: P0118	**Engine Coolant Temperature (ECT) Sensor 1 Circuit High:** Indicates the sensor signal is greater than the self-test maximum. The ECT sensor maximum is 4.6 volts or -50°C (-58°F).
DTC: P0119	**Engine Coolant Temperature (ECT) Sensor 1 Circuit Intermittent/Erratic:** Indicates the ECT circuit became intermittently open or short while the engine was running. On vehicles that are not equipped with an ECT sensor, the cylinder head temperature (CHT) sensor can be used and can set this DTC.
DTC: P011E	**Engine Coolant Temperature 1/Ambient Air Temperature Correlation:** The DTC indicates that the engine coolant temperature (ECT) and ambient air temperature (AAT) sensor readings differ by greater than a calibrated value.
DTC: P0121	**Throttle/Pedal Position Sensor A Circuit Range/Performance (For All Others):** The electronic throttle control (ETC) throttle position (TP) sensor 1 circuit was flagged as a concern by the powertrain control module (PCM) indicating an out of range in either the closed or wide open throttle (WOT) modes.
DTC: P0122	**Throttle/Pedal Position Sensor A Circuit Low:** The electronic throttle control (ETC) throttle position (TP) sensor 1 circuit was flagged as a concern by the powertrain control module (PCM) indicating a low voltage or open circuit.

DTC	Trouble Code Title & Conditions
DTC: P0123	**Throttle/Pedal Position Sensor A Circuit High:** The electronic throttle control (ETC) throttle position (TP) sensor 1 circuit was flagged as a concern by the powertrain control module (PCM) indicating a high voltage.
DTC: P0125	**Insufficient Coolant Temperature For Closed Loop Fuel Control:** Indicates the engine coolant temperature (ECT) or the cylinder head temperature (CHT) sensor has not achieved the required temperature level to enter closed loop operating conditions within a specified amount of time after starting the engine.
DTC: P0126	**Insufficient Coolant Temperature (ECT) For Stable Operation:** This DTC indicates that an ECT sensor range performance concern has been detected. The DTC sets when the vehicle has been operating at less than 1,000 RPM and less than 20 mg/stroke mass fuel desired (MFDES) with the ECT sensor signal reading above 110°C (230°F). The time to set the concern is dependent on the ECT and IAT temperatures and can vary between 15 and 45 minutes.
DTC: P0127	**Intake Air Temperature (IAT) Too High:** Indicates that the IAT2 sensor has detected a concern in the Charge Air Cooler (CAC) system **NOTE: Monitor the IAT2 PID. A typical IAT2 temperature should be greater than the IAT1 temperature**
DTC: P0128	**Coolant Thermostat (Coolant Temperature Below Thermostat Regulating Temperature):** Indicates that the thermostat monitor has not achieved the required engine operating temperature within a specified amount of time after starting the engine.
DTC: P012B	**Turbocharger/Supercharger Inlet Pressure Sensor Circuit Range/Performance:** Manifold absolute pressure (MAP) sensor input to the powertrain control module (PCM) is monitored and is not within the calibrated value.
DTC: P012C	**Turbocharger/Supercharger Inlet Pressure Sensor Circuit Low:** Manifold absolute pressure (MAP) sensor operating voltage is below the minimum calibrated parameter of 0.25 volt.
DTC: P012D	**Turbocharger/Supercharger Inlet Pressure Sensor Circuit High:** Manifold absolute pressure (MAP) sensor operating voltage is above the maximum calibrated parameter of 5 volts.
DTC: P012E	**Turbocharger/Supercharger Inlet Pressure Sensor Circuit Intermittent/Erratic:** The sensor signal to the Powertrain Control Module (PCM) is intermittent **NOTE: Check the harness and connection.**
DTC: P012F	**Engine Coolant Temperature/ Engine Oil Temperature Correlation:** This DTC sets when the maximum difference between the engine coolant temperature and the engine oil temperature exceeds the calibrated threshold for a prescribed amount of time.
DTC: P0130	**O2 Circuit (Bank 1, Sensor 1) (For Vehicles With HO2S (4-pin)):** The powertrain control module (PCM) monitors the heated oxygen sensor (HO2S) for a circuit concern. This DTC sets when the PCM detects a concern with one of the circuits used to determine the oxygen content in the exhaust gas.
DTC: P0130	**O2 Circuit (Bank 1, Sensor 1):** The powertrain control module (PCM) monitors the heated oxygen sensor (HO2S) for a circuit concern. This DTC sets when the PCM detects a concern with one of the circuits used to determine the oxygen content in the exhaust gas.
DTC: P0131	**O2 Circuit Low Voltage (Bank 1, Sensor 1):** The powertrain control module (PCM) monitors the heated oxygen sensor (HO2S) for a circuit concern. This DTC sets when the PCM detects a concern with one of the circuits used to determine the oxygen content in the exhaust gas.
DTC: P0132	**O2 Circuit High Voltage (Bank 1, Sensor 1) (For Vehicles With Universal HO2S):** The powertrain control module (PCM) monitors the heated oxygen sensor (HO2S) for a circuit concern. This DTC sets when the PCM detects a concern with one of the circuits used to determine the oxygen content in the exhaust gas.
DTC: P0133	**O2 Sensor Circuit Slow Response (Bank1 Sensor 1):** The nitrogen oxide (NOx) module monitors the NOx sensor oxygen (O2) response time during the transition from an engine load to deceleration fuel shut off (DFSO). This DTC sets when the actual O2 signal value does not reach a predicted O2 signal value within a calibrated amount of time.
DTC: P0134	**O2 Circuit No Activity Detected (Bank 1, Sensor 1):** The Powertrain Control Module (PCM) monitors the Heated Oxygen Sensor (HO2S) for a lack of movement concern. If the sensor signal value is not changing from the default value, the PCM commands an oscillating air/fuel ratio attempting to detect some movement in the signal value. The test fails when the PCM is unable to detect movement in the sensor signal while the air/fuel ratio is oscillating.
DTC: P0135	**O2 Heater Circuit (Bank 1, Sensor 1):** During testing the heated oxygen sensor (HO2S) heaters are checked for open and short circuits and excessive current draw. The test fails when the current draw exceeds a calibrated limit or an open or short circuit is detected.

DTC	Trouble Code Title & Conditions
DTC: P0136	**O2 Circuit (Bank 1, Sensor 2):** This DTC sets when the powertrain control module (PCM) detects a concern with one of the circuits used to determine the oxygen content in the exhaust gas.
DTC: P0137	**O2 Sensor Circuit Low Voltage (Bank 1 Sensor 2):** The powertrain control module (PCM) monitors the heated oxygen sensor (HO2S) for a circuit concern. This DTC sets when the PCM detects a concern with the circuit used to determine the oxygen content in the exhaust gas.
DTC: P0138	**O2 Circuit High Voltage (Bank 1, Sensor 2) (For Vehicles With HO2S (4-pin)):** The heated oxygen sensor (HO2S) signals are monitored for an over voltage condition. For Fiesta, this DTC sets if the HO2S signal voltage is 1.1 volts or greater. For all others, this DTC sets if the HO2S signal voltage is 1.5 volts or greater.
DTC: P0139	**O2 Circuit Slow Response (Bank 1, Sensor 2):** The Heated Oxygen Sensor (HO2S) monitor tracks the rate of voltage change during the rise and fall of the HO2S signal. When the rate of voltage change is less than a calibrated value, the Powertrain Control Module (PCM) begins to modify the fuel trim attempting to increase the HO2S voltage switch rate. The DTC sets when the PCM is at the allowable limit or has exceeded an allowable length of time for fuel trim modification, without detecting an acceptable rate of voltage change. **NOTE: Access the HO2S test results from the generic OBD menu to verify the DTC.**
DTC: P013A	**O2 Sensor Slow Response - Rich to Lean (Bank 1, Sensor 2):** During a Deceleration Fuel Shut-Off (DFSO) event, the powertrain control module (PCM) monitors how quickly the rear Heated Oxygen Sensor (HO2S) switches from rich to lean. The measured rate of the rich to lean switch is compared to a calibrated fault threshold value. The threshold value takes into account the level of oxygen in the catalyst, which has an impact on how quickly the rich to lean switch occurs. The test fails when the measured value is slower than the threshold value. **NOTE: Check for leaks in the exhaust system.**
DTC: P013B	**O2 Sensor Slow Response - Lean to Rich Bank 1, Sensor 2:** During a deceleration fuel shut-off (DFSO) event, the powertrain control module (PCM) monitors how quickly the rear heated oxygen sensor (HO2S) switches from lean to rich. The measured rate of the lean to rich switch is compared to a calibrated fault threshold value. The measured rate of the lean to rich switch is compared to a calibrated fault threshold value. This DTC sets if the measured value is slower than the threshold value.
DTC: P013C	**O2 Sensor Slow Response - Rich to Lean (Bank 2, Sensor 2):** During a Deceleration Fuel Shut-Off (DFSO) event, the powertrain control module (PCM) monitors how quickly the rear Heated Oxygen Sensor (HO2S) switches from rich to lean. The measured rate of the rich to lean switch is compared to a calibrated fault threshold value. The threshold value takes into account the level of oxygen in the catalyst, which has an impact on how quickly the rich to lean switch occurs. The test fails when the measured value is slower than the threshold value. **NOTE: Check for leaks in the exhaust system.**
DTC: P013E	**Sensor Delayed Response - Rich to Lean (Bank 1, Sensor 2):** During a deceleration fuel shut-off (DFSO) event, the powertrain control module (PCM) monitors the rear heated oxygen sensor (HO2S) signal to determine if the signal is stuck in range. The PCM expects the signal to exceed a calibrated rich or lean value within a calibrated amount of time. If the signal voltage remains less than the rich value after a number of occurrences, the PCM intrusively controls the fuel system rich over increasing time periods in an attempt to force the signal to greater than the calibrated rich value. The test fails when after three consecutive intrusive attempts the signal cannot be forced greater than the calibrated rich value. Also, if the signal voltage remains greater than the lean value after a calibrated amount of time with the fuel injectors off, a counter is incremented. The test fails when after three consecutive occurrences the signal is not less than the calibrated lean value.
DTC: P0140	**O2 Circuit No Activity Detected (Bank 1, Sensor 2):** The powertrain control module (PCM) monitors the heated oxygen sensor (HO2S) for a lack of movement concern. If the sensor signal value is not changing from the default value, the PCM commands an oscillating air/fuel ratio attempting to detect some movement in the signal value. The test fails when the PCM is unable to detect movement in the sensor signal while the air/fuel ratio is oscillating.
DTC: P0141	**O2 Heater Circuit (Bank 1, Sensor 2):** During testing the heated oxygen sensor (HO2S) heaters are checked for open and short circuits and excessive current draw. The test fails when the current draw exceeds a calibrated limit or an open or short circuit is detected.
DTC: P0144	**O2 Circuit High Voltage (Bank 1, Sensor 3):** The Heated Oxygen Sensor (HO2S) signals are monitored for an over voltage condition. The code is set when the HO2S signal voltage is 1.5 volts or greater. **NOTE: An HO2S PID switching across 0.45 volt from 0.2 to 0.9 volt indicates a normal switching HO2S. An HO2S PID voltage of 1.5 volts or greater indicates a short to voltage.**
DTC: P0147	**O2 Heater Circuit (Bank 1, Sensor 3):** During testing the Heated Oxygen Sensor (HO2S) heaters are checked for open and short circuits and excessive current draw. The test fails when the current draw exceeds a calibrated limit or an open or short circuit is detected. **NOTE: Inspect the connectors for signs of damage, water ingress, or corrosion.**

DTC	Trouble Code Title & Conditions
DTC: P0148	**Fuel Delivery Error:** At least one bank is lean at wide open throttle (WOT) or fuel flow is lower than expected.
DTC: P0149	**Fuel Timing Error:** The powertrain control module (PCM) monitors the injection timing from the injector driver feedback circuit during the vehicle deceleration. The PCM also compares the difference between actual fuel pressure and desired fuel pressure, to the calibrated value. The DTC is set when the injection timing or the difference between the actual and desired fuel pressure are out of the calibrated range.
DTC: P014A	**Sensor Delayed Response - Rich to Lean (Bank 2, Sensor 2):** During a Deceleration Fuel Shut-Off (DFSO) event, the Powertrain Control Module (PCM) monitors the rear Heated Oxygen Sensor (HO2S) signal to determine if the signal is stuck in range. The PCM expects the signal to exceed a calibrated rich or lean value within a calibrated amount of time. If the signal voltage remains less than the rich value after a number of occurrences, the PCM intrusively controls the fuel system rich over increasing time periods in an attempt to force the signal to greater than the calibrated rich value. The test fails when after three consecutive intrusive attempts the signal cannot be forced greater than the calibrated rich value. Also, if the signal voltage remains greater than the lean value after a calibrated amount of time with the fuel injectors off, a counter is incremented. The test fails when after three consecutive occurrences the signal is not less than the calibrated lean value. **NOTE: Check for leaks in the exhaust system. Check for an intermittent HO2S signal.**
DTC: P0150	**O2 Circuit (Bank 2, Sensor 1) (For Vehicles With HO2S (4-pin)):** The powertrain control module (PCM) monitors the heated oxygen sensor (HO2S) for a circuit concern. This DTC sets when the PCM detects a concern with one of the circuits used to determine the oxygen content in the exhaust gas.
DTC: P0151	**O2 Circuit Low Voltage (Bank 2, Sensor 1) (For Vehicles With HO2S (4-pin)):** The powertrain control module (PCM) monitors the heated oxygen sensor (HO2S) for a circuit concern. This DTC sets when the PCM detects a concern with the circuit used to determine the oxygen content in the exhaust gas.
DTC: P0152	**O2 Circuit High Voltage (Bank 2, Sensor 1) (For Vehicles With HO2S (4-pin)):** The heated oxygen sensor (HO2S) signals are monitored for an over voltage condition. For Fiesta, this DTC sets if the HO2S signal voltage is 1.1 volts or greater. For all others, this DTC sets if the HO2S signal voltage is 1.5 volts or greater.
DTC: P0153	**O2 Circuit Slow Response (Bank 2, Sensor 1):** The Powertrain Control Module (PCM) commands an air/fuel ratio that changes in the shape of a square wave. The PCM calculates the length of the resulting signal from the HO2S. The test fails when the length of the signal is less than a calibrated limit. For all others, the PCM checks the HO2S signal frequency and amplitude. The test fails when the frequency and amplitude less than a calibrated limit. **NOTE: Access the HO2S test results from the generic OBD menu to verify the DTC.**
DTC: P0154	**O2 Circuit No Activity Detected (Bank 2, Sensor 1):** The Powertrain Control Module (PCM) monitors the Heated Oxygen Sensor (HO2S) for a lack of movement concern. If the sensor signal value is not changing from the default value, the PCM commands an oscillating air/fuel ratio attempting to detect some movement in the signal value. The test fails when the PCM is unable to detect movement in the sensor signal while the air/fuel ratio is oscillating.
DTC: P0155	**O2 Heater Circuit (Bank 2, Sensor 1):** During testing the Heated Oxygen Sensor (HO2S) heaters are checked for open and short circuits and excessive current draw. The test fails when the current draw exceeds a calibrated limit or an open or short circuit is detected. **NOTE: Inspect the connectors for signs of damage, water ingress, or corrosion.**
DTC: P0157	**O2 Sensor Circuit Low Voltage (Bank 2 Sensor 2):** The powertrain control module (PCM) monitors the heated oxygen sensor (HO2S) for a circuit concern. This DTC sets when the PCM detects a concern with the circuit used to determine the oxygen content in the exhaust gas.
DTC: P0158	**O2 Circuit High Voltage (Bank 2, Sensor 2) (For Vehicles With HO2S (4-pin)):** The heated oxygen sensor (HO2S) signals are monitored for an over voltage condition. For Fiesta, this DTC sets if the HO2S signal voltage is 1.1 volts or greater. For all others, this DTC sets if the HO2S signal voltage is 1.5 volts or greater.
DTC: P0159	**O2 Circuit Slow Response (Bank 2, Sensor 2):** The heated oxygen sensor (HO2S) monitor tracks the rate of voltage change during the rise and fall of the HO2S signal. When the rate of voltage change is less than a calibrated value, the powertrain control module (PCM) begins to modify the fuel trim attempting to increase the HO2S voltage switch rate. This DTC sets when the PCM is at the allowable limit or has exceeded an allowable length of time for fuel trim modification, without detecting an acceptable rate of voltage change.
DTC: P0161	**O2 Heater Circuit (Bank 2, Sensor 2):** During testing the Heated Oxygen Sensor (HO2S) heaters are checked for open and short circuits and excessive current draw. The test fails when the current draw exceeds a calibrated limit or an open or short circuit is detected. **NOTE: Inspect the connectors for signs of damage, water ingress, or corrosion.**
DTC: P0168	**Engine Fuel Temperature Too High:** The powertrain control module (PCM) continuously monitors the fuel rail temperature (FRT) sensor input. The test fails when the fuel temperature exceeds a maximum calibrated value for a calibrated period of time.

DTC	Trouble Code Title & Conditions
DTC: P016A	**O2 Sensor Not Ready (Bank 1, Sensor 1):** The heated oxygen sensor (HO2S) monitor tracks the rate of voltage change during the rise and fall of the HO2S signal. When the rate of voltage change is less than a calibrated value, the powertrain control module (PCM) begins to modify the fuel trim attempting to increase the HO2S voltage switch rate. This DTC sets when the PCM is at the allowable limit or has exceeded an allowable length of time for fuel trim modification, without detecting an acceptable rate of voltage change.
DTC: P016B	**Closed Loop Air/Fuel Ratio Control at Limit - System Too Rich:** This DTC is set when the powertrain control module detects the fuel ratio control is at its limit indicating the fuel system is too rich.
DTC: P016C	**Closed Loop Air/Fuel Ratio Control at Limit - System Too Lean:** This DTC is set when the powertrain control module detects the fuel ratio control is at its limit indicating the fuel system is too lean.
DTC: P016D	**Excessive Time to Enter Closed Loop Fuel Pressure Control:** On every engine start with fuel temperature less than 40 °C (104 °F), the powertrain control module (PCM) checks the accuracy of the fuel rail pressure sensor by estimating the amount of effort required by the fuel pressure control valve to maintain pressure for a given fuel rail pressure reading. If the system is unable to successfully learn the effort required over a substantial period of time, this DTC sets. It likely indicates that some element of the fuel system is operating within plausible tolerances, but with too much variation to get a stable reading.
DTC: P0171	**System Too Lean (Bank 1):** The adaptive fuel strategy continuously monitors the fuel delivery hardware. The test fails when the adaptive fuel tables reach a rich calibrated limit.
DTC: P0172	**System Too Rich (Bank 1):** The adaptive fuel strategy continuously monitors the fuel delivery hardware. The test fails when the adaptive fuel tables reach a lean calibrated limit. Refer to Section 1, Powertrain Control Software Fuel Trim for more information.
DTC: P0174	**System Too Lean (Bank 2):** Engine started, engine running at cruise speed for 3 to 4 minutes, and the PCM detected the Bank 1 Adaptive Fuel Control System reached its rich correction limit (a lean A/F condition).
DTC: P0175	**System Too Rich (Bank 2):** The adaptive fuel strategy continuously monitors the fuel delivery hardware. The test fails when the adaptive fuel tables reach a lean calibrated limit.
DTC: P0180	**Fuel Temperature Sensor A Circuit:** The PCM or CCM monitors the fuel temperature sensor circuit to the powertrain control module (PCM) for low and high voltage. The test fails if the voltage falls below or exceeds a calibrated limit and amount of time during testing.
DTC: P0181	**Fuel Temperature Sensor A Circuit Range/Performance:** The PCM or CCM monitors the fuel temperature sensor for acceptable operating temperature. The test fails if the voltage falls below or exceeds a calibrated limit, for a calibrated amount of time during testing.
DTC: P0182	**Fuel Temperature Sensor 'A' Circuit Low:** The PCM or CCM monitors the fuel temperature sensor circuit to the Powertrain Control Module (PCM) for low voltage. The test fails if the voltage falls below a calibrated limit for a calibrated amount of time during testing **NOTE: Verify the FRT PID and VREF values to determine an open or short.**
DTC: P0183	**Fuel Temperature Sensor A Circuit High:** The PCM or CCM monitors the fuel temperature sensor circuit to the powertrain control module (PCM) for high voltage. The test fails if the voltage exceeds a calibrated limit for a calibrated amount of time during testing.
DTC: P018C	**Fuel Pressure Sensor B Circuit Low:** The PCM or CCM monitors the fuel pressure sensor circuit to the powertrain control module (PCM) for low voltage. The test fails if the voltage falls below a calibrated limit for a calibrated amount of time during testing.
DTC: P018D	**Fuel Pressure Sensor B Circuit High:** The PCM or CCM monitors the fuel pressure sensor circuit to the powertrain control module (PCM) for high voltage. The test fails if the voltage exceeds a calibrated limit for a calibrated amount of time during testing.
DTC: P0190	**Fuel Rail Pressure Sensor 'A' Circuit:** The PCM or CCM monitors the Fuel Rail Pressure (FRP) sensor to the Powertrain Control Module (PCM) for VREF voltage. The test fails when the VREF voltage from the PCM drops to a voltage less than a minimum calibrated value. **NOTE: The sensor VREF should be between 4.0 to 6.0v at all times.**
DTC: P0191	**Fuel Rail Pressure Sensor A Circuit Range/Performance:** The comprehensive component monitor (CCM) checks the fuel rail pressure (FRP) sensor for an acceptable fuel pressure. The test fails when the difference between the fuel rail pressure requested by the PCM and the fuel rail pressure delivered exceeds 138 kPa (20 psi) for greater than 8 seconds.

DTC	Trouble Code Title & Conditions
DTC: P0192	**Fuel Rail Pressure Sensor A Circuit Low:** The powertrain control module (PCM) continuously monitors the fuel rail pressure (FRP) sensor input to determine if the FRP signal is within an expected range. The test fails when FRP voltage is lower than expected.
DTC: P0193	**Fuel Rail Pressure Sensor A Circuit High:** The powertrain control module (PCM) continuously monitors the fuel rail pressure (FRP) sensor input to determine if the FRP signal is within an expected range. The test fails when FRP voltage is higher than expected.
DTC: P0194	**Fuel Rail Pressure Sensor A Circuit Intermittent/Erratic:** The powertrain control module (PCM) continuously monitors the fuel rail pressure (FRP) sensor input to determine if the FRP signal is within an expected range. The test fails when the PCM detects an intermittent concern with the FRP signal.
DTC: P0195	**Engine Oil Temperature Sensor Circuit:** Indicates the value from the engine oil temperature (EOT) sensor is not within the powertrain control module (PCM) predicted engine oil temperature range, based on other PCM inputs.
DTC: P0196	**Engine Oil Temperature Sensor Circuit Range/Performance:** Indicates the value from the engine oil temperature (EOT) sensor is not within the powertrain control module (PCM) predicted engine oil temperature range, based on other PCM inputs.
DTC: P0197	**Engine Oil Temperature Sensor Circuit Low:** Indicates the engine oil temperature (EOT) signal voltage is low (high temperature).
DTC: P0198	**Engine Oil Temperature Sensor Circuit High:** Indicates engine oil temperature (EOT) signal voltage is high (low temperature).
DTC: P0201	**Injector Circuit/Open - Cylinder 1:** The powertrain control module (PCM) monitors the charge and discharge time of the piezo actuator device during the fill stage, main injection and end of main injection stage. The DTC sets when the charge and discharge timing is not correct or when it is out of calibrated range.
DTC: P0202	**Injector Circuit/Open - Cylinder 2:** The powertrain control module (PCM) monitors the output of the fuel injector circuits and sets a DTC when it detects the output is not within a calibrated limit. This DTC sets when the PCM detects the output voltage of the fuel injector control circuit is outside of the calibrated limit.
DTC: P0203	**Injector Circuit/Open - Cylinder 3:** The powertrain control module (PCM) monitors the charge and discharge time of the piezo actuator device during the fill stage, main injection and end of main injection stage. The DTC sets when the charge and discharge timing is not correct or when it is out of calibrated range.
DTC: P0204	**Injector Circuit/Open - Cylinder 4:** The powertrain control module (PCM) monitors the charge and discharge time of the piezo actuator device during the fill stage, main injection and end of main injection stage. The DTC sets when the charge and discharge timing is not correct or when it is out of calibrated range.
DTC: P0205	**Injector Circuit/Open - Cylinder 5:** The powertrain control module (PCM) monitors the charge and discharge time of the piezo actuator device during the fill stage, main injection and end of main injection stage. The DTC sets when the charge and discharge timing is not correct or when it is out of calibrated range.
DTC: P0206	**Injector Circuit/Open - Cylinder 6:** The powertrain control module (PCM) monitors the charge and discharge time of the piezo actuator device during the fill stage, main injection and end of main injection stage. The DTC sets when the charge and discharge timing is not correct or when it is out of calibrated range.
DTC: P0207	**Injector Circuit/Open - Cylinder 7:** The powertrain control module (PCM) monitors the output of the fuel injector circuits and sets a DTC when it detects the output is not within a calibrated limit. This DTC sets when the PCM detects the output voltage of the fuel injector control circuit is outside of the calibrated limit.
DTC: P0208	**Injector Circuit/Open - Cylinder 8:** The powertrain control module (PCM) monitors the output of the fuel injector circuits and sets a DTC when it detects the output is not within a calibrated limit. This DTC sets when the PCM detects the output voltage of the fuel injector control circuit is outside of the calibrated limit.
DTC: P020x	**Injector Circuit/Open - Cylinder X (For All Others):** The PCM or CCM monitors the operation of the fuel injector drivers in the powertrain control module (PCM). The test fails when the fuel injector circuitry is inoperative. **NOTE: x represents injector numbers 1 through 9.**

DTC	Trouble Code Title & Conditions
DTC: P0210	**Injector Circuit/Open - Cylinder 10 (For Vehicles With Direct Fuel Injection):** The PCM or CCM monitors the operation of the fuel injector drivers in the powertrain control module (PCM). The test fails when the fuel injector circuitry is inoperative.
DTC: P0216	**Injector/Injection Timing Control Circuit:** Indicates that the piezo actuator device activates the fuel injectors at the wrong time when the certain conditions are met during the vehicle deceleration.
DTC: P0217	**Engine Coolant Over-Temperature Condition (For All Others):** Indicates an engine overheat condition was detected by the engine temperature sensor (CHT or ECT depending how the vehicle is equipped).
DTC: P0218	**Transmission Fluid Temperature Over-Temperature Condition:** Indicates a transmission overheat condition was sensed by the Transmission Fluid Temperature (TFT) sensor. **NOTE: Monitor the transmission temperature PID TFT for an overheat condition.**
DTC: P0219	**Engine Overspeed Condition:** Indicates the vehicle has been operated in a manner which caused the engine speed to exceed a calibrated limit. The engine RPM is continuously monitored and evaluated by the powertrain control module (PCM). The DTC sets when the RPM exceeds the calibrated limit set within the PCM.
DTC: P0221	**Throttle/Pedal Position Sensor/Switch B Circuit Range/Performance:** The Electronic Throttle Control (ETC) Throttle Position (TP) sensor 2 circuit was flagged as a concern by the Powertrain Control Module (PCM) indicating an out of range in either the closed or Wide Open Throttle (WOT) modes. **NOTE: This concern exhibits a symptom of limited power.**
DTC: P0222	**Throttle/Pedal Position Sensor/Switch B Circuit Low:** The Electronic Throttle Control (ETC) Throttle Position (TP) sensor 2 circuit was flagged as a concern by the Powertrain Control Module (PCM) indicating a low voltage, or open circuit. **NOTE: This concern exhibits a symptom of limited power. A TP2 PID reading less than 0.25 volt in key ON, engine OFF or key ON, engine running indicates a concern is present.**
DTC: P0223	**Throttle/Pedal Position Sensor/Switch B Circuit High:** The electronic throttle control (ETC) throttle position (TP) sensor 2 circuit was flagged as a concern by the powertrain control module (PCM) indicating a high voltage.
DTC: P0230	**Fuel Pump Primary Circuit:** The powertrain control module (PCM) monitors the fuel pump (FP) circuit output from the PCM. The test fails when the FP output is commanded ON (grounded) and excessive current draw is detected on the FP circuit. The test also fails when the FP output is commanded OFF and voltage is not detected on the FP circuit. The PCM expects to detect VPWR voltage coming through the fuel pump relay coil to the FP circuit.
DTC: P0231	**Fuel Pump Secondary Circuit Low:** The powertrain control module (PCM) monitors the fuel pump monitor (FPM) circuit. The test fails if the PCM commands the fuel pump ON and B+ voltage is not detected on the FPM circuit.
DTC: P0232	**Fuel Pump Secondary Circuit High:** The powertrain control module (PCM) monitors the fuel pump monitor (FPM) circuit. This test fails when the PCM detects voltage on the FPM circuit while the fuel pump is commanded OFF. The FPM circuit is wired to a pull-up voltage inside the PCM. The FPM circuit goes high if, with the ignition ON, engine OFF and the fuel pump commanded OFF, the FPM/FP PWR circuit loses its path to ground through the fuel pump. The FPM circuit also goes high if the FPM/FP PWR circuit is short to voltage.
DTC: P0234	**Turbocharger/Supercharger A Overboost Condition:** The powertrain control module (PCM) continuously monitors the turbocharger system for an overboost condition.Indicates that boost pressure is greater than the desired pressure value by more than a calibrated threshold.
DTC: P0236	**Turbocharger/Supercharger Boost Sensor A Circuit Range/Performance:** The powertrain control module (PCM) continuously monitors this sensor for concerns.This DTC sets when either of the following conditions are present.When the throttle intake pressure (TIP_PRS_BOOST) PID does not correlate with the barometric pressure (BARO) or the manifold absolute pressure (MAP) PIDs at ignition ON.When the turbocharger boost pressure (TCBP) sensor does not correlate with the BARO sensor at idle and the TCBP sensor and MAP sensor fail to correlate while driving.
DTC: P0237	**Turbo/Super Charger Boost Sensor A Circuit Low:** Sensor operating voltage is less than 0.25 volt (VREF). As a result it failed below the minimum allowable calibrated parameter.
DTC: P0238	**Turbocharger/Supercharger Boost Sensor A Circuit High:** The powertrain control module (PCM) continuously monitors the TCBP circuit for concerns. This DTC sets when the PCM detects an open circuit or high voltage in the circuit.

DTC	Trouble Code Title & Conditions
DTC: P0243	**Turbocharger/Supercharger Wastegate Solenoid A:** The powertrain control module (PCM) continuously monitors the TCWRVS circuit for concerns. This DTC sets when the PCM detects an open in the TCWRVS circuit.
DTC: P0245	**Turbocharger/Supercharger Wastegate Solenoid A Low:** The powertrain control module (PCM) continuously monitors the TCWRVS circuit for concerns. This DTC sets when the PCM detects a short to ground in the circuit.
DTC: P0246	**Turbocharger/Supercharger Wastegate Solenoid A High:** The powertrain control module (PCM) continuously monitors the TCWRVS circuit for concerns. This DTC sets when the PCM detects an open circuit or high voltage in the circuit.
DTC: P025A	**Fuel Pump Module Control Circuit/Open:** The Powertrain Control Module (PCM) monitors the Fuel Pump Command (FPC) circuit for a concern. When the PCM commands the Fuel Pump (FP) ON, the PCM is able to detect a short to voltage on the FPC circuit. When the PCM commands the FP OFF, the PCM is able to detect an open circuit or a short to ground on the FPC circuit. The test fails if the voltage is less than or greater than a calibrated limit, for a calibrated amount of time. **NOTE: Check for any harness concerns.**
DTC: P025B	**Fuel Pump Module Control Circuit Range/Performance:** The fuel pump control module monitors the duty cycle and frequency of the signal it receives from the Powertrain Control Module (PCM). The fuel pump control module determines if the signal from the PCM on the Fuel Pump Command (FPC) circuit is a valid duty cycle and frequency. If the duty cycle or frequency is invalid, the fuel pump control module sends a 20% duty cycle signal on the Fuel Pump Monitor (FPM) circuit to report the concern to the PCM. The test fails when the fuel pump control module is still reporting that it is receiving an invalid duty cycle or frequency from the PCM after a calibrated amount of time. **NOTE: Check the harness for routing, alterations, incorrect shielding, or electrical interference from other systems.**
DTC: P025C	**Fuel Pump Module A Control Circuit Low:** The powertrain control module (PCM) monitors the fuel pump command (FPC) circuit for a concern. When the PCM commands the fuel pump (FP) ON, the PCM is able to detect a short to voltage on the FPC circuit. When the PCM commands the FP OFF, the PCM is able to detect an open circuit or a short to ground on the FPC circuit. The test fails if the voltage is less than or greater than a calibrated limit, for a calibrated amount of time.
DTC: P025D	**Fuel Pump Module A Control Circuit High:** The powertrain control module (PCM) monitors the fuel pump command (FPC) circuit for a concern. When the PCM commands the fuel pump (FP) ON, the PCM is able to detect a short to voltage on the FPC circuit. When the PCM commands the FP OFF, the PCM is able to detect an open circuit or a short to ground on the FPC circuit. The test fails if the voltage is less than or greater than a calibrated limit, for a calibrated amount of time.
DTC: P025E	**Turbocharger/Supercharger Boost Sensor A Intermittent/Erratic:** The powertrain control module (PCM) continuously monitors the TCBP circuit for concerns. The test fails when the PCM detects ten intermittent events during a single drive cycle.
DTC: P0261	**Cylinder 1 Injector Circuit Low:** The powertrain control module (PCM) monitors the output of the fuel injector circuits and sets a DTC when it detects the output is not within a calibrated limit.
DTC: P0261	**Cylinder 1 Injector Circuit Low:** The fuel injector control module (FICM) continuously monitors the open/close coil power and ground circuits for continuity. When the open circuit condition is detected the FICM sends a message to the powertrain control module (PCM) through the FICM/PCM communication line. The DTC sets when the PCM receives a message from the FICM.
DTC: P0262	**Cylinder 1 Injector Circuit High:** The powertrain control module (PCM) or fuel injector control module (FICM) monitors the output of the fuel injector circuits and sets a DTC when it detects the output is not within a calibrated limit.
DTC: P0263	**Cylinder 1 Contribution/Balance:** The powertrain control module (PCM) monitors the crankshaft speed and acceleration for each cylinder event. The DTC sets when the acceleration rate of the crankshaft is below or above the calibrated value.
DTC: P0264	**Cylinder 2 Injector Circuit Low:** The fuel injector control module (FICM) continuously monitors the open/close coil power and ground circuits for continuity. When the open circuit condition is detected the FICM sends a message to the powertrain control module (PCM) through the FICM/PCM communication line. The DTC sets when the PCM receives a message from the FICM.
DTC: P0265	**Cylinder 2 Injector Circuit High:** The fuel injector control module (FICM) monitors the current flow on the open/close coil power and ground circuits. When the current draw exceeds the calibrated threshold the FICM sends a message to the powertrain control module (PCM) through the FICM/PCM communication line. The DTC sets when the PCM receives a message from the FICM.

DTC	Trouble Code Title & Conditions
DTC: P0266	**Cylinder 2 Contribution/Balance:** The powertrain control module (PCM) monitors the crankshaft speed and acceleration for each cylinder event. The DTC sets when the acceleration rate of the crankshaft is below the calibrated value.
DTC: P0267	**Cylinder 3 Injector Circuit Low:** The fuel injector control module (FICM) continuously monitors the open/close coil power and ground circuits for continuity. When the open circuit condition is detected the FICM sends a message to the powertrain control module (PCM) through the FICM/PCM communication line. The DTC sets when the PCM receives a message from the FICM.
DTC: P0268	**Cylinder 3 Injector Circuit High:** The fuel injector control module (FICM) monitors the current flow on the open/close coil power and ground circuits. When the current draw exceeds the calibrated threshold the FICM sends a message to the powertrain control module (PCM) through the FICM/PCM communication line. The DTC sets when the PCM receives a message from the FICM.
DTC: P0269	**Cylinder 3 Contribution/Balance:** The powertrain control module (PCM) monitors the crankshaft speed and acceleration for each cylinder event. This DTC sets when the acceleration rate of the crankshaft is below or above the calibrated value.
DTC: P026A	**Charge Air Cooler Efficiency Below Threshold:** The powertrain control module (PCM) continuously monitors the charge air cooler (CAC) efficiency. If the PCM detects that the modeled CAC efficiency differs from the measured CAC efficiency by more than a calibrated value for 10 seconds, the DTC sets.
DTC: P0270	**Cylinder 4 Injector Circuit Low:** The fuel injector control module (FICM) continuously monitors the open/close coil power and ground circuits for continuity. When the open circuit condition is detected the FICM sends a message to the powertrain control module (PCM) through the FICM/PCM communication line. The DTC sets when the PCM receives a message from the FICM.
DTC: P0271	**Cylinder 4 Injector Circuit High:** The fuel injector control module (FICM) monitors the current flow on the open/close coil power and ground circuits. When the current draw exceeds the calibrated threshold the FICM sends a message to the powertrain control module (PCM) through the FICM/PCM communication line. The DTC sets when the PCM receives a message from the FICM.
DTC: P0272	**Cylinder 4 Contribution/Balance:** The powertrain control module (PCM) monitors the crankshaft speed and acceleration for each cylinder event. This DTC sets when the acceleration rate of the crankshaft is below or above the calibrated value.
DTC: P0273	**Cylinder 5 Injector Circuit Low:** The fuel injector control module (FICM) continuously monitors the open/close coil power and ground circuits for continuity. When the open circuit condition is detected the FICM sends a message to the powertrain control module (PCM) through the FICM/PCM communication line. The DTC sets when the PCM receives a message from the FICM.
DTC: P0274	**Cylinder 5 Injector Circuit High:** The fuel injector control module (FICM) monitors the current flow on the open/close coil power and ground circuits. When the current draw exceeds the calibrated threshold the FICM sends a message to the powertrain control module (PCM) through the FICM/PCM communication line. The DTC sets when the PCM receives a message from the FICM.
DTC: P0275	**Cylinder 5 Contribution/Balance:** The powertrain control module (PCM) monitors the crankshaft speed and acceleration for each cylinder event. The DTC sets when the acceleration rate of the crankshaft is below or above the calibrated value.
DTC: P0276	**Cylinder 6 Injector Circuit Low:** The fuel injector control module (FICM) continuously monitors the open/close coil power and ground circuits for continuity. When the open circuit condition is detected the FICM sends a message to the powertrain control module (PCM) through the FICM/PCM communication line. The DTC sets when the PCM receives a message from the FICM.
DTC: P0277	**Cylinder 6 Injector Circuit High:** The fuel injector control module (FICM) monitors the current flow on the open/close coil power and ground circuits. When the current draw exceeds the calibrated threshold the FICM sends a message to the powertrain control module (PCM) through the FICM/PCM communication line. The DTC sets when the PCM receives a message from the FICM.
DTC: P0278	**Cylinder 6 Contribution/Balance:** The powertrain control module (PCM) monitors the crankshaft speed and acceleration for each cylinder event. This DTC sets when the acceleration rate of the crankshaft is below or above the calibrated value.
DTC: P0279	**Cylinder 7 Injector Circuit Low:** The fuel injector control module (FICM) continuously monitors the open/close coil power and ground circuits for continuity. When the open circuit condition is detected the FICM sends a message to the powertrain control module (PCM) through the FICM/PCM communication line. The DTC sets when the PCM receives a message from the FICM.

DTC	Trouble Code Title & Conditions
DTC: P027A	**Fuel Pump Module B Control Circuit/Open:** The powertrain control module (PCM) monitors the fuel pump command (FPC) circuit for a concern. When the PCM commands the fuel pump (FP) ON, the PCM is able to detect a short to voltage on the FPC circuit. When the PCM commands the FP OFF, the PCM is able to detect an open circuit or a short to ground on the FPC circuit. The test fails if the voltage is less than or greater than a calibrated limit, for a calibrated amount of time.
DTC: P027B	**Fuel Pump Module Control Circuit Range/Performance:** The fuel pump control module 2 monitors the duty cycle and frequency of the signal it receives from the powertrain control module (PCM). The fuel pump control module 2 determines if the signal from the PCM on the fuel pump command (FPC) circuit is a valid duty cycle and frequency. If the duty cycle or frequency is invalid, the fuel pump control module 2 sends a 20% duty cycle signal on the fuel pump monitor 2 (FPM2) circuit to report the concern to the PCM. The test fails when the fuel pump control module 2 is still reporting that it is receiving an invalid duty cycle or frequency from the PCM after a calibrated amount of time.
DTC: P0280	**Cylinder 7 Injector Circuit High:** The fuel injector control module (FICM) monitors the current flow on the open/close coil power and ground circuits. When the current draw exceeds the calibrated threshold the FICM sends a message to the powertrain control module (PCM) through the FICM/PCM communication line. The DTC sets when the PCM receives a message from the FICM.
DTC: P0281	**Cylinder 7 Contribution/Balance:** The powertrain control module (PCM) monitors the crankshaft speed and acceleration for each cylinder event. The DTC sets when the acceleration rate of the crankshaft is below or above the calibrated value.
DTC: P0282	**Cylinder 8 Injector Circuit Low:** The fuel injector control module (FICM) continuously monitors the open/close coil power and ground circuits for continuity. When the open circuit condition is detected the FICM sends a message to the powertrain control module (PCM) through the FICM/PCM communication line. The DTC sets when the PCM receives a message from the FICM.
DTC: P0283	**Cylinder 8 Injector Circuit High:** The fuel injector control module (FICM) monitors the current flow on the open/close coil power and ground circuits. When the current draw exceeds the calibrated threshold the FICM sends a message to the powertrain control module (PCM) through the FICM/PCM communication line. The DTC sets when the PCM receives a message from the FICM.
DTC: P0284	**Cylinder 8 Contribution/Balance:** The powertrain control module (PCM) monitors the crankshaft speed and acceleration for each cylinder event. This DTC sets when the acceleration rate of the crankshaft is below or above the calibrated value.
DTC: P0297	**Vehicle Over-Speed Condition:** Indicates the vehicle has been operated in a manner which caused the vehicle speed to exceed a calibration limit. The vehicle speed is continuously monitored and evaluated by the Powertrain Control Module (PCM). The DTC is set when the vehicle speed exceeds the calibrated limit set within the PCM. **NOTE: The DTC indicates the vehicle has been operated in a manner which caused the engine speed to exceed a calibrated limit.**
DTC: P0298	**Engine Oil Over Temperature Condition:** Indicates the engine oil temperature protection strategy in the powertrain control module (PCM) has been activated. This temporarily prohibits high engine speed operation by disabling injectors, to reduce the risk of engine damage from high engine oil temperature. The PCM uses an oil algorithm to determine actual engine oil temperature.
DTC: P0299	**Turbocharger/Supercharger A Underboost Condition:** The powertrain control module (PCM) continuously monitors the turbocharger system for an underboost condition. The PCM checks for a minimum throttle intake pressure (TIP) parameter identification (PID) reading during engine operation, which indicates an underboost condition. The DTC sets when the PCM detects that the actual throttle intake pressure is less than the desired throttle intake pressure by 27.6 kPa (4 psi) or more for 5 seconds.
DTC: P02CC	**Cylinder 1 Fuel Injector Offset Learning at Minimum Limit:** The powertrain control module (PCM) monitors the operation of fuel system and calculates parameters necessary for an ideal engine operation. These parameters are stored in the adaptive strategy table. The table is used as a correction factor when controlling engine operation and corrects for wear or aging of components. This DTC sets when the adaptive strategy has reached its minimum learning limit.
DTC: P02CD	**Cylinder 1 Fuel Injector Offset Learning at Maximum Limit:** The powertrain control module (PCM) monitors the operation of fuel system and calculates parameters necessary for an ideal engine operation. These parameters are stored in the adaptive strategy table. The table is used as a correction factor when controlling engine operation and corrects for wear or aging of components. The DTC is set when the adaptive strategy has reached its maximum learning limit.
DTC: P02CE	**Cylinder 2 Fuel Injector Offset Learning at Minimum Limit:** The powertrain control module (PCM) monitors the operation of fuel system and calculates parameters necessary for an ideal engine operation. These parameters are stored in the adaptive strategy table. The table is used as a correction factor when controlling engine operation and corrects for wear or aging of components. This DTC sets when the adaptive strategy has reached its minimum learning limit.

DTC	Trouble Code Title & Conditions
DTC: P02D0	**Cylinder 3 Fuel Injector Offset Learning at Minimum Limit:** The powertrain control module (PCM) monitors the operation of fuel system and calculates parameters necessary for an ideal engine operation. These parameters are stored in the adaptive strategy table. The table is used as a correction factor when controlling engine operation and corrects for wear or aging of components. The DTC is set when the adaptive strategy has reached its minimum learning limit.
DTC: P02D1	**Cylinder 3 Fuel Injector Offset Learning at Maximum Limit:** The powertrain control module (PCM) monitors the operation of fuel system and calculates parameters necessary for an ideal engine operation. These parameters are stored in the adaptive strategy table. The table is used as a correction factor when controlling engine operation and corrects for wear or aging of components. This DTC sets when the adaptive strategy has reached its maximum learning limit.
DTC: P02D2	**Cylinder 4 Fuel Injector Offset Learning at Minimum Limit:** The powertrain control module (PCM) monitors the operation of fuel system and calculates parameters necessary for an ideal engine operation. These parameters are stored in the adaptive strategy table. The table is used as a correction factor when controlling engine operation and corrects for wear or aging of components. This DTC sets when the adaptive strategy has reached its minimum learning limit.
DTC: P02D3	**Cylinder 4 Fuel Injector Offset Learning at Maximum Limit:** The powertrain control module (PCM) monitors the operation of fuel system and calculates parameters necessary for an ideal engine operation. These parameters are stored in the adaptive strategy table. The table is used as a correction factor when controlling engine operation and corrects for wear or aging of components. The DTC is set when the adaptive strategy has reached its maximum learning limit.
DTC: P02D4	**Cylinder 5 Fuel Injector Offset Learning at Minimum Limit:** The powertrain control module (PCM) monitors the operation of fuel system and calculates parameters necessary for an ideal engine operation. These parameters are stored in the adaptive strategy table. The table is used as a correction factor when controlling engine operation and corrects for wear or aging of components. This DTC sets when the adaptive strategy has reached its minimum learning limit.
DTC: P02D5	**Cylinder 5 Fuel Injector Offset Learning at Maximum Limit:** The powertrain control module (PCM) monitors the operation of fuel system and calculates parameters necessary for an ideal engine operation. These parameters are stored in the adaptive strategy table. The table is used as a correction factor when controlling engine operation and corrects for wear or aging of components. This DTC sets when the adaptive strategy has reached its maximum learning limit.
DTC: P02D6	**Cylinder 6 Fuel Injector Offset Learning at Minimum Limit:** The powertrain control module (PCM) monitors the operation of fuel system and calculates parameters necessary for an ideal engine operation. These parameters are stored in the adaptive strategy table. The table is used as a correction factor when controlling engine operation and corrects for wear or aging of components. This DTC sets when the adaptive strategy has reached its minimum learning limit.
DTC: P02D7	**Cylinder 6 Fuel Injector Offset Learning at Maximum Limit:** The powertrain control module (PCM) monitors the operation of fuel system and calculates parameters necessary for an ideal engine operation. These parameters are stored in the adaptive strategy table. The table is used as a correction factor when controlling engine operation and corrects for wear or aging of components. The DTC is set when the adaptive strategy has reached its maximum learning limit.
DTC: P02D8	**Cylinder 7 Fuel Injector Offset Learning at Minimum Limit:** The powertrain control module (PCM) monitors the operation of fuel system and calculates parameters necessary for an ideal engine operation. These parameters are stored in the adaptive strategy table. The table is used as a correction factor when controlling engine operation and corrects for wear or aging of components. This DTC sets when the adaptive strategy has reached its minimum learning limit.
DTC: P02D9	**Cylinder 7 Fuel Injector Offset Learning at Maximum Limit:** The powertrain control module (PCM) monitors the operation of fuel system and calculates parameters necessary for an ideal engine operation. These parameters are stored in the adaptive strategy table. The table is used as a correction factor when controlling engine operation and corrects for wear or aging of components. The DTC is set when the adaptive strategy has reached its maximum learning limit.
DTC: P02DA	**Cylinder 8 Fuel Injector Offset Learning at Minimum Limit:** The powertrain control module (PCM) monitors the operation of fuel system and calculates parameters necessary for an ideal engine operation. These parameters are stored in the adaptive strategy table. The table is used as a correction factor when controlling engine operation and corrects for wear or aging of components. The DTC is set when the adaptive strategy has reached its minimum learning limit.

DTC	Trouble Code Title & Conditions
DTC: P02DB	**Cylinder 8 Fuel Injector Offset Learning at Maximum Limit:** The powertrain control module (PCM) monitors the operation of fuel system and calculates parameters necessary for an ideal engine operation. These parameters are stored in the adaptive strategy table. The table is used as a correction factor when controlling engine operation and corrects for wear or aging of components. This DTC sets when the adaptive strategy has reached its maximum learning limit.
DTC: P02E0	**Diesel Intake Air Flow Control Circuit/Open:** The powertrain control module (PCM) monitors the status of the intake throttle actuator. If an intake throttle actuator position concern is detected, the PCM sets a DTC.
DTC: P02E1	**Diesel Intake Air Flow Control Performance:** The powertrain control module (PCM) monitors the status of the intake throttle actuator. If an intake throttle actuator position concern is detected, the PCM sets a DTC.
DTC: P02E2	**Diesel Intake Air Flow Control Circuit Low:** The powertrain control module (PCM) monitors the status of the intake throttle actuator. If an intake throttle actuator position concern is detected, the PCM sets a DTC.
DTC: P02E3	**Diesel Intake Air Flow Control Circuit High:** The powertrain control module (PCM) monitors the status of the intake throttle actuator. If an intake throttle actuator position concern is detected, the PCM sets a DTC.
DTC: P02E8	**Diesel Intake Air Flow Position Sensor Circuit Low:** The powertrain control module (PCM) monitors the status of the intake throttle actuator. If an intake throttle actuator position concern is detected, the PCM sets a DTC.
DTC: P02E9	**Diesel Intake Air Flow Position Sensor Circuit High:** The powertrain control module (PCM) monitors the status of the intake throttle actuator. If an intake throttle actuator position concern is detected, the PCM sets a DTC.
DTC: P02EC	**Diesel Intake Airflow Control System - High Airflow Detected:** The powertrain control module (PCM) sets this DTC when the desired mass air flow versus the actual mass air flow measured from the mass air flow (MAF) sensor is outside a calibrated limit.
DTC: P02ED	**Diesel Intake Airflow Control System - Low Airflow Detected:** The powertrain control module (PCM) sets this DTC when the desired mass air flow versus the actual mass air flow measured from the mass air flow (MAF) sensor is outside a calibrated limit.
DTC: P02EE	**Cylinder 1 Injector Circuit Range/Performance:** The powertrain control module (PCM) monitors the output of the fuel injector circuits and sets a DTC when it detects the output is not within a calibrated limit.
DTC: P02EF	**Cylinder 2 Injector Circuit Range/Performance:** The powertrain control module (PCM) monitors the output of the fuel injector circuits and sets a DTC when it detects the output is not within a calibrated limit.
DTC: P02F0	**Cylinder 3 Injector Circuit Range/Performance:** The powertrain control module (PCM) monitors the output of the fuel injector circuits and sets a DTC when it detects the output is not within a calibrated limit.
DTC: P02F1	**Cylinder 4 Injector Circuit Range/Performance:** The powertrain control module (PCM) monitors the output of the fuel injector circuits and sets a DTC when it detects the output is not within a calibrated limit.
DTC: P02F2	**Cylinder 5 Injector Circuit Range/Performance:** The powertrain control module (PCM) monitors the output of the fuel injector circuits and sets a DTC when it detects the output is not within a calibrated limit.
DTC: P02F3	**Cylinder 6 Injector Circuit Range/Performance:** The powertrain control module (PCM) monitors the output of the fuel injector circuits and sets a DTC when it detects the output is not within a calibrated limit.
DTC: P02F4	**Cylinder 7 Injector Circuit Range/Performance:** The powertrain control module (PCM) monitors the output of the fuel injector circuits and sets a DTC when it detects the output is not within a calibrated limit.
DTC: P02F5	**Cylinder 8 Injector Circuit Range/Performance:** The powertrain control module (PCM) monitors the output of the fuel injector circuits and sets a DTC when it detects the output is not within a calibrated limit.

DTC	Trouble Code Title & Conditions
DTC: P0301	**Cylinder 1 Misfire Detected:** The powertrain control module (PCM) continuously monitors the crankshaft speed and acceleration for each cylinder event. When the deceleration is detected the PCM uses the crankshaft position (CKP) and the camshaft position (CMP) signal information to determine which cylinder misfired. The DTC is set when the misfire event occurred in the cylinder due to a poor cylinder compression, fuel delivery concern or mechanical engine concern.
DTC: P0302	**Cylinder 2 Misfire Detected:** The powertrain control module (PCM) continuously monitors the crankshaft speed and acceleration for each cylinder event. When the deceleration is detected the PCM uses the crankshaft position (CKP) and the camshaft position (CMP) signal information to determine which cylinder misfired. The DTC is set when the misfire event occurred in the cylinder due to a poor cylinder compression, fuel delivery concern or mechanical engine concern.
DTC: P0303	**Cylinder 3 Misfire Detected:** The powertrain control module (PCM) continuously monitors the crankshaft speed and acceleration for each cylinder event. When the deceleration is detected the PCM uses the crankshaft position (CKP) and the camshaft position (CMP) signal information to determine which cylinder misfired. The DTC is set when the misfire event occurred in the cylinder due to a poor cylinder compression, fuel delivery concern or mechanical engine concern.
DTC: P0304	**Cylinder 4 Misfire Detected:** The misfire detection monitor is designed to monitor engine misfire and identify the specific cylinder in which the misfire has occurred. Misfire is defined as lack of combustion in a cylinder due to absence of spark, incorrect fuel metering, incorrect compression, or any other cause.
DTC: P0305	**Cylinder 5 Misfire Detected:** The powertrain control module (PCM) continuously monitors the crankshaft speed and acceleration for each cylinder event. When the deceleration is detected the PCM uses the crankshaft position (CKP) and the camshaft position (CMP) signal information to determine which cylinder misfired. The DTC is set when the misfire event occurred in the cylinder due to a poor cylinder compression, fuel delivery concern or mechanical engine concern.
DTC: P0306	**Cylinder 6 Misfire Detected:** The powertrain control module (PCM) continuously monitors the crankshaft speed and acceleration for each cylinder event. When the deceleration is detected the PCM uses the crankshaft position (CKP) and the camshaft position (CMP) signal information to determine which cylinder misfired. The DTC is set when the misfire event occurred in the cylinder due to a poor cylinder compression, fuel delivery concern or mechanical engine concern.
DTC: P0307	**Cylinder 7 Misfire Detected:** The powertrain control module (PCM) continuously monitors the crankshaft speed and acceleration for each cylinder event. When the deceleration is detected the PCM uses the crankshaft position (CKP) and the camshaft position (CMP) signal information to determine which cylinder misfired. The DTC is set when the misfire event occurred in the cylinder due to a poor cylinder compression, fuel delivery concern or mechanical engine concern.
DTC: P0308	**Cylinder 8 Misfire Detected:** The powertrain control module (PCM) continuously monitors the crankshaft speed and acceleration for each cylinder event. When the deceleration is detected the PCM uses the crankshaft position (CKP) and the camshaft position (CMP) signal information to determine which cylinder misfired. The DTC is set when the misfire event occurred in the cylinder due to a poor cylinder compression, fuel delivery concern or mechanical engine concern.
DTC: P0309	**Cylinder Number 9 Misfire Detected:** The misfire detection monitor is designed to monitor engine misfire and identify the specific cylinder in which the misfire has occurred. Misfire is defined as lack of combustion in a cylinder due to absence of spark, poor fuel metering, poor compression, or any other cause. **NOTE: The Malfunction Indicator Lamp (MIL) blinks once per second when a misfire severe enough to cause catalyst damage is detected. If the MIL is on steady state due to a misfire, this indicates the threshold for emissions was exceeded and caused the vehicle to fail an inspection and maintenance tailpipe test.**
DTC: P0310	**Cylinder 10 Misfire Detected:** The misfire detection monitor is designed to monitor engine misfire and identify the specific cylinder in which the misfire has occurred. Misfire is defined as lack of combustion in a cylinder due to absence of spark, poor fuel metering, poor compression, or any other cause. **NOTE: The Malfunction Indicator Lamp (MIL) blinks once per second when a misfire severe enough to cause catalyst damage is detected. If the MIL is on steady state due to a misfire, this indicates the threshold for emissions was exceeded and caused the vehicle to fail an inspection and maintenance tailpipe test.**
DTC: P0313	**Misfire Detected with Low Fuel:** The powertrain control module (PCM) continuously monitors the ignition system for concerns. This DTC sets if the PCM detects that the actual fuel volume is less than the requested fuel volume that results in a misfire condition.

DTC	Trouble Code Title & Conditions
DTC: P0315	**Crankshaft Position System Variation Not Learned.:** The Powertrain Control Module (PCM) is unable to learn and correct for mechanical inaccuracies in crankshaft pulse wheel tooth spacing. This DTC disables the misfire monitor. **NOTE: Requires visual inspection of the CKP sensor and the crankshaft pulse wheel teeth for damage.**
DTC: P0316	**Misfire Detected On Startup (First 1000 Revolutions):** DTC P0316 sets in addition to any type B misfire DTC which occurs in the first 1,000 revolution test interval following engine start.
DTC: P0320	**Ignition/Distributor Engine Speed Input Circuit:** The ignition engine speed sensor input signal to Powertrain Control Module (PCM) is continuously monitored. The test fails when the signal indicates two successive erratic Profile Ignition Pickup (PIP) pulses occurred. **NOTE: The DTC indicates two successive erratic PIP pulses occurred.**
DTC: P0322	**Ignition/Distributor Engine Speed Input Circuit No Signal:** The ignition engine speed sensor input signal to powertrain control module (PCM) is continuously monitored after one normal camshaft signal is detected and the starter motor is engaged, or the camshaft speed exceeds the equivalent speed of engine idle. The test fails when one or more full camshaft revolutions have elapsed without profile ignition pickup (PIP) pulses.
DTC: P0325	**Knock Sensor 1 Circuit (Bank 1):** The knock sensor (KS) detects vibrations upon increase and decrease in engine RPM. The KS generates a voltage based on this vibration. This DTC sets if the voltage goes outside a calibrated level.
DTC: P0326	**Knock Sensor 1 Circuit Range/Performance (Bank 1):** The knock sensor (KS) detects vibrations upon increase and decrease in engine RPM. The knock sensor generates a voltage based on this vibration. A DTC is set if the voltage goes outside a calibrated level.
DTC: P0327	**Knock Sensor 1 Circuit Low (Bank 1):** The knock sensor (KS) detects vibrations upon increase and decrease in engine RPM. The KS generates a voltage based on this vibration. This DTC sets if the voltage goes outside a calibrated level.
DTC: P0328	**Knock Sensor 1 Circuit High (Bank 1):** The knock sensor (KS) detects vibrations upon increase and decrease in engine RPM. The KS generates a voltage based on this vibration. This DTC sets if the voltage goes outside a calibrated level.
DTC: P0330	**Knock Sensor 2 Circuit (Bank 2).:** The Knock Sensor (KS) detects vibrations upon increase and decrease in engine RPM. The knock sensor generates a voltage based on this vibration. A DTC is set if the voltage goes outside a calibrated level. **NOTE: A knock sensor voltage greater than 0.5 volt with the key ON engine OFF indicates a concern is present.**
DTC: P0331	**Knock Sensor 2 Circuit Range/Performance (Bank 2):** The knock sensor (KS) detects vibrations upon increase and decrease in engine RPM. The KS generates a voltage based on this vibration. This DTC sets if the voltage goes outside a calibrated level.
DTC: P0332	**Knock Sensor 2 Circuit Low (Bank 2):** The knock sensor (KS) detects vibrations upon increase and decrease in engine RPM. The KS generates a voltage based on this vibration. This DTC sets if the voltage goes outside a calibrated level.
DTC: P0333	**Knock Sensor 2 Circuit High (Bank 2):** The knock sensor (KS) detects vibrations upon increase and decrease in engine RPM. The KS generates a voltage based on this vibration. This DTC sets if the voltage goes outside a calibrated level.
DTC: P0335	**Crankshaft Position Sensor A Circuit:** The powertrain control module (PCM) continuously monitors this sensor for concerns. This DTC sets when the PCM detects that the crankshaft position (CKP) sensor signal is missing for greater than a calibrated number of camshaft revolutions.
DTC: P0336	**Crankshaft Position Sensor A Circuit Range/Performance:** The DTC sets when the input signal to the powertrain control module (PCM) from the crankshaft position (CKP) sensor is erratic.
DTC: P0337	**Crankshaft Position Sensor A Circuit Low:** The powertrain control module (PCM) monitors the crankshaft position (CKP) and camshaft position (CMP) signals during engine cranking. The DTC is set when the CKP signal is inactive while the CMP signal indicates the engine is rotating. The PCM also monitors the CKP signal for electrical noise. When the electrical noise exceeds the calibrated threshold the DTC sets.
DTC: P0340	**Camshaft Position Sensor A Circuit (Bank 1 or single sensor):** This DTC sets when the powertrain control module (PCM) can no longer detect the signal from the camshaft position (CMP) sensor on bank 1 (vehicles with a single CMP sensor per bank) or bank 1, sensor 1 (vehicles with dual CMP sensors per bank).
DTC: P0341	**Camshaft Position Sensor A Circuit Range/Performance (Bank 1 or Single Sensor):** The powertrain control module (PCM) monitors the camshaft position (CMP) sensor for a noisy signal.

DTC	Trouble Code Title & Conditions
DTC: P0342	**Camshaft Position Sensor A Circuit Low (Bank 1 or Single Sensor):** The powertrain control module (PCM) monitors the camshaft position (CMP) and crankshaft position (CKP) signals during engine cranking. The DTC is set when the CMP signal is inactive while the CKP signal indicates the engine is rotating. The PCM also monitors the CMP signal for electrical noise. When the electrical noise exceeds the calibrated threshold the DTC sets.
DTC: P0344	**Camshaft Position Sensor A Circuit Intermittent (Bank 1 or single sensor):** The test fails when the Powertrain Control Module (PCM) detects an intermittent signal from the Camshaft Position (CMP) sensor. **NOTE: Harness routing, harness alterations, incorrect shielding, or electrical interference from other systems may have an intermittent impact on the CMP signal.**
DTC: P0345	**Camshaft Position Sensor A Circuit (Bank 2):** The test fails when the Powertrain Control Module (PCM) can no longer detect the signal from the Camshaft Position (CMP) sensor on bank 2. **NOTE: Harness routing, harness alterations, incorrect shielding, or electrical interference from other systems may have an intermittent impact on the CMP signal.**
DTC: P0346	**Camshaft Position Sensor A Circuit Range/Performance (Bank 2):** The Powertrain Control Module (PCM) monitors the Camshaft Position (CMP) sensor for a noisy signal. **NOTE: Harness routing, harness alterations, incorrect shielding, or electrical interference from other systems may have an intermittent impact on the CMP signal.**
DTC: P0349	**Camshaft Position Sensor A Circuit Intermittent (Bank 2):** The test fails when the Powertrain Control Module (PCM) detects an intermittent signal from the Camshaft Position (CMP) sensor. **NOTE: Harness routing, harness alterations, incorrect shielding, or electrical interference from other systems may have an intermittent impact on the CMP signal.**
DTC: P0350	**Ignition Coil Primary/Secondary Circuit Malfunction:** Each ignition primary circuit is continuously monitored. The test fails when the Powertrain Control Module (PCM) does not receive a valid Ignition Diagnostic Monitor (IDM) pulse signal from the ignition module (integrated in the PCM). **NOTE: The PCM may disable the fuel injector for a cylinder that is misfiring to protect the exhaust system catalyst. Use the 12-volt non-powered test lamp to verify START/RUN voltage at the ignition coil harness connector. Check the coil driver circuit for open, short to VPWR, or short to ground.**
DTC: P0351	**Ignition Coil 1 Primary/Secondary Circuit Malfunction:** Each ignition primary circuit is continuously monitored. The test fails when the Powertrain Control Module (PCM) does not receive a valid Ignition Diagnostic Monitor (IDM) pulse signal from the ignition module (integrated in the PCM). **NOTE: The PCM may disable the fuel injector for a cylinder that is misfiring to protect the exhaust system catalyst. Use the 12-volt non-powered test lamp to verify START/RUN voltage at the ignition coil harness connector. Check the coil driver circuit for open, short to VPWR, or short to ground.**
DTC: P0352	**Ignition Coil 2 Primary/Secondary Circuit Malfunction:** Each ignition primary circuit is continuously monitored. The test fails when the Powertrain Control Module (PCM) does not receive a valid Ignition Diagnostic Monitor (IDM) pulse signal from the ignition module (integrated in the PCM). **NOTE: The PCM may disable the fuel injector for a cylinder that is misfiring to protect the exhaust system catalyst. Use the 12-volt non-powered test lamp to verify START/RUN voltage at the ignition coil harness connector. Check the coil driver circuit for open, short to VPWR, or short to ground.**
DTC: P0353	**Ignition Coil 3 Primary/Secondary Circuit Malfunction:** Each ignition primary circuit is continuously monitored. The test fails when the Powertrain Control Module (PCM) does not receive a valid Ignition Diagnostic Monitor (IDM) pulse signal from the ignition module (integrated in the PCM). **NOTE: The PCM may disable the fuel injector for a cylinder that is misfiring to protect the exhaust system catalyst. Use the 12-volt non-powered test lamp to verify START/RUN voltage at the ignition coil harness connector. Check the coil driver circuit for open, short to VPWR, or short to ground.**
DTC: P0354	**Ignition Coil 4 Primary/Secondary Circuit Malfunction:** Each ignition primary circuit is continuously monitored. The test fails when the Powertrain Control Module (PCM) does not receive a valid Ignition Diagnostic Monitor (IDM) pulse signal from the ignition module (integrated in the PCM). **NOTE: The PCM may disable the fuel injector for a cylinder that is misfiring to protect the exhaust system catalyst. Use the 12-volt non-powered test lamp to verify START/RUN voltage at the ignition coil harness connector. Check the coil driver circuit for open, short to VPWR, or short to ground.**
DTC: P0355	**Ignition Coil 5 Primary/Secondary Circuit Malfunction:** Each ignition primary circuit is continuously monitored. The test fails when the Powertrain Control Module (PCM) does not receive a valid Ignition Diagnostic Monitor (IDM) pulse signal from the ignition module (integrated in the PCM). **NOTE: The PCM may disable the fuel injector for a cylinder that is misfiring to protect the exhaust system catalyst. Use the 12-volt non-powered test lamp to verify START/RUN voltage at the ignition coil harness connector. Check the coil driver circuit for open, short to VPWR, or short to ground.**

DTC	Trouble Code Title & Conditions
DTC: P0356	**Ignition Coil 6 Primary/Secondary Circuit Malfunction:** Each ignition primary circuit is continuously monitored. The test fails when the Powertrain Control Module (PCM) does not receive a valid Ignition Diagnostic Monitor (IDM) pulse signal from the ignition module (integrated in the PCM). **NOTE: The PCM may disable the fuel injector for a cylinder that is misfiring to protect the exhaust system catalyst. Use the 12-volt non-powered test lamp to verify START/RUN voltage at the ignition coil harness connector. Check the coil driver circuit for open, short to VPWR, or short to ground.**
DTC: P0357	**Ignition Coil 7 Primary/Secondary Circuit Malfunction:** Each ignition primary circuit is continuously monitored. The test fails when the Powertrain Control Module (PCM) does not receive a valid Ignition Diagnostic Monitor (IDM) pulse signal from the ignition module (integrated in the PCM). **NOTE: The PCM may disable the fuel injector for a cylinder that is misfiring to protect the exhaust system catalyst. Use the 12-volt non-powered test lamp to verify START/RUN voltage at the ignition coil harness connector. Check the coil driver circuit for open, short to VPWR, or short to ground.**
DTC: P0358	**Ignition Coil 8 Primary/Secondary Circuit Malfunction:** Each ignition primary circuit is continuously monitored. The test fails when the Powertrain Control Module (PCM) does not receive a valid Ignition Diagnostic Monitor (IDM) pulse signal from the ignition module (integrated in the PCM). **NOTE: The PCM may disable the fuel injector for a cylinder that is misfiring to protect the exhaust system catalyst. Use the 12-volt non-powered test lamp to verify START/RUN voltage at the ignition coil harness connector. Check the coil driver circuit for open, short to VPWR, or short to ground.**
DTC: P0359	**Ignition Coil I Primary/Secondary Circuit:** Each ignition primary circuit is continuously monitored. The test fails when the powertrain control module (PCM) does not receive a valid ignition diagnostic monitor (IDM) pulse signal from the ignition module (integrated in the PCM).
DTC: P0360	**Ignition Coil J Primary/Secondary Circuit:** Each ignition primary circuit is continuously monitored. The test fails when the powertrain control module (PCM) does not receive a valid ignition diagnostic monitor (IDM) pulse signal from the ignition module (integrated in the PCM).
DTC: P0365	**Camshaft Position Sensor B Circuit (Bank 1):** This DTC sets when the powertrain control module (PCM) can no longer detect the signal from the camshaft position (CMP) sensor (bank 1, sensor 2).
DTC: P0366	**Camshaft Position Sensor B Circuit Range/Performance (Bank 1):** The powertrain control module (PCM) monitors the camshaft position (CMP) sensor for a noisy signal.
DTC: P0369	**Camshaft Position Sensor B Circuit Intermittent (Bank 2):** The test fails when the powertrain control module (PCM) detects an intermittent signal from the camshaft position (CMP) sensor.
DTC: P0381	**Glow Plug/Heater Indicator Circuit:** The powertrain control module (PCM) measures the glow plug/heater indicator circuit for continuity. When the continuity exceeds programmed threshold, the PCM sets the DTC.
DTC: P0390	**Camshaft Position Sensor B Circuit (Bank 2):** This DTC sets when the powertrain control module (PCM) can no longer detect the signal from the camshaft position (CMP) sensor (bank 2, sensor 2).
DTC: P0391	**Camshaft Position Sensor B Circuit Range/Performance (Bank 2):** The powertrain control module (PCM) monitors the camshaft position (CMP) sensor for a noisy signal.
DTC: P0394	**Camshaft Position Sensor B Circuit Intermittent (Bank 2):** The test fails when the powertrain control module (PCM) detects an intermittent signal from the camshaft position (CMP) sensor.
DTC: P0400	**Exhaust Gas Recirculation (EGR) Flow:** The electric EGR (EEGR) system is monitored once per drive cycle at high and low load conditions. The test fails when a concern is detected by powertrain control module (PCM) calculations indicating the EGR flow is less or greater than expected.
DTC: P0401	**Exhaust Gas Recirculation (EGR) Flow Insufficient Detected:** The EGR system is monitored during steady state driving conditions while the EGR is commanded on. The test fails when the signal from the differential pressure feedback EGR sensor indicates that EGR flow is less than the desired minimum.
DTC: P0402	**Exhaust Gas Recirculation (EGR) Flow Excessive Detected:** Estimated EGR percent is greater than the maximum limit for the operating conditions.
DTC: P0403	**Exhaust Gas Recirculation (EGR) Control Circuit:** The powertrain control module (PCM) continuously monitors the EGR actuator and circuits for opens and shorts.
DTC: P0404	**Exhaust Gas Recirculation (EGR) Control Circuit Range/Performance:** The EGR valve commanded position compared to the actual position does not match within a calibrated range and time period.
DTC: P0405	**Exhaust Gas Recirculation (EGR) Sensor A Circuit Low:** The powertrain control module (PCM) continuously monitors the EGR valve position circuits for opens and shorts.

DTC	Trouble Code Title & Conditions
DTC: P0406	**Exhaust Gas Recirculation (EGR) Sensor A Circuit High:** The powertrain control module (PCM) continuously monitors the EGR valve position circuits for opens and shorts. This DTC sets when the EGRVP voltage is above the specified voltage, an increment counter advances.
DTC: P040B	**Exhaust Gas Recirculation Temperature (EGRT) Sensor A Circuit Range/Performance:** When the change in the EGRT is less than a calibrated threshold, an increment counter increments for that drive cycle. This DTC sets once the increment counter reaches a calibrated limit.
DTC: P040C	**Exhaust Gas Recirculation Temperature (EGRT) Sensor A Circuit Low:** When the EGRT sensor signal is lower than a specified value, an increment counter advances until the DTC is set.
DTC: P040D	**Exhaust Gas Recirculation Temperature (EGRT) Sensor A Circuit High:** When the EGRT sensor signal is higher than the specified value, an increment counter advances until the DTC is set.
DTC: P0410	**Secondary Air Injection (AIR) System:** The AIR system detected a lack of air flow with the secondary AIR pump ON. **NOTE: Measured air flow is less than expected. Visually inspect the secondary AIR inlet hose**
DTC: P0412	**Secondary Air Injection (AIR) System - Switching Valve A Circuit:** On the primary side of the AIR relay, open and short faults on the AIR command circuit are detected during normal operation by the Powertrain Control Module (PCM) output driver. **NOTE: For intermittent faults use the AIR PCM output driver fault PID (AIRF) during a harness wiggle test with the AIR PCM output driver in OFF and ON states. The AIR PCM output driver fault PID AIRF instantly detects open circuits and shorts to ground with the PCM output driver off. The AIR PCM output driver fault PID AIRF instantly detects open circuits and shorts to ground with the PCM output driver off. The AIR PCM output driver fault PID AIRF instantly detects a short to voltage or low resistance load with the PCM output driver on. Use the OTM to toggle the PCM output driver from OFF to ON.**
DTC: P041B	**Exhaust Gas Recirculation Temperature (EGRT) Sensor B Circuit Range/Performance:** When the change in the EGRT2 is less than the calibrated threshold, an increment counter increments for that drive cycle. The DTC is set once the increment counter reaches the calibrated limit.
DTC: P041C	**Exhaust Gas Recirculation Temperature (EGRT) Sensor B Circuit Low:** When the EGRT2 sensor signal is lower than a specified value, an increment counter advances until the DTC is set.
DTC: P041D	**Exhaust Gas Recirculation Temperature (EGRT) Sensor B Circuit High:** When the EGRT2 sensor signal is higher than a specified value, an increment counter advances until the DTC is set.
DTC: P0420	**Catalyst System Efficiency Below Threshold (Bank 1):** Indicates the catalyst system efficiency is below the acceptable threshold.
DTC: P042E	**Exhaust Gas Recirculation (EGR) Control Stuck Open:** When the EGR setpoint is less than a specified threshold, the actual EGR position is greater than a specified threshold, and the EGR control limit is less than a specified limit, this DTC sets.
DTC: P042F	**Exhaust Gas Recirculation (EGR) Control Stuck Closed:** When the EGR setpoint is greater than a specified threshold, the actual EGR position is less than a specified threshold, and the EGR control limit is greater than a specified limit, the DTC is set.
DTC: P0430	**Catalyst System Efficiency Below Threshold (Bank 2):** Indicates the bank 1 catalyst system efficiency is below the acceptable threshold. **NOTE: The signal line lengths of the downstream HO2Ss are compared against the signal line lengths of the upstream HO2Ss. Under normal closed loop fuel conditions, high efficiency catalysts have oxygen storage which reduces the frequency and amplitude of the downstream HO2S as compared with an upstream HO2S signal. As catalyst efficiency deteriorates, its ability to store oxygen declines and the downstream HO2S signal has an increased amplitude and frequency, approaching the amplitude and frequency of the upstream HO2S. Once beyond an acceptable limit the DTC is set.** Vehicles with universal HO2Ss compare the signal line length of the downstream HO2Ss to an expected signal line length of the downstream HO2Ss with a deteriorated catalytic converter.
DTC: P0442	**Evaporative Emission System Leak Detected (Small Leak):** The Powertrain Control Module (PCM) monitors the complete Evaporative Emission (EVAP) control system for the presence of a small fuel vapor leak. System failure occurs when a fuel vapor leak from an opening as small as 1.016 mm (0.040 in) is detected by the EVAP running loss monitor test. **NOTE: Check for a missing fuel filler cap or the integrity of the cap. Verify the capless fuel tank filler pipe is sealed correctly (if equipped). Check for loose or damaged vapor hoses. Visually inspect the EVAP canister inlet port, CV solenoid filter, and canister vent hose assembly for contamination or debris.**
DTC: P0443	**Evaporative Emission System Purge Control Valve Circuit:** The powertrain control module (PCM) monitors the state of the evaporative emission (EVAP) canister purge valve circuit output driver. The test fails when the signal moves outside the minimum or maximum limit for the commanded state.

DTC	Trouble Code Title & Conditions
DTC: P0443	**Evaporative Emission System Purge Control Valve Circuit:** The powertrain control module (PCM) monitors the state of the evaporative emission (EVAP) canister purge valve circuit output driver. The test fails when the signal moves outside the minimum or maximum limit for the commanded state.
DTC: P0443	**Evaporative Emission System Purge Control Valve Circuit:** The Powertrain Control Module (PCM) monitors the state of the Evaporative Emission (EVAP) canister purge valve circuit output driver. The test fails when the signal moves outside the minimum or maximum limit for the commanded state. **NOTE: To verify normal function, monitor the EVAP canister purge valve signal PID EVMV or EVAPCP and the signal voltage (PCM control side). With the valve closed, the EVMV indicates 0 mA (0% duty cycle for EVAPCP) and voltage approximately equal to battery voltage. When the valve is commanded fully open, EVMV indicates 1,000 mA (100% duty cycle for EVAPCP) and a voltage drop of 3 volts minimum is normal. Output test mode may be used to switch output on/off to verify function.**
DTC: P0444	**Evaporative Emission System Purge Control Valve A Circuit Open:** The powertrain control module (PCM) monitors the state of the evaporative emission (EVAP) canister purge valve circuit output driver. The test fails when the signal moves outside the minimum or maximum limit for the commanded state.
DTC: P0446	**Evaporative Emission System Vent Control Circuit:** Monitors the EVAP canister vent solenoid circuit for an electrical failure. The test fails when the signal moves outside the minimum or maximum allowable calibrated parameters for a specified EVAP canister vent duty cycle by powertrain control module (PCM) command.
DTC: P0450	**Evaporative Emission System Pressure Sensor/Switch:** The powertrain control module (PCM) monitors the evaporative emission (EVAP) system natural vacuum leak detection (NVLD) module vacuum switch input signal to the PCM. The test fails when the signal input is not responding as expected.
DTC: P0451	**Evaporative Emission System Pressure Sensor/Switch Range/Performance:** This DTC sets for a Fuel Tank Pressure (FTP) sensor range (offset) concern. The FTP sensor output is offset by greater than 1.7 inches of water or less than -1.7 inches of water. **NOTE: With the FTP sensor at atmospheric pressure, the FTP PID normally indicates 0 inches of water.**
DTC: P0452	**Evaporative Emission System Pressure Sensor/Switch Low:** The powertrain control module (PCM) monitors the evaporative emission (EVAP) control system fuel tank pressure (FTP) sensor input signal to the PCM. The test fails when the signal average drops below a minimum allowable calibrated parameter.
DTC: P0453	**Evaporative Emission System Pressure Sensor/Switch High:** The Powertrain Control Module (PCM) monitors the Evaporative Emission (EVAP) control system Fuel Tank Pressure (FTP) sensor input signal to the PCM. The test fails when the signal average jumps above a minimum allowable calibrated parameter. **NOTE: An FTP voltage PID reading greater than 4.85 volts in key ON, engine OFF or key ON, engine running indicates a concern is present.**
DTC: P0454	**Evaporative Emission System Pressure Sensor/Switch Intermittent:** The fuel tank pressure changes greater than 14 inches of water in 0.10 seconds.
DTC: P0455	**Evaporative Emission System Leak Detected (Gross Leak/No Flow):** The powertrain control module (PCM) monitors the complete evaporative emission (EVAP) control system for no purge flow, the presence of a large fuel vapor leak, or multiple small fuel vapor leaks. System failure occurs when no purge flow, which is attributed to fuel vapor blockages or restrictions, a large fuel vapor leak, or multiple fuel vapor leaks are detected by the EVAP running loss monitor test with the engine running, but not at idle.
DTC: P0456	**Evaporative Emission System Leak Detected (Very Small Leak):** The Powertrain Control Module (PCM) monitors the complete Evaporative Emission (EVAP) control system for the presence of a very small fuel vapor leak. The system failure occurs when a fuel vapor leak from an opening as small as 0.508 mm (0.020 inch) is detected by the EVAP running loss monitor test. **NOTE: Check for a missing fuel filler cap or the integrity of the cap. Verify the capless fuel tank filler pipe is sealed correctly (if equipped). Check for loose or damaged vapor hoses. Visually inspect the EVAP canister inlet port, CV solenoid filter, and canister vent hose assembly for contamination or debris.**
DTC: P0456	**Evaporative Emission System Leak Detected (Very Small Leak):** The powertrain control module (PCM) monitors the complete evaporative emission (EVAP) control system for the presence of a very small fuel vapor leak. The system failure occurs when a fuel vapor leak from an opening as small as 0.508 mm (0.020 inch) is detected by the EVAP running loss monitor test.
DTC: P0456	**Evaporative Emission System Leak Detected (Very Small Leak):** The powertrain control module (PCM) monitors the complete evaporative emission (EVAP) control system for the presence of a very small fuel vapor leak. The system failure occurs when a fuel vapor leak from an opening as small as 0.508 mm (0.020 inch) is detected by the EVAP running loss monitor test.

DTC	Trouble Code Title & Conditions
DTC: P0457	**Evaporative Emission System Leak Detected (Fuel Cap Loose/Off):** The Powertrain Control Module (PCM) continuously monitors the fuel level and retains the last updated value prior to the ignition switch being placed in the OFF position. After the ignition switch is placed in the ON position a new fuel level is taken and compared to the level recorded at key off. If the fuel level has increased, a flag is set in the PCM indicating the vehicle was refueled. If the Evaporative Emission (EVAP) monitor detects a gross leak while the refueling flag is set, a loose fuel filler cap or an incorrectly sealed fuel tank filler pipe (if equipped) is suspected and the DTC is set. On most vehicles when the DTC sets, either the check fuel cap indicator illuminates or a message on the instrument cluster displays to instruct the driver to check the fuel cap or capless fuel tank filler pipe (if equipped). **NOTE: Check for a missing fuel filler cap or the integrity of the cap. Verify the capless fuel tank filler pipe is sealed correctly (if equipped). If OK, clear the continuous memory DTCs and test the system for correct operation.**
DTC: P0458	**Evaporative Emission System Purge Control Valve Circuit Low:** The powertrain control module (PCM) monitors the state of the evaporative emission (EVAP) canister purge valve circuit output driver. The test fails when the signal moves outside the minimum or maximum limit for the commanded state.
DTC: P0459	**Evaporative Emission System Purge Control Valve Circuit High:** The powertrain control module (PCM) monitors the state of the evaporative emission (EVAP) canister purge valve circuit output driver. The test fails when the signal moves outside the minimum or maximum limit for the commanded state.
DTC: P0460	**Fuel Level Sensor A Circuit:** The Powertrain Control Module (PCM) monitors the Fuel Level Input (FLI) communications network message for a concern. The test fails when the PCM determines that the value of the FLI signal is stuck. The PCM calculates the amount of fuel used during operation. If the FLI signal does not change or does not correspond with the calculated fuel usage, the DTC is set. **NOTE: Check with the customer for driving and fueling habits that would keep the fuel level at approximately the same value. Monitor the FLI PIDs while attempting to move the fuel level float by adding or removing fuel as necessary.**
DTC: P0461	**Fuel Level Sensor A Circuit Range/Performance:** The powertrain control module (PCM) monitors the fuel level input (FLI) communications network message for a concern. The test fails when the FLI signal repeatedly moves in and out of range, exceeding the minimum or maximum allowable calibrated parameters for a specified fuel fill percentage in the fuel tank.
DTC: P0462	**Fuel Level Sensor A Circuit Low:** The Powertrain Control Module (PCM) monitors the Fuel Level Input (FLI) communications network message for a concern. The test fails when the FLI signal is less than the minimum allowable calibrated parameter for a specified fuel fill percentage in the fuel tank. **NOTE: Monitor the FLI PIDs in key ON, engine running. A concern is present if the FLI percentage PID is at 25% fill and the FLI voltage PID is less than 0.90 volt with a non-matching fuel gauge or the FLI percentage PID is at 75% fill and the FLI voltage PID is greater than 2.45 volts with a non-matching fuel gauge.**
DTC: P0463	**Fuel Level Sensor A Circuit High:** The powertrain control module (PCM) monitors the fuel level input (FLI) communications network message for a concern. The test fails when the FLI signal is greater than the maximum allowable calibrated parameter for a specified fuel fill percentage in the fuel tank.
DTC: P0470	**Exhaust Pressure Sensor A Circuit:** Indicates that a concern with the exhaust pressure (EP) sensor A circuit was present during the key on, engine running, (KOER) self test.
DTC: P0471	**Exhaust Pressure Sensor A Circuit Range/Performance:** Exhaust pressure (EP) sensor input to the powertrain control module (PCM) is monitored and is not within the calibrated value.
DTC: P0472	**Exhaust Pressure Sensor A Circuit Low:** This DTC indicates the exhaust pressure (EP) sensor signal is less than the self-test minimum.
DTC: P0473	**Exhaust Pressure Sensor A Circuit High:** This DTC indicates the exhaust pressure (EP) sensor signal is greater than the self-test maximum.
DTC: P0478	**Exhaust Pressure Control Valve High**
DTC: P0480	**Fan 1 Control Circuit:** This test checks the fan control variable (FCV) output circuit for the cooling fan clutch. This DTC sets if the powertrain control module (PCM) detects the voltage on the FCV circuit is not within the expected range.
DTC: P0481	**Fan 2 Control Circuit:** Monitors the high fan control (HFC) primary circuit output from the powertrain control module (PCM). The test fails when the HFC output is commanded on (grounded) and excessive current draw is detected on the HFC circuit; or when the HFC circuit is commanded off and voltage is not detected on the HFC circuit (the PCM expects to detect VPWR voltage through the high speed FC relay coil to the HFC circuit).

DTC	Trouble Code Title & Conditions
DTC: P0482	**Fan 3 Control Circuit:** Monitors the medium fan control (MFC) primary circuit output from the powertrain control module (PCM). The test fails if the MFC output commanded on (grounded), excessive current draw is detected on the MFC circuit or, with the MFC circuit commanded off, voltage is not detected on the MFC circuit (the PCM expects to detect IGN START/RUN voltage through the medium speed FC relay coil to the MFC circuit).
DTC: P0483	**Fan Performance:** The powertrain control module (PCM) uses the fan speed sensor (FSS) input to monitor the cooling fan clutch speed. If the indicated fan speed is higher than the calibrated value during continuous memory self-test, this DTC sets.
DTC: P0488	**Exhaust Gas Recirculation (EGR) Throttle Control Circuit A Range/Performance:** The intake throttle actuator monitors the status of the intake throttle. If an intake throttle position error is detected, a status message is sent to the powertrain control module (PCM) from the throttle actuator.
DTC: P0489	**Exhaust Gas Recirculation (EGR) A Control Circuit Low:** The powertrain control module (PCM) continuously monitors the EGR actuator and circuits for opens and shorts.
DTC: P0490	**Exhaust Gas Recirculation (EGR) A Control Circuit High:** The powertrain control module (PCM) continuously monitors the EGR actuator and circuits for opens and shorts.
DTC: P0491	**Secondary Air Injection (AIR) System Insufficient Flow (Bank 1):** The AIR system detected that there was insufficient mass air flow change during pump switching (ON/OFF). **NOTE: Measured air flow is less than expected. Visually inspect the secondary AIR inlet hose.**
DTC: P0494	**Fan Speed Low:** The powertrain control module (PCM) uses the fan speed sensor (FSS) input to monitor the cooling fan clutch speed. If the indicated fan speed is lower than the calibrated value during the key ON engine running (KOER) self-test, the DTC is set.
DTC: P0495	**Fan Speed High:** The powertrain control module (PCM) uses the fan speed sensor (FSS) input to monitor the cooling fan clutch speed. If the indicated fan speed is higher than the calibrated value during the key ON engine running (KOER) self-test, the DTC is set.
DTC: P0496	**Evaporative Emission System High Purge Flow:** The powertrain control module (PCM) monitors the complete evaporative emission (EVAP) control system for high purge flow.
DTC: P0497	**Evaporative Emission System Low Purge Flow:** The powertrain control module (PCM) monitors the complete evaporative emission (EVAP) control system for low purge flow.
DTC: P04D9	**Closed Loop EGR Control at Limit - Flow Too Low:** Estimated EGR percent is less than the minimum limit for the operating conditions.
DTC: P04DA	**Closed Loop EGR Control at Limit - Flow Too High:** Estimated EGR percent is greater than the maximum limit for the operating conditions.
DTC: P0500	**Vehicle Speed Sensor A:** Indicates the powertrain control module (PCM) detected an error in the vehicle speed information.
DTC: P0501	**Vehicle Speed Sensor (VSS) A Range/Performance:** Engine started; then with the engine speed more than the TCC stall speed, the PCM detected a problem with the vehicle speed data.
DTC: P0503	**Vehicle Speed Sensor (VSS) A Intermittent/Erratic/High:** Indicates incorrect or noisy VSS performance. Vehicle speed data is received from either the VSS, the transfer case speed sensor (TCSS), or the anti lock brake system (ABS) control module.
DTC: P0504	**Brake Switch Correlation:** The PCM does a comparison test between the Brake Pedal Switch (BPS) and the Brake Pedal Position (BPP) switch. **NOTE: Check the state of PID BPS and PID BPP. BPS is normally closed and BPP is normally open.**
DTC: P0505	**Idle Air Control (IAC) System (Vehicles Without IAC Valve):** The Powertrain Control Module (PCM) attempts to control engine speed during the Key On, Engine Running (KOER) self-test. The test fails when the desired RPM could not be reached or controlled during the self-test. **NOTE: This DTC may be accompanied by other DTCs. Diagnose other DTCs first. If other DTCs are not present inspect the intake air system for air restrictions, vacuum leaks, and damage. If no concerns are present, clear the DTC and carry out the KOER self-test.**
DTC: P0506	**Idle Air Control System RPM Lower Than Expected:** This DTC sets when the powertrain control module (PCM) detects an engine idle speed that is less than the desired RPM. If the PCM detects that the actual RPM is greater than 100 RPM below the desired RPM for more than 5 seconds, the DTC sets.
DTC: P0507	**Idle Air Control (IAC) System RPM Higher Than Expected (Vehicles With IAC Valve):** This DTC is set when the Powertrain Control Module (PCM) detects an engine idle speed that is greater than the desired RPM. **NOTE: Disconnect the IAC valve and look for little or no change in engine RPM as an indication of a stuck or damaged valve.**

DTC	Trouble Code Title & Conditions
DTC: P050A	**Cold Start Idle Air Control Performance (For Vehicles With An Idle Air Control (IAC) Valve):** The cold start emission reduction monitor has detected an airflow performance deficiency. The cold start emission reduction monitor validates the operation of the components of the system required to achieve the cold start emission reduction strategy, retarded spark timing (P050B) and elevated idle airflow (P050A). When the idle airflow test portion of the cold start emission reduction strategy is enabled, the idle air control system requests a higher idle RPM to increase the engine airflow. The cold start emission reduction monitor compares the actual airflow measured by the mass air flow (MAF) sensor to the requested powertrain control module (PCM) airflow. The DTC sets when the airflow is less than the calibrated limit.
DTC: P050A	**Cold Start Idle Air Control Performance:** The monitor compares the actual measured engine speed to the engine speed requested by the powertrain control module (PCM). When the difference between desired and actual engine speed exceeds the calibrated threshold, the DTC sets.
DTC: P050B	**Cold Start Ignition Timing Performance:** The cold start ignition timing performance has a functional response test of actual spark timing angle actual versus commanded spark timing in the Powertrain Control Module (PCM). **NOTE: Diagnose all other powertrain related DTCs first.**
DTC: P050E	**Cold Start Engine Exhaust Temperature Out of Range:** The powertrain control module (PCM) calculates the actual catalyst warm up temperature during a cold start. The PCM then compares the actual catalyst temperature to the expected catalyst temperature model. The difference between the actual and expected temperatures is a ratio. This DTC sets when this ratio exceeds the calibrated value and the malfunction indicator lamp (MIL) illuminates.
DTC: P0511	**Idle Air Control (IAC) Circuit:** This DTC is set when the Powertrain Control Module (PCM) detects an electrical load failure on the IAC output circuit.
DTC: P0512	**Starter Request Circuit:** Indicates the one touch integrated starting system voltage circuit to the starter relay has a short to voltage.
DTC: P0528	**Fan Speed Sensor Circuit No Signal:** The Powertrain Control Module (PCM) uses the Fan Speed Sensor (FSS) input to monitor the cooling fan clutch speed. If the indicated fan speed is lower than the calibrated value during the Key On Engine Running (KOER) self-test, the DTC is set. **NOTE: Visually inspect the cooling fan clutch for damage or obstruction.**
DTC: P0529	**Fan Speed Sensor Circuit Intermittent:** The purpose of this diagnostic test is to find an intermittent fan speed signal. This is done by comparing a previous calibrated fan speed to the current fan speed. If there is change from the previous calibrated fan speed to the current fan speed, the DTC set.
DTC: P052A	**Cold Start Camshaft Position Timing Over-Advanced (Bank 1):** The Powertrain Control Module (PCM) monitors the Variable Camshaft Timing (VCT) position for an over-advanced camshaft timing during cold start up. The test fails when the camshaft timing exceeds a maximum calibrated value or remains in an advanced position. **NOTE: This DTC is a functional check of the VCT unit. Diagnose any base engine concerns related to the engine oil pressure or engine timing**
DTC: P052B	**Cold Start Camshaft Position Timing Over-Retarded (Bank 1):** The Powertrain Control Module (PCM) monitors the Variable Camshaft Timing (VCT) position for over-retarded camshaft timing during cold start up. The test fails when the camshaft timing exceeds a maximum calibrated value or remains in a retarded position. **NOTE: This DTC is a functional check of the VCT unit. Diagnose any base engine concerns related to the engine oil pressure or engine timing.**
DTC: P052C	**Cold Start Camshaft Position Timing Over-Advanced (Bank 2):** The Powertrain Control Module (PCM) monitors the Variable Camshaft Timing (VCT) position for over-advanced camshaft timing during cold start up. The test fails when the camshaft timing exceeds a maximum calibrated value or remains in an advanced position. **NOTE: This DTC is a functional check of the VCT unit. Diagnose any base engine concerns related to the engine oil pressure or engine timing.**
DTC: P052D	**Cold Start Camshaft Position Timing Over-Retarded (Bank 2):** The Powertrain Control Module (PCM) monitors the Variable Camshaft Timing (VCT) position for over-retarded camshaft timing during cold start up. The test fails when the camshaft timing exceeds a maximum calibrated value or remains in a retarded position. **NOTE: This DTC is a functional check of the VCT unit. Diagnose any base engine concerns related to the engine oil pressure or engine timing.**
DTC: P0532	**A/C Pressure Refrigerant Sensor A Circuit Low:** The Air Conditioning Pressure (ACP) transducer sensor inputs a voltage to the Powertrain Control Module (PCM). If the voltage is below the calibrated level the DTC sets. **NOTE: Verify the VREF voltage is between 4 and 6 volts.**

DTC	Trouble Code Title & Conditions
DTC: P0533	**A/C Refrigerant Pressure Sensor A Circuit High:** The Air Conditioning Pressure (ACP) transducer sensor inputs a voltage to the Powertrain Control Module (PCM). If the voltage is above a calibrated level the DTC sets **NOTE: Verify the VREF voltage is between 4 and 6 volts.**
DTC: P0534	**A/C Refrigerant Charge Loss:** Indicates frequent A/C compressor clutch cycling. **NOTE: This test is designed to protect the transmission. In some strategies, the PCM unlocks the torque converter during A/C clutch engagement. If a concern is present that results in frequent A/C clutch cycling, damage could occur if the torque converter is cycled at these intervals. This test detects this condition, sets the DTC and prevents the torque converter from excessive cycling.**
DTC: P0537	**A/C Evaporator Temperature Sensor Circuit Low:** Indicates the air conditioning evaporator temperature (ACET) signal input was less than the self-test minimum. The self-test minimum is 0.13 volt. **NOTE: The Powertrain Control Module (PCM) sources a low current 5 volts on the ACET circuit (this voltage can be measured with the sensor disconnected). As the A/C evaporator air temperature changes, the ACET circuit resistance to SIG RTN (ground) changes (which changes the voltage the PCM detects). When the ACET signal is detected below the self-test minimum, check for shorts to the SIG RTN or ground, which would pull the voltage low.**
DTC: P0538	**A/C Evaporator Temperature Sensor Circuit High:** Indicates the Air Conditioning Evaporator Temperature (ACET) signal input was greater than the self-test maximum. The self-test maximum is 4.5 volts. **NOTE: The Powertrain Control Module (PCM) sources a low current 5 volts on the ACET circuit (this voltage can be measured with the sensor disconnected). As the A/C evaporator air temperature changes, the ACET circuit resistance to SIG RTN (ground) changes (which changes the voltage the PCM detects). When the ACET signal is detected above the self-test maximum, check for open circuits (ACET or SIG RTN), which would cause the voltage to remain high. Although not as probable, also check for a short to voltage VREF.**
DTC: P053A	**Positive Crankcase Ventilation (PCV) Heater Control Circuit / Open:** This DTC sets when the Powertrain Control Module (PCM) detects a Positive Crankcase Ventilation (PCV) heater circuit failure. **NOTE: Make sure the PCV valve is correct for the engine application and the PCV heater connector is correctly connected.**
DTC: P053F	**Cold Start Fuel Pressure Performance:** The PCM monitors fuel rail pressure to control split injection. This DTC sets if the fuel rail pressure falls outside a calibrated threshold limit for controlling split injection during a cold start.
DTC: P0544	**Exhaust Gas Temperature Sensor Circuit - Bank 1 Sensor 1:** The powertrain control module (PCM) monitors the operation of the exhaust gas temperature (EGT) sensor to determine if the EGT sensor responds to the increase in temperature of the exhaust gas, during vehicle operation. The test fails when after 10 minutes of driving, following an 8-hour soak, the EGT sensor does not indicate a temperature increase of 40°C (72°F).
DTC: P0545	**Exhaust Gas Temperature Sensor Circuit Low - Bank 1 Sensor 1:** The powertrain control module (PCM) monitors the exhaust gas temperature (EGT) sensor for a low voltage concern. The test fails when the sensor voltage is less than 0.10 volt for greater than 15 seconds. Some updated vehicles may use 0.20 volt instead of 0.10 volt.
DTC: P0546	**Exhaust Gas Temperature Sensor Circuit High - Bank 1 Sensor 1:** The powertrain control module (PCM) monitors the exhaust gas temperature (EGT) sensor for a high voltage concern. The test fails when the sensor voltage is greater than 4.75 volts for greater than 15 seconds. Some updated vehicles may use 2.50 volts instead of 4.75 volts.
DTC: P054A	**Cold Start Exhaust (B) Camshaft Position Timing Over-Advanced (Bank 1):** The powertrain control module (PCM) monitors the variable camshaft timing (VCT) position for an over-advanced camshaft timing during cold start up. The test fails when the camshaft timing exceeds a maximum calibrated value or remains in an advanced position.
DTC: P054B	**Cold Start Exhaust (B) Camshaft Position Timing Over-Retarded (Bank 1):** The powertrain control module (PCM) monitors the variable camshaft timing (VCT) position for over-retarded camshaft timing during cold start up. The test fails when the camshaft timing exceeds a maximum calibrated value or remains in a retarded position.
DTC: P054C	**Cold Start Exhaust (B) Camshaft Position Timing Over-Advanced (Bank 2):** The powertrain control module (PCM) monitors the variable camshaft timing (VCT) position for an over-advanced camshaft timing during cold start up. The test fails when the camshaft timing exceeds a maximum calibrated value or remains in an advanced position.
DTC: P054D	**Cold Start Exhaust (B) Camshaft Position Timing Over-Retarded (Bank 2):** The powertrain control module (PCM) monitors the variable camshaft timing (VCT) position for over-retarded camshaft timing during cold start up. The test fails when the camshaft timing exceeds a maximum calibrated value or remains in a retarded position.
DTC: P054E	**Idle Control System - Fuel Quantity Lower Than Expected:** When the powertrain control module (PCM) detects the fuel quantity needed for idle control is greater than 30% lower than lowest expected fuel rate, this DTC sets.

DTC	Trouble Code Title & Conditions
DTC: P054F	**Idle Control System - Fuel Quantity Higher Than Expected:** When the powertrain control module (PCM) detects the fuel quantity needed for idle control is greater than 30% higher than highest expected fuel rate, this DTC sets.
DTC: P0552	**Power Steering Pressure (PSP) Sensor/Switch Circuit Low:** Indicates the PSP sensor input signal was less than the self-test minimum **NOTE: View the PSP PID to monitor the PSP input.**
DTC: P0553	**Power Steering Pressure (PSP) Sensor Circuit High Input:** Indicates the PSP sensor input signal was greater than the self-test maximum. **NOTE: View the PSP PID to monitor the PSP input.**
DTC: P0560	**System Voltage:** This DTC is set when the powertrain control module (PCM) detects a low system voltage when operating above 1,000 RPM.
DTC: P0562	**System Voltage Low:** This DTC is set when the Powertrain Control Module (PCM) or Transaxle Control Module (TCM) detects low system voltage. **NOTE: System voltage is monitored by the PCM. When the voltage is above or below a calibrated value, internal counter increments until a DTC is set.**
DTC: P0563	**System Voltage High:** This DTC is set when the Powertrain Control Module (PCM) detects high system voltage. **NOTE: System voltage is monitored by the PCM. When the voltage is above or below a calibrated value, internal counter increments until a DTC is set.**
DTC: P0565	**Cruise Control ON Signal:** PCM detects a concern with the cruise control ON circuit.
DTC: P0566	**Cruise Control OFF Signal:** PCM detects a concern with the cruise control OFF circuit.
DTC: P0567	**Cruise Control RESUME Signal:** PCM detects a concern with the cruise control RESUME circuit.
DTC: P0568	**Cruise Control SET Signal:** PCM detects a concern with the cruise control SET circuit.
DTC: P0569	**Cruise Control COAST Signal:** PCM detects a concern with the cruise control COAST circuit.
DTC: P0571	**Brake Switch A Circuit:** The purpose of this DTC is to check whether the brake switch has toggled or not during the Key On Engine Running (KOER) test. **NOTE: Using the scan tool, check the BPP/BOO PID. The BPP/BOO PID should toggle on and off with brake pedal activation.**
DTC: P0572	**Brake Switch A Circuit Low:** This DTC indicates the brake switch is stuck in the ON position. **NOTE: Using the scan tool, check the BPP/BOO PID. The BPP/BOO PID should toggle on and off with brake pedal activation.**
DTC: P0573	**Brake Switch A Circuit High:** This DTC indicates the brake switch is stuck in the OFF position. **NOTE: Using the scan tool, check the BPP/BOO PID. The BPP/BOO PID should toggle on and off with brake pedal activation.**
DTC: P0579	**Cruise Control Multifunction Input A Circuit Range / Performance:** This DTC indicates the speed control is inoperative.
DTC: P0581	**Cruise Control Multifunction Input A Circuit High:** This DTC indicates the speed control is inoperative.
DTC: P0600	**Serial Communication Link:** Indicates an error occurred in the Powertrain Control Module (PCM). This DTC may be set alone or in combination with P2105.
DTC: P0601	**Internal Control Module Memory Checksum Error:** Indicates the powertrain control module (PCM) internal central processing unit (CPU) has encountered an error. The PCM monitors itself and carries out internal checks of its own CPU. If any of these checks returns an incorrect value, the DTC sets.
DTC: P0602	**Powertrain Control Module (PCM) Programming Error:** This DTC indicates a programming error within the Vehicle ID (VID) block. **NOTE: The VID block must be programmed.**

DTC	Trouble Code Title & Conditions
DTC: P0603	**Internal Control Module Keep Alive Memory (KAM) Error:** Indicates the Powertrain Control Module (PCM) has experienced an internal memory concern. However, there are external items that can cause this DTC. **NOTE: If KAPWR is interrupted to the PCM because of a battery or PCM disconnect, this DTC can be generated on the first power-up.**
DTC: P0604	**Internal Control Module Random Access Memory (RAM) Error:** Indicates the Powertrain Control Module (PCM) RAM has been corrupted. **NOTE: Reprogram or update the calibration. Check for other DTCs or drive symptoms for further action. Make sure to check for aftermarket performance products before installing a new PCM. If it is necessary to install a new PCM.**
DTC: P0605	**Internal Control Module Read Only Memory (ROM) Error:** The Powertrain Control Module (PCM) ROM has been corrupted. **NOTE: Reprogram the vehicle identification VID block (use as built data). Check for other DTCs or drive symptoms for further action. Make sure to check for aftermarket performance products before installing a new Powertrain Control Module (PCM). If it is necessary to install a new PCM.**
DTC: P0606	**Control Module Processor:** This DTC indicates an internal Powertrain Control Module (PCM) communication error. **NOTE: Reprogram or update the calibration. Check for other DTCs and diagnose those first. Make sure to check for aftermarket performance products before installing a new PCM. Clear the DTCs, repeat the self-test. If the DTC is retrieved again, install a new PCM.**
DTC: P0607	**Control Module Performance:** Indicates that the Powertrain Control Module (PCM) internal Central Processing Unit (CPU) has encountered an error. The PCM monitors itself and carries out internal checks of its own CPU. If any of these checks returns an incorrect value, the DTC is set. **NOTE: Reprogram or update the calibration. Check for other DTCs and diagnose those first. Make sure to check for aftermarket performance products before installing a new PCM. Clear the DTCs, repeat the self-test. If the DTC is retrieved again, install a new PCM.**
DTC: P060A	**Internal Control Module Monitoring Processor Performance:** Indicates an error occurred in the Powertrain Control Module (PCM). This DTC may set in combination with P2105. **NOTE: Verify the PCM is at the latest calibration level.**
DTC: P060B	**Internal Control Module A/D Processing Performance:** Indicates an error occurred in the Powertrain Control Module (PCM). This DTC may set in combination with P2104 or P2110. **NOTE: Inspect the harness for damage. Verify correct operation of the sensors using VREF and related circuits.**
DTC: P060C	**Internal Control Module Main Processor Performance:** Indicates an internal error occurred in the powertrain control module (PCM) or a transmission range (TR) sensor concern.
DTC: P060D	**Internal Control Module Accelerator Pedal Position Performance:** Indicates an error occurred in the Powertrain Control Module (PCM). If the PCM detects a concern identifying an issue with an Accelerator Pedal Position (APP) sensor signal or with processing the brake pedal sensor input, the DTC is set. **NOTE: Verify the PCM is at the latest calibration level.**
DTC: P0610	**Control Module Vehicle Options Error:** Indicates a Powertrain Control Module (PCM) vehicle options error. **NOTE: Reprogram or update the calibration. Check for other DTCs or drive symptoms for further action. Make sure to check for aftermarket performance products before installing a new PCM. If it is necessary to install a new PCM.**
DTC: P0611	**Fuel Injector Control Module Performance:** The fuel injectors are controlled by the powertrain control module (PCM). This DTC sets when the PCM detects the voltage necessary to control the fuel injectors is not within a calibrated range.
DTC: P0613	**Transmission Control Module (TCM) Read-Only Memory (ROM) Error.:** Indicates TCM has detected an internal software issue. Mechanical limp-home mode, default to 3rd or 5th gear. **NOTE: May turn on MIL, TCIL light on.**
DTC: P0616	**Starter Relay Circuit Low:** The PCM detects a malfunction in the starting system.
DTC: P0617	**Starter Relay Circuit High:** The PCM detects a malfunction in the starting system.
DTC: P061A	**Internal Control Module Torque Performance:** This DTC is set by the powertrain control module (PCM) when the measured engine torque value exceeds the maximum allowable engine torque value.

DTC	Trouble Code Title & Conditions
DTC: P061B	**Internal Control Module Torque Calculation Performance:** Indicates a calculation error occurred in the Powertrain Control Module (PCM). **NOTE: Check for sensor and circuit related DTCs. Do not install a new Electronic Throttle Body (ETB) for this DTC.**
DTC: P061C	**Internal Control Module Engine RPM Performance:** Indicates a calculation error occurred in the Powertrain Control Module (PCM). **NOTE: Verify correct operation of the CKP and CMP sensors and related circuits.**
DTC: P061D	**Internal Control Module Engine Air Mass Performance:** Indicates a calculation error occurred in the Powertrain Control Module (PCM). **NOTE: Verify the PCM is at the latest calibration level.**
DTC: P061F	**Internal Control Module Throttle Actuator Controller Performance:** Indicates a calculation error occurred in the Powertrain Control Module (PCM). **NOTE: Verify correct operation of the Electronic Throttle Control (ETC) components and related circuits**
DTC: P0620	**Generator Control Circuit:** The Powertrain Control Module (PCM) reads the GENLI and sends a DTC through the network when the signal frequency of GENLI indicates a concern.
DTC: P0622	**Generator Field Terminal Circuit:** The Powertrain Control Module (PCM) monitors the generator load from the generator/regulator in the form of frequency. The frequency range is determined by the temperature of the voltage regulator, where 97% indicates a full load, and less than 6% indicates no load.
DTC: P0623	**Generator Lamp Control Circuit:** The powertrain control module (PCM) monitors the generator lamp control circuit. When the PCM detects a concern it sets this DTC.
DTC: P0625	**Generator Field Terminal Circuit Low:** The Powertrain Control Module (PCM) monitors generator load from the generator/regulator in the form of frequency. The concern indicates the input is lower than the load should be in normal operation. The load input could be low when no generator output exists.
DTC: P0625	**Generator Field Terminal Circuit Low:** The Powertrain Control Module (PCM) monitors generator load from the generator/regulator in the form of frequency The concern indicates the input is lower than the load should be in normal operation The load input could be low when no generator output exists.
DTC: P0627	**Fuel Pump A Control Circuit/Open:** The fuel pump control module monitors the fuel pump assembly and secondary circuits for a concern. If the fuel pump control module detects a concern with the fuel pump assembly or secondary circuits, the fuel pump control module sends an 80% duty cycle signal on the fuel pump monitor (FPM) circuit to report the concern to the powertrain control module (PCM). The test fails when the fuel pump control module is still reporting a concern with the fuel pump assembly or secondary circuits after a calibrated amount of time.
DTC: P0628	**Fuel Pump A Control Circuit Low:** The powertrain control module (PCM) monitors the fuel pump (FP) circuit output from the PCM. The test fails if the FP output is commanded ON (grounded), excessive current draw is detected on the FP circuit, or with the FP output commanded OFF, voltage is not detected on the FP circuit and the PCM expects to detect VPWR voltage coming through the fuel pump relay coil to the FP circuit.
DTC: P0629	**Fuel Pump A Control Circuit High:** The powertrain control module (PCM) monitors the fuel pump (FP) circuit output from the PCM. The test fails if the FP output is commanded ON (grounded), excessive current draw is detected on the FP circuit, or with the FP output commanded OFF, voltage is not detected on the FP circuit and the PCM expects to detect VPWR voltage coming through the fuel pump relay coil to the FP circuit.
DTC: P062A	**Fuel Pump A Control Circuit Range/Performance:** The powertrain control module (PCM) monitors the fuel pump command (FPC) circuit output from the PCM. The test fails if the airbags deploy and the fuel pump monitor (FPM) shows the fuel pump is energized, or if the FPC request and FPM feedback do not correlate.
DTC: P062B	**Internal Control Module Fuel Injector Control Performance:** This DTC sets when the powertrain control module (PCM) detects the current fuel injector energizing time is greater than the permitted energizing time after overrun demand by the driver.
DTC: P062C	**Internal Control Module Vehicle Speed Performance:** Indicates an error occurred in the Powertrain Control Module (PCM). **NOTE: Repair any ABS DTCs, ABS-related DTCs in other modules, or vehicle communication concerns.**
DTC: P062D	**Fuel Injector Driver Circuit Performance Bank 1:** The powertrain control module (PCM) continuously monitors the operation of the fuel injectors and corresponding circuitry for cylinders 1, 4, 6 and 7. When the short to ground or short to power condition for those cylinders is detected the PCM sets the DTC.

DTC	Trouble Code Title & Conditions
DTC: P062E	**Fuel Injector Driver Circuit Performance Bank 2:** The powertrain control module (PCM) continuously monitors the operation of the fuel injectors and corresponding circuitry for cylinders 2, 3, 5 and 8. When the short to ground or short to power condition for those cylinders is detected the PCM sets the DTC. Monitor the PIDs to determine which cylinder number has an injector or injector circuit concern.
DTC: P062F (PCM)	**Internal Control Module EEPROM Error:** Indicates the powertrain control module (PCM) electrically erasable programmable read only memory (EEPROM) has been corrupted.
DTC: P062F (TCM)	**Internal Control Module EEPROM Error:** The Transmission control module (TCM) read only memory (ROM) has been corrupted.
DTC: P0630	**VIN Not Programmed or Incompatible - ECM/PCM:** The PCM has a programming error.
DTC: P0634	**TCM module temperature:** Internal temperature within TCM too high. Possible restriction in cooling circuit. Default to 3rd or 5th gear
DTC: P0641	**Transmission Control Module (TCM) sensor Range/Performance:** Indicates TCM internal temperature is too high. Mechanical limp-home mode, default to 3rd or 5th gear. **NOTE: May turn on MIL.** * Transmission cooler tubes for possible restrictions. (kinked or bent cooler)* Operation/orientation of the thermal bypass valve* Mechatronics unit failed* TFT has failed* TCM module sensor failed* TCM has failed
DTC: P0642	**Sensor Reference Voltage A Circuit Low:** Indicates the Reference Voltage (VREF) circuit is less than VREF minimum. **NOTE: This DTC is set due to an under voltage condition on the VREF circuit.**
DTC: P0643	**Sensor Reference Voltage A Circuit High:** Indicates the Reference Voltage (VREF) circuit is less than VREF minimum. **NOTE: This DTC is set due to an over voltage condition on the VREF circuit.**
DTC: P0645	**Air Conditioning Clutch Relay Control Circuit Malfunction:** Key on or engine running; and the PCM detected an unexpected low or high voltage condition A/C clutch relay control circuit.
DTC: P0646	**A/C Clutch Relay Control Circuit Low:** Key on or engine running; and the PCM detected an unexpected low voltage condition A/C clutch relay control circuit.
DTC: P0647	**A/C Clutch Relay Control Circuit High:** Key on or engine running; and the PCM detected an unexpected high voltage condition A/C clutch relay control circuit.
DTC: P0649	**Cruise Control Lamp Control Circuit:** Engine started, vehicle driven at cruise with the Cruise switch set, and the PCM detected a fault in the C/C lamp control circuit.
DTC: P064C	**Glow Plug Control Module:** This DTC sets by the glow plug control module (GPCM) to indicate an internal software error has occurred.
DTC: P064D	**Internal Control Module O2 Sensor Processor Performance (Bank 1):** The Powertrain Control Module (PCM) monitors the application-specific integrated circuit that controls and monitors the Heated Oxygen Sensor (HO2S). The test fails when the PCM detects an internal circuit or communication concern. **NOTE: Internal PCM concern.**
DTC: P064E	**Internal Control Module O2 Sensor Processor Performance (Bank 2):** The Powertrain Control Module (PCM) monitors the application-specific integrated circuit that controls and monitors the Heated Oxygen Sensor (HO2S). The test fails when the PCM detects an internal circuit or communication concern. **NOTE: Internal PCM concern.**
DTC: P0652	**Sensor Reference Voltage B Circuit Low:** Indicates the electronic throttle control reference voltage (ETCREF) circuit is less than VREF minimum.
DTC: P0653	**Sensor Reference Voltage B Circuit High:** Indicates the reference voltage (VREF) circuit is greater than VREF maximum.
DTC: P0653	**Sensor Reference Voltage B Circuit High:** Indicates the electronic throttle control reference voltage (ETCREF) circuit is greater than VREF maximum.
DTC: P0657	**Actuator Supply Voltage A Circuit/Low:** Voltage to all transmission solenoids has been interrupted. Mechanical limp-home mode, default to 3rd or 5th gear
DTC: P0658	**Actuator Supply Voltage A Circuit/Open:** Voltage to all transmission solenoids has been interrupted. Mechanical limp-home mode, default to 3rd or 5th gear

DTC	Trouble Code Title & Conditions
DTC: P0659	**Actuator Supply Voltage A Circuit/High:** Voltage to all transmission solenoids has been interrupted. Mechanical limp-home mode, default to 3rd or 5th gear
DTC: P065B	**Generator Control Circuit Range/Performance:** The Powertrain Control Module (PCM) reads the GENLI and sends a DTC through the network when the signal frequency of GENLI indicates a concern. **NOTE: An IMTVM PID reading may indicate a fault.**
DTC: P065C	**Generator Mechanical Performance:** The Powertrain Control Module (PCM) reads the GENLI and sends a DTC through the network when the signal frequency of GENLI indicates a concern. **NOTE: An IMTVM PID reading may indicate a fault.**
DTC: P0660	**Intake Manifold Tuning Valve (IMTV) Control Circuit Open (Bank 1):** The IMTV system is monitored for failure during continuous, Key On Engine Off (KOEO), or Key On Engine Running (KOER) self-tests. The test fails when the signal is more or less than an expected calibrated range.
DTC: P0663	**Intake Manifold Tuning Valve (IMTV) Control Circuit Open (Bank 2):** The IMTV system is monitored for failure during continuous, Key On Engine Off (KOEO), or Key On Engine Running (KOER) self-tests. The test fails when the signal is more or less than an expected calibrated range.
DTC: P0667	**Powertrain Control Module (PCM) Transmission Control Module (TCM) Internal Temperature Sensor Range/ Operation.:** Substrate temperature sensor malfunction.
DTC: P066A	**Cylinder 1 Glow Plug Circuit Low:** The powertrain control module (PCM) carries out a functional key ON, engine running (KOER) self-test for the glow plug system. During that test the PCM enables the glow plug control module (GPCM) which monitors each individual glow plug and harness for concerns. When the GPCM detects a concern with cylinder glow plug or harness, it sends a message to the PCM, which sets this DTC.
DTC: P066B	**Cylinder 1 Glow Plug Circuit High:** The powertrain control module (PCM) carries out a functional key ON, engine running (KOER) self-test for the glow plug system. During that test the PCM enables the glow plug control module (GPCM) which monitors each individual glow plug and harness for concerns. When the GPCM detects a concern with cylinder glow plug or harness, it sends a message to the PCM, which sets this DTC.
DTC: P066C	**Cylinder 2 Glow Plug Circuit Low:** The powertrain control module (PCM) carries out a functional key ON, engine running (KOER) self-test for the glow plug system. During that test the PCM enables the glow plug control module (GPCM) which monitors each individual glow plug and harness for concerns. When the GPCM detects a concern with cylinder glow plug or harness, it sends a message to the PCM, which sets this DTC.
DTC: P066D	**Cylinder 2 Glow Plug Circuit High:** The powertrain control module (PCM) carries out a functional key ON, engine running (KOER) self-test for the glow plug system. During that test the PCM enables the glow plug control module (GPCM) which monitors each individual glow plug and harness for concerns. When the GPCM detects a concern with cylinder glow plug or harness, it sends a message to the PCM, which sets this DTC.
DTC: P066E	**Cylinder 3 Glow Plug Circuit Low:** The powertrain control module (PCM) carries out a functional key ON, engine running (KOER) self-test for the glow plug system. During that test the PCM enables the glow plug control module (GPCM) which monitors each individual glow plug and harness for concerns. When the GPCM detects a concern with cylinder glow plug or harness, it sends a message to the PCM, which sets this DTC.
DTC: P066F	**Cylinder 3 Glow Plug Circuit High:** The powertrain control module (PCM) carries out a functional key ON, engine running (KOER) self-test for the glow plug system. During that test the PCM enables the glow plug control module (GPCM) which monitors each individual glow plug and harness for concerns. When the GPCM detects a concern with cylinder glow plug or harness, it sends a message to the PCM, which sets this DTC.
DTC: P0670	**Glow Plug Control Module (GPCM) Control Circuit/Open:** The powertrain control module (PCM) carries out a functional key ON, engine running (KOER) self-test for the glow plug system. During that test the PCM enables the GPCM which monitors glow plug control circuit for concerns. When the GPCM detects a concern with a glow plug control circuit, it sends a message to the PCM, which sets this DTC.

DTC	Trouble Code Title & Conditions
DTC: P0671	**Cylinder 1 Glow Plug Circuit/Open:** The powertrain control module (PCM) carries out a functional key ON, engine running (KOER) self-test for the glow plug system. During that test the PCM enables the glow plug control module (GPCM) which monitors each individual glow plug and harness for concerns. When the GPCM detects a concern with cylinder glow plug or harness, it sends a message to the PCM, which sets this DTC.
DTC: P0672	**Cylinder 2 Glow Plug Circuit/Open:** The powertrain control module (PCM) carries out a functional key ON, engine running (KOER) self-test for the glow plug system. During that test the PCM enables the GPCM which monitors each individual glow plug and harness for concerns. When the GPCM detects a concern with cylinder glow plug or harness, it sends a message to the PCM, which sets this DTC.
DTC: P0673	**Cylinder 3 Glow Plug Circuit/Open:** The powertrain control module (PCM) carries out a functional key ON, engine running (KOER) self-test for the glow plug system. During that test the PCM enables the glow plug control module (GPCM) which monitors each individual glow plug and harness for concerns. When the GPCM detects a concern with cylinder glow plug or harness, it sends a message to the PCM, which sets this DTC.
DTC: P0674	**Cylinder 4 Glow Plug Circuit/Open:** The powertrain control module (PCM) carries out a functional key ON, engine running (KOER) self-test for the glow plug system. During that test the PCM enables the GPCM which monitors each individual glow plug and harness for concerns. When the GPCM detects a concern with cylinder glow plug or harness, it sends a message to the PCM, which sets this DTC.
DTC: P0675	**Cylinder 5 Glow Plug Circuit/Open:** The powertrain control module (PCM) carries out a functional key ON, engine running (KOER) self-test for the glow plug system. During that test the PCM enables the glow plug control module (GPCM) which monitors each individual glow plug and harness for concerns. When the GPCM detects a concern with cylinder glow plug or harness, it sends a message to the PCM, which sets this DTC.
DTC: P0676	**Cylinder 6 Glow Plug Circuit/Open:** The powertrain control module (PCM) carries out a functional key ON, engine running (KOER) self-test for the glow plug system. During that test the PCM enables the GPCM which monitors each individual glow plug and harness for concerns. When the GPCM detects a concern with cylinder glow plug or harness, it sends a message to the PCM, which sets this DTC.
DTC: P0677	**Cylinder 7 Glow Plug Circuit/Open:** The powertrain control module (PCM) carries out a functional key ON, engine running (KOER) self-test for the glow plug system. During that test the PCM enables the glow plug control module (GPCM) which monitors each individual glow plug and harness for concerns. When the GPCM detects a concern with cylinder glow plug or harness, it sends a message to the PCM, which sets this DTC.
DTC: P0678	**Cylinder 8 Glow Plug Circuit/Open:** The powertrain control module (PCM) carries out a functional key ON, engine running (KOER) self-test for the glow plug system. During that test the PCM enables the GPCM which monitors each individual glow plug and harness for concerns. When the GPCM detects a concern with cylinder glow plug or harness, it sends a message to the PCM, which sets this DTC.
DTC: P067A	**Cylinder 4 Glow Plug Circuit Low:** The powertrain control module (PCM) carries out a functional key ON, engine running (KOER) self-test for the glow plug system. During that test the PCM enables the glow plug control module (GPCM) which monitors each individual glow plug and harness for concerns. When the GPCM detects a concern with cylinder glow plug or harness, it sends a message to the PCM, which sets this DTC.
DTC: P067B	**Cylinder 4 Glow Plug Circuit High:** The powertrain control module (PCM) carries out a functional key ON, engine running (KOER) self-test for the glow plug system. During that test the PCM enables the glow plug control module (GPCM) which monitors each individual glow plug and harness for concerns. When the GPCM detects a concern with cylinder glow plug or harness, it sends a message to the PCM, which sets this DTC.
DTC: P067C	**Cylinder 5 Glow Plug Circuit Low:** The powertrain control module (PCM) carries out a functional key ON, engine running (KOER) self-test for the glow plug system. During that test the PCM enables the glow plug control module (GPCM) which monitors each individual glow plug and harness for concerns. When the GPCM detects a concern with cylinder glow plug or harness, it sends a message to the PCM, which sets this DTC.
DTC: P067D	**Cylinder 5 Glow Plug Circuit High:** The powertrain control module (PCM) carries out a functional key ON, engine running (KOER) self-test for the glow plug system. During that test the PCM enables the glow plug control module (GPCM) which monitors each individual glow plug and harness for concerns. When the GPCM detects a concern with cylinder glow plug or harness, it sends a message to the PCM, which sets this DTC.

DTC	Trouble Code Title & Conditions
DTC: P067E	**Cylinder 6 Glow Plug Circuit Low:** The powertrain control module (PCM) carries out a functional key ON, engine running (KOER) self-test for the glow plug system. During that test the PCM enables the glow plug control module (GPCM) which monitors each individual glow plug and harness for concerns. When the GPCM detects a concern with cylinder glow plug or harness, it sends a message to the PCM, which sets this DTC.
DTC: P067F	**Cylinder 6 Glow Plug Circuit High:** The powertrain control module (PCM) carries out a functional key ON, engine running (KOER) self-test for the glow plug system. During that test the PCM enables the glow plug control module (GPCM) which monitors each individual glow plug and harness for concerns. When the GPCM detects a concern with cylinder glow plug or harness, it sends a message to the PCM, which sets this DTC.
DTC: P0683	**Glow Plug Control Module (GPCM) to Powertrain Control Module (PCM) Communication Circuit:** The PCM carries out a functional key ON, engine running (KOER) self-test for the glow plug system. During that test the PCM enables the GPCM and monitors the GPCM/PCM communication circuit for concerns. When the PCM detects a concern with a GPCM/PCM communication circuit, the DTC is set.
DTC: P0684	**Glow Plug Control Module (GPCM) to Powertrain Control Module (PCM) Communication Circuit Range/Performance:** During the glow plug system check, the PCM enables the GPCM and monitors the GPCM/PCM communication circuit for a response. The DTC sets when the PCM stops receiving messages or receives an error message from the GPCM over the communication circuit.
DTC: P0685	**Electronic Control Module (ECM)/Powertrain Control Module (PCM) Power Relay Control Circuit/Open:** This DTC sets when the Ignition Switch Position Run (ISP-R) circuit indicates the key is in the OFF, ACC, or LOCK position, and the amount of time the PCM remains powered through the PCM power relay exceeds a predetermined amount of time. **NOTE: Ability to communicate with the PCM when the key is in the OFF, ACC, or LOCK position indicates a hard fault.**
DTC: P0686	**Electronic Control Module (ECM)/Powertrain Control Module (PCM) Power Relay Control Circuit Low:** This DTC sets when the ignition switch position run (ISP-R) circuit indicates the ignition is in the OFF, ACC, or LOCK position, and the amount of time the PCM remains powered through the PCM power relay exceeds a predetermined amount of time.
DTC: P0687	**Electronic Control Module (ECM)/Powertrain Control Module (PCM) Power Relay Control Circuit High:** This DTC sets when the ignition switch position run (ISP-R) circuit indicates the ignition is in the OFF, ACC, or LOCK position, and the amount of time the PCM remains powered through the PCM power relay exceeds a predetermined amount of time.
DTC: P0689	**Electronic Control Module (ECM)/Powertrain Control Module (PCM) Power Relay Sense Circuit Low:** This DTC sets when the Passive Anti-Theft System (PATS) system indicates the key is in ON or START position and the ignition switch position run (ISP-R) circuit indicates OFF, ACC, or LOCK position. **NOTE: Diagnose and repair all PATS DTCs first.**
DTC: P068A	**Internal Control Module Non-Volatile Random Access Memory (NVRAM) write did not complete:** This DTC sets when the powertrain control module (PCM) power relay is de-energized too early.
DTC: P068A	**ECM/PCM Power Relay De-Energized - Too Early:** This DTC sets when the powertrain control module (PCM) power relay is de-energized too early.
DTC: P068C	**Cylinder 7 Glow Plug Circuit Low:** The powertrain control module (PCM) carries out a functional key ON, engine running (KOER) self-test for the glow plug system. During that test the PCM enables the glow plug control module (GPCM) which monitors each individual glow plug and harness for concerns. When the GPCM detects a concern with cylinder glow plug or harness, it sends a message to the PCM, which sets this DTC.
DTC: P068D	**Cylinder 7 Glow Plug Circuit High:** The powertrain control module (PCM) carries out a functional key ON, engine running (KOER) self-test for the glow plug system. During that test the PCM enables the glow plug control module (GPCM) which monitors each individual glow plug and harness for concerns. When the GPCM detects a concern with cylinder glow plug or harness, it sends a message to the PCM, which sets this DTC.
DTC: P068E	**Cylinder 8 Glow Plug Circuit Low:** The powertrain control module (PCM) carries out a functional key ON, engine running (KOER) self-test for the glow plug system. During that test the PCM enables the glow plug control module (GPCM) which monitors each individual glow plug and harness for concerns. When the GPCM detects a concern with cylinder glow plug or harness, it sends a message to the PCM, which sets this DTC.
DTC: P068F	**Cylinder 8 Glow Plug Circuit High:** The powertrain control module (PCM) carries out a functional key ON, engine running (KOER) self-test for the glow plug system. During that test the PCM enables the glow plug control module (GPCM) which monitors each individual glow plug and harness for concerns. When the GPCM detects a concern with cylinder glow plug or harness, it sends a message to the PCM, which sets this DTC.

DTC	Trouble Code Title & Conditions
DTC: P0690	**Electronic Control Module (ECM)/Powertrain Control Module (PCM) Power Relay Sense Circuit High:** This DTC sets when the Passive Anti-Theft System (PATS) system indicates the key is in the OFF, ACC, or LOCK position and the Ignition Switch Position Run (ISP-R) circuit indicates ON or START position. **NOTE: Diagnose and repair all PATS DTCs first.**
DTC: P0691	**Fan 1 Control Circuit Low:** The powertrain control module (PCM) monitors the fan control variable (FCV) circuit for an electrical concern. This DTC is set when the PCM detects a short to ground condition on the FCV circuit.
DTC: P0692	**Fan 1 Control Circuit High:** The powertrain control module (PCM) monitors the fan control variable (FCV) circuit for an electrical concern. This DTC is set when the PCM detects a short to voltage condition on FCV the circuit.
DTC: P06A6	**Sensor Reference Voltage A Circuit Range/Performance:** Indicates the reference voltage (VREF) circuit is out of range.
DTC: P06A7	**Sensor Reference Voltage B Circuit Range/Performance:** Indicates the reference voltage (VREF) circuit is out of range.
DTC: P06A8	**Sensor Reference Voltage C Circuit Range/Performance:** Indicates the reference voltage (VREF) circuit is out of range.
DTC: P06B6	**Internal Control Module Knock Sensor Processor 1 Performance:** The powertrain control module (PCM) has detected an error condition with the knock sensor (KS) processor integrated circuit.
DTC: P06B8	**Internal Control Module Non-Volatile Random Access Memory (NVRAM) Error:** This DTC indicates a concern with the ability of the Powertrain Control Module (PCM) to correctly store permanent DTCs. **NOTE: Check for other DTCs and diagnose those first. Make sure to check for aftermarket performance products. If an updated calibration is available, update the calibration to the latest level. Clear the DTCs and drive the vehicle. If an updated calibration is not available, install a new PCM.**
DTC: P06B9	**Cylinder 1 Glow Plug Circuit Range/Performance:** The powertrain control module (PCM) carries out a functional key ON, engine running (KOER) self-test for the glow plug system. During that test the PCM enables the glow plug control module (GPCM) which monitors each individual glow plug and harness for concerns. When the GPCM detects a concern with cylinder glow plug or harness, it sends a message to the PCM, which sets this DTC.
DTC: P06BA	**Cylinder 2 Glow Plug Circuit Range/Performance:** The powertrain control module (PCM) carries out a functional key ON, engine running (KOER) self-test for the glow plug system. During that test the PCM enables the glow plug control module (GPCM) which monitors each individual glow plug and harness for concerns. When the GPCM detects a concern with cylinder glow plug or harness, it sends a message to the PCM, which sets this DTC.
DTC: P06BB	**Cylinder 3 Glow Plug Circuit Range/Performance:** The powertrain control module (PCM) carries out a functional key ON, engine running (KOER) self-test for the glow plug system. During that test the PCM enables the glow plug control module (GPCM) which monitors each individual glow plug and harness for concerns. When the GPCM detects a concern with cylinder glow plug or harness, it sends a message to the PCM, which sets this DTC.
DTC: P06BC	**Cylinder 4 Glow Plug Circuit Range/Performance:** The powertrain control module (PCM) carries out a functional key ON, engine running (KOER) self-test for the glow plug system. During that test the PCM enables the glow plug control module (GPCM) which monitors each individual glow plug and harness for concerns. When the GPCM detects a concern with cylinder glow plug or harness, it sends a message to the PCM, which sets this DTC.
DTC: P06BD	**Cylinder 5 Glow Plug Circuit Range/Performance:** The powertrain control module (PCM) carries out a functional key ON, engine running (KOER) self-test for the glow plug system. During that test the PCM enables the glow plug control module (GPCM) which monitors each individual glow plug and harness for concerns. When the GPCM detects a concern with cylinder glow plug or harness, it sends a message to the PCM, which sets this DTC.
DTC: P06BE	**Cylinder 6 Glow Plug Circuit Range/Performance:** The powertrain control module (PCM) carries out a functional key ON, engine running (KOER) self-test for the glow plug system. During that test the PCM enables the glow plug control module (GPCM) which monitors each individual glow plug and harness for concerns. When the GPCM detects a concern with cylinder glow plug or harness, it sends a message to the PCM, which sets this DTC.

DTC	Trouble Code Title & Conditions
DTC: P06BF	**Cylinder 7 Glow Plug Circuit Range/Performance:** The powertrain control module (PCM) carries out a functional key ON, engine running (KOER) self-test for the glow plug system. During that test the PCM enables the glow plug control module (GPCM) which monitors each individual glow plug and harness for concerns. When the GPCM detects a concern with cylinder glow plug or harness, it sends a message to the PCM, which sets this DTC.
DTC: P06C0	**Cylinder 8 Glow Plug Circuit Range/Performance:** The powertrain control module (PCM) carries out a functional key ON, engine running (KOER) self-test for the glow plug system. During that test the PCM enables the glow plug control module (GPCM) which monitors each individual glow plug and harness for concerns. When the GPCM detects a concern with cylinder glow plug or harness, it sends a message to the PCM, which sets this DTC.
DTC: P06D1	**Internal Control Module Ignition Coil Control Module Performance:** The powertrain control module (PCM) has detected an error with the ignition coil driver and diagnostic circuit.
DTC: P06DF	**Glow Plug Control Module (GPCM) Memory Checksum Error:** This DTC is set by the GPCM to indicate an internal software error has occurred.
DTC: P06EA	**NOX Sensor Processor Performance (Bank 1 Sensor 1):** The nitrogen oxide (NOx) module monitors the internal NOx module temperature and the NOx sensor signal. This DTC sets when the internal NOx module temperature is out of range or when the NOx module can no longer process the signal from the NOx sensor.
DTC: P0700	**Transmission Control System (MIL Request):** This DTC indicates the powertrain control module (PCM) received a MIL request controller area network CAN message from the transaxle control module (TCM).
DTC: P0701	**Transmission control system range/performance:** The PCM has detected an intermittent clutch on fault and the control system keeps getting stuck on ratio changes but when it turns off the suspected clutch it releases.
DTC: P0701	**Transmission Control System. Range/Operation:** The TCM has detected a concern with the operational strategy. Dual DTC causing transmission default to a hydraulic limp-home mode. Mechanical limp-home mode, defaults to 3rd or 5th gear. **NOTE: Multiple DTC failure with conflicting failure mode actions. If other DTCs are present, REPAIR them first. MONITOR the appropriate PID. Turns on TCIL, may turn on MIL.**
DTC: P0702	**Battery voltage out of range:** The PCM detected a voltage level above or below the accepted voltage range. Wrench light illuminated. Maximum line pressure. DTCs P0882 and/or P0883 may set
DTC: P0703	**Brake Switch B Input Circuit:** Indicates the Powertrain Control Module (PCM) did not receive a Brake Pedal Position (BPP) input. **NOTE: Verify the brake pedal was applied and released during the Key On Engine Running (KOER) self-test.**
DTC: P0704	**Clutch Switch Input Circuit:** When the clutch pedal is applied the voltage goes to low. If the powertrain control module (PCM) does not see this change from high to low the DTC is set.
DTC: P0705	**Transmission Range (TR) Sensor A Circuit (PRNDL) Input:** The TCM has detected a TR signal (P, R, N, D, 3, 2 or 1) is out of normal range. Mechanical limp-home mode, defaults to 3rd or 5th gear. **NOTE: Turns on TCIL, may turn on MIL.**
DTC: P0706	**Transmission Range (TR) Sensor A Circuit Range/Performance:** TR sensor stuck in transition zone and possible no crank condition. Only PARK, REVERSE, NEUTRAL and 5th gear available. **NOTE: Will turn on wrench lamp.**
DTC: P0707	**Transmission Range (TR) Sensor A Circuit Low:** Key on or engine running; and the PCM detected the Digital Transmission Range (DTR) or Transmission Range sensor (TR) input was more than the self-test maximum range in the test.
DTC: P0708	**Transmission Range (TR) Sensor A Circuit High:** Key on or engine running; and the PCM detected the Digital Transmission Range (DTR) or Transmission Range sensor (TR) input was more than the self-test maximum range in the test.
DTC: P0709	**TR sensor A circuit intermittent:** The PCM detected a TR sensor signal duty cycle is not out of range but is invalid.

DTC	Trouble Code Title & Conditions
DTC: P0709	**Transmission Range (TR) Sensor A Circuit Range/Performance:** TR sensor stuck in transition zone and possible no crank condition. Only PARK, REVERSE, NEUTRAL and 5th gear available. **NOTE: Will turn on wrench lamp.**
DTC: P0710	**Transmission Fluid Temperature Sensor A Circuit:** The transaxle control module (TCM) uses the transmission fluid temperature (TFT) sensor to continuously monitor its temperature. This DTC indicates the concern in TFT sensor or circuit.
DTC: P0710	**Transmission Fluid Temperature (TFT) sensor:** *Torque Converter Clutch and stabilized shift schedule may be enabled sooner after cold start*Harsh or soft shifts
DTC: P0710	**Transmission Fluid Temperature (TFT) sensor A circuit:** The PCM detected a voltage drop across the TFT sensor exceeds scale.
DTC: P0710	**Transmission Fluid Temperature Sensor Circuit Input Voltage:** * Engine won't crank* Only Park, Neutral, Reverse and 5th Gear available* Harsh engagements* Extremely delayed engagements
DTC: P0711	**TFT Sensor Circuit Range/Performance:** Key on or engine running; and the PCM detected no change in the Transmission Fluid Temperature (TFT) sensor.
DTC: P0711	**TFT sensor A circuit range/performance:** PCM has detected no TFT sensor change during operation. The TFT sensor is stuck below 21°C (70°F) or above 107°C (225°F) or the temperature did not change by 8°F during a drive cycle. Transmission Control Indicator Lamp (TCIL) flashing Wrench light illuminated Default to 1st or 3rd gear
DTC: P0712	**TFT Sensor Circuit Circuit Low:** Key on or engine running; and the PCM detected low voltage in the Transmission Fluid Temperature (TFT) sensor. **NOTE: TCM has detected a voltage drop across TFT sensor exceeds scale set for temperature (grounded circuit).**
DTC: P0712	**TFT sensor A circuit low:** PCM detected a temperature greater than 171°C (340°F) for at least 2.5 seconds (grounded circuit).TCIL flashing Wrench light illuminated Default to 1st gea rDTC P0710 may set
DTC: P0713	**TFT sensor A circuit high:** PCM detected a temperature less than -45°C (-50°F) for at least 2.5 seconds (open circuit).TCIL flashing Wrench light illuminated Default to 1st gear DTC P0710 may set
DTC: P0713	**TFT Sensor Circuit High:** Key on or engine running; and the PCM detected high voltage in the Transmission Fluid Temperature (TFT) sensor.
DTC: P0714	**TFT sensor A circuit intermittent:** TCM has detected no TFT intermittent operation. No TCC
DTC: P0714	**TFT Sensor Circuit Intermittent/Erratic:** Key on or engine running; and the PCM detected intermittent condition in the Transmission Fluid Temperature (TFT) sensor.
DTC: P0715	**Turbine Shaft Speed (TSS) Sensor Error:** Engine started, vehicle speed sensor signal over 1 mph, and the PCM detected a short circuit to power on the TSS signal circuit. **NOTE: Will turn on TCIL, holds in 3rd gear.**
DTC: P0715	**Turbine Shaft Speed (TSS) sensor A circuit:** PCM indicated 0 rpm from the TSS sensor when the Output Shaft Speed (OSS) sensor indicated rpm greater than 0.Wrench light illuminated Default to 5th gear Maximum line pressure DTC P0717 may set
DTC: P0716	**Turbine Shaft Speed (TSS) Sensor Range/Performance:** Engine started, TSS signal more than 1 mph, and the PCM detected "noise" interference on the TSS sensor circuit. **NOTE: Will turn on TCIL, holds in 3rd gear.**
DTC: P0717	**Turbine Shaft Speed (TSS) Sensor No Signal:** Engine started, TCM has not detected a TSS signal. No TSS signal when Output Shaft Speed (OSS) signal is present. **NOTE: Will turn on TCIL, holds in 3rd gear.**
DTC: P0718	**TSS sensor signal noisy:** PCM has detected a noisy TSS signal. Harsh shifts, harsh TCC activation and harsh engagements.
DTC: P0718	**Turbine Shaft Speed (TSS) Sensor Erratic:** Engine started, TCM has detected erratic TSS signal. Erratic TSS signal when OSS signal is present.
DTC: P0720	**Output Shaft Speed (OSS) Sensor Circuit:** The OSS sensor inputs a signal to the Powertrain Control Module (PCM) based on the speed of the output shaft of the transmission. **NOTE: Verify the sensor signal output varies with the vehicle speed.**

DTC	Trouble Code Title & Conditions
DTC: P0721	**Output Shaft Speed (OSS) Sensor Circuit Range/Performance:** The OSS sensor signal is very sensitive to noise. This noise distorts the input to the Powertrain Control Module (PCM). **NOTE: Check the routing of the harness, and the wiring and the connector for damage.**
DTC: P0722	**Output Shaft Speed (OSS) Sensor Circuit No Signal:** The OSS sensor failed to provide a signal to the Powertrain Control Module (PCM) upon initial movement of vehicle. **NOTE: Check the wiring, connector, and sensor for damage.**
DTC: P0723	**Output Shaft Speed (OSS) Sensor Circuit Intermittent:** The OSS sensor signal to the Powertrain Control Module (PCM) is irregular or interrupted. **NOTE: Verify harness and connector integrity and correct installation of the OSS sensor. Will turn on TCIL.**
DTC: P0726	**Engine Speed Input Circuit Range/Performance:** The transaxle control module (TCM) calculates an engine speed and compares it to the engine speed received from the powertrain control module (PCM). This DTC is set when the RPM difference between the calculated and received speeds is greater than 1,000 RPM.
DTC: P0727	**Engine Speed Input Circuit No Signal:** The transaxle control module (TCM) continuously monitors the clean tachometer output (CTO) circuit from the powertrain control module (PCM) for an engine speed signal. This DTC is set when if there is a CTO circuit concern.
DTC: P0729	**Incorrect Sixth Gear Ratio:** Engine started, vehicle operating with 6th Gear commanded "on", and the PCM detected an incorrect 6th gear ratio during the test. **NOTE: Verify harness and connector integrity and correct installation of the OSS sensor. Will turn on TCIL.**
DTC: P072B	**Shift Drum 2 Unable to Disengage Reverse:** Shift drum 2 mechanical fault.* Shift drum 2 motor fault.* Electrical faults that prevent shift drum 2 from rotating (open circuits cannot be detected during operation).* Clutch 2 stuck on (if undetected may prevent shift drum 2 movement).* 2nd, 4th and 6th gears disabled
DTC: P072C	**Shift Drum Unable to Disengage 1st Gear:** * Shift drum 1 mechanical fault.* Shift drum 1 motor fault.* Electrical faults that prevent shift drum 1 from rotating (open circuits cannot be detected during operation).* Clutch 1 stuck on (if undetected may prevent shift drum 1 movement).* 3rd and 5th gears disabled.
DTC: P072D	**Shift drum 2 Unable to Disengage 2nd Gear:** * Shift drum 2 mechanical fault.* Shift drum 2 motor fault.* Electrical faults that prevent shift drum 2 from rotating (open circuits cannot be detected during operation).* Clutch 2 stuck on (if undetected may prevent shift drum 2 movement).* REVERSE, 4th and 6th gears disabled.
DTC: P072F	**Shift Drum 2 Unable to Disengage 4th Gear:** * Shift drum 2 mechanical fault.* Shift drum 2 motor fault.* Electrical faults that prevent shift drum 2 from rotating (open circuits cannot be detected during operation).* Clutch 2 stuck on (if undetected may prevent shift drum 2 movement).* REVERSE, 2nd and 6th gears disabled.
DTC: P0730	**Gear Ratio Error:** Engine running, vehicle in motionPCM has detected an incorrect gear ratio during the test
DTC: P0731	**Incorrect First Gear Ratio:** Engine started, vehicle operating with 1st Gear commanded "on", and the PCM detected an incorrect 1st gear ratio during the test. **NOTE: Verify harness and connector integrity and correct installation of the OSS sensor. Will turn on TCIL.**
DTC: P0732	**Incorrect Second Gear Ratio:** Engine started, vehicle operating with 2nd Gear commanded "on", and the PCM detected an incorrect 2nd gear ratio during the test. **NOTE: Verify harness and connector integrity and correct installation of the OSS sensor. Will turn on TCIL.**
DTC: P0733	**Incorrect Third Gear Ratio:** Engine started, vehicle operating with 3rd Gear commanded "on", and the PCM detected an incorrect 3rd gear ratio during the test. **NOTE: Verify harness and connector integrity and correct installation of the OSS sensor. Will turn on TCIL.**
DTC: P0734	**Incorrect Fourth Gear Ratio:** Engine started, vehicle operating with 4th Gear commanded "on", and the PCM detected an incorrect 4th gear ratio during the test. **NOTE: Verify harness and connector integrity and correct installation of the OSS sensor. Will turn on TCIL.**
DTC: P0735	**Incorrect Fifth Gear Ratio:** Engine started, vehicle operating with 5th Gear commanded "on", and the PCM detected an incorrect 5th gear ratio during the test.
DTC: P0736	**Incorrect Reverse Gear Ratio:** Engine started, vehicle operating in reverse, TCM detected no reverse gear ratio

DTC	Trouble Code Title & Conditions
DTC: P073A	**Shift Drum 1 Unable to Disengage 5th Gear:** * Shift drum 1 mechanical fault.* Shift drum 1 motor fault.* Electrical faults that prevent shift drum 1 from rotating (open circuits cannot be detected during operation).* Clutch 1 stuck on (if undetected may prevent shift drum 1 movement).* 1st and 3rd gears disabled.
DTC: P073B	**Shift Drum 2 Unable to Disengage 6th Gear:** * Shift drum 2 mechanical fault.* Shift drum 2 motor fault.* Electrical faults that prevent shift drum 2 from rotating (open circuits cannot be detected during operation).* Clutch 2 stuck on (if undetected may prevent shift drum 2 movement).* REVERSE, 2nd and 4th gears disabled.
DTC: P073E	**Shift Drum 2 Unable to Engage Reverse:** * Motor turns, but cannot synchronize and engage REVERSE gear.* Reverse gear is disabled.
DTC: P0740	**TCC Solenoid Circuit Malfunction:** Key on, KOEO Self-Test enabled and the PCM did not detect any voltage drop across the TCC solenoid circuit during the test period.
DTC: P0741	**Torque Converter Clutch (TCC) Failed Off:** * Non-electrical TCC solenoid stuck off.* TCC mechanical failure.* TCC regulator apply valve stuck in TCC release position.* TCC control valve stuck in TCC release position.* TCC failed to apply 3 consecutive times.
DTC: P0742	**Torque Converter Clutch (TCC) Circuit Short to Ground:** * Failure Mode Effects Management action opens the transaxle solenoid power control, removing power from all solenoids.* Harsh engagements* Poor launch performance (due to 5th gear drive away)
DTC: P0742	**TCC Solenoid Circuit Stuck On:** * Failure Mode Effect Management action opens the transaxle solenoid power control, removing power from all solenoids (get PARK, REVERSE, NEUTRAL and 5th gear as the only forward gear with TCC open).* Harsh engagements of gears* Poor launch performance (due to 5th gear drive away).* Does not shift* TCIL flashing
DTC: P0743	**TCC solenoid circuit failure during OBD:** TCC solenoid circuit fails to provide voltage drop across solenoid. Circuit open or shorted or PCM driver failure during OBD .
DTC: P0743	**Torque Converter Clutch (TCC) Electrical Fault:** *Failure Mode Effects Management action opens the transaxle solenoid power control, removing power from all solenoids* Harsh engagements.* Poor launch performance (due to 5th gear drive away)* No shifts
DTC: P0743	**TCC solenoid circuit failure during OBD test:** TCC solenoid circuit fails to provide voltage drop across solenoid. Circuit open or shorted or PCM driver failure during OBD test. Short circuit: engine stalls in second ((D), 2 range) at low idle speeds with brake applied.
DTC: P0744	**Torque Converter Clutch (TCC) Short to Voltage:** * TCC failed off* Vehicle engine temperature increased* Lower fuel economy
DTC: P0744	**TCC solenoid circuit intermittent:** The PCM has detected a TCC solenoid control circuit shorted to power.TCC is disabled. DTC P0743 may set
DTC: P0745	**Pressure Control Solenoid A or Circuit Fault:** PCA functional fault-low pressure
DTC: P0748	**Line Pressure Control (LPC) Solenoid Electrical Fault:** * Failed to minimum line pressure.* Failure Mode Effects Management action opens the transaxle solenoid power control, removing power from all solenoids* Harsh engagements.* Poor launch performance (due to 5th gear drive away).
DTC: P0748	**Pressure Control Solenoid A Inoperative:** Electrical failure of the solenoid detected. Possible slip in gear and/or 3rd gear ratio.
DTC: P0748	**Pressure Control Solenoid (PCA) A Electrical:** * Failure Mode Effect Management action* TCIL Flashing
DTC: P0748	**EPC solenoid circuit failure:** Voltage through EPC solenoid is checked. An error will be noted if tolerance is exceeded. Short circuit results in minimum EPC pressure (minimum capacity) and limits engine torque (alternate firm). Not all gears present. Open circuit: maximum Pressure Control Solenoid A (PCA) pressure, harsh engagements and shifts.
DTC: P074A	**Shift Drum 2 Unable to Engage 2nd Gear:** * Motor turns, but cannot synchronize and engage 2nd gear.* 2nd gear disabled.* For certain faults shift drum controls will not pass through a failed gear; reverse, 4th and 6th gears may also be disabled.
DTC: P074B	**Shift Drum 1 Unable to Engage 3rd Gear:** * Motor turns, but cannot synchronize and engage 3rd gear.* 3rd gear disabled.* For certain faults shift drum controls will not pass through a failed gear; 1st and 5th gears may also be disabled.

DTC	Trouble Code Title & Conditions
DTC: P074C	**Shift Drum 2 Unable to Engage 4th Gear:** * Motor turns, but cannot synchronize and engage 4th gear.* 4th gear disabled.* For certain faults shift drum controls will not pass through a failed gear; reverse, 2nd and 6th gears may also be disabled.
DTC: P074D	**Shift Drum 1 Unable to Engage 5th Gear:** * Motor turns, but cannot synchronize and engage 5th gear.* 5th gear disabled.
DTC: P074E	**Shift Drum 2 Unable to engage 6th gear:** * Motor turns, but cannot synchronize and engage 6th gear.* 6th gear disabled.
DTC: P074x	**Transmission Code:**
DTC: P0750	**A/T Shift Solenoid 1/A Circuit Malfunction:** Engine started, vehicle driven with the solenoid applied, and the PCM detected an unexpected voltage condition on the SS1/A solenoid circuit was incorrect during the test.
DTC: P0751	**A/T Shift Solenoid 2/B Circuit Malfunction:** Engine started, vehicle driven with the solenoid applied, and the PCM detected an unexpected voltage condition on the SS2/B solenoid circuit was incorrect during the test.
DTC: P0751	**SSA performance/stuck off:** PCM commanded SSA on but detected a ratio error (mechanical failure).5th and 6th gear only. Harsh reverse engagement. Neutral or flair condition on a downshift. Maximum line pressure. DTC P2700 may set
DTC: P0752	**SSA stuck on:** The PCM/ TCM commanded SSA off but detected a ratio error (mechanical failure).Disable 5th and 6th gear. Erratic shifts. Stuck in 4th gear. DTC P2700 may set
DTC: P0752	**Shift Solenoid A Functional Failure:** * PCM detected a mechanical or hydraulic failure while operating the Shift Solenoid A.* Not all gears present
DTC: P0752	**Shift Solenoid A Performance/Stuck On:** * Neutral conditions or flares on downshifts from 5th or 6th gear.* Gears 1 through 4 are disabled — leaving 5th and 6th gears as the only forward gears.* Erratic shifting* Harsh engagements* Neutral conditions* Poor launch performance* Harsh reverse engagements
DTC: P0753	**Shift Solenoid B Electrical:** * Failure Mode Effect Management action for DTC P0750, P0973 and P0974
DTC: P0753	**SSA electrical:** The PCM sets this DTC along with one or more specific electrical DTCs. TCIL flashing. Wrench light illuminated. 5th and 6th gear only. DTCs P0750, P0973 and/or P0974 may set
DTC: P0753	**A/T Shift Solenoid 2/B Function Range/Performance:** Engine started, vehicle driven with the solenoid applied, and the PCM detected a mechanical failure while operating the Shift Solenoid 2/B during the CCM test period.
DTC: P0753	**Shift Solenoid A Circuit Malfunction:** Engine started, vehicle driven with the solenoid applied, and the PCM detected an unexpected voltage condition on the SSA solenoid circuit was incorrect during the test. No reverse gear or no 4th gear.
DTC: P0754	**Shift Solenoid A Intermittent:** * Unexpected upshifts* Unexpected downshifts* Unexpected flairs* Neutral conditions.
DTC: P0754	**SSA intermittent :** The PCM sets this DTC when an intermittent condition (open, short to power or ground) occurs 3 times for less than 5 seconds with each occurrence. Unexpected upshifts, downshifts, flairs or neutral conditions
DTC: P0755	**A/T Shift Solenoid 2/B Circuit Malfunction:** Key on, KOEO Self-Test enabled, Shift Solenoid 2/B applied, and the PCM detected an unexpected voltage condition on the Shift Solenoid 2/B circuit during the CCM test period.
DTC: P0756	**A/T Shift Solenoid 3/C Circuit Malfunction:** Engine started, vehicle driven with Shift Solenoid 3/C applied, and the PCM detected an unexpected voltage condition on the Shift Solenoid 3/C circuit during the CCM test period.
DTC: P0756	**Shift Solenoid B Performance/Stuck Off:** * Flares or neutral conditions on shifts into 3rd or 5th gear.* PCM will command 3 shifts into 3rd or 5th gear* If direct clutch is failed off the driver will notice flares or neutral conditions that last one second or so.* 3rd and 5th gears are disabled,* Transmission hangs in 2nd on acceleration until driver tips out to closed pedal (done to protect overdrive clutch)

DTC	Trouble Code Title & Conditions
DTC: P0756	**Shift Solenoid B Functional Failure:** Engine started, vehicle driven with the solenoid applied, and the PCM detected an unexpected voltage condition on the SSB solenoid circuit was incorrect during the test.
DTC: P0757	**Shift Solenoid B Functional Failure:** * PCM detected a mechanical or hydraulic failure while operating the Shift Solenoid B.* Not all gears present
DTC: P0757	**Shift Solenoid B Stuck On:** * Vehicle deceleration on shift into 2nd, 4th or 6th gear.* Harsh 1-3 shift* Poor launch performance - lack of shifts
DTC: P0757	**A/T Shift Solenoid 3/C Function Range/Performance:** Engine started, vehicle driven with Shift Solenoid 3/C applied, and the PCM detected a mechanical failure occurred (stuck "off") while operating Shift Solenoid 3/C during the test.
DTC: P0758	**A/T Shift Solenoid 3/C Function Range/Performance:** Engine started, vehicle driven with Shift Solenoid 3/C applied, and the PCM detected a mechanical failure occurred (stuck "on") while operating Shift Solenoid 3/C during the test.
DTC: P0758	**Shift Solenoid B Circuit Malfunction:** Engine started, vehicle driven with the solenoid applied, and the PCM detected an unexpected voltage condition on the SSB solenoid circuit was incorrect during the test.
DTC: P0758	**SSB electrical:** The PCM sets this DTC along with one or more specific electrical DTCs. Wrench light illuminated Default to 3rd or 5th gear Maximum line pressure DTCs P0755, P0976 and/or P0977 may set
DTC: P0759	**Shift Solenoid B Intermittent:** * Unexpected upshifts* Unexpected downshifts* Unexpected flairs* Neutral conditions.
DTC: P0760	**A/T Shift Solenoid 4/D Circuit Malfunction:** Engine started, vehicle driven with Shift Solenoid 4/D applied, and the PCM detected an unexpected voltage condition on Shift Solenoid 4/D circuit during the CCM continuous test.
DTC: P0760	**Shift Solenoid C Circuit Malfunction:** Engine started, vehicle driven with the solenoid applied, and the PCM detected an unexpected voltage condition on the SSC solenoid circuit was incorrect during the test.
DTC: P0760	**Shift Solenoid C (SSC) Circuit Open:** The PCM detected that the SSC circuit failed open. Disable 2nd and 6th gear Erratic or harsh 1-3 shift DTC P0763 may set
DTC: P0761	**Shift Solenoid C Functional Failure:** * PCM detected a mechanical or hydraulic failure while operating the Shift Solenoid C.* Not all gears present
DTC: P0761	**A/T 1 to 2 Shift Error:** Engine started, vehicle driven in gear with VSS signals received, and the PCM detected the engine speed (rpm) did not decrease properly (i.e., an incorrect 1-2 gear ratio was detected during a shift event).
DTC: P0761	**Shift Solenoid C Performance/Stuck Off:** * Neutral conditions or flares on shifts to 2nd or 6th gear.* Disabled 2nd and 6th gears.* Erratic shifting, neutral conditions, flares, higher engine speeds on highway due to 6th gear being disabled.
DTC: P0762	**SSC stuck on:** The PCM/ TCM commanded SSC off but detected a ratio error (mechanical failure).2nd and 6th gear only. Harsh reverse engagement. Erratic shift or stuck in 6thDTC P2702 may set
DTC: P0762	**SSC stuck on :** PCM commanded SSC off but detected a ratio error (mechanical failure).2nd and 6th upshift only. Harsh reverse engagement. Erratic shift or stuck in 6thDTC P2702 may set
DTC: P0762	**Shift Solenoid C Stuck On:** * Vehicle deceleration on a shift into 3rd or 5th gear (intermediate clutch failing to release will cause a tie-up in 3rd or 5th gear).* Erratic shifting or being stuck in 6th gear.* 3rd, 4th and 5th gears are disabled.* Hangs in 2nd gear on acceleration since 2nd-6th upshifts only occur at closed pedal (due to energy limitations of overdrive clutch), harsh reverse engagements (since low/reverse clutch is not on in 2nd gear).
DTC: P0762	**A/T 2 to 3 Shift Error:** Engine started, vehicle driven in gear with VSS signals received, and the PCM detected the engine speed (rpm) did not decrease properly (i.e., an incorrect 2-3 gear ratio was detected during a shift event).
DTC: P0762	**Shift Solenoid C Functional Failure:** * PCM detected a mechanical or hydraulic failure while operating the Shift Solenoid C.* Not all gears present

DTC	Trouble Code Title & Conditions
DTC: P0763	**SSC electrical :** The PCM/ TCM sets this DTC along with one or more specific electrical DTCs. Wrench light illuminated. Default to 2nd and 6th gear or 1st and 3rd depending on other DTCs. Minimum or maximum line pressure depending on other DTCs (failed voltage high or voltage low)DTCs P0760, P0979 and/or P0980 may set
DTC: P0763	**Shift Solenoid C Circuit Malfunction:** Engine started, vehicle driven with the solenoid applied, and the PCM detected an unexpected voltage condition on the SSC solenoid circuit was incorrect during the test.
DTC: P0763	**SSC solenoid circuit failure:** SSC circuit failed to provide voltage drop across solenoid. Circuit open or shorted or PCM driver failure during OBD .
DTC: P0764	**SSC intermittent :** The PCM sets this DTC when an intermittent condition (open, short to power or ground) occurs three times for less than 5 seconds with each occurrence.Unexpected upshifts, downshifts, flairs or neutral conditions
DTC: P0764	**Shift Solenoid C Intermittent:** * Unexpected upshifts* Unexpected downshifts* Unexpected flairs* Neutral conditions.
DTC: P0765	**Shift Solenoid D Open Circuit:** * Shift Solenoid D applied, and the PCM detected an unexpected voltage condition on the Shift Solenoid D circuit during the CCM test period.* Overdrive clutch failed on, only 4th, 5th and 6th gears available.* Harsh engagements.* Poor launch due to 4th gear drive away.
DTC: P0765	**Shift Solenoid D Circuit Failure:** Engine started, vehicle driven with the solenoid applied, and the PCM detected an unexpected voltage condition on the SSD solenoid circuit was incorrect during the test.
DTC: P0765	**A/T 3 to 4 Shift Error:** Engine started, vehicle driven in gear with VSS signals received, and the PCM detected the engine speed (rpm) did not change properly (i.e., an incorrect 3-4 gear ratio was detected during the shift event).
DTC: P0766	**Shift Solenoid D Functional Failure:** * PCM detected a mechanical or hydraulic failure while operating the Shift Solenoid D.* Not all gears present
DTC: P0766	**Shift Solenoid D Performance/Stuck Off:** * Flares or neutral conditions on shifts into 4th, 5th or 6th gear.* Erratic shifting, flares, neutral conditions while the code is being set.* 1st, 4th, 5th and 6th gears are disabled* Delayed or no reverse engagement
DTC: P0767	**SSD stuck on:** PCM commanded SSD off but detected a ratio error (mechanical failure).4th, 5th and 6th gear only. Early upshifts. Stuck in 4thDTC P2704 may set
DTC: P0767	**A/T Shift Solenoid 4/D Functional Failure:** Functional Failure (Stuck ON) or Main Control System Failure. (shift valves, orifices and sealing)
DTC: P0768	**SSD electrical:** The PCM sets this DTC along with one or more specific electrical DTCs. Wrench light illuminated. Default to 3rd gear. DTCs P0765, P0982 and/or P0983 may set
DTC: P0768	**A/T Shift Solenoid 4/D Circuit Failure:** Functional Failure (Stuck ON) or Main Control System Failure. (shift valves, orifices and sealing)
DTC: P0768	**Shift Solenoid D Circuit Failure:** Engine started, vehicle driven with the solenoid applied, and the PCM detected an unexpected voltage condition on the SSD solenoid circuit was incorrect during the test.
DTC: P0769	**SSD intermittent:** The PCM sets this DTC when an intermittent condition (open, short to power or ground) occurs three times for less than 5 seconds with each occurrence. Unexpected upshifts, downshifts, flairs or neutral conditions
DTC: P0769	**Shift Solenoid D Intermittent:** * Unexpected upshifts* Unexpected downshifts* Unexpected flairs* Neutral conditions
DTC: P076x	**Transmission Code:**
DTC: P0770	**A/T Shift Solenoid 5/E Functional Failure:** Functional Failure (Stuck ON) or Main Control System Failure. (shift valves, orifices and sealing)
DTC: P0770	**Shift Solenoid E Functional Failure:** Engine started, vehicle driven with the solenoid applied, and the PCM detected an unexpected voltage condition on the SSE solenoid circuit was incorrect during the test.

DTC	Trouble Code Title & Conditions
DTC: P0770	**Shift Solenoid E (SSE) Circuit:** The PCM detected that the SSE circuit failed open, short to ground or short to power. No TCC If 1st, 2nd and 3rd gears are achieved than circuit is open or shorted to power (no pressure)If 5th gear launch than circuit is shorted to ground (pressure)DTC P0774 may set
DTC: P0771	**Shift Solenoid E Performance/Stuck Off:** Functional Failure (Stuck OFF) or Main Control System Failure. (shift valves, orifices and sealing)
DTC: P0771	**A/T Shift Solenoid 5/E Circuit Failure:** Functional Failure (Stuck ON) or Main Control System Failure. (shift valves, orifices and sealing)
DTC: P0772	**Shift Solenoid E Performance/Stuck On:** Functional Failure (Stuck ON) or Main Control System Failure. (shift valves, orifices and sealing)
DTC: P0772	**Shift Solenoid E Functional Failure:** * PCM detected a mechanical or hydraulic failure while operating the Shift Solenoid E.* Not all gears present
DTC: P0773	**Shift Solenoid E Electrical:** * Failure Mode Effect Management for P0770
DTC: P0773	**Shift Solenoid E Circuit Failure:** Engine started, vehicle driven with the solenoid applied, and the PCM detected an unexpected voltage condition on the SSE solenoid circuit was incorrect during the test.
DTC: P0774	**Shift Solenoid E Intermittent:** * Failure Mode Effect Management for P0770
DTC: P0774	**SSE intermittent:** The PCM sets this DTC when an intermittent condition (open, short to power or ground) occurs but does not set DTC P0770. Transmission hangs in 1st gear or may be stuck in 3rd gear
DTC: P0775	**Pressure Control Solenoid B (PCB):** Functional fault, Low pressure or circuit fault. Incorrect shift pattern indicating mechanical or hydraulic failure of the transmission
DTC: P0778	**Pressure Control Solenoid B (PCB) Circuit Failure:** Electrical failure of the solenoid detected, 2nd and 5th gear.
DTC: P0780	**Universal shifting Stuck Valve (Aisin AW21 Transmission):** Solenoid or valve internal to transaxle, valve stuck. Increase rpm during shifts. Slipping or erratic shifting.
DTC: P0780	**Transaxle Valve Stuck:** * Increased RPM during shifts* Slipping or erratic shifting
DTC: P0781	**A/T 4 to 5 Shift Error:** Engine started, vehicle driven in gear with VSS signals received, and the PCM detected the engine speed (rpm) did not change properly (i.e., an incorrect 4-5 gear ratio was detected during a shift event).
DTC: P0781	**Transmission 1-2 or 2-1 shift error:** Incorrect ratio calculated during shift 1-2 or 2-1. Incorrect gear selection depending on failure or mode and manual lever position. Shift errors may also be due to other internal transmission concerns (stuck valves, damaged friction material)No TCCNo adaptive learning strategy. Hold in 3rd, 2nd or 4th gear
DTC: P0782	**A/T Reverse Switch Circuit Malfunction:** Key on, engine off, KOEO Self Test enabled, and the PCM detected the reverse switch signal did not change as the selector was shifted in or out of reverse gear. **NOTE: The RS PID should change from ON to OFF while shifting.**
DTC: P0782	**Transmission 2-3 or 3-2 shift error:** Incorrect ratio calculated during shift 2-3. Incorrect gear selection depending on failure or mode and manual lever position. Shift errors may also be due to other internal transmission concerns (stuck valves, damaged friction material) No TCC No adaptive learning strategy. Hold in 4th, 3rd or 2nd gear
DTC: P0783	**Transmission 3-4 or 4-3 shift error:** Incorrect ratio calculated during shift 3-4 or 4-3. Incorrect gear selection depending on failure or mode and manual lever position. Shift errors may also be due to other internal transmission concerns (stuck valves, damaged friction material)No TCC No adaptive learning strategy Default to 3rd or 4th gear
DTC: P0783	**Transmission Control System Malfunction:** Engine started, vehicle speed more than 1 in gear, and the PCM detected a problem in the Transmission Control System operation.

DTC	Trouble Code Title & Conditions
DTC: P0784	**Transmission Control System Malfunction:** Key on, engine off, KOEO Self Test enabled, and the PCM detected the reverse switch input did not change as the selector was shifted in or out of reverse (i.e., it was high when it should have been low). **NOTE: The RS PID should change from ON to OFF while shifting.**
DTC: P0784	**Transmission 4-5 or 5-4 shift error:** Incorrect ratio calculated during shift 4-5 or 5-4. Incorrect gear selection depending on failure or mode and manual lever position. Shift errors may also be due to other internal transmission concerns (stuck valves, damaged friction material)No TCC. No adaptive learning strategy. Default to 4th or 5th gear
DTC: P0791	**Intermediate Shaft Speed Sensor No Signal:** Insufficient input from the intermediate shaft speed sensor. PCM has detected a loss of the intermediate shaft speed sensor signal during operation. Harsh shifts.
DTC: P0794	**Intermediate Shaft Speed Sensor Signal Noise:** Intermediate shaft speed sensor signal noisy. PCM has detected a loss of the intermediate shaft speed sensor signal during operation. Harsh shifts.
DTC: P0795	**Pressure Control Solenoid C (PCC) Circuit Fault:** Incorrect shift pattern indicating mechanical or hydraulic failure of the transmission.
DTC: P0798	**Pressure Control Solenoid C (PCC) Circuit Fault:** Electrical failure of the solenoid detected. Incorrect gear ratio in 4th and 5th gear.
DTC: P07A2	**Clutch A Stuck Off:** Clutch A (1st, 3rd and 5th gears) spring fault or clutch motor 1 is blocked, preventing it traveling its full range
DTC: P07A3	**Clutch A Stuck On:** Clutch A (1st, 3rd and 5th gears) spring fault or clutch motor 1 is blocked, preventing it traveling its full range
DTC: P07A4	**Clutch B Stuck Off:** Reverse, 2nd, 4th and 6th gears disabled
DTC: P07A5	**Clutch B Stuck On:** Clutch B (reverse, 2nd, 4th and 6th gears) spring fault or clutch motor 2 is blocked, preventing it traveling its full range
DTC: P07A8	**Friction element D performance/stuck off:** The Low/Reverse clutch failed off, ratio error (mechanical failure) Disable 1st gear. Delayed or no reverse engagement
DTC: P07A9	**Transmission friction element D stuck on:** Low reverse or One-Way Clutch (OWC) stuck on. No TCC1st gear only. High engine rpm
DTC: P07AA	**Transmission friction element E performance/stuck off:** PCM detected a ratio error (mechanical failure).1st, 2nd and 3rd gears onlyNeutral or flair condition. High engine rpm. Erratic shifts
DTC: P0805	**Clutch Motor 1 Fault:** 1st, 3rd and 5th gears disabled.
DTC: P0806	**Clutch Motor 1 Sensor Fault:** * 1st, 3rd and 5th gears disabled* Clutch motor 1 hall sensor fault detected
DTC: P0813	**Reverse Lamp Circuit Short/Open:** * Reverse lamps always illuminated* Reverse lamps inoperative
DTC: P0815	**Upshift Switch Circuit:** Key on or engine running; and the PCM detected an incorrect up shift.
DTC: P0816	**Downshift switch circuit:** The upshift and downshift switches are open in PARK, REVERSE and NEUTRAL. The PCM sets this DTC when it detects a downshift switch is closed (short to ground). Wrench light illuminated. Disable SelectShift™ scheduling to automatic shift scheduling. Upshifts request ignored. Unexpected downshifts
DTC: P0817	**Starter Lock Circuit Failed:** Ignition switch is ON, TCM and PCM communication is normal. No voltage is detected on the start lock circuit for more than 0.1 second or a continuous 12-volt output is detected for more than 0.1 second.
DTC: P0819	**Select Shift Switch Output Circuit Failure:** * No manual up/down shift available

DTC	Trouble Code Title & Conditions
DTC: P0826	**SelectShift™ switch Up and Down switch circuit :** The upshift and downshift switches are open in PARK, REVERSE and NEUTRAL. The PCM sets this DTC when it detects the select switch inputs do not match the selector lever position. Wrench light illuminated. Default to automatic shift scheduling. Upshifts and downshift request ignored
DTC: P0829	**Transmission 5-6 or 6-5 shift error:** Incorrect ratio calculated during shift 5-6 or 6-5. Incorrect gear selection depending on failure or mode and manual lever position. Shift errors may also be due to other internal transmission concerns (stuck valves, damaged friction material)No TCC. Default to 2nd or 3rd gear
DTC: P0830	**Clutch Pedal Switch A Circuit:** The powertrain control module (PCM) monitors the clutch pedal position (CPP) bottom of travel (CPP-BT) switch only during the calibrated engine speed range (cranking speed range). This DTC sets when the CPP-BT switch does not indicate that the clutch is disengaged (clutch pedal pressed) when the engine is cranked.
DTC: P0833	**Clutch Pedal Switch B Circuit:** The powertrain control module (PCM) monitors the clutch pedal position (CPP) top of travel (CPP-TT) switch only during the calibrated engine speed range (cranking speed range). This DTC sets when the CPP-TT does not indicate that the clutch is disengaged (clutch pedal pressed) when the engine is cranked.
DTC: P0840	**Transmission Fluid Pressure Sensor/Switch A Circuit:** The Transmission Control Module (TCM) monitors the transmission fluid pressure. This DTC sets when the TCC does not see the proper transmission fluid pressure. **NOTE: Check for the correct fluid level and condition.**
DTC: P0867	**Transmission Fluid Pressure:** The control valve test raises line pressure to insure that the clutch control bypass valve (multiplex valve) is latched, then turns on SSE to test for a stuck TCC control valve under steady state operation in 4th, 5th and 6th gear. If the ratio breaks away the test is aborted. If enough ratio break away occur, the DTC is set.
DTC: P087A	**Clutch Motor 2 Fault:** Reverse, 2nd, 4th and 6th gears disabled.
DTC: P087B	**Clutch Motor 2 Sensor :** Reverse, 2nd, 4th and 6th gears disabled.
DTC: P087E	**Clutch Motor 2 Sequence Fault:** Reverse, 2nd, 4th and 6th gears disabled. Clutch motor 2 hall sensor fault detected
DTC: P0882	**Transmission Control Module (TCM) power input signal low:** The TCM has detected a voltage level below 9 volts. Default to 3rd or 5th gear. Battery voltage below 9 volts. Maximum line pressure
DTC: P0883	**TCM power input signal high:** The TCM has detected a voltage level above 21 volts. Default to 3rd or 5th gear. Battery voltage above 21 volts. Maximum line pressure. May set DTC P0702
DTC: P0884	**PCM/ TCM power input signal intermittent :** The PCM/ TCM has detected a Non-Volatile Random Access Memory (NVRAM) write was interrupted at powerdown. This DTC may set when the PCM/ TCM is reprogrammed. Adaptive strategy set to default. Poor shift quality
DTC: P0885	**PCM/ TCM power relay control circuit/open:** The PCM/ TCM has detected that the actuator supply voltage circuit failed open. Wrench light illuminated. Maximum line pressure. Default to 5th gear. DTC P0657 and/or P2669 may set
DTC: P0900	**Clutch motor 1 Open Circuit:** 1st. 3rd and 5th gears disabled. Clutch motor 1 open circuit fault detected
DTC: P0901	**Clutch Motor 1 Fault**
DTC: P0902	**Clutch Motor 1 Short to Ground:** 1st, 3rd and 5th gears disabled.
DTC: P0903	**Clutch Motor 1 Short to Voltage :** 1st, 3rd and 5th gears disabled.
DTC: P090A	**Clutch Motor 2 Open Circuit:** Reverse, 2nd, 4th and 6th gears disabled.
DTC: P090B	**Clutch B Actuator Control**

DTC	Trouble Code Title & Conditions
DTC: P090C	**Clutch Motor 2 Short to Ground:** Reverse, 2nd, 4th and 6th gears disabled.
DTC: P090D	**Clutch Motor 2 Short to Voltage:** Reverse, 2nd, 4th and 6th gears disabled.
DTC: P0960	**Pressure Control Solenoid A (PCA):** PCA circuit or Variable Force Solenoid (VFS 5) failed during operation. Max line pressure. **NOTE: Will turn on the TCIL**
DTC: P0960	**Line Pressure Control (LPC) Solenoid Circuit Open:** * Maximum LPC pressure* Harsh engagements and shifts
DTC: P0961	**Pressure Control Solenoid A Circuit or Solenoid Failure:** * Incorrect current detected by the TCM* No engagements* No adaptive or self-learning strategy
DTC: P0961	**PCA control circuit range/performance:** The PCM has detected the PCA control circuit shorted to ground but not long enough to set DTC P0962.Wrench light illuminated. Intermittent condition. Minimum line pressure
DTC: P0961	**Pressure Control Solenoid Intermittent Short:** * Intermittent PCA short to ground. Fault not present long enough to store DTC for maximum line pressure.
DTC: P0962	**Line Pressure Control (LPC) Solenoid Short to Ground:** * Maximum LPC pressure* Harsh engagements and shifts
DTC: P0962	**Pressure Control Solenoid (PCA) Signal Fault:** PCA solenoid signal or ground circuits either short or open solenoid circuit failure. Voltage through PCA solenoid (VFS-5) is checked. An error will be noted if tolerance is exceeded. **NOTE: Will turn on the TCIL. Mechanical limp home mode, defaults to 3rd or 5th gear.**
DTC: P0963	**Pressure Control Solenoid (PCA) Short To Voltage (VFS-5):** Voltage through PCA solenoid (VFS-5) is checked. An error will be noted if tolerance is exceeded. Max line pressure. Mechanical limp-home mode, default to 3rd or 5th gear. May turn on MIL. **NOTE: Will turn on the TCIL.**
DTC: P0964	**PCB solenoid circuit open:** Voltage through PCB solenoid is checked. Error is noted if tolerance is exceeded.
DTC: P0966	**PCB solenoid circuit failure, short to ground:** Voltage through PCB solenoid is checked. An error will be noted if tolerance is exceeded. No 2nd and 5th gear.
DTC: P0967	**PCB solenoid short to battery voltage, short to ground:** Voltage through PCB solenoid is checked. An error will be noted if tolerance is exceeded. Short to battery power: harsh shift and engagements. Short to ground — No 2nd and 4th gear.
DTC: P0968	**PCC solenoid circuit open:** Voltage through PCC solenoid is checked. Error is noted if tolerance is exceeded.
DTC: P0970	**PCC solenoid circuit failure, short to ground:** Voltage through PCC solenoid is checked. An error will be noted if tolerance is exceeded. No 4th and 5th gear.
DTC: P0971	**PCC solenoid short to power, short to ground:** Voltage through PCC solenoid is checked. An error will be noted if tolerance is exceeded. Short to battery power: harsh shift and engagements. Short to ground — No 4th and 5th gear.
DTC: P0972	**Shift Solenoid A (SSA) control circuit range/performance:** SSA control circuit or solenoid failure. Default to 3rd or 5th gear
DTC: P0972	**Shift Solenoid A (SSA) Solenoid Failure (VFS-1):** SSA (VFS-1) circuit or solenoid failure. Mechanical limp-home mode, default to 3rd or 5th gear. May turn on MIL. **NOTE: Will turn on the TCIL.**
DTC: P0973	**Shift Solenoid (SSA) Short To Ground (VFS-1):** SSA (VFS-1) circuit or solenoid failure. Mechanical limp-home mode, default to 3rd or 5th gear. May turn on MIL. **NOTE: Will turn on the TCIL.**
DTC: P0973	**SSA control circuit low :** The PCM detected 0 volts on the SSA circuit. Short to ground detected. Wrench light illuminated. Default to 5th gear. Default to 3rd only, when the selector lever is shifted into Reverse then back into Drive. Maximum line pressure. DTC P0753 may set

DTC	Trouble Code Title & Conditions
DTC: P0974	**Shift Solenoid A (SSA) Short to Voltage:** * Forward clutch is failed off* Neutral condition or flare when fault occurs.* Poor launch due to 5th gear drive away
DTC: P0974	**Pressure Control Solenoid (PCA) Short To Voltage (VFS-1):** Voltage through PCA solenoid (VFS-1) is checked. An error will be noted if tolerance is exceeded. Max line pressure. Mechanical limp-home mode, default to 3rd or 5th gear. May turn on MIL. **NOTE: Will turn on the TCIL.**
DTC: P0974	**SSA control circuit high:** The PCM detected voltage on the SSA circuit. Short to power or open circuit detected. Wrench light illuminated5th and 6th gear only. DTC P0753 may set
DTC: P0975	**Shift Solenoid (SSA) Short To Ground (VFS-2):** SSA (VFS-2) circuit or solenoid failure. Mechanical limp-home mode, default to 3rd or 5th gear. May turn on MIL. **NOTE: Will turn on the TCIL.**
DTC: P0975	**Shift Solenoid B (SSA) Solenoid Failure (VFS-2):** SSA (VFS-2) circuit or solenoid failure. Mechanical limp-home mode, default to 3rd or 5th gear. May turn on MIL. **NOTE: Will turn on the TCIL.**
DTC: P0975	**Shift Solenoid B (SSB) control circuit range/performance:** SSB control circuit or solenoid failure. Default to 3rd or 5th gear
DTC: P0976	**Pressure Control Solenoid (PCA) Short To Voltage (VFS-2):** Voltage through PCA solenoid (VFS-2) is checked. An error will be noted if tolerance is exceeded. Max line pressure. **NOTE: Will turn on the TCIL.**
DTC: P0976	**Shift Solenoid B Short to Ground:** * Failure Mode Effects Management action opens the transaxle solenoid power control, removing power from all solenoids.* Harsh engagements.* Poor launch performance (due to 5th gear drive away).* No TCC apply.* No shifts.
DTC: P0976	**Shift Solenoid B Short to Ground:** * Failure Mode Effect Management action opens the transaxle solenoid power control relay, removing power from all solenoids.* Poor launch performance* No shifts
DTC: P0976	**SSB control circuit low:** The PCM detected 0 volts on the SSB circuit. Short to ground detected. Wrench light illuminated. Default to 5th gear. Default to 3rd only, when the selector lever is shifted into REVERSE then back into DRIVE. Maximum line pressure. DTC P0753 may set
DTC: P0977	**Shift Solenoid B Short to Voltage:** * Direct clutch failed on – only 3rd and 5th gears available.* Harsh 1-3 shift if failure occurs while in 1st.* Poor launch due to 3rd gear drive away.
DTC: P0977	**SSB control circuit high:** The PCM detected voltage on the SSB circuit. Short to power or open circuit. Wrench light illuminated. Default to 3rd and 5th gear. Harsh 1st to 3rd shift. Maximum line pressure. DTC P0758 may set
DTC: P0978	**Shift Solenoid C (SSA) Solenoid Failure (VFS-3):** SSA (VFS-3) circuit or solenoid failure. Mechanical limp-home mode, default to 3rd or 5th gear. May turn on MIL. **NOTE: Will turn on the TCIL.**
DTC: P0979	**Shift Solenoid C (SSC) Short to Ground:** * Failure Mode Effects Management action opens the transaxle solenoid power control, removing power from all solenoids.* Harsh engagements.* Poor launch performance (due to 5th gear drive away).* No TCC apply.* No shifts.
DTC: P0979	**Shift Solenoid (SSA) Short To Ground (VFS-3):** SSA (VFS-3) circuit or solenoid failure. Mechanical limp-home mode, default to 3rd or 5th gear. May turn on MIL. **NOTE: Will turn on the TCIL.**
DTC: P0980	**Shift Solenoid C Open Circuit:** * Erratic, delayed or harsh shifts.* If fault occurs while in 2nd or 6th gear, neutral condition will exist before diagnostics disables 2nd and 6th gears
DTC: P0980	**Pressure Control Solenoid (PCA) Short To Voltage (VFS-3):** Voltage through PCA solenoid (VFS-3) is checked. An error will be noted if tolerance is exceeded. Max line pressure. Mechanical limp-home mode, default to 3rd or 5th gear. May turn on MIL. **NOTE: Will turn on the TCIL.**
DTC: P0980	**Shift Solenoid C (SSC) Short to Voltage:** * Neutral condition before diagnostics disables 2nd and 6th gears* Erratic, delayed or harsh shifts

DTC	Trouble Code Title & Conditions
DTC: P0980	**SSC control circuit high:** The PCM detected voltage on the SSC circuit. Short to power detected. Wrench light illuminated2nd and 6th gears disabled. Harsh 1st to 3rd shift. Maximum line pressure. DTC P0763 may set
DTC: P0981	**Shift Solenoid D (SSA) Solenoid Failure (VFS-4):** SSA (VFS-4) circuit or solenoid failure. Mechanical limp-home mode, default to 3rd or 5th gear. May turn on MIL. **NOTE: Will turn on the TCIL.**
DTC: P0981	**Shift Solenoid D (SSD) control circuit range/performance:** SSD control circuit or solenoid failure. Default to 3rd or 5th gear
DTC: P0981	**Shift Solenoid D Circuit Failure:** * No shift engagements* No adaptive or self-learning strategy* Incorrect current detected by TCM
DTC: P0982	**SSD control circuit low:** The PCM detected 0 volts on the SSD circuit. Short to ground detected. Wrench light illuminated. Default to 5th gear. Default to 3rd only, when the selector lever is shifted into REVERSE then back into DRIVE. Maximum line pressure. DTC P0768 may set
DTC: P0982	**Shift Solenoid (SSA) Short To Ground (VFS-4):** SSA (VFS-4) circuit or solenoid failure. Mechanical limp-home mode, default to 3rd or 5th gear. May turn on MIL. **NOTE: Will turn on the TCIL.**
DTC: P0982	**Shift Solenoid D (SSD) Short to Ground:** * Failure Mode Effects Management action opens the transaxle solenoid power control, removing power from all solenoids.* Harsh engagements.* Poor launch performance (due to 5th gear drive away).* No TCC apply.* No shifts.
DTC: P0983	**SSD control circuit high:** The PCM detected voltage on the SSD circuit. Short to power detected.Wrench light illuminatedDisable 1st, 2nd and 3rd gearPoor launch performanceMaximum line pressureDTC P0768 may set
DTC: P0983	**Shift Solenoid D (SSD) Short to Voltage:** * O/D clutch failed on, only 4th, 5th and 6th gears available* Harsh engagements* Poor launch due to 4th gear drive away
DTC: P0983	**Shift Solenoid D Open Circuit:** * Only 4th, 5th and 6th gears available.* Harsh engagements.* Poor launch due to 4th gear drive away
DTC: P0983	**Pressure Control Solenoid (PCA) Short To Voltage (VFS-4):** Voltage through PCA solenoid (VFS-4) is checked. An error will be noted if tolerance is exceeded. Max line pressure. Mechanical limp-home mode, default to 3rd or 5th gear. May turn on MIL. **NOTE: Will turn on the TCIL.**
DTC: P0984	**Pressure Control Solenoid (PCA) Signal Circuit Short To Voltage (VFS-4):** Voltage through PCA solenoid (VFS-4) is checked. An error will be noted if tolerance is exceeded. Max line pressure. Mechanical limp-home mode, default to 3rd or 5th gear. May turn on MIL. **NOTE: Will turn on the TCIL.**
DTC: P0984 T PCM	**SSE control circuit range/performance:** The PCM commanded SSE ON or OFF but detected a ratio error (mechanical failure).Wrench light illuminated. DTC P0771 and/or DTC P0772 may set
DTC: P0985	**SSE control circuit low:** Voltage through SSE was not detected when the solenoid was commanded off. Short to ground detected. Default to 3rd or 5th gear
DTC: P0986	**SSE control circuit high:** The PCM/ TCM detected voltage on the SSE circuit. Short to power or open circuit detected. Maximum line pressure. Disable 1st, 2nd and 3rd gear4th gear launch. Delayed reverse engagement. DTC P0773 may set
DTC: P0986	**Shift Solenoid E Short to Voltage:** * During self test, voltage in SSE circuit tolerance is exceeded* No engagements* No adaptive or self-learning strategy
DTC: P0997	**Shift Solenoid F Circuit Failure:** * No engagements* No adaptive or self-learning strategy* Incorrect current detected by the TCM
DTC: P0998	**Shift Solenoid F Short to Ground:** * No engagements* No adaptive or self-learning strategy* SSF circuit voltage exceeded tolerance during self test
DTC: P0999	**Shift Solenoid F Short to Voltage:** * During self test, voltage in SSF circuit tolerance is exceeded* No engagements* No adaptive or self-learning strategy

DTC	Trouble Code Title & Conditions
DTC: P0A09	**DC/DC Converter Status Circuit Low:** This DTC indicates the DC/DC fault (DCF) circuit is shorted to ground, there is internal DC/DC damage, or the 12 volt bus voltage dropped below the calibrated threshold.
DTC: P0A0A (TBCM)	**High Voltage System Inter-lock Circuit:** The traction battery control module (TBCM) checks continuity of the high voltage interlock circuit. When the TBCM detects an open circuit condition this DTC is set.
DTC: P0A0A (TCM)	**High Voltage System Inter-lock Circuit:** The transaxle control module (TCM) checks continuity check of the high voltage interlock circuit. When the TCM detects an open circuit condition this DTC sets.
DTC: P0A10	**DC/DC Converter Status Circuit High:** This DTC indicates the DC/DC fault (DCF) circuit is open, shorted to VPWR, or there is internal DC/DC damage.
DTC: P0A5A	**Generator Current Sensor Circuit Range/Performance:** Engine running, the Powertrain Control Module (PCM) detects that the generator field control circuit has a malfunction.
DTC: P0A5B	**Generator Current Sensor Circuit Low:** Engine running, the Powertrain Control Module (PCM) detects that the generator field control circuit has a malfunction.
DTC: P0A5C	**Generator Current Sensor Circuit High:** Engine running, the Powertrain Control Module (PCM) detects that the generator field control circuit has a malfunction.

OBD II Trouble Code List (P1xxx Codes)

DTC	Trouble Code Title & Conditions
DTC: P1000	**On-Board Diagnostic (OBD) Systems Readiness Test Not Complete:** The OBD monitors are carried out during the OBD drive cycle. This DTC is stored in continuous memory if any of the OBD monitors do not carry out their full diagnostic check.
DTC: P1001	**KOER Self-Test Not Completed, KOER Test Aborted:** This non-Malfunction Indicator Lamp (MIL) DTC is set when the KOER self-test does not complete in the time allowed. **NOTE: Carry out the KOEO self-test.**
DTC: P1100	**Mass Air Flow (MAF) Sensor Circuit Intermittent:** The MAF sensor circuit is monitored by the powertrain control module (PCM) for sudden voltage (or airflow) input change through the comprehensive component monitor (CCM). If during the last 40 warm-up cycles in ignition ON, engine running the PCM detects a voltage (or airflow) change beyond the minimum or maximum calibrated limit, a continuous memory DTC is stored.
DTC: P1101	**Mass Air Flow (MAF) Sensor Out of Self-Test Range:** The MAF sensor circuit is monitored by the powertrain control module (PCM) for an out of range condition. This DTC sets if during ignition ON engine OFF, the output signal is greater than a calibrated limit or during ignition ON engine running, the output signal is not within the calibrated range.
DTC: P1102	**Mass Air Flow Sensor In Range But Lower Than Expected:** The powertrain control module (PCM) monitors a vehicle operation rationality check by comparing sensed throttle position to mass air flow readings. If, during a key on engine running (KOER) self-test, the comparison of the TP sensor and MAF sensor readings are not consistent with the calibrated load values, the test fails and a DTC is stored in continuous memory.
DTC: P1103	**Mass Air Flow Sensor In Range But Higher Than Expected:** The powertrain control module (PCM) monitors mass air flow values. If, during a key on engine running (KOER) self-test, the MAF sensor values are greater than the calibrated values, the test fails and a DTC is stored in continuous memory.
DTC: P1111	**System Pass:** Indicates all systems passed and no concerns are present.
DTC: P1112	**Intake Air Temperature (IAT) Circuit Intermittent:** Engine started, and the PCM detected an intermittent condition in the IAT sensor signal during the self-test. **NOTE: Select the IAT PID and monitor the signal for sudden changes when the harness is wiggled or the sensor is tapped.**
DTC: P1114	**Intake Air Temperature 2 (IAT2) Circuit Low (Supercharged/Turbocharged engines):** Indicates the sensor signal is less than the self-test minimum. The IAT2 sensor minimum is 0.2 volt.
DTC: P1114	**Intake Air Temperature 2 (IAT-2) Circuit Low:** Engine started, and the PCM detected the IAT sensor signal was less than the self-test minimum of 0.20v (equivalent to 250°F). Monitor the IAT PID for very low signal.
DTC: P1115	**Intake Air Temperature 2 (IAT2) Circuit High (Supercharged/Turbocharged engines):** Indicates the sensor signal is greater than the self-test maximum. The IAT2 sensor maximum is 4.6 volts.

DTC	Trouble Code Title & Conditions
DTC: P1115	**Intake Air Temperature 2 (IAT-2) Circuit High:** Engine started, and the PCM detected the IAT Sensor 2 signal was more than the self-test maximum of 4.60v (equivalent to 250°F). Monitor the IAT PID for very high signal. **NOTE: Monitor the IAT2 PID value. A typical IAT2 temperature should be greater than the IAT1 temperature**
DTC: P1116	**Engine Coolant Temperature (ECT) Sensor Out of Self-Test Range:** Indicates the ECT sensor is out of self-test range. The correct range is 0.3 to 3.7 volts.
DTC: P1117	**Engine Coolant Temperature (ECT) Sensor Circuit Intermittent:** Indicates the ECT circuit became intermittently open or short while the engine was running.
DTC: P1117	**CHT or ECT Sensor Signal Intermittent:** Engine started, and the PCM detected an intermittent loss of the CHT or ECT sensor signal (it may have an open circuit condition). **NOTE: Monitor the CHT or ECT on a scan tool. Look for sudden changes in the reading when the harness is wiggled or the sensor is tapped.**
DTC: P1120	**Throttle Position Sensor A Out Of Range Low (Range Too Low):** The throttle position (TP) sensor circuit is monitored by the powertrain control module (PCM) for a low TP rotation angle or voltage input below the closed throttle position through the comprehensive component monitor (CCM). The test fails if the TP rotation angle or voltage remains within the calibrated self-test range, but falls between 3.42-9.85% (0.17-0.49 volt).
DTC: P1121	**TP Sensor Inconsistent With MAF Sensor:** Engine started; and the PCM detected the MAF and TP sensor signals were not consistent the calibrated values expected for these two sensors during the self-test. **NOTE: Drive the vehicle and monitor the TP PID in all gears. A TP PID of less than 0.24v (4.82%) with a LOAD PID over 55%, or a TP PID over 2.44v (49.05%) with a LOAD PID under 30% will set this code.**
DTC: P1124	**TP Sensor Out of Self-Test Range:** Key on, KOEO Self-Test enabled, and the PCM detected the TP sensor signal was less than 0.66v (13.27%), or with the engine running, KOER Self-Test enabled, the PCM detected the TP sensor signal was approximately 1.17v (23.52%). **NOTE: A TP V PID less than 4.82 % (0.24 volt) with a LOAD PID more than 55%; or the TP V PID more than 49.05% (2.44 volts) with a LOAD PID less than 30% indicates a hard fault is present.**
DTC: P1124	**Throttle Position Sensor A Out Of Self-Test Range (For All Others):** During key on engine off (KOEO) and key on engine running (KOER) self-tests, the powertrain control module (PCM) monitors the electronic throttle control (ETC) throttle position (TP) sensor inputs to determine if the TP1 and TP2 signals are less than an expected value. If either TP1 or TP2 is greater than the expected value, the DTC is set.
DTC: P1124	**Throttle Position (TP) Sensor A Out Of Self-Test Range (Vehicles Without an IAC Valve):** During Key On Engine Off (KOEO) and Key On Engine Running (KOER) self-tests, the powertrain control module (PCM) monitors the Electronic Throttle Control (ETC) Throttle Position (TP) sensor inputs to determine if the TP1 and TP2 signals are less than an expected value. If either TP1 or TP2 is greater than the expected value, the DTC is set. **NOTE: Repeat the self-test without applying the accelerator pedal. Make sure the floor mat is not interfering with the accelerator pedal. Diagnose any TP circuit DTCs first.**
DTC: P1125	**TP Sensor Circuit Malfunction (Intermittent):** Engine started, and the PCM detected the TP sensor rotational angle changed beyond the minimum or maximum calibrated limit. **NOTE: Monitor the TP V PID, and tap lightly on the TP sensor housing and wiggle the wiring harness. Watch for the value to suddenly go below 0.49v or over 4.65v.**
DTC: P1127	**Exhaust Temperature Out of Range, O2 Sensor Tests Not Completed:** The heated oxygen sensor (HO2S) monitor uses an exhaust temperature model to determine when the HO2S heaters are cycled ON. The test fails when the inferred exhaust temperature is below a minimum calibrated value.
DTC: P1127	**Exhaust Temperature Out of Range, O2 Sensor Tests Not Completed:** The heated oxygen sensor (HO2S) monitor uses an exhaust temperature model to determine when the HO2S heaters are cycled ON. The test fails when the inferred exhaust temperature is below a minimum calibrated value.
DTC: P1140	**Water in Fuel Condition:** The water in fuel (WIF) sensor is monitored by the powertrain control module (PCM). If the PCM detects water in the fuel, this DTC sets and the WIF indicator lamp is illuminated.
DTC: P1145 (PCM)	**Calculated Torque Error:** This DTC indicates the engine was overproducing torque and overcharging the traction battery, when its operating temperature was below the calibrated threshold. To protect the traction battery the powertrain control module (PCM) disabled the fuel injectors.
DTC: P1145 (TCM)	**Calculated Torque Error:** The transaxle control module (TCM) continuously monitors the controller area network (CAN) for calculated torque message from the powertrain control module (PCM). This DTC is set when the calculated torque is not within the expected range.

DTC	Trouble Code Title & Conditions
DTC: P1148	**Generator 2 Control Circuit:** The powertrain control module (PCM) monitors the generator circuits and sets this DTC when the PCM detects a concern.
DTC: P1149	**Generator 2 Monitor Circuit High:** The powertrain control module (PCM) monitors the generator circuits and sets this DTC when the PCM detects a concern.
DTC: P115A	**Low Fuel Level - Forced Limited Power:** Fuel level information is sent from the instrument cluster to the powertrain control module (PCM) on the communication link. If an excessively low fuel level input message is received by the PCM from the instrument cluster, the PCM limits the fuel rail pressure (FRP) or Injection Control Pressure (ICP) and sets DTC P115A.
DTC: P115E	**Throttle Actuator Control (TAC) Throttle Body Air Flow Trim at Max Limit:** During idle, the Powertrain Control Module (PCM) monitors the throttle angle and air flow. If the air flow is determined to be less than expected, the PCM adjusts the throttle angle to compensate. The air flow reduction is typically the result of engine deposit buildup around the throttle plate. This DTC indicates the PCM has reached the maximum allowed compensation and is no longer able to compensate for the buildup.
DTC: P117A	**Engine Oil Over Temperature (Forced Limited Power):** Indicates the engine oil protection strategy is enabled when the Engine Oil Temperature (EOT) reaches a predetermined level in the Powertrain Control Module (PCM). The PCM then limits the engine RPMs until the EOT returns to normal. **NOTE: This DTC is an informational DTC and may be set by an engine overheating concern. If the engine overheats, check the cooling system.**
DTC: P117B	**Exhaust Gas Temperature Sensor Correlation - Bank 1:** The powertrain control module (PCM) monitors the 3 exhaust gas temperature (EGT) sensors at key ON, engine OFF, following an 8-hour soak to determine if a concern is present. The PCM compares the values of the 3 EGT sensors to verify the sensors correlate to each other. The test fails when the temperature difference at one of the EGT sensors is greater than 25°C (45°F).
DTC: P117F	**Fuel Pressure Regulator Control Exceeded Learning Limits:** The powertrain control module (PCM) monitors the operation of fuel pressure control valve and calculates parameters necessary for an ideal engine operation. These parameters are stored in the adaptive strategy table. The table is used as a correction factor when controlling engine operation and corrects for wear or aging of components. The DTC is set when the adaptive strategy has reached its minimum or maximum learning limits.
DTC: P1184	**Engine Oil Temperature (EOT) Sensor Out of Self-Test Range:** Indicates the EOT sensor signal was out of self-test range.
DTC: P1184	**Engine Oil Temperature (EOT) Sensor Out Of Self-Test Range:** Engine started, and the PCM detected the EOT sensor circuit was open or shorted to ground (i.e., this fault can be caused by an intermittent loss of this signal). **NOTE: The engine should be at operating temperature before carrying out the self-test**
DTC: P1201	**Cylinder 1 Injector Circuit Open/Shorted:** The powertrain control module (PCM) monitors the output of the fuel injector circuits and sets a DTC when it detects the output is not within a calibrated limit.
DTC: P1202	**Cylinder 2 Injector Circuit Open/Shorted:** The powertrain control module (PCM) monitors the output of the fuel injector circuits and sets a DTC when it detects the output is not within a calibrated limit.
DTC: P1203	**Cylinder 3 Injector Circuit Open/Shorted:** The powertrain control module (PCM) monitors the output of the fuel injector circuits and sets a DTC when it detects the output is not within a calibrated limit.
DTC: P1204	**Cylinder 4 Injector Circuit Open/Shorted:** The powertrain control module (PCM) monitors the output of the fuel injector circuits and sets a DTC when it detects the output is not within a calibrated limit.
DTC: P1205	**Cylinder 5 Injector Circuit Open/Shorted:** The powertrain control module (PCM) monitors the output of the fuel injector circuits and sets a DTC when it detects the output is not within a calibrated limit.
DTC: P1206	**Cylinder 6 Injector Circuit Open/Shorted:** The powertrain control module (PCM) monitors the output of the fuel injector circuits and sets a DTC when it detects the output is not within a calibrated limit.
DTC: P1207	**Cylinder 7 Injector Circuit Open/Shorted:** The powertrain control module (PCM) monitors the output of the fuel injector circuits and sets a DTC when it detects the output is not within a calibrated limit.

DTC	Trouble Code Title & Conditions
DTC: P1208	**Cylinder 8 Injector Circuit Open/Shorted:** The powertrain control module (PCM) monitors the output of the fuel injector circuits and sets a DTC when it detects the output is not within a calibrated limit.
DTC: P120F	**Fuel Pressure Regulator Excessive Variation:** The powertrain control module (PCM) adjusts the fuel rail pressure by controlling the fuel pressure control valve. This DTC sets when the actual fuel rail pressure varies too much from the desired fuel rail pressure for the calibrated fuel mass value.
DTC: P1227	**Wastegate Failed Closed (Over pressure):** Indicates that boost pressure is continuously higher than desired.
DTC: P1227	**Wastegate Failed Closed (Over pressure):** Key on or engine running; Indicates that boost pressure is continuously higher than desired. **NOTE: This DTC is informational only and it may be accompanied by other DTCs. Diagnose other DTCs first.**
DTC: P1229	**Charge Air Cooler (CAC) Pump Driver:** This DTC sets when the powertrain control module (PCM) commands the supercharger CAC pump to operate but no current is detected.
DTC: P1229	**Charge Air Cooler (CAC) Pump Driver:** Key on or engine running; This DTC sets when the Powertrain Control Module (PCM) commands the supercharger CAC pump to operate but no current is detected. **NOTE: Check for voltage at the relay. Check the fuse in the voltage circuit. Check the ground connection of the CAC pump motor.**
DTC: P1231	**Fuel Pump Secondary Low, High Speed Pump On:** Key on, KOEO Self-Test enabled; High Speed Fuel Pump (HFP) relay energized, fuel pump driver in VLCM off (to VLCM Pin 7) off, the PCM detected voltage on the FPM circuit.
DTC: P1232	**Low Speed Fuel Pump Primary Circuit Malfunction:** Engine started, Low Speed Fuel Pump (LFP) relay energized, the PCM detected excessive current on the LFP circuit; or with LFP commanded off it detected power on the LFP circuit.
DTC: P1233	**Fuel Pump Driver Module Disabled or Off Line:** The Powertrain Control Module (PCM) monitors the Fuel Pump Monitor (FPM) circuit from the Fuel Pump Driver Module (FPDM). With the key ON, engine OFF or key ON, engine running the FPDM continuously sends a duty cycle signal to the PCM through the FPM circuit. The test fails if the PCM stops receiving the duty cycle signal. **NOTE: The PCM expects to see one of the following duty cycle signals from the FPDM on the FPM circuit: 1) 50% (500 ms on, 500 ms off), all OK. 2) 25% (250 ms on, 750 ms off), FPDM did not receive a fuel pump (FP) duty cycle command from the PCM, or the duty cycle that was received was invalid. 3) 75% (750 ms on, 250 off), the FPDM detected a concern in the circuits between the FPDM and the fuel pump.**
DTC: P1234	**Fuel System Disabled Or Offline:** The Powertrain Control Module (PCM) monitors the Fuel Pump Monitor 2 (FPM2) circuit from the Fuel Pump Driver Module 2 (FPDM2). With the key ON, engine OFF or key ON, engine running the FPDM2 continuously sends a duty cycle signal to the PCM through the FPM2 circuit. The test fails if the PCM stops receiving the duty cycle signal. **NOTE: The PCM expects to see one of the following duty cycle signals from the FPDM2 on the FPM2 circuit: 1) 50% (500 ms on, 500 ms off), all OK. 2) 25% (250 ms on, 750 ms off), the FPDM2 did not receive a Fuel Pump (FP) duty cycle command from the PCM, or the duty cycle that was received was invalid. 3) 75% (750 ms on, 250 off), the FPDM2 detected a concern in the circuits between the FPDM2 and the fuel pump.**
DTC: P1235	**Fuel Pump Control Out Of Range:** Key on or engine running; and the PCM received a signal from the FPM over the SCP bus that the FPDM had received an invalid or missing fuel pump command from the PCM. **NOTE: The FPDM sends a 25% duty cycle (250 ms on, 750 ms off) through the FPM circuit to the PCM while the concern is being detected by the FPDM. If the concern is no longer detected, the FPDM returns to sending an all OK (50% duty cycle) message to the PCM. For ETC applications, check if ETC DTC P2105 is present. An ETC system concern could cause DTC P1235, and should be diagnosed first.**
DTC: P1235	**Fuel Pump Control Out Of Range:** This DTC indicates the fuel pump driver module (FPDM) detected an invalid or missing fuel pump (FP) duty cycle signal on the fuel pump control (FPC) circuit from the powertrain control module (PCM). The FPDM sends a message to the PCM through the fuel pump monitor (FPM) circuit, indicating this concern was detected. The PCM sets the DTC when the message is received.
DTC: P1236	**Fuel Pump Control Out Of Range:** This DTC indicates the Fuel Pump Driver Module 2 (FPDM2) detected an invalid or missing Fuel Pump (FP) duty cycle signal on the Fuel Pump Control (FPC) circuit from the Powertrain Control Module (PCM). The FPDM2 sends a message to the PCM through the Fuel Pump Monitor 2 (FPM2) circuit, indicating this concern was detected. The PCM sets the DTC when the message is received. **NOTE: The FPDM2 sends a 25% duty cycle (250 ms on, 750 ms off) through the FPM2 circuit to the PCM while the concern is being detected by the FPDM2. If the concern is no longer detected, the FPDM2 returns to sending an all OK (50% duty cycle) message to the PCM.**

DTC	Trouble Code Title & Conditions
DTC: P1237	**Fuel Pump Secondary Circuit Malfunction:** Key on or engine running; and the PCM received a signal from the FPDM that it had detected a fault in the fuel pump secondary circuit. **NOTE: The FPDM sends a 75% duty cycle (750 ms on, 250 ms off) through the FPM circuit to the PCM while the concern is being detected by the FPDM. If the concern is no longer detected, the PCM returns to sending an all OK (50% duty cycle) message to the PCM. The FPDM controls pump speed by supplying a variable ground on the FP RTN circuit.**
DTC: P1237	**Fuel Pump Secondary Circuit:** This DTC indicates the fuel pump driver module (FPDM) detected a fuel pump secondary circuit concern. The FPDM sends a message to the powertrain control module (PCM) through the fuel pump monitor (FPM) circuit indicating this concern was detected. The PCM sets the DTC when the message is received.
DTC: P1238	**Fuel Pump Secondary Circuit:** This DTC indicates the fuel pump driver module (FPDM2) detected a fuel pump secondary circuit concern. The FPDM2 sends a message to the powertrain control module (PCM) through the fuel pump monitor (FPM2) circuit, indicating this concern was detected. The PCM sets the DTC when the message is received.
DTC: P1238	**Fuel Pump Secondary Circuit Malfunction:** Key on or engine running; and the PCM received a signal from the FPDM that it had detected a fault in the fuel pump secondary circuit. **NOTE: The FPDM2 sends a 75% duty cycle (750 ms on, 250 ms off) through the FPM2 circuit to the PCM while the concern is being detected by the FPDM2. If the concern is no longer detected, the PCM returns to sending an all OK (50% duty cycle) message to the PCM. The FPDM2 controls pump speed by supplying a variable ground on the FP2RTN circuit.**
DTC: P123C	**Cold Start Turbo Protection - Forced Limited Power:** This DTC will set when the vehicle is started in temperatures below -26°C (-14.8°F). The vehicle will operate at reduced power to prevent damaging the turbocharger due to lack of lubrication. The vehicle will not operate at full power until the engine has had 30 seconds to warm up. A countdown timer is indicated on the instrument cluster to notify the driver when the engine is warmed up and operating at full power. The DTC will clear from the PCM when 40 ignition cycles have been completed.
DTC: P1244	**Alternator Load High Input:** The Powertrain Control Module (PCM) monitors generator load from the generator/regulator in the form of frequency. The concern indicates the input is higher than the load should be in normal operation. The load input could be high when a battery short to ground exists.
DTC: P1245	**Alternator Load High Low:** The Powertrain Control Module (PCM) monitors generator load from the generator/regulator in the form of frequency. The concern indicates the input is lower than the load should be in normal operation. The load input could be low when no generator output exists.
DTC: P1246	**Alternator Load Circuit Input:** The Powertrain Control Module (PCM) monitors the generator load from the generator/regulator in the form of frequency. The frequency range is determined by the temperature of the voltage regulator, where 97% indicates a full load, and less than 6% indicates no load.
DTC: P1247	**Turbocharger Boost Pressure Low:** The powertrain control module (PCM) continuously monitors the turbocharger system for an underboost condition. This DTC sets when the PCM detects that the difference between the desired and the measured boost pressure is not greater than a calibrated value for a specified period of time.
DTC: P1249	**Wastegate Control Valve Performance:** The powertrain control module (PCM) continuously monitors the turbocharger system for concerns. This DTC sets when the PCM detects that the difference between the manifold absolute pressure (MAP) pressure readings are not greater than a calibrated value for a specified period of time when the intrusive monitor runs at engine idle.
DTC: P1260	**Theft Detected, Vehicle Immobilized:** This DTC can be set if the passive anti-theft system (PATS) has determined a theft condition existed and the engine is disabled or an engine start was attempted using a non-PATS key. This DTC is a good indicator to check the PATS for DTCs. This DTC can also be set when a new instrument cluster (IC), instrument panel cluster (IPC) or powertrain control module (PCM) is installed without correctly programming either module even if the vehicle is not equipped with PATS.
DTC: P1260	**Theft Detected, Vehicle Immobilized:** Key on, and the PCM received a signal from the Anti-Theft System that a theft condition had occurred. The theft indicator on the dash will flash rapidly or remain on "solid" with the ignition switch in the "on" position. The engine may "start and stall", or may not crank if the vehicle is equipped with the PATS starter disable feature.
DTC: P1261	**Cylinder 1 High To Low Side Short:** The powertrain control module (PCM) monitors the output of the fuel injector circuits and sets a DTC when it detects the output is not within a calibrated limit.

DTC	Trouble Code Title & Conditions
DTC: P1263	**Cylinder 3 High To Low Side Short:** The powertrain control module (PCM) monitors the output of the fuel injector circuits and sets a DTC when it detects the output is not within a calibrated limit.
DTC: P1264	**Cylinder 4 High To Low Side Short:** The powertrain control module (PCM) monitors the output of the fuel injector circuits and sets a DTC when it detects the output is not within a calibrated limit.
DTC: P1265	**Cylinder 5 High To Low Side Short:** The powertrain control module (PCM) monitors the output of the fuel injector circuits and sets a DTC when it detects the output is not within a calibrated limit.
DTC: P1266	**Cylinder 6 High To Low Side Short:** The powertrain control module (PCM) monitors the output of the fuel injector circuits and sets a DTC when it detects the output is not within a calibrated limit.
DTC: P1267	**Cylinder 7 High To Low Side Short:** The powertrain control module (PCM) monitors the output of the fuel injector circuits and sets a DTC when it detects the output is not within a calibrated limit.
DTC: P1268	**Cylinder 8 High To Low Side Short:** The powertrain control module (PCM) monitors the output of the fuel injector circuits and sets a DTC when it detects the output is not within a calibrated limit.
DTC: P1270	**Engine RPM or Vehicle Speed Limiter Reached:** Indicates the vehicle has been operated in a manner which caused the engine or vehicle to exceed a calibration limit. The engine RPM and vehicle speed are continuously monitored and evaluated by the powertrain control module (PCM). This DTC sets when the RPM or vehicle speed falls out of a calibrated range. For additional information on the engine RPM/vehicle speed limiter, refer to Section 1, Powertrain Control Software.
DTC: P1270	**Engine RPM or Vehicle Speed Limiter Reached:** Engine started, and after the PCM monitored the engine speed and VSS signals, it detected the vehicle was operated in a manner where the engine or vehicle speed exceeded its limit.
DTC: P127A	**Aborted KOER - Fuel Pressure Failure:** The DTC indicates that the key on, engine running (KOER) self-test aborted because of the fuel rail pressure (FRP) out of self-test range.
DTC: P1284	**Aborted KOER - Injector Control Pressure Failure:** The DTC indicates that the key on, engine running (KOER) self-test aborted because of the injection control pressure (ICP) out of self-test range.
DTC: P1285	**Cylinder Head Over-Temperature Condition:** Key on or engine running; and the PCM detected an engine overheat condition through inputs from the cylinder head temperature sensor. **NOTE: On some applications when this fault occurs, the engine temperature warning indicator illuminates or forces the temperature gauge to the full H (hot) zone. The warning indicator can be triggered by either grounding the engine temperature warning circuit when wired to the Powertrain Control Module (PCM), or by sending a PCM network message to the Instrument Cluster (IC).**
DTC: P1288	**Cylinder Head Temperature Sensor Out of Self-Test Range:** Key on and KOEO Self-Test enabled, or engine running with the KOER Self-Test enabled, and the PCM detected the CHT sensor was out of its self-test range (i.e., the engine was too hot or it did not warm to its normal operating temperature) during the test period.
DTC: P1289	**Cylinder Head Temperature (CHT) Sensor Circuit High:** Indicates a CHT sensor circuit open.
DTC: P1289	**Cylinder Head Temperature Sensor Circuit High Input:** Key on or engine running; and the PCM detected a Cylinder Head Temperature (CHT) sensor signal that was more than 4.60v. This code may be due to an intermittent fault. Wiggle the CHT sensor wiring and connector while monitoring the CHT PID for a sudden change in voltage. DTC P0118 may also be reported when this code is set, and either code will cause the PCM to activate the MIL.
DTC: P1289	**Cylinder Head Temperature (CHT) Sensor Circuit High:** Indicates a CHT sensor circuit concern.
DTC: P128A	**Cylinder Head Temperature (CHT) Sensor Circuit Intermittent/Erratic:** Key on or engine running; Indicates the CHT circuit became intermittently open or shorted while the engine was running. **NOTE: Monitor the CHT on a scan tool. Look for sudden changes in the reading when the harness is wiggled or the sensor is tapped.**

DTC	Trouble Code Title & Conditions
DTC: P128A	**Cylinder Head Temperature (CHT) Sensor Circuit Intermittent/Erratic:** Indicates the CHT circuit became intermittently open or short while the engine was running.
DTC: P1290	**Cylinder Head Temperature (CHT) Sensor Circuit Low:** Indicates a CHT sensor circuit concern.
DTC: P1290	**Cylinder Head Temperature (CHT) Sensor Circuit Low:** Key on or engine running; and the PCM detected a Cylinder Head Temperature (CHT) sensor signal that was less than 0.2v. Note that this trouble code may be due to an intermittent type of fault. Wiggle the CHT sensor wiring and connector while monitoring the CHT V PID for signs of a sudden change in the voltage. DTC P0118 may also set along with this code (both codes will cause a MIL to be on).
DTC: P1291	**Injector High Side Short To GND Or VBATT - Bank 1:** The powertrain control module (PCM) monitors the output of the fuel injector circuits and sets a DTC when it detects the output is not within a calibrated limit. When diagnosing a fuel injector or fuel injector circuit concern, bank 1 refers to cylinder numbers 1, 4, 6 and 7.
DTC: P1292	**Injector High Side Short To GND Or VBATT - Bank 2:** The powertrain control module (PCM) monitors the output of the fuel injector circuits and sets a DTC when it detects the output is not within a calibrated limit. When diagnosing a fuel injector or fuel injector circuit concern, bank 2 refers to cylinder numbers 2, 3, 5 and 8.
DTC: P1299	**Cylinder Head Over-Temperature Protection Active:** Engine started, and after a period of time with the engine running, the PCM detected the engine was in an overheated condition. **NOTE: The PCM enables the Fail-Safe Cooling whenever this code is set to cool the engine (a Failure Mode Effects Strategy or FMEM).**
DTC: P1299	**Cylinder Head Over Temperature Protection Active:** Indicates an engine overheat condition was detected by the cylinder head temperature (CHT) sensor. A failure mode effects management (FMEM) strategy called fail-safe cooling was activated to cool the engine.
DTC: P130D	**Engine Knock/Combustion Performance - Forced Limited Power:** The powertrain control module (PCM) continuously monitors the knock system for concerns. This DTC sets when the PCM detects that the knock sensor (KS) voltage has exceeded a maximum value greater than a calibrated number of times within a set time period.
DTC: P132A	**Turbocharger/Supercharger Boost Control A Electrical:** The powertrain control module (PCM) continuously monitors the controller area network (CAN) for messages from the turbocharger actuator to set this DTC. The turbocharger actuator carries out a learn function to determine the minimum and maximum positions when the ignition is turned on and the engine is running. If, the actuator is unable to complete the learn mode, the test fails and a controller area network CAN message is sent to the PCM.
DTC: P132A	**Turbocharger/Supercharger Boost Control A Electrical:** The powertrain control module (PCM) continuously monitors the turbocharger system for concerns. This DTC sets when the PCM detects any circuit faults in the VGTC circuit.
DTC: P132B	**Turbocharger/Supercharger Boost Control A Performance:** The powertrain control module (PCM) continuously monitors the turbocharger system for concerns. This DTC sets when the PCM detects that the difference between the manifold absolute pressure (MAP) pressure readings are not greater than a calibrated value for a specified period of time when the intrusive monitor runs at engine idle.
DTC: P132B	**Turbocharger/Supercharger Boost Control A Performance:** The powertrain control module (PCM) continuously monitors the controller area network (CAN) for messages from the turbocharger actuator to set this DTC. The turbocharger actuator carries out a self-test to determine if it is operating according to design specifications. If the self-test fails, a CAN message is then sent to the PCM.
DTC: P132C	**Turbocharger/Supercharger Boost Control A Voltage:** The powertrain control module (PCM) continuously monitors the controller area network (CAN) for messages from the turbocharger actuator to set this DTC. The turbocharger actuator monitors the system voltage to determine if it is within a calibrated range. If the system voltage is outside of the calibrated range a CAN message is sent to the PCM.
DTC: P1335	**Exhaust Gas Recirculation (EGR) Position Sensor Minimum/Maximum Stop Performance:** This DTC is set when the voltage of the EGR valve position sensor greater than the bottom limit threshold.
DTC: P1336	**Crankshaft/Camshaft Sensor Range/Performance:** The DTC sets when the input signal to the powertrain control module (PCM) from the crankshaft position (CKP) sensor is erratic.
DTC: P1336	**Crankshaft/Camshaft Sensor Range/Performance:** The input signal to the powertrain control module (PCM) from the crankshaft position (CKP) sensor or the camshaft position (CMP) sensor is erratic.

DTC	Trouble Code Title & Conditions
DTC: P1336	**Crankshaft/Camshaft Sensor Range/Performance:** Engine started, and the PCM detected an erratic signal from CKP sensor or the CMP sensor. It is possible for EMI/RFI interference to cause this code when they occur on these circuits. **NOTE: Check the harness for routing, alterations, incorrect shielding, or electrical interference from other systems.**
DTC: P1378	**Fuel Injector Control Module System Voltage Low:** The DTC sets when the fuel injector control module (FICM) voltage drops below 7 volts at any time during the normal operation.
DTC: P1379	**Fuel Injector Control Module System Voltage High:** The DTC sets when the fuel injector control module (FICM) voltage exceeds 16 volts at any time during the normal operation.
DTC: P138B	**Glow Plug Control Module System Voltage:** The glow plug control module (GPCM) monitors the system supply voltage and sets this DTC when it detects an under voltage or over voltage condition.
DTC: P138D	**Turbocharger Boost Control A Temperature Too High:** The powertrain control module (PCM) continuously monitors the controller area network (CAN) for messages from the turbocharger actuator to set this DTC. The turbocharger actuator monitors the internal actuator temperature to determine if it is within a calibrated range. If the temperature is outside of the calibrated range a CAN message is sent to the PCM.
DTC: P1397	**System Voltage Out Of Self -Test Range:** This DTC indicates that the 12-volt system voltage is too high or too low during the Key On Engine Off (KOEO) or Key On Engine Running (KOER) self-test. It sets if the system voltage falls below or exceeds the calibrated threshold at any time during the KOEO or KOER self-test. **NOTE: Make sure the battery voltage is between 11 and 18 volts before running a KOEO or KOER self-test.**
DTC: P1405	**Differential Pressure Feedback (DPFE) Sensor Upstream Hose Off or Plugged:** While driving, the Exhaust Gas Recirculation (EGR) monitor commands the EGR valve closed and checks the differential pressure across the EGR orifice. The test fails when the signal from the differential pressure feedback EGR sensor indicates EGR flow is in the negative direction. **NOTE: Look for signs of water or icing in the hose. Verify the hose connection and routing (no excessive dips). Check the differential pressure feedback EGR sensor for correct mounting and function. View the DPFEGR PID while applying and releasing vacuum directly to the sensor with a hand pump.**
DTC: P1406	**Differential Pressure Feedback Sensor Downstream Hose Off or Plugged:** While driving, the exhaust gas recirculation (EGR) monitor commands the EGR valve closed and checks the differential pressure across the EGR orifice. The test fails when the signal from the differential pressure feedback EGR sensor continues to indicate EGR flow even after the EGR valve is commanded closed.
DTC: P1406	**Differential Pressure Feedback (DPFE) Sensor Downstream Hose Off Or Plugged:** Engine started; and the PCM detected the DPF EGR sensor signal indicated EGR flow existed with the EGR valve commanded closed.
DTC: P1408	**Exhaust Gas Recirculation (EGR) Flow Out of Self-Test Range (Non-MIL):** This test is carried out during the Key On Engine Running (KOER) on demand self-test only. The EGR system is commanded on at a fixed engine speed. The test does not pass and the DTC is set when the measured EGR flow falls above or below the required calibration. **NOTE: For EEGR, use the output state control function of the scan tool and monitor the Manifold Absolute Pressure (MAP) PID and the EEGR PID (EGRMDSD) while commanding the EEGR on. If EGR is introduced into the engine at idle, the RPM drops or stalls out. For vacuum systems see diagnostic aids for DTC P0401.**
DTC: P1409	**Exhaust Gas Recirculation (EGR) Vacuum Regulator Solenoid Circuit:** This test checks the electrical function of the EGR vacuum regulator solenoid. The test fails when the EVR circuit voltage is either too high or too low when compared to the expected voltage range. The EGR system must be enabled for the test to be completed.
DTC: P1409	**EGR Vacuum Regulator Solenoid Circuit Malfunction:** Engine started, and the PCM detected a fault in the EGR VR solenoid circuit (i.e., the VR circuit was too high or low when compared to its expected range with the solenoid enabled).
DTC: P1436	**A/C Evaporator Temperature (ACET) Circuit Low Input:** Key on or engine running; and the PCM detected the ACET signal was less than the self-test minimum amount of 0.13v in the self-test.
DTC: P1437	**A/C Evaporator Temperature (ACET) Circuit High Input:** Key on or engine running; Indicates the air conditioning evaporator temperature (ACET) signal input was less than the self-test minimum. The self-test minimum is 0.13 volt.
DTC: P1443	**Low Purge Flow Or No Purge Flow Condition Detected:** ECT sensor less than 90°Fat startup (cold engine), engine running at a steady cruise speed, and the PCM detected a fuel tank pressure change occurred of more than -7" H2O within 30 seconds with the purge flow less than 0.02 pounds per minute during testing.

DTC	Trouble Code Title & Conditions
DTC: P144A	**Evaporative Emission System Purge Vapor Line Restricted/Blocked:** The Powertrain Control Module (PCM) monitors the Evaporative Emission (EVAP) system for a blocked fuel vapor tube between the Fuel Tank Pressure (FTP) sensor and the fuel tank. During the initial phase of the EVAP monitor, the PCM closes the canister vent and a vacuum develops in the fuel vapor tubes and lines and in the fuel tank. The PCM monitors the FTP sensor to determine the amount of vacuum and how quickly the vacuum increases. The rate at which the vacuum increases is compared to an expected value. If the vacuum increases quicker than expected, a blocked fuel vapor tube is suspected and an intrusive test is carried out in the final phase of the EVAP monitor. If the intrusive test confirms a blockage a counter is incremented and once the counter reaches a calibrated number of completions, the DTC is. **NOTE: Check the fuel vapor tube for blockage between the fuel tank pressure FTP sensor and the fuel tank.**
DTC: P144C	**Evaporative Emission System Purge Check Valve Performance:** The powertrain control module (PCM) tests the EVAP canister purge check valve for a stuck open condition. The EVAP canister purge check valve test is performed during minimal boost conditions, once per drive cycle, when entry conditions are met. This DTC sets if the fuel tank pressure exceeds a calibrated amount within a specified amount of time during the test.
DTC: P1450	**Unable to Bleed Up Fuel Tank Vacuum:** Monitors the fuel vapor vacuum and pressure in the fuel tank. System failure occurs when the Evaporative Emission (EVAP) running loss monitor detects excessive fuel tank vacuum with the engine running, but not at idle. **NOTE: Visually inspect the EVAP canister inlet port, CV solenoid filter, and canister vent hose assembly for contamination or debris. Check EVAP canister purge valve for vacuum leak.**
DTC: P1450	**Unable to Bleed Up Fuel Tank Vacuum:** ECT sensor less than 90°F at startup (cold engine), engine running at a steady cruise speed, and the PCM detected a high fuel tank vacuum condition was present during the EVAP test.
DTC: P1451	**Evaporative Emission System Vent Control Circuit:** Monitors the EVAP canister vent solenoid circuit for an electrical failure. The test fails when the signal moves outside the minimum or maximum allowable calibrated parameters for a specified EVAP canister vent duty cycle by powertrain control module (PCM) command.
DTC: P1451	**Evaporative Emission System Vent Control Circuit:** Engine started, engine running at a steady cruise speed, canister vent solenoid enabled, and the PCM detected an unexpected voltage condition on the Canister Vent solenoid circuit. **NOTE: To verify normal functioning, monitor the Evaporative Emission (EVAP) CV solenoid signal PID EVAPCV and the signal voltage on the PCM control side. With the valve open, the EVAPCV PID indicates 0% duty cycle and a voltage approximately equal to battery voltage. When the valve is commanded fully closed, the EVAPCV PID indicates 100% duty cycle, and a minimum voltage drop of 4 volts is normal. Output Test Mode (OTM) may be used to switch the output on and off to verify function.**
DTC: P145B	**A/C Demand Not Activated During Self-Test:** The module senses no change from the pressure transducer when A/C is commanded on during the self-test. The PCM does not detect excessively high or low refrigerant pressure from the A/C pressure transducer. The PCM does not detect excessively high engine coolant temperature. The PCM does not detect an ambient air temperature below -1°C (30°F). The PCM has not detected a Wide Open Throttle (WOT) condition. The HVAC module does not detect an evaporator temperature below 2°C (36°F).
DTC: P145E	**PCV Heater Control B Circuit:** This DTC sets when the Powertrain Control Module (PCM) detects a Positive Crankcase Ventilation (PCV) heater circuit failure. **NOTE: Make sure the PCV valve is correct for the engine application and the PCV heater connector is correctly connected.**
DTC: P1460	**A/C clutch cycling pressure switch error:** A/C or defrost on condition may result from A/C clutch being on during OBD test. DTC set during OBD test, repeat with A/C off.Failed on, EPC pressure slightly low with A/C off.
DTC: P1460	**Wide Open Throttle A/C Cutout Relay Circuit Malfunction:** Key on, and the PCM detected a malfunction in the A/C Wide-Open Throttle (WOT) circuit during the test. **NOTE: If this code sets on vehicles without an A/C system, ignore this code.**
DTC: P1461	**A/C Pressure Sensor Circuit High Input:** Engine started, and the PCM detected the A/C Pressure sensor signal was over the test limit. **NOTE: Verify a VREF voltage between 4 and 6 volts.**
DTC: P1462	**Air Conditioning Pressure (A/CP) Sensor Low Voltage Detected:** Engine started, and the PCM detected the A/C Pressure sensor signal was under the test limit. **NOTE: Verify a VREF voltage between 4 and 6 volts.**
DTC: P1463	**A/C Pressure Sensor Insufficient Pressure Change:** Engine started, and with the A/C compressor operating, the PCM detected the A/C refrigerant pressure did not change as the compressor cycled during the self-test period.

DTC	Trouble Code Title & Conditions
DTC: P1464	**A/C Demand Out Of Self-Test Range:** This DTC is set when the powertrain control module (PCM) receives a request for A/C during the self-test.
DTC: P1464	**A/C Demand Out of Self-Test Range:** Key on, KOEO Self-Test enabled, or with the engine running, KOER Self-Test enabled, and the PCM detected the A/C demand switch signal was high during the self-test period.
DTC: P1469	**Low A/C Cycling Period:** Engine started, and with the A/C selected, PCM detected frequent cycling of the A/C compressor clutch. This test was designed to protect the transmission. In some strategies, the PCM will unlock the torque converter during A/C clutch engagement. If a concern is present that results in frequent A/C clutch cycling, damage could occur if the torque converter was cycled at these intervals. This test will detect this condition, set the code and prevent the torque converter from excessive cycling.
DTC: P1474	**Fan Control Primary Circuit:** Key on or engine running; Monitors the Low Fan Control (LFC) primary circuit output from the Powertrain Control Module (PCM). The test fails if the PCM grounds the LFC circuit. Excessive current draw is detected on the LFC circuit or with the LFC circuit not grounded by the PCM. Voltage is not detected on the LFC circuit (the PCM expects to detect VPWR voltage coming through the low speed FC relay coil to the LFC circuit).
DTC: P1474	**Fan Control Primary Circuit:** Monitors the low fan control (LFC) primary circuit output from the powertrain control module (PCM). The test fails if the PCM grounds the LFC circuit, excessive current draw is detected on the LFC circuit, or with the LFC circuit not grounded by the PCM, voltage is not detected on the LFC circuit (the PCM expects to detect VPWR voltage coming through the low speed FC relay coil to the LFC circuit).
DTC: P1477	**Additional Fan Relay Circuit:** Key on or engine running; Monitors the Medium Fan Control (MFC) primary circuit output from the Powertrain Control Module (PCM). The test fails if the MFC output commanded on (grounded), excessive current draw is detected on the MFC circuit or, with the MFC circuit commanded off, voltage is not detected on the MFC circuit (the PCM expects to detect IGN START/RUN voltage through the medium speed FC relay coil to the MFC circuit).
DTC: P1479	**High Fan Control Primary Circuit:** Monitors the high fan control (HFC) primary circuit output from the powertrain control module (PCM). The test fails if the HFC output commanded on (grounded), excessive current draw is detected on the HFC circuit or, with the HFC circuit commanded off, voltage is not detected on the HFC circuit (the PCM expects to detect VPWR voltage through the high speed FC relay coil to the HFC circuit).
DTC: P1479	**High Fan Control Primary Circuit Malfunction:** Key on, High Cooling Fan (HFC) enabled, and the PCM detected excessive current draw in the circuit; or with the HFC commanded off, it detected voltage present on the HFC circuit.
DTC: P1489	**PCV Heater Control Circuit:** This DTC sets when the powertrain control module (PCM) detects the actual PCVHC circuit voltage is less than or greater than the desired voltage.
DTC: P1489	**PCV Heater Control Circuit:** Key on or engine running; This DTC sets when the Powertrain Control Module (PCM) detects a Positive Crankcase Ventilation (PCV) heater circuit failure. **NOTE: Make sure the PCV valve is correct for the engine application and the PCV heater connector is correctly connected.**
DTC: P1500	**Vehicle Speed Sensor (VSS):** Indicates the VSS input signal was intermittent. This DTC sets when a VSS concern interferes with other on board diagnostics (OBD) tests, such as the catalyst efficiency monitor, the evaporative emission EVAP monitor or the heated oxygen sensor HO2S monitor.
DTC: P1500	**Vehicle Speed Sensor (VSS) Signal Intermittent:** Engine running in gear with a VSS signal present, and the PCM detected that the VSS signal was intermittent. **NOTE: Check the wiring, connector, and sensor for damage.**
DTC: P1501	**VSS Signal Out Of Self-Test Range:** Engine started, KOER Self-Test enabled, and the PCM detected a VSS signal during the self-test (i.e., with the vehicle not moving).
DTC: P1501	**Vehicle Speed Sensor Out Of Self-Test Range:** Indicates the vehicle speed sensor (VSS) input signal is out of self-test range. If the powertrain control module (PCM) detects a VSS input signal any time during the self-test, DTC P1501 is set and the test aborts. The anti-lock brake system (ABS) module provides the vehicle speed signal to the PCM.
DTC: P1502	**Vehicle Speed Sensor (VSS) Intermittent:** Indicates the powertrain control module (PCM) detected an error in the vehicle speed information. Vehicle speed data is received from either the VSS, transfer case speed sensor (TCSS) or anti-lock brake system (ABS) control module. This DTC sets the same way as P0500. However, it is intended to flash the transmission control indicator lamp (TCIL) for first time VSS circuit error.

DTC	Trouble Code Title & Conditions
DTC: P1502	**VSS Signal Intermittent:** Engine started, and the PCM detected an intermittent VSS signal. The TCIL will flash on the first trip that this code is set. The VSS signal is received from the VSS, transfer case speed sensor, ABS Control module, GEM or the Central Timer module (depends upon the vehicle).
DTC: P1502	**Invalid Test — Auxiliary Power Control Functioning:** The power take-off (PTO) system provides an input signal to the powertrain control module (PCM) indicating there is an additional load being applied to the engine. The PCM disables the on-board diagnostic (OBD) monitors and increases the engine RPM based on the PTO system or auxiliary idle control input. The following entry conditions are required to enable the PTO or auxiliary idle control: accelerator pedal released automatic transmission is in the PARK position brake pedal released engine at normal operating temperature parking brake applied
DTC: P1504	**Idle Air Control (IAC) Circuit Malfunction:** This DTC sets when the powertrain control module (PCM) detects an electrical load failure on the IAC output circuit.
DTC: P1506	**Idle Air Control (IAC) Overspeed Error:** This DTC sets when the powertrain control module (PCM) detects an engine idle speed that is greater than the desired RPM.
DTC: P1507	**Idle Air Control (IAC) Underspeed Error:** This DTC sets when the powertrain control module (PCM) detects an engine idle speed that is less than the desired RPM.
DTC: P1512	**Intake Manifold Runner Control (IMRC) Stuck Closed (Bank 1):** Key on or engine running; this DTC is set when the vacuum actuated IMRC is commanded open, but the IMRC monitor indicates closed. **NOTE: Monitor the IMRC and IMRCM PIDs. The IMRCM state should change when the IMRC is commanded open or closed.**
DTC: P1513	**Intake Manifold Runner Control (IMRC) Stuck Closed (Bank 2):** Key on or engine running; this DTC is set when the vacuum actuated IMRC is commanded open, but the IMRC monitor indicates closed. **NOTE: Monitor the IMRC and IMRCM PIDs. The IMRCM state should change when the IMRC is commanded open or closed.**
DTC: P1516	**Intake Manifold Runner Control Input Error (Bank 1):** Key on or engine running; and the PCM detected the IMRC Monitor signal for Bank 1 was outside of its expected calibrated range during the Continuous self test. **NOTE: Monitor the IMRC and IMRCM PIDs. The IMRCM state should change when the IMRC is commanded open or closed.**
DTC: P1517	**Intake Manifold Runner Control Input Error (Bank 2):** Key on or engine running; and the PCM detected the IMRC Monitor signal for Bank 2 was outside of its expected calibrated range during the Continuous self test. **NOTE: Monitor the IMRC and IMRCM PIDs. The IMRCM state should change when the IMRC is commanded open or closed.**
DTC: P1518	**Intake Manifold Runner Control (IMRC) Stuck Open (Bank 1):** Key on, and this DTC is set when the electrically actuated IMRC is commanded closed, but the IMRC monitor indicates open. **NOTE: Monitor the IMRC and IMRCM PIDs. The IMRCM state should change when the IMRC is commanded open or closed.**
DTC: P1519	**Intake Manifold Runner Control (IMRC) Stuck Closed (Bank 1):** Key on or engine running; and this DTC is set when the electrically actuated IMRC is commanded open, but the IMRC monitor indicates closed. **NOTE: Monitor the IMRC and IMRCM PIDs. The IMRCM state should change when the IMRC is commanded open or closed.**
DTC: P151A	**Intake Manifold Runner Controller Performance:** Key on or engine running; the Intake Manifold Runner Control (IMRC) system is monitored for failures. The test fails when the system detects a loss of bi-directional communication or signal(s) between the PCM and the IMRC solenoid. **NOTE: View the IMRCF PID to monitor for a fault.**
DTC: P1520	**Intake Manifold Runner Control (IMRC) Circuit:** Key on or engine running; this DTC indicates a failure in the IMRC primary control circuit. **NOTE: Monitor the IMRC and IMRCM PIDs. The IMRCM state should change when the IMRC is commanded open or closed.**
DTC: P1531	**Invalid Test - Accelerator Pedal Movement:** This DTC is set by the powertrain control module (PCM) when the PCM detects movement of the accelerator pedal during the key on engine running (KOER) self-test.
DTC: P1536	**Parking Brake Switch Circuit:** The parking brake applied switch provides an input signal to the powertrain control module (PCM) indicating the current status of the parking brake (applied or released). The parking brake signal circuit is pulled to ground with the application of the parking brake.
DTC: P1536	**Parking Brake Switch Circuit:** The parking brake applied switch provides an input signal to the powertrain control module (PCM) indicating the current status of the parking brake (applied or released). The parking brake signal circuit is pulled to ground with the parking brake applied.

DTC	Trouble Code Title & Conditions
DTC: P1537	**Intake Manifold Runner Control Stuck Open (Bank 1):** Key on or engine running; and the PCM detected the Bank 1 IMRC Monitor signal was more than its expected calibrated range at closed throttle (it may be stuck in open position). An IMRCM PID of VREF at 3000 rpm may indicate a fault is present. **NOTE: Monitor the IMRC and IMRCM PIDs. The IMRCM state should change when the IMRC is commanded open or closed.**
DTC: P1538	**Intake Manifold Runner Control Stuck Open (Bank 2):** Key on or engine running; and the PCM detected the Bank 2 IMRC Monitor signal was more than its expected calibrated range at closed throttle (it may be stuck in open position). An IMRCM PID of VREF at 3000 rpm may indicate a fault is present. **NOTE: Monitor the IMRC and IMRCM PIDs. The IMRCM state should change when the IMRC is commanded open or closed.**
DTC: P1548	**Engine Air Filter Restriction:** The powertrain control module (PCM) monitors the manifold absolute pressure at various engine speeds during wide open throttle (WOT) operation, and compares the information to a calibrated value. This DTC sets if the airflow is out of range.
DTC: P1548	**Engine Air Filter Restriction:** Key on or engine running and the PCM monitors the Manifold Absolute Pressure (MAP) at various engine speeds during Wide Open Throttle (WOT) operation, and compares the information to a calibrated value. If the air flow is out of range, the DTC is set. **NOTE: If this DTC is set, inspect the intake air system and replace the air filter if no obstructions are found.**
DTC: P1549	**Intake Manifold Communication Control (IMCC) Circuit (Bank 1):** KOER Self-Test enabled, and the IMCC or Intake Manifold Tuning Valve (IMTV) system is monitored for failure during continuous or Key On Engine Off (KOEO) self-test. The test fails when the Powertrain Control Module (PCM) detects a concern with the IMTV output circuit. **NOTE: An IMTV fault PID (IMTVF) displaying YES may indicate a fault.**
DTC: P1550	**Power Steering Pressure (PSP) Sensor Out of Self-Test Range:** The PSP sensor input signal to the powertrain control module (PCM) is continuously monitored. The test fails when the signal falls out of a maximum or minimum calibrated range.
DTC: P1551	**Cylinder 1 Injector Circuit Range/Performance:** The powertrain control module (PCM) monitors the output of the fuel injector circuits and sets a DTC when it detects the output is not within a calibrated limit.
DTC: P1551	**Cylinder 1 Injector Circuit Range/Performance:** The powertrain control module (PCM) monitors the charge and discharge voltage of the piezo actuator device during the fill stage, main injection and end of main injection stage. The DTC sets when the main injection and end of main injection stage voltages are out of calibrated range.
DTC: P1552	**Cylinder 2 Injector Circuit Range/Performance:** The powertrain control module (PCM) monitors the output of the fuel injector circuits and sets a DTC when it detects the output is not within a calibrated limit.
DTC: P1553	**Cylinder 3 Injector Circuit Range/Performance:** The powertrain control module (PCM) monitors the output of the fuel injector circuits and sets a DTC when it detects the output is not within a calibrated limit.
DTC: P1554	**Cylinder 4 Injector Circuit Range/Performance:** The powertrain control module (PCM) monitors the output of the fuel injector circuits and sets a DTC when it detects the output is not within a calibrated limit.
DTC: P1555	**Cylinder 5 Injector Circuit Range/Performance:** The powertrain control module (PCM) monitors the output of the fuel injector circuits and sets a DTC when it detects the output is not within a calibrated limit.
DTC: P1556	**Cylinder 6 Injector Circuit Range/Performance:** The powertrain control module (PCM) monitors the output of the fuel injector circuits and sets a DTC when it detects the output is not within a calibrated limit.
DTC: P1557	**Cylinder 7 Injector Circuit Range/Performance:** The powertrain control module (PCM) monitors the output of the fuel injector circuits and sets a DTC when it detects the output is not within a calibrated limit.
DTC: P1558	**Cylinder 8 Injector Circuit Range/Performance:** The powertrain control module (PCM) monitors the output of the fuel injector circuits and sets a DTC when it detects the output is not within a calibrated limit.
DTC: P1561	**Brake Line Pressure Sensor Circuit:** If a short to voltage or an open condition exists on any of the 3 circuits or if the transducer is indicating high pressure for more than 5 seconds while the Brake Pedal Position (BPP) switch (also known as the stoplamp switch) is indicating no brake application, DTC P1561 will be set.

DTC	Trouble Code Title & Conditions
DTC: P1572	**Brake Pedal Switch Circuit Malfunction:** KOER Self-Test enabled, the brake input rationality test for Brake Pedal Position (BPP) and Brake Pressure Switch (BPS) has detected a concern. One or both inputs to the Powertrain Control Module (PCM) did not change state when expected. On some vehicles with stability assist, the BPP switch is connected to the Anti lock Brake System (ABS) module and the ABS generates a driver brake application signal, which is then sent to the PCM. **NOTE: DTC P1572 sets when the PCM does not sense the correct sequence of the brake pedal input signal from both the BPP and BPS switches when the brake pedal is pressed and released.**
DTC: P1575	**Pedal Position Out Of Self Test Range:** During Key On Engine Off (KOEO) self-test, the Powertrain Control Module (PCM) monitors the Accelerator Pedal Position (APP) sensor inputs to determine if the APP1 and APP2 signals are less than an expected value. If either APP1 or APP2 is greater than the expected value, the DTC is set. **NOTE: Repeat the self-test without applying the accelerator pedal. Make sure the floor mat is not interfering with the accelerator pedal. Diagnose any APP circuit DTCs first.**
DTC: P1586	**Electronic Throttle to PCM Communication Error:** This DTC is set if there is no state change in the intake throttle control feedback circuit when the ignition is turned to the ON position. The intake throttle is cycled at ignition ON and the feedback signal should indicate a corresponding state change. If not, this DTC is set.
DTC: P1588	**Throttle Control Detected Loss Of Return Spring:** The powertrain control module (PCM) tests the electronic throttle for the ability of the throttle plate to return to the default (limp home) position from both the open and closed positions. This DTC sets if the throttle does not return to the default (limp home) position.
DTC: P160A	**Control Module Vehicle Options Reconfiguration Error:** Indicates a powertrain control module (PCM) vehicle reconfiguration error.
DTC: P160C	**Control Module Software Performance:** Indicates that the powertrain control module (PCM) internal central processing unit (CPU) has encountered an error. The PCM monitors itself and carries out internal checks of its own CPU. If any of these checks returns an incorrect value, this DTC sets.
DTC: P1610	**Interactive Reprogramming Code - Replace Module:** This DTC indicates an internal powertrain control module (PCM) error has been detected.
DTC: P1611	**Interactive Reprogramming Code — Diagnose Further:** This DTC indicates an internal powertrain control module (PCM) error has been detected.
DTC: P1615	**Interactive Reprogramming Code - Erase Error:** This DTC indicates an internal powertrain control module (PCM) error has been detected.
DTC: P1616	**Interactive Reprogramming Code - Erase Error, Low Voltage:** This DTC indicates an internal powertrain control module (PCM) error has been detected.
DTC: P1617	**Interactive Reprogramming Code - Block Program Error:** This DTC indicates an internal powertrain control module (PCM) error has been detected.
DTC: P1618	**Interactive Reprogramming Code - Block Program Error, Low Voltage:** This DTC indicates an internal powertrain control module (PCM) error has been detected.
DTC: P161A	**Incorrect Response from Immobilizer Control Module:** The BCM ID received by the PCM does not match the ID stored in the PCM memory. CARRY OUT a parameter reset. REFER to Passive Anti-Theft System (PATS) Parameter Reset. CLEAR the DTCs. REPEAT the self-test.
DTC: P162E	**Internal Control Module PTO Performance:** The DTC is set when the activation conditions of the power take off (PTO) are not met and the PTO is still being enabled by the PCM to run.
DTC: P1633	**Keep Alive Power (KAPWR) Voltage Too Low:** Key on, and the PCM detected that the KAPWR circuit has experienced a voltage interrupt. **NOTE: Loss of KAPWR to the Powertrain Control Module (PCM) results in immediate Malfunction Indicator Lamp (MIL) illumination and DTC P1633.**
DTC: P1635	**Tire Axle/Ratio Out Of Acceptable Range:** Key on, and the PCM detected the tire and axle information in the VID Block does not match the vehicle hardware. **NOTE: This code indicates that the PCM needs to be reprogrammed.**
DTC: P1636	**Inductive Signature Chip Communication Error:** Indicates the powertrain control module (PCM) has lost communication with the inductive signature chip.

DTC	Trouble Code Title & Conditions
DTC: P1639	**Vehicle ID Block Corrupted, Not Programmed:** This DTC indicates the vehicle identification (VID) block is not programmed or the information within is corrupt.
DTC: P163E	**TCM programming error:** The TCM has detected an invalid checksum.Default to 1st or 3rd gearMaximum line pressure
DTC: P163F	**Transmission ID block corrupted, not programmed:** The PCM has detected an invalid transmission identification.Default to 1st or 3rd gearMaximum line pressure
DTC: P1640	**Powertrain DTCs Available in Another Module:** Engine started, and the PCM received a request from another module to turn on the MIL due to a fault that could affect emissions. **NOTE: Vehicles using a secondary Engine Control Module can request that the PCM turn on the Check Engine Light when a failure occurs that could affect emissions. Request PID 0946 to determine which module made the request. Then select that module to read the related trouble code(s).**
DTC: P1640	**Powertrain DTCs Available in Another Module:** Vehicles using a secondary engine control module can request that the powertrain control module (PCM) illuminate the malfunction indicator lamp (MIL) when a failure occurs which affects emissions.
DTC: P1646	**Linear O2 Sensor Control Chip (Bank 1):** The powertrain control module (PCM) monitors the application-specific integrated circuit that controls and monitors the universal heated oxygen sensor (HO2S). The test fails when the PCM detects an internal circuit or communication concern.
DTC: P1646	**Linear O2 Sensor Control Chip (Bank 1):** The Powertrain Control Module (PCM) monitors the application-specific integrated circuit that controls and monitors the Heated Oxygen Sensor (HO2S). The test fails when the PCM detects an internal circuit or communication concern. **NOTE: Internal PCM concern.**
DTC: P1646	**Linear O2 Sensor Control Chip (Bank 1):** The powertrain control module (PCM) monitors the application-specific integrated circuit that controls and monitors the heated oxygen sensor (HO2S). The test fails when the PCM detects an internal circuit or communication concern.
DTC: P1647	**Linear O2 Sensor Control Chip (Bank 2):** The Powertrain Control Module (PCM) monitors the application-specific integrated circuit that controls and monitors the Heated Oxygen Sensor (HO2S). The test fails when the PCM detects an internal circuit or communication concern. **NOTE: Internal PCM concern.**
DTC: P164A	**O2 Sensor Positive Current Trim Circuit Performance (Bank 1 Sensor 1):** The nitrogen oxide (NOx) module monitors the NOx sensor O2 signal during an extended deceleration fuel shut off (DFSO) condition. This DTC sets when the actual O2 signal value does not match the expected O2 signal value.
DTC: P164A	**O2 Sensor Positive Current Trim Circuit Performance (Bank 1 Sensor 1):** A resistor is installed in the universal heated oxygen sensor (HO2S) connector for part to part variance. The powertrain control module (PCM) determines the value of this resistor by taking multiple measurements of the resistor during each key on event. The PCM uses this value in order to compensate for the variance in the pumping current signal. The test fails if the PCM receives an inconsistent or erratic measurement of the resistor.
DTC: P164B	**O2 Sensor Positive Current Trim Circuit Performance (Bank 2 Sensor 1):** A resistor is installed in the universal heated oxygen sensor (HO2S) connector for part to part variance. The powertrain control module (PCM) determines the value of this resistor by taking multiple measurements of the resistor during each key on event. The PCM uses this value in order to compensate for the variance in the pumping current signal. The test fails if the PCM receives an inconsistent or erratic measurement of the resistor.
DTC: P1650	**Power Steering Pressure (PSP) Switch Out of Self-Test Range:** Engine started, and the PCM detected the PSP switch signal did not change after a certain number of vehicle speed transitions. The PCM counts the number of times that the vehicle speed transitions from 0 mph to a calibrated speed. The PCM expects the PSP switch input to change after a certain number of transitions.
DTC: P1650	**Power Steering Pressure (PSP) Switch Out of Self-Test Range:** In the key on engine off (KOEO) self-test, this DTC indicates the PSP input to the powertrain control module (PCM) is high. In the key on engine running (KOER) self-test, this DTC indicates the PSP input did not change state.
DTC: P1651	**Power Steering Pressure (PSP) Switch Input:** Engine started, and the PCM detected the PSP switch signal did not change after a certain number of vehicle speed transitions. **NOTE: The PCM counts the number of times that the vehicle speed transitions from 0 mph to a calibrated speed. The PCM expects the PSP switch input to change after a certain number of transitions. Observe the PSP PID while checking the wires for intermittent concerns.**
DTC: P1674	**Control Module Software Corrupted:** Indicates an error occurred in the powertrain control module (PCM). This DTC sets in combination with P2105.

DTC	Trouble Code Title & Conditions
DTC: P1674	**Control Module Software Corrupted:** Engine started, and the PCM detected an error occurred in the Powertrain Control Module (PCM). This DTC is set in combination with P2105. **NOTE: Verify the PCM is at the latest calibration level.**
DTC: P167F	**Non-OEM Calibration Detected:** The powertrain control module (PCM) has detected an unauthorized calibration.
DTC: P1700	**Transmission indeterminate failure:** Internal component failure. Direct One-Way Clutch (OWC) failure. Failure Mode Effects Management becomes active — engine rpm limited to 4,000 rpm. Failed a neutral condition in 1st, 3rd or 4th gear in automatic Mode. Only 2nd and 5th gear available.
DTC: P1702	**Transmission Range Sensor Circuit Failure:** * Increased control pressure causes harsh shifts* Transmission defaults to Drive
DTC: P1702	**TR signal intermittent:** P0705, P0708 are set See P0705, P0708 conditions.
DTC: P1702	**Transmission Range Sensor Circuit:** * Possible no crank, only PARK, REVERSE, NEUTRAL and 5th gear available, harsh engagements.* Extremely delayed engagements (until a DTC is set).* After a DTC is set and the high side opened — harsh engagements, poor performance (due to a 5th gear drive away), no shifts.
DTC: P1703	**Brake Switch Circuit Out of Self-Test Range:** Key on, KOEO Self-Test enabled; and the PCM detected the brake switch signal was high, or with the KOER Self-Test enabled, the PCM detected the switch signal did not cycle On / Off. **NOTE: Check for correct function of the stoplamps. Using the scan tool, check the BPP PID. The stoplamps and PID should toggle on and off with brake pedal activation.**
DTC: P1704	**TR circuit reading in between gear position during KOEO and KOER:** TR sensor or selector lever cable incorrectly adjusted; or TR circuit failure. Wrong commanded EPC pressure. TR reading the wrong gear position.
DTC: P1704	**TR Sensor not in P or N positions during KOEO / KOER :** TR sensor or transmission selector lever cable incorrectly adjusted or TR circuit failure.
DTC: P1705	**Transmission Range Sensor Out of Self-Test Range:** Key on, KOEO Self Test enabled, and the PCM detected it did not receive a Transmission Range (TR) sensor signal in Park or Neutral position. **NOTE: Verify the gear selector is in PARK/NEUTRAL.**
DTC: P1705	**Transmission Range Circuit Not Indicating Park/Neutral During Self-Test:** The powertrain control module (PCM) checks the gear position when a KOER self-test is requested. The test fails when the gear indicated by the transmission range (TR) sensor is other than PARK.
DTC: P1707	**Park/Neutral (P/N) switch circuit failure:** Circuit or sensor failure high.Circuit or sensor failure low. Engine will not crank in P or N or engine will crank in all gears
DTC: P1709	**Park/Neutral Position (PNP) Switch Out of Self-Test Range:** This DTC indicates that the voltage is high when it should be low. Refer to Automatic Transmission/Transaxle Section.
DTC: P1709	**Park/Neutral Position (PNP) Switch Out of Self-Test Range:** Key on, KOEO Self-Test enabled, and the PCM detected the PNP switch was high when is should have been low (wrong gearshift position). **NOTE: When activating the PNP or CPP switch, the voltage should cycle from 5 volts to low.**
DTC: P1710	**TFT Sensor In-Range Circuit Malfunction:** Engine started, vehicle driven to a speed over 1 mph, TFT sensor signal in-range, and the PCM did not detect any change in the TFT signal in the self-test.
DTC: P1711	**TFT Sensor Out of Self-Test Range:** Key on, KOER Self Test enabled; or engine running with the KOER Self Test enabled, and the PCM detected the Transmission Fluid Temperature (TFT) sensor was more than or less than the calibrated range (25°F to 240°F) during the self-test.
DTC: P1712	**TFT Sensor Circuit Low Input:** Engine started, and the PCM detected the TFT sensor signal was less than 0.2v (equivalent to a temperature of more than 357°F).
DTC: P1713	**TFT Sensor No Activity or TFT Sensor Circuit Low Input:** Engine started, VSS over 1 mph, and the PCM did not detect any change in the TFT low range circuit during the self-test.
DTC: P1714	**Transmission Control System Malfunction:** Engine started, VSS over 1 mph, and the PCM did not detect any change in the TFT low range circuit during the self-test.

DTC	Trouble Code Title & Conditions
DTC: P1715	**Transmission Control System Malfunction:** Engine started, VSS over 1 mph, and the PCM detected a mechanical problem in the Shift Solenoid 'B' (SSB) during the test.
DTC: P1716	**Transmission Control System Malfunction:** Engine started, VSS over 1 mph, and the PCM detected a problem in the Transmission Control system during the self-test.
DTC: P1717	**Transmission Control System Malfunction:** Engine started, VSS over 1 mph, and the PCM detected a problem in the Transmission Control system during the self-test.
DTC: P1718	**TFT Sensor No Activity Or TFT Sensor Circuit High Input:** Engine started, VSS over 1 mph, and the PCM did not detect any change in the TFT high range circuit during the self-test.
DTC: P1719	**Transmission Control System Malfunction:** Engine started, VSS over 1 mph, and the PCM detected a problem in the Transmission Control system during the self-test.
DTC: P1725	**Insufficient Engine Speed Increase During Self-Test:** The powertrain control module (PCM) monitors the engine speed during the key ON engine running (KOER) self-test. When the PCM detects engine speed lower than a calibrated speed, the KOER self-test is aborted and the DTC is set.
DTC: P1726	**Insufficient Engine Speed Decrease During Self Test:** The powertrain control module (PCM) monitors the engine speed during the key on engine running (KOER) self-test. When the PCM detects engine speed higher than a calibrated speed, the KOER self-test is aborted and this DTC sets.
DTC: P1727	**Transmission Coast Clutch Solenoid Slip Malfunction:** Engine started, VSS over 1 mph in gear, and the PCM detected a signal that indicated the coast clutch solenoid had a slippage fault.
DTC: P1728	**Transmission Slip Malfunction:** Engine started, VSS over 1 mph in gear, and the PCM detected a signal that indicated the transmission was slipping while in gear.
DTC: P1729	**4x4L Switch:** The 4x4L switch is an on/off switch. If the powertrain control module (PCM) does not sense appropriate voltage when the switch is cycled on and off, a DTC sets for mechanical shift on the fly (MSOF) systems.
DTC: P1740	**Torque Converter Clutch (TCC) Solenoid Mechanical Malfunction:** Engine started, vehicle speed more than 20 mph, and the PCM detected that TCC lockup did not occur (the lockup event is inferred from other inputs).
DTC: P1741	**Torque Converter Clutch (TCC) Engagement Error:** Engine started, vehicle in gear at Cruise speed, and the PCM detected an error due to excessive TCC engagement. **NOTE: This problem can cause speed changes or vehicle surges.**
DTC: P1742	**Torque Converter Clutch (TCC) Solenoid Failed On (Electrical Or Mechanical Fault):** Engine started, vehicle in gear at Cruise speed, and the PCM detected that the Torque Converter Clutch system had failed "on".
DTC: P1744	**TCC solenoid circuit:** The PCM has detected that the TCC solenoid is stuck ON or OFF.TCIL flashing Wrench light illuminated DTC P0741 and/or P2758 may set
DTC: P1744	**Torque Converter Clutch (TCC) System Mechanically Stuck In Off Position:** Engine started, vehicle in gear at Cruise speed, and the PCM detected the Torque Converter Clutch system had failed with the TCC in the mechanically "off" position.
DTC: P1746	**EPC solenoid open circuit:** Voltage through EPC solenoid is checked. An error will be noted if tolerance is exceeded. Open circuit causes maximum EPC pressure, harsh engagements and shifts.
DTC: P1747	**EPC solenoid circuit failure, shorted circuit or output driver:** Voltage through EPC solenoid is checked. An error will be noted if tolerance is exceeded. Short circuit causes minimum EPC pressure (minimum capacity) and limits engine torque (alternate firm).
DTC: P174E	**Output Shaft Speed / ABS Wheel Speed Correlation:** This DTC detects a fault when the anti-lock brake system (ABS) module and the transmission control module (TCM) have different vehicle speed sensor (VSS) values.
DTC: P1760	**EPC solenoid circuit failure, shorted circuit or output driver:** PCM detected a loss of EPC during operation. Unexpected reduction in engine torque.
DTC: P1780	**Transmission Control Switch (TCS) Out of Self-Test Range:** During key on engine running (KOER) self-test the TCS must be cycled, or a DTC is set.

DTC	Trouble Code Title & Conditions
DTC: P1780	**Transmission Control Switch Out of Self-Test Range:** Engine started, KOER Self-Test enabled, and the PCM detected the Transmission Control Switch (TCS) was out of range during the test. **NOTE: Verify the TCS switch cycles on/off.**
DTC: P1781	**4x4L Switch Out of Self-Test Range:** The 4x4L switch is an on/off switch. If the powertrain control module (PCM) does not sense low voltage when the switch is on, the DTC sets.
DTC: P1781	**4x4 Low Switch Out Of Self-Test Range:** Key on, KOEO Self-Test enabled, and the PCM detected the 4x4 switch input was not low with the switch engaged or "on". **NOTE: Verify the 4x4L switch cycles on/off.**
DTC: P1783	**Transmission Over-Temperature Malfunction:** Engine started, engine runtime more than 5 minutes, vehicle in gear at Cruise speed, and the PCM detected the TFT sensor signal was more than 300°F during the CCM test period.
DTC: P1784	**Transmission System First Or Reverse Gear Malfunction:** Engine started, vehicle speed over 1 mph in gear, shift command received for First or Reverse gear, and the PCM detected a problem in the Transmission Control system.
DTC: P1785	**Transmission System First Or Second Gear Malfunction:** Engine started, vehicle speed over 1 mph in gear, shift command received for First or Second gear, and the PCM detected a problem in the Transmission Control system during the test.
DTC: P1786	**Transmission System Second Or Third Gear Malfunction:** Engine started, vehicle speed over 1 mph in gear, shift command received for Second or Third gear, and the PCM detected a problem in the Transmission Control system.
DTC: P1787	**Transmission System Third Or Fourth Gear Malfunction:** Engine started, vehicle speed over 1 mph in gear, shift command received for Third or Fourth gear, and the PCM detected a problem in the Transmission Control system during the test.
DTC: P1788	**3-2 Timing/Coast Clutch Solenoid Signal High Input:** Engine started, vehicle in gear at Cruise speed, and the PCM detected the malfunction 3-2 Timing or Coast Clutch solenoid circuit.
DTC: P1789	**3-2 Timing/Coast Clutch Solenoid Signal Low Input:** Engine started, vehicle in gear at Cruise speed, and the PCM detected the malfunction 3-2 Timing or Coast Clutch solenoid circuit.
DTC: P1793	**Ignition Supply Malfunction:** The powertrain control module (PCM) monitors the ignition switch position run (ISP-R) circuit. This DTC sets if the voltage drops below 7 volts or rises above 16 volts.
DTC: P179A	**Controller Area Network (CAN) Engine Control Module (ECM)/Turbocharger Boost Control A Actuator Circuit Malfunction:** The powertrain control module (PCM) continuously monitors the controller area network (CAN) for messages from the turbocharger actuator. This DTC sets when the PCM fails to receive the turbocharger actuator message within the defined amount of time.
DTC: P181F	**Clutch Control System Performance:** AWD operation may be limited
DTC: P1824	**4 Wheel Drive (4WD) Clutch Relay Circuit Failure:** The 4X4 control module detects a short to ground on the Active Torque Coupling (ATC) solenoid feedback circuit
DTC: P1825	**4 Wheel Drive (4WD) Clutch Relay Open Circuit:** The 4X4 control module detects an open or short to ground on the ATC solenoid command or feedback circuit for more than 2 seconds
DTC: P187B	**Tire/Axle Out of Acceptable Range:** -The PCM detects an inappropriate size mini spare or road wheels/tires (greater than 7% difference in size across the front and rear axle or greater than 14% difference in size at one wheel on either the front or rear axle) installed.-AWD Disabled or-AWD Limited Functionality
DTC: P188B	**All Wheel Drive (AWD) Clutch Control Circuit:** When the AWD relay module detects an open, a short to power or ground on the ATC solenoid voltage supply and or return circuit, this DTC is set and the AWD relay module shuts off current to the ATC solenoid.
DTC: P188C	**All Wheel Drive (AWD) Relay Module Communication Circuit:** The PCM detects an open, a short to ground or voltage on the command circuit.AWD operation may be disabled.

DTC	Trouble Code Title & Conditions
DTC: P188D	**All Wheel Drive (AWD) Relay Module Feedback Circuit:** - The PCM detects an open, a short to ground or voltage on the feedback circuit- The AWD relay module may not allow All-Wheel Drive (AWD) operation.
DTC: P1900	**Output Shaft Speed (OSS) Sensor Circuit Intermittent:** The OSS sensor signal to the Powertrain Control Module (PCM) is irregular or interrupted. **NOTE: Verify harness and connector integrity. Verify correct installation of the OSS sensor**
DTC: P1901	**Turbine Shaft Speed (TSS) Sensor Circuit Intermittent:** The TSS sensor signal to the Powertrain Control Module (PCM) is irregular or interrupted. **NOTE: Verify harness and connector integrity. Verify correct installation of the OSS sensor.**
DTC: P1910	**Reverse lamp control circuit/open:** The TR sensor sends a signal to the PCM when reverse is selected. The PCM then controls an output which energizes the reverse lamp relay. Reverse lamps do not function properly
DTC: P1910	**Reverse Lamp Control Circuit/Open:** Engine started, vehicle in reverse, and the PCM detected no backup lamps. Backup lamp driver control circuit failed.
DTC: P1911	**Reverse lamp circuit:** Reverse lamp control circuit shorted to ground. Circuit low Circuit or sensor failure.
DTC: P1912	**Reverse lamp control circuit shorted to power:** Circuit high Circuit or sensor failure. Park lock or interlock switched OFF
DTC: P1921	**Transmission Range Signal:** The transaxle control module (TCM) continuously monitors the controller area network (CAN) for a transmission range message from the powertrain control module (PCM). This DTC sets when the received message does not match the actual transmission range.
DTC: P1921	**TR signal:** The PCM has detected a TR signal duty cycle out of range. Engine will not crankDTC P1705, DTC P0706, DTC P0707, DTC P0708 or DTC P0709 may set
DTC: P1A03	**Drive Motor A Shutdown Circuit:** The transaxle control module (TCM) continuously monitors the motor shutdown (MSDN) circuit and the controller area network (CAN) signal for a MSDN request from the powertrain control module (PCM). This DTC sets when the PCM requests traction motor shutdown through the CAN signal or if there is an MSDN circuit concern. The traction motor inverter will be disabled.
DTC: P1A04	**Generator Shutdown Circuit:** The transaxle control module (TCM) continuously monitors the generator shutdown (GSDN) circuit and the controller area network (CAN) signal for a GSDN request from the powertrain control module (PCM). This DTC sets when the PCM requests generator shutdown through the CAN signal or if there is a GSDN circuit concern. The generator inverter will be disabled.
DTC: P1A05	**Desired Engine Speed Signal:** The transaxle control module (TCM) continuously monitors the controller area network (CAN) for a desired engine speed message from the powertrain control module (PCM). This DTC is set when the desired engine speed is not within the expected range.
DTC: P1A06	**Vehicle Mode Signal:** The transaxle control module (TCM) continuously monitors the controller area network (CAN) for a vehicle mode message from the powertrain control module (PCM). This DTC sets when the received message does not match the actual vehicle mode.
DTC: P1A07	**Inverter High Voltage Performance:** The transaxle control module (TCM) continuously monitors voltage at the motor and the generator inverters. It also checks the controller area network (CAN) communication bus for a voltage message from the traction battery control module (TBCM). This DTC indicates the measured voltage does not match the voltage received in the CAN message or is outside calibrated limits.
DTC: P1A08	**Generator Mode Signal:** The transaxle control module (TCM) continuously monitors the controller area network (CAN) communication bus for a generator mode message from the powertrain control module (PCM). This DTC sets when the received message does not match the actual generator mode.
DTC: P1A0A	**Immediate Shutdown Signal:** The transaxle control module (TCM) monitors two redundant immediate shutdown (ISDN) inputs from the traction battery control module (TBCM). When the TCM detects one or both inputs out of the expected range this DTC sets.
DTC: P1A0C	**Hybrid Powertrain Control Module - Engine Disabled:** This is an informational DTC and is set as the result of a limited operating strategy (LOS) or a failure mode effects management (FMEM) operating strategy that maintains limited vehicle function in the event of an engine start or stall concern.

DTC	Trouble Code Title & Conditions
DTC: P1A0D	**Hybrid Powertrain Control Module - Generator Disabled:** This is an informational DTC and is set as the result of a limited operating strategy (LOS) or a failure mode effects management (FMEM) operating strategy that maintains limited vehicle function in the event of an engine start or stall concern.
DTC: P1A0E	**Hybrid Powertrain Control Module - Motor Disabled:** This is an informational DTC and is set as the result of a limited operating strategy (LOS) or a failure mode effects management (FMEM) operating strategy that maintains limited vehicle function in the event of an engine start or stall concern.
DTC: P1A10	**Hybrid Powertrain Control Module - Battery Disabled:** This is an informational DTC and it can be set as a result of the vehicle operating with the engine disabled, the vehicle operating in neutral for an extended period of time, or the vehicle operating with a traction battery concern.
DTC: P1A13	**Hybrid Powertrain Control Module - Regenerative Braking Disabled:** This is an informational DTC and is set as a result of the torque monitor disabling the regenerative braking. This does not shutdown the vehicle but causes the fuel economy of the vehicle to decrease due to loss of regenerative braking.
DTC: P1A14	**Hybrid Powertrain Control Module - Transmission Disabled:** This is an informational DTC and is set as the result of a limited operating strategy (LOS) or a failure mode effects management (FMEM) operating strategy that maintains limited vehicle function in the event of an engine start or stall concern.
DTC: P1A1B	**Brake System Control Module - Forced Engine Running:** This DTC indicates the antilock braking system (ABS) module requested the engine on.

OBD II Trouble Code List (P2xxx Codes)

DTC	Trouble Code Title & Conditions
DTC: P2002	**Diesel Particulate Filter Efficiency Below Threshold (Bank 1):** The powertrain control module (PCM) monitors the efficiency of the diesel particulate filter for a concern. The efficiency of the filter is determined by the amount of restriction in the filter for a certain exhaust flow rate. The diesel particulate filter is preconditioned for 5,000 km (3,107 miles) before the PCM begins to monitor the level of restriction. The test fails when the measured level of restriction is less than the expected level calculated by the PCM.
DTC: P2004	**Intake Manifold Runner Control (IMRC) Stuck Open (Bank 1):** This DTC is set when the IMRC is commanded closed, but the IMRC monitor indicates open. **NOTE: Monitor the IMRC and IMRCM PIDs. The IMRCM state should change when the IMRC is commanded open or closed**
DTC: P2005	**Intake Manifold Runner Control (IMRC) Stuck Open (Bank 2):** This DTC is set when the IMRC is commanded closed, but the IMRC monitor indicates open. **NOTE: An IMRCM PID reading near approximately 1 volt at closed throttle may indicate a fault**
DTC: P2006	**Intake Manifold Runner Control (IMRC) Stuck Closed (Bank 1):** This DTC is set when the IMRC is commanded open, but the IMRC monitor indicates closed. **NOTE: Monitor the IMRC and IMRCM PIDs. The IMRCM state should change when the IMRC is commanded open or closed.**
DTC: P2007	**Intake Manifold Runner Control (IMRC) Stuck Closed (Bank 2):** Engine started, engine running the PCM detected the IMRC is commanded open, but the IMRC monitor indicates closed.
DTC: P2007	**Intake Manifold Runner Control (IMRC) Stuck Closed (Bank 2):** This DTC sets when the IMRC is commanded open, but the IMRC monitor indicates closed.
DTC: P2008	**Intake Manifold Runner Control (IMRC) Circuit Open (Bank 1):** Engine started, engine running the PCM detected a failure in the IMRC primary control circuit. **NOTE: Monitor the IMRC and IMRCM PIDs. The IMRCM state should change when the IMRC is commanded open or closed.**
DTC: P2008	**Intake Manifold Runner Control (IMRC) Circuit Open (Bank 1):** This DTC indicates a failure in the IMRC primary control circuit.
DTC: P200C	**Diesel Particulate Filter Over Temperature Bank 1:** The powertrain control module (PCM) monitors the diesel particulate filter temperature using compared EGT sensor values. This DTC sets if the diesel particulate filter temperature exceeds an expected threshold, if the temperature increase across any one catalyst exceeds 500°C (932°F), or if any EGT sensor downstream of the diesel particulate filter is disconnected.
DTC: P200E	**Catalyst System Over Temperature (Bank 1):** The powertrain control module (PCM) monitors the exhaust gas temperature bank 1, sensor 2 (EGT12) and exhaust gas temperature bank 1, sensor 3 (EGT13) sensors for an over temperature concern. If the EGT12 sensor temperature is greater than 830°C (1,526°F) or the EGT13 sensor temperature is greater than 950°C (1,742°F), the DTC is set. This DTC causes the PCM to immediately illuminate the malfunction indicator lamp (MIL) and enter a torque reduction failure mode effects management (FMEM), which may result in engine shutdown. Once the engine is shut down, the PCM prevents the engine from restarting for 1 hour. If the EGT13 sensor is not working, the engine will not start.

DTC	Trouble Code Title & Conditions
DTC: P2014	**Intake Manifold Runner Position Sensor/Switch Circuit (Bank 1):** The Intake Manifold Runner Control (IMRC) system is monitored for failure during continuous or Key On Engine Off (KOEO) self-test. Each DTC distinguishes the corresponding bank for IMRC actuator assemblies with dual monitor switches. The test fails when the signal on the monitor pin is outside an expected calibrated range. **NOTE: Monitor the IMRC and IMRCM PIDs. The IMRCM state should change when the IMRC is commanded open or closed.**
DTC: P2015	**Intake Manifold Runner Position Sensor/Switch Circuit Range/Performance (Bank 1):** The intake manifold runner control (IMRC) system is monitored for failures. Each DTC distinguishes the corresponding bank. The test fails when the system detects the presence of a broken or persistently out of range linkage.
DTC: P2019	**Intake Manifold Runner Position Sensor/Switch Circuit (Bank 2):** The Intake Manifold Runner Control (IMRC) system is monitored for failure during continuous or Key On Engine Off (KOEO) self-test. Each DTC distinguishes the corresponding bank for IMRC actuator assemblies with dual monitor switches. The test fails when the signal on the monitor pin is outside an expected calibrated range. **NOTE: Monitor the IMRC and IMRCM PIDs. The IMRCM state should change when the IMRC is commanded open or closed.**
DTC: P2020	**Intake Manifold Runner Position Sensor/Switch Circuit Range/Performance (Bank 2):** The intake manifold runner control (IMRC) system is monitored for failures. Each DTC distinguishes the corresponding bank. The test fails when the system detects the presence of a broken or persistently out of range linkage.
DTC: P2025	**Evaporative Emissions Fuel Vapor Temperature Sensor Circuit Performance:** The powertrain control module (PCM) monitors the natural vacuum leak detection (NVLD) module input for expected NVLD ambient temperature sensor values. This DTC sets when the input is outside a calibrated set of limits.
DTC: P2026	**Evaporative Emissions Fuel Vapor Temperature Sensor Circuit Low Voltage:** The powertrain control module (PCM) monitors the natural vacuum leak detection (NVLD) module input for expected NVLD ambient temperature sensor values. This DTC sets when the input is outside a calibrated set of limits.
DTC: P2027	**Evaporative Emissions Fuel Vapor Temperature Sensor Circuit High Voltage:** The powertrain control module (PCM) monitors the natural vacuum leak detection (NVLD) module input for expected NVLD ambient temperature sensor values. This DTC sets when the input is outside a calibrated set of limits.
DTC: P202D	**Reductant Leakage:** The PCM monitors the reductant pump motor when the selective catalytic reduction (SCR) system is active but the reductant injector is closed. If the PCM must output a duty cycle greater than 50% to the reductant pump motor to maintain system pressure, a leak is suspect and this DTC sets.
DTC: P2031	**Exhaust Gas Temperature Sensor Circuit Bank 1 Sensor 2:** The powertrain control module (PCM) monitors the operation of the exhaust gas temperature (EGT) sensor to determine if the EGT sensor responds to the increase in temperature of the exhaust gas, during vehicle operation. The PCM then compares the measured temperature to a modeled value. The test fails when after 5 minutes of driving, following a 6 hour soak, the EGT sensor temperature does not correlate to the modeled temperature of 150°C (302°F).
DTC: P2031	**Exhaust Gas Temperature Sensor Circuit Bank 1 Sensor 2:** The powertrain control module (PCM) monitors the operation of the exhaust gas temperature (EGT) sensor to determine if the EGT sensor responds to the increase in temperature of the exhaust gas, during vehicle operation. The test fails when after 10 minutes of driving, following an 8-hour soak, the EGT sensor does not indicate a temperature increase of 30°C (54°F).
DTC: P2032	**Exhaust Gas Temperature Sensor Circuit Low Bank 1 Sensor 2:** The powertrain control module (PCM) monitors the exhaust gas temperature (EGT) sensor for a low voltage concern. The test fails when the sensor voltage is less than 0.10 volt for greater than 15 seconds. Some updated vehicles may use 0.20 volt instead of 0.10 volt.
DTC: P2033	**Exhaust Gas Temperature Sensor Circuit High Bank 1 Sensor 2:** The powertrain control module (PCM) monitors the exhaust gas temperature (EGT) sensor for a high voltage concern. The test fails when the sensor voltage is greater than 4.75 volts for greater than 15 seconds. Some updated vehicles may use 2.50 volts instead of 4.75 volts.
DTC: P203A	**Reductant Level Sensor A Circuit:** The powertrain control module (PCM) continuously monitors the reductant level sensor voltage. This DTC sets when an open circuit condition is detected.
DTC: P203B	**Reductant Level Sensor Circuit Range/Performance:** The powertrain control module (PCM) monitors the RDL1, RDL2, and RDL3 circuits. This DTC sets if the PCM detects an irrational reading, such as RDL1 (top pin) indicating a full tank while RDL3 (bottom pin) is indicating an empty tank.
DTC: P203C	**Reductant Level Sensor Circuit Low:** The powertrain control module (PCM) monitors the reductant level sensor circuits to the PCM for high and low voltage. The test fails if the voltage exceeds or falls below a calibrated limit for a calibrated amount of time.

DTC	Trouble Code Title & Conditions
DTC: P203D	**Reductant Level Sensor Circuit High:** The powertrain control module (PCM) monitors the reductant level sensor circuits to the PCM for high and low voltage. The test fails if the voltage exceeds or falls below a calibrated limit for a calibrated amount of time.
DTC: P203F	**Reductant Level Too Low:** The powertrain control module (PCM) monitors the reductant level sensor for refill events. When the reductant level reaches a minimum amount, the PCM limits vehicle speed to 89 km/h (55 mph) and sets this DTC.
DTC: P2043	**Reductant Temperature Sensor Circuit Range/Performance:** The powertrain control module (PCM) completes a plausibility check on the reductant temperature sensor after a 6-hour cold soak by comparing the reductant temperature (RDT) signal to the ambient air temperature (AAT) and engine coolant temperature (ECT) signals on startup. This DTC sets if the RDT deviates more than 20°C (68°F) from the AAT and ECT.
DTC: P2047	**Reductant Injection Valve Circuit/Open Bank 1 Unit 1:** The powertrain control module (PCM) monitors the reductant injector circuits to the PCM for high and low voltage. The test fails if the voltage exceeds or falls below a calibrated limit for a calibrated amount of time.
DTC: P2048	**Reductant Injection Valve Circuit Low (Bank 1 Unit 1):** The powertrain control module (PCM) monitors the reductant injector circuits to the PCM for high and low voltage. The test fails if the voltage exceeds or falls below a calibrated limit for a calibrated amount of time.
DTC: P2049	**Reductant Injection Valve Circuit High (Bank 1 Unit 1):** The powertrain control module (PCM) monitors the reductant injector circuits to the PCM for high and low voltage. The test fails if the voltage exceeds or falls below a calibrated limit for a calibrated amount of time.
DTC: P204B	**Reductant Pressure Sensor Circuit Range/Performance:** The powertrain control module (PCM) completes a plausibility check on the reductant pressure sensor during startup after a successful purge cycle, when the reductant pressure line has been drained. This DTC sets if the reductant pressure sensor signal exceeds 30 kPa (4.4 psi).
DTC: P204C	**Reductant Pressure Sensor Circuit Low:** The powertrain control module (PCM) monitors the reductant pressure sensor circuits to the PCM for high and low voltage. The test fails if the voltage exceeds or falls below a calibrated limit for a calibrated amount of time.
DTC: P204D	**Reductant Pressure Sensor Circuit High:** The powertrain control module (PCM) monitors the reductant pressure sensor circuits to the PCM for high and low voltage. The test fails if the voltage exceeds or falls below a calibrated limit for a calibrated amount of time.
DTC: P204F	**Reductant System Performance (Bank 1):** The powertrain control module (PCM) monitors selective catalytic reduction (SCR) system performance by monitoring the rate of reductant flow and feedback from the nitrogen oxide (NOx) sensor. These values are compared to a calculated model. When the difference between the modeled and actual system performance exceeds a threshold, a restriction in the SCR system is suspect and this DTC sets.
DTC: P205C	**Reductant Tank Temperature Sensor Circuit Low:** The powertrain control module (PCM) monitors the reductant temperature sensor circuits to the PCM for high and low voltage. The test fails if the voltage exceeds or falls below a calibrated limit for a calibrated amount of time.
DTC: P205D	**Reductant Tank Temperature Sensor Circuit High:** The powertrain control module (PCM) monitors the reductant temperature sensor circuits to the PCM for high and low voltage. The test fails if the voltage exceeds or falls below a calibrated limit for a calibrated amount of time.
DTC: P2065	**Fuel Level Sensor B Circuit:** Fuel level information is sent to the powertrain control module (PCM) on the communication link.
DTC: P2066	**Fuel Level Sensor B Circuit Range/Performance:** Fuel level information is sent to the powertrain control module (PCM) on the communication link.
DTC: P2067	**Fuel Level Sensor B Circuit Low Input:** Fuel level information is sent to the powertrain control module (PCM) on the communication link.
DTC: P2068	**Fuel Level Sensor B Circuit High:** Fuel level information is sent to the Powertrain Control Module (PCM) on the communication link.
DTC: P2070	**Intake Manifold Tuning Valve (IMTV) Stuck Open (Bank 1):** The IMTV system is monitored for failure during continuous, Key On Engine Off (KOEO), or Key On Engine Running (KOER) self-tests. The test fails when the signal is more or less than an expected calibrated range. **NOTE: An IMTVM PID reading may indicate a fault.**

DTC	Trouble Code Title & Conditions
DTC: P2071	**Intake Manifold Tuning Valve (IMTV) Stuck Closed Bank 1:** The IMTV system is monitored for failure during continuous, Key On Engine Off (KOEO), or Key On Engine Running (KOER) self-tests. The test fails when the signal is more or less than an expected calibrated range. **NOTE: An IMTVM PID reading may indicate a fault.**
DTC: P2072	**Throttle Actuator Control (TAC) System (Ice Breakage):** This DTC only identifies that the strategy has carried out several open and close cycles to remove potential ice buildup. This DTC does not imply any system concerns, only that the mode has occurred, and that mode may be causing a long start time. **NOTE: Do not install a new Electronic Throttle Body (ETB) for this DTC. Check the PCV system for evidence of water or ice. Disconnect the intake air fresh air plenum from the throttle body. Check for water or oily residue at the PCV fresh air port. Disconnect the tube at the valve cover and check the tube for ice obstruction/ice. Start the engine and, to check the PCV system, place a piece of cardboard on the crankcase vent in the rocker cover. If the cardboard is held on the crankcase vent and fumes are not exiting, reconnect the tube to the valve cover and the intake air port. If the test passes, the PCV system is OK. If the cardboard is not held in place, turn off the engine and check the PCV valve side of the system for ice or obstruction and repair as necessary. If no obstruction is found there, isolate and repair any obstruction in the intake manifold connection. If no obstruction is found there, make sure the PCV coolant heater is functional and repair as necessary. If no concern is present, make sure the PCV valve is allowing the correct vacuum flow and repair as necessary.**
DTC: P2073	**Manifold Absolute Pressure/Mass Air Flow - Throttle Position Correlation at Idle:** The powertrain control module (PCM) continuously monitors the intake air system for concerns. If the PCM detects that the final air mass adaption stored value at idle is more than 15% above or below the calibrated threshold, this DTC sets.
DTC: P2074	**Manifold Absolute Pressure/Mass Air Flow - Throttle Position Correlation at Higher Load:** The powertrain control module (PCM) continuously monitors the intake air system for concerns. If the PCM detects that the final air mass adaption stored value at higher load is more than 15% above or below the calibrated threshold, this DTC sets.
DTC: P207F	**Reductant Quality Performance:** The powertrain control module (PCM) monitors selective catalytic reduction (SCR) system performance using the nitrogen oxide (NOx) sensor, in addition to other inputs. This DTC sets when overall NOx conversion drops suddenly.
DTC: P2080	**Exhaust Gas Temperature Sensor Circuit Range/Performance Bank 1 Sensor 1:** The powertrain control module (PCM) monitors the exhaust gas temperature (EGT) sensor for a biased signal value. Following an 8-hour soak, the PCM records the EGT sensor temperature value at key ON, engine OFF. After several minutes of vehicle operation at vehicle speeds greater than 40.2 km/h (25 mph) the PCM calculates an expected key ON, engine OFF value. The PCM determines what the expected EGT value at key ON, engine OFF should have been based on inputs from other sensors. The test fails when the difference between the expected calculated value and the actual recorded value is greater than 40°C (72°F).
DTC: P2081	**Exhaust Gas Temperature Sensor Circuit Intermittent Bank 1 Sensor 1:** The powertrain control module (PCM) monitors the exhaust gas temperature (EGT) sensor for an intermittent concern. The test fails when the sensor voltage fluctuates by greater than 0.25 volt for 20 seconds.
DTC: P2084	**Exhaust Gas Temperature Sensor Circuit Range/Performance Bank 1 Sensor 2:** The powertrain control module (PCM) monitors the exhaust gas temperature (EGT) sensor for a biased signal value. Following an 8-hour soak, the PCM records the EGT sensor temperature value at key ON, engine OFF. After several minutes of vehicle operation at vehicle speeds greater than 40.2 km/h (25 mph) the PCM calculates an expected key ON, engine OFF value. The PCM determines what the expected EGT value at key ON, engine OFF should have been based on inputs from other sensors. The test fails when the difference between the expected calculated value and the actual recorded value is greater than 40°C (72°F).
DTC: P2085	**Exhaust Gas Temperature Sensor Circuit Intermittent Bank 1 Sensor 2:** The powertrain control module (PCM) monitors the exhaust gas temperature (EGT) sensor for an intermittent concern. The test fails when the sensor voltage fluctuates by greater than 0.25 volt for 20 seconds.
DTC: P2088	**A Camshaft Position Actuator Control Circuit Low Bank 1:** The powertrain control module (PCM) monitors the variable camshaft timing (VCT) circuit for high and low voltage. The test fails if the voltage exceeds a calibrated limit for a calibrated amount of time.
DTC: P2089	**A Camshaft Position Actuator Control Circuit High Bank 1:** The powertrain control module (PCM) monitors the variable camshaft timing (VCT) circuit for high and low voltage. The test fails if the voltage exceeds a calibrated limit for a calibrated amount of time.
DTC: P208A	**Reductant Pump Control Circuit Open Load:** The powertrain control module (PCM) continuously monitors the reductant pump assembly circuit for concerns. The test fails if the voltage exceeds or falls below a calibrated limit for a calibrated amount of time.
DTC: P208B	**Reductant Pump A Control Range/Performance:** The powertrain control module (PCM) monitors the RDPC circuit for pump motor speed deviation. If the difference between the commanded and monitored pump speeds exceeds 300 rpm, this DTC sets and the selective catalytic reduction (SCR) system shuts down until the next key cycle.

DTC	Trouble Code Title & Conditions
DTC: P208C	**Reductant Pump Control Circuit Low:** The powertrain control module (PCM) monitors the reductant pump assembly circuits to the PCM for high and low voltage. The test fails if the voltage exceeds or falls below a calibrated limit for a calibrated amount of time.
DTC: P208D	**Reductant Pump Control Circuit High:** The powertrain control module (PCM) monitors the reductant pump assembly circuits to the PCM for high and low voltage. The test fails if the voltage exceeds or falls below a calibrated limit for a calibrated amount of time.
DTC: P208E	**Reductant Injection Valve Stuck Closed (Bank 1 Unit 1):** The powertrain control module (PCM) monitors reductant injector needle movement by monitoring the amount of current necessary to fire the injector solenoid. When the needle has reached its upper limit, the current ripples. If this ripple does not occur, the injector needle is stuck. The PCM then sets this DTC and shuts down the selective catalytic reduction (SCR) system until the next key cycle.
DTC: P2090	**B Camshaft Position Actuator Control Circuit Low Bank 1:** The powertrain control module (PCM) monitors the variable camshaft timing (VCT) circuit for high and low voltage. The test fails if the voltage exceeds a calibrated limit for a calibrated amount of time.
DTC: P2091	**B Camshaft Position Actuator Control Circuit High Bank 1:** The powertrain control module (PCM) monitors the variable camshaft timing (VCT) circuit for high and low voltage. The test fails if the voltage exceeds a calibrated limit for a calibrated amount of time.
DTC: P2096	**Post Catalyst Fuel Trim System Too Lean (Bank 1):** The Powertrain Control Module (PCM) monitors the correction value from downstream Heated Oxygen Sensor (HO2S) as part of the fore-aft oxygen sensor control routine. The test fails when the correction value is greater than a calibrated limit.
DTC: P2097	**Post Catalyst Fuel Trim System Too Rich Bank 1:** The powertrain control module (PCM) monitors the correction value from downstream heated oxygen sensor (HO2S) as part of the fore-aft oxygen sensor control routine. The test fails when the correction value is greater than a calibrated limit.
DTC: P2098	**Post Catalyst Fuel Trim System Too Lean (Bank 2):** The Powertrain Control Module (PCM) monitors the correction value from downstream Heated Oxygen Sensor (HO2S) as part of the fore-aft oxygen sensor control routine. The test fails when the correction value is greater than a calibrated limit.
DTC: P2099	**Post Catalyst Fuel Trim System Too Rich (Bank 2):** The Powertrain Control Module (PCM) monitors the correction value from downstream Heated Oxygen Sensor (HO2S) as part of the fore-aft oxygen sensor control routine. The test fails when the correction value is greater than a calibrated limit.
DTC: P209F	**Reductant Tank Heater Control Performance:** The reductant tank heater and reductant temperature sensor are in close proximity in the reductant tank. The powertrain control module (PCM) monitors reductant tank heater performance by monitoring the reductant temperature sensor signal. This DTC sets if the temperature does not rise more than 0.5°C (0.9°F) within a certain time frame after tank heat is requested.
DTC: P20A0	**Reductant Purge Control Valve Circuit Open Load:** The powertrain control module (PCM) continuously monitors the RDPGC circuit for concerns. The test fails if the voltage exceeds or falls below a calibrated limit for a calibrated amount of time.
DTC: P20A1	**Reductant Purge Control Valve Performance:** The powertrain control module (PCM) monitors reductant purge valve performance by monitoring the reductant pressure sensor. During a purge cycle, providing that the system pressure meets or exceeds 280 kPa (41 psi), if the system pressure does not drop by at least 230 kPa (33.3 psi), the PCM sets this DTC and shuts down the selective catalytic reduction (SCR) system.
DTC: P20A2	**Reductant Purge Control Valve Circuit Low:** The powertrain control module (PCM) continuously monitors the RDPGC circuit for concerns. The test fails if the voltage exceeds or falls below a calibrated limit for a calibrated amount of time.
DTC: P20A3	**Reductant Purge Control Valve Circuit High:** The powertrain control module (PCM) continuously monitors the RDPGC circuit for concerns. The test fails if the voltage exceeds or falls below a calibrated limit for a calibrated amount of time.
DTC: P20B9	**Reductant Heater A Control Circuit/Open:** The powertrain control module (PCM) carries out a functional key ON, engine running (KOER) self-test for the glow plug system. During that test the PCM enables the glow plug control module (GPCM) which monitors each individual reductant heater and harness for concerns. When the GPCM detects a concern with a reductant heater or harness, it sends a message to the PCM, which sets this DTC.
DTC: P20BA	**Reductant Heater A Control Performance:** The powertrain control module (PCM) carries out a functional key ON, engine running (KOER) self-test for the glow plug system. During that test the PCM enables the glow plug control module (GPCM) which monitors the conductance of each reductant heater during peak power and compares it to an expected threshold. When the GPCM detects that the reductant heater conductance is out of tolerance with this threshold, it sends a message to the PCM, which sets this DTC.

DTC	Trouble Code Title & Conditions
DTC: P20BB	**Reductant Heater A Control Circuit Low:** The powertrain control module (PCM) carries out a functional key ON, engine running (KOER) self-test for the glow plug system. During that test the PCM enables the glow plug control module (GPCM) which monitors the RDHTRC1 circuit. When the GPCM detects that the RDHTRC1 circuit is drawing more than 15 amps for more than 250 milliseconds, a short to ground is suspect. The GPCM sends a message to the PCM, which sets this DTC.
DTC: P20BC	**Reductant Heater A Control Circuit High:** The powertrain control module (PCM) carries out a functional key ON, engine running (KOER) self-test for the glow plug system. During that test the PCM enables the glow plug control module (GPCM) which monitors the reductant heater circuits. When the GPCM detects that the RDHTRC1 circuit is drawing 0 amps for more than 250 milliseconds, a short to voltage is suspect. The GPCM sends a message to the PCM, which sets this DTC.
DTC: P20BD	**Reductant Heater B Control Circuit/Open:** The powertrain control module (PCM) carries out a functional key ON, engine running (KOER) self-test for the glow plug system. During that test the PCM enables the glow plug control module (GPCM) which monitors each individual reductant heater and harness for concerns. When the GPCM detects a concern with a reductant heater or harness, it sends a message to the PCM, which sets this DTC.
DTC: P20BE	**Reductant Heater B Control Performance:** The powertrain control module (PCM) carries out a functional key ON, engine running (KOER) self-test for the glow plug system. During that test the PCM enables the glow plug control module (GPCM) which monitors the conductance of each reductant heater during peak power and compares it to an expected threshold. When the GPCM detects that the reductant heater conductance is out of tolerance with this threshold, it sends a message to the PCM, which sets this DTC.
DTC: P20BF	**Reductant Heater B Control Circuit Low:** The powertrain control module (PCM) carries out a functional key ON, engine running (KOER) self-test for the glow plug system. During that test the PCM enables the glow plug control module (GPCM) which monitors the RDHTRC2 circuit. When the GPCM detects that the RDHTRC2 circuit is drawing more than 15 amps for more than 250 milliseconds, a short to ground is suspect. The GPCM sends a message to the PCM, which sets this DTC.
DTC: P20C0	**Reductant Heater B Control Circuit High:** The powertrain control module (PCM) carries out a functional key ON, engine running (KOER) self-test for the glow plug system. During that test the PCM enables the glow plug control module (GPCM) which monitors the reductant heater circuits. When the GPCM detects that the RDHTRC2 circuit is drawing 0 amps for more than 250 milliseconds, a short to voltage is suspect. The GPCM sends a message to the PCM, which sets this DTC.
DTC: P20C1	**Reductant Heater C Control Circuit/Open:** The powertrain control module (PCM) carries out a functional key ON, engine running (KOER) self-test for the glow plug system. During that test the PCM enables the glow plug control module (GPCM) which monitors each individual reductant heater and harness for concerns. When the GPCM detects a concern with a reductant heater or harness, it sends a message to the PCM, which sets this DTC.
DTC: P20C2	**Reductant Heater C Control Performance:** The powertrain control module (PCM) carries out a functional key ON, engine running (KOER) self-test for the glow plug system. During that test the PCM enables the glow plug control module (GPCM) which monitors the RDHTRPWR circuit. When the GPCM detects that the RDHTRPWR circuit is less than 5 volts, it sends a message to the PCM, which sets this DTC.
DTC: P20C3	**Reductant Heater C Control Circuit Low:** The powertrain control module (PCM) carries out a functional key ON, engine running (KOER) self-test for the glow plug system. During that test the PCM enables the glow plug control module (GPCM) which monitors the RDHTRPWR circuit. When the GPCM detects that the RDHTRPWR circuit is drawing more than 6 amps for more than 250 milliseconds, a short to ground is suspect. The GPCM sends a message to the PCM, which sets this DTC.
DTC: P20C4	**Reductant Heater C Control Circuit High:** The powertrain control module (PCM) carries out a functional key ON, engine running (KOER) self-test for the glow plug system. During that test the PCM enables the glow plug control module (GPCM) which monitors the reductant heater circuits. When the GPCM detects that the RDHTRPWR circuit is drawing 0 amps for more than 250 milliseconds, a short to voltage is suspect. The GPCM sends a message to the PCM, which sets this DTC.
DTC: P20E2	**Exhaust Gas Temperature Sensor 1/2 Correlation Bank 1:** The powertrain control module (PCM) monitors the 3 exhaust gas temperature (EGT) sensors at key ON, engine OFF, following an 8-hour soak to determine if a concern is present. The PCM compares the values of the 3 EGT sensors to verify the sensors correlate to each other. The test fails when the temperature difference at EGT bank 1, sensor 1 (EGT11) is greater than 25°C (45°F).
DTC: P20E3	**Exhaust Gas Temperature Sensor 1/3 Correlation Bank 1:** The powertrain control module (PCM) monitors the 3 exhaust gas temperature (EGT) sensors at key ON, engine OFF, following an 8-hour soak to determine if a concern is present. The PCM compares the values of the 3 EGT sensors to verify the sensors correlate to each other. The test fails when the temperature difference at EGT bank 1, sensor 2 (EGT12) is greater than 25°C (45°F).

DTC	Trouble Code Title & Conditions
DTC: P20E4	**Exhaust Gas Temperature Sensor 2/3 Correlation Bank 1:** The powertrain control module (PCM) monitors the 3 exhaust gas temperature (EGT) sensors at key ON, engine OFF, following an 8-hour soak to determine if a concern is present. The PCM compares the values of the 3 EGT sensors to verify the sensors correlate to each other. The test fails when the temperature difference at EGT bank 1, sensor 3 (EGT13) is greater than 25°C (45°F).
DTC: P20E8	**Reductant Pressure Too Low:** The powertrain control module (PCM) monitors reductant pressure as the system primes for injection. If the system pressure does not exceed 350 kPa (51 psi) within 45 seconds after the reductant pump starts, this DTC sets.
DTC: P20E9	**Reductant Pressure Too High:** The powertrain control module (PCM) continuously monitors selective catalytic reduction (SCR) system pressure during closed-loop operation. If the system pressure exceeds 650 kPa (88 psi) for 10 seconds, or 790 kPa (115 psi) for 1 second, this DTC sets.
DTC: P20EE	**SCR NOX Catalyst Efficiency Below Threshold (Bank 1):** The efficiency of the selective catalytic reduction (SCR) catalyst to remove nitrogen oxides (NOx) from the exhaust gas is calculated based on an upstream estimate and the downstream measurement. The concentration of NOx upstream of the SCR catalyst is an estimate based on a calibrated model. The concentration of NOx downstream of the SCR catalyst is measured with the NOx sensor. This DTC sets when the SCR catalyst efficiency is below a calibrated threshold for a calibrated amount of time.
DTC: P2100	**Throttle Actuator Control (TAC) Motor Circuit/Open:** A Powertrain Control Module (PCM) fault flag is set indicating the motor circuit is open. May require cycling the key. **NOTE: A TAC motor circuit PID reading may indicate a concern, if available.**
DTC: P2101	**Throttle Actuator Control (TAC) Motor Range/Performance:** A Powertrain Control Module (PCM) fault flag is set indicating the motor circuit is open, and may require cycling the key. **NOTE: A TAC motor circuit PID reading may indicate a concern, if available.**
DTC: P2104	**Throttle Actuator Control System - Forced Idle:** This DTC is set when the powertrain control module (PCM) detects concerns with 2 of the accelerator pedal position (APP) sensor input signals. The PCM limits the engine to only operate at idle.
DTC: P2104	**Throttle Actuator Control (TAC) System (Forced Idle):** The TAC system is in the Failure Mode Effects Management (FMEM) mode of forced idle. **NOTE: This DTC is an informational DTC and may be set in combination with a number of other DTCs which are causing the FMEM. Diagnose other DTCs first.**
DTC: P2105	**Throttle Actuator Control (TAC) System (Forced Engine Shutdown):** The TAC system is in the Failure Mode Effects Management (FMEM) mode of forced idle. **NOTE: This DTC is an informational DTC and may be set in combination with a number of other DTCs which are causing the FMEM. Diagnose other DTCs first.**
DTC: P2107	**Throttle Actuator Control (TAC) Module Processor:** The Electronic Throttle Control (ETC) area of the Powertrain Control Module (PCM) failed the self-test. The concern could be the result of an incorrect Throttle Position (TP) command, or TAC motor wires shorted together. **NOTE: This DTC may be accompanied by other DTCs. If DTC P2110 is present along with other DTCs, disregard DTCs P2107 and P2110 at this time. Diagnose other DTCs first. A TAC motor circuit PID reading may indicate a concern, if available.**
DTC: P2109	**Throttle/Pedal Position Sensor A Minimum Stop Performance:** The powertrain control module (PCM) monitors the electronic throttle for the ability of the throttle plate to reach the lower mechanical stop position within a calibrated amount of time at ignition ON. This DTC sets if the throttle plate does not reach the lower mechanical stop position within a calibrated amount of time.
DTC: P2110	**Throttle Actuator Control (TAC) System (Forced Limited RPM):** The TAC system is in the Failure Mode Effects Management (FMEM) mode of forced limited RPM. **NOTE: This DTC is an informational DTC and may be set in combination with a number of other DTCs which are causing the FMEM. Diagnose other DTCs first.**
DTC: P2111	**Throttle Actuator Control (TAC) System - Stuck Open:** This powertrain control module (PCM) fault status indicates the throttle plate is at a greater angle than commanded.
DTC: P2112	**Throttle Actuator Control (TAC) System - Stuck Closed:** This Powertrain Control Module (PCM) fault status indicates the throttle plate is at a lower angle than commanded.
DTC: P2118	**Throttle Actuator A Control Motor Current Range/Performance:** The powertrain control module (PCM) monitors the electronic throttle control (ETC) operation for a high current condition. This DTC sets if the current necessary to operate the throttle actuator control (TAC) motor is higher than a calibrated limit.
DTC: P2119	**Throttle Actuator A Control Throttle Body Range/Performance:** This powertrain control module (PCM) fault status indicates the throttle plate is at an angle other than commanded.

DTC	Trouble Code Title & Conditions
DTC: P2121	**Throttle/Pedal Position Sensor/Switch D Circuit Range/Performance:** The Accelerator Pedal Position (APP) sensor fault flag is set for sensor 1 by the Powertrain Control Module (PCM), indicating the signal is out of the normal self-test operating range. **NOTE: An APP1 sensor PID reading may indicate a concern.**
DTC: P2121	**Throttle/Pedal Position Sensor/Switch D Circuit Range/Performance:** The accelerator pedal position (APP) sensor fault flag is set for sensor 1 by the powertrain control module (PCM), indicating the signal is out of the normal self-test operating range.
DTC: P2122	**Throttle/Pedal Position Sensor/Switch D Circuit Low:** The accelerator pedal position (APP) sensor 1 is out of self-test range low.
DTC: P2122	**Throttle/Pedal Position Sensor/Switch D Circuit Low:** The powertrain control module (PCM) monitors the accelerator pedal position (APP) sensor for a low voltage concern. The test fails when the APP1 circuit voltage is less than 0.25 volt (vehicles with an adjustable accelerator pedal or a fixed accelerator pedal with a white sensor housing) or 0.17 volt (all others).
DTC: P2122	**Throttle/Pedal Position Sensor/Switch D Circuit Low:** The Accelerator Pedal Position (APP) sensor 1 is out of self-test range low. **NOTE: An APP1 sensor PID reading may indicate a concern.**
DTC: P2123	**Throttle/Pedal Position Sensor/Switch D Circuit High:** The powertrain control module (PCM) monitors the accelerator pedal position (APP) sensor for a high voltage concern. This DTC sets when the APP1 circuit voltage is greater than 4.75 volts.
DTC: P2123	**Throttle/Pedal Position Sensor/Switch D Circuit High:** The accelerator pedal position (APP) sensor 1 is out of self-test range high. **NOTE: An APP1 sensor PID reading may indicate a concern.**
DTC: P2126	**Throttle/Pedal Position Sensor/Switch E Circuit Range/Performance:** The Accelerator Pedal Position (APP) sensor fault flag is set for sensor 2 by the Powertrain Control Module (PCM), indicating the signal is out of the normal self-test operating range. **NOTE: An APP2 sensor PID reading may indicate a concern.**
DTC: P2127	**Throttle/Pedal Position Sensor/Switch E Circuit Low:** The Accelerator Pedal Position (APP) sensor 2 is out of self-test range low. **NOTE: An APP2 sensor PID reading may indicate a concern.**
DTC: P2127	**Throttle/Pedal Position Sensor/Switch E Circuit Low:** The powertrain control module (PCM) monitors the accelerator pedal position (APP) sensor for a low voltage concern. The test fails when the APP2 circuit voltage is less than 0.25 volt (vehicles with an adjustable accelerator pedal or a fixed accelerator pedal with a white sensor housing) or 0.17 volt (all others).
DTC: P2128	**Throttle/Pedal Position Sensor/Switch E Circuit High:** The powertrain control module (PCM) monitors the accelerator pedal position (APP) sensor for a high voltage concern. This DTC sets when the APP2 circuit voltage is greater than 4.75 volts.
DTC: P2128	**Throttle/Pedal Position Sensor/Switch E Circuit High:** The Accelerator Pedal Position (APP) sensor 2 is out of self-test range high. **NOTE: An APP2 sensor PID reading may indicate a concern.**
DTC: P2128	**Throttle/Pedal Position Sensor/Switch E Circuit High:** The powertrain control module (PCM) monitors the accelerator pedal position (APP) sensor for a high voltage concern. The test fails when the APP2 circuit voltage is greater than 4.75 volts.
DTC: P2131	**Throttle/Pedal Position Sensor/Switch F Circuit Range/Performance:** The Accelerator Pedal Position (APP) sensor fault flag is set for sensor 3 by the Powertrain Control Module (PCM), indicating the signal is out of the normal self-test operating range. **NOTE: An APP3 sensor PID reading may indicate a concern.**
DTC: P2132	**Throttle/Pedal Position Sensor/Switch F Circuit Low:** The Accelerator Pedal Position (APP) sensor 3 is out of self-test range low. **NOTE: An APP3 sensor PID reading may indicate a concern.**
DTC: P2133	**Throttle/Pedal Position Sensor/Switch F Circuit High:** The Accelerator Pedal Position (APP) sensor 3 is out of self-test range high. **NOTE: An APP3 sensor PID reading may indicate a concern.**

DTC	Trouble Code Title & Conditions
DTC: P2135	**Throttle/Pedal Position Sensor/Switch A/B Voltage Correlation:** The Powertrain Control Module (PCM) flagged a concern indicating that Throttle Position (TP) 1 and TP2 disagree by more than a calibrated limit. **NOTE: Compare the TP1 and TP2 PID values for a full sweep and correlation. Check the wiring harness for an open or a short circuit. Check the TP sensor for an internal open or short circuit.**
DTC: P2138	**Throttle/Pedal Position Sensor/Switch D/E Voltage Correlation:** This DTC is set by the powertrain control module (PCM) when the accelerator pedal position (APP) sensor circuits 1 and 2 do not agree on the position of the pedal.
DTC: P2138	**Throttle/Pedal Position Sensor/Switch D/E Voltage Correlation:** The Powertrain Control Module (PCM) monitors the Accelerator Pedal Position (APP) sensor for a concern. The PCM compares the accelerator pedal position information from the APP sensor inputs, APP1 and APP2. If the APP sensor inputs APP1 and APP2 disagree on the position of the accelerator pedal by more than an expected value, the DTC is set. **NOTE: Monitor the APP_MAXDIFF PID while applying and releasing the accelerator pedal.**
DTC: P2139	**Throttle/Pedal Position Sensor/Switch D/F Voltage Correlation:** This DTC is set by the powertrain control module (PCM) when the accelerator pedal position (APP) sensor circuits 1 and 3 do not agree on the position of the pedal.
DTC: P2140	**Throttle/Pedal Position Sensor/Switch E/F Voltage Correlation:** This DTC is set by the powertrain control module (PCM) when the accelerator pedal position (APP) sensor circuits 2 and 3 do not agree on the position of the pedal.
DTC: P215A	**Vehicle Speed / Wheel Speed Correlation:** This DTC detects a concern in the vehicle speed signal being sent from the anti-lock brake system (ABS) module to the powertrain control module (PCM) over the controller area network (CAN).
DTC: P215B	**Vehicle Speed / Output Shaft Speed Correlation:** This DTC detects a concern in the vehicle speed signal being sent from the transmission control module (TCM) to the powertrain control module (PCM) over the controller area network (CAN).
DTC: P2163	**Throttle/Pedal Position Sensor A Maximum Stop Performance:** The powertrain control module (PCM) monitors the electronic throttle for the ability of the throttle plate to reach the upper mechanical stop position within a calibrated amount of time at ignition ON. This DTC sets if the throttle plate does not reach the upper mechanical stop position within a calibrated amount of time.
DTC: P2176	**Throttle Actuator A Control System - Idle Position Not Learned:** The electronic throttle control (ETC) system of the powertrain control module (PCM) detected a concern. This DTC sets if the PCM is unable to learn the calibrated throttle positions.
DTC: P2182	**Engine Coolant Temperature Sensor 2 Circuit:** The powertrain control module (PCM) continuously monitors this sensor for concerns. This DTC sets when the secondary cooling system engine coolant temperature 2 (ECT2) sensor reading does not correlate with the other temperature sensor readings at ignition on. The PCM runs this logic after an engine off and a calibrated soak period, typically 6 - 8 hours. This soak period allows the secondary cooling system ECT2 and the other temperature sensors to stabilize and not differ by more than a calibrated value, typically 17°C (30°F).
DTC: P2183	**Engine Coolant Temperature Sensor 2 Circuit Range/Performance:** This DTC indicates that an secondary cooling system engine coolant temperature 2 (ECT2) sensor range performance concern has been detected. The DTC sets when the vehicle has been driven above 1,250 RPM without the secondary cooling system ECT2 sensor signal increasing above 70°C (158°F). The time to set the concern depends on the secondary cooling system and intake air temperatures and can vary between 20 and 60 minutes.
DTC: P2184	**Engine Coolant Temperature Sensor 2 Circuit Low:** Indicates the sensor signal is less than the self-test minimum. The secondary cooling system engine coolant temperature 2 (ECT2) sensor minimum is 0.2 volt or 121°C (250°F).
DTC: P2185	**Engine Coolant Temperature Sensor 2 Circuit High:** Indicates the sensor signal is greater than the self-test maximum. The secondary cooling system engine coolant temperature 2 (ECT2) sensor maximum is 4.6 volts or -50°C (-58°F).
DTC: P2195	**O2 Sensor Signal Biased/Stuck Lean - Bank 1, Sensor 1:** A heated oxygen sensor (HO2S) indicating lean at the end of a test is trying to correct for an over-rich condition. The test fails when the fuel control system no longer detects switching for a calibrated amount of time.
DTC: P2195	**O2 Sensor Signal Biased/Stuck Lean - Bank 1, Sensor 1:** A heated oxygen sensor (HO2S) indicating lean at the end of a test is trying to correct for an over-rich condition. The test fails when the fuel control system no longer detects switching for a calibrated amount of time.

DTC	Trouble Code Title & Conditions
DTC: P2196	**O2 Sensor Signal Biased/Stuck Rich - Bank 1, Sensor 1:** A heated oxygen sensor (HO2S) indicating rich at the end of a test is trying to correct for an over-lean condition. The test fails when the fuel control system no longer detects switching for a calibrated amount of time.
DTC: P2197	**O2 Sensor Signal Biased/Stuck Lean - Bank 2, Sensor 1:** A heated oxygen sensor (HO2S) indicating lean at the end of a test is trying to correct for an over-rich condition. The test fails when the fuel control system no longer detects switching for a calibrated amount of time.
DTC: P2198	**O2 Sensor Signal Biased/Stuck Rich - Bank 2, Sensor 1:** A Heated Oxygen Sensor (HO2S) indicating lean at the end of a test is trying to correct for an over-lean condition. The test fails when the fuel control system no longer detects switching for a calibrated amount of time.
DTC: P2199	**Intake Air Temperature 1/2 Correlation:** The DTC indicates that the IAT and IAT2 sensor readings differ by more than a calibrated value.
DTC: P219A	**Bank 1 Air/Fuel Ratio Imbalance:** The air fuel imbalance monitor is designed to detect differences in the air fuel ratio between cylinders per engine bank. The test fails if the air fuel ratio difference per cylinder is greater than a calculated amount.
DTC: P219B	**Bank 2 Air/Fuel Ratio Imbalance:** The air fuel imbalance monitor is designed to detect differences in the air fuel ratio between cylinders per engine bank. The test fails if the air fuel ratio difference per cylinder is greater than a calculated amount.
DTC: P21AB	**Reductant Level Sensor B Circuit High:** The powertrain control module (PCM) monitors the reductant level sensor circuits to the PCM for high and low voltage. The test fails if the voltage exceeds or falls below a calibrated limit for a calibrated amount of time.
DTC: P21B0	**Reductant Level Sensor C Circuit High:** The powertrain control module (PCM) monitors the reductant level sensor circuits to the PCM for high and low voltage. The test fails if the voltage exceeds or falls below a calibrated limit for a calibrated amount of time.
DTC: P2200	**NOX Sensor Circuit (Bank 1 Sensor 1):** The nitrogen oxide (NOx) module monitors the NOx sensor for circuit concerns. This DTC sets when a concern is detected with one of the circuits used to determine the oxygen O2 content or the NOx content in the exhaust gas.
DTC: P2201	**NOx Sensor Circuit Range/Performance Bank 1:** The nitrogen oxide (NOx) module monitors the NOx sensor NOx concentration signal for an acceptable signal value. This DTC sets when the actual NOx signal value is not within the expected range for a calibrated amount of time.
DTC: P2209	**NOx Sensor Heater Sense Circuit Range/Performance (Bank 1 Sensor 1):** The powertrain control module (PCM) continuously monitors the controller area network (CAN) for messages from nitrogen oxide (NOx) module. This DTC sets when the PCM does not receive the NOx module message within a calibrated amount of time.
DTC: P220A	**NOX Sensor Supply Voltage Circuit (Bank 1 Sensor 1):** This DTC sets when the nitrogen oxide (NOx) module detects the battery voltage is out of range.
DTC: P220E	**NOX Sensor Heater Control Circuit Range/Performance (Bank 1 Sensor 1):** The nitrogen oxide (NOx) module monitors the temperature of the NOx sensor heater element and controls the heater voltage to maintain operating temperature. This DTC sets when the NOx sensor does not reach the required operating temperature in a calibrated amount of time or when the NOx module is not able to maintain the required operating temperature after the NOx sensor is warm.
DTC: P2227	**Barometric Pressure Sensor A Circuit Range/Performance:** The powertrain control module (PCM) continuously monitors this sensor for concerns. The test fails when the barometric pressure (BARO) parameter identification (PID) does not correlate with the throttle intake pressure (TIP) or the manifold absolute pressure (MAP) PIDs at ignition on. This DTC sets when the PCM detects an out of range condition in the control circuit.
DTC: P2227	**Barometric Pressure Sensor A Circuit Range/Performance:** The powertrain control module (PCM) continuously monitors this sensor for concerns. This DTC sets when the PCM detects that the barometric pressure (BARO) sensor reading is less than a calibrated value at key on engine off (KOEO).
DTC: P2228	**Barometric Pressure Circuit Low:** The powertrain control module (PCM) continuously monitors this sensor for concerns. Checks whether the signal from the barometric pressure (BARO) sensor is below the minimum threshold.
DTC: P2228	**Barometric Pressure Sensor A Circuit Low:** Checks whether the BARO reading is abnormally low indicating an extreme high altitude.
DTC: P2229	**Barometric Pressure Sensor A Circuit High:** Checks whether the BARO reading is abnormally high indicating an extreme low altitude.

DTC	Trouble Code Title & Conditions
DTC: P2229	**Barometric Pressure Sensor A Circuit High (For Fiesta):** The powertrain control module (PCM) continuously monitors this sensor for concerns. Checks whether the signal from the barometric pressure (BARO) sensor is above the maximum threshold.
DTC: P2229	**Barometric Pressure Circuit High:** Checks whether the signal from the BARO pressure sensor is above the maximum threshold.
DTC: P2230	**Barometric Pressure Circuit Intermittent:** A concern exists in the BARO sensor causing an incorrect pressure reading.
DTC: P2237	**O2 Sensor Positive Current Control Circuit Open - Bank 1, Sensor 1:** The powertrain control module (PCM) monitors the universal heated oxygen sensor (HO2S) for a circuit concern. This DTC sets when the PCM detects a concern with the circuit used to determine the oxygen content in the exhaust gas.
DTC: P2240	**O2 Sensor Positive Current Control Circuit Open - Bank 2, Sensor 1:** The powertrain control module (PCM) monitors the universal heated oxygen sensor (HO2S) for a circuit concern. This DTC sets when the PCM detects a concern with the circuit used to determine the oxygen content in the exhaust gas.
DTC: P2243	**O2 Sensor Reference Voltage Circuit Open - Bank 1, Sensor 1:** The powertrain control module (PCM) monitors the universal heated oxygen sensor (HO2S) for a circuit concern. This DTC sets when the PCM detects a concern with the circuit used to determine the oxygen content in the exhaust gas.
DTC: P2247	**O2 Sensor Reference Voltage Circuit Open - Bank 2, Sensor 1:** The powertrain control module (PCM) monitors the universal heated oxygen sensor (HO2S) for a circuit concern. This DTC sets when the PCM detects a concern with the circuit used to determine the oxygen content in the exhaust gas.
DTC: P2251	**O2 Sensor Negative Current Control Circuit Open - Bank 1, Sensor 1:** The powertrain control module (PCM) monitors the universal heated oxygen sensor (HO2S) for a circuit concern. This DTC sets when the PCM detects a concern with the circuit used to determine the oxygen content in the exhaust gas.
DTC: P2254	**O2 Sensor Negative Current Control Circuit Open - Bank 2, Sensor 1:** The powertrain control module (PCM) monitors the universal heated oxygen sensor (HO2S) for a circuit concern. This DTC sets when the PCM detects a concern with the circuit used to determine the oxygen content in the exhaust gas.
DTC: P2257	**Secondary Air Injection (AIR) System Control A Circuit Low:** The AIR system monitor circuit is low, indicating the secondary AIR pump is off although the secondary AIR pump was commanded on by the Powertrain Control Module (PCM). **NOTE: The AIR monitor circuit PCM input contains a pull up voltage through a resistance internal to the PCM. This voltage is normally held low by the resistance path through the secondary AIR pump when the secondary AIR pump is off. A single electrical open circuit component such as an AIR relay coil in this multi-component circuit is not detected by the PCM output driver, yet it sets DTC P2257.**
DTC: P2258	**Secondary Air Injection (AIR) System Control A Circuit High:** The AIR system monitor circuit is high, indicating the secondary AIR pump is on although the secondary AIR pump was commanded off by the Powertrain Control Module (PCM). **NOTE: The AIR monitor circuit PCM input contains a pull up voltage through a resistance internal to the PCM. This voltage is normally held low by the resistance path through the secondary AIR pump when the secondary AIR pump is off.**
DTC: P225A	**NOX Sensor Calibration Memory (Bank 1 Sensor 1):** The powertrain control module (PCM) continuously monitors the controller area network (CAN) for messages from nitrogen oxide (NOx) module. This DTC sets when the PCM receives an incorrect calibration message from the NOx module.
DTC: P2262	**Turbo/Super Charger Boost Pressure Not Detected — Mechanical:** The manifold absolute pressure (MAP) sensor is indicating a no boost condition while the turbocharger actuator is active and the turbocharger should be generating boost pressure.
DTC: P2262	**Turbo/Super Charger Boost Pressure Not Detected — Mechanical:** The manifold absolute pressure (MAP) sensor is indicating a no boost condition while the variable geometry actuator (VGT) solenoid is active and therefore should be generating boost pressure.
DTC: P2263	**Turbo/Super Charger Boost System Performance:** Indicates that boost pressure is not achieving the calibrated value by more than a calibrated threshold.
DTC: P2269	**Water in Fuel Condition:** The water in fuel (WIF) sensor is monitored by the powertrain control module (PCM). If the PCM detects water in the fuel, the DTC is set and the WIF indicator lamp is turned on.
DTC: P2270	**O2 Sensor Signal Stuck Lean - Bank 1, Sensor 2:** The downstream heated oxygen sensor (HO2S) is forced rich and lean and monitored by the powertrain control module (PCM). The test fails if the PCM does not detect the output of the HO2S in a calibrated amount of time.

DTC	Trouble Code Title & Conditions
DTC: P2271	**O2 Sensor Signal Stuck Rich (Bank 1, Sensor 2):** The downstream Heated Oxygen Sensor (HO2S) is forced rich and lean and monitored by the Powertrain Control Module (PCM). The test fails if the PCM does not detect the output of the HO2S in a calibrated amount of time.
DTC: P2272	**O2 Sensor Signal Stuck Lean - Bank 2, Sensor 2:** The downstream heated oxygen sensor (HO2S) is forced rich and lean and monitored by the powertrain control module (PCM). The test fails if the PCM does not detect the output of the HO2S in a calibrated amount of time.
DTC: P2273	**O2 Sensor Signal Stuck Rich - Bank 2, Sensor 2:** The downstream heated oxygen sensor (HO2S) is forced rich and lean and monitored by the powertrain control module (PCM). The test fails if the PCM does not detect the output of the HO2S in a calibrated amount of time.
DTC: P2274	**O2 Sensor Signal Stuck Lean (Bank 1, Sensor 3):** The downstream Heated Oxygen Sensor (HO2S) is forced rich and lean and monitored by the Powertrain Control Module (PCM). The test fails if the PCM does not detect the output of the HO2S in a calibrated amount of time.
DTC: P2275	**O2 Sensor Signal Stuck Rich (Bank 1, Sensor 3):** The downstream Heated Oxygen Sensor (HO2S) is forced rich and lean and monitored by the Powertrain Control Module (PCM). The test fails if the PCM does not detect the output of the HO2S in a calibrated amount of time.
DTC: P2279	**Intake Air System Leak:** This DTC indicates the engine was overproducing torque and overcharging the traction battery when its operating temperature was within normal range. To protect the traction battery the powertrain control module (PCM) disabled the fuel injectors.
DTC: P2282	**Air Leak Between Throttle Body and Intake Valve:** This DTC sets when the powertrain control module (PCM) detects an air leak that exceeds a predetermined limit for greater than 5 seconds. If the air flow entering the engine exceeds the air flow through the throttle, a leak is detected and this diagnostic fails.
DTC: P2284	**Injector Control Pressure Sensor Circuit Range/Performance:** The powertrain control module (PCM) monitors if the desired injection control pressure (ICP) is equal to the measured ICP while the engine is running. If the measured ICP does not reasonably compare to the desired ICP, the PCM sets the DTC, ignores the measured ICP sensor signal and attempts to control the engine with the desired value.
DTC: P2285	**Injector Control Pressure Sensor Circuit Low:** The powertrain control module (PCM) continuously monitors the signal of the injection control pressure (ICP) sensor to determine if the signal is within an expected range. If the PCM detects a higher or lower than expected voltage value, the PCM sets a DTC, illuminates the malfunction indicator lamp (MIL), ignores the ICP sensor signal, and uses a preset value based on engine operating conditions.
DTC: P2286	**Injector Control Pressure Sensor Circuit High:** The powertrain control module (PCM) continuously monitors the signal of the injection control pressure (ICP) sensor to determine if the signal is within an expected range. If the PCM detects a higher or lower than expected voltage value, the PCM sets a DTC, illuminates the malfunction indicator lamp (MIL), ignores the ICP sensor signal, and uses a preset value based on engine operating conditions.
DTC: P2287	**Injector Control Pressure Sensor Circuit Intermittent:** The powertrain control module (PCM) continuously monitors the injection control pressure (ICP) sensor signal to determine if the signal is within an expected range. If the PCM detects any intermittent concerns with the ICP signal the DTC sets, the malfunction indicator lamp (MIL) illuminates.
DTC: P2288	**Injector Control Pressure Too High:** The powertrain control module (PCM) monitors if the desired injection control pressure (ICP) is equal to the measured ICP while the engine is running. If the measured ICP does not reasonably compare to the desired ICP, the PCM sets the DTC, ignores the measured ICP sensor signal and attempts to control the engine with the desired value.
DTC: P2289	**Injector Control Pressure Too High - Engine Off:** The powertrain control module (PCM) monitors the injection control pressure (ICP) while the ignition is ON, and the engine is OFF. If the PCM detects an out of range high or low ICP sensor, the malfunction indicator lamp (MIL) is illuminated and the PCM functions from an estimated injection control pressure (open loop control of injection control pressure).
DTC: P2289	**Injector Control Pressure Too High - Engine Off:** The powertrain control module (PCM) monitors the fuel rail pressure (FRP) when the engine is turned OFF. If the FRP does not decrease below the calibrated threshold within the calibrated time, this DTC is set.
DTC: P228E	**Fuel Pressure Regulator 1 Exceeded Learning Limits - Too Low:** The powertrain control module (PCM) continuously monitors the fuel rail pressure sensor for concerns. If the PCM detects that the fuel rail pressure is 20% less than the calculated threshold, the DTC sets.

DTC	Trouble Code Title & Conditions
DTC: P228F	**Fuel Pressure Regulator 1 Exceeded Learning Limits - Too High:** The powertrain control module (PCM) continuously monitors the fuel rail pressure sensor for concerns. If the PCM detects that the fuel rail pressure is 20% greater than the calculated threshold, the DTC sets.
DTC: P2290	**Injector Control Pressure Too Low:** The powertrain control module (PCM) monitors if the desired injection control pressure (ICP) is equal to the measured ICP while the engine is running. If the measured ICP does not reasonably compare to the desired ICP, the PCM sets the DTC, ignores the measured ICP sensor signal and attempts to control the engine with the desired value.
DTC: P2291	**Injector Control Pressure Too Low - Engine Cranking:** The DTC sets when the PCM does not detect any ICP during crank (long crank time).
DTC: P2291	**Injector Control Pressure Too Low - Engine Cranking:** The powertrain control module (PCM) monitors the fuel rail pressure (FRP) during the engine cranking. If the FRP does not increase to the calibrated threshold while the engine is cranked this DTC is set.
DTC: P2297	**O2 Sensor Out of Range During Deceleration (Bank 1, Sensor 1):** During a deceleration fuel shut-off (DFSO) event, the powertrain control module (PCM) monitors how quickly the rear heated oxygen sensor (HO2S) switches from rich to lean. The measured rate of the rich to lean switch is compared to a calibrated threshold value. The threshold value takes into account the level of oxygen in the catalyst, which has an impact on how quickly the rich to lean switch occurs. The test fails when the measured value is slower than the threshold value.
DTC: P2300	**Ignition Coil A Primary Control Circuit Low:** The powertrain control module (PCM) continuously monitors the ignition system for concerns. This DTC sets when the PCM detects a short to ground in the circuit.
DTC: P2301	**Ignition Coil A Primary Control Circuit High:** The powertrain control module (PCM) continuously monitors the ignition system for concerns. This DTC sets when the PCM detects a short to voltage in the circuit.
DTC: P2303	**Ignition Coil B Primary Control Circuit Low:** The powertrain control module (PCM) continuously monitors the ignition system for concerns. This DTC sets when the PCM detects a short to ground in the circuit.
DTC: P2304	**Ignition Coil B Primary Control Circuit High:** The powertrain control module (PCM) continuously monitors the ignition system for concerns. This DTC sets when the PCM detects a short to voltage in the circuit.
DTC: P2306	**Ignition Coil C Primary Control Circuit Low:** The powertrain control module (PCM) continuously monitors the ignition system for concerns. This DTC sets when the PCM detects a short to ground in the circuit.
DTC: P2307	**Ignition Coil C Primary Control Circuit High:** The powertrain control module (PCM) continuously monitors the ignition system for concerns. This DTC sets when the PCM detects a short to voltage in the circuit.
DTC: P2309	**Ignition Coil D Primary Control Circuit Low:** The powertrain control module (PCM) continuously monitors the ignition system for concerns. This DTC sets when the PCM detects a short to ground in the circuit.
DTC: P2310	**Ignition Coil D Primary Control Circuit High:** The powertrain control module (PCM) continuously monitors the ignition system for concerns. This DTC sets when the PCM detects a short to voltage in the circuit.
DTC: P2312	**Ignition Coil E Primary Control Circuit Low:** The powertrain control module (PCM) continuously monitors the ignition system for concerns. This DTC sets when the PCM detects a short to ground in the circuit.
DTC: P2313	**Ignition Coil E Primary Control Circuit High:** The powertrain control module (PCM) continuously monitors the ignition system for concerns. This DTC sets when the PCM detects a short to voltage in the circuit.
DTC: P2315	**Ignition Coil F Primary Control Circuit Low:** The powertrain control module (PCM) continuously monitors the ignition system for concerns. This DTC sets when the PCM detects a short to ground in the circuit.
DTC: P2316	**Ignition Coil F Primary Control Circuit High:** The powertrain control module (PCM) continuously monitors the ignition system for concerns. This DTC sets when the PCM detects a short to voltage in the circuit.

DTC	Trouble Code Title & Conditions
DTC: P2418	**Evaporative Emission Control System Switching Valve Control Circuit/Open:** The powertrain control module (PCM) monitors the state of the fuel vapor vent valve circuit output driver. The test fails when the signal moves outside the minimum or maximum limit for the commanded state.
DTC: P2425	**Exhaust Gas Recirculation Cooling Valve Control Circuit/Open:** The powertrain control module (PCM) continuously monitors the EGRCBV circuit for concerns. This DTC sets when the PCM detects an open in the EGRCBV circuit.
DTC: P2426	**Exhaust Gas Recirculation Cooling Valve Control Circuit Low:** The powertrain control module (PCM) continuously monitors the EGRCBV circuit for concerns. This DTC sets when the PCM detects a short to ground in the EGRCBV circuit.
DTC: P2427	**Exhaust Gas Recirculation Cooling Valve Control Circuit High:** The powertrain control module (PCM) continuously monitors the EGRCBV circuit for concerns. This DTC sets when the PCM detects a short to voltage in the EGRCBV circuit.
DTC: P242A	**Exhaust Gas Temperature Sensor Circuit Bank 1 Sensor 3:** The powertrain control module (PCM) monitors the operation of the exhaust gas temperature (EGT) sensor to determine if the EGT sensor responds to the increase in temperature of the exhaust gas during vehicle operation. The PCM then compares the measured temperature to a modeled value. The test fails when after 5 minutes of driving, following a 6 hour soak, the EGT sensor temperature does not correlate to the modeled temperature of 130°C (266°F).
DTC: P242A	**Exhaust Gas Temperature Sensor Circuit Bank 1 Sensor 3:** The powertrain control module (PCM) monitors the operation of the exhaust gas temperature (EGT) sensor to determine if the EGT sensor responds to the increase in temperature of the exhaust gas, during vehicle operation. The test fails when after 10 minutes of driving, following an 8-hour soak, the EGT sensor does not indicate a temperature increase of 15°C (27°F).
DTC: P242B	**Exhaust Gas Temperature Sensor Circuit Range/Performance Bank 1 Sensor 3:** The powertrain control module (PCM) monitors the exhaust gas temperature (EGT) sensor for a biased signal value. Following an 8-hour soak, the PCM records the EGT sensor temperature value at key ON, engine OFF. After several minutes of vehicle operation at vehicle speeds greater than 40.2 km/h (25 mph) the PCM calculates an expected key ON, engine OFF value. The PCM determines what the expected EGT value at key ON, engine OFF should have been based on inputs from other sensors. The test fails when the difference between the expected calculated value and the actual recorded value is greater than 40°C (72°F).
DTC: P242C	**Exhaust Gas Temperature Sensor Circuit Low Bank 1 Sensor 3:** The powertrain control module (PCM) monitors the exhaust gas temperature (EGT) sensor for a low voltage concern. The test fails when the sensor voltage is less than 0.10 volt for greater than 15 seconds. Some updated vehicles may use 0.20 volt instead of 0.10 volt.
DTC: P242D	**Exhaust Gas Temperature Sensor Circuit High Bank 1 Sensor 3:** The powertrain control module (PCM) monitors the exhaust gas temperature (EGT) sensor for a high voltage concern. The test fails when the sensor voltage is greater than 4.75 volts for greater than 15 seconds. Some updated vehicles may use 2.50 volts instead of 4.75 volts.
DTC: P242E	**Exhaust Gas Temperature Sensor Circuit Intermittent/Erratic Bank 1 Sensor 3:** The powertrain control module (PCM) monitors the exhaust gas temperature (EGT) sensor for an intermittent concern. The test fails when the sensor voltage fluctuates by greater than 0.25 volt for 20 seconds.
DTC: P242F	**Diesel Particulate Filter Restriction - Ash Accumulation:** The powertrain control module (PCM) monitors the pressure decrease at the diesel particulate filter following a diesel particulate filter regeneration for a concern. The PCM calculates the amount of ash and the pressure increase the ash generates in the diesel particulate filter. During a regeneration the PCM expects the pressure to decrease. The amount of pressure decrease expected by the PCM is based on the temperature and flow of the exhaust gas. The test fails when the pressure reading at the diesel particulate filter pressure sensor does not decrease by the amount determined by the PCM.
DTC: P2448	**Secondary Air Injection System High Airflow (Bank 1):** The AIR system detects excessive mass air flow change with the pump on and a rich exhaust system air fuel ratio. **NOTE: Measured air flow is less than expected. Visually inspect the secondary AIR inlet hose.**
DTC: P244A	**Diesel Particulate Filter Differential Pressure Too Low:** The powertrain control module (PCM) monitors the diesel particulate filter for a concern. The diesel particulate filter is preconditioned for 5,000 km (3,107 miles) before the PCM begins to monitor the differential pressure. The test fails when the measured diesel particulate filter differential pressure is less than a minimum value for a certain exhaust flow rate.
DTC: P244C	**Exhaust Temperature Too Low For Particulate Filter Regeneration, Bank 1:** The powertrain control module (PCM) monitors the conditions necessary for diesel particulate filter regeneration. The test fails when the level of diesel particulate filter regeneration is at less than 10% of the target reduction after 13 minutes of active regeneration.

DTC	Trouble Code Title & Conditions
DTC: P244D	**Exhaust Temperature Too High For Particulate Filter Regeneration, Bank 1:** The powertrain control module (PCM) monitors the conditions necessary for diesel particulate filter regeneration. During vehicle operation if the diesel particulate filter temperature is greater than a calibrated limit, the PCM stores the amount of time the temperature is greater than the limit. The test fails when the temperature before or after the diesel particulate filter is greater than the calibrated limit for greater than 120 minutes over the life of the filter.
DTC: P2450	**Evaporative Emission Control System Switching Valve Performance or Stuck Open:** The powertrain control module (PCM) monitors the fuel vapor vent valve for correct operation. During the EVAP monitor cruise test after verifying a 1.02 mm (0.040 inch) leak is not present, the PCM commands the fuel vapor vent valve closed while a vacuum is present in the fuel tank and opens the canister vent. If the fuel vapor vent does not close, the vacuum in the tank is quickly lost. If the rate of loss exceeds a calibrated threshold the DTC is set.
DTC: P2452	**Diesel Particulate Filter Pressure Sensor A Circuit:** The powertrain control module (PCM) monitors the rationality of the diesel particulate filter pressure sensor during idle and part load operating conditions. The test fails when the diesel particulate filter pressure sensor signal value at idle is less than 0.15 kPa (0.022 psi). The test also fails when the diesel particulate filter pressure sensor signal value at part load is less than a minimum value or greater than a maximum value. These minimum and maximum values are based on the volume of exhaust.
DTC: P2453	**Diesel Particulate Filter Pressure Sensor A Circuit Range/Performance:** The powertrain control module (PCM) monitors the diesel particulate filter pressure sensor for offset and stuck signal value concerns. The test fails when the diesel particulate filter pressure sensor signal value at key ON, engine OFF is greater than 2.5 kPa (0.36 psi) or the key ON, engine running signal value changes less than 0.01 volt in 2 minutes.
DTC: P2454	**Diesel Particulate Filter Pressure Sensor A Circuit Low:** The powertrain control module (PCM) monitors the diesel particulate filter pressure sensor for a low voltage concern. The test fails when the sensor voltage is less than 0.10 volt for more than 15 seconds.
DTC: P2455	**Diesel Particulate Filter Pressure Sensor A Circuit High:** The powertrain control module (PCM) monitors the diesel particulate filter pressure sensor for a high voltage concern. The test fails when the sensor voltage is greater than 4.90 volts for more than 15 seconds.
DTC: P2455	**Diesel Particulate Filter Pressure Sensor A Circuit High:** The powertrain control module (PCM) monitors the diesel particulate filter pressure sensor for a high voltage concern. The test fails when the sensor voltage is greater than 4.90 volts for greater than 15 seconds.
DTC: P2456	**Diesel Particulate Filter Pressure Sensor A Circuit Intermittent/Erratic:** The powertrain control module (PCM) monitors the diesel particulate filter pressure sensor for an intermittent concern. The test fails when the sensor voltage fluctuates by greater than 3 kPa (0.44 psi) within 0.10 second for more than 30 seconds.
DTC: P2456	**Diesel Particulate Filter Pressure Sensor A Circuit Intermittent/Erratic:** The powertrain control module (PCM) monitors the diesel particulate filter pressure sensor for an intermittent concern. The test fails when the sensor voltage fluctuates by greater than 3 kPa (0.44 psi) within 0.10 second for greater than 30 seconds.
DTC: P2457	**Exhaust Gas Recirculation (EGR) Cooler System Performance:** Indicates excessive EGR cooler outlet temperature. Exhaust gases not being cooled effectively by the EGR coolers.
DTC: P2457	**Exhaust Gas Recirculation (EGR) Cooler System Performance:** The powertrain control module (PCM) monitors the EGR cooler outlet temperature for an under cooling condition or an over cooling condition. This DTC sets when the difference between the expected EGR gas temperature and the actual EGRT sensor value is greater than a calibrated amount.
DTC: P2457	**Exhaust Gas Recirculation (EGR) Cooler System Performance:** The low idle engine speed is between 600 and 750 RPM. The EGR valve position is greater than 0.08 volt. The mass fuel desired (MFDES) is between 4 and 16 mg/stroke, at low idle for a minimum of 30 seconds. No exhaust pressure (EP), barometric pressure (BARO), manifold absolute pressure (MAP), pressure signal, intake air temperature (IAT), IAT2 temperature signal, visctronic drive fan (VDF) fan DTC P0480, or EGR related concerns.
DTC: P2458	**Diesel Particulate Filter Regeneration Duration:** The powertrain control module (PCM) monitors the amount of time it takes for a diesel particulate filter regeneration to occur. The test fails when the diesel particulate filter regeneration has not completed after 25 minutes.
DTC: P2463	**Diesel Particulate Filter - Soot Accumulation:** The powertrain control module (PCM) monitors the diesel particulate filter for a very high restriction. The test fails during normal vehicle operation when the diesel particulate filter pressure is greater than a maximum amount. The PCM immediately illuminates the malfunction indicator lamp (MIL), limits engine performance, and sets the DTC. This DTC may inhibit the diesel particulate filter regeneration.

DTC	Trouble Code Title & Conditions
DTC: P246C	**Diesel Particulate Filter Restriction - Forced Limited Power:** The powertrain control module (PCM) monitors the diesel particulate filter for a high restriction. The test fails during normal vehicle operation when the diesel particulate filter pressure is greater than a calibrated amount. The PCM illuminates the powertrain malfunction indicator (wrench), limits engine performance, and sets the DTC.
DTC: P246E	**Exhaust Gas Temperature Sensor Circuit (Bank 1 Sensor 4):** The powertrain control module (PCM) monitors the operation of the exhaust gas temperature (EGT) sensor to determine if the EGT sensor responds to the increase in temperature of the exhaust gas, during vehicle operation. The PCM then compares the measured temperature to a modeled value. The test fails when after 5 minutes of driving, following a 6 hour soak, the EGT sensor temperature does not correlate to the modeled temperature of 110°C (230°F).
DTC: P2470	**Exhaust Gas Temperature Sensor Circuit Low (Bank 1 Sensor 4):** The powertrain control module (PCM) monitors the exhaust gas temperature (EGT) sensor for a low voltage concern. The test fails when the sensor voltage is less than 0.10 volt for more than 15 seconds.
DTC: P2471	**Exhaust Gas Temperature Sensor Circuit High (Bank 1 Sensor 4):** The powertrain control module (PCM) monitors the exhaust gas temperature (EGT) sensor for a high voltage concern. The test fails when the sensor voltage is greater than 4.90 volts for more than 15 seconds.
DTC: P2478	**Exhaust Gas Temperature Out of Range (Bank 1 Sensor 1):** The powertrain control module (PCM) monitors the exhaust gas temperature (EGT) sensor for an out-of-range concern. The test fails when the sensor temperature reads more than 1100°C (2012°F).
DTC: P2479	**Exhaust Gas Temperature Out of Range (Bank 1 Sensor 2):** The powertrain control module (PCM) monitors the exhaust gas temperature (EGT) sensor for an out-of-range concern. The test fails when the sensor temperature reads more than 1100°C (2012°F).
DTC: P247A	**Exhaust Gas Temperature Out of Range (Bank 1 Sensor 3):** The powertrain control module (PCM) monitors the exhaust gas temperature (EGT) sensor for an out-of-range concern. The test fails when the sensor temperature reads more than 1100°C (2012°F).
DTC: P247B	**Exhaust Gas Temperature Out of Range (Bank 1 Sensor 4):** The powertrain control module (PCM) monitors the exhaust gas temperature (EGT) sensor for an out-of-range concern. The test fails when the sensor temperature reads more than 1100°C (2012°F).
DTC: P249C	**SCR Time to Closed Loop:** The powertrain control module (PCM) monitors the amount of time elapsed until the selective catalytic reduction (SCR) system enters closed-loop control. This DTC sets when the time elapsed exceeds an expected threshold.
DTC: P249D	**Closed Loop Reductant Injection Control At Limit - Flow Too Low:** The powertrain control module (PCM) adapts a closed-loop correction factor to account for long term drift of the selective catalytic reduction (SCR) system. This correction factor is monitored continuously. This DTC sets if the correction factor reaches a negative threshold for 5 minutes.
DTC: P249E	**Closed Loop Reductant Injection Control At Limit - Flow Too High:** The powertrain control module (PCM) adapts a closed-loop correction factor to account for long term drift of the selective catalytic reduction (SCR) system. This correction factor is monitored continuously. This DTC sets if the correction factor reaches a positive threshold for 5 minutes.
DTC: P249F	**Excessive Time To Enter Closed Loop DPF Regeneration Control:** The powertrain control module (PCM) monitors the diesel particulate filter to determine that closed-loop control of a regeneration event occurs within a reasonable amount of time. This DTC sets if time in closed-loop operation is less than an expected threshold.
DTC: P24A0	**Closed Loop DPF Regeneration Control At Limit - Temperature Too Low:** The powertrain control module (PCM) monitors the exhaust gas temperature 12 (EGT12) sensor to make sure that diesel oxidation catalyst exit temperature is high enough to complete a regeneration. This DTC sets if the difference between the expected and actual diesel oxidation catalyst exit temperature exceeds 20°C (68°F).
DTC: P24A2	**Diesel Particulate Filter Regeneration Incomplete:** The powertrain control module (PCM) monitors diesel particulate filter regeneration. This DTC sets if a regeneration is aborted due to duration and the calculated restriction of the diesel particulate filter remains above a threshold. After the first occurrence of an incomplete regeneration, the PCM will force another regeneration in 150 miles (241 km) unless a normal regeneration occurs first.
DTC: P24A5	**Exhaust Gas Recirculation (EGR) Cooler Bypass Control Stuck (Bank 1):** The powertrain control module (PCM) monitors the EGR cooler outlet temperature for an over cooling condition. This DTC sets when the difference between the expected EGR gas temperature and the actual EGR gas temperature sensor value is greater than a calibrated amount.
DTC: P2506	**ECM / PCM Power Input Signal Range/Performance:** The powertrain control module (PCM) internal voltage is above or below a calibrated threshold.

DTC	Trouble Code Title & Conditions
DTC: P2507	**ECM / PCM Power Input Signal Low:** The powertrain control module (PCM) monitors the internal 5 volt power supply. When the 5 volt power supply voltage is less than a calibrated threshold this DTC sets.
DTC: P2508	**ECM / PCM Power Input Signal High:** The powertrain control module (PCM) monitors the internal 5 volt power supply. When the 5 volt power supply voltage is greater than a calibrated threshold this DTC sets.
DTC: P2510	**ECM / PCM Power Relay Sense Circuit Range/Performance:** The powertrain control module (PCM) monitors the voltage on the ignition switch position run (ISP-R) and the fuel injector power monitor (INJPWRM) circuits. This DTC sets when the voltage on the ISP-R and the INJPWRM circuit voltages do not correspond for a calibrated period of time.
DTC: P2531	**Ignition Switch Run Position Circuit Low:** The PCM carries out a logic check on the ISP-R and ISP-R/S circuits. When the powertrain control module (PCM) detects the ISP-R circuit low when it is expected to be high, this DTC sets.
DTC: P2533 (PCM)	**Ignition Switch Run/Start Position Circuit:** The powertrain control module (PCM) carries out a logic check on the ISP-R and ISP-R/S circuits. The PCM sets this DTC when a concern is detected.
DTC: P2533 (TBCM)	**Ignition Switch Run/Start Position Circuit:** At all times, the Traction Battery Control Module (TBCM) monitors the ignition run/start input circuit for voltage.* DTC P2533 sets if the TBCM does not detect voltage on the ignition run/start input circuit with the ignition switch in the ON position and the engine on or off.
DTC: P2535	**Ignition Switch Run/Start Position Circuit High:** The powertrain control module (PCM) carries out a logic check on the ISP-R and ISP-R/S circuits. If the ISP-R/S circuit stays high longer than a calibrated amount of time, or is high when the PCM when it is expected to be low, this DTC sets.
DTC: P2545	**Torque Management Request Input Signal A Range / Performance:** This DTC is set if there is a torque/engine speed request from the transmission control module (TCM), but at the same time, the powertrain control module (PCM) detects that this request should not be received.
DTC: P2552	**Throttle/Fuel Inhibit Circuit/Open:** The fuel injector control module monitor (FICMM) input line informs the diesel engine power monitor (DEPM) when the injectors are turned on and off. When the FICMM line is either shorted or open, the monitor strategy assumes that the fuel injectors are always turned on and sets DTC P2552.
DTC: P2560	**Engine Coolant Level Low:** The presence of this DTC may indicate that the vehicle is operating in derate mode and may experience a loss of power. Indicates the value from the engine coolant temperature (ECT) sensor is not within the powertrain control module (PCM) predicted engine coolant temperature range, based on other PCM inputs.
DTC: P2563	**Turbocharger Boost Control Position Sensor A Circuit Range/Performance:** The powertrain control module (PCM) monitors the difference between the turbocharger actuator commanded duty cycle and the actual duty cycle.
DTC: P2600	**Coolant Pump Control Circuit / Open:** The Powertrain Control Module (PCM) monitors the Heater Pump Control Relay (HPCR) primary circuit output. The test fails if the PCM grounds the HPCR circuit, and excessive current draw is detected on the HPCR circuit or, with the HPCR circuit not grounded by the PCM, voltage is not detected on the HPCR circuit. The PCM expects to detect VPWR voltage coming through the HPCR relay coil to the HPCR circuit.
DTC: P260F	**Evaporative System Monitoring Processor Performance:** This DTC sets when a concern is detected internal to the Powertrain Control Module (PCM). The microprocessor that controls the Engine Off Natural Vacuum (EONV) leak check monitor is separate from the main processor within the PCM. **NOTE: Verify the PCM is at the latest calibration level. Reprogram if necessary.**
DTC: P2610	**Electronic Control Module (ECM)/Powertrain Control Module (PCM) Internal Engine Off Timer Performance:** Indicates an error in the internal PCM engine off timer processor. The test fails when the difference between the engine off time and the central processing unit (CPU) time exceeds a calibrated limit for a calibrated amount of time.
DTC: P2610	**Electronic Control Module (ECM)/Powertrain Control Module (PCM) Internal Engine Off Timer Performance:** Indicates an error in the internal PCM engine off timer processor. **NOTE: Verify the PCM is at the latest calibration level.**
DTC: P2614	**Camshaft Position Output Circuit / Open:** This DTC is set by the powertrain control module (PCM) when no camshaft position output (CMPO) signal is present while the crankshaft position output (CKPO) is active.

DTC	Trouble Code Title & Conditions
DTC: P2617	**Crankshaft Position Output Circuit/Open:** The DTC is set by the powertrain control module (PCM) when no crankshaft position output (CKPO) signal is present while the camshaft position output (CMPO) is active.
DTC: P2623	**Injector Control Pressure Regulator/Open:** The powertrain control module (PCM) monitors the injection control pressure (ICP) while the engine is running and then compares it to the desired ICP. If the measured ICP does not reasonably compare to the desired ICP, the PCM ignores the measured ICP sensor signal and attempts to control the engine with the desired value.
DTC: P2626	**O2 Sensor Positive Current Trim Circuit/Open (Bank 1 Sensor 1):** During deceleration fuel shut-off (DFSO) the powertrain control module (PCM) monitors the integrity of the universal heated oxygen sensor (HO2S) UO2SPCT circuit by comparing the actual oxygen sensor voltage signal to an expected oxygen sensor voltage signal. The test fails when the actual oxygen sensor voltage exceeds the maximum expected voltage threshold for a specified amount of time.
DTC: P2627	**O2 Sensor Pumping Current Trim Circuit Low Bank 1, Sensor 1:** A resistor is installed in the universal heated oxygen sensor (HO2S) connector for part to part variance. The powertrain control module (PCM) determines the value of this resistor by taking multiple measurements of the resistor during each ignition ON event. The PCM uses this value in order to compensate for the variance in the pumping current signal. The test fails if the PCM determines the resistance value is too high.
DTC: P2628	**O2 Sensor Positive Current Trim Circuit High (Bank 1 Sensor 1):** The powertrain control module (PCM) monitors the universal heated oxygen sensor (HO2S) for a circuit concern. This DTC sets when the PCM detects a concern with the circuit used to determine the oxygen content in the exhaust gas.
DTC: P2629	**O2 Sensor Positive Current Trim Circuit/Open (Bank 2 Sensor 1):** During deceleration fuel shut-off (DFSO) the powertrain control module (PCM) monitors the integrity of the universal heated oxygen sensor (HO2S) UO2SPCT circuit by comparing the actual oxygen sensor voltage signal to an expected oxygen sensor voltage signal. The test fails when the actual oxygen sensor voltage exceeds the maximum expected voltage threshold for a specified amount of time.
DTC: P262A	**Fuel Injector - Pilot Injection Not Learned:** The powertrain control module (PCM) calibrates pilot injection during DFSO by commanding individual fuel injectors to spray a discrete amount of fuel and comparing the resulting crankshaft acceleration to an expected threshold. If the acceleration deviates from the threshold, the PCM then adjusts the injector until it matches the expected acceleration. This DTC sets if a fuel injector not currently set to fire causes a greater crankshaft acceleration than the injector that is currently firing.
DTC: P2630	**O2 Sensor Pumping Current Trim Circuit Low Bank 2, Sensor 1:** A resistor is installed in the universal heated oxygen sensor (HO2S) connector for part to part variance. The powertrain control module (PCM) determines the value of this resistor by taking multiple measurements of the resistor during each key on event. The PCM uses this value in order to compensate for the variance in the pumping current signal. The test fails if the PCM determines the resistance value is too high.
DTC: P2631	**O2 Sensor Positive Current Trim Circuit High (Bank 2 Sensor 1):** The powertrain control module (PCM) monitors the universal heated oxygen sensor (HO2S) for a circuit concern. This DTC sets when the PCM detects a concern with the circuit used to determine the oxygen content in the exhaust gas.
DTC: P2632	**Fuel Pump B Control Circuit/Open:** The fuel pump control module 2 monitors the fuel pump assembly and secondary circuits for a concern. If the fuel pump control module 2 detects a concern with the fuel pump assembly or secondary circuits, the fuel pump control module 2 sends an 80% duty cycle signal on the fuel pump monitor 2 (FPM2) circuit to report the concern to the powertrain control module (PCM). The test fails when the fuel pump control module 2 is still reporting a concern with the fuel pump assembly or secondary circuits after a calibrated amount of time.
DTC: P2669	**Actuator supply voltage B circuit open:** The PCM/ TCM detected the actuator supply voltage B high side power supply circuit failed. Maximum line pressureDefault to 5th gear
DTC: P268C	**Cylinder 1 Injector Data Incompatible:** Each injector has a code stored in the electronically erasable programmable read only memory (EEPROM) that provides information to the powertrain control module (PCM) about deviations of that fuel injector from a theoretical average fuel injector. If the fuel injector code is missing or invalid, this DTC sets.
DTC: P268D	**Cylinder 2 Injector Data Incompatible:** Each injector has a code stored in the electronically erasable programmable read only memory (EEPROM) that provides information to the powertrain control module (PCM) about deviations of that fuel injector from a theoretical average fuel injector. If the fuel injector code is missing or invalid, this DTC sets.

DTC	Trouble Code Title & Conditions
DTC: P268E	**Cylinder 3 Injector Data Incompatible:** Each injector has a code stored in the electronically erasable programmable read only memory (EEPROM) that provides information to the powertrain control module (PCM) about deviations of that fuel injector from a theoretical average fuel injector. If the fuel injector code is missing or invalid, this DTC sets.
DTC: P268F	**Cylinder 4 Injector Data Incompatible:** Each injector has a code stored in the electronically erasable programmable read only memory (EEPROM) that provides information to the powertrain control module (PCM) about deviations of that fuel injector from a theoretical average fuel injector. If the fuel injector code is missing or invalid, this DTC sets.
DTC: P2690	**Cylinder 5 Injector Data Incompatible:** Each injector has a code stored in the electronically erasable programmable read only memory (EEPROM) that provides information to the powertrain control module (PCM) about deviations of that fuel injector from a theoretical average fuel injector. If the fuel injector code is missing or invalid, this DTC sets.
DTC: P2691	**Cylinder 6 Injector Data Incompatible:** Each injector has a code stored in the electronically erasable programmable read only memory (EEPROM) that provides information to the powertrain control module (PCM) about deviations of that fuel injector from a theoretical average fuel injector. If the fuel injector code is missing or invalid, this DTC sets.
DTC: P2692	**Cylinder 7 Injector Data Incompatible:** Each injector has a code stored in the electronically erasable programmable read only memory (EEPROM) that provides information to the powertrain control module (PCM) about deviations of that fuel injector from a theoretical average fuel injector. If the fuel injector code is missing or invalid, this DTC sets.
DTC: P2693	**Cylinder 8 Injector Data Incompatible:** Each injector has a code stored in the electronically erasable programmable read only memory (EEPROM) that provides information to the powertrain control module (PCM) about deviations of that fuel injector from a theoretical average fuel injector. If the fuel injector code is missing or invalid, this DTC sets.
DTC: P2700	**Transmission Forward Clutch Performance:** * Wrench (TCIL) light is illuminated
DTC: P2700	**Transmission friction element A apply time range/performance:** The PCM commanded SSA on or off but detected a ratio error (mechanical failure).
DTC: P2701	**Transmission friction element B apply time range/performance:** The PCM commanded SSB on or off but detected a ratio error (mechanical failure).DTC P0756 or DTC P0757 will set
DTC: P2701	**Transmission Direct Clutch Performance:** * Wrench (TCIL) light is illuminated
DTC: P2702	**Transmission friction element C apply time range/performance :** The PCM commanded SSC on or off but detected a ratio error (mechanical failure).DTC P0761 and DTC P0762 will set
DTC: P2702	**Transmission Intermediate Clutch Performance:** * Wrench (TCIL) light is illuminated
DTC: P2703	**Transmission Low/Reverse Clutch Performance:** * No engine braking in 1st gear* Erratic shifting as the diagnostics isolates the fault to low/reverse clutch failed off.* Delayed or no reverse engagement.
DTC: P2703	**Transmission friction element D apply time range/performance:** The PCM commanded SSD on or off but detected a ratio error (mechanical failure).DTC P0766 will set
DTC: P2704	**Transmission friction element E apply time range/performance :** The PCM commanded SSE on or off but detected a ratio error (mechanical failure).DTC P0766 and P0767 will set
DTC: P2704	**Transmission Overdrive Clutch Performance:** * Overdrive clutch failed off
DTC: P2705	**Transmission One Way Clutch (OWC) Failed:** * Neutral conditions when 1st gear is commanded.* Erratic shifting as the diagnostic isolates the cause of the neutral condition to the OWC being failed.* Poor launch performance (due to 2nd gear drive away).* Harsh engagements.
DTC: P2705	**Transmission friction element F apply time range/performance:** The One-Way Clutch (OWC) failed OFF (OWC failure).Wrench light illuminated, Neutral condition when 1st gear is commanded. Poor launch performance. Harsh engagements

DTC	Trouble Code Title & Conditions
DTC: P2758	**TCC pressure control solenoid stuck on:** The PCM commanded TCC off but TCC did not release. (mechanical error)Wrench light illuminated. Engine stalls or is lugging. DTC P1744 may set
DTC: P2760	**TCC pressure control solenoid intermittent:** The PCM has detected that the TCC solenoid control circuit shorted to ground 3 times without setting DTC P0742.TCC disabled. Poor launch performance. Default to 5th gear
DTC: P2760	**TCC Pressure Control Solenoid Intermittent:** * Poor launch performance (due to 5th gear drive away).* No TCC apply.* No shifts.
DTC: P2763	**TCC pressure control solenoid control circuit high.:** Voltage through TCC was not detected when the solenoid was commanded on. Short to power detected. No TCC. No adaptive learning strategy. Default to 3rd or 5th gear
DTC: P2764	**TCC pressure control solenoid control circuit low.:** TCC was not detected when the solenoid was commanded on. Short to ground detected. No TCC. No adaptive learn strategy
DTC: P2765	**Input Speed Sensor Circuit:** 2nd, 4th and 6th gears disabled.
DTC: P2766	**Input Shaft Speed Sensor Circuit:** 2nd, 4th and 6th gears disabled.
DTC: P2767	**Input Speed Sensor 2 No Signal:** 2nd, 4th and 6th gears disabled. Vehicle in motion, speed sensor returns zero
DTC: P2768	**Input Speed Sensor Circuit:** 2nd, 4th and 6th gears disabled
DTC: P2783	**Torque Converter Temperature Too High:** * Torque converter temperature too high.* Erratic shifts, vehicle disengages at a stop while in drive or low, early TCC apply.* Test will run in 3rd gear or higher when valve 2 is in the latched position, pointing SSD at overdrive clutch when the TCC is commanded open. SSE is turned on, if the control valve is stuck, this will cause the TCC to apply even though the TCC solenoid is off.
DTC: P2800	**Transmission Range Sensor B Circuit (PRNDL Input):** The powertrain control module (PCM) checks the gear selector position by monitoring two independent voltage signals from the transmission range (TR) sensor. The TR voltages are then compared to an allowed voltage range for each gear. The test fails when the compared voltages are out of range. This DTC indicates that one TR signal is more than one band away from the majority.
DTC: P2801	**Transmission Range Sensor B Circuit Range/Performance:** The powertrain control module (PCM) checks the gear selector position by monitoring two independent voltage signals from the transmission range (TR) sensor. The TR voltages are then compared to an allowed voltage range for each gear. The test fails when the compared voltages are out of range. This DTC indicates that two or more TR signals are low or high.
DTC: P2802	**Transmission Range Sensor B Circuit Low:** The powertrain control module (PCM) checks the gear selector position by monitoring three independent voltage signals from the transmission range (TR) sensor. The TR voltages are then compared to an allowed voltage range for each gear. The test fails when the compared voltages are out of range. This DTC indicates that one TR signal is low.
DTC: P2803	**Transmission Range Sensor B Circuit High:** The powertrain control module (PCM) checks the gear selector position by monitoring two independent voltage signals from the transmission range (TR) sensor. The TR voltages are then compared to an allowed voltage range for each gear. The test fails when the compared voltages are out of range. This DTC indicates that one TR signal is high.
DTC: P2805	**Transmission Range Sensor A/B Correlation:** The powertrain control module (PCM) checks the gear selector position by monitoring two independent voltage signals from the transmission range (TR) sensor. The TR voltages are then compared to an allowed voltage range for each gear. The test fails when the compared voltages are out of range. This DTC indicates that all two TR sensors disagree but are still within range.
DTC: P2806 (PCM)	**Transmission Range Sensor Alignment:** The powertrain control module (PCM) checks the gear selector position by monitoring two independent voltage signals from the transmission range (TR) sensor. The TR voltages are then compared to an allowed voltage range for each gear. The test fails when the compared voltages are out of range. This DTC indicates that all two TR sensors disagree but are still within range.
DTC: P2806 (TCM)	**Transmission Range Sensor Alignment:** The transaxle control module (TCM) monitors vehicle speed and gear position. This DTC indicates that vehicle speed exceeded the maximum calibrated speed in PARK.

DTC	Trouble Code Title & Conditions
DTC: P2A00	**O2 Sensor Circuit Range/Performance (Bank 1 Sensor 1):** The nitrogen oxide (NOx) module estimates the expected exhaust oxygen (O2) content during certain fuel, boost and exhaust gas recirculation (EGR) conditions. This DTC sets when the actual NOx sensor O2 signal value is not within the expected range for a calibrated amount of time.
DTC: P2A01	**O2 Circuit Range / Performance Bank 1, Sensor 2:** The powertrain control module (PCM) monitors the heated oxygen sensor (HO2S) for an out of range low voltage concern. This DTC sets if the HO2S voltage is out of range low for a calibrated period of time.
DTC: P2A04	**O2 Circuit Range / Performance Bank 2, Sensor 2:** The powertrain control module (PCM) monitors the heated oxygen sensor (HO2S) for an out of range low voltage concern. This DTC sets if the HO2S voltage is out of range low for a calibrated period of time.

Commonly Used Abbreviations

2

2WD	Two Wheel Drive

4

4WD	Four Wheel Drive

A

A/C	Air Conditioning
ABDC	After Bottom Dead Center
ABS	Anti-lock Brakes
AC	Alternating Current
ACL	Air cleaner
ACT	Air Charge Temperature
AIR	Secondary Air Injection
ALCL	Assembly Line Communications Link
ALDL	Assembly Line Diagnostic Link
AT	Automatic Transaxle/Transmission
ATDC	After Top Dead Center
ATF	Automatic Transmission Fluid
ATS	Air Temperature Sensor
AWD	All Wheel Drive

B

BAP	Barometric Absolute Pressure
BARO	Barometric Pressure
BBDC	Before Bottom Dead Center
BCM	Body Control Module
BDC	Bottom Dead Center
BPT	Backpressure Transducer
BTDC	Before Top Dead Center
BVSV	Bimetallic Vacuum Switching Valve

C

CAC	Charge Air Cooler
CARB	California Air Resources Board
CAT	Catalytic Converter
CCC	Computer Command Control
CCCC	Computer Controlled Catalytic Converter
CCCI	Computer Controlled Coil Ignition
CCD	Computer Controlled Dwell
CDI	Capacitor Discharge Ignition
CEC	Computerized Engine Control
CFI	Continuous Fuel Injection
CIS	Continuous Injection System
CIS-E	Continuous Injection System - Electronic
CKP	Crankshaft Position
CL	Closed Loop
CMP	Camshaft Position
CPP	Clutch Pedal Position
CTOX	Continuous Trap Oxidizer System
CTP	Closed Throttle Position
CVC	Constant Vacuum Control
CYL	Cylinder

D

DBC	Dual Bed Catalyst
DC	Direct Current
DFI	Direct Fuel Injection
DIS	Distributorless Ignition System
DLC	Data Link Connector
DMM	Digital Multimeter
DOHC	Double Overhead Camshaft
DRB	Diagnostic Readout Box
DTC	Diagnostic Trouble Code
DTM	Diagnostic Test Mode
DVOM	Digital Volt/Ohmmeter

E

EBCM	Electronic Brake Control Module
ECM	Engine Control Module
ECT	Engine Coolant Temperature
ECU	Engine Control Unit or Electronic Control Unit
EDIS	Electronic Distributorless Ignition System
EEC	Electronic Engine Control
EEPROM	Electrically Erasable Programmable Read Only Memory
EFE	Early Fuel Evaporation
EGR	Exhaust Gas Recirculation
EGRT	Exhaust Gas Recirculation Temperature
EGRVC	EGR Valve Control
EPROM	Erasable Programmable Read Only Memory
EVAP	Evaporative Emissions
EVP	EGR Valve Position

F

FBC	Feedback Carburetor
FEEPROM	Flash Electrically Erasable Programmable Read Only Memory
FF	Flexible Fuel
FI	Fuel Injection
FT	Fuel Trim
FWD	Front Wheel Drive

GND	Ground

HAC	High Altitude Compensator
HEGO	Heated Exhaust Gas Oxygen Sensor
HEI	High Energy Ignition
HO2 Sensor	Heated Oxygen Sensor

I

IAC	Idle Air Control
IAT	Intake Air Temperature
ICM	Ignition Control Module
IFI	Indirect Fuel Injection
IFS	Inertia Fuel Shutoff
ISC	Idle Speed Control
IVSV	Idle Vacuum Switching Valve

Commonly Used Abbreviations

K

KOEO	Key On, Engine Off
KOER	Key ON, Engine Running
KS	Knock Sensor

M

MAF	Mass Air Flow
MAP	Manifold Absolute Pressure
MAT	Manifold Air Temperature
MC	Mixture Control
MDP	Manifold Differential Pressure
MFI	Multiport Fuel Injection
MIL	Malfunction Indicator Lamp or Maintenance
MST	Manifold Surface Temperature
MVZ	Manifold Vacuum Zone

N

NVRAM	Nonvolatile Random Access Memory

O

O2 Sensor	Oxygen Sensor
OBD	On-Board Diagnostic
OC	Oxidation Catalyst
OHC	Overhead Camshaft
OL	Open Loop

P

P/S	Power Steering
PAIR	Pulsed Secondary Air Injection
PCM	Powertrain Control Module
PCS	Purge Control Solenoid
PCV	Positive Crankcase Ventilation
PIP	Profile Ignition Pick-up
PNP	Park/Neutral Position
PROM	Programmable Read Only Memory
PSP	Power Steering Pressure
PTO	Power-Off
PTOX	Periodic Trap Oxidizer System

R

RABS	Anti-lock Brake System
RAM	Random Access Memory
ROM	Read Only Memory
RPM	Revolutions Per Minute
RWAL	Rear Wheel Anti-lock Brakes
RWD	Rear Wheel Drive

S

SBC	Single Bed Converter
SBEC	Single Board Engine Controller
SC	Supercharger
SCB	Supercharger Bypass
SFI	Sequential Multiport Fuel Injection
SIR	Supplemental Inflatible Restraint
SOHC	Single Overhead Camshaft
SPL	Smoke Puff Limiter
SPOUT	Spark Output
SRI	Service Reminder Indicator
SRS	Supplemental Restraint System
SRT	System Readiness Test
SSI	Solid State Ignition
ST	Scan Tool
STO	Self-Test Output

T

TAC	Thermostatic Air Cleaner
TBI	Throttle Body Fuel Injection
TC	Turbocharger
TCC	Torque Converter Clutch
TCM	Transmission Control Module
TDC	Top Dead Center
TFI	Thick Film Ignition
TP	Throttle Position
TR Sensor	Transaxle/Transmission Range Sensor
TVV	Thermal Vacuum Valve
TWC	Three-way Catalytic Converter

V

VAF	Volume Air Flow, or Vane Air Flow
VAPS	Variable Assist Power Steering
VRV	Vacuum Regulator Valve
VSS	Vehicle Speed Sensor
VSV	Vacuum Switching Valve

W

WOT	Wide Open Throttle
WU-TWC	Warm Up Three-way Catalytic Converter